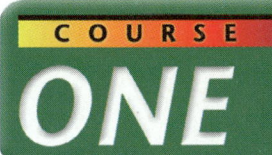

MICROSOFT®
Office
2003

Introductory Concepts and Techniques

COURSE ONE

WORD 2003   EXCEL 2003   ACCESS 2003   POWERPOINT 2003   OUTLOOK 2003

Gary B. Shelly
Thomas J. Cashman
Misty E. Vermaat

Contributing Authors
Steven G. Forsythe
Mary Z. Last
Philip J. Pratt
James S. Quasney
Jeffrey J. Quasney
Susan L. Sebok
Jeffrey J. Webb

THOMSON
COURSE TECHNOLOGY

COURSE TECHNOLOGY
25 THOMSON PLACE
BOSTON MA 02210

SHELLY
CASHMAN
SERIES®

Australia • Canada • Denmark • Japan • Mexico • New Zealand • Philippines • Puerto Rico • Singapore
South Africa • Spain • United Kingdom • United States

THOMSON
COURSE TECHNOLOGY

Microsoft Office 2003
Introductory Concepts and Techniques

Gary B. Shelly
Thomas J. Cashman
Misty E. Vermaat

Managing Editor:
Cheryl Costantini

Senior Product Manager:
Alexandra Arnold

Product Manager:
Erin Runyon

Associate Product Manager:
Reed Cotter

Signing Representative:
Cheryl Costantini

Development Editor:
Ginny Harvey

Editorial Assistant:
Selena Coppock

Print Buyer:
Denise Powers

Director of Production:
Becky Herrington

Production Editor:
Kristen Guevara

Production Assistant:
Jennifer Quiambao

Copy Editors/Proofreaders:
Ginny Harvey
Nancy Lamm
Lyn Markowicz
Lori Silfen
Lisa Jedlicka
Kim Kosmatka
Marilyn Martin

Interior Design:
Becky Herrington

Cover Design:
Richard Herrera

Illustrators:
Richard Herrera
Andrew Bartel
Ken Russo

Compositors:
Jeanne Black
Andrew Bartel
Kellee LaVars
Kenny Tran
Michelle French

Indexer:
Cristina Haley

Printer:
Banta Menasha

ISBN 0-619-25574-9 (perfect bound)
ISBN 0-619-20057-X (spiral bound)
ISBN 0-619-25558-7 (case bound)
ISBN 0-619-20024-3 (hard cover/ spiral bound)

PHOTO CREDITS: Microsoft Windows 2003 *Project 1, page* WIN 5 Dell computer, monitor, and printer, Courtesy of Dell Computers; *page* WIN 6 Dell computer and monitor, Courtesy of Dell Computers; **Microsoft PowerPoint 2003** *Project 1, page* PPT 6 laptop computer, Courtesy of PhotoDisc, Inc.

MICROSOFT®
Office 2003
Introductory Concepts and Techniques
WORD 2003   EXCEL 2003   ACCESS 2003   POWERPOINT 2003   OUTLOOK 2003

COURSE
ONE

Contents

MICROSOFT
Windows XP and Office 2003

Project One

Introduction to Microsoft Windows XP and Office 2003

Microsoft Office Word 2003

Project One

Creating and Editing a Word Document

Project Two

Creating a Research Paper

Project Two

Formulas, Functions, Formatting, and Web Queries

Project Three

What-If Analysis, Charting, and Working with Large Worksheets

MICROSOFT Office Access 2003

Project One

Creating and Using a Database

Project Two

Querying a Database Using the Select Query Window

Project Three

Maintaining a Database Using the Design and Update Features of Access

Web Feature

Creating a Presentation on the Web Using PowerPoint

MICROSOFT Office Outlook 2003

Project One

E-Mail and Contact Management with Outlook

MICROSOFT Office 2003 Integration

Project One

Integrating Office 2003 Applications and the World Wide Web

Appendix A

Microsoft Office Help System

Appendix B

Speech and Handwriting Recognition and Speech Playback

Appendix C

Publishing Office Web Pages to a Web Server

Appendix D

Changing Screen Resolution and Resetting the Word Toolbars and Menus

Appendix E

Microsoft Office Specialist Certification

Preface

The Shelly Cashman Series® offers the finest textbooks in computer education. We are proud of the fact that our series of Microsoft Office 4.3, Microsoft Office 95, Microsoft Office 97, Microsoft Office 2000, and Microsoft Office XP textbooks have been the most widely used books in education. With each new edition of our Office books, we have made significant improvements based on the software and comments made by the instructors and students. The *Microsoft Office 2003* books continue with the innovation, quality, and reliability that you have come to expect from the Shelly Cashman Series.

In this *Microsoft Office 2003* book, you will find an educationally sound, highly visual, and easy-to-follow pedagogy that combines a vastly improved step-by-step approach with corresponding screens. All projects and exercises in this book are designed to take full advantage of the Office 2003 enhancements. The popular Other Ways and More About features offer in-depth knowledge of the Office applications. The new Q&A feature offers students a way to solidify important application concepts. The Learn It Online page presents a wealth of additional exercises to ensure your students have all the reinforcement they need. The project material is developed to ensure that students will see the importance of learning how to use the Office applications for future coursework.

Objectives of This Textbook

Microsoft Office 2003: Introductory Concepts and Techniques is intended for a course that includes an in-depth introduction to Office 2003. No experience with a computer is assumed, and no mathematics beyond the high school freshman level is required. The objectives of this book are:

- To teach the fundamentals of Microsoft Office Word 2003, Microsoft Office Excel 2003, Microsoft Office Access 2003, Microsoft Office PowerPoint 2003, Microsoft Office Outlook 2003, and Microsoft Windows XP
- To expose students to practical examples of the computer as a useful tool
- To acquaint students with the proper procedures to create documents, worksheets, databases, and presentations suitable for coursework, professional purposes, and personal use
- To help students discover the underlying functionality of Office 2003 so they can become more productive
- To develop an exercise-oriented approach that allows learning by doing
- To serve as courseware in combination with the companion book *Microsoft Office 2003: Advanced Concepts and Techniques* for students interested in Microsoft Office Specialist certification
- To introduce students to new input technologies
- To encourage independent study, and help those who are working alone

Approved by Microsoft as Courseware for Microsoft Office Specialist Certification

Microsoft Office 2003: Introductory Concepts and Techniques, when used in combination with the companion textbook *Microsoft Office 2003: Advanced Concepts and Techniques* in a two-semester sequence, has been approved by Microsoft as courseware for Microsoft Office Specialist certification. After completing the projects and exercises in this book and its companion book, students will be prepared to take the specialist-level exams for the five basic Office applications.

By passing the certification exam for a Microsoft software application, students demonstrate their proficiency in that application to employers. This exam is offered at participating centers, participating corporations, and participating employment agencies. See Appendix E for additional information about obtaining Microsoft Office Specialist certification and for a table that includes the Word 2003, Excel 2003, Access 2003, PowerPoint 2003, and Outlook 2003 Microsoft Office Specialist skill sets and corresponding page numbers where a skill is discussed in the book, or visit the Web site microsoft.com/officespecialist.

The Shelly Cashman Series Microsoft Office Specialist Center (Figure 1) has links to valuable information on the certification program. The Web page (scsite.com/winoff2003/cert) includes links to general information about certification, choosing an application for certification, preparing for the certification exam, and taking and passing the certification exam.

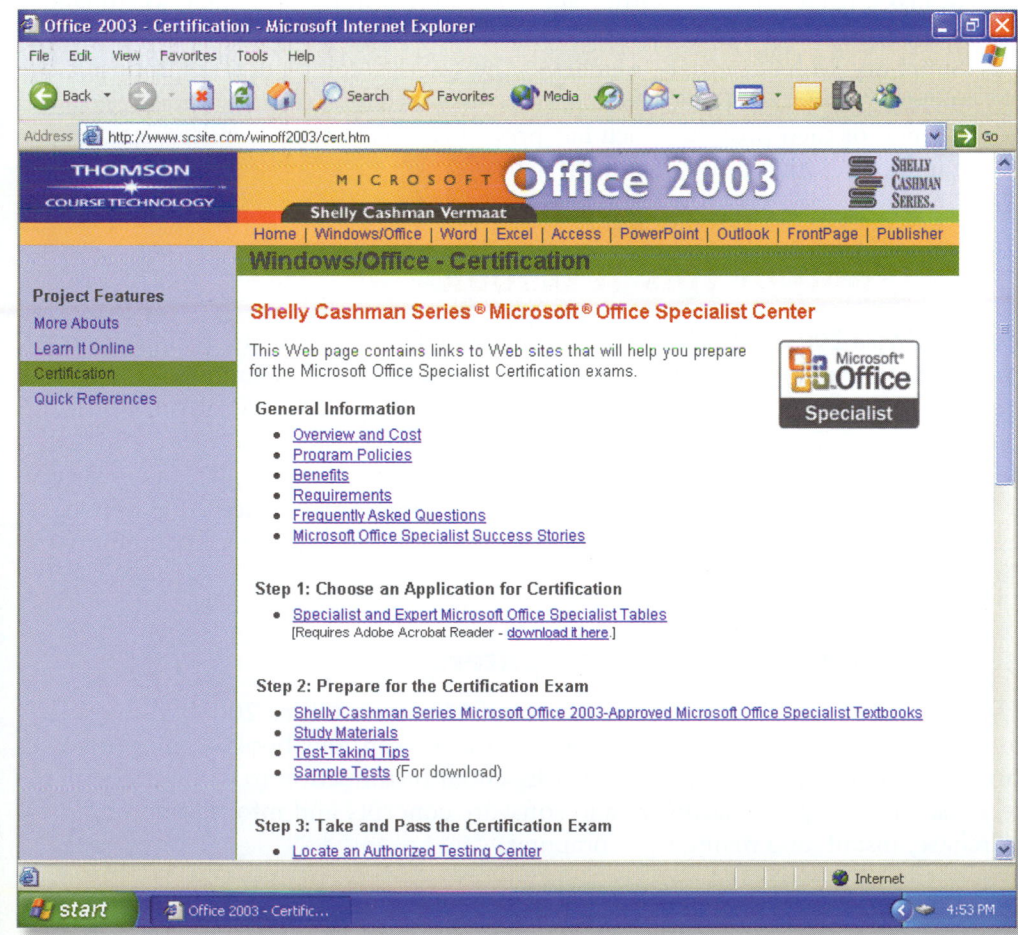

FIGURE 1

The Shelly Cashman Approach

Features of the Shelly Cashman Series *Microsoft Office 2003* books include:

- **Project Orientation:** Each project in the book presents a practical problem and complete solution in an easy-to-understand approach.
- **Step-by-Step, Screen-by-Screen Instructions:** Each of the tasks required to complete a project is identified throughout the project. Full-color screens with call outs accompany the steps.
- **Thoroughly Tested Projects:** Unparalleled quality is ensured because every screen in the book is produced by the author only after performing a step, and then each project must pass Course Technology's award-winning Quality Assurance program.
- **Other Ways Boxes and Quick Reference Summary:** The Other Ways boxes displayed at the end of most of the step-by-step sequences specify the other ways to do the task completed in the steps. Thus, the steps and the Other Ways box make a comprehensive reference unit.
- **More About and Q&A Features:** These marginal annotations provide background information, tips, and answers to common questions that complement the topics covered, adding depth and perspective to the learning process.
- **Integration of the World Wide Web:** The World Wide Web is integrated into the Office 2003 learning experience by (1) More About annotations that send students to Web sites for up-to-date information and alternative approaches to tasks; (2) a Microsoft Office Specialist Certification Web page so students can prepare for the certification examinations; (3) a Quick Reference Summary Web page that summarizes the ways to complete tasks (mouse, menu, shortcut menu, and keyboard); and (4) the Learn It Online page at the end of each project, which has project reinforcement exercises, learning games, and other types of student activities.

Organization of This Textbook

Microsoft Office 2003: Introductory Concepts and Techniques consists of a brief introduction to computers, a project that introduces Microsoft Windows XP and Office 2003, three projects each on Microsoft Office Word 2003, Microsoft Office Excel 2003, and Microsoft Office Access 2003, two projects on Microsoft Office PowerPoint 2003, four special features emphasizing Web-related topics, one project on Microsoft Office Outlook 2003, one project on integrating Office 2003 applications and the World Wide Web, five appendices, and a Quick Reference Summary. A short description of each follows.

Essential Introduction to Computers

Many students taking a course in the use of Microsoft Office 2003 will have little previous experience with computers. For this reason, this book begins with a completely updated 32-page section titled Essential Introduction to Computers that covers essential computer hardware and software concepts and information on how to purchase, install, and maintain a computer.

Other Ways

1. On Format menu click Cells, click Font tab, click Bold in Font style box, click OK button
2. Right-click cell, click Format Cells on shortcut menu, click Font tab, click Bold in Font style box, click OK button
3. Press CTRL+B
4. In Voice Command mode, say "Bold"

More About

The Office Assistant

The Office Assistant is an animated object that can answer questions for you. On some installations, the Office Assistant may appear when Word starts. If the Office Assistant appears on your screen and you do not want to use it, right-click it and then click Hide on the shortcut menu.

Q&A

Q: Why is the data type for Zip Code text instead of Number?

A: Zip codes are not used in arithmetic operations. You do not add Zip codes or find an average Zip code, for example.

Introduction to Microsoft Windows XP and Office 2003

In this project, students learn about user interfaces, Windows XP, Windows Explorer, and each Office 2003 application. Topics include using the mouse; minimizing, maximizing, and restoring windows; closing and reopening windows; sizing and scrolling windows; launching and quitting an application; displaying the contents of a folder; expanding and collapsing a folder; creating a folder; selecting and copying a group of files; renaming and deleting a file and a folder; using Windows XP Help and Support; and shutting down Windows XP. Topics pertaining to Office 2003 include a brief explanation of Word 2003; Excel 2003; Access 2003; PowerPoint 2003; Publisher 2003; FrontPage 2003; and Outlook 2003 and examples of how these applications take advantage of the Internet and World Wide Web.

Microsoft Office Word 2003

Project 1 – Creating and Editing a Word Document In Project 1, students are introduced to Word terminology and the Word window by preparing an announcement. Topics include starting and quitting Word; entering text; checking spelling while typing; saving a document; selecting characters, words, lines, and paragraphs; changing the font and font size of text; centering, right-aligning, bolding, and italicizing text; undoing commands and actions; inserting clip art in a document; resizing a graphic; printing a document; opening a document; correcting errors; and using the Word Help system.

Project 2 – Creating a Research Paper In Project 2, students use the MLA style of documentation to create a research paper. Topics include changing margins; adjusting line spacing; using a header to number pages; entering text using Click and Type; first-line indenting paragraphs; using the AutoCorrect feature and AutoCorrect Options button; adding a footnote; modifying a style; inserting a symbol automatically; inserting a manual page break; creating a hanging indent; creating a text hyperlink; sorting paragraphs; moving text; using the Paste Options button; finding a synonym; counting and recounting words in a document; checking spelling and grammar at once; e-mailing a document; and using the Research task pane.

Project 3 – Creating a Resume Using a Wizard and a Cover Letter with a Table In Project 3, students create a resume using Word's Resume Wizard and then create a cover letter with a letterhead. Topics include personalizing the resume; using print preview; adding color to characters; setting and using tab stops; collecting and pasting; adding a bottom border; clearing formatting; inserting the current date; inserting a nonbreaking space; creating and inserting an AutoText entry; creating a bulleted list while typing; inserting a Word table; entering data into a Word table; and formatting a Word table. Finally, students prepare and print an envelope address, use smart tags, and modify the document summary.

Web Feature – Creating Web Pages Using Word In the Web feature, students are introduced to creating Web pages in Word. Topics include saving a Word document as a Web page; formatting an e-mail address as a hyperlink; applying a theme to a Web page; previewing a Web page; creating and modifying a frames page; and inserting and modifying hyperlinks.

Microsoft Office Excel 2003

Project 1 - Creating a Worksheet and Embedded Chart In Project 1, students are introduced to starting Excel, quitting Excel, Excel terminology, the Excel window, and the basic characteristics of a worksheet and workbook. Topics include entering text and numbers; selecting a range; using the AutoSum button; copying using the fill

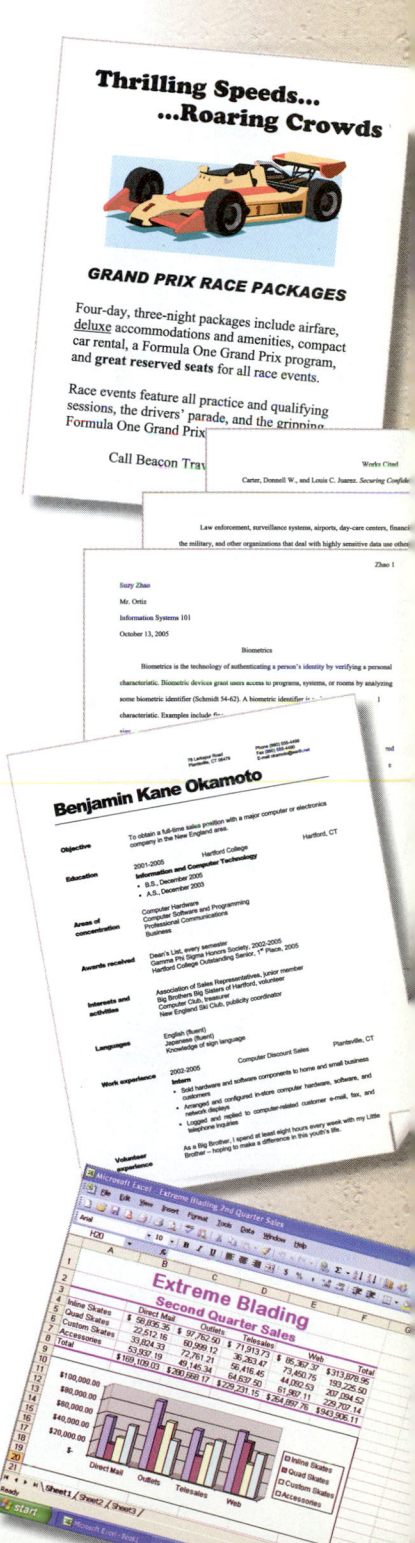

handle; changing font size; formatting in bold; centering across columns; using the AutoFormat command; charting using the ChartWizard; saving and opening a workbook; editing a worksheet; using the AutoCalculate area; and using the Excel Help system.

Project 2 – Formulas, Functions, Formatting, and Web Queries   In Project 2, students use formulas and functions to build a worksheet and learn more about formatting and printing a worksheet. Topics include entering formulas; using functions; verifying formulas; formatting text and numbers; conditional formatting; drawing borders; changing the widths of columns and rows; spell checking; previewing a worksheet; printing a section of a worksheet; and displaying and printing the formulas in a worksheet. This project also introduces students to accessing real-time data using Web Queries and sending the open workbook as an e-mail attachment directly from Excel.

Project 3 – What-If-Analysis, Charting, and Working with Large Worksheets In Project 3, students learn how to work with larger worksheets, how to create a worksheet based on assumptions, how to use the IF function and absolute cell references, charting techniques, and how to perform what-if analysis. Topics include assigning global formats; rotating text; using the fill handle to create a series; deleting, inserting, copying, and moving data on a worksheet; displaying and formatting the system date; displaying and docking toolbars; creating a 3-D Pie chart on a chart sheet, enhancing a 3-D Pie chart; freezing titles; changing the magnification of worksheets; displaying different parts of the worksheet using panes; and simple what-if analysis and goal seeking.

Web Feature - Creating Static and Dynamic Web Pages Using Excel   In the Web feature, students are introduced to creating static Web pages (noninteractive pages that do not change) and dynamic Web pages (interactive pages that offer Excel functionality). Topics include saving and previewing an Excel workbook as a Web page; viewing and manipulating a Web page created in Excel using a browser; file management tools in Excel; and using the Spreadsheet toolbar.

Microsoft Access Office 2003

Project 1 - Creating and Using a Database   In Project 1, students are introduced to the concept of a database and shown how to use Access to create a database. Topics include creating a database; creating a table; defining the fields in a table; opening a table; adding records to a table; closing a table; and previewing and printing the contents of a table. Other topics in this project include creating a query using the Simple Query Wizard, using a form to view data, using the Report Wizard to create a report, and using Access Help. Students also learn how to design a database to eliminate redundancy.

Project 2 - Querying a Database Using the Select Query Window   In Project 2, students learn to use queries to obtain information from the data in their databases. Topics include creating queries, running queries, saving queries, and printing the results. Specific query topics include displaying only selected fields; using character data in criteria; specifying parameter queries; using wildcards; using numeric data in criteria; using comparison operators; and creating compound criteria. Other related topics include sorting, joining tables, and restricting records in a join. Students also learn to use calculated fields, statistics, and grouping. They also learn how to create top-values queries and how to format fields in queries. Finally, they learn to create and use crosstab queries.

Project 3 - Maintaining a Database Using the Design and Update Features of Access

In Project 3, students learn the crucial skills involved in maintaining a database. These include using Datasheet view and Form view to add new records, to change existing records, to delete records, and to locate and filter records. Students also learn the processes of changing the structure of a table, adding additional fields, and changing characteristics of existing fields. They learn ways to change the appearance of a datasheet. They learn to create a variety of validation rules and to specify referential integrity. Students perform mass changes and deletions using queries, create single-field and multiple-field indexes, and use subdatasheets to view related data.

Integration Feature - Sharing Data among Applications

In this Integration feature, students learn how to embed an Excel worksheet in an Access database and how to link a worksheet to a database. Students also learn how to prepare Access data for use in other applications. Topics include embedding worksheets; linking worksheets; using the resulting tables; using the Export command to export database data to an Excel worksheet; using drag-and-drop to export data to a Word document; and using the Export command to create a snapshot of a report. They also learn how to export and import XML data.

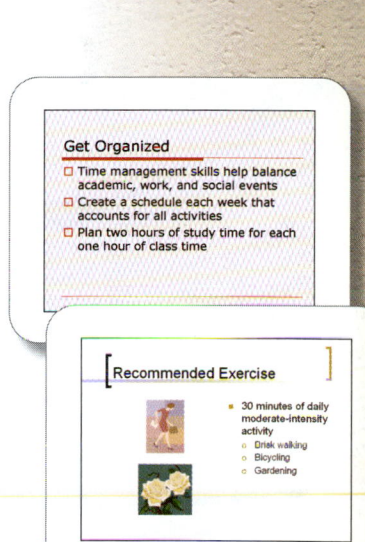

Microsoft Office PowerPoint 2003

Project 1 – Using a Design Template and Text Slide Layout to Create a Presentation

In Project 1, students are introduced to PowerPoint terminology, the PowerPoint window, and the basics of creating a bulleted list presentation. Topics include choosing a design template by using a task pane; creating a title slide and text slides with single and multi-level bulleted lists; changing the font size and font style; ending a slide show with a black slide; saving a presentation; viewing the slides in a presentation; checking a presentation for spelling errors; printing copies of the slides; and using the PowerPoint Help system.

Project 2 – Using the Outline Tab and Clip Art to Create a Slide Show

In Project 2, students create a presentation from an outline, insert clip art, and add animation effects. Topics include creating a slide presentation by indenting paragraphs on the Outline tab; changing slide layouts; inserting clip art; changing clip art size; adding an animation scheme; animating clip art; running an animated slide show; printing audience handouts from an outline; and e-mailing a slide show from within PowerPoint.

Web Feature – Creating a Presentation on the Web Using PowerPoint

In the Web feature, students are introduced to saving a presentation as a Web page. Topics include saving an existing PowerPoint presentation as an HTML file; viewing the presentation as a Web page; editing a Web page through a browser; and viewing the editing changes.

Microsoft Office Outlook 2003

Project 1 - E-Mail and Contact Management with Outlook

In Project 1, students learn to read and send e-mail messages and work with Contacts. Topics include reading, replying to, forwarding, and deleting e-mail messages; composing, formatting, and inserting a file attachment; sending new e-mail messages; flagging, sorting, and configuring e-mail options; generating and maintaining a contact list; and creating a personal folder for contacts.

Microsoft Office 2003 Integration

Project 1 - Integrating Office 2003 Applications and the World Wide Web   In Project 1, students are introduced to the seamless partnership of the Microsoft Office 2003 applications, which allows the sharing of information among Word, Excel, Access, PowerPoint, Outlook, and the World Wide Web. Topics include embedding an Excel chart into a Word document; creating a Web site home page from a Word document; creating a Web page from a PowerPoint presentation; creating a data access page Web page from an Access database; and creating hyperlinks from the home page created in Word to the Web pages created in PowerPoint and Access, as well as adding an e-mail hyperlink.

Appendices

The book includes five appendices. Appendix A presents an introduction to the Microsoft Office Help system. Appendix B describes how to use the Office speech and handwriting recognition and speech playback capabilities. Appendix C explains how to publish Web pages to a Web server. Appendix D shows how to change the screen resolution and reset the menus and toolbars. Appendix E introduces students to Microsoft Office Specialist certification.

Quick Reference Summary

In Office 2003, you can accomplish a task in a number of ways, such as using the mouse, menu, shortcut menu, and keyboard. The Quick Reference Summary at the back of the book provides a quick reference to each task presented.

End-of-Project Student Activities

A notable strength of the Shelly Cashman Series *Microsoft Office 2003* books is the extensive student activities at the end of each project. Well-structured student activities can make the difference between students merely participating in a class and students retaining the information they learn. The activities in the Shelly Cashman Series *Office* books include the following.

- **What You Should Know**   A listing of the tasks completed within a project together with the pages on which the step-by-step, screen-by-screen explanations appear.
- **Learn It Online**   Every project features a Learn It Online page that comprises twelve exercises. These exercises include True/False, Multiple Choice, Short Answer, Flash Cards, Practice Test, Learning Games, Tips and Tricks, Newsgroup usage, Expanding Your Horizons, Search Sleuth, Office Online Training, and Office Marketplace.
- **Apply Your Knowledge**   This exercise usually requires students to open and manipulate a file on the Data Disk that parallels the activities learned in the project. To obtain a copy of the Data Disk, follow the instructions on the inside back cover of this textbook.
- **In the Lab**   Three in-depth assignments per project require students to utilize the project concepts and techniques to solve problems on a computer.
- **Cases and Places**   Five unique real-world case-study situations, including one small-group activity.

Instructor Resources CD-ROM

The Shelly Cashman Series is dedicated to providing you with all of the tools you need to make your class a success. Information on all supplementary materials is available through your Course Technology representative or by calling one of the following telephone numbers: Colleges and Universities, 1-800-648-7450; High Schools, 1-800-824-5179; Private Career Colleges, 1-800-347-7707; Canada, 1-800-268-2222; Corporations with IT Training Centers, 1-800-648-7450; and Government Agencies, Health-Care Organizations, and Correctional Facilities, 1-800-477-3692.

The Instructor Resources CD-ROM for this textbook include both teaching and testing aids. The contents of each item on the Instructor Resources CD-ROM (ISBN 0-619-20048-0) are described below.

INSTRUCTOR'S MANUAL The Instructor's Manual is made up of Microsoft Word files, which include detailed lesson plans with page number references, lecture notes, teaching tips, classroom activities, discussion topics, projects to assign, and transparency references. The transparencies are available through the Figure Files described below.

LECTURE SUCCESS SYSTEM The Lecture Success System consists of intermediate files that correspond to certain figures in the book, allowing you to step through the creation of an application in a project during a lecture without entering large amounts of data.

SYLLABUS Sample syllabi, which can be customized easily to a course, are included. The syllabi cover policies, class and lab assignments and exams, and procedural information.

FIGURE FILES Illustrations for every figure in the textbook are available in electronic form. Use this ancillary to present a slide show in lecture or to print transparencies for use in lecture with an overhead projector. If you have a personal computer and LCD device, this ancillary can be an effective tool for presenting lectures.

POWERPOINT PRESENTATIONS PowerPoint Presentations is a multimedia lecture presentation system that provides slides for each project. Presentations are based on project objectives. Use this presentation system to present well-organized lectures that are both interesting and knowledge based. PowerPoint Presentations provides consistent coverage at schools that use multiple lecturers.

SOLUTIONS TO EXERCISES Solutions are included for the end-of-project exercises, as well as the Project Reinforcement exercises.

RUBRICS AND ANNOTATED SOLUTION FILES The grading rubrics provide a customizable framework for assigning point values to the laboratory exercises. Annotated solution files that correspond to the grading rubrics make it easy for you to compare students' results with the correct solutions whether you receive their homework as hard copy or via e-mail.

TEST BANK & TEST ENGINE The ExamView test bank includes 110 questions for every project (25 multiple-choice, 50 true/false, and 35 completion) with page number references, and when appropriate, figure references. A version of the test bank you can print also is included. The test bank comes with a copy of the test engine, ExamView, the ultimate tool for your objective-based testing needs. ExamView is a state-of-the-art test builder that is easy to use. ExamView enables you to create paper-, LAN-, or Web-based tests from test banks designed specifically for your Course Technology textbook. Utilize the ultra-efficient QuickTest Wizard to create tests in less than five minutes by taking advantage of Course Technology's question banks, or customize your own exams from scratch.

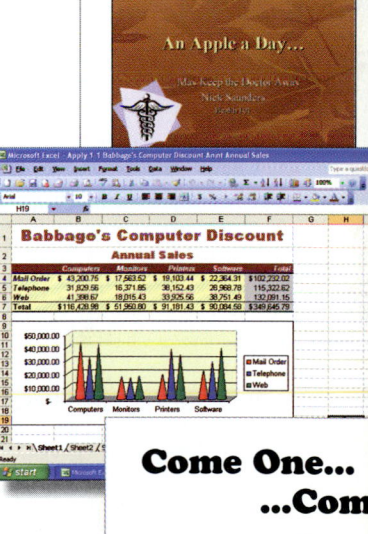

LAB TESTS/TEST OUT   The Lab Tests/Test Out exercises parallel the In the Lab assignments and are supplied for the purpose of testing students in the laboratory on the material covered in the project or testing students out of the course.

DATA FILES FOR STUDENTS   All the files that are required by students to complete the exercises are included. You can distribute the files on the Instructor Resources CD-ROM to your students over a network, or you can have them follow the instructions on the inside back cover of this book to obtain a copy of the Data Disk.

ADDITIONAL ACTIVITIES FOR STUDENTS   These additional activities consist of Project Reinforcement Exercises, which are true/false, multiple choice, and short answer questions that help students gain confidence in the material learned.

SAM 2003

SAM 2003 helps you energize your class exams and training assignments by allowing students to learn and test important computer skills in an active, hands-on environment.

SAM 2003 ASSESSMENT   With SAM 2003 Assessment, you create powerful interactive exams on critical applications such as Word, Excel, Access, PowerPoint, Windows, Outlook, and the Internet. The exams simulate the application environment, allowing your students to demonstrate their knowledge and think through the skill by performing real-world tasks. Build hands-on exams that allow students to work in the simulated application environment.

SAM 2003 TRAINING   Invigorate your lesson plan with SAM 2003 Training. Using highly interactive text, graphics, and sound, SAM 2003 Training gives your students the flexibility to learn computer applications by choosing the training method that fits them best. Create customized training units that employ various approaches to teaching computer skills.

SAM 2003 ASSESSMENT AND TRAINING   Designed to be used with the Shelly Cashman Series, SAM 2003 Assessment and Training includes built-in page references so students can create study guides that match the Shelly Cashman Series textbooks you use in class. Powerful administrative options allow you to schedule customized exams and assignments, secure your tests, and choose from more than one dozen reports to track testing and learning progress.

Online Content

Course Technology offers textbook-based content for Blackboard, WebCT, and MyCourse 2.1

BLACKBOARD AND WEBCT   As the leading provider of IT content for the Blackboard and WebCT platforms, Course Technology delivers rich content that enhances your textbook to give your students a unique learning experience. Course Technology has partnered with WebCT and Blackboard to deliver our market-leading content through these state-of-the-art online learning platforms. Course Technology offers customizable content in every subject area, from computer concepts to PC repair.

MYCOURSE 2.1 MyCourse 2.1 is Course Technology's powerful online course management and content delivery system. Completely maintained and hosted by Thomson, MyCourse 2.1 delivers an online learning environment that is completely secure and provides superior performance. MyCourse 2.1 allows nontechnical users to create, customize, and deliver World Wide Web-based courses; post content and assignments; manage student enrollment; administer exams; track results in the online gradebook; and more. With MyCourse 2.1, you easily can create a customized course that will enhance every learning experience.

Workbook for Microsoft Office 2003: Introductory Concepts and Techniques

This highly popular supplement (ISBN 0-619-20028-6) includes a variety of activities that help students recall, review, and master the concepts presented. The *Workbook* complements the end-of-project material with a guided project outline; a self-test consisting of true/false, multiple-choice, short answer, and matching questions; and activities calculated to help students develop a deeper understanding of the information presented.

Acknowledgments

The Shelly Cashman Series would not be the leading computer education series without the contributions of outstanding publishing professionals. First, and foremost, among them is Becky Herrington, director of production and book designer. She is the heart and soul of the Shelly Cashman Series, and it is only through her leadership, dedication, and tireless efforts that superior products are made possible.

Under Becky's direction, the following individuals made significant contributions to these books: Kristen Guevara, production editor; Jennifer Quiambao, production assistant; Ken Russo, senior Web and graphic designer; Richard Herrera, cover designer and illustrator; Andrew Bartel, Kellee LaVars, Phillip Hajjar, Kenny Tran, and Lisa Ikari, graphic artists; Jeanne Black, Andrew Bartel, Kellee LaVars, Kenny Tran, and Michelle French, QuarkXPress compositors; Ginny Harvey, Lisa Jedlicka, Nancy Lamm, Lyn Markowicz, Kim Kosmatka, Lori Silfen and Marilyn Martin, copy editors and proofreaders; and Cristina Haley, indexer.

We also would like to thank Kristen Duerr, executive vice president and publisher; Cheryl Costantini, executive editor; Jim Quasney, series consulting editor; Alexandra Arnold, senior product manager; Erin Runyon, product manager; Mark Ouellette and Heather McKinstry, online product managers; Reed Cotter, associate product manager; and Selena Coppock, editorial assistant.

Gary B. Shelly
Thomas J. Cashman
Misty E. Vermaat

To the Student... Getting the Most Out of Your Book

Welcome to *Microsoft Office 2003: Introductory Concepts and Techniques*. You can save yourself a lot of time and gain a better understanding of the Office 2003 applications if you spend a few minutes reviewing the figures and callouts in this section.

1 Project Orientation

Each project presents a practical problem and shows the solution in the first figure of the project. The project orientation lets you see firsthand how problems are solved from start to finish using application software and computers.

2 Consistent Step-by-Step, Screen-by-Screen Presentation

Project solutions are built using a step-by-step, screen-by-screen approach. This pedagogy allows you to build the solution on a computer as you read through the project. Generally, each step is followed by an italic explanation that indicates the result of the step.

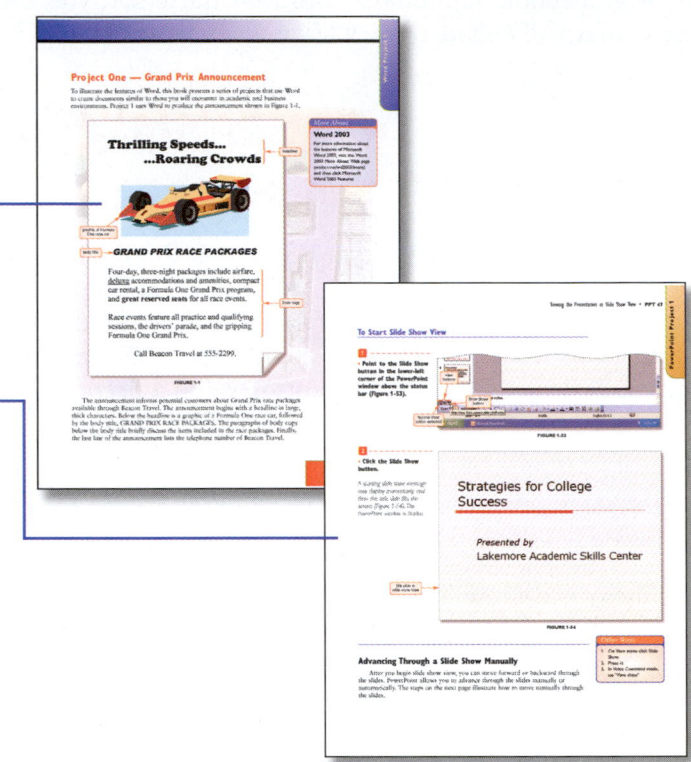

3 More Than Just Step-by-Step

More About and Q&A annotations in the margins of the book and substantive text in the paragraphs provide background information, tips, and answers to common questions that complement the topics covered, adding depth and perspective. When you finish with this book, you will be ready to use the Office applications to solve problems on your own.

4 Other Ways Boxes and Quick Reference Summary

Other Ways boxes that follow many of the step sequences and a Quick Reference Summary at the back of the book explain the other ways to complete the task presented, such as using the mouse, menu, shortcut menu, and keyboard.

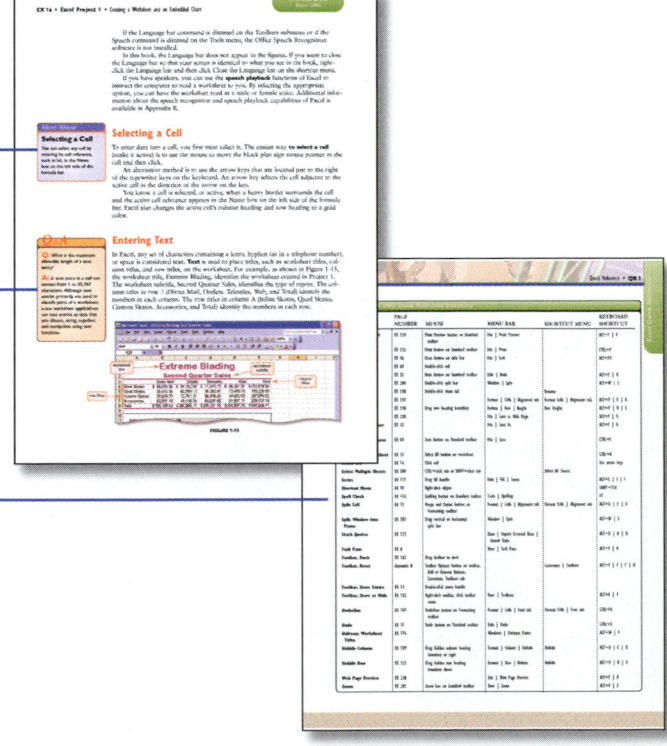

5 Emphasis on Getting Help When You Need It

The first project of each application and Appendix A show you how to use all the elements of the Office Help system. Being able to answer your own questions will increase your productivity and reduce your frustrations by minimizing the time it takes to learn how to complete a task.

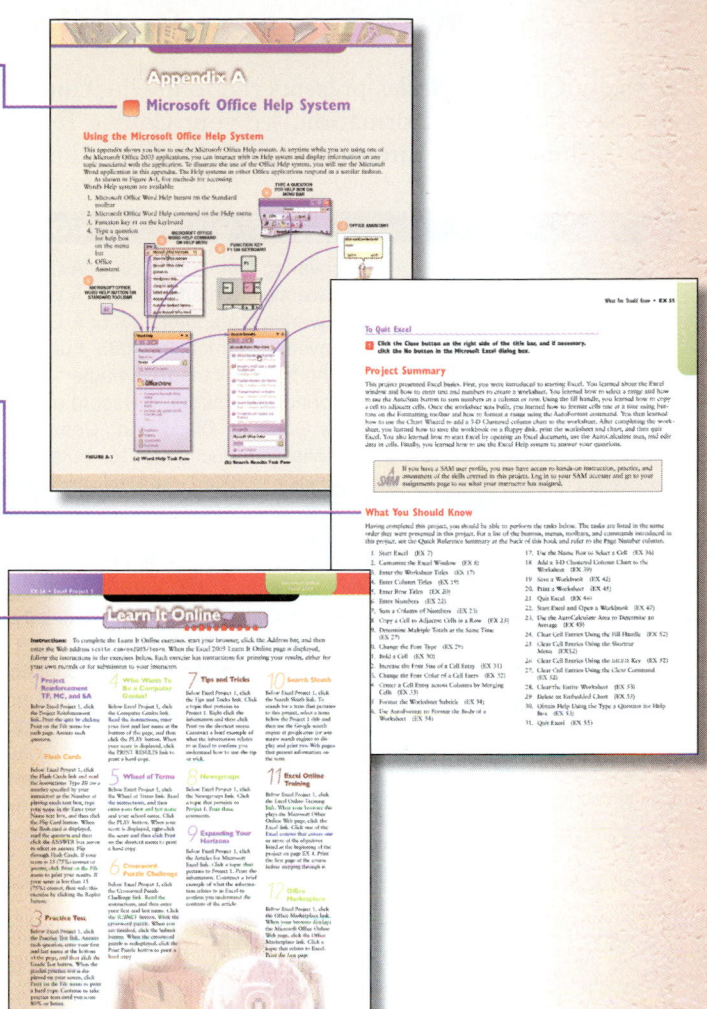

6 Review

After you successfully step through a project, a section titled What You Should Know summarizes the project tasks with which you should be familiar. Terms you should know for test purposes are bold in the text.

7 Reinforcement and Extension

The Learn It Online page at the end of each project offers reinforcement in the form of review questions, learning games, and practice tests. Also included are Web-based exercises that require you to extend your learning beyond the book.

8 Laboratory Exercises

If you really want to learn how to use the applications, then you must design and implement solutions to problems on your own. Every project concludes with several carefully developed laboratory assignments that increase in complexity.

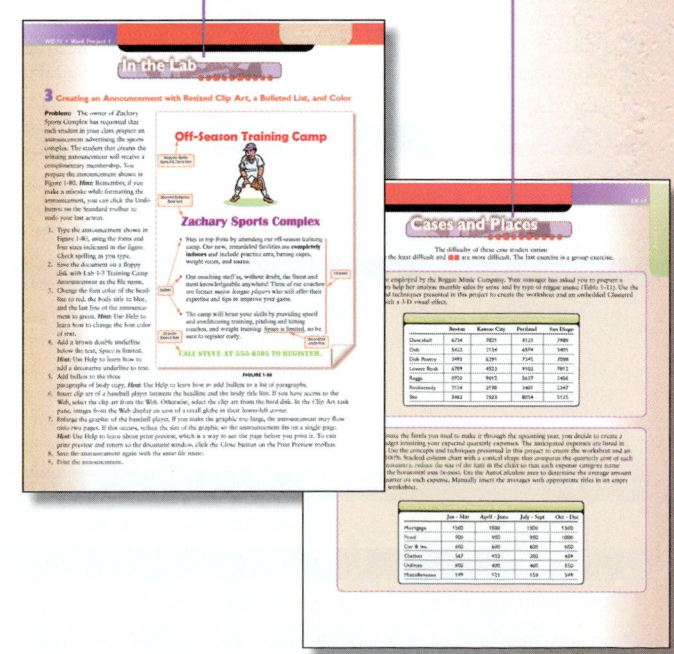

Shelly Cashman Series – Traditionally Bound Textbooks

The Shelly Cashman Series presents the following computer subjects in a variety of traditionally bound textbooks. For more information, see your Course Technology representative or call 1-800-648-7450. For Shelly Cashman Series information, visit Shelly Cashman Online at **scseries.com**

COMPUTERS	
Computers	Discovering Computers 2005: A Gateway to Information, Web Enhanced, Complete Edition
	Discovering Computers 2005: A Gateway to Information, Web Enhanced, Introductory Edition
	Discovering Computers 2005: A Gateway to Information, Web Enhanced, Brief Edition
	Discovering Computers 2005: Fundamentals Edition
	Teachers Discovering Computers: Integrating Technology in the Classroom 3e
	Exploring Computers: A Record of Discovery 4e
	Study Guide for Discovering Computers 2005: A Gateway to Information, Web Enhanced
	Essential Introduction to Computers 5e (40-page)

WINDOWS APPLICATIONS	
Microsoft Office	Microsoft Office 2003: Essential Concepts and Techniques (5 projects)
	Microsoft Office 2003: Brief Concepts and Techniques (9 projects)
	Microsoft Office 2003: Introductory Concepts and Techniques, (15 projects)
	Microsoft Office 2003: Advanced Concepts and Techniques (12 projects)
	Microsoft Office 2003: Post Advanced Concepts and Techniques (11 projects)
	Microsoft Office XP: Essential Concepts and Techniques (5 projects)
	Microsoft Office XP: Brief Concepts and Techniques (9 projects)
	Microsoft Office XP: Introductory Concepts and Techniques, Windows XP Edition
	Microsoft Office XP: Introductory Concepts and Techniques, Enhanced Edition (15 projects)[1]
	Microsoft Office XP: Advanced Concepts and Techniques (11 projects)
	Microsoft Office XP: Post Advanced Concepts and Techniques (11 projects)
Integration	Integrating Microsoft Office XP Applications and the World Wide Web: Essential Concepts and Techniques
PIM	Microsoft Outlook 2002: Essential Concepts and Techniques
Microsoft Works	Microsoft Works 6: Complete Concepts and Techniques[2] • Microsoft Works 2000: Complete Concepts and Techniques[2]
Microsoft Windows	Microsoft Windows XP: Complete Concepts and Techniques[3]
	Microsoft Windows XP: Brief Concepts and Techniques
	Microsoft Windows 2000: Complete Concepts and Techniques (6 projects)[3]
	Microsoft Windows 2000: Brief Concepts and Techniques (2 projects)
	Microsoft Windows 98: Essential Concepts and Techniques (2 projects)
	Microsoft Windows 98: Complete Concepts and Techniques (6 projects)[3]
	Introduction to Microsoft Windows NT Workstation 4
Word Processing	Microsoft Word 2003[3] • Microsoft Word 2002[3]
Spreadsheets	Microsoft Excel 2003[3] • Microsoft Excel 2002[3]
Database	Microsoft Access 2003[3] • Microsoft Access 2002[3]
Presentation Graphics	Microsoft PowerPoint 2003[3] • Microsoft PowerPoint 2002[3]
Desktop Publishing	Microsoft Publisher 2003[2] • Microsoft Publisher 2002[2]

PROGRAMMING	
Programming	Microsoft Visual Basic.NET: Complete Concepts and Techniques[3] • Microsoft Visual Basic 6: Complete Concepts and Techniques[2] • Programming in QBasic • Java Programming 2e: Complete Concepts and Techniques[3] • Structured COBOL Programming 2e

INTERNET	
Browser	Microsoft Internet Explorer 6: Introductory Concepts and Techniques • Microsoft Internet Explorer 5: An Introduction • Netscape Navigator 6: An Introduction
Web Page Creation and Design	Web Design: Introductory Concepts and Techniques • HTML: Complete Concepts and Techniques 2e[3] • Microsoft FrontPage 2003[3] • Microsoft FrontPage 2002[3] • Microsoft FrontPage 2002: Essential Concepts and Techniques • Java Programming: Complete Concepts and Techniques 2e[3] • JavaScript: Complete Concepts and Techniques 2e[2] • Macromedia Dreamweaver MX: Complete Concepts and Techniques[3]

SYSTEMS ANALYSIS	
Systems Analysis	Systems Analysis and Design 5e

DATA COMMUNICATIONS	
Data Communications	Business Data Communications: Introductory Concepts and Techniques 4e

[1]Available running under Windows XP or running under Windows 2000, [2]Also available as an Introductory Edition, which is a shortened version of the complete book, [3]Also available as an Introductory Edition, which is a shortened version of the complete book and also as a Comprehensive Edition, which is an extended version of the complete book

ESSENTIAL
Introduction to Computers
and How to Purchase, Install, and Maintain a Personal Computer

OBJECTIVES

After completing this material, you will be able to:

- Define the term computer and discuss the four basic computer operations: input, processing, output, and storage

- Define data and information

- Explain the principal components of the computer and their use

- Describe the use of floppy disks, hard disks, and other storage media

- Discuss computer software and explain the difference between system software and application software

- Identify several types of personal computer application software

- Discuss computer communications channels and equipment and the Internet and World Wide Web

- Explain how to purchase, install, and maintain a personal computer

- Define e-commerce

Everyday, computers impact how individuals work and how they live. The use of personal computers continues to increase and has made computing available to almost anyone. In addition, advances in communications technology allow people to use personal computers to access and send information easily and quickly to other computers and computer users. At home, at work, and in the field, computers are helping people to do their work faster, more accurately, and in some cases, in ways that previously would not have been possible.

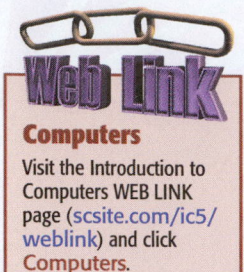

Computers

Visit the Introduction to Computers WEB LINK page (scsite.com/ic5/weblink) and click Computers.

WHAT IS A COMPUTER?

A **computer** is an electronic device, operating under the control of instructions stored in its own memory unit, that can accept data (input), manipulate the data according to specified rules (process), produce information (output) from the processing, and store the results for future use. Generally, the term is used to describe a collection of devices that function together as a system. An example of the devices that make up a personal computer is shown in Figure 1.

WHAT DOES A COMPUTER DO?

Whether small or large, computers can perform four general operations. These operations comprise the **information processing cycle** and are input, process, output, and storage. Collectively, these operations describe the procedures a computer performs to process data into information and store it for future use.

FIGURE 1 Common computer hardware components include a keyboard, mouse, microphone, scanner, digital camera, PC camera, printer, monitor, speakers, system unit, disk drives, card reader, and modem.

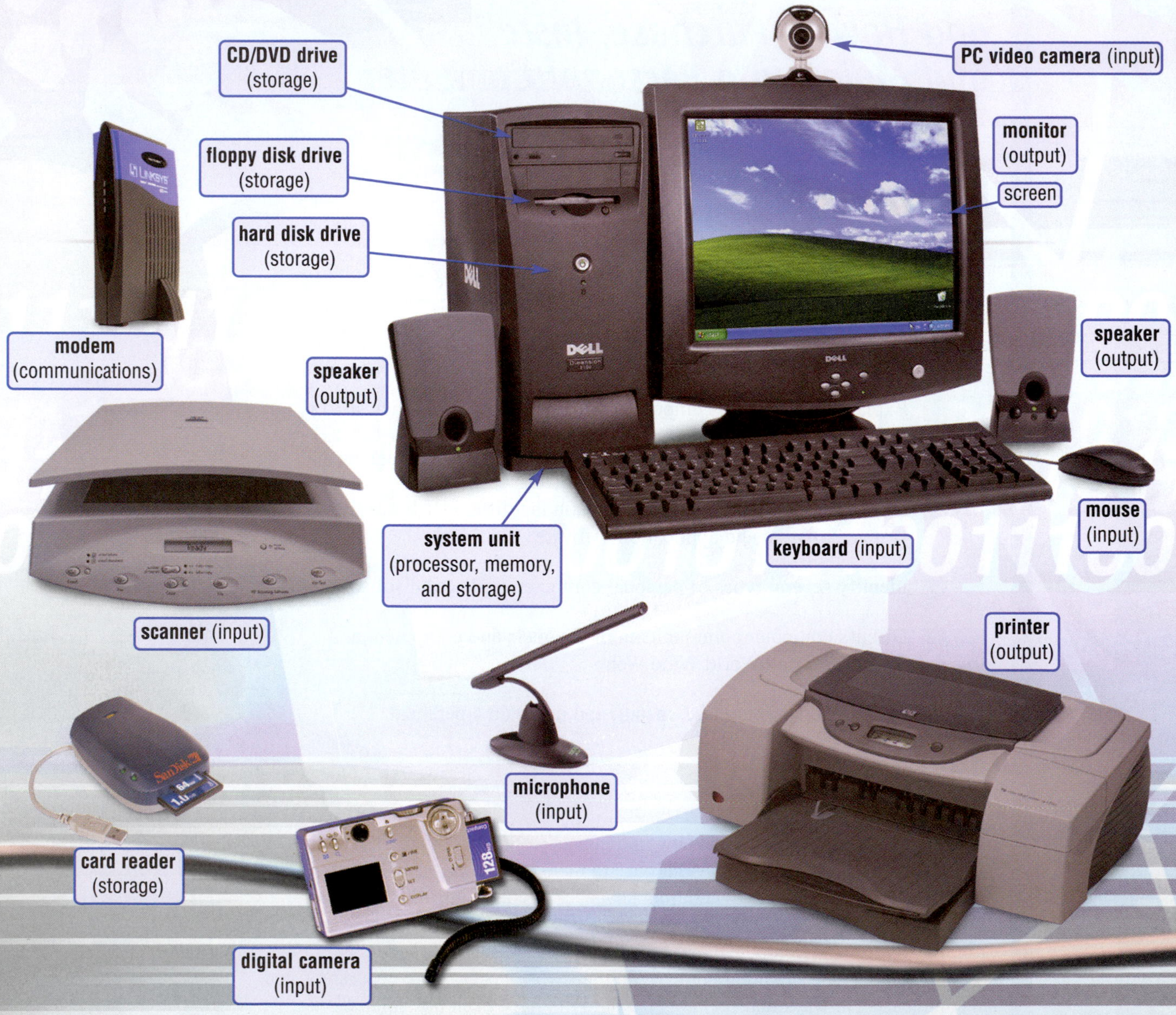

CD/DVD drive (storage)

floppy disk drive (storage)

hard disk drive (storage)

modem (communications)

speaker (output)

PC video camera (input)

monitor (output)

screen

speaker (output)

system unit (processor, memory, and storage)

keyboard (input)

mouse (input)

scanner (input)

printer (output)

card reader (storage)

microphone (input)

digital camera (input)

All computer processing requires **data**. Data is a collection of raw facts, figures, and symbols, such as numbers, words, images, video, and sounds, given to a computer during the input operation. Computers manipulate data to create information. **Information** is data that is organized, meaningful, and useful. During the output operation, the information that has been created is put into some form, such as a printed report, or it can be written to computer storage for future use. As shown in Figure 2, a computer processes several data items to produce a paycheck. Another example of information is a grade report, which is generated from data items such as a student name, course names, and course grades.

People who use the computer directly or use the information it provides are called **computer users**, **end users**, or sometimes, just **users**.

WHY IS A COMPUTER SO POWERFUL?

A computer derives its power from its capability to perform the information processing cycle with amazing speed, reliability (low failure rate), and accuracy; its capacity to store huge amounts of data and information; and its ability to communicate with other computers.

HOW DOES A COMPUTER KNOW WHAT TO DO?

For a computer to perform operations, it must be given a detailed set of instructions that tells it exactly what to do. These instructions are called a **computer program**, or **software**. Before processing for a specific job begins, the computer program corresponding to that job is stored in the computer. Once the program is stored, the computer can begin to operate by executing the program's first instruction. The computer executes one program instruction after another until the job is complete.

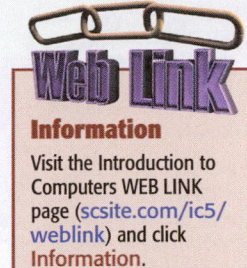

Information

Visit the Introduction to Computers WEB LINK page (scsite.com/ic5/weblink) and click **Information**.

Computer Programs

Visit the Introduction to Computers WEB LINK page (scsite.com/ic5/weblink) and click **Computer Programs**.

FIGURE 2 A computer processes data into information. In this example, the employee name, number of hours worked, and hourly pay rate each represent data. The computer processes these items to produce the desired information, in this case, a paycheck.

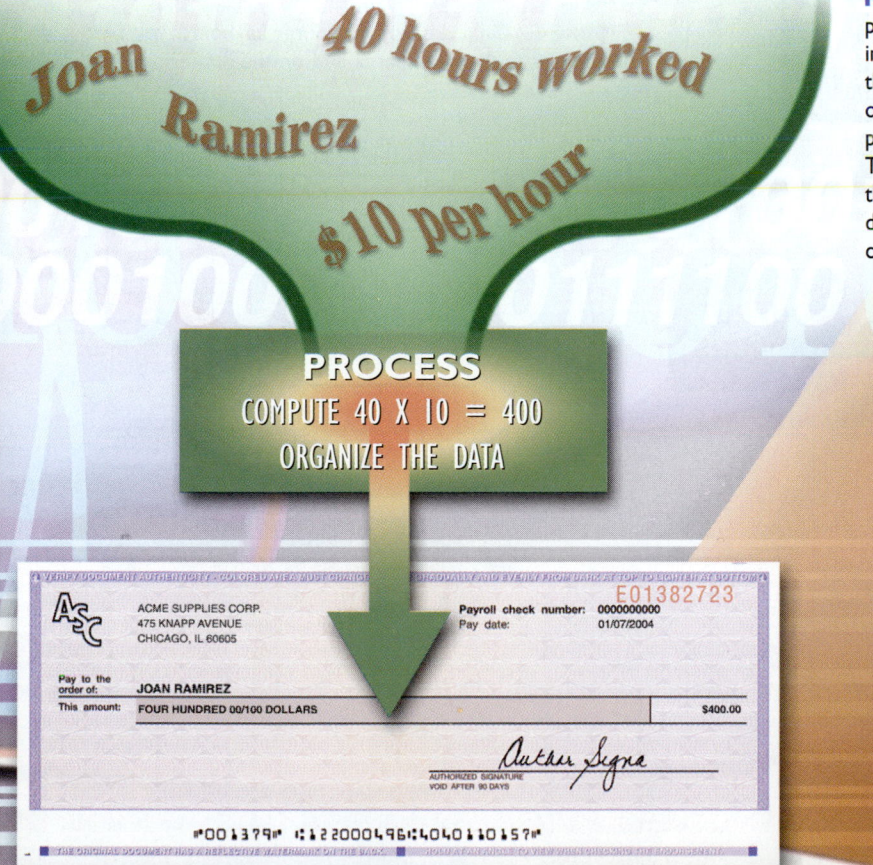

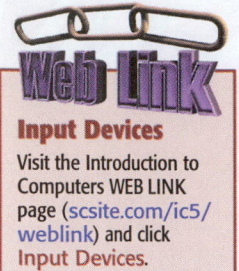

Input Devices

Visit the Introduction to Computers WEB LINK page (scsite.com/ic5/weblink) and click Input Devices.

WHAT ARE THE COMPONENTS OF A COMPUTER?

To understand how computers process data into information, you need to examine the primary components of the computer. The six primary components of a computer are input devices, the processor (control unit and arithmetic/logic unit), memory, output devices, storage devices, and communications devices. The processor, memory, and storage devices are housed in a box-like case called the **system unit**. Figure 3 shows the flow of data, information, and instructions between the first five components mentioned. The next six sections describe these primary components.

FIGURE 3 Most devices connected to the computer communicate with the processor to carry out a task. When a user starts a program, for example, its instructions transfer from a storage device to memory. Data needed by programs enters memory either from an input device or a storage device. The control unit interprets and executes instructions in memory and the ALU performs calculations on the data in memory. Resulting information is stored in memory, from which it can be sent to an output device or a storage device for future access, as needed.

INPUT DEVICES

An **input device** is any hardware component that allows you to enter data, programs, commands, and user responses into a computer. Depending on your particular application and requirement, the input device you use may vary. Popular input devices include the keyboard, mouse, digital camera, scanner, and microphone. The two primary input devices used are the keyboard and the mouse. This section discusses both of these input devices.

The Keyboard

A keyboard is an input device that contains keys you press to enter data into the computer. A desktop computer keyboard (Figure 4) typically has 101 to 105 keys. Keyboards for smaller computers, such as notebooks, contain fewer keys. A computer keyboard includes keys that allow you to type letters of the alphabet, numbers, spaces, punctuation marks, and other symbols such as the dollar sign ($) and asterisk (*). A keyboard also contains other keys that allow you to enter data and instructions into the computer.

FIGURE 4 On a desktop computer keyboard, you type using keys in the typing area and on the numeric keypad.

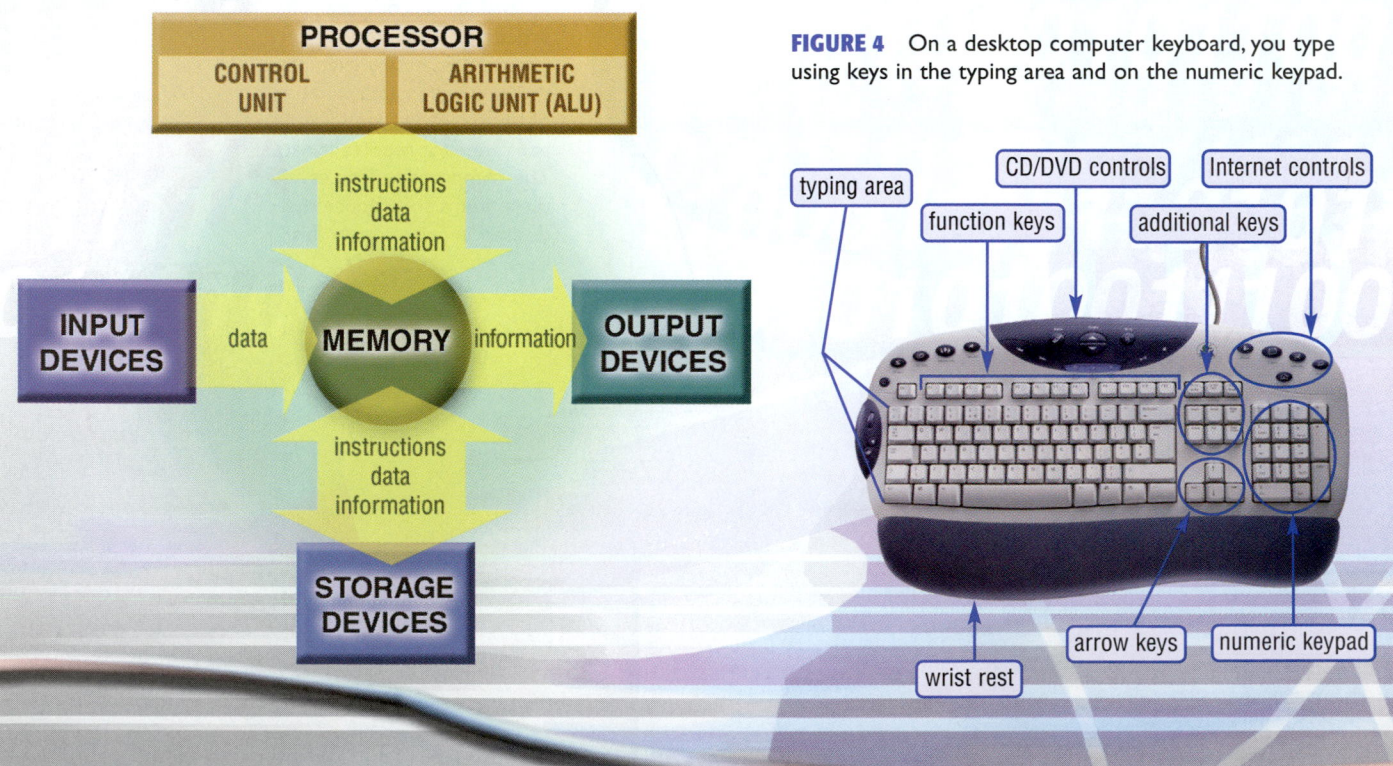

Most handheld computers (left in Figure 5) use an onscreen keyboard. With handheld computers, you use a stylus to select keys on the onscreen keyboard. A notebook computer (right in Figure 5) has the keyboard built into the top of the unit.

FIGURE 5 A handheld computer (left) employs an onscreen keyboard and stylus. A notebook computer (right) has the keyboard built into the unit.

The Mouse

A **mouse** (Figure 6) is a pointing device that fits comfortably under the palm of your hand. With a mouse, you control the movement of the **pointer**, often called the **mouse pointer**, on the screen and make selections from the screen. A mouse has one to five buttons. The bottom of a mouse is flat and contains a mechanism (optical sensor or ball) that detects movement of the mouse.

Notebook computers come with a pointing device built into the keyboard (Figure 7) so that you can select items on the screen without requiring additional desktop space.

FIGURE 7 Some notebook computers include a pointing device to allow a user to control the movement of the pointer.

FIGURE 6 This optical mouse uses an optical sensor. It also includes buttons to push with your thumb that enable forward and backward navigation through Web pages.

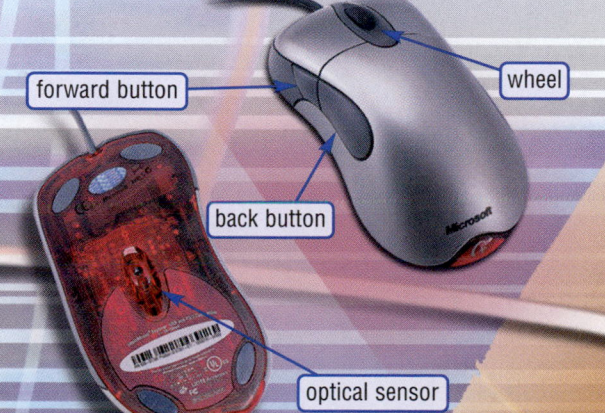

Processor

Visit the Introduction to Computers WEB LINK page (scsite.com/ic5/ weblink) and click Processor.

Memory

Visit the Introduction to Computers WEB LINK page (scsite.com/ic5/ weblink) and click Memory.

Output Devices

Visit the Introduction to Computers WEB LINK page (scsite.com/ic5/ weblink) and click Output Devices.

PROCESSOR

The **processor**, also called the **central processing unit** (**CPU**), interprets and carries out the basic instructions that operate a computer. The processor is made up of the control unit and arithmetic/logic unit (Figure 3 on page COM-4). The **control unit** interprets the instructions. The **arithmetic/logic unit** performs the logical and arithmetic processes. The personal computer processors shown in Figure 8 can fit in the palm of your hand. The high-end processors contain 42 million transistors and are capable of performing some operations 10 million times in a tenth of a second, or in the time it takes to blink your eye.

MEMORY

Memory, also called **random access memory**, or **RAM**, consists of electronic components that store instructions waiting to be executed by the processor, data needed by those instructions, and the results of processed data (information). Memory usually consists of one or more chips on the motherboard in the computer. The **motherboard** (Figure 9), sometimes

called a **system board**, is the main circuit board in the computer to which many electronic components are attached.

The amount of memory in computers typically is measured in kilobytes or megabytes. One **kilobyte** (**K or KB**) equals approximately 1,000 memory locations and one **megabyte** (**M or MB**) equals approximately one million memory locations. A **memory location**, or **byte**, usually stores one character. Therefore, a computer with 96 MB of memory can store approximately 96 million characters. One megabyte can hold approximately 500 pages of text information.

OUTPUT DEVICES

Output devices make the information resulting from processing available for use. The output from computers can be presented in many forms, such as a printed report or displaying it on a screen. When a computer is used for processing tasks such as word processing, spreadsheets, or database management, the two output devices more commonly used are the printer and a display device.

FIGURE 8 Less powerful personal computers have a Celeron processor. Higher-performance personal computers use Athlon XP and Pentium processors.

Celeron™

Athlon XP™

Pentium™

FIGURE 9 The motherboard is housed in the system unit of a desktop personal computer. It contains many electronic components, including adapter cards, a processor chip, memory chips, memory slots, and expansion slots. Memory slots hold memory cards (modules) and expansion slots hold adapter cards.

sound card

video card

modem card

network card

processor

memory chips

expansion slots for adapter cards

motherboard

memory slots

Printers

Printers used with computers can be either impact printers or nonimpact printers. An **impact printer** prints by striking an inked ribbon against the paper. One type of impact printer used with personal computers is the dot matrix printer (Figure 10).

Nonimpact printers, such as ink-jet printers (Figure 11) and laser printers (Figure 12), form characters by means other than striking a ribbon against paper. One advantage of using a nonimpact printer is that it can print higher-quality text and graphics than an impact printer, such as the dot matrix. Nonimpact printers also do a better job printing different fonts, are quieter, and can print in color. The popular and affordable ink-jet printer forms a character or graphic by using a nozzle that sprays drops of ink onto the page.

Ink-jet printers produce excellent images. The speed of an ink-jet printer is measured by the number of pages per minute (ppm) it can print. Most ink-jet printers print from three to nineteen pages per minute. Graphics and colors print at the slower rate.

Laser printers (Figure 12) work similarly to a copying machine by converting data from the computer into a beam of light that is focused on a photoconductor drum, forming the images to be printed. Laser printers produce high-quality black-and-white or color output and are used for applications that combine text and graphics such as desktop publishing. Laser printers for personal computers can cost from a few hundred dollars to several thousand dollars. The more expensive the laser printer, the more pages it can print per minute.

FIGURE 12 Laser printers are used with personal computers, as well as larger computers.

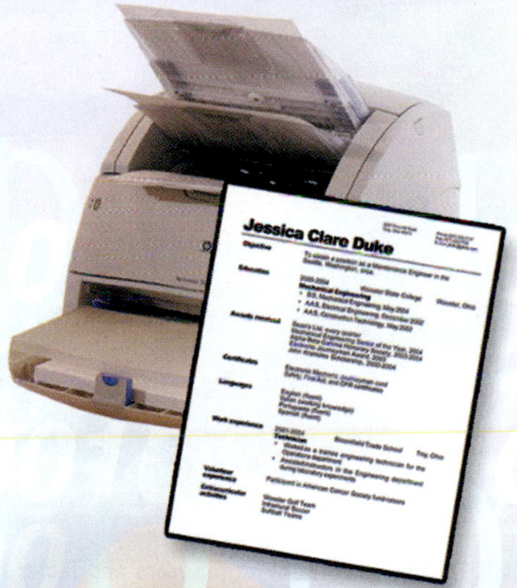

FIGURE 10 Dot matrix printers are capable of handling wide paper and printing multipart forms.

FIGURE 11 Ink-jet printers are the most popular type of printer used in the home.

Display Devices

A display device is an output device that visually conveys text, graphics, and video information. A **monitor** is a plastic or metal case that houses a display device. There are two basic types of monitors, CRT and LCD. The television-like **CRT (cathode ray tube)** monitor shown on the left in Figure 13 is the most common display device used with desktop computers. The **LCD monitor**, also called a **flat panel monitor**, shown on the right in Figure 13 uses a liquid display crystal, similar to a digital watch, to produce images on the screen. The flat panel monitor, although more expensive than the CRT monitor, takes up much less desk space. The surface of the screen of either a CRT monitor or LCD monitor is composed of individual picture elements called **pixels**. A screen set to a resolution of 800 x 600 pixels has a total of 480,000 pixels. Each pixel can be illuminated to form parts of a character or graphic shape on the screen.

Mobile computers, such as notebook computers and Tablet PCs, and mobile devices, such as PDAs and smart phones, have LCD screens (Figure 14).

FIGURE 13 The CRT monitor (left) and flat panel monitor (right) are used with desktop computers. The flat panel monitor is much thinner and weighs less than a CRT monitor.

FIGURE 14 Notebook computers and Tablet PCs have color LCD screens. Some PDAs have color displays and a few smart phones even have color displays.

STORAGE DEVICES

Storage devices are used to store instructions, data, and information when they are not being used in memory. Six common types of storage devices are floppy disks, zip disks, optical discs, tape, and miniature storage media. Figure 15 shows how different types of storage media and memory compare in terms of relative speeds and uses.

Floppy Disks

A **floppy disk**, or **diskette**, is a portable, inexpensive storage medium that consists of a thin, circular, flexible plastic disk with a magnetic coating enclosed in a square-shaped plastic shell (Figure 16). The most widely used floppy disk is 3.5 inches wide and typically can store up to 1.44 megabytes of data or 1,474,560 characters. Although the exterior of the 3.5-inch disk is not floppy, users still refer to them as floppy disks.

A floppy disk is a **portable storage medium**. When discussing a storage medium, the term portable means you can remove the medium from one computer and carry it to another computer. For example, you can insert a floppy disk into and remove it from a floppy disk drive on many types of computers (Figure 17). A **floppy disk drive** is a device that can read from and write to a floppy disk.

FIGURE 16 In a 3.5-inch floppy disk, a thin, circular, flexible Mylar film is enclosed between two liners. A piece of metal called a shutter covers an opening to the recording surface in the rigid plastic shell.

FIGURE 15 A comparison of different types of storage media and memory in terms of relative speed and uses. Memory is faster than storage, but is expensive and not practical for all storage requirements. Storage is less expensive than memory.

		Stores...
Primary Storage	Memory (most RAM)	Items waiting to be interpreted and executed by the processor
Secondary Storage	Hard Disk	Operating system, application software, user data and information
	CDs and DVDs	Software, backups, movies, music
	Miniature Storage Media	Digital pictures or small files to be transported
	Tape	Backups
	Floppy Disk	Small files to be transported

faster transfer rates ↑

slower access times ↓

FIGURE 17 On a personal computer, you insert and remove a floppy disk from a floppy disk drive.

FIGURE 17a (floppy disk drive built into a desktop computer)

FIGURE 17b (external floppy disk drive attaches to computer with cable)

A floppy disk is a type of magnetic disk, which means it uses magnetic patterns to store items such as data, instructions, and information on the disk's surface. Most magnetic disks are read/write storage media; that is, you can access (read) data from and place (write) data on a magnetic disk any number of times, just as you can with an audiocassette tape. Most floppy disks that you purchase are already formatted. If they are not formatted, then before you can write on a new floppy disk, it must be formatted.

Formatting is the process of preparing a disk (floppy disk or hard disk) for reading and writing by organizing the disk into storage locations called tracks and sectors (Figure 18). A **track** is a narrow recording band that forms a full circle on the surface of the disk. The disk's storage locations then are divided into pie-shaped sections, which break the tracks into small arcs called sectors. A **sector** is capable of holding 512 bytes of data. A typical floppy disk stores data on both sides and has 80 tracks on each side of the recording surface with 18 sectors per track.

Data stored in sectors on a floppy disk must be retrieved and placed into memory to be processed. The time required to access and retrieve data is called the **access time**. The access time for floppy disks varies from about 175 milliseconds (one millisecond equals 1/1000 of a second) to approximately 300 milliseconds. On average, data stored in a single sector on a floppy disk can be retrieved in approximately 1/15 to 1/3 of a second.

Zip Disks

A **Zip disk** is a type of portable magnetic media that can store up to 750 MB of data. Zip disks can be built-in to the system unit or it can be external (Figure 19). The Zip disk can hold about 500 times more than a standard floppy disk. These large capacities make it easy to transport many files or large items such as graphics, audio, or video files. Another popular use of Zip disks is to back up important data and information. A **backup** is a duplicate of a file, program, or disk that you can use in case the original is lost, damaged, or destroyed.

Hard Disks

Another form of storage is a hard disk. A **hard disk** (Figure 20) consists of one or more rigid metal platters coated with a metal oxide material that allows data to be recorded magnetically. Although hard disks are available in removable cartridge form, most disks cannot be removed from the computer. As with floppy disks, the data on hard disks is recorded on a series of tracks. The tracks are divided into sectors when the disk is formatted.

Web Link

Hard Disks

Visit the Introduction to Computers WEB LINK page (scsite.com/ic5/weblink) and click Hard Disks.

FIGURE 19   An external Zip drive has a cable that plugs into a port on a system unit.

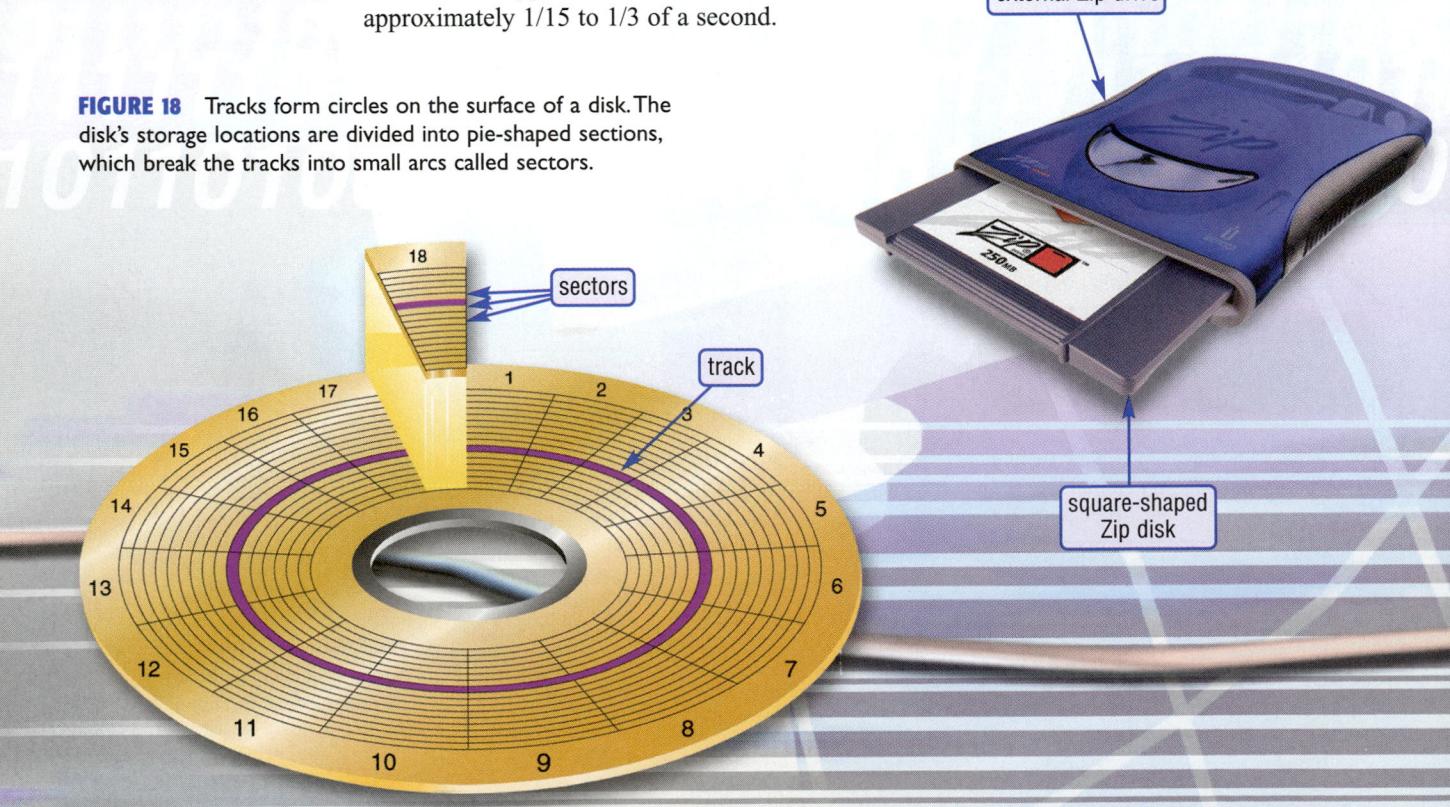

external Zip drive

square-shaped Zip disk

FIGURE 18   Tracks form circles on the surface of a disk. The disk's storage locations are divided into pie-shaped sections, which break the tracks into small arcs called sectors.

sectors

track

The hard disk platters spin at a high rate of speed, typically 5,400 to 7,200 revolutions per minute. When reading data from the disk, the read head senses the magnetic spots that are recorded on the disk along the various tracks and transfers that data to memory. When writing, the data is transferred from memory and is stored as magnetic spots on the tracks on the recording surface of one or more of the disk platters. When reading or writing, the read/write heads on a hard disk drive do not actually touch the surface of the disk.

The number of platters permanently mounted on the spindle of a hard disk varies. On most drives, each surface of the platter can be used to store data. Thus, if a hard disk drive uses one platter, two surfaces are available for data. If the drive uses two platters, four sets of read/write heads read and record data from the four surfaces. Storage capacities of internally mounted fixed disks for personal computers range from one billion characters to more than 200 billion characters. One billion bytes are called a **gigabyte** (**GB**). Typical hard disk sizes range from 40 GB to 200 GB.

Optical Discs

An **optical disc** is a storage medium that consists of a flat, round, portable, metal storage medium that usually is 4.75 inches in diameter and less than 1/20 of an inch thick. Two types of optical discs are CD and DVD. Just about every desktop computer and notebook computer includes some type of compact disc drive installed in a drive bay. Many computers come with both a CD and DVD drive. These drives read compact discs, including audio discs.

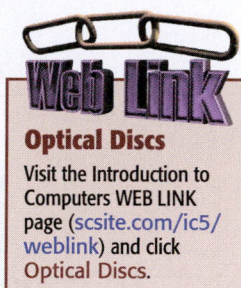

Web Link

Optical Discs
Visit the Introduction to Computers WEB LINK page (scsite.com/ic5/ weblink) and click Optical Discs.

FIGURE 20 The hard disk in a desktop computer is enclosed inside an airtight, sealed case inside the system unit.

hard disk installed in system unit

On a CD or DVD drive, you push a button to slide out a tray, insert your compact disc with the label side up, and then push the same button to close the tray (Figure 21). Other convenient features on most of these drives include a volume control button and a headphone jack so you can use stereo headphones to listen to audio without disturbing others nearby.

Compact discs are available in a variety of formats, including CD-ROM, CD-R, CD-RW, DVD-ROM, and DVD+RW.

CD-ROMs

A **CD-ROM** (pronounced SEE-DEE-rom), or **compact disc read-only memory**, is a type of optical disc that uses the same laser technology as audio CDs for recording music. In addition to audio, a CD-ROM can contain text, graphics, and video. The manufacturer writes, or records, the contents of standard CD-ROMs. You can only read the contents of these discs. That is, you cannot erase or modify their contents — hence the name read-only.

A typical CD-ROM holds from 650 MB to 1 GB of data, instructions, and information. This is 450 to 700 times more than you can store on a 3.5-inch floppy disk.

CD-R and CD-RW

A **CD-R** (**compact disc-recordable**) is a multisession optical disc onto which you can record your own items such as text, graphics, and audio. With a CD-R, you can write on part of the disc at one time and another part at a later time. Once you have recorded the CD-R, you can read from it as many times as you wish. You can write on each part only one time, and you cannot erase the disc's contents. Most CD-ROM drives can read a CD-R.

A **CD-RW** (**compact disc-rewritable**) is an erasable disc you can write on multiple times. Originally called an erasable CD (CD-E), a CD-RW overcomes the major disadvantage of CD-R discs, which is that you can write on them only once. With CD-RWs, the disc acts like a floppy or hard disk, allowing you to write and rewrite data, instructions, and information onto it multiple times.

DVDs

Although CDs have huge storage capacities, even a CD is not large enough for many of today's complex programs. Some software, for example, is sold on five or more CDs. To meet these tremendous storage requirements, some software companies have moved from CDs to the larger DVD — a technology that can be used to store large amounts of text and even cinema-like videos (Figure 22).

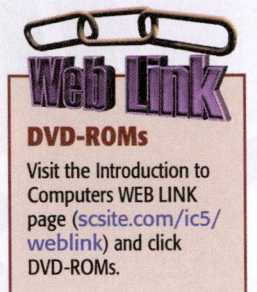

DVD-ROMs

Visit the Introduction to Computers WEB LINK page (scsite.com/ic5/weblink) and click DVD-ROMs.

FIGURE 21 On CD and DVD drives, you push a button to slide out a tray, insert the disc with the label side up, and then push the same button to close the tray.

headphone port (or jack)

volume control

Push the button to slide out the tray.

Insert the disc, label side up.

Push the same button to close the tray.

DVD-ROM

DVD drive

FIGURE 22 A DVD is an extremely high capacity optical disc.

A **DVD-ROM (digital video disc-ROM)** is a very high capacity optical disc capable of storing from 4.7 GB to 17 GB — more than enough to hold a telephone book containing every resident in the United States. As with the CD-ROM format, you cannot write to an optical disc that uses the DVD-ROM format. You can only read from it.

With optical discs that use the **DVD+RW (DVD-rewriteable)** format, a user can erase and record more than a 1,000 times. One major use of the high-capacity DVD+RW format is the ability to edit videos read from a video camera or VCR, stored and edited on your computer, and then written to a DVD+RW disc.

Tape

Tape is a magnetically coated ribbon of plastic housed in a tape cartridge (Figure 23) capable of storing large amounts of data and information at a low cost. A tape drive is used to read from and write to a tape. Tape is primarily used for long-term storage and backup.

Miniature Storage Media

Miniature storage media is rewritable media usually in the form of a flash memory card. Flash memory cards are solid-state devices, which means they consist entirely of electronics (chips, wires, etc.) and contain no moving parts. Miniature storage media (Figure 24) is the primary storage used with PDAs, digital cameras, music players, and smart phones to store digital images, music, or documents.

FIGURE 24 Digital cameras, music players, PDAs, smart phones, and notebook computers use miniature mobile storage media.

Web Link

Flash Memory Cards

Visit the Introduction to Computers WEB LINK page (scsite.com/ic5/weblink) and click Flash Memory Cards.

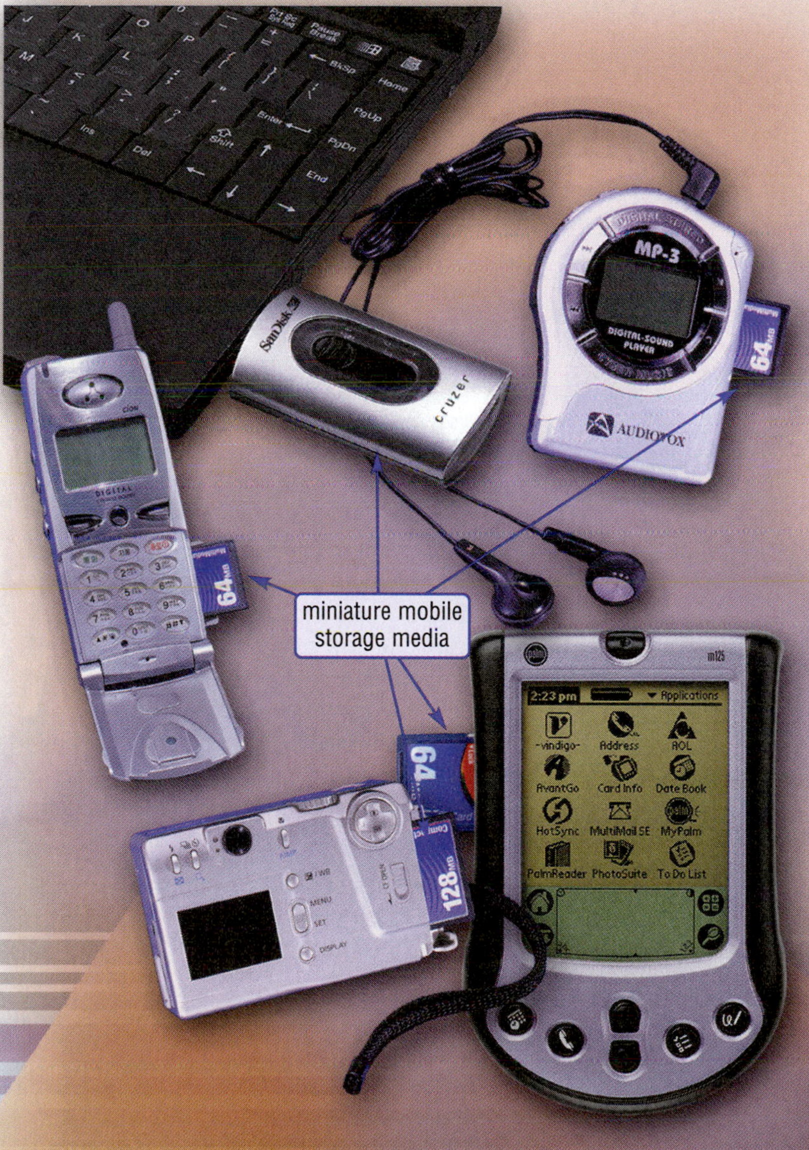

FIGURE 23 A tape cartridge and a tape drive.

miniature mobile storage media

COMMUNICATIONS DEVICES

A **communications device** is a hardware component that enables a computer to send (transmit) and receive data, instructions, and information to and from one or more computers. A widely used communication device is the modem (Figure 1 on page COM-2).

Communications occur over **transmission media**, such as cables, telephone lines, cellular radio networks, and satellites. Some transmission media, such as satellites and cellular radio networks, are wireless, which means they have no physical lines or wires. People around the world use computers and communications devices to communicate with each other using one or more transmission media.

COMPUTER SOFTWARE

Computer software is the key to productive use of computers. With the correct software, a computer can become a valuable tool. Software can be categorized into two types: system software and application software.

System Software

System software consists of programs to control the operations of computer equipment. An important part of system software is a set of programs called the operating system. Instructions in the **operating system** tell the computer how to perform the functions of loading, storing, and executing an application program and how to transfer data. For a computer to operate, an operating system must be stored in the computer's memory. When a computer is turned on, the operating system is loaded into the computer's memory from auxiliary storage. This process is called **booting**.

Today, most computers use an operating system that has a **graphical user interface (GUI)** that provides visual cues such as icon symbols to help the user. Each icon represents an application such as word processing, or a file or document where data is stored. Microsoft Windows (Figure 25) is a widely used graphical operating system. Apple Macintosh computers also have a graphical user interface operating system.

Application Software

Application software consists of programs that tell a computer how to produce information. Some widely used application software includes personal information manager, project management, accounting, computer-aided design, desktop publishing, paint/image editing, audio and video editing, multimedia authoring, Web page authoring, personal finance, legal, tax preparation, home design/landscaping, educational, reference, and entertainment (games, simulations, etc.). As shown in Figure 26, you often purchase application software from a store that sells computer products.

Personal computer users often use application software. Some of the more commonly used applications are word processing, electronic spreadsheet, presentation graphics, database, communications, and electronic mail software. Some software packages, such as Microsoft Office, also include access to the World Wide Web as an integral part of the application.

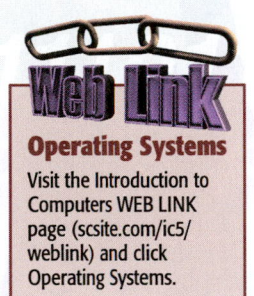

Web Link

Operating Systems

Visit the Introduction to Computers WEB LINK page (scsite.com/ic5/weblink) and click Operating Systems.

FIGURE 25 A graphical user interface such as Microsoft Windows makes the computer easier to use. The small pictures, or symbols, on the screen are called icons. Icons represent a program or data the user can choose. A window is a rectangular area of the screen that is used to display a program, data, and/or information.

Word Processing

Word processing software (Figure 27) is used to create, edit, format, and print documents. A key advantage of word processing software is that users easily can make changes in documents, such as correcting spelling, changing margins, and adding, deleting, or relocating entire paragraphs. These changes would be difficult and time consuming to make using manual methods such as a typewriter. With a word processor, documents can be printed quickly and accurately and easily stored on a disk for future use. Word processing software is oriented toward working with text, but most word processing packages also can include numeric and graphic information.

Spreadsheet

Electronic spreadsheet software (Figure 28) allows the user to add, subtract, and perform user-defined calculations on rows and columns of numbers. These numbers can be changed, and the spreadsheet quickly recalculates the new results. Electronic spreadsheet software eliminates the tedious recalculations required with manual methods. Spreadsheet information frequently is converted into a graphic form, such as charts. Graphics capabilities now are included in most spreadsheet packages.

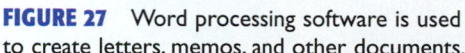

FIGURE 27 Word processing software is used to create letters, memos, and other documents.

FIGURE 26 Stores that sell computer products have shelves stocked with software for sale.

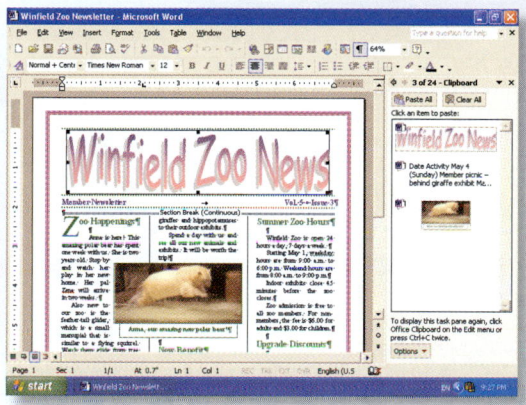

FIGURE 28 Electronic Spreadsheet software frequently is used by people who work with numbers. The user enters the data and the formulas to be used on the data, and the computer calculates the results.

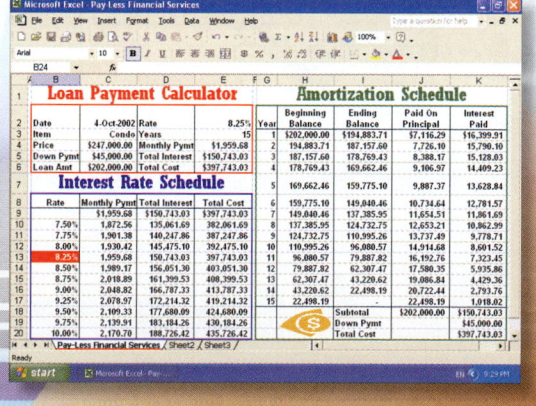

Word Processing Software

Visit the Introduction to Computers WEB LINK page (scsite.com/ic5/weblink) and click Word Processing Software.

Spreadsheet Software

Visit the Introduction to Computers WEB LINK page (scsite.com/ic5/weblink) and click Spreadsheet Software.

Web Link

Database Software

Visit the Introduction to Computers WEB LINK page (scsite.com/ic5/weblink) and click Database Software.

Web Link

Presentation Graphics Software

Visit the Introduction to Computers WEB LINK page (scsite.com/ic5/weblink) and click Presentation Graphics Software.

Database Database software (Figure 29) allows the user to enter, retrieve, and update data in an organized and efficient manner. These software packages have flexible inquiry and reporting capabilities that let users access the data in different ways and create custom reports that include some or all of the information in the database.

Presentation Graphics Presentation graphics software (Figure 30) allows the user to create documents called slides to be used in making presentations. Using special projection devices, the slides are projected directly from the computer.

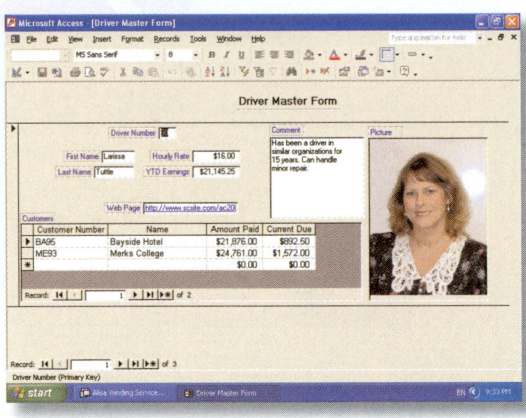

FIGURE 29 Database software allows the user to enter, retrieve, and update data in an organized and efficient manner.

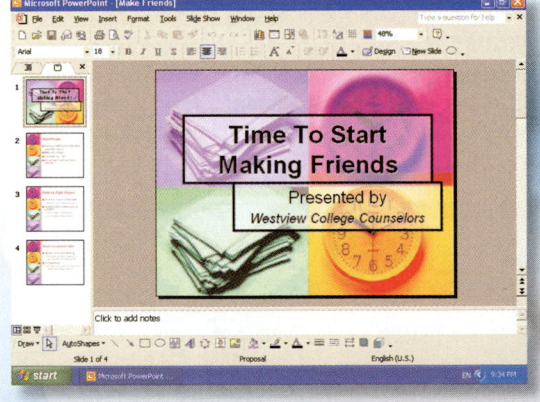

FIGURE 30 Presentation graphics software allows the user to create documents called slides for use in presentations.

NETWORKS AND THE INTERNET

A **network** is a collection of computers and devices connected via communications media and devices such as cables, telephone lines, modems, or other means.

Computers are networked together so users can share resources, such as hardware devices, software programs, data, and information. Sharing resources saves time and money. For example, instead of purchasing one printer for every computer in a company, the firm can connect a single printer and all computers via a network (Figure 31); the network enables all of the computers to access the same printer.

Most business computers are networked together. These networks can be relatively small or quite extensive. A network that connects computers in a limited geographic area, such as a school computer laboratory, office, or group of buildings, is called a **local area network** (**LAN**). A network that covers a large geographical area, such as one that connects the district offices of a national corporation, is called a **wide area network** (**WAN**) (Figure 32).

FIGURE 31 This local area network (LAN) enables two or more separate computers to share the same printer.

client   client

printer   server

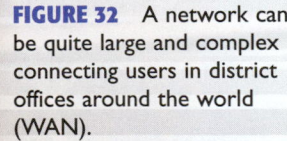

FIGURE 32 A network can be quite large and complex connecting users in district offices around the world (WAN).

The Internet

The world's largest network is the **Internet**, which is a worldwide collection of networks that links together millions of computers by means of modems, telephone lines, cables, and other communications devices and media. With an abundance of resources and data accessible via the Internet, more than 600 million users around the world are making use of the Internet for a variety of reasons (Figure 33). Some of these reasons include the following:

- Sending messages to other connected users (e-mail)

- Accessing a wealth of information, such as news, maps, airline schedules, and stock market data

- Shopping for goods and services

- Meeting or conversing with people around the world

- Accessing sources of entertainment and leisure, such as online games, magazines, and vacation planning guides

Most users connect to the Internet in one of two ways: through an Internet service provider or through an online service provider. An **Internet service provider** (**ISP**) is an organization that supplies connections to the Internet for a monthly fee. Like an ISP, an **online service provider** (**OSP**) provides access to the Internet, but it also provides a variety of other specialized content and services such as financial data, hardware and software guides, news, weather, legal information, and other similar commodities. For this reason, the fees for using an online service usually are slightly higher than fees for using an ISP. Two popular online services are America Online and The Microsoft Network.

The World Wide Web

One of the more popular segments of the Internet is the **World Wide Web**, also called the **Web**, which contains billions of documents called Web pages. A **Web page** is a document that contains text, graphics, sound, and/or video, and has built-in connections, or hyperlinks, to other Web documents. Web pages are stored on computers throughout the world. A **Web site** is a related collection of Web pages. You access and view Web pages using a software program called a **Web browser**. A Web page has a unique address, called a **Uniform Resource Locator** (**URL**).

Internet
Visit the Introduction to Computers WEB LINK page (scsite.com/ic5/weblink) and click Internet.

FIGURE 33 Users access the Internet for a variety of reasons: to send messages to other connected users, to access a wealth of information, to shop for goods and services, to meet or converse with people around the world, and for entertainment.

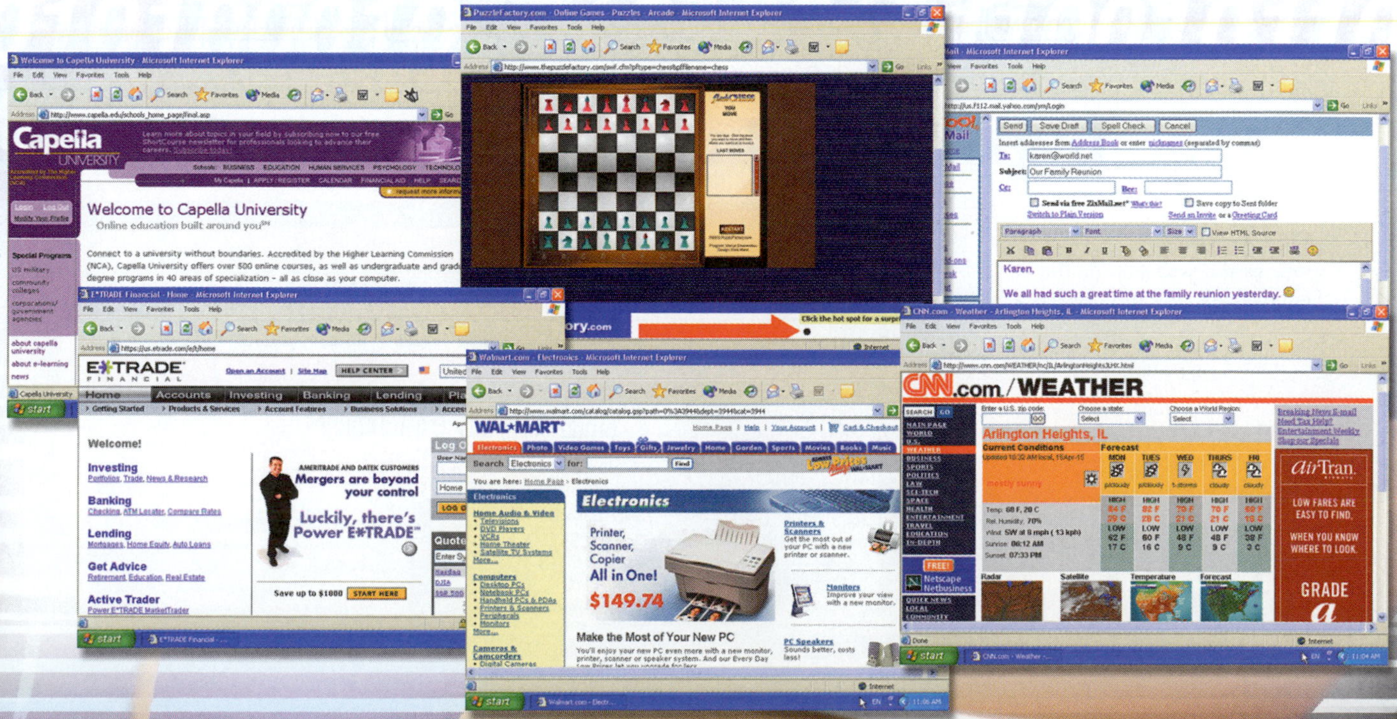

World Wide Web

Visit the Introduction to Computers WEB LINK page (scsite.com/ic5/weblink) and click World Wide Web.

E-Commerce

Visit the Introduction to Computers WEB LINK page (scsite.com/ic5/weblink) and click E-Commerce.

As shown in Figure 34, a URL consists of a protocol, domain name, and sometimes the path to a specific Web page or location in a Web page. Most Web page URLs begin with **http://**, which stands for hypertext transfer protocol, the communications standard used to transfer pages on the Web. The domain name identifies the Web site, which is stored on a Web server. A **Web server** is a computer that delivers (serves) requested Web pages.

Electronic Commerce

When you conduct business activities online, you are participating in **electronic commerce**, also known as **e-commerce**. These commercial activities include shopping, investing, and any other venture that represents a business transaction. Today, three types of e-commerce exist: business to consumer, consumer to consumer, and business to business. **Business to consumer (B2C)** involves the sale of goods to the general public. **Consumer to consumer (C2C)** involves one consumer selling directly to another. **Business to business (B2B)** provides goods and services to other businesses.

FIGURE 34   One method of connecting to the Web and displaying a Web page.

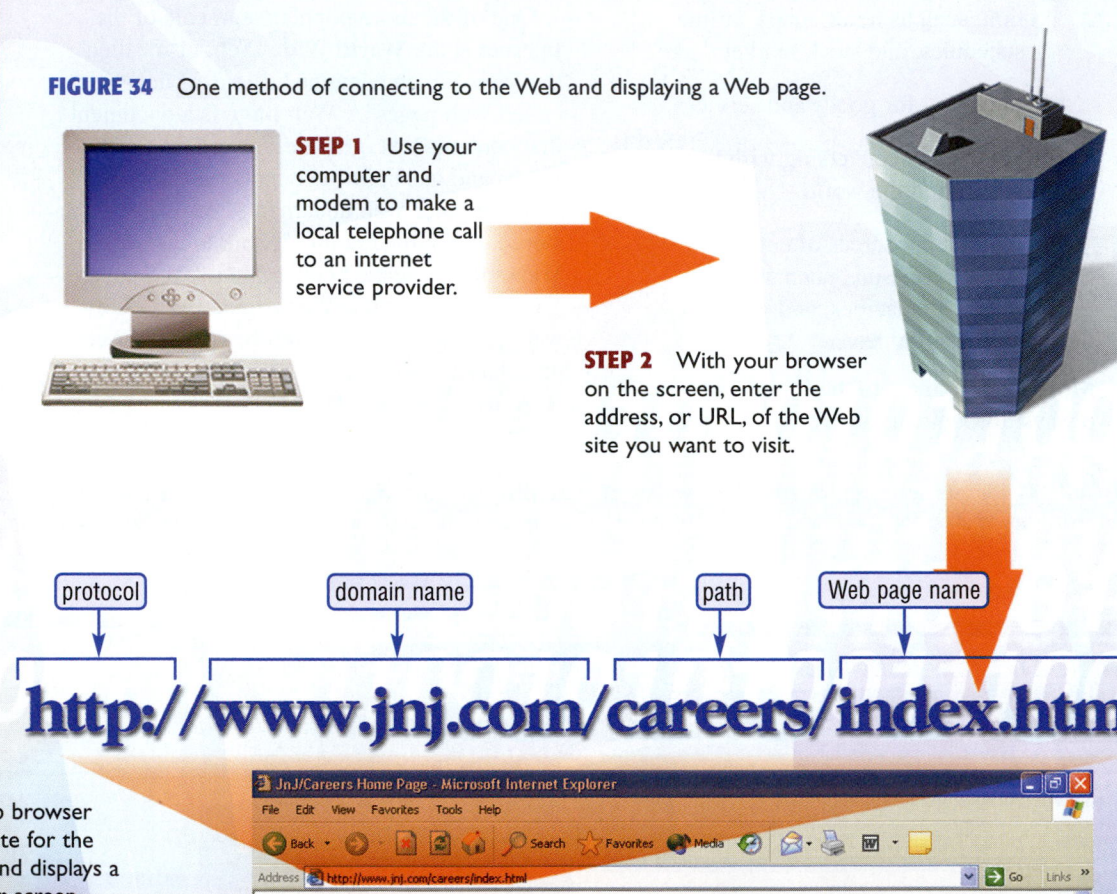

STEP 1   Use your computer and modem to make a local telephone call to an internet service provider.

STEP 2   With your browser on the screen, enter the address, or URL, of the Web site you want to visit.

| protocol | domain name | path | Web page name |

http://www.jnj.com/careers/index.html

STEP 3   The Web browser locates the web site for the entered address and displays a Web page on your screen.

How to Purchase, Install, and Maintain a Personal Computer

At some point, perhaps while you are taking this course, you may decide to buy a personal computer. The decision is an important one, which will require an investment of both time and money. As with many buyers, you may have little computer experience and find yourself unsure of how to proceed. You can get started by talking to your friends, coworkers, and instructors about their computers. What type of computers did they buy? Why? For what purposes do they use their computers? You also should answer the following four questions to help narrow your choices to a specific computer type, before reading the Buyer's Guide guidelines for purchasing a desktop computer, notebook computer, Tablet PC, or PDA.

Do you want a desktop or mobile computer?

A desktop computer (Figure 35a) is designed as a stationary device that sits on or below a desk or table in a location such as a home, office, or dormitory room. A desktop computer must be plugged into an electrical outlet to operate. A mobile computer or device, such as a notebook computer (Figure 35b), Tablet PC (Figure 35c), and PDA (Figure 35d), is smaller, more portable, and has a battery that allows you to operate it for a period without an electrical outlet.

Desktop computers are a good option if you work mostly in one place and have plenty of space in your work area. Desktop computers generally give you more performance for your money and are easier to upgrade than mobile computers.

Increasingly, more desktop computer users are buying notebook computers to take advantage of their portability to work in the library, while traveling, and at home. The past disadvantages of notebook computers, such as lower processor speeds, poor-quality monitors, weight, short battery life, and significantly higher prices, have all but disappeared when compared with desktop computers.

If you are thinking of using a mobile computer to take notes in class or in business meetings, then consider a Tablet PC with handwriting and drawing capabilities. Typically, note-taking involves writing text notes and drawing charts, schematics, and other illustrations. By allowing you to write and draw directly on the screen with a digital pen, a Tablet PC eliminates the distracting sound of the notebook keyboard tapping and allows you to capture drawings. Some notebook computers can convert to Tablet PCs.

FIGURE 35

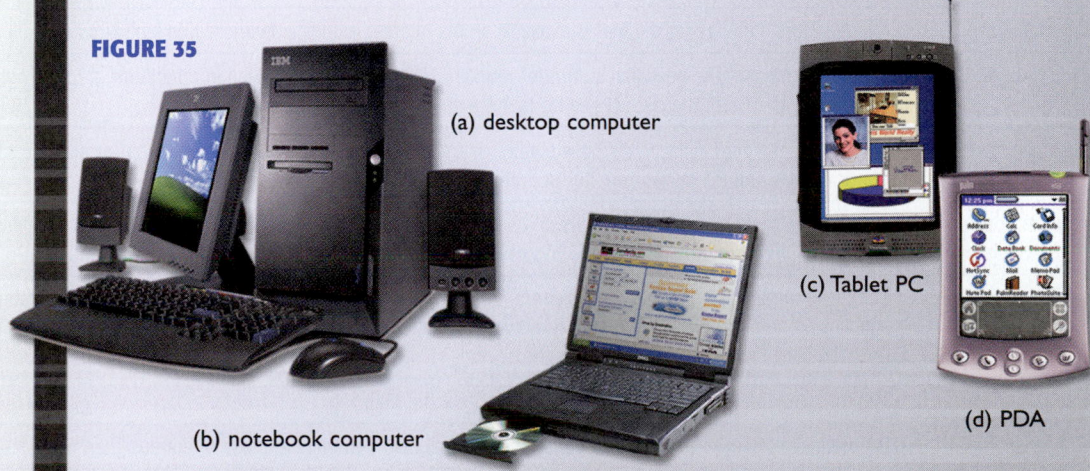

(a) desktop computer

(b) notebook computer

(c) Tablet PC

(d) PDA

A PDA (Personal Digital Assistant) is a lightweight mobile device that easily fits in your pocket, which makes it ideal if you require a mobile computing device as you move from place to place. PDAs provide personal organizer functions, such as a calendar, appointment book, address book, and thousands of other applications. Some PDAs also function as a cellular telephone. The small size of the processor, screen, and keyboard, however, limit a PDA's capabilities when compared with a desktop or notebook computer. For this reason, most people who purchase PDAs also have a desktop or notebook computer to handle heavy-duty applications.

Drawbacks of mobile computers and devices are that they tend to have a shorter useful lifetime than desktop computers, cost more than desktop computers, and lack the high-end capabilities. Their portability makes them susceptible to vibrations, heat or cold, and accidental drops, which can cause components such as hard disks or monitors to fail. Also, because of their size and portability, they are easy to lose and are the prime targets of thieves.

For what purposes will you use the computer?

Having a general idea of the purposes for which you want to use your computer will help you decide on the type of computer to buy. At this point in your research, it is not necessary to know the exact application software titles or version numbers you might want to use. Knowing that you plan to use the computer primarily to create word processing, spreadsheet, database, and presentation documents, however, will point you in the direction of a desktop or notebook computer. If you plan to use a mobile device to get organized, then a PDA may be your best choice. If you want the portability of a PDA, but need more computing power, then a Tablet PC may

be the best alternative. You also must consider that some application software runs only on a Mac, while others run only on a PC with the Windows operating system. Still other software may run only on a PC running the UNIX or Linux operating system.

Should the computer be compatible with the computers at school or work?

If you plan to bring work home, telecommute, or take distance education courses, then you should purchase a computer that is compatible with those at school or work. Compatibility is primarily a software issue. If your computer runs the same operating system version, such as Windows XP, and the same application software, such as Office XP, then your computer will be able to read documents created at school or work and vice versa. Incompatible hardware can become an issue if you plan to connect directly to a school or office network using a cable or wireless technology. You usually can obtain the minimum system requirements from the Information Technology department at your school or workplace.

Should the computer be a Mac or PC?

If you ask a friend, coworker, or instructor, which is better — a Mac or a PC — you may be surprised by the strong opinion expressed in the response. No other topic in the computer industry causes more heated debate. The Mac has strengths, especially in the areas of graphics, movies, photos, and music. The PC, however, has become the industry standard with 95 percent of the market share. Figure 36 compares features of the Mac and PC in several different areas. Overall, the Mac and PC have more similarities than differences, and you should consider cost, compatibility, and other factors when choosing whether to purchase a Mac or PC.

FIGURE 36 Comparison of Mac and PC features.

Area	Comparison
Cost and availability	A Mac has slightly higher prices than a PC. Mac peripherals also are more expensive. The PC offers more available models from a wide range of vendors. You can custom build, upgrade, and expand a PC for less money than a Mac.
Exterior design	The Mac has a more distinct and stylish appearance than most PCs.
Free software	Although free software for the Mac is available on the Internet, significantly more free software applications are available for the PC.
Market share	The PC dominates the personal computer market. While the Mac sells well in education, publishing, Web design, graphics, and music, the PC is the overwhelming favorite of businesses.
Operating system	Both Mac OS X and Windows XP are stable. Users claim that Mac OS X provides a better all-around user experience than Windows XP. The PC supports other operating systems, such as Linux and UNIX.
Program control	Both have simple and intuitive graphical user interfaces. The Mac relies more on the mouse and less on keyboard shortcuts than the PC. The mouse on the Mac has one button, whereas the mouse on a PC has a minimum of two buttons.
Software availability	The basic application software most users require, such as the Office suite, is available for both the Mac and PC. More specialized software, however, often is only available for PCs. Many programs are released for PCs long before they are released for Macs.
Speed	The PC has faster processors to choose from than the Mac.
Viruses	Dramatically fewer viruses attack Macs. Mac viruses also generally are less infectious than PC viruses.

After evaluating the answers to these four questions, you should have a general idea of how you plan to use your computer and the type of computer you want to buy. Once you have decided on the type of computer you want, you can follow the guidelines presented in this Buyer's Guide to help you purchase a specific computer of that type, along with software, peripherals, and other accessories.

This first set of guidelines will help you purchase, install, and maintain a desktop computer. Many of the guidelines presented also apply to the purchase of a mobile computer or device, such as a notebook computer, Tablet PC, and PDA. Later in this special feature, sections on purchasing a notebook computer, PDA, or Tablet PC address additional considerations specific to those computer types.

HOW TO PURCHASE A DESKTOP COMPUTER

Once you have decided that a desktop computer is most suited to your computing needs, the next step is to determine specific software, hardware, peripheral devices, and services to purchase, as well as where to buy the computer.

Determine the specific software you want to use on your computer.

Before deciding to purchase a particular program, be sure it contains the features necessary for the tasks you want to perform. Rely on the computer users in whom you have confidence to help you decide on the software to use. The minimum requirements of the application software you select may determine the operating system (Windows XP, Linux, UNIX, Mac OS X) you need. If you have decided to use a particular operating system that does not support application software you want to use, you may be able to purchase the similar application software from other manufacturers.

Many Web sites and trade magazines, such as those listed in Figure 37, provide reviews of software products. These Web sites frequently have articles that rate computers and software on cost, performance, and support.

Your hardware requirements depend on the minimum requirements of the application software you will run on your computer. Some application software requires more memory and disk space than others, as well as additional input, output, and storage devices. For example, suppose you want to run software that can copy one CD's or DVD's contents directly to another CD or DVD, without first copying the data to your hard disk. To support that, you should consider a desktop computer or a high-end notebook computer, because the computer will need two CD or DVD drives: one that reads from a CD or DVD, and one that reads from and writes on a CD or DVD. If you plan to run software that allows your computer to work as an entertainment system, then you will need a CD or DVD drive, quality speakers, and an upgraded sound card.

Look for bundled software.

When you purchase a computer, it may come bundled with several programs. Some sellers even let you choose which application software you want. Remember, however, that bundled software has value only if you would have purchased the software even if it had not come with the computer. At the very least, you probably will want word processing software and a browser to access the Internet. If you need additional applications, such as a spreadsheet, a database, or presentation graphics, consider purchasing a software suite, such as Microsoft Works, Microsoft Office, or Sun StarOffice™, which include several programs at a reduced price.

FIGURE 37 Hardware and software reviews.

Type of Computers	Web Site	URL
PC	Computer Shopper	shopper.cnet.com
	PC World Magazine	pcworld.com
	BYTE Magazine	byte.com
	PC Magazine	zdnet.com/reviews
	Yahoo! Computers	computers.yahoo.com
	Microsoft Network	eshop.msn.com
	Dave's Guide to Buying a Home Computer	css.msu.edu/PC-Guide
Mac	ZDNet News	zdnet.com/mac
	Macworld Magazine	macworld.com
	Apple	apple.com
	Switch to Mac Campaign	apple.com/switch

For an updated list of hardware and software reviews and their Web site addresses, visit scsite.com/dc2004/ch8/buyers.

Avoid buying the least powerful computer available.

Once you know the application software you want to use, you then can consider the following important criteria about the computer's components: (1) processor speed, (2) size and types of memory (RAM) and storage, (3) types of input/output devices, (4) types of ports and adapter cards, and (5) types of communications devices. The information in Figure 38 and Figure 39 (on page COM-24) can help you determine what system components are best for you. Figure 38 outlines considerations for specific hardware components. Figure 39 provides a Base Components worksheet that lists PC recommendations for each category of user discussed in this book: Home User, Small Office/Home Office User, Mobile User, Large Business User, and Power User. In the worksheet, the Home User category is divided into two groups: Application Home User and Game Home User. The Mobile User recommendations list criteria for a notebook computer, but do not include the PDA or Tablet PC options.

Computer technology changes rapidly, meaning a computer that seems powerful enough today may not serve your computing needs in a few years. In fact, studies show that many users regret not buying a more powerful computer. To avoid this, plan to buy a computer that will last you for two to three years. You can help delay obsolescence by purchasing the fastest processor, the most memory, and the largest hard disk you can afford. If you must buy a less powerful computer, be sure you can upgrade it with additional memory, components, and peripheral devices as your computer requirements grow.

FIGURE 38 Hardware guidelines.

CD/DVD Drives: Most computers come with a 32X to 48X speed CD-ROM drive that can read CDs. If you plan to write music, audio files, and documents on a CD or DVD, then you should consider upgrading to a CD-RW. An even better alternative is to upgrade to a DVD+RW/CD-RW combination drive. It allows you to read DVDs and CDs and to write data on (burn) a DVD or CD. A DVD has a capacity of at least 4.7 GB versus the 650 MB capacity of a CD.

Card Reader: A card reader is useful for transferring data directly from a removable flash memory card, such as the ones used in your camera or music player. Make sure the card reader can read the flash memory cards that you use.

Digital Camera: Consider an inexpensive point-and-shoot digital camera. They are small enough to carry around, usually operate automatically in terms of lighting and focus, and contain storage cards for storing photographs. A 1.3- to 2.2-megapixel camera with an 8 MB or 16 MB storage card is fine for creating images for use on the Web or to send via e-mail.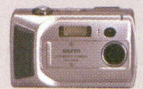

Digital Video Capture Device: A digital video capture device allows you to connect your computer to a camcorder or VCR and record, edit, manage, and then write video back to a VCR tape, a CD, or a DVD. The digital video capture device can be an external device or an adapter card. To create quality video (true 30 frames per second, full-sized TV), the digital video capture device should have a USB 2.0 or FireWire port. You will find that a standard USB port is too slow to maintain video quality. You also will need sufficient storage: an hour of data on a VCR tape takes up about 5 GB of disk storage.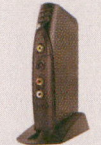

Floppy Disk Drive: Make sure the computer you purchase has a standard 3.5", 1.44 MB floppy disk drive. A floppy disk drive is useful for backing up and transferring files.

Hard Disk: It is recommended that you buy a computer with 40 to 60 GB if your primary interests are browsing the Web and using e-mail and Office suite-type applications; 60 to 80 GB if you also want to edit digital photographs; 80 to 100 GB if you plan to edit digital video or manipulate large audio files even occasionally; and 100 to 160 GB if you will edit digital video, movies, or photography often or store audio files and music or consider yourself to be a power user.

Joystick/Wheel: If you use your computer to play games, then you will want to purchase a joystick or a wheel. These devices, especially the more expensive ones, provide for realistic game play with force feedback, programmable buttons, and specialized levers and wheels.

Keyboard: The keyboard is one of the more important devices used to communicate with the computer. For this reason, make sure the keyboard you purchase has 101 to 105 keys, is comfortable, easy to use, and has a USB connection. A wireless keyboard should be considered, especially if you have a small desk area.

Microphone: If you plan to record audio or use speech recognition to enter text and commands, then purchase a close-talk headset with gain adjustment support.

Modem: Most computers come with a modem so that you can use your telephone line to dial out and access the Internet. Some modems also have fax capabilities. Your modem should be rated at 56 Kbps.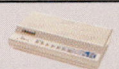

Monitor: The monitor is where you will view documents, read e-mail messages, and view pictures. A minimum of a 17" screen is recommended, but if you are planning to use your computer for graphic design or game playing, then you may want to purchase a 19" or 21" monitor. The LCD flat panel monitor should be considered, especially if space is an issue.

Mouse: As you work with your computer, you use the mouse constantly. For this reason, spend a few extra dollars, if necessary, and purchase a mouse with an optical sensor and USB connection. The optical sensor replaces the need for a mouse ball, which means you do not need a mouse pad. For a PC, make sure your mouse has a wheel, which acts as a third button in addition to the top two buttons on the left and right. An ergonomic design is also important because your hand is on the mouse most of the time when you are using your computer. A wireless mouse should be considered to eliminate the cord and allow you to work at short distances from your computer.

Network Card: If you plan to connect to a network or use broadband (cable or DSL) to connect to the Internet, then you will need to purchase a network card. Broadband connections require a 10/100 PCI Ethernet network card.

Printer: Your two basic printer choices are ink-jet and laser. Color ink-jet printers cost on average between $50 and $300. Laser printers cost from $300 to $2,000. In general, the cheaper the printer, the lower the resolution and speed, and the more often you are required to change the ink cartridge or toner. Laser printers print faster and with a higher quality than an ink-jet, and their toner on average costs less. If you want color, then go with a high-end ink-jet printer to ensure quality of print. Duty cycle (the number of pages you expect to print each month) also should be a determining factor. If your duty cycle is on the low end — hundreds of pages per month — then stay with a high-end ink-jet printer, rather than purchasing a laser printer. If you plan to print photographs taken with a digital camera, then you should purchase a photo printer. A photo printer is a dye-sublimation printer or an ink-jet printer with higher resolution and features that allow you to print quality photographs.

Processor: For a PC, a 2.0 GHz Intel or AMD processor is more than enough processor power for application home and small office/home office users. Game home, large business, and power users should upgrade to faster processors.

RAM: RAM plays a vital role in the speed of your computer. Make sure the computer you purchase has at least 256 MB of RAM. If you have extra money to invest in your computer, then consider increasing the RAM to 512 MB or more. The extra money for RAM will be well spent.

Scanner: The most popular scanner purchased with a computer today is the flatbed scanner. When evaluating a flatbed scanner, check the color depth and resolution. Do not buy anything less than a color depth of 48 bits and a resolution of 1200 x 2400 dpi. The higher the color depth, the more accurate the color. A higher resolution picks up the more subtle gradations of color.

Sound Card: Most sound cards today support the Sound Blaster and General MIDI standards and should be capable of recording and playing digital audio. If you plan to turn your computer into an entertainment system or are a game home user, then you will want to spend the extra money and upgrade from the standard sound card.

Speakers: Once you have a good sound card, quality speakers and a separate subwoofer that amplifies the bass frequencies of the speakers can turn your computer into a premium stereo system.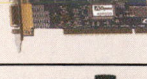

Video Graphics Card: Most standard video cards satisfy the monitor display needs of application home and small office users. If you are a game home user or a graphic designer, you will want to upgrade to a higher quality video card. The higher refresh rates will further enhance the display of games, graphics, and movies.

PC Video Camera: A PC video camera is a small camera used to capture and display live video (in some cases with sound), primarily on a Web page. You also can capture, edit, and share video and still photos. The camera sits on your monitor or desk. Recommended minimum specifications include 640 x 480 resolution, a video with a rate of 30 frames per second, and a USB 2.0 or FireWire connection.

Wireless LAN Access Point: A Wireless LAN Access Point allows you to network several computers, so they can share files and access the Internet through a single cable modem or DSL connection. Each device that you connect requires a wireless card. A Wireless LAN Access Point can offer a range of operation up to several hundred feet, so be sure the device has a high-powered antenna.

Zip® Drive: Consider purchasing a Zip® or Peerless® disk drive to back up important files. The Zip® drive, which has a capacity of up to 750 MB, is sufficient for most users. An alternative to purchasing a backup drive is to purchase a CD-RW or DVD+RW and burn backups of key files on a CD or DVD.

Consider upgrades to the mouse, keyboard, monitor, printer, microphone, and speakers.

You use these peripheral devices to interact with your computer, so you should make sure they are up to your standards. Review the peripheral devices listed in Figure 38 on the pages COM-22 and COM-23 and then visit both local computer dealers and large retail stores to test the computers on display. Ask the salesperson what input and output devices would be best for you and whether you should upgrade beyond what comes standard. A few extra dollars spent on these components when you initially purchase a computer can extend its usefulness by years.

Determine whether you want to use telephone lines or broadband (cable or DSL) to access the Internet.

If your computer has a modem, then you can access the Internet using a standard telephone line. Ordinarily, you call a local or toll-free 800 number to connect to an ISP (see Guideline 6). Using a dial-up Internet connection is relatively inexpensive, but slow.

DSL and cable connections provide much faster Internet connections, which are ideal if you want faster file download speeds for software, digital photos, and music. As you would expect, they also are more expensive. DSL, which is available through local telephone companies, also may require that you subscribe to an ISP. Cable is available through your local cable television provider and some online service providers (OSPs). If you get cable, then you would not use a separate Internet service provider or online service provider.

FIGURE 39 Base computer components and optional components. A copy of the Base Components worksheet is on the Data Disk. To obtain a copy of the Data Disk, see the inside back cover of this book for instructions.

BASE COMPONENTS

	Application Home User	Game Home User	Small Office/Home Office User	Mobile User	Large Business User	Power User
HARDWARE						
Processor	Pentium®4 at 2.0 GHz	Pentium®4 at 3.0 GHz	Pentium®4 at 2.0 GHz	Pentium®4 at 1.8 GHz	Pentium®4 at 3.0 GHz	Multiple Itanium™ at 2.5 GHz
RAM	256 MB	512 MB	256 MB	256 MB	512 MB	1 GB
Cache	256 KB L2	512 KB L2	512 KB L2	512 KB L2	512 KB L2	2 MB L3
Hard Disk	60 GB	120 GB	100 GB	40 GB	160 GB	160 GB
Monitor/LCD Flat Panel	17" or 19"	23"	19" or 21"	16.1" SuperVGA+ TFT	19" or 21"	23"
Video Graphics Card	64 MB	128 MB	64 MB	16 MB	64 MB	128 MB
CD/DVD Bay 1	48x CD-ROM	48x CD-ROM	48x CD-ROM	24x CD-ROM	48x CD-ROM	48x CD-ROM
CD/DVD Bay 2	32x/10x/40x CD-RW/DVD	DVD+RW/CD-RW	32x/10x/40x CD-RW/DVD	24x CD-RW/DVD	DVD+RW/CD-RW	DVD+RW/CD-RW
Floppy Disk Drive	3.5"	3.5"	3.5"	3.5"	3.5"	3.5"
Printer	Color Ink-Jet	Color Ink-Jet	10 ppm Laser	Portable Ink-Jet	24 ppm Laser	10 ppm Laser
PC Video Camera	Yes	Yes	Yes	Yes	Yes	Yes
Fax/Modem	Yes	Yes	Yes	Yes	Yes	Yes
Microphone	Close-Talk Headset with Gain Adjustment	Close-Talk Headset with Gain Adjustment	Close-Talk Headset with Gain Adjustment	Close-Talk Headset with Gain Adjustment	Close-Talk Headset with Gain Adjustment	Close-Talk Headset with Gain Adjustment
Speakers	Stereo	Full-Dolby Surround	Stereo	Stereo	Stereo	Full-Dolby
Pointing Device	IntelliMouse or Optical Mouse	Optical Mouse and Joystick	IntelliMouse or Optical Mouse	Touchpad or Pointing Stick and Optical Mouse	IntelliMouse or Optical Mouse	IntelliMouse or Optical Mouse and Joystick
Keyboard	Yes	Yes	Yes	Built-In	Yes	Yes
Backup Disk/Tape Drive	750 MB Zip®	10 GB Peerless™	10 GB Peerless™	10 GB Peerless™	20 GB Peerless™	20 GB Peerless™
Sound Card	Sound Blaster Compatible	Sound Blaster Compatible	Sound Blaster Compatible	Built-In	Sound Blaster Compatible	Sound Blaster
Network Card	Yes	Yes	Yes	Yes	Yes	Yes
TV-Out Connector	Yes	Yes	Yes	Yes	Yes	Yes
USB Port	Yes	Yes	Yes	Yes	Yes	Yes
FireWire Port	Yes	Yes	Yes	Yes	Yes	Yes
SOFTWARE						
Operating System	Windows XP Home Edition	Windows XP Home Edition	Windows XP Professional	Windows XP Professional	Windows XP Professional	Windows XP Professional
Application Suite	Office XP Standard Edition	Office XP Standard Edition	Office XP Small Business Edition	Office XP Small Business Edition	Office XP Professional with FrontPage 2002	Office XP Professional with FrontPage 2002
AntiVirus	Yes, 12-Mo. Subscription	Yes, 12-Mo. Subscription	Yes, 12-Mo. Subscription	Yes, 12-Mo. Subscription	Yes, 12-Mo. Subscription	Yes, 12-Mo. Subscription
Internet Access	Cable, DSL, or Dial-up	Cable, DSL, or Dial-up	Cable, DSL, or Dial-up	Satellite or Cellular	LAN/WAN (T1/T3)	Cable or DSL
OTHER						
Surge Protector	Yes	Yes	Yes	Portable	Yes	Yes
Warranty	3-Year Limited, 1-Year Next Next Business Day On-Site Service	3-Year Limited, 1-Year Next Next Business Day On-Site Service	3-year On-Site Service	3-Year Limited, 1-Year Next Business Day On-Site Service	3-year On-Site Service	3-year On-Site Service
Other	Wheel		Postage Printer	Docking Station Carrying Case		Graphics Tablet Plotter or Large-Format Printer

Optional Components for all Categories

802.11b Wireless Card	Graphics Tablet	
Bluetooth™ Enabled	iPod Music Player	
Biometric Input Device	IrDa Port	Fingerprint Scanner
Card Reader	Mouse Pad/Wrist Rest	Portable Data Projector
Digital Camera	Multifunction Peripheral	
Digital Video Capture	Photo Printer	
Digital Video Camera	Portable Data Projector	
Dual-Monitor Support with Second Monitor	Scanner	
Ergonomic Keyboard	TV/FM Tuner	
External Hard Disk	Uninterruptible Power Supply	
	USB Drive	

If you are using a dial-up or wireless connection to connect to the Internet, then select an ISP or OSP.

You can access the Internet via telephone lines in one of two ways: via an ISP or an OSP. Both provide Internet access for a monthly fee that ranges from $6 to $25. If you are using DSL, you will have to pay additional costs for a residential DSL line. Local ISPs offer Internet access to users in a limited geographic region, through local telephone numbers. National ISPs provide access for users nationwide (including mobile users), through local and toll-free telephone numbers and cable. Because of their size, national ISPs generally offer more services and have a larger technical support staff than local ISPs. OSPs furnish Internet access as well as members-only features for users nationwide. Figure 40 lists several national ISPs and OSPs. Before you choose an ISP or OSP, compare such features as the number of access hours, monthly fees, available services (e-mail, Web page hosting, chat), and reliability.

Use a worksheet to compare computers, services, and other considerations.

You can use a separate sheet of paper to take notes on each vendor's computer and then summarize the information on a worksheet, such as the one shown in Figure 41. You can use Figure 41 to compare prices for either a PC or a MAC. Most companies advertise a price for a base computer that includes components housed in the system unit (processor, RAM, sound card, video card), disk drives (floppy disk, hard disk, CD-ROM, CD-RW, DVD-ROM, and DVD+RW), a keyboard, mouse, monitor, printer, speakers, and modem. Be aware, however, that some advertisements list prices for computers with only some of these components.

Monitors and printers, for example, often are not included in a base computer's price. Depending on how you plan to use the computer, you may want to invest in additional or more powerful components. When you are comparing the prices of computers, make sure you are comparing identical or similar configurations.

 If you are buying a new computer, you have several purchasing options: buying from your school bookstore, a local computer dealer, a local large retail store, or ordering by mail via telephone or the Web.

Each purchasing option has certain advantages. Many college bookstores, for example, sign exclusive pricing agreements with computer manufacturers and, thus, can offer student discounts. Local dealers and local large retail stores, however, more easily can provide hands-on support. Mail-order companies that sell computers by telephone or online via the Web (Figure 42 on the next page) often provide the lowest prices, but extend less personal service. Some major mail-order companies, however, have started to provide next-business-day, on-site services. A credit card usually is required to buy from a mail-order company. Figure 43 on the next page lists some of the more popular mail-order companies and their Web site addresses.

FIGURE 41 A worksheet is an effective tool for summarizing and comparing the prices and components of different computer vendors. A copy of the Computer Cost Comparison Worksheet for the PC or Mac is on the Data Disk. To obtain a copy of the Data Disk, see the inside back cover of this book for instructions.

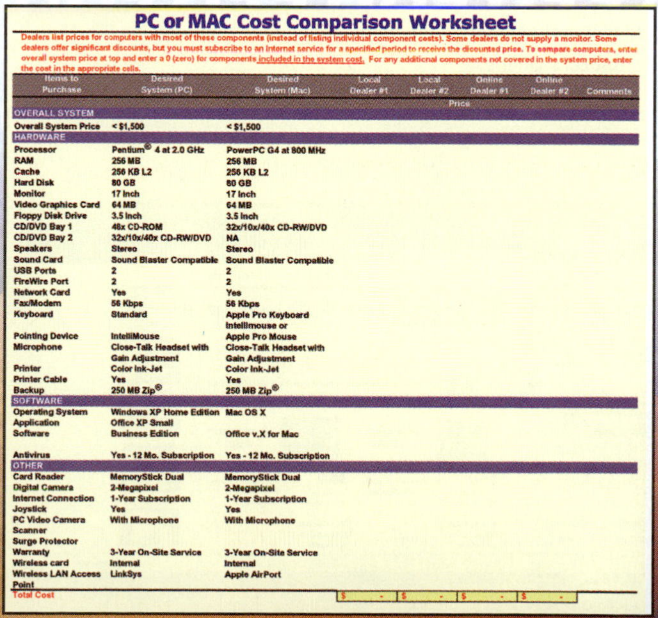

FIGURE 40 National ISPs and OSPs.

Company	Service	URL
America Online	OSP	aol.com
AT&T WorldNet	ISP	www.att.net
CompuServe	OSP	compuserve.com
EarthLink®	ISP	earthlink.net
Juno®	OSP	juno.com
NetZero®	OSP	netzero.com
Prodigy™	ISP/OSP	www.prodigy.net
MSN	OSP	msn.com

For an updated list of national ISPs and OSPs and their Web site addresses, visit scsite.com/dc2004/ch8/buyers.

PC or MAC Cost Comparison Worksheet

Dealers list prices for computers with most of these components (instead of listing individual component costs). Some dealers do not supply a monitor. Some dealers offer significant discounts, but you must subscribe to an Internet service for a specified period to receive the discounted price. To compare computers, enter overall system price at top and enter a 0 (zero) for components included in the system cost. For any additional components not covered in the system price, enter the cost in the appropriate cells.

Items to Purchase	Desired System (PC)	Desired System (Mac)	Local Dealer #1	Local Dealer #2	Online Dealer #1	Online Dealer #2	Comments
			Price				
OVERALL SYSTEM							
Overall System Price	< $1,500	< $1,500					
HARDWARE							
Processor	Pentium® 4 at 2.0 GHz	PowerPC G4 at 800 MHz					
RAM	256 MB	256 MB					
Cache	256 KB L2	256 KB L2					
Hard Disk	80 GB	60 GB					
Monitor	17 Inch	17 Inch					
Video Graphics Card	64 MB	64 MB					
Floppy Disk Drive	3.5 Inch	3.5 Inch					
CD/DVD Bay 1	48x CD-ROM	32x/10x/40x CD-RW/DVD					
CD/DVD Bay 2	32x/10x/40x CD-RW/DVD	NA					
Speakers	Stereo	Stereo					
Sound Card	Sound Blaster Compatible	Sound Blaster Compatible					
USB Ports	2	2					
FireWire Port	2	2					
Network Card	Yes	Yes					
Fax/Modem	56 Kbps	56 Kbps					
Keyboard	Standard	Apple Pro Keyboard					
Pointing Device	IntelliMouse	IntelliMouse or Apple Pro Mouse					
Microphone	Close-Talk Headset with Gain Adjustment	Close-Talk Headset with Gain Adjustment					
Printer	Color Ink-Jet	Color Ink-Jet					
Printer Cable	Yes	Yes					
Backup	250 MB Zip®	250 MB Zip®					
SOFTWARE							
Operating System	Windows XP Home Edition	Mac OS X					
Application Software	Office XP Small Business Edition	Office v.X for Mac					
Antivirus	Yes - 12 Mo. Subscription	Yes - 12 Mo. Subscription					
OTHER							
Card Reader	MemoryStick Dual	MemoryStick Dual					
Digital Camera	2-Megapixel	2-Megapixel					
Internet Connection	1-Year Subscription	1-Year Subscription					
Joystick	Yes	Yes					
PC Video Camera	With Microphone	With Microphone					
Scanner							
Surge Protector							
Warranty	3-Year On-Site Service	3-Year On-Site Service					
Wireless card	Internal	Internal					
Wireless LAN Access Point	LinkSys	Apple AirPort					
Total Cost			$ -	$ -	$ -	$ -	

If you are buying a used computer, stay with name brands such as Dell, Gateway, Hewlett-Packard, and Apple.

Although brand-name equipment can cost more, most brand-name computers have longer, more comprehensive warranties, are better supported, and have more authorized centers for repair services. As with new computers, you can purchase a used computer from local computer dealers, local large retail stores, or mail order via the telephone or the Web. Classified ads and used computer sellers offer additional outlets for purchasing used computers. Figure 44 lists several major used computer brokers and their Web site addresses.

If you have a computer and are upgrading to a new one, then consider selling or trading in the old one.

If you are a replacement buyer, your older computer still may have value. If you cannot sell the computer through the classified ads, via a Web site, or to a friend, then ask if the computer dealer will buy your old computer. An increasing number of companies are taking trade-ins, but do not expect too much money for your old computer.

Be aware of hidden costs.

Before purchasing, be sure to consider any additional costs associated with buying a computer, such as an additional telephone line, a cable or DSL modem, an uninterruptible power supply (UPS), computer furniture, floppy disks and paper, and computer training classes you may want to take. Depending on where you buy your computer, the seller may be willing to include some or all of these in the computer purchase price.

Consider more than just price.

The lowest-cost computer may not be the best long-term buy. Consider such intangibles as the vendor's time in business, the vendor's regard for quality, and the vendor's reputation for support. If you need to upgrade your computer often, you may want to consider a leasing arrangement, in which you pay monthly lease fees, but can upgrade or add on to your computer as your equipment needs change. No matter what type of buyer you are, insist on a 30-day, no-questions-asked return policy on your computer.

FIGURE 43 New computer mail-order companies.

Type of Computer	Company	URL
PC	Computer Shopper	shopper.cnet.com
	HP/Compaq	thenew.hp.com
	CompUSA	compusa.com
	dartek.com™	dartek.com
	Dell	dell.com
	Gateway	gateway.com
	Micron	micron.com
Macintosh	Apple Computer	store.apple.com
	Club Mac	clubmac.com
	MacConnection	macconnection.com
	MacExchange	macx.com

For an updated list of new computer mail-order companies and their Web site addresses, visit scsite.com/dc2004/ch8/buyers.

FIGURE 42 Mail-order companies, such as Dell, sell computers online.

FIGURE 44 Used computer mail-order companies.

Company	URL
Amazon.com	amazon.com
Off Lease Computer Supermarket	off-leasecomputers.com
American Computer Exchange	www.amcoex.com
U.S. Computer Exchange	uscomputerexchange.com
eBay	ebay.com

For an updated list of used computer mail-order companies and their Web site addresses, visit scsite.com/dc2004/ch8/buyers.

Avoid restocking fees.

Some companies charge a restocking fee of 10 to 20 percent as part of their money-back return policy. In some cases, no restocking fee for hardware is applied, but it is applied for software. Ask about the existence and terms of any restocking policies before you buy.

Consider purchasing an extended warranty or service plan.

If you use your computer for business or require fast resolution to major computer problems, consider purchasing an extended warranty or a service plan through a local dealer or third-party company. Most extended warranties cover the repair and replacement of computer components beyond the standard warranty. Most service plans ensure that your technical support calls receive priority response from technicians. You also can purchase an on-site service plan that states that a technician will come to your home, work, or school within 24 hours. If your computer includes a warranty and service agreement for a year or less, think about extending the service for two or three years when you buy the computer.

Use a credit card to purchase your new computer.

Many credit cards offer purchase protection and extended warranty benefits that cover you in case of loss of or damage to purchased goods. Paying by credit card also gives you time to install and use the computer before you have to pay for it. Finally, if you are dissatisfied with the computer and are unable to reach an agreement with the seller, paying by credit card gives you certain rights regarding withholding payment until the dispute is resolved. Check your credit card terms for specific details.

HOW TO PURCHASE A NOTEBOOK COMPUTER

If you need computing capability when you travel or to use in lecture or meetings, you may find a notebook computer to be an appropriate choice. The guidelines mentioned in the previous section also apply to the purchase of a notebook computer. The following are additional considerations unique to notebook computers.

Purchase a notebook computer with a sufficiently large active-matrix screen.

Active-matrix screens display high-quality color that is viewable from all angles. Less expensive, passive-matrix screens sometimes are difficult to see in low-light conditions and cannot be viewed from an angle. Notebook computers typically come with a 12.1-inch, 13.3-inch, 14.1-inch, 15-inch, or 16.1-inch display. For most users, a 14.1-inch display is satisfactory. If you intend to use your notebook computer as a desktop computer replacement, however, you may opt for a 15-inch or 16.1-inch display. Notebook computers with these larger displays weigh seven to ten pounds, however, so if you travel a lot and portability is essential, you might want a lighter computer with a smaller display. The lightest notebook computers, which weigh less than 3 pounds, are equipped with a 12.1-inch display. Regardless of size, the resolution of the display should be at least 1024 x 768 pixels. To compare the monitor size on various notebook computers, visit the company Web sites in Figure 45.

FIGURE 45 Companies that sell notebook computers.

Type of Notebook	Company	URL
PC	Acer	acer.com
	Dell	dell.com
	Fujitsu	fujitsu.com
	Gateway	gateway.com
	HP	hp.com
	IBM	ibm.com
	NEC	nec.com
	Sony	sony.com
	Sharp	sharp.com
	Toshiba	toshiba.com
Mac	Apple	apple.com

For an updated list of companies and their Web site addresses, visit scsite.com/dc2004/ch8/buyers.

 **Experiment with different keyboards and pointing devices.**

Notebook computer keyboards are far less standardized than those for desktop computers. Some notebook computers, for example, have wide wrist rests, while others have none. Notebook computers also use a range of pointing devices, including pointing sticks, touchpads, and trackballs. Before you purchase a notebook computer, try various types of keyboard and pointing devices to determine which is easiest for you to use. Regardless of the pointing device you select, you also may want to purchase a regular mouse to use when you are working at a desk or other large surface.

Make sure the notebook computer you purchase has a CD and/or DVD drive.

Loading and installing software, especially large Office suites, is much faster if done from a CD-ROM, CD-RW, DVD-ROM, or DVD+RW. Today, most notebook computers come with an internal or external CD-ROM drive. Some notebook computers even come with a CD-ROM drive and a CD-RW drive or a DVD-ROM drive and a CD-RW or DVD+RW/CD-RW drive. Although DVD drives are more expensive, they allow you to play CDs and DVD movies using your notebook computer and a headset.

If necessary, upgrade the processor, memory, and disk storage at the time of purchase.

As with a desktop computer, upgrading your notebook computer's memory and disk storage usually is less expensive at the time of initial purchase. Some disk storage is custom designed for notebook computer manufacturers, meaning an upgrade might not be available in the future. If you are purchasing a lightweight notebook computer, then it should include at least a 1.4 GHz processor, 256 MB RAM, and 40 GB of storage.

The availability of built-in ports on a notebook computer is important.

A notebook computer does not have a lot of room to add adapter cards. If you know the purpose for which you plan to use your notebook computer, then you can determine the ports you will need. Most notebooks come with common ports, such as a mouse port, IrDA port, serial port, parallel port, video port, and USB port. If you plan to connect your notebook computer to a TV, however, then you will need a PC-toTV port. If you want to connect to networks at school or in various offices, make sure the notebook computer you purchase has a built-in network card. If your notebook computer does not come with a network card built-in, then you will have to purchase an external network card that slides into an expansion slot in your notebook computer, as well as a network cable. If you expect to connect an iPod portable digital music player to your notebook computer, then you will need a FireWire port.

 If you plan to use your notebook computer for note-taking at school or in meetings, consider a notebook computer that converts to a Tablet PC.

Some computer manufacturers have developed convertible notebook computers that allow the screen to rotate 180 degrees on a central hinge and then fold down to cover the keyboard and become a Tablet PC (Figure 46). You then can use a pencil-like device to input text or drawings into the computer by writing on the screen.

 **Consider purchasing a notebook computer with a built-in wireless card to connect to your home network.**

Many users today are setting up wireless home networks. With a wireless home network, the desktop computer functions as the server and your notebook computer can access the desktop computer from any location in the house to share files and hardware, such as a printer, and browse the Web. If your notebook computer does not come with a built-in wireless card, you can purchase an external one that slides into your notebook computer. Most home wireless networks allow connections from distances of 150 to 800 feet.

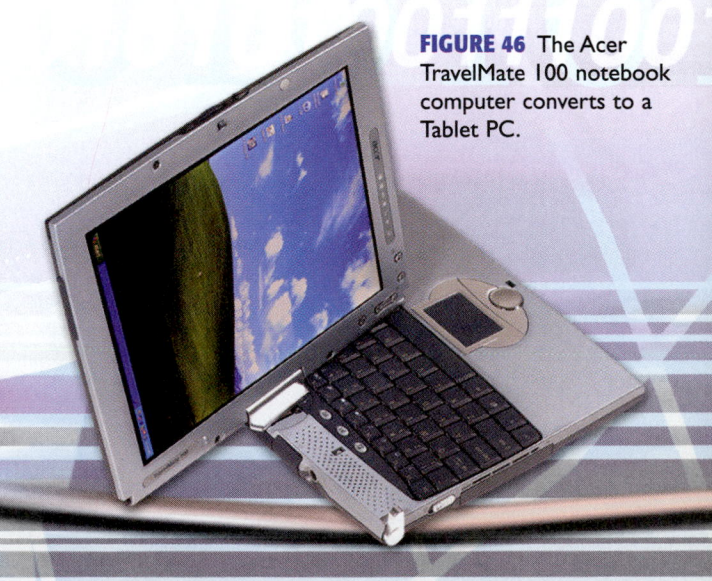

FIGURE 46 The Acer TravelMate 100 notebook computer converts to a Tablet PC.

8 **If you are going to use your notebook computer for long periods without access to an electrical outlet, purchase a second battery.**

The trend among notebook computer users today is power and size over battery life, and notebook computer manufacturers have picked up on this. Many notebook computer users today are willing to give up longer battery life for a larger screen, faster processor, and bigger storage. For this reason, you need to be careful in choosing a notebook computer if you plan to use it without access to electrical outlets for long periods, such as an airplane flight. You also might want to purchase a second battery as a backup. If you anticipate running your notebook computer on batteries frequently, choose a computer that uses lithium-ion batteries (they last longer than nickel cadmium or nickel hydride batteries).

9 **Purchase a well-padded and well-designed carrying case.**

An amply padded carrying case will protect your notebook computer from the bumps it will receive while traveling. A well-designed carrying case will have room for accessories such as spare floppy disks, CDs and DVDs, a user manual, pens, and paperwork (Figure 47).

10 **If you travel overseas, obtain a set of electrical and telephone adapters.**

Different countries use different outlets for electrical and telephone connections. Several manufacturers sell sets of adapters that will work in most countries (Figure 48).

FIGURE 47 Well-designed carrying case.

11 **If you plan to connect your notebook computer to a video projector, make sure the notebook computer is compatible with the video projector.**

You should check, for example, to be sure that your notebook computer will allow you to display an image on the computer screen and projection device at the same time (Figure 49). Also, ensure that your notebook computer has the ports required to connect to the video projector.

12 **For improved security, consider a fingerprint scanner.**

More than a quarter million notebook computers are stolen or lost each year. If you have critical information stored on your notebook computer, then consider purchasing one with a fingerprint scanner to protect the data if your computer is stolen or lost. Fingerprint security offers a level of protection that extends well beyond the standard password protection.

FIGURE 48 Set of electrical and telephone adapters for travel abroad.

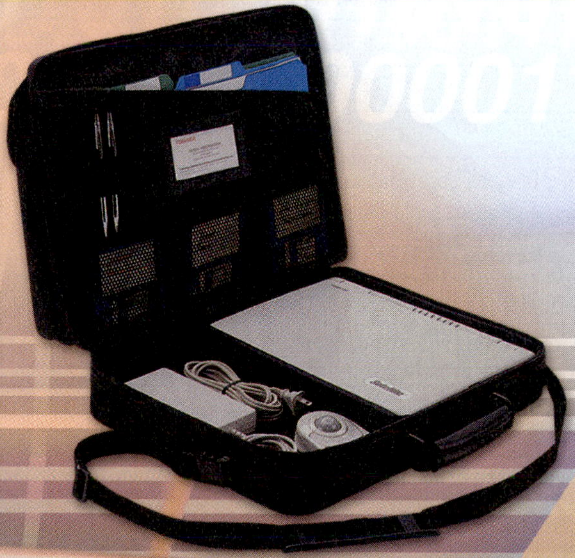

FIGURE 49 A notebook computer connected to a video projector to project what displays on the screen.

HOW TO PURCHASE A TABLET PC

The Tablet PC (Figure 50) combines the mobility features of a traditional notebook computer with the simplicity of pencil and paper, because you can create and save Office-type documents by writing and drawing directly on the screen with a digital pen. Tablet PCs use the Windows XP Tablet PC Edition operating system, which expands on Windows XP Professional by including digital pen and speech capabilities. A notebook computer and a Tablet PC have many similarities. For this reason, if you are considering purchasing a Tablet PC, review the guidelines for purchasing a notebook computer, as well as the guidelines below.

 ### Make sure the Tablet PC fits your mobile computing needs.

The Tablet PC is not for every mobile user. If you find yourself in need of a computer in class or you are spending more time in meetings than in your office, then the Tablet PC may be the answer. Before you invest money in a Tablet PC, however, determine the programs you plan to use it for. You should not buy a Tablet PC simply because it is a new and interesting type of computer. For additional information about the Tablet PC, visit the Web sites listed in Figure 51. You may have to use the search capabilities on the home page of the companies listed to locate information about the Tablet PC.

Decide whether you want a convertible or pure Tablet PC.

Convertible Tablet PCs have an attached keyboard and look like a notebook computer. You rotate the screen and lay it flat against the computer for note-taking. The pure Tablet PCs are slim and lightweight, weighing less than four pounds. They have the capability of easily docking at a desktop to gain access to a large monitor, keyboard, and mouse. If you spend a lot of time attending lectures or meetings, than the pure Tablet PC is ideal. Acceptable specifications for a Tablet PC are shown in Figure 52.

FIGURE 51 Companies involved with Tablet PCs and their Web sites.

Company	URL
Acer	acer.com/us
Fujitsu	fujitsu.com
Hewlett-Packard	hp.com
Microsoft	microsoft.com/windowsxp/tabletpc
ViewSonic	viewsonic.com
VIA Technologies	via.com

For an updated list of companies and their Web site addresses, visit scsite.com/dc2004/ch8/buyers.

FIGURE 52 Tablet PC specifications.

Tablet PC Specifications	
Dimensions	12" x 9" x 1.5"
Weight	Less than 4 Pounds
Processor	Pentium III at 2.0 GHz
RAM	128 MB
Hard Disk	20 GB
Display	10.4" XGA TFT 16-Bit Color
Digitizer	Electromagnetic Digitizer
Battery	4-Cell (3-Hour)
USB	2
FireWire	1
Docking Station	Grab and Go with CD-ROM, Keyboard, and Mouse
Bluetooth Port	Yes
802.11b Card	Yes
Network Card	10/100 Ethernet
Modem	56 Kbps
Speakers	Internal
Microphone	Internal
Operating System	Windows XP Tablet PC Edition
Application Software	Office XP Small Business Edition
Antivirus Software	Yes - 12 Month Subscription
Warranty	1-Year Limited Warranty Parts and Labor

FIGURE 50 The lightweight Tablet PC, with its handwriting capabilities, is the latest addition to the family of mobile computers.

 **Be sure the weight and dimensions are conducive to portability.**

The weight and dimensions of the Tablet PC are important because you carry it around like a notepad. The Tablet PC you buy should weigh in at four pounds or less. Its dimensions should be approximately 12 inches by 9 inches by 1.5 inches.

 **Port availability, battery life, and durability are even more important with a Tablet PC than they are with a notebook computer.**

Make sure the Tablet PC you purchase has the ports required for the applications you plan to run. As with any mobile computer, battery life is important, especially if you plan to use your Tablet PC for long periods without access to an electrical outlet. A Tablet PC must be durable because if you use it for what it was built for, then you will be handling it much like you handle a pad of paper.

 **Experiment with different models of the Tablet PC to find the digital pen that works best for you.**

The key to making use of the Tablet PC is to be comfortable with its handwriting capabilities and on-screen keyboard. Not only is the digital pen used to write on the screen (Figure 53), but you also use it to make gestures to complete tasks, in a manner similar to the way you use a mouse. Figure 54 compares the standard point-and-click of a mouse unit with the gestures made with a digital pen. Other gestures with the digital pen replicate some of the commonly used keys on a keyboard.

 Check out the comfort level of handwriting in different positions.

You should be able to handwrite on a Tablet PC with your hand resting on the screen. You also should be able to handwrite holding the Tablet PC in one hand, as well as with it sitting in your lap.

FIGURE 53 A Tablet PC lets you handwrite notes and draw on the screen using a digital pen.

 **Make sure the LCD display device has a resolution high enough to take advantage of Microsoft's ClearType technologies.**

Tablet PCs use a digitizer under a standard 10.4-inch motion-sensitive LCD display to make the digital ink on the screen look like real ink on paper. The Tablet PC also uses ClearType technology that makes the characters crisper on the screen, so your notes are easier to read and cause less fatigue to the eyes. To ensure you get the maximum benefits from the new ClearType technology, make sure the LCD display has a resolution of 800 x 600 in landscape mode and a 600 x 800 in portrait mode.

Test the built-in Tablet PC microphone and speakers.

With many application software packages recognizing human speech, such as the Microsoft Office XP, it is important that the Tablet PC's built-in microphone operates at an acceptable level. If the microphone is not to your liking, you may want to purchase a close-talk headset with your Tablet PC. Increasingly, more users are sending information as audio files, rather than relying solely on text. For this reason, you also should check the speakers on the Tablet PC to make sure they meet your standards.

Consider a Tablet PC with a built-in PC video camera.

A PC video camera adds streaming video and still photography capabilities to your Tablet PC, while still allowing you to take notes in lecture or in meetings.

FIGURE 54 Standard point-and-click of a mouse unit compared with the gestures made with a digital pen.

Mouse Unit	Digital Pen
Point	Point
Click	Tap
Double-click	Double-tap
Right-click	Tap and hold
Click and drag	Drag

10 Review the docking capabilities of the Tablet PC.

The Windows XP Tablet PC Edition operating system supports a grab-and-go form of docking, so you can pick up and take a docked Tablet PC with you, just as you would pick up a notepad on your way to a meeting. Two basic types of docking stations are available. One type of docking station (Figure 55) changes the Tablet PC into a desktop computer. It uses the Tablet PC as a monitor. The station has a CD or DVD drive, full-size keyboard, mouse, and other accessories. Another type of docking station lets you dock your PC to your desktop computer and use Windows XP Dual Monitor support. Windows XP Dual Monitor support allows you to work on one monitor, while using the Tablet PC monitor to display often-used applications, such as your calendar or address book.

11 Wireless access to the Internet and your e-mail is essential with a Tablet PC.

Make sure the Tablet PC has wireless networking, so you can access the Internet and your e-mail anytime and anywhere. Your Tablet PC also should include standard network connections, such as dial-up and Ethernet connections.

12 Review available accessories to purchase with your Tablet PC.

Tablet PC accessories include docking stations, mouse units, keyboards, security cables, additional memory and storage, protective handgrips, screen protectors, and various types of digital pens. You should review the available accessories when you purchase a Tablet PC.

HOW TO PURCHASE A PDA

If you need to stay organized when you are on the go, then a lightweight, palm-sized or pocket-sized mobile device, called a PDA, may be the right choice. PDAs typically are categorized by the operating system they run. Although several are available, the two primary operating systems are Palm OS® (Figure 56) or a Windows-based operating systems, such as Pocket PC 2002 (Figure 57).

This section lists guidelines you will want to consider when purchasing a PDA. You also should visit the Web sites listed in Figure 24 to gather more information about the type of PDA that best suits your computing needs.

FIGURE 56 Sony's NR70V PDA with Palm OS. The NR70V lets you take pictures with its digital camera, listen to MP3 files, display videos and images, plus keep your datebook and contact list organized.

FIGURE 55 A Tablet PC docked to create a desktop computer with the Tablet PC as the monitor.

FIGURE 57 Compaq's iPaq H3970 with Pocket PC 2002 includes Bluetooth wireless connectivity. The iPaq plays MP3 music or audio programs from the Web, as well as records and plays back voice notes or meeting notes.

Determine the programs you plan to run on your PDA.

All PDAs can handle basic organizer-type software such as a calendar, address book, and notepad. The availability of other software depends on the operating system you choose. The depth and breadth of software for the Palm OS is significant, with more than 11,000 basic programs and over 600 wireless programs. PDAs that run Windows-based operating systems, such as Pocket PC 2002, may have fewer programs available, but the operating system and application software are similar to those with which you are familiar, such as Word and Excel.

Consider how much you want to pay.

The price of a PDA can range from $100 to $800, depending on its capabilities. In general, Palm OS devices are at the lower end of the cost spectrum and Pocket PC and other Windows-based devices are at the higher end. For the latest PDA prices, capabilities, and accessories, visit the Web sites listed in Figure 58.

Determine whether you need wireless access to the Internet and e-mail or mobile telephone capabilities with your PDA.

Some PDAs offer wireless access to the Internet, instant messaging, and e-mail for a monthly network connection fee. To run the wireless, the functionality of the PDAs often is stripped down to conserve battery power. Some wireless PDAs, such as Handspring's Treo 270, come with a mobile telephone built-in (Figure 59). These features and services allow PDA users to access real-time information from anywhere to help make decisions while on the go.

Make sure your PDA has enough memory.

Memory (RAM) is not a major issue with low-end PDAs with monochrome displays and basic organizer functions. Memory is a major issue, however, for high-end PDAs that have color displays and wireless features. Without enough memory, the performance level of your PDA will drop dramatically. If you plan to purchase a high-end PDA running the Palm OS operating system, the PDA should have at least 16 MB of RAM. If you plan to purchase a high-end PDA running the Pocket PC 2002 operating system, the PDA should have at least 48 MB of RAM.

Practice with the touch screen, handwriting recognition, and built-in keyboard before deciding on a model.

To enter data into a PDA, you use a pen-like stylus to handwrite on the screen or a keyboard. The keyboard either is mounted on the front of the PDA or it slides out. The Handspring Treo shown in Figure 59, comes with a small, built-in keyboard that works like a mobile telephone keypad. With handwriting recognition, the PDA translates the handwriting into a computerized font. You also can use the stylus as a pointing device to select items on the screen and enter data by tapping on an on-screen keyboard. By practicing data entry before buying a PDA, you can learn if one PDA may be easier for you to use than another. You also can buy third-party software to improve a PDA's handwriting recognition.

FIGURE 59 The Handspring Treo 270 running Palm OS has a full-color display and can be used as a telephone, an organizer, or to access e-mail and the Web.

FIGURE 58 Reviews and information about PDAs.

Web Site	URL
Compaq	compaq.com/products/handhelds
Computer Shopper	shopper.cnet.com
Handspring	handspring.com
Microsoft	pocketpc.com
Palm	palm.com
PDA Buyers Guide	pdabuyersguide.com
Sony	sonystyle.com
Wireless Developer Network	wirelessdevnet.com

For an updated list of reviews and information about PDAs and their Web site addresses, visit scsite.com/dc2004/ch8/buyers.

Decide whether you want a color display.

Pocket PC devices usually come with a color display that supports as many as 65,536 colors. Palm OS devices also have a color display, but the less expensive ones have a monochrome display in 4 to 16 shades of gray. Having a color display does result in greater on-screen detail, but it also requires more memory and uses more power. Resolution also influences the quality of the display.

Compare battery life.

Any mobile device is good only if it has the power required to run. Palm OS devices with monochrome screens typically have a much longer battery life than Pocket PC devices with color screens. To help alleviate this problem, many Palm OS and Pocket PC devices have incorporated rechargeable batteries that can be recharged by placing the PDA in a cradle or connecting it to a charger.

Even with PDAs, seriously consider the importance of ergonomics.

Will you put the PDA in your pocket, a carrying case, wear it on your belt? How does it feel in your hand? Will you use it indoors or outdoors? Many screens are unreadable outdoors. Do you need extra ruggedness, such as would be required in construction, in a plant, or a warehouse?

Check out the accessories.

Determine which accessories you want for your PDA. PDA accessories include carrying cases, portable mini- and full-size keyboards, removable storage, modems, synchronization cradles and cables, car chargers, wireless communications, global positioning system modules, digital camera modules, expansion cards, dashboard mounts, replacement styli, and more.

Decide whether you want additional functionality.

In general, off-the-shelf Pocket PC devices have broader functionality than Palm OS devices. For example, voice-recording capability, e-book players, MP3 players, and video players are standard on most Pocket PC devices. If you are leaning towards a Palm OS device and want these additional functions, you can purchase additional software or expansion modules to add them later.

Determine whether synchronization of data with other PDAs or personal computers is important.

Most PDAs come with a cradle that connects to the USB or serial port on your computer so you can synchronize data on your PDA with your desktop or notebook computer. Increasingly, more PDAs are Bluetooth and/or 802.11b enabled, which gives them the capability of synchronizing wirelessly. Most PDAs today also have an infrared port that allows you to synchronize data with any device that has a similar infrared port, including desktop and notebook computers or other PDAs.

HOW TO INSTALL A COMPUTER

It is important that you spend time planning for the installation of your computer. Follow these steps to ensure your installation experience will be a pleasant one and that your work area is safe, healthy, and efficient.

Read the installation manuals before you start to install your equipment.

Many manufacturers include separate installation manuals that contain important information with their equipment. You can save a great deal of time and frustration if you make an effort to read the manuals before starting the installation process.

Do some additional research.

To locate additional instructions or advice about installing your computer, review the computer magazines or Web sites listed in Figure 60 to search for articles about installing a computer.

Web Site	URL
Getting Started/Installation	
HelpTalk Online	www.helptalk.com
Ergonomics	
Ergonomic Computing	cobweb.creighton.edu/training/ergo.htm
HealthyComputing.com	healthycomputing.com
IBM Healthy Computing	www.pc.ibm.com/ww/healthycomputing
Apple Ergonomics	apple.com/about/ergonomics/
Healthy Choices for Computer Users	www-ehs.ucsd.edu/ergo/ergobk/ vdt.htm
Video Display Terminal Health and Safety Guidelines	uhs.berkeley.edu/Facstaff/Ergonomics
For an updated list of reference materials, visit scsite.com/dc2004/ ch8/buyers.	

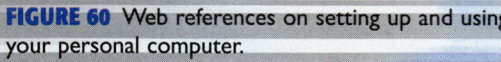

FIGURE 60 Web references on setting up and using your personal computer.

 **Set up your computer in a well-designed work area and remain aware of health issues as you work.**

Ergonomic studies have shown that using the correct type and configuration of chair, keyboard, monitor, and work surface will help you work comfortably and efficiently, and help protect your health. For your computer work space, experts recommend an area of at least two feet by four feet. You also should set up a document holder that keeps documents at the same height and distance as your computer screen to minimize neck and eye discomfort. Finally, use non-glare light bulbs that illuminate your entire work area to reduce eyestrain. Figure 61 illustrates additional guidelines for setting up your work area. Figure 62 provides computer user health guidelines.

 **Install your computer in a work space where you can control the temperature and humidity.**

You should keep the computer in an area with a constant temperature between 60°F and 80°F. High temperatures and humidity can damage electronic components. Be careful when using space heaters, for example, as the hot, dry air they generate can cause disk problems.

FIGURE 61 A well-designed work area should be flexible to allow adjustments to the height and build of different individuals. Good lighting and air quality also are important considerations.

 **Set up your work space near an available electrical outlet and set aside a proper location for the electrical wires.**

Your computer and peripheral devices, such as the monitor and printer, require an electrical outlet. To maintain safety and simplify the connections, purchase a surge protector to connect the computer and peripheral devices to the electrical outlet. Place the electrical wires in a location where they are not a fire risk and you can avoid tripping on them. After you turn your computer off, turn the master switch on the surge protector to off.

 Have a telephone outlet and telephone or cable connection near your work space, so you can connect your modem and/or place calls while using your computer.

To plug in your modem to dial up and access the Internet, you will need a telephone outlet or cable connection close to your computer. Having a telephone nearby also helps if you need to place business or technical support calls while you are working on your computer. Often, if you call a vendor about a hardware or software problem, the support person can talk you through a correction while you are on the telephone. To avoid data loss, however, do not place floppy disks on the telephone or near any other electrical or electronic equipment.

FIGURE 62 Following these health guidelines can help computer users maintain their health.

1. Work in a well-designed work area, as shown in Figure 61.

2. Alternate work activities to prevent physical and mental fatigue. If possible, change the order of your work to provide some variety.

3. Take frequent breaks. Every 15 minutes, look away from the screen to give your eyes a break. At least once per hour, get out of your chair and move around. Every two hours, take at least a 15-minute break.

4. Incorporate hand, arm, and body stretching exercises into your breaks. During your lunch break, try to get outside and walk.

5. Make sure your computer monitor is designed to minimize electro-magnetic radiation (EMR).

6. Try to eliminate or minimize surrounding noise that contributes to stress and tension.

7. If you frequently use the telephone and the computer at the same time, consider using a telephone headset. Cradling the telephone between your head and shoulder can cause muscle strain.

8. Be aware of symptoms of repetitive strain injuries: soreness, pain, numbness, or weakness in neck, shoulders, arms, wrists, and hands. Do not ignore early signs; seek medical advice.

If you plan to set up a wireless network, choose an area that is free from potential signal interference.

Low-level basement areas, doors, trees, and walls, for example, can affect the signals between wireless devices. The signal pattern for most wireless antenna is circular, with the strongest signal closest to the antenna. The best advice is to give the antenna ample room and determine its placement by trial and error.

 **Install bookshelves.**

When you set up your work space, install bookshelves above and/or to the side of your computer area to keep manuals and other reference materials handy.

 **Obtain a computer tool set.**

Computer tool sets include any screwdrivers and other tools you might need to work on your computer. Computer dealers, office supply stores, and mail-order companies sell these tool sets. To keep all the tools together, get a tool set that comes in a zippered carrying case.

 **Save all the paperwork that comes with your computer.**

Keep the documents that come with your computer in an accessible place, along with the paperwork from your other computer-related purchases. To keep different-sized documents together, consider putting them in a manila file folder, large envelope, or sealable plastic bag.

 **Record the serial numbers of all your equipment and software.**

Write the serial numbers of your equipment and software on the outside of the manuals packaged with these items. As noted in the next section, you also should create a single, comprehensive list that contains the serial numbers of all your equipment and software.

 **Complete and mail your equipment and software registration cards or register online.**

When you register your equipment and software, the vendor usually enters you in its user database. Being a registered user not only can save you time when you call with a support question, it also makes you eligible for special pricing on software upgrades.

 Keep the shipping containers and packing materials for all your equipment.

Shipping containers and packing materials will come in handy if you have to return your equipment for servicing or must move it to another location.

 **Identify device connectors.**

At the back or front of your computer, you will find a number of connectors for your printer, monitor, mouse, telephone line, and so forth (Figure 63). If the manufacturer has not identified them for you, use a marking pen to write the purpose of each connector on the back or front of the computer case, or photograph or draw the connectors and label them in a notebook.

 **Keep your computer area clean.**

Avoid eating and drinking around your computer. Also avoid smoking, because cigarette smoke can damage floppy disk drives and floppy disk surfaces.

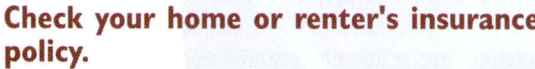 **Check your home or renter's insurance policy.**

Some renter's insurance policies have limits on the amount of computer equipment they cover. Other policies do not cover computer equipment at all if it is used for business. In this instance, you may want to obtain a separate insurance policy.

FIGURE 63 Adapter cards have a connector that is positioned in the back of the computer when the card is inserted in an expansion slot on the motherboard.

How to Maintain Your Computer

Even with the most sophisticated hardware and software, you may need to do some type of maintenance to keep your computer working properly. You can simplify and minimize the maintenance by following the steps listed in this section.

 **Start a notebook or file using a simple outline that includes information about your computer.**

Keep a notebook that provides a single source of information about your entire computer, both hardware and software and network connectivity. Each time you make a change to your computer, such as adding or removing hardware or software or altering computer parameters, record the change in your notebook. Include the following items in your notebook:

- Vendor support numbers from your user manuals

- Serial numbers of all equipment and software

- User IDs, passwords, and nicknames for your ISP or OSP, network access, Web sites, and so on

- Vendor and date of purchase for all software and equipment

- Trouble log that provides a chronological history of equipment or software problems

- Notes on any discussions with vendor support personnel

Figure 64 provides a suggested outline for the contents of your Computer Owner's Notebook.

 Before you work inside your computer, turn off the power and disconnect the equipment from the power source.

Working inside your computer with the power on can affect both you and the computer adversely. In addition, before you touch anything inside the computer, you should touch an unpainted metal surface, such as the power supply. Doing so will help discharge any static electricity that could damage internal components. As an added protection, for less than $10 from an electronics or computer store, buy an antistatic wristband to prevent static electricity from damaging the computer's circuitry while you replace components. Do not twist, bend, or force components into place. Gently work around existing cables.

Keep the area surrounding your computer dirt and dust free.
Reducing the dirt and dust around your computer will reduce the need to clean the inside of your computer. If dust builds up inside the computer, remove it carefully with compressed air and a small vacuum. Do not touch the components with the vacuum.

FIGURE 64 To keep important information about your computer on hand and organized, use an outline such as this sample outline.

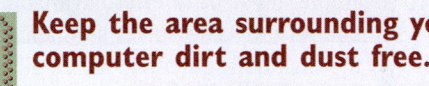

OUTLINE FOR COMPUTER OWNER'S NOTEBOOK

1. List of Vendors
Vendor
Product(s)
City/State
URL
E-mail address
Telephone number
Technical support telephone number

2. Internet and online services information
Service provider name
URL
E-mail address
Logon telephone number
Alternate logon telephone number
Technical support telephone number
User ID
Password

3. Serial numbers
Product
Manufacturer
Serial number

4. Hardware purchase history
Date
Product
Manufacturer
Vendor
Cost
Warranty information

5. Software purchase history
Product
Manufacturer
Vendor
Cost
Date purchased
Date installed/uninstalled
Product keys/registration numbers

6. Trouble Log
Date
Time
Problem
Resolution

7. Support Calls
Date
Time
Company
Contact
Problem
Comments

8. Vendor paperwork

Back up important files and data.

Use a utility program included with the operating system or from a third-party to create a recovery or rescue disk to help you restart your computer if it crashes. Regularly copy important data files to disks, tape, or another computer.

 ### Protect your computer from viruses.

You can protect your computer from viruses by installing an antivirus program and then periodically updating the program by connecting to the manufacturer's Web site. Also, never open a file from an unknown user, particularly those received as e-mail attachments.

 ### Keep your computer tuned.

Most operating systems include several computer utilities that provide basic maintenance functions. In Windows, for example, these utilities are available via the System Tools submenu on the Accessories submenu. One important utility is the disk defragmenter, which allows you to reorganize files, so they are in contiguous (adjacent) clusters, making disk operations faster (Figure 65). Some programs allow you to schedule maintenance tasks for times when you are not using your computer. If necessary, leave your computer on at night so it can run the required maintenance programs. If your operating system does not provide the tools, you can purchase a stand-alone utility program to perform basic maintenance functions.

 ### Learn to use diagnostic tools.

Diagnostic tools help you identify and resolve problems, thereby helping to reduce your need for technical assistance. Diagnostic tools help you test components, monitor resources such as memory and processing power, undo changes made to files, and more. As with basic maintenance tools, most operating systems include diagnostic tools; you also can purchase or download many stand-alone diagnostic tools.

 ### Conserve energy wherever possible.

A simple way to conserve energy is to avoid animated screen savers, which use additional power and prevent your computer from going into hibernation. Fortunately, many of the recent computer, monitor, and printer models go into a very low power mode when not in use for a few minutes. If your printer does not go into a very low power mode, then keep it turned off until you need to print a document or report. Finally, shut your computer system down at night and turn off the main switch on your surge protector.

FIGURE 65 The Disk Defragmenter utility defragments the hard disk by reorganizing the files, so they are in contiguous (adjacent) clusters, making disk operations faster.

Learn It Online

INSTRUCTIONS

To complete these exercises, start your browser, click the Address box, and then enter scsite.com/ic5/exs.htm. When the Introduction to Computers Web page displays, follow the instructions in the exercises below.

I. Project Reinforcement - True/False, Multiple Choice, and Short Answer

Click Project Reinforcement. Print the quiz by clicking Print on the File menu. Answer each question. Write your first and last name at the top of each page, and then hand in the printout to your instructor.

2. Practice Test

Click Practice Test. Answer each question, enter your first and last name at the bottom of the page, and then click the Grade Test button. When the graded practice test displays on your screen, click Print on the File menu to print a hard copy. Continue to take practice tests until you score 80% or better. Hand in a printout of the final practice test to your instructor.

3. Who Wants to Be a Computer Genius?

Click Computer Genius. Read the instructions, enter your first and last name at the bottom of the page, and then click the PLAY button. Submit your score to your instructor.

4. Wheel of Terms

Click Wheel of Terms. Read the instructions, and then enter your first and last name and your school name. Click the VERY HIGH SCORES link to see other student scores. Close the HIGH SCORES window. Click the PLAY button. Submit your score to your instructor.

5. Crossword Puzzle Challenge

Click Crossword Puzzle Challenge. Read the instructions, and then enter your first and last name. Click the PLAY button. Work the crossword puzzle. When you are finished, click the Submit button. When the crossword puzzle re-displays, click the Print button. Hand in the printout to your instructor.

6. Using the Web Guide

Click Web Guide. Click the Computers and Computing link, and then take a tour of the Virtual Museum of Computing. When you are finished, close the window, and then use your word processing program to prepare a brief report on your tour. Visit four other Web sites listed in the Web Guide and print the main page of each. Hand in the printouts to your instructor.

7. Visiting Web Link Sites

Visit 10 of the 18 Web Link sites in the margins of pages COM-2 to COM-18. Print the main Web page for each of the 10 Web sites you visit and hand them in to your instructor.

8. Scavenger Hunt

Click Scavenger Hunt. Print a copy of the Scavenger Hunt page; use this page to write down your answers as you search the Web. Hand in your completed page to your instructor.

9. Search Sleuth

Click Search Sleuth to learn search techniques that will help make you a research expert. Hand in your completed assignment to your instructor.

INDEX

PHOTO CREDITS

Page 1a Courtesy of Intel Corporation; *Page 1b* Photo courtesy of Iomega Corporation; *Page 1c* Courtesy of International Business Machines Corporation; *Page 1d* Courtesy of Microsoft® Corporation; *Page 1e* Courtesy of Handspring, Inc; *Figure 1a* Courtesy of Dell Computer Corporation; *Figure 1b* Courtesy of Logitech, Inc.; *Figure 1c* Courtesy of Hewlett-Packard Company; *Figure 1d* Courtesy of Telex Communications, Inc.; *Figure 1e* Courtesy of SanDisk; *Figure 1f* Courtesy of SanDisk; *Figure 1g* Courtesy of Hewlett-Packard Company; *Figure 1h* Photo Courtesy of Linksys; *Figure 3* © Scott Goodwin Photography; *Figure 4* Courtesy of Logitech, Inc.; *Figure 5a* Courtesy of Palm, Inc., Palm is a trademark of Palm, Inc.; Figure 5b © 2002 PhotoDisc; *Figure 6* Courtesy of Microsoft® Corporation; *Figure 7* Courtesy of International Business Machines Corporation; *Figure 8* Courtesy of Intel Corporation; *Figure 11 collage* Inkjet printer and output pictures provided by Epson America, Inc.; *Figure 12* Courtesy of Hewlett-Packard Company; *Figure 13* Courtesy of ViewSonic Corporation; *Figure 14a* Courtesy of Dell Computer Corporation; *Figure 14b* Courtesy of ViewSonic Corporation; *Figure 14c* Courtesy of Sony Electronics Inc.; *Figure 14d* Courtesy of Handspring, Inc.; *Figure 14e* Siemens press photo © Siemens AG, Munich/Berlin; *Figure 19* Photo courtesy of Iomega Corporation; *Figure 17b* Courtesy of International Business Machines Corporation; *Figure 20a* Courtesy of International Business Machines Corporation; *Figure 20b* © Scott Goodwin Photography; *Figure 22* Courtesy of International Business Machines Corporation; *Figure 23* Courtesy of Seagate Removable Storage Solutions LLC; *Figure 24a* Courtesy of SanDisk; *Figure 24b* Courtesy of Palm, Inc., Palm is a trademark of Palm, Inc.; *Figure 24c* Courtesy of SanDisk; *Figure 24d* Courtesy of SanDisk; *Figure 24e* Courtesy of SanDisk; *Figure 26* © Scott Goodwin Photography; *Figure 35a* Courtesy of Dell Computer Corporation; *Figure 35c* Courtesy of ViewSonic Corporation; *Figure 35d* Courtesy of Palm, Inc., Palm is a trademark of Palm, Inc.; *Figure 46* © 2002 Acer, Inc.; *Figure 47* Courtesy of Toshiba America; *Figure 48* Courtesy of Toshiba America; Figure 49 © Jon Feingersh/ CORBIS; *Figure 50* © 2002 Acer Inc.; *Figure 53* AP/ Wide World Photos; *Figure 55* Courtesy of Fujitsu PC Corporation; *Figure 56* Courtesy of Sony Electronics, Inc.; *Figure 57* Courtesy of Compaq Computer Corporation; *Figure 59* Courtesy of Handspring, Inc.; *Figure 65* Courtesy of Seagate Technology LLC.

MICROSOFT

Windows XP and Office 2003

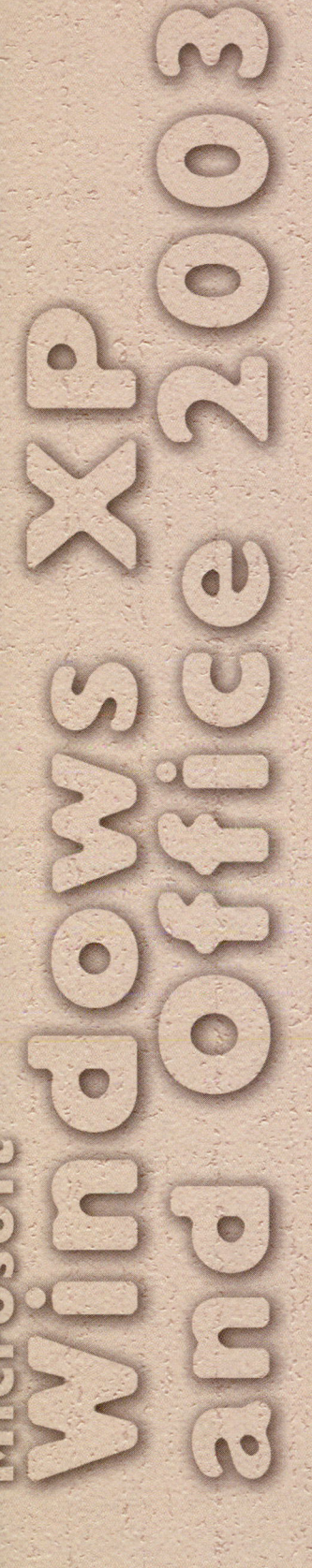

Microsoft Windows XP and Office 2003

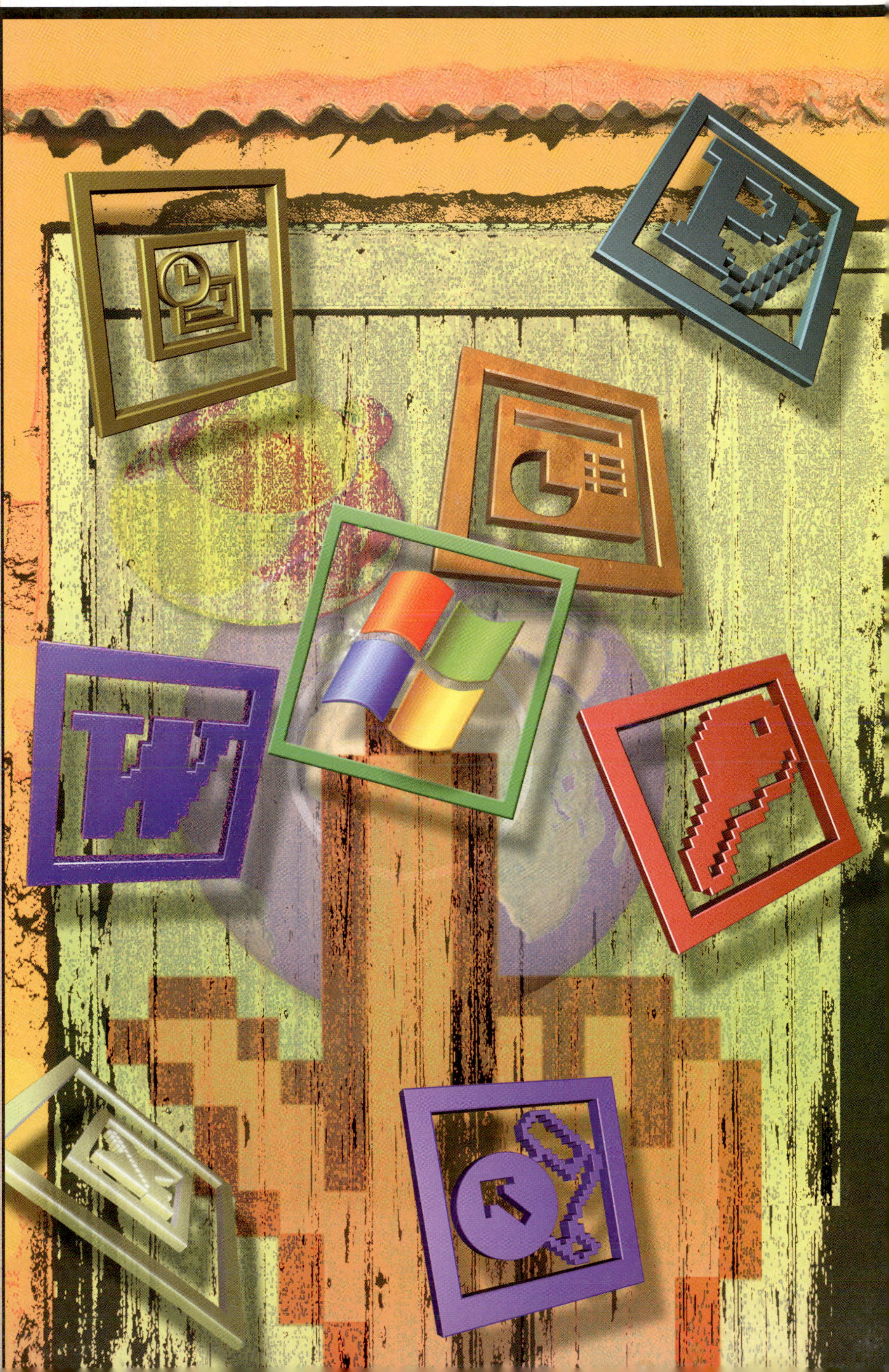

Introduction to Microsoft Windows XP and Office 2003

PROJECT

1

CASE PERSPECTIVE

After weeks of planning, your organization finally installed Microsoft Windows XP Professional on all workstations. As the computer trainer for the upcoming in-house seminar, you realize you should know more about Microsoft Windows XP Professional but have had little time to learn. Since installing Windows XP Professional, many employees have come to you with questions. You have taken the time to answer their questions by sitting down with them at their computers and searching for the answers using the Help and Support feature.

From their questions, you determine that you should customize the seminar to cover the basics of Windows XP Professional, including basic mouse operations, working with windows, launching an application, and searching for answers using Help and Support. Your goal is to become familiar with Microsoft Windows XP Professional in order to teach the seminar more effectively to the participants.

As you read through this project, you will learn how to use the Windows XP operating system to perform basic operating system tasks and become familiar with the Microsoft Office 2003 applications.

Introduction to Microsoft Windows XP and Office 2003

Objectives

You will have mastered the material in this project when you can:

- Launch Microsoft Windows XP, log on to the computer, and identify the objects on the desktop
- Perform the basic mouse operations: point, click, right-click, double-click, drag, and right-drag
- Display the Start menu and launch an application program
- Add and remove a desktop icon
- Open, minimize, maximize, restore, and close a window
- Move, size, and scroll a window
- Launch and quit an application using Windows Explorer
- Expand and collapse a folder
- Display the contents of a drive and folder
- Copy, move, rename, and delete files
- Use Help and Support
- Log off from the computer and turn it off

Introduction

An **operating system** is the set of computer instructions, called a computer program, that controls the allocation of computer hardware such as memory, disk devices, printers, and CD and DVD drives, and provides the capability for you to communicate with the computer. The most popular and widely used operating system is **Microsoft Windows**. **Microsoft Windows XP**, the newest version of Microsoft Windows, allows you to easily communicate with and control your computer.

Windows XP is easy to use and can be customized to fit individual needs. Windows XP simplifies the processes of working with documents and applications, transferring data between documents, organizing the manner in which you interact with the computer, and using the computer to access information on the Internet or an intranet. The **Internet** is a worldwide group of connected computer networks that allows public access to information on thousands of subjects and gives users the means to use this information, send messages, and obtain products and services.

Microsoft Windows XP Operating Systems

The Microsoft Windows XP operating systems consist of Microsoft Windows XP Professional and Microsoft Windows XP Home Edition. **Microsoft Windows XP Professional** is the operating system designed for businesses of all sizes and for advanced home computing. In business, Windows XP Professional is commonly used on computer workstations and portable computers. A **workstation** is a computer connected to a server. A **server** is a computer that controls access to the hardware and software on a network and provides a centralized storage area for programs, data, and information. Figure 1-1 illustrates a simple computer network consisting of a server and three computers (called workstations) and a laser printer connected to the server (Figure 1-1).

Microsoft
Windows XP

Microsoft
Windows XP

Microsoft
Windows XP

workstation

workstation

workstation

server

laser
printer

FIGURE 1-1

More About

Microsoft Windows XP

Microsoft Windows XP combines the best features of Microsoft Windows 98 with the power and reliability of Microsoft Windows 2000. Windows 98, which was designed for use on personal computers, is the most popular operating system for PCs. Windows 2000, designed for use on a computer network, is the most widely used business version of Windows.

Microsoft Windows XP Home Edition contains many of the features of the Microsoft Windows XP Professional operating system but is designed for entertainment and home use. Home Edition allows you to establish in the home a network of computers that share a single Internet connection, share a device such as a printer or a scanner, share files and folders, and play multi-computer games. The network can be created using Ethernet cable or telephone wire, or it can be wireless.

More About

Microsoft
Windows XP

A vast amount of information about Microsoft Windows XP is available on the Internet. For additional information about Microsoft Windows XP, visit the Windows XP More About Web Page (scsite.com/winoff2003/more) and then click Microsoft Windows XP.

Microsoft Windows XP Professional

Microsoft Windows XP Professional (called **Windows XP** for the rest of the book) is an operating system that performs every function necessary for you to communicate with and use the computer. Windows XP is called a **32-bit operating system** because it uses 32 bits for addressing and other purposes, which means the operating system can address more than four gigabytes of RAM (random-access memory) and perform tasks faster than older operating systems. A **Windows XP 64-Bit Edition** is also available for individuals solving complex scientific problems, developing high-performance design and engineering applications, or creating 3-D animations.

Windows XP is easy to use and can be customized to fit individual needs. Windows XP simplifies the process of working with documents and applications by transferring data between documents, organizing the manner in which you interact with the computer, and using the computer to access information on the Internet or an intranet. Windows XP is used to run **application programs**, which are programs that perform an application-related function such as word processing. To use the application programs that can be launched under Windows XP, you must know about the Windows XP user interface.

What Is a User Interface?

A **user interface** is the combination of hardware and software that you use to communicate with and control the computer. Through the user interface, you are able to make selections on the computer, request information from the computer, and respond to messages displayed by the computer. Thus, a user interface provides the means for dialogue between you and the computer.

Hardware and software together form the user interface. Among the hardware devices associated with a user interface are the monitor, keyboard, and mouse (Figure 1-2). The **monitor** displays messages and provides information. You respond by entering data in the form of a command or other response using the **keyboard** or **mouse**. Among the responses available to you are ones that specify which application program to run, what document to open, when to print, and where to store data for future use.

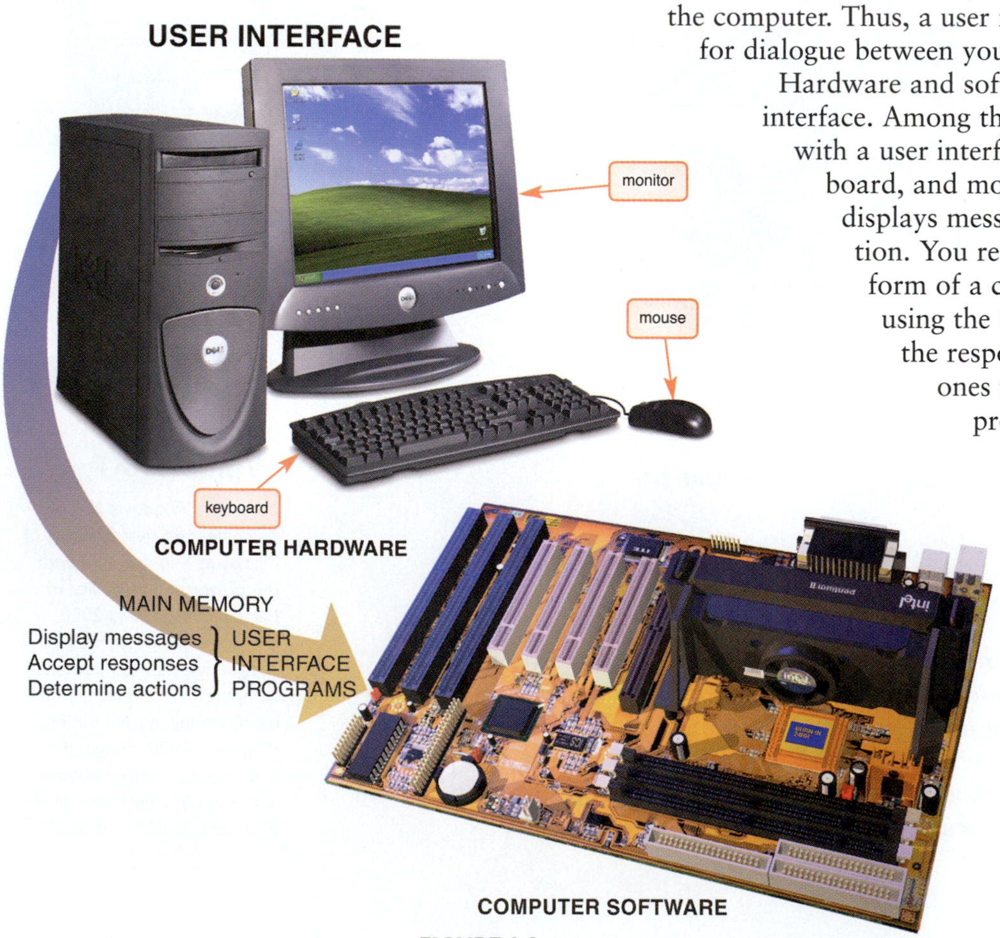

USER INTERFACE

monitor

mouse

keyboard

COMPUTER HARDWARE

MAIN MEMORY

Display messages } USER
Accept responses } INTERFACE
Determine actions } PROGRAMS

COMPUTER SOFTWARE

FIGURE 1-2

The computer software associated with the user interface consists of the programs that engage you in dialogue (Figure 1-2). The computer software determines the messages you receive, the manner in which you should respond, and the actions that occur, based on your responses.

The goal of an effective user interface is to be **user-friendly**, which means the software can be used easily by individuals with limited training. Research studies have indicated that the use of graphics can play an important role in aiding users to interact effectively with a computer. A **graphical user interface**, or **GUI** (pronounced gooey), is a user interface that displays graphics in addition to text when it communicates with the user.

The Windows XP graphical user interface was designed carefully to be easier to set up, simpler to learn, faster, more powerful, and better integrated with the Internet than previous versions of Microsoft Windows.

Launching Microsoft Windows XP

When you turn on the computer, an introductory black screen consisting of the Microsoft Windows XP logo, progress bar, copyright messages (Copyright © 1985–2001 and Microsoft Corporation), and the word, Microsoft, are displayed. The progress bar indicates the progress of the Windows XP operating system launch. After approximately one minute, the Welcome screen displays (Figure 1-3).

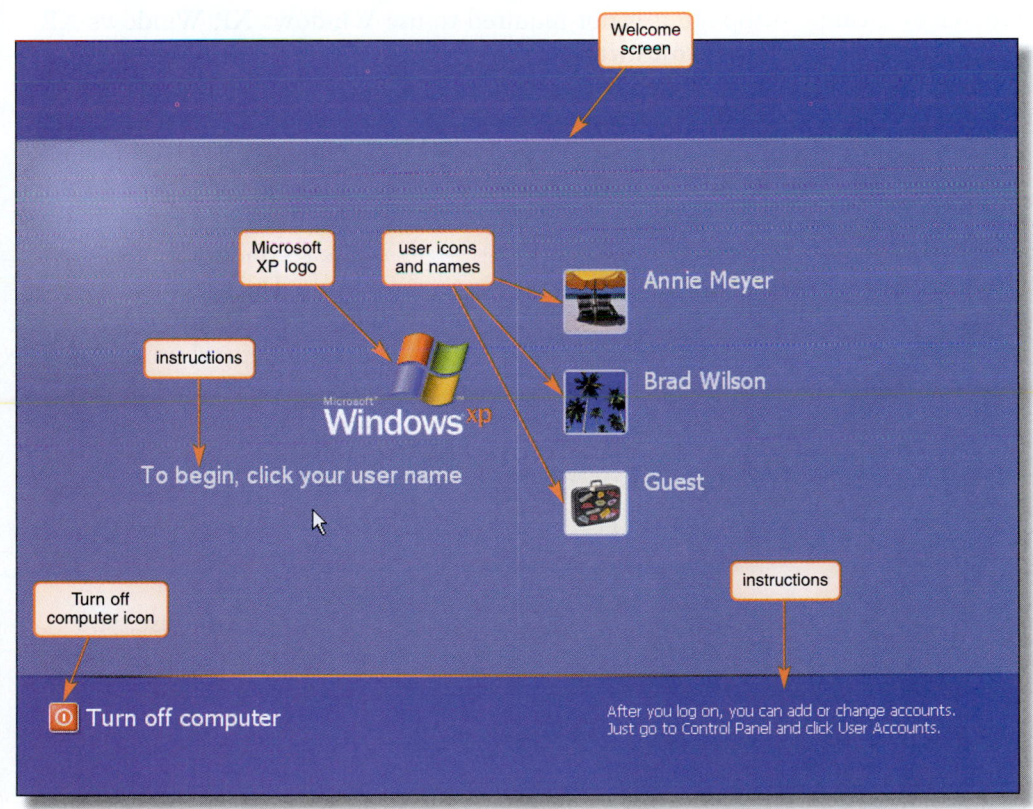

FIGURE 1-3

More About

User Names and Passwords

A unique user name identifies each computer user. In the past, users often entered a variation of their name as the user name. For example, Brad Wilson might have chosen bradwilson or bwilson. Today, most Windows XP users use their first and last names without variation as the user name. A password is a combination of characters that allows a user access to certain computer resources on the network. Passwords should be kept confidential.

More About

Microsoft Mice

For additional information about Microsoft Mice, visit the Microsoft Windows XP More About Web Page (scsite.com/winoff2003/more) and then click Microsoft Mice.

More About

The Mouse

The mouse, although invented in the 1960s, was not used widely until the Apple Macintosh computer became available in 1984. Even then, some highbrows called mouse users wimps. Today, the mouse is an indispensable tool for every computer user.

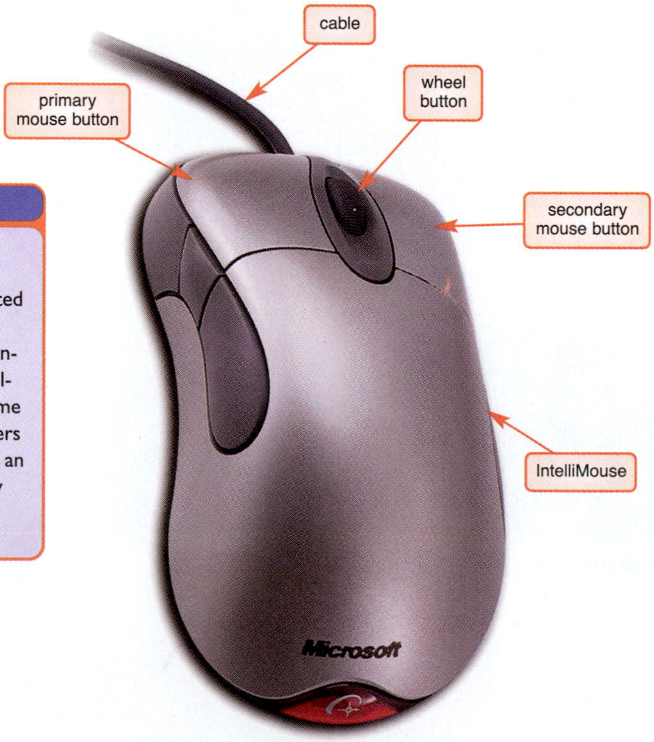

The **Welcome screen** shows the names of every computer user on the computer. On the left side of the Welcome screen, the Microsoft XP logo and the instructions, To begin, click your user name, appear. On the right side of the Welcome screen is a list of the **user icons** and **user names** for all authorized computer users (Annie Meyer, Brad Wilson, and Guest). Clicking the user icon or user name begins the process of logging on to the computer. The list of user icons and names on the Welcome screen on your computer may be different.

At the bottom of the Welcome screen is the Turn off computer icon and the instructions, After you log on, you can add or change accounts. Just go to Control Panel and click User Accounts. Clicking the Turn off computer icon initiates the process of shutting down the computer. The **Control Panel** allows you to create a new user, change or remove an existing user, and change user information. The user information that can be changed consists of the user icon and user name, user password, and account type (Administrator, Limited, and Guest).

The Windows XP User Interface

The Windows XP interface provides the means for dialogue between you and the computer. Part of this dialogue involves requesting information from the computer and responding to messages displayed by the computer. You can request information and respond to messages by using either the mouse or the keyboard.

A **mouse** is a pointing device used with Windows XP that is attached to the computer by a cable. Although it is not required to use Windows XP, Windows XP supports the use of the **Microsoft IntelliMouse** (Figure 1-4). The IntelliMouse contains three buttons: the primary mouse button, the secondary mouse button, and the wheel button between the primary and secondary mouse buttons. Typically, the **primary mouse button** is the left mouse button and the **secondary mouse button** is the right mouse button, although Windows XP allows you to switch them. In this book, the left mouse button is the primary mouse button and the right mouse button is the secondary mouse button. The functions the **wheel button** and wheel perform depend on the software application being used. If the mouse connected to the computer is not an IntelliMouse, it will not have a wheel button between the primary and secondary mouse buttons.

Using the mouse, you can perform the following operations: (1) point; (2) click; (3) right-click; (4) double-click; (5) drag; and (6) right-drag. These operations are demonstrated on the following pages.

FIGURE 1-4

Many common tasks, such as logging on to the computer or logging off, are performed by pointing to an item and then clicking the item. **Point** means you move the mouse across a flat surface until the mouse pointer rests on the item of choice. As you move the mouse across a flat surface, the IntelliEye optical sensor on the underside of the mouse senses the movement of the ball on the mouse (Figure 1-5), and the mouse pointer moves across the desktop in the same direction.

Click means you press and release the primary mouse button, which in this book is the left mouse button. In most cases, you must point to an item before you click.

Logging On to the Computer

After launching Windows XP but before working with Windows XP, you must log on to the computer. **Logging on** to the computer opens your user account and makes the computer available for use.

In the following steps, the Brad Wilson icon and the Next button are used to log on to the computer. In a school environment, you will want to log on to the computer by pointing to and clicking *your user icon* on the Welcome screen and typing *your password* in the text box instead of the password shown in the steps.

The following steps illustrate how to log on to the computer by pointing to and clicking your icon on the Welcome screen, typing your password, and then pointing to and clicking the Next button.

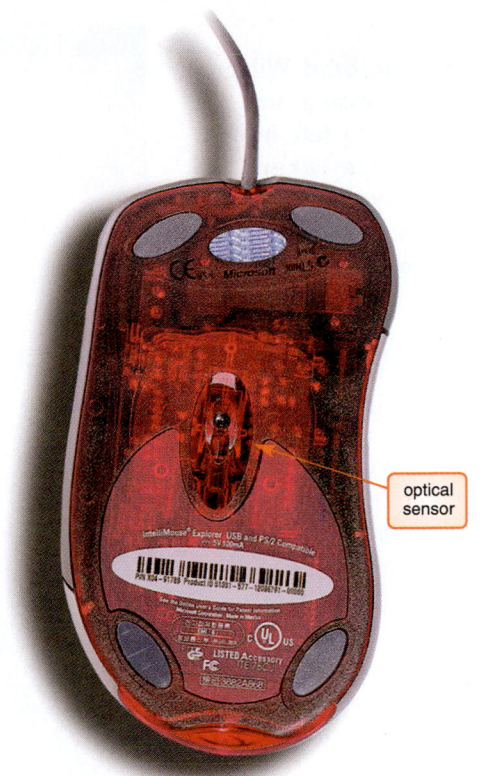

optical sensor

FIGURE 1-5

To Log On to the Computer

1

• Point to the Brad Wilson icon on the Welcome screen by moving the mouse across a flat surface until the mouse pointer rests on the icon.

Pointing to the Brad Wilson icon displays a yellow border on the icon and dims the other user icons and names (Figure 1-6).

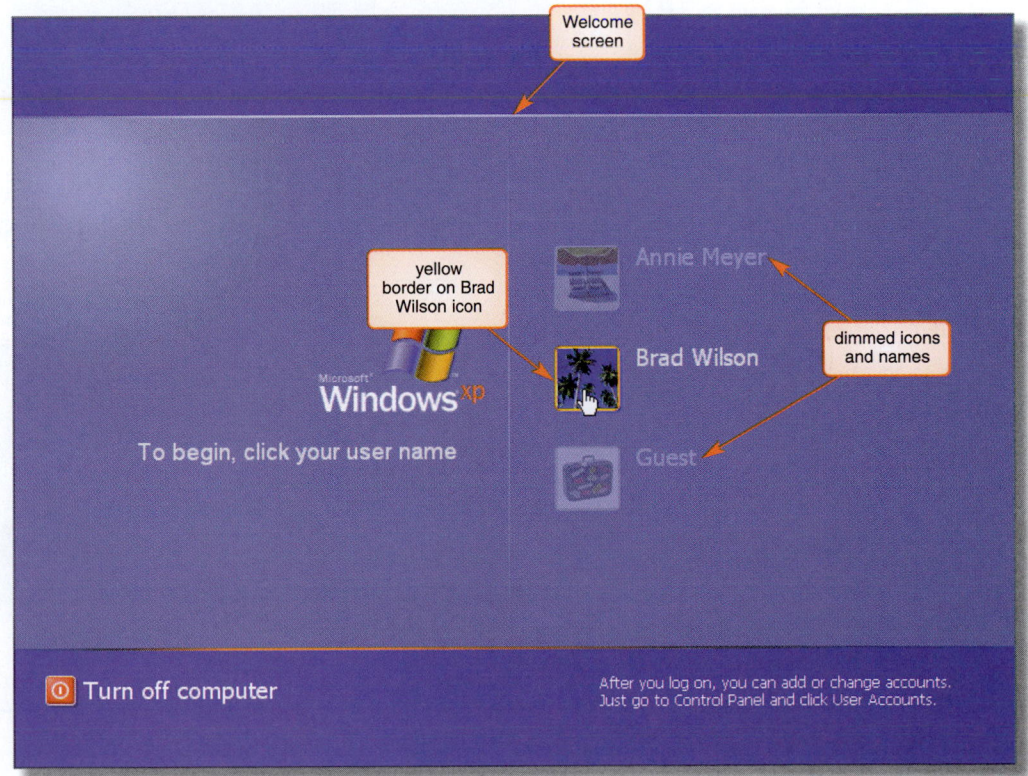

Welcome screen

yellow border on Brad Wilson icon

Annie Meyer

dimmed icons and names

Brad Wilson

Microsoft
Windowsxp

To begin, click your user name

Guest

Turn off computer

After you log on, you can add or change accounts. Just go to Control Panel and click User Accounts.

FIGURE 1-6

2

• **Click the Brad Wilson icon by pressing and releasing the left mouse button, type** lakers **in the Type your password text box, and then point to the Next button.**

Windows XP highlights the Brad Wilson icon and name, displays the Type your password text box containing a series of bullets (•••••) and an insertion point, and the Next and Help buttons (Figure 1-7). A text box is a rectangular area in which you can enter text. The bullets in the text box hide the password entered by the user.

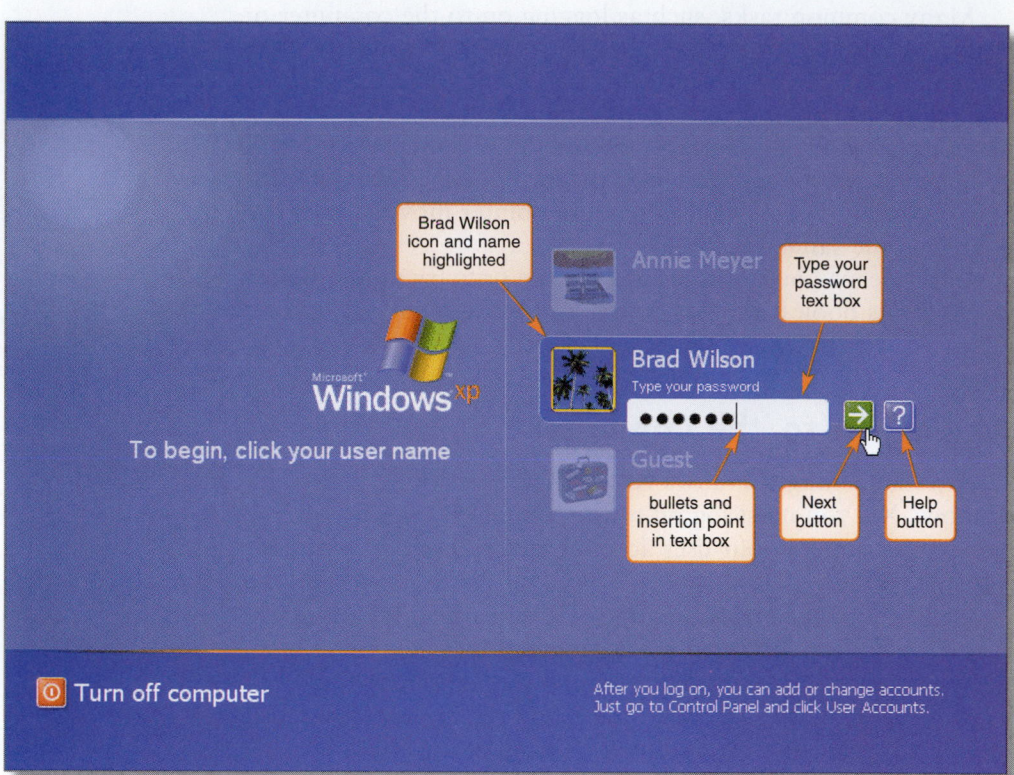

FIGURE 1-7

3

• **Click the Next button.**

The contents of the Welcome screen change to contain the word, Welcome, on the left side of the screen and the user name, user icon, and message, Loading your personal settings..., on the right side. This screen appears momentarily while the user is logged on to the computer and then several items appear on a background called the desktop (Figure 1-8). The background design of the desktop is Bliss, but your computer may display a different design.

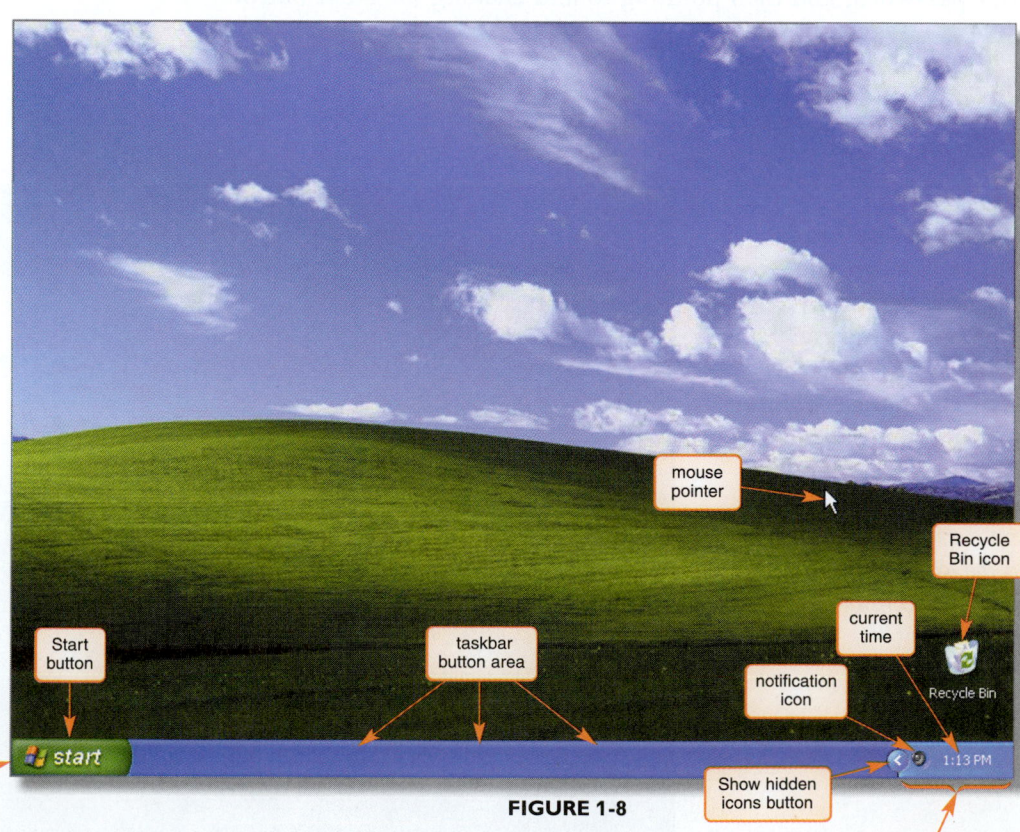

FIGURE 1-8

The items on the desktop in Figure 1-8 include the Recycle Bin icon and its name in the lower-right corner of the desktop and the taskbar across the bottom of the desktop. The Recycle Bin icon (Recycle Bin) allows you to discard unneeded objects. Your computer's desktop may contain more, fewer, or different icons because you can customize the desktop of the computer.

The **taskbar** shown at the bottom of the screen in Figure 1-8 contains the Start button, taskbar button area, and notification area. The **Start button** allows you to launch a program quickly, find or open a document, change the computer's settings, obtain Help, shut down the computer, and perform many more tasks. The **taskbar button area** contains buttons to indicate which windows are open on the desktop. In Figure 1-8, no windows are displayed on the desktop and no buttons appear in the taskbar button area.

The **notification area** contains the Show hidden icons button, one notification icon, and the current time. The **Show hidden icons button** indicates that one or more inactive icons are hidden from view in the notification area. The **notification icon** in the notification area provides quick access to programs on the computer. Other icons that provide information about the status of the computer appear temporarily in the notification area. For example, the Printer icon appears when a document is sent to the printer and is removed when printing is complete. The notification area on your desktop may contain more, fewer, or different icons because the contents of the notification area can change.

The mouse pointer appears on the desktop. On the desktop, the **mouse pointer** is the shape of a block arrow. The mouse pointer allows you to point to objects on the desktop and may change shape when it points to different objects. A shadow may be displayed behind the mouse pointer to make the mouse pointer appear in a three-dimensional form.

When you click an object, such as the Brad Wilson icon (or your icon) or the Next button shown in Figure 1-7, you must point to the object before you click. In the steps that follow, the instruction that directs you to point to a particular item and then click is, Click the particular item. For example, Click the Next button means point to the Next button and then click.

The Windows XP Desktop

Nearly every item on the Windows XP desktop is considered an object. Even the desktop itself is an object. Every **object** has properties. The **properties** of an object are unique to that specific object and may affect what can be done to the object or what the object does. For example, a property of an object may be the color of the object, such as the color of the desktop.

The Windows XP desktop and the objects on the desktop emulate a work area in an office. You may think of the Windows desktop as an electronic version of the top of your desk. You can place objects on the desktop, move the objects around on the desktop, look at them, and then put them aside, and so on. In this project, you will learn how to interact and communicate with the Windows XP desktop.

Displaying the Start Menu

A **menu** is a list of related commands and each **command** on a menu performs a specific action, such as searching for files or obtaining Help. The **Start menu** allows you to access easily the most useful items on the computer. The Start menu contains commands that allow you to connect to and browse the Internet, launch an e-mail program, launch application programs, store and search for documents, customize the computer, and obtain Help on thousands of topics.

The following steps show how to display the Start menu.

To Display the Start Menu

1

• **Point to the Start button on the taskbar.**

The mouse pointer on the Start button causes the color of the Start button to change to light green and displays a ToolTip (Click here to begin) (Figure 1-9). The ToolTip provides instructions for using the Start button.

FIGURE 1-9

2

• **Click the Start button.**

The Start menu appears, the color of the Start button changes to dark green, and the Start button becomes recessed (Figure 1-10). The top section of the Start menu contains the user icon and name, the middle section contains two columns of commands, and the bottom section contains two icons (Log Off and Turn Off Computer).

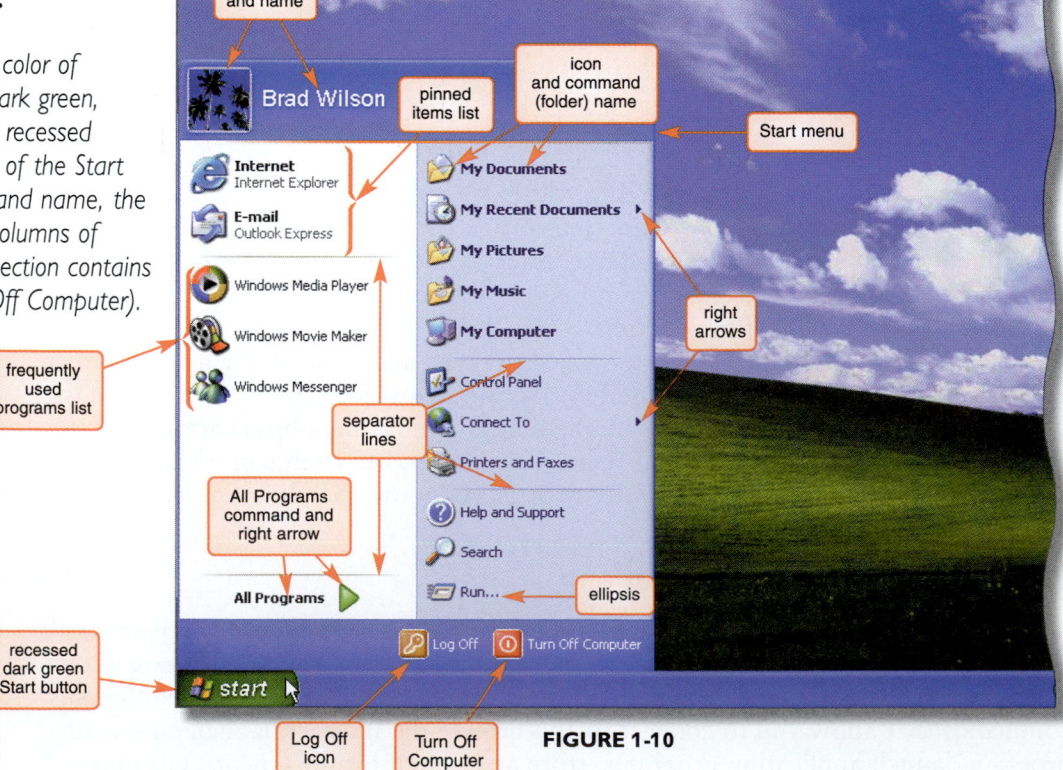

FIGURE 1-10

3

• **Point to All Programs on the Start menu.**

When you point to All Programs, Windows XP highlights the All Programs command on the Start menu by displaying the All Programs command name in white text on a blue background and displays the All Programs submenu (Figure 1-11). A submenu is a menu that appears when you point to a command followed by a right arrow. Whenever you point to a command on a menu or submenu, the command name is highlighted.

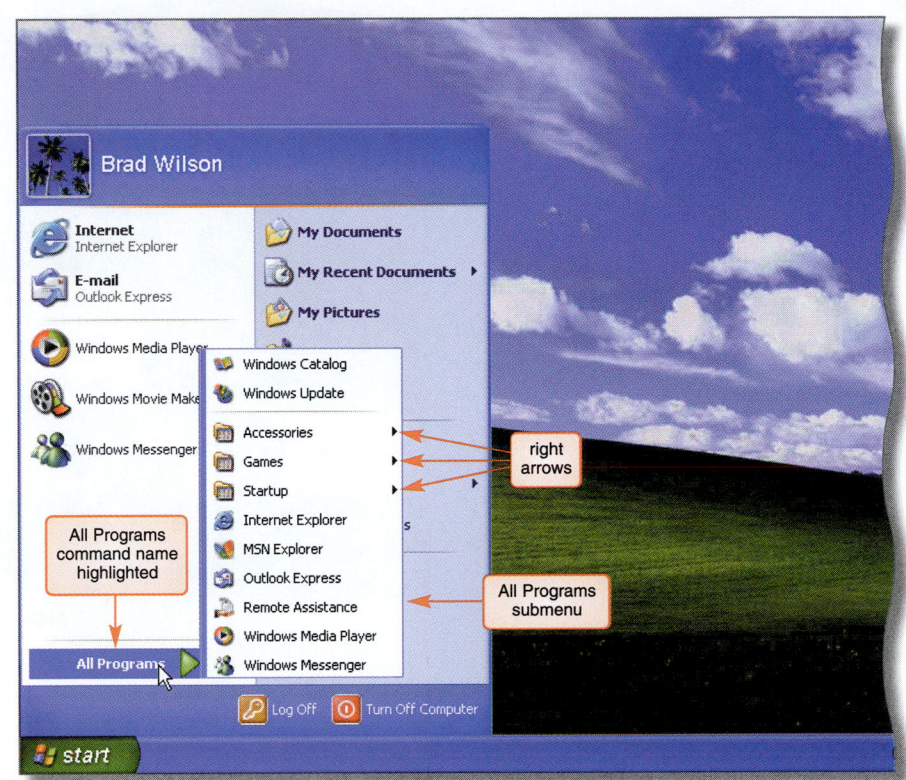

FIGURE 1-11

4

• **Point to Accessories on the All Programs submenu.**

When you point to Accessories, Windows XP highlights the Accessories command on the All Programs submenu and displays the Accessories submenu (Figure 1-12). Clicking a command on the Accessories submenu that contains an application name launches that application. For example, to launch Notepad, you would click the Notepad command on the Accessories submenu.

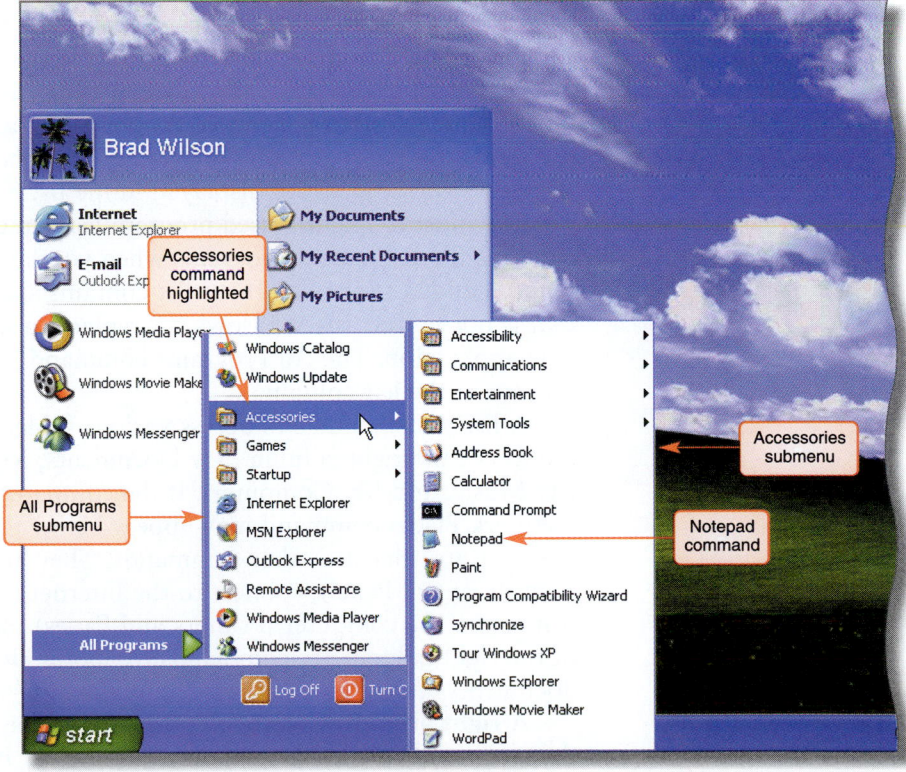

FIGURE 1-12

5

• **Point to an open area of the desktop and then click the open area to close the Start menu, Accessories submenu, and All Programs submenu.**

The Start menu, Accessories submenu, and All Programs submenu close, and the recessed dark green Start button changes to its original light green color (Figure 1-13). The mouse pointer points to the desktop. To close a menu, click any area of the desktop except the menu itself.

Start menu, Accessories submenu, and All Programs submenu close

mouse pointer

non-recessed light green Start button

FIGURE 1-13

Other Ways

1. Press CTRL+ESC
2. Press WINDOWS

More About

Desktop Icons

In the past, rows and rows of icons could be seen on Windows desktops. That was the past! Today, the Windows XP desktop contains only the Recycle Bin icon. The Recycle Bin icon, the lone desktop icon, vigilantly waits to dispose of your trash. Yes, the word of the day at Microsoft is uncluttered.

The middle section of the Start menu shown in Figure 1-10 on page WIN 12 consists of two columns of commands. Each command is identified by a unique icon and name. Commands may represent an application program, folder, or operation.

The list of commands above the separator line at the top of the left column, called the **pinned items list**, consists of the default Web browser program (Internet Explorer) and default e-mail program (Outlook Express). The list of commands below the separator line, called the **most frequently used programs list**, contains the most frequently used programs. Programs are added to the list when you use them. Currently, three programs (Windows Media Player, Windows Movie Maker, and Windows Messenger) are displayed in the list.

The most frequently used program list can contain up to six programs. If the list contains fewer than six programs when you launch a new program, the program name is added to the list. If the list contains six names when you launch a program that is not on the list, Windows XP replaces a less frequently used program with the new application. The All Programs command appears below the separator line at the bottom of the left column.

A list of commands to access various folders appears above the separator line at the top of the right column (My Documents, My Recent Documents, My Pictures, My Music, and My Computer). If the computer is connected to a network, the My Network Places command may appear below the My Computer command. Below the separator line are other commands. They are commands to customize the computer (Control Panel), connect to the Internet (Connect To), and add printers and fax printers to the computer (Printers and Faxes). Below the separator line at the bottom of the right column are commands to obtain Help (Help and Support), search for documents and folders (Search), and launch programs (Run).

A **right arrow** following a command on the Start menu indicates that pointing to the command will display a submenu. The All Programs command is followed by a green right arrow, and the My Recent Documents and Connect To commands are followed by smaller black arrows. One command (Run) is followed by an **ellipsis** (…) to indicate more information is required to execute the command.

Windows XP provides a number of ways in which to accomplish a particular task. In the remainder of this book, a specific set of steps will illustrate how to accomplish each task. These steps may not be the only way in which the task can be completed. If you can perform the same task using other means, the Other Ways box specifies the methods. In each case, the method shown in the steps is the preferred method, but it is important for you to be aware of all the techniques you can use.

Adding an Icon to the Desktop

Although the Windows XP desktop may contain only the Recycle Bin icon (see Figure 1-8 on page WIN 10), you may want to add additional icons to the desktop. For example, you may want to add the My Computer icon to the desktop so you can view the contents of the computer easily. One method of viewing the contents of the computer is to click the My Computer command on the Start menu to open the My Computer window. If you use My Computer frequently, you may want to place the My Computer icon on the desktop where it is easier to find.

One method of adding the My Computer icon to the desktop is to right-click the My Computer command on the Start menu. **Right-click** means you press and release the secondary mouse button, which in this book is the right mouse button. As directed when using the primary mouse button to click an object, normally you will point to the object before you right-click it. The following steps illustrate how to add the My Computer icon to the desktop.

To Add an Icon to the Desktop

1

• **Click the Start button, point to My Computer on the Start menu, and then press and release the right mouse button.**

Windows XP highlights the My Computer command and displays a shortcut menu containing nine commands (Figure 1-14). Right-clicking an object, such as the My Computer command, displays a shortcut menu that contains commands specifically for use with that object.

FIGURE 1-14

2

• **Point to Show on Desktop on the shortcut menu.**

When you point to Show on Desktop, Windows XP highlights the Show on Desktop command (Figure 1-15).

FIGURE 1-15

3

• **Click Show on Desktop.**

The shortcut menu closes and the My Computer icon is displayed on the desktop (Figure 1-16). The Start menu remains on the desktop.

4

• **Click an open area on the desktop to close the Start menu.**

The Start menu closes.

FIGURE 1-16

Whenever you right-click an object, a shortcut menu is displayed. As you will see, the use of shortcut menus speeds up your work and adds flexibility to your interaction with the computer.

Opening a Window Using a Desktop Icon

Double-click means you quickly press and release the left mouse button twice without moving the mouse. In most cases, you must point to an item before you double-click. The following step shows how to open the My Computer window on the desktop by double-clicking the My Computer icon on the desktop.

To Open a Window Using a Desktop Icon

1

• **Point to the My Computer icon on the desktop and then double-click by quickly pressing and releasing the left mouse button twice without moving the mouse.**

The My Computer window opens and the recessed dark blue My Computer button is displayed in the taskbar button area (Figure 1-17). The My Computer window allows you to view the contents of the computer.

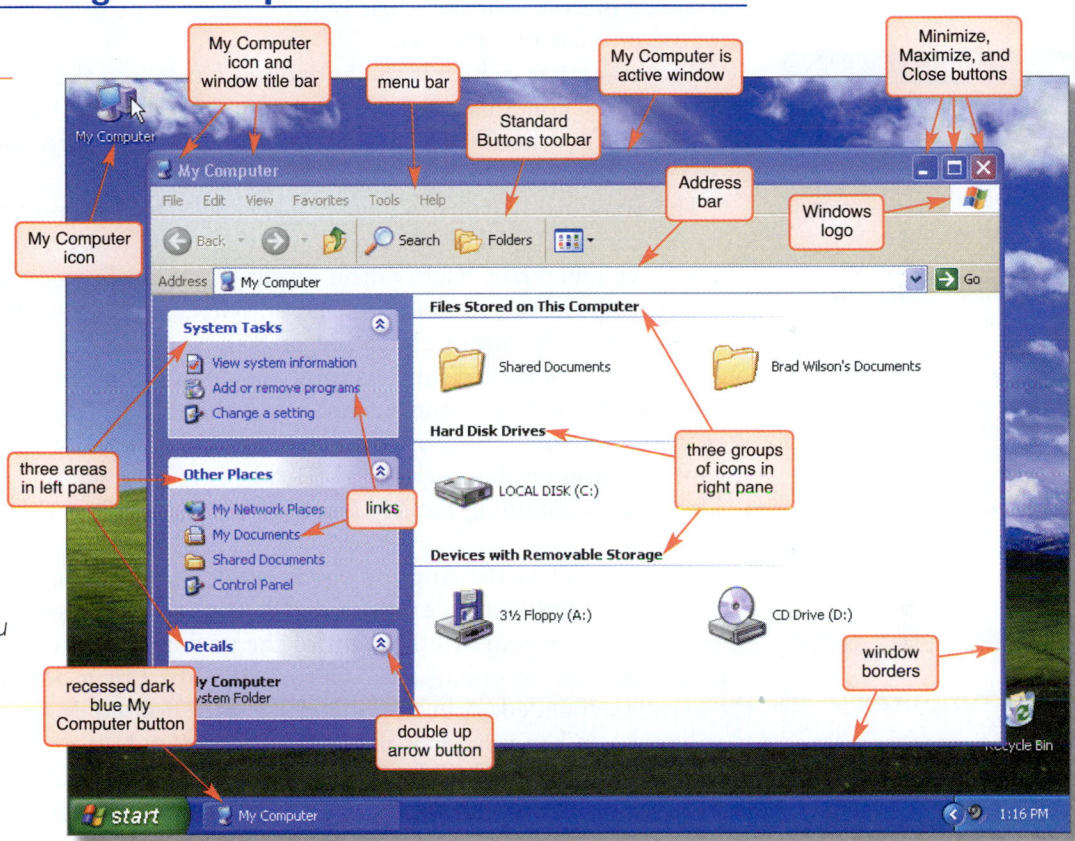

FIGURE 1-17

The My Computer window, the only open window, is the active window. The **active window** is the window you currently are using or that currently is selected. Whenever you click an object that opens a window, such as the My Computer icon, Windows XP will open the window and a recessed dark blue button in the taskbar button area will identify the open window. The recessed dark blue button identifies the active window. The contents of the My Computer window on your computer may be different from the contents of the My Computer window shown in Figure 1-17.

Other Ways

1. Right-click desktop icon, click Open on shortcut menu
2. Press WINDOWS+E

More About

Double-Clicking

Double-clicking is the most difficult mouse skill to learn. Many people have a tendency to move the mouse before they click a second time, even when they do not want to move the mouse. With a little practice, you should find double-clicking without moving the mouse becomes quite natural.

More About

The Contents of the My Computer Window

Because windows can be easily customized, your My Computer window may not resemble the window shown in Figure 1-17. For example, different toolbars may appear below the menu bar, icons may appear smaller, icons may not be grouped, and different areas may be displayed in the left pane of the window.

More About

My Computer

While the trade press and media once poked fun at the My Computer name, Microsoft continues to expand the concept. Windows XP now showcases the My Computer, My Documents, My Pictures, and My Music names by placing them on the Start menu. In addition, the new My Videos folder was added to the operating system. Microsoft contends that beginners find these names easier to understand.

The My Computer Window

The thin blue line, or **window border**, surrounding the My Computer window shown in Figure 1-17 on the previous page determines its shape and size. The **title bar** at the top of the window contains a small icon that is similar to the icon on the desktop, and the **window title** (My Computer) identifies the window. The color of the title bar (dark blue) and the recessed dark blue My Computer button in the taskbar button area indicate that the My Computer window is the active window. The color of the active window on your computer may be different from the color shown in Figure 1-17.

Clicking the icon at the left on the title bar will display the **System menu**, which contains commands to carry out the actions associated with the My Computer window. At the right on the title bar are three buttons (the Minimize button, the Maximize button, and the Close button) that can be used to specify the size of the window or close the window.

The **menu bar**, which is the horizontal bar below the title bar of a window, in Figure 1-17 contains a list of menu names for the My Computer window: File, Edit, View, Favorites, Tools, and Help. The Windows logo appears on the far right of the menu bar.

The Standard buttons toolbar displays below the menu bar. The **Standard Buttons toolbar** allows you to perform often-used tasks more quickly than when you use the menu bar. Each button on the Standard Buttons toolbar contains an icon. Three buttons contain a **text label** (Back, Search, and Folders) that identifies the function of the button. Each button will be explained in detail as it is used. The buttons on the Standard Buttons toolbar on your computer may be different.

Below the Standard Buttons toolbar is the Address bar. The **Address bar** allows you to launch an application, display a document, open another window, and search for information on the Internet. The Address bar shown in Figure 1-17 displays the Address box containing the My Computer icon, window title, down arrow, and the Go button.

The area below the Address bar is divided into two panes. The System Tasks, Other Places, and Details areas are displayed in the left pane. A title identifies each area. A button appears to the right of the title in each area to indicate whether the area is expanded or collapsed. A button identified by a **double up arrow** indicates the area is expanded. A button identified by a **double down arrow** indicates the area is collapsed. When you click the double up arrow button, the area collapses and only the title and the double down arrow button appear. When you click the double down arrow button, the area expands and the entire contents of the area are visible.

All three areas in the left pane are expanded. The **System Tasks area** contains a title (System Tasks) and three tasks (View system information, Add or remove programs, and Change a setting) associated with the My Computer window. The **Other Places area** contains a title (Other Places) and links to four folders (My Network Places, My Documents, Shared Documents, and Control Panel) associated with the My Computer folder. The **Details area** contains a title (Details), the window title (My Computer), and the folder type (System Folder) of the My Computer window. Clicking the double up arrow collapses the area and leaves only the title and arrow button.

Pointing to a task in the System Tasks area or a folder name in the Other Places area underlines the task or folder name and displays the task or folder name in light blue. Underlined text, such as the task and folder names, is referred to as a **hyperlink**, or simply a **link**. Pointing to a link changes the mouse pointer to a hand icon, and clicking a link displays information associated with the link. For example, clicking the Add or remove programs task in the System Tasks area allows you to install or remove application programs, and clicking the My Documents link in the Other Places area opens the My Documents window.

The right pane of the My Computer window contains three groups of icons. The top group, Files Stored on This Computer, contains Shared Documents and Brad Wilson's Documents icons. The **Shared Documents folder** contains documents and folders that are available (shared) to other computer users on the network, and the Brad Wilson's Documents folder contains his personal documents. On your computer, your name will replace the Brad Wilson name in the Brad Wilson's Documents icon.

The middle group, Hard Disk Drives, contains the LOCAL DISK (C:) drive icon. A title to the right of the icon identifies the drive name, LOCAL DISK (C:). The bottom group, Devices with Removable Storage, contains the 3½ Floppy (A:) and CD Drive (D:) icons and labels. The three icons in the Hard Disk Drives and Devices with Removable Storage sections, called **drive icons**, represent a hard disk drive, 3½ floppy disk drive, and a Compact Disc drive. The number of groups in the right pane and the icons in the groups on your computer may be different.

Clicking a drive or folder icon selects the icon in the right pane and displays details about the drive or folder in the areas in the left pane. Double-clicking a drive or folder icon allows you to display the contents of the corresponding drive or folder in the right pane and details about the drive or folder in the areas in the left pane. You may find more, fewer, or different drive and folder icons in the My Computer window on your computer.

Minimizing a Window

Two buttons on the title bar of a window, the Minimize button and the Maximize button, allow you to control the way a window is displayed or is not displayed on the desktop. When you click the **Minimize button** (see Figure 1-18 on the next page), the My Computer window no longer is displayed on the desktop and the recessed dark blue My Computer button in the taskbar button area changes to a non-recessed medium blue button. A minimized window still is open but is not displayed on the screen. To minimize and then redisplay the My Computer window, complete the steps on the next page.

More About

Minimizing Windows

Windows management on the Windows XP desktop is important in order to keep the desktop uncluttered. You will find yourself frequently minimizing windows and then later reopening them with a click of a button in the taskbar button area.

To Minimize and Redisplay a Window

1

• **Point to the Minimize button on the title bar of the My Computer window.**

The mouse pointer points to the Minimize button on the My Computer window title bar, the color of the Minimize button changes to light blue, a ToolTip is displayed below the Minimize button, and the recessed dark blue My Computer button appears on the taskbar (Figure 1-18).

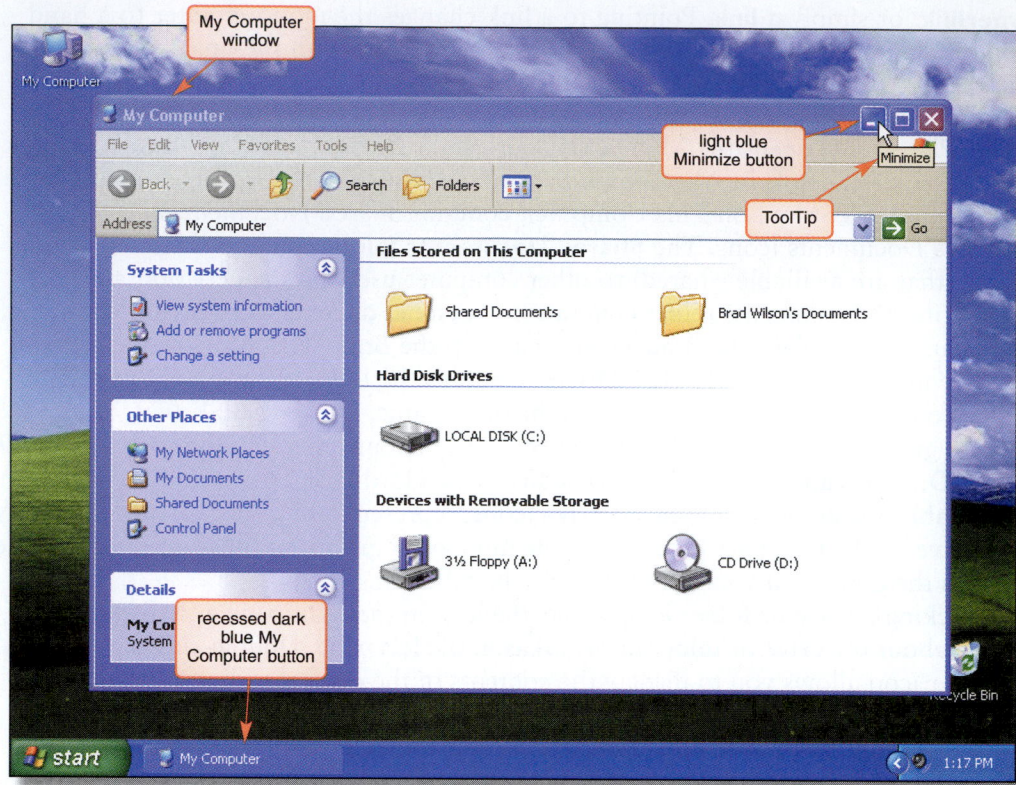

FIGURE 1-18

2

• **Click the Minimize button.**

When you minimize the My Computer window, Windows XP removes the My Computer window from the desktop, the My Computer button changes to a non-recessed button, and the color of the button changes to medium blue (Figure 1-19).

FIGURE 1-19

3

• **Click the My Computer button in the taskbar button area.**

The My Computer window is displayed in the same place with the same size as it was before being minimized, and the My Computer button on the taskbar is recessed (Figure 1-20). With the mouse pointer pointing to the My Computer button, the color of the button is medium blue. Moving the mouse pointer off the button changes its color to dark blue. The My Computer window is the active window because it contains the dark blue title bar.

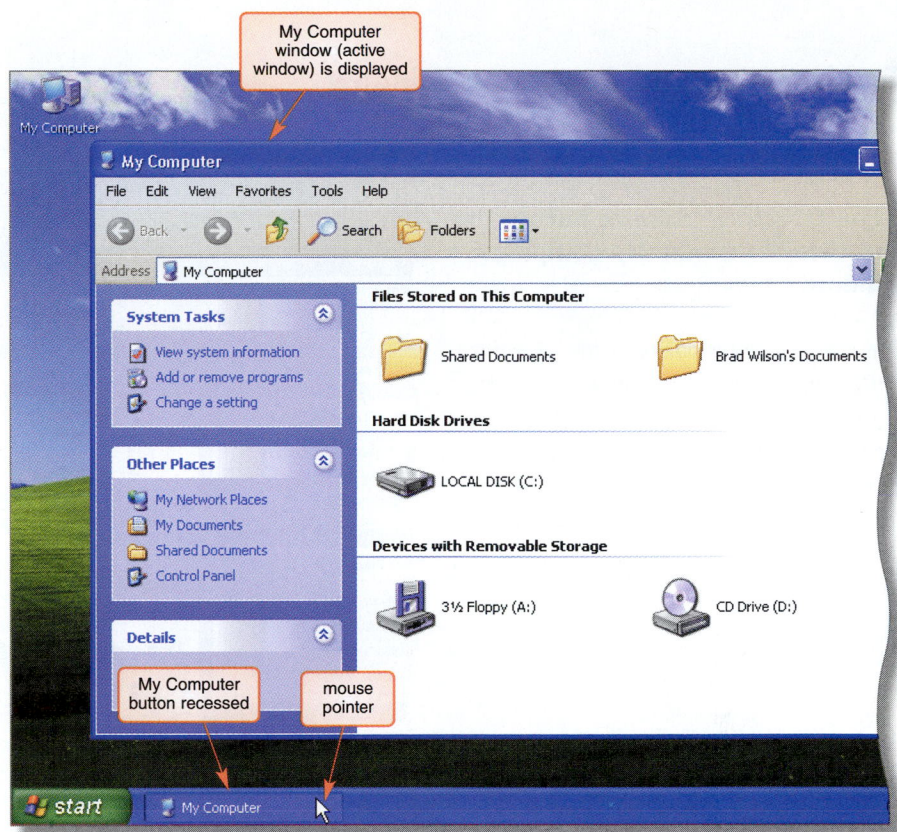

FIGURE 1-20

Whenever a window is minimized, it is not displayed on the desktop, but a non-recessed dark blue button for the window is displayed in the taskbar button area. Whenever you want a minimized window to display and be the active window, click its button in the taskbar button area.

As you point to many objects, such as a button or command, when you work with Windows XP, Windows XP displays a ToolTip. A **ToolTip** is a short on-screen note associated with the object to which you are pointing. ToolTips display on the desktop for approximately five seconds. Examples of ToolTips are shown in Figure 1-9 on page WIN 12, Figure 1-18 on the previous page, Figure 1-21 on the next page, Figure 1-23 on page WIN 23, and Figure 1-25 on page WIN 24. To reduce clutter on the screen, the ToolTips will not be shown on the remaining screens in this book.

Maximizing and Restoring a Window

Sometimes when information is displayed in a window, the information is not completely visible. One method of displaying the entire contents of a window is to enlarge the window using the **Maximize button**. The Maximize button maximizes a window so the window fills the entire screen, making it easier to see the contents of the window. When a window is maximized, the **Restore Down button** replaces the Maximize button on the title bar. Clicking the Restore Down button will return the window to its size before maximizing. To maximize and restore the My Computer window, complete the steps on the next page.

To Maximize and Restore a Window

1

• **Point to the Maximize button on the title bar of the My Computer window.**

The mouse pointer points to the Maximize button on the My Computer window title bar and the color of the Maximize button changes to light blue (Figure 1-21). A ToolTip identifying the button name is displayed below the Maximize button.

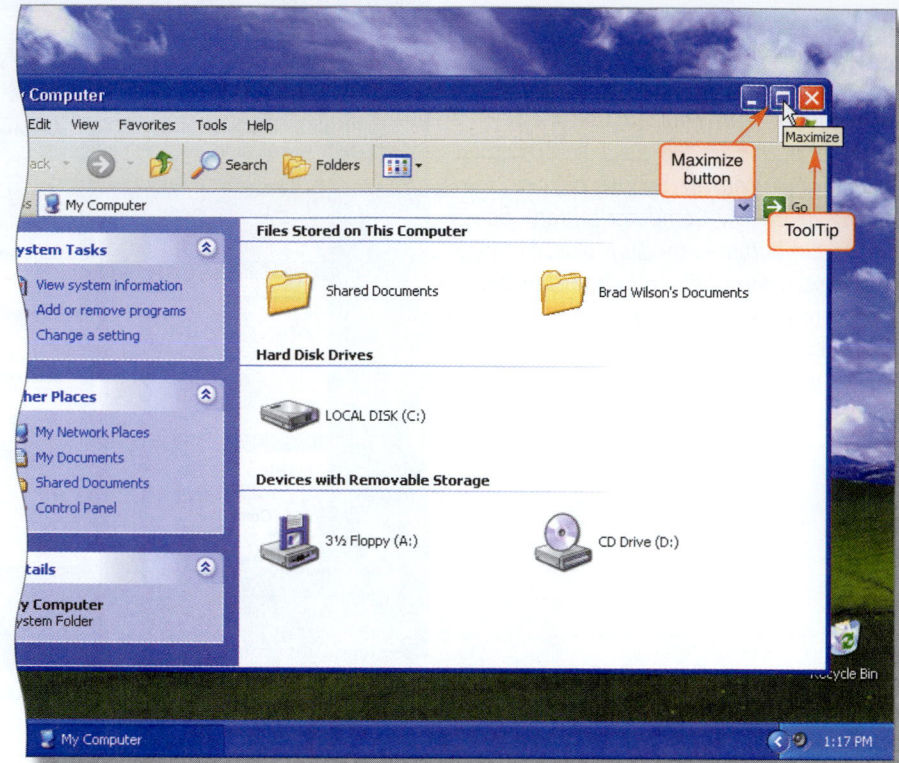

FIGURE 1-21

2

• **Click the Maximize button.**

The My Computer window expands so it and the taskbar fill the desktop (Figure 1-22). The Restore Down button replaces the Maximize button, the My Computer button in the taskbar button area does not change, and the My Computer window still is the active window.

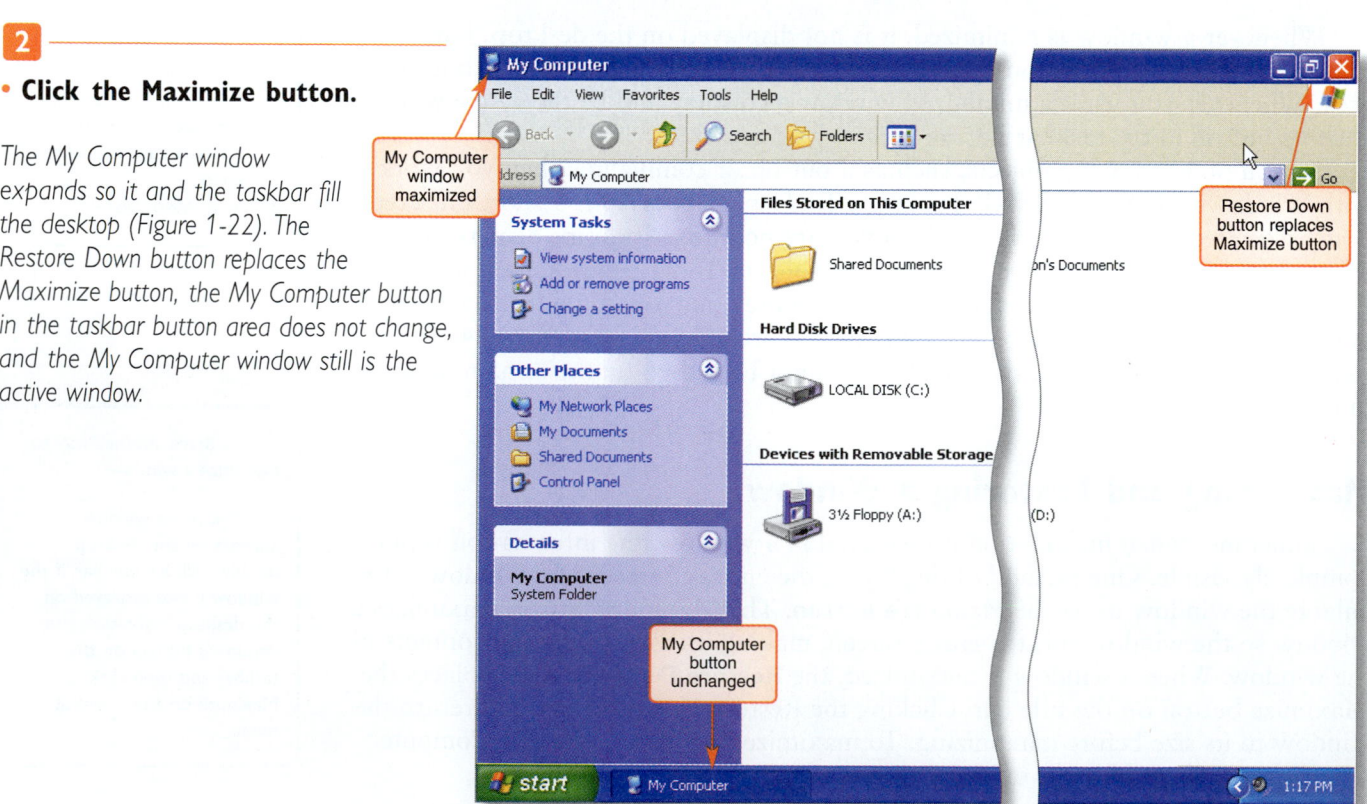

FIGURE 1-22

3

• **Point to the Restore Down button on the title bar of the My Computer window.**

The mouse pointer points to the Restore Down button on the My Computer window title bar and the color of the Restore Down button changes to light blue (Figure 1-23). A ToolTip is displayed below the Restore Down button identifying it.

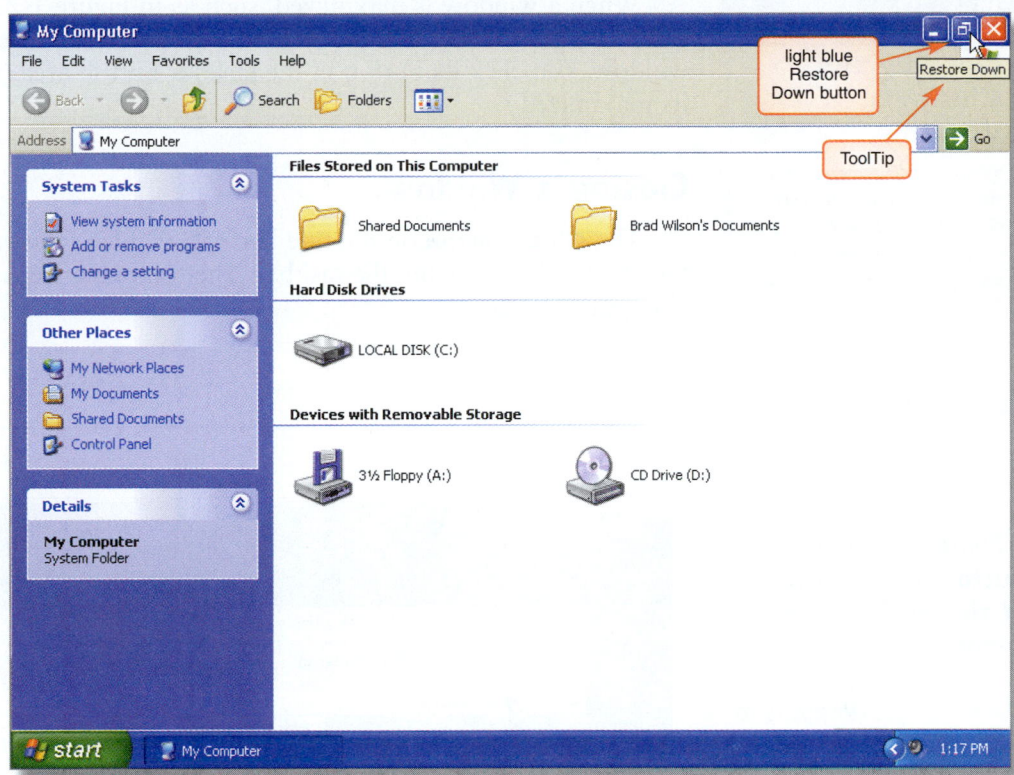

FIGURE 1-23

4

• **Click the Restore Down button.**

The My Computer window returns to the size and position it occupied before being maximized (Figure 1-24). The My Computer button does not change. The Maximize button replaces the Restore Down button.

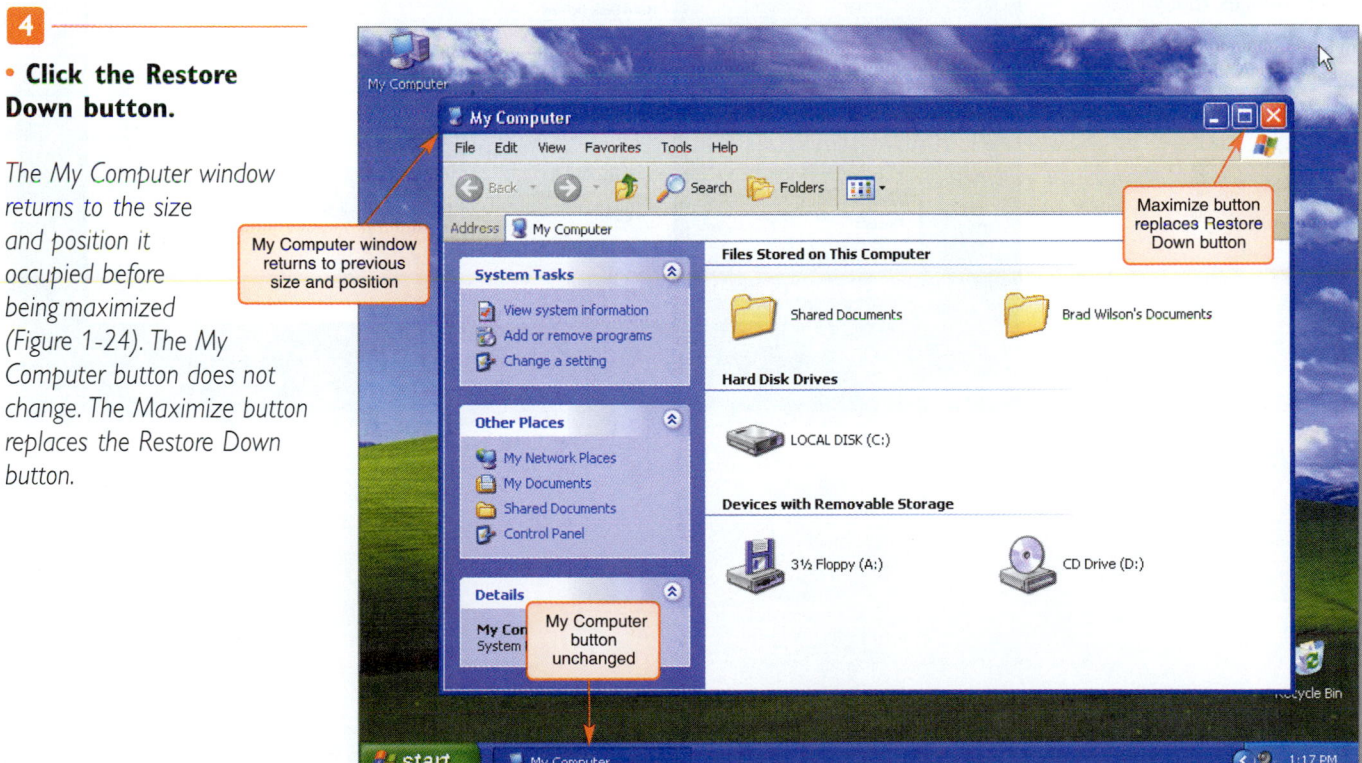

FIGURE 1-24

When a window is maximized, such as in Figure 1-22 on page WIN 22, you also can minimize the window by clicking the Minimize button. If, after minimizing the window, you click its button in the taskbar button area, the window will return to its maximized size.

Closing a Window

The **Close button** on the title bar of a window closes the window and removes the taskbar button from the taskbar. The following steps show how to close the My Computer window.

More About

Opening and Closing a Window

Windows XP remembers the size of a window when you close the window. When you reopen the window, it will display in the same size you closed it.

To Close a Window

1

• **Point to the Close button on the title bar of the My Computer window.**

The mouse pointer points to the Close button on the My Computer window title bar and the color of the Close button changes to light red (Figure 1-25). A ToolTip is displayed below the Close button.

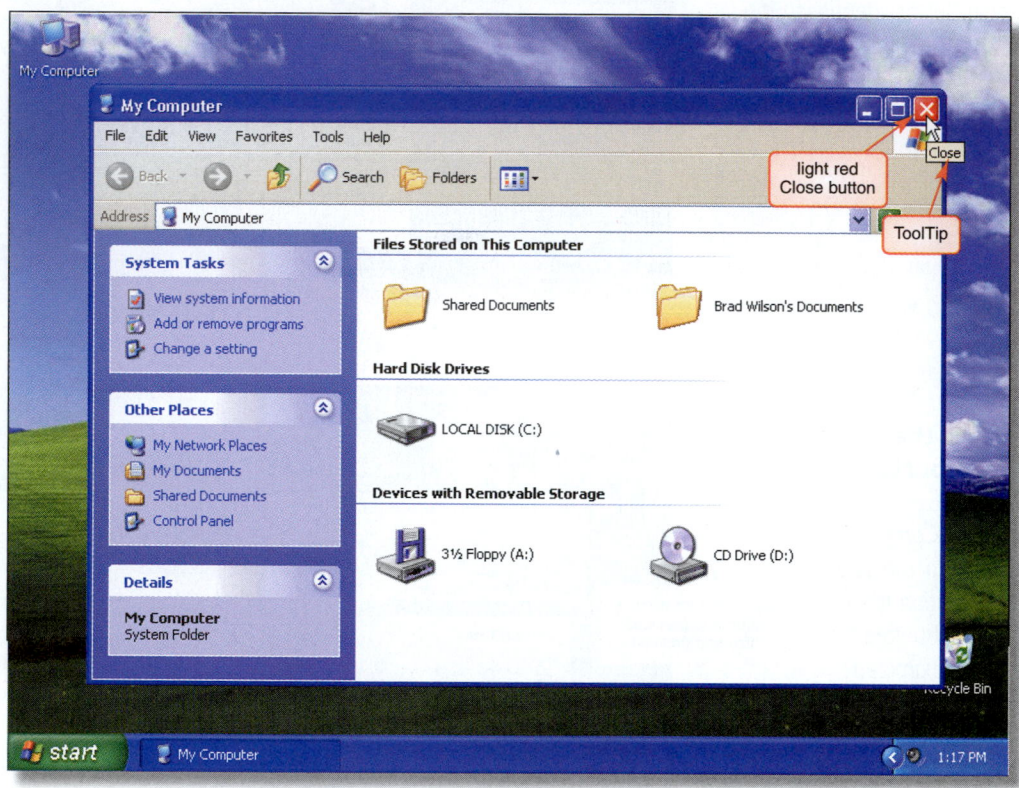

FIGURE 1-25

2

• **Click the Close button.**

The My Computer window closes and the My Computer button no longer is displayed in the taskbar button area (Figure 1-26).

My Computer window closes

My Computer button no longer appears

FIGURE 1-26

Opening a Window Using the Start Menu

Previously, you opened the My Computer window by double-clicking the My Computer icon on the desktop. Another method of opening a window and viewing the contents of the window is to click a command on the Start menu. The steps on the next page show how to open the My Documents window using the My Documents command on the Start menu.

More About

Opening a Window

Although the preferred method of opening a window in previous Windows versions was double-clicking a desktop icon, using the redesigned Start menu now makes it easier to open those windows.

To Open a Window Using the Start Menu

1

• **Click the Start button on the taskbar and then point to the My Documents command on the Start menu.**

The Start menu is displayed, the Start button is recessed on the taskbar, the color of the button changes to dark green, and the mouse pointer points to the highlighted My Documents command on the Start menu (Figure 1-27).

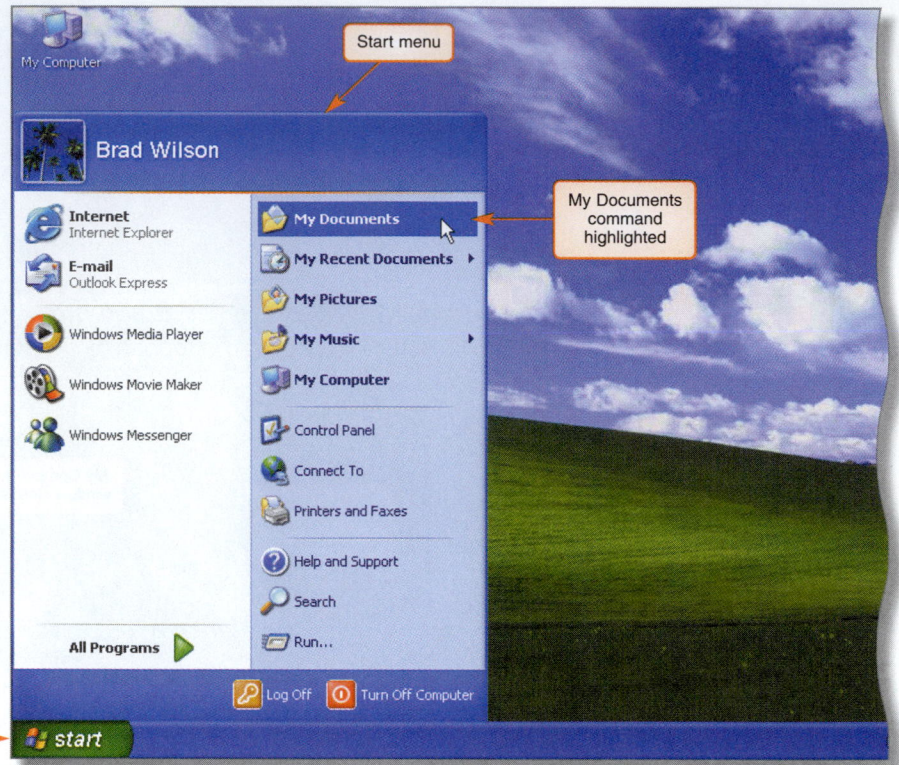

FIGURE 1-27

2

• **Click My Documents on the Start menu.**

The My Documents window opens, the recessed dark blue My Documents button is displayed in the taskbar button area, and the My Documents window is the active window (Figure 1-28). You may find more, fewer, or different folder icons in the right pane on your computer.

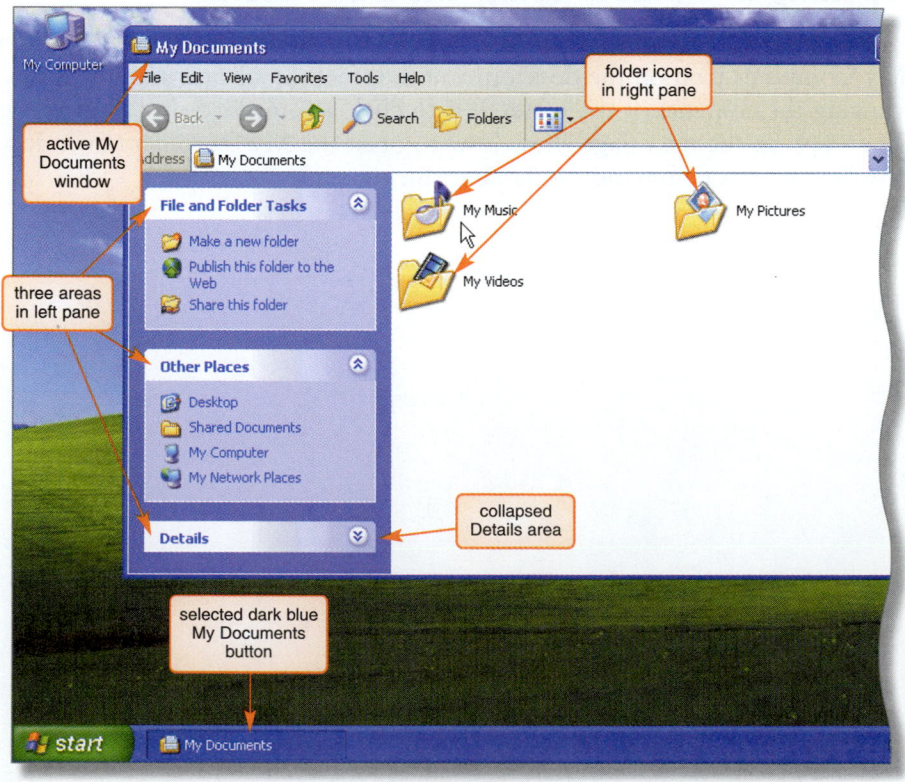

FIGURE 1-28

Other Ways

1. Click Start button, right-click window icon, click Open on shortcut menu

The My Documents Window

The **My Documents window** shown in Figure 1-28 is a central location for the storage and management of documents. The title bar at the top of the My Documents window identifies the window and the color of the title bar (dark blue) and the recessed dark blue My Documents button in the taskbar button area indicate the My Documents window is the active window.

The File and Folders Tasks, Other Places, and Details areas display in the left pane. The **File and Folders Tasks area** contains three tasks (Make a new folder, Publish this folder to the Web, and Share this folder). The **Other Places area** contains links to four folders (Desktop, Shared Documents, My Computer, and My Network Places). The **Details area** is collapsed and only the title and a double down arrow button appear in the area.

The right pane of the My Documents window contains the My Music, My Pictures, and My Videos folders. Clicking a folder icon in the right pane highlights the icon in the right pane and changes the files and folder tasks in the File and Folder Tasks area in the left pane. Double-clicking a folder icon displays the contents of the corresponding folder in the right pane, adds another area to the folder (My Music Tasks area, My Pictures Tasks area, or My Videos Tasks area) in the left pane, and changes the file and folder information in the left pane.

Moving a Window by Dragging

Drag means you point to an item, hold down the left mouse button, move the item to the desired location, and then release the left mouse button. You can move any open window to another location on the desktop by pointing to the title bar of the window and then dragging the window. The following steps illustrate dragging the My Documents window to the center of the desktop.

To Move a Window by Dragging

1

• Point to the My Documents window title bar (Figure 1-29).

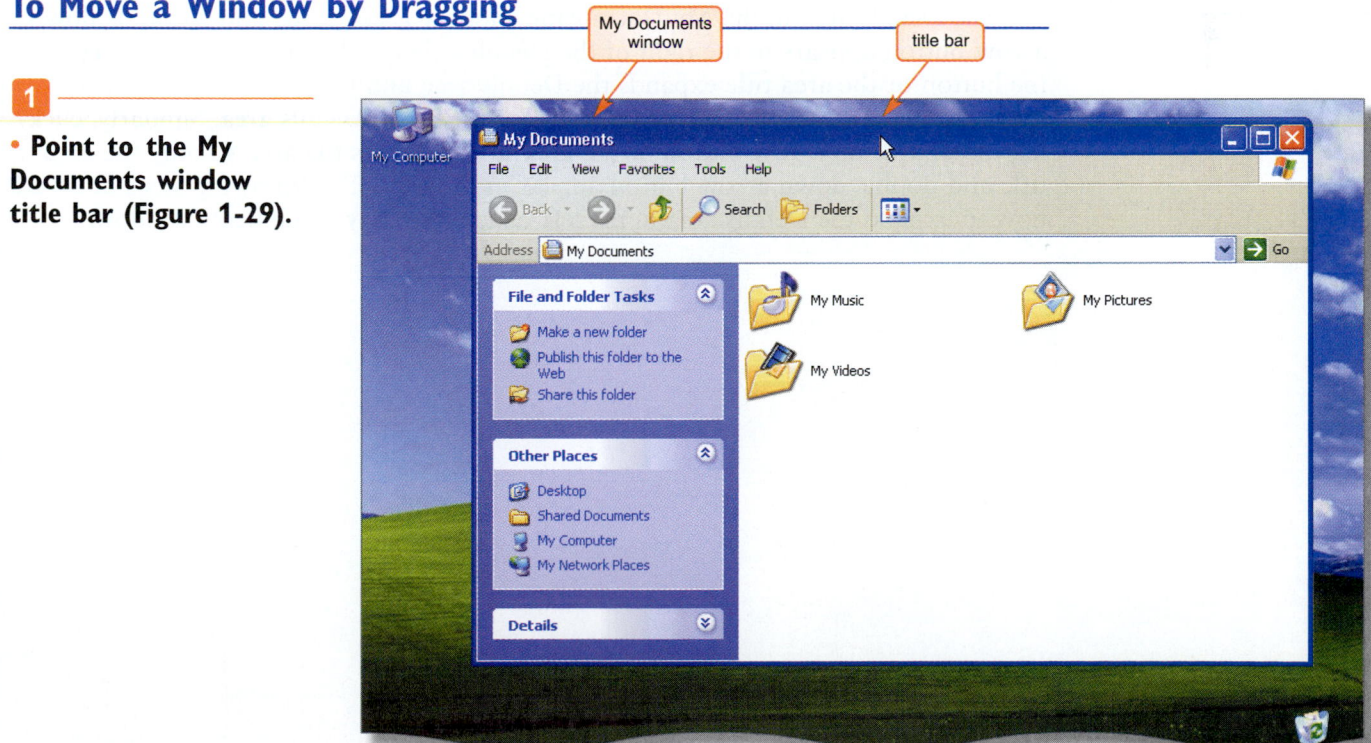

FIGURE 1-29

2

• **Hold down the left mouse button, move the mouse down so the window moves to the center of the desktop, and then release the left mouse button.**

As you drag the My Documents window, the window moves across the desktop. When you release the left mouse button, the window is displayed in its new location on the desktop (Figure 1-30).

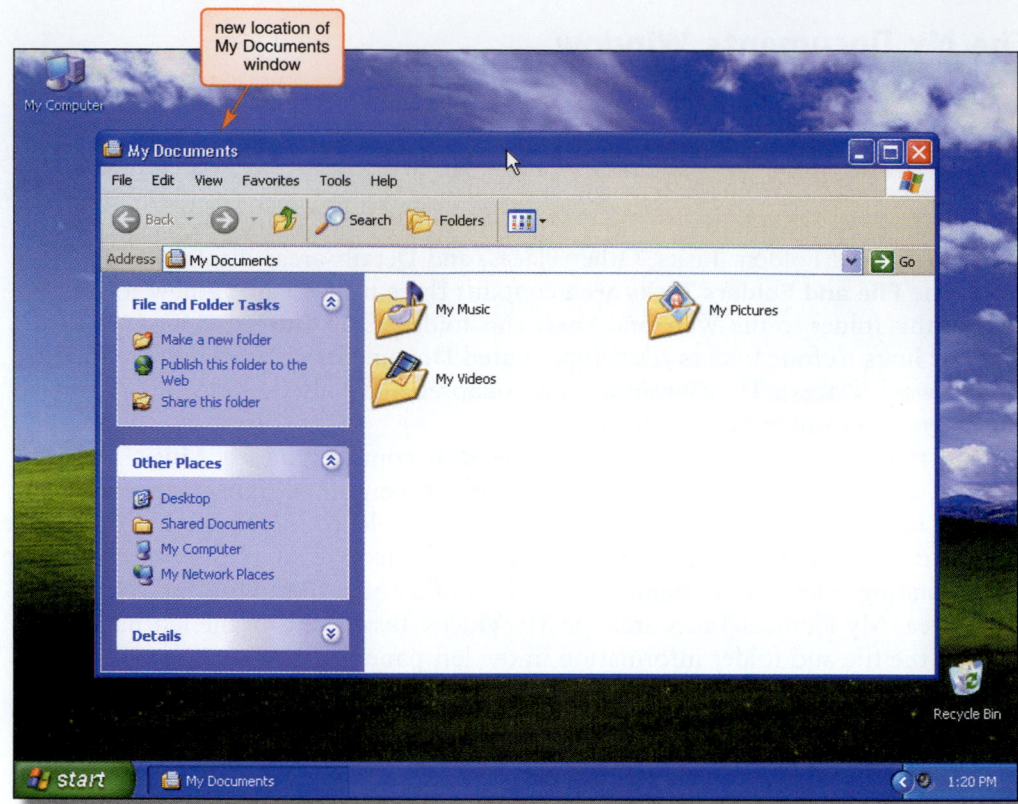

FIGURE 1-30

Expanding an Area

The Details area in the My Documents window is collapsed and a double down arrow button appears to the right of the Details title (see Figure 1-31). Clicking the button or the area title expands the Details area and reveals the window title (My Documents) and folder type (System Folder) in the Details area. Similarly, clicking the double up arrow button or the area title collapses the area so only the area title and double down arrow button appear in the area. The following steps illustrate how to expand the Details area in the left pane of the My Documents window.

To Expand an Area

1

• Point to the double down arrow button in the Details area.

The mouse pointer changes to a hand icon and points to the double down arrow button in the Details area and the color of the Details title and button changes to light blue (Figure 1-31).

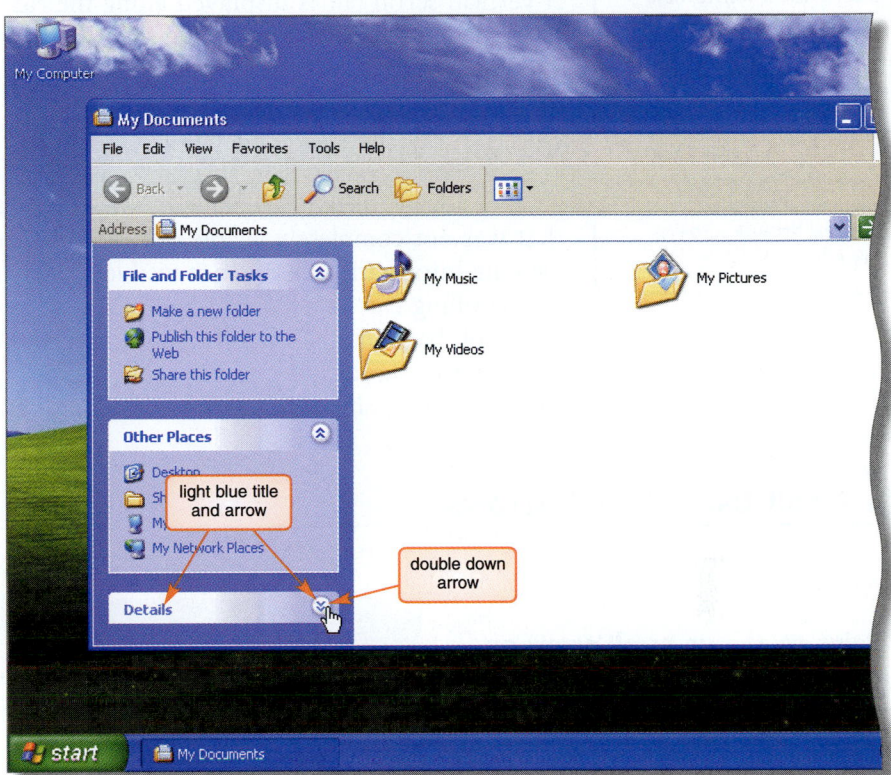

FIGURE 1-31

2

• Click the double down arrow button.

The Details area expands, the window title (My Documents) and folder type (System Folder) is displayed in the area, the double down arrow on the button changes to a double up arrow, a portion of the left pane is not visible, and a scroll bar is displayed in the area (Figure 1-32).

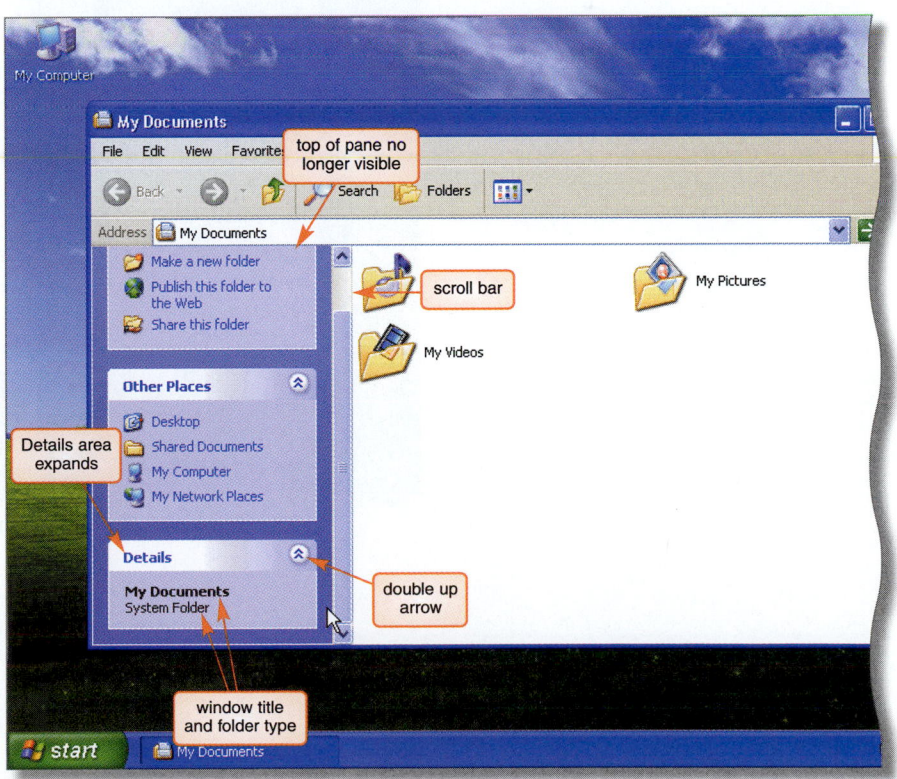

FIGURE 1-32

Microsoft
Windows XP

Q&A

Q: Is scrolling a window the most efficient way to view objects in a window?

A: No. There are other more efficient methods. You can either maximize a window or size it so that all the objects in the window are visible. It is better to avoid scrolling because scrolling takes time.

A **scroll bar** is a bar that appears when the contents of a pane or window are not completely visible. A vertical scroll bar contains an **up scroll arrow**, a **down scroll arrow**, and a **scroll box** that enable you to view areas that currently are not visible. A vertical scroll bar is displayed along the right side of the left pane in the My Documents window shown in Figure 1-32 on the previous page. In some cases, the vertical scroll bar also may appear along the right side of the right pane in a window.

Scrolling in a Window

Previously, the My Documents window was maximized to display information that was not completely visible in the My Documents window. Another method of viewing information that is not visible in a window is to use the scroll bar.

Scrolling can be accomplished in three ways: (1) click the scroll arrows; (2) click the scroll bar; and (3) drag the scroll box. On the following pages, you will use the scroll bar to scroll the contents of the left pane of the My Documents window. The following steps show how to scroll the left pane using the scroll arrows.

To Scroll Using Scroll Arrows

1

• **Point to the up scroll arrow on the vertical scroll bar.**

The color of the up scroll arrow changes to light blue (Figure 1-33).

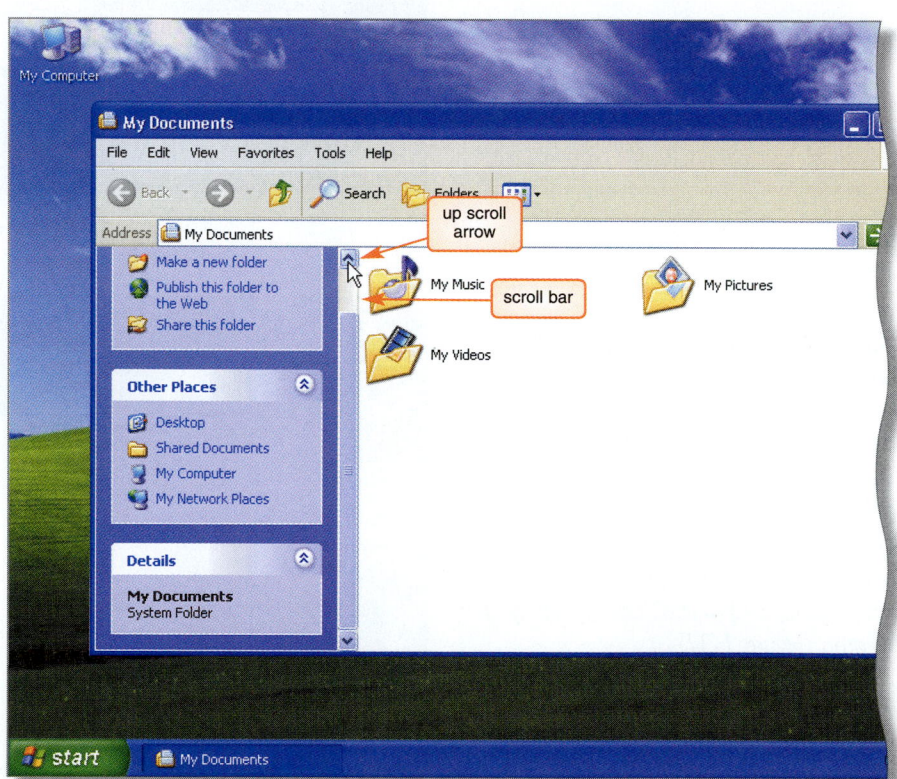

FIGURE 1-33

2

• **Click the up scroll arrow two times.**

The left pane scrolls down (the contents in the left pane move up) and displays a portion of the text in the File and Folder Tasks area at the top of the pane that previously was not visible (Figure 1-34). Because the size of the left pane does not change when you scroll, the contents in the left pane will change, as seen in the difference between Figure 1-33 and Figure 1-34.

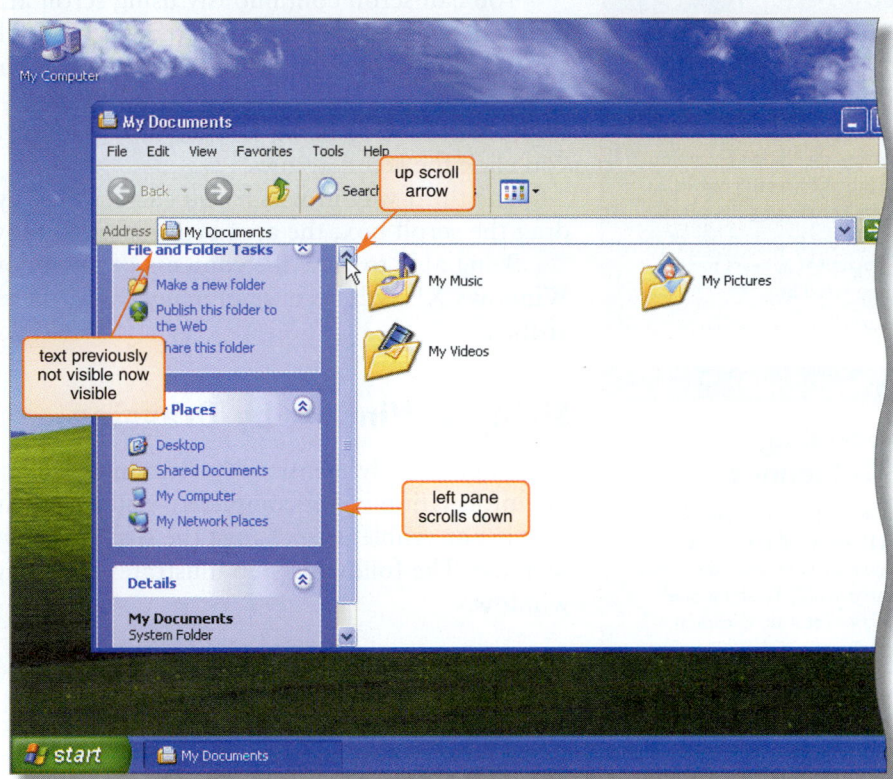

FIGURE 1-34

3

• **Click the up scroll arrow three more times.**

The scroll box moves to the top of the scroll bar and the remaining text in the File and Folder Tasks area is displayed (Figure 1-35).

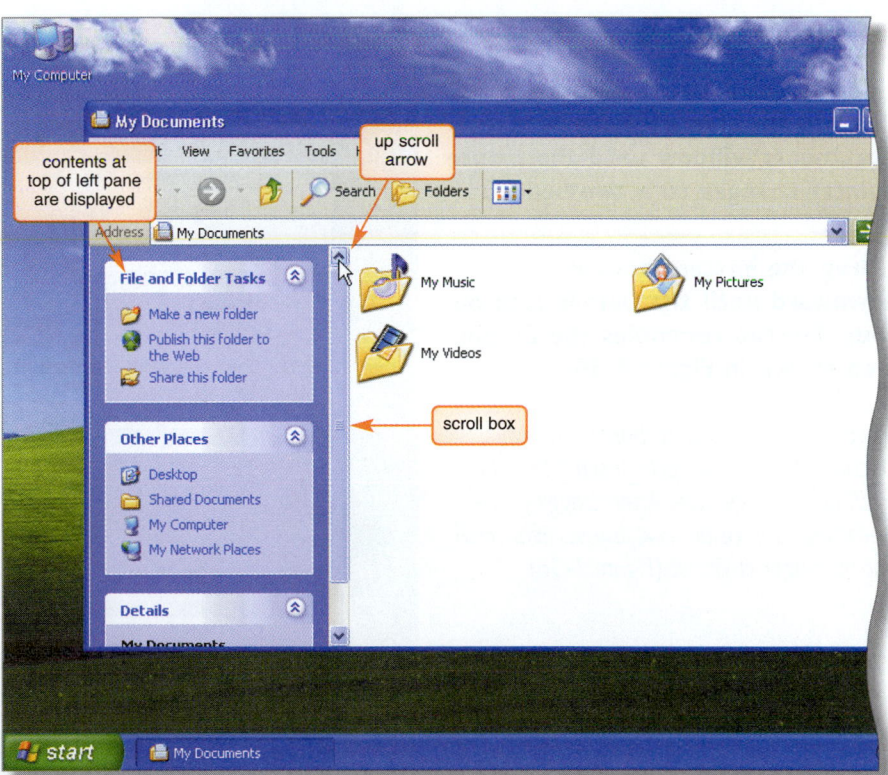

FIGURE 1-35

More About

The Scroll Box

Dragging the scroll box is the most efficient technique to scroll long distances. In many application programs, such as Microsoft Word, as you scroll using the scroll box, the page number of the document appears next to the scroll box.

More About

Scrolling Guidelines

General scrolling guidelines: (1) To scroll short distances (line by line), click the scroll arrows; (2) To scroll one screen at a time, click the scroll bar; and (3) To scroll long distances, drag the scroll box.

You can scroll continuously using scroll arrows by pointing to the up or down scroll arrow and holding down the left mouse button. The area being scrolled continues to scroll until you release the left mouse button or you reach the top or bottom of the area. You also can scroll by clicking the scroll bar itself. When you click the scroll bar, the area being scrolled moves up or down a greater distance than when you click the scroll arrows.

The third way in which you can scroll is by dragging the scroll box. When you drag the scroll box, the area being scrolled moves up or down as you drag.

Being able to view the contents of a window by scrolling is an important Windows XP skill because in many cases, the entire contents of a window are not visible.

Sizing a Window by Dragging

As previously mentioned, sometimes when information is displayed in a window, the information is not completely visible. A third method of displaying information that is not visible is to change the size of the window by dragging the border of a window. The following step illustrates changing the size of the My Documents window.

To Size a Window by Dragging

1

• **Position the mouse pointer over the bottom border of the My Documents window until the mouse pointer changes to a two-headed arrow.**

• **Drag the bottom border downward until the Details area on your desktop resembles the Details area shown in Figure 1-36.**

As you drag the bottom border, the My Documents window, vertical scroll bar, and scroll box change size. After dragging, the Details area is visible and the vertical scroll bar no longer is visible (Figure 1-36).

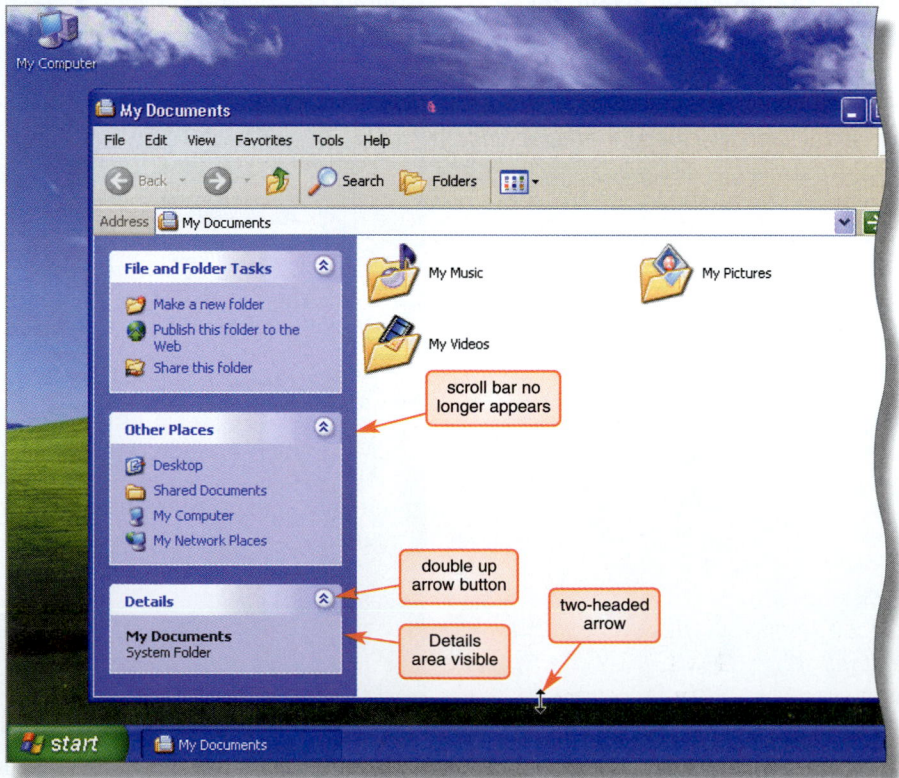

FIGURE 1-36

In addition to dragging the bottom border of a window, you also can drag the other borders (left, right, and top) and any window corner. If you drag a vertical border (left or right), you can move the border left or right. If you drag a horizontal border (top or bottom), you can move the border of the window up or down. If you drag a corner, you can move the corner up, down, left, or right.

Collapsing an Area

The Details area in the My Documents window is expanded and a double up arrow button displays to the right of the Details title (Figure 1-36). Clicking the button or the area title collapses the Details area and removes the window title (My Documents) and folder type (System Folder) from the Details area. The following steps show how to collapse the Details area in the My Documents window.

To Collapse an Area

1

• **Point to the double up arrow button in the Details area.**

The mouse pointer changes to a hand icon, points to the double up arrow button in the Details area, and the color of the Details title and button changes to light blue (Figure 1-37).

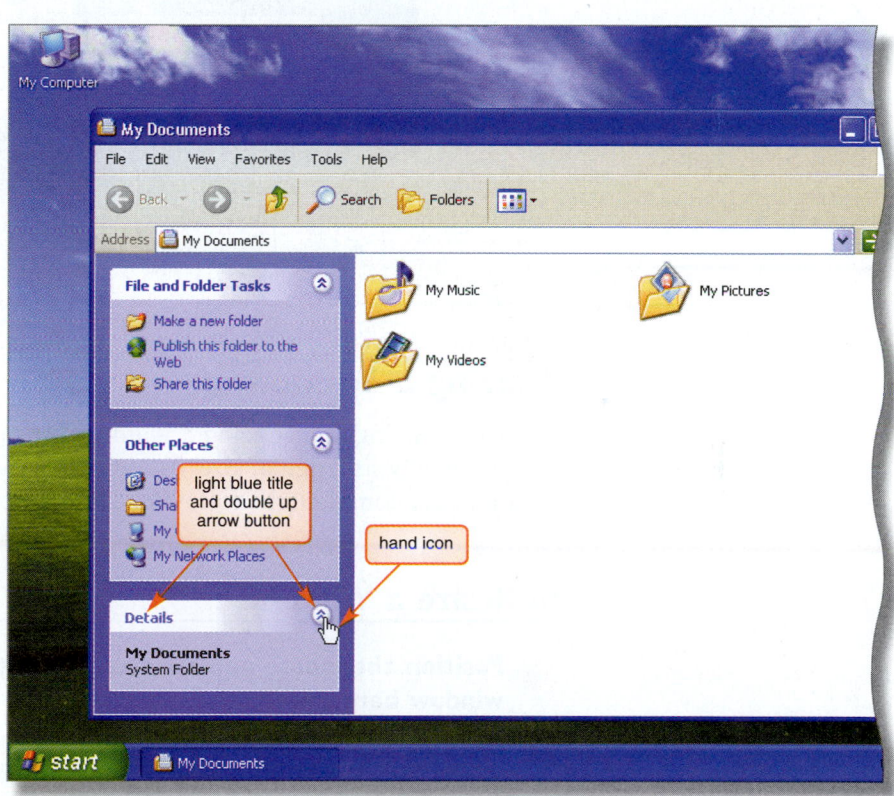

FIGURE 1-37

2

• **Click the double up arrow button.**

The Details area collapses and only the Details title and the double down arrow button are displayed (Figure 1-38).

FIGURE 1-38

Resizing a Window

After moving and resizing a window, you may wish to return the window to approximately its original size. To return the My Documents window to about its original size, complete the following steps.

To Resize a Window

1 Position the mouse pointer over the bottom border of the My Documents window border until the mouse pointer changes to a two-headed arrow.

2 Drag the bottom border of the My Documents window up until the window is the same size as shown in Figure 1-28 on page WIN 26 and then release the mouse button.

The My Documents window is approximately the same size as it was before you made it smaller.

Closing a Window

After you have completed work in a window, normally you will close the window. The following steps show how to close the My Documents window.

To Close a Window

1 Point to the Close button on the right of the title bar in the My Documents window.

2 Click the Close button.

The My Documents window closes and the desktop contains no open windows.

Deleting a Desktop Icon by Right-Dragging

The My Computer icon remains on the desktop. In many cases after you have placed an icon on the desktop, you will want to delete the icon. Although Windows XP has many ways to delete desktop icons, one method of removing the My Computer icon from the desktop is to right-drag the My Computer icon to the Recycle Bin icon on the desktop. **Right-drag** means you point to an item, hold down the right mouse button, move the item to the desired location, and then release the right mouse button. When you right-drag an object, a shortcut menu is displayed. The shortcut menu contains commands specifically for use with the object being dragged.

When you delete an icon from the desktop, Windows XP places the item in the **Recycle Bin**, which is an area on the hard disk that contains all the items you have deleted not only from the desktop but also from the hard disk. When the Recycle Bin becomes full, you can empty it. Up until the time you empty the Recycle Bin, you can recover deleted items from the Recycle Bin. The following steps illustrate how to delete the My Computer icon by right-dragging the icon to the Recycle Bin icon.

More About

Right-Dragging

Right-dragging was not available on some earlier versions of Windows, so you might find people who are familiar with Windows not even considering right-dragging. Because it always produces a shortcut menu, right-dragging is the safest way to drag.

To Delete a Desktop Icon by Right-Dragging

1

• **Point to the My Computer icon on the desktop, hold down the right mouse button, drag the My Computer icon over the Recycle Bin icon.**

• **Release the right mouse button and then point to Move Here on the shortcut menu.**

The My Computer icon is displayed on the desktop as you drag the icon. When you release the right mouse button, a shortcut menu is displayed on the desktop (Figure 1-39). Pointing to the Move Here command on the shortcut menu highlights the Move Here command.

FIGURE 1-39

2

• **Click Move Here and then point to the Yes button in the Confirm Delete dialog box.**

The shortcut menu closes, and the Confirm Delete dialog box is displayed on the desktop (Figure 1-40). A dialog box is displayed whenever Windows XP needs to supply information to you or wants you to enter information or select among several options. The Confirm Delete dialog box contains a question, a message, and the Yes and No buttons.

3

• **Click the Yes button.**

The Confirm Delete dialog box closes, the My Computer icon no longer is displayed on the desktop, and the My Computer icon now is contained in the Recycle Bin.

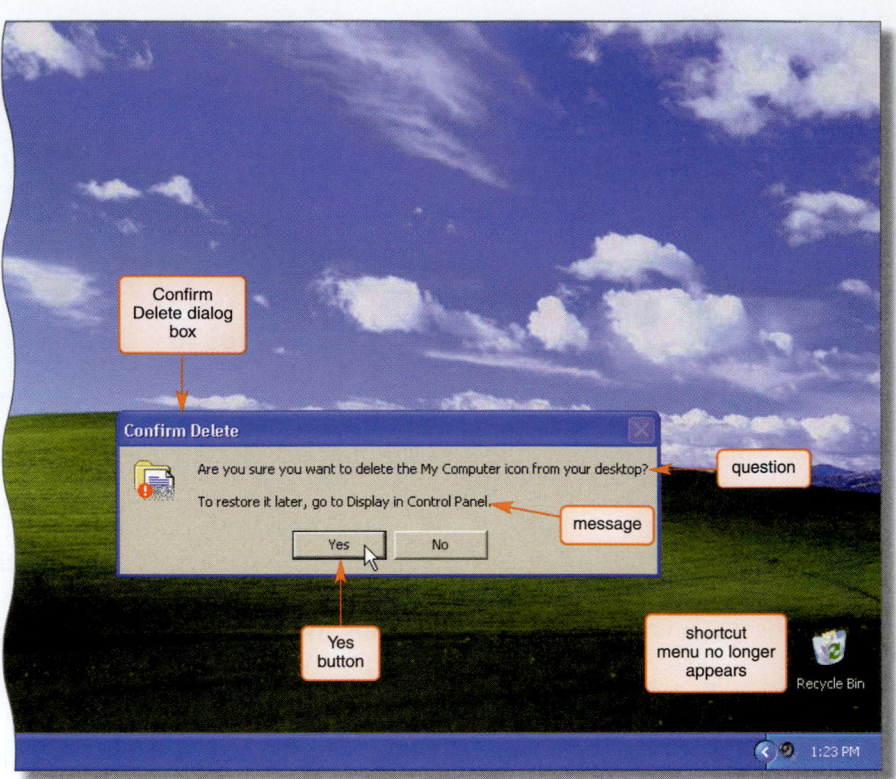

FIGURE 1-40

Other Ways

1. Drag icon to Recycle Bin, click Yes button
2. Right-click icon, click Delete, click Yes button

If you click **Move Here** on the shortcut menu shown in Figure 1-39 on the previous page, Windows XP will move the icon from its current location to the new location. If you click Cancel, the operation will be terminated, and the **Cancel command** will reset anything you have done during the operation.

In Figure 1-40, the Confirm Delete dialog box contains the Yes button and the No button. Clicking the Yes button completes the operation and clicking the No button terminates the operation.

Although you can move icons by dragging with the primary (left) mouse button and by right-dragging with the secondary (right) mouse button, it is strongly suggested you right-drag because a shortcut menu appears and, in most cases, you can specify the exact operation you want to occur. When you drag using the left mouse button, a default operation takes place and that operation may not be the operation you intended to perform.

Summary of Mouse and Windows Operations

You have seen how to use the mouse to point, click, right-click, double-click, drag, and right-drag in order to accomplish certain tasks on the desktop. The use of a mouse is an important skill when using Windows XP. In addition, you have learned how to move around and use windows on the Windows XP desktop.

The Keyboard and Keyboard Shortcuts

The **keyboard** is an input device on which you manually key in, or type, data. Figure 1-41 shows the Microsoft Office keyboard designed specifically for use with Microsoft Office and the Internet. The Single Touch pad along the left side of the keyboard contains keys to browse the Internet, copy and paste text, and switch between applications. A scroll wheel allows you to move quickly within a document window. The Hot Keys along the top of the keyboard allow you to launch a Web browser or e-mail program, play multimedia, and adjust the system volume.

Hot Keys

Single Touch pad

FIGURE 1-41

Many tasks you accomplish with a mouse also can be accomplished using a keyboard. To perform tasks using the keyboard, you must understand the notation used to identify which keys to press. This notation is used throughout Windows XP to identify a **keyboard shortcut**.

Keyboard shortcuts consist of (1) pressing a single key (such as press the ENTER key); or (2) pressing and holding down one key and pressing a second key, as shown by two key names separated by a plus sign (such as press CTRL+ESC). For example, to obtain help about Windows XP, you can press the F1 key and to display the Start menu, hold down the CTRL key and then press the ESC key (press CTRL+ESC).

Often, computer users will use keyboard shortcuts for operations they perform frequently. For example, many users find pressing the F1 key to launch Help and Support easier than using the Start menu as shown later in this project. As a user, you probably will find the combination of keyboard and mouse operations that particularly suits you, but it is strongly recommended that generally you use the mouse.

Launching an Application Program

One of the basic tasks you can perform using Windows XP is launching an application program. A **program** is a set of computer instructions that carries out a task on the computer. An **application program** is a set of specific computer instructions that is designed to allow you to accomplish a particular task. For example, a **word processing program** is an application program that allows you to create written documents; a **presentation graphics program** is an application

More About

Application Programs

Several application programs (Internet Explorer, Movie Maker, Media Player, and Windows Messenger) are part of Windows XP. Most application programs, such as the Microsoft Office applications, must be purchased separately from Windows XP, however.

program that allows you to create graphic presentations for display on a computer; and a **Web browser program** is an application program that allows you to search for and display Web pages.

The **default Web browser program** (Internet Explorer) appears in the pinned items list on the Start menu shown in Figure 1-42. Because the default **Web browser** is selected during the installation of the Windows XP operating system, the default Web browser on your computer may be different. In addition, you can easily select another Web browser as the default Web browser. Another frequently used Web browser program is **MSN Explorer**.

Launching an Application Using the Start Menu

The most common activity performed on a computer is launching an application program to accomplish specific tasks. You can launch an application program by using the Start menu. To illustrate the use of the Start menu to launch an application program, the default Web browser program (Internet Explorer) will be launched. The following steps illustrate launching Internet Explorer using the Internet command on the Start menu.

To Launch a Program Using the Start Menu

1

• **Click the Start button on the taskbar and then point to Internet on the pinned items list on the Start menu.**

The Start menu is displayed (Figure 1-42). The pinned items list on the Start menu contains the Internet command to launch the default Web browser program and the name of the default Web browser program (Internet Explorer). The default Web browser program on your computer may be different.

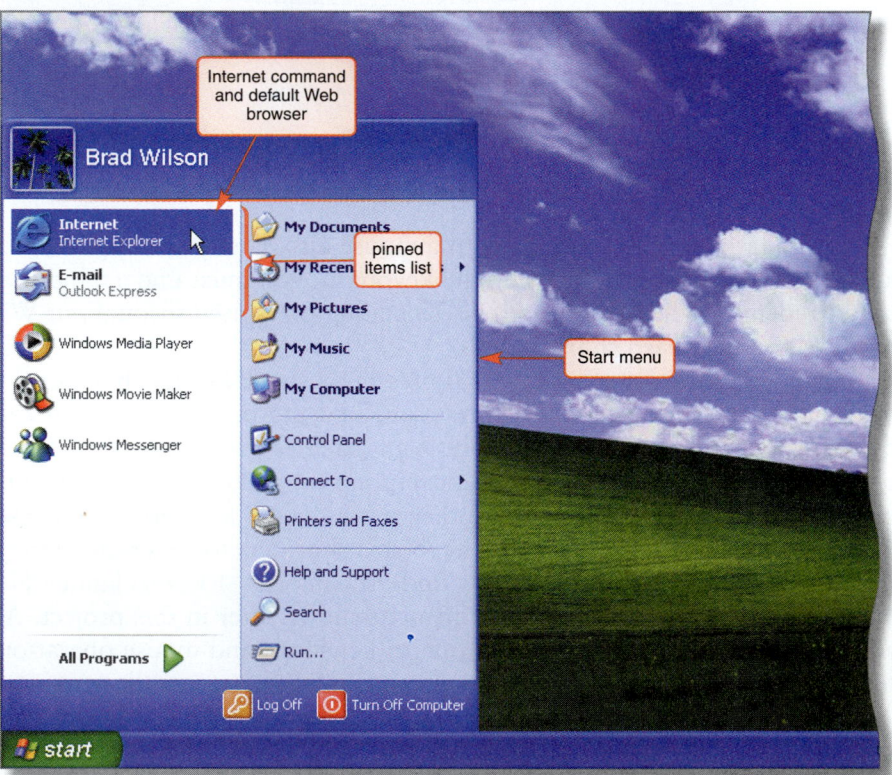

FIGURE 1-42

2

• **Click Internet.**

Windows XP launches the Internet Explorer program by displaying the Welcome to MSN.com – Microsoft Internet Explorer window, displaying the MSN home page in the window, and adding a recessed button on the taskbar (Figure 1-43). The URL for the Web page is displayed in the Address bar. Because you can select the default Web browser and the Web page to display when you launch the Web browser, the Web page that is displayed on your desktop may be different.

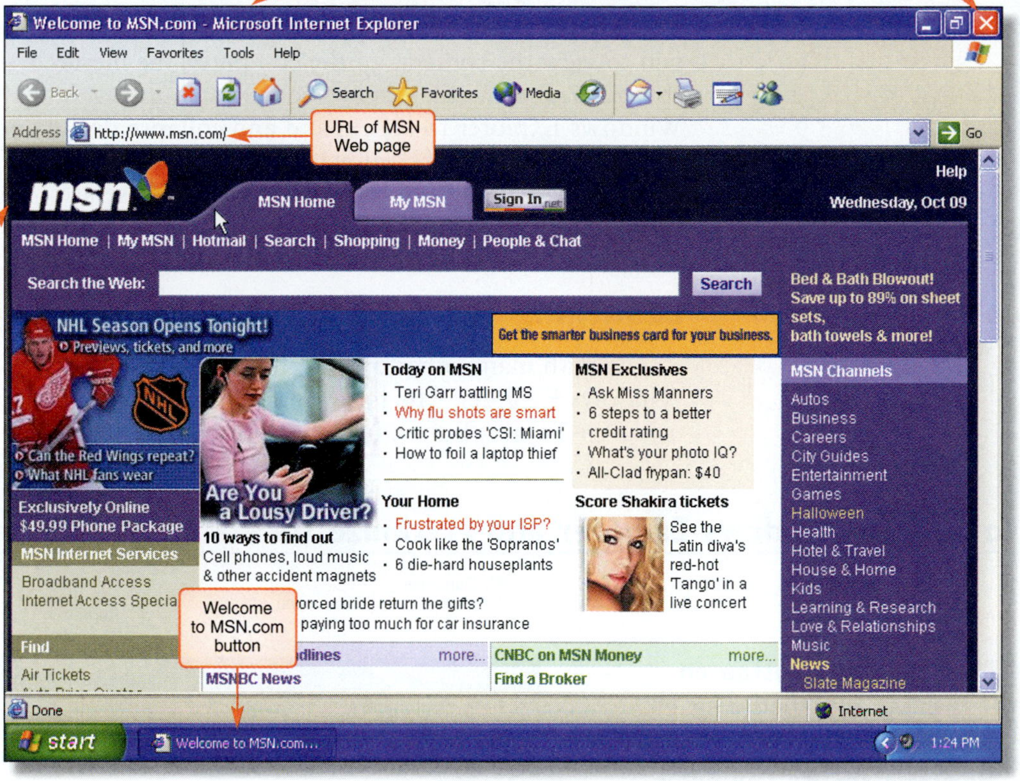

3

• **Click the Close button in the Microsoft Internet Explorer window.**

The Microsoft Internet Explorer window closes.

FIGURE 1-43

Other Ways

1. Click Start button, in frequently used program list click Internet Explorer
2. Click Start button, point to All Programs, click Internet Explorer
3. Press CTRL+ESC, press I

Any computer connected to the Internet that contains Web pages you can reference is called a **Web site**. The **MSN.com Web site**, one of millions of Web sites around the world, is stored on a computer operated by Microsoft Corporation and can be accessed using a Web browser. The Welcome to MSN.com **Web page** shown in Figure 1-43 is the first Web page you see when you access the MSN.com Web site and is, therefore, referred to as a **home page**, or **start page.**

After you have launched a Web browser, you can use the program to search for and display additional Web pages located on different Web sites around the world.

In the preceding section, you launched Internet Explorer and then quit the Internet Explorer program by closing the Microsoft Internet Explorer window. In the next section, you will launch the Windows Explorer application program.

Windows Explorer

Windows Explorer is an application program included with Windows XP. It allows you to view the contents of the computer, the hierarchy of drives and folders on the computer, and the files and folders in each folder. In this project, you will use Windows Explorer to (1) expand and collapse drives and folders; (2) display drive and folder contents; (3) launch an application program; (4) copy a file between folders; and (5) rename and then delete a file. These are common operations that you should understand how to perform.

Launching Windows Explorer

As with many other operations, Windows XP offers a variety of ways to launch Windows Explorer. The following steps show how to launch Windows Explorer using the Folders button in the My Computer window.

To Launch Windows Explorer and Maximize Its Window

1

• **Click the Start button on the taskbar and then click My Computer on the Start menu.**

• **Maximize the My Computer window.**

• **If the status bar does not appear at the bottom of the My Computer window, click View on the menu bar and then click Status Bar.**

• **Point to the Folders button on the Standard Buttons toolbar.**

The maximized My Computer window is displayed (Figure 1-44). The status bar is located at the bottom of the window. Pointing to the Folders button on the Standard Buttons toolbar displays a three-dimensional button.

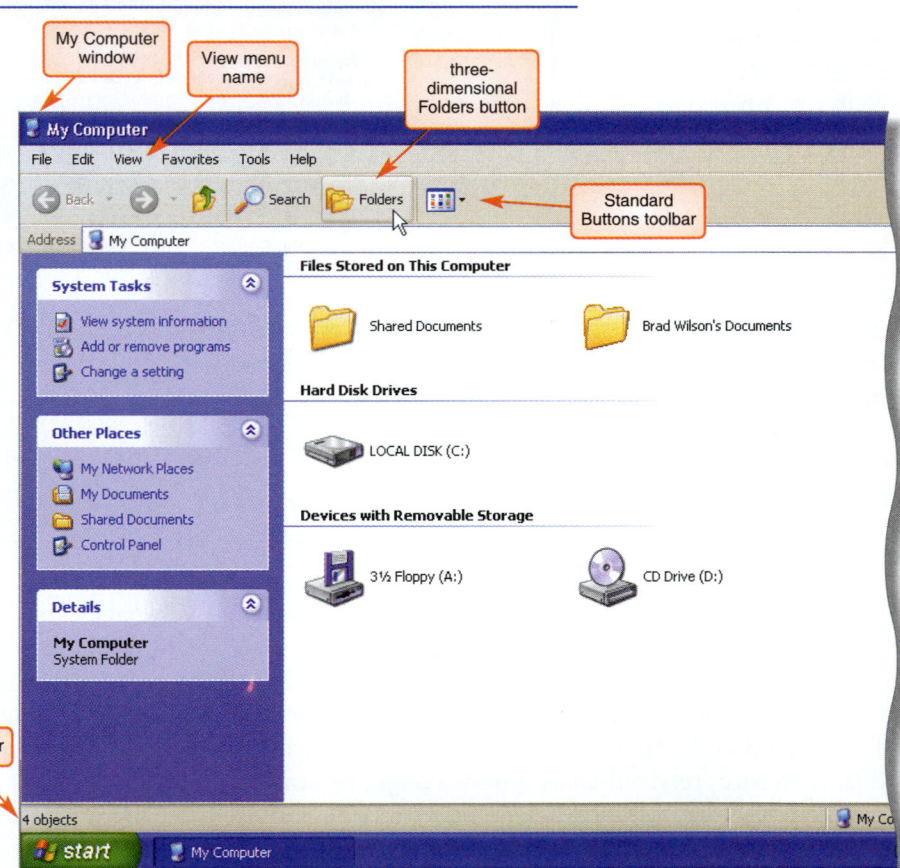

FIGURE 1-44

Windows XP Project 1

2

• **Click the Folders button.**

The Folders pane is displayed in place of the left pane in the My Computer window (Figure 1-45).

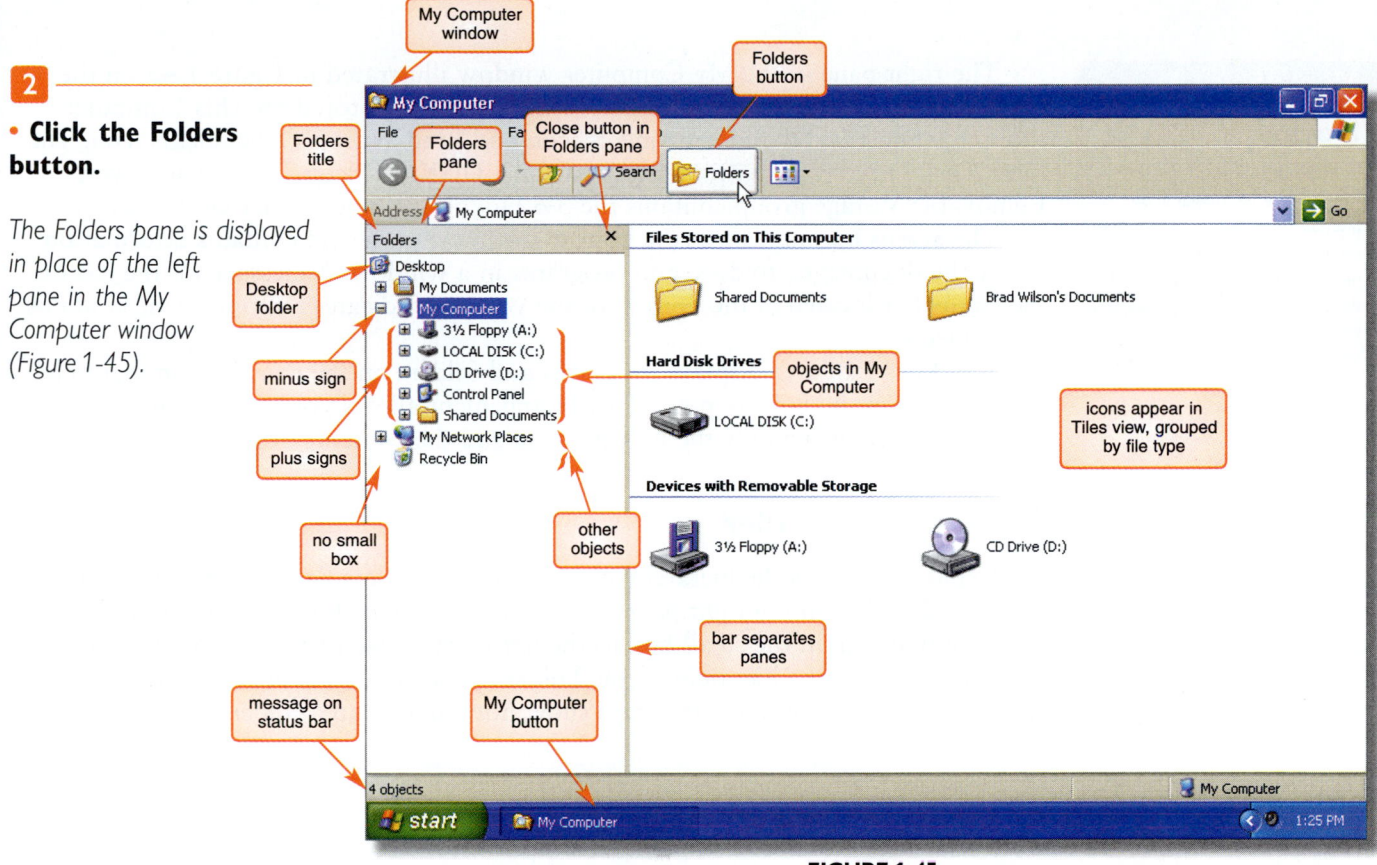

FIGURE 1-45

Clicking the Folders button in the My Computer window selects the Folders button, displays the Folders pane shown in Figure 1-45, and allows you to use Windows Explorer. The **Folders pane** (or **Folder bar**) displays the **hierarchical structure** of folders and drives on the computer. The title bar in the Folders pane contains a title (Folders) and Close button. Clicking the Close button removes the Folders pane from the My Computer window and deselects the Folders button. A bar separates the Folders pane and the right pane of the My Computer window. You can drag the bar left or right to change the size of the Folders pane.

The top level of the hierarchy in the Folders pane is the Desktop. Below the Desktop are the My Documents, My Computer, My Network Places, and Recycle Bin icons. The icons on your computer may be different.

To the left of the My Computer icon is a minus sign in a small box. The **minus sign** indicates that the drive or folder represented by the icon next to it, in this case My Computer, contains additional folders or drives and these folders or drives appear below the icon. Thus, below the My Computer icon are the 3½ Floppy (A:), LOCAL DISK (C:), CD Drive (D:), Control Panel, and Shared Documents icons. Each of these icons has a small box with a plus sign next to it. The **plus sign** indicates that the drive or folder represented by the icon has more folders within it but the folders do not appear in the Folders pane. As you will see shortly, clicking the box with the plus sign will display the folders within the drive or folder represented by the icon. If an item contains no folders, such as the Recycle Bin, no hierarchy exists and no small box is displayed next to the icon.

Other Ways

1. Click Start button, right-click My Computer, click Explore on shortcut menu
2. Right-click Start button or any desktop icon, click Explore on shortcut menu
3. Click Start button, point to All Programs, point to Accessories, click Windows Explorer, click My Computer

More About

Icons

In many cases, you may not recognize a particular icon because hundreds of icons are developed by software vendors to represent their products. Each icon is supposed to be unique and eye-catching. You can purchase thousands of icons on floppy disk or CD-ROM to use to represent the documents you create.

The right pane in the My Computer window illustrated in Figure 1-45 on the previous page contains three groups of icons. The Files Stored on This Computer group contains the Shared Documents icon and Brad Wilson's Documents icon. The Hard Disk Drives group contains the LOCAL DISK (C:) icon. The Devices with Removable Storage group contains the 3½ Floppy (A:) and CD Drive (D:) icons.

The **status bar** appears at the bottom of the window and contains information about the documents, folders, and programs in a window. A message on the left of the status bar located at the bottom of the window indicates the right pane contains four objects.

Windows Explorer displays the drives and folders on the computer in hierarchical structure in the Folders pane. This arrangement allows you to move and copy files and folders using only the Folders pane and the contents of the right pane.

Expanding a Folder

Explorer displays the hierarchy of items in the Folders pane and the contents of drives and folders in the right pane. To expand a drive or folder in the Folders pane, click the plus sign in the small box to the left of the drive or folder icon. Clicking the plus sign expands the hierarchy in the Folders pane. The contents of the right pane remain the same. The following steps show how to expand a folder.

To Expand a Folder

1

• **Point to the plus sign in the small box to the left of the My Documents icon in the Folders pane (Figure 1-46).**

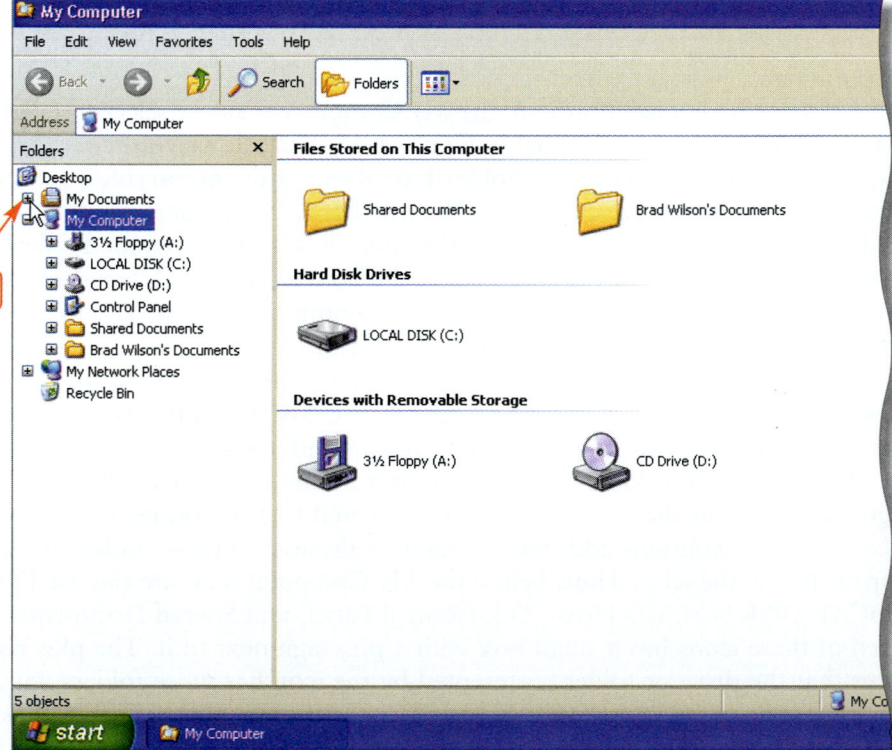

plus sign

FIGURE 1-46

2

• **Click the plus sign.**

The hierarchy below the My Documents icon expands to display the My Music folder, My Pictures folder, and My Videos folder (Figure 1-47). The minus sign to the left of the My Documents folder indicates the folder is expanded. No sign to the left of the My Music, My Pictures, and My Videos folders indicates the folders contain no additional folders.

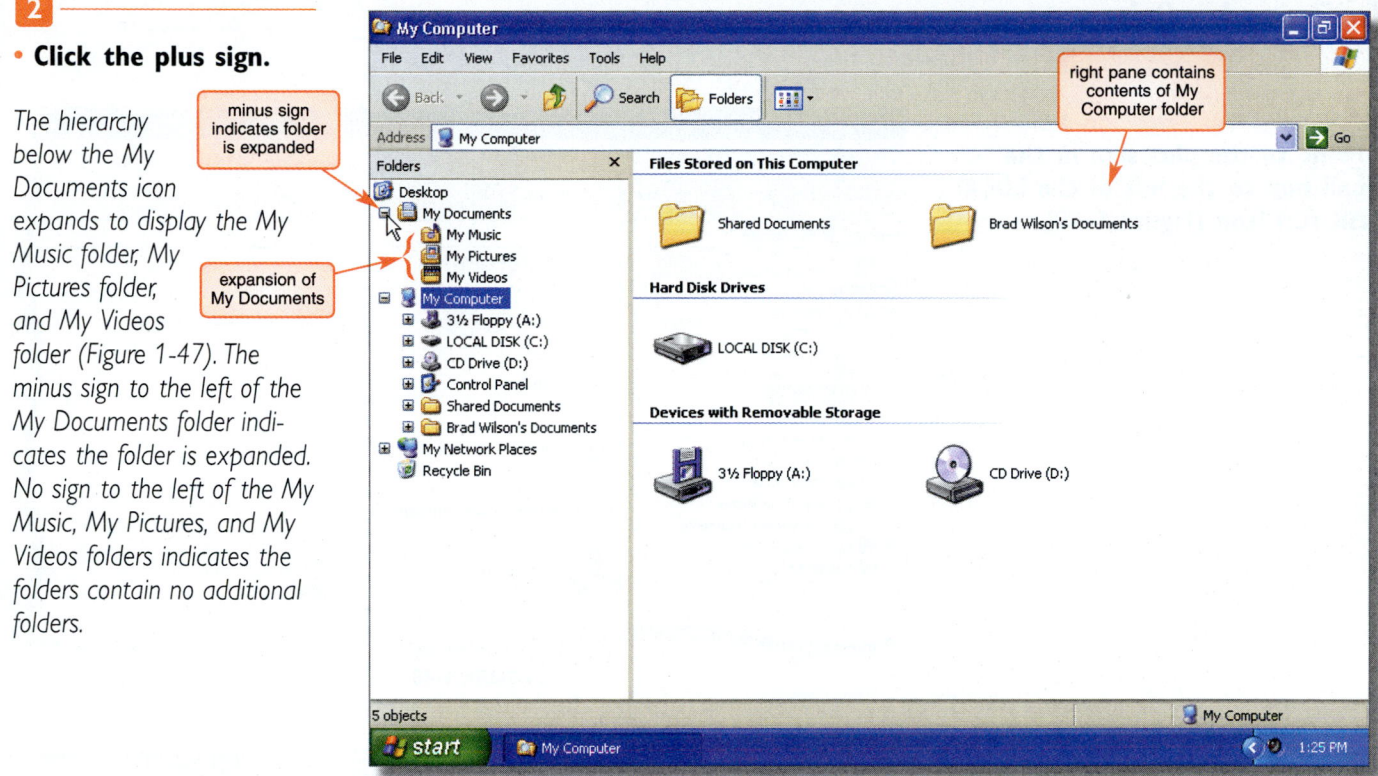

FIGURE 1-47

In Figure 1-47, the My Documents folder is expanded and the right pane still contains the contents of the My Computer folder. Clicking the plus sign next to a folder icon expands the hierarchy but does not change the contents of the right pane.

Expanding a Drive

When a plus sign in a small box displays to the left of a drive icon in the Folders pane, you can expand the drive to show all the folders it contains. The steps on the next page illustrate expanding drive C to view the folders on drive C.

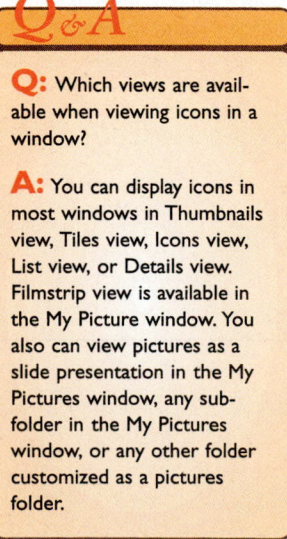

Q: Which views are available when viewing icons in a window?

A: You can display icons in most windows in Thumbnails view, Tiles view, Icons view, List view, or Details view. Filmstrip view is available in the My Picture window. You also can view pictures as a slide presentation in the My Pictures window, any subfolder in the My Pictures window, or any other folder customized as a pictures folder.

To Expand a Drive

1

• **Point to the plus sign in the small box to the left of the LOCAL DISK (C:) icon (Figure 1-48).**

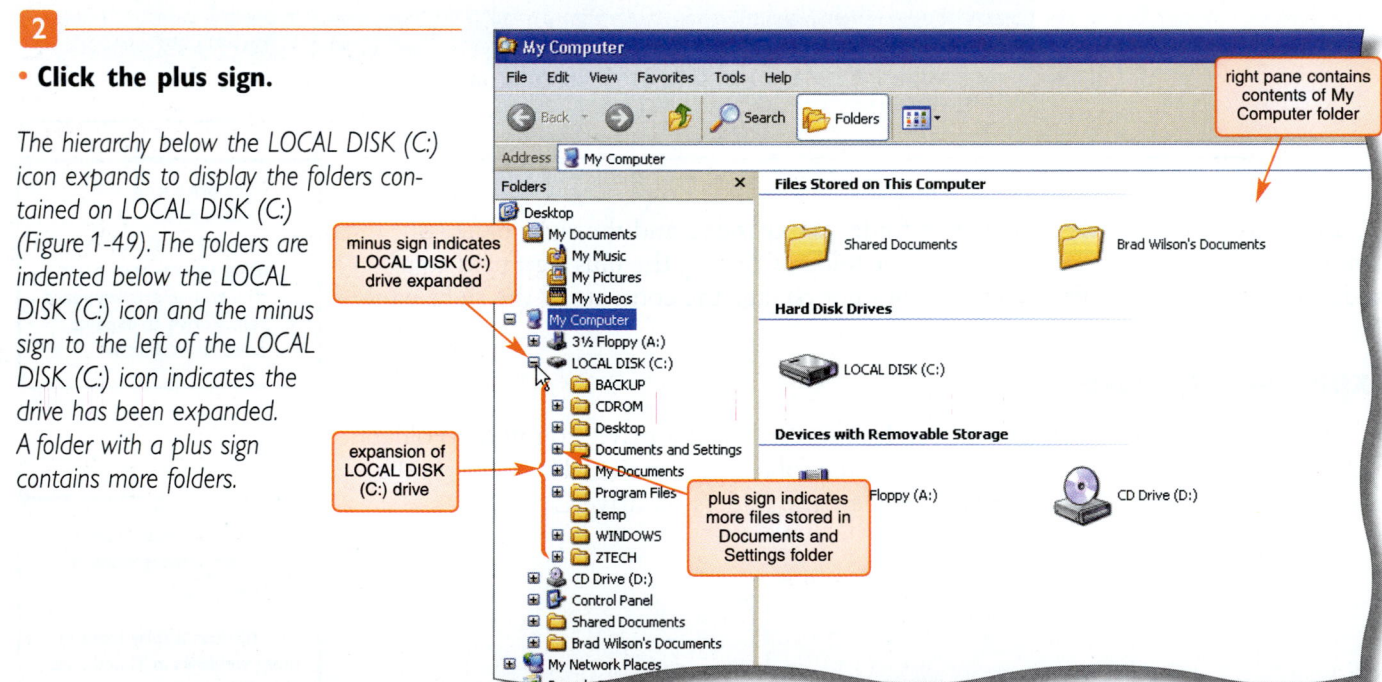

plus sign

FIGURE 1-48

2

• **Click the plus sign.**

The hierarchy below the LOCAL DISK (C:) icon expands to display the folders contained on LOCAL DISK (C:) (Figure 1-49). The folders are indented below the LOCAL DISK (C:) icon and the minus sign to the left of the LOCAL DISK (C:) icon indicates the drive has been expanded. A folder with a plus sign contains more folders.

right pane contains contents of My Computer folder

minus sign indicates LOCAL DISK (C:) drive expanded

expansion of LOCAL DISK (C:) drive

plus sign indicates more files stored in Documents and Settings folder

FIGURE 1-49

In Figure 1-49, the LOCAL DISK (C:) drive is expanded and the right pane still contains the contents of the My Computer folder. Clicking the plus sign next to a drive icon expands the hierarchy but does not change the contents of the right pane.

When a drive is expanded, the folders contained within the expanded drive display in the Folders pane. You can continue this expansion to view further levels of the hierarchy.

Displaying Files and Folders in Windows Explorer

You can display files and folders in the right pane in several different views. Currently, the files and folders in the My Computer folder display in Tiles view using Large Icons format and are grouped based upon file type. Other folders may display in a different view. The manner in which you display drive or folder contents in the right pane is a matter of personal preference.

Displaying Drive and Folder Contents

Explorer displays the hierarchy of items in the left, or Folders, pane and the contents of drives and folders in the right pane. To display the contents of a drive or folder in the right pane, click the drive or folder icon in the Folders pane. Clicking the icon displays the contents of the drive or folder in the right pane and expands the hierarchy in the Folders pane. The following step shows how to display the contents of the Shared Documents folder.

To Display the Contents of a Folder

1

• **Click the Shared Documents icon in the Folders pane.**

The highlighted Shared Documents name is displayed in the Folders pane, the hierarchy below the Shared Documents icon expands, and the right pane contains the contents of the Shared Documents folder (Figure 1-50). The window title changes to Shared Documents, the Shared Documents button replaces the My Computer button on the taskbar, and the status bar indicates two objects are displayed in the right pane.

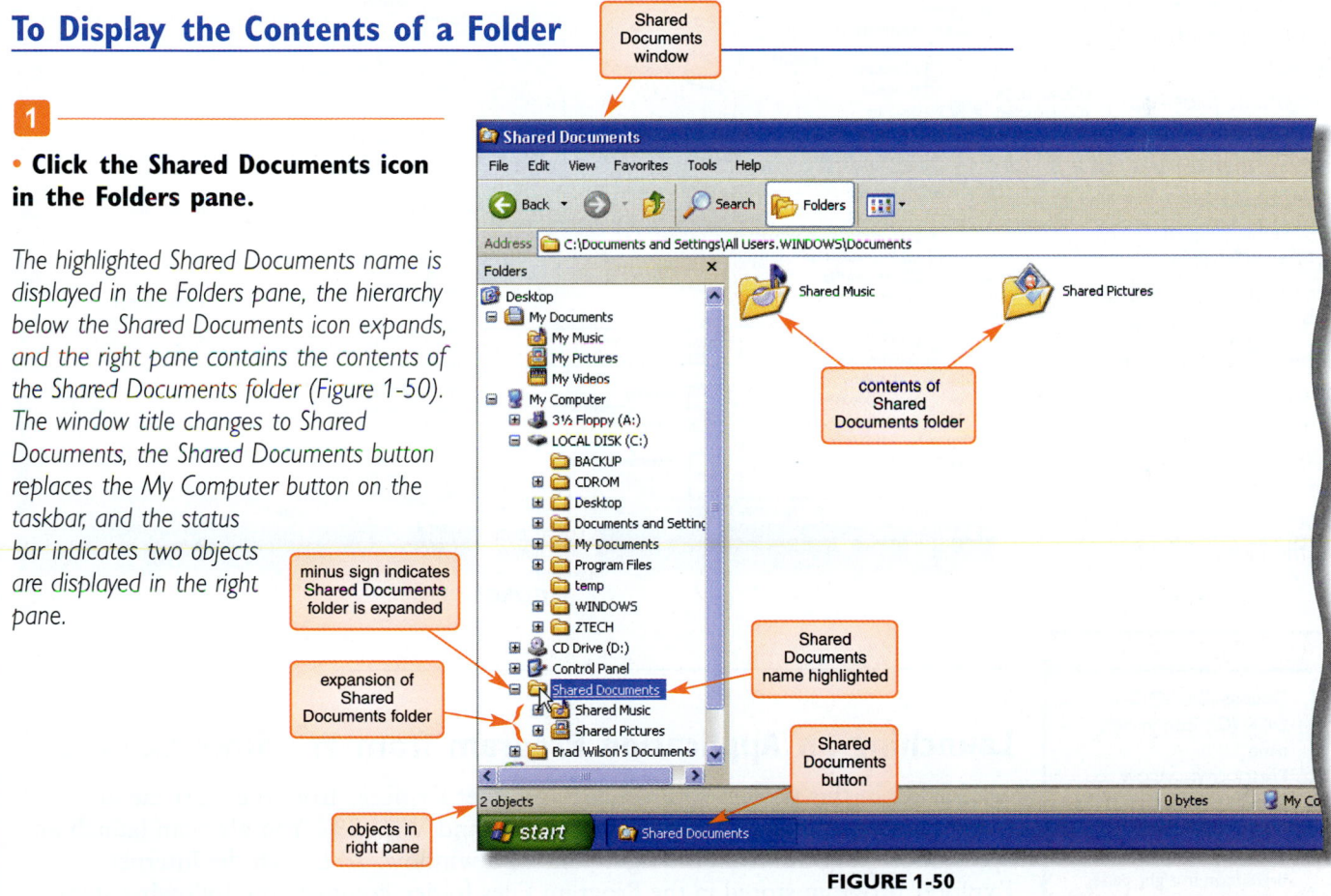

FIGURE 1-50

Whenever files or folders display in the right pane of a window, you can display the contents of the file or folder by double-clicking the icon of the file or folder.

Other Ways

1. Right-click Shared Documents icon, click Explore on shortcut menu

In Figure 1-50 on the previous page, you clicked the Shared Documents icon in the Folders pane and the contents of the Shared Documents folder displayed in the right pane and the hierarchy below the Shared Documents icon expanded. If you click the icon of an expanded drive or folder, the contents of the drive or folder are displayed in the right pane The hierarchy below the icon will not expand because it is already expanded. The step below shows how to display the contents of the expanded LOCAL DISK (C:) drive.

To Display the Contents of an Expanded Drive

1

• **Click the LOCAL DISK (C:) icon in the Folders pane.**

The LOCAL DISK (C:) entry is selected in the Folders pane, the expanded Shared Documents folder collapses, and the contents of the LOCAL DISK (C:) folder are displayed in the right pane (Figure 1-51). Notice that all the folder icons appear first and then the file icons appear. The status bar indicates 21 objects and 8 hidden objects occupy 328 kilobytes and the amount of space that is not being used on the disk is 9.02 gigabytes.

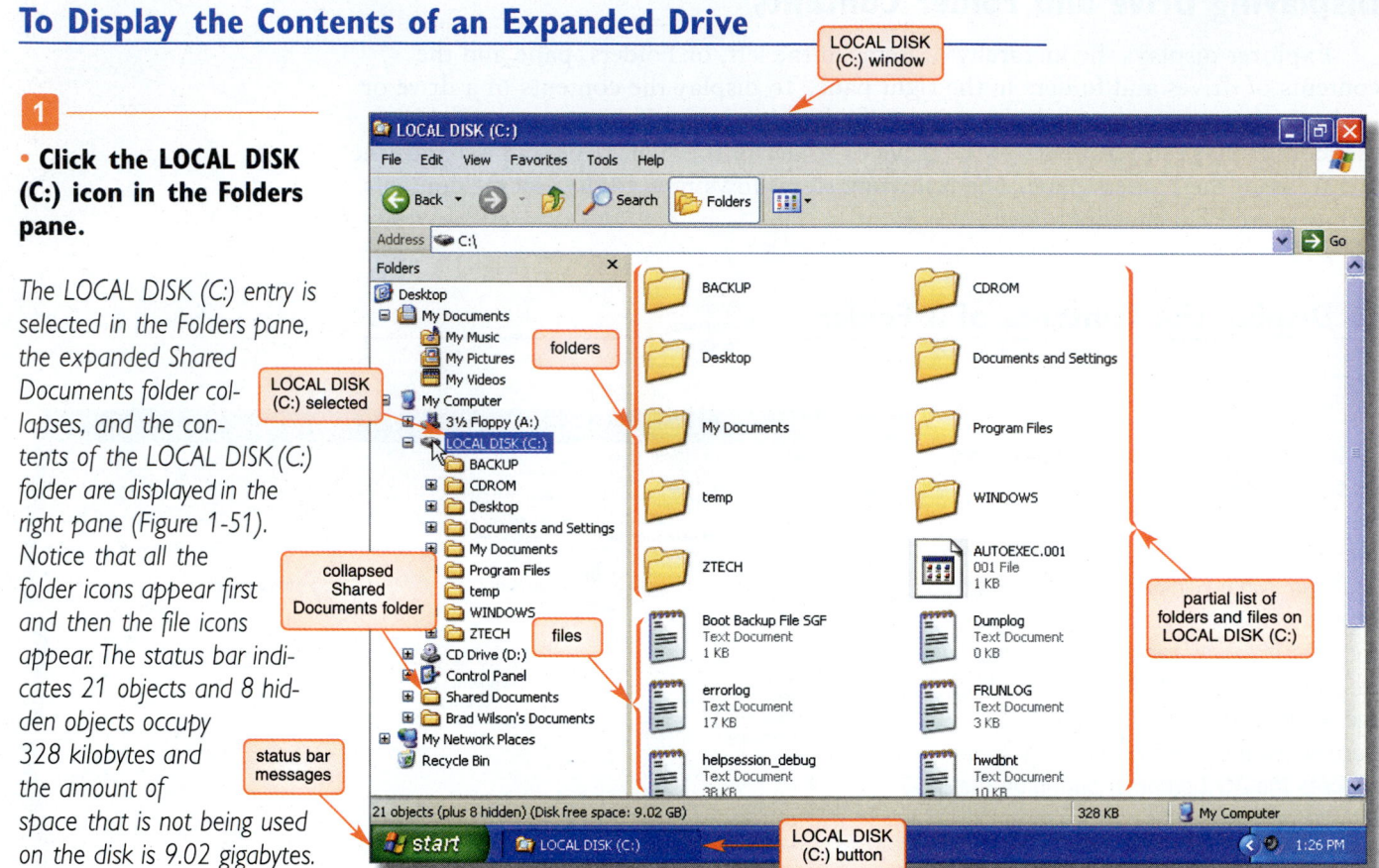

FIGURE 1-51

Other Ways

1. Double-click LOCAL DISK (C:) icon in right pane
2. Press DOWN ARROW to select LOCAL DISK (C:) icon in Folders pane
3. Press TAB to select any drive icon in right pane, press DOWN ARROW or RIGHT ARROW to select LOCAL DISK (C:) icon, press ENTER

Launching an Application Program from Windows Explorer

Earlier in this project you launched Internet Explorer from the Start menu (see Figures 1-42 and 1-43 on pages WIN 38 and WIN 39). You also can launch an application program from the right pane of a window. To launch the Internet Explorer program stored in the Program Files folder, complete the following steps.

To Launch an Application Program from Explorer

1

• **Click the plus sign to the left of the Program Files icon in the Folders pane.**

• **Click the Internet Explorer icon in the Folders pane.**

• **Point to the IEXPLORE (Internet Explorer) icon in the right pane of the Internet Explorer window.**

The Program Files and Internet Explorer folders expand, the Internet Explorer folder is selected, the window title changes to Internet Explorer, the Internet Explorer button replaces the LOCAL DISK (C:) button on the taskbar, and the contents of the Internet Explorer folder are displayed in the right pane (Figure 1-52). The status bar indicates 6 objects and 1 hidden object consume 124 kilobytes on drive C.

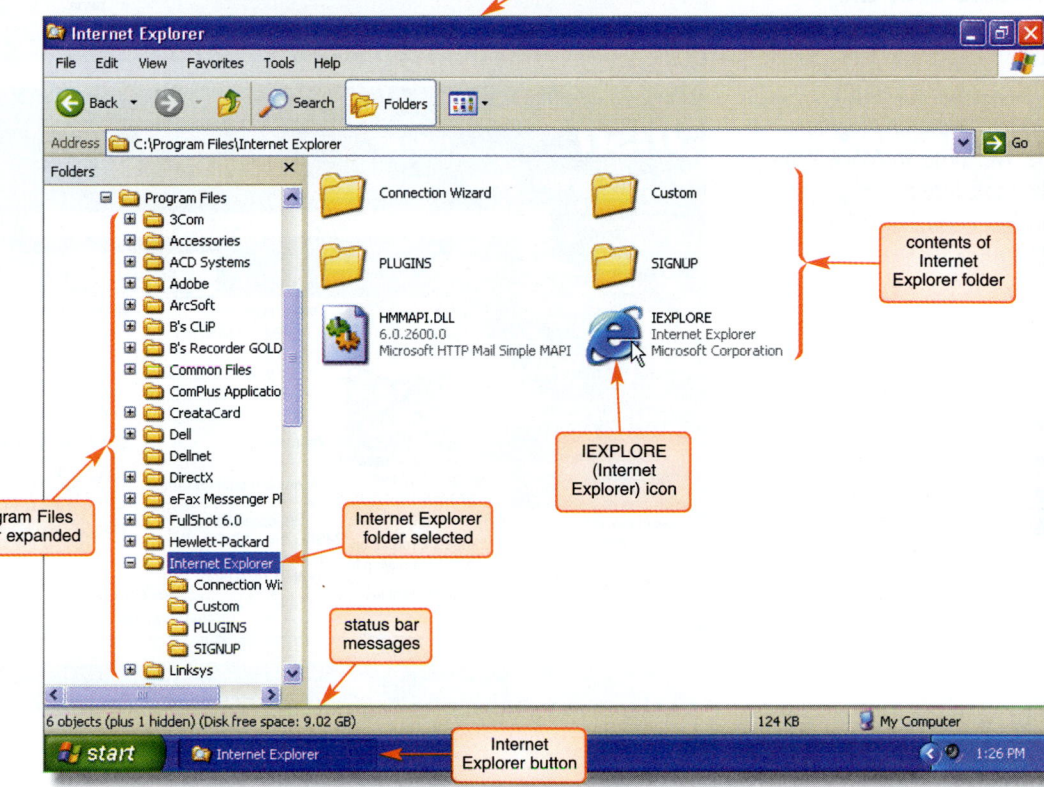

FIGURE 1-52

2

• **Double-click the IEXPLORE icon.**

Windows launches the Internet Explorer program. The Welcome to MSN.com - Microsoft Internet Explorer window, containing the MSN page, is displayed (Figure 1-53). Because Web pages are modified frequently, the Web page that is displayed on your desktop may be different from the Web page shown in Figure 1-53. The URL for the Web page is displayed in the Address bar.

FIGURE 1-53

You can use the Internet Explorer program for any purpose you wish, just as if you had launched it from the Start menu. When you are finished with the Internet Explorer program, you should quit the program. The step below shows how to quit the Internet Explorer program.

To Quit an Application Program

1 **Click the Close button on the Welcome to MSN.com - Microsoft Internet Explorer title bar.**

The Welcome to MSN.com - Microsoft Internet Explorer window closes.

Closing Folder Expansions

Sometimes, after you have completed work with expanded folders, you will want to close the expansions while still leaving the Explorer window open. The following steps illustrate how to close the expanded folders shown in Figure 1-52 on page WIN 47.

To Close Expanded Folders

1

• **Click the minus sign to the left of the Internet Explorer icon.**

The expansion of the Internet Explorer folder collapses and the minus sign changes to a plus sign (Figure 1-54). The contents of the right pane do not change.

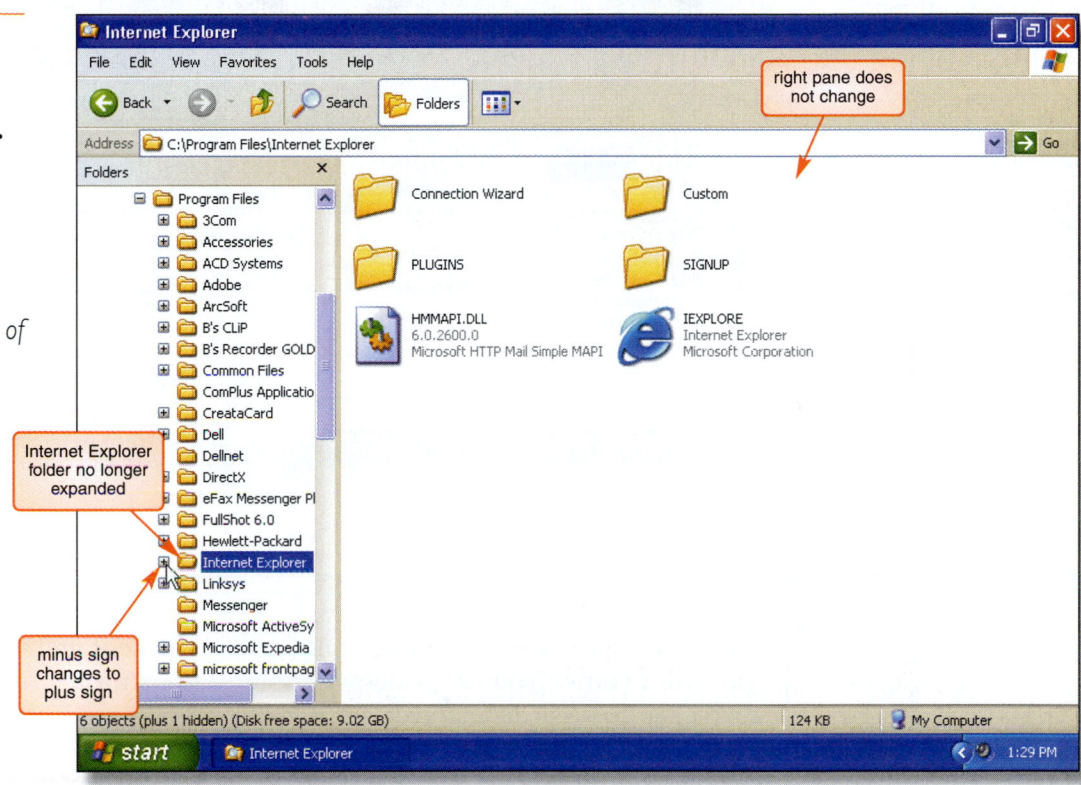

FIGURE 1-54

2

● **Click the minus sign to the left of the Program Files icon.**

The expansion of the Program Files folder collapses, the minus sign changes to a plus sign, the window title changes to Program Files, the Program Files button replaces the Internet Explorer button on the taskbar, and the right pane contains the files and folders in the Program Files folder (Figure 1-55).

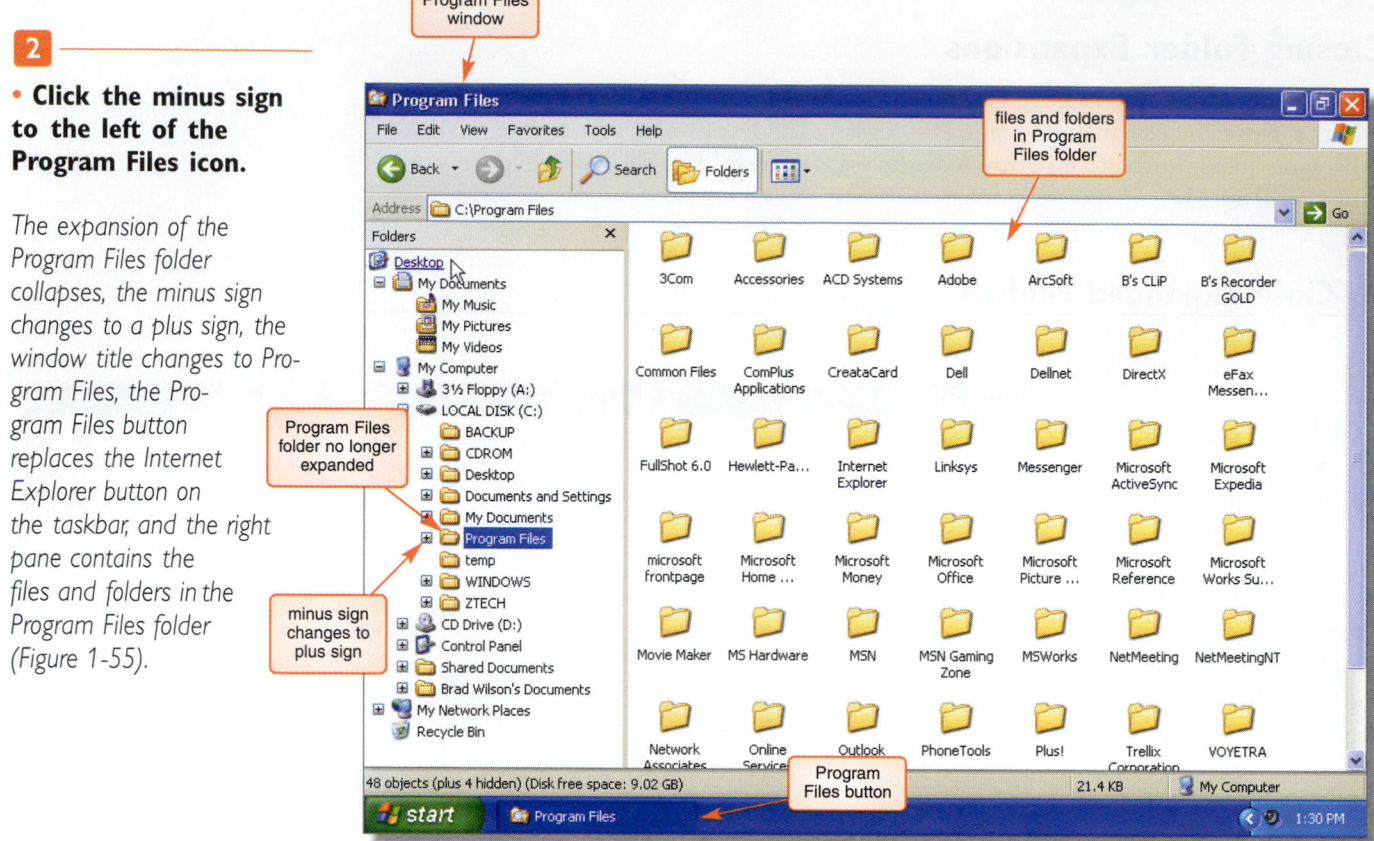

FIGURE 1-55

Moving through the Folders pane and right pane is an important skill because you will find that you use Windows Explorer to perform a significant amount of file maintenance on the computer.

Copying, Moving, Renaming, and Deleting Files in Windows Explorer

Three common operations that every student should understand how to perform are copying a file, renaming a file, and deleting a file. On the following pages, you will use Windows Explorer to copy a file from the WINDOWS folder on drive C to the My Pictures folder on drive C, rename a file in the My Pictures folder, and then delete a file in the My Pictures folder.

More About

The WINDOWS Folder

The WINDOWS folder appears in the LOCAL DISK (C:) window if the computer has been upgraded to Windows XP from Windows 98 or Windows Me. The WINNT folder appears if the computer has been upgraded to Windows XP from Windows 2000. WINNT is an abbreviation for Windows NT, an older operating system designed for business networks.

Copying Files in Windows Explorer

When copying files, the drive and folder containing the files to be copied are called the **source drive** and **source folder**, respectively. The drive and folder to which the files are copied are called the **destination drive** and **destination folder**, respectively. In the following steps, the WINDOWS folder is the source folder, the My Pictures folder is the destination folder, and drive C is both the source drive and the destination drive.

One method of copying files in Windows Explorer is to right-drag a file icon from the right pane to a folder or drive icon in the Folders pane. The following steps show how to copy the Prairie Wind file from the WINDOWS folder (source folder) to the My Pictures folder (destination folder).

To Copy a File in Windows Explorer by Right-Dragging

1

• **Click the WINDOWS icon in the Folders pane.**

• **Scroll the right pane to display the Prairie Wind icon. If the Prairie Wind file is not available, display another icon.**

• **Scroll the Folders pane to display the expanded My Documents folder.**

The contents of the WINDOWS folder, including the Prairie Wind icon, are displayed in the right pane and the My Pictures folder is displayed in the expanded My Documents folder in the Folders pane (Figure 1-56).

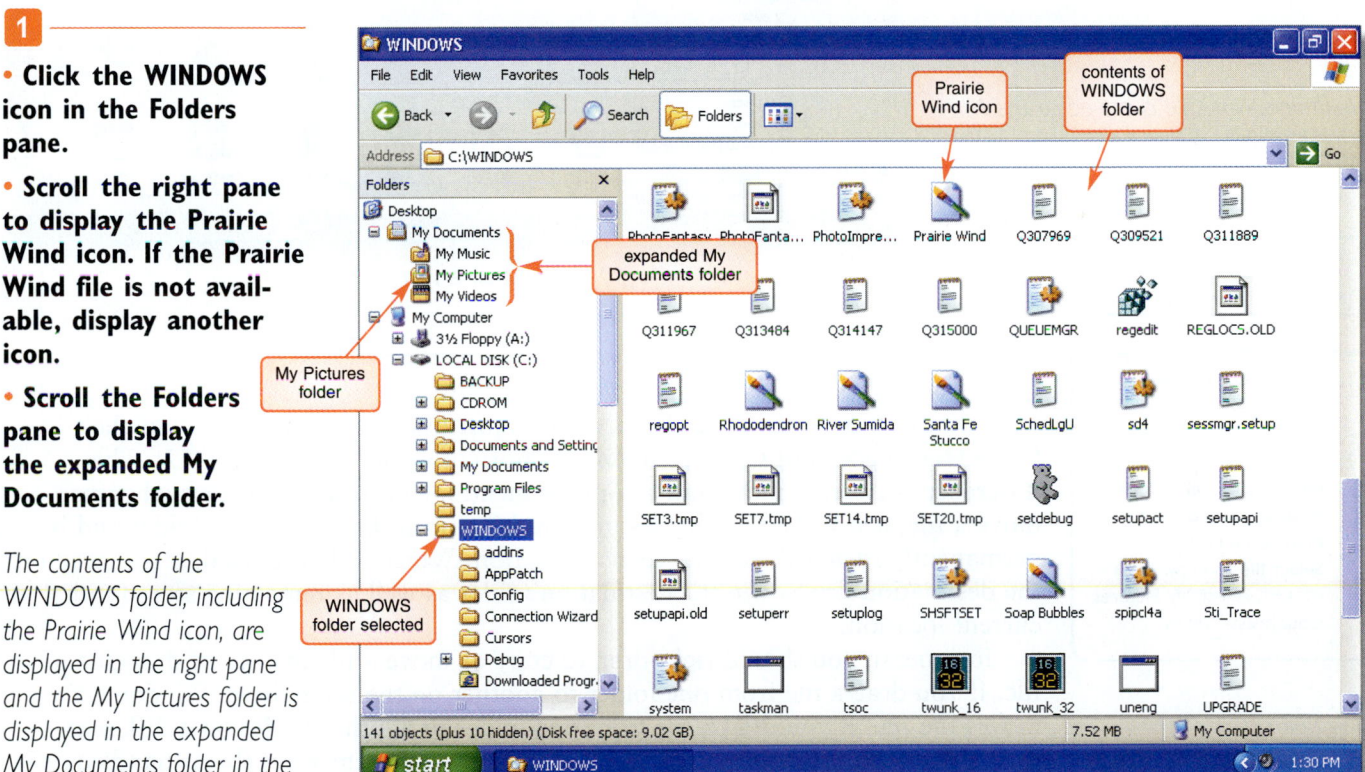

FIGURE 1-56

2

• **Right-drag the Prairie Wind icon onto the top of the My Pictures icon.**

• **Point to Copy Here on the shortcut menu.**

The dimmed image of the Prairie Wind icon is displayed as you right-drag the icons onto the top of the My Pictures icon, a shortcut menu is displayed, and the dimmed image no longer is displayed (Figure 1-57).

3

• **Click Copy Here.**

The Prairie Wind file is copied to the My Pictures folder.

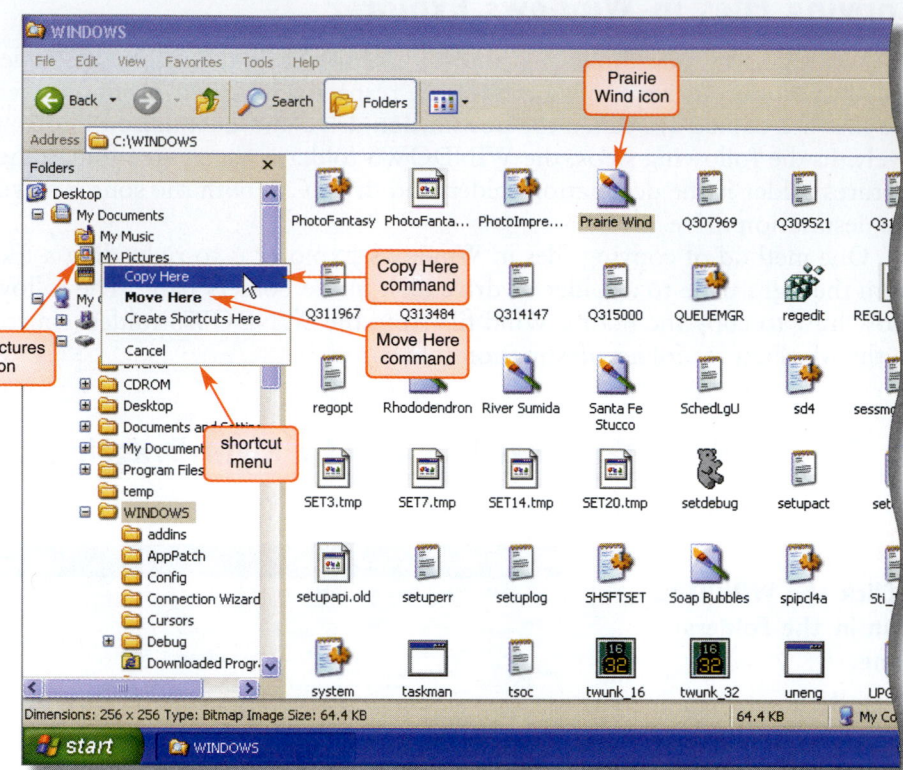

FIGURE 1-57

Q&A

Q: Are copying and moving the same?

A: No! When you copy a file, it will be located in both the place to which it was copied and the place from which it was copied. When you move a file, it will be located in only the location to which it was moved. You will be sorry if you do not know the difference, and a file you thought was copied was moved instead.

You can move files using the techniques just discussed except that you click **Move Here** instead of Copy Here on the shortcut menu (see Figure 1-57). The difference between a move and a copy, as mentioned previously, is that when you move a file, it is placed on the destination drive or in the destination folder and is permanently removed from its current location. When a file is copied, it is placed on the destination drive or in the destination folder as well as remaining stored in its current location.

In general, you should right-drag to copy or move a file instead of dragging a file. If you drag a file from one folder to another on the same drive, Windows XP moves the file. If you drag a file from one folder to another folder on a different drive, Windows XP copies the file. Because of the different ways this is handled, it is strongly suggested you right-drag when moving or copying files.

Displaying the Contents of the My Pictures Folder

After copying a group of files, you might want to examine the folder or drive where the files were copied to ensure they were copied properly. The following step shows how to display the contents of the My Pictures folder.

To Display the Contents of a Folder

1

• **Click the My Pictures icon in the Folders pane.**

The contents of the My Pictures folder, including the Prairie Wind file, are displayed in the right pane (Figure 1-58). If additional files or folders are contained in the My Pictures folder, their icons and titles also are displayed.

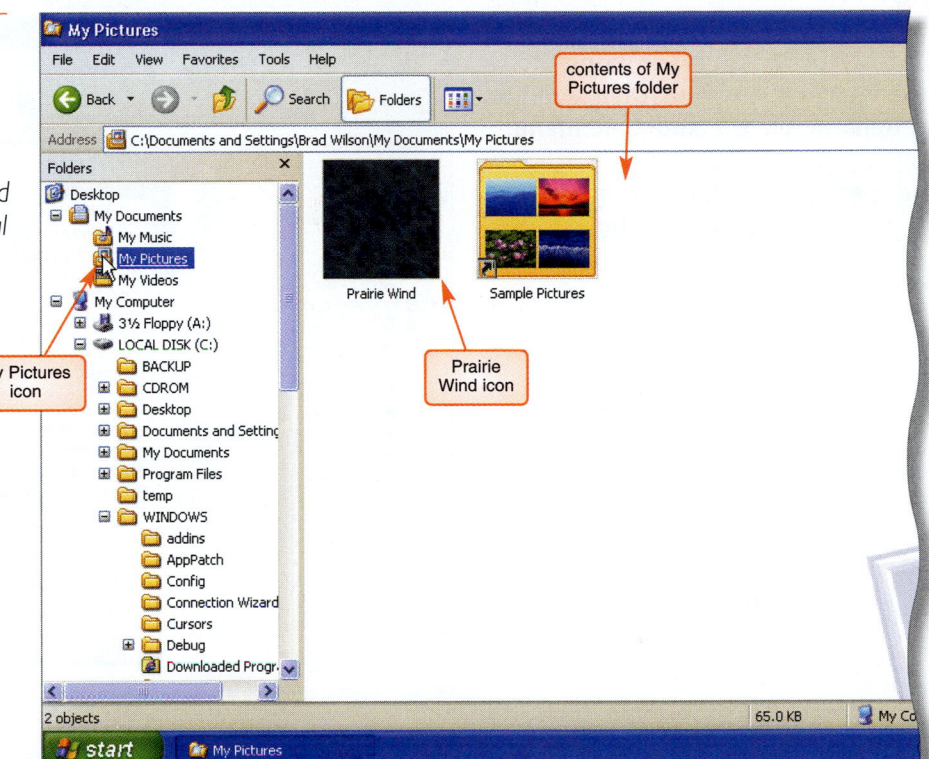

FIGURE 1-58

Renaming Files and Folders

In some circumstances, you may want to **rename** a file or a folder. This could occur when you want to distinguish a file in one folder or drive from a copy, or if you decide you need a better name to identify a file. The steps on the next page illustrate how to change the name of the Prairie Wind file in the My Pictures folder to Blue Prairie Wind.

To Rename a File

1

• **Right-click the Prairie Wind icon in the right pane and then point to Rename on the shortcut menu.**

The selected Prairie Wind icon and a shortcut menu are displayed (Figure 1-59).

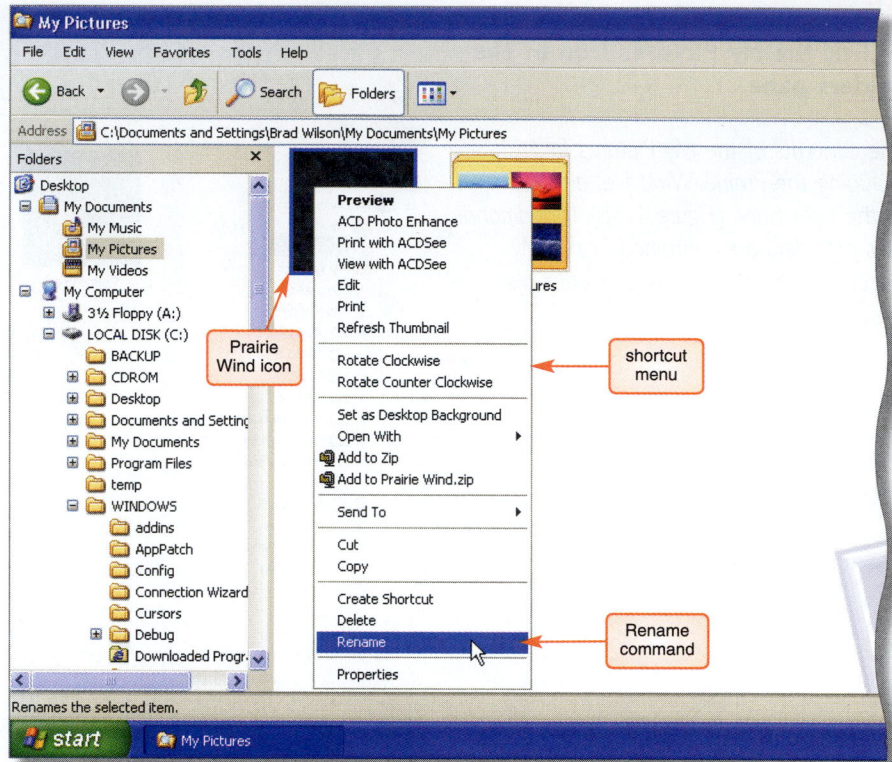

FIGURE 1-59

2

• **Click Rename.**

• **Type** Blue Prairie Wind **and then press the enter key.**

The file is renamed Blue Prairie Wind (Figure 1-60). Notice that the file in the My Pictures folder is renamed, but the original file in the WINDOWS folder in drive C is not renamed.

Other Ways

1. Right-click icon, press M, type name, press ENTER
2. Click icon, press F2, type name, press ENTER
3. Click icon, on File menu click Rename, type name, press ENTER
4. Select icon, press ALT+F, press M, type name, press ENTER

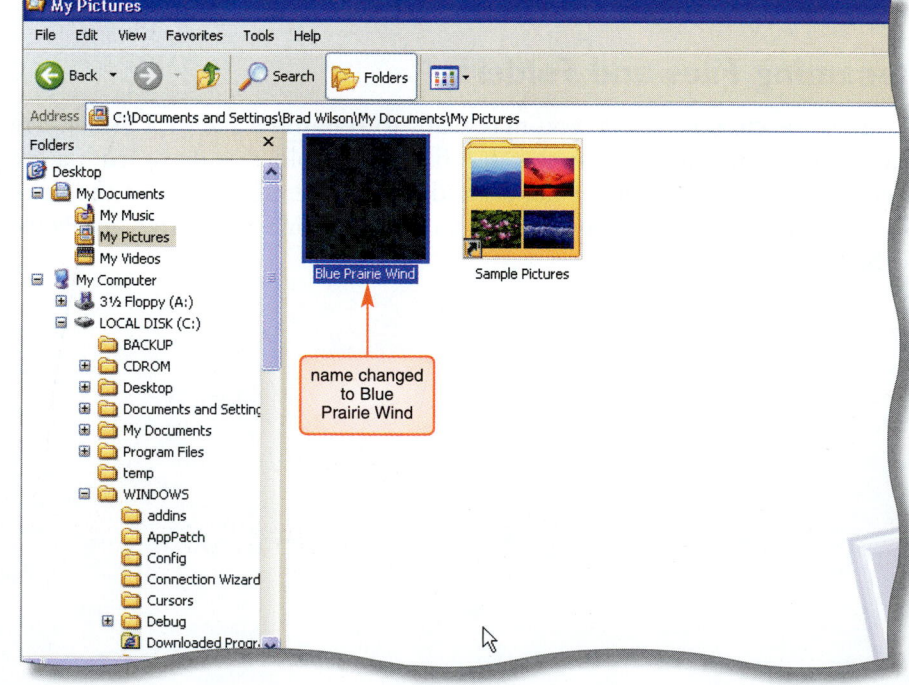

FIGURE 1-60

Renaming files by this method also can be accomplished in other windows. For example, if you open the My Computer window and then open the My Music window, you can rename any file stored in the My Music window using the technique just presented.

Use caution when renaming files on the hard disk. If you inadvertently rename a file that is associated with certain programs, the programs may not be able to find the file and, therefore, may not execute properly.

Deleting Files in Windows Explorer

A final operation that you may want to perform in Windows Explorer is to delete a file. Exercise extreme caution when deleting a file or files. When you delete a file from a hard drive, the deleted file is stored in the Recycle Bin where you can recover it until you empty the Recycle Bin. If you delete a file from a floppy disk, the file is gone permanently once you delete it.

Assume you have decided to delete the Blue Prairie Wind file from the My Pictures window. The following steps illustrate how to delete the Blue Prairie Wind file.

More About

Deleting Files

Someone proposed that the Delete command be removed from operating systems after an employee, who thought he knew what he was doing, deleted an entire database, which cost the company millions of dollars to replace. You should regard the Delete command as something to be used with extreme caution.

To Delete a File by Right-Dragging to the Recycle Bin

1

• **Scroll the Folders pane to display the Recycle Bin icon.**

• **Right-drag the Blue Prairie Wind icon to the Recycle Bin icon in the Folders pane and then point to Move Here on the shortcut menu.**

The Blue Prairie Wind icon in the right pane is right-dragged to the Recycle Bin icon in the Folders pane and a shortcut menu is displayed (Figure 1-61). The Move Here command is highlighted on the shortcut menu.

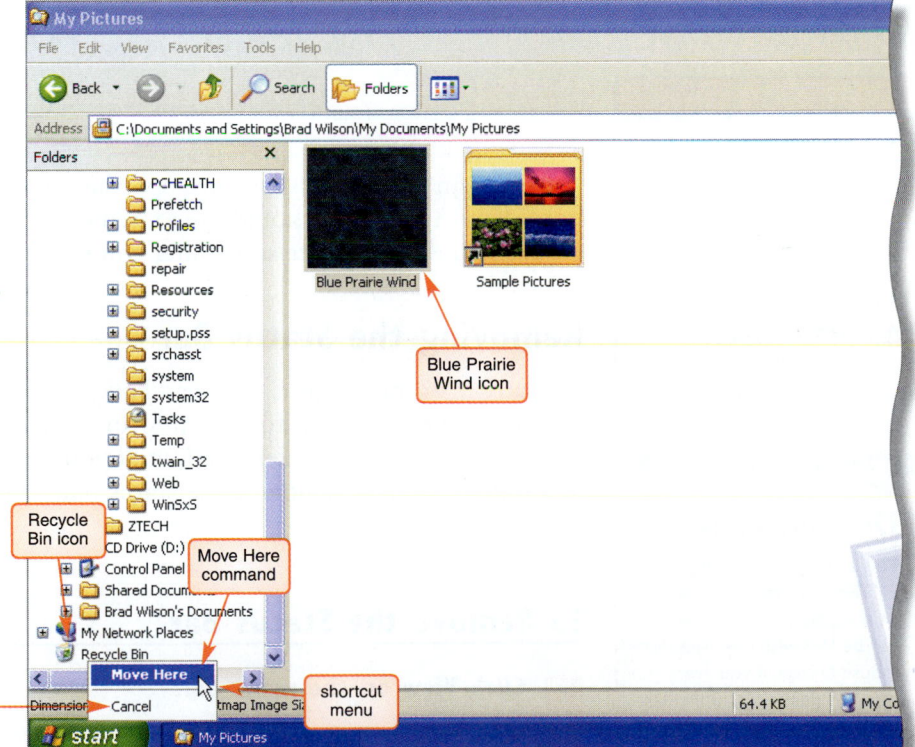

FIGURE 1-61

2

• **Click Move Here.**

The Blue Prairie Wind icon is removed from the right pane and moved to the Recycle Bin (Figure 1-62). If you wish to terminate the deleting process before it is complete, you can click the Cancel command on the shortcut menu.

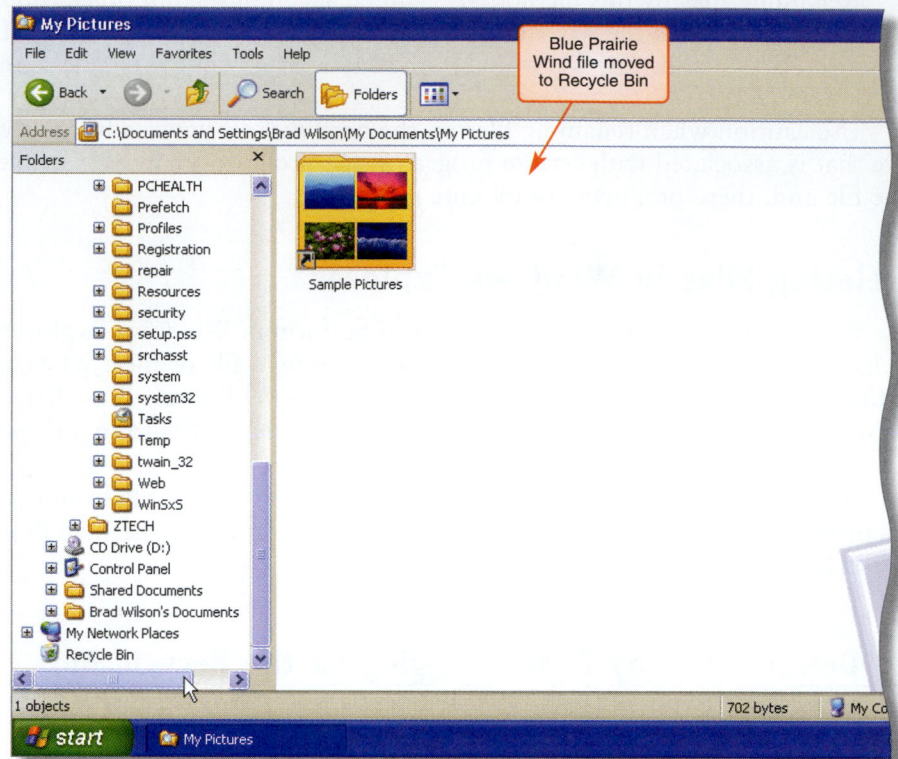

FIGURE 1-62

You can use the methods just specified to delete folders on a floppy disk or a hard disk. Again, you should use extreme caution when deleting files and folders to ensure you do not delete something you may not be able to recover.

Removing the Status Bar

Earlier in this project, you may have used the View command on the menu bar to display the status bar to view information about the folders, programs, and documents in the My Computer window. If you did, you should return the status bar to its original state by removing the status bar. The following steps remove the status bar.

To Remove the Status Bar

1 **Click View on the menu bar.**

2 **Click Status Bar on the View menu.**

The status bar no longer is displayed.

Quitting Windows Explorer

When you have finished working with Windows Explorer, you can quit Windows Explorer by closing the Folders pane or by closing the Windows Explorer (My Pictures) window. The following step shows how to quit Windows Explorer by closing the My Pictures window.

To Quit Windows Explorer

1   **Click the Close button on the My Pictures window title bar.**

Windows XP closes the My Pictures window and quits Windows Explorer.

Using Help and Support

One of the more powerful Windows XP features is Help and Support. **Help and Support** is available when using Windows XP, or when using any application program running under Windows XP. It contains answers to many questions you may ask with respect to Windows XP.

Launching Help and Support

Before you can access the Help and Support Center services, you must launch Help and Support. One method of launching Help and Support uses the Start menu. The following steps show how to launch Help and Support.

To Launch Help and Support

1

• **Click the Start button on the taskbar and then point to Help and Support on the Start menu.**

Windows XP displays the Start menu and highlights the Help and Support command (Figure 1-63).

> **More About**
>
> ### Windows XP Help and Support
>
> If you purchased an operating system or application program nine years ago, you received at least one, and more often several, heavy thick technical manuals that explained the software. With Windows XP, you receive a booklet with only 34 pages. The Help and Support feature of Windows XP replaces the reams and reams of printed pages in hard-to-understand technical manuals.

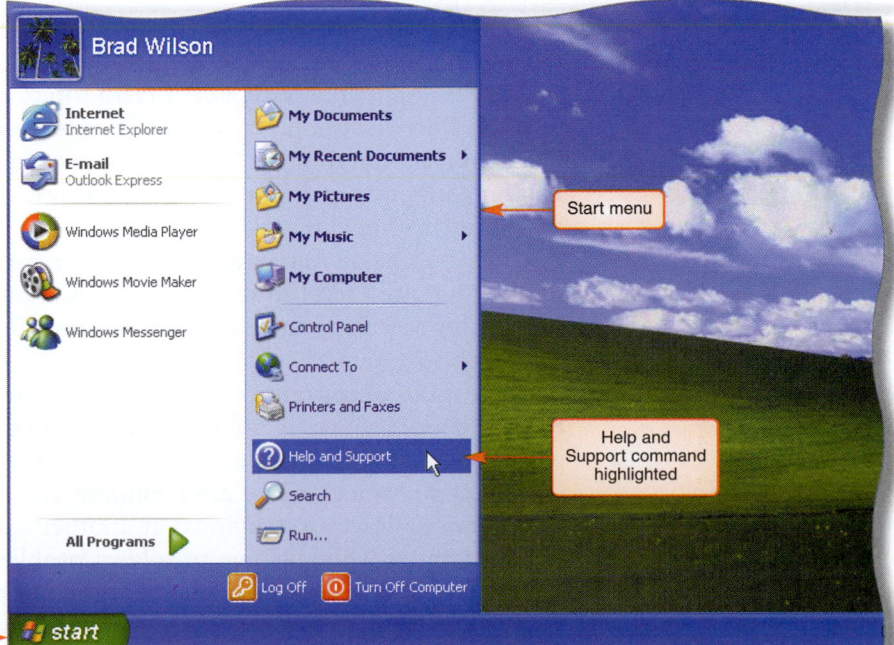

FIGURE 1-63

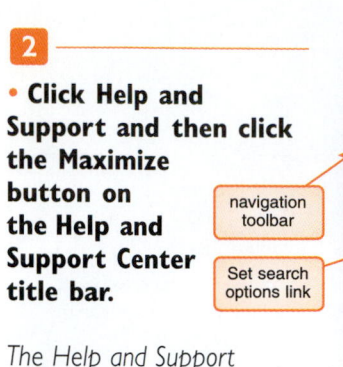

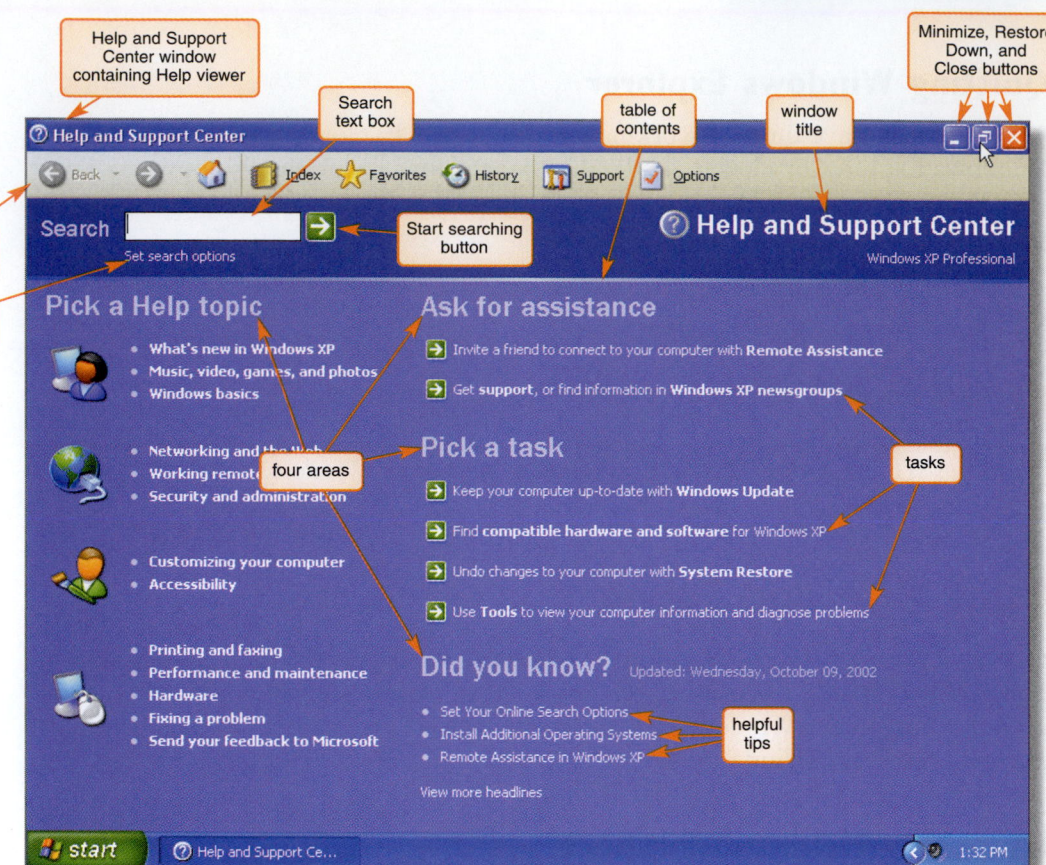

2

• **Click Help and Support and then click the Maximize button on the Help and Support Center title bar.**

The Help and Support Center window opens and maximizes (Figure 1-64). The window contains the Help viewer. The Help viewer includes the navigation toolbar, Search text box and Set search options link, and table of contents. The table of contents contains four areas (Pick a Help topic, Ask for assistance, Pick a task, and Did you know?).

FIGURE 1-64

Other Ways

1. Press F1
2. Press CTRL+ESC, press H
3. Press WINDOWS+F1

The Help and Support Center title bar shown in Figure 1-64 contains a Minimize button, Restore Down button, and Close button. You can minimize or restore the Help and Support Center window as needed and also close the Help and Support Center window.

The navigation toolbar is displayed below the title bar. The **navigation toolbar** allows you to navigate through Help topics and pages, browse and save Help topics and pages, view previously saved Help topics and pages, get online support for questions and problems, and customize the Help viewer. An icon identifies each button on the navigation toolbar. Six buttons contain a text label (Back, Index, Favorites, History, Support, and Options). The buttons on the navigation toolbar on your computer may be different.

The area below the navigation toolbar contains the Search text box and Start searching button used to search for Help, the Set search options link to set the criteria for searching the Help and Support Center, and the window's title (Help and Support Center).

The **table of contents** contains four areas. The **Pick a Help topic area** contains four category groups. A unique icon identifies each group. Clicking a category in a group displays a list of subcategories and Help topics related to the category.

The **Ask for assistance area** contains two tasks. The first task (**Remote Assistance**) allows an individual at another computer to connect and control your computer while helping to solve a problem. The second task (**Windows XP newsgroups**) allows you to obtain Help from product support experts or discuss your questions with other Windows XP users in newsgroups.

The **Pick a task area** contains four tasks. The first task (**Windows Update**) allows you to access a catalog of items such as device drivers, security fixes, critical updates, the latest Help files, and Internet products that you can download to keep your computer up-to-date. The second task (**compatible hardware and software**) allows you to search for hardware and software that are compatible with Windows XP. The third task (**System Restore**) allows you to store the current state of your computer and restore your computer to that state without losing important information. The fourth task (**Tools**) contains a collection of eight helpful tools to keep your computer running smoothly. The **Did you know? area** is updated daily with helpful tips for using Windows XP.

Browsing for Help Topics in the Table of Contents

After launching Help and Support, the next step is to find the Help topic in which you are interested. Assume you want to know more about finding information using the Help and Support Center. The following steps illustrate how to use the table of contents to find a Help topic that describes how to find what you need in the Help and Support Center.

To Browse for Help Topics in the Table of Contents

1

• **Point to Windows basics in the Pick a Help topic area.**

The mouse pointer changes to a hand icon when positioned on the Windows basics category, and the category is underlined (Figure 1-65).

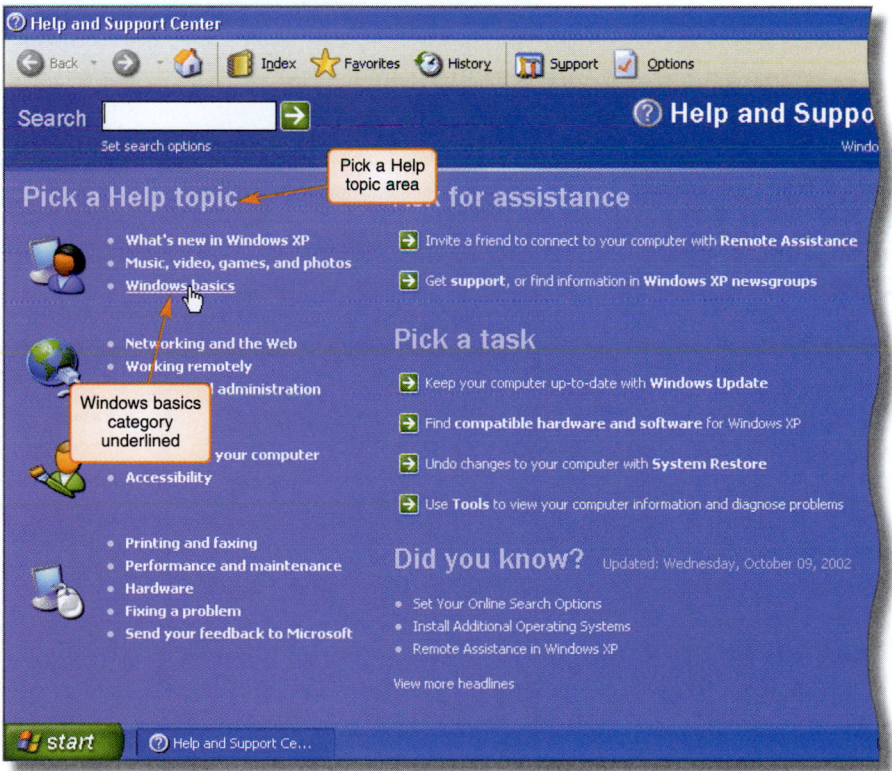

FIGURE 1-65

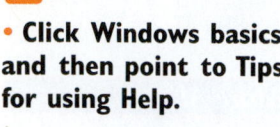

2

• **Click Windows basics and then point to Tips for using Help.**

The navigation pane and topic pane are displayed in the Help and Support Center window (Figure 1-66). The Windows basics area in the navigation pane contains five categories and the underlined Tips for using Help category. The See Also area contains four Help topics. The topic pane contains the Help and Support toolbar and the Windows basics page.

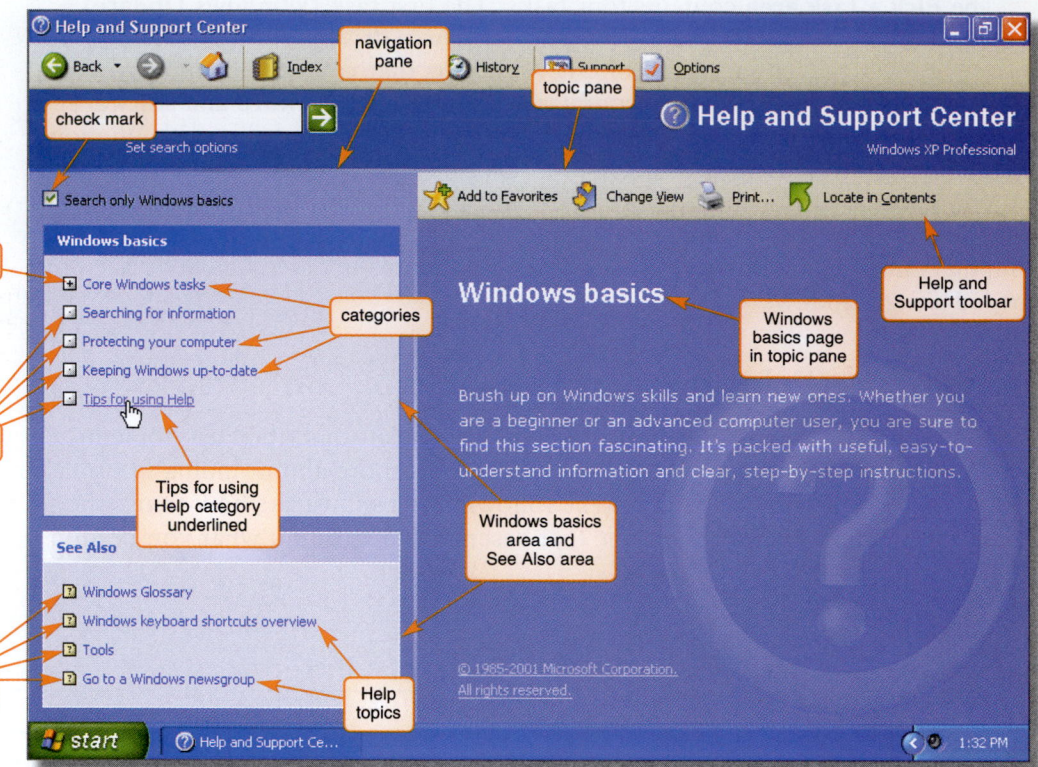

FIGURE 1-66

3

• **Click Tips for using Help and then point to Find what you need in Help and Support Center in the topic pane.**

Windows XP highlights the Tips for using Help category in the Windows basics area, displays the Tips for using Help page in the topic pane, and underlines the Find what you need in Help and Support Center task (Figure 1-67). The Add to Favorites button and Print button on the Help and Support Center toolbar are dimmed to indicate the page cannot be added to the favorites list or printed.

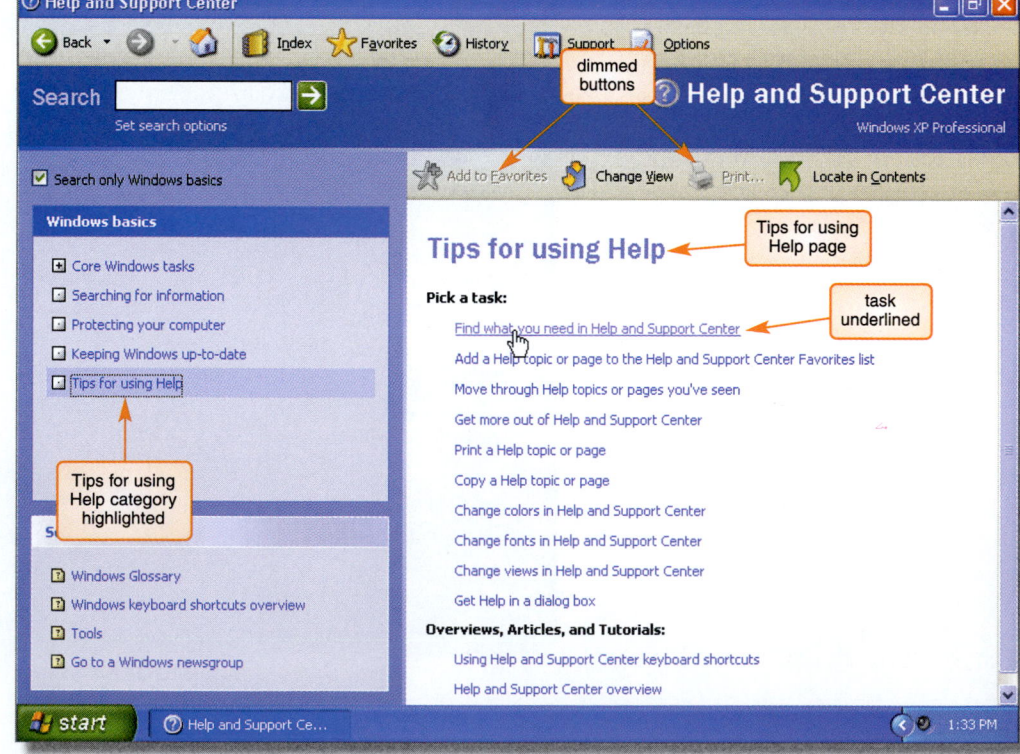

FIGURE 1-67

4
• **Click Find what you need in Help and Support Center and then read the information in the To find what you need in Help and Support Center topic in the topic pane.**

Windows XP removes the dotted rectangle surrounding the Tips for using Help category in the Windows basics area and displays the To find what you need in Help and Support Center topic in the topic pane (Figure 1-68). Clicking the Related Topics link displays a list of related Help topics.

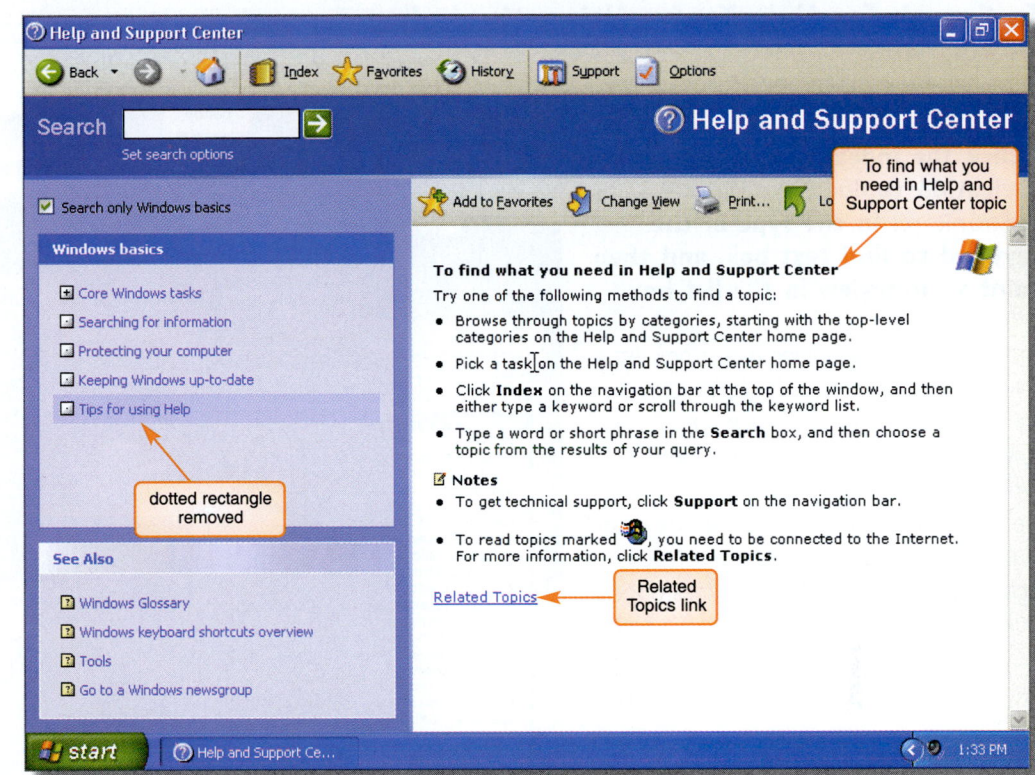

FIGURE 1-68

The check mark in the Search only Windows basics check box shown in Figure 1-66 indicates topics in the Windows basics category will be searched.

In the Windows basics area, the **plus sign** in the small box to the left of the Core Windows tasks category indicates the category contains subcategories but the subcategories do not appear in the area. Clicking the box with the plus sign displays a list of subcategories below the Core Windows category. A **bullet** in a small box indicates a category. Clicking the bullet within a small box displays a list of tasks in the topic pane.

Each of the four Help topics in the See Also area is identified by a question mark in a document icon. The **question mark** indicates a Help topic without further subdivision.

The Help and Support Center toolbar in the topic pane shown in Figure 1-66 contains four buttons. An icon and text label identify each button on the toolbar. The buttons allow you to add a Help topic to the favorites list, display only the Help and Support Center toolbar and topic pane in the Help and Support Center window, print a Help topic in the topic pane, and locate a Help topic in the topic pane in the table of contents.

Using the Help and Support Center Index

A second method of finding answers to your questions about Windows XP is to use the Help and Support Center Index. The **Help and Support Center Index** contains a list of index entries, each of which references one or more Help topics. Assume you want more information about home networking. The steps on the next page illustrate how to learn more about home networking.

Other Ways

1. Press TAB until category or topic is highlighted, press ENTER, repeat for each category or topic

More About

The Index

The Index is probably the best source of information in Windows Help and Support, because you can enter the name of the subject in which you are interested. Sometimes, however, you will have to be creative to discover the index entry that answers your question, because the most obvious entry will not always lead to your answer.

To Search for Help Topics Using the Index

1

• **Click the Index button on the navigation toolbar, type** home networking **in the Type in the keyword to find text box, and then point to overview in the list box.**

The Index area, containing a text box, list box, and Display button, is displayed in the navigation pane and the Index page is displayed in the topic pane (Figure 1-69). When you type an entry in the text box, the list of index entries in the list box automatically scrolls and the entry you type is highlighted in the list. Several entries appear indented below the home networking entry.

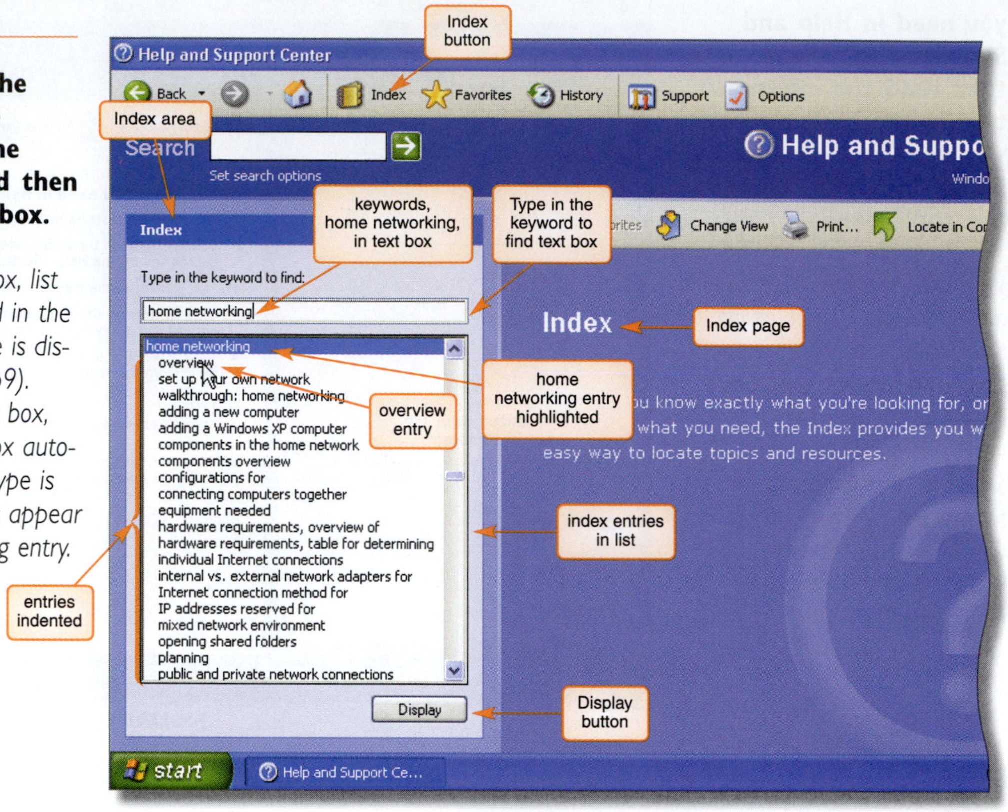

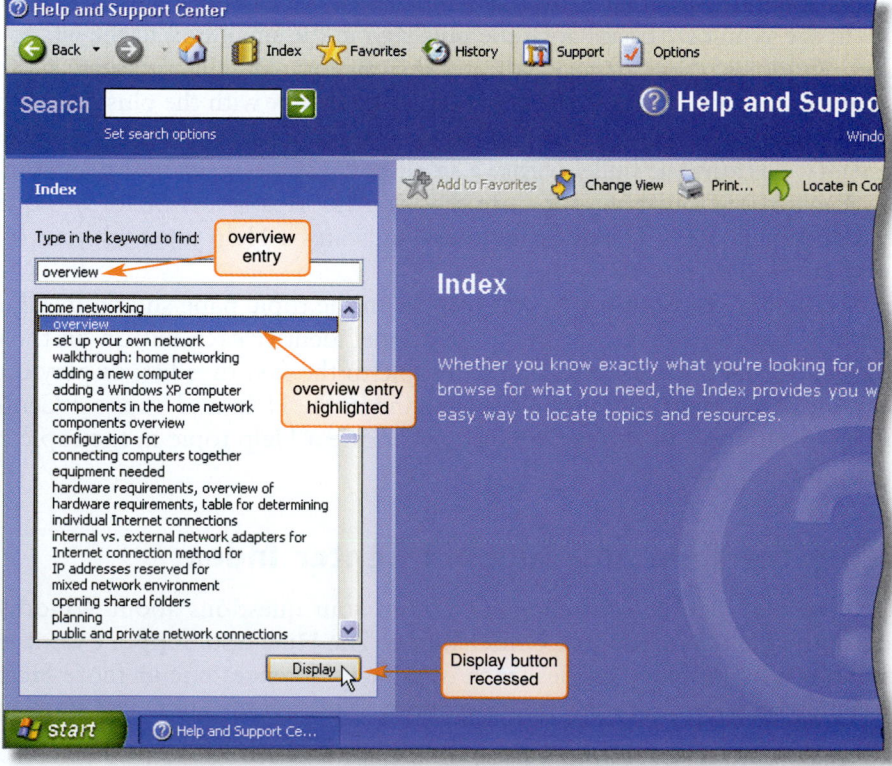

FIGURE 1-69

2

• **Click overview in the list and then point to the Display button.**

Windows XP displays the overview entry in the text box and highlights the overview entry in the list (Figure 1-70). The yellow outline surrounding the Display button indicates the button is recessed.

FIGURE 1-70

3

• **Click the Display button.**

The Home or small office network overview topic is displayed in the topic pane (Figure 1-71). The topic contains an overview of home and small office networks. Additional information is available by using the vertical scroll bar in the topic pane.

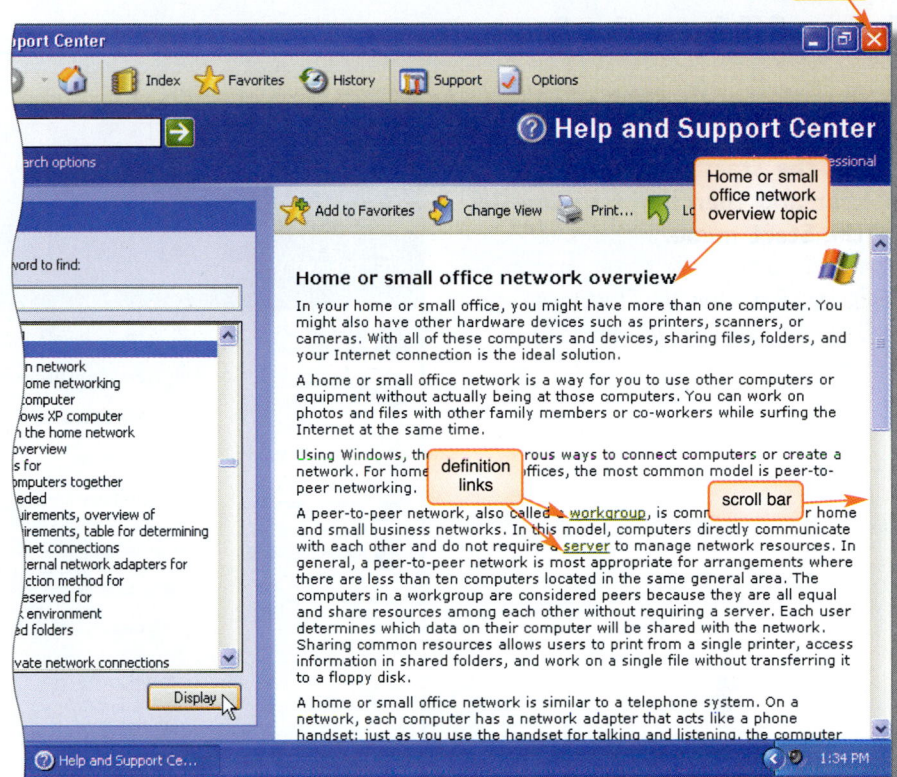

FIGURE 1-71

In Figure 1-71, the workgroup and server links are underlined and displayed in green font to indicate that clicking the link will display its definition. To remove the definition, click anywhere off the definition. Although not visible in Figure 1-71, other links, such as the Related Topics link, appear at the bottom of the page, underlined, and in blue font. Clicking the Related Topics link displays a pop-up window that contains topics related to the home or small office network overview.

After using the Help and Support Center, normally you will close the Help and Support Center. The following step shows how to close the Help and Support Center.

To Close the Help and Support Center

1 **Click the Close button on the title bar of the Help and Support Center window.**

Windows XP closes the Help and Support Center window.

Logging Off and Turning Off the Computer

After completing your work with Windows XP, you should close your user account by logging off from the computer. Logging off from the computer closes any open applications, allows you to save any unsaved documents, ends the Windows XP session, and makes the computer available for other users. Perform the steps on the next page to log off from the computer.

Other Ways

1. Press ALT+N, type keyword, press DOWN ARROW until topic is highlighted, press ALT+D (or ENTER)

Q&A

Q: Why is it important to log off the computer?

A: It is important to log off the computer so you do not lose your work. Some users of Windows XP have turned off their computers without following the log off procedure only to find data they thought they had stored on disk was lost.

To Log Off from the Computer

1

• **Click the Start button on the taskbar and then point to Log Off on the Start menu.**

Windows XP displays the Start menu and highlights the Log Off command (Figure 1-72).

FIGURE 1-72

2

• **Click Log Off.**

• **Point to the Log Off button in the Log Off Windows dialog box.**

Windows XP displays the Log Off Windows dialog box (Figure 1-73). The dialog box contains three buttons (Switch User, Log Off, and Cancel). Pointing to the Log Off button changes the color of the button to light orange and displays the Log Off balloon. The balloon contains the balloon name, Log Off, and the text, Closes your programs and ends your Windows session. The Cancel button is hidden behind the balloon.

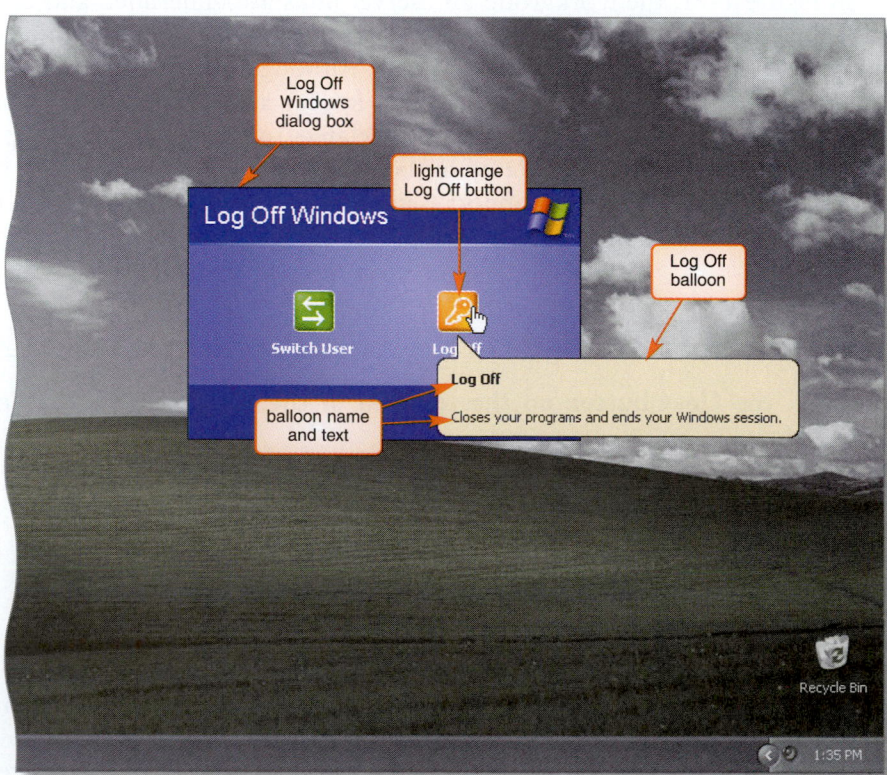

FIGURE 1-73

3

• **Click the Log Off button.**

Windows XP logs off from the computer and displays the Welcome screen (Figure 1-74). A message is displayed below the Brad Wilson name on the Welcome screen to indicate the user has unread e-mail messages. Your user name will be displayed instead of the Brad Wilson name on the Welcome screen.

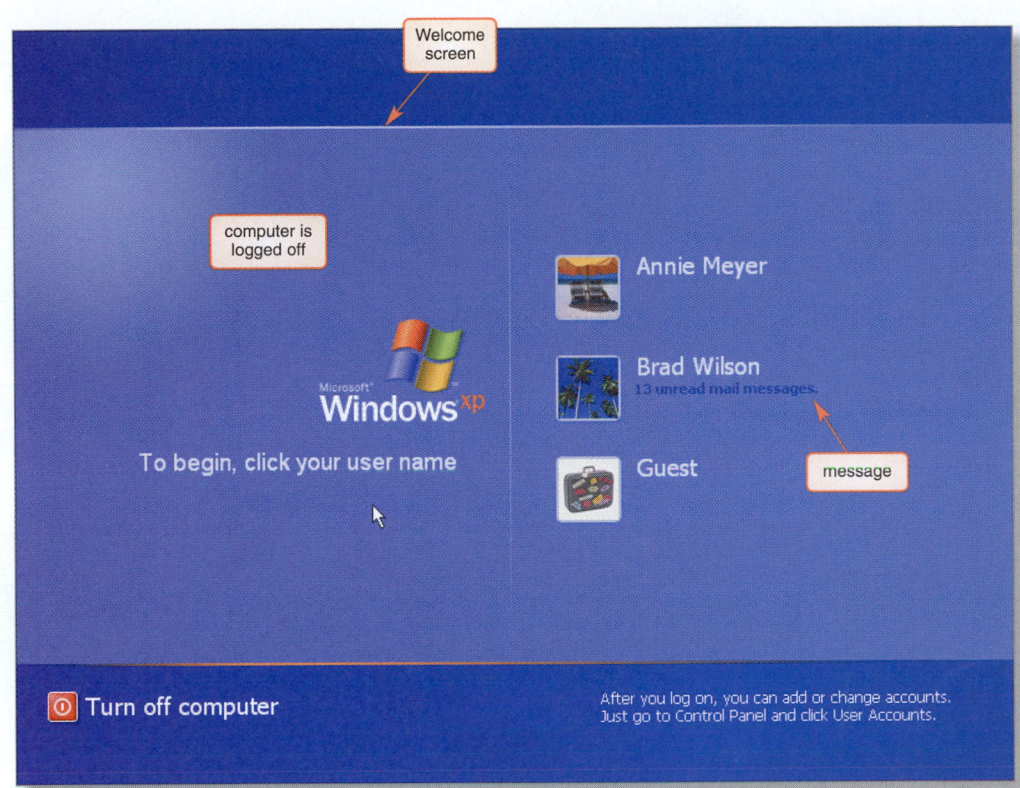

FIGURE 1-74

Other Ways

1. Press CTRL+ESC, press L, press L

While Windows XP is logging off, a blue screen containing the word, Welcome, appears on the desktop and the messages, Logging off..., and Saving your settings..., appear on the screen momentarily. The blue screen closes and the Welcome screen (Figure 1-74) appears on the desktop. At this point, another user can log on.

If you accidentally click Log Off on the Start menu as shown in Figure 1-72 and you do not want to log off, click the Cancel button in the Log Off Windows dialog box to return to normal Windows XP operation.

After logging off, you also may want to turn off the computer using the **Turn off computer link** on the Welcome screen. Turning off the computer shuts down Windows XP so you can turn off the power to the computer. Many computers turn the power off automatically. The steps on the next page illustrate how to turn off the computer. If you are not sure about turning off the computer, simply read the steps.

To Turn Off the Computer

1

• **Point to the Turn off computer link on the Welcome screen.**

Pointing to the Turn off computer link underlines the Turn off computer link (Figure 1-75).

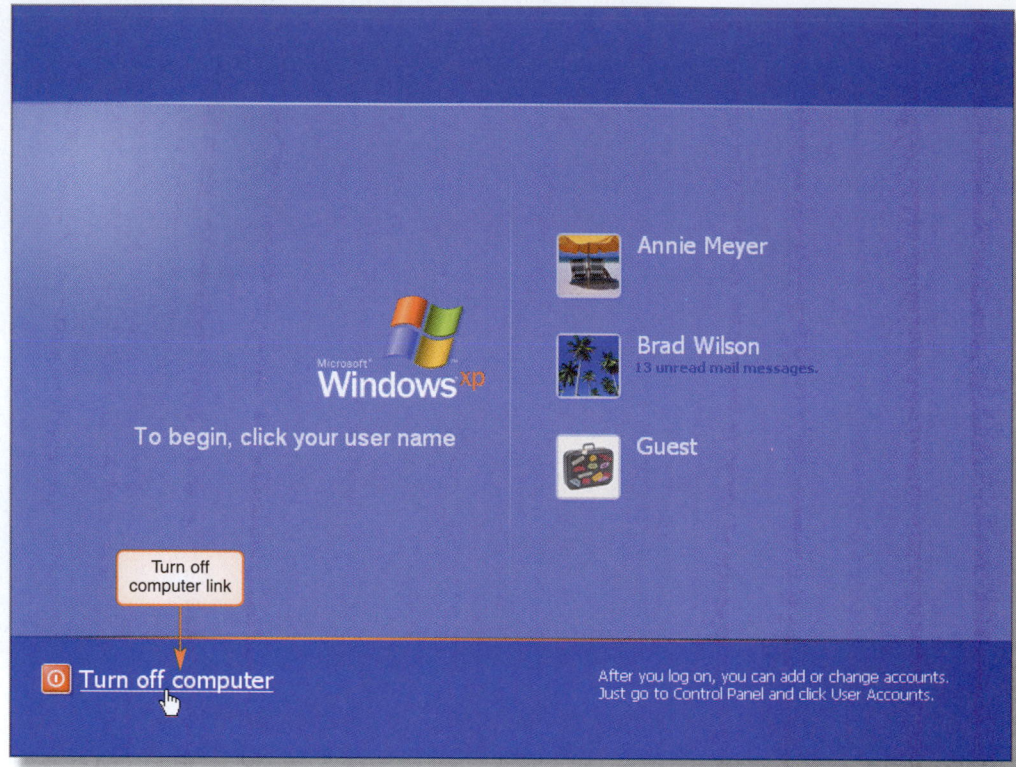

FIGURE 1-75

2

• **Click Turn off computer.**

The Welcome screen darkens and the Turn off computer dialog box is displayed (Figure 1-76). The dialog box contains four buttons (Stand By, Turn Off, Restart, and Cancel). The buttons allow you to perform different operations, such as placing the computer in stand by mode (Stand By), shutting down Windows XP (Turn Off), restarting the computer (Restart), and canceling the process of shutting down Windows XP (Cancel).

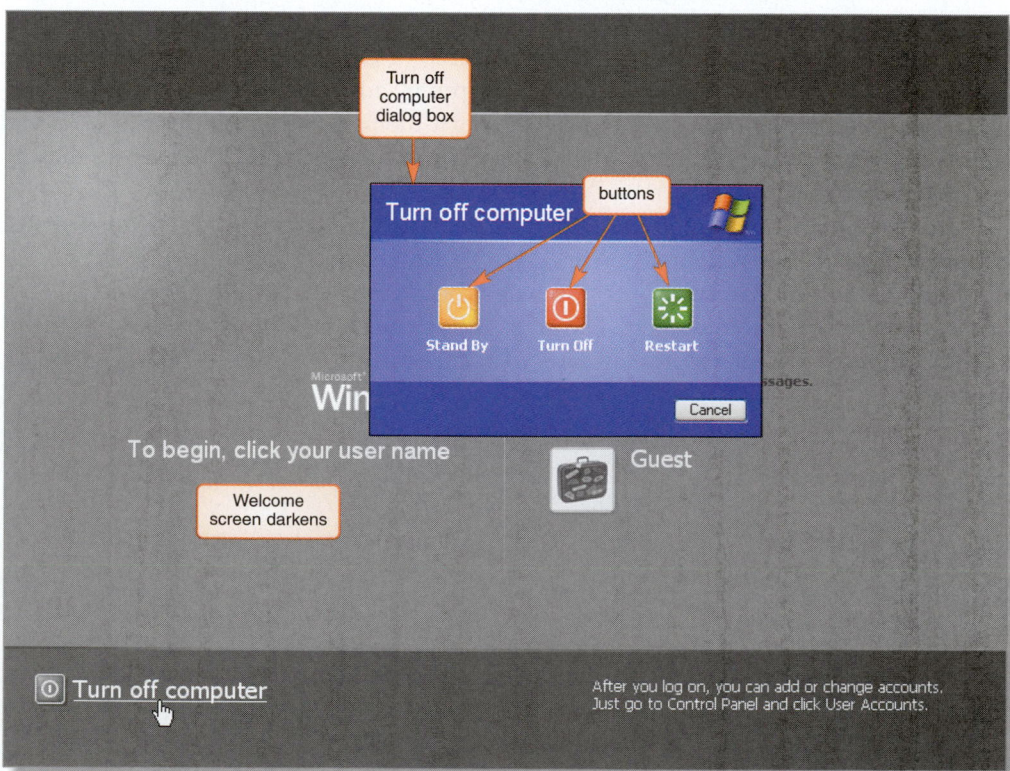

FIGURE 1-76

3

• **Point to the Turn Off button in the Turn off computer dialog box.**

The color of the Turn Off button changes to light red and the Turn Off balloon is displayed (Figure 1-77). The balloon contains the balloon name, Turn Off, and the text, Shuts down Windows so that you can safely turn off the computer.

4

• **Click the Turn Off button.**

Windows XP is shut down.

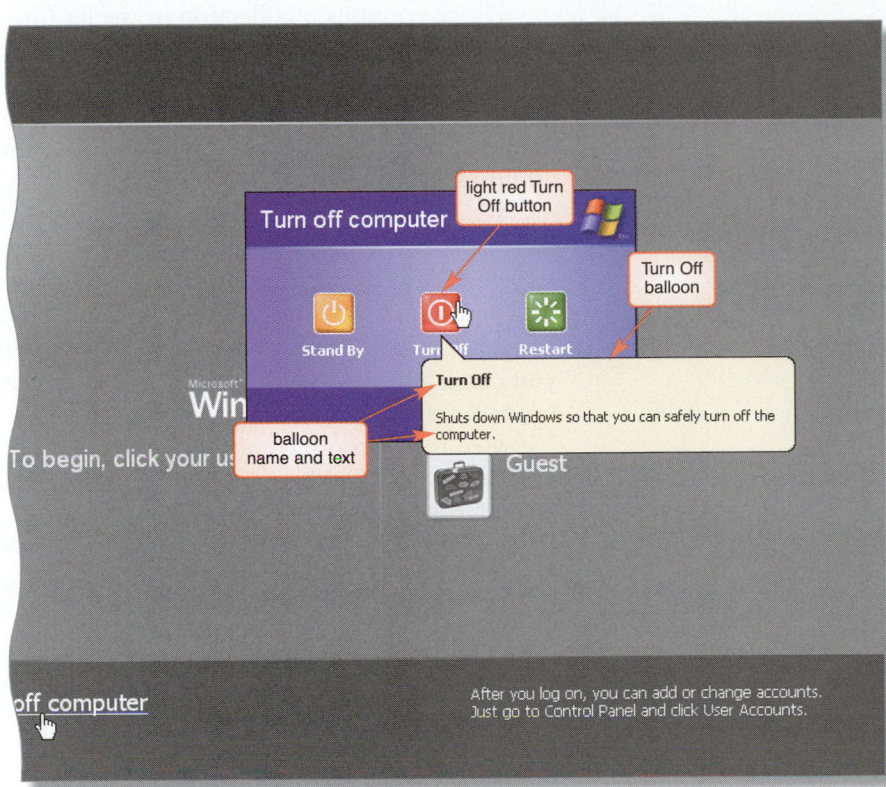

FIGURE 1-77

While Windows XP is shutting down, a blue screen containing the word, Welcome, is displayed on the desktop and the message, Windows is shutting down…, appears momentarily. At this point, you can turn off the computer. When shutting down Windows XP, you should never turn off the computer before these messages appear.

If you accidentally click Turn off computer on the Welcome screen as shown in Figure 1-75 on page WIN 66 and you do not want to shut down Windows XP, click the Cancel button in the Turn off computer dialog box shown in Figure 1-76 to return to normal Windows XP operation.

What Is Microsoft Office 2003?

Microsoft Office 2003 is a collection of the more popular Microsoft application software products and is available in Standard, Small Business, Professional, Student and Teacher, and Developer editions. The **Microsoft Office Professional Edition 2003** includes the five basic applications, which are Microsoft Office Word 2003, Microsoft Office Excel 2003, Microsoft Office Access 2003, Microsoft Office PowerPoint 2003, and Microsoft Office Outlook 2003. Office allows you to work more efficiently, communicate more effectively, and improve the appearance of each document you create.

Office contains a collection of media files (art, sound, animation, and movies) that you can use to enhance documents. **Microsoft Clip Organizer** allows you to organize the media files on your computer and search for specific files, as well as search for and organize media files located on the Internet. Clip art and media files are accessible from the Microsoft Office Online Web site and contains thousands of additional media files.

With the **Office Speech Recognition** software installed and a microphone, you can speak the names of toolbar buttons, menus, and menu commands, and list items, screen alerts, and dialog box controls, such as OK and Cancel. You also can dictate text and numbers to insert them as well as delete them. If you have speakers, you can instruct the computer to speak a document or worksheet to you. In addition, you can translate a word, phrase, or an entire document from English into Japanese, Chinese, French, Spanish, or German.

Menus and toolbars adjust to the way in which you work. As Office detects which commands you use more frequently, these commands are displayed at the top of the menu, and the infrequently used commands are placed in reserve. A button at the bottom of the menu allows you to expand the menu in order to view all its commands. More frequently used buttons on a toolbar appear on the toolbar, while less frequently used buttons are not displayed.

In addition, Office integrates its applications with the power of the Internet so you can share information, communicate and collaborate on projects over long distances, and conduct online meetings.

The Internet, World Wide Web, and Intranets

Office allows you to take advantage of the Internet, the World Wide Web, and intranets. The **Internet** is a worldwide network of thousands of computer networks and millions of commercial, educational, government, and personal computers. The **World Wide Web** is an easy-to-use graphical interface for exploring the Internet. The World Wide Web consists of many individual Web sites. A **Web site** consists of a single **Web page** or multiple Web pages linked together. The first Web page in the Web site is called the **home page** and a unique address, called a **Uniform Resource Locator** (**URL**), identifies each Web page. Web sites are located on computers called Web servers.

A software tool, called a **browser**, allows you to locate and view a Web page. One method of viewing a Web page is to use the browser to enter the URL for the Web page. A widely used browser, called **Internet Explorer**, is included with Office. Another method of viewing a Web page is clicking a hyperlink. A **hyperlink** is colored or underlined text or a graphic that, when clicked, connects to another Web page.

An **intranet** is a special type of Web site that is available only to the users of a particular type of computer network, such as a network used within a company or organization for internal communication. Like the Internet, hyperlinks are used within an intranet to access documents, pages, and other destinations on the intranet.

Office and the Internet

Office was designed in response to customer requests to streamline the process of information sharing and collaboration within their organizations. Organizations that, in the past, made important information available only to a select few, now want their information accessible to a wider range of individuals who are using tools such as Office and Internet Explorer. Office allows users to utilize the Internet or an intranet as a central location to view documents, manage files, and work together.

Each of the Office applications makes publishing documents on a Web server as simple as saving a file on a hard disk. Once the file is placed on the Web server, users can view and edit the documents, and conduct Web discussions and live online meetings.

An explanation of each Office application along with how it is used to access an intranet or the Internet is given on the following pages.

Microsoft Office Word 2003

Microsoft Office Word 2003 is a full-featured word processing program that allows you to create many types of personal and business communications, including announcements, letters, resumes, business documents, and academic reports, as well as other forms of written documents. Figure 1-78 illustrates the top portion of the announcement that students create in Project 1 of the Word section of this book. The steps to create the announcement also are shown in Project 1 of the Word section of this book.

FIGURE 1-78

The Word AutoCorrect, Spelling, and Grammar features allow you to proofread documents for errors in spelling and grammar by identifying the errors and offering corrections as you type. As you create a specific document, such as a business letter or resume, Word provides wizards, which ask questions and then use your answers to format the document before you type the text of the document.

Word automates many often-used tasks and provides you with powerful desktop publishing tools to use as you create professional looking brochures, advertisements, and newsletters. The drawing tools allow you to design impressive 3-D effects by including shadows, textures, and curves.

Word makes it easier for you to share documents in order to collaborate on a document. The Send for Review and Markup features allow you to send a document for review and easily track the changes made to the document.

Word and the Internet

Word makes it possible to design and publish Web pages on an intranet or the Internet, insert a hyperlink to a Web page in a word processing document, as well as access other Web pages to search for and retrieve information and pictures from them. Figure 1-79 illustrates the top portion of a cover letter that contains a hyperlink (e-mail address) that allows you to send an e-mail message to the sender.

Clicking the hyperlink starts the Outlook mail program, through which you can send an e-mail message to the author of the cover letter. In Figure 1-80, the Resume and Cover Letter - Message window that allows you to compose a new e-mail message contains the recipient's e-mail address (okamoto@earth.net), subject of the e-mail message (Resume and Cover Letter), and a brief message.

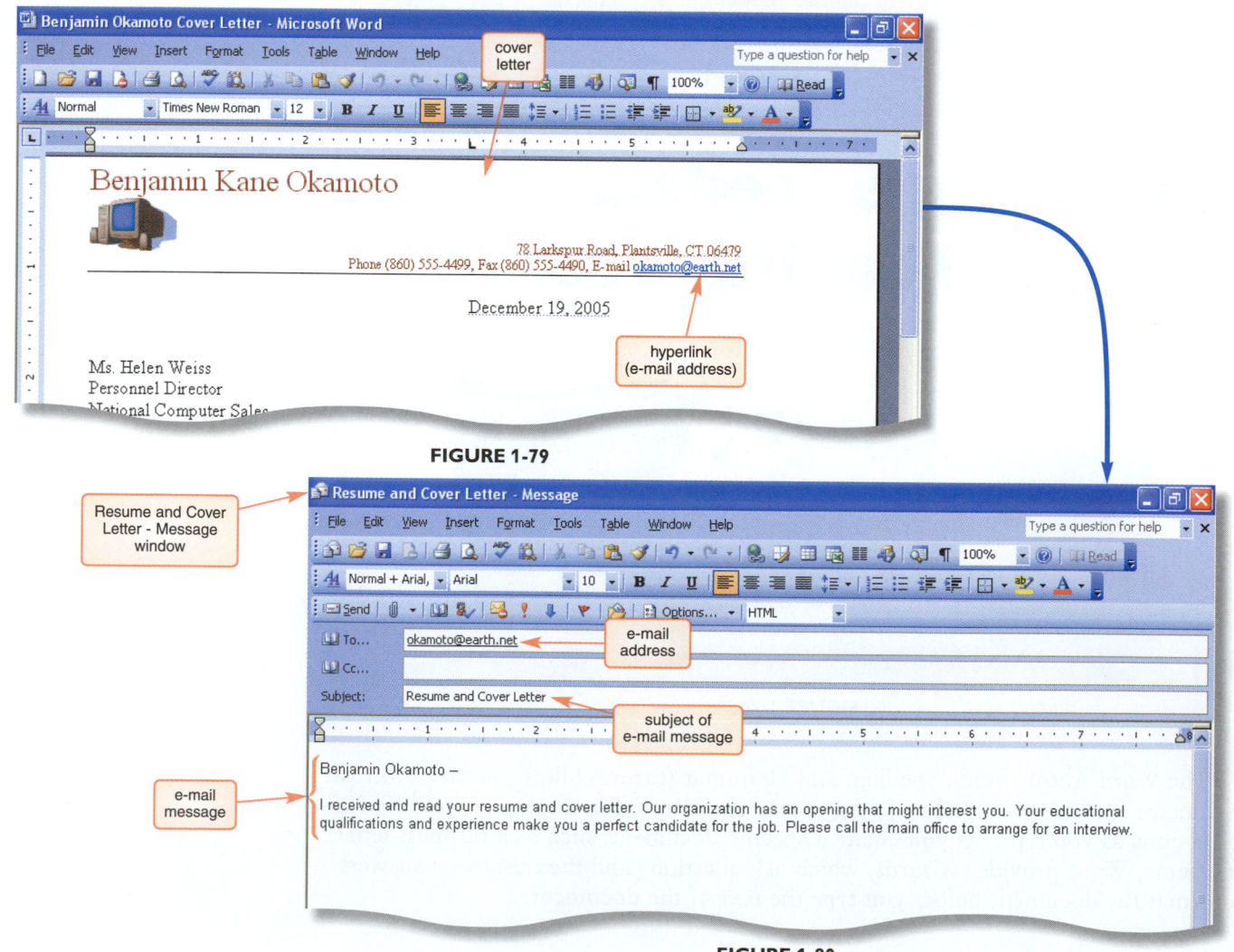

FIGURE 1-79

FIGURE 1-80

Microsoft Office Excel 2003

Microsoft Office Excel 2003 is a spreadsheet program that allows you to organize data, complete calculations, graph data, develop professional looking reports, publish organized data to the Web, access real-time data from Web sites, and make decisions. Figure 1-81 illustrates the Excel window that contains the worksheet and 3-D Column chart created in one of the exercises in Project 1 of the Excel section of this book.

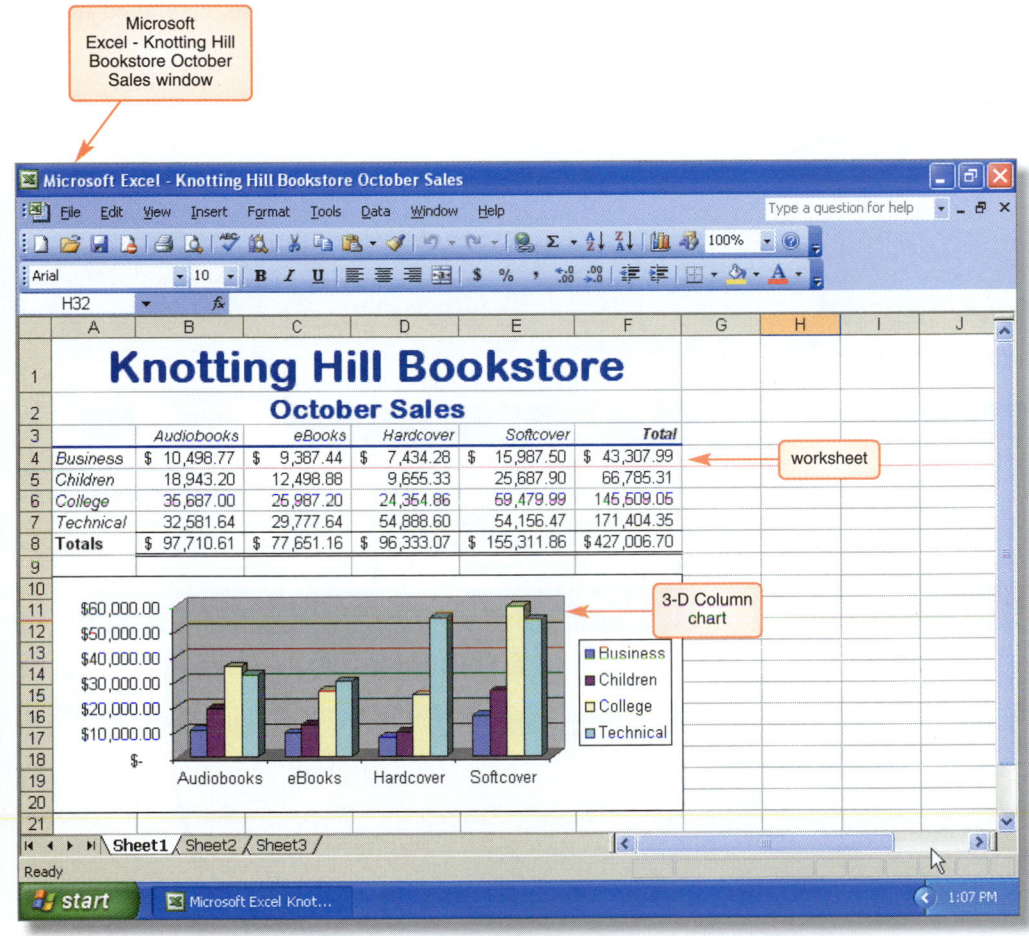

FIGURE 1-81

Excel and the Internet

Using Excel, you can create hyperlinks within a worksheet to access other Office documents on the network, an organization's intranet, or the Internet. You also can save worksheets as static or dynamic Web pages that can be viewed using a browser. Static Web pages cannot be changed by the person viewing them. Dynamic Web pages give the person viewing them in their browser many capabilities to modify them using Excel. In addition, you can create and run queries to retrieve information from a Web page directly into a worksheet.

Figure 1-82 illustrates a worksheet created by running a Web query to retrieve stock market information for two stocks (XM Satellite Radio Holdings Inc. and Sirius Satellite Radio Inc.). The two hyperlinks were created using the Insert Hyperlink button on the Standard toolbar, and the information in the worksheet was obtained from the MSN Money Web site.

The Refresh All button on the External Data toolbar allows you to update the last price of the stocks (Last). Clicking the Refresh All button locates the MSN Money Web site, retrieves current information for the stocks listed in the worksheet, and displays the updated information in the worksheet (Figure 1-83). Notice that the stock prices and information in this worksheet differ from what was displayed in the worksheet shown in Figure 1-82.

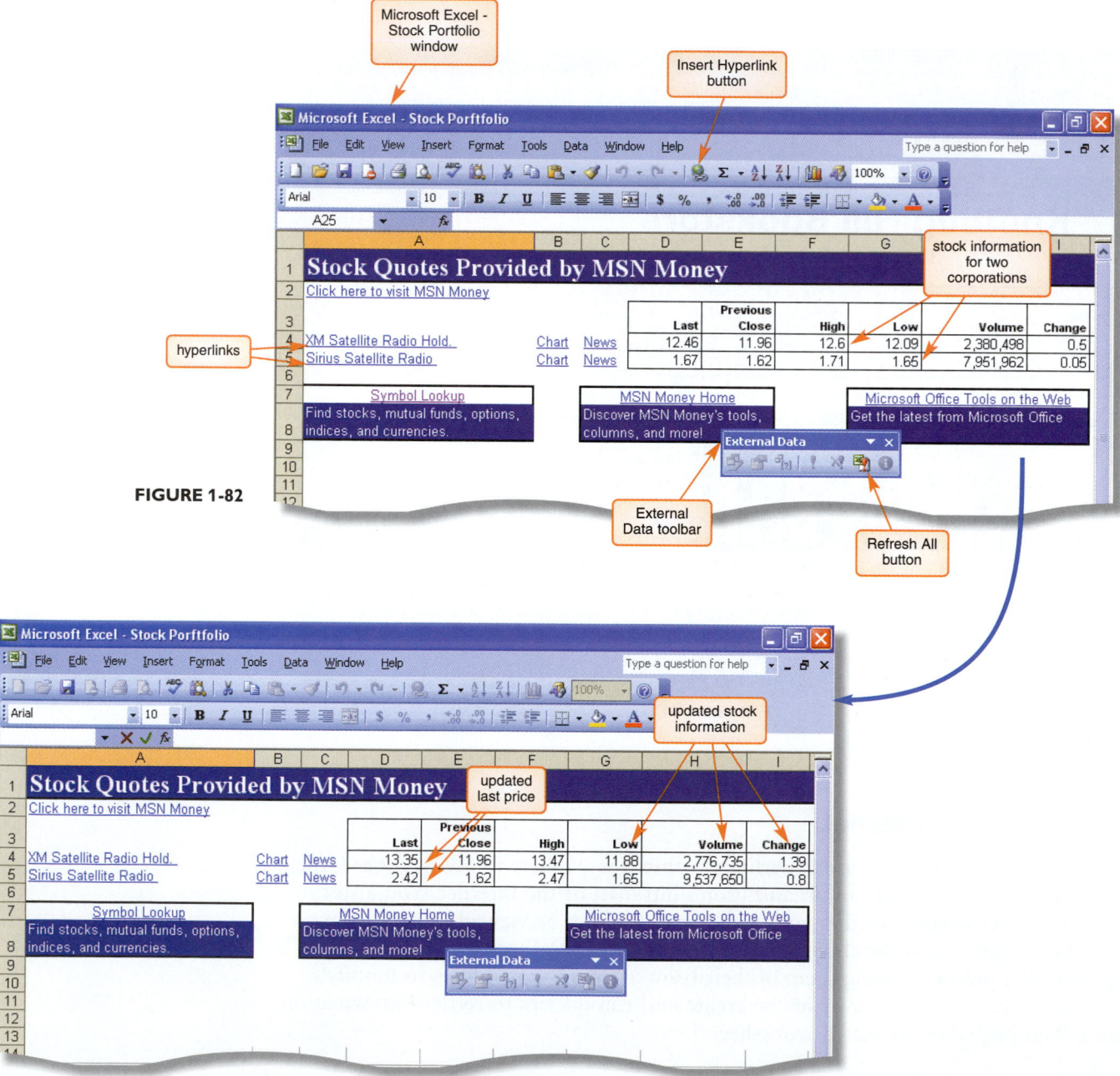

FIGURE 1-82

FIGURE 1-83

Microsoft Office Access 2003

Microsoft Office Access 2003 is a comprehensive database management system (DBMS). A **database** is a collection of data organized in a manner that allows access, retrieval, and use of that data. Access allows you to create a database; add, change, and delete data in the database; sort data in the database; retrieve data from the database; and create forms and reports using the data in the database.

The database created in Project 1 of the Access section of this book is displayed in the Microsoft Access - [Client : Table] window illustrated in Figure 1-84. The steps to create this database are shown in Project 1 of Access.

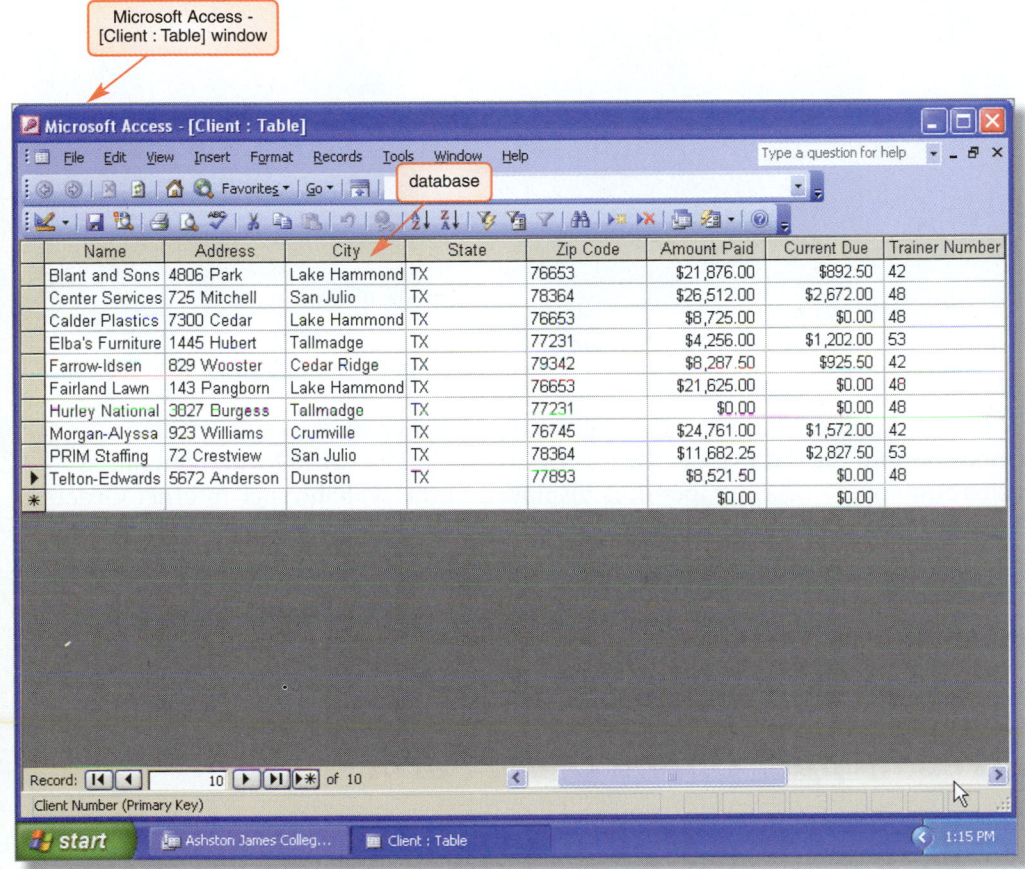

FIGURE 1-84

Access and the Internet

Databases provide a central location to store related pieces of information. Access simplifies the creation of a database with a wizard that quickly can build one of more than a dozen types of databases. You also can transform lists or worksheets into databases using Access wizards. Data access pages permit you to share a database with other computer users on a network, intranet, or over the Internet, as well as allowing the users to view and edit the database. The database shown in Figure 1-85 on the next page contains information (order number, customer number, order date, product number, and quantity) about three orders entered over the Internet using the Internet Explorer browser.

Microsoft Access - [WebShopper Internet Orders : Table] window

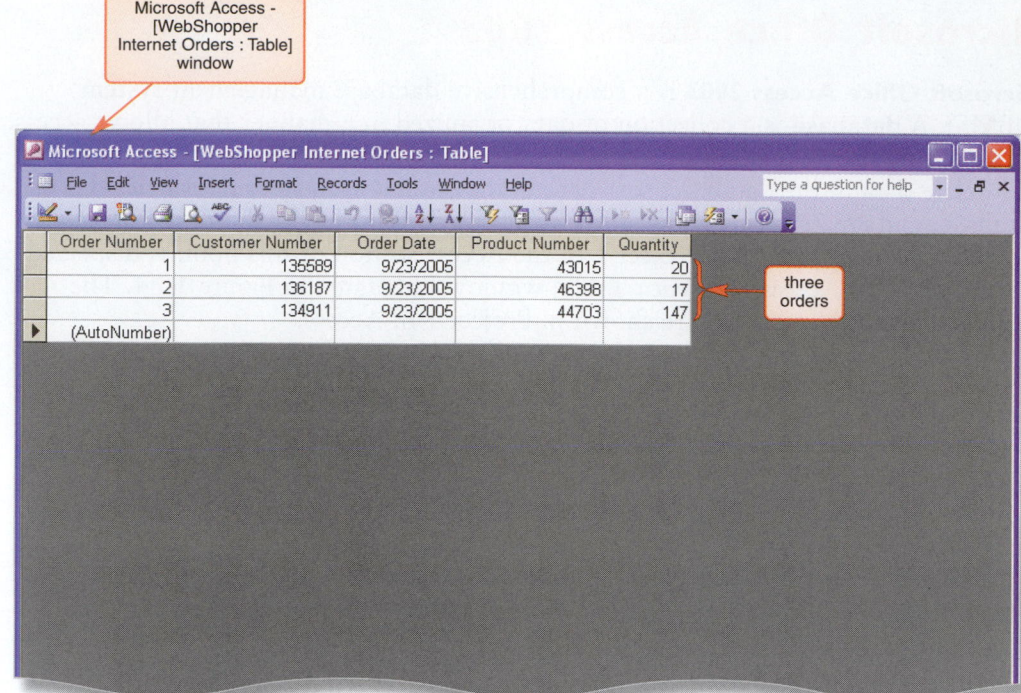

three orders

FIGURE 1-85

Figure 1-86 illustrates a simple online order form created to enter order information into the database shown in Figure 1-85. The order form, containing information about order number 4, is displayed in the WebShopper Internet Orders - Microsoft Internet Explorer window.

WebShopper Internet Orders - Microsoft Internet Explorer window

online order form

information about order number 4

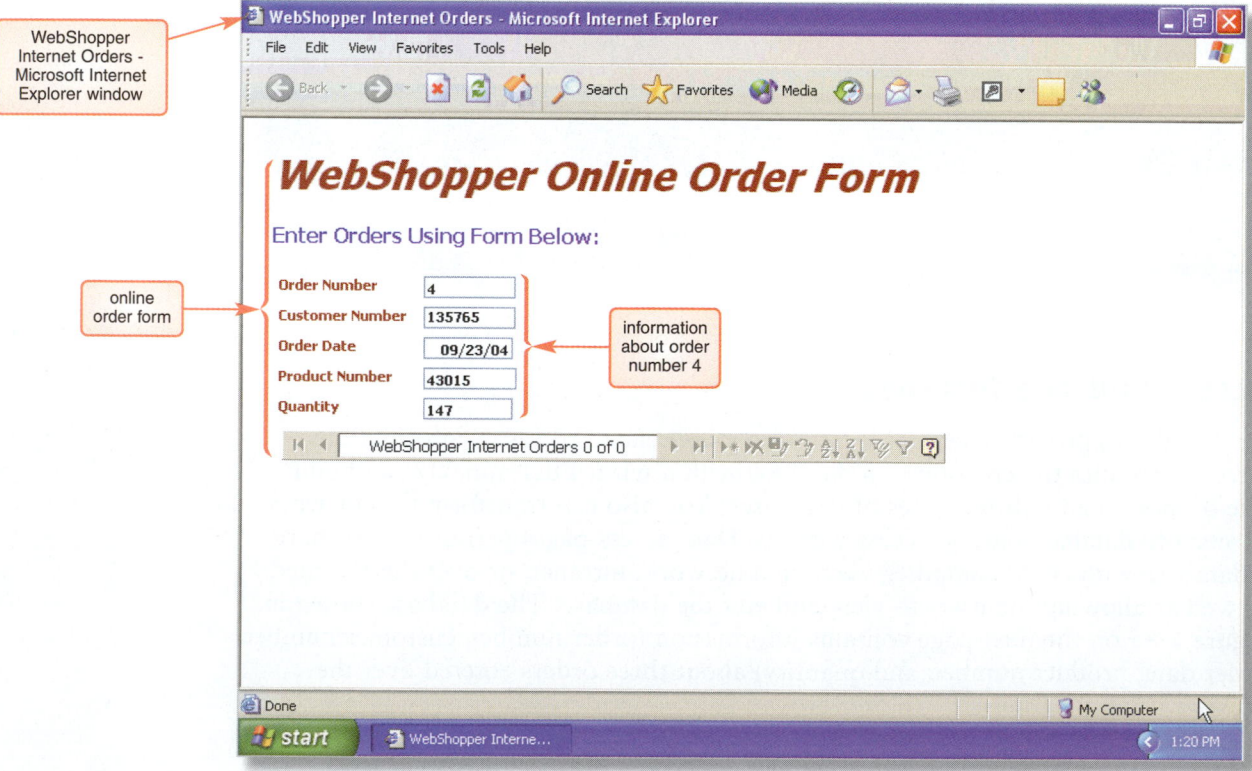

FIGURE 1-86

Microsoft Office PowerPoint 2003

Microsoft Office PowerPoint 2003 is a complete presentation graphics program that allows you to produce professional looking presentations. PowerPoint provides the flexibility that lets you make informal presentations using overhead transparencies, make electronic presentations using a projection device attached to a personal computer, make formal presentations using 35mm slides or a CD, or run virtual presentations on the Internet.

In PowerPoint, you create a presentation in Normal view. **Normal view** allows you to view the tabs pane, slide pane, and notes pane at the same time. The first slide in the presentation created in one of the exercises in Project 1 of the PowerPoint section of this book appears in the Microsoft PowerPoint - [Rivercrest Community Center] window illustrated in Figure 1-87. The full window contains the Outline tab with the presentation outline, the slide pane displaying the first slide in the presentation, and the notes pane showing a note about the presentation.

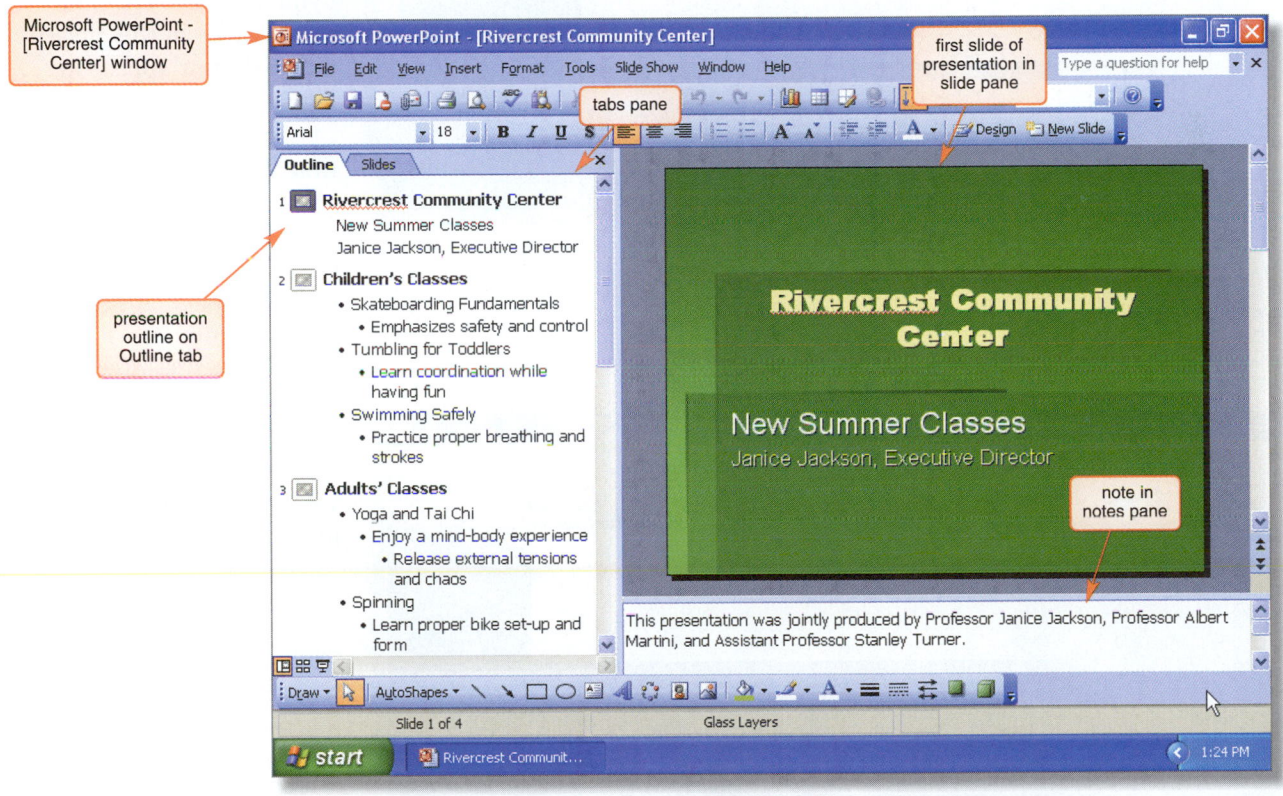

FIGURE 1-87

PowerPoint allows you to create dynamic presentations easily that include multimedia features such as sounds, movies, and pictures. PowerPoint comes with templates that assist you in designing a presentation that you can use to create a slide show. PowerPoint also contains formatting for tables, so that you do not have to create the tables using Excel or Word. The Table Draw tool used in Word to draw tables also is available in PowerPoint.

PowerPoint makes it easier for you to share presentations and collaborate on those presentations. The Send for Review feature and Compare and Merge feature allow you to send a presentation for review and easily merge comments and revisions from multiple reviewers.

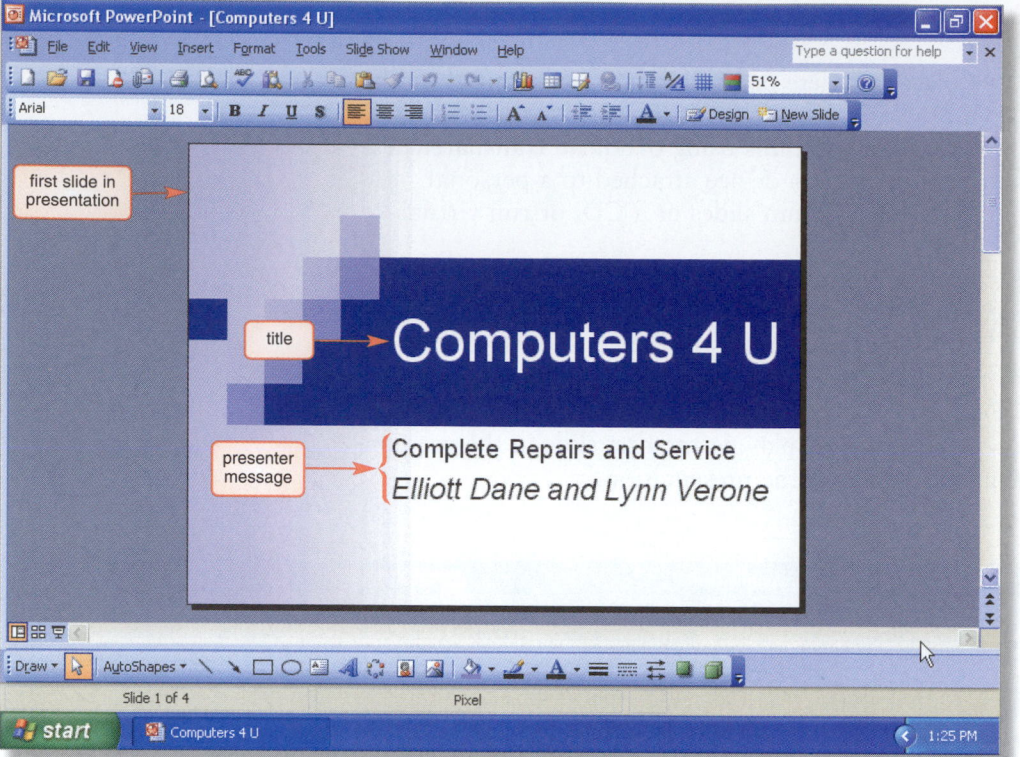

FIGURE 1-88

PowerPoint and the Internet

PowerPoint allows you to publish presentations on the Internet or an intranet. Figure 1-88 illustrates the first slide in a presentation to be published on the Internet. The slide appears in slide view and contains a title (Computers 4 U), a subtitle (Complete Repairs and Service), and a presenter message (Elliott Dane and Lynn Verone). The additional slides in this presentation do not appear in Figure 1-88.

Figure 1-89 shows the first Web page in a series of Web pages created from the presentation illustrated in Figure 1-88. The Web page appears in the Computers 4 U window in the Internet Explorer browser window. Navigation buttons below the Web page allow you to view additional Web pages in the presentation.

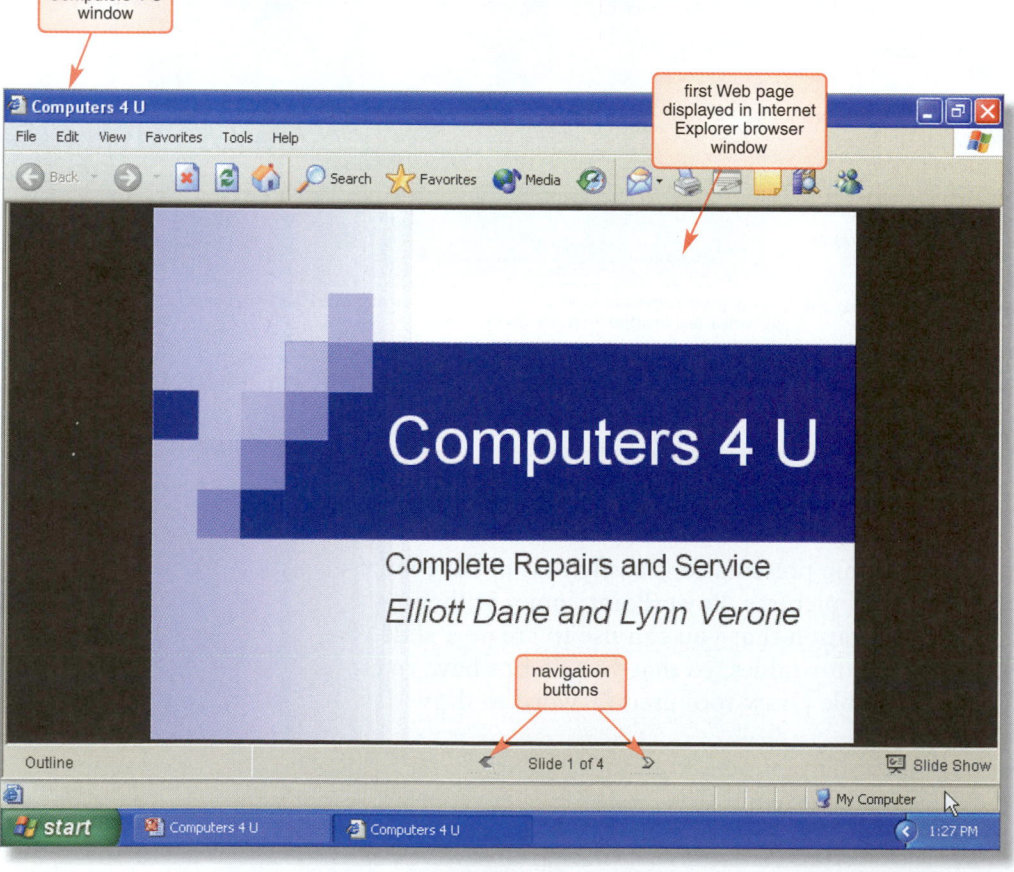

FIGURE 1-89

The Web Toolbar

The easiest method of navigating an intranet or the Internet is to use the Web toolbar. The Web toolbar allows you to search for and open Office documents that you have placed on an intranet or the Internet. The Web toolbar in the Benjamin Okamoto Cover Letter - Microsoft Word window shown in Figure 1-90 is available in all Office applications except FrontPage. Currently, a Word document (cover letter) is displayed in the window, and the path and file name of the document appear in the text box on the Web toolbar.

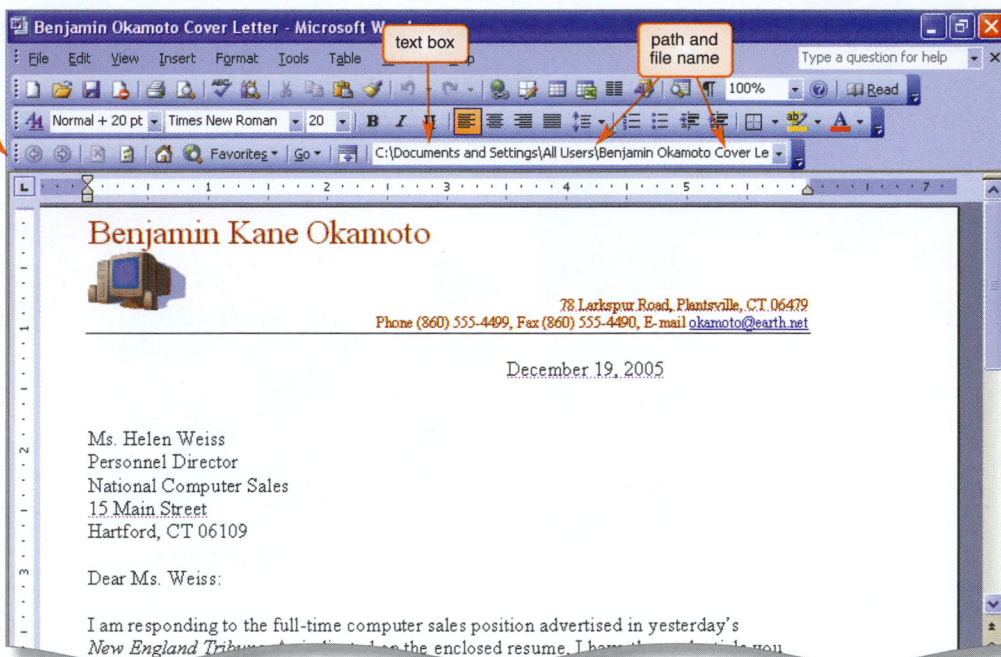

FIGURE 1-90

The buttons and text box on the Web toolbar allow you to jump to Web pages you have viewed previously, cancel a jump to a Web page, update the contents of the current Web page, or replace all other toolbars with the Web toolbar. In addition, you can view the first Web page displayed, search the Web for new Web sites, and add any Web pages you select to the Favorites folder, so you can return to them quickly in the future.

Microsoft Office Publisher 2003

Microsoft Office Publisher 2003 is a desktop publishing program (DTP) that allows you to design and produce professional quality documents (newsletters, flyers, brochures, business cards, Web sites, and so on) that combine text, graphics, and photographs. Desktop publishing software provides a variety of tools, including design templates, graphic manipulation tools, color schemes or libraries, and various page wizards and templates. For large jobs, businesses use desktop publishing software to design publications that are **camera ready**, which means the files are suitable for production by outside commercial printers. Publisher also allows you to locate commercial printers, service bureaus, and copy shops willing to accept customer files created in Publisher.

Publisher allows you to design a unique image, or logo, using one of more than 45 master design sets. This, in turn, permits you to use the same design for all your printed documents (letters, business cards, brochures, and advertisements) and Web pages. Publisher includes 60 coordinated color schemes, more than 10,000 high-quality clip art images, 1,500 photographs, 1,000 Web-art graphics, 175 fonts, 340 animated graphics, and hundreds of unique Design Gallery elements (quotations, sidebars, and so on). If you wish, you also can download additional images from the Microsoft Office Online Web page on the Microsoft Web site.

In the Business Card - Hank Landers - Microsoft Publisher window illustrated in Figure 1-91 on the next page, a business card that was created using the Business Card wizard and the Arcs design set is displayed.

Business Card - Hank Landers - Microsoft Publisher - Print Publication window

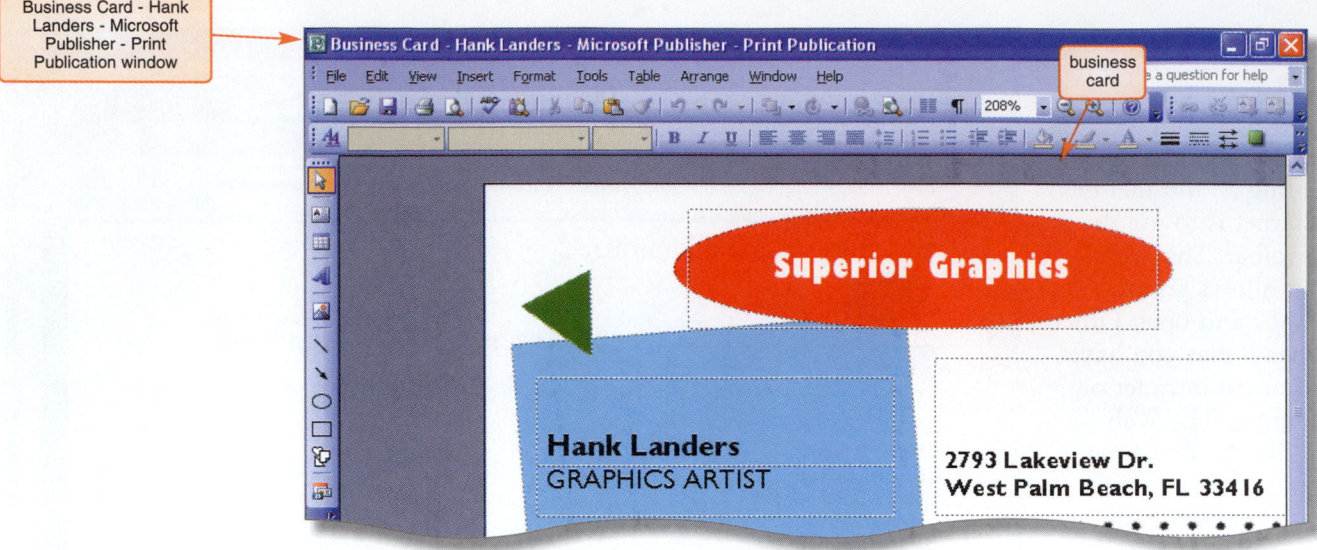

FIGURE 1-91

Publisher and the Internet

Publisher allows you easily to create a multipage Web site with custom color schemes, photo images, animated images, and sounds. Figure 1-92 illustrates the Superior Graphics - Microsoft Internet Explorer window displaying the top portion of the home page in a Web site created using the Web page wizard and Arcs design set.

The home page in the Superior Graphics Web site contains text, graphic images, animated graphic images, and displays using the same design set (Arcs) as the business card illustrated in Figure 1-91.

Superior Graphics - Microsoft Internet Explorer window

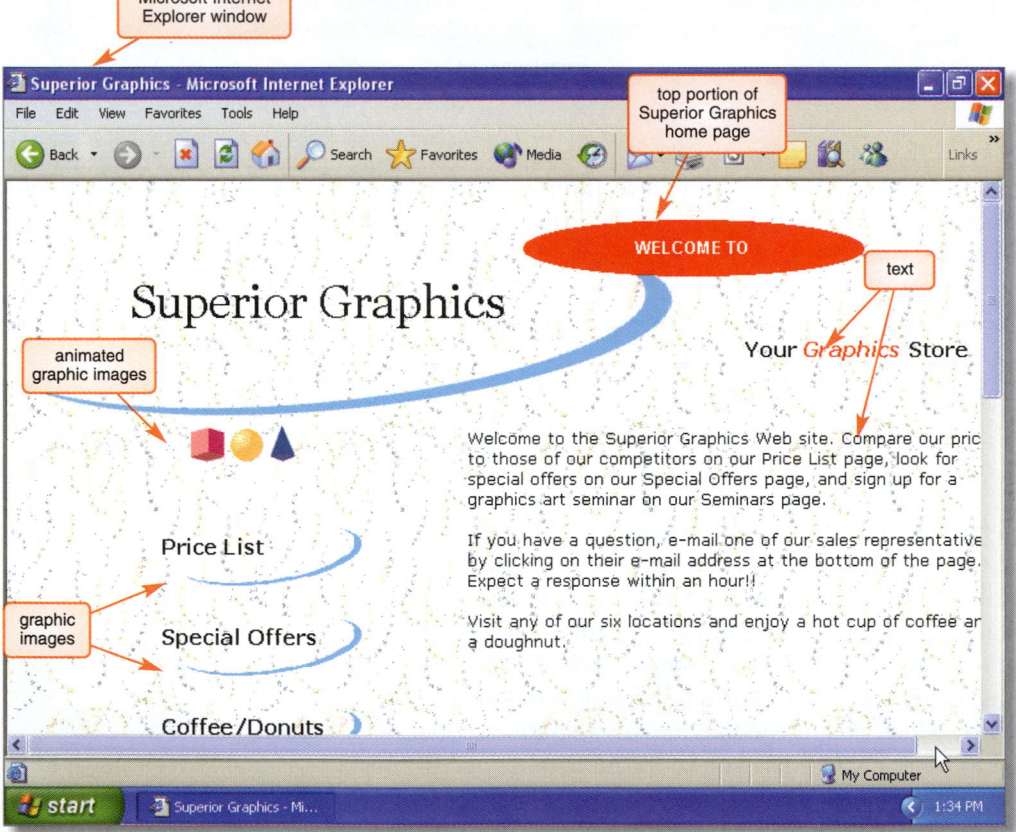

FIGURE 1-92

Microsoft Office FrontPage 2003

Microsoft Office FrontPage 2003 is a Web page authoring and site management program that lets you create and manage professional looking Web sites on the Internet or an intranet. You can create and edit Web pages without knowing HyperText Markup Language (HTML), view the pages and files in the Web site and control their organization, manage existing Web sites, import and export files, and diagnose and correct problems. A variety of templates, including the Workgroup Web template that allows you to set up and maintain the basic structure of a workgroup Web, are available to facilitate managing the Web site.

Figure 1-93 illustrates the top portion of a Web page created using FrontPage that contains information about the Shelly Cashman Series developed by Course Technology. It appears in the SCSITE.COM Shelly Cashman Series Student Resources - Microsoft Internet Explorer window.

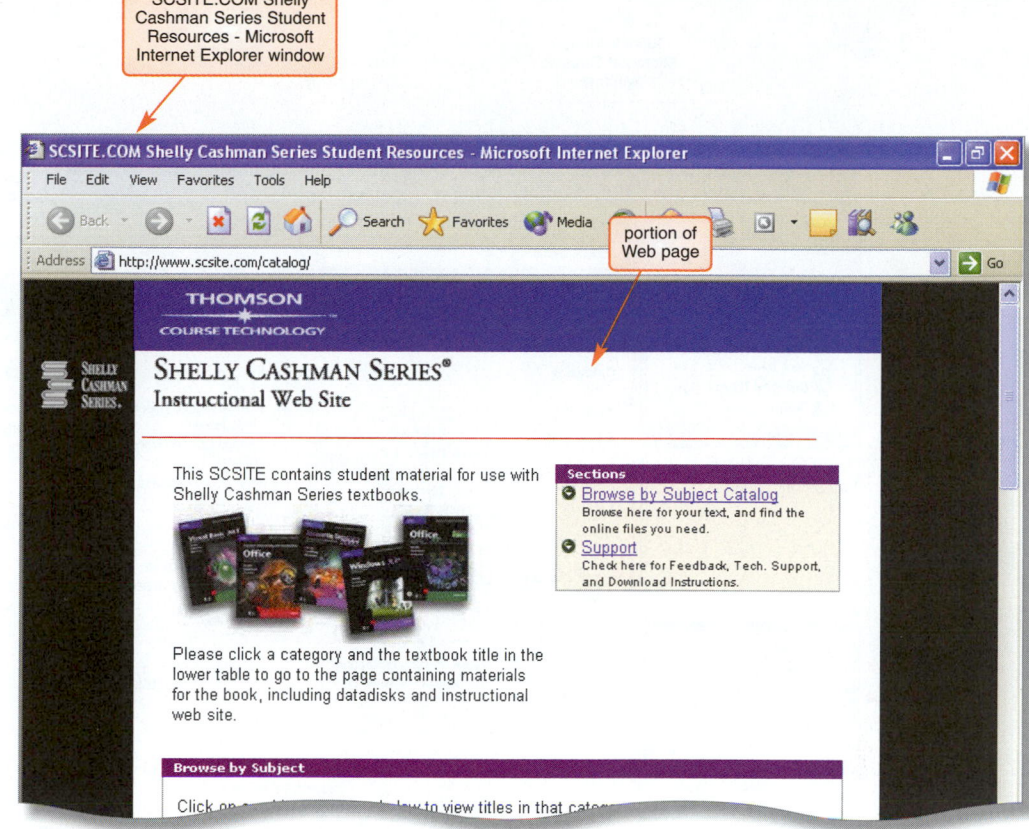

SCSITE.COM Shelly Cashman Series Student Resources - Microsoft Internet Explorer window

portion of Web page

FIGURE 1-93

Microsoft Office Outlook 2003

Microsoft Office Outlook 2003 is a powerful communications and scheduling program that helps you communicate with others, keep track of your contacts, and organize your busy schedule. Outlook allows you to send and receive electronic mail and permits you to engage in real-time messaging with family, friends, or coworkers using instant messaging. Outlook also provides you with the means to organize your contacts. Users easily can track e-mail messages, meetings, and notes with a particular contact. Outlook's Calendar, Contacts, Tasks, and Notes components aid in this organization. Contact information readily is available from the Outlook Calendar, Mail, Contacts, and Task components by accessing the Find a Contact feature. **Personal information management** (**PIM**) programs such as Outlook provide a way for individuals and workgroups to organize, find, view, and share information easily.

Figure 1-94 on the next page shows the Outlook Today - Microsoft Outlook window with the Navigation Pane on the left side of the window and the **Outlook Today page** on the right side of the window. The Outlook Today page contains the current date (Friday, September 23, 2005); the Calendar area with the currently scheduled events; the Tasks area with a list of tasks to perform; and the Messages area that summarizes the users e-mail messages by folder. You can customize this page by clicking the Customize Outlook Today button in the upper-right corner of the Outlook Today page.

The **Navigation Pane** is a new feature in Outlook. It is set up to help you navigate Outlook while using any of the components. It comprises one or more panes and two sets of buttons. Although the two sets of buttons remain constant, the area of the Navigation Pane above the buttons changes depending on the active component (Mail, Calendar, Contacts, or Tasks). In Figure 1-94, the expanded Mail pane displays the Favorite Folders pane and the All Mail Folders pane. Clicking a button in the Navigation Pane displays the contents of the component's folder with its associated panes in the Outlook window.

Microsoft
Windows XP

Outlook Today -
Microsoft Outlook
window

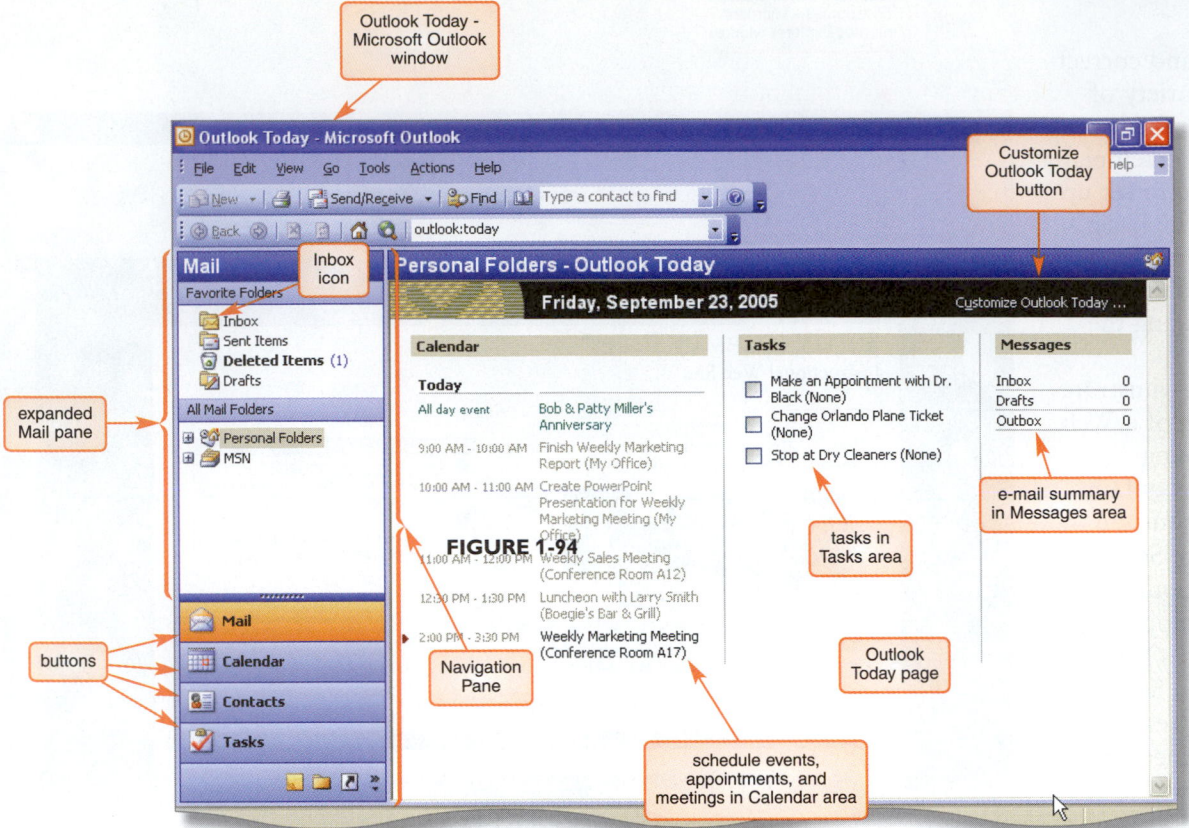

Customize
Outlook Today
button

Inbox
icon

expanded
Mail pane

e-mail summary
in Messages area

FIGURE 1-94

tasks in
Tasks area

Navigation
Pane

buttons

Outlook
Today page

schedule events,
appointments, and
meetings in Calendar area

FIGURE 1-94

Inbox - Microsoft
Outlook window

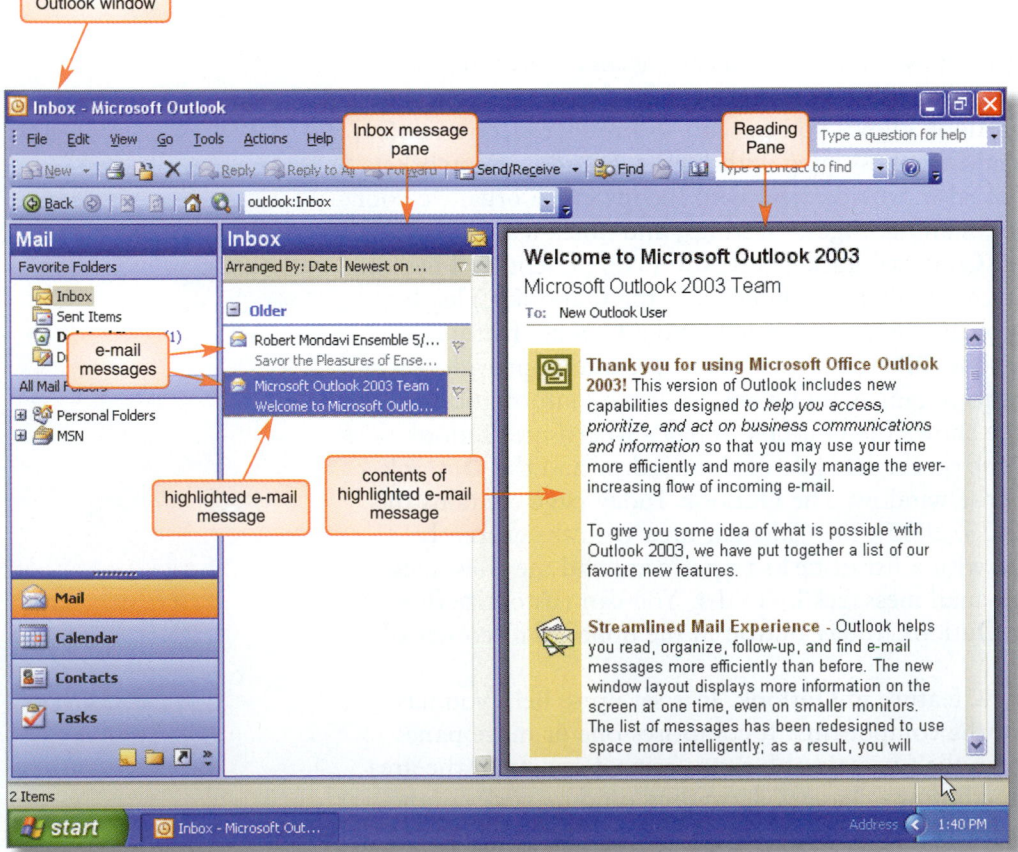

Inbox message
pane

Reading
Pane

e-mail
messages

highlighted e-mail
message

contents of
highlighted e-mail
message

FIGURE 1-95

Outlook allows you to click the Mail button in the Navigation Pane to view e-mail messages, click the Calendar button to schedule activities (events, appointments, and meetings), click the Contacts button to maintain a list of contacts and e-mail addresses, and click the Tasks button to view a detailed list of tasks.

When you click the Inbox icon in the Mail pane, the Inbox - Microsoft Outlook window is displayed and the contents of the Inbox folder (your e-mail messages) and the Reading Pane are displayed in the window (Figure 1-95).

The Inbox message pane contains two e-mail messages. The second e-mail message is highlighted. The contents of the highlighted e-mail message are displayed in the Reading Pane.

The Microsoft Office 2003 Help System

At any time while you are using one of the Office applications, you can interact with the **Microsoft Office 2003 Help system** for that application and display information on any topic associated with the application. Several categories of help are available to you. One of the easiest methods to obtain help is to use the Type a question for help box. The **Type a question for help box** on the right side of the menu bar lets you type free-form questions, such as how do I save or how do I create a Web page, or you can type terms, such as template, smart tags, or speech. The Help system responds by displaying a list of topics relating to the question or term in the Search Results task pane. The Type a question for help box that appears in the Grand Prix Announcement – Microsoft Word window is illustrated in Figure 1-96.

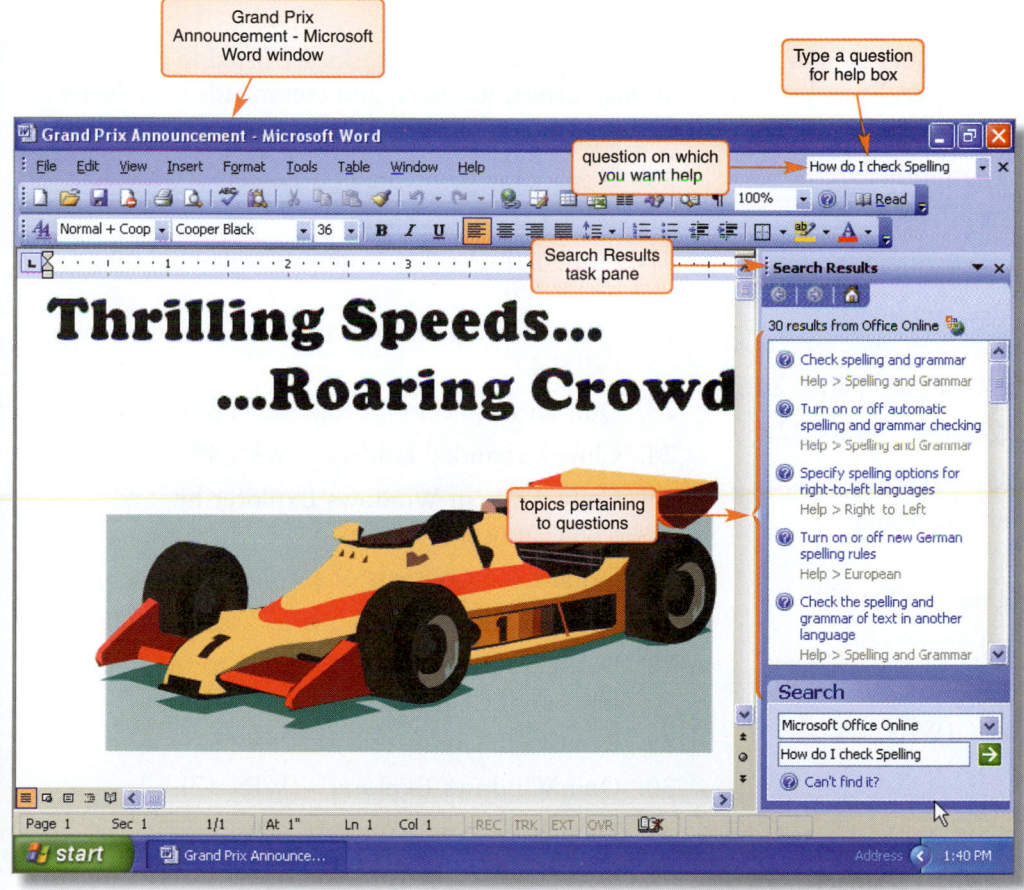

FIGURE 1-96

When you type the question, How do I check Spelling, in the Type a question for help box shown in Figure 1-96, the Help system displays a list of topics relating to the question. Clicking a topic in the list opens a Help window that provides Help information about spell checking. Detailed instructions for using the Type a question for help box and the other categories of Help are explained in Appendix A of this book.

Project Summary

Project 1 illustrated the Microsoft Windows XP graphical user interface and the Microsoft Office 2003 applications. You started Windows XP, learned the components of the desktop and the six mouse operations. You opened, closed, moved, resized, minimized, maximized, and scrolled a window. You used Windows Explorer to copy a file, display the contents of a folder, expand and collapse a folder, and then rename and delete a file. You obtained help about using Microsoft Windows XP and shut down Windows XP.

Brief explanations of the Word, Excel, Access, PowerPoint, Publisher, FrontPage, and Outlook applications and examples of how these applications interact with the Internet were given. With this introduction, you now are ready to begin a more in-depth study of each Office application explained in this book.

 If you have a SAM user profile, you may have access to hands-on instruction, practice, and assessment of the skills covered in this project. Log in to your SAM account and go to your assignments page to see what your instructor has assigned.

What You Should Know

Having completed this project, you should be able to perform the tasks below. The tasks are listed in the same order they were presented in this project. For a list of the buttons, menus, toolbars, and commands introduced in this project, see the Quick Reference Summary at the back of this book and refer to the Page Number column.

1. Log On to the Computer   (WIN 9)
2. Display the Start Menu   (WIN 12)
3. Add an Icon to the Desktop   (WIN 15)
4. Open a Window Using a Desktop Icon (WIN 17)
5. Minimize and Redisplay a Window   (WIN 20)
6. Maximize and Restore a Window   (WIN 22)
7. Close a Window   (WIN 24, WIN 35)
8. Open a Window Using the Start Menu (WIN 26)
9. Move a Window by Dragging   (WIN 27)
10. Expand an Area   (WIN 29)
11. Scroll Using Scroll Arrows   (WIN 30)
12. Size a Window by Dragging   (WIN 32)
13. Collapse an Area   (WIN 33)
14. Resize a Window   (WIN 34)
15. Delete a Desktop Icon by Right-Dragging (WIN 35)
16. Launch a Program Using the Start Menu (WIN 38)
17. Launch Windows Explorer and Maximize Its Window   (WIN 40)
18. Expand a Folder   (WIN 42)
19. Expand a Drive   (WIN 44)
20. Display the Contents of a Folder   (WIN 45, WIN 53)
21. Display the Contents of an Expanded Drive (WIN 46)
22. Launch an Application Program from Explorer (WIN 47)
23. Quit an Application Program   (WIN 48)
24. Close Expanded Folders   (WIN 49)
25. Copy a File in Windows Explorer by Right-Dragging   (WIN 51)
26. Display the Contents of a Folder (WIN 53)
27. Rename a File   (WIN 54)
28. Delete a File by Right-Dragging to the Recycle Bin   (WIN 55)
29. Remove the Status Bar   (WIN 56)
30. Quit Windows Explorer   (WIN 57)
31. Launch Help and Support   (WIN 57)
32. Browse for Help Topics in the Table of Contents (WIN 59)
33. Search for Help Topics Using the Index (WIN 62)
34. Close the Help and Support Center   (WIN 63)
35. Log Off from the Computer   (WIN 64)
36. Turn Off the Computer   (WIN 66)

Learn It Online

Instructions: To complete the Learn It Online exercises, start your browser, click the Address bar, and then enter the Web address scsite.com/winoff2003/learn. When the Window XP Learn It Online page is displayed, follow the instructions in the exercises below. Each exercise has instructions for printing your results, either for your own records or for submission to your instructor.

1 Project Reinforcement TF, MC, and SA

Below Windows XP Project 1, click the Project Reinforcement link. Print the quiz by clicking Print on the File menu for each page. Answer each question.

2 Flash Cards

Below Windows XP Project 1, click the Flash Cards link and read the instructions. Type 20 (or a number specified by your instructor) in the Number of playing cards text box, type your name in the Enter your Name text box, and then click the Flip Card button. When the flash card is displayed, read the question and then click the ANSWER box arrow to select an answer. Flip through Flash Cards. If your score is 15 (75%) correct or greater, click Print on the File menu to print your results. If your score is less than 15 (75%) correct, then redo this exercise by clicking the Replay button.

3 Practice Test

Below Windows XP Project 1, click the Practice Test link. Answer each question, enter your first and last name at the bottom of the page, and then click the Grade Test button. When the graded practice test is displayed on your screen, click Print on the File menu to print a hard copy. Continue to take practice tests until you score 80% or better.

4 Who Wants To Be a Computer Genius?

Below Windows XP Project 1, click the Computer Genius link. Read the instructions, enter your first and last name at the bottom of the page, and then click the PLAY button. When your score is displayed, click the PRINT RESULTS link to print a hard copy.

5 Wheel of Terms

Below Windows XP Project 1, click the Wheel of Terms link. Read the instructions, and then enter your first and last name and your school name. Click the PLAY button. When your score is displayed, right-click the score and then click Print on the shortcut menu to print a hard copy.

6 Crossword Puzzle Challenge

Below Windows XP Project 1, click the Crossword Puzzle Challenge link. Read the instructions, and then enter your first and last name. Click the SUBMIT button. Work the crossword puzzle. When you are finished, click the Submit button. When the crossword puzzle is redisplayed, click the Print Puzzle button to print a hard copy.

7 Tips and Tricks

Below Windows XP Project 1, click the Tips and Tricks link. Click a topic that pertains to Project 1. Right-click the information and then click Print on the shortcut menu. Construct a brief example of what the information relates to in Windows XP to confirm you understand how to use the tip or trick.

8 Newsgroups

Below Windows XP Project 1, click the Newsgroups link. Click a topic that pertains to Project 1. Print three comments.

9 Expanding Your Horizons

Below Windows XP Project 1, click the Expanding Your Horizons link. Click a topic that pertains to Project 1. Print the information. Construct a brief example of what the information relates to in Windows XP to confirm you understand the contents of the article.

10 Search Sleuth

Below Windows XP Project 1, click the Search Sleuth link. To search for a term that pertains to this project, select a term below the Project 1 title and then use the Google search engine at google.com (or any major search engine) to display and print two Web pages that present information on the term.

11 Windows XP Online Training

Below Windows XP Project 1, click the Windows XP Online Training link. When your browser displays the Microsoft Office Online Web page, click the Windows XP link. Click one of the Windows XP courses that covers one or more of the objectives listed at the beginning of the project on page WIN 4. Print the first page of the course before stepping through it.

12 Office Marketplace

Below Windows XP Project 1, click the Office Marketplace link. When your browser displays the Microsoft Office Online Web page, click the Office Marketplace link. Click a topic that relates to one of the Office 2003 applications. Print the first page.

In the Lab

1 Taking the Windows XP Tour

Instructions: Use a computer to perform the following tasks.

Part 1: Launching the Windows XP Tour

1. If necessary, start Microsoft Windows XP and log on to the computer.
2. Click the Start button and then click Help and Support on the Start menu.
3. Click the Maximize button on the Help and Support Center title bar.
4. Click What's new in Windows XP in the navigation pane.
5. Click Taking a tour or tutorial in the navigation pane. The Taking a tour or tutorial page appears in the topic pane.
6. Click Take the Windows XP tour in the topic pane. The Windows XP Tour dialog box appears.
7. If your computer does not have speakers or earphones, proceed to step 8 below. If your computer has speakers or earphones, follow the steps in Part 2.
8. If your computer does not have speakers or earphones, follow the steps in Part 3.

Part 2: Taking the Windows XP Tour with Sound and Animation

1. Verify the Play the animated tour that features text, animation, music, and voice narration button is selected in the Windows XP Tour dialog box and then click the Next button.
2. Listen to the voice narration of the introduction to the Windows XP tour.
3. Click the gray Windows XP Basics button and answer the following questions.
   a. What is the narrow band at the bottom of the desktop called? _____
   b. What identifies a shortcut icon? _____
   c. What icons appear on the desktop the first time you launch Windows? _____
   d. What is contained in the notification area? _____
   e. How does Windows keep the taskbar tidy? _____
   f. What does a right-facing arrow on a Start menu command signify? _____
   _____
   g. In which folders are text, image, and music files placed? _____
   _____
   h. What does the Restore Down button do? _____
   i. What appears when a program needs some information from you before it can complete a command?
   _____
   j. What do you use to set up user accounts? _____
   k. Where do you go when you want to interrupt your Windows session and let someone else use the computer? _____
4. Click the Skip Intro button in the lower corner of the desktop to skip the introduction to the Windows XP tour.
5. Click the yellow Best for Business button and listen to the narration.
6. Click the red Safe and Easy Personal Computing button and listen to the narration.
7. Click the green Unlock the World of Digital Media button and listen to the narration.
8. Click the blue The Connected Home and Office button and listen to the narration.

In the Lab

9. Click the red Exit Tour button on the desktop to exit the Windows XP tour.
10. Click the Close button in the Help and Support center window.
11. You have completed this lab assignment.

Part 3: Taking the Windows XP Tour without Sound or Animation

1. Click the Play the non-animated tour that features text and images only button in the Windows XP Tour dialog box and then click the Next button.
2. Click the Start Here button to read about the basics of the Windows XP operating system.
3. Scroll the Windows XP Basics window and read the paragraph below the Windows Desktop heading. Click the Next button to display the next topic.
4. Scroll the Windows XP Basics window and read the paragraph below the Icons heading. Answer the following questions.
   a. What icon displays on the desktop the first time you launch Windows? _____
   b. Does deleting a shortcut icon affect the actual program or file? _____
5. Click the Next button to display the next topic. Scroll the Windows XP Basics window and read the paragraphs below the Taskbar heading. Answer the following question.
   a. Where is the notification area located? _____
6. Click the Next button to display the next topic. Scroll the Windows XP Basics window and read the paragraph below the Start Menu heading. Answer the following question.
   a. What does a right-facing arrow mean? _____
7. Click the Next button to display the next topic. Scroll the Windows XP Basics window and read the paragraph below the Files and Folder heading. Answer the following question.
   a. In which folders are text, image, and music files placed?

   _____
8. Click the Next button to display the next topic. Scroll the Windows XP Basics window and read the paragraphs below the Windows heading. Answer the following question.
   a. What appears if a program needs some information from you before it can complete a command?

   _____
9. Click the Next button to display the next topic. Scroll the Windows XP Basics window and read the paragraphs below the Control Panel heading. Answer the following questions.
   a. What Windows feature do you use to customize computer settings? _____
   b. Where is this feature located? _____
10. Click the Next button to display the next topic. Scroll the Windows XP Basics window and read the paragraphs below the Ending Your Session heading. Answer the following question.
    a. What do you do when you want to interrupt your Windows session and let someone else use the computer? _____
11. Click the Next button repeatedly to display the topics in the remaining four sections of the Windows XP tour.
12. Click the Close button in the window to end the tour.
13. Click the Close button in the Help and Support Center window.
14. You have completed this lab assignment.

2 Windows Explorer

Instructions: Use a computer to perform the following tasks.

1. Start Microsoft Windows XP and connect to the Internet.
2. Right-click the Start button on the Windows taskbar, click Explore on the shortcut menu, and then maximize the Start Menu window.
3. If necessary, scroll to the left in the Folders pane so the Start Menu and Programs icons are visible.
4. Click the Programs icon in the Start Menu folder.
5. Double-click the Internet Explorer Shortcut icon in the Contents pane to launch the Internet Explorer application. What is the URL of the Web page that appears in the Address bar in the Microsoft Internet Explorer window? _____
6. Click the URL in the Address bar in the Internet Explorer window to select it. Type scsite.com and then press the ENTER key.
7. Scroll the Web page to display the Browse by Subject area containing the subject categories. Clicking a subject category displays the book titles in that category.
8. Click Operating Systems in the Browse by Subject area.
9. Click the Microsoft Windows XP Comprehensive Concepts and Techniques link.
10. Right-click the Microsoft Windows XP textbook cover image on the Web page, click Save Picture As on the shortcut menu, type Windows XP Cover in the File name box, and then click the Save button in the Save Picture dialog box to save the image in the My Pictures folder.
11. Click the Close button in the Microsoft Internet Explorer window.
12. If necessary, scroll to the top of the Folders pane to make the drive C icon visible.
13. Click the minus sign in the box to the left of the drive C icon. The 3½ Floppy (A:) and My Documents icons should be visible in the Folders pane.
14. Click the plus sign in the box to the left of the My Documents icon.
15. Click the My Pictures folder name in the Folders pane.
16. Right-click the Windows XP Cover icon and then click Properties on the shortcut menu.
    a. What type of file is the Windows XP Cover file? _____
    b. When was the file last modified? _____
    c. With what application does this file open? _____
17. Click the Cancel button in the Windows XP Cover Properties dialog box.
18. Insert a formatted floppy disk in drive A of your computer.
19. Right-drag the Windows XP Cover icon to the 3½ Floppy (A:) icon in the Folders pane. Click Move Here on the shortcut menu. Click the 3½ Floppy (A:) icon in the Folders pane.
    a. Is the Windows XP Cover file stored on drive A? _____
20. Click the Close button in the 3½ Floppy (A:) window.

In the Lab

3 Using the Help and Support Center

Instructions: Use Windows Help and Support to perform the following tasks.

Part 1: Using the Question Mark Button

1. If necessary, launch Microsoft Windows XP and then log on to the computer.
2. Right-click an open area of the desktop to display a shortcut menu.
3. Click Properties on the shortcut menu to display the Display Properties dialog box.
4. Click the Desktop tab in the Display Properties dialog box.
5. Click the Help button on the title bar. The mouse pointer changes to a block arrow with a question mark.
6. Click the list box in the Desktop sheet. A pop-up window displays explaining the list box. Read the information in the pop-up window and then summarize the function of the list box.

   _____

7. Click an open area of the Desktop sheet to remove the pop-up window.
8. Click the Help button on the title bar and then click the Customize Desktop button. A pop-up window displays explaining what happens when you click this button. Read the information in the pop-up window and then summarize the function of the button.

   _____

9. Click an open area in the Desktop sheet to remove the pop-up window.
10. Click the Help button on the title bar and then click the monitor icon in the Desktop sheet. A pop-up window displays explaining the function of the monitor. Read the information in the pop-up window and then summarize the function of the monitor.

    _____

11. Click an open area in the Desktop sheet to remove the pop-up window.
12. Click the Help button on the title bar and then click the Cancel button. A pop-up window displays explaining what happens when you click the button. Read the information in the pop-up window and then summarize the function of the Cancel button.

    _____

13. Click an open area in the Desktop sheet to remove the pop-up window.
14. Click the Cancel button in the Display Properties dialog box.

Part 2: Finding What's New in Windows XP

1. Click the Start button and then click Help and Support on the Start menu.
2. Click the Maximize button on the Help and Support Center title bar.
3. Click What's new in Windows XP in the navigation pane.
4. Click What's new topics in the navigation pane. Ten topics display in the topic pane.
5. Click What's new on your desktop in the topic pane.
6. Click Start menu (or the plus sign in the small box preceding Start menu) to expand the entry. Read the information about the Start menu.
7. Click the Using the Start menu link.
8. Click the Print button on the Help and Support toolbar to print the topic. Click the Print button in the Print dialog box.

(continued)

Using Help and Support Center *(continued)*

9. Scroll the topic pane to display the Related Topics link. Click the Related Topics link to display a pop-up window containing three related topics. List the three topics.

_____

_____

10. Click Display a program at the top of the Start menu in the pop-up window.
11. Click the Print button on the Help and Support toolbar to print the topic. Click the Print button in the Print dialog box.

Part 3: *Viewing Windows XP Articles*

1. Click Windows XP articles: Walk through ways to use your PC in the What's new in Windows XP area in the navigation pane. A list of overviews, articles, and tutorials displays in the topic pane.
2. Click Walkthrough: Making music in the topic pane. Read the Making music article in the topic pane. List four ways in which you can use Windows XP musically.

_____

_____

3. Click Play music in the Making Music area. Scroll to display the Display details about a CD area. List the three steps to display details about a CD.

_____

_____

4. Scroll to the top of the window to display the Making Music area.
5. Click Create CDs in the Making Music area. Scroll to display the steps to burn your own CD. List the six steps to burn a CD.

_____

_____

_____

_____

_____

6. Read other articles of interest to you in the Making music area.
7. Click the Close button in the Help and Support Center window.

MICROSOFT
Office Word 2003

MICROSOFT
Office Word 2003

Creating and Editing a Word Document

PROJECT

1

CASE PERSPECTIVE

Racing fans everywhere proclaim the Formula One Grand Prix as the most exhilarating racing competition in the world. Formula One Grand Prix events typically run for three days in a variety of countries including Brazil, Canada, England, Germany, Italy, Spain, and the United States. On the first day of each event, drivers practice on the tracks. Qualifying sessions begin on the second day. The fastest 26 drivers participate in a drivers' parade and then compete in the Formula One Grand Prix race on Sunday. During the race of nearly 200 miles, Formula One cars reach speeds that exceed 220 miles per hour.

When the Formula One Grand Prix season approaches, travel agents begin taking reservations for race packages. Jill Hall is a senior travel agent at Beacon Travel, where you are employed as a summer intern. Jill knows you have learned the guidelines for designing announcements in your marketing classes and has asked you to prepare a one-page flier announcing Beacon's Grand Prix race packages. You decide to use thick, bold characters to emphasize the headline and title. To attract attention to the announcement, you plan to include a large graphic of a Formula One race car. When you show the finished document to Jill, she is quite impressed. After Jill approves the completed flier, she wants you to distribute it to businesses for display on bulletin boards and in window fronts.

As you read through this project, you will learn how to use Word to create, save, and print a document that includes a graphical image.

MICROSOFT
Office Word 2003

Creating and Editing a Word Document

Objectives

You will have mastered the material in this project when you can:

- Start and quit Word
- Describe the Word window
- Enter text in a document
- Check spelling as you type
- Save a document
- Format text and paragraphs

- Undo and redo commands or actions
- Insert clip art in a document
- Print a document
- Open a document
- Correct errors in a document
- Use Word's Help to answer questions

What Is Microsoft Office Word 2003?

Microsoft Office Word 2003 is a full-featured word processing program that allows you to create professional looking documents and revise them easily. With Word, you can develop announcements, letters, memos, resumes, reports, fax cover sheets, mailing labels, newsletters, and many other types of documents. Word also provides tools that enable you to create Web pages with ease. From within Word, you can place these Web pages directly on a Web server.

Word has many features designed to simplify the production of documents and make documents look visually appealing. Using Word, you easily can change the shape, size, and color of text. You also can include borders, shading, tables, images, pictures, and Web addresses in documents. With proper hardware, you can dictate or handwrite text instead of typing it in Word. You also can speak instructions to Word.

While you are typing, Word performs many tasks automatically. For example, Word detects and corrects spelling and grammar errors in several languages. Word's thesaurus allows you to add variety and precision to your writing. Word also can format text such as headings, lists, fractions, borders, and Web addresses as you type them. Within Word, you can e-mail a copy of a Word document to an e-mail address.

This latest version of Word has many new features to make you more productive. It supports XML documents, improves readability of documents, supports ink input from devices such as the Tablet PC, provides more control for protecting documents, allows two documents to be compared side by side, and includes the capability to search a variety of reference information.

Project One — Grand Prix Announcement

To illustrate the features of Word, this book presents a series of projects that use Word to create documents similar to those you will encounter in academic and business environments. Project 1 uses Word to produce the announcement shown in Figure 1-1.

FIGURE 1-1

More About

Word 2003

For more information about the features of Microsoft Word 2003, visit the Word 2003 More About Web page (scsite.com/wd2003/more) and then click Microsoft Word 2003 Features.

The announcement informs potential customers about Grand Prix race packages available through Beacon Travel. The announcement begins with a headline in large, thick characters. Below the headline is a graphic of a Formula One race car, followed by the body title, GRAND PRIX RACE PACKAGES. The paragraphs of body copy below the body title briefly discuss the items included in the race packages. Finally, the last line of the announcement lists the telephone number of Beacon Travel.

Starting and Customizing Word

If you are stepping through this project on a computer and you want your screen to match the figures in this book, then you should change your computer's resolution to 800 × 600. For more information about how to change the resolution on your computer, read Appendix D.

To start Word, Windows must be running. The following steps show how to start Word. You may need to ask your instructor how to start Word for your system.

To Start Word

1

• **Click the Start button on the Windows taskbar, point to All Programs on the Start menu, point to Microsoft Office on the All Programs submenu, and then point to Microsoft Office Word 2003 on the Microsoft Office submenu.**

Windows displays the commands on the Start menu above the Start button and then displays the All Programs and Microsoft Office submenus (Figure 1-2).

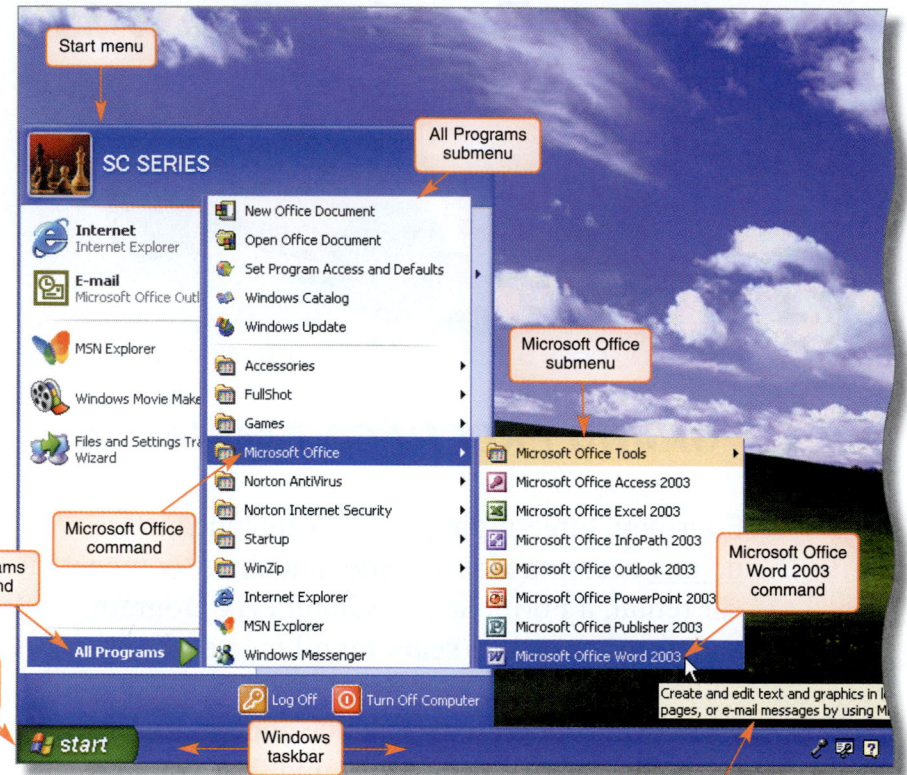

FIGURE 1-2

2

- **Click Microsoft Office Word 2003.**

Word starts. After a few moments, Word displays a new blank document titled Document1 in the Word window (Figure 1-3). The Windows taskbar displays the Word program button, indicating Word is running.

3

- **If the Word window is not maximized, double-click its title bar to maximize it.**

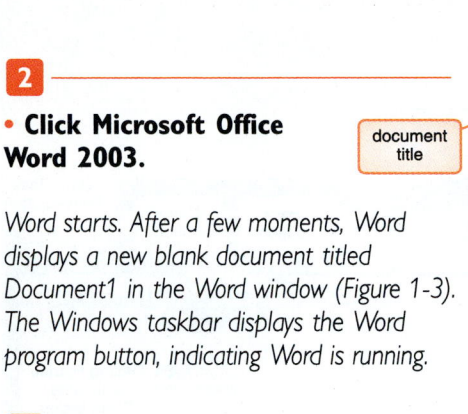
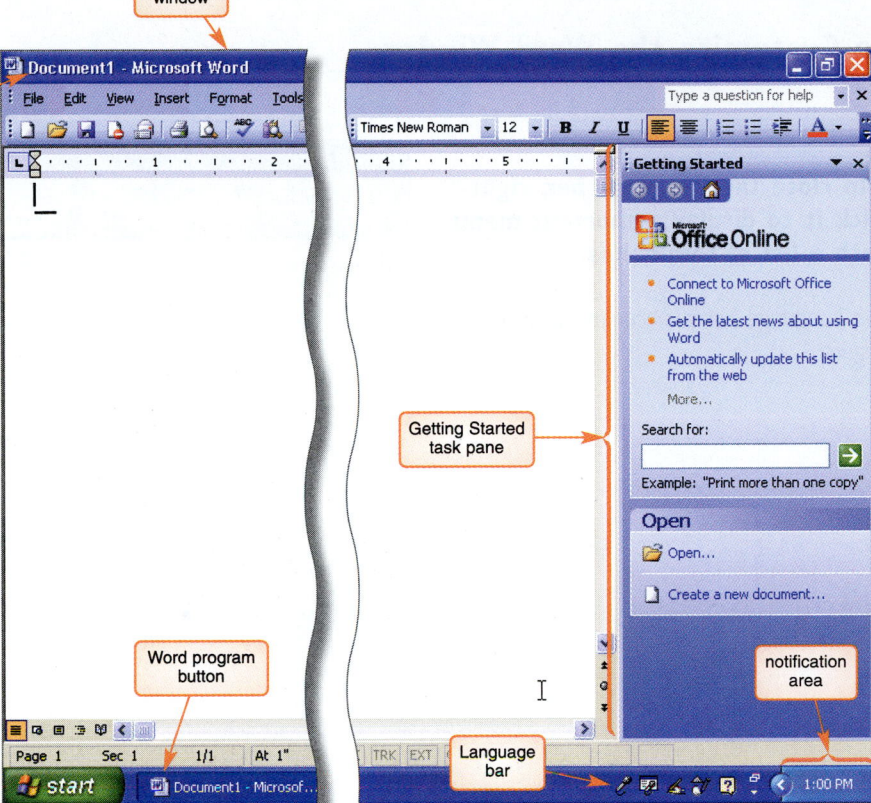

FIGURE 1-3

More About

Task Panes

When you first start Word, a small window called a task pane may be displayed docked on the right side of the screen. You can drag a task pane title bar to float the pane in your work area or dock it on either the left or right side of a screen, depending on your personal preference.

The screen in Figure 1-3 shows how the Word window looks the first time you start Word after installation on most computers. If the Office Speech Recognition software is installed and active on your computer, then when you start Word the Language bar is displayed on the screen. The **Language bar** contains buttons that allow you to speak commands and dictate text. It usually is located on the right side of the Windows taskbar next to the notification area, and it changes to include the speech recognition functions available in Word. In this book, the Language bar is closed because it takes up computer resources and with the Language bar active, the microphone can be turned on accidentally by clicking the Microphone button, causing your computer to act in an unstable manner. For additional information about the Language bar, see page WD 16 and Appendix B.

As shown in Figure 1-3, Word may display a task pane on the right side of the screen. A **task pane** is a separate window that enables users to carry out some Word tasks more efficiently. When you start Word, it automatically may display the Getting Started task pane, which is a task pane that allows you to search for Office-related topics on the Microsoft Web site, open files, or create new documents. In this book, the Getting Started task pane is closed to allow the maximum typing area in Word.

After installation, Word displays the toolbar buttons on a single row. A **toolbar** contains buttons and boxes that allow you to perform frequent tasks quickly. For more efficient use of the buttons, the toolbars should be displayed on two separate rows instead of sharing a single row.

The steps on the next page show how to customize the Word window by closing the Language bar, closing the Getting Started task pane, and displaying the toolbar buttons on two separate rows.

To Customize the Word Window

1

• **To close the Language bar, right-click it to display a shortcut menu with a list of commands.**

The Language bar shortcut menu appears (Figure 1-4).

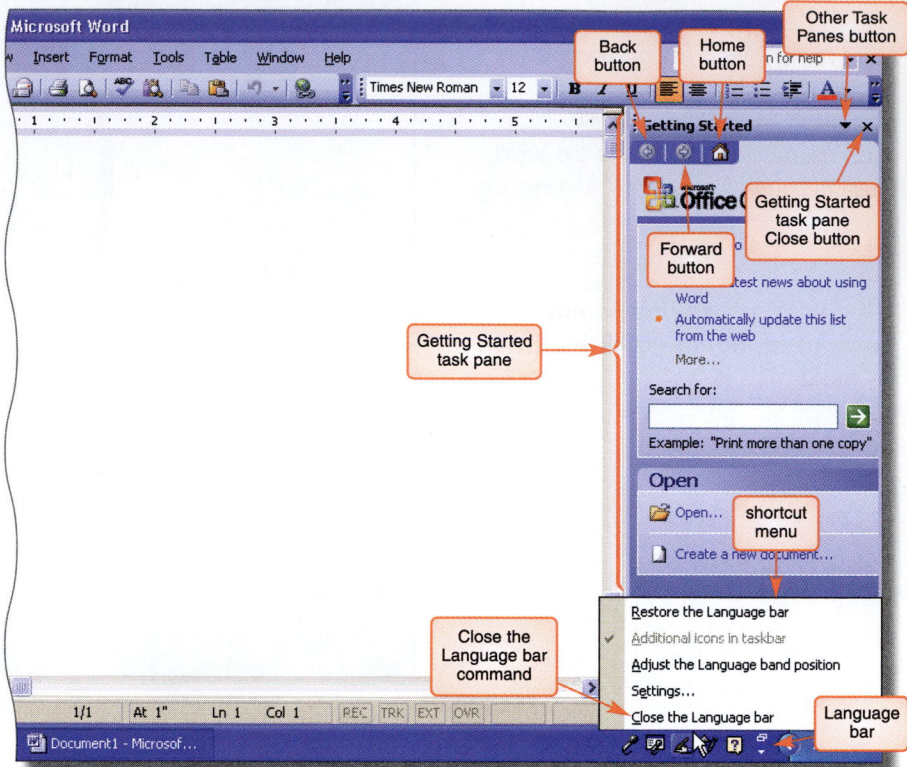

FIGURE 1-4

2

• **Click Close the Language bar on the shortcut menu.**

• **If the Getting Started task pane is displayed, click the Close button in the upper-right corner of the task pane.**

The Language bar disappears. Word removes the Getting Started task pane from the screen (Figure 1-5).

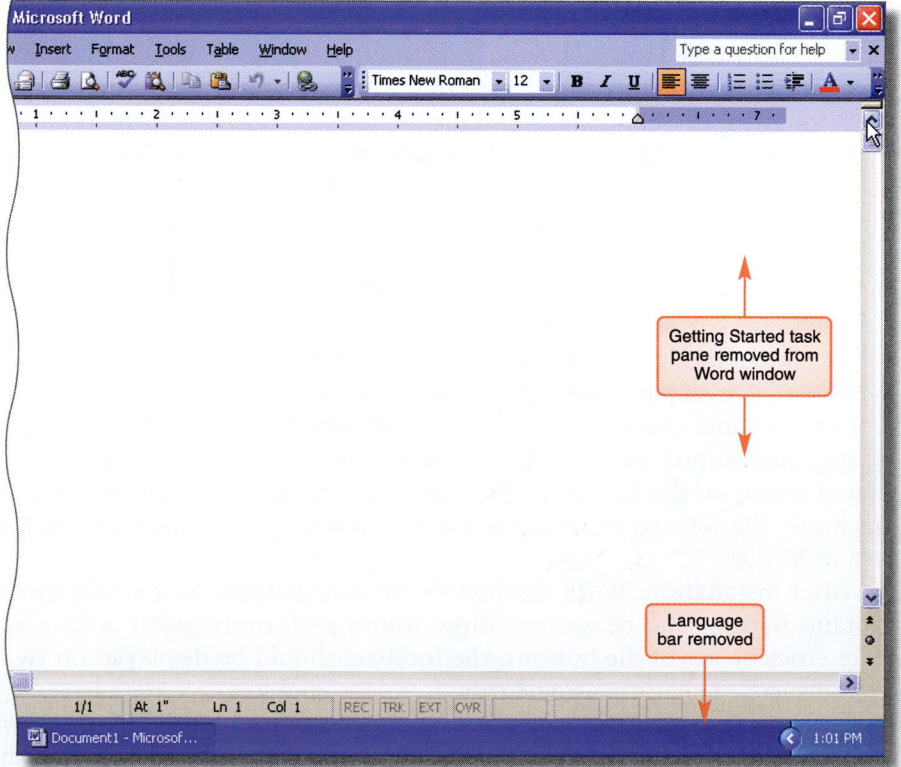

FIGURE 1-5

3

• If the toolbar buttons are displayed on one row, click the Toolbar Options button.

Word displays the Toolbar Options list, which shows the buttons that do not fit on the toolbars when they are displayed on one row (Figure 1-6).

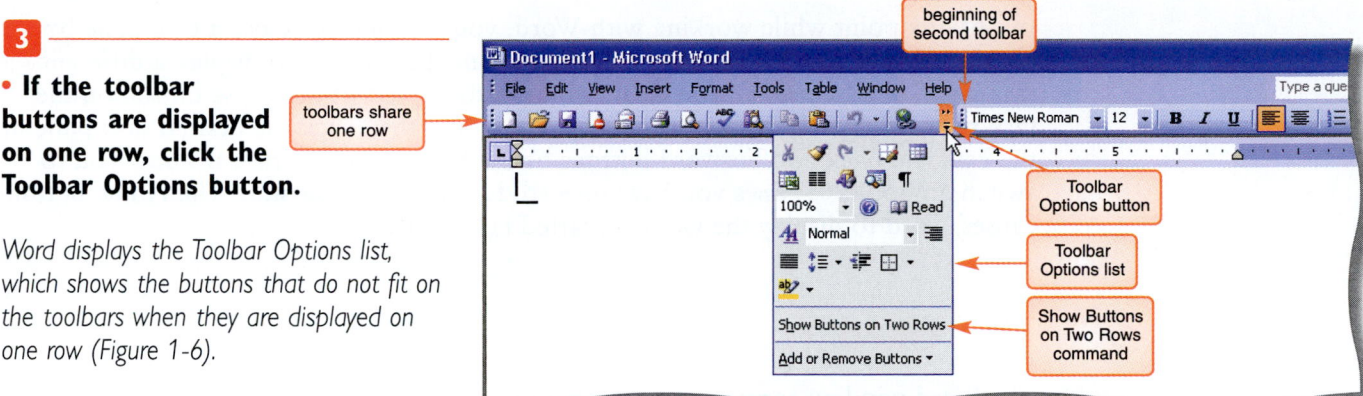

FIGURE 1-6

4

• Click Show Buttons on Two Rows in the Toolbar Options list.

• If your screen differs from Figure 1-7, click the Normal View button on the horizontal scroll bar.

Word displays the toolbars on two separate rows (Figure 1-7). The Toolbar Options list now is empty because all of the buttons fit on the toolbars when they display on two rows.

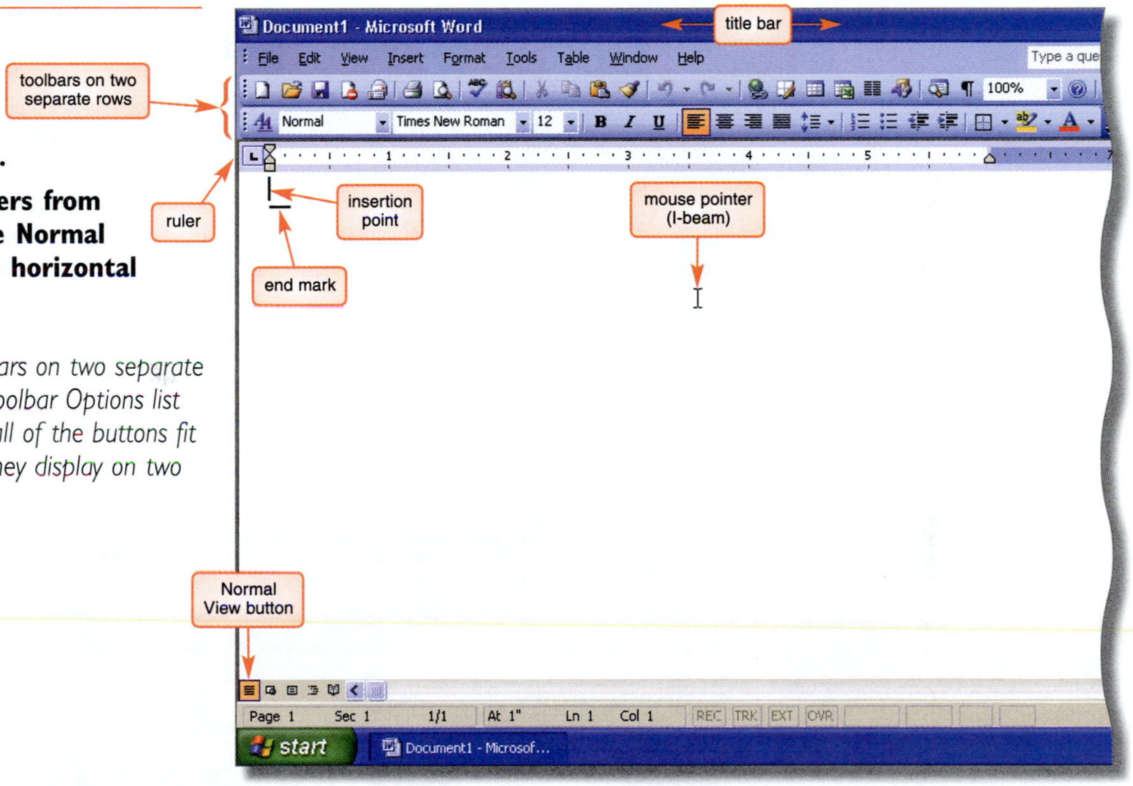

FIGURE 1-7

As an alternative to Steps 3 and 4 above, you can point to the beginning of the second toolbar (Figure 1-6), and when the mouse pointer changes to a four-headed arrow, drag the toolbar down to create two rows of toolbars.

Each time you start Word, the Word window appears the same way it did the last time you used Word. If the toolbar buttons are displayed on one row, then they will be displayed on one row the next time you start Word.

As you work through creating a document, you will find that certain Word operations automatically display a task pane. In addition to the Getting Started task pane shown in Figure 1-4, Word provides 13 other task panes. Some of the more important ones are the Help, Clip Art, Clipboard, and Research task panes. These task panes are discussed as they are used throughout the book.

More About

The Office Assistant

The Office Assistant is an animated object that can answer questions for you. On some installations, the Office Assistant may appear when Word starts. If the Office Assistant appears on your screen and you do not want to use it, right-click it and then click Hide on the shortcut menu.

At any point while working with Word, you can open or close a task pane by clicking View on the menu bar and then clicking Task Pane. To display a different task pane, click the Other Task Panes button to the left of the Close button on the task pane title bar (Figure 1-4 on page WD 8) and then click the desired task pane in the list. The Back and Forward buttons below the task pane title bar allow you to switch among task panes you have opened during a Word session. The Home button causes Word to display the Getting Started task pane.

The Word Window

The Word window consists of a variety of components to make your work more efficient and documents more professional. The following sections discuss these components, which are identified in either Figure 1-7 on the previous page or Figure 1-8.

Document Window

The **document window** displays text, tables, graphics, and other items as you type or insert them in a document. Only a portion of a document, however, appears on the screen at one time. You view the portion of the document displayed on the screen through a document window (Figure 1-8).

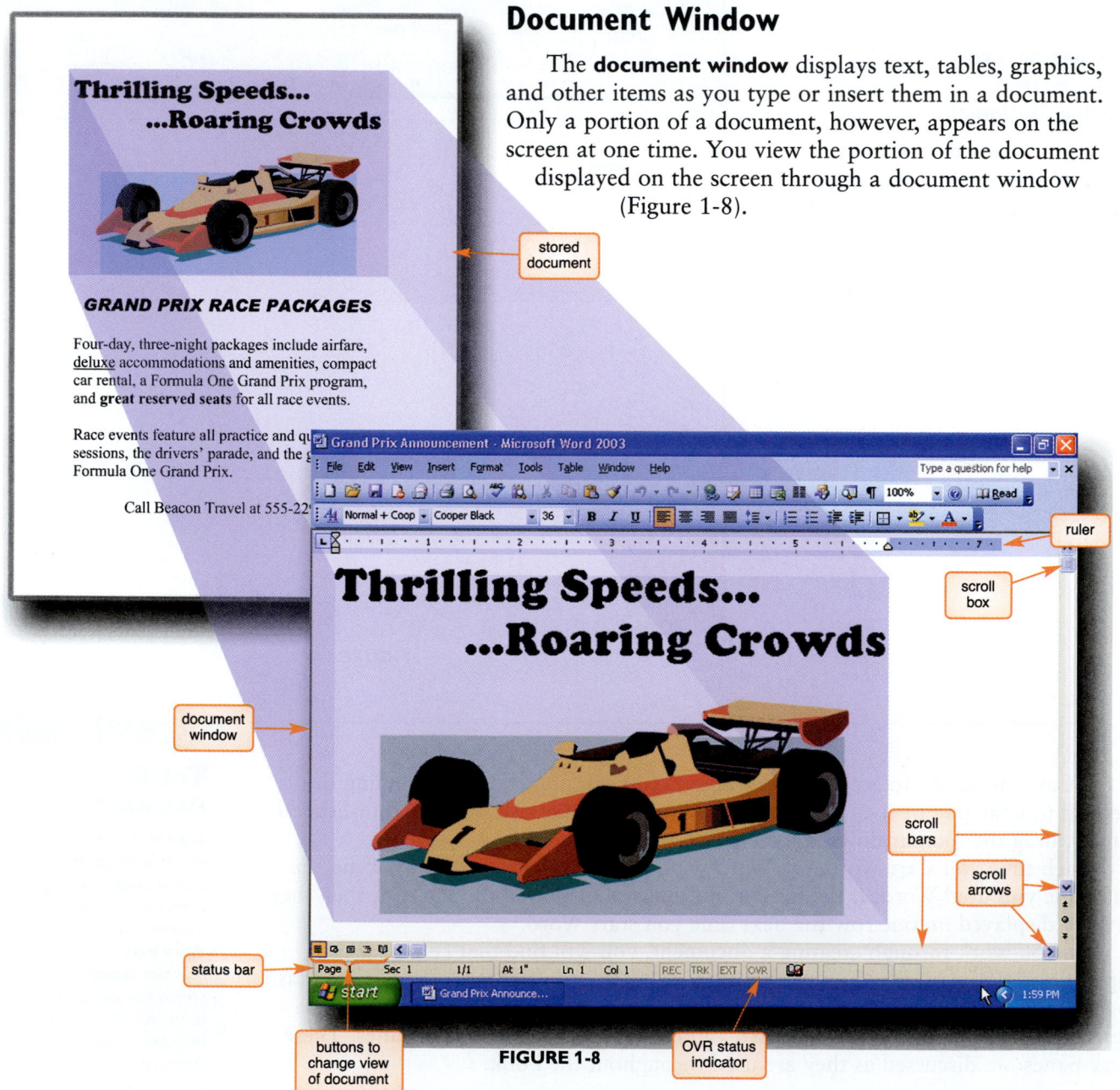

FIGURE 1-8

A document window contains several elements commonly found in other application software, as well as some elements unique to Word. The main elements of the Word document window are the insertion point, end mark, mouse pointer, rulers, scroll bars, and status bar.

INSERTION POINT   The **insertion point** (Figure 1-7 on page WD 9) is a blinking vertical bar that indicates where text will be inserted as you type. As you type, the insertion point moves to the right and, when you reach the end of a line, it moves downward to the beginning of the next line. You also insert graphics, tables, and other items at the location of the insertion point.

END MARK   The **end mark** (Figure 1-7) is a short horizontal line that indicates the end of the document. Each time you begin a new line, the end mark moves downward.

MOUSE POINTER   The **mouse pointer** becomes different shapes depending on the task you are performing in Word and the pointer's location on the screen (Figure 1-7). The mouse pointer in Figure 1-7 has the shape of an I-beam. Other mouse pointer shapes are described as they appear on the screen during this and subsequent projects.

RULERS   At the top edge of the document window is the horizontal ruler (Figure 1-8). You use the **horizontal ruler,** usually simply called the **ruler,** to set tab stops, indent paragraphs, adjust column widths, and change page margins.

An additional ruler, called the **vertical ruler,** sometimes is displayed at the left edge of the Word window when you perform certain tasks. The purpose of the vertical ruler is discussed in a later project. If your screen displays a vertical ruler, click View on the menu bar and then click Normal.

SCROLL BARS   By using the **scroll bars,** you display different portions of your document in the document window (Figure 1-8). At the right edge of the document window is a vertical scroll bar. At the bottom of the document window is a horizontal scroll bar. On both the vertical and horizontal scroll bars, the position of the **scroll box** reflects the location of the portion of the document that is displayed in the document window.

On the left edge of the horizontal scroll bar are five buttons that change the view of a document. On the bottom of the vertical scroll bar are three buttons you can use to scroll through a document. These buttons are discussed as they are used in later projects.

STATUS BAR   The **status bar** displays at the bottom of the document window, above the Windows taskbar (Figure 1-8). The status bar presents information about the location of the insertion point and the progress of current tasks, as well as the status of certain commands, keys, and buttons.

From left to right, Word displays the following information on the status bar in Figure 1-8: the page number, the section number, the page containing the insertion point followed by the total number of pages in the document, the position of the insertion point in inches from the top of the page, the line number and column number of the insertion point, and then several status indicators.

More About

The Horizontal Ruler

If the horizontal ruler is not displayed on your screen, click View on the menu bar and then click Ruler. To hide the ruler, also click View on the menu bar and then click Ruler.

More About

Scroll Bars

You can use the vertical scroll bar to scroll through multi-page documents. As you drag the scroll box up or down the scroll bar, Word displays a page indicator to the left of the scroll box. When you release the mouse button, the document window displays the page shown in the page indicator.

More About

Languages

If multiple languages have been installed on your computer, the status bar also displays the language format, which shows the name of the language you are using to create the document. You add languages through the Control Panel in Windows.

You use the **status indicators** to turn certain keys or modes on or off. Word displays the first four status indicators (REC, TRK, EXT, and OVR) darkened when they are on and dimmed when they are off. For example, the dimmed OVR indicates overtype mode is off. To turn these four status indicators on or off, double-click the status indicator on the status bar. Each of these status indicators is discussed as it is used in the projects.

The remaining status indicators display icons as you perform certain tasks. For example, when you begin typing in the document window, Word displays a Spelling and Grammar Status icon. When Word is saving your document, it displays a Background Save icon. When you print a document, Word displays a Background Print icon. If you perform a task that requires several seconds (such as saving a document), the status bar usually displays a message informing you of the progress of the task.

Menu Bar and Toolbars

The menu bar and toolbars display at the top of the screen just below the title bar (Figure 1-9).

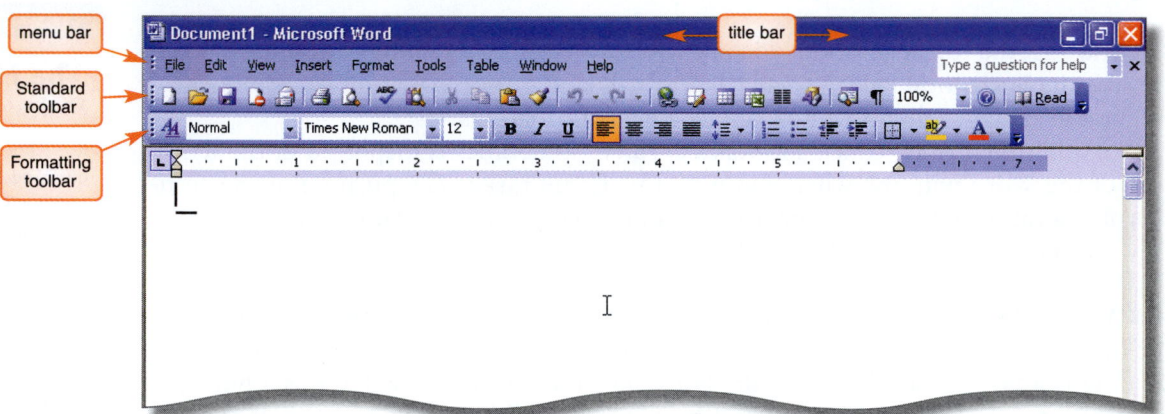

FIGURE 1-9

MENU BAR   The **menu bar** is a special toolbar that displays the Word menu names. Each menu name represents a menu. A **menu** contains a list of commands you use to perform tasks such as retrieving, storing, printing, and formatting data in a document.

When you point to a menu name on the menu bar, the area of the menu bar containing the name is displayed as a selected button. Word shades selected buttons in light orange and surrounds them with a blue outline.

To display a menu, click the menu name on the menu bar. For example, to display the Edit menu, click the Edit menu name on the menu bar. When you click a menu name on the menu bar, Word initially displays a **short menu** listing your most recently used commands (Figure 1-10a). If you wait a few seconds or click the arrows at the bottom of the short menu, it expands into a full menu. A **full menu** lists all the commands associated with a menu (Figure 1-10b). You also can display a full menu immediately by double-clicking the menu name on the menu bar.

More About

Menus

Right-clicking an object displays a shortcut menu (also called a context-sensitive or object menu). Depending on the object, the commands in the shortcut menu vary.

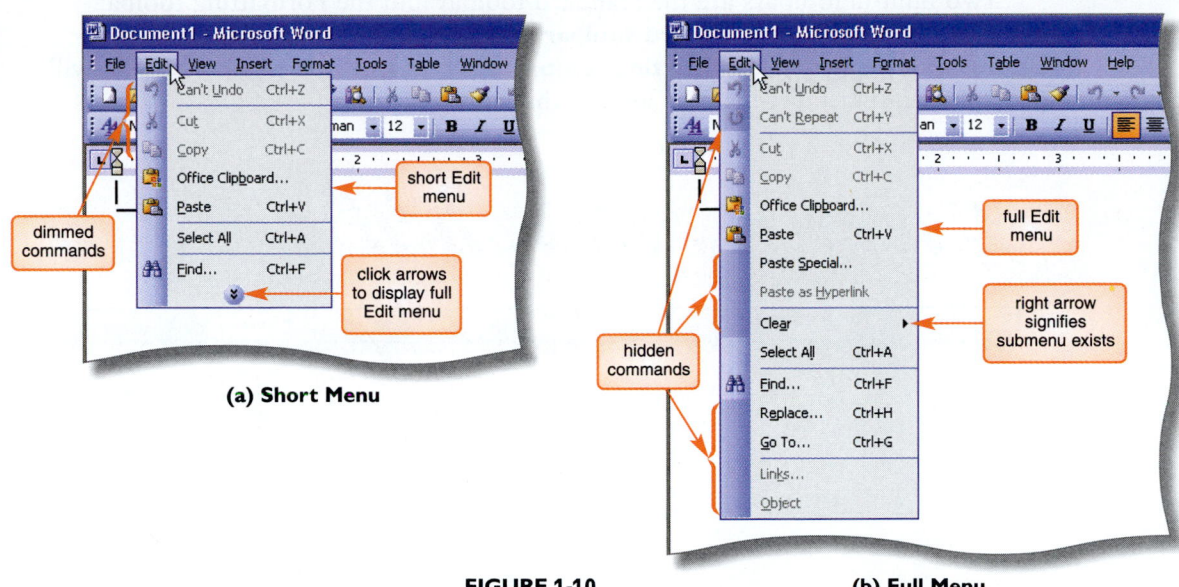

FIGURE 1-10

(a) Short Menu   (b) Full Menu

In this book, when you display a menu, use one of the following techniques to ensure that Word always displays a full menu:

1. Click the menu name on the menu bar and then wait a few seconds.
2. Click the menu name on the menu bar and then click the arrows at the bottom of the short menu.
3. Click the menu name on the menu bar and then point to the arrows at the bottom of the short menu.
4. Double-click the menu name on the menu bar.

Both short and full menus may display some dimmed commands. A **dimmed command** appears gray, or dimmed, instead of black, which indicates it is not available for the current selection. A command with medium blue shading in the rectangle to its left on a full menu is called a **hidden command** because it does not appear on a short menu. As you use Word, it automatically personalizes the short menus for you based on how often you use commands. That is, as you use hidden commands on the full menu, Word *unhides* them and places them on the short menu.

Some commands have an arrow at the right edge of the menu. If you point to this arrow, Word displays a **submenu**, which is a list of additional commands associated with the selected command.

TOOLBARS Word has many predefined, or built-in, toolbars. A toolbar contains buttons, boxes, and menus that allow you to perform tasks more quickly than using the menu bar. For example, to print a document, you can click the Print button on a toolbar instead of navigating through the File menu to reach the Print command.

Each button on a toolbar displays an image to help you remember its function. Also, when you position the mouse pointer on, or point to, a button or box, Word displays the name of the button or box in a ScreenTip. A **ScreenTip** is a short on-screen note associated with the object to which you are pointing.

Two built-in toolbars are the Standard toolbar and the Formatting toolbar. Figure 1-11a shows the **Standard toolbar** and identifies its buttons and boxes. Figure 1-11b shows the **Formatting toolbar**. Each of these buttons and boxes will be explained in detail when it is used in this book.

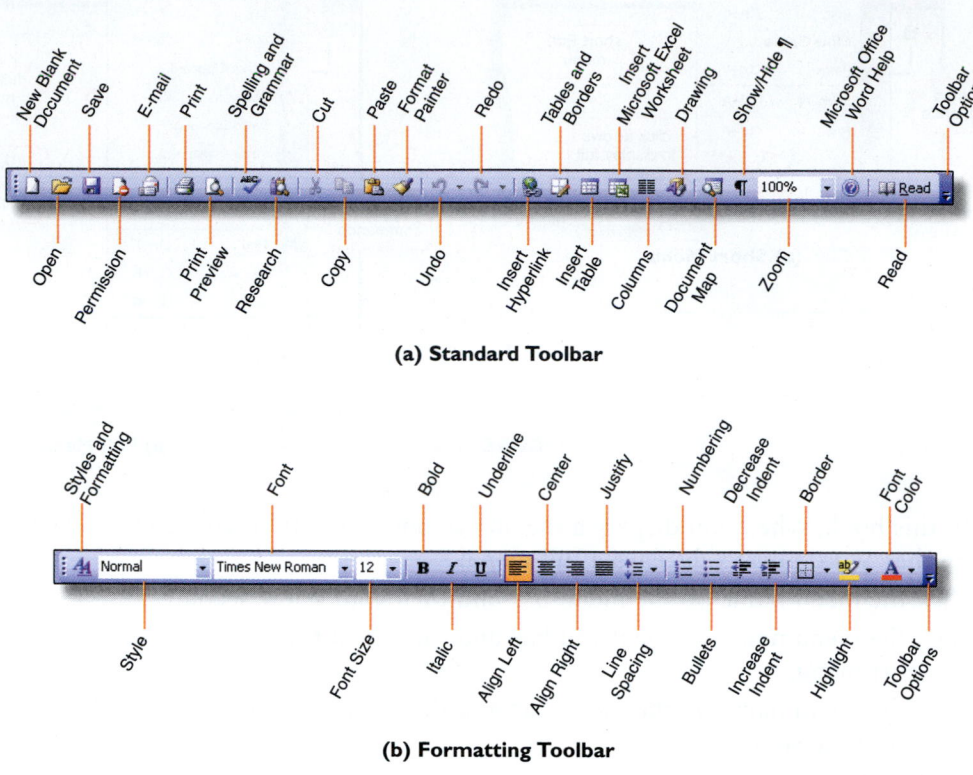

(a) Standard Toolbar

(b) Formatting Toolbar

FIGURE 1-11

More About

The Word Help System

Need Help? It is no further away than the Type a question for help box on the menu bar in the upper-right corner of the window. Click the box that contains the text, Type a question for help (Figure 1-12c), type help, and then press the ENTER key. Word responds with a list of topics you can click to learn about obtaining help on any Word-related topic. To find out what is new in Word 2003, type what is new in Word in the Type a question for help box.

When you first install Word, the buttons on both the Standard and Formatting toolbars are preset to display on the same row immediately below the menu bar (Figure 1-12a). Unless the resolution of your display device is greater than 800 × 600, many of the buttons that belong to these toolbars are hidden when the two toolbars share one row. The buttons that display on the toolbar are the more frequently used buttons. Hidden buttons display in the Toolbar Options list (Figure 1-12b). You can display all the buttons on either toolbar by double-clicking the **move handle**, which is the vertical dotted line on the left edge of the toolbar.

As an alternative, you can instruct Word to display the buttons on the Standard and Formatting toolbars on separate rows, one below the other, by clicking the Show Buttons on Two Rows command in the Toolbar Options list (Figure 1-12b). In this book, the Standard and Formatting toolbars are shown on separate rows so that all buttons are displayed on a screen with the resolution set to 800 × 600 (Figure 1-12c).

In the previous figures, the Standard and Formatting toolbars are docked. A **docked toolbar** is a toolbar that is attached to an edge of the Word window. Depending on the task you are performing, Word may display additional toolbars on the screen. These additional toolbars either are docked or floating in the Word window. A **floating toolbar** is not attached to an edge of the Word window; that is, it appears in the middle of the Word window. You can rearrange the order of docked toolbars and can move floating toolbars anywhere in the Word window. Later in this book, steps are presented that show you how to float a docked toolbar or dock a floating toolbar.

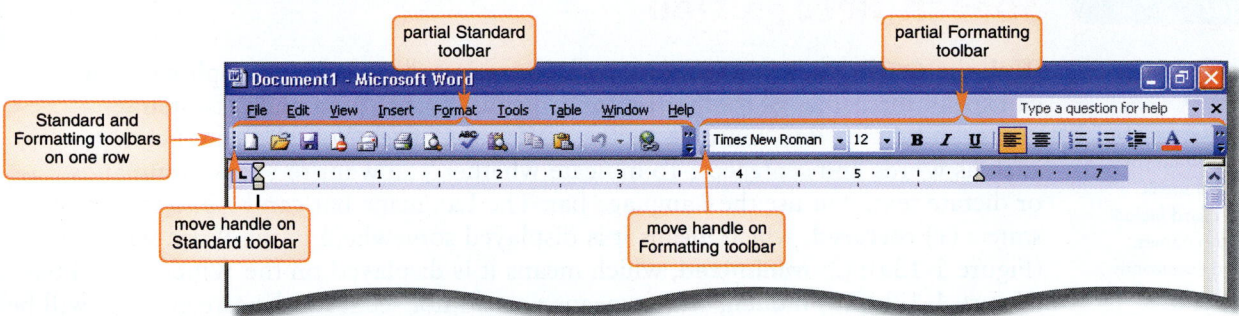

(a) Standard and Formatting Toolbars on One Row

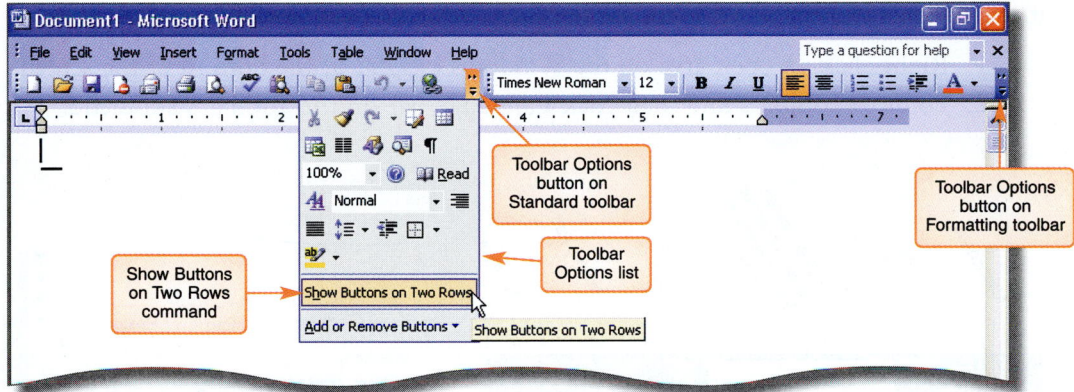

(b) Toolbar Options List

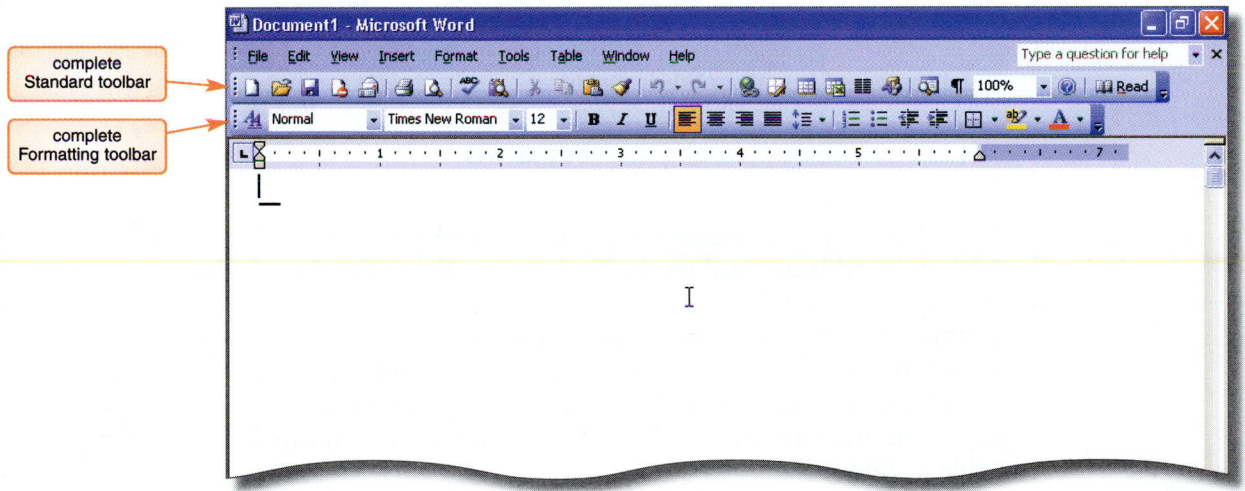

(c) Standard and Formatting Toolbars on Two Rows

FIGURE 1-12

Resetting Menus and Toolbars

Each project in this book begins with the menus and toolbars appearing as they did at the initial installation of the software. If you are stepping through this project on a computer and you want your menus and toolbars to match the figures in this book, then you should reset your menus and toolbars. For more information about how to reset menus and toolbars, read Appendix D.

More About

Speech Recognition

If Office Speech Recognition software is installed on your computer, you can speak instructions to Word including toolbar button names, menu names and commands, and items in dialog boxes and task panes. You also can dictate so Word writes exactly what you say. The microphone picks up others' voices and background sounds, so speech recognition is most effective when used in a quiet environment.

Speech Recognition

With the **Office Speech Recognition software** installed and a microphone, you can speak the names of toolbar buttons, menus, menu commands, list items, alerts, and dialog box controls, such as OK and Cancel. You also can dictate text, such as words and sentences. To indicate whether you want to speak commands or dictate text, you use the Language bar. The Language bar can be in one of four states: (1) **restored**, which means it is displayed somewhere in the Word window (Figure 1-13a); (2) **minimized**, which means it is displayed on the Windows taskbar (Figure 1-13b); (3) **hidden**, which means you do not see it on the screen but it will be displayed the next time you start your computer; or (4) **closed**, which means it is hidden permanently until you enable it. If the Language bar is hidden and you want it to be displayed, then do the following:

1. Right-click an open area on the Windows taskbar at the bottom of the screen.
2. Point to Toolbars and then click Language bar on the Toolbars submenu.

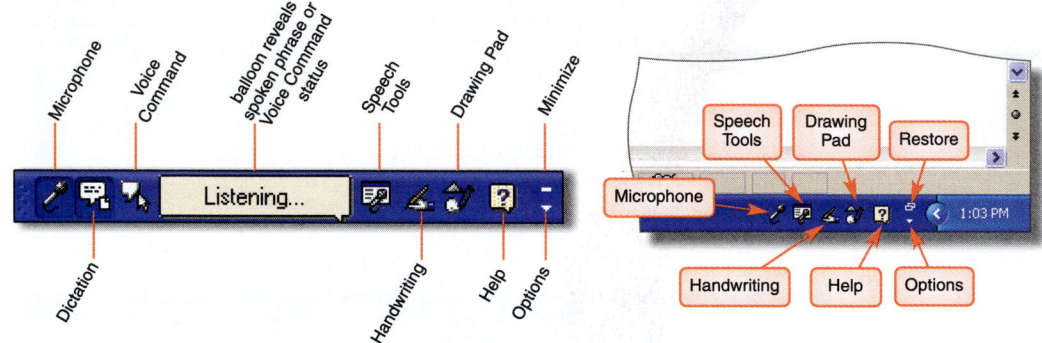

(a) Language Bar in Word Window with Microphone Enabled

(b) Language Bar Minimized on Windows Taskbar

FIGURE 1-13

If the Language bar command is dimmed on the Toolbars submenu or if the Speech command is dimmed on the Tools menu, the Office Speech Recognition software is not installed.

In this book, the Language bar does not appear in the figures. If you want to close the Language bar so that your screen is identical to what you see in the book, right-click the Language bar and then click Close the Language bar on the shortcut menu. Additional information about the speech recognition capabilities of Word is available in Appendix B.

Q&A

Q: What font size should I use in an announcement?

A: An announcement usually is posted on a bulletin board. Thus, its font size should be as large as possible so that all potential readers easily can see the announcement.

Entering Text

Characters that display on the screen are a specific shape, size, and style. The **font**, or typeface, defines the appearance and shape of the letters, numbers, and special characters. The preset, or **default**, font is Times New Roman (Figure 1-14). **Font size** specifies the size of the characters and is determined by a measurement system called points. A single **point** is about 1/72 of one inch in height. Thus, a character with a font size of 12 is about 12/72 or 1/6 of one inch in height. On most computers, the default font size in Word is 12.

If more of the characters in your document require a larger font size than the default, you easily can change the font size before you type. In Project 1, many of the characters in the body copy of the announcement are a font size of 22. The following steps show how to increase the font size before you begin typing text.

To Increase the Font Size before Typing

1

• **Click the Font Size box arrow on the Formatting toolbar.**

Word displays a list of available font sizes in the Font Size list (Figure 1-14). The available font sizes depend on the current font, which is Times New Roman.

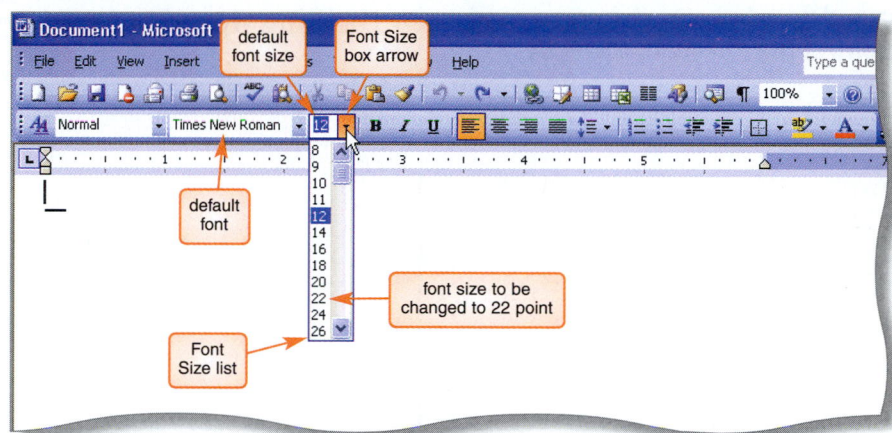

FIGURE 1-14

2

• **Click 22 in the Font Size list.**

The font size for characters to be entered in this document changes to 22 (Figure 1-15). The size of the insertion point increases to reflect the new font size.

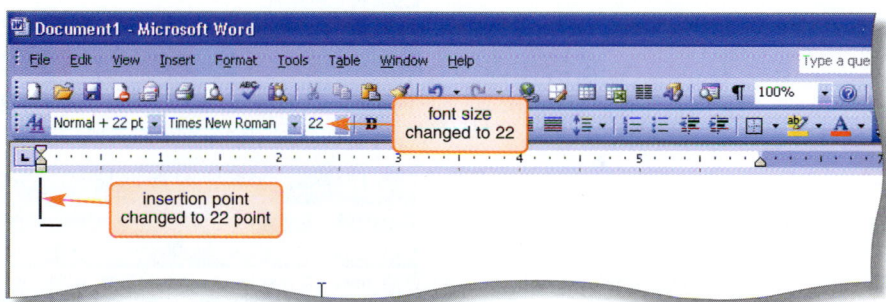

FIGURE 1-15

The new font size takes effect immediately in the document. Word uses this font size for characters you enter in this announcement.

Typing Text

To enter text in a document, you type on the keyboard or speak into the microphone. The example on the next page illustrates the steps required to type both lines of the headline in the announcement. By default, Word positions these lines at the left margin. In a later section, this project will show how to make all of the characters in the headline larger and thicker, and how to position the second line of the headline at the right margin.

The steps on the next page show how to begin typing text in the announcement.

Other Ways

1. On Format menu click Font, click Font tab, select desired font size in Size list, click OK button
2. Right-click paragraph mark above end mark, click Font on shortcut menu, click Font tab, select desired font size in Size list, click OK button
3. Press CTRL+SHIFT+P, type desired font size, press ENTER
4. Press CTRL+SHIFT+> repeatedly
5. In Voice Command mode, say "Font Size, [select font size]"

To Type Text

1

• **Type** Thrilling Speeds **and then press the** PERIOD **(.) key three times. If you make an error while typing, press the** BACKSPACE **key until you have deleted the text in error and then retype the text correctly.**

As you type, the insertion point moves to the right (Figure 1-16).

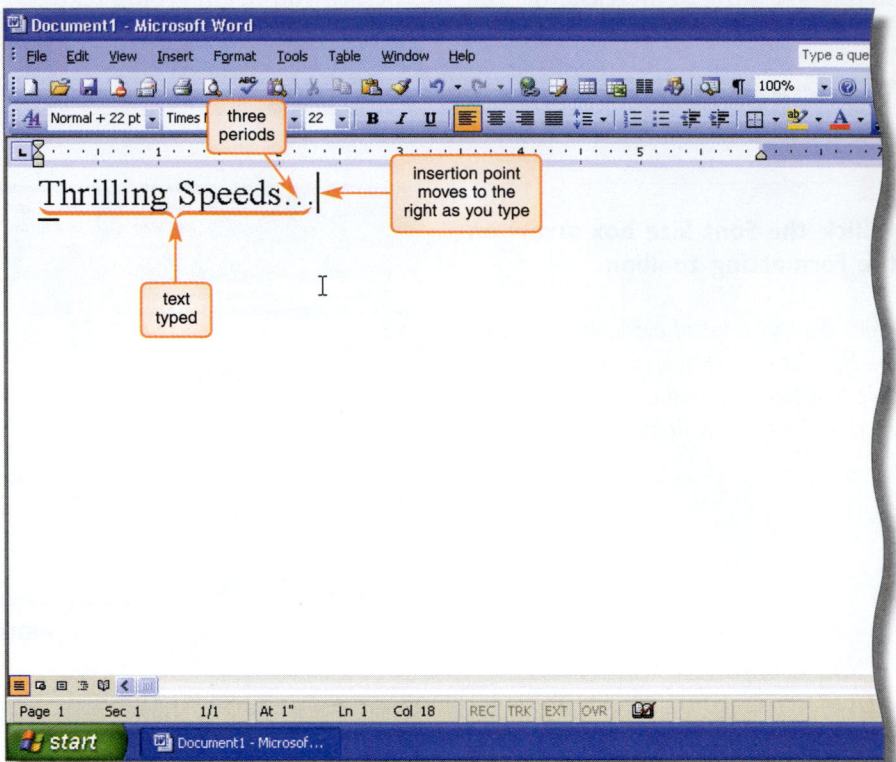

FIGURE 1-16

2

• **Press the** ENTER **key.**

Word moves the insertion point to the beginning of the next line (Figure 1-17). Notice the status bar indicates the current position of the insertion point. That is, the insertion point currently is on line 2 column 1.

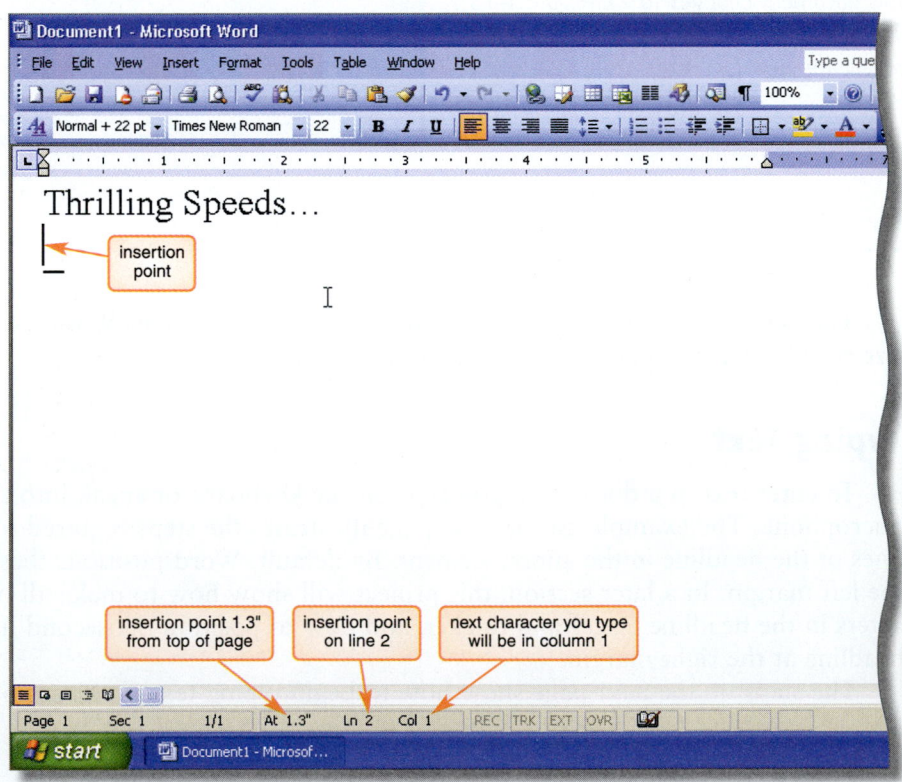

FIGURE 1-17

3

• **Press the PERIOD key three times.**

• **Type** Roaring Crowds **and then press the ENTER key.**

The headline is complete (Figure 1-18). The insertion point is on line 3.

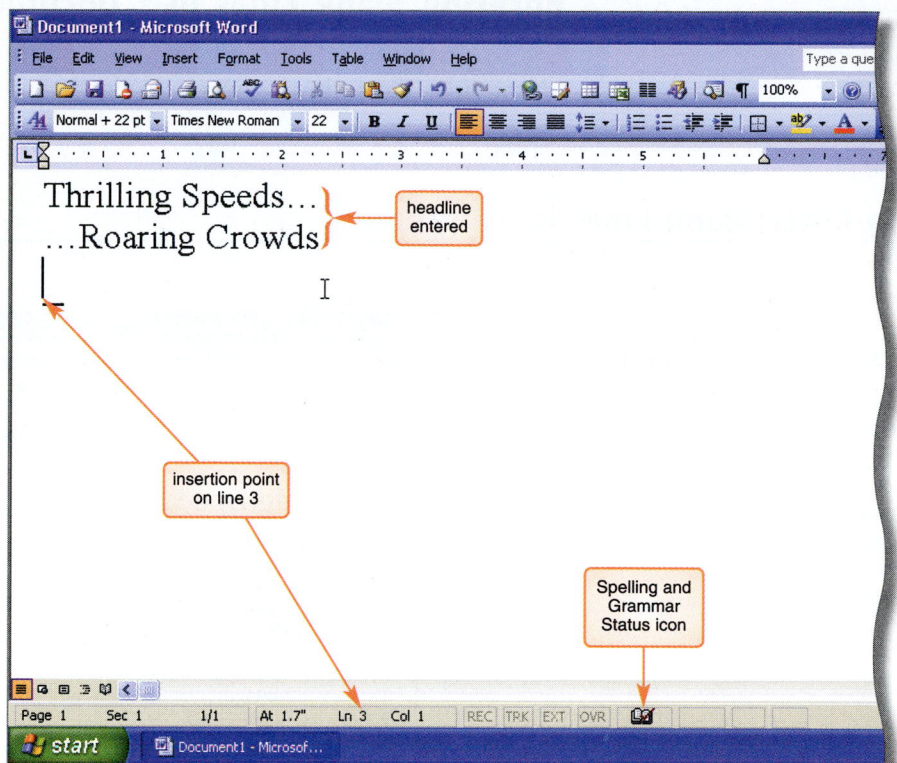

FIGURE 1-18

Other Ways

1. In Dictation mode, say "Thrilling Speeds, Period, Period, Period, New Line, Period, Period, Period, Roaring Crowds, New Line"

When you begin entering text in a document, the **Spelling and Grammar Status icon** appears at the right of the status bar (Figure 1-18). As you type, the Spelling and Grammar Status icon shows an animated pencil writing on paper, which indicates Word is checking for possible errors. When you stop typing, the pencil changes to either a red check mark or a red X. In Figure 1-18, the Spelling and Grammar Status icon contains a red check mark.

In general, if all of the words you have typed are in Word's dictionary and your grammar is correct, the Spelling and Grammar Status icon contains a red check mark. If you type a word not in the dictionary (because it is a proper name or misspelled), a red wavy underline appears below the word. If you type text that may be incorrect grammatically, a green wavy underline appears below the text. When Word flags a possible spelling or grammar error, it also changes the red check mark on the Spelling and Grammar Status icon to a red X. As you enter text in a document, your Spelling and Grammar Status icon may show a red X instead of a red check mark. Later, this project will show how to check the spelling of these flagged words. At that time, the red X returns to a red check mark.

More About

Entering Text

In the days of typewriters, the letter l was used for both the letter l and the numeral one. Keyboards, however, have both a numeral one and the letter l. Keyboards also have both a numeral zero and the letter o. Be careful to press the correct keyboard character when creating a word processing document.

Entering Blank Lines in a Document

To enter a blank line in a document, press the ENTER key without typing any text on the line. The following example shows how to enter three blank lines below the headline.

To Enter Blank Lines in a Document

1

• **Press the ENTER key three times.**

Word inserts three blank lines in the document below the headline (Figure 1-19).

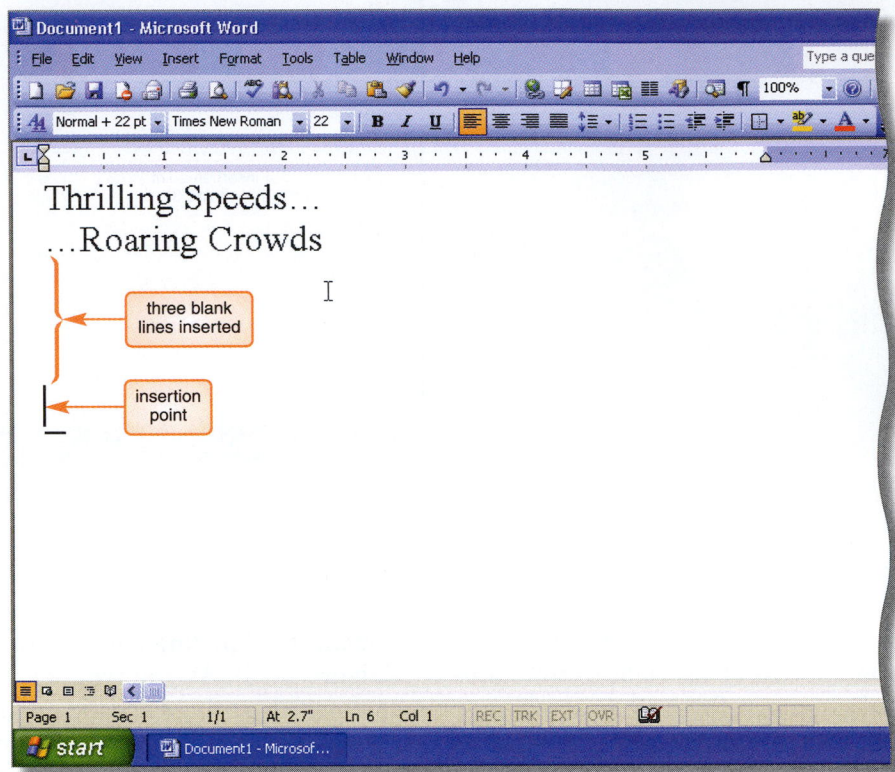

FIGURE 1-19

Displaying Formatting Marks

To indicate where in a document you press the ENTER key or SPACEBAR, you may find it helpful to display formatting marks. A **formatting mark**, sometimes called a **nonprinting character**, is a character that Word displays on the screen but is not visible on a printed document. For example, the paragraph mark (¶) is a formatting mark that indicates where you pressed the ENTER key. A raised dot (•) shows where you pressed the SPACEBAR. Other formatting marks are discussed as they appear on the screen.

More About

Hidden Text

When you display formatting marks, Word also displays hidden text. Text formatted as hidden shows on the screen but does not print. Hidden text is useful if you want to write a note to yourself in a document. To format text as hidden, select the text, click Format on the menu bar, click Font, click the Font tab, place a check mark in the Hidden check box, and then click the OK button.

Depending on settings made during previous Word sessions, the Word screen already may display formatting marks (Figure 1-20). The following step shows how to display formatting marks, if they are not displayed already on the screen.

To Display Formatting Marks

1

• **If it is not selected already, click the Show/Hide ¶ button on the Standard toolbar.**

Word displays formatting marks on the screen (Figure 1-20). The Show/Hide ¶ button is selected. That is, the button is light orange and surrounded with a blue outline.

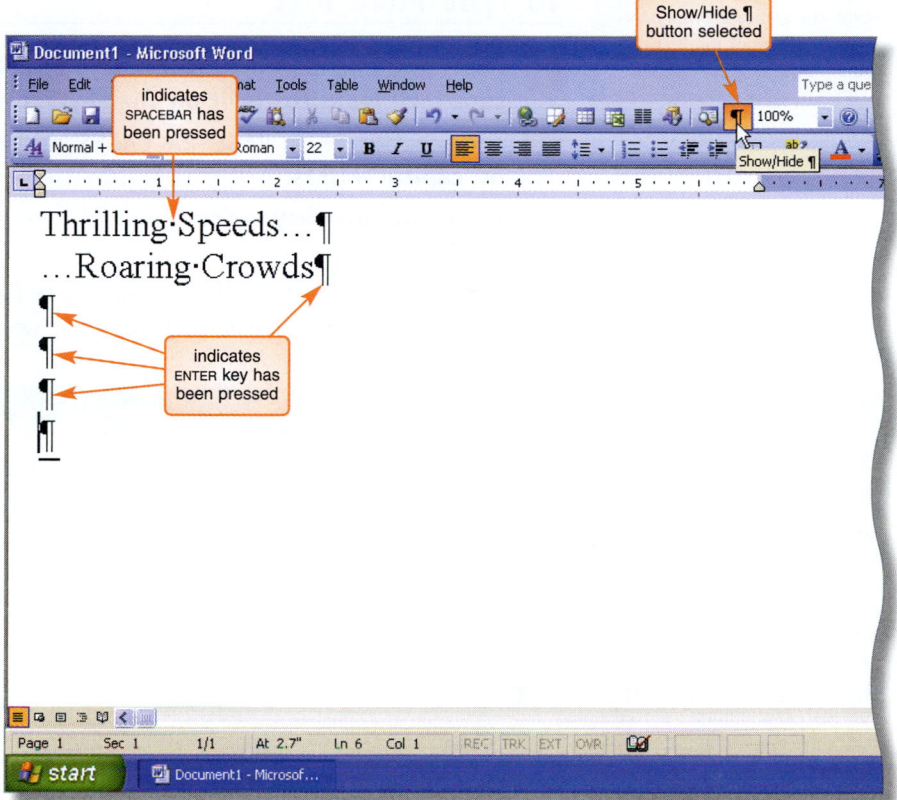

FIGURE 1-20

Notice several changes to the Word document window (Figure 1-20). A paragraph mark appears at the end of each line to indicate you pressed the ENTER key. Each time you press the ENTER key, Word creates a new paragraph. The size of paragraph marks is 22 point because the font size was changed earlier in the project. Between each word, a raised dot appears, indicating you pressed the SPACEBAR. Finally, the Show/Hide ¶ button changes from blue to light orange and has a blue outline, which indicates it is selected.

If you feel the formatting marks clutter the screen, you can hide them by clicking the Show/Hide ¶ button again. It is recommended that you display formatting marks; therefore, the document windows presented in this book show the formatting marks.

Other Ways

1. On Tools menu click Options, click View tab, click All check box, click OK button
2. Press CTRL+SHIFT+ASTERISK (*)
3. In Voice Command mode, say "Show Hide Paragraph"

More About

Zooming

If text is too small to read on the screen, you can zoom the document by clicking View on the menu bar, clicking Zoom, selecting the desired percentage, and then clicking the OK button. Changing the zoom percent has no effect on the printed document.

More About

Caps Lock

If you leave the CAPS LOCK key on and begin typing a new sentence, Word automatically corrects the problem for you. That is, it disengages the CAPS LOCK key and capitalizes only the first letter of the first word in the next sentence.

Entering More Text

Every character in the body title (GRAND PRIX RACE PACKAGES) of the announcement is in capital letters. The next step is to enter this body title in all capital letters in the document window, as explained below.

To Type More Text

1 Press the CAPS LOCK key on the keyboard to turn on capital letters. Verify the caps lock indicator is lit on the keyboard.

2 Type GRAND PRIX RACE PACKAGES and then press the CAPS LOCK key to turn off capital letters.

3 Press the ENTER key twice.

Word displays the body title on line 6 (Figure 1-21). Depending on your Word settings, your screen may not display the smart tag indicator below the word, RACE.

More About

Smart Tags

A smart tag is a button that automatically appears on the screen when Word performs a certain action. You then can use the smart tag to perform tasks more efficiently. Word notifies you of a smart tag by displaying a smart tag indicator, such as the purple dotted underline shown in Figure 1-21.

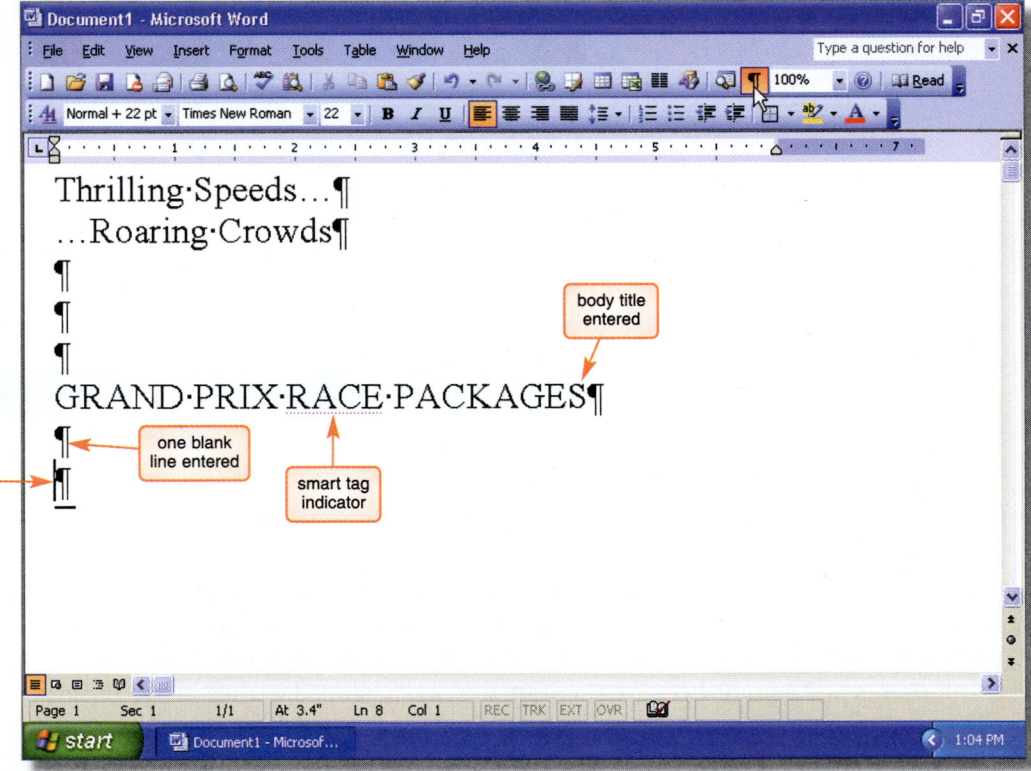

FIGURE 1-21

Using Wordwrap

Wordwrap allows you to type words in a paragraph continually without pressing the ENTER key at the end of each line. When the insertion point reaches the right margin, Word automatically positions the insertion point at the beginning of the next line. As you type, if a word extends beyond the right margin, Word also automatically positions that word on the next line with the insertion point.

As you type text in the document window, do not press the ENTER key when the insertion point reaches the right margin. Word creates a new paragraph each time you press the ENTER key. Thus, press the ENTER key only in these circumstances:

1. To insert blank lines in a document
2. To begin a new paragraph
3. To terminate a short line of text and advance to the next line
4. In response to certain Word commands

The following step illustrates wordwrap.

To Wordwrap Text as You Type

1

• **Type** Four-day, three-night packages include airfare, deluxe **and then press the SPACEBAR.**

The word, deluxe, wraps to the beginning of line 9 because it is too long to fit on line 8 (Figure 1-22). Your document may wordwrap differently depending on the type of printer you are using.

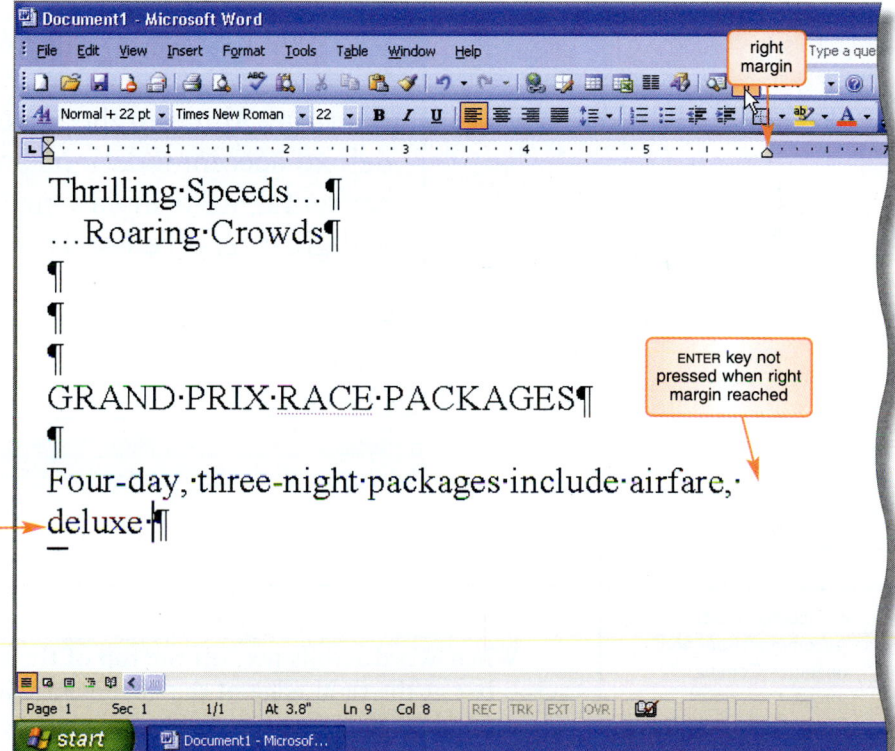

the word, deluxe, could not fit on line 8, so it wrapped to beginning of line 9

right margin

ENTER key not pressed when right margin reached

FIGURE 1-22

Entering Text that Scrolls the Document Window

As you type more lines of text than Word can display in the document window, Word **scrolls** the top portion of the document upward off the screen. Although you cannot see the text once it scrolls off the screen, it remains in the document. As previously discussed, the document window allows you to view only a portion of your document at one time (Figure 1-8 on page WD 10).

Microsoft Office
Word 2003

The following step shows how Word scrolls text through the document window.

To Enter Text that Scrolls the Document Window

1

• **Type** accommodations and amenities, compact car rental, a Formula One Grand Prix program, and great reserved seats for all race events.

• **Press the ENTER key twice.**

Word scrolls the headline off the top of the screen (Figure 1-23). Your screen may scroll differently depending on the type of monitor you are using.

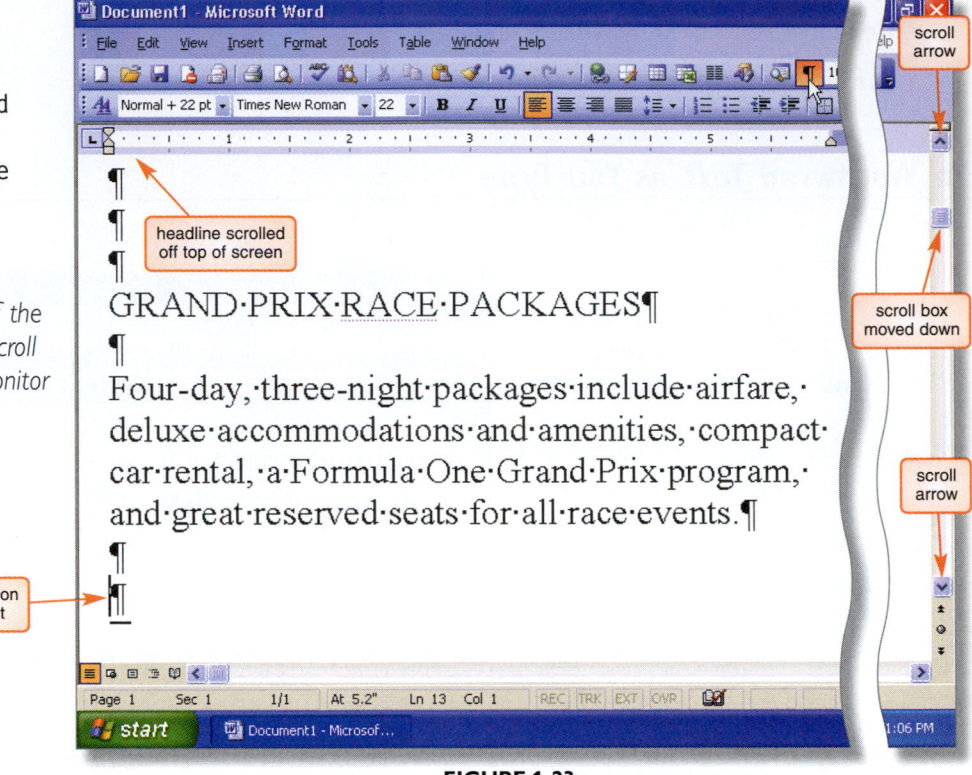

FIGURE 1-23

When Word scrolls text off the top of the screen, the scroll box on the vertical scroll bar at the right edge of the document window moves downward (Figure 1-23). The scroll box indicates the current relative location of the portion of the document that is displayed in the document window. You may use either the mouse or the keyboard to scroll to a different location in a document.

With the mouse, you can use the scroll arrows or the scroll box on the scroll bar to display a different portion of the document in the document window, and then click the mouse to move the insertion point to that location. Table 1-1 explains various techniques for using the scroll bar to scroll vertically with the mouse.

More About

Healthy Computing

For more information about healthy computing, visit the Word 2003 More About Web page (scsite.com/wd2003/more) and then click Healthy Computing.

Table 1-1	Using the Scroll Bar to Scroll with the Mouse
SCROLL DIRECTION	**MOUSE ACTION**
Up	Drag the scroll box upward.
Down	Drag the scroll box downward.
Up one screen	Click anywhere above the scroll box on the vertical scroll bar.
Down one screen	Click anywhere below the scroll box on the vertical scroll bar.
Up one line	Click the scroll arrow at the top of the vertical scroll bar.
Down one line	Click the scroll arrow at the bottom of the vertical scroll bar.

When you use the keyboard to scroll, the insertion point automatically moves when you press the appropriate keys. Table 1-2 outlines various techniques to scroll through a document using the keyboard.

Table 1-2	Scrolling with the Keyboard
SCROLL DIRECTION	**KEY(S) TO PRESS**
Left one character	LEFT ARROW
Right one character	RIGHT ARROW
Left one word	CTRL+LEFT ARROW
Right one word	CTRL+RIGHT ARROW
Up one line	UP ARROW
Down one line	DOWN ARROW
To end of a line	END
To beginning of a line	HOME
Up one paragraph	CTRL+UP ARROW
Down one paragraph	CTRL+DOWN ARROW
Up one screen	PAGE UP
Down one screen	PAGE DOWN
To top of document window	ALT+CTRL+PAGE UP
To bottom of document window	ALT+CTRL+PAGE DOWN
To beginning of a document	CTRL+HOME
To end of a document	CTRL+END

Q&A

Q: How can I help prevent wrist injury while working on a computer?

A: Typical computer users frequently switch between the keyboard and the mouse during a word processing session, an action that strains the wrist. To help prevent wrist injury, minimize switching. If your fingers already are on the keyboard, use keyboard keys to scroll. If your hand already is on the mouse, use the mouse to scroll.

Checking Spelling and Grammar as You Type

As you type text in the document window, Word checks your typing for possible spelling and grammar errors. If a word you type is not in the dictionary, a red wavy underline appears below the word. Similarly, if text you type contains a possible grammar error, a green wavy underline appears below the text. In both cases, the Spelling and Grammar Status icon on the status bar shows a red X, instead of a check mark. Although you can check the entire document for spelling and grammar errors at once, you also can check these flagged errors immediately.

To verify that the check spelling as you type feature is enabled, right-click the Spelling and Grammar Status icon on the status bar and then click Options on the shortcut menu. When Word displays the Spelling & Grammar dialog box, be sure Check spelling as you type has a check mark and Hide spelling errors in this document does not have a check mark.

When a word is flagged with a red wavy underline, it is not in Word's dictionary. To display a list of suggested corrections for a flagged word, you right-click the word. A flagged word, however, is not necessarily misspelled. For example, many names, abbreviations, and specialized terms are not in Word's main dictionary. In these cases, you tell Word to ignore the flagged word. As you type, Word also detects duplicate words. For example, if your document contains the phrase, to the the store, Word places a red wavy underline below the second occurrence of the word, the.

In the example on the next page, the word, feature, has been misspelled intentionally as feture to illustrate Word's check spelling as you type. If you are doing this project on a personal computer, your announcement may contain different misspelled words, depending on the accuracy of your typing.

To Check Spelling and Grammar as You Type

1

• **Type** Race events feture **and then press the SPACEBAR.**

• **Position the mouse pointer in the flagged word (feture, in this case).**

Word flags the misspelled word, feture, by placing a red wavy underline below it (Figure 1-24). The Spelling and Grammar Status icon on the status bar now contains a red X, indicating Word has detected a possible spelling or grammar error.

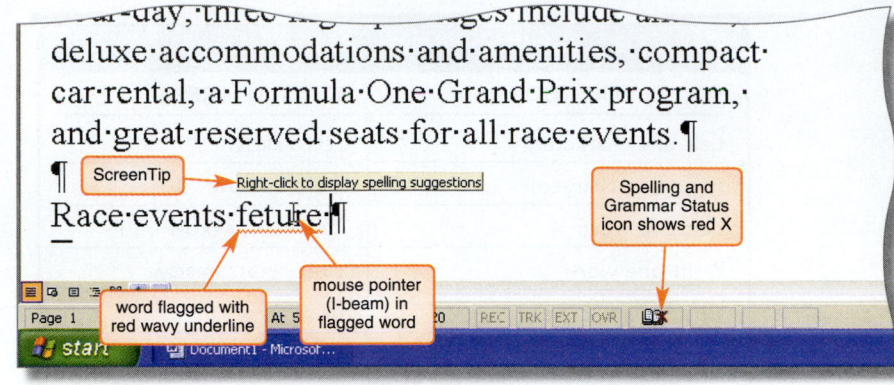

FIGURE 1-24

2

• **Right-click the flagged word, feture.**

Word displays a shortcut menu that lists suggested spelling corrections for the flagged word (Figure 1-25).

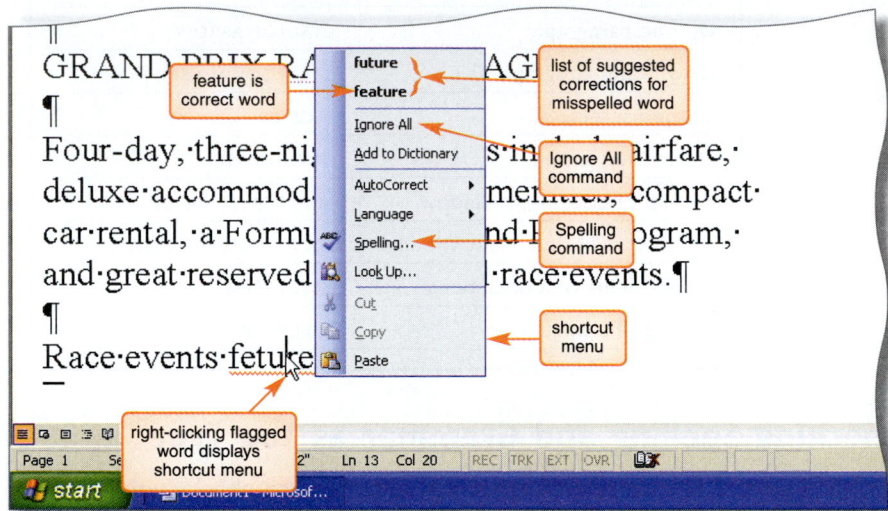

FIGURE 1-25

3

• **Click feature on the shortcut menu.**

Word replaces the misspelled word with the word selected on the shortcut menu (Figure 1-26). The Spelling and Grammar Status icon once again contains a red check mark.

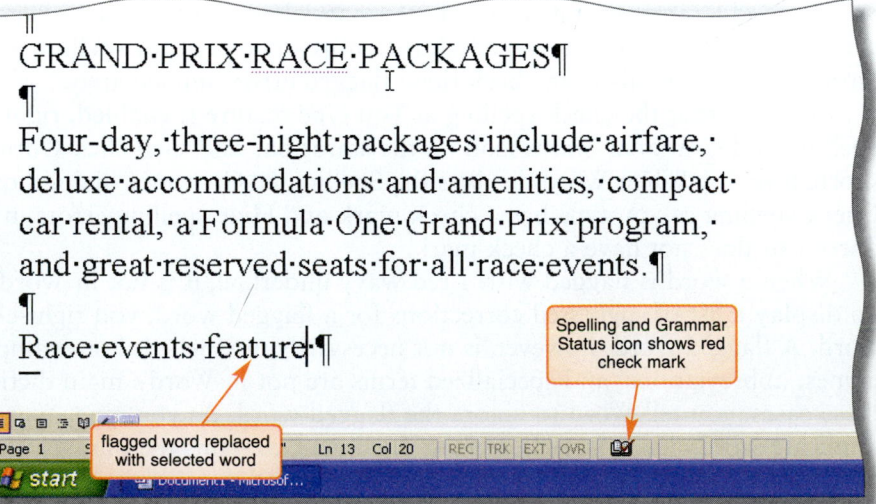

FIGURE 1-26

Other Ways

1. Double-click Spelling and Grammar Status icon on status bar, click correct word on shortcut menu
2. In Voice Command mode, say "Spelling and Grammar"

If a flagged word actually is spelled correctly and, for example, is a proper name, you can right-click it and then click Ignore All on the shortcut menu (Figure 1-25). If, when you right-click the misspelled word, your desired correction is not in the list on the shortcut menu, you can click outside the shortcut menu to close the menu and then retype the correct word, or you can click Spelling on the shortcut menu to display the Spelling dialog box. Project 2 discusses the Spelling dialog box.

If you feel the wavy underlines clutter the document window, you can hide them temporarily until you are ready to check for spelling and grammar errors. To hide spelling errors, right-click the Spelling and Grammar Status icon on the status bar and then click Hide Spelling Errors on the shortcut menu. To hide grammar errors, right-click the Spelling and Grammar Status icon on the status bar and then click Hide Grammatical Errors on the shortcut menu.

The next step is to type the remainder of text in the announcement, as described in the following steps.

To Enter More Text

1 Press the END key to move the insertion point to the end of the line.

2 Type all practice and qualifying sessions, the drivers' parade, and the gripping Formula One Grand Prix.

3 Press the ENTER key twice.

4 Type Call Beacon Travel at 555-2299.

The text of the announcement is complete (Figure 1-27).

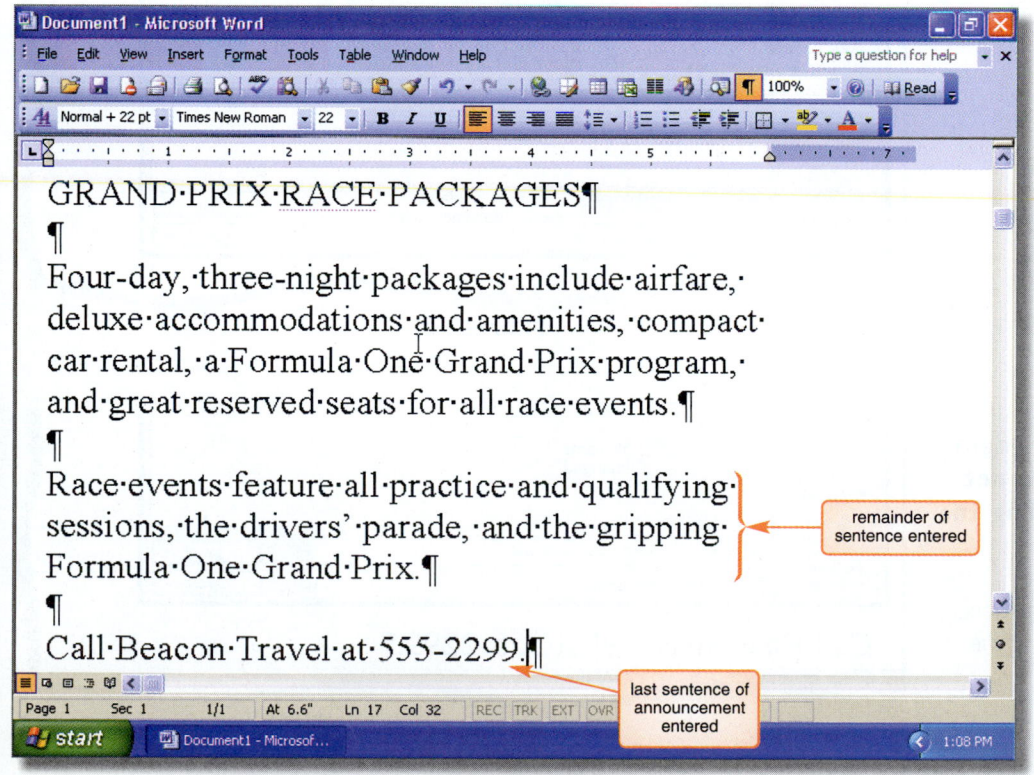

FIGURE 1-27

Saving a Document

As you create a document in Word, the computer stores it in memory. If the computer is turned off or if you lose electrical power, the document in memory is lost. Hence, if you plan to use the document later, you must save it on disk.

A saved document is called a **file**. A **file name** is the name assigned to a file when it is saved. This project saves the announcement with the file name, Grand Prix Announcement. Depending on your Windows settings, the file type .doc may display immediately after the file name. The file type **.doc** indicates the file is a Word document.

The following steps illustrate how to save a document on a floppy disk in drive A using the Save button on the Standard toolbar.

To Save a New Document

1

• **With a formatted floppy disk in drive A, click the Save button on the Standard toolbar.**

Word displays the Save As dialog box (Figure 1-28). The first line from the document (Thrilling Speeds) is selected in the File name text box as the default file name. You can change this selected file name by immediately typing the new name.

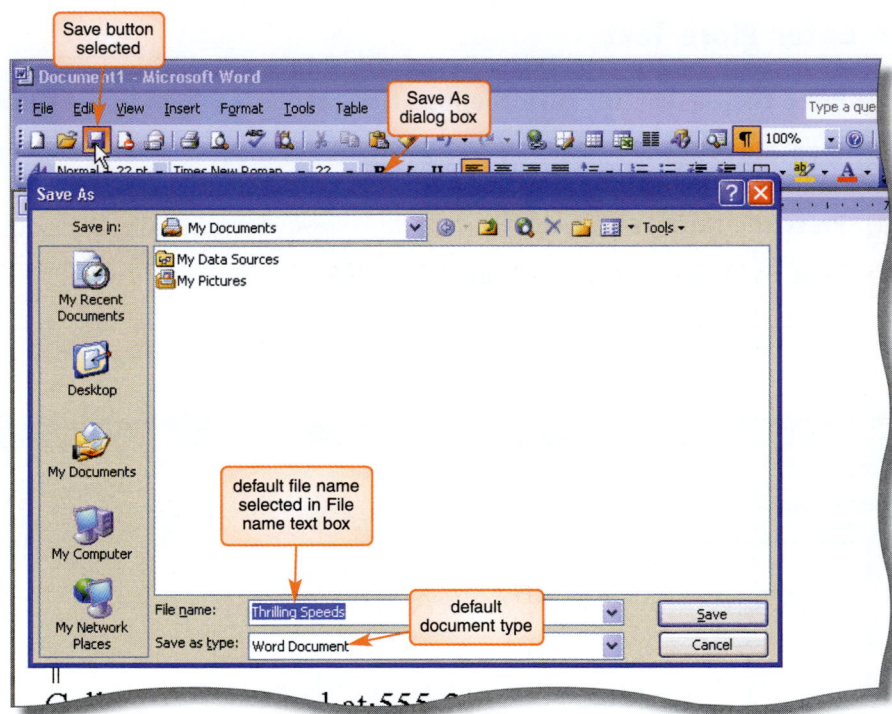

FIGURE 1-28

2

• **Type** Grand Prix Announcement **in the File name text box. Do not press the ENTER key after typing the file name.**

The file name, Grand Prix Announcement, replaces the text, Thrilling Speeds, in the File name text box (Figure 1-29).

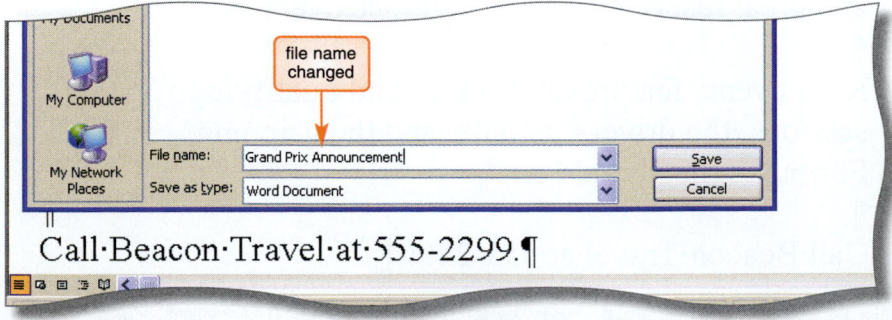

FIGURE 1-29

3

• **Click the Save in box arrow.**

Word displays a list of the available drives and folders in which you can save the document (Figure 1-30). A **folder** is a specific location on a disk. Your list may differ depending on your computer's configuration.

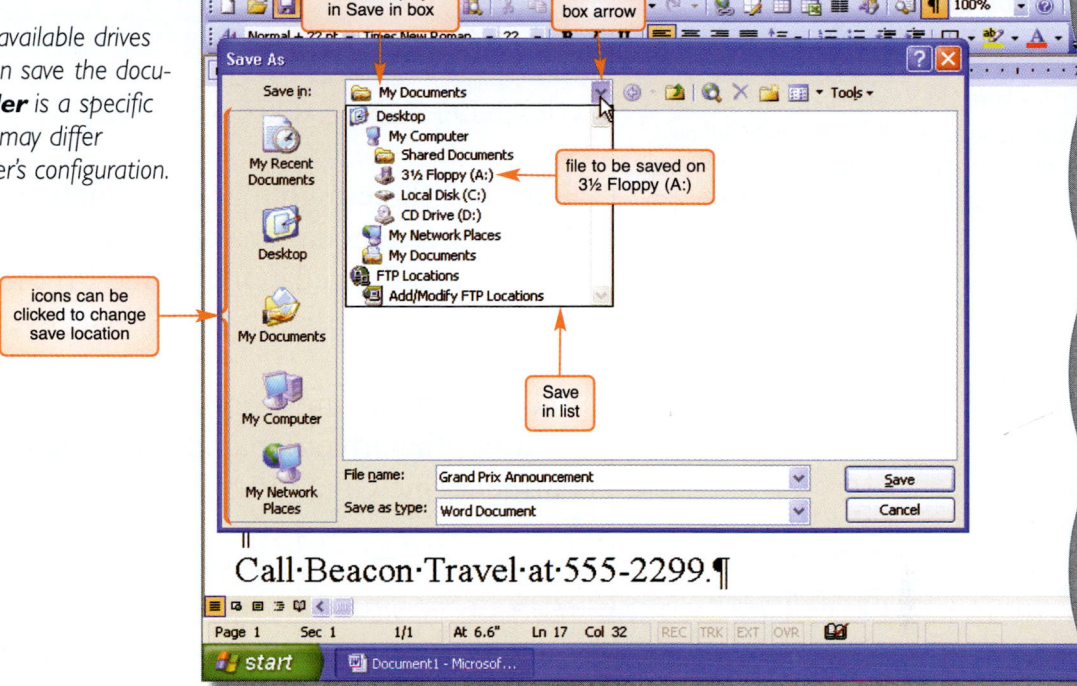

FIGURE 1-30

4

• **Click 3½ Floppy (A:) in the Save in list.**

Drive A becomes the new save location (Figure 1-31). The Save As dialog box now shows names of existing files stored on the floppy disk in drive A. In Figure 1-31, the list is empty because no Word files currently are stored on the floppy disk in drive A.

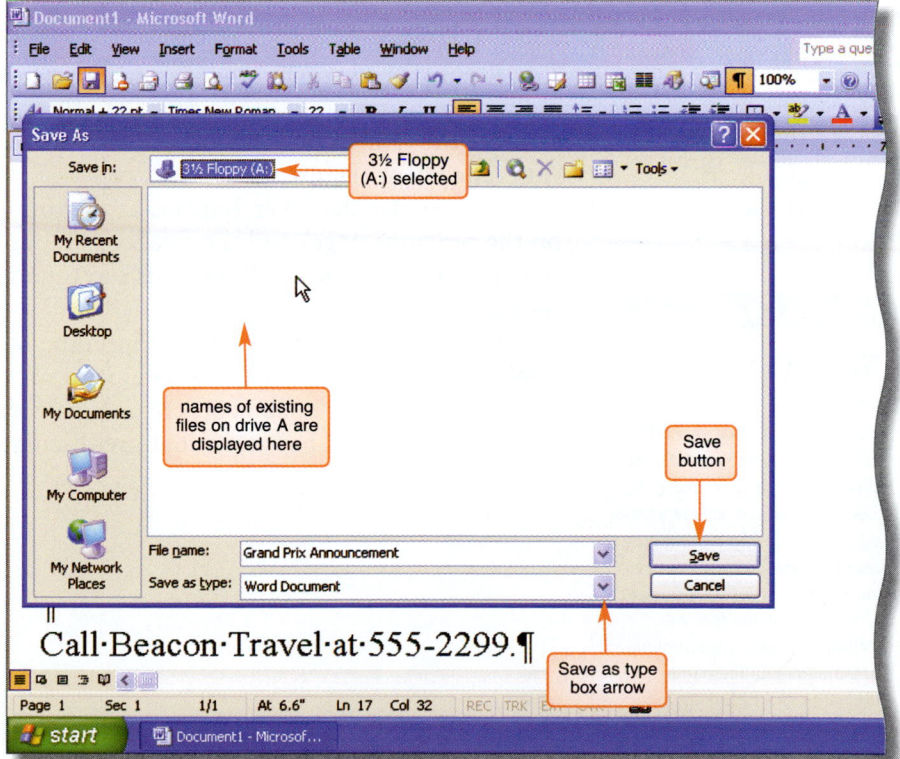

FIGURE 1-31

5

• **Click the Save button in the Save As dialog box.**

Word saves the document on the floppy disk in drive A with the file name, Grand Prix Announcement (Figure 1-32). Although the announcement is saved on a floppy disk, it also remains in main memory and on the screen.

title bar displays file name

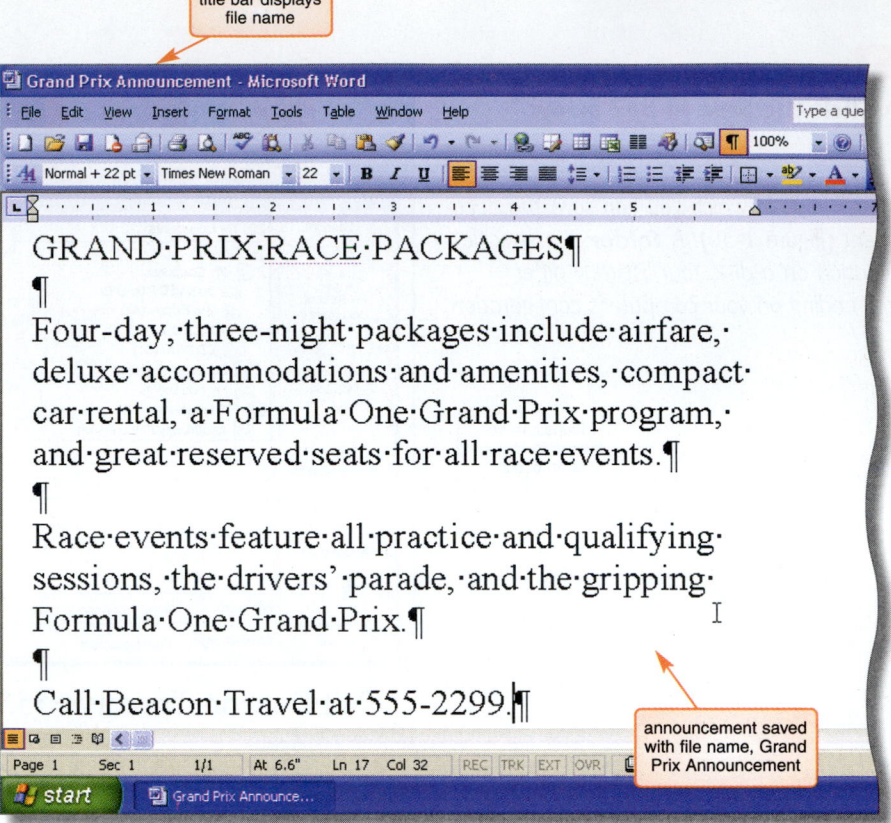

GRAND·PRIX·RACE·PACKAGES¶
¶
Four-day,·three-night·packages·include·airfare,· deluxe·accommodations·and·amenities,·compact· car·rental,·a·Formula·One·Grand·Prix·program,· and·great·reserved·seats·for·all·race·events.¶
¶
Race·events·feature·all·practice·and·qualifying· sessions,·the·drivers'·parade,·and·the·gripping· Formula·One·Grand·Prix.¶
¶
Call·Beacon·Travel·at·555-2299.¶

announcement saved with file name, Grand Prix Announcement

FIGURE 1-32

While Word is saving the document, it displays a message on the status bar indicating the progress of the save. After the save operation is complete, Word changes the name of the document on the title bar from Document1 to Grand Prix Announcement (Figure 1-32).

You can use the seven buttons at the top of the Save As dialog box (Figure 1-30 on the previous page) and the five icons along the left edge to change the save location and other tasks. Table 1-3 lists the function of the buttons and icons in the Save As dialog box.

When you click the Tools button in the Save As dialog box, Word displays the Tools menu. The Save Options command on the Tools menu allows you to save a backup copy of the document, create a password to limit access to the document, and carry out other functions that are discussed later.

Table 1-3	Save As Dialog Box Buttons and Icons	
BUTTON OR ICON	**BUTTON OR ICON NAME**	**FUNCTION**
	Default File Location	Displays contents of default file location
	Up One Level	Displays contents of folder one level up from current folder
	Search the Web	Starts Web browser and displays search engine
	Delete	Deletes selected file or folder
	Create New Folder	Creates new folder
	Views	Changes view of files and folders
Tools	Tools	Lists commands to print or modify file names and folders
My Recent Documents	My Recent Documents	Displays contents of My Recent Documents in Save in list (you cannot save to this location)

Table 1-3	Save As Dialog Box Buttons and Icons	
BUTTON OR ICON	**BUTTON OR ICON NAME**	**FUNCTION**
Desktop	Desktop	Displays contents of Windows desktop folder in Save in list to save quickly to the Windows desktop
My Documents	My Documents	Displays contents of My Documents in Save in list to save quickly to the My Documents folder
My Computer	My Computer	Displays contents of My Computer in Save in list to save quickly to another drive on the computer
My Network Places	My Network Places	Displays contents of My Network Places in Save in list to save quickly to My Network Places

Formatting Paragraphs and Characters in a Document

The text for Project 1 now is complete. The next step is to format the paragraphs and characters in the announcement.

Paragraphs encompass the text up to and including a paragraph mark (¶). **Paragraph formatting** is the process of changing the appearance of a paragraph. For example, you can center or indent a paragraph.

Characters include letters, numbers, punctuation marks, and symbols. **Character formatting** is the process of changing the way characters appear on the screen and in print. You use character formatting to emphasize certain words and improve readability of a document. For example, you can italicize or underline characters.

In many cases, you apply both paragraph and character formatting to the same text. For example, you may center a paragraph (paragraph formatting) and bold the characters in a paragraph (character formatting).

With Word, you can format paragraphs and characters before you type, or you can apply new formats after you type. Earlier, this project showed how to change the font size (character formatting) before you typed any text. This section shows how to format existing text.

Q & **A**

Q: What is the difference between character formatting and paragraph formatting?

A: Character formatting includes changing the font, font style, font size; adding an underline, color, strike-through, shadow, or outline; embossing; engraving; making a superscript or subscript; and changing the case of the letters. Paragraph formatting includes alignment; indentation; and spacing above, below, and in between lines.

Figure 1-33a shows the announcement before formatting its paragraphs and characters. Figure 1-33b shows the announcement after formatting. As you can see from the two figures, a document that is formatted is easier to read and looks more professional.

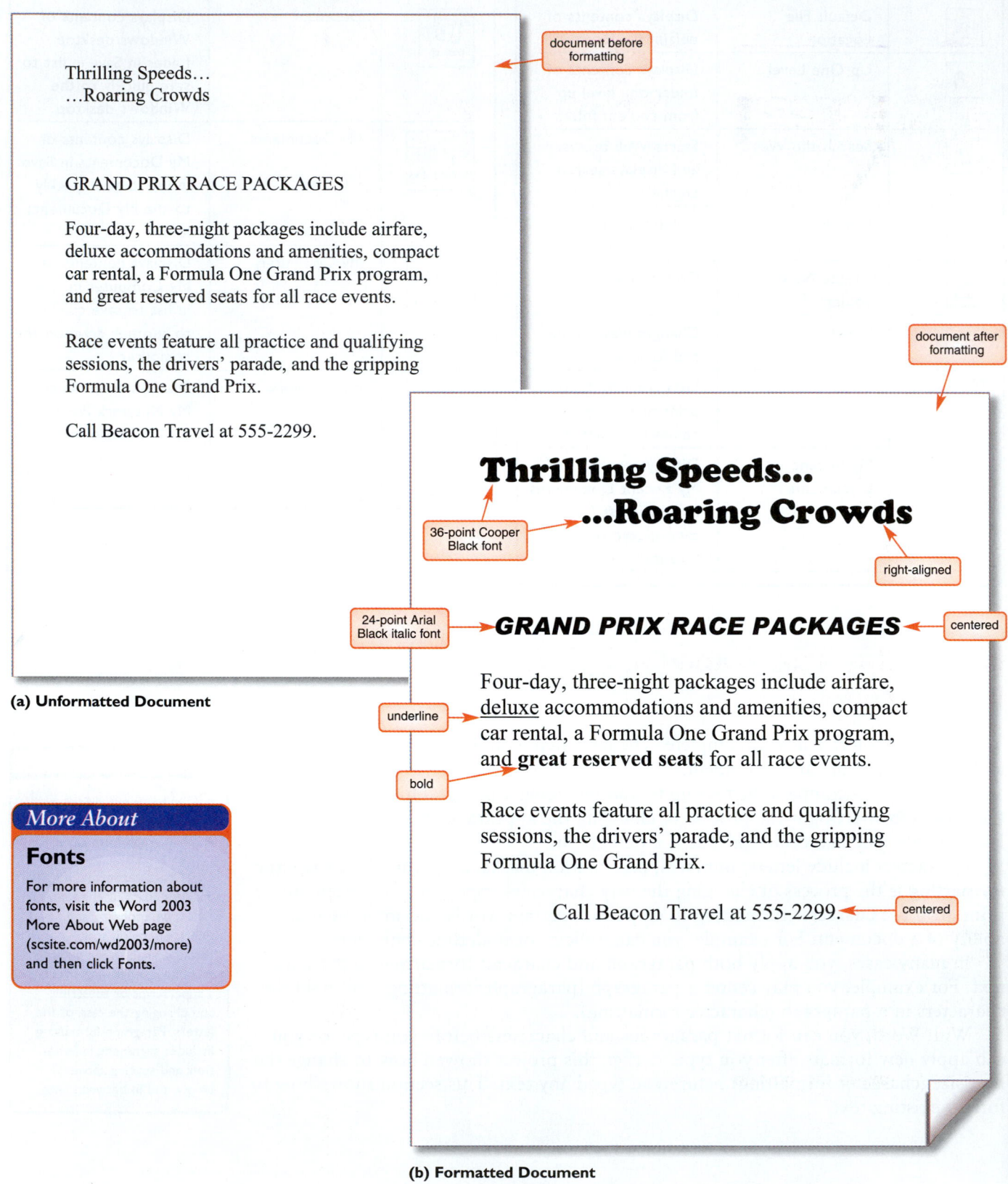

(a) Unformatted Document

(b) Formatted Document

FIGURE 1-33

Selecting and Formatting Paragraphs and Characters

To format a single paragraph, move the insertion point in the paragraph and then format the paragraph. That is, you do not need to select a single paragraph to format it. To format *multiple* paragraphs, however, you first must select the paragraphs you want to format and then format them. In the same manner, to format a single word, position the insertion point in the word and then format the word. To format multiple characters or words, however, you first must select the characters or words to be formatted and then format the selection.

Selected text is highlighted text. If your screen normally displays dark letters on a light background, then selected text displays light letters on a dark background.

Selecting Multiple Paragraphs

The first formatting step in this project is to change the font size of the characters in the headline. The headline consists of two separate lines, each ending with a paragraph mark. As previously discussed, Word creates a new paragraph each time you press the ENTER key. Thus, the headline actually is two separate paragraphs.

To change the font size of the characters in the headline, you first must **select** (highlight) both paragraphs in the headline, as shown in the following steps.

To Select Multiple Paragraphs

1

• **Press CTRL+HOME; that is, press and hold down the CTRL key, press the HOME key, and then release both keys.**

• **Move the mouse pointer to the left of the first paragraph to be selected until the mouse pointer changes to a right-pointing block arrow.**

CTRL+HOME is a keyboard shortcut that positions the insertion point at the top of the document. The mouse pointer changes to a right-pointing block arrow when positioned to the left of a paragraph (Figure 1-34).

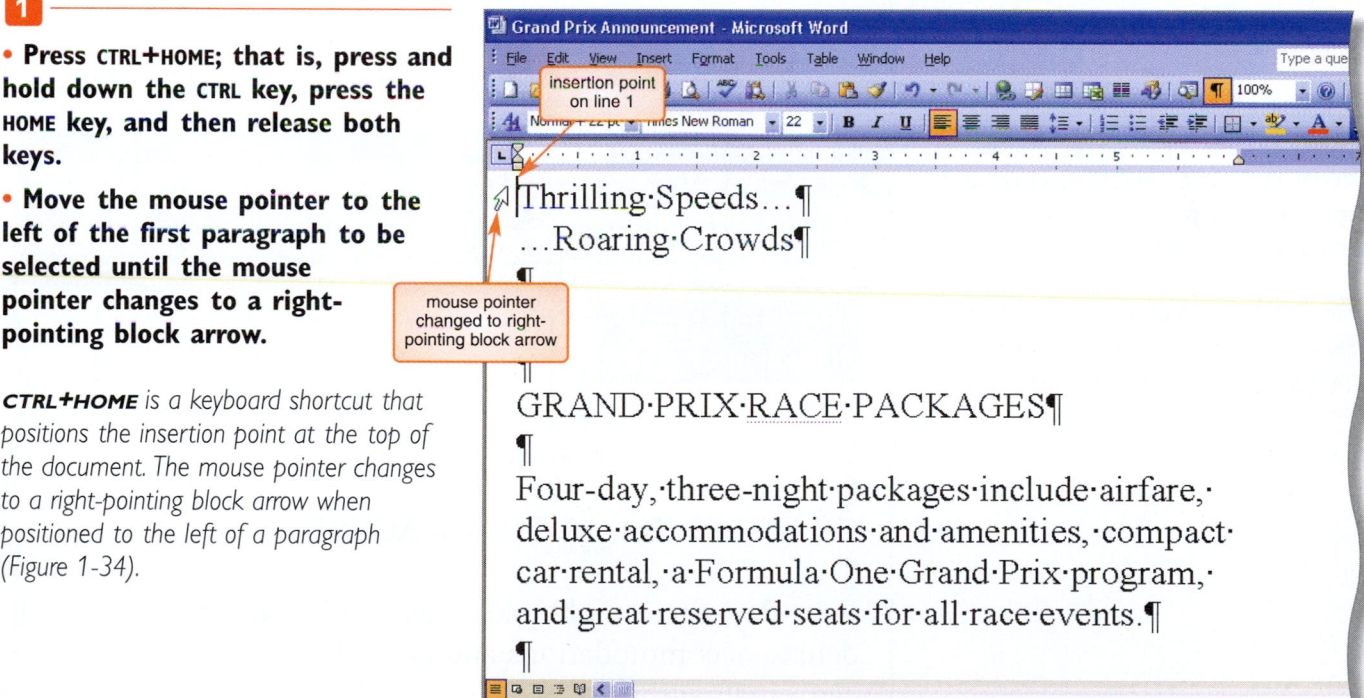

FIGURE 1-34

2

• **Drag downward until both paragraphs are selected.**

Word selects (highlights) both of the paragraphs (Figure 1-35). Dragging is the process of holding down the mouse button while moving the mouse and then releasing the mouse button.

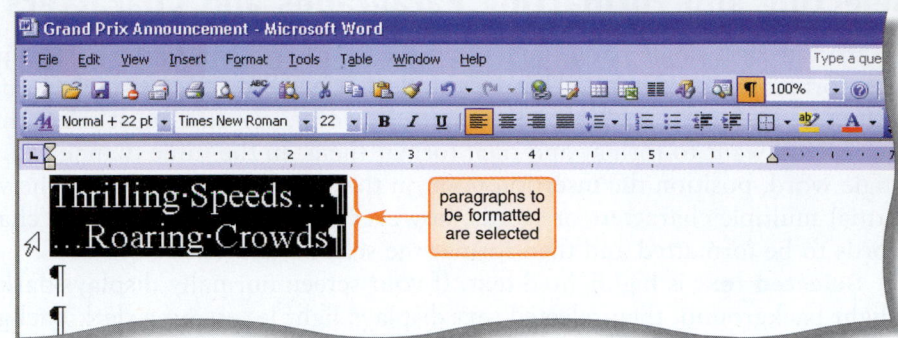

FIGURE 1-35

Changing the Font Size of Text

The next step is to increase the font size of the characters in the selected headline. Recall that the font size specifies the size of the characters. Earlier, this project showed how to change the font size to 22 for characters typed in the entire announcement. To give the headline more impact, it has a font size larger than the body copy. The following steps show how to increase the font size of the headline from 22 to 36 point.

To Change the Font Size of Text

1

• **With the text selected, click the Font Size box arrow on the Formatting toolbar.**

Word displays a list of available font sizes (Figure 1-36). Available font sizes vary depending on the current font and the printer driver.

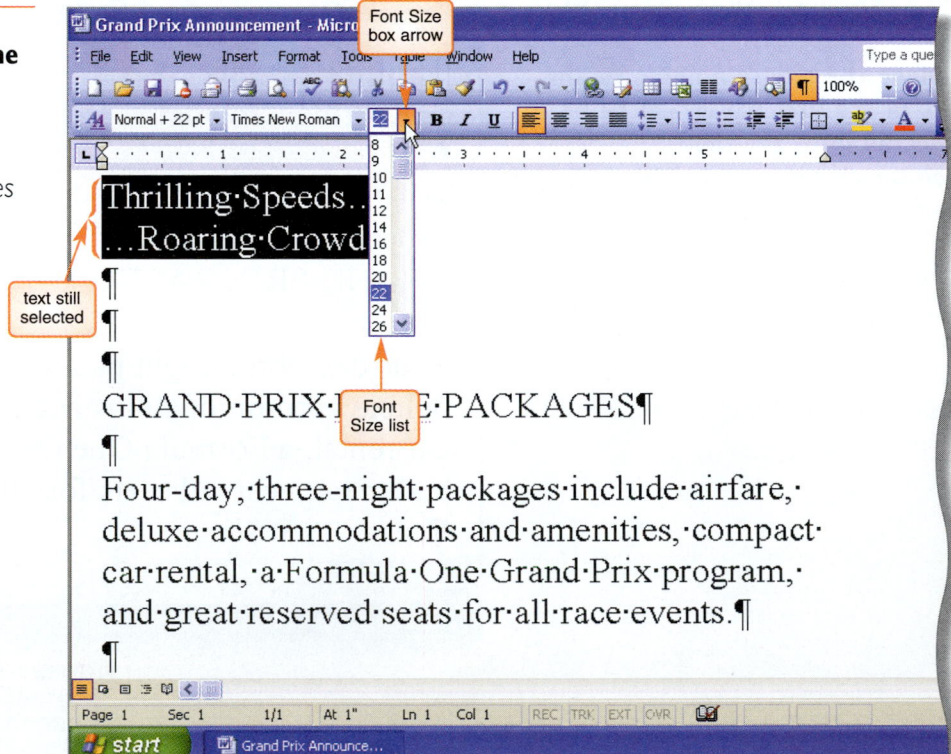

FIGURE 1-36

2

• **Click the down scroll arrow on the Font Size scroll bar until 36 appears in the list (Figure 1-37).**

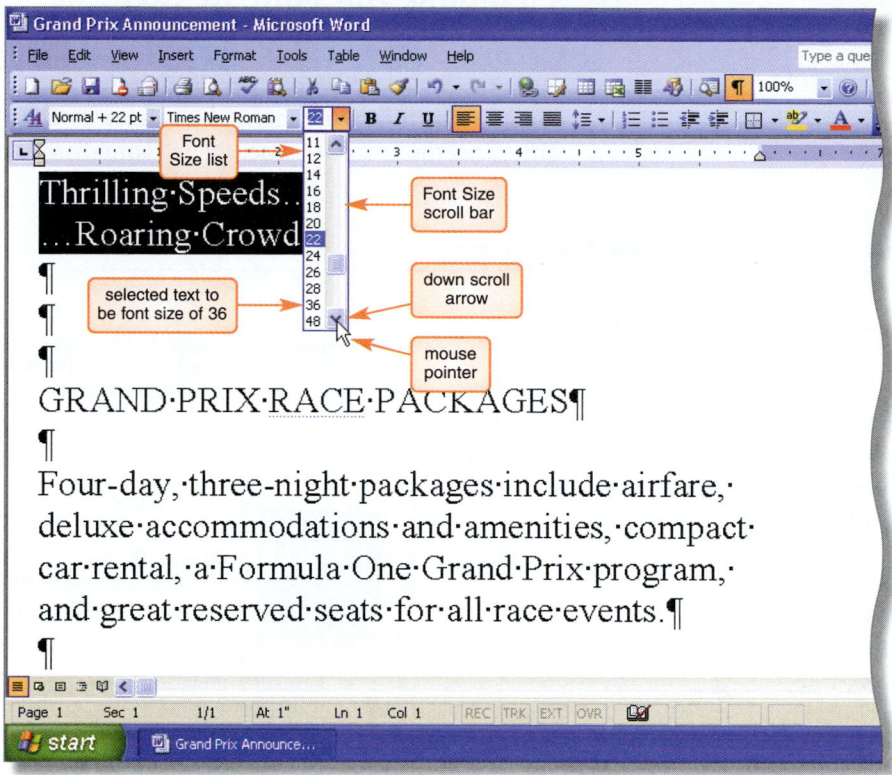

FIGURE 1-37

3

• **Click 36 in the Font Size list.**

Word increases the font size of the headline to 36 (Figure 1-38). The Font Size box on the Formatting toolbar displays 36, indicating the selected text has a font size of 36. Notice that when the mouse pointer is positioned in selected text, its shape is a left-pointing block arrow.

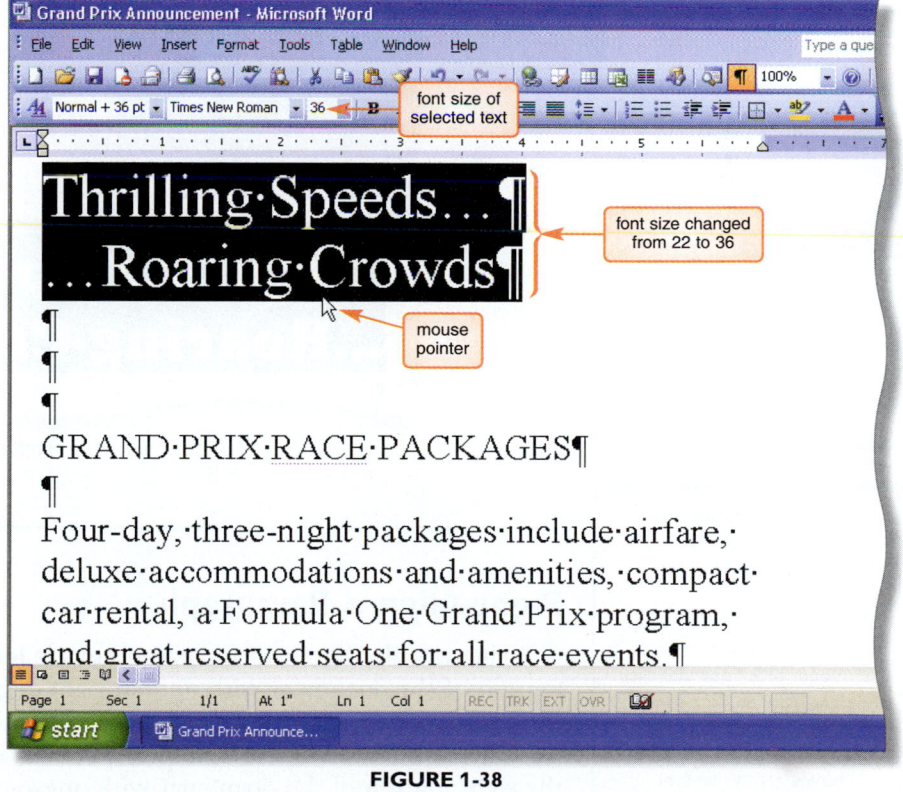

FIGURE 1-38

Changing the Font of Text

As mentioned earlier in this project, the default font in Word is Times New Roman. Word, however, provides many other fonts to add variety to your documents. The following steps show how to change the font of the headline in the announcement from Times New Roman to Cooper Black.

To Change the Font of Text

1

• **With the text selected, click the Font box arrow on the Formatting toolbar and then scroll through the Font list until Cooper Black (or a similar font) is displayed.**

Word displays a list of available fonts (Figure 1-39). Your list of available fonts may differ, depending on the type of printer you are using.

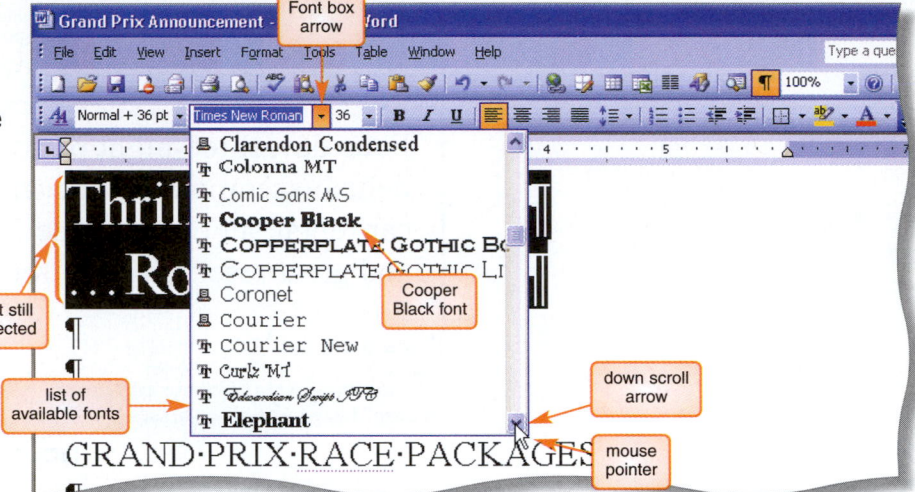

FIGURE 1-39

2

• **Click Cooper Black (or a similar font).**

Word changes the font of the selected text to Cooper Black (Figure 1-40).

FIGURE 1-40

Right-Align a Paragraph

The default alignment for paragraphs is **left-aligned**, that is, flush at the left margin of the document with uneven right edges. In Figure 1-41, the Align Left button is selected to indicate the paragraph containing the insertion point is left-aligned.

The second line of the headline, however, is to be **right-aligned**, that is, flush at the right margin of the document with uneven left edges. Recall that the second line of the headline is a paragraph, and paragraph formatting does not require you to select the paragraph prior to formatting. Just position the insertion point in the paragraph to be formatted and then format it accordingly.

The following steps show how to right-align the second line of the headline.

To Right-Align a Paragraph

1

• **Click somewhere in the paragraph to be right-aligned.**

Word positions the insertion point at the location you clicked (Figure 1-41).

FIGURE 1-41

2

• **Click the Align Right button on the Formatting toolbar.**

The second line of the headline now is right-aligned (Figure 1-42). Notice that you did not have to select the paragraph before right-aligning it. Formatting a single paragraph requires only that the insertion point be positioned somewhere in the paragraph.

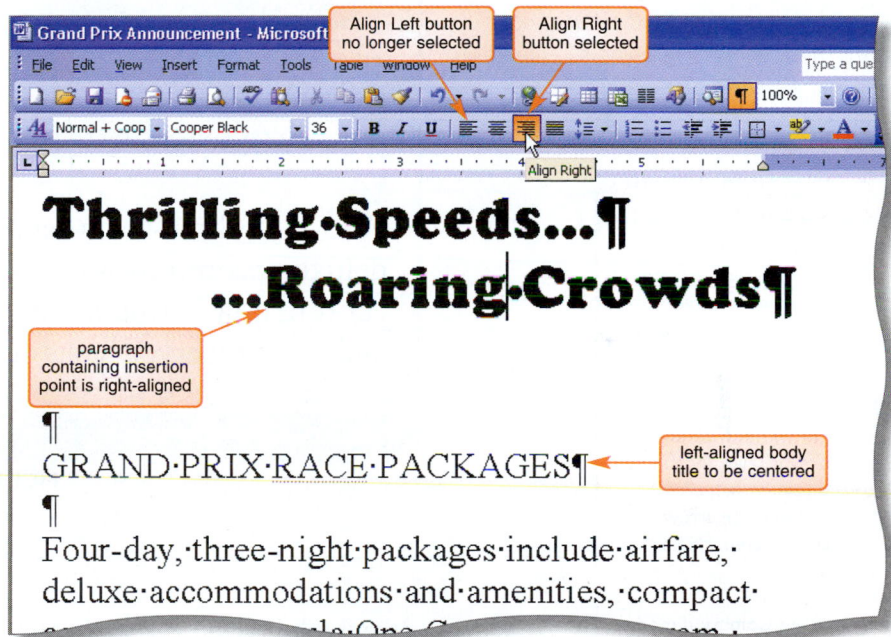

FIGURE 1-42

When a paragraph is right-aligned, the Align Right button on the Formatting toolbar is selected. If, for some reason, you wanted to return the paragraph to left-aligned, you would click the Align Left button on the Formatting toolbar.

Other Ways

1. On Format menu click Paragraph, click Indents and Spacing tab, click Alignment box arrow, click Right, click OK button
2. Right-click paragraph, click Paragraph on short-cut menu, click Indents and Spacing tab, click Alignment box arrow, click Right, click OK button
3. Press CTRL+R
4. In Voice Command mode, say "Align Right"

Center a Paragraph

The body title currently is left-aligned (Figure 1-42 on the previous page). The following step shows how to **center** the paragraph, that is, position its text horizontally between the left and right margins on the page.

To Center a Paragraph

1

• **Click somewhere in the paragraph to be centered.**

• **Click the Center button on the Formatting toolbar.**

Word centers the body title between the left and right margins (Figure 1-43). The Center button on the Formatting toolbar is selected, which indicates the paragraph containing the insertion point is centered.

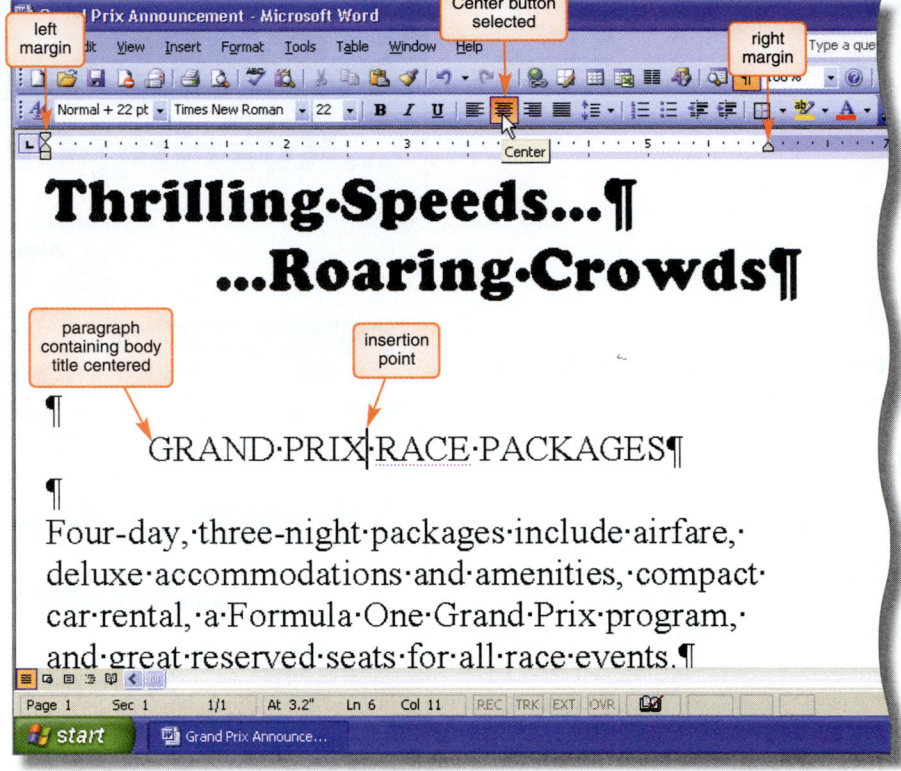

FIGURE 1-43

Other Ways

1. On Format menu click Paragraph, click Indents and Spacing tab, click Alignment box arrow, click Centered, click OK button
2. Right-click paragraph, click Paragraph on short-cut menu, click Indents and Spacing tab, click Alignment box arrow, click Centered, click OK button
3. Press CTRL+E
4. In Voice Command mode, say "Center"

More About

Centering

The Center button on the Formatting toolbar centers text horizontally between the left and right margins. You also can center text vertically between the top and bottom margins. To do this, click File on the menu bar, click Page Setup, click the Layout tab, click the Vertical alignment box arrow, click Center in the list, and then click the OK button.

When a paragraph is centered, the Center button on the Formatting toolbar is selected. If, for some reason, you wanted to return the paragraph to left-aligned, you would click the Align Left button on the Formatting toolbar.

Undoing, Redoing, and Repeating Commands or Actions

Word provides an Undo button on the Standard toolbar that you can use to cancel your recent command(s) or action(s). For example, if you format text incorrectly, you can undo the format and try it again. If, after you undo an action, you decide you did not want to perform the undo, you can use the Redo button to redo the undo. Word prevents you from undoing or redoing some actions, such as saving or printing a document.

The following steps show how to undo the center format to the body title using the Undo button and then re-center it using the Redo button.

To Undo and Redo an Action

 1

• **Click the Undo button on the Standard toolbar.**

Word returns the body title to its formatting before you issued the center command (Figure 1-44). That is, Word left-aligns the body title.

 2

• **Click the Redo button on the Standard toolbar.**

Word reapplies the center format to the body title (shown in Figure 1-43).

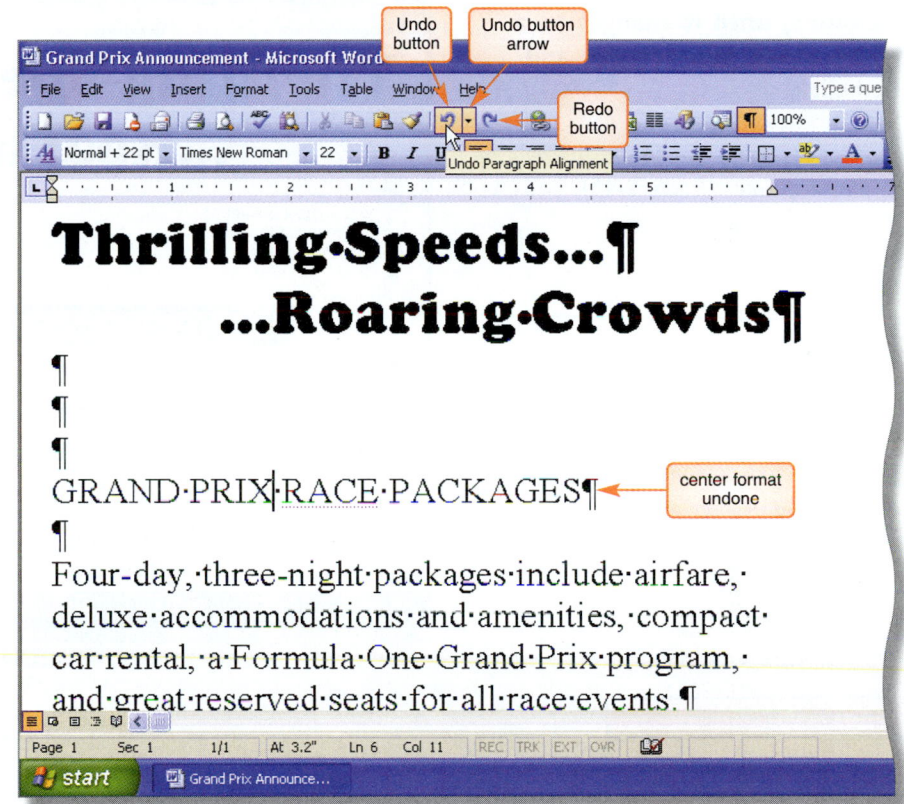

FIGURE 1-44

Other Ways

1. On Edit menu click Undo
2. Press CTRL+Z
3. In Voice Command mode, say "Undo"

You also can cancel a series of prior actions by clicking the Undo button arrow on the Standard toolbar (Figure 1-44) to display the list of undo actions and then dragging through the actions you wish to undo.

Whereas the Undo command cancels an action you did not want to perform, Word also provides a **Repeat command** on the Edit menu, which duplicates your last command so you can perform it again. For example, if you centered a paragraph and wish to format another paragraph the exact same way, you could click in the second paragraph to format, click Edit on the menu bar, and then click Repeat Paragraph Alignment. The text listed after Repeat varies, depending on your most recent action. If the action cannot be repeated, Word displays the text, Can't Repeat, on the Edit menu.

Selecting a Line and Formatting It

The characters in the body title, GRAND PRIX RACE PACKAGES, are to be a different font, larger font size, and italicized. To make these changes, you must select the line of text containing the body title, as shown in the following step.

To Select a Line

1

• **Move the mouse pointer to the left of the line to be selected (in this case, GRAND PRIX RACE PACKAGES) until it changes to a right-pointing block arrow and then click.**

Word selects the entire line to the right of the mouse pointer (Figure 1-45).

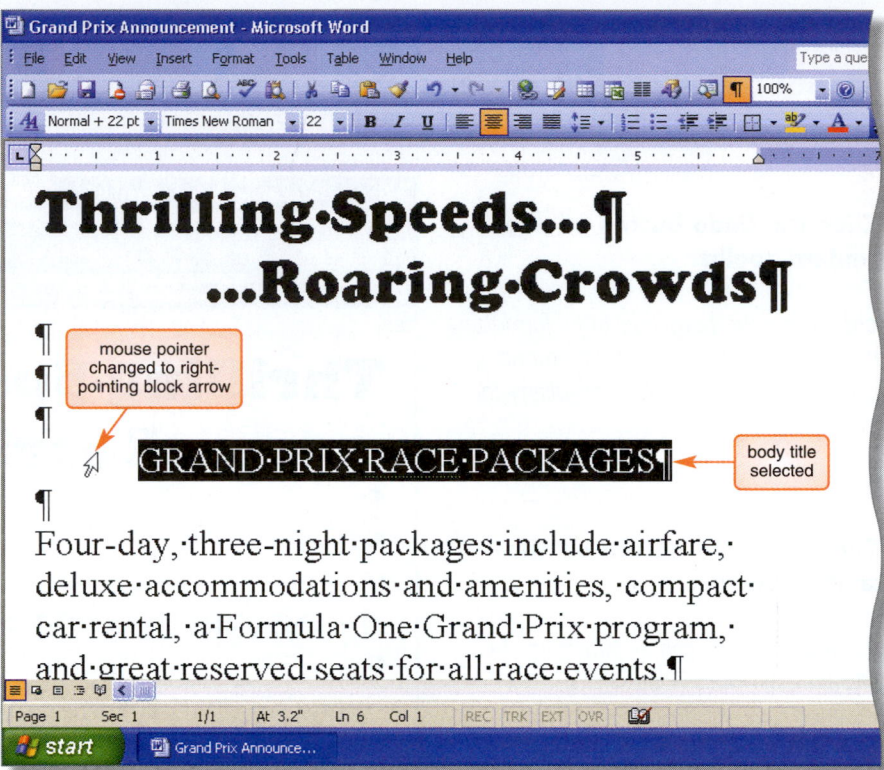

mouse pointer changed to right-pointing block arrow

body title selected

FIGURE 1-45

The next step is to change the font of the selected characters from Times New Roman to Arial Black and increase the font size of the selected characters from 22 to 24, as explained below.

To Format a Line of Text

1 **With the text selected, click the Font box arrow on the Formatting toolbar and then scroll to Arial Black (or a similar font) in the list. Click Arial Black (or a similar font).**

2 **With the text selected, click the Font Size box arrow on the Formatting toolbar and then click 24 in the list.**

Word changes the characters in the body title to 24-point Arial Black (Figure 1-46).

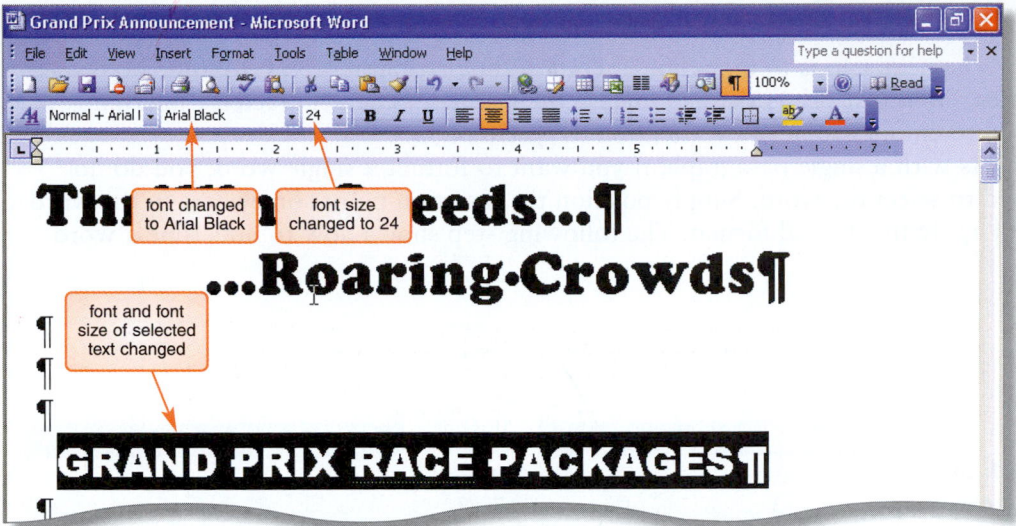

FIGURE 1-46

More About

Fonts

With some fonts, the formatting marks are not displayed on the screen properly. For example, the raised dot in each space may be displayed behind a character instead of in the space between two characters, causing the characters to look incorrect. Notice in Figure 1-46 that the formatting marks in the body title run into the characters. Recall that formatting marks do not print. Thus, the line will print fine.

Italicizing Text

Italicized text has a slanted appearance. The following step shows how to italicize the selected characters in the body title.

To Italicize Text

1

• **With the text still selected, click the Italic button on the Formatting toolbar.**

Word italicizes the text (Figure 1-47). The Italic button on the Formatting toolbar is selected.

FIGURE 1-47

When the selected text is italicized, the Italic button on the Formatting toolbar is selected. If, for some reason, you wanted to remove the italic format from the selected text, you would click the Italic button a second time, or you immediately could click the Undo button on the Standard toolbar.

Other Ways

1. On Format menu click Font, click Font tab, click Italic in Font style list, click OK button
2. Right-click selected text, click Font on shortcut menu, click Font tab, click Italic in Font style list, click OK button
3. Press CTRL+I
4. In Voice Command mode, say "Italic"

Underlining Text

The next step is to underline a word in the first paragraph below the body title. **Underlined** text prints with an underscore (_) below each character. Underlining is used to emphasize or draw attention to specific text.

As with a single paragraph, if you want to format a single word, you do not need to select the word. Simply position the insertion point somewhere in the word and apply the desired format. The following step shows how to underline a word.

To Underline a Word

1

• **Click somewhere in the word to be underlined (deluxe, in this case).**

• **Click the Underline button on the Formatting toolbar.**

Word underlines the word containing the insertion point (Figure 1-48). The Underline button on the Formatting toolbar is selected.

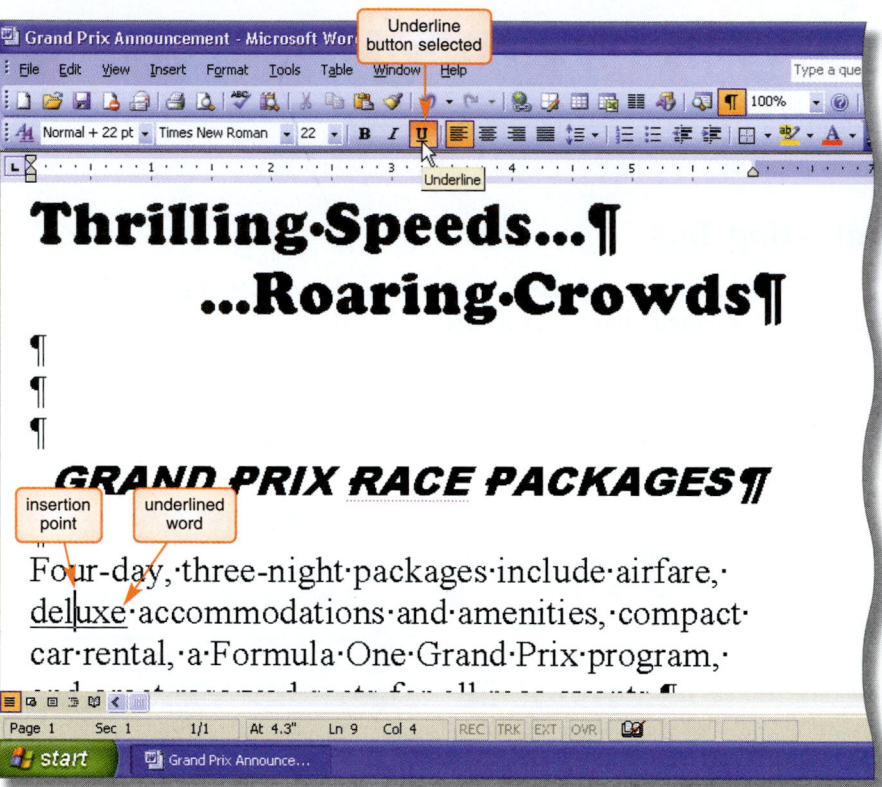

FIGURE 1-48

When the text containing the insertion point is underlined, the Underline button on the Formatting toolbar is selected. If, for some reason, you wanted to remove the underline from the text, you would click the Underline button a second time, or you immediately could click the Undo button on the Standard toolbar.

In addition to the basic underline shown in Figure 1-48, Word has many decorative underlines that are available through the Font dialog box. For example, you can use double underlines, dotted underlines, and wavy underlines. In the Font dialog box, you also can change the color of an underline and instruct Word to underline only the words and not the spaces between the words. To display the Font dialog box, click Format on the menu bar and then click Font.

Scrolling

The next text to format is in the lower portion of the announcement, which currently is not showing in the document window. To continue formatting the document, scroll down so the lower portion of the announcement is displayed in the document window, as shown in the following step.

To Scroll through a Document

- **Click the down scroll arrow on the vertical scroll bar nine times.**

Word scrolls through the document (Figure 1-49). Depending on your monitor type, your screen may scroll differently.

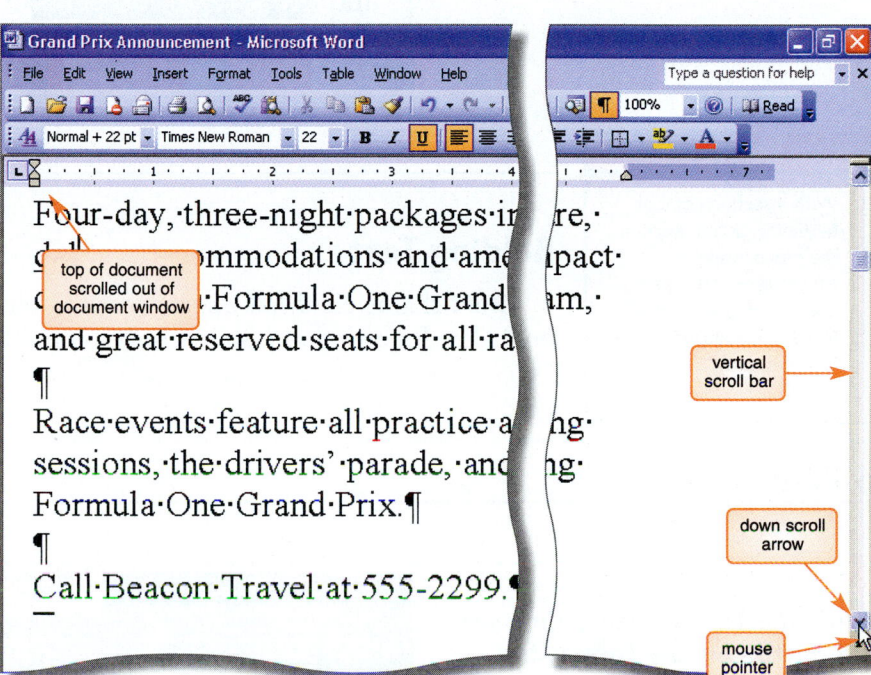

FIGURE 1-49

Other Ways

1. See Tables 1-1 and 1-2 on pages WD 24 and WD 25
2. In Dictation mode, say key name(s) in Table 1-2

Selecting a Group of Words

The next step is to bold the words, great reserved seats, in the announcement. To do this, you first must select this group of words. The following steps show how to select a group of words.

To Select a Group of Words

- **Position the mouse pointer immediately to the left of the first character of the text to be selected (in this case, the g in great).**

The mouse pointer's shape is an I-beam when positioned in unselected text in the document window (Figure 1-50).

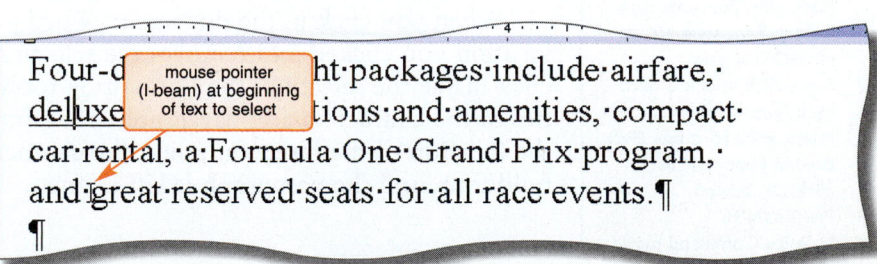

FIGURE 1-50

Microsoft Office Word 2003

2

• **Drag the mouse pointer through the last character of the text to be selected (in this case, the second s in seats).**

Word selects the phrase, great reserved seats (Figure 1-51).

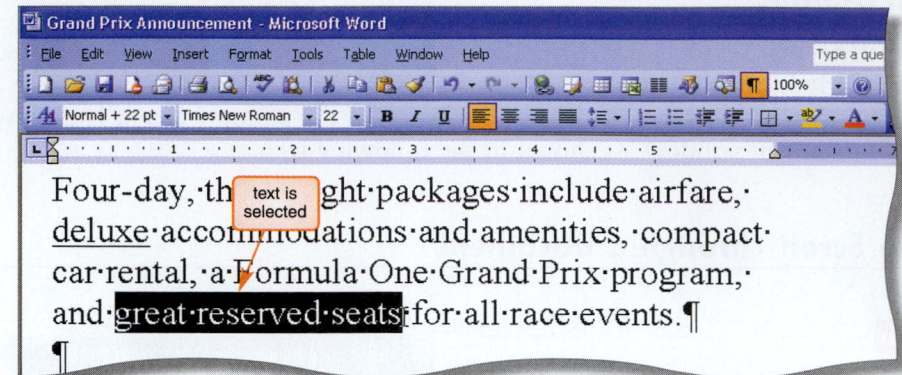

FiGURE 1-51

Bolding Text

Bold characters display somewhat thicker and darker than those that are not bold. The following step shows how to bold the selected phrase, great reserved seats.

To Bold Text

1

• **With the text selected, click the Bold button on the Formatting toolbar.**

• **Click inside the selected text to remove the selection (highlight).**

Word formats the selected text in bold and positions the insertion point inside the bold text (Figure 1-52). The Bold button on the Formatting toolbar is selected.

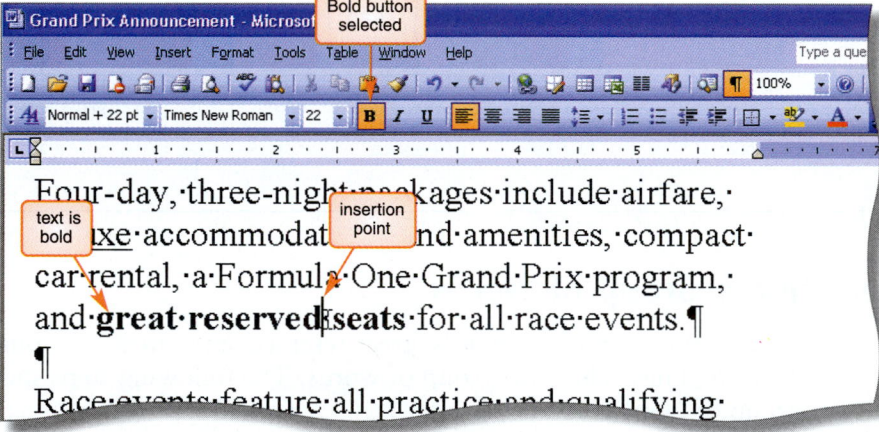

FIGURE 1-52

When you click in the document, Word positions the insertion point at the location you clicked and removes the selection (highlight) from the screen. If you click inside the selection, the Formatting toolbar displays the formatting characteristics of the characters and paragraphs containing the insertion point. For example, at the location of the insertion point, the characters are a 22-point Times New Roman bold font, and the paragraph is left-aligned.

When the selected text is bold, the Bold button on the Formatting toolbar is selected. If, for some reason, you wanted to remove the bold format from the selected text, you would click the Bold button a second time, or you immediately could click the Undo button on the Standard toolbar.

The next step is to center the last line of the announcement, as described in the following steps.

To Center a Paragraph

1 Click somewhere in the paragraph to be centered (in this case, the last line of the announcement).

2 Click the Center button on the Formatting toolbar.

Word centers the last line of the announcement (Figure 1-53).

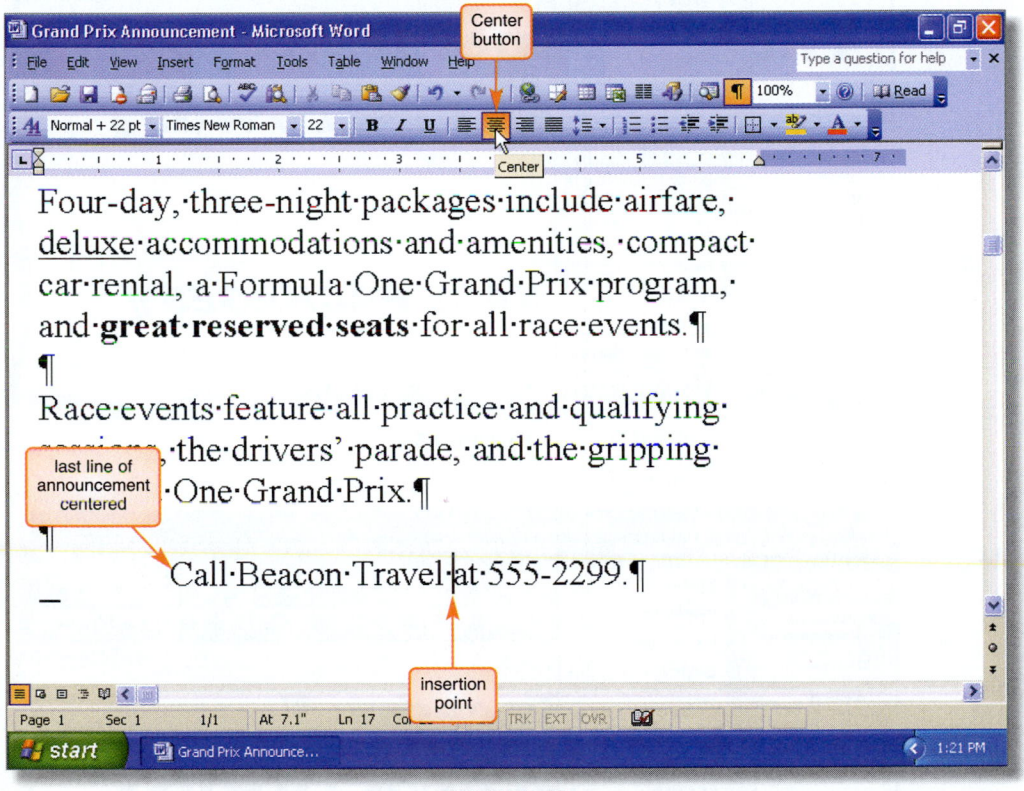

FIGURE 1-53

The formatting for the announcement now is complete.

Inserting Clip Art in a Word Document

Files containing graphical images, also called **graphics**, are available from a variety of sources. Word includes many predefined graphics, called **clip art**, that you can insert in a document. Clip art is located in the **Clip Organizer**, which contains a collection of clips, including clip art, as well as photographs, sounds, and video clips.

Inserting Clip Art

The next step in the project is to insert clip art of a race car in the announcement between the headline and the body title. Recall that Word has 14 task panes, some of which automatically appear as you perform certain operations. When you use the Clip Art command, Word automatically displays the Clip Art task pane. The following steps show how to use the Clip Art task pane to insert clip art in a document.

To Insert Clip Art in a Document

1

• **To position the insertion point where you want the clip art to be located, press CTRL+HOME and then press the DOWN ARROW key three times.**

• **Click Insert on the menu bar.**

Word positions the insertion point on the second paragraph mark below the headline, and displays the Insert menu (Figure 1-54). Remember that a short menu initially displays, which expands into a full menu after a few seconds.

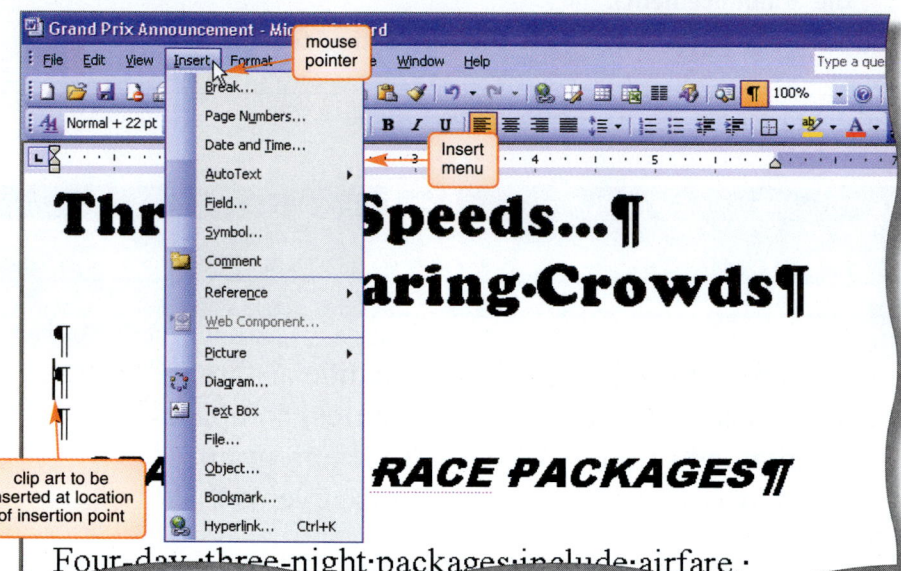

FIGURE 1-54

2

• **Point to Picture on the Insert menu.**

Word displays the Picture submenu (Figure 1-55). As discussed earlier, when you point to a command that has a small arrow to its right, Word displays a submenu associated with that command.

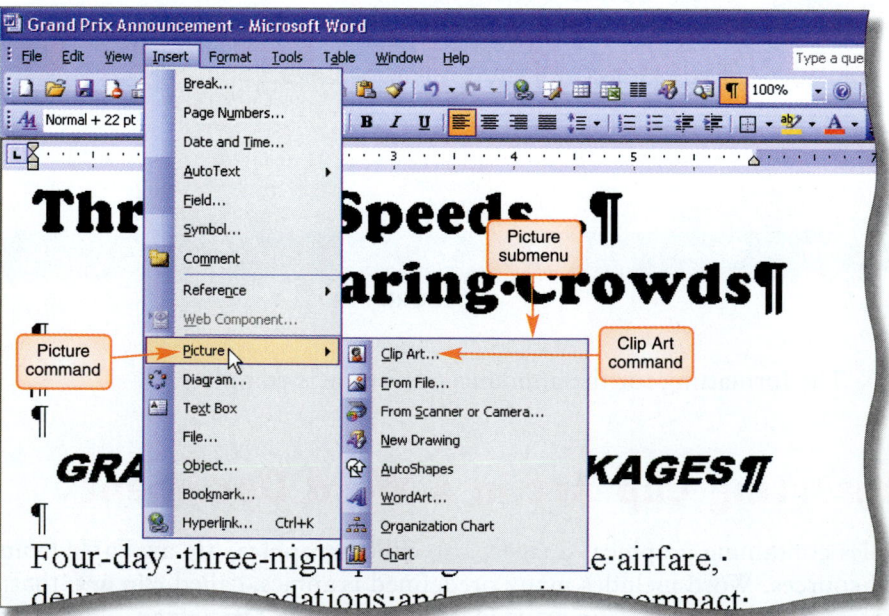

FIGURE 1-55

3

• **Click Clip Art on the Picture submenu.**

• **If the Search for text box contains text, drag through the text to select it.**

• **Type** race car **in the Search for text box.**

Word displays the Clip Art task pane at the right edge of the Word window (Figure 1-56). Recall that a task pane is a separate window that enables you to carry out some Word tasks more efficiently. When you click the Go button, Word searches the Clip Organizer for clips that match the description you type in the Search for text box.

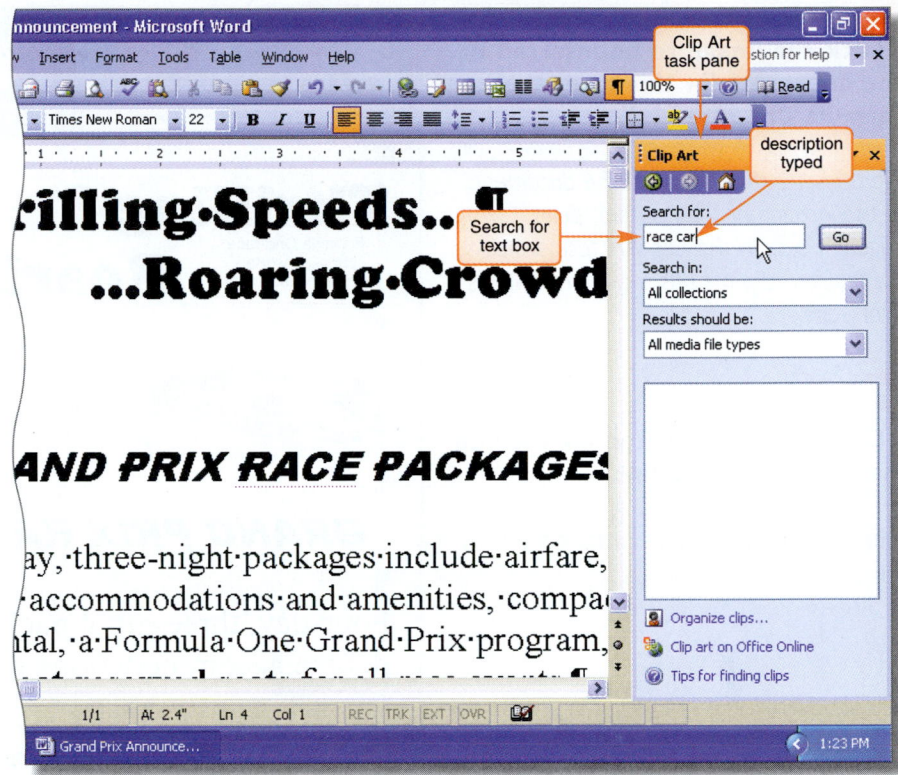

FIGURE 1-56

4

• **Click the Go button.**

Word displays a list of clips that match the description, race car (Figure 1-57). If you are connected to the Web, the Clip Art task pane displays clips from the Web, as well as those installed on your hard disk.

FIGURE 1-57

5

• **Click the image to be inserted in the document (in this case, the Formula One race car).**

Word inserts the clip art in the document at the location of the insertion point (Figure 1-58). In the Clip Art task pane, the selected clip art has a box arrow at its right edge.

6

• **Click the Close button on the Clip Art task pane title bar.**

Word removes the Clip Art task pane from the screen.

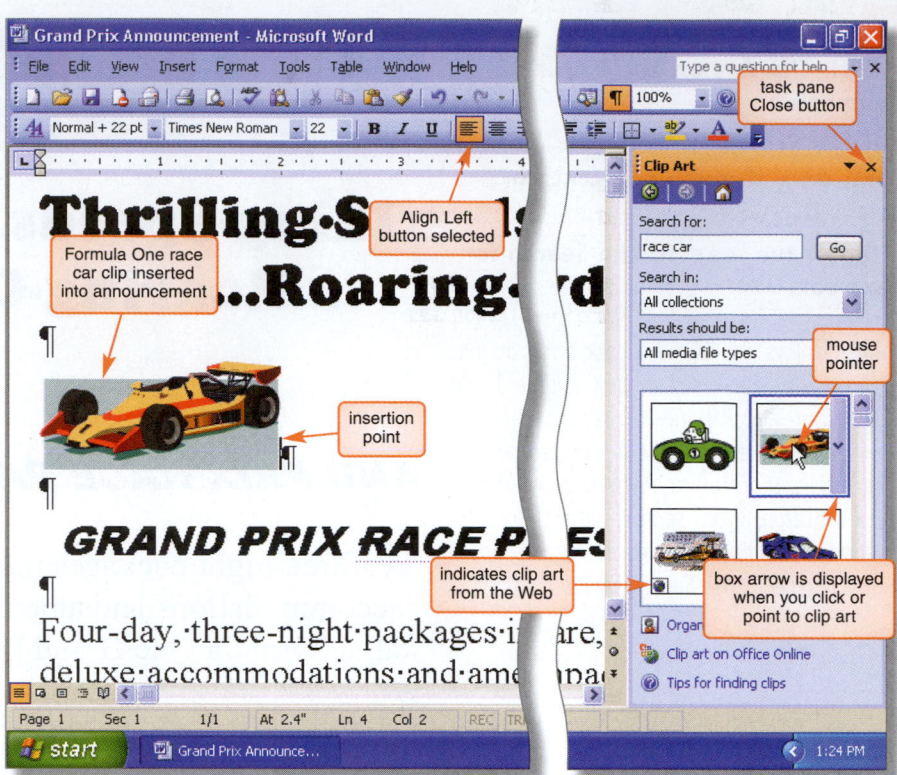

FIGURE 1-58

The clip art in the announcement is part of a paragraph. Because that paragraph is left-aligned, the clip art also is left-aligned. Notice the Align Left button on the Formatting toolbar is selected (Figure 1-58). You can use any of the paragraph alignment buttons on the Formatting toolbar to reposition the clip art. The following step shows how to center a graphic that is part of a paragraph.

To Center a Paragraph Containing a Graphic

1 **With the insertion point on the paragraph mark containing the clip art, click the Center button on the Formatting toolbar.**

Word centers the paragraph, which also centers the graphic in the paragraph (Figure 1-59).

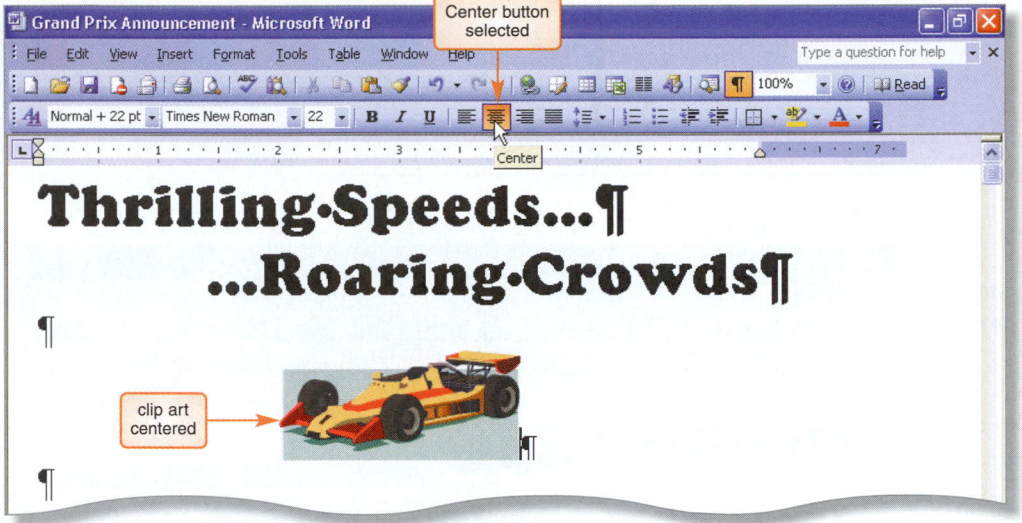

FIGURE 1-59

More About

Clip Art Packages

For more information about the clip art available for purchase, visit the Word 2003 More About Web page (scsite.com/wd2003/more) and then click Clip Art.

Resizing a Graphic

The clip art in this announcement is to be a larger size. Once you have inserted a graphic in a document, you easily can change its size. **Resizing** includes both enlarging and reducing the size of a graphic. To resize a graphic, you first must select it. Thus, the following step shows how to select a graphic.

Q: Where should a graphic be positioned in an announcement?

A: Emphasize a graphic by placing it at the optical center of the page. To determine optical center, divide the page in half horizontally and vertically. The optical center is located one third of the way up the vertical line from the point of intersection of the two lines.

To Select a Graphic

1

• **Click anywhere in the graphic.**

• **If your screen does not display the Picture toolbar, click View on the menu bar, point to Toolbars, and then click Picture.**

*Word selects the graphic (Figure 1-60). A selected graphic is displayed surrounded by a **selection rectangle**, which has small squares, called **sizing handles**, at each corner and middle location. You use the sizing handles to change the size of the graphic. When a graphic is selected, the Picture toolbar automatically should appear on the screen.*

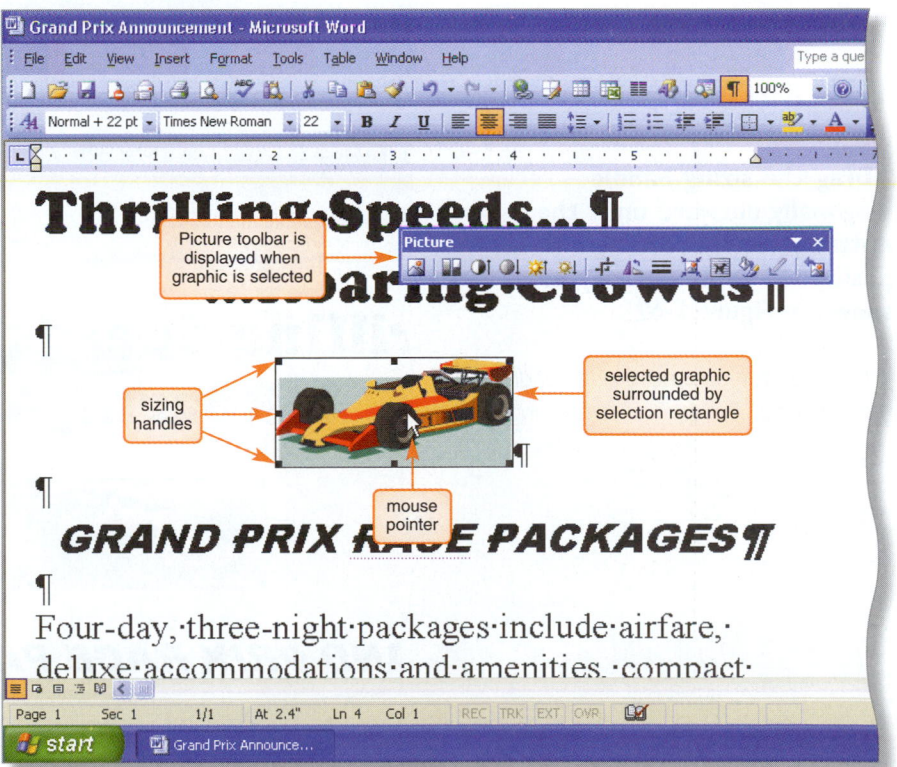

FIGURE 1-60

The following steps show how to resize the graphic just inserted and selected.

To Resize a Graphic

1

• **With the graphic still selected, point to the upper-right corner sizing handle.**

The mouse pointer shape changes to a two-headed arrow when it is on a sizing handle (Figure 1-61). To resize a graphic, you drag the sizing handle(s) until the graphic is the desired size.

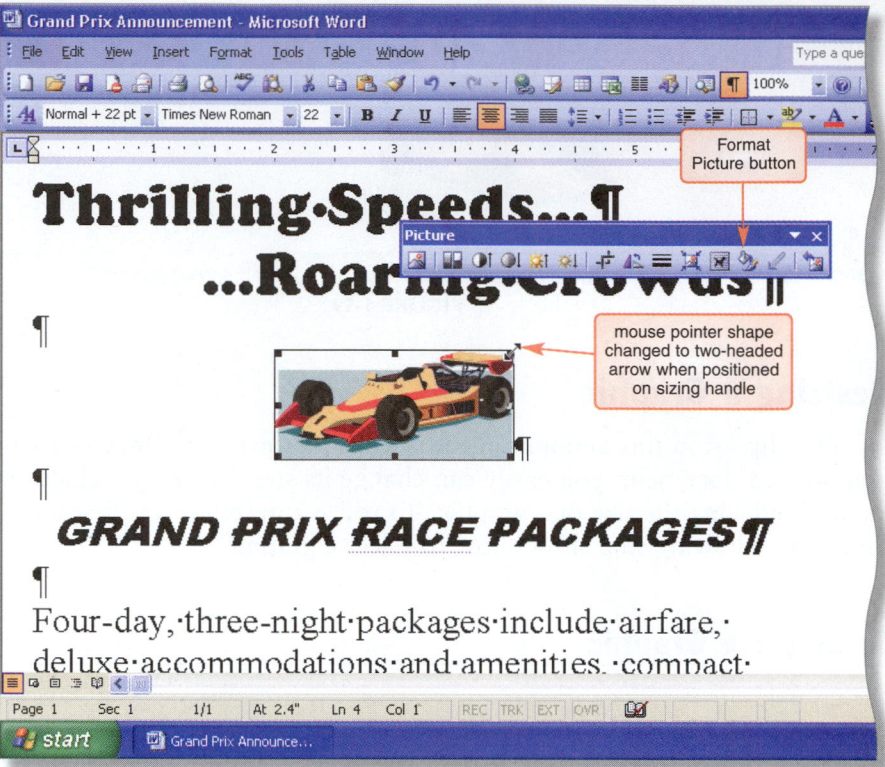

FIGURE 1-61

2

• **Drag the sizing handle diagonally outward until the dotted selection rectangle is positioned approximately as shown in Figure 1-62.**

When you drag a corner sizing handle, the proportions of the graphic remain intact.

FIGURE 1-62

3

• **Release the mouse button. Press CTRL+HOME.**

Word resizes the graphic (Figure 1-63). When you click outside of a graphic or press a key to scroll through a document, Word deselects the graphic. The Picture toolbar disappears from the screen when you deselect a graphic.

graphic resized

FIGURE 1-63

Instead of resizing a selected graphic by dragging a sizing handle with the mouse, you also can use the Format Picture dialog box to resize a graphic by clicking the Format Picture button on the Picture toolbar (Figure 1-61) and then clicking the Size tab. In the Size sheet, you can enter exact height and width measurements. If you have a precise measurement for a graphic, use the Format Picture dialog box; otherwise, drag the sizing handles to resize a graphic.

Sometimes, you might resize a graphic and realize it is the wrong size. In this case, you may want to return the graphic to its original size and start again. To restore a resized graphic to its exact original size, click the graphic to select it and then click the Format Picture button on the Picture toolbar to display the Format Picture dialog box. Click the Size tab, click the Reset button, and then click the OK button.

Saving an Existing Document with the Same File Name

The announcement for Project 1 now is complete. To transfer the modified document with the formatting changes and graphic to the floppy disk in drive A, you must save the document again. When you saved the document the first time, you assigned a file name to it (Grand Prix Announcement). When you use the procedure on the next page, Word automatically assigns the same file name to the document each time you subsequently save it.

To Save an Existing Document with the Same File Name

1

• **Click the Save button on the Standard toolbar.**

Word saves the document on a floppy disk inserted in drive A using the currently assigned file name, Grand Prix Announcement (Figure 1-64).

FIGURE 1-64

While Word is saving the document, the Background Save icon appears near the right edge of the status bar. When the save is complete, the document remains in memory and on the screen.

If, for some reason, you want to save an existing document with a different file name, click Save As on the File menu to display the Save As dialog box. Then, fill in the Save As dialog box as discussed in Steps 2 through 5 on pages WD 28 through WD 30.

Printing a Document

The next step is to print the document you created. A printed version of the document is called a **hard copy** or **printout**. The following steps show how to print the announcement created in this project.

To Print a Document

1

• **Ready the printer according to the printer instructions.**

• **Click the Print button on the Standard toolbar.**

The mouse pointer briefly changes to an hourglass shape as Word prepares to print the document. While the document is printing, a printer icon appears in the notification area on the Windows taskbar (Figure 1-65).

2

• **When the printer stops printing the document, retrieve the printout, which should look like Figure 1-1 on page WD 5.**

FIGURE 1-65

When you use the Print button to print a document, Word prints the entire document automatically. You then may distribute the printout or keep it as a permanent record of the document.

If you wanted to print multiple copies of the document, display the Print dialog box by clicking File on the menu bar and then clicking Print. In addition to the number of copies, the Print dialog box has several printing options.

If you wanted to cancel your job that is printing or one you have waiting to be printed, double-click the printer icon on the taskbar (Figure 1-65). In the printer window, click the job to be canceled and then click Cancel on the Document menu.

Other Ways

1. On File menu click Print, click OK button
2. Press CTRL+P, press ENTER
3. In Voice Command mode, say "Print"

Q&A

Q: How can I save ink, print faster, or decrease printer overrun errors?

A: Print a draft. Click File on the menu bar, click Print, click the Options button, place a check mark in the Draft output check box, and then click the OK button in each dialog box.

Quitting Word

After you create, save, and print the announcement, Project 1 is complete. The following steps show how to quit Word and return control to Windows.

To Quit Word

1

• **Position the mouse pointer on the Close button on the right side of the title bar (Figure 1-66).**

2

• **Click the Close button.**

The Word window closes.

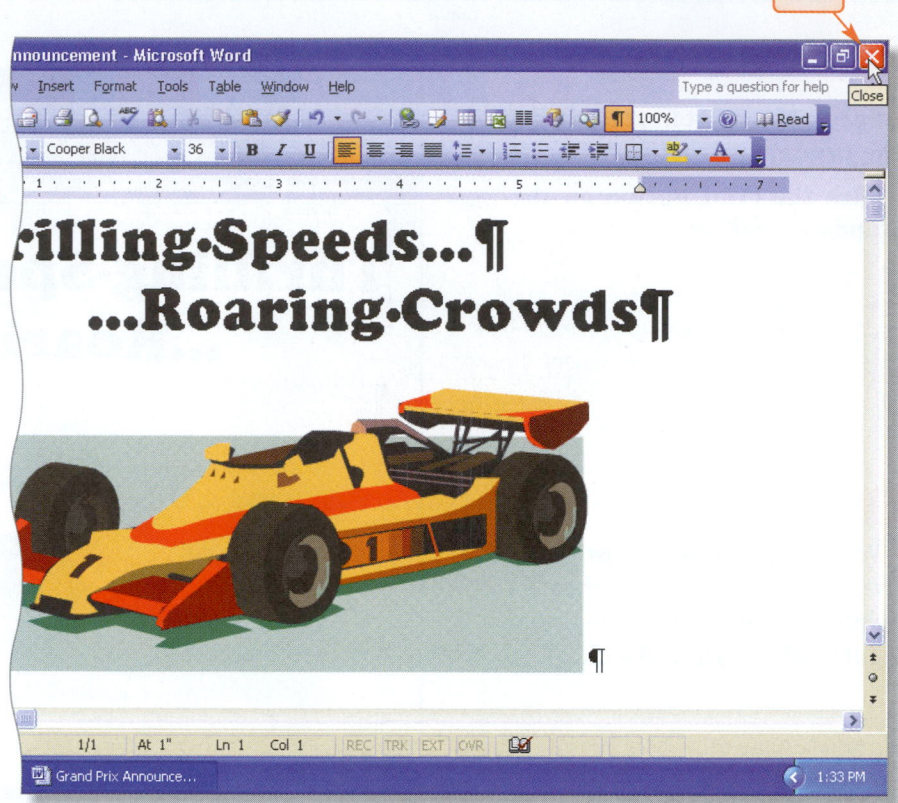

FIGURE 1-66

When you quit Word, a dialog box may display asking if you want to save the changes. This occurs if you made changes to the document since the last save. Clicking the Yes button in the dialog box saves the changes; clicking the No button ignores the changes; and clicking the Cancel button returns to the document. If you did not make any changes since you saved the document, this dialog box usually is not displayed.

Starting Word and Opening a Document

Once you have created and saved a document, you often will have reason to retrieve it from disk. For example, you might want to revise the document or print it again. Earlier, you saved the Word document created in Project 1 on a floppy disk using the file name, Grand Prix Announcement.

The following steps, which assume Word is not running, show how to open the Grand Prix Announcement file from a floppy disk in drive A.

To Open a Document

1

• **With your floppy disk in drive A, click the Start button on the Windows taskbar, point to All Programs on the Start menu, point to Microsoft Office on the All Programs submenu, and then click Microsoft Office Word 2003 on the Microsoft Office submenu.**

Word starts. The Open area of the Getting Started task pane lists up to four of the most recently used files (Figure 1-67).

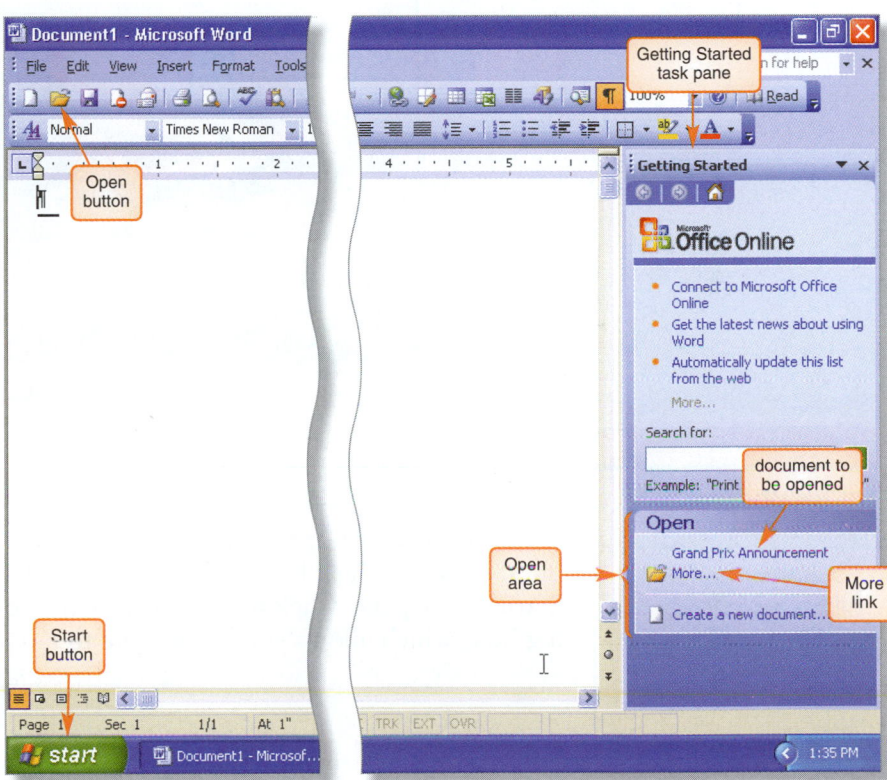

FIGURE 1-67

More About

Opening Files

In Word, you can open a recently used file by clicking File on the menu bar and then clicking the file name on the File menu. To instruct Word to show the recently used documents on the File menu, click Tools on the menu bar, click Options, click the General tab, click Recently used file list to place a check mark in the check box, and then click the OK button.

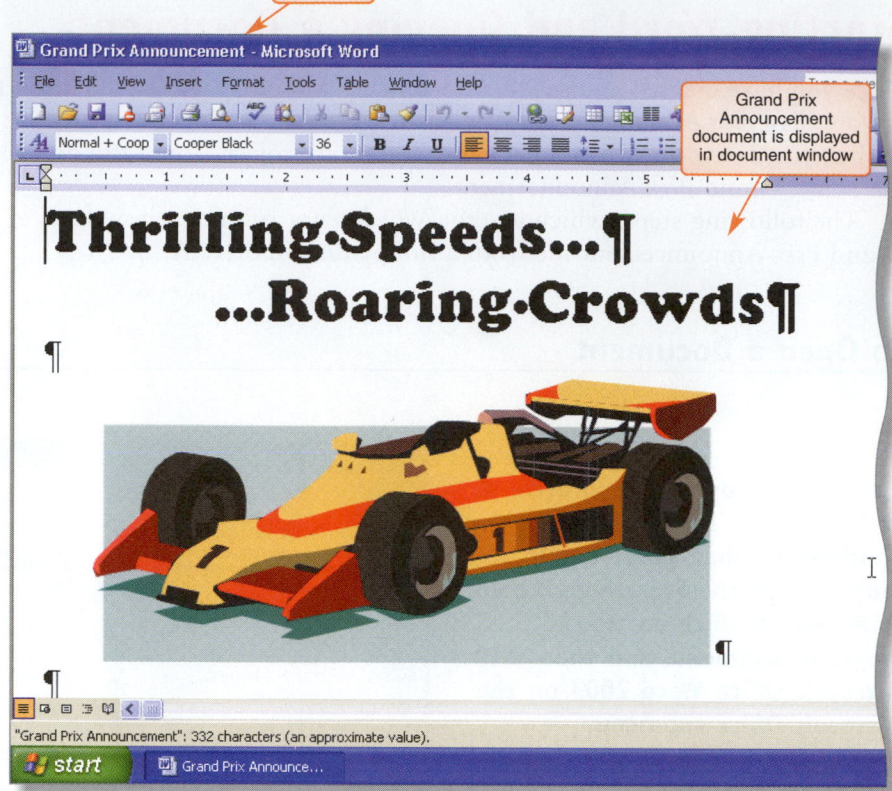

FIGURE 1-68

2

• **Click Grand Prix Announcement in the Getting Started task pane.**

Word opens the document, Grand Prix Announcement, from the floppy disk in drive A and displays it in the Word window (Figure 1-68). The Getting Started task pane closes.

Other Ways

1. Click Start Button, point to All Programs on Start menu, click Open Office Document, select desired drive, double-click file name
2. Right-click Start button, click Explore, display contents of desired drive and folder, double-click file name
3. In Word, click Open button on Standard toolbar, select file name, click Open button in dialog box
4. In Word, on File menu click Open, select file name, click Open button in dialog box
5. In Word, press CTRL+O, select file name, press ENTER
6. In Word, in Voice Command mode, say "Open, [select file name], Open"

If you want to open a document other than one of the four most recently opened ones, click the Open button on the Standard toolbar or the More link in the Getting Started task pane. Clicking the Open button or the More link displays the Open dialog box, which allows you to navigate to a document stored on disk.

Correcting Errors

After creating a document, you often will find you must make changes to it. For example, the document may contain an error or new circumstances may require you add text to the document.

Types of Changes Made to Documents

The types of changes made to documents normally fall into one of the three following categories: additions, deletions, or modifications.

ADDITIONS Additional words, sentences, or paragraphs may be required in a document. Additions occur when you omit text from a document and want to insert it later. For example, the travel agency may decide to add breakfast as part of its Grand Prix race packages.

DELETIONS Sometimes, text in a document is incorrect or is no longer needed. For example, the travel agency may stop including car rental in their Grand Prix race packages. In this case, you would delete the words, compact car rental, from the announcement.

MODIFICATIONS If an error is made in a document or changes take place that affect the document, you might have to revise a word(s) in the text. For example, the travel agency might change the Grand Prix race packages from four-day, three-night to five-day, four-night.

Inserting Text in an Existing Document

Word inserts text to the left of the insertion point. The text to the right of the insertion point moves to the right and downward to fit the new text. The following steps show how to insert the word, fun, to the left of the word, drivers', in the announcement.

To Insert Text in an Existing Document

1

• **Scroll through the document and then click to the left of the location of text to be inserted (in this case, the d in drivers').**

Word positions the insertion point at the clicked location (Figure 1-69).

FIGURE 1-69

2

• **Type** fun **and then press the SPACEBAR.**

Word inserts the word, fun, to the left of the insertion point (Figure 1-70).

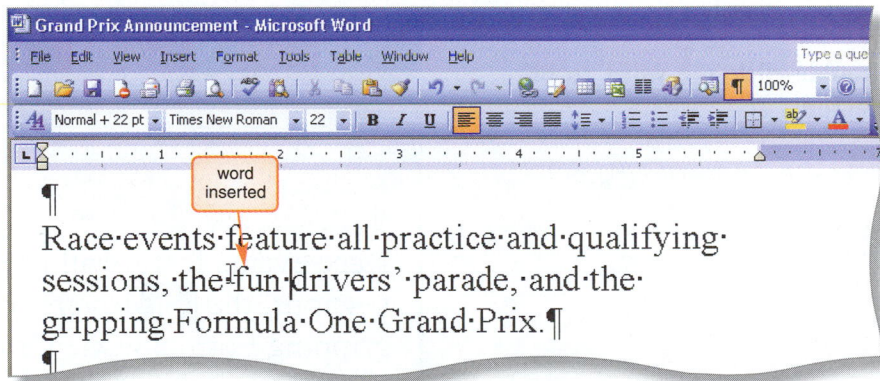

FIGURE 1-70

In Word, the default typing mode is insert mode. In **insert mode**, as you type a character, Word inserts the character and moves all the characters to the right of the typed character one position to the right. You can change to overtype mode by double-clicking the OVR status indicator on the status bar (Figure 1-8 on page WD 10). In **overtype mode**, Word replaces characters to the right of the insertion point. Double-clicking the OVR status indicator again returns Word to insert mode.

More About

Overtype

As you type, if existing text is overwritten with new text, you probably are in overtype mode. Double-click the OVR status indicator to turn overtype mode off. You also can press the INSERT key on the keyboard to turn off overtype mode.

More About

The Clipboard Task Pane

If you click the Cut button (or Copy button) twice in a row, Word displays the Clipboard task pane. You use the Clipboard task pane to copy and paste items within a document or from one Office document to another. To close the Clipboard task pane, click the Close button on the task pane title bar.

Deleting Text from an Existing Document

It is not unusual to type incorrect characters or words in a document. As discussed earlier in this project, you can click the Undo button on the Standard toolbar to immediately undo a command or action — this includes typing. Word also provides other methods of correcting typing errors.

To delete an incorrect character in a document, simply click next to the incorrect character and then press the BACKSPACE key to erase to the left of the insertion point, or press the DELETE key to erase to the right of the insertion point.

To delete a word or phrase you first must select the word or phrase. The following steps show how to select the word, fun, that was just added in the previous steps and then delete the selection.

To Select a Word

1

• **Position the mouse pointer somewhere in the word to be selected (in this case, fun), as shown in Figure 1-71.**

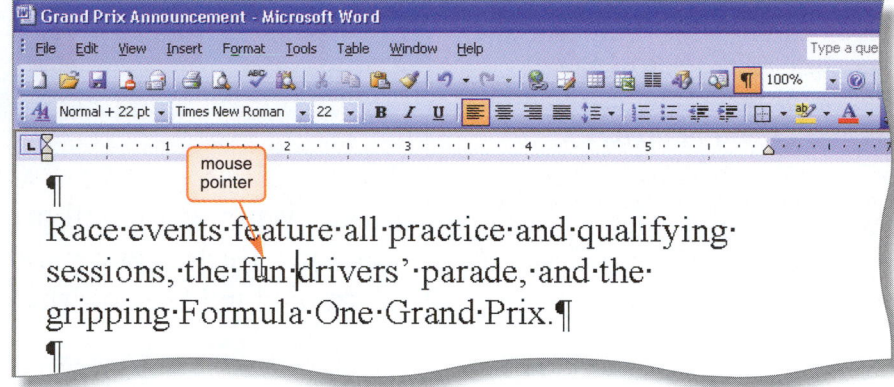

FIGURE 1-71

2

• **Double-click the word to be selected.**

The word, fun, is selected (Figure 1-72).

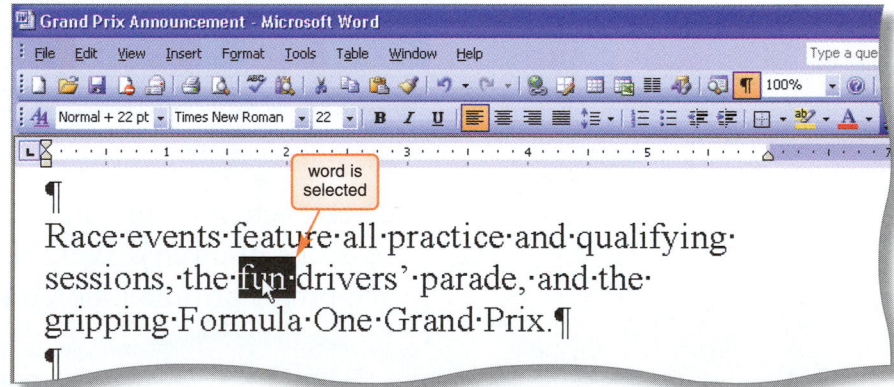

FIGURE 1-72

Other Ways

1. Drag through the word
2. With insertion point at beginning of desired word, press CTRL+SHIFT+RIGHT ARROW
3. With insertion point at beginning of desired word, in Voice Command mode, say "Select Word"

The next step is to delete the selected text.

To Delete Text

1

• **With the text selected, press the DELETE key.**

Word deletes the selected word from the document (Figure 1-73).

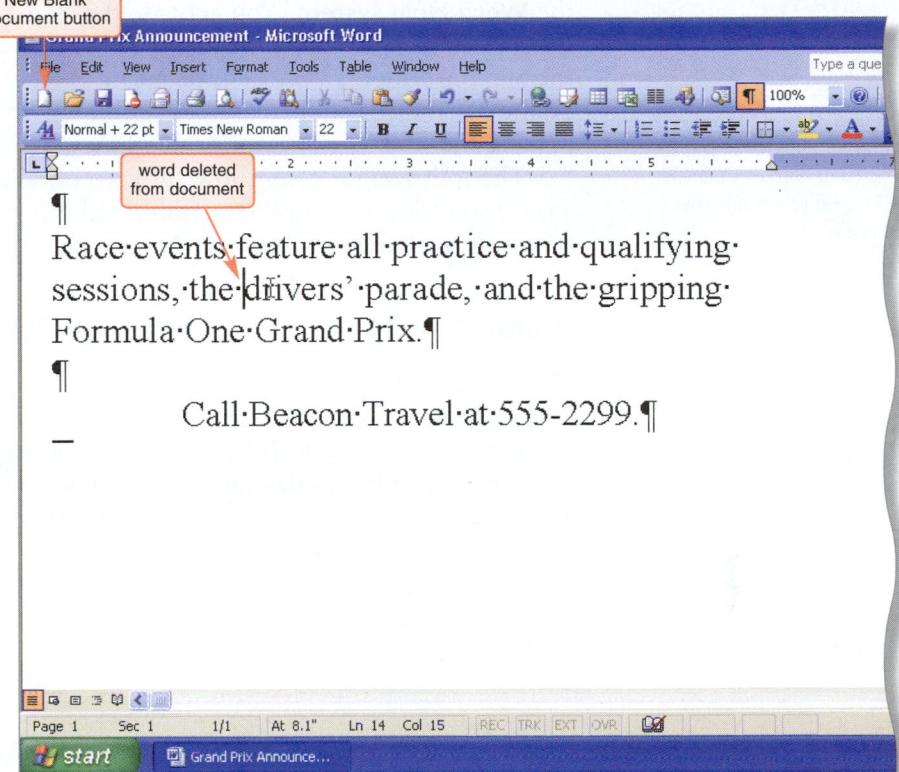

FIGURE 1-73

Closing the Entire Document

Sometimes, everything goes wrong. If this happens, you may want to close the document entirely and start over. You also may want to close a document when you are finished with it so you can begin your next document.

To Close the Entire Document and Start Over

1. Click File on the menu bar and then click Close.
2. If Word displays a dialog box, click the No button to ignore the changes since the last time you saved the document.
3. Click the New Blank Document button (Figure 1-73) on the Standard toolbar.

You also can close the document by clicking the Close button at the right edge of the menu bar.

More About

The Word Help System

The best way to become familiar with the Word Help system is to use it. Appendix A includes detailed information on the Word Help system and exercises that will help you gain confidence in using it.

Word Help System

At anytime while you are using Word, you can get answers to questions through the **Word Help system**. You activate the Word Help system by using the Type a question for help box on the menu bar, the Microsoft Office Word Help button on the Standard toolbar, or the Help menu (Figure 1-74). Used properly, this form of online assistance can increase your productivity and reduce your frustrations by minimizing the time you spend learning how to use Word.

The following section shows how to obtain answers to your questions using the Type a question for help box. Additional information about using the Word Help system is available in Appendix A.

Using the Type a Question for Help Box

Through the Type a question for help box on the right side of the menu bar (Figure 1-66 on page WD 54), you type free-form questions, such as *how do I save* or *how do I create a Web page*, or you type terms, such as *copy*, *save*, or *format*. Word responds by displaying a list of topics related to the word or phrase you typed. The following steps show how to use the Type a question for help box to obtain information about shortcut keys.

To Use the Type a Question for Help Box

1

• **Click the Type a question for help box on the right side of the menu bar and then type** shortcut keys **(Figure 1-74).**

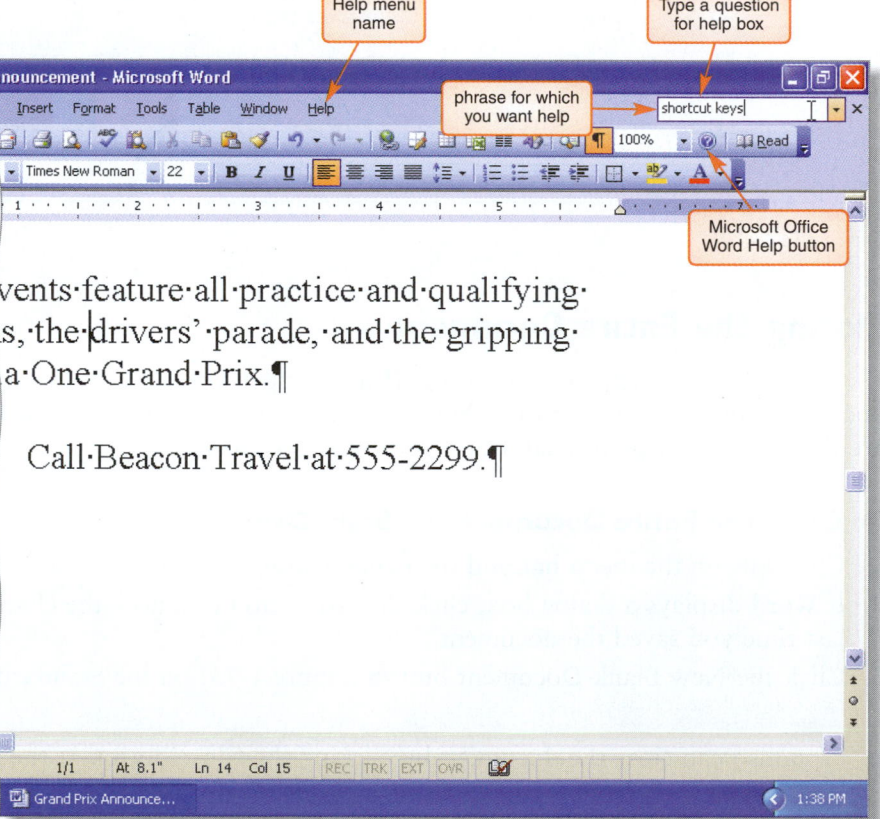

FIGURE 1-74

2

- Press the ENTER key.
- When Word displays the Search Results task pane, if necessary, scroll to display the topic, About shortcut keys.
- Click About shortcut keys.
- If the Microsoft Office Help window has an Auto Tile button, click it so the Word window and Help window display side-by-side.

Word displays the Search Results task pane with a list of topics relating to the phrase, shortcut keys. When the About shortcut keys link is clicked, Word opens the Microsoft Office Word Help window on the right side of the screen (Figure 1-75).

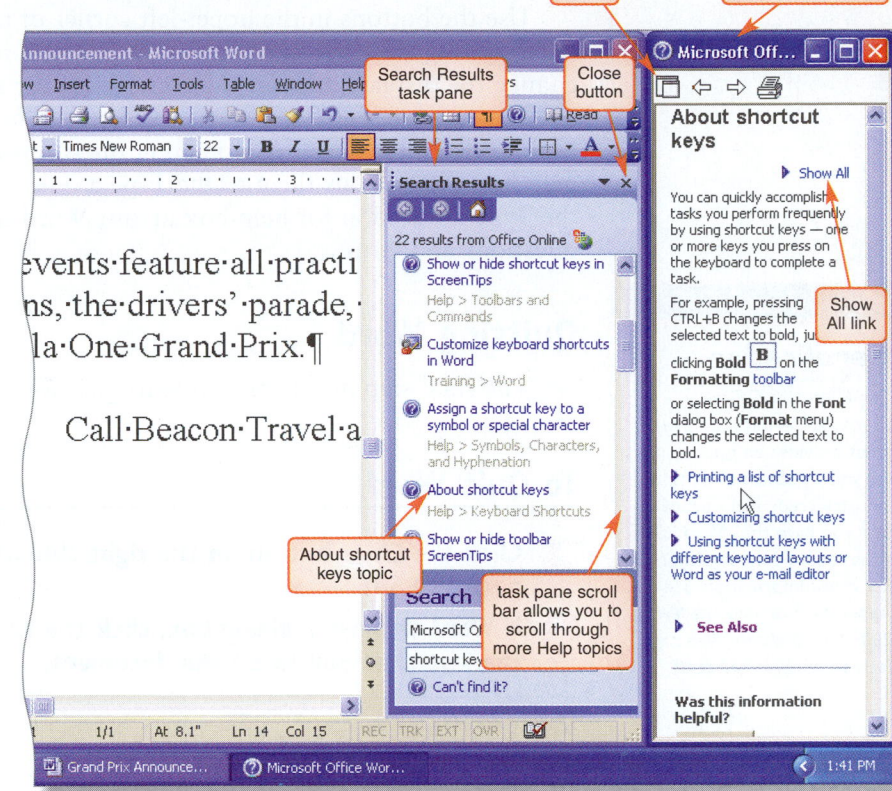

FIGURE 1-75

3

- Click the Show All link on the right side of the Microsoft Office Word Help window to expand the links in the window.
- Double-click the Microsoft Office Word Help window title bar to maximize the window.

The links in the Microsoft Office Word Help window are expanded and the window is maximized (Figure 1-76).

4

- Click the Close button on the Microsoft Office Word Help window title bar.
- Click the Close button on the Search Results task pane.

Word closes the Microsoft Office Word Help window. The Word document window again is active.

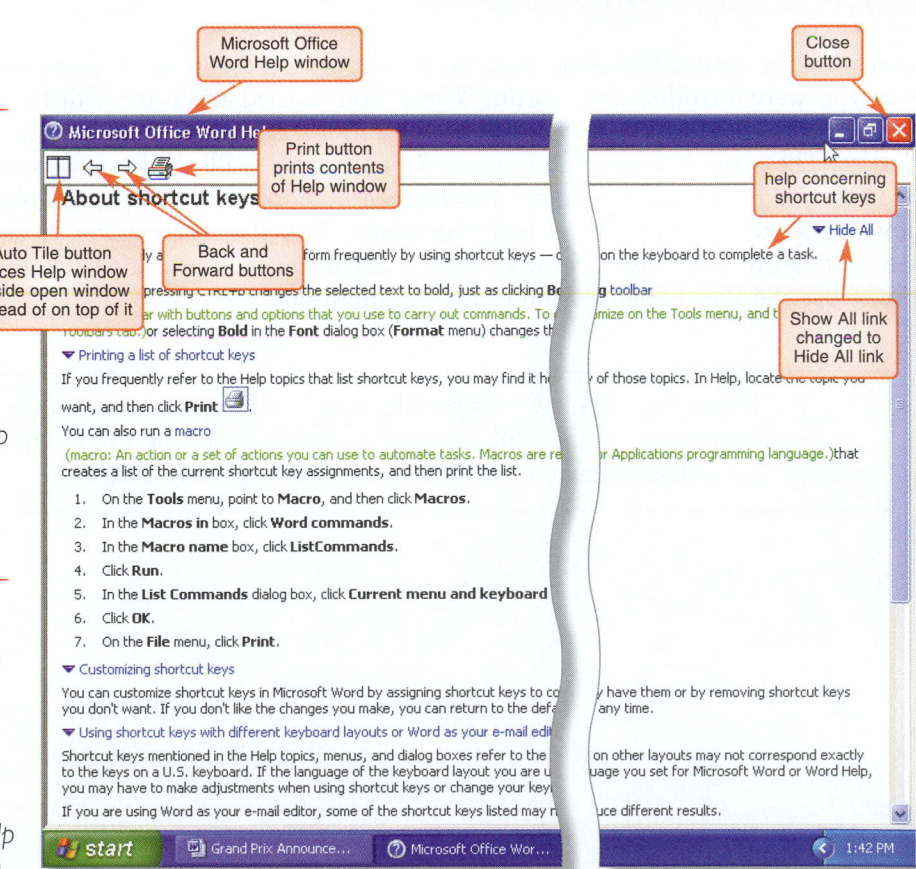

FIGURE 1-76

Use the buttons in the upper-left corner of the Microsoft Office Word Help window (Figure 1-76 on the previous page) to navigate through the Help system, change the display, or print the contents of the window.

You can use the Type a question for help box to search for Help about any topic concerning Word. As you enter questions and terms in the Type a question for help box, Word adds them to the Type a question for help list. Thus, if you click the Type a question for help box arrow, Word displays a list of previously typed questions and terms.

Quitting Word

The final step in this project is to quit Word.

To Quit Word

1 Click the Close button on the right side of the Word title bar (Figure 1-66 on page WD 54).

2 If Word displays a dialog box, click the No button to ignore the changes since the last time you saved the document.

The Word window closes.

More About

Certification

The Microsoft Office Specialist Certification program provides an opportunity for you to obtain a valuable industry credential - proof that you have the Word 2003 skills required by employers. For more information, see Appendix E or visit the Word 2003 Certification Web page (scsite.com/wd2003/cert).

Project Summary

In creating the Grand Prix Announcement document in this project, you gained a broad knowledge of Word. First, you were introduced to starting Word. You learned about the Word window. Before entering any text in the document, you learned how to change the font size. You then learned how to type in the Word document window. The project showed how to use Word's check spelling as you type feature.

Once you saved the document, you learned how to format its paragraphs and characters. Then, the project showed how to insert and resize a clip art image. You also learned how to save the document again, print it, and then quit Word. You learned how to open a document, and insert, delete, and modify text. Finally, you learned how to use the Word Help system to answer questions.

 If you have a SAM user profile, you may have access to hands-on instruction, practice, and assessment of the skills covered in this project. Log in to your SAM account and go to your assignments page to see what your instructor has assigned.

What You Should Know

Having completed this project, you should be able to perform the tasks below. The tasks are listed in the same order they were presented in this project. For a list of the buttons, menus, toolbars, and commands introduced in this project, see the Quick Reference Summary at the back of this book and refer to the Page Number column.

1. Start Word   (WD 6)
2. Customize the Word Window   (WD 8)
3. Increase the Font Size before Typing   (WD 17)
4. Type Text   (WD 18)
5. Enter Blank Lines in a Document   (WD 20)
6. Display Formatting Marks   (WD 21)
7. Type More Text   (WD 22)
8. Wordwrap Text as You Type   (WD 23)
9. Enter Text that Scrolls the Document Window (WD 24)
10. Check Spelling and Grammar as You Type (WD 26)
11. Enter More Text   (WD 27)
12. Save a New Document   (WD 28)
13. Select Multiple Paragraphs   (WD 33)
14. Change the Font Size of Text   (WD 34)
15. Change the Font of Text   (WD 36)
16. Right-Align a Paragraph   (WD 37)
17. Center a Paragraph   (WD 38)
18. Undo and Redo an Action   (WD 39)
19. Select a Line   (WD 40)
20. Format a Line of Text   (WD 40)
21. Italicize Text   (WD 41)
22. Underline a Word   (WD 42)
23. Scroll through a Document   (WD 43)
24. Select a Group of Words   (WD 43)
25. Bold Text   (WD 44)
26. Center a Paragraph   (WD 45)
27. Insert Clip Art in a Document   (WD 46)
28. Center a Paragraph Containing a Graphic (WD 48)
29. Select a Graphic   (WD 49)
30. Resize a Graphic   (WD 50)
31. Save an Existing Document with the Same File Name   (WD 52)
32. Print a Document   (WD 53)
33. Quit Word   (WD 54, WD 62)
34. Open a Document   (WD 55)
35. Insert Text in an Existing Document   (WD 57)
36. Select a Word   (WD 58)
37. Delete Text   (WD 59)
38. Close the Entire Document and Start Over (WD 59)
39. Use the Type a Question for Help Box   (WD 60)

More About

Quick Reference

For a table that lists how to complete the tasks covered in this book using the mouse, menu, shortcut menu, and keyboard, see the Quick Reference Summary at the back of this book, or visit the Word 2003 Quick Reference Web page (scsite.com/ wd2003/qr).

Learn It Online

Instructions: To complete the Learn It Online exercises, start your browser, click the Address bar, and then enter the Web address scsite.com/wd2003/learn. When the Word 2003 Learn It Online page is displayed, follow the instructions in the exercises below. Each exercise has instructions for printing your results, either for your own records or for submission to your instructor.

1 Project Reinforcement TF, MC, and SA

Below Word Project 1, click the Project Reinforcement link. Print the quiz by clicking Print on the File menu for each page. Answer each question.

2 Flash Cards

Below Word Project 1, click the Flash Cards link and read the instructions. Type 20 (or a number specified by your instructor) in the Number of playing cards text box, type your name in the Enter your Name text box, and then click the Flip Card button. When the flash card is displayed, read the question and then click the ANSWER box arrow to select an answer. Flip through Flash Cards. If your score is 15 (75%) correct or greater, click Print on the File menu to print your results. If your score is less than 15 (75%) correct, then redo this exercise by clicking the Replay button.

3 Practice Test

Below Word Project 1, click the Practice Test link. Answer each question, enter your first and last name at the bottom of the page, and then click the Grade Test button. When the graded practice test is displayed on your screen, click Print on the File menu to print a hard copy. Continue to take practice tests until you score 80% or better.

4 Who Wants To Be a Computer Genius?

Below Word Project 1, click the Computer Genius link. Read the instructions, enter your first and last name at the bottom of the page, and then click the PLAY button. When your score is displayed, click the PRINT RESULTS link to print a hard copy.

5 Wheel of Terms

Below Word Project 1, click the Wheel of Terms link. Read the instructions, and then enter your first and last name and your school name. Click the PLAY button. When your score is displayed, right-click the score and then click Print on the shortcut menu to print a hard copy.

6 Crossword Puzzle Challenge

Below Word Project 1, click the Crossword Puzzle Challenge link. Read the instructions, and then enter your first and last name. Click the SUBMIT button. Work the crossword puzzle. When you are finished, click the Submit button. When the crossword puzzle is redisplayed, click the Print Puzzle button to print a hard copy.

7 Tips and Tricks

Below Word Project 1, click the Tips and Tricks link. Click a topic that pertains to Project 1. Right-click the information and then click Print on the shortcut menu. Construct a brief example of what the information relates to in Word to confirm you understand how to use the tip or trick.

8 Newsgroups

Below Word Project 1, click the Newsgroups link. Click a topic that pertains to Project 1. Print three comments.

9 Expanding Your Horizons

Below Word Project 1, click the Expanding Your Horizons link. Click a topic that pertains to Project 1. Print the information. Construct a brief example of what the information relates to in Word to confirm you understand the contents of the article.

10 Search Sleuth

Below Word Project 1, click the Search Sleuth link. To search for a term that pertains to this project, select a term below the Project 1 title and then use the Google search engine at google.com (or any major search engine) to display and print two Web pages that present information on the term.

11 Word Online Training

Below Word Project 1, click the Word Online Training link. When your browser displays the Microsoft Office Online Web page, click the Word link. Click one of the Word courses that covers one or more of the objectives listed at the beginning of the project on page WD 4. Print the first page of the course before stepping through it.

12 Office Marketplace

Below Word Project 1, click the Office Marketplace link. When your browser displays the Microsoft Office Online Web page, click the Office Marketplace link. Click a topic that relates to Word. Print the first page.

Apply Your Knowledge

1 Checking Spelling and Grammar, Modifying Text, and Formatting a Document

Instructions: Start Word. Open the document, Apply 1-1 Paris Announcement Unformatted, on the Data Disk. See the inside back cover of this book for instructions for downloading the Data Disk or see your instructor for information about accessing files required in this book.

The document on the Data Disk is an unformatted announcement that contains some spelling errors. You are to fix the spelling mistakes, modify text, format paragraphs and characters, and insert clip art in the announcement, so it looks like Figure 1-77 on the next page.

1. Correct each spelling and grammar error by right-clicking the flagged word and then clicking the appropriate correction on the shortcut menu, so the announcement text matches Figure 1-77 on the next page. The unformatted announcement on the Data Disk contains several spelling errors (red wavy underline) and grammar errors (green wavy underline). Word may flag some proper names that are spelled correctly. In these cases, click Ignore Once or Ignore All on the shortcut menu. If your screen does not display the wavy underlines, right-click the Spelling and Grammar Status icon on the status bar and be sure Hide Spelling Errors and Hide Grammatical Errors do not have check marks beside them. If they do, remove the check mark(s) by the appropriate command. If your screen still does not display the wavy underlines, right-click the Spelling and Grammar Status icon on the status bar, click Options on the shortcut menu, click the Recheck Document button, and then click the OK button.
2. At the end of the first sentence of body copy, change the period to an exclamation point. The sentence should read: See Paris this spring – on a shoestring!
3. Delete the word, morning, in the first sentence of the second paragraph of body copy.
4. Insert the word, event, between the text, Discount tickets, in the second sentence of the second paragraph of body copy. The text should read: Discount event tickets...
5. Change the font and font size of the first line of the headline to 72-point Lucida Calligraphy, or a similar font.
6. Change the font and font size of the second line of the headline to 48-point Lucida Calligraphy, or a similar font.
7. Right-align the second line of the headline.
8. Change the font size of the two paragraphs of body copy to 20 point.
9. Change the font and font size of the last line of the announcement to 24-point Arial.
10. Italicize the word, shoestring, in the first paragraph of body copy.
11. Bold the phrase, unbelievably low price, in the same paragraph.
12. Underline the telephone number in the last line of the announcement.
13. Italicize the text in the last line of the announcement.
14. Center the last line of the announcement.
15. Insert the clip art between the first and second lines of the headline. Use the search text, Paris, to locate this, or a similar, clip art image. Center the clip art.
16. Click File on the menu bar and then click Save As. Save the document using Apply 1-1 Paris Announcement Formatted as the file name.
17. Print the revised document, shown in Figure 1-77.

(continued)

Apply Your Knowledge

Checking Spelling and Grammar, Modifying Text, and Formatting a Document *(continued)*

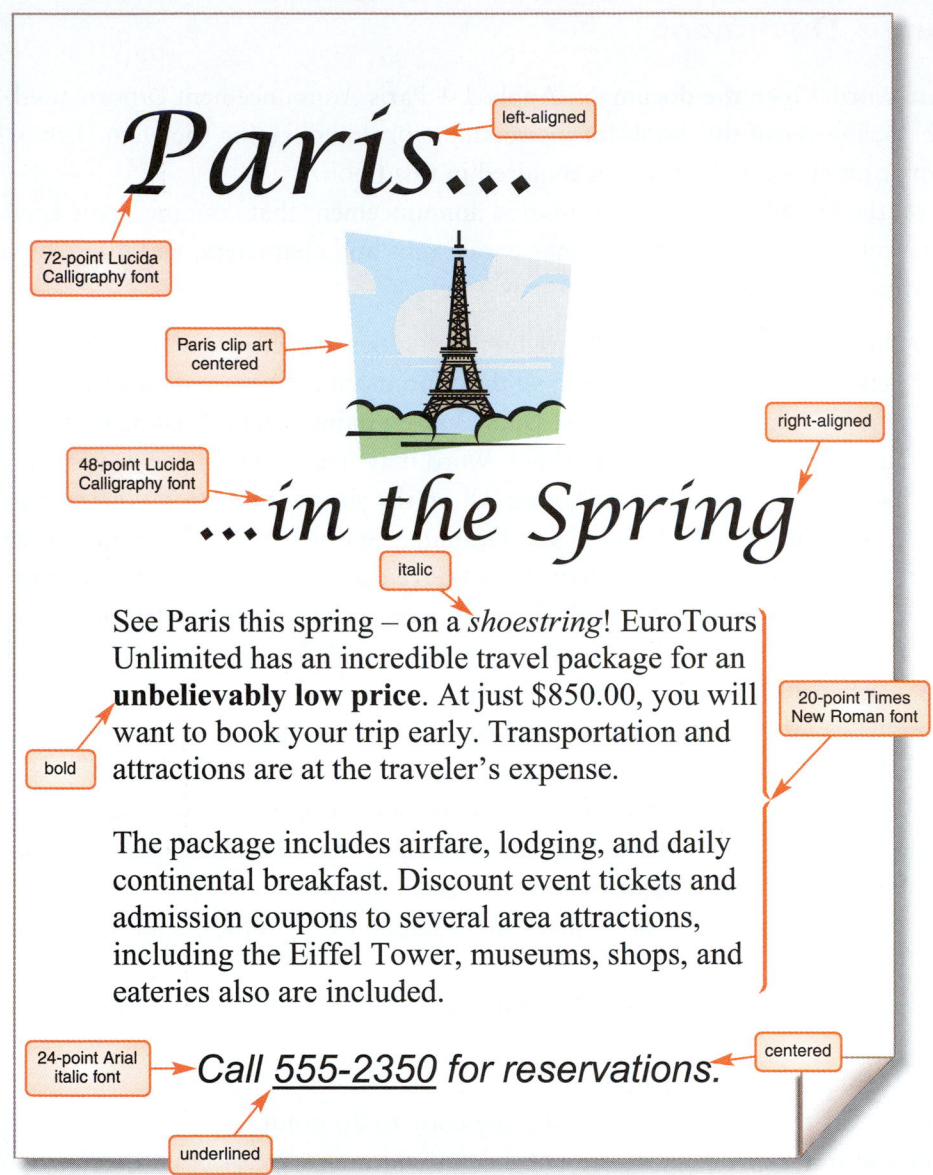

FIGURE 1-77

In the Lab

1 Creating an Announcement with Clip Art

Problem: You work part-time for the events coordinator at Memorial Hall. She has asked you to prepare an announcement for the upcoming annual charity costume ball. First, you prepare the unformatted announcement shown in Figure 1-78a, and then you format it so it looks like Figure 1-78b on the next page. *Hint:* Remember, if you make a mistake while formatting the announcement, you can click the Undo button on the Standard toolbar to undo your last action.

1. Before entering any text, change the font size from 12 to 20.
2. Display formatting marks on the screen.
3. Type the unformatted announcement shown in Figure 1-78a. If Word flags any misspelled words as you type, check the spelling of these words and correct them.
4. Save the document on a floppy disk with Lab 1-1 Costume Ball Announcement as the file name.

Come One...
...Come All

Charity Costume Ball

Mark your calendar for a fun-filled gala on Saturday, August 6, at 8:00 p.m. at Memorial Hall. Tickets are $50.00 per couple, with dinner prepared by Chef Jeffery Vincent of Le Chic and live entertainment by The Class Act. All proceeds go to charity.

As in past years, this event includes prizes for the best costumes, door prizes, a silent auction, and the traditional unmasking at midnight. Have an enjoyable evening while promoting a good cause.

Call 555-6344 for reservations.

(a) Unformatted Document

FIGURE 1-78

5. Change the font of both lines of the headline to Cooper Black, or a similar font. Change the font size from 20 to 48.
6. Right-align the second line of the headline.
7. Center the body title line.

(continued)

In the Lab

Creating an Announcement with Clip Art *(continued)*

8. Change the font of the body title line to Harrington, or a similar font. Change the font size to 36. Bold the body title line.

9. In the first paragraph of the body copy, bold the text, fun-filled.

10. In the same paragraph, italicize the word, live.

11. In the same paragraph, underline the word, All.

12. Center the last line of the announcement.

13. Insert the clip art of a mask between the headline and the body title line. Search for the text, mask, in the Clip Art task pane to locate this, or a similar, graphic.

14. Center the clip art.

15. Save the announcement again with the same file name.

16. Print the formatted announcement, as shown in Figure 1-78b.

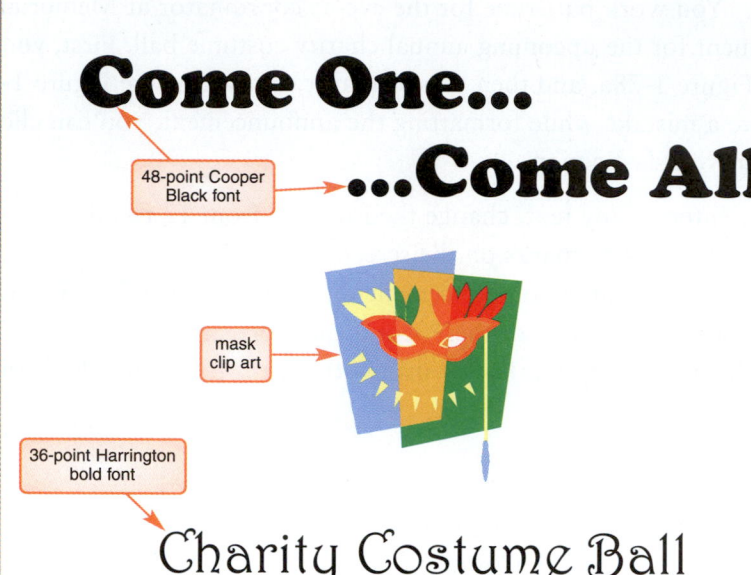

**Come One...
...Come All**

48-point Cooper Black font

mask clip art

36-point Harrington bold font

Charity Costume Ball

Mark your calendar for a **fun-filled** gala on Saturday, August 6, at 8:00 p.m. at Memorial Hall. Tickets are $50.00 per couple, with dinner prepared by Chef Jeffery Vincent of Le Chic and *live* entertainment by The Class Act. <u>All</u> proceeds go to charity.

As in past years, this event includes prizes for the best costumes, door prizes, a silent auction, and the traditional unmasking at midnight. Have an enjoyable evening while promoting a good cause.

Call 555-6344 for reservations.

20-point

(b) Formatted Document

FIGURE 1-78

2 Creating an Announcement with Resized Clip Art

Problem: Your boss at Southside Physicians Group has requested that you prepare an announcement for the upcoming Public Health Clinic. You prepare the announcement shown in Figure 1-79. *Hint:* Remember, if you make a mistake while formatting the announcement, you can click the Undo button on the Standard toolbar to undo your last action.

1. Before entering any text, change the font size from 12 to 20.

2. Display formatting marks on the screen.

In the Lab

3. Create the announcement shown in Figure 1-79. Enter the text of the document first without the clip art and unformatted; that is, without any bold, underlined, italicized, right-aligned, or centered text. If Word flags any misspelled words as you type, check the spelling of these words and correct them.

4. Save the document on a floppy disk with Lab 1-2 Health Clinic Announcement as the file name.

5. Change the font of both lines of the headline to Brush Script MT, or a similar font. Change the font size from 20 to 48.

6. Right-align the second line of the headline.

7. Center the body title line.

8. Change the font and font size of the body title line to 28-point Bookman Old Style. Bold the body title line.

9. Underline the word, free, in the first paragraph of the body copy.

10. In the next paragraph, italicize these words: Qualified, licensed physicians and nurse practitioners.

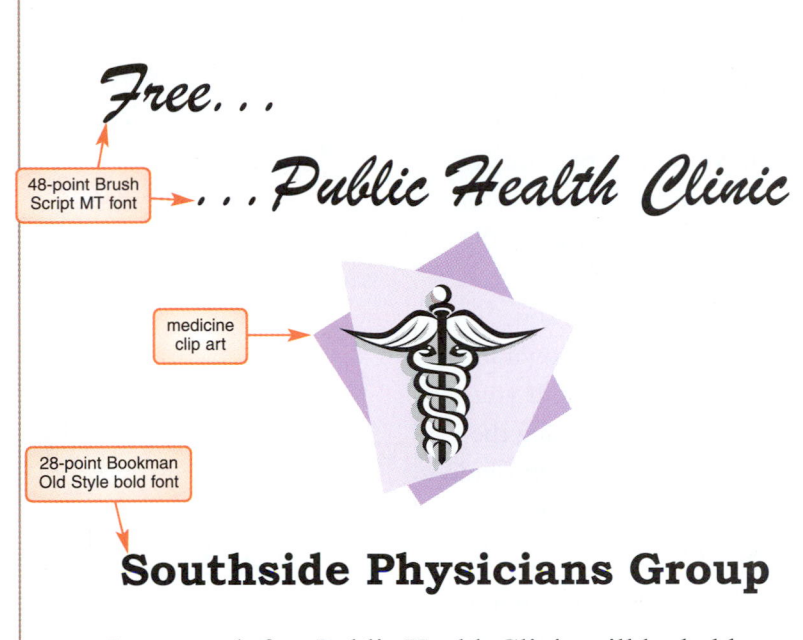

48-point Brush Script MT font

medicine clip art

28-point Bookman Old Style bold font

Free...

...Public Health Clinic

Southside Physicians Group

Our annual, <u>free</u> Public Health Clinic will be held at the concourse of Woodstar Mall from 9:30 a.m. until 6:30 p.m. on Thursday, November 3. No appointment is necessary.

Flu shots, cholesterol tests, hearing and eye exams, and blood pressure screening will be offered to the public. *Qualified, licensed physicians and nurse practitioners* conduct the exams and dispense advice.

Call 555-7225 for more information.

20-point

FIGURE 1-79

11. Center the last line of the announcement.

12. Insert the clip art between the headline and the body title line. Search for the text, medicine, in the Clip Art task pane to locate this, or a similar, graphic. Center the graphic.

13. Enlarge the graphic. If you make the graphic too large, the announcement may flow onto two pages. If this occurs, reduce the size of the graphic so the announcement fits on a single page. *Hint:* Use Help to learn about print preview, which is a way to see the page before you print it. To exit print preview and return to the document window, click the Close button on the Print Preview toolbar.

14. Save the announcement again with the same file name.

15. Print the announcement.

In the Lab

3 Creating an Announcement with Resized Clip Art, a Bulleted List, and Color

Problem: The owner of Zachary Sports Complex has requested that each student in your class prepare an announcement advertising the sports complex. The student that creates the winning announcement will receive a complimentary membership. You prepare the announcement shown in Figure 1-80. *Hint:* Remember, if you make a mistake while formatting the announcement, you can click the Undo button on the Standard toolbar to undo your last action.

1. Type the announcement shown in Figure 1-80, using the fonts and font sizes indicated in the figure. Check spelling as you type.
2. Save the document on a floppy disk with Lab 1-3 Training Camp Announcement as the file name.
3. Change the font color of the headline to red, the body title to blue, and the last line of the announcement to green. *Hint:* Use Help to learn how to change the font color of text.
4. Add a brown double underline below the text, Space is limited. *Hint:* Use Help to learn how to add a decorative underline to text.
5. Add bullets to the three paragraphs of body copy. *Hint:* Use Help to learn how to add bullets to a list of paragraphs.
6. Insert clip art of a baseball player between the headline and the body title line. If you have access to the Web, select the clip art from the Web. Otherwise, select the clip art from the hard disk. In the Clip Art task pane, images from the Web display an icon of a small globe in their lower-left corner.
7. Enlarge the graphic of the baseball player. If you make the graphic too large, the announcement may flow onto two pages. If this occurs, reduce the size of the graphic so the announcement fits on a single page. *Hint:* Use Help to learn about print preview, which is a way to see the page before you print it. To exit print preview and return to the document window, click the Close button on the Print Preview toolbar.
8. Save the announcement again with the same file name.
9. Print the announcement.

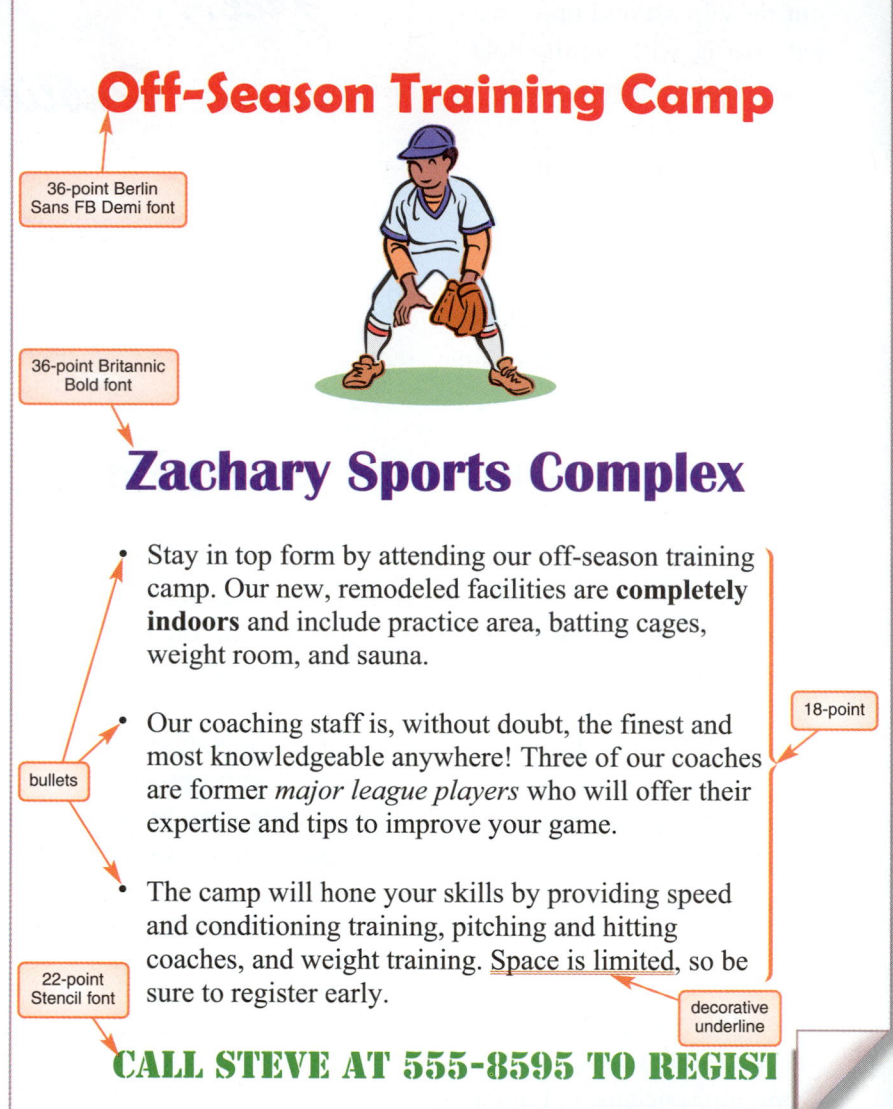

FIGURE 1-80

Cases and Places

The difficulty of these case studies varies:
■ are the least difficult and ■■ are more difficult. The last exercise is a group exercise.

1 ■ You have been assigned the task of preparing an announcement for The Gridiron Club. The announcement is to contain clip art related to football. Use the following text: first line of headline – Gridiron Club…; second line of headline – …Tailgate Party; body title – GO TROJANS!; first paragraph of body copy – Join us on Friday, October 28, for a pre-game tailgate party. Help us celebrate our beloved Trojans' undefeated season! The Gridiron Club will provide grills, brats, hamburgers, hot dogs, and buns. Please bring a side dish to share and your own nonalcoholic beverages.; second paragraph of body copy – The party starts at 5:30 p.m. in the parking lot by the Administration Center. Kick-off for the first playoff game is at 7:00 p.m.; last line – Call 555-1995 for more information. Use the concepts and techniques presented in this project to create and format this announcement. Be sure to check spelling and grammar in the announcement.

2 ■ You have been assigned the task of preparing an announcement for an upcoming camp at the Sherman Planetarium. The announcement is to contain clip art of a telescope. Use the following text: first line of headline – Reach for…; second line of headline – …the Stars; body title – Space, Stars, and Skies Camp; first paragraph of body copy – Have you always been fascinated by the planets, stars, and space travel? Enroll in our Space, Stars, and Skies Camp to learn more about the cosmos. The camp will meet June 6 through June 9 from 8:30 a.m. until 12:30 p.m. at the Sherman Planetarium.; second paragraph of body copy – Our facilities include simulators, lecture halls, virtual rooms, and a planetarium. Learn about space travel from our staff, two of whom are former astronauts.; third paragraph of body copy – Register early to reserve your seat. Space is limited to 25 participants.; last line – Call 555-9141 to register. Use the concepts and techniques presented in this project to create and format this announcement. Be sure to check spelling and grammar in the announcement.

3 ■■ Your boss at Cornucopia Health Foods has asked you to prepare an announcement for a grand opening. You are to include appropriate clip art. He gives you the following information for the announcement. The doors of its newest store will open in Centerbrook Mall at 9:00 a.m. on Monday, September 26. You will find great deals throughout the store. Discount coupons and free samples will be distributed all day. The first 50 customers at the register will receive a free bottle of vitamin C tablets. Cornucopia Health Foods offers a huge selection of health food and organics. Tofu, carob, soy products, herbal teas, vitamin supplements, and organically grown produce are just a few items in our extensive product line. The store's slogan is as follows: Cornucopia ~ good food for good health! Use the concepts and techniques presented in this project to create the announcement. Change the color of text in the headline, body title, and last line of the announcement. Use a decorative underline in the announcement. Add bullets to the paragraphs of the body copy. Be sure to check spelling and grammar in the announcement.

Cases and Places

4 ■■ You have been assigned the task of preparing an announcement for Stone Bay Apartments advertising an apartment for rent. You are to include appropriate clip art. These details have been provided. Stone Bay Apartments has a two-bedroom apartment available for rent now. This upper-level unit has an eat-in kitchen, central air, and a large living room with southern exposure. Rent is $925.00 a month. Utilities are included in rent. Pets are welcome. Interested parties should call 555-8265 to arrange a showing. Stone Bay Apartments provide amenities galore, including laundry facilities, garage parking, clubhouse, pool, and tennis courts. We are located close to Lake Park Mall, grocery stores, restaurants, and Victor Community College. Use the concepts and techniques presented in this project to create the announcement. Change the color of text in the headline, body title, and last line of the announcement. Use a decorative underline in the announcement. Add bullets to some of the paragraphs of the body copy. Be sure to check spelling and grammar in the announcement.

5 ■■ **Working Together** Schools, churches, libraries, grocery stores, and other public places have bulletin boards for announcements and other postings. Often, these bulletin boards have so many announcements that some go unnoticed. Look at a bulletin board at one of the locations mentioned above and find a posted announcement that you think might be overlooked. Copy the text from the announcement and distribute it to each team member. Each member then independently should use this text, together with the techniques presented in this project, to create an announcement that would be more likely to catch a reader's eye. Be sure to check spelling and grammar. As a group, critique each announcement and have each member redesign their announcement based on the group's recommendations. Hand in printouts of each team member's original and final announcements.

Creating a Research Paper

CASE PERSPECTIVE

Suzy Zhao is a full-time college student, majoring in Finance. Mr. Ortiz, the instructor in her introductory computer class, has assigned a short research paper that should contain a minimum of 325 words. The paper must discuss some aspect of computer security. It also must be written according to the MLA documentation style, which specifies guidelines for report preparation. The paper is to contain one footnote and three references — one of which must be obtained from the World Wide Web. Finally, all students are to submit their papers electronically via e-mail to Mr. Ortiz.

When Suzy graduates from college, she plans to work in the banking sector. She is interested in ways to ensure that users are legitimate before allowing them access to a computer. Suzy recently read a short article about computer security that mentioned computers can use biometrics to authenticate a person's identity by verifying a personal characteristic. Examples include fingerprints, hand geometry, facial features, voice, signatures, and eye patterns. Suzy decides to write her research paper about biometrics. She intends to review computer magazines at the school's library, surf the Internet, and e-mail a few biometrics vendors for information about their products. She also plans to use the Internet to obtain the guidelines for the MLA style of documentation. Suzy knows that you are a computer major and quite skilled at searching the Internet. She asks you to assist her with the Web searches. You immediately agree to help your friend.

As you read through this project, you will learn how to use Word to create a research paper and e-mail a copy of the finished paper.

MICROSOFT
Office Word 2003

Creating a Research Paper

Objectives

You will have mastered the material in this project when you can:

- Describe the MLA documentation style for research papers
- Change the margin settings and line spacing in a document
- Use a header to number pages of a document
- Apply formatting using shortcut keys
- Modify paragraph indentation
- Add a footnote to a document

- Count the words in a document
- Insert a manual page break
- Create a hyperlink
- Sort selected paragraphs
- Proof and revise a document
- Display the Web page associated with a hyperlink
- E-mail a copy of a document
- Use the Research task pane to locate information

Introduction

In both academic and business environments, you will be asked to write reports. Business reports range from proposals to cost justifications to five-year plans to research findings. Academic reports focus mostly on research findings. Whether you are writing a business report or an academic report, you should follow a standard style when preparing it.

Many different styles of documentation exist for report preparation, depending on the nature of the report. Each style requires the same basic information; the differences among styles relates to how the information is presented. For example, one documentation style may use the term bibliography, whereas another uses references, and yet a third prefers works cited. Two popular documentation styles for research papers are the **Modern Language Association of America** (**MLA**) and **American Psychological Association** (**APA**) styles. This project uses the MLA documentation style.

Project 2 — Biometrics Research Paper

Project 2 illustrates the creation of a short research paper about biometrics. As shown in Figure 2-1, the paper follows the MLA documentation style. The first two pages present the research paper, and the third page alphabetically lists the works cited.

Zhao 3

Works Cited

Carter, Donnell W., and Louis C. Juarez. *Securing Confidential Data Entered into a Computer*.

Boston: Thomas Publishing, 2005.

Computers and Biometrics. Shelly Cashman Series®. Course Technology. 3 Oct. 2005.

http://www.scsite.com/wd2003/pr2/wc.htm.

Schmidt, Karl J. "Biometrics and Authenticating Computer Users." *Computers and the Internet*

Aug. 2005: 54-62.

> **paragraphs in alphabetical order**

Zhao 2

Law enforcement, surveillance systems, airports, day-care centers, financial institutions,

the military, and other organizations that deal with highly sensitive data use other types of

biometrics. A face recognition system captures a live face image and compares it with a stored

image. A hand geometry system measures the shape and size of a person's hand (*Computers and*

Biometrics). A voice verification system compares a person's live speech with his or her stored

voice pattern. A signature verification system recognizes the shape of a handwritten signature, as

well as measures the pressure exerted and the motion used to write the signature. Finally, an iris

recognition system reads patterns in the iris of the eye.

> **parenthetical citation**

Zhao 1

> **header contains last name followed by page number**

Suzy Zhao

Mr. Ortiz

Information Systems 101

October 13, 2005

Biometrics

> **parenthetical citation**

Biometrics is the technology of authenticating a person's identity by verifying a personal

characteristic. Biometric devices grant users access to programs, systems, or rooms by analyzing

some biometric identifier (Schmidt 54-62). A biometric identifier is a physical or behavioral

characteristic. Examples include fingerprints, facial features, hand geometry, voice patterns,

signatures, and eye patterns.

A biometric device translates a personal characteristic into a digital code that is compared

with a digital code stored in the computer. If the digital code in the computer does not match the

personal characteristic's code, the computer denies access to the individual.

The most widely used biometric device today is a fingerprint scanner. A fingerprint

scanner captures curves and indentations of a fingerprint. With the cost of fingerprint scanners

less than $100, experts believe this technology will become the home user's authentication

device for e-commerce transactions. To conduct a credit-card transaction, the Web site would

require users to hold a finger on the scanner. External fingerprint scanners usually plug into a

parallel or USB port.[1] Businesses use fingerprint scanners to authenticate users before they can

access a personal computer. Grade schools use fingerprint scanners as an alternative to lunch

money. Students' account balances adjust for each lunch purchased.

> **superscripted note reference mark**

---

[1] According to Carter and Juarez, newer keyboards and notebook computers have a

fingerprint scanner built into them (42-53).

> **explanatory note positioned as footnote**

FIGURE 2-1

More About

MLA and APA

The MLA documentation style is the standard in the humanities, and the APA style is preferred in the social sciences. For more information about the MLA and APA guidelines, visit the Word 2003 More About Web page (scsite.com/wd2003/more) and then click MLA or APA, respectively.

MLA Documentation Style

When writing papers, you should adhere to some style of documentation. The research paper in this project follows the guidelines presented by the MLA. To follow the MLA style, double-space text on all pages of the paper using one-inch top, bottom, left, and right margins. Indent the first word of each paragraph one-half inch from the left margin. At the right margin of each page, place a page number one-half inch from the top margin. On each page, precede the page number by your last name.

The MLA style does not require a title page. Instead, place your name and course information in a block at the left margin beginning one inch from the top of the page. Center the title one double-space below your name and course information.

In the body of the paper, place author references in parentheses with the page number(s) of the referenced information. The MLA style uses in-text **parenthetical citations** instead of noting each source at the bottom of the page or at the end of the paper. In the MLA style, notes are used only for optional explanatory notes.

If used, explanatory notes elaborate on points discussed in the body of the paper. Use a superscript (raised number) to signal that an explanatory note exists, and also sequence the notes. Position explanatory notes either at the bottom of the page as footnotes or at the end of the paper as endnotes. Indent the first line of each explanatory note one-half inch from the left margin. Place one space following the superscripted number before beginning the note text. Double-space the note text. At the end of the note text, you may list bibliographic information for further reference.

The MLA style uses the term **works cited** for the bibliographical references. The works cited page alphabetically lists works that are referenced directly in the paper. List works by each author's last name, or, if the author's name is not available, by the title of the work. Italicize or underline the title of the work. Place the works cited on a separate numbered page. Center the title, Works Cited, one inch from the top margin. Double-space all lines. Begin the first line of each entry at the left margin, indenting subsequent lines of the same entry one-half inch from the left margin.

Starting and Customizing Word

To start and customize Word, Windows must be running. If you are stepping through this project on a computer and you want your screen to match the figures in this book, then you should change your computer's resolution to 800 × 600 and reset the toolbars and menus. For information about changing the resolution and resetting toolbars and menus, read Appendix D.

The next steps show how to start Word and customize the Word window. You may need to ask your instructor how to start Word for your system.

More About

Titles of Works

Titles of books, periodicals, and Web sites typically are underlined when a research paper is submitted in printed form. Some instructors require that Web addresses be hyperlinks for online access. Word formats hyperlinks with an underline. To distinguish hyperlinks from titles, the MLA allows titles to be italicized, if approved by the instructor.

Q&A

Q: How does the APA style differ from the MLA style?

A: In the APA style, double-space all pages of the paper with 1.5" top, bottom, left, and right margins. Indent the first word of each paragraph .5" from the left margin. In the upper-right margin of each page, place a running head that consists of the page number double-spaced below a summary of the paper title.

To Start and Customize Word

1 Click the **Start** button on the Windows taskbar, point to **All Programs** on the **Start** menu, point to **Microsoft Office** on the **All Programs** submenu, and then click **Microsoft Office Word 2003** on the **Microsoft Office** submenu.

2 If the Word window is not maximized, double-click its title bar to maximize it.

3 If the **Language** bar appears, right-click it and then click **Close the Language bar** on the shortcut menu.

4 If the **Getting Started** task pane is displayed in the Word window, click its **Close** button.

5 If the Standard and Formatting toolbar buttons are displayed on one row, click the **Toolbar Options** button and then click **Show Buttons on Two Rows** in the Toolbar Options list.

6 If your screen differs from Figure 2-2 on the next page, click **View** on the menu bar and then click **Normal**.

7 If your zoom percent is not 100 (shown in Figure 2-2), click **View** on the menu bar, click **Zoom** on the View menu, click **100%**, and then click the **OK** button.

Word starts and, after a few moments, displays an empty document titled Document1 in the Word window (shown in Figure 2-2).

Displaying Formatting Marks

As discussed in Project 1, it is helpful to display formatting marks that indicate where in the document you pressed the ENTER key, SPACEBAR, and other keys. The following step discusses how to display formatting marks.

To Display Formatting Marks

1 If the **Show/Hide ¶** button on the Standard toolbar is not selected already, click it.

Word displays formatting marks in the document window, and the Show/Hide ¶ button on the Standard toolbar is selected (shown in Figure 2-2).

Changing the Margins

Word is preset to use standard 8.5-by-11-inch paper, with 1.25-inch left and right margins and 1-inch top and bottom margins. These margin settings affect every page in the document.

Periodically, you may want to change the default margin settings. The MLA documentation style, for example, requires one-inch top, bottom, left, and right margins throughout the paper. Thus, the steps on the next page show how to change the margin settings for a document when the window is in normal view. To verify the document window is in normal view, click View on the menu bar and then click Normal.

To Change the Margin Settings

1

• **Click File on the menu bar (Figure 2-2).**

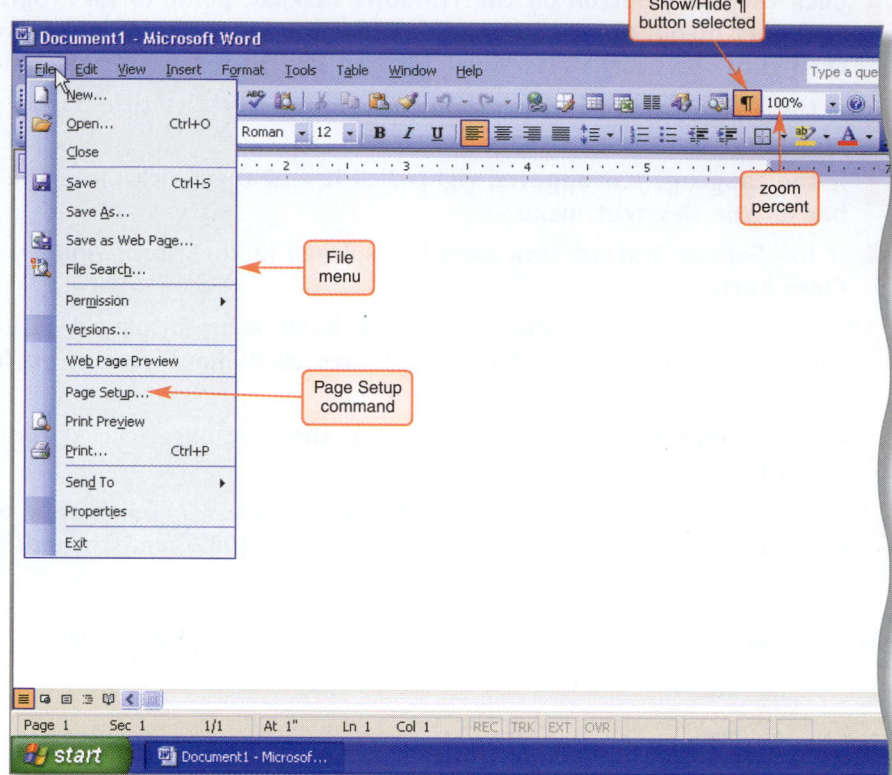

FIGURE 2-2

2

• **Click Page Setup on the File menu.**

• **When Word displays the Page Setup dialog box, if necessary, click the Margins tab.**

Word displays the current margin settings in the text boxes of the Page Setup dialog box (Figure 2-3).

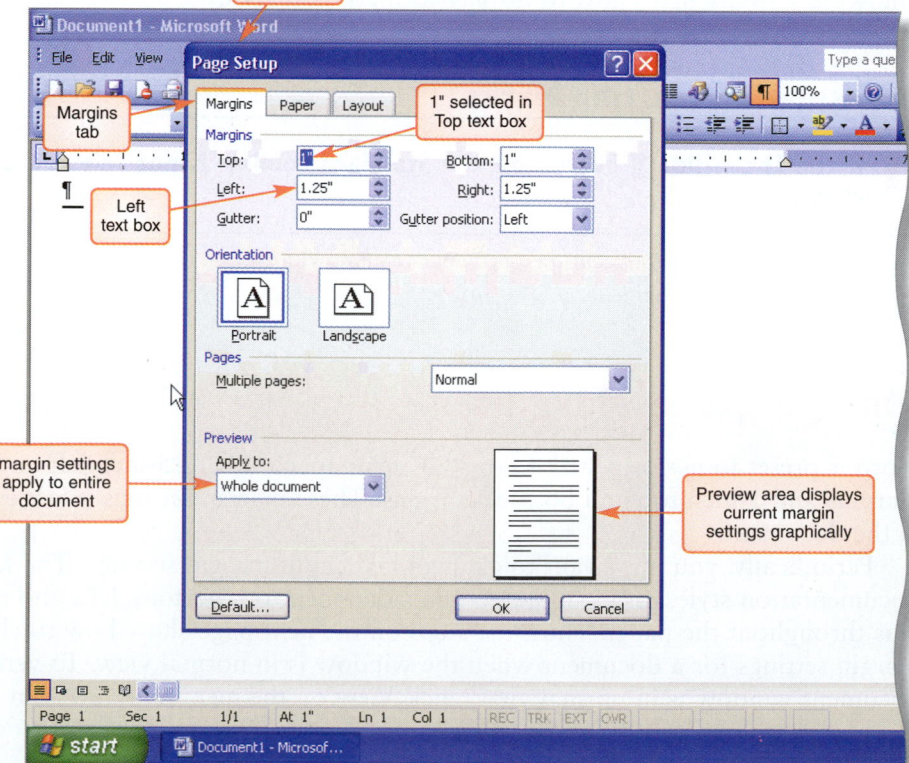

FIGURE 2-3

3

• **With 1" selected in the Top text box, press the TAB key twice to select 1.25" in the Left text box.**

• **Type** 1 **and then press the TAB key.**

• **Type** 1 **in the Right text box.**

The new left and right margin settings are 1 inch (Figure 2-4). Instead of typing margin values, you can click the text box arrows to increase or decrease the number in the text box.

4

• **Click the OK button in the Page Setup dialog box.**

Word changes the left and right margins.

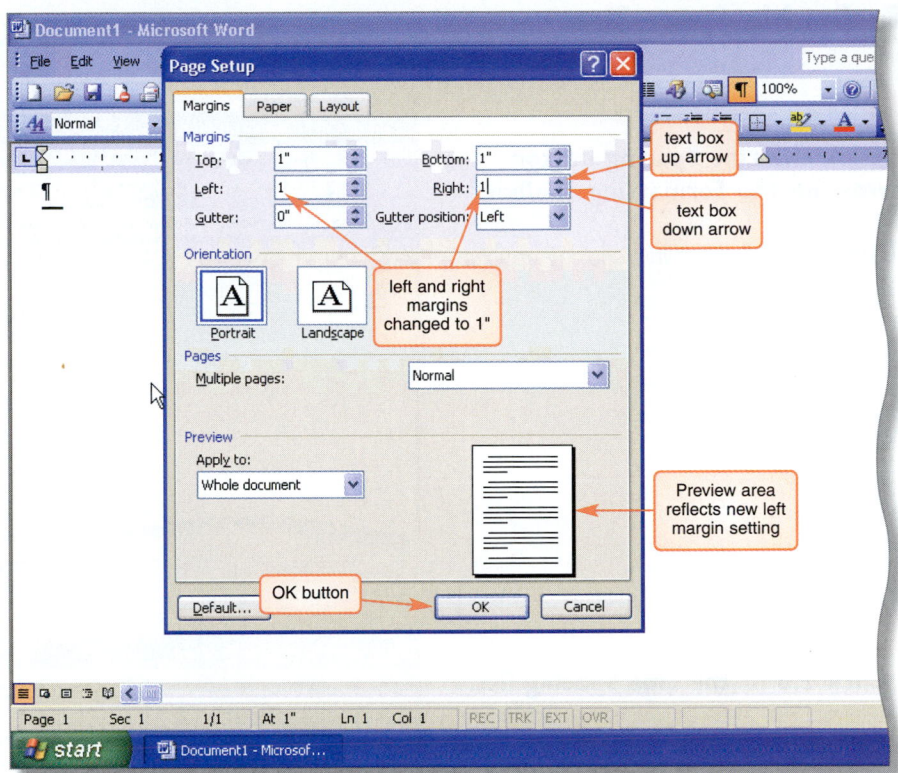

FIGURE 2-4

The new margin settings take effect immediately in the document. Word uses these margins for the entire document.

When you change the margin settings in the text boxes in the Page Setup dialog box, the Preview area (Figure 2-4) does not adjust to reflect a changed margin setting until the insertion point leaves the respective text box. That is, you must press the TAB or ENTER key or click another text box if you want to view a changed margin setting in the Preview area.

Adjusting Line Spacing

Line spacing is the amount of vertical space between lines of text in a document. By default, Word single-spaces between lines of text and automatically adjusts line height to accommodate various font sizes and graphics.

The MLA documentation style requires that you **double-space** the entire paper; that is, one blank line should be between each line of text. The steps on the next page show how to adjust the line spacing from single to double.

More About

The Page Setup Dialog Box

A document printed in portrait orientation is taller than it is wide. A document printed in landscape orientation is wider than it is tall. If you want to change the orientation of a printout from portrait to landscape, click Landscape in the Orientation area in the Page Setup dialog box (Figure 2-4).

To Double-Space Text

1

• **Click the Line Spacing button arrow on the Formatting toolbar.**

Word displays a list of line spacing options (Figure 2-5).

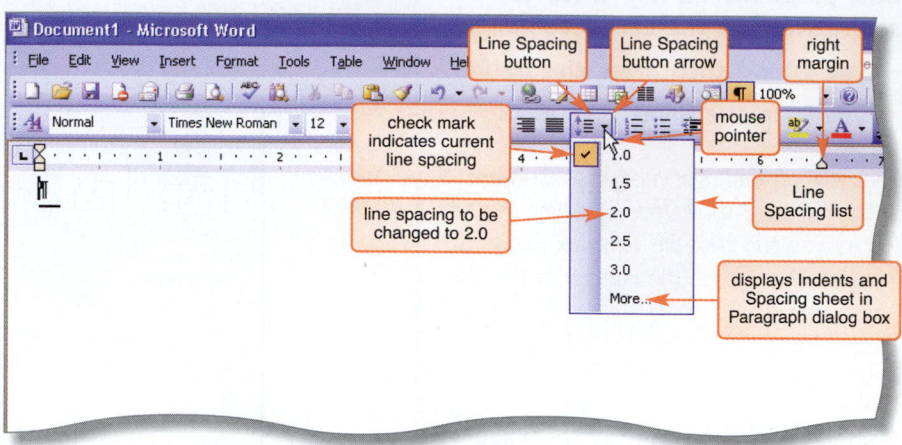

FIGURE 2-5

2

• **Click 2.0 in the Line Spacing list.**

Word changes the line spacing to double at the location of the insertion point (Figure 2-6).

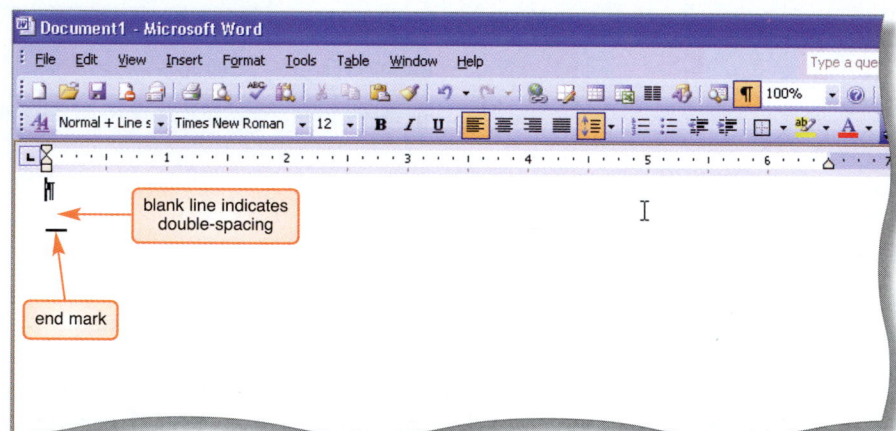

FIGURE 2-6

Notice when line spacing is double (Figure 2-6), the end mark displays one blank line below the insertion point.

The Line Spacing list (Figure 2-5) contains a variety of settings for the line spacing. The default, 1 (for single), and the options 1.5, 2 (for double), 2.5, and 3 (for triple) instruct Word to adjust line spacing automatically to accommodate the largest font or graphic on a line. For additional line spacing options, click More in the Line Spacing list and then click the Line spacing box arrow in the Indents and Spacing sheet in the Paragraph dialog box.

If you wanted to apply the most recently set line spacing to the current or selected paragraphs, you would click the Line Spacing button instead of the Line Spacing button arrow.

To change the line spacing of existing text, select the text first and then change the line spacing. For example, to change an existing paragraph to double-spacing, triple-click the paragraph to select it, click the Line Spacing button arrow on the Formatting toolbar, and then click 2.0 in the list.

Using a Header to Number Pages

In Word, you easily can number pages by clicking Insert on the menu bar and then clicking Page Numbers. Using the Page Numbers command, you can specify the location (top or bottom of the page) and alignment (right, left, or centered) of the page numbers.

The MLA style requires that your last name display to the left of the page number on each page. The Page Numbers command, however, does not allow you to enter text along with the page number. Thus, to place your name to the left of the page number, you must create a header that contains the page number.

Headers and Footers

A **header** is text you want printed at the top of each page in a document. A **footer** is text you want printed at the bottom of every page. In Word, headers print in the top margin one-half inch from the top of every page, and footers print in the bottom margin one-half inch from the bottom of each page, which meets the MLA style. Headers and footers can include text and graphics, as well as the page number, total number of pages, current date, and current time.

In this project, you are to precede the page number with your last name placed one-half inch from the top of each page. Your last name and the page number should print right-aligned; that is, at the right margin.

To create the header, first you display the header area in the document window. Then, you can enter the header text into the header area. The procedures on the following pages show how to create the header with page numbers, according to the MLA documentation style.

To Display the Header Area

1

• **Click View on the menu bar (Figure 2-7).**

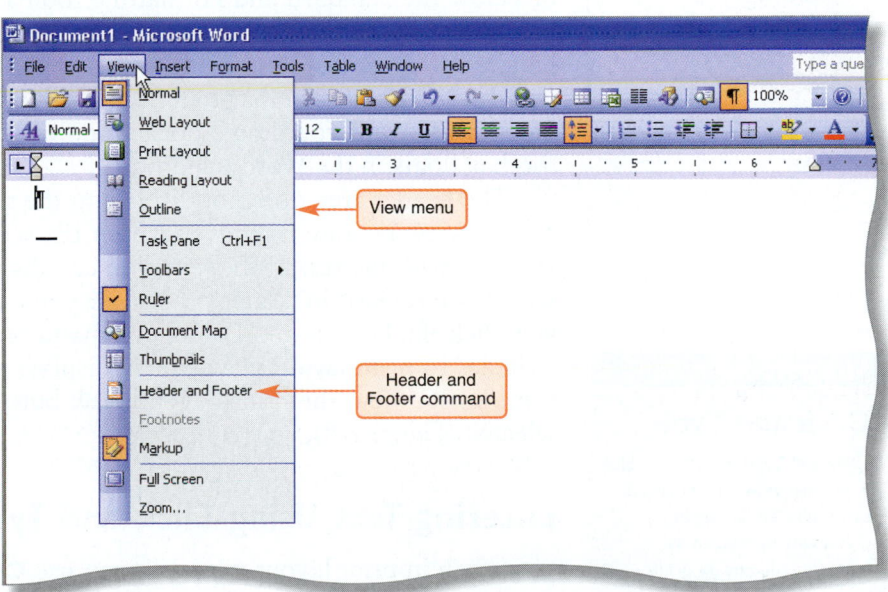

FIGURE 2-7

2

- **Click Header and Footer on the View menu.**

- **If your zoom percent is not 100, click View on the menu bar, click Zoom on the View menu, click 100%, and then click the OK button.**

Word switches from normal view to print layout view and displays the Header and Footer toolbar (Figure 2-8). You type header text in the header area.

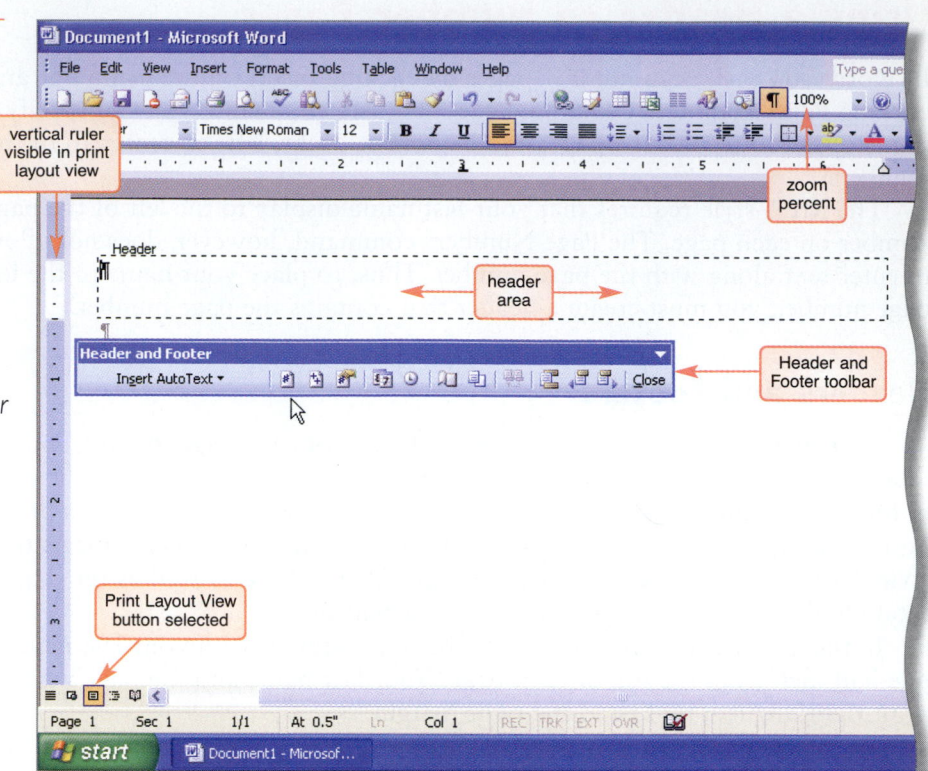

FIGURE 2-8

The Header and Footer toolbar initially floats in the document window. To move a floating toolbar, drag its title bar. You can **dock**, or attach, a floating toolbar above or below the Standard and Formatting toolbars by double-clicking the floating toolbar's title bar. To move a docked toolbar, drag its move handle. Recall that the move handle is the vertical dotted bar to the left of the first button on a docked toolbar. If you drag a floating toolbar to an edge of the window, the toolbar snaps to the edge of the window. If you drag a docked toolbar to the middle of the window, the toolbar floats in the Word window.

The header area does not display on the screen when the document window is in normal view because it tends to clutter the screen. To see the header in the document window with the rest of the text, you can display the document in print preview, which is discussed in a later project, or you can switch to print layout view. When you click the Header and Footer command on the View menu, Word automatically switches to **print layout view**, which displays the document exactly as it will print. In print layout view, the Print Layout View button on the horizontal scroll bar is selected (Figure 2-8).

Entering Text Using Click and Type

When in print layout view, you can use **Click and Type** to format and enter text, graphics, and other items. To use Click and Type, you double-click a blank area of the document window. Word automatically formats the item you enter according to the location where you double-click. The next steps show how to use Click and Type to right-align and then type the last name into the header area.

To Click and Type

1

• **Position the mouse pointer at the right edge of the header area to display a right-align icon next to the I-beam.**

As you move the Click and Type pointer around the window, the icon changes to represent formatting that will be applied if you double-click at that location (Figure 2-9).

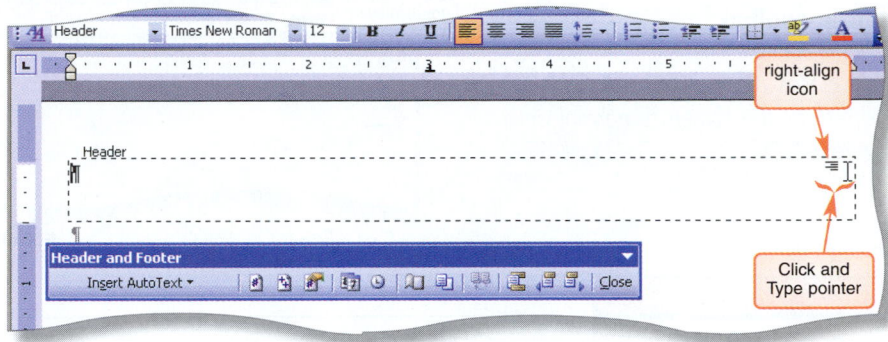

FIGURE 2-9

2

• **Double-click.**

• **Type** Zhao **and then press the SPACEBAR.**

Word displays the last name, Zhao, right-aligned in the header area (Figure 2-10).

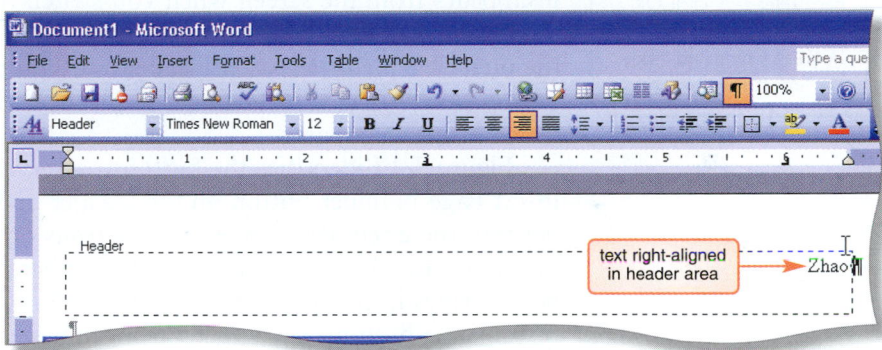

FIGURE 2-10

Entering a Page Number into the Header

The next task is to enter the page number into the header area, as shown in the following steps.

To Enter a Page Number

1

• **Click the Insert Page Number button on the Header and Footer toolbar.**

Word displays the page number 1 in the header area (Figure 2-11).

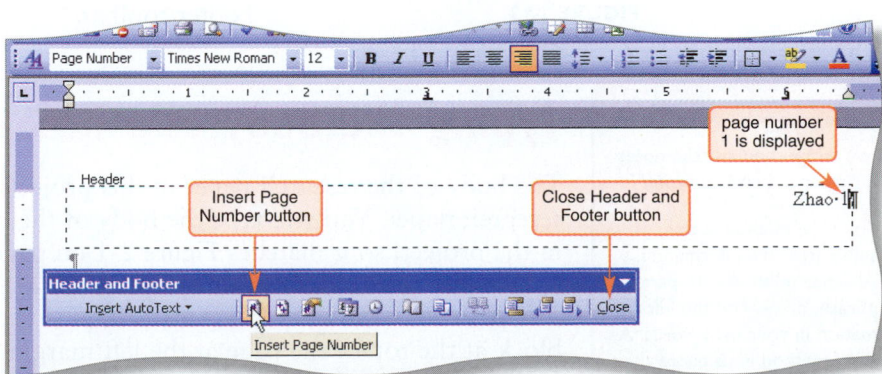

FIGURE 2-11

2

• **Click the Close Header and Footer button on the Header and Footer toolbar.**

Word closes the Header and Footer toolbar and returns the screen to normal view (Figure 2-12).

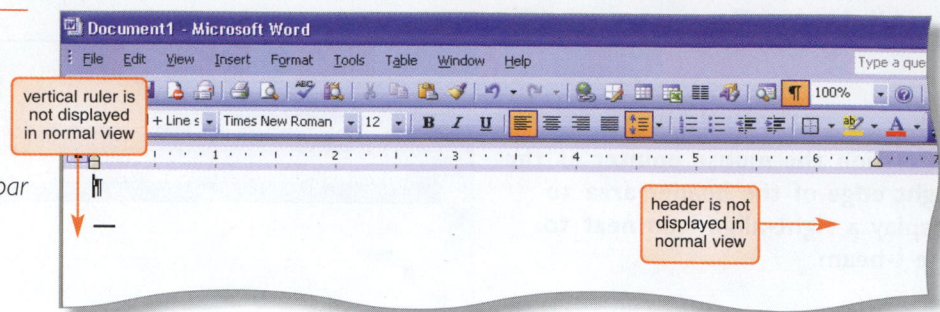

vertical ruler is not displayed in normal view

header is not displayed in normal view

FIGURE 2-12

Word does not display the header on the screen in normal view. Although it disappears from the screen when you switch from print layout view to normal view, the header still is part of the document. To view the header, you can click View on the menu bar and then click Header and Footer; you can switch to print layout view; or you can display the document in print preview. Project 3 discusses print layout view and print preview.

Figure 2-13 identifies the buttons on the Header and Footer toolbar. Just as the Insert Page Number button on the Header and Footer toolbar inserts the page number into the document, three other buttons on the Header and Footer toolbar insert items into the document. The Insert Number of Pages button inserts the total number of pages in the document; the Insert Date button inserts the current date; and the Insert Time button inserts the current time.

To edit an existing header, you can follow the same procedure that you use to create a new header. That is, click View on the menu bar and then click Header and Footer to display the header area. If you have multiple headers, click the Show Next button on the Header and Footer toolbar until the appropriate header displays in the header area. Edit the header as you would any Word text and then click the Close Header and Footer button on the Header and Footer toolbar.

To create a footer, click View on the menu bar, click Header and Footer, click the Switch Between Header and Footer button on the Header and Footer toolbar, and then follow the same procedure as you would to create a header.

Later projects explain other buttons on the Header and Footer toolbar.

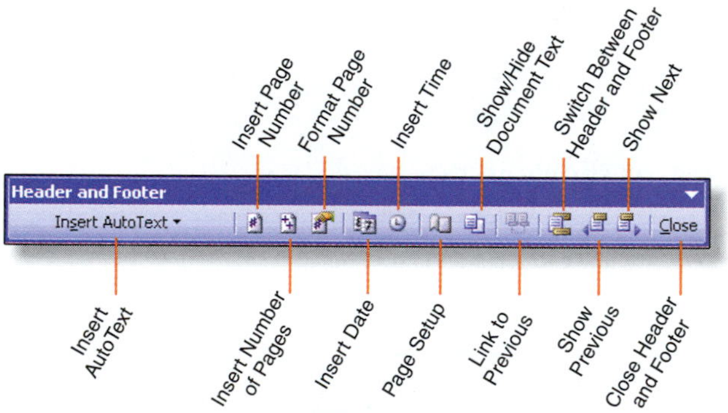

Insert Page Number · Format Page Number · Insert Time · Show/Hide Document Text · Switch Between Header and Footer · Show Next

Header and Footer
Insert AutoText ▾   Close

Insert AutoText · Insert Number of Pages · Insert Date · Page Setup · Link to Previous · Show Previous · Close Header and Footer

FIGURE 2-13

Typing the Body of a Research Paper

The body of the research paper in this project encompasses the first two pages of the research paper. You will type the body of the research paper and then modify it later in the project, so it matches Figure 2-1 on page WD 75.

As discussed earlier in this project, the MLA style does not require a separate title page for research papers. Instead, place your name and course information in a block at the top of the page at the left margin. The next steps describe how to begin typing the body of the research paper.

To Enter Name and Course Information

1 **Type** `Suzy Zhao` **and then press the** ENTER **key.**

2 **Type** `Mr. Ortiz` **and then press the** ENTER **key.**

3 **Type** `Information Systems 101` **and then press the** ENTER **key.**

4 **Type** `October 13, 2005` **and then press the** ENTER **key.**

Word displays the student name on line 1, the instructor name on line 2, the course name on line 3, and the paper due date on line 4 (Figure 2-14). Depending on your Word settings, the smart tag indicator may not appear below the date on the screen.

Q&A

Q: Does the APA style require a title page?

A: Yes, a separate title page is required instead of placing name and course information on the paper's first page. The running head (header), which contains a brief summary of the title and the page number, also is on the title page.

More About

Smart Tags

Word notifies you of a smart tag by displaying a smart tag indicator, such as the purple dotted underline shown in Figure 2-14. You then can use the smart tag to perform tasks more efficiently. For example, you can schedule an appointment on the under-lined date in Outlook Calendar. Smart tags are discussed later in this project.

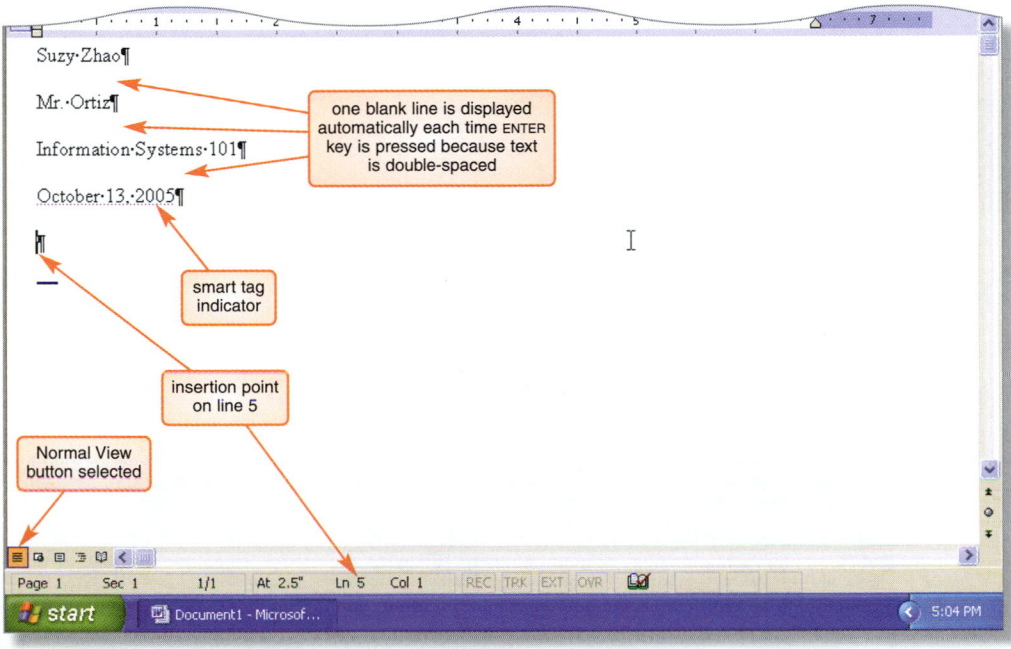

one blank line is displayed automatically each time ENTER key is pressed because text is double-spaced

smart tag indicator

insertion point on line 5

Normal View button selected

FIGURE 2-14

Notice in Figure 2-14 that the insertion point currently is on line 5. Each time you press the ENTER key, Word advances two lines on the screen. The line counter on the status bar is incremented by only one, however, because earlier you set line spacing to double.

If you watch the screen as you type, you may have noticed that as you typed the first few characters in the month, Octo, Word displayed the **AutoComplete tip**, October, above the characters. To save typing, you could press the ENTER key while the AutoComplete tip appears, which instructs Word to place the text of the AutoComplete tip at the location of your typing.

Applying Formatting Using Shortcut Keys

The next step is to enter the title of the research paper centered between the page margins. As you type text, you may want to format paragraphs and characters as you type them, instead of typing the text and then formatting it later. In Project 1, you typed the entire document, selected the text to be formatted, and then applied the desired formatting using toolbar buttons. When your fingers are already on the keyboard, it often is more efficient to use **shortcut keys**, or keyboard key combinations, to format text as you type it.

The following steps show how to center a paragraph using the shortcut keys CTRL+E and then left-align a paragraph using the shortcut keys CTRL+L. (Recall from Project 1 that a notation such as CTRL+E means to press the letter e on the keyboard while holding down the CTRL key.)

To Format Text Using Shortcut Keys

1

• **Press CTRL+E.**

• **Type** Biometrics **and then press the ENTER key.**

Word centers the title between the left and right margins (Figure 2-15). The paragraph mark and insertion point are centered because the formatting specified in the previous paragraph is carried forward to the next paragraph.

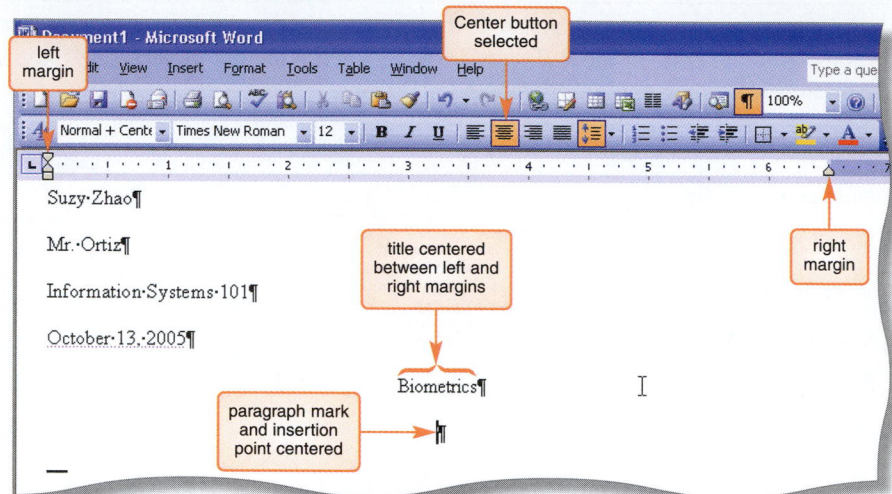

FIGURE 2-15

2

• **Press CTRL+L.**

Word positions the paragraph mark and the insertion point at the left margin (Figure 2-16). The next text you type will be left-aligned.

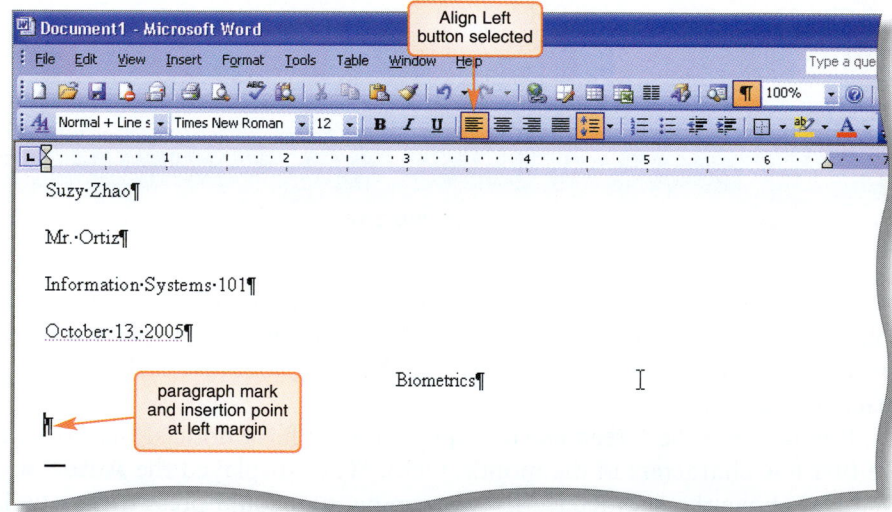

FIGURE 2-16

Word has many shortcut keys for your convenience while typing. Table 2-1 lists the common shortcut keys for formatting characters. Table 2-2 lists common shortcut keys for formatting paragraphs.

Table 2-1 Shortcut Keys for Formatting Characters	
CHARACTER FORMATTING TASK	**SHORTCUT KEYS**
All capital letters	CTRL+SHIFT+A
Bold	CTRL+B
Case of letters	SHIFT+F3
Decrease font size	CTRL+SHIFT+<
Decrease font size 1 point	CTRL+[
Double-underline	CTRL+SHIFT+D
Increase font size	CTRL+SHIFT+>
Increase font size 1 point	CTRL+]
Italic	CTRL+I
Remove character formatting (plain text)	CTRL+SPACEBAR
Small uppercase letters	CTRL+SHIFT+K
Subscript	CTRL+=
Superscript	CTRL+SHIFT+PLUS SIGN
Underline	CTRL+U
Underline words, not spaces	CTRL+SHIFT+W

Table 2-2 Shortcut Keys for Formatting Paragraphs	
PARAGRAPH FORMATTING TASK	**SHORTCUT KEYS**
1.5 line spacing	CTRL+5
Add/remove one line above	CTRL+0 (zero)
Center paragraph	CTRL+E
Decrease paragraph indent	CTRL+SHIFT+M
Double-space lines	CTRL+2
Hanging indent	CTRL+T
Increase paragraph indent	CTRL+M
Justify paragraph	CTRL+J
Left-align paragraph	CTRL+L
Remove hanging indent	CTRL+SHIFT+T
Remove paragraph formatting	CTRL+Q
Right-align paragraph	CTRL+R
Single-space lines	CTRL+1

Saving the Research Paper

You now should save the research paper. For a detailed example of the procedure summarized below, refer to pages WD 28 through WD 30 in Project 1.

To Save a Document

1 Insert a floppy disk into drive A.

2 Click the Save button on the Standard toolbar.

3 Type `Biometrics Paper` in the File name text box.

4 Click the Save in box arrow and then click 3½ Floppy (A:).

5 Click the Save button in the Save As dialog box.

Word saves the document with the file name, Biometrics Paper (shown in Figure 2-17 on the next page).

Indenting Paragraphs

According to the MLA style, the first line of each paragraph in the research paper is to be indented one-half inch from the left margin. You can instruct Word to indent just the first line of a paragraph, called **first-line indent**, using the horizontal ruler. The left edge of the horizontal ruler contains two triangles above a square. The **First Line Indent marker** is the top triangle at the 0" mark on the ruler (Figure 2-17). The bottom triangle is discussed later in this project. The small square at the 0" mark is the Left Indent marker. The **Left Indent marker** allows you to change the entire left margin, whereas the First Line Indent marker indents only the first line of the paragraph.

The following steps show how to first-line indent paragraphs in the research paper.

To First-Line Indent Paragraphs

1

• **If the horizontal ruler is not displayed on your screen, click View on the menu bar and then click Ruler.**

• **With the insertion point on the paragraph mark in line 6, point to the First Line Indent marker on the ruler (Figure 2-17).**

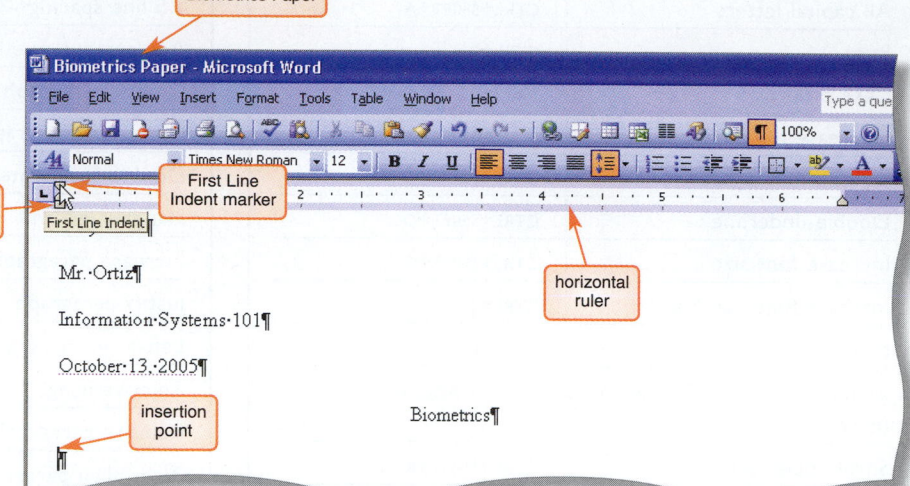

FIGURE 2-17

2

• **Drag the First Line Indent marker to the .5" mark on the ruler.**

As you drag the mouse, Word displays a vertical dotted line in the document window, indicating the proposed location of the first line of the paragraph (Figure 2-18).

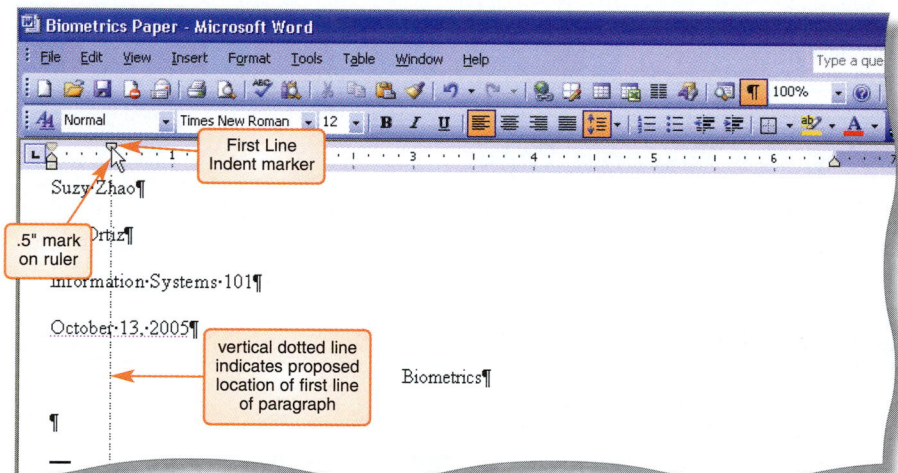

FIGURE 2-18

3

• **Release the mouse button.**

Word displays the First Line Indent marker at the .5" mark on the ruler, or one-half inch from the left margin (Figure 2-19). The paragraph mark containing the insertion point in the document window also moves one-half inch to the right.

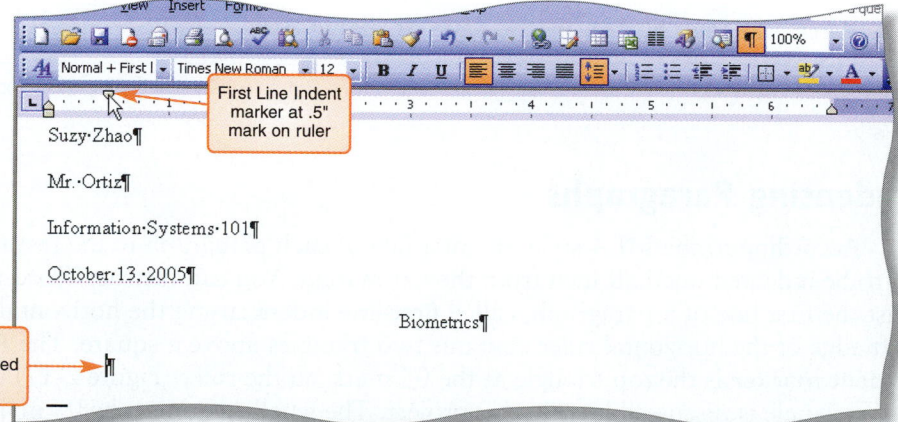

FIGURE 2-19

4

• **Type the first paragraph of the research paper body, as shown in Figure 2-20.**

• **Press the ENTER key.**

• **Type** A biometric device translates a personal characteristic into a digital code that is compared with a digital code stored in the computer.

Word automatically indents the first line of the second paragraph by one-half inch (Figure 2-20).

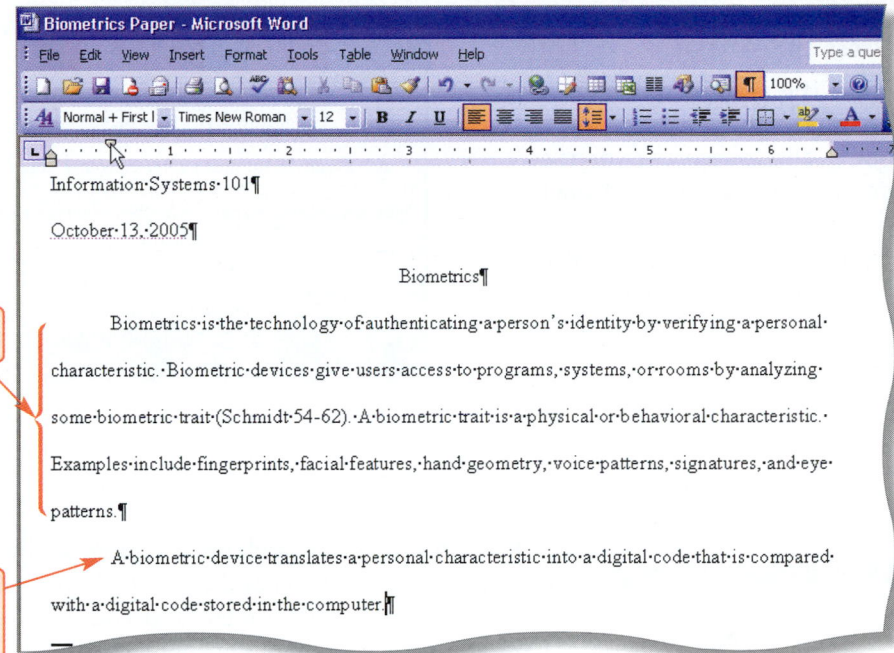

FIGURE 2-20

Recall that each time you press the ENTER key, the paragraph formatting in the previous paragraph is carried forward to the next paragraph. Thus, once you set the first-line indent, its format carries forward automatically to each subsequent paragraph you type.

Using Word's AutoCorrect Feature

As you type, you may make typing, spelling, capitalization, or grammar errors. For this reason, Word provides an **AutoCorrect** feature that automatically corrects these kinds of errors as you type them in the document. For example, if you type the text, ahve, Word automatically changes it to the correct spelling, have, when you press the SPACEBAR or a punctuation mark key such as a period or comma.

Word has predefined many commonly misspelled words, which it automatically corrects for you. In the following steps the word, the, is misspelled intentionally as teh to illustrate the AutoCorrect as you type feature.

Other Ways

1. On Format menu click Paragraph, click Indents and Spacing tab, click Special box arrow, click First line, click OK button
2. Right-click paragraph, click Paragraph on shortcut menu, click Indents and Spacing tab, click Special box arrow, click First line, click OK button
3. Press TAB key at beginning of paragraph
4. In Voice Command mode, say "Format, Paragraph, Indents and Spacing, Special, First line, OK"

To AutoCorrect as You Type

1

• **Press the SPACEBAR.**

• **Type the beginning of the next sentence, misspelling the word, the, as follows:** If the digital code in the computer does not match teh **(Figure 2-21).**

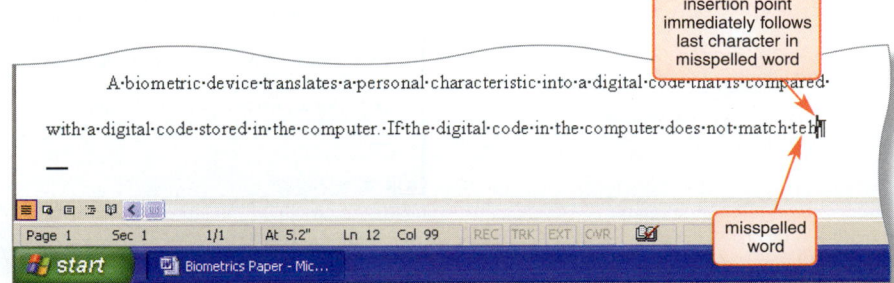

FIGURE 2-21

2

• **Press the SPACEBAR.**

• **Type the rest of the sentence:** personal characteristic's code, the computer denies access to the individual.

As soon as the SPACEBAR is pressed, Word's AutoCorrect feature detects the misspelling and corrects the misspelled word (Figure 2-22).

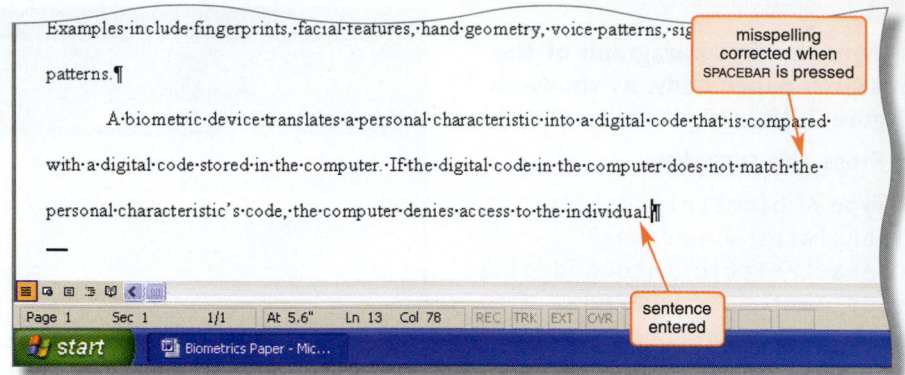

FIGURE 2-22

Word has a list of predefined typing, spelling, capitalization, and grammar errors that AutoCorrect detects and corrects. If you do not like a change that Word automatically makes in a document and you immediately notice the automatic correction, you can undo the change by clicking the Undo button on the Standard toolbar; clicking Edit on the menu bar and then clicking Undo; or pressing CTRL+Z.

If you do not immediately notice the change, you still can undo a correction automatically made by Word through the AutoCorrect Options button. When you position the mouse pointer on text that Word automatically corrected, a small blue box appears below the text. If you point to the small blue box, Word displays the AutoCorrect Options button. When you click the **AutoCorrect Options button**, Word displays a menu that allows you to undo a correction or change how Word handles future automatic corrections of this type. The following steps show how to use the AutoCorrect Options button and menu.

To Use the AutoCorrect Options Button

1

• **Position the mouse pointer at the beginning of the text automatically corrected by Word (in this case, the t in the).**

Word displays a small blue box below the automatically corrected word (Figure 2-23).

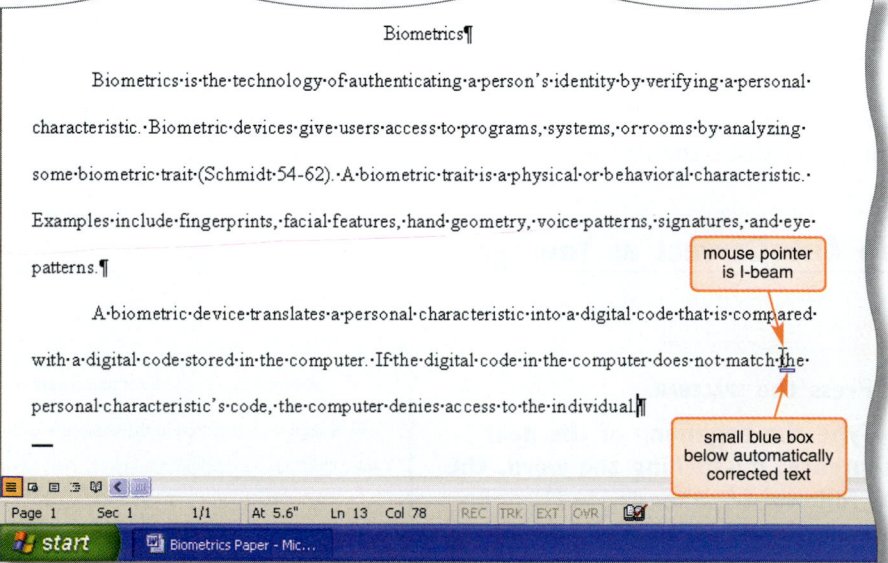

FIGURE 2-23

2

• **Point to the small blue box to display the AutoCorrect Options button.**

• **Click the AutoCorrect Options button.**

Word displays the AutoCorrect Options menu (Figure 2-24).

3

• **Press the ESCAPE key to remove the AutoCorrect Options menu from the screen.**

When you move the mouse pointer, the AutoCorrect Options button disappears from the screen, or you can press the ESCAPE key a second time to remove the AutoCorrect Options button from the screen.

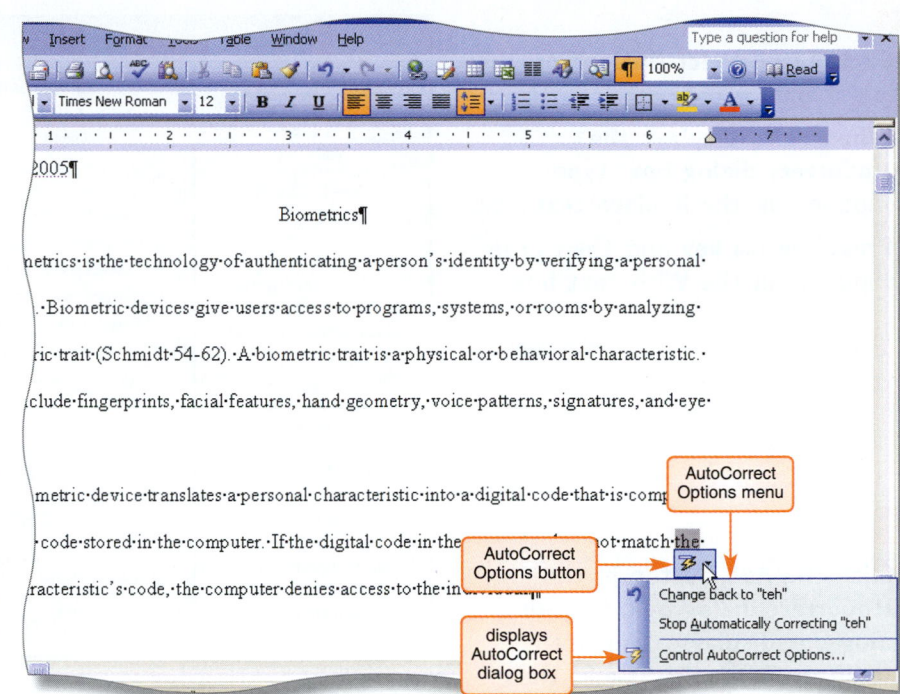

FIGURE 2-24

More About

AutoCorrect Options

The small blue box that appears below the automatically corrected text (Figure 2-23) is another type of smart tag indicator. Smart tags are discussed later in this project.

In addition to the predefined list of AutoCorrect spelling, capitalization, and grammar errors, you can create your own AutoCorrect entries to add to the list. For example, if you tend to type the word, computer, as comptuer, you should create an AutoCorrect entry for it, as shown in these steps.

To Create an AutoCorrect Entry

1

• **Click Tools on the menu bar (Figure 2-25).**

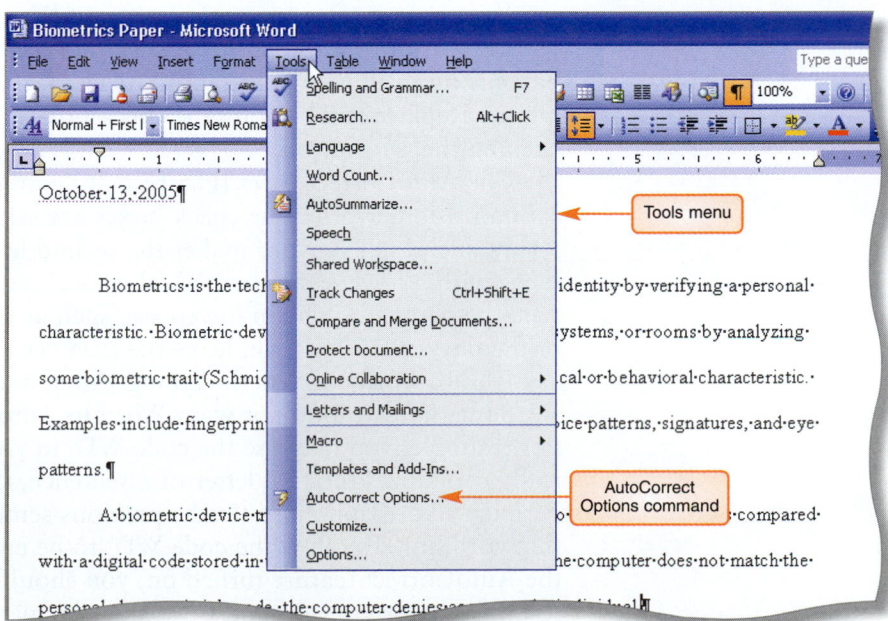

FIGURE 2-25

2

• **Click AutoCorrect Options on the Tools menu.**

• **When Word displays the AutoCorrect dialog box, type** comptuer **in the Replace text box.**

• **Press the TAB key and then type** computer **in the With text box.**

In the AutoCorrect dialog box, the Replace text box contains the misspelled word, and the With text box contains its correct spelling (Figure 2-26).

3

• **Click the Add button in the AutoCorrect dialog box. (If your dialog box displays a Replace button instead, click it and then click the Yes button in the Microsoft Office Word dialog box.)**

• **Click the OK button.**

Word adds the entry alphabetically to the list of words to correct automatically as you type.

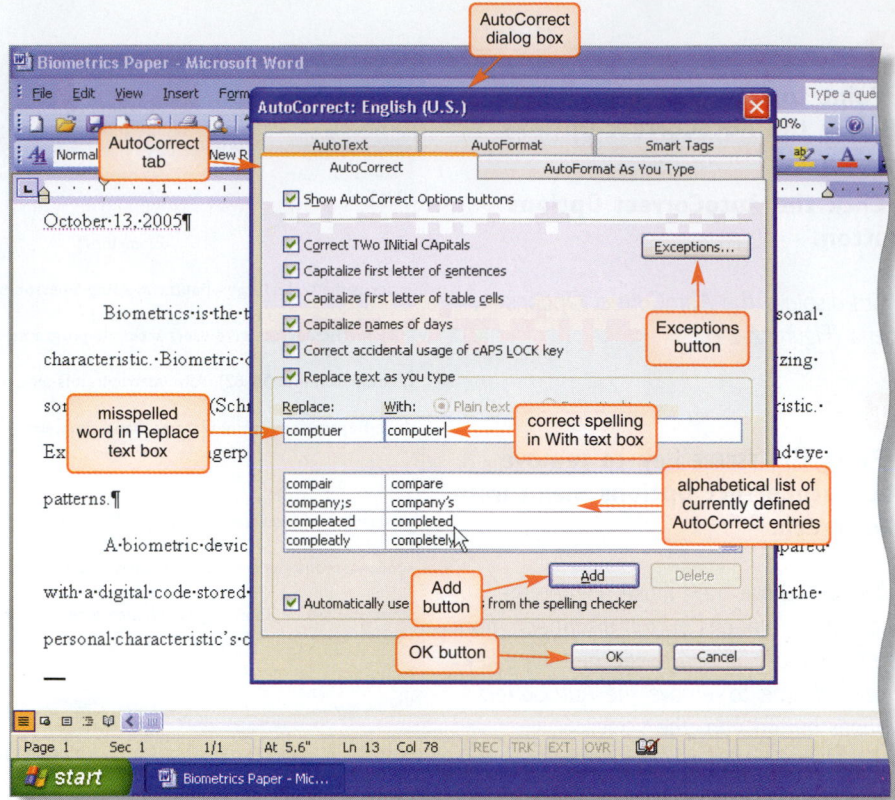

FIGURE 2-26

In addition to creating AutoCorrect entries for words you commonly misspell or mistype, you can create entries for abbreviations, codes, and so on. For example, you could create an AutoCorrect entry for asap, indicating that Word should replace this text with the phrase, as soon as possible.

If, for some reason, you do not want Word to correct automatically as you type, you can turn off the Replace text as you type feature by clicking Tools on the menu bar, clicking AutoCorrect Options, clicking the AutoCorrect tab (Figure 2-26), clicking the Replace text as you type check box to remove the check mark, and then clicking the OK button.

The AutoCorrect sheet (Figure 2-26) contains other check boxes that correct capitalization errors if the check boxes are selected. If you type two capital letters in a row, such as TH, Word makes the second letter lowercase, Th. If you begin a sentence with a lowercase letter, Word capitalizes the first letter of the sentence. If you type the name of a day in lowercase, such as tuesday, Word capitalizes the first letter of the day, Tuesday. If you leave the CAPS LOCK key on and begin a new sentence such as aFTER, Word corrects the typing, After, and turns off the CAPS LOCK key.

Sometimes you do not want Word to AutoCorrect a particular word or phrase. For example, you may use the code WD. in your documents. Because Word automatically capitalizes the first letter of a sentence, the character you enter following the period will be capitalized (in the previous sentence, it would capitalize the letter i in the word, in). To allow the code WD. to be entered into a document and still leave the AutoCorrect feature turned on, you should set an exception. To set an exception to an AutoCorrect rule, click Tools on the menu bar, click AutoCorrect Options, click the AutoCorrect tab, click the Exceptions button in the AutoCorrect sheet (Figure 2-26), click the appropriate tab in the AutoCorrect Exceptions dialog box, type the exception entry in the text box, click the Add button, click the Close button in the AutoCorrect Exceptions dialog box, and then click the OK button in the AutoCorrect dialog box.

The next step is to continue typing text in the body of the research paper, up to the location of the footnote, as described below.

To Enter More Text

1 Press the ENTER key.

2 Type the first five sentences in the third paragraph of the paper as shown in Figure 2-27.

Word displays the first five sentences in the third paragraph in the document window (Figure 2-27).

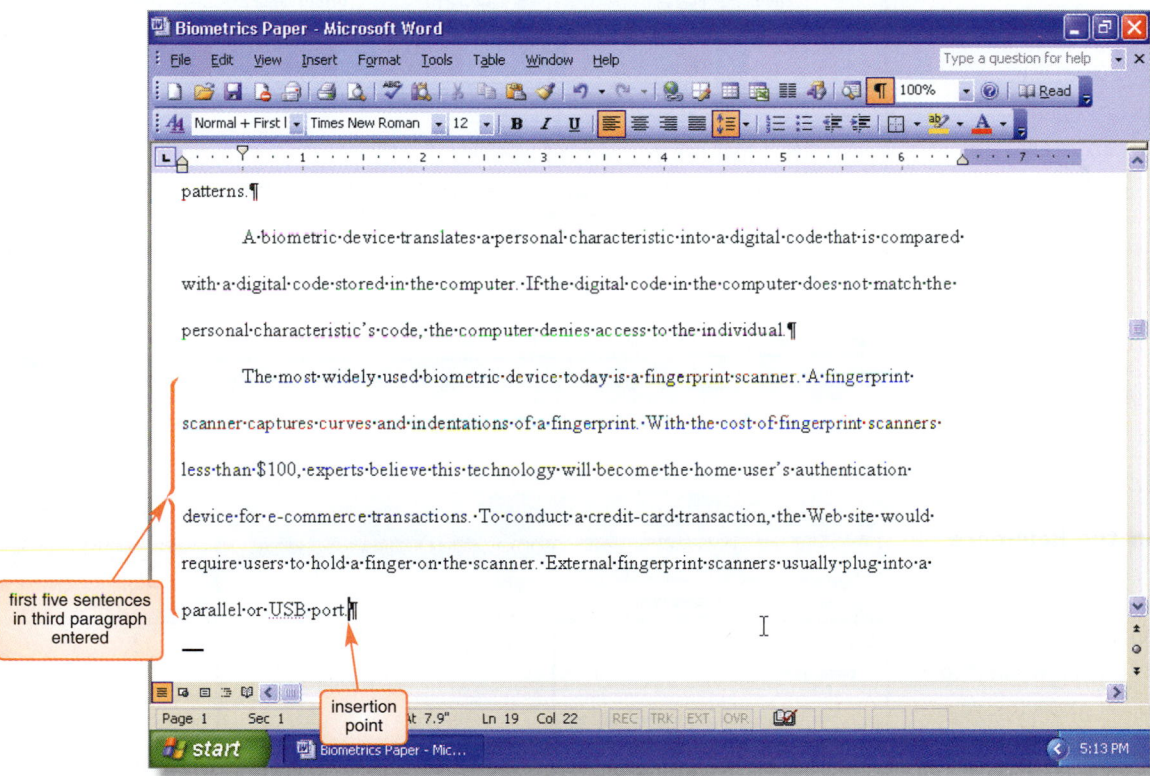

FIGURE 2-27

Adding Footnotes

As discussed earlier in this project, explanatory notes are optional in the MLA documentation style. They are used primarily to elaborate on points discussed in the body of a research paper. The MLA style specifies that a superscript (raised number) be used for a **note reference mark** to signal that an explanatory note exists either at the bottom of the page as a **footnote** or at the end of the document as an **endnote**.

Word, by default, places notes at the bottom of each page as footnotes. In Word, **note text** can be any length and format. Word automatically numbers notes sequentially by placing a note reference mark in the body of the document and also to the left of the note text. If you insert, rearrange, or remove notes, Word renumbers any subsequent note reference marks according to their new sequence in the document.

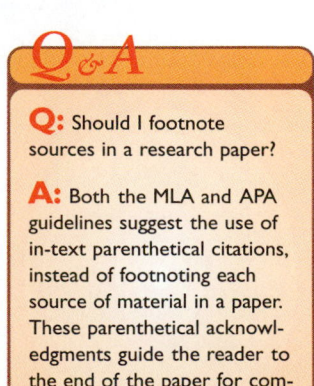

Q: Should I footnote sources in a research paper?

A: Both the MLA and APA guidelines suggest the use of in-text parenthetical citations, instead of footnoting each source of material in a paper. These parenthetical acknowledgments guide the reader to the end of the paper for complete information on the source.

The following steps show how to add a footnote to the research paper.

To Add a Footnote

1

• **With the insertion point positioned as shown in Figure 2-28, click Insert on the menu bar and then point to Reference (Figure 2-28).**

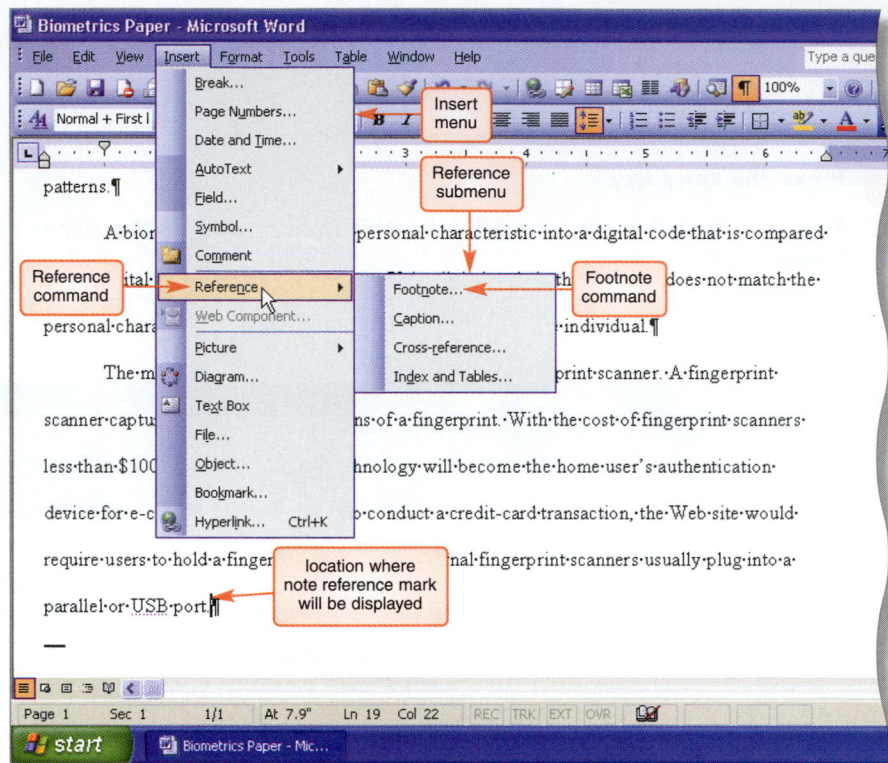

FIGURE 2-28

2

• **Click Footnote on the Reference submenu.**

Word displays the Footnote and Endnote dialog box (Figure 2-29). If you wanted to create endnotes instead of footnotes, you would click Endnotes in the Footnote and Endnote dialog box.

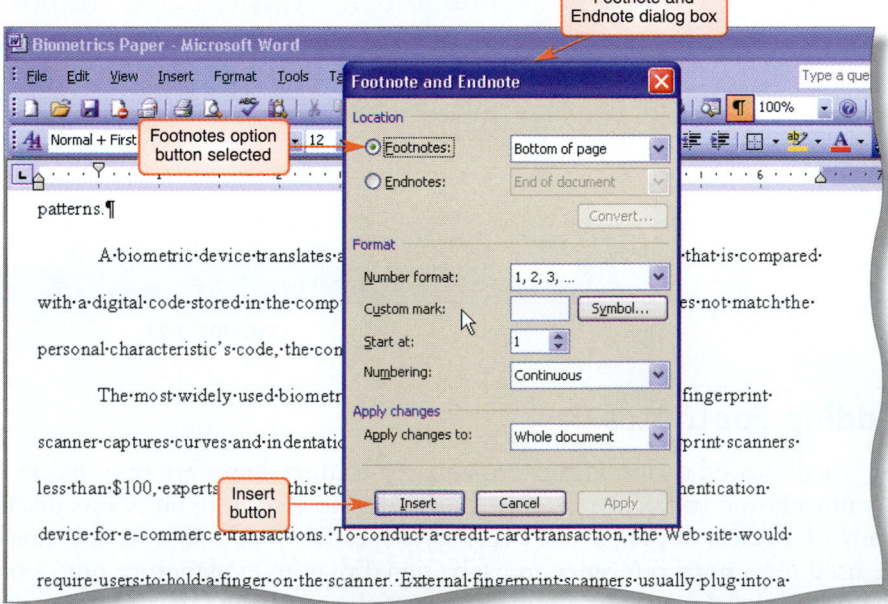

FIGURE 2-29

3

• **Click the Insert button in the Footnote and Endnote dialog box.**

Word opens a note pane in the lower portion of the Word window with the note reference mark (a superscripted 1) positioned at the left margin of the note pane (Figure 2-30). Word also displays the note reference mark in the document window at the location of the insertion point. Note reference marks are, by default, superscripted; that is, raised above other letters.

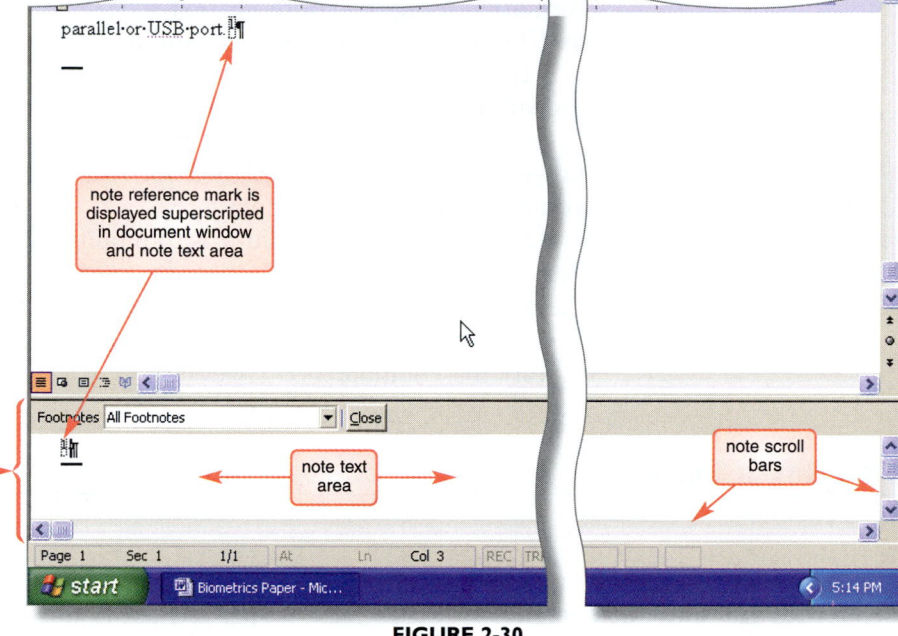

FIGURE 2-30

4

• **Type** According to Carter and Juarez, newer keyboards and notebook computers have a fingerprint scanner built into them (42-53).

Word displays the note text in the note pane (Figure 2-31).

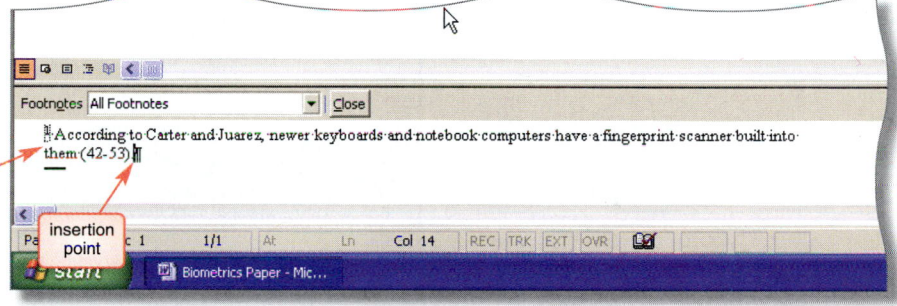

FIGURE 2-31

The footnote is not formatted according to the MLA requirements. Thus, the next step is to modify the style of the footnote.

Modifying a Style

A **style** is a named group of formatting characteristics that you can apply to text. Word has many built-in, or predefined, styles that you may use to format text. The formats defined by these styles include character formatting, such as the font and font size; paragraph formatting, such as line spacing and text alignment; table formatting; and list formatting.

Whenever you create a document, Word formats the text using a particular style. The underlying style, called the **base style**, for a new Word document is the Normal style. For a new installation of Word 2003, the **Normal style** most likely uses 12-point Times New Roman font for characters and single-spaced, left-aligned paragraphs. As you type, you can apply different predefined styles to the text or you can create your own styles. A later project discusses applying and creating styles.

Other Ways

1. In Voice Command mode, say "Insert, Reference, Footnote, Insert, Dictation, [note text]"

More About

Styles

To view the list of styles associated with the current document, click the Style box arrow on the Formatting toolbar or display the Styles and Formatting task pane by clicking the Styles and Formatting button on the Formatting toolbar. To apply a style, click the desired style name in the Style list or in the Styles and Formatting task pane.

When the insertion point is in the note text area, the entered note text is formatted using the Footnote Text style. The Footnote Text style defines characters as 10-point Times New Roman and paragraphs as single-spaced and left-aligned.

You could change the paragraph formatting of the footnote text to first-line indent and double-spacing as you did for the text in the body of the research paper. Then, you would change the font size from 10 to 12 point. If you use this technique, however, you will need to change the format of the footnote text for each footnote you enter into the document.

A more efficient technique is to modify the format of the Footnote Text style to first-line indent and double-spaced paragraphs and a 12-point font size. By changing the formatting of the Footnote Text style, every footnote you enter into the document will use the formats defined in this style. The following steps show how to modify the Footnote Text style.

To Modify a Style

1

• **Right-click the note text in the note pane.**

Word displays a shortcut menu related to footnotes (Figure 2-32).

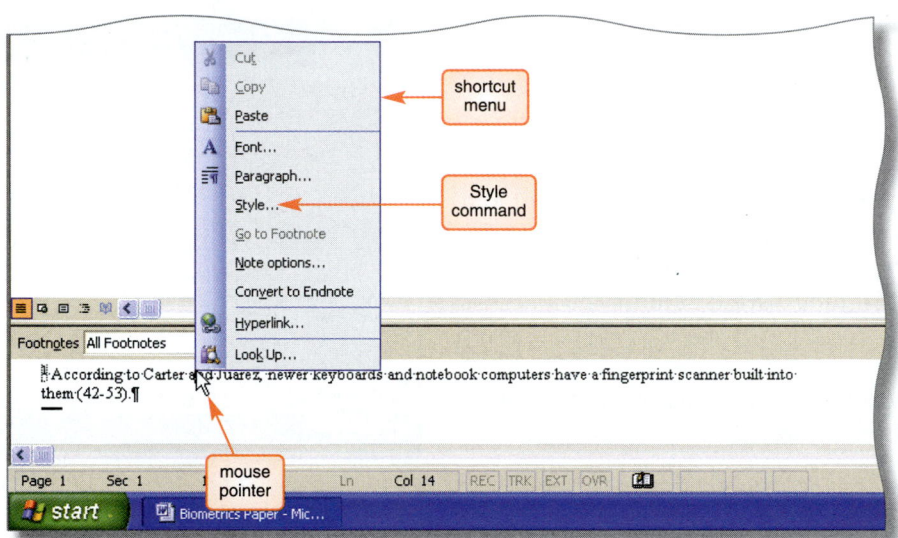

FIGURE 2-32

2

• **Click Style on the shortcut menu.**
• **When Word displays the Style dialog box, if necessary, click Footnote Text in the Styles list.**

The Preview area of the Style dialog box shows the formatting associated with the selected style (Figure 2-33). The selected style is Footnote Text.

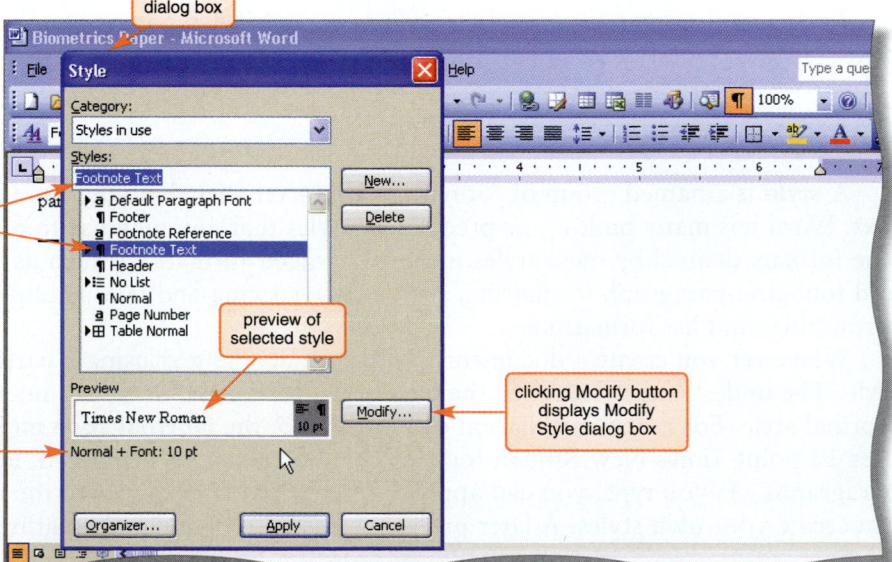

FIGURE 2-33

3

• **Click the Modify button in the Style dialog box.**

• **When Word displays the Modify Style dialog box, click the Font Size box arrow in the Formatting area and then click 12 in the Font Size list.**

• **Click the Double Space button in the Modify Style dialog box.**

In the Modify Style dialog box, the font size for the Footnote Text style is changed to 12, and paragraph spacing is changed to double (Figure 2-34). The first-line indent still must be set.

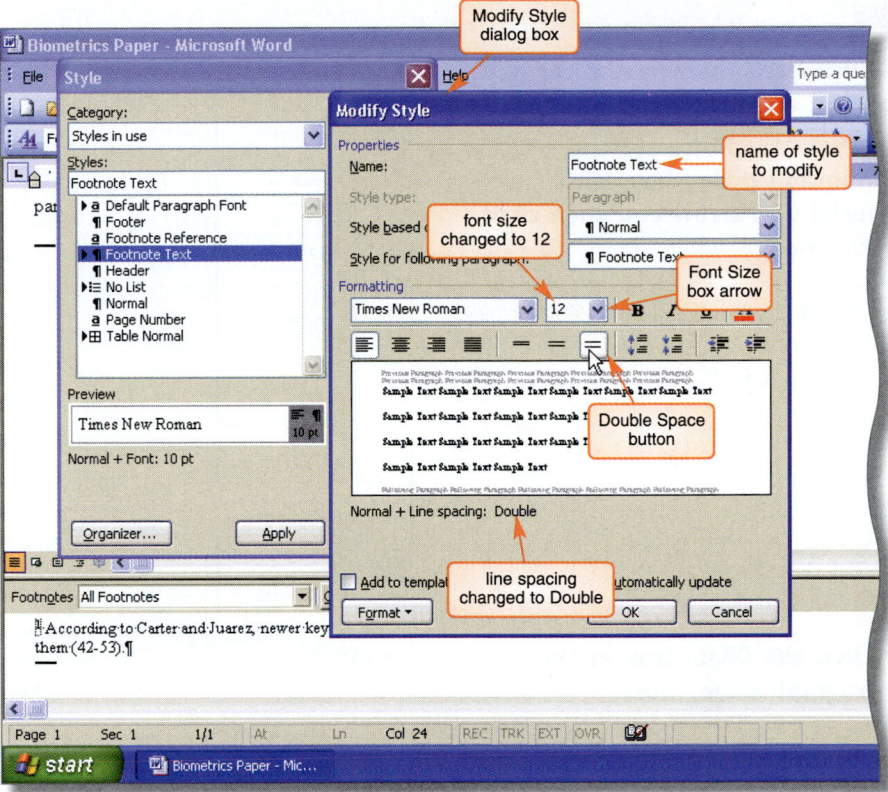

FIGURE 2-34

4

• **Click the Format button in the Modify Style dialog box.**

Word displays the Format button menu above the Format button (Figure 2-35).

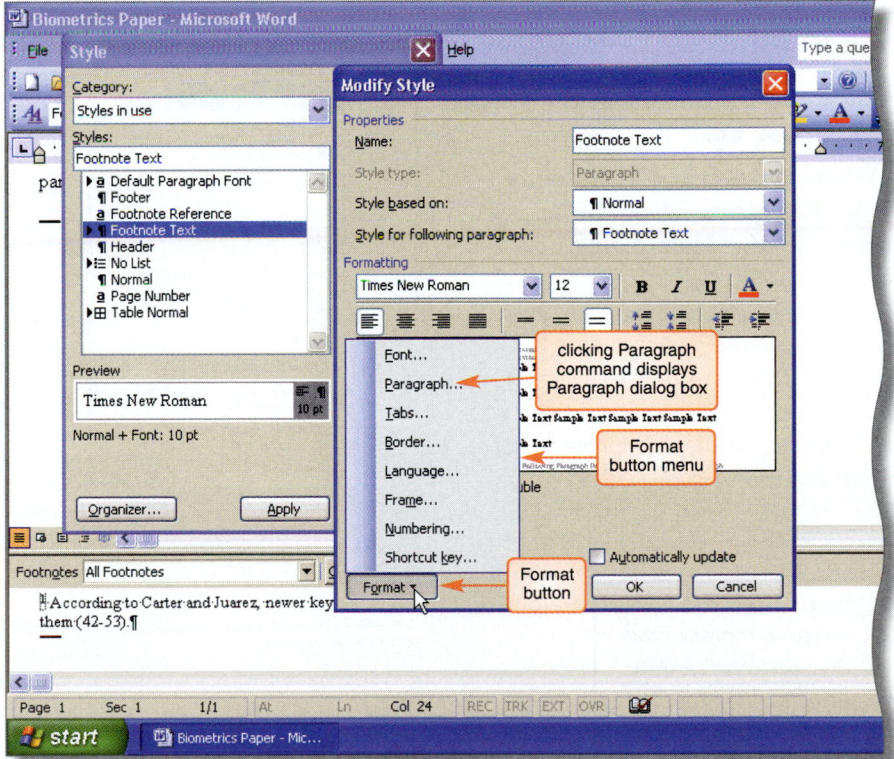

FIGURE 2-35

5

• **Click Paragraph on the Format button menu.**

• **When Word displays the Paragraph dialog box, click the Special box arrow and then click First line.**

In the Paragraph dialog box, Word displays First line in the Special box (Figure 2-36). Notice the default first-line indent is 0.5".

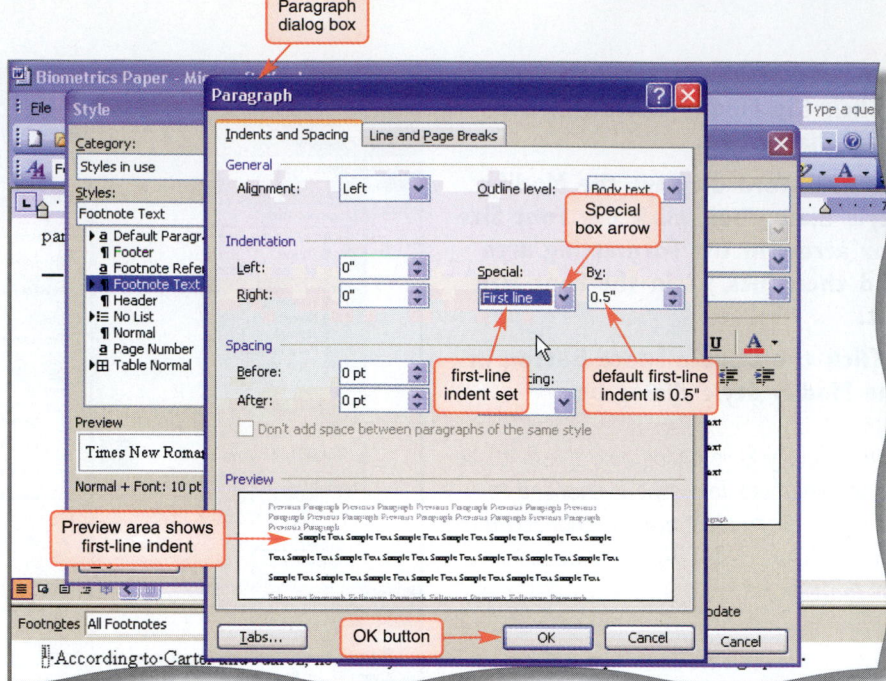

FIGURE 2-36

6

• **Click the OK button in the Paragraph dialog box.**

Word modifies the Footnote Text style to first-line indented paragraphs and closes the Paragraph dialog box (Figure 2-37). The Modify Style dialog box is visible again.

7

• **Click the OK button in the Modify Style dialog box.**

• **When Word closes the Modify Style dialog box, click the Apply button in the Style dialog box.**

Word displays the note text using the modified Footnote Text style, that is, the font size of the note text is changed to 12, the line spacing for the note is set to double, and the first line of the note is indented by one-half inch (Figure 2-38).

FIGURE 2-37

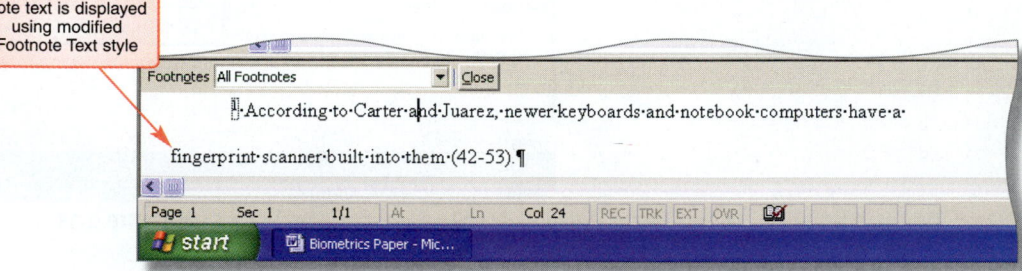

FIGURE 2-38

Any future footnotes entered into the document will use a 12-point font with the paragraphs first-line indented and double-spaced. The footnote now is complete. The next step is to close the note pane.

To Close the Note Pane

1

• **Position the mouse pointer on the Close button in the note pane (Figure 2-39).**

2

• **Click the Close button to remove the note pane from the document window.**

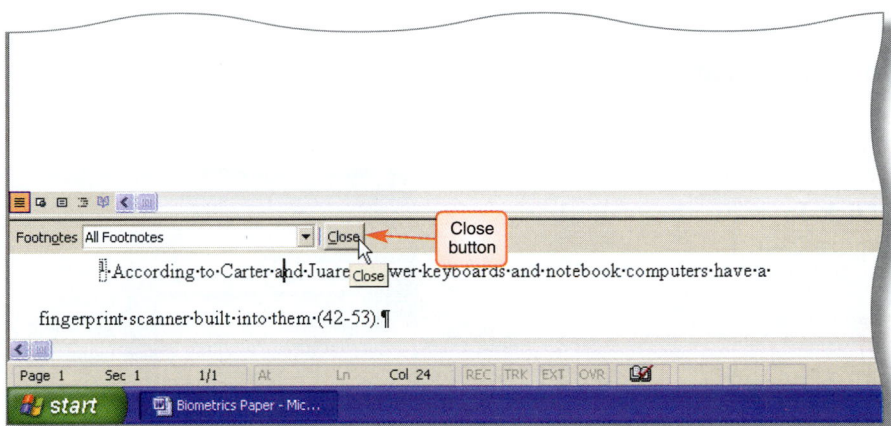

FIGURE 2-39

Other Ways

1. Press ALT+C
2. In Voice Command mode, say "Close"

When Word closes the note pane and returns to the document window, the note text disappears from the screen. Although the note text still exists, it usually is not visible as a footnote in normal view. If, however, you position the mouse pointer on the note reference mark, the note text displays above the note reference mark as a ScreenTip. To remove the ScreenTip, move the mouse pointer.

If you want to verify that the note text is positioned correctly on the page, you must switch to print layout view or display the document in print preview. Project 3 discusses print preview and print layout view.

To delete a note, select the note reference mark in the document window (not in the note pane) by dragging through the note reference mark and then click the Cut button on the Standard toolbar. Another way to delete a note is to click immediately to the right of the note reference mark in the document window and then press the BACKSPACE key twice, or click immediately to the left of the note reference mark in the document window and then press the DELETE key twice.

To move a note to a different location in a document, select the note reference mark in the document window (not in the note pane), click the Cut button on the Standard toolbar, click the location where you want to move the note, and then click the Paste button on the Standard toolbar. When you move or delete notes, Word automatically renumbers any remaining notes in the correct sequence.

You edit note text using the note pane that is displayed at the bottom of the Word window. To display the note text in the note pane, double-click the note reference mark in the document window, or click View on the menu bar and then click Footnotes. In the note pane, you can edit the note as you would any Word text. When finished editing the note text, click the Close button in the note pane.

If you want to change the format of note reference marks in footnotes or endnotes (i.e., from 1, 2, 3, to A, B, C), click Insert on the menu bar, point to Reference, and then click Footnote. When Word displays the Footnote and Endnote dialog box, click the Number format box arrow, click the desired number format in the list, and then click the OK button.

More About

Notes

To convert existing footnotes to endnotes, click Insert on the menu bar, point to Reference, and then click Footnote. Click the Convert button in the Footnote and Endnote dialog box. Make sure the Convert all footnotes to endnotes option button is selected and then click the OK button. Click the Close button in the Footnote and Endnote dialog box.

Using Word Count

Often when you write papers, you are required to compose the papers with a minimum number of words. The minimum requirement for the research paper in this project is 325 words. Word provides a command that displays the number of words, as well as the number of pages, characters, paragraphs, and lines in the current document. The following steps show how to use word count and display the Word Count toolbar, which allows you easily to recount words as you type more text.

To Count Words

 1

• Click **Tools** on the menu bar (Figure 2-40).

2

• Click **Word Count** on the Tools menu.

• When Word displays the Word Count dialog box, if necessary, click **Include footnotes and endnotes** to place a check mark in the check box.

• Click the **Show Toolbar** button in the Word Count dialog box.

In the Word Count dialog box, the number of pages, words, characters, paragraphs, and lines is displayed (Figure 2-41). The Word Count toolbar is displayed floating in the Word window.

3

• Click the **Close** button in the Word Count dialog box.

Word removes the Word Count dialog box from the screen, but the Word Count toolbar remains on the screen (Figure 2-42). Your Word Count toolbar may be displayed at a different location on the screen.

Other Ways

1. Click Recount button on Word Count toolbar
2. On File menu click Properties, click Statistics tab, click OK button
3. In Voice Command mode, say "Tools, Word Count, Include footnotes and endnotes, Show Toolbar, Close"

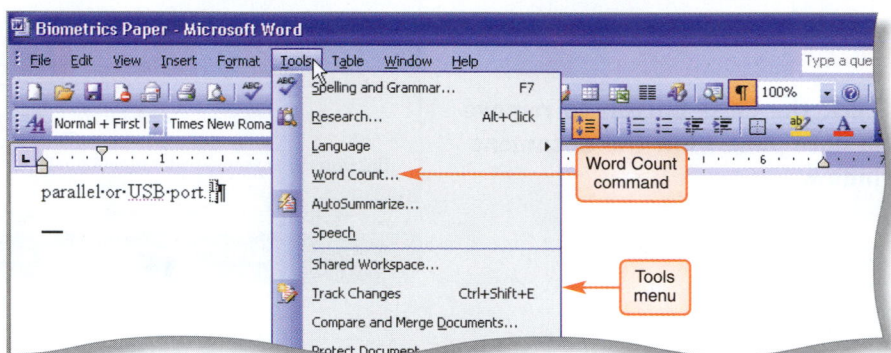

FIGURE 2-40

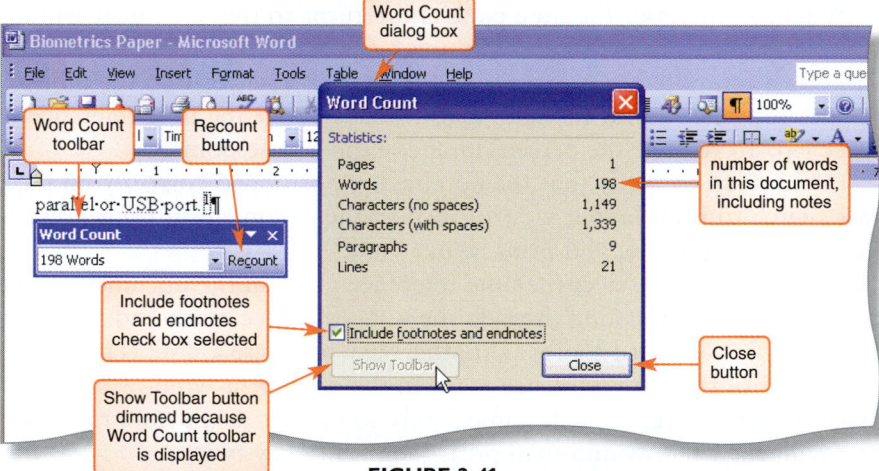

FIGURE 2-41

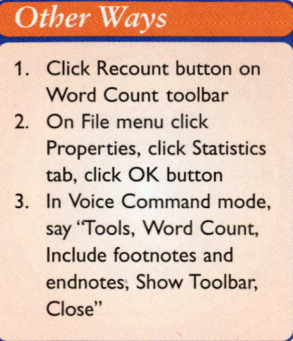

FIGURE 2-42

The Word Count toolbar floats on the screen. As discussed earlier in this project, you can move a floating toolbar by dragging its title bar.

The Word Count dialog box (Figure 2-41) presents a variety of statistics about the current document, including number of pages, words, characters, paragraphs, and lines. You can choose to have note text included or not included in these statistics. If you want statistics on only a section of the document, select the section and then issue the Word Count command.

At anytime, you can recount the number of words in a document by clicking the Recount button on the Word Count toolbar.

Automatic Page Breaks

As you type documents that exceed one page, Word automatically inserts page breaks, called **automatic page breaks** or **soft page breaks**, when it determines the text has filled one page according to paper size, margin settings, line spacing, and other settings. If you add text, delete text, or modify text on a page, Word recomputes the location of automatic page breaks and adjusts them accordingly.

Word performs page recomputation between the keystrokes, that is, in between the pauses in your typing. Thus, Word refers to the automatic page break task as **background repagination**. In normal view, automatic page breaks display on the Word screen as a single dotted horizontal line. The following step illustrates Word's automatic page break feature.

To Page Break Automatically

1

• **With the insertion point positioned as shown in Figure 2-42, press the SPACEBAR and then type the last three sentences of the third paragraph of the paper, as shown in Figure 2-43.**

• **Press the ENTER key and then type the fourth paragraph. Italicize the text in the parenthetical citation.**

• **Drag the title bar of the Word Count toolbar to the location shown in Figure 2-43.**

As you type, Word places an automatic page break between the third and fourth paragraphs in the paper (Figure 2-43). The status bar now displays Page 2 as the current page.

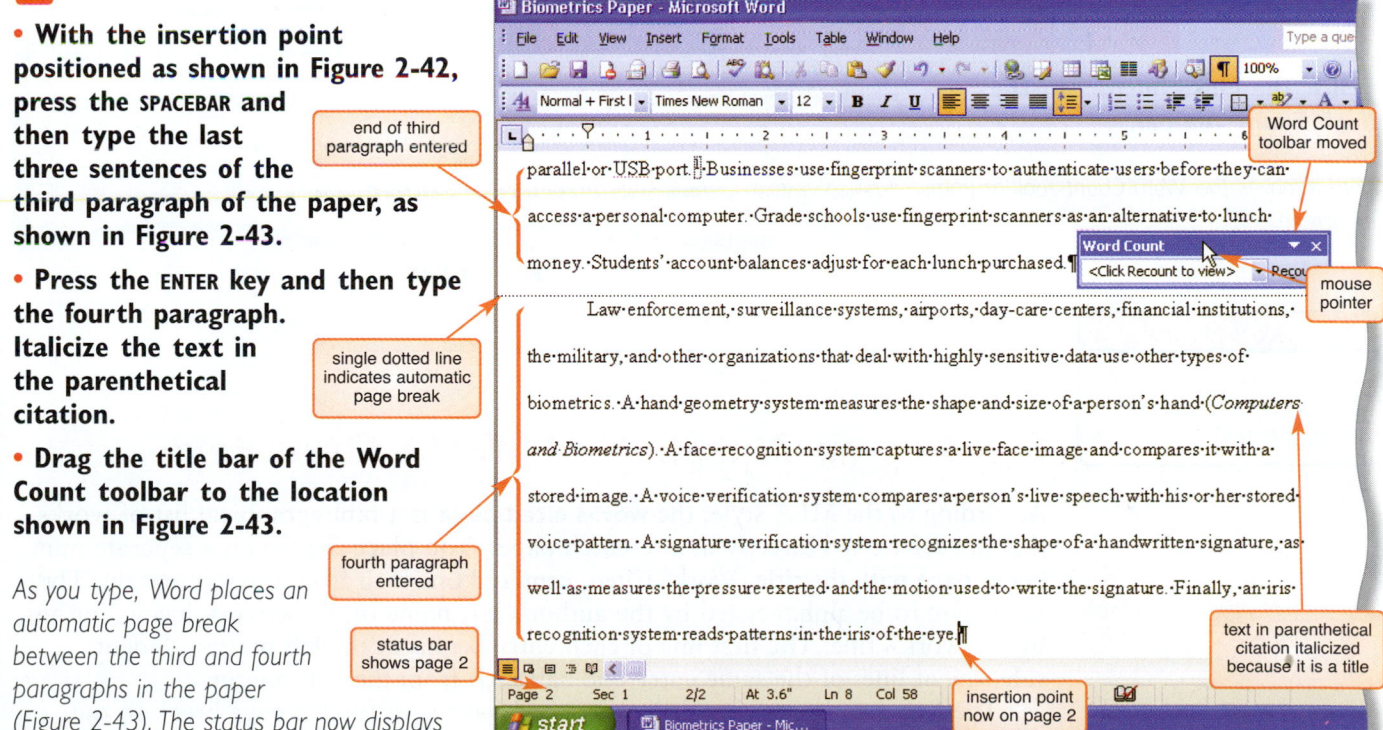

FIGURE 2-43

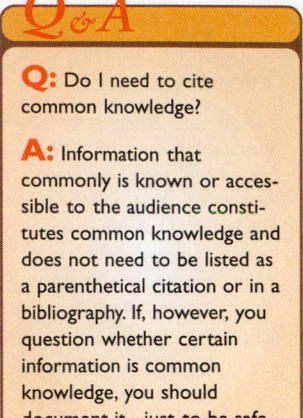

Your page break may occur at a different location, depending on the type of printer connected to the computer.

The header, although not shown in normal view, contains the name Zhao followed by the page number 2. If you wanted to view the header, click View on the menu bar and then click Header and Footer. Then, click the Close Header and Footer button on the Header and Footer toolbar to return to normal view.

Recounting Words in a Document

Now that the last paragraph of the body of the paper is typed, you want to recount the number of words to see if you have met the minimum requirement of 325 words. The following steps show how to use the Word Count toolbar to recount words in a document.

To Recount Words

1

• **Click the Recount button on the Word Count toolbar.**

The Word Count toolbar displays the number of words in the document (Figure 2-44). You now close the Word Count toolbar because the research paper contains the required minimum of 325 words.

2

• **Click the Close button on the Word Count toolbar.**

Word removes the Word Count toolbar from the screen.

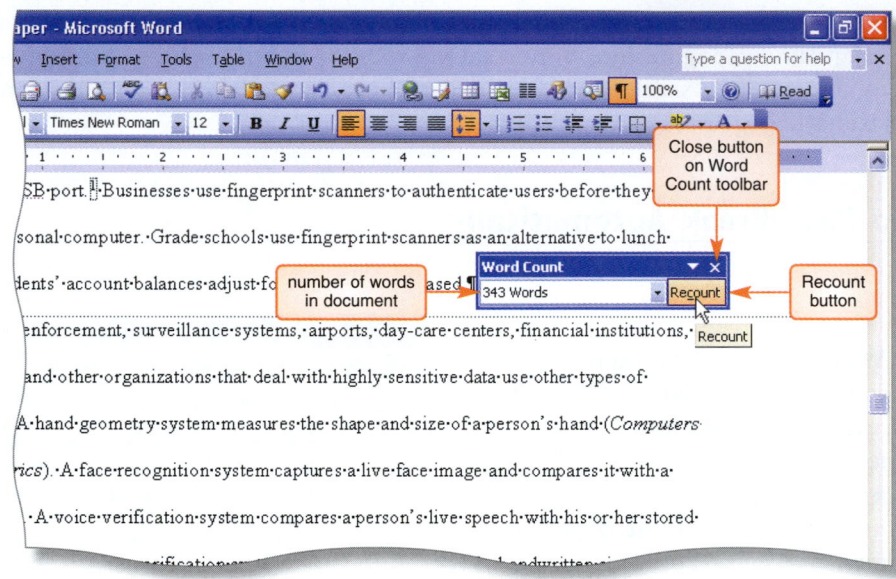

FIGURE 2-44

Creating an Alphabetical Works Cited Page

According to the MLA style, the **works cited page** is a bibliographical list of works that are referenced directly in a research paper. You place the list on a separate numbered page with the title, Works Cited, centered one inch from the top margin. The works are to be alphabetized by the author's last name or, if the work has no author, by the work's title. The first line of each entry begins at the left margin. Indent subsequent lines of the same entry one-half inch from the left margin.

The first step in creating the works cited page is to force a page break so the works cited display on a separate page.

Manual Page Breaks

The works cited are to display on a separate numbered page. Thus, you must insert a manual page break following the body of the research paper. A **manual page break**, or **hard page break**, is one that you force into the document at a specific location. Word displays a manual page break on the screen as a horizontal dotted line, separated by the words, Page Break. Word never moves or adjusts manual page breaks; however, Word adjusts any automatic page breaks that follow a manual page break. Word inserts manual page breaks just before the location of the insertion point.

The following step shows how to insert a manual page break after the body of the research paper.

To Page Break Manually

1

• **With the insertion point at the end of the body of the research paper, press the ENTER key.**

• **Then, press CTRL+ENTER.**

*The shortcut keys, **CTRL+ENTER**, instruct Word to insert a manual page break immediately above the insertion point and position the insertion point immediately below the manual page break (Figure 2-45). The status bar indicates the insertion point now is on page 3.*

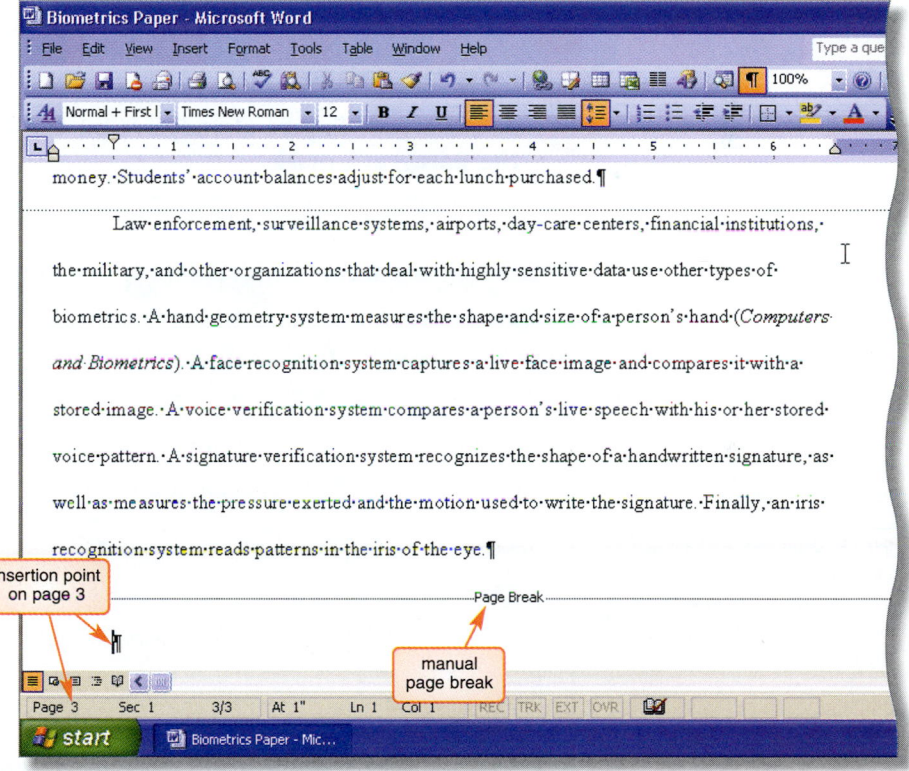

FIGURE 2-45

Other Ways

1. On Insert menu click Break, click OK button
2. In Voice Command mode, say "Insert, Break, OK"

Word displays the manual page break as a horizontal dotted line with the words, Page Break, in the middle of the line. The header, although not shown in normal view, contains the name Zhao followed by the page number 3. If you wanted to view the header, click View on the menu bar and then click Header and Footer. Then, click the Close Header and Footer button on the Header and Footer toolbar to return to normal view.

If, for some reason, you wanted to remove a manual page break from a document, you must first select the page break by double-clicking it. Then, press the DELETE key; or click the Cut button on the Standard toolbar; or right-click the selection and then click Cut on the shortcut menu.

Centering the Title of the Works Cited Page

The works cited title is to be centered between the margins of the paper. If you simply click the Center button on the Formatting toolbar, the title will not be centered properly. Instead, it will be one-half inch to the right of the center point because earlier you set first-line indent at one-half inch. That is, Word indents the first line of every paragraph one-half inch.

To properly center the title of the works cited page, you must move the First Line Indent marker back to the left margin before clicking the Center button, as described in the following steps.

To Center the Title of the Works Cited Page

1 **Drag the First Line Indent marker to the 0" mark on the ruler, which is at the left margin.**

2 **Click the Center button on the Formatting toolbar.**

3 **Type** Works Cited **as the title.**

4 **Press the ENTER key.**

5 **Because your fingers already are on the keyboard, press CTRL+L to left-align the paragraph mark.**

Word centers the title properly, and the insertion point is left-aligned (Figure 2-46).

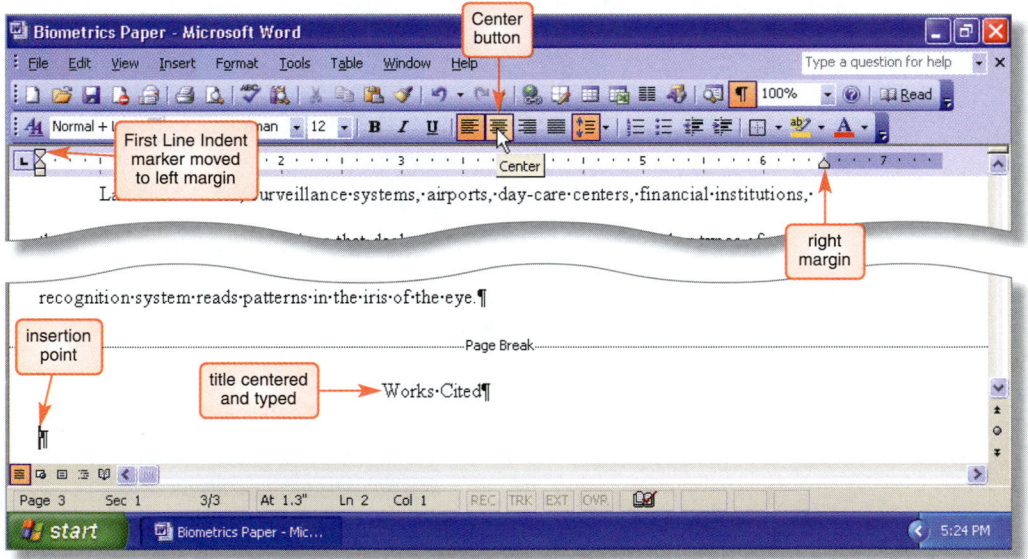

FIGURE 2-46

Creating a Hanging Indent

On the works cited page, the first line of each entry begins at the left margin. Subsequent lines in the same paragraph are to be indented one-half inch from the left margin. In essence, the first line hangs to the left of the rest of the paragraph; thus, this type of paragraph formatting is called a **hanging indent**.

One method of creating a hanging indent is to use the horizontal ruler. The **Hanging Indent marker** is the bottom triangle at the 0" mark on the ruler (Figure 2-47). The next steps show how to create a hanging indent using the horizontal ruler.

To Create a Hanging Indent

1

• **With the insertion point in the paragraph to format, point to the Hanging Indent marker on the ruler (Figure 2-47).**

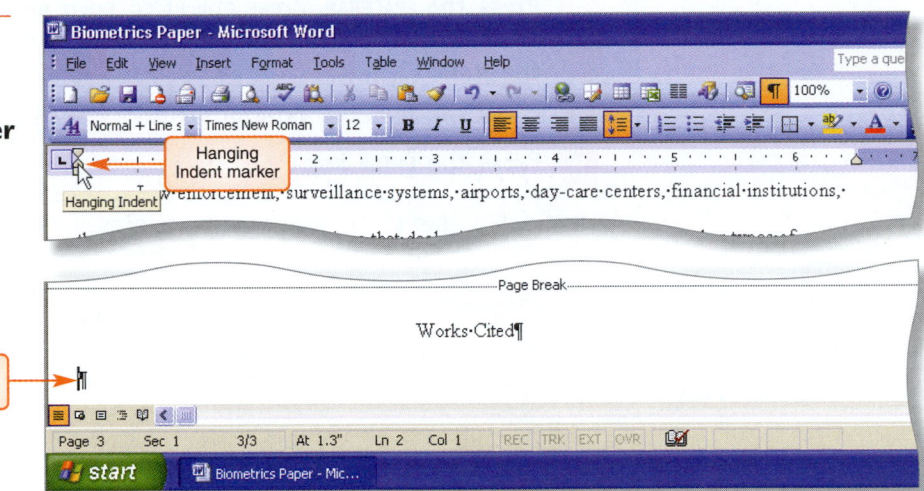

FIGURE 2-47

2

• **Drag the Hanging Indent marker to the .5" mark on the ruler.**

The Hanging Indent marker and Left Indent marker display one-half inch from the left margin (Figure 2-48). When you drag the Hanging Indent marker, the Left Indent marker moves with it. The insertion point in the document window remains at the left margin because only subsequent lines in the paragraph are to be indented.

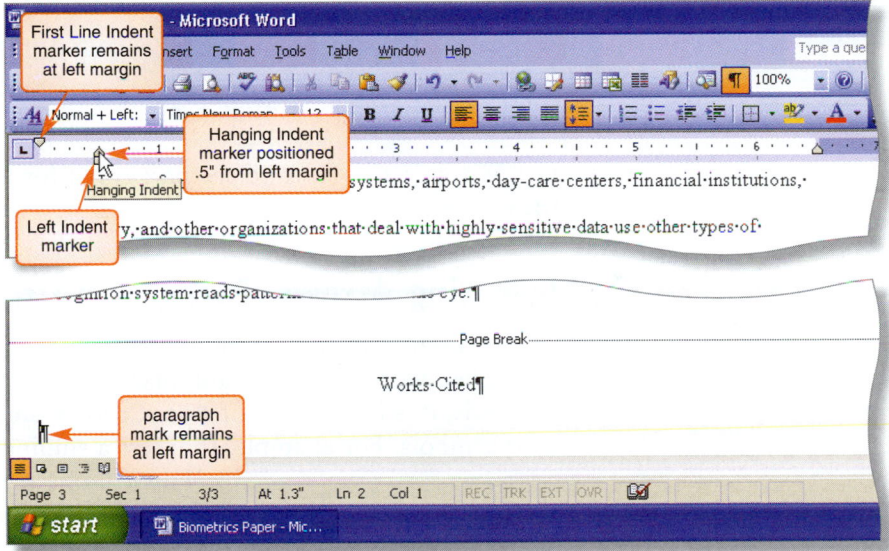

FIGURE 2-48

The next step is to enter the works in the works cited. As you type the works, Word will format them with a hanging indent. The following steps describe how to type the first two works in the works cited.

To Enter Works Cited Paragraphs

1 **Type** Schmidt, Karl J. "Biometrics and Authenticating Computer Users."

2 **Press the SPACEBAR. Press CTRL+I to turn on the italic format. Type** Computers and the Internet **and then press CTRL+I to turn off the italic format.**

3 **Press the SPACEBAR. Type** Aug. 2005: 54-62.

4 Press the ENTER key.

5 Type Carter, Donnell W., and Louis C. Juarez.

6 Press the SPACEBAR. Press CTRL+I to turn on the italic format. Type Securing Confidential Data Entered into a Computer. Press CTRL+I to turn off the italic format.

7 Press the SPACEBAR. Type Boston: Thomas Publishing, 2005.

8 Press the ENTER key.

Word displays two of the works cited paragraphs in the document window (Figure 2-49).

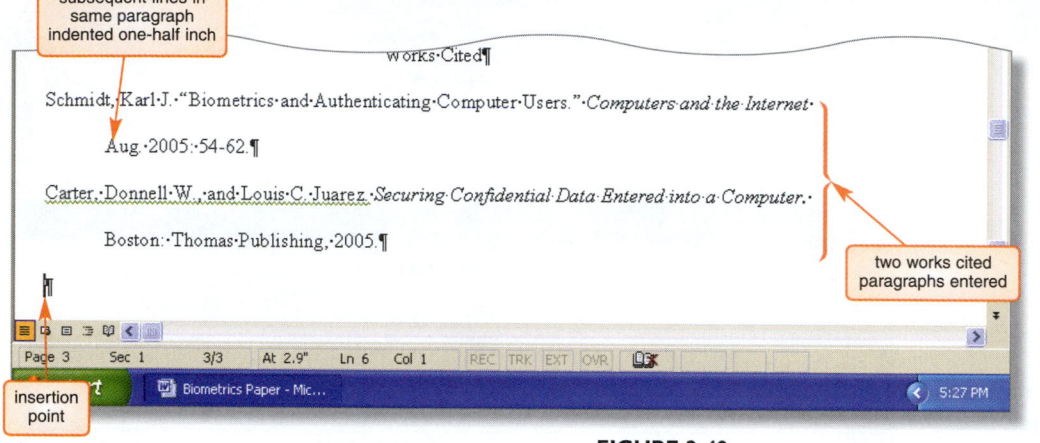

subsequent lines in same paragraph indented one-half inch

two works cited paragraphs entered

insertion point

FIGURE 2-49

When Word wraps the text in each works cited paragraph, it automatically indents the second line of the paragraph by one-half inch. When you press the ENTER key at the end of the first paragraph of text, the insertion point returns automatically to the left margin for the next paragraph. Recall that each time you press the ENTER key, Word carries forward the paragraph formatting from the previous paragraph to the next paragraph.

Inserting Arrows, Faces, and Other Symbols Automatically

As discussed earlier in this project, Word has predefined many commonly misspelled words, which it automatically corrects for you as you type. In addition to words, this built-in list of **AutoCorrect entries** also contains some commonly used symbols. For example, to insert a smiling face in a document, you type :) and Word automatically changes it to ☺. Table 2-3 lists the characters you type to insert arrows, faces, and other symbols in a Word document.

You also can enter the first four symbols in Table 2-3 and other symbols by clicking Insert on the menu bar, clicking Symbol, clicking the Special Characters tab, clicking the desired symbol in the Character list, clicking the Insert button, and then clicking the Close button in the Symbol dialog box.

As discussed earlier in this project, if you do not like a change that Word automatically makes in a document and you immediately notice the automatic correction, you can undo the change by clicking the Undo button on the Standard toolbar; clicking Edit on the menu bar and then clicking Undo; or pressing CTRL+Z.

If you do not immediately notice the change, you can undo a correction automatically made by Word using the AutoCorrect Options button. Figures 2-23 and 2-24 on pages WD 90 and WD 91 illustrated how to display and use the AutoCorrect Options button.

Table 2-3	Word's Automatic Symbols	
TO DISPLAY	DESCRIPTION	TYPE
©	copyright symbol	(c)
®	registered trademark symbol	(r)
™	trademark symbol	(tm)
…	ellipsis	...
☺	smiling face	:) or :-)
☺	indifferent face	:| or :-|
☹	frowning face	:(or :-(
→	thin right arrow	-->
←	thin left arrow	<
➜	thick right arrow	==>
⬅	thick left arrow	<==
⇔	double arrow	<=>

The next step in the research paper is to enter text that uses the registered trademark symbol. The following steps show how to insert automatically the registered trademark symbol in the research paper.

To Insert a Symbol Automatically

1

- **With the insertion point positioned as shown in Figure 2-49, press CTRL+I to turn on the italic format.**

- **Type** Computers and Biometrics.

- **Press CTRL+I to turn off the italic format.**

- **Press the SPACEBAR.**

- **Type** Shelly Cashman Series(r **as shown in Figure 2-50.**

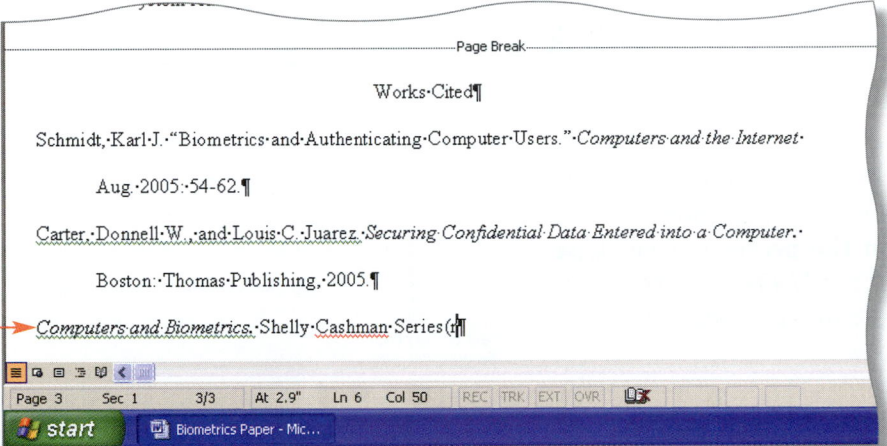

FIGURE 2-50

2

- **Press the RIGHT PARENTHESIS key.**

Word automatically converts the typed (r) to ®, the registered trademark symbol (Figure 2-51).

3

- **Press the PERIOD key.**

- **Press the SPACEBAR.**

- **Type** Course Technology. 3 Oct. 2005.

- **Press the SPACEBAR.**

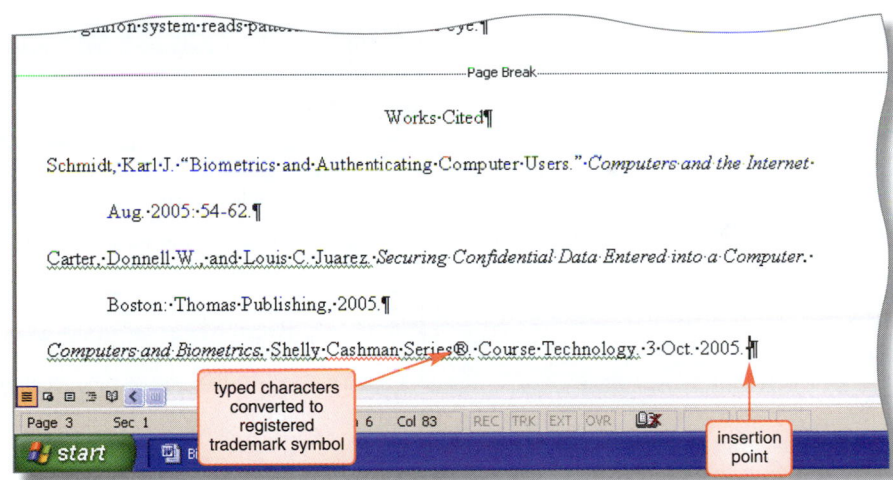

FIGURE 2-51

Creating a Hyperlink

A **hyperlink** is a shortcut that allows a user to jump easily and quickly to another location in the same document or to other documents or Web pages. **Jumping** is the process of following a hyperlink to its destination. For example, by clicking a hyperlink in the document window while pressing the CTRL key (called **CTRL+clicking**), you jump to another document on your computer, on your network, or on the World Wide Web. When you close the hyperlink destination page or document, you return to the original location in your Word document. In Word, you can create a hyperlink simply by typing the address of the file or Web page to which you want to link and then pressing the SPACEBAR or the ENTER key.

In this project, one of the works cited is from a Web page on the Internet. When someone displays your research paper on the screen, you want him or her to be able to CTRL+click the Web address in the work to jump to the associated Web page for more information.

To create a hyperlink to a Web page in a Word document, you do not have to be connected to the Internet. The following steps show how to create a hyperlink as you type.

To Create a Hyperlink

1

• **With the insertion point positioned as shown in Figure 2-51 on the previous page, type** `http://www.scsite.com/wd2003/pr2/wc.htm.`

Word does not format the entry as a hyperlink until you press the ENTER key or SPACEBAR (Figure 2-52).

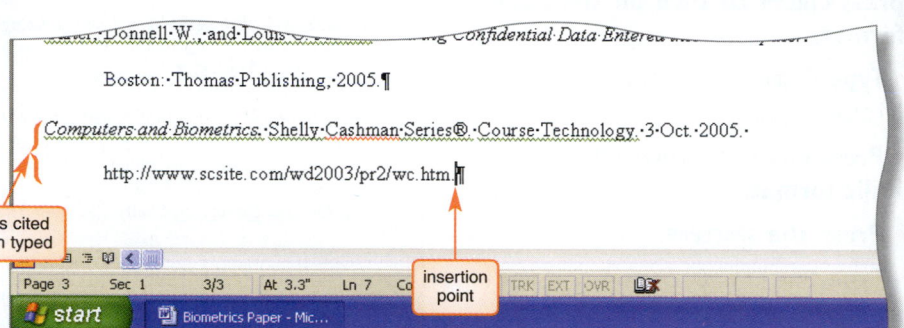

FIGURE 2-52

2

• **Press the ENTER key.**

As soon as you press the ENTER key after typing the Web address, Word formats it as a hyperlink (Figure 2-53). That is, the Web address is underlined and colored blue.

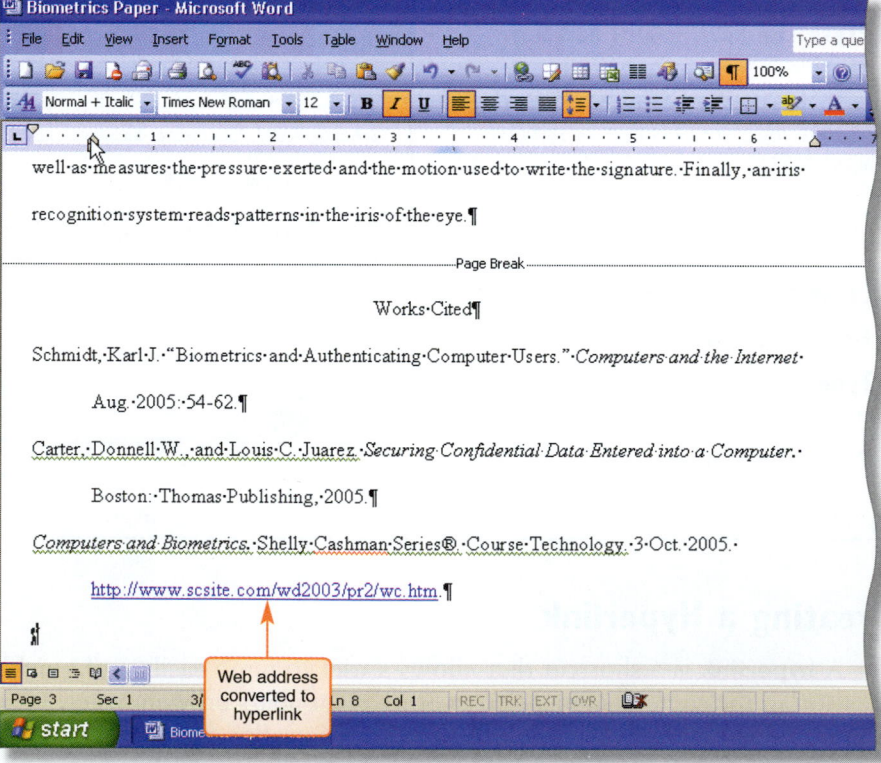

FIGURE 2-53

Other Ways

1. Select text, click Insert Hyperlink button on Standard toolbar, click Existing File or Web Page in the Link to bar, type Web address in Address text box, click OK button

2. Right-click selected text, click Hyperlink on short-cut menu, click Existing File or Web Page in the Link to bar, type Web address in Address text box, click OK button

Later, this project will show how to jump to the hyperlink just created.

Sorting Paragraphs

The MLA style requires that the works cited be listed in alphabetical order by the first character in each work. In Word, you can arrange paragraphs in alphabetic, numeric, or date order based on the first character in each paragraph. Ordering characters in this manner is called **sorting**.

The following steps show how to sort the works cited paragraphs alphabetically.

To Sort Paragraphs

1

• **Select all the works cited paragraphs by pointing to the left of the first paragraph and then dragging down.**

• **Click Table on the menu bar.**

Word displays the Table menu (Figure 2-54). All of the paragraphs to be sorted are selected.

FIGURE 2-54

2

• **Click Sort on the Table menu.**

Word displays the Sort Text dialog box (Figure 2-55). In the Sort by area, Ascending, the default, is selected. The term, ascending, means to sort in alphabetic, numeric, or earliest to latest date order.

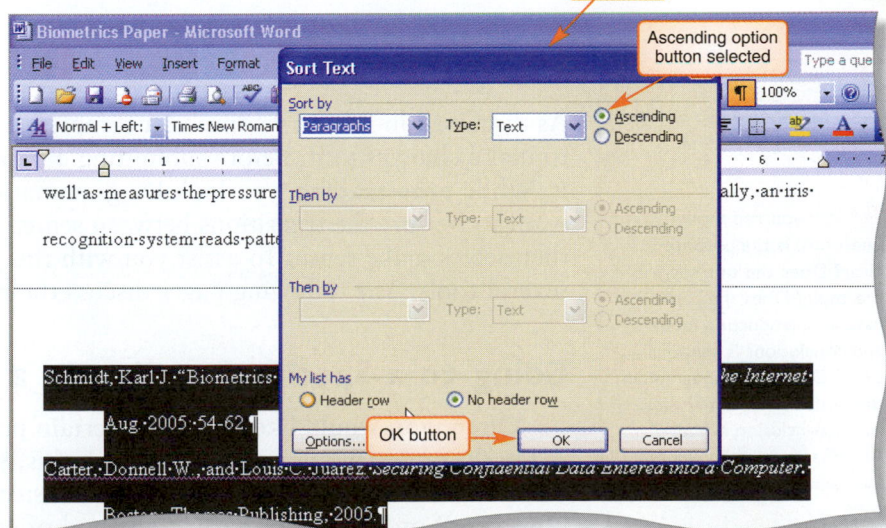

FIGURE 2-55

3

- **Click the OK button in the Sort Text dialog box.**
- **Click inside the selected text to remove the selection.**

Word sorts the works cited paragraphs alphabetically (Figure 2-56).

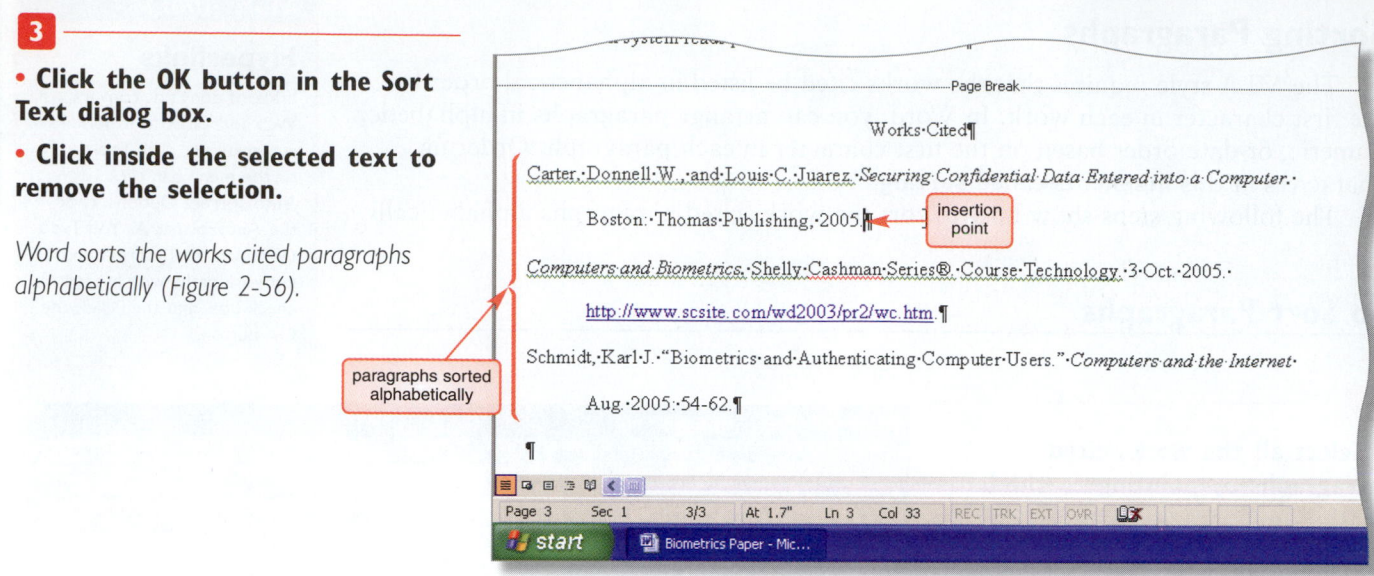

FIGURE 2-56

Other Ways

1. In Voice Command mode, say "Table, Sort, OK"

If you accidentally sort the wrong paragraphs, you can undo a sort by clicking the Undo button on the Standard toolbar.

In the Sort Text dialog box (Figure 2-55 on the previous page), the default sort order is Ascending. By default, Word orders in **ascending sort order**, which means from the beginning of the alphabet to the end of the alphabet, smallest number to the largest number, or earliest date to the most recent date. For example, if the first character of each paragraph to be sorted is a letter, Word sorts the selected paragraphs alphabetically.

You also can sort in descending order by clicking Descending in the Sort Text dialog box. **Descending sort order** means sorting from the end of the alphabet to the beginning of the alphabet, the largest number to the smallest number, or the most recent date to the earliest date.

Q: How should I go about proofreading a research paper?

A: Ask yourself these questions: Is the purpose clear? Does the title suggest the topic? Does the paper have an introduction, body, and conclusion? Is the thesis clear? Does each paragraph in the body relate to the thesis? Is the conclusion effective? Are all sources acknowledged?

Proofing and Revising the Research Paper

As discussed in Project 1, once you complete a document, you might find it necessary to make changes to it. Before submitting a paper to be graded, you should proofread it. While **proofreading**, you look for grammatical errors and spelling errors. You want to be sure the transitions between sentences flow smoothly and the sentences themselves make sense. To assist you with the proofreading effort, Word provides several tools. The following pages discuss these tools.

Going to a Specific Location in a Document

Often, you would like to bring a certain page, footnote, or other object into view in the document window. To accomplish this, you could scroll through the document to find a desired page, footnote, or item. Instead of scrolling through the document, however, Word provides an easier method of going to a specific location via the Select Browse Object menu.

The next steps show how to go to the top of page two in the research paper using the Select Browse Object menu.

To Browse by Page

1

• **Click the Select Browse Object button on the vertical scroll bar.**

• **When Word displays the Select Browse Object menu, position the mouse pointer on the Browse by Page icon.**

When you point to an icon on the Select Browse Object menu, Word displays the associated command name at the bottom of the menu (Figure 2-57).

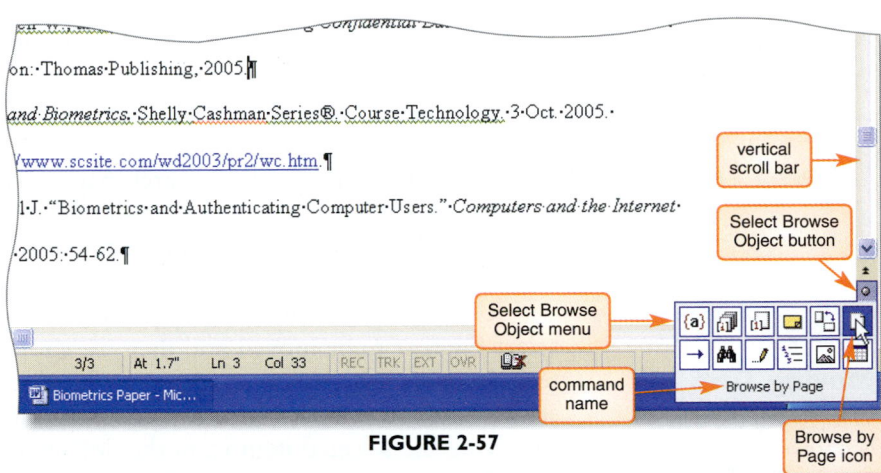

FIGURE 2-57

2

• **Click the Browse by Page icon.**

• **Position the mouse pointer on the Previous Page button on the vertical scroll bar.**

Word closes the Select Browse Object menu and displays the top of page 3 at the top of the document window (Figure 2-58).

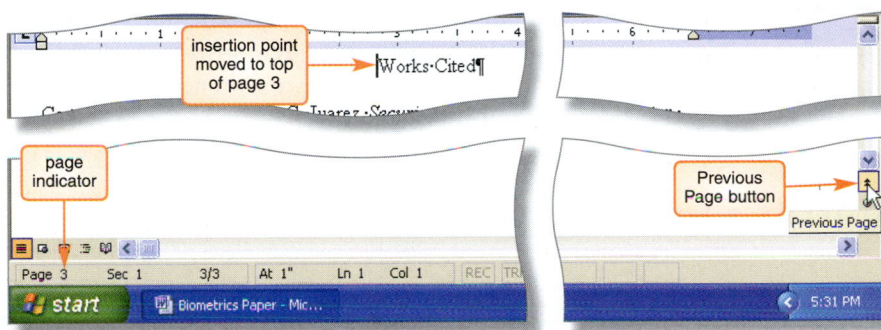

FIGURE 2-58

3

• **Click the Previous Page button.**

Word places the top of page 2 (the previous page) at the top of the document window (Figure 2-59).

Other Ways

1. Double-click page indicator on status bar (Figure 2-59), click Page in Go to what list, type page number in Enter page number text box, click Go To button, click Close button
2. On Edit menu click Go To, and then proceed as described in 1 above starting with click Page in Go to what list
3. Press CTRL+G, and then proceed as described in 1 above starting with click Page in Go to what list

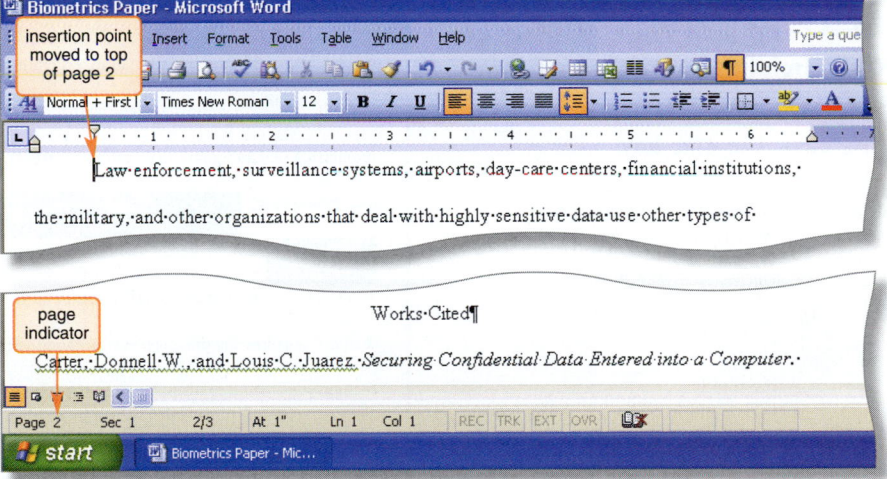

FIGURE 2-59

Depending on the icon you click on the Select Browse Object menu, the function of the buttons above and below the Select Browse Object button on the vertical scroll bar changes. When you select Browse by Page, the buttons become Previous Page and Next Page buttons. If you select Browse by Footnote, however, the buttons become Previous Footnote and Next Footnote buttons, and so on.

Moving Text

While proofreading the research paper, you realize that text in the fourth paragraph would flow better if the third sentence was moved so it followed the first sentence. That is, you want to move the third sentence so it is the second sentence in the fourth paragraph.

To move text, such as words, characters, sentences, or paragraphs, you first select the text to be moved and then use drag-and-drop editing or the cut-and-paste technique to move the selected text. With **drag-and-drop editing**, you drag the selected item to the new location and then insert, or *drop*, it there. **Cutting** involves removing the selected item from the document and then placing it on the Clipboard. The **Clipboard** is a temporary Windows storage area. **Pasting** is the process of copying an item from the Clipboard into the document at the location of the insertion point. The next steps demonstrate drag-and-drop editing.

To drag-and-drop a sentence in the research paper, first select a sentence as shown in the next step.

To Select a Sentence

1

• **Position the mouse pointer (an I-beam) in the sentence to be moved (shown in Figure 2-60).**

• **Press and hold down the CTRL key. While holding down the CTRL key, click the sentence.**

• **Release the CTRL key.**

Word selects the entire sentence (Figure 2-60). Notice that Word includes the space following the period in the selection.

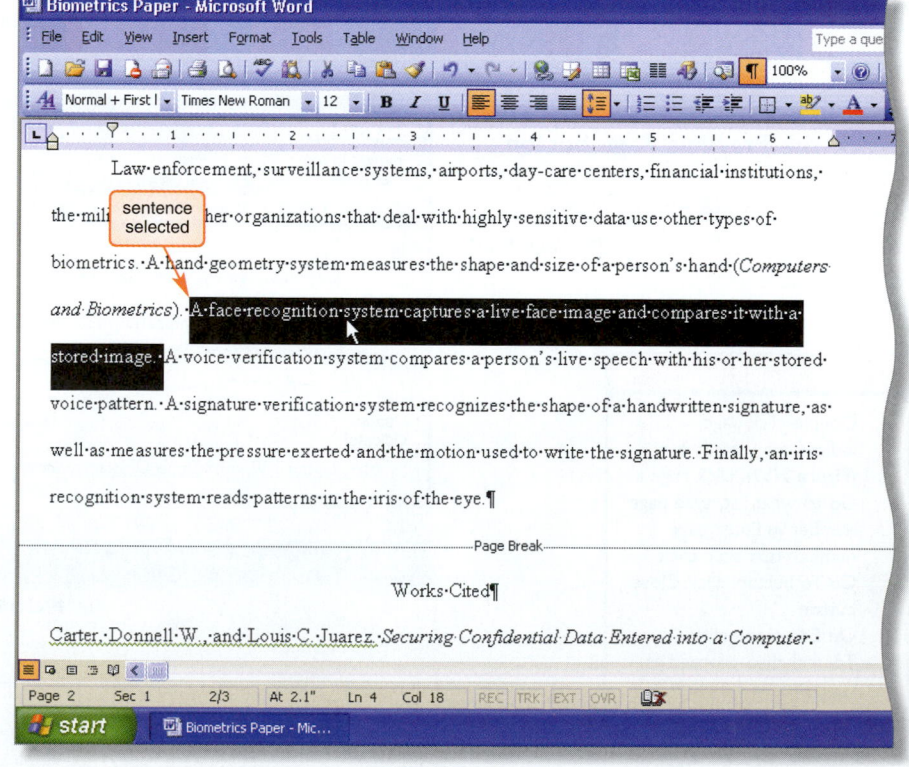

FIGURE 2-60

In the previous steps and throughout Projects 1 and 2, you have selected text. Table 2-4 summarizes the techniques used to select various items with the mouse.

Table 2-4 Techniques for Selecting Items with the Mouse	
ITEM TO SELECT	**MOUSE ACTION**
Block of text	Click at beginning of selection, scroll to end of selection, position mouse pointer at end of selection, hold down SHIFT key and then click; or drag through the text
Character(s)	Drag through character(s)
Document	Move mouse to left of text until mouse pointer changes to a right-pointing block arrow and then triple-click
Graphic	Click the graphic
Line	Move mouse to left of line until mouse pointer changes to a right-pointing block arrow and then click
Lines	Move mouse to left of first line until mouse pointer changes to a right-pointing block arrow and then drag up or down
Paragraph	Triple-click paragraph; or move mouse to left of paragraph until mouse pointer changes to a right-pointing block arrow and then double-click
Paragraphs	Move mouse to left of paragraph until mouse pointer changes to a right-pointing block arrow, double-click and then drag up or down
Sentence	Press and hold down CTRL key and then click sentence
Word	Double-click the word
Words	Drag through words

With the sentence to be moved selected, you can use drag-and-drop editing to move it. You should be sure that drag-and-drop editing is enabled by clicking Tools on the menu bar, clicking Options, clicking the Edit tab, verifying the Drag-and-drop text editing check box is selected, and then clicking the OK button.

The following steps show how to move the selected sentence so it becomes the second sentence in the paragraph.

To Move Selected Text

1

• **With the mouse pointer in the selected text, press and hold down the mouse button.**

When you begin to drag the selected text, the insertion point changes to a dotted insertion point (Figure 2-61).

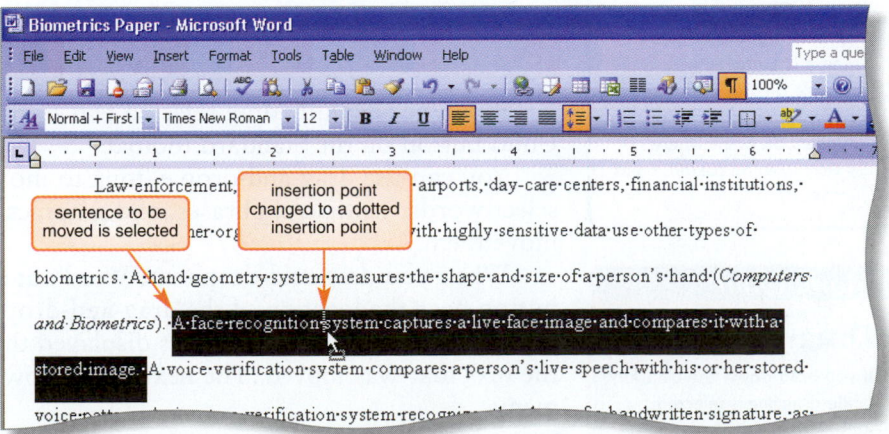

FIGURE 2-61

2

• **Drag the dotted insertion point to the location where the selected text is to be moved, as shown in Figure 2-62.**

The dotted insertion point follows the space after the first sentence in the paragraph (Figure 2-62).

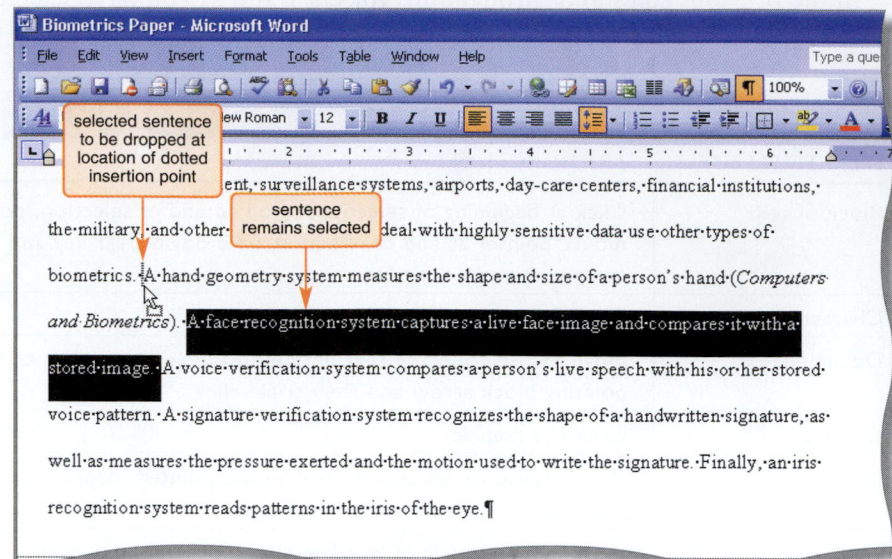

FIGURE 2-62

3

• **Release the mouse button. Click outside the selected text to remove the selection.**

Word moves the selected text to the location of the dotted insertion point (Figure 2-63).

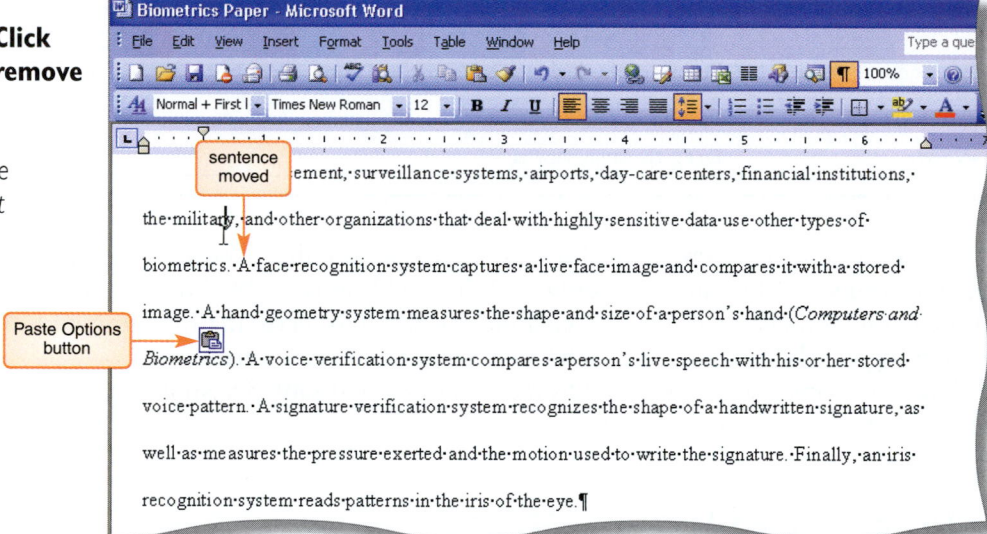

FIGURE 2-63

Other Ways

1. Click Cut button on Standard toolbar, click where text is to be pasted, click Paste button on Standard toolbar
2. On Edit menu click Cut, click where text is to be pasted, on Edit menu click Paste
3. Right-click selected text, click Cut on shortcut menu, right-click where text is to be pasted, click Paste on shortcut menu
4. Press CTRL+X, position insertion point where text is to be pasted, press CTRL+V

More About

Drag-and-Drop

If you hold down the CTRL key while dragging a selected item, Word copies the item instead of moving it.

If you accidentally drag selected text to the wrong location, you can click the Undo button on the Standard toolbar.

You can use drag-and-drop editing to move any selected item. That is, you can select words, sentences, phrases, and graphics and then use drag-and-drop editing to move them.

When you drag-and-drop text, Word automatically displays a Paste Options button near the location of the drag-and-dropped text (Figure 2-63). If you click the **Paste Options button**, a menu is displayed that allows you to change the format of the text that was moved. The next steps show how to display the Paste Options menu.

To Display the Paste Options Menu

1

• **Click the Paste Options button.**

Word displays the Paste Options menu (Figure 2-64).

2

• **Press the ESCAPE key to remove the Paste Options menu from the window.**

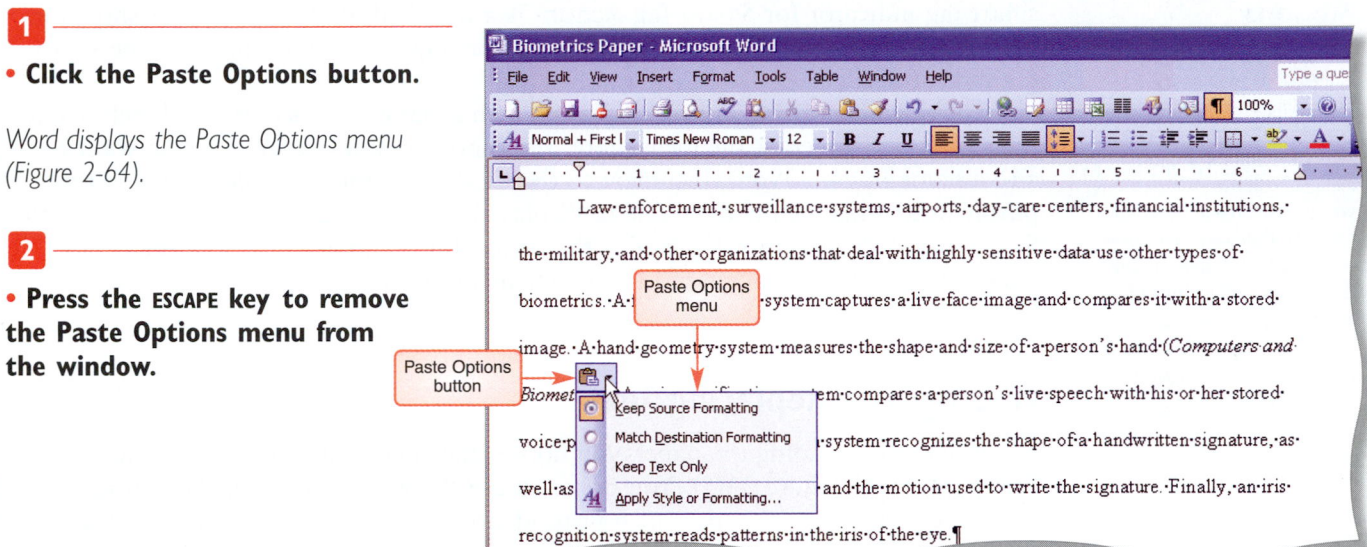

FIGURE 2-64

Smart Tags

A **smart tag** is a button that automatically appears on the screen when Word performs a certain action. In this project, you used two smart tags: AutoCorrect Options (Figures 2-23 and 2-24 on pages WD 90 and WD 91) and Paste Options (Figure 2-64). In addition to AutoCorrect Options and Paste Options, Word provides other smart tags. Table 2-5 summarizes the smart tags available in Word.

Table 2-5	Smart Tags in Word	
BUTTON	**NAME**	**MENU FUNCTION**
	AutoCorrect Options	Undoes an automatic correction, stops future automatic corrections of this type, or displays the AutoCorrect Options dialog box
	Paste Options	Specifies how moved or pasted items should display, e.g., with original formatting, without formatting, or with different formatting
	Smart Tag Actions	
	• Person name	Adds this name to Outlook Contacts folder, sends an e-mail, or schedules a meeting in Outlook Calendar with this person
	• Date or time	Schedules a meeting in Outlook Calendar at this date or time or displays your calendar
	• Address	Adds this address to Outlook Contacts folder or displays a map or driving directions
	• Place	Adds this place to Outlook Contacts folder or schedules a meeting in Outlook Calendar at this location

More About

Smart Tag Actions

The commands in the Smart Tag Actions menu vary depending on the smart tag. For example, the Smart Tag Actions menu for a date includes commands that allow you to schedule a meeting in Outlook Calendar or display your Outlook Calendar. The Smart Tag Actions menu for an address includes commands for displaying a map of the address or driving directions to or from the address.

With the AutoCorrect Options and Smart Tag Actions, Word notifies you that the smart tag is available by displaying a **smart tag indicator** on the screen. The smart tag indicator for the AutoCorrect Options smart tag is a small blue box. The smart tag indicator for Smart Tag Actions is a purple dotted underline, as shown in Figure 2-14 on page WD 85. To display a smart tag button, you point to the smart tag indicator.

Clicking a smart tag button displays a menu that contains commands relative to the action performed at the location of the smart tag. For example, if you want to add a name in your Word document to the Outlook Contacts folder, point to the purple dotted line below the name to display the Smart Tag Actions button, click the Smart Tag Actions button to display the Smart Tag Actions menu, and then click Add to Contacts on the Smart Tag Actions menu to display the Contact window in Outlook.

Finding and Replacing Text

While proofreading the paper, you notice that it contains the word, trait, in the first paragraph (Figure 2-65). You prefer to use the word, identifier. Therefore, you wish to change all occurrences of trait to identifier. To do this, you can use Word's find and replace feature, which automatically locates each occurrence of a word or phrase and then replaces it with specified text, as shown in these steps.

To Find and Replace Text

1

• **Press CTRL+HOME to position the insertion point at the top of the document.**

• **Double-click the status bar anywhere to the left of the status indicators.**

• **When Word displays the Find and Replace dialog box, click the Replace tab.**

• **Type** trait **in the Find what text box.**

• **Press the TAB key. Type** identifier **in the Replace with text box.**

Word displays entered text in the Find and Replace dialog box (Figure 2-65).

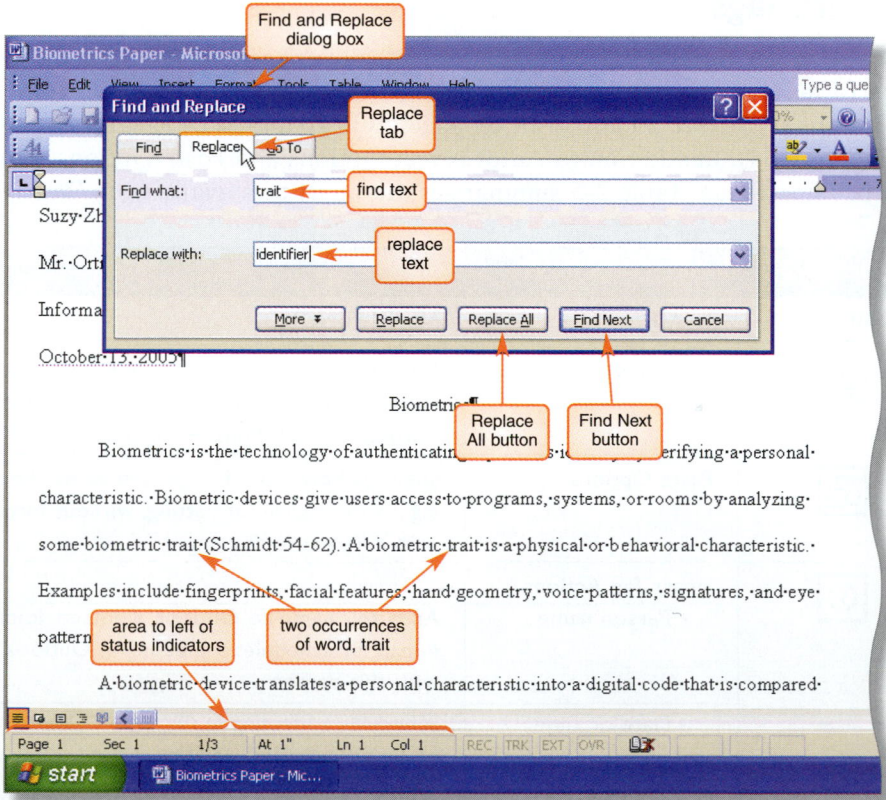

FIGURE 2-65

2

• **Click the Replace All button in the Find and Replace dialog box.**

A Microsoft Office Word dialog box displays indicating the total number of replacements made (Figure 2-66). The word, identifier, displays in the document instead of the word, trait.

3

• **Click the OK button in the Microsoft Office Word dialog box.**

• **Click the Close button in the Find and Replace dialog box.**

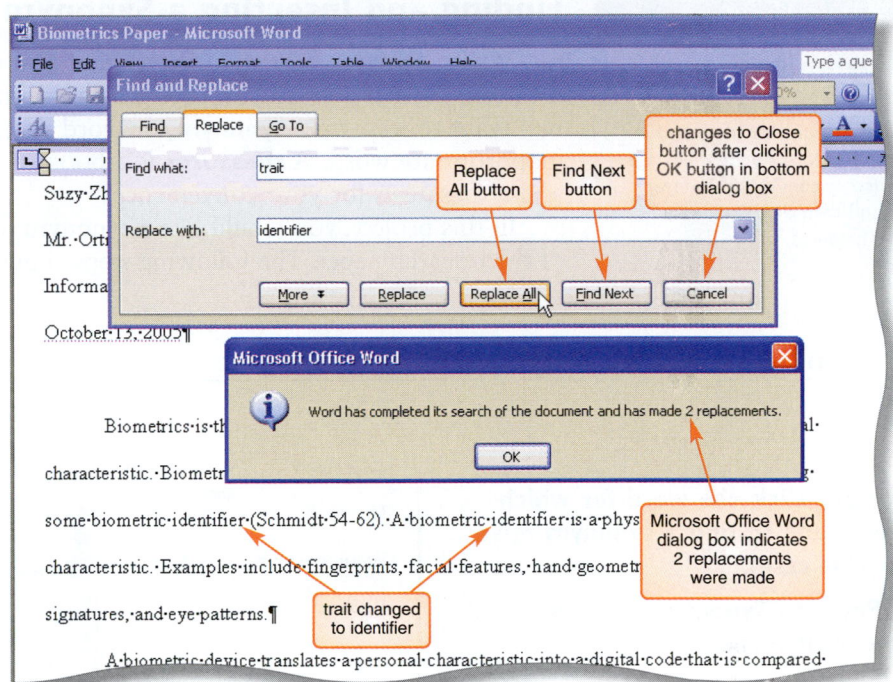

FIGURE 2-66

The Replace All button replaces all occurrences of the Find what text with the Replace with text. In some cases, you may want to replace only certain occurrences of a word or phrase, not all of them. To instruct Word to confirm each change, click the Find Next button in the Find and Replace dialog box (Figure 2-65), instead of the Replace All button. When Word locates an occurrence of the text, it pauses and waits for you to click either the Replace button or the Find Next button. Clicking the Replace button changes the text; clicking the Find Next button instructs Word to disregard the replacement and look for the next occurrence of the Find what text.

If you accidentally replace the wrong text, you can undo a replacement by clicking the Undo button on the Standard toolbar. If you used the Replace All button, Word undoes all replacements. If you used the Replace button, Word undoes only the most recent replacement.

Finding Text

Sometimes, you may want only to find text, instead of finding *and* replacing text. To search for just a single occurrence of text, you would follow these steps.

To Find Text

1. Click the Select Browse Object button on the vertical scroll bar and then click the Find icon on the Select Browse Object menu; or click Edit on the menu bar and then click Find; or press CTRL+F.

2. Type the text to locate in the Find what text box and then click the Find Next button. To edit the text, click the Cancel button in the Find and Replace dialog box; to find the next occurrence of the text, click the Find Next button.

More About

Synonyms

For access to an online thesaurus, visit the Word 2003 More About Web page (scsite.com/wd2003/more) and then click Online Thesaurus.

Finding and Inserting a Synonym

When writing, you may discover that you used the same word in multiple locations or that a word you used was not quite appropriate. In these instances, you will want to look up a **synonym**, or word similar in meaning, to the duplicate or inappropriate word. A **thesaurus** is a book of synonyms. Word provides synonyms and a thesaurus for your convenience.

In this project, you would like a synonym for the word, give, in the first paragraph of the research paper. The following steps show how to find an appropriate synonym.

To Find and Insert a Synonym

1

• **Right-click the word for which you want to find a synonym (give, in this case).**

• **Point to Synonyms on the shortcut menu.**

Word displays a list of synonyms for the word that you right-clicked (Figure 2-67).

2

• **Click the synonym you want (grant) on the Synonyms submenu.**

Word replaces the word, give, in the document with the word, grant (Figure 2-68).

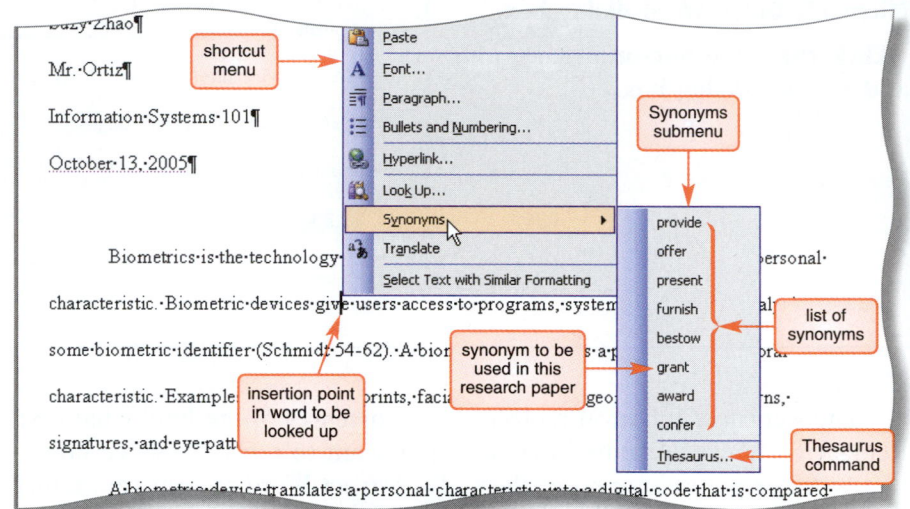

FIGURE 2-67

Other Ways

1. Select word, on Tools menu point to Language, on Language submenu click Thesaurus, scroll to appropriate meaning in Research task pane, point to desired synonym in Research task pane, click the box arrow to the right of the synonym, click Insert on submenu, close Research task pane

2. Select word, press SHIFT+F7, scroll to appropriate meaning in Research task pane, point to desired synonym in Research task pane, click the box arrow to the right of the synonym, click Insert on submenu, close Research task pane

3. In Voice Command mode, with insertion point in word, say "Right Click, Synonyms, [select synonym]"

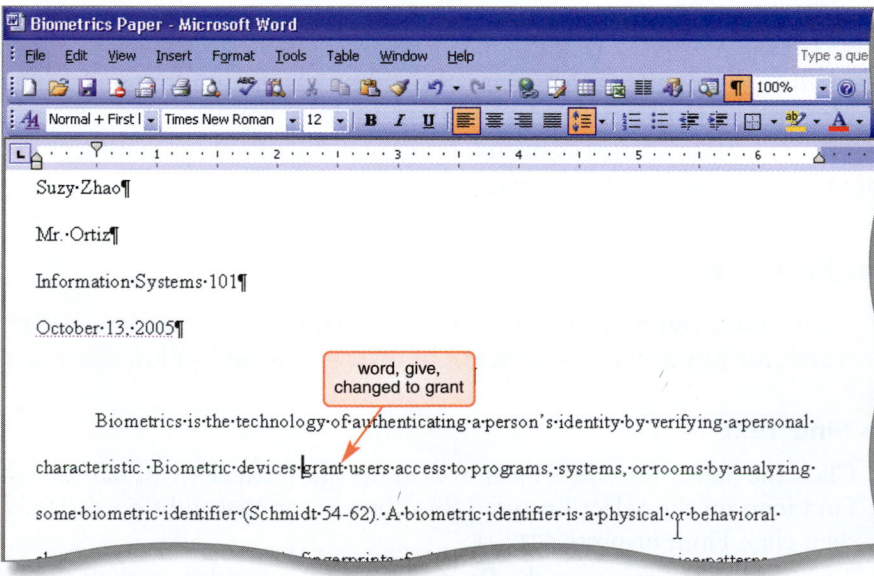

FIGURE 2-68

If the synonyms list on the shortcut menu does not display an appropriate word, you can display the thesaurus in the Research task pane by clicking Thesaurus on the Synonyms submenu (Figure 2-67). The Research task pane displays a complete thesaurus, in which you can look up synonyms for various meanings of a word. You also can look up an **antonym**, or word with an opposite meaning. The Research task pane is discussed later in this project.

Checking Spelling and Grammar at Once

As discussed in Project 1, Word checks spelling and grammar as you type and places a wavy underline below possible spelling or grammar errors. Project 1 illustrated how to check these flagged words immediately. As an alternative, you can wait and check the entire document for spelling and grammar errors at once.

The following steps illustrate how to check spelling and grammar in the Biometrics Paper at once. In the following example the word, hand, has been misspelled intentionally as han to illustrate the use of Word's check spelling and grammar at once feature. If you are completing this project on a personal computer, your research paper may contain different misspelled words, depending on the accuracy of your typing.

To Check Spelling and Grammar at Once

1

• **Press CTRL+HOME to move the insertion point to the beginning of the document.**

• **Click the Spelling and Grammar button on the Standard toolbar.**

Word displays the Spelling and Grammar dialog box (Figure 2-69). The spelling and grammar check begins at the location of the insertion point, which, in this case, is at the beginning of the document. Word did not find the misspelled word, han, in its dictionary. The Suggestions list displays suggested corrections for the flagged word.

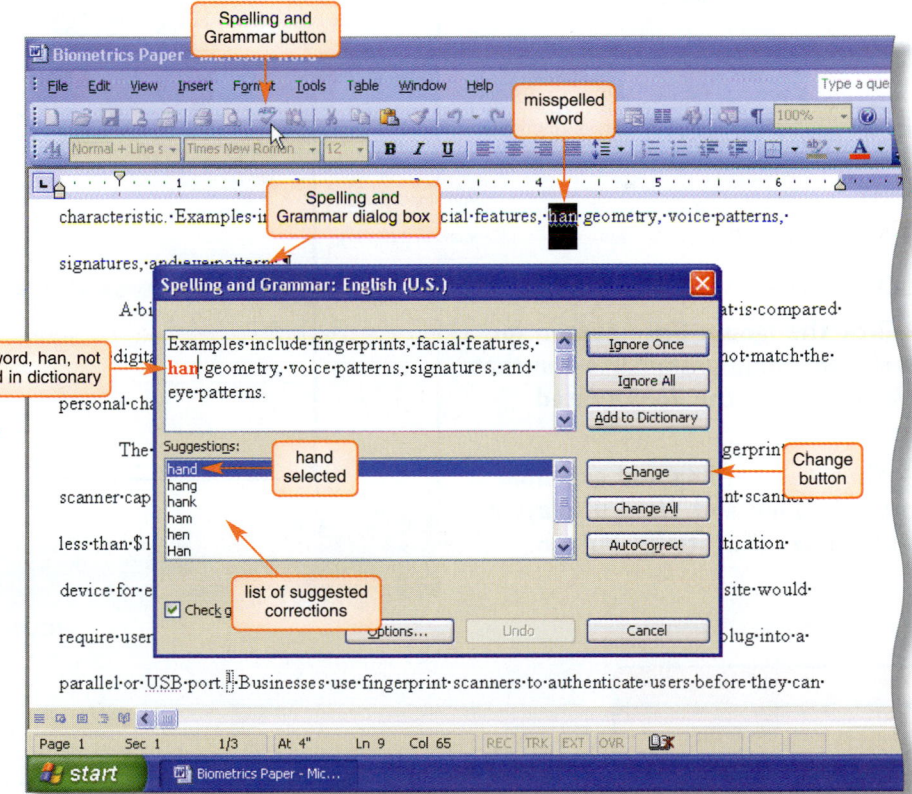

FIGURE 2-69

2

• **Click the Change button in the Spelling and Grammar dialog box.**

Word corrects the misspelled word and then continues the spelling and grammar check until it finds the next error or reaches the end of the document. In this case, it flags an error on the Works Cited page (Figure 2-70). The entry is correct, so you instruct Word to ignore it.

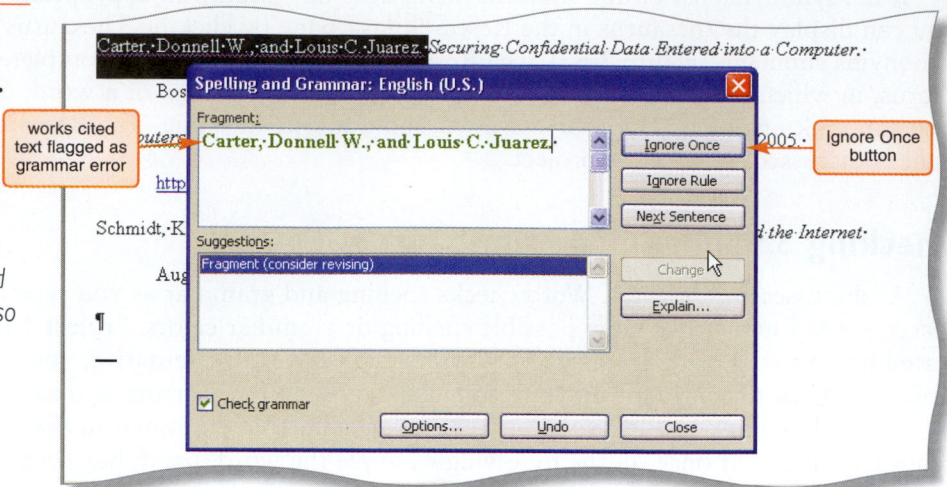

FIGURE 2-70

3

• **Click the Ignore Once button.**

• **Click the Ignore Once button for the next grammar error that Word flags on the Works Cited page.**

Word continues the spelling and grammar check and does not find Cashman in its dictionary (Figure 2-71). Cashman is a proper name and is spelled correctly.

4

• **Click the Ignore All button.**

• **Click the Ignore Once button for each remaining grammar error that Word flags on the Works Cited page.**

• **When the spelling and grammar check is done and Word displays a dialog box, click its OK button.**

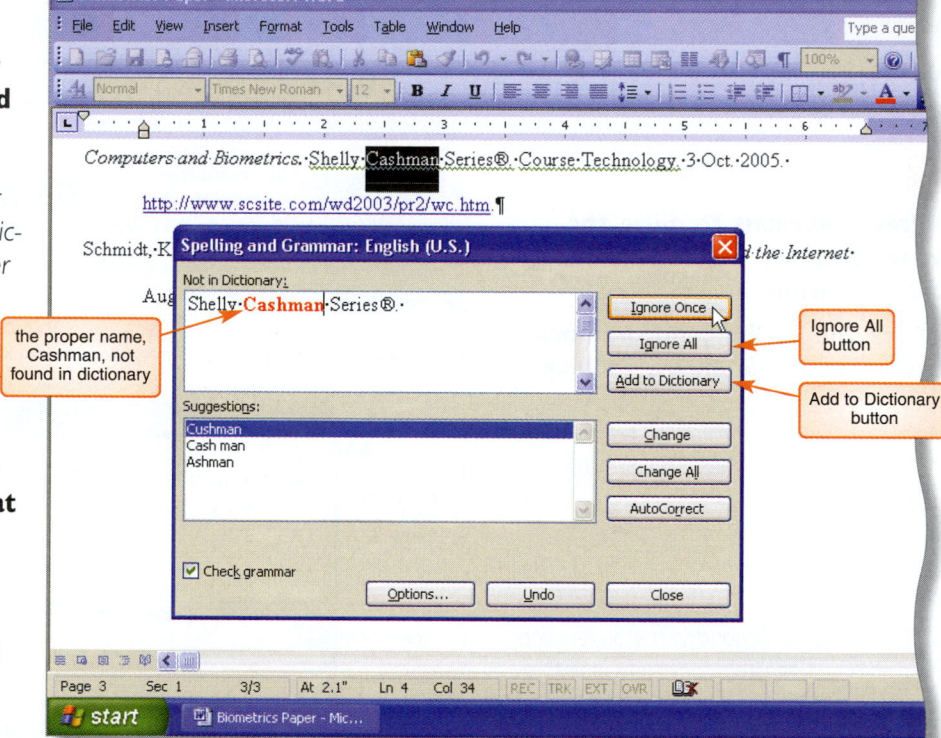

FIGURE 2-71

Your document no longer displays red and green wavy underlines below words and phrases. In addition, the red X on the Spelling and Grammar Status icon has returned to a red check mark.

Saving Again and Printing the Document

The document now is complete. You should save the research paper again and print it, as described in the following steps.

To Save a Document Again and Print It

1 Click the Save button on the Standard toolbar.

2 Click the Print button on the Standard toolbar.

Word saves the research paper with the same file name, Biometrics Paper. The completed research paper prints as shown in Figure 2-1 on page WD 75.

Working with Main and Custom Dictionaries

As shown in the previous steps, Word often flags proper names as errors because these names are not in its main dictionary. To prevent Word from flagging proper names as errors, you can add the names to the custom dictionary. To add a correctly spelled word to the custom dictionary, click the Add to Dictionary button in the Spelling and Grammar dialog box (Figure 2-71) or right-click the flagged word and then click Add to Dictionary on the shortcut menu. Once you have added a word to the custom dictionary, Word no longer will flag it as an error. To view or modify the list of words in a custom dictionary, you would follow these steps.

To View or Modify Entries in a Custom Dictionary

1. Click Tools on the menu bar and then click Options.
2. Click the Spelling & Grammar tab in the Options dialog box.
3. Click the Custom Dictionaries button.
4. When Word displays the Custom Dictionaries dialog box, place a check mark next to the dictionary name to view or modify. Click the Modify button. (In this dialog box, you can add or delete entries to and from the selected custom dictionary.)
5. When finished viewing and/or modifying the list, click the OK button in the dialog box.
6. Click the OK button in the Custom Dictionaries dialog box.
7. If the Suggest from main dictionary only check box is selected in the Spelling & Grammar sheet in the Options dialog box, remove the check mark. Click the OK button in the Options dialog box.

If you have multiple custom dictionaries, you can specify which one Word should use when checking spelling. The following steps describe how to set the default custom dictionary.

To Set the Default Custom Dictionary

1. Click Tools on the menu bar and then click Options.
2. Click the Spelling & Grammar tab in the Options dialog box.
3. Click the Custom Dictionaries button.
4. When the Custom Dictionaries dialog box displays, place a check mark next to the desired dictionary name. Click the Change Default button.
5. Click the OK button in the Custom Dictionaries dialog box.
6. If the Suggest from main dictionary only check box is selected in the Spelling & Grammar dialog box, remove the check mark. Click the OK button in the Spelling & Grammar dialog box.

More About

Certification

The Microsoft Office Specialist Certification program provides an opportunity for you to obtain a valuable industry credential - proof that you have the Word 2003 skills required by employers. For more information, see Appendix E or visit the Word 2003 Certification Web page (scsite.com/wd2003/cert).

Navigating to a Hyperlink

Recall that a requirement of this research paper is that one of the works be a Web page and be formatted as a hyperlink. The following steps show how to check the hyperlink in the document.

To Navigate to a Hyperlink

1

• **Display the third page of the research paper in the document window and then position the mouse pointer in the hyperlink.**

When you position the mouse pointer in a hyperlink in a Word document, a ScreenTip is displayed above the hyperlink (Figure 2-72).

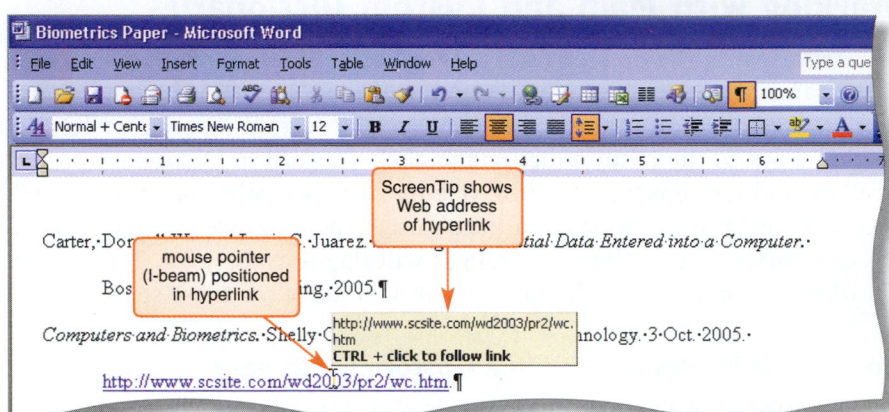

FIGURE 2-72

2

• **While holding down the CTRL key, click the hyperlink. Release the CTRL key.**

If you currently are not connected to the Web, Word connects you using your default browser. The www.scsite.com/wd2003/pr2/wc.htm Web page is displayed in a browser window (Figure 2-73).

3

• **Close the browser window.**

• **If necessary, click the Microsoft Word program button on the taskbar to redisplay the Word window.**

• **Press CTRL+HOME.**

Word displays the first page of the research paper on the screen.

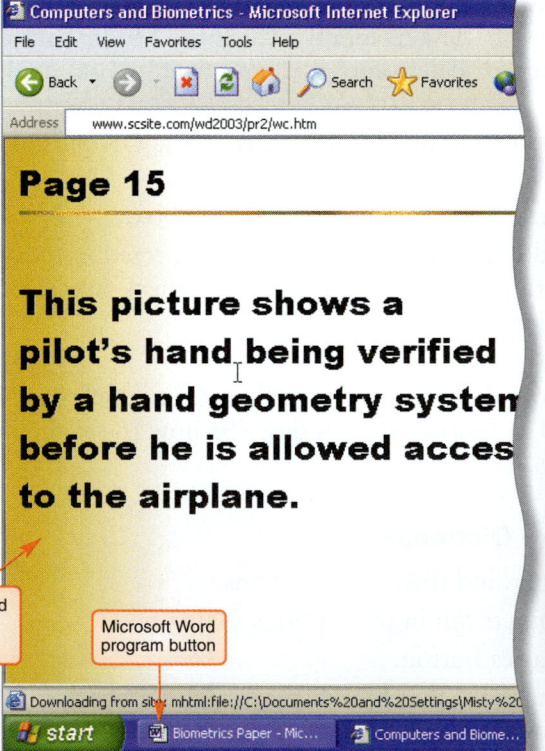

FIGURE 2-73

The hyperlink in the document changes color, which indicates you CTRL+clicked the hyperlink to display its associated Web page.

E-Mailing a Copy of the Research Paper

Your instructor, Mr. Ortiz, has requested you e-mail him a copy of your research paper so he can verify your hyperlink. The following steps show how to e-mail the document from within Word if you use Outlook as your e-mail program.

To E-Mail a Document

1

• **Click the E-mail button on the Standard toolbar.**

• **Fill in the To text box with Mr. Ortiz's e-mail address and the Introduction text box as shown in Figure 2-74.**

Word displays certain buttons and boxes from the e-mail editor inside the Word window. The file name is displayed automatically in the Subject text box.

2

• **Click the Send a Copy button.**

The document is e-mailed to the recipient named in the To text box.

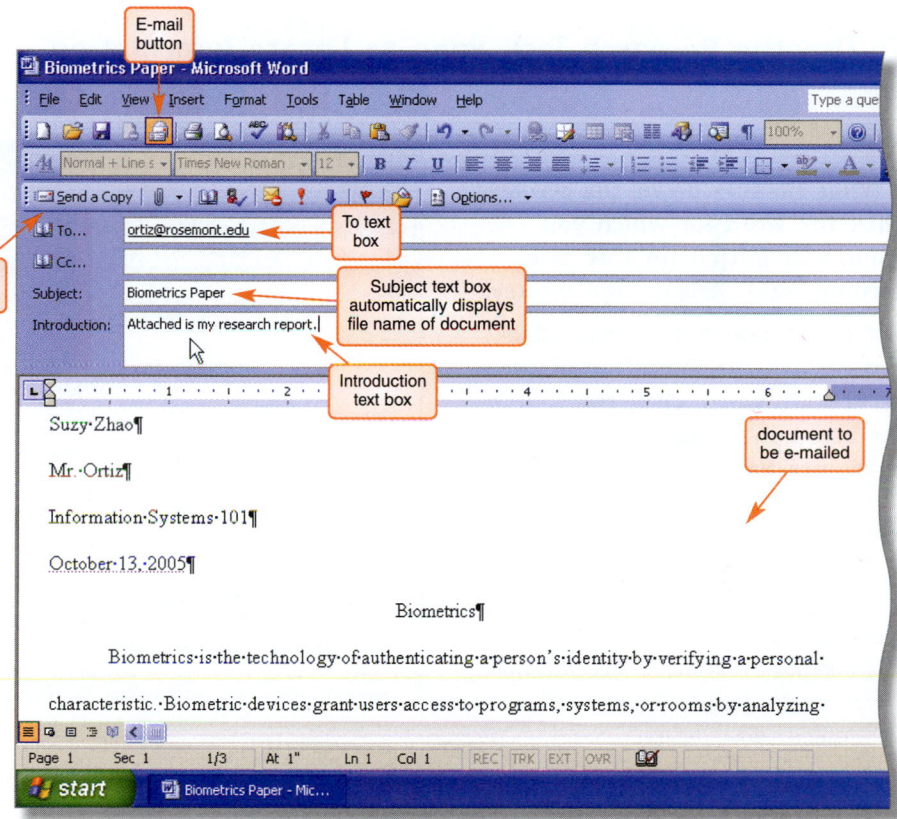

FIGURE 2-74

Other Ways

1. On File menu point to Send To, on Send To submenu click Mail Recipient
2. In Voice Command mode, say "E-mail"

If you want to cancel the e-mail operation, click the E-mail button again.

In the steps above, the Word document becomes part of the e-mail message. If you wanted to send the Word document as an attachment to the e-mail message instead, do the following.

To E-Mail a Document as an Attatchment

1. Click File on the menu bar, point to Send To, and then click Mail Recipient (as Attachment).
2. Fill in the text boxes.
3. Click the Send button.

Microsoft Office
Word 2003

Using the Research Task Pane

From within Word, you can search through various forms of online reference information. Earlier, this project discussed the Research task pane with respect to looking up a synonym in a thesaurus. Other services available in the Research task pane include the Microsoft Encarta English dictionary, bilingual dictionaries, the Microsoft Encarta Encyclopedia (with a Web connection), and Web sites that provide information such as stock quotes, news articles, and company profiles.

After reading a document you create, you might want to know the meaning of a certain word. For example, in the research paper, you might want to look up the definition of the word, e-commerce. The following step shows how to use the Research task pane to look up the definition of a word.

To Use the Research Task Pane to Locate Information

1

• **While holding down the ALT key, click the word for which you want a definition (in this case, e-commerce). Release the ALT key.**

• **If the Research task pane does not display the definition of the ALT+CLICKED word, click the Search for box arrow and then click All Reference Books.**

Word displays the Research task pane with the ALT+CLICKED word in the Search for text box (Figure 2-75). The Research button on the Standard toolbar is selected and the insertion point is in the ALT+CLICKED word. The contents of your reference book entry in the Research task pane may be different.

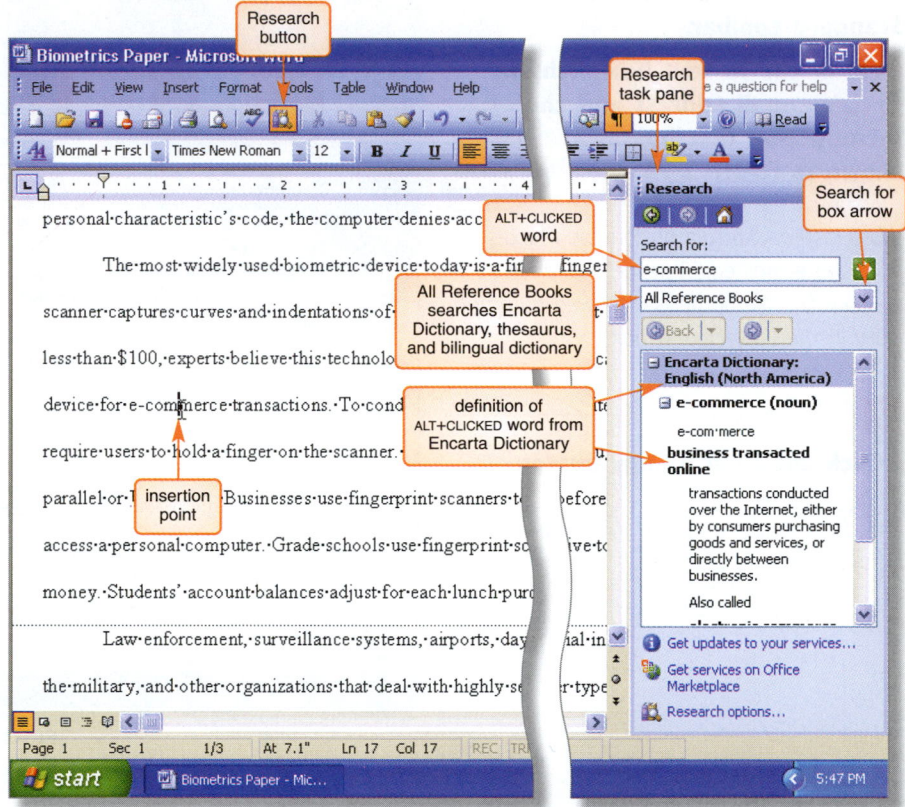

FIGURE 2-75

After you have looked up information in the Research task pane, you either can close the task pane or you can insert certain pieces of the information into the document. The next steps illustrate the procedure of copying information displayed in the Research task pane and inserting the copied text in a Word document.

To Insert Text from the Research Task Pane in a Word Document

1

• **In the Research task pane, double-click the word, Internet.**

• **Right-click the selected word.**

The word, Internet, is selected in the Research task pane and a shortcut menu is displayed (Figure 2-76).

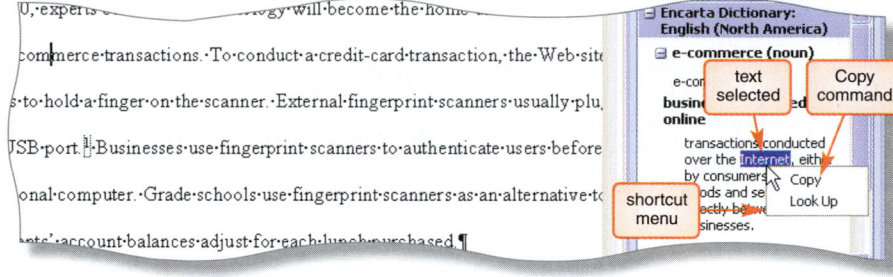

FIGURE 2-76

2

• **Click Copy on the shortcut menu to copy the selected text to the Clipboard.**

• **Drag through the word, e-commerce, in the research paper.**

• **Right-click the selected text in the document (Figure 2-77).**

The word, e-commerce, is selected in the document and a shortcut menu is displayed.

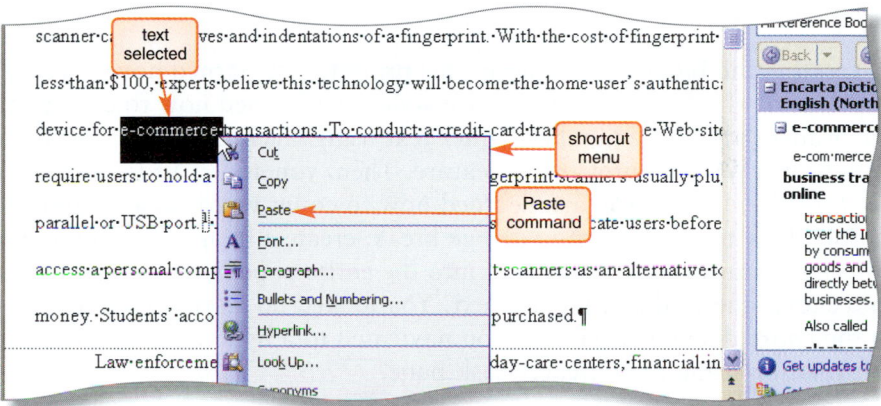

FIGURE 2-77

3

• **Click Paste on the shortcut menu.**

• **If necessary, press the SPACEBAR to insert a space after the inserted word.**

• **Click the Close button in the Research task pane.**

Word removes the selected word, e-commerce, and inserts the word, Internet, in its place (Figure 2-78).

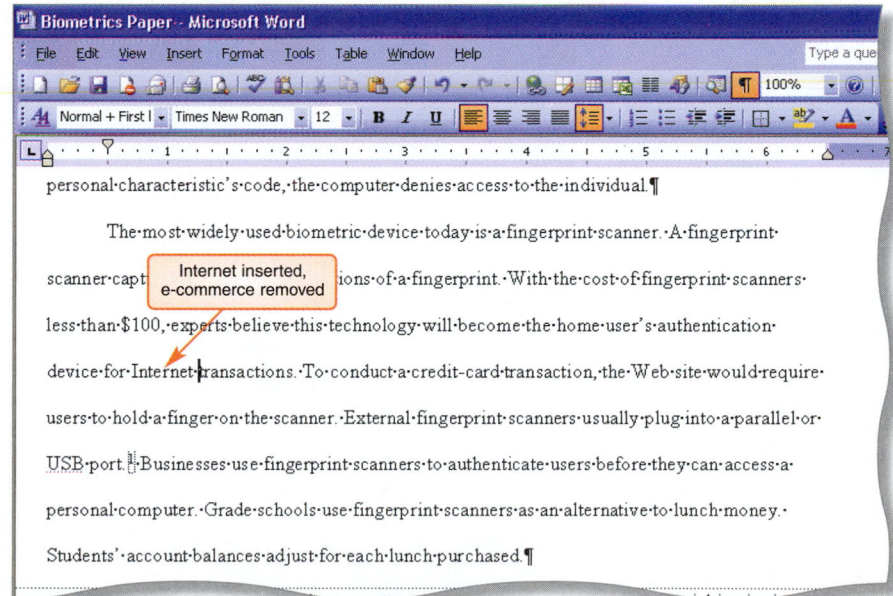

FIGURE 2-78

When using Word to insert material from the Research task pane or any other online reference, be very careful not to plagiarize, or copy other's work and use it as your own. Not only is plagiarism unethical, but it is considered an academic crime that can have severe punishments such as failing a course or being expelled from school.

The final step in this project is to quit Word, as described below.

To Quit Word

1 **Click the Close button in the Word window.**

2 **If Word displays a dialog box, click the No button.**

The Word window closes.

Project Summary

In creating the Biometrics Paper in this project, you learned how to use Word to enter and format a research paper using the MLA documentation style. You learned how to change margin settings, adjust line spacing, create headers with page numbers, enter text using Click and Type, and first-line indent paragraphs. You learned how to use Word's AutoCorrect feature. Then, you added a footnote in the research paper and modified the Footnote Text style. You also learned how to count words in a document. In creating the Works Cited page, you learned how to insert a manual page break, create a hanging indent, create a hyperlink, and sort paragraphs.

Once you finished typing text into the entire paper, you learned how to browse through a Word document, move text, and find and replace text. You looked up a synonym for a word and checked spelling and grammar in the entire document. Finally, you navigated to a hyperlink, e-mailed a copy of a document, and looked up information using the Research task pane.

If you have a SAM user profile, you may have access to hands-on instruction, practice, and assessment of the skills covered in this project. Log in to your SAM account and go to your assignments page to see what your instructor has assigned.

What You Should Know

Having completed this project, you should be able to perform the tasks below. The tasks are listed in the same order they were presented in this project. For a list of the buttons, menus, toolbars, and commands introduced in this project, see the Quick Reference Summary at the back of this book and refer to the Page Number column.

1. Start and Customize Word   (WD 77)
2. Display Formatting Marks   (WD 77)
3. Change the Margin Settings   (WD 78)
4. Double-Space Text   (WD 80)
5. Display the Header Area   (WD 81)
6. Click and Type   (WD 83)
7. Enter a Page Number   (WD 83)
8. Enter Name and Course Information   (WD 85)
9. Format Text Using Shortcut Keys   (WD 86)
10. Save a Document   (WD 87)
11. First-Line Indent Paragraphs   (WD 88)
12. AutoCorrect as You Type   (WD 89)
13. Use the AutoCorrect Options Button   (WD 90)
14. Create an AutoCorrect Entry   (WD 91)
15. Enter More Text   (WD 93)
16. Add a Footnote   (WD 94)
17. Modify a Style   (WD 96)
18. Close the Note Pane   (WD 99)
19. Count Words   (WD 100)
20. Page Break Automatically   (WD 101)
21. Recount Words   (WD 102)
22. Page Break Manually   (WD 103)
23. Center the Title of the Works Cited Page (WD 104)
24. Create a Hanging Indent   (WD 105)
25. Enter Works Cited Paragraphs   (WD 105)
26. Insert a Symbol Automatically   (WD 107)
27. Create a Hyperlink   (WD 108)
28. Sort Paragraphs   (WD 109)
29. Browse by Page   (WD 111)
30. Select a Sentence   (WD 112)
31. Move Selected Text   (WD 113)
32. Display the Paste Options Menu   (WD 115)
33. Find and Replace Text   (WD 116)
34. Find Text   (WD 117)
35. Find and Insert a Synonym   (WD 118)
36. Check Spelling and Grammar at Once (WD 119)
37. Save a Document Again and Print It   (WD 121)
38. View or Modify Entries in a Custom Dictionary (WD 121)
39. Set the Default Custom Dictionary   (WD 121)
40. Navigate to a Hyperlink   (WD 122)
41. E-Mail a Document   (WD 123)
42. E-Mail a Document as an Attachment (WD 123)
43. Use the Research Task Pane to Locate Information   (WD 124)
44. Insert Text from the Research Task Pane in a Word Document   (WD 125)
45. Quit Word   (WD 126)

Learn It Online

Instructions: To complete the Learn It Online exercises, start your browser, click the Address bar, and then enter the Web address scsite.com/wd2003/learn. When the Word 2003 Learn It Online page is displayed, follow the instructions in the exercises below. Each exercise has instructions for printing your results, either for your own records or for submission to your instructor.

1 Project Reinforcement TF, MC, and SA

Below Word Project 2, click the Project Reinforcement link. Print the quiz by clicking Print on the File menu for each page. Answer each question.

2 Flash Cards

Below Word Project 2, click the Flash Cards link and read the instructions. Type 20 (or a number specified by your instructor) in the Number of playing cards text box, type your name in the Enter your Name text box, and then click the Flip Card button. When the flash card is displayed, read the question and then click the ANSWER box arrow to select an answer. Flip through Flash Cards. If your score is 15 (75%) correct or greater, click Print on the File menu to print your results. If your score is less than 15 (75%) correct, then redo this exercise by clicking the Replay button.

3 Practice Test

Below Word Project 2, click the Practice Test link. Answer each question, enter your first and last name at the bottom of the page, and then click the Grade Test button. When the graded practice test is displayed on your screen, click Print on the File menu to print a hard copy. Continue to take practice tests until you score 80% or better.

4 Who Wants To Be a Computer Genius?

Below Word Project 2, click the Computer Genius link. Read the instructions, enter your first and last name at the bottom of the page, and then click the PLAY button. When your score is displayed, click the PRINT RESULTS link to print a hard copy.

5 Wheel of Terms

Below Word Project 2, click the Wheel of Terms link. Read the instructions, and then enter your first and last name and your school name. Click the PLAY button. When your score is displayed, right-click the score and then click Print on the shortcut menu to print a hard copy.

6 Crossword Puzzle Challenge

Below Word Project 2, click the Crossword Puzzle Challenge link. Read the instructions, and then enter your first and last name. Click the SUBMIT button. Work the crossword puzzle. When you are finished, click the Submit button. When the crossword puzzle is redisplayed, click the Print Puzzle button to print a hard copy.

7 Tips and Tricks

Below Word Project 2, click the Tips and Tricks link. Click a topic that pertains to Project 2. Right-click the information and then click Print on the shortcut menu. Construct a brief example of what the information relates to in Word to confirm you understand how to use the tip or trick.

8 Newsgroups

Below Word Project 2, click the Newsgroups link. Click a topic that pertains to Project 2. Print three comments.

9 Expanding Your Horizons

Below Word Project 2, click the Expanding Your Horizons link. Click a topic that pertains to Project 2. Print the information. Construct a brief example of what the information relates to in Word to confirm you understand the contents of the article.

10 Search Sleuth

Below Word Project 2, click the Search Sleuth link. To search for a term that pertains to this project, select a term below the Project 2 title and then use the Google search engine at google.com (or any major search engine) to display and print two Web pages that present information on the term.

11 Word Online Training

Below Word Project 2, click the Word Online Training link. When your browser displays the Microsoft Office Online Web page, click the Word link. Click one of the Word courses that covers one or more of the objectives listed at the beginning of the project on page WD 74. Print the first page of the course before stepping through it.

12 Office Marketplace

Below Word Project 2, click the Office Marketplace link. When your browser displays the Microsoft Office Online Web page, click the Office Marketplace link. Click a topic that relates to Word. Print the first page.

Apply Your Knowledge

1 Revising a Document

Instructions: Start Word. Open the document, Apply 2-1 Authentication Paragraph, on the Data Disk. See the inside back cover of this book for instructions for downloading the Data Disk or see your instructor for information about accessing the files in this book.

The document on the Data Disk is a paragraph of text. You are to revise the paragraph as follows: move a sentence; change the format of the moved sentence; change paragraph indentation, change line spacing, change margin settings, replace all occurrences of the word, memorized, with the word, remembered; add a sentence; remove an automatic hyperlink format, and modify the header. The revised paragraph is shown in Figure 2-79.

Perform the following tasks:

1. Select the first sentence of the paragraph. Use drag-and-drop editing to move this sentence to the end of the paragraph, so it is the last sentence in the paragraph.

2. Click the Paste Options button that displays to the right of the moved sentence. Remove the italic format from the moved sentence by clicking Keep Text Only on the shortcut menu.

3. Use first-line indent to indent the first line of the paragraph.

> Revised Authentication Paragraph
> 10/17/2005 12:35:34 PM
>
> Three common types of authentication are remembered information, biometric devices, and possessed objects. With remembered information, the user enters a word or series of characters that match an entry in the computer's security file. Examples of remembered information are passwords, user IDs, and logon codes. A password is confidential, usually known only by the user and possibly the system administrator. A user ID typically identifies the user, and a logon code identifies an application program. A possessed object is any item the user must carry to access the computer facility. Some examples are keys, badges, and cards. Possessed objects often are used together with a personal identification number (PIN), which is a numeric password. For more information about passwords, visit www.scsite.com/dc2003/apply.htm and click Apply It #1 below Chapter 11.

FIGURE 2-79

4. Change the line spacing of the paragraph from single to double.

5. Change the left and right margins of the document to .75".

6. Use the Find and Replace dialog box to replace all occurrences of the word, memorized, with the word, remembered.

7. Use Word's thesaurus to change the word, usually, to the word, typically, in the sentence that starts, A user ID usually…

8. At the end of the paragraph, press the SPACEBAR and then type this sentence: For more information about passwords, visit www.scsite.com/dc2003/apply.htm and click Apply It #1 below Chapter 11.

9. Remove the hyperlink automatic format from the Web address by positioning the mouse pointer at the beginning of the Web address (that is, the w in www), pointing to the small blue box below the w, clicking the AutoCorrect Options button, and then clicking Undo Hyperlink on the shortcut menu.

10. Display the header on the screen. Change the alignment of the text in the header from left to centered. Insert the word, Revised, in the text so it reads: Revised Authentication Paragraph. On the second line of the header, insert and center the current date and the current time using buttons on the Header and Footer toolbar. Place one space between the current date and current time.

11. Click File on the menu bar and then click Save As. Save the document using the file name, Apply 2-1 Revised Authentication Paragraph.

12. Print the revised paragraph, shown in Figure 2-79.

13. Use the Research task pane to look up the definition of the word, passwords, in the third sentence of the paragraph. Handwrite the definition on your printout.

1 Preparing a Short Research Paper

Problem: You are a college student currently enrolled in an introductory computer class. Your assignment is to prepare a short research paper (350-400 words) about a computer component. The requirements are that the paper be presented according to the MLA documentation style and have three references. One of the three references must be from the Web and formatted as a hyperlink on the Works Cited page. You prepare the paper shown in Figure 2-80, which discusses the system unit.

Marks 1

Nicholas Marks

Ms. White

Computer Literacy 100

August 6, 2005

The System Unit

The system unit is a case that houses the electronic components of the computer used to process data. Although many system units resemble a box, they are available in many shapes and sizes. The case of the system unit, sometimes called a chassis, is made of metal or plastic and protects the internal electronic components from damage. All computers have a system unit (Alvarez 102).

Components of the system unit include the processor, memory modules, adapter cards, drive bays, power supply, ports, and connectors. The processor interprets and carries out the basic instructions that operate a computer. A memory module houses memory chips. An adapter card is a circuit board that provides connections and functions not built into the motherboard.[1] A drive bay holds a disk drive. The power supply allows electricity to travel into a computer.

On a personal computer, the electronic components and most storage devices reside inside the system unit. Other devices, such as a keyboard, mouse, microphone, monitor, printer, speakers, scanner, and digital camera, normally occupy space outside the system unit (*How to Use a Computer*). On a desktop personal computer, the system unit usually is a device separate from the monitor and keyboard. Some system units sit on top of a desk. Other models, called tower models, can stand vertically on the floor.

---

[1] According to Wilson, four adapter cards most commonly found in desktop personal computers today are sound cards, modem cards, video cards, and network cards (18-32).

FIGURE 2-80a

In the Lab

Marks 2

     To conserve space, an all-in-one computer houses the system unit in the same physical case as the monitor. On notebook computers, the keyboard and pointing device often occupy the area on the top of the system unit. The display attaches to the system unit by hinges. The system unit on a PDA (personal digital assistant) or handheld computer usually consumes the entire device. On these small mobile devices, the display is part of the system unit, too.

FIGURE 2-80b

Marks 3

Works Cited

Alvarez, Juan. *Understanding Computer Basics: Stepping Toward Literacy*. Chicago: Martin
Publishing, 2005.

How to Use a Computer. Shelly Cashman Series®. Course Technology. 3 Aug. 2005.
www.scsite.com/wd2003/pr2/wc1.htm.

Wilson, Tracey M. "Personal Computers and their Applications." *Computing and Information
Systems Weekly* May 2005: 18-32.

FIGURE 2-80c

Instructions:

1. If necessary, display formatting marks on the screen.
2. Change all margins to one inch.
3. Adjust line spacing to double.
4. Create a header to number pages.
5. Type the name and course information at the left margin. Center and type the title.
6. Set first-line indent for paragraphs in the body of the research paper.
7. Type the body of the paper as shown in Figure 2-80a and Figure 2-80b. Add the footnote as shown in Figure 2-80a. At the end of the body of the research paper, press the ENTER key and then insert a manual page break.
8. Create the works cited page (Figure 2-80c).
9. Check the spelling of the paper at once.
10. Save the document on a floppy disk using Lab 2-1 System Unit Paper as the file name.
11. Use the Select Browse Object button to go to page 3. If you have access to the Web, CTRL+click the hyperlink to test it.
12. Print the research paper. Handwrite the number of words, paragraphs, and characters in the research paper above the title of your printed research paper.

In the Lab

2 Preparing a Research Report with a Footnote(s)

Problem: You are a college student currently enrolled in an introductory computer class. Your assignment is to prepare a short research paper in any area of interest to you. The requirements are that the paper be presented according to the MLA documentation style, contain at least one explanatory note positioned as a footnote, and have three references. One of the three references must be from the Internet and formatted as a hyperlink on the works cited page. You decide to prepare a paper about employee monitoring (Figure 2-81).

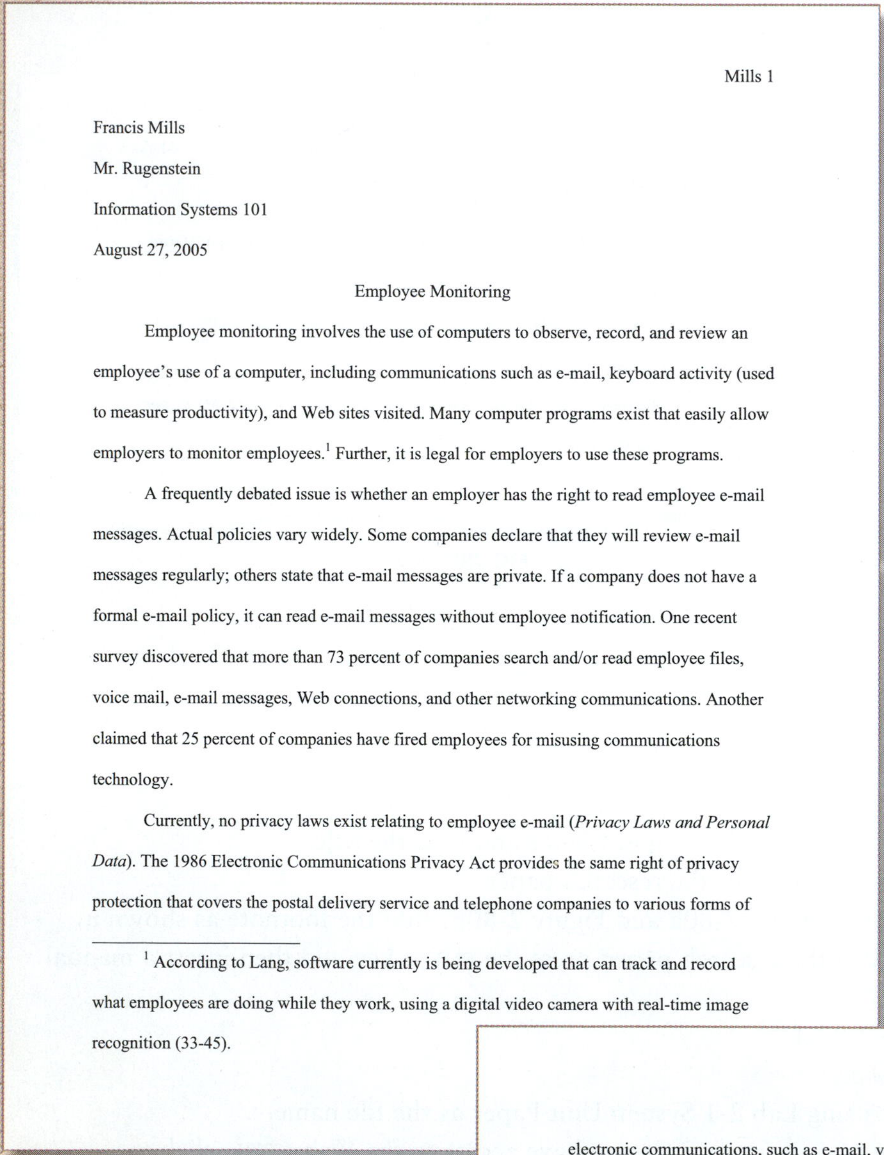

Mills 1

Francis Mills

Mr. Rugenstein

Information Systems 101

August 27, 2005

Employee Monitoring

Employee monitoring involves the use of computers to observe, record, and review an employee's use of a computer, including communications such as e-mail, keyboard activity (used to measure productivity), and Web sites visited. Many computer programs exist that easily allow employers to monitor employees.[1] Further, it is legal for employers to use these programs.

A frequently debated issue is whether an employer has the right to read employee e-mail messages. Actual policies vary widely. Some companies declare that they will review e-mail messages regularly; others state that e-mail messages are private. If a company does not have a formal e-mail policy, it can read e-mail messages without employee notification. One recent survey discovered that more than 73 percent of companies search and/or read employee files, voice mail, e-mail messages, Web connections, and other networking communications. Another claimed that 25 percent of companies have fired employees for misusing communications technology.

Currently, no privacy laws exist relating to employee e-mail (*Privacy Laws and Personal Data*). The 1986 Electronic Communications Privacy Act provides the same right of privacy protection that covers the postal delivery service and telephone companies to various forms of

---

[1] According to Lang, software currently is being developed that can track and record what employees are doing while they work, using a digital video camera with real-time image recognition (33-45).

FIGURE 2-81a

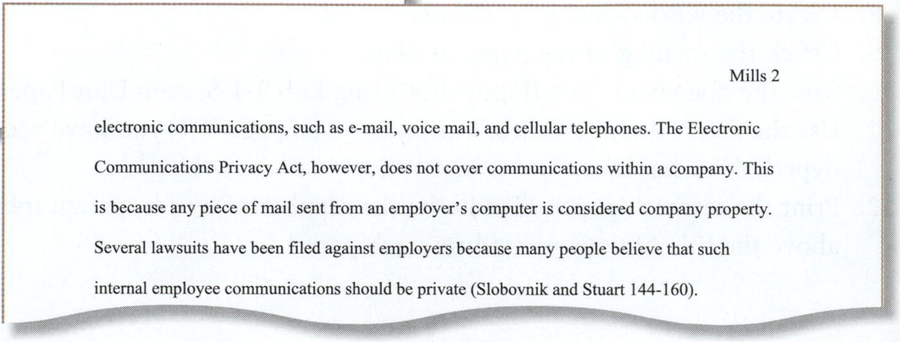

Mills 2

electronic communications, such as e-mail, voice mail, and cellular telephones. The Electronic Communications Privacy Act, however, does not cover communications within a company. This is because any piece of mail sent from an employer's computer is considered company property. Several lawsuits have been filed against employers because many people believe that such internal employee communications should be private (Slobovnik and Stuart 144-160).

FIGURE 2-81b

In the Lab

Instructions Part 1: Perform the following tasks to create the research paper:

1. If necessary, display formatting marks on the screen. Change all margin settings to one inch. Adjust line spacing to double. Create a header to number pages. Type the name and course information at the left margin. Center and type the title. Set first-line indent for paragraphs in the body of the research paper.

2. Type the body of the paper as shown in Figure 2-81a and Figure 2-81b. Add the footnote as shown in Figure 2-81a. Change the Footnote Text style to the format specified in the MLA style. At the end of the body of the research paper, press the ENTER key once and insert a manual page break.

3. Create the works cited page. Enter the works cited shown below as separate paragraphs. Format the works according to the MLA documentation style and then sort the works cited paragraphs.
    (a) Slobovnik, Victor W., and Janel K. Stuart. Workplace Challenges. Dallas: Techno-Cyber Publishing, 2005.
    (b) Privacy Laws and Personal Data. Shelly Cashman Series®. Course Technology. 3 Aug. 2005. www.scsite.com/wd2003/pr2/wc2.htm.
    (c) Lang, Stefanie. "The New Invasion: Employee Monitoring and Privacy Issues." Technology Issues Aug. 2005: 33-45.

4. Check the spelling of the paper.

5. Save the document on a floppy disk using Lab 2-2 Employee Monitoring Paper as the file name.

6. If you have access to the Web, CTRL+click the hyperlink to test it.

7. Print the research paper. Handwrite the number of words, including the footnotes, in the research paper above the title of your printed research paper.

Instructions Part 2: Perform the following tasks to modify the research paper:

1. Use Word to find a synonym of your choice for the word, issue, in the first sentence of the second paragraph.

2. Change all occurrences of the word, employers, to the word, companies.

3. Insert a second footnote at the end of the fourth sentence in the last paragraph of the research paper. Use the following footnote text: Some companies even use automated software that searches e-mail messages for derogatory language. One unidentified woman, for example, was fired for using her office e-mail to complain about her boss.

4. In the first footnote, find the word, developed, and change it to the word, written.

5. Save the document on a floppy disk using Lab 2-2 Employee Monitoring Paper - Part 2 as the file name.

6. Print this revised research paper that has notes positioned as footnotes. Handwrite the number of words, including the footnotes, in the research paper above the title of the printed research paper.

Instructions Part 3: Perform the following tasks to modify the research paper created in Part 2:

1. Convert the footnotes to endnotes. Recall that endnotes display at the end of a document. Switch to print layout view to see the endnotes. *Hint:* Use Help to learn about print layout view and converting footnotes to endnotes.

2. Modify the Endnote text style to 12-point font, double-spaced text with a first-line indent. Insert a page break so the endnotes are placed on a separate, numbered page. Center the title, Endnotes, double-spaced above the notes.

3. Change the format of the note reference marks to capital letters (A, B, etc.). *Hint:* Use Help to learn about changing the number format of note reference marks.

4. Save the document on a floppy disk using Lab 2-2 Employee Monitoring Paper - Part 3 as the file name.

5. Print the revised research paper with notes positioned as endnotes. Handwrite the number of words, including the endnotes, in the research paper above the title of the printed research paper.

In the Lab

3 Composing a Research Paper from Notes

Problem: You have drafted the notes shown in Figure 2-82. Your assignment is to prepare a short research paper from these notes.

Instructions: Perform the following tasks:

1. Review the notes in Figure 2-82 and then rearrange and reword them. Embellish the paper as you deem necessary. Present the paper according to the MLA documentation style. Create an AutoCorrect entry that automatically corrects the spelling of the misspelled word, softare, to the correct spelling, software. Add a footnote that refers the reader to the Web for more information. Create the works cited page from the listed sources. Be sure to sort the works.

2. Check the spelling and grammar of the paper. Save the document on a floppy disk using Lab 2-3 Computer Software Paper as the file name.

3. Use the Research task pane to look up a definition. Copy and insert the definition into the document as a footnote. Be sure to quote the definition and cite the source.

4. Print the research paper. Hand-write the number of words, including the footnotes, in the research paper above the title of the printed research paper. Circle the definition inserted into the document from the Research task pane.

5. Use Word to e-mail the research paper to your instructor, if your instructor gives you permission to do so.

Software, also called a program, is a series of instructions that tells the computer hardware what to do and how to do it. Two categories of software are system software and application software.

System software (source: "The Future of Application Software," an article on page 39-55 in the May 2005 issue of Computers and Peripherals, authors James A. Naylor and Joseph I. Vincent.)
- System software is an interface between the application software, the user, and the computer's hardware.
- An operating system is a popular type of system software. Microsoft Windows is an operating system that has a graphical user interface. Users interact with software through its user interface.
- System software consists of the programs that control or maintain the operations of the computer and its devices.

Application software (source: a Web site titled Guide to Application Software, sponsored by the Shelly Cashman Series® at Course Technology, site visited on October 3, 2005, Web address is www.scsite.com/wd2003/pr2/wc3.htm)
- Application software consists of programs that perform specific tasks for users. Examples are word processing software, spreadsheet software, database software, presentation graphics software, and Web browsers.
- Database software - store data in an organized fashion, and retrieve, manipulate, and display that data in a variety of formats.
- Word processing software - create documents such as letters, reports, and brochures.
- Spreadsheet software - calculate numbers arranged in rows and columns.
- Web browser - connect to the Internet to access and view Web pages.
- Presentation graphics software - create documents called slides that add visual appeal to presentations.
- Other types of application software are available that enable users to perform a variety of tasks, including personal information management, project management, accounting, desktop publishing, photo and video editing, personal finance, tax preparation, reference, education, entertainment, and communications.

Software suites (source: Hardware and Software Made Simple, a book published by Cyber Press Publishing in New York, 2005, written by Nanette Allen and Clint Muhr.)
- When installing the software suite, you install the entire collection of programs at once instead of installing each one individually. Business software suites typically include word processing, spreadsheet, e-mail, and presentation graphics programs.
- Software vendors often bundle and sell individual programs together as a single package called a software suite. This costs much less than buying the applications individually.
- Two widely used business software suites are Microsoft Office and Sun StarOffice.

FIGURE 2-82

Cases and Places

The difficulty of these case studies varies:
■ are the least difficult and ■■ are more difficult. The last exercise is a group exercise.

1 ■ This project discussed the requirements of the MLA documentation style on page WD 76 and in several More About boxes dispersed throughout the project. Using the material presented in this project, write a short research paper (400-450 words) that describes the requirements of the MLA documentation style. Include at least two references and one explanatory note positioned as a footnote. Add an AutoCorrect entry to correct a word you commonly mistype. Use the concepts and techniques presented in this project to format the paper. Type the paper with the Word screen in normal view. Switch to print layout view to proof the paper.

2 ■■ The ever-increasing presence of computers in everyone's lives has generated an awareness of the need to address computing requirements for those who have or may develop physical limitations. The Americans with Disabilities Act (ADA) requires any company with 15 or more employees to make reasonable attempts to accommodate the needs of physically challenged workers. Whether at work or at home, you may find it necessary to acquire devices that address physical limitations. Using Word's Research task pane, the school library, other textbooks, magazines, the Internet, friends and family, or other resources, research the types of input and/or output devices designed for physically challenged computer users. Then, prepare a brief research paper (400-450 words) that discusses your findings. Include at least one explanatory note and two references, one of which must be a Web site on the Internet. Use the concepts and techniques presented in this project to format the paper.

3 ■■ Computers process input (data) into output (information). A computer often holds data, information, and instructions in storage for future use. Most computers today also can communicate with other computers. Computers perform input, output, storage, and communications operations with amazing speed, reliability, consistency, and accuracy. Using Word's Research task pane, the school library, other textbooks, the Internet, magazines, or other resources, research one of the following computer operations: input, output, storage, or communications. Then, prepare a brief research paper (400-450 words) that discusses how the computer operation works and/or the types of devices used for that activity. Include at least one explanatory note and two references, one of which must be a Web site on the Internet. Use the concepts and techniques presented in this project to format the paper.

4 ■■ A programming language is a set of words, symbols, and codes that enables a programmer to communicate instructions to a computer. Just as humans speak a variety of languages (English, Spanish, French, and so on), programmers use a variety of programming languages and program development tools to write computer programs. Using Word's Research task pane, the school library, other textbooks, the Internet, magazines, interviews with programmers, or other resources, research the types of programming languages or program development tools on the market today. Then, prepare a brief research paper (400-450 words) that discusses one or more programming languages or program development tools. Include at least one explanatory note and two references, one of which must be a Web site on the Internet. Use the concepts and techniques presented in this project to format the paper.

Cases and Places

5 ■■ **Working Together**   PDAs are one of the more popular lightweight mobile devices in use today. A PDA (personal digital assistant) can provide a variety of personal information management functions including calendar, appointment book, address book, calculator, and notepad, as well as access to the Internet and telephone capabilities. Many different PDAs are on the market. Each team member is to research the features, price, and accessories of one type of PDA by looking through newspapers, magazines, searching the Web, and/or visiting an electronics or computer store. Each team member is to write a minimum of 200 words summarizing his or her findings. Each team member also is to write at least one explanatory note and supply his or her reference for the works cited page. Then, the team should meet as a group to compose a research paper that includes all team members' write-ups. Start by copying and pasting the text into a single document and then write an introduction and conclusion as a group. Use the concepts and techniques presented in this project to format the paper according to the MLA documentation style. Set the default dictionary. If Word flags any of your last names as an error, add the name(s) to the custom dictionary. Hand in printouts of each team member's original write-up, as well as the final research paper.

MICROSOFT
Office Word 2003

Creating a Resume Using a Wizard and a Cover Letter with a Table

P R O J E C T

3

CASE PERSPECTIVE

Hartford College offers many educational courses of study, such as certificate (vocational training), associate, and bachelor degree programs. Benjamin Kane Okamoto recently graduated from Hartford with a bachelor's degree in information and computer technology. You had classes with Benjamin and counseled him while you worked as an intern in Hartford College's Office of Career Development.

Benjamin is ready to embark on a full-time career in computer sales. He buys several local newspapers to begin his job hunt. While reading through the classified section of the *New England Tribune*, Benjamin notices a computer sales position available at National Computer Sales that seems perfect. The ad requests that all applicants send a resume and a cover letter to the personnel director, Ms. Helen Weiss. Benjamin contacts you and asks you to help him create a professional resume and cover letter. You immediately agree to help your schoolmate.

With Benjamin's educational background, work experience, and communications skills, and your resume-writing abilities, Benjamin will be prepared for success in acquiring the computer sales position. You suggest he use Word's Resume Wizard to create the resume because the wizard saves time by formatting much of the document. You also advise Benjamin to include all essential business letter components in the cover letter. Then, you mention he can use Word to prepare and print an envelope, so the entire presentation looks professional.

As you read through this project, you will learn how to use Word to create a resume, a cover letter, and an addressed envelope.

Office Word 2003

Creating a Resume Using a Wizard and a Cover Letter with a Table

PROJECT

3

Objectives

You will have mastered the material in this project when you can:

- Create a resume using Word's Resume Wizard
- Fill in a document template
- Use print preview to view and print a document
- Set and use tab stops
- Collect and paste using the Clipboard task pane
- Format paragraphs and characters
- Remove formatting from text
- Identify the components of a business letter

- Insert the current date
- Create and insert an AutoText entry
- Insert a Word table, enter data into the table, and format the table
- Address and print an envelope
- Work with smart tags
- Modify file properties

Introduction

At some time in your professional life, you will prepare a resume along with a personalized cover letter to send to a prospective employer(s). In addition to some personal information, a **resume** usually contains the applicant's educational background and job experience. Employers review many resumes for each vacant position. Thus, you should design your resume carefully so it presents you as the best candidate for the job. You also should attach a personalized cover letter to each resume you send. A **cover letter** enables you to elaborate on positive points in your resume; it also provides you with an opportunity to show a potential employer your written communications skills. Accordingly, it is important that your cover letter is written well and follows proper business letter rules.

Composing documents from scratch can be a difficult process for many people. To assist with this task, Word provides wizards and templates. A **wizard** asks you several basic questions and then, based on your responses, uses a template to prepare and format a document for you. A **template** is similar to a form with prewritten text; that is, Word prepares the requested document with text and/or formatting common to all documents of this nature. After Word creates a document from a template, you fill in the blanks or replace prewritten words in the document. In addition to templates used by wizards, Word provides other templates you can use to create documents.

Project Three — Resume and Cover Letter

Benjamin Kane Okamoto, a recent college graduate, is seeking a full-time position in computer sales. Project 3 uses Word to produce his resume, shown in Figure 3-1, and a personalized cover letter and an envelope, shown in Figure 3-2 on the next page.

resume

78 Larkspur Road
Plantsville, CT 06479

Phone (860) 555-4499
Fax (860) 555-4490
E-mail okamoto@earth.net

Benjamin Kane Okamoto

Objective
To obtain a full-time sales position with a major computer or electronics company in the New England area.

Education
2001-2005   Hartford College   Hartford, CT
Information and Computer Technology
- B.S., December 2005
- A.S., December 2003

Areas of concentration
Computer Hardware
Computer Software and Programming
Professional Communications
Business

Awards received
Dean's List, every semester
Gamma Phi Sigma Honors Society, 2002-2005
Hartford College Outstanding Senior, 1st Place, 2005

Interests and activities
Association of Sales Representatives, junior member
Big Brothers Big Sisters of Hartford, volunteer
Computer Club, treasurer
New England Ski Club, publicity coordinator

Languages
English (fluent)
Japanese (fluent)
Knowledge of sign language

Work experience
2002-2005   Computer Discount Sales   Plantsville, CT
Intern
- Sold hardware and software components to home and small business customers
- Arranged and configured in-store computer hardware, software, and network displays
- Logged and replied to computer-related customer e-mail, fax, and telephone inquiries

Volunteer experience
As a Big Brother, I spend at least eight hours every week with my Little Brother – hoping to make a difference in this youth's life.

FIGURE 3-1

More About

Resumes and Cover Letters

The World Wide Web contains a host of information, tips, and suggestions about writing resumes and cover letters. For links to Web sites about writing resumes and cover letters, visit the Word 2003 More About Web page (scsite.com/wd2003/more) and then click one of the Writing Research Papers and Cover Letters links.

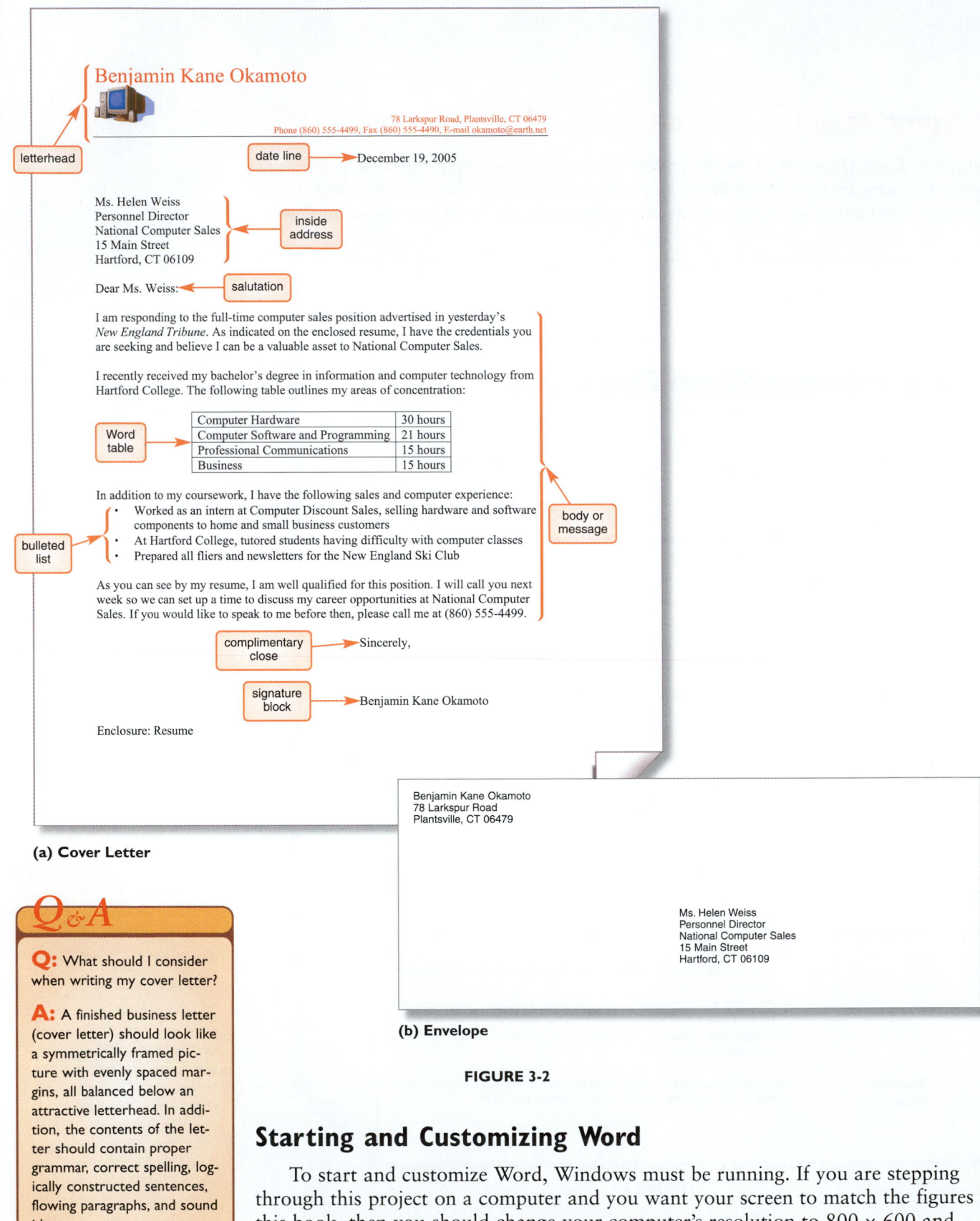

(a) Cover Letter

(b) Envelope

FIGURE 3-2

Starting and Customizing Word

To start and customize Word, Windows must be running. If you are stepping through this project on a computer and you want your screen to match the figures in this book, then you should change your computer's resolution to 800 × 600 and reset the toolbars and menus. For information about changing the resolution and resetting toolbars and menus, read Appendix D.

The following steps describe how to start Word and customize the Word window. You may need to ask your instructor how to start Word for your system.

To Start and Customize Word

1 Click the Start button on the Windows taskbar, point to All Programs on the Start menu, point to Microsoft Office on the All Programs submenu, and then click Microsoft Office Word 2003 on the Microsoft Office submenu.

2 If the Word window is not maximized, double-click its title bar to maximize it.

3 If the Language bar appears, right-click it and then click Close the Language bar on the shortcut menu.

4 If the Getting Started task pane is displayed in the Word window, click its Close button.

5 If the Standard and Formatting toolbar buttons are displayed on one row, click the Toolbar Options button and then click Show Buttons on Two Rows in the Toolbar Options list.

6 If your screen differs from Figure 3-3 on the next page, click View on the menu bar and then click Normal.

Word starts and, after a few moments, displays an empty document in the Word window (shown in Figure 3-3).

Displaying Formatting Marks

As discussed in Project 1, it is helpful to display formatting marks that indicate where in the document you pressed the ENTER key, SPACEBAR, and other keys. The following step describes how to display formatting marks.

To Display Formatting Marks

1 If the Show/Hide ¶ button on the Standard toolbar is not selected already, click it.

Word displays formatting marks in the document window, and the Show/Hide ¶ button on the Standard toolbar is selected (shown in Figure 3-3).

Using Word's Resume Wizard to Create a Resume

You can type a resume from scratch into a blank document window, or you can use the **Resume Wizard** and let Word format the resume with appropriate headings and spacing. After answering several questions, you customize the resume created by the Resume Wizard by filling in blanks or selecting and replacing text.

When you use a wizard, Word displays a dialog box with the wizard's name on its title bar. A wizard's dialog box displays a list of **panel names** along its left side with the currently selected panel displaying on the right side of the dialog box (shown in Figure 3-6 on page WD 143). Each panel presents a different set of options, in which you select preferences or enter text. To move from one panel to the next within the wizard's dialog box, click the Next button or click the panel name on the left side of the dialog box.

The following steps show how to create a resume using the Resume Wizard. A wizard retains the settings selected by the last person who used the wizard. Thus, the wizard initially may display some text and selections different from the figures shown here. If you are stepping through this project on a computer, be sure to verify that your settings match the screens shown in the following steps before clicking the Next button in each dialog box.

To Create a Resume Using Word's Resume Wizard

1

• **Click File on the menu bar (Figure 3-3).**

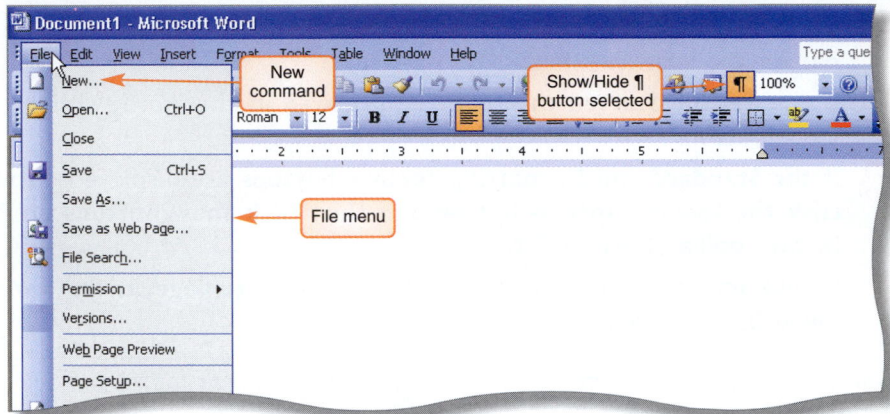

FIGURE 3-3

2

• **Click New on the File menu.**

Word displays the New Document task pane (Figure 3-4). You access wizards through the Templates area in the task pane.

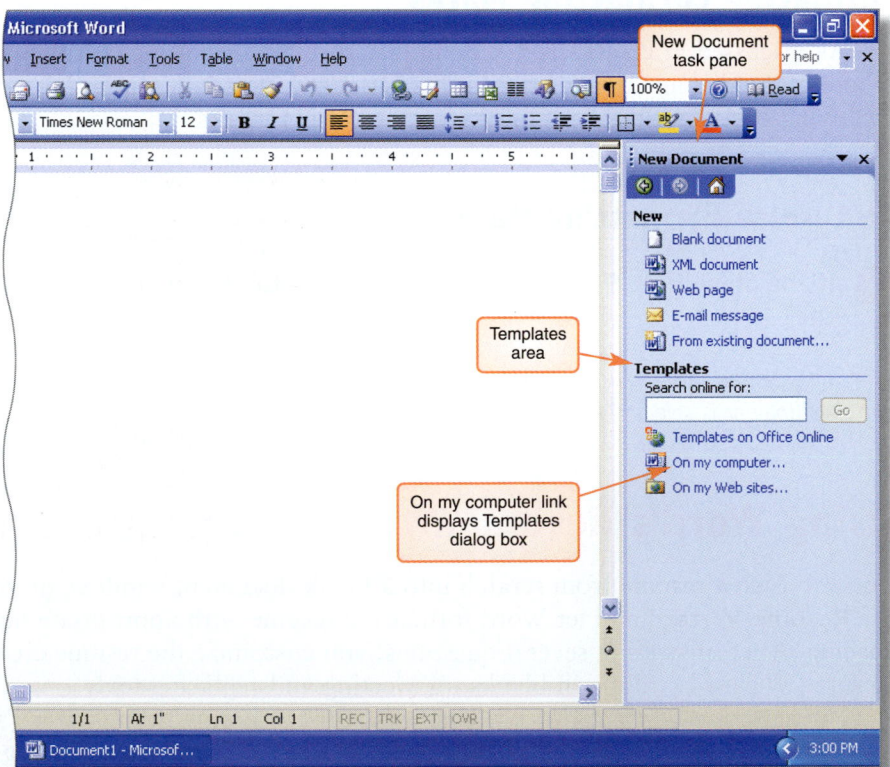

FIGURE 3-4

3

• Click the **On my computer** link in the Templates area in the New Document task pane.

• When Word displays the Templates dialog box, click the Other Documents tab.

• Click the Resume Wizard icon.

Word displays several wizard and template icons in the Other Documents sheet in the Templates dialog box (Figure 3-5). Icons without the word, wizard, are templates. If you click an icon, the Preview area shows a sample of the resulting document.

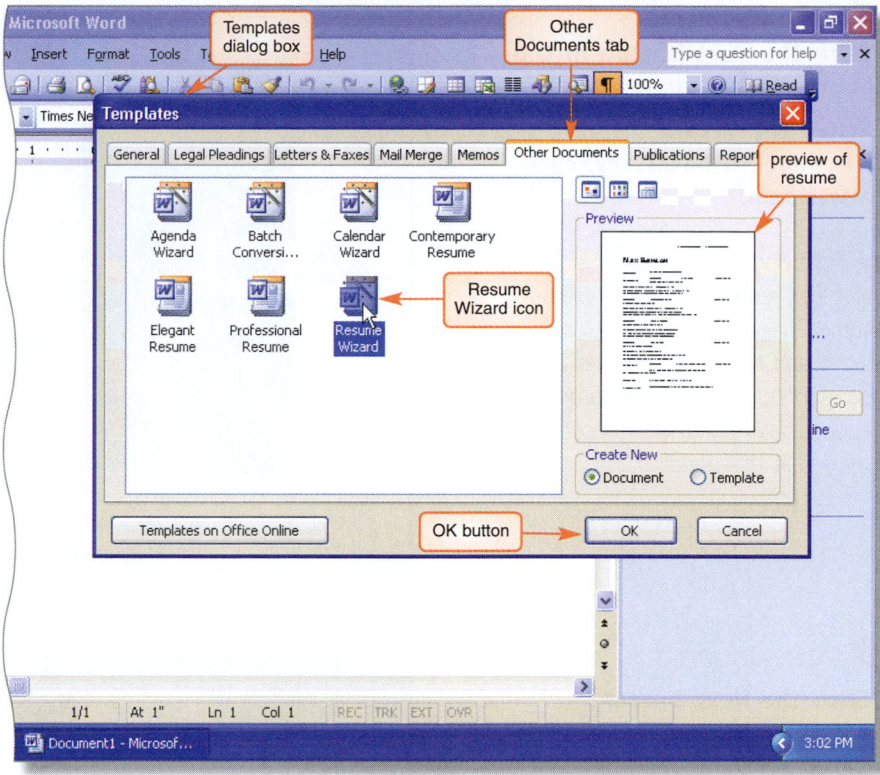

FIGURE 3-5

4

• Click the **OK** button.

After a few seconds, Word displays the Start panel in the Resume Wizard dialog box, informing you the Resume Wizard has started (Figure 3-6). This dialog box has a Microsoft Word Help button you can click to obtain help while using the wizard. When you create a document based on a wizard, Word creates a new document window, which is called Document2 in this figure.

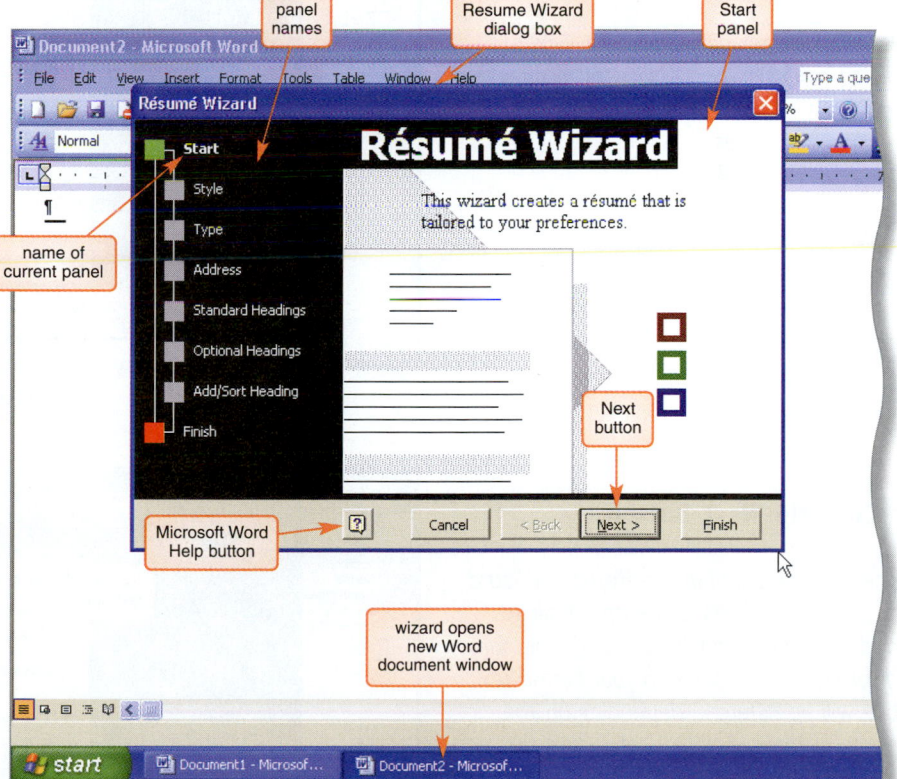

FIGURE 3-6

5

• **Click the Next button in the Resume Wizard dialog box.**

• **When the wizard displays the Style panel, if necessary, click Professional.**

The Style panel in the Resume Wizard dialog box requests the style of your resume (Figure 3-7). Three styles of wizards and templates are available in Word: Professional, Contemporary, and Elegant. A sample of each resume style is displayed in this panel.

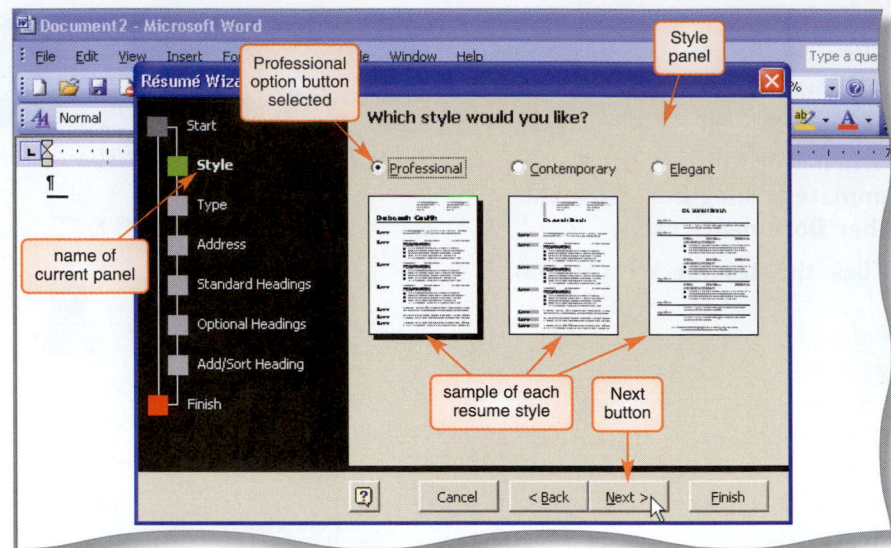

FIGURE 3-7

6

• **Click the Next button.**

• **When the wizard displays the Type panel, if necessary, click Entry-level resume.**

The Type panel in the Resume Wizard dialog box asks for the type of resume that you want to create (Figure 3-8).

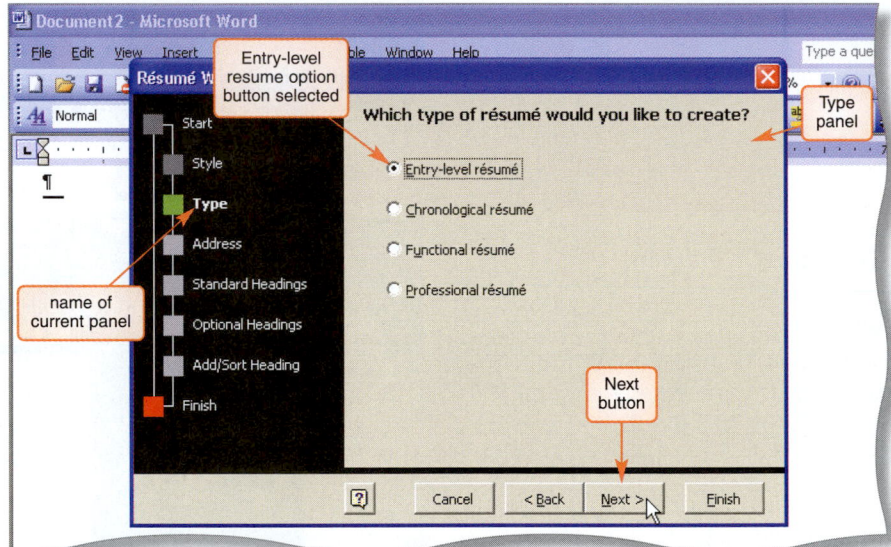

FIGURE 3-8

7

• **Click the Next button.**

The Address panel in the Resume Wizard dialog box requests name and mailing address information (Figure 3-9). The name displayed and selected in your Name text box will be different, depending on the name of the last person who used the Resume Wizard.

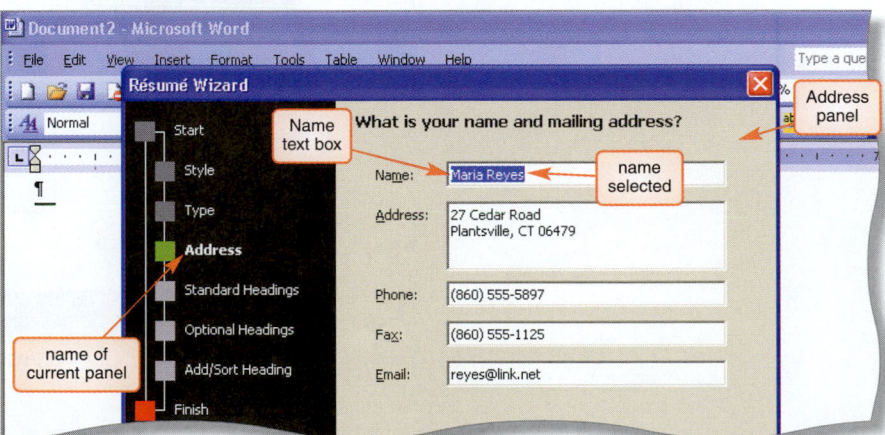

FIGURE 3-9

8

• **With the name in the Name text box selected, type** Benjamin Kane Okamoto **and then press the TAB key.**

• **Type** 78 Larkspur Road **and then press the ENTER key.**

• **Type** Plantsville, CT 06479 **and then press the TAB key.**

• **Type** (860) 555-4499 **and then press the TAB key.**

• **Type** (860) 555-4490 **and then press the TAB key.**

• **Type** okamoto@earth.net **as the e-mail address.**

As you type the new text, it automatically replaces any selected text (Figure 3-10).

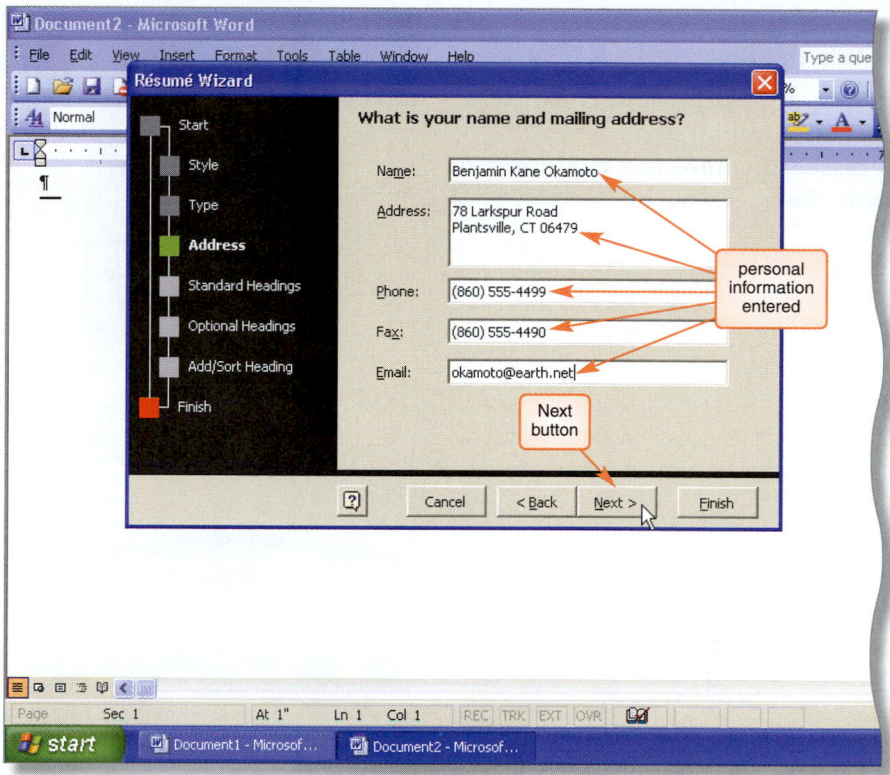

FIGURE 3-10

9

• **Click the Next button.**

• **When the wizard displays the Standard Headings panel, if necessary, click Hobbies and References to remove the check marks. All other check boxes should have check marks. If any do not, place a check mark in the check box by clicking it.**

The Standard Headings panel in the Resume Wizard dialog box requests the headings you want on your resume (Figure 3-11). You want all headings, except for these two: Hobbies and References.

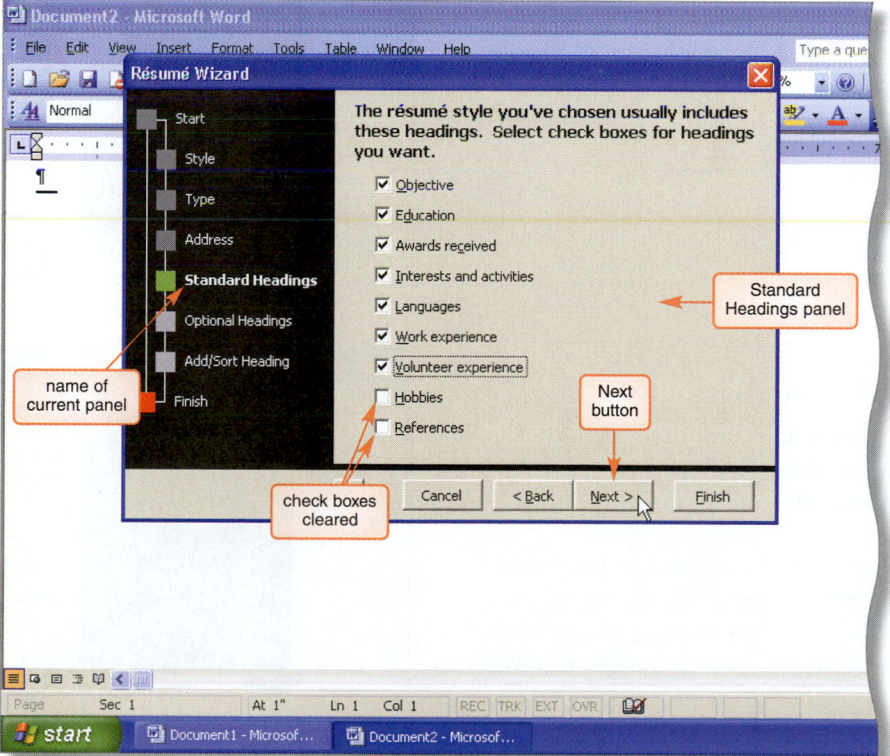

FIGURE 3-11

10

• **Click the Next button.**

• **When the wizard displays the Optional Headings panel, if necessary, remove any check marks from the check boxes.**

The Optional Headings panel in the Resume Wizard dialog box allows you to choose additional headings for your resume (Figure 3-12). All of these check boxes should be empty because none of these headings are on the resume in this project.

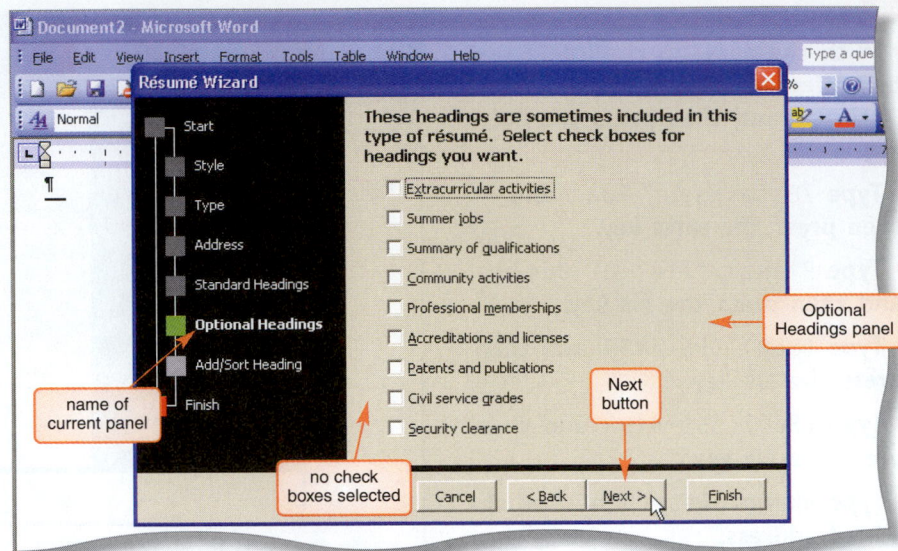

FIGURE 3-12

11

• **Click the Next button.**

• **When the wizard displays the Add/Sort Heading panel, type** Areas of concentration **in the additional headings text box.**

The Add/Sort Heading panel in the Resume Wizard dialog box allows you to enter any additional headings you want on the resume (Figure 3-13).

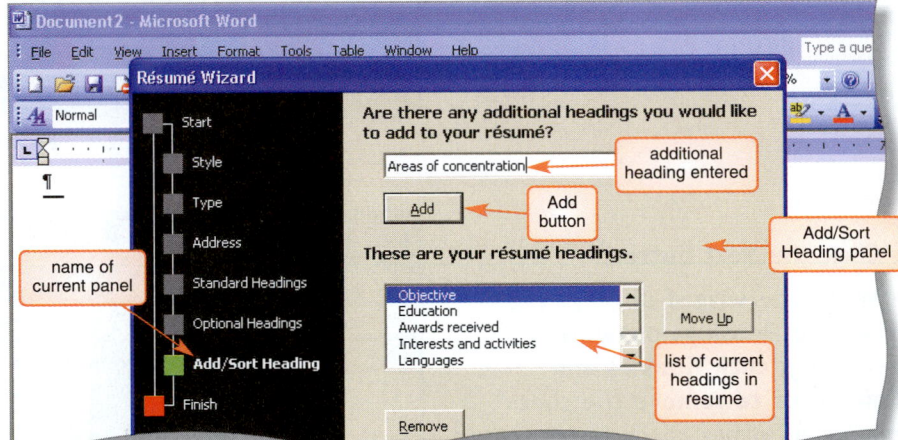

FIGURE 3-13

12

• **Click the Add button.**

• **Scroll to the bottom of the list of resume headings and then click Areas of concentration.**

The Areas of concentration heading is selected (Figure 3-14). You can rearrange the order of the headings on your resume by selecting a heading and then clicking the appropriate button (Move Up button or Move Down button).

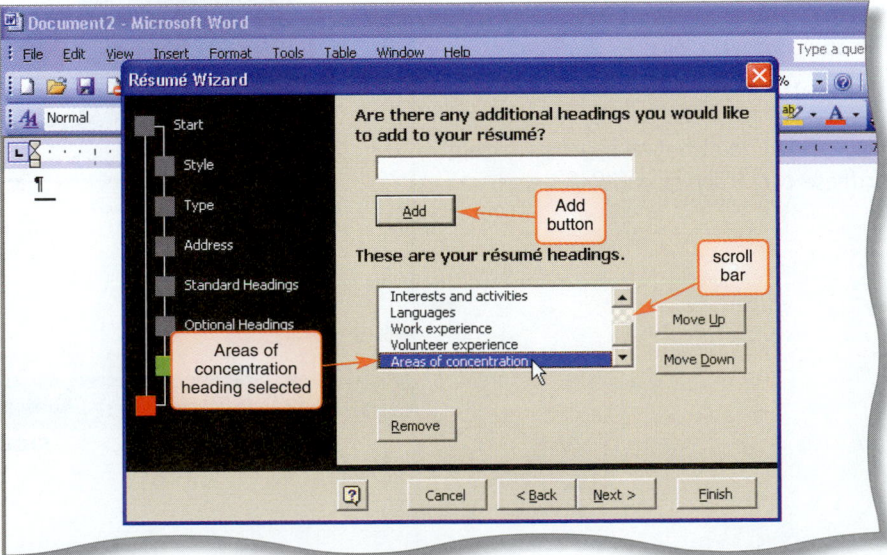

FIGURE 3-14

13

• **Click the Move Up button five times.**

The wizard moves the heading, Areas of concentration, above the Awards received heading (Figure 3-15).

14

• **If the last person using the Resume Wizard included additional headings, you may have some unwanted headings. Your heading list should be as follows: Objective, Education, Areas of concentration, Awards received, Interests and activities, Languages, Work experience, and Volunteer experience. If you have an additional heading(s), click the unwanted heading and then click the Remove button.**

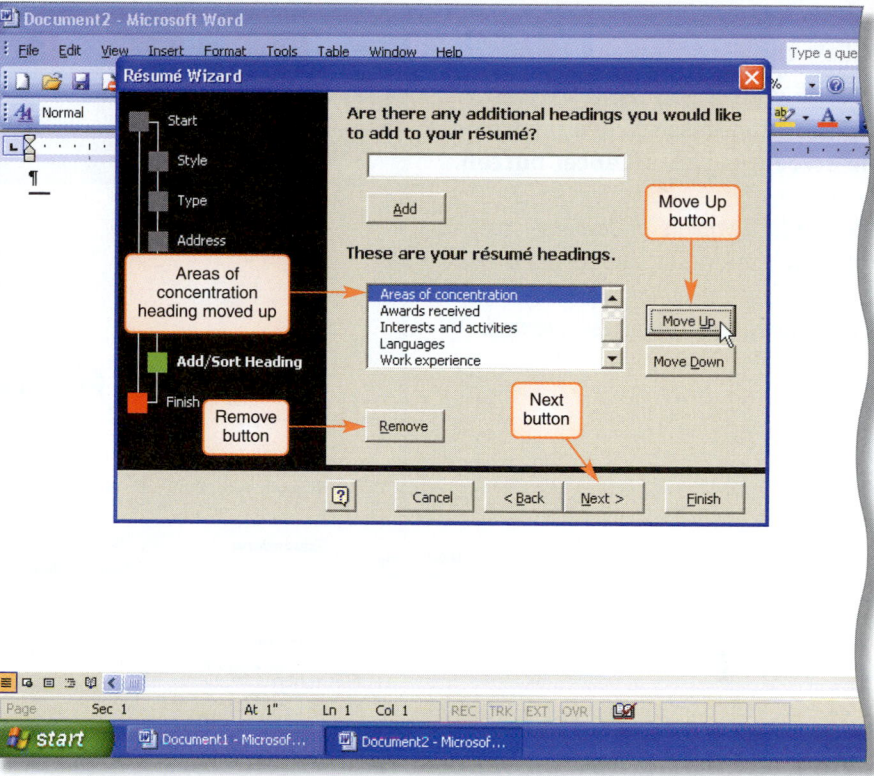

FIGURE 3-15

15

• **Click the Next button.**

The Finish panel in the Resume Wizard dialog box indicates the wizard is ready to create your document (Figure 3-16).

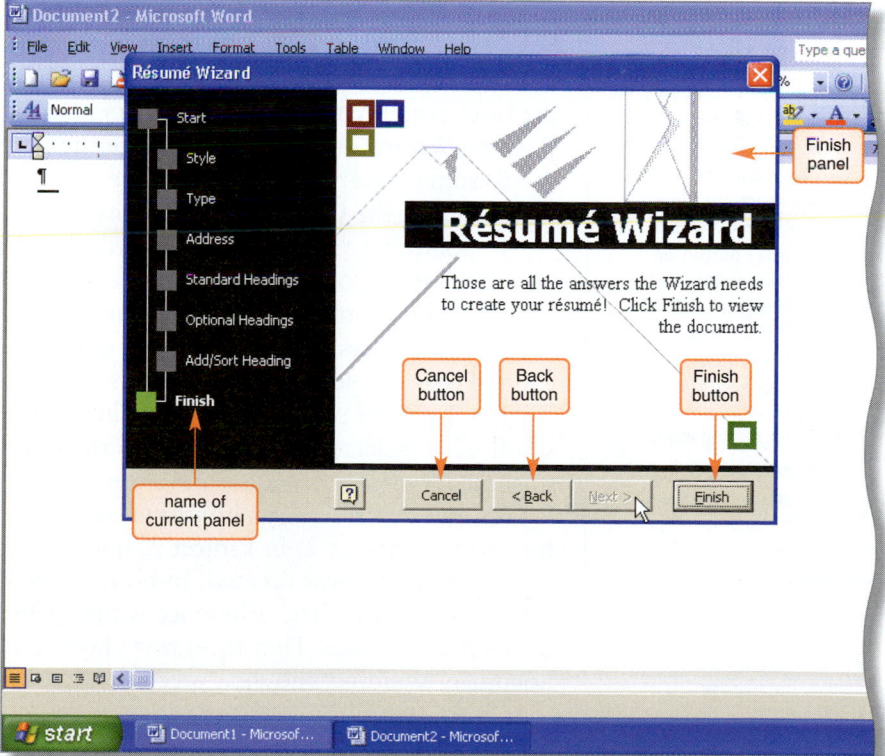

FIGURE 3-16

16

- Click the **Finish** button in the Resume Wizard dialog box.
- If the Office Assistant appears on the screen, click its Cancel button.

Word uses a template of an entry-level professional style resume to format a resume on the screen (Figure 3-17). You are to personalize the resume as indicated.

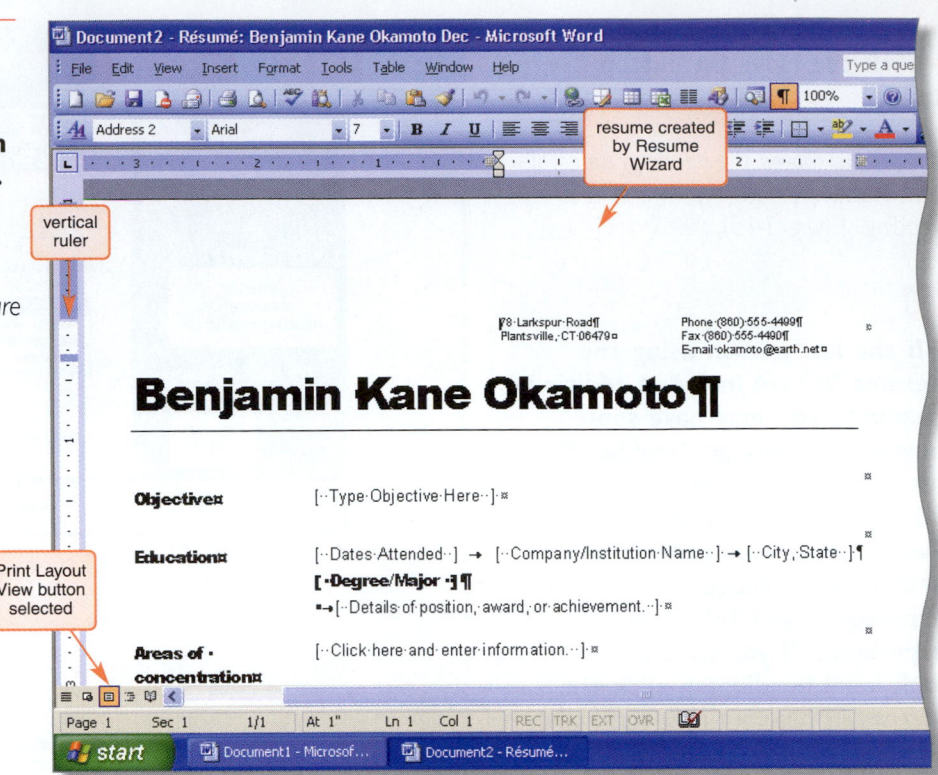

FIGURE 3-17

When you create a resume using the Resume Wizard (Figure 3-16 on the previous page), you can click the panel name or the Back button in any panel of the Resume Wizard dialog box to change the previously selected options. To exit from the Resume Wizard and return to the document window without creating the resume, click the Cancel button in any panel of the Resume Wizard dialog box.

In addition to the Resume Wizard, Word provides many other wizards to assist you in creating documents: agenda for a meeting, calendar, envelope, fax cover sheet, legal pleading, letter, mailing label, and memorandum.

Word displays the resume in the document window in print layout view. You can tell that the document window is in print layout view by looking at the screen (Figure 3-17). In print layout view, the Print Layout View button on the horizontal scroll bar is selected. Also, a vertical ruler is displayed at the left edge of the document window, in addition to the horizontal ruler at the top of the window.

The Word screen was in normal view while creating documents in Project 1 and for most of Project 2. In Project 2, the Word window switched to print layout view when the header was created. In both normal view and print layout view, you can type and edit text. The difference is that **print layout view** shows you an exact view of the printed page. That is, in print layout view, Word places a piece of paper in the document window, showing precisely the positioning of the text, margins, headers, footers, and footnotes.

To display more of the document on the screen in print layout view, you can hide the white space at the top and bottom of the pages and the gray space between pages. The next steps show how to hide the white space, if your screen displays it.

To Hide White Space

1

• **Point to the top of the page in the document window until the Hide White Space button appears.**

The mouse pointer changes to the Hide White Space button when positioned at the top of the page (Figure 3-18).

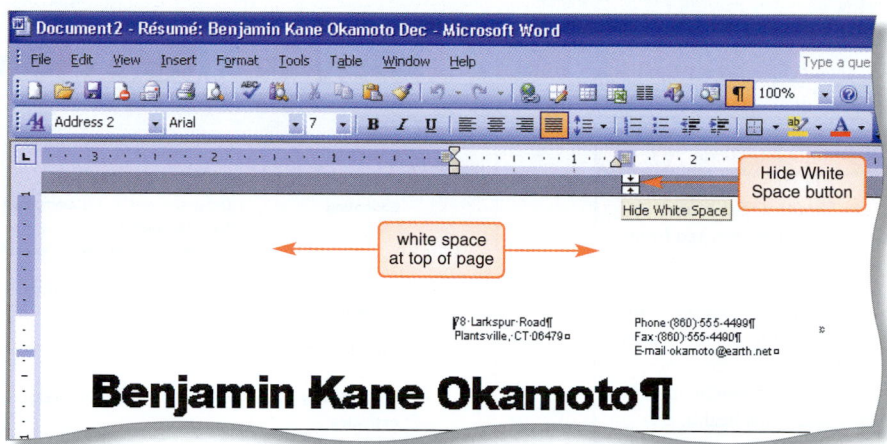

FIGURE 3-18

2

• **Click the Hide White Space button.**

Word removes white space, which causes the page to move up in the document window (Figure 3-19).

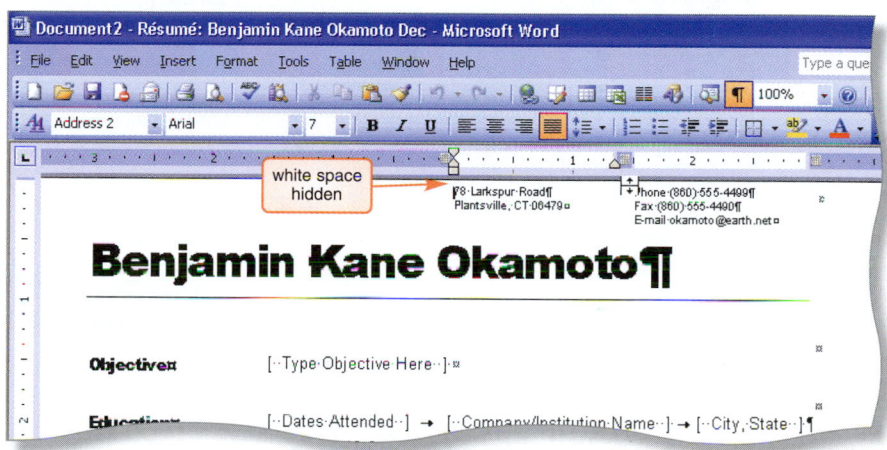

FIGURE 3-19

If you wanted to show the white space again, you would point between two pages and click when the mouse pointer changes to a Show White Space button.

To see the entire resume created by the Resume Wizard, print the document shown in the Word window, as described in the following steps.

To Print the Resume Created by the Resume Wizard

1 Ready the printer and then click the Print button on the Standard toolbar.

2 When the printer stops, retrieve the hard copy resume from the printer.

The printed resume is shown in Figure 3-20 on the next page.

More About

Hiding White Space

If you want Word always to hide white space, click Tools on the menu bar, click Options, click the View tab, remove the check mark from the White space between pages check box, and then click the OK button. This command is available only in print layout view.

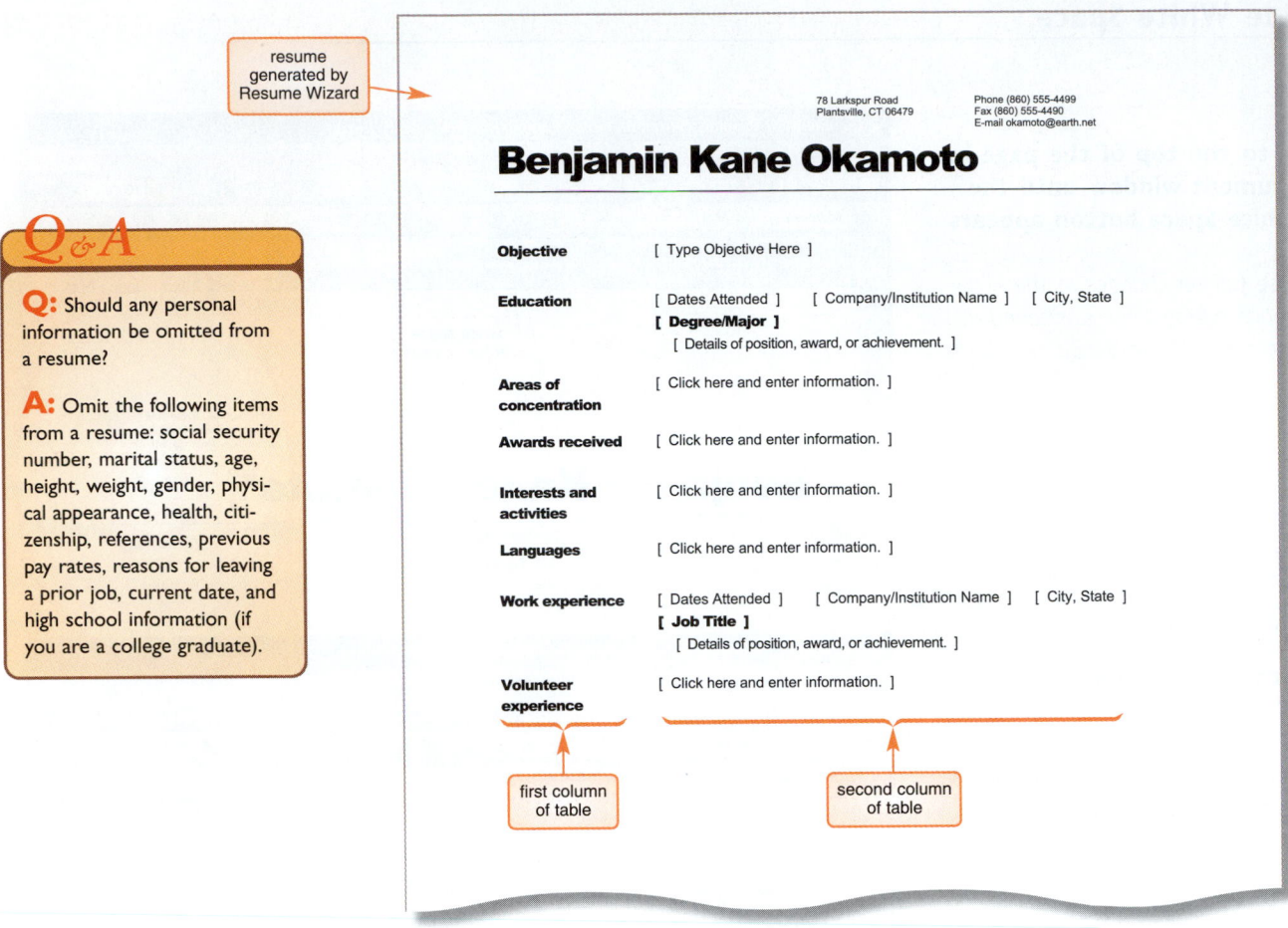

FIGURE 3-20

Personalizing the Resume

The next step is to personalize the resume. Where Word has indicated, you type the objective, education, areas of concentration, awards received, interests and activities, languages, work experience, and volunteer experience next to the respective headings. The following pages show how to personalize the resume generated by the Resume Wizard.

Tables

When the Resume Wizard prepares a resume, it arranges the body of the resume as a table. A Word **table** is a collection of rows and columns. As shown in Figure 3-21, the first column of the table in the resume contains the section headings (Objective, Education, Areas of concentration, Awards received, Interests and activities, Languages, Work experience, and Volunteer experience). The second column of the table contains the details for each of these sections. Thus, this table contains two columns. It also contains eight rows — one row for each section of the resume.

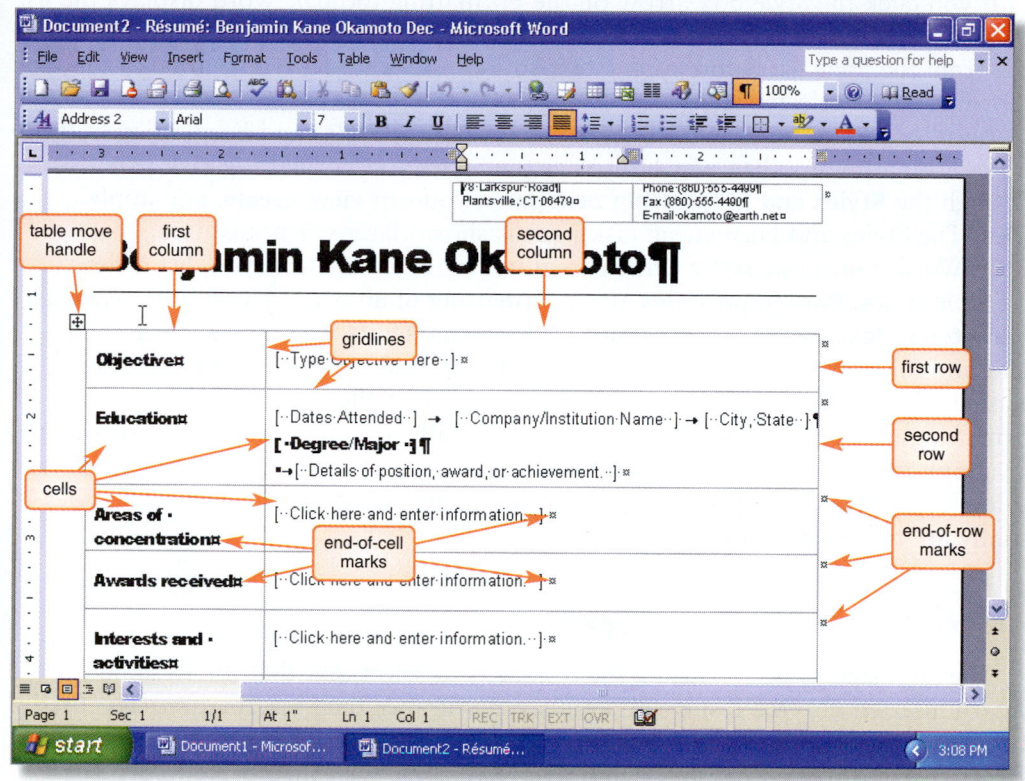

FIGURE 3-21

The intersection of a row and a column is called a **cell**, and cells are filled with text. Each cell has an **end-of-cell mark**, which is a formatting mark that assists you with selecting and formatting cells. Recall that formatting marks do not print on a hard copy.

To see the rows, columns, and cells clearly in a Word table, some users prefer to show gridlines. As illustrated in Figure 3-21, **gridlines** help identify the rows and columns in a table. If you want to display gridlines in a table, position the insertion point somewhere in the table, click Table on the menu bar, and then click Show Gridlines. If you want to hide the gridlines, click somewhere in the table, click Table on the menu bar, and then click Hide Gridlines.

You can resize a table, add or delete rows or columns in a table, and format a table. When you point to the upper-left corner of the table, the table move handle appears. Using the table move handle, you can select or move a table. To select a table, click the table move handle; to move the table to a new location, drag the table move handle. These and other features of tables are discussed in more depth later in this project.

Styles

When you use a wizard to create a document, Word formats the document using styles. As discussed in Project 2, a **style** is a named group of formatting characteristics that you can apply to text. The Style box on the Formatting toolbar displays the name of the style associated with the location of the insertion point or selection. You can identify many of the characteristics assigned to a style by looking at the Formatting toolbar. For example, in Figure 3-22 on the next page, the characters in the selected paragraph are formatted with the Objective style, which uses 10-point Arial font.

More About

The Ruler

When the insertion point is in a table, the ruler shows the boundaries of each column in the table. For example, in Figure 3-21, the address information at the top of the resume is a separate table of one row and two columns. The ruler shows the width of each column.

If you click the Style box arrow on the Formatting toolbar, Word displays the list of styles associated with the current document. You also can select the appropriate style from the Style list before typing text so that the text you type will be formatted according to the selected style.

Another way to work with styles is by clicking the Styles and Formatting button on the Formatting toolbar, which displays the Styles and Formatting task pane. Through the **Styles and Formatting task pane**, you can view, create, and apply styles. The Styles and Formatting task pane is shown later when it is used.

In Word, four basic styles exist: paragraph styles, character styles, list styles, and table styles. **Paragraph styles** affect formatting of an entire paragraph, whereas **character styles** affect formats of only selected characters. **List styles** affect alignment and fonts in a numbered or bulleted list, and **table styles** affect the borders, shading, alignment, and fonts in a Word table. In the Style list and Styles and Formatting task pane, paragraph style names usually are followed by a proofreader's paragraph mark (¶); character style names usually are followed by an underlined letter a (a); list styles usually are followed by a bulleted list icon (≡); and table styles usually are followed by a table icon (⊞).

Selecting and Replacing Text

The next step in personalizing the resume is to select text that the Resume Wizard inserted into the resume and replace it with personal information. The first heading on the resume is the objective. You enter the objective where the Resume Wizard inserted the words, Type Objective Here, which is called **placeholder text**.

To replace text in Word, select the text to be removed and then type the desired text. To select the placeholder text, Type Objective Here, you click it. Then, type the objective. As soon as you begin typing, Word deletes the selected placeholder text. Thus, you do not need to delete the selection before you begin typing.

The following steps show how to enter the objective into the resume.

To Select and Replace Placeholder Text

1

• **Click the placeholder text, Type Objective Here.**

Word selects the placeholder text in the resume (Figure 3-22). Notice the style is Objective in the Style box on the Formatting toolbar.

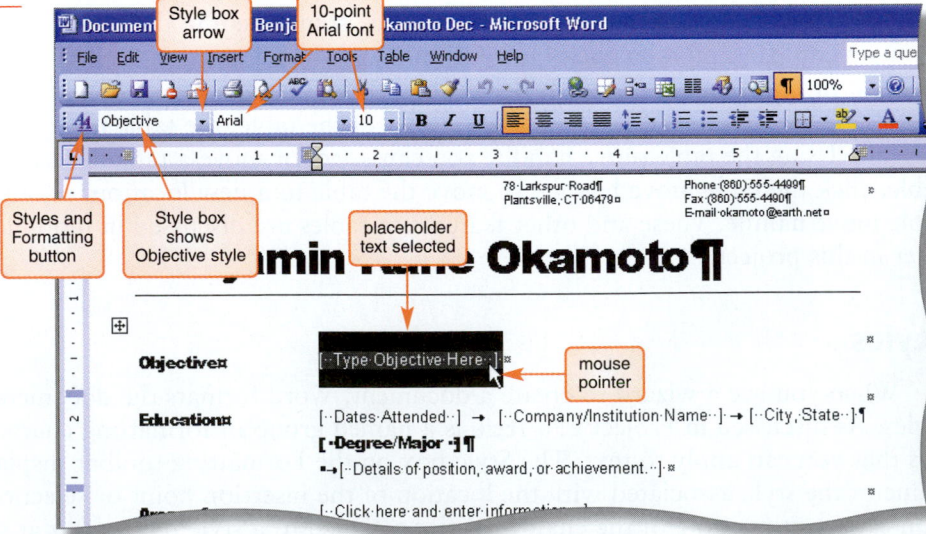

FIGURE 3-22

2

• **Type** To obtain a full-time sales position with a major computer or electronics company in the New England area.

Word replaces the selected placeholder text, Type Objective Here, with the typed objective (Figure 3-23). Your document may wordwrap differently depending on the type of printer you are using.

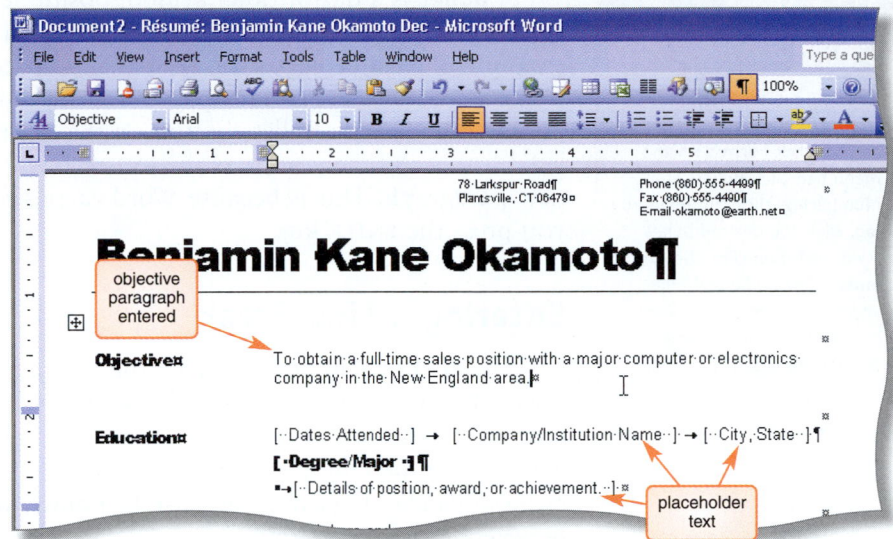

FIGURE 3-23

The next step in personalizing the resume is to replace the placeholder text in the education section of the resume with your own words and phrases, as described in the following steps.

To Select and Replace More Placeholder Text

1 If necessary, scroll down to display the entire education section of the resume. Click, or if necessary drag through, the placeholder text, Dates Attended. **Type** 2001-2005 and then click the placeholder text, Company/Institution Name.

2 **Type** Hartford College and then click the placeholder text, City, State. **Type** Hartford, CT and then click the placeholder text, Degree/Major. **Type** Information and Computer Technology and then click the placeholder text, Details of position, award, or achievement.

3 **Type** B.S., December 2005 and then press the ENTER key. **Type** A.S., December 2003 as the last item in the list.

The education section is entered (Figure 3-24).

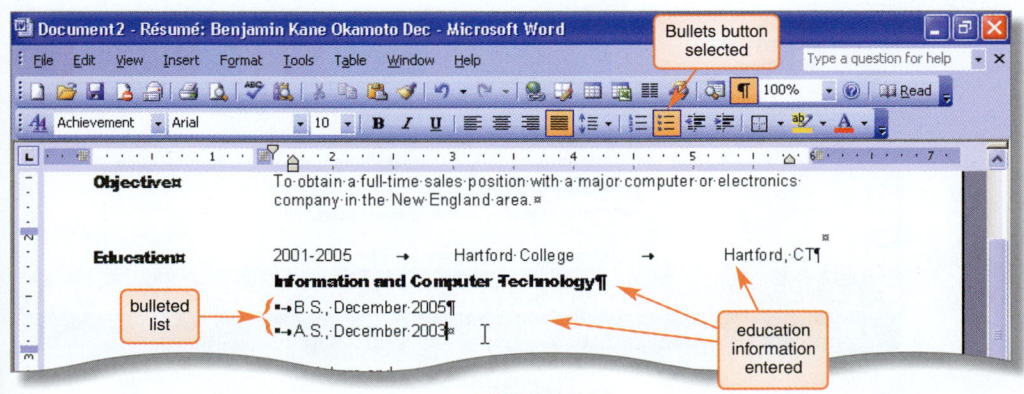

FIGURE 3-24

A **bullet** is a dot or other symbol positioned at the beginning of a paragraph. A **bulleted list** is a list of paragraphs that each begin with a bullet character. For example, the list of degrees in the education section of the resume is a bulleted list (Figure 3-24 on the previous page). When the insertion point is in a paragraph containing a bullet, the Bullets button on the Formatting toolbar is selected. In a bulleted list, each time you press the ENTER key, a bullet displays at the beginning of the new paragraph. This is because Word carries forward paragraph formatting when you press the ENTER key.

Entering a Line Break

The next step in personalizing the resume is to enter four lines of text in the areas of concentration section. The style used for the characters in the areas of concentration section of the resume is the Objective style. A paragraph formatting characteristic of the Objective style is that when you press the ENTER key, the insertion point advances downward at least 11 points, which leaves nearly an entire blank line between each paragraph.

You want the lines within the areas of concentration section to be close to each other, as shown in Figure 3-1 on page WD 139. Thus, you will not press the ENTER key between each area of concentration. Instead, you press SHIFT+ENTER to create a **line break**, which advances the insertion point to the beginning of the next physical line.

The following steps show how to enter text in the areas of concentration section using a line break, instead of a paragraph break, between each line.

To Enter a Line Break

1

• **If necessary, scroll down to display the areas of concentration section of the resume.**

• **In the areas of concentration section, click the placeholder text, Click here and enter information.**

• **Type** Computer Hardware **and then press** SHIFT+ENTER.

*Word inserts a **line break character**, which is a formatting mark for a line break at the end of a line, and moves the insertion point to the beginning of the next physical line (Figure 3-25).*

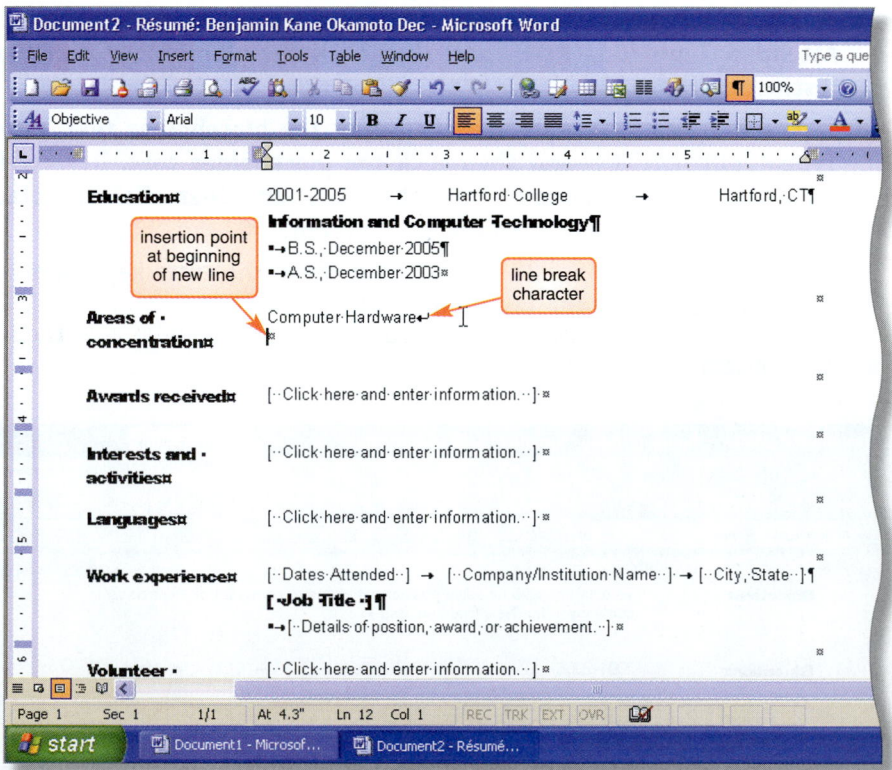

FIGURE 3-25

2

• **Type** Computer Software and Programming **and then press** SHIFT+ENTER.

• **Type** Professional Communications **and then press** SHIFT+ENTER.

• **Type** Business **as the last entry. Do not press** SHIFT+ENTER **at the end of this line.**

The areas of concentration section is entered (Figure 3-26).

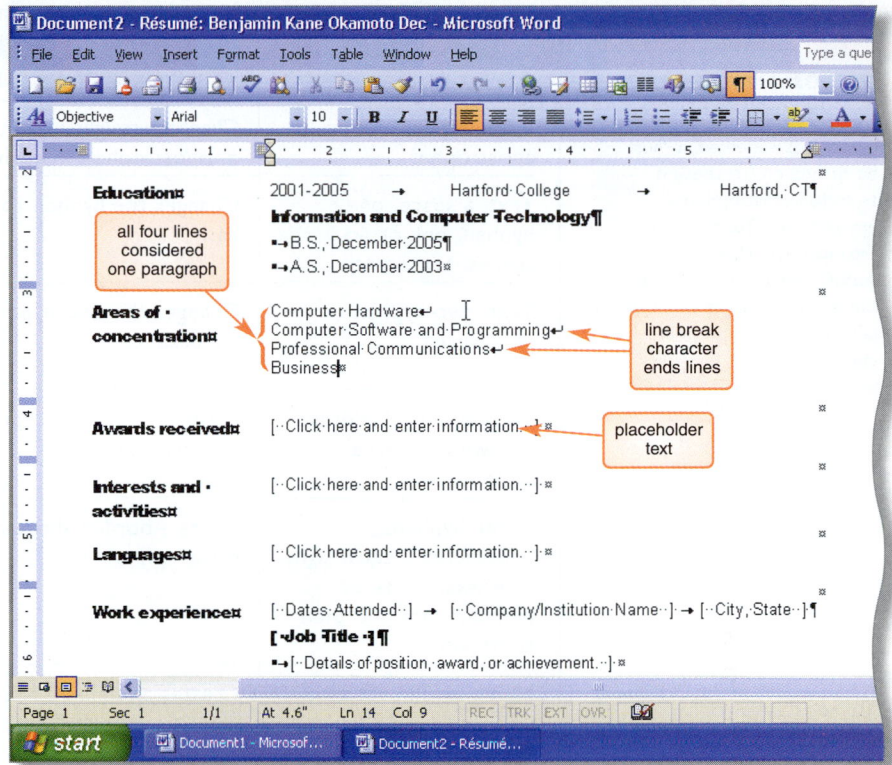

FIGURE 3-26

The next step is to enter the first two awards in the awards received section of the resume.

To Enter More Text with Line Breaks

1 **If necessary, scroll down to display the awards received section of the resume. In the awards received section, click the placeholder text, Click here and enter information. Type** Dean's List, every semester **and then press** SHIFT+ENTER.

2 **Type** Gamma Phi Sigma Honors Society, 2002-2005 **and then press** SHIFT+ENTER.

The first two awards are entered in the awards received section (shown in Figure 3-27 on the next page).

AutoFormat As You Type

As you type text in a document, Word automatically formats it for you. Table 3-1 on the next page outlines commonly used AutoFormat As You Type options and their results.

More About

AutoFormat

For an AutoFormat option to work as expected, it must be turned on. To check if an AutoFormat option is enabled, click Tools on the menu bar, click AutoCorrect Options, click the AutoFormat As You Type tab, select the appropriate check boxes, and then click the OK button.

Table 3-1	Commonly Used AutoFormat As You Type Options	
TYPED TEXT	**AUTOFORMAT FEATURE**	**EXAMPLE**
Quotation marks or apostrophes	Changes straight quotation marks or apostrophes to curly ones	"the" becomes "the"
Text, a space, one hyphen, one or no spaces, text, space	Changes the hyphen to an en dash	ages 20 - 45 becomes ages 20 – 45
Text, two hyphens, text, space	Changes the two hyphens to an em dash	Two types--yellow and red becomes Two types—yellow and red
Web or e-mail address followed by space or ENTER key	Formats Web or e-mail address as a hyperlink	www.scsite.com becomes www.scsite.com
Three hyphens, underscores, equal signs, asterisks, tildes, or number signs and then ENTER key	Places a border above a paragraph	--- This line becomes ⎯⎯⎯ This line
Number followed by a period, hyphen, right parenthesis, or greater than sign and then a space or tab followed by text	Creates a numbered list when you press the ENTER key	1. Word 2. Excel becomes 1. Word 2. Excel
Asterisk, hyphen, or greater than sign and then a space or tab followed by text	Creates a bulleted list when you press the ENTER key	* Standard toolbar * Formatting toolbar becomes • Standard toolbar • Formatting toolbar
Fraction and then a space or hyphen	Converts the entry to a fraction-like notation	1/2 becomes ½
Ordinal and then a space or hyphen	Makes the ordinal a superscript	3rd becomes 3rd

The next step in this project is to enter an ordinal (1st) and see how Word automatically makes the ordinal a superscript.

To AutoFormat As You Type

1

• **Type** Hartford College Outstanding Senior, 1st (Figure 3-27).

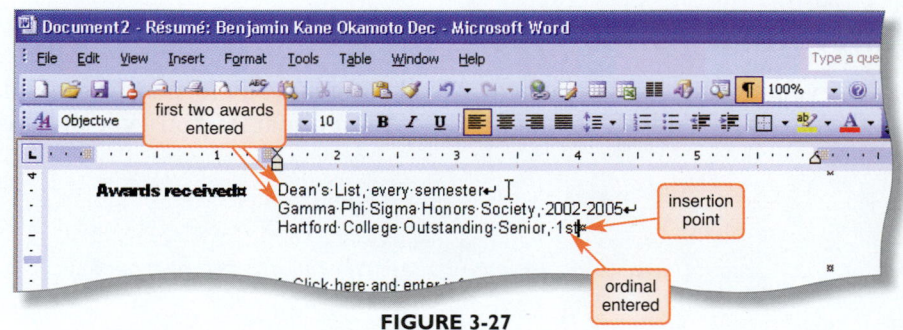

FIGURE 3-27

2

- Press the SPACEBAR.
- Type Place, 2005 as the end of the award.

Word automatically converts the st in 1st to a superscript (Figure 3-28).

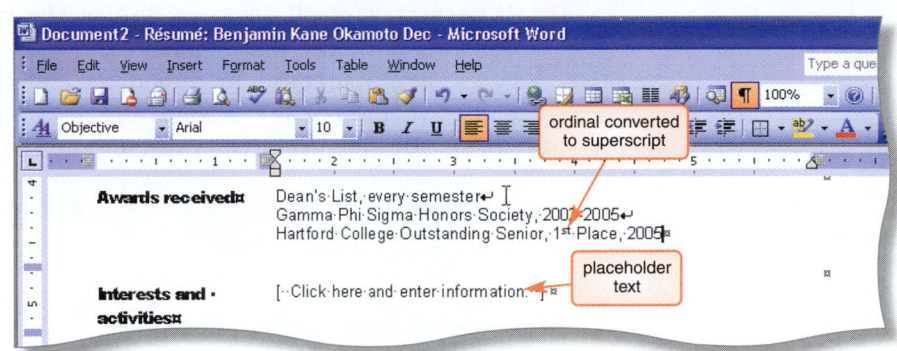

FIGURE 3-28

The next step is to enter the remaining text for the resume, as described below.

To Enter the Remaining Sections of the Resume

1 If necessary, scroll down to display the interests and activities section of the resume. Click the placeholder text, Click here and enter information. Type Association of Sales Representatives, junior member and then press SHIFT+ENTER.

2 Type Big Brothers Big Sisters of Hartford, volunteer and then press SHIFT+ENTER.

3 Type Computer Club, treasurer and then press SHIFT+ENTER.

4 Type New England Ski Club, publicity coordinator as the last activity. Do not press SHIFT+ENTER at the end of this line.

5 If necessary, scroll down to display the languages section of the resume. Click the placeholder text, Click here and enter information. Type English (fluent) and then press SHIFT+ENTER.

6 Type Japanese (fluent) and then press SHIFT+ENTER.

7 Type Knowledge of sign language as the last language. Do not press SHIFT+ENTER at the end of this line.

8 If necessary, scroll down to display the work experience section of the resume. Click, or if necessary drag through, the placeholder text, Dates Attended. Type 2002-2005 as the years.

9 Click the placeholder text, Company/Institution Name. Type Computer Discount Sales and then click the placeholder text, City, State. Type Plantsville, CT and then click the placeholder text, Job Title. Type Intern as the title.

10 Click the placeholder text, Details of position, award, or achievement. Type Sold hardware and software components to home and small business customers and then press the ENTER key.

11 Type Arranged and configured in-store computer hardware, software, and network displays and then press the ENTER key.

12 Type Logged and replied to computer-related customer e-mail, fax, and telephone inquiries as the last item in the list.

Q & A

Q: Should my resume contain references?

A: Do not list references on your resume, and do not state "References Available Upon Request." Employers assume you will give references, if asked, and this information simply clutters a resume. Often you are asked to list references on your application. Be sure to give your references a copy of your resume.

13 **If necessary, scroll down to display the volunteer experience section of the resume. Click the placeholder text, Click here and enter information. Type** As a Big Brother, I spend at least eight hours every week with my Little Brother - hoping to make a difference in this youth's life. **Do not press the ENTER key at the end of this line.**

The interests and activities, languages, work experience, and volunteer experience sections of the resume are complete (Figure 3-29).

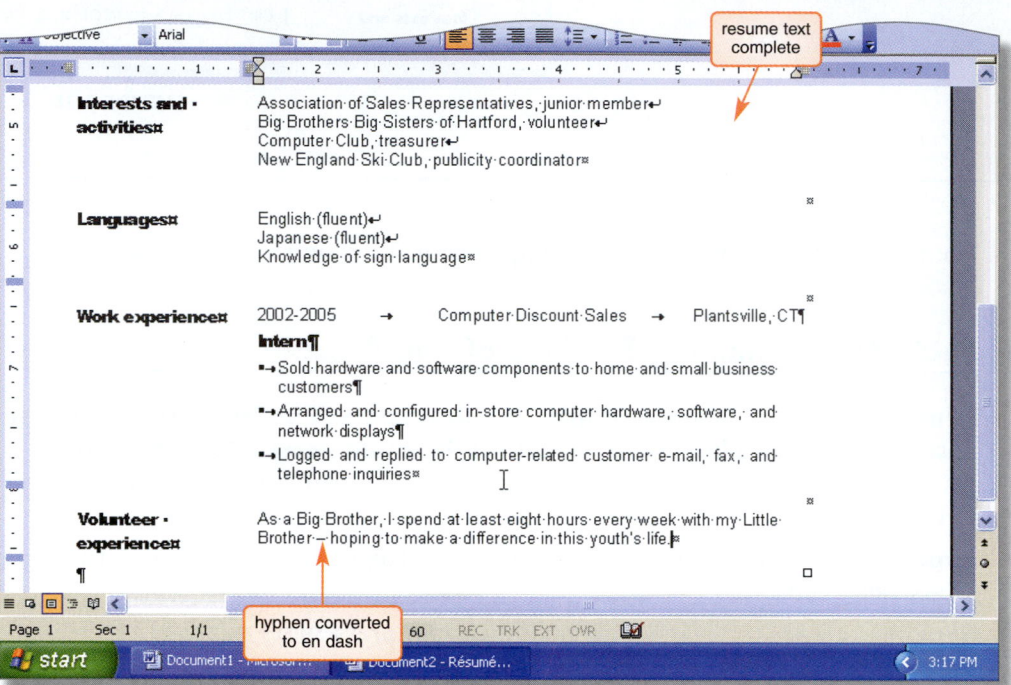

FIGURE 3-29

Notice when you typed the hyphen in the volunteer experience section of the resume (Step 13) that Word automatically formatted it as an en dash as you typed.

Viewing and Printing the Resume in Print Preview

To see exactly how a document will look when you print it, you could display it in print preview. **Print preview** displays the entire document in reduced size on the Word screen. In print preview, you can edit and format text, adjust margins, view multiple pages, reduce the document to fit on a single page, and print the document. The following steps show how to view and print the resume in print preview.

To Print Preview a Document

1

• **Point to the Print Preview button on the Standard toolbar (Figure 3-30).**

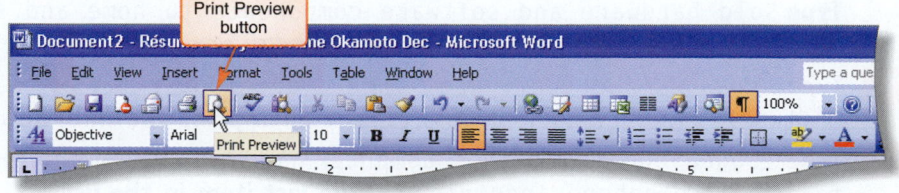

FIGURE 3-30

2

• **Click the Print Preview button.**

Word displays the document in print preview (Figure 3-31). The Print Preview toolbar is displayed below the menu bar; the Standard and Formatting toolbars disappear from the screen.

3

• **Click the Print button on the Print Preview toolbar.**

• **Click the Close Preview button on the Print Preview toolbar.**

Word prints the resume, as shown in Figure 3-1 on page WD 139. When you close print preview, Word redisplays the resume in the document window.

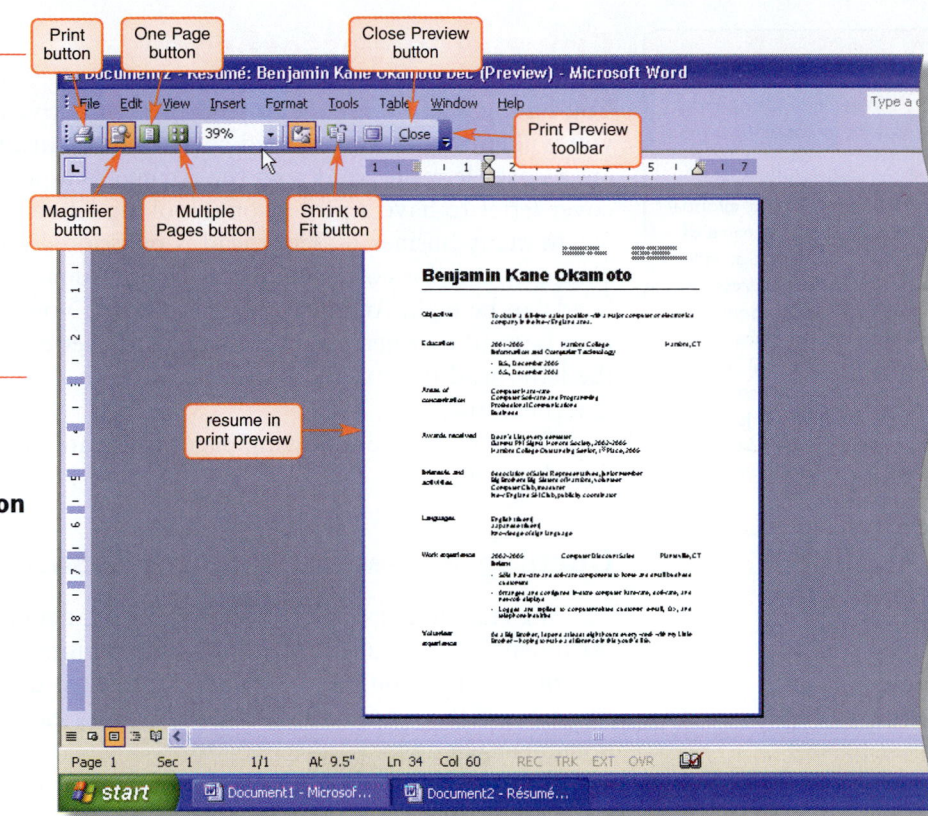

FIGURE 3-31

Other Ways

1. On File menu click Print Preview
2. Press CTRL+F2
3. In Voice Command mode, say "Print Preview"

Saving the Resume

The resume now is complete. Thus, you should save it. For a detailed example of the procedure summarized below, refer to pages WD 28 through WD 30 in Project 1.

To Save a Document

1 **Insert your floppy disk into drive A.**

2 **Click the Save button on the Standard toolbar.**

3 **Type** `Okamoto Resume` **in the File name text box. Do not press the ENTER key.**

4 **Click the Save in box arrow and then click 3½ Floppy (A:).**

5 **Click the Save button in the Save As dialog box.**

Word saves the document on a floppy disk in drive A with the file name, Okamoto Resume.

Do not close the Okamoto Resume. You will use it again later in this project to copy the address, telephone, fax, and e-mail information.

More About

Print Preview

If the page is not centered in the Print Preview window, click the One Page button on the Print Preview toolbar. With the Magnifier button on the Print Preview toolbar selected, you can click in the document to zoom in or out. Magnifying a page does not affect the printed document. To edit a document, click the Magnifier button to deselect it and then edit the text. If a document spills onto a second page by a line or two, click the Shrink to Fit button and Word will try to fit it all on a single page.

Q&A

Q: What information should a letterhead contain?

A: A letterhead should contain the following information: complete legal name of the company, group, or individual; full street address including building, room, suite number, or post office box; city; state; and postal code. Some letterheads also include a logo, department name, telephone and fax number, Web address, and e-mail address.

Creating a Letterhead

You have created a resume to send to prospective employers. Along with the resume, you will enclose a personalized cover letter. Thus, the next step in Project 3 is to create a cover letter to send with the resume to a potential employer. You would like the cover letter to have a professional looking letterhead (Figure 3-2a on page WD 140).

In many businesses, letterhead is preprinted on stationery that everyone in a company uses for correspondence. For personal letters, the cost of preprinted letterhead can be high. An alternative is to create your own letterhead and save it in a file. At a later time, when you want to create a letter using the letterhead, simply open the letterhead file and then save the file with a new name – to preserve the original letterhead file.

The steps on the following pages illustrate how to use Word to create a personal letterhead file.

Opening a New Document Window

The resume currently is displayed in the document window. The resume document should remain open because you intend to use it again during this Word session. That is, you will be working with two documents at the same time: the resume and the letterhead. Word will display each of these documents in a separate document window.

The following step opens a new document window for the letterhead file.

To Open a New Document Window

1

• **Click the New Blank Document button on the Standard toolbar.**

Word opens a new document window (Figure 3-32).

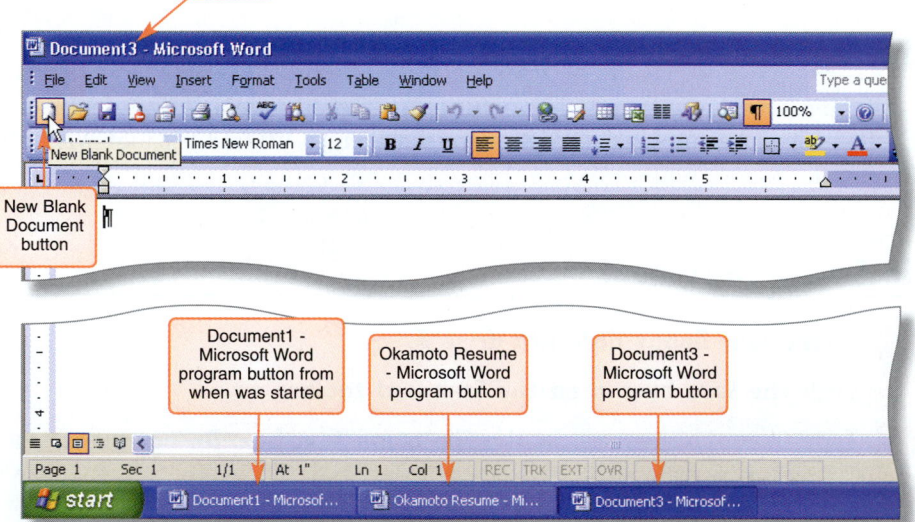

FIGURE 3-32

Other Ways

1. On File menu click New, click Blank document in New area in New Document task pane
2. Press CTRL+N
3. In Voice Command mode, say "New Blank Document"

The Okamoto Resume document still is open. The program buttons on the taskbar display the names of the open Word document windows. The Document3 button on the taskbar is selected, indicating that it is the active document currently displayed in the Word document window.

The next step is to change the font size to 20 because you want the name in the letterhead to be a larger font size than the body of the letter. The next steps describe how to change the font size.

To Change the Font Size

1 Click the Font Size box arrow on the Formatting toolbar.

2 Click 20 in the Font Size list.

Word changes the font size to 20 (shown in Figure 3-33 below).

Changing Color of Text

The text in the letterhead is to be brown. The following steps show how to change the color of the text before you type.

To Color Text

1

• **Click the Font Color button arrow on the Formatting toolbar.**

Word displays a list of available colors on the color palette (Figure 3-33). The color that displays below the letter A on the Font Color button is the most recently used text color. Your button may show a different color.

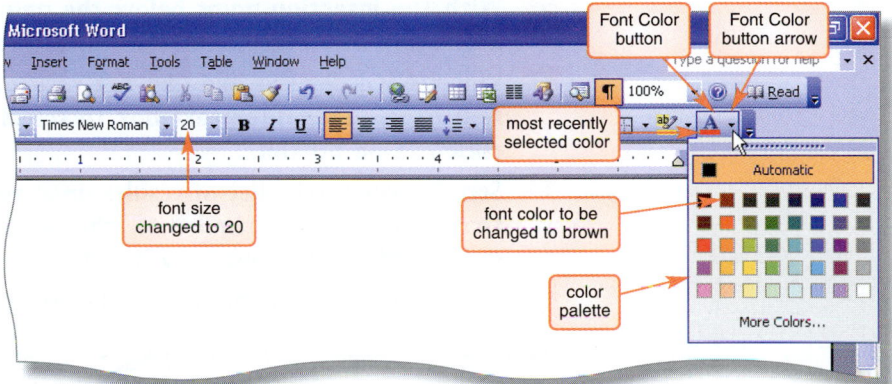

FIGURE 3-33

2

• **Click Brown, which is the second color on the first row of the color palette.**

• **Type** Benjamin Kane Okamoto **and then press the ENTER key.**

Word displays the first line of the letterhead in brown (Figure 3-34).

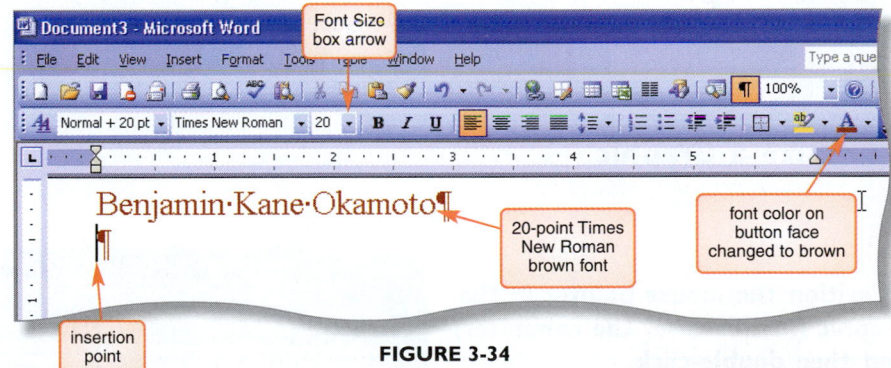

FIGURE 3-34

More About

Program Buttons

If the Windows taskbar does not display a separate program button for each open Word document (Figure 3-32), click Tools on the menu bar, click Options, click the View tab, place a check mark in the Windows in Taskbar check box, and then click the OK button.

Other Ways

1. On Format menu click Font, click Font tab, click Font color box arrow, click desired color, click OK button
2. In Voice Command mode, say "Font Color, [select font color]"

Notice the paragraph mark on line 2 is brown. Recall that each time you press the ENTER key, Word carries forward formatting to the next paragraph. If, for some reason, you wanted to change the text back to black at this point, you would click the Font Color button arrow on the Formatting toolbar and then click Automatic on the color palette. Automatic is the default color, which usually is black.

The next step is to reduce the font size of text entered into the second line in the letterhead. The address, telephone, fax, and e-mail information is to be a font size of 9. The steps on the next page describe how to change the font size.

To Change the Font Size

1 With the insertion point on line 2 as shown in Figure 3-34 on the previous page, click the Font Size box arrow on the Formatting toolbar.

2 Click 9 in the Font Size list.

At the location of the insertion point, Word changes the font size to 9 (shown in Figure 3-37).

Inserting and Resizing a Graphic

The letterhead has a graphic of a computer on line 2 below the job seeker's name. The following steps describe how to insert this graphic.

To Insert a Graphic

1 With the insertion point below the name on line 2, click Insert on the menu bar, point to Picture, and then click Clip Art on the Picture submenu.

2 When Word displays the Clip Art task pane, if necessary, drag through any text in the Search for text box to select the text. Type `computer` and then click the Go button.

3 Scroll through the list of results until you locate the graphic of a computer that matches, or is similar to, the one shown in Figure 3-35. Click the graphic of the computer to insert it in the document.

4 Click the Close button on the Clip Art task pane title bar.

Word inserts the graphic of the computer at the location of the insertion point (shown in Figure 3-35).

The next step is to reduce the size of the graphic to 40 percent of its current size. Instead of dragging the sizing handle, you can use the Format Picture dialog box to set exact size measurements. The following steps show how to resize a graphic using the Format Picture dialog box.

To Resize a Graphic

1

• **Position the mouse pointer in the graphic (in this case, the computer) and then double-click.**

• **When Word displays the Format Picture dialog box, click the Size tab.**

The Size sheet allows you to specify exact measurements of the selected graphic (Figure 3-35).

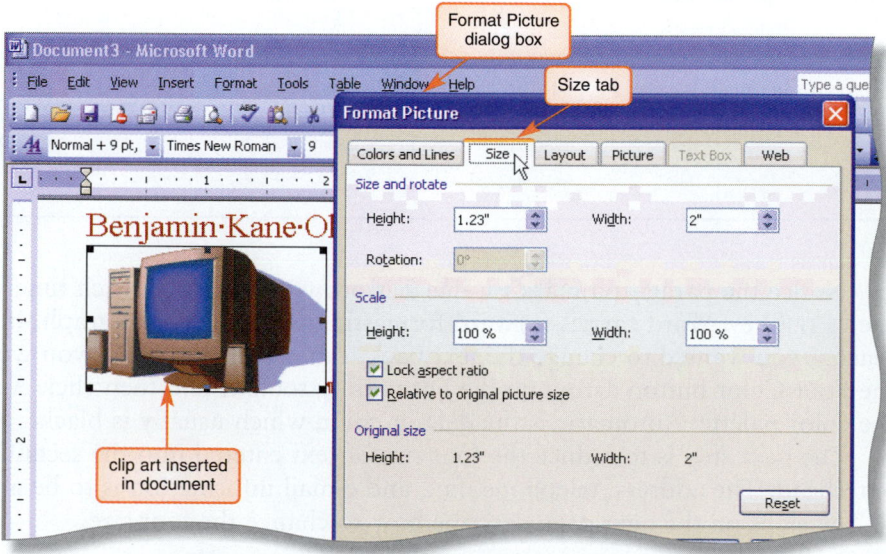

FIGURE 3-35

2

• **In the Scale area, double-click the Height box to select it.**

• **Type** 40 **and then press the TAB key.**

Word displays 40 % in the Height and Width boxes (Figure 3-36). When you press the TAB key from the Height box, the insertion point moves to the Width box and automatically changes the width to 40 % - to match the height proportionately.

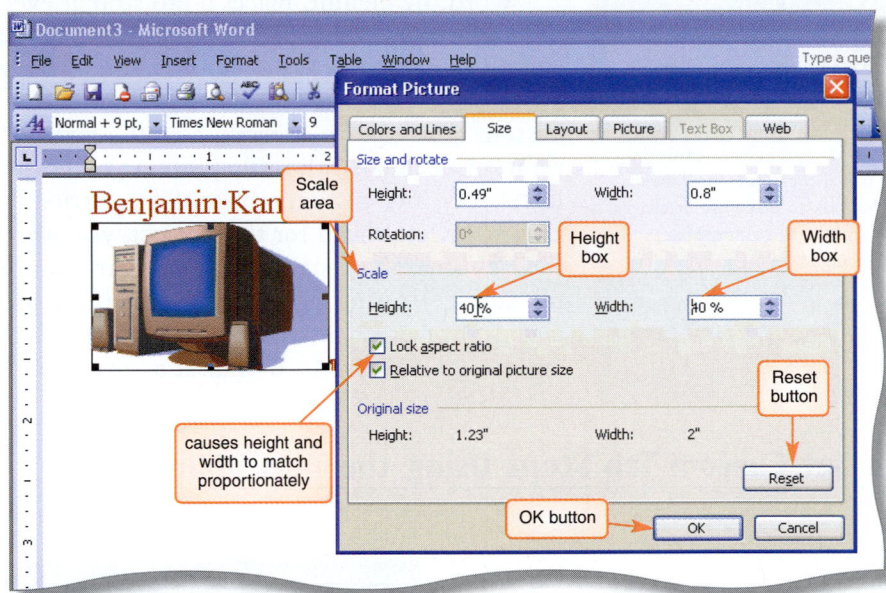

FIGURE 3-36

3

• **Click the OK button in the Format Picture dialog box.**

• **Press the END key to move the insertion point to the paragraph mark to the right of the graphic.**

Word resizes the graphic to 40 percent of its original size (Figure 3-37).

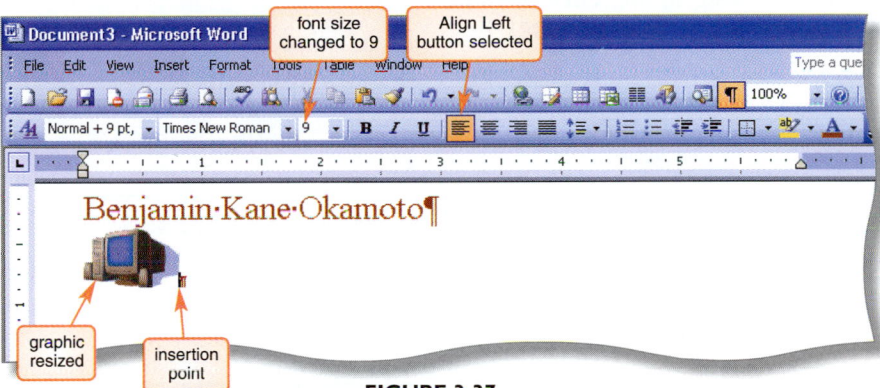

FIGURE 3-37

Sometimes, you might resize a graphic and realize it is the wrong size. In this case, you may want to return the graphic to its original size and start again. To restore a resized graphic to its exact original size, click the Reset button in the Format Picture dialog box (Figure 3-36).

Setting Tab Stops Using the Tabs Dialog Box

The graphic of the computer is left-aligned (Figure 3-37). The address information in the letterhead is to be positioned at the right margin of the same line. If you click the Align Right button, the graphic will be right-aligned. In Word, a paragraph cannot be both left-aligned and right-aligned. To place text at the right margin of a left-aligned paragraph, you set a tab stop at the right margin.

A **tab stop** is a location on the horizontal ruler that tells Word where to position the insertion point when you press the TAB key on the keyboard. A tab stop is useful for indenting and aligning text.

Other Ways

1. Select the graphic, drag the graphic's sizing handle
2. Click Format Picture button on Picture toolbar, click Size tab, enter desired height and width, click OK button
3. In Voice Command mode, say "Format, Picture"

More About

Tabs

You can use the Tabs dialog box to change an existing tab stop's alignment or position. You also can use the Tabs dialog box to place leader characters in the empty space occupied by the tab. Leader characters, such as a series of dots, often are used in a table of contents to precede the page number.

Word, by default, places a tab stop at every .5" mark on the ruler (shown in Figure 3-39). These default tab stops are indicated at the bottom of the horizontal ruler by small vertical tick marks. You also can set your own custom tab stops. When you set a **custom tab stop**, Word clears all default tab stops to the left of the custom tab stop. You specify how the text will align at a tab stop: left, centered, right, or decimal. Tab settings are a paragraph format. Thus, each time you press the ENTER key, any custom tab stops are carried forward to the next paragraph.

In the letterhead for this project, you want the tab stop to be right-aligned with the right margin, that is, at the 6" mark on the ruler. One method of setting custom tab stops is to click the ruler at the desired location of the tab stop. You cannot click, however, at the right margin location. Thus, use the Tabs dialog box to set a custom tab stop at the 6" mark, as shown in the following steps.

To Set Custom Tab Stops Using the Tabs Dialog Box

1

• **With the insertion point positioned between the paragraph mark and the graphic, click Format on the menu bar (Figure 3-38).**

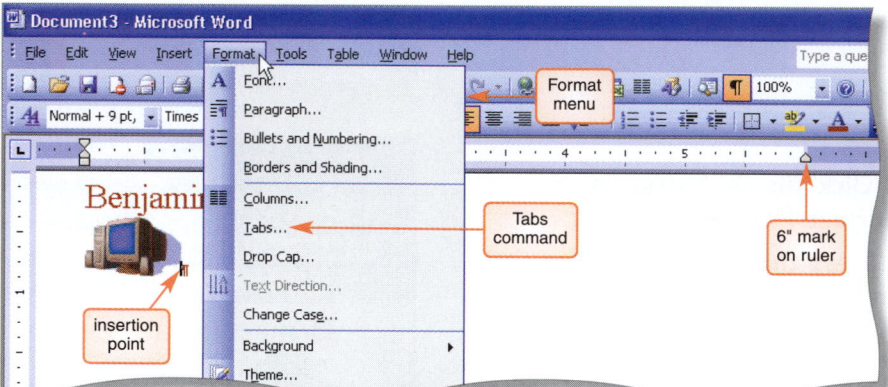

FIGURE 3-38

2

• **Click Tabs on the Format menu.**

• **When Word displays the Tabs dialog box, type 6 in the Tab stop position text box.**

• **Click Right in the Alignment area.**

The Tabs dialog box allows you to set and clear custom tabs (Figure 3-39).

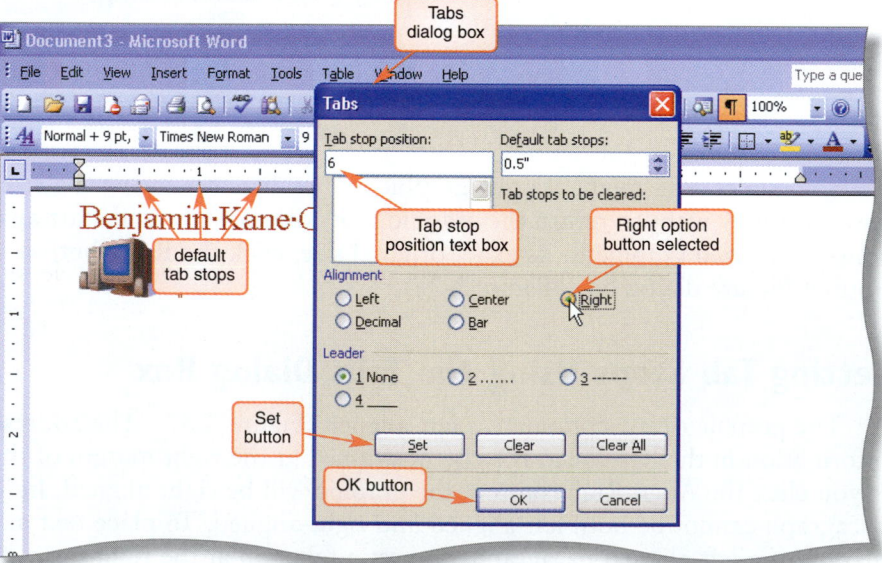

FIGURE 3-39

3

• **Click the Set button in the Tabs dialog box.**

• **Click the OK button.**

Word places a right tab marker at the 6" mark on the ruler and removes all default tab stops to the left of the tab marker on the ruler (Figure 3-40).

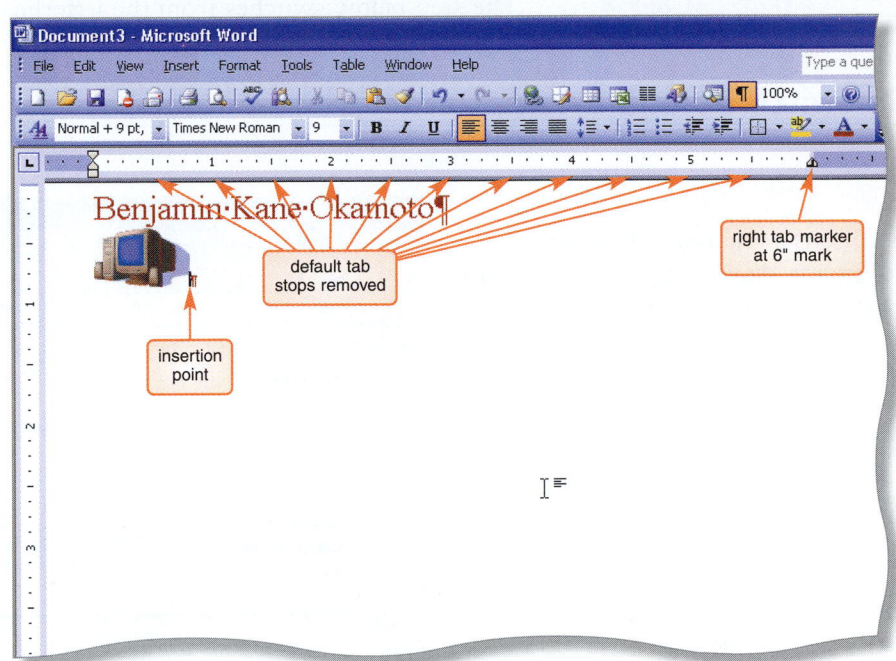

FIGURE 3-40

When you set a custom tab stop, the tab marker on the ruler reflects the alignment of the characters at the location of the tab stop. A capital letter L ( ) indicates a left-aligned tab stop. A mirror image of a capital letter L ( ) indicates a right-aligned tab stop. An upside down T ( ) indicates a centered tab stop. An upside down T with a dot next to it ( ) indicates a decimal-aligned tab stop. Specific tab markers are discussed as they are presented in these projects. The tab marker on the ruler in Figure 3-40 indicates text entered at that tab stop will be right-aligned.

To move the insertion point from one tab stop to another, press the TAB key on the keyboard. When you press the TAB key, a **tab character** formatting mark appears in the empty space between the tab stops.

Collecting and Pasting

The next step in creating the letterhead is to copy the address, telephone, fax, and e-mail information from the resume to the letterhead. To copy multiple items from one Office document to another, you use the Office Clipboard. The **Office Clipboard** is a temporary storage area that holds up to 24 items (text or graphics) copied from any Office application. You copy, or **collect**, items and then paste them in a new location. **Pasting** is the process of copying an item from the Office Clipboard into the document at the location of the insertion point. When you paste an item into a document, the contents of the Office Clipboard are not erased.

To copy the address, telephone, fax, and e-mail information from the resume to the letterhead, you first switch to the resume document, copy the items from the resume to the Office Clipboard, switch back to the letterhead document, and then paste the information from the Office Clipboard into the letterhead. The following pages illustrate this process.

Other Ways

1. Click button on left of ruler until desired tab stop alignment displays and then click ruler
2. In Voice Command mode, say "Format, Tabs"

More About

Tab Alignment

If you have a series of numbers that you want aligned on the decimal point, such as dollar amounts, use a decimal-aligned tab stop for the data.

Q&A

Q: Is the Windows Clipboard the same as the Office Clipboard?

A: The Windows Clipboard, which can hold only one item at a time, is separate from the Office Clipboard. When you collect multiple items on the Office Clipboard, the last copied item also is copied to the Windows Clipboard. When you clear the Office Clipboard, the Windows Clipboard also is cleared.

The step below switches from the letterhead document to the resume document.

To Switch from One Open Document to Another

1

• **Click the Okamoto Resume - Microsoft Word program button on the Windows taskbar.**

Word switches from the letterhead document to the resume document (Figure 3-41). The letterhead document (Document3) still is open.

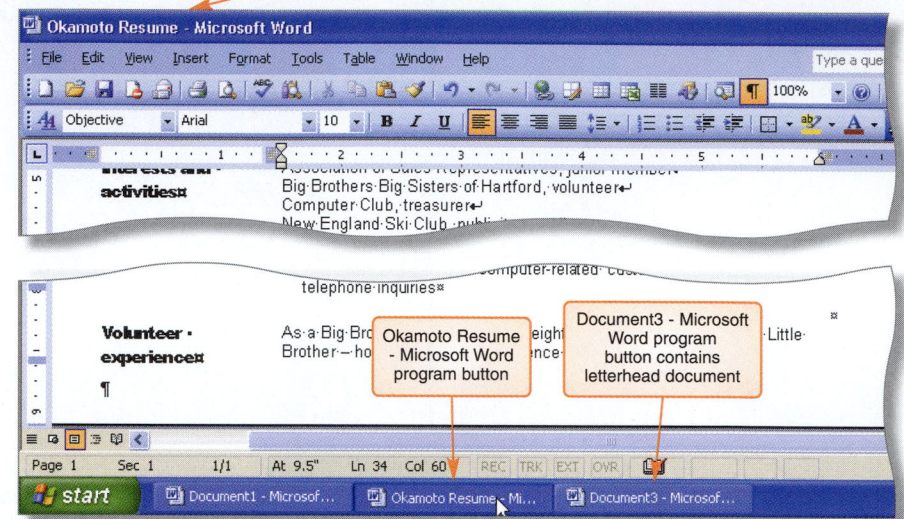

FIGURE 3-41

Other Ways

1. On Window menu click document name
2. Press ALT+TAB
3. In Voice Command mode, say "Window [document number]"

You can copy multiple items to the Office Clipboard and then can paste them later. Each copied item appears as an entry in the Office Clipboard gallery in the Clipboard task pane. The entry displays an icon that indicates the Office program from which the item was copied. The entry also displays a portion of text that was copied or a thumbnail of a graphic that was copied. The most recently copied item is displayed at the top of the gallery.

The following steps show how to copy five items to the Office Clipboard.

To Copy Items to the Office Clipboard

1

• **Press CTRL+HOME to display the top of the resume in the document window.**

• **Click Edit on the menu bar (Figure 3-42).**

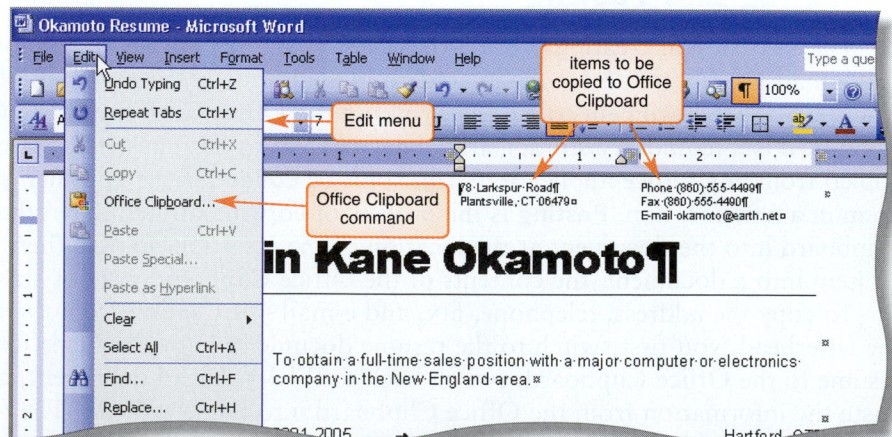

FIGURE 3-42

2

• **Click Office Clipboard on the Edit menu.**

• **If the Office Clipboard gallery in the Clipboard task pane is not empty, click the Clear All button in the Clipboard task pane.**

• **Scroll to the right to display all of the telephone, fax, and e-mail information in the resume.**

• **In the resume, drag through the street address, 78 Larkspur Road.**

Word displays the Clipboard task pane on the screen (Figure 3-43). The Office Clipboard icon appears in the notification area on the Windows taskbar, indicating the Office Clipboard is displayed in at least one open Office program.

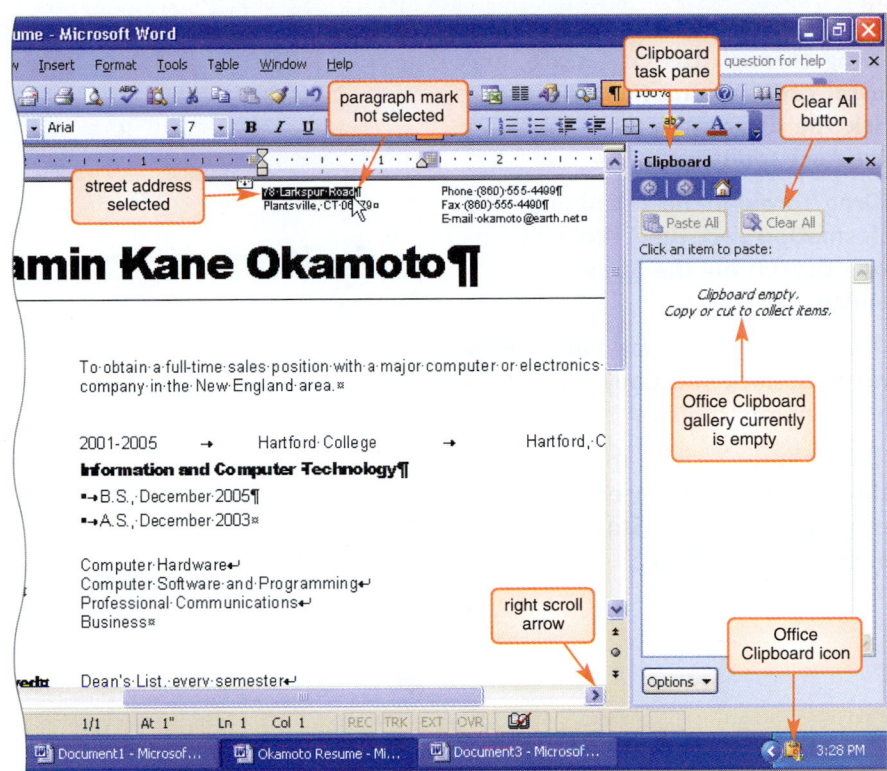

FIGURE 3-43

3

• **Click the Copy button on the Standard toolbar.**

Word copies the selection to the Office Clipboard and places an entry in the Office Clipboard gallery in the Clipboard task pane (Figure 3-44).

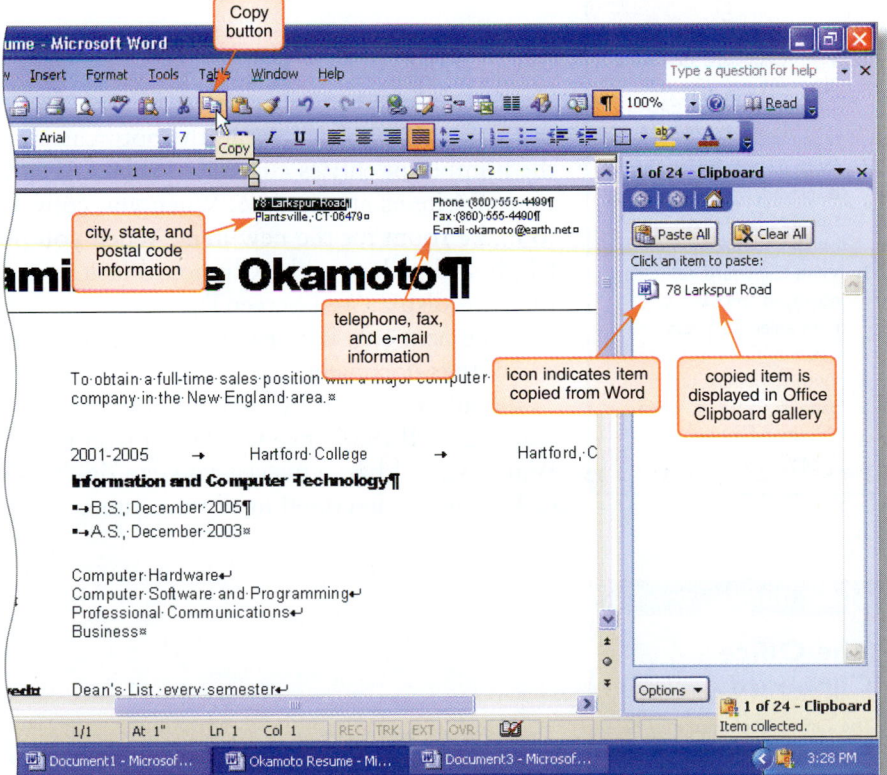

FIGURE 3-44

4

• Drag through the city, state, and postal code information and then click the Copy button on the Standard toolbar.

• Drag through the telephone information and then click the Copy button on the Standard toolbar.

• Drag through the fax information and then click the Copy button on the Standard toolbar.

• Drag through the e-mail information and then click the Copy button on the Standard toolbar (Figure 3-45).

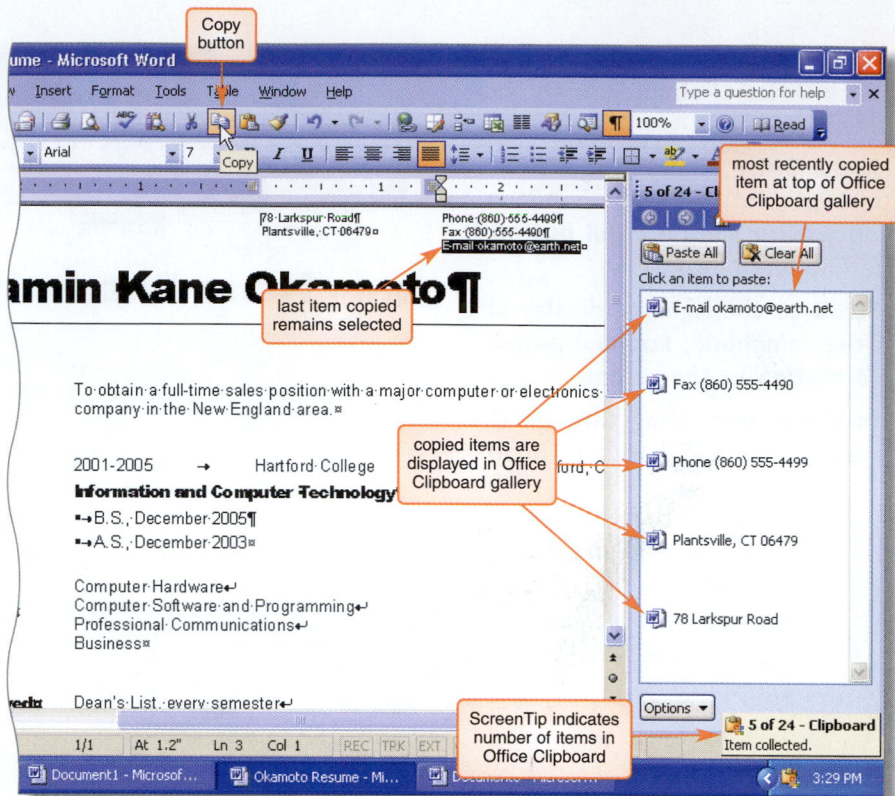

FIGURE 3-45

Other Ways

1. With Clipboard task pane displayed and item to copy selected, on Edit menu click Copy
2. With Clipboard task pane displayed, right-click selected item, click Copy on shortcut menu
3. With Clipboard task pane displayed and item to copy selected, press CTRL+C
4. With Clipboard task pane displayed, in Voice Command mode, say "Copy"

Each time you copy an item to the Office Clipboard, a ScreenTip appears above the Office Clipboard icon in the notification area on the Windows taskbar, indicating the number of entries currently in the Office Clipboard. The Office Clipboard stores up to 24 items at one time. When you copy a 25th item, Word deletes the first item to make room for the new item. When you point to a text entry in the Office Clipboard gallery in the Clipboard task pane, the first several characters of text in the item display as a ScreenTip.

The next step is to paste the copied items into the letterhead. When you switch to another document, the Clipboard task pane might not be displayed on the screen. You could display it by clicking Edit on the menu bar and then clicking Office Clipboard. If the Office Clipboard icon is displayed in the notification area on the Windows taskbar, however, you can double-click the icon to display the Clipboard task pane, as described in the next step.

More About

The Office Clipboard

The Office Clipboard may be displayed automatically on the Word screen if you click the Copy button or the Cut button on the Standard toolbar twice in succession, or if you copy and paste an item and then copy another item.

To Display the Clipboard Task Pane

1

• **Click the Document3 - Microsoft Word button on the Windows taskbar to display the letterhead.**

• **Double-click the Office Clipboard icon in the notification area on the Windows taskbar.**

Word displays the Clipboard task pane on the screen (Figure 3-46). The Office Clipboard gallery shows the items contained on the Clipboard.

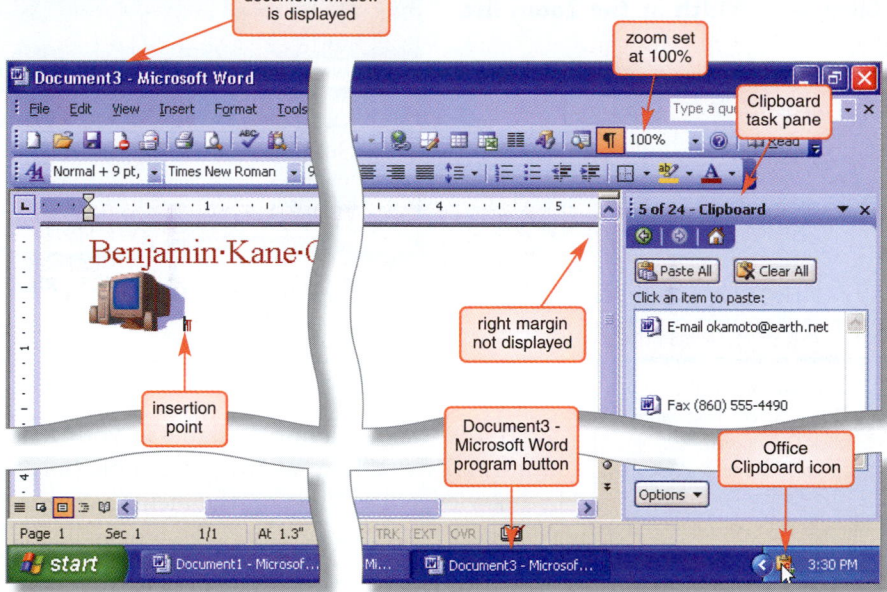

FIGURE 3-46

More About

The Office Clipboard Icon

If the Office Clipboard icon does not appear on the Windows taskbar, click the Options button at the bottom of the Clipboard task pane and then click Show Office Clipboard icon on Taskbar.

The next step is to press the TAB key to position the insertion point at the location where the text will be copied. Recall that the address information is to be located at the right margin of the document window. Notice in Figure 3-46 that the right margin is not displayed on the screen when the task pane also is on the screen.

Depending on your Windows and Word settings, the horizontal ruler at the top of the document window may show more inches or fewer inches than the ruler shown in Figure 3-46. Two factors that affect how much of the ruler displays in the document window are the Windows screen resolution and the Word zoom percentage. The more inches of ruler that display, the smaller the text will be on the screen. The fewer inches of ruler that display, the larger the text will be on the screen.

To view both the right and left margins on the screen beside the Clipboard task pane, you need to change the zoom percent, which in this project is set at 100 percent. The following steps show how to let Word determine the best percentage to zoom when showing both the left and right margins at the same time.

To Zoom Text Width

1

• **Click the Zoom box arrow on the Standard toolbar (Figure 3-47).**

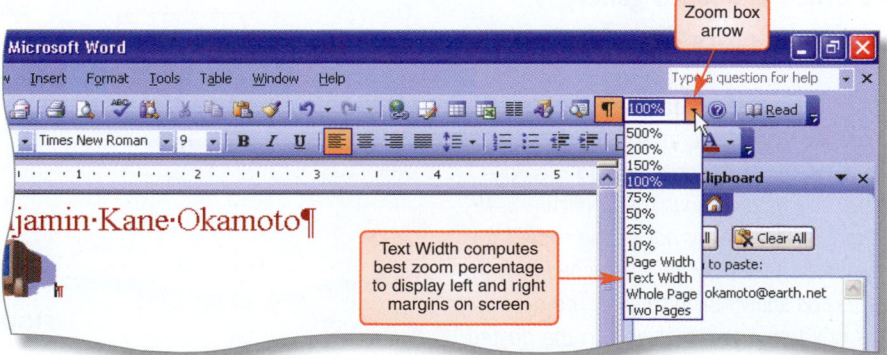

FIGURE 3-47

2

- **Click Text Width in the Zoom list.**

Word places the margins of the document in the window (Figure 3-48).

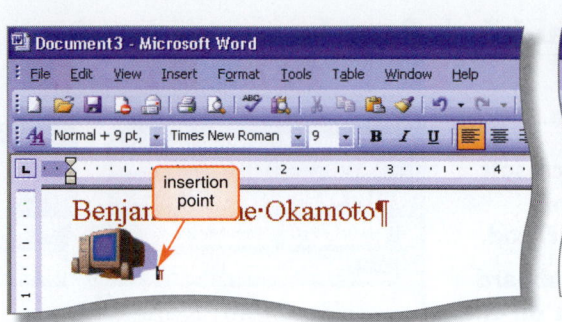

FIGURE 3-48

If Text Width is not available in your Zoom list, then your document window is in normal view. Text Width is available only in print layout view. To switch to print layout view, click View on the menu bar and then click Print Layout.

The Zoom box in Figure 3-48 displays 89%, which Word computes based on a variety of settings. Your percentage may be different depending on your computer configuration.

When you paste items into a document, Word displays the Paste Options button on the screen. The Paste Options button allows you to change the format of pasted items. For example, you can instruct Word to format the pasted text the same as the text from where it was copied or format it the same as the text to where it was pasted. You also can have Word remove all extra non-text characters that were pasted. For example, if you included a paragraph mark when copying at the end of a line in the address of the resume, the Paste Options button allows you to remove the paragraph marks from the pasted text.

The following steps show how to paste the address information from the Office Clipboard into the letterhead – removing any extraneous paragraph marks after pasting.

To Paste from the Office Clipboard

1

- **With the insertion point between the paragraph mark and the computer graphic (shown in Figure 3-48), press the TAB key.**

- **Click the bottom (first) entry in the Office Clipboard gallery.**

- **Click the Paste Options button.**

Word pastes the contents of the clicked item at the location of the insertion point, which is at the 6" mark on the ruler, and then displays the Paste Options menu (Figure 3-49). Depending on the format of the copied text, the pasted text may not be aligned or formatted as shown in this figure. The next step fixes any formatting problems in the pasted text.

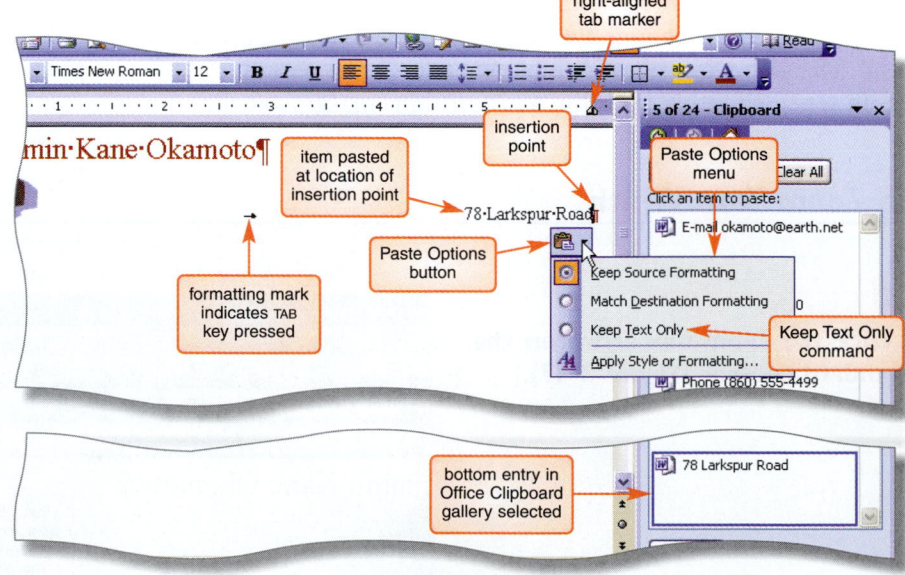

FIGURE 3-49

2

- **Click Keep Text Only on the Paste Options menu.**
- **Press the COMMA key. Press the SPACEBAR.**
- **Click the second entry (city, state, postal code) in the Office Clipboard gallery.**
- **Click the Paste Options button and then click Keep Text Only.**

The city, state, and postal code from the Office Clipboard are pasted into the letterhead (Figure 3-50). The Keep Text Only command removes any extraneous paragraph marks from the pasted text.

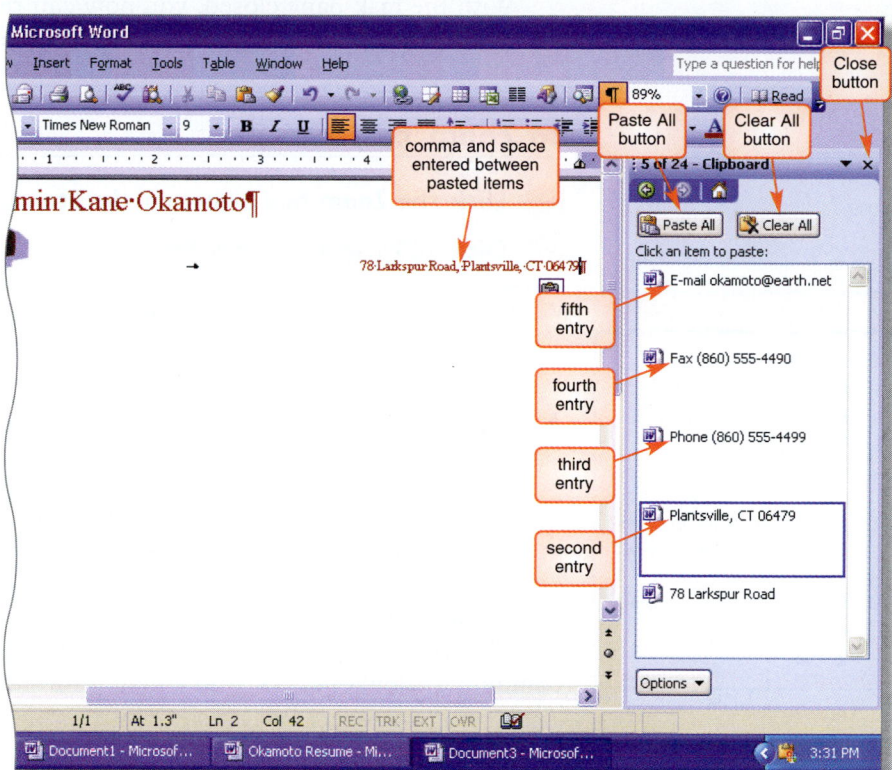

FIGURE 3-50

If you wanted to paste all items in a row without any characters in between them, you would click the Paste All button in the Clipboard task pane. If you wanted to erase all items on the Office Clipboard, you would click the Clear All button in the Clipboard task pane.

The following steps discuss how to paste the telephone, fax, and e-mail information into the letterhead from the resume.

To Paste More Information from the Office Clipboard

1 Press the ENTER key. Press the TAB key. Click the third entry (telephone) in the Office Clipboard gallery. Click the Paste Options button and then click Keep Text Only.

2 Press the COMMA key. Press the SPACEBAR. Click the fourth entry (fax) in the Office Clipboard gallery. Click the Paste Options button and then click Keep Text Only.

3 Press the COMMA key. Press the SPACEBAR. Click the fifth entry (e-mail) in the Office Clipboard gallery. Click the Paste Options button and then click Keep Text Only.

4 Click the Close button in the upper-right corner of the Clipboard task pane title bar to close the task pane.

All items are pasted from the Office Clipboard into the letterhead (shown in Figure 3-51 on the next page). The Clipboard task pane is closed.

Other Ways

1. With Clipboard task pane displayed, on Edit menu click Paste
2. With Clipboard task pane displayed, right-click selected item, click Paste on shortcut menu
3. With Clipboard task pane displayed, press CTRL+V
4. With Clipboard task pane displayed, in Voice Command mode, say "Paste"

More About

The Office Clipboard Gallery

To delete an item from the Office Clipboard gallery, point to the item in the gallery, click the box arrow to the right of the item, and then click Delete.

With the task pane closed, you now can return the zoom percentage of the document window to 100 percent, as described in the following steps.

To Zoom to 100%

1 Click the Zoom box arrow on the Standard toolbar.

2 Click 100% in the Zoom list.

Word changes the zoom to 100% (shown in Figure 3-51).

Adding a Bottom Border to a Paragraph

To add professionalism to the letterhead, you can draw a horizontal line from the left margin to the right margin immediately below the telephone, fax, and e-mail information. In Word, you draw a solid line, called a **border**, at any edge of a paragraph. That is, borders may be added above or below a paragraph, to the left or right of a paragraph, or any combination of these sides.

The following steps show how to add a bottom border to the paragraph containing telephone, fax, and e-mail information.

To Bottom Border a Paragraph

1

• **With the insertion point in the paragraph to border, click the Border button arrow on the Formatting toolbar.**

Word displays the border palette either horizontally or vertically below the Border button (Figure 3-51). Using the border palette, you can add a border to any edge of a paragraph.

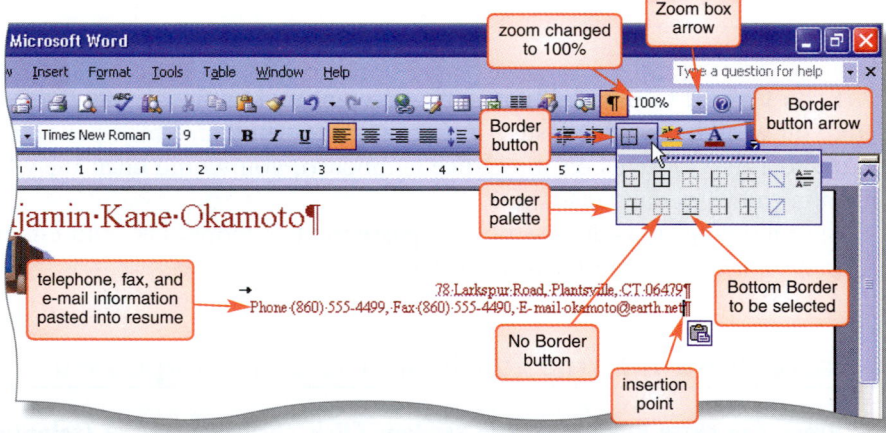

FIGURE 3-51

2

• **Click Bottom Border on the border palette.**

Word places a border below the paragraph containing the insertion point (Figure 3-52). The Border button on the Formatting toolbar now displays the icon for a bottom border.

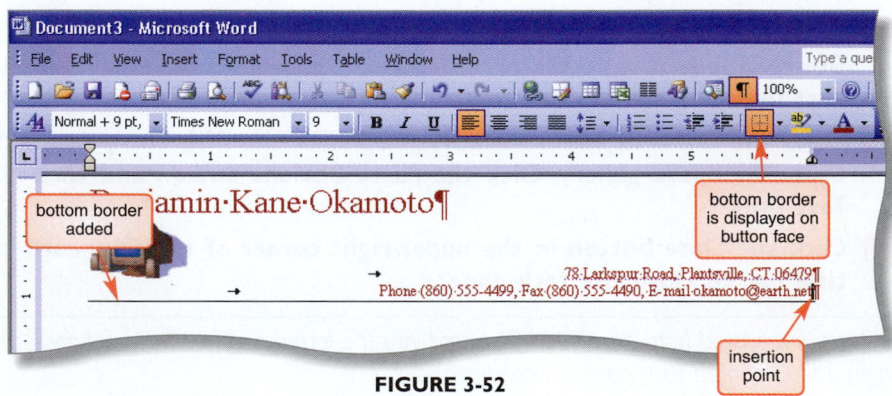

FIGURE 3-52

If, for some reason, you wanted to remove a border from a paragraph, you would position the insertion point in the paragraph, click the Border button arrow on the Formatting toolbar, and then click the No Border button (Figure 3-51) on the border palette.

Clearing Formatting

The next step is to position the insertion point below the letterhead, so that you can type the content of the letter. When you press the ENTER key at the end of a paragraph containing a border, Word moves the border forward to the next paragraph. It also retains all current settings. That is, the paragraph text will be brown and will have a bottom border. Instead, you want the paragraph and characters on the new line to use the Normal style: black font with no border. In Word the term, **clear formatting**, refers to returning the formatting to the Normal style.

The following steps show how to clear formatting at the location of the insertion point.

To Clear Formatting

- **With the insertion point at the end of line 3 (Figure 3-52), press the ENTER key.**
- **Click the Styles and Formatting button on the Formatting toolbar.**

Word displays the Styles and Formatting task pane (Figure 3-53). The insertion point is on line 4. Formatting at the insertion point consists of a bottom border and a brown font. You want to clear this formatting.

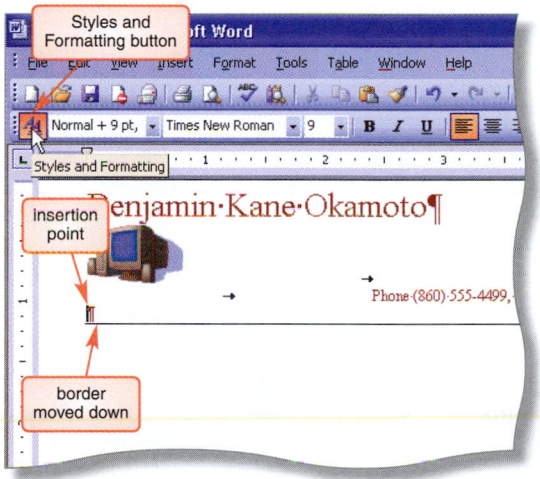
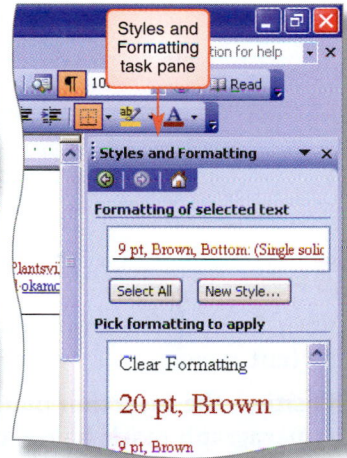

FIGURE 3-53

- **Click Clear Formatting in the Pick formatting to apply area in the Styles and Formatting task pane.**

Word applies the Normal style to the location of the insertion point (Figure 3-54).

- **Click the Close button in the upper-right corner of the Styles and Formatting task pane title bar.**

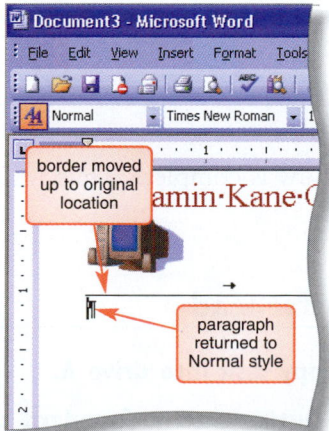
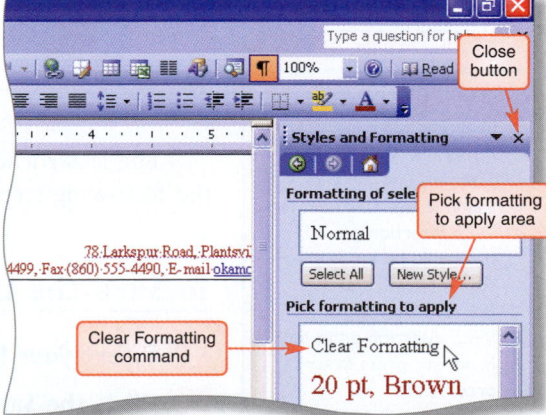

FIGURE 3-54

The next step is to remove the hyperlink autoformat from the e-mail address in the letterhead. As discussed earlier in this project, Word automatically formats text as you type. When you press the ENTER key or SPACEBAR after entering an e-mail address or Web address, Word automatically formats the address as a hyperlink, that is, colored blue and underlined. In Step 1 on the previous page, Word formatted the e-mail address as a hyperlink because you pressed the ENTER key at the end of the line. You want to remove the hyperlink format from the e-mail address.

The following steps show how to convert the e-mail address from a hyperlink to regular text.

To Convert a Hyperlink to Regular Text

1

• **Right-click the hyperlink, in this case, the e-mail address (Figure 3-55).**

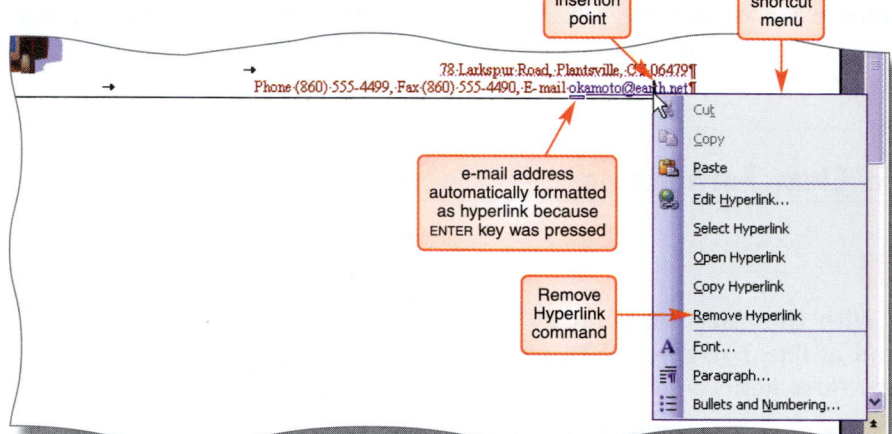

FIGURE 3-55

2

• **Click Remove Hyperlink on the shortcut menu.**

• **Position the insertion point on the paragraph mark below the border.**

Word removes the hyperlink format from the e-mail address (Figure 3-56).

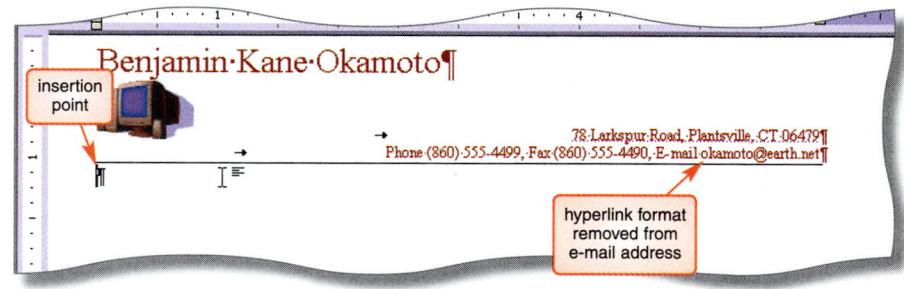

FIGURE 3-56

Other Ways

1. With insertion point in hyperlink, click Insert Hyperlink button on Standard toolbar, click Remove Link button
2. With insertion point in hyperlink, on Insert menu click Hyperlink, click Remove Link button
3. With insertion point in hyperlink, press CTRL+K, press ALT+R
4. With insertion point in hyperlink, in Voice Command mode, say "Right Click, Remove Hyperlink"

The letterhead now is complete. Thus, you should save it in a file, as described in the following steps.

To Save the Letterhead

1 **Insert your floppy disk into drive A.**

2 **Click the Save button on the Standard toolbar.**

3 **Type the file name** Okamoto Letterhead **in the File name text box.**

4 **If necessary, click the Save in box arrow and then click 3½ Floppy (A:).**

5 Click the Save button in the Save As dialog box.

Word saves the document on a floppy disk in drive A with the file name, Okamoto Letterhead.

Each time you wish to create a letter, you would open the letterhead file (Okamoto Letterhead) and then immediately save it with a new file name. By doing this, the letterhead file will remain unchanged for future use.

Creating a Cover Letter

You have created a letterhead for the cover letter. The next step is to compose the cover letter. The following pages outline how to use Word to compose a cover letter that contains a table and a bulleted list.

Components of a Business Letter

During your professional career, you most likely will create many business letters. A cover letter is one type of business letter. All business letters contain the same basic components.

When preparing business letters, you should include all essential elements. Essential business letter elements include the date line, inside address, message, and signature block (Figure 3-2a on page WD 140). The **date line**, which consists of the month, day, and year, is positioned two to six lines below the letterhead. The **inside address**, placed three to eight lines below the date line, usually contains the addressee's courtesy title plus full name, business affiliation, and full geographical address. The **salutation**, if present, begins two lines below the last line of the inside address. The body of the letter, the message, begins two lines below the salutation. Within the **message**, paragraphs are single-spaced with double-spacing between paragraphs. Two lines below the last line of the message, the **complimentary close** is displayed. Capitalize only the first word in a complimentary close. Type the **signature block** at least four lines below the complimentary close, allowing room for the author to sign his or her name.

You can follow many different styles when you create business letters. The cover letter in this project follows the modified block style. Table 3-2 outlines the differences among three common styles of business letters.

Table 3-2	Common Business Letter Styles
LETTER STYLES	**FEATURES**
Block	All components of the letter begin flush with the left margin.
Modified Block	The date, complimentary close, and signature block are positioned approximately ½" to the right of center, or at the right margin. All other components of the letter begin flush with the left margin.
Modified Semi-Block	The date, complimentary close, and signature block are centered, positioned approximately ½" to the right of center, or at the right margin. The first line of each paragraph in the body of the letter is indented ½" to 1" from the left margin. All other components of the letter begin flush with the left margin.

Saving the Cover Letter with a New File Name

The document in the document window currently has the name Okamoto Letterhead, the name of the personal letterhead. You want the letterhead to remain intact. Thus, you should save the document with a new file name, as described in steps on the next page.

To Save the Document with a New File Name

1 If necessary, insert your floppy disk into drive A.

2 Click File on the menu bar and then click Save As.

3 Type the file name `Okamoto Cover Letter` in the File name text box.

4 If necessary, click the Save in box arrow and then click 3½ Floppy (A:).

5 Click the Save button in the Save As dialog box.

Word saves the document on a floppy disk in drive A with the file name, Okamoto Cover Letter (shown in Figure 3-57).

Setting Tab Stops Using the Ruler

The first required element of the cover letter is the date line, which in this letter is to be positioned two lines below the letterhead. The date line contains the month, day, and year, and begins 3.5 inches from the left margin, or one-half inch to the right of center. Thus, you should set a custom tab stop at the 3.5" mark on the ruler.

Earlier you used the Tabs dialog box to set a tab stop because you could not use the ruler to set a tab stop at the right margin. The following steps show how to set a left-aligned tab stop using the ruler.

To Set Custom Tab Stops Using the Ruler

1

• **With the insertion point on the paragraph mark below the border, press the ENTER key.**

• **If necessary, click the button at the left edge of the horizontal ruler until it displays the Left Tab icon.**

• **Position the mouse pointer on the 3.5" mark on the ruler.**

Each time you click the button at the left of the horizontal ruler, its icon changes (Figure 3-57). The left tab icon looks like a capital letter L ( ).

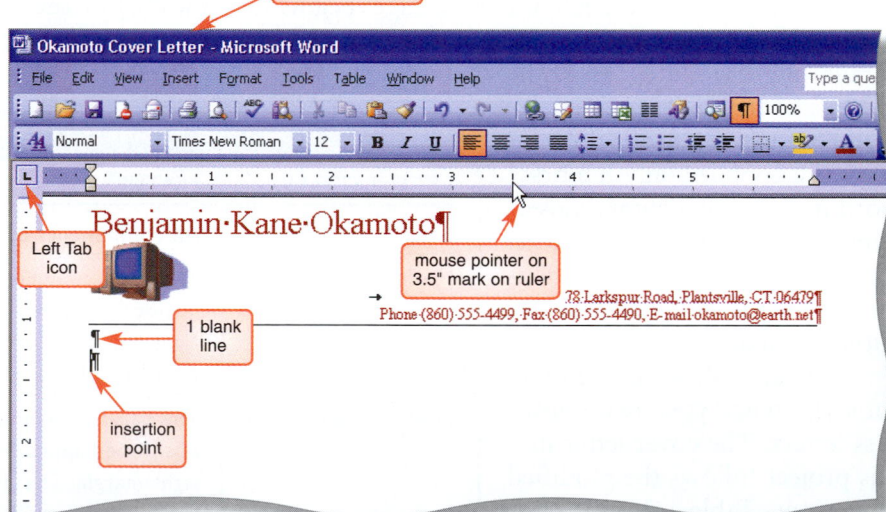

FIGURE 3-57

2

• **Click the 3.5" mark on the ruler.**

Word places a left tab marker at the 3.5" mark on the ruler (Figure 3-58). The text you type at this tab stop will be left-aligned.

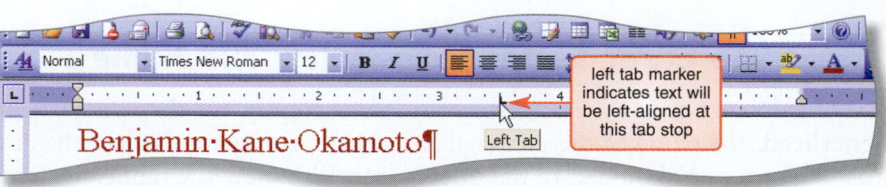

FIGURE 3-58

If, for some reason, you wanted to move a custom tab stop, you would drag the tab marker to the desired location on the ruler.

If you wanted to change the alignment of a custom tab stop, you could remove the existing tab stop and then insert a new one as described in the previous steps. To remove a custom tab stop, point to the tab marker on the ruler and then drag the tab marker down and out of the ruler. You also could use the Tabs dialog box to change an existing tab stop's alignment or position. As discussed earlier in this project, you click Format on the menu bar and then click Tabs to display the Tabs dialog box. To remove all tab stops, click the Clear All button in the Tabs dialog box.

Inserting the Current Date in a Document

The next step is to enter the current date at the 3.5" tab stop in the document. Word provides a method of inserting a computer's system date in a document. The following steps show how to insert the current date in the cover letter.

To Insert the Current Date in a Document

1

• **Press the TAB key.**

• **Click Insert on the menu bar (Figure 3-59).**

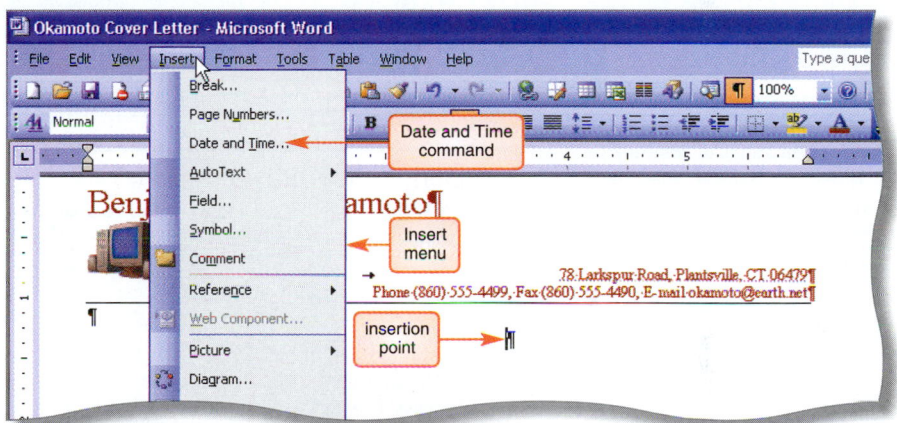

FIGURE 3-59

2

• **Click Date and Time on the Insert menu.**

• **When Word displays the Date and Time dialog box, click the desired format (in this case, December 19, 2005).**

• **If the Update automatically check box is selected, click the check box to remove the check mark.**

The Date and Time dialog box lists a variety of date and time formats (Figure 3-60). Your dialog box will differ, showing the current system date stored in your computer.

3

• **Click the OK button.**

Word inserts the current date at the location of the insertion point (shown in Figure 3-61 on the next page).

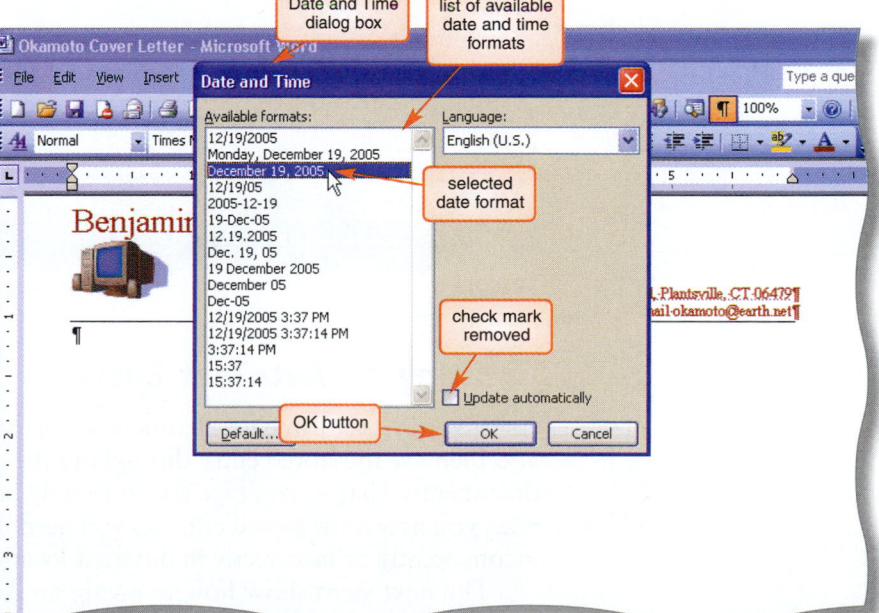

FIGURE 3-60

More About

Dates

A field is a set of codes that instructs Word to perform a certain action. If you want Word to display the current date or time when you print a document, make it a field. That is, place a check mark in the Update automatically check box in the Date and Time dialog box (Figure 3-60 on the previous page) when you insert the current date or time.

The next step is to type the inside address and salutation in the cover letter, as described in the following steps.

To Enter the Inside Address and Salutation

1 **With the insertion point at the end of the date, press the** ENTER **key three times.**

2 **Type** Ms. Helen Weiss **and then press the** ENTER **key.**

3 **Type** Personnel Director **and then press the** ENTER **key.**

4 **Type** National Computer Sales **and then press the** ENTER **key.**

5 **Type** 15 Main Street **and then press the** ENTER **key.**

6 **Type** Hartford, CT 06109 **and then press the** ENTER **key twice.**

7 **Type** Dear Ms. Weiss **and then press the** COLON **key (:).**

The inside address and salutation are entered (Figure 3-61).

More About

Inside Addresses

Pay close attention to the spelling, punctuation, and official abbreviations of company names. For example, does the company name spell out the word, and, or does it use the ampersand character (&)? Is the word, Company, spelled out or abbreviated?

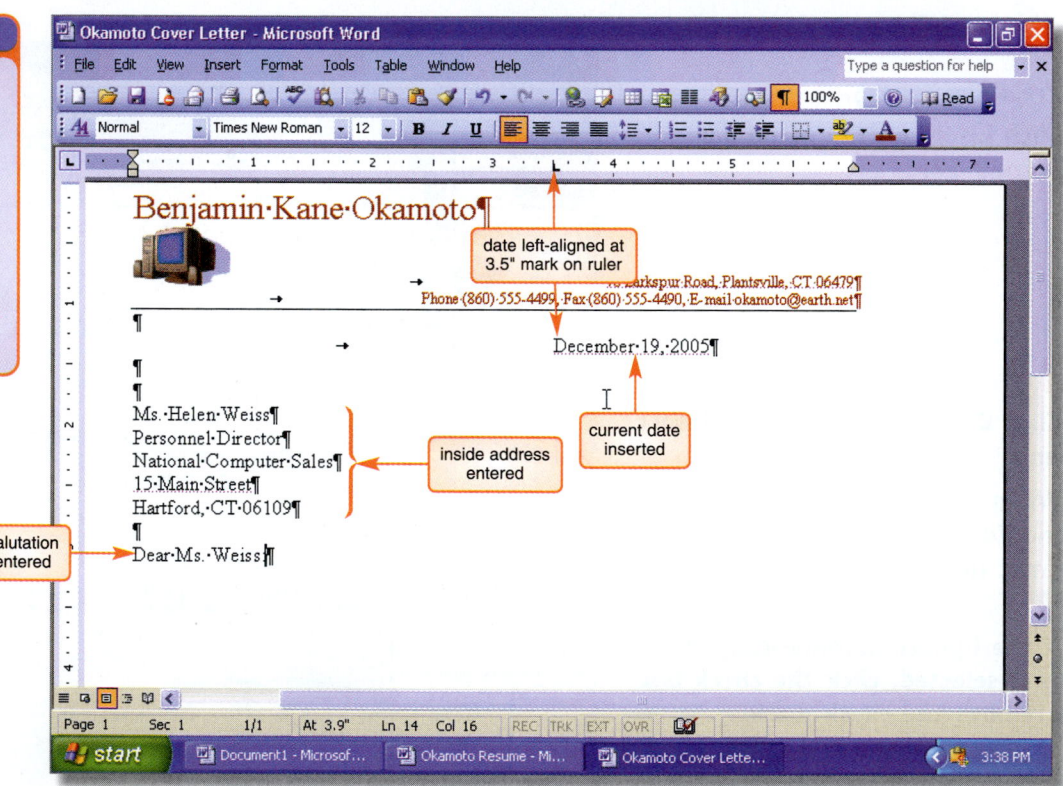

FIGURE 3-61

Creating an AutoText Entry

If you use the same text frequently, you can store the text in an **AutoText entry** and then use the stored entry throughout the open document, as well as future documents. That is, you type the entry only once, and for all future occurrences of the text, you access the stored entry as you need it. In this way, you avoid entering the text inconsistently or incorrectly in different locations throughout the same document.

The next steps show how to create an AutoText entry for the prospective employer's name.

To Create an AutoText Entry

1

• **Drag through the text to be stored, in this case, National Computer Sales. Do not select the paragraph mark at the end of the text.**

• **Click Insert on the menu bar and then point to AutoText.**

The employer name, National Computer Sales, in the inside address is selected (Figure 3-62). Notice the paragraph mark is not part of the selection.

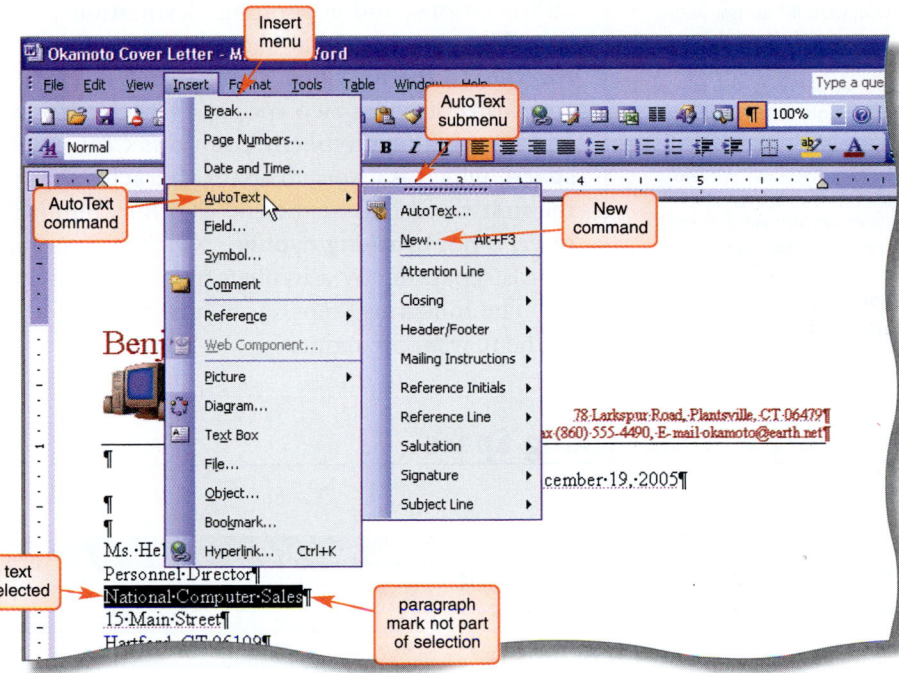

FIGURE 3-62

2

• **Click New on the AutoText submenu.**

• **When Word displays the Create AutoText dialog box, type** ncs **as the AutoText entry name.**

When the Create AutoText dialog box first appears, Word proposes a name for the AutoText entry. You change Word's suggestion to ncs (Figure 3-63).

3

• **Click the OK button.**

• **If Word displays another dialog box, click the Yes button.**

Word stores the AutoText entry and closes the AutoText dialog box.

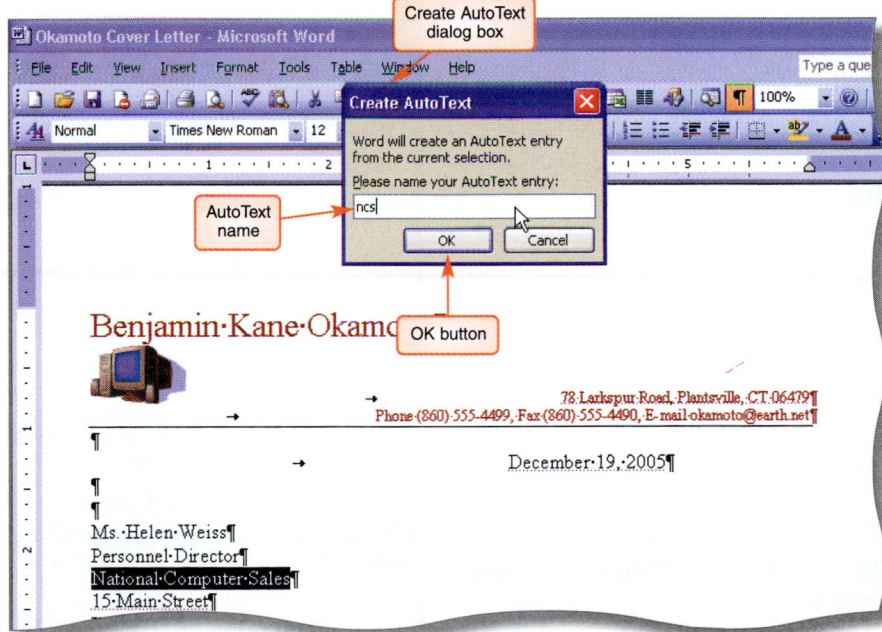

FIGURE 3-63

The name, ncs, has been stored as an AutoText entry. Later in the project, you will use the AutoText entry, ncs, instead of typing the employer name, National Computer Sales.

Other Ways

1. Select text, press ALT+F3, type AutoText name, click OK button
2. In Voice Command mode, say "Insert, AutoText, New, [AutoText name], OK"

Entering a Nonbreaking Space

Some compound words, such as proper names, dates, units of time and measure, abbreviations, and geographic destinations, should not be divided at the end of a line. These words either should fit as a unit at the end of a line or be wrapped together to the next line.

Word provides two special characters to assist with this task: nonbreaking space and nonbreaking hyphen. You press CTRL+SHIFT+SPACEBAR to insert a **nonbreaking space**, which is a special space character that prevents two words from splitting if the first word falls at the end of a line. Similarly, you press CTRL+SHIFT+HYPHEN to insert a **nonbreaking hyphen**, which is a special type of hyphen that prevents two words separated by a hyphen from splitting at the end of a line.

The following steps show how to enter a nonbreaking space between the words in the newspaper name.

To Insert a Nonbreaking Space

1

• **Scroll the salutation to the top of the document window. Click after the colon in the salutation and then press the ENTER key twice.**

• **Type** I am responding to the full-time computer sales position advertised in yesterday's **and then press the SPACEBAR.**

• **Press CTRL+I to turn on italics. Type** New **and then press CTRL+SHIFT+SPACEBAR.**

Word inserts a nonbreaking space after the word, New (Figure 3-64).

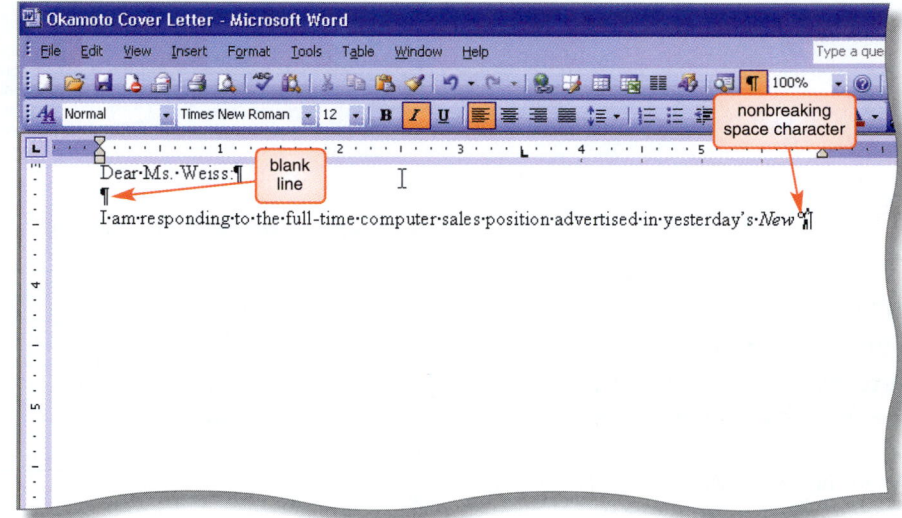

FIGURE 3-64

2

• **Type** England **and then press CTRL+SHIFT+SPACEBAR.**

• **Type** Tribune **and then press CTRL+I to turn off italics. Press the PERIOD key.**

Word wraps the words in the newspaper title, New England Tribune, to the next line (Figure 3-65).

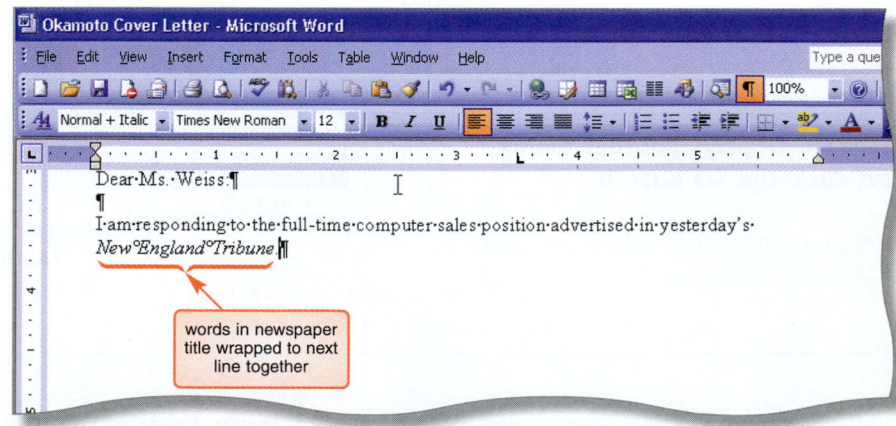

FIGURE 3-65

Inserting an AutoText Entry

At the end of the next sentence in the body of the cover letter, you want the prospective employer name, National Computer Sales, to be displayed. Recall that earlier in this project, you created an AutoText entry name of ncs for National Computer Sales. Thus, you will type the AutoText entry's name and then instruct Word to replace the AutoText entry's name with the stored entry of National Computer Sales.

The following steps show how to insert an AutoText entry.

To Insert an AutoText Entry

1

• **Press the SPACEBAR. Type** As indicated on the enclosed resume, I have the credentials you are seeking and believe I can be a valuable asset to ncs **as shown in Figure 3-66.**

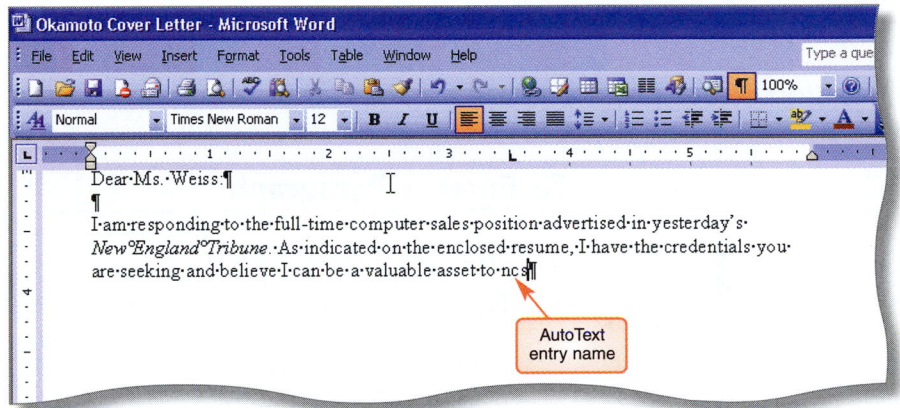

FIGURE 3-66

2

• **Press the F3 key.**
• **Press the PERIOD key.**

Word replaces the characters, ncs, with the stored AutoText entry, National Computer Sales, when you press the F3 key (Figure 3-67).

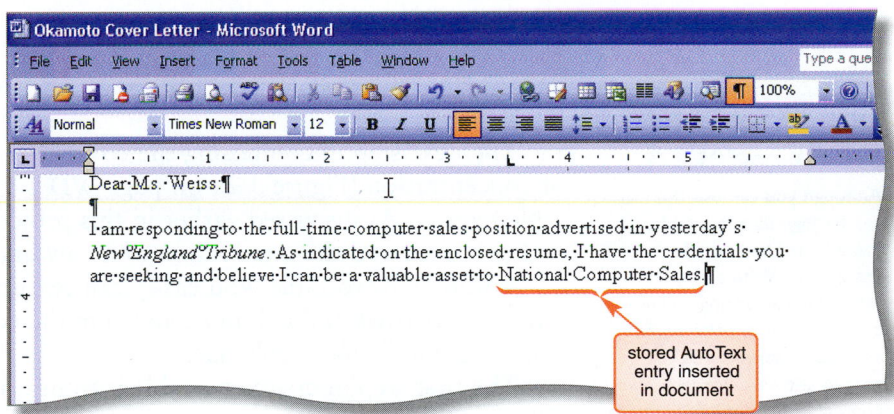

FIGURE 3-67

Pressing the **F3** key instructs Word to replace the AutoText entry name with the stored AutoText entry. In Project 2, you learned how to use the AutoCorrect feature, which enables you to insert and also create AutoCorrect entries (just as you did for this AutoText entry). The difference between an AutoCorrect entry and an AutoText entry is that the AutoCorrect feature makes corrections for you automatically as soon as you press the SPACEBAR or type a punctuation mark, whereas you must press the F3 key or click the AutoText command to instruct Word to make an AutoText correction.

More About

AutoText

Word provides many AutoText categories of entries for business letters. Categories include attention line, closing, mailing instructions, salutation, and subject line. To insert an AutoText entry, click Insert on the menu bar, point to AutoText, point to the desired category, and then click the desired entry. Or, click the All Entries button on the AutoText toolbar, point to the desired category, and then click the desired entry.

If you watch the screen as you type, you may discover that AutoComplete tips appear on the screen. As you type, Word searches the list of AutoText entry names, and if one matches your typing, Word displays its complete name above your typing as an **AutoComplete tip**. If you press the ENTER key while an AutoComplete tip is displayed on the screen, Word places the text in the AutoComplete tip at the location of your typing. To ignore an AutoComplete tip proposed by Word, simply continue typing to remove the AutoComplete tip from the screen.

In addition to AutoText entries, Word proposes AutoComplete tips for the current date, days of the week, months, and so on. If your screen does not display AutoComplete tips, click Tools on the menu bar, click AutoCorrect Options, click the AutoText tab, click Show AutoComplete suggestions, and then click the OK button. To view the complete list of entries, click Tools on the menu bar, click AutoCorrect Options, click the AutoText tab, and then scroll through the list of entries.

The next step is to enter a paragraph of text into the cover letter, as described below.

To Enter a Paragraph

1 **Press the ENTER key twice.**

2 **Type** I recently received my bachelor's degree in information and computer technology from Hartford College. The following table outlines my areas of concentration **and then press the COLON key.**

3 **Press the ENTER key twice.**

The paragraph is entered (shown in Figure 3-68).

More About

Word Tables

Although you can use the TAB key to align data in a table, many Word users prefer to use a table. With a Word table, you can arrange numbers and text in columns. For emphasis, tables can be shaded and have borders. The contents of Word tables can be sorted, and you can have Word sum the contents of an entire row or column.

Creating a Table with the Insert Table Button

The next step in composing the cover letter is to place a table listing your areas of concentration (Figure 3-2a on page WD 140). You create this table using Word's table feature. As discussed earlier in this project, a Word table is a collection of rows and columns, and the intersection of a row and a column is called a cell.

Within a Word table, you easily can rearrange rows and columns, change column widths, sort rows and columns, and sum the contents of rows and columns. You also can format and chart table data.

The first step in creating a table is to insert an empty table into the document. When inserting a table, you must specify the total number of rows and columns required, which is called the **dimension** of the table. The table in this project has two columns. You often do not know the total number of rows in a table. Thus, many Word users create one row initially and then add more rows as needed. The first number in a dimension is the number of rows, and the second is the number of columns.

The following steps show how to insert a 1 × 2 (pronounced one by two) table; that is, a table with one row and two columns.

To Insert an Empty Table

1

• **Click the Insert Table button on the Standard toolbar.**

• **Position the mouse pointer on the cell in the first row and second column of the grid.**

Word displays a grid so you can select the desired table dimension (Figure 3-68). Word will insert the table immediately above the insertion point.

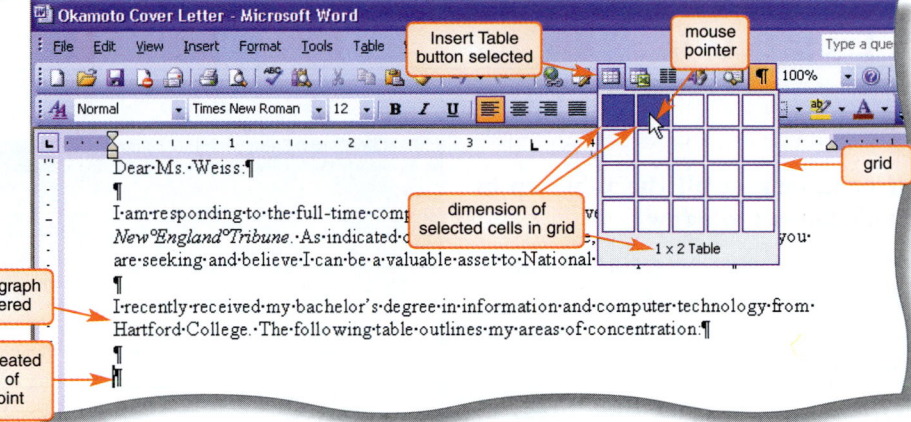

FIGURE 3-68

2

• **Click the cell in the first row and second column of the grid.**

Word inserts an empty 1 × 2 table in the document (Figure 3-69). The insertion point is in the first cell (row 1 and column 1) of the table.

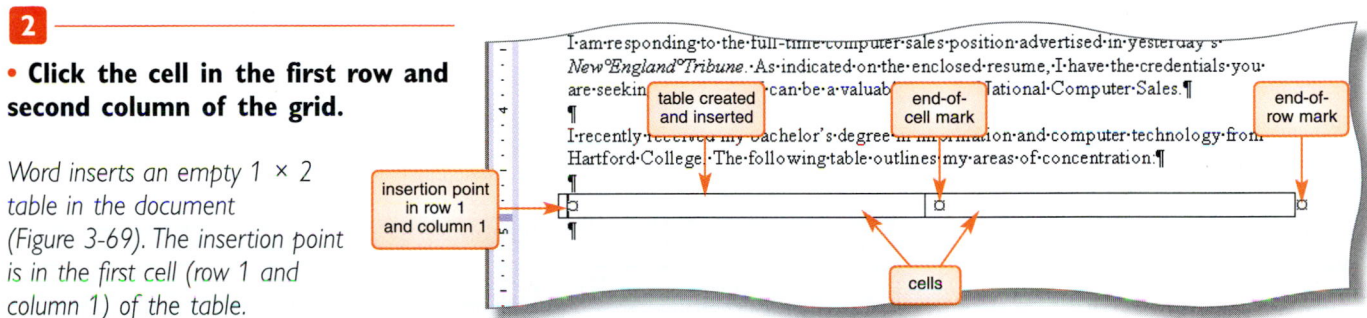

FIGURE 3-69

As discussed earlier in this project, each row of a table has an end-of-row mark, which you can use to add columns to the right of a table. Each cell has an end-of-cell mark, which you can use to select a cell. The end-of-cell mark currently is left-aligned; thus, it is positioned at the left edge of each cell. You can use any of the paragraph formatting buttons on the Formatting toolbar to change the alignment of the text within the cells. For example, if you click the Align Right button on the Formatting toolbar, the end-of-cell mark and any entered text will be displayed at the right edge of the cell.

For simple tables, such as the one just created, Word users click the Insert Table button to create a table. For more complex tables, such as one with a varying number of columns per row, Word has a Draw Table feature that allows you to use a pencil pointer to draw a table on the screen.

Entering Data in a Word Table

The next step is to enter data into the cells of the empty table. The data you enter within a cell wordwraps just as text does between the margins of a document. To place data in a cell, you click the cell and then type. To advance rightward from one cell to the next, press the TAB key. When you are at the rightmost cell in a row, also press the TAB key to move to the first cell in the next row; do not press the ENTER key. The ENTER key is used to begin a new paragraph within a cell.

Other Ways

1. On Table menu point to Insert, click Table on Insert submenu, enter number of columns, enter number of rows, click OK button
2. In Voice Command mode, say "Insert Table, [select table dimension]"

More About

Draw Table

To use Draw Table, click the Tables and Borders button on the Standard toolbar to change the mouse pointer to a pencil. Use the pencil to draw from one corner to the opposite diagonal corner to define the perimeter of the table. Then, draw the column and row lines inside the perimeter. To remove a line, use the Eraser button on the Tables and Borders toolbar.

To add new rows to a table, press the TAB key with the insertion point positioned in the bottom-right corner cell of the table.

The following steps show how to enter data in the table.

To Enter Data in a Table

1

• **If necessary, scroll the table up in the document window.**

• **With the insertion point in the left cell of the table, type** Computer Hardware **and then press the TAB key.**

• **Type** 30 hours **and then press the TAB key.**

Word enters the table data in the first row of the table and adds a second row to the table (Figure 3-70). The insertion point is positioned in the first cell of the second row.

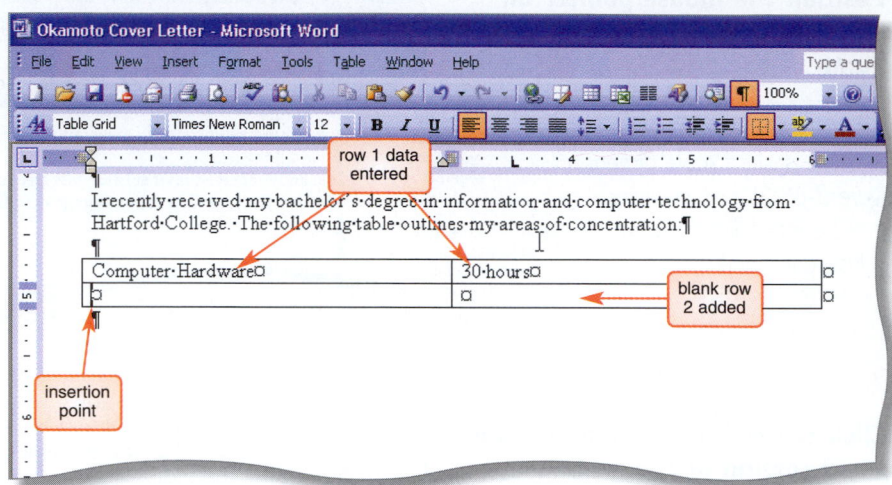

FIGURE 3-70

2

• **Type** Computer Software and Programming **and then press the TAB key. Type** 21 hours **and then press the TAB key.**

• **Type** Professional Communications **and then press the TAB key. Type** 15 hours **and then press the TAB key.**

• **Type** Business **and then press the TAB key. Type** 15 hours **as shown in Figure 3-71.**

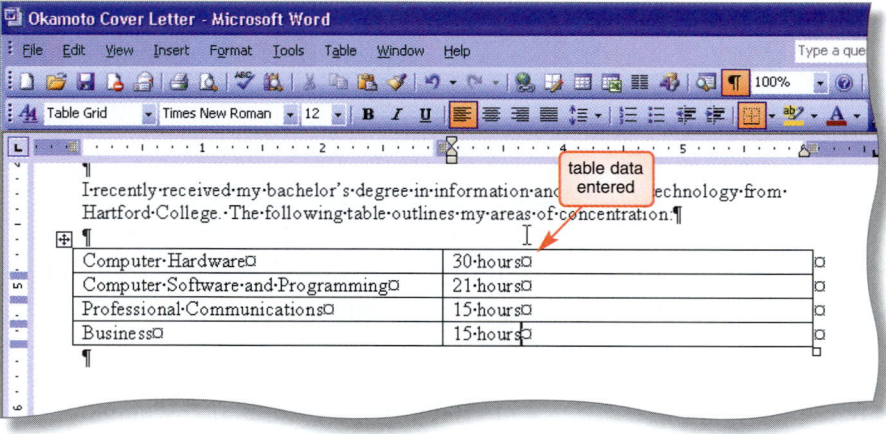

FIGURE 3-71

You modify the contents of cells just as you modify text in a document. To delete the contents of a cell, select the cell contents by pointing to the left edge of a cell and clicking when the mouse pointer changes direction, and then press the DELETE key. To modify text in a cell, click in the cell and then correct the entry. You can double-click the OVR indicator on the status bar to toggle between insert and overtype modes. You also can drag and drop or cut and paste the contents of cells.

As discussed in the previous steps, you add a row to the end of a table by positioning the insertion point in the bottom-right corner cell and then pressing the TAB key. To add a row in the middle of a table, select the row below where the new row is to be inserted, then click the Insert Rows button on the Standard toolbar (the same button you clicked to insert a table); or click Insert Rows on the shortcut menu; or click Table on the menu bar, point to Insert, and then click Rows Above.

To add a column in the middle of a table, select the column to the right of where the new column is to be inserted and then click the Insert Columns button on the Standard toolbar (the same button you clicked to insert a table); or click Insert Columns on the shortcut menu; or click Table on the menu bar, point to Insert, and then click Columns to the Left. To add a column to the right of a table, select the end-of-row marks at the right edge of the table, then click the Insert Columns button; or click Insert Columns on the shortcut menu; or click Table on the menu bar, point to Insert, and then click Columns to the Right.

If you want to delete row(s) or delete column(s) from a table, select the row(s) or column(s) to delete and then click Delete Rows or Delete Columns on the shortcut menu, or click Table on the menu bar, click Delete, and then click the appropriate item to delete.

Resizing Table Columns

The table in this project currently extends from the left margin to the right margin of the document. You want each column only to be as wide as the longest entry in the table. That is, the first column must be wide enough to accommodate the words, Computer Software and Programming; and the second column must be wide enough for the phrase, 30 hours.

The following steps show how to instruct Word to fit the width of the columns to the contents of the table automatically.

To Fit Columns to Table Contents

1

• **Right-click the table and then point to AutoFit on the shortcut menu (Figure 3-72).**

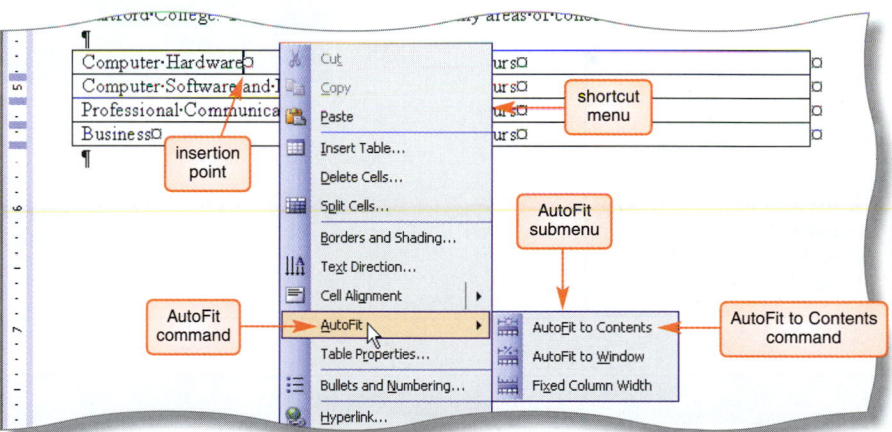

FIGURE 3-72

2

• **Click AutoFit to Contents on the AutoFit submenu.**

Word automatically adjusts the widths of the columns based on the text in the table (Figure 3-73). In this case, Word reduces the widths of the columns.

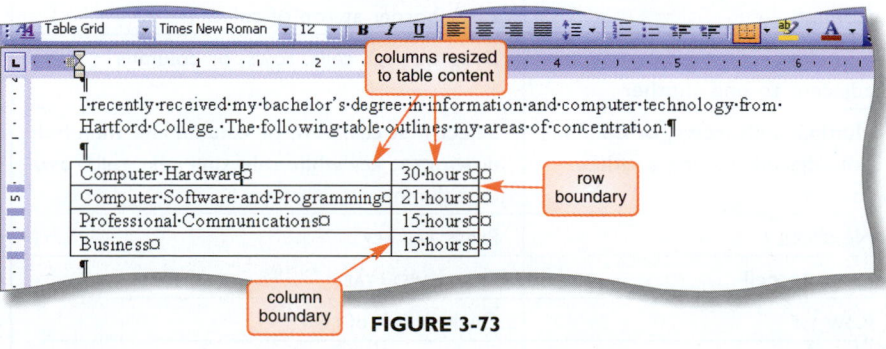

FIGURE 3-73

More About

Table Formats

You can change the width of a column to an exact measurement. Hold down the ALT key while dragging markers on the ruler. Or, click Table on the menu bar, click Table Properties, click the Column tab, enter desired measurements, and then click the OK button. Similarly, to change the row height to an exact measurement, click the Row tab in the Table Properties dialog box, enter desired measurements, and then click the OK button.

If you do not want to resize the columns to the table widths, Word provides other options. You can drag a **column boundary**, the border to the right of a column (Figure 3-73 on the previous page), until the column is the desired width. Similarly, you can resize a row by dragging the **row boundary**, the border at the bottom of a row, until the row is the desired height. You also can resize the entire table by dragging the **table resize handle**, which is a small square that appears when you point to the bottom-right corner of the table (shown in Figure 3-74).

Changing the Table Alignment

When you first create a table, it is left-aligned; that is, flush with the left margin. In this cover letter, the table should be centered. To center a table, select the entire table and then center it using the Center button on the Formatting toolbar, as shown in the following series of steps.

To Select a Table

1

• **Position the mouse pointer in the table so the table move handle appears.**

• **Click the table move handle.**

Word selects the entire table (Figure 3-74).

Other Ways

1. On Table menu point to Select, click Table
2. With insertion point in table, press ALT+5 (using the 5 on the numeric keypad with NUM LOCK off)
3. In Voice Command mode, say "Table, Select, Table"

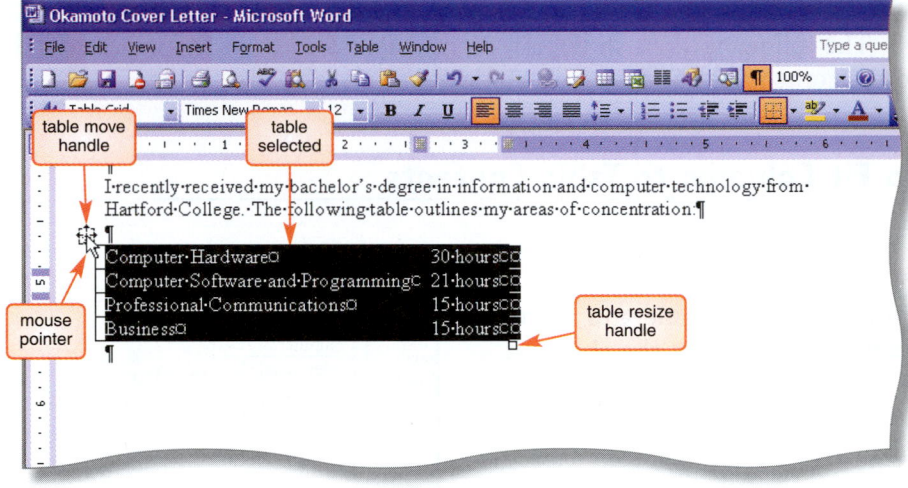

FIGURE 3-74

Table 3-3 Selecting Items in a Table	
ITEM TO SELECT	**ACTION**
Cell	Click left edge of cell
Column	Click border at top of column
Multiple cells, rows, or columns adjacent to one another	Drag through cells, rows, or columns
Multiple cells, rows, or columns not adjacent to one another	Select first cell, row, or column and then hold down CTRL key while selecting next cell, row, or column
Next cell	Press TAB key
Previous cell	Press SHIFT+TAB
Row	Click to left of row
Table	Click table move handle

When working with tables, you may need to select the contents of cells, rows, columns, or the entire table. Table 3-3 identifies ways to select various items in a table.

The following step centers the selected table between the margins.

To Center a Selected Table

1 **Click the Center button on the Formatting toolbar.**

Word centers the selected table between the left and right margins (shown in Figure 3-75).

When an entire table is selected and you click the Center button on the Formatting toolbar, Word centers the entire table. If you wanted to center the contents of the cells, you would select the cells by dragging through them and then click the Center button.

The next step is to add more text below the table, as described here.

To Add More Text

1 **If necessary, scroll up. Click the paragraph mark below the table.**

2 **Press the ENTER key.**

3 **Type** In addition to my coursework, I have the following sales and computer experience **and then press the COLON key. Press the ENTER key.**

The text is entered (shown in Figure 3-75).

Bulleting a List

You can type a list and then add bullets to the paragraphs at a later time, or you can use Word's AutoFormat As You Type feature to bullet the paragraphs as you type them (Table 3-1 on page WD 156).

The following steps show how to add bullets automatically to a list as you type.

To Bullet a List as You Type

1

• **Press the ASTERISK key (*).**

• **Press the SPACEBAR.**

• **Type** Worked as an intern at Computer Discount Sales, selling hardware and software components to home and small business customers **(Figure 3-75).**

More About

Table AutoFormat

Word has many predefined table formats that you can apply to tables. With the insertion point positioned in the table, click Table on the menu bar, click Table AutoFormat, click the desired format, and then click the Apply button. Or, click the Styles and Formatting button on the Formatting toolbar, click the Show box arrow, click All styles in the list, and then click the desired style in the Pick formatting to apply area.

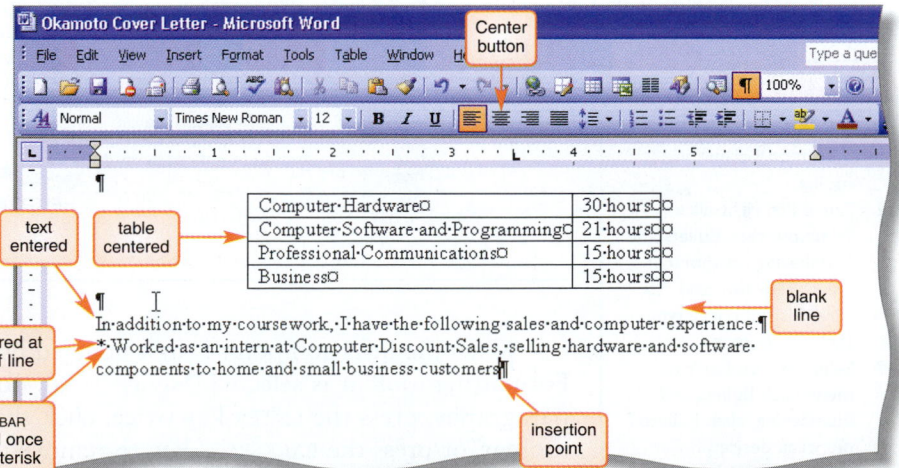

FIGURE 3-75

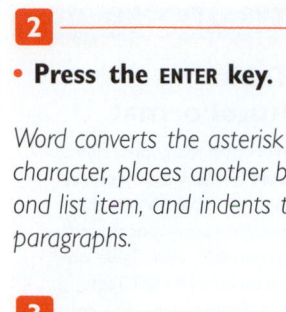

2

• **Press the ENTER key.**

Word converts the asterisk to a bullet character, places another bullet on the second list item, and indents the two bulleted paragraphs.

3

• **Type** At Hartford College, tutored students having difficulty with computer classes **and then press the ENTER key.**

• **Type** Prepared all fliers and newsletters for the New England Ski Club **and then press the ENTER key.**

Word places a bullet on the next line (Figure 3-76).

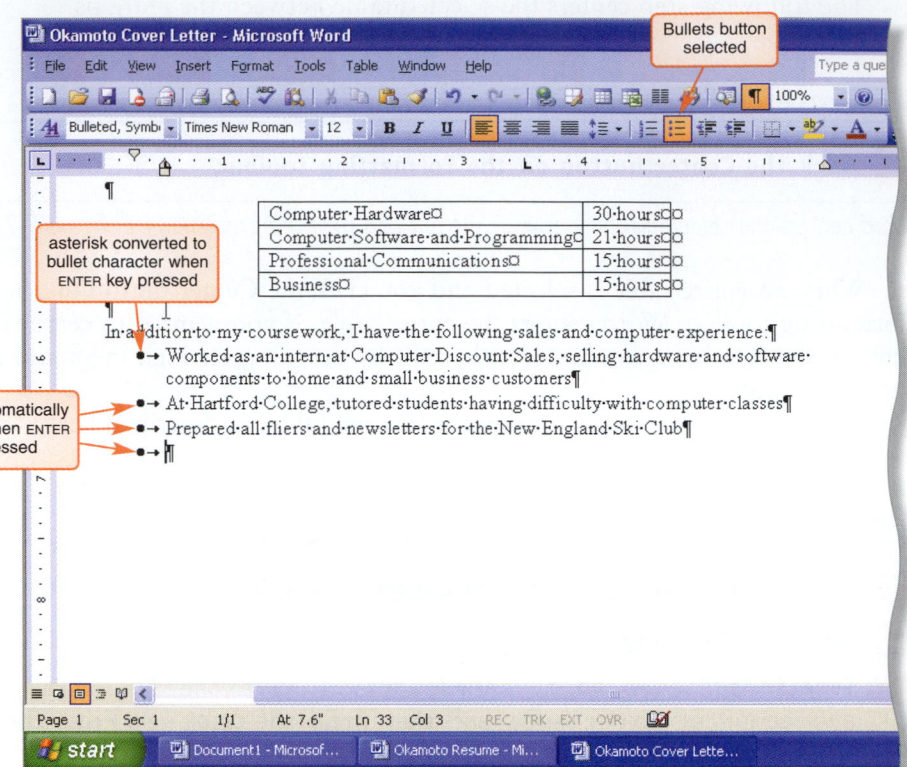

FIGURE 3-76

4

• **Press the ENTER key.**

Word removes the lone bullet because you pressed the ENTER key twice (Figure 3-77). The Bullets button no longer is selected.

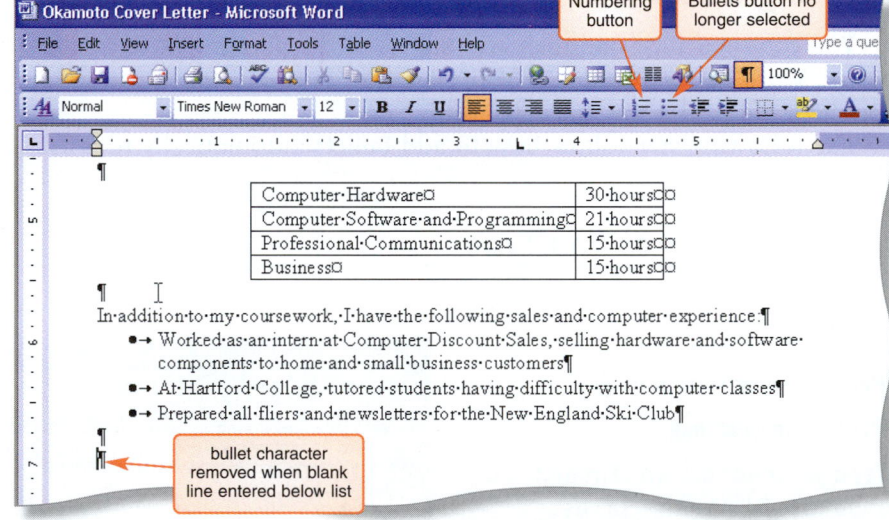

FIGURE 3-77

When the insertion point is in a bulleted list, the Bullets button on the Formatting toolbar is selected (Figure 3-76). To instruct Word to stop bulleting paragraphs, press the ENTER key twice, click the Bullets button on the Formatting toolbar, or press the BACKSPACE key to remove the bullet.

You may have noticed that Word displayed the AutoCorrect Options button when it formatted the list automatically as a bulleted list. If you did not want the list to be a bulleted list, you could click the AutoCorrect Options button and then click Undo Automatic Bullets on the shortcut menu.

You can add numbers as you type, just as you can add bullets as you type. To number a list, type the number one followed by a period and then a space (1.) at the beginning of the first item and then type your text. When you press the ENTER key, Word places the number two (2.) at the beginning of the next line automatically. As with bullets, press the ENTER key twice at the end of the list or click the Numbering button (Figure 3-77) on the Formatting toolbar to stop numbering.

The next step is to enter the remainder of the cover letter, as described below.

More About

Outline Numbered Lists

To create an outline numbered list, click Format on the menu bar, click Bullets and Numbering, click the Outline Numbered tab, and then click a style that does not contain the word, Heading. To promote or demote a list item to the next or previous levels, click the Increase Indent and Decrease Indent buttons on the Formatting toolbar.

To Enter the Remainder of the Cover Letter

1. **Type the paragraph shown in Figure 3-78, making certain you use the AutoText entry, ncs, to insert the employer name.**
2. **Press the ENTER key twice. Press the TAB key. Type** `Sincerely` **and then press the COMMA key.**
3. **Press the ENTER key four times. Press the TAB key. Type** `Benjamin Kane Okamoto` **and then press the ENTER key twice.**
4. **Type** `Enclosure: Resume` **as the final text.**

The cover letter text is complete (Figure 3-78).

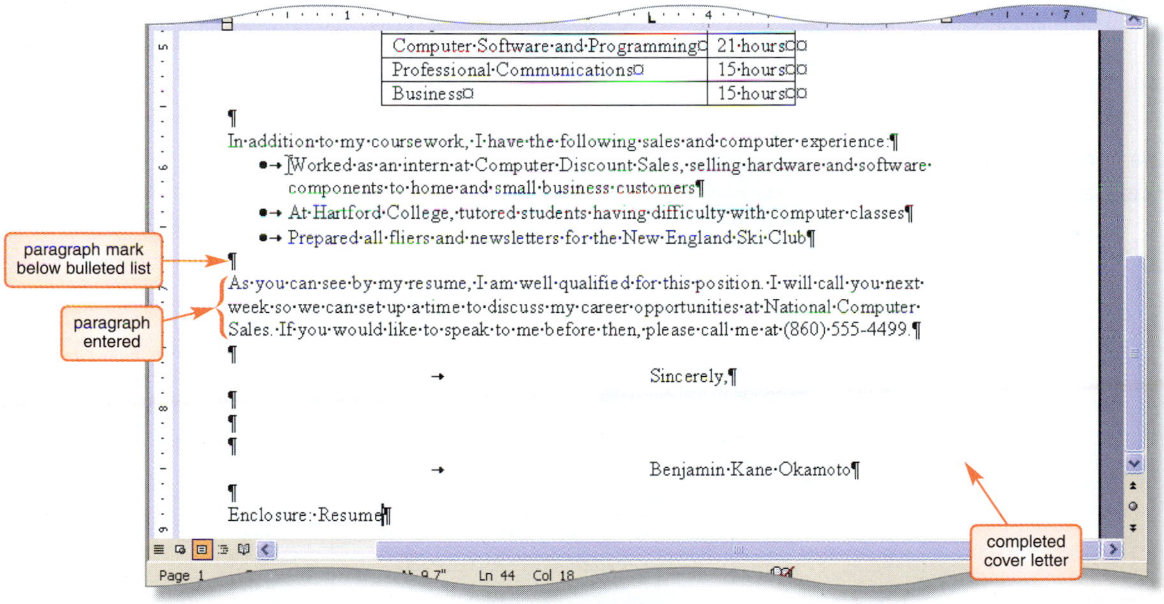

FIGURE 3-78

Saving Again and Printing the Cover Letter

The cover letter for the resume now is complete. You should save the cover letter again and then print it, as described in the following steps.

Q&A

Q: Should I proofread the resume and cover letter?

A: You should be absolutely certain that your resume and cover letter are error free. Check spelling and grammar using Word. Proofread for errors. Set the resume and cover letter aside for a couple of days and then proofread them again. Ask others, such as a friend or teacher, to proofread them also.

To Save a Document Again

1. **Click the Save button on the Standard toolbar.**

Word saves the cover letter with the same file name, Okamoto Cover Letter.

To Print a Document

1 **Click the Print button on the Standard toolbar.**

The completed cover letter prints as shown in Figure 3-2a on page WD 140.

Addressing and Printing Envelopes and Mailing Labels

With Word, you can print address information on an envelope or on a mailing label. Computer-printed addresses look more professional than handwritten ones. Thus, the following steps show how to address and print an envelope.

To Address and Print an Envelope

1

• **Scroll through the cover letter to display the inside address in the document window.**

• **Drag through the inside address to select it.**

• **Click Tools on the menu bar and then point to Letters and Mailings (Figure 3-79).**

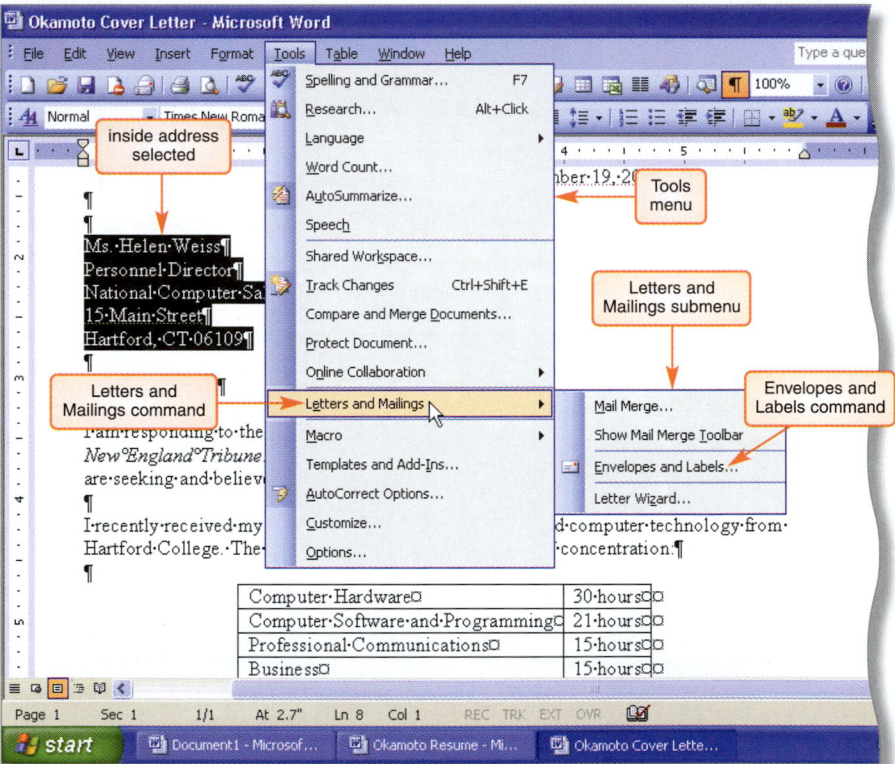

FIGURE 3-79

2

- **Click Envelopes and Labels on the Letters and Mailings submenu.**
- **When Word displays the Envelopes and Labels dialog box, if necessary, click the Envelopes tab.**
- **Click the Return address text box.**
- **Type** `Benjamin Kane Okamoto` **and then press the ENTER key.**
- **Type** `78 Larkspur Road` **and then press the ENTER key.**
- **Type** `Plantsville, CT 06479` **(Figure 3-80).**

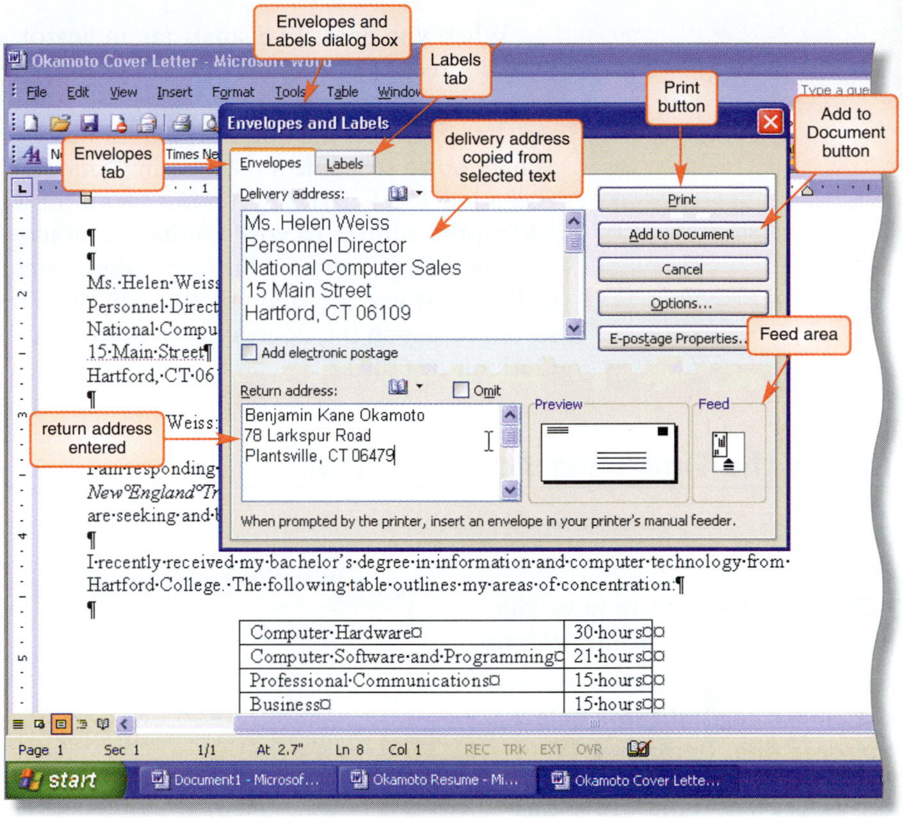

FIGURE 3-80

3

- **Insert an envelope into your printer, as shown in the Feed area of the dialog box (your Feed area may be different depending on your printer).**
- **Click the Print button in the Envelopes and Labels dialog box.**
- **If a dialog box is displayed, click the No button.**

Word prints the envelope (shown in Figure 3-2b on page WD 140).

Instead of printing the envelope immediately, you can add it to the document by clicking the Add to Document button in the Envelopes and Labels dialog box. To specify a different envelope or label type (identified by a number on the box of envelopes or labels), click the Options button in the Envelopes and Labels dialog box.

Instead of printing an envelope, you can print a mailing label. To do this, click the Labels tab in the Envelopes and Labels dialog box (Figure 3-80). Type the delivery address in the Address box. To print the same address on all labels on the page, click Full page of the same label. Click the Print button in the dialog box.

More About

Office Supplies

For more information about where to obtain supplies for printing documents, visit the Word 2003 More About Web page (scsite.com/wd2003/more) and then click Online Office Supplies.

Smart Tags

A **smart tag** is a button that automatically appears on the screen when Word performs a certain action. In this and previous projects, you worked with the AutoCorrect Options and Paste Options smart tags. This section discusses the third type of smart tag, called Smart Tag Actions, which performs various functions depending on the object identified by the smart tag indicator.

The smart tag indicator for Smart Tag Actions is a purple dotted underline. As shown throughout this project, a smart tag indicator appears below addresses and dates. A smart tag indicator also may appear below names, places, times, and financial symbols. To view or change the list of objects recognized as smart tags, click Tools on the menu bar, click AutoCorrect Options, and then click the Smart Tags tab.

When you point to a smart tag indicator, the Smart Tag Actions button appears on the screen. Clicking the Smart Tag Actions button displays a Smart Tag Actions menu. The commands in the Smart Tag Actions menu vary depending on the smart tag. For example, the Smart Tag Actions menu for a date includes commands that allow you to schedule a meeting in Outlook Calendar or display your Outlook Calendar. The Smart Tag Actions menu for an address includes commands for adding the address to your Outlook contacts list.

The following steps illustrate using a smart tag to display your Outlook Calendar. If you are stepping through this project on a computer and you want your screen to match the figures in the following steps, then your computer must have Outlook installed.

To Use the Smart Tag Actions Button

1

• **Click anywhere to remove the highlight from the inside address.**

• **Position the mouse pointer on the smart tag indicator below the date line, December 19, 2005, in the cover letter. (If the smart tag indicator is not displayed, click Tools on the menu bar, click AutoCorrect Options, click the Smart Tags tab, click Date, and then click the OK button.)**

Word displays the Smart Tag Actions button (Figure 3-81).

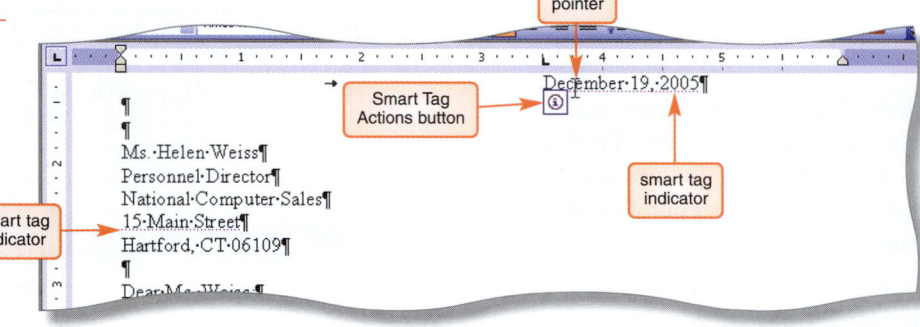

FIGURE 3-81

2

• **Click the Smart Tag Actions button.**

Word displays the Smart Tag Actions menu (Figure 3-82).

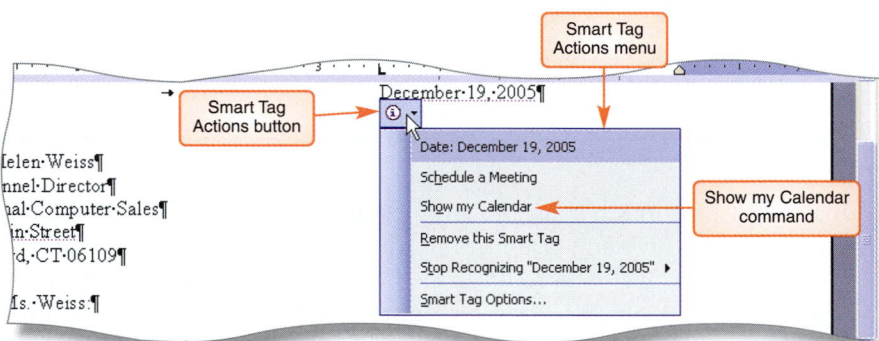

FIGURE 3-82

3

• **Click Show my Calendar on the Smart Tag Actions menu.**

Outlook starts and displays your calendar for today's date (Figure 3-83). Your date will differ, depending on the computer's system date.

4

• **Click the Close button on the Outlook title bar to close Outlook.**

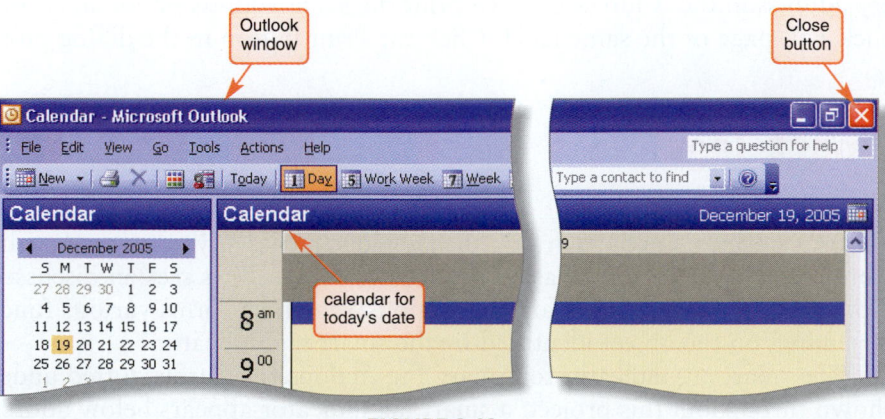

FIGURE 3-83

Document Summary

When you create and save many documents on a computer, you may not remember the name of each individual document. To help locate documents at a later time, you can store additional information about the document, called **file properties** or the **document summary**, when you save it. For example, you can specify items such as a title, subject, category, keyword(s), and comment(s).

The following steps show how to modify and view the document summary for the cover letter.

To Modify the Document Summary

1

• Click File on the menu bar (Figure 3-84).

2

• Click Properties on the File menu.

• When Word displays the Okamoto Cover Letter Properties dialog box, if necessary, click the Summary tab.

• **Type** National Computer Sales **in the Title text box.**

• **Type** Cover Letter **in the Subject text box.**

• **Type** Cover Letter **in the Category text box.**

• **Type** cover letter, National Computer Sales **in the Keywords text box.**

• **Type** Cover letter to Ms. Helen Weiss at National Computer Sales **in the Comments text box (Figure 3-85).**

3

• Click the OK button to close the dialog box.

• Click the Save button on the Standard toolbar.

• Click File on the menu bar and then click Close to close the cover letter document window.

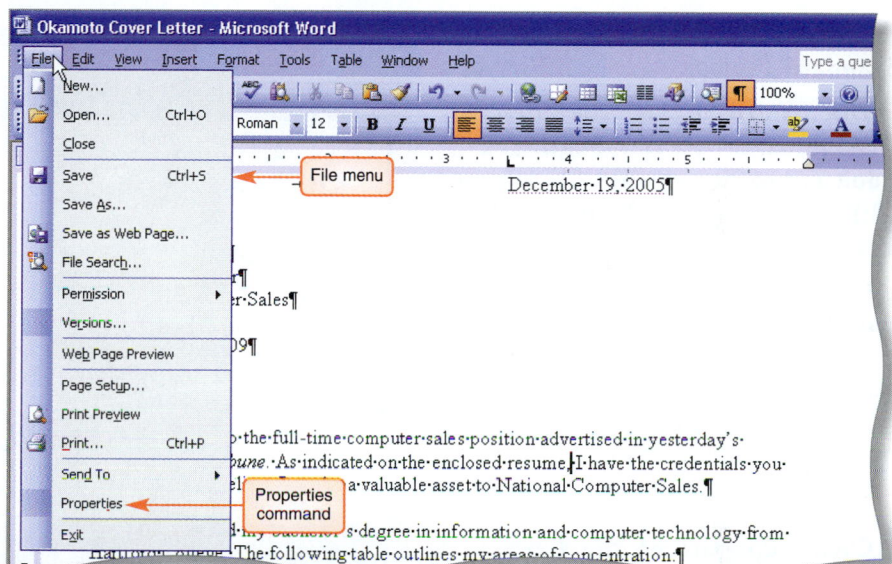

FIGURE 3-84

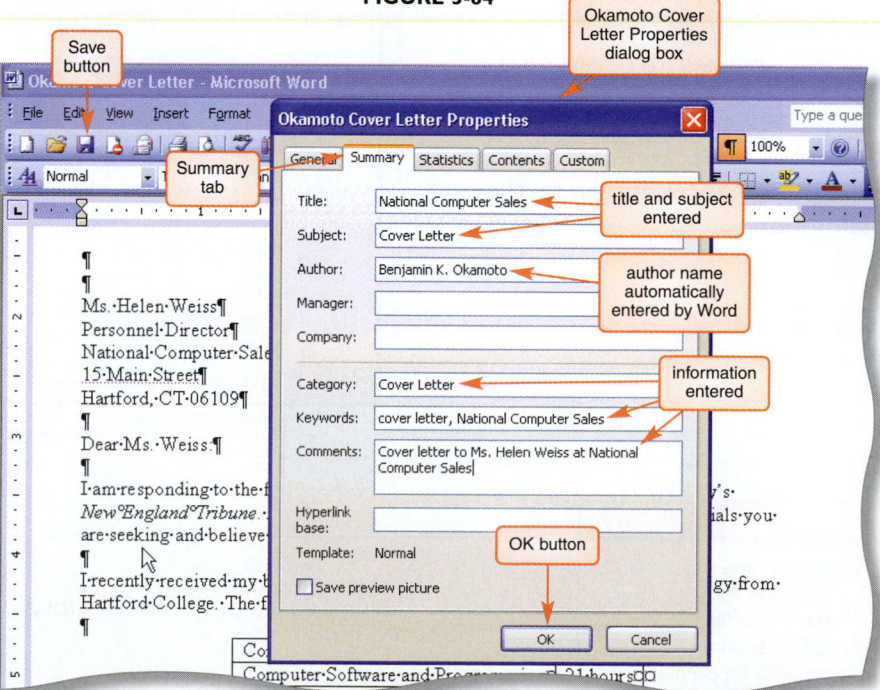

FIGURE 3-85

The updated file properties become part of the document when you save the document.

Word automatically pulls the author information from the user information stored on the computer. To change the user information, click Tools on the menu bar, click Options, click the User Information tab, enter the new information in the text boxes, and then click the OK button.

When opening a document at a later time, you can display the document properties to help you locate a particular file, as shown in the following steps.

To Display File Properties in the Open Dialog Box

1

• **Click the Open button on the Standard toolbar.**

• **When Word displays the Open dialog box, if necessary, click the Look in box arrow, click 3½ Floppy (A:), and then click Okamoto Cover Letter.**

• **Click the Views button arrow in the Open dialog box.**

Word displays the Views menu in the Open dialog box (Figure 3-86).

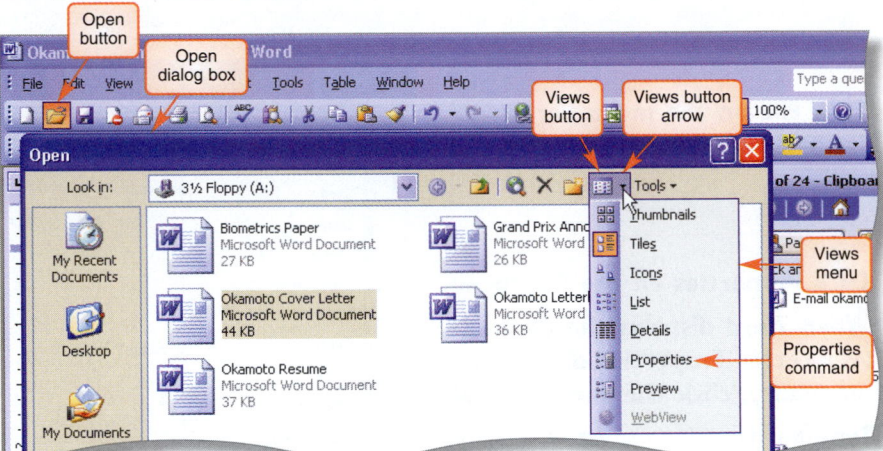

FIGURE 3-86

2

• **Click Properties on the Views menu.**

Word displays the file properties to the right of the selected file (Figure 3-87).

3

• **Click the Cancel button in the dialog box.**

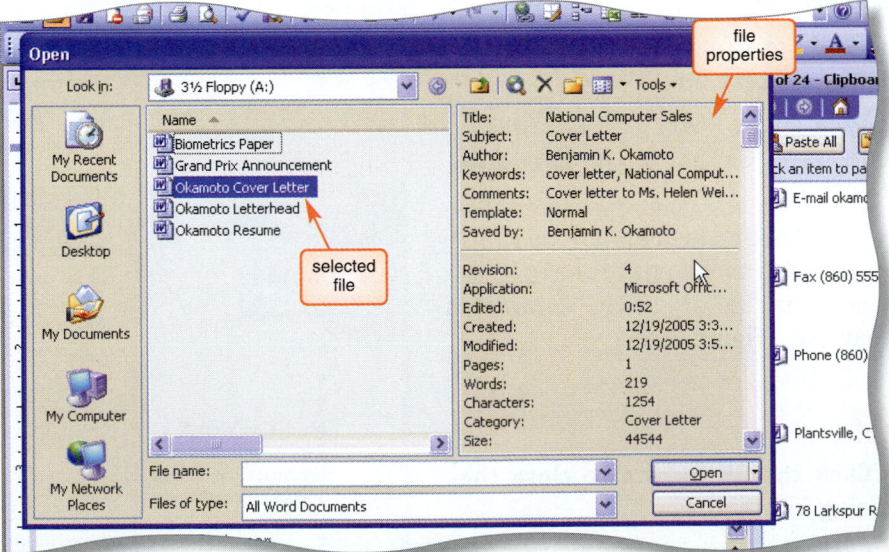

FIGURE 3-87

The final step in this project is to quit Word, as described in the next step.

To Quit Word

1 **Click File on the menu bar and then click Exit. (If Word displays a dialog box about saving changes, click the No button.)**

Word closes any open documents (in this case, the resume) and then the Word window closes.

More About

Job Searches

For links to Web sites about job searches, visit the Word 2003 More About Web page (scsite.com/wd2003/more) and then click one of the Job Searches links.

Project Summary

In creating the Okamoto Resume and Okamoto Cover Letter in this project, you learned how to use Word to enter and format a resume and cover letter. You learned how to use the Resume Wizard to create a resume. Then, you selected and replaced placeholder text in the document created by the resume. In personalizing the resume, you learned how to hide white space, enter a line break, and use Word's AutoFormat As You Type feature. This project also discussed how to view and print the resume in print preview.

Next, this project showed how to create a letterhead and then the cover letter. While creating the letterhead, you learned how to add color to characters, set custom tab stops, collect and paste between documents, add a border to a paragraph, and clear formatting. In the cover letter, this project showed how to insert a date, create and insert an AutoText entry, create and format a table, and enter a bulleted list. Finally, the project showed how to address and print an envelope, use smart tags, and modify the document summary.

 If you have a SAM user profile, you may have access to hands-on instruction, practice, and assessment of the skills covered in this project. Log in to your SAM account and go to your assignments page to see what your instructor has assigned.

What You Should Know

Having completed this project, you should be able to perform the tasks below. The tasks are listed in the same order they were presented in this project. For a list of the buttons, menus, toolbars, and commands introduced in this project, see the Quick Reference Summary at the back of this book and refer to the Page Number column.

1. Start and Customize Word   (WD 141)
2. Display Formatting Marks   (WD 141)
3. Create a Resume Using Word's Resume Wizard (WD 142)
4. Hide White Space   (WD 149)
5. Print the Resume Created by the Resume Wizard (WD 149)
6. Select and Replace Placeholder Text   (WD 152)
7. Select and Replace More Placeholder Text (WD 153)
8. Enter a Line Break   (WD 154)
9. Enter More Text with Line Breaks   (WD 155)
10. AutoFormat As You Type   (WD 156)
11. Enter the Remaining Sections of the Resume (WD 157)
12. Print Preview a Document   (WD 158)
13. Save a Document   (WD 159)
14. Open a New Document Window   (WD 160)
15. Change the Font Size   (WD 161, WD 162)
16. Color Text   (WD 161)
17. Insert a Graphic   (WD 162)
18. Resize a Graphic   (WD 162)
19. Set Custom Tab Stops Using the Tabs Dialog Box (WD 164)
20. Switch from One Open Document to Another (WD 166)
21. Copy Items to the Office Clipboard   (WD 166)
22. Display the Clipboard Task Pane   (WD 169)
23. Zoom Text Width   (WD 169)
24. Paste from the Office Clipboard   (WD 170)
25. Paste More Information from the Office Clipboard   (WD 171)

26. Zoom to 100% (WD 172)
27. Bottom Border a Paragraph (WD 172)
28. Clear Formatting (WD 173)
29. Convert a Hyperlink to Regular Text (WD 174)
30. Save the Letterhead (WD 174)
31. Save the Document with a New File Name (WD 176)
32. Set Custom Tab Stops Using the Ruler (WD 176)
33. Insert the Current Date in a Document (WD 177)
34. Enter the Inside Address and Salutation (WD 178)
35. Create an AutoText Entry (WD 179)
36. Insert a Nonbreaking Space (WD 180)
37. Insert an AutoText Entry (WD 181)
38. Enter a Paragraph (WD 182)

39. Insert an Empty Table (WD 183)
40. Enter Data in a Table (WD 184)
41. Fit Columns to Table Contents (WD 185)
42. Select a Table (WD 186)
43. Center a Selected Table (WD 187)
44. Add More Text (WD 187)
45. Bullet a List as You Type (WD 187)
46. Enter the Remainder of the Cover Letter (WD 189)
47. Save a Document Again (WD 189)
48. Print a Document (WD 190)
49. Address and Print an Envelope (WD 190)
50. Use the Smart Tag Actions Button (WD 192)
51. Modify the Document Summary (WD 193)
52. Display File Properties in the Open Dialog Box (WD 194)
53. Quit Word (WD 195)

More About

Certification

The Microsoft Office Specialist Certification program provides an opportunity for you to obtain a valuable industry credential - proof that you have the Word 2003 skills required by employers. For more information, see Appendix E or visit the Word 2003 Certification Web page (scsite.com/wd2003/cert).

More About

Quick Reference

For a table that lists how to complete the tasks covered in this book using the mouse, menu, shortcut menu, and keyboard, see the Quick Reference Summary at the back of this book, or visit the Word 2003 Quick Reference Web page (scsite.com/wd2003/qr).

Learn It Online

Instructions: To complete the Learn It Online exercises, start your browser, click the Address bar, and then enter the Web address scsite.com/wd2003/learn. When the Word 2003 Learn It Online page is displayed, follow the instructions in the exercises below. Each exercise has instructions for printing your results, either for your own records or for submission to your instructor.

1 Project Reinforcement TF, MC, and SA

Below Word Project 3, click the Project Reinforcement link. Print the quiz by clicking Print on the File menu for each page. Answer each question.

2 Flash Cards

Below Word Project 3, click the Flash Cards link and read the instructions. Type 20 (or a number specified by your instructor) in the Number of playing cards text box, type your name in the Enter your Name text box, and then click the Flip Card button. When the flash card is displayed, read the question and then click the ANSWER box arrow to select an answer. Flip through Flash Cards. If your score is 15 (75%) correct or greater, click Print on the File menu to print your results. If your score is less than 15 (75%) correct, then redo this exercise by clicking the Replay button.

3 Practice Test

Below Word Project 3, click the Practice Test link. Answer each question, enter your first and last name at the bottom of the page, and then click the Grade Test button. When the graded practice test is displayed on your screen, click Print on the File menu to print a hard copy. Continue to take practice tests until you score 80% or better.

4 Who Wants To Be a Computer Genius?

Below Word Project 3, click the Computer Genius link. Read the instructions, enter your first and last name at the bottom of the page, and then click the PLAY button. When your score is displayed, click the PRINT RESULTS link to print a hard copy.

5 Wheel of Terms

Below Word Project 3, click the Wheel of Terms link. Read the instructions, and then enter your first and last name and your school name. Click the PLAY button. When your score is displayed, right-click the score and then click Print on the shortcut menu to print a hard copy.

6 Crossword Puzzle Challenge

Below Word Project 3, click the Crossword Puzzle Challenge link. Read the instructions, and then enter your first and last name. Click the SUBMIT button. Work the crossword puzzle. When you are finished, click the Submit button. When the crossword puzzle is redisplayed, click the Print Puzzle button to print a hard copy.

7 Tips and Tricks

Below Word Project 3, click the Tips and Tricks link. Click a topic that pertains to Project 3. Right-click the information and then click Print on the shortcut menu. Construct a brief example of what the information relates to in Word to confirm you understand how to use the tip or trick.

8 Newsgroups

Below Word Project 3, click the Newsgroups link. Click a topic that pertains to Project 3. Print three comments.

9 Expanding Your Horizons

Below Word Project 3, click the Expanding Your Horizons link. Click a topic that pertains to Project 3. Print the information. Construct a brief example of what the information relates to in Word to confirm you understand the contents of the article.

10 Search Sleuth

Below Word Project 3, click the Search Sleuth link. To search for a term that pertains to this project, select a term below the Project 3 title and then use the Google search engine at google.com (or any major search engine) to display and print two Web pages that present information on the term.

11 Word Online Training

Below Word Project 3, click the Word Online Training link. When your browser displays the Microsoft Office Online Web page, click the Word link. Click one of the Word courses that covers one or more of the objectives listed at the beginning of the project on page WD 138. Print the first page of the course before stepping through it.

12 Office Marketplace

Below Word Project 3, click the Office Marketplace link. When your browser displays the Microsoft Office Online Web page, click the Office Marketplace link. Click a topic that relates to Word. Print the first page.

Apply Your Knowledge

1 Working with Tabs and a Table

Instructions: Start Word. Open the document, Apply 3-1 Expenses Table, on the Data Disk. See the inside back cover of this book for instructions for downloading the Data Disk or see your instructor for information about accessing the files in this book.

The document is a Word table that you are to edit and format. The revised table is shown in Figure 3-88.

Perform the following tasks:

1. In the line containing the table title, Personal Expenses Table, remove the tab stop at the 1" mark on the ruler.

2. Set a centered tab at the 3" mark on the ruler.

3. Bold the characters in the title. Change their color to dark red.

4. Add a new row to the bottom of the table. In the first cell of the new row, type `Total` as the entry.

Personal Expenses Table

	January	February	March	April
Rent	425.00	425.00	425.00	425.00
Utilities	130.92	126.33	99.12	96.54
Entertainment	88.95	75.50	91.17	101.49
Telephone	33.24	36.22	35.67	34.80
Cable/Internet	62.19	62.19	62.19	62.19
Car Payment	205.14	205.14	205.14	205.14
Total	**945.44**	**930.38**	**918.29**	**925.16**

FIGURE 3-88

5. Delete the row containing the Miscellaneous expenses.

6. Insert a column between the February and April columns. Fill in the column as follows: Column Title – March; Rent – 425.00; Utilities – 99.12; Entertainment – 91.17; Telephone – 35.67; Cable/Internet – 62.19; Car Payment – 205.14.

7. Click the Tables and Borders button on the Standard toolbar to display the Tables and Borders toolbar. If necessary, click the Draw Table button on the Tables and Borders toolbar to deselect the button. Position the insertion point in the January Total cell (second column, last row). Click the AutoSum button on the Tables and Borders toolbar to sum the contents of the column. Repeat for February, March, and April totals. Click the Tables and Borders button on the Standard toolbar to remove the Tables and Borders toolbar from the screen. Leave the screen in print layout view.

8. Right-align all cells containing numbers.

9. Apply the Table Contemporary style to the table. *Hint:* You may need to click the Show box arrow in the Styles and Formatting task pane and then click All styles to display all available styles.

10. Make all columns as wide as their contents (AutoFit to Contents).

11. Center the table between the left and right margins of the page.

12. Change the color of the table contents to dark blue.

13. Bold the last row of the table, which contains the totals.

14. Click File on the menu bar and then click Save As. Save the document using the file name, Apply 3-1 Modified Expenses Table.

15. Print the revised table.

In the Lab

1 Using Word's Resume Wizard to Create a Resume

Problem: You are a student at Midway University expecting to receive your Bachelor of Arts degree in Technical Writing this May. As graduation is approaching quickly, you prepare the resume shown in Figure 3-89 using Word's Resume Wizard.

Instructions:

1. Use the Resume Wizard to create a Professional style resume. Use your own name and address information when the Resume Wizard requests it.
2. Hide white space on the screen. Personalize the resume as shown in Figure 3-89. When entering multiple lines in the areas of concentration, awards received, interests and activities, and languages sections, be sure to enter a line break at the end of each line, instead of a paragraph break.
3. Check the spelling of the resume.
4. Save the resume with Lab 3-1 Malone Resume as the file name.
5. View and print the resume from within print preview.

2 Creating a Cover Letter with a Table

Problem: You prepared the resume shown in Figure 3-89 and now are ready to create a cover letter to send to a prospective employer (Figure 3-90 on the next page).

Instructions:

1. Create the letterhead shown at the top of Figure 3-90. If you completed In the Lab 1, use the Office Clipboard to copy and paste the address information from the resume to the letterhead. Save the letterhead with the file name, Lab 3-2 Malone Letterhead.

	1225 Schilton Court Chicago, IL 60602	Phone (312) 555-6380 Fax (312) 555-6391 E-mail malone@earthnet.com

Leah A. Malone

Objective	To obtain a full-time editorial position with a publishing company in the Chicago area.
Education	2001-2005 Midway University Chicago, IL **Technical Writing** ▪ B.A., May 2005 ▪ A.A., May 2003
Areas of concentration	Technical Publications Journalism Research Writing and Techniques Information Technology
Awards received	Dean's List, 2002-2005 Excellence in Student Publications Award, 1st Place, 2004-2005 Alpha Omega Honors Society, 2003-2005
Interests and activities	Reading Buddy program, participant Technical Buzz, contributor Regional Writers Association, member Literacy Council, member
Languages	English (fluent) Spanish (fluent)
Work experience	2001-2005 Midway Community Center Chicago, IL **Assistant Program Coordinator** ▪ Assisted with developing programs aimed at increasing literacy and reading skills ▪ Conducted reading programs aimed at children, adults, and seniors, as well as new readers ▪ Composed, proofread, and edited the center's monthly newsletter advertising new offerings and services
Volunteer experience	Participant in Midway Library's Reading Buddy program, in which adults read to school-aged children on a weekly basis.

FIGURE 3-89

(continued)

In the Lab

Creating a Cover Letter with a Table *(continued)*

2. Create the letter shown in Figure 3-90. Set a tab stop at the 3.5" mark on the ruler for the date line, complimentary close, and signature block. Insert the current date. After entering the inside address, create an AutoText entry for Greyton Publications, and insert the AutoText entry whenever you have to enter the company name. Remove the hyperlink format from the e-mail address. Insert and center the table.

3. Modify the document summary as follows: Title – Greyton Publications; Subject – Cover Letter; Category – Cover Letter; Keywords – cover letter, Greyton Publications; Comments – Cover letter to Mr. Roger Grandy at Greyton Publications.

4. Check the spelling. Save the letter with Lab 3-2 Malone Cover Letter as the file name.

5. View and print the cover letter from within print preview.

6. View the document summary. On the printout, write down the edited time.

7. Address and print an envelope and a mailing label using the inside and return addresses in the cover letter.

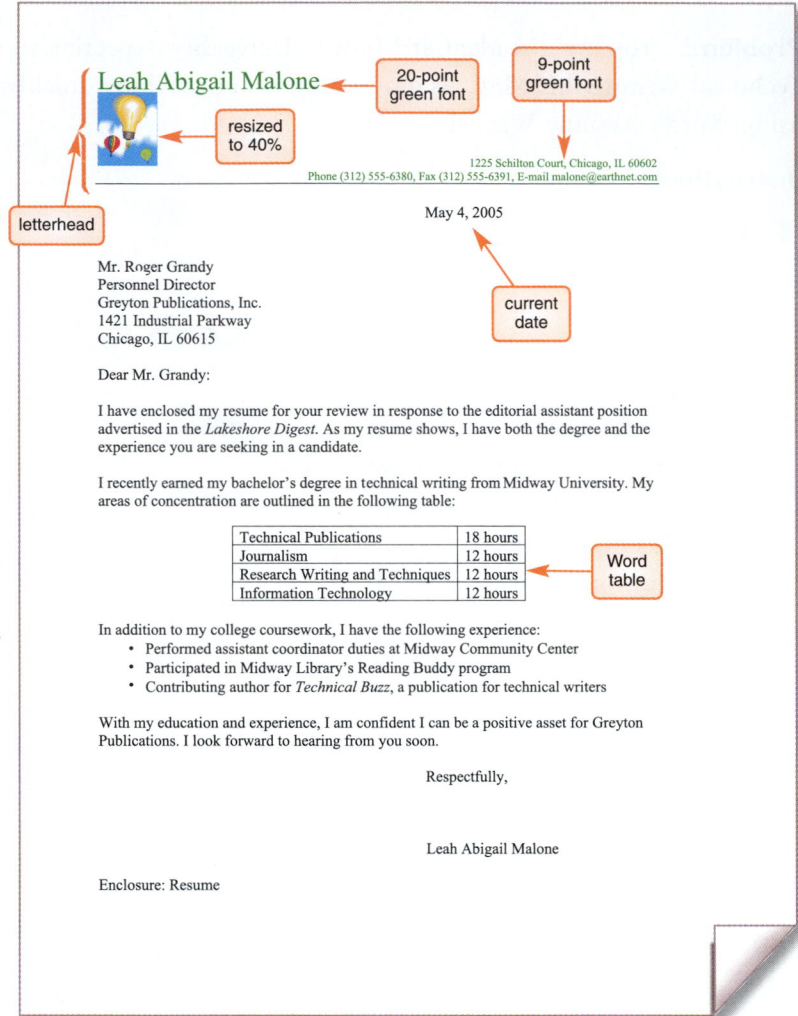

FIGURE 3-90

3 Creating a Resume and Cover Letter

Problem: You are to create a personal resume and cover letter. Assume you are graduating this semester.

Instructions:

1. Use the Resume Wizard to create a personal resume using whichever style you desire. Try to be as accurate as possible when personalizing the resume. Check spelling and grammar in the resume.

2. Obtain a copy of last Sunday's newspaper. Look through the classified section and cut out a want ad in an area of your major. Create a cover letter for your resume, gearing the letter to the job advertised in the newspaper. Use the job advertisement information for the inside address and your personal information for the return address. After setting tabs at the 3.5" mark, change them to the 3" mark. Include a table and a numbered list in the cover letter. *Hint:* Use Help to learn how to create a numbered list.

3. Address and print an envelope. Then, print an entire page of mailing labels using your home address. Submit the want ad with your cover letter, resume, envelope, and mailing labels.

Cases and Places

The difficulty of these case studies varies:
■ are the least difficult and ■■ are more difficult. The last exercise is a group exercise.

1 ■ Your boss has asked you to create a calendar for June so he can post it on the office bulletin board. Use the Calendar Wizard in the Other Documents sheet in the Templates dialog box. Use the following settings in the wizard: Boxes & borders style, portrait print direction, leave room for a picture, June 2005 for both the start and end date. With the calendar on the screen, click the current graphic and delete it. Insert a clip art image of a sailboat graphic (he loves to sail) and then resize the image so it fits in the entire space for the graphic.

2 ■ You have been asked to prepare the agenda for an insurance benefits meeting. Use the Agenda Wizard in the Other Documents sheet in the Templates dialog box. Use the following settings in the wizard: style – standard; meeting date – September 15, 2005; meeting time – 8:00 a.m. to 10:15 a.m.; title – Insurance Benefits Meeting; meeting location – Conference Room G; include Type of meeting and Special notes headings; include these names on agenda – Meeting called by and Attendees; Topics, People, and Minutes – Introduction, Keith Brazil, 10; New information system, Kelly Walters, 60; Benefits update, Sharon Gonzalez, 20; Break, 15; Updated claim forms, Bryant Jenkins, 30; do not add a form for recording the minutes. On the agenda created by the wizard, add the following names in the appropriate spaces: Marsha Goldfarb, Employee Insurance and Benefits director called the meeting; all people listed in this assignment will be attending – along with T. Ryan, D. Bleuer, M. Kiddle, and you. The meeting is an informational meeting. As a special note, remind attendees to bring paper and pen to the meeting.

3 ■ A customer has asked you to fax information about a rental home in Panama City, Florida so he can review it for an upcoming vacation. Use the Fax Wizard and the following settings: create the fax cover sheet with a note and print the fax so you can send it on a separate fax machine. It must be faxed to Terrell Bryce. His fax number is (317) 555-2202 and his telephone number is (317) 555-2214. You will fax him a total of four pages of information using the subject of Vacation home rental inquiry. In the fax notes, write a message informing Terrell that the following pages contain the information he requested on the rental home in Panama City, Florida, and that he should let you know if you can help with any other part of his vacation planning. Use your own name, address, and telephone information in the fax and use whichever fax style you like best.

4 ■■ As director of employee insurance and benefits, you are responsible for keeping all Employee Insurance and Benefits staff members informed of changes in procedures or policies. You will be scheduling a meeting on Thursday, September 15, at 8:30 a.m. in Conference Room G to discuss the new information system, along with new claim forms and benefits. It is important all staff members attend. If they will be on vacation or are unavailable, they need to contact you to arrange to receive the informational packet that will be distributed at the meeting. You prepare a memorandum about the meeting. A copy of the memo should be sent to Marsha Goldfarb. Use the Memo Wizard or a memo template, together with the concepts and techniques presented in this project, to create and format the interoffice memorandum.

Cases and Places

5 ■■ **Working Together**   The office of career development at your school is looking for a team of students to create a sample resume to be used as a reference for other students in your major. The department also would like you to submit a list of resume-writing tips they could share with other students. Each member of your team is to identify a minimum of five resume-writing tips by searching the Web, visiting a library, and/or talking to an expert in the area of human resources. Then, the team should meet as a group to create a numbered list of resume-writing tips. Next, all team members are to look through the headings available in the Resume Wizard and select the ones best suited to students in your major, adding any not included in the wizard. Then, the members should divide up the headings among the team. After each team member writes his or her section(s) of the resume, the group should meet to copy and paste the individual sections into a single resume. Finally, write a memo indicating the work the team has completed. Use the concepts and techniques presented in this project to format the memo, resume-writing tips, and resume.

MICROSOFT
Office Word 2003

Creating Web Pages Using Word

CASE PERSPECTIVE

In Project 3, Benjamin Kane Okamoto created his resume with your assistance (Figure 3-1 on page WD 139). Recently, Benjamin has been surfing the Internet and has discovered that many people have their own personal Web pages. Their Web pages contain links to other Web sites and also to personal Web pages such as resumes and schedules. These personal Web pages are very impressive.

To make himself more marketable to a potential employer, Benjamin has asked you to help him create a personal Web page. He wants his Web page to contain a hyperlink to his resume – with the hyperlink on the left side of the page and his resume on the right side of the page. On the left side of the Web page, Benjamin would like another hyperlink called My Favorite Site. When a Web site visitor clicks this link, Benjamin's favorite Web site (www.scsite.com) will be displayed on the right side of his personal Web page. Finally, Benjamin wants the e-mail address on his resume Web page to be a hyperlink to an e-mail program. This way, potential employers easily can send him an e-mail message to schedule an interview or request additional information. You show Benjamin how to save his resume as a Web page and incorporate frames and hyperlinks into a Web page.

As you read through this Web Feature, you will learn how to use Word to create a Web page. If you are stepping through this feature on a computer, you will need the resume document created in Project 3. (If you did not create the resume, see your instructor for a copy of it.)

Objectives

You will have mastered the material in this feature when you can:

- Save a Word document as a Web page
- Format and preview a Web page
- Create and modify a frames page
- Insert and modify hyperlinks

Introduction

Word provides two techniques for creating Web pages. If you have an existing Word document, you can save it as a Web page. If you do not have an existing Word document, you can use Word to create a Web page from scratch. Word has many Web page authoring tools that allow you to incorporate objects such as frames, hyperlinks, sounds, videos, pictures, scrolling text, bullets, horizontal lines, check boxes, option buttons, list boxes, text boxes, and scripts on Web pages.

This Web Feature illustrates how to save the resume created in Project 3 as a Web page. Then, it uses Word to create another Web page that contains two frames (Figure 1a on the next page). A **frame** is a rectangular section of a Web page that can display another separate Web page. Thus, a Web page with multiple frames can display multiple Web pages simultaneously. Word stores all frames associated with a Web page in a single file called the **frames page**. When you open the frames page in Word or a Web browser, all frames associated with the Web page are displayed on the screen.

In this Web Feature, the file name of the frames page is Okamoto Personal Web Page. When you initially open this frames page, the left frame contains the title, Benjamin Okamoto, and two hyperlinks — My Resume and My Favorite Site; the right frame displays Benjamin's resume (Figure 1a). As discussed in Project 3, a hyperlink is a shortcut that allows a user to jump easily and quickly to another location in the same document or to other documents or Web pages. In the left frame, the My Resume hyperlink is a link to the resume Web page, and the My Favorite Site hyperlink is a link to www.scsite.com.

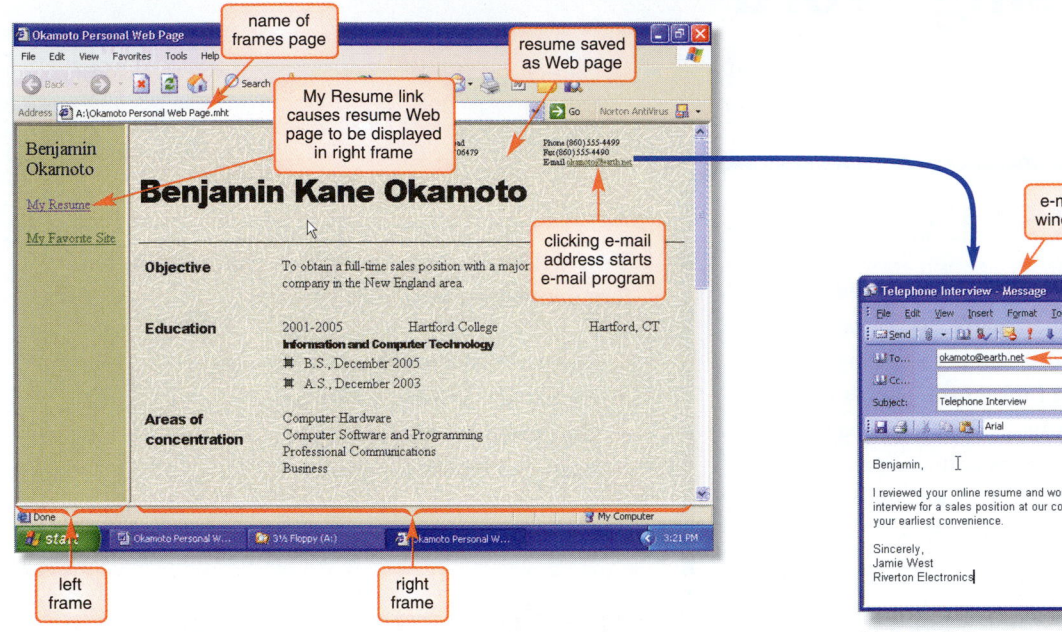

(a) Web Page Displaying Resume

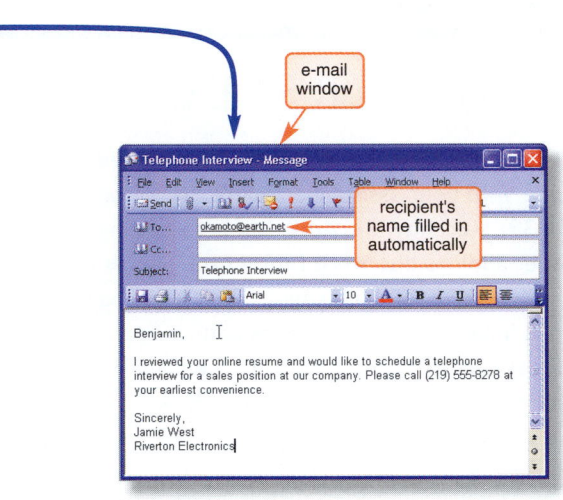

(c) E-Mail Program

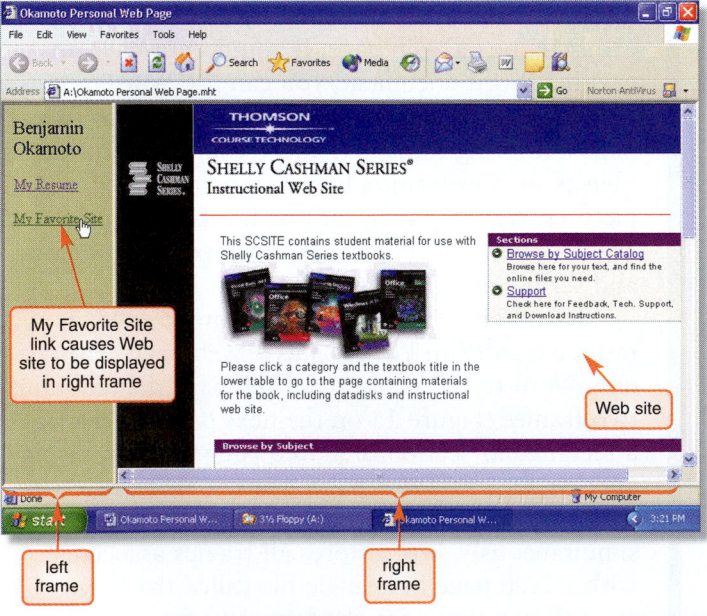

(b) Web Page Displaying Web Site

FIGURE 1

When you click the My Favorite Site hyperlink in the left frame, the www.scsite.com Web site is displayed in the right frame (Figure 1b). When you click the My Resume hyperlink in the left frame, the resume Web page is displayed in the right frame. The resume itself contains a hyperlink to an e-mail address. When you click the e-mail address, Word starts your e-mail program automatically with the recipient's address (okamoto@earth.net) already filled in (Figure 1c). You simply type a subject and message and then click the Send button, which places the message in the Outbox or sends it if you are connected to an e-mail server.

Once you have created Web pages, you can publish them. **Publishing** is the process of making Web pages available to others, for example on the World Wide Web or on a company's intranet. In Word, you can publish Web pages by saving them to a Web folder or to an FTP location. The procedures for publishing Web pages in Microsoft Office are discussed in Appendix C.

This Web Feature is for instructional purposes. Thus, you create and save your frames page and associated Web pages to a floppy disk rather than to the Web.

Saving a Word Document as a Web Page

Once you have created a Word document, you can save it as a Web page so that it can be published and then viewed by a Web browser, such as Internet Explorer. The following steps show how to save the resume created in Project 3 as a Web page.

To Save a Word Document as a Web Page

1

• **Start Word and then open the file named Okamoto Resume created in Project 3. Click File on the menu bar (Figure 2).**

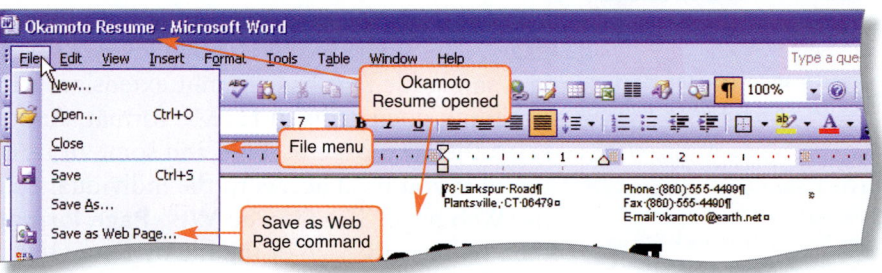

FIGURE 2

2

• **Click Save as Web Page on the File menu.**

• **When Word displays the Save As dialog box, type** Okamoto Resume Web Page **in the File name text box and then, if necessary, change the Save in location to 3½ Floppy (A:).**

• **Click the Change Title button.**

• **When Word displays the Set Page Title dialog box, type** Okamoto Resume Web Page **in the Page title text box (Figure 3).**

When the Web page is displayed in a browser, it will show the text, Okamoto Resume Web Page, on the title bar.

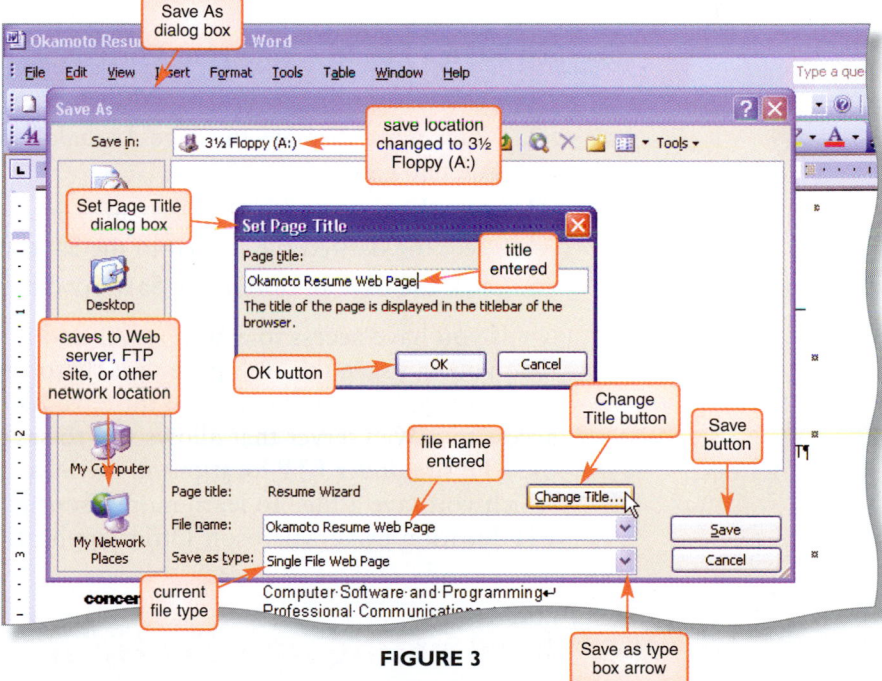

FIGURE 3

3

• **Click the OK button in the Set Page Title dialog box.**

• **Click the Save button in the Save As dialog box.**

Word saves the resume as a Web page and displays it in the Word window (Figure 4).

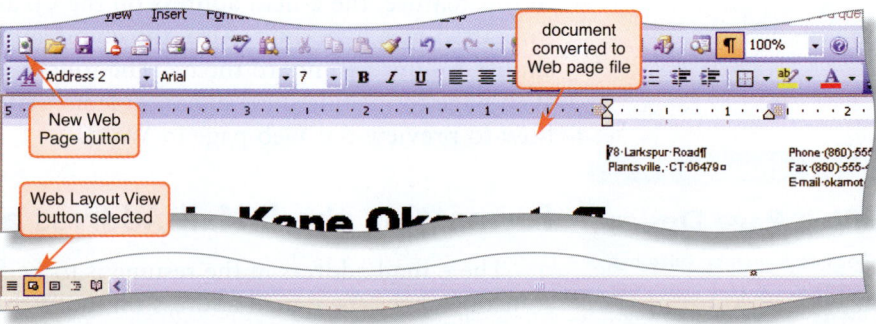

FIGURE 4

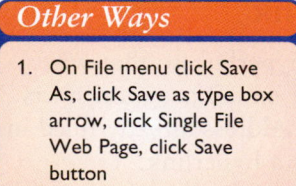

Other Ways

1. On File menu click Save As, click Save as type box arrow, click Single File Web Page, click Save button

Word switches to Web layout view and also changes some of the toolbar buttons and menu commands to provide Web page authoring features. For example, the Standard toolbar now displays a New Web Page button (Figure 4 on the previous page). The Web Layout View button on the horizontal scroll bar is selected.

The resume is displayed in the Word window much like it will be displayed in a Web browser. Some of Word's formatting features are not supported by Web pages. Thus, your Web page may look slightly different from the original Word document.

When you save a file as a Web page, Word converts the contents of the document into **HTML** (hypertext markup language), which is a language that browsers can interpret. The Save as Web Page command, by default, saves the document in a format called single file Web page (shown in Figure 3 on the previous page). The **single file Web page format** saves all of the components of the Web page in a single file that has an .mht extension. This format is particularly useful for e-mailing documents in HTML format. Another format, called **Web Page format**, saves the Web page in a file and some of its components in a folder. This format is useful if you need access to the individual components, such as images, that make up the Web page. The **filtered Web Page format** saves the file in Web page format and then reduces the size of the file by removing specific Microsoft Office formats.

If you wanted to save a file using the Web Page format or the filtered Web page format, or any other type of format, you would follow these steps.

To Save a File in a Different Format

1. Click File on the menu bar and then click Save As.
2. When Word displays the Save As dialog box, type the desired file name in the File name box.
3. Click the Save as type box arrow.
4. Select the desired file format in the Save as type list.
5. Click the Save button in the Save As dialog box.

If you have access to a Web server and it allows you to save files to a Web folder, then you can save the Web page directly to the Web server by clicking My Network Places in the lower-left corner of the Save As dialog box (Figure 3). If you have access to a Web server that allows you to save to an FTP site, then you can select the FTP site under FTP locations in the Save in box just as you select any folder to which you save a file. To learn more about publishing Web pages to a Web folder or FTP location using Microsoft Office applications, refer to Appendix C.

Formatting and Previewing a Web Page

In this feature, the e-mail address on the Okamoto Resume Web page is to be formatted as a hyperlink. Also, the colors and formats of elements on the Web page should follow a standard theme. The following sections describe how to modify the Web page to include these enhancements. After modifying the Web page, you will see how to preview the Web page in Word.

Formatting the E-Mail Address as a Hyperlink

The e-mail address in the resume is to be formatted as a hyperlink so that when someone clicks the e-mail address on the Web page, his or her e-mail program starts automatically and displays an e-mail window with the e-mail address already filled in.

The next steps show how to format the e-mail address as a hyperlink.

More About

HTML

If you wish to view the HTML source code associated with a Web page, click View on the menu bar and then click HTML Source, which starts the Script Editor. To close the Script Editor, click File on the menu bar and then click Exit.

More About

Web Page Design

For information on guidelines for designing Web pages, visit the Word 2003 More About Web page (scsite.com/wd2003/more) and then click Web Page Design.

To Format Text as a Hyperlink

1

• Select the e-mail address (okamoto@earth.net) and then right-click the selected text (Figure 5).

2

• Click **Hyperlink** on the shortcut menu.

• When Word displays the Insert Hyperlink dialog box, click **E-mail Address** in the Link to bar.

• In the Text to display text box, type **okamoto@earth.net** and then click the E-mail address text box.

• Type **okamoto@earth.net** in the E-mail address text box.

As soon as you begin typing the e-mail address, Word inserts mailto: in front of the address, which connects the hyperlink to your e-mail program (Figure 6). The text in the Text to display text box will be displayed as the hyperlink text on the screen.

3

• Click the **OK** button.

Word formats the e-mail address as a hyperlink; that is, it is colored blue and underlined (shown in Figure 7 on the next page).

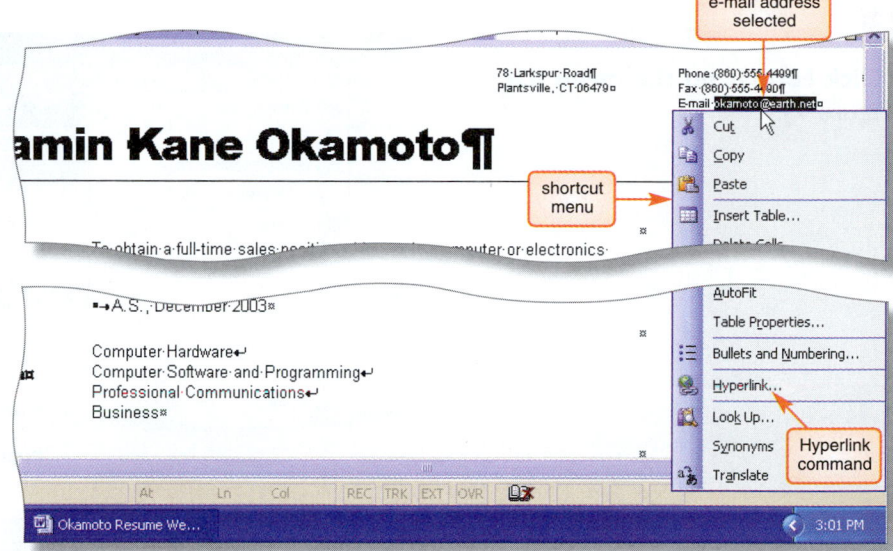

FIGURE 5

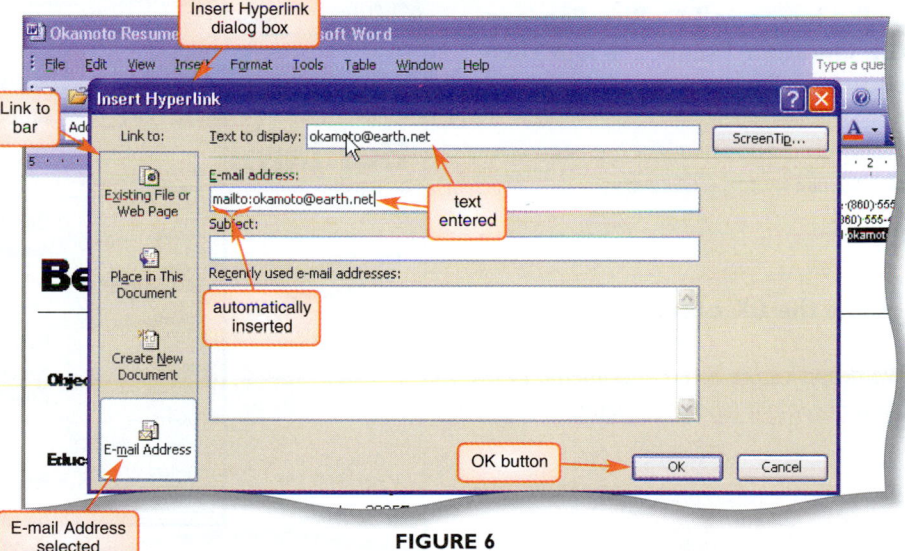

FIGURE 6

Other Ways

1. Click Insert Hyperlink button on Standard toolbar
2. On Insert menu click Hyperlink
3. Press CTRL+K
4. In Voice Command mode, say "Insert, Hyperlink"

If you want to test the e-mail address hyperlink, CTRL+click the mouse while pointing to the hyperlink. This should open an e-mail window.

To edit a hyperlink, right-click the hyperlink and then click Edit Hyperlink on the shortcut menu.

Applying a Theme to the Web Page

The next step is to apply a theme to the Web page. A **theme** is a predefined set of colors, fonts, and other design elements for backgrounds, graphics, headings, lists, lines, hyperlinks, and tables. By using themes, you easily can make Web pages and other online documents consistent with one another.

The steps on the next page show how to apply a theme to the Okamoto Resume Web Page document.

To Apply a Theme

1

• **Click Format on the menu bar (Figure 7).**

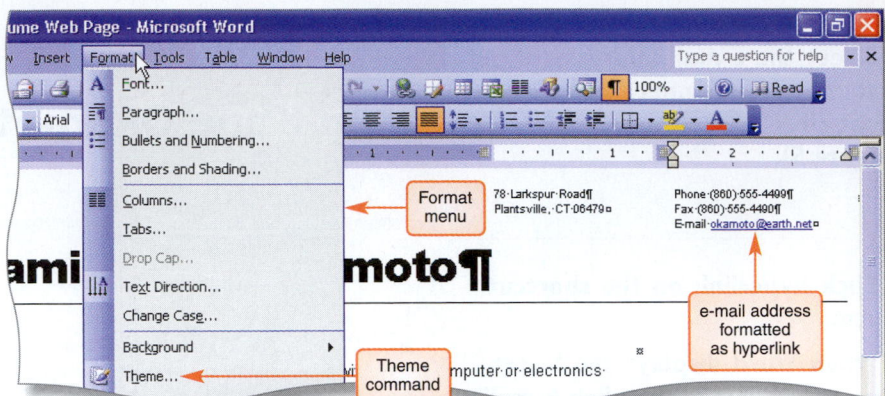

FIGURE 7

2

• **Click Theme on the Format menu.**

• **When Word displays the Theme dialog box, scroll to Rice Paper in the Choose a Theme list and then click Rice Paper.**

Word presents a variety of themes in the Theme dialog box (Figure 8).

3

• **Click the OK button.**

Word applies the Rice Paper theme to the open document (shown in Figure 9).

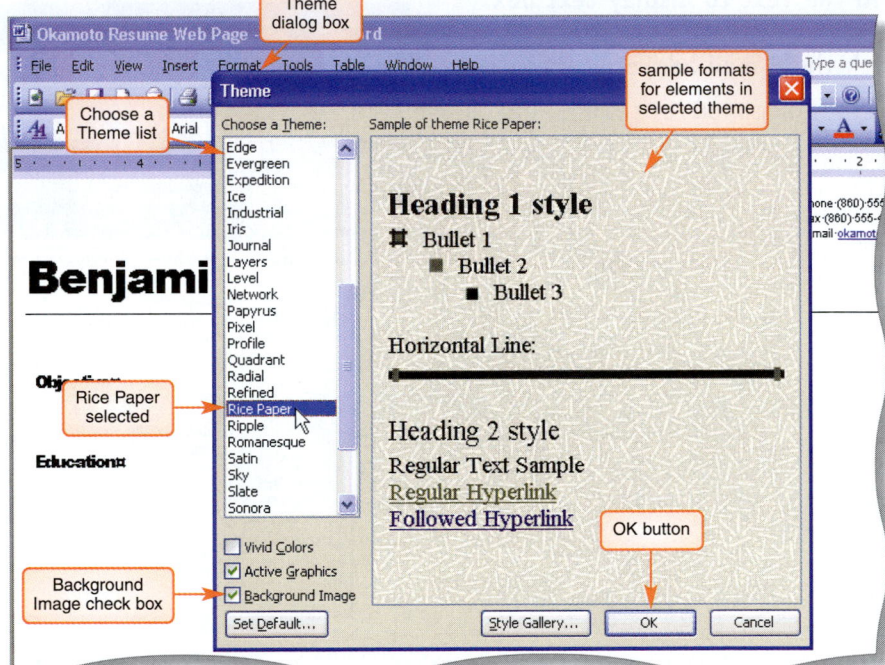

FIGURE 8

Other Ways

1. In Voice Command mode, say "Format, Theme"

If you like all elements except for the background in a theme, remove the check mark from the Background Image check box in the Theme dialog box (Figure 8) before clicking the OK button.

Viewing the Web Page in Your Default Browser

In Word, you can see how a Web page looks in your default browser – before publishing it and without actually connecting to the Internet. To do this, use the Web Page Preview command, which displays on the File menu when Word is in Web layout view. The next steps show how to preview a Web page in Word.

To Preview a Web Page

1

• **Click File on the menu bar (Figure 9).**

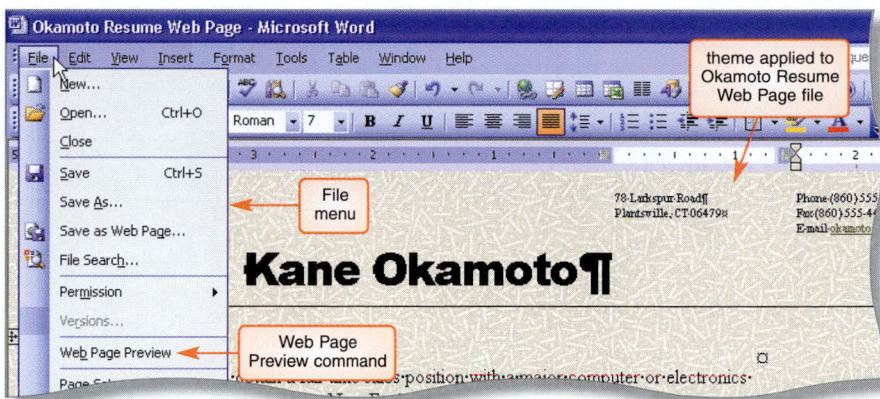

FIGURE 9

2

• **Click Web Page Preview on the File menu.**

• **If necessary, maximize the browser window.**

Word opens the Web browser in a separate window and displays the open Web page file in the browser window (Figure 10).

3

• **Click the Close button on the browser title bar to close the browser window.**

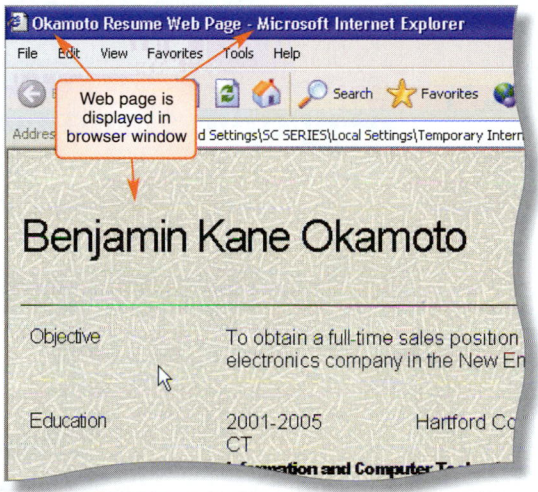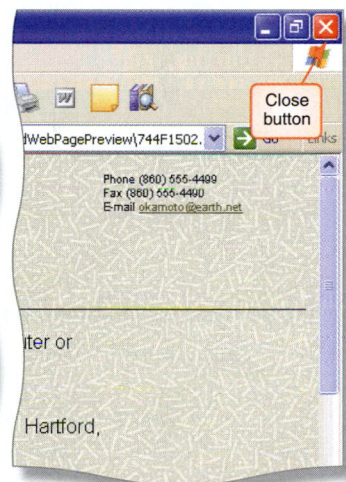

FIGURE 10

Other Ways

1. In Windows Explorer, double-click Web page file name
2. In Voice Command mode, say "File, Web Page Preview"

You now are finished modifying the Okamoto Resume Web Page file. The following step describes saving the file again.

To Save a Web Page

1 **Click the Save button on the Standard toolbar.**

Word saves the file.

Creating and Modifying a Frames Page

In the previous section, you saved an existing Word document as a Web page. Next, you want to create the frames page that will be divided into two separate frames. The left frame is to contain two links: one to the Okamoto Resume Web Page file just created and one to www.scsite.com.

The following steps show how to create a frames page and then add a frame so the frames page contains two frames side-by-side.

To Create a Frames Page

1

- **Click Format on the menu bar and then point to Frames (Figure 11).**

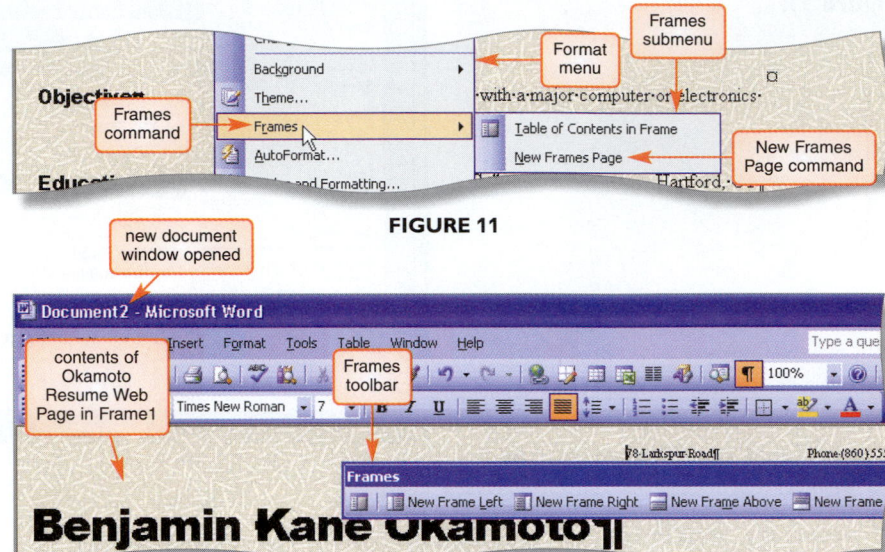

FIGURE 11

2

- **Click New Frames Page on the Frames submenu.**

Word opens a new document window that contains the Okamoto Resume Web Page in the current frame (called Frame1) and displays the Frames toolbar on the screen (Figure 12).

FIGURE 12

3

- **Click the New Frame Left button on the Frames toolbar.**

Word opens a new frame to the left of the current frame (Figure 13). The new frame is called Frame2.

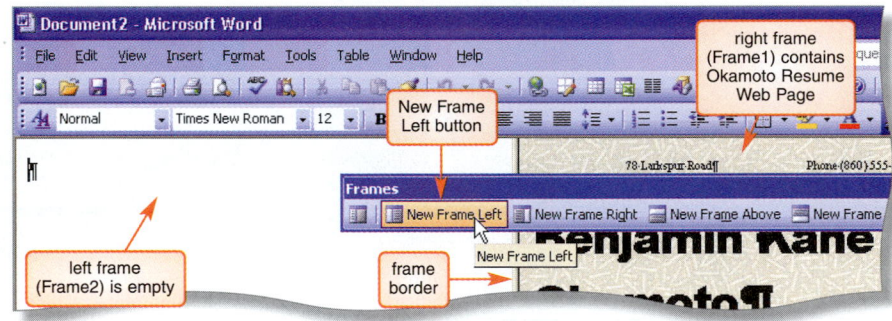

FIGURE 13

> ***More About***
>
> **Web Pages**
>
> You can use horizontal lines to separate sections of a Web page. To add a horizontal line at the location of the insertion point, click Format on the menu bar, click Borders and Shading, click the Horizontal Line button, click the desired line type in the Horizontal Line dialog box, and then click the OK button.

The frames page is divided into two frames, one on the left and one on the right. A **frame border** separates the frames. The next step is to add text to the left frame, as described below.

To Add Text to a Frame

1. **With the insertion point in the left frame (Frame2), click the Font Size box arrow. Click 16 in the Font Size list. Type** `Benjamin Okamoto` **and then click the Font Size box arrow. Click 12 in the Font Size list. Press the ENTER key twice.**
2. **Type** `My Resume` **and then press the ENTER key twice.**
3. **Type** `My Favorite Site` **as the last entry in the left frame.**

Word displays the text in the left frame (shown in Figure 14).

The next step is to make the left frame narrower. To do this, you drag the frame border. When you point to and drag the frame border, the mouse pointer shape changes to a double-headed arrow. The following step shows how to resize a Web page frame.

To Resize a Web Page Frame

1

• **Drag the frame border to the left until it is positioned between the letters a and m in Okamoto in the left frame (Figure 14).**

Word narrows the left frame and widens the right frame (shown in Figure 15).

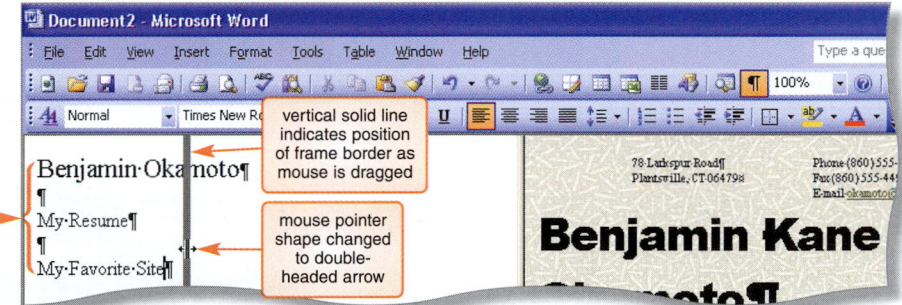

FIGURE 14

In this feature the left frame uses the Rice Paper theme, except it does not contain a background image. The following steps describe how to apply a theme, without a background image.

To Apply a Theme

1 **With the insertion point in the left frame, click Format on the menu bar and then click Theme.**

2 **When the Theme dialog box is displayed, scroll to and then click Rice Paper in the Choose a Theme list.**

3 **Place a check mark in the Vivid Colors check box.**

4 **Remove the check mark from the Background Image check box (Figure 15).**

5 **Click the OK button.**

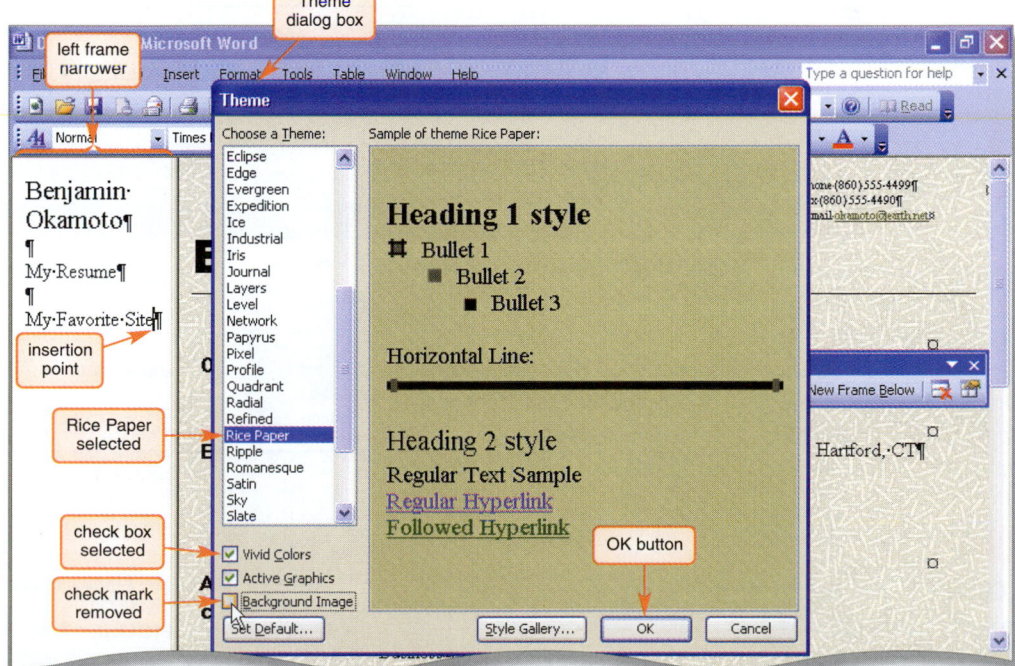

FIGURE 15

Word applies the Rice Paper theme, without a background image (shown in Figure 16 on the next page).

In the left frame, you want the text, My Resume, to be a hyperlink to the Okamoto Resume Web Page document. This means when you click the My Resume link in the left frame, the Okamoto Resume Web Page file will be displayed in the right frame. Similarly, you want the My Favorite site text to be a hyperlink. That is, when you click the hyperlink in the left frame, the www.scsite.com Web site should be displayed in the right frame.

The following steps describe how to link the My Resume text in the left frame to an existing Web Page file that will be displayed in the right frame (Frame1) when the user clicks the My Resume link in the left frame (Frame2).

To Insert and Modify a Hyperlink

1

• **Drag through the text, My Resume, in the left frame to select it.**

• **Click the Insert Hyperlink button on the Standard toolbar.**

• **When Word displays the Insert Hyperlink dialog box, if necessary, click Existing File or Web Page in the Link to bar.**

• **If necessary, click the Look in box arrow and then click 3½ Floppy (A:).**

• **Click Okamoto Resume Web Page.**

Word displays the Okamoto Resume Web Page file name in the Address box (Figure 16).

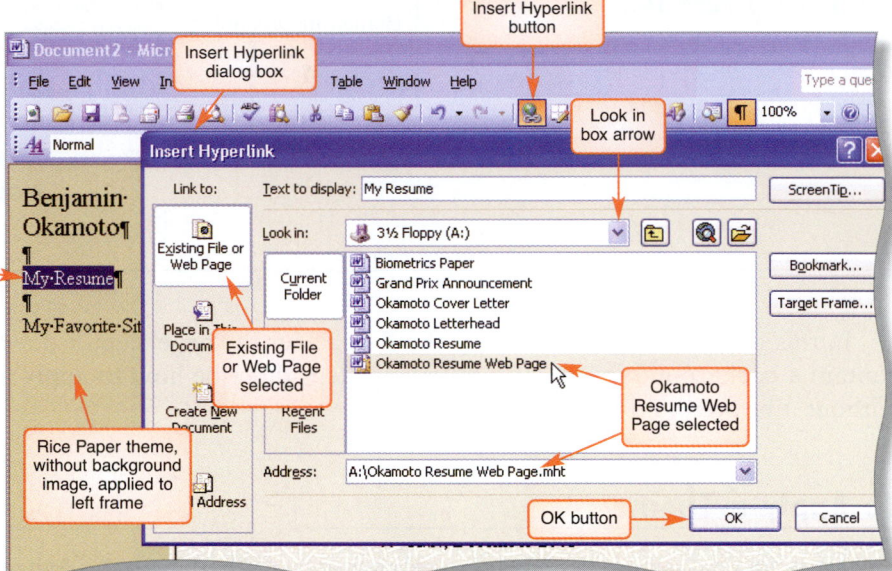

FIGURE 16

2

• **Click the Target Frame button.**

• **When Word displays the Set Target Frame dialog box, click the right frame in the Current frames page diagram.**

The Set Target Frame dialog box displays a diagram of the left and right frames in the frames page (Figure 17).

3

• **Click the OK button in the Set Target Frame dialog box.**

• **Click the OK button in the Insert Hyperlink dialog box.**

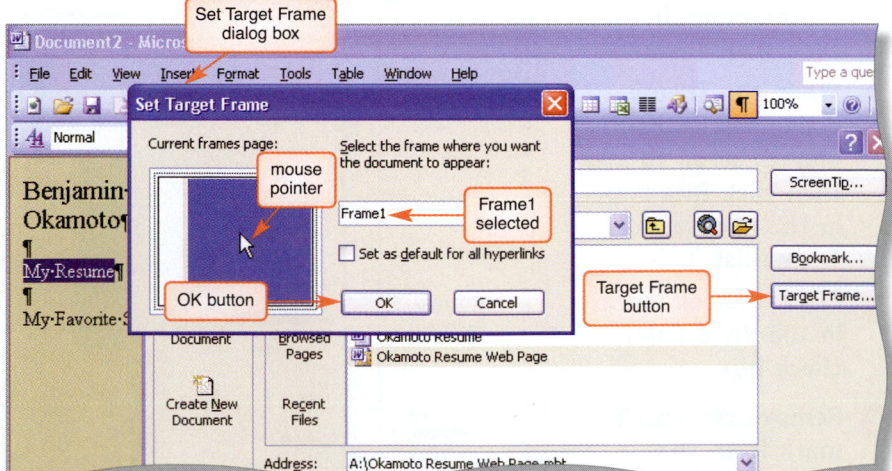

FIGURE 17

Word formats the selected text as a hyperlink (shown in Figure 18). When you click the My Resume link in the left frame, the Okamoto Resume Web Page file will be displayed in the right frame.

The following steps describe how to link the My Favorite Site text in the left frame to a Web site that will be displayed in the right frame.

To Insert and Modify a Hyperlink

1 Drag through the text, My Favorite Site, in the left frame.

2 Click the Insert Hyperlink button on the Standard toolbar.

3 When Word displays the Insert Hyperlink dialog box, if necessary, click Existing File or Web Page in the Link to bar. Type `www.scsite.com` in the Address text box.

4 Click the Target Frame button. When Word displays the Set Target Frame dialog box, click the right frame in the diagram (Figure 18).

5 Click the OK button in each dialog box.

Word formats the text, My Favorite Site, as a hyperlink that, when clicked, displays the associated Web site in the right frame (shown in Figure 1b on page WD 204).

(shown in Figure 1b on page WD 204).

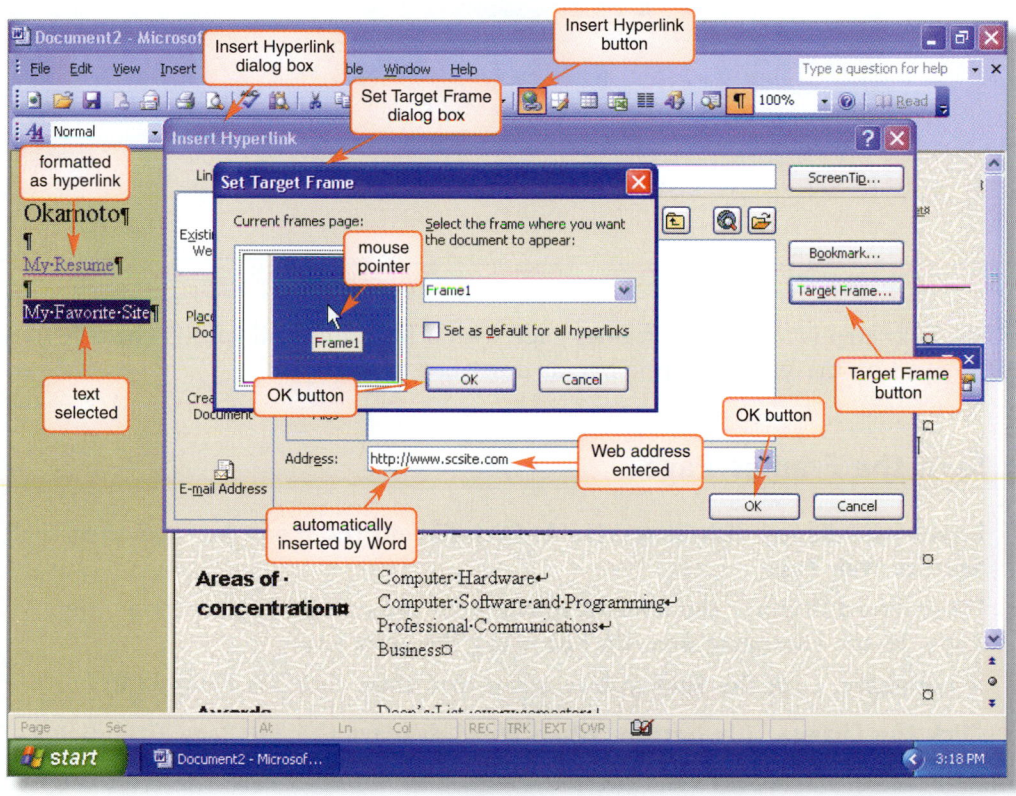

FIGURE 18

If you wanted to edit an existing hyperlink, you right-click the hyperlink text and then click Edit Hyperlink on the shortcut menu. Word will display the Edit Hyperlink dialog box instead of the Insert Hyperlink dialog box. Other than the title bar, these two dialog boxes are the same.

The next task is to modify the frame properties of the left frame so it does not display a scroll bar between the left and right frames, as shown on the next page.

as shown on the next page.

Other Ways

1. Right-click selected text, click Hyperlink on short-cut menu
2. With text selected, click Hyperlink on Insert menu
3. With text selected, press CTRL+K
4. In Voice Command mode, say "Insert, Hyperlink"

More About

Quick Reference

For a table that lists how to complete the tasks covered in this book using the mouse, menu, shortcut menu, and keyboard, see the Quick Reference Summary at the back of this book, or visit the Word 2003 Quick Reference Web page (scsite.com/wd2003/qr).

More About

Highlighting

To add color to an online document or e-mail message, highlight the text. Highlighting alerts the reader to the text's importance, much like a high-light marker does in a text-book. To highlight text, select it, click the Highlight button arrow on the Formatting toolbar, and then click the desired highlight color.

To Modify Frame Properties

1

• **With the insertion point in the left frame, click the Frame Properties button on the Frames toolbar.**

• **When Word displays the Frame Properties dialog box, if necessary, click the Borders tab.**

• **Click the Show scrollbars in browser box arrow and then click Never.**

The Borders sheet in the Frame Properties dialog box allows you to set options related to the frame borders (Figure 19).

2

• **Click the OK button.**

Word formats the border to no scroll bar.

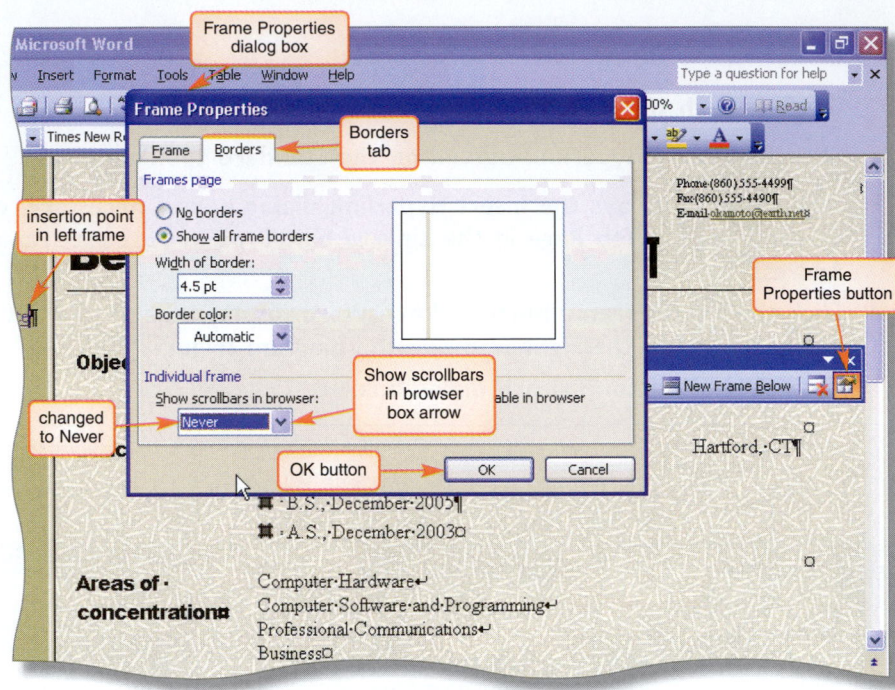

FIGURE 19

The next step is to save the frames page with a file name and specify the title to be displayed on the Web page title bar, as described below.

To Save the Frames Page

1 **Insert your floppy disk into drive A. Click File on the menu bar and then click Save as Web Page.**

2 **When Word displays the Save As dialog box, type** `Okamoto Personal Web Page` **in the File name box. Do not press the ENTER key.**

3 **If necessary, click the Save in box arrow and then click 3½ Floppy (A:).**

4 **Click the Change Title button. When Word displays the Set Page Title dialog box, type** `Okamoto Personal Web Page` **in the Page title text box.**

5 **Click the OK button in the Set Page Title dialog box. Click the Save button in the Save As dialog box.**

Word saves the frames page on a floppy disk in drive A with the file name, Okamoto Personal Web Page. When a user displays the Web page in a browser, the title bar also will show this same name.

The final step is to quit Word, as described next.

To Quit Word

1 **Click the Close button on the Word title bar.**

The Word window closes.

You can start Windows Explorer and double-click the file name, Okamoto Personal Web Page to display the Web page in your browser. From the browser window (Figure 1a on page WD 204), you can test your hyperlinks to be sure they work — before publishing them to the Web. For example, in the left frame, click the My Favorite Site link to display the Web site www.scsite.com in the right frame. (If you are not connected to the Internet, your browser will connect you and then display the Web site.) Click the My Resume link to display the Okamoto Resume Web Page in the right frame. Click the e-mail address to start your e-mail program with the address, okamoto@earth.net, entered in the recipient's address box.

The final step is to make your Web pages and associated files available to others on a network, on an intranet, or on the World Wide Web. Read Appendix C for instructions about publishing Web pages and then talk to your instructor about how you should do this for your system.

Web Feature Summary

This Web Feature introduced you to creating a Web page by illustrating how to save an existing Word document as a Web page file. The feature then showed how to modify and format the Web page file. Next, you learned how to create a new Web page with frames and then modify the frames page. Finally, the project showed how to create one hyperlink to an e-mail address, one to a Web page file, and another to a Web site.

 If you have a SAM user profile, you may have access to hands-on instruction, practice, and assessment of the skills covered in this project. Log in to your SAM account and go to your assignments page to see what your instructor has assigned.

What You Should Know

Having completed this feature, you should be able to perform the tasks below. The tasks are listed in the same order they were presented in this project. For a list of the buttons, menus, toolbars, and commands introduced in this feature, see the Quick Reference Summary at the back of this book and refer to the Page Number column.

1. Save a Word Document as a Web Page (WD 205)
2. Save a File in a Different Format (WD 206)
3. Format Text as a Hyperlink (WD 207)
4. Apply a Theme (WD 208, WD 211)
5. Preview a Web Page (WD 209)
6. Save a Web Page (WD 209)
7. Create a Frames Page (WD 210)
8. Add Text to a Frame (WD 210)
9. Resize a Web Page Frame (WD 211)
10. Insert and Modify a Hyperlink (WD 212, WD 213)
11. Modify Frame Properties (WD 214)
12. Save the Frames Page (WD 214)
13. Quit Word (WD 215)

In the Lab

1 Saving a Word Document as a Web Page and in Other Formats

Problem: You created the research paper shown in Figure 2-80 on pages WD 130 and WD 131 in Project 2. You decide to save this research paper in a variety of formats.

Instructions:

1. Open the Lab 2-1 System Unit Paper shown in Figure 2-80. (If you did not create the research paper, see your instructor for a copy.)
2. Save the paper as a single file Web page using the file name, Lab WF-1 System Unit Paper Web Page A. Print the Web page.
3. Use the Web Page Preview command to view the Web page.
4. If you have access to a Web server or FTP site, save the Web page to the server or site (see Appendix C for instructions).
5. Using Windows Explorer, look at the contents of the disk containing the Web page. Write down the names of the files. Open the original Lab 2-1 System Unit Paper. Save it as a Web page (not single file) using the file name, Lab WF-1 System Unit Paper Web Page B. That is, change the file type in the Save as type box to Web Page. Again, look at the contents of the disk using Windows Explorer. Write down any additional file names. How many more files and folders are created by the Web Page format?
6. Open the original Lab 2-1 System Unit Paper. Save it as plain text using the file name, Lab WF-1 System Unit Paper Plain Text. That is, change the file type in the Save as type box to Plain Text. Click the OK button when Word displays the File Conversion dialog box. Open the plain text file. *Hint:* In the Open dialog box, click the Files of type box arrow and then click All Files. Write down the difference between the plain text file and the original file.

2 Creating a Web Page with Frames and Hyperlinks

Problem: You created the resume shown in Figure 3-89 on page WD 199 in Project 3. You decide to create a personal Web page with a link to this resume. Thus, you also must save the resume as a Web page.

Instructions:

1. Open the Lab 3-1 Malone Resume shown in Figure 3-89. (If you did not create the resume, see your instructor for a copy.)
2. Save the resume as a single file Web page using the file name, Lab WF-2 Malone Resume Web Page. Convert the e-mail address to a hyperlink. Apply the Blends theme to the Web page. Preview the Web page using the Web Page Preview command. Save the Web page again.
3. Create a frames page. Insert a left frame. Add the following text to the left frame on three separate lines: Leah Malone, My Resume, My Favorite Site. Apply the Blends theme to the left frame. Resize the left frame to the width of its text.
4. In the left frame of the frames page, format the text, My Resume and My Favorite Site, as hyperlinks. When clicked, the My Resume hyperlink should display the Lab WF-2 Malone Resume Web Page in the right frame. The My Favorite Site hyperlink, when clicked, should display your favorite Web site in the right frame.
5. Modify the properties of the left frame to never display a scroll bar. Save the frames page using the file name, Lab WF-2 Malone Personal Web Page and change the title of the Web page. Use the Web Page Preview command to view the Web page in your browser.
6. In Windows Explorer, double-click the name of the frames page. Test your Web page links. Print the Web page.
7. If you have access to a Web server or FTP site, save the Web page to the server or site (see Appendix C).

MICROSOFT

Office Excel 2003

xcel

=AVERAGE(C4:C10) =MIN(D4:D10) =SUM(B8,C4,D6,E8)

=IF(AND(1<A3, A3<100),

NORTH AMERICA

Microsoft Office EXCEL

Creating a Worksheet and an Embedded Chart

CASE PERSPECTIVE

In the late 1970s, Extreme Blading pioneered the sport of inline skating as an off-season training tool for hockey players. The sport quickly caught on with fitness enthusiasts, aggressive skaters, and the population in general. Today, nearly 50 million inline skaters participate in the activity worldwide and the sport continues to grow.

The Extreme Blading product line includes a variety of skates, including inline, quad, and custom models for all age levels, as well as a complete line of protective gear and other accessories.

For years, the company sold their goods via direct mail, telesales, and company-owned outlets in major cities across the country. Thanks to the popularity of personal computers and the World Wide Web, the company added an e-commerce Web site last year. This new sales channel has given the company access to more than 600 million people worldwide and has resulted in a significant increase in sales.

Sales continued to grow during the first half of this year, thus driving senior management to ask their financial analyst, Maria Lopez, to develop a better sales tracking system. As a first step, Maria has asked you to prepare an easy-to-read worksheet that shows product sales for the second quarter by sales channel (Figure 1-1 on page EX 5). In addition, Maria has asked you to create a chart showing second quarter sales, because the president of the company likes to have a graphical representation of sales that allows her quickly to identify stronger and weaker product groups by sales channel.

As you read through this project, you will learn how to use Excel to create, save, and print a financial report that includes a 3-D Column chart.

Creating a Worksheet and an Embedded Chart

Objectives

You will have mastered the material in this project when you can:

- Start and Quit Excel
- Describe the Excel worksheet
- Enter text and numbers
- Use the AutoSum button to sum a range of cells
- Copy a cell to a range of cells using the fill handle
- Format a worksheet
- Create a 3-D Clustered column chart
- Save a workbook and print a worksheet
- Open a workbook
- Use the AutoCalculate area to determine statistics
- Correct errors on a worksheet
- Use the Excel Help system to answer questions

What Is Microsoft Office Excel 2003?

Microsoft Office Excel 2003 is a powerful spreadsheet program that allows users to organize data, complete calculations, make decisions, graph data, develop professional looking reports (Figure 1-1), publish organized data to the Web, and access real-time data from Web sites. The four major parts of Excel are:

- **Worksheets**   Worksheets allow users to enter, calculate, manipulate, and analyze data such as numbers and text. The term worksheet means the same as spreadsheet.
- **Charts**   Excel can draw a variety of charts.
- **Lists**   Lists organize and store data. For example, once a user enters data into a worksheet, Excel can sort the data, search for specific data, and select data that satisfies defined criteria.
- **Web Support**   Web support allows users to save Excel worksheets or parts of a worksheet in HTML format, so a user can view and manipulate the worksheet using a browser. Excel Web support also provides access to real-time data, such as stock quotes, using Web queries.

This latest version of Excel makes it much easier to create and manipulate lists of data. It also offers industry-standard XML support that simplifies the sharing of data within and outside an organization; improved statistical functions; smart documents that automatically fill with data; information rights management; allows two workbooks to be compared side by side; and includes the capability of searching a variety of reference information.

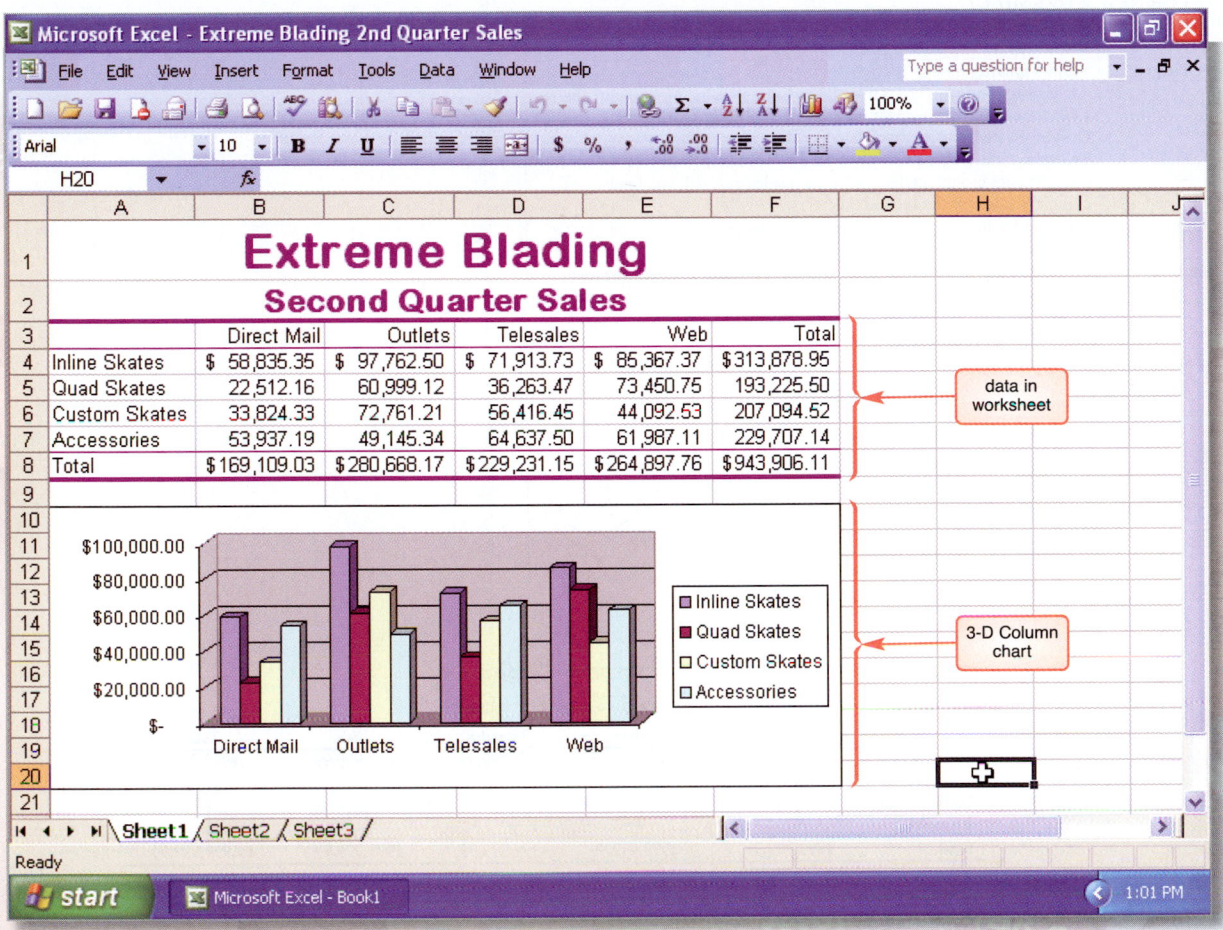

FIGURE 1-1

Project One — Extreme Blading Second Quarter Sales

The first step in creating an effective worksheet is to make sure you understand what is required. The person or persons requesting the worksheet should supply their requirements in a requirements document. A **requirements document** includes a needs statement, source of data, summary of calculations, and any other special requirements for the worksheet, such as charting and Web support. Figure 1-2 on the next page shows the requirements document for the new worksheet to be created in this project.

After carefully reviewing the requirements document, the next step is to design a solution or draw a sketch of the worksheet based on the requirements, including titles, column and row headings, location of data values, and the 3-D Column chart, as shown in Figure 1-3 on the next page. The dollar signs, 9s, and commas that you see in the sketch of the worksheet indicate formatted numeric values.

More About

Worksheet Development Cycle

Spreadsheet specialists do not sit down and start entering text, formulas, and data into a blank Excel worksheet as soon as they have a spreadsheet assignment. Instead, they follow an organized plan, or methodology, that breaks the development cycle into a series of tasks. The recommended methodology for creating worksheets includes (1) analyze requirements (supplied in a requirements document); (2) design solution; (3) validate design; (4) implement design; (5) test solution; and (6) document solution.

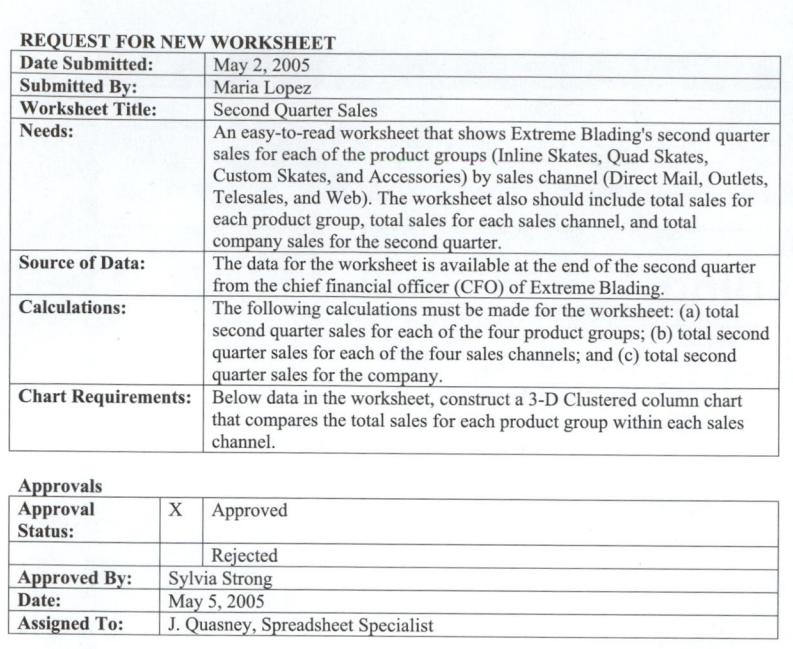

REQUEST FOR NEW WORKSHEET

Date Submitted:	May 2, 2005
Submitted By:	Maria Lopez
Worksheet Title:	Second Quarter Sales
Needs:	An easy-to-read worksheet that shows Extreme Blading's second quarter sales for each of the product groups (Inline Skates, Quad Skates, Custom Skates, and Accessories) by sales channel (Direct Mail, Outlets, Telesales, and Web). The worksheet also should include total sales for each product group, total sales for each sales channel, and total company sales for the second quarter.
Source of Data:	The data for the worksheet is available at the end of the second quarter from the chief financial officer (CFO) of Extreme Blading.
Calculations:	The following calculations must be made for the worksheet: (a) total second quarter sales for each of the four product groups; (b) total second quarter sales for each of the four sales channels; and (c) total second quarter sales for the company.
Chart Requirements:	Below data in the worksheet, construct a 3-D Clustered column chart that compares the total sales for each product group within each sales channel.

Approvals

Approval Status:	X	Approved
		Rejected
Approved By:	Sylvia Strong	
Date:	May 5, 2005	
Assigned To:	J. Quasney, Spreadsheet Specialist	

requirements document

FIGURE 1-2

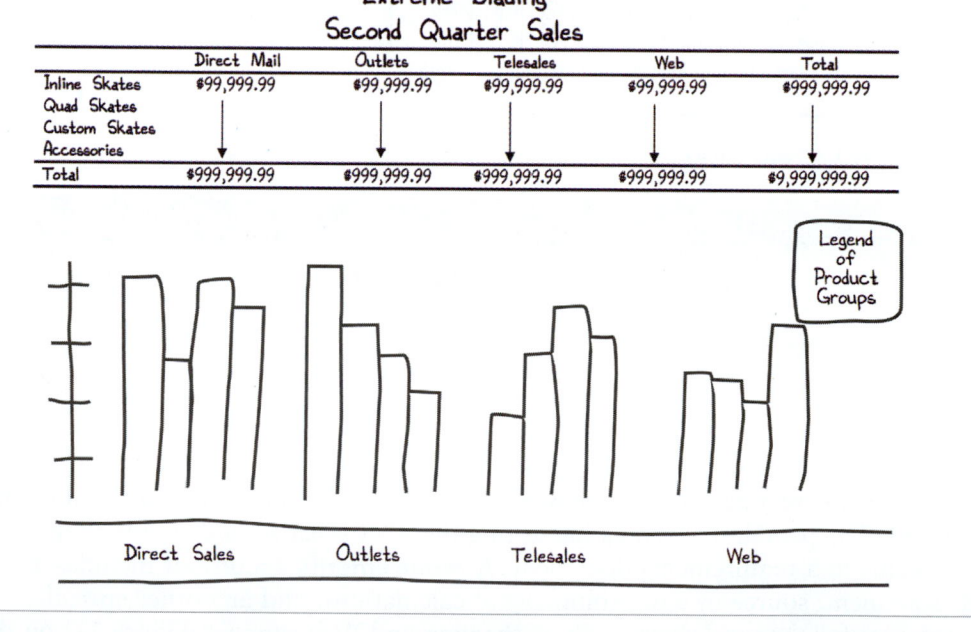

sketch of worksheet

FIGURE 1-3

With a good understanding of the requirements document and a sketch of the worksheet, the next step is to use Excel to create the worksheet and chart.

Starting and Customizing Excel

If you are stepping through this project on a computer and you want your screen to match the figures in this book, then you should change your computer's resolution to 800 × 600. For more information on how to change the resolution on your computer, see Appendix D. The following steps show how to start Excel.

To Start Excel

1

• **Click the Start button on the Windows taskbar, point to All Programs on the Start menu, point to Microsoft Office on the All Programs submenu, and then point to Microsoft Office Excel 2003 on the Microsoft Office submenu.**

Windows displays the Start menu, the All Programs submenu, and the Microsoft Office submenu (Figure 1-4).

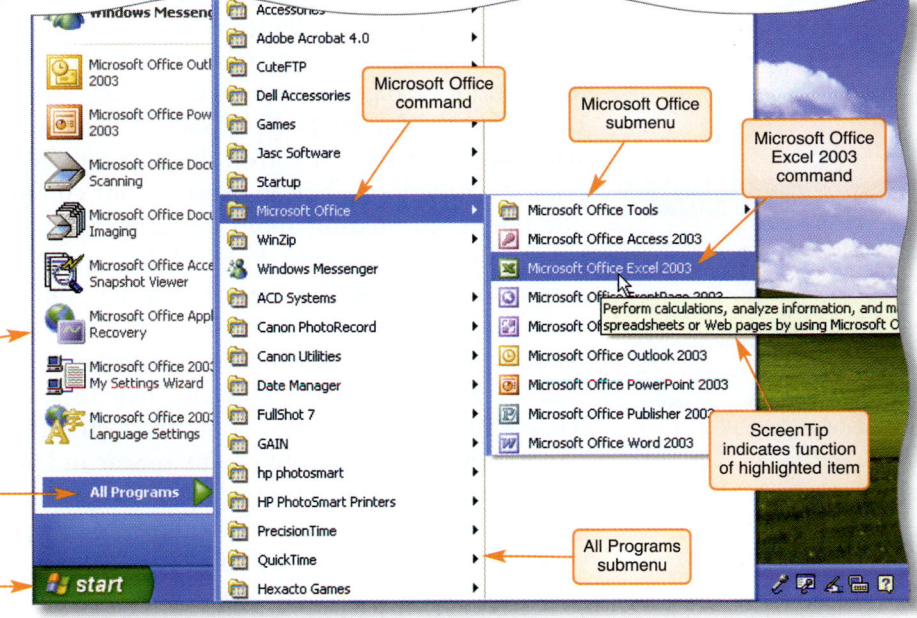

FIGURE 1-4

2

• **Click Microsoft Office Excel 2003.**

Excel starts. After several seconds, Excel displays a blank workbook titled Book1 in the Excel window (Figure 1-5).

3

• **If the Excel window is not maximized, double-click its title bar to maximize it.**

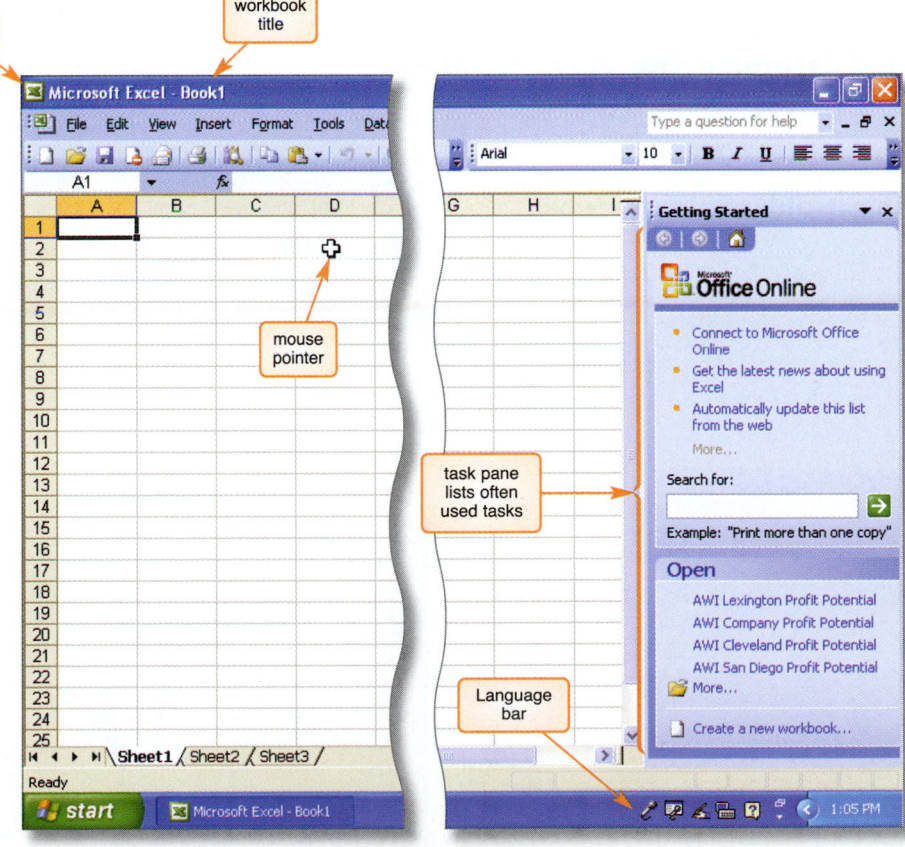

FIGURE 1-5

The screen shown in Figure 1-5 on the previous page illustrates how the Excel window looks the first time you start Excel after installation on most computers. If the Office Speech Recognition software is installed and active on your computer, then when you start Excel, the Language bar is displayed on the screen. The **Language bar** contains buttons that allow you to speak commands and dictate text. It usually is located on the right side of the Windows taskbar next to the notification area, and it changes to include the speech recognition functions available in Excel. In this book, the Language bar is closed because it takes up computer resources and with the Language bar active, the microphone can be turned on accidentally by clicking the Microphone button causing your computer to act in an unstable manner. For additional information about the Language bar, see page EX 15 and Appendix B.

As shown in Figure 1-5, Excel displays a task pane on the right side of the screen. A **task pane** is a separate window that enables users to carry out some Excel tasks more efficiently. When you start Excel, it displays the Getting Started task pane, which is a small window that provides commonly used links and commands that allow you to open files, create new files, or search Office-related topics on the Microsoft Web site. In this book, the Getting Started task pane is hidden to allow the maximum number of columns to appear in Excel.

At startup, Excel also displays two toolbars on a single row. A **toolbar** contains buttons, boxes, and menus that allow you to perform tasks quickly. To allow for more efficient use of the buttons, the toolbars should appear on two separate rows, instead of sharing a single row. The following steps show how to close the Language bar, close the Getting Started task pane, and instruct Excel to display the toolbars on two separate rows.

More About

Task Panes

You can drag a task pane title bar to float the pane in your work area or dock it on either the left or right side of a screen, depending on your personal preference.

To Customize the Excel Window

1

• **Right-click the Language bar.**

The Language bar shortcut menu appears (Figure 1-6).

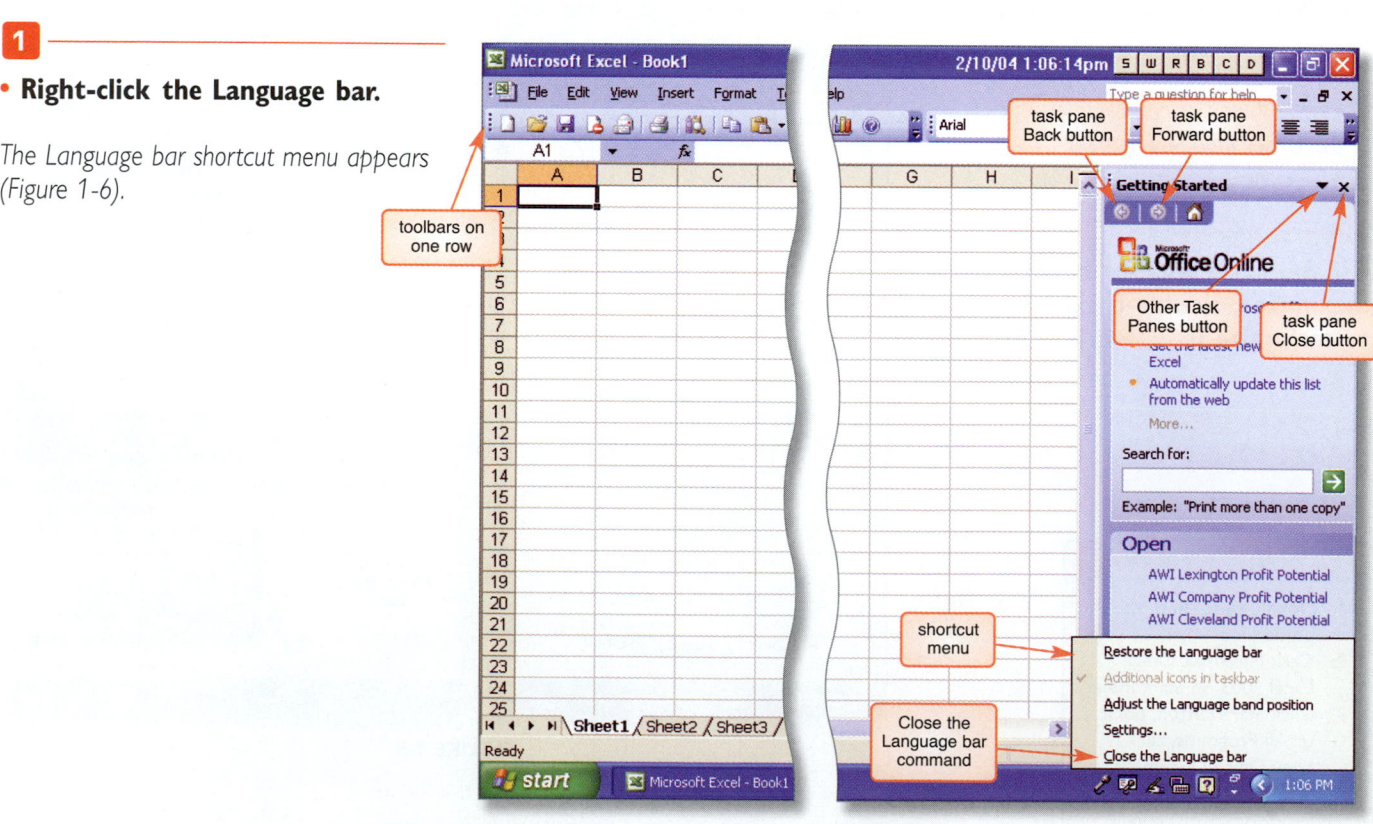

FIGURE 1-6

2

• **Click Close the Language bar.**

• **Click the Getting Started task pane Close button in the upper-right corner of the task pane.**

• **If the toolbars are positioned on the same row, click the Toolbar Options button.**

The Language bar disappears. Excel closes the Getting Started task pane and displays additional columns. Excel also displays the Toolbar Options list showing the buttons that do not fit on the toolbars when toolbars appear on one row (Figure 1-7).

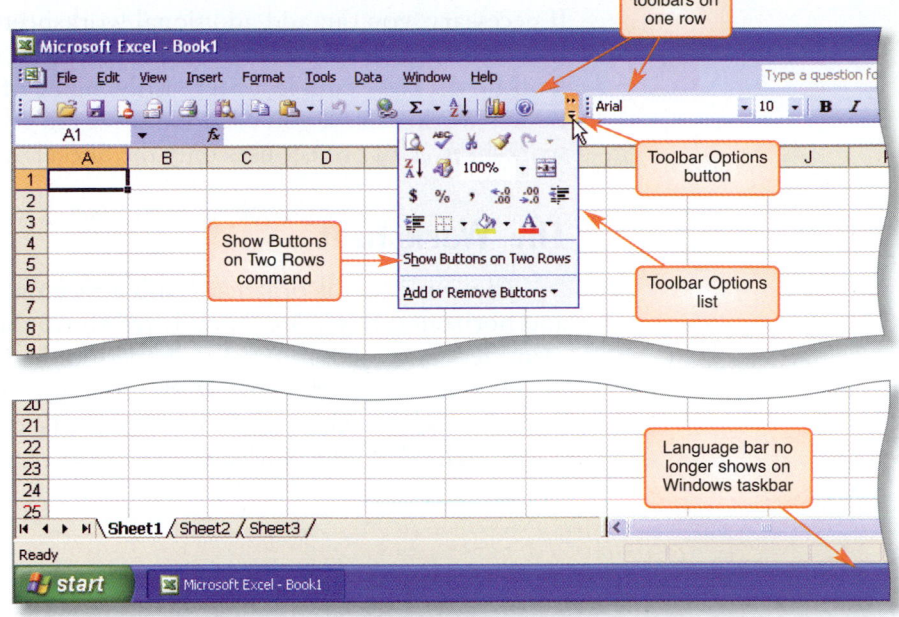

FIGURE 1-7

3

• **Click Show Buttons on Two Rows.**

Excel displays the toolbars on two separate rows (Figure 1-8). With the toolbars on two separate rows, all of the buttons fit on the two toolbars.

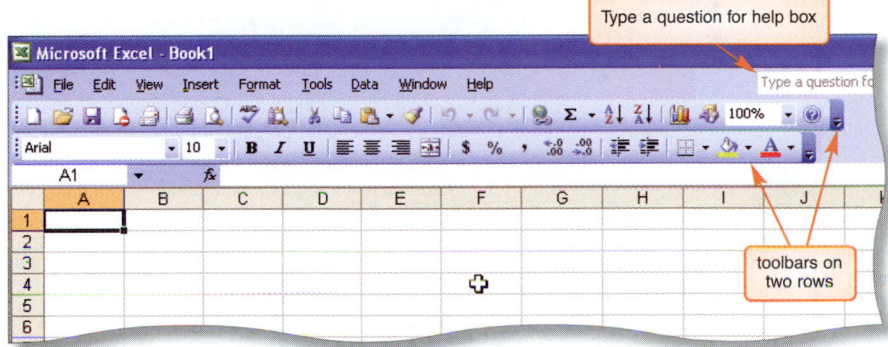

FIGURE 1-8

As you work through creating a worksheet, you will find that certain Excel operations cause Excel to display a task pane. Excel provides eleven task panes, in addition to the Getting Started task pane shown in Figure 1-6. Some of the more important ones are the Clipboard task pane, the Excel Help task pane, and the Clip Art task pane. Throughout the book, these task panes are discussed when they are used.

At any point while working with an Excel worksheet, you can open or close a task pane by clicking the Task Pane command on the View menu. You can activate additional task panes by clicking the Other Task Panes button to the left of the Close button on the task pane title bar (Figure 1-6) and then selecting a task pane in the Other Task Panes list. The Back and Forward buttons below the task pane title bar allow you to switch between task panes that you opened during a session.

The Excel Worksheet

When Excel starts, it creates a new blank workbook, called Book1. The **workbook** (Figure 1-9 on the next page) is like a notebook. Inside the workbook are sheets, each of which is called a **worksheet**. Excel opens a new workbook with three worksheets.

If necessary, you can add additional worksheets to a maximum of 255. Each worksheet has a sheet name that appears on a **sheet tab** at the bottom of the workbook. For example, Sheet1 is the name of the active worksheet displayed in the Book1 workbook. If you click the sheet tab labeled Sheet2, Excel displays the Sheet2 worksheet. This project uses only the Sheet1 worksheet.

The Worksheet

The worksheet is organized into a rectangular grid containing vertical columns and horizontal rows. A column letter above the grid, also called the **column heading**, identifies each column. A row number on the left side of the grid, also called the **row heading**, identifies each row. With the screen resolution set to 800 × 600 and the Excel window maximized, Excel displays 12 columns (A through L) and 23 rows (1 through 23) of the worksheet on the screen, as shown in Figure 1-9.

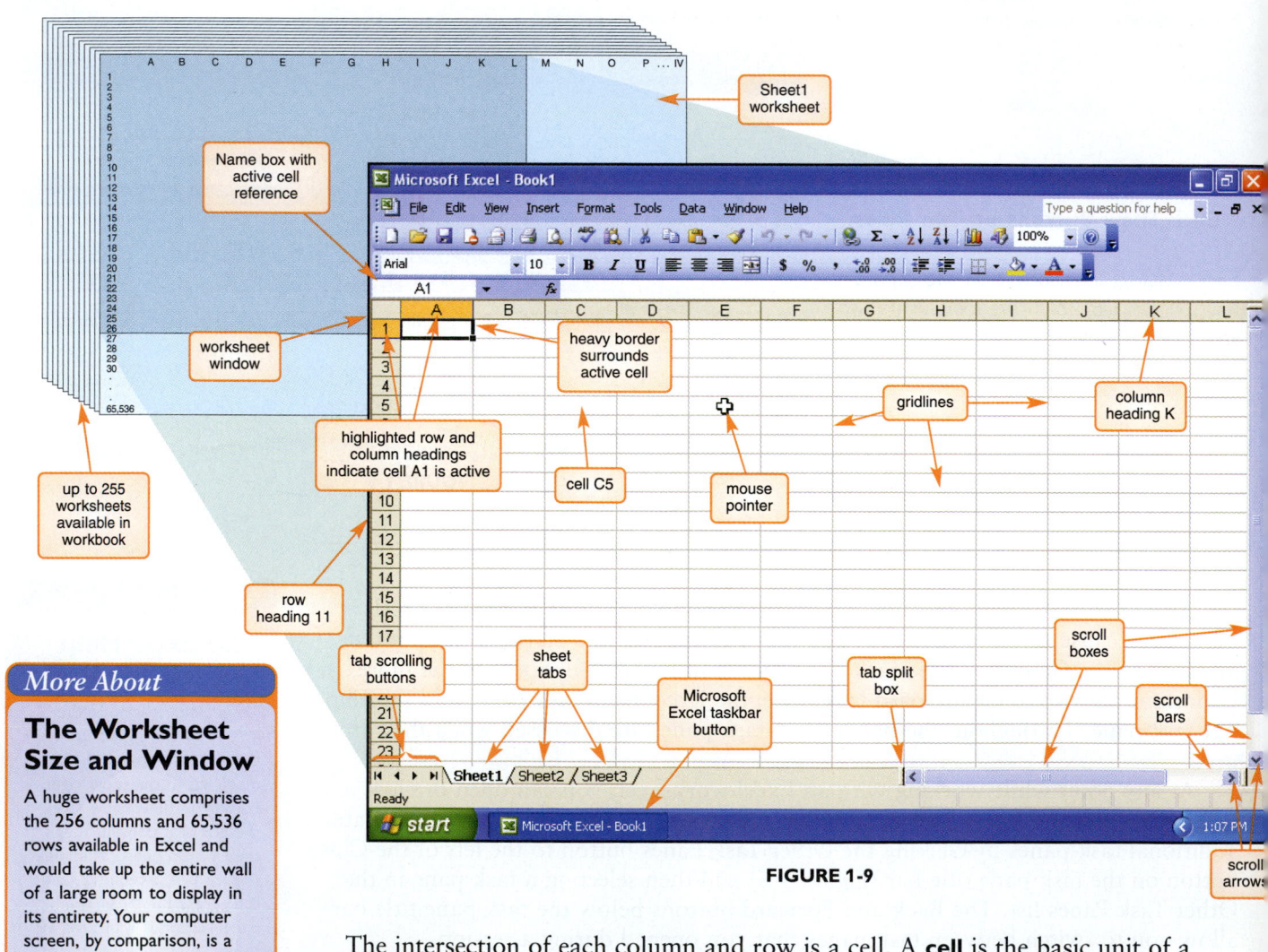

FIGURE 1-9

The intersection of each column and row is a cell. A **cell** is the basic unit of a worksheet into which you enter data. Each worksheet in a workbook has 256 columns and 65,536 rows for a total of 16,777,216 cells. The column headings begin with A and end with IV. The row headings begin with 1 and end with 65,536. Only a small fraction of the active worksheet appears on the screen at one time.

A cell is referred to by its unique address, or **cell reference**, which is the coordinates of the intersection of a column and a row. To identify a cell, specify the column letter first, followed by the row number. For example, cell reference C5 refers to the cell located at the intersection of column C and row 5 (Figure 1-9).

One cell on the worksheet, designated the **active cell**, is the one into which you can enter data. The active cell in Figure 1-9 is A1. The active cell is identified in three ways. First, a heavy border surrounds the cell; second, the active cell reference shows immediately above column A in the Name box; and third, the column heading A and row heading 1 are highlighted so it is easy to see which cell is active (Figure 1-9).

The horizontal and vertical lines on the worksheet itself are called **gridlines**. Gridlines make it easier to see and identify each cell in the worksheet. If desired, you can turn the gridlines off so they do not show on the worksheet, but it is recommended that you leave them on for now.

The mouse pointer in Figure 1-9 has the shape of a block plus sign. The mouse pointer appears as a block plus sign whenever it is located in a cell on the worksheet. Another common shape of the mouse pointer is the block arrow. The mouse pointer turns into the block arrow whenever you move it outside the worksheet or when you drag cell contents between rows or columns. The other mouse pointer shapes are described when they appear on the screen.

More About

The Mouse Pointer

The mouse pointer can change to one of more than 15 different shapes, such as a block arrow, cross hair, or chart symbol, depending on the task you are performing in Excel and the mouse pointer's location on the screen.

Worksheet Window

You view the portion of the worksheet displayed on the screen through a **worksheet window** (Figure 1-9). Below and to the right of the worksheet window are **scroll bars**, **scroll arrows**, and **scroll boxes** that you can use to move the worksheet window around to view different parts of the active worksheet. To the right of the sheet tabs at the bottom of the screen is the tab split box. You can drag the **tab split box** to increase or decrease the view of the sheet tabs (Figure 1-9). When you decrease the view of the sheet tabs, you increase the length of the horizontal scroll bar, and vice versa.

The menu bar, Standard toolbar, Formatting toolbar, and formula bar appear at the top of the screen, above the worksheet window and below the title bar.

Menu Bar

The **menu bar** is a special toolbar that includes the menu names as shown in Figure 1-10a on the next page. Each **menu name** represents a menu. A **menu** is a list of commands that you can use to retrieve, store, print, and manipulate data on the worksheet. When you point to a menu name on the menu bar, the area of the menu bar containing the name changes to a button. To display a menu, such as the Edit menu, click the Edit menu name on the menu bar (Figures 1-10b and 1-10c on the next page). If you point to a menu command with an arrow to its right, Excel displays a **submenu** from which you can choose a command.

Q&A

Q: Can the Excel window or viewing area be increased to show more of the worksheet?

A: Yes. Two ways exist to increase what you can see in the viewing area: (1) on the View menu, click Full Screen; and (2) change to a higher resolution. See Appendix D for information about how to change to a higher resolution.

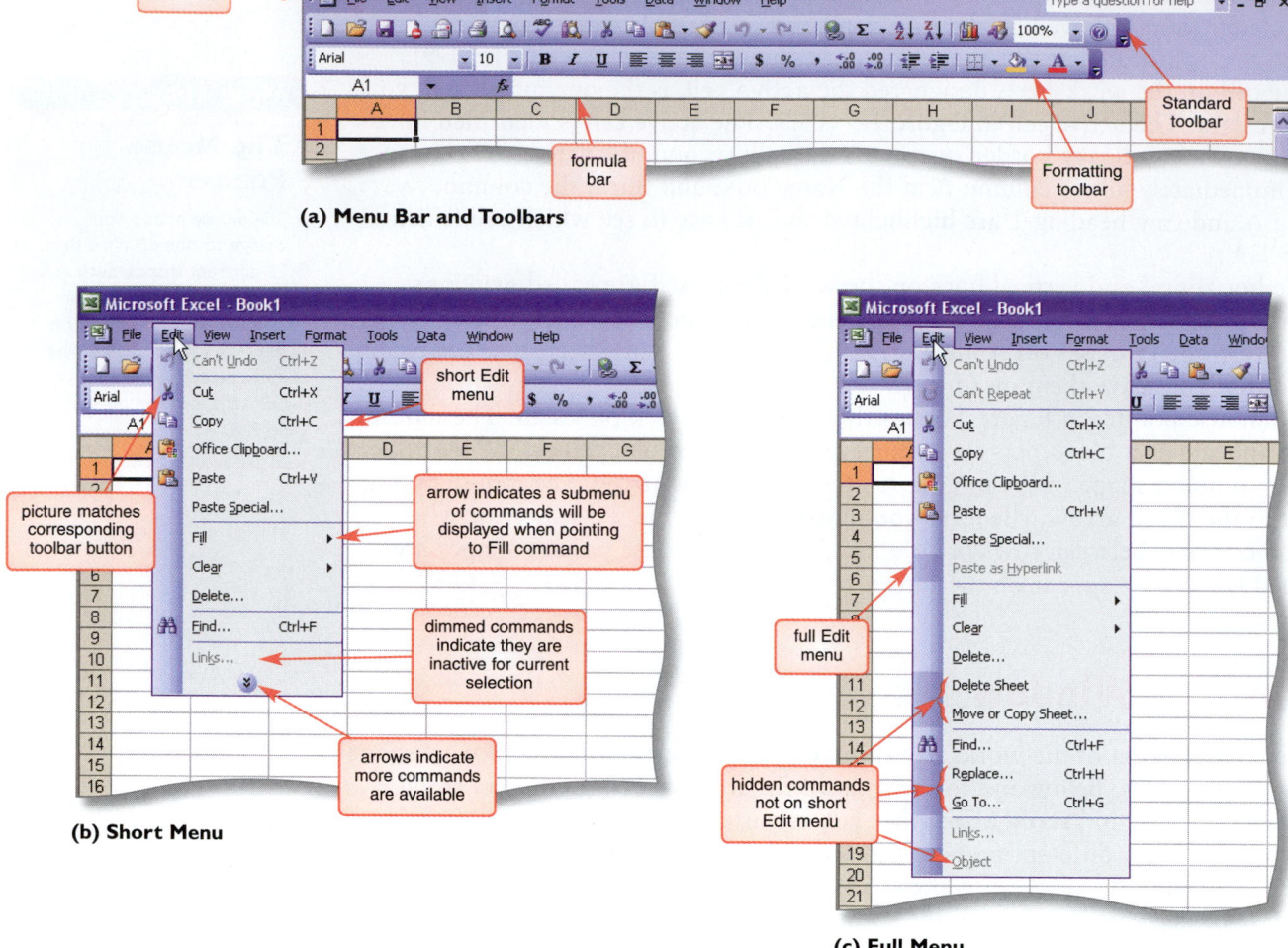

FIGURE 1-10

When you click a menu name on the menu bar, Excel displays a **short menu** listing the most recently used commands (Figure 1-10b). If you wait a few seconds or click the arrows at the bottom of the short menu, Excel displays the full menu. The **full menu** lists all of the commands associated with a menu (Figure 1-10c). You also can display a full menu immediately by double-clicking the menu name on the menu bar. In this book, use one of the following techniques to ensure that Excel always displays the full menu.

1. Click the menu name on the menu bar and then wait a few seconds.
2. Click the menu name on the menu bar and then click the arrows at the bottom of the short menu.
3. Click the menu name on the menu bar and then point to the arrows at the bottom of the short menu.
4. Double-click the menu name on the menu bar.

Both short and full menus display some dimmed commands. A **dimmed command** appears gray, or dimmed, instead of black, which indicates it is not available for the current selection. A command with medium blue shading to the left of it on a full menu is called a **hidden command** because it does not appear on a short menu. As you use Excel, it automatically personalizes the short menus for you based on how often you use commands. That is, as you use hidden commands, Excel *unhides* them and places them on the short menu.

The menu bar can change to include other menu names depending on the type of work you are doing in Excel. For example, if you are working with a chart sheet rather than a worksheet, Excel displays the Chart menu bar with menu names that reflect charting commands.

Standard Toolbar and Formatting Toolbar

The Standard toolbar and the Formatting toolbar (Figure 1-11) contain buttons and boxes that allow you to perform frequent tasks more quickly than when using the menu bar. For example, to print a worksheet, you click the Print button on the Standard toolbar. Each button has a picture on the button face to help you remember the button's function. Also, when you move the mouse pointer over a button or box, Excel displays the name of the button or box below it in a **ScreenTip**.

Figures 1-11a and 1-11b illustrate the Standard and Formatting toolbars and describe the functions of the buttons. Each of the buttons and boxes will be explained in detail when they are used.

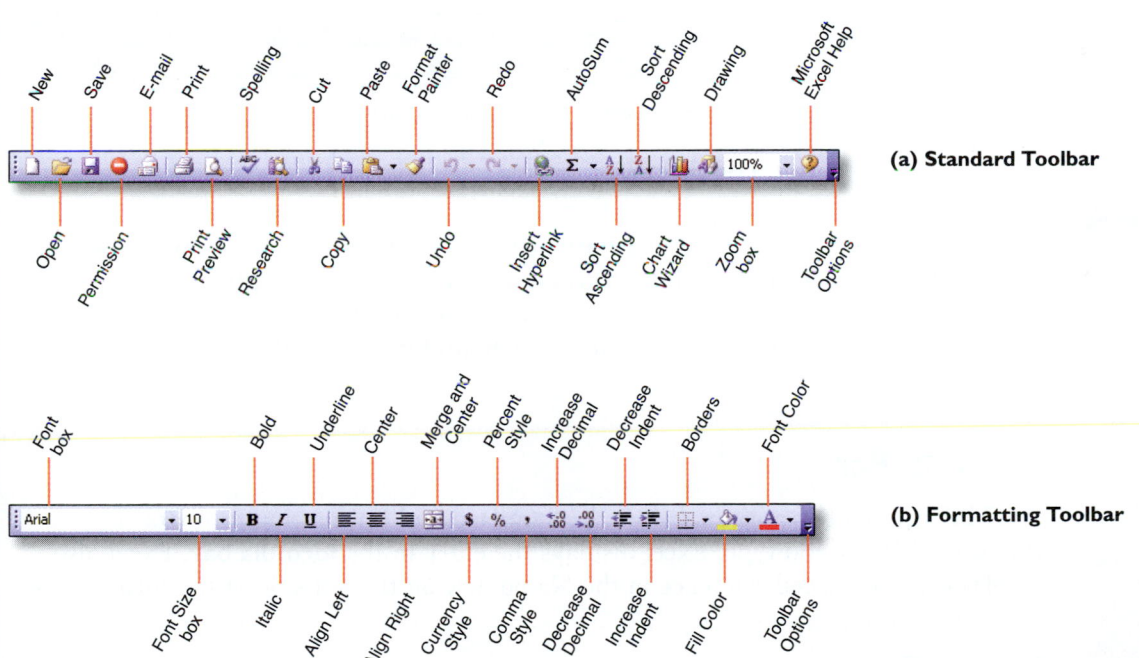

FIGURE 1-11

When you first install Excel, both the Standard and Formatting toolbars are preset to display on the same row (Figure 1-12a on the next page), immediately below the menu bar. Unless the resolution of your display device is greater than 800 × 600, many of the buttons that belong on these toolbars are hidden. Hidden buttons appear in the Toolbar Options list (Figure 1-12b on the next page). In this mode, you also can display all the buttons on either toolbar by double-clicking the **move handle** on the left of each toolbar (Figure 1-12a).

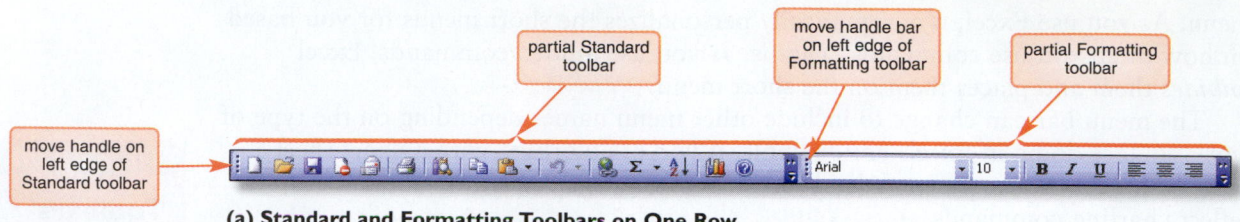

(a) Standard and Formatting Toolbars on One Row

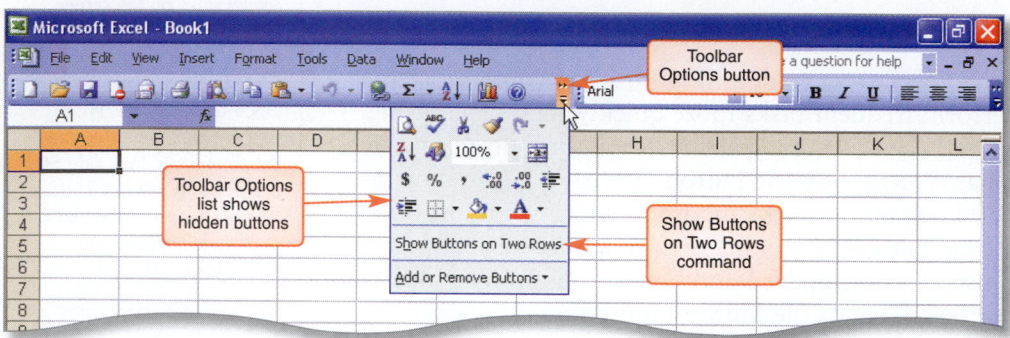

(b) Toolbar Options List

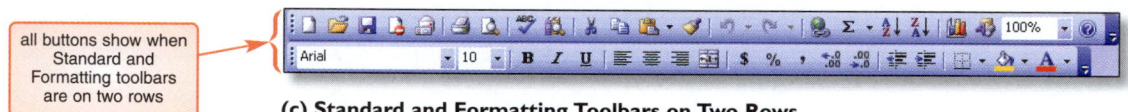

(c) Standard and Formatting Toolbars on Two Rows

FIGURE 1-12

In this book, the Standard and Formatting toolbars are shown on two rows, one below the other, so that all buttons appear on a screen with the resolution set to 800 × 600 (Figure 1-12c). You can show the two toolbars on two rows by clicking the Show Buttons on Two Rows command in the Toolbar Options list (Figure 1-12b).

Formula Bar

The formula bar appears below the Standard and Formatting toolbars (Figure 1-13). As you type, Excel displays the entry in the **formula bar**. Excel also displays the active cell reference in the Name box on the left side of the formula bar.

Status Bar

The status bar is located immediately above the Windows taskbar at the bottom of the screen (Figure 1-13). The **status bar** displays a brief description of the command selected (highlighted) on a menu, the function of the button the mouse pointer is pointing to, or the mode of Excel. **Mode indicators**, such as Enter and Ready, appear on the status bar and specify the current mode of Excel. When the mode is **Ready**, Excel is ready to accept the next command or data entry. When the mode indicator reads **Enter**, Excel is in the process of accepting data through the keyboard into the active cell.

In the middle of the status bar is the AutoCalculate area. The **AutoCalculate area** can be used in place of a calculator or formula to view the sum, average, or other types of totals of a group of numbers on the worksheet. The AutoCalculate area is discussed in detail later in this project.

Keyboard indicators, such as CAPS (Caps Lock), NUM (Num Lock), and SCRL (Scroll), show which keys are engaged. Keyboard indicators appear in the small rectangular boxes on the right side of the status bar (Figure 1-13).

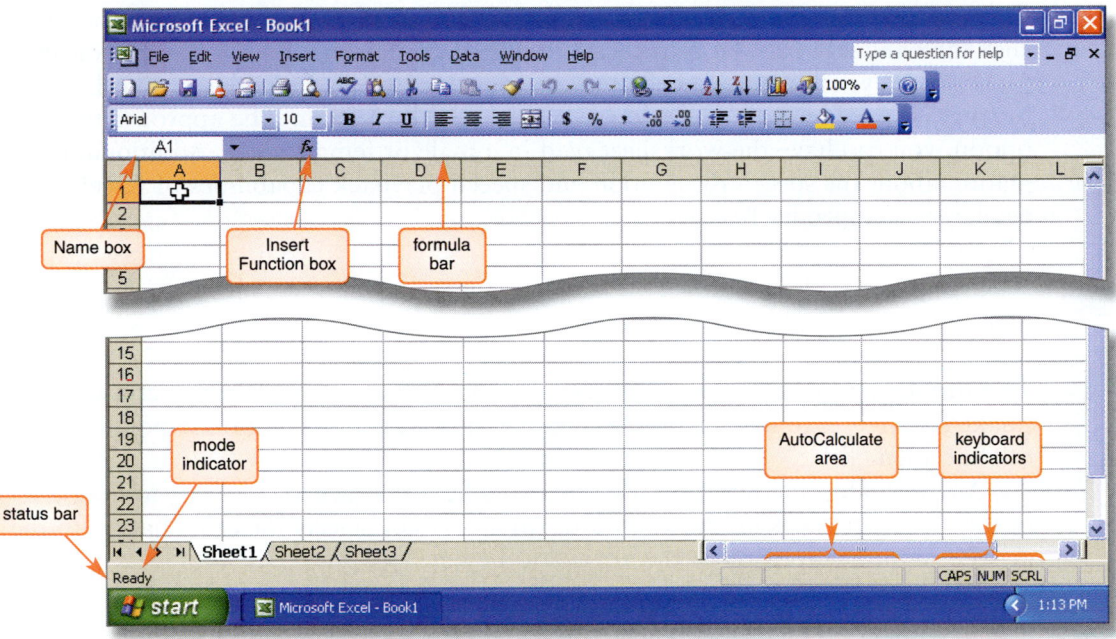

FIGURE 1-13

Speech Recognition and Speech Playback

With the **Office Speech Recognition software** installed and a microphone, you can speak the names of toolbar buttons, menus, menu commands, list items, alerts, and dialog box controls, such as OK and Cancel. You also can dictate cell entries, such as text and numbers. To indicate whether you want to speak commands or dictate cell entries, you use the Language bar. The Language bar can be in one of four states: (1) **restored**, which means it is displayed somewhere in the Excel window (Figure 1-14a); (2) **minimized**, which means it is displayed on the Windows taskbar (Figure 1-14b); (3) **hidden**, which means you do not see it on the screen but it will be displayed the next time you start your computer; (4) **closed**, which means it is hidden permanently until you enable it. If the Language bar is hidden or closed and you want it to display, then do the following:

1. Right-click an open area on the Windows taskbar at the bottom of the screen.
2. Point to Toolbars on the shortcut menu and then click Language bar on the Toolbars submenu.

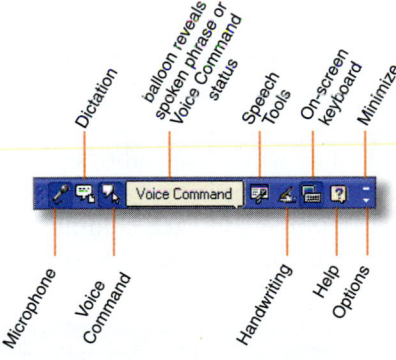

(a) Language Bar in Excel Window with Microphone Enabled

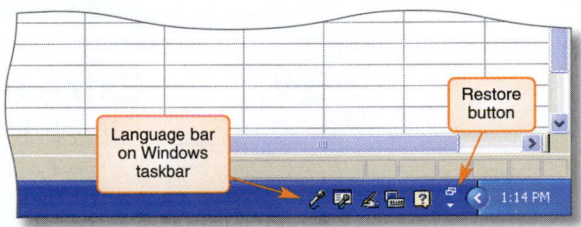

(b) Language Bar Minimized on Windows Taskbar

FIGURE 1-14

If the Language bar command is dimmed on the Toolbars submenu or if the Speech command is dimmed on the Tools menu, the Office Speech Recognition software is not installed.

In this book, the Language bar does not appear in the figures. If you want to close the Language bar so that your screen is identical to what you see in the book, right-click the Language bar and then click Close the Language bar on the shortcut menu.

If you have speakers, you can use the **speech playback** functions of Excel to instruct the computer to read a worksheet to you. By selecting the appropriate option, you can have the worksheet read in a male or female voice. Additional information about the speech recognition and speech playback capabilities of Excel is available in Appendix B.

Selecting a Cell

To enter data into a cell, you first must select it. The easiest way **to select a cell** (make it active) is to use the mouse to move the block plus sign mouse pointer to the cell and then click.

An alternative method is to use the arrow keys that are located just to the right of the typewriter keys on the keyboard. An arrow key selects the cell adjacent to the active cell in the direction of the arrow on the key.

You know a cell is selected, or active, when a heavy border surrounds the cell and the active cell reference appears in the Name box on the left side of the formula bar. Excel also changes the active cell's column heading and row heading to a gold color.

Entering Text

In Excel, any set of characters containing a letter, hyphen (as in a telephone number), or space is considered text. **Text** is used to place titles, such as worksheet titles, column titles, and row titles, on the worksheet. For example, as shown in Figure 1-15, the worksheet title, Extreme Blading, identifies the worksheet created in Project 1. The worksheet subtitle, Second Quarter Sales, identifies the type of report. The column titles in row 3 (Direct Mail, Outlets, Telesales, Web, and Total) identify the numbers in each column. The row titles in column A (Inline Skates, Quad Skates, Custom Skates, Accessories, and Total) identify the numbers in each row.

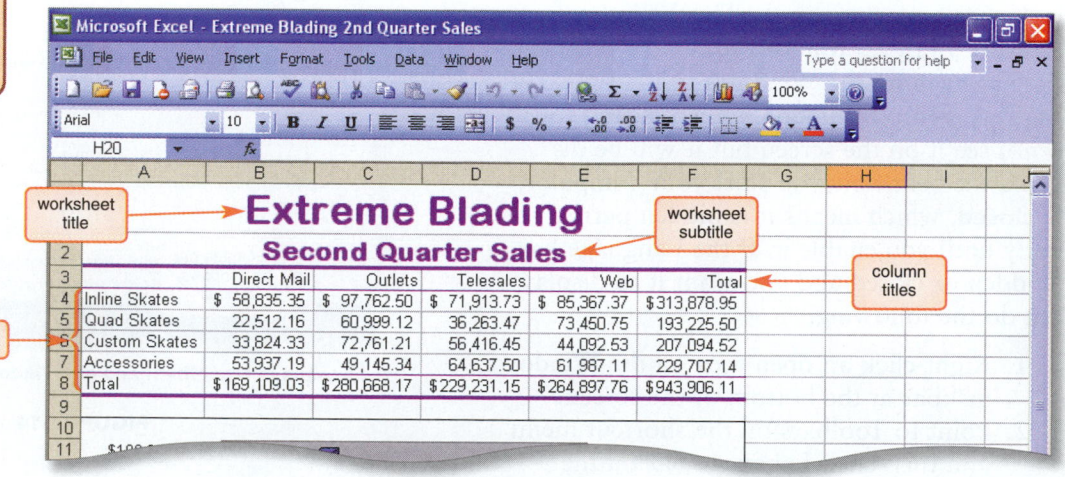

FIGURE 1-15

Entering the Worksheet Titles

The following steps show how to enter the worksheet titles in cells A1 and A2. Later in this project, the worksheet titles will be formatted so they appear as shown in Figure 1-15.

To Enter the Worksheet Titles

1

• **Click cell A1.**

Cell A1 becomes the active cell and a heavy border surrounds it (Figure 1-16).

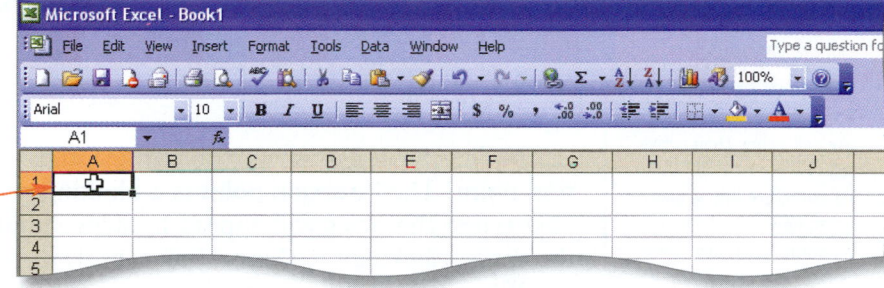

FIGURE 1-16

2

• **Type** Extreme Blading **in cell A1 and then point to the Enter box in the formula bar.**

Excel displays the title in the formula bar and in cell A1 (Figure 1-17). When you begin typing a cell entry, Excel displays two additional boxes in the formula bar: the Cancel box and the Enter box.

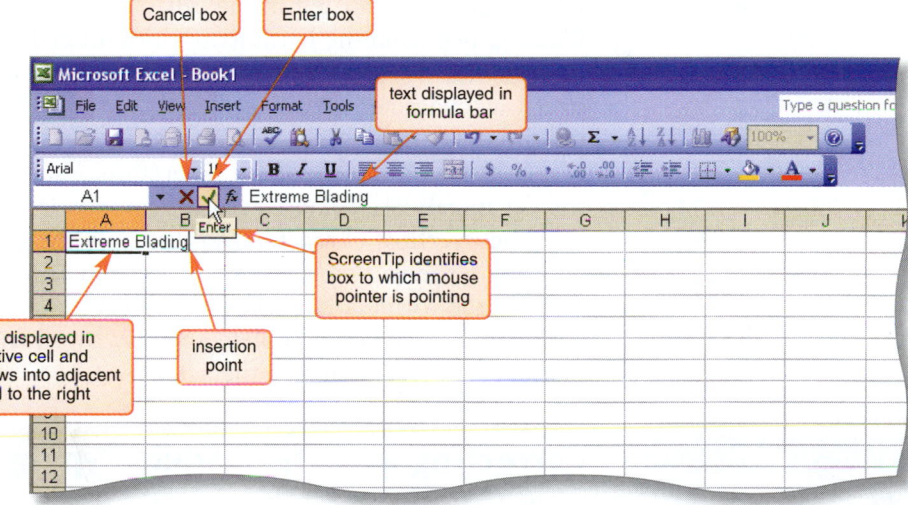

FIGURE 1-17

3

• **Click the Enter box to complete the entry.**

Excel enters the worksheet title in cell A1 (Figure 1-18).

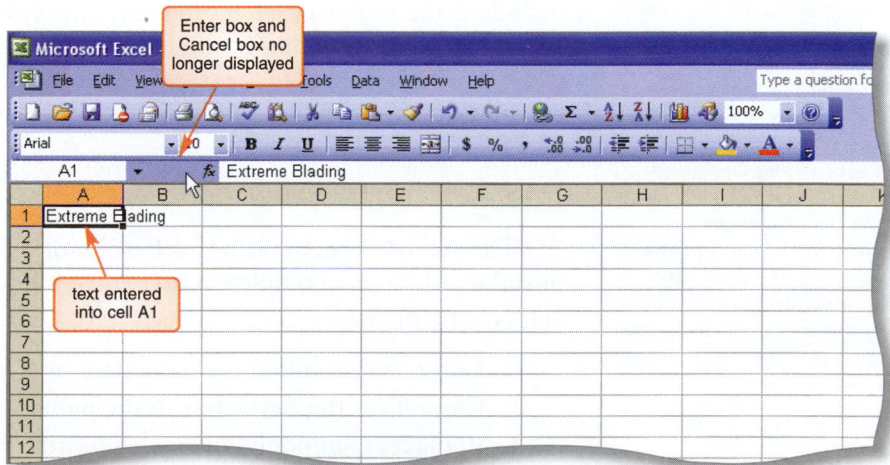

FIGURE 1-18

4

• **Click cell A2 to select it. Type** Second Quarter Sales **as the cell entry. Click the Enter box to complete the entry.**

Excel enters the worksheet subtitle in cell A2 (Figure 1-19).

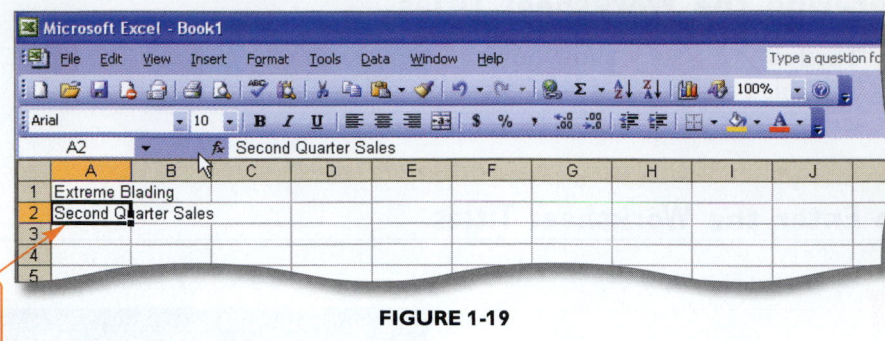

worksheet subtitle entered into cell A2

FIGURE 1-19

Other Ways

1. To complete entry, click any cell other than active cell
2. To complete entry, press ENTER key
3. To complete entry, press HOME, PAGE UP, PAGE DOWN, or END key
4. To complete entry, in Voice Command mode, say "Enter"

In Figure 1-17 on the previous page, the text in cell A1 is followed by the insertion point. The **insertion point** is a blinking vertical line that indicates where the next typed character will appear. In Steps 3 and 4, clicking the **Enter box** completes the entry. Clicking the **Cancel box** cancels the entry.

When you complete a text entry into a cell, a series of events occurs. First, Excel positions the text left-aligned in the cell. **Left-aligned** means the cell entry is positioned at the far left in the cell. Therefore, the E in the worksheet title, Extreme Blading, begins in the leftmost position of cell A1.

Second, when the text is longer than the width of a column, Excel displays the overflow characters in adjacent cells to the right as long as these adjacent cells contain no data. In Figure 1-19, the width of cell A1 is approximately 9 characters. The text consists of 15 characters. Therefore, Excel displays the overflow characters from cell A1 in cell B1, because cell B1 is empty. If cell B1 contained data, Excel would hide the overflow characters, so that only the first 9 characters in cell A1 would appear on the worksheet. Excel stores the overflow characters in cell A1 and displays them in the formula bar whenever cell A1 is the active cell.

Third, when you complete an entry by clicking the Enter box, the cell in which the text is entered remains the active cell.

Correcting a Mistake while Typing

If you type the wrong letter and notice the error before clicking the Enter box or pressing the ENTER key, use the BACKSPACE key to delete all the characters back to and including the incorrect letter. To cancel the entire entry before entering it into the cell, click the Cancel box in the formula bar or press the ESC key. If you see an error in a cell after entering the text, select the cell and retype the entry. Later in this project, additional error-correction techniques are discussed.

AutoCorrect

The **AutoCorrect feature** of Excel works behind the scenes, correcting common mistakes when you complete a text entry in a cell. AutoCorrect makes three types of corrections for you:

1. Corrects two initial capital letters by changing the second letter to lowercase.
2. Capitalizes the first letter in the names of days.
3. Replaces commonly misspelled words with their correct spelling. For example, it will change the misspelled word *recieve* to *receive* when you complete the entry. AutoCorrect will correct the spelling of hundreds of commonly misspelled words automatically.

More About

The ENTER Key

When you first install Excel, the ENTER key not only completes the entry, but it also moves the selection to an adjacent cell. You can instruct Excel not to move the selection after pressing the ENTER key by clicking Options on the Tools menu, clicking the Edit tab, removing the check mark from the Move Selection after Enter check box, and then clicking the OK button.

Entering Column Titles

To enter the column titles in row 3, select the appropriate cell and then enter the text, as described in the following steps.

To Enter Column Titles

1

• **Click cell B3.**

Cell B3 becomes the active cell. The active cell reference in the Name box changes from A2 to B3 (Figure 1-20).

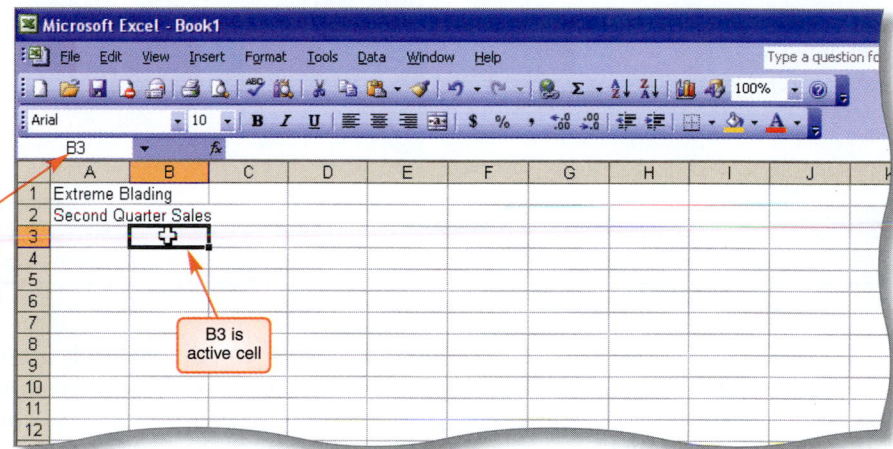

FIGURE 1-20

2

• **Type** Direct Mail **in cell B3.**

Excel displays Direct Mail in the formula bar and in cell B3 (Figure 1-21).

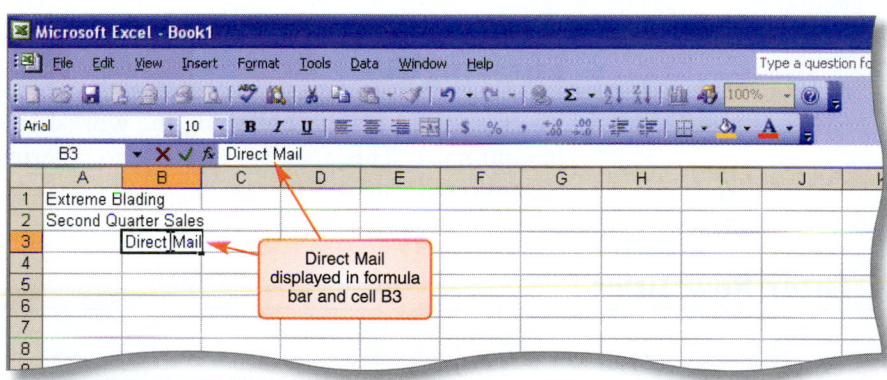

FIGURE 1-21

3

• **Press the RIGHT ARROW key.**

Excel enters the column title, Direct Mail, in cell B3 and makes cell C3 the active cell (Figure 1-22).

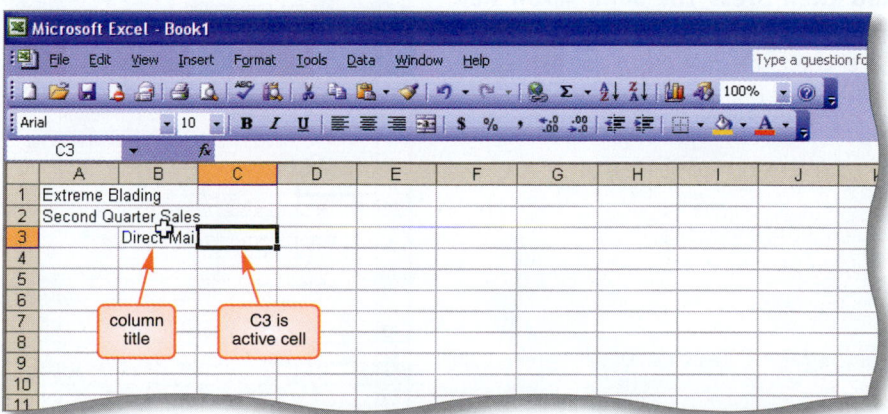

FIGURE 1-22

4

- **Repeat Steps 2 and 3 for the remaining column titles in row 3; that is, enter** Outlets **in cell C3,** Telesales **in cell D3,** Web **in cell E3, and** Total **in cell F3 (complete the last entry in cell F3 by clicking the Enter box in the formula bar).**

Excel displays the column titles left-aligned as shown in Figure 1-23.

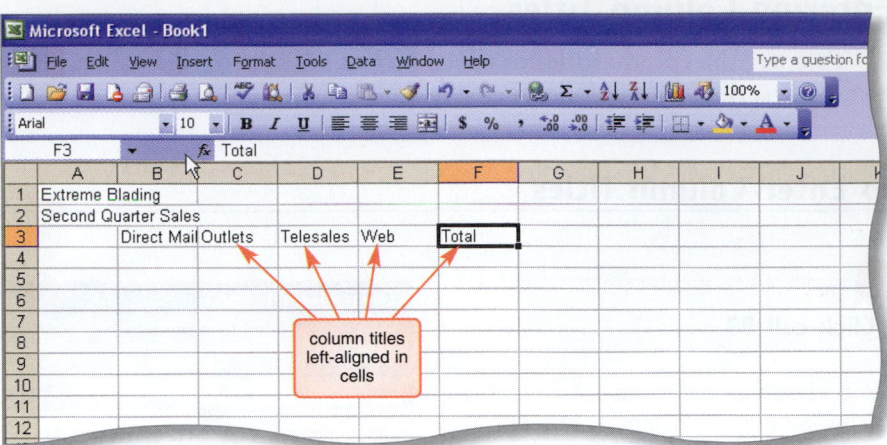

FIGURE 1-23

If the next entry is in an adjacent cell, use the arrow keys to complete the entry in a cell. When you press an arrow key to complete an entry, the adjacent cell in the direction of the arrow (up, down, left, or right) becomes the active cell. If the next entry is in a nonadjacent cell, complete an entry by clicking the next cell in which you plan to enter data. You also can click the Enter box or press the ENTER key and then click the appropriate cell for the next entry.

Entering Row Titles

The next step in developing the worksheet in Project 1 is to enter the row titles in column A. This process is similar to entering the column titles and is described in the following steps.

To Enter Row Titles

1

- **Click cell A4. Type** Inline Skates **and then press the DOWN ARROW key.**

Excel enters the row title, Inline Skates, in cell A4, and cell A5 becomes the active cell (Figure 1-24).

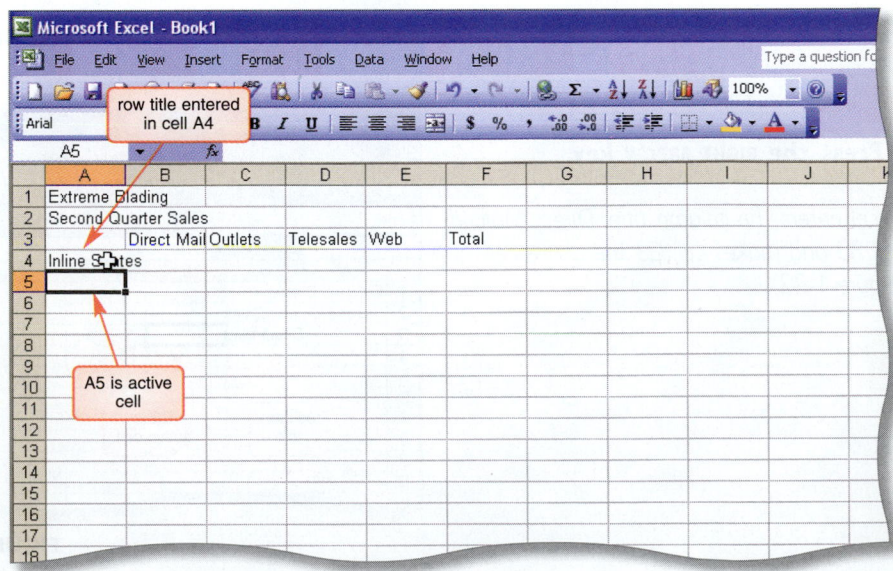

FIGURE 1-24

2

• **Repeat Step 1 for the remaining row titles in column A; that is, enter** Quad Skates **in cell A5,** Custom Skates **in cell A6,** Accessories **in cell A7, and** Total **in cell A8.**

Excel displays the row titles as shown in Figure 1-25.

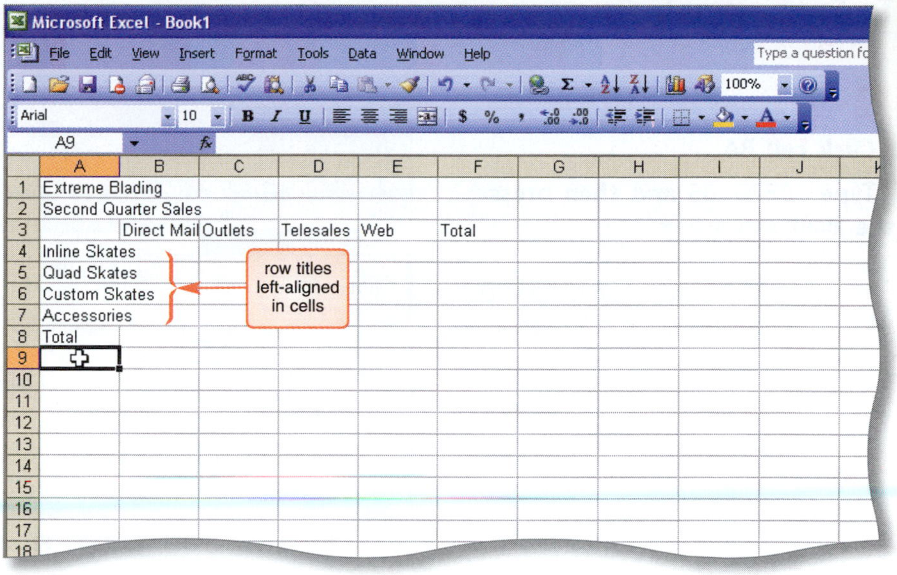

FIGURE 1-25

When you enter text, Excel automatically left-aligns the text in the cell. Excel treats any combination of numbers, spaces, and nonnumeric characters as text. For example, the following entries are text:

401AX21, 921-231, 619 321, 883XTY

You can change the text alignment in a cell by realigning it. Several alignment techniques are discussed later in the project.

Entering Numbers

In Excel, you can enter numbers into cells to represent amounts. A **number** can contain only the following characters:

0 1 2 3 4 5 6 7 8 9 + - ( ) , / . $ % E e

If a cell entry contains any other keyboard character (including spaces), Excel interprets the entry as text and treats it accordingly. The use of the special characters is explained when they are used in the project.

The Extreme Blading Second Quarter numbers used in Project 1 are summarized in Table 1-1. These numbers, which represent second quarter sales for each of the sales channels and product groups, must be entered in rows 4, 5, 6, and 7. The steps on the next page enter the numbers in Table 1-1 one row at a time.

> *More About*
>
> **Entering Numbers as Text**
>
> Sometimes, you will want Excel to treat numbers, such as Zip codes and telephone numbers, as text. To enter a number as text, start the entry with an apostrophe (').

Table 1-1 Extreme Blading Second Quarter Data				
	Direct Mail	**Outlets**	**Telesales**	**Web**
Inline Skates	58835.35	97762.50	71913.73	85367.37
Quad Skates	22512.16	60999.12	36263.47	73450.75
Custom Skates	33824.33	72761.21	56416.45	44092.53
Accessories	53937.19	49145.34	64637.50	61987.11

To Enter Numbers

1

• **Click cell B4.**

• **Type** 58835.35 **and then press the RIGHT ARROW key.**

Excel enters the number 58835.35 in cell B4 and changes the active cell to cell C4 (Figure 1-26).

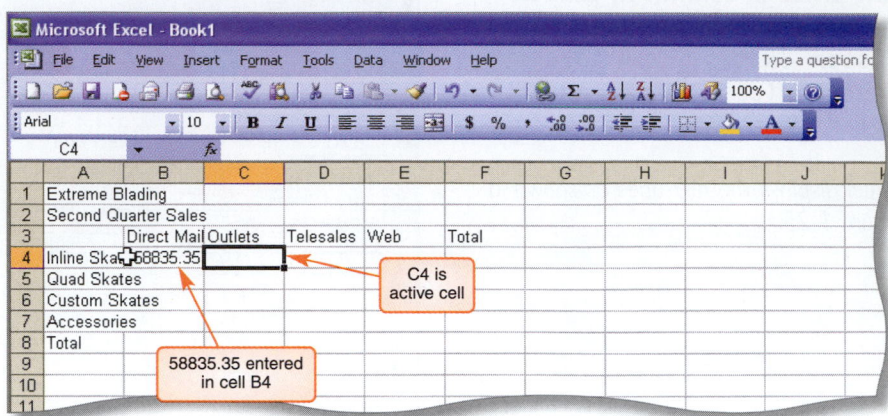

FIGURE 1-26

2

• **Enter** 97762.50 **in cell C4,** 71913.73 **in cell D4, and** 85367.37 **in cell E4.**

Row 4 now contains the second quarter sales by sales channel for the Inline Skates product group (Figure 1-27). The numbers in row 4 are right-aligned, which means Excel displays the cell entry to the far right in the cell.

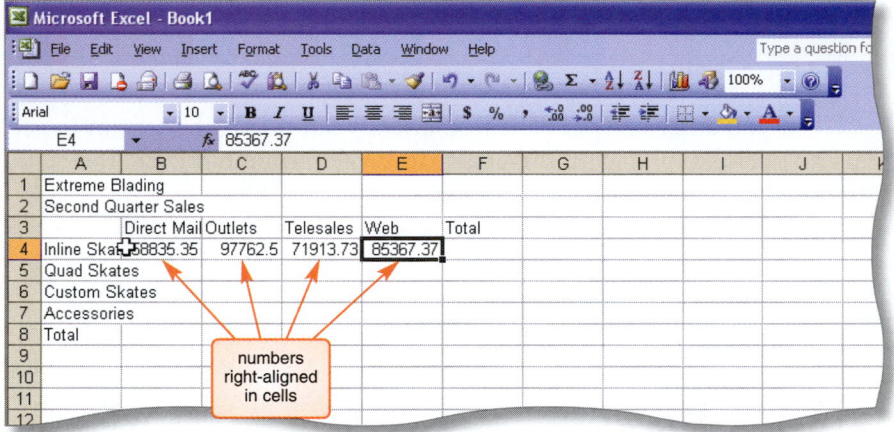

FIGURE 1-27

3

• **Click cell B5.**

• **Enter the remaining second quarter sales provided in Table 1-1 on the previous page for each of the three remaining product groups in rows 5, 6, and 7.**

Excel displays the second quarter sales as shown in Figure 1-28.

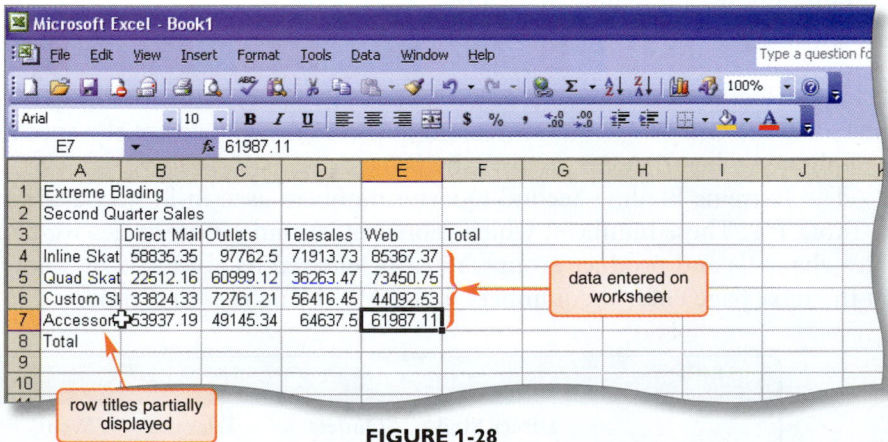

FIGURE 1-28

When the numbers are entered into the cells in column B, Excel only partially displays the row titles in column A. When the worksheet is formatted later in the project, the row titles will appear in their entirety.

Steps 1 through 3 complete the numeric entries. As shown in Figure 1-28, Excel does not display trailing zeros in cells C4 and D7. You are not required to type dollar signs, commas, or trailing zeros. When you enter a dollar value that has cents, however, you must add the decimal point and the numbers representing the cents. Later in this project, the numbers will be formatted to use dollar signs, commas, and trailing zeros to improve the appearance and readability of the numbers.

Calculating a Sum

The next step in creating the worksheet is to determine the total second quarter sales for the Direct Mail sales channel in column B. To calculate this value in cell B8, Excel must add, or sum, the numbers in cells B4, B5, B6, and B7. Excel's **SUM function**, which adds all of the numbers in a range of cells, provides a convenient means to accomplish this task.

A **range** is a series of two or more adjacent cells in a column or row or a rectangular group of cells. For example, the group of adjacent cells B4, B5, B6, and B7 is called a range. Many Excel operations, such as summing numbers, take place on a range of cells.

The following steps show how to sum the numbers in column B.

Q&A

Q: What are the limits on numeric entries in Excel?

A: In Excel, a number can be between approximately -1×10^{308} and 1×10^{308} — that is, between a negative 1 followed by 308 zeros and a positive 1 followed by 308 zeros. To enter a number such as 6,000,000,000,000,000, you can type 6,000,000,000,000,000, or you can type 6E15, which stands for 6×10^{15}.

To Sum a Column of Numbers

1

• **Click cell B8.**

Cell B8 becomes the active cell (Figure 1-29).

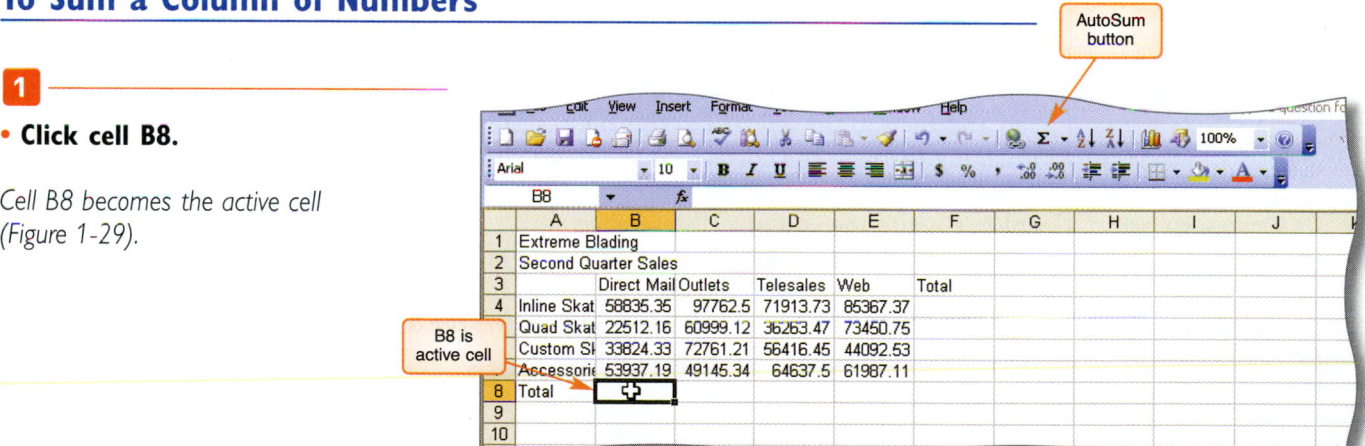

FIGURE 1-29

2

• **Click the AutoSum button on the Standard toolbar.**

Excel responds by displaying =SUM(B4:B7) in the formula bar and in the active cell B8 (Figure 1-30). Excel displays a ScreenTip below the active cell. The B4:B7 within parentheses following the function name SUM is Excel's way of identifying that the SUM function will add the numbers in the range B4 through B7. Excel also surrounds the proposed cells to sum with a moving border, called a **marquee***.*

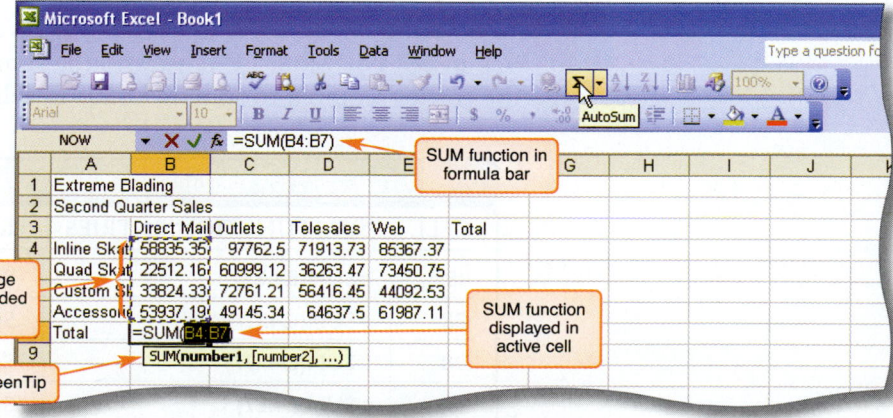

FIGURE 1-30

3

• **Click the AutoSum button a second time.**

Excel enters the sum of the second quarter sales for the Direct Mail sales channel in cell B8 (Figure 1-31). The SUM function assigned to cell B8 appears in the formula bar when cell B8 is the active cell.

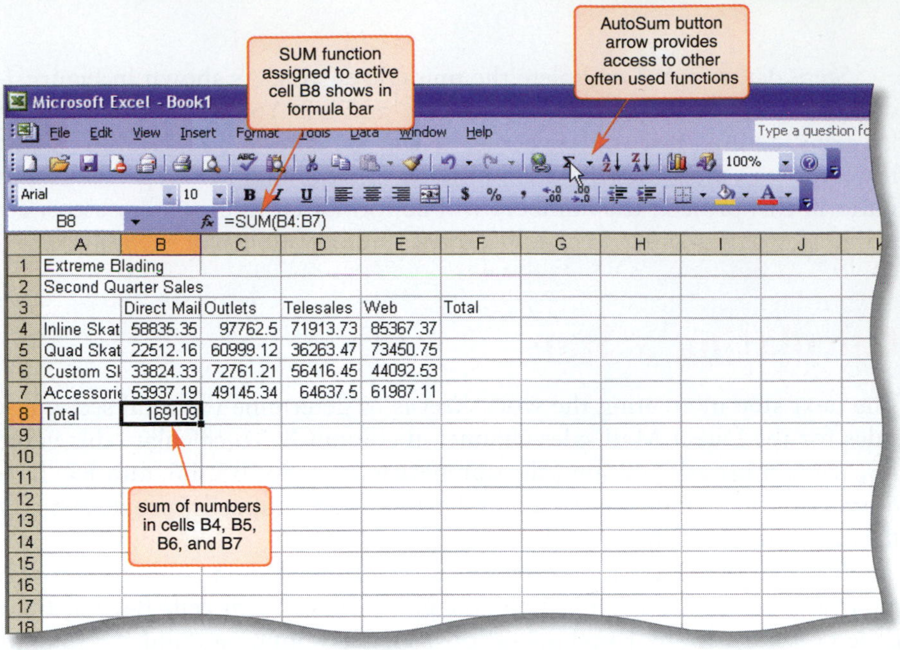

FIGURE 1-31

Other Ways

1. Click Insert Function button in formula bar, select SUM in Select a function list, click OK button, select range, click OK button
2. On Insert menu click Function, select SUM in Select a function list, click OK button, select range, click OK button
3. Press ALT+EQUAL SIGN (=) twice
4. In Voice Command mode, say "AutoSum, Sum, Enter"

When you enter the SUM function using the AutoSum button, Excel automatically selects what it considers to be your choice of the range to sum. When proposing the range to sum, Excel first looks for a range of cells with numbers above the active cell and then to the left. If Excel proposes the wrong range, you can correct it by dragging through the correct range before clicking the AutoSum button a second time. You also can enter the correct range by typing the beginning cell reference, a colon (:), and the ending cell reference.

If you click the AutoSum button arrow on the right side of the AutoSum button, Excel displays a list of often used functions from which you can choose. The list includes functions that allow you to determine the average, the minimum value, or the maximum value of a range of numbers.

Using the Fill Handle to Copy a Cell to Adjacent Cells

Excel also must calculate the totals for Outlets in cell C8, Telesales in cell D8, and for Web in cell E8. Table 1-2 illustrates the similarities between the entry in cell B8 and the entries required to sum the totals in cells C8, D8, and E8.

Table 1-2	Sum Function Entries in Row 8	
CELL	**SUM FUNCTION ENTRIES**	**REMARK**
B8	=SUM(B4:B7)	Sums cells B4, B5, B6, and B7
C8	=SUM(C4:C7)	Sums cells C4, C5, C6, and C7
D8	=SUM(D4:D7)	Sums cells D4, D5, D6, and D7
E8	=SUM(E4:E7)	Sums cells E4, E5, E6, and E7

To place the SUM functions in cells C8, D8, and E8, follow the same steps shown previously in Figures 1-29 through 1-31. A second, more efficient method is to copy the SUM function from cell B8 to the range C8:E8. The cell being copied is called the **source area** or **copy area**. The range of cells receiving the copy is called the **destination area** or **paste area**.

Although the SUM function entries in Table 1-2 are similar, they are not exact copies. The range in each SUM function entry uses cell references that are one column to the right of the previous column. When you copy cell references, Excel automatically adjusts them for each new position, resulting in the SUM function entries illustrated in Table 1-2. Each adjusted cell reference is called a **relative reference**.

The easiest way to copy the SUM formula from cell B8 to cells C8, D8, and E8 is to use the fill handle. The **fill handle** is the small black square located in the lower-right corner of the heavy border around the active cell. The following steps show how to use the fill handle to copy cell B8 to the adjacent cells C8:E8.

To Copy a Cell to Adjacent Cells in a Row

1

• **With cell B8 active, point to the fill handle.**

The mouse pointer changes to a cross hair (Figure 1-32).

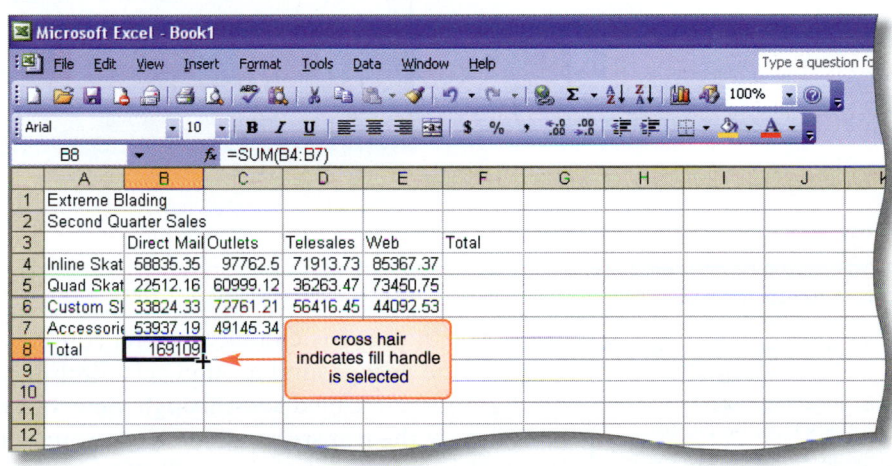

FIGURE 1-32

2

• **Drag the fill handle to select the destination area, range C8:E8. Do not release the mouse button.**

Excel displays a shaded border around the destination area, range C8:E8, and the source area, cell B8 (Figure 1-33).

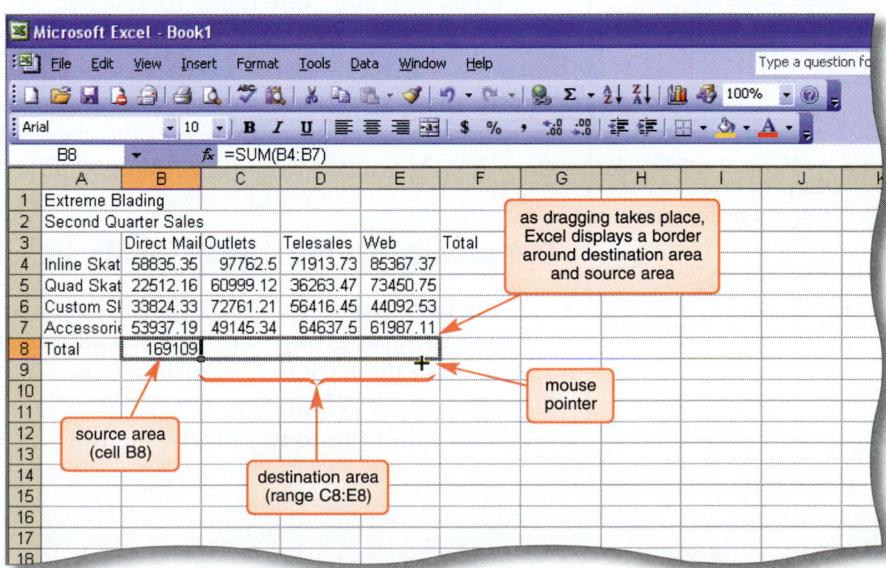

FIGURE 1-33

3

• **Release the mouse button.**

Excel copies the SUM function in cell B8 to the range C8:E8 (Figure 1-34). In addition, Excel calculates the sums and enters the results in cells C8, D8, and E8. The Auto Fill Options button appears to the right and below the destination area.

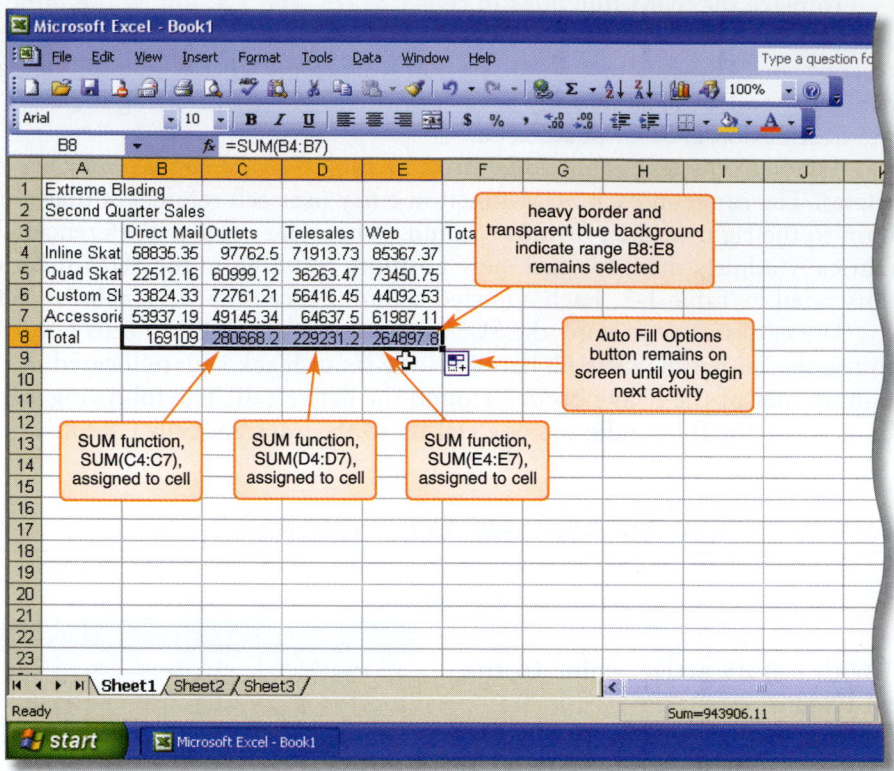

FIGURE 1-34

Once the copy is complete, Excel continues to display a heavy border and transparent blue background around cells B8:E8. The heavy border and transparent blue background are called **see-through view** and indicates a selected range. Excel does not display the transparent blue background around cell B8, the first cell in the range, because it is the active cell. If you click any cell, Excel will remove the heavy border and transparent blue background of the see-through view.

When you copy one range to another, Excel displays an Auto Fill Options button to the right and below the destination area (Figure 1-34). The Auto Fill Options button allows you to choose whether you want to copy the values from the source area to the destination area with formatting, without formatting, or only copy the format. To view the available fill options, click the Auto Fill Options button. The Auto Fill Options button disappears when you begin another activity.

Determining Multiple Totals at the Same Time

The next step in building the worksheet is to determine total second quarter sales for each product group and total second quarter sales for the company in column F. To calculate these totals, you can use the SUM function much as you used it to total the sales by sales channel in row 8. In this example, however, Excel will determine totals for all of the rows at the same time. The following steps illustrate this process.

To Determine Multiple Totals at the Same Time

1

• **Click cell F4.**

Cell F4 becomes the active cell (Figure 1-35).

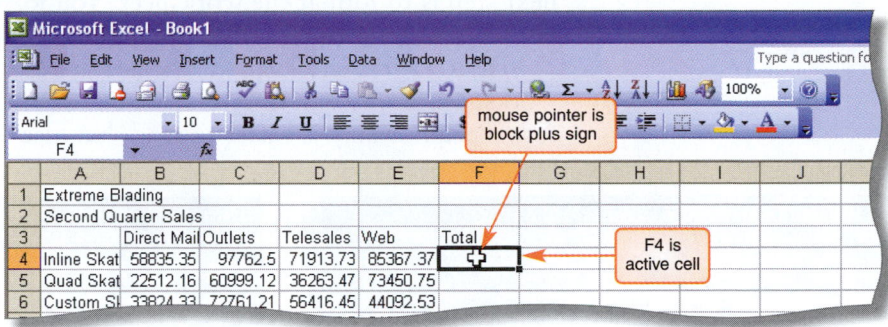

FIGURE 1-35

2

• **With the mouse pointer in cell F4 and in the shape of a block plus sign, drag the mouse pointer down to cell F8.**

Excel highlights the range F4:F8 with a see-through view (Figure 1-36).

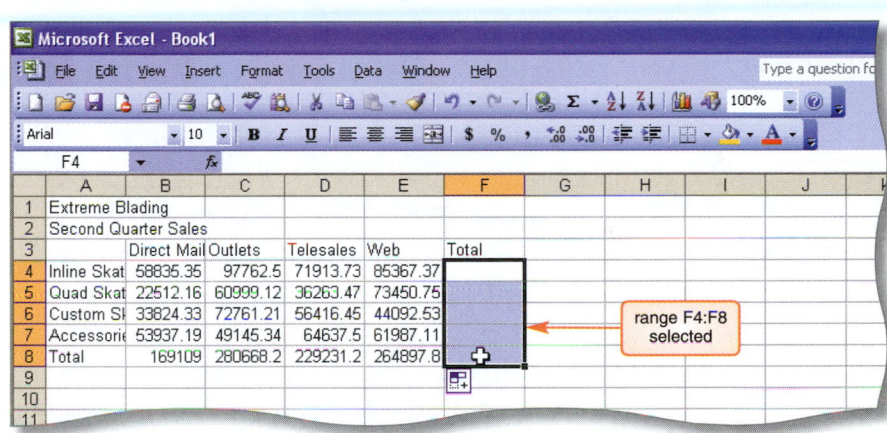

FIGURE 1-36

3

• **Click the AutoSum button on the Standard toolbar.**

Excel assigns the appropriate SUM functions to cells F4, F5, F6, F7, and F8, and then calculates and displays the sums in the respective cells (Figure 1-37).

 4

• **Select cell A9 to deselect the range F4:F8.**

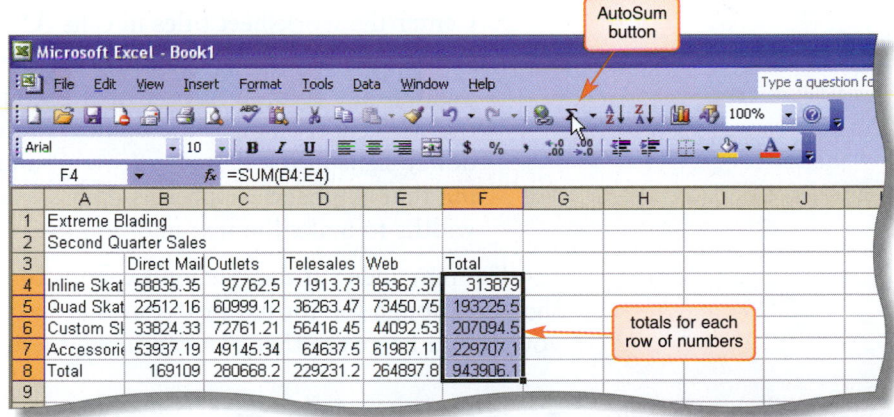

FIGURE 1-37

If each cell in a selected range is next to a row of numbers, Excel assigns the SUM function to each cell when you click the AutoSum button. Thus, as shown in the previous steps, each of the five cells in the selected range is assigned a SUM function with a different range, based on its row. This same procedure could have been used earlier to sum the columns. That is, instead of clicking cell B8, clicking the AutoSum button twice, and then copying the SUM function to the range C8:E8, the range B8:E8 could have been selected and then the AutoSum button clicked once, which would have assigned the SUM function to the entire range.

More About

Summing Columns and Rows

A more efficient way to determine the totals in row 8 and column F in Figure 1-37 is to select the range (B4:F8) and then click the AutoSum button on the Standard toolbar.

Formatting the Worksheet

The text, numeric entries, and functions for the worksheet now are complete. The next step is to format the worksheet. You **format** a worksheet to emphasize certain entries and make the worksheet easier to read and understand.

Figure 1-38a shows the worksheet before formatting. Figure 1-38b shows the worksheet after formatting. As you can see from the two figures, a worksheet that is formatted not only is easier to read, but also looks more professional.

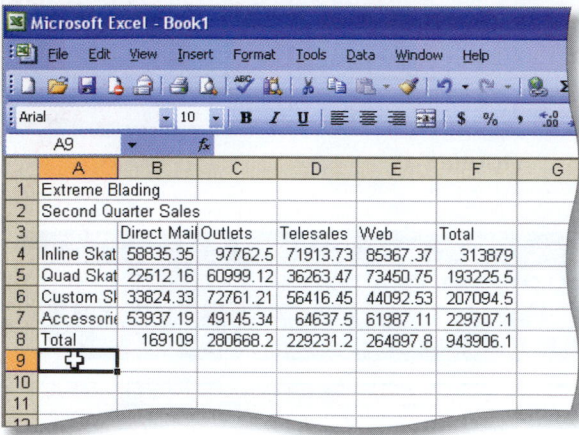

(a) Before Formatting

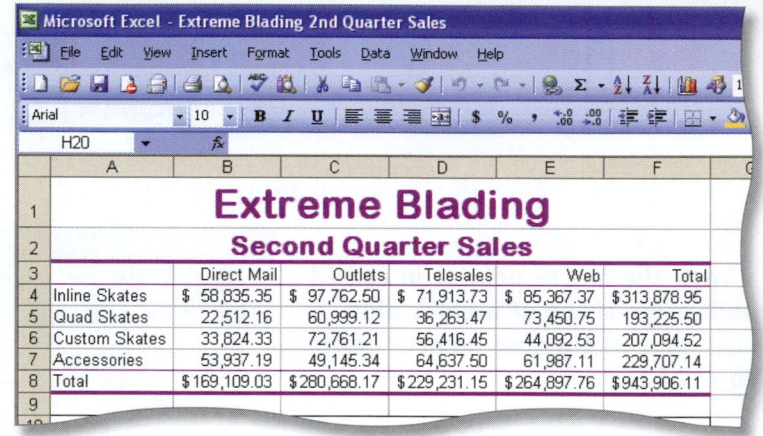

(b) After Formatting

FIGURE 1-38

To change the unformatted worksheet in Figure 1-38a to the formatted worksheet in Figure 1-38b, the following tasks must be completed:

1. Change the font type, change the font style to bold, increase the font size, and change the font color of the worksheet titles in cells A1 and A2.
2. Center the worksheet titles in cells A1 and A2 across columns A through F.
3. Format the body of the worksheet. The body of the worksheet, range A3:F8, includes the column titles, row titles, and numbers. Formatting the body of the worksheet changes the numbers to use a dollars-and-cents format, with dollar signs in the first row (row 4) and the total row (row 8); adds underlining that emphasizes portions of the worksheet; and modifies the column widths to make the text and numbers readable.

The remainder of this section explains the process required to format the worksheet. Although the format procedures are explained in the order described above, you should be aware that you can make these format changes in any order.

Font Type, Style, Size, and Color

The characters that Excel displays on the screen are a specific font type, style, size, and color. The **font type**, or font face, defines the appearance and shape of the letters, numbers, and special characters. Examples of font types include Times New Roman, Arial, and Courier. **Font style** indicates how the characters are formatted. Common font styles include regular, bold, underline, or italic. The **font size** specifies the size of the characters on the screen. Font size is gauged by a measurement system called points. A single point is about 1/72 of one inch in height. Thus, a character with a **point size** of 10 is about 10/72 of one inch in height. The **font color** defines the color of the characters. Excel can display characters in a wide variety of colors, including black, red, orange, and blue.

When Excel begins, the preset font type for the entire workbook is Arial, with a font size and font style of 10-point regular black. Excel allows you to change the font characteristics in a single cell, a range of cells, the entire worksheet, or the entire workbook.

Changing the Font Type

Different font types often are used in a worksheet to make it more appealing to the reader. The following steps show how to change the worksheet title font type from Arial to Arial Rounded MT Bold.

To Change the Font Type

1

• **Click cell A1 and then point to the Font box arrow on the Formatting toolbar.**

Cell A1 is the active cell (Figure 1-39).

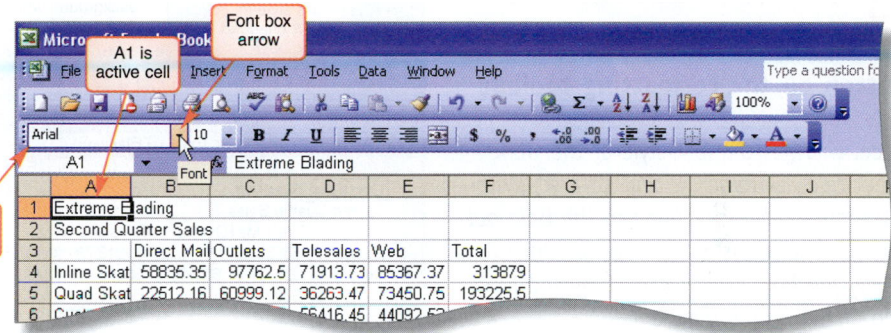

FIGURE 1-39

2

• **Click the Font box arrow and then point to Arial Rounded MT Bold.**

Excel displays the Font list with Arial Rounded MT Bold highlighted (Figure 1-40).

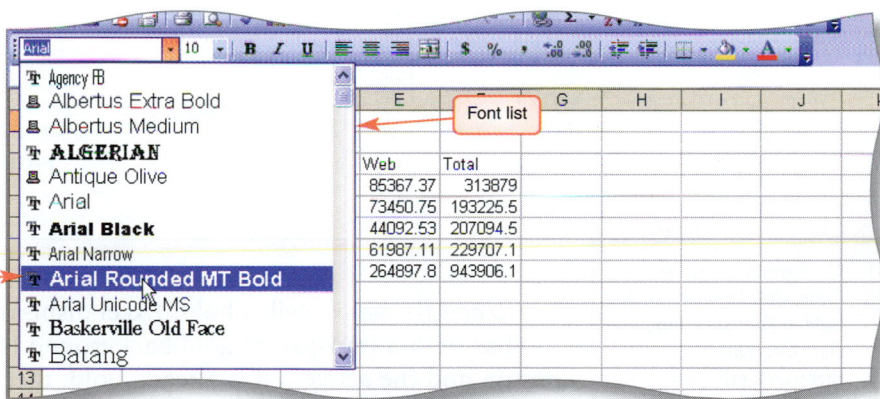

FIGURE 1-40

3

• **Click Arial Rounded MT Bold.**

Excel changes the font type of cell A1 from Arial to Arial Rounded MT Bold (Figure 1-41).

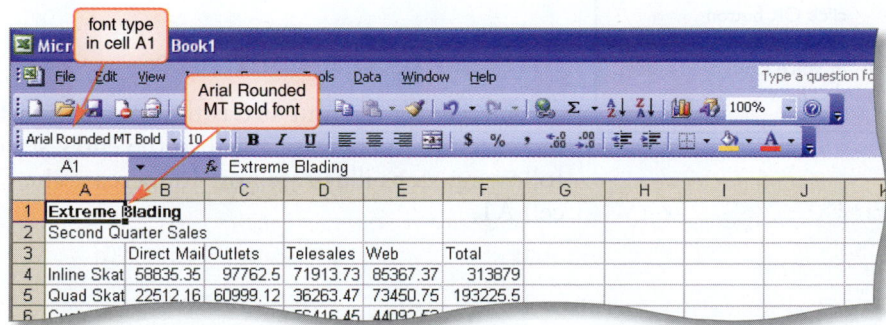

FIGURE 1-41

Because many applications supply additional font types beyond what comes with the Windows operating system, the number of font types available on your computer will depend on the applications installed. This book only uses font types that come with the Windows operating system.

Bolding a Cell

You **bold** an entry in a cell to emphasize it or make it stand out from the rest of the worksheet. The following step shows how to bold the worksheet title in cell A1.

To Bold a Cell

- **With cell A1 active, click the Bold button on the Formatting toolbar.**

Excel changes the font style of the worksheet title, Extreme Blading, to bold. With the mouse pointer pointing to the Bold button, Excel displays a ScreenTip immediately below the Bold button to identify the function of the button (Figure 1-42).

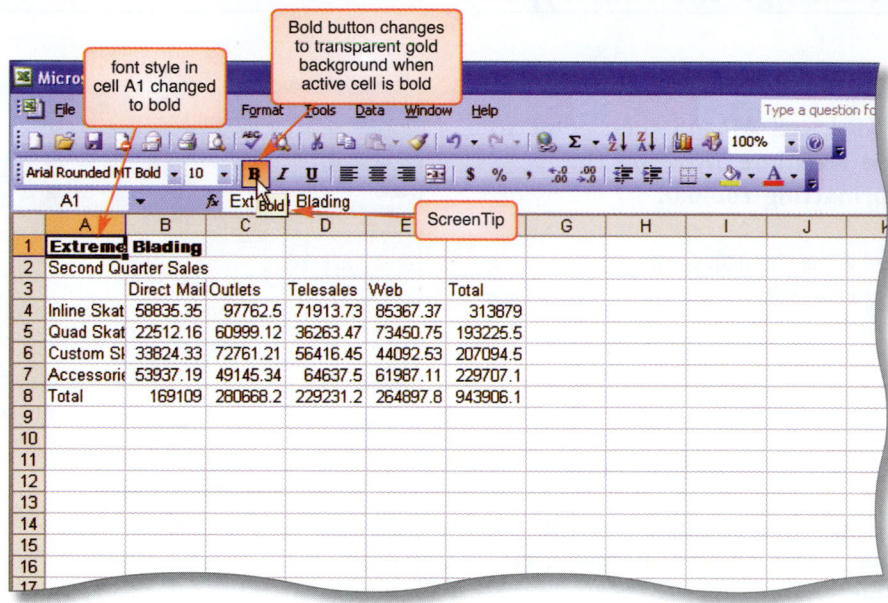

FIGURE 1-42

When the active cell is bold, Excel displays the Bold button on the Formatting toolbar with a transparent gold background (Figure 1-42). If you point to the Bold button and the active cell is already bold, then Excel displays the button with a transparent red background. Clicking the Bold button a second time removes the bold font style.

Increasing the Font Size

Increasing the font size is the next step in formatting the worksheet title. You increase the font size of a cell so the entry stands out and is easier to read. The following steps illustrate how to increase the font size of the worksheet title in cell A1.

To Increase the Font Size of a Cell Entry

1

• **With cell A1 selected, click the Font Size box arrow on the Formatting toolbar.**

Excel displays the Font Size list as shown in Figure 1-43.

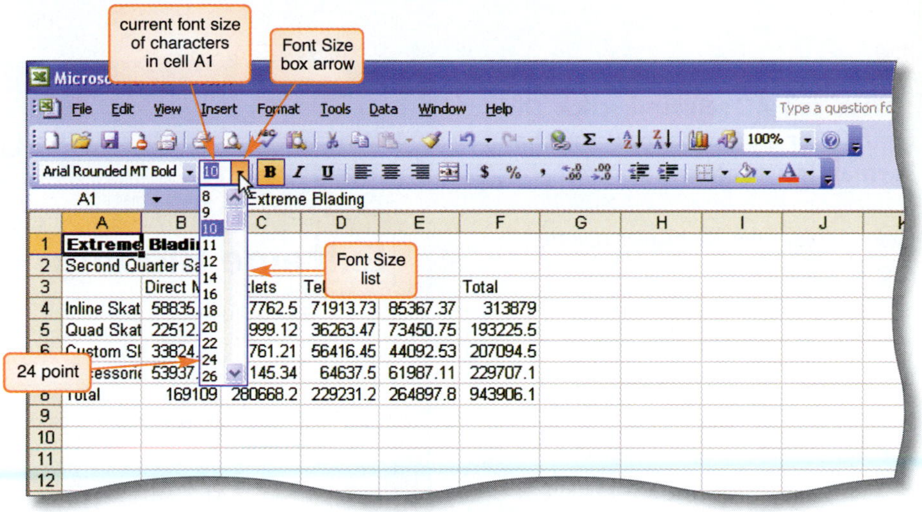

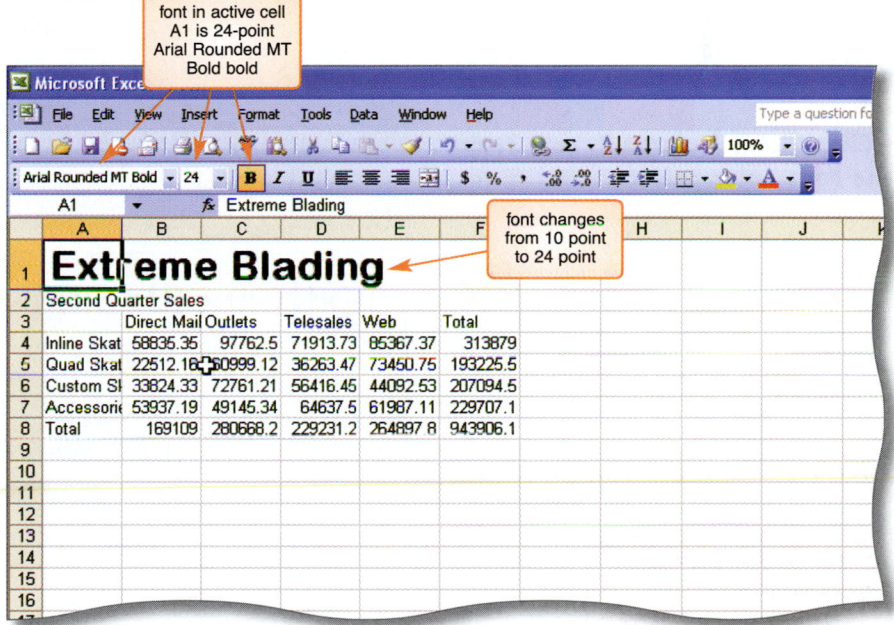

FIGURE 1-43

2

• **Click 24 in the Font Size list.**

The font size of the characters in cell A1 increase from 10 point to 24 point (Figure 1-44). The increased font size makes the worksheet title easier to read.

FIGURE 1-44

An alternative to clicking a font size in the Font Size list is to click the Font Size box, type the font size, and then press the ENTER key. This procedure allows you to assign a font size not available in the Font Size list to a selected cell entry. With cell A1 selected (Figure 1-44), the Font Size box shows that the new font size is 24 and the transparent gold Bold button shows that the font style is bold.

Changing the Font Color of a Cell Entry

The next step is to change the color of the font in cell A1 from black to violet. The steps on the next page show how to change the font color of a cell entry.

> **Other Ways**
>
> 1. On Format menu click Cells, click Font tab, select font size in Size box, click OK button
> 2. Right-click cell, click Format Cells on shortcut menu, click Font tab, select font size in Size box, click OK button
> 3. In Voice Command mode, say "Font Size, [desired font size]"

To Change the Font Color of a Cell Entry

1

• **With cell A1 selected, click the Font Color button arrow on the Formatting toolbar.**

Excel displays the Font Color palette (Figure 1-45).

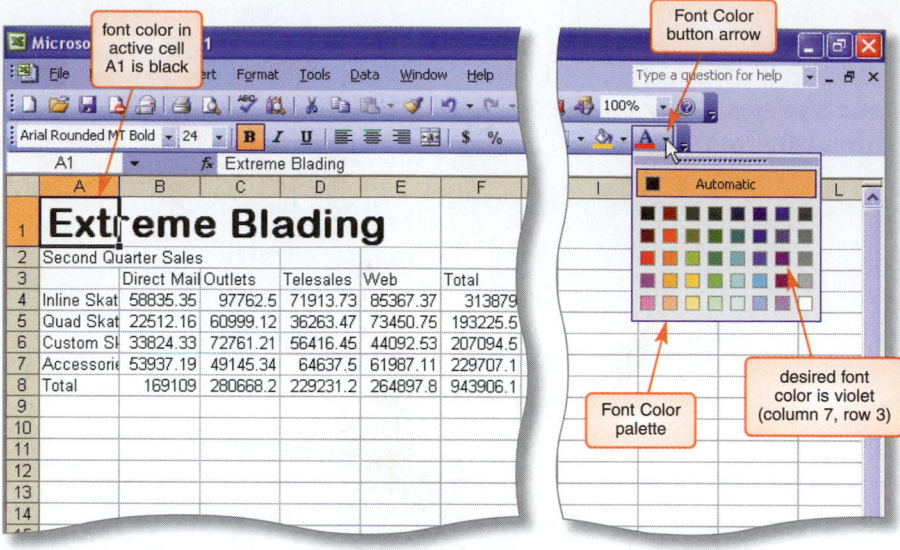

FIGURE 1-45

2

• **Click Violet (column 7, row 3) on the Font Color palette.**

The font in the worksheet title in cell A1 changes from black to violet (Figure 1-46).

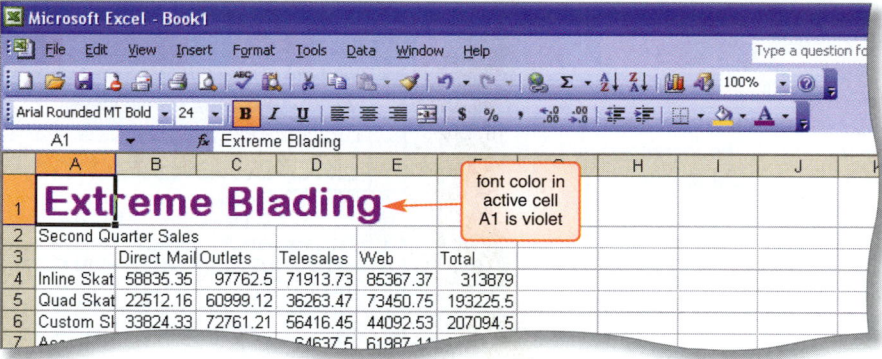

FIGURE 1-46

Other Ways

1. On Format menu click Cells, click Font tab, click Color box arrow, select color on Color palette, click OK button
2. Right-click cell, click Format Cells on shortcut menu, click Font tab, click Color box arrow, select color on Color palette, click OK button
3. In Voice Command mode, say "Font Color, [desired color]"

As shown in Figure 1-45, you can choose from 40 different font colors on the Font Color palette. Your Font Color palette may have more or fewer colors, depending on color settings of your operating system. When you choose a color on the Font Color palette, Excel changes the Font Color button on the Formatting toolbar to the chosen color. Thus, to change the font color of the cell entry in another cell to the same color, you only need to select the cell and then click the Font Color button.

Centering a Cell Entry across Columns by Merging Cells

The final step in formatting the worksheet title is to center it across columns A through F. Centering a worksheet title across the columns used in the body of the worksheet improves the worksheet's appearance. To do this, the six cells in the range A1:F1 are combined, or merged, into a single cell that is the width of the columns in the body of the worksheet. **Merging cells** involves creating a single cell by combining two or more selected cells. The following steps illustrate how to center the worksheet title across columns by merging cells.

To Center a Cell Entry across Columns by Merging Cells

1

- **With cell A1 selected, drag to cell F1.**

Excel highlights the selected cells (Figure 1-47).

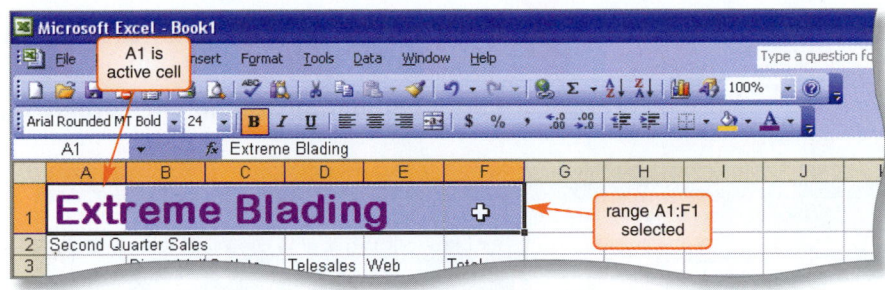

FIGURE 1-47

2

- **Click the Merge and Center button on the Formatting toolbar.**

Excel merges the cells A1 through F1 to create a new cell A1 and centers the contents of cell A1 across columns A through F (Figure 1-48). After the merge, cells B1 through F1 no longer exist on the worksheet.

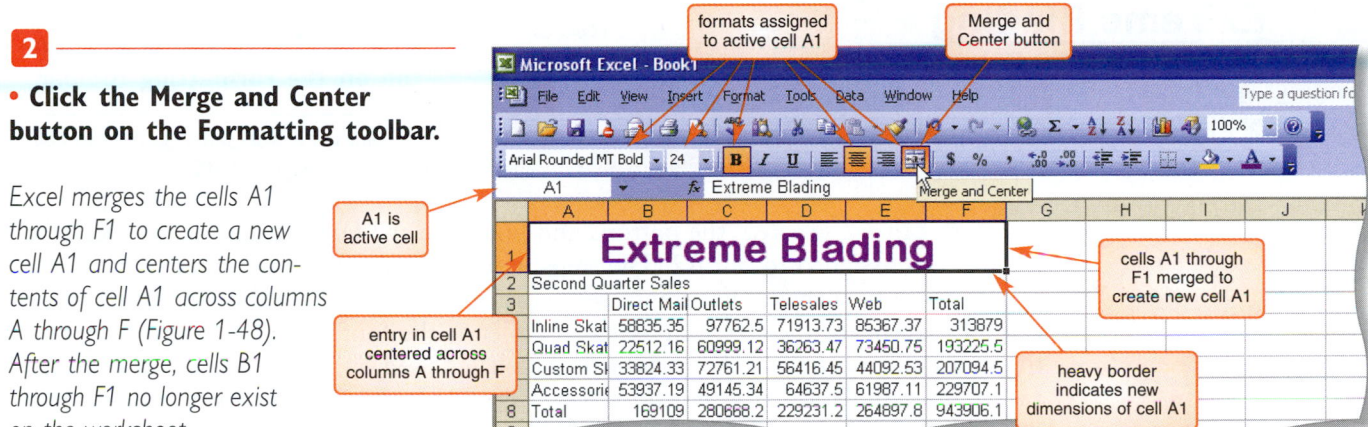

FIGURE 1-48

Excel not only centers the worksheet title across the range A1:F1, but it also merges cells A1 through F1 into one merged cell, cell A1. For the Merge and Center button to work properly, all the cells except the leftmost cell in the selected range must be empty.

The opposite of merging cells is **splitting a merged cell**. After you have merged multiple cells to create one merged cell, you can unmerge, or split, the merged cell to display the original cells on the worksheet. You split a merged cell by selecting it and clicking the Merge and Center button. For example, if you click the Merge and Center button a second time in Step 2, it will split the merged cell A1 to cells A1, B1, C1, D1, E1, and F1.

Most formats assigned to a cell will appear on the Formatting toolbar when the cell is selected. For example, with cell A1 selected in Figure 1-48, Excel displays the font type and font size of the active cell in their appropriate boxes. Transparent gold buttons on the Formatting toolbar indicate other assigned formatting. To determine if less frequently used formats are assigned to a cell, right-click the cell, click Format Cells on the shortcut menu, and then click each of the tabs in the Format Cells dialog box.

Formatting the Worksheet Subtitle

The worksheet subtitle in cell A2 is to be formatted the same as the worksheet title in cell A1, except that the font size should be 16 rather than 24. The steps on the next page show how to format the worksheet subtitle in cell A2.

Other Ways

1. On Format menu click Cells, click Alignment tab, select Center in Horizontal list, click Merge cells check box, click OK button
2. Right-click cell, click Format Cells on shortcut menu, click Alignment tab, select Center in Horizontal list, click Merge cells check box, click OK button
3. In Voice Command mode, say "Merge and Center"

To Format the Worksheet Subtitle

1 Select cell A2.

2 Click the Font box arrow on the Formatting toolbar and then click Arial Rounded MT Bold.

3 Click the Bold button on the Formatting toolbar.

4 Click the Font Size box arrow on the Formatting toolbar and then click 16.

5 Click the Font Color button on the Formatting toolbar.

6 Select the range A2:F2 and then click the Merge and Center button on the Formatting toolbar.

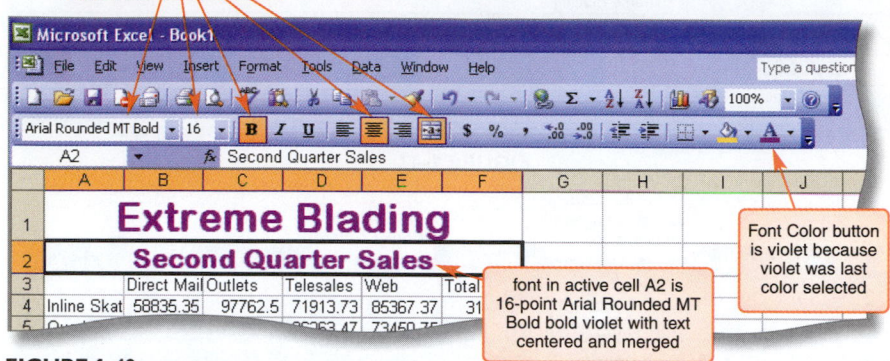

buttons and boxes on Formatting toolbar identify formats assigned to active cell A2

font in active cell A2 is 16-point Arial Rounded MT Bold bold violet with text centered and merged

Font Color button is violet because violet was last color selected

FIGURE 1-49

Excel displays the worksheet subtitle in cell A2 as shown in Figure 1-49.

With cell A2 selected, the buttons and boxes on the Formatting toolbar describe the formats assigned to cell A2. The steps used to format the worksheet subtitle in cell A2 were the same as the steps used to assign the formats to the worksheet title in cell A1, except for the step that assigned violet as the font color. The step to change the font color of the worksheet subtitle in cell A2 used only the Font Color button, rather than the Font Color button arrow. Recall that, when you choose a color on the Font Color palette, Excel assigns the last font color used (in this case, violet) to the Font Color button.

Using AutoFormat to Format the Body of a Worksheet

Excel has customized autoformats that allow you to format the body of the worksheet to give it a professional look. An **autoformat** is a built-in collection of formats such as font style, font color, borders, and alignment, which you can apply to a range of cells. The following steps format the range A3:F8 using the AutoFormat command on the Format menu.

To Use AutoFormat to Format the Body of a Worksheet

1

• Select cell A3, the upper-left corner cell of the rectangular range to format.

• Drag the mouse pointer to cell F8, the lower-right corner cell of the range to format.

Excel highlights the range to format with a heavy border and transparent blue background (Figure 1-50).

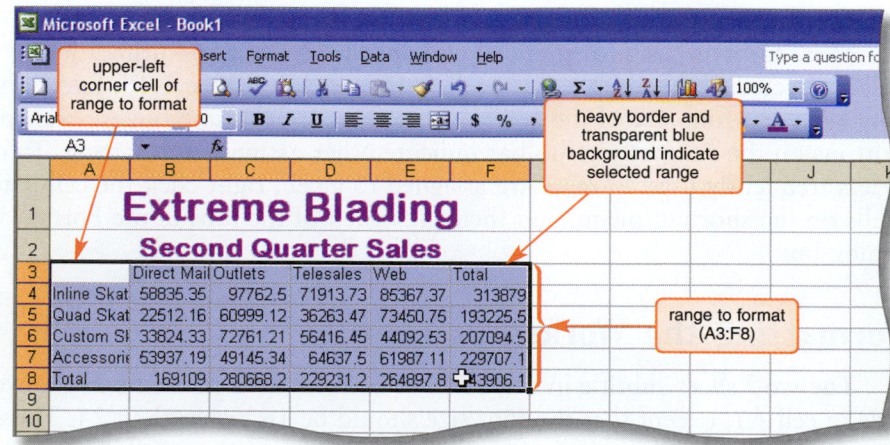

upper-left corner cell of range to format

heavy border and transparent blue background indicate selected range

range to format (A3:F8)

FIGURE 1-50

2

• **Click Format on the menu bar.**

Excel displays the Format menu (Figure 1-51).

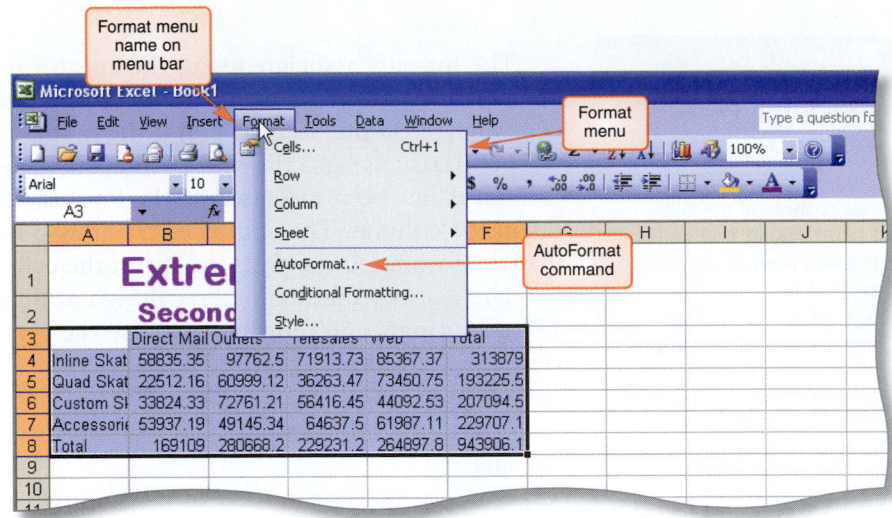

Format menu name on menu bar

Format menu

AutoFormat command

FIGURE 1-51

3

• **Click AutoFormat on the Format menu.**

• **When Excel displays the AutoFormat dialog box, click the Accounting 2 format.**

Excel displays the AutoFormat dialog box with a list of available autoformats (Figure 1-52). For each autoformat, Excel provides a sample to illustrate how the body of the worksheet will appear if that autoformat is chosen.

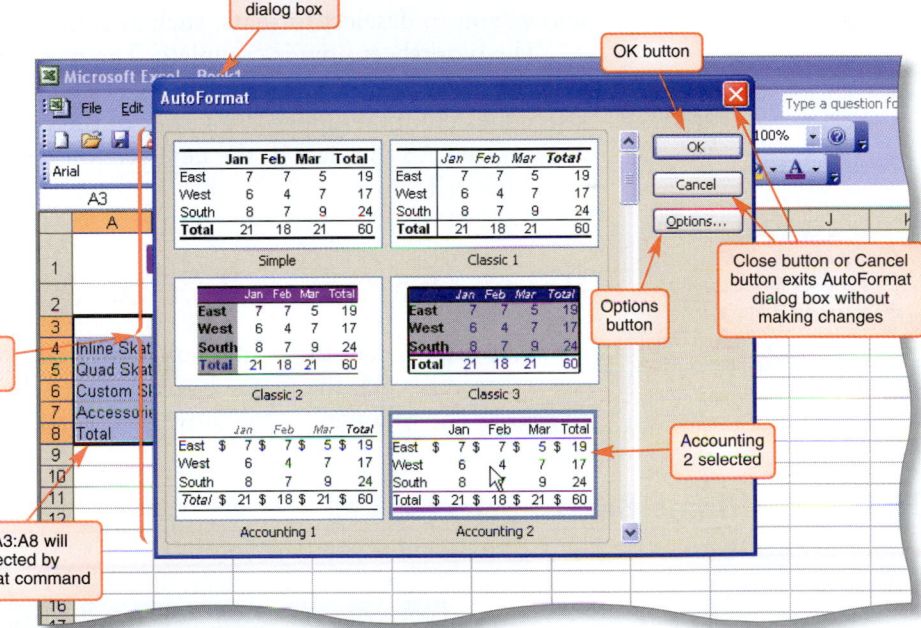

AutoFormat dialog box

OK button

available autoformats

Options button

Close button or Cancel button exits AutoFormat dialog box without making changes

Accounting 2 selected

range A3:A8 will be affected by AutoFormat command

FIGURE 1-52

4

• **Click the OK button.**

• **Select cell A10 to deselect the range A3:F8.**

Excel displays the worksheet with the range A3:F8 formatted using the autoformat, Accounting 2 (Figure 1-53).

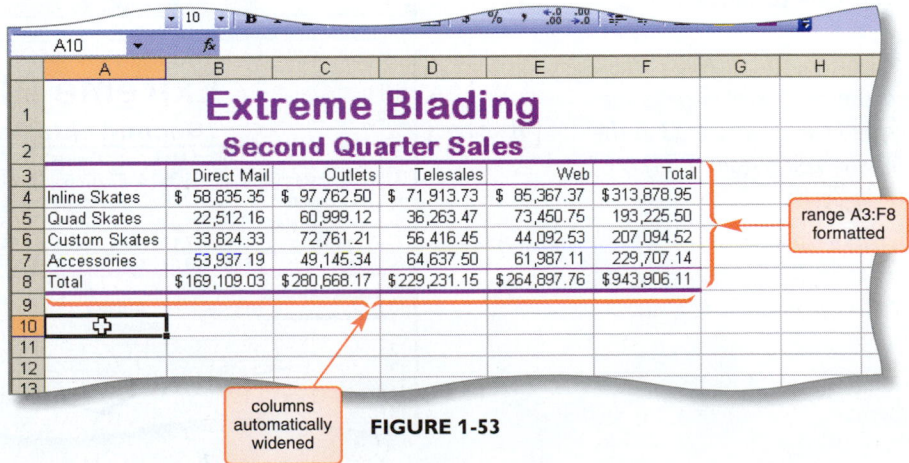

range A3:F8 formatted

columns automatically widened

FIGURE 1-53

More About

Merging Table Formats

It is not uncommon to apply two or more of the table formats (Figure 1-52 on the previous page) to the same range. If you assign two table formats to a range, Excel does not remove the original format from the range; it simply adds the second table format to the first. Thus, if you decide to change a table format to another, select the table format None from the bottom of the list to clear the first table format.

More About

Navigation

For more information about selecting cells that contain certain entries, such as constants or formulas, visit the Excel 2003 More About Web page (scsite.com/ex2003/more) and click Using Go To Special.

The formats associated with the autoformat Accounting 2 include right-aligned column titles; numbers displayed as dollars and cents with comma separators; numbers aligned on the decimal point; the first row and total row of numbers displayed with dollar signs; and top and bottom rows displayed with borders. The width of column A has been increased so the longest row title in cell A6, Custom Skates, just fits in the column. The widths of columns B through F also have been increased so that the formatted numbers will fit in the cells.

The AutoFormat dialog box shown in Figure 1-52 on the previous page includes 17 autoformats and four buttons. Use the vertical scroll bar in the dialog box to view the autoformats that are not displayed when the dialog box first opens. Each one of these autoformats offers a different look. The one you choose depends on the worksheet you are creating. The last autoformat in the list, called None, removes all formats.

The four buttons in the AutoFormat dialog box allow you to complete the entries, modify an autoformat, or cancel changes and close the dialog box. The Close button on the title bar and the Cancel button both terminate the current activity and close the AutoFormat dialog box without making changes. The Options button allows you to deselect formats, such as fonts or borders, within an autoformat.

The worksheet now is complete. The next step is to chart the second quarter sales for the four product groups by sales channel. To create the chart, you must select the cell in the upper-left corner of the range to chart (cell A3). Rather than clicking cell A3 to select it, the next section describes how to use the Name box to select the cell.

Using the Name Box to Select a Cell

As previously noted, the Name box is located on the left side of the formula bar. To select any cell, click the Name box and enter the cell reference of the cell you want to select. The following steps show how to select cell A3.

To Use the Name Box to Select a Cell

1

• **Click the Name box in the formula bar and then type** a3 **as the cell to select.**

Even though cell A10 is the active cell, Excel displays the typed cell reference a3 in the Name box (Figure 1-54).

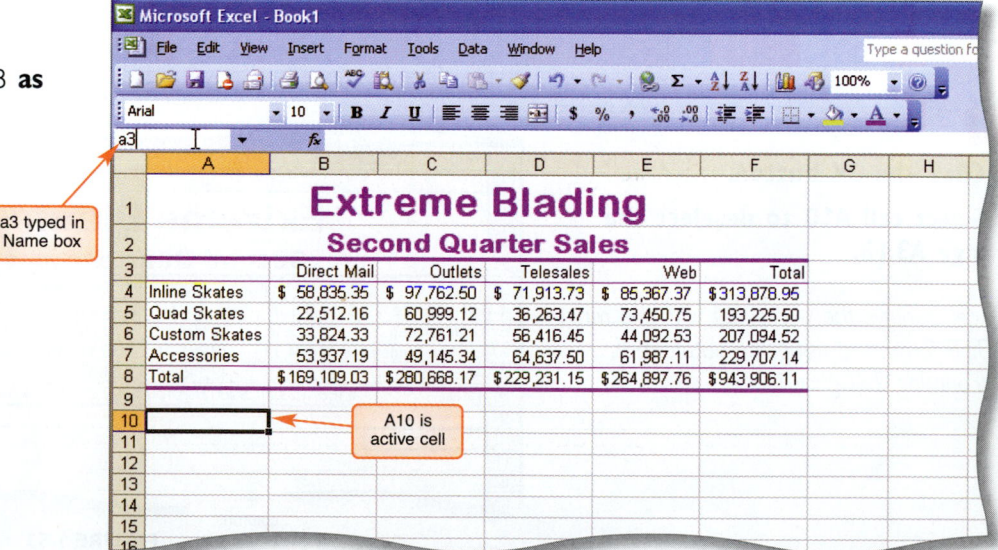

FIGURE 1-54

2

• **Press the ENTER key.**

Excel changes the active cell from cell A10 to cell A3 (Figure 1-55).

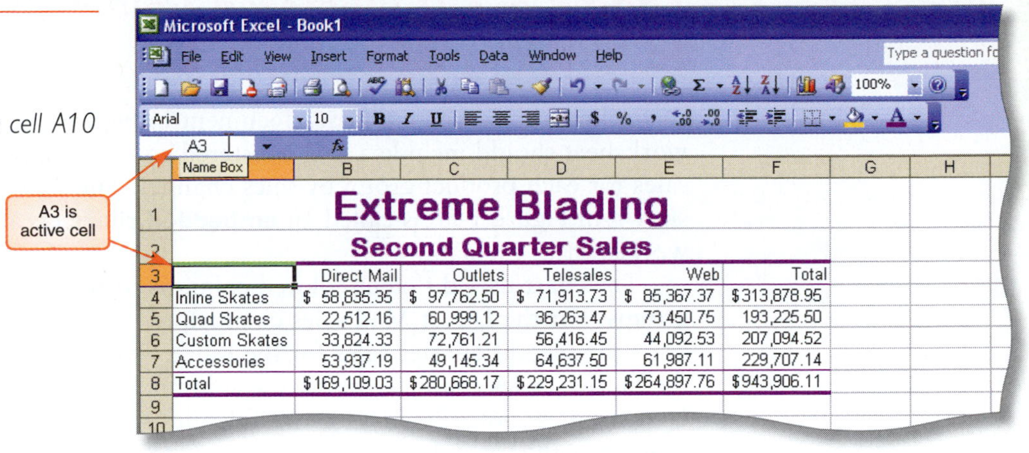

FIGURE 1-55

As you will see in later projects, in addition to using the Name box to select any cell in a worksheet, you also can use it to assign names to a cell or range of cells. Excel supports several additional ways to select a cell, as summarized in Table 1-3.

Table 1-3	Selecting Cells in Excel
KEY, BOX, OR COMMAND	**FUNCTION**
ALT+PAGE DOWN	Selects the cell one worksheet window to the right and moves the worksheet window accordingly.
ALT+PAGE UP	Selects the cell one worksheet window to the left and moves the worksheet window accordingly.
ARROW	Selects the adjacent cell in the direction of the arrow on the key.
CTRL+ARROW	Selects the border cell of the worksheet in combination with the arrow keys and moves the worksheet window accordingly. For example, to select the rightmost cell in the row that contains the active cell, press CTRL+RIGHT ARROW. You also can press the END key, release it, and then press the appropriate arrow key to accomplish the same task.
CTRL+HOME	Selects cell A1 or the cell one column and one row below and to the right of frozen titles and moves the worksheet window accordingly.
Find command on Edit menu or SHIFT+F5	Finds and selects a cell that contains specific contents that you enter in the Find dialog box. If necessary, Excel moves the worksheet window to display the cell. You also can press CTRL+F to display the Find dialog box.
Go To command on Edit menu or F5	Selects the cell that corresponds to the cell reference you enter in the Go To dialog box and moves the worksheet window accordingly. You also can press CTRL+G to display the Go To dialog box.
HOME	Selects the cell at the beginning of the row that contains the active cell and moves the worksheet window accordingly.
Name box	Selects the cell in the workbook that corresponds to the cell reference you enter in the Name box.
PAGE DOWN	Selects the cell down one worksheet window from the active cell and moves the worksheet window accordingly.
PAGE UP	Selects the cell up one worksheet window from the active cell and moves the worksheet window accordingly.

Adding a 3-D Clustered Column Chart to the Worksheet

As outlined in the requirements document in Figure 1-2 on page EX 6, the worksheet should include a 3-D Clustered column chart to graphically represent sales for each product group by sales channel. The 3-D Clustered column chart shown in Figure 1-56 is called an **embedded chart** because it is drawn on the same worksheet as the data.

The chart uses different colored columns to represent sales for different product groups. For the Direct Mail sales channel, for example, the light blue column represents the second quarter sales for the Inline Skates product group ($58,835.35); for the Outlets sales channel, the purple column represents the second quarter sales for Quad Skates ($60,999.12); for the Telesales sales channel, the light yellow column represents the second quarter sales for Custom Skates ($56,416.45); and for the Web sales channel, the turquoise column represents the second quarter sales for Accessories ($61,987.11). For the Outlets, Telesales, and Web sales channels, the columns follow the same color scheme to represent the comparable second quarter sales. The totals from the worksheet are not represented because the totals are not in the range specified for charting.

Excel derives the chart scale based the values in the worksheet and then displays the scale along the vertical axis (also called the **y-axis** or **value axis**) of the chart. For example, no value in the range B4:E7 is less than 0 or greater than $100,000.00, so the scale ranges from 0 to $100,000.00. Excel also determines the $20,000.00 increments of the scale automatically. For the numbers along the y-axis, Excel uses a format that includes representing the 0 value with a dash (Figure 1-56).

Q&A

Q: If I change a cell value on which the chart is dependent, will Excel redraw the chart?

A: Yes. Excel redraws the chart instantaneously, unless automatic recalculation is disabled. If automatic recalculation is disabled, then you must press function key F9 to redraw the chart. To enable or disable automatic recalculation, invoke the Options command on the Tools menu and click the Calculation tab.

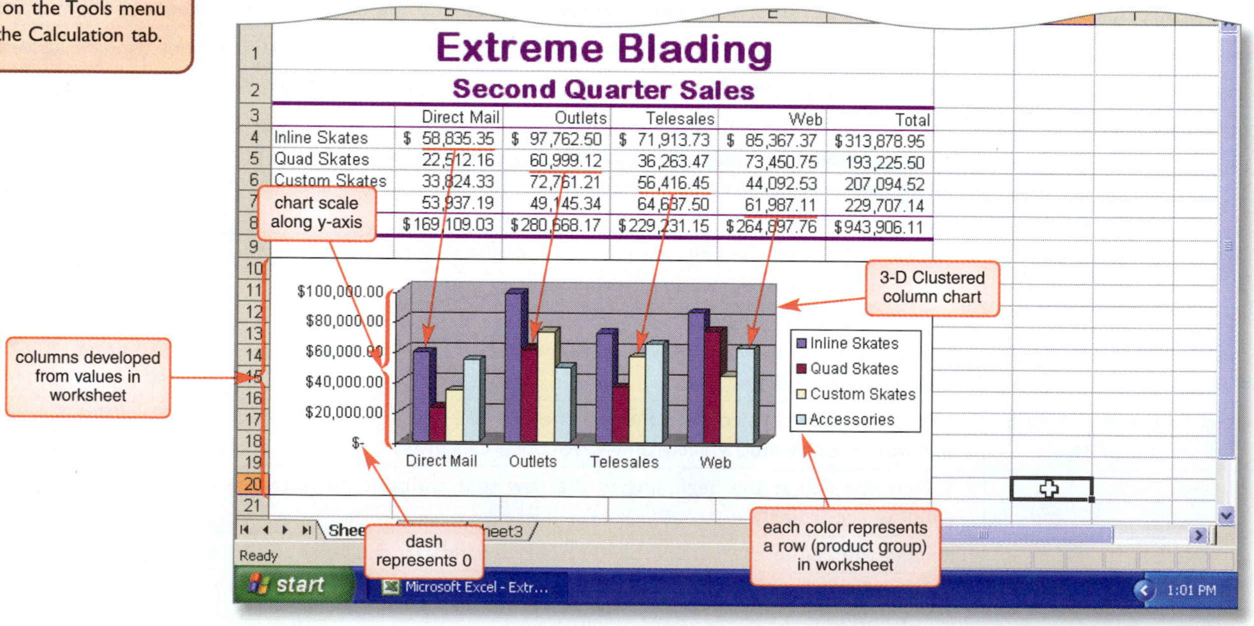

FIGURE 1-56

With the range to chart selected, you click the Chart Wizard button on the Standard toolbar to initiate drawing the chart. The area on the worksheet where the chart appears is called the **chart location**. As shown in Figure 1-56, the chart location in this worksheet is the range A10:F20, immediately below the worksheet data.

The following steps show how to draw a 3-D Clustered column chart that compares the second quarter sales by product group for the four sales channels.

To Add a 3-D Clustered Column Chart to the Worksheet

1

• **With cell A3 selected, position the block plus sign mouse pointer within the cell's border and drag the mouse pointer to the lower-right corner cell (cell E7) of the range to chart (A3:E7).**

Excel highlights the range to chart (Figure 1-57).

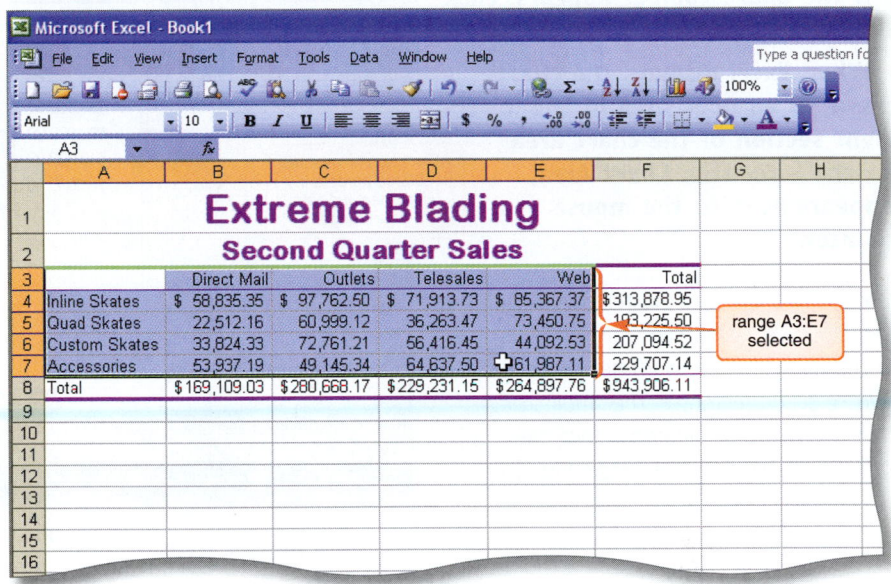

FIGURE 1-57

2

• **Click the Chart Wizard button on the Standard toolbar.**

• **When Excel displays the Chart Wizard - Step 1 of 4 - Chart Type dialog box, and with Column selected in the Chart type list, click Clustered column with a 3-D visual effect (column 1, row 2) in the Chart sub-type area.**

Excel displays the Chart Wizard - Step 1 of 4 - Chart Type dialog box as shown in Figure 1-58.

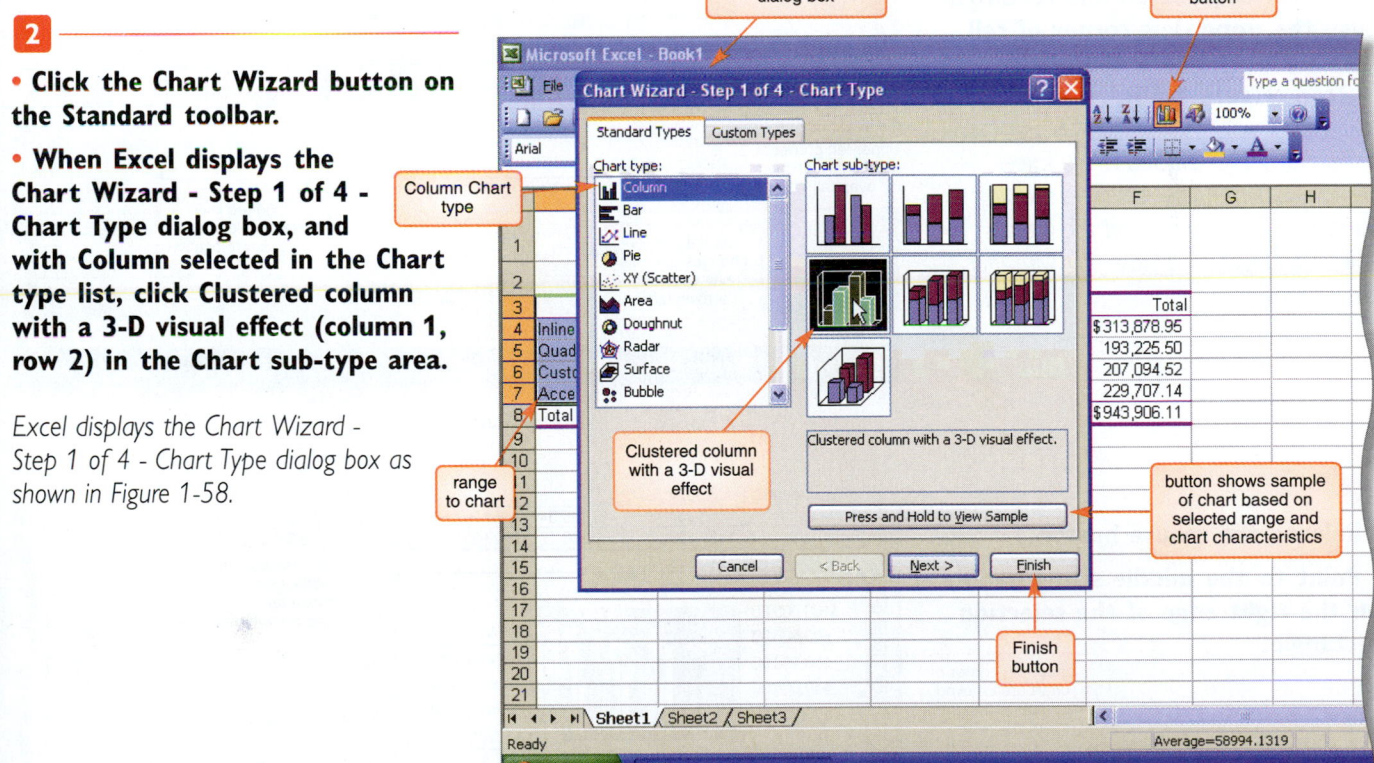

FIGURE 1-58

3

• **Click the Finish button.**

• **If the Chart toolbar appears, click its Close button.**

• **When Excel displays the chart, point to an open area in the lower-right section of the chart area so the ScreenTip, Chart Area, appears next to the mouse pointer.**

Excel draws the 3-D Clustered column chart (Figure 1-59). The chart appears in the middle of the worksheet window in a selection rectangle. The small sizing handles at the corners and along the sides of the selection rectangle indicate the chart is selected.

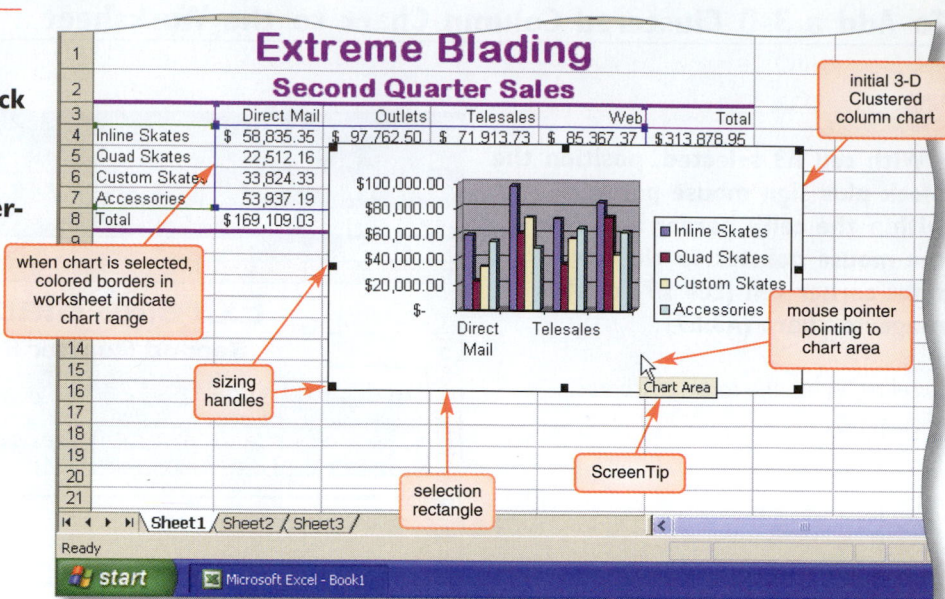

FIGURE 1-59

4

• **Drag the chart down and to the left to position the upper-left corner of the dotted line rectangle over the upper-left corner of cell A10. Do not release the mouse button (Figure 1-60).**

As you drag the selected chart, Excel displays a dotted line rectangle showing the new chart location and the mouse pointer changes to a cross hair with four arrowheads.

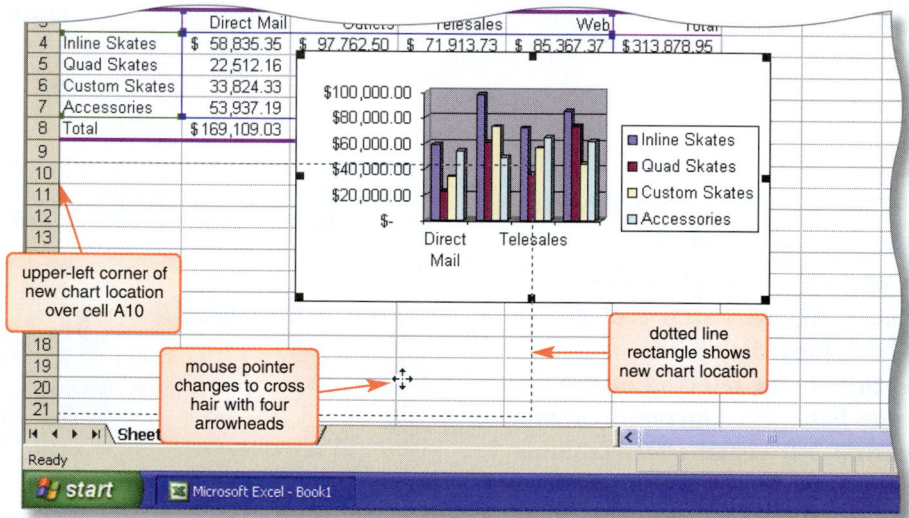

FIGURE 1-60

5

• **Release the mouse button.**

• **Point to the middle sizing handle on the right edge of the selection rectangle.**

The chart appears in a new location (Figure 1-61). The mouse pointer changes to a horizontal line with two arrowheads when it points to a sizing handle.

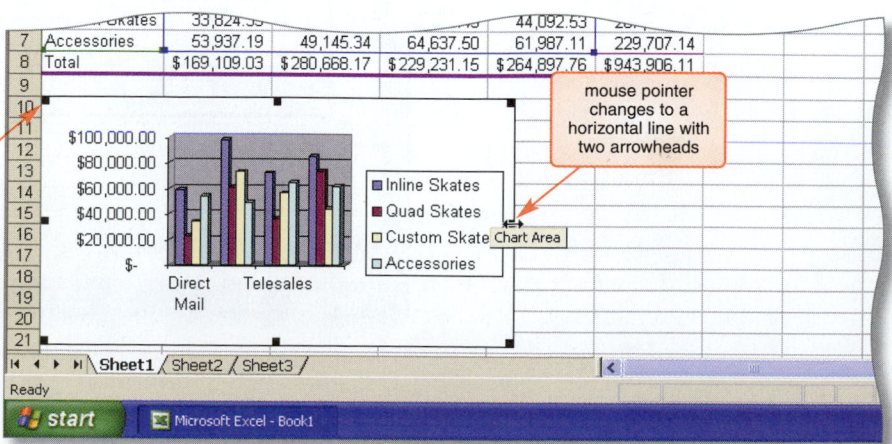

FIGURE 1-61

6

• While holding down the ALT key, drag the sizing handle to the right edge of column F.

While you drag, the dotted line rectangle shows the new chart location (Figure 1-62). Holding down the ALT key while you drag a chart snaps (aligns) the edge of the chart area to the worksheet gridlines.

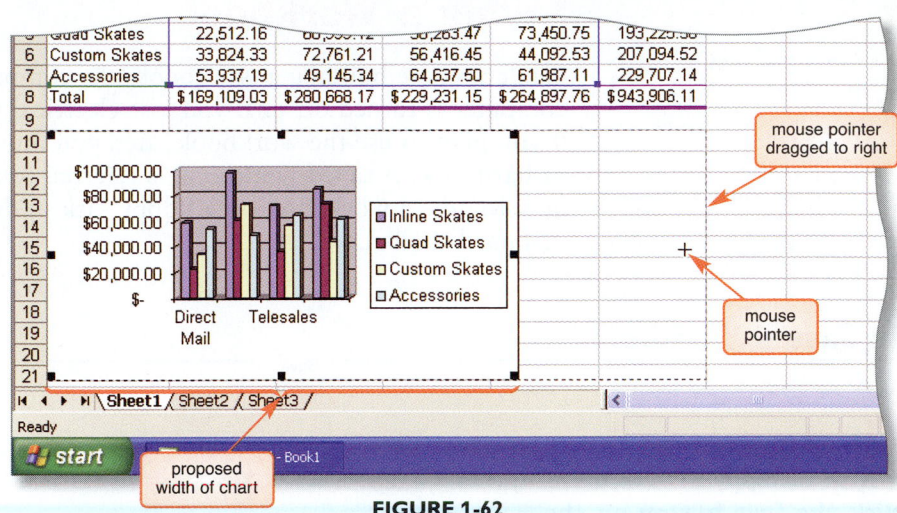

FIGURE 1-62

7

• If necessary, hold down the ALT key and drag the lower-middle sizing handle up to the bottom border of row 20.

• Click cell H20 to deselect the chart.

The new chart location extends from the top of cell A10 to the bottom of cell F20 (Figure 1-63).

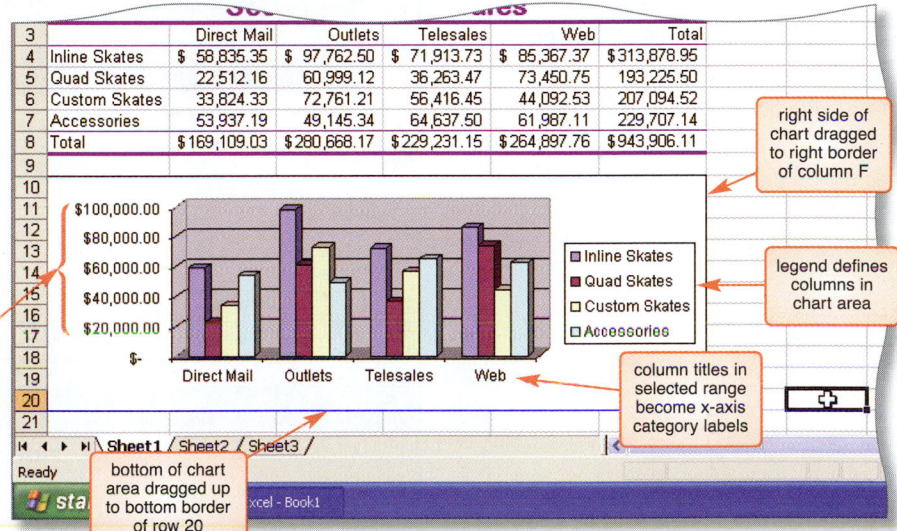

FIGURE 1-63

The embedded 3-D Clustered column chart in Figure 1-63 compares the second quarter sales for the four product groups by each sales channel. It also allows you to compare second quarter sales for the four product groups among the sales channels.

Excel automatically selects the entries in the topmost row of the chart range (row 3) as the titles for the horizontal axis (also called the **x-axis** or **category axis**) and draws a column for each of the 16 cells in the range containing numbers. The small box to the right of the column chart in Figure 1-63 contains the **legend**, which identifies the colors assigned to each bar in the chart. Excel automatically selects the entries in the leftmost column of the chart range (column A) as titles within the legend. As indicated earlier, Excel also automatically derives the chart scale on the y-axis based on the highest and lowest numbers in the chart range.

Excel offers 14 different chart types (Figure 1-58 on page EX 39). The **default chart type** is the chart Excel draws if you click the Finish button in the first Chart Wizard dialog box. When you install Excel on a computer, the default chart type is the 2-D (two-dimensional) Column chart.

Other Ways

1. On Insert menu click Chart
2. Press F11
3. In Voice Command mode, say "Chart Wizard"

More About

Printing Only the Chart

To print the embedded chart without printing the work-sheet, select the chart, click File on the menu bar, click Page Setup, click the Chart tab, click the Scale to fit page in the Printed chart size area, click the Print button, and then click the OK button.

Saving a Workbook

While you are building a workbook, the computer stores it in memory. If the computer is turned off or if you lose electrical power, the workbook is lost. Hence, if you plan to use the workbook later, you must save the workbook on a floppy disk or hard disk. A saved workbook is referred to as a **file**. The following steps illustrate how to save a workbook on a floppy disk in drive A using the Save button on the Standard toolbar.

To Save a Workbook

1

• **With a floppy disk in drive A, click the Save button on the Standard toolbar.**

Excel displays the Save As dialog box (Figure 1-64). The default Save in folder is Documents (your Save in folder may be different), the default file name is Book1, and the default file type is Microsoft Office Excel Workbook.

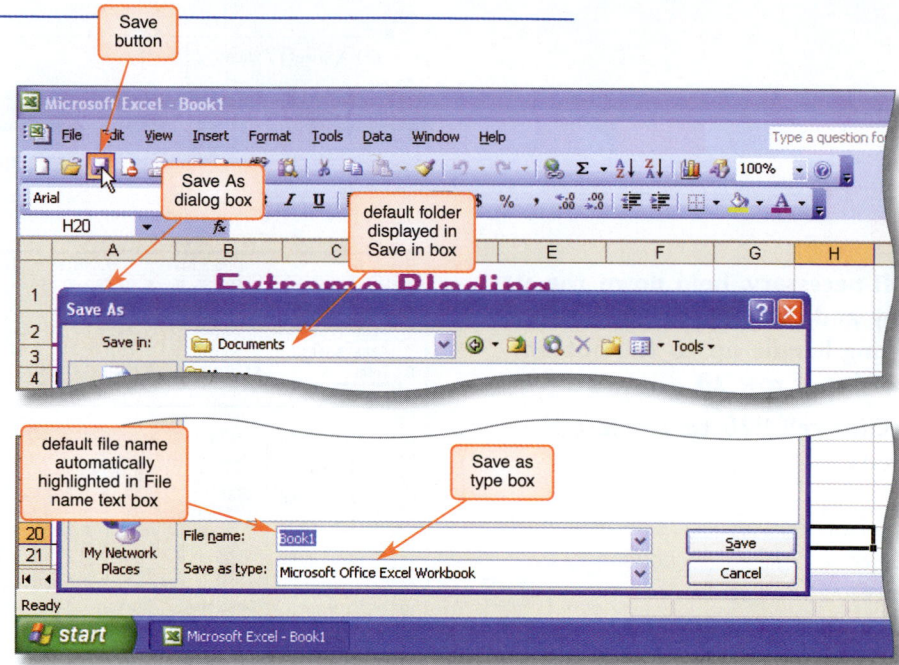

FIGURE 1-64

2

• **Type** Extreme Blading 2nd Quarter Sales **in the File name text box.**

• **Click the Save in box arrow.**

The new file name replaces Book1 in the File name text box (Figure 1-65). A file name can be up to 255 characters and can include spaces. Excel displays a list of available drives and folders.

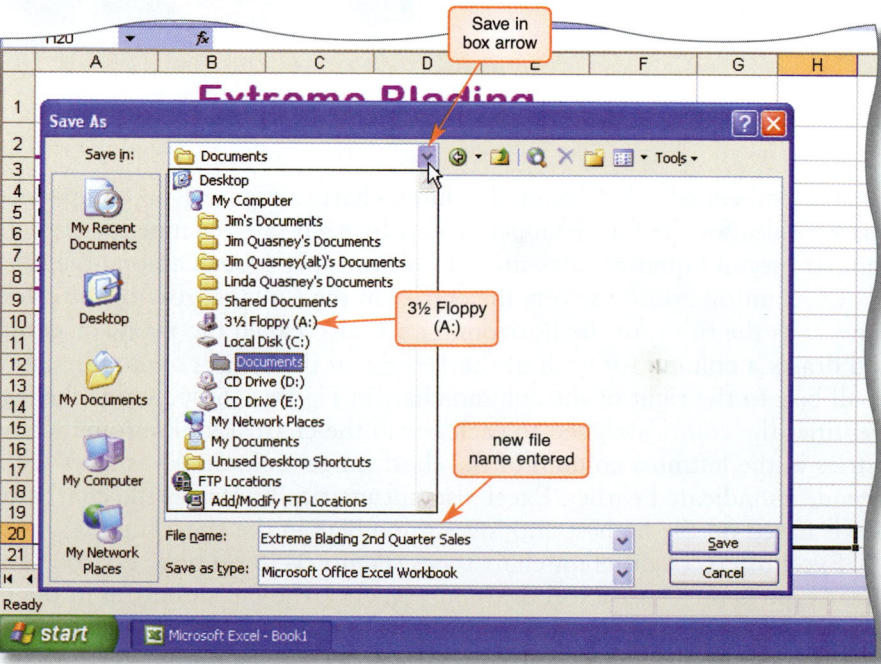

FIGURE 1-65

3

- **Click 3½ Floppy (A:) in the Save in list.**

Drive A becomes the selected drive (Figure 1-66). The buttons on the top and on the side of the dialog box are used to select folders, change the appearance of file names, and complete other tasks.

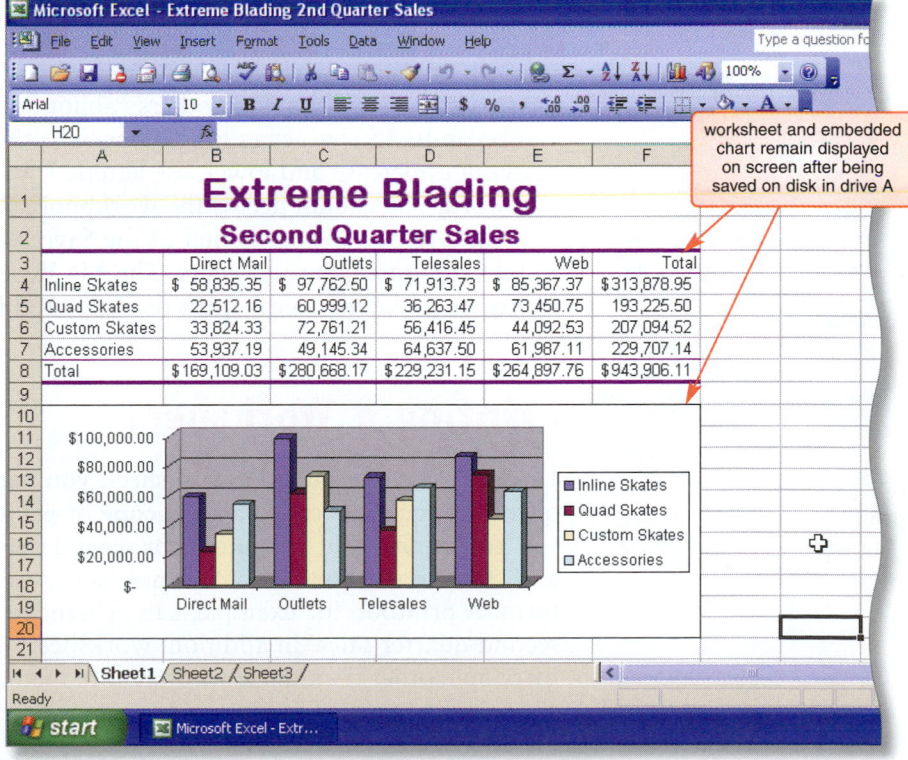

drive A selected

buttons select folders, change display, and perform other tasks

displays a list of most recently used files in a folder titled Recent

commonly used folders

new file name

Save button

FIGURE 1-66

4

- **Click the Save button in the Save As dialog box.**

Excel saves the workbook on the floppy disk in drive A using the file name, Extreme Blading 2nd Quarter Sales. Excel automatically appends the extension .xls to the file name you entered in Step 2, which stands for Excel workbook. Although the workbook is saved on a floppy disk, it also remains in memory and is displayed on the screen (Figure 1-67). Excel displays the new file name on the title bar.

title bar displays new workbook file name Extreme Blading 2nd Quarter Sales

worksheet and embedded chart remain displayed on screen after being saved on disk in drive A

FIGURE 1-67

Other Ways

1. On File menu click Save As, type file name, select drive or folder, click Save button
2. Right-click workbook Control-menu icon on menu bar, click Save As on shortcut menu, type file name, select drive or folder, click Save button
3. Press CTRL+S, type file name, select drive or folder, click Save button
4. In Voice Command mode, say "File, Save As", [type desired file name], say "Save"

While Excel is saving the workbook, it momentarily changes the word Ready on the status bar to Saving. It also displays a horizontal bar on the status bar indicating the amount of the workbook saved. After the save operation is complete, Excel changes the name of the workbook on the title bar from Book1 to Extreme Blading 2nd Quarter Sales (Figure 1-67 on the previous page).

The seven buttons at the top of the Save As dialog box in Figure 1-66 on the previous page and their functions are summarized in Table 1-4.

Table 1-4	Save As Dialog Box Toolbar Buttons	
BUTTON	**BUTTON NAME**	**FUNCTION**
⊕	Default File Location	Displays contents of default file location
📁	Up One Level	Displays contents of folder one level up from current folder
🔍	Search the Web	Starts browser and displays search engine
✕	Delete	Deletes selected file or folder
📁	Create New Folder	Creates new folder
▦	Views	Changes view of files and folders
Tools ▾	Tools	Lists commands to print or modify file names and folders

When you click the Tools button in the Save As dialog box, Excel displays the Tools menu. The General Options command on the menu allows you to save a backup copy of the workbook, create a password to limit access to the workbook, and carry out other functions that are discussed later. Saving a **backup copy** of the workbook means that each time you save a workbook, Excel copies the current version of the workbook on disk to a file with the same name, but with the words, Backup of, appended to the front of the file name. In the case of a power failure or some other problem, you can use the backup copy to restore your work.

You also can use the General Options command on the Tools menu to assign a password to a workbook so others cannot open it. A password is case-sensitive and can be up to 15 characters long. **Case-sensitive** means Excel can differentiate between uppercase and lowercase letters. If you assign a password and forget the password, you cannot access the workbook.

The five buttons on the left of the Save As dialog box in Figure 1-66 allow you to select frequently used folders. The My Recent Documents button displays a list of shortcuts (pointers) to the most recently used files in a folder titled Recent.

Printing a Worksheet

Once you have created the worksheet, you might want to print it. A printed version of the worksheet is called a **hard copy** or **printout**.

You might want a printout for several reasons. First, to present the worksheet and chart to someone who does not have access to a computer, it must be in printed form. A printout, for example, can be handed out in a management meeting about second quarter sales. In addition, worksheets and charts often are kept for reference by people other than those who prepare them. In many cases, worksheets and charts are printed and kept in binders for use by others. The following steps illustrate how to print the worksheet.

More About

Saving

Excel allows you to save a workbook in more than 30 different file formats. Choose the file format by clicking the Save as type box arrow at the bottom of the Save As dialog box (Figure 1-66). Microsoft Office Excel Workbook is the default file format.

To Print a Worksheet

1

• **Ready the printer according to the printer instructions and then click the Print button on the Standard toolbar (Figure 1-68).**

Print button

Microsoft Excel - Extreme Blading 2nd Quarter Sales

File Edit View Insert Format Tools Data Window Help

Type a question for

Arial

Print (HP LaserJet 4MP)

H20

	A	B	C	D	E	F	G	H
1		**Extreme Blading**						
2		**Second Quarter Sales**						
3		Direct Mail	Outlets	Telesales	Web	Total		
4	Inline Skates	$ 58,835.35	$ 97,762.50	$ 71,913.73	$ 85,367.37	$313,878.95		
5	Quad Skates	22,512.16	60,999.12	36,263.47	73,450.75	193,225.50		
6	Custom Skates	33,824.33	72,761.21	56,416.45	44,092.53	207,094.52		
7	Accessories	53,937.19	49,145.34	64,637.50	61,987.11	229,707.14		
8	Total	$169,109.03	$280,668.17	$229,231.15	$264,897.76	$943,906.11		
9								
10								

FIGURE 1-68

2

• **When the printer stops printing the worksheet and the chart, retrieve the printout.**

Excel sends the worksheet to the printer, which prints it (Figure 1-69).

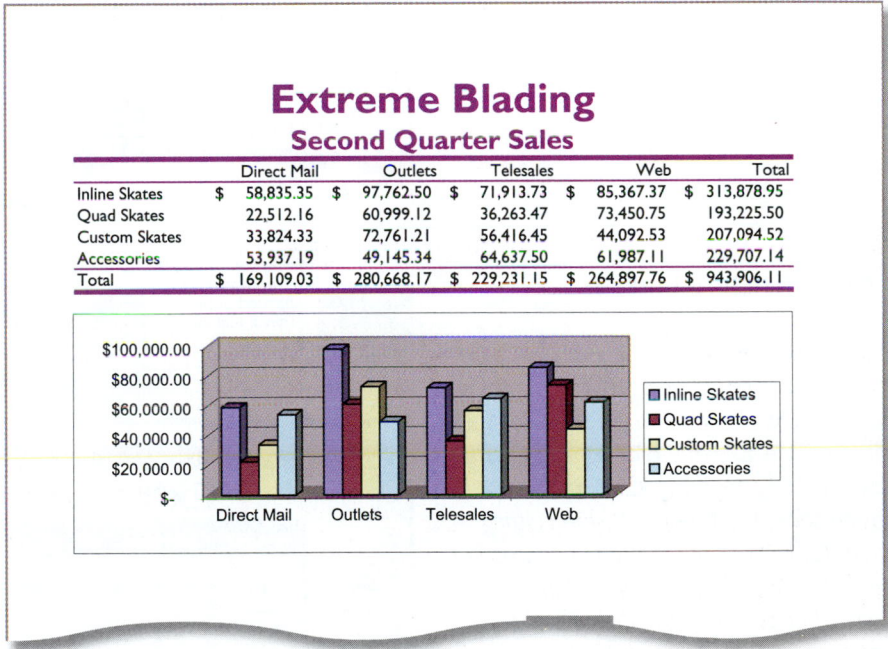

FIGURE 1-69

Prior to clicking the Print button, you can select which columns and rows in the worksheet to print. The range of cells you choose to print is called the **print area**. If you do not select a print area, as was the case in the previous set of steps, Excel automatically selects a print area on the basis of used cells. As you will see in future projects, Excel has many different print options, such as allowing you to preview the printout on the screen to see if the printout is satisfactory before sending it to the printer.

Other Ways

1. On File menu click Print, click OK button
2. Right-click workbook Control-menu icon on menu bar, click Print on shortcut menu, click OK button
3. Press CTRL+P, click OK button
4. In Voice Command mode, say "Print"

Quitting Excel

The Project 1 worksheet and embedded chart are complete. The following steps show how to quit Excel.

To Quit Excel

1

• **Point to the Close button on the right side of the title bar (Figure 1-70).**

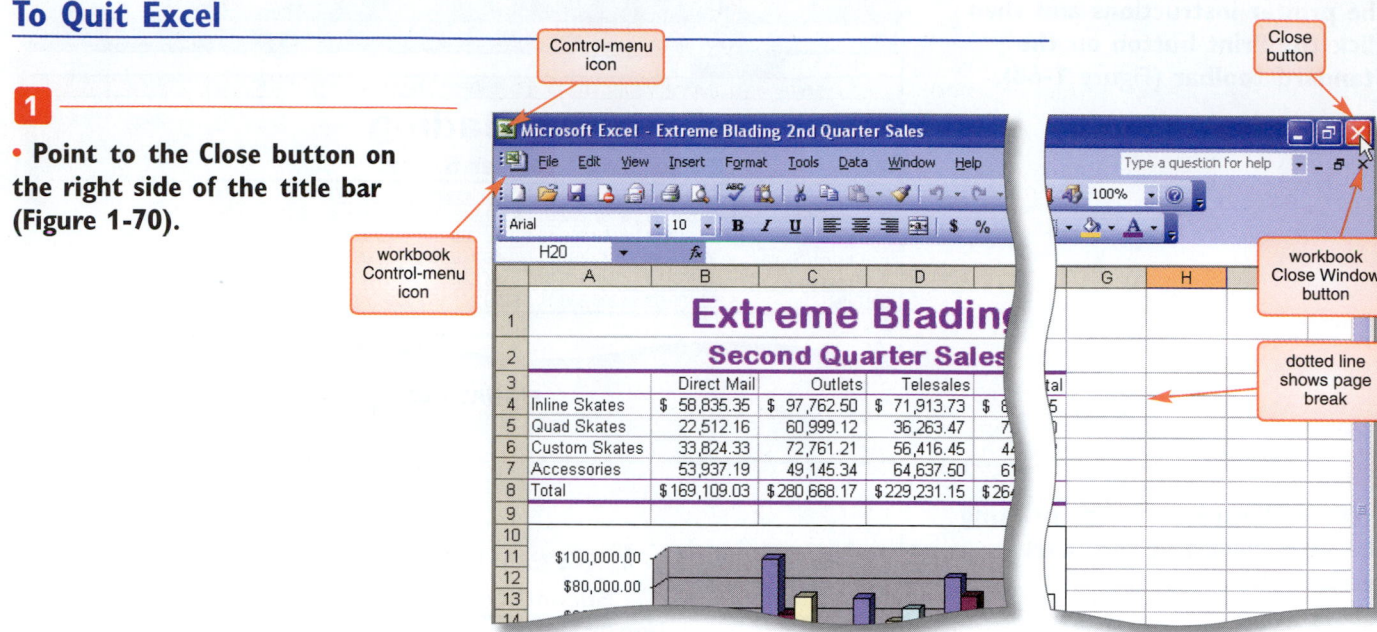

FIGURE 1-70

2

• **Click the Close button.**

If the worksheet was changed or printed, the Microsoft Excel dialog box displays the question, Do you want to save the changes you made to 'Extreme Blading 2nd Quarter Sales.xls'? (Figure 1-71). Clicking the Yes button saves the changes before quitting Excel. Clicking the No button quits Excel without saving the changes. Clicking the Cancel button closes the dialog box and returns control to the worksheet without saving the changes.

3

• **Click the No button.**

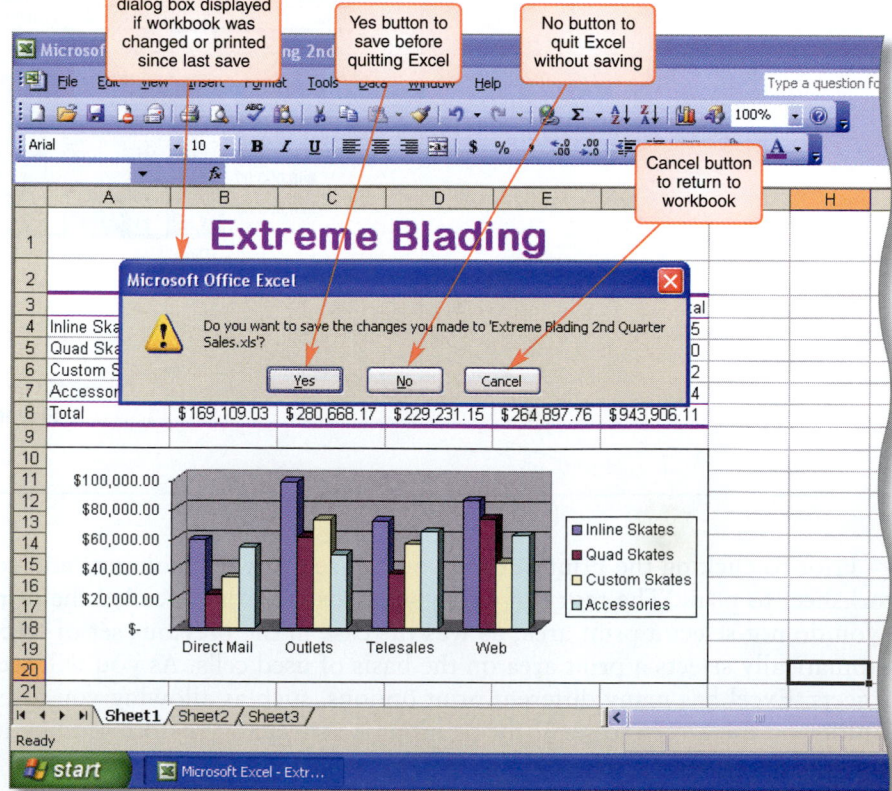

FIGURE 1-71

Other Ways

1. On File menu click Exit
2. Right-click Microsoft Excel button on taskbar, click Close on shortcut menu
3. Double-click Control-menu icon
4. In Voice Command mode, say "File, Exit"

In Figure 1-70, you can see that the Excel window includes two Close buttons and two Control-menu icons. The Close button and Control-menu icon on the title bar can be used to quit Excel. The Close Window button and Control-menu icon on the menu bar can be used to close the workbook, but not to quit Excel.

Starting Excel and Opening a Workbook

After creating and saving a workbook, you often will have reason to retrieve it from a floppy disk. For example, you might want to review the calculations on the worksheet and enter additional or revised data. The following steps assume Excel is not running.

To Start Excel and Open a Workbook

1

• **With your floppy disk in drive A, click the Start button on the Windows taskbar, point to All Programs on the Start menu, point to Microsoft Office on the All Programs submenu, and then click Microsoft Office Excel 2003 on the Microsoft Office submenu.**

Excel starts. The Getting Started task pane lists the four most recently used files in the Open area (Figure 1-72).

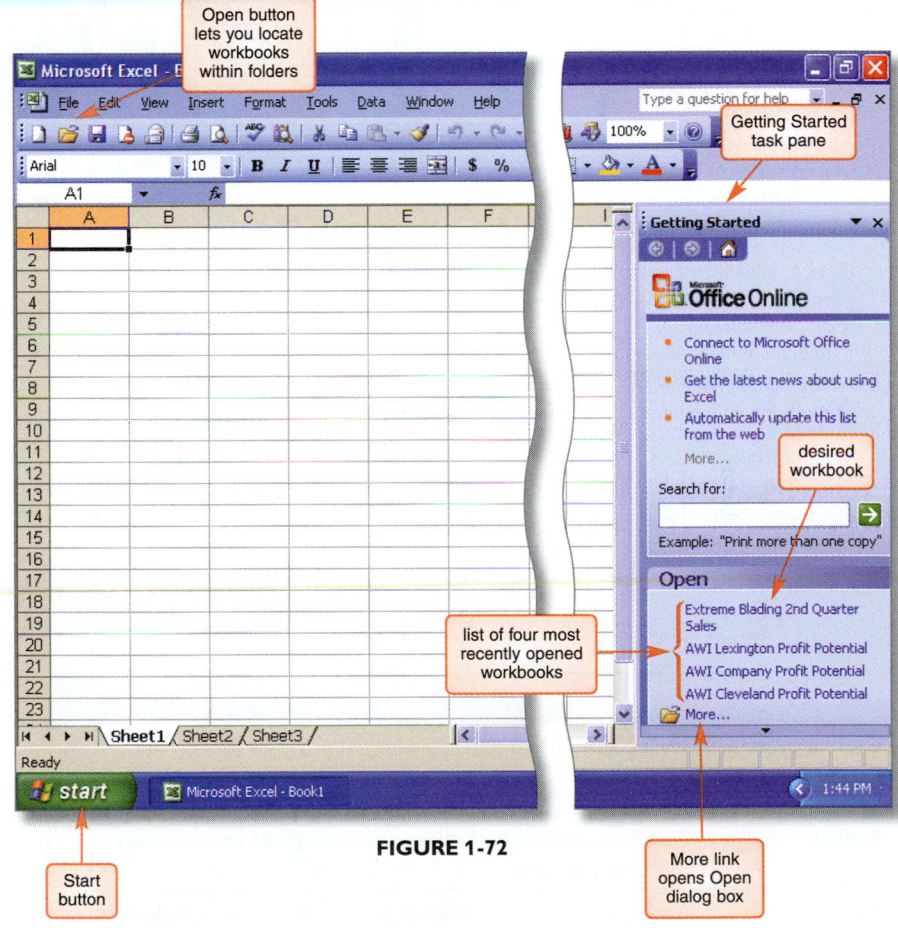

Open button lets you locate workbooks within folders

Getting Started task pane

desired workbook

list of four most recently opened workbooks

Start button

FIGURE 1-72

More link opens Open dialog box

2

• **Click Extreme Blading 2nd Quarter Sales in the Open area in the Getting Started task pane.**

Excel opens the workbook Extreme Blading 2nd Quarter Sales (Figure 1-73). The Getting Started task pane closes.

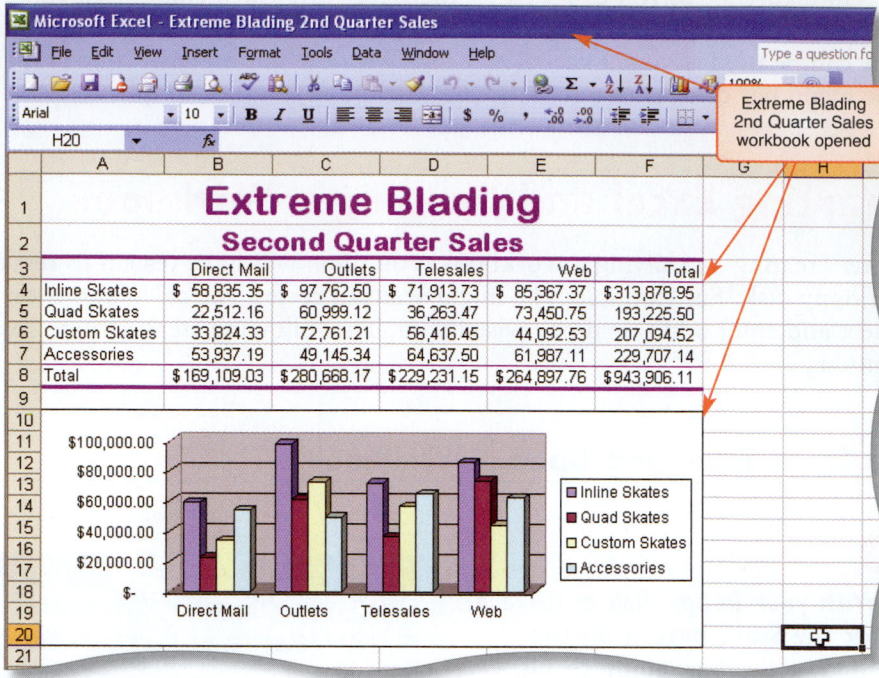

FIGURE 1-73

If you want to open a workbook other than one of the four most recently opened ones, click the Open button on the Standard toolbar or the More link in the Getting Started task pane. Clicking the Open button or the More link displays the Open dialog box, which allows you to navigate to a workbook stored on disk.

AutoCalculate

You easily can obtain a total, an average, or other information about the numbers in a range by using the **AutoCalculate area** on the status bar. First, select the range of cells containing the numbers you want to check. Next, right-click the AutoCalculate area to display the shortcut menu (Figure 1-74). The check mark to the left of the active function (Sum) indicates that the sum of the selected range is displayed in the AutoCalculate area on the status bar. The function of the commands on the AutoCalculate shortcut menu are described in Table 1-5.

The following steps show how to display the average second quarter sales for the Custom Skates product group.

Table 1-5 AutoCalculate Shortcut Menu Commands	
COMMAND	**FUNCTION**
None	No value is displayed in the AutoCalculate area
Average	AutoCalculate area displays the average of the numbers in the selected range
Count	AutoCalculate area displays the number of nonblank cells in the selected range
Count Nums	AutoCalculate area displays the number of cells containing numbers in the selected range
Max	AutoCalculate area displays the highest value in the selected range
Min	AutoCalculate area displays the lowest value in the selected range
Sum	AutoCalculate area displays the sum of the numbers in the selected range

To Use the AutoCalculate Area to Determine an Average

1

• **Select the range B6:E6 and then right-click the AutoCalculate area on the status bar.**

The sum of the numbers in the range B6:E6 is displayed (207,094.52) in the AutoCalculate area, because Sum is the active function (Figure 1-74). Excel displays a shortcut menu listing the other available functions above the AutoCalculate area. If another function is active on your shortcut menu, you may see a different value in the AutoCalculate area.

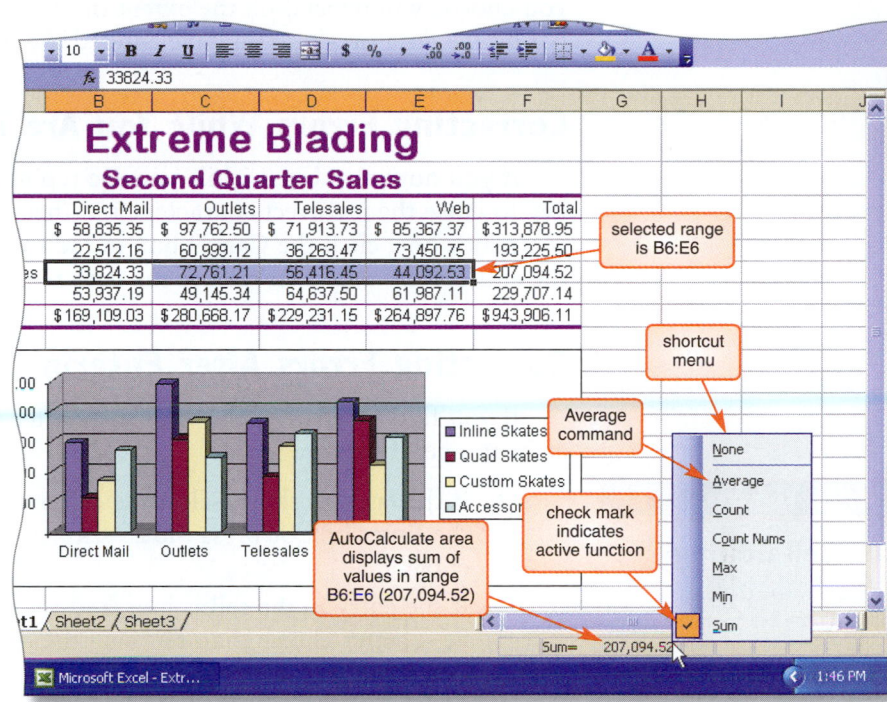

FIGURE 1-74

2

• **Click Average on the shortcut menu.**

Excel displays the average of the numbers in the range B6:E6 (51,773.63) in the AutoCalculate area (Figure 1-75).

3

• **Right-click the AutoCalculate area and then click Sum on the shortcut menu.**

The AutoCalculate area displays the sum as shown earlier in Figure 1-74.

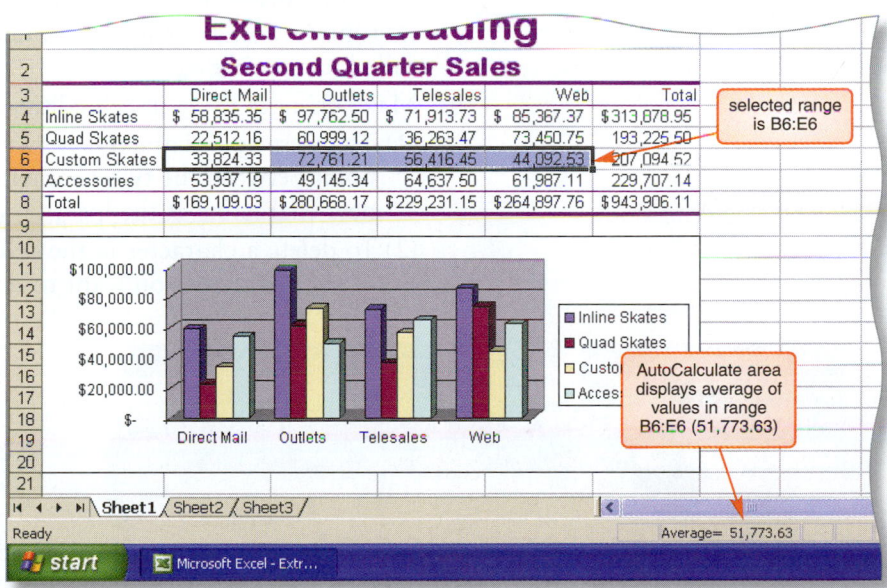

FIGURE 1-75

To change to any one of the other five functions for the range B6:E6, right-click the AutoCalculate area and then click the desired function. Clicking None at the top of the AutoCalculate shortcut menu in Figure 1-74 turns off the AutoCalculate area. Thus, if you select None, then no value will be displayed in the AutoCalculate area when you select a range.

> ### *More About*
>
> ## Shortcut Menus
>
> Shortcut menus contain the most frequently used commands that relate to the object to which the mouse pointer is pointing.

Correcting Errors

You can correct errors on a worksheet using one of several methods. The method you choose will depend on the extent of the error and whether you notice it while typing the data or after you have entered the incorrect data into the cell.

Correcting Errors While You Are Typing Data into a Cell

If you notice an error while you are typing data into a cell, press the BACKSPACE key to erase the incorrect characters and then type the correct characters. If the error is a major one, click the Cancel box in the formula bar or press the ESC key to erase the entire entry and then reenter the data from the beginning.

Correcting Errors After Entering Data into a Cell

If you find an error in the worksheet after entering the data, you can correct the error in one of two ways:

1. If the entry is short, select the cell, retype the entry correctly, and then click the Enter box or press the ENTER key. The new entry will replace the old entry.

2. If the entry in the cell is long and the errors are minor, using Edit mode may be a better choice than retyping the cell entry. Use the Edit mode as described below.

   a. Double-click the cell containing the error to switch Excel to Edit mode. In **Edit mode**, Excel displays the active cell entry in the formula bar and a flashing insertion point in the active cell (Figure 1-76). With Excel in Edit mode, you can edit the contents directly in the cell — a procedure called **in-cell editing**.

   b. Make changes using in-cell editing, as indicated below.

      (1) To insert new characters between two characters, place the insertion point between the two characters and begin typing. Excel inserts the new characters at the location of the insertion point.

      (2) To delete a character in the cell, move the insertion point to the left of the character you want to delete and then press the DELETE key or place the insertion point to the right of the character you want to delete and then press the BACKSPACE key. You also can use the mouse to drag through the character or adjacent characters you want to delete and then press the DELETE key or click the Cut button on the Standard toolbar.

      (3) When you are finished editing an entry, click the Enter box or press the ENTER key.

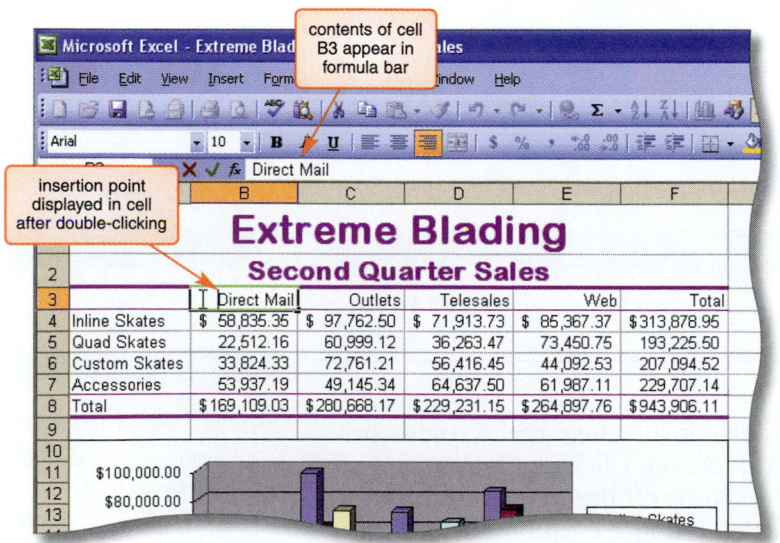

contents of cell B3 appear in formula bar

insertion point displayed in cell after double-clicking

FIGURE 1-76

When Excel enters the Edit mode, the keyboard usually is in Insert mode. In **Insert mode**, as you type a character, Excel inserts the character and moves all characters to the right of the typed character one position to the right. You can change to Overtype mode by pressing the INSERT key. In **Overtype mode**, Excel overtypes, or replaces, the character to the right of the insertion point. The INSERT key toggles the keyboard between Insert mode and Overtype mode.

While in Edit mode, you may have reason to move the insertion point to various points in the cell, select portions of the data in the cell, or switch from inserting characters to overtyping characters. Table 1-6 summarizes the more common tasks used during in-cell editing.

Table 1-6   Summary of In-Cell Editing Tasks

	TASK	MOUSE	KEYBOARD
1	Move the insertion point to the beginning of data in a cell.	Point to the left of the first character and click.	Press HOME
2	Move the insertion point to the end of data in a cell.	Point to the right of the last character and click.	Press END
3	Move the insertion point anywhere in a cell.	Point to the appropriate position and click the character.	Press RIGHT ARROW or LEFT ARROW
4	Highlight one or more adjacent characters.	Drag the mouse pointer through adjacent characters.	Press SHIFT+RIGHT ARROW or SHIFT+LEFT ARROW
5	Select all data in a cell.	Double-click the cell with the insertion point in the cell.	
6	Delete selected characters.	Click the Cut button on the Standard toolbar.	Press DELETE
7	Delete characters to the left of the insertion point.		Press BACKSPACE
8	Toggle between Insert and Overtype modes.		Press INSERT

Undoing the Last Cell Entry

Excel provides the Undo command on the Edit menu and the Undo button on the Standard toolbar (Figure 1-77), both of which allow you to erase recent cell entries. Thus, if you enter incorrect data in a cell and notice it immediately, click the Undo command or Undo button and Excel changes the cell entry to what it was prior to the incorrect data entry.

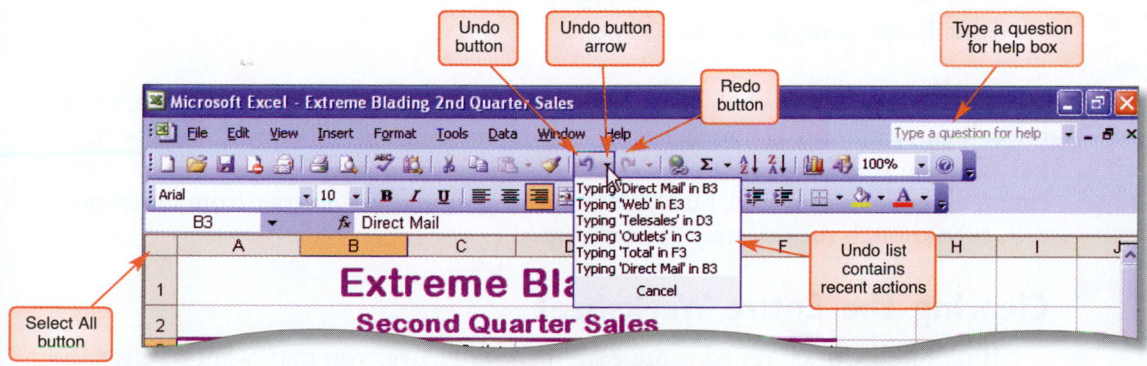

FIGURE 1-77

More About

The Undo Button

The Undo button can undo far more complicated worksheet activities than just removing the latest entry from a cell. In fact, most commands can be undone if you click the Undo button before you make another entry or issue another command. You cannot undo a save or print, but, as a rule, the Undo button can restore the worksheet data and settings to what they were the last time Excel was in Ready mode. With Excel, you have multiple-level undo and redo capabilities.

Excel remembers the last 16 actions you have completed. Thus, you can undo up to 16 previous actions by clicking the Undo button arrow to display the Undo list and then clicking the action to be undone (Figure 1-77 on the previous page). You can drag through several actions in the Undo list to undo all of them at once. If no actions are available for Excel to undo, then the Undo button is dimmed and inoperative.

The Redo button, next to the Undo button on the Standard toolbar, allows you to repeat previous actions. You also can click Redo on the Edit menu, instead of using the Redo button.

Clearing a Cell or Range of Cells

If you enter data into the wrong cell or range of cells, you can erase, or clear, the data using one of the first four methods listed below. The fifth method clears the formatting from the selected cells.

To Clear Cell Entries Using the Fill Handle

1. Select the cell or range of cells and then point to the fill handle so the mouse pointer changes to a cross hair.
2. Drag the fill handle back into the selected cell or range until a shadow covers the cell or cells you want to erase. Release the mouse button.

To Clear Cell Entries Using the Shortcut Menu

1. Select the cell or range of cells to be cleared.
2. Right-click the selection.
3. Click Clear Contents on the shortcut menu.

To Clear Cell Entries Using the DELETE Key

1. Select the cell or range of cells to be cleared.
2. Press the DELETE key.

To Clear Cell Entries Using the Clear Command

1. Select the cell or range of cells to be cleared.
2. Click Edit on the menu bar and then point to Clear.
3. Click All on the Clear submenu.

More About

Getting Back to Normal

If you accidentally assign unwanted formats to a range of cells, you can use the Clear command on the Edit menu to delete the formats of a selected range. Doing so changes the format to Normal style. To view the characteristics of the Normal style, click Style on the Format menu or press ALT+APOSTROPHE (').

To Clear Formatting Using the Clear Command

1. Select the cell or range of cells that you want to remove the formatting from.
2. Click Edit on the menu bar and then point to Clear.
3. Click Formats on the Clear submenu.

The All command on the Clear submenu is the only command that clears both the cell entry and the cell formatting. As you are clearing cell entries, always remember that you should *never press the* SPACEBAR *to clear a cell*. Pressing the SPACEBAR enters a blank character. A blank character is text and is different from an empty cell, even though the cell may appear empty.

More About

The Quick Reference

For a table that lists how to complete the tasks covered in this book using the mouse, menu, shortcut menu, and keyboard, see the Quick Reference Summary at the back of this book, or visit the Excel 2003 Quick Reference Web page (scsite.com/ex2003/qr).

Clearing the Entire Worksheet

If required worksheet edits are extremely extensive, you may want to clear the entire worksheet and start over. To clear the worksheet or delete an embedded chart, use the following steps.

To Clear the Entire Worksheet

1. Click the Select All button on the worksheet (Figure 1-77 on page EX 51).
2. Press the DELETE key to delete all the entries. Click Edit on the menu bar, point to Clear, and then click All on the Clear submenu to delete both the entries and formats.

The Select All button selects the entire worksheet. Instead of clicking the Select All button, you also can press CTRL+A. To clear an unsaved workbook, click the workbook's Close Window button or click the Close command on the File menu. Click the No button if the Microsoft Excel dialog box asks if you want to save changes. To start a new, blank workbook, click the New button on the Standard toolbar or click the New command on the File menu and begin working on a new workbook.

To delete an embedded chart, complete the following steps.

To Delete an Embedded Chart

1. Click the chart to select it.
2. Press the DELETE key.

Excel Help System

At any time while you are using Excel, you can get answers to questions using the **Excel Help** system. You can activate the Excel Help system by using the Type a question for help box on the menu bar, the Microsoft Excel Help button on the Standard toolbar, or by clicking Help on the menu bar (Figure 1-78). Used properly, this form of online assistance can increase your productivity and reduce your frustrations by minimizing the time you spend learning how to use Excel.

The following section shows how to get answers to your questions using the Type a question for help box. Additional information on using the Excel Help system is available in Appendix A.

Obtaining Help Using the Type a Question for Help Box on the Menu Bar

The Type a question for help box on the right side of the menu bar (see Figure 1-77 on page EX 51) lets you type free-form questions such as, how do I save or how do I create a Web page, phrases such as save a workbook or print a worksheet, or key terms such as, copy, save, or formatting. Excel responds by displaying a list of topics related to the question or terms you entered in the Search Results task pane. The following steps show how to use the Type a question for help box to obtain information on saving a workbook.

To Obtain Help Using the Type a Question for Help Box

• **Type** save a workbook **in the Type a question for help box on the right side of the menu bar (Figure 1-78).**

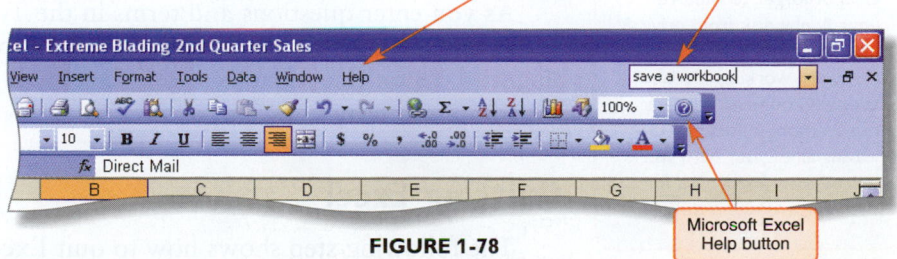

FIGURE 1-78

2

- **Press the ENTER key.**
- **When Excel displays the Search Results task pane, scroll down and then click the link Save a file.**
- **If necessary, click the AutoTile button (see Figure 1-80) to tile the windows.**

Excel displays the Search Results task pane with a list of topics related to the term, save. Excel found 30 search results (Figure 1-79). When the Save a file link is clicked, Excel opens the Microsoft Excel Help window on the left side of the screen.

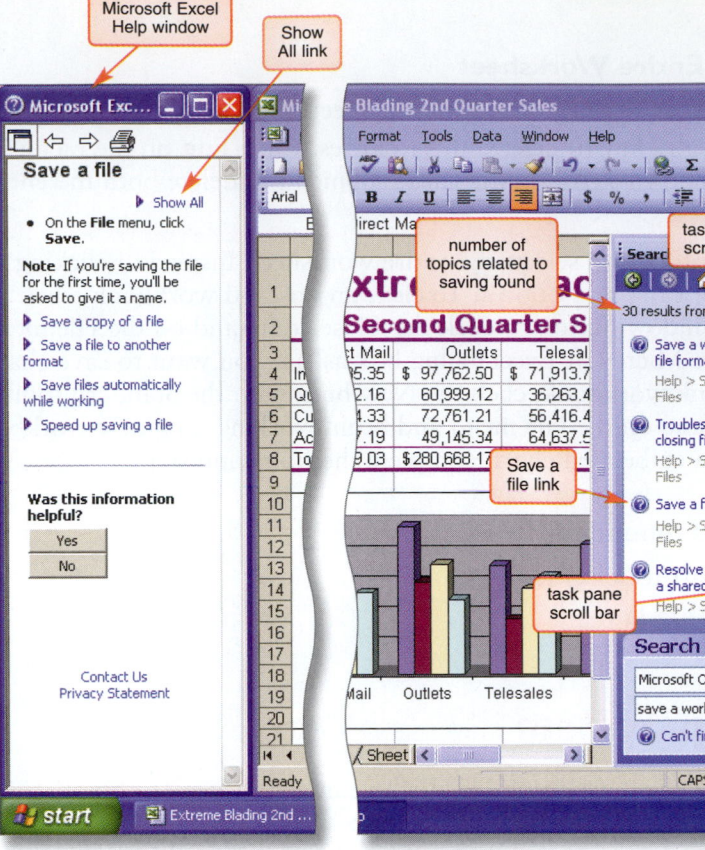

FIGURE 1-79

3

- **Click the Show All link on the right side of the Microsoft Excel Help window to expand the links in the window.**
- **Double-click the Microsoft Excel Help title bar to maximize it.**

The links in the Microsoft Excel Help window are expanded. Excel maximizes the window that provides Help information about saving a file (Figure 1-80).

4

- **Click the Close button on the Microsoft Excel Help window title bar.**

The Microsoft Excel Help window closes and the worksheet is active.

FIGURE 1-80

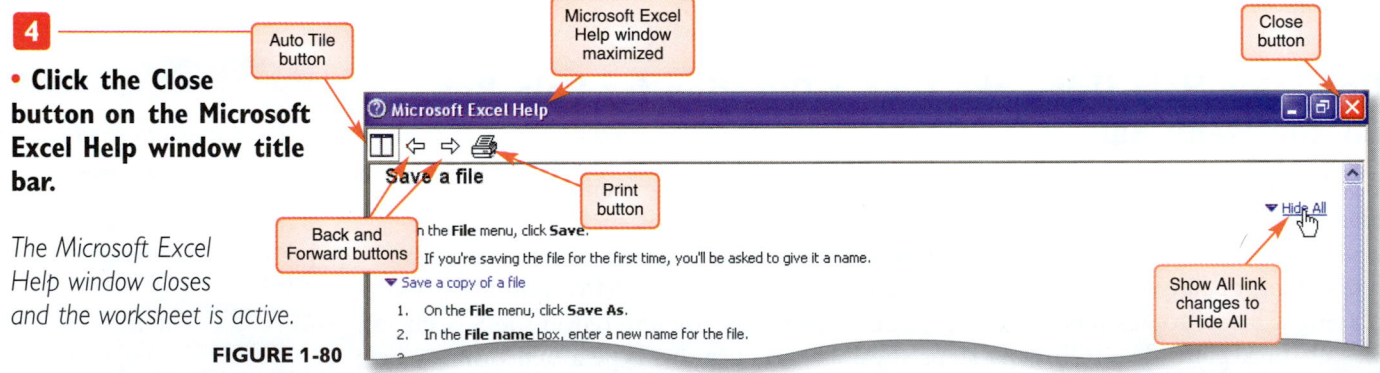

More About

Quitting Excel

Do not forget to remove your floppy disk from drive A after quitting Excel, especially if you are working in a laboratory environment. Nothing can be more frustrating than leaving all of your hard work behind on a floppy disk for the next user.

Use the buttons in the upper-left corner of the Microsoft Excel Help window (Figure 1-80) to navigate through the Help system, change the display, and print the contents of the window.

As you enter questions and terms in the Type a question for help box, Excel adds them to its list. Thus, if you click the Type a question for help box arrow (Figure 1-78 on the previous page), Excel will display a list of previously entered questions and terms.

Quitting Excel

The following step shows how to quit Excel.

To Quit Excel

1 Click the Close button on the right side of the title bar, and if necessary, click the No button in the Microsoft Excel dialog box.

Project Summary

This project presented Excel basics. First, you were introduced to starting Excel. You learned about the Excel window and how to enter text and numbers to create a worksheet. You learned how to select a range and how to use the AutoSum button to sum numbers in a column or row. Using the fill handle, you learned how to copy a cell to adjacent cells. Once the worksheet was built, you learned how to format cells one at a time using buttons on the Formatting toolbar and how to format a range using the AutoFormat command. You then learned how to use the Chart Wizard to add a 3-D Clustered column chart to the worksheet. After completing the worksheet, you learned how to save the workbook on a floppy disk, print the worksheet and chart, and then quit Excel. You also learned how to start Excel by opening an Excel document, use the AutoCalculate area, and edit data in cells. Finally, you learned how to use the Excel Help system to answer your questions.

 If you have a SAM user profile, you may have access to hands-on instruction, practice, and assessment of the skills covered in this project. Log in to your SAM account and go to your assignments page to see what your instructor has assigned.

What You Should Know

Having completed this project, you should be able to perform the tasks below. The tasks are listed in the same order they were presented in this project. For a list of the buttons, menus, toolbars, and commands introduced in this project, see the Quick Reference Summary at the back of this book and refer to the Page Number column.

1. Start Excel   (EX 7)
2. Customize the Excel Window   (EX 8)
3. Enter the Worksheet Titles   (EX 17)
4. Enter Column Titles   (EX 19)
5. Enter Row Titles   (EX 20)
6. Enter Numbers   (EX 22)
7. Sum a Column of Numbers   (EX 23)
8. Copy a Cell to Adjacent Cells in a Row   (EX 25)
9. Determine Multiple Totals at the Same Time (EX 27)
10. Change the Font Type   (EX 29)
11. Bold a Cell   (EX 30)
12. Increase the Font Size of a Cell Entry   (EX 31)
13. Change the Font Color of a Cell Entry   (EX 32)
14. Center a Cell Entry across Columns by Merging Cells   (EX 33)
15. Format the Worksheet Subtitle   (EX 34)
16. Use AutoFormat to Format the Body of a Worksheet   (EX 34)
17. Use the Name Box to Select a Cell   (EX 36)
18. Add a 3-D Clustered Column Chart to the Worksheet   (EX 39)
19. Save a Workbook   (EX 42)
20. Print a Worksheet   (EX 45)
21. Quit Excel   (EX 46)
22. Start Excel and Open a Workbook   (EX 47)
23. Use the AutoCalculate Area to Determine an Average   (EX 49)
24. Clear Cell Entries Using the Fill Handle   (EX 52)
25. Clear Cell Entries Using the Shortcut Menu   (EX 52)
26. Clear Cell Entries Using the DELETE Key   (EX 52)
27. Clear Cell Entries Using the Clear Command (EX 52)
28. Clear the Entire Worksheet   (EX 53)
29. Delete an Embedded Chart   (EX 53)
30. Obtain Help Using the Type a Question for Help Box   (EX 53)
31. Quit Excel   (EX 55)

Learn It Online

Instructions: To complete the Learn It Online exercises, start your browser, click the Address bar, and then enter the Web address scsite.com/ex2003/learn. When the Excel 2003 Learn It Online page is displayed, follow the instructions in the exercises below. Each exercise has instructions for printing your results, either for your own records or for submission to your instructor.

1 Project Reinforcement TF, MC, and SA

Below Excel Project 1, click the Project Reinforcement link. Print the quiz by clicking Print on the File menu for each page. Answer each question.

2 Flash Cards

Below Excel Project 1, click the Flash Cards link and read the instructions. Type 20 (or a number specified by your instructor) in the Number of playing cards text box, type your name in the Enter your Name text box, and then click the Flip Card button. When the flash card is displayed, read the question and then click the ANSWER box arrow to select an answer. Flip through Flash Cards. If your score is 15 (75%) correct or greater, click Print on the File menu to print your results. If your score is less than 15 (75%) correct, then redo this exercise by clicking the Replay button.

3 Practice Test

Below Excel Project 1, click the Practice Test link. Answer each question, enter your first and last name at the bottom of the page, and then click the Grade Test button. When the graded practice test is displayed on your screen, click Print on the File menu to print a hard copy. Continue to take practice tests until you score 80% or better.

4 Who Wants To Be a Computer Genius?

Below Excel Project 1, click the Computer Genius link. Read the instructions, enter your first and last name at the bottom of the page, and then click the PLAY button. When your score is displayed, click the PRINT RESULTS link to print a hard copy.

5 Wheel of Terms

Below Excel Project 1, click the Wheel of Terms link. Read the instructions, and then enter your first and last name and your school name. Click the PLAY button. When your score is displayed, right-click the score and then click Print on the shortcut menu to print a hard copy.

6 Crossword Puzzle Challenge

Below Excel Project 1, click the Crossword Puzzle Challenge link. Read the instructions, and then enter your first and last name. Click the SUBMIT button. Work the crossword puzzle. When you are finished, click the Submit button. When the crossword puzzle is redisplayed, click the Print Puzzle button to print a hard copy.

7 Tips and Tricks

Below Excel Project 1, click the Tips and Tricks link. Click a topic that pertains to Project 1. Right-click the information and then click Print on the shortcut menu. Construct a brief example of what the information relates to in Excel to confirm you understand how to use the tip or trick.

8 Newsgroups

Below Excel Project 1, click the Newsgroups link. Click a topic that pertains to Project 1. Print three comments.

9 Expanding Your Horizons

Below Excel Project 1, click the Expanding Your Horizons link. Click a topic that pertains to Project 1. Print the information. Construct a brief example of what the information relates to in Excel to confirm you understand the contents of the article.

10 Search Sleuth

Below Excel Project 1, click the Search Sleuth link. To search for a term that pertains to this project, select a term below the Project 1 title and then use the Google search engine at google.com (or any major search engine) to display and print two Web pages that present information on the term.

11 Excel Online Training

Below Excel Project 1, click the Excel Online Training link. When your browser displays the Microsoft Office Online Web page, click the Excel link. Click one of the Excel courses that covers one or more of the objectives listed at the beginning of the project on page EX 4. Print the first page of the course before stepping through it.

12 Office Marketplace

Below Excel Project 1, click the Office Marketplace link. When your browser displays the Microsoft Office Online Web page, click the Office Marketplace link. Click a topic that relates to Excel. Print the first page.

Apply Your Knowledge

1 Changing the Values in a Worksheet

Instructions: Start Excel. Open the workbook Apply 1-1 Watson's Computer Discount Annual Sales from the Data Disk. See the inside back cover of this book for instructions for downloading the Data Disk or see your instructor for information on accessing the files required in this book.

Make the changes to the worksheet described in Table 1-7 so that the worksheet appears as shown in Figure 1-81. As you edit the values in the cells containing numeric data, watch the totals in row 7, the totals in column F, and the chart change.

Change the worksheet title in cell A1 to 20-point Arial Black brown, bold font and then center it across columns A through F. Change the worksheet subtitle in cell A2 to 14-point Arial Black brown, bold font and then center it across columns A through F.

Enter your name, course, laboratory assignment number, date, and instructor name in cells A21 through A25. Save the workbook using the file name, Apply 1-1 Babbage's Computer Discount Annual Sales. Print the revised worksheet and hand in the printout to your instructor.

Table 1-7 New Worksheet Data	
CELL	**CHANGE CELL CONTENTS TO**
A1	Babbage's Computer Discount
B4	43200.75
C4	17563.52
D5	38152.43
E5	28968.78
E6	38751.49

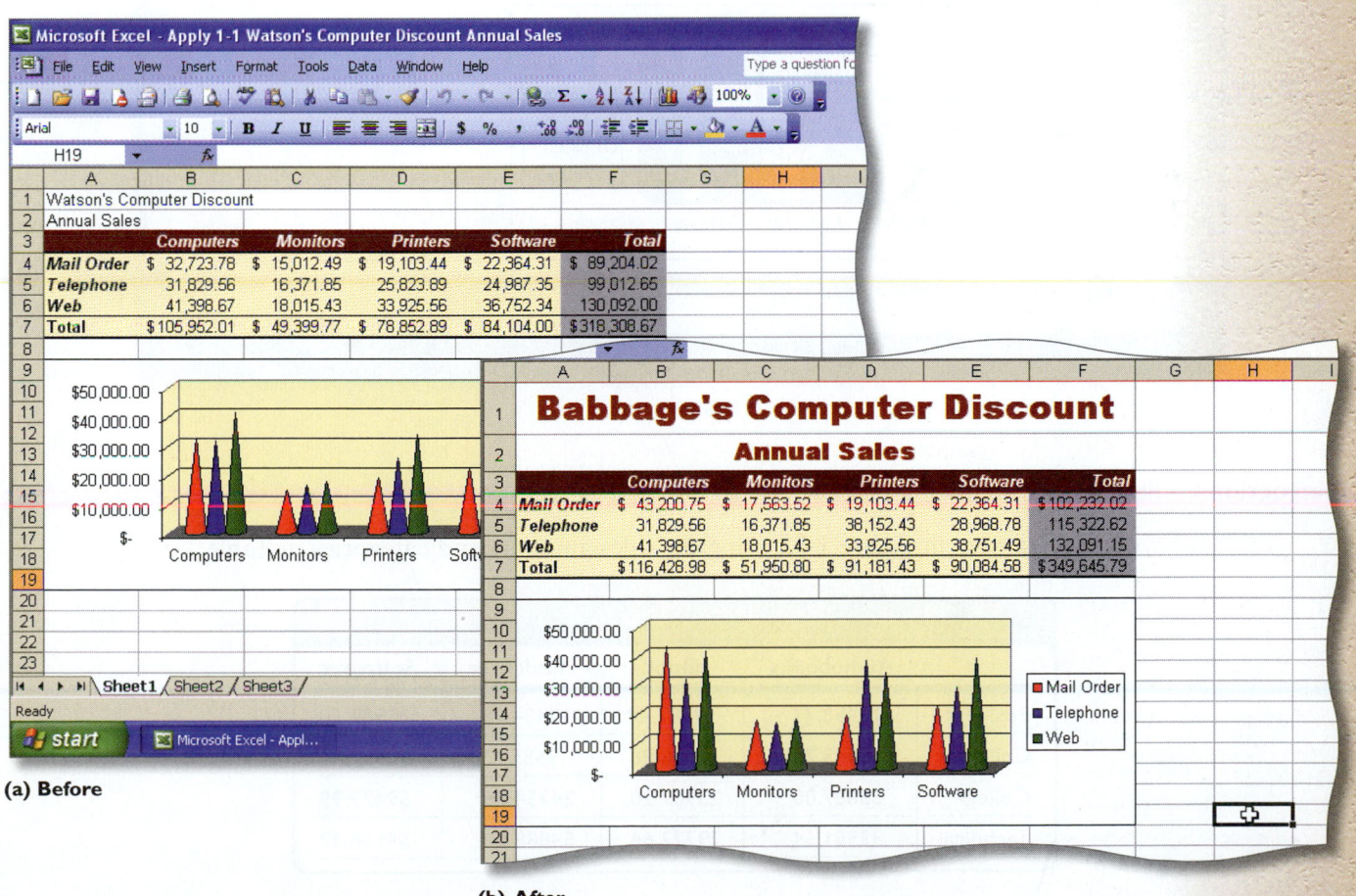

(a) Before

(b) After

FIGURE 1-81

In the Lab

1 Monthly Sales Analysis Worksheet

Problem: You work part-time as a spreadsheet specialist for Knotting Hill Bookstore, one of the larger bookstores in the world. Your manager has asked you to develop a monthly sales analysis worksheet similar to the one shown in Figure 1-82.

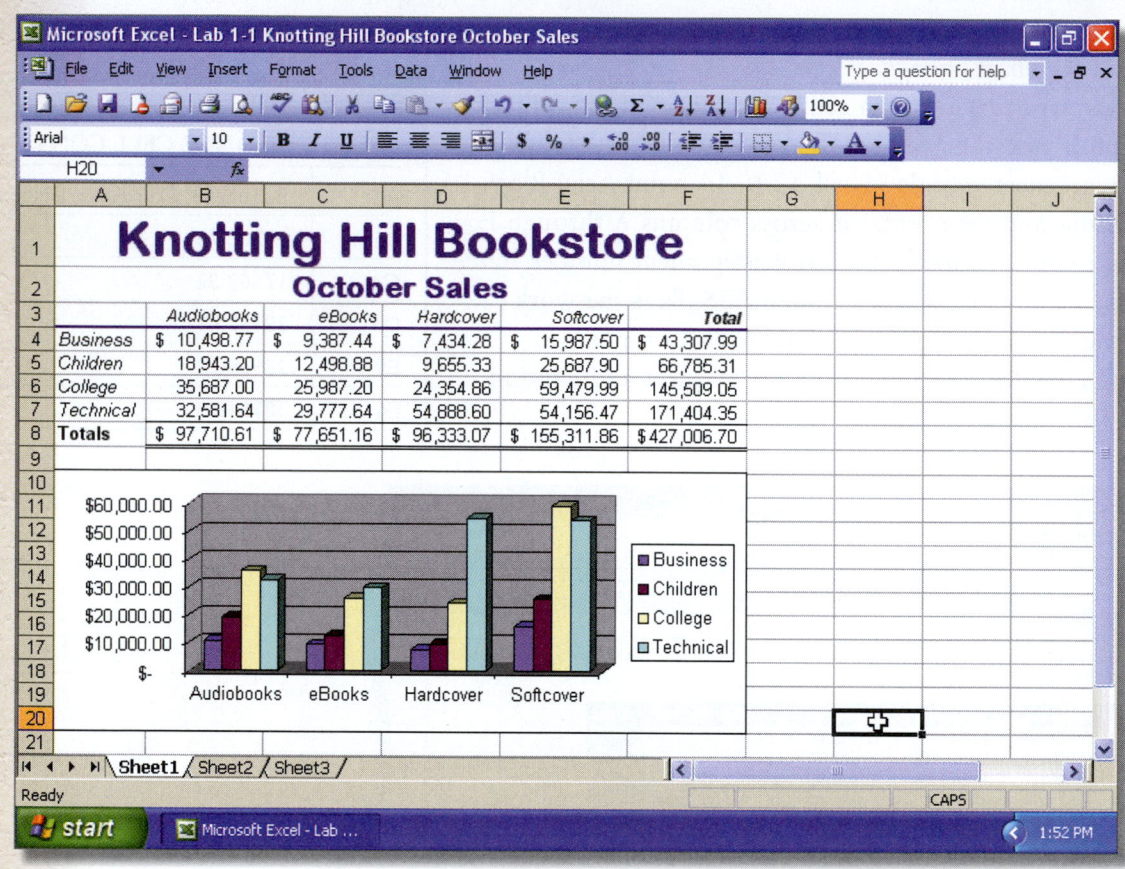

FIGURE 1-82

Instructions: Perform the following tasks.

1. Create the worksheet shown in Figure 1-82 using the sales amounts and categories in Table 1-8.

Table 1-8 Knotting Hill Bookstore October Sales				
	Audiobooks	**eBooks**	**Hardcover**	**Softcover**
Business	10498.77	9387.44	7434.28	15987.50
Children	18943.20	12498.88	9655.33	25687.90
College	35687.00	25987.20	24354.86	59479.99
Technical	32581.64	29777.64	54888.60	54156.47

In the Lab

2. Use the SUM function to determine the totals for the types of books, subject area, and company totals.

3. Format the worksheet title to 26-point Arial Rounded MT Bold dark blue, bold font and center it across columns A through F. Do not be concerned if the edges of the worksheet title are not displayed.

4. Format the worksheet subtitle to 16-point Arial Rounded MT Bold dark blue, bold font and center it across columns A through F.

5. Format the range A3:F8 using the AutoFormat command. Select the Accounting 3 autoformat.

6. Select the range A3:E7 and then use the Chart Wizard button on the Standard toolbar to draw a Clustered column with a 3-D visual effect chart (column 1, row 2 in the Chart sub-type list). Move and resize the chart so that it appears in the range A10:F20. If the labels along the horizontal axis (x-axis) do not appear as shown in Figure 1-82, then drag the right side of the chart so that it is displayed in the range A10:H20.

7. Enter your name, course, laboratory assignment number, date, and instructor name in cells A22 through A26.

8. Save the workbook using the file name Lab 1-1 Knotting Hill Bookstore October Sales.

9. Print the worksheet.

10. Make the following two corrections to the sales amounts: $14,785.21 for Children eBooks (cell C5), $57,752.54 for Technical Softcover books (cell E7). After you enter the corrections, the company totals in cell F8 should equal $432,889.10.

11. Print the revised worksheet. Close the workbook without saving the changes.

2 Quarterly Expense Analysis Worksheet

Problem: As the chief accountant for College Travel, Inc., you have been asked by the vice president to create a worksheet to analyze the 4th quarter expenses for the company by office and expense category (Figure 1-83 on the next page). The office locations and corresponding expenses for the 4th quarter are shown in Table 1-9.

Table 1-9 College Travel 4th Quarter Expenses				
	Atlanta	Nashville	New Orleans	Orlando
Marketing	42502.23	19231.56	32012.40	14012.00
Rent	43970.50	57510.00	29089.32	31765.23
Supplies	31892.70	18429.34	26723.15	22914.50
Travel	9512.45	12323.21	9012.56	8910.32
Wages	83463.30	72135.45	63908.55	92364.50

Instructions: Perform the following tasks.

1. Create the worksheet shown in Figure 1-83 using the data in Table 1-9.

2. Use the SUM function to determine totals expenses for the four offices, the totals for each expense category, and the company total. Add column and row headings for the totals, as appropriate.

(continued)

In the Lab

Quarterly Expense Analysis Worksheet *(continued)*

3. Change the worksheet title to 26-point Arial Black dark red, bold font, and center it across columns A through F. Format the worksheet subtitle to 16-point Arial dark red, bold font, and center it across columns A through F.

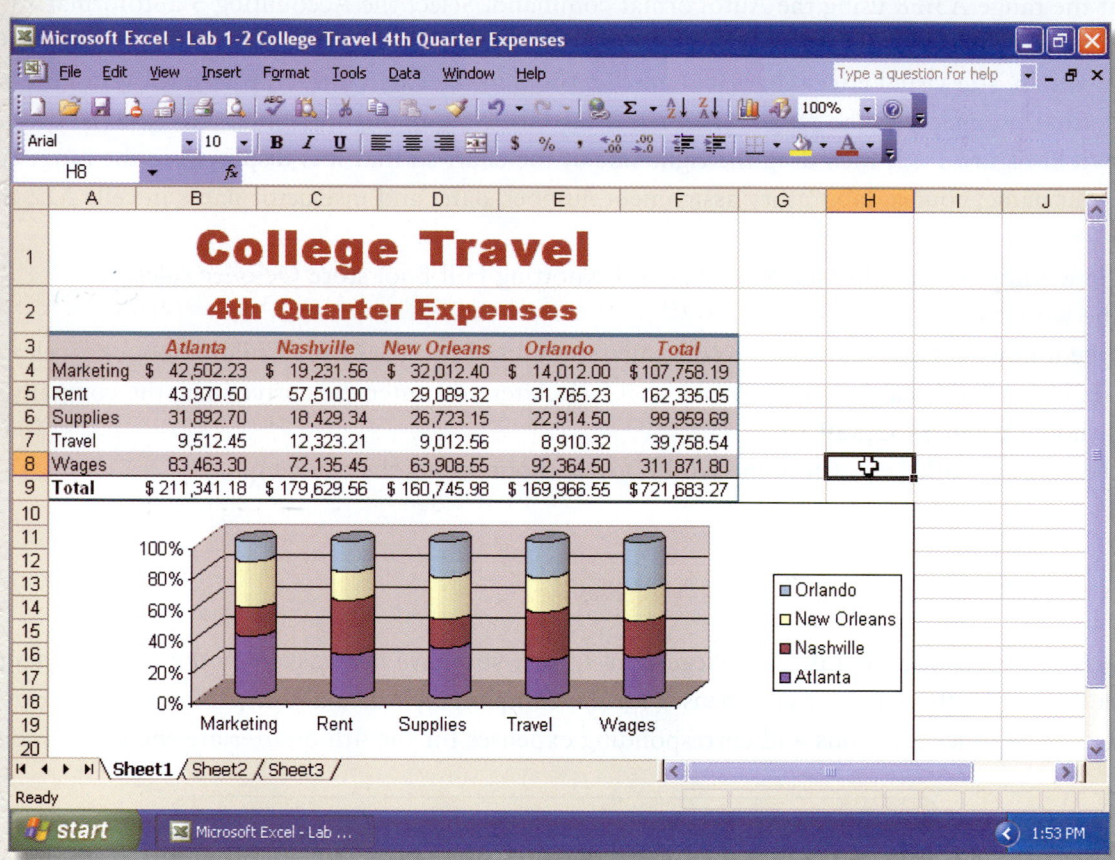

FIGURE 1-83

4. Format the range A3:F9 using the AutoFormat command on the Format menu as follows: (a) apply the autoformat Accounting 1; and (b) with the range A3:F9 still selected, apply the autoformat List 1. If you make a mistake, apply the autoformat None and then apply the autoformats again.

5. Chart the range A3:E8. Draw the 100% Stacked column with a cylindrical shape chart, as shown in Figure 1-83, by clicking the Chart Wizard button on the Standard toolbar. When Excel displays the Chart Wizard dialog box, select Cylinder in the Chart type list, and then select column 3, row 1 in the Chart sub-type list. Use the chart location A10:H20.

6. Enter your name, course, laboratory assignment number, date, and instructor name in cells A23 through A27.

7. Save the workbook using the file name, Lab 1-2 College Travel 4th Quarter Expenses. Print the worksheet.

8. Two corrections to the expenses were sent in from the accounting department. The correct expenses are $62,345.12 for the Nashville's quarterly rent (cell C5) and $18,615.42 for Orlando's quarterly travel expenses (cell E7). After you enter the two corrections, the company total in cell F9 should equal $736,223.49. Print the revised worksheet.

In the Lab

9. Use the Undo button to change the worksheet back to the original numbers in Table 1-9. Use the Redo button to change the worksheet back to the revised state.

10. Close Excel without saving the latest changes. Start Excel and open the workbook saved in step 7. Double-click cell D6 and use in-cell editing to change the New Orleans quarterly supplies expense to $29,098.32. Write the company total in cell F9 at the top of the first printout. Click the Undo button.

11. Click cell A1 and then click the Merge and Center button to split cell A1 into cells A1, B1, C1, D1, E1, and F1. To re-merge the cells into one, select the range A1:F1 and then click the Merge and Center button.

12. Hand in the two printouts to your instructor. Close the workbook without saving the changes.

3 College Expenses and Resources Worksheet

Problem: Attending college is an expensive proposition and your resources are limited. To plan for your four-year college career, you have decided to organize your anticipated resources and expenses in a worksheet. The data required to prepare your worksheet is shown in Table 1-10.

Table 1-10 College Expenses and Resources				
Expenses	Freshman	Sophomore	Junior	Senior
Room & Board	3390.00	3627.30	3881.21	4152.90
Tuition & Books	4850.00	5189.50	5552.77	5941.46
Clothes	540.00	577.80	618.25	661.52
Entertainment	635.00	679.45	727.01	777.90
Miscellaneous	325.00	347.75	372.09	398.14
Resources	Freshman	Sophomore	Junior	Senior
Savings	1700.00	1819.00	1946.33	2082.57
Parents	2390.00	2557.30	2736.31	2927.85
Job	1450.00	1551.50	1660.11	1776.32
Financial Aid	4200.00	4494.00	4808.58	5145.18

Instructions Part 1: Using the numbers in Table 1-10, create the worksheet shown in columns A through F in Figure 1-84 on the next page. Format the range A3:F9 using the AutoFormat command on the Format menu as follows: (a) select the range A3:F9 and then apply the autoformat Accounting 1; and (b) with the range A3:F9 still selected, apply the autoformat Colorful 2. Use the same autoformats for the range A11:F16.

Enter your identification on the worksheet and save the workbook using the file name Lab 1-3 Part 1 College Expenses and Resources. Print the worksheet in landscape orientation. You print in landscape orientation by invoking the Page Setup command on the File menu and then clicking Landscape in the Page sheet in the Page Setup dialog box. Click the Save button on the Standard toolbar to save the workbook with the new print settings.

(continued)

In the Lab

College Expenses and Resources Worksheet *(continued)*

After reviewing the numbers, you realize you need to increase manually each of the Junior-year expenses in column D by $400. Change the Junior-year expenses to reflect this change. Manually change the financial aid for the Junior year by the amount required to cover the increase in expenses. The totals in cells F9 and F16 should equal $45,245.05. Print the worksheet. Close the workbook without saving changes. Hand in the two printouts to your instructor.

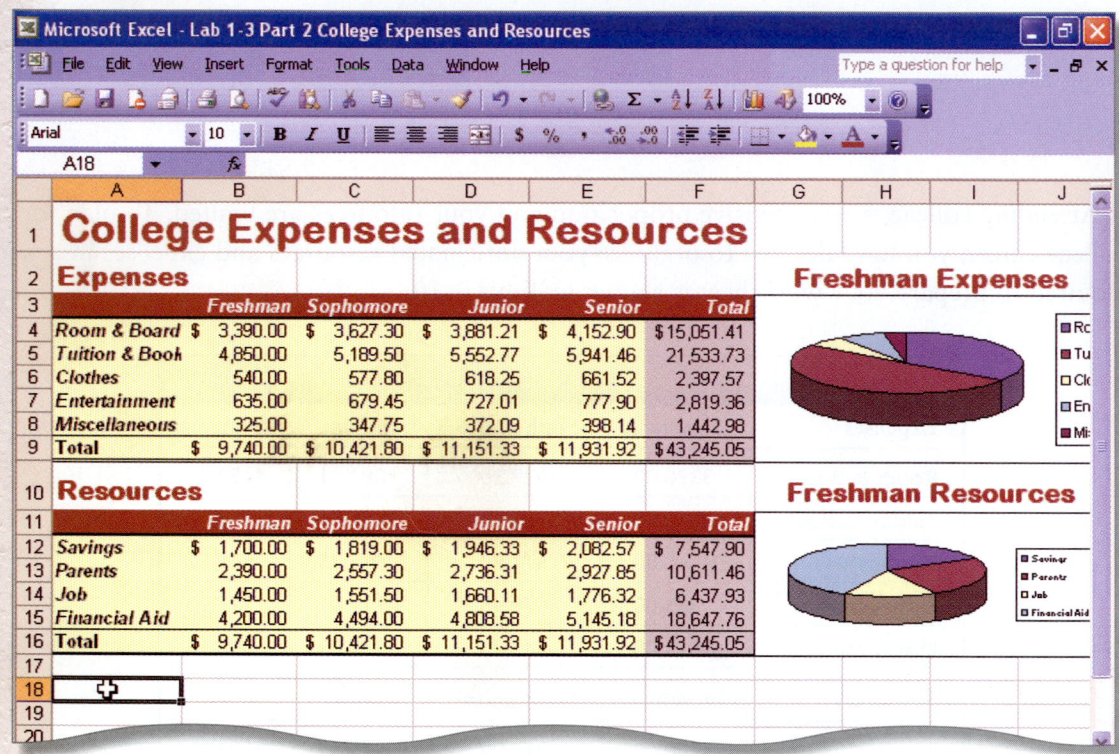

FIGURE 1-84

Instructions Part 2: Open the workbook Lab 1-3 Part 1 College Expenses and Resources. Draw a 3-D Pie chart in the range G3:J9 to show the contribution of each category of expenses for the Freshman year. Chart the range A4:B8. Add the Pie chart title as shown in cell G2 in Figure 1-84. Draw a 3-D Pie chart in the range G11:J16 to show the contribution of each category of resources for the Freshman year. Chart the range A12:B15. Add the Pie chart title shown in cell G10 in Figure 1-84. Save the workbook using the file name, Lab 1-3 Part 2 College Expenses and Resources. Print the worksheet. Hand in the printout to your instructor.

Instructions Part 3: Open the workbook Lab 1-3 Part 2 College Expenses and Resources. A close inspection of Table 1-10 shows that both expenses and resources increase 7% each year. Use the Type a question for help box on the menu bar to learn how to enter the data for the last three years using a formula and the Copy command. For example, the formula to enter in cell C4 is =B4 * 1.07. Enter formulas to replace all the numbers in the range C4:E8 and C12:E15. If necessary, reformat the tables using the autoformats, as described in Part 1. The worksheet should appear as shown in Figure 1-84, except that some of the totals will be off by 0.01 due to rounding errors. Save the worksheet using the file name, Lab 1-3 Part 3 College Expenses and Resources. Print the worksheet. Press CTRL+ACCENT MARK(`) to display the formulas. Print the formulas version. Close the workbook without saving changes. Hand in both printouts to your instructor.

Cases and Places

The difficulty of these case studies varies:
■ are the least difficult and ■■ are more difficult. The last exercise is a group exercise.

1 ■ You are employed by the Reggae Music Company. Your manager has asked you to prepare a worksheet to help her analyze monthly sales by store and by type of reggae music (Table 1-11). Use the concepts and techniques presented in this project to create the worksheet and an embedded Clustered bar chart with a 3-D visual effect.

Table 1-11	Reggae Music Company Monthly Sales			
	Boston	**Kansas City**	**Portland**	**San Diego**
Dancehall	6734	7821	4123	7989
Dub	5423	2134	6574	3401
Dub Poetry	3495	6291	7345	7098
Lovers Rock	6789	4523	9102	7812
Ragga	8920	9812	5637	3456
Rocksteady	2134	2190	3401	2347
Ska	5462	2923	8034	5135

2 ■ To estimate the funds you need to make it through the upcoming year, you decide to create a personal budget itemizing your expected quarterly expenses. The anticipated expenses are listed in Table 1-12. Use the concepts and techniques presented in this project to create the worksheet and an embedded 100% Stacked column chart with a conical shape that compares the quarterly cost of each expense. If necessary, reduce the size of the font in the chart so that each expense category name appears on the horizontal axis (x-axis). Use the AutoCalculate area to determine the average amount spent per quarter on each expense. Manually insert the averages with appropriate titles in an empty area on the worksheet.

Table 1-12	Quarterly Personal Budget			
	Jan - Mar	**April - June**	**July - Sept**	**Oct - Dec**
Mortgage	1500	1500	1500	1500
Food	900	950	950	1000
Car & Ins.	600	600	600	600
Clothes	567	433	200	459
Utilities	600	400	400	550
Miscellaneous	149	121	159	349

Cases and Places

3 ◼◼ The Magic Theater is a movie house that shows movies at weekday evening, weekend matinee, and weekend evening screenings. Three types of tickets are sold at each presentation: general admission, senior citizen, and children. The theater management has asked you to prepare a worksheet, based on the revenue from a typical week, that can be used to reevaluate its ticket structure. During an average week, weekday evening shows generate $7,250 from general admission ticket sales, $6,715 from senior citizen ticket sales, and $1,575 from children ticket sales. Weekend matinee shows make $6,723 from general admission ticket sales, $2,050 from senior citizen ticket sales, and $2,875 from children ticket sales. Weekend evening shows earn $9,415 from general admission ticket sales, $9,815 from senior citizen ticket sales, and $1,235 from children ticket sales. Use the concepts and techniques presented in this project to prepare a worksheet that includes total revenues for each type of ticket and for each presentation time, and a Clustered Bar chart illustrating ticket revenues.

4 ◼◼ Jasmine's Floral Shop on Michigan Avenue in Chicago sells floral arrangments to an exclusive clientele. The company is trying to decide whether it is feasible to open another boutique in the Chicago area. You have been asked to develop a worksheet totaling all the revenue received last year from customers living in the Chicago area. The revenue from customers living in the Chicago area by quarter is: Quarter 1, $221,565.56; Quarter 2, $182,704.34; Quarter 3, $334,116.31; and Quarter 4, $421,333.50. Create a Pie chart with a 3-D visual effect to illustrate Chicago-area revenue contribution by quarter. Use the AutoCalculate area to find the average, maximum, and minimum quarterly revenue and manually enter them and their corresponding identifiers in an empty area on the worksheet.

5 ◼◼ **Working Together** Visit the Registrar's office at your school and obtain data, such as age, gender, and resident status, for the students majoring in at least five different academic departments this semester. Have each member of your team divide the data into different categories. For example, separate the data by:

1. Age, divided into four different age groups
2. Gender, divided into male and female
3. Resident status, divided into resident and nonresident

After coordinating the data as a group, have each member independently use the concepts and techniques presented in this project to create a worksheet and appropriate chart to show the total students by characteristics by academic department. As a group, critique each worksheet and have each member re-do his or her worksheet based on the group recommendations. Hand in printouts of your original worksheet and final worksheet.

MICROSOFT
Office Excel 2003

Formulas, Functions, Formatting, and Web Queries

PROJECT

2

CASE PERSPECTIVE

Several years ago, while Alisha Wright was taking an Investment course as a sophomore in college, she persuaded six of her classmates to start a stock club geared towards researching and investing in stocks of large, well-established, and consistently profitable companies, which are referred to as blue chip stocks. They decided to call themselves the Blue Chip Stock Club. While in college, each member of the club contributed $20 per month.

Now, the club members are out of college, married, and have taken jobs around the country. They continue to invest in the stock market as a group, however, using e-mail, chat rooms, and Web cams to communicate and conduct their monthly meetings via the Internet. A few years ago, they increased their monthly contribution to $100.

At the end of each month, Alisha, the Blue Chip Stock Club's permanent treasurer, summarizes the club's financial status. Alisha plans to use Excel to create a worksheet summarizing the club's stock activities, which she can use to track and analyze the investment portfolio, answer questions posed by club members in their e-mails, and e-mail a monthly closing report to the club members. She also plans to use its Web query capabilities to access real-time stock quotes.

Alisha knows little about Excel 2003 and has asked you to show her how to create the worksheet (Figure 2-1a) and access real-time stock quotes over the Internet (Figure 2-1b).

As you read through this project, you will learn how to enter formulas and functions, how to improve the appearance of a worksheet, how to perform Web queries, and how to e-mail from within Excel.

MICROSOFT
Office Excel 2003

Formulas, Functions, Formatting, and Web Queries

PROJECT

2

Objectives

You will have mastered the material in this project when you can:

- Enter formulas using the keyboard and Point mode
- Recognize smart tags and option buttons
- Apply the AVERAGE, MAX, and MIN functions
- Verify a formula using Range Finder
- Format a worksheet using buttons and commands
- Add conditional formatting to a range of cells
- Change the width of a column and height of a row
- Check the spelling of a worksheet
- Preview how a printed copy of the worksheet will look
- Print a partial or complete worksheet
- Display and print the formulas version of a worksheet
- Use a Web query to get real-time data from a Web site
- Rename sheets in a workbook
- E-mail the active workbook from within Excel

Introduction

In Project 1, you learned how to enter data, sum values, format the worksheet to make it easier to read, and draw a chart. You also learned about online Help and saving, printing, and opening a workbook. This project continues to emphasize these topics and presents some new ones.

The new topics covered in this project include using formulas and functions to create the worksheet shown in Figure 2-1a. Other new topics include smart tags and option buttons, verifying formulas, adding borders, formatting numbers and text, using conditional formatting, changing the widths of columns and heights of rows, spell checking, e-mailing from within an application, renaming worksheets, and using alternative types of worksheet displays and printouts. One alternative worksheet display and printout shows the formulas in the worksheet, instead of the values. When you display the formulas in the worksheet, you see exactly what text, data, formulas, and functions you have entered into it. Finally, this project covers Web queries to obtain real-time data from a Web site (Figure 2-1b).

(a) Worksheet

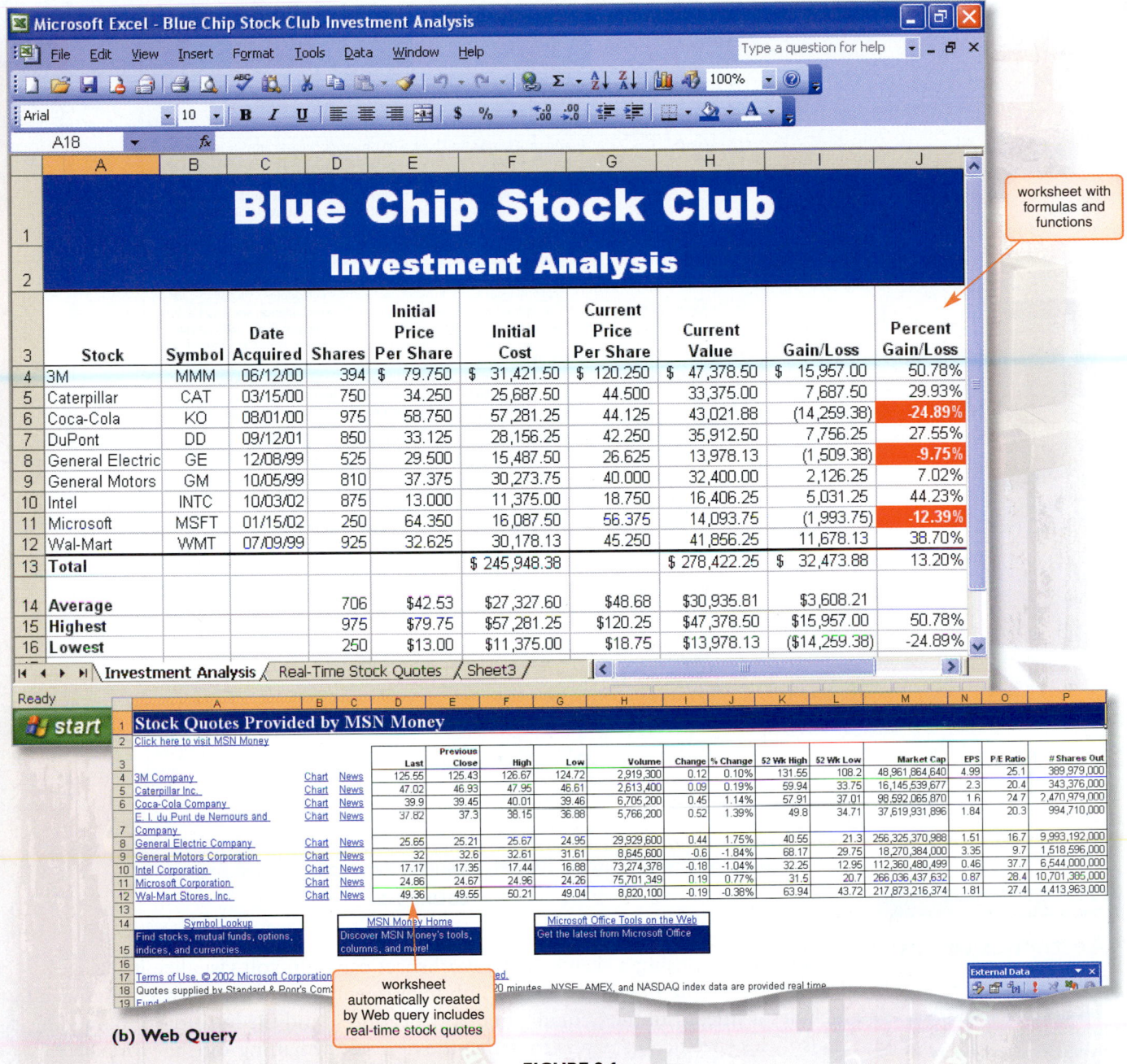

worksheet with formulas and functions

(b) Web Query

worksheet automatically created by Web query includes real-time stock quotes

FIGURE 2-1

Project Two — Blue Chip Stock Club Investment Analysis

Recall that the first step in creating an effective worksheet is to make sure you understand what is required. Requirements usually are provided by the people who will use the worksheet. The requirements document for the Blue Chip Stock Club Investment Analysis worksheet includes the following: needs, source of data, summary of calculations, Web requirements, and other facts about its development (Figure 2-2 on the next page).

REQUEST FOR NEW WORKBOOK

Date Submitted:	July 1, 2005
Submitted By:	Alisha Wright
Worksheet Title:	Blue Chip Stock Club Investment Analysis
Needs:	An easy-to-read workbook with two worksheets to provide information on the current investment portfolio and updated stock quote data. The first worksheet will summarize the club's investment portfolio (Figure 2-3). For each stock, the worksheet will include the stock name, stock symbol, date acquired, shares, initial price per share, initial cost, current price per share, current value, gain/loss, and percent gain/loss. The worksheet also will include (1) totals for initial cost, current value, and gain loss and (2) the average, highest value, and lowest value for each column of numbers. The second worksheet will use the import data capabilities of Excel to access real-time stock quotes using Web queries.
Source of Data:	The data supplied by Alisha includes the stock names, stock symbols, dates acquired, number of shares, initial price per share, and current price per share. This data is shown in Table 2-1, Blue Chip Stock Club Portfolio.
Calculations:	1. Complete the following calculations for each of the stocks: a. Initial Cost = Shares _ Initial Price Per Share b. Current Value = Shares _ Current Price Per Share c. Gain/Loss = Current Value – Initial Cost d. Percent Gain/Loss = Gain/Loss / Initial Cost 2. Compute the totals for initial cost, current value, and gain/loss. 3. Use the AVERAGE function to determine the average for the number of shares, initial price per share, initial cost per share, current price per share, current value, and gain/loss. 4. Use the MAX and MIN functions to determine the highest and lowest values for the number of shares, initial price per share, initial cost per share, current price per share, current value, gain/loss, and percent gain/loss.
Web Requirements:	Use the Web query feature of Excel to get real-time stock quotes for the stocks owned by the Blue Chip Stock Club.

Approvals

Approval Status:	X	Approved
		Rejected
Approved By:	Members of the Blue Chip Stock Club	
Date:	July 6, 2005	
Assigned To:	J. Quasney, Spreadsheet Specialist	

FIGURE 2-2

In addition, using a sketch of the worksheet can help you visualize its design. The sketch for the Blue Chip Stock Club Investment Analysis worksheet (Figure 2-3) includes a title, a subtitle, column and row headings, and the location of data values. It also uses specific characters to define the desired formatting for the worksheet as follows:

1. The row of Xs below the two leftmost columns defines the cell entries as text, such as stock names and stock symbols.

2. The rows of Zs and 9s with slashes, dollar signs, decimal points, commas, and percent signs in the remaining columns define the cell entries as numbers. The Zs indicate that the selected format should instruct Excel to suppress leading 0s. The 9s indicate that the selected format should instruct Excel to display any digits, including 0s.

3. The decimal point means that a decimal point should appear in the cell entry and indicates the number of decimal places to use.

4. The commas indicate that the selected format should instruct Excel to display a comma separator only if the number has enough digits to the left of the decimal point.

5. The slashes in the third column identify the cell entry as a date.

6. The dollar signs that are not adjacent to the Zs in the first row below the column headings and in the total row signify a fixed dollar sign. The dollar signs that are adjacent to the Zs below the total row signify a floating dollar sign, or one that appears next to the first significant digit.

7. The percent sign (%) in the far right column indicates a percent sign should appear after the number.

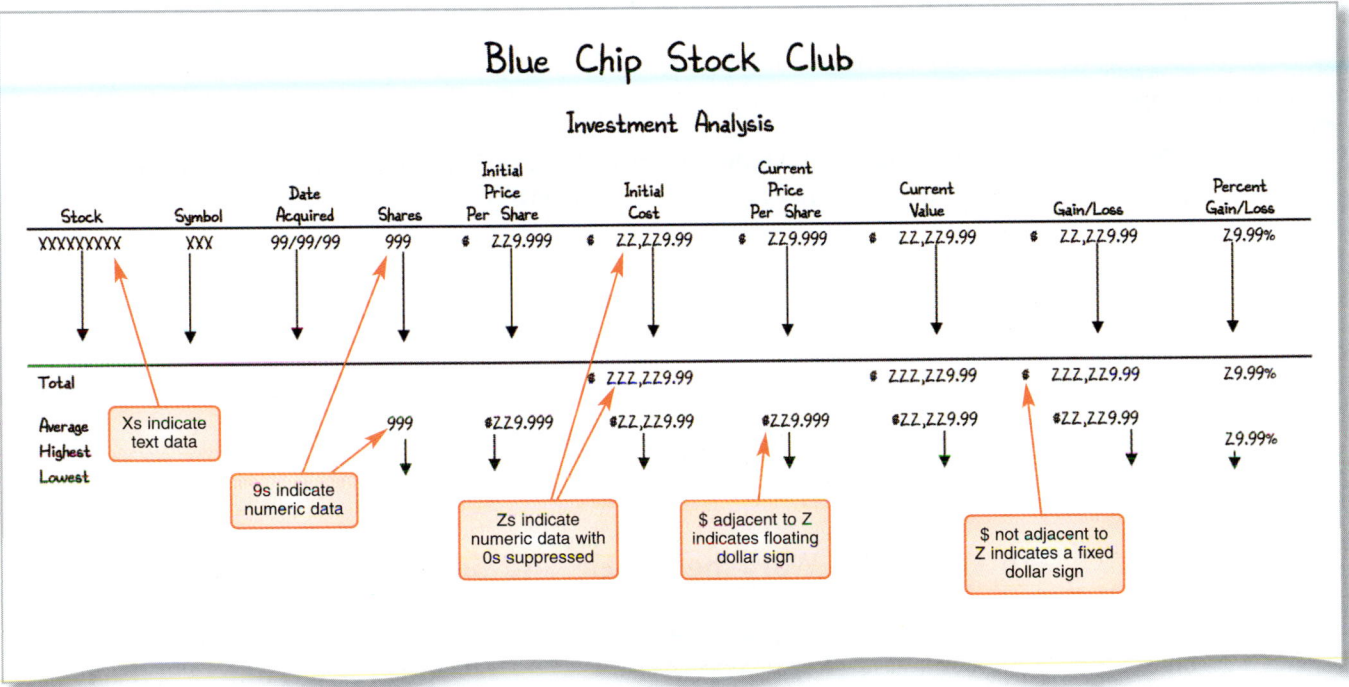

FIGURE 2-3

The real-time stock quotes (shown in Figure 2-1b on page EX 67) will be accessed via a Web query. The stock quotes will be returned to the active workbook on a separate worksheet. Microsoft determines the content and format of the Real-Time Stock Quotes worksheet.

Starting and Customizing Excel

With the requirements document and sketch of the worksheet complete, the next step is to use Excel to create the worksheet. To start and customize Excel, Windows must be running. If you are stepping through this project on a computer and you want your screen to match the figures in this book, then you should change your computer's resolution to 800 × 600. For more information on how to change the resolution on your computer, see Appendix B. The steps on the next page start Excel and customize the Excel window.

More About

Starting Excel

You can use a command-line switch to start Excel and control how it starts. First, click the Start button on the Windows taskbar and then click Run. Next, enter the complete path to Excel's application file including the switch (for example, "C:\ Program Files\Microsoft Office\Office\Excel.exe" /e). The switch /e opens Excel without opening a new workbook; /i starts Excel with a maximized window; /p "folder" sets the active path to folder and ignores the default folder; /r "filename" opens filename in read-only mode; and /s starts Excel in safe mode.

To Start and Customize Excel

1 Click the Start button on the Windows taskbar, point to All Programs on the Start menu, point to Microsoft Office on the All Programs submenu, and then click Microsoft Office Excel 2003 on the Microsoft Office submenu.

2 If the Excel window is not maximized, double-click its title bar to maximize it.

3 If the Language bar appears, right-click it and then click Close the Language bar on the shortcut menu.

4 If the Getting Started task pane appears in the Excel window, click its Close button in the upper-right corner.

5 If the Standard and Formatting toolbars are positioned on the same row, click the Toolbar Options button and then click Show Buttons on Two Rows.

The Excel window with the Standard and Formatting toolbars on two rows appears as shown in Figure 2-1a on page EX 67.

After the Excel window is opened, Steps 3 through 5 close the Getting Started task pane, close the Language bar, and ensure that the Standard and Formatting toolbars appear on two rows.

Entering the Titles and Numbers into the Worksheet

The following steps show how to enter the worksheet title and subtitle into cells A1 and A2.

To Enter the Worksheet Title and Subtitle

1 Select cell A1. Type Blue Chip Stock Club in the cell and then press the DOWN ARROW key.

2 Type Investment Analysis in cell A2 and then press the DOWN ARROW key.

Excel displays the worksheet title in cell A1 and the worksheet subtitle in cell A2, as shown in Figure 2-4 on page EX 73.

The column titles in row 3 begin in cell A3 and extend through cell J3. The column titles in Figure 2-3 include multiple lines of text. To start a new line in a cell, press ALT+ENTER after each line, except for the last line, which is completed by clicking the Enter box, pressing the ENTER key, or pressing one of the arrow keys. When you see ALT+ENTER in a step, press the ENTER key while holding down the ALT key and then release both keys.

The stock names and the row titles Total, Average, Highest, and Lowest in the leftmost column begin in cell A4 and continue down to cell A16.

The stock club's investments are summarized in Table 2-1. This data is entered into rows 4 through 12 of the worksheet. The remainder of this section explains the steps required to enter the column titles, stock data, and row titles as shown in Figure 2-4 and then save the workbook.

Table 2-1	Blue Chip Stock Club Portfolio				
Stock	Symbol	Date Acquired	Shares	Initial Price Per Share	Current Price Per Share
3M	MMM	6/12/00	394	79.75	120.25
Caterpillar	CAT	3/15/00	750	34.25	44.50
Coca-Cola	KO	8/01/00	975	58.75	44.125
DuPont	DD	9/12/01	850	33.125	42.25
General Electric	GE	12/08/99	525	29.50	26.625
General Motors	GM	10/05/99	810	37.375	40.00
Intel	INTC	10/03/02	875	13.00	18.75
Microsoft	MSFT	1/15/02	250	64.35	56.375
Wal-Mart	WMT	7/09/99	925	32.625	45.25

To Enter the Column Titles

1. **With cell A3 selected, type** Stock **and then press the RIGHT ARROW key.**

2. **Type** Symbol **in cell B3 and then press the RIGHT ARROW key.**

3. **In cell C3, type** Date **and then press ALT+ENTER. Type** Acquired **and then press the RIGHT ARROW key.**

4. **Type** Shares **in cell D3 and then press the RIGHT ARROW key.**

5. **In cell E3, type** Initial **and then press ALT+ENTER. Type** Price **and then press ALT+ENTER. Type** Per Share **and then press the RIGHT ARROW key.**

6. **In cell F3, type** Initial **and then press ALT+ENTER. Type** Cost **and then press the RIGHT ARROW key.**

7. **In cell G3, type** Current **and then press ALT+ENTER. Type** Price **and then press ALT+ENTER. Type** Per Share **and then press the RIGHT ARROW key.**

8. **In cell H3, type** Current **and then press ALT+ENTER. Type** Value **and then press the RIGHT ARROW key.**

9. **Type** Gain/Loss **in cell I3 and then press the RIGHT ARROW key.**

10. **In cell J3, type** Percent **and then press ALT+ENTER. Type** Gain/Loss **and then click cell A4.**

The column titles appear as shown in row 3 of Figure 2-4 on page EX 73. When you press ALT+ENTER to add more lines to a cell, Excel automatically increases the height of the entire row.

The stock data in Table 2-1 includes a date on which each stock was acquired. Excel considers a date to be a number and, therefore, it displays the date right-aligned in the cell. The steps on the next page describe how to enter the stock data shown in Table 2-1.

More About

Two-Digit Years

When you enter a two-digit year value, Excel changes a two-digit year less than 30 to 20xx and a two-digit year of 30 and greater to 19xx. Use four-digit years to ensure that Excel interprets year values the way you intend, if necessary.

To Enter the Stock Data

1 With cell A4 selected, type 3M and then press the RIGHT ARROW key. Type MMM in cell B4 and then press the RIGHT ARROW key.

2 Type 6/12/00 in cell C4 and then press the RIGHT ARROW key. Type 394 in cell D4 and then press the RIGHT ARROW key.

3 Type 79.75 in cell E4 and then press the RIGHT ARROW key twice. Type 120.25 in cell G4 and then press the ENTER key.

4 Click cell A5. Enter the data in Table 2-1 for the eight remaining stocks in rows 5 through 12.

The stock data appears in rows 4 through 12 as shown in Figure 2-4.

To Enter the Row Titles

More About

Formatting a Worksheet

With early worksheet packages, users often skipped rows to improve the appearance of the worksheet. With Excel it is not necessary to skip rows because you can increase row heights to add white space between information.

1 Click cell A13. Type Total and then press the DOWN ARROW key. Type Average in cell A14 and then press the DOWN ARROW key.

2 Type Highest in cell A15 and then press the DOWN ARROW key. Type Lowest in cell A16 and then press the ENTER key. Click cell F4.

The row titles appear in rows 13 through 16 as shown in Figure 2-4.

With the data entered into the worksheet, the next step is to save the workbook using the file name Blue Chip Stock Club Investment Analysis. As you are building a workbook, it is a good idea to save it often so that you do not lose your work if the computer is turned off or if you lose electrical power.

To Save the Workbook

1 With a floppy disk in drive A, click the Save button on the Standard toolbar.

2 When Excel displays the Save As dialog box, type Blue Chip Stock Club Investment Analysis in the File name text box.

3 If necessary, click 3½ Floppy (A:) in the Save in list. Click the Save button in the Save As dialog box.

More About

Entering Numbers into a Range

An efficient way to enter data into a range of cells is to select a range and then enter the first number in the upper-left cell of the range. Excel responds by entering the value and moving the active cell selection down one cell. When you enter the last value in the first column, Excel moves the active cell selection to the top of the next column.

Excel saves the workbook on the floppy disk in drive A using the file name, Blue Chip Stock Club Investment Analysis.

This concludes entering the data into the worksheet. After saving the file, the worksheet remains on the screen with the file name, Blue Chip Stock Club Investment Analysis, on the title bar.

Entering Formulas

The initial cost for each stock, which appears in column F, is equal to the number of shares in column D times the initial price per share in column E. Thus, the initial cost for 3M in cell F4 is obtained by multiplying 394 (cell D4) by 79.75 (cell E4).

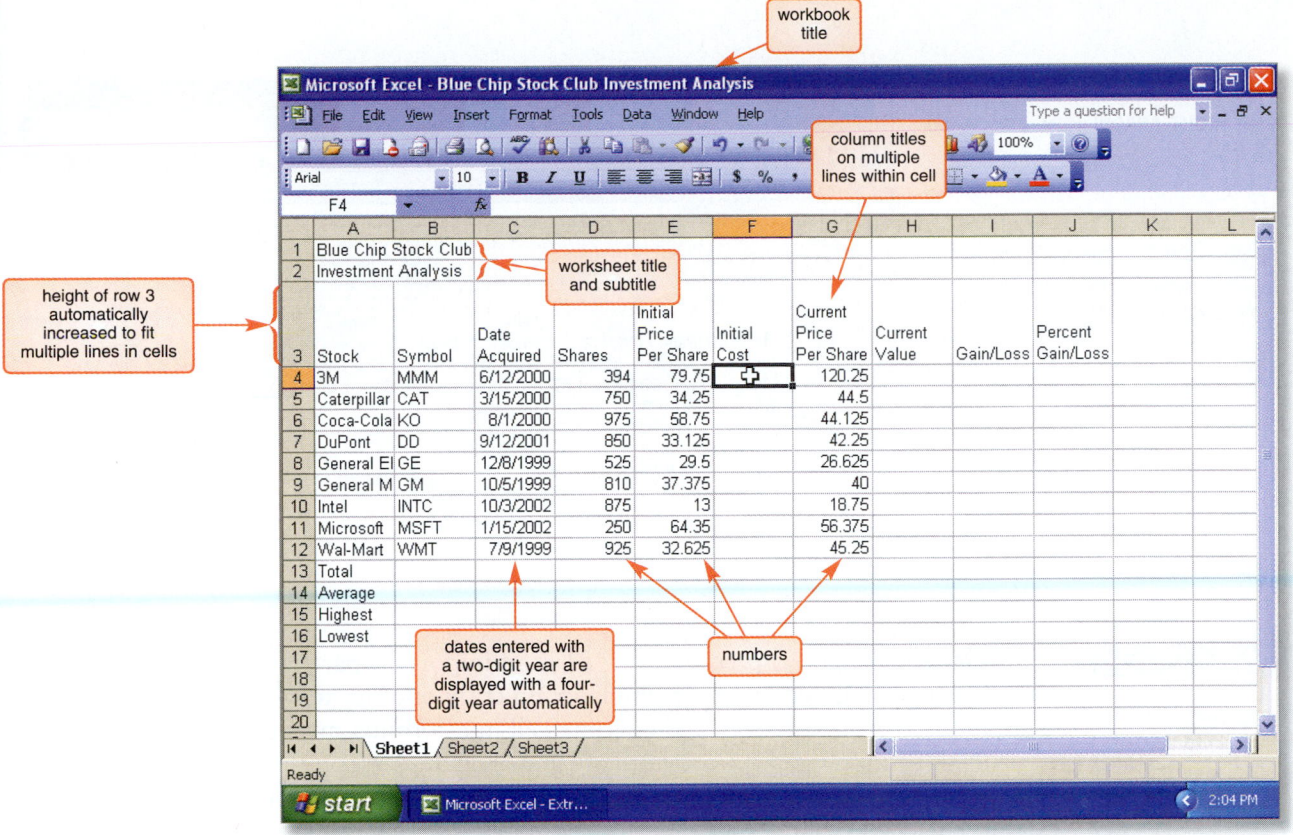

FIGURE 2-4

One of the reasons Excel is such a valuable tool is that you can assign a **formula** to a cell and Excel will calculate the result. Consider, for example, what would happen if you had to multiply 394 × 79.75 and then manually enter the product, 31421.5, in cell F4. Every time the values in cells D4 or E4 changed, you would have to recalculate the product and enter the new value in cell F4. By contrast, if you enter a formula in cell F4 to multiply the values in cells D4 and E4, Excel recalculates the product whenever new values are entered into those cells and displays the result in cell F4. The following steps enter the initial cost formula in cell F4 using the keyboard.

To Enter a Formula Using the Keyboard

1

• **With cell F4 selected, type =d4*e4 in the cell.**

Excel displays the formula in the formula bar and in cell F4 (Figure 2-5). Excel also displays colored borders around the cells referenced in the formula.

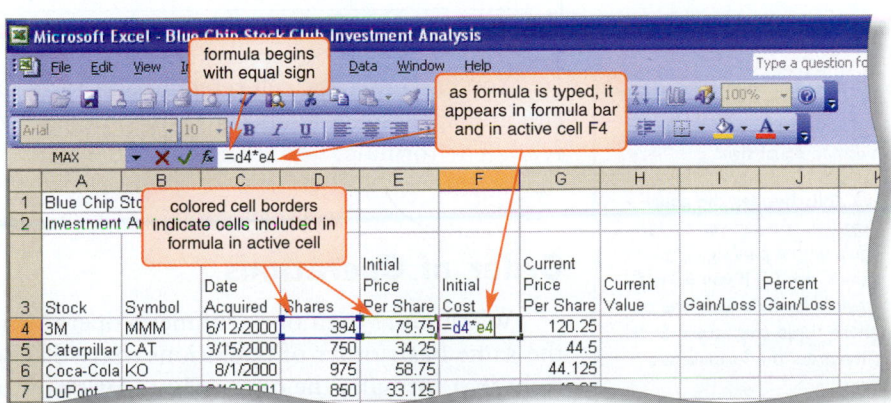

FIGURE 2-5

2

• **Press the RIGHT ARROW key twice to select cell H4.**

Instead of displaying the formula in cell F4, Excel completes the arithmetic operation indicated by the formula and displays the result, 31421.5 (Figure 2-6).

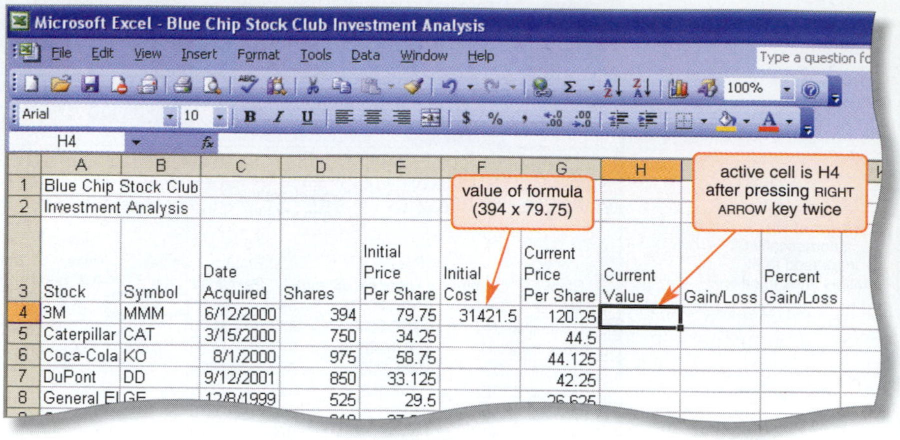

FIGURE 2-6

> ***More About***
>
> **Automatic Recalculation**
>
> Every time you enter a value into a cell in the worksheet, Excel automatically recalculates all formulas. You can change to manual recalculation by clicking Options on the Tools menu and then clicking Manual on the Calculation sheet. In manual calculation mode, press F9 to instruct Excel to recalculate all formulas.

The **equal sign** (=) preceding d4*e4 is an important part of the formula: it alerts Excel that you are entering a formula or function and not text. Because the most common error is to reference the wrong cell in a formula mistakenly, Excel colors the borders of the cells referenced in the formula (Figure 2-5 on the previous page). The coloring helps in the reviewing process to ensure the cell references are correct. The **asterisk** (*) following d4 is the arithmetic operator that directs Excel to perform the multiplication operation. Table 2-2 describes multiplication and other valid Excel arithmetic operators.

Table 2-2 Summary of Arithmetic Operators

ARITHMETIC OPERATOR	MEANING	EXAMPLE OF USAGE	MEANING
–	Negation	–63	Negative 63
%	Percentage	=13%	Multiplies 13 by 0.01
^	Exponentiation	=5 ^ 2	Raises 5 to the second power
*	Multiplication	=17.5 * E4	Multiplies the contents of cell E4 by 17.5
/	Division	=A2 / A4	Divides the contents of cell A2 by the contents of cell A4
+	Addition	=4 + 8	Adds 4 and 8
–	Subtraction	=K15 – 13	Subtracts 13 from the contents of cell K15

> ***Q&A***
>
> **Q:** Must all formulas begin with an equal sign?
>
> **A:** No. Besides the equal sign (=), you can start a formula with a plus sign (+) or a minus sign (-). If you do not begin a formula with one of these three characters, Excel interprets the formula as text.

You can enter the cell references in formulas in uppercase or lowercase, and you can add spaces before and after arithmetic operators to make the formulas easier to read. The formula, =d4*e4, is the same as the formulas, =d4 * e4, =D4 * e4, or =D4 * E4.

Order of Operations

When more than one arithmetic operator is involved in a formula, Excel follows the same basic order of operations that you use in algebra. Moving from left to right in a formula, the **order of operations** is as follows: first negation (–), then all percentages (%), then all exponentiations (^), then all multiplications (*) and divisions (/), and finally, all additions (+) and subtractions (–).

You can use parentheses to override the order of operations. For example, if Excel follows the order of operations, 8 * 3 + 2 equals 26. If you use parentheses, however, to change the formula to 8 * (3 + 2), the result is 40, because the parentheses instruct Excel to add 3 and 2 before multiplying by 8. Table 2-3 illustrates several examples of valid Excel formulas and explains the order of operations.

Table 2-3 Examples of Excel Formulas	
FORMULA	**MEANING**
=M5	Assigns the value in cell M5 to the active cell.
=12 + − 3^2	Assigns the sum of 12 + 9 (or 21) to the active cell.
=6 * E22 or =E22 * 6 or =(6 * E22)	Assigns six times the contents of cell E22 to the active cell.
=70% * 6	Assigns the product of 0.70 times 6 (or 4.2) to the active cell.
= − (G7 * V67)	Assigns the negative value of the product of the values contained in cells G7 and V67 to the active cell.
=5 * (P4 − G4)	Assigns the product of five times the difference between the values contained in cells P4 and G4 to the active cell.
=K5 / Y7 − D6 * L9 + W4 ^ V10	Instructs Excel to complete the following arithmetic operations, from left to right: first exponentiation (W4 ^ V10), then division (K5 / Y7), then multiplication (D6 * L9), then subtraction (K5 / Y7) − (D6 * L9), and finally addition (K5 / Y7 − D6 * L9) + (W4 ^ V10). If cells K5 = 10, D6 = 6, L9 = 2, W4 = 5, V10 = 2, and Y7 = 2, then Excel assigns the active cell the value 18; that is, 10 / 2 − 6 * 2 + 5 ^ 2 = 18.

Entering Formulas Using Point Mode

The sketch of the worksheet in Figure 2-3 on page EX 69 calls for the current value, gain/loss, and percent gain/loss of each stock to appear in columns H, I, and J, respectively. All three of these values are calculated using formulas. The formula used to calculate the current value for 3M in cell H4 multiples the number of shares in cell D4 by the current price per share in cell G4 (=D4*G4). The formula used to calculate the gain/loss for 3M in cell I4 is equal to the current value in cell H4 minus the initial cost in cell F4 (=H4 − F4). The formula used to calculate the percent gain/loss for 3M in cell J4 is equal to the gain/loss in cell I4 divided by the initial cost in cell F4 (=I4/F4).

An alternative to entering the formulas in cell H4, I4, and J4 using the keyboard is to enter the formulas using the mouse and Point mode. **Point mode** allows you to select cells for use in a formula by using the mouse. The following steps illustrate how to enter formulas using Point mode.

More About

Using Point Mode

Point mode allows you to create formulas using the mouse. You can enter arithmetic operators using the mouse and on-screen keyboard that is available through the Language bar (see Appendix B). Thus, with Excel, you can enter entire formulas without ever touching the keyboard.

To Enter Formulas Using Point Mode

1

• **With cell H4 selected, type = (equal sign) to begin the formula and then click cell D4.**

Excel surrounds cell D4 with a marquee and appends D4 to the equal sign (=) in cell H4 (Figure 2-7).

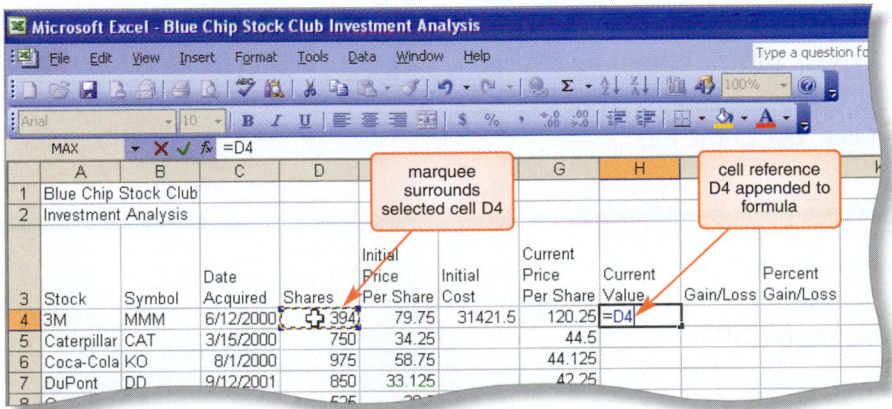

FIGURE 2-7

2

• **Type * (asterisk) and then click cell G4.**

Excel surrounds cell G4 with a marquee and appends G4 to the asterisk (*) in cell H4. The formula =D4*G4 appears in cell H4 and in the formula bar (Figure 2-8).

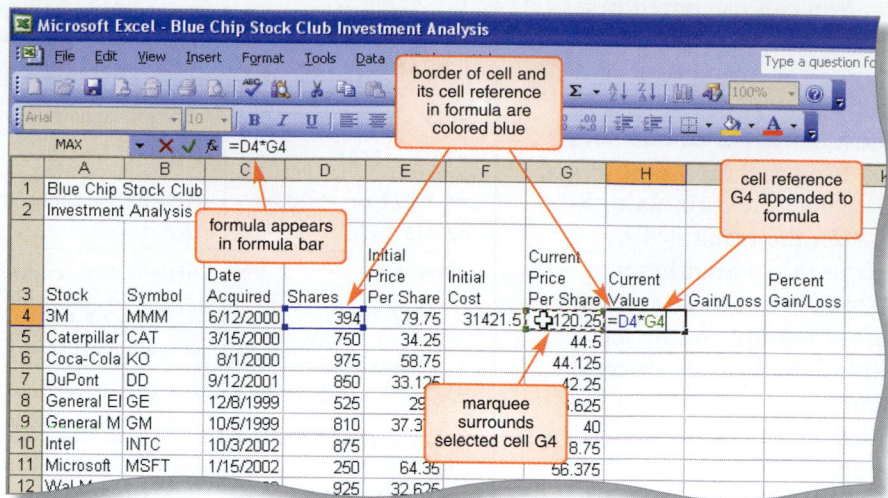

FIGURE 2-8

3

• **Click the Enter box and then click cell I4.**

• **Type = (equal sign) and then click cell H4.**

• **Type – (minus sign) and then click cell F4.**

Excel determines the result of the formula =D4*G4 and displays the result, 47378.5, in cell H4. The formula =H4–F4 appears in cell I4 and in the formula bar (Figure 2-9).

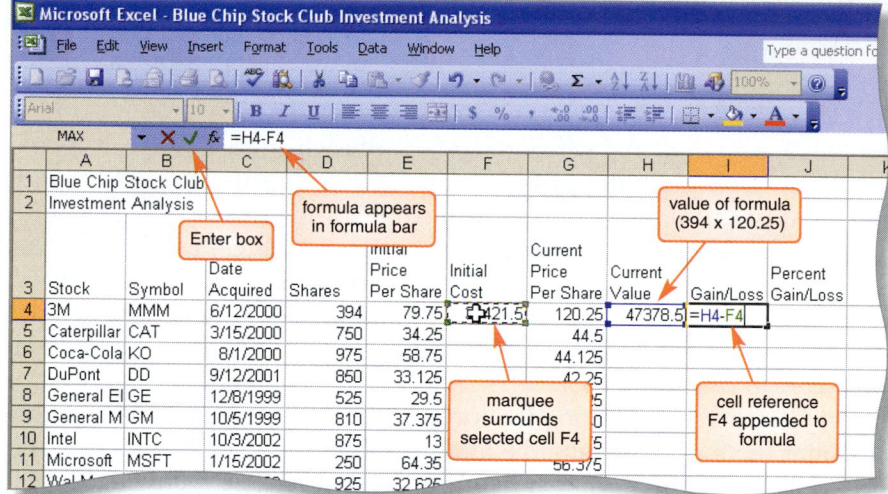

FIGURE 2-9

4

• **Click the Enter box.**

• **Click cell J4. Type = (equal sign) and then click cell I4.**

• **Type / (division sign) and then click cell F4.**

• **Click the Enter box.**

Excel calculates and then displays the gain/loss for 3M (15957) in cell I4 and the Percent gain/loss for 3M (0.507837) in cell J4 (Figure 2-10). The 0.507837 represents approximately 50.78%.

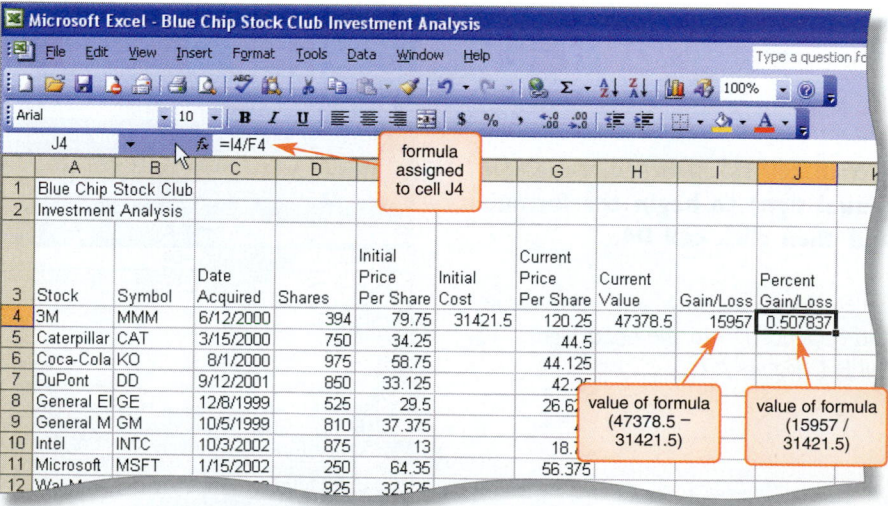

FIGURE 2-10

Depending on the length and complexity of the formula, using Point mode to enter formulas often is faster and more accurate than using the keyboard to type the entire formula. In many instances, as in the previous steps, you may want to use both the keyboard and mouse when entering a formula in a cell. You can use the keyboard to begin the formula, for example, and then use the mouse to select a range of cells.

The actual value assigned by Excel to cell J4 from the division operation in Step 4 is 0.507836990595611. While all the decimal places do not appear in Figure 2-10, Excel maintains all of them for computational purposes. Thus, if cell J4 is referenced in a formula, the value used for computational purposes is 0.507836990595611, not 0.507837. Excel displays the value in cell J4 as 0.507837 because the cell formatting is set to display only 6 digits after the decimal point. If you change the cell formatting of column J to display 15 digits after the decimal point, then Excel displays the true value 0.507836990595611. It is important to recognize this difference between the value Excel displays in a cell and the actual value to understand why the sum of data in a column sometimes is a tenth or hundredth off from the expected value.

Copying Formulas Using the Fill Handle

The four formulas for 3M in cells F4, H4, I4, and J4 now are complete. You could enter the same four formulas one at a time for the eight remaining stocks, Caterpillar, Coca-Cola, DuPont, General Electric, General Motors, Intel, Microsoft, and Wal-Mart. A much easier method of entering the formulas, however, is to select the formulas in row 4 and then use the fill handle to copy them through row 12. Recall from Project 1 that the fill handle is a small rectangle in the lower-right corner of the active cell. The following steps show how to copy the formulas using the fill handle.

To Copy Formulas Using the Fill Handle

1

• **Click cell F4 and then point to the fill handle.**

• **Drag the fill handle down through cell F12 and continue to hold down the mouse button.**

A border surrounds the source and destination areas (range F4:F12) and the mouse pointer changes to a cross hair (Figure 2-11).

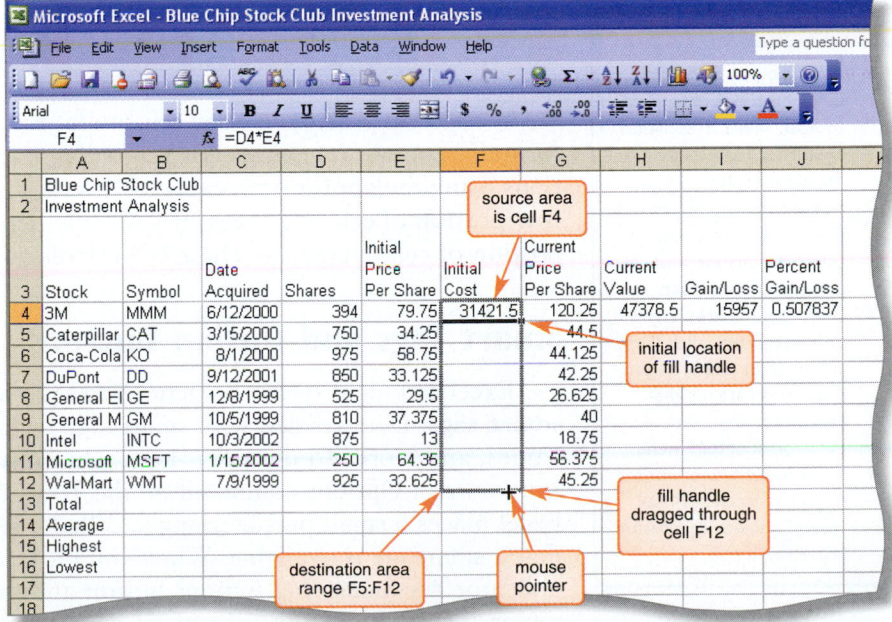

FIGURE 2-11

2

- **Release the mouse button.**
- **Select the range H4:J4 and then point to the fill handle.**

Excel copies the formula =D4*E4 to the range F5:F12 and displays the initial costs for the remaining eight stocks. Excel highlights the selected range H4:J4 (Figure 2-12). The Auto Fill Options button, which allows you to refine the copy, appears at the lower right of the destination range.

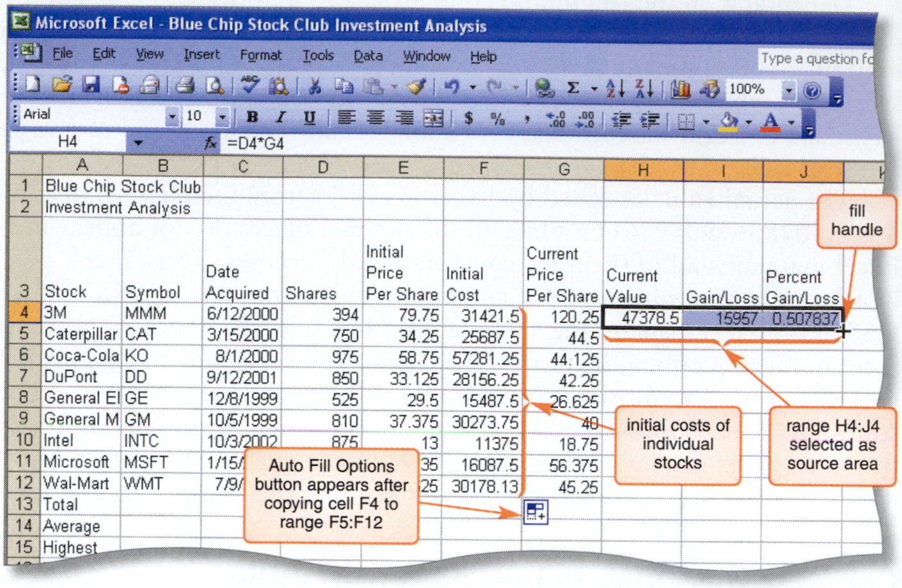

FIGURE 2-12

3

- **Drag the fill handle down through the range H5:J12.**

Excel copies the three formulas =D4*G4 in cell H4, =H4-F4 in cell I4, and =I4/F4 in cell J4 to the range H5:J12. The worksheet now displays the current value, gain/loss, and percent gain/loss for the remaining eight stocks (Figure 2-13).

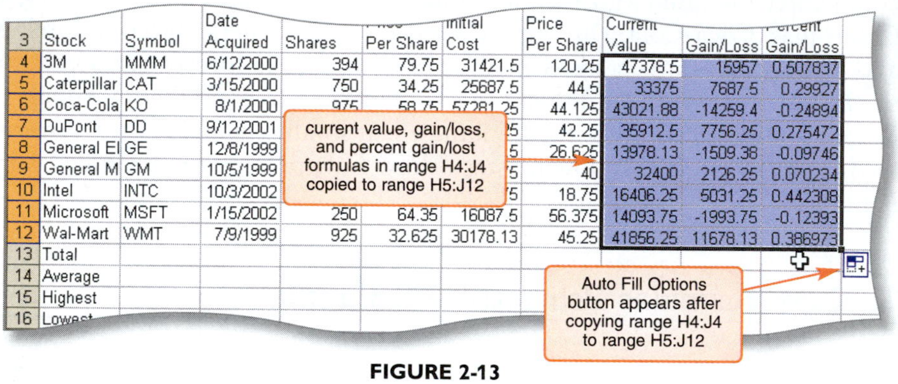

FIGURE 2-13

Other Ways

1. Select source area, click Copy button on Standard toolbar, select destination area, click Paste button on Standard toolbar
2. Select source area, on Edit menu click Copy, select destination area, on Edit menu click Paste
3. Select source area, right-click copy area, click Copy on shortcut menu, select destination area, right-click paste area, click Paste on shortcut menu
4. In Voice Command mode, [select source area], say "Copy", [select destination area], say "Paste"

Recall that when you copy a formula, Excel adjusts the cell references so the new formulas contain references corresponding to the new location and performs calculations using the appropriate values. Thus, if you copy downward, Excel adjusts the row portion of cell references. If you copy across, then Excel adjusts the column portion of cell references. These cell references are called **relative references**.

Smart Tags and Option Buttons

Excel can identify certain actions to take on specific data in workbooks using **smart tags**. Data labeled with smart tags includes dates, financial symbols, people's names, and more. To use smart tags, you must turn on smart tags using the AutoCorrect Options command on the Tools menu. Once smart tags are turned on, Excel places a small purple triangle, called a **smart tag indicator**, in a cell to indicate that a smart tag is available. When you move the insertion point over the smart tag indicator, the Smart Tag Actions button appears. Clicking the Smart Tag Actions button arrow produces a list of actions you can perform on the data in that specific cell.

In addition to smart tags, Excel also displays Options buttons in a workbook while you are working on it to indicate that you can complete an operation using automatic features such as AutoCorrect, Auto Fill, error checking, and others. For example, the Auto Fill Options button shown in Figures 2-12 and 2-13 appears after a fill operation, such as dragging the fill handle. When an error occurs in a formula in a cell, Excel displays the Trace Error button next to the cell and identifies the cell with the error by placing a green triangle in the upper left of the cell.

Table 2-4 summarizes the smart tag and Options buttons available in Excel. When one of these buttons appears on your worksheet, click the button arrow to produce the list of options for modifying the operation or to obtain additional information.

Table 2-4	Smart Tag and Options Buttons in Excel	
BUTTON	**NAME**	**MENU FUNCTION**
	Auto Fill Options	Gives options for how to fill cells following a fill operation, such as dragging the fill handle
	AutoCorrect Options	Undoes an automatic correction, stops future automatic corrections of this type, or causes Excel to display the AutoCorrect Options dialog box
	Insert Options	Lists formatting options following an insert of cells, rows, or columns
	Paste Options	Specifies how moved or pasted items should appear (for example, with original formatting, without formatting, or with different formatting)
	Smart Tag Actions	Lists information options for a cell containing data recognized by Excel, such as a stock symbol (see In the Lab 3, Part 4 on Page EX 139)
	Trace Error	Lists error checking options following the assignment of an invalid formula to a cell

Determining Totals Using the AutoSum Button

The next step is to determine the totals in row 13 for the initial cost in column F, current value in column H, and gain/loss in column I. To determine the total initial cost in column F, the values in the range F4 through F12 must be summed. To do so, enter the function =sum(f4:f12) in cell F13 or select cell F13 and then click the AutoSum button on the Standard toolbar twice. Similar SUM functions or the AutoSum button can be used in cells H13 and I13 to determine total current value and total gain/loss, respectively. Recall from Project 1 that when you select one cell and use the AutoSum button, you must click the AutoSum button twice. If you select a range, then you need only click the AutoSum button once.

To Determine Totals Using the AutoSum Button

1. Select cell F13. Click the AutoSum button on the Standard toolbar twice.

2. Select the range H13:I13. Click the AutoSum button.

Excel displays the three totals in row 13 as shown in Figure 2-14.

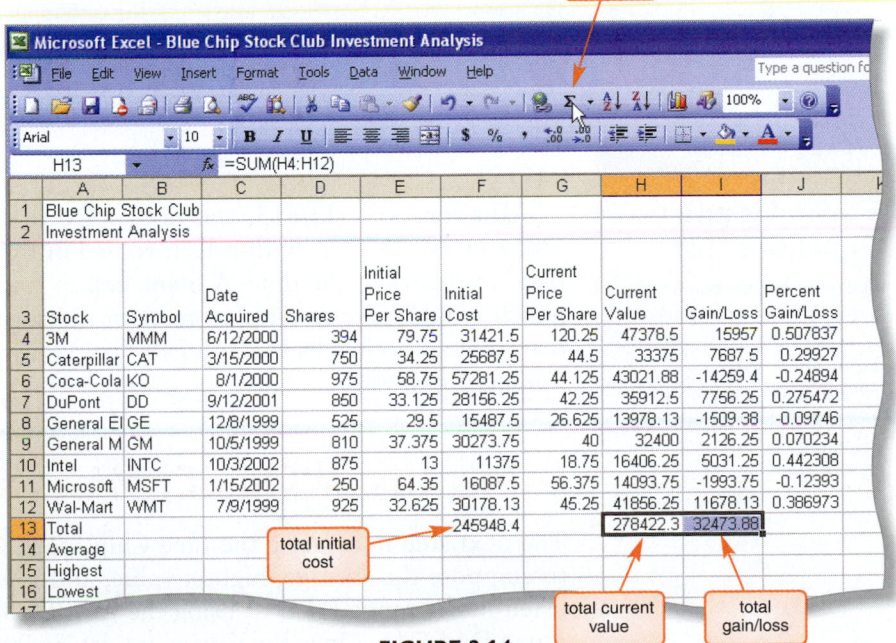

FIGURE 2-14

More About

Selecting a Range

You can select a range using the keyboard. Press F8 and then use the arrow keys to select the desired range. After you are finished, make sure to press F8 to turn the selection off or you will continue to select ranges.

Rather than using the AutoSum button to calculate column totals individually, you can select all three cells before clicking the AutoSum button to calculate all three column totals at one time. To select the nonadjacent range F13, H13, and I13, select cell F13, and then, while holding down the CTRL key, drag through the range H13:I13. Next, click the AutoSum button on the Standard toolbar.

Determining the Total Percent Gain/Loss

With the totals in row 13 determined, the next step is to copy the percent gain/loss formula in cell J12 to cell J13 as shown in the following steps.

To Determine the Total Percent Gain/Loss

1 Select cell J12 and then point to the fill handle.

2 Drag the fill handle down through cell J13.

Excel copies the formula, =I12/F12, in cell J12 to cell J13 and then adjusts the row references. The resulting formula in cell J13 is =I13/F13, which shows the club's holdings had a total gain of 0.132035 or 13.2035% (Figure 2-15).

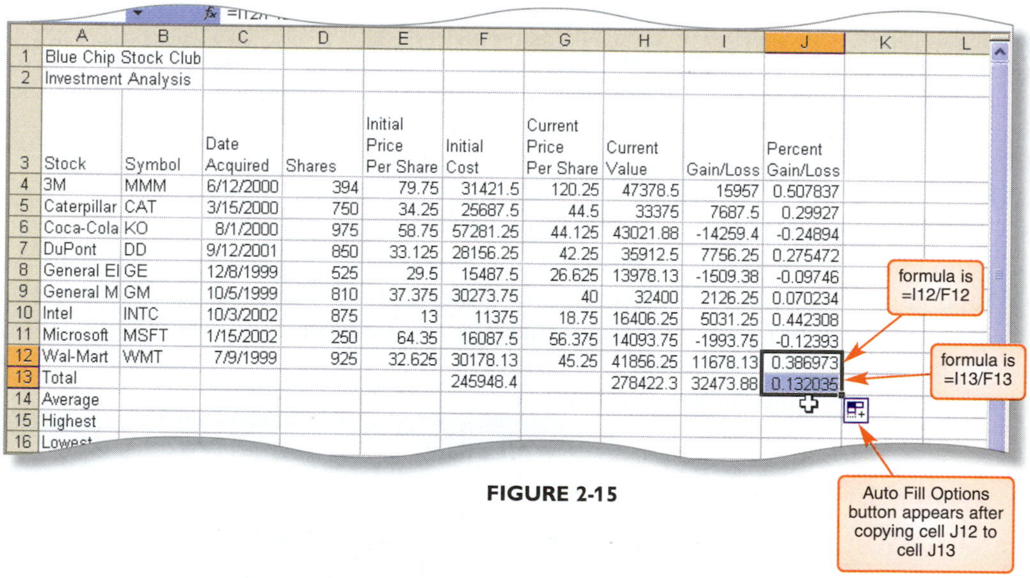

FIGURE 2-15

formula is =I12/F12

formula is =I13/F13

Auto Fill Options button appears after copying cell J12 to cell J13

More About

Formulas and Functions

For more information on entering formulas and functions, visit the Excel 2003 More About Web page (scsite.com/ex2003/more) and click Using Formulas and Functions.

The formula, I13/F13, was not copied to cell J13 when cell J4 was copied to the range J5:J12 because both cells involved in the computation (I13 and F13) were blank, or zero, at the time. A **blank cell** in Excel has a numerical value of zero, which would have resulted in an error message in cell J13. Once the totals were determined, both cells I13 and F13 (especially F13, because it is the divisor) had non-zero numerical values.

Using the AVERAGE, MAX, and MIN Functions

The next step in creating the Blue Chip Stock Club Investment Analysis worksheet is to compute the average, highest value, and lowest value for the number of shares listed in the range D4:D12 using the AVERAGE, MAX, and MIN functions in the range D14:D16. Once the values are determined for column D, the entries can be copied across to the other columns.

Excel includes prewritten formulas called functions to help you compute these statistics. A **function** takes a value or values, performs an operation, and returns a result to the cell. The values that you use with a function are called **arguments**. All functions begin with an equal sign and include the arguments in parentheses after the function name. For example, in the function =AVERAGE(D4:D12), the function name is AVERAGE, and the argument is the range D4:D12.

With Excel, you can enter functions using one of six methods: (1) the keyboard or mouse; (2) the Insert Function box in the formula bar; (3) the AutoSum button menu; (4) the Function command on the Insert menu; (5) the Name box area in the formula bar (Figure 2-16); and (6) Voice Command mode. The method you choose will depend on your typing skills and whether you can recall the function name and required arguments.

The following pages uses each of the first three methods. The keyboard and mouse method will be used to determine the average number of shares (cell D14). The Insert Function button in the formula bar method will be used to determine the highest number of shares (cell D15). The AutoSum button menu method will be used to determine the lowest number of shares (cell D16).

Determining the Average of a Range of Numbers

The **AVERAGE function** sums the numbers in the specified range and then divides the sum by the number of non-zero cells in the range. To determine the average of the numbers in the range D4:D12, use the AVERAGE function, as shown in the following steps.

To Determine the Average of a Range of Numbers Using the Keyboard and Mouse

1

• Select cell D14.

• Type =average(in the cell.

• Click cell D4, the first endpoint of the range to average and drag through cell D12, the second endpoint of the range to average. Do not release the mouse button.

A marquee surrounds the range D4:D12. When you click cell D4, Excel appends cell D4 to the left parenthesis in the formula bar and surrounds cell D4 with a marquee. When you begin dragging, Excel appends to the argument a colon (:) and the cell reference of the cell where the mouse pointer is located (Figure 2-16).

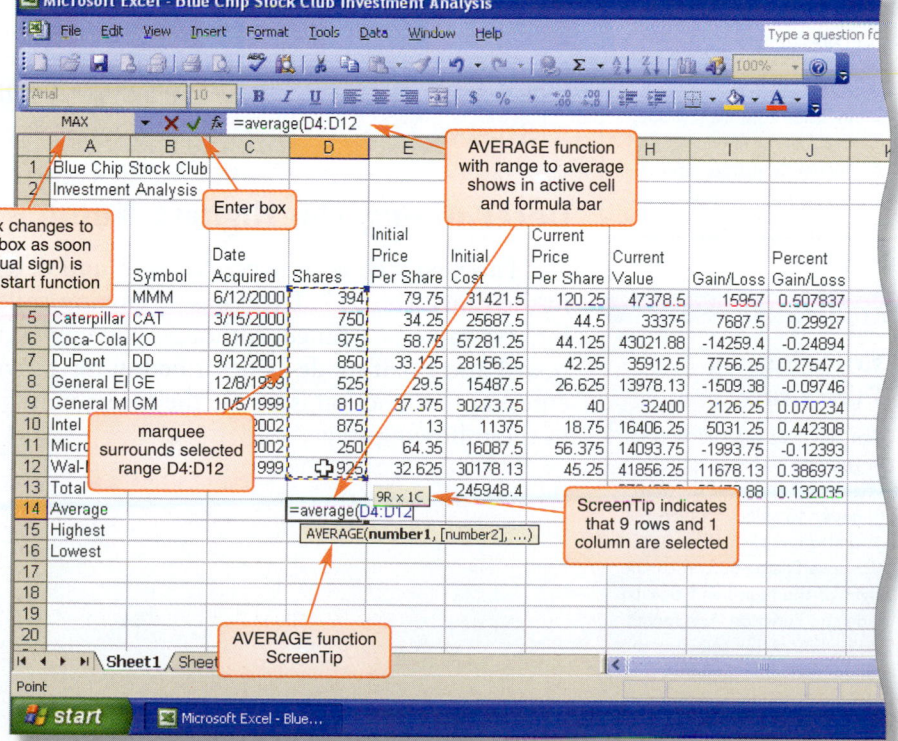

FIGURE 2-16

2

• **Release the mouse button and then click the Enter box.**

Excel computes the average of the nine numbers in the range D4:D12 and displays the result, 706, in cell D14 (Figure 2-17). Thus, the average number of shares owned in the nine companies is 706.

when cell D14 is active cell, formula bar displays AVERAGE function

right parenthesis automatically appended when Enter box is clicked or ENTER key pressed

D14   fx =AVERAGE(D4:D12)

	A	B	C	D	E	F	G	H	I	J
1	Blue Chip Stock Club									
2	Investment Analysis									
3	Stock	Symbol	Date Acquired	Shares	Initial Price Per Share	Initial Cost	Current Price Per Share	Current Value	Gain/Loss	Percent Gain/Loss
4	3M	MMM	6/12/2000	394	79.75	31421.5	120.25	47378.5	15957	0.507837
5	Caterpillar	CAT	3/15/2000	750	34.25	25687.5	44.5	33375	7687.5	0.29927
6	Coca-Cola	KO	8/1/2000	975	58.75	57281.25	44.125	43021.88	-14259.4	-0.24894
7	DuPont	DD	9/12/2001	850	33.125	28156.25	42.25	35912.5	7756.25	0.275472
8	General El	GE	12/8/1999	525	29.5	15487.5	26.625	13978.13	-1509.38	-0.09746
9	General M	GM	10/5/1999	810	37.375	30273.75	40	32400	2126.25	0.070234
10	Intel	INTC	10/3/2002	875	13	11375	18.75	16406.25	5031.25	0.442308
11	Microsoft	MSFT	1/15/2002	250	64.35	16087.5	56.375	14093.75	-1993.75	-0.12393
12	Wal-Mart	WMT	7/9/1999	925	32.625	30178.13	45.25	41856.25	11678.13	0.386973
13	Total					245948.4		278422.3	32473.88	0.132035
14	Average			706						
15	Highest									
16	Lowest									
17										
18										
19										
20										

average shares per stock

FIGURE 2-17

Other Ways

1. Click Insert Function box in formula bar, click AVERAGE function
2. Click AutoSum button arrow on Standard toolbar, click Average function
3. On Insert menu click Function, click AVERAGE in Select a function list
4. Type = (equal sign), click Functions box arrow, click AVERAGE
5. In Voice command mode, say "Insert Function", [select Statistical category], say "Average, OK"

More About

Entering Functions

You can drag the Function Arguments dialog box (Figure 2-19) out of the way in order to select a range. You also can click the Collapse Dialog button to the right of the Number 1 box to hide the Function Arguments dialog box. After selecting the range, click the Collapse Dialog button a second time.

The AVERAGE function requires that the argument (in this case, the range D4:D12) be included within parentheses following the function name. Excel automatically appends the right parenthesis to complete the AVERAGE function when you click the Enter box or press the ENTER key. When you use Point mode, as in the previous steps, you cannot use the arrow keys to complete the entry. While in Point mode, the arrow keys change the selected cell reference in the range you are selecting.

Determining the Highest Number in a Range of Numbers

The next step is to select cell D15 and determine the highest (maximum) number in the range D4:D12. Excel has a function called the **MAX function** that displays the highest value in a range. Although you could enter the MAX function using the keyboard and Point mode as described in the previous steps, an alternative method to entering the function is to use the Insert Function box in the formula bar, as shown in the following steps.

To Determine the Highest Number in a Range of Numbers Using the Insert Function Box

1

• **Select cell D15.**

• **Click the Insert Function box in the formula bar.**

• **When Excel displays the Insert Function dialog box, click MAX in the Select a function list.**

Excel displays the Insert Function dialog box (Figure 2-18).

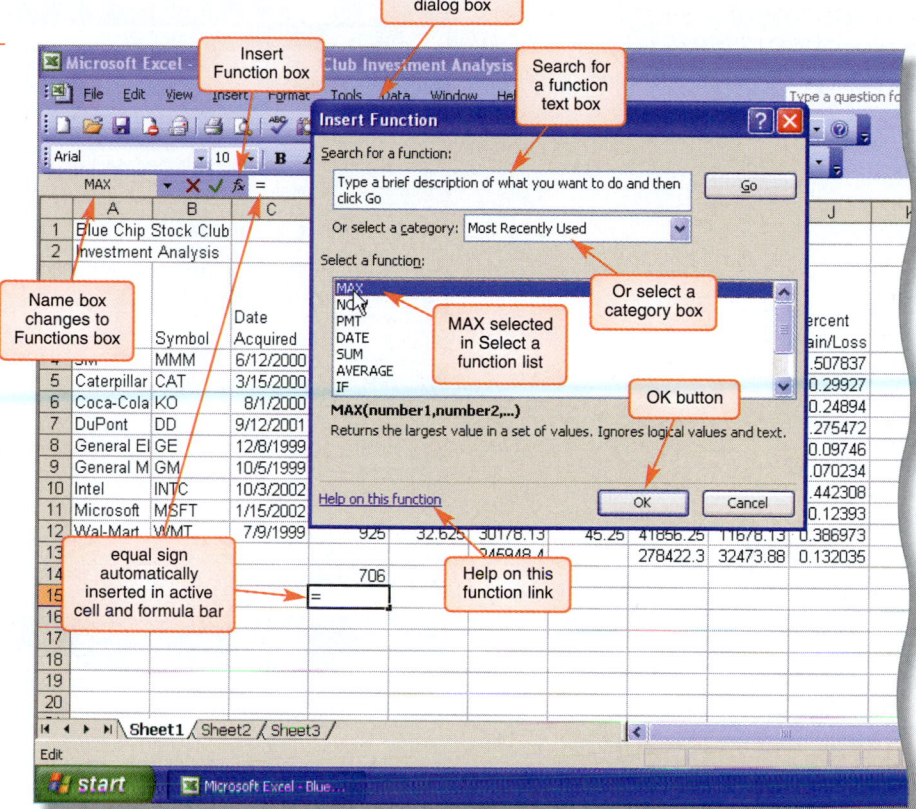

FIGURE 2-18

2

• **Click the OK button.**

• **When Excel displays the Function Arguments dialog box, type** d4:d12 **in the Number 1 box.**

Excel displays the Function Arguments dialog box with the range d4:d12 entered in the Number 1 box (Figure 2-19). The completed MAX function appears in the formula bar, and the last part of the function appears in the active cell, D15.

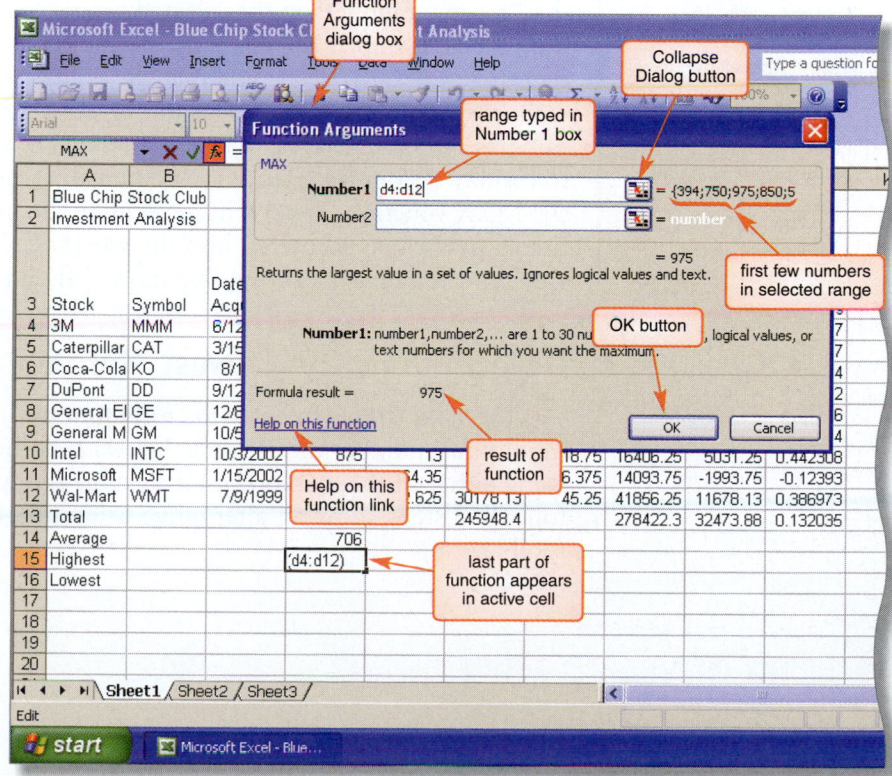

FIGURE 2-19

3

- **Click the OK button.**

Excel determines that the highest value in the range D4:D12 is 975 (value in cell D6) and displays it in cell D15 (Figure 2-20).

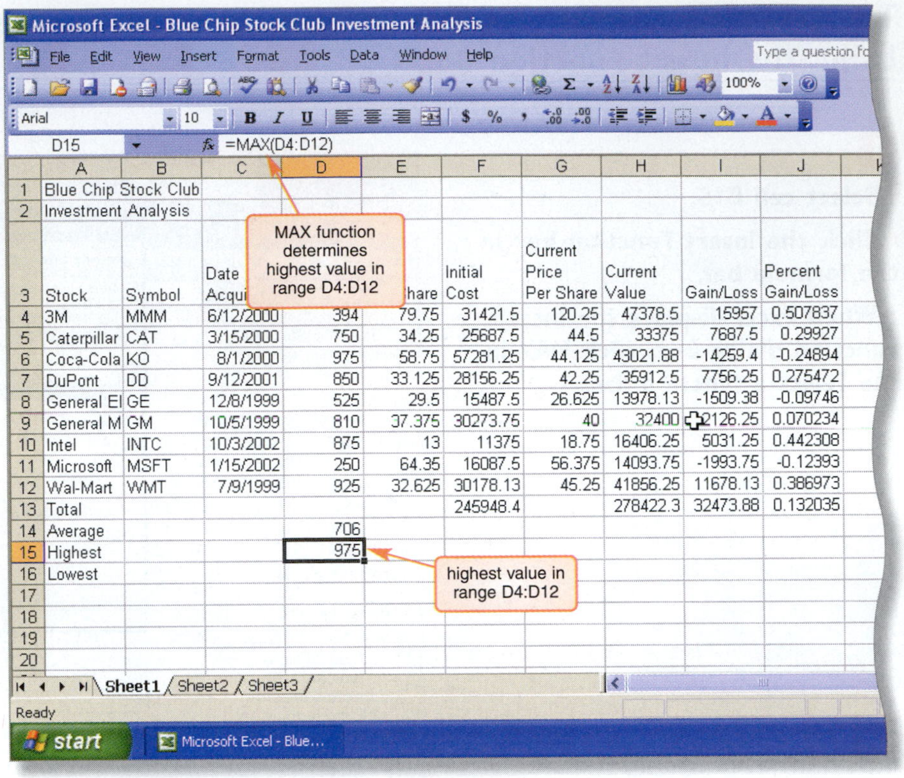

FIGURE 2-20

Other Ways

1. Click AutoSum button arrow on Standard toolbar, click Max function
2. On Insert menu click Function, click MAX in Select a function list
3. Type MAX function in cell
4. Type = (equal sign), click Functions box arrow, click MAX
5. In Voice command mode, say "Insert Function", [select Statistical category], say "Max, OK"

As shown in Figure 2-19 on the previous page, Excel displays the value the MAX function will return to cell D15 in the Function Arguments dialog box. It also lists the first few numbers in the selected range, next to the Number 1 box.

In this example, rather than entering the MAX function, you easily could scan the range D4:D12, determine that the highest number of shares is 975, and manually enter the number 975 as a constant in cell D15. Excel would display the number the same as in Figure 2-20. Because it contains a constant, however, Excel will continue to display 975 in cell D15, even if the values in the range D4:D12 change. If you use the MAX function, Excel will recalculate the highest value in the range D4:D12 each time a new value is entered into the worksheet. Manually determining the highest value in the range also would be more difficult if the club owned more stocks.

Determining the Lowest Number in a Range of Numbers

The next step is to enter the **MIN function** in cell D16 to determine the lowest (minimum) number in the range D4:D12. Although you can enter the MIN function using either of the methods used to enter the AVERAGE and MAX functions, the following steps show an alternative using the AutoSum button menu on the Standard toolbar.

To Determine the Lowest Number in a Range of Numbers Using the AutoSum Button Menu

1

- **Select cell D16.**
- **Click the AutoSum button arrow on the Standard toolbar.**

Excel displays the AutoSum button menu (Figure 2-21).

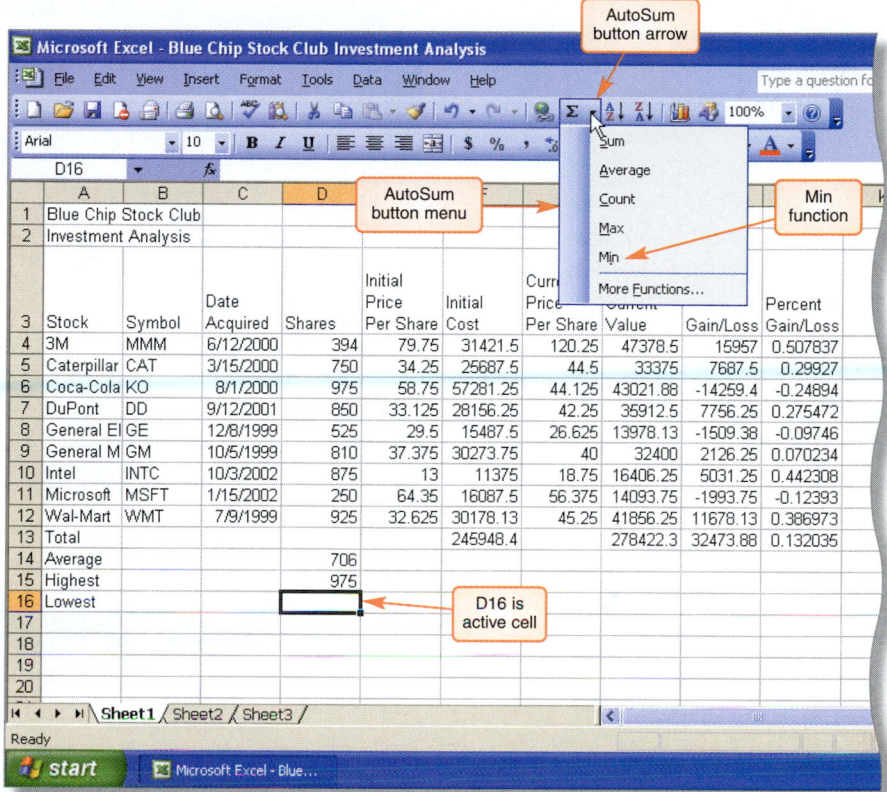

FIGURE 2-21

2

- **Click Min.**

The function =MIN(D14:D15) appears in the formula bar and in cell D16. A marquee surrounds the range D14:D15 (Figure 2-22). The range D14:D15 automatically selected by Excel is not correct.

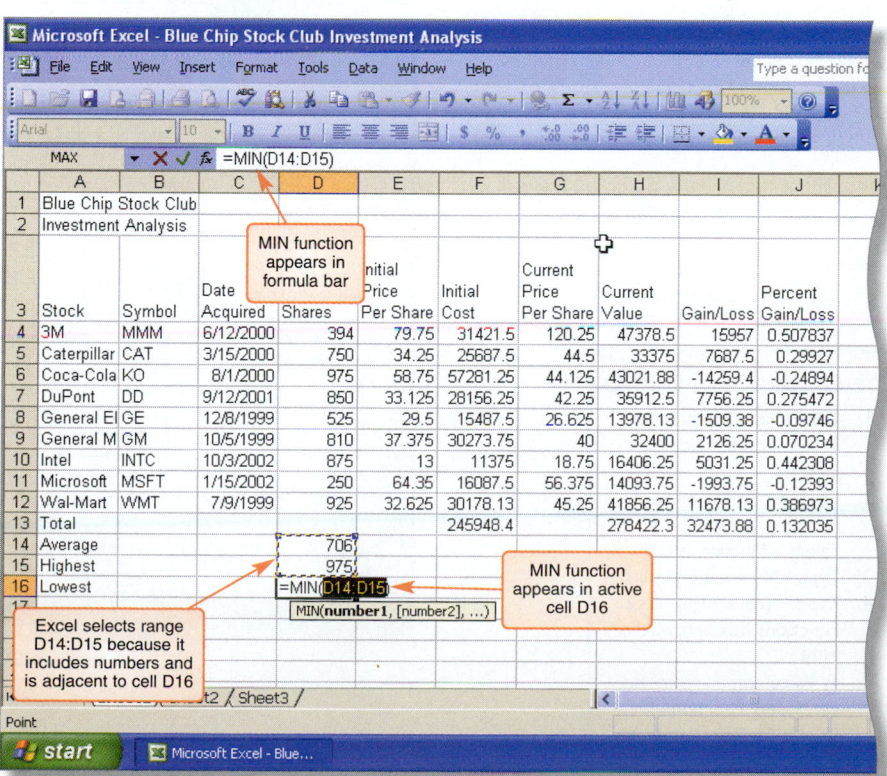

FIGURE 2-22

3

• **Click cell D4 and then drag through cell D12.**

Excel displays the function in the formula bar and in cell D14 with the new range D4:D12 (Figure 2-23).

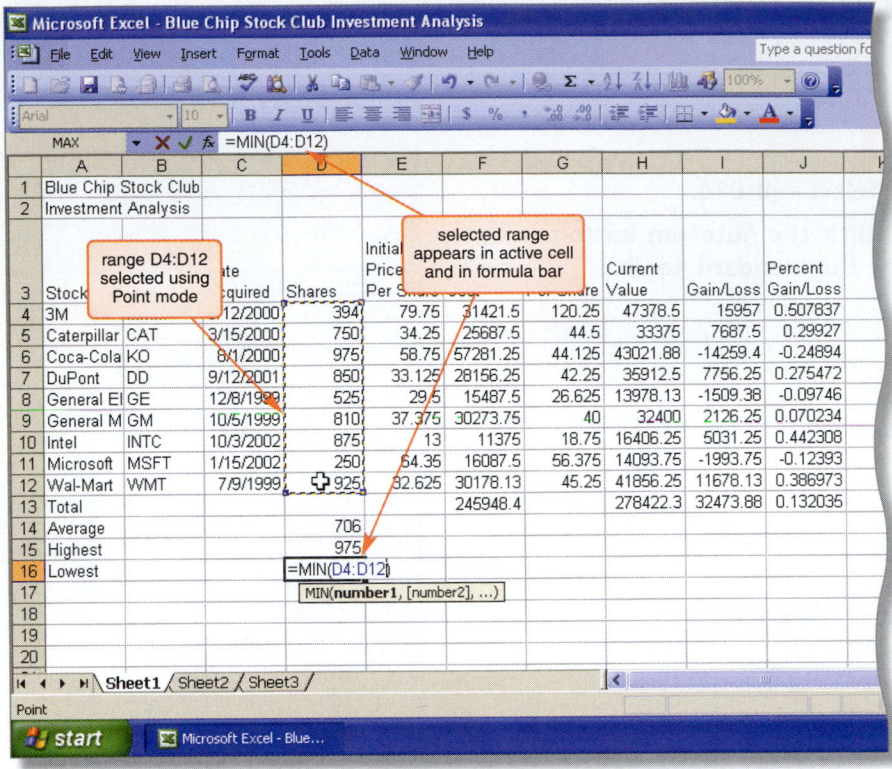

FIGURE 2-23

4

• **Click the Enter box.**

Excel determines that the lowest value in the range D4:D12 is 250 and displays it in cell D16 (Figure 2-24).

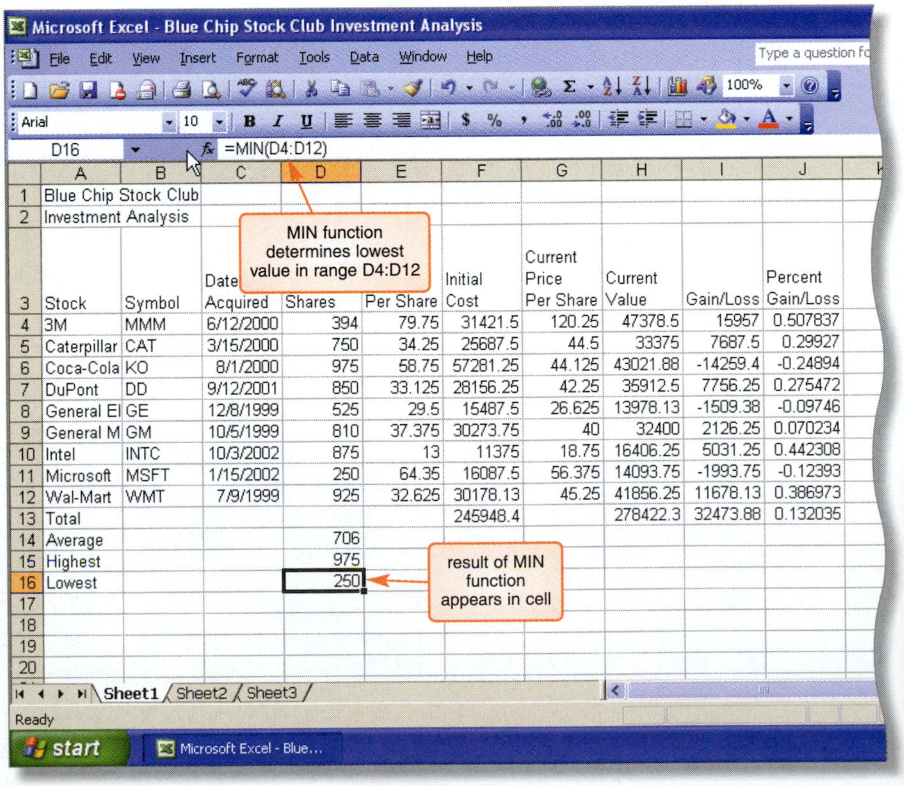

FIGURE 2-24

Other Ways

1. Click Insert Function box in formula bar, click MIN function
2. On Insert menu click Function, click MIN in Select a function list
3. Type MIN function in cell
4. Type = (equal sign), click Functions box arrow, click MIN
5. In Voice command mode, say "Insert Function", [select Statistical category], say "Min, OK"

You can see from the previous example that using the AutoSum button menu allows you to enter one of five often-used functions easily into a cell, without having to memorize its name or the required arguments. If you need to enter a function not available on the AutoSum button menu and cannot remember its name, then click More Functions on the AutoSum button menu or click the Insert Function box in the formula bar.

Thus far, you have learned to use the SUM, AVERAGE, MAX, and MIN functions. In addition to these four functions, Excel has more than 400 additional functions that perform just about every type of calculation you can imagine. These functions are categorized in the Insert Function dialog box shown in Figure 2-18 on page EX 83. To view the categories, click the Or select a category box arrow. To obtain a description of a selected function, select its name in the Insert Function dialog box. Excel displays the description of the function below the Select a function list in the dialog box.

Copying the AVERAGE, MAX, and MIN Functions

The next step is to copy the AVERAGE, MAX, and MIN functions in the range D14:D16 to the adjacent range E14:J16. The fill handle again will be used to complete the copy. The following steps illustrate this procedure.

To Copy a Range of Cells across Columns to an Adjacent Range Using the Fill Handle

1

• **Select the range D14:D16.**

• **Drag the fill handle in the lower-right corner of the selected range through cell J16 and continue to hold down the mouse button.**

Excel displays an outline around the source and destination areas (range D14:J16) as shown in Figure 2-25.

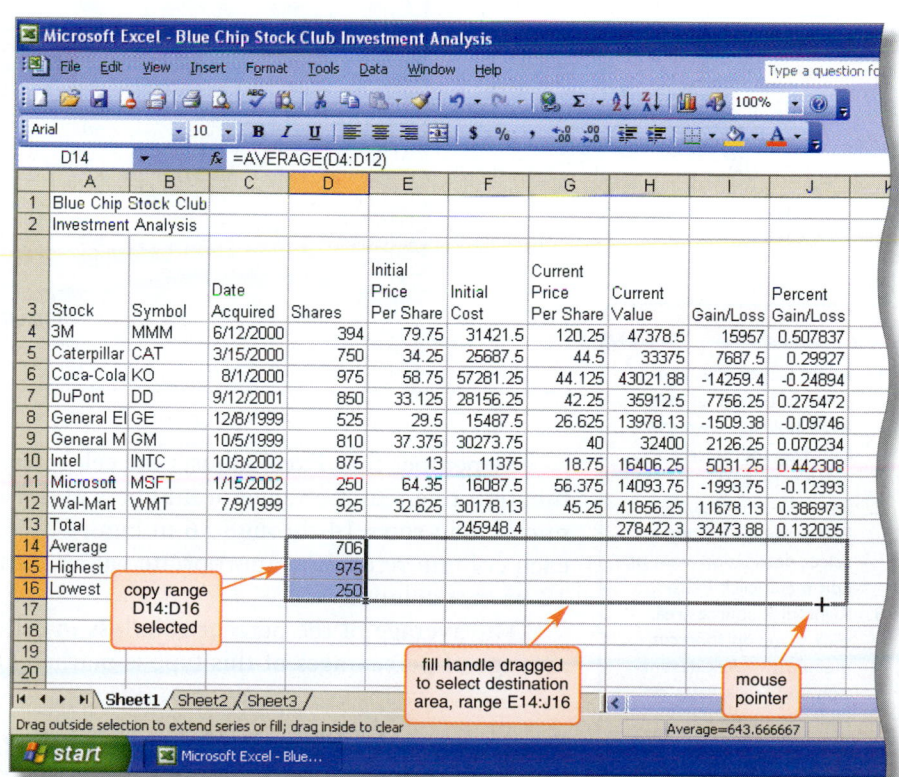

FIGURE 2-25

2

• **Release the mouse button.**

Excel copies the three functions to the range E14:J16 (Figure 2-26). The Auto Fill Options button appears to allow you to refine the copy.

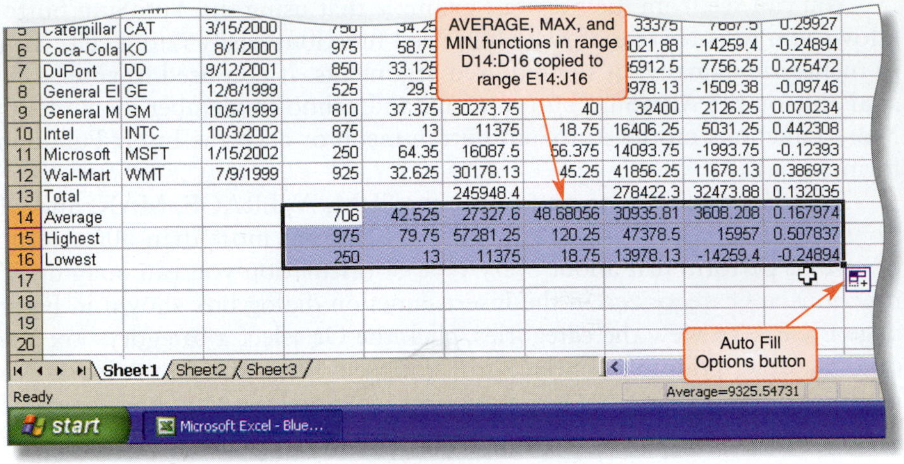

FIGURE 2-26

3

• **Select cell J14 and press the DELETE key to delete the average of the percent gain/loss.**

Cell J14 is blank (Figure 2-27).

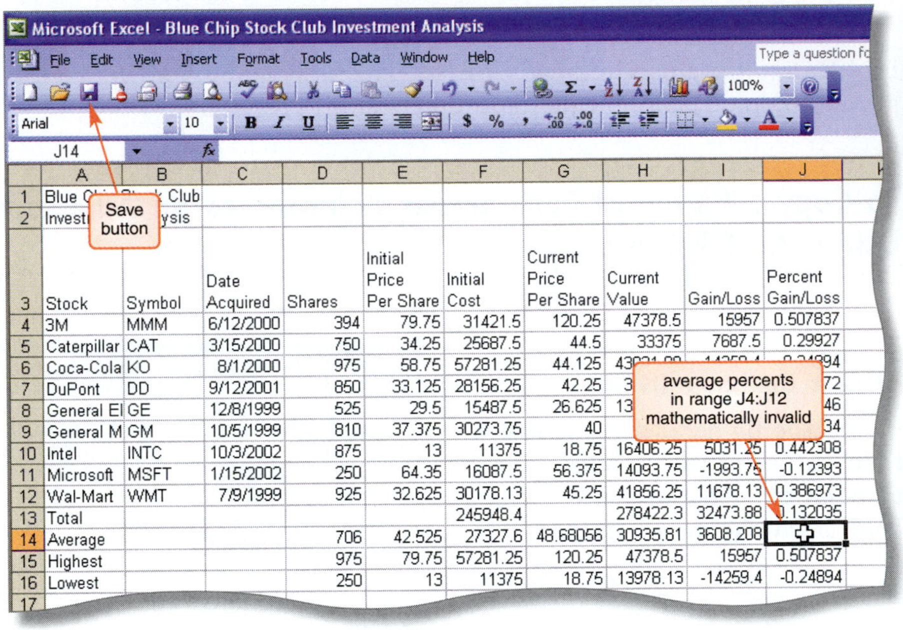

FIGURE 2-27

Other Ways

1. Select source area and point to border of range, while holding down CTRL key, drag source area to destination area
2. Select source area, on Edit menu click Copy, select destination area, on Edit menu click Paste
3. Right-click source area, click Copy on shortcut menu, right-click destination area, click Paste on shortcut menu
4. Select source area, press CTRL+C, select destination area, press CTRL+V
5. In Voice Command mode, [select source area], say "Copy", [select destination area], say "Paste"

Remember that Excel adjusts the cell references in the copied functions so each function refers to the range of numbers above it in the same column. Review the numbers in rows 14 through 16 in Figure 2-26. You should see that the functions in each column return the appropriate values, based on the numbers in rows 4 through 12 of that column.

The average of the percent gain/loss in cell J14 was deleted in Step 3 because an average of percentages of this type is mathematically invalid.

Saving a Workbook Using the Same File Name

Earlier in this project, an intermediate version of the workbook was saved using the file name, Blue Chip Stock Club Investment Analysis. The following step saves the workbook a second time using the same file name.

To Save a Workbook Using the Same File Name

1 **Click the Save button on the Standard toolbar.**

Excel saves the workbook on the floppy disk in drive A using the file name Blue Chip Stock Club Investment Analysis.

Excel automatically stores the latest version of the workbook using the same file name, Blue Chip Stock Club Investment Analysis. When you save a workbook a second time using the same file name, Excel will not display the Save As dialog box as it does the first time you save the workbook. You also can click Save on the File menu or press SHIFT+F12 or CTRL+S to save a workbook again.

If you want to save the workbook using a new name or on a different drive, click Save As on the File menu. Some Excel users, for example, use the Save button to save the latest version of the workbook on the default drive. Then, they use the Save As command to save a copy of the workbook on another drive.

Verifying Formulas Using Range Finder

One of the more common mistakes made with Excel is to include a wrong cell reference in a formula. An easy way to verify that a formula references the cells you want it to reference is to use Excel's Range Finder. **Range Finder** can be used to check which cells are referenced in the formula assigned to the active cell. Range Finder allows you to make immediate changes to the cells referenced in a formula.

To use Range Finder to verify that a formula contains the intended cell references, double-click the cell with the formula you want to check. Excel responds by highlighting the cells referenced in the formula so you can check that the cell references are correct. The following steps use Range Finder to check the formula in cell J4.

To Verify a Formula Using Range Finder

1

• **Double-click cell J4.**

Excel responds by displaying different colored borders around the cells referenced by the formula in cell J4 (Figure 2-28). The different colors allow you to see easily which cells are referenced by the formula in cell J4.

2

• **Press the ESC key to quit Range Finder.**

• **Select cell A18.**

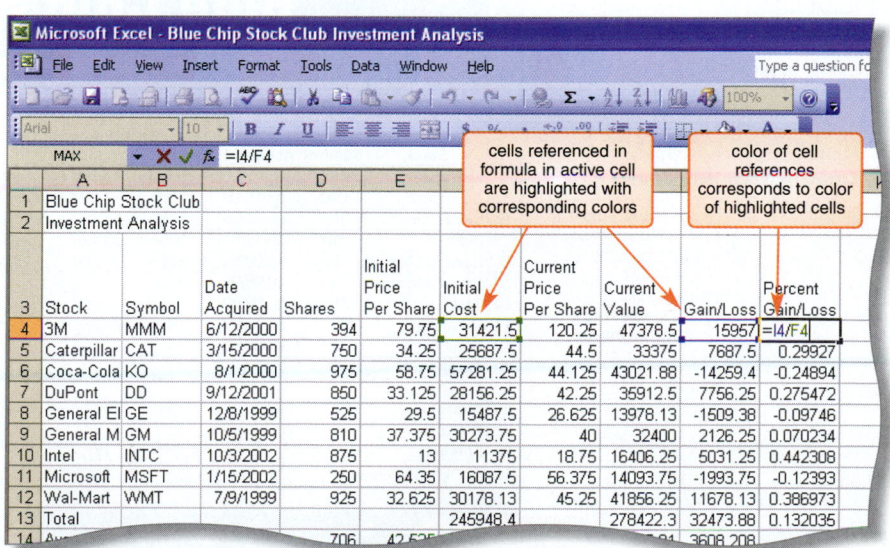

FIGURE 2-28

Not only does Range Finder show you the cells referenced in the formula in cell J4, but it also allows you to drag the colored borders to other cells to instruct Excel to change the cell references in the formula to the newly selected cells. If you use Range Finder to change the cells referenced in a formula, press the ENTER key to complete the edit.

Formatting the Worksheet

Although the worksheet contains the appropriate data, formulas, and functions, the text and numbers need to be formatted to improve their appearance and readability.

In Project 1, the AutoFormat command was used to format the majority of the worksheet. This section describes how to change the unformatted worksheet in Figure 2-29a to the formatted worksheet in Figure 2-29b using the Formatting toolbar and Format Cells command.

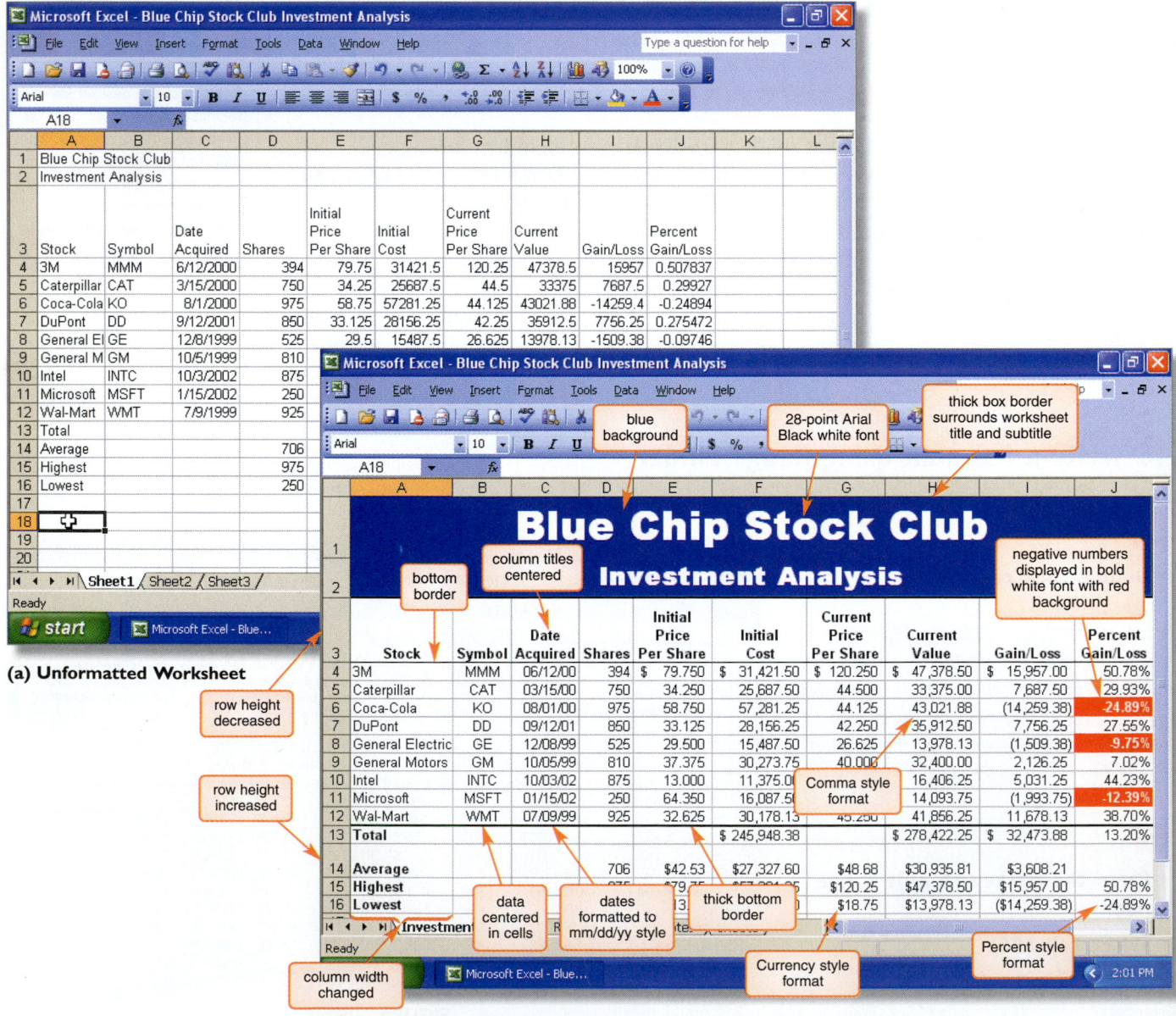

(a) Unformatted Worksheet

(b) Formatted Worksheet

FIGURE 2-29

The following outlines the formatting suggested in the sketch of the worksheet in Figure 2-3 on page EX 69:

1. Worksheet title and subtitle
   a. Font type — Arial Black
   b. Font size — title 28; subtitle 18
   c. Font style — bold
   d. Alignment — center across columns A through J and center vertically
   e. Background color (range A1:J2) — blue
   f. Font color — white
   g. Border — thick box border around range A1:J2
2. Column titles
   a. Font style — bold
   b. Alignment — center
   c. Border — bottom border on row 3
3. Data
   a. Alignment — center data in column B
   b. Dates in column C — mm/dd/yy format
   c. Numbers in top row (range E4:I4) — Currency style
   d. Numbers below top row (range E5:I12) — Comma style
   e. Border — thick bottom border on row 12
4. Total line
   a. Font style of row title in cell A13 — bold
   b. Numbers — Currency style
5. Average, Highest, and Lowest lines
   a. Font style of row titles in range A14:A16 — bold
   b. Numbers — Currency style with floating dollar sign in the range E14:I16
6. Percentages in column J
   a. Numbers — Percent style with two decimal places; if a cell in range J4:J12 is less than 0, then cell appears with bold white font and background color of red
7. Column widths
   a. Column A — 13.00 characters
   b. Columns B through D — best fit
   c. Column E, G, and J — 10.00 characters
   d. Columns F, H, and I — 12.00 characters
8. Row heights
   a. Row 3 — 45.00 points
   b. Row 14 — 24.00 points
   c. Remaining rows — default

Except for vertically centering the worksheet title in row 1, the Date format assigned to the dates in column C, the Currency style assigned to the functions in rows 14 through 16, and the conditional formatting in column J, all of the listed formats can be assigned to cells using the Formatting toolbar and mouse.

Changing the Font and Centering the Worksheet Title and Subtitle

When developing presentation-quality worksheets, different fonts often are used in the same worksheet. Excel allows you to change the font of individual characters in a cell or all the characters in a cell, in a range of cells, or in the entire worksheet. To emphasize the worksheet title and subtitle in cells A1 and A2, the font type, size, and style are changed and the title and subtitle are centered as described in the following two sets of steps.

More About

Colors

Knowing how people perceive colors helps you emphasize parts of your worksheet. Warmer colors (red and orange) tend to reach toward the reader. Cooler colors (blue, green, and violet) tend to pull away from the reader. Bright colors jump out of a dark background and are easiest to see. White or yellow text on a dark blue, green, purple, or black background is ideal.

More About

Toolbars

You can remove a button from a toolbar by holding down the ALT key and dragging the button off the toolbar. See Appendix D for information on resetting a toolbar to its default settings.

To Change the Font and Center the Worksheet Title

- **Click cell A1.**
- **Click the Font box arrow on the Formatting toolbar.**

Excel displays the Font list with Arial highlighted (Figure 2-30).

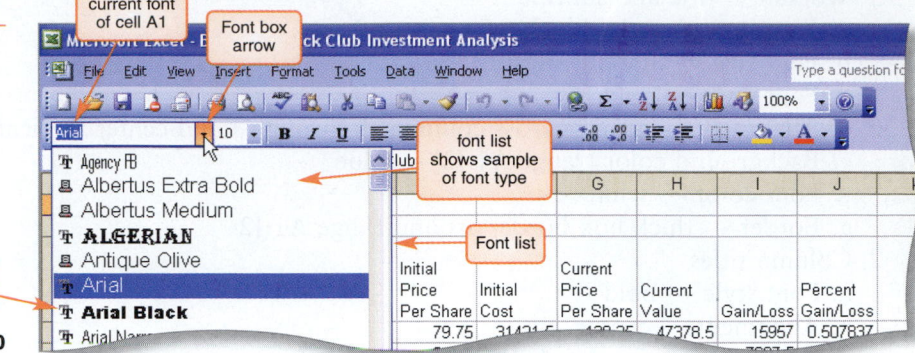

FIGURE 2-30

- **Click Arial Black (or Impact if Arial Black is not available).**
- **Click the Font Size box arrow on the Formatting toolbar and then click 28 in the Font Size list.**
- **Click the Bold button on the Formatting toolbar.**
- **Select the range A1:J1. Right-click the selection.**

Excel displays the text in cell A1 in 28-point Arial Black bold font. Excel automatically increases the height of row 1 so that the taller characters fit in the cell. Excel displays the shortcut menu for the selected range A1:J1 (Figure 2-31).

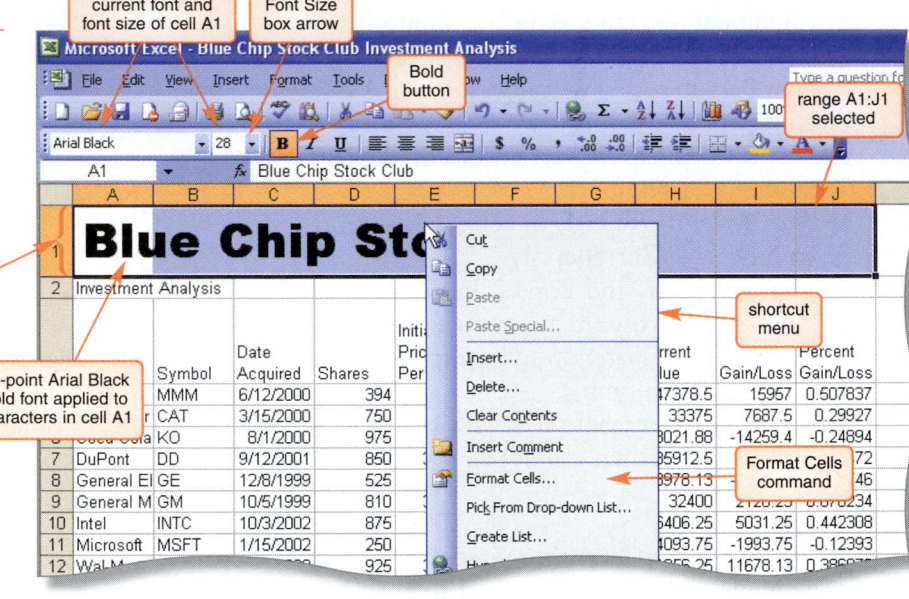

FIGURE 2-31

- **Click Format Cells on the shortcut menu.**
- **When Excel displays the Format Cells dialog box, click the Alignment tab.**
- **Click the Horizontal box arrow and select Center in the Horizontal list.**
- **Click the Vertical box arrow and select Center in the Vertical list.**
- **Click Merge cells in the Text control area.**

Excel displays the Format Cells dialog box as shown in Figure 2-32.

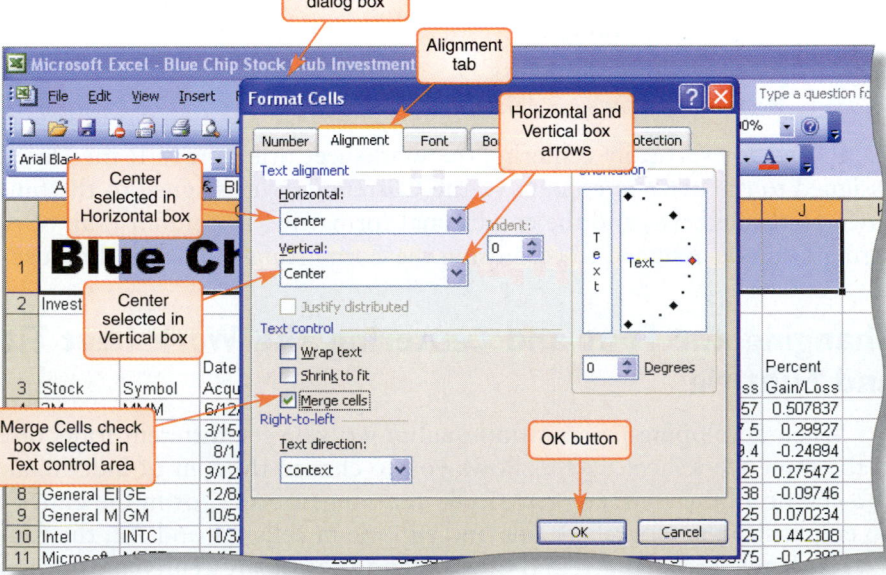

FIGURE 2-32

4

- **Click the OK button.**

Excel merges the cells A1 through J1 to create a new cell A1 and then centers the worksheet title horizontally across columns A through J and centers it vertically in row 1 (Figure 2-33).

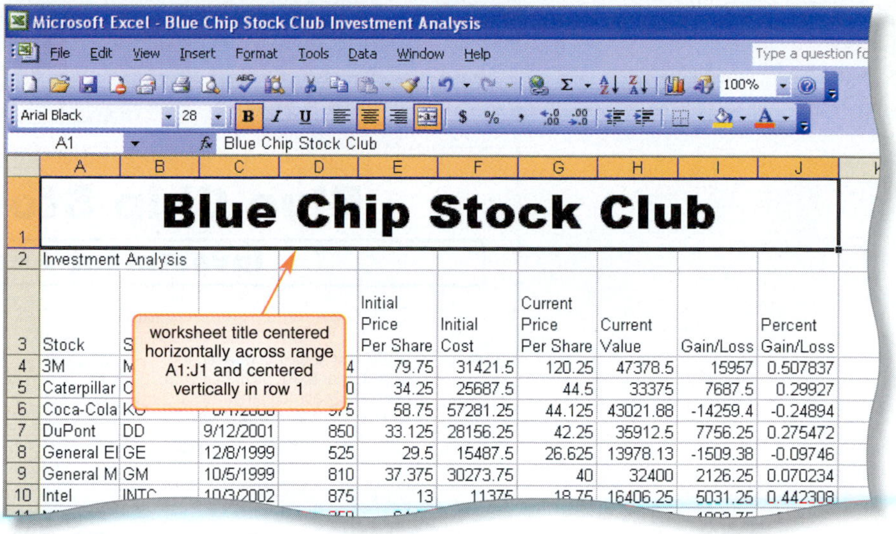

FIGURE 2-33

You can change a font type, size, or style at any time while the worksheet is active. Some Excel users prefer to change fonts before they enter any data. Others change the font while they are building the worksheet or after they have entered all the data.

In Project 1, the Merge and Center button on the Formatting toolbar was used to center the worksheet title across columns. In Step 3 of the previous steps, the Alignment tab in the Format Cells dialog box is used to center the worksheet title across columns, because the project also called for vertically centering the worksheet title in row 1.

The next step is to format the worksheet subtitle in the same fashion as the worksheet title, except that the font size will be changed to 18 rather than 28.

Other Ways

1. On Format menu click Cells, click appropriate tab, select formats, click OK button
2. Press CTRL+1, click appropriate tab, select formats, click OK button
3. In Voice Command mode, say "Format Cells, [desired tab], [desired format], OK"

To Change the Font and Center the Worksheet Subtitle

1. **Click cell A2. Click the Font box arrow on the Formatting toolbar.**
2. **Click Arial Black (or Impact if Arial Black is not available).**
3. **Click the Font Size box arrow on the Formatting toolbar and then click 18 in the Font Size list.**
4. **Click the Bold button on the Formatting toolbar.**
5. **Select the range A2:J2. Right-click the selection. Click Format Cells on the shortcut menu. When Excel displays the Format Cells dialog box, click the Alignment tab. Click the Horizontal box arrow and select Center in the Horizontal list. Click the Vertical box arrow and select Center in the Vertical list. Click Merge cells in the Text control area. Click the OK button.**

Excel increases the font size of the worksheet subtitle to 18, centers it horizontally across columns A through J, centers it vertically in row 2, and merges the cells A2 through J2 to create a new cell A2 (Figure 2-34 on the next page).

Q&A

Q: What is the most popular background color?

A: Blue. Research shows that the color blue is used most often because this color connotes serenity, reflection, and proficiency.

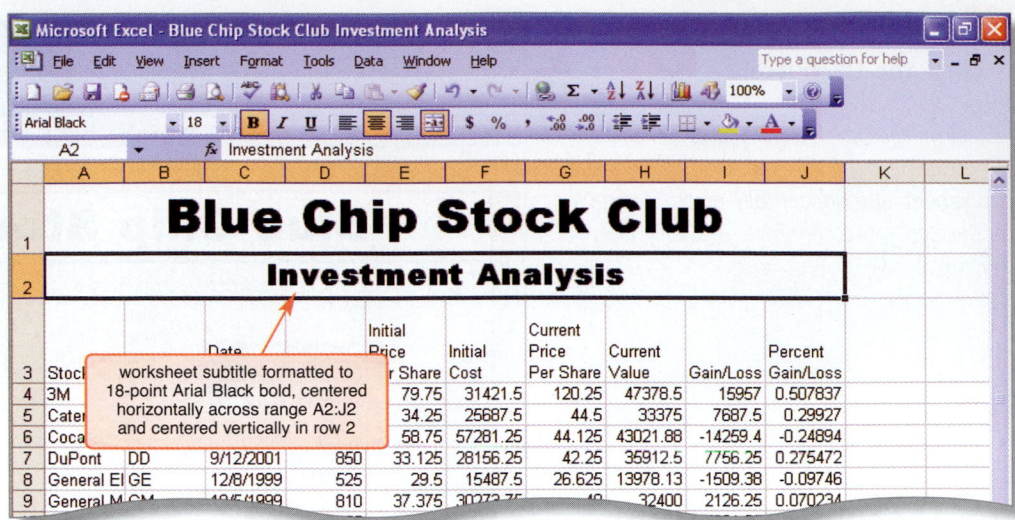

FIGURE 2-34

Some of the formatting, such as the font type, font style, and alignment, could have been done to both titles at the same time by selecting the range A1:A2 before assigning the formats. The font size, which is different, and the merging of cells, however, cannot be done to both titles at the same time.

Changing the Background and Font Colors and Applying a Box Border to the Worksheet Title and Subtitle

The final formats to be assigned to the worksheet title and subtitle are the blue background color, white font color, and thick box border (Figure 2-29b on page EX 90). The following steps complete the formatting of the worksheet titles.

To Change the Background and Font Colors and Apply a Box Border to the Worksheet Title and Subtitle

1

• **Select the range A1:A2, and then click the Fill Color button arrow on the Formatting toolbar.**

Excel displays the Fill Color palette (Figure 2-35).

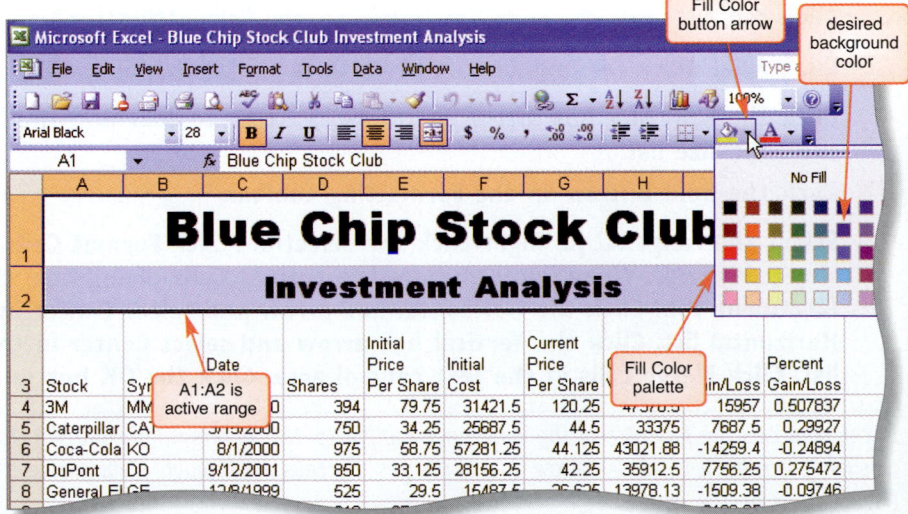

FIGURE 2-35

More About

Adding Colors and Borders

Colors and borders can change a boring worksheet into an interesting and easy-to-read worksheet. Colors and borders also can be used to make important information stand out.

2

- **Click Blue (column 6, row 2) on the Fill Color palette.**
- **Click the Font Color button arrow on the Formatting toolbar.**

Excel changes the background color of cells A1 and A2 from white to blue and displays the Font Color palette (Figure 2-36).

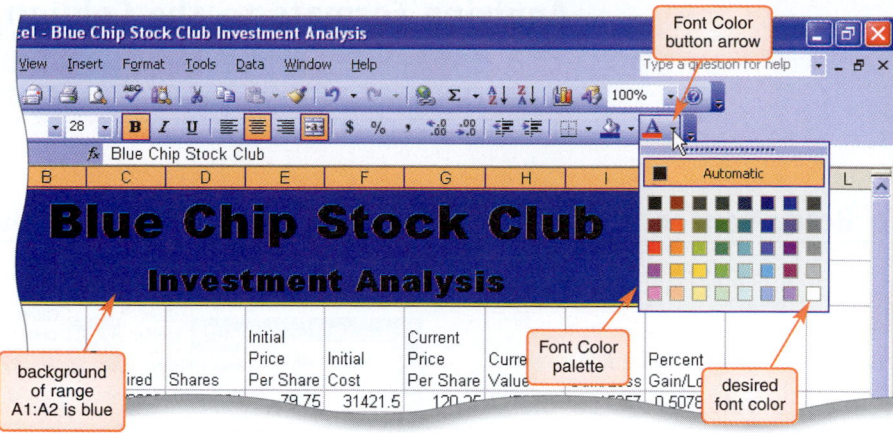

FIGURE 2-36

3

- **Click White (column 8, row 5) on the Font Color palette.**
- **Click the Borders button arrow on the Formatting toolbar.**

Excel changes the font in the worksheet titles from black to white and displays the Borders palette (Figure 2-37).

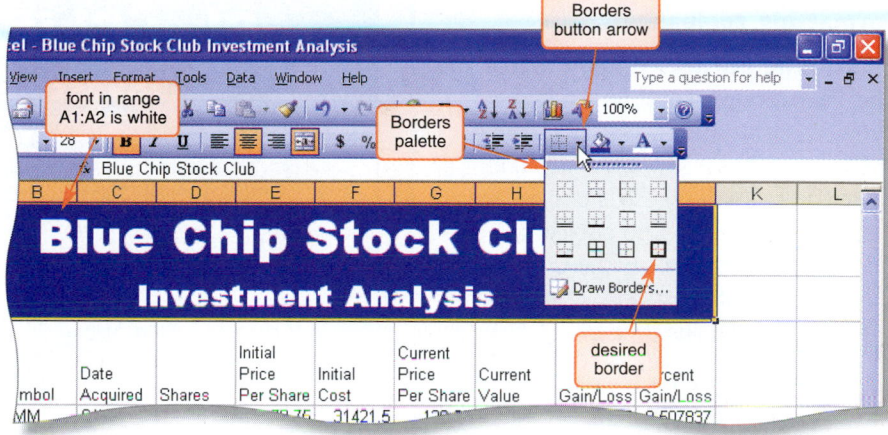

FIGURE 2-37

4

- **Click the Thick Box Border button (column 4, row 3) on the Borders palette.**
- **Click cell B16 to deselect the range A1:A2.**

Excel displays a thick box border around the range A1:A2 (Figure 2-38).

FIGURE 2-38

You can remove borders, such as the thick box border around the range A1:A2, by selecting the range and clicking the No Border button on the Borders palette. You can remove a background color by selecting the range, clicking the Fill Color button arrow on the Formatting toolbar, and then clicking the No Fill button on the Fill Color palette. The same technique allows you to change the font color back to Excel's default color, except you use the Font Color button arrow and click the Automatic button on the Font Color palette.

Other Ways

1. On Format menu click Cells, click appropriate tab, click desired format, click OK button
2. Right-click range, click Format Cells on shortcut menu, click appropriate tab, click desired format, click OK button
3. In Voice Command mode, say "Format Cells, [desired tab], [desired format], OK"

Applying Formats to the Column Titles

As shown in Figure 2-29b on page EX 90, the column titles are bold, centered, and have a bottom border (underline). The following steps assign these formats to the column titles.

To Bold, Center, and Apply a Bottom Border to the Column Titles

1

- **Select the range A3:J3.**
- **Click the Bold button on the Formatting toolbar.**
- **Click the Center button on the Formatting toolbar.**
- **Click the Borders button arrow on the Formatting toolbar.**

The column titles in row 3 are bold and centered (Figure 2-39). Excel displays the Borders palette. Excel also displays the column titles in columns E and G on four lines. In cell J3, the last letter of the column title appears on a line by itself.

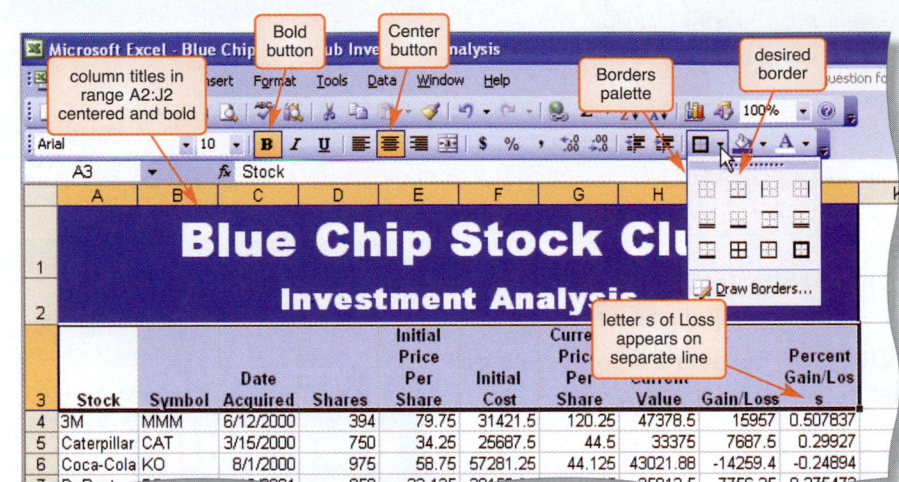

FIGURE 2-39

2

- **Click the Bottom Border button (column 2, row 1) on the Borders palette.**

Excel adds a bottom border to the range A3:J3.

You can align the contents of cells in several different ways. Left alignment, center alignment, and right alignment are the more frequently used horizontal alignments. In fact, these three horizontal alignments are used so often that Excel has Align Left, Center, and Align Right buttons on the Formatting toolbar. In addition to aligning the contents of a cell horizontally, you also can align the contents of a cell vertically, as shown earlier. In addition, you can change the orientation of a cell to display the cell contents at various angles (see the Format Cells dialog box in Figure 2-32 on page EX 92).

Centering the Stock Symbols and Formatting the Dates and Numbers in the Worksheet

With the column titles formatted, the next step is to center the stock symbols in column B and format the dates in column C. If a cell entry is short, such as the stock symbols in column B, centering the entries within their respective columns improves the appearance of the worksheet. The following steps center the data in the range B4:B12 and format the dates in the range C4:C12.

To Center Data in Cells and Format Dates

1

• **Select the range B4:B12.**

• **Click the Center button on the Formatting toolbar.**

Excel centers the stock symbols in column B.

2

• **Select the range C4:C12.**

• **Right-click the selected range and then click Format Cells on the shortcut menu.**

• **When Excel displays the Format Cells dialog box, click the Number tab, click Date in the Category list, and then click 03/14/01 in the Type list.**

Excel displays the Format Cells dialog box as shown in Figure 2-40.

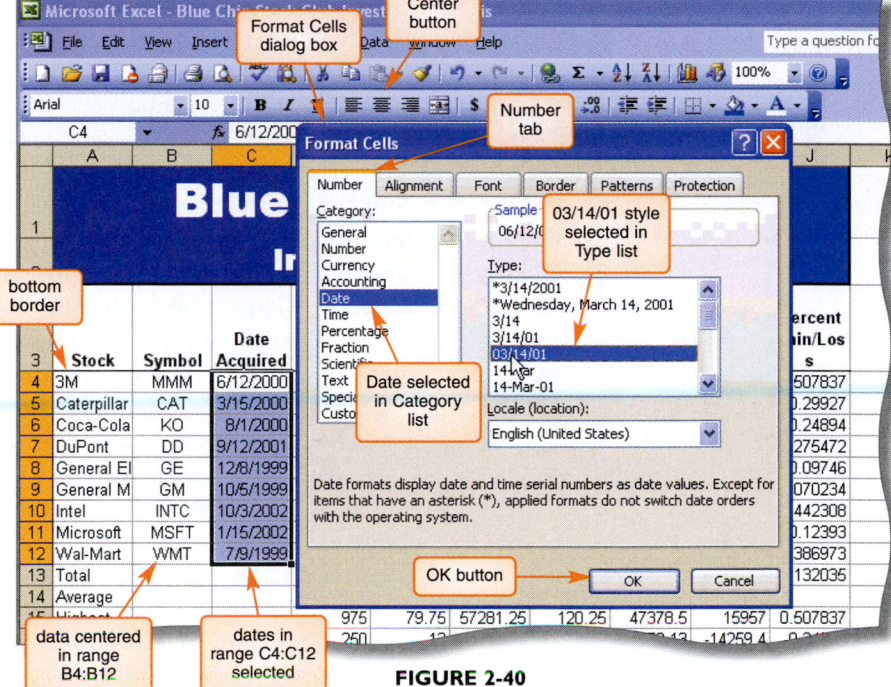

FIGURE 2-40

3

• **Click the OK button.**

• **Select cell E4 to deselect the range C4:C12.**

Excel displays the dates in column C using the date format style, mm/dd/yy (Figure 2-41).

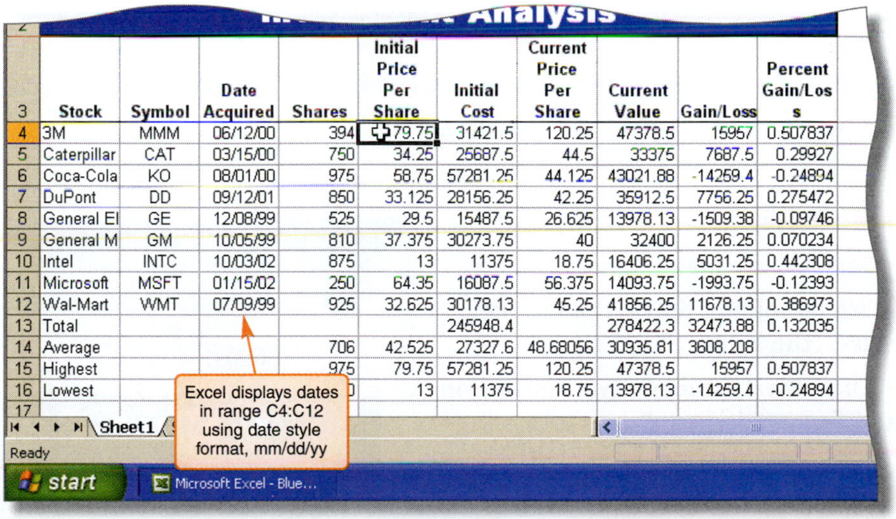

FIGURE 2-41

Other Ways

1. On Format menu click Cells, click appropriate tab, click desired format, click OK button
2. Right-click range, click Format Cells on shortcut menu, click appropriate tab, click desired format, click OK button
3. In Voice Command mode, say "Format Cells, [desired tab], [desired format], OK"

Rather than selecting the range B4:B12 in Step 1, you could have clicked the column B heading immediately above cell B1, and then clicked the Center button on the Formatting toolbar. In this case, all cells in column B down to cell B65536 would have been formatted to use center alignment. This same procedure could have been used to format the dates in column C.

Formatting Numbers Using the Formatting Toolbar

As shown in Figure 2-29b on page EX 90, the worksheet is formatted to resemble an accounting report. For example, in columns E through I, the numbers in the first row (row 4), the totals row (row 13), and the rows below the totals (rows 14 through 16) have dollar signs, while the remaining numbers (rows 5 through 12) in columns E through I do not.

To append a dollar sign to a number, you should use the Currency style format. Excel displays numbers using the **Currency style format** with a dollar sign to the left of the number, inserts a comma every three positions to the left of the decimal point, and displays numbers to the nearest cent (hundredths place). Clicking the Currency Style button on the Formatting toolbar assigns the desired Currency style format. When you use the Currency Style button to assign the Currency style format, Excel displays a **fixed dollar sign** to the far left in the cell, often with spaces between it and the first digit. To assign a **floating dollar sign** that appears immediately to the left of the first digit with no spaces, you must use the Cells command on the Format menu or the Format Cells command on the shortcut menu. The sketch of the worksheet in Figure 2-3 on page EX 69 calls for the Currency style format with a fixed dollar sign to be assigned to the numbers in the ranges E4:I4 and F13:I13, and the Currency style format with a floating dollar sign to be assigned to the numbers in the range E14:I16.

The Comma style format is used to instruct Excel to display numbers with commas and no dollar signs. The **Comma style format**, which can be assigned to a range of cells by clicking the Comma Style button on the Formatting toolbar, inserts a comma every three positions to the left of the decimal point and causes numbers to be displayed to the nearest hundredths.

The following steps show how to assign formats using the Currency Style button and the Comma Style button on the Formatting toolbar.

To Apply a Currency Style Format and Comma Style Format Using the Formatting Toolbar

1

• **Select the range E4:I4.**

• **While holding down the CTRL key, select the range F13:I13.**

• **Click the Currency Style button on the Formatting toolbar.**

Excel applies the Currency style format with fixed dollar signs to the nonadjacent ranges E4:I4 and F13:I13 as shown in Figure 2-42. Excel automatically increases the width of columns F, H, and I to best fit, so the numbers assigned the Currency style format will fit in the cells.

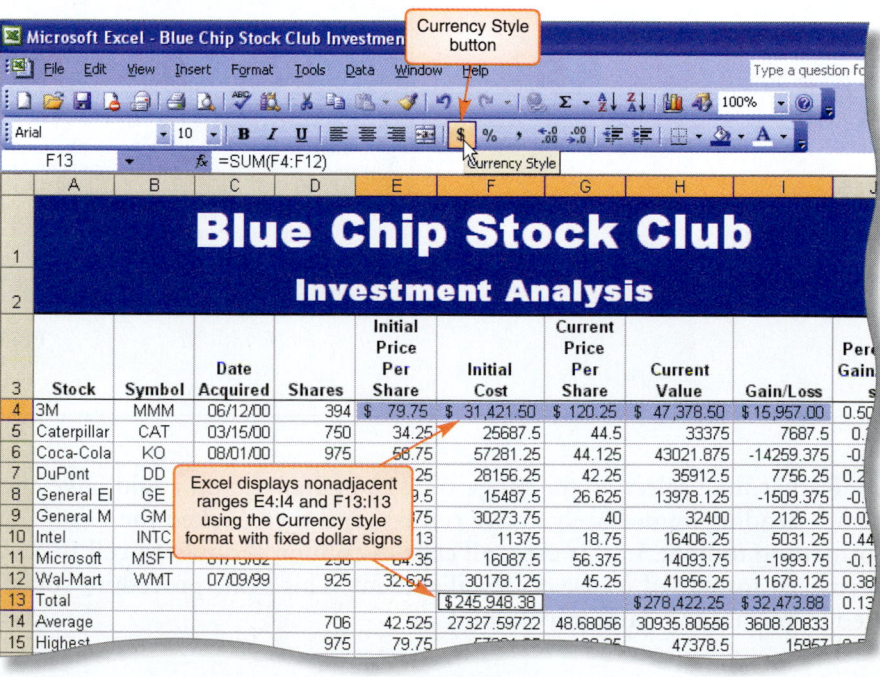

FIGURE 2-42

2

- Select the range E5:I12.
- Click the Comma Style button on the Formatting toolbar.

Excel assigns the Comma style format to the range E5:I12 (Figure 2-43).

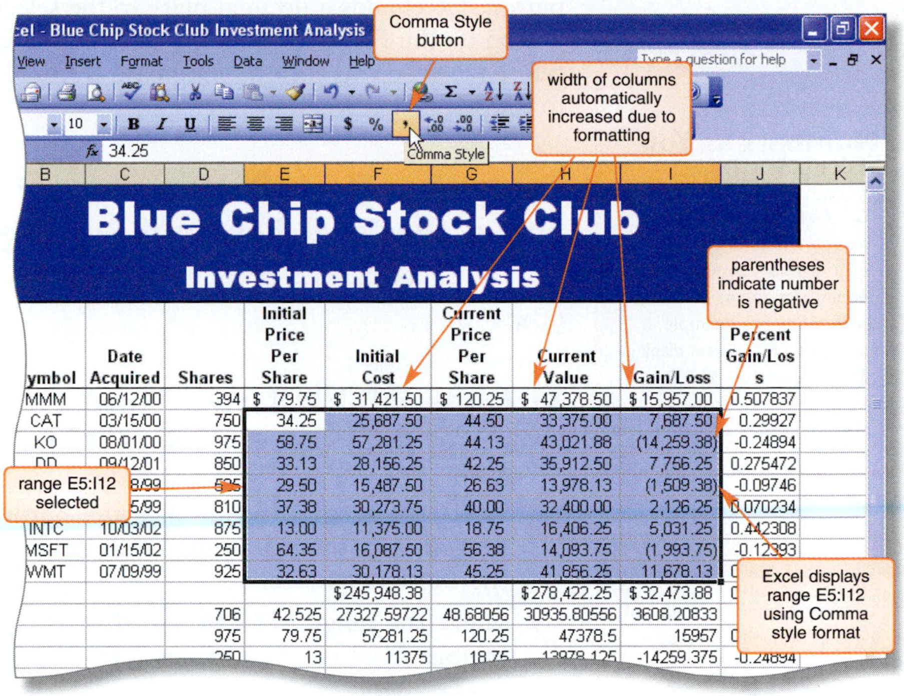

FIGURE 2-43

3

- Click cell E4.
- While holding down the CTRL key, select cell G4.
- Click the Increase Decimal button on the Formatting toolbar.
- Select the range E5:E12. While holding down the CTRL key, select the range G5:G12.
- Click the Increase Decimal button on the Formatting toolbar.
- Click cell A12 to deselect the range G5:G12.

Excel displays the initial prices and current prices with three decimal positions (Figure 2-44).

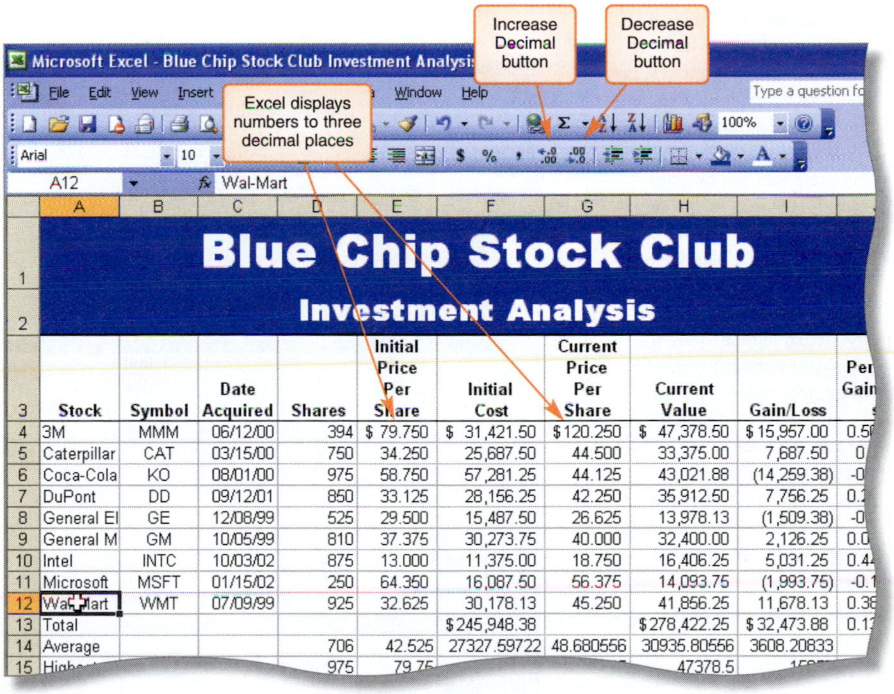

FIGURE 2-44

The Currency Style button assigns a fixed dollar sign to the numbers in the ranges E4:I4 and F13:I13. In each cell in these ranges, Excel displays the dollar sign to the far left with spaces between it and the first digit in the cell. Excel automatically rounds a number to fit the selected format.

Using the Increase Decimal button on the Formatting toolbar instructs Excel to display additional decimal places in a cell. Each time you click the Increase Decimal

More About

Formatting Numbers as You Enter Them

You can format numbers as you enter them by entering a dollar sign ($), comma (,), or percent sign (%) as part of the number. For example, if you enter 1500, Excel displays 1500. If you enter $1500, however, Excel displays $1,500.

Q&A

Q: What causes the sum of a group of numbers to be a penny or two off from an expected result?

A: If the numbers being summed are the result of multiplication or division of decimal fraction numbers, or the sum or difference of numbers with different numbers of decimal places, then the numbers you see on your screen may not be the same as the numbers used in calculations. When a number has more decimal places than Excel displays on the screen, the actual number (not the displayed number) is used in the computation. This can cause the sum to be a penny or two off from an expected result. You can eliminate this problem by using the ROUND function in formulas involving decimal fraction numbers.

button, Excel adds a decimal place to the selected cell. Using the Decrease Decimal button on the Formatting toolbar instructs Excel to display fewer decimal places in a cell. Each time you click the Decrease Decimal button, Excel removes a decimal place to the selected cell.

Applying a Thick Bottom Border to the Row above the Total Row and Bolding the Total Row Titles

The following steps add a thick bottom border to row 12 and bold the total row titles.

To Apply a Thick Bottom Border to the Row above the Total Row and Bold the Total Row Titles

1 Select the range A12:J12, click the Borders button arrow on the Formatting toolbar, and then click the Thick Bottom Border button (column 2, row 2) on the Borders palette.

2 Select the range A13:A16 and then click the Bold button on the Formatting toolbar. Click cell E14 to deselect the range A13:A16.

The row immediately above the total row (row 12) has a thick bottom border, signifying the last stock in the worksheet. The row titles in the range A13:A16 are bold (Figure 2-45).

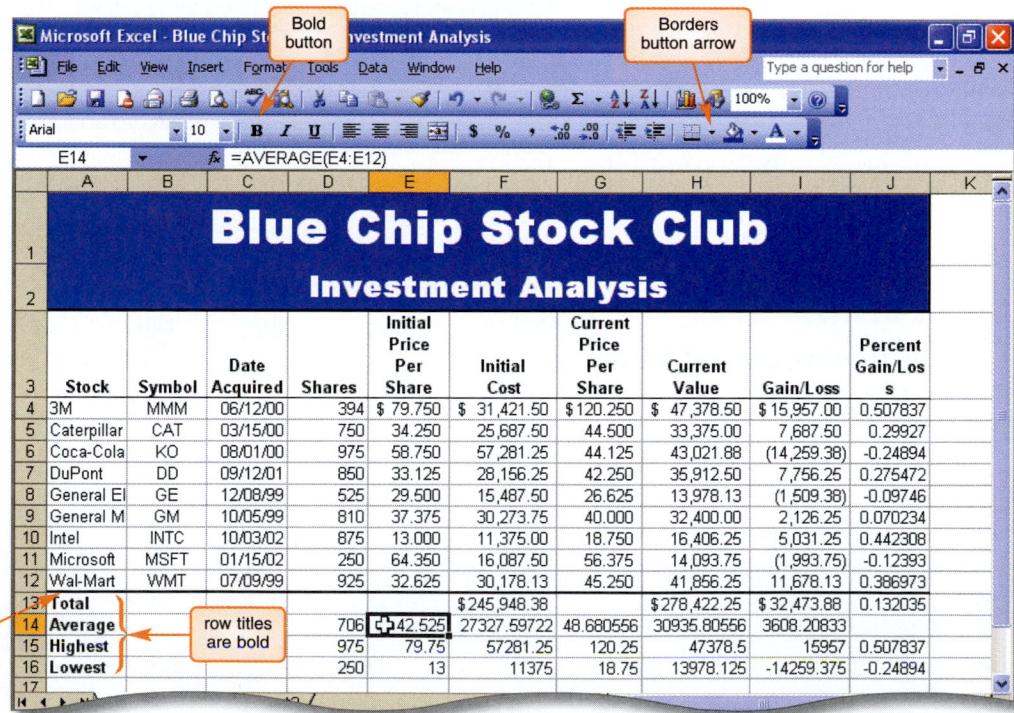

FIGURE 2-45

Formatting Numbers Using the Format Cells Command on the Shortcut Menu

The following steps show you how to use the Format Cells command on the shortcut menu to apply the Currency style format with a floating dollar sign to the numbers in the range E14:I16.

To Apply a Currency Style Format with a Floating Dollar Sign Using the Format Cells Command

1

• **Select the range E14:I16. Right-click the selected range.**

Excel displays the shortcut menu (Figure 2-46).

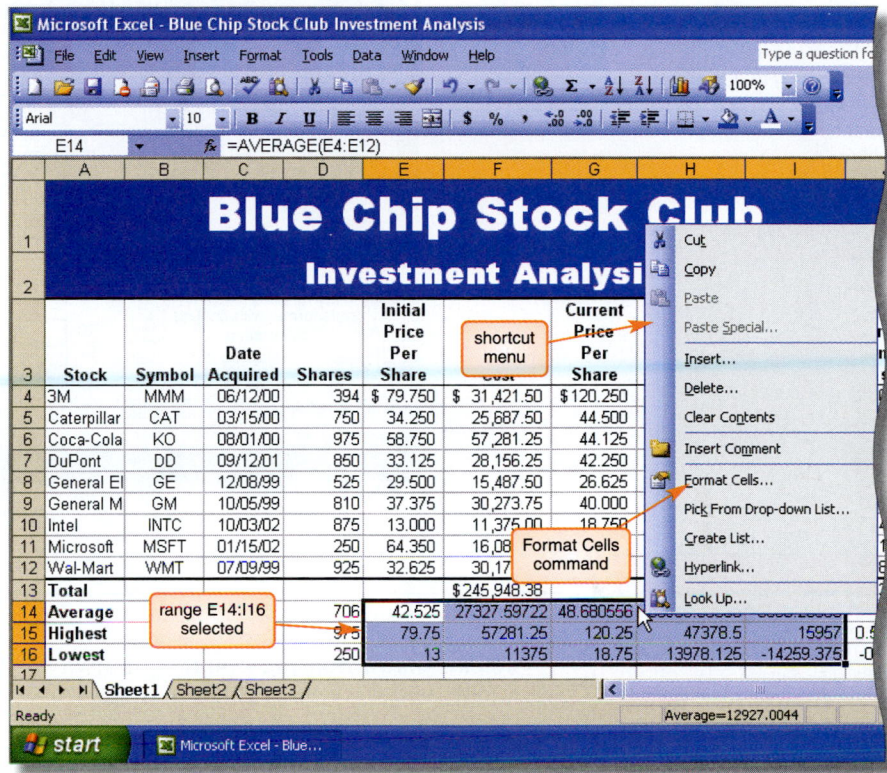

FIGURE 2-46

2

• **Click Format Cells on the shortcut menu.**

• **Click the Number tab in the Format Cells dialog box.**

• **Click Currency in the Category list and then click the third style ($1,234.10) in the Negative numbers list.**

Excel displays the Format Cells dialog box as shown in Figure 2-47.

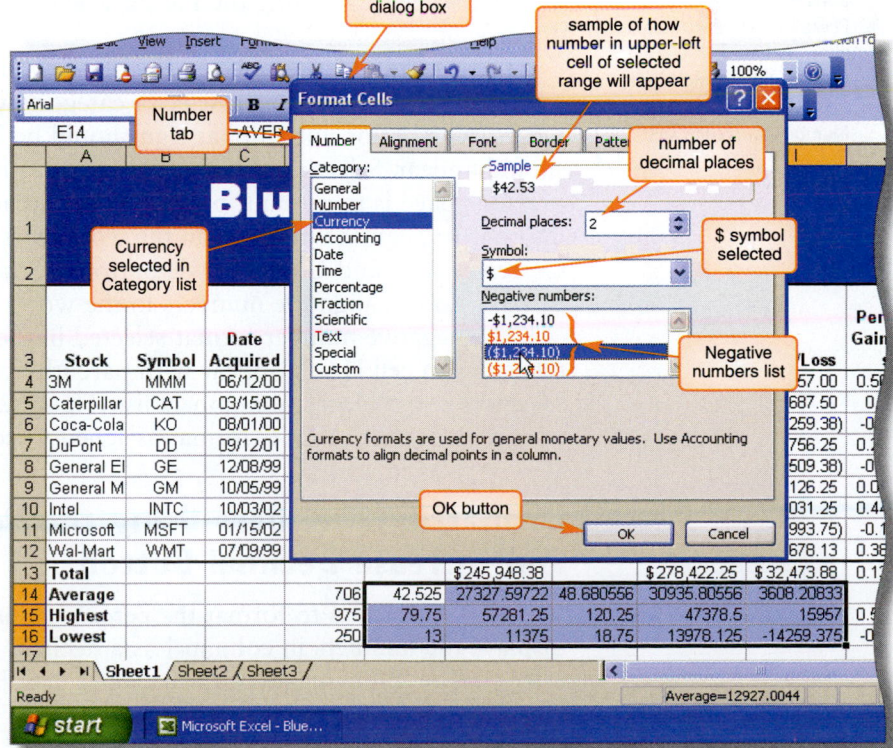

FIGURE 2-47

3

• **Click the OK button.**

Excel displays the worksheet with the numbers in rows 14 through 16 assigned the Currency style format with a floating dollar sign (Figure 2-48).

Blue Chip Stock Club
Investment Analysis

	Stock	Symbol	Date Acquired	Shares	Initial Price Per Share	Initial Cost	Current Price Per Share	Current Value	Gain/Loss	Per Gain
4	3M	MMM	06/12/00	394	$ 79.750	$ 31,421.50	$120.250	$ 47,378.50	$15,957.00	0.50
5	Caterpillar	CAT	03/15/00	750	34.250	25,687.50	44.500	33,375.00	7,687.50	0.
6	Coca-Cola	KO	08/01/00	975	58.750	57,281.25	44.125	43,021.88	(14,259.38)	-0
7	DuPont	DD	09/12/01	850	33.125	28,156.25	42.250	35,912.50	7,756.25	0.2
8	General El	GE	12/08/99	525	29.500	15,487.50	26.625	13,978.13	(1,509.38)	-0
9	General M	GM	10/05/99	810	37.375	30,273.75	40.000	32,400.00	2,126.25	0.0
10	Intel	INTC	10/03/02	875	13.000	11,375.00	18.750	16,406.25	5,031.25	0.44
11	M			250	64.350	16,087.50	56.375	14,093.75	(1,993.75)	-0.1
12	W			925	32.625	30,178.13	45.250	41,856.25	11,678.13	0.38
13	T					$245,948.38		$278,422.25	$ 32,473.88	0.1
14	A			706	$42.53	$27,327.60	$48.68	$30,935.81	$3,608.21	
15	Hi			975	$79.75	$57,281.25	$120.25	$47,378.50	$15,957.00	0.5
16	Lowest			250	$13.00	$11,375.00	$18.75	$13,978.13	($14,259.38)	-0

Excel displays range E14:I16 using Currency style format with floating dollar signs

parentheses surround negative numbers

=$12,927.00

FIGURE 2-48

Other Ways

1. On Format menu click Cells, click Number tab, click Currency in Category list, select format, click OK button
2. Press CTRL+1, click Number tab, click Currency in Category list, select format, click OK button
3. Press CTRL+SHIFT+DOLLAR SIGN
4. In Voice Command mode, say "Format Cells, Number, Currency, OK"

Recall that a floating dollar sign always appears immediately to the left of the first digit, and the fixed dollar sign always appears on the left side of the cell. Cell E4, for example, has a fixed dollar sign, while cell E14 has a floating dollar sign. Also recall that, while cells E4 and E14 both were assigned a Currency style format, the Currency style was assigned to cell E4 using the Currency Style button on the Formatting toolbar and the result is a fixed dollar sign. The Currency style was assigned to cell E14 using the Format Cells dialog box and the result is a floating dollar sign.

As shown in Figure 2-47 on the previous page, you can choose from 12 categories of formats. Once you select a category, you can select the number of decimal places, whether or not a dollar sign should be displayed, and how negative numbers should appear. Selecting the appropriate negative numbers format in Step 2 on the previous page is important, because doing so adds a space to the right of the number in order to align the numbers in the worksheet on the decimal points (as do the Currency Style and Comma Style buttons). Some of the available negative number formats do not align the numbers in the worksheet on the decimal points.

The negative number format selected in the previous set of steps causes the negative entry in cell I16 to appear with parentheses surrounding the number. The third selection in the Negative numbers list (Figure 2-47) purposely was chosen to agree with the negative number format assigned to cell I6 using the Comma Style button.

Formatting Numbers Using the Percent Style Button and Increase Decimal Button

The next step is to format the percent gain/loss in column J. Currently, Excel displays the numbers in column J as a decimal fraction (for example, 0.507837 in cell J4). The following steps format the range J4:J16 to the Percent style format with two decimal places.

To Apply a Percent Style Format

1

- **Select the range J4:J16.**
- **Click the Percent Style button on the Formatting toolbar.**

Excel displays the numbers in column J as a rounded whole percent.

2

- **Click the Increase Decimal button on the Formatting toolbar twice.**

Excel displays the numbers in column J with the Percent style format with two decimal places (Figure 2-49).

Percent Style button — Increase Decimal button — Decrease Decimal button

=I4/F4

Excel displays range J4:J16 using Percent style format with two decimal places

Blue Chip Stock Club
Investment Analysis

Symbol	Date Acquired	Shares	Initial Price Per Share	Initial Cost	Current Price Per Share	Current Value	Gain/Loss	Percent Gain/Loss
MMM	06/12/00	394	$ 79.750	$ 31,421.50	$120.250	$ 47,378.50	$ 15,957.00	50.78%
CAT	03/15/00	750	34.250	25,687.50	44.500	33,375.00	7,687.50	29.93%
KO	08/01/00	975	58.750	57,281.25	44.125	43,021.88	(14,259.38)	-24.89%
DD	09/12/01	850	33.125	28,156.25	42.250	35,912.50	7,756.25	27.55%
GE	12/08/99	525	29.500	15,487.50	26.625	13,978.13	(1,509.38)	-9.75%
GM	10/05/99	810	37.375	30,273.75	40.000	32,400.00	2,126.25	7.02%
INTC	10/03/02	875	13.000	11,375.00	18.750	16,406.25	5,031.25	44.23%
MSFT	01/15/02	250	64.350	16,087.50	56.375	14,093.75	(1,993.75)	-12.39%
WMT	07/09/99	925	32.625	30,178.13	45.250	41,856.25	11,678.13	38.70%
				$245,948.38		$278,422.25	$ 32,473.88	13.20%
		706	$42.53	$27,327.60	$48.68	$30,935.81	$3,608.21	
		975	$79.75	$57,281.25	$120.25	$47,378.50	$15,957.00	50.78%
		250	$13.00	$11,375.00	$18.75	$13,978.13	($14,259.38)	-24.89%

FIGURE 2-49

The Percent Style button on the Formatting toolbar is used to instruct Excel to display a value as a percentage, determined by multiplying the cell entry by 100, rounding the result to the nearest percent, and adding a percent sign. For example, when cell J4 is formatted using the Percent Style and Increase Decimal buttons, Excel displays the actual value -0.507836990595611 as 50.78%.

Conditional Formatting

The next step is to emphasize the negative percentages in column J by formatting them to appear with white bold text on a red background. The Conditional Formatting command on the Format menu will be used to complete this task.

Excel lets you apply formatting that appears only when the value in a cell meets conditions that you specify. This type of formatting is called **conditional formatting**. You can apply conditional formatting to a cell, a range of cells, the entire worksheet, or the entire workbook. Usually, you apply conditional formatting to a range of cells that contains values you want to highlight, if conditions warrant. For example, you can instruct Excel to use the bold font style and change the color of the background of a cell if the value in the cell meets a condition, such as being less than 0 as shown below.

condition

cell value is less than 0

value 1   relational operator   value 2

Other Ways

1. On Format menu click Cells, click Number tab, click Percentage in Category list, select format, click OK button
2. Right-click range, click Format Cells on shortcut menu, click Number tab, click Percentage in Category list, select format, click OK button
3. Press CTRL+I, click Number tab, click Percentage in Category list, select format, click OK button
4. Click CTRL+SHIFT+PERCENT SIGN (%)
5. In Voice Command mode, say "Format Cells, Number, Percentage, OK"

A **condition**, which is made up of two values and a relational operator, is true or false for each cell in the range. If the condition is true, then Excel applies the formatting. If the condition is false, then Excel suppresses the formatting. What makes conditional formatting so powerful is that the cell's appearance can change as you enter new values in the worksheet.

The following steps show how to assign conditional formatting to the range J4:J12, so that any cell value less than 0 will cause Excel to display the number in the cell in white bold text with a red background.

To Apply Conditional Formatting

1

• **Select the range J4:J12.**

• **Click Format on the menu bar.**

Excel displays the Format menu (Figure 2-50).

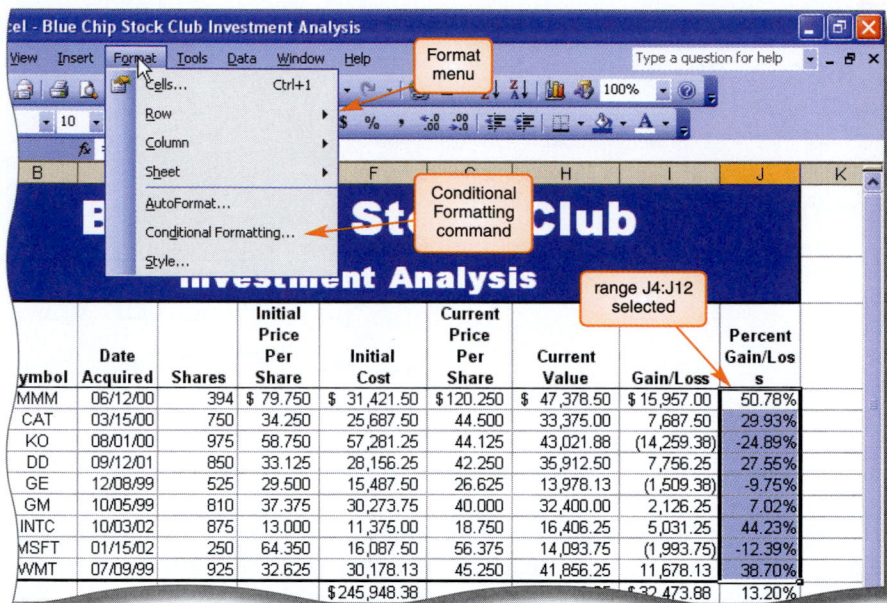

FIGURE 2-50

2

• **Click Conditional Formatting.**

• **When the Conditional Formatting dialog box appears, if necessary, click the leftmost text box arrow and then click Cell Value Is.**

• **Click the middle text box arrow and then click less than.**

• **Type 0 in the rightmost text box.**

Excel displays the Conditional Formatting dialog box as shown in Figure 2-51.

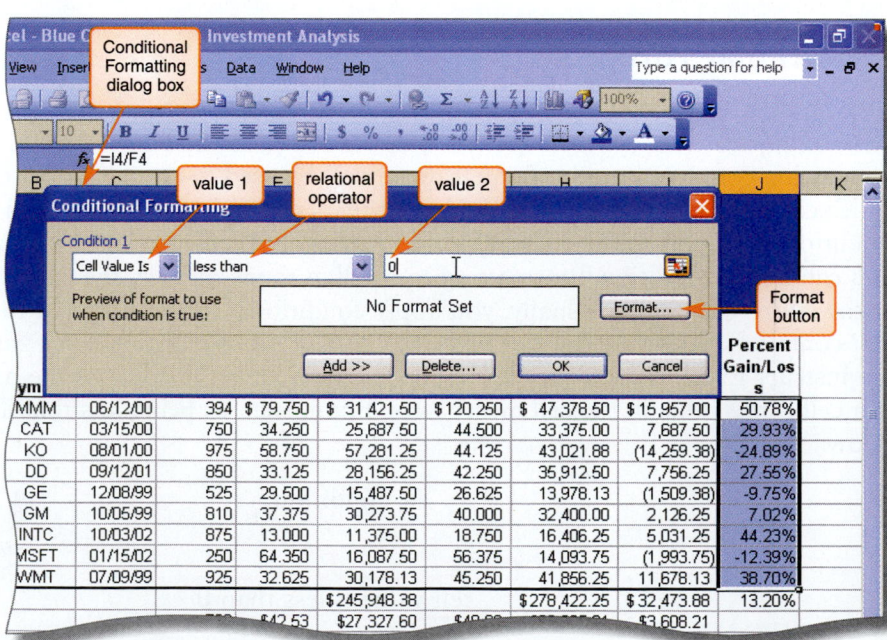

FIGURE 2-51

3

• **Click the Format button.**

• **When Excel displays the Format Cells dialog box, click the Patterns tab and then click Red (column 1, row 3).**

• **Click the Font tab and then click Bold in the Font style list.**

• **Click the Color box arrow.**

Excel displays the Format Cells dialog box as shown in Figure 2-52.

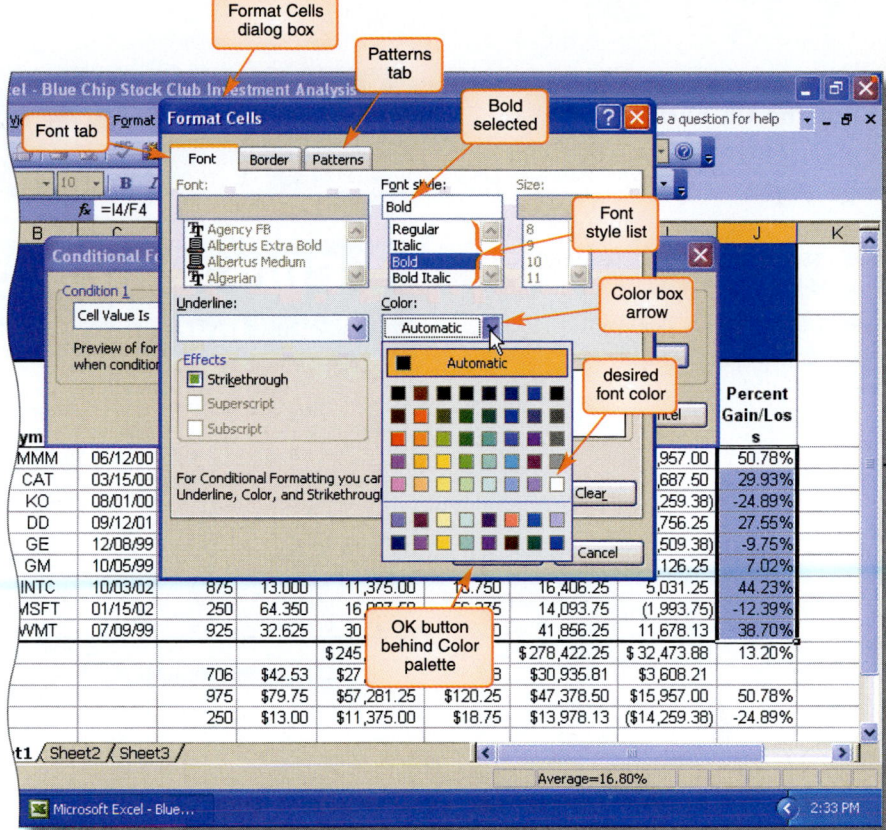

FIGURE 2-52

4

• **Click White (column 8, row 5) and then click the OK button.**

Excel displays the Conditional Formatting dialog box as shown in Figure 2-53. In the middle of the dialog box, Excel displays a preview of the format that Excel will use when the condition is true.

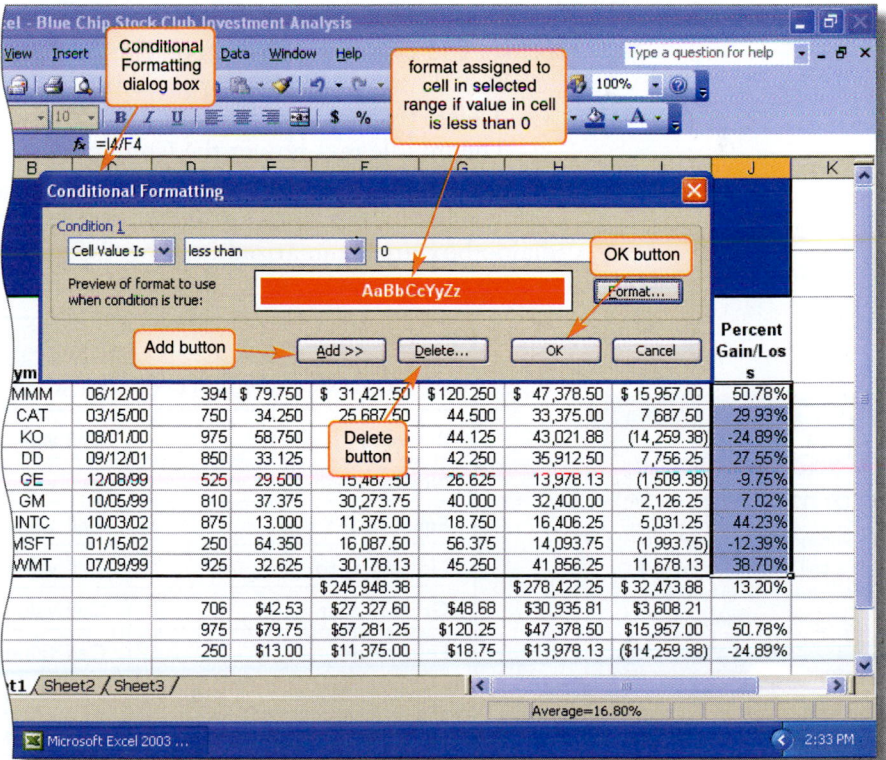

FIGURE 2-53

5

- **Click the OK button.**
- **Click cell B16 to deselect the range J4:J12.**

Excel assigns the conditional format to the range J4:J12. Excel displays any negative value in this range in bold with a red background (Figure 2-54).

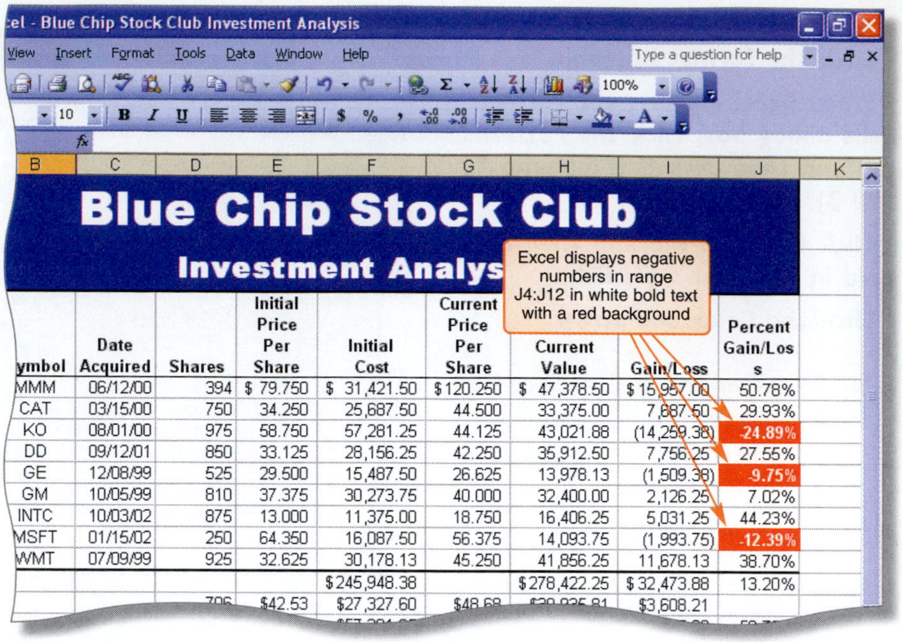

FIGURE 2-54

> **Other Ways**
>
> 1. Press ALT+O, D
> 2. In Voice Command mode, say "Format, Conditional Formatting"

In Figure 2-53 on the previous page, the preview box in the Conditional Formatting dialog box shows the format that will be assigned to all cells in the range J4:J12 that have a value less than 0. This preview allows you to review the format before you click the OK button. The Add button in the Conditional Formatting dialog box allows you to add two additional conditions for a total of three conditions. The Delete button allows you to delete one or more active conditions.

The middle text box in the Conditional Formatting dialog box allows you to select a relational operator, such as less than, to use in the condition. The eight different relational operators from which you can choose in the Conditional Formatting dialog box are summarized in Table 2-5.

> **More About**
>
> **Conditional Formatting**
>
> You can assign any format to a cell, a range of cells, a worksheet, or an entire workbook conditionally. If the value of the cell changes and no longer meets the specified condition, Excel suppresses the conditional formatting.

Table 2-5 Summary of Conditional Formatting Relational Operators

RELATIONAL OPERATOR	DESCRIPTION
Between	Cell value is between two numbers
Not between	Cell value is not between two numbers
Equal to	Cell value is equal to a number
Not equal to	Cell value is not equal to a number
Greater than	Cell value is greater than a number
Less than	Cell value is less than a number
Greater than or equal to	Cell value is greater than or equal to a number
Less than or equal to	Cell value is less than or equal to a number

With the conditional formatting complete, the next step is to change the column widths and row heights to make the worksheet easier to read.

Changing the Widths of Columns and Heights of Rows

When Excel starts and displays a blank worksheet on the screen, all of the columns have a default width of 8.43 characters, or 64 pixels. A **character** is defined as a letter, number, symbol, or punctuation mark in 10-point Arial font, the default font used by Excel. An average of 8.43 characters in 10-point Arial font will fit in a cell.

Another measure is pixels, which is short for picture element. A **pixel** is a dot on the screen that contains a color. The size of the dot is based on your screen's resolution. At a common resolution of 800 × 600, 800 pixels appear across the screen and 600 pixels appear down the screen for a total of 480,000 pixels. It is these 480,000 pixels that form the font and other items you see on the screen.

The default row height in a blank worksheet is 12.75 points (or 17 pixels). Recall from Project 1 that a point is equal to 1/72 of an inch. Thus, 12.75 points is equal to about 1/6 of an inch. You can change the width of the columns or height of the rows at any time to make the worksheet easier to read or to ensure that Excel displays an entry properly in a cell.

Changing the Widths of Columns

When changing the column width, you can set the width manually or you can instruct Excel to size the column to best fit. **Best fit** means that the width of the column will be increased or decreased so the widest entry will fit in the column. Sometimes, you may prefer more or less white space in a column than best fit provides. Excel thus allows you to change column widths manually.

When the format you assign to a cell causes the entry to exceed the width of a column, Excel automatically changes the column width to best fit. This happened earlier when the Currency style format was used (Figure 2-43 on page EX 99). If you do not assign a format to a cell or cells in a column, the column width will remain 8.43 characters, as is the case in columns A and B. To set a column width to best fit, double-click the right boundary of the column heading above row 1.

The following steps change the column widths: column A to 13.00 characters; columns B through D to best fit; columns E, G, and J to 10.00 characters; and columns F, H, and I to 12.00 characters.

To Change the Widths of Columns

1

• **Point to the boundary on the right side of the column A heading above row 1.**

• **When the mouse pointer changes to a split double arrow, drag to the right until the ScreenTip indicates Width: 13.00 (96 pixels). Do not release the mouse button.**

A dotted line shows the proposed right border of column A (Figure 2-55).

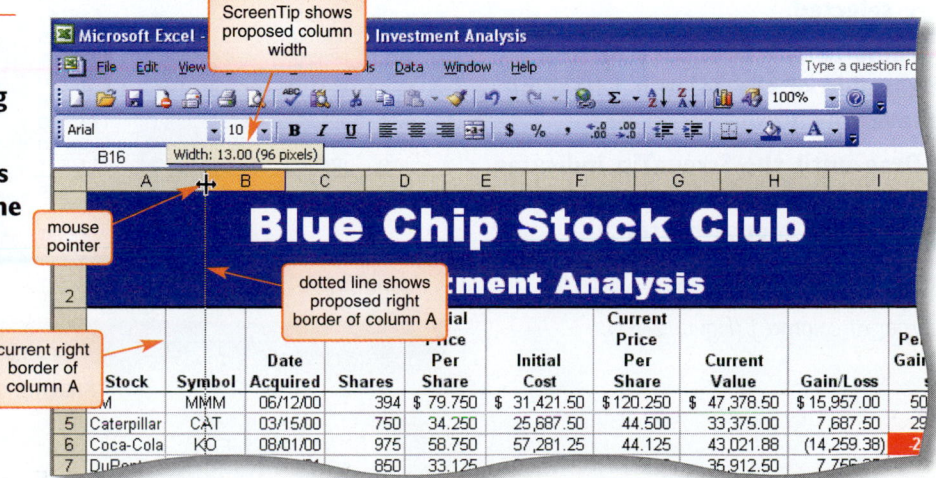

FIGURE 2-55

2

• Release the mouse button.

• Drag through column headings B through D above row 1.

• Point to the boundary on the right side of column heading D.

The mouse pointer becomes a split double arrow (Figure 2-56).

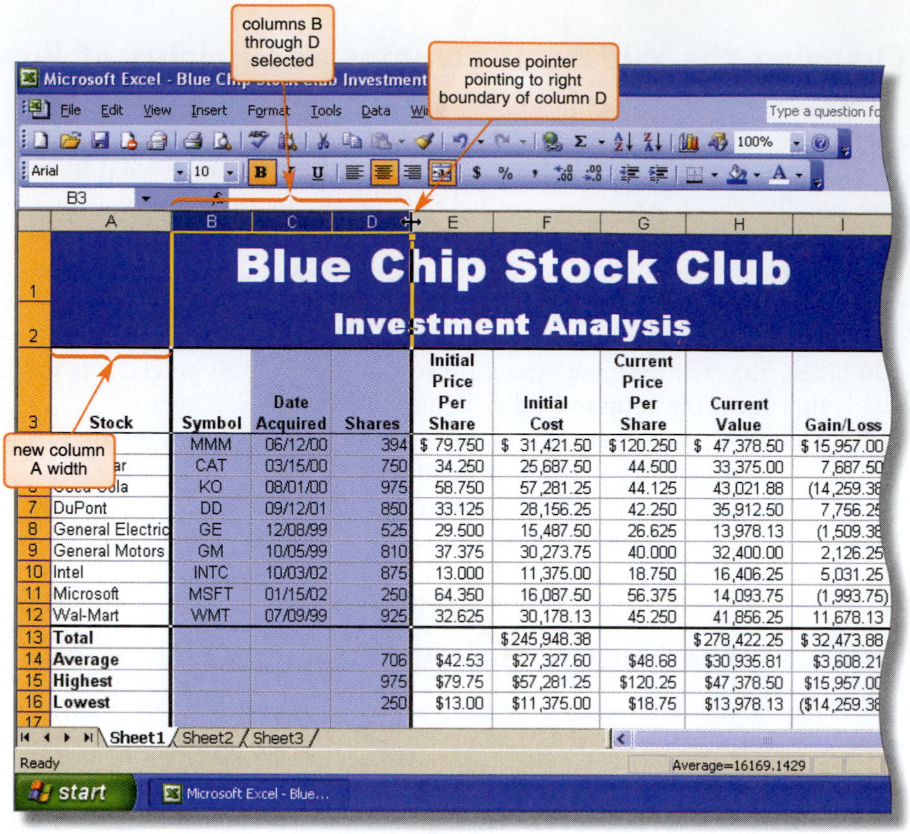

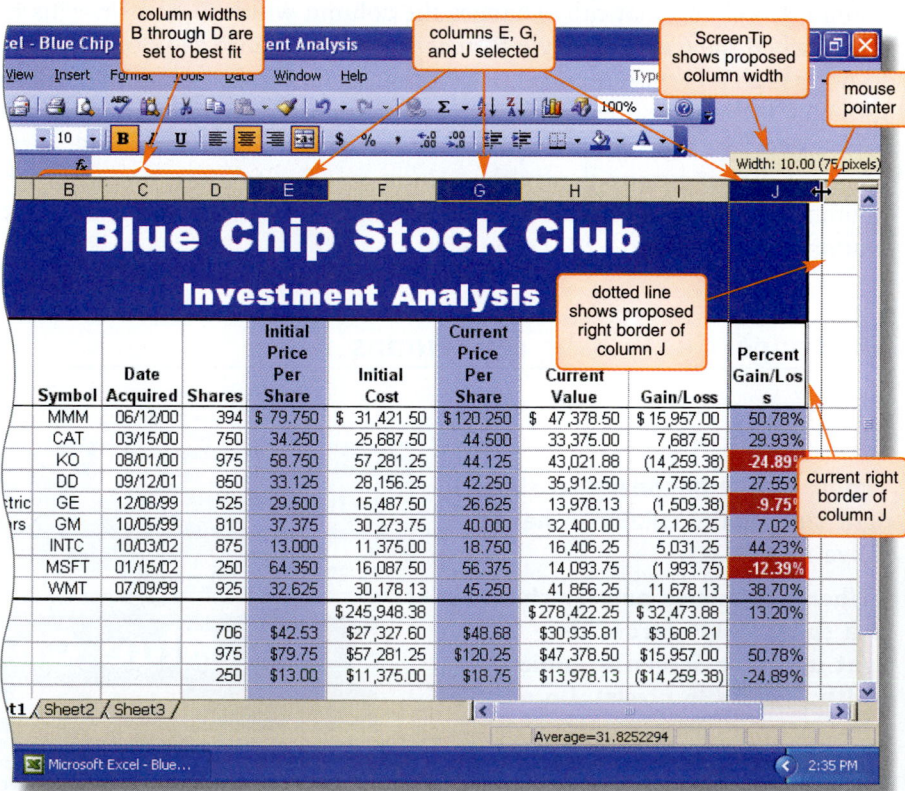

FIGURE 2-56

3

• Double-click the right boundary of column heading D to change the width of columns B, C, and D to best fit.

• Click the column E heading above row 1.

• While holding down the CTRL key, click the column G heading and then the column J heading above row 1 so that columns E, G, and J are selected.

• Point to the boundary on the right side of the column J heading above row 1.

• Drag until the ScreenTip indicates Width: 10.00 (75 pixels). Do not release the mouse button.

A dotted line shows the proposed right border of column J (Figure 2-57).

FIGURE 2-57

4

- Release the mouse button.
- Click the column F heading above row 1 to select column F.
- While holding down the CTRL key, click the column H and I headings above row 1 so that columns F, H, and I are selected.
- Point to the boundary on the right side of the column I heading above row 1.
- Drag to the right until the ScreenTip indicates Width: 12.00 (89 pixels). Do not release the mouse button.

A dotted line shows the proposed right border of column I (Figure 2-58).

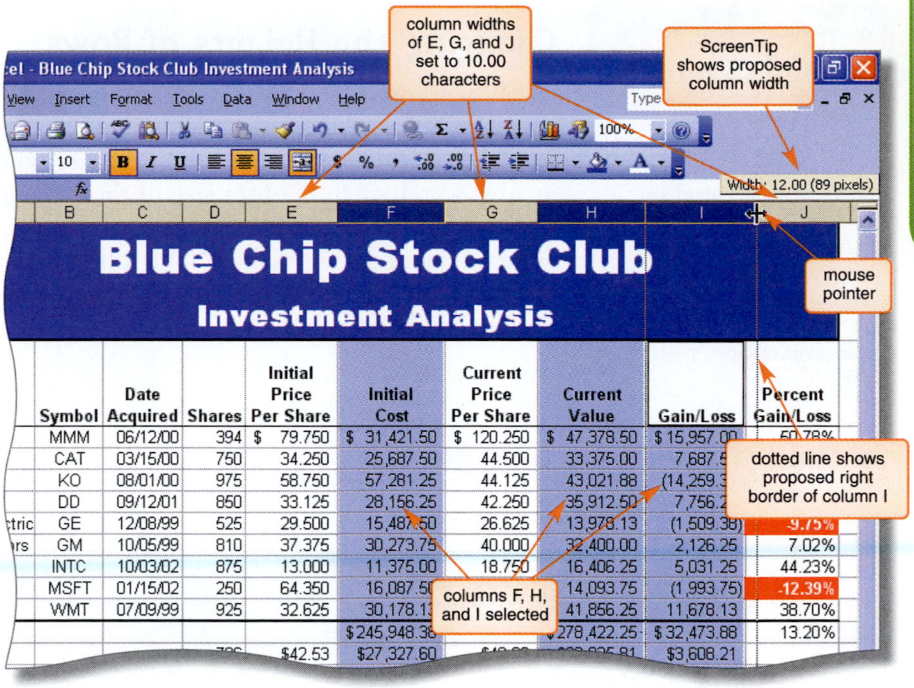

FIGURE 2-58

5

- Release the mouse button.
- Click cell B16 to deselect columns F, H, and I.

Excel displays the worksheet with the new column widths (Figure 2-59).

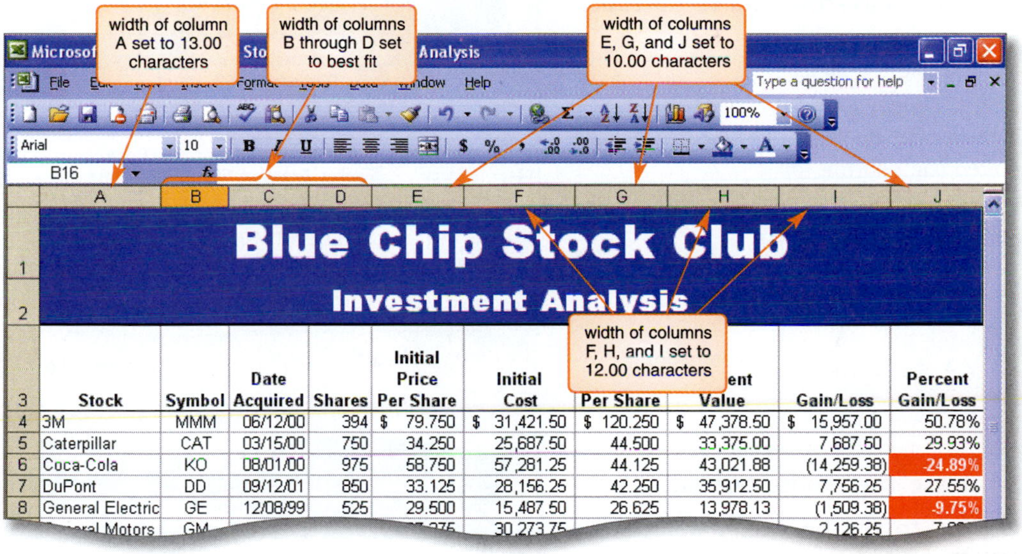

FIGURE 2-59

If you want to increase or decrease column width significantly, you can right-click a column heading and then use the Column Width command on the shortcut menu to change the column's width. To use this command, however, you must select one or more entire columns. As shown in the previous set of steps, you select entire columns by dragging through the column headings above row 1.

A column width can vary from zero (0) to 255 characters. If you decrease the column width to 0, the column is hidden. **Hiding cells** is a technique you can use to hide data that might not be relevant to a particular report or sensitive data that you do not want others to see. When you print a worksheet, hidden columns do not print. To instruct Excel to display a hidden column, position the mouse pointer to the right of the column heading boundary where the hidden column is located and then drag to the right.

Other Ways

1. Select cell or range of cells, on Format menu point to Column, click Width on Column sub-menu, enter desired column width, click OK button
2. Right-click column heading or drag through multiple column headings and right-click, click Column Width on shortcut menu, enter desired column width, click OK button
3. In Voice Command mode, say Format, Column, Width, [enter width], OK"

More About

Hidden Columns

Trying to unhide a range of columns using the mouse can be frustrating. An alternative is to use the keyboard, by selecting the columns to the right and left of the hidden columns and then pressing CTRL+SHIFT+RIGHT PARENTHESIS. To use the keyboard to hide a range of columns, press CTRL+0.

Changing the Heights of Rows

When you increase the font size of a cell entry, such as the title in cell A1, Excel automatically increases the row height to best fit so it can display the characters properly. Recall that Excel did this earlier when multiple lines were entered in a cell in row 3 and when the font size of the worksheet title and subtitle were increased.

You also can increase or decrease the height of a row manually to improve the appearance of the worksheet. The following steps show how to improve the appearance of the worksheet by decreasing the height of row 3 to 45.00 points and increasing the height of row 14 to 24.00 points.

To Change the Heights of Rows

1

• **Point to the boundary below row heading 3.**

• **Drag up until the ScreenTip indicates Height: 45.00 (60 pixels). Do not release the mouse button.**

Excel displays a horizontal dotted line (Figure 2-60). The distance between the dotted line and the top of row 3 indicates the proposed height for row 3.

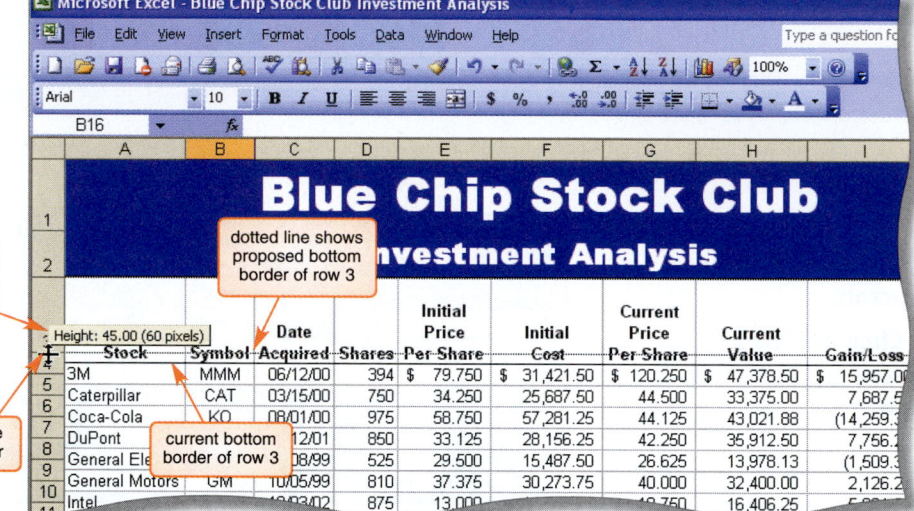

FIGURE 2-60

2

• **Release the mouse button.**

• **Point to the boundary below row heading 14.**

• **Drag down until the ScreenTip indicates Height: 24.00 (32 pixels). Do not release the mouse button.**

Excel displays a horizontal dotted line (Figure 2-61). The distance between the dotted line and the top of row 14 indicates the proposed height for row 14.

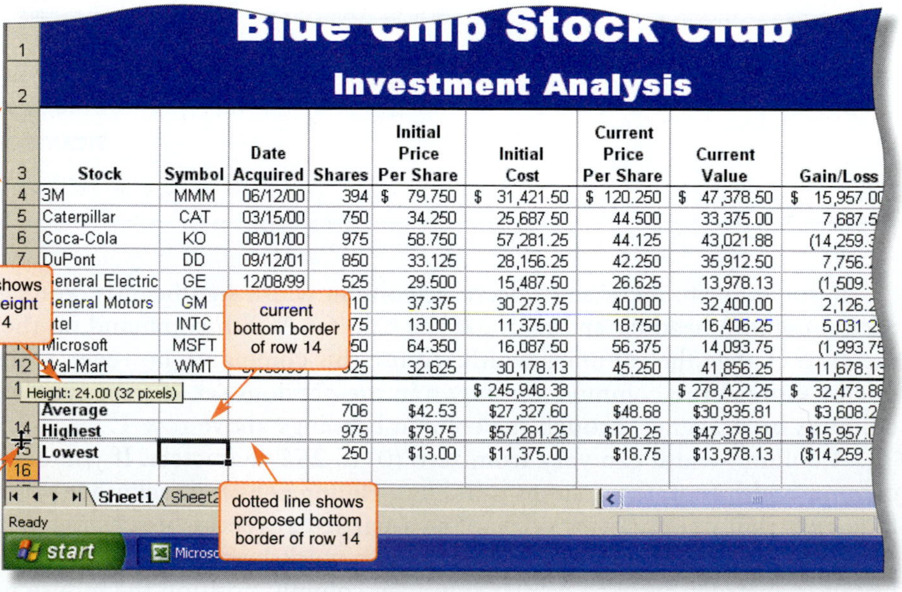

FIGURE 2-61

3

• **Release the mouse button and then select cell B16.**

The Total row and the Average row have additional white space between them, which improves the appearance of the worksheet (Figure 2-62). The formatting of the worksheet is complete.

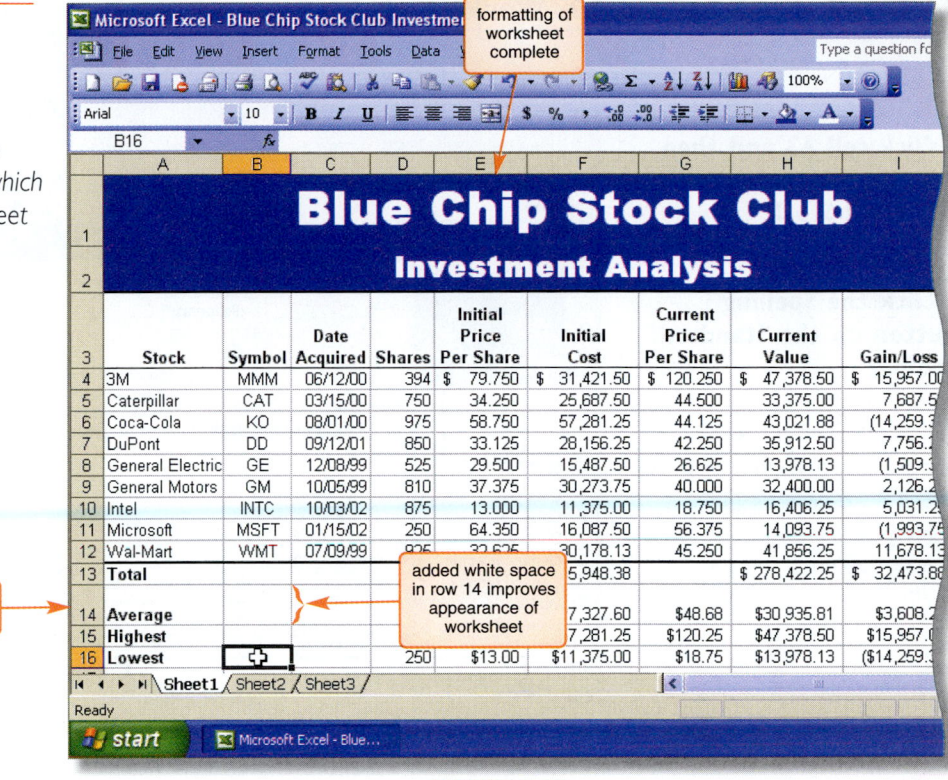

row 14 height is 24.00 points

FIGURE 2-62

The row height can vary between 0 and 409 points. As with column widths, when you decrease the row height to 0, the row is hidden. To instruct Excel to display a hidden row, position the mouse pointer just below the row heading boundary where the row is hidden and then drag down. To set a row height to best fit, double-click the bottom boundary of the row heading.

The task of formatting the worksheet is complete. The next step is to check the spelling of the worksheet.

Checking Spelling

Excel has a **spell checker** you can use to check the worksheet for spelling errors. The spell checker looks for spelling errors by comparing words on the worksheet against words contained in its standard dictionary. If you often use specialized terms that are not in the standard dictionary, you may want to add them to a custom dictionary using the Spelling dialog box.

When the spell checker finds a word that is not in either dictionary, it displays the word in the Spelling dialog box. You then can correct it if it is misspelled.

To illustrate how Excel responds to a misspelled word, the word, Stock, in cell A3 is misspelled purposely as the word, Stcok, as shown in Figure 2-63 on the next page.

To Check Spelling on the Worksheet

1

- Click cell **A3** and then type `Stcok` to misspell the word Stock.

- Click cell **A1**.

- Click the **Spelling** button on the Standard toolbar.

When the spell checker identifies the misspelled word, Stcok, in cell A3 it displays the Spelling dialog box (Figure 2-63).

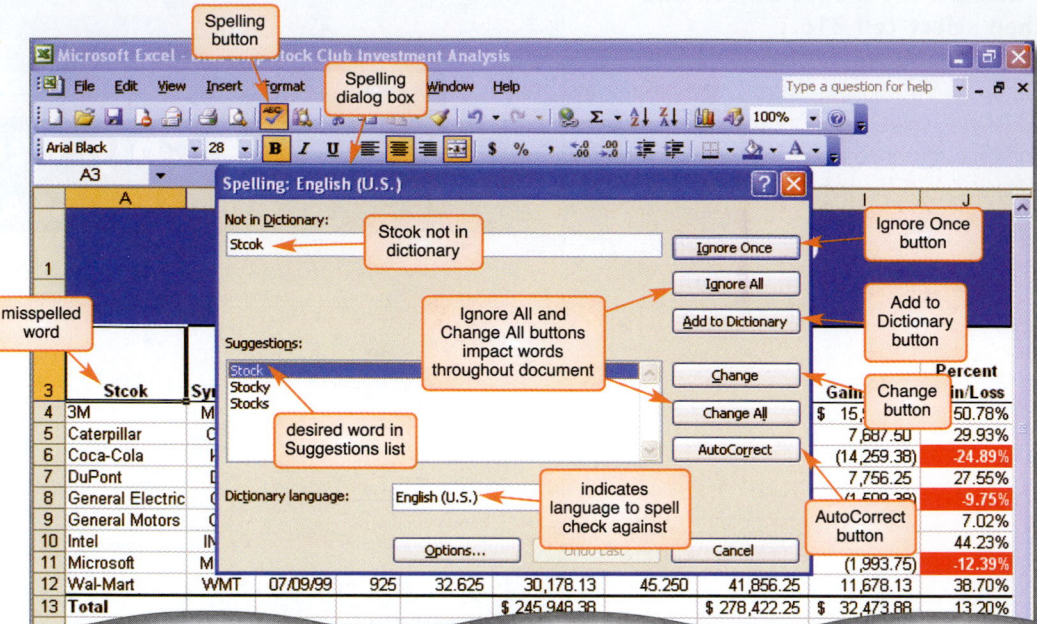

FIGURE 2-63

2

- With the word **Stock** highlighted in the Suggestions list, click the **Change** button.

- As the spell checker checks the remainder of the worksheet, click the **Ignore All** and **Change** buttons as needed.

The spell checker changes the misspelled word, Stcok, to the correct word, Stock, and continues spell checking the worksheet. When the spell checker is finished, it displays the Microsoft Office Excel dialog box with a message indicating that the spell check is complete (Figure 2-64).

3

- Click the **OK** button.

- Click the **Save** button on the Standard toolbar to save the workbook.

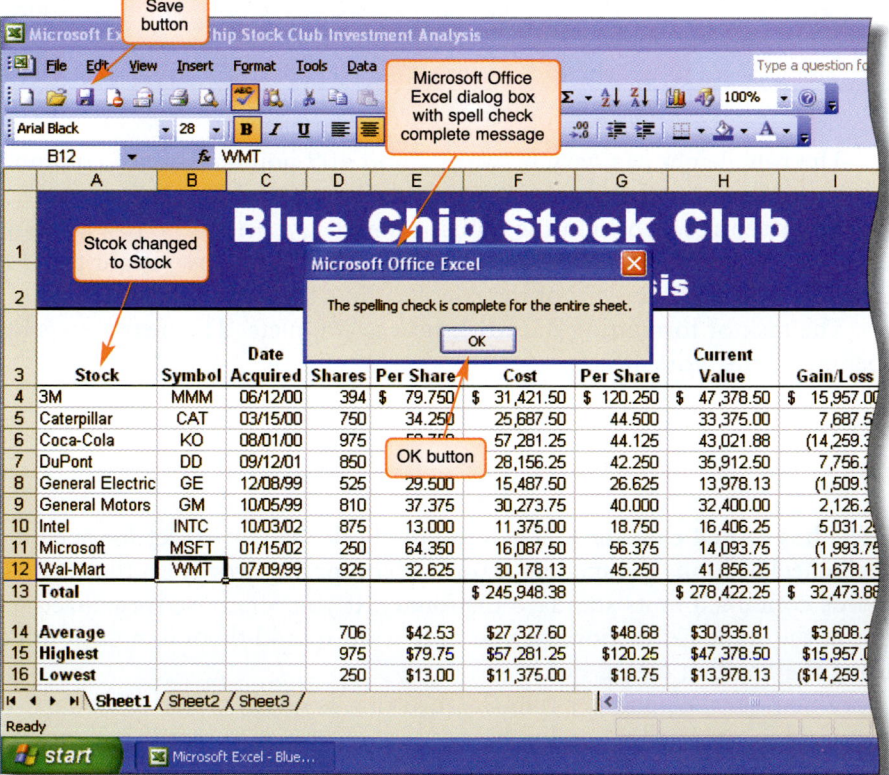

FIGURE 2-64

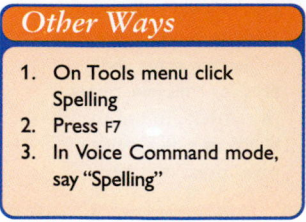

Other Ways

1. On Tools menu click Spelling
2. Press F7
3. In Voice Command mode, say "Spelling"

When the spell checker identifies that a cell contains a word not in its standard or custom dictionary, it selects that cell as the active cell and displays the Spelling dialog box. The Spelling dialog box (Figure 2-63) lists the word not found in the dictionary, a suggested correction, and a list of alternative suggestions. If one of the words in the Suggestions list is correct, click it and then click the Change button. If none of the suggestions is correct, type the correct word in the Not in Dictionary text box and then click the Change button. To change the word throughout the worksheet, click the Change All button instead of the Change button. To skip correcting the word, click the Ignore Once button. To have Excel ignore the word for the remainder of the worksheet, click the Ignore All button.

Consider these additional guidelines when using the spell checker:

- To check the spelling of the text in a single cell, double-click the cell to make the formula bar active and then click the Spelling button on the Standard toolbar.
- If you select a single cell so that the formula bar is not active and then start the spell checker, Excel checks the remainder of the worksheet, including notes and embedded charts.
- If you select a range of cells before starting the spell checker, Excel checks the spelling of the words only in the selected range.
- To check the spelling of all the sheets in a workbook, click Select All Sheets on the sheet tab shortcut menu and then start the spell checker. To instruct Excel to display the sheet tab shortcut menu, right-click any sheet tab.
- If you select a cell other than cell A1 before you start the spell checker, Excel will display a dialog box when the spell checker reaches the end of the worksheet, asking if you want to continue checking at the beginning.
- To add words to the dictionary such as your last name, click the Add to Dictionary button in the Spelling dialog box (Figure 2-63) when Excel identifies the word as not in the dictionary.
- Click the AutoCorrect button (Figure 2-63) to add the misspelled word and the correct version of the word to the AutoCorrect list. For example, suppose you misspell the word, do, as the word, dox. When the spell checker displays the Spelling dialog box with the correct word, do, in the Change to box, click the AutoCorrect button. Then, anytime in the future that you type the word, dox, Excel automatically will change it to the word, do.

Previewing and Printing the Worksheet

In Project 1, the worksheet was printed without first previewing it on the screen. By **previewing the worksheet**, however, you see exactly how it will look without generating a printout. Previewing allows you to see if the worksheet will print on one page in portrait orientation. **Portrait orientation** means the printout is printed across the width of the page. **Landscape orientation** means the printout is printed across the length of the page. Previewing a worksheet using the Print Preview command on the File menu or Print Preview button on the Standard toolbar can save time, paper, and the frustration of waiting for a printout only to discover it is not what you want.

The steps on the next page preview and then print the worksheet.

To Preview and Print a Worksheet

1

• **Point to the Print Preview button on the Standard toolbar (Figure 2-65).**

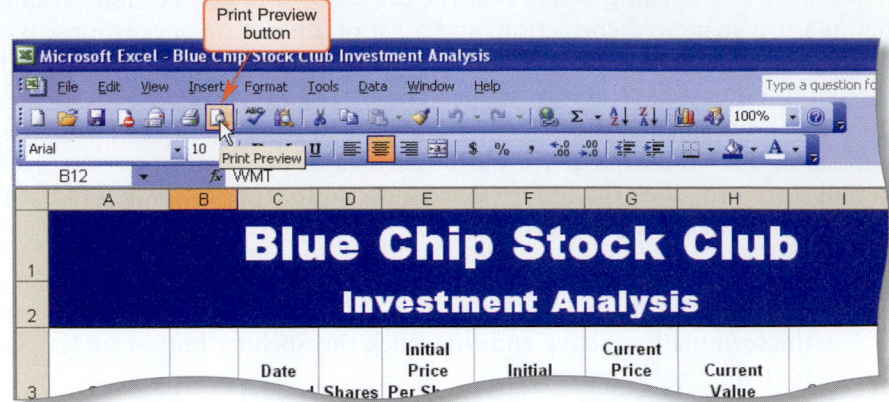

FIGURE 2-65

2

• **Click the Print Preview button.**

Excel displays a preview of the worksheet in portrait orientation, because portrait is the default orientation. In portrait orientation, the worksheet does not fit on one page (Figure 2-66).

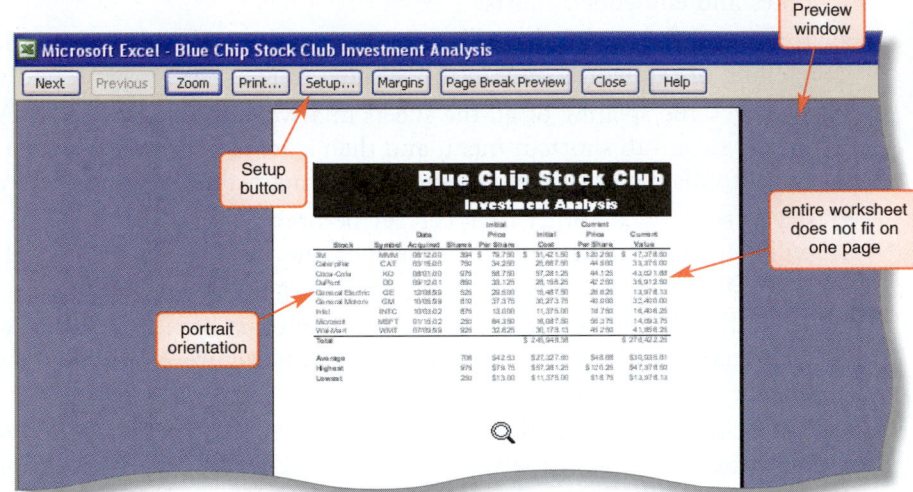

FIGURE 2-66

3

• **Click the Setup button.**

• **When Excel displays the Page Setup dialog box, click the Page tab and then click Landscape in the Orientation area.**

Excel displays the Page Setup dialog box. The Orientation area contains two option buttons, Portrait and Landscape. The Landscape option button is selected (Figure 2-67).

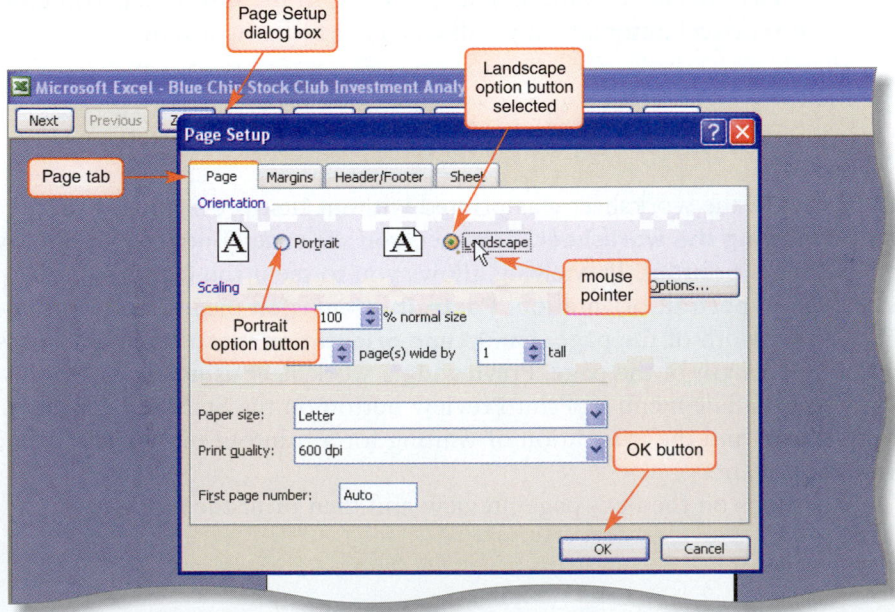

FIGURE 2-67

4

• **Click the OK button.**

Excel displays the worksheet in the Preview window. In landscape orientation, the entire worksheet fits on one page (Figure 2-68).

worksheet fits on one page in landscape orientation

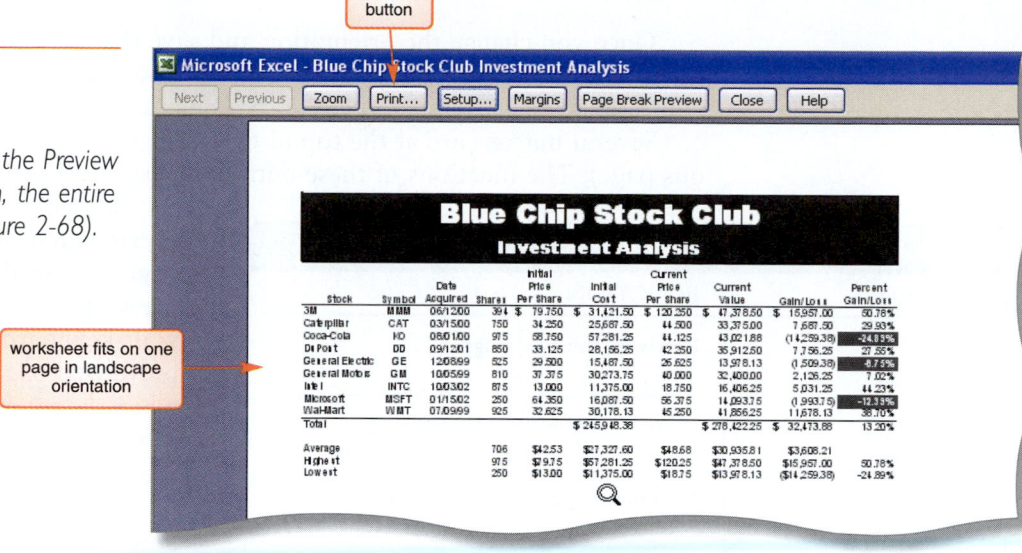

FIGURE 2-68

5

• **Click the Print button.**

Excel displays the Print dialog box as shown in Figure 2-69.

Print dialog box

All option button in Print range area instructs Excel to print entire worksheet

OK button

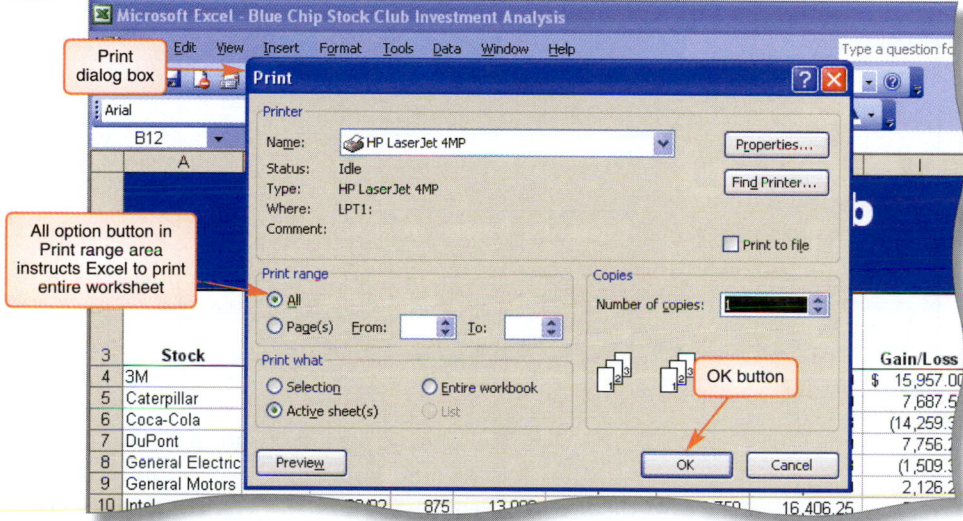

FIGURE 2-69

6

• **Click the OK button.**

• **Click the Save button on the Standard toolbar.**

Excel prints the worksheet (Figure 2-70). Excel saves the workbook with the landscape orientation print setting.

Other Ways

1. On File menu click Print Preview
2. On File menu click Page Setup, click Print Preview button
3. On File menu click Print, click Entire Workbook, click Preview button
4. In Voice Command mode, say "Print Preview"

landscape orientation

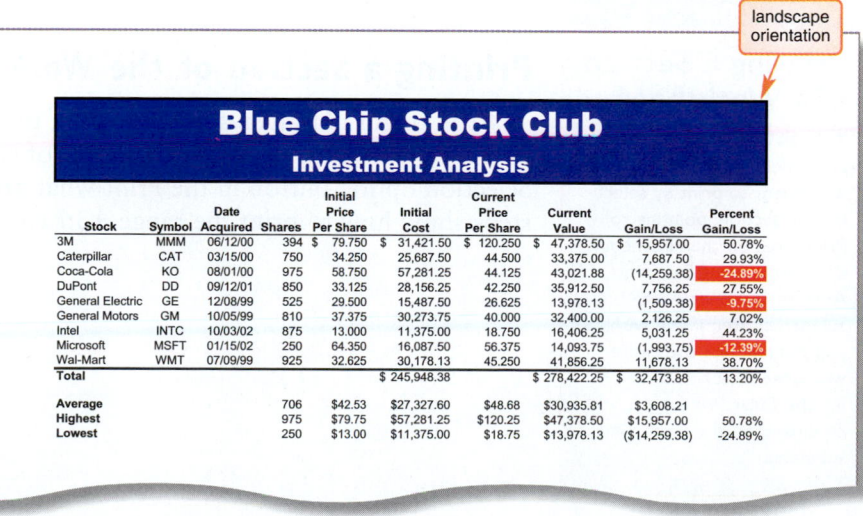

FIGURE 2-70

Once you change the orientation and save the workbook, Excel will save the orientation setting for that workbook until you change it. When you open a new workbook, Excel sets the orientation to portrait.

Several buttons are at the top of the Preview window (Figure 2-68 on the previous page). The functions of these buttons are summarized in Table 2-6.

Table 2-6	Print Preview Buttons
BUTTON	**FUNCTION**
Next	Previews the next page
Previous	Previews the previous page
Zoom	Magnifies or reduces the print preview
Print...	Prints the worksheet
Setup...	Instructs Excel to display the Print Setup dialog box
Margins	Changes the print margins
Page Break Preview	Previews page breaks
Close	Closes the Preview window
Help	Instructs Excel to display Help about the Preview window

Rather than click the Next and Previous buttons to move from page to page as described in Table 2-6, you can press the PAGE UP and PAGE DOWN keys on your keyboard. You also can click the previewed page in the Preview window when the mouse pointer shape is a magnifying glass to carry out the function of the Zoom button.

The Page Setup dialog box shown in Figure 2-67 on page EX 114 allows you to make changes to the default settings for a printout. For example, on the Page tab, you can set the page orientation, as shown in the previous set of steps; scale the printout so it fits on one page; and set the page size and print quality. Scaling, which can be used to fit a wide worksheet on one page, will be discussed later in the project. The Margins tab, Header/ Footer tab, and Sheet tab in the Page Setup dialog box provide additional options that allow for even more control of the way the printout will appear. These tabs will be discussed when they are used.

When you click the Print command on the File menu or a Print button in a dialog box or Preview window, Excel displays the Print dialog box shown in Figure 2-69 on the previous page. Excel does not display the Print dialog box when you use the Print button on the Standard toolbar, as was the case in Project 1. The Print dialog box allows you to select a printer, instruct Excel what to print, and indicate how many copies of the printout you want.

Printing a Section of the Worksheet

You might not always want to print the entire worksheet. You can print portions of the worksheet by selecting the range of cells to print and then clicking the Selection option button in the Print what area in the Print dialog box. The following steps show how to print the range A3:F16.

To Print a Section of the Worksheet

1

• **Select the range A3:F16.**

• **Click File on the menu bar and then click Print.**

• **Click Selection in the Print what area.**

Excel displays the Print dialog box (Figure 2-71). Because the Selection option button is selected, Excel will print only the selected range.

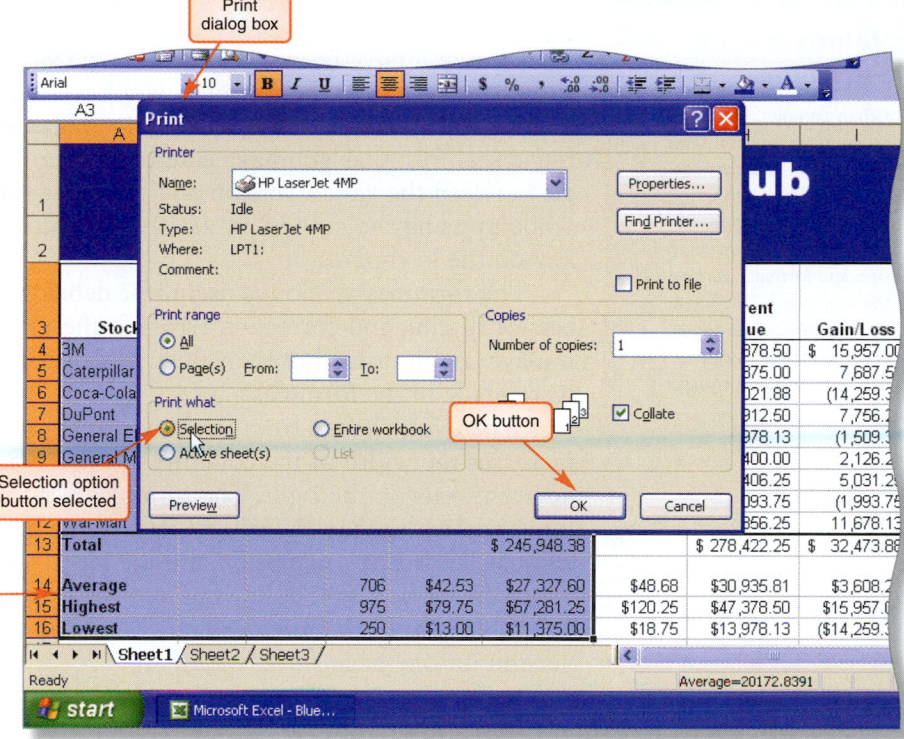

FIGURE 2-71

2

• **Click the OK button.**

• **Click cell B16 to deselect the range A3:F16.**

Excel prints the selected range of the worksheet on the printer (Figure 2-72).

only selected range prints

Stock	Symbol	Date Acquired	Shares	Initial Price Per Share	Initial Cost
3M	MMM	06/12/00	394	$ 79.750	$ 31,421.50
Caterpillar	CAT	03/15/00	750	34.250	25,687.50
Coca-Cola	KO	08/01/00	975	58.750	57,281.25
DuPont	DD	09/12/01	850	33.125	28,156.25
General Electric	GE	12/08/99	525	29.500	15,487.50
General Motors	GM	10/05/99	810	37.375	30,273.75
Intel	INTC	10/03/02	875	13.000	11,375.00
Microsoft	MSFT	01/15/02	250	64.350	16,087.50
Wal-Mart	WMT	07/09/99	925	32.625	30,178.13
Total					**$ 245,948.38**
Average			706	$42.53	$27,327.60
Highest			975	$79.75	$57,281.25
Lowest			250	$13.00	$11,375.00

FIGURE 2-72

The Print what area of the Print dialog box includes three option buttons (Figure 2-71). As shown in the previous steps, the Selection option button instructs Excel to print the selected range. The Active sheet(s) option button instructs Excel to print the active worksheet (the worksheet currently on the screen) or the selected worksheets. Finally, the Entire workbook option button instructs Excel to print all of the worksheets in the workbook.

Other Ways

1. Select range to print, on File menu point to Print Area, click Set Print Area, click Print button on Standard toolbar; on File menu point to Print Area, click Clear Print Area
2. Select range to print, in Voice Command mode, say "File, Print Area, Set Print Area"

Displaying and Printing the Formulas Version of the Worksheet

More About

Values versus Formulas

When completing class assignments, do not enter numbers in cells that require formulas. Most instructors require their students to hand in both the values version and formulas version of the worksheet. The formulas version verifies that you entered formulas, rather than numbers, in formula-based cells.

Thus far, you have been working with the **values version** of the worksheet, which shows the results of the formulas you have entered, rather than the actual formulas. Excel also can display and print the **formulas version** of the worksheet, which shows the actual formulas you have entered, rather than the resulting values. You can toggle between the values version and formulas version by holding down the CTRL key while pressing the ACCENT MARK (`) key, which is located to the left of the number 1 key on the keyboard.

The formulas version is useful for debugging a worksheet. **Debugging** is the process of finding and correcting errors in the worksheet. Viewing and printing the formulas version instead of the values version makes it easier to see if any mistakes were made in the formulas.

When you change from the values version to the formulas version, Excel increases the width of the columns so the formulas and text do not overflow into adjacent cells on the right. The formulas version of the worksheet thus usually is significantly wider than the values version. To fit the wide printout on one page, you can use landscape orientation and the Fit to option in the Page sheet in the Page Setup dialog box. The following steps change the view of the worksheet from the values version to the formulas version of the worksheet and then print the formulas version on one page.

To Display the Formulas in the Worksheet and Fit the Printout on One Page

1

• Press CTRL+ACCENT MARK (`).

• When Excel displays the formulas version of the worksheet, click the right horizontal scroll arrow until column J appears.

• If the Formula Auditing toolbar appears, click its Close button.

Excel changes the display of the worksheet from values to formulas (Figure 2-73). It displays the formulas in the worksheet showing unformatted numbers, formulas, and functions that were assigned to the cells. Excel automatically increases the column widths.

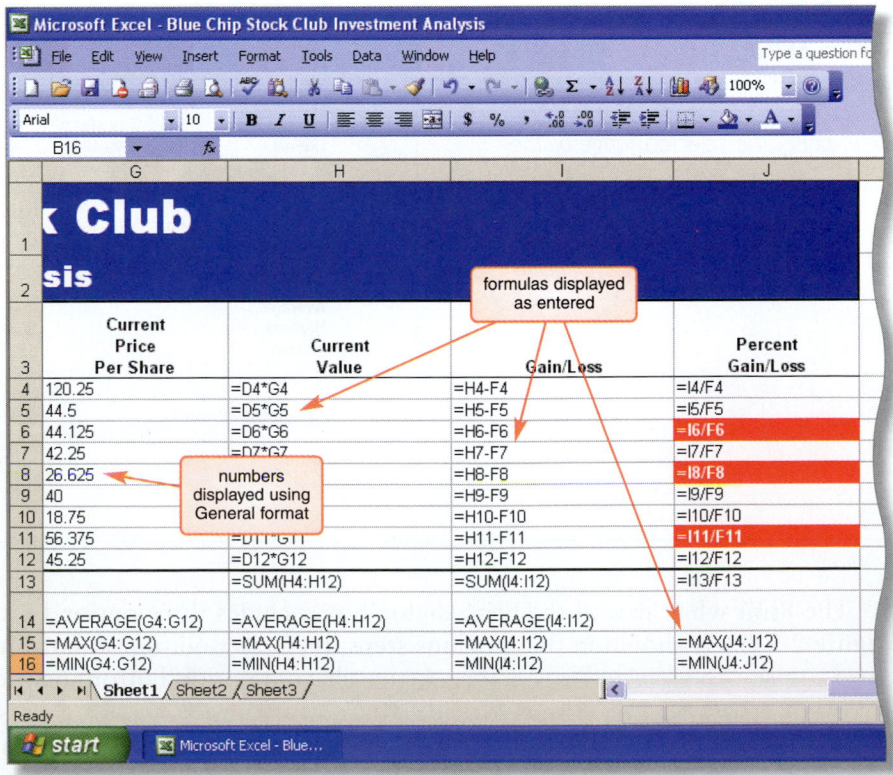

FIGURE 2-73

2

• **Click File on the menu bar and then click Page Setup.**

• **When Excel displays the Page Setup dialog box, click the Page tab.**

• **If necessary, click Landscape to select it and then click Fit to in the Scaling area.**

Excel displays the Page Setup dialog box with the Landscape and Fit to option buttons selected (Figure 2-74).

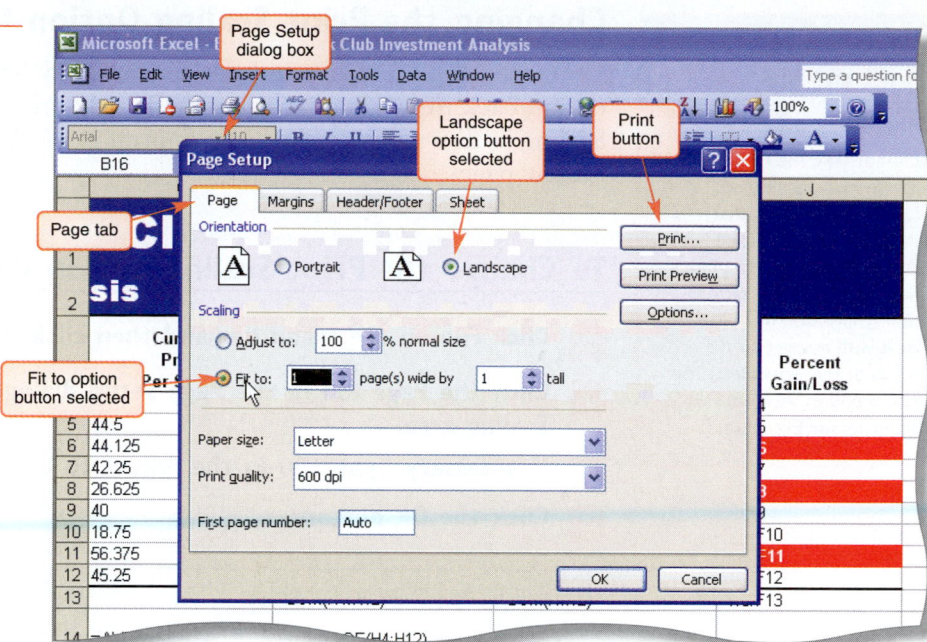

FIGURE 2-74

3

• **Click the Print button in the Page Setup dialog box.**

• **When Excel displays the Print dialog box, click the OK button.**

• **After viewing and printing the formulas version, press CTRL+ACCENT mark (`) to instruct Excel to display the values version.**

Excel prints the formulas in the worksheet on one page in landscape orientation (Figure 2-75). Excel displays the values version of the worksheet.

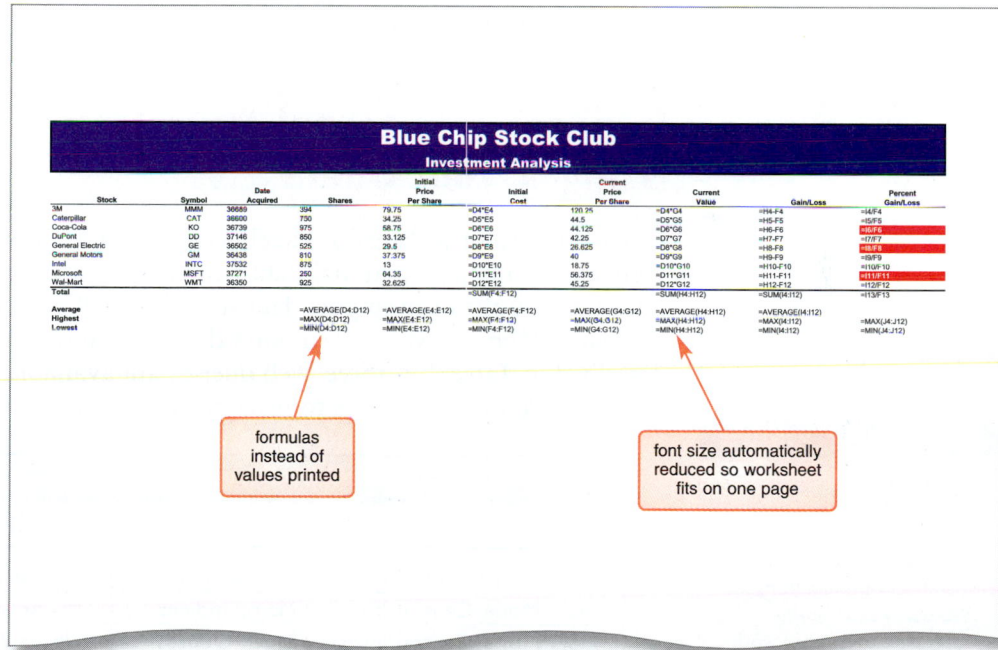

FIGURE 2-75

Although the formulas version of the worksheet was printed in the previous example, you can see from Figure 2-73 that you can review the formulas on the screen.

Other Ways

1. On Tools menu click Options, click View tab, click Formulas check box, click OK button
2. In Voice Command mode, say "Tools, Options, View, Formulas, OK"

More About

The Fit To Option

Do not take the Fit To option lightly. Most applications involve worksheets that extend well beyond the 8½"- by-11" page. Most users, however, want the information to print on one page, at least with respect to the width of the worksheet. The Fit To option thus is a valuable tool for Excel users.

Changing the Print Scaling Option Back to 100%

Depending on your printer driver, you may have to change the Print Scaling option back to 100% after using the Fit to option. The following steps reset the Print Scaling option so future worksheets print at 100%, instead of being resized to print on one page.

To Change the Print Scaling Option Back to 100%

1 Click File on the menu bar and then click Page Setup.

2 Click the Page tab in the Page Setup dialog box. Click Adjust to in the Scaling area.

3 If necessary, type 100 in the Adjust to box.

4 Click the OK button.

The print scaling is set to normal.

The Adjust to box allows you to specify the percentage of reduction or enlargement in the printout of a worksheet. The default percentage is 100%. When you click the Fit to option, this percentage automatically changes to the percentage required to fit the printout on one page.

Importing External Data from a Web Source Using a Web Query

One of the major features of Excel is its capability of importing external data from Web sites. To import external data from a Web site, you must have access to the Internet. You then can import data stored on a Web site using a **Web query**. When you run a Web query, Excel imports the external data in the form of a worksheet. As described in Table 2-7, three Web queries are available when you first install Excel. All three Web queries relate to investment and stock market activities.

More About

Web Queries

Most Excel specialists that build Web queries use the worksheet returned from the Web query as an engine to supply data to another worksheet in the workbook. With 3-D cell references, you can create a worksheet similar to the Blue Chip Stock Club worksheet to feed the Web query stock symbols and get refreshed stock prices in return.

Table 2-7 Excel Web Queries	
QUERY	**EXTERNAL DATA RETURNED**
MSN MoneyCentral Investor Currency Rates	Currency rates
MSN MoneyCentral Investor Major Indices	Major indices
MSN MoneyCentral Investor Stock Quotes	Up to 20 stocks of your choice

The data returned by the stock-related Web queries is real time in the sense that it is no more than 20 minutes old during the business day. The following steps show how to get the most recent stock quotes for the nine stocks owned by the Blue Chip Stock Club — 3M, Caterpillar, Coca-Cola, DuPont, General Electric, General Motors, Intel, Microsoft, and Wal-Mart. Although you can have a Web query return data to a blank workbook, the following steps have the data returned to a blank worksheet in the Blue Chip Stock Club Investment Analysis workbook.

To Import Data from a Web Source Using a Web Query

1

- With the Blue Chip Stock Club Investment Analysis workbook open, click the Sheet2 tab at the bottom of the window.

- With cell A1 active, click Data on the menu bar, and then point to Import External Data on the Data menu.

Excel displays the Data menu and Import External Data submenu as shown in Figure 2-76.

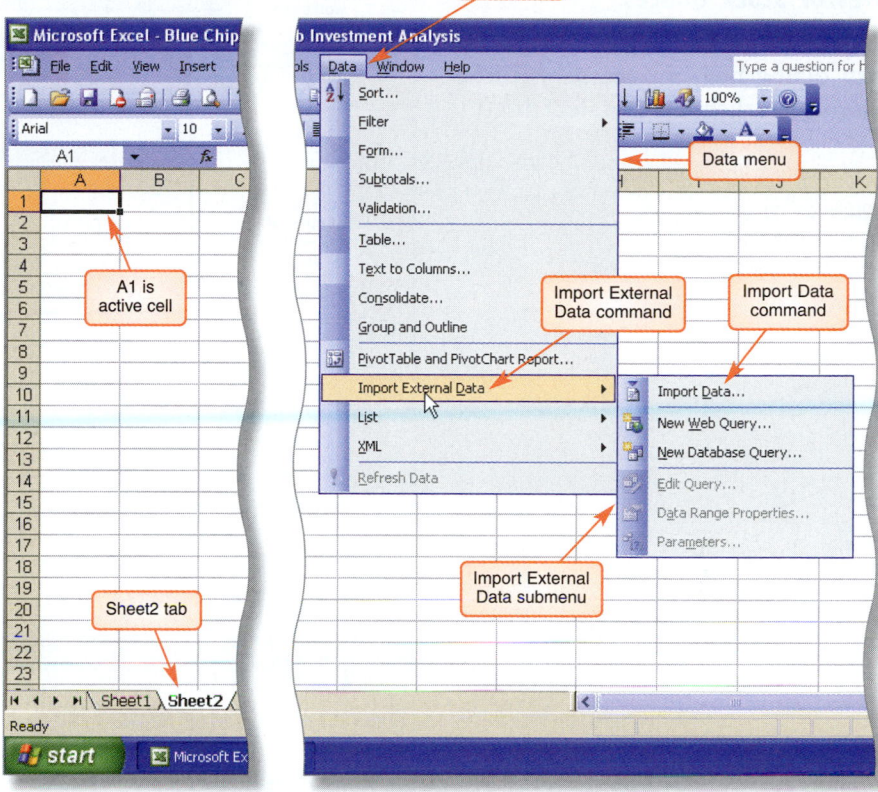

FIGURE 2-76

2

- Click Import Data on the Import External Data submenu.

Excel displays the Select Data Source dialog box (Figure 2-77). If your screen is different, ask your instructor for the folder location of the Web queries.

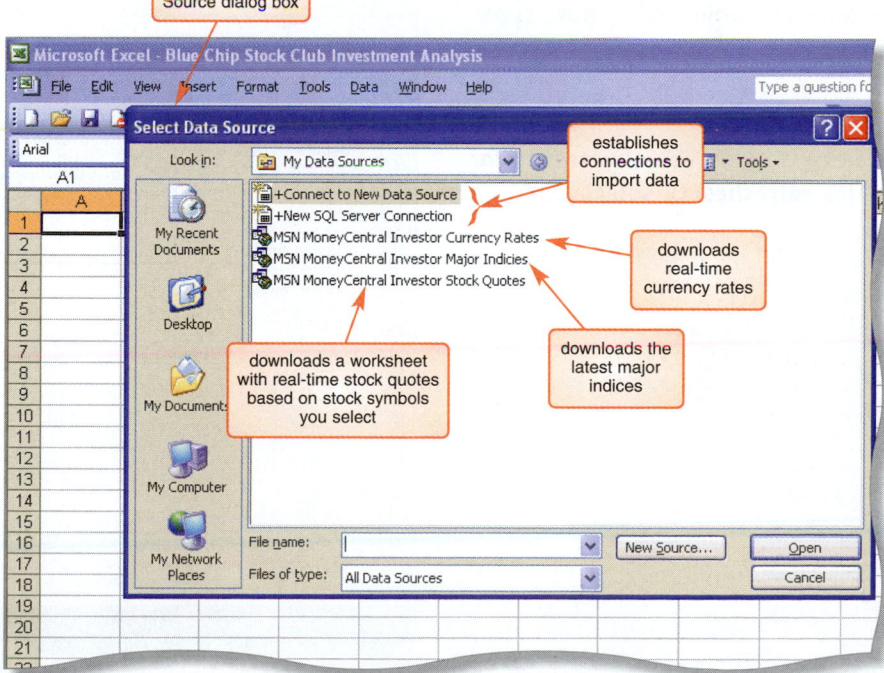

FIGURE 2-77

3

• **Double-click MSN MoneyCentral Investor Stock Quotes.**

• **When Excel displays the Import Data dialog box, if necessary, click Existing worksheet to select it.**

Excel displays the Import Data dialog box (Figure 2-78).

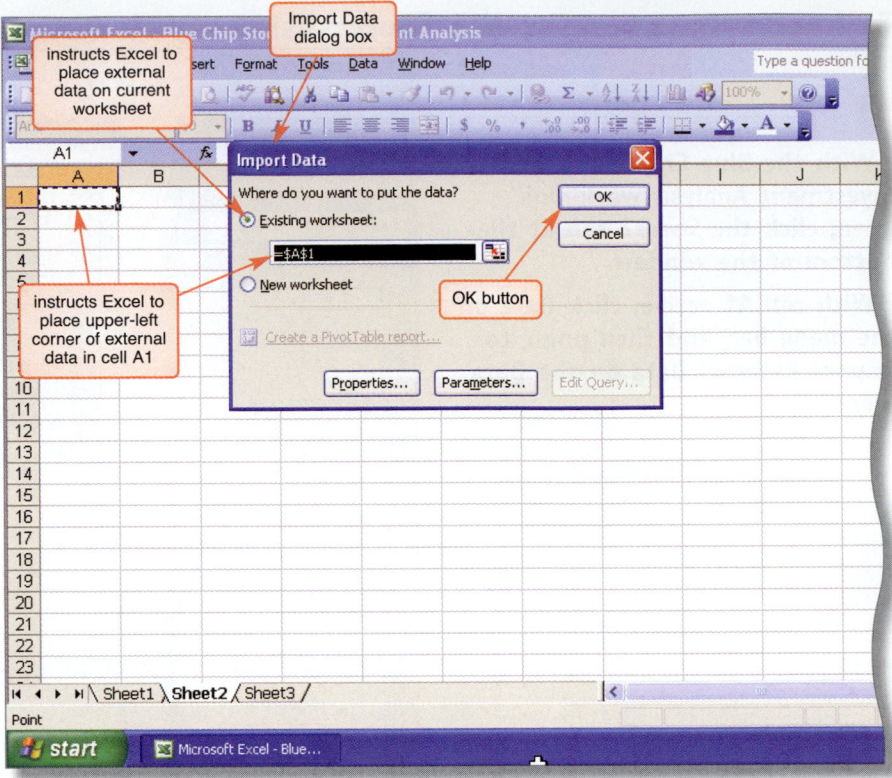

FIGURE 2-78

4

• **Click the OK button.**

• **When Excel displays the Enter Parameter Value dialog box, type the eight stock symbols** mmm cat ko dd ge gm intc msft wmt **in the text box.**

• **Click Use this value/reference for future refreshes to select it.**

Excel displays the Enter Parameter Value dialog box (Figure 2-79). You can enter up to 20 stock symbols separated by spaces (or commas).

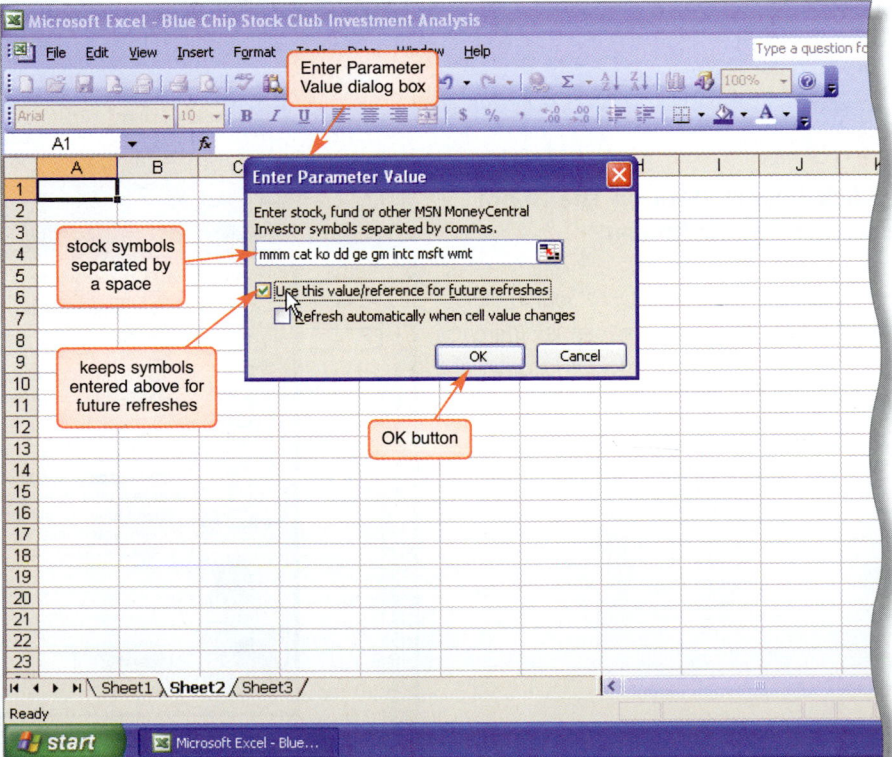

FIGURE 2-79

5

• **Click the OK button.**

Once your computer connects to the Internet, a message appears informing you that Excel is getting external data. After a short period, Excel displays a new worksheet with the desired data (Figure 2-80). The complete worksheet is shown in Figure 2-1b on page EX 67.

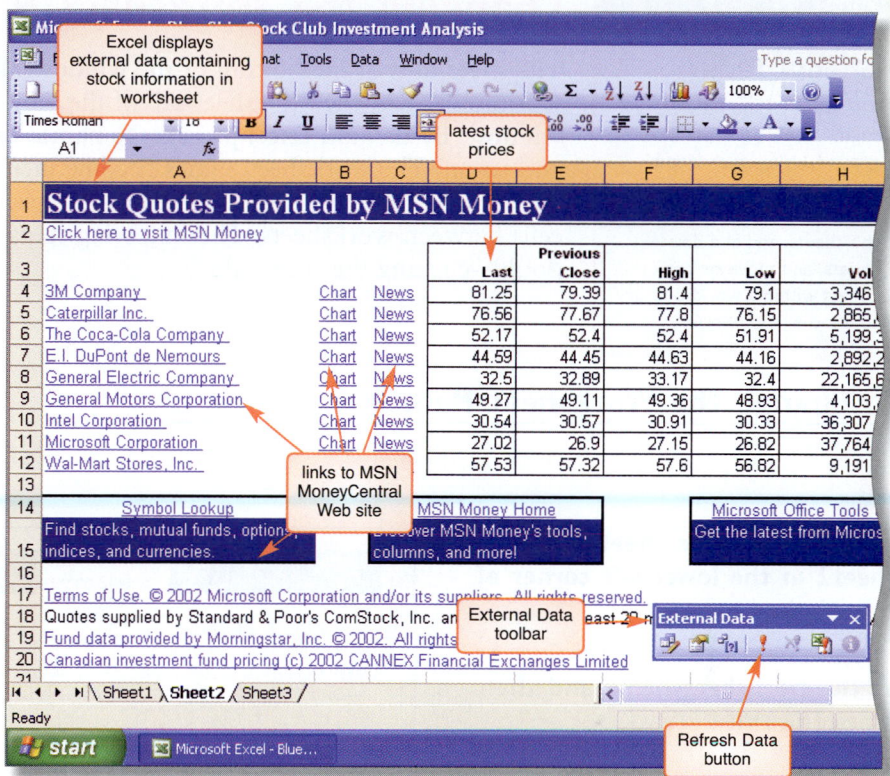

FIGURE 2-80

As shown in Figure 2-80, Excel displays the data returned from the Web query in an organized, formatted worksheet, which has a worksheet title, column titles, and a row of data for each stock symbol entered. Other than the first column, which contains the stock name and stock symbol, you have no control over the remaining columns of data returned. The latest price of each stock appears in column D.

Once Excel displays the worksheet, you can refresh the data as often as you want. To refresh the data for all the stocks, click the Refresh All button on the External Data toolbar (Figure 2-81). Because the Use this value/reference for future refreshes check box was selected in Step 4 of the previous steps (Figure 2-79), Excel will continue to use the same stock symbols each time it refreshes. You can change the symbols by clicking the Query Parameters button on the External Data toolbar.

If the External Data toolbar does not appear, right-click any toolbar and then click External Data. Instead of using the External Data toolbar, you also can invoke any Web query command by right-clicking any cell in the returned worksheet to display a shortcut menu with several of the same commands as the External Data toolbar.

This section gives you an idea of the potential of Web queries by having you use just one of Excel's Web queries. To reinforce the topics covered here, work through In the Lab 3 on page EX 136.

The workbook is nearly complete. The final step is to change the names of the sheets located on the sheet tabs at the bottom of the Excel window.

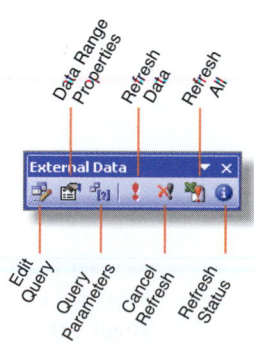

FIGURE 2-81

More About

Sheets Tabs

The name of the active sheet is bold on a white background. Using its shortcut menu, you can rename the sheets, color the tab, reorder the sheets, add and delete sheets, and move or copy sheets within a workbook or to another workbook.

Changing the Worksheet Names

The sheet tabs at the bottom of the window allow you to view any worksheet in the workbook. You click the sheet tab of the worksheet you want to view in the Excel window. By default, Excel presets the names of the worksheets to Sheet1, Sheet2, and so on. The worksheet names become increasingly important as you move towards more sophisticated workbooks, especially those in which you reference cells between worksheets. The following steps show how to rename worksheets by double-clicking the sheet tabs.

To Change the Worksheet Names

1

- **Double-click the sheet tab labeled Sheet2 in the lower-left corner of the window.**

- **Type** Real-Time Stock Quotes **as the worksheet name and then press the ENTER key.**

The new worksheet name appears on the sheet tab (Figure 2-82).

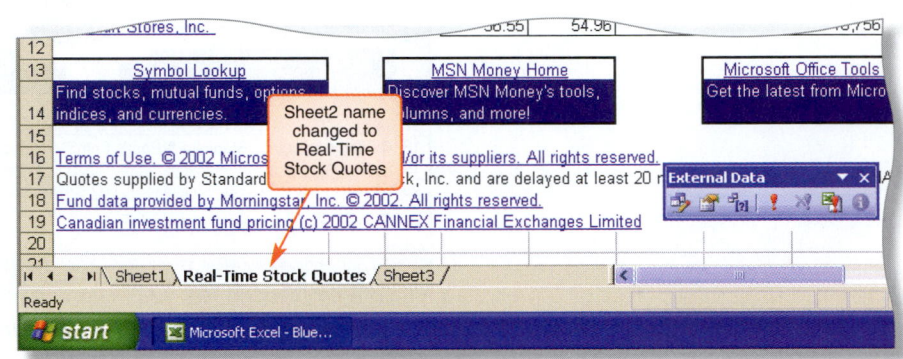

FIGURE 2-82

2

- **Double-click the sheet tab labeled Sheet1 in the lower-left corner of the window.**

- **Type** Investment Analysis **as the worksheet name and then press the ENTER key.**

Excel changes the worksheet name from Sheet1 to Investment Analysis (Figure 2-83).

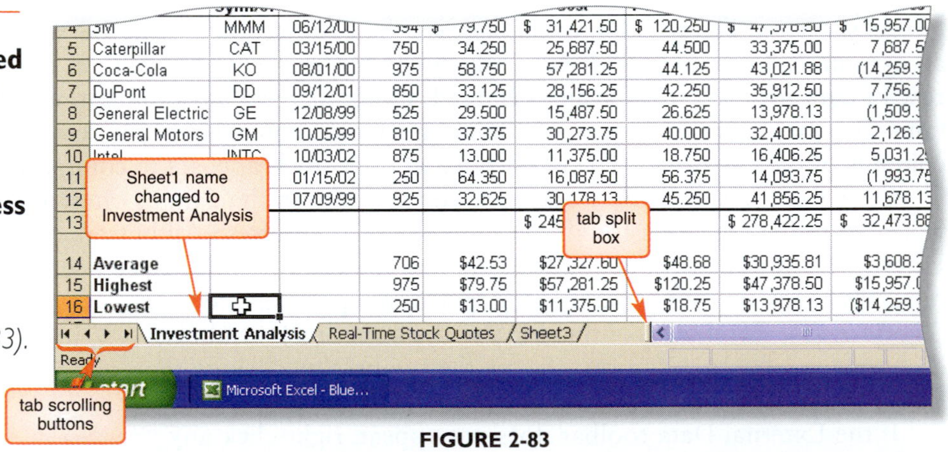

FIGURE 2-83

Worksheet names can be up to 31 characters (including spaces) in length. Longer worksheet names, however, mean that fewer sheet tabs will show. To view more sheet tabs, you can drag the tab split box (Figure 2-83) to the right. This will reduce the size of the scroll bar at the bottom of the screen. Double-click the tab split box to reset it to its normal position.

You also can use the tab scrolling buttons to the left of the sheet tabs (Figure 2-83) to move between worksheets. The leftmost and rightmost scroll buttons move to the first or last worksheet in the workbook. The two middle scroll buttons move one worksheet to the left or right.

E-Mailing a Workbook from within Excel

The most popular service on the Internet is electronic mail, or **e-mail**, which is the electronic transmission of messages and files to and from other computers using the Internet. Using e-mail, you can converse with friends across the room or on another continent. One of the features of e-mail is the ability to attach Office files, such as Word documents or Excel workbooks, to an e-mail message and send it to a coworker. In the past, if you wanted to e-mail a workbook, you saved the workbook, closed the file, started your e-mail program, and then attached the workbook to the e-mail message before sending it. With Excel you have the capability of e-mailing a worksheet or workbook directly from within Excel. For these steps to work properly, you must have an e-mail address and one of the following as your e-mail program: Microsoft Outlook, Microsoft Outlook Express, Microsoft Exchange Client, or another 32-bit e-mail program compatible with Messaging Application Programming Interface. The following steps show how to e-mail the Blue Chip Stock Club Investment Analysis workbook from within Excel to Alisha Wright at the e-mail address wright_alisha@hotmail.com.

To E-Mail a Workbook from within Excel

1

• **With the Blue Chip Stock Club Investment Analysis workbook open, click File on the menu bar and then point to Send To.**

Excel displays the File menu and Send To submenu as shown in Figure 2-84.

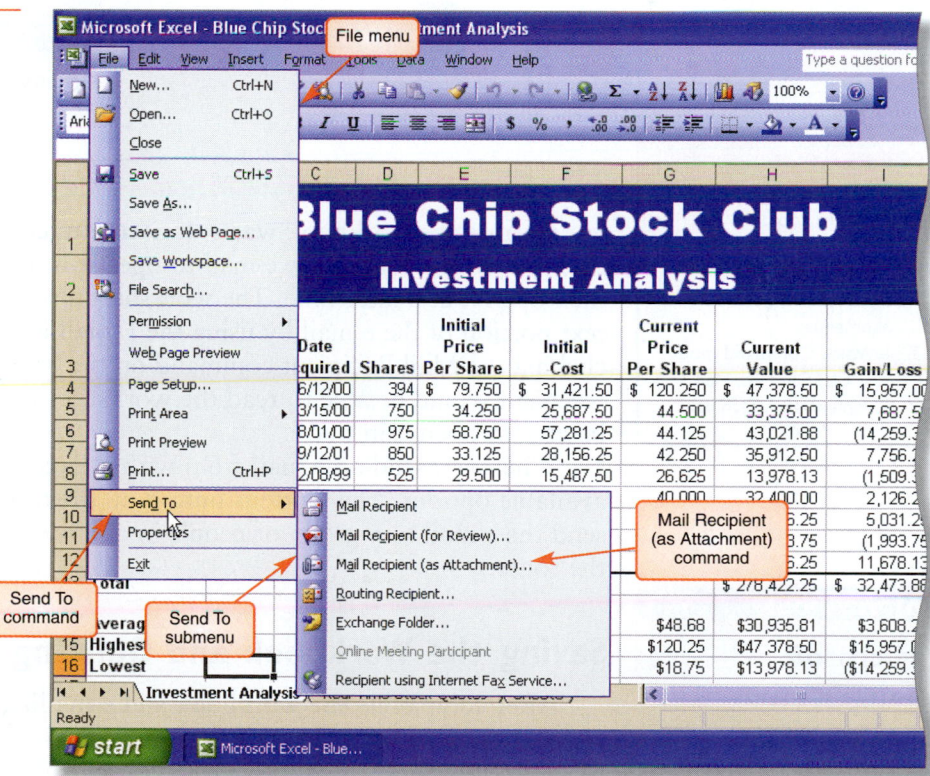

FIGURE 2-84

2

• **Click Mail Recipient (as Attachment) on the Send To submenu.**

• **When the e-mail Message window appears, type** wright_alisha@hotmail.com **in the To text box.**

• **Type the message shown in the message area in Figure 2-85.**

Excel displays the e-mail Message window. The workbook is included as an attachment (Figure 2-85).

3

• **Click the Send button.**

The e-mail with the attached workbook is sent to wright_alisha@hotmail.com.

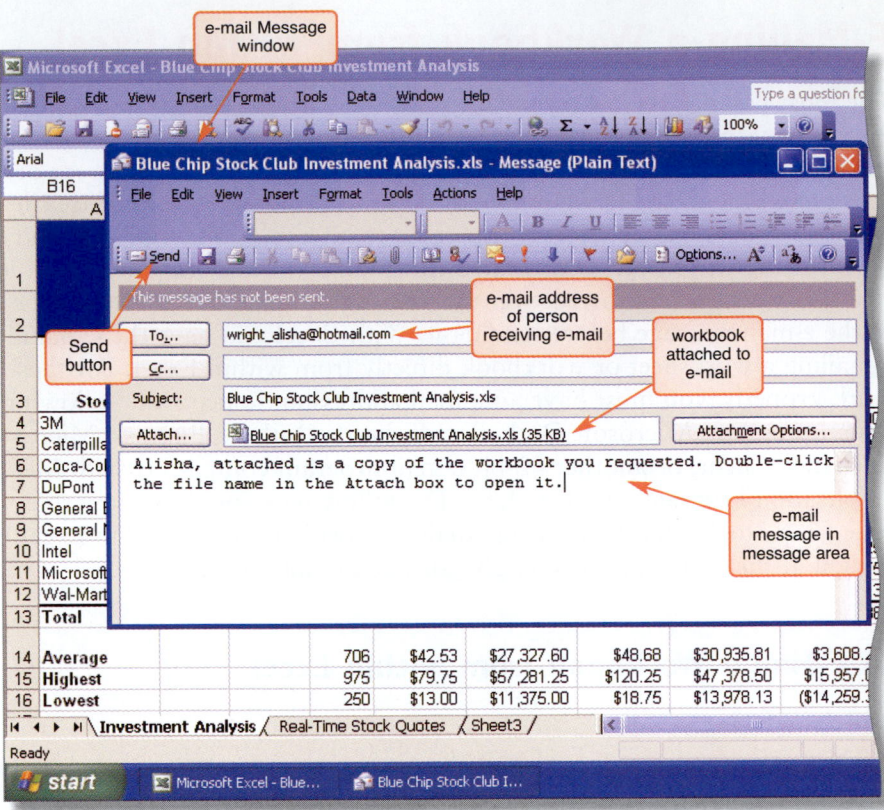

FIGURE 2-85

Because the workbook was sent as an attachment, Alisha Wright can double-click the attachment in the e-mail to open it in Excel, or she can save it on disk and then open it at a later time. The worksheet also could have been sent as part of the text portion of the e-mail by using the E-mail button on the Standard toolbar or by clicking the Mail Recipient command on the Send To submenu. In this case, the recepient would be able to read the worksheet in the e-mail message, but would not be able to open it in Excel.

When you send an e-mail from within Excel, you can choose from many other available options. The Options button on the toolbar, for example, allows you to send the e-mail to a group of people in a particular sequence and get responses along the route.

Saving the Workbook and Quitting Excel

After completing the workbook and e-mailing a copy of the workbook, the final steps are to save the workbook and quit Excel.

To Save the Workbook and Quit Excel

1 Click the Save button on the Standard toolbar.

2 Click the Close button on the upper-right corner of the title bar.

Project Summary

In creating the Blue Chip Stock Club Investment Analysis workbook, you learned how to enter formulas, calculate an average, find the highest and lowest numbers in a range, verify formulas using Range Finder, change fonts, draw borders, align text, format numbers, change column widths and row heights, and add conditional formatting to a range of numbers. You learned how to spell check a worksheet, preview a worksheet, print a worksheet, print a section of a worksheet, and display and print the formulas version of the worksheet using the Fit to option. You also learned how to complete a Web query to generate a worksheet using external data obtained from the Web and rename sheet tabs. Finally, you learned how to send an e-mail directly from within Excel with the opened workbook as an attachment.

 If you have a SAM user profile, you may have access to hands-on instruction, practice, and assessment of the skills covered in this project. Log in to your SAM account and go to your assignments page to see what your instructor has assigned.

What You Should Know

Having completed this project, you should be able to perform the tasks below. The tasks are listed in the same order they were presented in this project. For a list of the buttons, menus, toolbars, and commands introduced in this project, see the Quick Reference Summary at the back of this book and refer to the Page Number column.

1. Start and Customize Excel (EX 70)
2. Enter the Worksheet Title and Subtitle (EX 70)
3. Enter the Column Titles (EX 71)
4. Enter the Stock Data (EX 72)
5. Enter the Row Titles (EX 72)
6. Save the Workbook (EX 72)
7. Enter a Formula Using the Keyboard (EX 73)
8. Enter Formulas Using Point Mode (EX 75)
9. Copy Formulas Using the Fill Handle (EX 77)
10. Determine Totals Using the AutoSum Button (EX 79)
11. Determine the Total Percent Gain/Loss (EX 80)
12. Determine the Average of a Range of Numbers Using the Keyboard and Mouse (EX 81)
13. Determine the Highest Number in a Range of Numbers Using the Insert Function Box (EX 83)
14. Determine the Lowest Number in a Range of Numbers Using the AutoSum Button Menu (EX 85)
15. Copy a Range of Cells across Columns to an Adjacent Range Using the Fill Handle (EX 87)
16. Save a Workbook Using the Same File Name (EX 89)
17. Verify a Formula Using Range Finder (EX 89)
18. Change the Font and Center the Worksheet Title (EX 92)
19. Change the Font and Center the Worksheet Subtitle (EX 93)
20. Change the Background and Font Colors and Apply a Box Border to the Worksheet Title and Subtitle (EX 94)
21. Bold, Center, and Apply a Bottom Border to the Column Titles (EX 96)
22. Center Data in Cells and Format Dates (EX 97)
23. Apply a Currency Style Format and Comma Style Format Using the Formatting Toolbar (EX 98)
24. Apply a Thick Bottom Border to the Row above the Total Row and Bold the Total Row Titles (EX 100)
25. Apply a Currency Style Format with a Floating Dollar Sign Using the Format Cells Command (EX 101)
26. Apply a Percent Style Format (EX 103)
27. Apply Conditional Formatting (EX 104)

(continued)

What You Should Know *(continued)*

28. Change the Widths of Columns   (EX 107)

29. Change the Heights of Rows   (EX 110)

30. Check Spelling on the Worksheet   (EX 112)

31. Preview and Print a Worksheet   (EX 114)

32. Print a Section of the Worksheet   (EX 117)

33. Display the Formulas in the Worksheet and Fit the Printout on One Page   (EX 118)

34. Change the Print Scaling Option Back to 100%   (EX 120)

35. Import Data from a Web Source Using a Web Query   (EX 121)

36. Change the Worksheet Names   (EX 124)

37. E-Mail a Workbook from within Excel   (EX 125)

38. Save the Workbook and Quit Excel   (EX 126)

More About

The Quick Reference

For a table that lists how to complete the tasks covered in this book using the mouse, menu, shortcut menu, and keyboard, see the Quick Reference Summary at the back of this book or visit the Excel 2003 Quick Reference Web page (scsite.com/ex2003/qr).

Learn It Online

Instructions: To complete the Learn It Online exercises, start your browser, click the Address bar, and then enter the Web address scsite.com/ex2003/learn. When the Excel 2003 Learn It Online page is displayed, follow the instructions in the exercises below. Each exercise has instructions for printing your results, either for your own records or for submission to your instructor.

1 Project Reinforcement TF, MC, and SA

Below Excel Project 2, click the Project Reinforcement link. Print the quiz by clicking Print on the File menu for each page. Answer each question.

2 Flash Cards

Below Excel Project 2, click the Flash Cards link and read the instructions. Type 20 (or a number specified by your instructor) in the Number of playing cards text box, type your name in the Enter your Name text box, and then click the Flip Card button. When the flash card is displayed, read the question and then click the ANSWER box arrow to select an answer. Flip through Flash Cards. If your score is 15 (75%) correct or greater, click Print on the File menu to print your results. If your score is less than 15 (75%) correct, then redo this exercise by clicking the Replay button.

3 Practice Test

Below Excel Project 2, click the Practice Test link. Answer each question, enter your first and last name at the bottom of the page, and then click the Grade Test button. When the graded practice test is displayed on your screen, click Print on the File menu to print a hard copy. Continue to take practice tests until you score 80% or better.

4 Who Wants To Be a Computer Genius?

Below Excel Project 2, click the Computer Genius link. Read the instructions, enter your first and last name at the bottom of the page, and then click the PLAY button. When your score is displayed, click the PRINT RESULTS link to print a hard copy.

5 Wheel of Terms

Below Excel Project 2, click the Wheel of Terms link. Read the instructions, and then enter your first and last name and your school name. Click the PLAY button. When your score is displayed, right-click the score and then click Print on the shortcut menu to print a hard copy.

6 Crossword Puzzle Challenge

Below Excel Project 2, click the Crossword Puzzle Challenge link. Read the instructions, and then enter your first and last name. Click the SUBMIT button. Work the crossword puzzle. When you are finished, click the Submit button. When the crossword puzzle is redisplayed, click the Print Puzzle button to print a hard copy.

7 Tips and Tricks

Below Excel Project 2, click the Tips and Tricks link. Click a topic that pertains to Project 2. Right-click the information and then click Print on the shortcut menu. Construct a brief example of what the information relates to in Excel to confirm you understand how to use the tip or trick.

8 Newsgroups

Below Excel Project 2, click the Newsgroups link. Click a topic that pertains to Project 2. Print three comments.

9 Expanding Your Horizons

Below Excel Project 2, click the Expanding Your Horizons link. Click a topic that pertains to Project 2. Print the information. Construct a brief example of what the information relates to in Excel to confirm you understand the contents of the article.

10 Search Sleuth

Below Excel Project 2, click the Search Sleuth link. To search for a term that pertains to this project, select a term below the Project 2 title and then use the Google search engine at google.com (or any major search engine) to display and print two Web pages that present information on the term.

11 Excel Online Training

Below Excel Project 2, click the Excel Online Training link. When your browser displays the Microsoft Office Online Web page, click the Excel link. Click one of the Excel courses that covers one or more of the objectives listed at the beginning of the project on page EX 66. Print the first page of the course before stepping through it.

12 Office Marketplace

Below Excel Project 2, click the Office Marketplace link. When your browser displays the Microsoft Office Online Web page, click the Office Marketplace link. Click a topic that relates to Excel. Print the first page.

Profit Analysis Worksheet

Instructions Part 1: Start Excel. Open the workbook Apply 2-1 e-cove Profit Analysis from the Data Disk. See the inside back cover of this book for instructions for downloading the Data Disk or see your instructor for information on accessing the files required in this book. The purpose of this exercise is to open a partially completed workbook, enter formulas and functions, copy the formulas and functions, and then format the worksheet titles and numbers. As shown in Figure 2-86, the completed worksheet analyzes profits by item. Use the following formulas:

Total Sales (cell F3) = Units Sold * (Unit Cost + Unit Profit) or =C3 * (D3 + E3)

Total Profit (cell G3) = Units Sold * Unit Profit or = C3 * E3

% Total Profit (cell H3) = Total Profit / Total Sales or = G3 / F3

e-cove Auction
Profit Analysis

Item Number	Item Description	Units Sold	Unit Cost	Unit Profit	Total Sales	Total Profit	% Total Profit
A4T5	FTP Software	32,435	$ 92.95	$ 19.75	$ 3,655,424.50	$ 640,591.25	17.524%
C812	Game Software	16,534	175.99	45.65	3,664,595.76	754,777.10	20.596%
H4TT	Hard Disk	32,102	110.60	62.50	5,556,856.20	2,006,375.00	36.106%
K890	Monitor	34,391	121.35	38.75	5,505,999.10	1,332,651.25	24.204%
MM34	PDA	23,910	200.23	95.15	7,062,535.80	2,275,036.50	32.213%
NK34	Printer	45,219	50.65	12.85	2,871,406.50	581,064.15	20.236%
R567	Stereo Speakers	63,213	34.20	14.35	3,068,991.15	907,106.55	29.557%
SH67	System Unit	52,109	43.00	12.75	2,905,076.75	664,389.75	22.870%
Z345	Tax Software	76,145	38.25	13.00	3,902,431.25	989,885.00	25.366%
Totals		376,058			$ 38,193,317.01	$ 10,151,876.55	
Lowest		16,534	$34.20	$12.75	$2,871,406.50	$581,064.15	17.524%
Highest		76,145	$200.23	$95.15	$7,062,535.80	$2,275,036.50	36.106%
Average		41,784	$96.36	$34.97	$4,243,701.89	$1,127,986.28	

FIGURE 2-86

Use the fill handle to copy the three formulas in the range F3:H3 to the range F4:H11. After the copy is complete, click the Auto Fill Options button and then click the Fill Without Formatting command to maintain the bottom double border in the range F11:H11. Determine totals for the units sold, total sales, and total profit in row 12. In the range C13:C15, determine the lowest value, highest value, and average value, respectively, for the values in the range C3:C11. Use the fill handle to copy the three functions to the range D13:H15. Delete the average from cell H15, because an average of percentages of this type is mathematically invalid.

Apply Your Knowledge

Format the worksheet as follows:

(1) cell A1 – change to Impact font (or a font of your choice) with a dark red (column 1, row 2) background
(2) cells D3:G3 and F12:G12 – apply Currency style format with fixed dollar signs
(3) cells C3, C4:G11, and C13:C15 – apply Comma style format
(4) cells C3:C15 – format numbers to appear with no decimal places
(5) cells H3:H14 – apply Percent style format with three decimal places
(6) cells D13:G15 – apply Currency style format with floating dollar signs

Enter your name, course, laboratory assignment number (Apply 2-1), date, and instructor name in the range A20:A24. Preview and print the worksheet in landscape orientation. Save the workbook using the file name, Apply 2-1 e-cove Profit Analysis Complete.

Use Range Finder to verify the formula in cell G3. Print the range A2:F15. Press CTRL+ACCENT MARK (`) to change the display from the values version of the worksheet to the formulas version. Print the formulas version in landscape orientation on one page with gridlines showing (Figure 2-87) by (1) using the Fit to option in the Page sheet in the Page Setup dialog box and (2) clicking Gridlines on the Sheet sheet in the Page Setup dialog box. Press CTRL+ACCENT MARK (`) to change the display of the worksheet back to the values version. Do not save the workbook. Hand in the three printouts to your instructor.

Instructions Part 2: In column E, use the keyboard to add manually $3.00 to the profit of each product with a unit profit less than $40.00 and $4.00 to the profits of all other products. You should end up with $11,352,596.55 in cell G12. Print the worksheet. Do not save the workbook. Hand in the printout to your instructor.

Report

e-cove Auction
Profit Analysis

Item Number	Item Description	Units Sold	Unit Cost	Unit Profit	Total Sales	Total Profit	% Total Profit
A4T5	FTP Software	32435	92.95	19.75	=C3*(D3+E3)	=C3*E3	=G3/F3
C812	Game Software	16534	175.99	45.65	=C4*(D4+E4)	=C4*E4	=G4/F4
H4TT	Hard Disk	32102	110.6	62.5	=C5*(D5+E5)	=C5*E5	=G5/F5
K890	Monitor	34391	121.35	38.75	=C6*(D6+E6)	=C6*E6	=G6/F6
MM34	PDA	23910	200.23	95.15	=C7*(D7+E7)	=C7*E7	=G7/F7
NK34	Printer	45219	50.65	12.85	=C8*(D8+E8)	=C8*E8	=G8/F8
R567	Stereo Speakers	63213	34.2	14.35	=C9*(D9+E9)	=C9*E9	=G9/F9
SH67	System Unit	52109	43	12.75	=C10*(D10+E10)	=C10*E10	=G10/F10
Z345	Tax Software	76145	38.25	13	=C11*(D11+E11)	=C11*E11	=G11/F11
Totals		=SUM(C3:C11)			=SUM(F3:F11)	=SUM(G3:G11)	
Lowest		=MIN(C3:C11)	=MIN(D3:D11)	=MIN(E3:E11)	=MIN(F3:F11)	=MIN(G3:G11)	=MIN(H3:H11)
Highest		=MAX(C3:C11)	=MAX(D3:D11)	=MAX(E3:E11)	=MAX(F3:F11)	=MAX(G3:G11)	=MAX(H3:H11)
Average		=AVERAGE(C3:C11)	=AVERAGE(D3:D11)	=AVERAGE(E3:E11)	=AVERAGE(F3:F11)	=AVERAGE(G3:G11)	

FIGURE 2-87

In the Lab

1 Weekly Payroll Worksheet

Problem: Illiana Custom Homes has hired you as an intern in its software applications department. Because you took an Excel course last semester, the assistant manager has asked you to prepare a weekly payroll report for the six employees listed in Table 2-8.

Table 2-8 Illiana Custom Homes Weekly Payroll Data			
Employee	Rate	Hours	Dep.
Jedi, Hubert	24.90	40.00	3
Kaden, Hadef	33.50	38.75	5
Pancer, Dion	12.90	66.00	8
Rifken, Felix	29.75	27.25	3
Sanchez, Maria	21.35	45.00	5
Scarff, Heidi	17.85	39.75	1

Microsoft Excel - Lab 2-1 Illiana Custom Homes Weekly Payroll Report

File   Edit   View   Insert   Format   Tools   Data   Window   Help   Type a question for help

Arial   10   B   I   U   ≡ ≡ ≡ $ %   ,   *.0 .00 | A15

Illiana Custom Homes
Weekly Payroll Report

Employee	Rate	Hours	Dep.	Gross Pay	Fed. Tax	State Tax	Net Pay	% Taxes
Jedi, Hubert	$24.90	40.00	3	$ 996.00	$ 176.12	$ 31.87	$ 788.00	20.883%
Kaden, Hadef	33.50	38.75	5	1,298.13	221.17	41.54	1,035.42	20.237%
Pancer, Dion	12.90	66.00	8	851.40	108.74	27.24	715.41	15.972%
Rifken, Felix	29.75	27.25	3	810.69	139.06	25.94	645.68	20.354%
Sanchez, Maria	21.35	45.00	5	960.75	153.69	30.74	776.32	19.197%
Scarff, Heidi	17.85	39.75	1	709.54	134.22	22.71	552.62	22.116%
Totals		256.75		$5,626.50	$ 933.00	$ 180.05	$4,513.45	19.782%
Average	$23.38	42.79	4	$937.75	$155.50	$30.01	$752.24	
Highest	$33.50	66.00	8	$1,298.13	$221.17	$41.54	$1,035.42	22.116%
Lowest	$12.90	27.25	1	$709.54	$108.74	$22.71	$552.62	15.972%

Sheet1 Sheet2 Sheet3

Ready

start   Microsoft Excel - Lab ...   2:57 PM

FIGURE 2-88

Instructions Part 1: Perform the following tasks to create a worksheet similar to the one shown in Figure 2-88.

1. Enter the worksheet titles Illiana Custom Homes in cell A1 and Weekly Payroll Report in cell A2. Enter the column titles in row 3, the data in Table 2-8 in columns A through D, and the row titles in the range A10:A13.

In the Lab

2. Use the following formulas to determine the gross pay, federal tax, state tax, and net pay for the first employee:

   a. Gross Pay (cell E4) = Rate*Hours or =B4 * C4

   b. Fed. Tax (cell F4) = 20% * (Gross Pay – Dep. * 38.46) or =20% *(E4 – D4 * 38.46)

   c. State Tax (cell G4) = 3.2% * Gross Pay or =3.2% * E4

   d. Net Pay (cell H4) = Gross Pay – (Fed. Tax + State Tax) or =E4 – (F4 + G4)

   e. % Taxes (I4) = (Fed. Tax + State Tax) / Gross Pay or =(F4 + G4) / E4

   Copy the formulas for the first employee to the remaining employees.

3. Calculate totals for hours, gross pay, federal tax, state tax, net pay, and % taxes paid in row 10.

4. Use the appropriate functions to determine the average, highest, and lowest values of each column in rows 11 through 13. Delete the value in cell I11.

5. Use Range Finder to verify each of the formulas entered in row 4.

6. Select the range A1:A2 and change its background color to red. Change the worksheet title to 26-point Broadway white, bold font (or a font of your choice). Center the worksheet title across columns A through I. Vertically center the worksheet title. Format the worksheet subtitle in a similar fashion, except change its font size to 18. Assign the range A1:A2 a border (column 4, row 4 on the Borders palette). Assign the Comma style format with two decimal places to the ranges B5:H9 and C4:C13. Assign a Currency style format with a fixed dollar sign to the ranges B4, E4:H4, and E10:H10. Assign a Currency style format with a floating dollar sign to the ranges B11:B13 and E11:H13. Assign the Number style format with 0 decimals to the range D4:D13 and center the range. Assign a Percent style format with three decimal places to the range I4:I13. Bold, italicize, and assign a bottom border (column 2, row 1 on the Borders palette) to the range A3:I3. Align right the column titles in the range B3:I3. Bold and italicize the range A10:A13. Assign a top and thick bottom border (column 1, row 3 on the Borders palette) to the range A10:I10.

7. Change the width of column A to 18.00 characters. If necessary, change the widths of columns B through H to best fit. Change the heights of row 1 to 39.75 points and rows 2, 3, and 11 to 30.00 points.

8. Use the Conditional Formatting command on the Format menu to display white, bold font on a blue background for any rate in the range B4:B9 greater than $25.00.

9. Enter your name, course, laboratory assignment number (Lab 2-1), date, and instructor name in the range A15:A19.

10. Spell check the worksheet. Save the workbook using the file name Lab 2-1 Illiana Custom Homes Weekly Payroll Report. Preview and then print the worksheet.

11. Press CTRL+ACCENT MARK (`) to change the display from the values version to the formulas version. Print the formulas version of the worksheet in landscape orientation using the Fit to option in the Page sheet in the Page Setup dialog box. After the printer is finished, press CTRL+ACCENT MARK (`) to reset the worksheet to the values version. Reset the Scaling option to 100% by clicking the Adjust to option button in the Page sheet in the Page Setup dialog box and then setting the percent value to 100%. Hand in the printouts to your instructor.

Instructions Part 2:   Use the keyboard to increase manually the number of hours worked for each employee by 12 hours. The total net pay in cell H10 should equal $5,806.00. If necessary, increase the width of column F to best fit to view the new federal tax total. Preview and print the worksheet with the new values. Do not save the workbook. Hand in the printout to your instructor.

In the Lab

2 Accounts Receivable Balance Sheet

Problem: You are a spreadsheet specialist in the Accounting department of Fife's Finer Furniture, a popular Virginia Beach-based furniture company with several outlets in major cities across the United States. You have been asked to use Excel to generate a report (Figure 2-89) that summarizes the monthly accounts receivable balance. A graphic breakdown of the data also is desired. The customer accounts receivable data in Table 2-9 is available for test purposes.

Table 2-9	Fife's Finer Furniture Accounts Receivable Data				
Customer ID	Customer Name	Beginning Balance	Purchases	Payments	Credits
A421	Sri, Oranu	32548.30	3291.50	6923.00	785.25
H861	Agarwall, Bikash	9351.55	4435.10	5000.00	75.00
K190	Amigo, Julio	5909.50	750.30	2350.00	0.00
M918	Wang, Shiela	18761.60	5560.00	1875.00	905.25
P415	Davis, Jasmine	14098.20	1596.10	3250.00	236.45
R623	Smith, John	18433.60	200.20	1375.00	196.00
U111	Gupta, Arjun	13462.75	2026.00	750.00	25.00

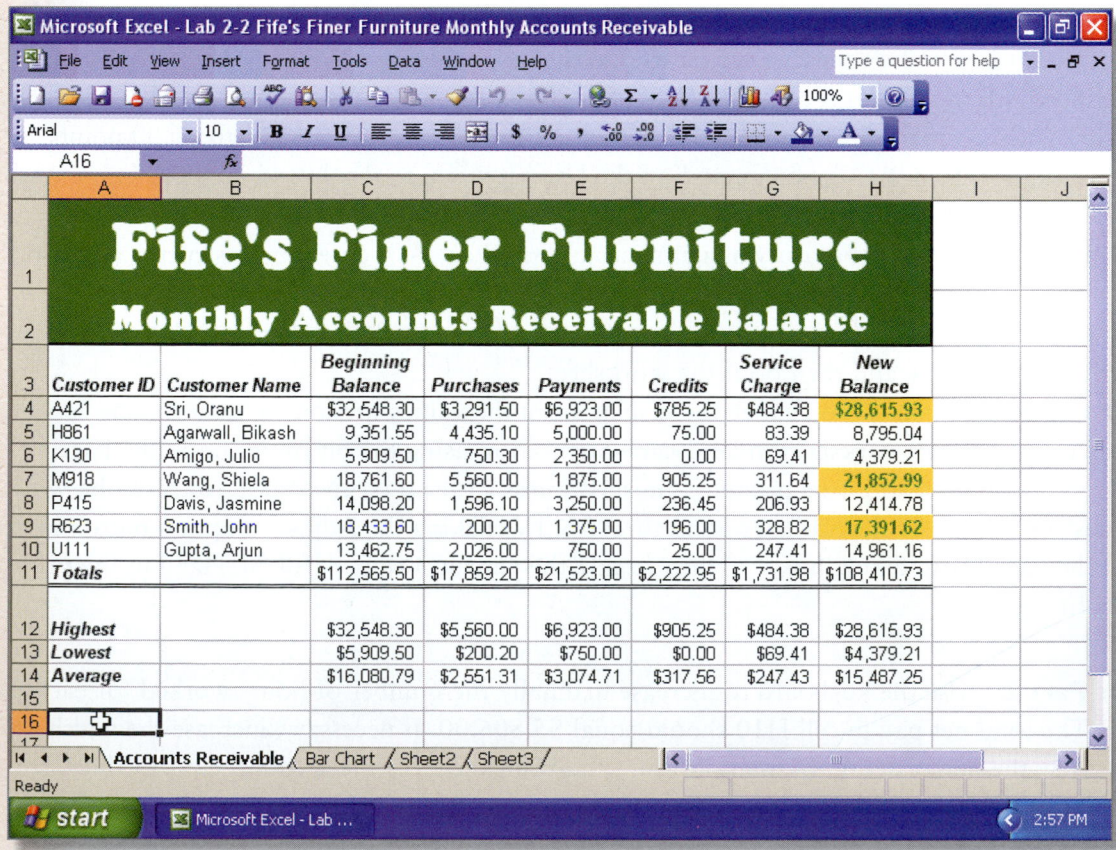

FIGURE 2-89

In the Lab

Instructions Part 1: Create a worksheet similar to the one shown in Figure 2-89. Include the six columns of customer data in Table 2-9 in the report, plus two additional columns to compute a service charge and a new balance for each customer. Assume no negative unpaid monthly balances. Perform the following tasks.

1. Enter and format the worksheet title, worksheet subtitle, column titles and row titles. Use a font type of your choice for the worksheet titles. The Cooper Black font is shown in Figure 2-89. Bold and italicize the column titles in row 3. Add a bottom border to the column titles in row 3. Center the column titles in the range B3:H3. Bold and italicize the titles in the range A11:A14. Add a top and double bottom border to the range A11:H11.

2. Enter the data in Table 2-9.

3. Use the following formulas to determine the service charge in column G and the new balance in column H for the first customer. Copy the two formulas down through the remaining customers.

   a. Service Charge (cell G4) = 1.95% * (Beginning Balance – Payments – Credits) or = 0.0195 * (C4 - E4 - F4)

   b. New Balance (H4) = Beginning Balance + Purchases – Payments – Credits + Service Charge or C4 + D4 - E4 - F4 + G4

4. Determine the totals in row 11.

5. Determine the maximum, minimum, and average values in cells C12:C14 for the range C4:C10 and then copy the range C12:C14 to D12:H14.

6. Change the width of column A to 11.00 characters. Change the widths of columns B through H to best fit. Change the heights of row 3 to 27.75 and row 12 to 30.00 points.

7. Assign the Currency style with a floating dollar sign to the cells containing numeric data in the ranges C4:H4 and C11:H14. Assign the Comma style (currency with no dollar sign) to the range C5:H10.

8. Use conditional formatting to change the formatting to green bold font on a yellow background in any cell in the range H4:H10 that contains a value greater than or equal to 15000.

9. Change the widths of columns C through H to best fit again, if necessary.

10. Change the worksheet name from Sheet1 to Accounts Receivable.

11. Enter your name, course, laboratory assignment number (Lab 2-2), date, and instructor name in the range A16:A20.

12. Spell check the worksheet. Preview and then print the worksheet in landscape orientation. Save the workbook using the file name Lab 2-2 Fife's Finer Furniture Monthly Accounts Receivable.

13. Print the range A3:D14. Print the formulas version on one page. Close the workbook without saving the changes. Hand in the three printouts to your instructor.

Instructions Part 2: This part requires that you use the Chart Wizard button on the Standard toolbar to draw a 3-D Bar chart. If necessary, use the Type a question for help box on the menu bar to obtain information on drawing a Bar chart on a separate sheet in the workbook.

With the Lab 2-2 Fife's Finer Furniture Monthly Accounts Receivable workbook open, draw the 3-D Bar chart showing each customer's total new balance as shown in Figure 2-90 on the next page. Use the CTRL key and mouse to select the nonadjacent chart ranges B4:B10 and H4:H10. The customer names in the range B4:B10 will identify the bars, while the data series in the range H4:H10 will determine the length of the bars. Click the Chart Wizard button on the Standard toolbar. When the Chart Wizard - Step 1 of 4 - Chart Type dialog box is displayed, select the Bar Chart type and Chart sub-type Clustered bar with a 3-D visual effect (column 1, row 2). Click the Next button twice to display the Chart Wizard - Step 3 of 4 - Chart Options dialog box. Add the chart title Accounts Receivable. Click the Next button and select As new sheet to draw the bar chart on a new worksheet.

(continued)

In the Lab

Accounts Receivable Balance Sheet (continued)

Change the worksheet name from Chart1 to Bar Chart. Drag the Accounts Receivable tab to the left of the Bar Chart tab to reorder the sheets in the workbook. Save the workbook using the same file name as in Part 1. Preview and print the chart. Hand in the printout to your instructor.

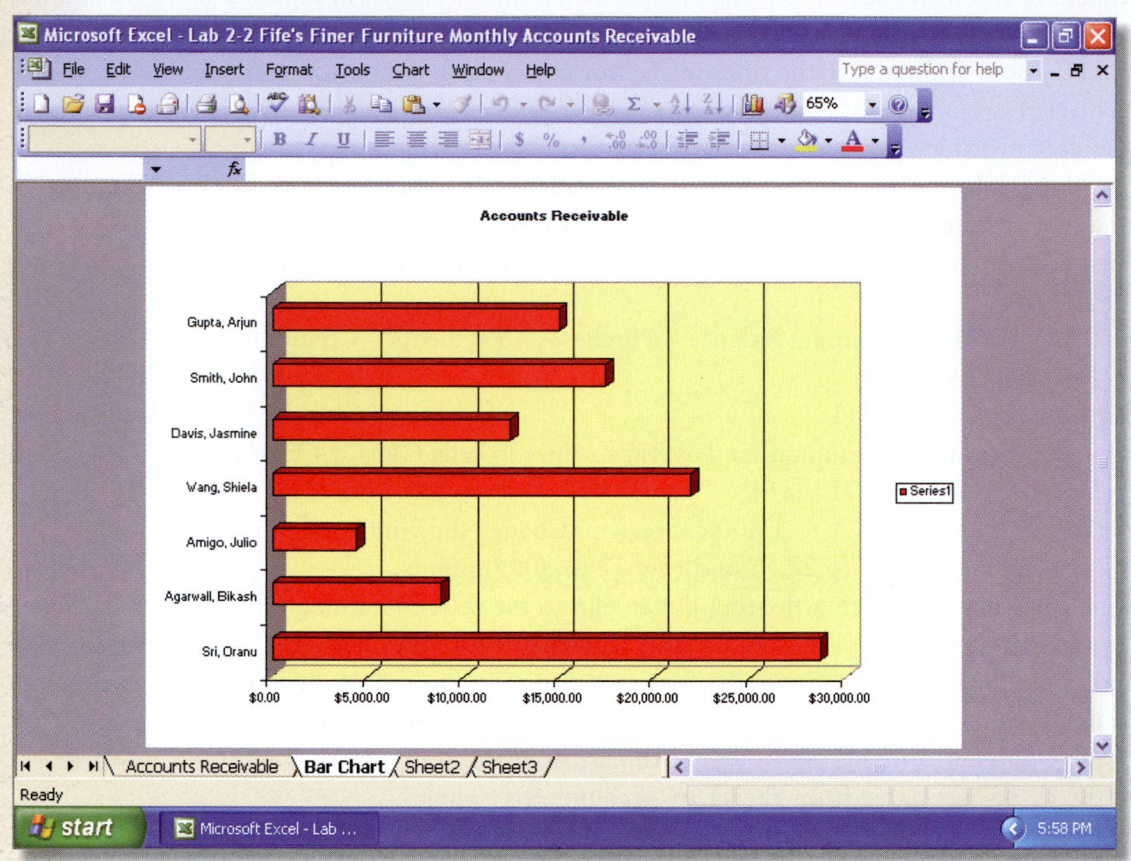

FIGURE 2-90

Instructions Part 3: With the Lab 2-2 Fife's Finer Furniture Monthly Accounts Receivable workbook open, click the Accounts Receivable tab. Change the following purchases: account number K190 to $6,500.00; account number R623 to $3,000.00. The total new balance in cell H11 should equal $116,960.23. Select both sheets by holding down the SHIFT key and then clicking the Bar Chart tab. Preview and print the selected sheets. Hand in the printouts to your instructor. Save the worksheet using the file name Lab 2-2 Fife's Finer Furniture Monthly Accounts Receivable 2.

Instructions Part 4: With your instructor's permission, e-mail the workbook created in this exercise with the changes indicated in Part 2 as an attachment to your instructor. Close the workbook without saving the changes.

3 Equity Web Queries

Problem: Esmeralda Dominga, president of Pro Cards, Inc., recently attended a Microsoft Office seminar at the local community college and learned that Excel can connect to the Web, download real-time stock data into

In the Lab

a worksheet, and then refresh the data as often as needed. Because you have had courses in Excel and the Internet, she has hired you as a consultant to develop a stock analysis workbook. Her portfolio is listed in Table 2-10.

Instructions Part 1: If necessary, connect to the Internet. Open a new Excel workbook and select cell A1. Perform a Web query to obtain multiple stock quotes (Figure 2-91), using the stock symbols in Table 2-10. Enter your name, course, laboratory assignment number (Lab 2-3a), date, and instructor

Table 2-10 Esmeralda Dominga's Stock Portfolio	
Company	Stock Symbol
International Business Machines	IBM
Oracle	ORCL
Johnson & Johnson	JNJ
Boeing	BA
Home Depot	HD
Citigroup	C

name in the range A22:A26. Rename the worksheet Multiple Quotes. Save the workbook using the file name Lab 2-3 Esmeralda Dominga Equities Online. Preview and then print the worksheet in landscape orientation using the Fit to option.

Click the following links and print the Web page that appears in the browser window: Click here to visit MSN Money; Oracle Corporation; Chart to the right of Home Depot, Inc., and News to the right of Citigroup Inc. Hand in the printouts to your instructor.

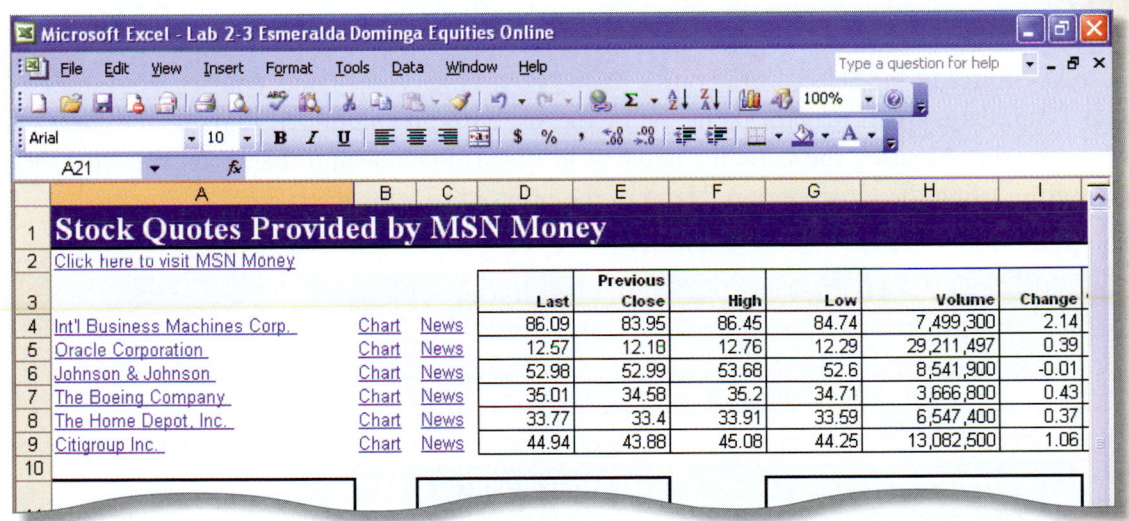

FIGURE 2-91

Instructions Part 2: Create a worksheet listing the major indices and their current values on Sheet 2 of the Lab 2-3 Esmeralda Dominga Equities Online workbook (Figure 2-92 on the next page). To create this worksheet, double-click MSN MoneyCentral Investor Major Indices in the Select Data Source dialog box. Enter your name, course, laboratory assignment number (Lab 2-3b), date, and instructor name below the last entry in column A. Rename the worksheet Major Indices. Save the workbook using the same file name as in Part 1. Preview and then print the worksheet in landscape orientation using the Fit to option. Hand in the printout to your instructor.

(continued)

Equity Web Queries (continued)

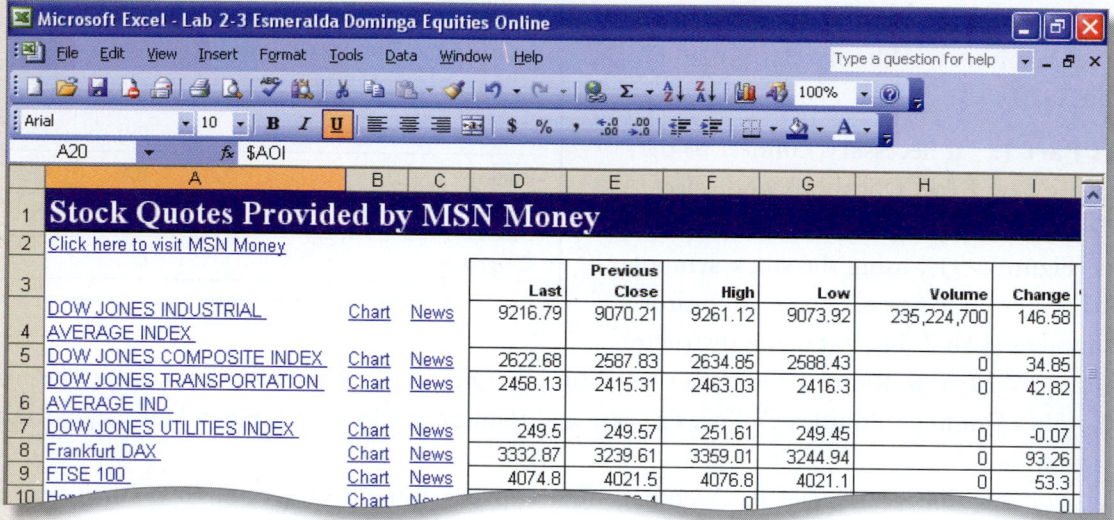

FIGURE 2-92

Instructions Part 3: Create a worksheet listing the latest currency rates on Sheet 3 of the Lab 2-3 Esmeralda Dominga Equities Online workbook (Figure 2-93). To create this worksheet, double-click MSN MoneyCentral Investor Currency Rates in the Select Data Source dialog box. Enter your name, course, laboratory assignment number (Lab 2-3c), date, and instructor name below the last entry in column A. Rename the sheet Currency Rates. Save the workbook using the same file name as in Part 1. Preview and then print the worksheet in portrait orientation using the Fit to option. Hand in the printout to your instructor.

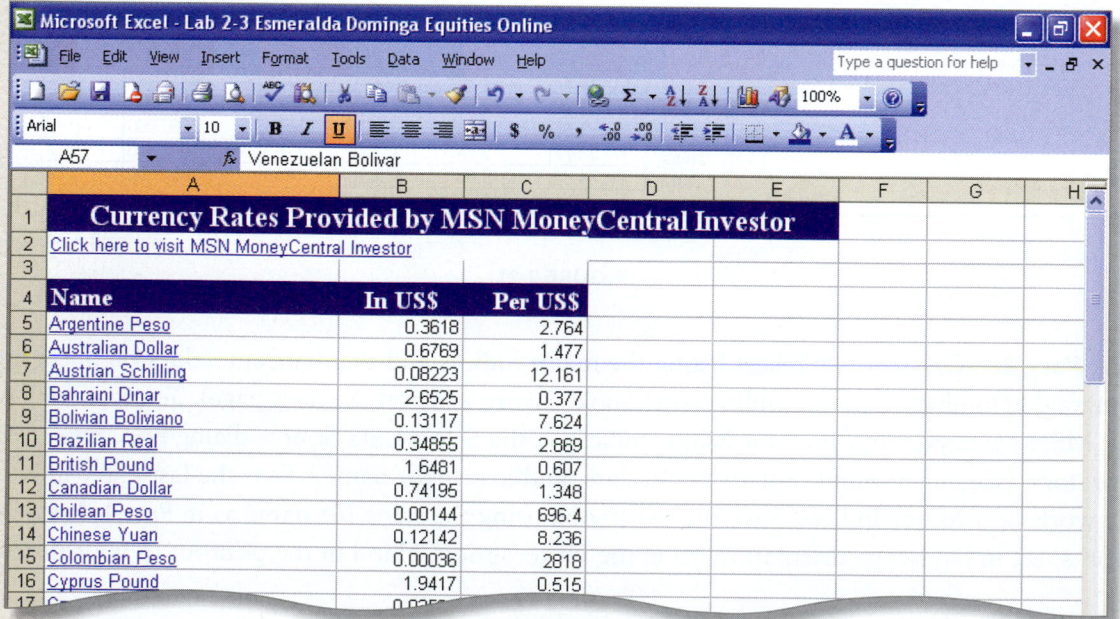

FIGURE 2-93

In the Lab

Instructions Part 4: Excel recognizes certain types of data in a cell, such as stock symbols. To indicate that it recognizes the data, Excel then inserts a smart tag indicator (a small purple triangle) in the lower-right corner of those cells. If you click the cell with the smart tag indicator, Excel displays the Smart Tag Actions button. If you click the Smart Tag Actions button arrow, Excel displays a menu (Figure 2-94) that can be used to gain instant access to information about the data. To ensure Excel options are set to label data with smart tags, click AutoCorrect Options on the Tools menu and then click the Smart Tags tab when the AutoCorrect dialog box appears. If necessary, select the three check boxes, Label data with smart tags, Smart tag lists (MSN MoneyCentral Financial Symbols), and Embed smart tags in this workbook.

With a new workbook opened, enter the column title, Stock Symbols, in cell A1 as shown in Figure 2-94. Enter the three stock symbols, JPM (J.P. Morgan Chase), MCD (McDonald's Corporation), and SBC (SBC Communications) in the range A2:A4. Save the workbook using the file name Lab 2-3 Smart Tags.

Click cell A4. When Excel displays the Smart Tag Actions button, click the arrow to display the Smart Tag Actions list (Figure 2-94). One at a time, click the first three commands below Financial Symbol: SBC. Print the Web pages that your browser displays when you click these three commands and then print the worksheet. Repeat these steps, clicking the first three commands in the Smart Tag Actions list for the stock symbols in cells A2 and A3. Hand in the printouts to your instructor.

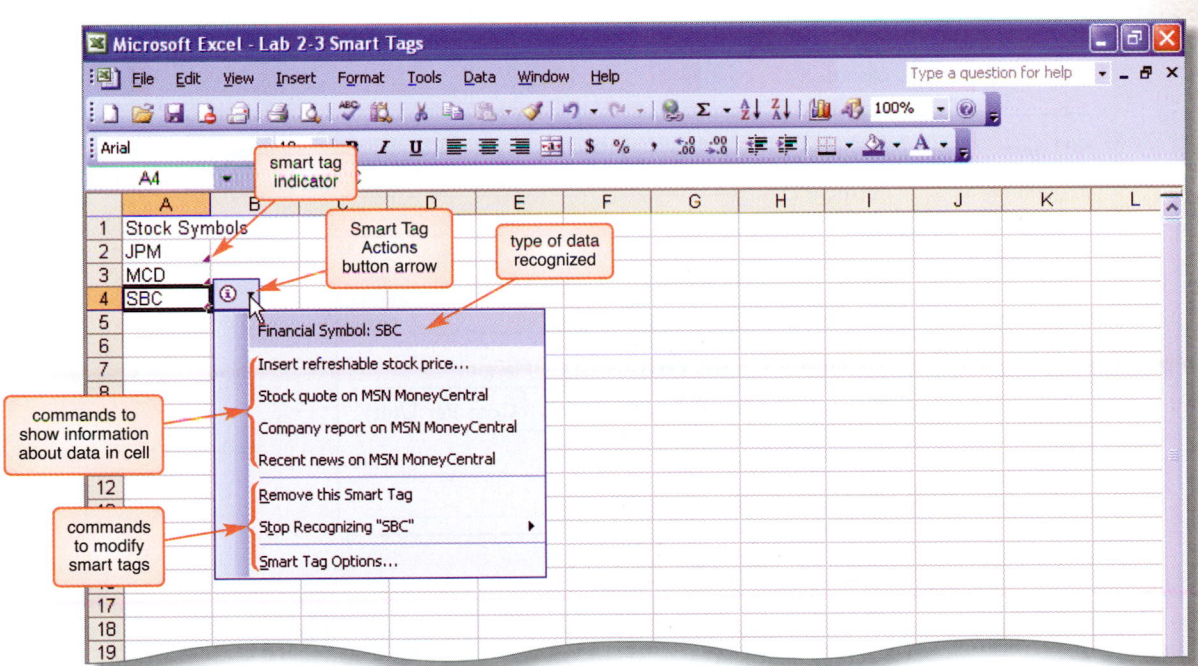

FIGURE 2-94

Cases and Places

The difficulty of these case studies varies:
■ are the least difficult and ■■ are more difficult. The last exercise is a group exercise.

1 ■ You are the cochairman of the fund-raising committee for the school's band. You want to compare various fund-raising ideas to determine which will give you the best profit. You obtain information from six businesses about their products (Table 2-11). Using the formulas in Table 2-12 and the general worksheet layout in Table 2-11, produce a worksheet to share the information with your committee. Use the concepts and techniques presented in this project to create and format the worksheet.

Table 2-11   Band Fund-Raising Data and Worksheet Layout

Company	Product	Cost Per Unit	Margin	Selling Price	Profit Per 3000 Sales
T&S	T-shirts	$2.50	60%	Formula A	Formula B
Aunt Mame's	Coffee	2.00	55%		
Wong Lo	Green Tea	1.75	65%		
Pen & Pencil	Pens	1.60	50%		
Gum-It	Gum	1.75	53%		
Dip-N-Donuts	Donuts	2.60	45%		
Minimum	Formula C				
Maximum	Formula D				

Table 2-12   Band Fund-Raising Formulas

Formula A = Cost Per Unit / (1 − Margin)

Formula B = 3000 * (Selling Price − Cost Per Unit)

Formula C = MIN function

Formula D = MAX function

Cases and Places

2 ■■ To determine the effectiveness of their endangered species recovery plan, the Fish and Wildlife Department traps and releases red wolves in selected sections of the state and records how many are pregnant. To obtain a representative sample, the department tries to trap and release approximately 20% of the population. The sample for eight sections is shown in Table 2-13. Use the following formula to determine the total red wolf population for each section:

Wolves in a Section = 5 * (Wolves Caught + Pregnant Wolves) – 5 * Death Rate * (Wolves Caught + Pregnant Wolves)

Use the concepts and techniques presented in this project to create the worksheet. Determine appropriate totals. Finally, estimate the total state red wolf population if 925 sections are in the state.

Table 2-13	Red Wolf Catch Data		
Section	Wolves Caught	Wolves Pregnant	Annual Death Rate
1	7	3	51%
2	8	6	67%
3	7	1	51%
4	6	4	61%
5	3	1	60%
6	4	2	54%
7	4	2	44%
8	4	1	53%

Cases and Places

3 ■■ You are a spreadsheet specialist consultant for Super Store Furniture. The owners of the store want to know the profit potential of their furniture inventory. The data and the format of the desired report are shown in Table 2-14. The required formulas are shown in Table 2-15.

Use the concepts and techniques developed in this project to create and format the worksheet and chart. Hand in a printout of the values version and formulas version of the worksheet. The company just received a shipment of 100 additional loveseats and 250 end tables. Update the appropriate cells in the Units on Hands column. The additional inventory yields a total profit potential of $3,878,742.96.

Table 2-14 Super Store Profit Potential Data and Worksheet Layout

Item	Units On Hand	Unit Cost	Total Cost	Average Unit Price	Total Value	Potential Profit
Rugs	983	$89.00	Formula A	Formula B	Formula C	Formula D
Sofas	1,980	678.00				
Loveseats	2,187	189.00				
End Tables	2,354	65.45				
Lamps	2,346	23.85				
Total	—		—		—	—
Average	Formula E					
Lowest	Formula F					
Highest	Formula G					

Table 2-15 Super Store Profit Potential Formulas

Formula A = Units on Hand * Unit Cost
Formula B = Unit Cost * (1 / (1 − .65))
Formula C = Units on Hand * Average Unit Price
Formula D = Total Value − Total Cost
Formula E = AVERAGE function
Formula F = MIN function
Formula G = MAX function

Cases and Places

4 ■■ LUV Steel Company pays a 3.25% commission to its salespeople to stimulate sales. The company also pays each employee a base salary. The management has projected each employee's sales for the next quarter. This information — employee name, employee base salary, and projected sales — is as follows: Meeks, Tyrone, $12,500.00, $542,413.00; Mandinka, Al-Jabbar, $10,250.00, $823,912.00; Silverstein, Aaron, $9,150.00, $362,750.00; Chronowski, John, $6,950.00, $622,165.00; Putin, Nikita, $9,500.00, $750,450.00.

With this data, you have been asked to develop a worksheet calculating the amount of commission and the projected quarterly salary for each employee. The following formulas can be used to obtain this information:

Commission Amount = 3.25% × Projected Sales

Quarterly Salary = Base Salary + Commission Amount

Include a total, average value, highest value, and lowest value for employee base salary, commission amount, and quarterly salary. Use the concepts and techniques presented in this project to create and format the worksheet.

Create a 3-D Pie chart on a separate sheet illustrating the portion each employee's quarterly salary contributes to the total quarterly salary. Use the Microsoft Excel Help system to create a professional looking 3-D Pie chart with title and data labels.

5 ■■ **Working Together** Have each member of your team select six stocks — two technology stocks, two bank stocks, and two retail stocks. Each member should submit the stock names, stock symbols, and an approximate 12-month-old price. Create a worksheet that lists the stock names, symbols, price, and number of shares for each stock (use 500 shares as number of shares for all stocks). Format the worksheet so that it has a professional appearance and is as informative as possible.

Have the group do research on the use of 3-D references, which is a reference to a range that spans two or more worksheets in a workbook (use Microsoft Excel Help). Use what the group learns to create a Web query on the Sheet2 worksheet by referencing the stock symbols on the Sheet1 worksheet. Change the cells that list current price per share numbers on the Sheet1 worksheet to use 3-D cell references that refer to the worksheet created by the Web query on the Sheet2 worksheet. Present your workbook and findings to the class.

What-If Analysis, Charting, and Working with Large Worksheets

PROJECT

3

CASE PERSPECTIVE

Aquatics Wear is a global provider of swimming accessories, including swimsuits, water exercise gear, swim caps, goggles, and water polo equipment. The Aquatics Wear sales force sells these products in bulk to large retail stores. The company also sells directly to customers via catalog sales and the Web.

Each June and December, the chief financial officer (CFO) of Aquatics Wear, Adriana Romaro, submits a plan to the board of directors to show projected monthly revenues, cost of goods sold, expenses, and operating income for the next six months.

Last December, Adriana used pencil, paper, and a calculator to complete the report and draw a Pie chart. When she presented her report, the directors asked for the effect on the projected operating income if the percentage of expenses allocated to the marketing department was changed. While the directors anxiously waited, Adriana calculated the answers by hand. Once she changed the percentage of expenses allocated to marketing, the Pie chart no longer matched the projections and thus was meaningless. Adriana now wants to use a computer and spreadsheet software to address what-if questions so she can take advantage of its instantaneous recalculation feature.

Adriana has asked you to assist her in preparing an easy-to-read worksheet that shows financial projections for the next six months (Figure 3-1a). In addition, she wants a 3-D Pie chart (Figure 3-1b) that shows the projected operating income contribution for each of the six months, because the directors prefer a graphical representation to numbers.

As you read through this project, you will learn how to create large worksheets, develop professional looking charts, and complete what-if analyses.

MICROSOFT
Office Excel 2003

What-If Analysis, Charting, and Working with Large Worksheets

Objectives

You will have mastered the material in this project when you can:

- Rotate text in a cell
- Create a series of month names
- Use the Format Painter button to format cells
- Copy, paste, insert, and delete cells
- Format numbers using format symbols
- Freeze and unfreeze titles
- Show and format the system date

- Use absolute cell references in a formula
- Use the IF function to perform a logical test
- Show and dock toolbars
- Create a 3-D Pie chart on a separate chart sheet
- Color and rearrange worksheet tabs
- Change the worksheet view
- Goal seek to answer what-if questions

Introduction

Worksheets normally are much larger than those created in the previous projects, often extending beyond the size of the window (Figure 3-1a). Because you cannot see the entire worksheet on the screen at one time, working with a large worksheet sometimes can be frustrating to work with. This project introduces several Excel commands that allow you to control what displays on the screen so you can view critical parts of a large worksheet at one time. One command lets you freeze the row and column titles so Excel always displays them on the screen. Another command splits the worksheet into separate window panes so you can view different parts of a worksheet on the screen at one time.

When you set up a worksheet, you should use as many cell references in formulas as possible, rather than constant values. The cell references in a formula are called assumptions. **Assumptions** are values in cells that you can change to determine new values for formulas. This project emphasizes the use of assumptions and shows how to use Excel to answer what-if questions such as, what happens to the six-month total operating income (cell H16 in Figure 3-1a) if you decrease the marketing expenses assumption (cell B22 in Figure 3-1a) by 2%? Being able to analyze quickly the effect of changing values in a worksheet is an important skill in making business decisions.

This project also introduces you to techniques that will enhance your ability to create worksheets and draw charts. From your work in Project 1, you are aware of how easily charts can be created. This project covers additional charting techniques that allow you to convey your message in a dramatic pictorial fashion (Figure 3-1b). This project also covers other methods for entering values in cells and formatting these values. In addition, you will learn how to use absolute cell references and how to use the IF function to assign a value to a cell based on a logical test.

In the previous projects, you learned how to use the Standard and Formatting toolbars. Excel has several other toolbars that can make your work easier. One such toolbar is the Drawing toolbar, which allows you to draw shapes and arrows and add drop shadows to cells you want to emphasize.

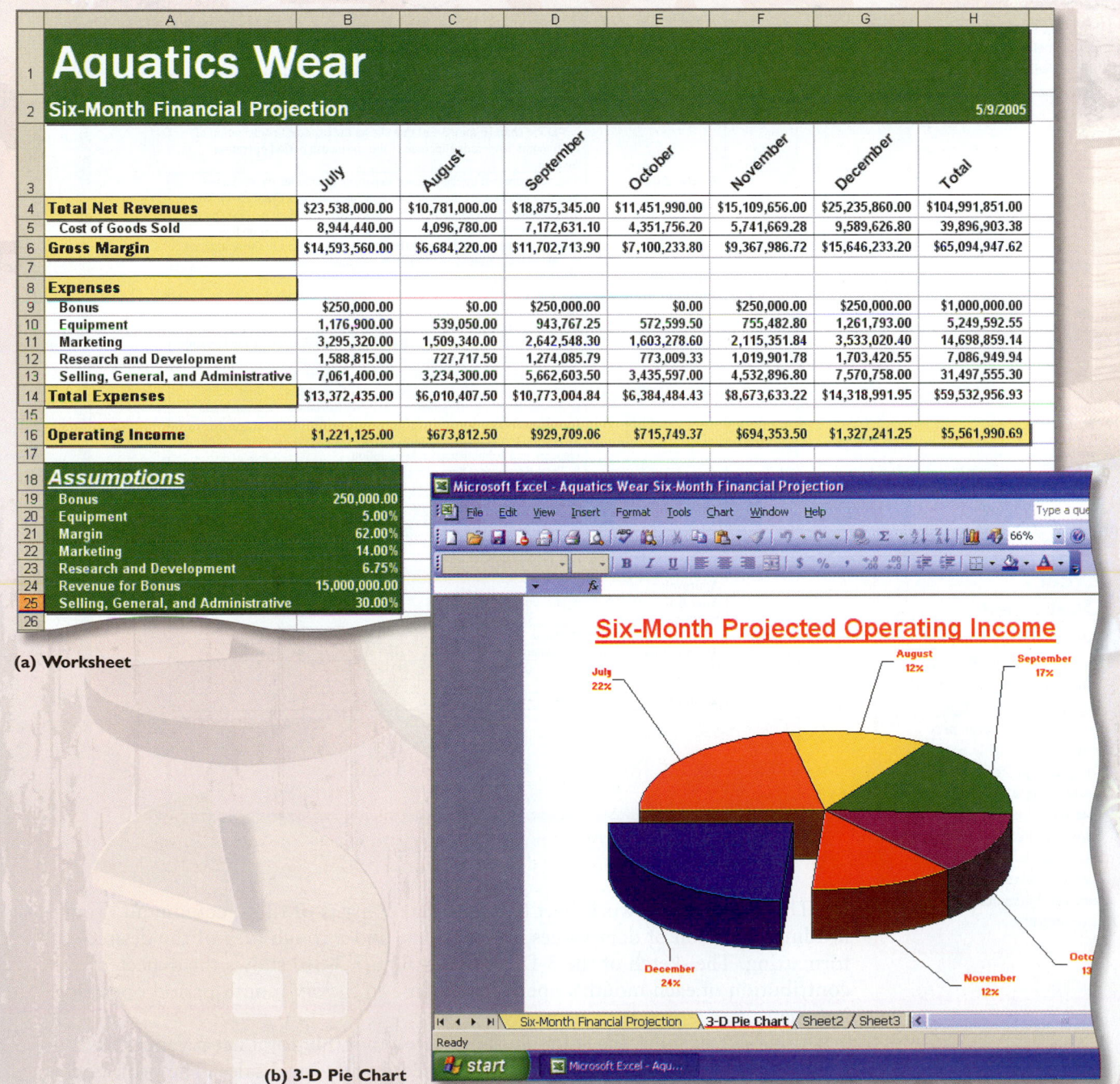

(a) Worksheet

(b) 3-D Pie Chart

FIGURE 3-1

More About

Correctness

Studies have shown that more than 25 percent of all business worksheets have errors. If you are not careful entering data and formulas, then your worksheet is prone to errors. You can ensure correctness in your formulas by carefully checking them using Range Finder and the Error Checking command on the Tools menu. The Formula Auditing command on the Tools menu also can be helpful when verifying formulas.

Project Three — Aquatics Wear Six-Month Financial Projection

The requirements document for the Aquatics Wear Six-Month Financial Projection worksheet is shown in Figure 3-2. It includes the needs, source of data, summary of calculations, chart requirements, and other facts about its development.

REQUEST FOR NEW WORKBOOK

Date Submitted:	May 2, 2005
Submitted By:	Adriana Romaro
Worksheet Title:	Aquatics Wear Six-Month Financial Projection
Needs:	The needs are: (1) a worksheet (Figure 3-3a) that shows Aquatics Wear's projected monthly total net revenues, cost of goods sold, gross margin, expenses, and operating income for a six-month period; and (2) a 3-D Pie chart (Figure 3-3b) that shows the expected contribution of each month's operating income to the six-month period operating income.
Source of Data:	The data supplied by the Finance department includes the projected monthly total net revenues and expense assumptions (Table 3-1). The six projected monthly total net revenues (row 4 of Figure 3-3a) and the seven assumptions at the bottom of Figure 3-3a are based on the company's historical data. All the remaining numbers in the worksheet are determined from these 13 numbers using formulas.
Calculations:	The following calculations must be made for each month: 1. Cost of Goods Sold = Total Net Revenues - Total Net Revenues * Margin 2. Gross Margin = Total Net Revenues - Cost of Goods Sold 3. Bonus = $250,000.00 if the Total Net Revenues exceeds the Revenue for Bonus; otherwise, Bonus = 0 4. Equipment = Total Net Revenues × Equipment Assumption 5. Marketing = Total Net Revenues × Marketing Assumption 6. Research and Development = Total Net Revenues × Research and Development Assumption 7. Selling, General, and Administrative = Total Net Revenues × Selling, General, and Administrative Assumption 8. Total Expenses = Sum of Expenses 9. Operating Income = Gross Margin - Total Expenses
Chart Requirements:	A 3-D Pie chart is required on a separate sheet (Figure 3-3b) to show the contribution of each month's operating income to the six-month period operating income. The chart also should emphasize the month with the greatest operating income.

Approvals

Approval Status:	X	Approved
		Rejected
Approved By:		Adriana Romaro
Date:		May 3, 2005
Assigned To:		J. Quasney, Spreadsheet Specialist

FIGURE 3-2

More About

Excel's Usefulness

Just a few short years ago, a what-if question of any complexity only could be answered using a large, expensive computer programmed by highly paid computer professionals. Generating a result could take days. Excel gives the noncomputer professional the ability to get complex business-related questions answered instantaneously and economically.

The sketch of the worksheet (Figure 3-3a) consists of titles, column and row headings, location of data values, calculations, and a rough idea of the desired formatting. The sketch of the 3-D Pie chart (Figure 3-3b) shows the expected contribution of each month's operating income to the six-month period operating income.

Table 3-1 includes the company's projected monthly total net revenues and expense assumptions for the six months based on historical sales. The projected monthly total net revenues will be entered in row 4 of the worksheet. The

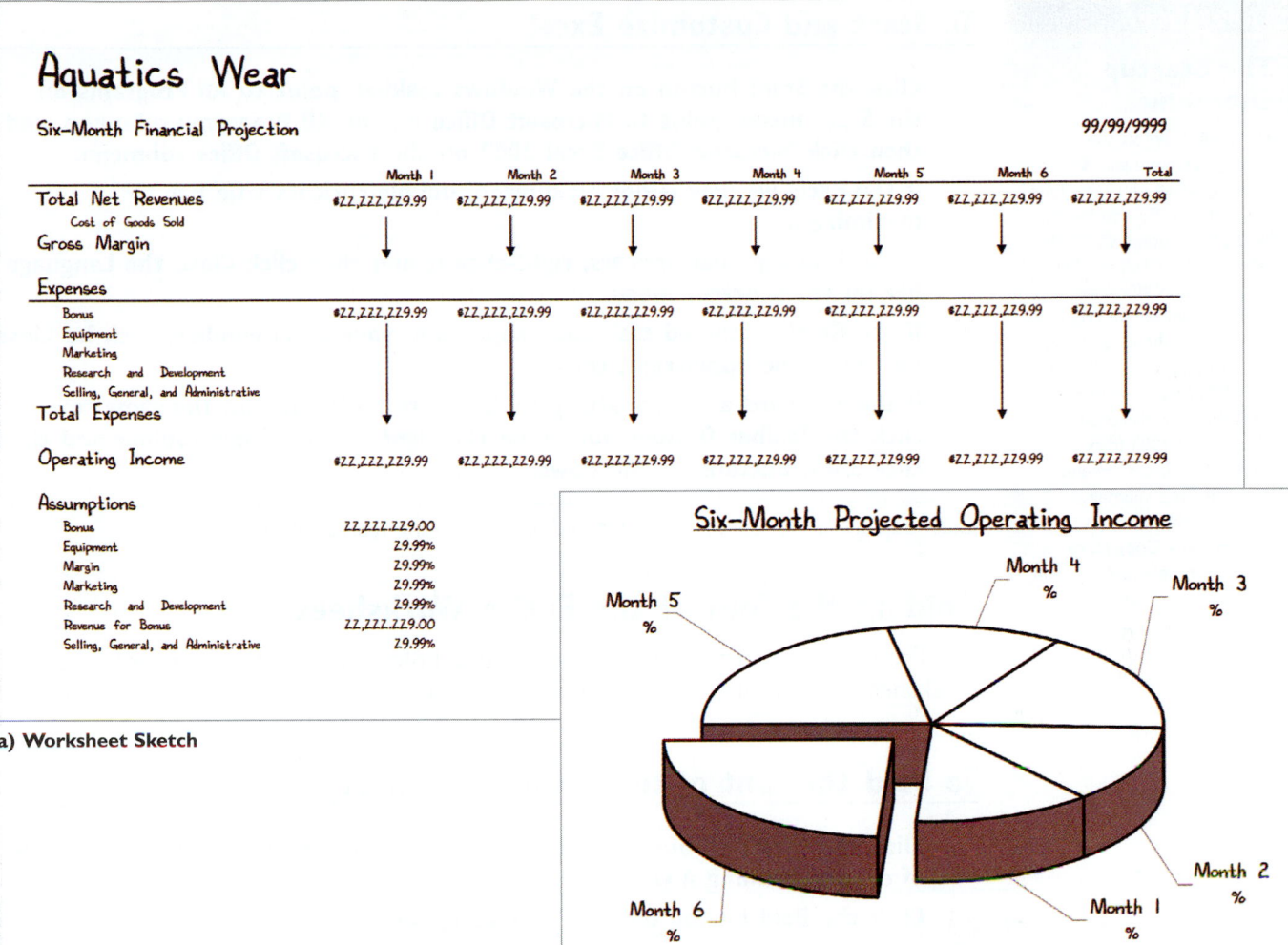

(a) Worksheet Sketch

(b) 3-D Pie Chart Sketch

FIGURE 3-3

assumptions will be entered in the range A18:B25 below the operating income (Figure 3-3a). The projected monthly total revenues and the assumptions will be used to calculate the remaining numbers in the worksheet.

Starting and Customizing Excel

With the requirements document and sketch of the worksheet and chart complete, the next step is to start and customize Excel. If you are stepping through this project on a computer and you want your screen to agree with the figures in this book, then you should change your computer's resolution to 800 × 600. For information on changing the resolution on your computer, see Appendix B. The steps on the next page start Excel and customize the Excel window.

Table 3-1 Aquatics Wear Six-Month Financial Projections Data and Assumptions	
PROJECTED MONTHLY TOTAL NET REVENUES	
July	$23,538,000
August	10,781,000
September	18,875,345
October	11,451,990
November	15,109,656
December	25,235,860
ASSUMPTIONS	
Bonus	$250,000.00
Equipment	5.00%
Margin	62.00%
Marketing	14.00%
Research and Development	6.75%
Revenue for Bonus	$15,000,000.00
Selling, General, and Administrative	30.00%

More About

The Startup Submenu

Any application on the Startup submenu starts automatically when you turn your computer on. To add Excel to the Startup submenu, do the following: (1) Click the Start button on the Windows taskbar, point to All Programs on the Start menu, and then point to Microsoft Office on the All Programs submenu; (2) Right-drag Microsoft Office Excel 2003 from the Microsoft Office submenu to the Startup submenu; (3) When the shortcut menu appears, click Copy Here. The next time you turn your computer on, Excel will start automatically.

To Start and Customize Excel

1. Click the Start button on the Windows taskbar, point to All Programs on the Start menu, point to Microsoft Office on the All Programs submenu, and then click Microsoft Office Excel 2003 on the Microsoft Office submenu.

2. If the Excel window is not maximized, double-click its title bar to maximize it.

3. If the Language bar appears, right-click it and then click Close the Language bar on the shortcut menu.

4. If the Getting Started task pane appears in your Excel window, click its Close button in the upper-right corner.

5. If the Standard and Formatting toolbars are positioned on the same row, click the Toolbar Options button on the right side of either toolbar and then click Show Buttons on Two Rows.

Excel displays its window with the Standard and Formatting toolbars on two rows.

Bolding the Font of the Entire Worksheet

The following steps show how to assign a bold format to the font for the entire worksheet so that all entries will be emphasized.

To Bold the Font of the Entire Worksheet

1. Click the Select All button immediately above row heading 1 and to the left of column heading A (Figure 3-4).

2. Click the Bold button on the Formatting toolbar.

No immediate change takes place on the screen. As you enter text and numbers into the worksheet, however, Excel will display them in bold.

Entering the Worksheet Titles and Saving the Workbook

The worksheet contains two titles, one in cell A1 and another in cell A2. In the previous projects, titles were centered across the worksheet. With large worksheets that extend beyond the size of a window, it is best to enter titles in the upper-left corner as shown in the sketch of the worksheet in Figure 3-3a on the previous page. The following steps enter the worksheet titles and save the workbook.

Q&A

Q: What are three alternatives to bolding to make it easier for users to read a worksheet on the screen?

A: Select easy-to-read font styles, increase the font size, or increase the percentage in the Zoom box. The latter is particularly useful if users have less-than-average eyesight.

To Enter the Worksheet Titles and Save the Workbook

1. Click cell A1 and then enter Aquatics Wear as the worksheet title.

2. Click cell A2 and then enter Six-Month Financial Projection as the worksheet subtitle.

3. With a floppy disk in drive A, click the Save button on the Standard toolbar.

4 **When Excel displays the Save As dialog box, type** `Aquatics Wear Six-Month Financial Projection` **in the File name text box.**

5 **If necessary, click 3½ Floppy (A:) in the Save in list. Click the Save button in the Save As dialog box.**

Excel responds by displaying the worksheet titles in cells A1 and A2 in bold as shown in Figure 3-4. Excel saves the workbook on the floppy disk in drive A using the file name Aquatics Wear Six-Month Financial Projection.

More About

Rotating Text in a Cell

In Excel, you use the Alignment sheet of the Format Cells dialog box, as shown in Figure 3-5 on the next page, to position data in a cell by centering, left-aligning, or right-aligning; indenting; aligning at the top, bottom, or center; and rotating. If you enter 90 in the Degrees box in the Orientation area, the text will appear vertically and read from bottom to top in the cell.

Rotating Text and Using the Fill Handle to Create a Series

When you first enter text, its angle is zero degrees (0°), and it reads from left to right in a cell. Text in a cell can be rotated counterclockwise by entering a number between 1° and 90° on the Alignment sheet in the Format Cells dialog box.

Projects 1 and 2 used the fill handle to copy a cell or a range of cells to adjacent cells. The fill handle also can be used to create a series of numbers, dates, or month names automatically. The following steps illustrate how to enter the month name, July, in cell B3; format cell B3 (including rotating the text); and then use the fill handle to enter the remaining month names in the range C3:G3.

To Rotate Text and Use the Fill Handle to Create a Series of Month Names

1

- **Select cell B3.**
- **Type** `July` **as the cell entry and then click the Enter box.**
- **Click the Font Size box arrow on the Formatting toolbar and then click 11 in the Font Size list.**
- **Click the Borders button arrow on the Formatting toolbar and then click the Bottom Border button (column 2, row 1) on the Borders palette.**
- **Right-click cell B3.**

Excel displays the text, July, in cell B3 using the assigned formats and it displays the shortcut menu (Figure 3-4).

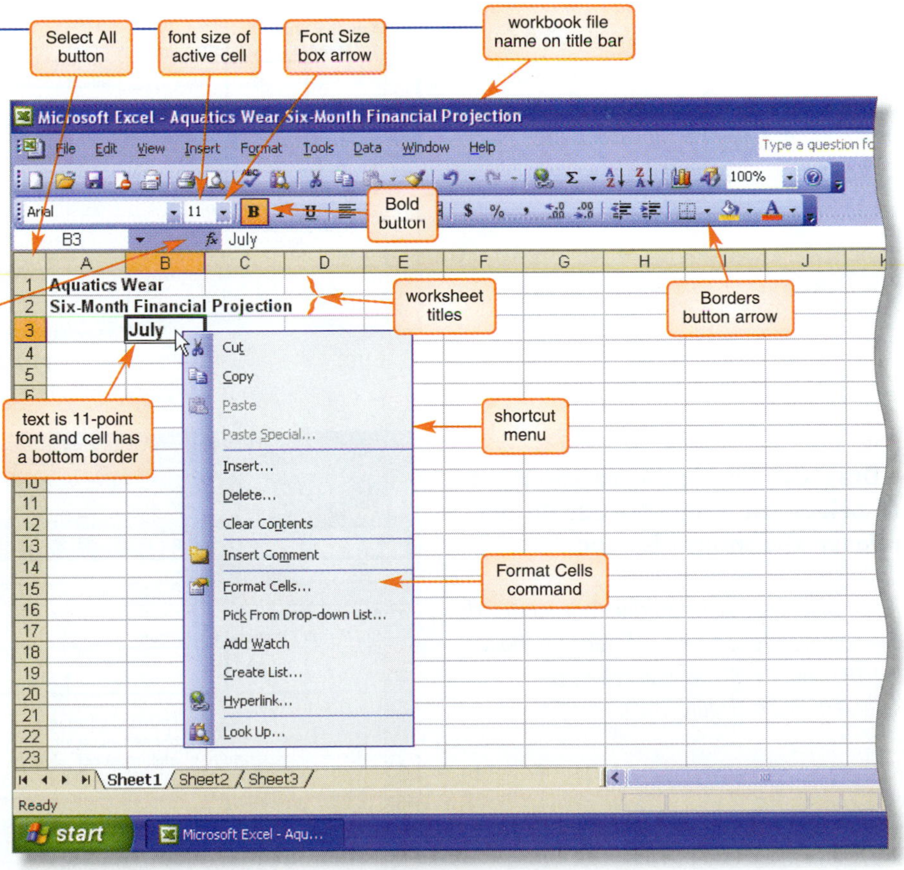

FIGURE 3-4

2

• **Click Format Cells on the shortcut menu.**

• **When the Format Cells dialog box is displayed, click the Alignment tab.**

• **Click the 45° point in the Orientation area.**

Excel displays the Alignment sheet in the Format Cells dialog box. The Text hand in the Orientation area points to the 45° point and 45 appears in the Degrees box (Figure 3-5).

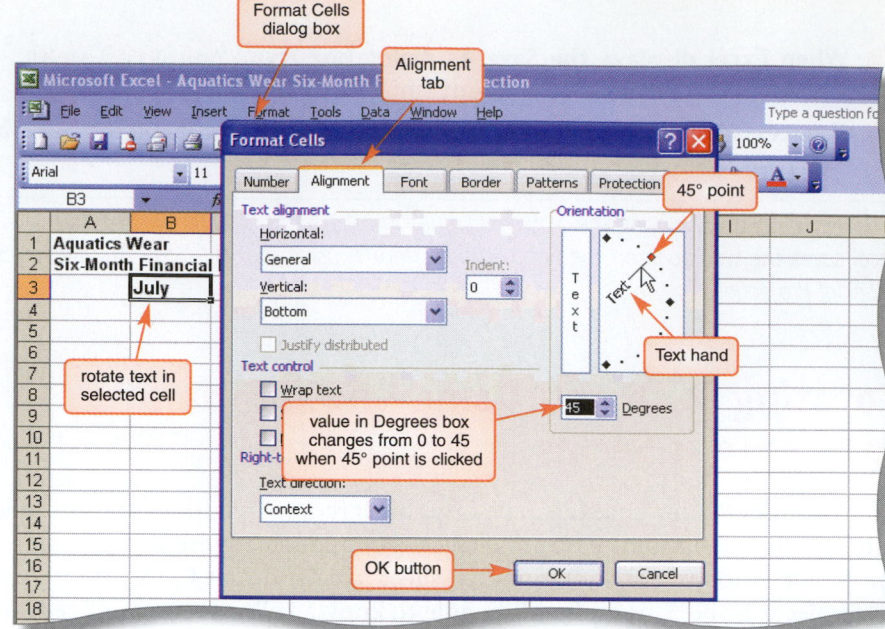

FIGURE 3-5

3

• **Click the OK button.**

• **Point to the fill handle on the lower-right corner of cell B3.**

Excel displays the text, July, in cell B3 at a 45° angle and automatically increases the height of row 3 to best fit the rotated text (Figure 3-6). The mouse pointer changes to a crosshair.

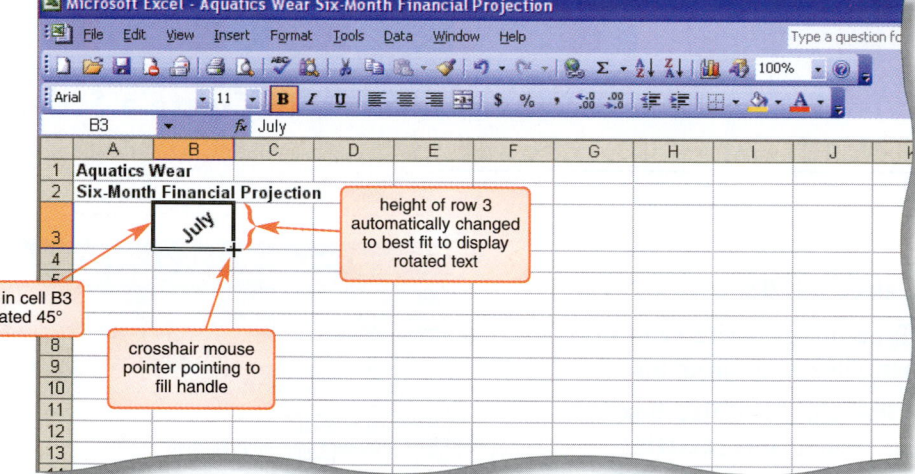

FIGURE 3-6

4

• **Drag the fill handle to the right to select the range C3:G3. Do not release the mouse button.**

Excel displays a light border that surrounds the selected range and a ScreenTip indicating the month of the last cell in the selected range (Figure 3-7).

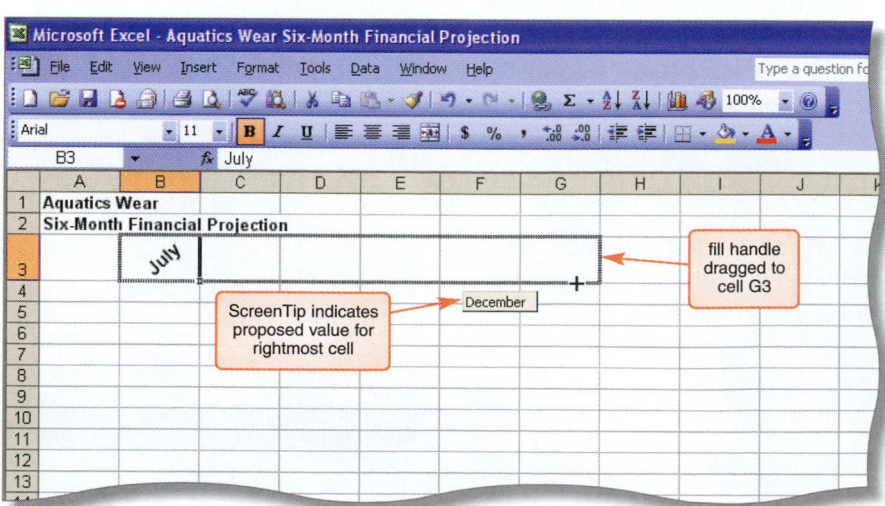

FIGURE 3-7

5

• **Release the mouse button.**

• **Click the Auto Fill Options button below the lower-right corner of the fill area.**

Using July in cell B3 as the basis, Excel creates the month name series August through December in the range C3:G3 (Figure 3-8). The formats assigned to cell B3 earlier in the previous steps (11-point font, bottom border, and text rotated 45°) also are copied to the range C3:G3. The Auto Fill Options menu shows the available fill options.

6

• **Click the Auto Fill Options button to hide the Auto Fill Options menu.**

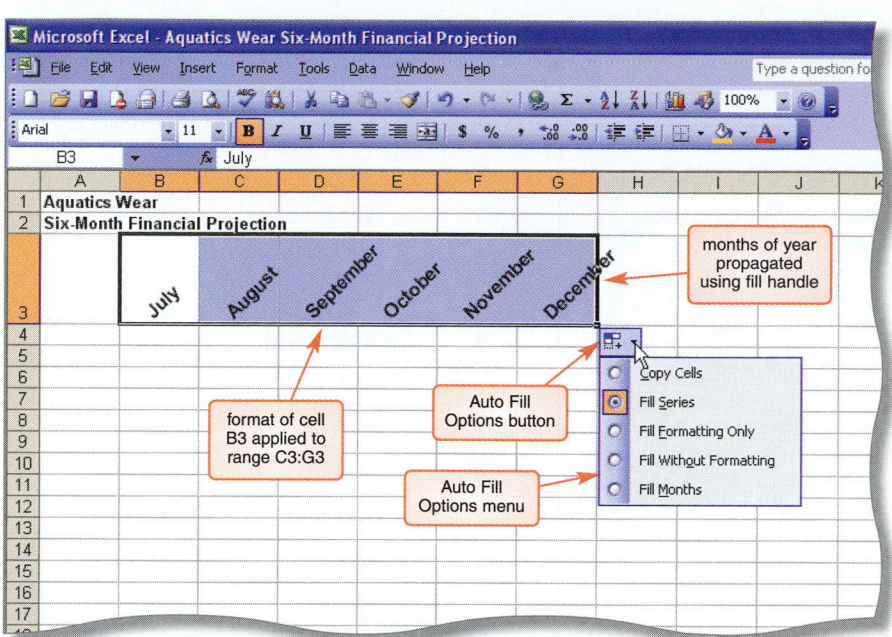

FIGURE 3-8

Other Ways

1. Enter start month in cell, right-drag fill handle in direction to fill, click Fill Months on shortcut menu
2. Select range to fill, in Voice Command mode, say "Edit, Fill, Series, AutoFill"

In addition to creating a series of values, dragging the fill handle instructs Excel to copy the format of cell B3 to the range C3:G3. With some fill operations, you may not want to copy the formats of the source cell or range to the destination cell or range. If this is the case, click the Auto Fill Options button after the range fills (Figure 3-8) and then select the option you desire on the Auto Fill Options menu. As shown in Figure 3-8, Fill Series is the default option that Excel uses to fill the area, which means it fills the destination area with a series, using the same formatting as the source area. If you choose another option on the Auto Fill Options menu, then Excel immediately changes the contents of the destination range. Following the use of the fill handle, the Auto Fill Options button remains active until you begin the next Excel operation. Table 3-2 summarizes the options on the Auto Fill Options menu.

You can use the fill handle to create a series longer than the one shown in Figure 3-8. If you drag the fill handle past cell G3 in Step 4, Excel continues to increment the months and logically will repeat July, August, and so on, if you extend the range far enough to the right.

You can create several different types of series using the fill handle. Table 3-3 on the next page illustrates several examples. Notice in examples 4 through 7 that, if you use the fill handle to create a series of numbers or non-sequential months, you must enter the first item in the series in one cell and the second item in the series in an adjacent cell. Next, select both cells and drag the fill handle through the destination area.

Table 3-2 Options Available on the Auto Fill Options Menu	
AUTO FILL OPTION	**DESCRIPTION**
Copy Cells	Fill destination area with contents using format of source area. Do not create a series.
Fill Series	Fill destination area with series using format of source area. This option is the default.
Fill Formatting Only	Fill destination area using format of source area. No content is copied unless fill is series.
Fill Without Formatting	Fill destination area with contents, without the formatting of source area.
Fill Months	Fill destination area with series of months using format of source area. Same as Fill Series and shows as an option only if source area contains a month.

More About

The Mighty Fill Handle

If you drag the fill handle to the left or up, Excel will decrement the series rather than increment the series. To copy a word, such as January or Monday, which Excel might interpret as the start of a series, hold down the CTRL key while you drag the fill handle to a destination area. If you drag the fill handle back into the middle of a cell, Excel erases the contents.

Table 3-3	Examples of Series Using the Fill Handle	
EXAMPLE	CONTENTS OF CELL(S) COPIED USING THE FILL HANDLE	NEXT THREE VALUES OF EXTENDED SERIES
1	2:00	3:00, 4:00, 5:00
2	Qtr3	Qtr4, Qtr1, Qtr2
3	Quarter 1	Quarter 2, Quarter 3, Quarter 4
4	5-Jan, 5-Mar	5-May, 5-Jul, 5-Sep
5	2005, 2006	2007, 2008, 2009
6	1, 2	3, 4, 5
7	430, 410	390, 370, 350
8	Sun	Mon, Tue, Wed
9	Sunday, Tuesday	Thursday, Saturday, Monday
10	4th Section	5th Section, 6th Section, 7th Section
11	-205, -208	-211, -214, -217

More About

Painting a Format to Nonadjacent Ranges

Double-click the Format Painter button on the Standard toolbar and then drag through the nonadjacent ranges to paint the formats to the ranges. Click the Format Painter button to deactivate it.

Copying a Cell's Format Using the Format Painter Button

Because the last column title, Total, is not part of the series, it must be entered separately in cell H3 and formatted to match the other column titles. Imagine how many steps it would take, however, to assign the formatting of the other column titles to this cell — first, you have to change the font to 11 point, and then add a bottom border, and finally, rotate the text 45°. Using the Format Painter button on the Standard toolbar, however, you can format a cell quickly by copying a cell's format to another cell. The following steps enter the column title, Total, in cell H3 and format the cell using the Format Painter button.

To Copy a Cell's Format Using the Format Painter Button

 1

• **Click cell H3.**

• **Type** Total **and then press the LEFT ARROW key.**

• **With cell G3 selected, click the Format Painter button on the Standard toolbar.**

• **Point to cell H3.**

The mouse pointer changes to a block plus sign with a paint brush (Figure 3-9).

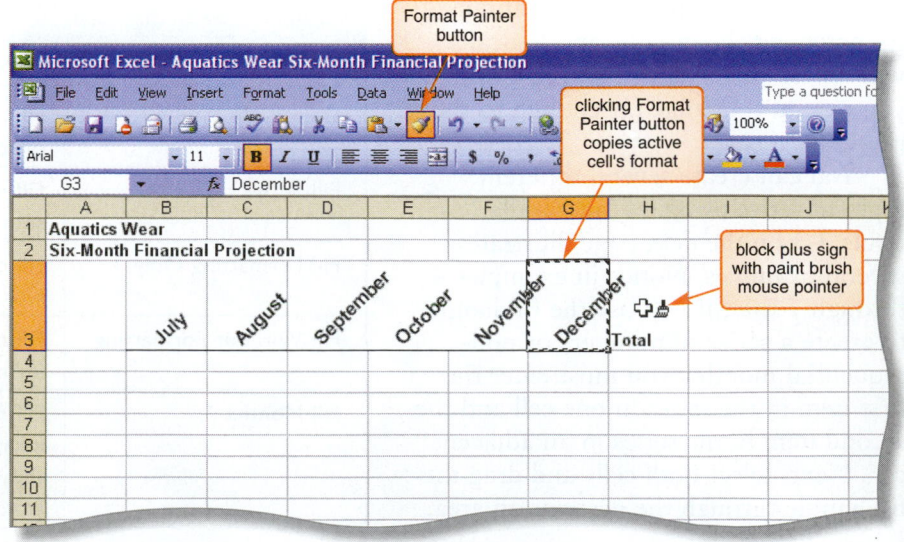

FIGURE 3-9

2

• **Click cell H3 to assign the format of cell G3 to cell H3.**

• **Click cell A4.**

Excel copies the format of cell G3 (11-point font, bottom border, text rotated 45°) to cell H3 (Figure 3-10). Cell A4 is now the active cell.

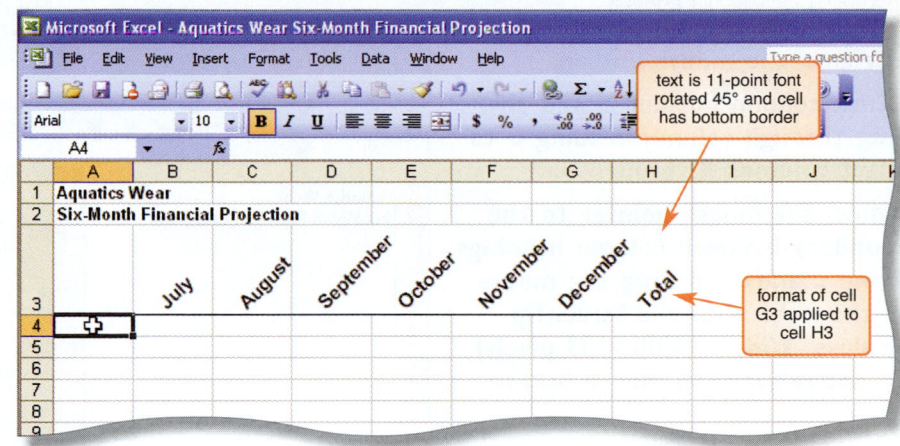

FIGURE 3-10

The Format Painter button also can be used to copy the formats of a cell to a range of cells. To copy formats to a range of cells, select the cell or range with the desired format, click the Format Painter button on the Standard toolbar, and then drag through the range to which you want to paste the formats.

Increasing the Column Widths and Indenting Row Titles

In Project 2, the column widths were increased after the values were entered into the worksheet. Sometimes, you may want to increase the column widths before you enter the values and, if necessary, adjust them later. The following steps increase the column widths and then enter the row titles in column A down to Assumptions in cell A18.

To Increase Column Widths and Enter Row Titles

1

• **Move the mouse pointer to the boundary between column heading A and column heading B so that the mouse pointer changes to a split double arrow.**

• **Drag the mouse pointer to the right until the ScreenTip displays, Width: 35.00 (250 pixels). Do not release the mouse button.**

The distance between the left edge of column A and the vertical dotted line below the mouse pointer shows the proposed column width (Figure 3-11). The ScreenTip displays the proposed width in points and pixels.

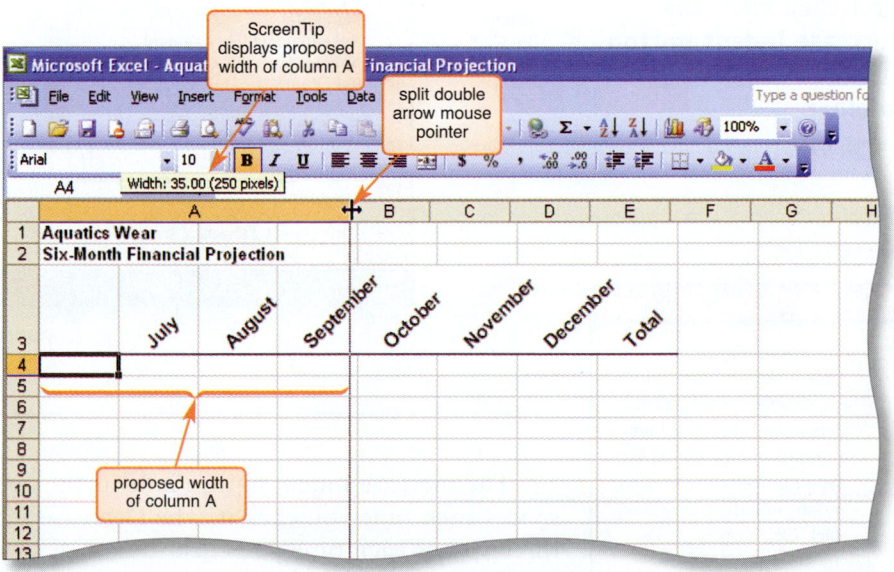

FIGURE 3-11

2

• **Release the mouse button.**

• **Click column heading B and then drag through column heading G to select columns B through G.**

• **Move the mouse pointer to the boundary between column headings B and C and then drag the mouse to the right until the ScreenTip displays, Width: 14.00 (103 pixels). Do not release the mouse button.**

The distance between the left edge of column B and the vertical line below the mouse pointer shows the proposed width of columns B through G (Figure 3-12). The ScreenTip displays the proposed width in points and pixels.

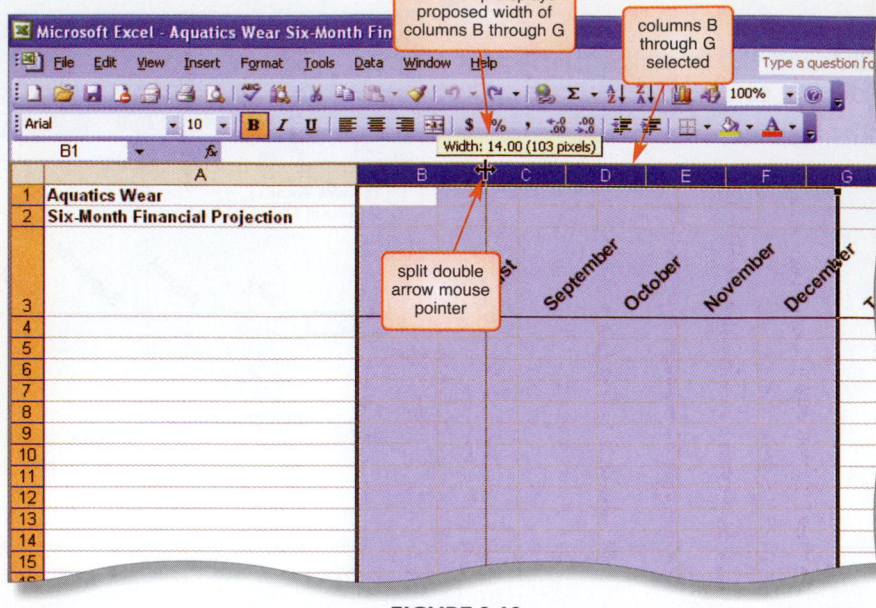

FIGURE 3-12

3

• **Release the mouse button.**

• **Use the technique described in Step 1 to increase the width of column H to 15.00.**

• **Enter the row titles in the range A4:A18 as shown in Figure 3-13, but without the indents.**

• **Click cell A5 and then click the Increase Indent button on the Formatting toolbar.**

• **Select the range A9:A13 and then click the Increase Indent button on the Formatting toolbar.**

• **Click cell A19.**

Excel displays the row titles as shown in Figure 3-13.

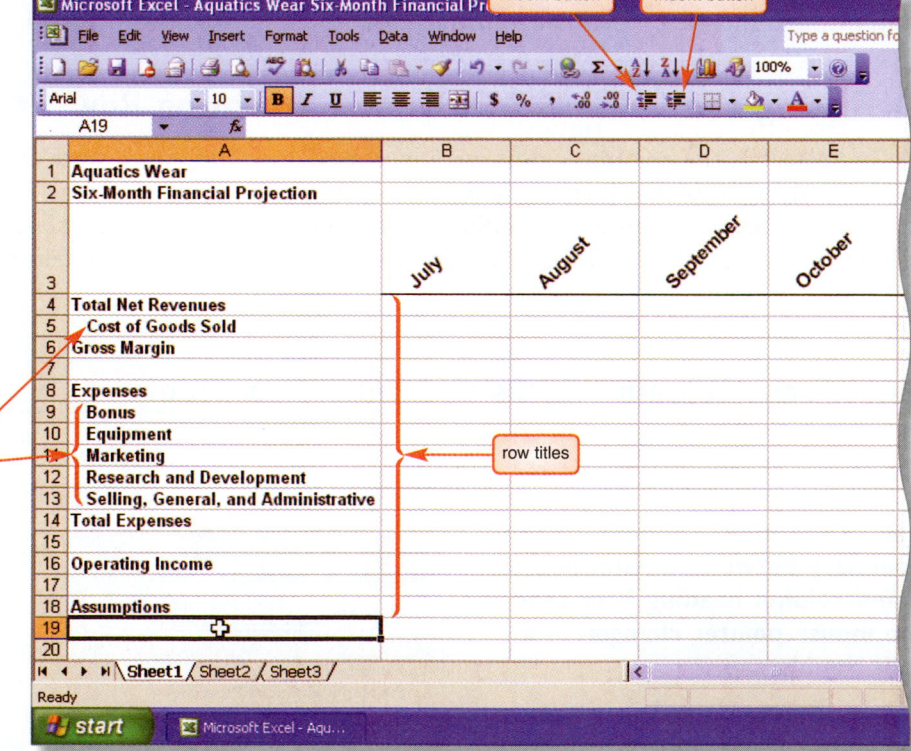

FIGURE 3-13

Other Ways

1. To indent, right-click range, click Format cells on shortcut menu, click Alignment tab, click Left (Indent) in Horizontal list, type number of spaces to indent in Indent text box, click OK button

2. To indent, in Voice Command mode, say "Increase Indent"

The Increase Indent button indents the contents of a cell to the right by three spaces each time you click it. The Decrease Indent button decreases the indent by three spaces each time you click it.

Copying a Range of Cells to a Nonadjacent Destination Area

As shown in the sketch of the worksheet (Figure 3-3a on page EX 149), the row titles in the range A9:A13 are the same as the row titles in the Assumptions table in the range A19:A25, with the exception of the two additional entries in cells A21 (Margin) and A24 (Revenue for Bonus). Hence, the Assumptions table row titles can be created by copying the range A9:A13 to the range A19:A23 and then inserting two rows for the additional entries in cells A21 and A24. The source area (range A9:A13) is not adjacent to the destination area (range A19:A23). The first two projects used the fill handle to copy a source area to an adjacent destination area. To copy a source area to a nonadjacent destination area, however, you cannot use the fill handle.

A more versatile method of copying a source area is to use the Copy button and Paste button on the Standard toolbar. You can use these two buttons to copy a source area to an adjacent or nonadjacent destination area.

The Copy button copies the contents and format of the source area to the **Office Clipboard**, a special place in the computer's memory that allows you to collect text and graphic items from an Office document and then paste them into any Office document. The Copy command on the Edit menu or shortcut menu works the same as the Copy button. The Paste button copies the item from the Office Clipboard to the destination area. The Paste command on the Edit menu or shortcut menu works the same as the Paste button.

The following steps use the Copy and Paste buttons to copy the range A9:A13 to the nonadjacent range A19:A23.

To Copy a Range of Cells to a Nonadjacent Destination Area

1

• **Select the range A9:A13 and then click the Copy button on the Standard toolbar.**

• **Click cell A19, the top cell in the destination area.**

Excel surrounds the source area A9:A13 with a marquee (Figure 3-14). Excel also copies the values and formats of the range A9:A13 to the Office Clipboard.

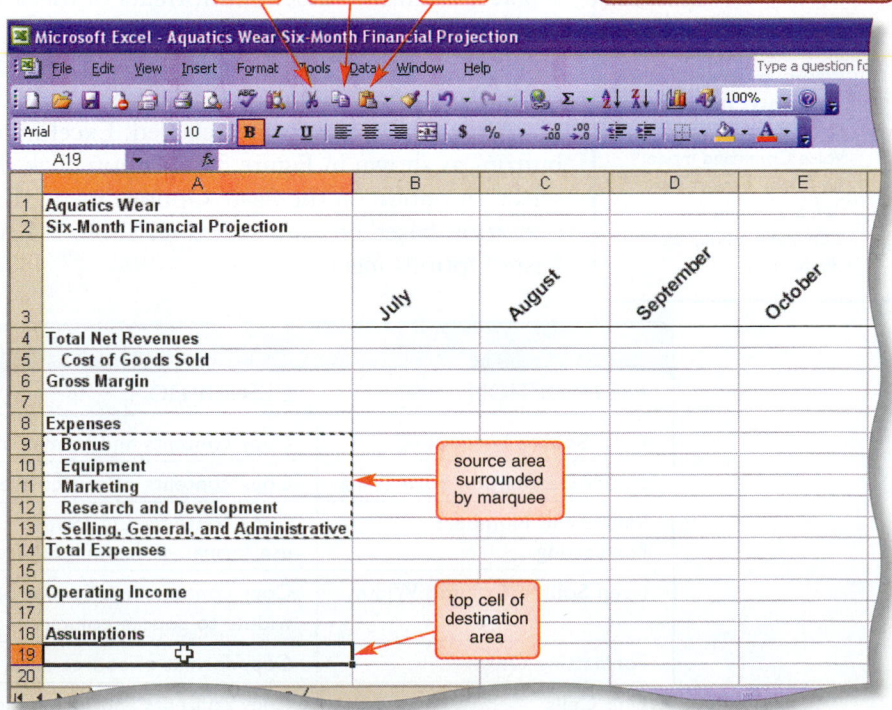

FIGURE 3-14

2

• **Click the Paste button on the Standard toolbar.**

• **Scroll down so row 5 appears at the top of the window.**

Excel copies the values and formats of the last item placed on the Office Clipboard (range A9:A13) to the destination area A19:A23 (Figure 3-15). The Paste Options button appears.

3

• **Press the ESC key.**

Excel removes the marquee from the source area and disables the Paste button on the Standard toolbar.

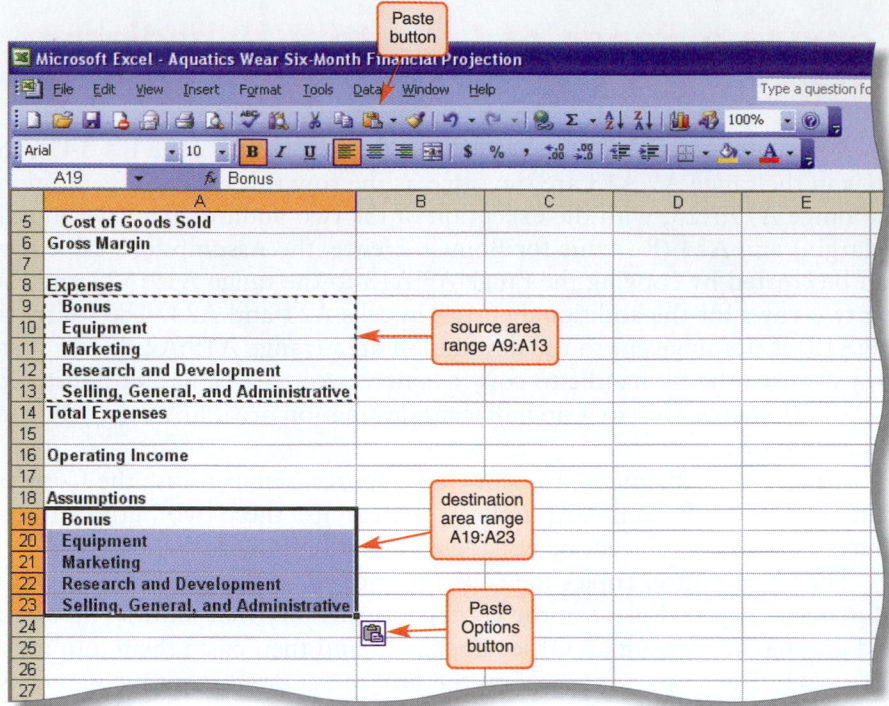

FIGURE 3-15

Other Ways

1. Select source area, on Edit menu click Copy, select destination area, on Edit menu click Paste
2. Right-click source area, click Copy on shortcut menu, right-click destination area, click Paste on shortcut menu
3. Select source area and point to border of range; while holding down CTRL key, drag source area to destination area
4. Select source area, press CTRL+C, select destination area, press CTRL+V
5. Select source area, in Voice Command mode, say "Copy" [select destination area], in Voice Command mode, say "Paste"

As shown in Step 1 and Figure 3-14 on the previous page, you are not required to select the entire destination area (range A19:A23) before clicking the Paste button. Excel only needs to know the upper-left cell of the destination area. In the case of a single column range, such as A19:A23, the top cell of the destination area (cell A19) also is the upper-left cell of the destination area.

When you complete a copy, the values and formats in the destination area are replaced with the values and formats of the source area. Any data contained in the destination area prior to the copy and paste is lost. If you accidentally delete valuable data, immediately click the Undo button on the Standard toolbar or click the Undo Paste command on the Edit menu to undo the paste.

After the Paste button is clicked, Excel immediately displays the Paste Options button, as shown in Figure 3-15. If you click the Paste Options button arrow and select an option on the Paste Options menu, Excel modifies the most recent paste operation based on your selection. Table 3-4 summarizes the options available on the Paste Options menu.

Table 3-4 Options Available on the Paste Options Menu	
PASTE OPTION	**DESCRIPTION**
Keep Source Formatting	Copy contents and format of source area. This option is the default.
Match Destination Formatting	Copy contents of source area, but not the format.
Values and Numbers Formatting	Copy contents and format of source area for numbers or formulas, but use format of destination area for text.
Keep Source Column Widths	Copy contents and format of source area. Change destination column widths to source column widths.
Formatting Only	Copy format of source area, but not the contents.
Link Cells	Copy contents and format and link cells so that a change to the cells in source area updates the corresponding cells in destination area.

The Paste button on the Standard toolbar (Figure 3-15) includes an arrow, which displays a list of advanced paste options (Formulas, Values, No Borders, Transpose, Paste Link, and Paste Special). These options will be discussed when they are used.

An alternative to clicking the Paste button is to press the ENTER key. The ENTER key completes the paste operation, removes the marquee from the source area, and disables the Paste button so that you cannot paste the copied source area to other destination areas. The ENTER key was not used in the previous set of steps so that the capabilities of the Paste Options button could be discussed. The Paste Options button does not appear on the screen when you use the ENTER key to complete the paste operation.

As previously indicated, the Office Clipboard allows you to collect text and graphic items from an Office document and then paste them into any Office document. You can use the Office Clipboard to collect up to 24 different items. To collect multiple items, you first must display the Clipboard task pane by clicking Office Clipboard on the Edit menu. If you want to paste an item on the Office Clipboard into a document, such as a spreadsheet, click the icon representing the item in the Clipboard task pane.

Using Drag and Drop to Move or Copy Cells

You also can use the mouse to move or copy cells. First, you select the source area and point to the border of the cell or range. You know you are pointing to the border of the cell or range when the mouse pointer changes to a block arrow. To move the selected cell or cells, drag the selection to the destination area. To copy a selection, hold down the CTRL key while dragging the selection to the destination area. You know Excel is in copy mode when a small plus sign appears next to the block arrow mouse pointer. Be sure to release the mouse button before you release the CTRL key. Using the mouse to move or copy cells is called **drag and drop**.

Using Cut and Paste to Move or Copy Cells

Another way to move cells is to select them, click the Cut button on the Standard toolbar (Figure 3-14 on page EX 157) to remove them from the worksheet and copy them to the Office Clipboard, select the destination area, and then click the Paste button on the Standard toolbar or press the ENTER key. You also can use the Cut command on the Edit menu or shortcut menu, instead of the Cut button.

Inserting and Deleting Cells in a Worksheet

At anytime while the worksheet is on the screen, you can insert cells to enter new data or delete cells to remove unwanted data. You can insert or delete individual cells, a range of cells, entire rows, entire columns, or entire worksheets.

Inserting Rows

The Rows command on the Insert menu or the Insert command on the shortcut menu allows you to insert rows between rows that already contain data. According to the sketch of the worksheet in Figure 3-3a on page EX 149, two rows must be inserted in the Assumptions table, one between rows 20 and 21 for the Margin assumption and another between rows 22 and 23 for the Revenue for Bonus assumption. The steps on the next page show how to accomplish the task of inserting the new rows into the worksheet.

To Insert a Row

1

• **Right-click row heading 21, the row below where you want to insert a row.**

Excel highlights row 21 and displays the shortcut menu (Figure 3-16).

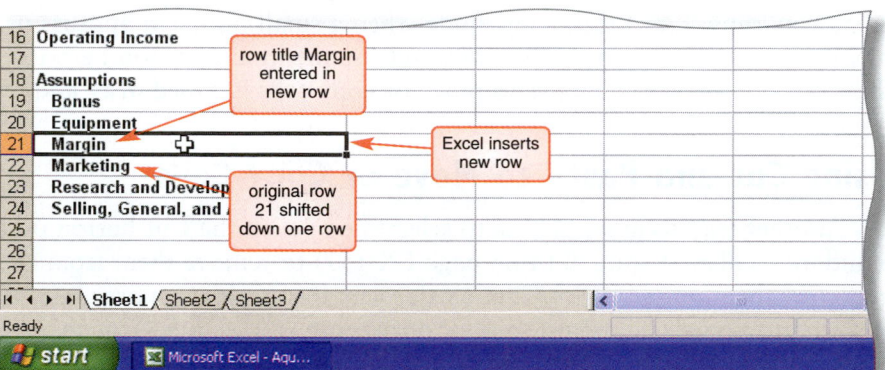

FIGURE 3-16

2

• **Click Insert on the shortcut menu.**

• **Click cell A21 in the new row and then enter Margin as the row title.**

Excel inserts a new row in the worksheet by shifting the selected row 21 and all rows below it down one row (Figure 3-17). Excel displays the new row title in cell A21. The cells in the new row inherit the formats of the cells in the row above them.

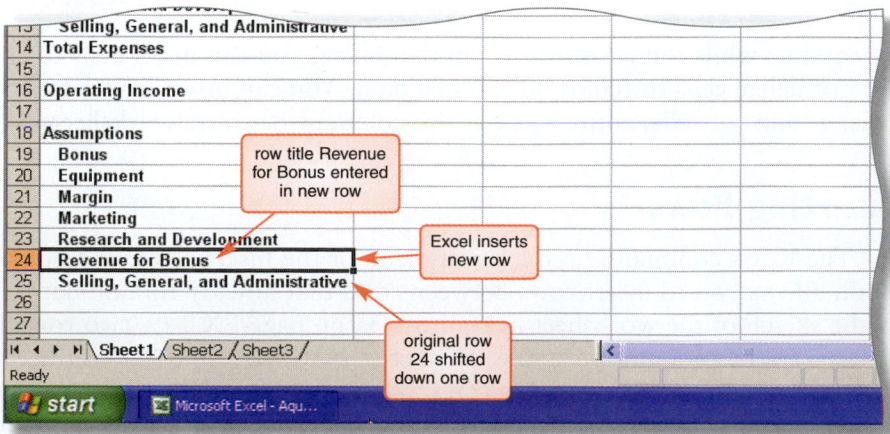

FIGURE 3-17

3

• **Right-click row heading 24 and then click Insert on the shortcut menu.**

• **Click cell A24 in the new row and then enter Revenue for Bonus as the row title.**

Excel inserts a new row in the worksheet and displays the new row title in cell A24 (Figure 3-18).

FIGURE 3-18

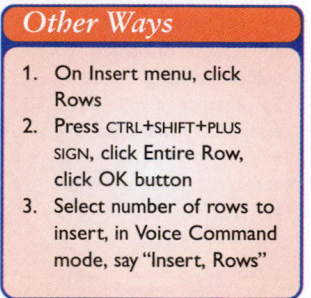

Other Ways

1. On Insert menu, click Rows
2. Press CTRL+SHIFT+PLUS SIGN, click Entire Row, click OK button
3. Select number of rows to insert, in Voice Command mode, say "Insert, Rows"

To insert multiple adjacent rows, first select as many rows as you want to insert by dragging through the row headings immediately below where you want the new rows inserted before invoking the Insert command.

When you insert a row, it inherits the format of the row above it. You can change this by clicking the Insert Options button that appears immediately above the inserted row. Following the insertion of a row, the Insert Options button lets you select from the following options: (1) Format Same As Above; (2) Format Same As Below; and (3) Clear Formatting. The Format Same as Above option is the default. The Insert Options button remains active until you begin the next Excel operation.

If the rows that are shifted down include cell references in formulas located in the worksheet, Excel automatically adjusts the cell references in the formulas to their new locations. Thus, in Step 2 in the previous steps, if a formula in the worksheet references a cell in row 21 before the insert, then the cell reference in the formula is adjusted to row 22 after the insert.

The primary difference between the Insert command on the shortcut menu and the Rows command on the Insert menu is that the Insert command on the shortcut menu requires that you select an entire row (or rows) in order to insert a row (or rows). The Rows command on the Insert menu requires that you select a single cell in a row to insert one row or a range of cells to insert multiple rows.

Inserting Columns

You insert columns into a worksheet in the same way you insert rows. To insert columns, select one or more columns immediately to the right of where you want Excel to insert the new column or columns. Select the number of columns you want to insert. Next, click Columns on the Insert menu or click Insert on the shortcut menu. The primary difference between these two commands is this: The Columns command on the Insert menu requires that you select a single cell in a column to insert one column or a range of cells to insert multiple columns. The Insert command on the shortcut menu, however, requires that you select an entire column (or columns) to insert a column (or columns). Following the insertion of a column, Excel displays the Insert Options button, which allows you to modify the insertion in a fashion similar to that discussed earlier when inserting rows.

Inserting Single Cells or a Range of Cells

The Insert command on the shortcut menu or the Cells command on the Insert menu allows you to insert a single cell or a range of cells. You should be aware that if you shift a single cell or a range of cells, however, it no longer may be lined up with its associated cells. To ensure that the values in the worksheet do not get out of order, it is recommended that you insert only entire rows or entire columns. When you insert a single cell or a range of cells, Excel displays the Insert Options button so that you can change the format of the inserted cell, using options similar to those for inserting rows and columns.

Deleting Columns and Rows

The Delete command on the Edit menu or shortcut menu removes cells (including the data and format) from the worksheet. Deleting cells is not the same as clearing cells. The Clear command, which was described earlier in Project 1 on page EX 52, clears the data from the cells, but the cells remain in the worksheet. The Delete command removes the cells from the worksheet and shifts the remaining

More About

Dragging Ranges

You can move and insert a selected cell or range between existing cells by holding down the SHIFT key while you drag the selection to the gridline where you want to insert. You also can copy and insert by holding down the CTRL+SHIFT keys while you drag the selection to the desired gridline.

More About

The Insert Options Button

When you insert columns or rows, Excel only displays the Insert Options button if formats are assigned to the left-most column or top row of the selection.

Q&A

Q: Can you undo copying, deleting, inserting, and moving ranges of cells?

A: Yes. Copying, deleting, inserting, and moving ranges of cells have the potential to render a worksheet useless. Carefully review these actions before continuing on to the next task. If you are not sure the action is correct, click the Undo button on the Standard toolbar.

rows up (when you delete rows) or shifts the remaining columns to the left (when you delete columns). If formulas located in other cells reference cells in the deleted row or column, Excel does not adjust these cell references. Excel displays the error message **#REF!** in those cells to indicate a cell reference error. For example, if cell A7 contains the formula =A4+A5 and you delete row 5, Excel assigns the formula =A4+#REF! to cell A6 (originally cell A7) and displays the error message #REF! in cell A6. It also displays an Error Options button when you select the cell containing the error message #REF!, which allows you to select options to determine the nature of the problem.

Deleting Individual Cells or a Range of Cells

Although Excel allows you to delete an individual cell or range of cells, you should be aware that if you shift a cell or range of cells on the worksheet, it no longer may be lined up with its associated cells. For this reason, it is recommended that you delete only entire rows or entire columns.

Entering Numbers with Format Symbols

The next step in creating the Six-Month Financial Projection worksheet is to enter the assumption values in the range B19:B25. The assumption numbers can be entered and then formatted as in Projects 1 and 2, or each one can be entered with format symbols. When a number is entered with a **format symbol**, Excel immediately displays it with the assigned format. Valid format symbols include the dollar sign ($), comma (,), and percent sign (%).

If you enter a whole number, it appears without any decimal places. If you enter a number with one or more decimal places and a format symbol, Excel displays the number with two decimal places. Table 3-5 illustrates several examples of numbers entered with format symbols. The number in parentheses in column 4 indicates the number of decimal places.

Table 3-5	Numbers Entered with Format Symbols		
FORMAT SYMBOL	**TYPED IN FORMULA BAR**	**DISPLAYS IN CELL**	**COMPARABLE FORMAT**
,	83,341	83,341	Comma (0)
	1,675.8	1,675.80	Comma (2)
$	$278	$278	Currency (0)
	$3818.54	$3,818.54	Currency (2)
	$45,612.3	$45,612.3	Currency (2)
%	23%	23%	Percent (0)
	97.5%	97.50%	Percent (2)
	39.833%	39.83%	Percent (2)

The following step enters the numbers in the Assumptions table with format symbols.

To Enter Numbers with Format Symbols

1

• **Enter** 250,000.00 **in cell B19,** 5.00% **in cell B20,** 62.00% **in cell B21,** 14.00% **in cell B22,** 6.75% **in cell B23,** 15,000,000.00 **in cell B24, and** 30.00% **in cell B25.**

Excel displays the entries using a format based on the format symbols entered with the numbers (Figure 3-19).

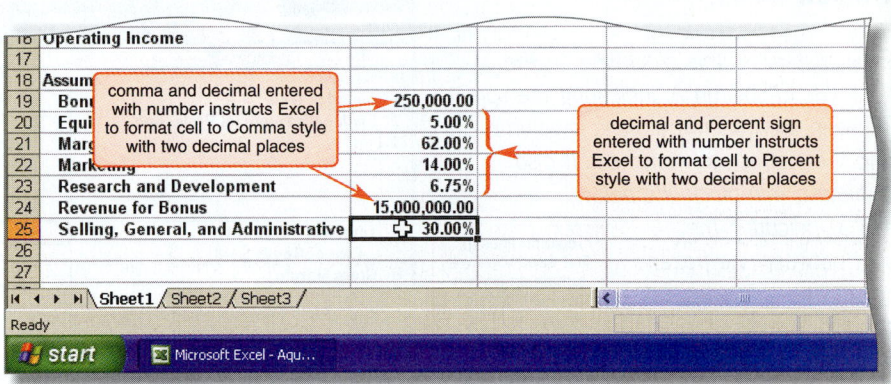

FIGURE 3-19

Freezing Worksheet Titles

Freezing worksheet titles is a useful technique for viewing large worksheets that extend beyond the window. Normally, when you scroll down or to the right, the column titles in row 3 and the row titles in column A that define the numbers no longer appear on the screen. This makes it difficult to remember what the numbers in these rows and columns represent. To alleviate this problem, Excel allows you to **freeze the titles,** so that Excel displays the titles on the screen, no matter how far down or to the right you scroll.

The following steps show how to use the Freeze Panes command on the Window menu to freeze the worksheet title and column titles in rows 1, 2, and 3, and the row titles in column A.

To Freeze Column and Row Titles

1

• **Press CTRL+HOME to select cell A1 and ensure that Excel displays row 1 and column A on the screen.**

• **Select cell B4.**

• **Click Window on the menu bar.**

Excel displays the Window menu (Figure 3-20).

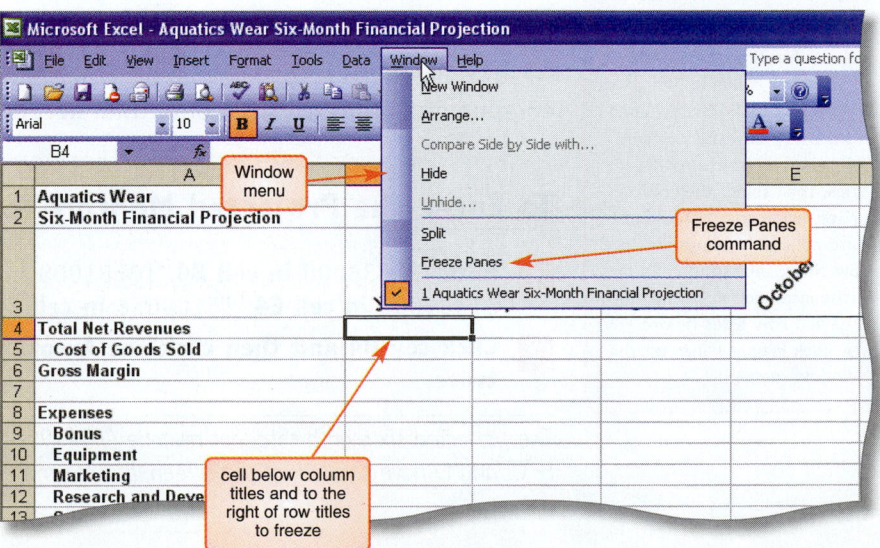

FIGURE 3-20

2

• **Click Freeze Panes on the Window menu.**

Excel displays a thin black line on the right side of column A, indicating the split between the frozen row titles in column A and the rest of the worksheet. It also displays a thin black line below row 3, indicating the split between the frozen column titles in rows 1 through 3 and the rest of the worksheet (Figure 3-21).

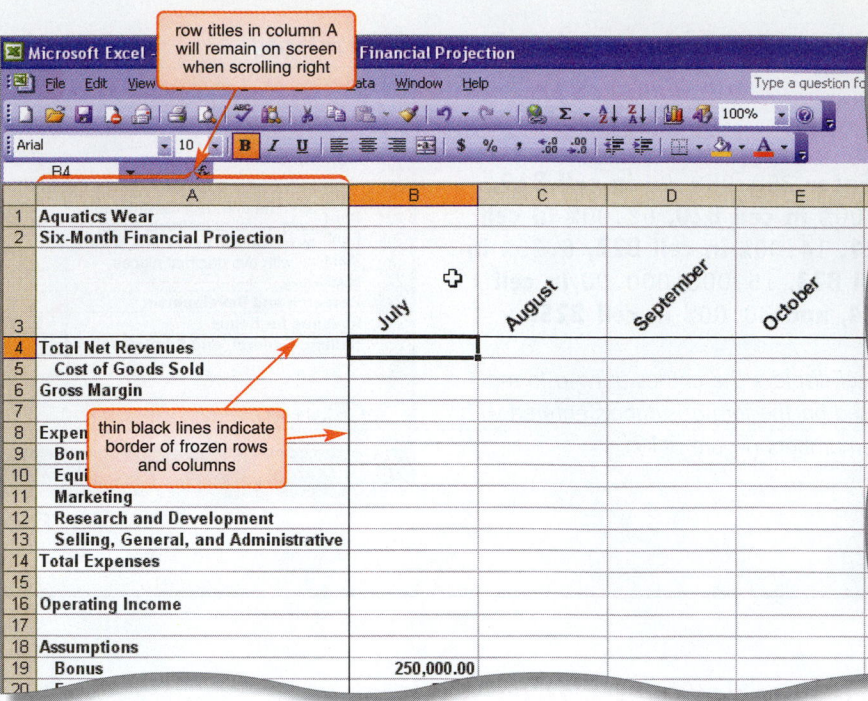

FIGURE 3-21

Other Ways

1. Press ALT+W, F
2. In Voice Command mode, say "Window, Freeze Panes"

Once frozen, the column titles in rows 1 through 3 and the row titles in column A will remain on the screen even when you scroll to the right. The titles remain frozen until you unfreeze them. You unfreeze the titles by clicking the Unfreeze Panes command on the Window menu. You will learn how to use the Unfreeze Panes command later in this project.

Before freezing the titles, it is important that Excel displays cell A1 in the upper-left corner of the screen. For example, if in Step 1 on the previous page, cell B4 was selected without first selecting cell A1 to ensure Excel displays the upper-left corner of the screen, then Excel would have frozen the titles and also hidden rows 1 and 2. Excel thus would not be able to display rows 1 and 2 until they are unfrozen.

Entering the Projected Monthly Total Net Revenues

The next step is to enter the projected monthly total net revenues in row 4 and compute the projected six-month total net revenue in cell H4.

To Enter the Projected Monthly Total Net Revenue

1 Enter 23538000 **in cell B4,** 10781000 **in cell C4,** 18875345 **in cell D4,** 11451990 **in cell E4,** 15109656 **in cell F4, and** 25235860 **in cell G4.**

2 Click cell H4 and then click the AutoSum button on the Standard toolbar twice.

The projected six-month total net revenue (104991851) appears in cell H4 (Figure 3-22). Columns B, C, and D have scrolled off the screen, but column A remains because it was frozen earlier.

More About

Freezing Titles

If you only want to freeze column headings, select the appropriate cell in column A before you click Freeze Panes on the Window menu. If you only want to freeze row titles, then select the appropriate cell in row 1. To freeze both column headings and row titles, select the cell that is the intersection of the column and row titles before you click Freeze Panes on the Window menu.

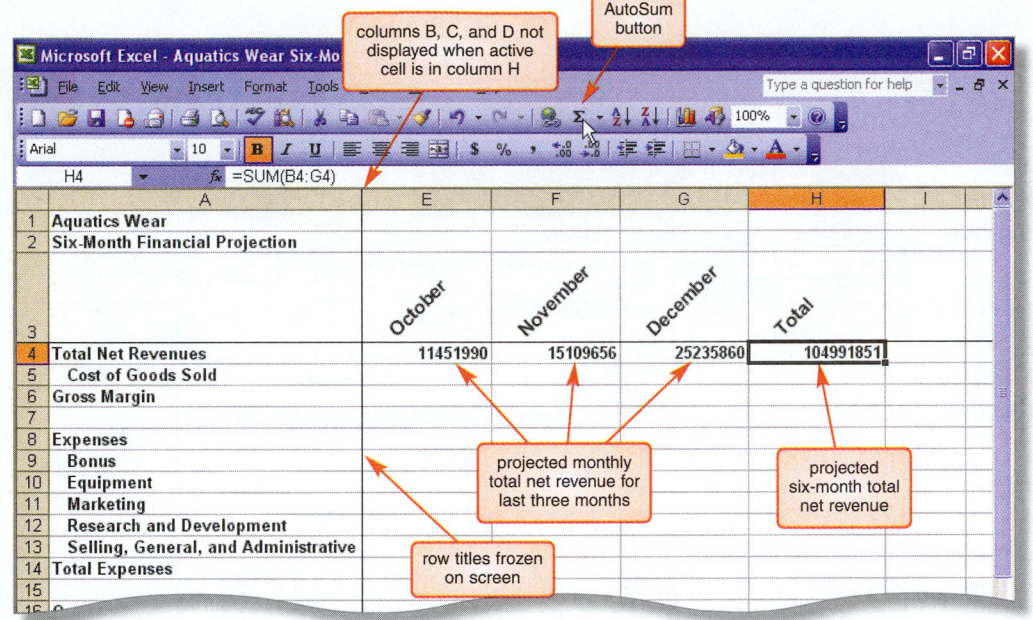

columns B, C, and D not displayed when active cell is in column H

AutoSum button

projected monthly total net revenue for last three months

projected six-month total net revenue

row titles frozen on screen

FIGURE 3-22

Recall from Projects 1 and 2 that if you select a single cell below or to the right of a range of numbers, you must click the AutoSum button twice to instruct Excel to display the sum. If you select a range of cells below or to the right of a range of numbers, you only need to click the AutoSum button once to instruct Excel to display the sums.

Displaying a System Date

The sketch of the worksheet in Figure 3-3a on page EX 149 includes a date stamp on the right side of the heading section. A **date stamp** shows the date a workbook, report, or other document was created or the period it represents. In business, a report often is meaningless without a date stamp. For example, if a printout of the worksheet in this project were distributed to the company's analysts, the date stamp would show when the six-month projections were made, as well as what period the report represents.

A simple way to create a date stamp is to use the NOW function to enter the system date tracked by your computer in a cell in the worksheet. The **NOW function** is one of 14 date and time functions available in Excel. When assigned to a cell, the NOW function returns a number that corresponds to the system date and time beginning with December 31, 1899. For example, January 1, 1900 equals 1, January 2, 1900 equals 2, and so on. Noon equals .5. Thus, noon on January 1, 1900 equals 1.5 and 6 P.M. on January 1, 1900 equals 1.75. If the computer's system date is set to the current date, which normally it is, then the date stamp is equivalent to the current date.

Excel automatically formats this number as a date, using the date and time format, mm/dd/yyyy hh:mm, where the first mm is the month, dd is the day of the month, yyyy is the year, hh is the hour of the day, and mm is the minutes past the hour.

The steps on the next page show how to enter the NOW function and change the format from mm/dd/yyyy hh:mm to mm/dd/yyyy.

To Enter and Format the System Date

1

• **Click cell H2 and then click the Insert Function box in the formula bar.**

• **When Excel displays the Insert Function dialog box, click the Or select a category box arrow, and then select Date & Time in the list.**

• **Scroll down in the Select a function list and then click NOW.**

An equal sign appears in the active cell and in the formula bar. Excel displays the Insert Function dialog box as shown in Figure 3-23.

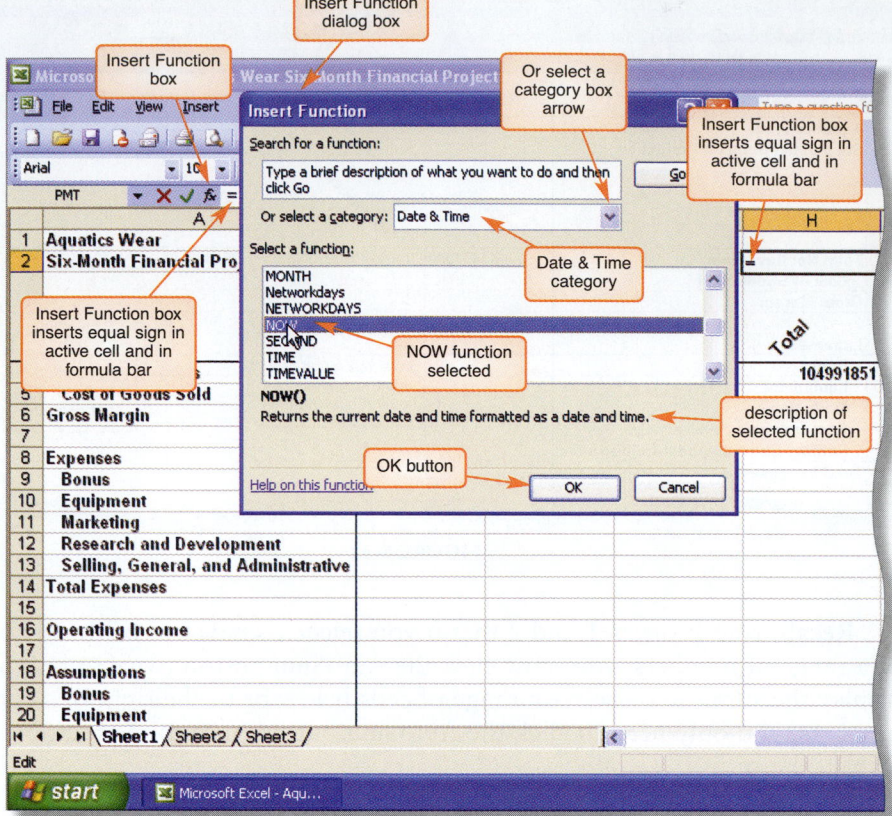

FIGURE 3-23

2

• **Click the OK button.**

• **When Excel displays the Function Arguments dialog box, click the OK button.**

• **Right-click cell H2.**

Excel displays the system date and time in cell H2, using the default date and time format mm/dd/yyyy hh:mm. It also displays the shortcut menu (Figure 3-24). The system date on your computer may be different.

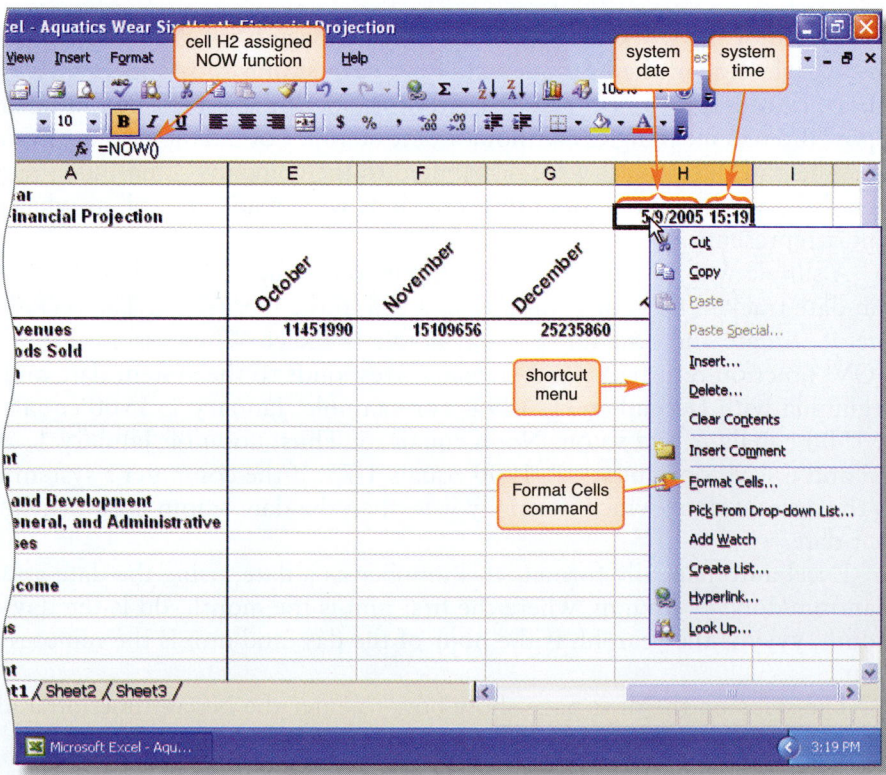

FIGURE 3-24

3

• **Click Format Cells on the shortcut menu.**
• **When Excel displays the Format Cells dialog box, if necessary, click the Number tab.**
• **Click Date in the Category list. Scroll down in the Type list and then click 3/14/2001.**

Excel displays the Format Cells dialog box with Date selected in the Category list and 3/14/2001 (mm/dd/yyyy) selected in the Type list (Figure 3-25). A sample of the data in the active cell (H2) using the selected format appears in the Sample area.

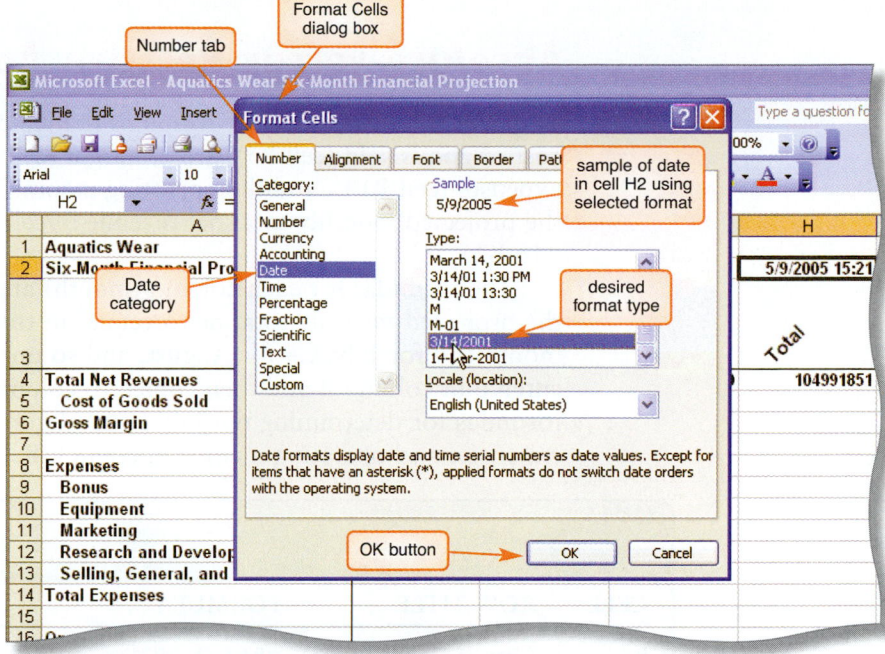

FIGURE 3-25

4

• **Click the OK button.**

Excel displays the system date in the form mm/dd/yyyy (Figure 3-26).

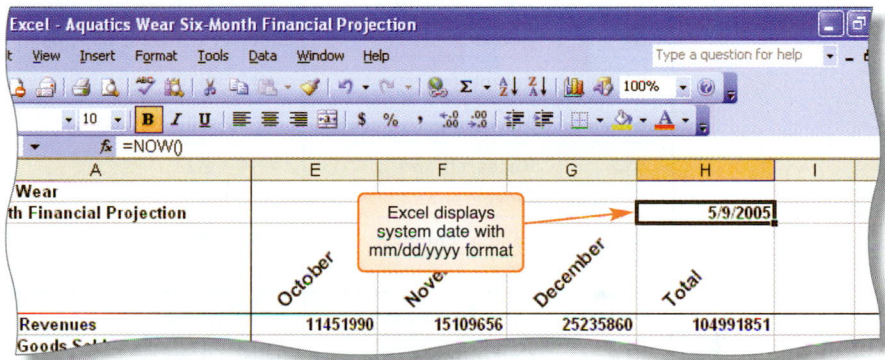

FIGURE 3-26

In Figure 3-26, the date is displayed right-aligned in the cell because Excel treats a date as a number formatted to display as a date. If you assign the General format (Excel's default format for numbers) to a date in a cell, the date is displayed as a number with two decimal places. For example, if the system time and date is 6:00 P.M. on September 12, 2005 and the cell containing the NOW function is assigned the General format, then Excel displays the following number in the cell:

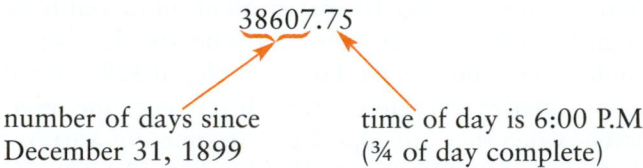

38607.75

number of days since   time of day is 6:00 P.M.
December 31, 1899   (¾ of day complete)

The whole number portion of the number (38607) represents the number of days since December 31, 1899. The decimal portion of the number (.75) represents 6:00 P.M. as the time of day, at which point ¾ of the day is complete. To assign the General format to a cell, click General in the Category list in the Format Cells dialog box (Figure 3-25).

Other Ways

1. On Insert menu click Function, click Date & Time in Or select a category list, click NOW, click OK button
2. Press CTRL+SEMICOLON (not a volatile date)
3. Press CTRL+SHIFT+# to format date to day-month-year
4. In Voice Command mode, say "Insert, Function, [select Date & Time category], NOW, OK"

Absolute versus Relative Addressing

The next step is to enter the formulas that calculate the following values for July: cost of goods sold (cell B5), gross margin (cell B6), expenses (range B9:G13), total expenses (cell B14), and the operating income (cell B16). The formulas are based on the projected monthly total net revenue in cell B4 and the assumptions in the range B19:B25.

The formulas for each column (month) are the same, except for the reference to the projected monthly total net revenues in row 4, which varies according to the month (B4 for July, C4 for August, and so on). Thus, the formulas for July can be entered in column B and then copied to columns C through G. Table 3-6 shows the formulas for determining the July costs of goods sold, gross margin, expenses, total expenses, and operating income in column B.

Table 3-6   Formulas for Determining Cost of Goods Sold, Gross Margin, Expenses, Total Expenses, and Operating Income for July

CELL	ROW TITLE	FORMULA	COMMENT
B5	Cost of Goods Sold	=B4 * (1 – B21)	Total Net Revenues * (1 – Margin %)
B6	Gross Margin	= B4 – B5	Total Net Revenues minus Cost of Goods Sold
B9	Bonus	=IF(B4 >= B24, B19, 0)	Bonus equals value in B19 or 0
B10	Equipment	=B4 * B20	Total Net Revenues times Equipment %
B11	Marketing	=B4 * B22	Total Net Revenues times Marketing %
B12	Research and Development	=B4 * B23	Total Net Revenues times Research and Development %
B13	Selling, General, and Administrative	=B4 * B25	Total Net Revenues times Selling, General, and Administrative %
B14	Total Expenses	=SUM(B9:B13)	Sum of July Expenses
B16	Operating Income	=B6 – B14	Gross Margin minus Total Expenses

If the formulas are entered as shown in Table 3-6 in column B for July and then copied to columns C through G (August through December) in the worksheet, Excel will adjust the cell references for each column automatically. Thus, after the copy, the August Equipment expense in cell C10 would be =C4 * C20. While the cell reference C4 (August Revenue) is correct, the cell reference C20 references an empty cell. The formula for cell C7 should read =C4 * B20, rather than =C4 * C20, because B20 references the Equipment % value in the Assumptions table. In this instance, a way is needed to keep a cell reference in a formula the same, or constant, when it is copied.

To keep a cell reference constant when copying a formula or function, Excel uses a technique called absolute cell referencing. To specify an absolute cell reference in a formula, enter a dollar sign ($) before any column letters or row numbers you want to keep constant in formulas you plan to copy. For example, $B$20 is an absolute cell reference, while B20 is a relative cell reference. Both reference the same cell. The difference becomes apparent when they are copied to a destination area. A formula using the **absolute cell reference** $B$20 instructs Excel to keep the cell reference B20 constant (absolute) in the formula as it copies it to the destination area. A formula using the **relative cell reference** B20 instructs Excel to adjust the cell reference as it copies it to the destination area. A cell reference with only one dollar sign before either the column or the row is called a **mixed cell reference**. Table 3-7 gives some additional examples of absolute, relative, and mixed cell references.

More About

Absolute Referencing

Absolute referencing is one of the more difficult worksheet concepts to understand. One point to keep in mind is that the paste operation is the only operation affected by an absolute cell reference. An absolute cell reference instructs the paste operation to keep the same cell reference as it copies a formula from one cell to another.

Table 3-7	Examples of Absolute, Relative, and Mixed Cell References	
CELL REFERENCE	**TYPE OF REFERENCE**	**MEANING**
$B$20	Absolute cell reference	Both column and row references remain the same when you copy this cell, because the cell references are absolute.
B$20	Mixed reference	This cell reference is mixed. The column reference changes when you copy this cell to another column because it is relative. The row reference does not change because it is absolute.
$B20	Mixed reference	This cell reference is mixed. The row reference changes when you copy this cell reference to another row because it is relative. The column reference does not change because it is absolute.
B20	Relative cell reference	Both column and row references are relative. When copied to another cell, both the row and column in the cell reference are adjusted to reflect the new location.

Entering a Formula Containing Absolute Cell References

The following steps show how to enter the cost of goods sold formula =B4 * (1 − $B$21) in cell B5 using Point mode. To enter an absolute cell reference, you can type the dollar sign ($) as part of the cell reference or enter it by pressing F4 with the insertion point in or to the right of the cell reference to change to absolute.

To Enter a Formula Containing Absolute Cell References

1

• **Press CTRL+HOME and then click cell B5.**

• **Type = (equal sign), click cell B4, type *(1-b21 and then press F4 to change b21 from a relative cell reference to an absolute cell reference.**

• **Type) to complete the formula.**

Excel displays the formula =B4*(1−$B$21) in cell B5 and in the formula bar (Figure 3-27). The formula always will reference the Margin value in cell B21, even if it is copied.

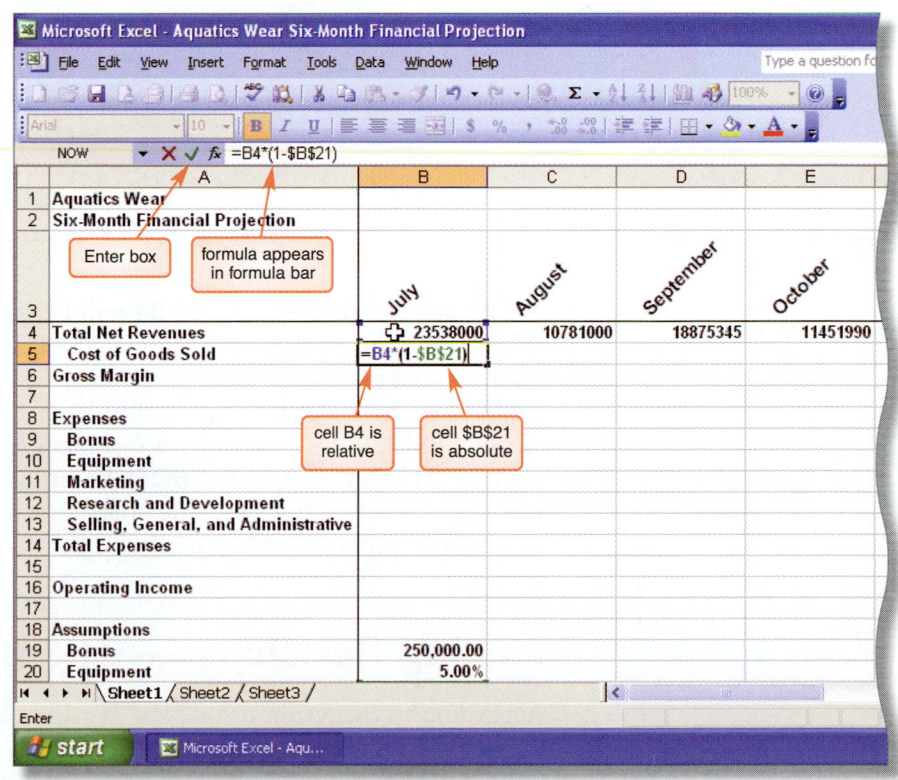

FIGURE 3-27

2

• **Click the Enter box in the formula bar.**

Excel displays the result, 8944440, in cell B5, instead of the formula (Figure 3-28). With cell B5 selected, the formula assigned to it appears in the formula bar.

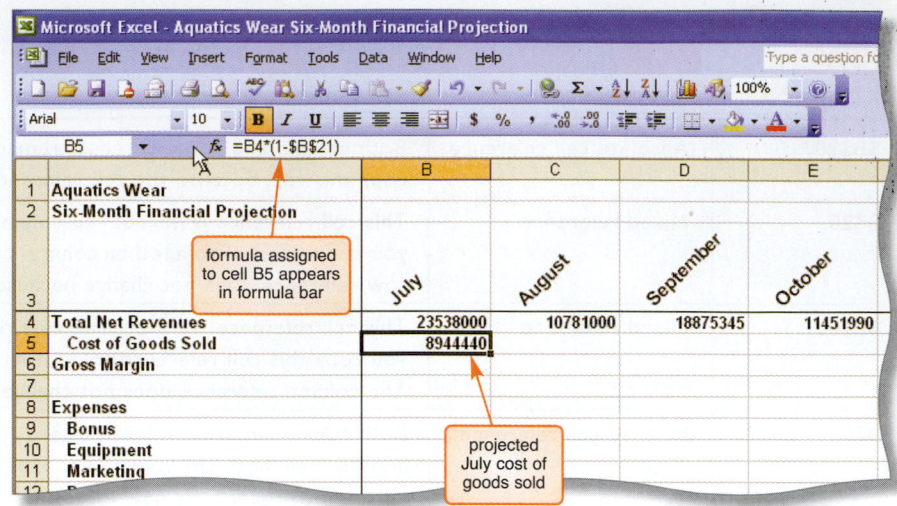

FIGURE 3-28

3

• **Click cell B6, type = (equal sign), click cell B4, type − and then click cell B5.**
• **Click the Enter box in the formula bar.**

Excel displays the gross margin for July, 14593560, in cell B6.

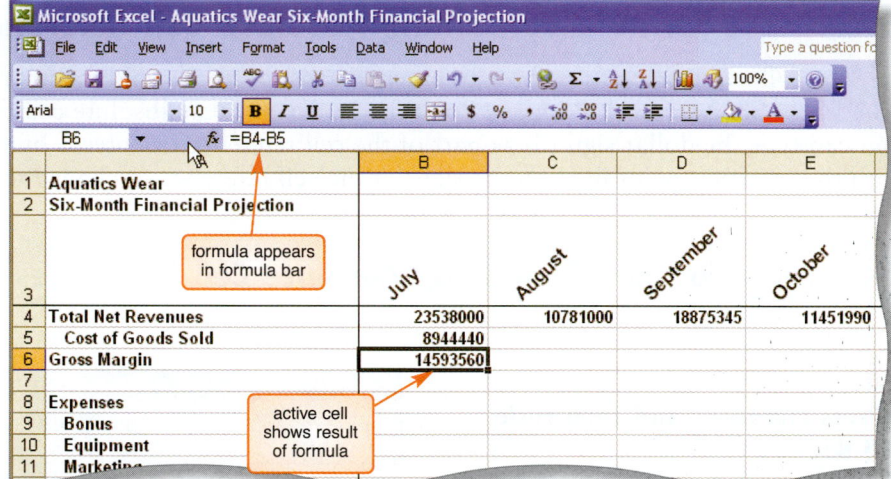

FIGURE 3-29

Because the formula in cell B4 will be copied across columns, rather than down rows, the formula entered in cell B4 in Step 1 on the previous page could have been entered as =B4*(1–$B21), rather than =B4*(1–$B$21). That is, the formula could have included the mixed cell reference $B21, rather than the absolute cell reference $B$21. When you copy a formula across columns, the row does not change anyway. The key is to ensure that column B remains constant as you copy the formula across rows. To change the absolute cell reference to a mixed cell reference, continue to press the F4 key until you get the desired cell reference.

Making Decisions — The If Function

According to the Request for New Workbook in Figure 3-2 on page EX 148, if the projected July total net revenues in cell B4 is greater than or equal to the revenue for bonus in cell B24 (15,000,000.00), then the July bonus value in cell B9 is equal to the bonus value in cell B19 (250,000.00); otherwise, cell B9 is equal to 0. One way to assign the monthly bonus value in cell B9 is to check to see if the total net revenues in cell B4 equal or exceed the revenue for bonus amount in cell B24 and, if so, then to enter 250,000.00 in cell B9. You can use this manual process for all six months by checking the values for the corresponding month.

Because the data in the worksheet changes each time a report is prepared or the figures are adjusted, however, it is preferable to have Excel assign the monthly bonus to the entries in the appropriate cells automatically. To do so, cell B9 must include a formula or function that displays 250,000.00 or 0.00 (zero), depending on whether the projected July total net revenues in cell B4 is greater than or equal to or less than the revenue for bonus value in cell B24.

The **IF function** is useful when you want to assign a value to a cell based on a logical test. For example, using the IF function, cell B9 can be assigned the following IF function:

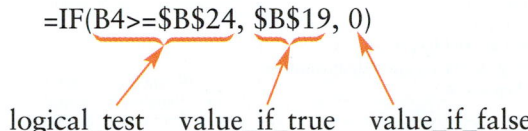

=IF(B4>=$B$24, $B$19, 0)

logical_test   value_if_true   value_if_false

The IF function instructs Excel that, if the projected July total net revenues in cell B4 is greater than or equal to the revenue for bonus value in cell B24, then Excel should display the value 250000 in cell B19, in cell B9. If the projected July total net revenues in cell B4 is less than the revenue for bonus value in cell B24, then Excel displays a 0 (zero) in cell B9.

The general form of the IF function is:

=IF(logical_test, value_if_true, value_if_false)

The argument, logical_test, is made up of two expressions and a comparison operator. Each expression can be a cell reference, a number, text, a function, or a formula. Valid comparison operators, their meaning, and examples of their use in IF functions are shown in Table 3-8. The argument, value_if_true, is the value you want Excel to display in the cell when the logical test is true. The argument, value_if_false, is the value you want Excel to display in the cell when the logical test is false.

Table 3-8 Comparison Operators		
COMPARISON OPERATOR	**MEANING**	**EXAMPLE**
=	Equal to	=IF(H7 = 0, J6 ^ H4, L9 + D3)
<	Less than	=IF(C34 * W3 < K7, $K$6, L33 − 5)
>	Greater than	=IF(MIN(K8:K12) > 75, 1, 0)
>=	Greater than or equal to	=IF(P8 >= $H$6, J7 / V4, 7.5)
<=	Less than or equal to	=IF(G7 − G2 <= 23, L$9, 35 / Q2)
<>	Not equal to	=IF(B1 <> 0, ''No'',''Yes'')

The steps on the next page assign the IF function =IF(B4>=$B$24,$B$19,0) to cell B9. This IF function determines whether or not the worksheet assigns a bonus for July.

To Enter an IF Function

1

• **Click cell B9. Type**
=if(b4>=b24,b19,0) in the
cell.

Excel displays the IF function in the formula bar and in the active cell B9. Excel also displays a ScreenTip showing the general form of the IF function (Figure 3-30).

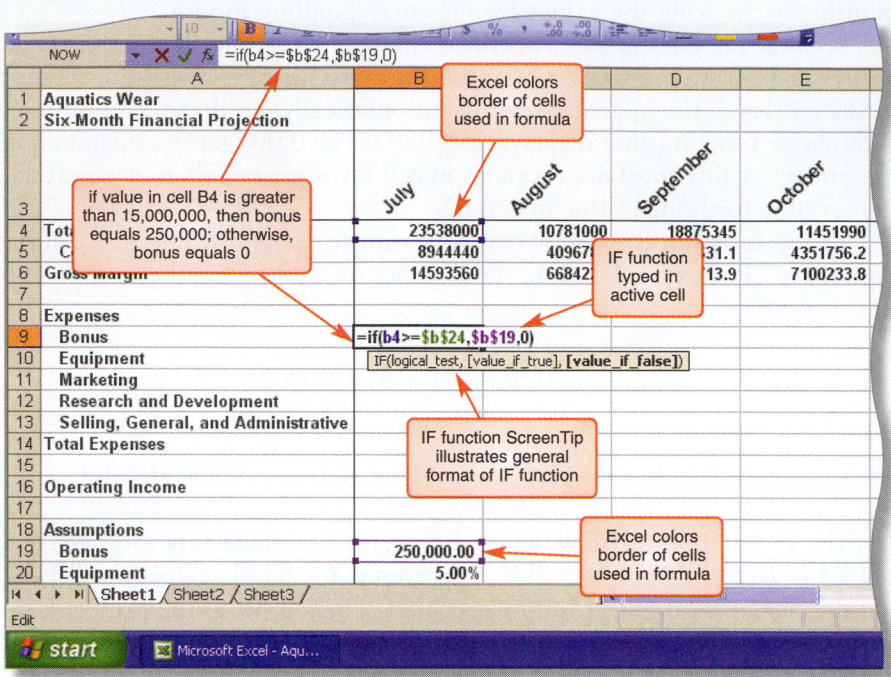

FIGURE 3-30

2

• **Click the Enter box in the**
formula bar.

Excel displays 250000 in cell B9 (Figure 3-31), because the value in cell B4 (23538000) is greater than or equal to the value in cell B24 (15,000,000.00).

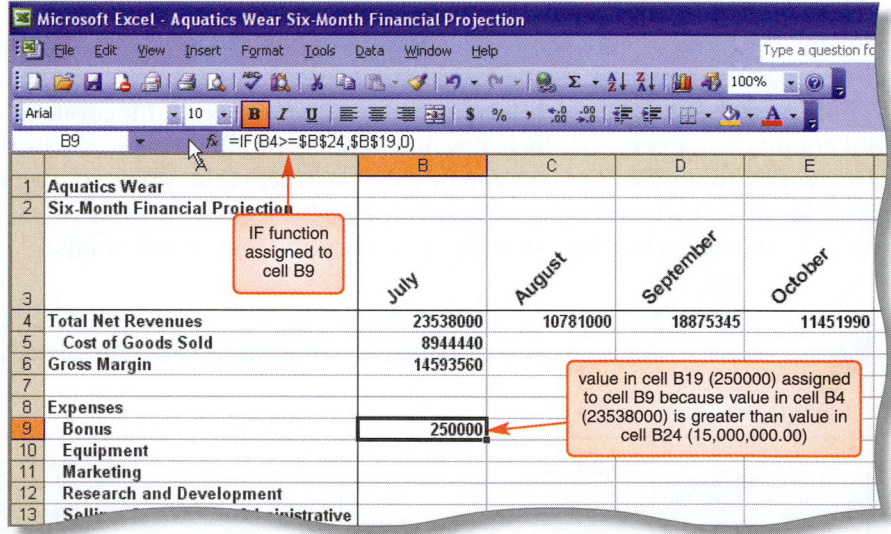

FIGURE 3-31

Other Ways

1. On Insert menu click Function, click Logical in Or select a category list, click IF, click OK button
2. Click Insert Function box in formula bar, click Logical in Or select a category list, click IF, click OK button
3. In Voice Command mode, say "Insert, Function", [select Logical category], in Voice Command mode, say "IF, OK"

The value that Excel displays in cell B9 depends on the values assigned to cells B4, B19, and B24. For example, if the value for July total net revenues in cell B4 is reduced below 15,000,000.00, then the IF function in cell B9 will cause Excel to display a 0. If you change the bonus in cell B19 from 250,000.00 to another number and the value in cell B4 greater than or equal to the value in cell B24, it will change the results in cell B9 as well. Finally, increasing the revenue for bonus in cell B24 so that it is greater than the value in cell B4 will change the result in cell B9.

Entering the Remaining Formulas

The July equipment expense in cell B10 is equal to the total net revenues in cell B4 times the equipment assumption in cell B20 (5.00%). The July marketing expense in cell B11 is equal to the projected July total net revenue in cell B4 times the marketing assumption in cell B22 (14.00%). Similar formulas determine the remaining July expenses in cells B12 and B13.

The total expenses value in cell B14 is equal to the sum of the expenses in the range B9:B13. The operating income in cell B16 is equal to the gross margin in cell B6 minus the total expenses in cell B14. The formulas are short, and therefore, they are typed in the following steps, rather than entered using Point mode.

To Enter the Remaining July Formulas

1 Click cell B10. Type =b4*b20 and then press the DOWN ARROW key. Type =b4*b22 and then press the down arrow key. Type =b4*b23 and then press the DOWN ARROW key. Type =b4*b25 and then press the DOWN ARROW key.

2 With cell B14 selected, click the AutoSum button on the Standard toolbar twice. Click cell B16. Type =b6-b14 and then press the ENTER key.

3 Press CTRL+ACCENT MARK(`) to instruct Excel to display the formulas version of the worksheet.

4 When you are finished viewing the formulas version, press CTRL+ACCENT MARK(`) to instruct Excel to display the values version of the worksheet.

Following Step 2 and Step 4, Excel displays the results of the remaining July formulas (Figure 3-32a). Following Step 3, Excel displays the formulas version of the worksheet (Figure 3-32b).

More About

Replacing a Formula with a Constant

You can replace a formula with its result so it remains constant. Do the following: (1) click the cell with the formula; (2) press F2 or click in the formula bar; (3) press F9 to display the value in the formula bar; and (4) press the ENTER key.

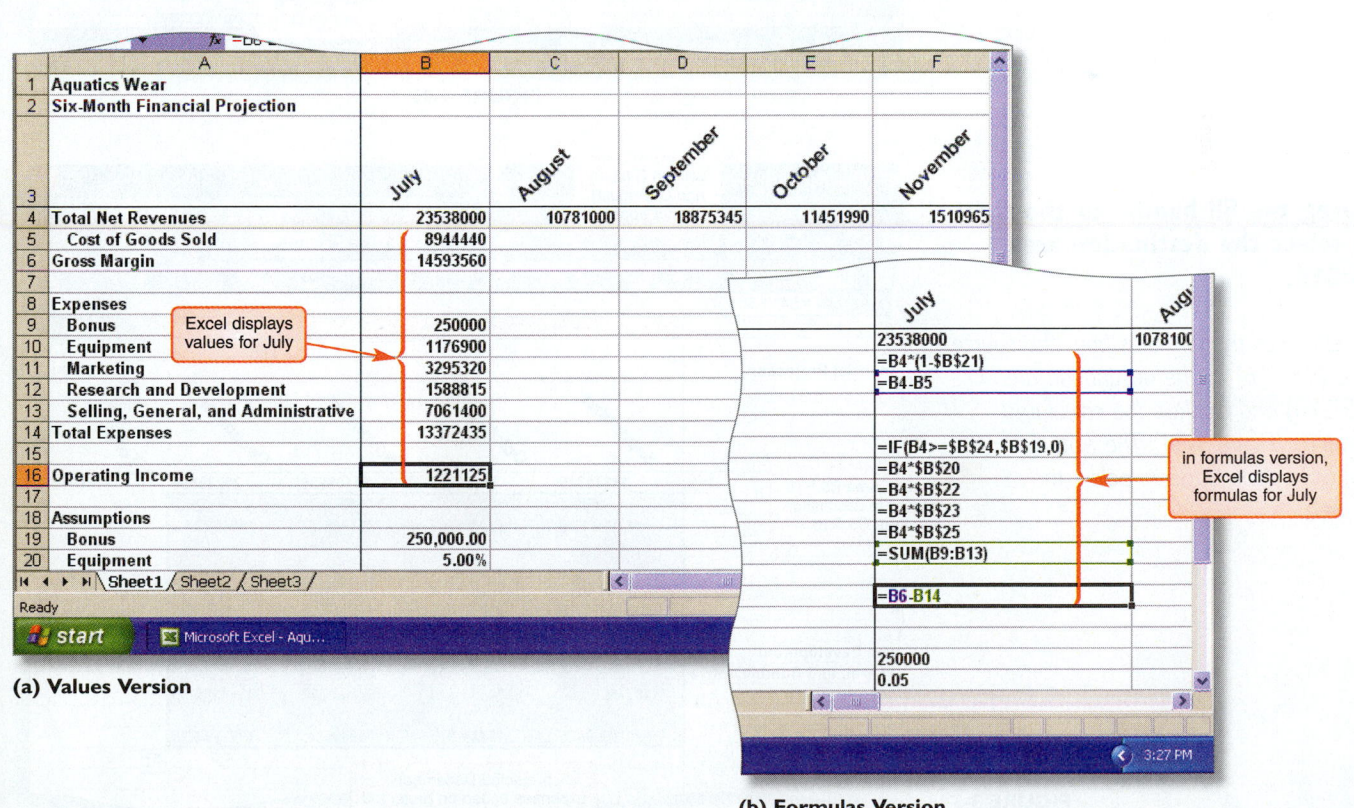

(a) Values Version

(b) Formulas Version

FIGURE 3-32

Viewing the formulas version (Figure 3-32b on the previous page) of the worksheet allows you to check the formulas assigned to the range B5:B16. You can see that Excel converts all the formulas from lowercase to uppercase.

Copying Formulas with Absolute Cell References

The following steps show how to use the fill handle to copy the July formulas in column B to the other five months in columns C through G.

To Copy Formulas with Absolute Cell References Using the Fill Handle

1

• **Select the range B5:B16 and then point to the fill handle in the lower-right corner of cell B16.**

Excel highlights the range B5:B16 and the mouse pointer changes to a crosshair (Figure 3-33).

3		July	August	Septe	Octob
4	Total Net Revenues	23538000	10781000	18875345	11451990
5	Cost of Goods Sold	8944440			
6	Gross Margin	14593560			
7					
8	Expenses				
9	Bonus	250000			
10	Equipment	1176900			
11	Marketing	3295320			
12	Research and Development	1588815			
13	Selling, General, and Administrative	7061400			
14	Total Expenses	13372435			
15					
16	Operating Income	1221125			
17					
18	Assumptions				
19	Bonus	250,000.00			
20	Equipment	5.00%			

source area is B5:B16

mouse pointer changes to a crosshair

Ready   Sum=51503995

FIGURE 3-33

2

• **Drag the fill handle to the right to select the destination area C5:G16.**

Excel copies the formulas from the source area (B5:B16) to the destination area (C5:G16) and displays the calculated amounts (Figure 3-34). The Auto Fill Options button appears below the fill area.

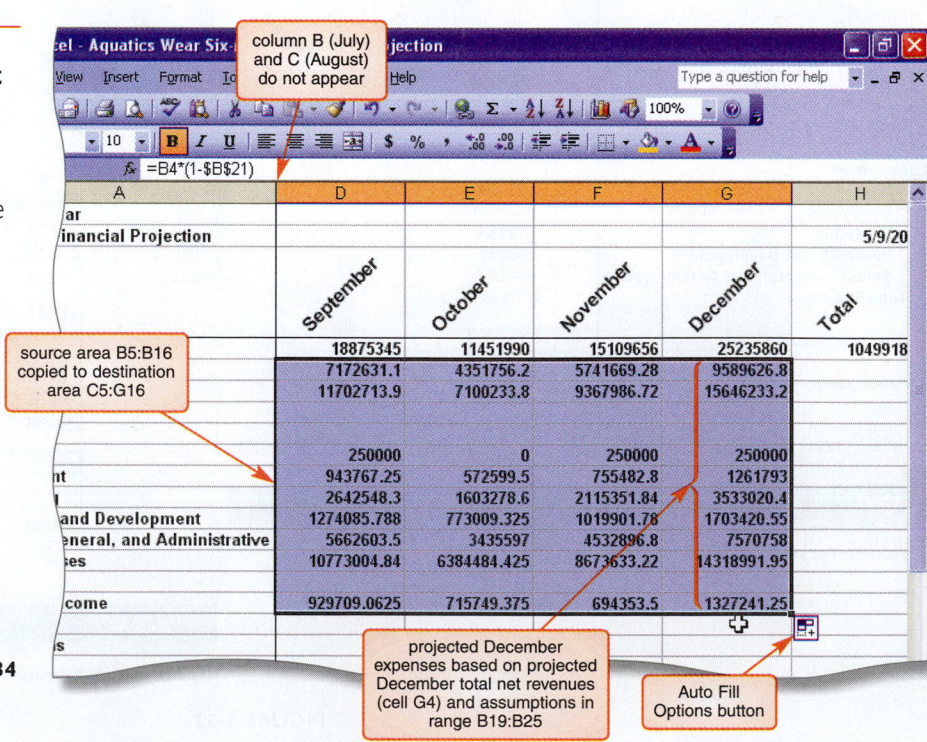

column B (July) and C (August) do not appear

fx =B4*(1-$B$21)

source area B5:B16 copied to destination area C5:G16

projected December expenses based on projected December total net revenues (cell G4) and assumptions in range B19:B25

Auto Fill Options button

FIGURE 3-34

Because the formulas in the range B5:B16 use absolute cell references, the formulas still refer to the current values in the Assumptions table when the formulas are copied to the range C5:G16.

As shown in Figure 3-34, as the fill handle is dragged to the right, columns B and C no longer appear on the screen. Column A, however, remains on the screen, because the row titles were frozen earlier in this project.

Determining Row Totals in Nonadjacent Cells

The following steps determine the row totals in column H. To determine the row totals using the AutoSum button, select only the cells in column H containing numbers in adjacent cells to the left. If, for example, you select the range H5:H16, Excel will display 0s as the sum of empty rows in cells H7, H8, and H15.

To Determine Row Totals in Nonadjacent Cells

1 Select the range H5:H6. Hold down the CTRL key and select the range H9:H14 and cell H16 as shown in Figure 3-35.

2 Click the AutoSum button on the Standard toolbar.

Excel displays the row totals in column H (Figure 3-35).

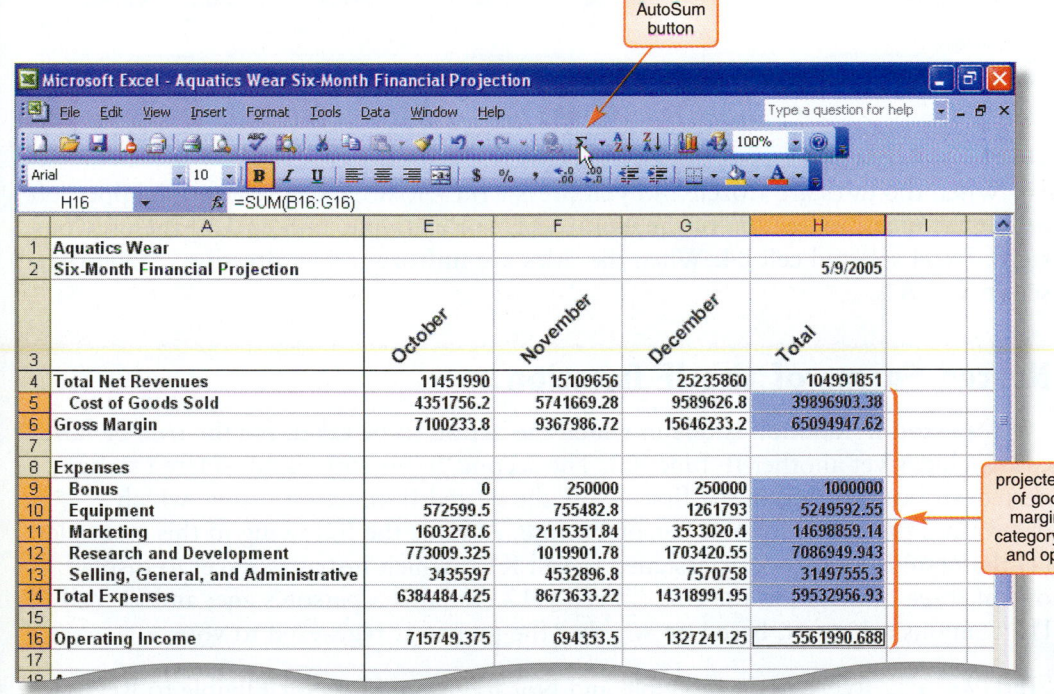

FIGURE 3-35

Unfreezing Worksheet Titles and Saving the Workbook

All the text, data, and formulas have been entered into the worksheet. The steps on the next page unfreeze the titles and save the workbook using its current file name, Aquatics Wear Six-Month Financial Projection.

More About

Error Messages

When Excel cannot calculate a formula, it displays an error message in a cell. These error messages always begin with a number sign (#). The more commonly occurring error messages are: #DIV/0! (tries to divide by zero); #NAME? (uses a name Excel does not recognize); #N/A (refers to a value not available); #NULL! (specifies an invalid intersection of two areas); #NUM! (uses a number incorrectly); #REF (refers to a cell that is not valid); #VALUE! (uses an incorrect argument or operand); and ##### (cell not wide enough to display entire entry).

More About

Toggle Commands

Many of the commands on menus and the shortcut keys function as a toggle. For example, if you invoke the Freeze Panes command, the command changes to Unfreeze Panes the next time you view the Window menu. These types of commands work like an on-off switch or toggle.

To Unfreeze the Worksheet Titles and Save the Workbook

1 Press CTRL+HOME to select cell B4 and view the upper-left corner of the screen.

2 Click Window on the menu bar (Figure 3-36) and then click Unfreeze Panes.

3 Click the Save button on the Standard toolbar.

Excel unfreezes the titles so that column A scrolls off the screen when you scroll to the right and the first three rows scroll off the screen when you scroll down. The latest changes to the workbook are saved on disk using the file name, Aquatics Wear Six-Month Financial Projection.

More About

Work Days

Assume that you have two dates: one in cell F3 and the other in cell F4. The date in cell F3 is your starting date and the date in cell F4 is the ending date. To calculate the work days between the two dates (excludes weekends), use the following formula: =NETWORKDAYS(F3, F4). For this function to work, make sure the Analysis ToolPak add-in is installed. You can install it by clicking Add-Ins on the Tools menu.

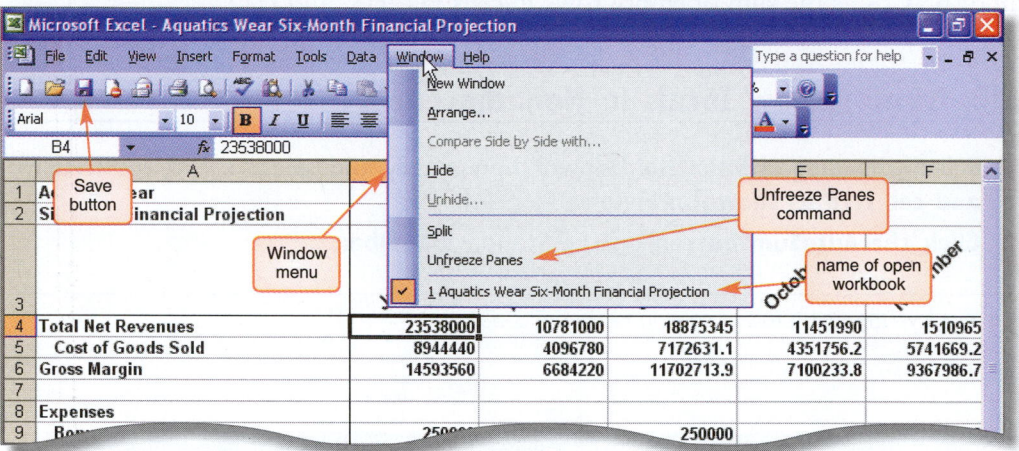

FIGURE 3-36

When the titles are frozen and you press CTRL+HOME, Excel selects the upper-left cell of the unfrozen section of the worksheet. For example, in Step 1 of the previous steps, Excel selected cell B4. When the titles are unfrozen, then pressing CTRL+HOME selects cell A1.

Nested Forms of the IF function

A **nested IF function** is one in which the action to be taken for the true or false case includes yet another IF function. The second IF function is considered to be nested, or layered, within the first. Study the nested IF function below, which determines the eligibility of a person to vote. Assume the following in this example: (1) the nested IF function is assigned to cell K12, which instructs Excel to display one of three messages in the cell; (2) cell H12 contains a person's age; and (3) cell I12 contains a Y or N, based on whether the person is registered to vote.

=IF(H12>=18, IF(I12="Y","Registered","Eligible and Not Registered"),"Not Eligible to Register")

The nested IF function instructs Excel to display one, and only one, of the following three messages in cell K12: (1) Registered; or (2) Eligible and Not Registered; or (3) Not Eligible to Register.

You can nest IF functions as deep as you want, but after you get beyond a nest of three IF functions, the logic becomes difficult to follow and alternative solutions, such as the use of multiple cells and simple IF functions, should be considered.

Formatting the Worksheet

The worksheet created thus far shows the financial projections for the six-month period, from July to December. Its appearance is uninteresting, however, even though some minimal formatting (bolding the worksheet, formatting assumptions numbers, changing the column widths, and formatting the date) was performed earlier. This section will complete the formatting of the worksheet to make the numbers easier to read and to emphasize the titles, assumptions, categories, and totals. The worksheet will be formatted in the following manner so it appears as shown in Figure 3-37: (1) format the numbers; (2) format the worksheet title, column titles, row titles, and operating income row; and (3) format the assumptions table.

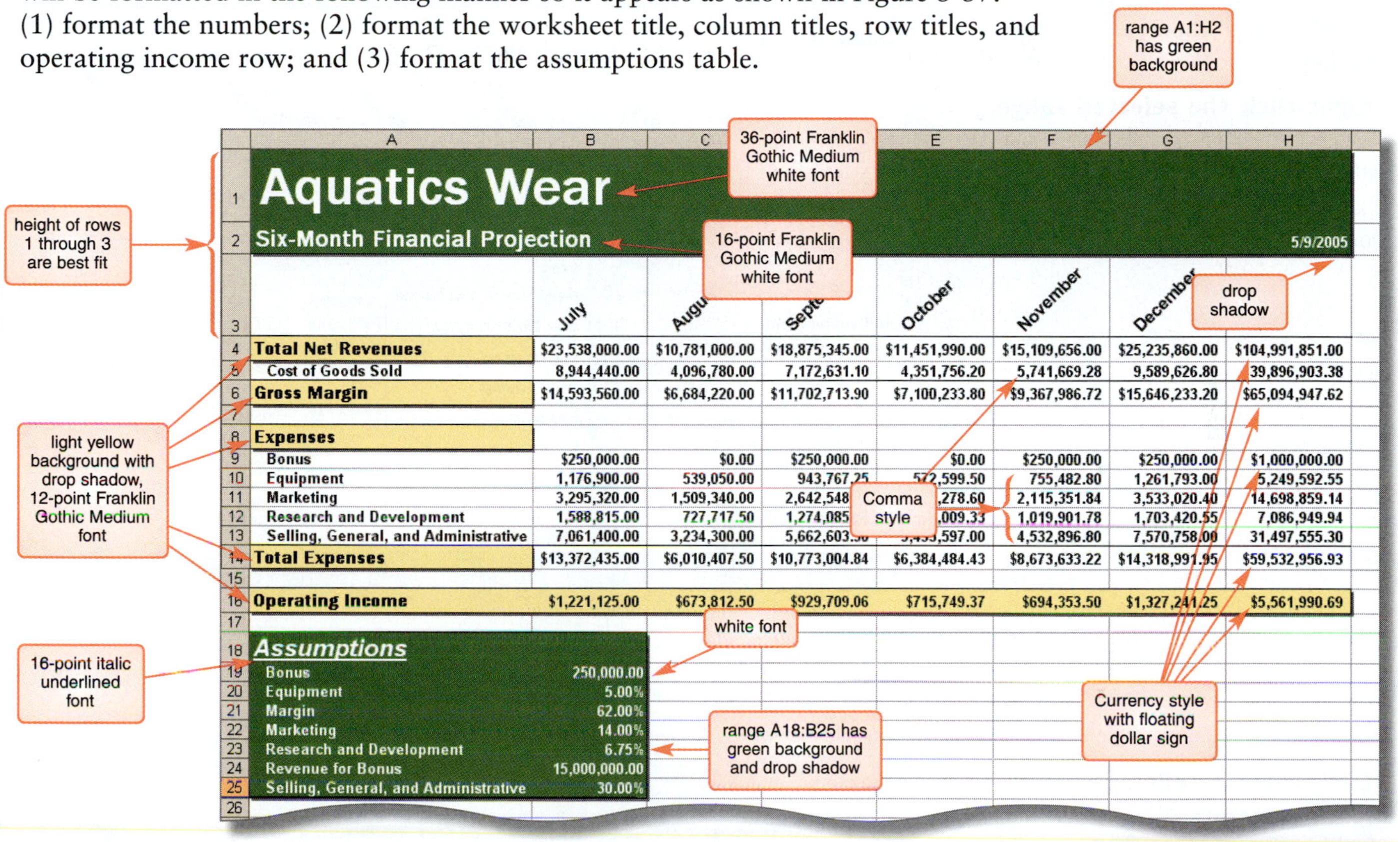

FIGURE 3-37

Formatting the Numbers

The numbers in the range B4:H16 are to be formatted as follows:

1. Assign the Currency style with a floating dollar sign to rows 4, 6, 9, 14, and 16.

2. Assign a customized Comma style to rows 5 and 10 through 13.

To assign a Currency style with a floating dollar sign, the Format Cells command will be used, rather than the Currency Style button on the Formatting toolbar, which assigns a fixed dollar sign. The Comma style also must be assigned using the Format Cells command, because the Comma Style button on the Formatting toolbar assigns a format that displays a dash (-) when a cell has a value of 0. The specifications for this worksheet call for displaying a value of 0 as 0.00 (see cell C9 in Figure 3-37), rather than as a dash. To create a Comma style using the Format Cells command, you can assign a Currency style with no dollar sign. The steps on the next page show how to assign formats to the numbers in rows 4 through 16.

More About

Selecting Nonadjacent Ranges

One of the more difficult tasks to learn is selecting nonadjacent ranges. To complete this task, do not hold down the CTRL key when you select the first range because Excel will consider the current active cell to be the first selection. Once the first range is selected, hold down the CTRL key and drag through the nonadjacent ranges. If a desired range is not visible in the window, use the scroll arrows to view the range. It is not necessary to hold down the CTRL key while you scroll.

To Assign Formats to Nonadjacent Ranges

1

- **Select the range B4:H4.**

- **While holding down the CTRL key, select the nonadjacent ranges B6:H6, B9:H9, B14:H14, and B16:H16, and then release the CTRL key.**

- **Right-click the selected range.**

Excel highlights the selected nonadjacent ranges and displays the shortcut menu as shown in Figure 3-38.

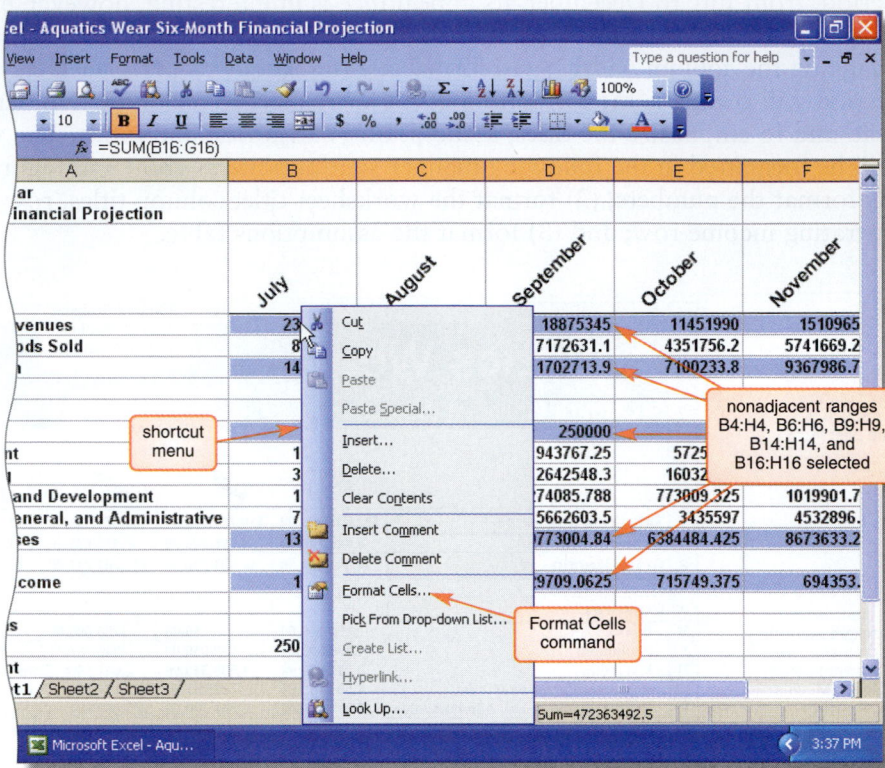

FIGURE 3-38

2

- **Click Format Cells on the shortcut menu.**

- **When Excel displays the Format Cells dialog box, click the Number tab, click Currency in the Category list, select 2 in the Decimal places box, click $ in the Symbol list to ensure a dollar sign shows, and click ($1,234.10) in the Negative numbers list.**

Excel displays the cell format settings in the Number sheet in the Format Cells dialog box as shown in Figure 3-39.

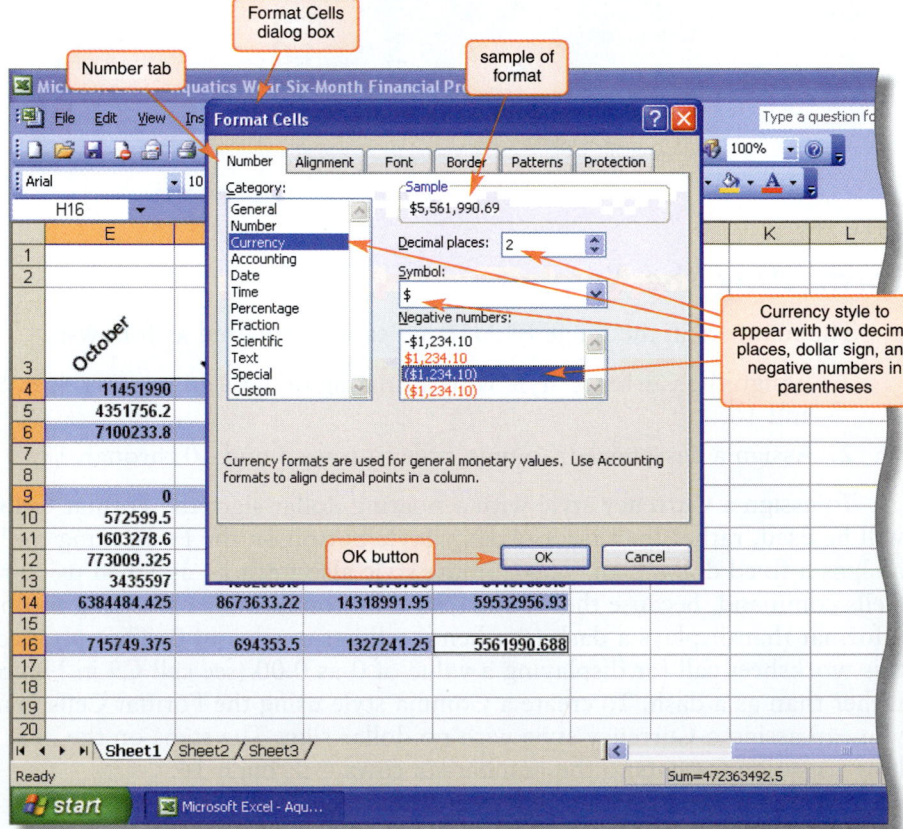

FIGURE 3-39

3

- Click the OK button.
- Select the range B5:H5.
- While holding down the CTRL key, select the range B10:H13, and then release the CTRL key.
- Right-click the selected range.
- Click Format Cells on the shortcut menu.

4

- When Excel displays the Format Cells dialog box, click Currency in the Category list, select 2 in the Decimal places box, click None in the Symbol list so a dollar sign does not show, click (1,234.10) in the Negative numbers list.

Excel displays the format settings in the Number sheet in the Format Cells dialog box as shown in Figure 3-40.

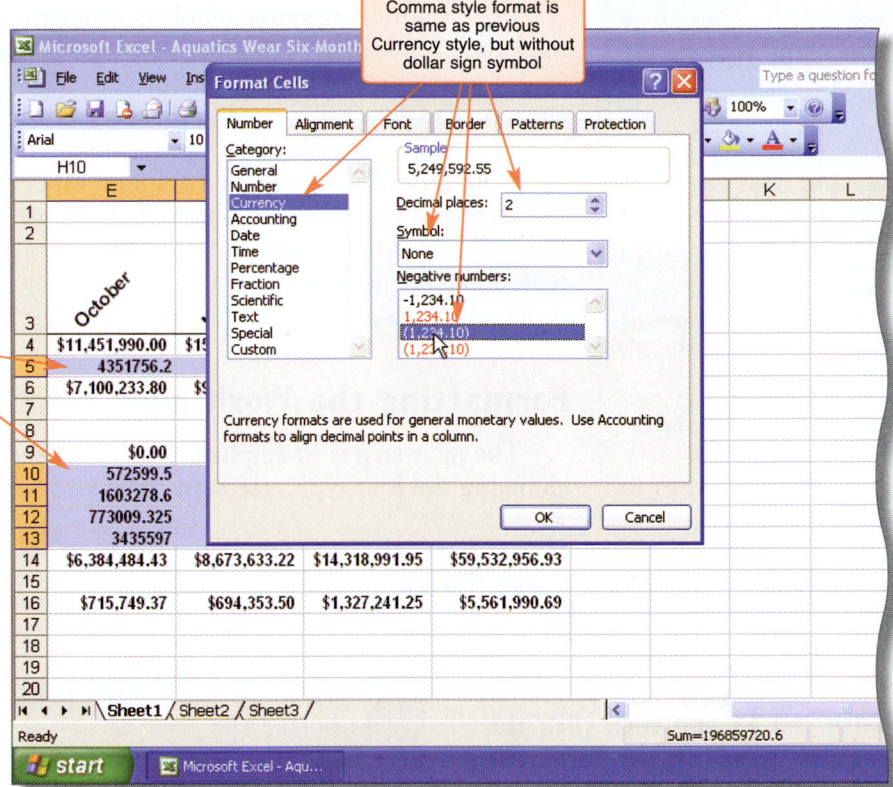

FIGURE 3-40

5

- Click the OK button.
- Press CTRL+HOME to select cell A1.

Excel displays the formatted numbers as shown in Figure 3-41.

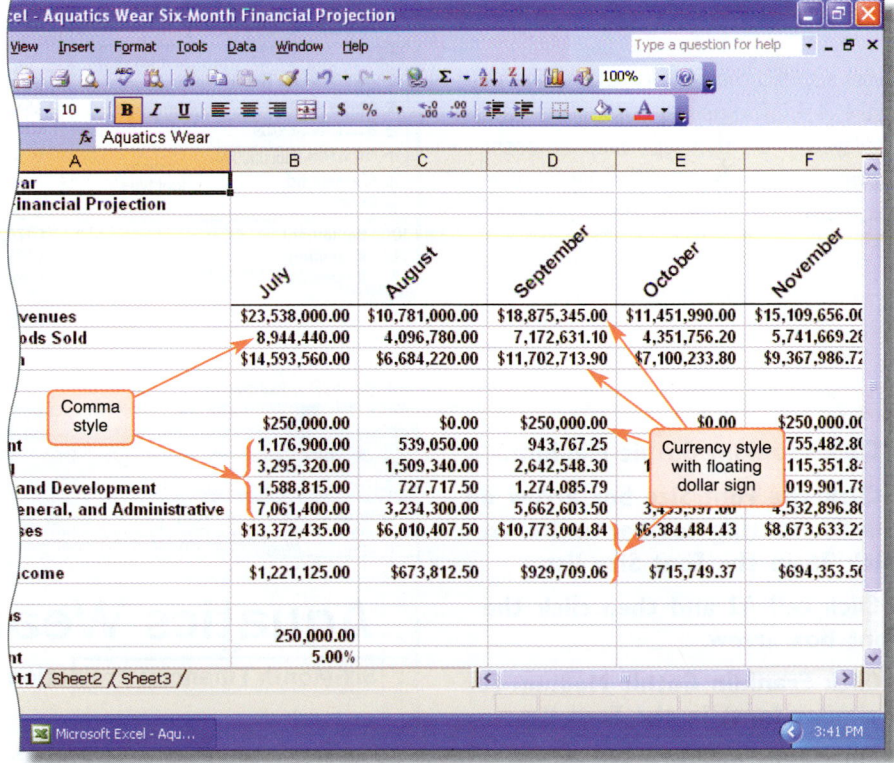

FIGURE 3-41

More About

The Fill and Font Color Buttons

You may have noticed that the color bar at the bottom of the Fill Color and Font Color buttons on the Formatting toolbar (Figure 3-44) changes to the most recently selected color. To apply this same color to a cell background or text, select a cell and then click the Fill Color button to use the color as a background or click the Font Color button to use the color as a font color.

In accounting, negative numbers often are shown with parentheses surrounding the value rather than with a negative sign preceding the value. Thus, in Step 2 and Step 4 of the previous steps, the format (1,234.10) in the Negative numbers list was clicked. The data being used in this project contains no negative numbers. You must, however, select a format for negative numbers, and you must be consistent if you are choosing different formats in a column, otherwise the decimal points may not line up.

In Step 2 (Figure 3-39) and Step 4 (Figure 3-40), the Accounting category could have been selected to generate the same format, rather than Currency. You should review the formats available in each category. Thousands of combinations of format styles can be created using the options in the Format Cells dialog box.

Formatting the Worksheet Titles

The next step is to emphasize the worksheet titles in cells A1 and A2 by changing the font type, size, and color as described in the following steps.

To Format the Worksheet Titles

1

• Click cell A1 and then click the Font box arrow on the Formatting toolbar.

• Scroll down and point to Franklin Gothic Medium (or a similar font) in the Font list.

Excel displays the Font list as shown in Figure 3-42. The names in the Font list are displayed in the font type they represent, allowing you to view the font type before you assign it to a cell or range of cells.

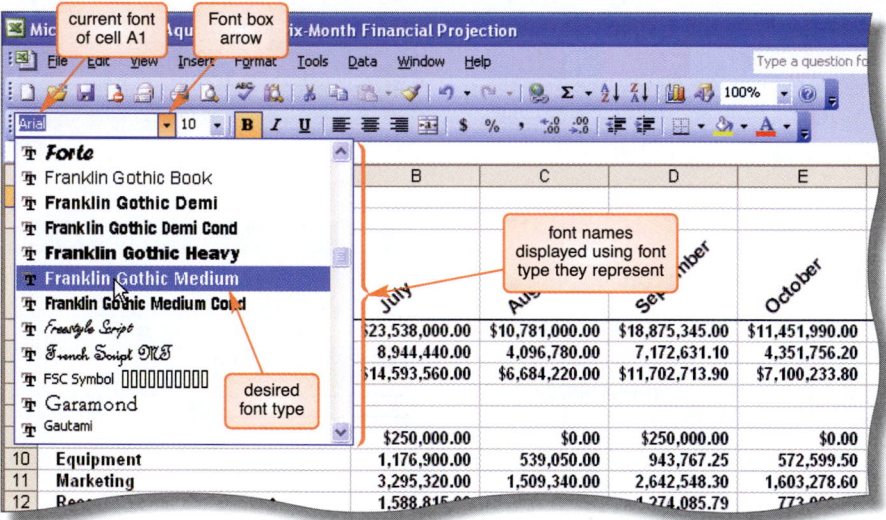

FIGURE 3-42

2

• Click Franklin Gothic Medium.

• Click the Font Size box arrow on the Formatting toolbar and then click 36 in the Font Size list.

• Click cell A2 and then click the Font box arrow.

• Click Franklin Gothic Medium (or a similar font) in the Font list.

• Click the Font Size box arrow and then click 16 in the Font Size list.

Excel displays the worksheet titles in cells A1 and A2 as shown in Figure 3-43.

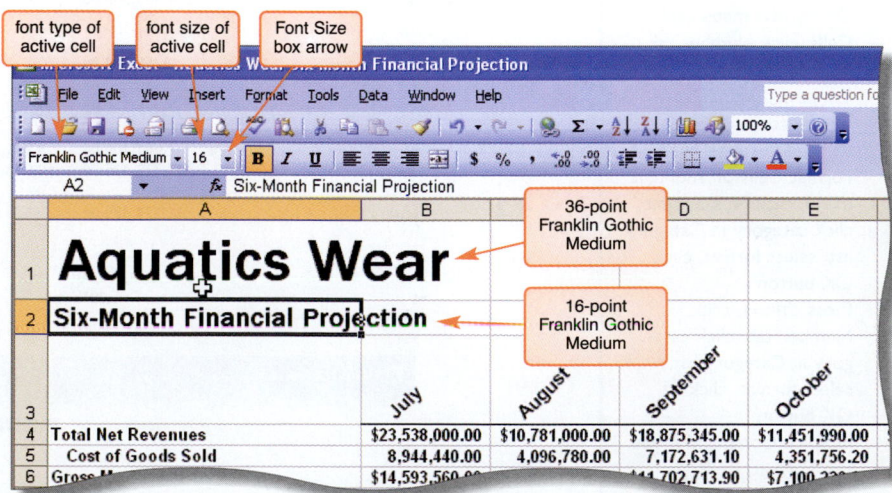

FIGURE 3-43

3

• **Select the range A1:H2 and then click the Fill Color button arrow on the Formatting toolbar.**

• **Click Green (column 4, row 2) on the Fill Color palette and then click the Font Color button arrow on the Formatting toolbar.**

Excel assigns a green background to the selected range and displays the Font Color palette (Figure 3-44).

4

• **Click White (column 8, row 5) on the Font Color palette.**

Excel changes the color of the font in the range A1:H2 from black to white (see Figure 3-37 on page EX 177).

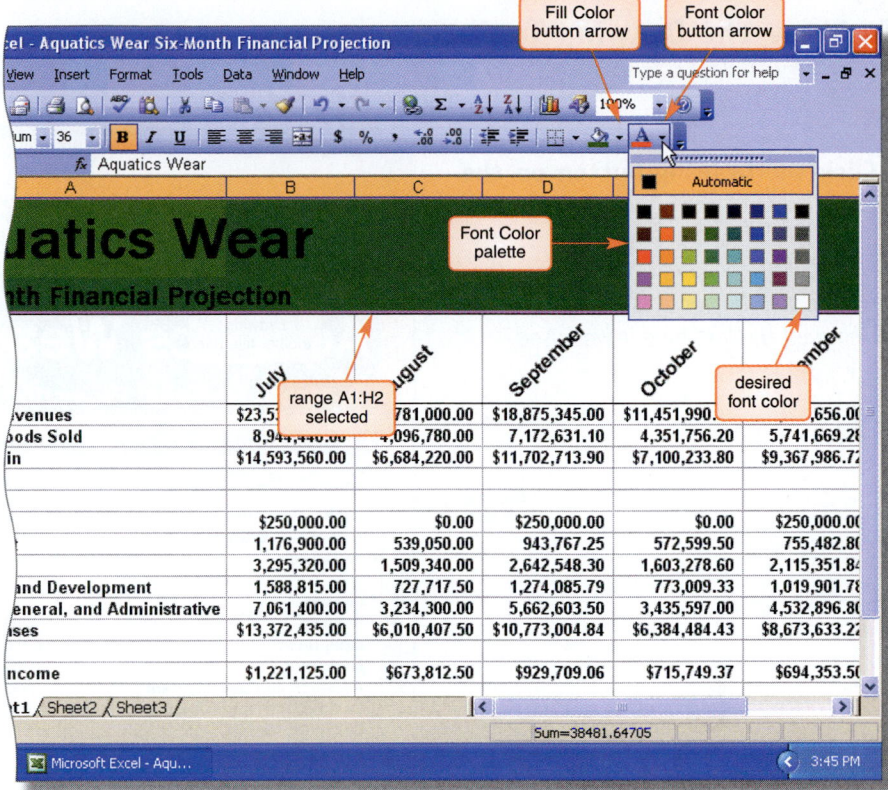

FIGURE 3-44

Showing the Drawing Toolbar

The next step is to add a drop shadow to the selected range A1:H2 using the Shadow button on the Drawing toolbar. The Drawing toolbar currently is hidden. Before using the Drawing toolbar, Excel must be instructed to display the Drawing toolbar on the screen. This section describes how to show an inactive (hidden) toolbar and then dock it.

Excel has hundreds of toolbar buttons, most of which it displays on 22 built-in toolbars. Two of these 22 built-in toolbars are the Standard toolbar and Formatting toolbar, which usually appear at the top of the screen. Another built-in toolbar is the Drawing toolbar. The **Drawing toolbar** provides tools that can simplify adding lines, boxes, and other geometric figures to a worksheet. You also can create customized toolbars containing the buttons that you use often.

To show or hide any Excel toolbar, you can use the shortcut menu that Excel displays when you right-click a toolbar, or you can use the Toolbars command on the View menu. The Drawing toolbar also can be displayed or hidden by clicking the Drawing button on the Standard toolbar.

The step on the next page illustrates how to show the Drawing toolbar.

Other Ways

1. On Format menu click Cells, click Patterns tab to color background (or click Font tab to color font), click OK button
2. Right-click range, click Format Cells on shortcut menu, click Patterns tab to color background (or click Font tab to color font), click OK button
3. Press CTRL+1, click Patterns tab to color background (or click Font tab to color font), click OK button
4. In Voice Command mode, say "Format, Cells, Patterns (or Font), [desired color], OK"

To Show the Drawing Toolbar

1

• **Click the Drawing button on the Standard toolbar.**

Excel displays the Drawing toolbar in the same location and with the same shape as it displayed the last time it was used (Figure 3-45).

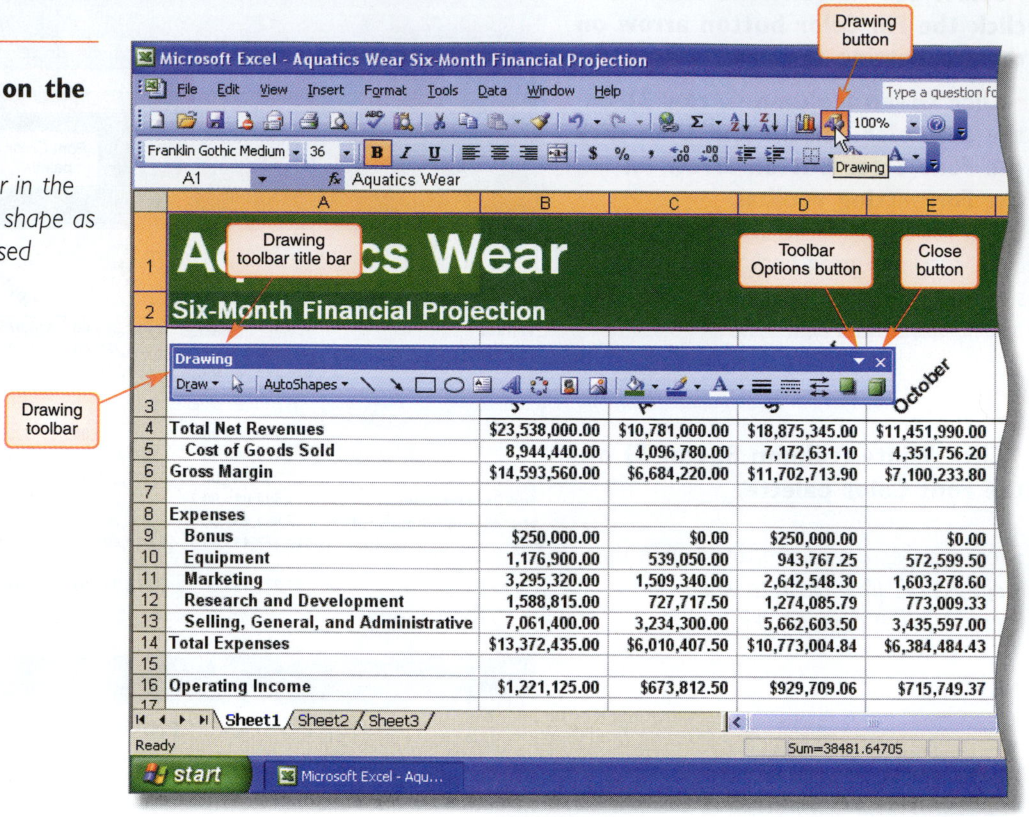

FIGURE 3-45

Other Ways

1. On View menu point to Toolbars, click Drawing
2. Right-click Standard or Formatting toolbar, click Drawing on shortcut menu
3. In Voice Command mode, say "View, Toolbars, Drawing"

Q&A

Q: What happens when you dock a toolbar with a box or a button with a list on the left or right edge of the window?

A: If you dock a toolbar that includes a box or a button with a list on the left or right edge of the window, the box and its list will not appear on the toolbar and will not be available.

When a toolbar is displayed in the middle of the screen as shown in Figure 3-45, the toolbar includes a title bar. The Toolbar Options button and Close button are on the right side of the title bar.

Moving and Docking a Toolbar

The Drawing toolbar in Figure 3-45 is called a **floating toolbar** because it is displayed in its own window and can be moved anywhere in the Excel window. You move the toolbar by pointing to the toolbar title bar or to a blank area within the toolbar window (not a button) and then dragging the toolbar to its new location. As with any window, you also can resize the toolbar by dragging the toolbar window borders.

Sometimes a floating toolbar gets in the way no matter where you move it or how you resize it. You can hide the floating toolbar by clicking the Close button on the toolbar title bar. At times, however, you will want to keep the toolbar available for use. For this reason, Excel allows you to position toolbars on the edge of its window. If you drag the toolbar close to the edge of the window, Excel positions the toolbar in a **toolbar dock**.

Excel has four toolbar docks, one on each of the four sides of the window. You can add as many toolbars to a toolbar dock as you want. Each time you dock a toolbar, however, the Excel window slightly decreases in size to compensate for the room occupied by the toolbar. The following step shows how to dock the Drawing toolbar at the bottom of the screen below the scroll bar.

To Move and Dock a Toolbar

1

• **Point to the Drawing toolbar title bar or to a blank area in the Drawing toolbar.**

• **Drag the Drawing toolbar over the status bar at the bottom of the screen.**

Excel docks the Drawing toolbar at the bottom of the screen (Figure 3-46).

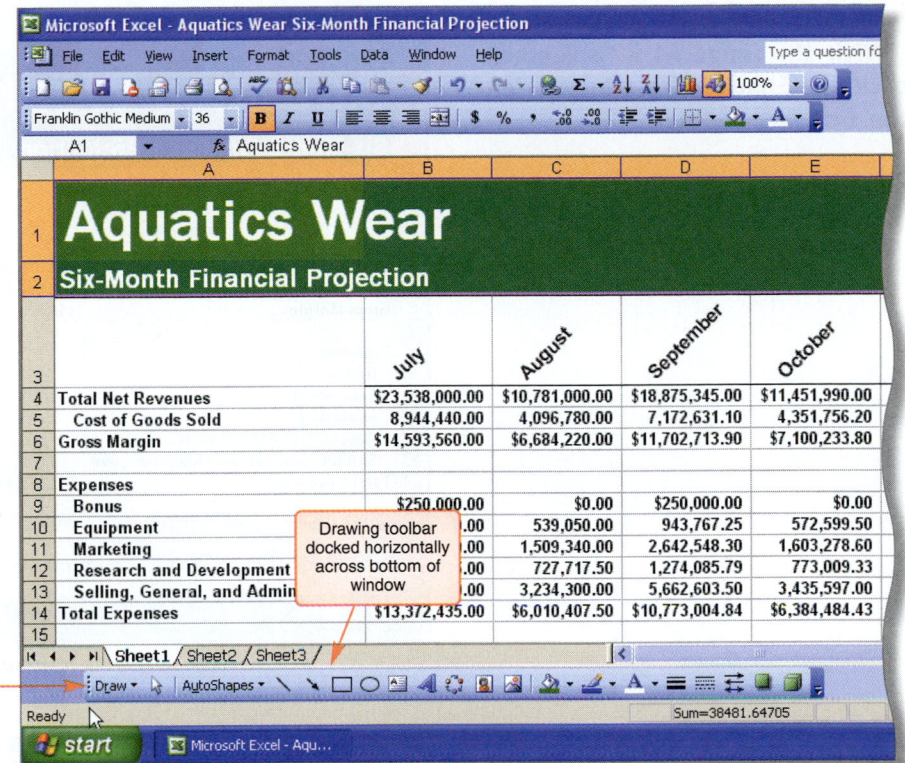

FIGURE 3-46

Compare Figure 3-46 with Figure 3-45. The heavy window border that surrounded the floating toolbar has changed to a light border and the title bar no longer appears.

To move a toolbar to any of the other three toolbar docks, drag the toolbar from its current position to the desired side of the window. To move a docked toolbar, it is easiest to point to the move handle and, when the mouse pointer changes to a cross with four arrowheads, drag it to the desired location.

Adding a Drop Shadow

With the Drawing toolbar docked at the bottom of the screen, the next step is to add the drop shadow to the range A1:H2, as shown in the steps on the next page.

To Add a Drop Shadow

1

• **With the range A1:H2 selected, click the Shadow Style button on the Drawing toolbar.**

Excel displays the Shadow Style palette of drop shadows with varying shadow depths (Figure 3-47).

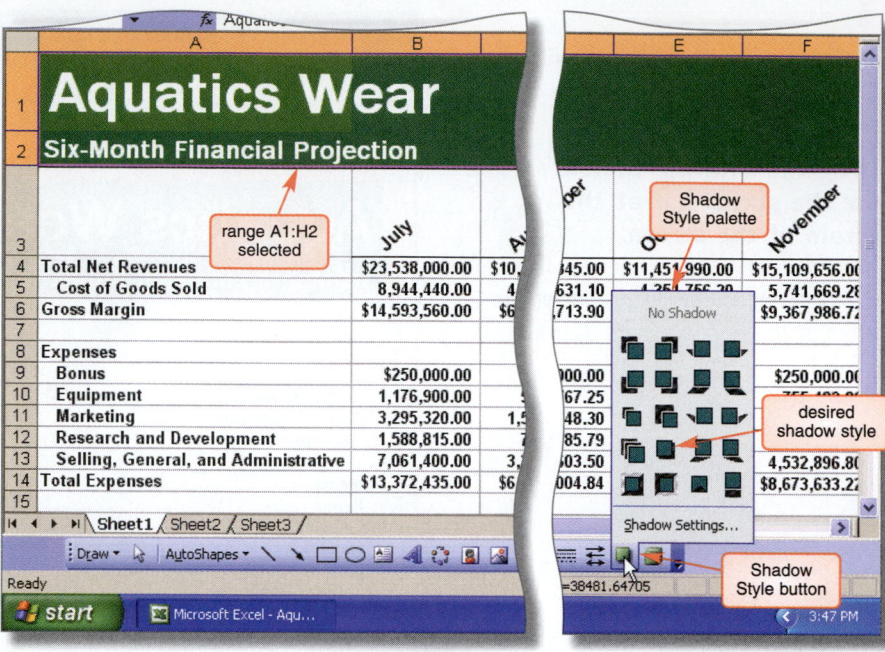

FIGURE 3-47

2

• **Click Shadow Style 14 (column 2, row 4) on the Shadow Style palette.**

• **Click cell A4 to deselect the range A1:H2.**

Excel adds a drop shadow to the range A1:H2 (Figure 3-48).

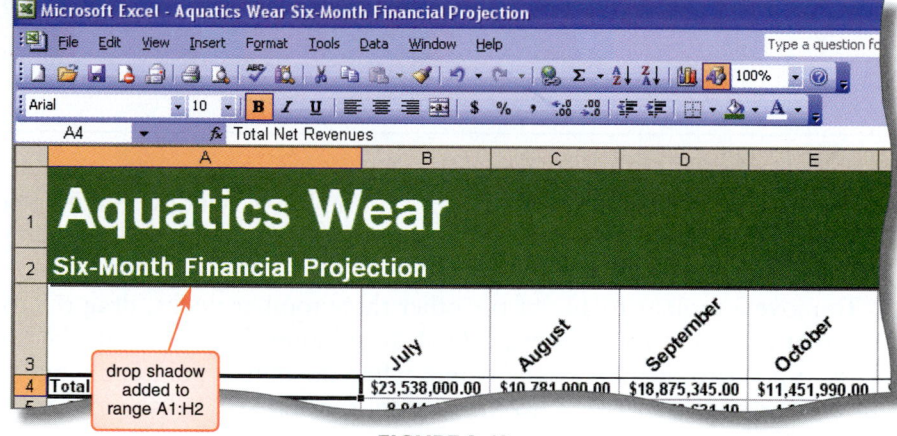

FIGURE 3-48

When you add a drop shadow to a range of cells, Excel selects the drop shadow and surrounds it with handles. To deselect the drop shadow, click any cell, as described in Step 2 above.

Formatting Nonadjacent Cells

The following steps change the font type and font size of the nonadjacent cells A4, A6, A8, A14, and A16 to 12-point Franklin Gothic Medium. The steps then add the light yellow background color and drop shadows to the nonadjacent cells A4, A6, A8, A14, and the range A16:H16.

To Change Font, Add Underlines, Add Background Colors, and Add Drop Shadows to Nonadjacent Cells

1

• **With cell A4 selected, hold down the CTRL key, click cells A6, A8, A14, and A16.**

• **Click the Font box arrow on the Formatting toolbar, scroll down and click Franklin Gothic Medium (or a similar font) in the Font list.**

• **Click the Font Size box arrow on the Formatting toolbar and then click 12 in the Font Size list.**

• **Use the CTRL key to select the nonadjacent ranges B5:H5 and B13:H13 and then click the Borders button on the Formatting toolbar.**

• **Click cell A4 and then while holding down the CTRL key, click cells A6, A8, A14, and select the range A16:H16.**

• **Click the Fill Color button arrow on the Formatting toolbar and then click Light Yellow (column 3, row 5).**

• **Click the Shadow Style button on the Drawing toolbar**

Excel displays the worksheet with the new formats (Figure 3-49). The Shadow Style palette appears at the bottom of the window.

2

• **Click Shadow Style 14 (column 2, row 4) on the Shadow palette.**

Excel adds a drop shadow to cells A4, A6, A8, A14, and the range A16:H16 (Figure 3-50).

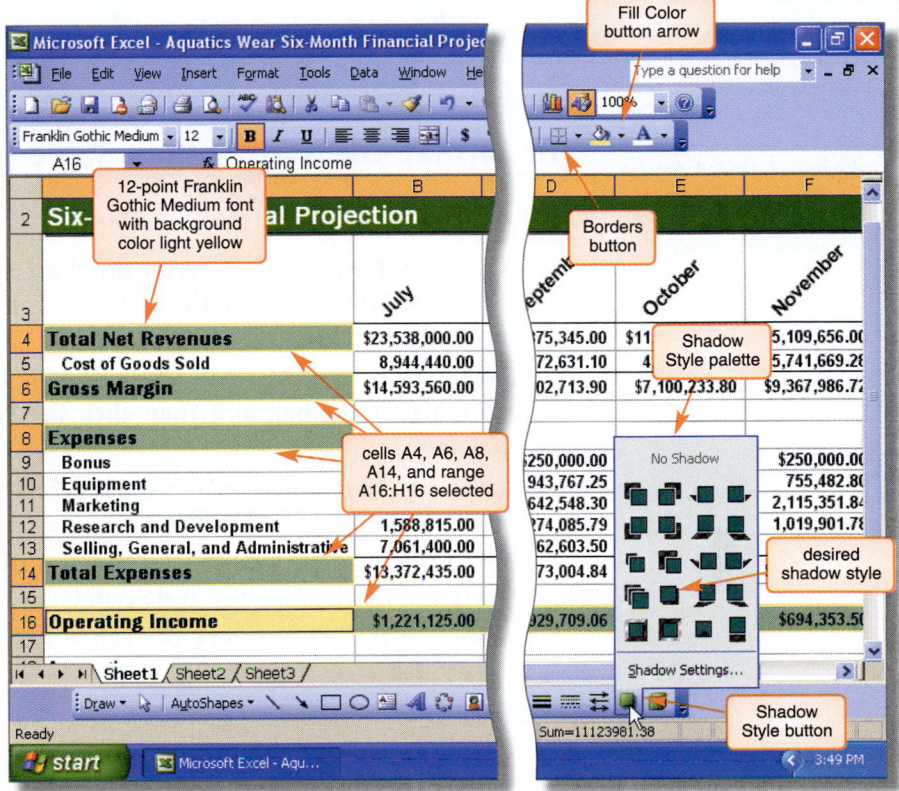

FIGURE 3-49

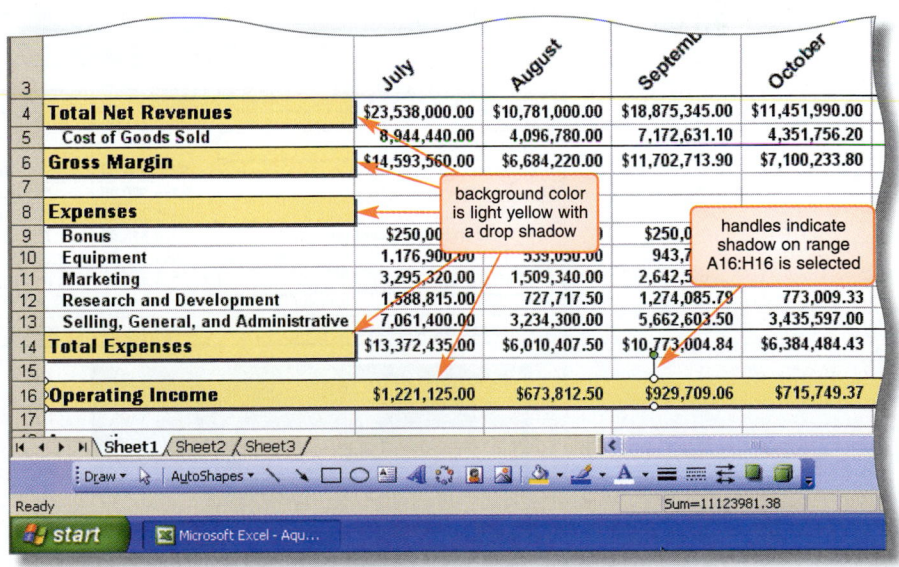

FIGURE 3-50

An alternative to formatting the nonadjacent ranges at once is to select each range separately and then apply the formats.

Formatting the Assumptions Table

The last step to improving the appearance of the worksheet is to format the Assumptions table in the range A18:B25. The specifications in Figure 3-37 on page EX 177 require a 16-point italic underlined font for the title in cell A18. The range A18:B25 has a white font, green background color, and a drop shadow that surrounds it. The following steps format the Assumptions table.

To Format the Assumptions Table

1 Scroll down to view rows 18 through 25 and then click cell A18.

2 Click the Font Size box arrow on the Formatting toolbar and then click 16 in the Font Size list. Click the Italic button and then click the Underline button on the Formatting toolbar.

3 Select the range A18:B25, click the Fill Color button arrow on the Formatting toolbar, and then click Green (column 4, row 2) on the Fill Color palette.

4 Click the Font Color button on the Formatting toolbar to change the font in the selected range to white.

5 Click the Shadow Style button on the Drawing toolbar and then click Shadow Style 14 on the Shadow Style palette.

6 Click cell D25 to deselect the range A18:B25.

Excel displays the Assumptions table as shown in Figure 3-51.

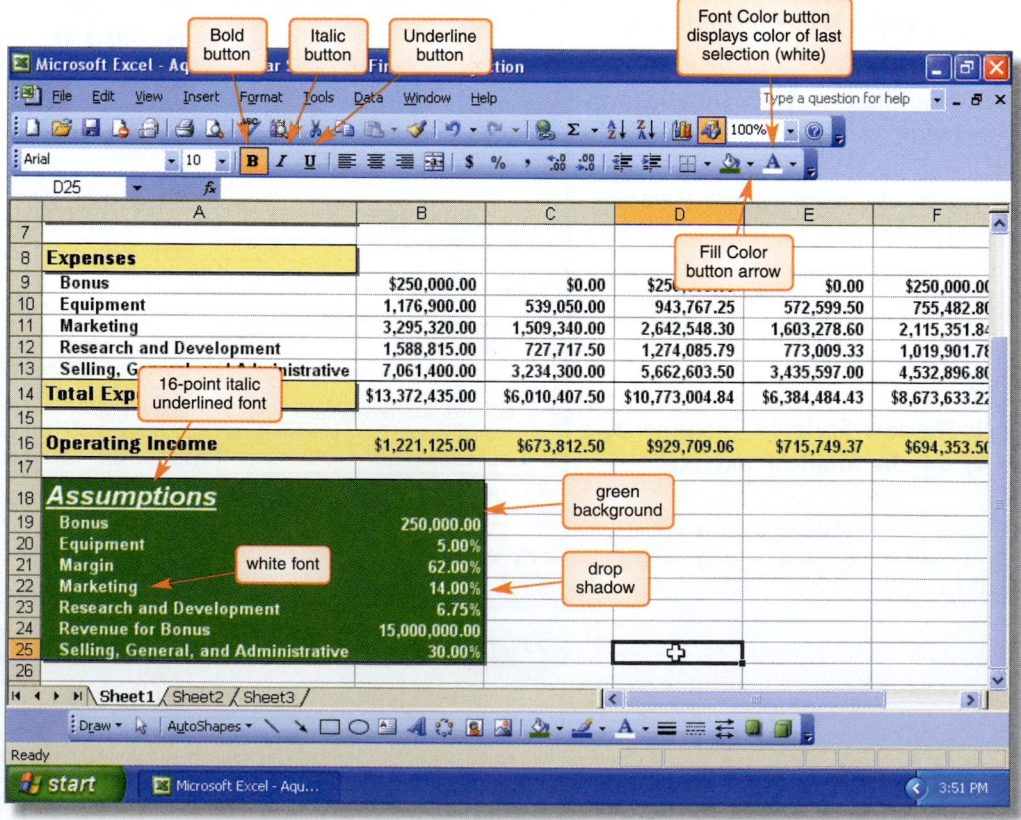

FIGURE 3-51

The previous steps introduced you to two new formats: italic and underline. When you assign the **italic** font style to a cell, Excel slants the characters slightly to the right as shown in cell A18 in Figure 3-51. The **underline** format underlines only the characters in the cell, rather than the entire cell, as is the case when you assign a cell a bottom border.

Hiding the Drawing Toolbar and Saving the Workbook

The formatting of the worksheet is complete. The following steps hide the Drawing toolbar and save the workbook.

To Hide the Drawing Toolbar and Save the Workbook

1. Click the Drawing button on the Standard toolbar.

2. Click the Save button on the Standard toolbar.

Excel hides the Drawing toolbar (Figure 3-52) and saves the workbook using the file name Aquatics Wear Six-Month Financial Projection.

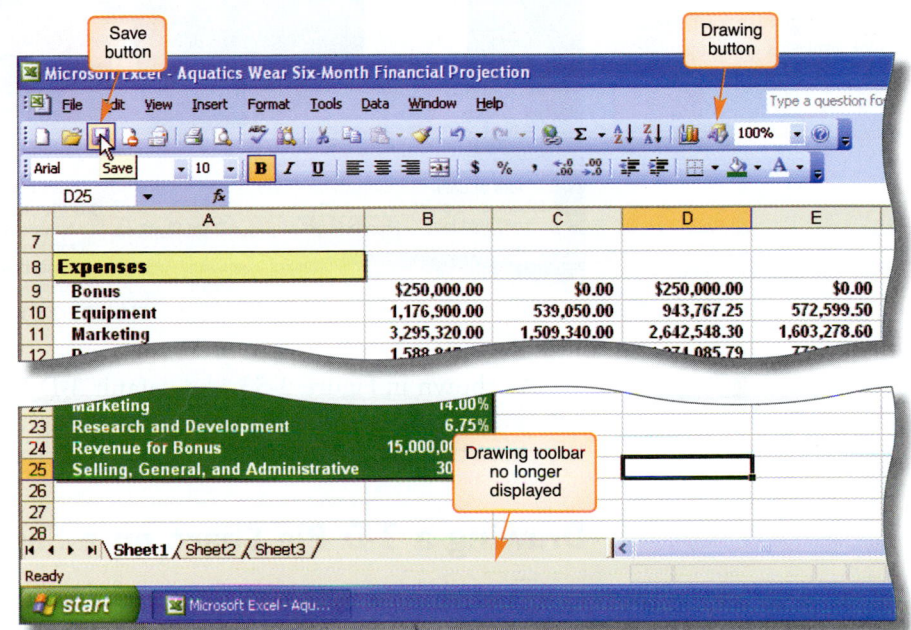

FIGURE 3-52

Adding a 3-D Pie Chart to the Workbook

The next step in the project is to draw the 3-D Pie chart on a separate sheet in the workbook, as shown in Figure 3-53 on the next page. A **Pie chart** is used to show the relationship or proportion of parts to a whole. Each slice (or wedge) of the pie shows what percent that slice contributes to the total (100%). The 3-D Pie chart in Figure 3-53 shows the contribution of each month's projected operating income to the six-month projected operating income. The 3-D Pie chart makes it easy to evaluate the contribution of one month to the six-month projected operating income in comparison to the other months.

Unlike the 3-D Column chart created in Project 1, the 3-D Pie chart shown in Figure 3-53 is not embedded in the worksheet. Instead, the Pie chart resides on a separate sheet, called a **chart sheet**, which contains only the chart.

In this worksheet, the ranges to chart are the nonadjacent ranges B3:G3 (month names) and B16:G16 (monthly operating incomes). The month names in the range B3:G3 will identify the slices of the Pie chart; these entries are called **category names**. The range B16:G16 contains the data that determines the size of the slices in the pie; these entries are called the **data series**. Because six months are being charted, the 3-D Pie chart contains six slices.

The sketch of the 3-D Pie chart in Figure 3-3b on page EX 149 also calls for emphasizing the month with the greatest contribution to the six-month projected operating income (in this case, December) by offsetting its slice from the main portion. A Pie chart with one or more slices offset is called an **exploded Pie chart**.

More About

Charts

You are aware that, when you change a value on which a chart is dependent, Excel immediately redraws the chart based on the new value. Did you know that, with bar charts, you can drag the bar in the chart in one direction or another to change the corresponding value in the worksheet, as well?

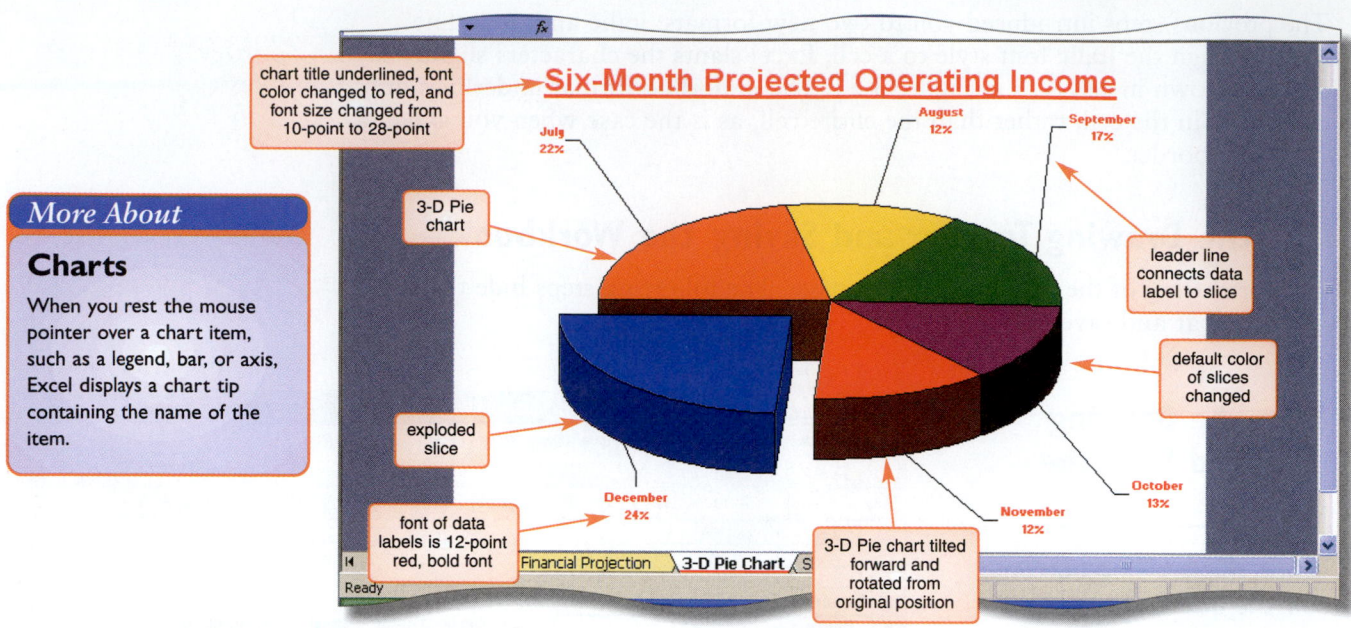

More About

Charts

When you rest the mouse pointer over a chart item, such as a legend, bar, or axis, Excel displays a chart tip containing the name of the item.

FIGURE 3-53

As shown in Figure 3-53, the default 3-D Pie chart also has been enhanced by rotating and tilting the pie forward, changing the colors of the slices, and modifying the chart title and labels that identify the slices.

Drawing a 3-D Pie Chart on a Separate Chart Sheet

The following steps show how to draw the 3-D Pie chart on a separate chart sheet using the Chart Wizard button on the Standard toolbar.

To Draw a 3-D Pie Chart on a Separate Chart Sheet

1

• **Select the range B3:G3.**

• **While holding down the CTRL key, select the range B16:G16.**

• **Click the Chart Wizard button on the Standard toolbar.**

• **When Excel displays the Chart Wizard - Step 1 of 4 - Chart Type dialog box, click Pie in the Chart type list and then click the 3-D Pie chart (column 2, row 1) in the Chart sub-type box.**

Excel displays the Chart Wizard - Step 1 of 4 - Chart Type dialog box, which allows you to select one of the 14 types of charts available in Excel (Figure 3-54).

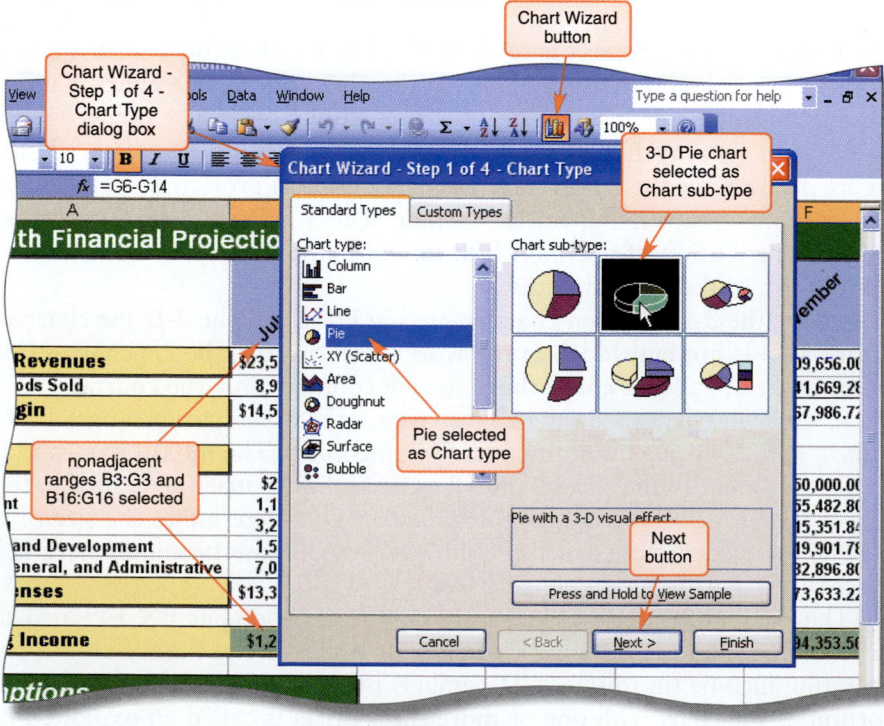

FIGURE 3-54

2

• **Click the Next button.**

Excel displays the Chart Wizard - Step 2 of 4 - Chart Source Data dialog box showing a sample of the 3-D Pie chart and the chart data range. A marquee surrounds the selected nonadjacent ranges on the worksheet (Figure 3-55).

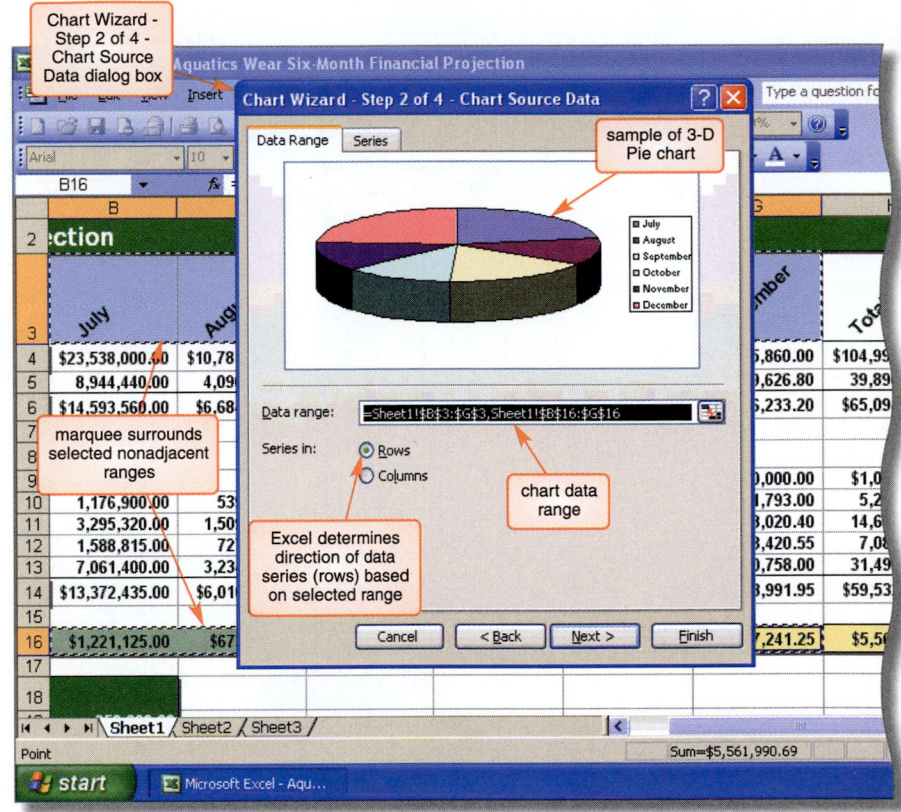

FIGURE 3-55

3

• **Click the Next button.**

• **When Excel displays the Chart Wizard - Step 3 of 4 - Chart Options dialog box, type** Six-Month Projected Operating Income **in the Chart title text box.**

Excel redraws the sample 3-D Pie chart with the chart title, Six-Month Projected Operating Income (Figure 3-56). Excel automatically bolds the chart title.

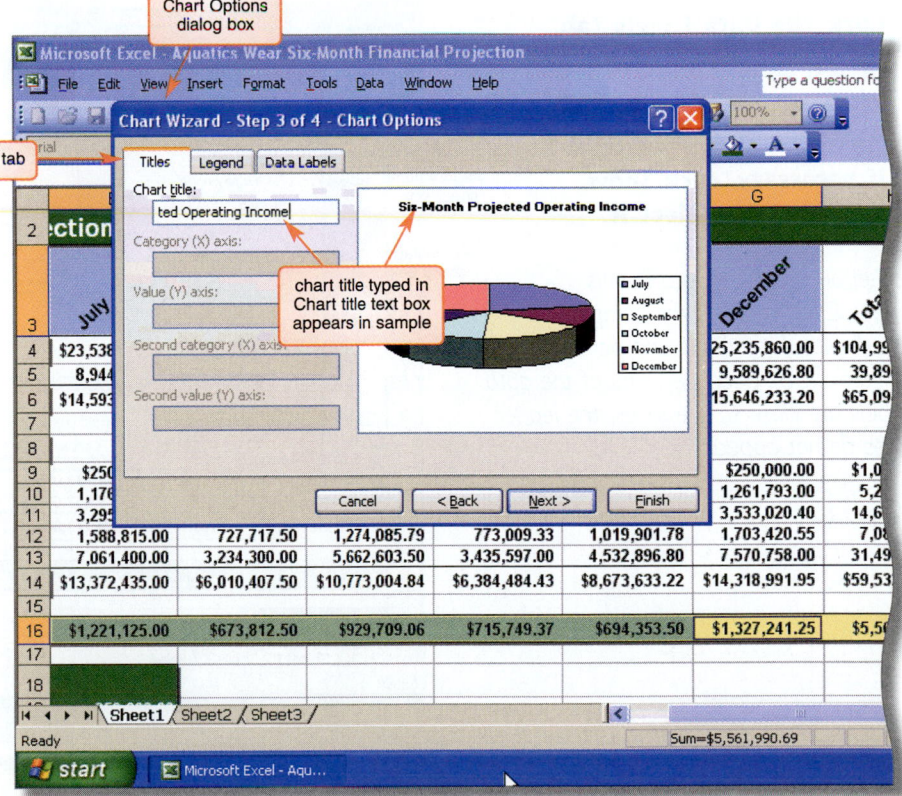

FIGURE 3-56

4

• **Click the Legend tab and then click Show legend to remove the check mark.**

Excel displays the Legend tab. Excel redraws the sample 3-D Pie chart without the legend (Figure 3-57).

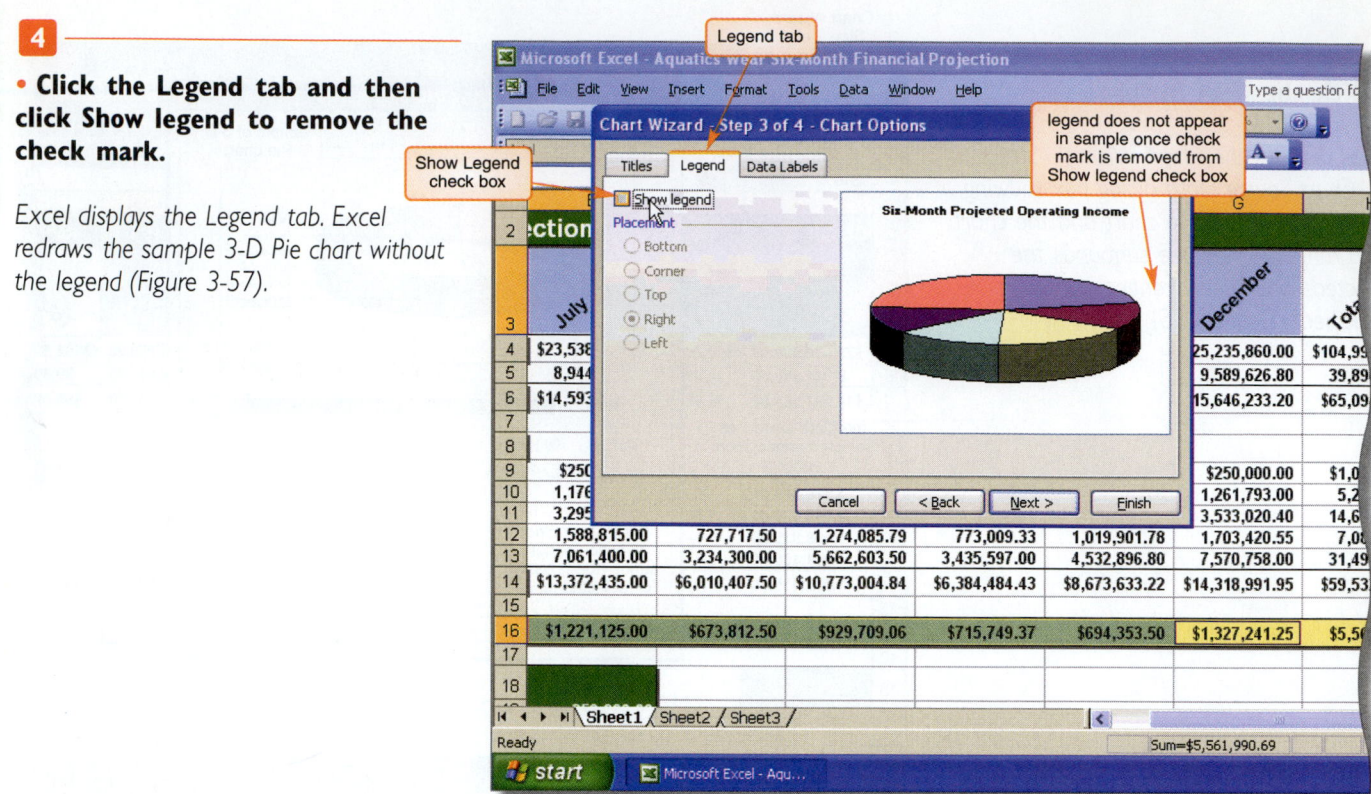

FIGURE 3-57

5

• **Click the Data Labels tab.**

• **In the Label Contains area, click Category name and click Percentage to select them.**

• **If necessary, click Show leader lines to select it.**

Excel displays the Data Labels sheet. Excel redraws the sample 3-D Pie chart with data labels and percentages (Figure 3-58). Because some of the data labels are close to the slices, the leader lines do not appear.

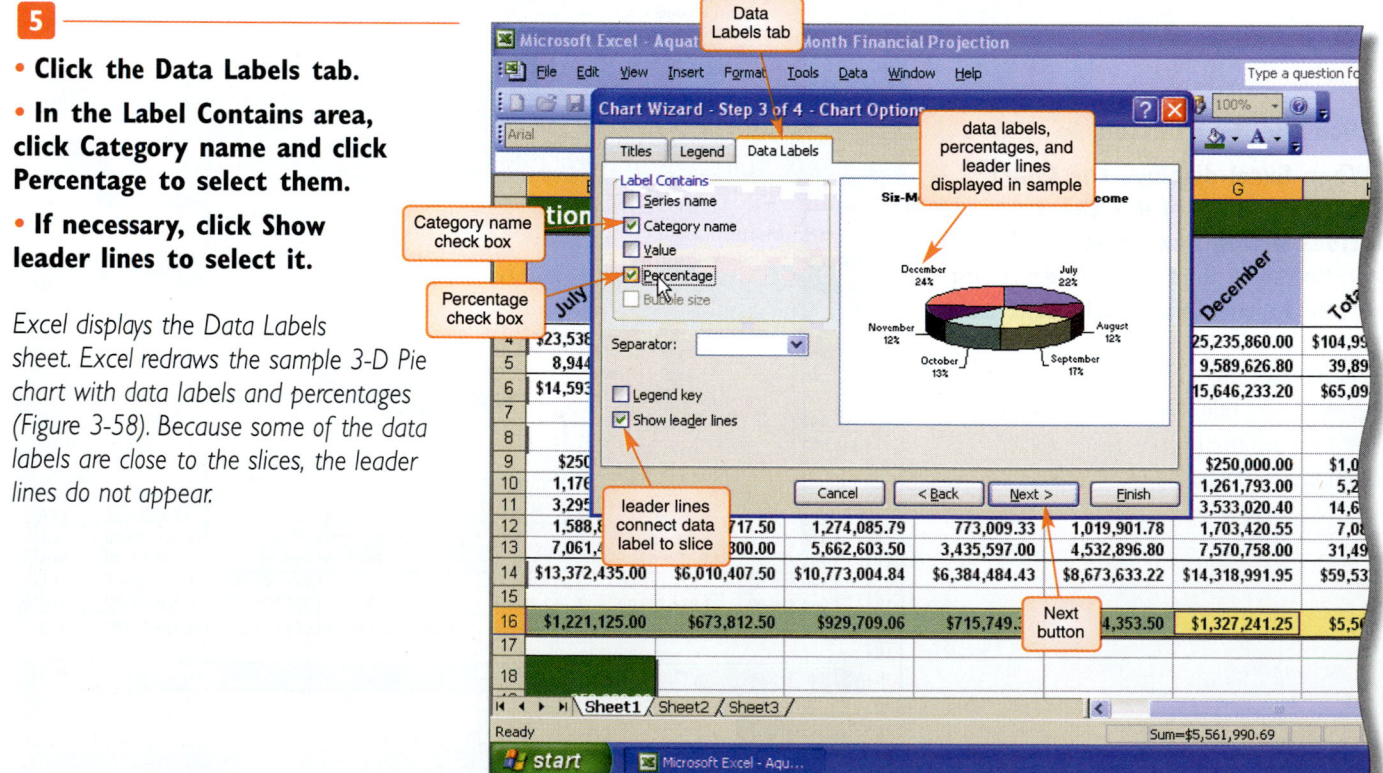

FIGURE 3-58

6

• **Click the Next button.**

• **When Excel displays the Chart Wizard - Step 4 of 4 - Chart Location dialog box, click As new sheet.**

Excel displays the Chart Wizard - Step 4 of 4 - Chart Location dialog box (Figure 3-59). It offers two chart location options: to draw the chart on a new sheet in the workbook or to draw it as an object in an existing worksheet.

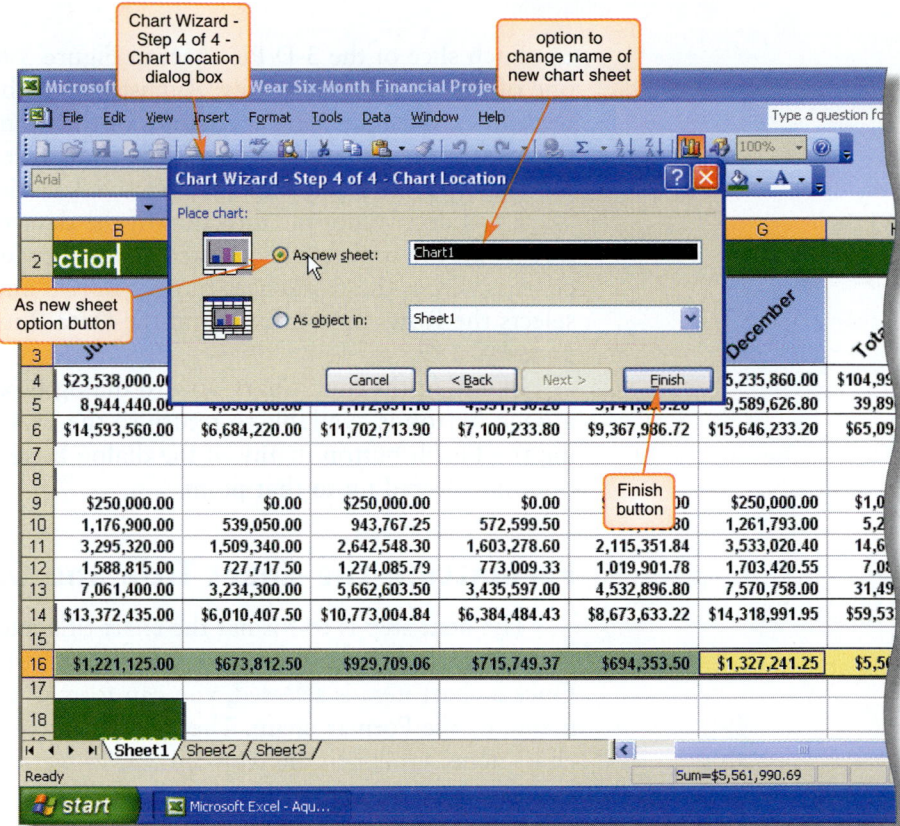

FIGURE 3-59

7

• **Click the Finish button.**

• **If the Chart toolbar appears, click its Close button.**

Excel draws the 3-D Pie chart on a separate chart sheet (Chart1) in the Aquatics Wear Six-Month Financial Projection workbook (Figure 3-60).

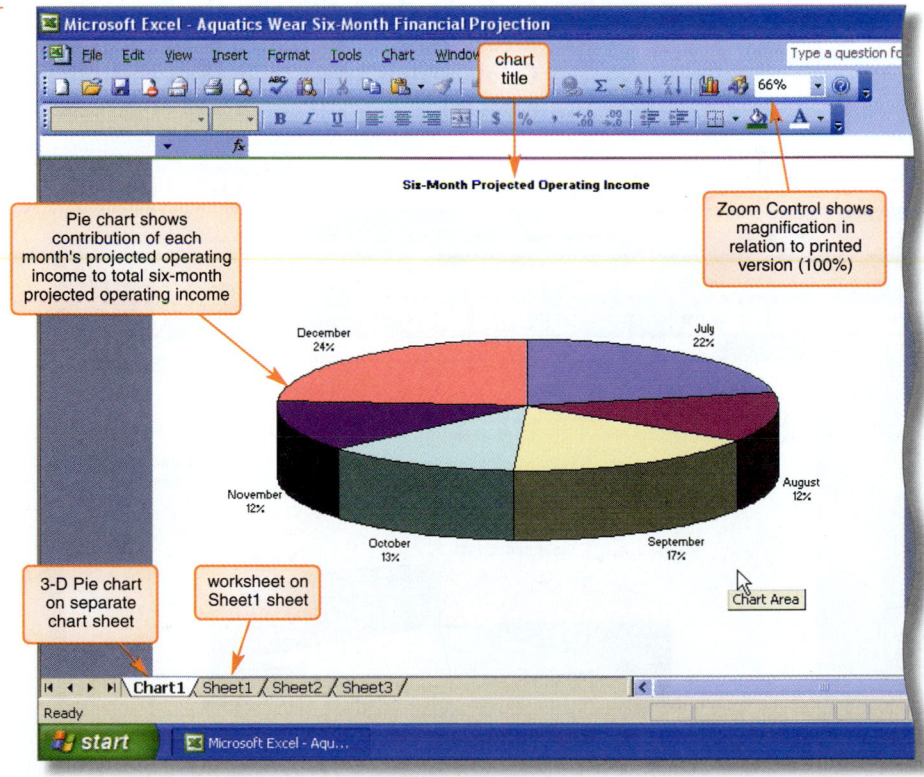

FIGURE 3-60

Other Ways

1. Select range to chart, press F11
2. Select range to chart, in Voice Command mode, say "Chart Wizard, [desired chart type]"

Each slice of the 3-D Pie chart in Figure 3-60 on the previous page represents one of the six months — July, August, September, October, November, and December. Excel displays the names of the months and the percent contribution to the total value outside the slices. The chart title, Six-Month Projected Operating Income, appears immediately above the 3-D Pie chart.

Excel determines the direction of the data series range (down a column or across a row) on the basis of the selected range. Because the range selected for the 3-D Pie chart is across the worksheet (ranges B3:G3 and B16:G16), Excel automatically selects the Rows option button in the Data Range sheet as shown in Figure 3-55 on page EX 189.

In any of the four Chart Wizard dialog boxes (Figure 3-54 through Figure 3-59), a Back button is available to return to the previous Chart Wizard dialog box. Clicking the Finish button in any of the dialog boxes creates the 3-D Pie chart with the options selected up to that point.

Formatting the Chart Title and Data Labels

The next step is to format the chart title and labels that identify the slices. Before you can format a chart item, such as the chart title or data labels, you must select it. Once a chart item is selected, you can format it using the Formatting toolbar, shortcut menu, or the Format menu. The following steps use the Formatting toolbar to format chart items similar to the way cell entries were formatted earlier in this project.

To Format the Chart Title and Data Labels

1 Click the chart title. On the Formatting toolbar, click the Font Size box arrow, click 28 in the Font Size list, click the Underline button, click the Font Color button arrow, and then click Red (column 1, row 3) on the Font Color palette.

2 Click one of the five data labels that identify the slices. On the Formatting toolbar, click the Font Size box arrow, click 12 in the Font Size list, click the Bold button, and then click the Font Color button to change the font to the color red.

Excel increases the font size of the chart title, underlines the chart title, and displays the chart title and data labels in red as shown in Figure 3-61. The data labels are selected.

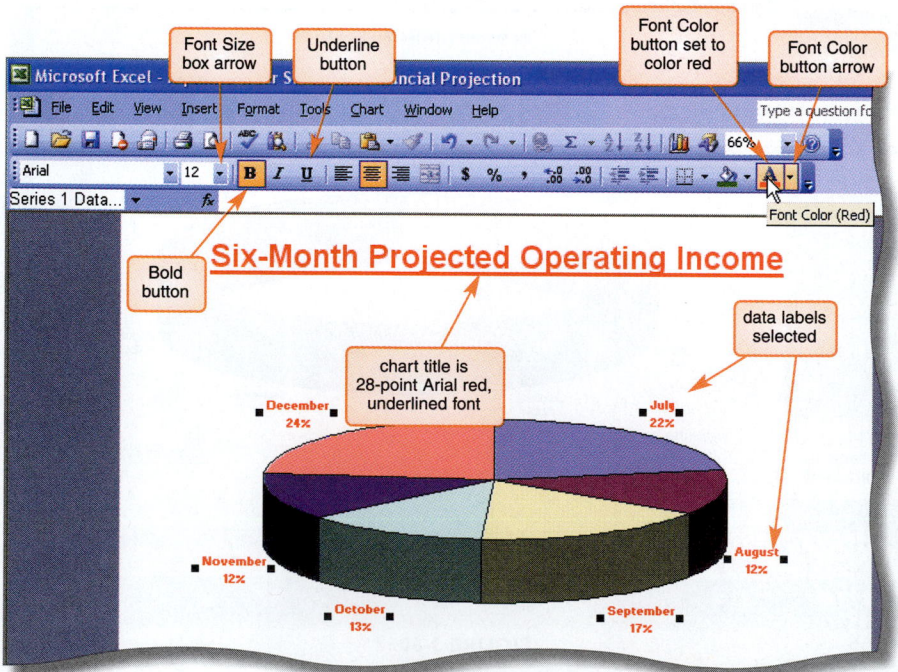

FIGURE 3-61

If you compare Figure 3-61 with Figure 3-60, you can see that the labels and chart title are easier to read and make the chart sheet look more professional.

Changing the Colors of Slices in a Pie Chart

The next step is to change the colors of the slices of the pie. The colors shown in Figure 3-61 are the default colors Excel uses when you first create a 3-D Pie chart. Project 3 requires that the colors be changed to those shown in Figure 3-53 on page EX 188. The following steps show how to change the colors of the slice by selecting them one at a time and using the Fill Color button arrow on the Formatting toolbar.

To Change the Colors of Slices in a Pie Chart

1

• **Click the July slice twice (do not double-click). Click the Fill Color button arrow on the Formatting toolbar.**

Excel displays sizing handles around the July slice. Excel also displays the Fill Color palette (Figure 3-62).

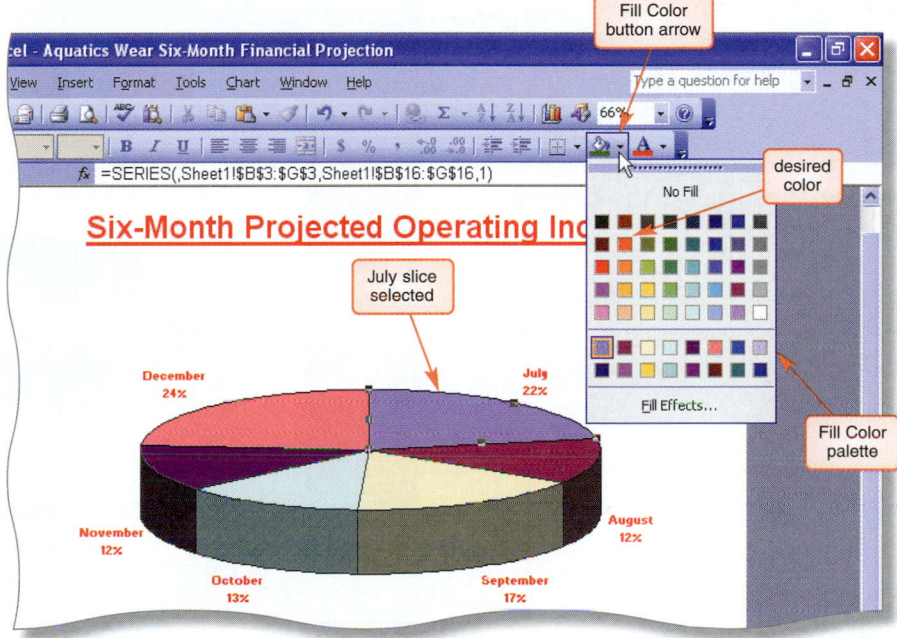

FIGURE 3-62

2

• **Click Orange (column 2, row 2). One at a time, click the remaining slices and then use the Fill Color button arrow on the Formatting toolbar to change each slice to the following colors: August – Yellow (column 3, row 4); September – Green (column 4, row 2); October – Plum (column 7, row 4); November – Red (column 1, row 3); and December – Blue (column 6, row 2). Click outside the chart area.**

Excel displays the 3-D Pie chart as shown in Figure 3-63.

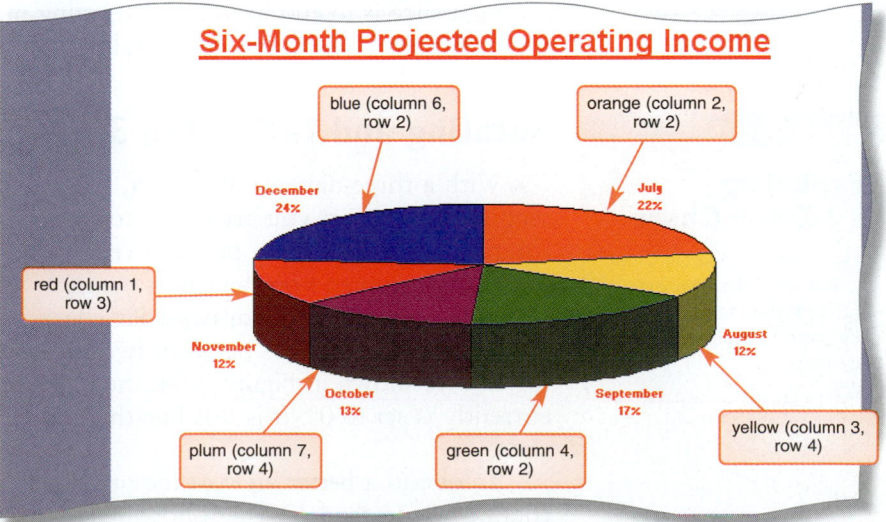

FIGURE 3-63

Exploding the 3-D Pie Chart

The next step is to emphasize the slice representing December, the month with the greatest contribution to the operating income, by **offsetting**, or exploding, it from the rest of the slices so that it stands out. The following steps show how to explode a slice of the 3-D Pie chart.

To Explode the 3-D Pie Chart

1

• **Click the slice labeled December twice (do not double-click).**

Excel displays sizing handles around the December slice.

2

• **Drag the slice to the desired position.**

Excel redraws the 3-D Pie chart with the December slice offset from the rest of the slices (Figure 3-64).

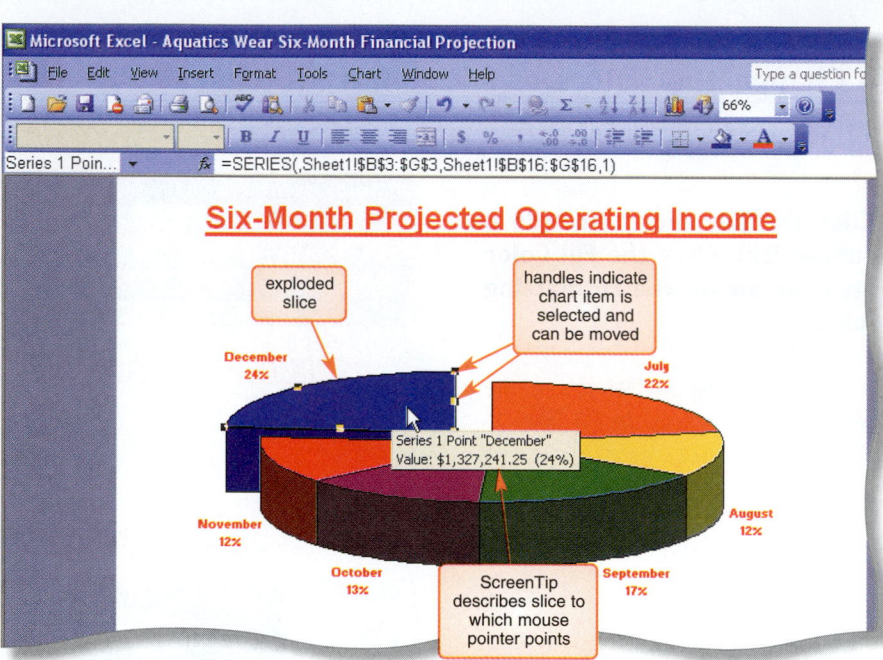

FIGURE 3-64

You can offset as many slices as you want, but remember that the reason for offsetting a slice is to emphasize it. Offsetting multiple slices tends to reduce the impact on the reader and reduces the overall size of the Pie chart.

Rotating and Tilting the 3-D Pie Chart

With a three-dimensional chart, you can change the view to better show the section of the chart you are trying to emphasize. Excel allows you to control the rotation angle, elevation, perspective, height, and angle of the axes by using the 3-D View command on the Chart menu.

When Excel initially draws a Pie chart, it always positions the chart so that one of the dividing lines between two slices is a straight line pointing to 12 o'clock (or 0°). As shown in Figure 3-64, the line that divides the July and December slices currently is set to 0°. It is this line that defines the rotation angle of the 3-D Pie chart.

To obtain a better view of the offset December slice, the 3-D Pie chart can be rotated 90° to the left. The following steps show how to rotate the 3-D Pie chart and change, or tilt, the elevation so the 3-D Pie chart is at less of an angle to the viewer.

To Rotate and Tilt the 3-D Pie Chart

1

• **With the December slice selected, click Chart on the menu bar.**

Excel displays the Chart menu (Figure 3-65).

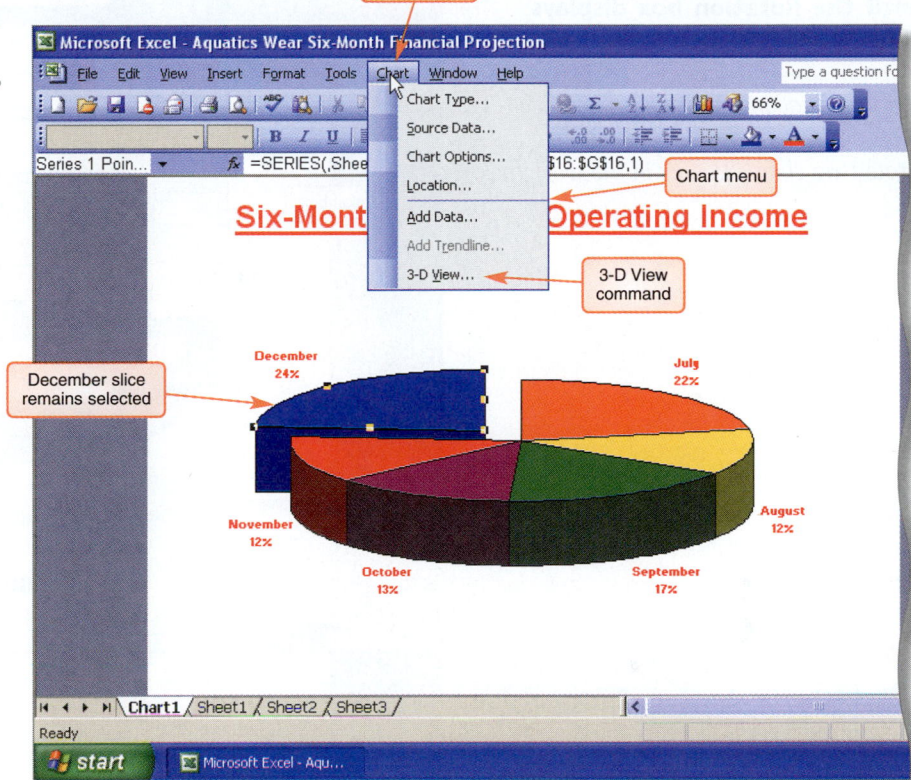

FIGURE 3-65

2

• **Click 3-D View.**

• **When Excel displays the 3-D View dialog box, click the Up Arrow button until 25 shows in the Elevation box.**

Excel displays the 3-D View dialog box, which includes a sample of the 3-D Pie chart (Figure 3-66). Increasing the elevation of the 3-D Pie chart causes it to tilt forward.

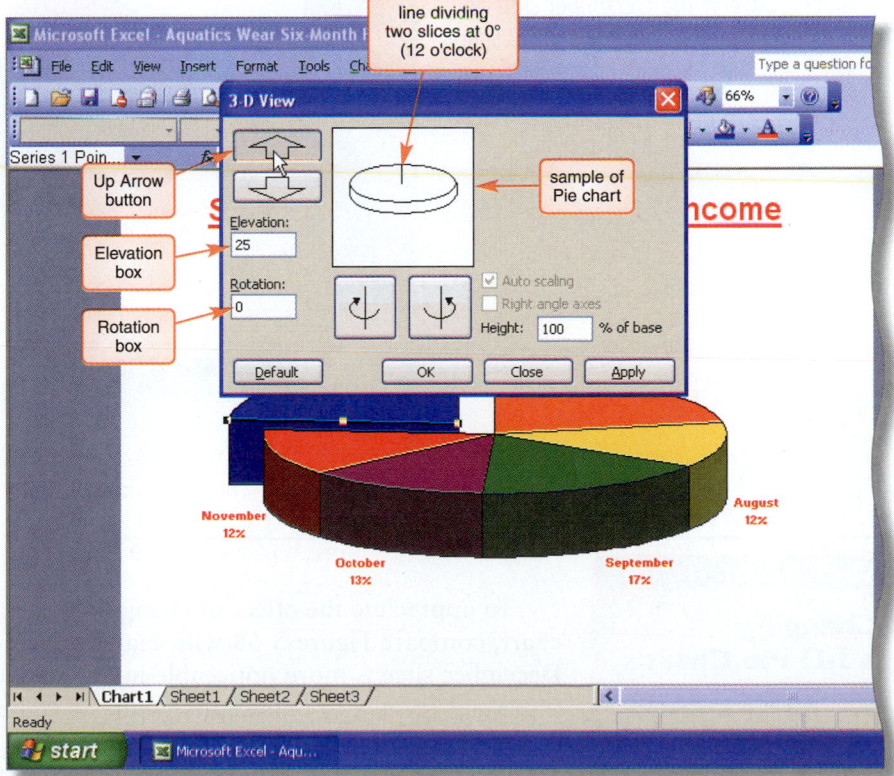

FIGURE 3-66

3

• **Click the Left Rotation button until the Rotation box displays 270.**

The new rotation setting (270) shows in the Rotation box (Figure 3-67). A sample of the rotated Pie chart appears in the dialog box.

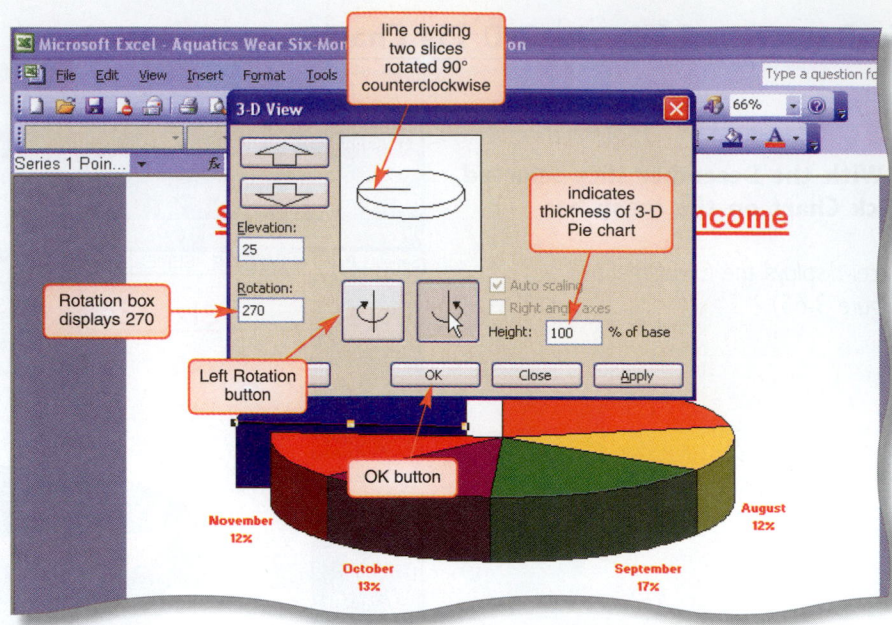

FIGURE 3-67

4

• **Click the OK button. Click outside the chart area.**

Excel displays the 3-D Pie chart tilted forward and rotated to the left, which makes the space between the December slice and the main portion of the pie more prominent (Figure 3-68).

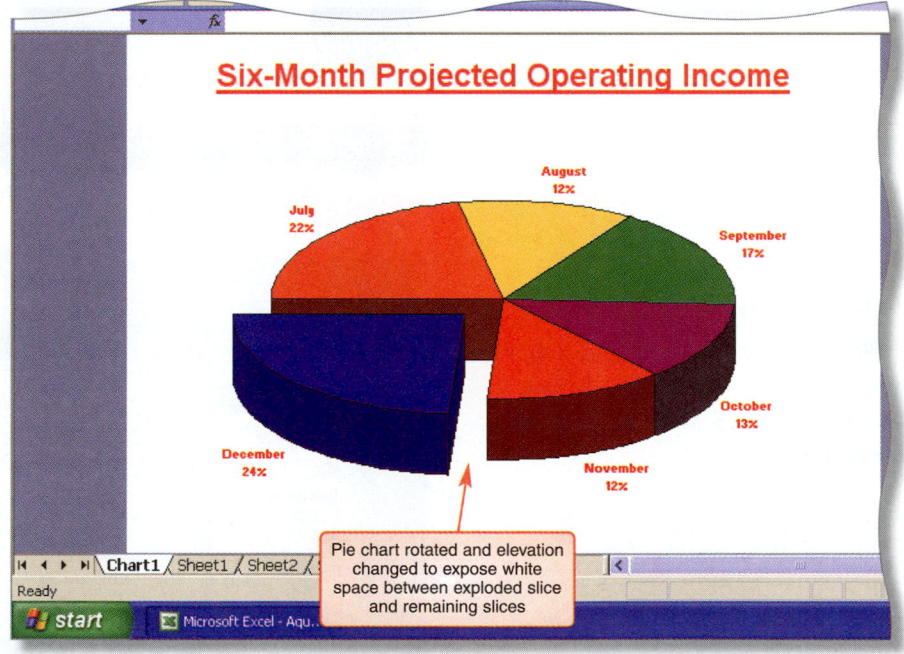

FIGURE 3-68

More About

Changing a 3-D Pie Chart's Thickness

You can increase or decrease the thickness of the 3-D Pie chart by changing the height to base ratio in the 3-D View dialog box (Figure 3-67).

To appreciate the effect of changing the elevation and rotation of the 3-D Pie chart, compare Figure 3-68 with Figure 3-65 on the previous page. The offset of the December slice is more noticeable in Figure 3-68, because the Pie chart has been tilted and rotated to expose the white space between the December slice and the rest of the Pie chart.

In addition to controlling the rotation angle and elevation, you also can control the thickness of the 3-D Pie chart by entering a percent smaller or larger than the default 100% in the Height box (Figure 3-67).

Showing Leader Lines with the Data Labels

In Step 5 on page EX 190 in the Data Labels sheet of the Chart Wizard - Step 3 of 4 - Chart Options dialog box, the Show leader lines option was selected to instruct Excel to display leader lines. As the data labels are dragged away from each slice, Excel draws thin leader lines that connect each data label to its corresponding slice. The following steps show how to add leader lines to the data labels.

To Show Leader Lines with the Data Labels

1

• **Click the December data label twice (do not double-click).**

Excel displays a box with handles around the December data label.

2

• **Point to the upper-left sizing handle on the box border and drag the December data label away from the December slice.**

• **Select and drag the remaining data labels away from their corresponding slices as shown in Figure 3-69.**

• **Click outside the chart area.**

Excel displays the data labels with leader lines as shown in Figure 3-69.

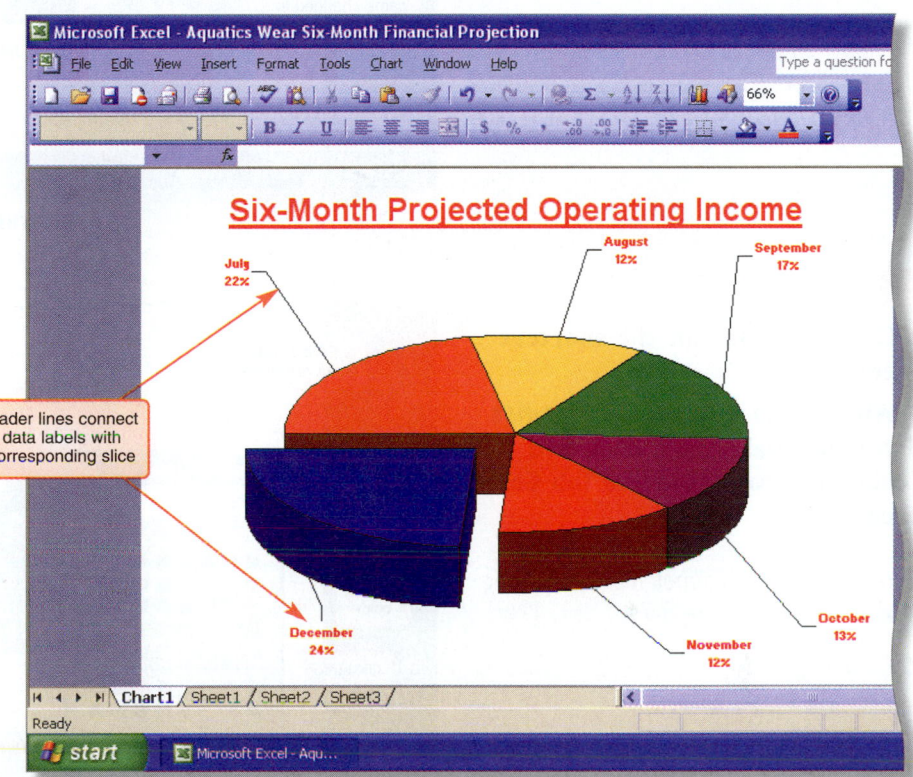

FIGURE 3-69

You also can select and format individual labels by clicking a specific data label after all the data labels have been selected. Making an individual data label larger or a different color, for example, helps emphasize a small or large slice in a Pie chart.

Renaming and Reordering the Sheets and Coloring Their Tabs

The final step in creating the workbook is to reorder the sheets and modify the tabs at the bottom of the screen. The steps on the next page show how to rename the sheets, color the tabs, and reorder the sheets so the worksheet precedes the chart sheet in the workbook.

To Rename and Reorder the Sheets and Color Their Tabs

1

• **Double-click the tab labeled Chart1 at the bottom of the screen.**

• **Type** 3-D Pie Chart **and then press the ENTER key.**

• **Right-click the tab.**

The label on the Chart1 tab changes to 3-D Pie Chart (Figure 3-70). Excel displays the tab's shortcut menu.

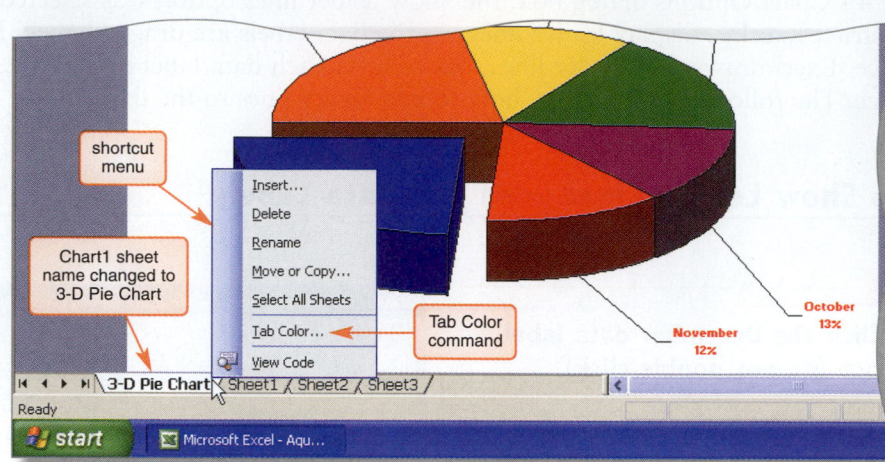

FIGURE 3-70

2

• **Click Tab Color on the shortcut menu.**

• **When Excel displays the Format Tab Color dialog box, click Red (column 1, row 3) in the Tab Color area.**

Excel displays the Format Tab Color dialog box as shown in Figure 3-71.

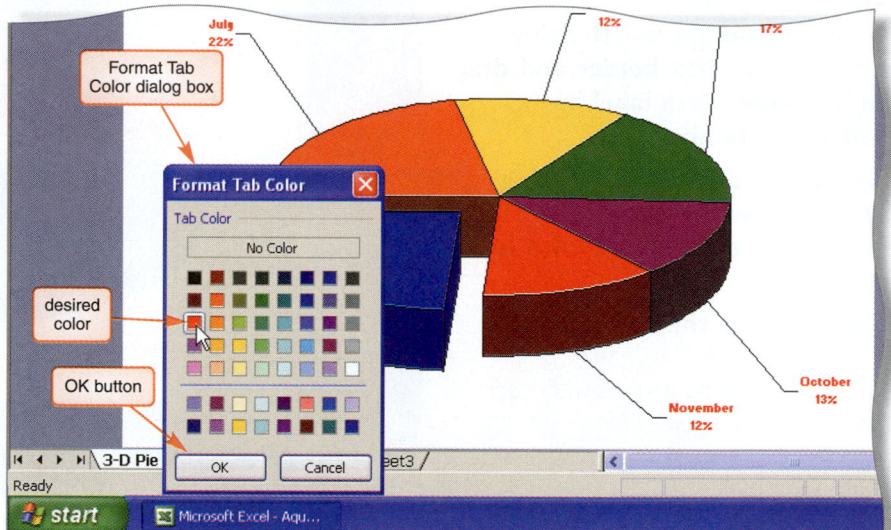

FIGURE 3-71

3

• **Click the OK button.**

Excel displays the name on the tab with a red underline (Figure 3-72). The red underline indicates the sheet is active. When the sheet is inactive, Excel displays the tab with a red background.

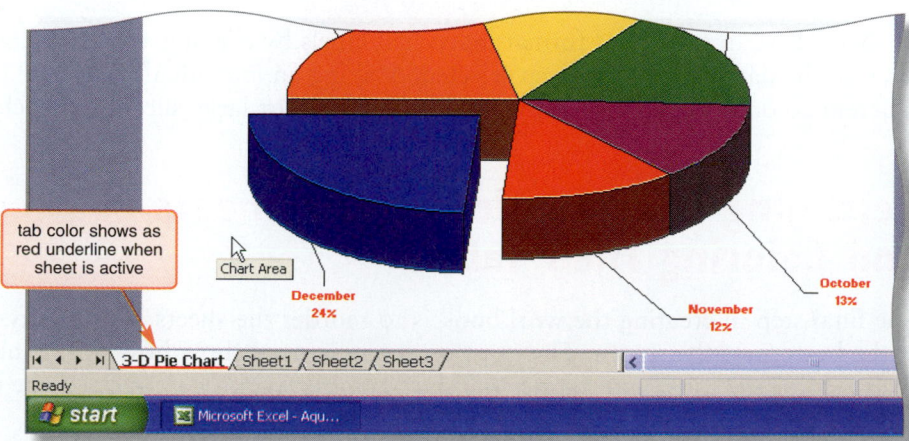

FIGURE 3-72

4

- Double-click the tab labeled **Sheet1** at the bottom of the screen.

- Type Six-Month Financial Projection as the new sheet name and then press the ENTER key.

- Right-click the tab and then click **Tab Color** on the shortcut menu.

- When Excel displays the Format Tab Color dialog box, click Light Yellow (column 3, row 5) in the Tab Color area, and then click the OK button.

- Drag the Six-Month Financial Projection tab to the left in front of the 3-D Pie Chart tab and then click cell E18.

Excel rearranges the sequence of the sheets and displays the Six-Month Financial Projection worksheet (Figure 3-73). The yellow underline indicates the sheet is active.

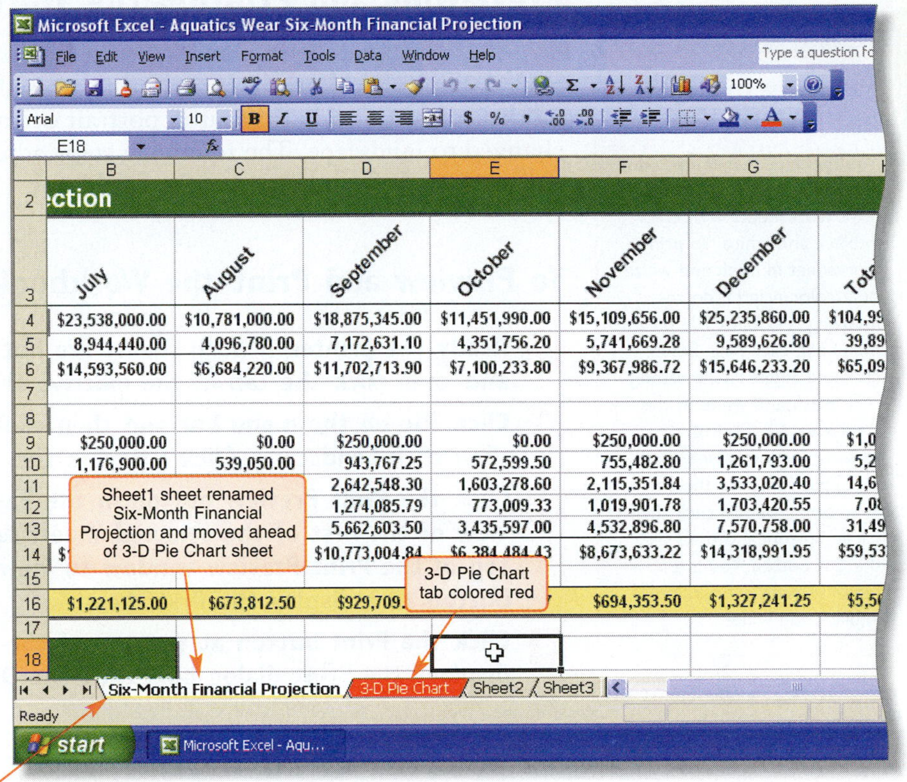

Sheet1 sheet renamed Six-Month Financial Projection and moved ahead of 3-D Pie Chart sheet

3-D Pie Chart tab colored red

tab color shows as light yellow underline when sheet is active

FIGURE 3-73

Checking Spelling, Saving, Previewing, and Printing the Workbook

With the workbook complete, this section checks spelling, saves, previews, and then prints the workbook. Each set of steps concludes with saving the workbook to ensure that the latest changes are saved.

Checking Spelling in Multiple Sheets

By default, the spell checker checks the spelling only in the selected sheets. It will check all the cells in the selected sheets, unless you select a range of two or more cells. Before checking the spelling, the following steps select the 3-D Pie Chart sheet so that the entire workbook is checked for spelling errors.

To Check Spelling in Multiple Sheets

1 With the Six-Month Financial Projection sheet active, hold down the CTRL key and then click the 3-D Pie Chart tab.

2 Click the Spelling button on the Standard toolbar.

3 Correct any errors and then click the OK button when the spell check is complete.

4 Click the Save button on the Standard toolbar.

Previewing and Printing the Workbook

After checking the spelling, the next step is to preview and print the sheets. As with spelling, Excel previews and prints only the selected sheets. Also, because the worksheet is too wide to print in portrait orientation, the orientation must be changed to landscape. The following steps adjust the orientation and scale, preview the workbook, and then print the workbook.

To Preview and Print the Workbook

1 Ready the printer. If both sheets are not selected, hold down the CTRL key and then click the tab of the inactive sheet.

2 Click File on the menu bar and then click Page Setup. Click the Page tab and then click Landscape. Click Fit to in the Scaling area.

3 Click the Print Preview button in the Page Setup dialog box. When the preview of the first of the selected sheets appears, click the Next button at the top of the Print Preview window to view the next sheet. Click the Previous button to redisplay the first sheet.

4 Click the Print button at the top of the Print Preview window. When Excel displays the Print dialog box, click the OK button.

5 Right-click the Six-Month Financial Projection tab. Click Ungroup Sheets on the shortcut menu to deselect the 3-D Pie Chart tab.

6 Click the Save button on the Standard toolbar.

The worksheet and 3-D Pie chart print as shown in Figures 3-74a and 3-74b. Excel saves the print settings with the workbook.

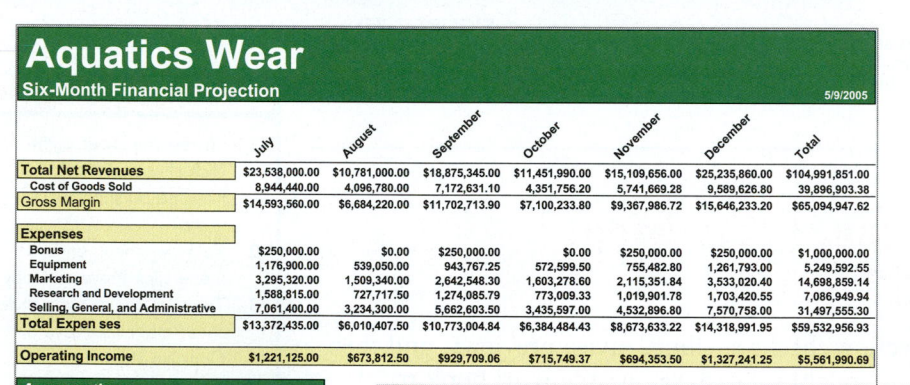

(a) Worksheet

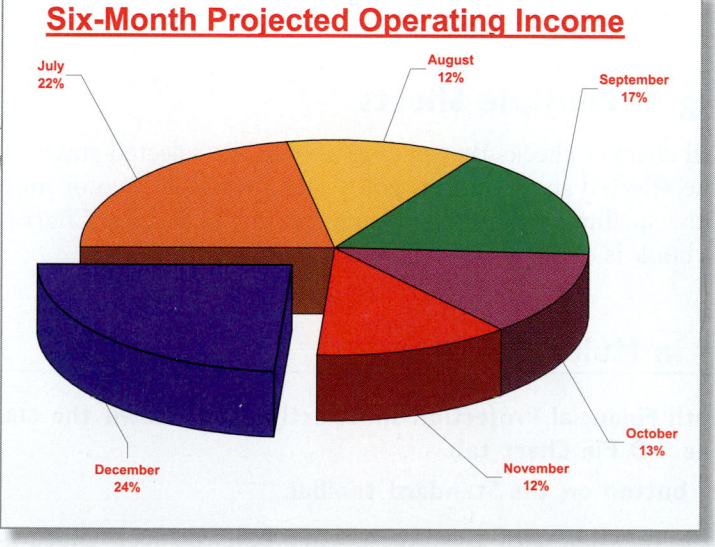
(b) 3-D Pie Chart

FIGURE 3-74

Changing the View of the Worksheet

With Excel, you easily can change the view of the worksheet. For example, you can magnify or shrink the worksheet on the screen. You also can view different parts of the worksheet through window panes.

More About

Zooming

You can type any number between 10 and 400 in the Zoom box on the Standard toolbar to reduce or enlarge the display of the worksheet.

Shrinking and Magnifying the View of a Worksheet or Chart

You can magnify (zoom in) or shrink (zoom out) the appearance of a worksheet or chart by using the Zoom box on the Standard toolbar. When you magnify a worksheet, Excel enlarges the view of the characters on the screen, but displays fewer columns and rows. Alternatively, when you shrink a worksheet, Excel is able to display more columns and rows. Magnifying or shrinking a worksheet affects only the view; it does not change the window size or printout of the worksheet or chart. The following steps shrink and magnify the view of the worksheet.

To Shrink and Magnify the View of a Worksheet or Chart

1

- If cell A1 is not active, press CTRL+HOME.

- Click the Zoom box arrow on the Standard toolbar.

Excel displays a list of percentages in the Zoom list (Figure 3-75).

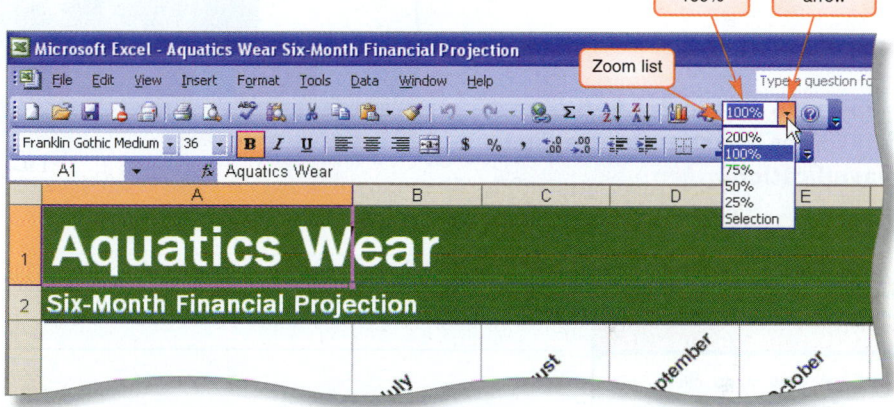

FIGURE 3-75

2

- Click 75%.

Excel shrinks the display of the worksheet to 75% of its normal display (Figure 3-76). With the worksheet zoomed out to 75%, you can see more rows and columns than you did at 100% magnification. Some of the numbers, however, appear as a series of number signs (#), because the columns are not wide enough to show the formatted numbers.

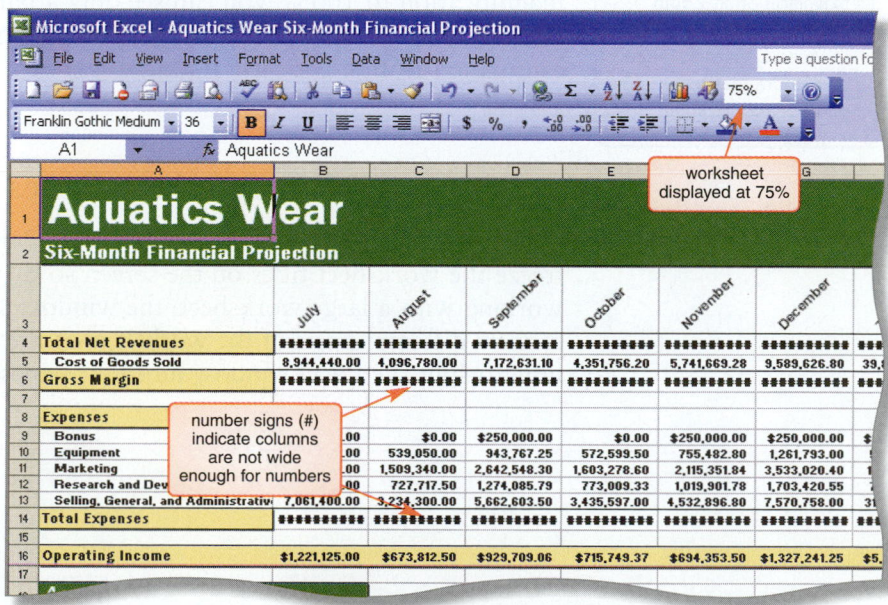

FIGURE 3-76

3

• **Click the Zoom box arrow on the Standard toolbar and then click 100%.**

Excel displays the worksheet at 100%.

4

• **Click the 3-D Pie Chart tab at the bottom of the screen. Click the Zoom box arrow on the Standard toolbar and then click 100%.**

Excel changes the magnification of the chart from 66% (shown in Figure 3-69 on page EX 197) to 100% (Figure 3-77). Excel displays the chart at the same size as the printout of the chart.

5

• **Enter 66 in the Zoom box to return the chart to its original magnification.**

Excel changes the magnification of the chart back to 66%.

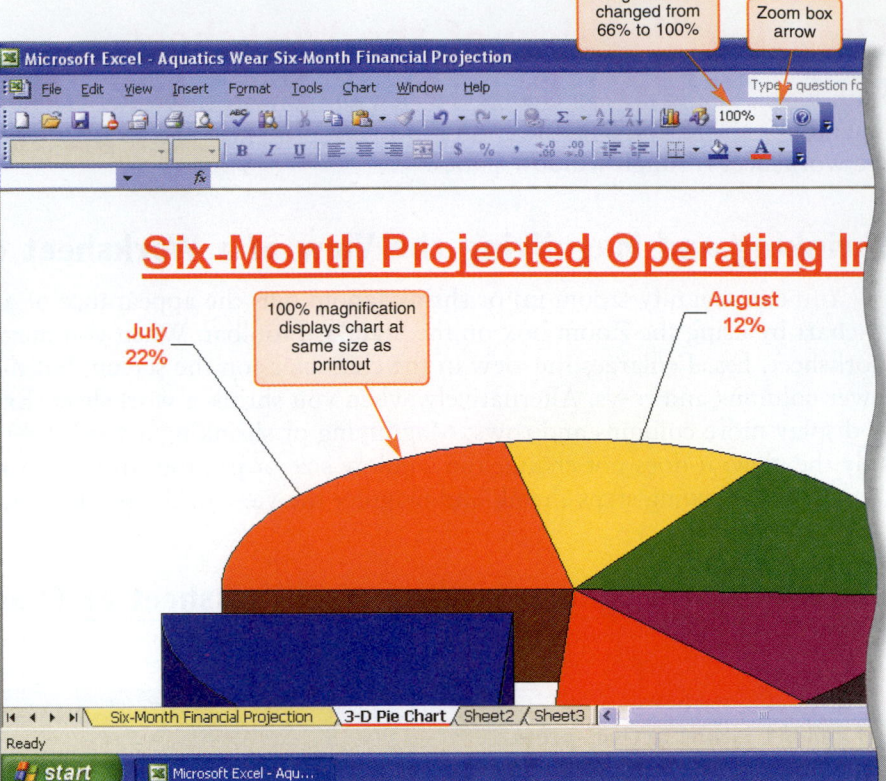

FIGURE 3-77

At 800 × 600 resolution, Excel normally displays a chart in the range of 65% to 70% magnification, so that the entire chart appears on the screen. By changing the magnification to 100%, you can see only a part of the chart, but at a magnification that corresponds with the chart's size on a printout. Excel allows you to enter a percent magnification between 10 and 400 in the Zoom box for worksheets and chart sheets.

Splitting the Window into Panes

This project previously used the Freeze Panes command to instruct Excel to freeze the worksheet titles on the screen so they always show when you scroll. When working with a large worksheet, the window also can be split into two or four panes to view different parts of the worksheet at the same time. The following steps show how to split the Excel window into four panes.

To Split a Window into Panes

1

- **Click the Six-Month Financial Projection tab at the bottom of the screen.**
- **Select cell D7, the intersection of the four proposed panes.**
- **Click Window on the menu bar.**

Excel displays the Window menu (Figure 3-78). Cell D7 is the active cell.

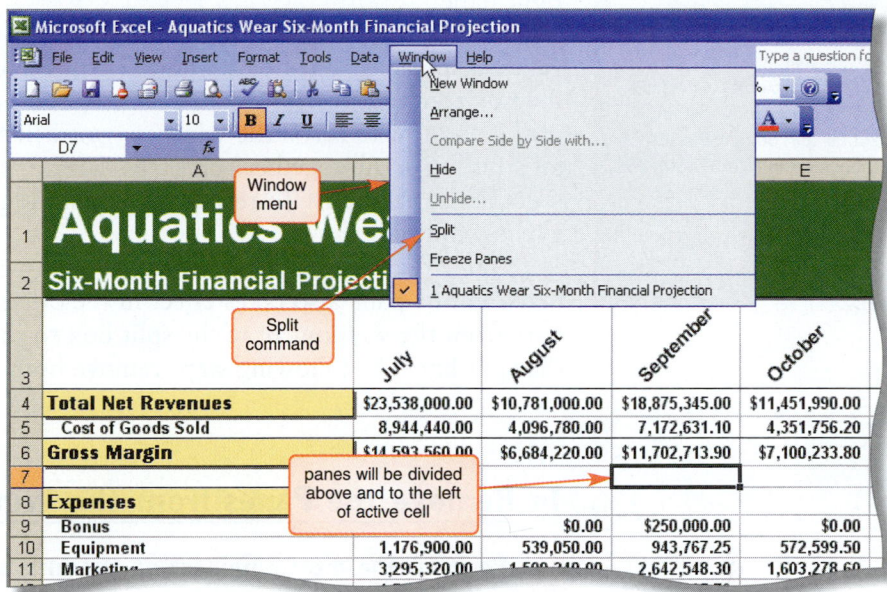

FIGURE 3-78

2

- **Click Split on the Window menu.**
- **Use the scroll arrows to show the four corners of the worksheet at the same time.**

Excel divides the window into four panes and displays the four corners of the worksheet (Figure 3-79).

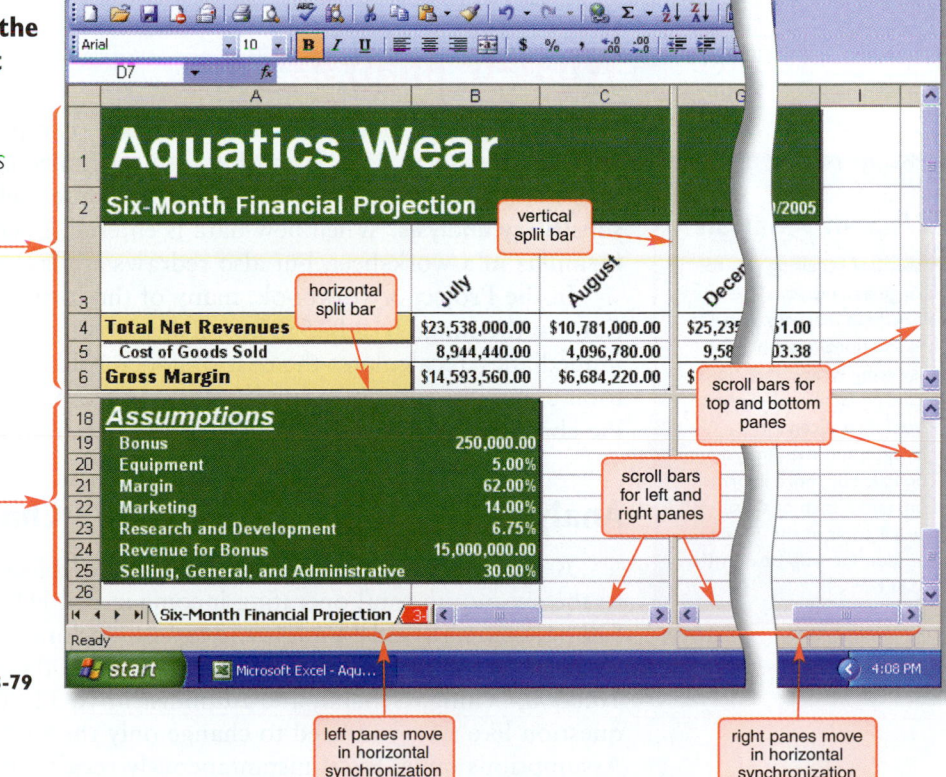

FIGURE 3-79

Other Ways

1. Drag horizontal split box and vertical split box to desired locations
2. In Voice Command mode, say "Window, Split"

More About

Window Panes

If you want to split the window into two panes, rather than four, drag the vertical split box to the far left of the window or horizontal split box to the top of the window (Figure 3-80). You also can drag the center of the four panes in any direction to change the size of the panes.

The four panes in Figure 3-79 on the previous page are used to show the following: (1) range A1:B6 in the upper-left pane; (2) range F1:I6 in the upper-right pane; (3) range A18:B26 in the lower-left pane; and (4) range F18:I26 in the lower-right pane.

The vertical bar going up and down the middle of the window is called the **vertical split bar**. The horizontal bar going across the middle of the window is called the **horizontal split bar**. If you use the scroll bars below the window and to the right of the window to scroll the window, you will see that the panes split by the horizontal split bar scroll together vertically. The panes split by the vertical split bar scroll together horizontally. To resize the panes, drag either split bar to the desired location in the window.

You can change the values of cells in any of the four panes. Any change you make in one pane also takes effect in the other panes. To remove one of the split bars from the window, drag the split box to the edge of the window or double-click the split bar. The following steps remove both split bars to remove the four panes from the window.

To Remove the Panes from the Window

1 Position the mouse pointer at the intersection of the horizontal and vertical split bars.

2 When the mouse pointer changes to a four-headed arrow, double-click.

Excel removes the four panes from the window.

What-If Analysis

More About

What-If Analysis

Instead of requiring you to change assumptions in a worksheet manually, Excel has additional methods for answering what-if questions, including Goal Seek, Solver, PivotTables, Scenario Manager, and the Analysis ToolPak. For more information, enter each of these what-if tools in the Type a question for help box on the menu bar.

The automatic recalculation feature of Excel is a powerful tool that can be used to analyze worksheet data. Using Excel to scrutinize the impact of changing values in cells that are referenced by a formula in another cell is called **what-if analysis** or **sensitivity analysis**. When new data is entered, Excel not only recalculates all formulas in a worksheet, but also redraws any associated charts.

In the Project 3 workbook, many of the formulas are dependent on the assumptions in the range B19:B25. Thus, if you change any of the assumption values, Excel immediately recalculates the cost of goods sold, gross margin, monthly expenses, total expenses, and operating income in rows 5 through 16. Excel redraws the 3-D Pie chart as well, because it is based on these numbers.

Analyze Data in a Worksheet by Changing Values

A what-if question for the worksheet in Project 3 might be *what* would happen to the six-month total operating income in cell H16 *if* the Bonus, Marketing, and Selling, General, and Administrative assumptions in the Assumptions table are changed as follows: Bonus $250,000.00 to $100,000.00; Marketing 14.00% to 10.00%; Selling, General, and Administrative 32.00% to 30.00%? To answer a question like this, you need to change only the first, fourth, and seventh values in the Assumptions table. Excel instantaneously recalculates the formulas in the worksheet and redraws the 3-D Pie chart to answer the question.

The following steps change the three assumptions as indicated in the previous paragraph to determine the new six-month operating income in cell H16. To ensure that the Assumptions table and the six-month operating income in cell H16 show on the screen at the same time, the steps also divide the window into two vertical panes.

To Analyze Data in a Worksheet by Changing Values

1

• **Use the vertical scroll bar to move the window so cell A6 is in the upper-left corner of the screen.**

• **Drag the vertical split box from the lower-right corner of the screen to the left so that the vertical split bar is positioned as shown in Figure 3-80.**

• **Use the right scroll arrow to view the totals in column H in the right pane.**

• **Click cell B19 in the left pane.**

Excel divides the window into two vertical panes and shows the totals in column H in the pane on the right side of the window (Figure 3-80).

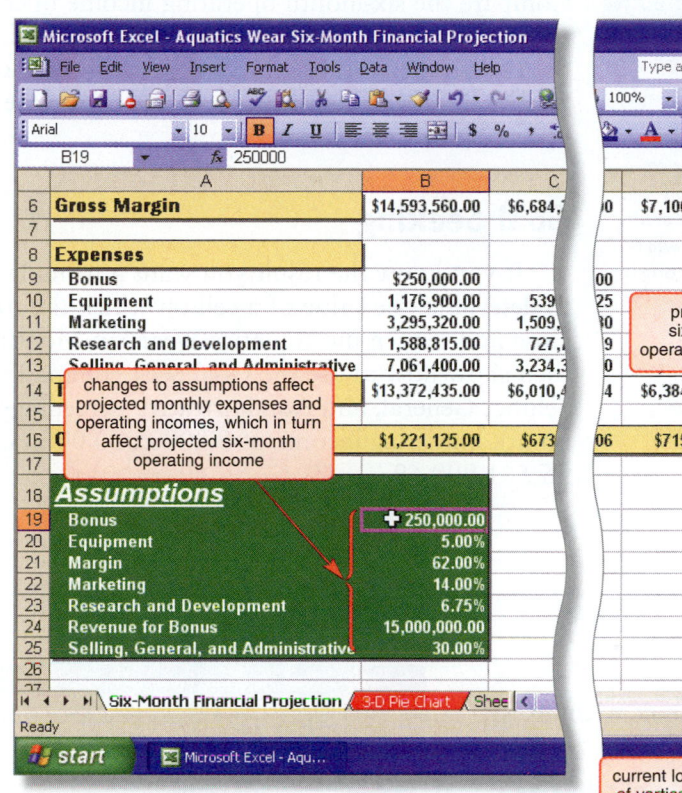
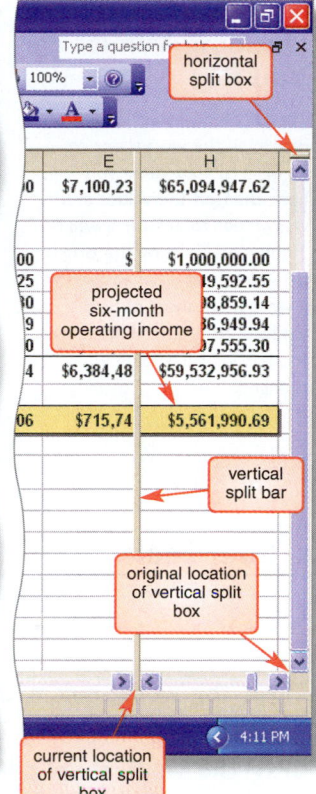

FIGURE 3-80

2

• **Enter 100000 in cell B19, 10 in cell B22, and 32 in cell B25.**

Excel immediately recalculates all the formulas in the worksheet (Figure 3-81).

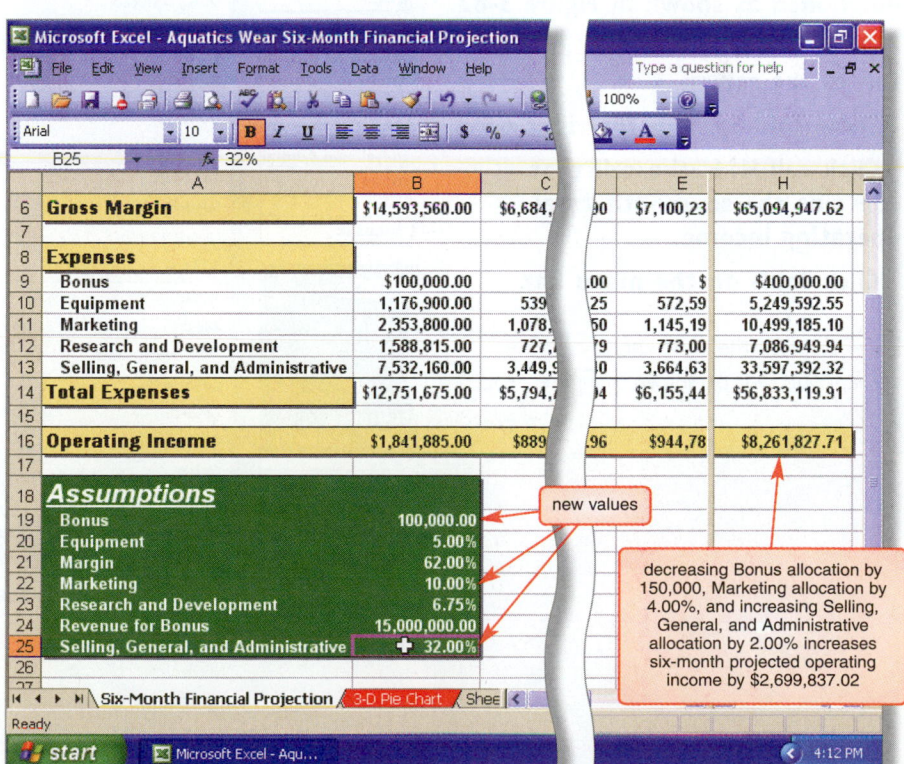

FIGURE 3-81

Microsoft Office
Excel 2003

Each time you enter a new assumption, Excel recalculates the worksheet and redraws the 3-D Pie chart. This process usually takes less than one second, depending on how many calculations must be performed and the speed of your computer. Compare the six-month operating income in cell H16 in Figures 3-80 and 3-81 on the previous page. By changing the values of the three assumptions (Figure 3-81), the six-month operating income in cell H16 increases from $5,561,990.69 to $8,261,827.71. This translates into an increase of $2,699,837.71 for the six-month operating income.

Goal Seeking

If you know the result you want a formula to produce, you can use **goal seeking** to determine the value of a cell on which the formula depends. The following steps close and reopen the Aquatics Wear Six-Month Financial Projection workbook. They then show how to use the Goal Seek command on the Tools menu to determine the Selling, General, and Administrative percentage in cell B25 that will yield a six-month operating income of $7,000,000.00 in cell H16, rather than the original $5,561,990.69.

To Goal Seek

1

• **Close the workbook without saving changes and then reopen it.**

• **Drag the vertical split box so that the vertical split bar is positioned as shown in Figure 3-82.**

• **Scroll down so row 6 is at the top of the screen.**

• **Show column H in the right pane.**

• **Click cell H16, the cell that contains the six-month total operating income.**

• **Click Tools on the menu bar.**

Excel displays the Tools menu and the vertical split bar as shown in Figure 3-82.

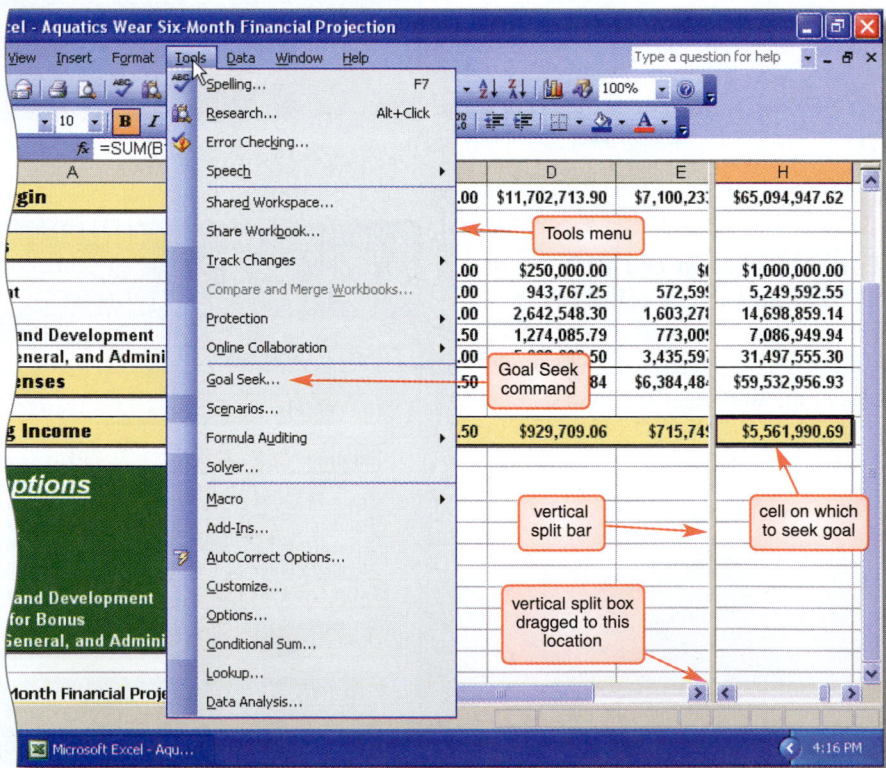

FIGURE 3-82

2

• **Click Goal Seek.**

• **When Excel displays the Goal Seek dialog box, click the To value text box, type** `7,000,000` **and then click the By changing cell box.**

• **Click cell B25 on the worksheet.**

Excel displays the Goal Seek dialog box as shown in Figure 3-83. Excel automatically assigns the Set cell box the cell reference of the active cell in the worksheet (cell H16). A marquee surrounds cell B25, which is set as the cell reference in the By changing cell box.

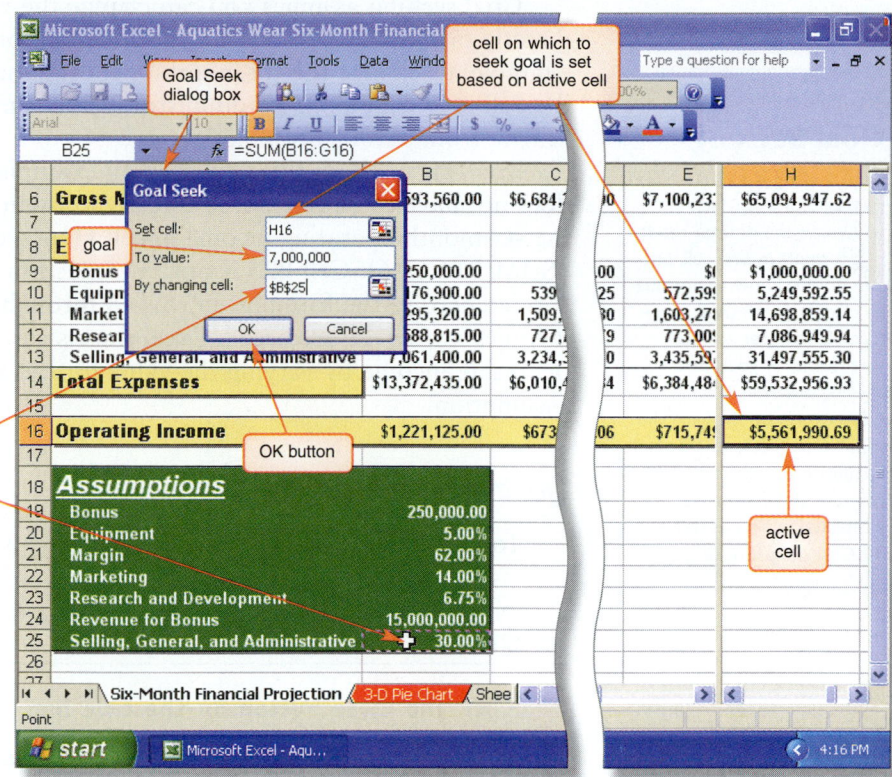

FIGURE 3-83

3

• **Click the OK button.**

Excel immediately changes cell H16 from $5,561,990.69 to the desired value of $7,000,000.00. More importantly, Excel changes the Selling, General, and Administrative assumption in cell B25 from 30.00% to 28.63% (Figure 3-84). Excel also displays the Goal Seek Status dialog box. If you click the OK button, Excel keeps the new values in the worksheet. If you click the Cancel button, Excel redisplays the original values.

4

• **Click the Cancel button in the Goal Seek Status dialog box.**

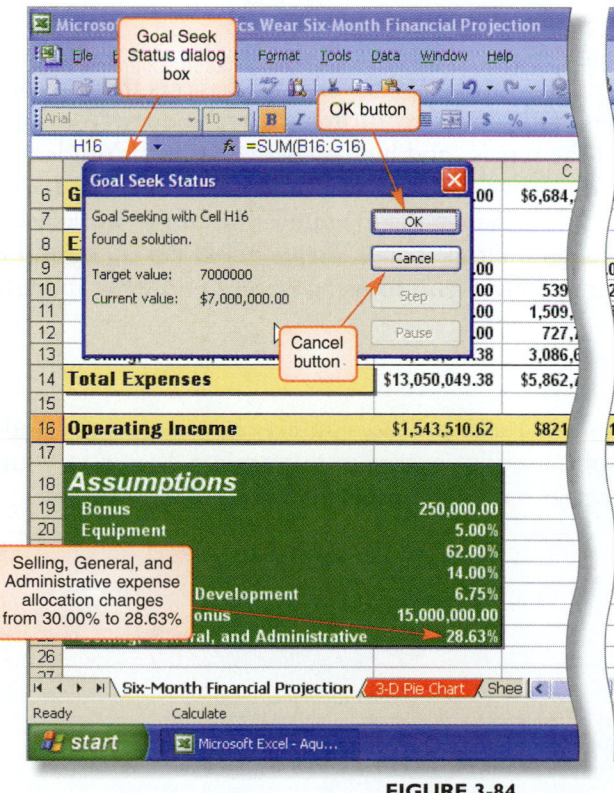
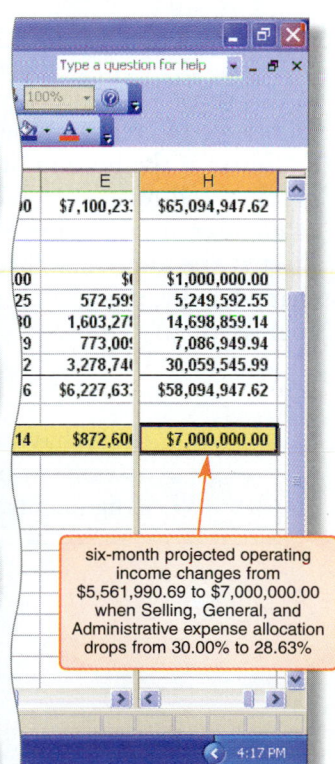

FIGURE 3-84

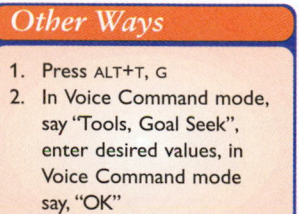

Other Ways

1. Press ALT+T, G
2. In Voice Command mode, say "Tools, Goal Seek", enter desired values, in Voice Command mode say, "OK"

More About

Goal Seeking

Goal seeking is a methodology in which you know the desired result of a formula in one cell, but you do not know what value to place in a cell used in the formula in order to reach that result, or goal. Goal seeking determines what value to use by changing the value in that cell, so that the formula returns the desired result in the first cell, as illustrated in Figures 3-83 and 3-84 on the previous page.

Goal seeking assumes you can change the value of only one cell referenced directly or indirectly to reach a specific goal for a value in another cell. In this example, to change the six-month operating income in cell H16 to $7,000,000.00, the Selling, General, and Administrative percentage in cell B25 must decrease by 1.37% from 30.00% to 28.63%.

You can see from this goal seeking example that the cell to change (cell B25) does not have to be referenced directly in the formula or function. For example, the six-month operating income in cell H16 is calculated by the function =SUM(B16:G16). Cell B25 is not referenced in this function. Instead, cell B25 is referenced in the formulas in rows 8 through 13, on which the monthly operating incomes in row 16 are based. Excel thus is capable of goal seeking on the six-month operating income by varying the value for the Selling, General, and Administrative assumption.

Quitting Excel

To quit Excel, complete the following steps.

To Quit Excel

1 Click the Close button on the title bar.

2 If the Microsoft Excel dialog box is displayed, click the No button.

Project Summary

In this project, you learned how to work with large worksheets that extend beyond the window, how to use the fill handle to create a series, and some new formatting techniques. You learned to show hidden toolbars, dock a toolbar at the bottom of the screen, and hide an active toolbar. You learned about the difference between absolute cell references and relative cell references and how to use the IF function. You also learned how to rotate text in a cell, freeze titles, change the magnification of the worksheet, show different parts of the worksheet at the same time through multiple panes, create a 3-D Pie chart, and improve the appearance of a 3-D Pie chart. Finally, this project introduced you to using Excel to do what-if analysis by changing values in cells and goal seeking.

 If you have a SAM user profile, you may have access to hands-on instruction, practice, and assessment of the skills covered in this project. Log in to your SAM account and go to your assignments page to see what your instructor has assigned.

What You Should Know

Having completed this project, you should be able to perform the tasks below. The tasks are listed in the same order they were presented in this project. For a list of the buttons, menus, toolbars, and commands introduced in this project, see the Quick Reference Summary at the back of this book and refer to the Page Number column.

1. Start and Customize Excel   (EX 150)
2. Bold the Font of the Entire Worksheet   (EX 150)
3. Enter the Worksheet Titles and Save the Workbook   (EX 150)
4. Rotate Text and Use the Fill Handle to Create a Series of Month Names   (EX 151)
5. Copy a Cell's Format Using the Format Painter Button   (EX 154)
6. Increase Column Widths and Enter Row Titles   (EX 155)
7. Copy a Range of Cells to a Nonadjacent Destination Area   (EX 157)
8. Insert a Row   (EX 160)
9. Enter Numbers with Format Symbols   (EX 163)
10. Freeze Column and Row Titles   (EX 163)
11. Enter the Projected Monthly Total Net Revenue   (EX 164)
12. Enter and Format the System Date   (EX 166)
13. Enter a Formula Containing Absolute Cell References   (EX 169)
14. Enter an IF Function   (EX 172)
15. Enter the Remaining July Formulas   (EX 173)
16. Copy Formulas with Absolute Cell References Using the Fill Handle   (EX 174)
17. Determine Row Totals in Nonadjacent Cells   (EX 175)
18. Unfreeze the Worksheet Titles and Save the Workbook   (EX 176)
19. Assign Formats to Nonadjacent Ranges (EX 178)
20. Format the Worksheet Titles   (EX 180)
21. Show the Drawing Toolbar   (EX 182)
22. Move and Dock a Toolbar   (EX 183)
23. Add a Drop Shadow   (EX 184)
24. Change Font, Add Underlines, Add Background Colors, and Add Drop Shadows to Nonadjacent Cells   (EX 185)
25. Format the Assumptions Table   (EX 186)
26. Hide the Drawing Toolbar and Save the Workbook   (EX 187)
27. Draw a 3-D Pie Chart on a Separate Chart Sheet   (EX 188)
28. Format the Chart Title and Data Labels (EX 192)
29. Change the Colors of the Slices in a Pie Chart   (EX 193)
30. Explode the 3-D Pie Chart   (EX 194)
31. Rotate and Tilt the 3-D Pie Chart   (EX 195)
32. Show Leader Lines with the Data Labels (EX 197)
33. Rename and Reorder the Sheets and Color Their Tabs   (EX 198)
34. Check Spelling in Multiple Sheets   (EX 199)
35. Preview and Print the Workbook   (EX 200)
36. Shrink and Magnify the View of a Worksheet or Chart   (EX 201)
37. Split a Window into Panes   (EX 203)
38. Remove the Panes from the Window   (EX 204)
39. Analyze Data in a Worksheet by Changing Values   (EX 205)
40. Goal Seek   (EX 206)
41. Quit Excel   (EX 208)

More About

The Quick Reference

For a table that lists how to complete the tasks covered in this book using the mouse, menu, shortcut menu, and keyboard, see the Quick Reference Summary at the back of this book or visit the Excel 2003 Quick Reference Web page (scsite.com/ex2003/qr).

More About

Microsoft Certification

The Microsoft Office Specialist Certification program provides an opportunity for you to obtain a valuable industry credential — proof that you have the Excel 2003 skills required by employers. For more information, see Appendix E or visit the Excel 2003 Certification Web page (scsite.com/ex2003/cert).

Learn It Online

Instructions: To complete the Learn It Online exercises, start your browser, click the Address bar, and then enter the Web address scsite.com/ex2003/learn. When the Excel 2003 Learn It Online page is displayed, follow the instructions in the exercises below. Each exercise has instructions for printing your results, either for your own records or for submission to your instructor.

1 Project Reinforcement TF, MC, and SA

Below Excel Project 3, click the Project Reinforcement link. Print the quiz by clicking Print on the File menu for each page. Answer each question.

2 Flash Cards

Below Excel Project 3, click the Flash Cards link and read the instructions. Type 20 (or a number specified by your instructor) in the Number of playing cards text box, type your name in the Enter your Name text box, and then click the Flip Card button. When the flash card is displayed, read the question and then click the ANSWER box arrow to select an answer. Flip through Flash Cards. If your score is 15 (75%) correct or greater, click Print on the File menu to print your results. If your score is less than 15 (75%) correct, then redo this exercise by clicking the Replay button.

3 Practice Test

Below Excel Project 3, click the Practice Test link. Answer each question, enter your first and last name at the bottom of the page, and then click the Grade Test button. When the graded practice test is displayed on your screen, click Print on the File menu to print a hard copy. Continue to take practice tests until you score 80% or better.

4 Who Wants To Be a Computer Genius?

Below Excel Project 3, click the Computer Genius link. Read the instructions, enter your first and last name at the bottom of the page, and then click the PLAY button. When your score is displayed, click the PRINT RESULTS link to print a hard copy.

5 Wheel of Terms

Below Excel Project 3, click the Wheel of Terms link. Read the instructions, and then enter your first and last name and your school name. Click the PLAY button. When your score is displayed, right-click the score and then click Print on the shortcut menu to print a hard copy.

6 Crossword Puzzle Challenge

Below Excel Project 3, click the Crossword Puzzle Challenge link. Read the instructions, and then enter your first and last name. Click the SUBMIT button. Work the crossword puzzle. When you are finished, click the Submit button. When the crossword puzzle is redisplayed, click the Print Puzzle button to print a hard copy.

7 Tips and Tricks

Below Excel Project 3, click the Tips and Tricks link. Click a topic that pertains to Project 3. Right-click the information and then click Print on the shortcut menu. Construct a brief example of what the information relates to in Excel to confirm you understand how to use the tip or trick.

8 Newsgroups

Below Excel Project 3, click the Newsgroups link. Click a topic that pertains to Project 3. Print three comments.

9 Expanding Your Horizons

Below Excel Project 3, click the Expanding Your Horizons link. Click a topic that pertains to Project 3. Print the information. Construct a brief example of what the information relates to in Excel to confirm you understand the contents of the article.

10 Search Sleuth

Below Excel Project 3, click the Search Sleuth link. To search for a term that pertains to this project, select a term below the Project 3 title and then use the Google search engine at google.com (or any major search engine) to display and print two Web pages that present information on the term.

11 Excel Online Training

Below Excel Project 3, click the Excel Online Training link. When your browser displays the Microsoft Office Online Web page, click the Excel link. Click one of the Excel courses that covers one or more of the objectives listed at the beginning of the project on page EX 146. Print the first page of the course before stepping through it.

12 Office Marketplace

Below Excel Project 3, click the Office Marketplace link. When your browser displays the Microsoft Office Online Web page, click the Office Marketplace link. Click a topic that relates to Excel. Print the first page.

Apply Your Knowledge

1 Understanding the IF Function and Absolute Cell Referencing

Instructions: Fill in the correct answers.

1. Determine the truth value (true or false) of the following logical tests, given the following cell values: A2 = 20; B6 = 17; L8 = 100; S2 = 25; and W9 = 42. Enter true or false.

   a. B6 < A2   Truth value: _____

   b. 5 * A2 = L8 - 10   Truth value: _____

   c. W9 + 12 * S2 / 5 <> 2 * L8   Truth value: _____

   d. L8 / S2 > A2 – B6   Truth value: _____

   e. B6 * 2 – 42 < (S2 – W9 +8) / 4   Truth value: _____

   f. A2 + 300 <= B6 * S2 + 10   Truth value: _____

   g. W9 + L8 + 100 > 8 * (S2 + 10)   Truth value: _____

   h. A2 + B6 – 27 <> 2 * (S2 / 5)   Truth value: _____

2. Write an IF function for cell H3 that assigns the value of cell A7 to cell H3 if the value in cell J7 is less than the value in cell Q2; otherwise, have the IF function assign zero (0) to cell H3.

   Function: _____

3. Write an IF function for cell P8 that assigns the text "OK" if the value in cell S3 is five times greater than the value in cell F4; otherwise, have the IF function assign the text "Not OK" to cell P8.

   Function: _____

4. A nested IF function is an IF function that contains another IF function in the value_if_true or value_if_false arguments. For example, =IF(A1 = "IN","Region 1", IF(A1 = "OH", "Region 2", "Not Applicable")) is a valid nested IF function. Start Excel and enter this IF function in cell B1 and then use the fill handle to copy the function down through cell B7. Enter the following data in the cells in the range A1:A7 and then write down the results in cells B1 through B7 for each set. Set 1: A1 = IL; A2 = IN; A3 = IN; A4 = OH; A5 = IN; A6 = OH; A7 = IN. Set 2: A1= WI; A2 = KY; A3 = IN; A4 = IL; A5 = IN; A6 = IN; A7 = OH.

   Set 1 Results: _____

   Set 2 Results: _____

5. Write cell G3 as a relative cell reference, absolute cell reference, mixed cell reference with the row varying, and mixed cell reference with the column varying.

   _____ _____ _____ _____

6. Write the formula for cell B8 that divides cell D5 by the sum of cells N10 through N13. Write the formula so that when it is copied to cells C8 and D8, cell D5 remains absolute.

   Formula: _____

7. Write the formula for cell Y6 that divides cell P7 by the sum of cells H4, I4, and J4. Write the formula so that when it is copied to cells Y7, Y8, and Y9, cell P7 remains absolute.

   Formula: _____

8. Write the formula for cell M4 that multiplies cell T7 by the sum of cells D4 through D10. Write the formula so that when it is copied to cells M5 and M6, Excel adjusts all the cell references according to the new locations.

   Formula: _____

1 Seven-Year Financial Projection

Problem: As the spreadsheet specialist at Shawshank Manufacturing, you have been asked to create a worksheet that will project the annual gross margin, expenses, operating income, income taxes, and net income for the next seven years based on the assumptions in Table 3-9. The desired worksheet is shown in Figure 3-85.

Table 3-9 Shawshank Manufacturing Assumptions	
Units Sold in Year 2003	12,459,713
Unit Cost	$12.96
Annual Sales Growth	4.25%
Annual Price Decrease	3.75%
Margin	39.25%

Instructions Part 1: Complete the following steps to create the worksheet shown in Figure 3-85.

1. Bold the entire worksheet. Enter the worksheet titles in cells A1 and A2. Enter the system date in cell H2 using the NOW function. Format the date to the 3/14/2001 style.

2. Enter the seven column titles 2004 through 2010 in the range B3:H3 by entering 2004 in cell B3, and then, while holding down the CTRL key, dragging cell B3's fill handle. Format cell B3 as follows: (a) change the number in cell B3 to text by assigning it the format Text in the Format Cells dialog box; (b) center and italicize cell B3; (c) rotate its contents 45°. Use the Format Painter button to copy the format assigned to cell B3 to the range C3:H3.

3. Enter the row titles in the range A4:A24. Add heavy bottom borders to the ranges A3:H3 and B5:H5.

4. Change the following column widths: A = 24.71; B through H = 11.00. Change the heights of rows 7, 13, 15, 16, and 17 to 24.00.

5. Enter the assumptions values in Table 3-9 in the range B20:B24. Use format symbols.

6. Assign the Comma style format with no decimal places to the range B4:H17.

7. Complete the following entries:
   a. 2004 Total Net Revenue (cell B4) = Units Sold in Year 2003 * (Unit Cost / (1 – Margin)) or =B20 * (B21 / (1 – B24))
   b. 2005 Total Net Revenue (cell C4) = 2004 Total Net Revenue * (1 + Annual Sales Growth) * (1 – Annual Price Decrease) or =B4 * (1 + $B$22) * (1 – $B$23)
   c. Copy cell C4 to the range D4:H4.
   d. 2004 Cost of Goods Sold (cell B5) = 2004 Total Net Revenue – (2004 Total Net Revenue * Margin) or =B4 * (1 – $B$24)
   e. Copy cell B5 to the range C5:H5.
   f. 2004 Gross Margin (cell B6) = 2004 Total Net Revenue – 2004 Cost of Goods Sold or =B4 – B5
   g. Copy cell B6 to the range C6:H6.
   h. 2004 Advertising (cell B8) = 500 + 13% * 2004 Total Net Revenue or =500 + 13% * B4
   i. Copy cell B8 to the range C8:H8.
   j. Maintenance (row 9): 2004 = 1,900,000; 2005 = 5,397,000; 2006 = 4,200,000; 2007 = 5,150,000; 2008 = 2,500,000; 2009 = 3,150,000; 2010 = 2,960,000
   k. 2004 Rent (cell B10) = 1,800,000
   l. 2005 Rent (cell C10) = 2004 Rent + 10% * 2004 Rent or =B10 * (1 + 10%)
   m. Copy cell C10 to the range D10:H10.
   n. 2004 Salaries (cell B11) = 22% * 2004 Total Net Revenue or =22% * B4

In the Lab

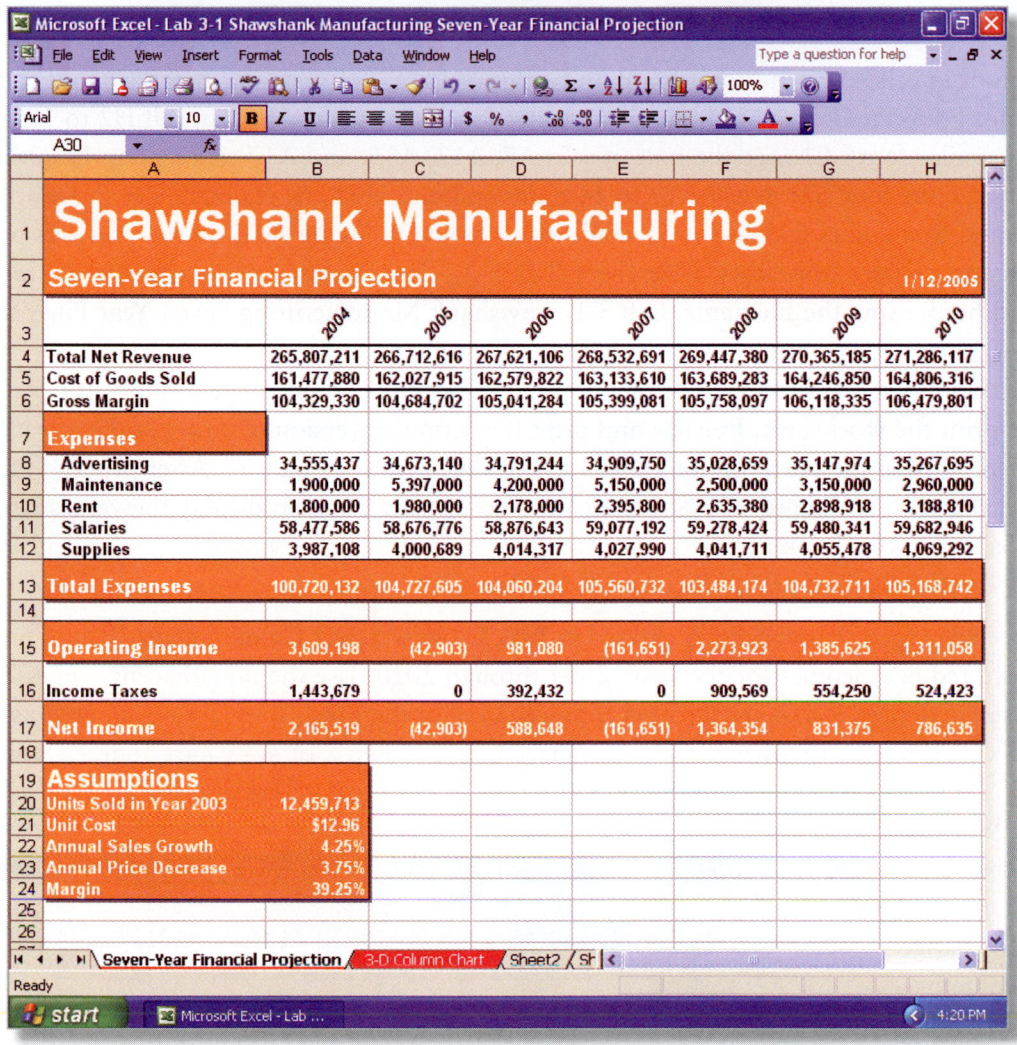

FIGURE 3-85

o. Copy cell B11 to the range C11:H11.

p. 2004 Supplies (cell B12) = 1.5% * 2004 Total Net Revenue or =1.5% * B4

q. Copy cell B12 to the range C12:H12.

r. 2004 Total Expenses (cell B13) = SUM(B8:B12)

s. Copy cell B13 to the range C13:H13.

t. 2004 Operating Income (cell B15) = 2004 Gross Margin – 2004 Total Expenses or =B6 – B13

u. Copy cell B15 to the range C15:H15.

v. 2004 Income Taxes (cell B16): If 2004 Operating Income is less than 0, then 2004 Income Taxes equal 0; otherwise 2004 Income Taxes equal 40% * 2004 Operating Income or =IF(B15 < 0, 0, 40% * B15)

w. Copy cell B16 to the range C16:H16.

x. 2004 Net Income (cell B17) = 2004 Operating Income – 2004 Income Taxes or =B15 – B16

y. Copy cell B17 to the range C17:H17.

(continued)

In the Lab

Seven-Year Financial Projection *(continued)*

8. Change the font in cell A1 to 36-point Franklin Gothic Medium (or a similar font). Change the font in cell A2 to 16-point Franklin Gothic Medium (or a similar font). Change the font in cell H2 to 10-point Century Gothic (or a similar font). Change the font in cells A7, A13, A15, and A17 to 12-point Franklin Gothic Medium. Change the font size in cell A19 to 14 point and underline the characters in the cell. Change the background and font colors and add drop shadows as shown in Figure 3-85 on the previous page.

9. Enter your name, course, laboratory assignment (Lab 3-1), date, and instructor name in the range A27:A31. Save the workbook using the file name, Lab 3-1 Shawshank Manufacturing Seven-Year Financial Projection.

10. Use the Page Setup command on the File menu to fit the printout on one page in portrait orientation. Preview and print the worksheet. Preview and print the formulas version (CTRL+`) of the worksheet in landscape orientation using the Fit to option button in the Page Setup dialog box. After printing the formulas version, reset the print scaling to 100%. Press CTRL+` to instruct Excel to display the values version of the worksheet. Save the workbook again.

11. Zoom to: (a) 200%; (b) 75%; (c) 25%; and (d) 100%.

Instructions Part 2: Open the workbook created in Part 1. Draw a 3-D Column chart (Figure 3-86) that compares the projected net incomes for the years 2004 through 2010. Use the nonadjacent ranges B3:H3 and B17:H17. Because the desired x-axis labels 2004 through 2010 in the range B3:H3 were entered as numbers in Step 2 on page EX 212, do the following when the ChartWizard – Step 2 of 4 – Chart Source Data dialog box appears: (1) click the Series tab; (2) remove Series 1 from the Series list if necessary; and (3) type =sheet1!b3:h3 in the Category (X) axis labels box. Add the chart title and format it as shown in Figure 3-86. To change the color of the columns, right-click a column and then click Format Data Series on the shortcut menu. To change the color of the walls behind and to the left of the columns, right-click a wall and then click Format Walls on the shortcut menu. Rename and rearrange the sheets, and color their tabs as shown in Figure 3-86. Save the workbook using the same file name (Lab 3-1 Shawshank Manufacturing Seven-Year Financial Projection) as defined in Part 1. Print both sheets.

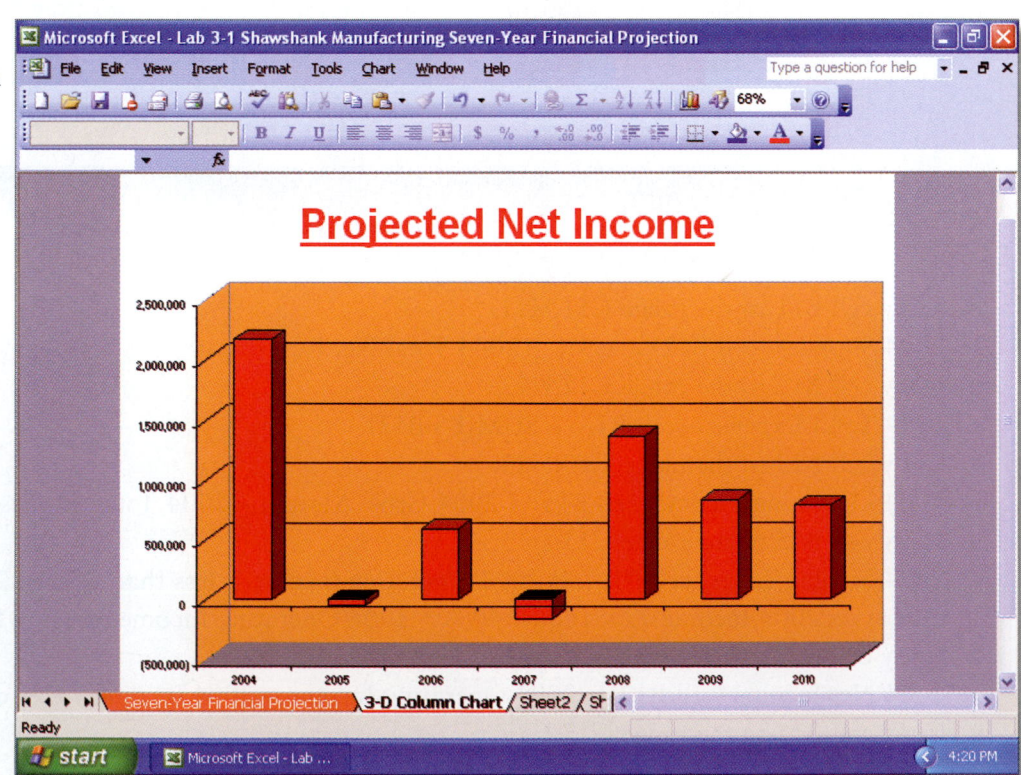

FIGURE 3-86

Instructions Part 3: Open the workbook created in Part 2. If the 3-D Column chart is on the screen, click the Seven-Year Financial Projection tab to view the worksheet. Divide the window into two panes by dragging the horizontal split box between rows 6 and 7. Use the scroll bars to show both the top and bottom of the worksheet.

Using the numbers in columns 2 and 3 of Table 3-10, analyze the effect of changing the annual sales growth (cell B22) and annual price decrease (cell B23) on the annual net incomes in row 17. The resulting answers are in column 4 of Table 3-10. Print both the worksheet and chart for each case.

Table 3-10 Shawshank Manufacturing Data to Analyze and Results			
Case	Annual Sales Growth	Annual Price Decrease	2010 Resulting Net Income
1	18.25%	2.75%	6,454,088
2	20.25%	−2.75%	11,914,998
3	34.35%	15.45%	5,732,746

Close the workbook without saving it, and then reopen it. Use the Goal Seek command to determine a margin (cell B24) that would result in a net income in 2010 of $5,000,000 (cell H17). You should end up with a margin of 41.63% in cell B24. After you complete the goal seeking, print only the worksheet. Do not save the workbook with the latest changes.

2 Profit Center Analysis of Indirect Expense Allocations

Problem: You are a summer intern at the elegant five-star Casa Grande Resort & Spa. Your work-study advisor at school and your supervisor have agreed on a challenging Excel project for you to do. They want you to create an indirect expense allocation worksheet (Figure 3-87 on the next page) that will help the resort and spa administration better evaluate the profit centers described in Table 3-11.

Table 3-11 Casa Grande Resort & Spa Worksheet Data								
	Spa	Lounge	Banquet Room	Restaurant	Business Center	Conference Rooms	Gift Shop	Children's Game Room
Total Net Revenue	78865	492800	486725	592500	225125	196475	88450	19450
Cost of Sales	36715	136500	106500	325600	14790	45125	37000	8650
Direct Expenses	14750	152975	53890	252975	8435	22475	31800	6940
Square Footage	2500	5100	8800	6000	900	5700	750	1200

(continued)

In the Lab

Profit Center Analysis of Indirect Expense Allocations *(continued)*

Casa Grande Resort & Spa
Profit Center Analysis of Indirect Expenses

1/12/2004

	Spa	Lounge	Banquet Room	Restaurant	Business Center	Conference Rooms	Gift Shop	Children's Game Room	Total
Total Net Revenue	$78,865.00	$492,800.00	$486,725.00	$592,500.00	$225,125.00	$196,475.00	$88,450.00	$19,450.00	$2,180,390.00
Cost of Sales	36,715.00	136,500.00	106,500.00	325,600.00	14,790.00	45,125.00	37,000.00	8,650.00	710,880.00
Direct Expenses	14,750.00	152,975.00	53,890.00	252,975.00	8,435.00	22,475.00	31,800.00	6,940.00	544,240.00
Indirect Expenses									
Administrative	$2,622.33	$16,386.06	$16,184.06	$19,701.18	$7,485.62	$6,532.98	$2,941.04	$646.73	$72,500.00
Depreciation	4,947.50	10,092.89	17,415.19	11,873.99	1,781.10	11,280.29	1,484.25	2,374.80	61,250.00
Energy	1,663.83	10,396.67	10,268.51	12,500.06	4,749.49	4,145.06	1,866.04	410.34	46,000.00
Insurance	1,009.69	2,059.77	3,554.12	2,423.26	363.49	2,302.10	302.91	484.65	12,500.00
Maintenance	2,100.16	4,284.33	7,392.57	5,040.39	756.06	4,788.37	630.05	1,008.08	26,000.00
Marketing	1,889.89	11,809.26	11,663.68	14,198.43	5,394.81	4,708.25	2,119.58	466.09	52,250.00
Total Indirect Expenses	$14,233.40	$55,028.99	$66,478.13	$65,737.31	$20,530.56	$33,757.05	$9,343.87	$5,390.69	$270,500.00
Net Income	$13,166.60	$148,296.01	$259,856.87	($51,812.31)	$181,369.44	$95,117.95	$10,306.13	($1,530.69)	$654,770.00
Square Footage	2,500	5,100	8,800	6,000	900	5,700	750	1,200	30,950
Planned Indirect Expenses									
Administrative	$72,500.00								
Depreciation	$61,250.00								
Energy	$46,000.00								
Insurance	$12,500.00								
Maintenance	$26,000.00								
Marketing	$52,250.00								

FIGURE 3-87

Instructions Part 1: Do the following to create the worksheet shown in Figure 3-87.

1. Bold the entire worksheet. Enter the worksheet titles in cells A1 and A2 and the system date in cell J2. Format the date to the 3/14/2001 style.

2. Enter the column titles and the first three rows of numbers in Table 3-11 on the previous page in rows 3 through 6. In row 3, use ALT+ENTER so the column titles show on two lines in a cell. Center and italicize the column headings in the range B3:J3. Add a bottom border to the range B3:J3. Select the range J4:J6 and click the AutoSum button. Freeze rows 1 through 3 and column A.

3. Enter the Square Footage row in Table 3-11 in row 16. Select cell J16 and use the AutoSum button to determine the sum of the values in the range B16:I16. Change the height of row 16 to 39.00 and vertically center the range A16:J16.

4. Change the following column widths: A = 26.00; B through I = 12.00, and J = 13.00.

5. Enter the remaining row titles in the range A7:A17 as shown in Figure 3-87. Increase the font size in cells A7, A14, and A15 to 12-point.

6. Copy the row titles in range A8:A13 to the range A18:A23. Enter the numbers shown in the range B18:B23 of Figure 3-87 with format symbols.

7. The planned indirect expenses in the range B18:B23 are to be prorated across the profit center as follows: Administrative (row 8), Energy (row 10), and Marketing (row 13) on the basis of Total Net Revenue (row 4); Depreciation (row 9), Insurance (row 11), and Maintenance (row 12) on the basis of Square Footage (row 16). Use the following formulas to accomplish the prorating.

In the Lab

a. Spa Administrative (cell B8) = Administrative Expenses * Spa Total Net Revenue / Resort Total Net Revenue or =$B$18 * B4 / $J$4

b. Spa Depreciation (cell B9) = Depreciation Expenses * Spa Square Footage / Total Square Footage or =$B$19 * B16 / $J$16

c. Spa Energy (cell B10) = Energy Expenses * Spa Total Net Revenue / Resort Total Net Revenue or =$B$20 * B4 / $J$4

d. Spa Insurance (cell B11) = Insurance Expenses * Spa Square Feet / Total Square Footage or =$B$21 * B16 / $J$16

e. Spa Maintenance (cell B12) = Maintenance Expenses * Spa Square Footage / Total Square Footage or =$B$22 * B16 / $J$16

f. Spa Marketing (cell B13) = Marketing Expenses * Spa Total Net Revenue / Resort Total Net Revenue or =$B$23 * B4 / $J$4

g. Spa Total Indirect Expenses (cell B14) = SUM(B8:B13)

h. Spa Net Income (cell B15) = Revenue – (Cost of Sales + Direct Expenses + Total Indirect Expenses) or =B4 – (B5 + B6 + B14)

i. Use the fill handle to copy the range B8:B15 to the range C8:I15.

j. Select the range J8:J15 and click the AutoSum button on the Standard toolbar.

8. Add a bottom border to the range B13:J13. Assign the Currency style with two decimal places and show negative numbers in parentheses to the following ranges: B4:J4; B8:J8; and B14:J15. Assign the Comma style with two decimal places and show negative numbers in parentheses to the following ranges: B5:J6 and B9:J13.

9. Change the font in cell A1 to 36-point Arial Black (or a similar font). Change the font in cell A2 to 18-point Arial Black (or a similar font). Change the font in cell A17 to 14-point italic underlined font.

10. Use the background color red, the font color white, and a drop shadow (Shadow Style 14) for the ranges A1:J2; A7; A15:J15; and A17:B23 as shown in Figure 3-87.

11. Rename the Sheet1 sheet, Indirect Expenses, and color its tab red. Unfreeze the worksheet.

12. Enter your name, course, laboratory assignment (Lab 3-2), date, and instructor name in the range A27:A31. Save the workbook using the file name, Lab 3-2 Casa Grande Profit Center Analysis of Indirect Expenses.

13. Use the Page Setup command on the File menu to change the orientation to landscape. Preview and print the worksheet. Preview and print the formulas version (CTRL+`) of the worksheet in landscape orientation using the Fit to option button in the Page Setup dialog box. After printing the formulas version, reset the print scaling to 100%. Press CTRL+` to show the values version of the worksheet. Save the workbook again.

14. Divide the window into four panes and show the four corners of the worksheet. Remove the four panes.

15. Add white space to the worksheet by inserting blank rows between rows 6 and 7 and 15 and 16. Move the range A19:B25 down three rows. Print the worksheet and then close the workbook without saving changes.

Instructions Part 2: Open the workbook created in Part 1. Draw a 3-D Pie chart (Figure 3-88 on the next page) that shows the contribution of each category of indirect expense to the total indirect expenses. That is, chart the nonadjacent ranges A8:A13 (category names) and J8:J13 (data series). Show labels that include category names and percentages. Do not show the legend. Format the 3-D Pie chart as shown in Figure 3-88. Rename the chart sheet 3-D Pie Chart and color the tab blue. Move the chart tab to the right of the worksheet tab. Save the workbook using the file name Lab 3-2 Casa Grande Profit Center Analysis of Indirect Expenses. Preview and print both sheets.

(continued)

In the Lab

Profit Center Analysis of Indirect Expense Allocations (continued)

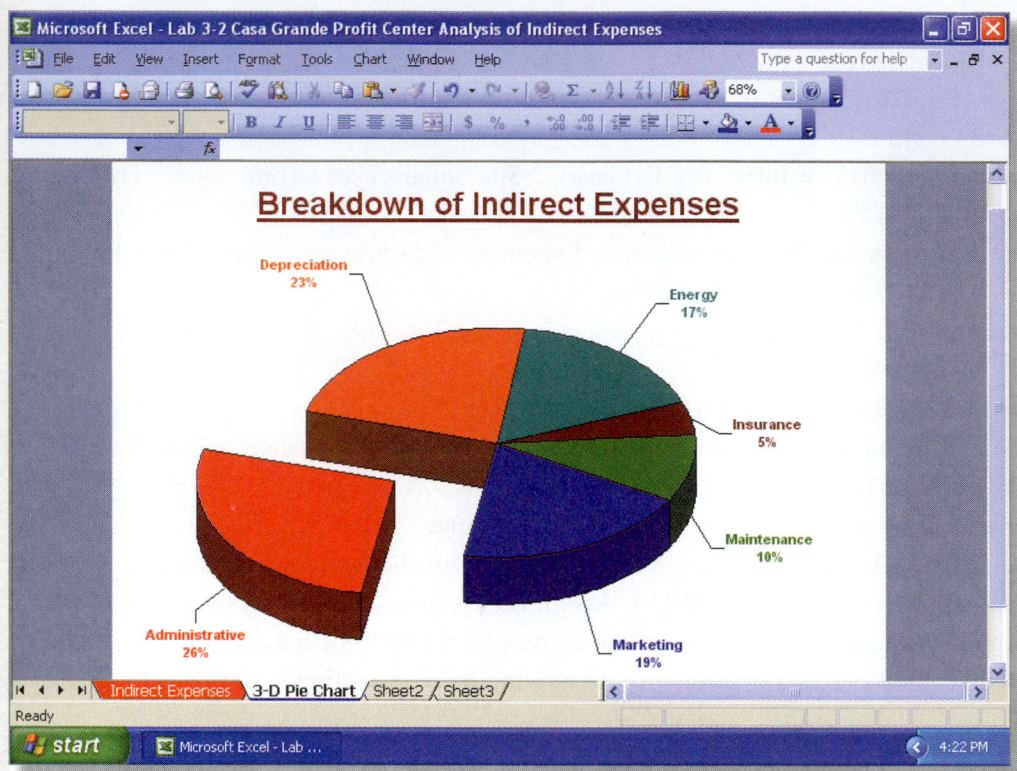

FIGURE 3-88

Instructions Part 3: Using the numbers in Table 3-12, analyze the effect of changing the planned indirect expenses in the range B18:B23 on the net incomes for each profit center. Print the worksheet for each case. You should end with the following totals in cell J15: Case 1 = $538,570.00 and Case 2 = $654,020.00. When you have finished, close the workbook without saving the latest changes.

Table 3-12 Casa Grande Resort & Spa What-If Data		
	Case 1	Case 2
Administrative	110000	66250
Depreciation	96500	63000
Energy	48750	31500
Insurance	32450	22500
Maintenance	38000	28000
Marketing	61000	60000

3 Modifying the Weekly Payroll Worksheet

Problem: Your supervisor in the Payroll department has asked you to modify the payroll workbook developed in Exercise 1 of the Project 2 In the Lab section on page EX 132, so that it appears as shown in Figure 3-89. If you did not complete Exercise 1 in Project 2, ask your instructor for a copy of Lab 2-1 Illiana Custom Homes Weekly Payroll Report workbook or complete that exercise before you begin this one.

In the Lab

	A	B	C	D	E	F	G	H	I	J	K	L	M
1	**Illiana Custom Homes**												
2	Weekly Payroll Report	2/7/2005											
3	Employee	Rate	Hours	Dep.	YTD Soc. Sec.	Gross Pay	Soc. Sec.	Medicare	Fed. Tax	State Tax	Net Pay	% Taxes	
4	Jedi, Hubert	24.90	40.00	3	4,974.00	996.00	61.75	14.44	176.12	31.87	711.81	28.53%	
5	Kaden, Hadef	8.00	38.75	10	5,340.20	310.00	19.22	4.50	0.00	9.92	276.37	10.85%	
6	Pancer, Dion	12.90	66.00	8	4,254.00	1,019.10	63.18	14.78	142.28	32.61	766.24	24.81%	
7	Sanchez, Maria	21.35	45.00	5	5,393.00	1,014.13	1.00	14.70	164.37	32.45	801.60	20.96%	
8	Scarff, Heidi	17.85	39.75	1	4,825.50	709.54	43.99	10.29	134.22	22.71	498.34	29.77%	
9	Ho, Lee	25.50	6.00	7	250.00	153.00	9.49	2.22	0.00	4.90	136.40	10.85%	
10	Mil, Tyrone	31.50	32.50	5	5,394.00	1,023.75	0.00	14.84	166.29	32.76	809.86	20.89%	
11	Totals		268.00		30,430.70	5,225.51	198.63	75.77	783.28	167.22	4,000.61	23.44%	
12													
13	Social Security Tax	6.20%											
14	Medicare Tax	1.45%											
15	Maximum Social Security	$5,394.00											
16													

FIGURE 3-89

The major modifications requested by your supervisor include: (1) reformatting the worksheet; (2) adding computations of time-and-a-half for hours worked greater than 40; (3) removing the conditional formatting assigned to the range B4:B9; (4) adding calculations to charge no federal tax in certain situations; (5) adding Social Security and Medicare deductions; (6) adding and deleting employees; and (7) changing employee information.

Instructions Part 1: Open the workbook, Lab 2-1 Illiana Custom Homes Weekly Payroll Report, created in Project 2 (Figure 2-88 on page EX 132). Perform the following tasks.

1. Delete rows 11 through 13. Change all the row heights back to the default height (12.75). Select the entire sheet using the Select All button and then clear all remaining formats using the Formats command on the Clear submenu of the Edit menu. Bold the entire worksheet. Enhance the worksheet title as shown in Figure 3-89.

2. Insert a new column between columns D and E. Enter the new column E title YTD Soc. Sec. in cell E3. Insert two new columns between columns E and F. Enter the new column G title Soc. Sec. in cell G3. Enter the new column H title Medicare in cell H3.

3. Change the column widths as follows: A = 25.00; B = 9.43; C = 7.00; D = 6.00; E = 13.14; F through K = 9.71; and L = 8.43. Change the row heights as follows: row 1 = 41.25; rows 2 and 3 = 18.00.

4. Assign the NOW function to cell B2 and format it to the 3/14/2001 style.

5. Delete row 7 (Rifken, Felix). Change Hadef Kaden's (row 5) rate of pay to $8.00 and number of dependents to 10.

6. Freeze column A and rows 1 through 3. In column E, enter the YTD Soc. Sec. values listed in Table 3-13.

Table 3-13 Illiana Custom Homes Employee YTD Social Security Values	
Employee	YTD Soc. Sec.
Jedi, Hubert	4,974.00
Kaden, Hadef	5,340.20
Pancer, Dion	4,254.00
Sanchez, Maria	5,393.00
Scarff, Heidi	4,825.50

(continued)

In the Lab

Modifying the Weekly Payroll Worksheet *(continued)*

7. Insert two new rows immediately above the Totals row. Add the new employee data as listed in Table 3-14.

Table 3-14 New Employee Data				
Employee	**Rate**	**Hours**	**Dep.**	**YTD Soc. Sec.**
Ho, Lee	25.50	6.00	7	250.00
Mil, Tyrone	31.50	32.50	5	5,394.00

8. Assign a Comma style with two decimal places to the ranges B4:C11 and E4:K11. Assign a Percent style and two decimal places to the range L4:L11. Center the range D4:D10.

9. As shown in Figure 3-89 on the previous page, enter and format the Social Security and Medicare tax information in the range A13:B15. Use format symbols where applicable.

10. Change the formulas to determine the gross pay in column F and the federal tax in column I as follows:

    a. In cell F4, enter an IF function that applies the following logic and then copy it to the range F5:F10.

    If Hours <= 40, then Gross Pay = Rate * Hours, otherwise Gross Pay = Rate * Hours + 0.5 * Rate * (Hours - 40)

    b. In cell I4, enter the IF function that applies the following logic and then copy it to the range I5:I10.

    If (Gross Pay – Dependents * 38.46) > 0, then Federal Tax = 20% * (Gross Pay – Dependents * 38.46), otherwise Federal Tax = 0

11. An employee pays Social Security tax only if his or her YTD Soc. Sec. in column E is less than the Maximum Social Security in cell B15. Use the following logic to determine the Social Security tax for Hubert Jedi in cell G4 and then copy it to the range G5:G10.

    If Social Security Tax * Gross Pay + YTD Soc. Sec. > Maximum Social Security, then Maximum Social Security – YTD Soc. Sec., otherwise Social Security Tax * Gross Pay

    Use absolute cell references for the Social Security Tax and Maximum Social Security values.

12. In cell H4, enter the following formula and then copy it to the range H5:H10:

    Medicare = Medicare Tax * Gross Pay

    Use absolute cell references for the Medicare Tax values.

13. In cell K4, enter the following formula and copy it to the range K5:K10:

    Gross Pay - (Soc. Sec. + Medicare + Fed. Tax + State Tax)

14. In cell L4, enter the following formula and copy it to the range L5:L11:

    (Soc. Sec. + Medicare + Fed. Tax + State Tax) / Gross Pay

15. Determine any new totals as shown in row 11 of Figure 3-89.

16. Use alignment, borders, and drop shadows to format the worksheet as shown in Figure 3-89.

17. Enter your name, course, laboratory assignment (Lab 3-3), date, and instructor name in the range A17:A21.

18. Save the workbook using the file name Lab 3-3 Illiana Custom Homes Weekly Payroll Report.

19. Use the Zoom box on the Standard toolbar to change the view of the worksheet. One by one, select all the percents in the Zoom list. When you are done, return the worksheet to 100% magnification.

20. Use the Page Setup command on the File menu to change the orientation to landscape. Preview the worksheet. If number signs appear in place of numbers in any columns, adjust the column widths. Print the worksheet. Save the worksheet using the same file name.

21. Preview and print the formulas version (CTRL+`) in landscape orientation using the Fit to option button in the Page Setup dialog box. Close the worksheet without saving the latest changes.

Instructions Part 2: Open Lab 3-3 Illiana Custom Homes Weekly Payroll Report. Using the numbers in Table 3-15, analyze the effect of changing the Social Security tax in cell B13 and the Medicare tax in cell B14. Print the worksheet for each case. The first case should result in a total Social Security tax in cell G11 of $240.07. The second case should result in a total Social Security tax of $319.76. Close the workbook and do not save any changes.

Table 3-15 Illiana Custom Homes Social Security and Medicare Tax Cases		
Case	Social Security Tax	Medicare Tax
1	7.50%	2.45%
2	10.00%	3.00%

Instructions Part 3: Hand in your handwritten results for this exercise to your instructor. Open Lab 3-3 Illiana Custom Homes Weekly Payroll Report.

1. Select cell F4. Write down the formula that Excel displays in the formula bar. Select the range C4:C10. Point to the border surrounding the range and drag the selection to the range D13:D19. Click cell F4, and write down the formula that Excel displays in the formula bar below the one you wrote down earlier. Compare the two formulas. What can you conclude about how Excel responds when you move cells involved in a formula? Click the Undo button on the Standard toolbar.

2. Right-click the range C4:C10 and then click Delete on the shortcut menu. When Excel displays the Delete dialog box, click Shift cells left and then click the OK button. What does Excel display in cell F4? Use the Type a question for help box on the menu bar to find a definition of the result in cell F4. Write down the definition. Click the Undo button on the Standard toolbar.

3. Right-click the range C4:C10 and then click Insert on the shortcut menu. When Excel displays the Insert dialog box, click Shift cells right and then click the OK button. What does Excel display in the formula bar when you click cell F4? What does Excel display in the formula bar when you click cell G4? What can you conclude about how Excel responds when you insert cells next to cells involved in a formula? Close the workbook without saving the changes.

Cases and Places

The difficulty of these case studies varies:
■ are the least difficult and ■■ are more difficult. The last exercise is a group exercise.

■ Ester's Sweet Shop is open all year, but most of the shop's sales revolves around four holidays: Valentine's Day (18,330 pounds of candy), Easter (12,925 pounds of candy), Halloween (14,275 pounds of candy), and Christmas (15,975 pounds of candy). On and around these holidays, 31% of the store's output is Chocolate Creams, 27% is Gummy Bears, 18% is Jelly Beans, and the remaining 24% is Mints. The Chocolate Creams sell for $4.50 per pound, the Gummy Bears for $2.75 per pound, the Jelly Beans for $2.50 per pound, and the Mints for $1.75 per pound. Ester's management is considering revising its production figures. They have asked you to create a worksheet they can use in making this decision. The worksheet should show the total number of pounds of each candy ordered for each holiday, total candy ordered for the four holidays, potential dollar sales for each type of candy, total potential dollar sales for each holiday, and total potential dollar sales from each type of candy. Include an appropriate chart illustrating total potential dollar sales for each candy type. Use the concepts and techniques presented in this project to create and format the worksheet and chart.

■ Vashon's IT Hardware & Services is one of the largest Information Technology hardware and services company in the Southwest. The company generates revenue from the sale of hardware and consulting. A fixed percentage of the total net revenue is spent on marketing, payroll, equipment, quarterly bonus if the total net revenue for the quarter exceeds $150,000,000, production, and administrative expenses. The company's projected receipts and expenditures for the next four quarters are shown in Table 3-16.

With this data, you have been asked to prepare a worksheet and chart similar to Figure 3-1 on page EX 147 for the next shareholders' meeting. The worksheet should show total net revenues, total expenditures, and operating income for each quarterly period. Include a 3-D Pie chart on a separate sheet that compares the quarterly contributions to the operating income. Use the concepts and techniques presented in this project to create and format the worksheet and chart. During the meeting, one shareholder lobbied to reduce marketing expenditures by 1.25% and payroll costs by 3.65%. Perform a what-if analysis reflecting the proposed changes in expenditures. The changes should result in an operating income of $153,310,217 for the year.

Table 3-16 Vashon's IT Hardware & Services Projected Revenues and Expenses				
Revenues	**Quarter 1**	**Quarter 2**	**Quarter 3**	**Quarter 4**
Sales	77,230,192	82,822,010	79,401,034	73,010,304
Consulting	67,023,910	62,912,013	80,771,819	62,010,498
Expenditures				
Marketing	13.25%			
Payroll	23.65%			
Equipment	21.75%			
Production	6.50%			
Bonus	300,000.00			
Revenue for Bonus	150,000,000.00			
Administrative	13.50%			

Cases and Places

3 ■ You are the product manager for JB Smyth Publishers, a company that produces textbooks for the career school market. One of your responsibilities is to submit income projections to your publisher for the books you plan to sign. The projected first year net sales for the three books you plan to sign are shown in Table 3-17. Also included in the table are the percent of net sales for payment of royalty, manufacturing, and administrative costs. Use the concepts and techniques presented in this project to create and format a worksheet that shows the projected royalty, manufacturing costs, administrative costs, net income for each book, and totals for the five columns in Table 3-17. The net income for a book is equal to the net sales minus the royalty, manufacturing, and administrative costs. Also create an embedded 3-D Pie chart that shows the contributions of each book to the total net income.

Table 3-17	JB Smyth Publishers 1st Year Net Sales and Cost Allocations				
Book Title	Net Sales	Royalty	Manu. Costs	Adm. Costs	Net Income
Book 1	4,123,489.00	—	—	—	—
Book 2	2,275,546.50	—	—	—	—
Book 3	1,678,925.75	—	—	—	—
Total	—	—	—	—	—
Assumptions					
Royalty	16.25%				
Manu. Costs	23.5%				
Adm. Costs	20.00%				

Your publisher reviewed your plan and returned it, requesting printouts of the worksheet for the following set of values: Set 1 – Royalty - 12.5%; Manu. Costs - 30.5%, and Adm. Costs - 18.50% (answer Total Net Income = $3,110,015.08); Set 2 – Royalty - 18.5%; Manu. Costs - 32%, and Adm. Costs - 20.50% (answer Total Net Income = $2,342,608.76).

4 ■■ Uncle Harry and Aunt Matilda own a plumbing company and run a farm part-time. They want to save enough money over the next six months to buy a used tractor for the spring planting season. They have job orders at their plumbing company for the next six months: $15,200 in January, $18,560 in February, $29,560 in March, $32,019 in April, $43,102 in May, and $29,955 in June. Each month, they spend 36.35% of the job order income on material, 3.15% on patterns, 5.25% on their retirement account, and 42.5% on food and clothing. 25% of the remaining profits (orders – total expenses) will be put aside for the tractor. Aunt Matilda's parents have agreed to provide a bonus of $150 whenever the monthly savings exceeds $750. Uncle Harry has asked you to create a worksheet that shows orders, expenses, profits, bonuses, and savings for the next six months, and totals for each category. Aunt Matilda would like you to (a) perform a what-if analysis to determine the total savings by reducing the percentage spent on material to 25% (answer total savings = $11,045.86), and (b) with the original assumptions, goal seek to determine what percentage of profits to spend on food and clothing if $7,000 is needed for the used tractor (answer = 40.05%). Use the concepts and techniques presented in this project to create and format the worksheet.

Cases and Places

5 ■■ **Working Together** Your group has been asked to develop a worksheet that shows quarterly growth for the year based on Quarter 1 sales and growth data. The data and general layout of the worksheet, including the totals, are shown in Table 3-18.

Table 3-18 Working Together Data and General Layout					
	Qtr 1	Qtr 2	Qtr 3	Qtr 4	Total
Total Net Revenue	Formula A	Formula D ———————————————→			—
Cost of Goods Sold	Formula B ——————————————→				—
Gross Margin	Formula C ——————————————→				—
Assumptions					
Qtr 1 Revenue	$18,645,830.00				
Qtr Growth Rate	0.00%	−3.50%	5.00%	3.75%	
Qtr Cost Rate	42.50%	46.00%	52.00%	53.75%	
Extra	2.90%	3.10%	4.95%	2.50%	

Enter the formulas shown in Table 3-19 in the locations shown in Table 3-18. Copy Formula B, C, and D to the remaining quarters.

Table 3-19 Working Together Formulas
Formula A = Qtr 1 Revenue
Formula B = IF(Qtr Growth Rate < 0, Revenue * (Qtr Cost Rate + Extra), Revenue * Qtr Cost Rate)
Formula C = Revenue − Cost
Formula D = Qtr 1 Total Net Revenue * (1 + Qtr Growth Rate)

Have each member of your team submit a sketch of the proposed worksheet and 3-D Pie chart (see Figure 3-3b on page EX 149) and then implement the best one. The gross margin for the four quarters should equal $38,014,124.00. Include an embedded exploded 3-D Pie chart that shows the contribution of each quarter to the gross margin. Use the concepts and techniques developed in the first three projects to create and format the worksheet and embedded 3-D Pie chart. Use the Goal Seek command to determine the Qtr 1 Revenue (first value in the Assumptions area) that will generate a total gross margin of $40,000,000.00. Your team should end up with a Qtr 1 Revenue of $19,619,897.07. Hand in the sketches submitted by each team member and a printout of the modified worksheet and 3-D Pie chart.

MICROSOFT
Office Excel 2003

Creating Static and Dynamic Web Pages Using Excel

CASE PERSPECTIVE

Home Wireless Fidelity, a network company that specializes in the installation of wireless home networks, has experienced significant growth since it developed the first wireless home network system. In two years, the company has grown from a single owner, garage-based company to one with annual sales in the millions.

Sergio Autohbon is a spreadsheet specialist for Home Wireless Fidelity. One of Sergio's responsibilities is a workbook that summarizes quarterly sales by store location (Figure 1a on the next page). In the past, Sergio printed the worksheet and chart, sent it out to make copies of it, and then mailed it to his distribution list.

Home Wireless Fidelity recently upgraded to Office 2003 because of its Web and collaboration capabilities. After attending an Office 2003 training session, Sergio had a great idea and called you for help. He would like to save the Excel worksheet and Pie chart (Figure 1a) on the company's intranet as a static Web page (Figure 1b), so the lower-level management on the distribution list can display it using a browser. He also suggested publishing the same workbook on the company's intranet as a dynamic (interactive) Web page (Figure 1c), so the higher-level management could use its browser to manipulate the data in the worksheet without requiring Excel.

Finally, Sergio wants both the static and dynamic Web pages saved as single files, also called Single File Web Page format, rather than in the traditional file and folder format, called Web Page format.

As you read through this Web feature, you will learn how to create static and dynamic Web pages from workbooks in Excel and then display the results using a browser.

Objectives

You will have mastered the material in this Web feature when you can:

- Publish a worksheet and chart as a static or a dynamic Web page
- Display Web pages published in Excel in a browser
- Manipulate the data in a published Web page using a browser
- Complete file management tasks within Excel

Introduction

Excel provides fast, easy methods for saving workbooks as Web pages that can be stored on the World Wide Web, a company's intranet, or a local hard disk. A user then can display the workbook using a browser, rather than Excel.

You can save a workbook, or a portion of a workbook, as a static Web page or a dynamic Web page. A **static Web page**, also called a **noninteractive Web page** or **view-only Web page**, is a snapshot of the workbook. It is similar to a printed report in that you can view it through your browser, but you cannot modify it. In the browser window, the workbook appears as it would in Microsoft Excel, including sheet tabs that you can click to switch between worksheets. A **dynamic Web page**, also called an **interactive Web page**, includes the interactivity and functionality of the workbook. For example, with a dynamic Web page, you can view a copy of the worksheet in your browser and then enter formulas, reformat cells, and change values in the worksheet to perform what-if analysis. A user does not need Excel on his or her computer to complete these tasks.

As illustrated in Figure 1, this Web feature shows you how to save a workbook (Figure 1a) as a static Web page (Figure 1b) and view it using your browser. Then, using the same workbook, the steps show how to save it as a dynamic Web page (Figure 1c), view it using your browser, and then change values to test the Web page's interactivity and functionality.

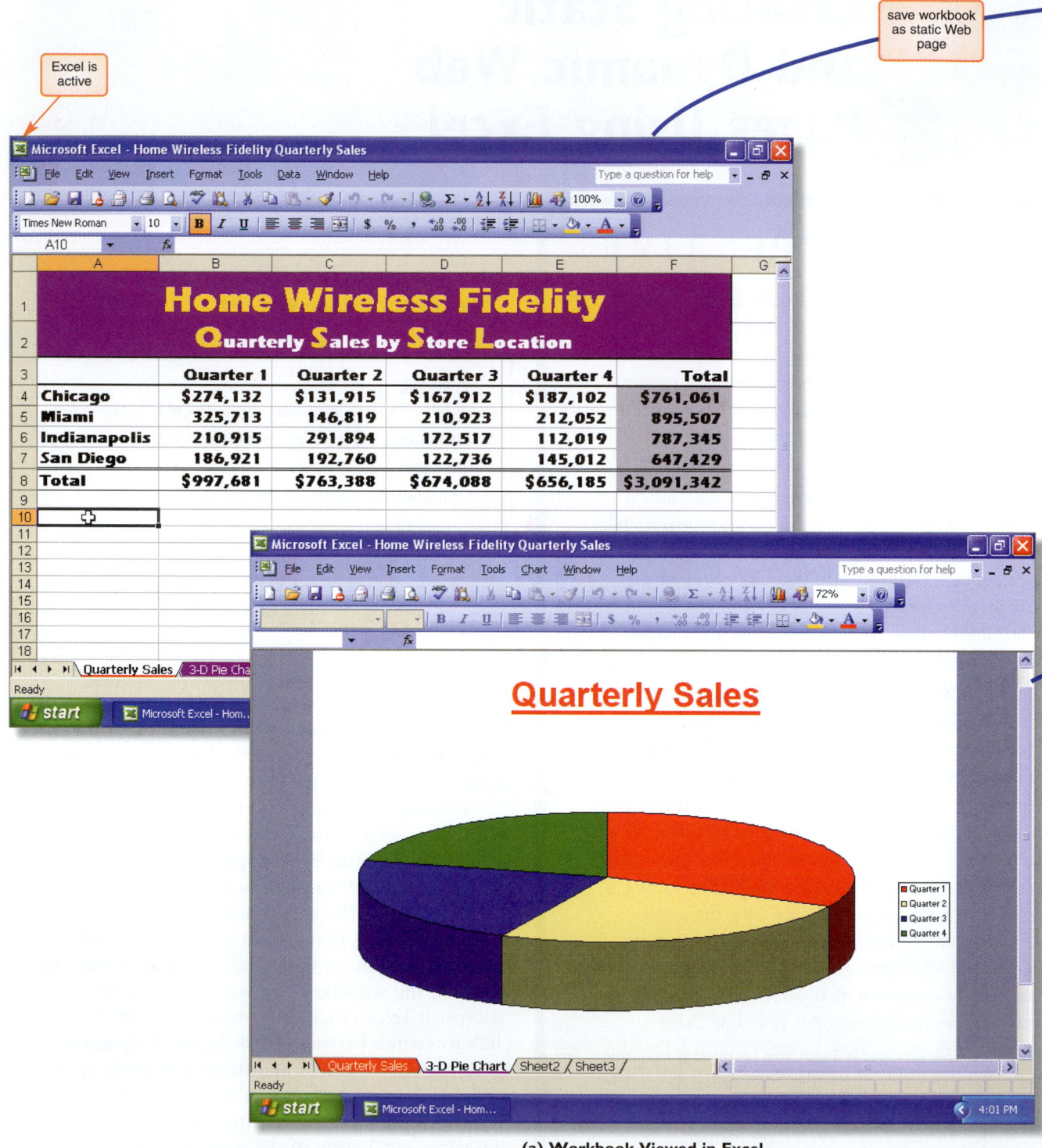

(a) Workbook Viewed in Excel

FIGURE 1

browser
is active

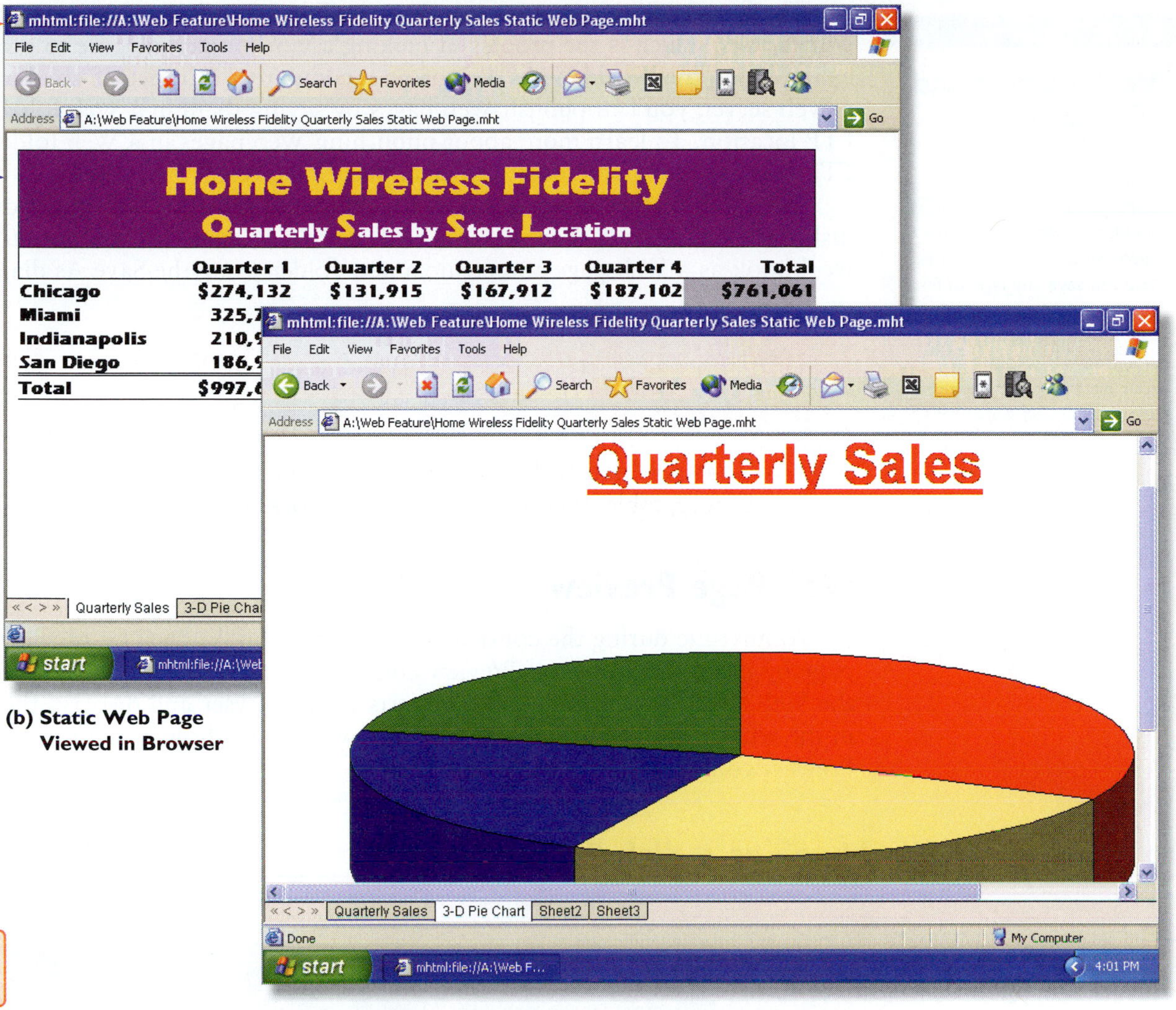

mhtml:file://A:\Web Feature\Home Wireless Fidelity Quarterly Sales Static Web Page.mht

File Edit View Favorites Tools Help

Back · · Search Favorites Media

Address A:\Web Feature\Home Wireless Fidelity Quarterly Sales Static Web Page.mht Go

Home Wireless Fidelity
Quarterly Sales by Store Location

	Quarter 1	Quarter 2	Quarter 3	Quarter 4	Total
Chicago	$274,132	$131,915	$167,912	$187,102	$761,061
Miami	325,7				
Indianapolis	210,9				
San Diego	186,9				
Total	$997,6				

« < > » Quarterly Sales | 3-D Pie Chart

start mhtml:file://A:\Web

**(b) Static Web Page
Viewed in Browser**

mhtml:file://A:\Web Feature\Home Wireless Fidelity Quarterly Sales Static Web Page.mht

File Edit View Favorites Tools Help

Back · · Search Favorites Media

Address A:\Web Feature\Home Wireless Fidelity Quarterly Sales Static Web Page.mht Go

Quarterly Sales

« < > » Quarterly Sales | 3-D Pie Chart | Sheet2 | Sheet3

Done My Computer

start mhtml:file://A:\Web F... 4:01 PM

save 3-D Pie chart
and worksheet as
dynamic Web page

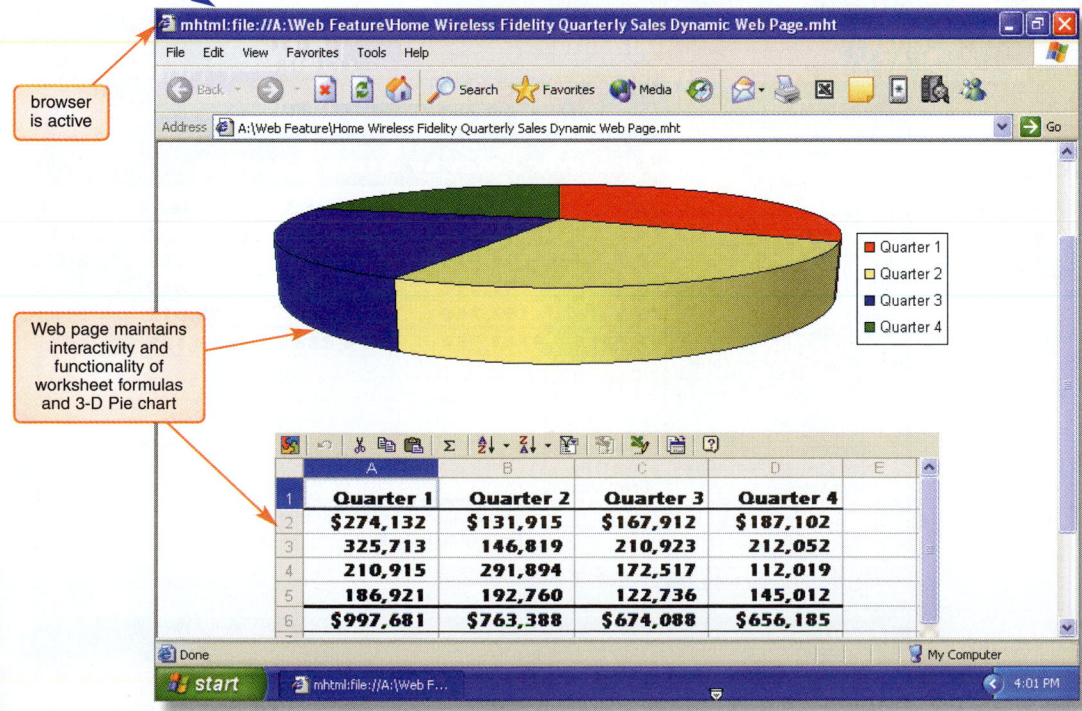

mhtml:file://A:\Web Feature\Home Wireless Fidelity Quarterly Sales Dynamic Web Page.mht

File Edit View Favorites Tools Help

Back · · Search Favorites Media

Address A:\Web Feature\Home Wireless Fidelity Quarterly Sales Dynamic Web Page.mht Go

browser
is active

Quarter 1
Quarter 2
Quarter 3
Quarter 4

Web page maintains
interactivity and
functionality of
worksheet formulas
and 3-D Pie chart

	A	B	C	D	E
1	**Quarter 1**	**Quarter 2**	**Quarter 3**	**Quarter 4**	
2	**$274,132**	**$131,915**	**$167,912**	**$187,102**	
3	325,713	146,819	210,923	212,052	
4	210,915	291,894	172,517	112,019	
5	186,921	192,760	122,736	145,012	
6	$997,681	$763,388	$674,088	$656,185	

Done My Computer

start mhtml:file://A:\Web F... 4:01 PM

**(c) Dynamic Web Page
Viewed in Browser**

The Save as Web Page command on the File menu allows you to **publish workbooks**, which is the process of making a workbook available to others; for example, on the World Wide Web or on a company's intranet. If you have access to a Web server, you can publish Web pages by saving them in a Web folder or on an FTP location. To learn more about publishing Web pages in a Web folder or on an FTP location using Microsoft Office applications, refer to Appendix C.

This Web feature illustrates how to create and save the Web pages on a floppy disk, rather than on a Web server. This feature also demonstrates how to preview a workbook as a Web page and create a new folder using the Save As dialog box.

Using Web Page Preview and Saving an Excel Workbook as a Static Web Page

After you have created an Excel workbook, you can preview it as a Web page. If the preview is acceptable, then you can save the workbook as a Web page.

Web Page Preview

At anytime during the construction of a workbook, you can preview it as a Web page by using the Web Page Preview command on the File menu. When you invoke the Web Page Preview command, it starts your browser and displays the active sheet in the workbook as a Web page. The following steps show how to use the Web Page Preview command.

To Preview the Workbook as a Web Page

1

• **Insert the Data Disk in drive A.**

• **Start Excel and then open the workbook, Home Wireless Fidelity Quarterly Sales, on drive A.**

• **Click File on the menu bar.**

Excel starts and opens the workbook, Home Wireless Fidelity Quarterly Sales. The workbook is made up of two sheets: a worksheet and a chart. Excel displays the File menu (Figure 2).

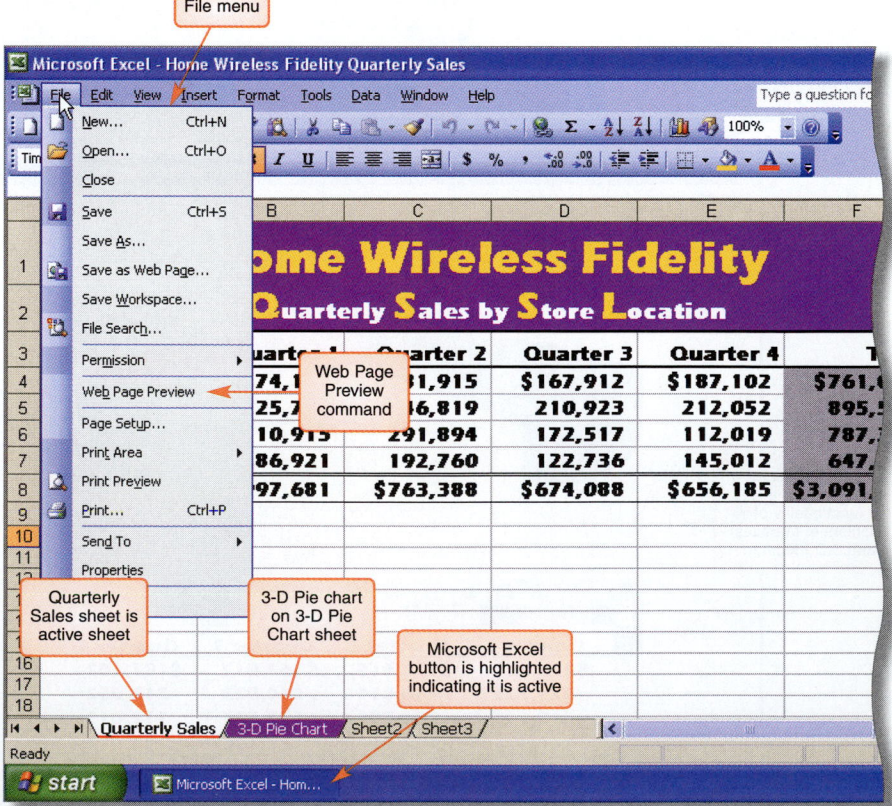

FIGURE 2

2

• **Click Web Page Preview.**

Excel starts your browser. The browser displays a preview of how the Quarterly Sales sheet will appear as a Web page (Figure 3). The Web page preview in the browser is nearly identical to the display of the worksheet in Excel. A highlighted browser button appears on the Windows taskbar indicating it is active. The Excel button on the Windows taskbar no longer is highlighted.

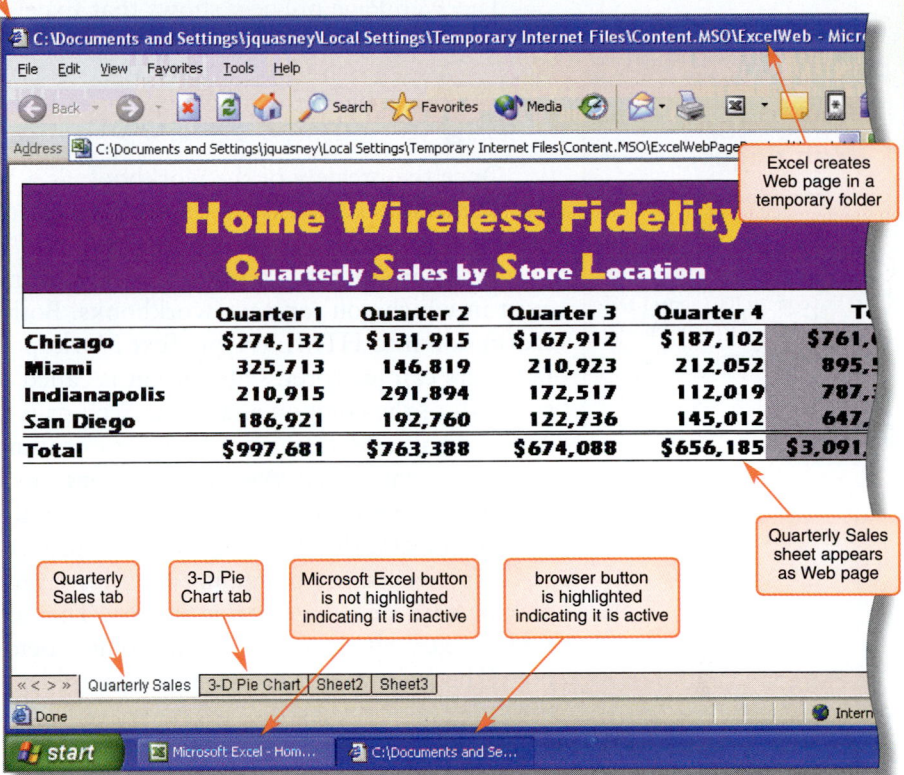

FIGURE 3

3

• **Click the 3-D Pie Chart tab at the bottom of the Web page.**

The browser displays the 3-D Pie chart (Figure 4).

4

• **After viewing the Web page preview of the Home Wireless Fidelity Quarterly Sales workbook, click the Close button on the right side of the browser title bar.**

The browser closes. Excel becomes active and again displays the Home Wireless Fidelity Quarterly Sales worksheet.

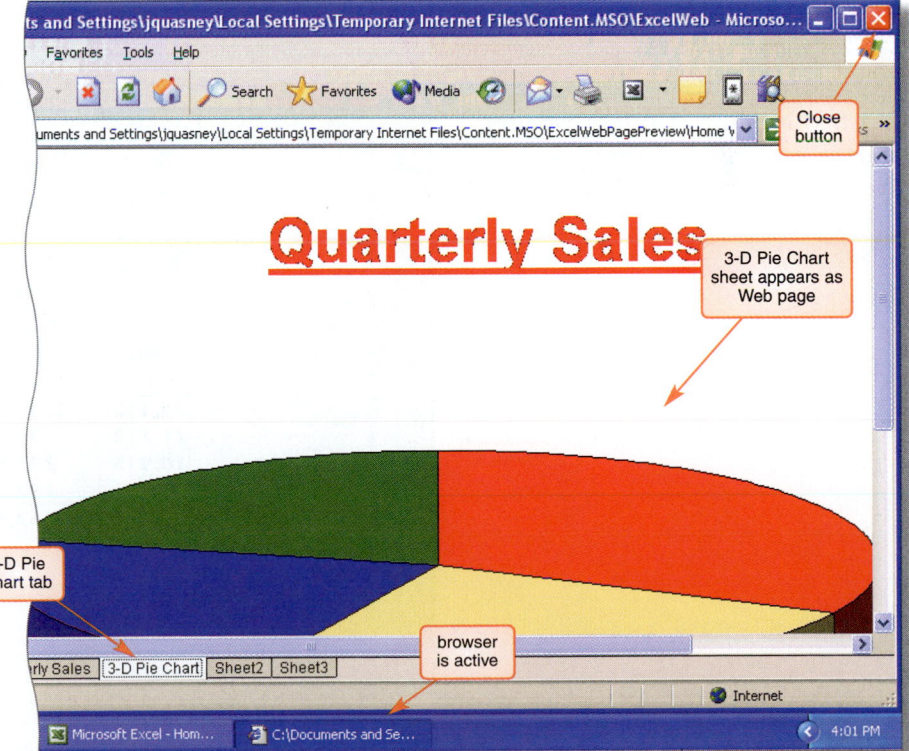

FIGURE 4

The Web Page preview shows that Excel has the capability of producing professional looking Web pages from workbooks.

Saving a Workbook as a Static Web Page in a New Folder

Once the preview of the workbook as a Web page is acceptable, you can save the workbook as a Web page so that others can view it using a Web browser, such as Internet Explorer or Netscape Navigator.

Whether you plan to save static or dynamic Web pages, two Web page formats exist in which you can save workbooks. Both formats convert the contents of the workbook into HTML (HyperText Markup Language), which is a language browsers can interpret. One format is called **Single File Web Page format**, which saves all of the components of the Web page in a single file with an .mht extension. This format is useful particularly for e-mailing workbooks in HTML format. The second format, called **Web Page format,** saves the Web page in a file and some of its components in a folder. This format is useful if you need access to the components, such as images, that make up the Web page.

Experienced users organize the files saved on a storage medium, such as a floppy disk or hard disk, by creating folders. They then save related files in a common folder. Excel allows you to create folders before saving a file using the Save As dialog box. The following steps create a new folder on the Data Disk in drive A and save the workbook as a static Web page in the new folder.

More About

Publishing Web Pages

For more information about publishing Web pages using Excel, visit the Excel 2003 More About Web page (scsite.com/ex2003/more) and then click Publishing Web Pages Using Excel.

To Save an Excel Workbook as a Static Web Page in a Newly Created Folder

1

• **With the Home Wireless Fidelity Quarterly Sales workbook open, click File on the menu bar.**

Excel displays the File menu (Figure 5).

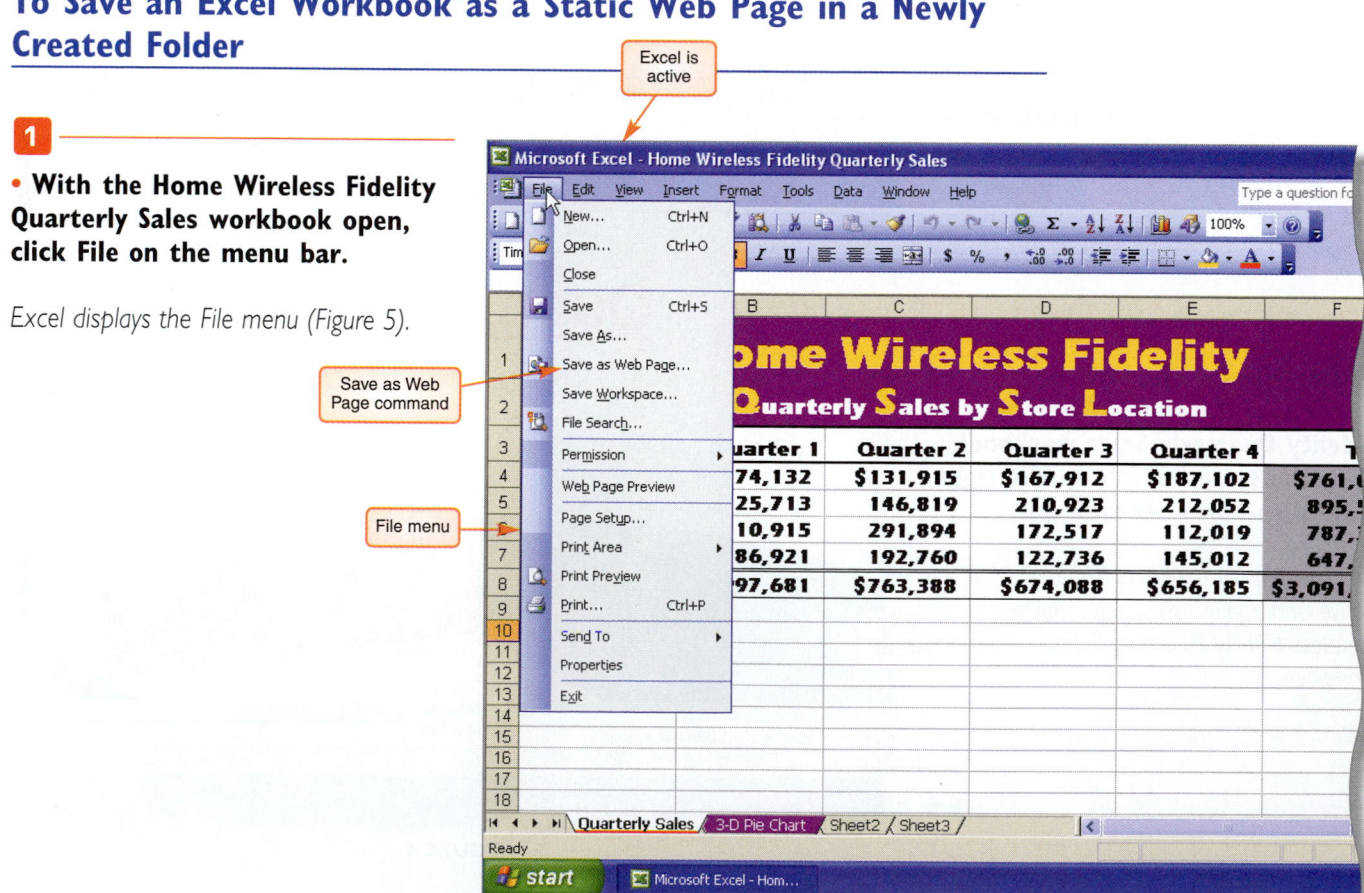

FIGURE 5

• Click Save as Web Page.

• When Excel displays the Save As dialog box, type Home Wireless Fidelity Quarterly Sales Static Web Page **in the File name text box.**

• Click the Save as type box arrow and then click Single File Web Page.

• Click the Save in box arrow, select 3½ Floppy (A:), and then click the Create New Folder button.

• When Excel displays the New Folder dialog box, type Web Feature **in the Name text box.**

Excel displays the Save As dialog box and New Folder dialog box as shown in Figure 6.

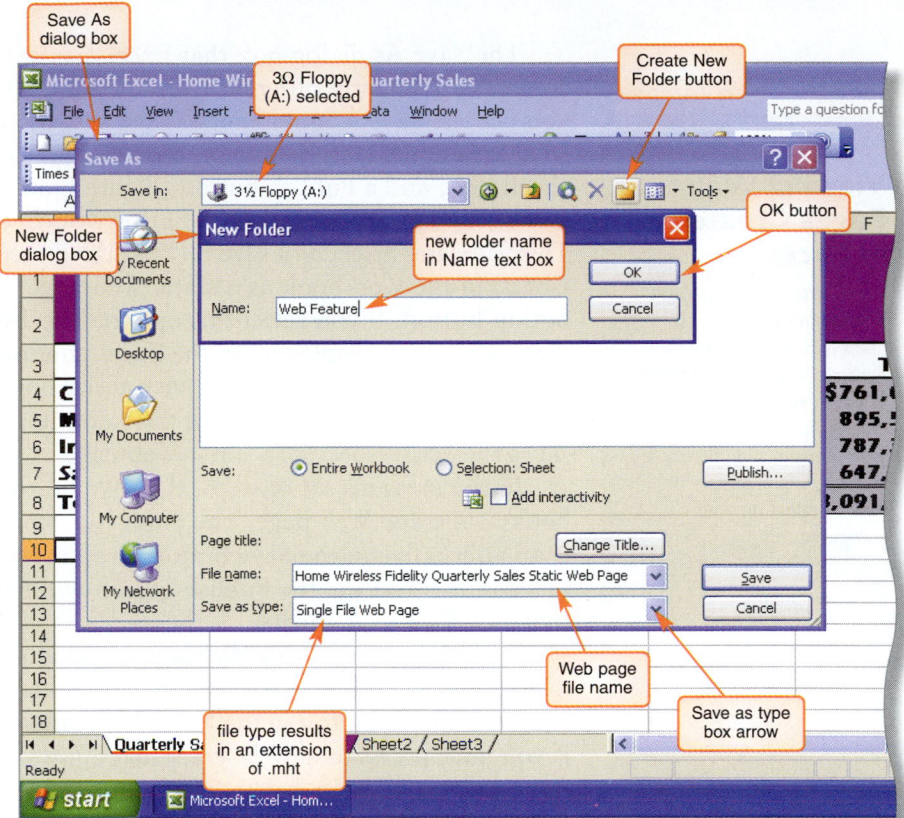

FIGURE 6

• Click the OK button in the New Folder dialog box.

Excel automatically selects the new folder Web Feature in the Save in box (Figure 7). The Entire Workbook option in the Save area instructs Excel to save all sheets in the workbook as static Web pages.

• Click the Save button in the Save As dialog box.

• Click the Close button on the right side of the Excel title bar to quit Excel.

Excel saves the workbook in a single file in HTML format in the Web Feature folder on the Data Disk in drive A.

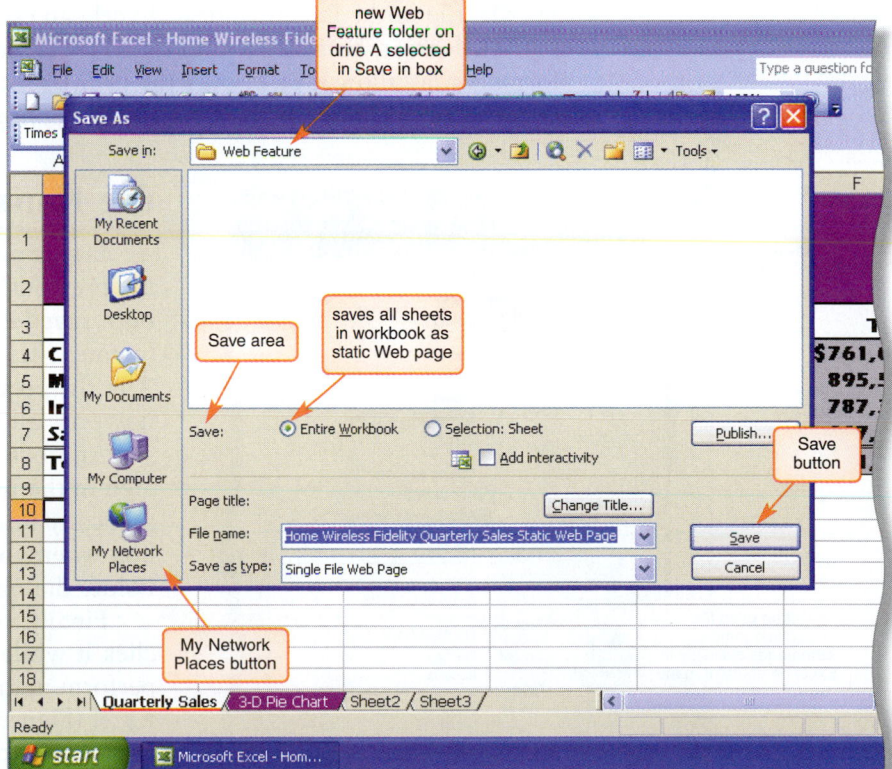

FIGURE 7

The Save As dialog box that Excel displays when you use the Save as Web Page command is slightly different from the Save As dialog box that Excel displays when you use the Save As command. When you use the Save as Web Page command, a Save area appears in the dialog box. Within the Save area are two option buttons, a check box, and a Publish button (Figure 7 on the previous page). You can select only one of the option buttons. The Entire Workbook option button is selected by default. This indicates Excel will save all the active sheets (Quarterly Sales and 3-D Pie Chart) in the workbook as a static Web page. The alternative is the Selection Sheet option button. If you select this option, Excel will save only the active sheet (the one that currently is displaying in the Excel window) in the workbook. If you add a check mark to the Add interactivity check box, then Excel saves the active sheet as a dynamic Web page. If you leave the Add interactivity check box unchecked, Excel saves the active sheet as a static Web page.

In the previous set of steps, the Save button was used to save the Excel workbook as a static Web page. The Publish button in the Save As dialog box in Figure 7 is an alternative to the Save button. It allows you to customize the Web page further. Later in this feature, the Publish button will be used to explain how you can customize a Web page further.

If you have access to a Web server and it allows you to save files in a Web folder, then you can save the Web page directly on the Web server by clicking the My Network Places button in the lower-left corner of the Save As dialog box (Figure 7). If you have access to a Web server that allows you to save on an FTP site, then you can select the FTP site below FTP locations in the Save in box just as you select any folder on which to save a file. To learn more about publishing Web pages in a Web folder or on an FTP location using Office applications, refer to Appendix C.

After Excel saves the workbook in Step 4 on the previous page, it displays the HTML file in the Excel window. Excel can continue to display the workbook in HTML format, because, within the HTML file that it created, it also saved the Excel formats that allow it to display the HTML file in Excel. This is referred to as **round tripping** the HTML file back to the application in which it was created.

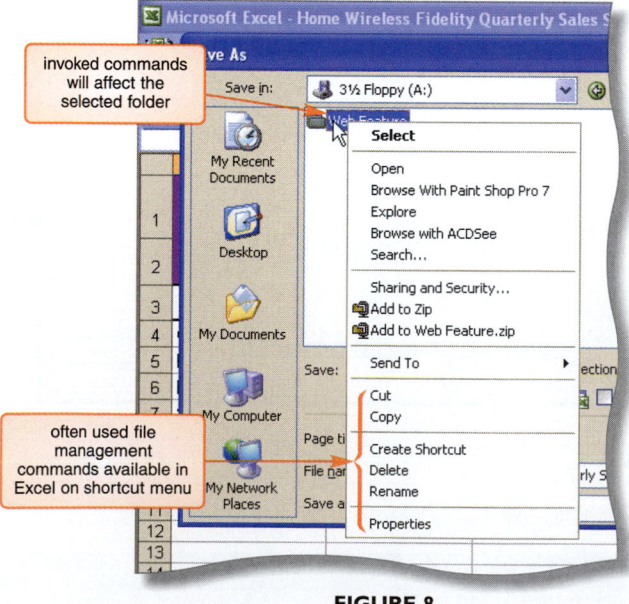

invoked commands will affect the selected folder

often used file management commands available in Excel on shortcut menu

FIGURE 8

File Management Tools in Excel

It was not necessary to create a new folder in the previous set of steps. The Web page could have been saved on the Data Disk in drive A in the same manner files were saved on the Data Disk in drive A in the previous projects. Creating a new folder, however, allows you to organize your work.

Another point concerning the new folder created in the previous set of steps is that Excel automatically inserts the new folder name in the Save in box when you click the OK button in the New Folder dialog box (Figure 7).

Finally, once you create a folder, you can right-click it while the Save As dialog box is active and perform many file management tasks directly in Excel (Figure 8). For example, once the shortcut menu appears, you can rename the selected folder, delete it, copy it, display its properties, and perform other file management functions.

Viewing the Static Web Page Using a Browser

With the static Web page saved in the Web Feature folder on drive A, the next step is to view it using a browser as shown in the following steps.

To View and Manipulate the Static Web Page Using a Browser

1

• **If necessary, insert the Data Disk in drive A.**

• **Click the Start button on the Windows taskbar, point to All Programs on the Start menu, and then click Internet Explorer on the All Programs submenu.**

• **When the Internet Explorer window appears, type** a:\web feature\home wireless fidelity quarterly sales static web page.mht **in the Address box and then press the ENTER key.**

The browser displays the Web page, Home Wireless Fidelity Quarterly Sales Static Web Page.mht, with the Quarterly Sales sheet active (Figure 9).

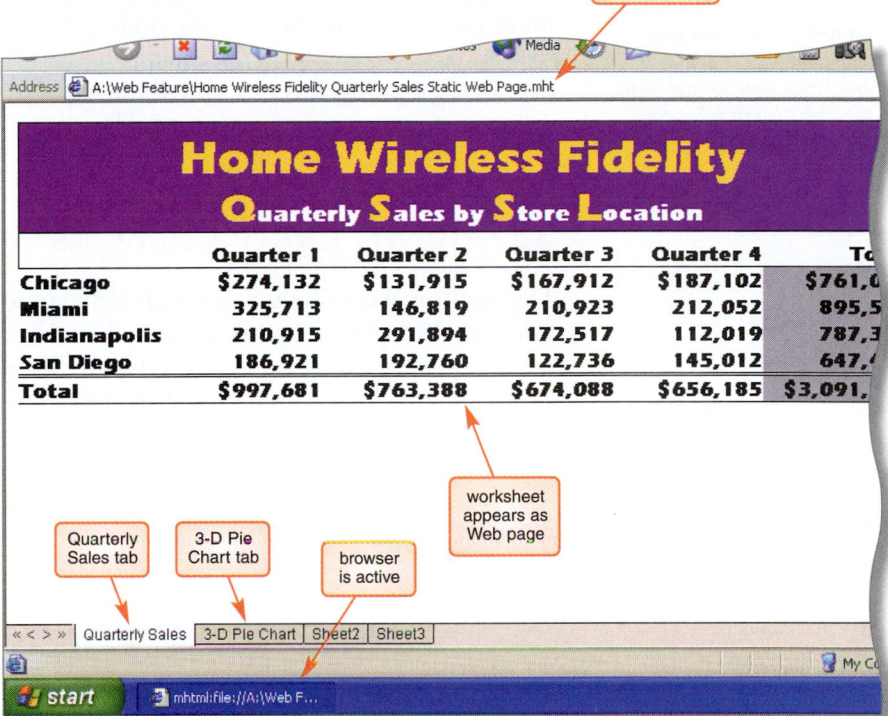

FIGURE 9

2

• **Click the 3-D Pie Chart tab at the bottom of the window.**

• **Use the scroll arrows to display the lower portion of the chart.**

The browser displays the 3-D Pie chart as shown in Figure 10.

3

• **Click the Close button on the right side of the browser title bar to close the browser.**

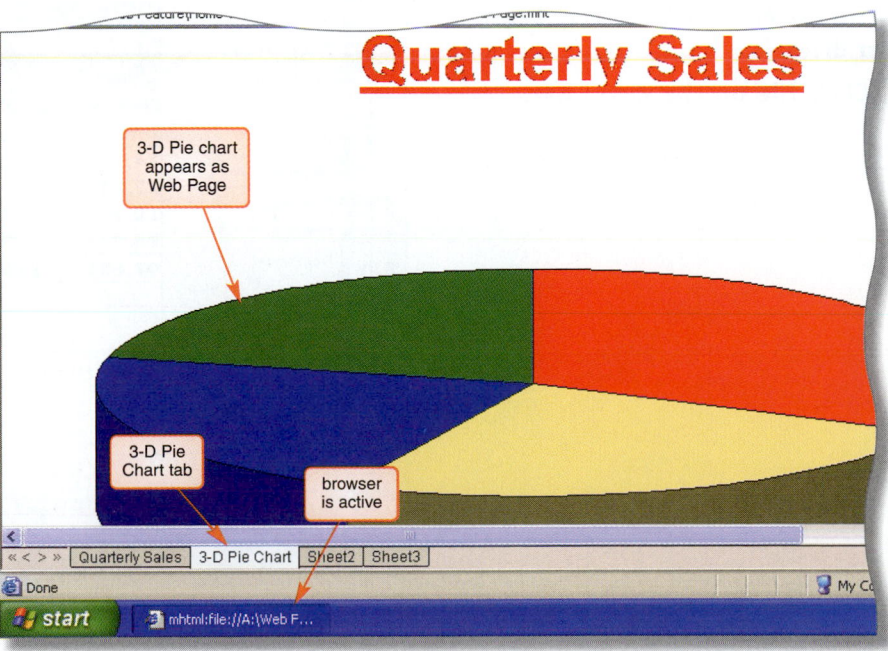

FIGURE 10

Q: Can I view the source code of a static Web page created in Excel?

A: Yes. To view the HTML source code for a Web page created in Excel, use your browser to display the Web page, click View on the menu bar, and then click Source.

You can see from Figures 9 and 10 on the previous page that a static Web page is an ideal way to distribute information to a large group of people. For example, the static Web page could be published on a Web server connected to the Internet and made available to anyone with a computer, browser, and the address of the Web page. It also can be e-mailed easily, because the Web page resides in a single file, rather than in a file and folder. Publishing a static Web page of a workbook thus is an excellent alternative to distributing printed copies of the workbook.

Figures 9 and 10 show that, when you instruct Excel to save the entire workbook (see the Entire Workbook option button in Figure 7 on page EX 231), it creates a Web page with tabs for each sheet in the workbook. Clicking a tab displays the corresponding sheet. If you want, you can use the Print command on the File menu in your browser to print the sheets one at a time.

Saving an Excel Chart as a Dynamic Web Page

This section shows how to publish a dynamic Web page that includes Excel functionality and interactivity. The objective is to publish the 3-D Pie chart that is on the 3-D Pie Chart sheet in the Home Wireless Fidelity Quarterly Sales workbook. The following steps use the Publish button in the Save As dialog box, rather than the Save button, to illustrate the additional publishing capabilities of Excel.

To Save an Excel Chart as a Dynamic Web Page

1

• **If necessary, insert the Data Disk in drive A.**

• **Start Excel and then open the workbook, Home Wireless Fidelity Quarterly Sales, on drive A.**

• **Click File on the menu bar.**

Excel opens the workbook and displays the File menu (Figure 11).

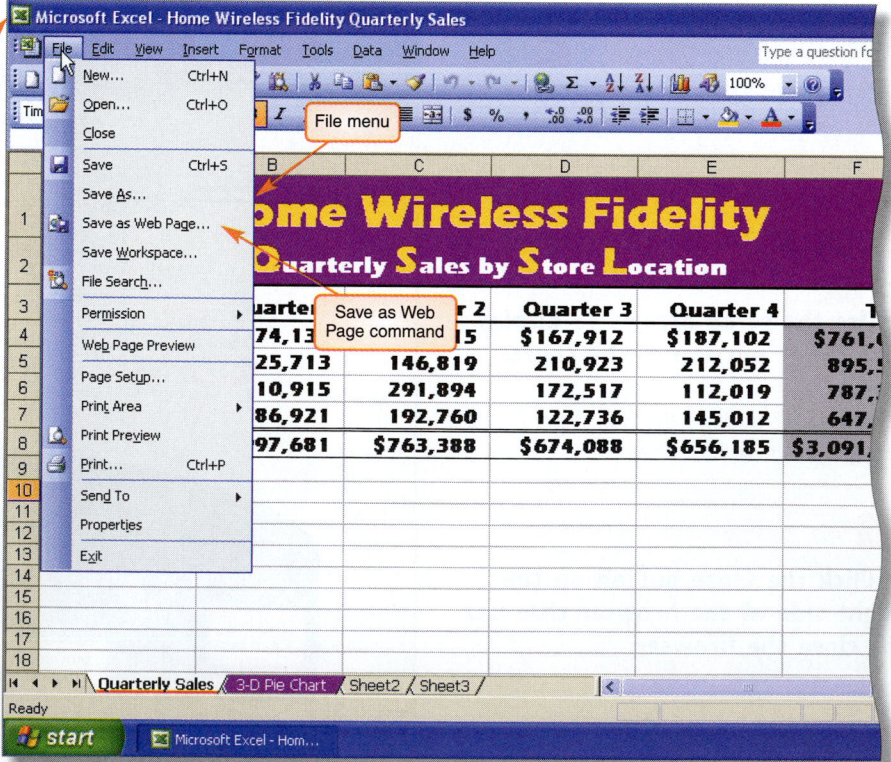

FIGURE 11

2

• Click **Save as Web Page.**

• When Excel displays the **Save As dialog box, type** Home Wireless Fidelity Quarterly Sales Dynamic Web Page **in the File name text box.**

• Click the **Save as type box arrow** and then click **Single File Web Page.**

• If necessary, click the **Save in box arrow, select 3½ Floppy (A:) in the Save in list, and then select the Web Feature folder.**

Excel displays the Save As dialog box as shown in Figure 12.

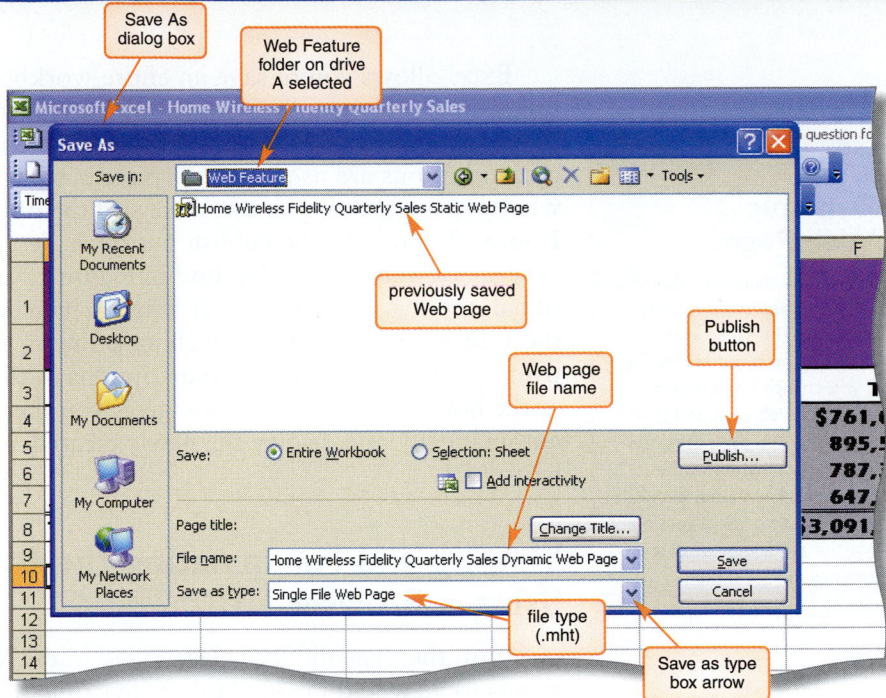

FIGURE 12

3

• Click the **Publish button.**

• When Excel displays the **Publish as Web Page dialog box, click the Choose box arrow and then click Items on 3-D Pie Chart.**

• Click the **Add interactivity with check box in the Viewing options area.**

• If necessary, click the **Add interactivity with box arrow and then click Chart functionality.**

Excel displays the Publish as Web Page dialog box as shown in Figure 13.

4

• Click the **Publish button, click the Close button on the right side of the Excel title bar, and if necessary, click the No button in the Microsoft Excel dialog box.**

Excel saves the dynamic Web page in the Web Feature folder on the Data Disk in drive A. The Excel window is closed.

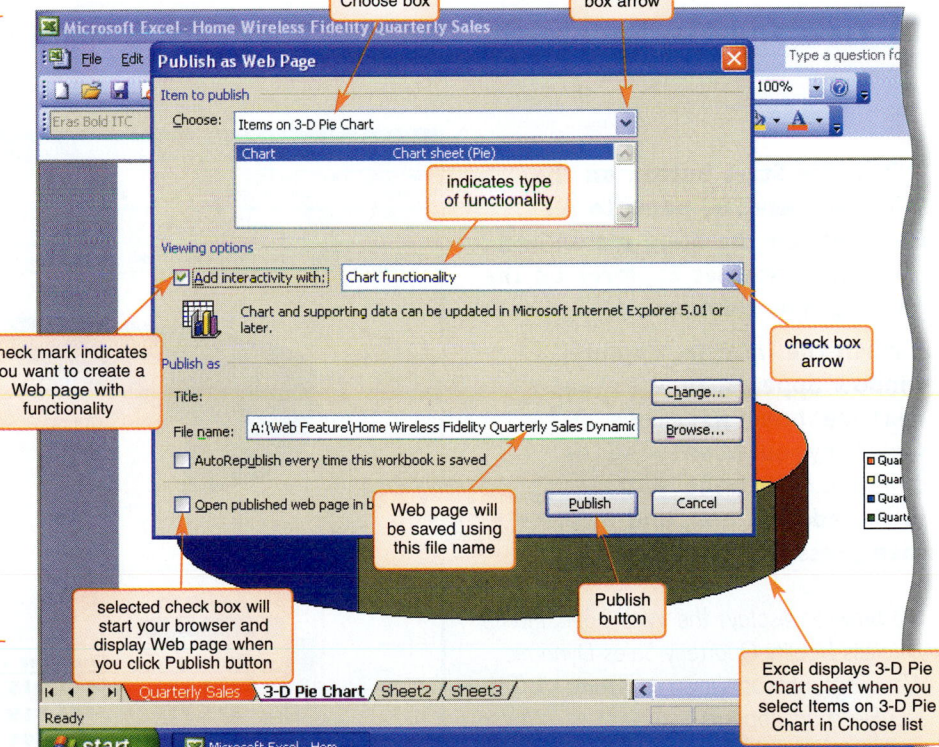

FIGURE 13

Excel allows you to save an entire workbook, a sheet in the workbook, or a range on a sheet as a Web page. In Figure 12 on the previous page, the Save area provides options that allow you to save the entire workbook or only a sheet. These option buttons are used with the Save button. If you want to be more selective in what you save, then you can disregard the option buttons in the Save area in Figure 12 and click the Publish button as described in Step 3. The Choose box in the Publish as Web Page dialog box in Figure 13 on the previous page provides addi-tional options for you to select what to include on the Web page. You also may save the Web page as a dynamic Web page (interactive) or a static Web page (noninterac-tive) by selecting the appropriate options in the Viewing options area. The check box at the bottom of the dialog box gives you the opportunity to start your browser automatically and display the newly created Web page when you click the Publish button.

Viewing and Manipulating the Dynamic Web Page Using a Browser

With the dynamic Web page saved in the Web Feature folder on drive A, the next step is to view and manipulate the dynamic Web page using a browser, as shown in the following steps.

To View and Manipulate the Dynamic Web Page Using a Browser

1

• **Click the Start button on the Windows taskbar, point to All Programs on the Start menu, and then click Internet Explorer on the All Programs submenu.**

• **When the Internet Explorer window appears, type** a:\web feature\home wireless fidelity quarterly sales dynamic web page.mht **in the Address box, and then press the ENTER key.**

The browser displays the Web page, Home Wireless Fidelity Quarterly Sales Dynamic Web Page.mht, as shown in Figure 14. The 3-D Pie chart appears at the top of the Web page. The rows and columns of the worksheet that determine the size of the slices appear immediately below the 3-D Pie chart.

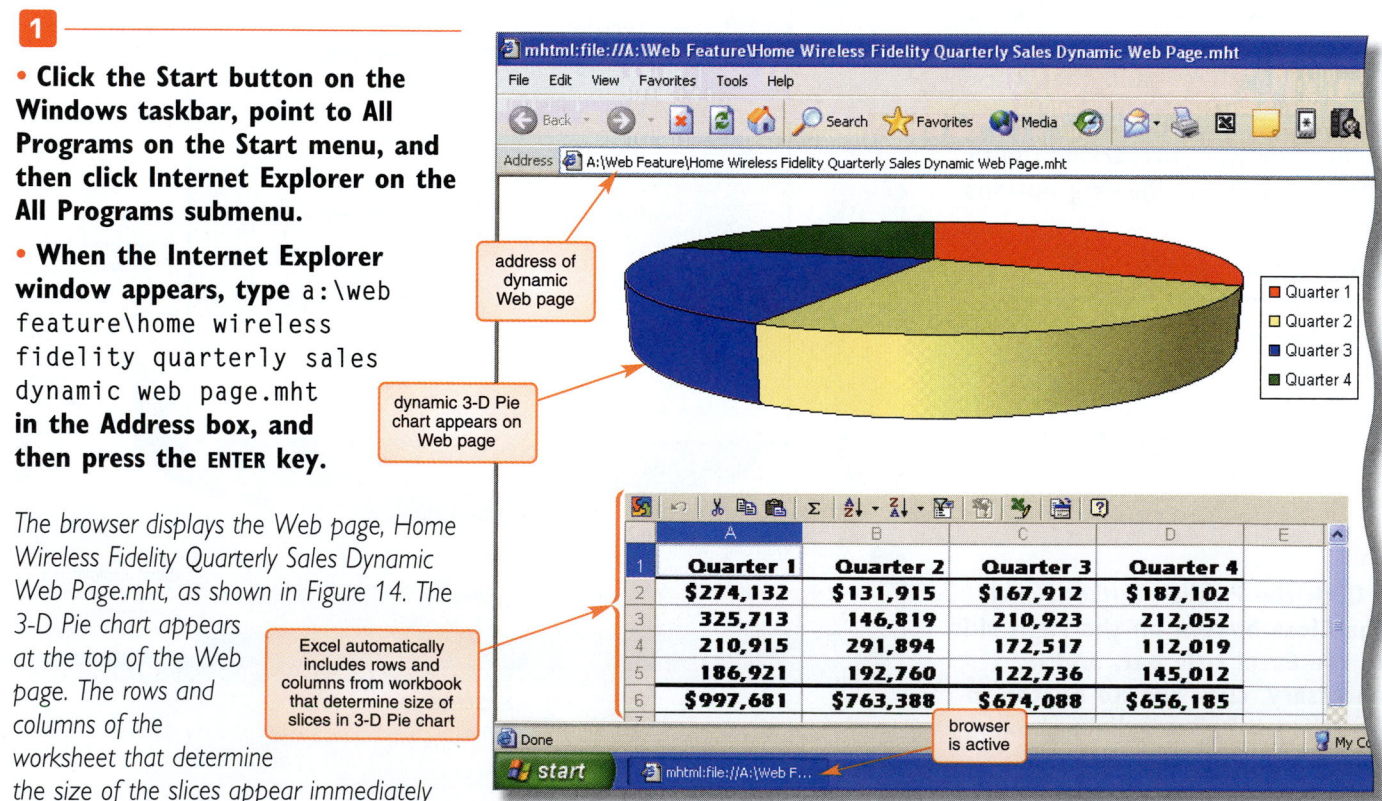

FIGURE 14

2

• **Click cell A2 and then enter**
1600000 **as the new value.**

The number 1,600,000 replaces the number 274,132 in cell A2. The formulas in the worksheet portion recalculate the totals in row 6 and the slices in the 3-D Pie chart change to agree with the new totals (Figure 15).

3

• **Click the Close button on the right side of the browser title bar to close the browser.**

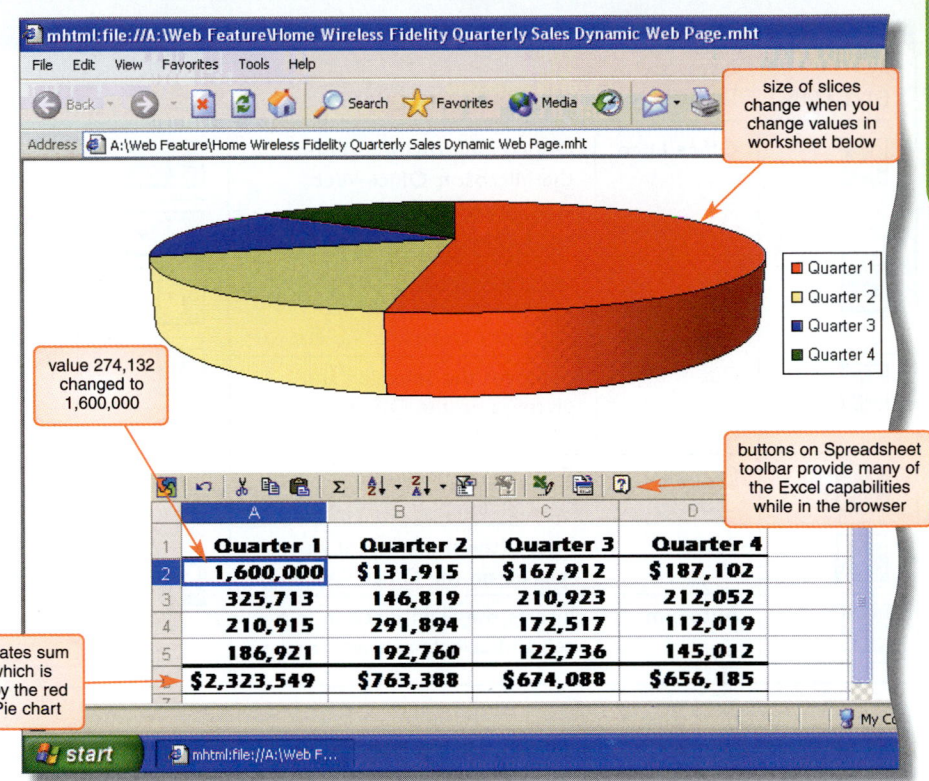

FIGURE 15

Figure 14 shows the result of saving the 3-D Pie chart as a dynamic Web page. Excel displays a slightly rounded version of the 3-D Pie chart and automatically adds the columns and rows from the worksheet that affect the chart directly below the chart. As shown in Figure 15, when a number in the worksheet that determines the size of the slices in the 3-D Pie chart is changed, the Web page instantaneously recalculates all formulas and redraws the 3-D Pie chart. For example, when cell A2 is changed from 274,132 to 1,600,000, the Web page recalculates the totals in row 6. The slice representing Quarter 1 is based on the number in cell A6. Thus, when the number in cell A6 changes from 997,681 to 2,323,549 because of the change made in cell A2, the slice representing Quarter 1 changes to a much larger slice in relation to the others. The interactivity and functionality allow you to share a workbook's formulas and charts with others who may not have access to Excel, but do have access to a browser.

Modifying the Worksheet on a Dynamic Web Page

As shown in Figure 15, the Web page displays a toolbar immediately above the rows and columns in the worksheet. This toolbar, called the Spreadsheet toolbar, allows you to invoke the most commonly used worksheet commands. For example, you can select a cell immediately below a column of numbers and click the AutoSum button to sum the numbers in the column. Cut, copy, and paste capabilities also are available. Table 1 on the next page summarizes the functions of the buttons on the Spreadsheet toolbar shown in Figure 15.

Table 1 Spreadsheet Toolbar Options

BUTTON	NAME OF BUTTON	FUNCTION	BUTTON	NAME OF BUTTON	FUNCTION
	Office Logo	Displays information about the Microsoft Office Web component, including the version number installed		Sort Ascending	Sorts the selected items in ascending sequence
	Undo	Reverses the last command or action, or deletes the last entry typed		Sort Descending	Sorts the selected items in descending sequence
	Cut	Removes the selection and places it on the Office Clipboard		AutoFilter	Selects specific items you want to display in a list
	Copy	Copy the selection to the Office Clipboard		Refresh All	Refreshes data when connected to the Web
	Paste	Inserts the most recent item placed on the Office Clipboard		Export to Excel	Opens the Web page as a workbook in Excel
	AutoSum	Inserts the SUM function in a cell and selects a range to sum		Commands and Options	Displays the Commands and Options dialog box
				Help	Displays Microsoft Office 2003 Spreadsheet Components Help

In general, the Spreadsheet toolbar allows you to add formulas, format, sort, and export the Web page to Excel. Many additional Excel capabilities are available through the Commands and Options dialog box. You display the Commands and Options dialog box by clicking the Commands and Options button on the Spreadsheet toolbar. When Excel displays the Command and Options dialog box, click the Format tab. The Format sheet makes formatting options, such as bold, italic, underline, font color, font style, and font size, available through your browser for the purpose of formatting cells in the worksheet below the 3-D Pie chart on the Web page.

Modifying the dynamic Web page does not change the makeup of the original workbook or the Web page stored on disk, even if you use the Save As command on the browser's File menu. If you do use the Save As command in your browser, it will save the original mht file without any changes you might have made. You can, however, use the Export to Excel button on the Spreadsheet toolbar to create a workbook that will include any changes you made in your browser. The Export to Excel button only saves the worksheet and not the chart.

Web Feature Summary

This Web feature introduced you to previewing a workbook as a Web page, creating a new folder on disk, and publishing and viewing two types of Web pages: static and dynamic. Whereas the static Web page is a snapshot of the workbook, a dynamic Web page adds functionality and interactivity to the Web page. Besides changing the data and generating new results with a dynamic Web page, you also learned how to use your browser to add formulas and change the formats to improve the appearance of the Web page.

 If you have a SAM user profile, you may have access to hands-on instruction, practice, and assessment of the skills covered in this project. Log in to your SAM account and go to your assignments page to see what your instructor has assigned.

What You Should Know

Having completed this Web feature, you should be able to perform the tasks listed below. The tasks are listed in the same order they were presented in this Web feature. For a list of the buttons, menus, toolbars, and commands introduced in this Web feature, see the Quick Reference Summary at the back of this book and refer to the Page Number column.

1. Preview the Workbook as a Web Page   (EX 228)
2. Save an Excel Workbook as a Static Web Page in a Newly Created Folder   (EX 230)
3. View and Manipulate the Static Web Page Using a Browser   (EX 233)
4. Save an Excel Chart as a Dynamic Web Page   (EX 234)
5. View and Manipulate the Dynamic Web Page Using a Browser   (EX 236)

1 Creating Static and Dynamic Web Pages I

Problem: You are a student employed part-time as a spreadsheet specialist by Awesome Intranets. Your supervisor has asked you to create a static Web page and dynamic Web page from the company's annual sales workbook.

Instructions Part 1:   Start Excel and open the Lab WF-1 Awesome Intranets Annual Sales workbook from the Data Disk. Perform the following tasks:

1. Review the worksheet and chart so you have an idea of what the workbook contains. Preview the workbook as a Web page. Close the browser.
2. Save the workbook as a single file Web page in a new folder titled Web Feature Exercises on the Data Disk in drive A using the file name, Lab WF-1 Awesome Intranets Annual Sales Static Web Page. Make sure you select Entire Workbook in the Save area before you click the Save button. Quit Excel.
3. Start your browser. Type a:\web feature exercises\lab wf-1 awesome intranets annual sales static web page.mht in the Address box. When the browser displays the Web page, click the tabs at the bottom of the window to view the sheets. As you view each sheet, print it in landscape orientation. Close the browser.

Instructions Part 2:   Start Excel and open the Lab WF-1 Awesome Intranets Annual Sales workbook from the Data Disk. Perform the following tasks:

1. Click File on the menu bar and then click Save as Web Page. Use the Publish button to save the workbook as a single file Web page in the Web Feature Exercises folder on the Data Disk in drive A using the file name, Lab WF-1 Awesome Intranets Annual Sales Dynamic Web Page. In the Publish as Web Page dialog box, select Items on Bar Chart in the Choose list and click the Add Interactivity with check box to add chart functionality. Click the Publish button. Quit Excel.
2. Start your browser. Type a:\web feature exercises\lab wf-1 awesome intranets annual sales dynamic web page.mht in the Address box. When the browser displays the Web page, click cell B6 and then click the AutoSum button on the Spreadsheet toolbar twice. Cell B6 should equal $8,948,686. Print the Web page.
3. Update the range B1:B5 by entering the following gross sales: East = 1,545,000; North = 1,111,250; South = 1,500,300; West = 1,400,000; and International = 1,250,000. Cell B6 should equal $6,806,550. Print the Web page. Close the browser.

In the Lab

2 Creating Static and Dynamic Web Pages II

Problem: You are the spreadsheet analyst for Hard Disk Storage Plus. You have been asked to create a static Web page and dynamic Web page from the workbook that the company uses to project sales and payroll expenses.

Instructions Part 1: Start Excel and open the Lab WF-2 Hard Disk Storage Plus Projections workbook from the Data Disk. Perform the following tasks:

1. Display the 3-D Pie Chart sheet. Redisplay the Projected Expenses sheet. Preview the workbook as a Web page. Close the browser.

2. Save the workbook as a Web page (select Web Page in the Save as type box) in the Web Feature Exercises folder on the Data Disk in drive A using the file name, Lab WF-2 Hard Disk Storage Plus Projections Static Web Page. Make sure you select Entire Workbook in the Save area before you click the Save button. Quit Excel. Saving the workbook as a Web page, rather than a single file Web page, will result in an additional folder being added to the Web Feature Exercises folder.

3. Start your browser. Type a:\web feature exercises\lab wf-2 hard disk storage plus projections static web page.htm in the Address box. When the browser displays the Web page, click the tabs at the bottom of the window to view the sheets. Print each sheet in landscape orientation. Close the browser.

Instructions Part 2: Start Excel and open the Lab WF-2 Hard Disk Storage Plus Projections workbook from the Data Disk. Perform the following tasks:

1. Click File on the menu bar and then click Save as Web Page. Use the Publish button to save the workbook as a single file Web page in the Web Feature Exercises folder on the Data Disk in drive A using the file name, Lab WF-2 Hard Disk Storage Plus Projections Dynamic Web Page. In the Publish as Web Page dialog box, select Items on 3-D Pie Chart in the Choose list and click the Add Interactivity with check box to add chart functionality. Click the Publish button. Quit Excel.

2. Start your browser. Type a:\web feature exercises\lab wf-2 hard disk storage plus projections dynamic web page.mht in the Address box. When the browser displays the Web page, print it in landscape orientation.

3. Scroll down and change the values of the following cells: cell B15 = 28%; cell B16 = 4.5%; cell B17 = 25,000; cell B19 = 20.25%; and cell B20 = 7.75%. Cell H12 should equal $3,555,899.49. The 3-D Pie chart should change to show the new contributions to the projected payroll expenses. Close the browser.

3 File Management within Excel

Problem: Your manager at Hard Disk Storage Plus as asked you to teach him to complete basic file management tasks from within Excel.

Instructions: Start Excel and click the Open button on the Standard toolbar. When Excel displays the Open dialog box, create a new folder called In the Lab 3 on the Data Disk in drive A. Click the Up One Level button to reselect 3½ Floppy (A:) in the Look in box. Use the shortcut menu to complete the following tasks: (1) rename the In the Lab 3 folder to In the Lab 4; (2) show the properties of the In the Lab 4 folder; and (3) delete the In the Lab 4 folder.

MICROSOFT
Office Access 2003

ESS

NORTH
AMERICA

Time Card E...

Expense

Time Cards

mployees

Payments

Payments

Time Card H...

Work Codes

MICROSOFT OFFICE
ACCESS

MICROSOFT
Office Access 2003

Creating and Using a Database

PROJECT

1

CASE PERSPECTIVE

Ashton James College (AJC) has a solid reputation in the community, delivers quality computer courses, and has a faculty of highly professional, dedicated instructors. Its graduates are among the top achievers in the state. Recently, at the urging of area businesses that depend on the college-educated workforce, AJC has begun to offer corporate computer training through its Continuing Education department. The programs have proved to be very popular, and the client list is growing rapidly.

AJC employs several trainers to teach these corporate courses. It assigns each client to a specific trainer. The trainer contacts the client to determine the particular course the client requires. The trainer then customizes a program for that particular client. The trainer will schedule all the necessary training sessions.

To ensure that operations run smoothly, Ashton James College needs to maintain data on its trainers and their clients. The AJC administration wants to organize the data in a database, managed by a database management system such as Access. In this way, AJC can keep its data current and accurate while program administrators analyze the data for trends and produce a variety of useful reports. Your task is to help the director of continuing education at Ashton James College, Dr. Robert Gernaey, create and use the database.

As you read through this project, you will learn how to use Access to create a database.

MICROSOFT

Office Access 2003

Creating and Using a Database

PROJECT

1

Objectives

You will have mastered the material in this project when you can:

- Describe databases and database management systems
- Start Access
- Describe the features of the Access desktop
- Create a database
- Create a table and add records
- Close a table
- Close a database and quit Access
- Open a database
- Print the contents of a table
- Create and use a simple query
- Create and use a simple form
- Create and print a custom report
- Design a database to eliminate redundancy

What Is Microsoft Office Access 2003?

Microsoft Office Access 2003 is a powerful database management system (DBMS) that functions in the Windows environment and allows you to create and process data in a database. Some of the key features are:

- **Data entry and update** Access provides easy mechanisms for adding, changing, and deleting data, including the capability of making mass changes in a single operation.
- **Queries (questions)** Access makes it possible to ask complex questions concerning the data in the database and then receive instant answers.
- **Forms** Access allows the user to produce attractive and useful forms for viewing and updating data.
- **Reports** Access report creation tools make it easy to produce sophisticated reports for presenting data.
- **Web support** Access allows you to save objects, reports, and tables in HTML format so they can be viewed using a browser. You also can import and export documents in XML format. Access's capability of creating data access pages allows real-time access to data in the database via the Internet.

What Is New in Access?

This latest version of Access has many new features to make you more productive. You can view information on dependencies between various database objects. You can enable error checking for many common errors in forms and reports. You can add smart tags to fields in tables, queries, forms, or data access pages. Access now has a command to backup a database. Many wizards provide more options for sorting data. You can export to, import from, or link to a Windows SharePoint Services list. Access now offers enhanced XML support.

Project One — Ashton James College Database

Creating, storing, sorting, and retrieving data are important tasks. In their personal lives, many people keep a variety of records such as names, addresses, and telephone numbers of friends and business associates, records of investments, records of expenses for tax purposes, and so on. For effective use of this data, users must have quick access to it. Businesses also must be able to store and access information quickly and easily.

The term **database** describes a collection of data organized in a manner that allows access, retrieval, and use of that data. A **database management system**, such as Access, is a software tool that allows you to use a computer to create a database; add, change, and delete data in the database; sort the data in the database; retrieve data in the database; and create forms and reports using the data in the database.

In Access, a database consists of a collection of tables. Figure 1-1 shows a sample database for Ashton James College, which consists of two tables. The Client table contains information about the clients to which Ashton James College provides services. The college assigns each client to a specific trainer. The Trainer table contains information about the trainers to whom these clients are assigned.

Client table

fields

CLIENT NUMBER	NAME	ADDRESS	CITY	STATE	ZIP CODE	AMOUNT PAID	CURRENT DUE	TRAINER NUMBER
BS27	Blant and Sons	4806 Park	Lake Hammond	TX	76653	$21,876.00	$892.50	42
CE16	Center Services	725 Mitchell	San Julio	TX	78364	$26,512.00	$2,672.00	48
CP27	Calder Plastics	7300 Cedar	Lake Hammond	TX	76653	$8,725.00	$0.00	48
EU28	Elba's Furniture	1445 Hubert	Tallmadge	TX	77231	$4,256.00	$1,202.00	53
FI28	Farrow-Idsen	829 Wooster	Cedar Ridge	TX	79342	$8,287.50	$925.50	42
FL93	Fairland Lawn	143 Pangborn	Lake Hammond	TX	76653	$21,625.00	$0.00	48
HN83	Hurley National	3827 Burgess	Tallmadge	TX	77231	$0.00	$0.00	48
MC28	Morgan-Alyssa	923 Williams	Crumville	TX	76745	$24,761.00	$1,572.00	42
PS82	PRIM Staffing	72 Crestview	San Julio	TX	78364	$11,682.25	$2,827.50	53
TE26	Telton-Edwards	5672 Anderson	Dunston	TX	77893	$8,521.50	$0.00	48

records

clients of trainer Belinda Perry

Trainer table

TRAINER NUMBER	LAST NAME	FIRST NAME	ADDRESS	CITY	STATE	ZIP CODE	HOURLY RATE	YTD EARNINGS
42	Perry	Belinda	261 Porter	Burdett	TX	76734	$23.00	$27,620.00
48	Stevens	Michael	3135 Gill	Rockwood	TX	78884	$21.00	$23,567.50
53	Gonzalez	Manuel	265 Maxwell	Camino	TX	76574	$24.00	$29,885.00
67	Danville	Marty	1827 Maple	Dunston	TX	77893	$20.00	$0.00

trainer Belinda Perry

FIGURE 1-1

More About

Databases in Access 2003

In some DBMSs, every table, query, form, or report is stored in a separate file. This is not the case in Access 2003, in which a database is stored in a single file on disk. The file contains all the tables, queries, forms, reports, and programs created for this database.

The rows in the tables are called **records**. A record contains information about a given person, product, or event. A row in the Client table, for example, contains information about a specific client.

The columns in the tables are called fields. A **field** contains a specific piece of information within a record. In the Client table, for example, the fourth field, City, contains the city where the client is located.

The first field in the Client table is the Client Number. Ashton James College assigns a number to each client. As is common to the way in which many organizations format client numbers, Ashton James College calls it a *number*, although it actually contains letters. The AJC client numbers consist of two uppercase letters followed by a two-digit number.

These numbers are unique; that is, no two clients are assigned the same number. Such a field can be used as a **unique identifier**. This simply means that a given client number will appear only in a single record in the table. Only one record exists, for example, in which the client number is CP27. A unique identifier also is called a **primary key**. Thus, the Client Number field is the primary key for the Client table.

The next seven fields in the Client table are Name, Address, City, State, Zip Code, Amount Paid, and Current Due. The Amount Paid field contains the amount that the client has paid Ashton James College year-to-date (YTD), but before the current period. The Current Due field contains the amount due to AJC for the current period.

For example, client BS27 is Blant and Sons. The address is 4806 Park in Lake Hammond, Texas. The Zip code is 76653. The client has paid $21,876.00 for training services so far this year. The amount due for the current period is $892.50.

AJC assigns each client a single trainer. The last field in the Client table, Trainer Number, gives the number of the client's trainer.

The first field in the Trainer table, Trainer Number, is the number Ashton James College assigns to the trainer. These numbers are unique, so Trainer Number is the primary key of the Trainer table.

The other fields in the Trainer table are Last Name, First Name, Address, City, State, Zip Code, Hourly Rate, and YTD Earnings. The Hourly Rate field gives the trainer's hourly billing rate, and the YTD Earnings field contains the total amount that AJC has paid the trainer for services so far this year.

For example, Trainer 42 is Belinda Perry. Her address is 261 Porter in Burdett, Texas. The Zip code is 76734. Her hourly billing rate is $23.00, and her YTD earnings are $27,620.00.

The trainer number appears in both the Client table and the Trainer table. It relates clients and trainers. For example, in the Client table, you see that the trainer number for client BS27 is 42. To find the name of this trainer, look for the row in the Trainer table that contains 42 in the Trainer Number field. After you have found it, you know the client is assigned to Belinda Perry. To find all the clients assigned to Belinda Perry, however, you must look through the Client table for all the clients that contain 42 in the Trainer Number field. Her clients are BS27 (Blant and Sons), FI28 (Farrow-Idsen), and MC28 (Morgan-Alyssa).

The last trainer in the Trainer table, Marty Danville, has not been assigned any clients yet; therefore, his trainer number, 67, does not appear on any row in the Client table.

Figure 1-1 on page AC 5 shows the data that must be maintained in the database. The first step is to create the database and the tables it contains. In the process, you must define the fields included in the two tables, as well as the type of data each field will contain. Then, you must add the appropriate records to the tables. Finally, you will print the contents of the tables. After you have completed these tasks, you will create a query, a form, and a report.

Starting Access

If you are stepping through this project on a computer, and you want your screen to agree with the figures in this book, then you should change your computer's resolution to 800 × 600. For more information on how to change the resolution on your computer, see Appendix D. To start Access, Windows must be running. The following steps show how to start Access.

To Start Access

1

• **Click the Start button on the Windows taskbar, point to All Programs on the Start menu and then point to Microsoft Office on the All Programs submenu.**

Windows displays the Start menu, the All Programs submenu, and the Microsoft Office submenu (Figure 1-2).

More About

The Access Help System

Need Help? It is no further than the Type a question for help box on the menu bar in the upper-right corner of the window. Click the box that contains the text, Type a question for help (Figure 1-3 on the next page), type help, and then press the ENTER key. Access responds with a list of topics you can click to learn about obtaining help on any Access-related topic. To find out what is new in Access 2003, type what is new in Access in the Type a question for help box.

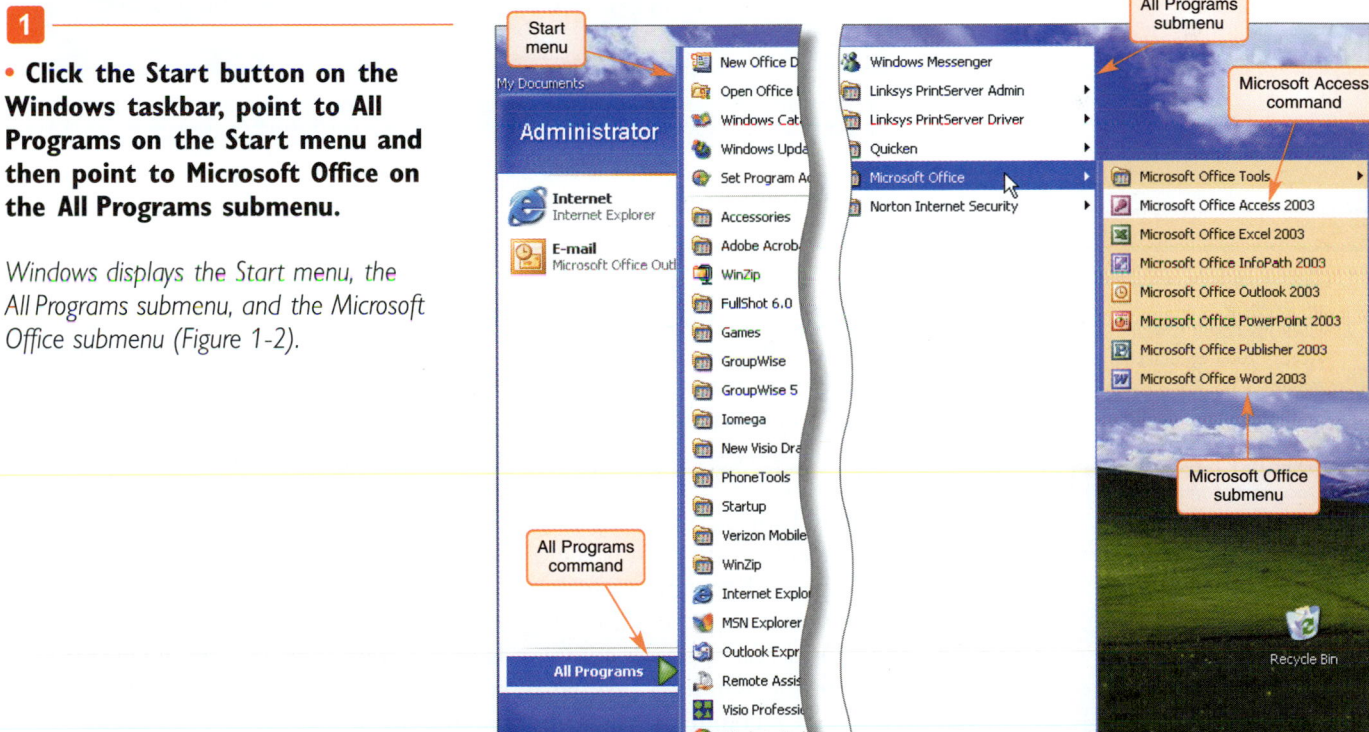

FIGURE 1-2

2

• **Click Microsoft Office Access 2003.**

*Access starts. After several seconds, the
Access window appears (Figure 1-3).*

3

• **If the Access window is not
maximized, double-click its title
bar to maximize it.**

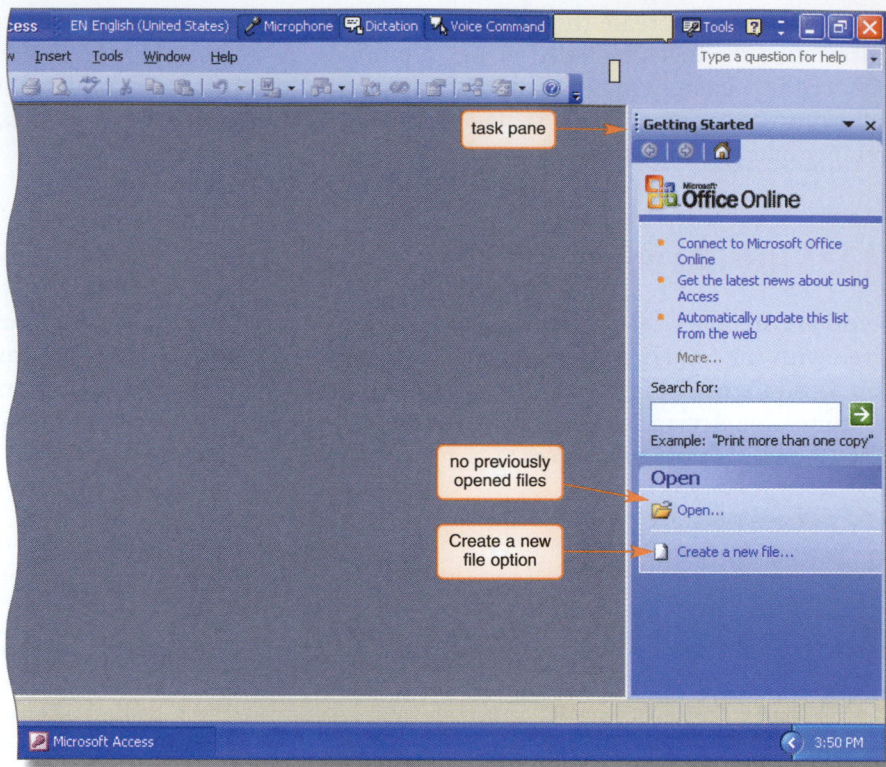

FIGURE 1-3

More About

Task Panes

You can drag a task pane title
bar to float the pane in your
work area or dock it on
either the left or right side of
a screen, depending on your
personal preference.

The screen in Figure 1-3 illustrates how the Access window looks the first time you
start Access after installation on most computers. Access displays a task pane on the
right side of the screen at startup. A **task pane** is a separate window that enables
users to carry out some Access tasks more efficiently. When you start Access, it
displays the Getting Started task pane, which is a small window that provides commonly used links and commands that allow you to open files, create new files, or
search Office-related topics on the Microsoft Web site. The task pane is used only
to create a new database and then it is closed.

If the Office Speech Recognition software is installed and active on your computer, then when you start Access the Language bar is displayed on the screen. The
Language bar allows you to speak commands and dictate text. It usually is located
on the right side of the Windows taskbar next to the notification area and changes
to include the speech recognition functions available in Access. In this book, the
Language bar is closed. For additional information about the Language bar, see the
next page and Appendix B. The following steps show how to close the Language bar
if it appears on the screen.

To Close the Language Bar

1

- **Right-click the Language bar to display a list of commands.**

The Language bar shortcut menu appears (Figure 1-4).

2

- **Click Close the Language bar.**
- **Click the OK button.**

The Language bar disappears.

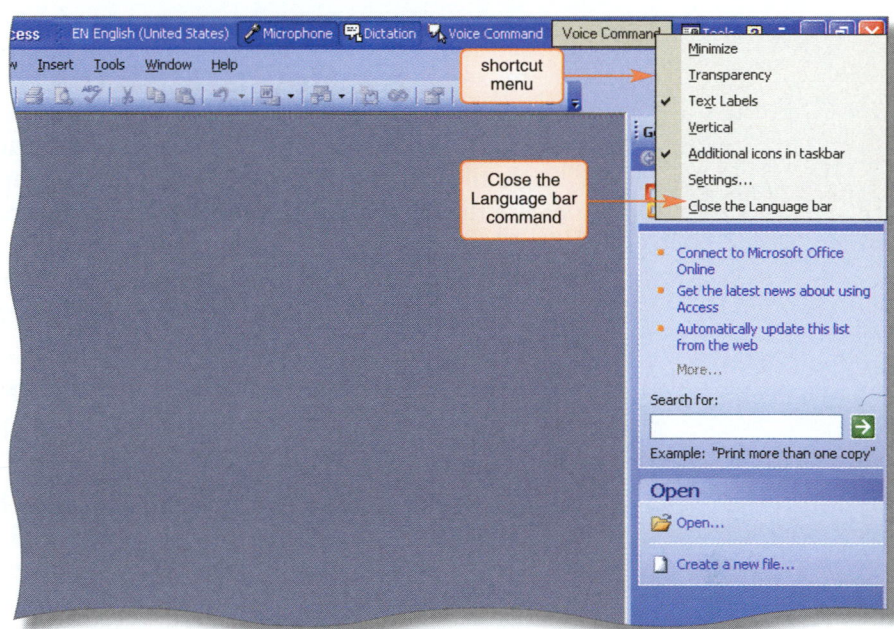

FIGURE 1-4

Speech Recognition

With the **Office Speech Recognition software** installed and a microphone, you can speak the names of toolbar buttons, menus, menu commands, list items, alerts, and dialog box controls, such as OK and Cancel. You also can dictate field entries, such as text and numbers. To indicate whether you want to speak commands or dictate cell entries, you use the Language bar. The Language bar can be in one of three states: (1) **restored**, which means it is displayed somewhere in the Access window (Figure 1-5a); (2) **minimized**, which means it is displayed on the Windows taskbar (Figure 1-5b); or (3) **hidden**, which means you do not see it on the screen. If the Language bar is hidden and you want it to display, then do the following:

1. Right-click an open area on the Windows taskbar at the bottom of the screen.
2. Point to Toolbars and then click Language bar on the Toolbars submenu.

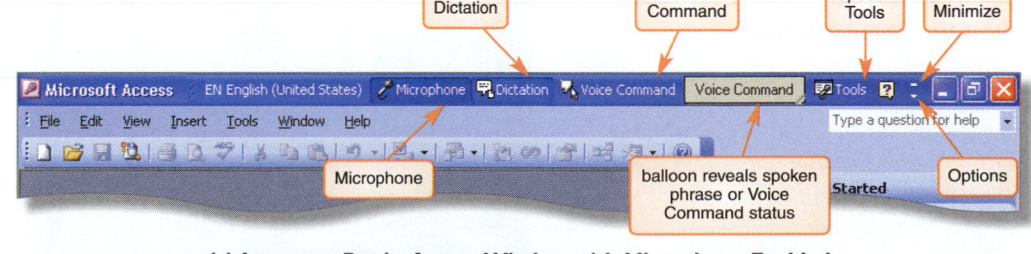

(a) Language Bar in Access Window with Microphone Enabled

(b) Language Bar Minimized on Windows Taskbar

FIGURE 1-5

If the Language bar command is dimmed on the Toolbars submenu or if the Speech command is dimmed on the Tools menu, the Office Speech Recognition software is not installed.

Creating a New Database

In Access, all the tables, reports, form, and queries that you create are stored in a single file called a database. Thus, before creating any of these objects, you first must create the database that will hold them. You can use either the Database Wizard or the Blank database option in the task pane to create a new database. The Database Wizard can guide you by suggesting some commonly used databases. If you choose to create a database using the Database Wizard, you would use the following steps.

To Create a Database Using the Database Wizard

1. Click the New button on the Database toolbar and then click the On my computer link in the New File task pane.
2. When Access displays the Template dialog box, click the Databases tab, and then click the database that is most appropriate for your needs.
3. Follow the instructions in the Database Wizard dialog box to create the database.

Because you already know the tables and fields you want in the Ashton James College database, you would use the Blank database option in the task pane rather than the Database Wizard. The following steps illustrate how to use the Blank database option to create a database on a floppy disk in drive A.

To Create a New Database

1

• **Insert a formatted floppy disk in drive A.**

• **Click the New button on the Database toolbar to display the task pane.**

• **Click the Blank database option in the task pane, and then click the Save in box arrow.**

Access displays the File New Database dialog box and the Save in list appears (Figure 1-6a). Your File name text box may display db1.mdb, rather than db1.

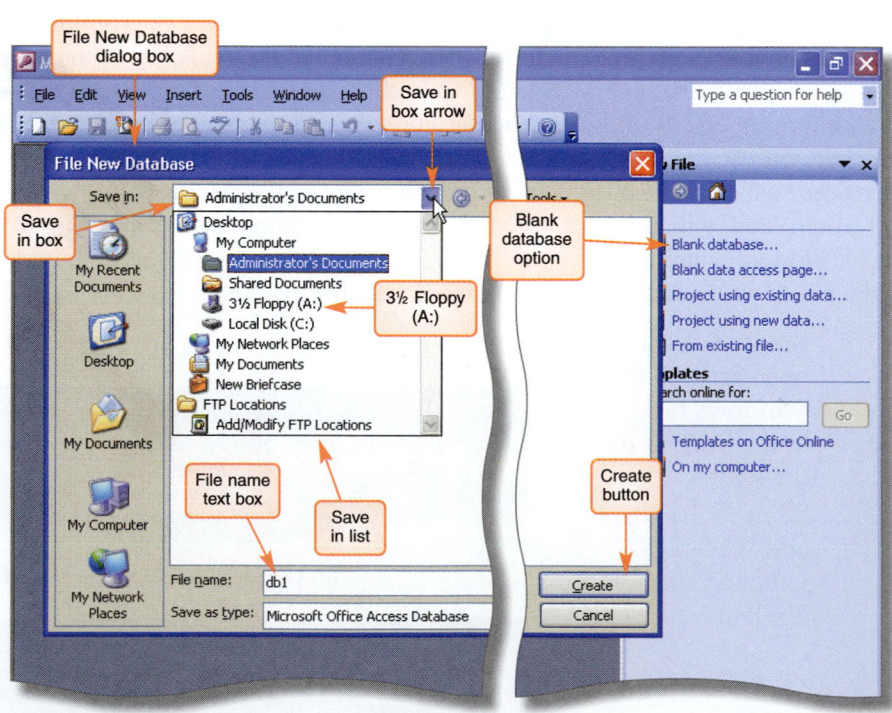

FIGURE 1-6a

2

• **Click 3½ Floppy (A:).**

• **Click the File name text box.**

• **Use the BACKSPACE key or the DELETE key to delete db1 and then type** Ashton James College **as the file name.**

The file name is changed to Ashton James College (Figure 1-6b).

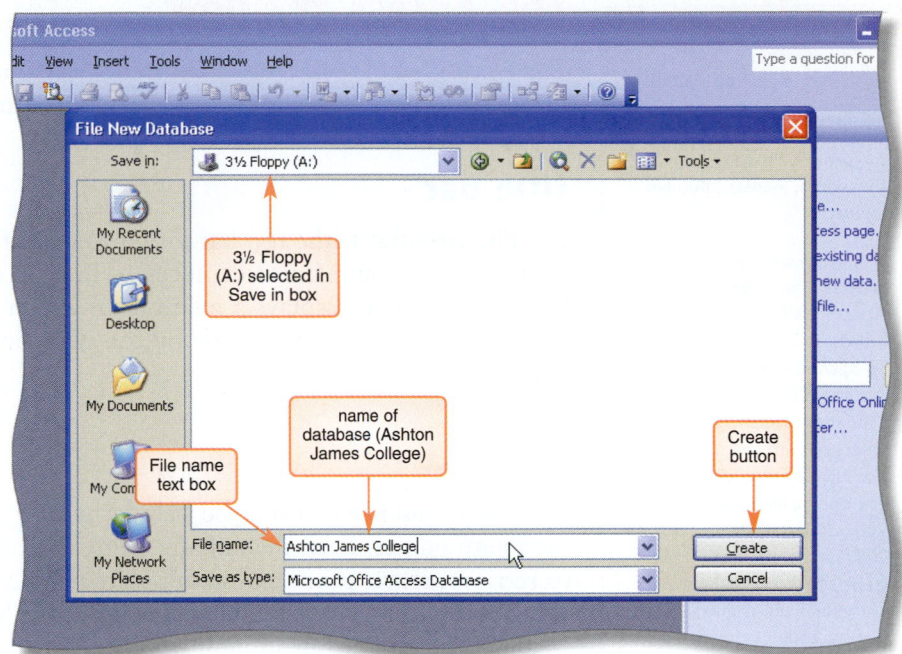

FIGURE 1-6b

3

• **Click the Create button to create the database.**

The Ashton James College database is created. The Ashton James College : Database window appears in the Microsoft Access window (Figure 1-7). The task pane does not appear.

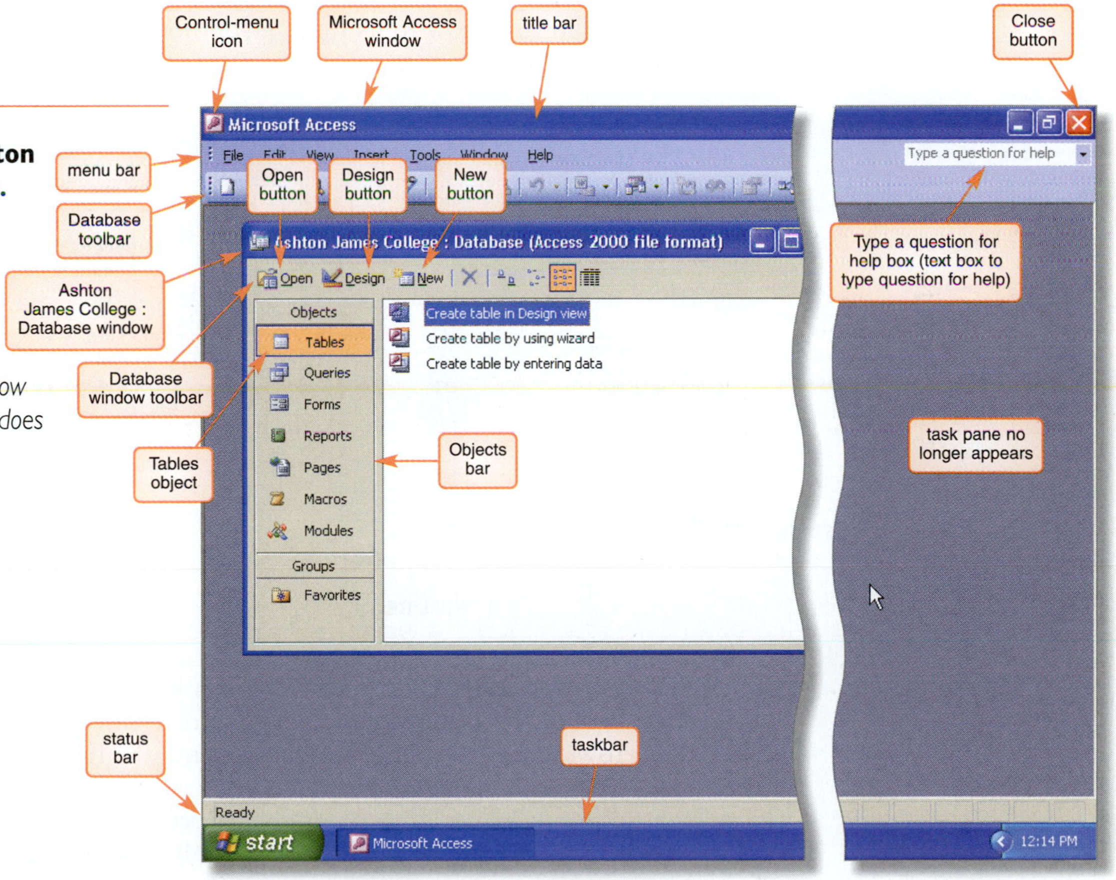

FIGURE 1-7

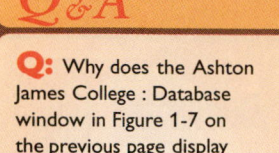

Q: Why does the Ashton James College : Database window in Figure 1-7 on the previous page display the words, Access 2000 file format?

A: By default, Access creates a new database in Access 2000 format. A file in Access 2000 format can be opened in Access 2000, Access 2002, or Access 2003. This allows you to share your database with users who do not have Access 2003. You can open a file in Access 2002-2003 only in Access 2002 or later. Certain features of Access 2003 are not available if the database is in Access 2000 file format.

The Access Window

The Access window (Figure 1-7 on the previous page) contains a variety of features that play important roles when you are working with a database.

Title Bar

The **title bar** is the top bar in the Microsoft Access window. It includes the title of the application, Microsoft Access. The icon on the left is the Control-menu icon. Clicking this icon displays a menu from which you can close the Access window. The button on the right is the Close button. Clicking the Close button closes the Access window.

Menu Bar

The **menu bar** is displayed below the title bar. It is a special toolbar that displays the menu names. Each menu name represents a menu of commands that you can use to retrieve, store, print, and manipulate data. When you point to a menu name on the menu bar, the area of the menu bar is displayed as a selected button. Access shades selected buttons in light orange and surrounds them with a blue outline. To display a menu, such as the Edit menu, click the Edit menu name on the menu bar (Figures 1-8a and 1-8b). A **menu** is a list of commands. If you point to a command on the menu with an arrow to its right, a **submenu** is displayed from which you can choose a command.

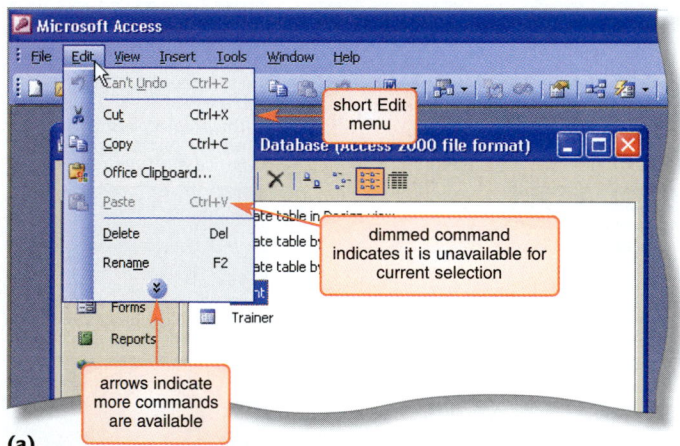

(a)

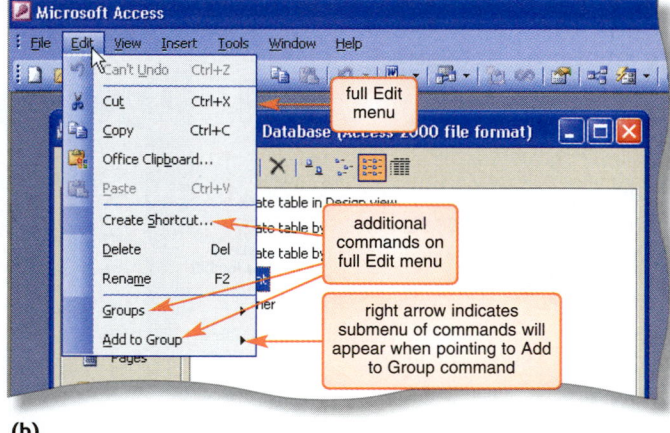

(b)

FIGURE 1-8

When you click a menu name on the menu bar, Access displays a **short menu** listing the most recently used commands (Figure 1-8a). If you wait a few seconds or click the arrows at the bottom of the short menu, the full menu appears. The **full menu** lists all the commands associated with a menu (Figure 1-8b). You also can display a full menu immediately by double-clicking the menu name on the menu bar. In this book, always have Access display the full menu using one of the following techniques.

1. Click the menu name on the menu bar and then wait a few seconds.
2. Click the menu name and then click the arrows at the bottom of the short menu.

3. Click the menu name and then point to the arrows at the bottom of the short menu.
4. Double-click the menu name.

Both short and full menus display some **dimmed commands** that appear gray, or dimmed, instead of black, which indicates they are not available for the current selection. A command with a medium blue shading to the left of it on a full menu is called a **hidden command** because it does not display on a short menu. As you use Access, it automatically personalizes the short menus for you based on how often you use commands. That is, as you use hidden commands, Access *unhides* them and places them on the short menu.

Toolbars

Below the menu bar is a toolbar. A **toolbar** contains buttons that allow you to perform certain tasks more quickly than using the menu bar. Each button contains a picture, or **icon**, depicting its function. When you move the mouse pointer over a button, the name of the button appears below it in a **ScreenTip**. The toolbar shown in Figure 1-7 on page AC 11 is the Database toolbar. The specific toolbar or toolbars that appear will vary, depending on the task on which you are working. Access routinely displays the toolbar or toolbars you will need for the task. If you want to change these or simply to determine what toolbars are available for the given task, consult Appendix D.

Taskbar

The Windows **taskbar** at the bottom of the screen displays the Start button, any active windows, and the current time.

Status Bar

Immediately above the Windows taskbar is the **status bar**. It contains special information that is appropriate for the task on which you are working. Currently, it contains the word, Ready, which means Access is ready to accept commands.

Database Window

The **Database window**, referred to in Figure 1-7 as the Ashton James College : Database window, is a special window that allows you to access easily and rapidly a variety of objects such as tables, queries, forms, and reports. To do so, you will use the various components of the window.

Shortcut Menus

Rather than use toolbars to accomplish a given task, you also can use **shortcut menus**, which are menus that display the actions available for a particular item. To display the shortcut menu for an item, right-click the item; that is, point to the item and then click the right mouse button. Figures 1-9a and 1-9b on the next page illustrate the use of toolbars and shortcut menus to perform the same task, namely to print the contents of the Client table. In the figure, the tables you will create in this project already have been created.

More About

Toolbars

Normally, the correct Access 2003 toolbar will display automatically. If it does not, click View on the menu bar, and then click Toolbars. On the Toolbars submenu, select the toolbar for the activity in which you are engaged. See Appendix D for additional details.

More About

Shortcut Menus

Shortcut menus contain the most frequently used commands that relate to the object to which the mouse pointer is pointing.

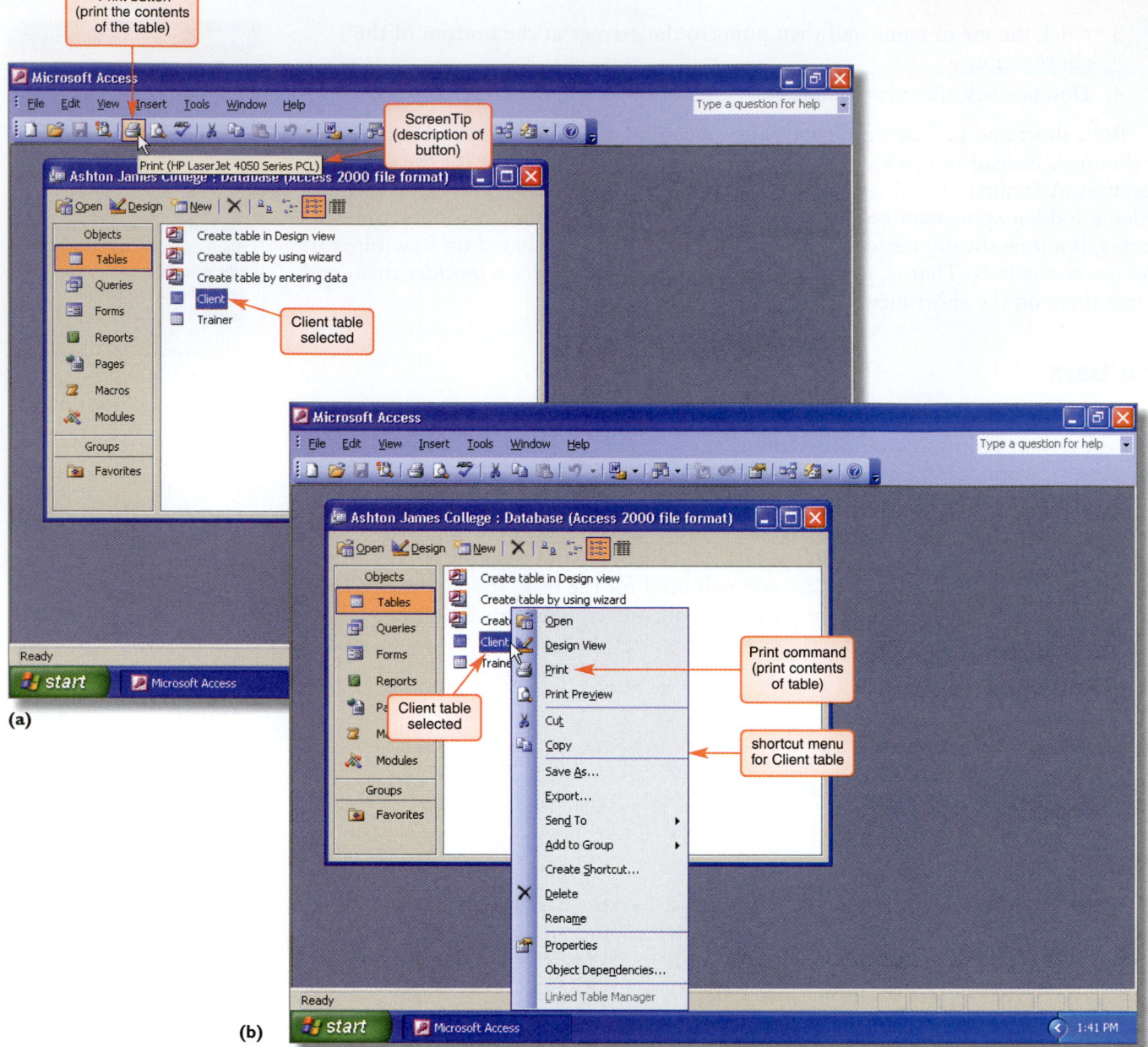

FIGURE 1-9

Before the action illustrated in Figure 1-9a, you would have to select the Client table by clicking it. Then, you would point to the Print button on the toolbar as shown in the figure. When you point to a button on a toolbar, the ScreenTip appears, indicating the purpose of the button, in this case Print. When you click the button, the corresponding action takes place. In this case, Access will print the contents of the Client table.

To use a shortcut menu to perform the same task, you would right-click the Client table, which produces the shortcut menu shown in Figure 1-9b. You then would click the desired command, in this case the Print command, on the shortcut menu. The corresponding action then takes place.

You can use whichever option you prefer. Many professionals who use Access will use a combination. If it is simplest to use the shortcut menu, which often is the case, they will use the shortcut menu. If it is simpler just to click a toolbar button, they will do that. The steps in this text follow this approach; that is, using a combination of both options. The text indicates how to accomplish the task using the other approach, as well. Thus, if the steps use a shortcut menu, the Other Ways box at the end of the steps will indicate how you could accomplish the task using a toolbar button. If the steps use a button, the Other Ways box will indicate how you could accomplish the task with a shortcut menu.

AutoCorrect

Not visible in the Access window, the **AutoCorrect** feature of Access works behind the scenes, correcting common mistakes when you complete a text entry in a cell. AutoCorrect makes three types of corrections for you:

1. Corrects two initial capital letters by changing the second letter to lowercase.
2. Capitalizes the first letter in the names of days.
3. Replaces commonly misspelled words with their correct spelling. For example, it will change the misspelled word *recieve* to *receive* when you complete the entry. AutoCorrect will correct the spelling automatically of more than 400 commonly misspelled words.

Creating a Table

An Access database consists of a collection of tables. After you have created the database, you must create each of the tables within it. In this project, for example, you must create both the Client and Trainer tables shown in Figure 1-1 on page AC 5.

To create a table, you describe the structure of the table to Access by describing the fields within the table. For each field, you indicate the following:

1. **Field name** — Each field in the table must have a unique name. In the Client table (Figure 1-10a and 1-10b on the next page), for example, the field names are Client Number, Name, Address, City, State, Zip Code, Amount Paid, Current Due, and Trainer Number.

More About

AutoCorrect

Using the Office AutoCorrect feature, you can create entries that will replace abbreviations with spelled-out names and phrases automatically. For example, you can create the abbreviated entry *dbms* for *database management system*. Whenever you type dbms followed by a space or punctuation mark, Access automatically replaces dbms with database management system. AutoCorrect works with text in a datasheet or in a form. To specify AutoCorrect rules and exceptions to the rules, click Tools on the menu bar and then click AutoCorrect Options.

More About

Creating a Table: The Table Wizard

Access includes a Table Wizard that guides you by suggesting some commonly used tables and fields. To use the Table Wizard, click Tables on the Objects bar and then click Create table by using wizard. Follow the directions in the Table Wizard dialog boxes. After you create the table, you can modify it at any time by opening the table in Design view.

Structure of Client table				
FIELD NAME	DATA TYPE	FIELD SIZE	PRIMARY KEY?	DESCRIPTION
Client Number	Text	4	Yes	Client Number (Primary Key)
Name	Text	20		Client Name
Address	Text	15		Street Address
City	Text	15		City
State	Text	2		State (Two-Character Abbreviation)
Zip Code	Text	5		Zip Code (Five-Character Version)
Amount Paid	Currency			Amount Paid by Client This Year
Current Due	Currency			Current Due from Client This Period
Trainer Number	Text	2		Number of Client's Trainer

FIGURE 1-10a

Client table

CLIENT NUMBER	NAME	ADDRESS	CITY	STATE	ZIP CODE	AMOUNT PAID	CURRENT DUE	TRAINER NUMBER
BS27	Blant and Sons	4806 Park	Lake Hammond	TX	76653	$21,876.00	$892.50	42
CE16	Center Services	725 Mitchell	San Julio	TX	78364	$26,512.00	$2,672.00	48
CP27	Calder Plastics	7300 Cedar	Lake Hammond	TX	76653	$8,725.00	$0.00	48
EU28	Elba's Furniture	1445 Hubert	Tallmadge	TX	77231	$4,256.00	$1,202.00	53
FI28	Farrow-Idsen	829 Wooster	Cedar Ridge	TX	79342	$8,287.50	$925.50	42
FL93	Fairland Lawn	143 Pangborn	Lake Hammond	TX	76653	$21,625.00	$0.00	48
HN83	Hurley National	3827 Burgess	Tallmadge	TX	77231	$0.00	$0.00	48
MC28	Morgan-Alyssa	923 Williams	Crumville	TX	76745	$24,761.00	$1,572.00	42
PS82	PRIM Staffing	72 Crestview	San Julio	TX	78364	$11,682.25	$2,827.50	53
TE26	Telton-Edwards	5672 Anderson	Dunston	TX	77893	$8,521.50	$0.00	48

FIGURE 1-10b

Q&A

Q: Do all database management systems use the same data types?

A: No. Different database management systems have different available data types. Even data types that are essentially the same can have different names. The Access 2003 Text data type, for example, is referred to as Character in some systems and Alpha in others.

More About

Primary Keys

In some cases, the primary key consists of a combination of fields rather than a single field. For more information about determining primary keys in such situations, visit the Access 2003 More About Web page (scsite.com/ac2003/more) and click Primary Keys.

2. **Data type** — Data type indicates to Access the type of data the field will contain. Some fields can contain only numbers. Others, such as Amount Paid and Current Due, can contain numbers and dollar signs. Still others, such as Name and Address, can contain letters.

3. **Description** — Access allows you to enter a detailed description of the field.

You also can assign field widths to text fields (fields whose data type is Text). This indicates the maximum number of characters that can be stored in the field. If you do not assign a width to such a field, Access assumes the width is 50.

You also must indicate which field or fields make up the primary key; that is, the unique identifier, for the table. In the Ashton James College database, the Client Number field is the primary key of the Client table and the Trainer Number field is the primary key of the Trainer table.

The rules for field names are:

1. Names can be up to 64 characters in length.

2. Names can contain letters, digits, and spaces, as well as most of the punctuation symbols.

3. Names cannot contain periods, exclamation points (!), accent graves (`), or square brackets ([ ]).

4. The same name cannot be used for two different fields in the same table.

Each field has a **data type**. This indicates the type of data that can be stored in the field. The data types you will use in this project are:

1. **Text** — The field can contain any characters. A maximum number of 255 characters is allowed in a field whose data type is Text.

2. **Number** — The field can contain only numbers. The numbers either can be positive or negative. Fields are assigned this type so they can be used in arithmetic operations. Fields that contain numbers but will not be used for arithmetic operations usually are assigned a data type of Text. The Trainer Number field, for example, is a text field because the trainer numbers will not be involved in any arithmetic.

3. **Currency** — The field can contain only monetary data. The values will appear with currency symbols, such as dollar signs, commas, decimal points, and with two digits following the decimal point. Like numeric fields, you can use currency fields in arithmetic operations. Access assigns a size to currency fields automatically.

Table 1-1 shows the other data types that are available.

Table 1-1	Additional Data Types
DATA TYPE	**DESCRIPTION**
Memo	Field can store a variable amount of text or combinations of text and numbers where the total number of characters may exceed 255.
Number	Field can store numeric data that can be used in mathematical calculations.
Date/Time	Field can store dates and times.
AutoNumber	Field can store a unique sequential number that Access assigns to a record. Access will increment the number by 1 as each new record is added.
Yes/No	Field can store only one of two values. The choices are Yes/No, True/False, or On/Off.
OLE Object	Field can store an OLE object, which is an object linked to or embedded in the table.
Hyperlink	Field can store text that can be used as a hyperlink address.
Lookup Wizard	Field can store a value from another table or from a list of values by using a list box or combo box. Choosing this data type starts the Lookup Wizard, which assists in the creation of the field. The field then is a Lookup field. The data type is set based on the values you selected in the wizard. If the values are text for example, the field is assigned the Text data type.

The field names, data types, field widths, primary key information, and descriptions for the Client table are shown in Figure 1-10a on page AC 15.

With the information in Figures 1-10a and 1-10b, you are ready to begin creating the table. The following steps illustrate how to create a table.

To Create a Table

1

• **Click the New button on the Database window toolbar.**

The New Table dialog box appears (Figure 1-11).

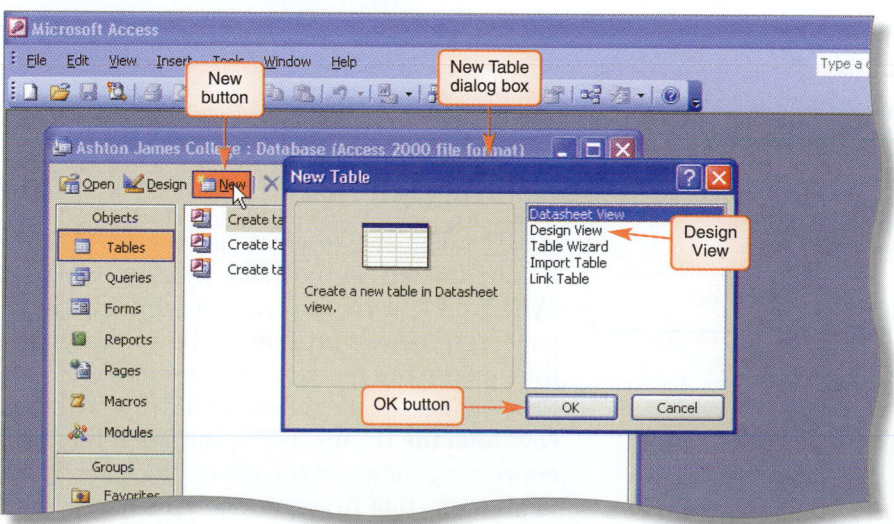

FIGURE 1-11

2

- **Click Design View and then click the OK button.**

The Table1 : Table window appears (Figure 1-12).

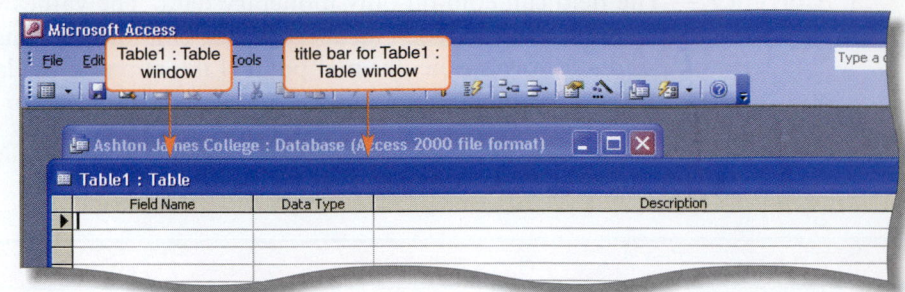

FIGURE 1-12

3

- **Double-click the title bar of the Table1 : Table window to maximize the window.**

Access displays the maximized Table1 : Table window (Figure 1-13).

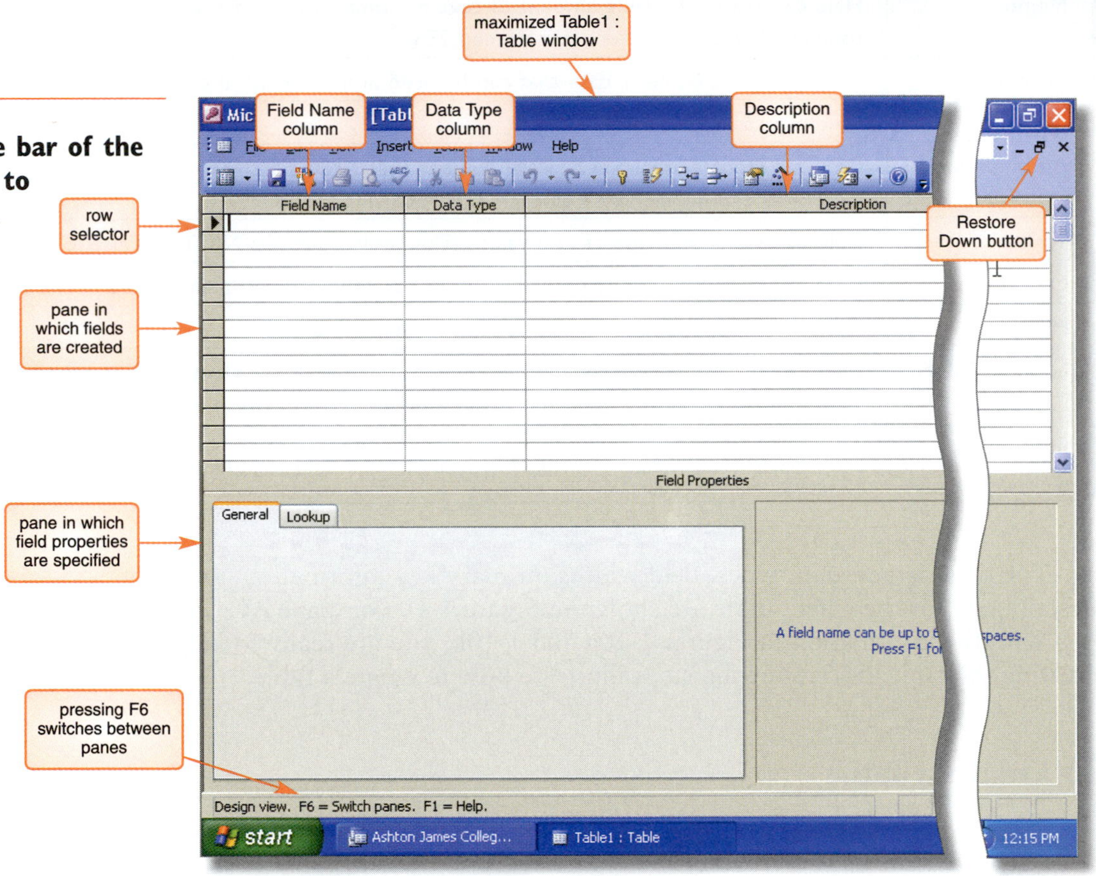

FIGURE 1-13

Other Ways

1. On Insert menu click Table
2. Double-click Create table in Design view
3. Press ALT+N
4. In Voice Command mode, say "Insert, Table"

Defining the Fields

The next step in creating the table is to define the fields by specifying the required details in the Table window, which include entries in the Field Name, Data Type, and Description columns and additional information in the Field Properties pane in the lower portion of the Table window. You press the F6 key to move from the upper **pane** (portion of the screen), the one where you define the fields, to the lower pane, the one where you define field properties. As you define the fields, the **row selector** (Figure 1-13), the small box or bar that, when you click it, selects the entire row, indicates the field you currently are describing. It is positioned on the first field, indicating Access is ready for you to enter the name of the first field in the Field Name column.

The following steps show how to define the fields in the table.

To Define the Fields in a Table

1

• **Type** Client Number **(the name of the first field) in the Field Name column, and then press the TAB key.**

The words, Client Number, appear in the Field Name column and the insertion point advances to the Data Type column, indicating you can enter the data type (Figure 1-14). The word, Text, one of the possible data types, currently appears. The arrow indicates a list of data types is available by clicking the arrow.

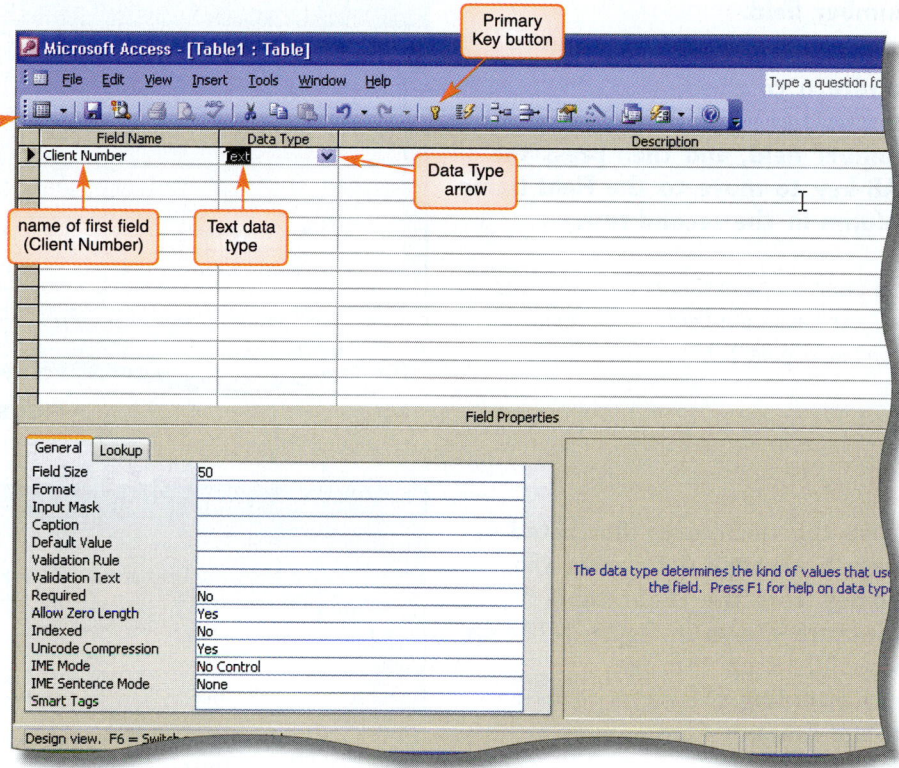

FIGURE 1-14

2

• **Because Text is the correct data type, press the TAB key to move the insertion point to the Description column, type** Client Number (Primary Key) **as the description, and then click the Primary Key button on the Table Design toolbar.**

The Client Number field is the primary key as indicated by the key symbol that appears in the row selector (Figure 1-15). A ScreenTip, which is a description of the button, appears.

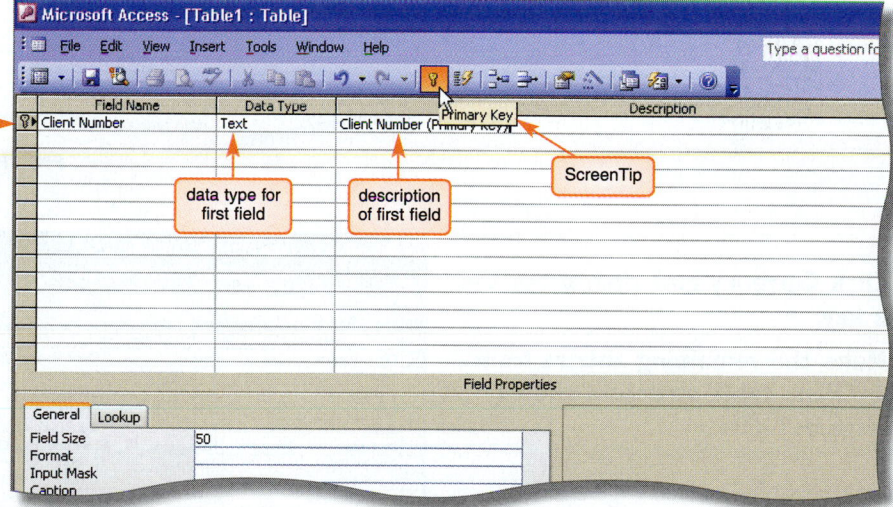

FIGURE 1-15

3

• **Press the F6 key.**

The current entry in the Field Size property box (50) is selected (Figure 1-16).

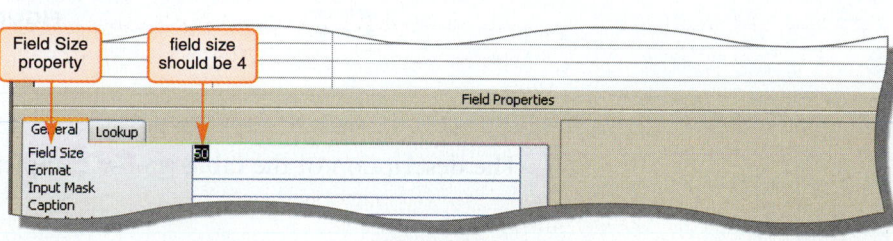

FIGURE 1-16

4

• **Type** 4 **as the size of the Client Number field.**

• **Press the** F6 **key to return to the Description column for the Client Number field, and then press the TAB key to move to the Field Name column in the second row.**

The insertion point moves to the second row just below the field name Client Number (Figure 1-17).

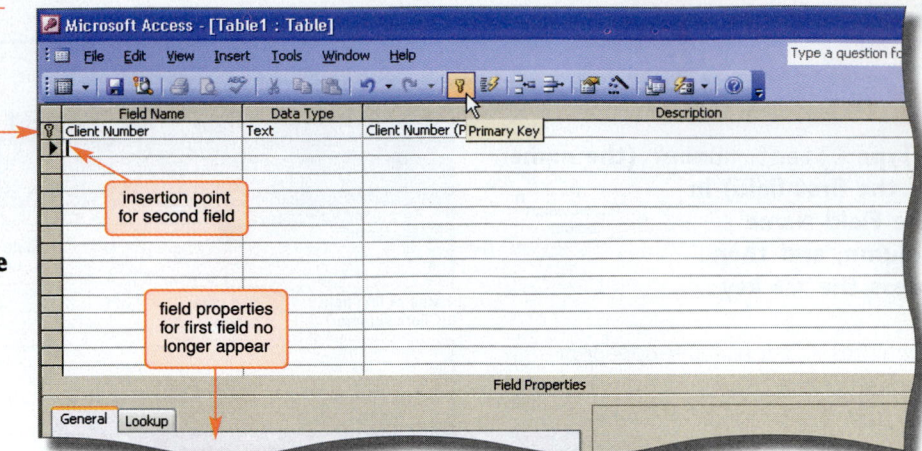

FIGURE 1-17

5

• **Use the techniques illustrated in Steps 1 through 4 to make the entries from the Client table structure shown in Figure 1-10a on page AC 15 up through and including the name of the Amount Paid field.**

• **Click the Data Type box arrow.**

The additional fields are entered (Figure 1-18). A list of available data types appears in the Data Type column for the Amount Paid field.

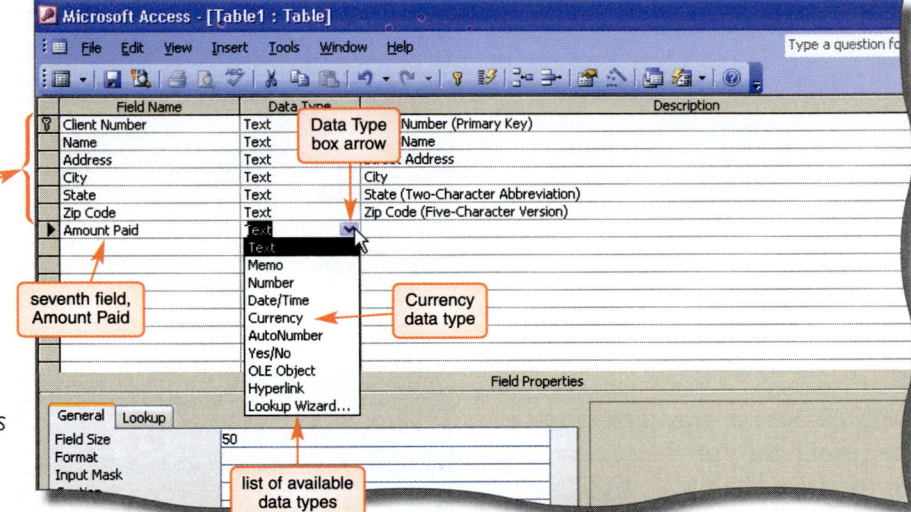

FIGURE 1-18

6

• **Click Currency and then press the** TAB **key.**

• **Make the remaining entries from the Client table structure shown in Figure 1-10a.**

All the fields are entered (Figure 1-19).

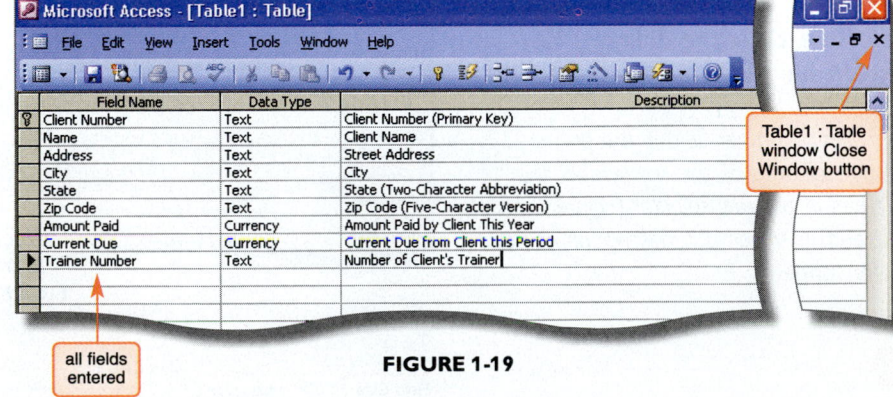

FIGURE 1-19

The description of the table is now complete.

Correcting Errors in the Structure

When creating a table, check the entries carefully to ensure they are correct. If you make a mistake and discover it before you press the TAB key, you can correct the error by repeatedly pressing the BACKSPACE key until the incorrect characters are removed. Then, type the correct characters. If you do not discover a mistake until later, you can click the entry, type the correct value, and then press the ENTER key.

If you accidentally add an extra field to the structure, select the field by clicking the row selector (the leftmost column on the row that contains the field to be deleted). After you have selected the field, press the DELETE key. This will remove the field from the structure.

If you forget a field, select the field that will follow the field you want to add by clicking the row selector, and then press the INSERT key. The remaining fields move down one row, making room for the missing field. Make the entries for the new field in the usual manner.

If you made the wrong field a primary key field, click the correct primary key entry for the field and then click the Primary Key button on the Table Design toolbar.

As an alternative to these steps, you may want to start over. To do so, click the Close Window button for the Table1 : Table window and then click the No button in the Microsoft Office Access dialog box. The initial Microsoft Access window is displayed and you can repeat the process you used earlier.

More About

Correcting Errors in the Structure

You also can correct errors by using the Undo button on the Table Design toolbar. Access displays a list of the 20 most recent actions you can undo. When you undo an action, you also undo all actions above it in the list. If you later decide you did not want to undo an action, click Redo.

Q&A

Q: Why is the data type for Zip Code Text instead of Number?

A: Zip codes are not used in arithmetic operations. You do not add Zip codes or find an average Zip code, for example.

Closing and Saving a Table

The Client table structure now is complete. The final step is to close and save the table within the database. At this time, you should give the table a name.

Table names are from 1 to 64 characters in length and can contain letters, numbers, and spaces. The two table names in this project are Client and Trainer.

The following steps close and save the table.

To Close and Save a Table

1

• **Click the Close Window button for the Table1 : Table window (see Figure 1-19). (Be sure not to click the Close button on the Microsoft Access title bar, because this would close Microsoft Access.)**

The Microsoft Office Access dialog box appears (Figure 1-20).

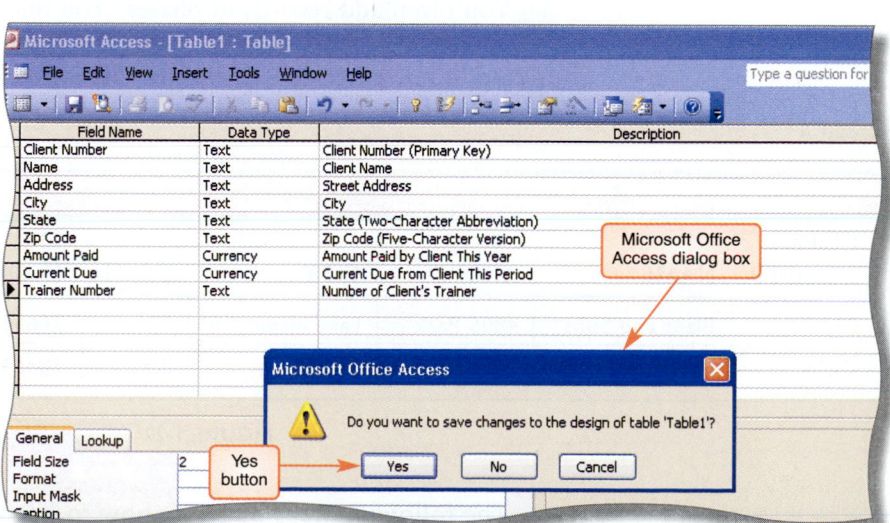

FIGURE 1-20

2

• **Click the Yes button in the Microsoft Office Access dialog box, and then type** Client **as the name of the table.**

The Save As dialog box appears (Figure 1-21). The table name is entered.

3

• **Click the OK button in the Save As dialog box.**

The table is saved. The window containing the table design no longer is displayed.

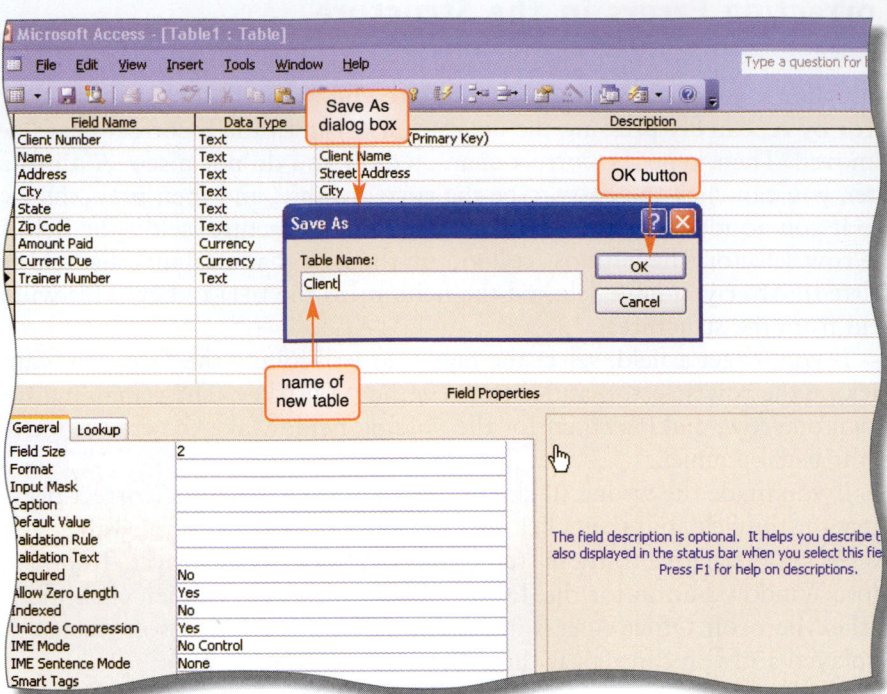

FIGURE 1-21

Other Ways

1. On File menu click Save
2. Press CTRL+S
3. In Voice Command mode, say "Save"

Adding Records to a Table

Creating a table by building the structure and saving the table is the first step in a two-step process. The second step is to add records to the table. To add records to a table, the table must be open. When making changes to tables, you work in Datasheet view. In **Datasheet view**, the table is represented as a collection of rows and columns called a **datasheet**. It looks very much like the tables shown in Figure 1-1 on page AC 5.

You often add records in phases. You may, for example, not have enough time to add all the records in one session. To illustrate this process, this project begins by adding the first two records in the Client table (Figure 1-22). The remaining records are added later.

Client table (first 2 records)

CLIENT NUMBER	NAME	ADDRESS	CITY	STATE	ZIP CODE	AMOUNT PAID	CURRENT DUE	TRAINER NUMBER
BS27	Blant and Sons	4806 Park	Lake Hammond	TX	76653	$21,876.00	$892.50	42
CE16	Center Services	725 Mitchell	San Julio	TX	78364	$26,512.00	$2,672.00	48

FIGURE 1-22

The following steps illustrate how to open the Client table and then add records.

To Add Records to a Table

1

• **Right-click the Client table in the Ashton James College : Database window.**

The shortcut menu for the Client table appears (Figure 1-23). The Ashton James College : Database window is maximized because the previous window, the Client : Table window, was maximized. (If you wanted to restore the Database window to its original size, you would click the Restore Window button.)

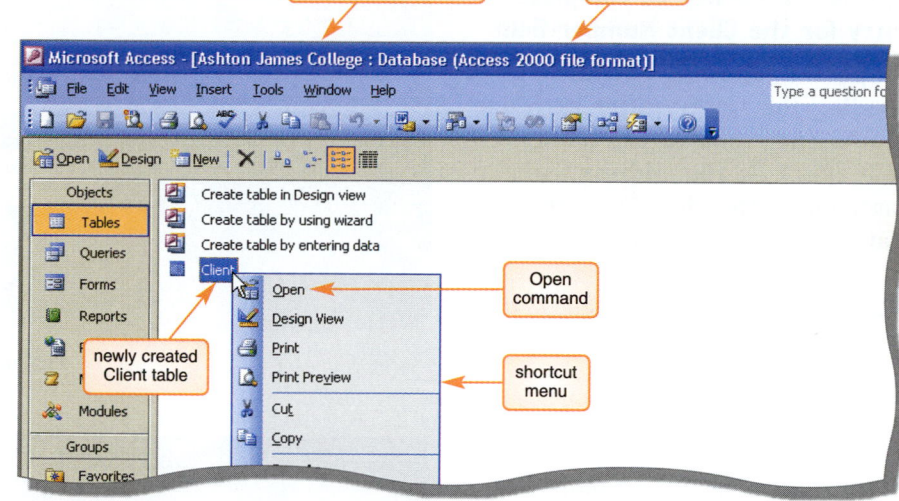

FIGURE 1-23

2

• **Click Open on the shortcut menu.**

*Access displays the Client : Table window (Figure 1-24). The window contains the Datasheet view for the Client table. The **record selector**, the small box or bar that, when clicked, selects the entire record, is positioned on the first record. The status bar at the bottom of the window also indicates that the record selector is positioned on record 1.*

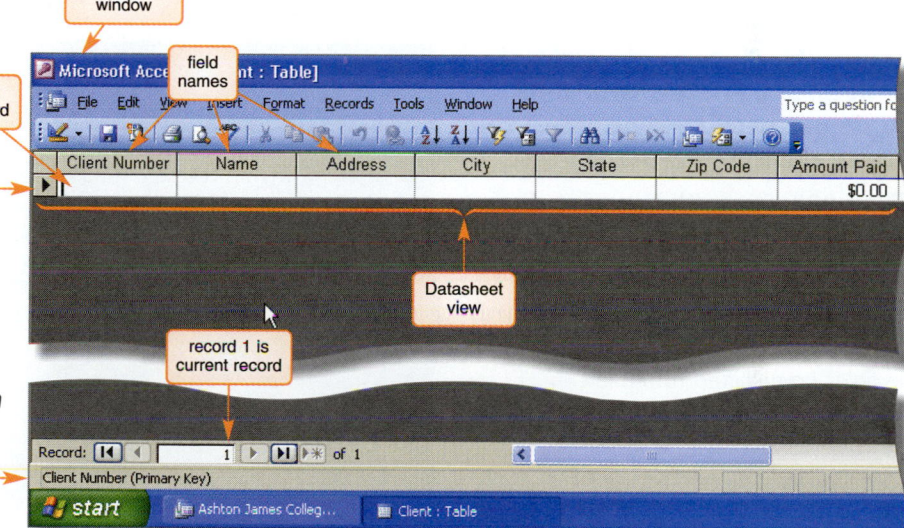

FIGURE 1-24

3

• **Type BS27 as the first client number (see Figure 1-22). Be sure you type the letters in uppercase as shown in the table in Figure 1-22 so they are entered in the database correctly.**

The client number is entered, but the insertion point is still in the Client Number field (Figure 1-25). The pencil icon in the record selector column indicates that the record is being edited but changes to the record are not saved yet. Microsoft Access also creates a row for a new record.

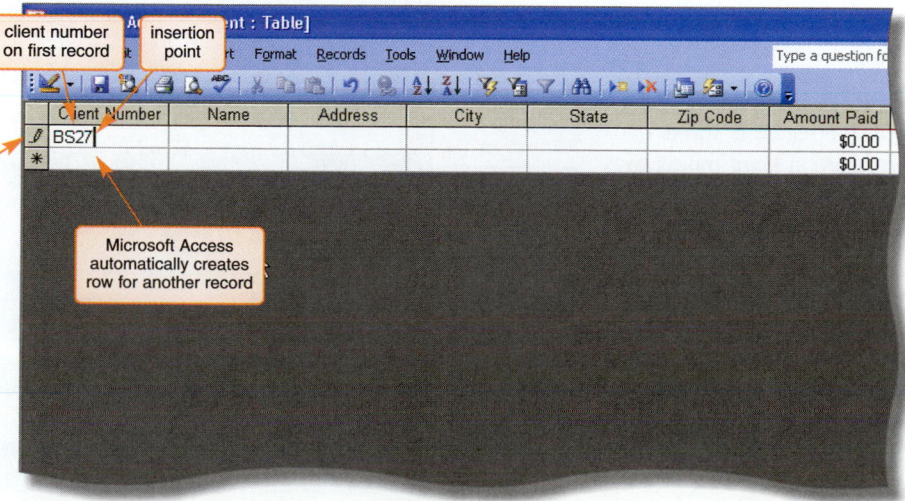

FIGURE 1-25

4

• **Press the TAB key to complete the entry for the Client Number field.**

• **Type the following entries, pressing the TAB key after each one:** Blant and Sons **as the name,** 4806 Park **as the address,** Lake Hammond **as the city,** TX **as the state, and** 76653 **as the Zip code.**

The Name, Address, City, State, and Zip Code fields are entered (Figure 1-26).

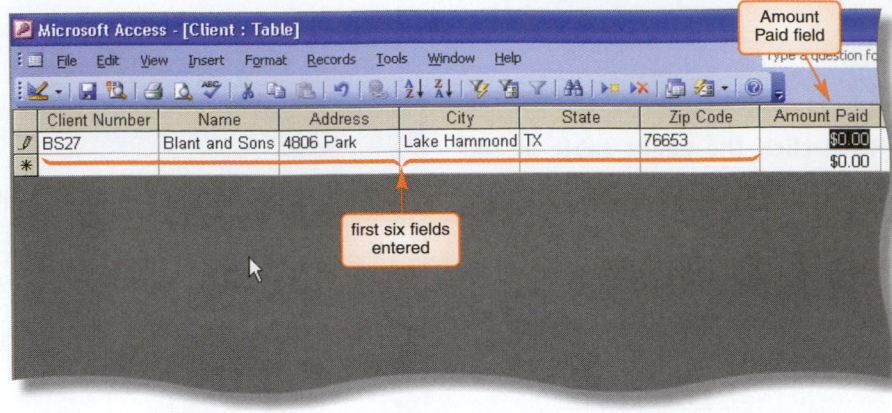

FIGURE 1-26

5

• **Type** 21876 **as the Amount Paid amount and then press the TAB key. (You do not need to type dollar signs or commas. In addition, because the digits to the right of the decimal point are both zeros, you do not need to type either the decimal point or the zeros.)**

• **Type** 892.50 **as the current due amount and then press the TAB key.**

• **Type** 42 **as the trainer number to complete data entry for the record.**

The fields have shifted to the left (Figure 1-27). The Amount Paid and Current Due values appear with dollar signs and decimal points. The insertion point is positioned in the Trainer Number field.

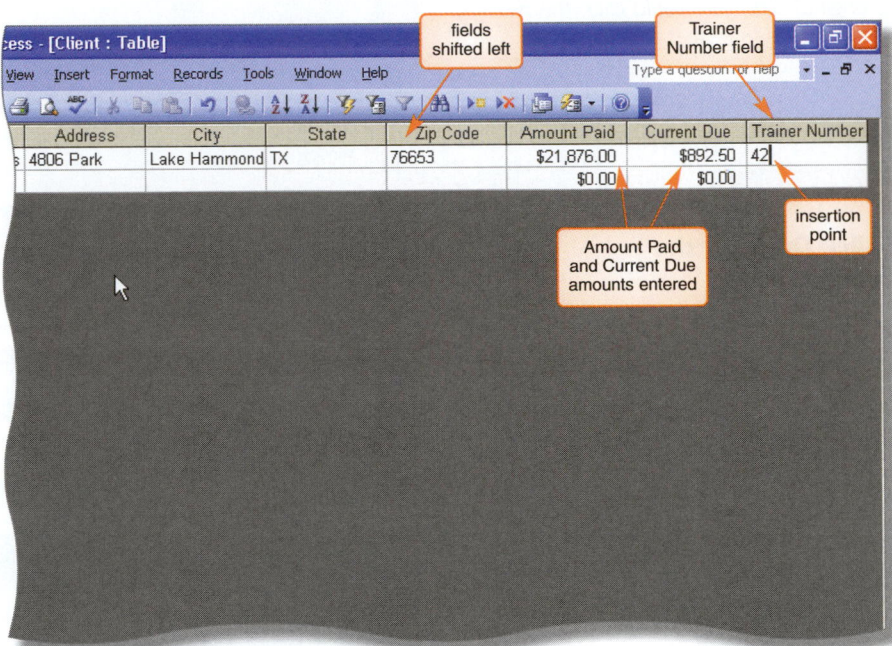

FIGURE 1-27

6

• **Press the TAB key.**

The fields shift back to the right, the record is saved, and the insertion point moves to the client number field on the second row (Figure 1-28).

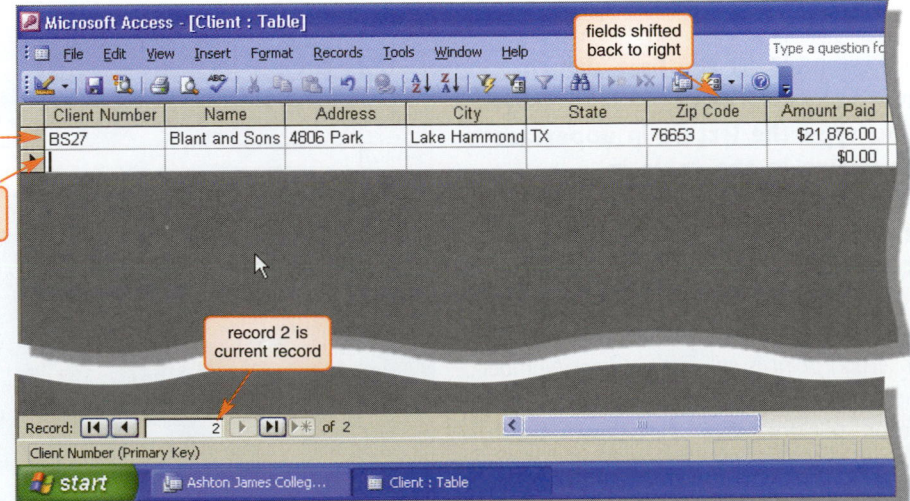

FIGURE 1-28

7

• **Use the techniques shown in Steps 3 through 6 to add the data for the second record shown in Figure 1-22 on page AC 22.**

The second record is added and the insertion point moves to the Client Number field on the third row (Figure 1-29).

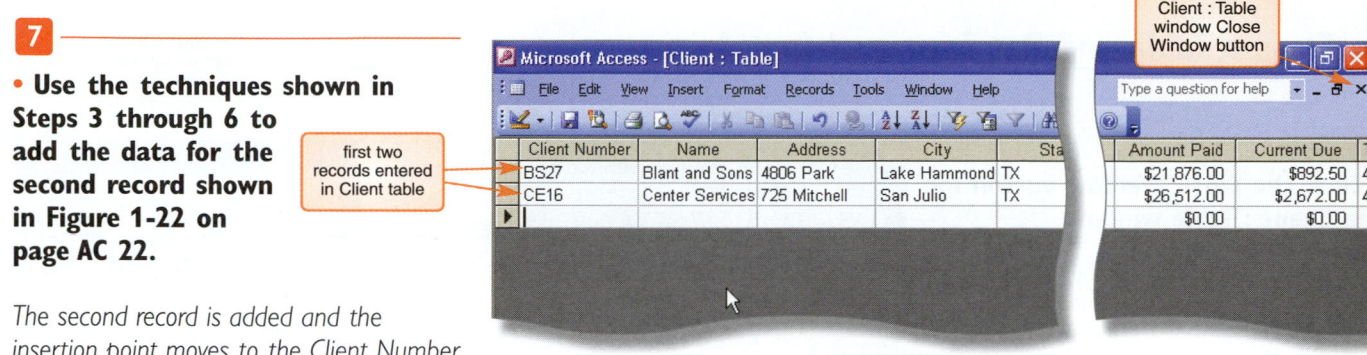

first two records entered in Client table

Client : Table window Close Window button

FIGURE 1-29

As soon as you have entered or modified a record and moved to another record, the original record is saved. This is different from other applications. The rows entered in a spreadsheet, for example, are not saved until the entire spreadsheet is saved.

Correcting Errors in the Data

Check your entries carefully to ensure they are correct. If you make a mistake and discover it before you press the TAB key, correct it by pressing the BACKSPACE key until the incorrect characters are removed and then typing the correct characters.

If you discover an incorrect entry later, correct the error by clicking the incorrect entry and then making the appropriate correction. If the record you must correct is not on the screen, use any technique, such as the UP ARROW and DOWN ARROW keys to move to it. If the field you want to correct is not visible on the screen, use the horizontal scroll bar along the bottom of the screen to shift all the fields until the one you want appears. Then make the correction.

If you add an extra record accidentally, select the record by clicking the record selector that immediately precedes the record. Then, press the DELETE key. This will remove the record from the table. If you forget a record, add it using the same procedure as for all the other records. Access will place it in the correct location in the table automatically.

If you cannot determine how to correct the data, you are, in effect, stuck on the record. Access neither allows you to move to any other record until you have made the correction, nor allows you to close the table. If you encounter this situation, simply press the ESC key. Pressing the ESC key will remove from the screen the record you are trying to add. You then can move to any other record, close the table, or take any other action you desire.

Closing a Table and Database and Quitting Access

It is a good idea to close a table as soon as you have finished working with it. It keeps the screen from getting cluttered and prevents you from making accidental changes to the data in the table. If you no longer will work with the database, you should close the database as well. With the creation of the Client table complete, you also can quit Access at this point.

The steps on the next page close the table and the database and then quit Access.

To Close a Table and Database and Quit Access

1

• **Click the Close Window button for the Client : Table window.**

The datasheet for the Client table no longer appears (Figure 1-30).

2

• **Click the Close Window button for the Ashton James College : Database window.**

The Ashton James College : Database window no longer appears.

3

• **Click the Close button for the Microsoft Access window.**

The Microsoft Access window closes and the Windows desktop appears.

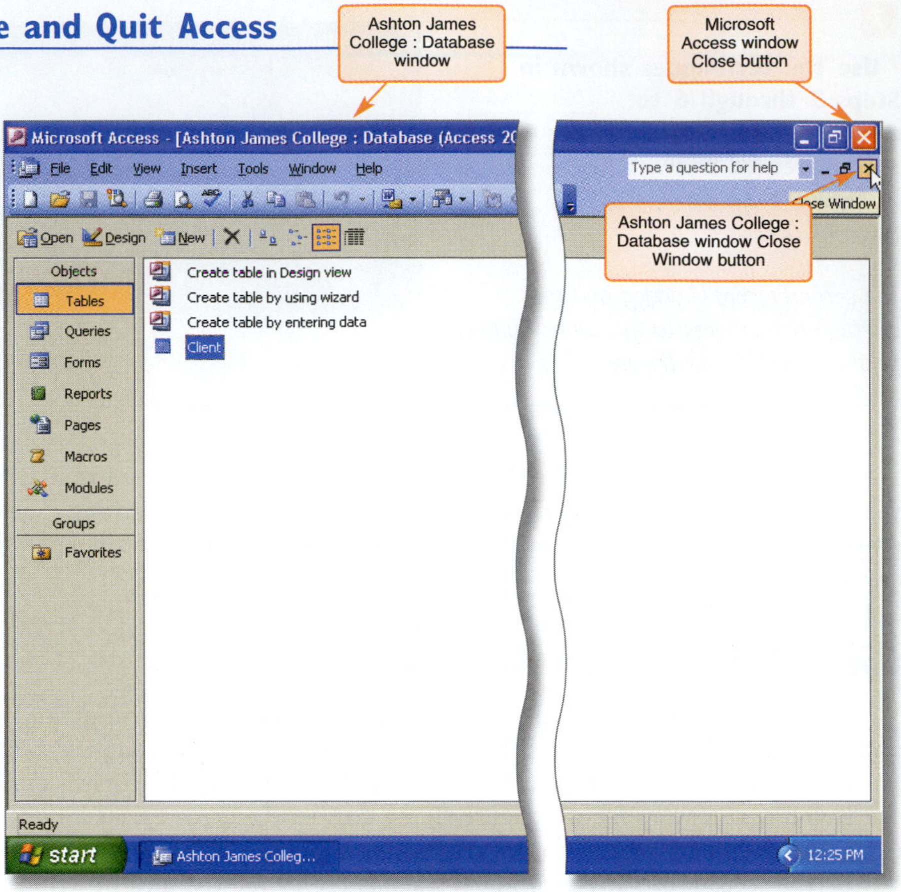

Ashton James College : Database window

Microsoft Access window Close button

Ashton James College : Database window Close Window button

FIGURE 1-30

Opening a Database

To work with any of the tables, reports, or forms in a database, the database must be open. The following steps open the database from within Access.

To Open a Database

1

• **Start Access following the steps on pages AC 7 and AC 8.**

• **If the task pane appears, click its Close button.**

• **Click the Open button on the Database toolbar.**

The Open dialog box appears (Figure 1-31).

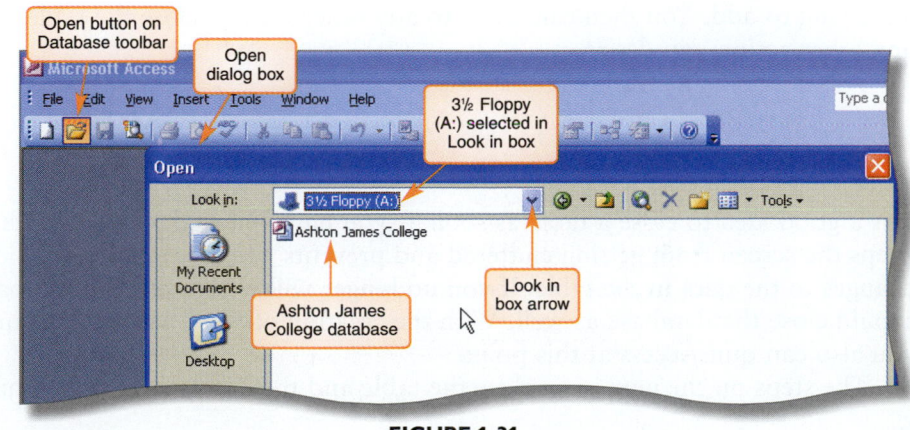

Open button on Database toolbar

Open dialog box

3½ Floppy (A:) selected in Look in box

Ashton James College database

Look in box arrow

FIGURE 1-31

2

• **Be sure 3½ Floppy (A:) folder appears in the Look in box. If not, click the Look in box arrow and click 3½ Floppy (A:).**

• **Click Ashton James College.**

Access displays the Open dialog box (Figure 1-32). The 3½ Floppy (A:) folder appears in the Look in box and the files on the floppy disk in drive A are displayed. (Your list may be different.)

3

• **Click the Open button in the Open dialog box.**

• **If a Security Warning dialog box appears, click the Open button.**

The database opens and the Ashton James College : Database window appears.

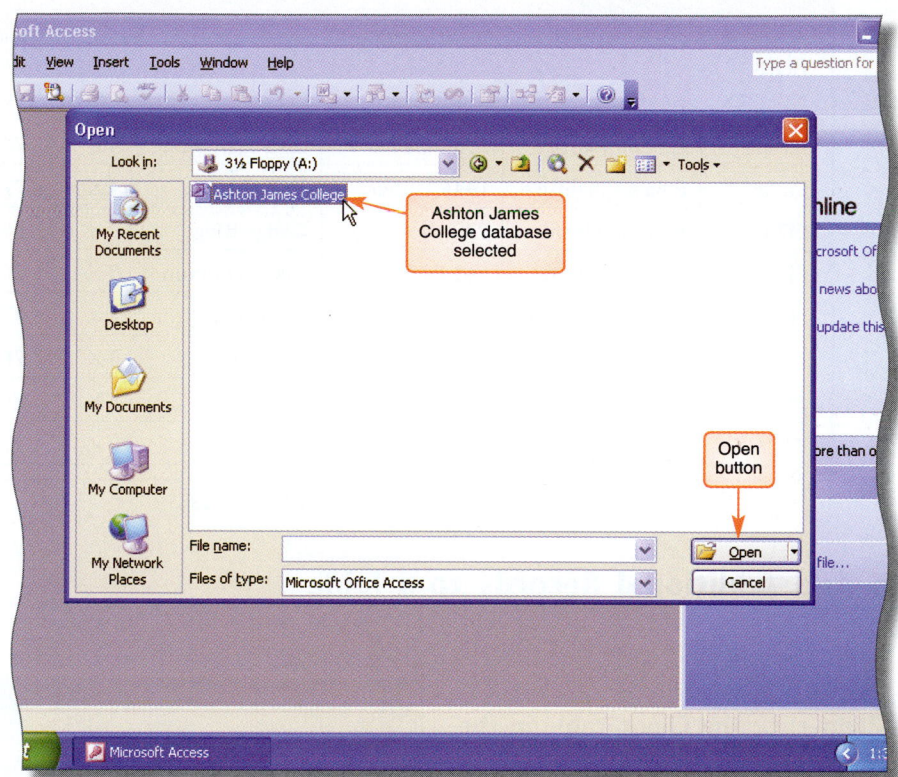

FIGURE 1-32

Other Ways

1. On File menu click Open
2. In Getting Started task pane, click name of database
3. Press CTRL + O
4. In Voice Command mode, say "Open"

Adding Additional Records

You can add records to a table that already contains data using a process almost identical to that used to add records to an empty table. The only difference is that you place the insertion point after the last data record before you enter the additional data. To do so, use the **Navigation buttons**, which are buttons used to move within a table, found near the lower-left corner of the screen shown in Figure 1-34 on the next page. The purpose of each of the Navigation buttons is described in Table 1-2.

Table 1-2 Navigation Buttons in Datasheet View	
BUTTON	PURPOSE
First Record	Moves to the first record in the table
Previous Record	Moves to the previous record
Next Record	Moves to the next record
Last Record	Moves to the last record in the table
New Record	Moves to the end of the table to a position for entering a new record

Q&A

Q: Why click the New Record button? Could you just click the Client Number on the first open record and then add the record?

A: You could click the Client Number on the first open record, provided that record appears on the screen. With only two records in the table, this is not a problem. Once a table contains more records than will fit on the screen, it is easier to click the New Record button.

The steps on the next page add the remaining records (Figure 1-33 on the next page) to the Client table.

Client table (last 8 records)

CLIENT NUMBER	NAME	ADDRESS	CITY	STATE	ZIP CODE	AMOUNT PAID	CURRENT DUE	TRAINER NUMBER
CP27	Calder Plastics	7300 Cedar	Lake Hammond	TX	76653	$8,725.00	$0.00	48
EU28	Elba's Furniture	1445 Hubert	Tallmadge	TX	77231	$4,256.00	$1,202.00	53
FI28	Farrow-Idsen	829 Wooster	Cedar Ridge	TX	79342	$8,287.50	$925.50	42
FL93	Fairland Lawn	143 Pangborn	Lake Hammond	TX	76653	$21,625.00	$0.00	48
HN83	Hurley National	3827 Burgess	Tallmadge	TX	77231	$0.00	$0.00	48
MC28	Morgan-Alyssa	923 Williams	Crumville	TX	76745	$24,761.00	$1,572.00	42
PS82	PRIM Staffing	72 Crestview	San Julio	TX	78364	$11,682.25	$2,827.50	53
TE26	Telton-Edwards	5672 Anderson	Dunston	TX	77893	$8,521.50	$0.00	48

FIGURE 1-33

To Add Additional Records to a Table

1

• **Right-click the Client table in the Ashton James College : Database window, and then click Open on the shortcut menu.**

• **When the Client table appears, maximize the window by double-clicking its title bar.**

The datasheet appears (Figure 1-34).

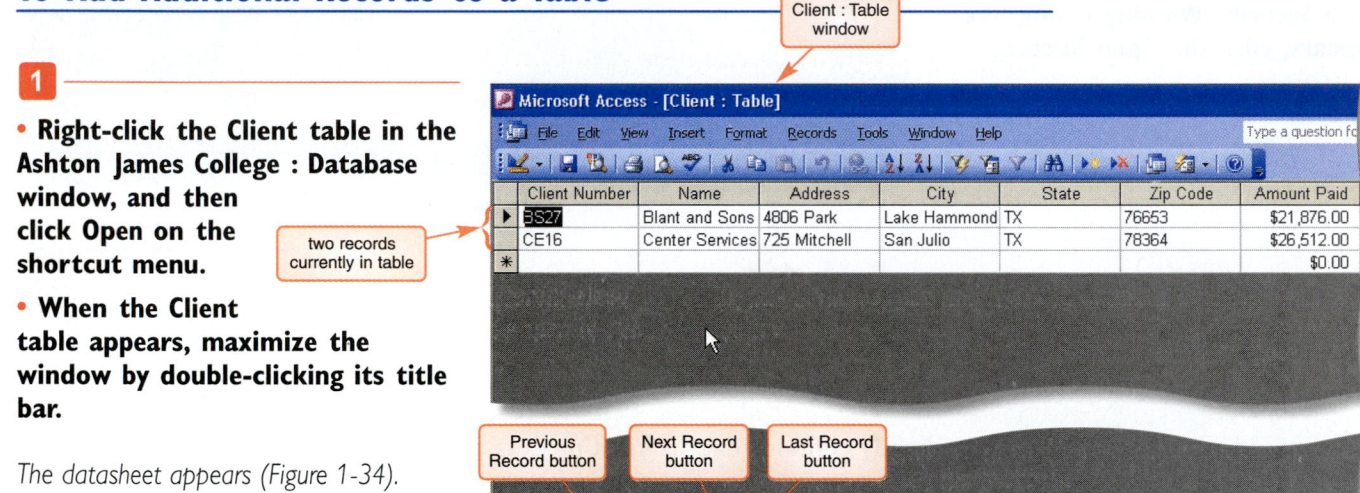

FIGURE 1-34

2

• **Click the New Record button.**

Access places the insertion point in position to enter a new record (Figure 1-35).

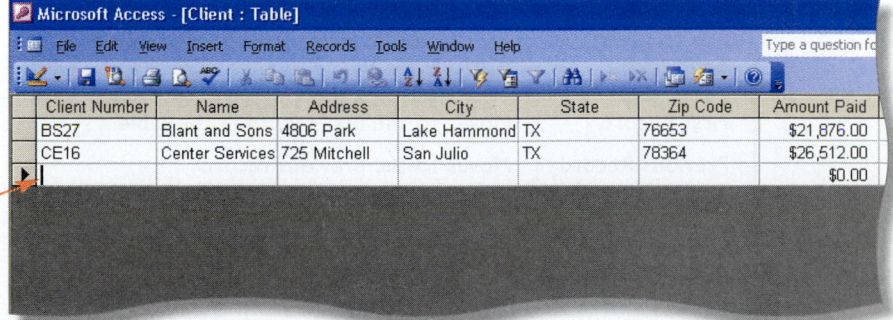

FIGURE 1-35

3

• **Add the records from Figure 1-33 using the same techniques you used to add the first two records.**

The additional records are added (Figure 1-36).

4

• **Click the Close Window button for the datasheet.**

The window containing the table closes and the Ashton James College : Database window appears.

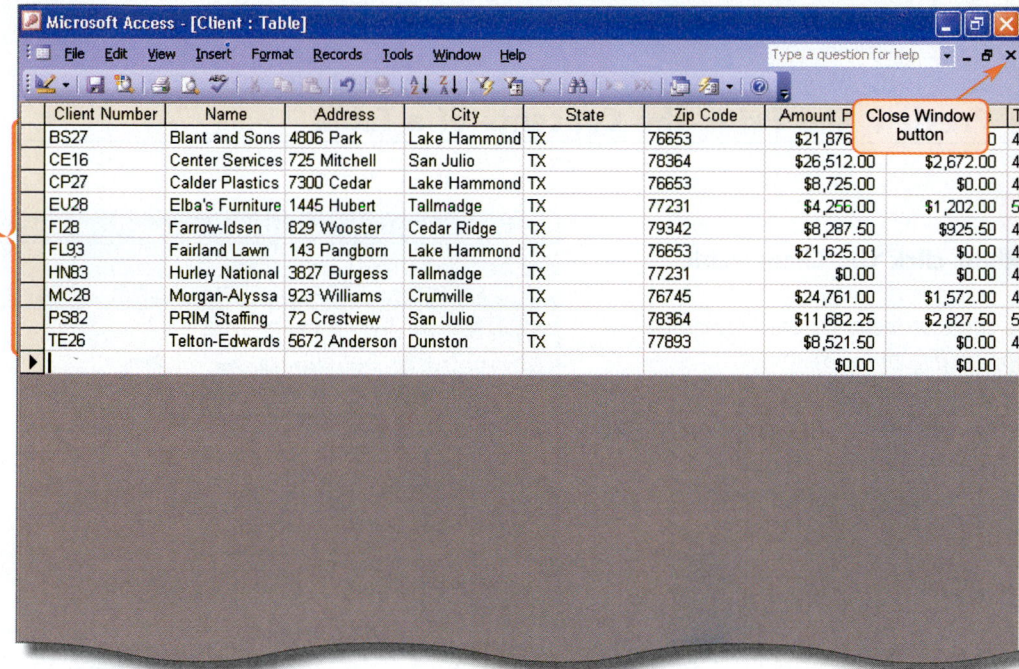

all 10 records entered

Close Window button

Client Number	Name	Address	City	State	Zip Code	Amount P...	...	T
BS27	Blant and Sons	4806 Park	Lake Hammond	TX	76653	$21,876...	...	4
CE16	Center Services	725 Mitchell	San Julio	TX	78364	$26,512.00	$2,672.00	4
CP27	Calder Plastics	7300 Cedar	Lake Hammond	TX	76653	$8,725.00	$0.00	4
EU28	Elba's Furniture	1445 Hubert	Tallmadge	TX	77231	$4,256.00	$1,202.00	5
FI28	Farrow-Idsen	829 Wooster	Cedar Ridge	TX	79342	$8,287.50	$925.50	4
FL93	Fairland Lawn	143 Pangborn	Lake Hammond	TX	76653	$21,625.00	$0.00	4
HN83	Hurley National	3827 Burgess	Tallmadge	TX	77231	$0.00	$0.00	4
MC28	Morgan-Alyssa	923 Williams	Crumville	TX	76745	$24,761.00	$1,572.00	4
PS82	PRIM Staffing	72 Crestview	San Julio	TX	78364	$11,682.25	$2,827.50	5
TE26	Telton-Edwards	5672 Anderson	Dunston	TX	77893	$8,521.50	$0.00	4
						$0.00	$0.00	

FIGURE 1-36

Previewing and Printing the Contents of a Table

When working with a database, you often will need to print a copy of the table contents. Figure 1-37 shows a printed copy of the contents of the Client table. (Yours may look slightly different, depending on your printer.) Because the Client table is wider substantially than the screen, it also will be wider than the normal printed page in portrait orientation. **Portrait orientation** means the printout is across the width of the page. **Landscape orientation** means the printout is across the length of the page. Thus, to print the wide database table, use landscape orientation. If you are printing the contents of a table that fit on the screen, you will not need landscape orientation. A convenient way to change to landscape orientation is to preview what the printed copy will look like by using Print Preview. This allows you to determine whether landscape orientation is necessary and, if it is, to change the orientation easily to landscape. In addition, you also can use Print Preview to determine whether any adjustments are necessary to the page margins.

			Client			9/15/05		

Client Number	Name	Address	City	State	Zip Code	Amount Paid	Current Due	Trainer Number
BS27	Blant and Sons	4806 Park	Lake Hammond	TX	76653	$21,876.00	$892.50	42
CE16	Center Service	725 Mitchell	San Julio	TX	78364	$26,512.00	$2,672.00	48
CP27	Calder Plastics	7300 Cedar	Lake Hammond	TX	76653	$8,725.00	$0.00	48
EU28	Elba's Furniture	1445 Hubert	Tallmadge	TX	77231	$4,256.00	$1,202.00	53
FI28	Farrow-Idsen	829 Wooster	Cedar Ridge	TX	79342	$8,287.50	$925.50	42
FL93	Fairland Lawn	143 Pangborn	Lake Hammond	TX	76653	$21,625.00	$0.00	48
HN83	Hurley National	3827 Burgess	Tallmadge	TX	77231	$0.00	$0.00	48
MC28	Morgan-Alyssa	923 Williams	Crumville	TX	76745	$24,761.00	$1,572.00	42
PS82	PRIM Staffing	72 Crestview	San Julio	TX	78364	$11,682.25	$2,827.50	53
TE26	Telton-Edwards	5672 Anderson	Dunston	TX	77893	$8,521.50	$0.00	48

FIGURE 1-37

The following steps illustrate using Print Preview to preview and then print the Client table.

To Preview and Print the Contents of a Table

1

• **Right-click the Client table.**

The shortcut menu for the Client table appears (Figure 1-38).

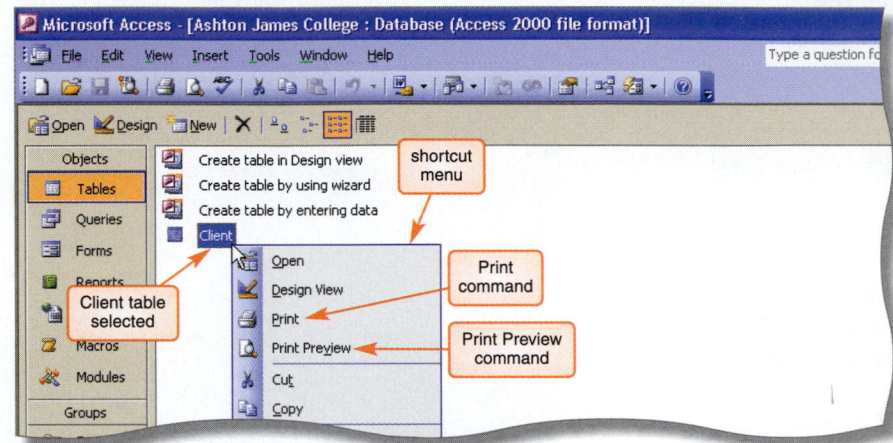

FIGURE 1-38

2

• **Click Print Preview on the shortcut menu.**

• **Point to the approximate position shown in Figure 1-39.**

The preview of the report appears. The mouse pointer shape changes to a magnifying glass, indicating you can magnify a portion of the report.

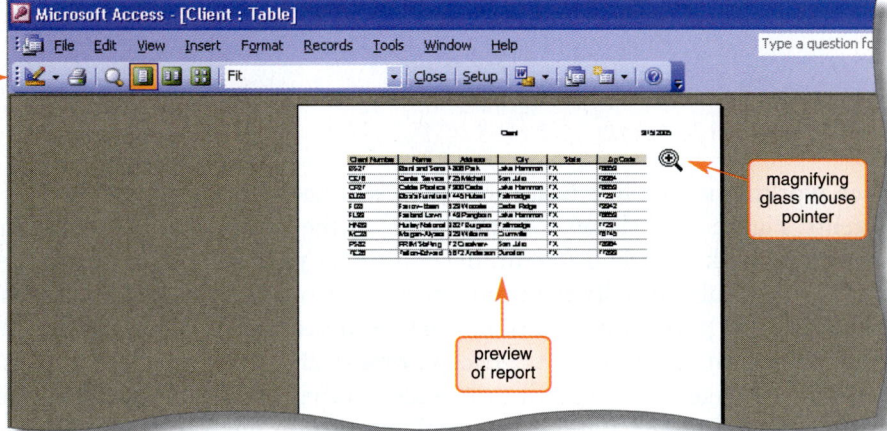

FIGURE 1-39

3

• **Click the magnifying glass mouse pointer in the approximate position shown in Figure 1-39.**

The portion surrounding the mouse pointer is magnified (Figure 1-40). The last field that appears is the Zip Code field. The Amount Paid, Current Due, and Trainer Number fields do not appear. To display the additional fields, you will need to switch to landscape orientation.

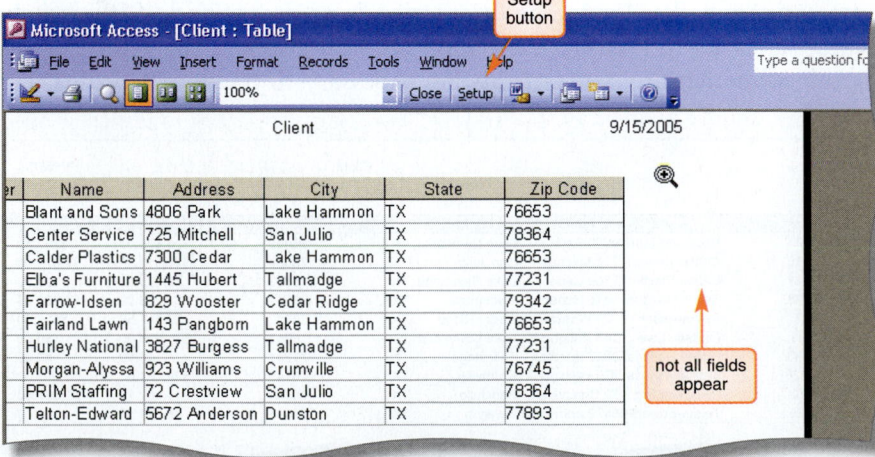

FIGURE 1-40

4

• **Click the Setup button on the Print Preview toolbar.**

Access displays the Page Setup dialog box (Figure 1-41).

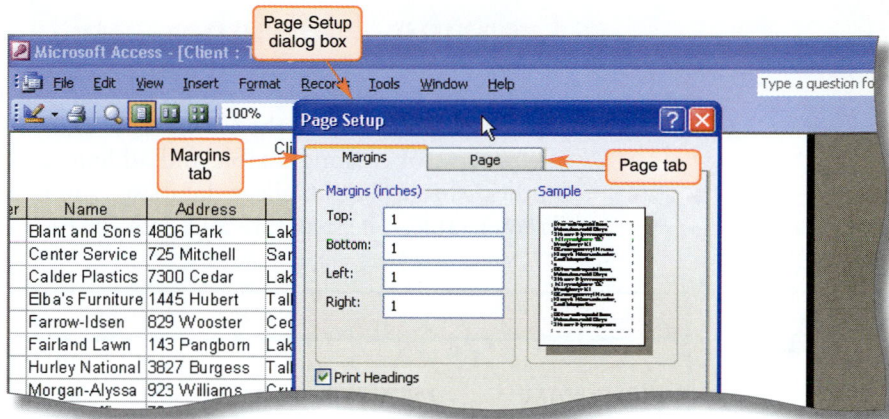

FIGURE 1-41

5

• **Click the Page tab.**

The Page sheet appears (Figure 1-42). The Portrait option button currently is selected. (Option button refers to the round button that indicates choices in a dialog box. When the corresponding option is selected, the button contains within it a solid circle. Clicking an option button selects it, and deselects all others.)

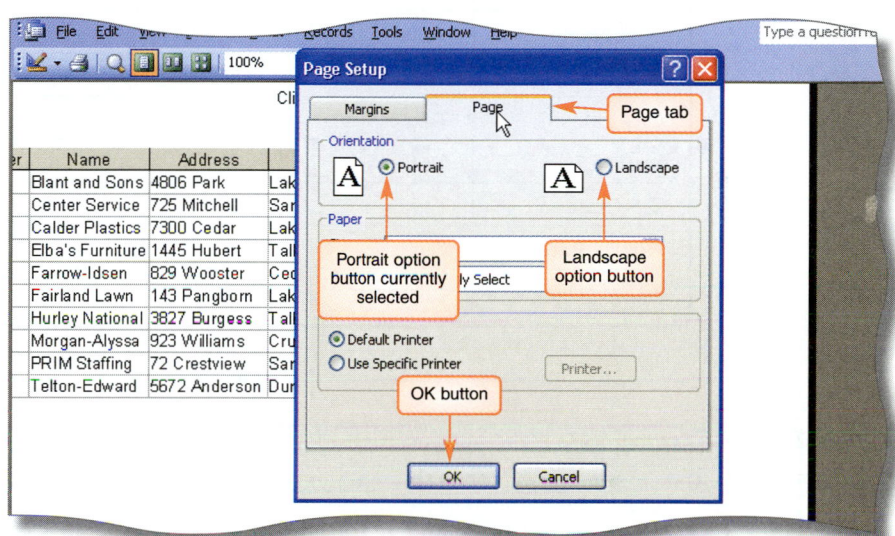

FIGURE 1-42

6

• **Click Landscape, and then click the OK button.**

The orientation is changed to landscape as shown by the report that appears on the screen (Figure 1-43). The last field that is displayed is the Trainer Number field; so all fields currently appear. If they did not, you could decrease the left and right margins; that is, the amount of space left by Access on the left and right edges of the report.

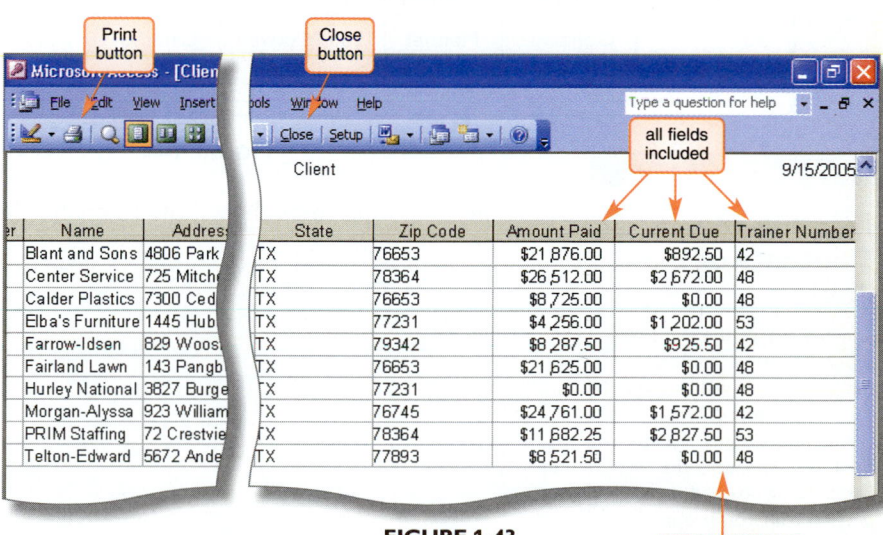

FIGURE 1-43

7

• **Click the Print button to print the report, and then click the Close button on the Print Preview toolbar.**

The report prints. It looks like the report shown in Figure 1-37 on page AC 29. The Print Preview window closes and the Ashton James College : Database window appears.

Creating Additional Tables

A database typically consists of more than one table. The Ashton James College database contains two, the Client table and the Trainer table. You need to repeat the process of creating a table and adding records for each table in the database. In the Ashton James College database, you need to create and add records to the Trainer table. The structure and data for the table are given in Figure 1-44.

Structure of Trainer table

FIELD NAME	DATA TYPE	FIELD SIZE	PRIMARY KEY?	DESCRIPTION
Trainer Number	Text	2	Yes	Trainer Number (Primary Key)
Last Name	Text	10		Last Name of Trainer
First Name	Text	8		First Name of Trainer
Address	Text	15		Street Address
City	Text	15		City
State	Text	2		State (Two-Character Abbreviation)
Zip Code	Text	5		Zip Code (Five-Character Version)
Hourly Rate	Currency			Hourly Rate of Trainer
YTD Earnings	Currency			YTD Earnings of Trainer

Trainer table

TRAINER NUMBER	LAST NAME	FIRST NAME	ADDRESS	CITY	STATE	ZIP CODE	HOURLY RATE	YTD EARNINGS
42	Perry	Belinda	261 Porter	Burdett	TX	76734	$23.00	$27,620.00
48	Stevens	Michael	3135 Gill	Rockwood	TX	78884	$21.00	$23,567.50
53	Gonzalez	Manuel	265 Maxwell	Camino	TX	76574	$24.00	$29,885.00
67	Danville	Marty	1827 Maple	Dunston	TX	77893	$20.00	$0.00

FIGURE 1-44

The following steps show how to create the table.

More About

Printing the Contents of a Table

You can change the margins, paper size, paper source, or the printer that will be used to print the report. To change the margins, select the Margins sheet in the Page Setup dialog box and then enter the appropriate margin size. To change the paper size, paper source, or the printer, select the Page sheet in the Page Setup dialog box, click the appropriate down arrow, and then select the desired option.

To Create an Additional Table

1

• **Make sure the Ashton James College database is open.**

• **Click the New button on the Database window toolbar, click Design View, and then click the OK button.**

all fields entered for Trainer table

• **Enter the data for the fields for the Trainer table from Figure 1-44. Be sure to click the Primary Key button when you enter the Trainer Number field.**

The entries appear (Figure 1-45).

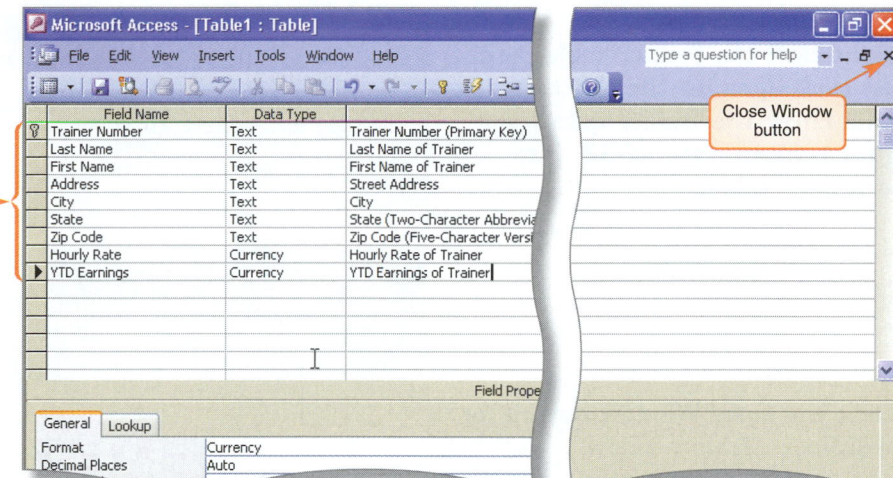

FIGURE 1-45

2

• **Click the Close Window button, click the Yes button in the Microsoft Office Access dialog box when asked if you want to save the changes, and then type** Trainer **as the name of the table.**

The Save As dialog box appears (Figure 1-46). The table name is entered.

3

• **Click the OK button.**

The table is saved in the Ashton James College database. The window containing the table structure no longer appears.

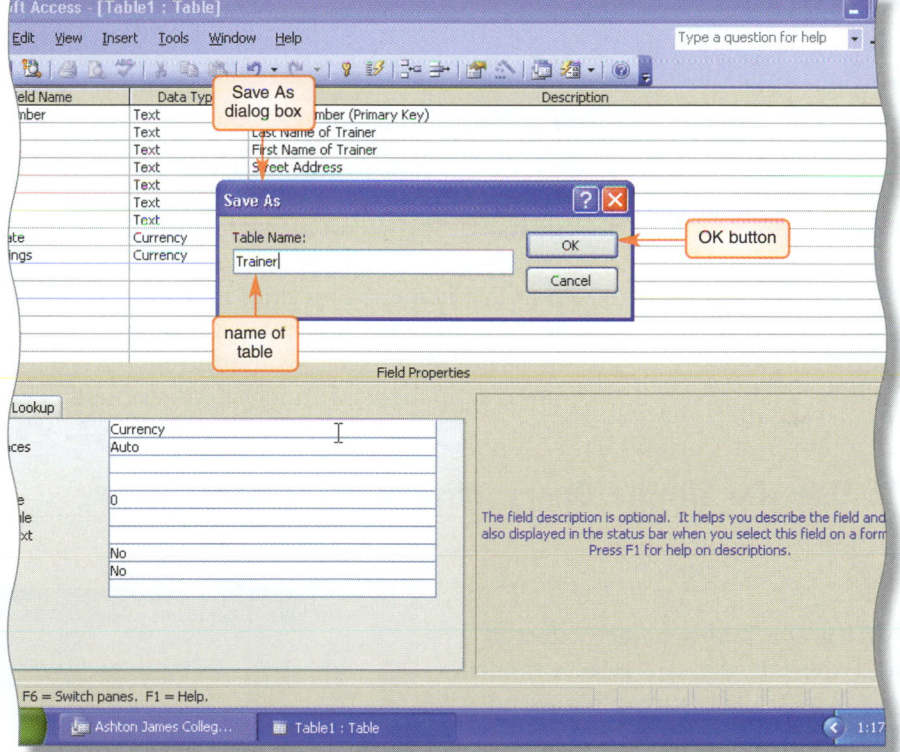

FIGURE 1-46

Adding Records to the Additional Table

Now that you have created the Trainer table, use the steps on the next page to add records to it.

To Add Records to an Additional Table

1

• **Right-click the Trainer table, and then click Open on the shortcut menu. Enter the Trainer data from Figure 1-44 on page AC 32 into the Trainer table.**

all records entered

The datasheet displays the entered records (Figure 1-47).

2

• **Click the Close Window button for the Trainer : Table window.**

Access closes the table and removes the datasheet from the screen.

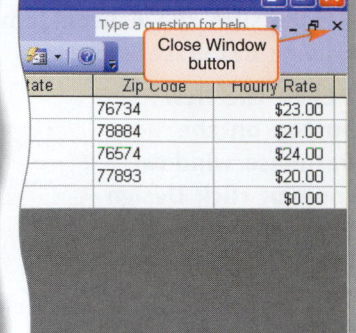

FIGURE 1-47

The records are now in the table.

Using Queries

Queries are simply questions, the answers to which are in the database. Access contains a powerful query feature. Through the use of this feature, you can ask a wide variety of complex questions. For simple requests, however, such as listing the number, name, and trainer number of all clients, you do not need to use the query feature, but instead can use the Simple Query wizard.

The following steps use the Simple Query wizard to create a query to display the number, name, and trainer number of all clients.

To Use the Simple Query Wizard to Create a Query

1

• **With the Tables object selected and the Client table selected, click the New Object button arrow on the Database toolbar.**

A list of objects that can be created is displayed (Figure 1-48).

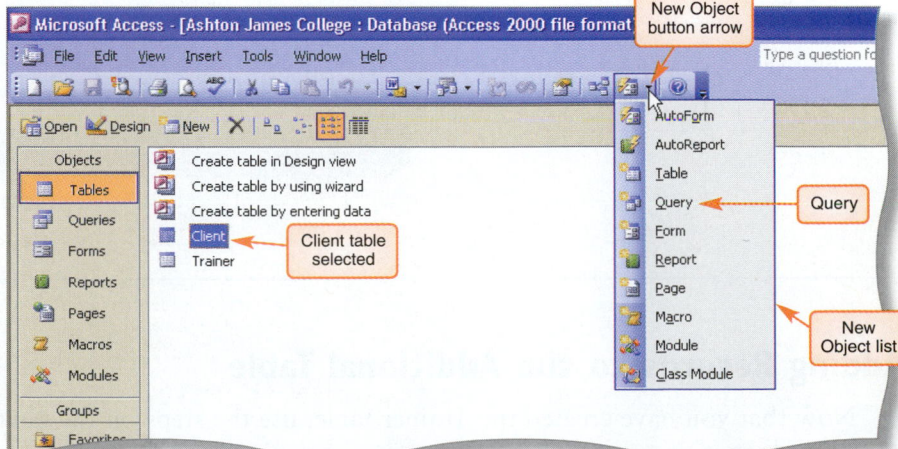

FIGURE 1-48

2

• **Click Query on the New Object list.**

The New Query dialog box appears (Figure 1-49).

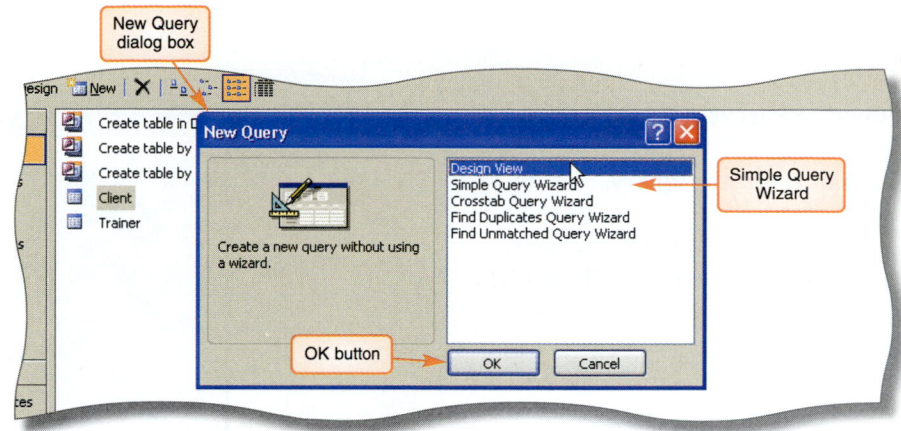

FIGURE 1-49

3

• **Click Simple Query Wizard, and then click the OK button.**

Access displays the Simple Query Wizard dialog box (Figure 1-50). It contains a list of available fields and a list of selected fields. Currently no fields are selected for the query.

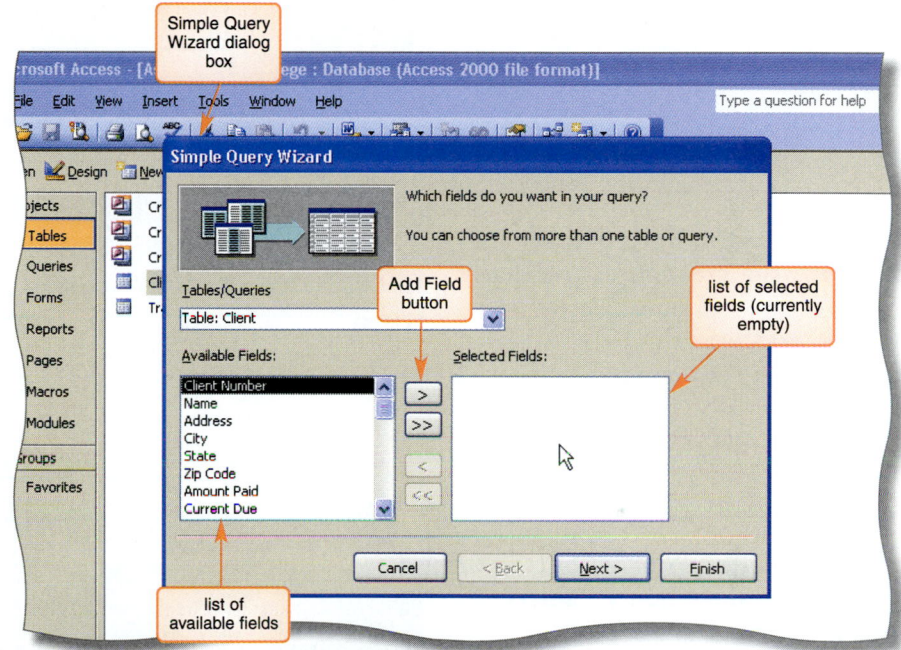

FIGURE 1-50

• **Click the Add Field button to add the Client Number field.**

• **Click the Add Field button a second time to add the Name field.**

• **Click the Trainer Number field, and then click the Add Field button to add the Trainer Number field.**

The fields are selected (Figure 1-51).

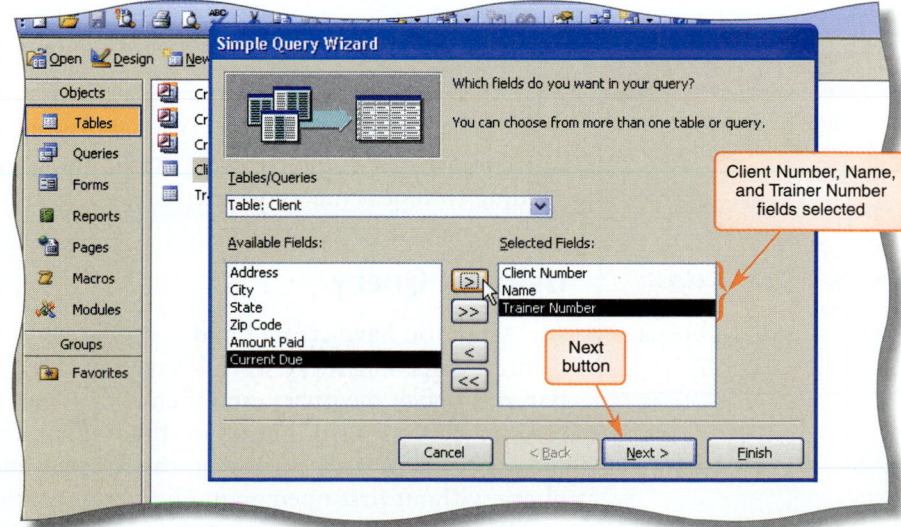

FIGURE 1-51

5

• **Click the Next button, and then type** Client-Trainer Query **as the name for the query.**

The Simple Query Wizard dialog box displays the new query name (Figure 1-52).

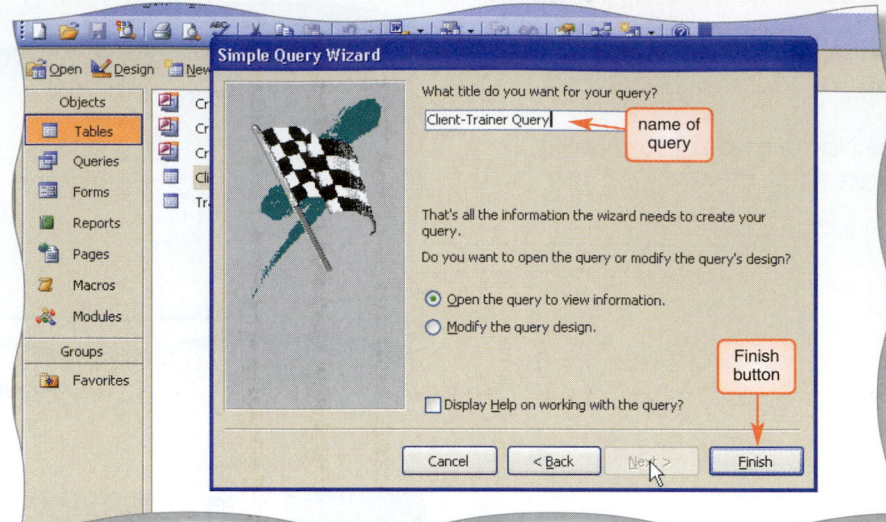

FIGURE 1-52

6

• **Click the Finish button to complete the creation of the query.**

Access displays the query results (Figure 1-53). The results contain all records, but only contain the Client Number, Name, and Trainer Number fields.

7

• **Click the Close Window button for the Client-Trainer Query : Select Query window.**

Access closes the query and the Ashton James College : Database window appears.

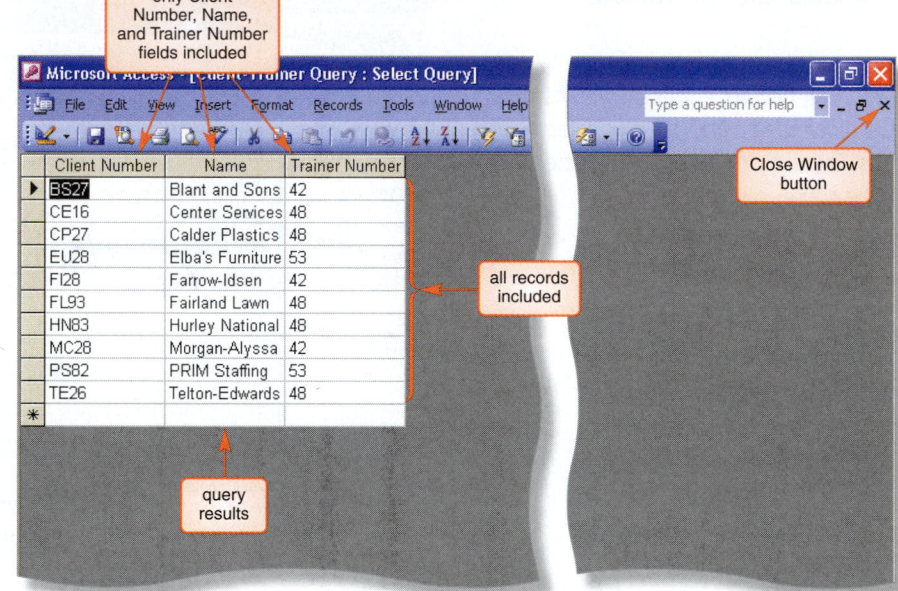

FIGURE 1-53

Other Ways

1. Click Queries object, double-click Create query by using wizard
2. Click Queries object, click New button on Database window toolbar
3. On Insert menu click Query
4. In Voice Command mode, say "Insert, Query"

The query is complete. You can use it at any time you like in the future without needing to repeat the above steps.

Using a Query

After you have created and saved a query, you can use it at any time in the future by opening it. To open a saved query, click the Queries object on the Objects bar, right-click the query, and then click Open on the shortcut menu. To print the results, click the Print button on the toolbar. If you want to change the design of the query, click Design View on the shortcut menu rather than Open. To print the query without first opening it, click Print on the shortcut menu.

You often want to restrict the records that are included. For example, you might only want to include those clients whose trainer number is 42. In such a case, you

need to enter the 42 as a **criterion**, which is a condition that the records to be
included must satisfy. To do so, you will open the query in Design view, enter the
criterion below the appropriate field, and then run the query. The following steps
show how to enter a criterion to include only clients of trainer 42 and then run
the query.

To Use a Query

1

• **If necessary, click the Queries object. Right-click the Client-Trainer Query.**

The shortcut menu for the Client-Trainer Query is displayed (Figure 1-54).

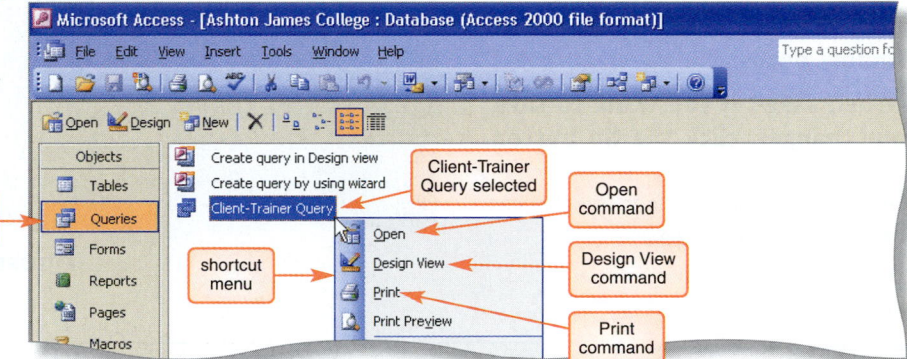

FIGURE 1-54

2

• **Click Design View on the shortcut menu.**

The query appears in Design view (Figure 1-55).

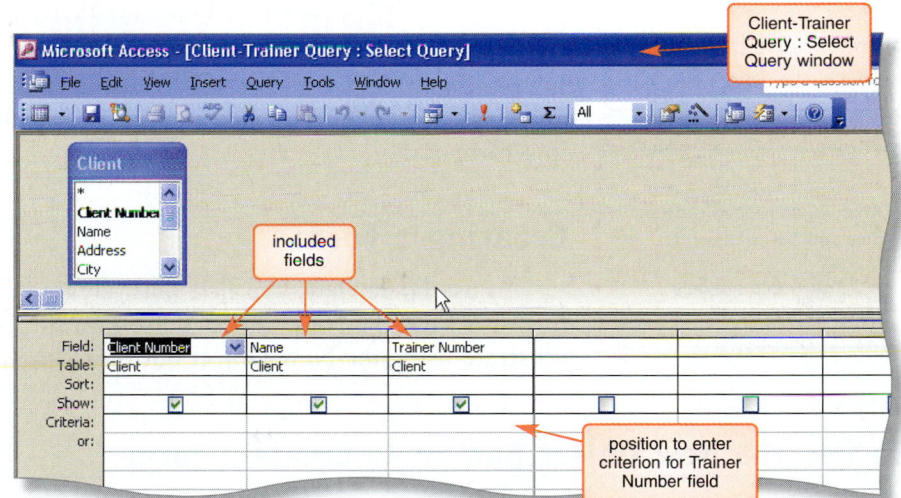

FIGURE 1-55

3

• **Click the Criteria row in the Trainer Number column of the grid, and then type 42 as the criterion.**

The criterion is typed (Figure 1-56).

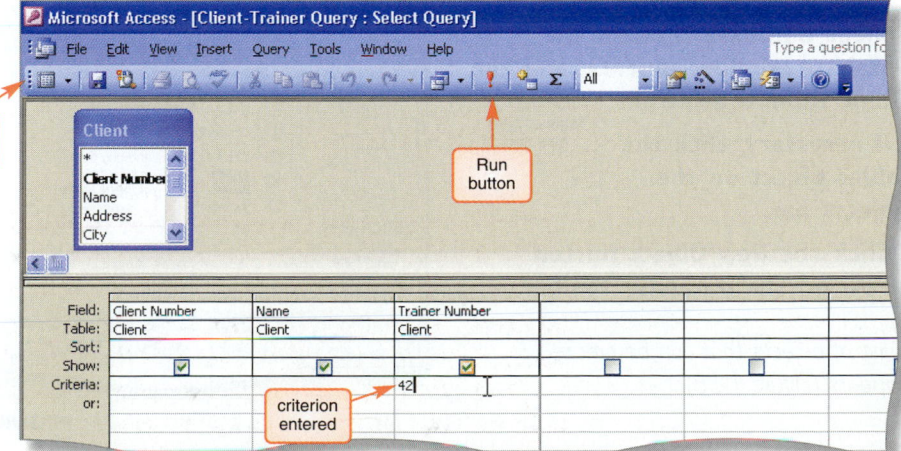

FIGURE 1-56

4

• **Click the Run button on the Query Design toolbar.**

Access displays the results (Figure 1-57). Only the clients of trainer 42 are included.

5

• **Close the window containing the query results by clicking its Close Window button.**

• **When asked if you want to save your changes, click the No button.**

The results no longer appear. The changes to the query are not saved.

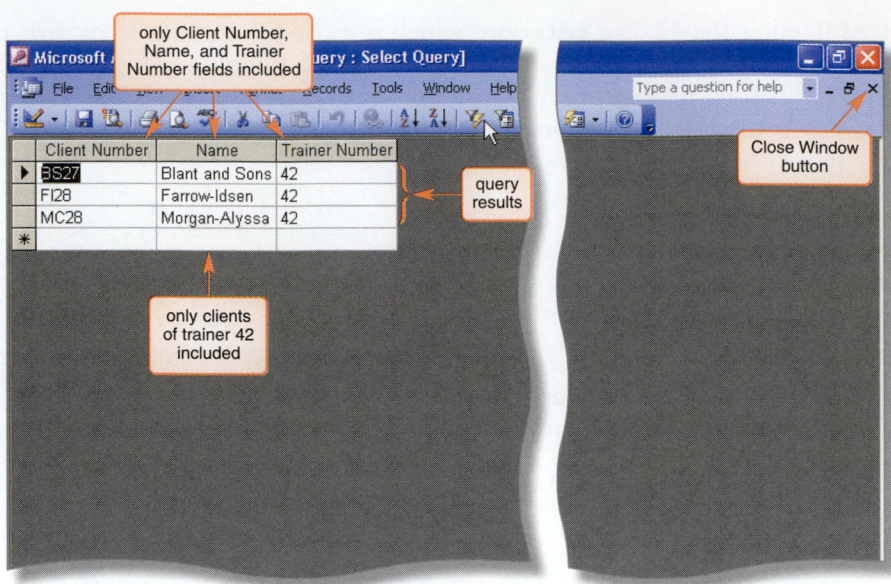

FIGURE 1-57

Other Ways

1. On Query menu click Run
2. In Voice Command mode, say "Run"

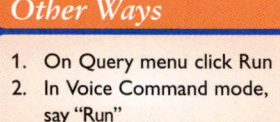

Q: If you saved the query, what would happen the next time you ran the query?

A: You would see only clients of trainer 42.

Using a Form to View Data

In creating tables, you have used Datasheet view; that is, the data on the screen appeared as a table. You also can use **Form view**, in which you see data contained in a form.

Creating a Form

To use Form view, you first must create a form. The simplest way to create a form is to use the New Object button on the Database toolbar. The following steps illustrate using the New Object button to create a form for the Client table.

To Use the New Object Button to Create a Form

1

• **Make sure the Ashton James College database is open, the Database window appears, and the Client table is selected.**

• **If necessary, click the Tables object on the Objects bar.**

• **Click the New Object button arrow on the Database toolbar.**

A list of objects that can be created appears (Figure 1-58).

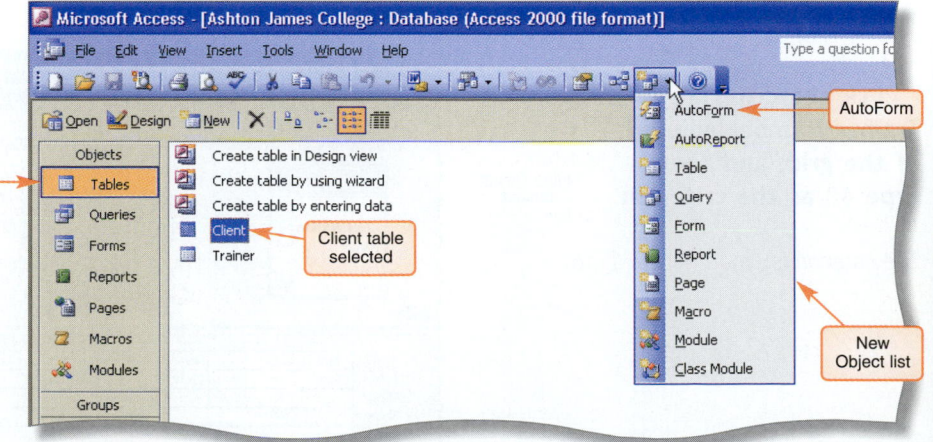

FIGURE 1-58

2

• **Click AutoForm on the New Object list.**

After a brief delay, the form appears (Figure 1-59). If you do not move the mouse pointer after clicking the New Object button, the ScreenTip for the Properties button may appear when the form opens. Access displays the Formatting toolbar when a form is created. (When you close the form, this toolbar no longer appears.)

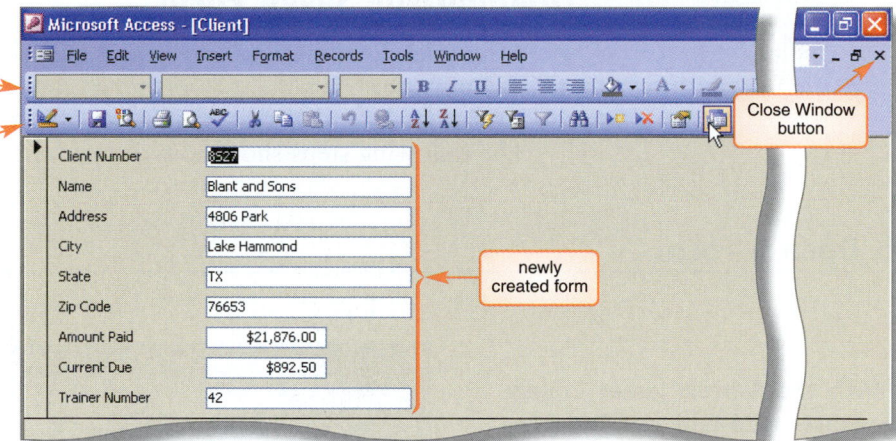

FIGURE 1-59

Closing and Saving the Form

Closing a form is similar to closing a table. The only difference is that you will be asked if you want to save the form unless you previously have saved it. The following steps close the form and save it as Client.

To Close and Save a Form

1

• **Click the Close Window button for the Client window (see Figure 1-59).**

Access displays the Microsoft Office Access dialog box (Figure 1-60).

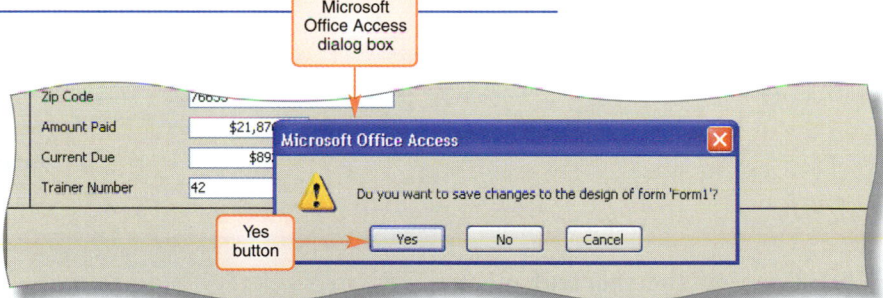

FIGURE 1-60

2

• **Click the Yes button.**

The Save As dialog box appears (Figure 1-61). The name of the table (Client) becomes the name of the form automatically. This name could be changed, if desired.

3

• **Click the OK button.**

The form is saved as part of the database and the form closes. The Ashton James College : Database window is redisplayed.

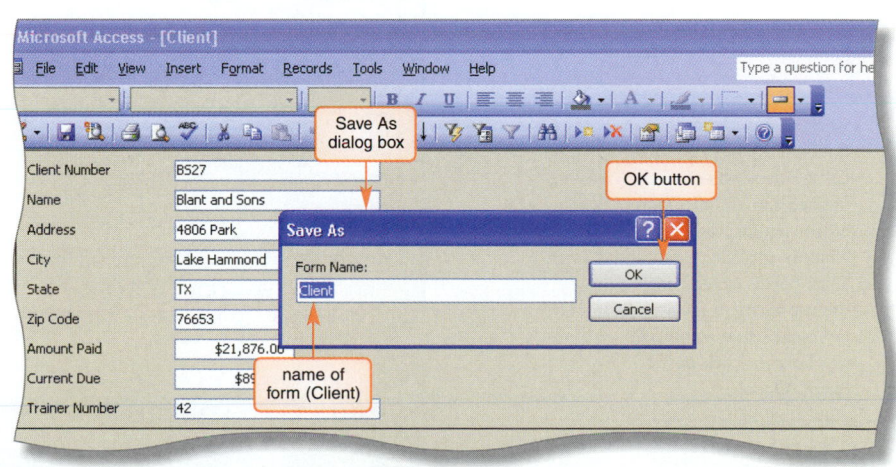

FIGURE 1-61

Opening the Saved Form

After you have saved a form, you can use it at any time in the future by opening it. Opening a form is similar to opening a table. Before opening the form, however, the Forms object, rather than the Tables object, must be selected.

The following steps show how to open the Client form.

To Open a Form

1

• **With the Ashton James College database open and the Database window on the screen, click Forms on the Objects bar, and then right-click the Client form.**

The list of forms appears (Figure 1-62). The shortcut menu for the Client form appears.

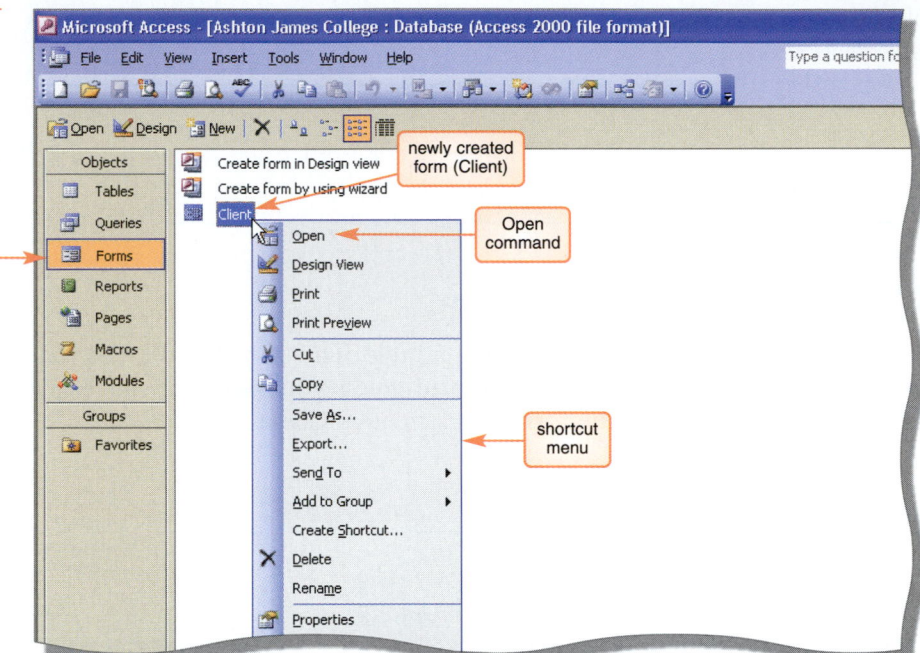

FIGURE 1-62

2

• **Click Open on the shortcut menu.**

The Client form appears (Figure 1-63).

Other Ways

1. Click Forms object, double-click desired form
2. Click Forms object, click desired form, click Open button on Database window toolbar
3. Click Forms object, click desired form, press ALT+O
4. In Voice Command mode, say "Forms, [click desired form], Open"

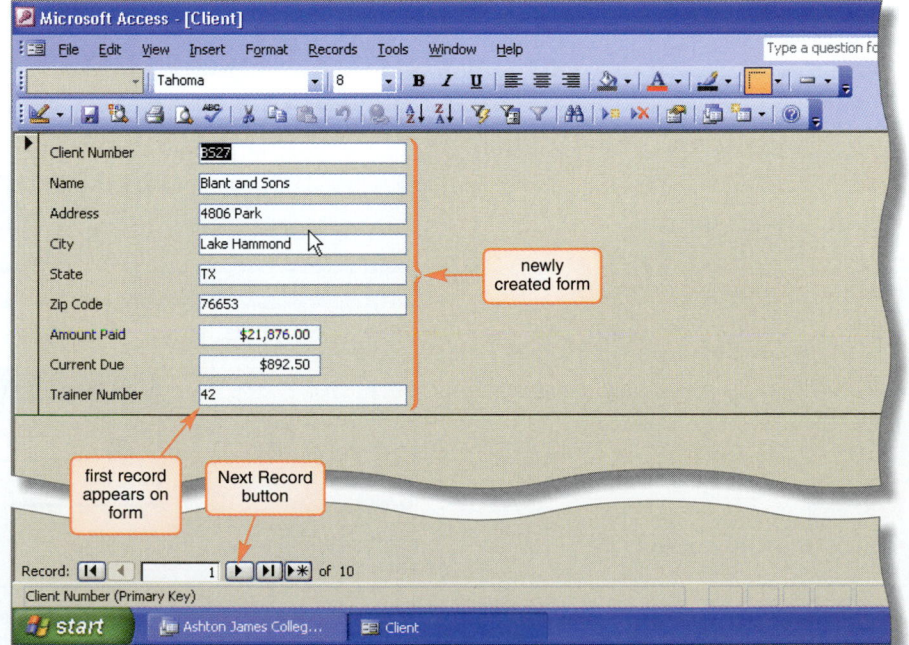

FIGURE 1-63

Using the Form

You can use the form just as you used Datasheet view. You use the Navigation buttons to move between records. You can add new records or change existing ones. To delete the record appearing on the screen, after selecting the record by clicking its record selector, press the DELETE key. Thus, you can perform database operations using either Form view or Datasheet view.

Because you can see only one record at a time in Form view, to see a different record, such as the fifth record, you must use the Navigation buttons to move to it. The following step illustrates moving from record to record in Form view.

To Use a Form

1

• **Click the Next Record button four times.**

Access displays the fifth record on the form (Figure 1-64).

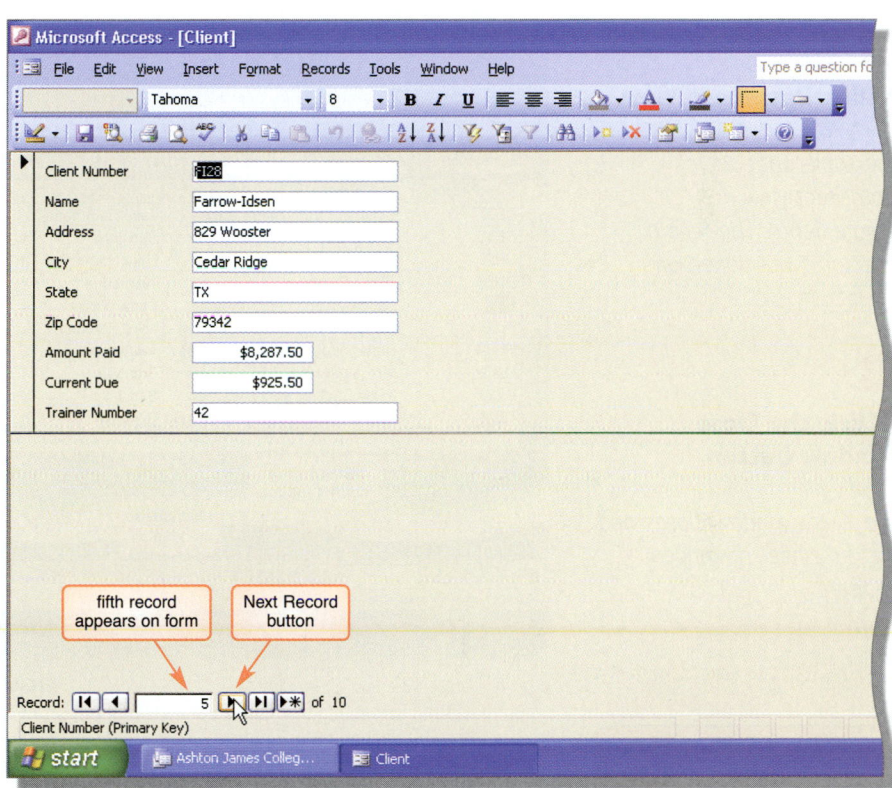

FIGURE 1-64

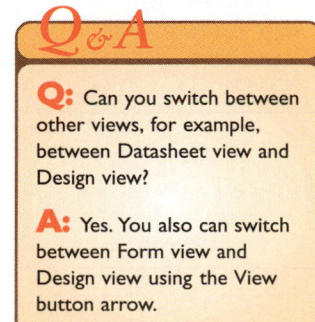

Q: Can you switch between other views, for example, between Datasheet view and Design view?

A: Yes. You also can switch between Form view and Design view using the View button arrow.

Switching Between Form View and Datasheet View

In some cases, after you have seen a record in Form view, you will want to switch to Datasheet view to see the collection of records. The steps on the next page show how to switch from Form view to Datasheet view.

To Switch from Form View to Datasheet View

1

• **Click the View button arrow on the Form View toolbar.**

The list of available views appears (Figure 1-65).

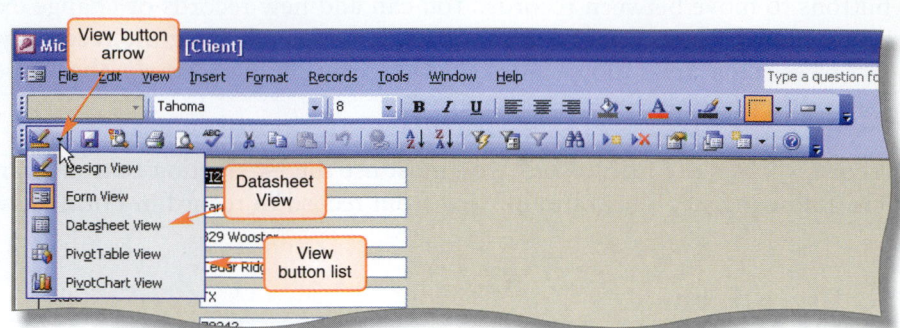

FIGURE 1-65

2

• **Click Datasheet View.**

The table appears in Datasheet view (Figure 1-66). The record selector is positioned on the fifth record.

3

• **Click the Close Window button.**

The Client window closes and the datasheet no longer appears.

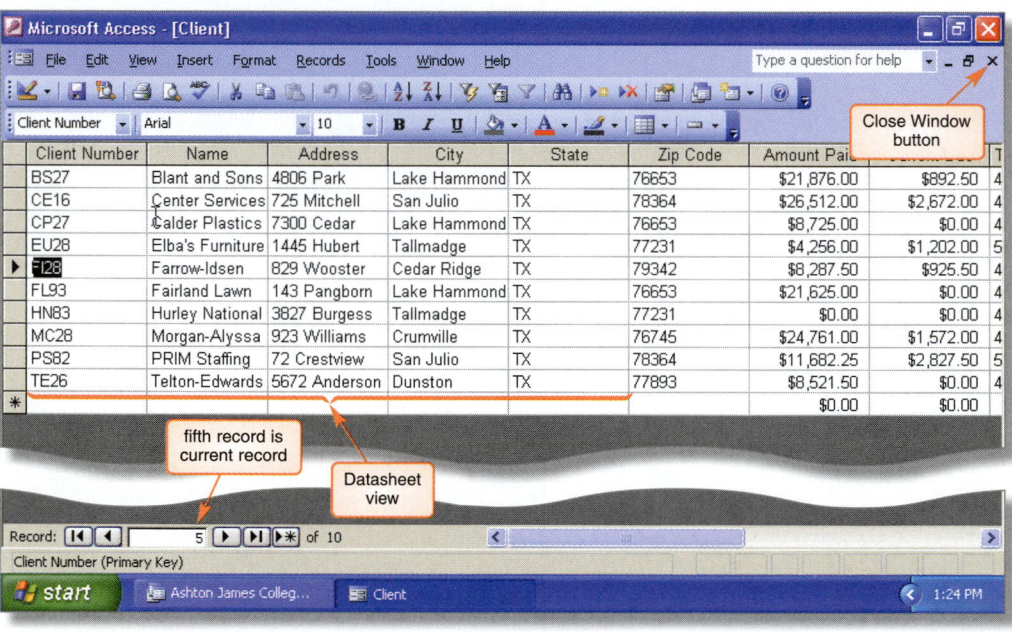

FIGURE 1-66

Creating a Report

Earlier in this project, you printed a table using the Print button. The report you produced was shown in Figure 1-37 on page AC 29. While this type of report presented the data in an organized manner, the format is very rigid. You cannot select the fields to appear, for example; the report automatically includes all the fields and they appear in precisely the same order as in the table. A way to change the title of the table is not available. Therefore, it will be the same as the name of the table.

In this section, you will create the report shown in Figure 1-67. This report features significant differences from the one in Figure 1-37. The portion at the top of the report in Figure 1-67, called a **page header**, contains a custom title. The contents of this page header appear at the top of each page. The **detail lines**, which are the lines that are printed for each record, contain only those fields you specify and in the order you specify.

Client Amount Report

Client Number	Name	Amount Paid	Current Due
BS27	Blant and Sons	$21,876.00	$892.50
CE16	Center Services	$26,512.00	$2,672.00
CP27	Calder Plastics	$8,725.00	$0.00
EU28	Elba's Furniture	$4,256.00	$1,202.00
FI28	Farrow-Idsen	$8,287.50	$925.50
FL93	Fairland Lawn	$21,625.00	$0.00
HN83	Hurley National	$0.00	$0.00
MC28	Morgan-Alyssa	$24,761.00	$1,572.00
PS82	PRIM Staffing	$11,682.25	$2,827.50
TE26	Telton-Edwards	$8,521.50	$0.00

FIGURE 1-67

The following steps show how to create the report in Figure 1-67.

To Create a Report

1

• **Click Tables on the Objects bar, and then make sure the Client table is selected.**

• **Click the New Object button arrow on the Database toolbar.**

The list of available objects appears (Figure 1-68).

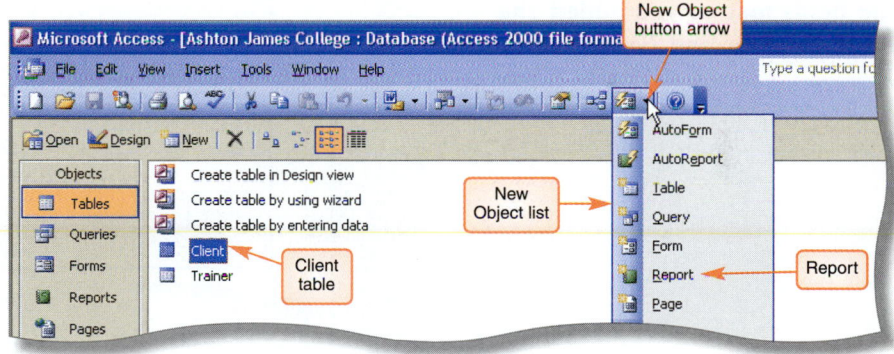

FIGURE 1-68

2

• **Click Report.**

Access displays the New Report dialog box (Figure 1-69).

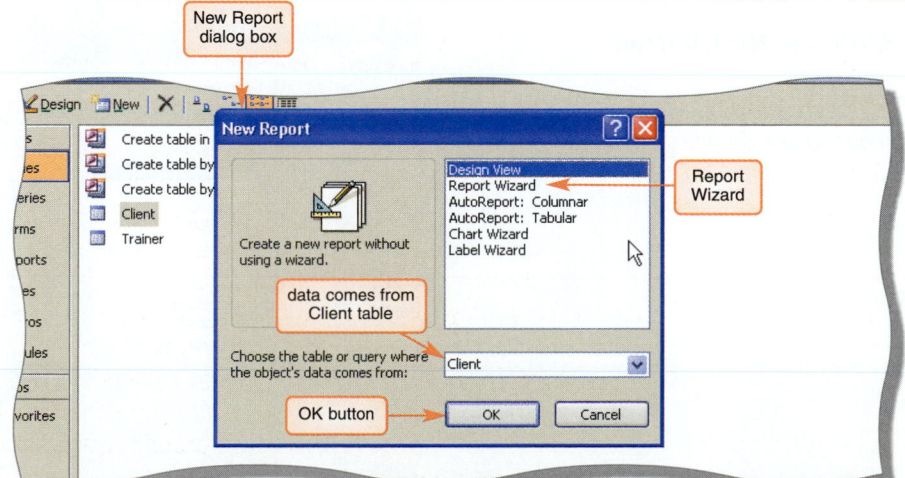

FIGURE 1-69

3

• **Click Report Wizard, and then click the OK button.**

Access displays the Report Wizard dialog box (Figure 1-70). As you click the Next button in this dialog box, a series of options helps you create the report.

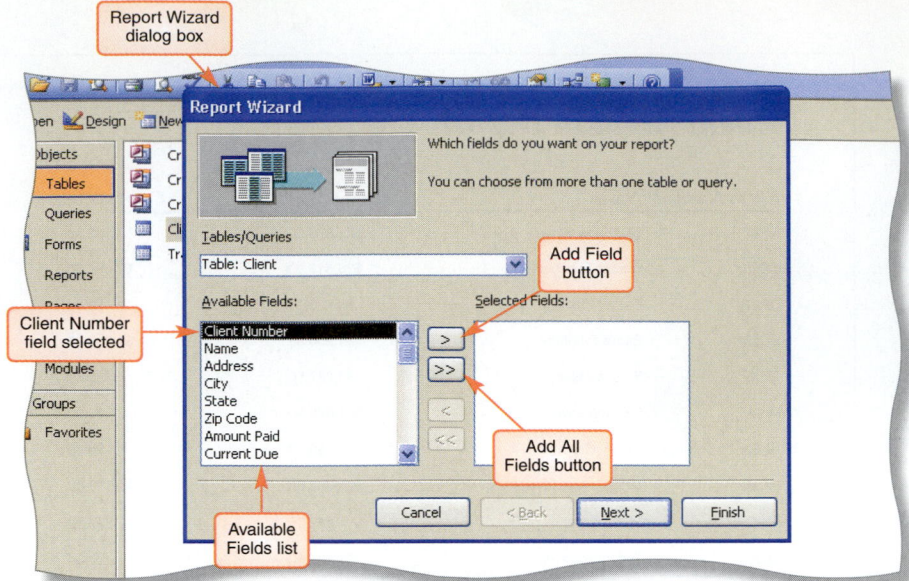

FIGURE 1-70

4

• **Click the Add Field button to add the Client Number field.**

• **Click the Add Field button to add the Name field.**

• **Add the Amount Paid and Current Due fields just as you added the Client Number and Name fields.**

The fields for the report appear in the Selected Fields box (Figure 1-71).

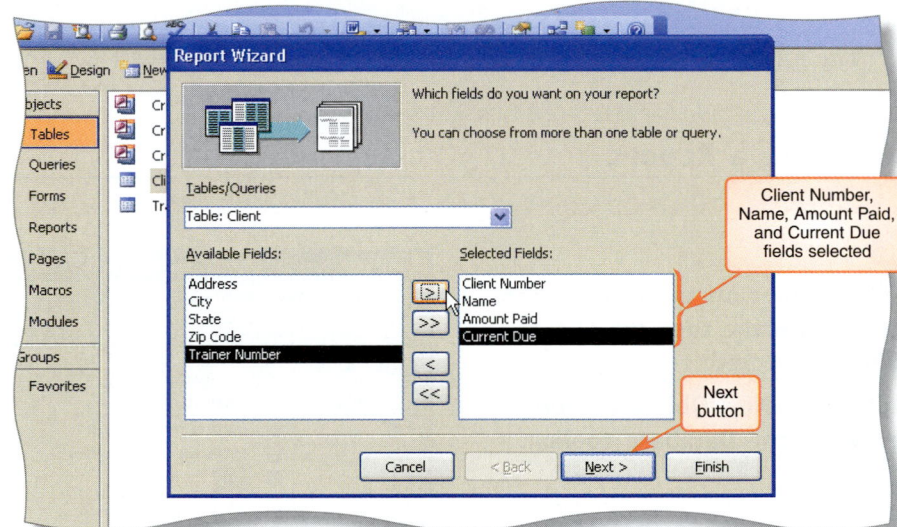

FIGURE 1-71

5

• **Click the Next button.**

The Report Wizard dialog box displays options to specify any grouping that is to take place (Figure 1-72).

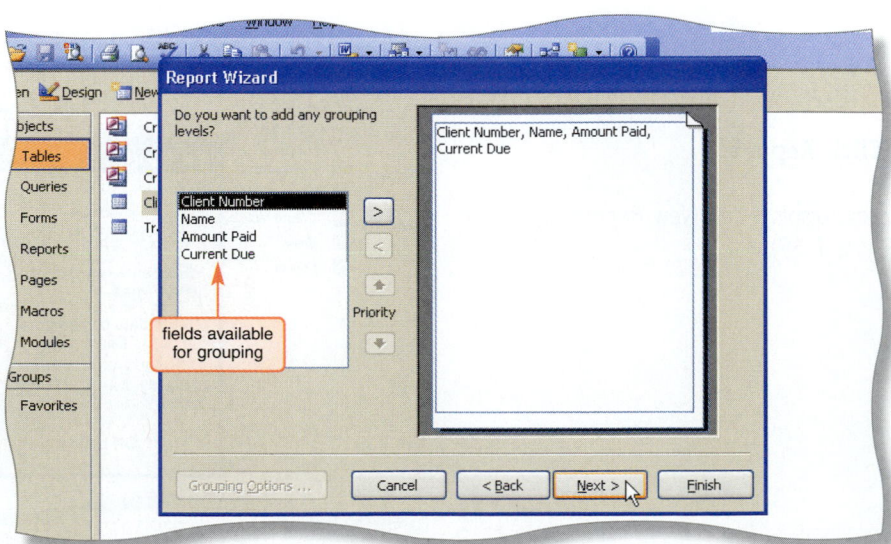

FIGURE 1-72

6

• **Because you will not specify any grouping, click the Next button in the Report Wizard dialog box.**

• **Click the Next button a second time because you will not need to change the sort order for the records.**

The Report Wizard dialog box displays options for changing the layout and orientation of the report (Figure 1-73).

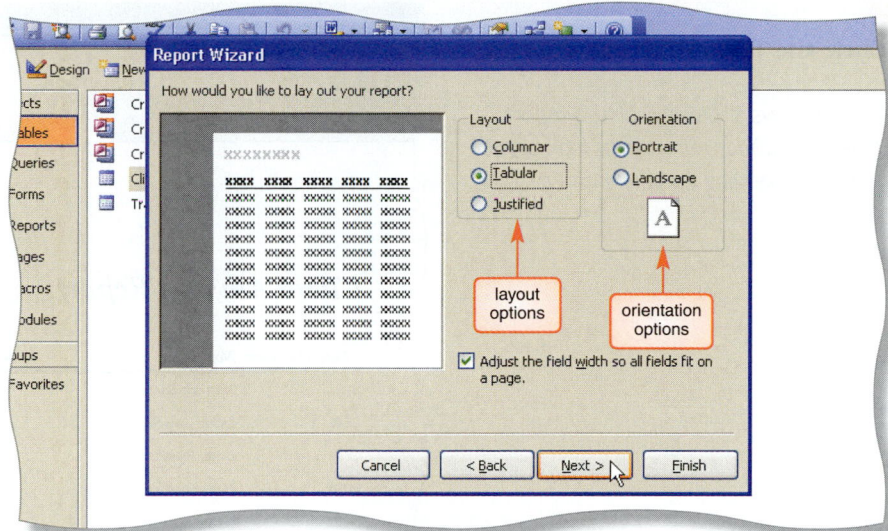

FIGURE 1-73

7

• **Make sure that Tabular is selected as the Layout and Portrait is selected as the Orientation, and then click the Next button.**

The Report Wizard dialog box displays options you can select for the style of the report (Figure 1-74).

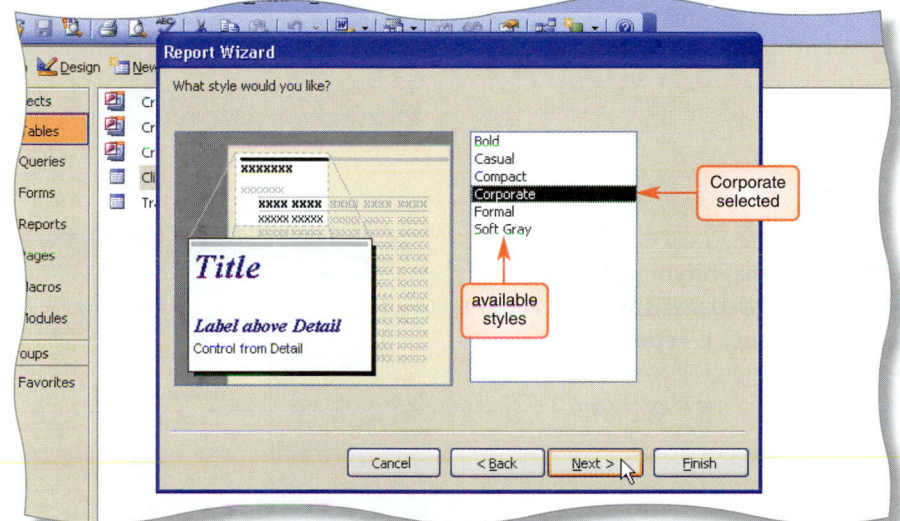

FIGURE 1-74

8

• **Be sure the Corporate style is selected, click the Next button, and then type** Client Amount Report **as the new title.**

The Report Wizard dialog box displays the new title of the report (Figure 1-75).

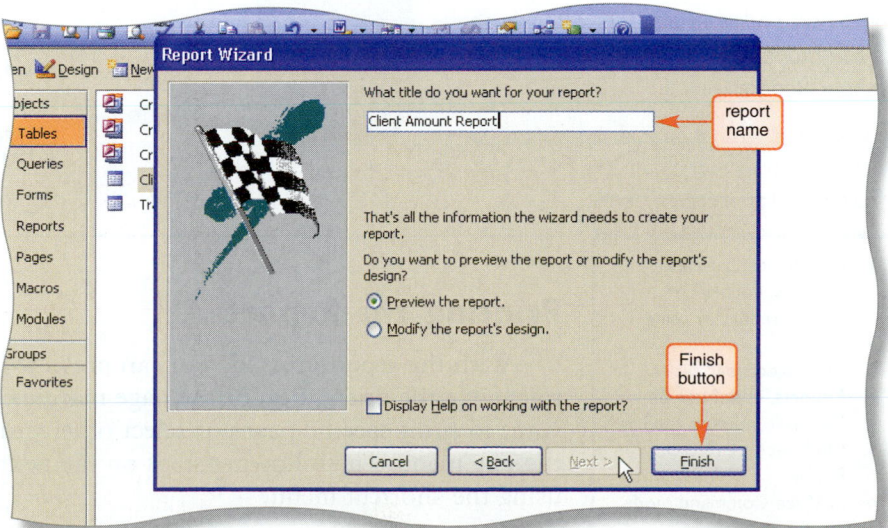

FIGURE 1-75

9

• **Click the Finish button.**

Access displays a preview of the report (Figure 1-76). Your report may look slightly different, depending on your printer.

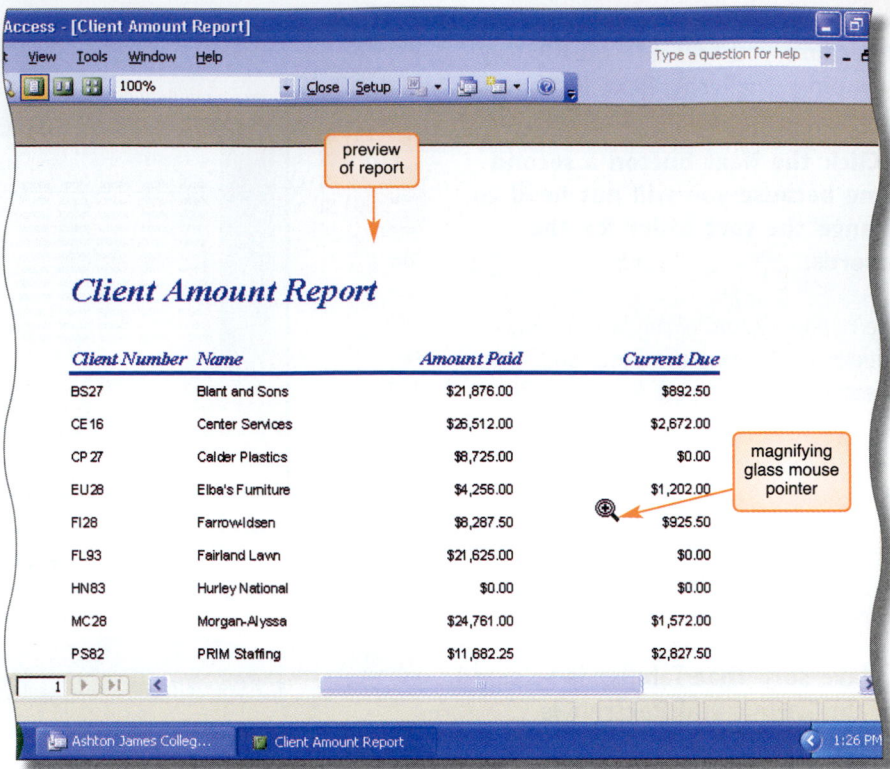

FIGURE 1-76

10

• **Click the magnifying glass mouse pointer anywhere within the report to see the entire report.**

The entire report appears (Figure 1-77).

11

• **Click the Close Window button in the Client Amount Report window.**

The report no longer appears. It has been saved automatically using the name Client Amount Report.

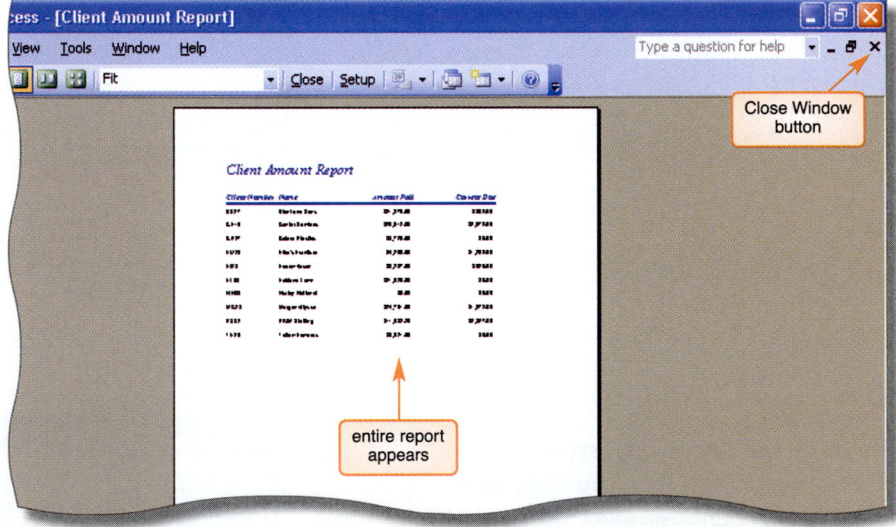

FIGURE 1-77

Other Ways

1. On Objects bar click Reports, double-click Create report by using wizard
2. On Objects bar click Reports, click New on Database window toolbar
3. On Insert menu click Report
4. In Voice Command mode, say "Insert, Report"

Printing the Report

With the report created, you can preview the report to determine if you need to change the orientation or the page margins. You also can print the report. If you want to print specific pages or select other print options, use the Print command on the File menu. The following steps on the next page show how to print a report using the shortcut menu.

To Print a Report

1

• **If necessary, click Reports on the Objects bar in the Database window.**

• **Right-click the Client Amount Report.**

The Client Amount Report is selected and the shortcut menu appears (Figure 1-78).

2

• **Click Print on the shortcut menu.**

The report prints. It should look similar to the one shown in Figure 1-67 on page AC 43.

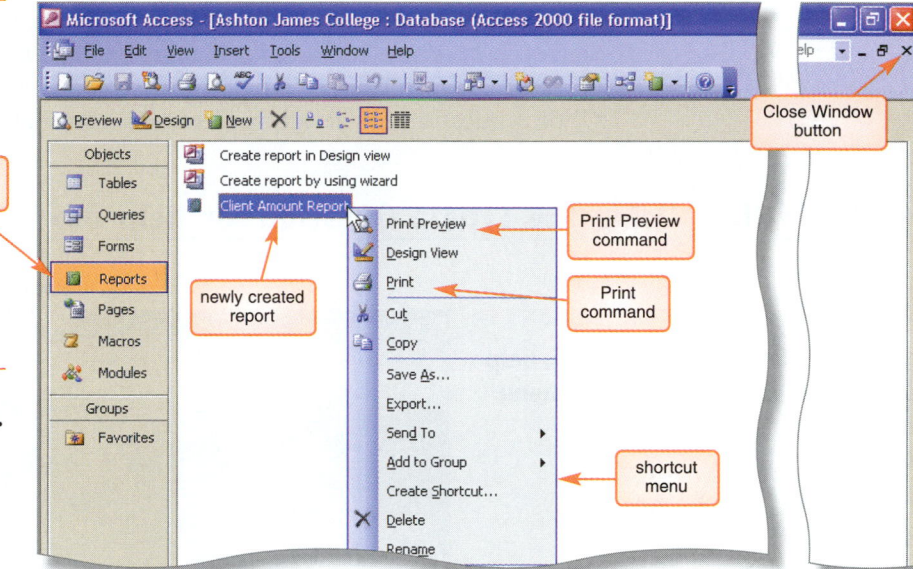

FIGURE 1-78

Closing the Database

After you have finished working with a database, you should close it. The following step closes the database by closing its Database window.

To Close a Database

1 **Click the Close Window button for the Ashton James College : Database window.**

Access Help System

At any time while you are using Access, you can get answers to questions by using the Access Help system. You can activate the Access Help system by using the Type a question for help box on the menu bar, by clicking the Microsoft Access Help button on the toolbar, or by clicking Help on the menu bar (Figure 1-79 on the next page). Used properly, this form of online assistance can increase your productivity and reduce your frustrations by minimizing the time you spend learning how to use Access.

The section on the next page shows how to get answers to your questions using the Type a question for help box. Additional information about using the Access Help system is available in Appendix A.

More About

The Access Help System

The best way to become familiar with the Access Help system is to use it. Appendix A includes detailed information on the Access Help system and exercises that will help you gain confidence in using it.

Obtaining Help Using the Type a Question for Help Box on the Menu Bar

The Type a question for help box on the right side of the menu bar lets you type in free-form questions, such as *how do I save* or *how do I create a Web page* or, you can type in terms, such as *copy*, *save*, or *formatting*. Access responds by displaying a list of topics related to what you entered. The following steps show how to use the Type a question for help box to obtain information on removing a primary key.

To Obtain Help Using the Type a Question for Help Box

1

• **Click the Type a question for help box on the right side of the menu bar.**

• **Type** how do I remove a primary key **in the box (Figure 1-79).**

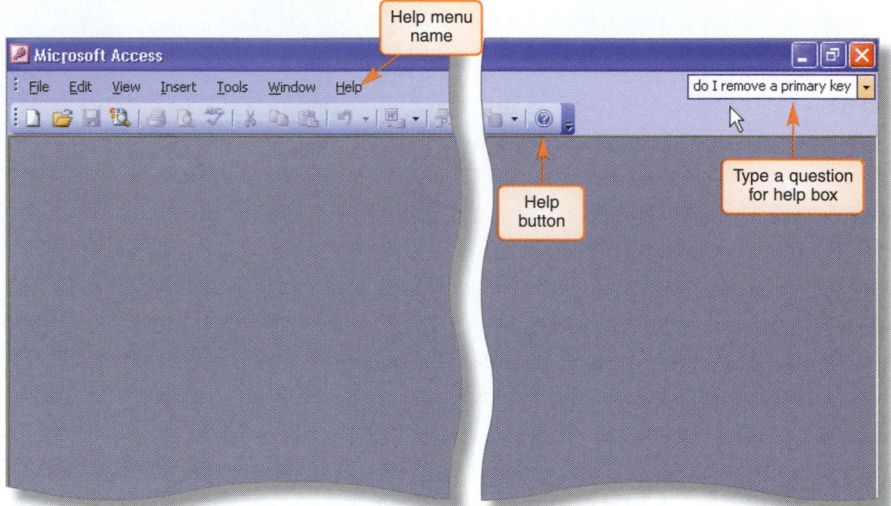

FIGURE 1-79

2

• **Press the ENTER key.**

Access displays the Search Results task pane, which includes a list of topics relating to the question, how do I remove a primary key (Figure 1-80). Your list may be different.

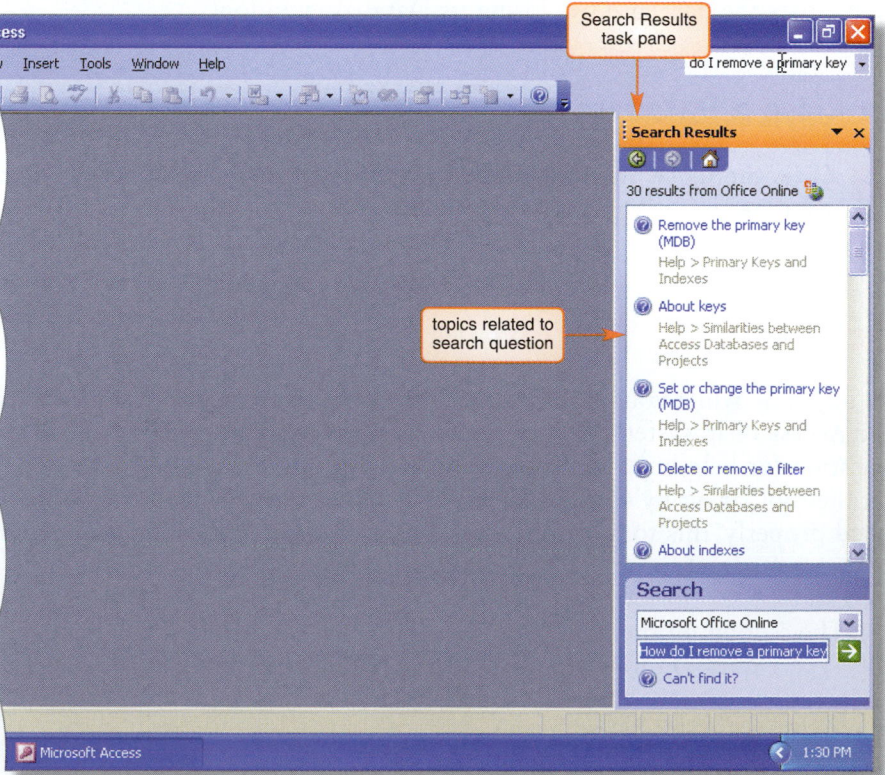

FIGURE 1-80

3

• **Point to the Remove the primary key (MDB) topic.**

The mouse pointer changes to a hand indicating it is pointing to a link (Figure 1-81).

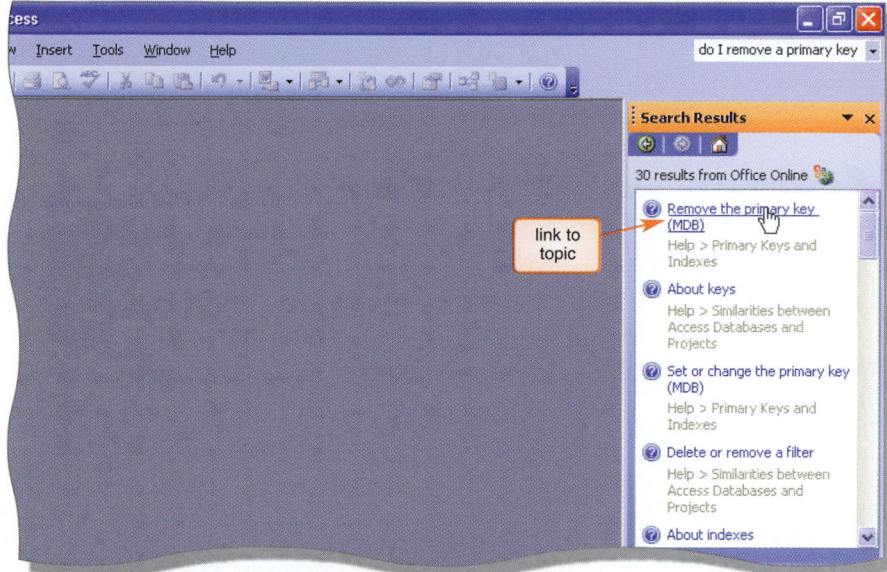

FIGURE 1-81

4

• **Click Remove the primary key (MDB).**

Access displays a Microsoft Office Access Help window that provides Help information about removing the primary key (Figure 1-82). Your window may be in a different position.

5

• **Click the Close button on the Microsoft Office Access Help window title bar.**

The Microsoft Access Help window closes.

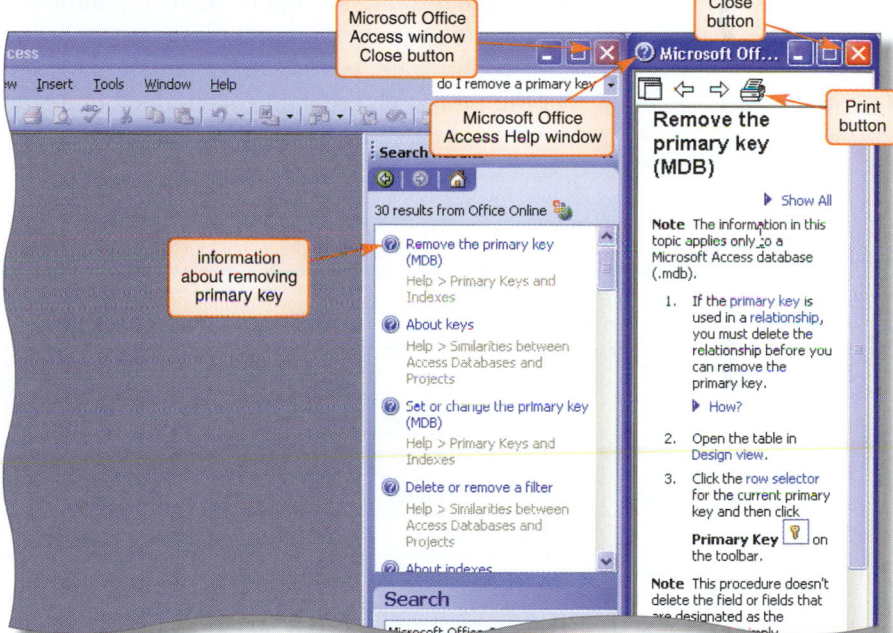

FIGURE 1-82

Use the buttons in the upper-left corner of the Microsoft Office Access Help window (Figure 1-82) to navigate through the Help system, and change the appearance and print the contents of the window.

As you enter questions and terms in the Type a question for help box, Access adds them to its list. Thus, if you click the Type a question for help box arrow, a list of previously asked questions and terms will appear.

Quitting Access

After you close a database, you can open another database, create a new database, or simply quit Access and return to the Windows desktop. The following step quits Access.

To Quit Access

1 **Click the Close button in the Microsoft Access window (see Figure 1-82 on the previous page).**

Designing a Database

Database design refers to the arrangement of data into tables and fields. In the example in this project, the design is specified, but in many cases, you will have to determine the design based on what you want the system to accomplish.

With large, complex databases, the database design process can be extensive. Major sections of advanced database textbooks are devoted to this topic. Often, however, you should be able to design a database effectively by keeping one simple principle in mind: design to remove redundancy. **Redundancy** means storing the same fact in more than one place.

To illustrate, you need to maintain the following information shown in Figure 1-83. In the figure, all the data is contained in a single table. Notice that the data for a given trainer (number, name, address, and so on) occurs on more than one record.

Client table

duplicate trainer names

CLIENT NUMBER	NAME	ADDRESS	...	CURRENT DUE	TRAINER NUMBER	LAST NAME	FIRST NAME	...
BS27	Blant and Sons	4806 Park	...	$892.50	42	Perry	Belinda	...
CE16	Center Services	725 Mitchell	...	$2,672.00	48	Stevens	Michael	...
CP27	Calder Plastics	7300 Cedar	...	$0.00	48	Stevens	Michael	...
EU28	Elba's Furniture	1445 Hubert	...	$1,202.00	53	Gonzalez	Manuel	...
FI28	Farrow-Idsen	829 Wooster	...	$925.50	42	Perry	Belinda	...
FL93	Fairland Lawn	143 Pangborn	...	$0.00	48	Stevens	Michael	...
HN83	Hurley National	3827 Burgess	...	$0.00	48	Stevens	Michael	...
MC28	Morgan-Alyssa	923 Williams	...	$1,572.00	42	Perry	Belinda	...
PS82	PRIM Staffing	72 Crestview	...	$2,827.50	53	Gonzalez	Manuel	...
TE26	Telton-Edwards	5672 Anderson	...	$0.00	48	Stevens	Michael	...

FIGURE 1-83

Storing this data on multiple records is an example of redundancy, which causes several problems, including:

1. Redundancy wastes space on the disk. The name of trainer 42 (Belinda Perry), for example, should be stored only once. Storing this fact several times is wasteful.

2. Redundancy makes updating the database more difficult. If, for example, Belinda Perry's name changes, her name would need to be changed in several different places.

3. A possibility of inconsistent data exists. If, for example, you change the name of Belinda Perry on client FI28's record to Belinda Martin, but do not change it on client BS27's record, the data is inconsistent. In both cases, the trainer number is 42, but the names are different.

The solution to the problem is to place the redundant data in a separate table, one in which the data no longer will be redundant. If, for example, you place the data for trainers in a separate table (Figure 1-84), the data for each trainer will appear only once.

More About

Database Design: Normalization

A special technique, called normalization, identifies and eliminates redundancy. For more information about normalization, visit the Access 2003 More About Web page (scsite.com/ac2003/more) and click Normalization.

trainer data is in separate table

Trainer table

TRAINER NUMBER	LAST NAME	FIRST NAME	ADDRESS	CITY	STATE	ZIP CODE	HOURLY RATE	YTD EARNINGS
42	Perry	Belinda	261 Porter	Burdett	TX	76734	$23.00	$27,620.00
48	Stevens	Michael	3135 Gill	Rockwood	TX	78884	$21.00	$23,567.50
53	Gonzalez	Manuel	265 Maxwell	Camino	TX	76574	$24.00	$29,885.00

Client table

CLIENT NUMBER	NAME	ADDRESS	CITY	STATE	ZIP CODE	AMOUNT PAID	CURRENT DUE	TRAINER NUMBER
BS27	Blant and Sons	4806 Park	Lake Hammond	TX	76653	$21,876.00	$892.50	42
CE16	Center Services	725 Mitchell	San Julio	TX	78364	$26,512.00	$2,672.00	48
CP27	Calder Plastics	7300 Cedar	Lake Hammond	TX	76653	$8,725.00	$0.00	48
EU28	Elba's Furniture	1445 Hubert	Tallmadge	TX	77231	$4,256.00	$1,202.00	53
FI28	Farrow-Idsen	829 Wooster	Cedar Ridge	TX	79342	$8,287.50	$925.50	42
FL93	Fairland Lawn	143 Pangborn	Lake Hammond	TX	76653	$21,625.00	$0.00	48
HN83	Hurley National	3827 Burgess	Tallmadge	TX	77231	$0.00	$0.00	48
MC28	Morgan-Alyssa	923 Williams	Crumville	TX	76745	$24,761.00	$1,572.00	42
PS82	PRIM Staffing	72 Crestview	San Julio	TX	78364	$11,682.25	$2,827.50	53
TE26	Telton-Edwards	5672 Anderson	Dunston	TX	77893	$8,521.50	$0.00	48

FIGURE 1-84

Notice that you need to have the trainer number in both tables. Without it, no way exists to tell which trainer is associated with which client. The remaining trainer data, however, was removed from the Client table and placed in the Trainer table. This new arrangement corrects the problems of redundancy in the following ways:

1. Because the data for each trainer is stored only once, space is not wasted.
2. Changing the name of a trainer is easy. You have only to change one row in the Trainer table.
3. Because the data for a trainer is stored only once, inconsistent data cannot occur.

Designing to omit redundancy will help you to produce good and valid database designs.

More About

Microsoft Certification

The Microsoft Office Specialist Certification program provides an opportunity for you to obtain a valuable industry credential — proof that you have the Access 2003 skills required by employers. For more information, see Appendix E, or visit the Access 2003 Certification Web page (scsite.com/ac2003/cert).

Project Summary

In Project 1, you learned about databases and database management systems. You learned how to create a database and how to create the tables within a database. You saw how to define the fields in a table by specifying the characteristics of the fields. You learned how to open a table, how to add records to it, and how to close it. You also printed the contents of a table. You learned how to use the Simple Query wizard to create a query that included columns from a table as well as how to enter a criterion to restrict the rows that were included. You created a form to view data on the screen and also created a custom report. You learned how to use Microsoft Access Help. Finally, you learned how to design a database to eliminate redundancy.

If you have a SAM user profile, you may have access to hands-on instruction, practice, and assessment of the skills covered in this project. Log in to your SAM account and go to your assignments page to see what your instructor has assigned.

What You Should Know

Having completed this project, you should be able to perform the tasks below. The tasks are listed in the same order they were presented in this project. For a list of the buttons, menus, toolbars, and commands introduced in this project, see the Quick Reference Summary at the back of this book and refer to the Page Number column.

1. Start Access   (AC 7)
2. Close the Language Bar   (AC 9)
3. Create a New Database   (AC 10)
4. Create a Table   (AC 17)
5. Define the Fields in a Table   (AC 19)
6. Close and Save a Table   (AC 21)
7. Add Records to a Table   (AC 23)
8. Close a Table and Database and Quit Access (AC 26)
9. Open a Database   (AC 26)
10. Add Additional Records to a Table   (AC 28)
11. Preview and Print the Contents of a Table (AC 30)
12. Create an Additional Table   (AC 33)
13. Add Records to an Additional Table   (AC 34)

14. Use the Simple Query Wizard to Create a Query (AC 34)
15. Use a Query   (AC 37)
16. Use the New Object Button to Create a Form (AC 38)
17. Close and Save a Form   (AC 39)
18. Open a Form   (AC 40)
19. Use a Form   (AC 41)
20. Switch from Form View to Datasheet View (AC 42)
21. Create a Report   (AC 43)
22. Print a Report   (AC 47)
23. Close a Database   (AC 47)
24. Obtain Help Using the Type a Question for Help Box   (AC 48)
25. Quit Access   (AC 50)

Learn It Online

Instructions: To complete the Learn It Online exercises, start your browser, click the Address bar, and then enter the Web address scsite.com/ac2003/learn. When the Access 2003 Learn It Online page is displayed, follow the instructions in the exercises below. Each exercise has instructions for printing your results, either for your own records or for submission to your instructor.

1 Project Reinforcement TF, MC, and SA

Below Access Project 1, click the Project Reinforcement link. Print the quiz by clicking Print on the File menu for each page. Answer each question.

2 Flash Cards

Below Access Project 1, click the Flash Cards link and read the instructions. Type 20 (or a number specified by your instructor) in the Number of playing cards text box, type your name in the Enter your Name text box, and then click the Flip Card button. When the flash card is displayed, read the question and then click the ANSWER box arrow to select an answer. Flip through Flash Cards. If your score is 15 (75%) correct or greater, click Print on the File menu to print your results. If your score is less than 15 (75%) correct, then redo this exercise by clicking the Replay button.

3 Practice Test

Below Access Project 1, click the Practice Test link. Answer each question, enter your first and last name at the bottom of the page, and then click the Grade Test button. When the graded practice test is displayed on your screen, click Print on the File menu to print a hard copy. Continue to take practice tests until you score 80% or better.

4 Who Wants To Be a Computer Genius?

Below Access Project 1, click the Computer Genius link. Read the instructions, enter your first and last name at the bottom of the page, and then click the PLAY button. When your score is displayed, click the PRINT RESULTS link to print a hard copy.

5 Wheel of Terms

Below Access Project 1, click the Wheel of Terms link. Read the instructions, and then enter your first and last name and your school name. Click the PLAY button. When your score is displayed, right-click the score and then click Print on the shortcut menu to print a hard copy.

6 Crossword Puzzle Challenge

Below Access Project 1, click the Crossword Puzzle Challenge link. Read the instructions, and then enter your first and last name. Click the SUBMIT button. Work the crossword puzzle. When you are finished, click the Submit button. When the crossword puzzle is redisplayed, click the Print Puzzle button to print a hard copy.

7 Tips and Tricks

Below Access Project 1, click the Tips and Tricks link. Click a topic that pertains to Project 1. Right-click the information and then click Print on the shortcut menu. Construct a brief example of what the information relates to in Access to confirm you understand how to use the tip or trick.

8 Newsgroups

Below Access Project 1, click the Newsgroups link. Click a topic that pertains to Project 1. Print three comments.

9 Expanding Your Horizons

Below Access Project 1, click the Expanding Your Horizons link. Click a topic that pertains to Project 1. Print the information. Construct a brief example of what the information relates to in Access to confirm you understand the contents of the article.

10 Search Sleuth

Below Access Project 1, click the Search Sleuth link. To search for a term that pertains to this project, select a term below the Project 1 title and then use the Google search engine at google.com (or any major search engine) to display and print two Web pages that present information on the term.

11 Access Online Training

Below Access Project 1, click the Access Online Training link. When your browser displays the Microsoft Office Online Web page, click the Access link. Click one of the Access courses that covers one or more of the objectives listed at the beginning of the project on page AC 4. Print the first page of the course before stepping through it.

12 Office Marketplace

Below Access Project 1, click the Office Marketplace link. When your browser displays the Microsoft Office Online Web page, click the Office Marketplace link. Click a topic that relates to Access. Print the first page.

1 Changing Data, Creating Queries, and Creating Reports

Instructions: Start Access. Open the database Begon Pest Control from the Data Disk. See the inside back cover for instructions for downloading the Data Disk or see your instructor for information about accessing the files required in this book.

Begon Pest Control is a company that performs pest control services for commercial businesses. Begon has a database that keeps track of its technicians and customers. The database has two tables. The Customer table contains data on the customers who use the services of Begon. The Technician table contains data on the individuals employed by Begon. The structure and data are shown for the Customer table in Figure 1-85 and for the Technician table in Figure 1-86.

Structure of Customer table

FIELD NAME	DATA TYPE	FIELD SIZE	PRIMARY KEY?	DESCRIPTION
Customer Number	Text	4	Yes	Customer Number (Primary Key)
Name	Text	20		Customer Name
Address	Text	15		Street Address
City	Text	15		City
State	Text	2		State (Two-Character Abbreviation)
Zip Code	Text	5		Zip Code (Five-Character Version)
Balance	Currency			Amount Owed by Customer
Technician Number	Text	3		Number of Customer's Technician

Customer table

CUSTOMER NUMBER	NAME	ADDRESS	CITY	STATE	ZIP CODE	BALANCE	TECHNICIAN NUMBER
AT23	Atlas Repair	220 Beard	Kady	TN	42514	$335.00	203
AZ01	AZ Auto	412 Beechwood	Conradt	TN	42547	$300.00	210
BL35	Blanton Shoes	443 Chedder	Kady	TN	42514	$290.00	210
CJ45	C Joe Diner	87 Fletcher	Carlton	TN	52764	$0.00	214
CM90	Cramden Co.	234 Fairlawn	Conradt	TN	42546	$355.00	203
HI25	Hill Crafts	245 Beard	Kady	TN	42514	$334.00	210
KL50	Klean n Dri	378 Stout	Carlton	TN	52764	$365.00	210
MC10	Moss Carpet	109 Fletcher	Carlton	TN	52764	$398.00	203
PV83	Prime Video	734 Lanton	Conradt	TN	42547	$0.00	214
SE05	Servete Mfg Co.	879 Redfern	Kady	TN	42515	$343.00	210

FIGURE 1-85

Apply Your Knowledge

Structure of Technician table

FIELD NAME	DATA TYPE	FIELD SIZE	PRIMARY KEY?	DESCRIPTION
Technician Number	Text	3	Yes	Technician Number (Primary Key)
Last Name	Text	10		Last Name of Technician
First Name	Text	8		First Name of Technician
Address	Text	15		Street Address
City	Text	15		City
State	Text	2		State (Two-Character Abbreviation)
Zip Code	Text	5		Zip Code (Five-Character Version)
Hourly Rate	Currency			Hourly Pay Rate

Technician table

TECHNICIAN NUMBER	LAST NAME	FIRST NAME	ADDRESS	CITY	STATE	ZIP CODE	HOURLY RATE
203	Estevez	Miguel	467 Clay	Kady	TN	42517	$11.50
210	Hillsdale	Rachel	78 Parkton	Conradt	TN	42547	$11.75
214	Liu	Chou	897 North	Carlton	TN	52764	$11.65
220	Short	Chris	111 Maple	Conradt	TN	42547	$11.50

FIGURE 1-86

Instructions: Perform the following tasks:

1. Open the Customer table and change the Technician Number for customer KL50 to 214.
2. Print the Customer table.
3. Use the Simple Query Wizard to create a new query to display and print the customer number, name, and technician number for records in the Customer table as shown in Figure 1-87 on the next page.
4. Save the query as Customer-Technician Query and then close the query.
5. Open the Customer-Technician Query in Design View and restrict the query results to only those customers whose technician number is 210.
6. Print the query but do not save the changes.
7. Create the report shown in Figure 1-88 on the next page for the Customer table.
8. Print the report.

(continued)

Apply Your Knowledge

Changing Data, Creating Queries, and Creating Reports *(continued)*

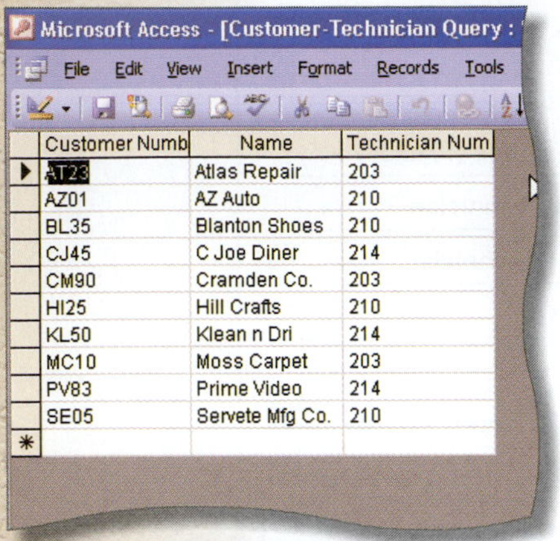

Microsoft Access - [Customer-Technician Query :

File Edit View Insert Format Records Tools

Customer Numb	Name	Technician Num
AT23	Atlas Repair	203
AZ01	AZ Auto	210
BL35	Blanton Shoes	210
CJ45	C Joe Diner	214
CM90	Cramden Co.	203
HI25	Hill Crafts	210
KL50	Klean n Dri	214
MC10	Moss Carpet	203
PV83	Prime Video	214
SE05	Servete Mfg Co.	210
*		

FIGURE 1-87

Customer Amount Report

Customer Number	Name	Balance
AT23	Atlas Repair	$335.00
AZ01	AZ Auto	$300.00
BL35	Blanton Shoes	$290.00
CJ45	C Joe Diner	$0.00
CM90	Cramden Co.	$355.00
HI25	Hill Crafts	$334.00
KL50	Klean n Dri	$365.00
MC10	Moss Carpet	$398.00
PV83	Prime Video	$0.00
SE05	Servete Mfg Co.	$343.00

FIGURE 1-88

In the Lab

1 Creating the Birds2U Database

Problem: Birds2U is a new online retailer. The company specializes in products for bird and nature enthusiasts. The database consists of two tables. The Item table contains information on items available for sale. The Supplier table contains information on the companies that supply the items.

Instructions: Perform the following tasks:

1. Create a new database in which to store all the objects related to the items for sale. Call the database Birds2U.
2. Create the Item table using the structure shown in Figure 1-89. Use the name Item for the table.
3. Add the data shown in Figure 1-89 to the Item table.
4. Print the Item table.

In the Lab

Structure of Item table

FIELD NAME	DATA TYPE	FIELD SIZE	PRIMARY KEY?	DESCRIPTION
Item Code	Text	4	Yes	Item Code (Primary Key)
Description	Text	20		Description of Item
On Hand	Number			Number of Units On Hand
Cost	Currency			Cost of Item
Selling Price	Currency			Selling Price of Item
Supplier Code	Text	2		Code of Item's Supplier

Item table

ITEM CODE	DESCRIPTION	ON HAND	COST	SELLING PRICE	SUPPLIER CODE
BA35	Bat House	14	$43.50	$45.50	21
BB01	Bird Bath	2	$82.10	$86.25	13
BE19	Bee Box	7	$39.80	$42.50	21
BL06	Bluebird House	9	$14.35	$15.99	13
BU24	Butterfly Box	6	$36.10	$37.75	21
GF12	Globe Feeder	12	$14.80	$16.25	05
HF01	Hummingbird Feeder	5	$11.35	$14.25	05
PM05	Purple Martin House	3	$67.10	$69.95	13
SF03	Suet Feeder	7	$8.05	$9.95	05
WF10	Window Feeder	10	$14.25	$15.95	05

FIGURE 1-89

5. Create the Supplier table using the structure shown in Figure 1-90 on the next page. Use the name Supplier for the table.
6. Add the data shown in Figure 1-90 to the Supplier table.
7. Print the Supplier table.
8. Create a form for the Supplier table. Use the name Supplier for the form.
9. Open the form you created and change the address for Supplier Code 17 to 56 Beechwood.
10. Create and print the report shown in Figure 1-91 on the next page for the Item table.

(continued)

In the Lab

Creating the Birds2U Database *(continued)*

Structure of Supplier table

FIELD NAME	DATA TYPE	FIELD SIZE	PRIMARY KEY?	DESCRIPTION
Supplier Code	Text	2	Yes	Supplier Code (Primary Key)
Name	Text	20		Supplier Name
Address	Text	15		Street Address
City	Text	15		City
State	Text	2		State (Two-Character Abbreviation)
Zip Code	Text	5		Zip Code (Five-Character Version)
Telephone Number	Text	12		Telephone Number (999-999-9999 Version)

Supplier table

SUPPLIER CODE	NAME	ADDRESS	CITY	STATE	ZIP CODE	TELEPHONE NUMBER
05	All Birds Supply	234 Southward	Elgin	AZ	85165	602-555-6756
13	Bird Casa Ltd	38 Junction	Grandber	TX	78628	512-555-3402
17	Lawn Fixtures	56 Beecham	Holligan	CA	95418	707-555-4545
21	Natural Woods	67 Main	Ghostman	MI	49301	610-555-3333

FIGURE 1-90

Inventory Report

Item Code	Description	On Hand	Cost
BA35	Bat House	14	$43.50
BB01	Bird Bath	2	$82.10
BE19	Bee Box	7	$39.80
BL06	Bluebird House	9	$14.35
BU24	Butterfly Box	6	$36.10
GF12	Globe Feeder	12	$14.80
HF01	Hummingbird Feeder	5	$11.35
PM05	Purple Martin House	3	$67.10
SF03	Suet Feeder	7	$8.05
WF10	Window Feeder	10	$14.25

FIGURE 1-91

In the Lab

2 Creating the Babbage Bookkeeping Database

Problem: Babbage Bookkeeping is a local company that provides bookkeeping services to several small businesses in the area. The database consists of two tables. The Client table contains information on the businesses that use Babbage's services. The Bookkeeper table contains information on the bookkeeper assigned to the business.

Instructions: Perform the following tasks:

1. Create a new database in which to store all the objects related to the bookkeeping data. Call the database Babbage Bookkeeping.
2. Create and print the Client table using the structure and data shown in Figure 1-92. Then, create and print the Bookkeeper table using the structure and data shown in Figure 1-93 on the next page.

Structure of Client table

FIELD NAME	DATA TYPE	FIELD SIZE	PRIMARY KEY?	DESCRIPTION
Client Number	Text	3	Yes	Client Number (Primary Key)
Name	Text	20		Name of Client
Address	Text	15		Street Address
City	Text	15		City
Zip Code	Text	5		Zip Code (Five-Character Version)
Balance	Currency			Amount Currently Owed for Services
Bookkeeper Number	Text	2		Number of Client's Bookkeeper

Client table

CLIENT NUMBER	NAME	ADDRESS	CITY	ZIP CODE	BALANCE	BOOKKEEPER NUMBER
A54	Afton Mills	612 Revere	Grant City	58120	$315.50	22
A62	Atlas Suppliers	227 Dandelion	Empeer	58216	$525.00	24
B26	Blake-Scripps	557 Maum	Grant City	58120	$229.50	24
D76	Dege Grocery	446 Linton	Portage	59130	$485.75	34
G56	Grand Cleaners	337 Abelard	Empeer	58216	$265.00	22
H21	Hill Shoes	247 Fulton	Grant City	58121	$228.50	24
J77	Jones Plumbing	75 Getty	Portage	59130	$0.00	24
M26	Mohr Crafts	665 Maum	Empeer	58216	$312.50	22
S56	SeeSaw Ind.	31 Liatris	Portage	59130	$362.50	34
T45	Tate Repair	824 Revere	Grant City	58120	$254.00	24

FIGURE 1-92

(continued)

In the Lab

Creating the Babbage Bookkeeping Database *(continued)*

Structure of Bookkeeper table

FIELD NAME	DATA TYPE	FIELD SIZE	PRIMARY KEY?	DESCRIPTION
Bookkeeper Number	Text	2	Yes	Bookkeeper Number (Primary Key)
Last Name	Text	10		Last Name of Bookkeeper
First Name	Text	8		First Name of Bookkeeper
Address	Text	15		Street Address
City	Text	15		City
Zip Code	Text	5		Zip Code (Five-Character Version)
Hourly Rate	Currency			Hourly Rate
YTD Earnings	Currency			Year-to-Date Earnings

Bookkeeper table

BOOKKEEPER NUMBER	LAST NAME	FIRST NAME	ADDRESS	CITY	ZIP CODE	HOURLY RATE	YTD EARNINGS
22	Lewes	Johanna	26 Cotton	Portage	59130	$14.50	$18,245.00
24	Rodriguez	Mario	79 Marsden	Grant City	58120	$13.50	$17,745.50
34	Wong	Choi	263 Topper	Empeer	58216	$14.00	$16,750.25

FIGURE 1-93

3. Change the Bookkeeper Number for client J77 to 34.
4. Use the Simple Query Wizard to create a new query to display and print the Client Number, Name, and Bookkeeper Number for all clients where the bookkeeper number is 24.
5. Create and print the report shown in Figure 1-94 for the Client table.

Balance Due Report

Client Number	Name	Balance
A54	Afton Mills	$315.50
A62	Atlas Suppliers	$525.00
B26	Blake-Scripps	$229.50
D76	Dege Grocery	$485.75
G56	Grand Cleaners	$265.00
H21	Hill Shoes	$228.50
J77	Jones Plumbing	$0.00
M26	Mohr Crafts	$312.50
S56	SeeSaw Ind.	$362.50
T45	Tate Repair	$254.00

FIGURE 1-94

In the Lab

3 Creating the City Guide Database

Problem: The local chamber of commerce publishes a guide for newcomers. To help finance the guide, the chamber includes advertisements from local businesses. Advertising representatives receive a commission based on the advertising revenues they generate. The database consists of two tables. The Advertiser table contains information on the businesses that advertise in the guide. The Ad Rep table contains information on the advertising representative assigned to the account.

Instructions Part 1: Using the data shown in Figures 1-95 and 1-96 on the next page create the City Guide database, the Advertiser table, and the Ad Rep table. Note that the Ad Rep table uses the number data type. Print the tables. Then, create a form for the Advertiser table.

Structure of Advertiser table

FIELD NAME	DATA TYPE	FIELD SIZE	PRIMARY KEY?	DESCRIPTION
Advertiser Number	Text	4	Yes	Advertiser Number (Primary Key)
Name	Text	20		Name of Advertiser
Address	Text	15		Street Address
Zip Code	Text	5		Zip Code (Five-Character Version)
Telephone Number	Text	8		Telephone Number (999-9999 Version)
Balance	Currency			Amount Currently Owed
Amount Paid	Currency			Amount Paid Year-to-Date
Ad Rep Number	Text	2		Number of Advertising Representative

Data for Advertiser table

ADVERTISER NUMBER	NAME	ADDRESS	ZIP CODE	TELEPHONE NUMBER	BALANCE	AMOUNT PAID	AD REP NUMBER
A228	Adam's Music	47 Berton	19363	555-0909	$90.00	$565.00	26
B103	Barbecue Joint	483 Cantor	19363	555-8990	$185.00	$825.00	29
C048	Chloe's Salon	10 Main	19362	555-2334	$0.00	$375.00	29
C135	Creative Toys	26 Jefferson	19362	555-1357	$130.00	$865.00	32
D217	Dog Groomers	33 Maple	19362	555-2468	$290.00	$515.00	26
G346	Gold's Clothes	196 Lincoln	19364	555-3579	$0.00	$805.00	29
M321	Meat Shoppe	234 Magnolia	19363	555-6802	$215.00	$845.00	29
P124	Palace Theatre	22 Main	19364	555-8024	$65.00	$180.00	26
S111	Suds n Spuds	10 Jefferson	19365	555-5791	$465.00	$530.00	32
W456	Western Wear	345 Oaktree	19363	555-7913	$105.00	$265.00	26

FIGURE 1-95

(continued)

Creating the City Guide Database (continued)

Structure for Ad Rep table

FIELD NAME	DATA TYPE	FIELD SIZE	PRIMARY KEY?	DESCRIPTION
Ad Rep Number	Text	2	Yes	Advertising Rep Number (Primary Key)
Last Name	Text	10		Last Name of Advertising Rep
First Name	Text	8		First Name of Advertising Rep
Address	Text	15		Street Address
City	Text	15		City
Zip Code	Text	5		Zip Code (Five-Character Version)
Comm Rate	Number	Double		Commission Rate on Advertising Sales
Commission	Currency			Year-to-Date Total Commissions

Data for Ad Rep table

AD REP NUMBER	LAST NAME	FIRST NAME	ADDRESS	CITY	ZIP CODE	COMM RATE	COMMISSION
26	Febo	Jen	57 Barton	Crescent	19111	0.09	$6,500.00
29	Martinson	Kyle	87 Pearl	Newton	19124	0.08	$6,250.00
32	Rogers	Elena	45 Magret	San Luis	19362	0.09	$7,000.00

FIGURE 1-96

Instructions Part 2: Correct the following error. The ad rep assigned to the Meat Shoppe account should be Elena Rogers. Use the form you created to make the correction, and then print the form showing the corrected record. To print the form, open the form, click File on the menu bar, and then click Print. Click Selected Records(s) as the Print Range. Click the OK button.

Instructions Part 3: Create a query to find which accounts Kyle Martinson represents. Print the results. Prepare an advertiser status report that lists the advertiser's number, name, balance currently owed, and amount paid to date.

Cases and Places

The difficulty of these case studies varies:
■ are the least difficult and ■■ are more difficult. The last exercise is a group exercise.

1 ■   To help finance your college education, you formed a small business. You provide dog-walking services to local residents. Dog walkers are paid by the walk for each dog they walk. The business has grown rapidly and you now have several other students working for you. You realize that you need to computerize your business.

Design and create a database to store the data that College Dog Walkers needs to manage its business. Then create the necessary tables and enter the data from the Case 1-1 College Dog Walkers Word document on the Data Disk. Print the tables. See the inside back cover of this book for instructions for downloading the Data Disk or see your instructor for information on accessing the files required in this book.

2 ■   The Health and Physical Education department at your college recognized early that personal training would be a growth field. One of your friends graduated from the program and has started a company, InPerson Fitness Company. The company specializes in personal training in the comfort of the customer's home. It designs exercise programs for clients based on each person's health history, abilities, and fitness objectives. The company is expanding rapidly and you have been hired to computerize the business.

Design and create a database to store the data that InPerson Fitness needs to manage its business. Then create the necessary tables and enter the data from the Case 1-2 InPerson Fitness Word document on the Data Disk. Print the tables. See the inside back cover of this book for instructions for downloading the Data Disk or see your instructor for information on accessing the files required in this book.

3 ■■   Regional Books is a local bookstore that specializes in books that are of local interest. These are books that are set in the region or are written by authors who live in the area. The owner has asked you to create and update a database that she can use to keep track of the books she has in stock.

Design and create a database to store the book data. To create the Books table, use the Table Wizard and select the Books table. You do not need to select all the fields the Table Wizard provides and you can rename the fields in the table. (*Hint*: See More About Creating a Table: The Table Wizard on page AC 15.) Enter the data from the Case 1-3 Regional Books Word document on the Data Disk. Print the tables. Prepare a sample query and a sample report to illustrate to the owner the types of tasks that can be done with a database management system. See the inside back cover of this book for instructions for downloading the Data Disk or see your instructor for information on accessing the files required in this book.

Cases and Places

4 ■■　The Campus Housing office at the local university provides a listing of available off-campus rentals by private owners. The office would like to make this listing available on the campus Web site. The administrator has asked you to create and update a database that can store information about available off-campus housing. The housing list is in the Case 1-4 Campus Housing Word document on the Data Disk. A listing that has 0 bedrooms is either an efficiency apartment or a room for rent in a home. Distance indicates the rental unit's distance in miles from the university. Parking signifies whether reserved parking is available with the unit.

Design and create a database to meet the needs of the Campus Housing office. Then create the necessary tables, enter the data from the Case 1-4 Campus Housing Word document on the Data Disk. Print the tables. Prepare a sample form, sample query, and sample report to illustrate to the office the types of tasks that can be done with a database management system. See the inside back cover of this book for instructions for downloading the Data Disk or see your instructor for information on accessing the files required in this book.

5 ■■　**Working Together**　Conducting a job search requires careful preparation. In addition to preparing a resume and cover letter, you will need to research the companies for which you are interested in working and contact these companies to let them know of your interest and qualifications. Microsoft Access can help you manage the job search process. The Database Wizard includes a Contact Management template that can create a database that will help you keep track of your job contacts.

Have each member of your team explore the features of the Database Wizard and determine individually which fields should be included in a Contact Management database. As a group, review your choices and decide on one common design. Prepare a short paper for your instructor that explains why your team chose those particular fields to include in the database.

After agreeing on the database design, assign one member to create the database using the Database Wizard. Every other team member should research a company and add the data to the database. Print the alphabetical contact listing that the Database Wizard creates. Turn in the short paper and the report to your instructor.

Querying a Database Using the Select Query Window

PROJECT

2

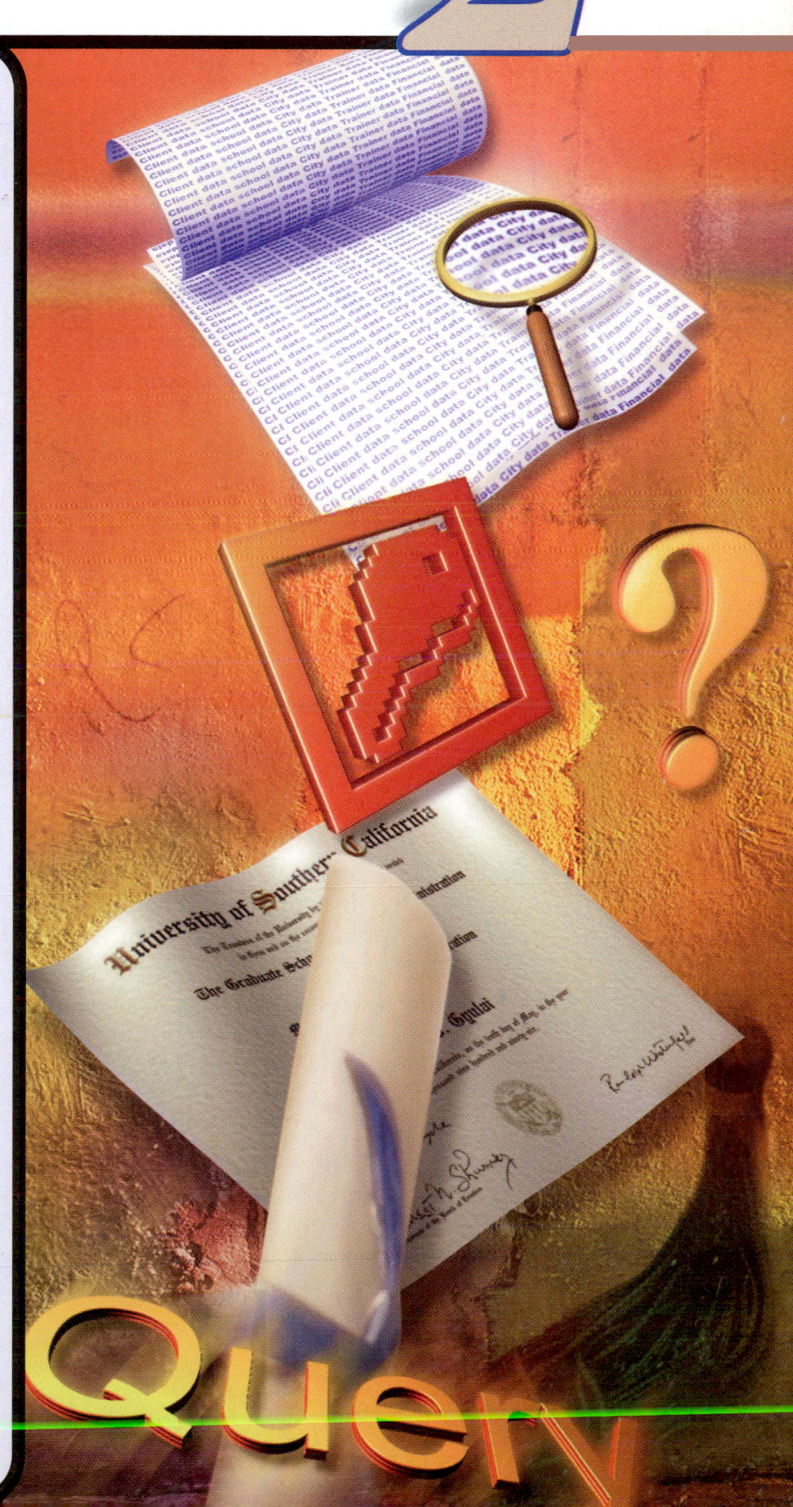

CASE PERSPECTIVE

Dr. Gernaey and his colleagues are eager for Ashton James College (AJC) to obtain the benefits they anticipated when they set up the database of client and trainer data. One immediate benefit they expect is the capability of easily asking questions such as the following concerning the data in the database and rapidly getting the answers.

1. What are the name, the amount paid, and the current due of client CP27?

2. Which clients' names begin with Fa?

3. Which clients are located in Lake Hammond?

4. Which clients have a current due of $0.00?

5. Which clients have an amount paid that is more than $20,000.00?

6. Which clients of trainer 48 have an amount paid that is more than $20,000.00?

7. In what cities are all the clients located?

8. How many hours has each trainer worked so far this year?

9. What is the client number and name of each client, and what is the number and name of the trainer to whom each client is assigned?

AJC needs to find information about clients located in a specific city, but they want to enter a different city each time they ask the question. A parameter query would enable this. They also have a special way they want to summarize their data and a crosstab query will present the data in the desired form.

Your task is to assist the administration of AJC in obtaining answers to these and other questions using Access query features.

As you read through this project, you will learn how to query a database and use the Select Query window.

Querying a Database Using the Select Query Window

PROJECT

2

Objectives:

You will have mastered the material in this project when you can:

- Create and run queries
- Print query results
- Include fields in the design grid
- Use text and numeric data in criteria
- Create and use parameter queries
- Save a query and use the saved query
- Use compound criteria in queries
- Sort data in queries
- Join tables in queries
- Perform calculations in queries
- Use grouping in queries
- Create crosstab queries

Introduction

A database management system such as Access offers many useful features, among them the capability of answering questions such as those posed by the administration of Ashton James College (Figure 2-1). The answers to these questions, and many more, are found in the database, and Access can find the answers quickly. When you pose a question to Access, or any other database management system, the question is called a query. A **query** is simply a question represented in a way that Access can understand.

Thus, to find the answer to a question, you first create a corresponding query using the techniques illustrated in this project. After you have created the query, you instruct Access to run the query; that is, to perform the steps necessary to obtain the answer. Access then will display the answer in Datasheet view.

Project Two — Querying the Ashton James College Database

The steps in this project obtain answers to the questions posed by the administration of Ashton James College. These include the questions shown in Figure 2-1, as well as many other questions that may be deemed important.

What are the name, the amount paid, and the current due for client CP27?

Which clients' names begin with Fa?

In what cities are all the clients located?

Which clients are located in Lake Hammond?

Which clients of trainer 48 have an amount paid that is more than $20,000.00?

Client table

CLIENT NUMBER	NAME	ADDRESS	CITY	STATE	ZIP CODE	AMOUNT PAID	CURRENT DUE	TRAINER NUMBER
BS27	Blant and Sons	4806 Park	Lake Hammond	TX	76653	$21,876.00	$892.50	42
CE16	Center Services	725 Mitchell	San Julio	TX	78364	$26,512.00	$2,672.00	48
CP27	Calder Plastics	7300 Cedar	Lake Hammond	TX	76653	$8,725.00	$0.00	48
EU28	Elba's Furniture	1445 Hubert	Tallmadge	TX	77231	$4,256.00	$1,202.00	53
FI28	Farrow-Idsen	829 Wooster	Cedar Ridge	TX	79342	$8,287.50	$925.50	42
FL93	Fairland Lawn	143 Pangborn	Lake Hammond	TX	76653	$21,625.00	$0.00	48
HN83	Hurley National	3827 Burgess	Tallmadge	TX	77231	$0.00	$0.00	48
MC28	Morgan-Alyssa	923 Williams	Crumville	TX	76745	$24,761.00	$1,572.00	42
PS82	PRIM Staffing	72 Crestview	San Julio	TX	78364	$11,682.25	$2,827.50	53
TE26	Telton-Edwards	5672 Anderson	Dunston	TX	77893	$8,521.50	$0.00	48

CLIENT NUMBER	NAME	AMOUNT PAID	CURRENT DUE
FI28	Farrow-Idsen	$8,287.50	$925.50
FL93	Fairland Lawn	$21,625.00	$0.00

CLIENT NUMBER	NAME	ADDRESS
BS27	Blant and Sons	4806 Park
CP27	Calder Plastics	7300 Cedar
FL93	Fairland Lawn	143 Pangborn

CLIENT NUMBER	NAME	AMOUNT PAID	CURRENT DUE
CP27	Calder Plastics	$8,725.00	$0.00

CITY
Cedar Ridge
Crumville
Dunston
Lake Hammond
Tallmadge

CLIENT NUMBER	NAME	AMOUNT PAID	CURRENT DUE	TRAINER NUMBER
CE16	Center Services	$26,512.00	$2,672.00	48
FL93	Fairland Lawn	$21,625.00	$0.00	48

FIGURE 2-1

More About

Queries: Query Languages

Before the advent of query languages in the mid-1970s, obtaining answers to questions concerning data in a database was very difficult, requiring that someone write lengthy (several hundred line) programs in languages such as COBOL. Query languages made it easy to obtain answers to such questions.

More About

The Access Help System

Need Help? It is no further than the Type a question for help box on the menu bar in the upper-right corner of the window. Click the box that contains the text, Type a question for help (Figure 2-5), type help, and then press the ENTER key. Access responds with a list of topics you can click to learn about obtaining help on any Access-related topic. To find out what is new in Access 2003, type what is new in Access in the Type a question for help box.

Opening the Database

If you are stepping through this project on a computer, and you want your screen to agree with the figures in this book, then you should change your computer's resolution to 800 × 600. For more information on how to change the resolution on your computer, see Appendix D. Before creating queries, first you must open the database. The following steps summarize the procedure to complete this task, once you have started Access.

To Open a Database

1 Click the Open button on the Database toolbar.

2 If necessary, click the Look in box arrow and then click 3½ Floppy (A:). Click Ashton James College, the database created in Project 1. (If you did not complete the steps in Project 1, see your instructor for a copy of the database.)

3 Click the Open button in the Open dialog box. If a Security Warning dialog box appears, click the Open button.

The database opens and the Ashton James College : Database window appears.

Creating and Running Queries

You create a query by making entries in a special window called a **Select Query window**. Once the database is open, the first step in creating a query is to select the table for which you are creating a query in the Database window. Then, you use the New Object button to design the new query in the Select Query window. It typically is easier to work with the Select Query window if it is maximized. Thus, as a standard practice, maximize the Select Query window as soon as you have created it. In addition, it often is useful to resize both panes within the window. This enables you to resize the field list that appears in the upper pane so more fields appear.

The following steps initiate creating a query.

To Create a Query

1

• **Be sure the Ashton James College database is open, the Tables object is selected, and the Client table is selected.**

• **Click the New Object button arrow on the Database toolbar.**

The list of available objects appears (Figure 2-2).

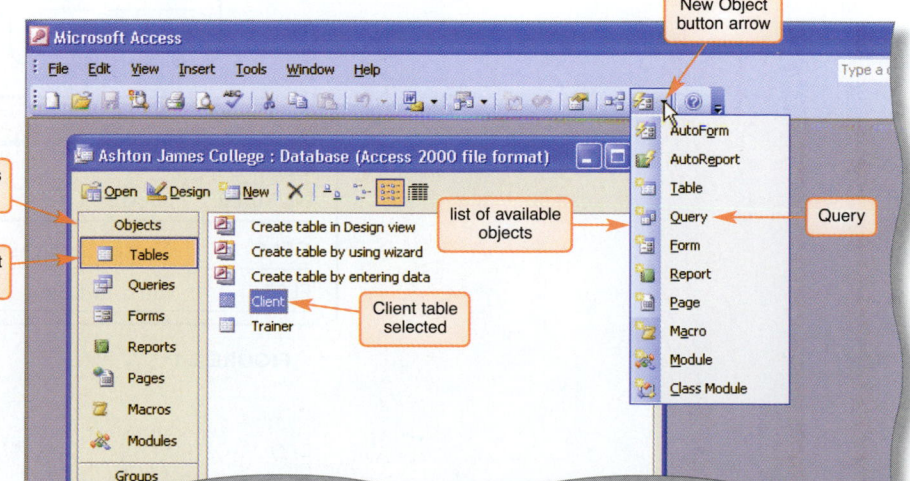

FIGURE 2-2

2

• **Click Query.**

Access displays the New Query dialog box (Figure 2-3).

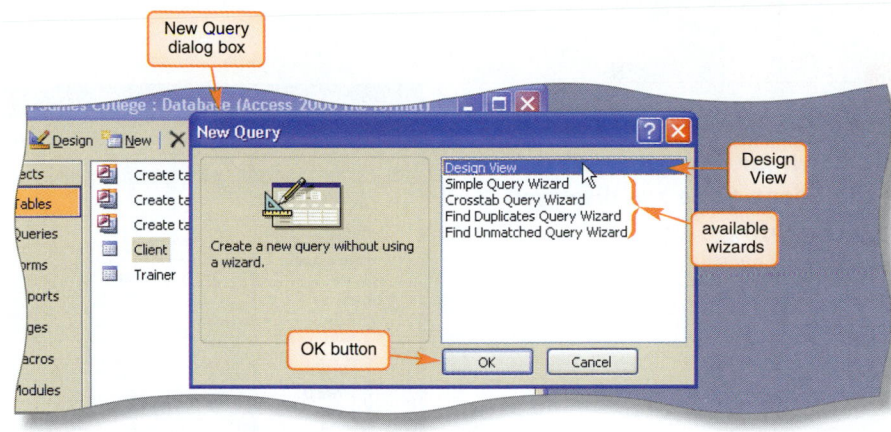

FIGURE 2-3

3

• **With Design View selected, click the OK button.**

The Query1 : Select Query window appears (Figure 2-4).

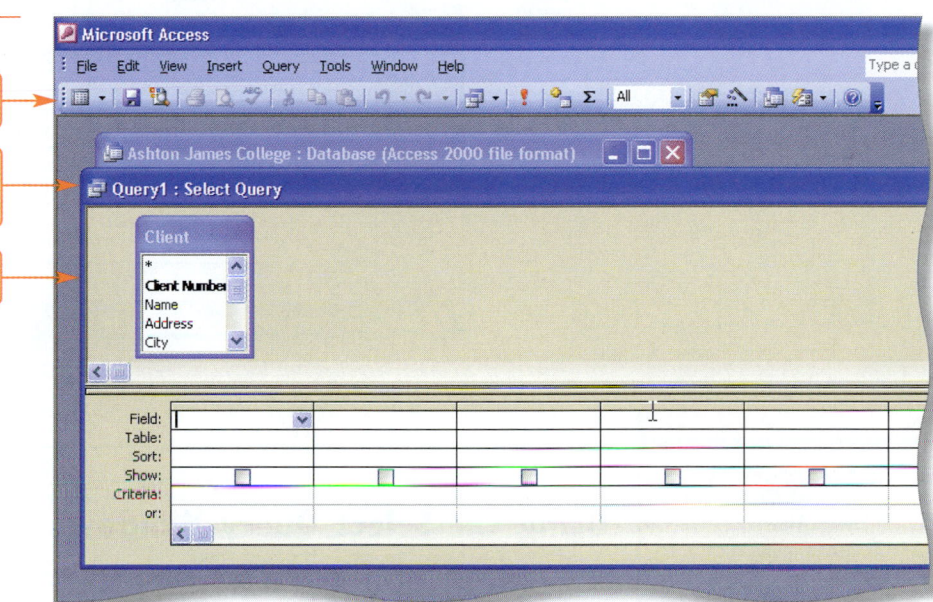

FIGURE 2-4

4

• **Maximize the Query1 : Select Query window by double-clicking its title bar, and then drag the line separating the two panes to the approximate position shown in Figure 2-5.**

*The Query1 : Select Query window is maximized. The upper pane contains a field list for the Client table. The lower pane contains the **design grid**, which is the area where you specify fields to be included, sort order, and the criteria the records you are looking for must satisfy. The mouse pointer shape indicates you can drag the line.*

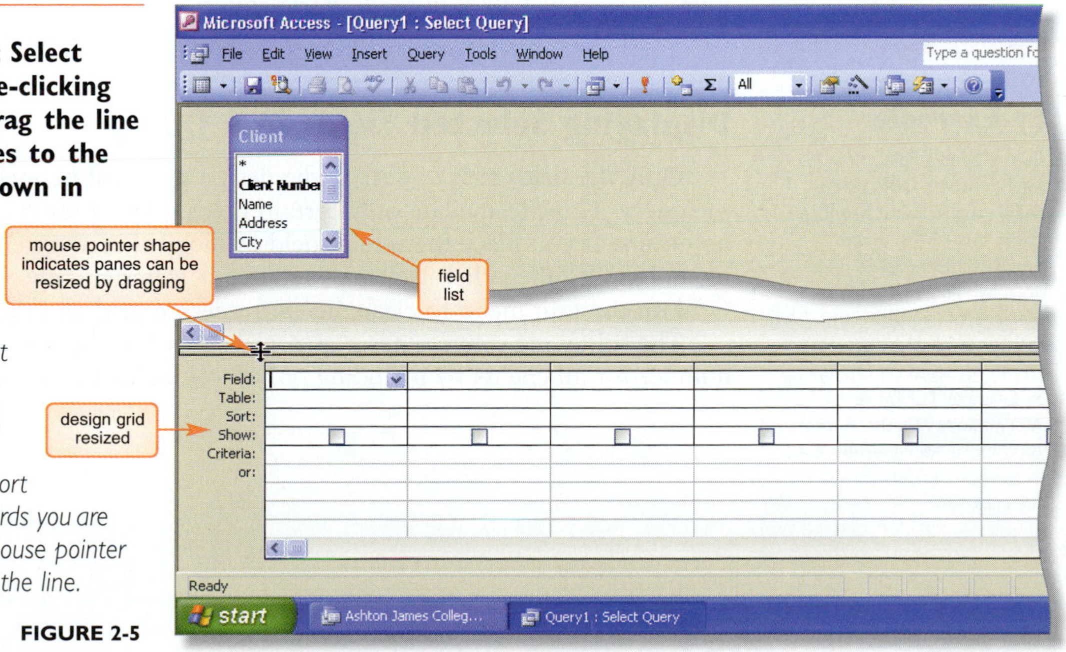

FIGURE 2-5

5

• Drag the lower edge of the field box down far enough so all fields in the Client table are displayed (Figure 2-6).

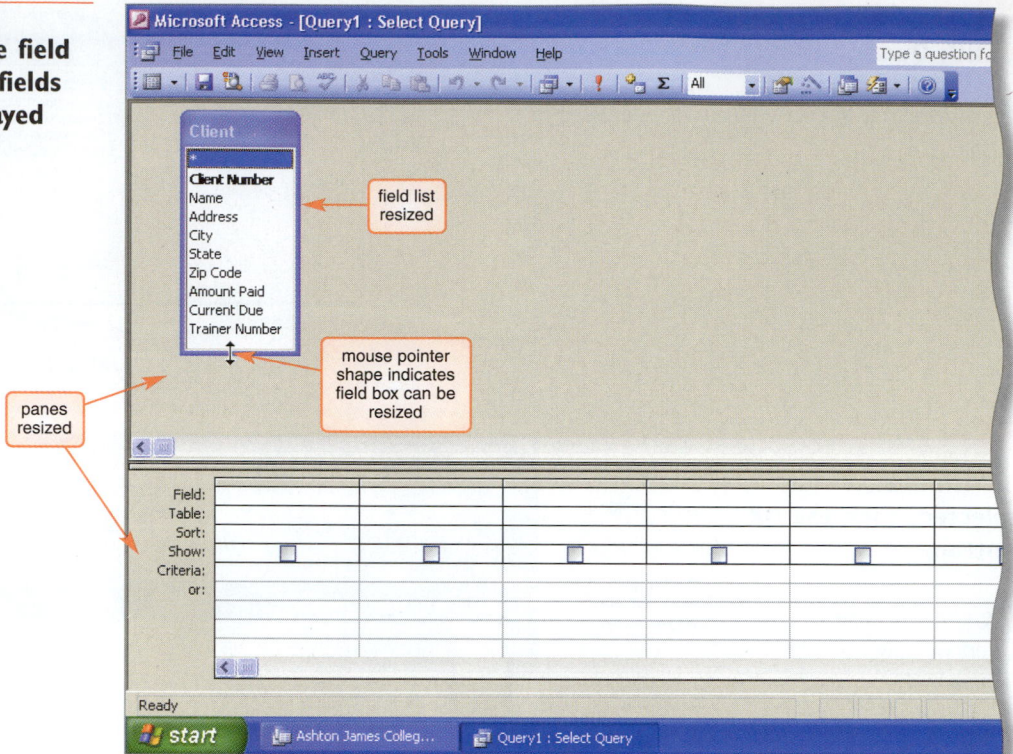

FIGURE 2-6

More About

Queries: Query-by-Example

Query-by-Example, often referred to as QBE, was a query language first proposed in the mid-1970s. In this approach, users asked questions by filling in a table on the screen. The approach to queries taken by several DBMSs is based on Query-by-Example. For more information, visit the Access 2003 More About Web page (scsite.com/ac2003/more) and click QBE.

Using the Select Query Window

Once you have created a new Select Query window, you are ready to create the actual query by making entries in the design grid in the lower pane of the window. You enter the names of the fields you want included in the Field row in the grid. You also can enter criteria, such as the fact that the client number must be a specific number, such as CP27, in the Criteria row of the grid. When you do so, only the record or records that match the criterion will be included in the answer.

Displaying Selected Fields in a Query

Only the fields that appear in the design grid will be included in the results of the query. Thus, to include only certain fields, place only these fields in the grid, and no others. If you place the wrong field in the grid inadvertently, click Edit on the menu bar and then click Delete to remove it. Alternatively, you could click Clear Grid on the Edit menu to clear the entire design grid and then start over.

The following step creates a query to show the client number, name, and trainer number for all clients by including only those fields in the design grid.

To Include Fields in the Design Grid

1

• If necessary, maximize the **Query1 : Select Query** window containing the field list for the Client table in the upper pane of the window and an empty design grid in the lower pane.

• Double-click the **Client Number** field in the field list to include it in the query.

• Double-click the **Name** field to include it in the query, and then double-click the **Trainer Number** field to include it as well.

The Client Number, Name, and Trainer Number fields are included in the query (Figure 2-7).

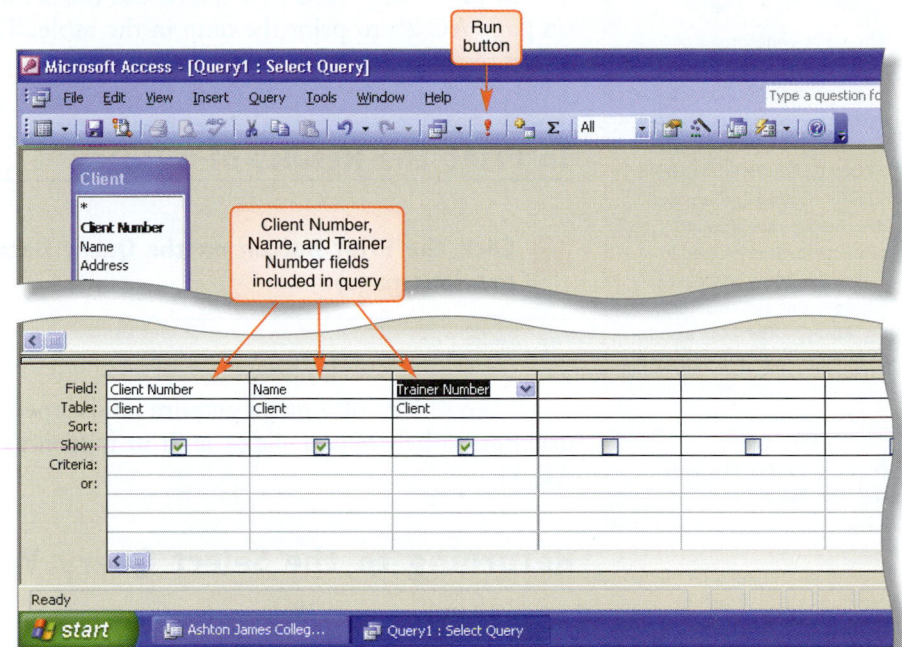

FIGURE 2-7

Running a Query

Once you have created the query, you run the query to produce the results using the Run button on the Query Design toolbar. Access performs the steps necessary to obtain and display the answer. The set of records that makes up the answer will be displayed in Datasheet view. Although it looks like a table that is stored on your disk, it really is not. The records are constructed from data in the existing Client table. If you were to change the data in the Client table and then rerun this same query, the results would reflect the changes. The following step runs the query.

To Run the Query

1

• Click the **Run** button on the Query Design toolbar (see Figure 2-7).

The query is executed and the results appear (Figure 2-8).

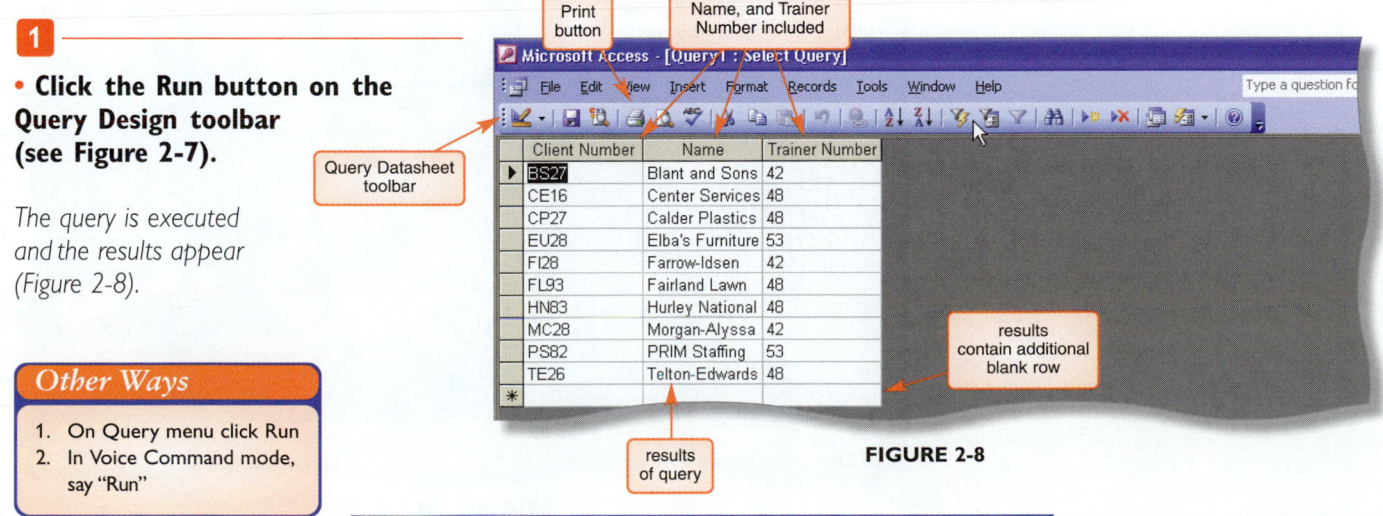

FIGURE 2-8

More About

Queries: SQL

The most widespread of all the query languages is a language called SQL. In SQL, users type commands such as SELECT CURRENT DUE FROM CUSTOMER WHERE CITY = "Tallmadge" to find the current due amounts of all customers located in Tallmadge. Many database management systems, including Access, offer SQL as one option for querying databases. For more information, visit the Access 2003 More About Web page (scsite.com/ac2003/more) and click SQL.

Printing the Results of a Query

To print the results of a query, use the same techniques you learned in Project 1 on page AC 29 to print the data in the table. The following step prints the current query results.

To Print the Results of a Query

1 **Click the Print button on the Query Datasheet toolbar (see Figure 2-8 on the previous page).**

The results print.

If the results of a query require landscape orientation, switch to landscape orientation before you click the Print button as indicated in Project 1 on page AC 31.

Returning to the Select Query Window

You can examine the results of a query on your screen to see the answer to your question. You can scroll through the records, if necessary, just as you scroll through the records of any other table. You also can print a copy of the table. In any case, once you are finished working with the results, you can return to the Select Query window to ask another question. The following steps illustrate how to return to the Select Query window.

To Return to the Select Query Window

1

• **Click the View button arrow on the Query Datasheet toolbar.**

The Query View list appears (Figure 2-9).

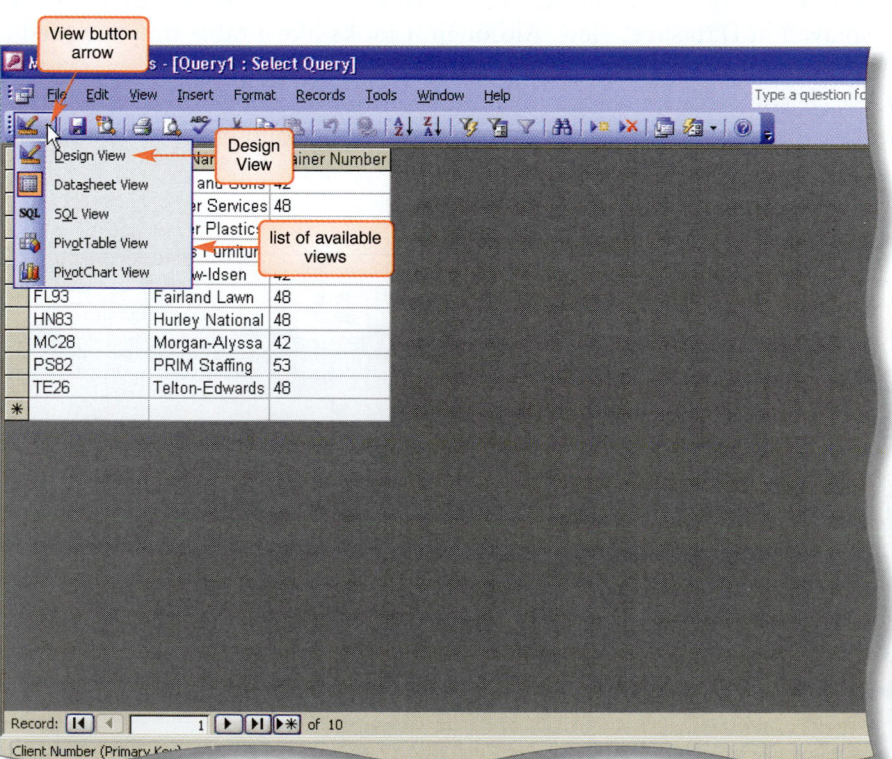

FIGURE 2-9

2

• **Click Design View.**

The Query1 : Select Query window is redisplayed (Figure 2-10).

FIGURE 2-10

Notice that the icon on the View button is the Design View icon. This indicates that the next time you want to display the window in Design view, you need only click the View button.

Closing a Query

To close a query, close the Select Query window. When you do so, Access displays the Microsoft Office Access dialog box asking if you want to save your query for future use. If you think you will need to create the same exact query often, you should save the query. For now, you will not save any queries. You will see how to save them later in the project. The following steps close a query without saving it.

To Close the Query

1

• **Click the Close Window button for the Query1 : Select Query window (see Figure 2-10).**

Access displays the Microsoft Office Access dialog box (Figure 2-11). Clicking the Yes button saves the query and clicking the No button closes the query without saving.

2

• **Click the No button in the Microsoft Office Access dialog box.**

The Query1 : Select Query window closes. The query is not saved.

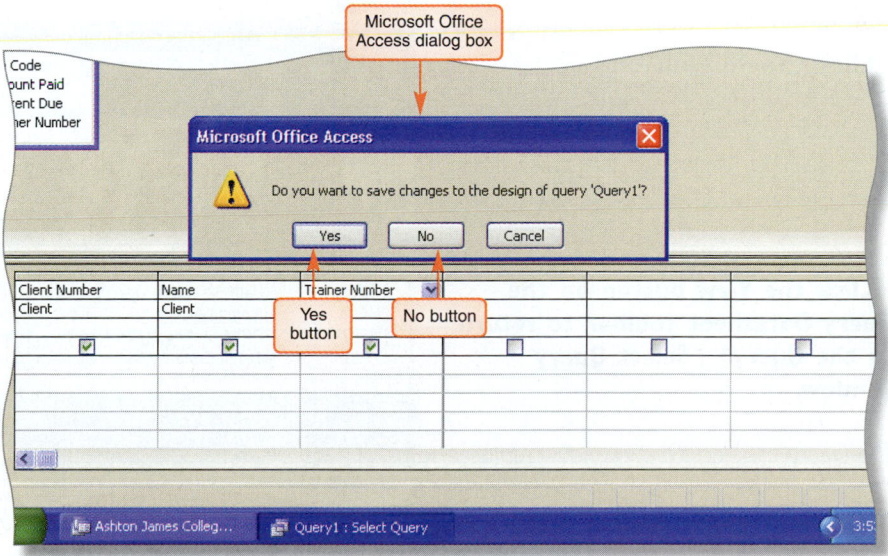

FIGURE 2-11

Including All Fields in a Query

If you want to include all fields in a query, you could select each field individually. A simpler way to include all fields is available, however. By selecting the asterisk (*) in the field list, you are indicating that all fields are to be included. The following steps use the asterisk to include all fields.

To Include All Fields in a Query

1

• **Be sure you have a maximized Query1 : Select Query window with resized upper and lower panes, an expanded field list for the Client table in the upper pane, and an empty design grid in the lower pane. (See Steps 1 through 5 on pages AC 68 through AC 70 to create the query and resize the window.)**

• **Double-click the asterisk at the top of the field list.**

The maximized Query1 : Select Query window displays two resized panes. The table name, Client, followed by a period and an asterisk is added to the design grid, indicating all fields are included (Figure 2-12).

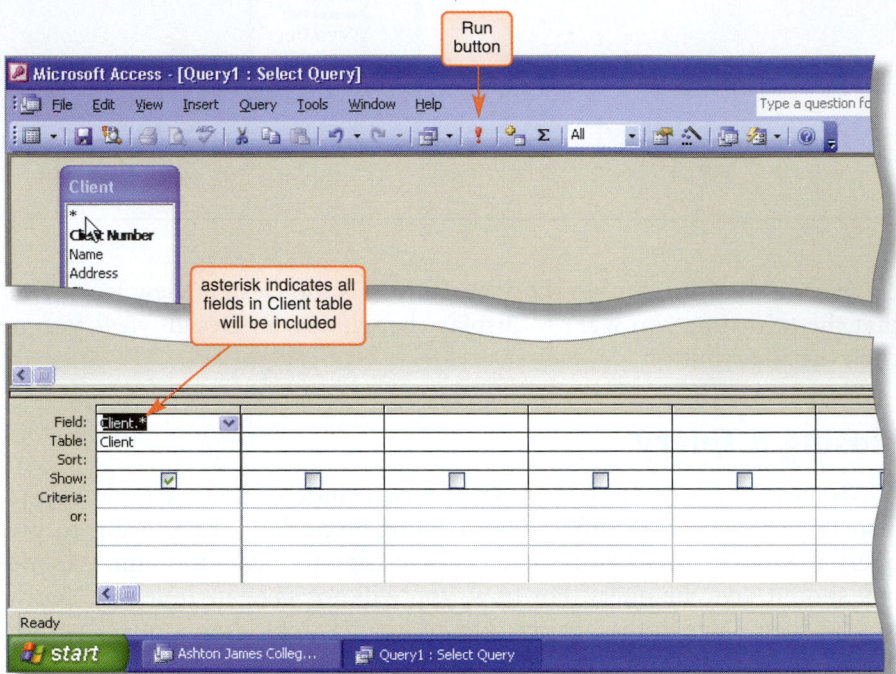

FIGURE 2-12

2

• **Click the Run button.**

The results appear and all fields in the Client table are included (Figure 2-13).

3

• **Click the View button on the Query Datasheet toolbar to return to the Query1 : Select Query window.**

The Query1 : Select Query window replaces the datasheet.

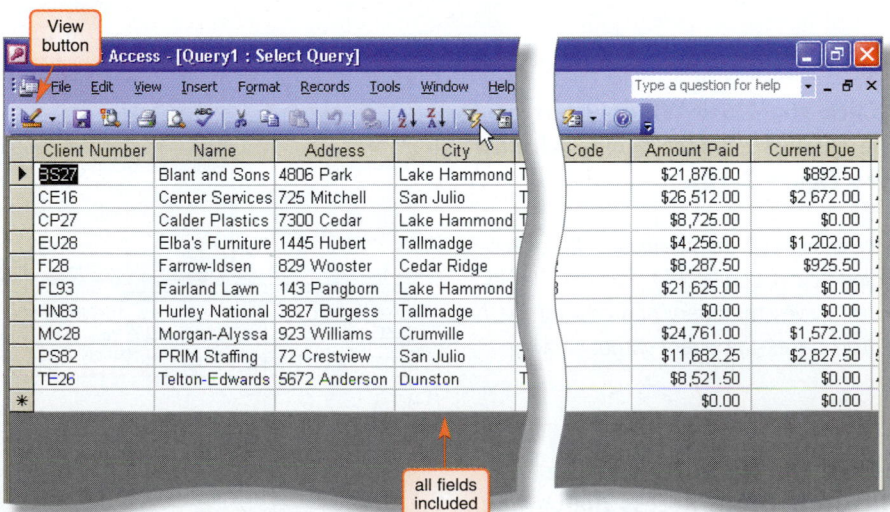

FIGURE 2-13

Other Ways

1. Drag asterisk from field list to design grid
2. Click column in grid, click arrow, click Client.*

Clearing the Design Grid

If you make mistakes as you are creating a query, you can fix each one individually. Alternatively, you simply may want to clear the query; that is, clear out the entries in the design grid and start over. One way to clear out the entries is to close the Select Query window and then start a new query just as you did earlier. A simpler approach, however, is to use the Clear Grid command on the Edit menu. The following steps clear the design grid.

To Clear the Design Grid

1

• **Click Edit on the menu bar.**

The Edit menu appears (Figure 2-14).

2

• **Click Clear Grid.**

Access clears the design grid so you can enter your next query.

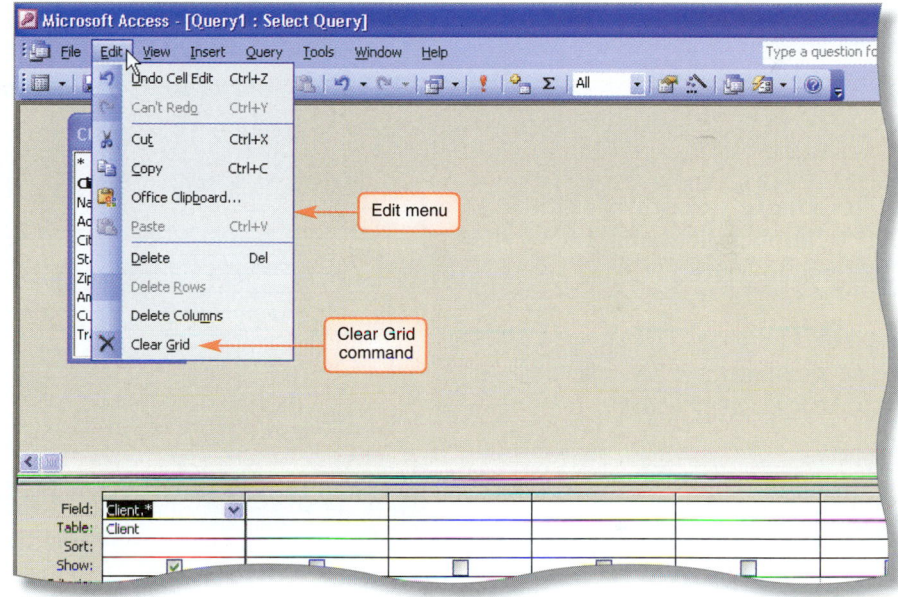

FIGURE 2-14

Entering Criteria

When you use queries, usually you are looking for those records that satisfy some criterion. You might want the name, amount paid, and current due amounts of the client whose number is CP27, for example, or of those clients whose names start with the letters, Fa. To enter criteria, enter them in the Criteria row in the design grid below the field name to which the criterion applies. For example, to indicate that the client number must be CP27, you first must add the Client Number field to the design grid. You then would type CP27 in the Criteria row below the Client Number field.

The next examples illustrate the types of criteria that are available.

Using Text Data in Criteria

To use **text data** (data in a field whose data type is Text) in criteria, simply type the text in the Criteria row below the corresponding field name. The steps on the next page query the Client table and display the client number, name, amount paid, and current due amount of client CP27.

To Use Text Data in a Criterion

1

• **One by one, double-click the Client Number, Name, Amount Paid, and Current Due fields to add them to the query.**

The Client Number, Name, Amount Paid, and Current Due fields are added to the design grid (Figure 2-15).

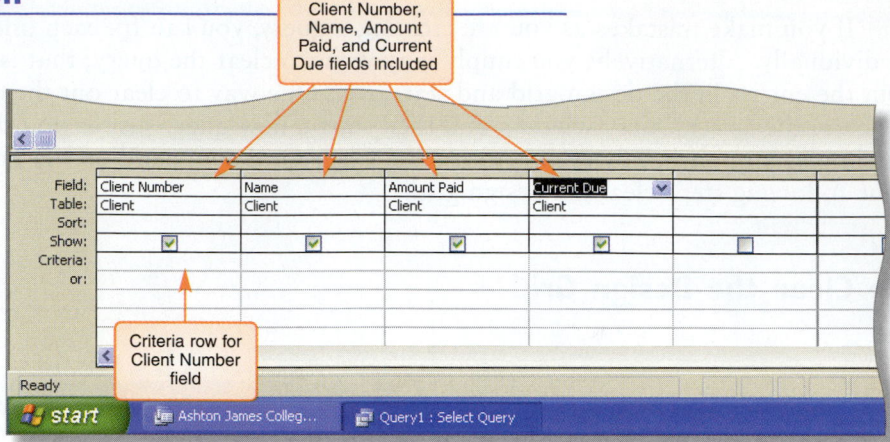

FIGURE 2-15

2

• **Click the Criteria row for the Client Number field and then type CP27 as the criterion.**

The criterion is entered (Figure 2-16). When the mouse pointer is in the Criteria box, its shape changes to an I-beam.

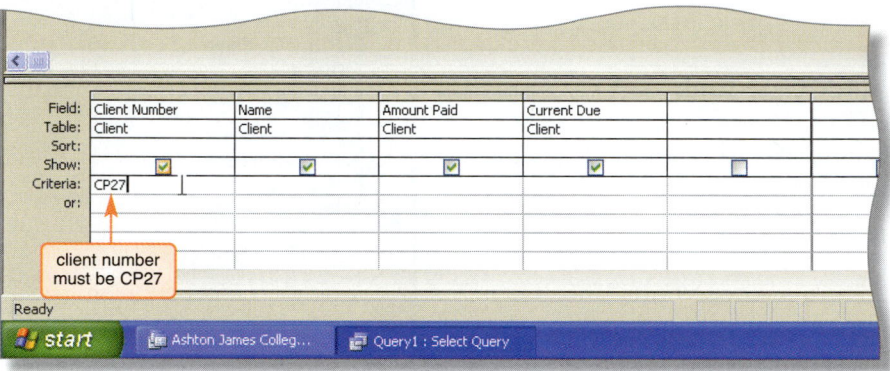

FIGURE 2-16

3

• **Click the Run button to run the query.**

The results appear (Figure 2-17). Only client CP27 is included. (The extra blank row contains $0.00 in the Amount Paid and Current Due fields. Unlike text fields, which are left blank, number and currency fields in the extra row contain 0. Because the Amount Paid and Current Due fields are currency fields, the values are displayed as $0.00.)

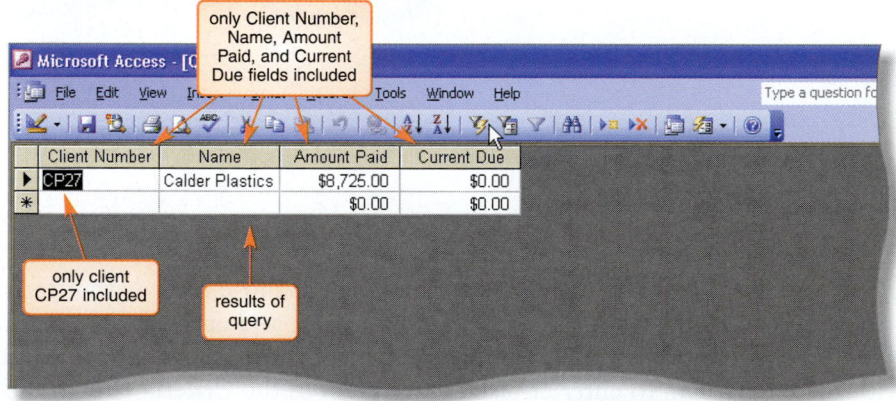

FIGURE 2-17

Using Wildcards

Two special wildcards are available in Microsoft Access. **Wildcards** are symbols that represent any character or combination of characters. The first of the two wildcards, the **asterisk** (*), represents any collection of characters. Thus Fa* represents the letters, Fa, followed by any collection of characters. The other wildcard symbol is the **question mark** (?), which represents any individual character. Thus t?m represents the letter, T, followed by any single character followed by the letter, m, such as Tim or Tom.

The following steps use a wildcard to find the number, name, and address of those clients whose names begin with Fa. Because you do not know how many characters will follow the Fa, the asterisk is appropriate.

To Use a Wildcard

 1

- **Click the View button on the Query Datasheet toolbar to return to the Query1 : Select Query window.**

- **If necessary, click the Criteria row below the Client Number field.**

- **Use the DELETE or BACKSPACE key as necessary to delete the current entry (CP27).**

- **Click the Criteria row below the Name field.**

- **Type Fa* as the criterion.**

The criterion is entered (Figure 2-18).

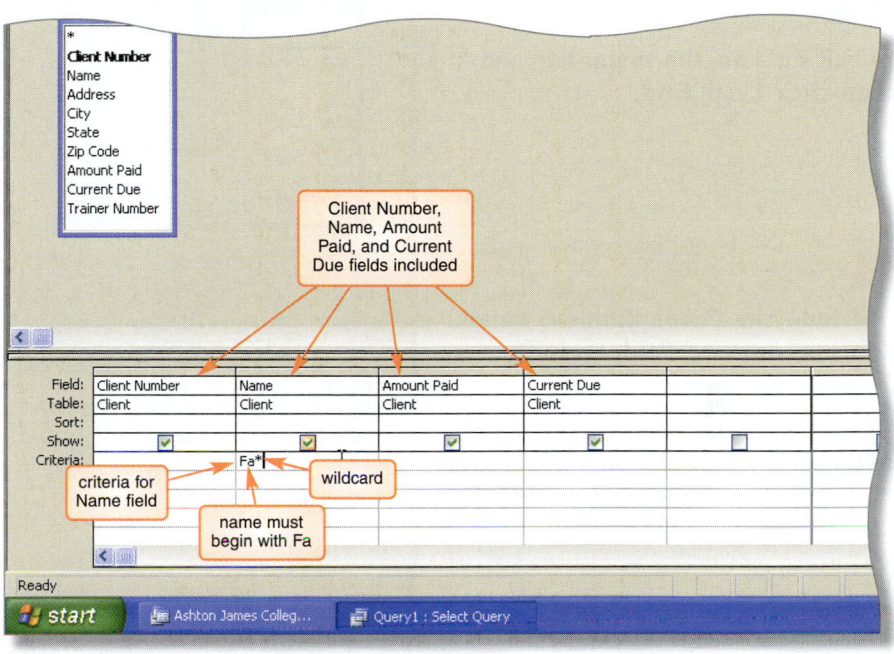

FIGURE 2-18

 2

- **Click the Run button to run the query.**

- **If instructed to do so, print the results by clicking the Print button on the Query Datasheet toolbar.**

The results appear (Figure 2-19). Only the clients whose names start with Fa are included.

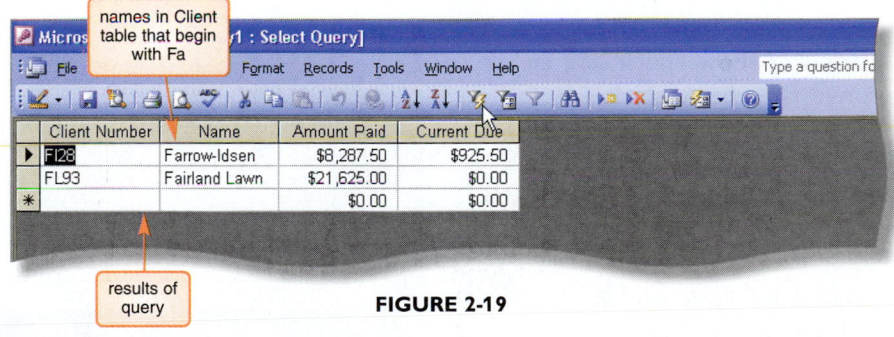

FIGURE 2-19

Criteria for a Field Not in the Result

In some cases, you may have criteria for a particular field that should not appear in the results of the query. For example, you may want to see the client number, name, address, and amount paid for all clients located in Lake Hammond. The criteria involve the City field, which is not one of the fields to be included in the results.

To enter a criterion for the City field, it must be included in the design grid. Normally, this also would mean it would appear in the results. To prevent this from happening, remove the check mark from its Show check box in the Show row of the grid. The steps on the next page illustrate the process by displaying the client number, name, and amount paid for clients located in Lake Hammond.

Q & A

Q: Can you add records or edit records in Query Datasheet view?

A: Yes. If the data in the query result is based on one table, you can add and edit records just as you did when the table was displayed in Table Datasheet view.

To Use Criteria for a Field Not Included in the Results

1

• **Click the View button on the Query Datasheet toolbar to return to the Query1 : Select Query window.**

• **Click Edit on the menu bar and then click Clear Grid.**

Access clears the design grid so you can enter the next query.

2

• **Include the Client Number, Name, Address, Amount Paid, and City fields in the query.**

• **Type** Lake Hammond **as the criterion for the City field.**

The fields are included in the grid, and the criterion for the City field is entered (Figure 2-20).

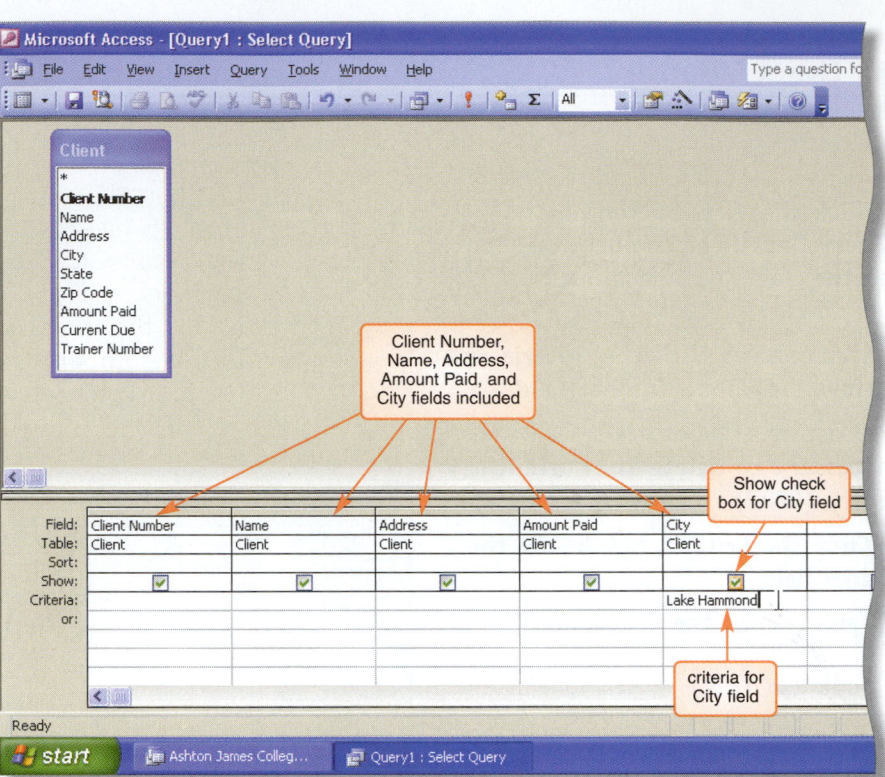

FIGURE 2-20

3

• **Click the Show check box to remove the check mark.**

The check mark is removed from the Show check box for the City field (Figure 2-21), indicating it will not show in the result. Because the City field is a text field, Access has added quotation marks before and after Lake Hammond automatically.

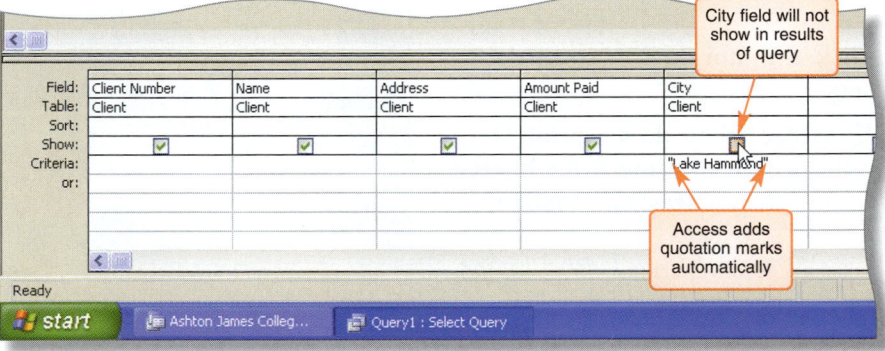

FIGURE 2-21

4

• **Click the Run button to run the query.**

• **If instructed to do so, print the results by clicking the Print button.**

The results appear (Figure 2-22). The City field does not appear. The only clients included are those located in Lake Hammond.

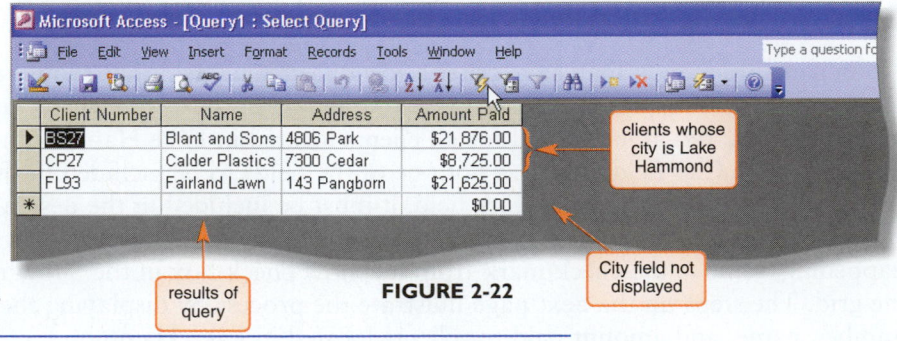

FIGURE 2-22

Creating a Parameter Query

Rather than giving a specific criterion when you first create the query, on occasion, you may want to be able to enter part of the criterion when you run the query and then have the appropriate results appear. For example, to include all the clients located in Tallmadge, you could enter Tallmadge as a criterion in the City field. From that point on, every time you ran the query, only the clients in Tallmadge would appear.

A better way is to allow the user to enter the city at the time the query is run. Thus a user could run the query, enter Tallmadge as the city and then see all the clients in Tallmadge. Later, the user could run the same query, but enter Lake Hammond as the city, and then see all the clients in Lake Hammond. To do this, you create a **parameter query**, which is a query that prompts for input whenever it is run. You enter a parameter, rather than a specific value as the criterion. You create one by enclosing a value in a criterion in square brackets. It is important that the value in the brackets does not match the name of any field. If you enter a field name in square brackets, Access assumes you want that particular field and will not prompt the user for input. For example, you could place [Enter City] as the criterion in the City field.

The following steps create a parameter query that will prompt the user to enter a city, and then display the client number, name, address, and amount paid for all clients located in that city.

To Create and Run a Parameter Query

1

• **Click the View button on the Query Datasheet toolbar to return to the Query1 : Select Query window.**

• **Erase the current criterion in the City column, and then type** [Enter City] **as the new criterion.**

The criterion is entered (Figure 2-23).

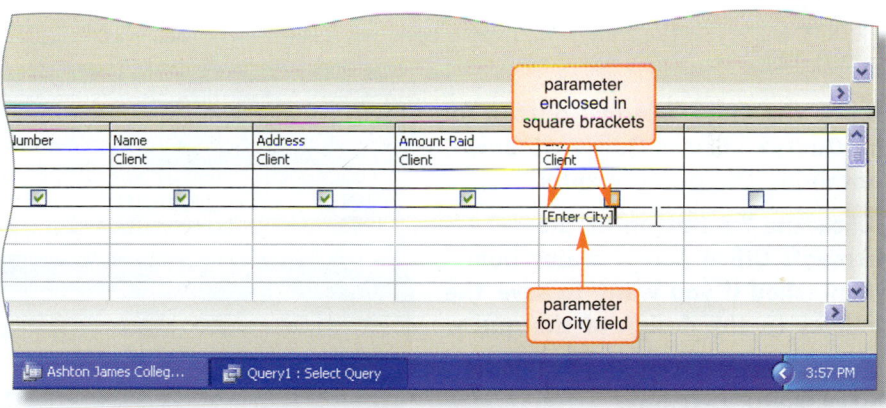

FIGURE 2-23

2

• **Click the Run button to run the query.**

Access displays the Enter Parameter Value dialog box (Figure 2-24). The value (Enter City) previously entered in brackets appears in the dialog box.

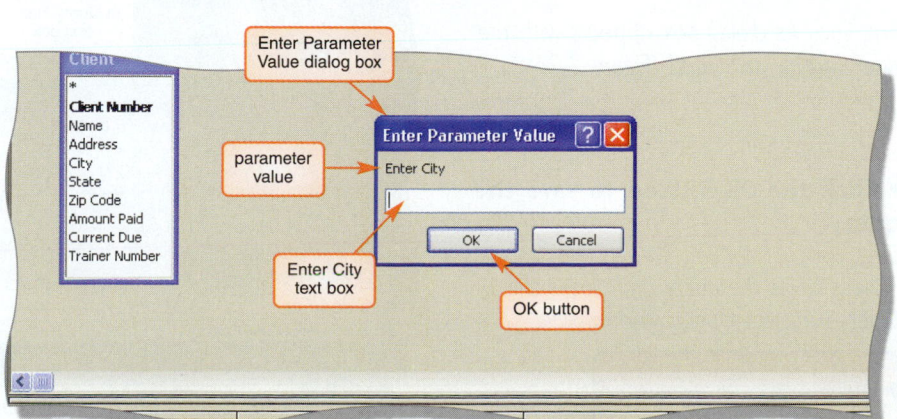

FIGURE 2-24

3

• **Type** `Tallmadge` **in the Enter City text box and then click the OK button.**

The results appear (Figure 2-25). Only clients whose city is Tallmadge are included. The city name is not displayed in the results.

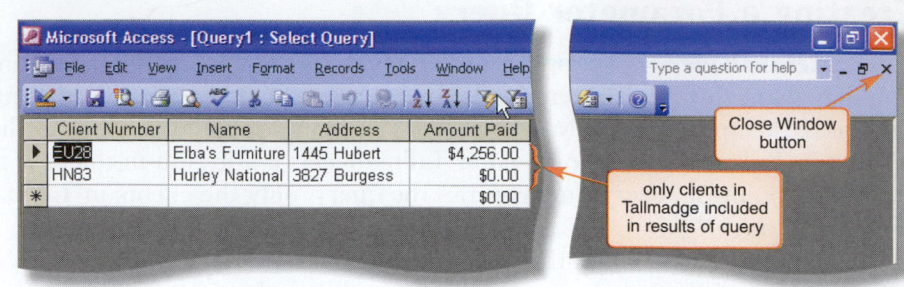

FIGURE 2-25

Each time you run this query, you will be asked to enter a city. Only clients in the city you enter will be included in the results.

Saving a Query

In many cases, you will construct a query you will want to use again. By saving the query, you will eliminate the need to repeat all your entries. The following steps illustrate the process by saving the query you just have created and assigning it the name Client-City Query. You can save with either the query design or the query results appearing on the screen.

To Save a Query

1

• **Click the Close Window button for the Query1 : Select Query window containing the query results.**

• **Click the Yes button in the Microsoft Office Access dialog box when asked if you want to save the changes to the design of the query.**

• **Type** `Client-City Query` **in the Query Name text box.**

The Save As dialog box appears with the query name you typed (Figure 2-26).

2

• **Click the OK button to save the query.**

Access saves the query and closes the Query1 : Select Query window.

Other Ways

1. On File menu click Save
2. Press CTRL+S

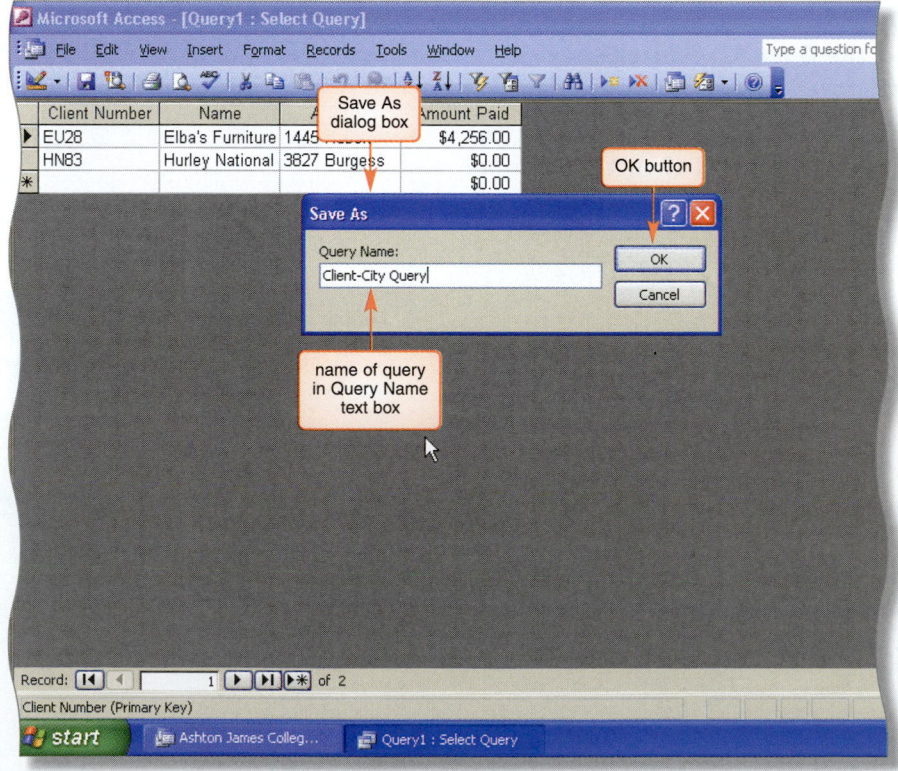

FIGURE 2-26

Using a Saved Query

Once you have saved a query, you can use and manipulate it at any time in the future by opening it. When you right-click the query in the Database window, Access displays a shortcut menu containing commands that allow you to open, print, and change the design of the query. You also can print the results by clicking the Print button on the toolbar. If you want to print the query results without first opening the query, you would click Print on the shortcut menu.

The query is run against the current database. Thus, if changes have been made to the data since the last time you ran it, the results of the query may be different. The following steps use the query named Client-City Query.

To Use a Saved Query

1

• Click Queries on the Objects bar, and then right-click Client-City Query.

The shortcut menu for Client-City Query appears (Figure 2-27).

2

• Click Open on the shortcut menu, type `Tallmadge` in the Enter City text box, and then click the OK button.

The results appear. They look like the results shown in Figure 2-25.

3

• Click the Close Window button for the Client-City Query : Select Query window containing the query results.

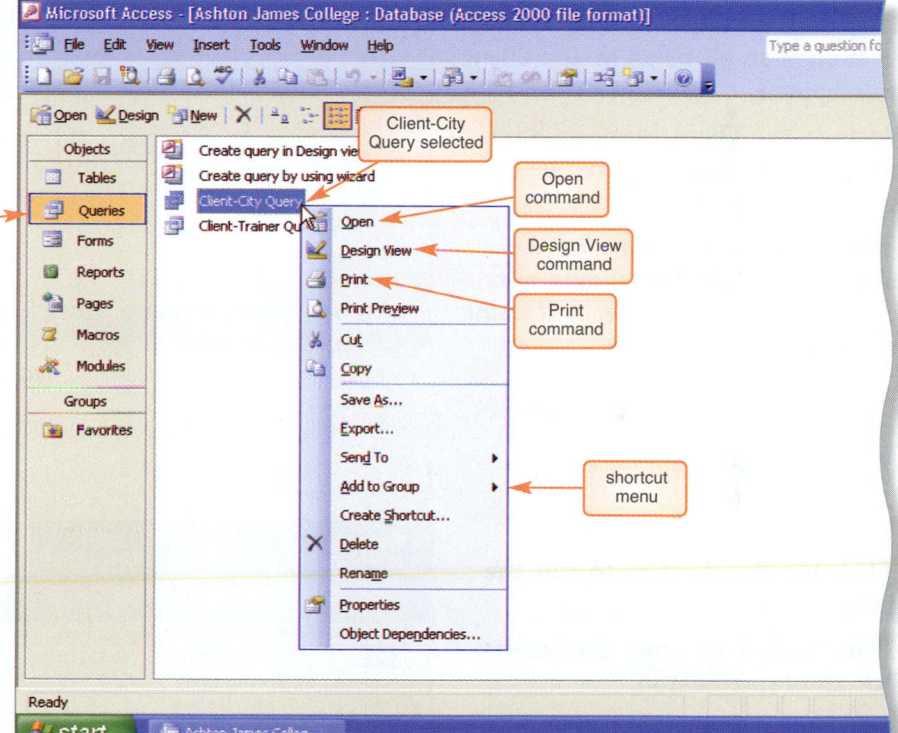

FIGURE 2-27

You can use the query at any time by following the above steps. Each time you do so, you will be prompted to enter a city. Only the clients in that city will be displayed in the results.

Using Numeric Data in Criteria

To enter a number in a criterion, type the number without any dollar signs or commas. The steps on the next page display all clients whose current due amount is $0.00.

To Use a Number in a Criterion

1

• Click the Tables object on the Objects bar and ensure the Client table is selected.

• Click the New Object button arrow on the Database toolbar, click Query, and then click the OK button in the New Query dialog box.

• Drag the line separating the two panes to the approximate position shown in Figure 2-28, and drag the lower edge of the field box down far enough so all fields in the Client table appear.

• Include the Client Number, Name, Amount Paid, and Current Due fields in the query.

• Type 0 as the criterion for the Current Due field. You should not enter a dollar sign or decimal point in the criterion.

The fields are selected and the criterion is entered (Figure 2-28).

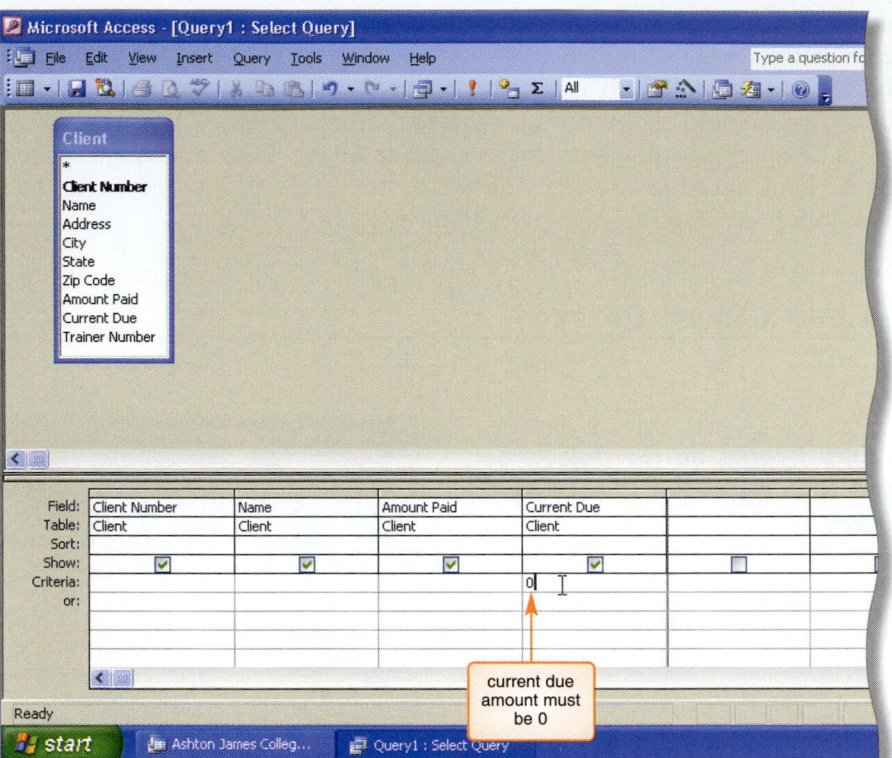

FIGURE 2-28

2

• Click the Run button to run the query.

• If instructed to print the results, click the Print button.

The results appear (Figure 2-29). Only those clients that have a current due amount of $0.00 are included.

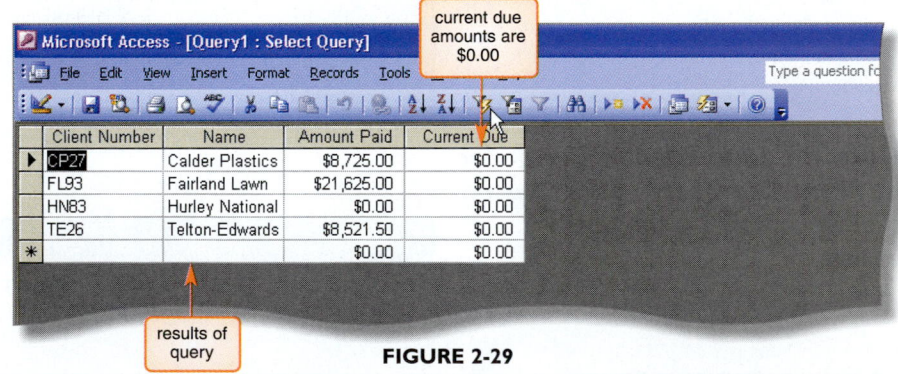

FIGURE 2-29

Using Comparison Operators

Unless you specify otherwise, Access assumes that the criteria you enter involve equality (exact matches). In the last query, for example, you were requesting those clients whose current due amount is equal to 0 (zero). If you want something other than an exact match, you must enter the appropriate **comparison operator**. The comparison operators are > (greater than), < (less than), >= (greater than or equal to), <= (less than or equal to), and NOT (not equal to).

The following steps use the > operator to find all clients whose amount paid is more than $20,000.00.

To Use a Comparison Operator in a Criterion

1

• **Click the View button on the Query Datasheet toolbar to return to the Query1 : Select Query window.**

• **Erase the 0 in the Current Due column.**

• **Type >20000 as the criterion for the Amount Paid field. Remember that you should not enter a dollar sign, a comma, or decimal point in the criterion.**

The fields are selected and the criterion is entered (Figure 2-30).

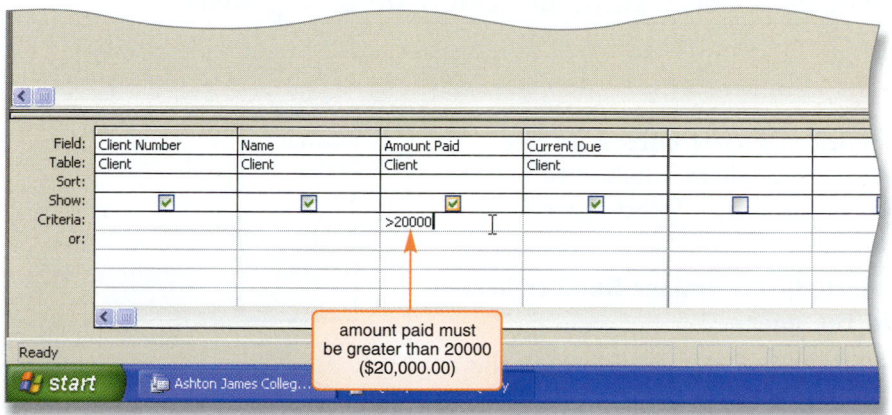

amount paid must be greater than 20000 ($20,000.00)

FIGURE 2-30

2

• **Click the Run button to run the query.**

• **If instructed to print the results, click the Print button.**

The results appear (Figure 2-31). Only those clients who have an amount paid greater than $20,000.00 are included.

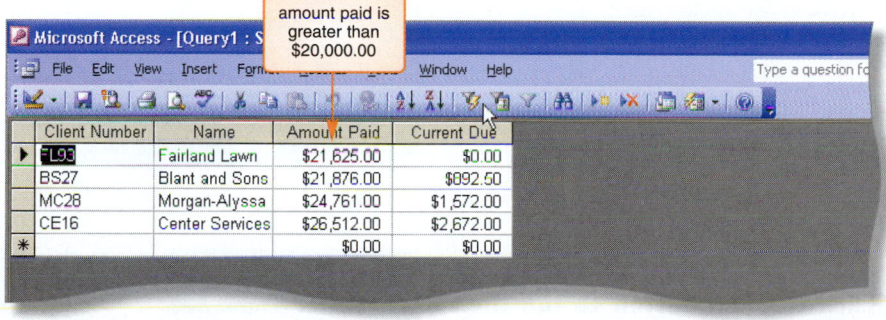

amount paid is greater than $20,000.00

FIGURE 2-31

Using Compound Criteria

Often you will have more than one criterion that the data for which you are searching must satisfy. This type of criterion is called a **compound criterion**. Two types of compound criteria exist.

In an **AND criterion**, each individual criterion must be true in order for the compound criterion to be true. For example, an AND criterion would allow you to find those clients that have an amount paid greater than $20,000.00 and whose trainer is trainer 48.

Conversely, an **OR criterion** is true provided either individual criterion is true. An OR criterion would allow you to find those clients that have an amount paid greater than $20,000.00 or whose trainer is trainer 48. In this case, any client whose amount paid is greater than $20,000.00 would be included in the answer whether or not the client's trainer is trainer 48. Likewise, any client whose trainer is trainer 48 would be included whether or not the client had an amount paid greater than $20,000.00.

More About

Compound Criteria

The BETWEEN operator allows you to search for a range of values in one field. For example, to find all clients whose amount paid amount is between $5,000 and $10,000, you would enter Between 5000 and 10000 in the Criteria row for the Amount Paid field. It also is possible to create compound criteria involving both OR and AND operators. For more information, visit the Access 2003 More About Web page (scsite.com/ac2003/more) and click Compound Criteria.

Using AND Criteria

To combine criteria with AND, place the criteria on the same line. The following steps use an AND criterion to find those clients whose amount paid is greater than $20,000.00 and whose trainer is trainer 48.

To Use a Compound Criterion Involving AND

1

• **Click the View button on the Query Datasheet toolbar to return to the Query1 : Select Query window.**

• **Include the Trainer Number field in the query.**

• **Type 48 as the criterion for the Trainer Number field.**

Criteria have been entered for the Amount Paid and Trainer Number fields (Figure 2-32).

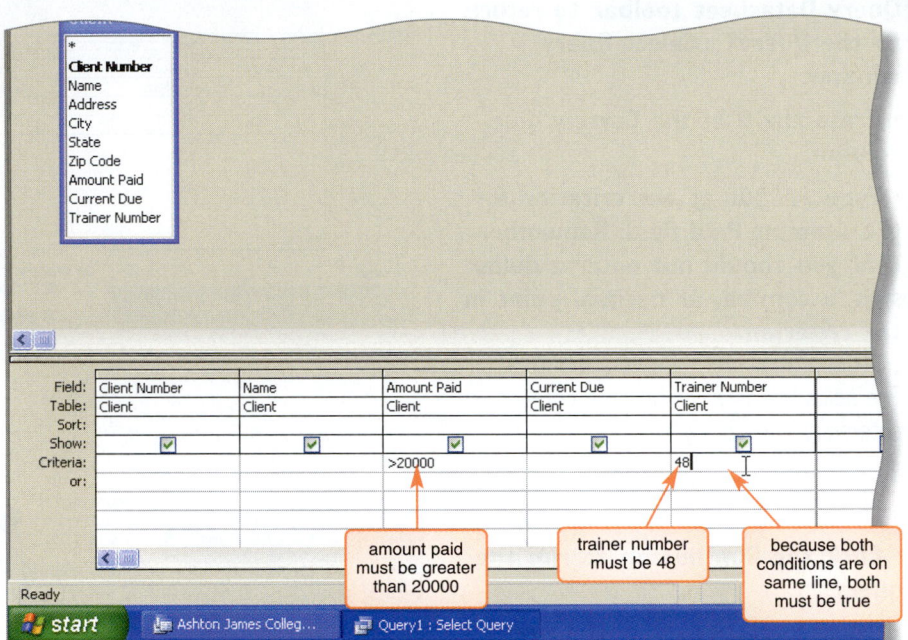

FIGURE 2-32

2

• **Click the Run button to run the query.**

• **If instructed to print the results, click the Print button.**

The results appear (Figure 2-33). Only the clients whose amount paid is greater than $20,000.00 and whose trainer number is 48 are included.

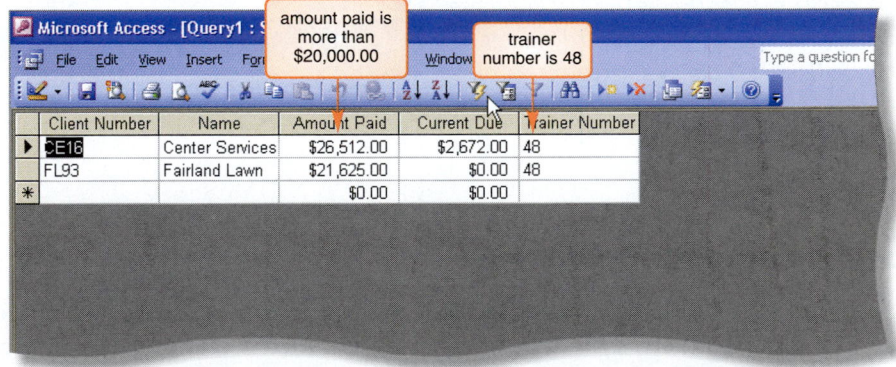

FIGURE 2-33

Using OR Criteria

To combine criteria with OR, the criteria must go on separate lines in the Criteria area of the grid. The following steps use an OR criterion to find those clients whose amount paid is greater than $20,000.00 or whose trainer is trainer 48 (or both).

To Use a Compound Criterion Involving OR

1

• **Click the View button on the Query Datasheet toolbar to return to the Query1 : Select Query window.**

2

• **If necessary, click the Criteria entry for the Trainer Number field and then use the BACKSPACE key or the DELETE key to erase the entry ("48").**

• **Click the or row (below the Criteria row) for the Trainer Number field and then type 48 as the entry.**

The criteria are entered for the Amount Paid and Trainer Number fields on different lines (Figure 2-34).

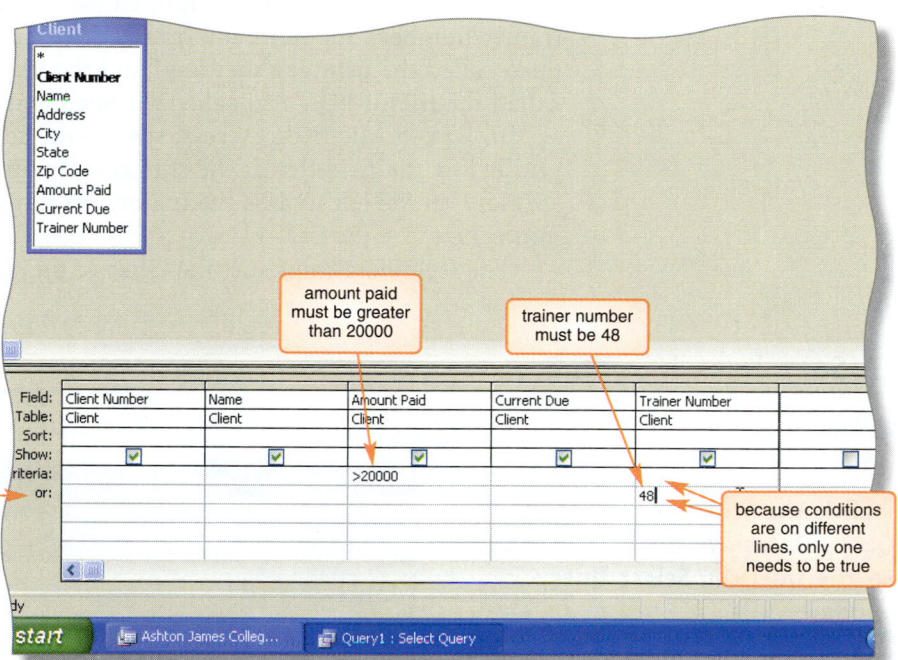

FIGURE 2-34

3

• **Click the Run button to run the query.**

• **If instructed to print the results, click the Print button.**

The results appear (Figure 2-35). Only those clients whose amount paid is greater than $20,000.00 or whose trainer number is 48 are included.

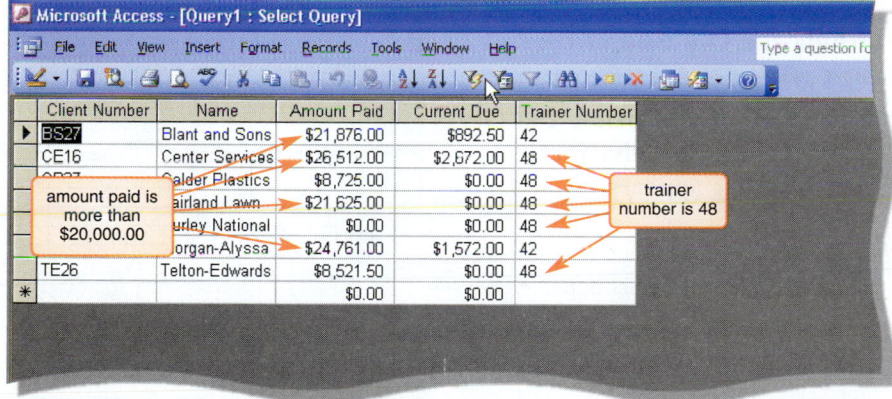

FIGURE 2-35

Sorting Data in a Query

In some queries, the order in which the records appear really does not matter. All you need be concerned about are the records that appear in the results. It does not matter which one is first or which one is last.

In other queries, however, the order can be very important. You may want to see the cities in which clients are located and would like them arranged alphabetically. Perhaps you want to see the clients listed by trainer number. Further, within all the clients of any given trainer, you might want them to be listed by amount paid.

More About

Sorting Data in a Query

When sorting data in a query, the records in the underlying tables (the tables on which the query is based) are not actually rearranged. Instead, the DBMS will determine the most efficient method of simply displaying the records in the requested order. The records in the underlying tables remain in their original order.

To order the records in the answer to a query in a particular way, you **sort** the records. The field or fields on which the records are sorted is called the **sort key**. If you are sorting on more than one field (such as sorting by amount paid within trainer number), the more important field (Trainer Number) is called the **major key** (also called the **primary sort key**) and the less important field (Amount Paid) is called the **minor key** (also called the **secondary sort key**).

To sort in Microsoft Access, specify the sort order in the Sort row of the design grid below the field that is the sort key. If you specify more than one sort key, the sort key on the left will be the major sort key and the one on the right will be the minor key.

The following steps sort the cities in the Client table.

To Sort Data in a Query

1

• **Click the View button on the Query Datasheet toolbar to return to the Query1 : Select Query window.**

• **Click Edit on the menu bar and then click Clear Grid.**

2

• **Include the City field in the design grid.**

• **Click the Sort row below the City field, and then click the Sort row arrow that appears.**

The City field is included (Figure 2-36). A list of available sort orders appears.

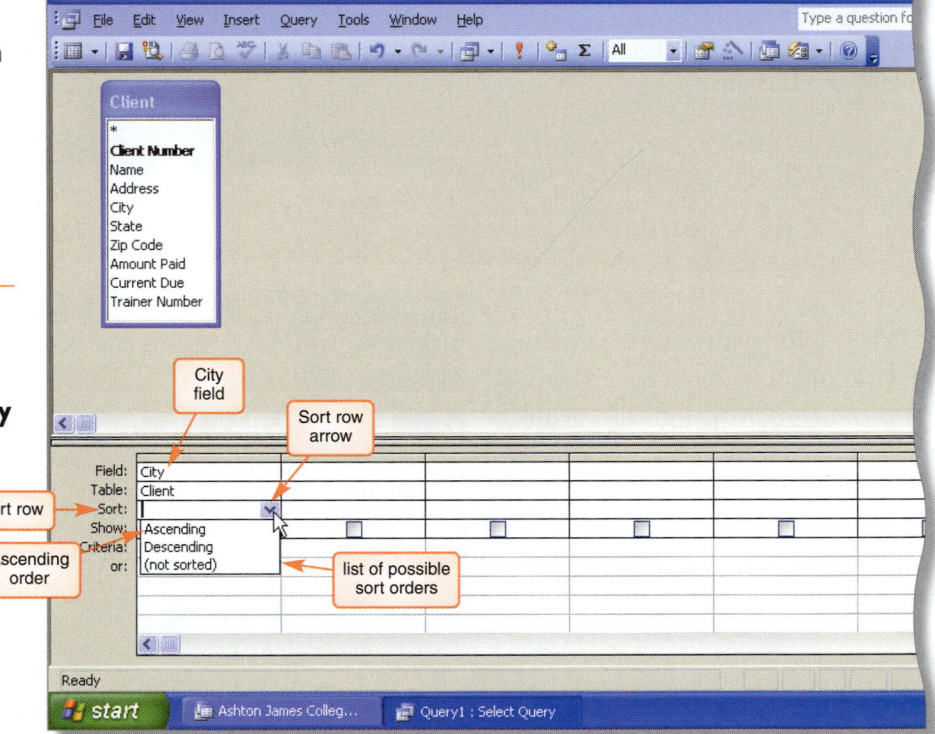

FIGURE 2-36

3

• **Click Ascending.**

Ascending is selected as the order (Figure 2-37).

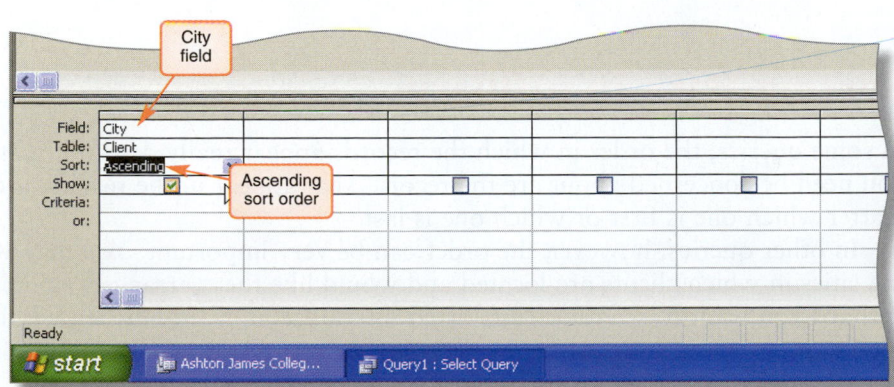

FIGURE 2-37

4

- **Click the Run button to run the query.**
- **If instructed to print the results, click the Print button.**

The results contain the cities from the Client table (Figure 2-38). The cities appear in alphabetical order. Duplicates, also called **identical rows**, *are included.*

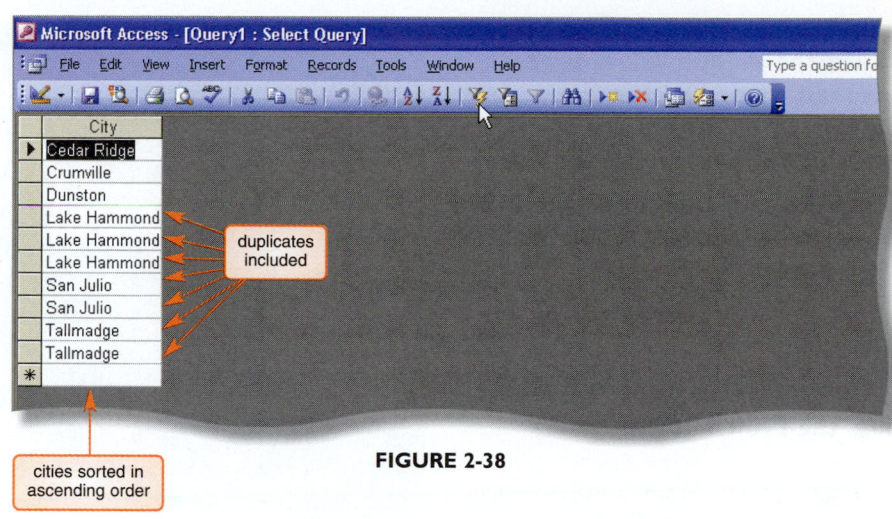

FIGURE 2-38

Omitting Duplicates

When you sort data, duplicates normally are included. In Figure 2-38, for example, San Julio appeared twice, Lake Hammond appeared three times, and Tallmadge appeared twice. To sort to eliminate duplicates, use the Properties button on the Query Design toolbar or the Properties command on the shortcut menu to display the item's property sheet. A **property sheet** is a window containing the various properties of the object. To omit duplicates, you will use the property sheet to change the Unique Values property.

The following steps produce a sorted list of the cities in the Client table in which each city is listed only once.

To Omit Duplicates

1

- **Click the View button on the Query Datasheet toolbar to return to the Query1 : Select Query window.**
- **Click the second field in the design grid (the empty field following City). You must click the second field or you will not get the correct results and will have to repeat this step.**
- **Click the Properties button on the Query Design toolbar.**

Access displays the Query Properties sheet (Figure 2-39). (If your sheet looks different, you clicked the wrong place and will have to repeat the step.)

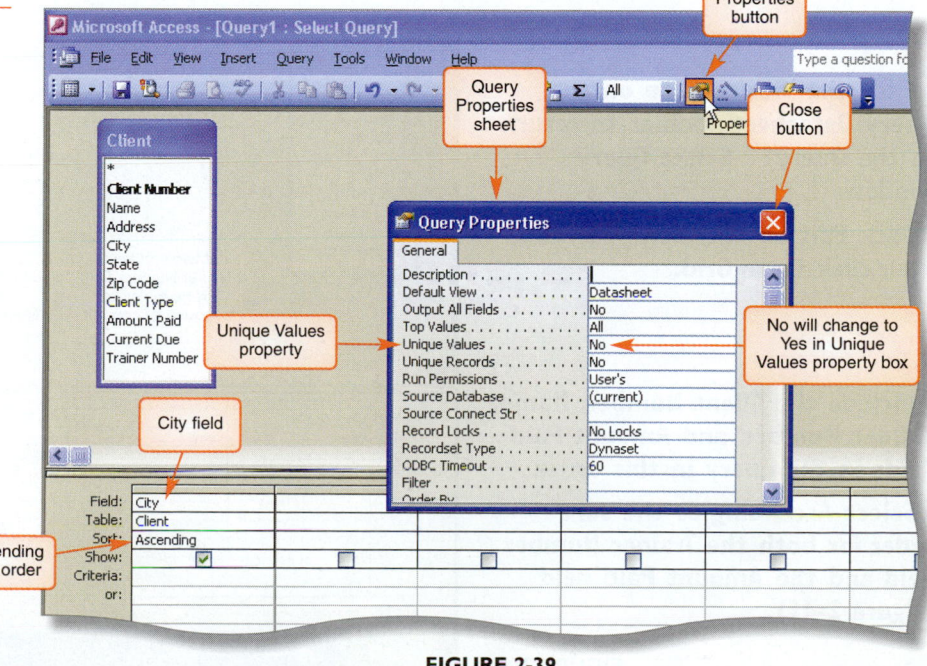

FIGURE 2-39

2

• Click the Unique Values property box, and then click the arrow that appears to produce a list of available choices for Unique Values.

• Click Yes and then close the Query Properties sheet by clicking its Close button.

• Click the Run button to run the query.

• If instructed to print the results, click the Print button.

The results appear (Figure 2-40). The cities are sorted alphabetically. Each city is included only once.

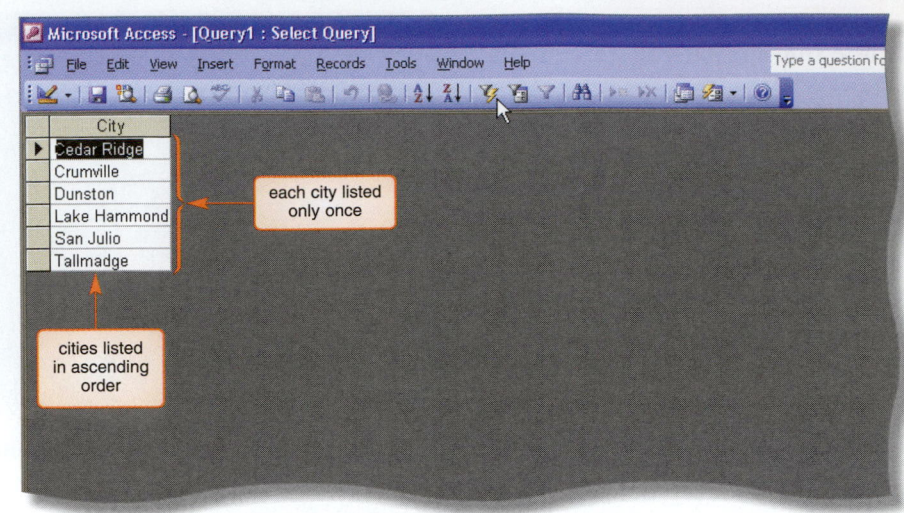

FIGURE 2-40

Other Ways

1. On View menu click Properties
2. Right-click second field in design grid, click Properties on shortcut menu
3. In Voice Command mode, say "Properties"

Sorting on Multiple Keys

The next example lists the number, name, trainer number, and amount paid for all clients. The data is to be sorted by amount paid (low to high) within trainer number, which means that the Trainer Number field is the major key and the Amount Paid field is the minor key.

The following steps accomplish this sorting by specifying the Trainer Number and Amount Paid fields as sort keys.

To Sort on Multiple Keys

1

• Click the View button on the Query Datasheet toolbar to return to the Query1 : Select Query window.

• Click Edit on the menu bar and then click Clear Grid.

2

• Include the Client Number, Name, Trainer Number, and Amount Paid fields in the query in this order.

• Select Ascending as the sort order for both the Trainer Number field and the Amount Paid field (Figure 2-41).

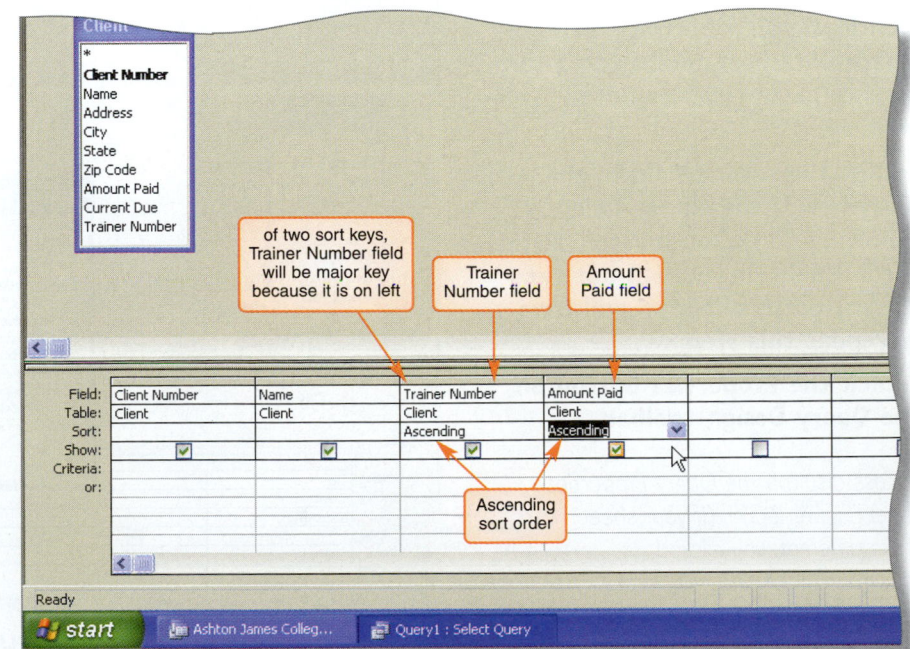

FIGURE 2-41

3

- **Click the Run button to run the query.**
- **If instructed to print the results, click the Print button.**

The results appear (Figure 2-42). The clients are sorted by trainer number. Within the collection of clients having the same trainer, the clients are sorted by amount paid.

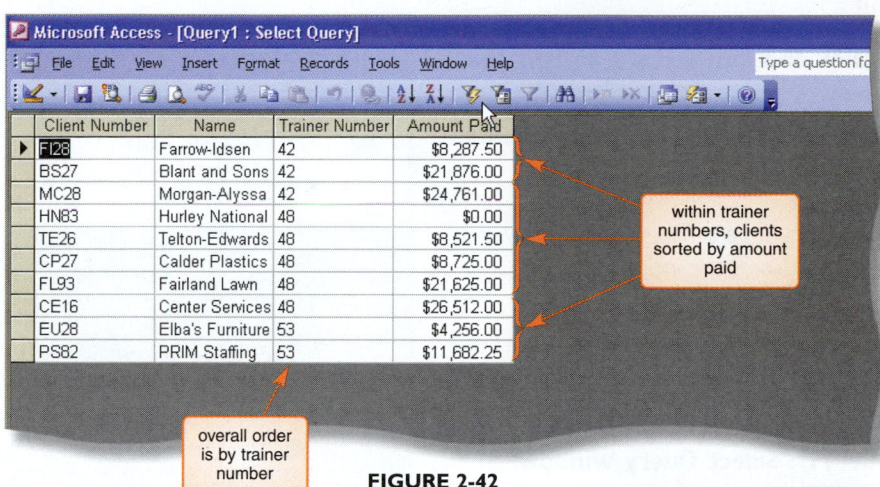

within trainer numbers, clients sorted by amount paid

overall order is by trainer number

FIGURE 2-42

It is important to remember that the major sort key must appear to the left of the minor sort key in the design grid. If you attempted to sort by amount paid within trainer number, but placed the Amount Paid field to the left of the Trainer Number field, your results would be incorrect.

Creating a Top-Values Query

Rather than show all the results of a query, you may want to show only a specified number of records or a percentage of records. Creating a **top-values query** allows you to quantify the results. When you sort records, you can limit results to those records having the highest (descending sort) or lowest (ascending sort) values. To do so, first create a query that sorts the data in the desired order. Next, use the Top Values box on the Query Design toolbar to change the number of records to be included from All to the desired number. The following steps show the first four records that were included in the results of the previous query.

To Create a Top-Values Query

1

- **Click the View button on the Query Datasheet toolbar to return to the Query1 : Select Query window.**
- **Click the Top Values box on the Query Design toolbar, and then type 4 as the new value.**

The value in the Top Values box is changed from All to 4 (Figure 2-43).

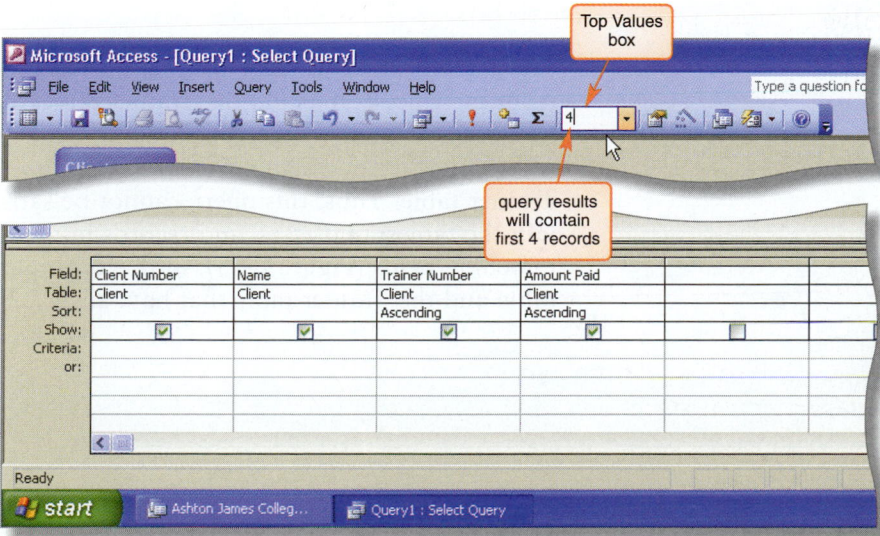

Top Values box

query results will contain first 4 records

FIGURE 2-43

2

• **Click the Run button to run the query.**

• **If instructed to print the results, click the Print button.**

The results appear (Figure 2-44). Only the first four records are included.

3

• **Close the query by clicking the Close Window button for the Query1 : Select Query window.**

• **When asked if you want to save your changes, click the No button.**

The Query1 : Select Query window closes. The query is not saved.

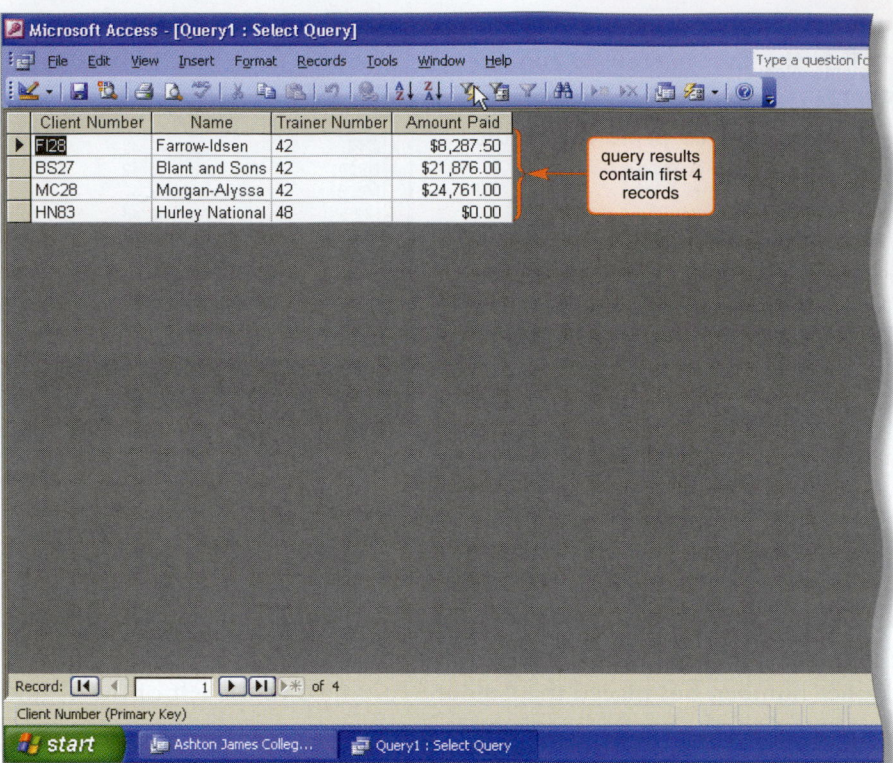

FIGURE 2-44

When you run a top-values query, it is important to change the value in the Top Values box back to All. If you do not change the Top Values value back to all, the previous value will remain in force. Consequently, you may very well not get all the records you should in the next query.

A good practice whenever you use a top-values query is to close the query as soon as you are done. That way, you will begin your next query from scratch, which guarantees that the value is set back to All.

Joining Tables

The Ashton James College database needs to satisfy a query that requires values from the Client table and the Trainer table. Specifically, the query needs to list the number and name of each client along with the number and name of the client's trainer. The client's name is in the Client table, whereas the trainer's name is in the Trainer table. Thus, this query cannot be satisfied using a single table. You need to **join** the tables; that is, to find records in the two tables that have identical values in matching fields (Figure 2-45). In this example, you need to find records in the Client table and the Trainer table that have the same value in the Trainer Number fields.

Give me the number and name of each client along with the number and name of each client's trainer.

Client table

CLIENT NUMBER	NAME	...	TRAINER NUMBER
BS27	Blant and Sons	...	42
CE16	Center Services	...	48
CP27	Calder Plastics	...	48
EU28	Elba's Furniture	...	53
FI28	Farrow-Idsen	...	42
FL93	Fairland Lawn	...	48
HN83	Hurley National	...	48
MC28	Morgan-Alyssa	...	42
PS82	PRIM Staffing	...	53
TE26	Telton-Edwards	...	48

Trainer table

TRAINER NUMBER	LAST NAME	FIRST NAME	...
42	Perry	Belinda	...
48	Stevens	Michael	...
53	Gonzalez	Manuel	...
67	Danville	Marty	...

Trainer table

CLIENT NUMBER	NAME	...	TRAINER NUMBER	LAST NAME	FIRST NAME	...
BS27	Blant and Sons	...	42	Perry	Belinda	...
CE16	Center Services	...	48	Stevens	Michael	...
CP27	Calder Plastics	...	48	Stevens	Michael	...
EU28	Elba's Furniture	...	53	Gonzalez	Manuel	...
FI28	Farrow-Idsen	...	42	Perry	Belinda	...
FL93	Fairland Lawn	...	48	Stevens	Michael	...
HN83	Hurley National	...	48	Stevens	Michael	...
MC28	Morgan-Alyssa	...	42	Perry	Belinda	...
PS82	PRIM Staffing	...	53	Gonzalez	Manuel	...
TE26	Telton-Edwards	...	48	Stevens	Michael	...

FIGURE 2-45

To join tables in Access, first you bring field lists for both tables to the upper pane of the Select Query window. Access will draw a line, called a **join line**, between matching fields in the two tables indicating that the tables are related. You then can select fields from either table. Access will join the tables automatically.

The first step is to select the Trainer table in the Database window and create a new query. Then, add the Client table to the query. A join line will appear connecting the Trainer Number fields in the two field lists. This join line indicates how the tables are related; that is, linked through these matching fields. (If you fail to give the matching fields the same name, Access will not insert the line. You can insert it manually, however, by clicking one of the two matching fields and dragging the mouse pointer to the other matching field.)

The steps on the next page create a new query, add the Client table and then select the appropriate fields.

Q&A

Q: Assuming you want the Trainer Number field to be the major key and the Amount Paid field to be the minor key as in the previous steps, how could you display the Amount Paid field before the Trainer Number field?

A: Include the Trainer Number field, the Amount Paid field, and then the Trainer Number field a second time. Select Ascending as the sort order for the first Trainer Number field and for the Amount Paid field. Remove the check mark from the Show check box for the first Trainer Number field. Thus, the first Trainer Number field will be part of the sort key, but will not appear in the results. The second Trainer Number field will appear in the results after the Amount Paid field.

To Join Tables

1

• **With the Tables object selected and the Trainer table selected, click the New Object button arrow on the Database toolbar.**

• **Click Query, and then click the OK button.**

• **Drag the line separating the two panes to the approximate position shown in Figure 2-46, and then drag the lower edge of the field list box down far enough so all fields in the Trainer table appear.**

• **Click the Show Table button on the Query Design toolbar.**

Access displays the Show Table dialog box (Figure 2-46).

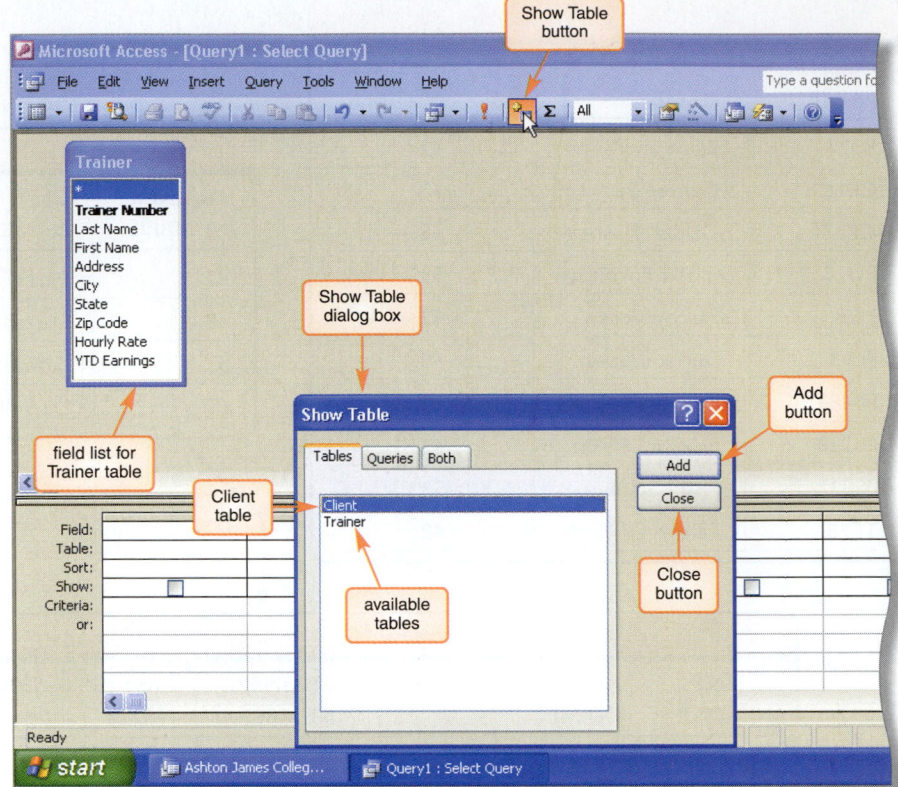

FIGURE 2-46

2

• **Be sure the Client table is selected, and then click the Add button.**

• **Close the Show Table dialog box by clicking the Close button.**

• **Expand the size of the field list so all the fields in the Client table appear.**

The field lists for both tables appear (Figure 2-47). A join line connects the two field lists.

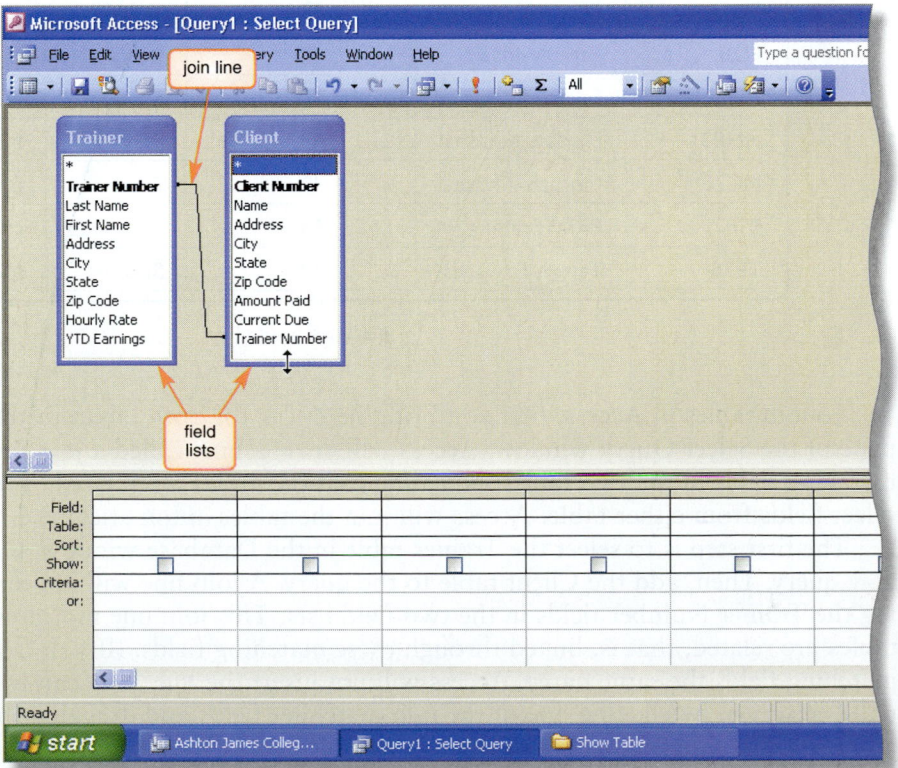

FIGURE 2-47

3

• **Include the Trainer Number, Last Name, and First Name fields from the Trainer table as well as the Client Number and Name fields from the Client table.**

• **Select Ascending as the sort order for both the Trainer Number field and the Client Number field.**

The fields from both tables are selected (Figure 2-48).

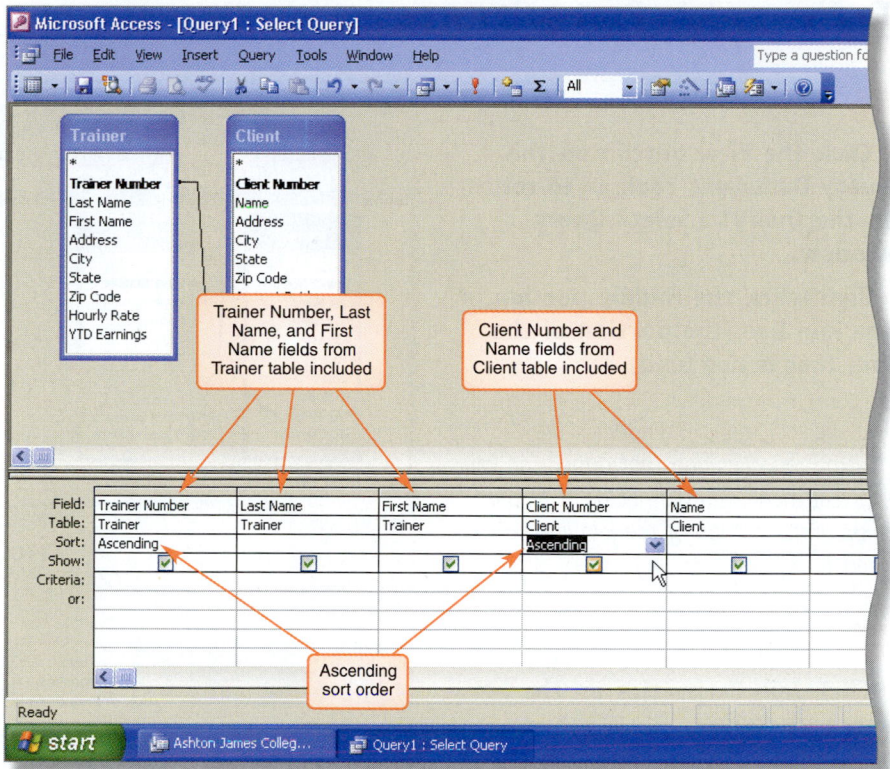

FIGURE 2-48

4

• **Click the Run button to run the query.**

• **If instructed to print the results, click the Print button.**

The results appear (Figure 2-49). They contain data from both the Trainer and Client tables. The records are sorted by trainer number and within trainer number by client number.

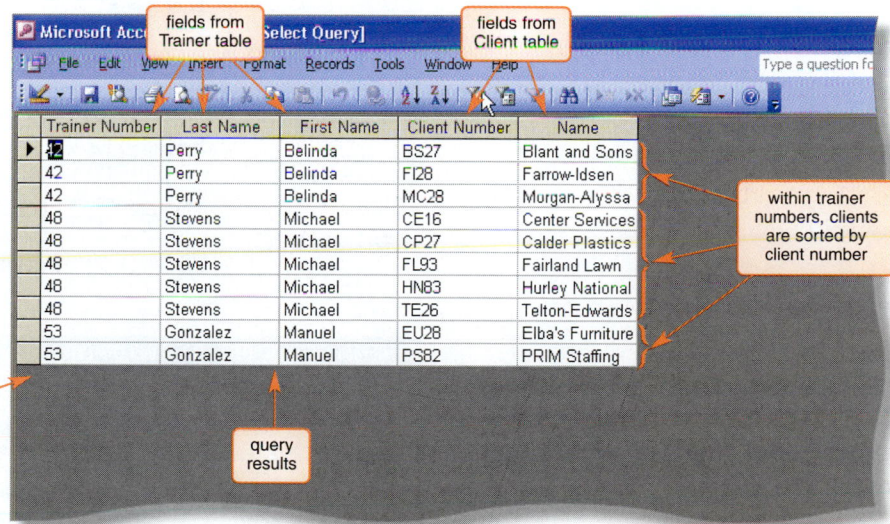

FIGURE 2-49

Changing Join Properties

Normally records that do not match will not appear in the results of a join query. A trainer such as Marty Danville, for whom no clients currently exist, for example, would not appear. To cause such a record to be displayed, you need to change the **join properties**, which are the properties that indicate which records appear in a join, of the query as the steps on the next page illustrate.

Other Ways

1. On Query menu click Show Table
2. Right-click any open area in upper pane, click Show Table on shortcut menu
3. In Voice Command mode, say "Show Table"

To Change Join Properties

1

• **Click the View button on the Query Datasheet toolbar to return to the Query1 : Select Query window.**

• **Right-click the middle portion of the join line (the portion of the line that is not bold).**

The shortcut menu appears (Figure 2-50). (If Join Properties does not appear on your shortcut menu, you did not point to the appropriate portion of the join line. You will need to right-click again.)

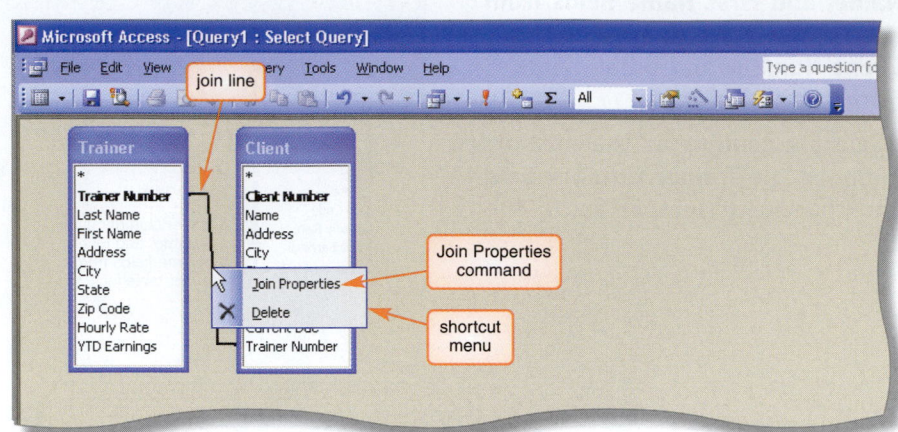

FIGURE 2-50

2

• **Click Join Properties on the shortcut menu.**

Access displays the Join Properties dialog box (Figure 2-51).

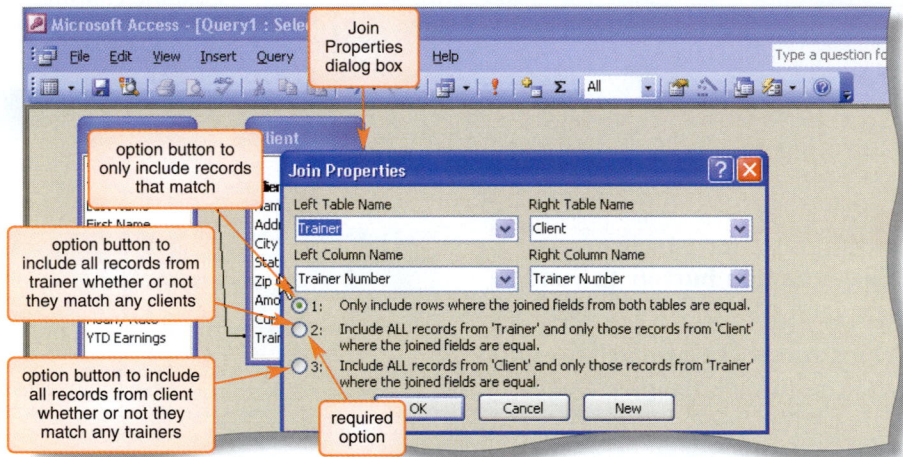

FIGURE 2-51

3

• **Click option button 2 to include all records from the Trainer table regardless of whether or not they match any clients.**

• **Click the OK button.**

• **Run the query by clicking the Run button.**

• **If instructed to print the results, click the Print button.**

The results appear (Figure 2-52).

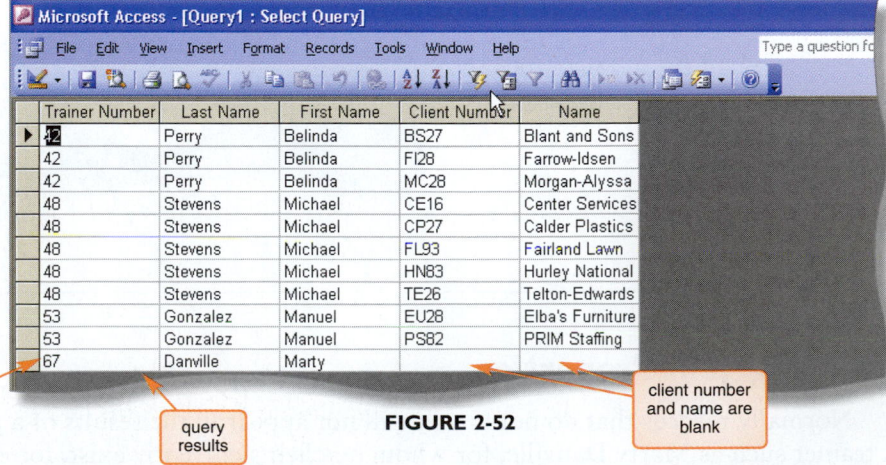

FIGURE 2-52

With the change to the join properties, trainer 67 is included, even though the trainer does not have any clients.

Restricting Records in a Join

Sometimes you will want to join tables, but you will not want to include all possible records. In such cases, you will relate the tables and include fields just as you did before. You also will include criteria. For example, to include the same fields as in the previous query, but only those clients whose amount paid is more than $20,000.00, you will make the same entries as before, but also include >20000 as a criterion for the Amount Paid field.

The following steps modify the query from the previous example to restrict the records that will be included in the join.

To Restrict the Records in a Join

1

• **Click the View button on the Query Datasheet toolbar to return to the Query1 : Select Query window.**

• **Add the Amount Paid field to the query.**

• **Type >20000 as the criterion for the Amount Paid field and then click the Show check box for the Amount Paid field to remove the check mark.**

The Amount Paid field appears in the design grid (Figure 2-53). A criterion is entered for the Amount Paid field, and the Show check box is empty, indicating that the field will not appear in the results of the query.

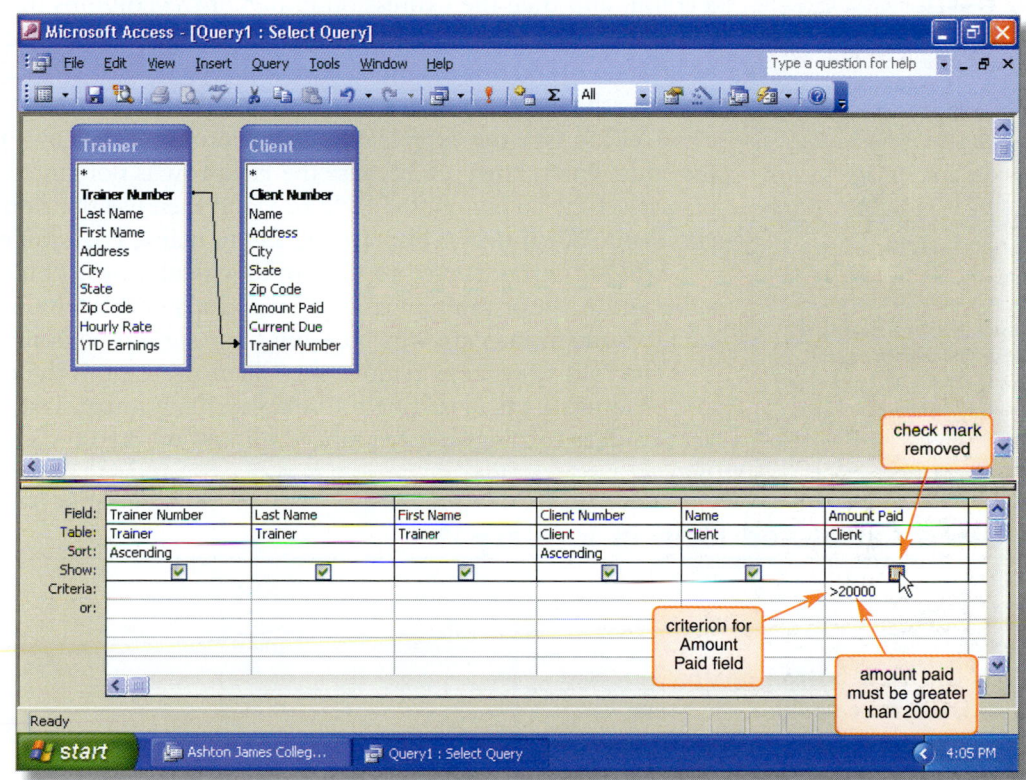

FIGURE 2-53

2

• **Click the Run button to run the query.**

• **If instructed to print the results, click the Print button.**

The results appear (Figure 2-54). Only those clients with an amount paid greater than $20,000.00 are displayed in the result. The Amount Paid field does not appear.

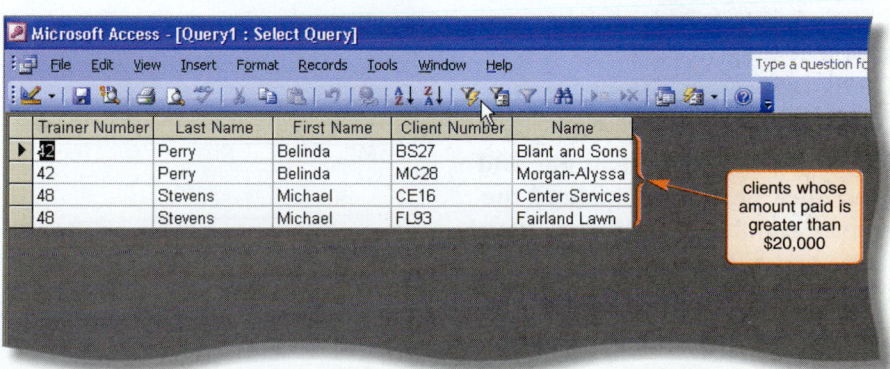

FIGURE 2-54

Calculations

Many types of calculations are available for use in queries. For example, you can add the values in two fields together, or you can calculate the sum or average of the values in one field.

Using Calculated Fields

Suppose that Ashton James College wants to know the number of hours worked by each trainer. This poses a problem because the Trainer table does not include a field for hours worked. You can calculate it, however, because the number of hours worked is equal to the YTD earnings divided by the hourly rate. A field that can be computed from other fields is called a **calculated field**.

To include calculated fields in queries, you enter a name for the calculated field, a colon, and then the expression in one of the columns in the Field row. Any fields included in the expression must be enclosed in square brackets ([ ]). For the number of hours worked, for example, you will type Hours Worked:[YTD Earnings]/[Hourly Rate] as the expression.

You can type the expression directly into the Field row. You will not be able to see the entire entry, however, because the Field row is not large enough. The preferred way is to select the column in the Field row and then use the Zoom command on its shortcut menu. When Access displays the Zoom dialog box, you can enter the expression.

You are not restricted to division in calculations. You can use addition (+), subtraction (-), or multiplication (*). You also can include parentheses in your calculations to indicate which calculations should be done first.

The following steps remove the Client table from the query (it is not needed), and then use a calculated field to display the number, last name, hourly rate, year-to-date earnings, and number of hours worked for all trainers.

To Use a Calculated Field in a Query

1

• **Click the View button on the Query Datasheet toolbar to return to the Query1 : Select Query window.**

• **Right-click any field in the Client table field list.**

• **Click Remove Table on the shortcut menu to remove the Client table from the Query1 : Select Query window.**

• **Click Edit on the menu bar and then click Clear Grid. Include the Trainer Number, Last Name, Hourly Rate, and YTD Earnings.**

• **Right-click the Field row in the first open column in the design grid.**

The shortcut menu appears (Figure 2-55).

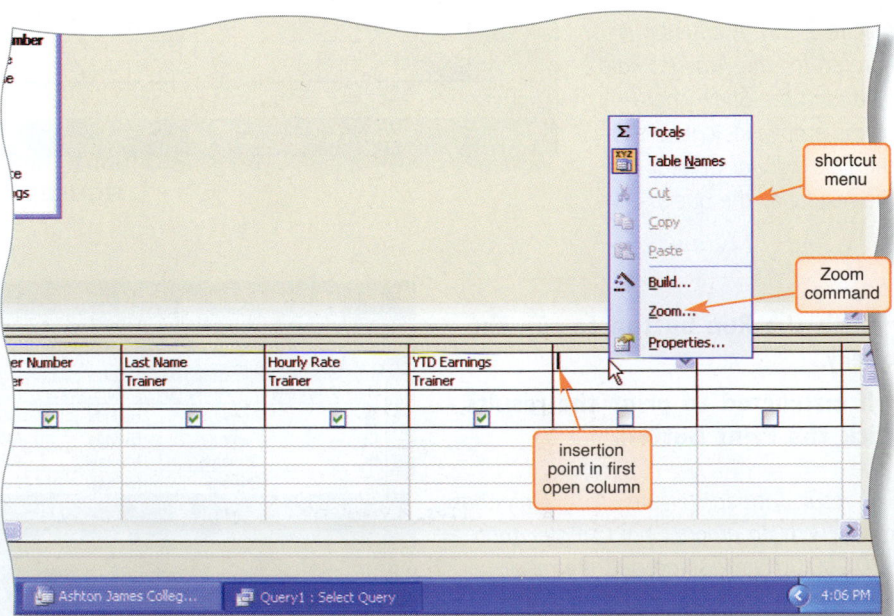

FIGURE 2-55

2

• **Click Zoom on the shortcut menu.**

• **Type** Hours Worked:[YTD Earnings]/[Hourly Rate] **in the Zoom dialog box that appears.**

Access displays the Zoom dialog box (Figure 2-56). The expression you typed appears within the dialog box.

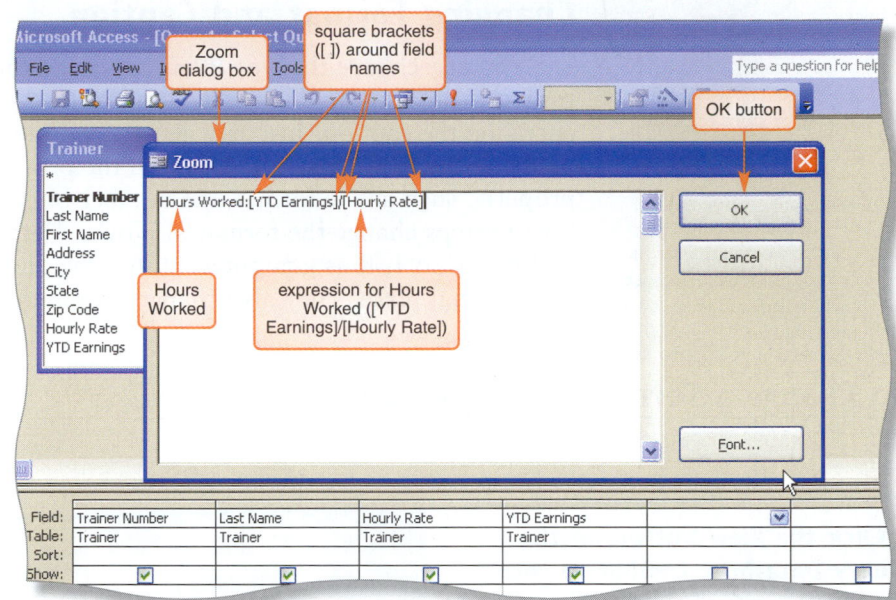

FIGURE 2-56

3

• **Click the OK button.**

A portion of the expression you entered appears in the fifth field in the design grid (Figure 2-57).

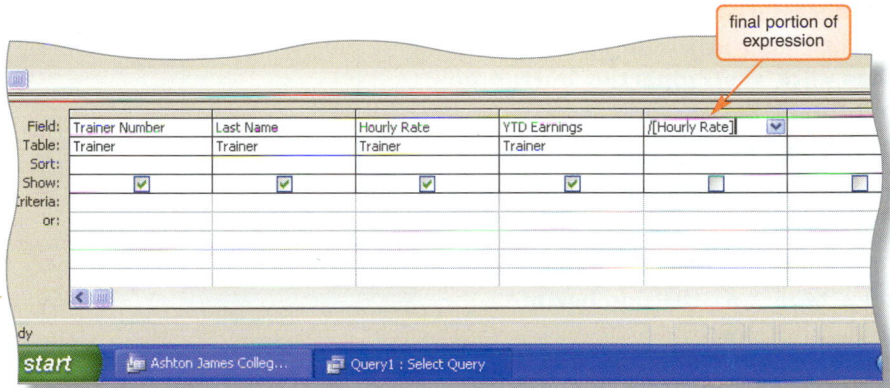

FIGURE 2-57

4

• **Click the Run button to run the query.**

• **If instructed to print the results, click the Print button.**

The results appear (Figure 2-58). Microsoft Access has calculated and displayed the number of hours worked for each trainer.

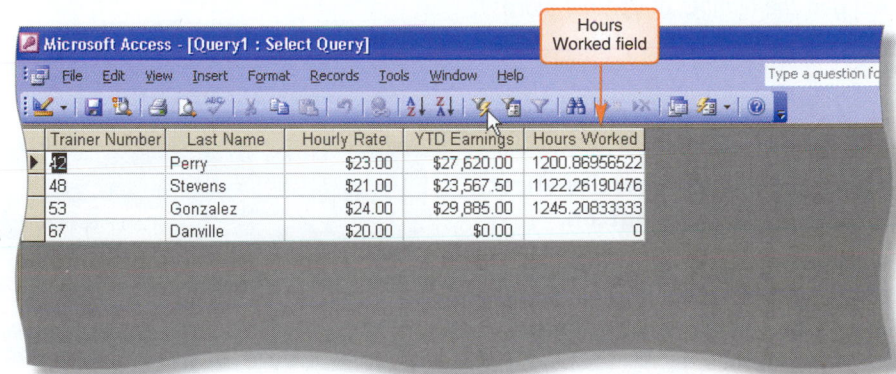

FIGURE 2-58

Trainer Number	Last Name	Hourly Rate	YTD Earnings	Hours Worked
42	Perry	$23.00	$27,620.00	1200.86956522
48	Stevens	$21.00	$23,567.50	1122.26190476
53	Gonzalez	$24.00	$29,885.00	1245.20833333
67	Danville	$20.00	$0.00	0

Other Ways

1. Press SHIFT+F2

Instead of clicking Zoom on the shortcut menu, you can click Build. Access displays the Expression Builder dialog box that provides assistance in creating the expression. If you know the expression you will need, however, usually it is easier to enter it using the Zoom command.

More About

Calculated Fields

Because it is easy to compute values in a query, it is not necessary to store calculated fields, also called computed fields, in a database. It is not necessary, for example, to store the total amount (the amount paid amount plus the current due amount), because it can be calculated whenever it is required.

Changing Format and Caption

You can change the way items appear in the results of a query by changing their format. You also can change the heading at the top of a column in the results by changing the caption. Just as when you omitted duplicates, you will make this change by using the field's property sheet. In the property sheet, you can change the desired property, such as the format, the number of decimal places, or the caption. The following steps change the format of Hours Worked to Fixed and the number of decimal places to 1, thus guaranteeing that the number on each row will contain exactly one decimal place. They also change the caption of the Hourly Rate field to Rate.

To Change a Format and a Caption

1

• **Click the View button on the Query Datasheet toolbar to return to the Query1 : Select Query window.**

• **If necessary, click the Hours Worked field in the design grid, and then click the Properties button on the Query Design toolbar.**

• **Click the Format box, click the Format box arrow, and then click Fixed.**

• **Click the Decimal Places box, and then type 1 as the number of decimal places.**

Access displays the Field Properties sheet (Figure 2-59). The format is changed to Fixed and the number of decimal places is set to 1.

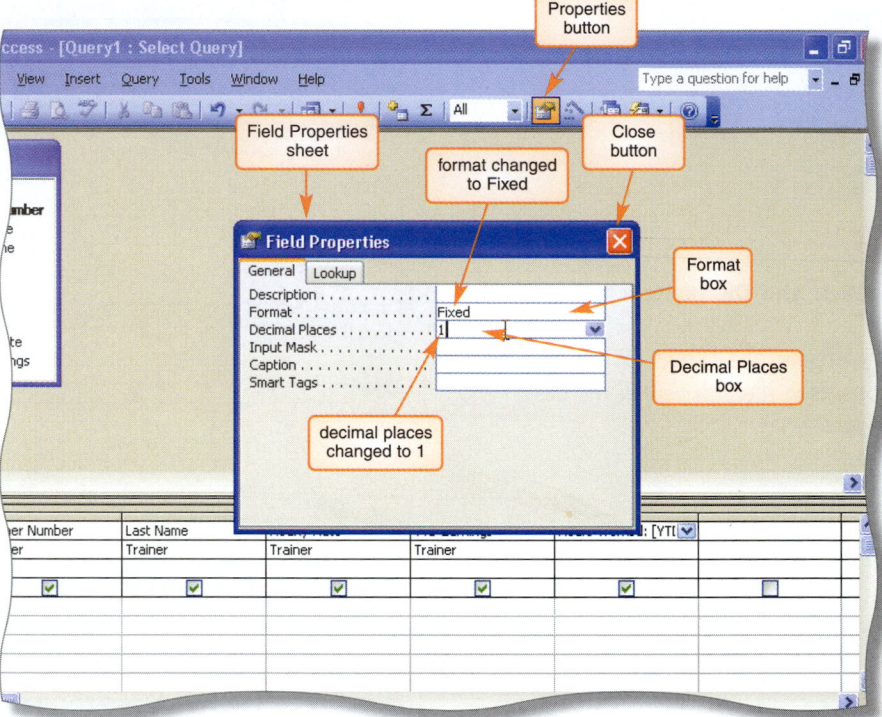

FIGURE 2-59

2

• **Close the Field Properties sheet by clicking its Close button.**

• **Click the Hourly Rate field in the design grid, and then click the Properties button on the Query Design toolbar.**

• **Click the Caption box, and then type Rate as the caption.**

Access displays the Field Properties sheet (Figure 2-60). The caption is changed to Rate.

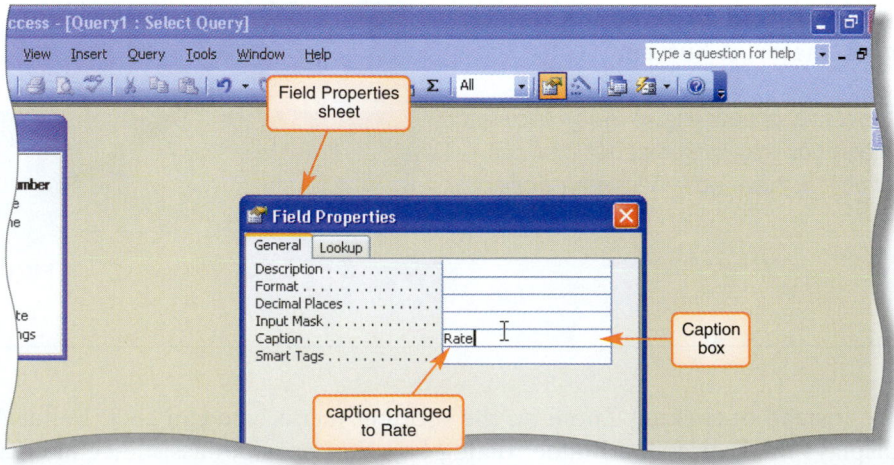

FIGURE 2-60

3

• **Click the Run button to run the query.**

• **If instructed to print the results, click the Print button.**

The results appear (Figure 2-61). The Hourly Rate caption is changed to Rate. The numbers in the Hours Worked column all contain exactly one decimal place.

4

• **Click the Close Window button for the Query1 : Select Query window.**

• **When asked if you want to save your changes, click the No button.**

The Query1 : Select Query window closes. The query is not saved.

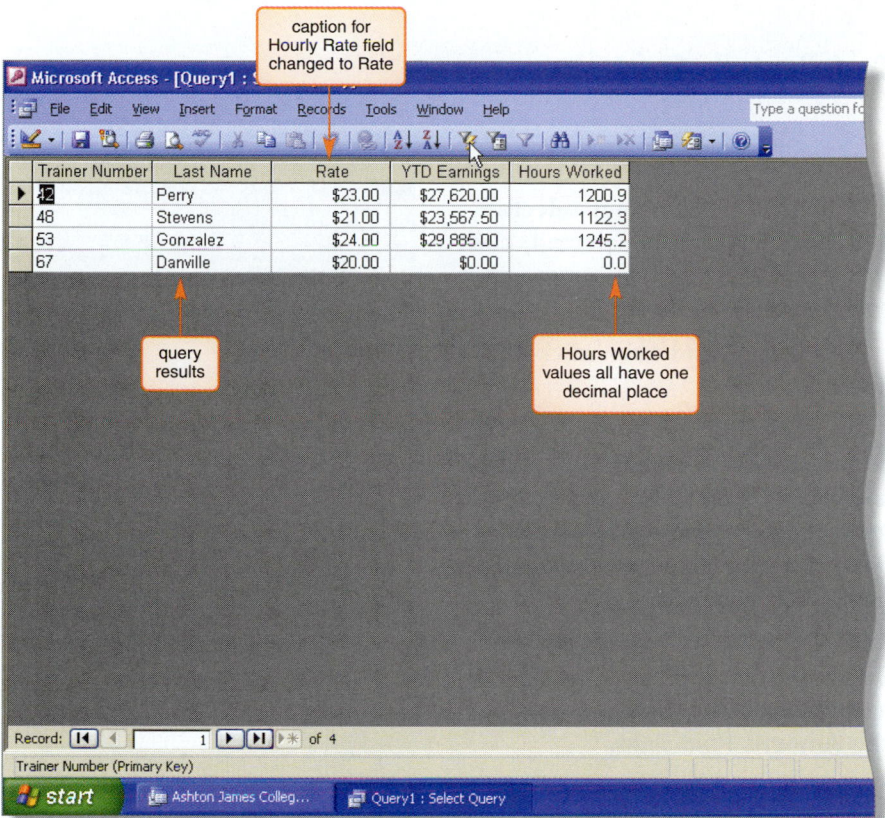

caption for Hourly Rate field changed to Rate

query results

Hours Worked values all have one decimal place

FIGURE 2-61

If you had saved the query, the changes you made to the properties would be saved along with the query.

Calculating Statistics

Microsoft Access supports the built-in statistics: COUNT, SUM, AVG (average), MAX (largest value), MIN (smallest value), STDEV (standard deviation), VAR (variance), FIRST, and LAST. These statistics are called aggregate functions. An **aggregate function** is a function that performs some mathematical function against a group of records. To use any of these aggregate functions in a query, you include it in the Total row in the design grid. The Total row routinely does not appear in the grid. To include it, click the Totals button on the Query Design toolbar.

The steps on the next page create a new query for the Client table and then calculate the average amount paid for all clients.

To Calculate Statistics

- **With the Tables object selected and the Client table selected, click the New Object button arrow on the Database toolbar.**

- **Click Query, and then click the OK button.**

- **Drag the line separating the two panes to the approximate position shown in Figure 2-62, and drag the lower edge of the field list box down far enough so all fields in the Client table appear.**

- **Click the Totals button on the Query Design toolbar, and then double-click the Amount Paid field.**

The Total row now is included in the design grid (Figure 2-62). The Amount Paid field is included, and the entry in the Total row is Group By.

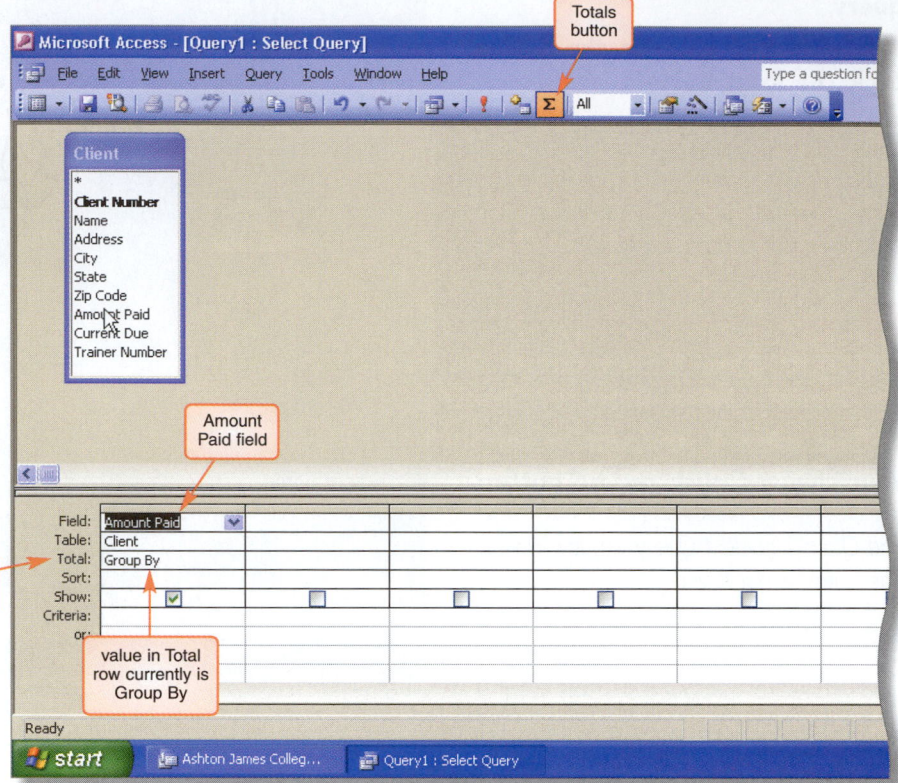

FIGURE 2-62

- **Click the Total row in the Amount Paid column, and then click the Total row arrow that appears.**

The list of available options appears (Figure 2-63).

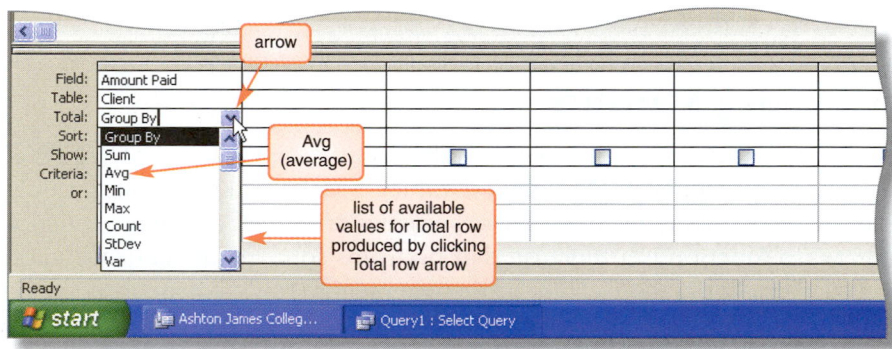

FIGURE 2-63

- **Click Avg.**

Avg is selected (Figure 2-64).

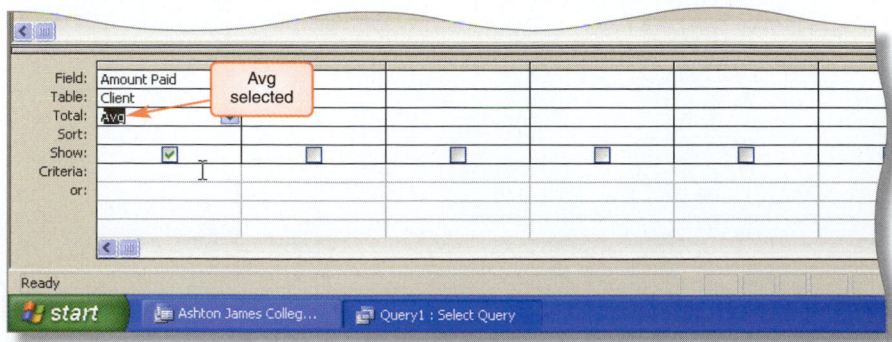

FIGURE 2-64

4

• **Click the Run button to run the query.**

• **If instructed to print the results, click the Print button.**

The result appears (Figure 2-65), showing the average amount paid for all clients.

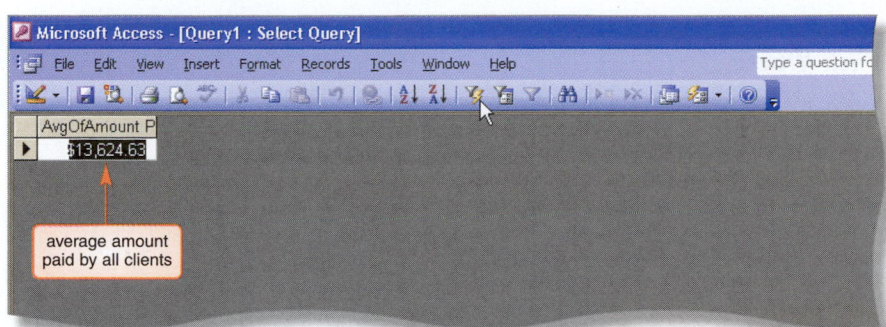

FIGURE 2-65

Other Ways

1. On View menu click Totals
2. Right-click any open area in upper pane, click Totals on shortcut menu
3. In Voice Command mode, say "Totals"

Using Criteria in Calculating Statistics

Sometimes calculating statistics for all the records in the table is appropriate. In other cases, however, you will need to calculate the statistics for only those records that satisfy certain criteria. To enter a criterion in a field, first you select Where as the entry in the Total row for the field and then enter the criterion in the Criteria row. The following steps use this technique to calculate the average amount paid for clients of trainer 48.

To Use Criteria in Calculating Statistics

1

• **Click the View button on the Query Datasheet toolbar to return to the Query1 : Select Query window.**

2

• **Include the Trainer Number field in the design grid.**

• **Produce the list of available options for the Total row entry just as you did when you selected Avg for the Amount Paid field.**

• **Use the vertical scroll bar to move through the options until the Where option appears.**

The list of available options appears (Figure 2-66). The Group By entry in the Trainer Number field may not be highlighted on your screen depending on where you clicked in the Total row.

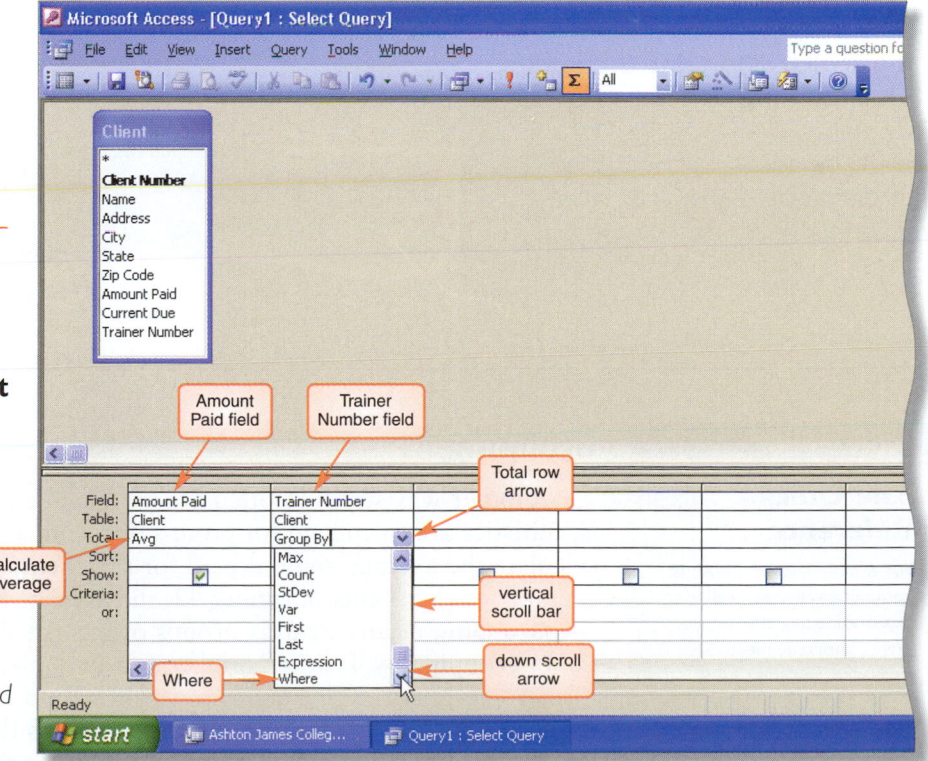

FIGURE 2-66

Microsoft Office
Access 2003

3

• **Click Where.**

• **Type** 42 **as the criterion for the Trainer Number field.**

Where is selected as the entry in the Total row for the Trainer Number field and 42 is entered in the Criteria row (Figure 2-67).

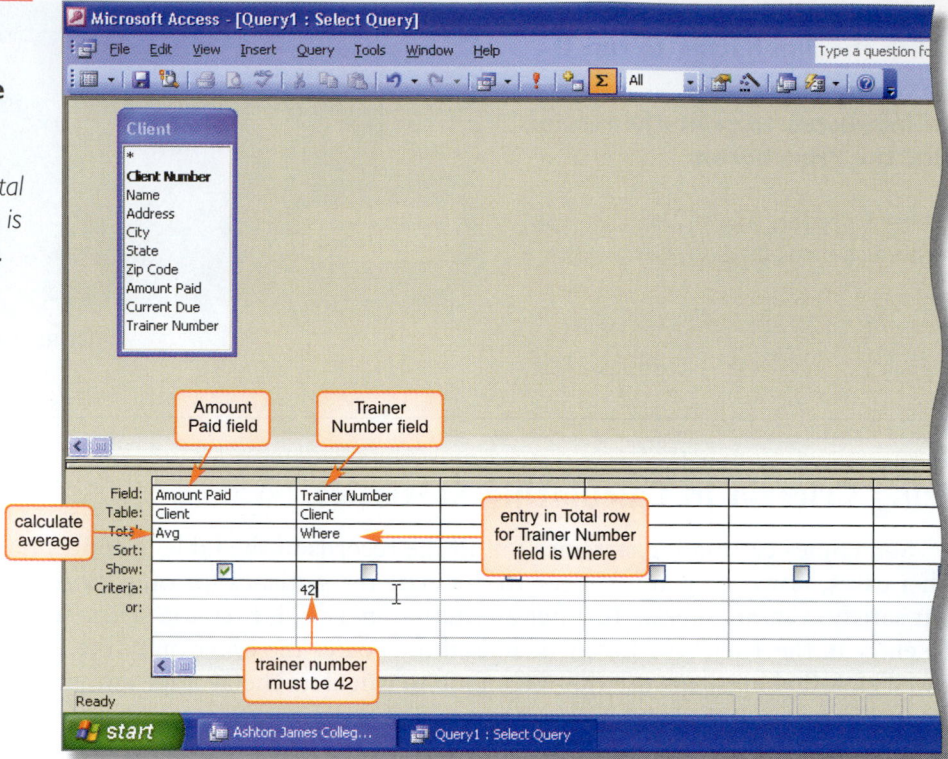

FIGURE 2-67

4

• **Click the Run button to run the query.**

• **If instructed to print the results, click the Print button.**

The results appear (Figure 2-68), giving the average amount paid for clients of trainer 42.

FIGURE 2-68

More About

The Quick Reference

For a table that lists how to complete tasks covered in this book using the mouse, menu, shortcut menu, and keyboard, see the Quick Reference Summary at the back of this book, or visit the Access 2003 Quick Reference Web page (scsite.com/ac2003/qr).

Grouping

Another way statistics often are used is in combination with grouping; that is, statistics are calculated for groups of records. You may, for example, need to calculate the average amount paid for the clients of each trainer. You will want the average for the clients of trainer 42, the average for clients of trainer 48, and so on.

Grouping means creating groups of records that share some common characteristic. In grouping by Trainer Number, for example, the clients of trainer 42 would form one group, the clients of trainer 48 would be a second, and the clients of trainer 53 form a third group. The calculations then are made for each group. To indicate grouping in Access, select Group By as the entry in the Total row for the field to be used for grouping.

The following steps calculate the average amount paid for clients of each trainer.

To Use Grouping

1

• **Click the View button on the Query Datasheet toolbar to return to the Query1 : Select Query window.**

• **Click Edit on the menu bar and then click Clear Grid.**

• **Include the Trainer Number field.**

• **Include the Amount Paid field, and then click Avg as the calculation in the Total row.**

The Trainer Number and Amount Paid fields are included (Figure 2-69). Group By currently is the entry in the Total row for the Trainer Number field, which is correct; thus, it was not changed.

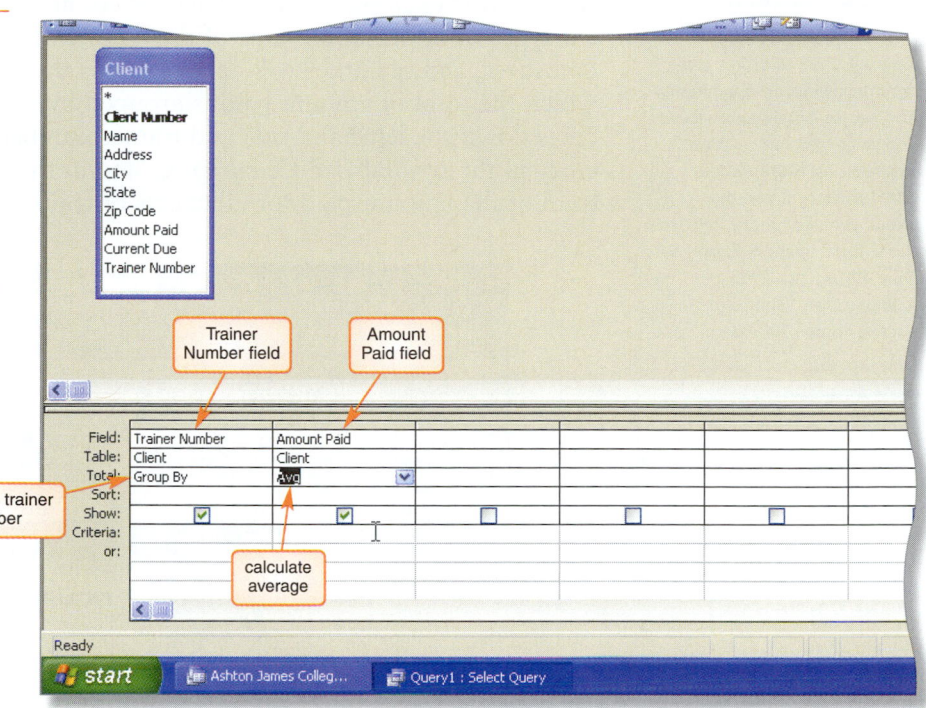

FIGURE 2-69

2

• **Click the Run button to run the query.**

• **If instructed to print the results, click the Print button.**

The results appear (Figure 2-70), showing each trainer's number along with the average amount paid for the clients of that trainer. Because the results are grouped by trainer number, a single row exists for each trainer summarizing all the clients of that trainer.

3

• **Close the query by clicking the Close Window button for the Query1 : Select Query window.**

• **When asked if you want to save your changes, click the No button.**

The Query1 : Select Query window closes. The query is not saved.

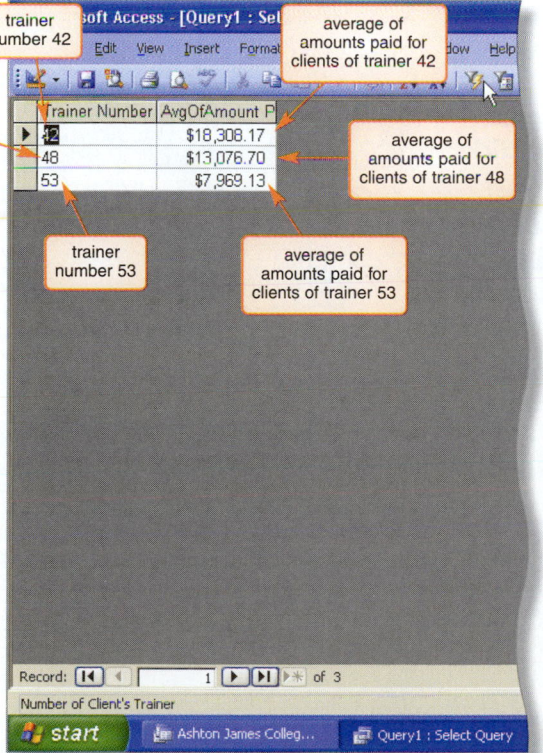

FIGURE 2-70

More About

Microsoft Certification

The Microsoft Office Specialist Certification program provides an opportunity for you to obtain a valuable industry credential — proof that you have the Access 2003 skills required by employers. For more information, see Appendix E, or visit the Access 2003 Certification Web page (scsite.com/ac2003/cert).

Crosstab Queries

Crosstab queries are useful for summarizing data. A **crosstab query** calculates a statistic (for example, sum, average, or count) for data that is grouped by two different types of information. One of the types will appear down the side of the resulting datasheet, and the other will appear across the top. Figure 2-71 shows a crosstab in which the total of amount paid is grouped by both city and trainer number with cities down the left-hand side and trainer numbers across the top. For example, the entry in the row labeled Cedar Ridge and in the column labeled 42 represents the total of the amount paid for all clients of trainer 42 who live in Cedar Ridge.

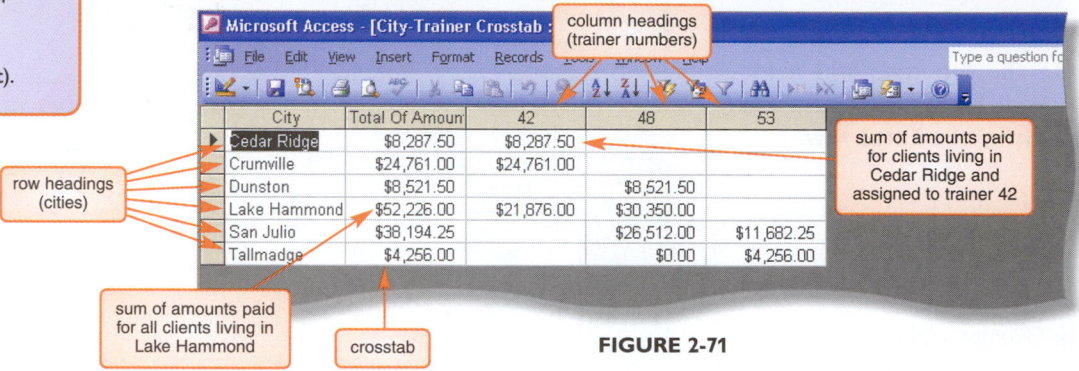

FIGURE 2-71

The following steps use the Crosstab Query wizard to create a crosstab query.

To Create a Crosstab Query

1

- **With the Tables object selected and the Client table selected, click the New Object button arrow.**

- **Click Query, click Crosstab Query Wizard in the New Query dialog box, and then click the OK button.**

Access displays the Crosstab Query Wizard dialog box (Figure 2-72).

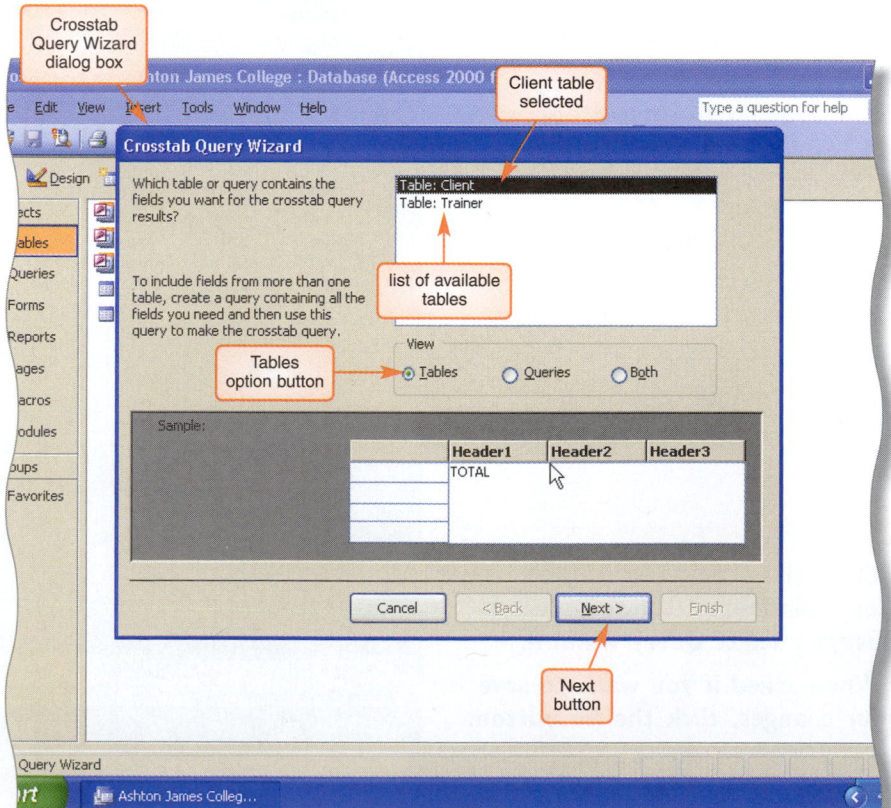

FIGURE 2-72

2

• **With the Tables option button selected and the Client table selected, click the Next button.**

• **Click the City field, and then click the Add Field button.**

The Crosstab Query Wizard dialog box displays options for selecting field values as row headings (Figure 2-73). The City field is selected as the field whose values will provide the row headings.

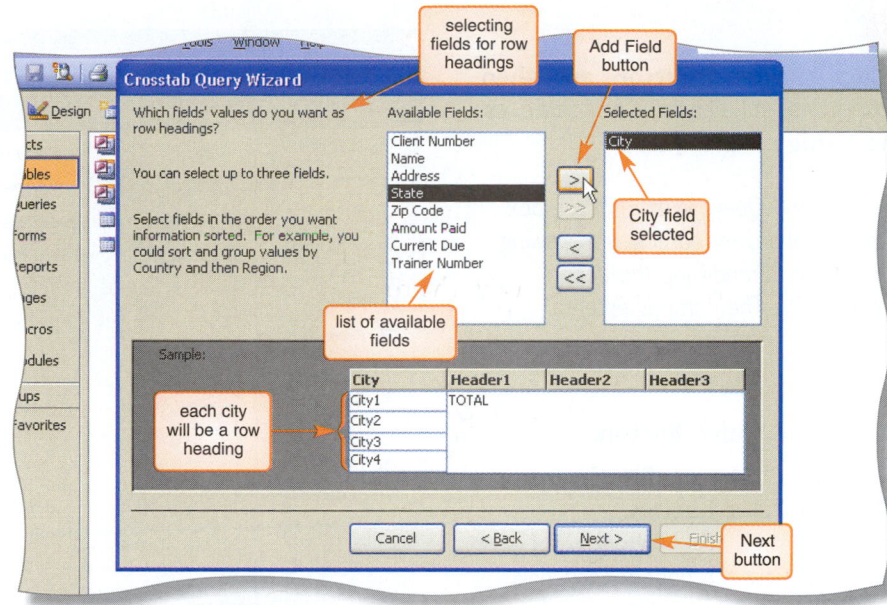

FIGURE 2-73

3

• **Click the Next button, and then click the Trainer Number field.**

The Crosstab Query Wizard dialog box displays options for selecting field values as column headings (Figure 2-74). The Trainer Number field is selected as the field whose values will provide the column headings.

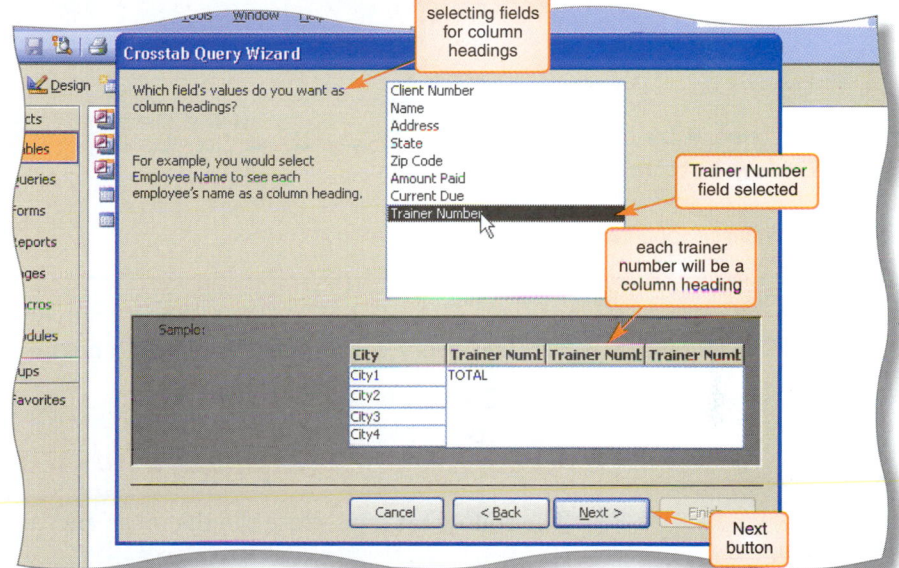

FIGURE 2-74

4

• **Click the Next button, click the Amount Paid field, and then click Sum.**

The Crosstab Query Wizard dialog box displays options for selecting fields for calculations for column and row intersections (Figure 2-75). The Amount Paid field is selected as the field whose value will be calculated for each row and column intersection. Because Sum is the selected function, the calculation will be the total amount paid.

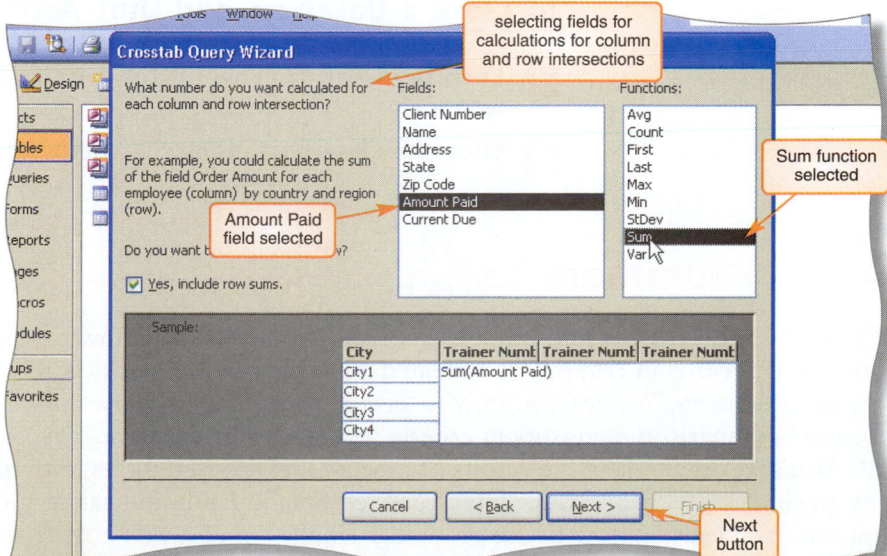

FIGURE 2-75

5

• **Click the Next button, and then type** City-Trainer Crosstab **as the name of the query.**

The Crosstab Query Wizard dialog box displays options for naming and viewing the query and modifying the design (Figure 2-76). The name is entered.

6

• **Click the Finish button.**

• **If instructed to print the results, click the Print button.**

The results now can appear. They look like the results shown in Figure 2-71 on page AC 104.

7

• **Close the query by clicking its Close Window button.**

The query no longer appears.

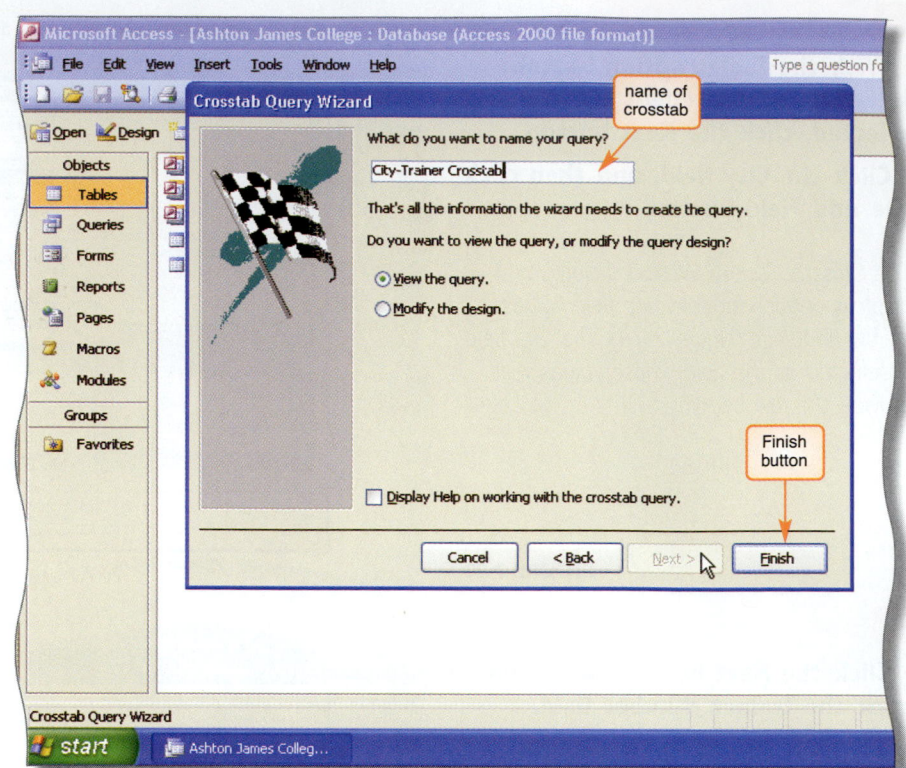

FIGURE 2-76

The query containing the crosstab now can be run just like any other query.

Closing a Database and Quitting Access

The following steps close the database and quit Access.

To Close a Database and Quit Access

1 Click the Close Window button for the Ashton James College : Database window.

2 Click the Close button for the Microsoft Access window.

Project Summary

In Project 2, you created and ran a variety of queries. You saw how to select fields in a query. You used text data and wildcards in criteria. You created a parameter query, which allowed users to enter a criterion when they run the query. You learned how to save a query for future use and how to use a query you have saved. You also used comparison operators in criteria involving numeric data. You combined criteria with both AND and OR. You saw how to sort the results of a query, how to join tables, how to restrict the records in a join, and how to change join properties. You created computed fields and calculated statistics. You changed formats and captions. You learned how to use grouping. Finally, you learned how to create a crosstab query.

If you have a SAM user profile, you may have access to hands-on instruction, practice, and assessment of the skills covered in this project. Log in to your SAM account and go to your assignments page to see what your instructor has assigned.

What You Should Know

Having completed this project, you should be able to perform the tasks below. The tasks are listed in the same order they were presented in this project. For a list of the buttons, menus, toolbars, and commands introduced in this project, see the Quick Reference Summary at the back of this book and refer to the Page Number column.

1. Open a Database   (AC 68)
2. Create a Query   (AC 68)
3. Include Fields in the Design Grid   (AC 71)
4. Run the Query   (AC 71)
5. Print the Results of a Query   (AC 72)
6. Return to the Select Query Window   (AC 72)
7. Close the Query   (AC 73)
8. Include All Fields in a Query   (AC 74)
9. Clear the Design Grid   (AC 75)
10. Use Text Data in a Criterion   (AC 76)
11. Use a Wildcard   (AC 77)
12. Use Criteria for a Field Not Included in the Results   (AC 78)
13. Create and Run a Parameter Query   (AC 79)
14. Save a Query   (AC 80)
15. Use a Saved Query   (AC 81)
16. Use a Number in a Criterion   (AC 82)
17. Use a Comparison Operator in a Criterion   (AC 83)
18. Use a Compound Criterion Involving AND   (AC 84)
19. Use a Compound Criterion Involving OR   (AC 85)
20. Sort Data in a Query   (AC 86)
21. Omit Duplicates   (AC 87)
22. Sort on Multiple Keys   (AC 88)
23. Create a Top-Values Query   (AC 89)
24. Join Tables   (AC 92)
25. Change Join Properties   (AC 94)
26. Restrict the Records in a Join   (AC 95)
27. Use a Calculated Field in a Query   (AC 96)
28. Change a Format and a Caption   (AC 98)
29. Calculate Statistics   (AC 100)
30. Use Criteria in Calculating Statistics   (AC 101)
31. Use Grouping   (AC 103)
32. Create a Crosstab Query   (AC 104)
33. Close a Database and Quit Access   (AC 106)

Learn It Online

Instructions: To complete the Learn It Online exercises, start your browser, click the Address bar, and then enter the Web address scsite.com/ac2003/learn. When the Access 2003 Learn It Online page is displayed, follow the instructions in the exercises below. Each exercise has instructions for printing your results, either for your own records or for submission to your instructor.

1 Project Reinforcement TF, MC, and SA

Below Access Project 2, click the Project Reinforcement link. Print the quiz by clicking Print on the File menu for each page. Answer each question.

2 Flash Cards

Below Access Project 2, click the Flash Cards link and read the instructions. Type 20 (or a number specified by your instructor) in the Number of playing cards text box, type your name in the Enter your Name text box, and then click the Flip Card button. When the flash card is displayed, read the question and then click the ANSWER box arrow to select an answer. Flip through Flash Cards. If your score is 15 (75%) correct or greater, click Print on the File menu to print your results. If your score is less than 15 (75%) correct, then redo this exercise by clicking the Replay button.

3 Practice Test

Below Access Project 2, click the Practice Test link. Answer each question, enter your first and last name at the bottom of the page, and then click the Grade Test button. When the graded practice test is displayed on your screen, click Print on the File menu to print a hard copy. Continue to take practice tests until you score 80% or better.

4 Who Wants To Be a Computer Genius?

Below Access Project 2, click the Computer Genius link. Read the instructions, enter your first and last name at the bottom of the page, and then click the PLAY button. When your score is displayed, click the PRINT RESULTS link to print a hard copy.

5 Wheel of Terms

Below Access Project 2, click the Wheel of Terms link. Read the instructions, and then enter your first and last name and your school name. Click the PLAY button. When your score is displayed, right-click the score and then click Print on the shortcut menu to print a hard copy.

6 Crossword Puzzle Challenge

Below Access Project 2, click the Crossword Puzzle Challenge link. Read the instructions, and then enter your first and last name. Click the SUBMIT button. Work the crossword puzzle. When you are finished, click the Submit button. When the crossword puzzle is redisplayed, click the Print Puzzle button to print a hard copy.

7 Tips and Tricks

Below Access Project 2, click the Tips and Tricks link. Click a topic that pertains to Project 2. Right-click the information and then click Print on the shortcut menu. Construct a brief example of what the information relates to in Access to confirm you understand how to use the tip or trick.

8 Newsgroups

Below Access Project 2, click the Newsgroups link. Click a topic that pertains to Project 2. Print three comments.

9 Expanding Your Horizons

Below Access Project 2, click the Expanding Your Horizons link. Click a topic that pertains to Project 2. Print the information. Construct a brief example of what the information relates to in Access to confirm you understand the contents of the article.

10 Search Sleuth

Below Access Project 2, click the Search Sleuth link. To search for a term that pertains to this project, select a term below the Project 2 title and then use the Google search engine at google.com (or any major search engine) to display and print two Web pages that present information on the term.

11 Access Online Training

Below Access Project 2, click the Access Online Training link. When your browser displays the Microsoft Office Online Web page, click the Access link. Click one of the Access courses that covers one or more of the objectives listed at the beginning of the project on page AC 66. Print the first page of the course before stepping through it.

12 Office Marketplace

Below Access Project 2, click the Office Marketplace link. When your browser displays the Microsoft Office Online Web page, click the Office Marketplace link. Click a topic that relates to Access. Print the first page.

Apply Your Knowledge

1 Querying the Begon Pest Control Database

Instructions: Start Access. Open the Begon Pest Control database that you modified in Apply Your Knowledge 1 in Project 1 on page AC 54. (If you did not complete this exercise, see your instructor for a copy of the modified database.) Perform the following tasks:

1. Create a query for the Customer table and add the Name and Address fields to the design grid.
2. Find only those records where the client has an address on Fletcher. Run the query and change the address for the client on 109 Fletcher to 190 Fletcher. Print the results. Return to Design view and clear the grid.
3. Add the Customer Number, Name, City, and Balance fields to the design grid. Sort the records in ascending order by City and descending by Balance. Run the query and print the results. Return to Design view.
4. Modify the query to allow the user to enter a different city each time the query is run. Run the query to find all customers who live in Kady. Print the query results. Save the query as Customer-City Query.
5. Open the Customer-City Query in Design view. Run the query to find all customers who live in Carlton but restrict retrieval to the top two records. Print the results. Close the query without saving it.
6. Create a new query for the Technician table and then join the Technician and Customer tables. Add the Technician Number, First Name and Last Name fields from the Technician table and the Customer Number, and Name fields from the Customer table. Sort the records in ascending order by Technician Number and Customer Number. All technicians should appear in the result even if they currently have no customers. Run the query and print the results.
7. Restrict the records retrieved in task 6 above to only those customers who have a balance greater than $350.00. Run the query and print the results. Close the query without saving it.
8. Create and print the crosstab shown in Figure 2-77. The crosstab groups total of customers' balances by city and technician number.

FIGURE 2-77

In The Lab

1 Querying the Birds2U Database

Problem: The management of Birds2U has determined a number of questions it wants the database management system to answer. You must obtain the answers to the questions posed by management.

Instructions: Use the database created in the In the Lab 1 of Project 1 on page AC 57 for this assignment or see your instructor for information on accessing the files required for this book. Perform the following tasks:

1. Open the Birds2U database and create a new query to display and print the Item Code, Description, On Hand, and Selling Price for all records in the Item table.
2. Display and print the Item Code, Description, Cost, and Supplier Code fields for all products where the Supplier Code is 13.

(continued)

In the Lab

1 Querying the Birds2U Database *(continued)*

3. Display and print the Item Code and Description fields for all items where the description includes the letters "bird."

4. Display and print the Item Code and Description fields for all items with a cost less than $15.00.

5. Display and print the Item Code and Description fields for all products that have a selling price greater than $50.00.

6. Display and print all fields for those items with a selling price greater than $30.00 and where the number on hand is at least 5.

7. Display and print all fields for those items that have a supplier code of 13 or a selling price less than $16.00.

8. Include the Item Code, Description, On Hand, and Selling Price in the design grid. Change the caption for the On Hand column to In Stock and sort the records in descending order by selling price. Run the query and print the results. Run the query again but this time limit retrieval to the top 3 records.

9. Join the Supplier table and the Item table. Display the Supplier Code and Name from the Supplier table and the Item Code, Description, On Hand, and Cost from the Item table. Sort the records in ascending order by Supplier Code and by Item Code. All suppliers should display in the result even if they currently supply no items. Run the query and print the results. Save the query as Suppliers and Items.

10. Restrict the records retrieved in task 9 above to only those products where number on hand is less than 5. Run the query and print the results. Close the query and do not save the changes.

11. Create a new query for the Item table and include the Item Code and Description fields in the design grid. Calculate the on-hand value (on hand * cost) for all records in the table. Run the query and print the results.

12. Display and print the average selling price of all items.

13. Display and print the average selling price of items grouped by supplier code.

2 Querying the Babbage Bookkeeping Database

Problem: Babbage Bookkeeping has determined a number of questions it wants the database management system to answer. You must obtain the answers to the questions posed by the bookkeeping service.

Instructions: Use the database created in the In the Lab 2 of Project 1 on page AC 59 for this assignment or see your instructor for information on accessing the files required for this book. Perform the following tasks:

1. Open the Babbage Bookkeeping database and create a new query for the Client table.

2. Display and print the Name and Balance fields for all clients where the bookkeeper number is 24.

3. Display and print the Client Number, Name, and Balance fields for all clients located in Empeer with a balance greater than $300.00.

4. Display and print the Client Number, Name, and Address fields for all clients with an address on Maum.

5. Display and print the cities in ascending order. Each city should appear only once.

6. Create a query that will allow the user to enter the city to search when the query is run. The query results should display the Client Number, Name, and Bookkeeper Number. Test the query by searching for those records where the client is located in Portage. Save the query as Client-City Query.

7. Include the Client Number, Name, and Balance fields in the design grid. Sort the records in descending order by the Balance field. Display and print the top half of the records.

In the Lab

8. Display and print the Client Number, Name, and Balance fields for all clients where the bookkeeper number is 24 or 34 and the balance is greater than $300.00. (*Hint:* Use Microsoft Access Help to solve this problem.)

9. Display and print the First Name, Last Name, and Hourly Rate fields from the Bookkeeper table and the Client Number, Name, and Balance fields from the Client table. Sort the records in ascending order by bookkeeper's last name and client's name.

10. Create a new query for the Bookkeeper table and include the Bookkeeper Number, First Name, Last Name, and Hourly Rate in the design grid. Calculate the number of hours each bookkeeper has worked (YTD Earnings/ Hourly Rate). Display hours worked as an integer (0 decimal places). Run the query and print the results.

11. Display and print the following statistics: the total balance for all clients; the total balance for clients of bookkeeper 22; and the total balance for each bookkeeper.

12. Create the crosstab shown in Figure 2-78. The crosstab groups total of clients' balances by city and bookkeeper number. Save the crosstab as City-Bookkeeper Crosstab. Print the crosstab.

City	Total Of Balance	22	24	34
Empeer	$1,102.50	$577.50	$525.00	
Grant City	$1,027.50	$315.50	$712.00	
Portage	$848.25			$848.25

FIGURE 2-78

3 Querying the City Guide Database

Problem: The chamber of commerce has determined a number of questions it wants the database management system to answer. You must obtain the answers to the questions posed by the chamber.

Instructions: Use the database created in the In the Lab 3 of Project 1 on page AC 61 for this exercise or see your instructor for information on accessing the files required for this book. Print the answers to each question.

Instructions Part 1: Create a new query for the Advertiser table and include the Advertiser Number, Name, Balance, and Amount Paid fields in the design grid. Answer the following questions: (1) Which advertisers' names begin with C? (2) Which advertisers are located on Main? (3) Which advertisers have a current balance of $0.00? (4) Which advertisers have a balance greater than $150.00 and have an amount paid greater than $800.00? (5) Which five advertisers have the highest balances? (6) For each advertiser, what is the total of the current balance and the amount paid?

Instructions Part 2: Join the Ad Rep table and the Advertiser table. Include the Ad Rep Number, First Name, and Last Name from the Ad Rep table and the Advertiser Number, Name, and Balance from the Advertiser table in the design grid. Sort the records in ascending order by Ad Rep Number and Advertiser Number. Perform the following: (1) Calculate the pending commission (comm rate * balance) for each ad rep. The pending commission should display as currency. (2) Restrict retrieval to only those records where the pending commission is greater than $20.00.

Instructions Part 3: Calculate the following statistics: (1) What is the average balance for advertisers assigned to ad rep 26? (2) What is the total amount paid of all advertisers? (3) What is the total balance for each ad rep?

Cases and Places

The difficulty of these case studies varies:
■ are the least difficult and ■■ are more difficult. The last exercise is a group exercise.

1 ■ Use the College Dog Walkers database you created in Cases and Places 1 in Project 1 on page AC 63 for this assignment or see your instructor for information on accessing the files required for this book. Perform the following: (a) Display and print the number and name of all customers who live on Easton. (b) Display and print the number, name, telephone number, and balance for all customers who have a balance of at least $40.00. (c) Display and print the number, name, balance, walker first name, and walker last name for all customers. Sort the records in ascending order by walker last name. (d) Display and print the average balance of all customers. (e) Display and print the average balance of customers grouped by walker. (f) Display and print the total balance of all customers.

2 ■ Use the InPerson Fitness Company database you created in Cases and Places 2 in Project 1 on page AC 63 for this assignment or see your instructor for information on accessing the files required for this book. Perform the following: (a) Display and print the number, client name, and balance for all clients of a particular trainer. The owner should be able to enter a different trainer number each time the query is run. (b) Display and print the number, client name, and total of balance due and amount paid. (c) Display and print the number, client name, and balance of all clients whose amount paid is greater than $400.00. (d) Display and print the trainer number, trainer name, client number, client name, client address, and client telephone number for all clients. Sort the data ascending by trainer number and client number. (e) Display and print the total amount paid and total balance grouped by trainer.

3 ■■ Use the Regional Books database you created in Cases and Places 3 in Project 1 on page AC 63 for this assignment or see your instructor for information on accessing the files required for this book. Perform the following: (a) List the book code, title, and on-hand value (units on hand * price) of all books. (b) List the book code, title, and price of all paperback books. (c) List the book code, title, price, and publisher name for all books where there are less than 3 books on hand. (d) Display and print the book code, title, and author for all books. (e) Find the lowest priced book and the highest priced book.

4 ■■ Use the Campus Housing database you created in Cases and Places 4 in Project 1 on page AC 64 for this assignment or see your instructor for information on accessing the files required for this book. Display and print the following: (a) List all rental units that are located two miles or less from campus. (b) List all rental units that have parking and allow pets. (c) List all three-bedroom apartments that rent for less than $1,000.00 a month. (d) Find the average rent for two-bedroom apartments. (e) List the owners of all units that are efficiencies or rooms for rent. (f) List the different lease terms in ascending order. Each lease term should display only once.

5 ■■ **Working Together** Create an additional query for each of the four databases described in the Cases and Places. Each team must create a parameter query, a top values query, a crosstab query, and an aggregate query. Select the database to use to create each specific query type. Use all four databases, that is, one database per specific query type. Run each of the queries and print the results. Write a one-page paper that lists the queries the team created and explains why the team chose those queries.

Maintaining a Database Using the Design and Update Features of Access

PROJECT

3

CASE PERSPECTIVE

Dr. Gernaey and his colleagues at Ashton James College have received many benefits from the database they created and loaded, including the ability to ask questions concerning the data in the database. They now face the task of keeping the database up-to-date. As they take on new clients and trainers, they will need to add new records and make changes to existing records.

Access offers many features for maintaining a database that they want to utilize. For example, they must change the structure of the database to categorize the clients by type. They will do this by adding a Client Type field to the Client table. They discovered the Name field was too short to contain the name of one of the clients, so they will enlarge the size of the field. Along with these changes, they want to change the appearance of a datasheet when displaying data.

They would like the ability to make mass updates, that is, to update many records in a single operation. They want rules that make sure users can enter only valid data into the database, and they want to ensure that it is not possible for the database to contain a client who is not associated with a specific trainer. Finally, they want to improve the efficiency of certain types of processing, specifically sorting and retrieving data. Your task is to help the administration accomplish these goals.

As you read through this project, you will learn how to use the Access design and update features to maintain a database.

MICROSOFT
Office Access 2003

Maintaining a Database Using the Design and Update Features of Access

PROJECT

3

Objectives

You will have mastered the material in this project when you can:

- Add, change, and delete records
- Search for records
- Filter records
- Update a table design
- Format a datasheet
- Use queries to update records

- Specify validation rules, default values, and formats
- Create and use a Lookup field
- Specify referential integrity
- Use a subdatasheet
- Sort records
- Create indexes

Introduction

Once a database has been created and loaded with data, it must be maintained. **Maintaining the database** means modifying the data to keep it up-to-date, such as adding new records, changing the data for existing records, and deleting records. Updating can include mass updates or mass deletions; that is, updates to, or deletions of, many records at the same time.

In addition to adding, changing, and deleting records, maintenance of a database can involve the need to **restructure the database** periodically; that is, to change the database structure. This can include adding new fields to a table, changing the characteristics of existing fields, and removing existing fields. It also can involve the creation of indexes, which are similar to indexes found in the back of books. Indexes are used to improve the efficiency of certain operations.

Figure 3-1 summarizes some of the various types of activities involved in maintaining a database.

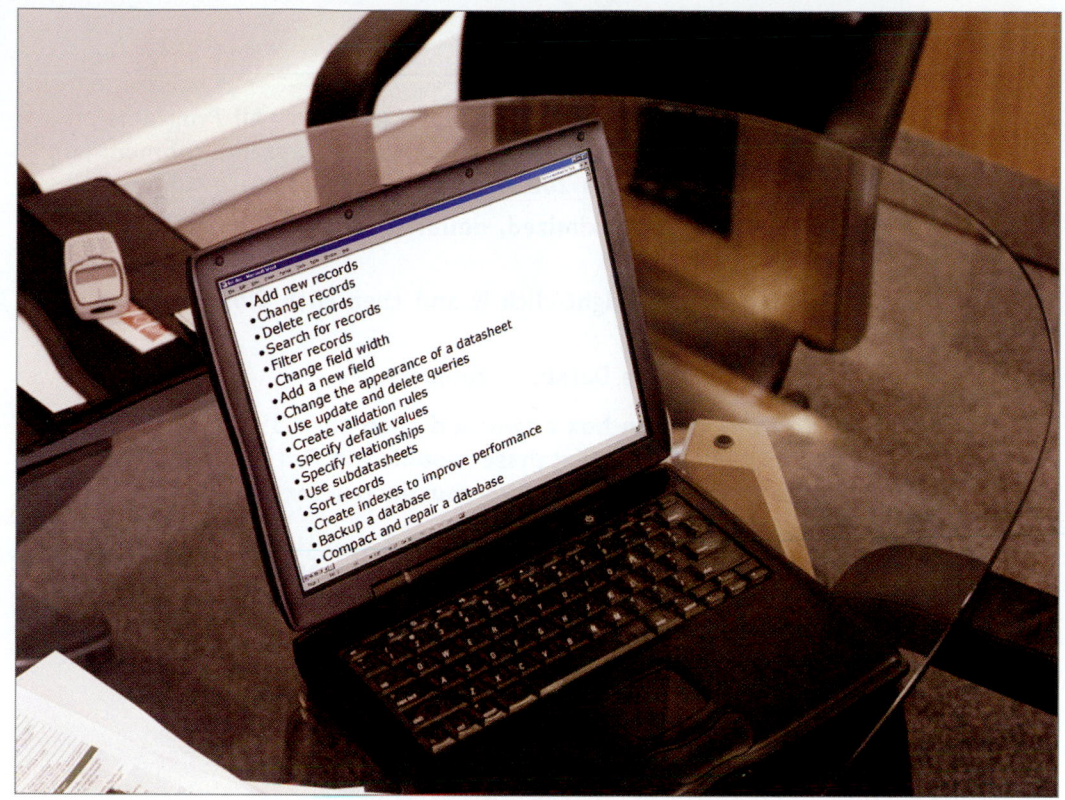

FIGURE 3-1

Project Three — Maintaining the Ashton James College Database

The steps in this project show how to make changes to the data in the Ashton James College database. They also illustrate how to search for records as well as filter records. The steps restructure the database, that is, make changes that meet the needs of the user, in this case, Ashton James College. This includes adding an additional field as well as increasing the width of one of the existing fields. Other changes modify the structure of the database in a way that prevents users from entering invalid data. Steps are presented to create indexes that reduce the time it takes for some operations, for example, those involving sorting the data.

Opening the Database

If you are stepping through this project on a computer and you want your screen to match the figures in this book, then you should change your computer's resolution to 800 × 600. For more information on how to change the resolution on your computer, see Appendix D. Before carrying out the steps in this project, first you must open the database. The steps on the next page start Access and open the database. The steps assume that the Ashton James College database is located on a disk in drive A. If your database is located anywhere else, you will need to adjust the appropriate steps.

More About

The Access Help System

Need Help? It is no further than the Type a question for help box on the menu bar in the upper-right corner of the window. Click the box that contains the text, Type a question for help (Figure 3-3), type help, and then press the ENTER key. Access responds with a list of topics you can click to learn about obtaining help on any Access-related topic. To find out what is new in Access 2003, type what is new in Access in the Type a question for help box.

To Open a Database

1 Click the Start button on the Windows taskbar, point to All Programs on the Start menu, point to Microsoft Office on the All Programs submenu, and then click Microsoft Office Access 2003 on the Microsoft Office submenu.

2 If the Access window is not maximized, double-click its title bar to maximize it.

3 If the Language bar appears, right-click it and then click Close the Language bar on the shortcut menu.

4 Click the Open button on the Database toolbar.

5 If necessary, click the Look in box arrow and then click 3½ Floppy (A:). Click Ashton James College, the database modified in Project 2. (If you did not complete the steps in Project 2, see your instructor for a copy of the database.)

6 Click the Open button in the Open dialog box. If the Security Warning dialog box appears, click the Open button.

The database opens and the Ashton James College : Database window appears.

Updating Records

Keeping the data in a database up-to-date requires updating records in three ways: adding new records, changing the data in existing records, and deleting existing records.

Adding Records

In Project 1, you added records to a database using Datasheet view; that is, as you were adding records, the records were appearing on the screen in the form of a datasheet, or table. When you need to add additional records, you can use the same techniques.

In Project 1, you used a form to view records. This is called Form view. You also can use **Form view** to update the data in a table. To add new records, change existing records, or delete records, you will use the same techniques you used in Datasheet view. The following steps add a record to the Client table with a form, for example. These steps use the Client form created in Project 1.

To Use a Form to Add Records

1

• **With the Ashton James College database open, click Forms on the Objects bar, and then right-click the Client form.**

The list of forms appears (Figure 3-2). The shortcut menu for the Client form also appears.

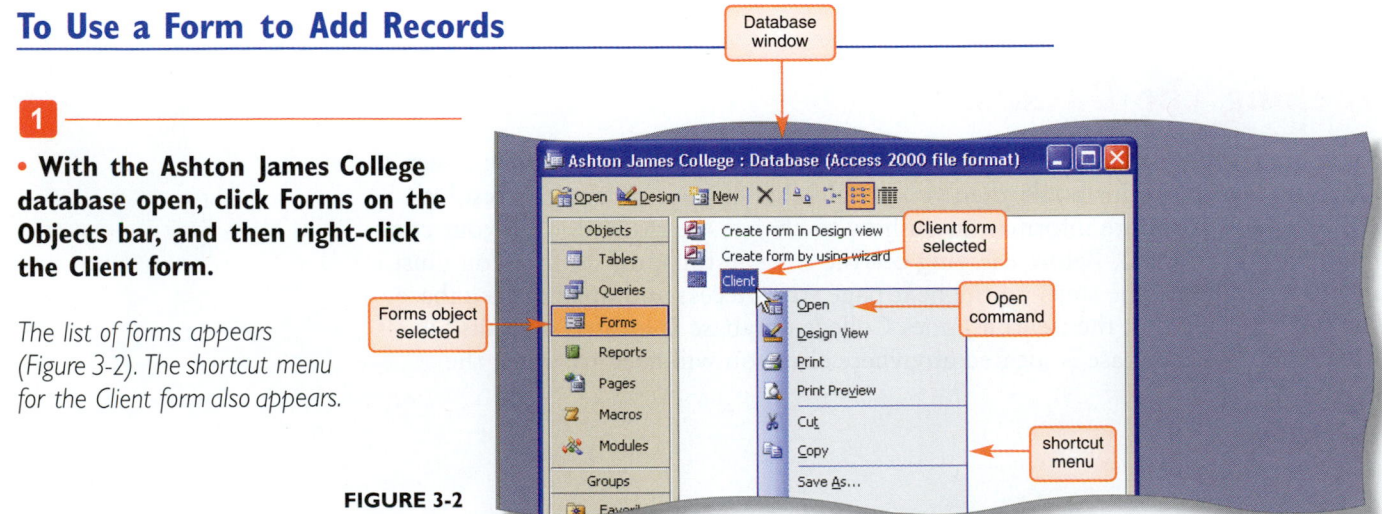

FIGURE 3-2

2

• **Click Open on the shortcut menu.**

The form for the Client table appears (Figure 3-3). Your toolbars may be arranged differently.

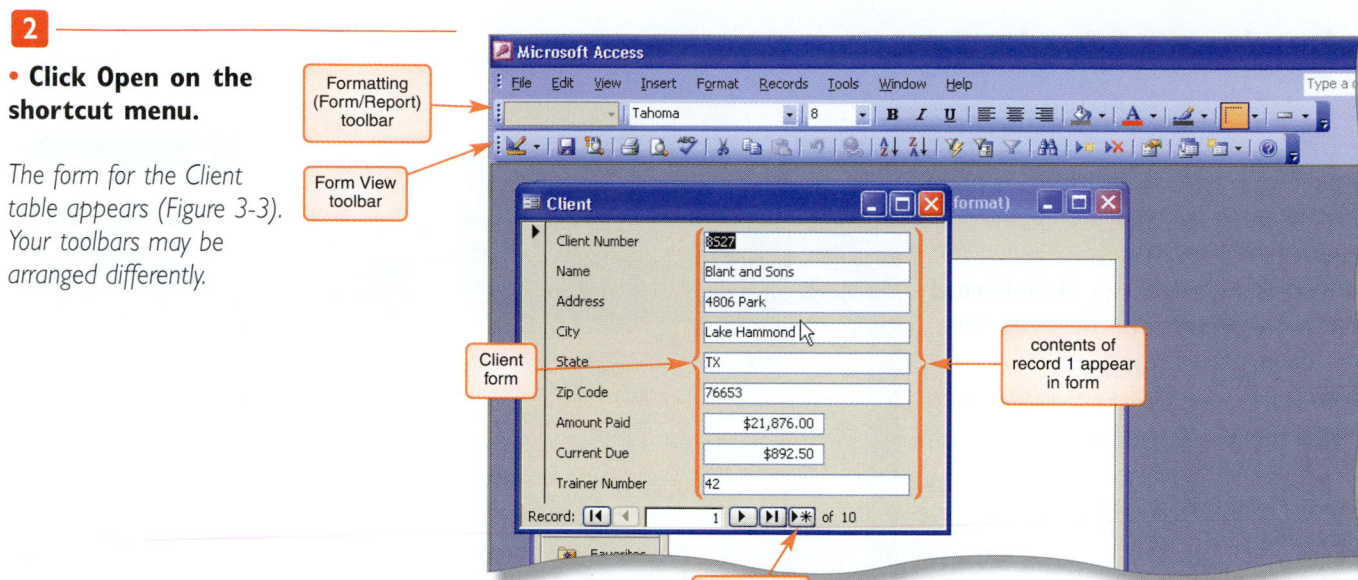

Formatting (Form/Report) toolbar

Form View toolbar

Client form

contents of record 1 appear in form

New Record button

FIGURE 3-3

3

• **Click the New Record button on the Navigation bar, and then type the data for the new record as shown in Figure 3-4. Press the TAB key after typing the data in each field, except after typing the data for the final field (Trainer Number).**

The record appears.

4

• **Press the TAB key.**

The record now is added to the Client table and the contents of the form are erased.

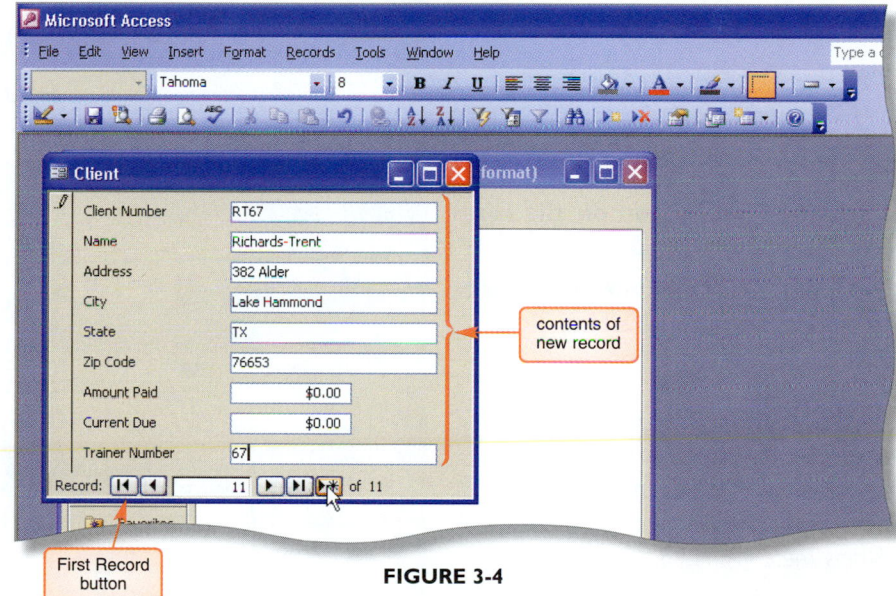

contents of new record

First Record button

FIGURE 3-4

Searching for a Record

In the database environment, **searching** means looking for records that satisfy some criteria. Looking for the client whose number is FL93 is an example of searching. The queries in Project 2 also were examples of searching. Access had to locate those records that satisfied the criteria.

A need for searching also exists when using Form view or Datasheet view. To update client FL93, for example, first you need to find the client.

You need a way to be able to go directly to a record just by giving the value in some field. This is the function of the Find button. Before clicking the Find button, select the field for the search.

The steps on the next page show how to search for the client whose number is FL93.

To Search for a Record

1

• Make sure the Client table is open and the form for the Client table is displayed.

• If necessary, click the First Record button to display the first record.

• If the Client Number field currently is not selected, select it by clicking the field name.

The first record appears on the form (Figure 3-5).

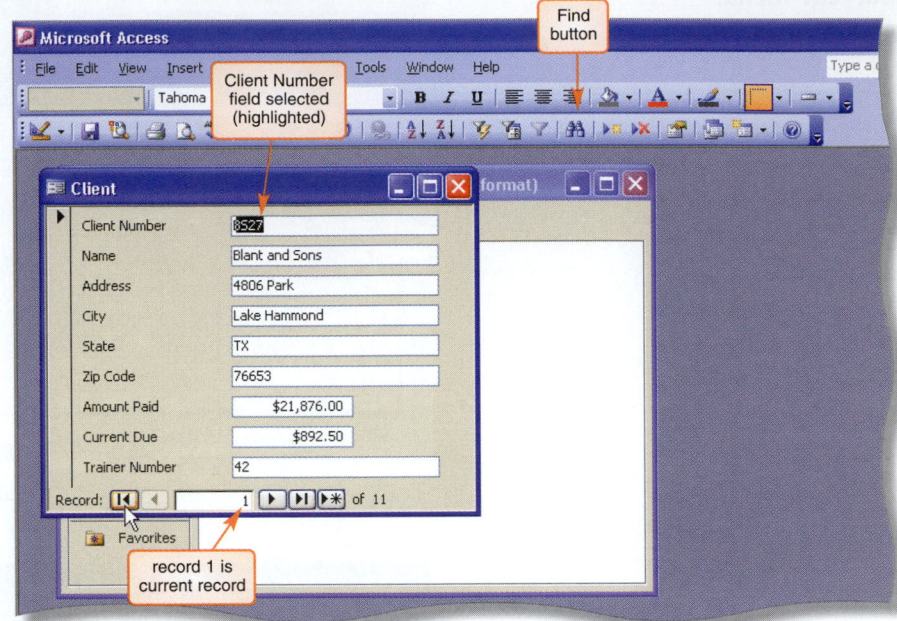

FIGURE 3-5

2

• Click the Find button on the Form View toolbar.

• Type FL93 in the Find What text box and then click the Find Next button.

Access displays the Find and Replace dialog box, locates the record for client FL93, and displays it in the Client form (Figure 3-6). The Find What text box contains the entry, FL93.

3

• Click the Cancel button in the Find and Replace dialog box.

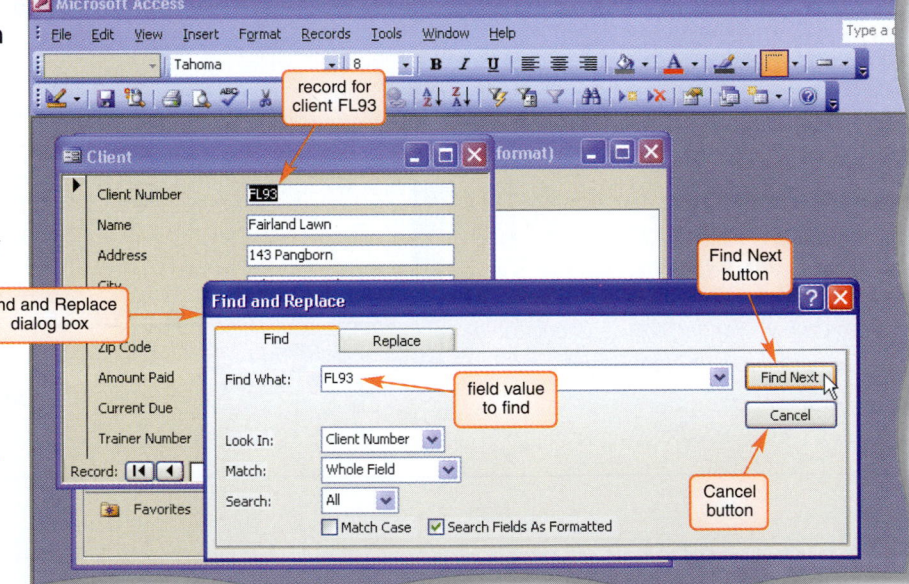

FIGURE 3-6

In some cases, after locating a record that satisfies a criterion, you might need to find the next record that satisfies the same criterion. For example, if you just found the first client whose trainer number is 42, you then may want to find the second such client, then the third, and so on. To do so, repeat the same process. You will not need to retype the value each time, however.

Changing the Contents of a Record

After locating the record to be changed, select the field to be changed by clicking the field. You also can press the TAB key repeatedly. Then make the appropriate changes. (Clicking the field automatically produces an insertion point. If you use the TAB key, you will need to press F2 to produce an insertion point.)

Normally, Access is in **Insert mode**, so the characters typed will be inserted at the appropriate position. To change to **Overtype mode**, press the INSERT key. The letters, OVR, will appear near the bottom right edge of the status bar. To return to Insert mode, press the INSERT key. In Insert mode, if the data in the field completely fills the field, no additional characters can be inserted. In this case, you would need to increase the size of the field before inserting the characters. You will see how to do this later in the project.

The following steps use Form view to change the name of client FL93 to Fairland Lawns by inserting the letter s after Lawn. Sufficient room exists in the field to make this change.

Q&A

Q: Why can you not use the Next Record button to find client FL93?

A: In a small table, repeatedly clicking the Next Record button until client FL93 is on the screen may not be particularly difficult. In a large table with many records, however, this would be extremely cumbersome.

To Update the Contents of a Field

1

• **Click in the Name field text box for client FL93 after the word Lawn, and then type s (the letter s) to change the name.**

The name is changed. The mouse pointer shape is an I-beam (Figure 3-7).

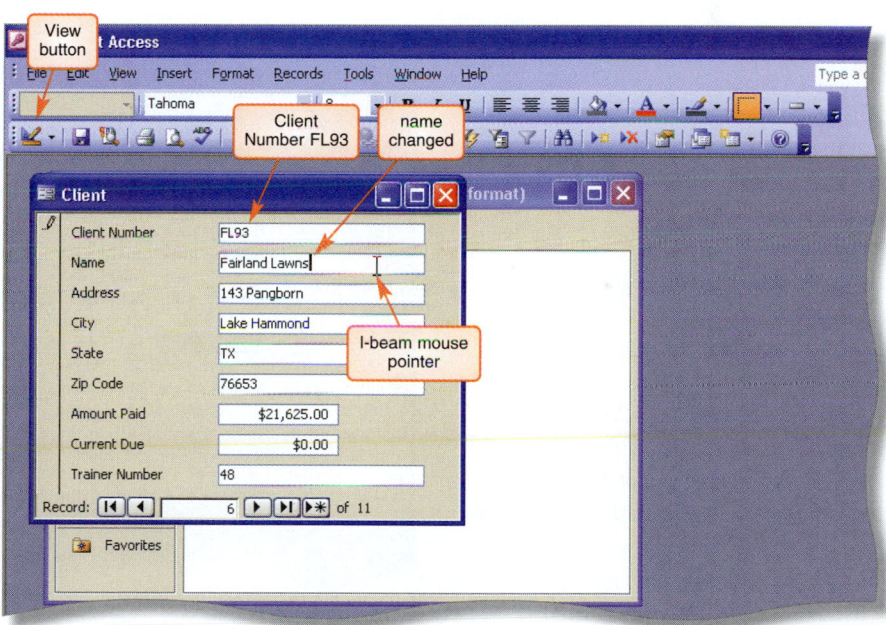

FIGURE 3-7

Once you move to another record or close this table, the change to the name will become permanent.

Switching Between Views

Sometimes, after working in Form view where you can see all fields, but only one record, it is helpful to see several records at a time. To do so, switch to Datasheet view. The steps on the next page switch from Form view to Datasheet view.

More About

The View Button

You can use the View button to switch easily between viewing the form, called Form view, and viewing the design of the form, called Design view. To switch to Datasheet view, you *must* click the down arrow, and then click Datasheet view in the list that appears.

To Switch from Form View to Datasheet View

1

• **Click the View button arrow on the Form View toolbar (see Figure 3-7 on the previous page).**

The View button list appears (Figure 3-8).

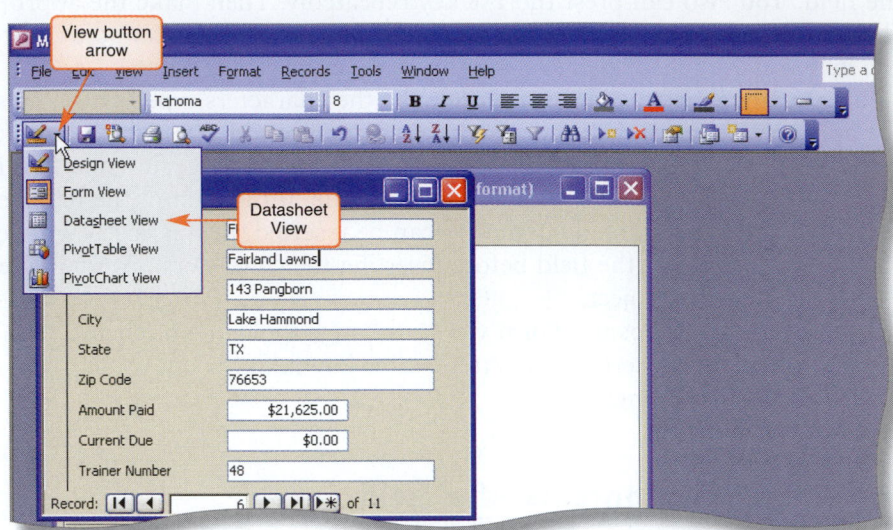

FIGURE 3-8

2

• **Click Datasheet View, and then maximize the window containing the datasheet by double-clicking its title bar.**

The datasheet appears (Figure 3-9). The position in the table is maintained. The current record selector points to client FL93, the client that appeared on the screen in Form view. The Name field, the field in which the insertion point appears, is selected. The new record for client RT67 is currently the last record in the table. When you close the table and open it later, client RT67 will be in its appropriate location.

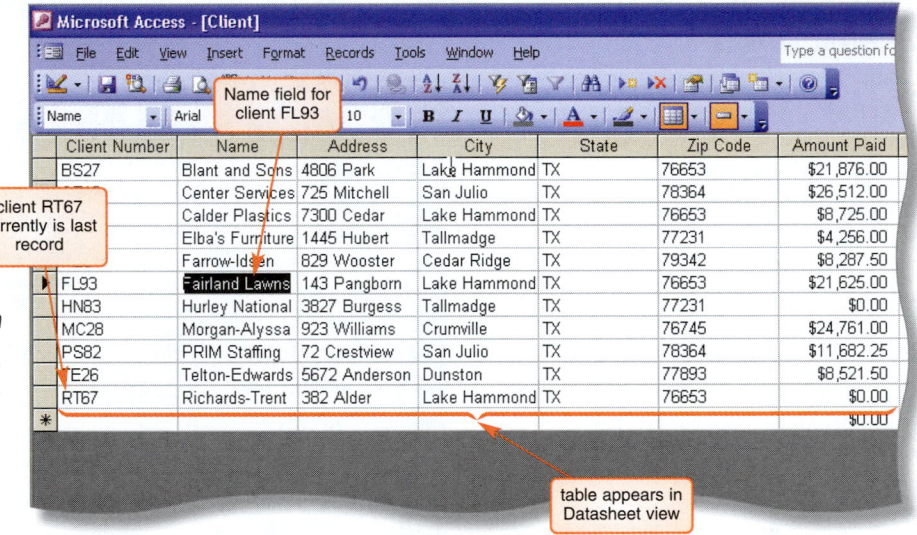

FIGURE 3-9

If you want to return to Form view, use the same process. The only difference is that you click Form View rather than Datasheet View.

Filtering Records

You can use the Find button in either Datasheet view or Form view to locate a record quickly that satisfies some criterion (for example, the client number is FL93). All records appear, however, not just the record or records that satisfy the criterion. To have only the record or records that satisfy the criterion appear, use a **filter**. Three types of filters are available: Filter By Selection, Filter By Form, and Advanced Filter/Sort. You can use a filter in either Datasheet view or Form view.

Using Filter By Selection

The simplest type of filter is called **Filter By Selection**. To use Filter By Selection, you first must give Access an example of the data you want by selecting the data within the table. The following steps use Filter By Selection in Datasheet view to display only the records for clients in San Julio.

To Use Filter By Selection

1

• **Click the City field on the second record.**

The insertion point appears in the City field on the second record (Figure 3-10). The city on this record is San Julio.

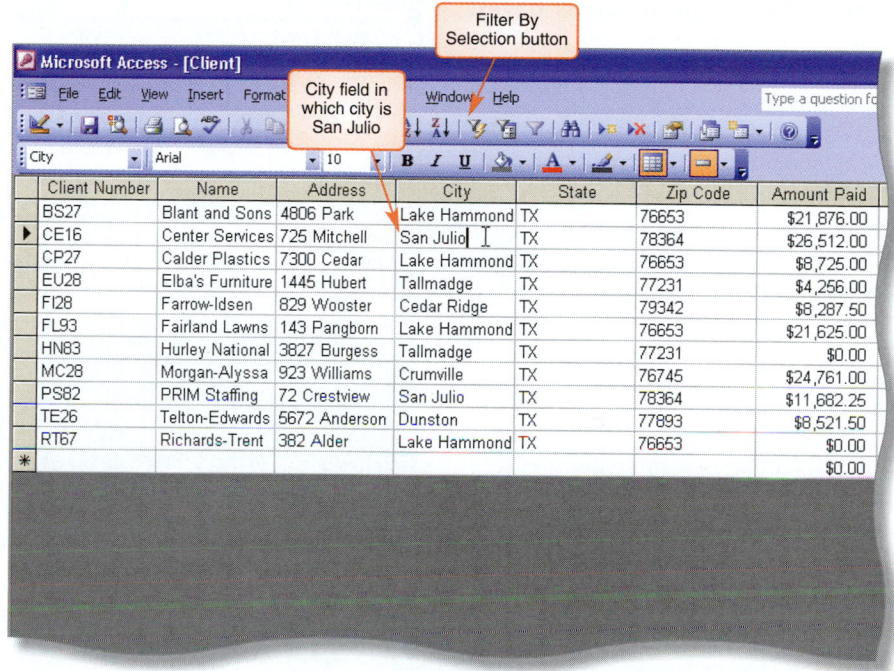

FIGURE 3-10

2

• **Click the Filter By Selection button on the Table Datasheet toolbar (see Figure 3-10).**

• **If instructed to do so, print the results by clicking the Print button on the Table Datasheet toolbar.**

Only the clients located in San Julio appear (Figure 3-11).

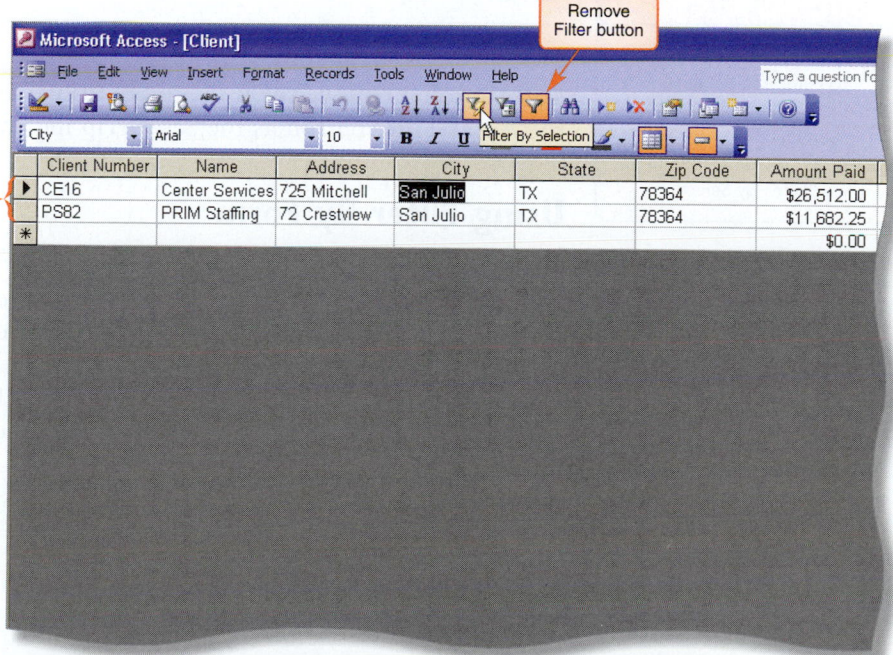

FIGURE 3-11

To redisplay all the records, remove the filter as shown in the following step.

To Remove a Filter

1

• **Click the Remove Filter button on the Table Datasheet toolbar (see Figure 3-11 on the previous page).**

All records appear (Figure 3-12).

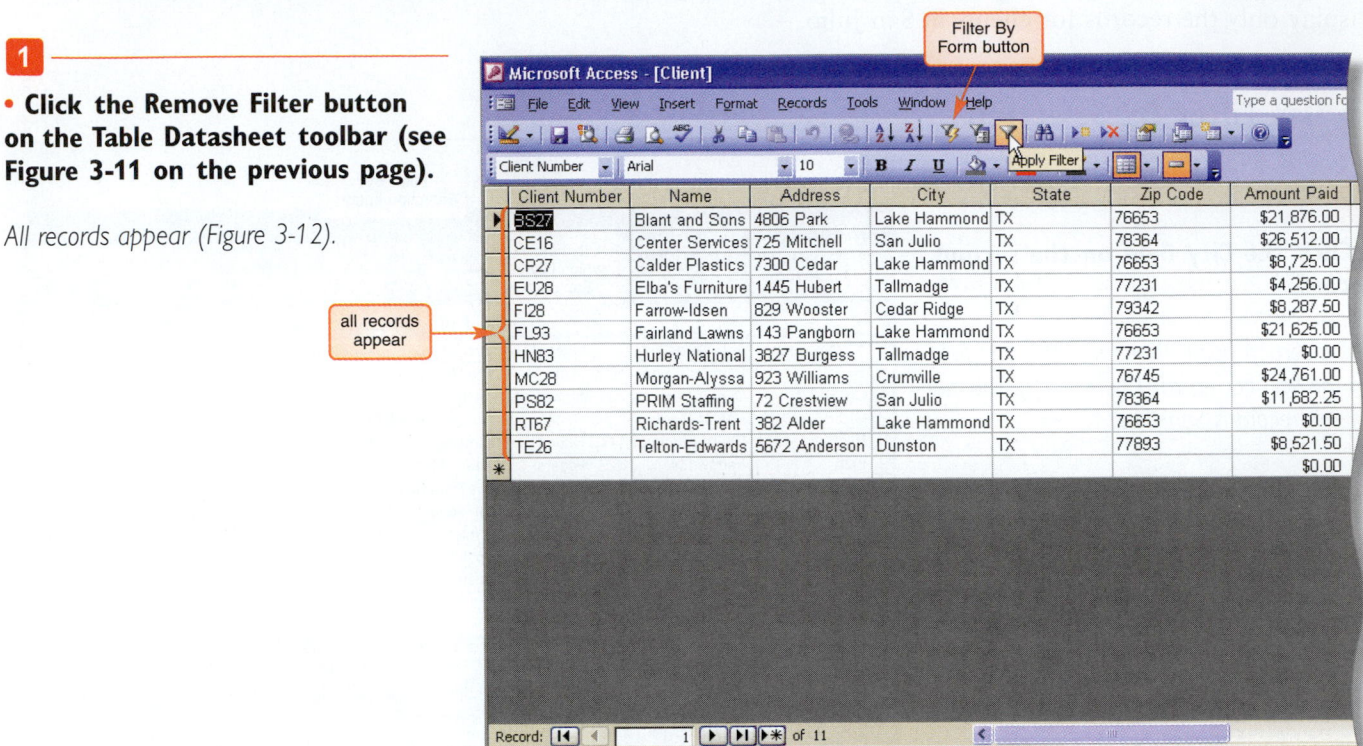

FIGURE 3-12

After you remove the filter, the button changes from the Remove Filter button to the Apply Filter button as the ScreenTip indicates.

Using Filter By Form

Filter By Selection is a quick and easy way to filter by the value in a single field. For more complex criteria, however, it is not appropriate. For example, you could not use Filter By Selection to restrict the records to those for which the city is Lake Hammond and the trainer number is 42. For this type of query, in which you want to specify multiple criteria, you can use **Filter By Form**. The following steps illustrate using this filtering method in Datasheet view.

To Use Filter By Form

1

• Click the **Filter By Form** button on the Table Datasheet toolbar (see Figure 3-12).

• Click the **City** field (San Julio may appear in the field), click the arrow that appears, and then click **Lake Hammond**.

• Click the right scroll arrow so the Trainer Number field is on the screen, click the **Trainer Number** field, click the down arrow that appears, and then click **42**.

The form for filtering appears (Figure 3-13). Lake Hammond is selected as the city, and 42 is selected as the trainer number.

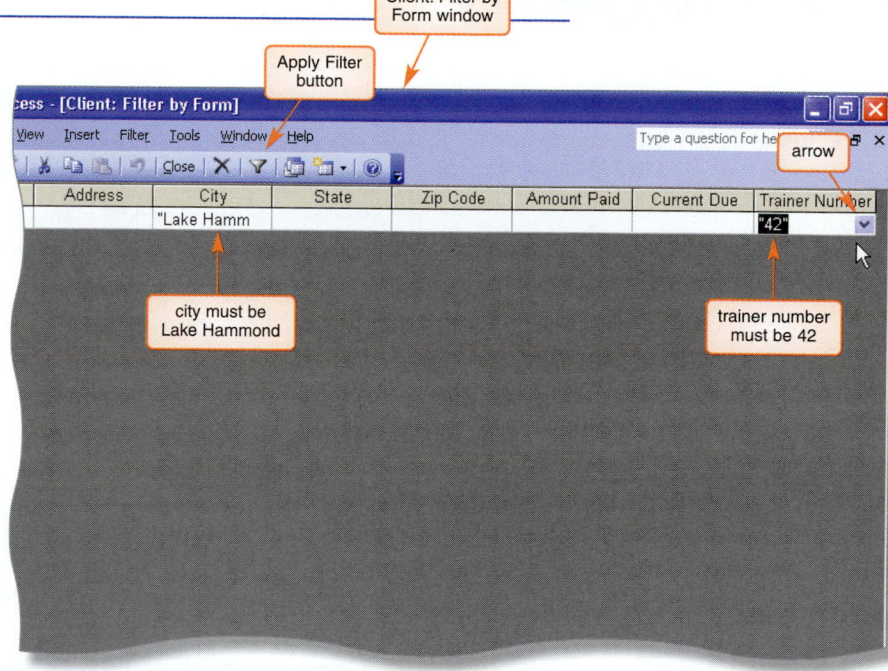

FIGURE 3-13

2

• Click the **Apply Filter** button on the Filter/Sort toolbar.

• If instructed to do so, print the results by clicking the **Print** button on the Table Datasheet toolbar.

The only record included is the record on which the city is Lake Hammond and the trainer number is 42 (Figure 3-14).

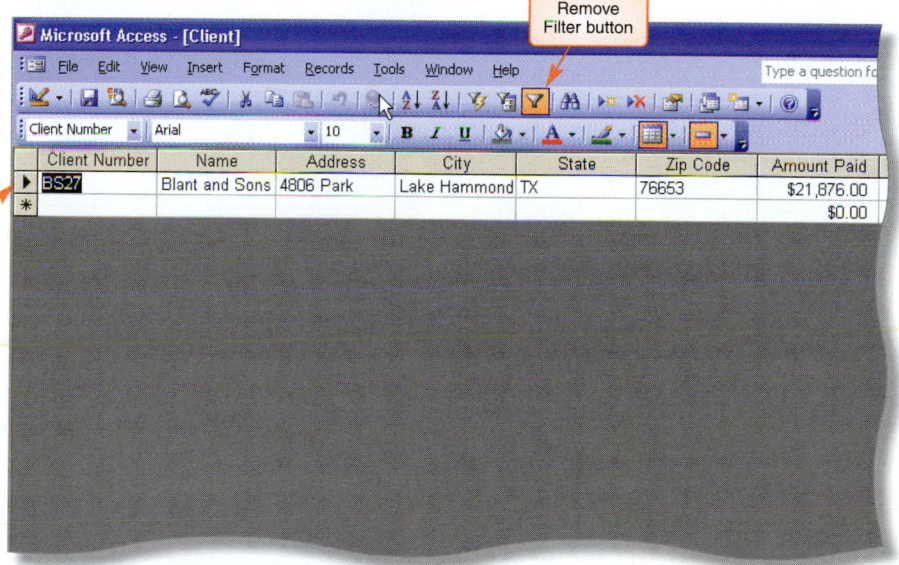

FIGURE 3-14

3

• Click the **Remove Filter** button on the Table Datasheet toolbar.

All records are shown.

Other Ways

1. On Records menu point to Filter, click Filter By Form on Filter submenu
2. In Voice Command mode, say "Filter By Form"

Using Advanced Filter/Sort

In some cases, your criteria may be too complex even for Filter By Form. For example, you might want to include any client for which the city is Lake Hammond and the trainer is number 42. You also may want to include any client of trainer 48, no matter where the client is located. Further, you might want to have the results sorted by name. To filter records using complex criteria, you need to use **Advanced Filter/Sort** as illustrated in the steps on the next page.

To Use Advanced Filter/Sort

1

• **Click Records on the menu bar, and then point to Filter.**

The Filter submenu appears (Figure 3-15).

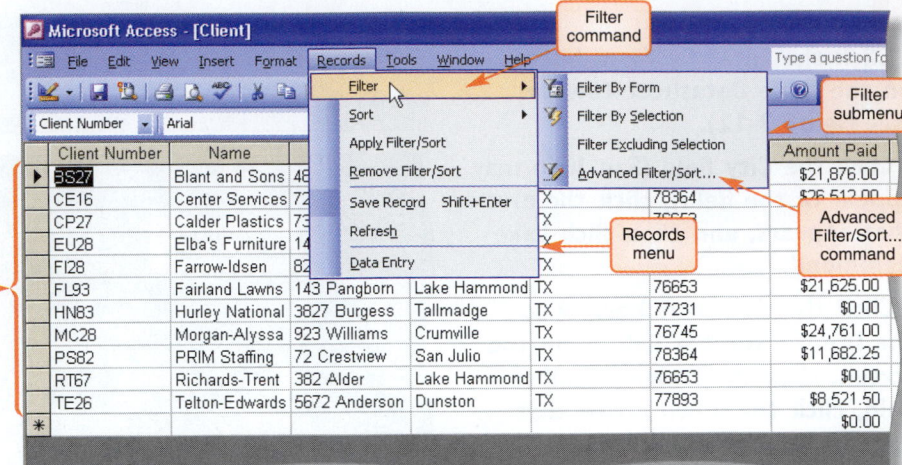

FIGURE 3-15

2

• **Click Advanced Filter/Sort.**

Access displays the ClientFilter1 : Filter window (Figure 3-16). The screen looks just like the screens you used to create queries. The city and trainer number criteria from the previous filter appear. If you were creating a different filter, you could delete these.

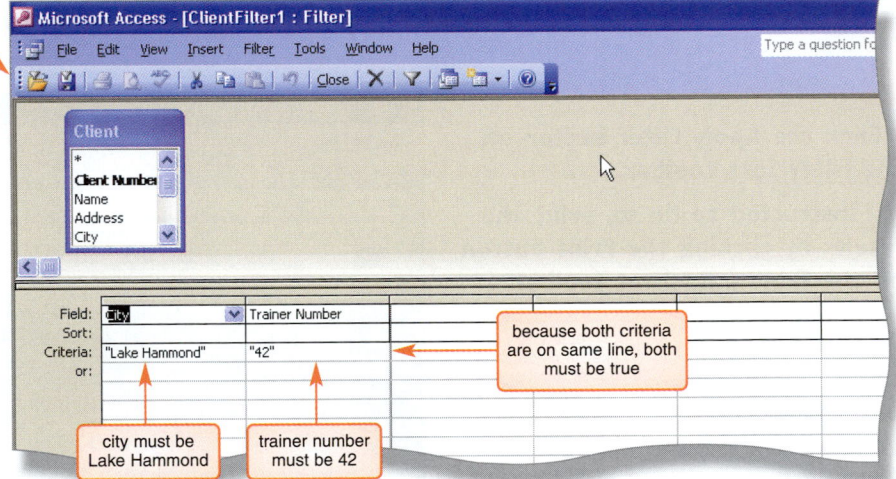

FIGURE 3-16

3

• **Type 48 as the criterion in the second Criteria row (the or row) of the Trainer Number column, double-click the Name field to add the field to the filter, click the Sort row for the Name column, click the arrow that appears, and then click Ascending.**

The additional criteria for the Trainer Number field are entered (Figure 3-17). The data will be sorted on Name in ascending order.

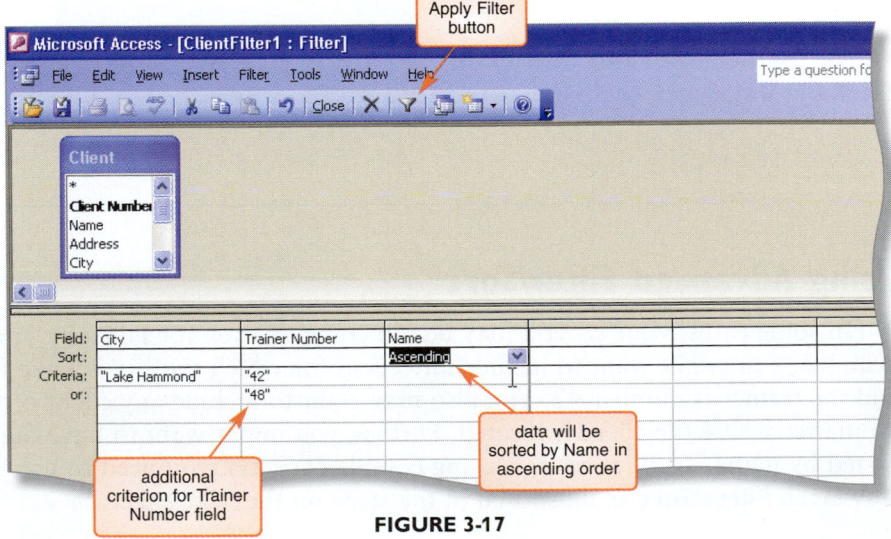

FIGURE 3-17

4

• Click the Apply Filter button on the Filter/Sort toolbar.

• If instructed to do so, print the results by clicking the Print button on the Table Datasheet toolbar.

The filtered data appears (Figure 3-18). Only the clients who satisfy the criteria in the filter are included. The clients are ordered by name.

5

• Click the Remove Filter button on the Table Datasheet toolbar.

All records are shown.

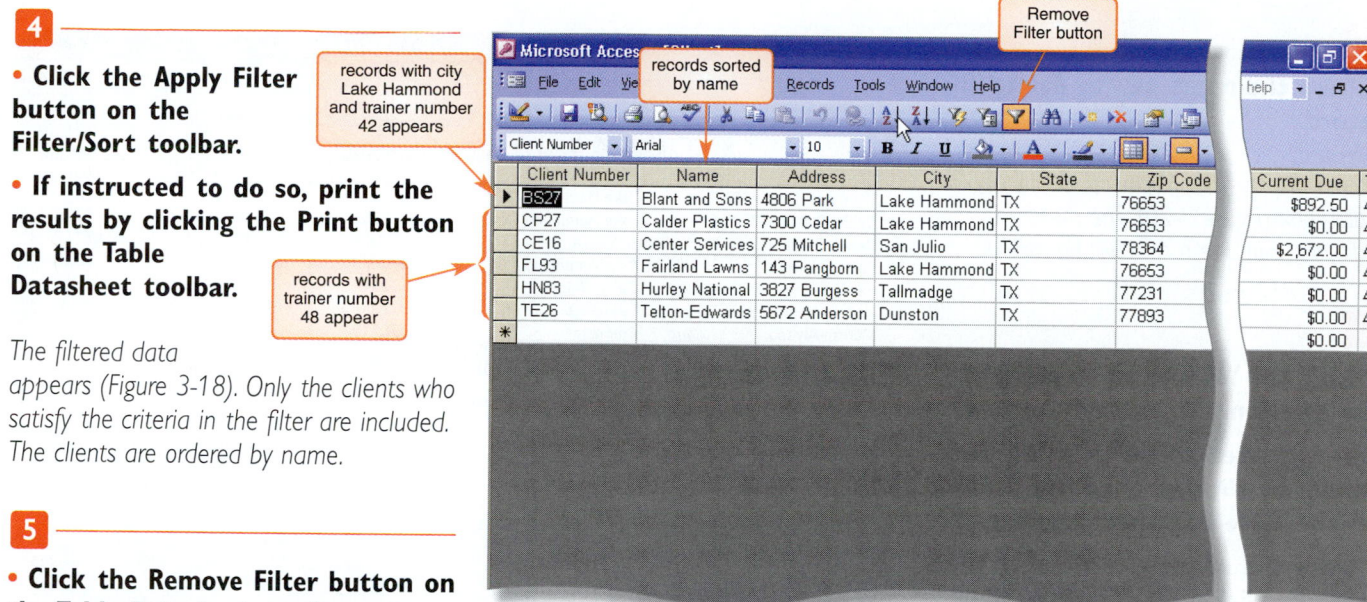

FIGURE 3-18

Deleting Records

When records no longer are needed, **delete the records** (remove them) from the table. For example, suppose client EU28 no longer is served by Ashton James College and its final payment is made. The record for that client should be deleted. The following steps delete client EU28.

To Delete a Record

1

• With the datasheet for the Client table on the screen, click the record selector of the record in which the client number is EU28.

The record is selected (Figure 3-19).

Q&A

Q: Can you filter records that have been retrieved as the result of a query?

A: Yes. You can use Filter By Selection, Filter By Form, and Advanced Filter/Sort in the Query Datasheet window just as you did in the Table Datasheet window. You also can use the command in Form view.

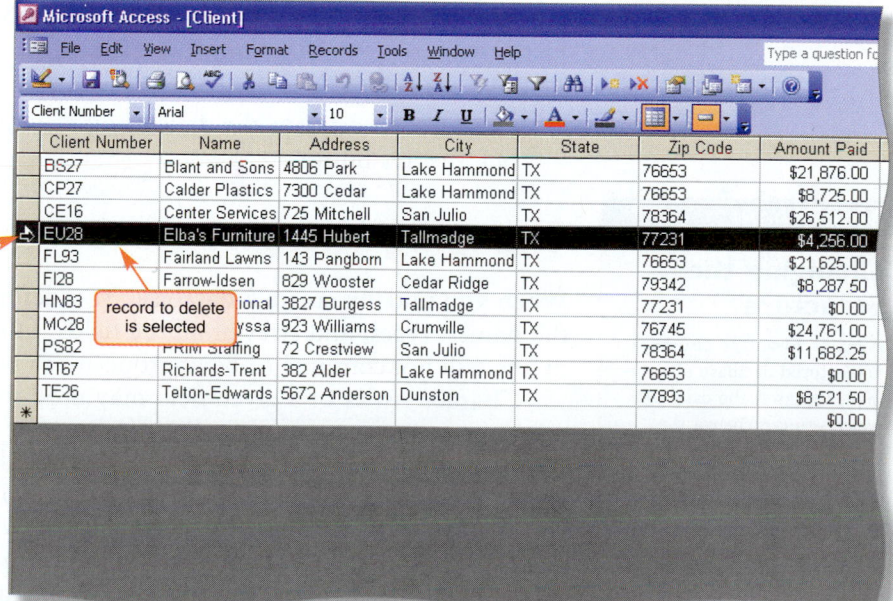

FIGURE 3-19

2

• **Press the DELETE key to delete the record.**

Access displays the Microsoft Office Access dialog box (Figure 3-20). The message indicates that one record will be deleted.

3

• **Click the Yes button to complete the deletion.**

• **If instructed to do so, print the results by clicking the Print button on the Table Datasheet toolbar.**

• **Close the window containing the table by clicking its Close Window button.**

The record is deleted and the table no longer appears.

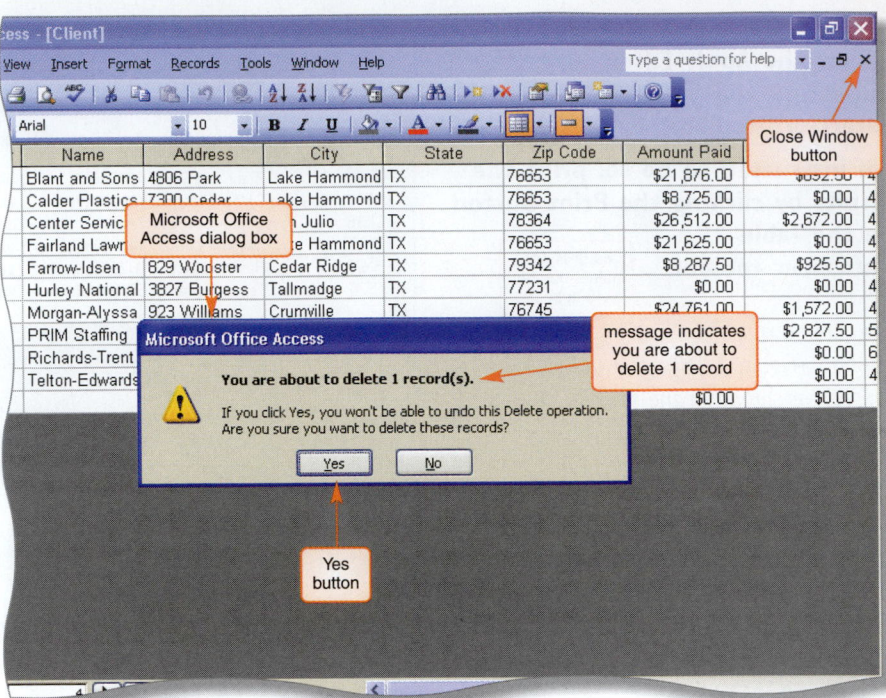

FIGURE 3-20

You can delete records using a form just as you delete records using a datasheet. To do so, first navigate to the record to be deleted. For example, you can use the Navigation buttons or you can locate the desired record using the Find button. The following steps illustrate how to delete a record in Form view after you have located the record to be deleted.

To Delete a Record in Form View

1. Click the Record Selector (the triangle in front of the record) to select the entire record.
2. Press the DELETE key.
3. When Access displays the dialog box asking if you want to delete the record, click the Yes button.

Changing the Structure

When you initially create a database, you define its **structure**; that is, you indicate the names, types, and sizes of all the fields. In many cases, the structure you first define will not continue to be appropriate as you use the database.

Characteristics of a given field may need to change. For example, a client name might be stored incorrectly in the database. In this example, the name Morgan-Alyssa actually should be Morgan-Alyssa Academy. The Name field is not large enough, however, to hold the correct name. To accommodate this change, you need to restructure the database by increasing the width of the Name field.

It may be that a field currently in the table no longer is necessary. If no one ever uses a particular field, it is not needed in the table. Because it is occupying space and serving no useful purpose, it should be removed from the table. You also would need to delete the field from any forms, reports, or queries that include it.

To make any of these changes, you first must open the table in Design view.

Changing the Size of a Field

The following steps change the size of the Name field from 20 to 25 to accommodate the change of name from Morgan-Alyssa to Morgan-Alyssa Academy.

To Change the Size of a Field

1

• **In the Database window, click Tables on the Objects bar, and then right-click Client.**

The shortcut menu for the Client table appears (Figure 3-21).

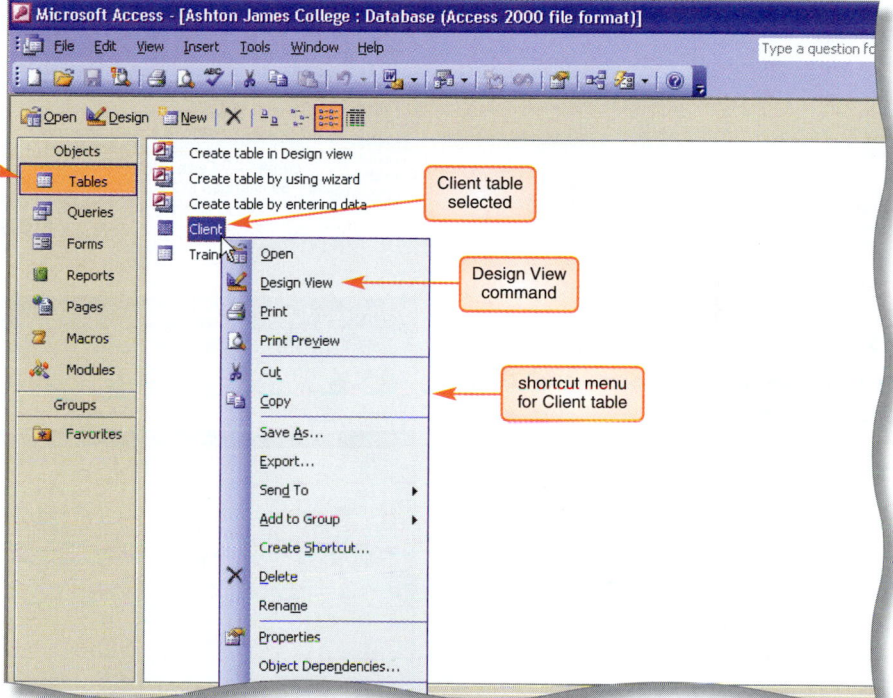

FIGURE 3-21

2

• **Click Design View on the shortcut menu.**

Access displays the Client : Table window (Figure 3-22).

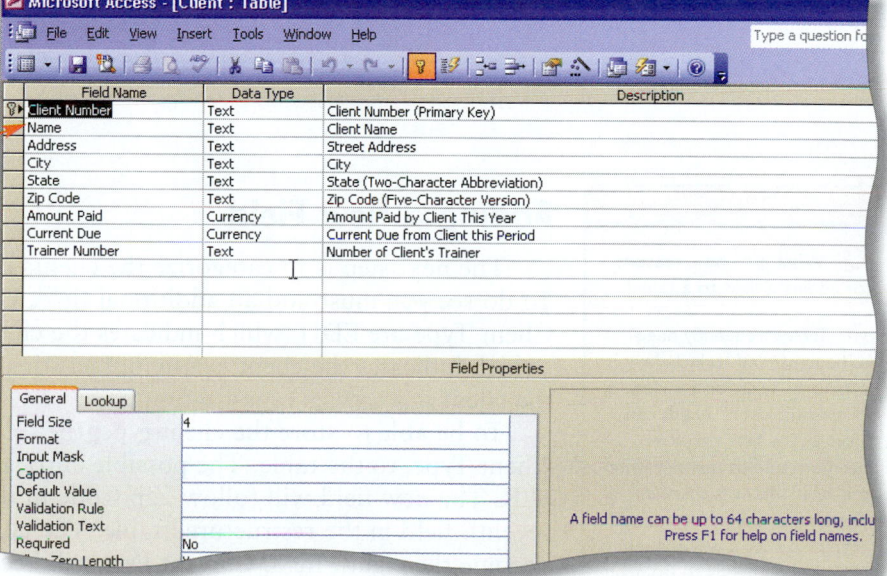

FIGURE 3-22

3

• **Click the row selector for the Name field.**

The Name field is selected (Figure 3-23).

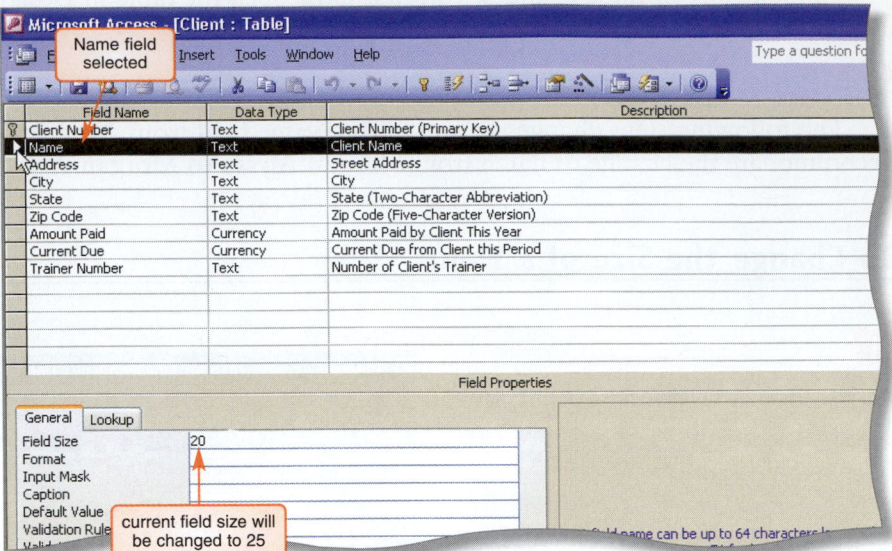

FIGURE 3-23

4

• **Press F6 to select the field size, type 25 as the new size, and then press F6 again.**

The field size is changed (Figure 3-24).

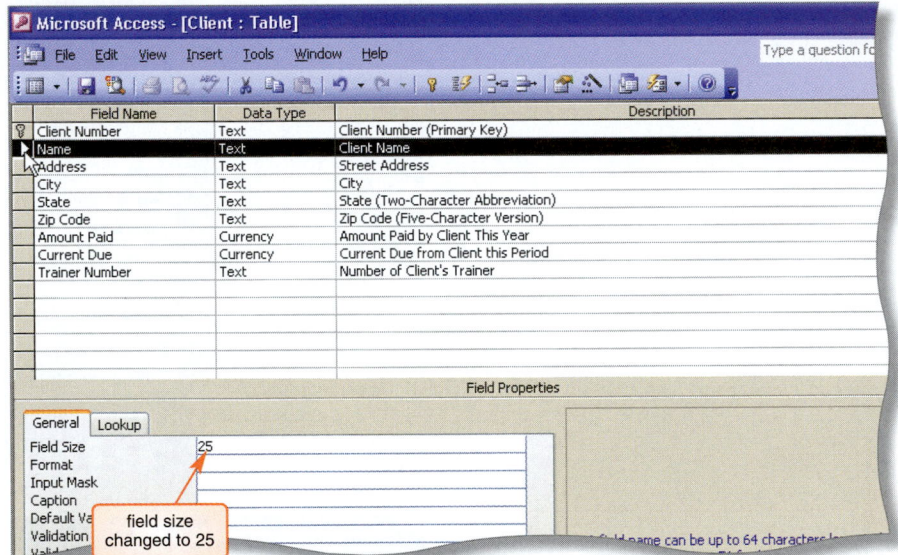

FIGURE 3-24

Q: What are some reasons for adding a field to a table?

A: Tables frequently need to be expanded to include additional fields for a variety of reasons. Users' needs can change. The field may have been omitted by mistake when the table first was created. Government regulations may change in such a way that an organization needs to maintain additional information.

Adding a New Field

The next step is to categorize the clients of the Ashton James College database. To do so, you must add an additional field, Client Type. The possible values for Client Type are EDU (which indicates the client is an educational institution), MAN (which indicates the client is a manufacturing organization), or SER (which indicates the client is a service organization).

To be able to store the client type, the following steps add a new field, called Client Type, to the table. The possible entries in this field are EDU, MAN, and SER. The new field will follow Zip Code in the list of fields; that is, it will be the seventh field in the restructured table. The current seventh field (Amount Paid) will become the eighth field, Current Due will become the ninth field, and so on. The following steps add the field.

To Add a Field to a Table

1

• **Click the row selector for the Amount Paid field, and then press the INSERT key to insert a blank row.**

A blank row appears in the position for the new field (Figure 3-25).

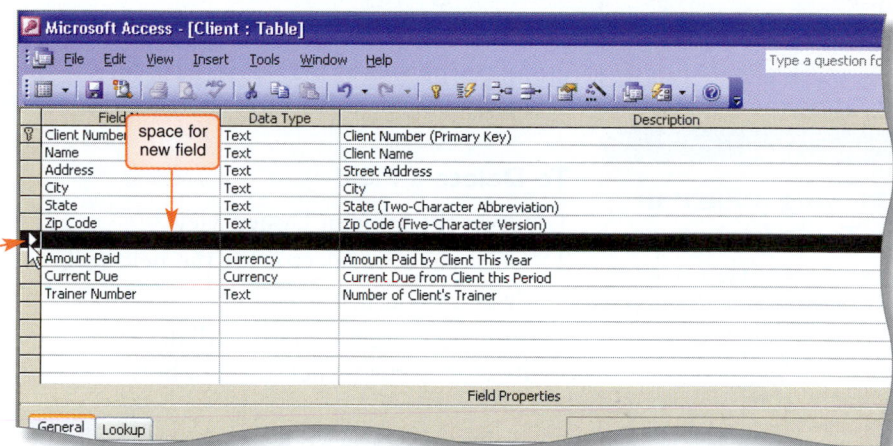

FIGURE 3-25

2

• **Click the Field Name column for the new field.**

• **Type** Client Type **as the field name and then press the TAB key. Select the Text data type by pressing the TAB key.**

• **Type** Client Type (EDU - Education, MAN - Manufacturing, SER - Service) **as the description.**

• **Press F6 to move to the Field Size text box, type** 3 **(the size of the Client Type field), and then press F6 again.**

The entries for the new field are complete (Figure 3-26).

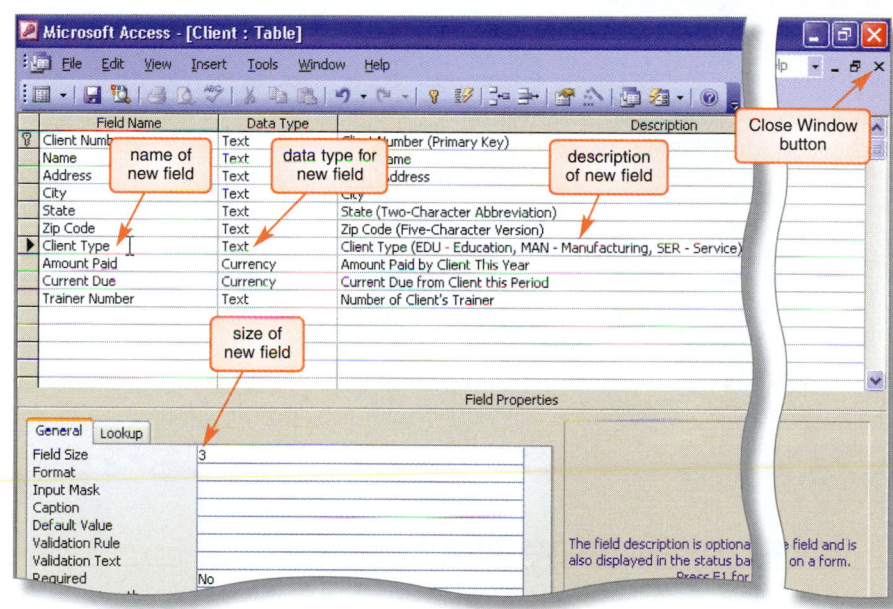

FIGURE 3-26

3

• **Close the Client : Table window by clicking its Close Window button.**

The Microsoft Office Access dialog box is displayed (Figure 3-27).

4

Click the Yes button to save the changes.

The changes are saved.

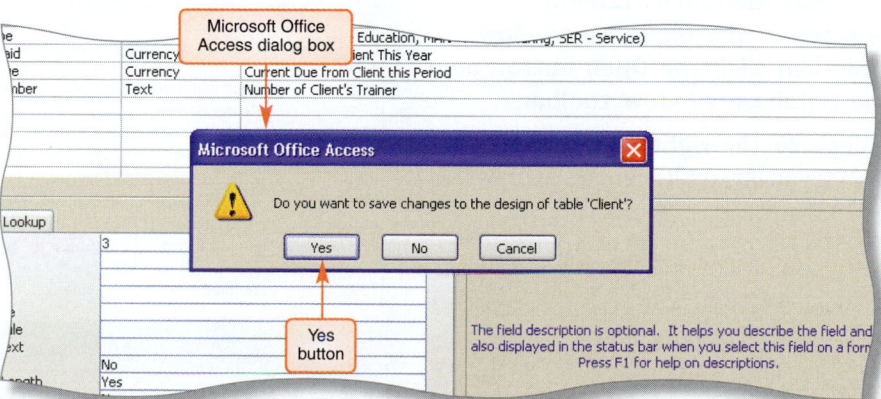

FIGURE 3-27

Other Ways

1. Click Insert Rows button on Table Design toolbar
2. On Insert menu click Rows
3. In Voice Command mode, say "Insert Rows"

The Client Type field now is included in the table and available for use.

Deleting a Field

If a field in one of your tables no longer is needed; for example, it serves no useful purpose or it may have been included by mistake, you should delete the field. The following steps illustrate how to delete a field.

To Delete a Field

1. Open the table in Design view.
2. Click the row selector for the field to be deleted.
3. Press the DELETE key.
4. When Access displays the dialog box requesting confirmation that you want to delete the field, click the Yes button.

When you save your changes to the table structure, the field will be removed from the table.

Updating the Restructured Database

Changes to the structure are available immediately. The Name field is longer, although it does not appear that way on the screen, and the new Client Type field is included.

To make a change to a single field, such as changing the name from Morgan-Alyssa to Morgan-Alyssa Academy, click the field to be changed, and then make the necessary correction. If the record to be changed is not on the screen, use the Navigation buttons (Next Record, Previous Record) to move to it. If the field to be corrected simply is not visible on the screen, use the horizontal scroll bar along the bottom of the screen to shift all the fields until the correct one appears. Then make the change.

The following step changes the name of Morgan-Alyssa to Morgan-Alyssa Academy.

More About

Moving a Field in a Table Structure

If you add a field to a table and later realize the field is in the wrong location, you can move the field. To do so, click the row selector for the field twice, and then drag the field to the new location.

More About

Changing Data Types

It is possible to change the data type for a field that already contains data. Before you change a data type, however, you should consider what effect the change will have on other database objects, such as forms, queries, and reports. For example, you could convert a Text field to a Memo field or to a Hyperlink field. You also could convert a Number field to a Currency field or vice versa.

To Update the Contents of a Field

1

• **Be sure the Client table is selected in the Database window, and then click the Open button on the Database window toolbar.**

• **Click to the right of the final a in Morgan-Alyssa (client MC28), press the SPACEBAR, and then type** Academy **to change the name.**

The name is changed from Morgan-Alyssa to Morgan-Alyssa Academy (Figure 3-28). Only the final portion of the name currently appears.

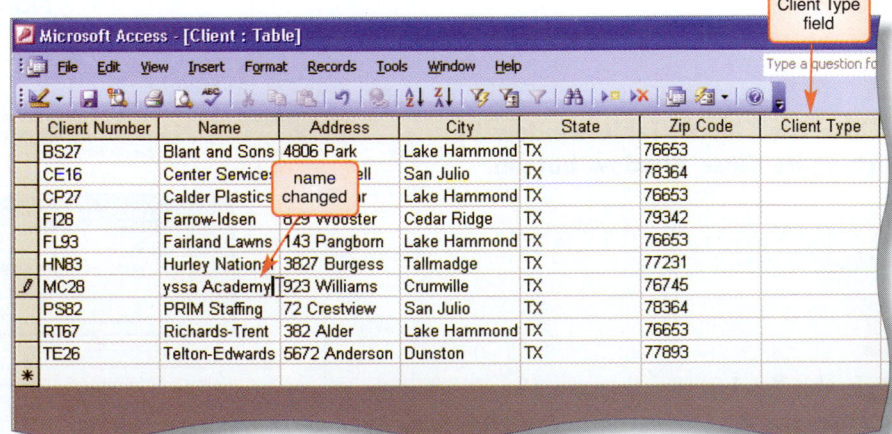

FIGURE 3-28

Changing the Appearance of a Datasheet

You can change the appearance of a datasheet in a variety of ways. You can resize columns and rows. You can change the font, the font size, the font style, and the color. You also can change the color of the gridlines in the datasheet as well as the cell effects.

Resizing Columns

The Access default column sizes do not always allow all the data in the field to appear. You can correct this problem by **resizing** the column (changing its size) in the datasheet. In some instances, you actually may want to reduce the size of a column. The State field, for example, is short enough that it does not require all the space on the screen that is allotted to it.

Both types of changes are made the same way. Position the mouse pointer on the right boundary of the column's **field selector** (the line in the column heading immediately to the right of the name of the column to be resized). The mouse pointer will change to a two-headed arrow with a vertical bar. You then can drag the line to resize the column. In addition, you can double-click in the line, in which case Access will determine the **best fit** for the column.

The following steps illustrate the process for resizing the Name column to the size that best fits the data.

Q&A

Q: Why would you need to change a data type?

A: You may need to change a data type because you imported data from another tool and Access imported the data type incorrectly. Also, you may find that a data type no longer is appropriate for a field. For example, a Text field can contain a maximum of 255 characters. If the data stored in a Text field exceeds 255 characters, you could change the data type to Memo.

To Resize a Column

1

• **Point to the right boundary of the field selector for the Name field.**

The mouse pointer shape changes to a bar with a double-arrow, indicating that the column can be resized (Figure 3-29).

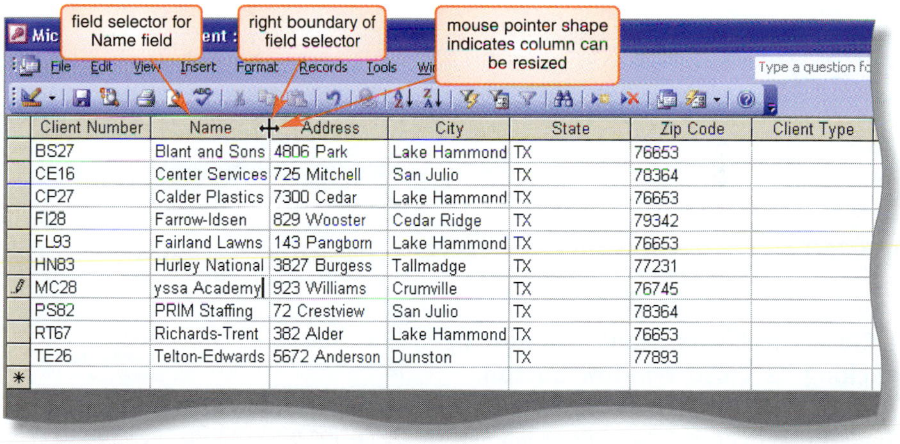

FIGURE 3-29

2

• **Double-click the right boundary of the field selector for the Name field.**

The Name column has been resized (Figure 3-30).

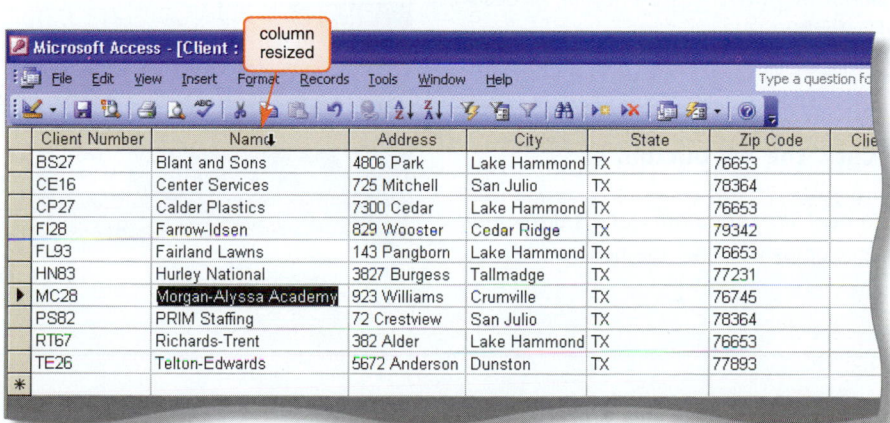

FIGURE 3-30

3

• **Use the same technique to resize the Client Number, Address, City, State, Zip Code, Client Type, and Amount Paid columns to best fit the data.**

The columns have been resized (Figure 3-31).

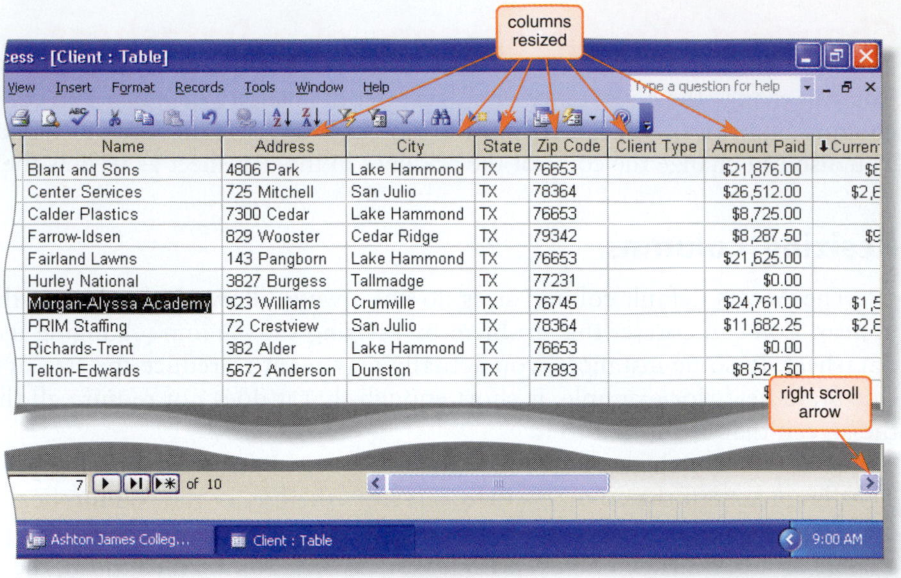

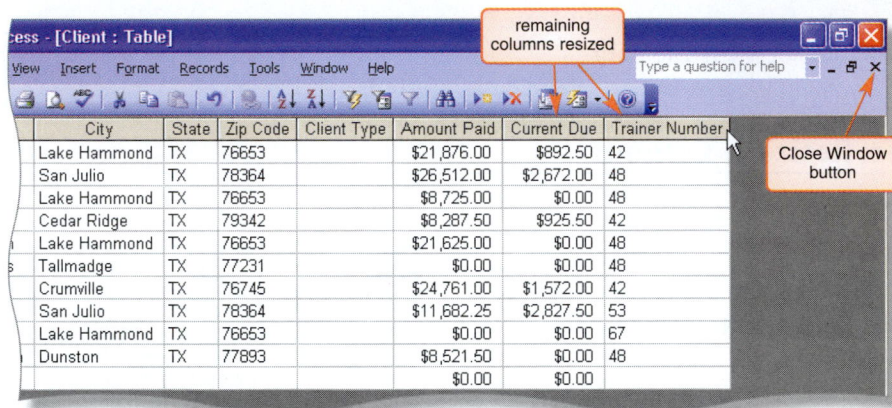

FIGURE 3-31

4

• **If necessary, click the right scroll arrow to display the Current Due and Trainer Number columns, and then resize the columns to best fit the data.**

All the columns have been resized (Figure 3-32).

FIGURE 3-32

5

• **Close the Client : Table window by clicking its Close Window button.**

The Microsoft Office Access dialog box is displayed (Figure 3-33). Changing a column width changes the layout, or design, of a table.

6

• **Click the Yes button.**

The next time the datasheet is displayed, the columns will have the new widths.

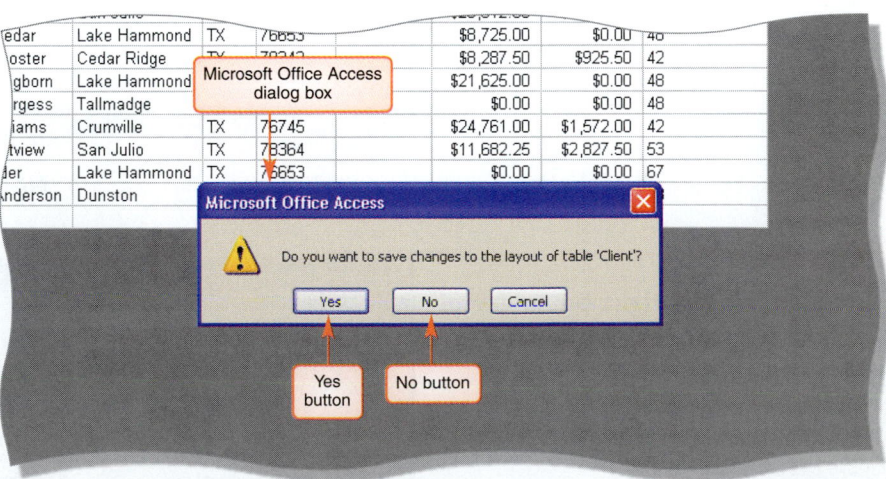

FIGURE 3-33

The change to the layout is saved.

Formatting a Datasheet

In addition to changing the column size, you can format a datasheet in other ways. You can change various aspects of the font, including the font itself, the font style, the size, and the color. You can change the cell effects to make the cells appear raised or sunken, and you can change the gridline color.

The changes to the datasheet will be reflected not only on the screen, but also when you print or preview the datasheet.

In this section, the following steps illustrate how to change the font in the datasheet and the format of the datasheet grid. You then will preview what the datasheet would look like when it is printed. At this point, you can print the datasheet if you so desire. Finally, you will close the datasheet without saving the changes. That way, the next time you view the datasheet, it will appear in its original format.

These steps show how to open the Trainer table in Datasheet view and then change the font.

> **Other Ways**
>
> 1. On Format menu click Column Width
> 2. In Voice Command mode, say "Format, Column Width"

To Change the Font in a Datasheet

1

• **With the Tables object selected and the Trainer table selected, click the Open button on the Database Window toolbar.**

• **Click Format on the menu bar.**

Access displays the Trainer table in Datasheet view (Figure 3-34). The Format menu appears.

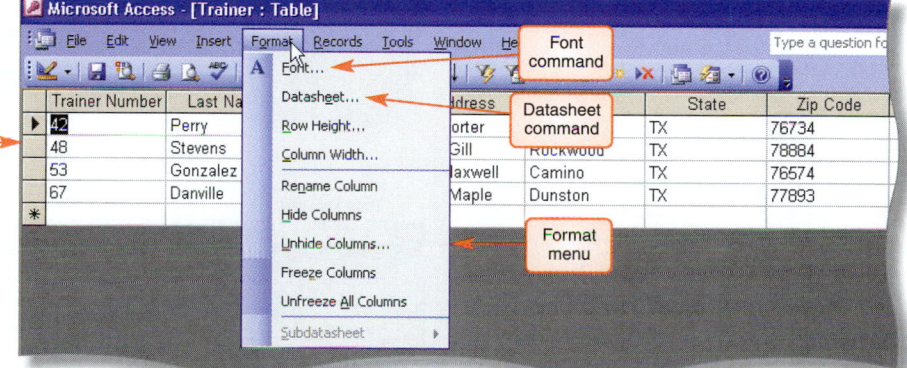

FIGURE 3-34

2

• **Click Font, click Arial Rounded MT Bold in the Font list, and then click 9 in the Size list. (If you do not have Arial Rounded MT Bold available, click another similar font.)**

Access displays the Font dialog box (Figure 3-35). Arial Rounded MT Bold is selected as the font style and 9 is selected as the font size.

3

• **Click the OK button.**

The font is changed.

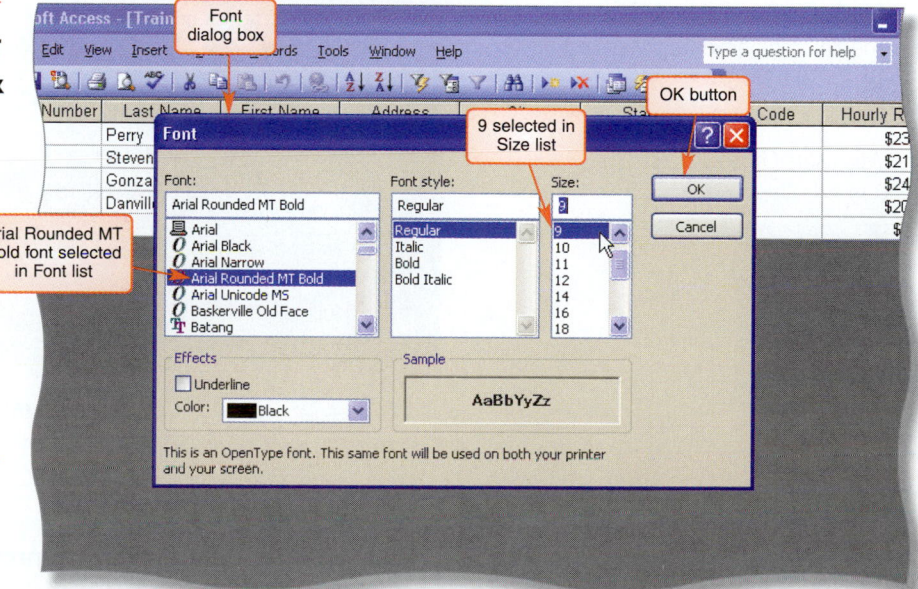

FIGURE 3-35

The following steps change the format of the grid.

To Change the Format of the Datasheet Grid

1

• **Click Format on the menu bar, and then click Datasheet.**

Access displays the Datasheet Formatting dialog box (Figure 3-36).

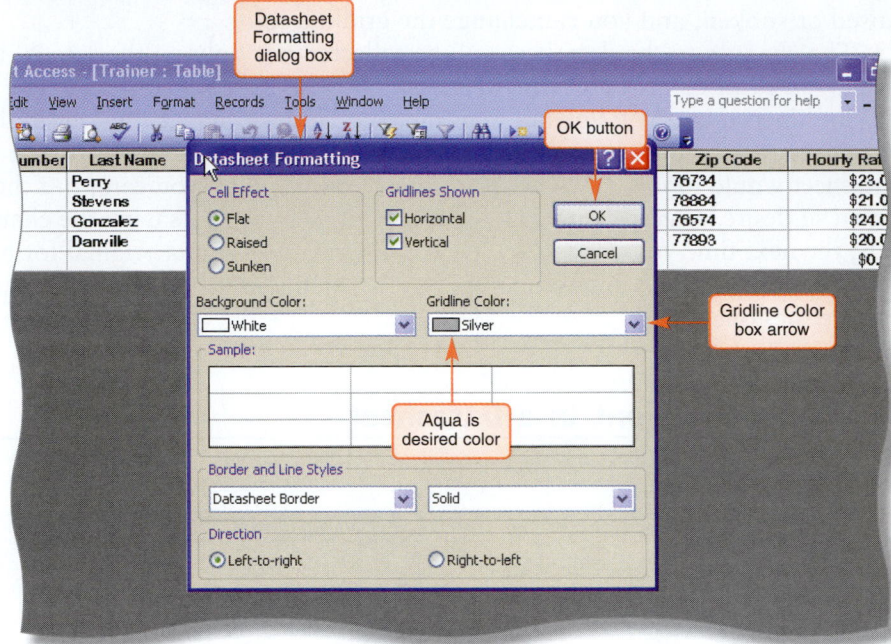

FIGURE 3-36

2

• **Click the Gridline Color box arrow, click Aqua, and then click the OK button.**

• **Resize the columns to best fit the data.**

The gridline color is changed to aqua and the columns have been resized (Figure 3-37).

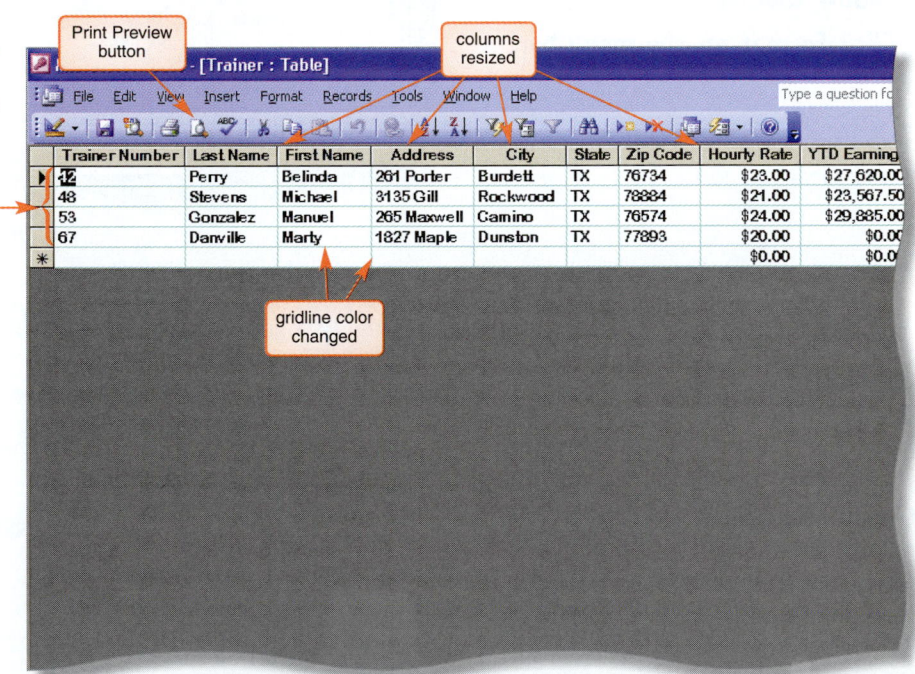

FIGURE 3-37

Other Ways

1. Right-click any open area outside datasheet, click Font on shortcut menu
2. In Voice Command mode, say "Format, Font"

The following steps use Print Preview to preview the changes to the datasheet.

To Use Print Preview

1

• **Click the Print Preview button on the Table Datasheet toolbar.**

• **If instructed to do so, print the results by clicking the Print button on the Print Preview toolbar.**

Access displays the pre-view window (Figure 3-38). The changes in the datasheet format are reflected in the preview.

2

• **Click the Close button on the Print Preview toolbar.**

The preview no longer appears.

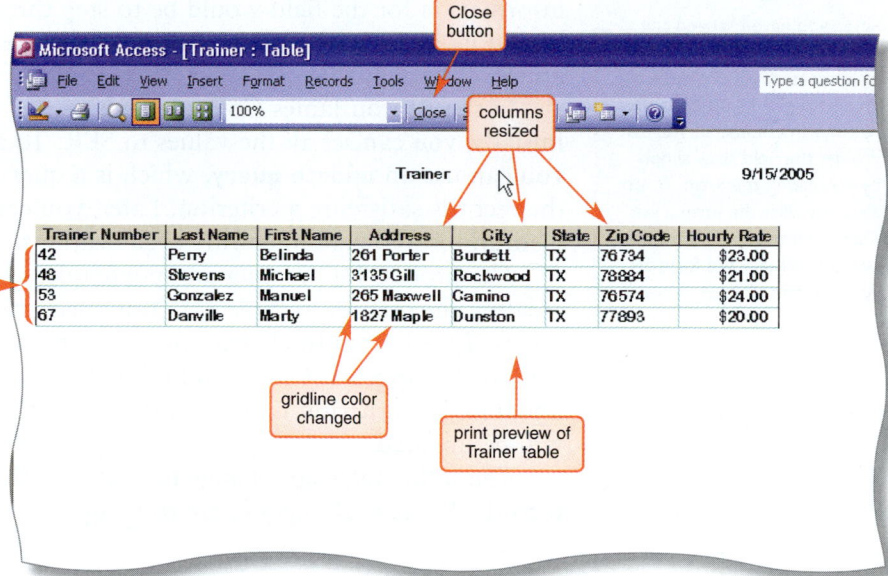

FIGURE 3-38

To print the datasheet, click the Print button on either the Table Datasheet toolbar or the Print Preview toolbar. The changes to the format are reflected in the printout.

The following steps show how to close the datasheet without saving the changes to the format.

To Close the Datasheet Without Saving the Format Changes

1 **Click the Close Window button for the Trainer : Table window.**

2 **Click the No button in the Microsoft Office Access dialog box when asked if you want to save your changes.**

Because the changes are not saved, the next time you open the Trainer table it will appear in the original format (see Figure 3-34 on page AC 133). If you had saved the changes, the changes would be reflected in its appearance.

Mass Changes

In some cases, rather than making individual changes, you will want to make mass changes. That is, you will want to add, change, or delete many records in a single operation. You can do this with queries. An update query allows you to make the same change to all records satisfying some criterion. If you omit the criterion, you will make the same changes to all records in the table. A delete query allows you to delete all the records satisfying some criterion. You can add the results of a query to an existing table by using an append query. You also can add the results to a new table by using a make-table query.

More About

Resizing Columns

After you have changed the size of a field, the forms you have created will not reflect your changes. If you used the AutoForm command, you can change the field sizes simply by recreating the form. To do so, right-click the form, click Delete on the shortcut menu, and then create the form as you did in Project 1.

Using an Update Query

The Client Type field is blank on every record. One approach to entering the information for the field would be to step through the entire table, assigning each record its appropriate value. If most of the clients have the same type, a simpler approach is available.

In the Ashton James College database, for example, most clients are type SER. Initially, you can set all the values to SER. To accomplish this quickly and easily, you can use an **update query**, which is a query that makes the same change to all the records satisfying a criterion. Later, you can change the type for educational institutions and manufacturing organizations.

The process for creating an update query begins the same as the process for creating the queries in Project 2. You select the table for the query and then use the Query Type button to change to an update query. In the design grid, an extra row, Update To, appears. Use this additional row to indicate the way the data will be updated. If a criterion is entered, then only those records that satisfy the criterion will be updated.

The following steps change the value in the Client Type field to SER for all the records. Because all records are to be updated, criteria are not required.

To Use an Update Query to Update All Records

1

• **With the Client table selected, click the New Object button arrow on the Database toolbar and then click Query. With Design View selected in the New Query dialog box, click the OK button.**

• **Be sure the Query1 : Select Query window is maximized.**

• **Resize the upper and lower panes of the window as well as the Client field list so all fields in the Client table field list appear (see Figure 2-6 on page AC 70 in Project 2).**

Click the Query Type button arrow on the Query Design toolbar.

The list of available query types appears (Figure 3-39).

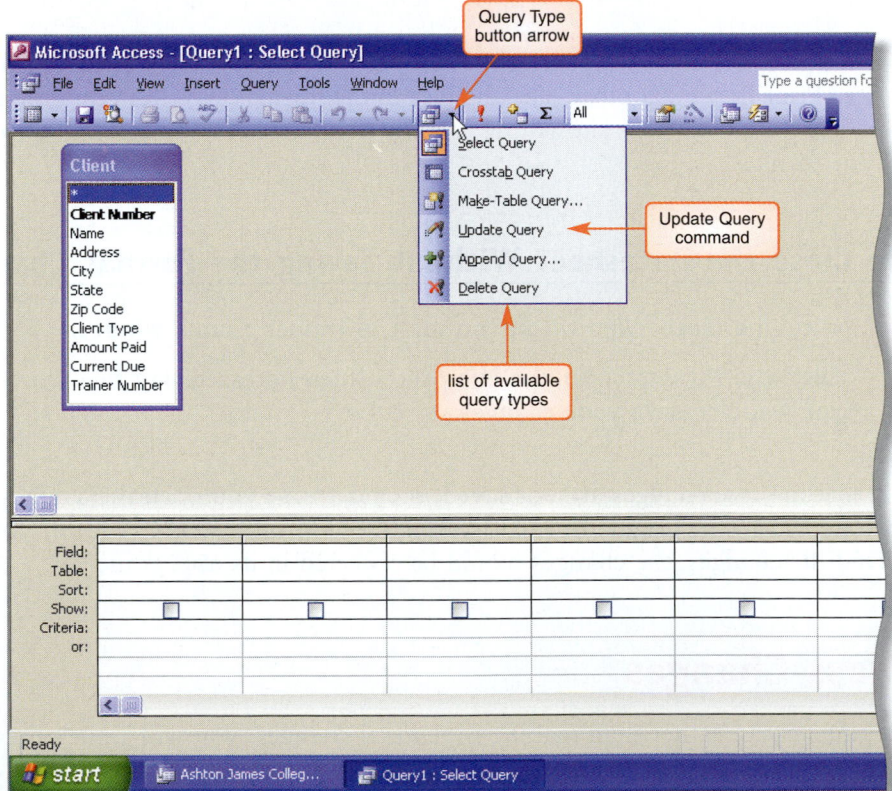

FIGURE 3-39

2

• **Click Update Query, double-click the Client Type field to select the field, click the Update To row in the first column of the design grid, and then type** SER **as the new value.**

The Client Type field is selected (Figure 3-40). In an update query, the Update To row appears in the design grid. The value to which the field is to be changed is entered as SER. Because no criteria are entered, the Client Type value on every row will be changed to SER.

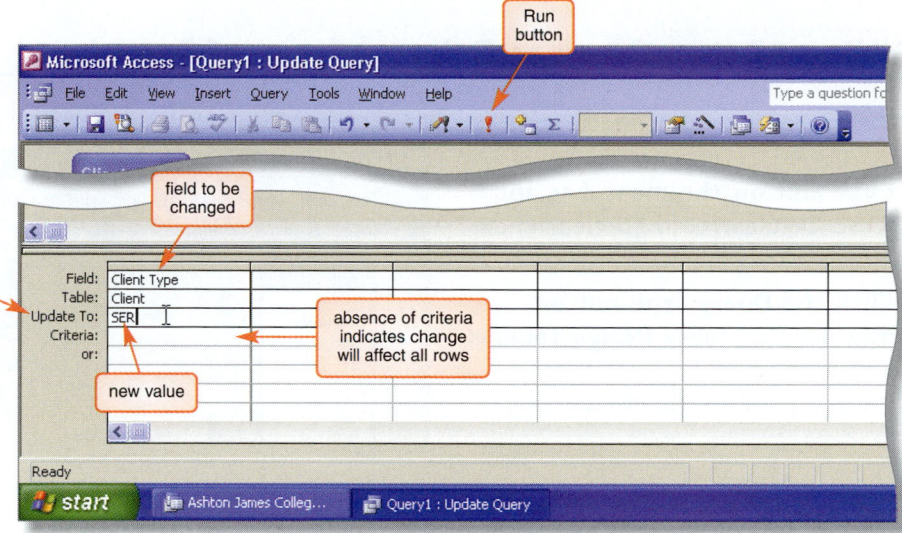

FIGURE 3-40

3

• **Click the Run button on the Query Design toolbar.**

The Microsoft Office Access dialog box is displayed (Figure 3-41). The message indicates that 10 rows (records) will be updated by the query.

4

• **Click the Yes button.**

The changes are made.

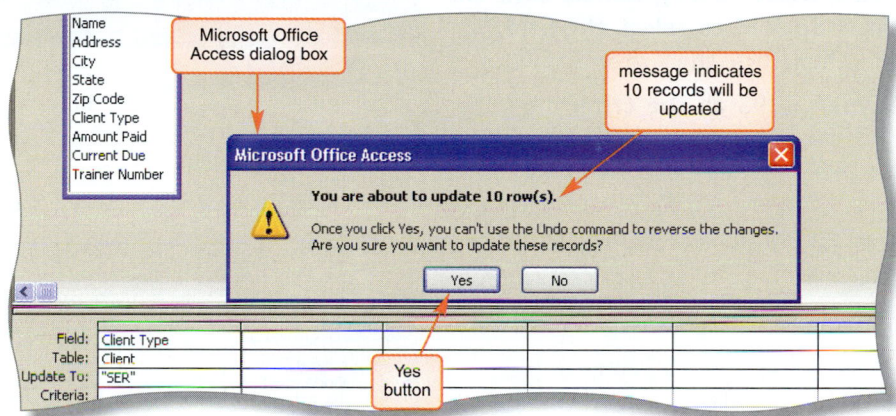

FIGURE 3-41

Using a Delete Query

In some cases, you may need to delete several records at a time. If, for example, all clients in a particular Zip code are to be serviced by another firm, the clients with this Zip code can be deleted from the Ashton James College database. Instead of deleting these clients individually, which could be very time-consuming in a large database, you can delete them in one operation by using a **delete query**, which is a query that will delete all the records satisfying the criteria entered in the query.

You can preview the data to be deleted in a delete query before actually performing the deletion. To do so, click the View button arrow on the Query Design toolbar and then click Datasheet View after you create the query, but before you run it. The records to be deleted then would appear in Datasheet view. To delete the records, click the View button arrow on the Query Datasheet toolbar and then click Design View to return to Design view. Click the Run button on the Query Design toolbar, and then click the Yes button in the Microsoft Office Access dialog box when asked if you want to delete the records.

The steps on the next page use a delete query to delete any client whose Zip code is 77893 without first previewing the data to be deleted. (Only one such client currently exists in the database.)

Other Ways

1. On Query menu click Update Query
2. Right-click any open area in upper pane, point to Query Type on shortcut menu, click Update Query on Query Type submenu
3. In Voice Command mode, say "Query, Update Query"

Q&A

Q: Why should you preview the data before running a delete query?

A: If you inadvertently enter the wrong criterion and do not realize it before you click the Yes button, you will delete the incorrect set of records. Worse yet, you might not even realize that you have done so.

To Use a Delete Query to Delete a Group of Records

1

• Click Edit on the menu bar and then click Clear Grid to clear the grid.

• Click the Query Type button arrow on the Query Design toolbar.

The list of available query types appears (Figure 3-42).

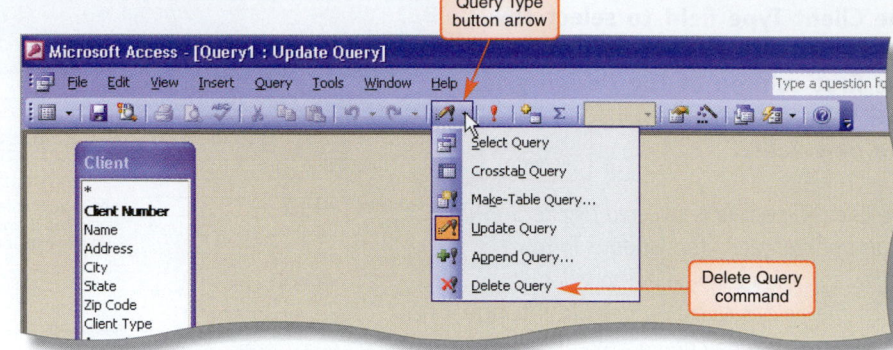

FIGURE 3-42

2

• Click Delete Query, double-click the Zip Code field to select the field, and then click the Criteria row.

• Type 77893 as the criterion.

The criterion is entered in the Zip Code column (Figure 3-43). In a delete query, the Delete row appears in the design grid.

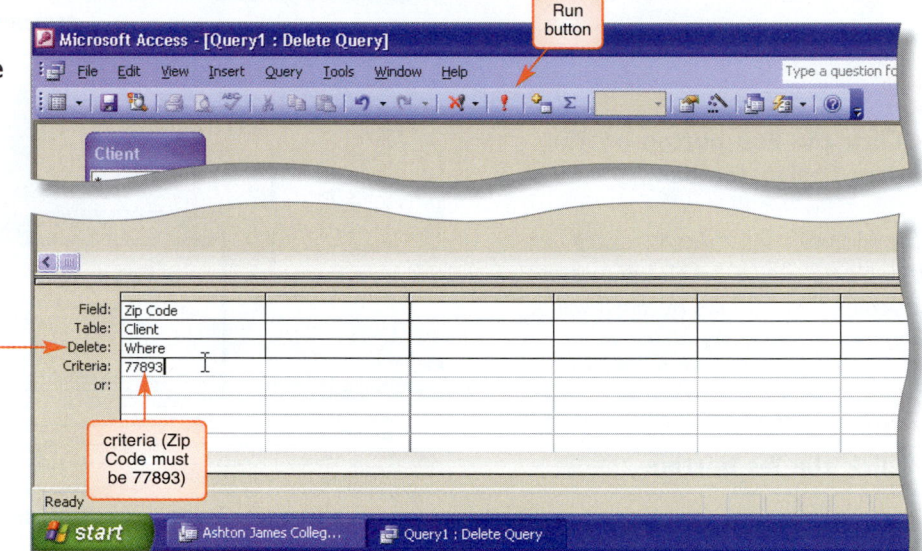

FIGURE 3-43

3

• Click the Run button on the Query Design toolbar to run the query.

The Microsoft Office Access dialog box is displayed (Figure 3-44). The message indicates the query will delete 1 row (record).

4

• Click the Yes button.

• Close the Query window. Do not save the query.

The client with Zip code 77893 has been removed from the table.

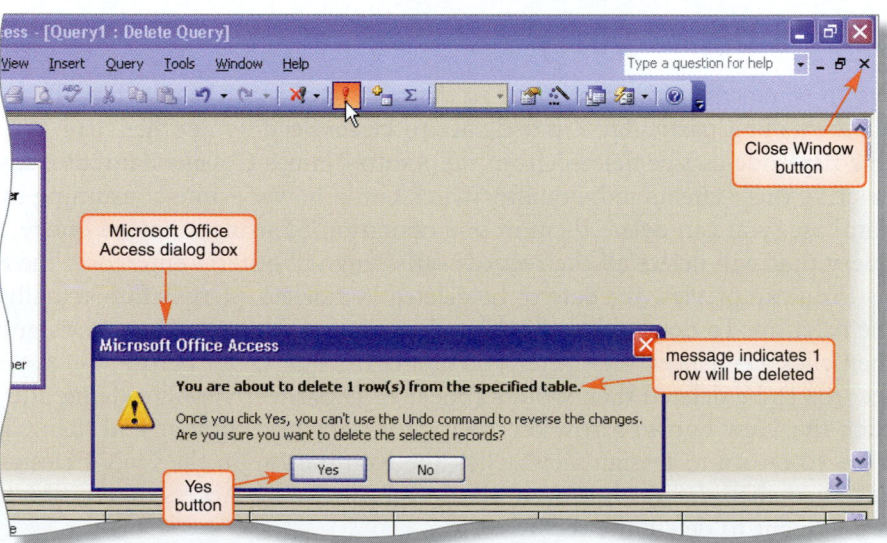

FIGURE 3-44

Using Append and Make-Table Queries

An **append query** adds a group of records from one table to the end of another table. For example, suppose that Ashton James College acquires some new clients and a database containing a table with those clients. To avoid entering all this information manually, you can append it to the Client table in the Ashton James College database using the append query. The following steps illustrate how to create an append query.

To Create an Append Query

1. Create a select query for the table containing the records to append.
2. In the design grid, indicate the fields to include, and then enter any necessary criteria.
3. Run the query to be sure you have specified the correct data, and then return to the design grid.
4. Click the Query Type button arrow on the Query Design toolbar, and then click Append Query.
5. When Access displays the Append Query dialog box, specify the name of the table to receive the new records and its location. Run the query by clicking the OK button.
6. When Access indicates the number of records to be appended, click the OK button.

The records then are added to the indicated table.

In some cases, you might want to add the records to a new table, that is, a table that has not yet been created. If so, use a **make-table query** to add the records to a new table. Access will create this table as part of the process and add the records to it.

Other Ways

1. On Query menu click Delete Query
2. Right-click any open area in upper pane, point to Query Type on shortcut menu, click Delete Query on Query Type submenu
3. In Voice Command mode, say "Query, Delete Query"

Validation Rules

You now have created, loaded, queried, and updated a database. Nothing you have done so far, however, makes sure that users enter only valid data. To ensure the entry of valid data, you create **validation rules**; that is, rules that a user must follow when entering the data. As you will see, Access will prevent users from entering data that does not follow the rules. The steps also specify **validation text**, which is the message that will appear if a user violates the validation rule.

Validation rules can indicate a **required field**, a field in which the user actually must enter data. For example, by making the Name field a required field, a user actually must enter a name (that is, the field cannot be blank). Validation rules can make sure a user's entry lies within a certain **range of values**; for example that the values in the Amount Paid field are between $0.00 and $90,000.00. They can specify a **default value**; that is, a value that Access will display on the screen in a particular field before the user begins adding a record. To make data entry of client numbers more convenient, you also can have lowercase letters appear automatically as uppercase letters. Finally, validation rules can specify a collection of acceptable values; for example, that the only legitimate entries for the Client Type field are EDU, MAN, and SER.

Specifying a Required Field

To specify that a field is to be required, change the value for the Required property from No to Yes. The steps on the next page specify that the Name field is to be a required field.

To Specify a Required Field

1

• **With the Database window open, the Tables object selected, and the Client table selected, click the Design button on the Database Window toolbar.**

• **Select the Name field by clicking its row selector.**

Access displays the Client : Table window (Figure 3-45). The Name field is selected.

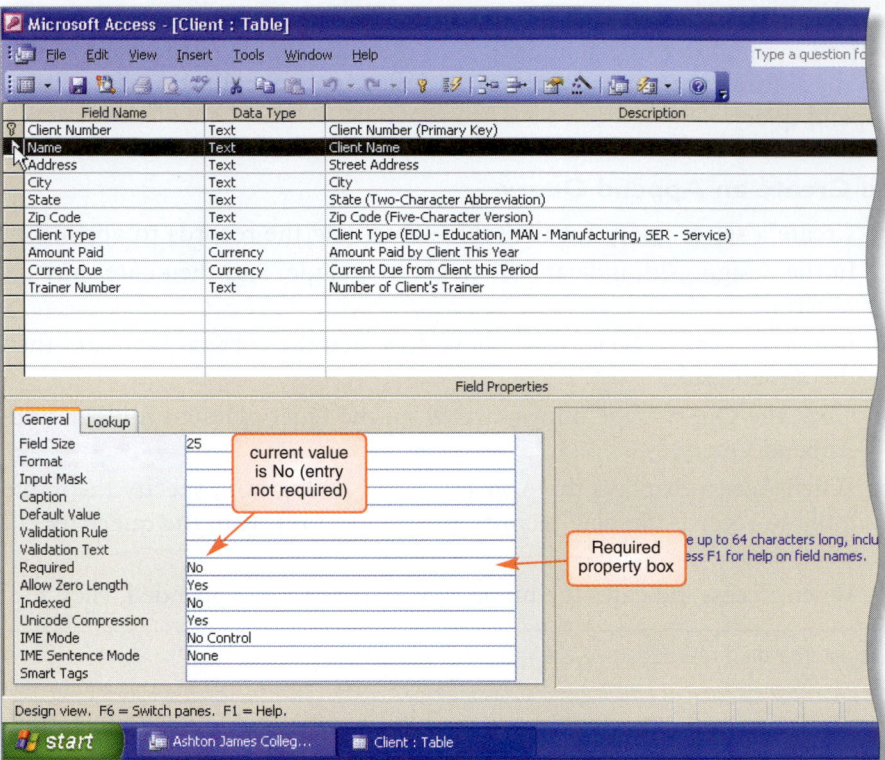

FIGURE 3-45

2

• **Click the Required property box in the Field Properties pane, and then click the down arrow that appears.**

• **Click Yes in the list.**

The value in the Required property box changes to Yes (Figure 3-46). It now is required that the user enter data into the Name field when adding a record.

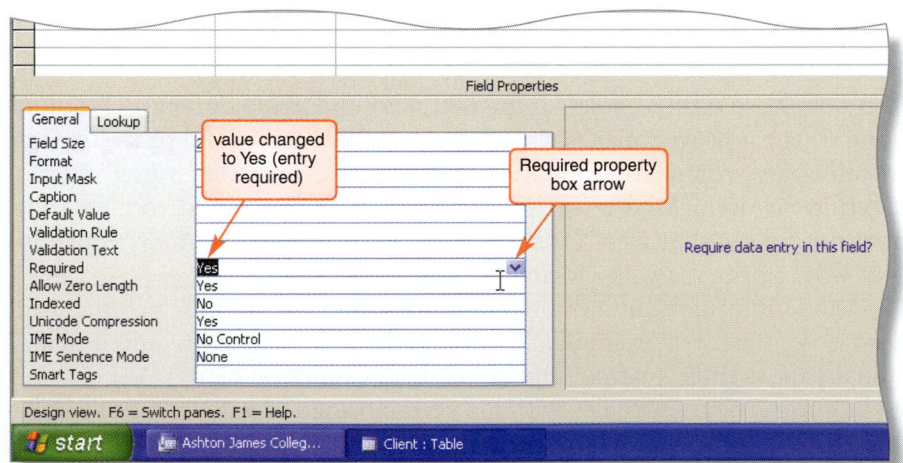

FIGURE 3-46

Specifying a Range

The following step specifies that entries in the Amount Paid field must be between $0.00 and $90,000.00. To indicate this range, the criterion specifies that the amount paid amount must be both >= 0 (greater than or equal to 0) and <= 90000 (less than or equal to 90000).

To Specify a Range

1

• **Select the Amount Paid field by clicking its row selector. Click the Validation Rule property box to produce an insertion point, and then type** `>=0` `and` `<=90000` **as the rule.**

• **Click the Validation Text property box to produce an insertion point, and then type** `Must` `be` `between` `$0.00` `and` `$90,000.00` **as the text.**

The validation rule and text are entered (Figure 3-47). In the Validation Rule property box, Access automatically changed the lowercase letter, a, to uppercase in the word, and. In the Validation Text property box, you should type all the text, including the dollar signs, decimal points, and comma.

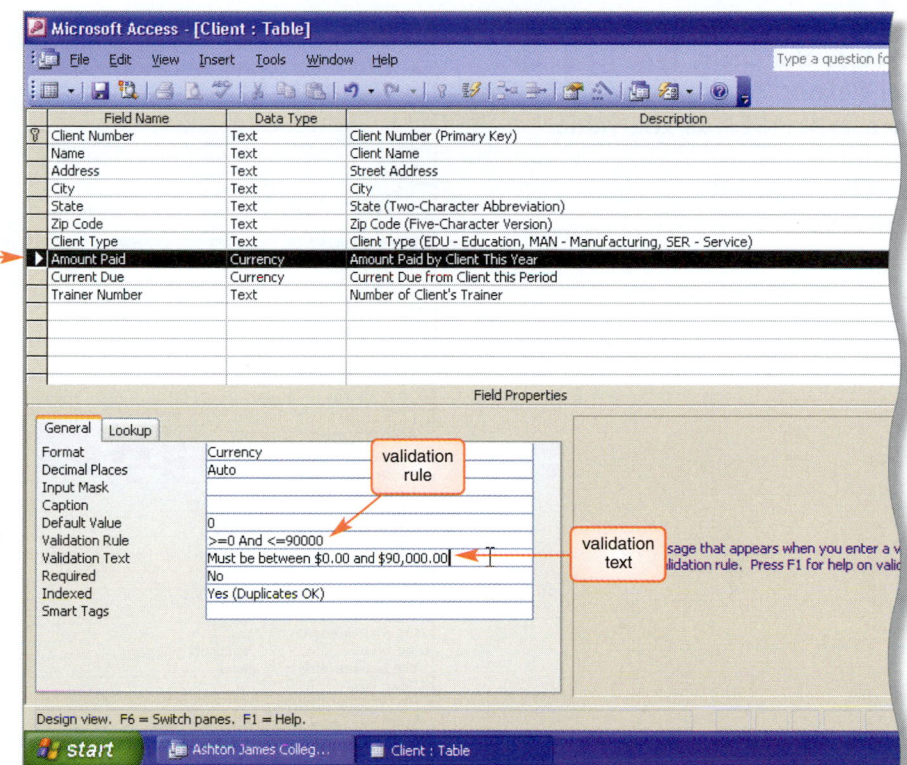

FIGURE 3-47

Users now will be prohibited from entering an amount paid amount that either is less than $0.00 or greater than $90,000.00 when they add records or change the value in the Amount Paid field.

Specifying a Default Value

To specify a default value, enter the value in the Default Value property box. The step on the next page specifies SER as the default value for the Client Type field. This simply means that if users do not enter a client type, the type will be SER.

To Specify a Default Value

1

• **Select the Client Type field. Click the Default Value property box, and then type** =SER **as the value.**

The Client Type field is selected. The default value is entered in the Default Value property box (Figure 3-48).

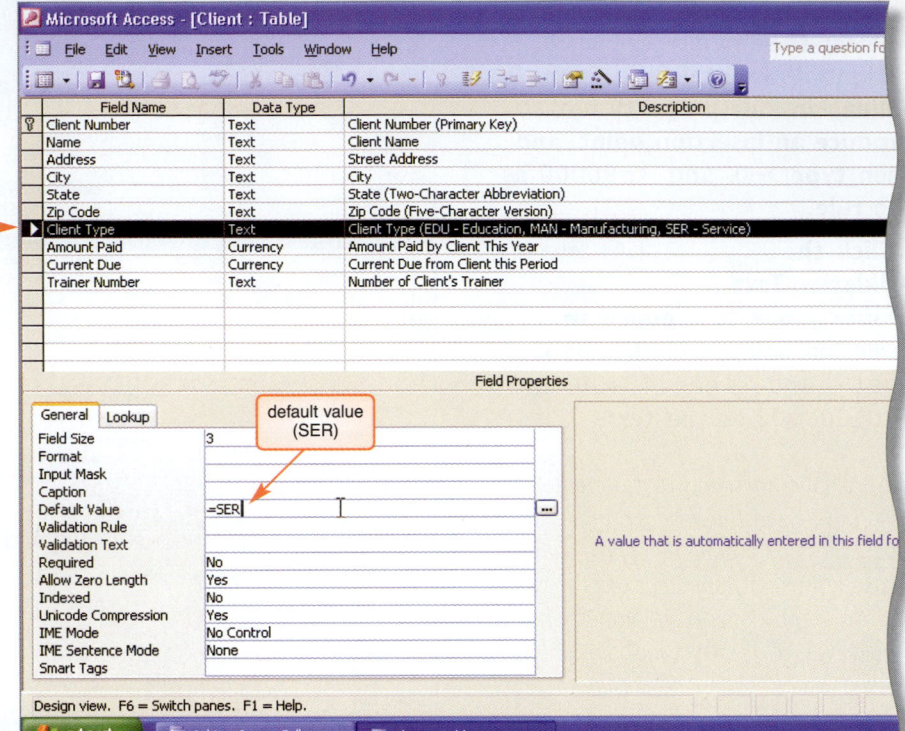

FIGURE 3-48

From this point on, if users do not make an entry in the Client Type field when adding records, Access will set the value equal to SER.

Specifying a Collection of Legal Values

The only **legal values** for the Client Type field are EDU, MAN, and SER. An appropriate validation rule for this field can direct Access to reject any entry other than these three possibilities. The following step specifies the legal values for the Client Type field.

To Specify a Collection of Legal Values

1

• **Make sure the Client Type field is selected.**

• **Click the Validation Rule property box and then type** =EDU or =MAN or =SER **as the validation rule.**

• **Click the Validation Text property box and then type** Must be EDU, MAN, or SER **as the validation text.**

The Client Type field is selected. The validation rule and text have been entered (Figure 3-49). In the Validation Rule property box, Access automatically inserted quotation marks around the EDU, MAN, and SER values and changed the lowercase letter, o, to uppercase in the word, or.

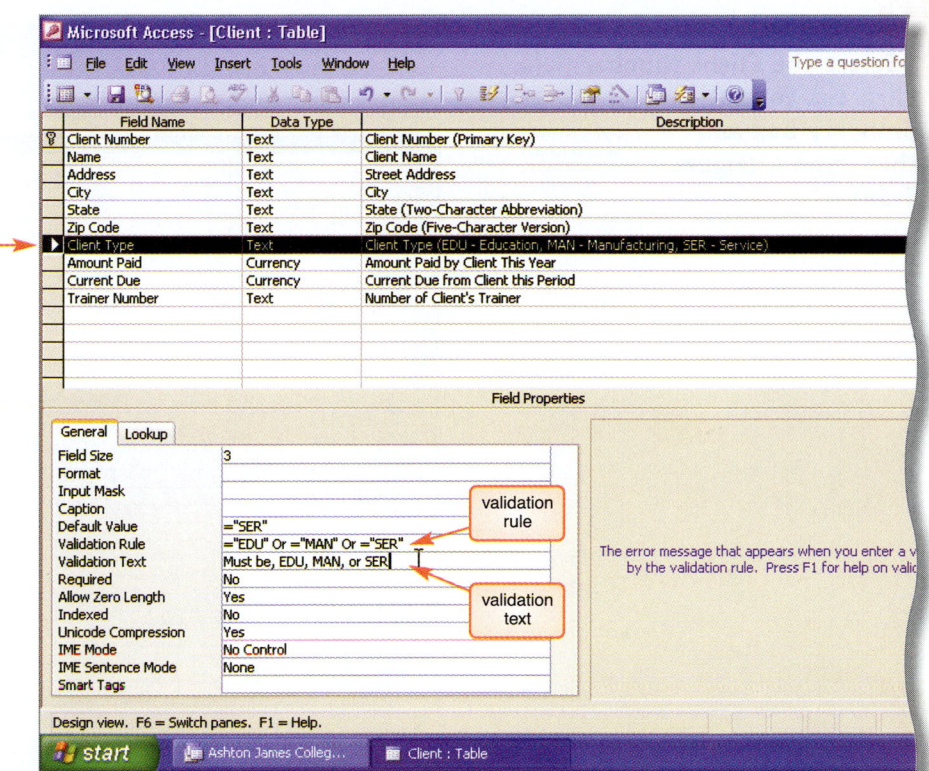

FIGURE 3-49

Users now will be allowed to enter only EDU, MAN, or SER in the Client Type field when they add records or make changes to this field.

Using a Format

To affect the way data appears in a field, you can use a **format**. To use a format with a Text field, you enter a special symbol, called a **format symbol**, in the field's Format property box. The Format property uses different settings for different data types. The following step specifies a format for the Client Number field in the Client table and illustrates the way you enter a format. The format symbol used in the example is >, which causes Access to display lowercase letters automatically as uppercase letters. The format symbol < causes Access to display uppercase letters automatically as lowercase letters.

To Specify a Format

1

• **Select the Client Number field. Click the Format property box and then type > (Figure 3-50).**

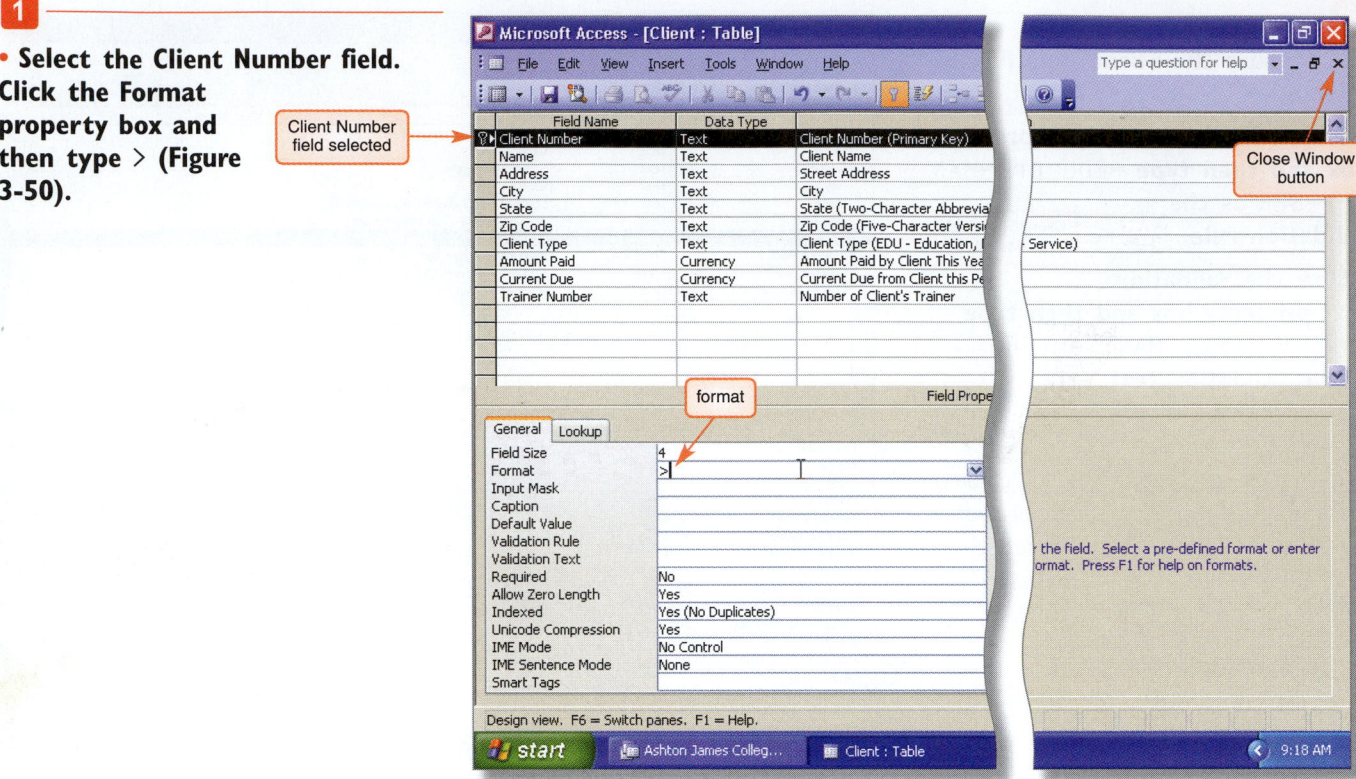

FIGURE 3-50

From this point on, any lowercase letters will appear automatically as uppercase when users add records or change the value in the Client Number field.

Saving Rules, Values, and Formats

The following steps save the validation rules, default values, and formats.

To Save the Validation Rules, Default Values, and Formats

1

• **Click the Close Window button for the Client : Table window to close the window (see Figure 3-50).**

The Microsoft Office Access dialog box is displayed, asking if you want to save your changes (Figure 3-51).

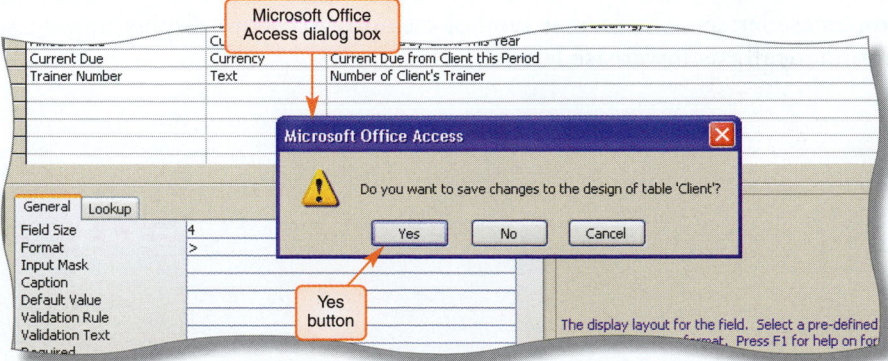

FIGURE 3-51

2

• **Click the Yes button to save the changes.**

The Microsoft Office Access dialog box is displayed (Figure 3-52). This message asks if you want the new rules applied to current records. If this were a database used to run a business or to solve some other critical need, you would click Yes. You would want to be sure that the data already in the database does not violate the rules.

3

• **Click the No button.**

The changes are saved. Existing data is not tested.

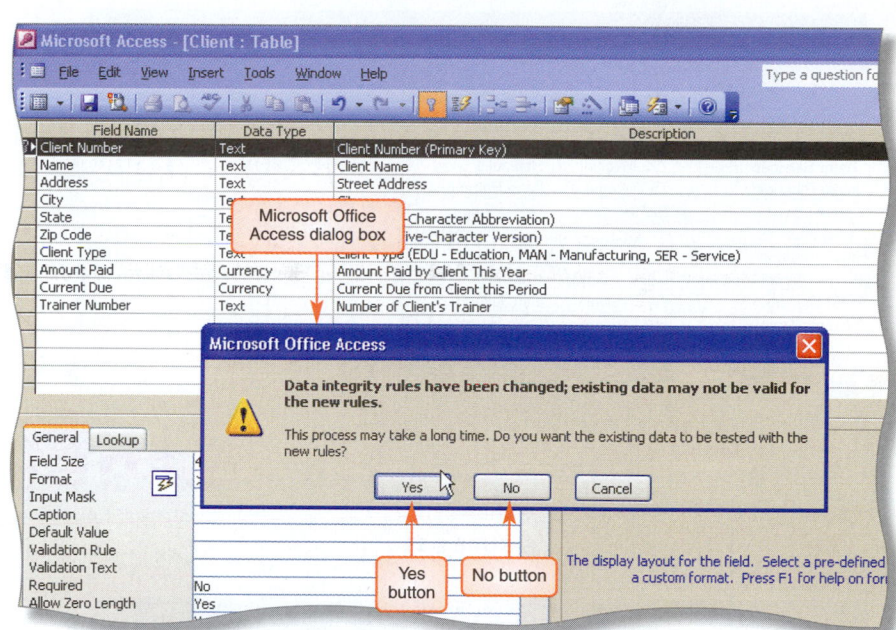

FIGURE 3-52

Updating a Table that Contains Validation Rules

When updating a table that contains validation rules, Access provides assistance in making sure the data entered is valid. It helps in making sure that data is for-matted correctly. Access also will not accept invalid data. Entering a number that is out of the required range, for example, or entering a value that is not one of the possible choices, will pro-duce an error message in the form of a dialog box. The database will not be updated until the error is corrected.

If the client number entered contains lowercase letters, such as st21 (Figure 3-53), Access will display the data automatically as ST21 (Figure 3-54).

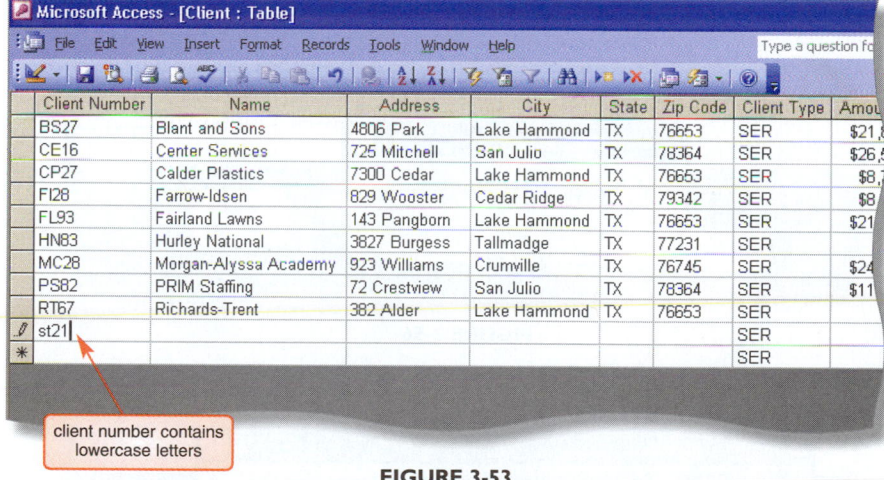

FIGURE 3-53

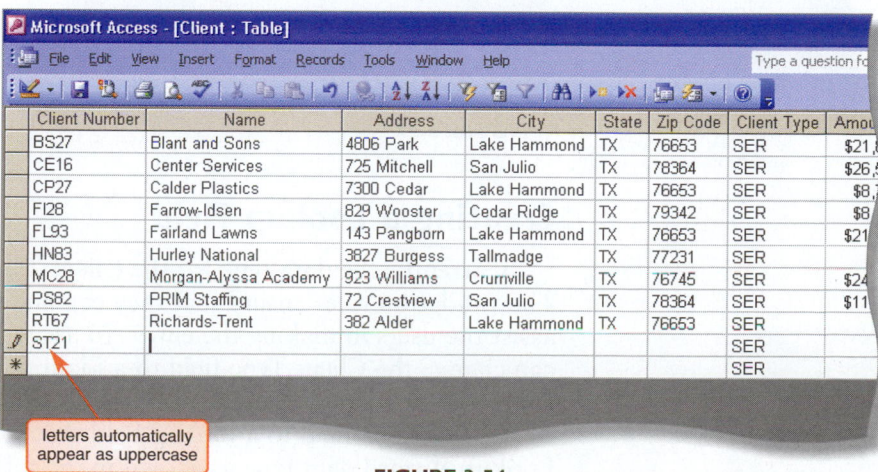

FIGURE 3-54

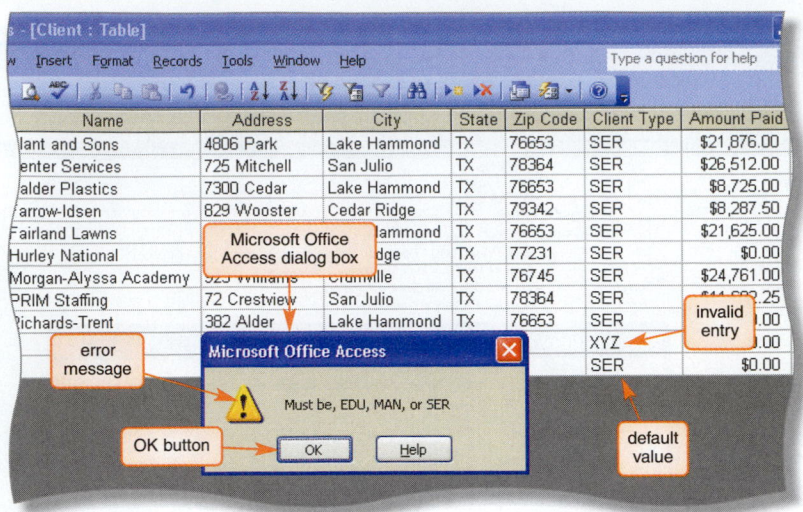

FIGURE 3-55

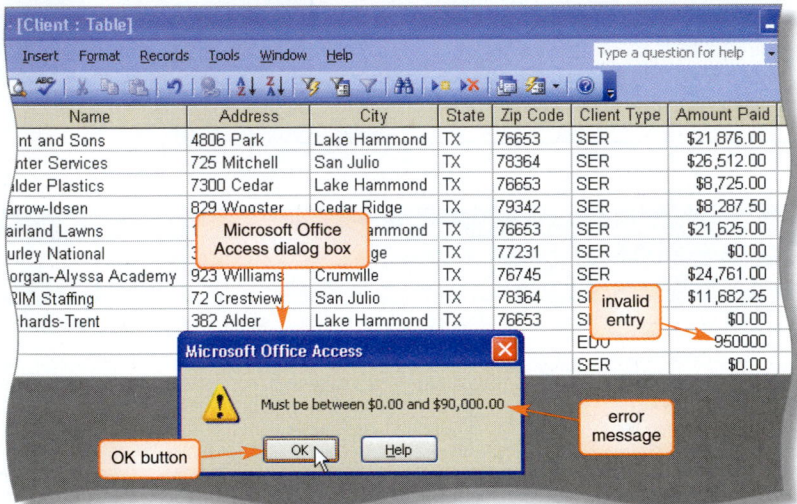

FIGURE 3-56

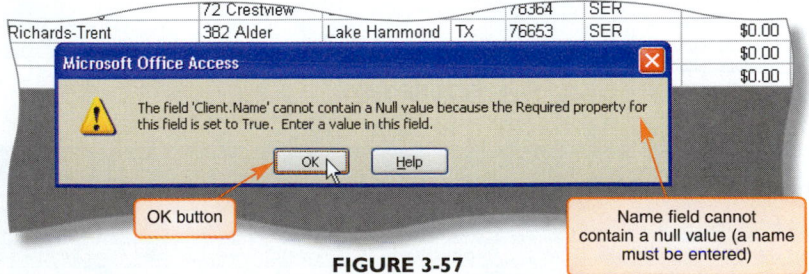

FIGURE 3-57

If the client type is not valid, such as XYZ, Access will display the text message you specified (Figure 3-55) and not allow the data to enter the database.

If the amount paid value is not valid, such as 950000, which is too large, Access also displays the appropriate message (Figure 3-56) and refuses to accept the data.

If a required field contains no data, Access indicates this by displaying an error message as soon as you attempt to leave the record (Figure 3-57). The field must contain a valid entry before Access will move to a different record.

When entering data into a field with a validation rule, you may find that Access displays the error message and you are unable to make the necessary correction. It may be that you cannot remember the validation rule you created or it was created incorrectly. In such a case, you neither can leave the field nor close the table because you have entered data into a field that violates the validation rule.

If this happens, first try again to type an acceptable entry. If this does not work, repeatedly press the BACKSPACE key to erase the contents of the field and then try to leave the field. If you are unsuccessful using this procedure, press the ESC key until the record is removed from the screen. The record will not be added to the database.

Should the need arise to take this drastic action, you probably have a faulty validation rule. Use the techniques of the previous sections to correct the existing validation rules for the field.

Creating a Lookup Field

Currently, the data type for the Client Type field is text. Users must enter a type. The validation rules ensure that they can enter only a valid type, but they do not assist the users in making the entry. To assist them in the data-entry process, you can change the Client Type field to a lookup field. A **Lookup field** allows the user to select from a list of values.

To change a field to a lookup field that selects from a list of values, use the Lookup Wizard data type as shown in the following steps.

To Create a Lookup Field

1

• **If necessary, click the Tables object. Click Client and then click the Design button on the Database Window toolbar.**

• **Click the Data Type column for the Client Type field, and then click the arrow.**

The list of available data types appears (Figure 3-58).

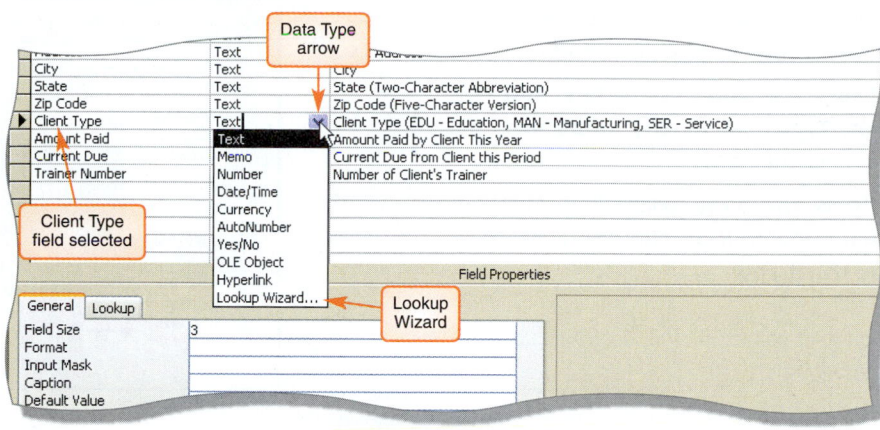

FIGURE 3-58

2

• **Click Lookup Wizard, and then click the "I will type in the values that I want" option button.**

Access displays the Lookup Wizard dialog box with options for creating a lookup column (Figure 3-59).

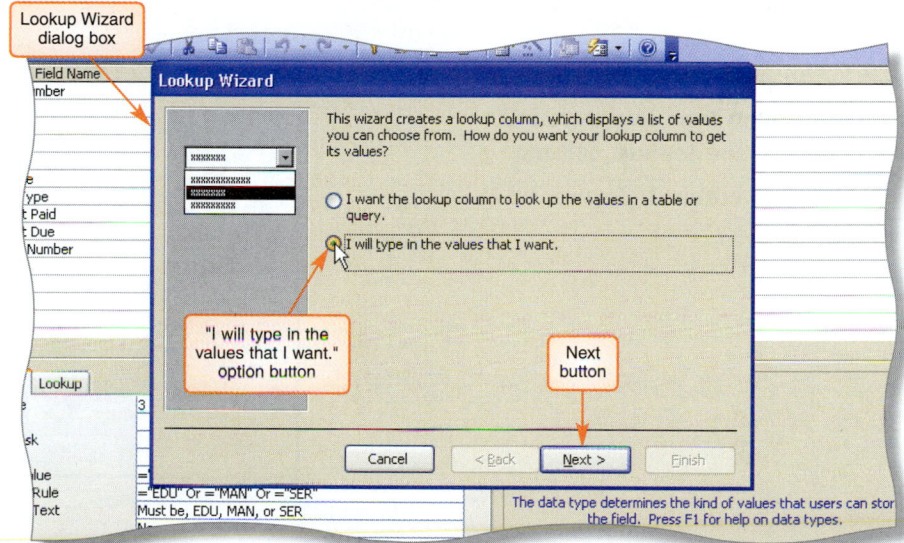

FIGURE 3-59

3

• **Click the Next button.**

The Lookup Wizard dialog box displays options for the number of columns and their values (Figure 3-60). In this screen, you enter the list of values.

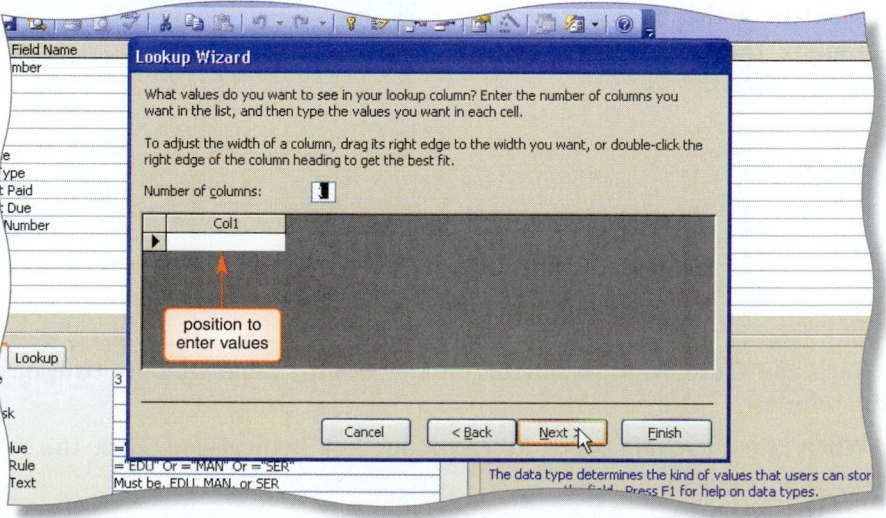

FIGURE 3-60

4

• **Click the first row of the table (below Col1), and then type** EDU **as the value in the first row.**

• **Press the** DOWN ARROW **key, and then type** MAN **as the value in the second row.**

• **Press the** DOWN ARROW **key, and then type** SER **as the value in the third row.**

The list of values for the lookup column is entered (Figure 3-61).

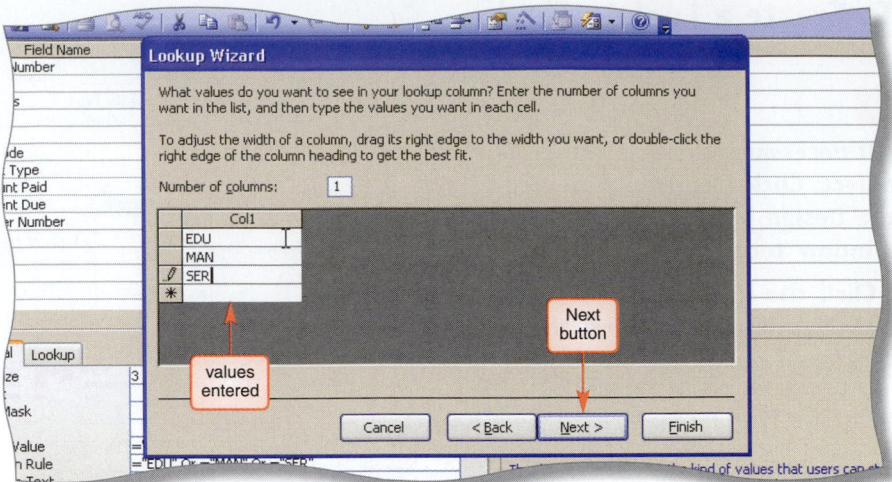

FIGURE 3-61

5

• **Click the Next button.**

• **Ensure Client Type is entered as the label for the lookup column.**

• **The label is entered (Figure 3-62).**

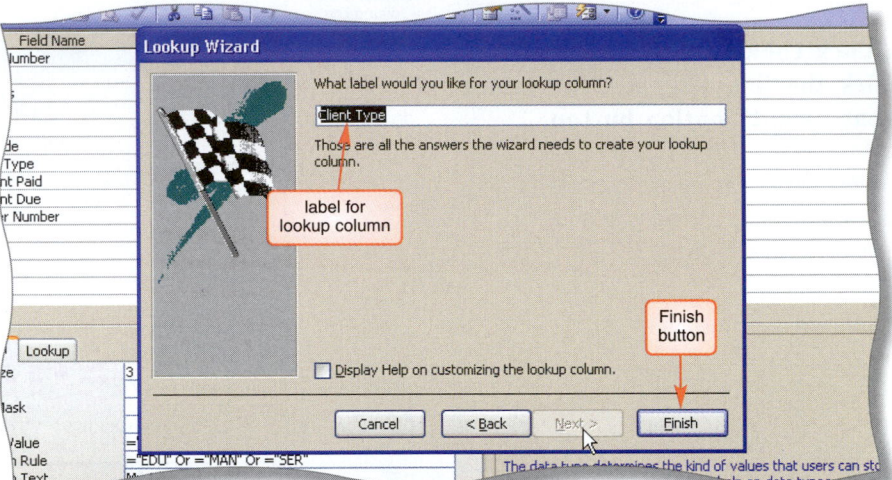

FIGURE 3-62

6

• **Click the Finish button to complete the definition of the Lookup Wizard field.**

Client Type is now a Lookup Wizard field, but the data type still is Text because the values entered in the wizard were entered as text (Figure 3-63).

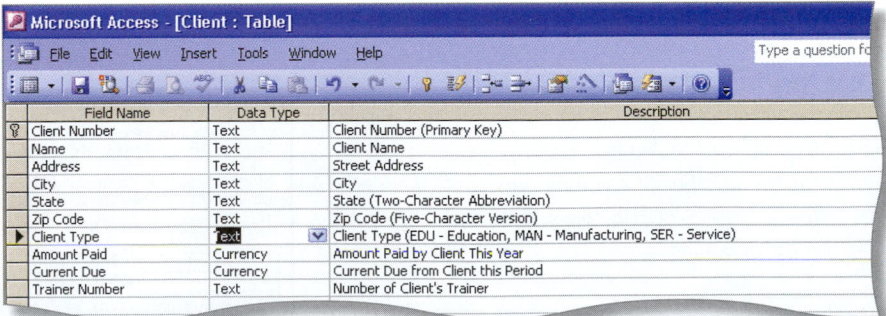

Field Name	Data Type	Description
Client Number	Text	Client Number (Primary Key)
Name	Text	Client Name
Address	Text	Street Address
City	Text	City
State	Text	State (Two-Character Abbreviation)
Zip Code	Text	Zip Code (Five-Character Version)
Client Type	Text	Client Type (EDU - Education, MAN - Manufacturing, SER - Service)
Amount Paid	Currency	Amount Paid by Client This Year
Current Due	Currency	Current Due from Client this Period
Trainer Number	Text	Number of Client's Trainer

FIGURE 3-63

7

• **Click the Close Window button on the Client : Table window title bar to close the window.**

• **When the Microsoft Office Access dialog box is displayed, click the Yes button to save your changes.**

The Client Type field is now a lookup field and the changes are saved.

Using a Lookup Field

Earlier, you changed all the entries in the Client Type field to SER. Thus, you have created a rule that will ensure that only legitimate values (EDU, MAN, or SER) can be entered in the field. You also made Client Type a Lookup field. You can make changes to a Lookup field by clicking the field to be changed, clicking the arrow that appears in the field, and then selecting the desired value from the list.

The following steps change the Client Type value on the second and sixth records to MAN and on the seventh and ninth records to SER.

To Use a Lookup Field

1

• **Make sure the Client table is displayed in Datasheet view.**

• **Click to the right of the SER entry in the Client Type field on the second record.**

An insertion point and down arrow appear in the Client Type field on the second record (Figure 3-64).

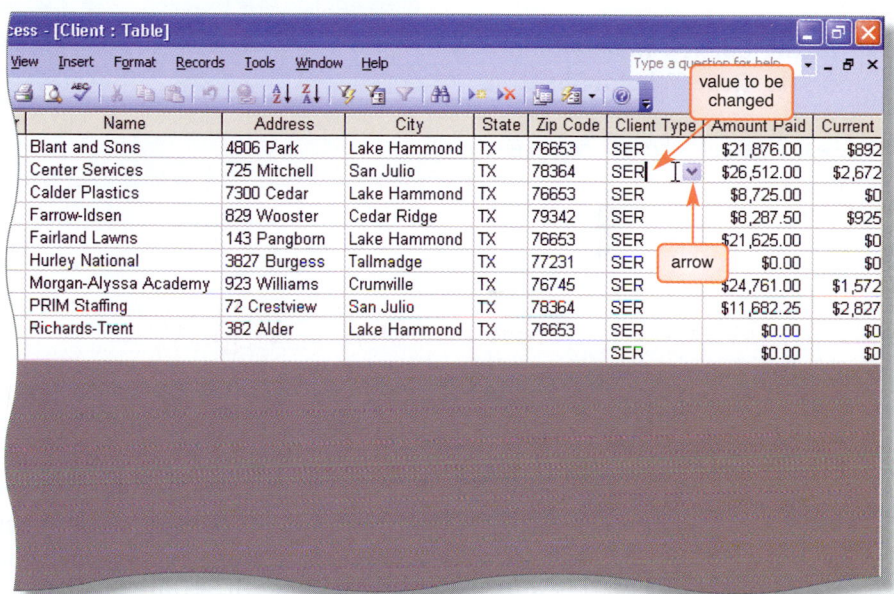

FIGURE 3-64

2

• **Click the down arrow.**

The list of values for the Client Type field appears (Figure 3-65).

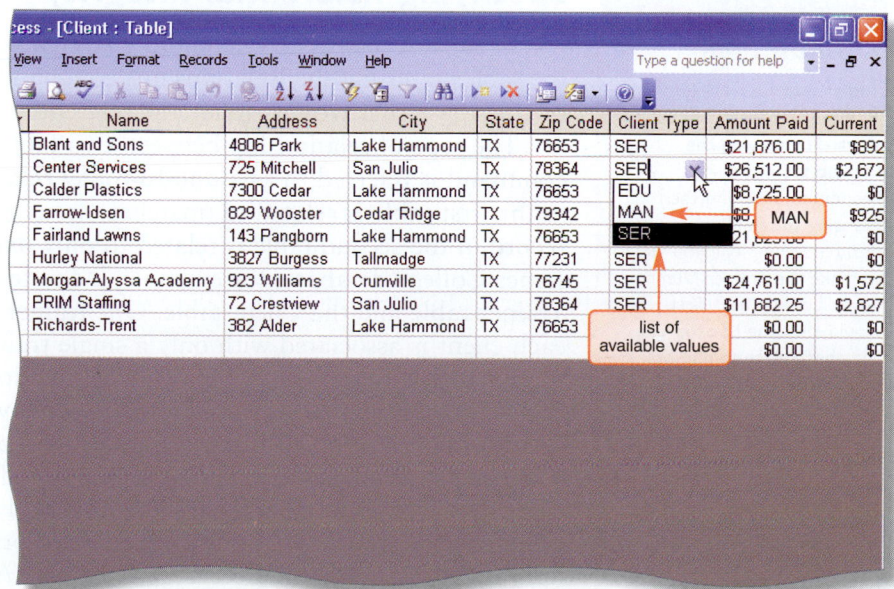

FIGURE 3-65

Microsoft Office
Access 2003

3

• Click **MAN** to change the value.

• In a similar fashion, change the SER on the sixth record to MAN, on the seventh record to EDU, and on the ninth record to EDU (Figure 3-66).

• If instructed to do so, print the results by clicking the Print button on the Table Datasheet.

4

• Close the Client : Table window by clicking its Close Window button.

The Client Type field changes now are complete.

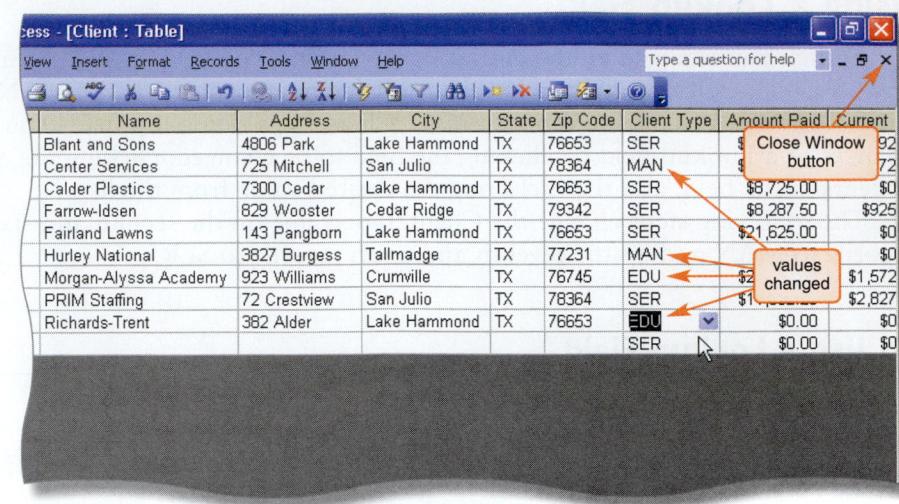

FIGURE 3-66

Referential Integrity

The property that ensures that the value in a foreign key must match that of another table's primary key is called **referential integrity**. A **foreign key** is a field in one table whose values are required to match the *primary key* of another table. In the Client table, the Trainer Number field is a foreign key that must match the primary key of the Trainer table; that is, the trainer number for any client must be a trainer currently in the Trainer table. A client whose trainer number is 92, for example, should not be stored because no such trainer exists.

Specifying Referential Integrity

In Access, to specify referential integrity, you must define a relationship between the tables by using the Relationships command. Access then prohibits any updates to the database that would violate the referential integrity.

The type of relationship between two tables specified by the Relationships command is referred to as a **one-to-many relationship**. This means that *one* record in the first table is related to (matches) *many* records in the second table, but each record in the second table is related to only *one* record in the first. In the Ashton James College database, for example, a one-to-many relationship exists between the Trainer table and the Client table. *One* trainer is associated with *many* clients, but each client is associated with only a single trainer. In general, the table containing the foreign key will be the *many* part of the relationship.

When specifying referential integrity, two ways exist to handle deletions. In the relationship between clients and trainers, for example, deletion of a trainer for whom clients exist, such as trainer number 42, would violate referential integrity. Any clients for trainer number 42 no longer would relate to any trainer in the database. The normal way to avoid this problem is to prohibit such a deletion. The other option is to **cascade the delete**, that is, have Access allow the deletion but then automatically delete any clients related to the deleted trainer.

Two ways also exist to handle the update of the primary key of the Trainer table. In the relationship between trainers and clients, for example, changing the trainer number for trainer 42 to 62 in the Trainer table would cause a problem. Clients are in the Client table on which the trainer number is 42. These clients no longer would relate to any trainer. Again, the normal way of avoiding the problem is to prohibit this type of update. The other option is to **cascade the update**; that is, have Access allow the update but then automatically make the corresponding change for any client whose trainer number was 42. It now will be 62.

The following steps use the Relationships command to specify referential integrity by specifying a relationship between the Trainer and Client tables. The steps also ensure that update will cascade, but that delete will not.

To Specify Referential Integrity

More About

**Relationships:
Printing
Relationships**

You can obtain a printed copy of your relationships after you have created them. To do so, first click the Relationships button to display the relationships. Next click File on the menu bar and then click Print Relationships. When Access displays the Print Preview window, click the Print button on the Print Preview toolbar

1

• **With the Database window displaying, click the Relationships button on the Database toolbar.**

Access displays the Show Table dialog box (Figure 3-67).

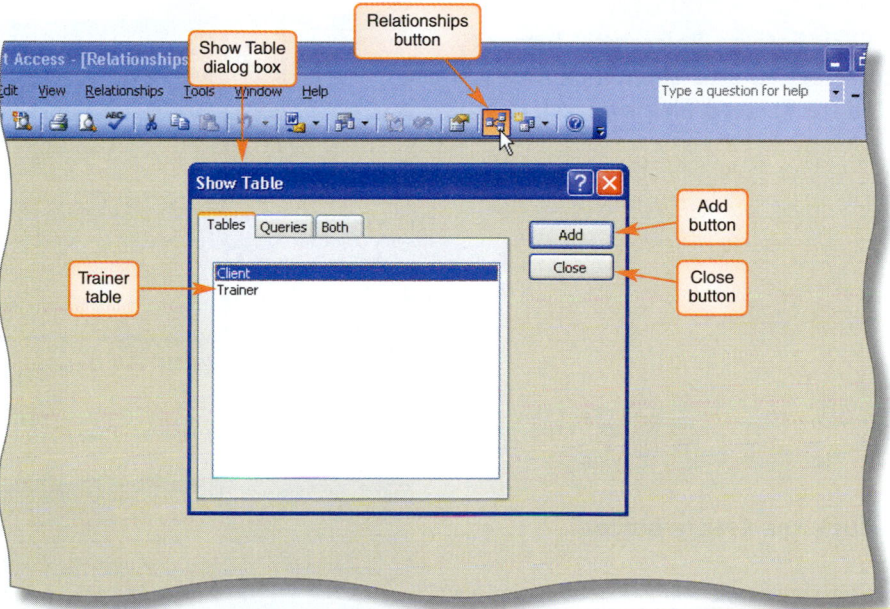

FIGURE 3-67

2

• **Click the Trainer table and then click the Add button. Click the Client table, click the Add button again, and then click the Close button in the Show Table dialog box.**

• **Resize the field lists that appear so all fields are visible.**

Field lists for the Trainer and Client tables appear (Figure 3-68). The lists have been resized so all fields are visible.

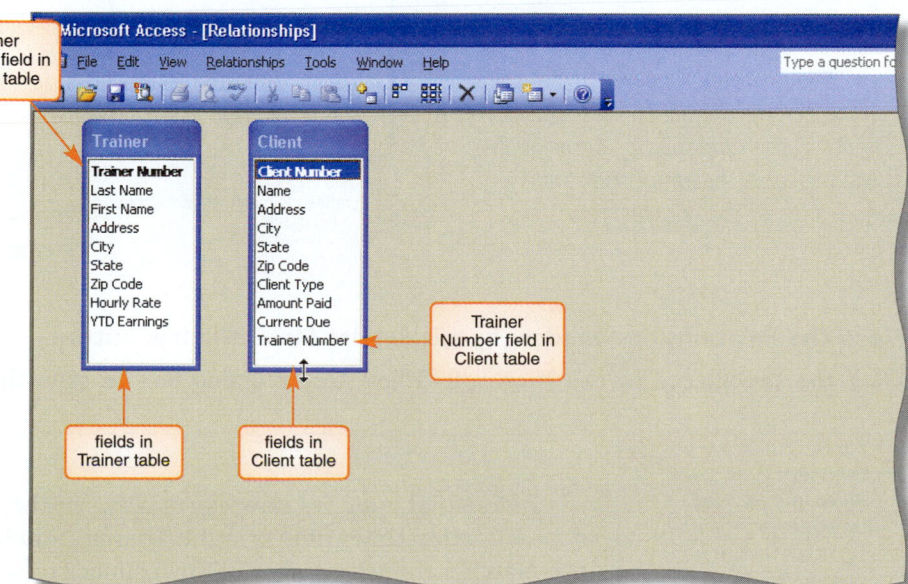

FIGURE 3-68

3

• **Drag the Trainer Number field in the Trainer table field list to the Trainer Number field in the Client table field list.**

Access displays the Edit Relationships dialog box (Figure 3-69). The correct fields (the Trainer Number fields) have been identified as the matching fields.

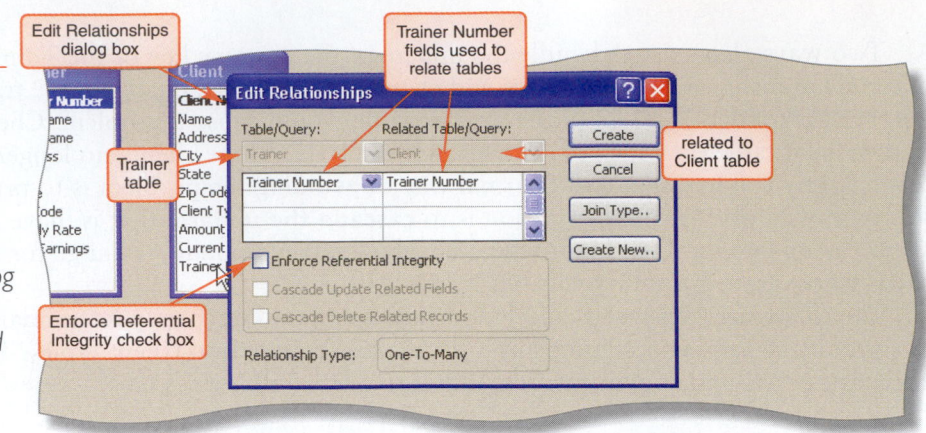

FIGURE 3-69

4

• **Click Enforce Referential Integrity to select it, and then click Cascade Update Related Fields to select it.**

The Enforce Referential Integrity and Cascade Update Related Fields check boxes are selected (Figure 3-70).

FIGURE 3-70

5

• **Click the Create button.**

*Access creates the relationship and displays it visually with the **relationship line** joining the two Trainer Number fields (Figure 3-71). The number 1 at the top of the relationship line close to the Trainer Number field in the Trainer table indicates that the Trainer table is the one part of the relationship. The infinity symbol at the other end of the relationship line indicates that the Client table is the many part of the relationship.*

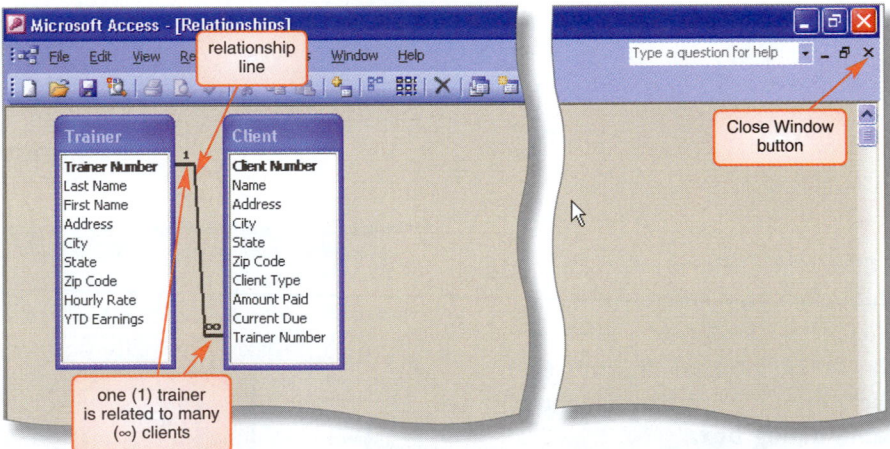

FIGURE 3-71

6

• **Close the Relationships window by clicking its Close Window button.**

• **Click the Yes button in the Microsoft Office Access dialog box to save the relationship you created.**

Referential integrity now exists between the Trainer and Client tables. Access now will reject any number in the Trainer Number field in the Client table that does not match a trainer number in the Trainer table. Attempting to add a client whose

Trainer Number field does not match would result in the error message shown in Figure 3-72.

A deletion of a trainer for whom related clients exist also would be rejected. Attempting to delete trainer 53 from the Trainer table, for example, would result in the message shown in Figure 3-73.

Access would, however, allow the change of a trainer number in the Trainer table. Then it automatically makes the corresponding change to the trainer number for all the trainer's clients. For example, if you changed the trainer number of trainer 42 to 62, the same 62 would appear in the trainer number field for clients.

Using Subdatasheets

Now that the Trainer table is related to the Client table, it is possible to view the clients of a given trainer when you are viewing the datasheet for the Trainer table. The clients for the trainer will appear below the trainer in a **subdatasheet**. The fact that such a subdatasheet is available is indicated by a plus sign that appears in front of the rows in the Trainer table. The following steps display the subdatasheet for trainer 48.

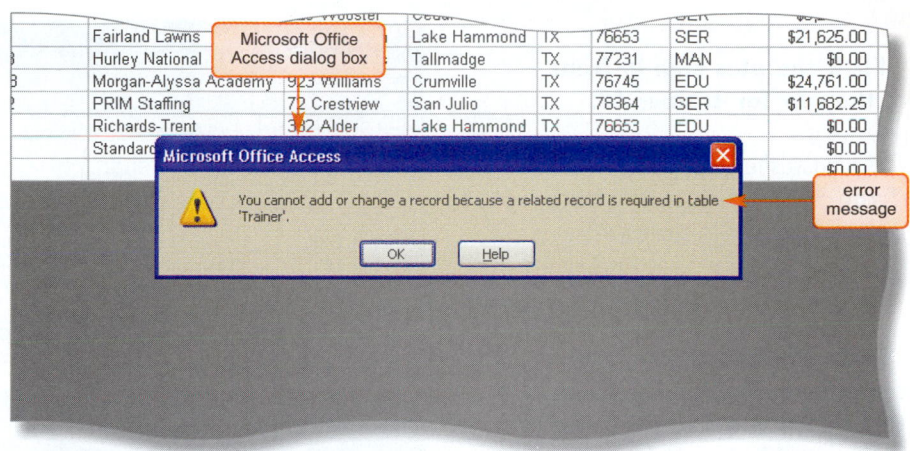

FIGURE 3-72

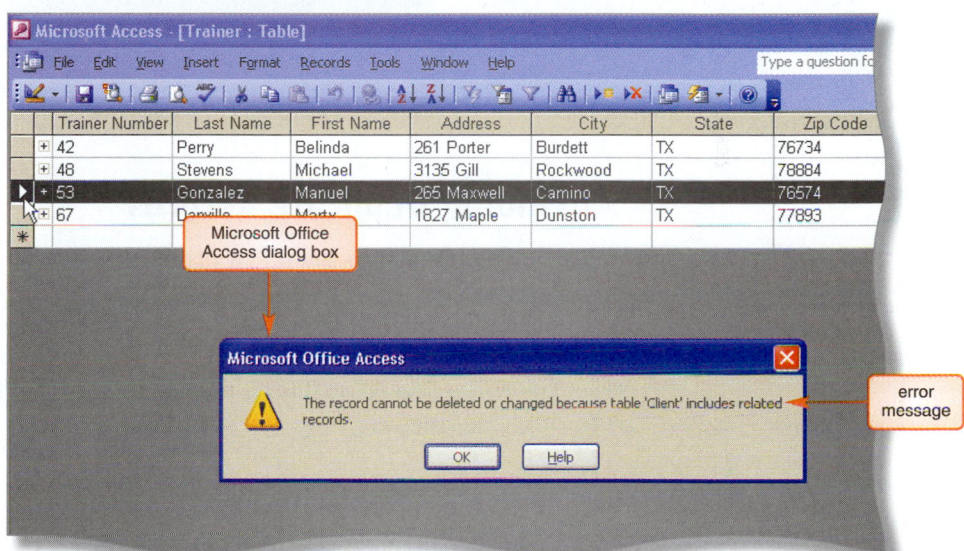

FIGURE 3-73

To Use a Subdatasheet

1

• **With the Database window on the screen, the Tables object selected, and the Trainer table selected, click the Open button on the Database Window toolbar.**

The datasheet for the Trainer table appears (Figure 3-74).

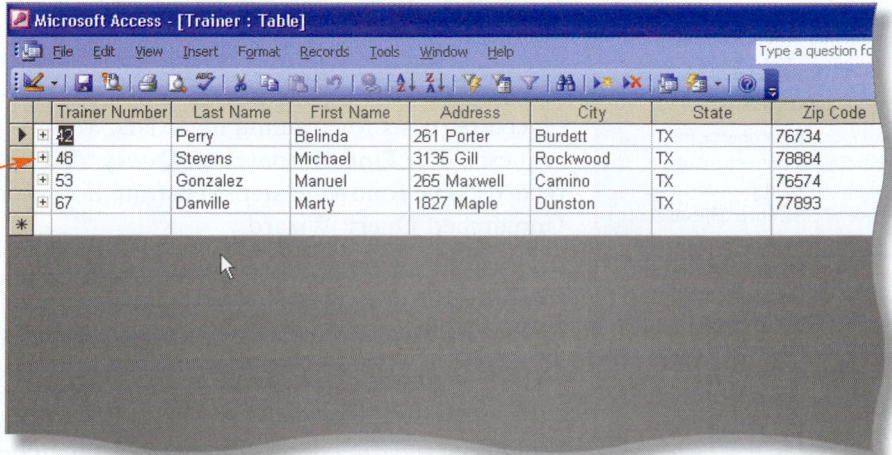

FIGURE 3-74

2

• **Click the plus sign in front of the row for trainer 48.**

The subdatasheet appears (Figure 3-75). It contains only those clients that are assigned to trainer 48.

3

• **Click the minus sign to remove the subdatasheet, and then close the datasheet for the Trainer table by clicking its Close Window button.**

The datasheet no longer appears.

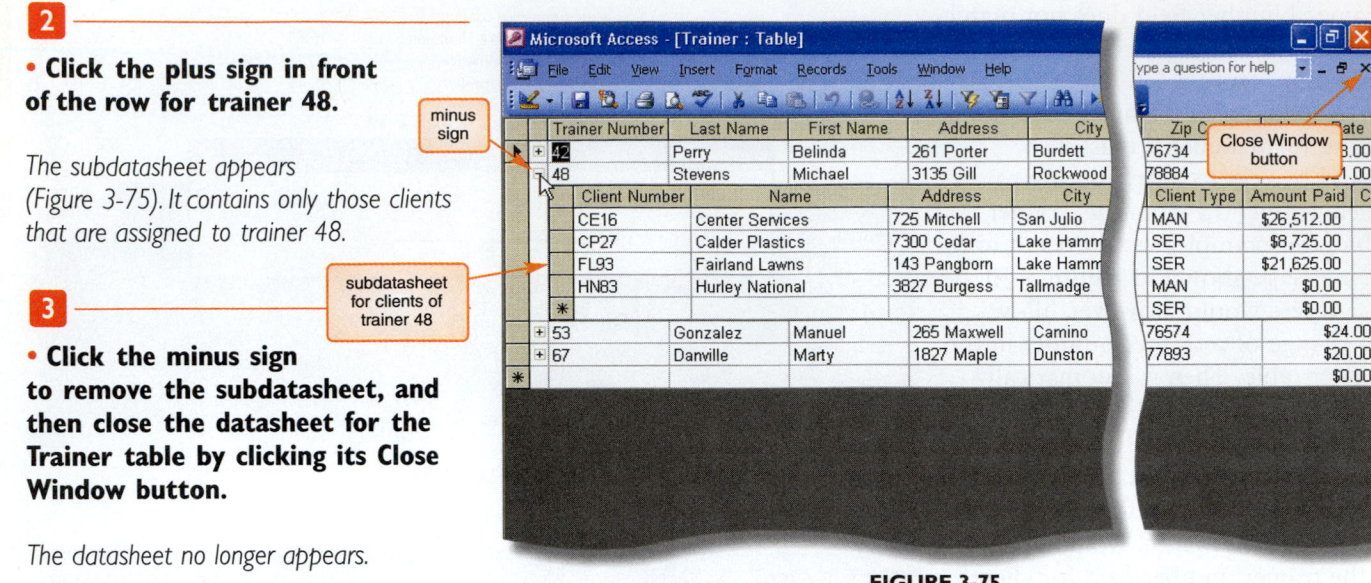

minus sign

subdatasheet for clients of trainer 48

Close Window button

FIGURE 3-75

Finding Duplicate Records

One reason to include a primary key for a table is to eliminate duplicate records. A possibility still exists, however, that duplicate records can get into your database. Perhaps, a client's name was misspelled and the data entry person assumed it was a new client. The **Find Duplicates Query Wizard** allows you to find duplicate records. The following steps illustrate how to use the Find Duplicates Query Wizard to find duplicate records.

To Find Duplicate Records

1. Select the table that you want to query.
2. Click the New Object button arrow, and then click Query.
3. When Access displays the New Query dialog box, click the Find Duplicates Query Wizard and then click the OK button.
4. Follow the directions in the Find Duplicates Query Wizard dialog boxes.

Finding Unmatched Records

Occasionally, you may want to find records in one table that have no matching records in another table. For example, suppose the clients of Ashton James College placed requests for training materials. You may want to know which clients have no requests. The **Find Unmatched Query Wizard** allows you to find unmatched records. The following steps illustrate how to find unmatched records using the Find Unmatched Query Wizard.

To Find Unmatched Records

1. Click the New Object button arrow, and then click Query.
2. When Access displays the New Query dialog box, click Find Unmatched Query Wizard and then click the OK button.
3. Follow the directions in the Find Unmatched Query Wizard dialog boxes.

Ordering Records

Normally, Access sequences the records in the Client table by client number whenever listing them because the Client Number field is the primary key. You can change this order, if desired.

Using the Sort Ascending Button to Order Records

To change the order in which records appear, use the Sort Ascending or Sort Descending buttons. Either button reorders the records based on the field in which the insertion point is located.

The following steps order the records by city using the Sort Ascending button.

To Use the Sort Ascending Button to Order Records

1

• **With the Database window on the screen, the Tables object selected, and the Client table selected, click the Open button on the Database Window toolbar.**

• **Click the City field on the first record (any other record would do as well).**

An insertion point appears in the City field (Figure 3-76).

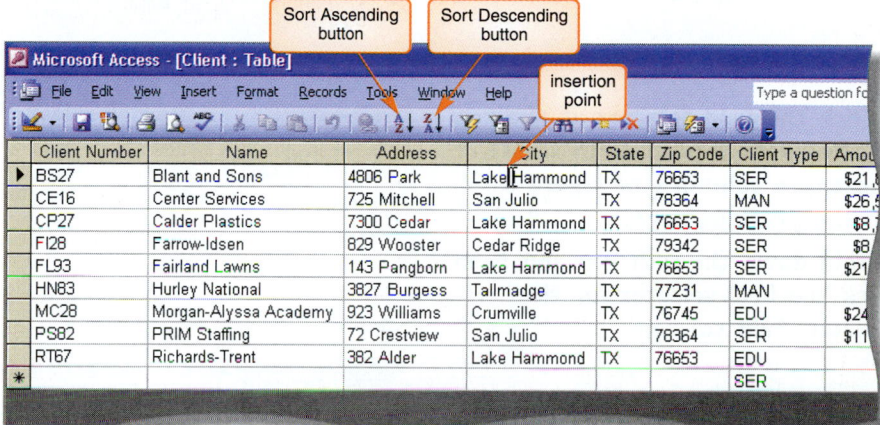

FIGURE 3-76

2

• **Click the Sort Ascending button on the Table Datasheet toolbar.**

• **If instructed to do so, print the table by clicking the Print button on the Table Datasheet toolbar.**

The rows now are ordered by city (Figure 3-77).

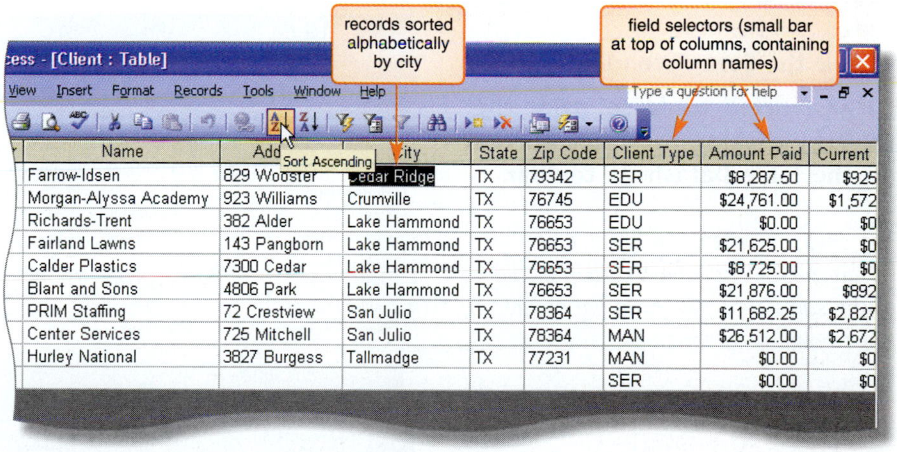

FIGURE 3-77

If you wanted to sort the data in reverse order, you would use the Sort Descending button instead of the Sort Ascending button.

Other Ways

1. On Records menu point to Sort, click Sort Ascending on Sort submenu
2. In Voice Command mode, say "Sort Ascending"

Ordering Records on Multiple Fields

Just as you are able to sort the answer to a query on multiple fields, you also can sort the data that appears in a datasheet on multiple fields. To do so, the major and minor keys must be next to each other in the datasheet with the major key on the left. (If this is not the case, you can drag the columns into the correct position. Instead of dragging, however, usually it will be easier to use a query that has the data sorted in the desired order.)

The following steps order records that have the major and minor keys in the correct position on the combination of the Client Type and Amount Paid fields. To select the fields, use the field selector, which is the small bar at the top of the column that you click to select an entire field in a datasheet.

To Use the Sort Ascending Button to Order Records on Multiple Fields

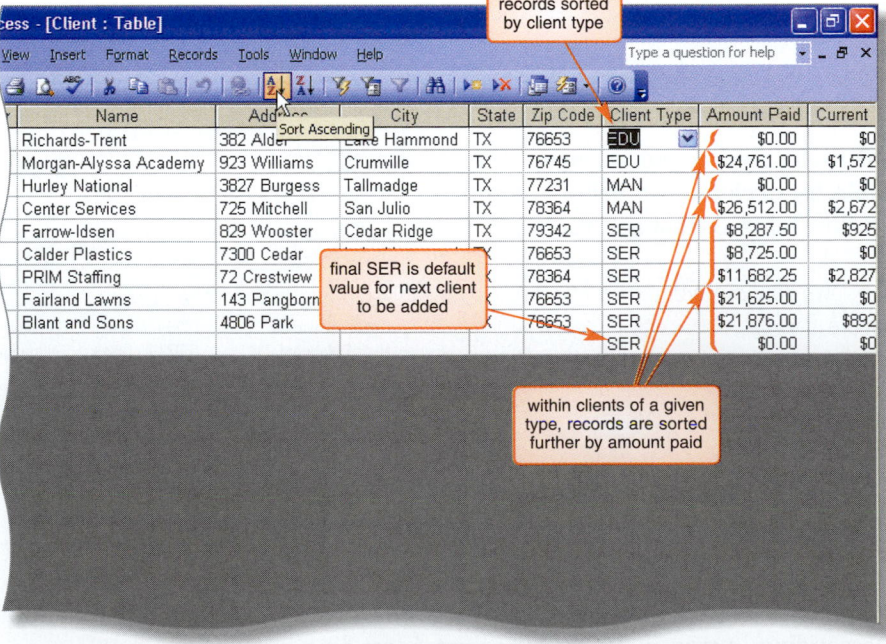

FIGURE 3-78

FIGURE 3-79

 1

• **Click the field selector at the top of the Client Type column to select the entire column (see Figure 3-77 on the previous page).**

• **Hold down the SHIFT key and then click the field selector for the Amount Paid column.**

The Client Type and Amount Paid columns both are selected (Figure 3-78).

 2

• **Click the Sort Ascending button.**

• **If instructed to do so, print the table by clicking the Print button on the Table Datasheet toolbar.**

The rows are ordered by client type (Figure 3-79). Within each group of clients of the same type, the rows are ordered by the amount paid amount.

3

• **Close the Client : Table window by clicking its Close Window button.**

• **Click the No button in the Microsoft Office Access dialog box to abandon the changes.**

The next time the table is open, the records will appear in their original order.

Creating and Using Indexes

You already are familiar with the concept of an index. The index in the back of a book contains important words or phrases together with a list of pages on which the given words or phrases can be found. An **index** for a table is similar. Figure 3-80, for example, shows the Client table along with an index built on client names. In this case, the items of interest are names instead of keywords or phrases as is the case in the back of this book. The field or fields on which the index is built is called the **index key**. Thus, in Figure 3-80, the Name field is the index key. (The structure of an index actually is a little more complicated than the one shown in the figure and is beyond the scope of this book. The concept is the same, however, and the structure shown in the figure illustrates the important concepts.)

Index on Name			Client Table						
NAME	RECORD NUMBER		RECORD NUMBER	CLIENT NUMBER	NAME	ADDRESS	CITY	STATE	ZIP CODE ...
Blant and Sons	1		1	BS27	Blant and Sons	4806 Park	Lake Hammond	TX	76653 ...
Calder Plastics	3		2	CE16	Center Services	725 Mitchell	San Julio	TX	78364 ...
Center Services	2		3	CP27	Calder Plastics	7300 Cedar	Lake Hammond	TX	76653 ...
Fairland Lawns	5		4	FI28	Farrow-Idsen	829 Wooster	Cedar Ridge	TX	79342 ...
Farrow-Idsen	4		5	FL93	Fairland Lawns	143 Pangborn	Lake Hammond	TX	76653 ...
Hurley National	6		6	HN83	Hurley National	3827 Burgess	Tallmadge	TX	77231 ...
Morgan-Alyssa Academy	7		7	MC28	Morgan-Alyssa Academy	923 Williams	Crumville	TX	76745 ...
PRIM Staffing	8		8	PS82	PRIM Staffing	72 Crestview	San Julio	TX	78364 ...
Richards-Trent	9		9	RT67	Richards-Trent	382 Alder	Lake Hammond	TX	76653 ...

FIGURE 3-80

Each name occurs in the index along with the number of the record on which the corresponding client is located. Further, the names appear in the index in alphabetical order. If Access were to use this index to find the record on which the name is Farrow-Idsen, for example, it could scan the names in the index rapidly to find Farrow-Idsen. Once it did, it would determine the corresponding record number (4) and then go immediately to record 4 in the Client table, thus finding this client more quickly than if it had to look through the entire Client table one record at a time. Indexes make the process of retrieving records very fast and efficient. (With relatively small tables, the increased efficiency associated with indexes will not be as apparent as in larger tables. In practice, it is common to encounter tables with thousands, tens of thousands, or even hundreds of thousands of records. In such cases, the increase in efficiency is dramatic. In fact, without indexes, many operations in such databases simply would not be practical. They would take too long to complete.)

Because no two clients happen to have the same name, the Record Number column contains only single values. This may not always be the case. Consider the index on the Zip Code field shown in Figure 3-81 on the next page. In this index, the Record Number column contains several values, namely all the records on which the corresponding Zip code appears. The first row, for example, indicates that Zip code 76653 is found on records 1, 3, 5, and 9; the fourth row indicates that Zip code 78364 is found on records 2 and 8. If Access were to use this index to find all clients in Zip code 78364, it could scan the Zip codes in the index rapidly to find

More About

Indexes

The most common structure for high-performance indexes is called a B-tree. It is a highly efficient structure that supports very rapid access to records in the database as well as a rapid alternative to sorting records. Virtually all systems use some version of the B-tree structure. For more information about B-tree indexes, visit the Access 2003 More About Web page (scsite.com/ac2003/more) and click B-tree.

78364. Once it did, it would determine the corresponding record numbers (2 and 8) and then go immediately to these records. It would not have to examine any other records in the Client table.

Index on Zip Code

ZIP CODE	RECORD NUMBER
76653	1, 3, 5, 9
76745	7
77231	6
78364	2, 8
79342	4

Client Table

RECORD NUMBER	CLIENT NUMBER	NAME	ADDRESS	CITY	STATE	ZIP CODE	...
1	BS27	Blant and Sons	4806 Park	Lake Hammond	TX	76653	...
2	CE16	Center Services	725 Mitchell	San Julio	TX	78364	...
3	CP27	Calder Plastics	7300 Cedar	Lake Hammond	TX	76653	...
4	FI28	Farrow-Idsen	829 Wooster	Cedar Ridge	TX	79342	...
5	FL93	Fairland Lawns	143 Pangborn	Lake Hammond	TX	76653	...
6	HN83	Hurley National	3827 Burgess	Tallmadge	TX	77231	...
7	MC28	Morgan-Alyssa Academy	923 Williams	Crumville	TX	76745	...
8	PS82	PRIM Staffing	72 Crestview	San Julio	TX	78364	...
9	RT67	Richards-Trent	382 Alder	Lake Hammond	TX	76653	...

FIGURE 3-81

Another benefit of indexes is that they provide an efficient way to order records. That is, if the records are to appear in a certain order, Access can use an index instead of physically having to rearrange the records in the database. Physically rearranging the records in a different order can be a very time-consuming process.

To use the index to order records, use record numbers in the index; that is, simply follow down the Record Number column, listing the corresponding clients. In this index, you would first list the client on record 1 (Blant and Sons), then the client on record 3 (Calder Plastics), then the client on record 2 (Center Services), and so on. The clients would be listed alphabetically by name without actually sorting the table.

To gain the benefits from an index, you first must create one. Access automatically creates an index on the primary key as well as some other special fields. If, as is the case with both the Client and Trainer tables, a table contains a field called Zip Code, for example, Access will create an index for it automatically. You must create any other indexes you feel you need, indicating the field or fields on which the index is to be built.

Although the index key usually will be a single field, it can be a combination of fields. For example, you might want to sort records by amount paid within client type. In other words, the records are ordered by a combination of fields: Client Type and Amount Paid. An index can be used for this purpose by using a combination of fields for the index key. In this case, you must assign a name to the index. It is a good idea to assign a name that represents the combination of fields. For example, an index whose key is the combination of the Client Type and Amount Paid fields might be called TypePaid.

How Does Access Use an Index?

Access creates an index whenever you request that it do so. It takes care of all the work in setting up and maintaining the index. In addition, Access will use the index automatically.

If you request that data be sorted in a particular order and Access determines that an index is available that it can use to make the process efficient, it will do so. If no index is available, it still will sort the data in the order you requested; it will just take longer.

Similarly, if you request that Access locate a particular record that has a certain value in a particular field, Access will use an index if an appropriate one exists. If not, it will have to examine each record until it finds the one you want.

In both cases, the added efficiency provided by an index will not be apparent readily in tables that have only a few records. As you add more records to your tables, however, the difference can be dramatic. Even with only 50 to 100 records, you will notice a difference. You can imagine how dramatic the difference would be in a table with 50,000 records.

When Should You Create an Index?

An index improves efficiency for sorting and finding records. On the other hand, indexes occupy space on your disk. They also require Access to do extra work. Access must keep all the indexes that have been created up-to-date. Thus, both advantages and disadvantages exist to using indexes. Consequently, the decision as to which indexes to create is an important one. The following guidelines should help you in this process.

Create an index on a field (or combination of fields) if one or more of the following conditions are present:

1. The field is the primary key of the table (Access will create this index automatically).
2. The field is the foreign key in a relationship you have created.
3. You frequently will need your data to be sorted on the field.
4. You frequently will need to locate a record based on a value in this field.

Because Access handles 1 automatically, you need only to concern yourself about 2, 3, and 4. If you think you will need to see client data arranged in order of amount paid amounts, for example, you should create an index on the Amount Paid field. If you think you will need to see the data arranged by amount paid within trainer number, you should create an index on the combination of the Trainer Number field and the Amount Paid field. Similarly, if you think you will need to find a client given the client's name, you should create an index on the Name field.

Creating Single-Field Indexes

A **single-field index** is an index whose key is a single field. In this case, the index key is to be the Name field. In creating an index, you need to indicate whether to allow duplicates in the index key; that is, two records that have the same value. For example, in the index for the Name field, if duplicates are not allowed, Access would not allow the addition of a client whose name is the same as the name of a client already in the database. In the index for the Name field, duplicates will be allowed. The steps on the next page create a single-field index.

More About

Changing Table Properties

You can change the properties of a table by opening the table in Design view and then clicking the Properties button on the Table Design toolbar. Access will display the property sheet for the table. To display the records in a table in an order other than primary key order (the default sort order), use the Order By property. For example, to display the Client table automatically in Name order, click the Order By property box, type `Client.Name` in the property box, close the property sheet, and save the change to the table design. When you open the Client table in Datasheet view, the records will be sorted in Name order.

To Create a Single-Field Index

1

• **With the Database window on the screen, the Tables object selected, and the Client table selected, click the Design button on the Database Window toolbar.**

• **Be sure the Client : Table window is maximized.**

• **Click the row selector to select the Name field.**

• **Click the Indexed property box in the Field Properties pane.**

• **Click the down arrow that appears.**

The Indexed list appears (Figure 3-82). The items in the list are No (no index), Yes (Duplicates OK) (create an index and allow duplicates), and Yes (No Duplicates) (create an index but reject (do not allow) duplicates).

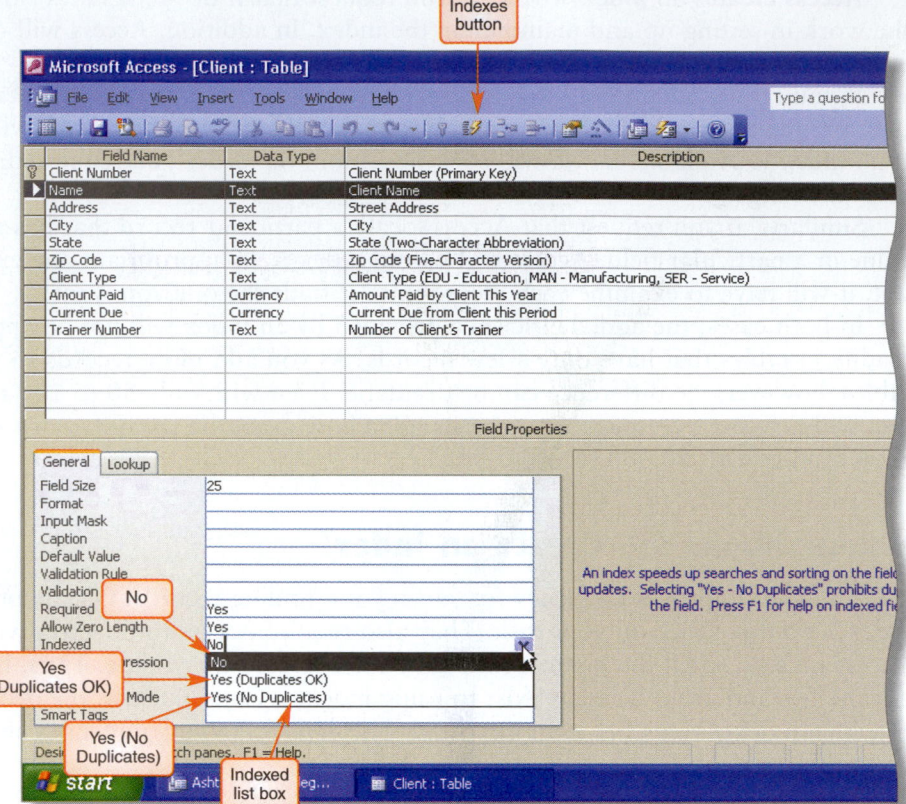

FIGURE 3-82

2

• **Click the Yes (Duplicates OK) item in the list.**

The index on the Name field now will be created and is ready for use as soon as you save your work.

Creating Multiple-Field Indexes

Creating **multiple-field indexes**, that is, indexes whose key is a combination of fields, involves a different process from creating single-field indexes. To create multiple-field indexes, you will use the Indexes button, enter a name for the index, and then enter the combination of fields that make up the index key. The following steps create a multiple-field index with the name TypePaid. The key will be the combination of the Client Type field and the Amount Paid field.

To Create a Multiple-Field Index

1

• Click the Indexes button on the Table Design toolbar (see Figure 3-82).

• Click the blank row (the row following Name) in the Index Name column in the Indexes: Client dialog box.

• Type `TypePaid` as the index name, and then press the TAB key.

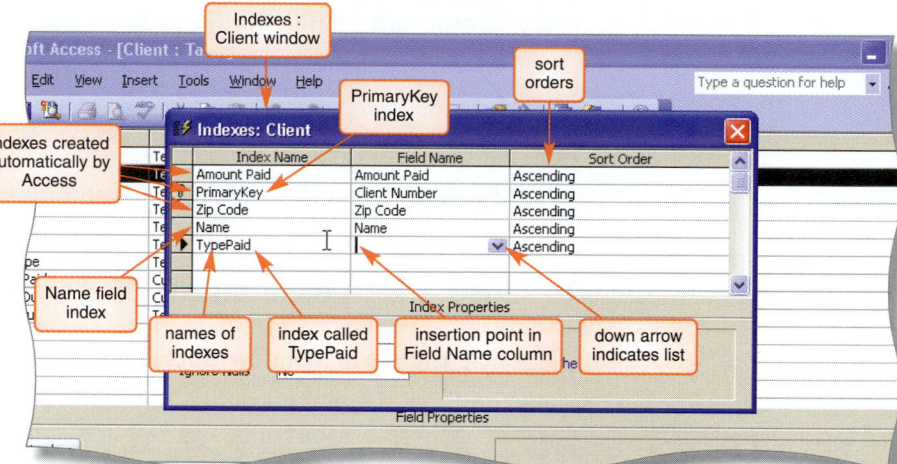

FIGURE 3-83

Access displays the Indexes: Client dialog box. It shows the indexes that already have been created and allows you to create additional indexes (Figure 3-83). The index name has been entered as TypePaid. An insertion point appears in the Field Name column. The index on the Client Number field is the primary index and was created automatically by Access. The index on the Name field is the one just created. Access created other indexes (for example, the Zip Code and Amount Paid fields) automatically. In this dialog box, you can create additional indexes.

2

• Click the down arrow in the Field Name column to produce a list of fields in the Client table. Select Client Type.

• Press the TAB key three times to move to the Field Name column on the following row.

• Select the Amount Paid field in the same manner as the Client Type field.

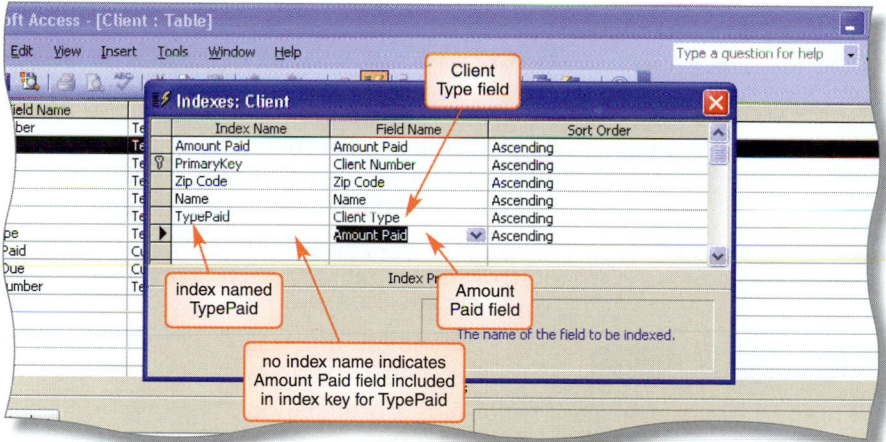

FIGURE 3-84

Client Type and Amount Paid are selected as the two fields for the TypePaid index (Figure 3-84). The absence of an index name on the row containing the Amount Paid field indicates that it is part of the previous index, TypePaid.

3

• Close the Indexes: Client dialog box by clicking its Close button, and then close the Client : Table window by clicking its Close Window button.

• Click the Yes button in the Microsoft Office Access dialog box to save your changes.

The indexes are created and Access displays the Database window.

Other Ways

1. On View menu click Indexes
2. In Voice Command mode, say "Indexes"

The indexes are created. Access will use them automatically whenever possible to improve efficiency of ordering or finding records. Access also will maintain them automatically. That is, whenever the data in the Client table is changed, Access will make appropriate changes in the indexes automatically.

Closing the Database and Quitting Access

The following steps close the database and quit Access.

To Close a Database and Quit Access

1 Click the Close Window button for the Ashton James College : Database window.

2 Click the Close button for the Microsoft Access window.

The database and Access close.

Special Database Operations

More About

The Quick Reference

For a table that lists how to complete tasks covered in this book using the mouse, menu, shortcut menu, and keyboard, see the Quick Reference Summary at the back of this book, or visit the Access 2003 Quick Reference Web page (scsite.com/ac2003/qr).

The special operations involved in maintaining a database are backup, recovery, compacting a database, and repairing a database.

Backup and Recovery

It is possible to damage or destroy a database. Users can enter data that is incorrect; programs that are updating the database can end abnormally during an update; a hardware problem can occur; and so on. After any such event has occurred, the database may contain invalid data. It even may be totally destroyed.

Obviously, you cannot allow a situation in which data has been damaged or destroyed to go uncorrected. You must somehow return the database to a correct state. This process is called **recovery**; that is, you say that you **recover** the database.

The simplest approach to recovery involves periodically making a copy of the database (called a **backup copy** or a **save copy**). This is referred to as **backing up** the database. If a problem occurs, you correct the problem by copying this backup copy over the actual database, often referred to as the **live database**.

More About

Microsoft Certification

The Microsoft Office Specialist Certification program provides an opportunity for you to obtain a valuable industry credential — proof that you have the Access 2003 skills required by employers. For more information, see Appendix E, or visit the Access 2003 Certification Web page (scsite.com/ac2003/cert).

To backup the database that is currently open, you use the Back Up Database command on the File menu. In the process, Access suggests a name that is a combination of the database name and the current date. For example, if you back up the Ashton James College database on April 20, 2005, Access will suggest the name Ashton James College_2005-04-20. You can change this name if you desire, although it is a good idea to use this name. By doing so, it will be easy to distinguish between all the backup copies you have made to determine which is the most recent. In addition, if you discover that a critical problem occurred on April 18, 2005, you may want to go back to the most recent backup before April 18. If, for example, the database was not backed up on April 17 but was backed up on April 16, you would use Ashton James College_2005-04-16.

The following steps back up a database to a file on a hard disk or high-capacity removable disk. You should check with your instructor before completing these steps.

To Backup a Database

1. Open the database to be backed up.
2. Click File on the menu bar, and then click Back Up Database.
3. Selected the desired location in the Save in box. If you do not want the name Access has suggested, enter the desired name in the File name text box.
4. Click the Save button.

Access creates a backup copy with the desired name in the desired location. Should you ever need to recover the database using this backup copy, you can simply copy it over the live version.

Compacting and Repairing a Database

As you add more data to a database, it naturally grows larger. Pictures will increase the size significantly. When you delete objects (for example, records, tables, forms, or pictures), the space previously occupied by the object does not become available for additional objects. Instead, the additional objects are given new space, that is, space that was not already allocated. If you decide to change a picture, for example, the new picture will not occupy the same space as the previous picture, but instead it will be given space of its own.

To remove this wasted space from the database, you must **compact** the database. Compacting the database makes an additional copy of the database, one that contains the same data, but does not contain the wasted space that the original does. The original database will still exist in its unaltered form.

A typical three-step process for compacting a database is as follows:

1. Compact the original database (for example, Ashton James College) and give the compacted database a different name (for example, Ashton James College Compacted).
2. Assuming that the compacting operation completed successfully, delete the original database (Ashton James College).
3. Also assuming that the compacting operation completed successfully, rename the compacted database (Ashton James College Compacted) with the name of the original database (Ashton James College).

Of course, if a problem occurs in the compacting operation, you should continue to use the original database; that is, do not complete Steps 2 and 3.

The operation can be carried out on a floppy disk, provided sufficient space is available. If the database to be compacted occupies more than half the floppy disk, however, Access may not have enough room to create the compacted database. In such a case, you should first copy the database to a hard disk or network drive. (You can use whatever Windows technique you prefer for copying files to do so.) You then can complete the process on the hard disk or network drive.

In addition to compacting the database, the same operation is used to **repair** the database in case of problems. If Microsoft Access reports a problem with the database or if some aspect of the database seems to be behaving in an unpredictable fashion, you should run the Compact and Repair operation to attempt to correct the problem. If Access is unable to repair the database, you will need to revert to your most recent backup copy.

More About

Compacting and Repairing a Database

You can require Access to compact a database automatically whenever the database is closed. To do so, click Tools on the menu bar and then click Options. When Access displays the Options dialog box, click the General tab. Click the Compact on Close check box.

More About

Backup and Recovery

Before making changes to the database, such as the changes made in this project, it is a good idea to make a copy of the database. Then, if a problem occurs that damages either the data in the database or the structure of the database, you can recover the database by copying the backup copy over it.

Q&**A**

Q: Is it possible to compact an open database?

A: Yes, to do so, click Tools on the menu bar, point to Database Utilities, and then click Compact and Repair Database on the Database Utilities submenu.

The following steps compact a database and repair any problems after you have copied the database to a hard disk. If you have not copied the database to a hard disk, check with your instructor before completing these steps.

To Compact and Repair a Database

1. Be sure the database is closed. Click Tools on the menu bar, point to Database Utilities, and then click Compact and Repair Database on the Database Utilities submenu.
2. In the Database to Compact From dialog box, select the database to be compacted and then click the Compact button.
3. In the Compact Database Into dialog box, enter a new name for the compacted database and then click the Save button in the Database to Compact From dialog box.
4. Assuming the operation is completed successfully, delete the original database and rename the compacted database as the original name.

The database now is the compacted form of the original.

Project Summary

In Project 3, you learned how to maintain a database. You saw how to use Form view to add records to a table. You learned how to locate and filter records. You saw how to change the contents of records in a table and how to delete records from a table. You restructured a table, both by changing field characteristics and by adding a new field. You saw how to make a variety of changes to the appearance of a datasheet. You learned how to make changes to groups of records and delete a group of records. You created a variety of validation rules that specified a required field, a range, a default value, legal values, and a format. You examined the issues involved in updating a table with validation rules. You also saw how to specify referential integrity. You learned how to view related data by using subdatasheets. You learned how to order records. You saw how to improve performance by creating single-field and multiple-field indexes.

If you have a SAM user profile, you may have access to hands-on instruction, practice, and assessment of the skills covered in this project. Log in to your SAM account and go to your assignments page to see what your instructor has assigned.

What You Should Know

Having completed this project, you should be able to perform the tasks below. The tasks are listed in the same order they were presented in this project. For a list of the buttons, menus, toolbars, and commands introduced in this project, see the Quick Reference Summary at the back of this book and refer to the Page Number column.

1. Open a Database   (AC 115)
2. Use a Form to Add Records   (AC 116)
3. Search for a Record   (AC 118)
4. Update the Contents of a Field   (AC 119)
5. Switch from Form View to Datasheet View   (AC 120)
6. Use Filter By Selection   (AC 121)
7. Remove a Filter   (AC 122)
8. Use Filter By Form   (AC 123)
9. Use Advanced Filter/Sort   (AC 124)
10. Delete a Record   (AC 125)
11. Delete a Record in Form View   (AC 126)
12. Change the Size of a Field   (AC 127)
13. Add a Field to a Table   (AC 129)
14. Delete a Field   (AC 130)
15. Update the Contents of a Field   (AC 130)
16. Resize a Column   (AC 131)
17. Change the Font in a Datasheet   (AC 133)
18. Change the Format of the Datasheet Grid   (AC 134)
19. Use Print Preview   (AC 135)
20. Close the Datasheet Without Saving the Format Changes   (AC 135)
21. Use an Update Query to Update All Records   (AC 136)
22. Use a Delete Query to Delete a Group of Records   (AC 138)
23. Create an Append Query   (AC 139)
24. Specify a Required Field   (AC 140)
25. Specify a Range   (AC 141)
26. Specify a Default Value   (AC 142)
27. Specify a Collection of Legal Values   (AC 143)
28. Specify a Format   (AC 144)
29. Save the Validation Rules, Default Values, and Formats   (AC 144)
30. Create a Lookup Field   (AC 147)
31. Use a Lookup Field   (AC 149)
32. Specify Referential Integrity   (AC 151)
33. Use a Subdatasheet   (AC 153)
34. Find Duplicate Records   (AC 154)
35. Find Unmatched Records   (AC 154)
36. Use the Sort Ascending Button to Order Records   (AC 155)
37. Use the Sort Ascending Button to Order Records on Multiple Fields   (AC 156)
38. Create a Single-Field Index   (AC 160)
39. Create a Multiple-Field Index   (AC 161)
40. Close a Database and Quit Access   (AC 162)
41. Backup a Database   (AC 163)
42. Compact and Repair a Database   (AC 164)

Learn It Online

Instructions: To complete the Learn It Online exercises, start your browser, click the Address bar, and then enter the Web address scsite.com/ac2003/learn. When the Access 2003 Learn It Online page is displayed, follow the instructions in the exercises below. Each exercise has instructions for printing your results, either for your own records or for submission to your instructor.

1 Project Reinforcement TF, MC, and SA

Below Access Project 3, click the Project Reinforcement link. Print the quiz by clicking Print on the File menu for each page. Answer each question.

2 Flash Cards

Below Access Project 3, click the Flash Cards link and read the instructions. Type 20 (or a number specified by your instructor) in the Number of playing cards text box, type your name in the Enter your Name text box, and then click the Flip Card button. When the flash card is displayed, read the question and then click the ANSWER box arrow to select an answer. Flip through Flash Cards. If your score is 15 (75%) correct or greater, click Print on the File menu to print your results. If your score is less than 15 (75%) correct, then redo this exercise by clicking the Replay button.

3 Practice Test

Below Access Project 3, click the Practice Test link. Answer each question, enter your first and last name at the bottom of the page, and then click the Grade Test button. When the graded practice test is displayed on your screen, click Print on the File menu to print a hard copy. Continue to take practice tests until you score 80% or better.

4 Who Wants To Be a Computer Genius?

Below Access Project 3, click the Computer Genius link. Read the instructions, enter your first and last name at the bottom of the page, and then click the PLAY button. When your score is displayed, click the PRINT RESULTS link to print a hard copy.

5 Wheel of Terms

Below Access Project 3, click the Wheel of Terms link. Read the instructions, and then enter your first and last name and your school name. Click the PLAY button. When your score is displayed, right-click the score and then click Print on the shortcut menu to print a hard copy.

6 Crossword Puzzle Challenge

Below Access Project 3, click the Crossword Puzzle Challenge link. Read the instructions, and then enter your first and last name. Click the SUBMIT button. Work the crossword puzzle. When you are finished, click the Submit button. When the crossword puzzle is redisplayed, click the Print Puzzle button to print a hard copy.

7 Tips and Tricks

Below Access Project 3, click the Tips and Tricks link. Click a topic that pertains to Project 3. Right-click the information and then click Print on the shortcut menu. Construct a brief example of what the information relates to in Access to confirm you understand how to use the tip or trick.

8 Newsgroups

Below Access Project 3, click the Newsgroups link. Click a topic that pertains to Project 3. Print three comments.

9 Expanding Your Horizons

Below Access Project 3, click the Expanding Your Horizons link. Click a topic that pertains to Project 3. Print the information. Construct a brief example of what the information relates to in Access to confirm you understand the contents of the article.

10 Search Sleuth

Below Access Project 3, click the Search Sleuth link. To search for a term that pertains to this project, select a term below the Project 3 title and then use the Google search engine at google.com (or any major search engine) to display and print two Web pages that present information on the term.

11 Access Online Training

Below Access Project 3, click the Access Online Training link. When your browser displays the Microsoft Office Online Web page, click the Access link. Click one of the Access courses that covers one or more of the objectives listed at the beginning of the project on page AC 114. Print the first page of the course before stepping through it.

12 Office Marketplace

Below Access Project 3, click the Office Marketplace link. When your browser displays the Microsoft Office Online Web page, click the Office Marketplace link. Click a topic that relates to Access. Print the first page.

Apply Your Knowledge

1 Maintaining the Begon Pest Control Database

Instructions: Start Access. Open the Begon Pest Control database that you modified in Apply Your Knowledge 1 in Project 2 on page AC 109. (If you did not complete this exercise, see your instructor for a copy of the modified database.) Perform the following tasks:

1. Open the Customer table in Design view as shown in Figure 3-85.

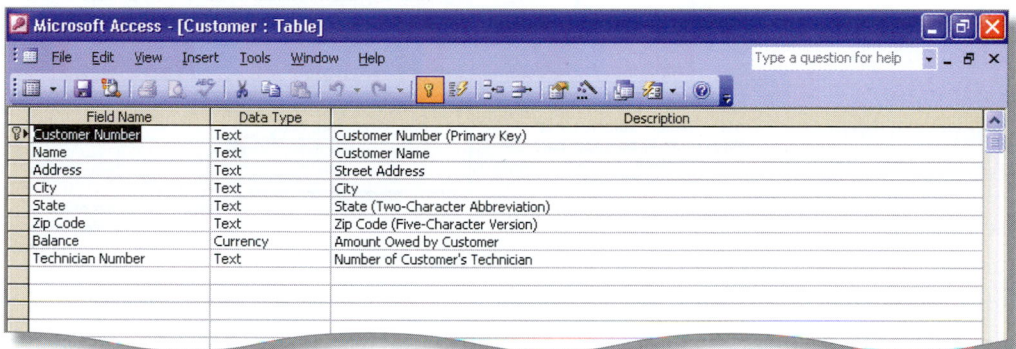

FIGURE 3-85

2. Increase the size of the Name field to 25.
3. Format the Customer Number and State fields so any lowercase letters appear in uppercase.
4. Make the Name field a required field.
5. Specify that balance amounts must be less than or equal to $2,000.00. Include validation text.
6. Create an index that allows duplicates for the Name field.
7. Save the changes to the structure.
8. Open the Customer table in Datasheet view.
9. Change the name of customer SE05 to Servete Manufacturing and the address of customer MC10 to 109 Fletcher.
10. Resize the Name column so the complete name for customer SE05 appears. Resize the remaining columns to the best fit.
11. Close the table and click the Yes button to save the changes to the layout of the table.
12. Print the table. If necessary, change the margins so the table prints on one page in landscape orientation.
13. Open the Customer table and use Filter By Selection to find the record for client CM90. Delete the record.
14. Remove the filter and then print the table.
15. Sort the data in descending order by balance.
16. Print the table in landscape orientation. Close the table. If you are asked to save changes to the design of the table, click the No button.
17. Establish referential integrity between the Technician table (the one table) and the Customer table (the many table). Cascade the update but do not cascade the delete. Print the Relationships window by making sure the Relationships window is open, clicking File on the menu bar, and then clicking Print Relationships. When Access displays the Print Preview window, click the Print button on the Print Preview toolbar. Do not save the report.
18. Backup the database.

In the Lab

1 Maintaining the Birds2U Database

Problem: The management of Birds2U recently acquired some items from a store that is going out of business. You now need to append these new items to the current item table. Because the business has expanded, you also need to change the database structure and add some validation rules to the database.

Instructions: Use both the Birds2U database created in the In the Lab 1 of Project 1 on page AC 56 and the More Birds database for this assignment. Perform the following tasks:

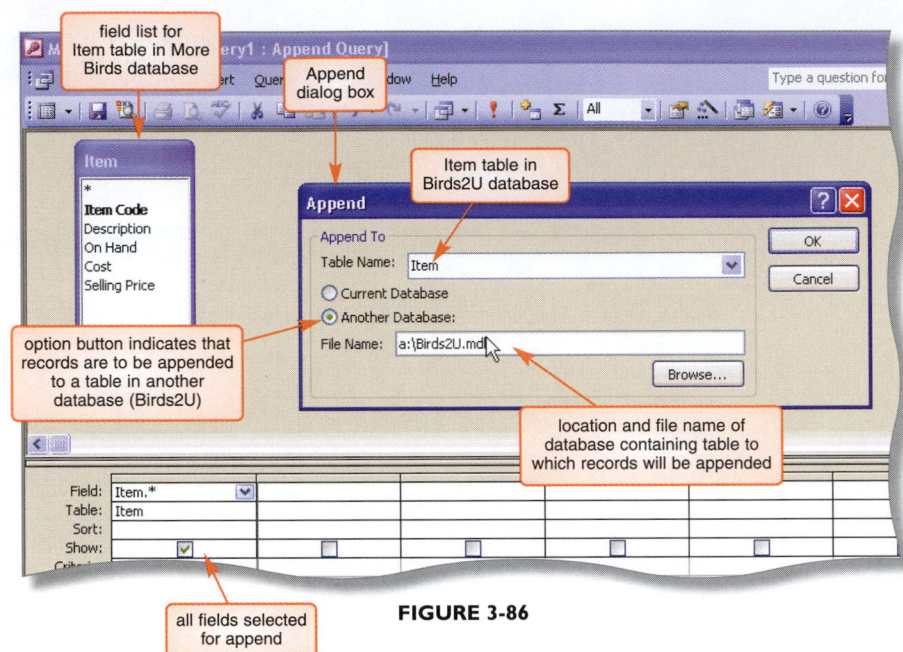

field list for Item table in More Birds database

Append dialog box

Item table in Birds2U database

option button indicates that records are to be appended to a table in another database (Birds2U)

location and file name of database containing table to which records will be appended

all fields selected for append

FIGURE 3-86

1. Open the More Birds database from the Data Disk.
2. Create a new query for the Item table and double-click the asterisk in the field list to add all fields to the query.
3. Change the query type to an Append Query. When Access displays the Append dialog box, make the entries shown in Figure 3-86 and then click the OK button. If your Birds2U database is not located on the floppy disk in drive A, you will need to enter the appropriate information in the File name text box.
4. Click the Run button on the Query Design toolbar to run the append query. Click the Yes button in the Microsoft Office Access dialog box that displays the message that you are about to append 4 rows.
5. Close the append query without saving it, and then close the More Birds database. Open the Birds2U database, and then open the Item table in Datasheet view. The table should contain 14 records.
6. The items added from the More Birds database do not have a supplier assigned to them. Assign items BS10, FS11, and LM05 to supplier 17. Assign item BO22 to supplier 21.
7. Resize the columns to best fit the data and print the Item table. Save the changes to the layout.
8. Using a query, delete all records in the Item table where the description starts with the letter S. (*Hint:* Use Help to solve this problem.) Close the query without saving it. Print the Item table.
9. Open the Supplier table in Design view and add a new field to the end of the table. Name the field, Fax Number. This new field has the same data type and length as Telephone Number. Enter the same comment as Telephone Number but replace Telephone with Fax. Save the change to the table design.
10. Add the following data to the Fax Number field.
11. Resize all columns in the Supplier table to the best fit.
12. Print the table on one page in landscape orientation. Save the change to the layout.
13. Specify referential integrity between the Supplier table (the one table) and the Item table (the many table). Cascade the update but not the delete. Print the Relationships window.
14. Compact the database.

05	602-555-6574
13	512-555-8967
17	707-555-9991
21	610-555-3344

In the Lab

2 Maintaining the Babbage Bookkeeping Database

Problem: Babbage Bookkeeping is expanding rapidly and needs to make some database changes to handle the expansion. The company needs to know more about its clients, such as the type of business and it needs to ensure that data that is entered in the database is valid. It also needs to add some new clients to the database.

Instructions: Use the Babbage Bookkeeping database created in the In the Lab 2 of Project 1 on page AC 59 or see your instructor for information about accessing the files required for this book. Perform the following tasks:

1. Open the Babbage Bookkeeping database and then open the Client table in Design view.
2. Add the field, Client Type, to the Client table. The field should appear after the Zip Code field. Define the field as text with a width of 3. This field will contain data on the type of client. The client types are MAN (Manufacturing), RET (Retail), and SER (Service). Save these changes to the structure.
3. Using a query, change all the entries in the Client Type column to RET. This will be the type of most clients. Do not save the query.
4. Open the Client table and resize all columns to best fit the data. Print the table in landscape orientation. Save the changes to the layout of the table.
5. Create the following validation rules for the Client table and save the changes to the table. List the steps involved on your own paper.
   a. Increase the size of the Name field to 25 and make the Name field a required field.
   b. Specify the legal values MAN, RET, and SER for the Client Type field. Include validation text.
   c. Assign a default value of RET to the Client Type field.
   d. Ensure that any letters entered in the Client Number field appear as uppercase.
   e. Specify that balance must be less than or equal to $1,500.00. Include validation text.
   f. Make the Client Type field a Lookup field.
6. Make the following changes to the Client table. You can use either the Find button or Filter By Selection to locate the records to change:
   a. Change the client type for clients G56, J77, and T45 to SER.
   b. Change the client type for clients B26 and S56 to MAN.
   c. Change the name of client S56 to SeeSaw Industries.
7. Add the following clients to the Client table:

| C21 | Crompton Meat Market | 72 Main | Empeer | 58216 | RET | $0.00 | 24 |
| L50 | Lou's Salon | 124 Fulton | Grant City | 58121 | SER | $125.00 | 34 |

8. Resize the Name column to best fit the new data, and save the changes to the layout of the table.
9. Open the Client table and use Filter By Form to find all records where the client has a balance of $0.00 and has the Client Type of SER. Delete these records.
10. Remove the filter, change the font to Courier New and the font size to 9. Change the gridline color to blue. Print the table in landscape orientation. Close the Client table and do not save any changes.
11. Specify referential integrity between the Bookkeeper table (the one table) and the Client table (the many table). Cascade the update but not the delete. Print the Relationships window. Do not save the report.
12. Compact the database and then backup the database.

In the Lab

3 Maintaining the City Guide Database

Problem: The chamber of commerce has determined that some changes must be made to the database structure. Another field must be added. Because several individuals update the data, the chamber also would like to add some validation rules to the database. Finally, some additions and deletions are required to the database.

Instructions: Use the database created in the In the Lab 3 of Project 1 on page AC 61 for this exercise or see your instructor for information about accessing the files required for this book.

Instructions Part 1: Several changes must be made to the database structure. For example, the chamber would like to categorize the businesses that advertise in the guide. It has determined that the businesses should be categorized as Retail, Dining, or Service establishments and suggest you use the advertiser types RET, DIN, and SER, respectively. Further, the chamber has identified advertisers A228, C135, G346, M321, and W456 as retail businesses. Advertisers C048, D217, P124, and S111 are service establishments and advertiser B103 is a restaurant. The chamber wants to ensure that only those types are entered and it wants to provide some type of lookup to help the individuals that do the data entry. It also wants to ensure that an entry always appears in the Name field and that any letters entered in the Advertiser Number field appear in uppercase. Because it often sorts the data by advertiser name, it wants to make the sorting process more efficient. Make the changes to the database structure and then print the Advertiser table. Place the Advertiser Type field after the Telephone Number field. To ensure that the table prints on one page, adjust the column widths to best fit the data and print the table in landscape orientation.

Instructions Part 2: The chamber has acquired three new advertisers. These advertisers are:

A245	AAA Diner	23 Berton	19363	555-0998	DIN	$50.00	$0.00	26
F410	Fran's Nails	145 Lincoln	19362	555-4218	SER	$75.00	$0.00	32
M111	Main Street Grille	20 Main	19364	555-4455	DIN	$0.00	$0.00	29

Also, the owner of Chloe's Salon has sold the business and the new owner now wants to advertise under the name, Clara for Hair. Another advertiser, Gold's Clothes, has gone out of business. Use the Advertiser form you created in Project 1 to make these changes. To show the chamber that you have made the appropriate changes, adjust column widths, and print the Advertiser table. Be sure the table prints on one page.

Instructions Part 3: Because the ad reps work on commission, the chamber wants to make sure that advertisers are not assigned to an ad rep that is not in the database. It also wants the ability to change an ad rep number in the Ad Rep table and have the change applied to the Advertiser table. Create the appropriate relationship that would satisfy the chamber's needs and print the relationship. Then, change the ad rep number for ad rep 26 to 21. Print the Advertiser table. Be sure the table prints on one page.

Cases and Places

The difficulty of these case studies varies:
■ are the least difficult and ■■ are more difficult. The last exercise is a group exercise.

1 ■ Use the College Dog Walkers database you created in Case Study 1 of Project 1 on page AC 63 for this assignment or see your instructor for information about accessing the files required for this book. Perform each of the following tasks and then print the results:

(a) Melissa Menteer recently married. Her new name is Melissa MacFarlandson.

(b) Frank Bishop adopted a stray dog and now has two dogs that are walked. Frank's per walk amount has been increased to $12.00. Frank's new balance is $30.00.

(c) The minimum per walk amount is now $8.00. The new minimum per walk amount should be the default for all new customers. No per walk amount should be less than $8.00 or more than $24.00.

(d) Specify referential integrity. Cascade the update but not the delete.

(e) Compact and then backup the database.

2 ■ Use the InPerson Fitness Company database you created in Case Study 2 of Project 1 on page AC 63 for this assignment or see your instructor for information about accessing the files required for this book. Perform each of these tasks and then print the results:

(a) Create an index on the Amount Paid and Balance fields in the Client table. Sort the records in the table in descending order by amount paid and balance.

(b) Add a Telephone Number field to the Trainer table. The field should appear after the First Name field. The field should have the same length and the same comment as the Telephone Number field in the Client table. The telephone number for trainer 203 is 555-0101. For trainer 205 and 207, the telephone numbers are 555-1243 and 555-2662, respectively.

(c) Resize the columns in both tables to best fit the data.

(d) Change the cell effect for the Trainer table to Sunken and change the gridline color to red.

(e) Specify referential integrity. Cascade the update but not the delete.

(f) Compact and then backup the database.

3 ■■ Use the Regional Books database you created in Case Study 3 of Project 1 on page AC 63 for this assignment or see your instructor for information about accessing the files required for this book:

(a) The bookstore has added a used book section. Add a field to the database to indicate whether a book is used or new. All books currently in the database are new books.

(b) All books must have a title and the units on hand should never be less than 0.

(c) The default sort order for the Books table should be by title rather than book code (**Hint**: See More About Changing Table Properties on page AC 159 to solve this problem.)

(d) The title for the book 5890 actually is Great Regional Recipes and Food.

(e) Add the used book, County Politics to the database and use 9867 as the book code. County Politics was written by Estelle Dearling and published by VanNestor. The book is a hardback and sells for $7.95. There is only one copy of the book.

(f) The owner sold the last copy of Quirky Architecture, and the book is now out of print.

(g) Determine whether any records are in one table that do not have related records in another table.

(h) Analyze the database and determine if you have a one-to-many relationship between any tables. If so, specify referential integrity between the tables. Cascade the update but not the delete.

Cases and Places

4 ◼◼ Use the Campus Housing database you created in Case Study 4 of Project 1 on page AC 64 for this assignment or see your instructor for information about accessing the files required for this book:

(a) Determine which units are located less than 2 miles from campus and have parking or which units allow pets. Sort the records by distance.

(b) All units must have at least one bathroom.

(c) The only valid lease terms are 3, 6, 9, and 12 months. Most units have a lease term of 9 months.

(d) Many users sort the data in ascending order by bedroom and bathroom. The users are complaining about the length of time it takes to sort the records.

(e) The unit that is located .25 miles from campus no longer is for rent.

(f) Alan Kindall has increased the rent on all his units by $25.00.

(g) Determine whether your database contains any duplicate records.

(h) Analyze the database and determine if you have a one-to-many relationship between any tables. If so, specify referential integrity. Cascade the update but not the delete.

5 ◼◼ **Working Together** With a make-table query, a user can create a new table from one or more tables in the database. The table can be stored in the same database or a new database. As a team, use the Access Help system to learn more about make-table queries. Then, choose one of the Cases and Places databases and create a make-table query. The query must use two tables to create one new table and must store the table in a new database that your team must create. For example, for the Birds2U database, the owner could create a table named Supplier Call List that would include the item code, description, and cost of each item as well as the supplier name and telephone number. Write a one-page paper that (1) explains the purpose for which the new table is intended and (2) suggests at least two additional uses for make-table queries.

Open the Contact Management database that you created in Project 1. As a team, review the data types for each of the fields that are in the database. Do any of these data types need to be changed? For example, is there a Text field that is storing notes about the company? Change the data types as necessary and write a one-page paper that explains your reasons for changing (or not changing) the data types in the Contact Management database.

Make a copy of the College Dog Walkers database and name it University Dog Walkers. Research the purpose of the Find Unmatched Query Wizard and the Find Duplicates Query Wizard. Create queries using each of these wizards. Did the queries perform as expected? Open each query in Design view and modify it, for example, add another field to the query. What happened to the query results? Write a one-page paper that explains the purpose of each query wizard and describes your experiences with creating and modifying the queries.

MICROSOFT
Office Access 2003

Sharing Data among Applications

CASE PERSPECTIVE

Harton-Janes Clinic specializes in physical therapy. Employees have been using Microsoft Excel to automate a variety of tasks for several years. When deciding to maintain patient data, the administrators decided to maintain the data as an Excel worksheet. Employees recently completed Microsoft Office training at Ashton James College (AJC) and now have decided they need to maintain the data in an Access database. They need an easy way to copy the data to Access.

AJC has determined that it needs to export (copy) some of the data in its database to other formats. Some users need the data in Excel, others want it placed in a Microsoft Word document, and still others want the ability to send a report via e-mail.

AJC would like to export the Client and Trainer tables in such a way that they can be imported easily to a database of a related organization, AJ Consulting, which handles various accounting functions for AJC. The users have learned that the easiest way to do this is to use XML (Extensible Markup Language).

As you read through this Integration Feature, you will learn how to use Access to convert data in the manner desired by Harton-Janes Clinic and Ashton James College.

Objectives

You will have mastered the material in this Integration Feature when you can:

- Import or link an Excel worksheet
- Export data to Excel and Word
- Create report snapshots
- Export and import XML data

Introduction

It is not uncommon for people to use an application for some specific purpose, only to find later that another application may be better suited. For example, an organization such as Harton-Janes Clinic initially might keep data in an Excel worksheet, only to discover later that the data would be better maintained in an Access database. The following are some common reasons for using a database instead of a worksheet:

1. The worksheet contains a great deal of redundant data. As discussed in Project 1 on pages AC 50 and AC 51, databases can be designed to eliminate redundant data.

2. The worksheet would need to be larger than Excel can handle. Excel has a limit of 16,384 rows. In Access, no such limit exists.

3. The data to be maintained consists of multiple interrelated items. For example, the Ashton James College database maintains data on two items, clients and trainers, and these items are interrelated. A client has a single trainer and each trainer is responsible for several clients. The Ashton James College database is a very simple one. Databases easily can contain thirty or more interrelated items.

4. You want to use the extremely powerful query and report capabilities of Microsoft Access.

Regardless of the reasons for making the change from a worksheet to a database, it is important to be able to make the change easily. In the not-too-distant past, converting data from one tool to another often could be a very difficult, time-consuming task. Fortunately, an easy way of converting data from Excel to Access is available.

Figures 1a and 1b illustrate the conversion process. The type of worksheet that can be converted is one in which the data is stored as a **list**, that is, a labeled series of rows in which each row contains the same type of data. For example, in the worksheet in Figure 1a, the first row contains the labels, which are entries indicating the type of data found in the column. The entry in the first column, for example, is Patient Number, indicating that all the other values in the column are patient numbers. The entry in the second column is Last Name, indicating that all the other values in the column are last names. Other than the first row, which contains the labels, all the rows contain precisely the same type of data shown in the Access database in Figure 1b: a patient number in the first column, a last name in the second column, a first name in the third column, and so on.

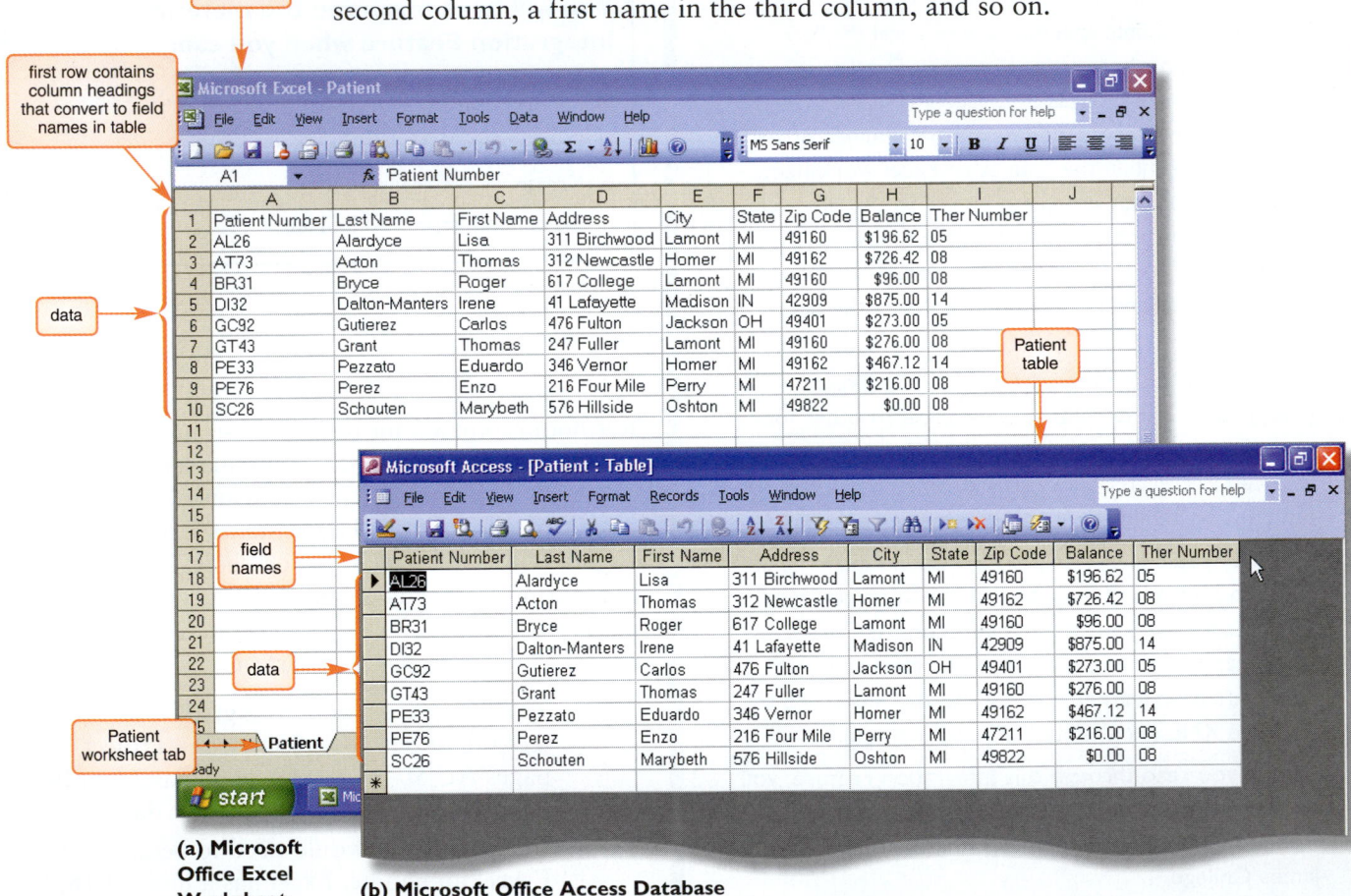

(a) Microsoft Office Excel Worksheet

(b) Microsoft Office Access Database

FIGURE 1

As the figures illustrate, the worksheet, shown in Figure 1a, is copied to a database table, shown in Figure 1b. The columns in the worksheet become the fields. The column headings in the first row of the worksheet become the field names. The rows of the worksheet, other than the first row, which contains the labels, become the records in the table. In the process, each field will be assigned the data type that seems the most reasonable, given the data currently in the worksheet.

Conversely, you can copy data from an Access database so that another application (for example, Excel) can use the data. Several different ways exist to export data. The two most common are to use the Export command on the File menu, which you will use to export a query to an Excel worksheet (Figure 2a), and to use drag-and-drop, which you will use to export a query to a Word document (Figure 2b).

At times you may want to send a report to a user via e-mail. It would be prohibitive to send the whole database to the other user, just so the user could print or view the report. In addition, doing so would require the other user to have Microsoft Access installed. A better way is to create a snapshot of the report. A **snapshot** is a special file that contains the report exactly as it appears when printed (Figure 2c). The other user then can use the Snapshot Viewer, which is a Microsoft Office tool, to view or print the report.

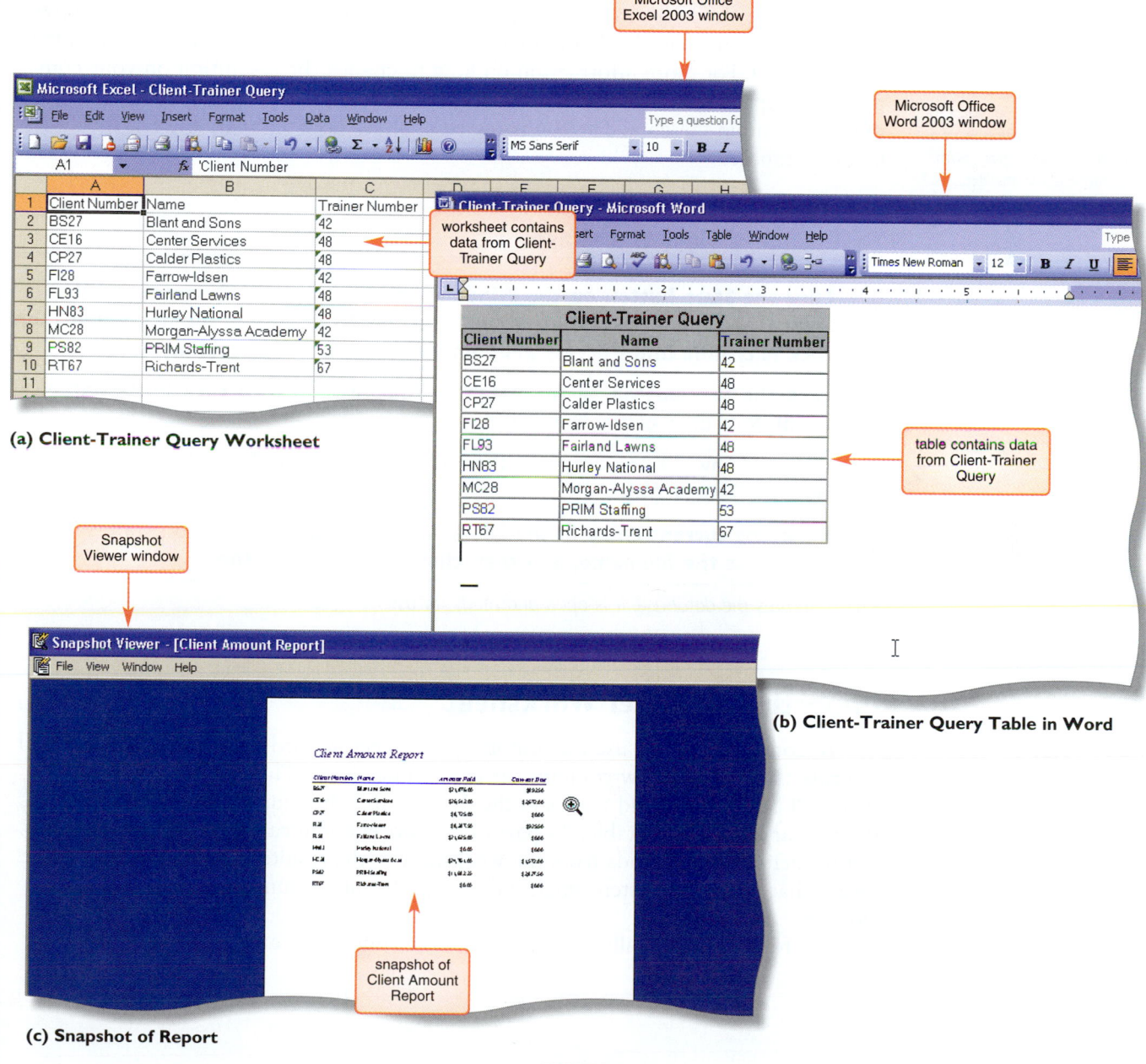

(a) Client-Trainer Query Worksheet

(b) Client-Trainer Query Table in Word

(c) Snapshot of Report

FIGURE 2

You also can export and import data using XML, which is a format for exchanging data between dissimilar applications. The XML format allows you to export and import both data and structure of multiple related tables in a single operation.

Convert Data from Other Applications to Access

More About

Importing Data: Databases

You can use the Import command to import objects, such as tables, queries, reports, and forms from other databases. When you select a database in the Import dialog box, Access displays the Import Objects dialog box. You then can select the type of object to import. Click the Options button in the Import Objects dialog box to display a list of options. For example, you can import only the structure of a table or you can import both the structure and the data.

The process of converting data to an Access database, referred to as **importing**, uses an Import wizard. Specifically, if the data is copied from an Excel worksheet, the process will use the **Import Spreadsheet Wizard**. The wizard takes you through some basic steps, asking a few simple questions. After you have answered the questions, the wizard will perform the conversion, creating an appropriate table in the database and filling it with the data from the worksheet.

Creating an Access Database

If you are stepping through this project on a computer and you want your screen to match the figures in this book, then you should change your computer's resolution to 800 × 600. For more information on how to change the resolution on your computer, see Appendix D. Before converting the data, you need to create the database that will contain the data. The following steps show how to create the Harton-Janes Clinic database.

To Create a New Database

1 Click the Start button on the Windows taskbar, click All Programs on the Start menu, point to Microsoft Office on the All Programs submenu, and then click Microsoft Office Access 2003 on the Microsoft Office submenu.

2 Click the New button on the Database toolbar, and then click Blank database in the New area of the New File task pane.

3 Click the Save in box arrow in the File New Database dialog box and then click 3½ Floppy (A:).

4 Erase the current entry in the File name text box, type Harton-Janes Clinic as the file name, and then click the Create button.

Access creates the database. It is open and ready for use.

Importing an Excel Worksheet

To convert the data, use the Import Spreadsheet Wizard. In the process, you will indicate that the first row contains the column headings. These column headings then will become the field names in the Access table. In addition, you will indicate the primary key for the table. As part of the process, you can, if you desire, choose not to include all the fields from the worksheet in the resulting table. You should be aware that some of the steps might take a significant amount of time for Access to execute.

The following steps illustrate the process of importing an Excel worksheet.

To Import an Excel Worksheet

1

• **With the Harton-Janes Clinic database open, right-click in the open area of the Database window.**

The shortcut menu appears (Figure 3).

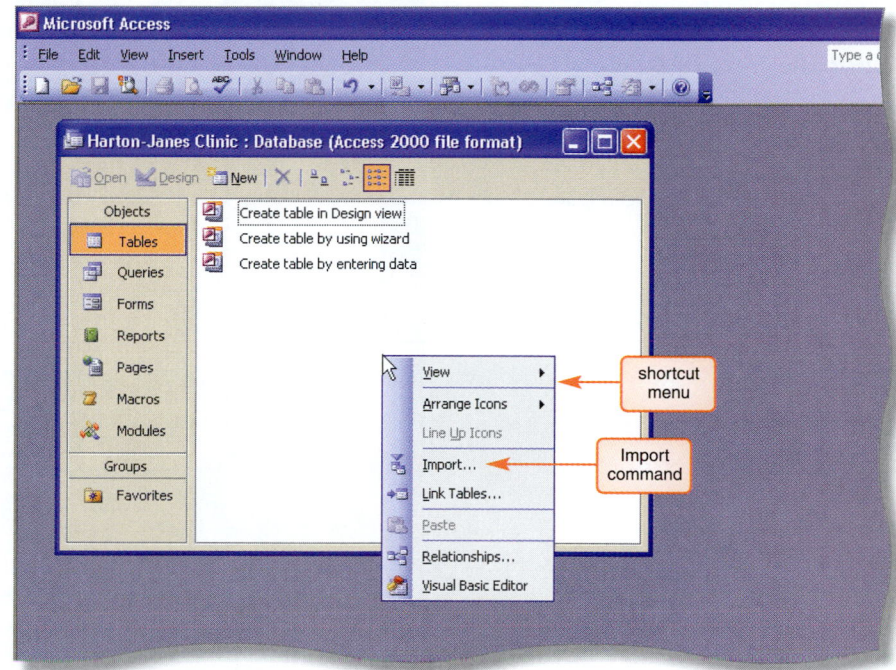

FIGURE 3

2

• **Click Import.**

• **When Access displays the Import dialog box, click the Files of type box arrow and then click Microsoft Excel.**

• **If necessary, select 3½ Floppy (A:) in the Look in list.**

• **Make sure the Patient workbook is selected, and then click the Import button.**

• **When Access displays the Import Spreadsheet Wizard dialog box, if necessary, click Show Worksheets and then click the Next button.**

• **Be sure the Patient worksheet is selected, and then click the Next button.**

Access displays the Import Spreadsheet Wizard dialog box requesting you to indicate whether the first row contains column headings (Figure 4).

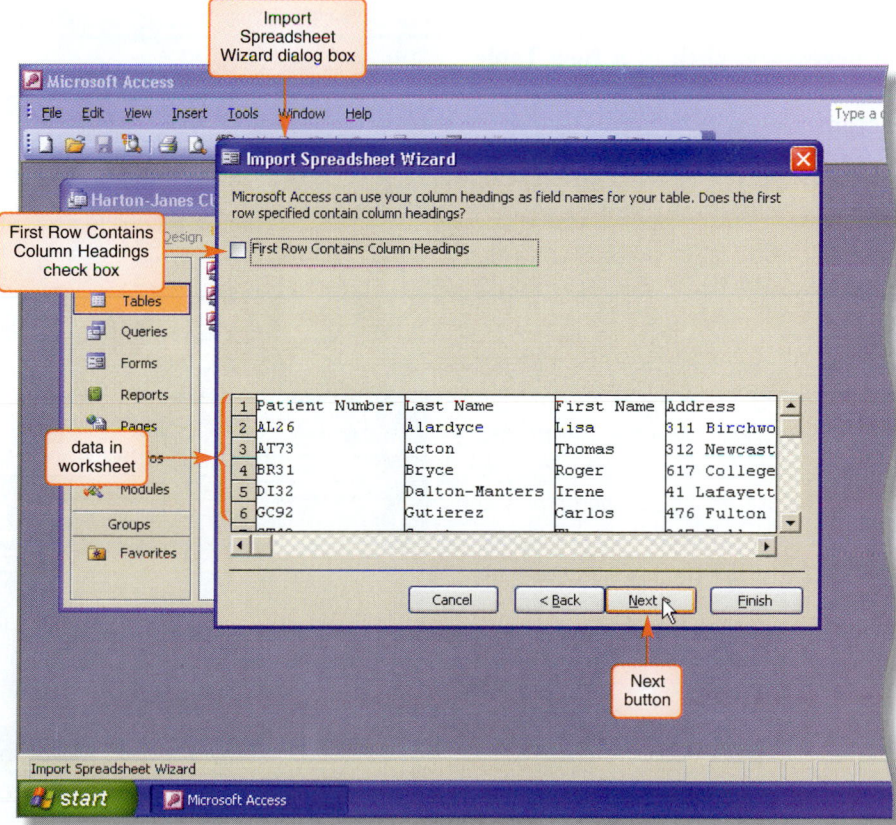

FIGURE 4

3

• **If necessary, click First Row Contains Column Headings to select it.**

• **Click the Next button.**

The Import Spreadsheet Wizard dialog box displays options for storing data in a new table or in an existing table (Figure 5).

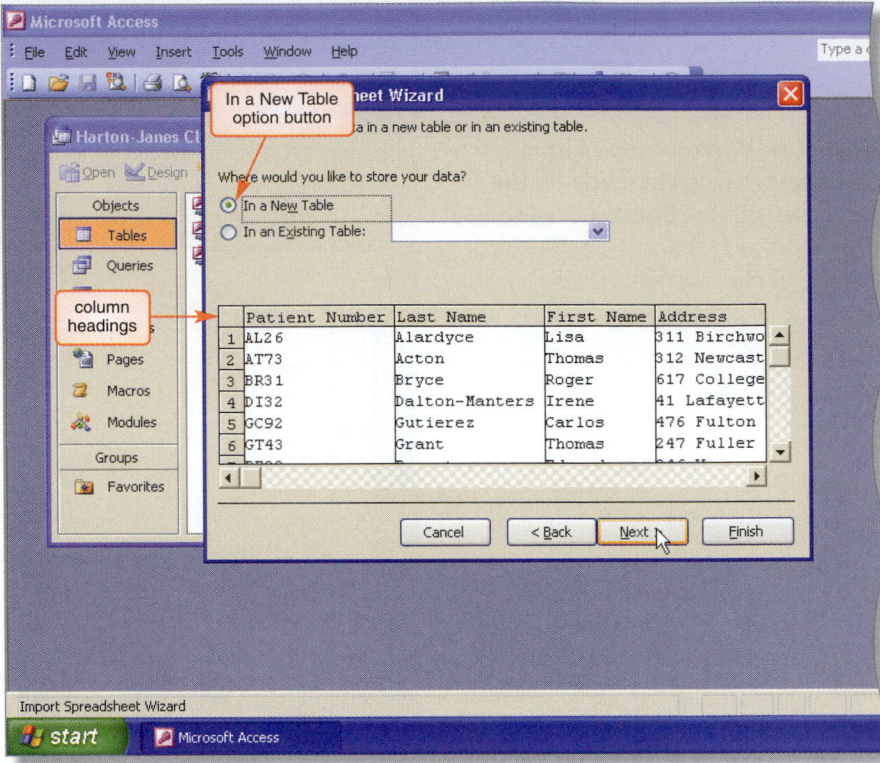

FIGURE 5

4

• **If necessary, click In a New Table to select it and then click the Next button.**

• **Because the Field Options need not be specified, click the Next button.**

The Import Spreadsheet Wizard dialog box displays options for defining a primary key for the new Access table (Figure 6). Options allow Access to add a special field to serve as the primary key, allow the user to choose an existing field to serve as the primary key, or allow the user to indicate no primary key. Most of the time, one of the existing fields will serve as the primary key. In this work- sheet, for example, the Patient Number serves as the primary key.

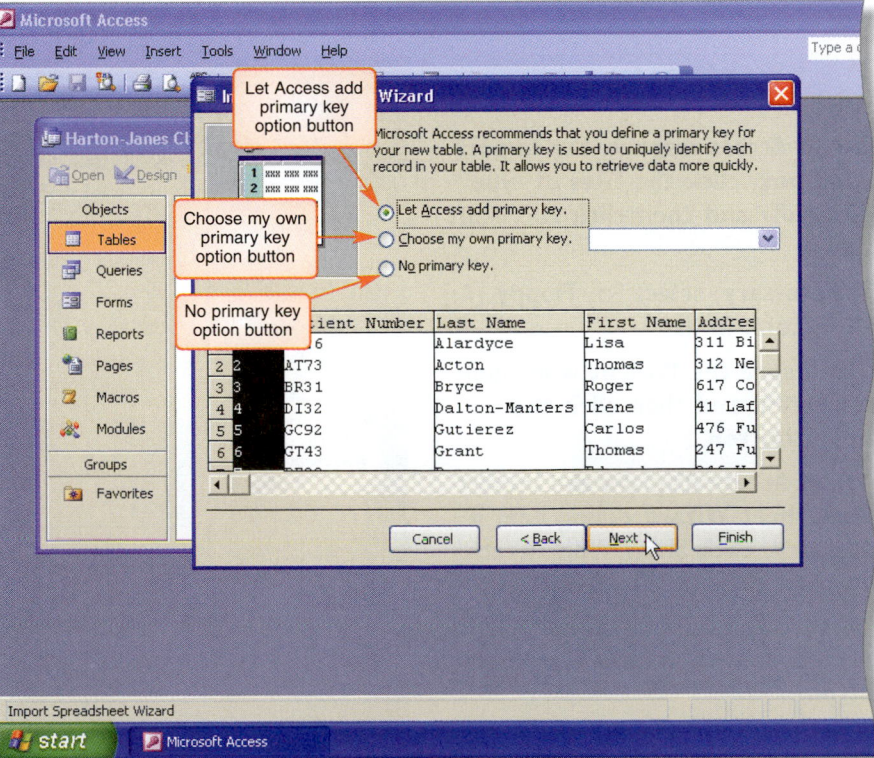

FIGURE 6

5

• **Click Choose my own primary key.**

• **Because the Patient Number field, which is the correct field, is already selected as the primary key, click the Next button. (If some other field were to be the primary key, you could click the down arrow and select the other field from the list of available fields.)**

• **Be sure Patient appears in the Import to Table text box.**

• **Click the Finish button.**

The worksheet is converted into an Access table named Patient. When the process is completed, Access displays the Import Spreadsheet Wizard dialog box (Figure 7).

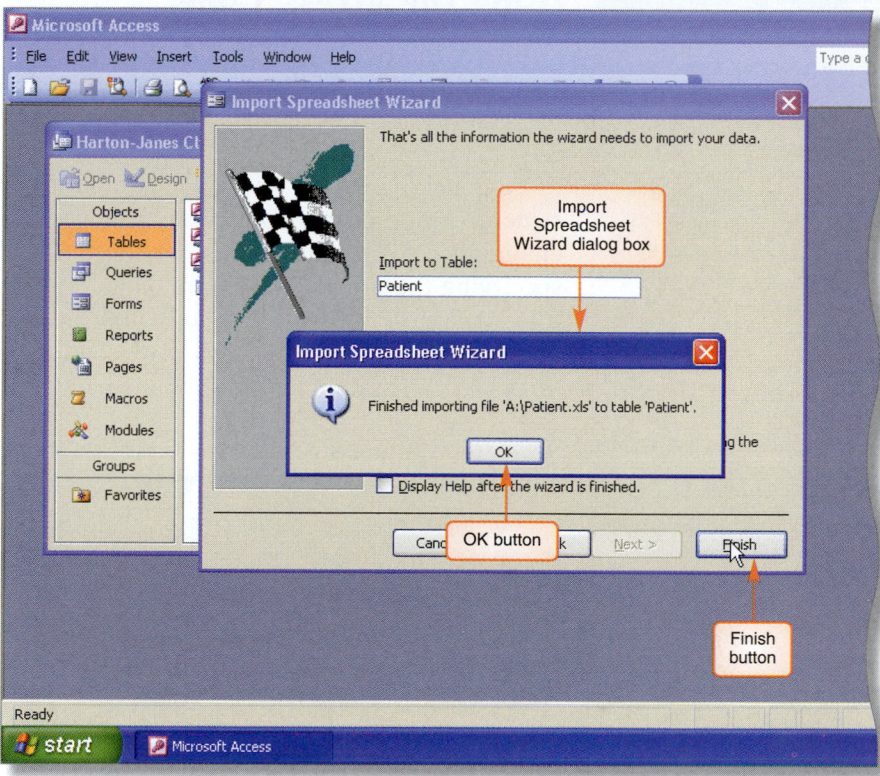

FIGURE 7

6

• **Click the OK button.**

Access has created the table (Figure 8). The table name appears in the Database window.

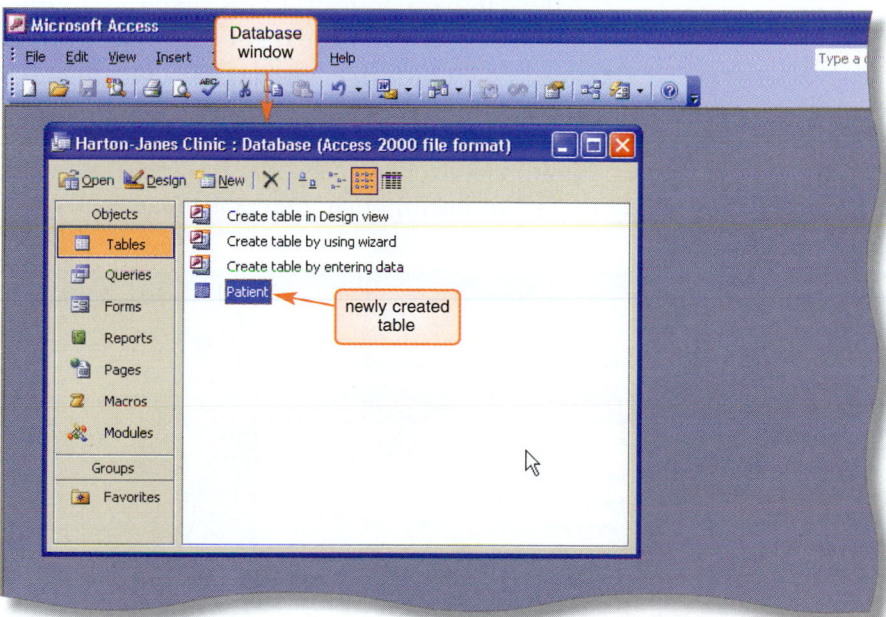

FIGURE 8

Other Ways

1. On File menu click Get External Data, click Import
2. In Voice Command mode, say "File, Get External Data, Import"

Using the Access Table

After the Access version of the table has been created, you can treat it as you would any other table. You can open the table in Datasheet view (Figure 1b on page AC 174). You can make changes to the data. You can create queries that use the data in the table.

By clicking Design View on the table's shortcut menu, you can view the table's structure and make any necessary changes to the structure. The changes may include changing field sizes and types (for those that may not be correct), creating indexes, specifying the primary key, or adding additional fields. If you have imported multiple tables that are to be related, you will need to relate the tables. To accomplish any of these tasks, use the same steps you used in Project 3. In the Patient table shown in Figure 1b, for example, the columns have been resized to best fit the data.

Linking versus Importing

When an external table or worksheet is imported, or converted, into an Access database, a copy of the data is placed as a table in the database. The original data still exists, just as it did before, but no further connection exists between it and the data in the database. Changes to the original data do not affect the data in the database. Likewise, changes in the database do not affect the original data.

It also is possible to **link** data stored in a variety of formats to Access databases by selecting Link instead of Import on the shortcut menu. (The available formats include several other database management systems as well as a variety of nondatabase formats, including Excel worksheets.) With linking, the connection is maintained.

When an Excel worksheet is linked, for example, the worksheet is not stored in the database. Instead Access simply establishes a connection to the worksheet so you can view or edit the data in either Access or Excel. Any change made in either one will be immediately visible in the other. For example, if you would change an address in Access and then view the worksheet in Excel, you would see the new address. If you add a new row in Excel and then view the table in Access, the row would appear as a new record.

To identify that a table is linked to other data, Access places an arrow in front of the table (Figure 9). In addition, the Excel icon in front of the name identifies the fact that the data is linked to an Excel worksheet.

After you link tables between a worksheet and a database or between two databases, you can modify many of the linked table's features. For example, you can rename the linked table, set view properties, and set links between tables in queries. If you move, rename, or modify linked tables, you can use the **Linked Table Manager** to update the links. To do so, use the Tools menu, click Database Utilities, and then click Linked Table Manager. The Linked Table Manager dialog box that appears includes instructions on how to update the links.

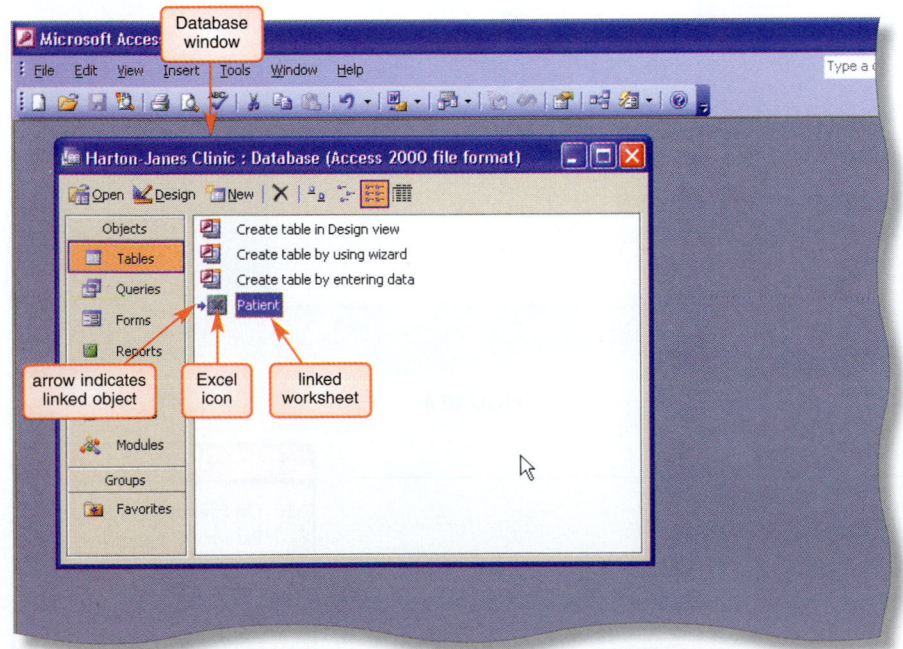

FIGURE 9

Closing the Database

The following step shows how to close the database by closing its Database window.

To Close a Database

1 Click the Close button for the Harton-Janes Clinic : Database window.

Copy Data from Access to Other Applications

Exporting is the process of copying database objects to another database, to a worksheet, or to some other format so another application (for example, Excel) can use the data. Several ways exist for exporting data. The two most common are to use the Export command, which you will use to export a query to Excel, and to use drag-and-drop, which you will use to export a query to a Word document. You also will use the Export command to export a report as a snapshot.

Opening the Database

Before exporting the Ashton James College data, you first must open the database. The following steps show how to open a database.

To Open a Database

1 Click the Open button on the Database toolbar.

2 If necessary, click the Look in box arrow and then click 3½ Floppy (A:). Click Ashton James College, the database modified in Project 3. (If you did not complete the steps in Project 3, see your instructor for a copy of the database.)

3 Click the Open button in the Open dialog box. If a Security Warning dialog box appears, click the Open button.

Access opens the Ashton James College database in the Database window.

Using the Export Command to Export Data to Excel

One way to export data to Excel, as well as to a variety of other formats, is to select the database object to be exported and then select the Export command on the shortcut menu. After you have selected the command, indicate the file type (for example, Microsoft Excel 97-2003) and then click the Save button. For some of the formats, including Excel, you can select Save formatted, in which case the export process will attempt to preserve as much of the Access formatting of the data as possible. You also can select Autostart in which case, the application receiving the data will start automatically once the data is exported. The resulting data then will appear in the application.

The steps on the next page show how to use the Export command to export the Client-Trainer Query to Excel.

Q: How could you export records from a table?

A: The process of exporting records from a table is identical to that of exporting records from a query. Simply select the Tables object and then the table containing the records to be exported before selecting the Export command. All records and fields from the table then will be exported.

To Use the Export Command to Export Data to Excel

1

• **Click Queries on the Objects bar, and then right-click Client-Trainer Query.**

The shortcut menu appears (Figure 10).

2

• **Click Export.**

• **If necessary, click the Save in box arrow and then click 3½ Floppy (A:).**

• **Click the Save as type box arrow, and then click Microsoft Excel 97-2003 in the Save as type list.**

• **Be sure the file name is Client-Trainer Query, and then click the Export button.**

The worksheet is created.

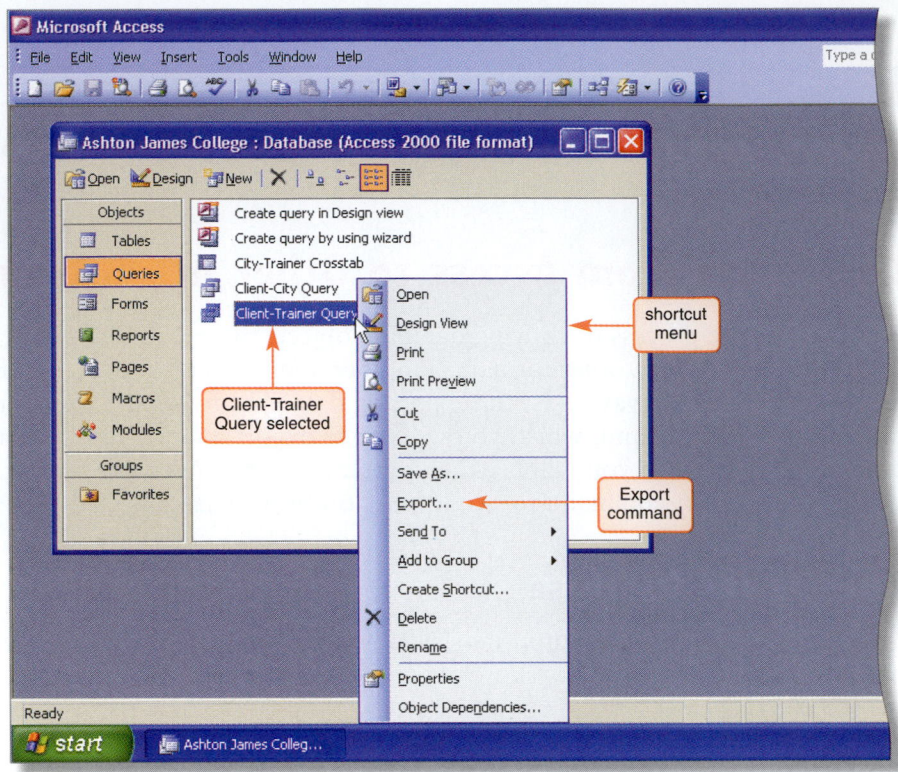

FIGURE 10

Other Ways

1. On File menu click Export
2. In Voice Command mode, say "File, Export"

Q&A

Q: Can you use drag-and-drop to export data to Excel?

A: Yes. You can use drag-and-drop to export data to Excel just as you can to export data to Word. Be sure that Excel is running instead of Word. Drag the table or query from the Database window in Access to the Excel worksheet. The records will be converted to rows in the worksheet and the fields will be converted to columns.

To view the worksheet, you could open it in Excel. You then could make any changes to it. For example, you could resize the columns to best fit the data by double-clicking the right edge of the column heading. Figure 2a on page AC 175 shows the worksheet displayed in Excel with the columns resized.

Using Drag-and-Drop to Export Data to Word

When using the Export command, Microsoft Word is not one of the available file types. You would need to select one of the file types that can be imported into Word, export from Access to the selected file type, and then import the file that is created into Word. A simpler way to export to Word is to use the drag-and-drop method. In this method, both Access and Word must be open simultaneously. You then drag the object to be imported from Access to the Word document. The following steps show how to export the Client-Trainer Query to Word using the drag-and-drop method.

To Use Drag-and-Drop to Export Data to Word

1

• **Click the Start button on the Windows taskbar, point to All Programs on the Start menu, point to Microsoft Office on the All Programs submenu, and then click Microsoft Office Word 2003 on the Microsoft Office submenu.**

• **Close the Getting Started task pane.**

• **Click the Microsoft Access button on the taskbar to return to Microsoft Access.**

• **Click the Restore Down button or resize the Access window so the Access window does not occupy the full screen.**

• **Be sure the Queries object is selected.**

• **Drag the Client-Trainer Query icon to the upper-left corner of the Word document. Do not release the mouse button.**

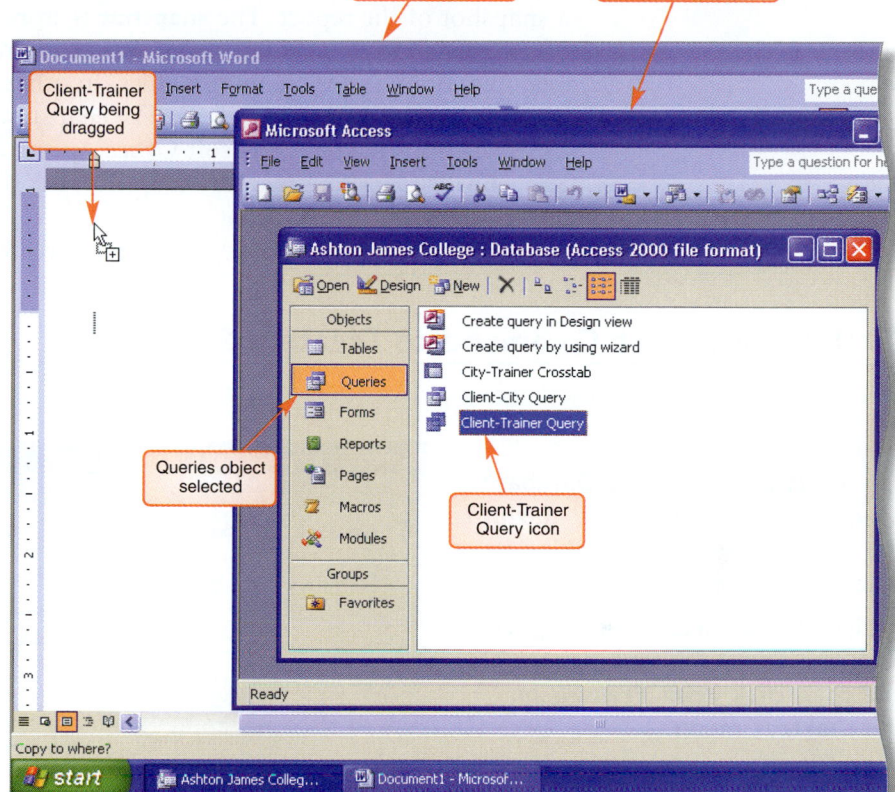

FIGURE 11

Microsoft Office Word is displayed in a maximized window (Figure 11). Microsoft Office Access is displayed in a resized, smaller window. The Queries object is selected and the Client-Trainer Query is selected. The mouse pointer indicates that the Client-Trainer Query is being dragged to Word.

2

• **Release the mouse button and then click the Save button on the Standard toolbar in Microsoft Word.**

• **Type** Client-Trainer Query **in the File name text box, and then click the Save button in the Save As dialog box.**

• **Click in the Word window to deselect the table.**

The data from the query is inserted in the Word document. The title of the query appears in bold at the top of the document. The data is inserted as a Word table. The document is saved. It looks like the one shown in Figure 2b on page AC 175.

3

• **Quit Word by clicking its Close button.**

• **Maximize the Microsoft Office Access window by double-clicking its title bar.**

Microsoft Word no longer appears. The file is saved and available for use.

Using the Export Command to Create a Snapshot

If you want to send a report to someone via e-mail, the simplest way is to create a snapshot of the report. The **snapshot** is stored in a separate file with an extension of snp. This file contains all the details of the report, including fonts, effects (for example, bold or italic), and graphics. In other words, the contents of the snapshot file look precisely like the report. The snapshot file can be viewed by anyone having the Snapshot Viewer; Microsoft Office Access 2003 is *not* required. You can use the **Snapshot Viewer** to e-mail the snapshot; the recipient can use the Snapshot Viewer to view or print the snapshot.

The following steps illustrate how to create a snapshot.

To Use the Export Command to Create a Snapshot

1

• **If the Microsoft Access Database window is not maximized, maximize the window by double-clicking its title bar.**

• **Click the Reports object, right-click the Client Amount Report, and then click Print Preview on the shortcut menu.**

• **Right-click the preview of the report.**

Access displays the Client Amount Report window with a preview of the report (Figure 12). The shortcut menu appears.

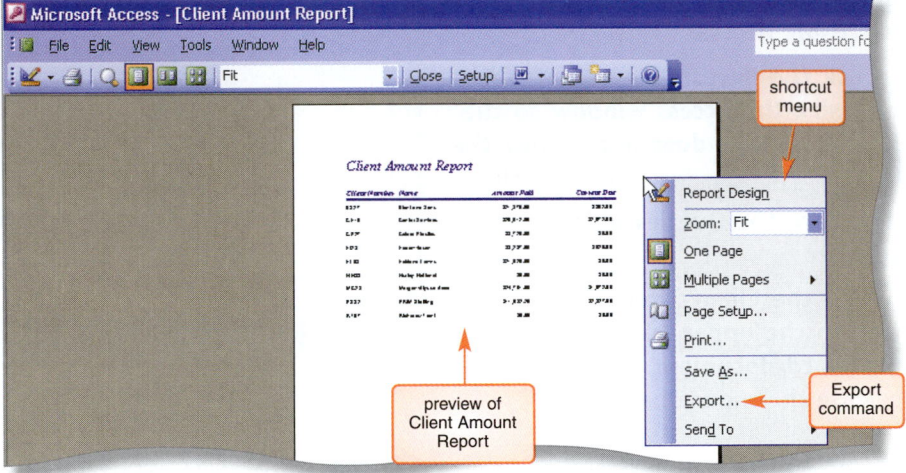

FIGURE 12

2

• **Click Export.**

• **If necessary, click the Save in box arrow and then click 3½ Floppy (A:).**

• **Click the Save as type box arrow, select Snapshot Format, be sure the Autostart check box is checked, and then click the Export button.**

• **If a Microsoft Office Access dialog box is displayed asking if you want to install Snapshot Viewer, click the No button and see your instructor.**

The snapshot of the report is created. It looks similar to the one in Figure 2c on page AC 175.

3

• **Click the Close button for the Snapshot Viewer - [Client Amount Report] window.**

• **Click the Close button on the Print Preview toolbar.**

The Snapshot Viewer and Print Preview windows close. Access displays the Database window.

You can e-mail the snapshot to other users. The other users can use the Snapshot Viewer to view the report online or to print the report.

XML

Just as Hypertext Markup Language (HTML) is the standard language for creating and displaying Web pages, **Extensible Markup Language** (**XML**) is the standard language for describing and delivering data on the Web. XML is a data interchange format that allows you to exchange data between dissimilar systems or applications. With XML, you can describe both the data and the structure (**schema**) of the data. You can export tables, queries, forms, or reports.

When exporting XML data, you can choose to export multiple related tables in a single operation to a single XML file. If you later import this XML data to another database, you will import all the tables in a single operation. Thus, the new database would contain each of the tables. All the fields would have all the correct data types and sizes. The primary keys would be correct, and the tables would be related exactly as they were in the original database.

Exporting XML Data

To export XML data, you use the same Export command you used to export to other formats. You then select XML as the Save as type. You indicate whether to just save the data or to save both the data and the schema (that is, the structure). If you have made changes to the appearance of the data, such as changing the font, and want these changes saved as well, you save what is termed the **presentation**. The data is saved in a file with the XML extension, the schema is saved in a file with the XSD extension, and the presentation is saved in a file with the XSL extension. The default choice, which usually is appropriate, is to save both the data and schema, but not the presentation. If multiple tables are related, such as the Client and Trainer tables in the Ashton James College data, you can export both tables to a single file.

The following steps export both the Client and Trainer tables to a single XML file called Client. The steps save the data and the schema, but do not save the presentation.

More About

The Quick Reference

For a table that lists how to complete tasks covered in this book using the mouse, menu, shortcut menu, and keyboard, see the Quick Reference Summary at the back of this book, or visit the Access 2003 Quick Reference Web page (scsite.com/ac2003/qr).

Q&A

Q: What are some advantages of report snapshots?

A: When you use Access to create a report snapshot, you can distribute reports electronically to users both inside and outside your organization. You do not need to photocopy or mail printed reports. Instead, users can view the reports online and print only the reports they need.

To Export XML Data

1

• **Click the Tables object, and then right-click Client.**

The shortcut menu for the Client table appears (Figure 13).

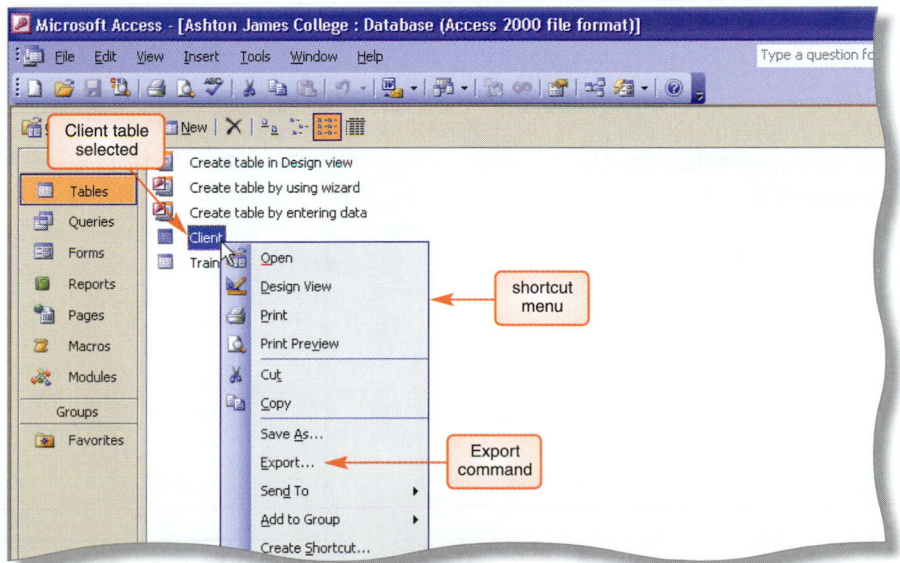

FIGURE 13

2

• **Click Export on the shortcut menu.**

• **Click the Save as type box arrow, scroll down, and then click XML in the list.**

• **If necessary, select 3½ Floppy (A:) in the Save in list.**

Access displays the Export Table 'Client' As dialog box (Figure 14). The file name is Client and the Save as type is XML.

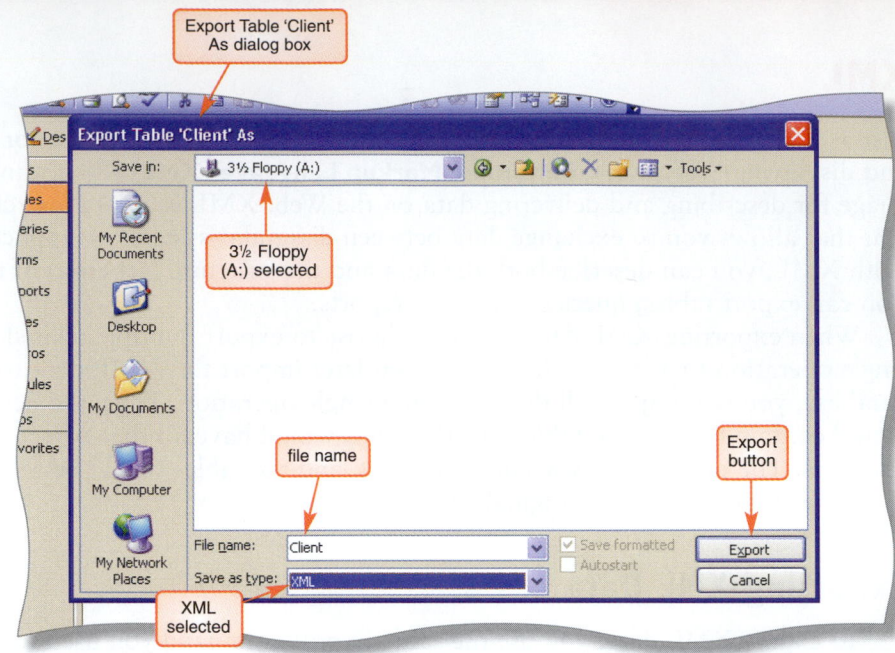

FIGURE 14

3

• **Click the Export button.**

Access displays the Export XML dialog box (Figure 15). The current selections call for the data and schema to be exported. The presentation will not be exported.

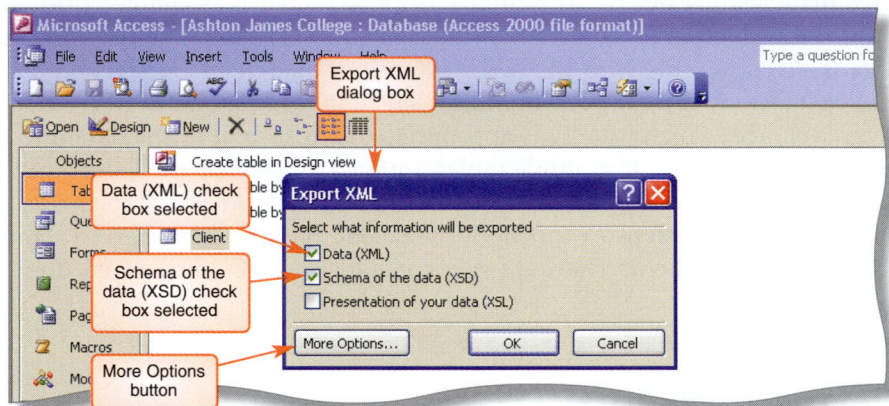

FIGURE 15

4

• **Click the More Options button.**

Access displays the Export XML dialog box (Figure 16). The Data tab is selected.

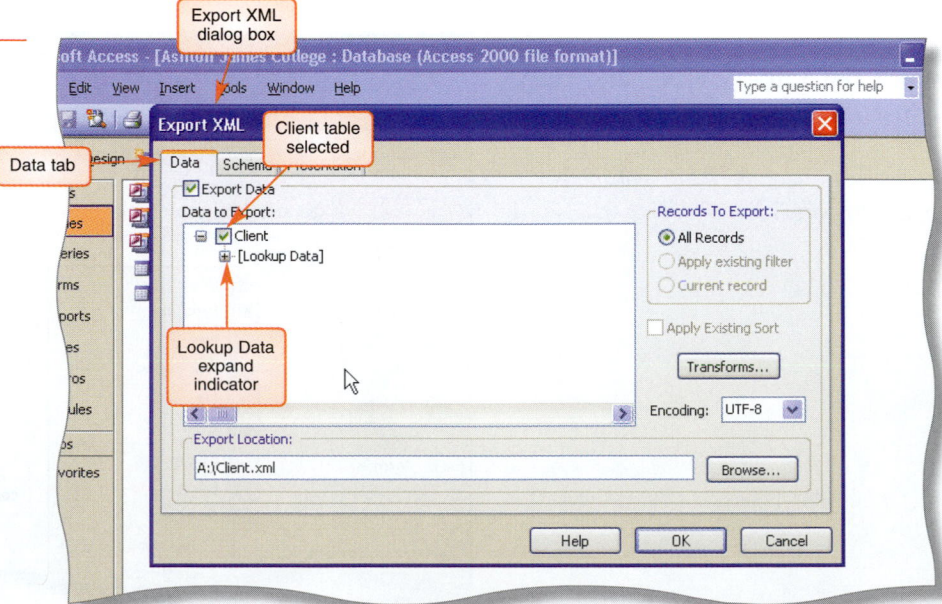

FIGURE 16

5

• Click the expand indicator (the plus sign) to the left of [Lookup Data], and then click the Trainer check box to select the Trainer table.

Both the Client table and the Trainer table are selected (Figure 17). The export location is A:\Client.xml.

6

• Click the OK button.

• Click the Close button for the Microsoft Access [Ashton James College : Database (Access 2000 file format)] window.

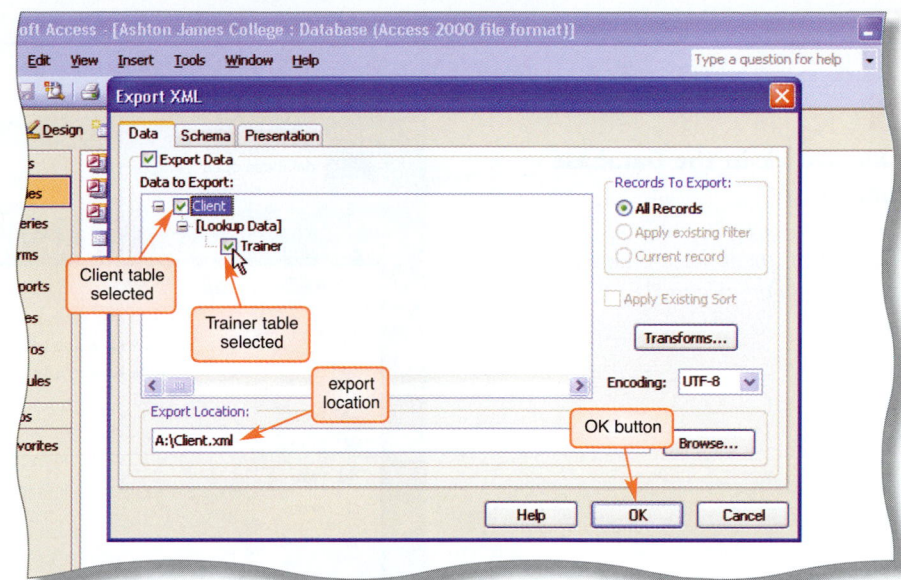

FIGURE 17

The data and structure for both the Client table and the Trainer table are exported to the file named Client. The file also contains the relationship between the two tables. The Ashton James College database is closed.

Creating an Access Database

Before importing the data, you need to create the database that will contain the data. The following steps create the AJ Consulting database.

To Create a New Database

1 Click the New button on the Database toolbar, and then click Blank database in the New area of the New File task pane.

2 If necessary, click the Save in box arrow in the File New Database dialog box and then click 3½ Floppy (A:).

3 Type AJ Consulting in the File name text box and then click the Create button.

Access creates the database. It is open and ready for use.

Importing XML Data

To import XML data, use the Import command and select XML as the type. You then select the XML file that contains the data to be imported. The steps on the next page import the Client and Trainer tables stored in the XML file called Client.

To Import XML Data

1

• **Right-click in the Database window.**

The shortcut menu for the Database window appears (Figure 18).

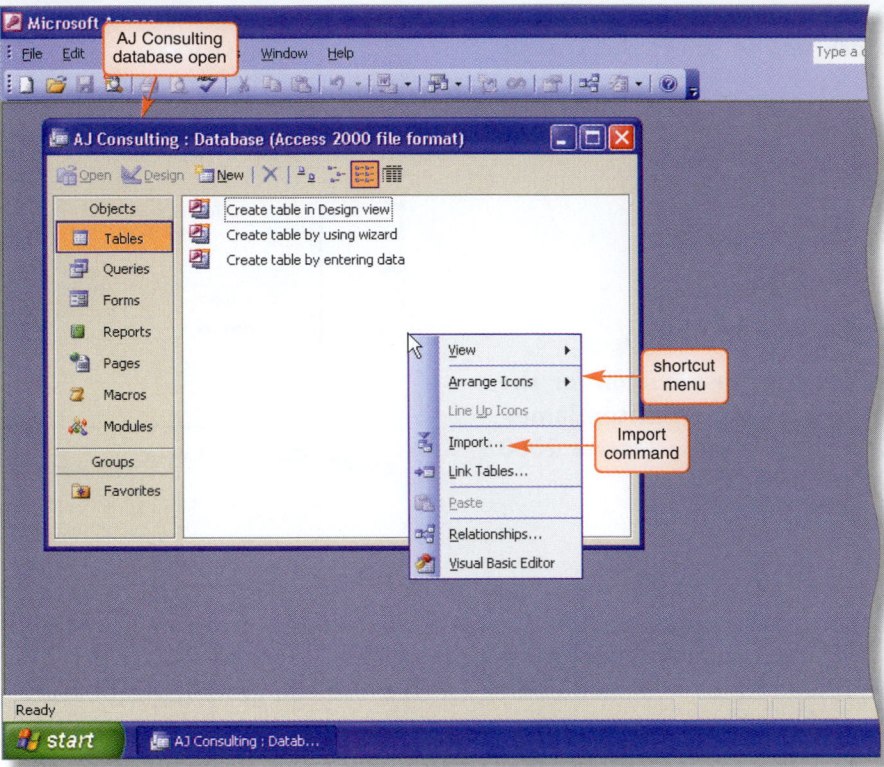

FIGURE 18

2

• **Click Import on the shortcut menu.**

• **Click the Files of type box arrow, scroll down, and then click XML in the list.**

• **If necessary, select 3½ Floppy (A:) in the Look in list.**

• **Click the Client file. (Do not click the xsd version. If you do, you will import both tables, but none of the data. That is, the tables will be empty.)**

Access displays the Import dialog box (Figure 19). The Client file is selected. XML is the file type.

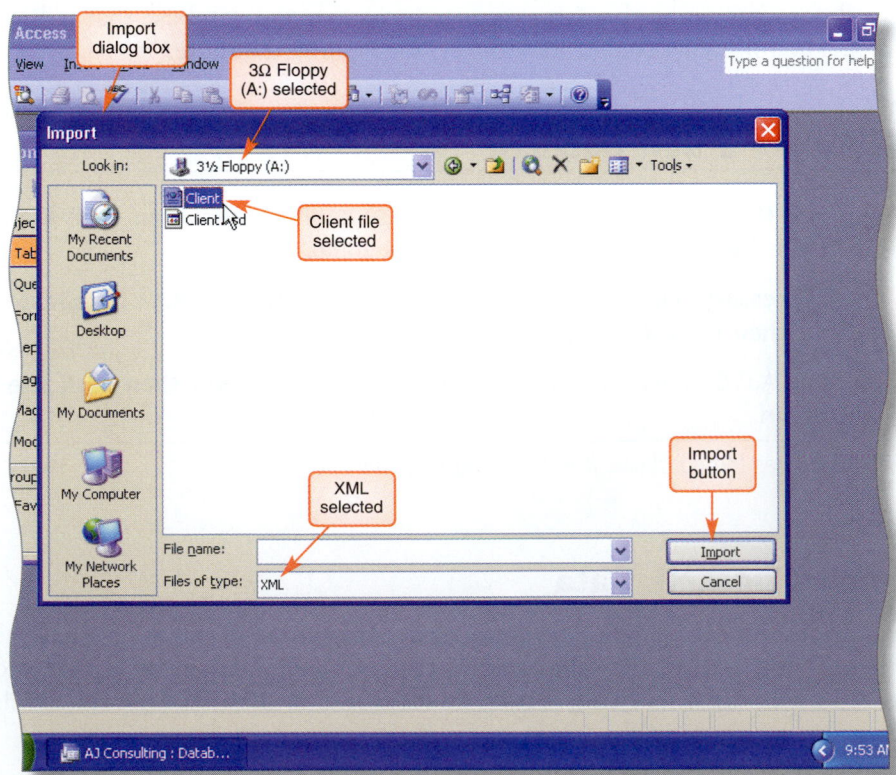

FIGURE 19

3

• **Click the Import button.**

Access displays the Import XML dialog box (Figure 20). Both the Client and Trainer tables will be imported. Clicking the expand indicator to the left of either table will display a list of fields in the table.

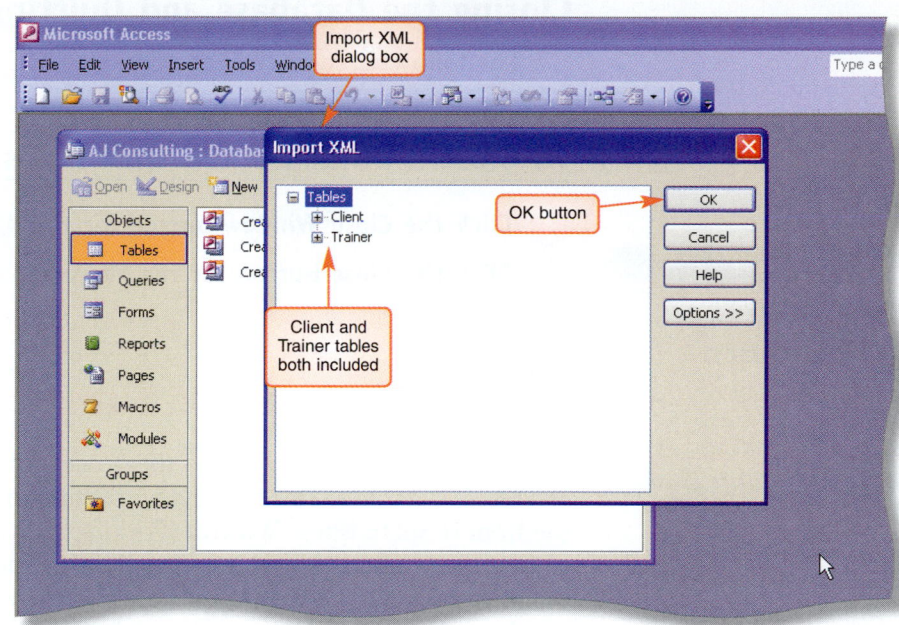

FIGURE 20

4

• **Click the OK button.**

The data is imported and the Microsoft Office Access dialog box is displayed (Figure 21).

5

• **Click the OK button.**

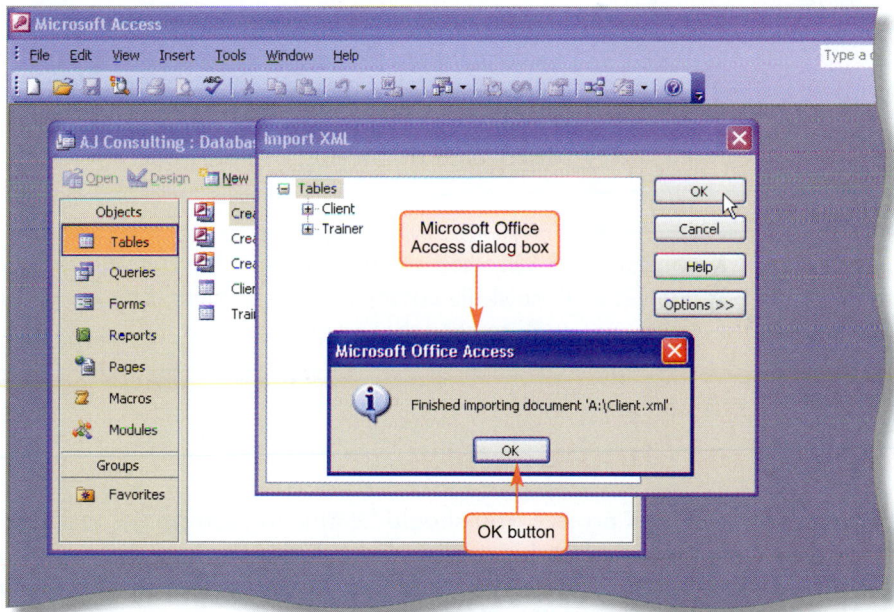

FIGURE 21

Both tables have been imported as part of this single Import operation. In addition to having the same data, the fields in both tables have precisely the same data types and sizes as in the original database. Also, the same fields have been designated primary keys.

Closing the Database and Quitting Access

The following steps close the database and quit Access.

To Close a Database and Quit Access

1 Click the **Close Window** button for the **AJ Consulting : Database** window.

2 Click the **Close** button for the **Microsoft Access window.**

More About

Microsoft Certification

The Microsoft Office Specialist Certification program provides an opportunity for you to obtain a valuable industry credential — proof that you have the Access 2003 skills required by employers. For more information, see Appendix E, or visit the Access 2003 Certification Web page (scsite.com/ac2003/cert).

Integration Feature Summary

The Integration Feature covered the process of integrating an Excel worksheet into an Access database. To convert a worksheet to an Access table, you learned to use the Import Spreadsheet Wizard. Working with the wizard, you identified the first row of the worksheet as the row containing the column headings and you indicated the primary key. The wizard then created the table for you and placed it in a new database. You also saw how you could link data instead of importing it.

You learned to use the Export command and used it to export data to an Excel worksheet. You also learned to use the drag-and-drop feature and used it to export data to a Word document. The project illustrated how to use the Export command to create a snapshot of a report. You learned how to export XML data. You exported both structure and data for multiple related tables in a single operation. Finally, you learned how to import the XML data to a separate database and discovered that a single import operation imported both tables and their structures.

If you have a SAM user profile, you may have access to hands-on instruction, practice, and assessment of the skills covered in this project. Log in to your SAM account and go to your assignments page to see what your instructor has assigned.

What You Should Know

Having completed this project, you should be able to perform the tasks below. The tasks are listed in the same order they were presented in this project. For a list of the buttons, menus, toolbars, and commands introduced in this project, see the Quick Reference Summary at the back of this book and refer to the Page Number column.

1. Create a New Database   (AC 176)
2. Import an Excel Worksheet   (AC 177)
3. Close a Database   (AC 181)
4. Open a Database   (AC 181)
5. Use the Export Command to Export Data to Excel   (AC 182)
6. Use Drag-and-Drop to Export Data to Word (AC 183)
7. Use the Export Command to Create a Snapshot (AC 184)
8. Export XML Data   (AC 185)
9. Create a New Database   (AC 187)
10. Import XML Data   (AC 188)
11. Close a Database and Quit Access   (AC 190)

In the Lab

1 Importing Data to an Access Database

Problem: CAC Logo Company has been using Excel for a number of tasks. The company sells logo-imprinted novelty items and clothing to organizations. CAC uses several worksheets to keep track of inventory, and customers. CAC realizes that the customer data would be better handled if maintained in an Access database. The company wants to maintain the items inventory in Excel worksheets but also would like to be able to use the query and report features of Access.

Instructions: For this assignment, you will need two files: Customer.xls and Logo Items.xls. These files are on the Data Disk. See the inside back cover of this book for instructions for downloading the Data Disk or see your instructor for information about accessing the files required for this book. Perform the following tasks:

1. Start Access and create a new database in which to store all the objects for CAC Logo Company. Call the database CAC Logo Company.
2. Import the Customer worksheet shown in Figure 22 into Access. The worksheet is in the Customer workbook on the Data Disk.
3. Use Customer as the name of the Access table and Customer Number as the primary key.
4. Open the Customer table in Datasheet view and resize the columns to best fit the data. Print the table.
5. Link the Logo Items worksheet shown in Figure 23 to the database. The worksheet is in the Logo Items workbook on the Data Disk.
6. Open the linked Logo Items table in Datasheet view and resize the columns to best fit the data. Print the table.
7. Rename the linked Logo Items table as Items. Then, use the Linked Table Manager to update the link between the Excel worksheet and the Access table. (If the Linked Table Manager wizard is not installed on your computer, see your instructor before continuing.)

	A	B	C	D	E	F
1	Customer Number	Name	Address	City	Telephone Number	Balance
2	AD23	Adson Cleaners	407 Mallery	Enders	512-555-4070	$105.00
3	AR76	Artur's Mfg	200 Wymberly	Cedar Estates	510-555-0200	$80.00
4	BE29	Becker's Autos	224 Harbor Oak	Cedar Estates	510-555-2024	$70.00
5	CR67	Cricket Store	506 Mallery	Enders	512-555-6050	$0.00
6	DL61	Del Sol	123 Village	Kingston	513-555-1231	$135.00
7	GR36	Great Foods	1345 Frederic	Kingston	513-555-5431	$104.00
8	HA09	Halyards Mfg	5689 Demerre	Enders	512-555-6895	$145.00
9	ME17	Merry Café	879 Vinca	Kingston	513-555-9780	$168.00
10	RO45	Royal Palms	678 Liatris	Enders	512-555-4567	$0.00
11	ST21	Steedman's	809 Lantana	Cedar Estates	510-555-9080	$123.00
12						

FIGURE 22

	A	B	C	D	E	F
1	Item Id	Description	On Hand	Cost	Selling Price	Vendor Code
2	A663	Baseball Cap	50	$9.25	$15.50	LG
3	A683	Coffee Mug	30	$1.85	$4.50	BH
4	B563	Glasses (4)	24	$8.20	$10.75	BH
5	B593	Golf Shirt	45	$18.20	$23.75	AC
6	C923	Jacket	24	$49.23	$57.70	LG
7	C953	Knit Cap	48	$4.95	$6.95	AC
8	D189	Sports Towel	64	$3.58	$5.10	LG
9	D343	Sweatpants	24	$21.45	$24.95	AC
10	E810	Sweatshirt	48	$27.50	$34.95	AC
11	E930	Tee Shirt	72	$8.90	$10.25	LG
12						

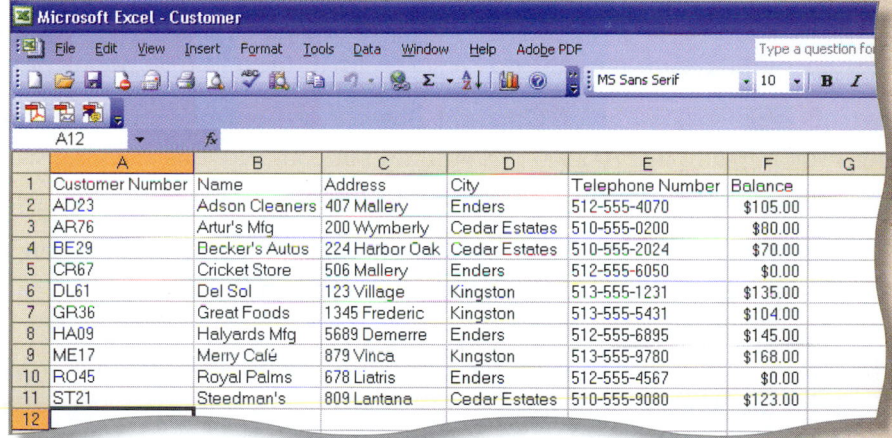

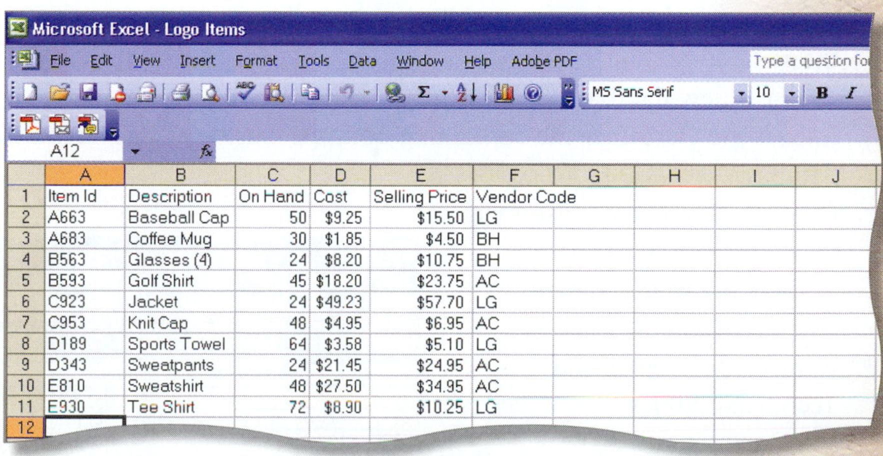

FIGURE 23

(continued)

In the Lab

Importing Data to an Access Database *(continued)*

8. Print the Items table.
9. Link the Trainer table in the AJ Consulting database to the CAC Logo database. Trainers of AJ Consulting may become potential sales reps for CAC Logo.
10. Rename the Trainer table as Potential Sales Reps. Then, use the Linked Table Manager to update the link between the two tables.
11. Print the Potential Sales Rep table.

2 Exporting Data to Other Applications

Problem: Begon Pest Control wants to be able to export some of the data in the Access database to other applications. The company wants to export the City-Technician Crosstab query for further processing in Excel. It also wants to use the Customer-Technician query in a Word document as well as e-mail the Customer Amount Report to the company's accounting firm. The company has decided to branch out and offer pest control services that will focus on outside pest control, that is, pest control for lawns and gardens. It wants to export the Customer and Technician tables as a single XML file and then import it to a new database.

Instructions: Start Access. Open the Begon Pest Control database that you modified in Apply Your Knowledge 1 in Project 3 on page AC 167. (If you did not complete this exercise, see your instructor for a copy of the modified database.) Perform the following tasks:

1. Export the City-Technician Crosstab query to Excel as shown in Figure 24.
2. Resize the columns to best fit the data as shown in Figure 24.
3. Print the Excel worksheet.
4. Use drag-and-drop to place the Customer-Technician query in a Word document.
5. Print the Word document.
6. Preview the Customer Amount Report and then export the report as a snapshot.
7. Open the report in the Snapshot Viewer and print it. (If a Microsoft Office Access dialog box is displayed asking if you want to install Snapshot Viewer, click the No button and see your instructor.)
8. Export both the Customer and Technician tables in XML format. Be sure that both tables are exported to the same file.
9. Create a new database called Begon Garden Services.
10. Import the Customer file containing both the Customer and Technician tables to the Begon Garden Services database.
11. Change the name of customer CJ45 to C Joseph Diner.
12. Change the first name of technician 220 to Christy.
13. Print the Customer and Technician tables.

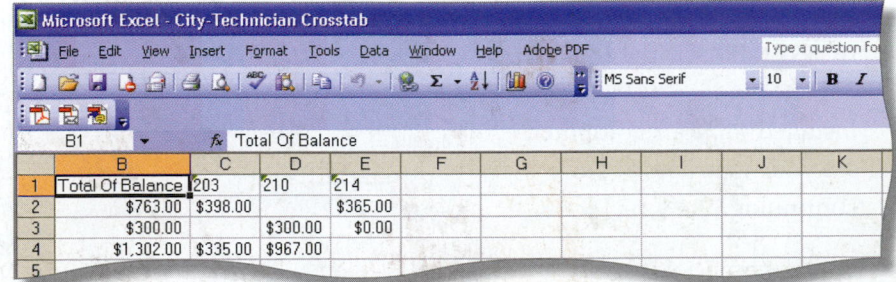

FIGURE 24

MICROSOFT
Office PowerPoint 2003

Using a Design Template and Text Slide Layout to Create a Presentation

CASE PERSPECTIVE

Do you use the 168 hours in each week effectively? From attending class, doing homework, attending school events, exercising, eating, watching television, and sleeping, juggling the demands of school and personal lives can be daunting. Odds are that one of every three students will fail a course at one point in their college career due to poor study habits.

The ability to learn effectively is the key to college success. What matters is not how long people study but how well they use their time in the classroom and while preparing for class assignments and tests. Students with good academic skills maximize their time and, consequently, achieve the highest grades on exams and homework assignments. They ultimately earn higher incomes than their less organized peers because good academic practices carry over to the working environment.

Advisers in the Academic Skills Center at your college are aware of this fact and are developing seminars to help students succeed. Their first presentation focuses on getting organized, enhancing listening skills, and taking tests effectively. Dr. Traci Johnson, the dean of the Academic Skills Center, has asked you to help her create a PowerPoint slide show to use at next month's lunchtime study skills session (Figure 1-1 on page PPT 5). In addition, she would like handouts of the slides to distribute to these students.

As you read through this project, you will learn how to use PowerPoint to create, save, and print a slide show that is composed of single- and multi-level bulleted lists.

Using a Design Template and Text Slide Layout to Create a Presentation

P R O J E C T

Objectives

You will have mastered the material in this project when you can:

- Start and customize PowerPoint
- Describe the PowerPoint window
- Select a design template
- Create a title slide and text slides with single- and multi-level bulleted lists
- Change the font size and font style

- Save a presentation
- End a slide show with a black slide
- View a presentation in slide show view
- Quit PowerPoint and then open a presentation
- Display and print a presentation in black and white
- Use the PowerPoint Help system

What Is Microsoft Office PowerPoint 2003?

Microsoft Office PowerPoint 2003 is a complete presentation graphics program that allows you to produce professional-looking presentations (Figure 1-1). A PowerPoint **presentation** also is called a **slide show**.

PowerPoint contains several features to simplify creating a slide show. For example, you can instruct PowerPoint to create a predesigned presentation, and then you can modify the presentation to fulfill your requirements. You quickly can format a slide show using one of the professionally designed presentation design templates. To make your presentation more impressive, you can add tables, charts, pictures, video, sound, and animation effects. Additional PowerPoint features include the following:

- **Word processing** create bulleted lists, combine words and images, find and replace text, and use multiple fonts and type sizes.
- **Outlining** develop your presentation using an outline format. You also can import outlines from Microsoft Word or other word processing programs.
- **Charting** create and insert charts into your presentations. The two chart types are: standard, which includes bar, line, pie, and xy (scatter) charts; and custom, which shows such objects as floating bars and colored lines.
- **Drawing** form and modify diagrams using shapes such as arcs, arrows, cubes, rectangles, stars, and triangles.
- **Inserting multimedia** insert artwork and multimedia effects into your slide show. The Microsoft Clip Organizer contains hundreds of media files, including pictures, photos, sounds, and movies.

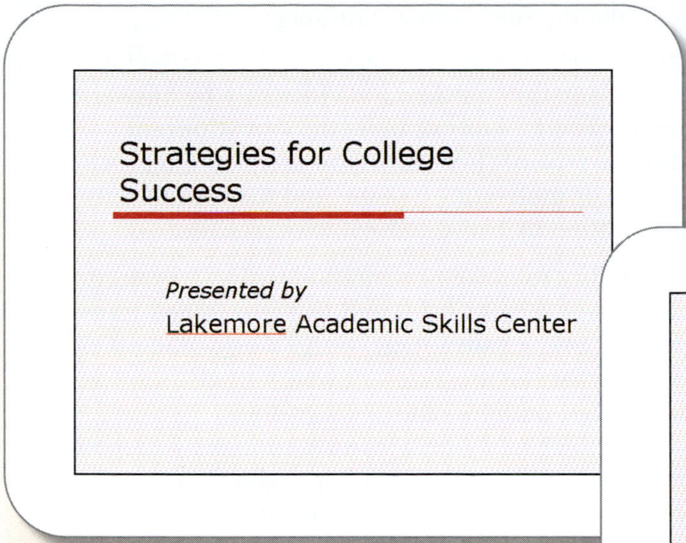

(a) Slide 1 (Title Slide)

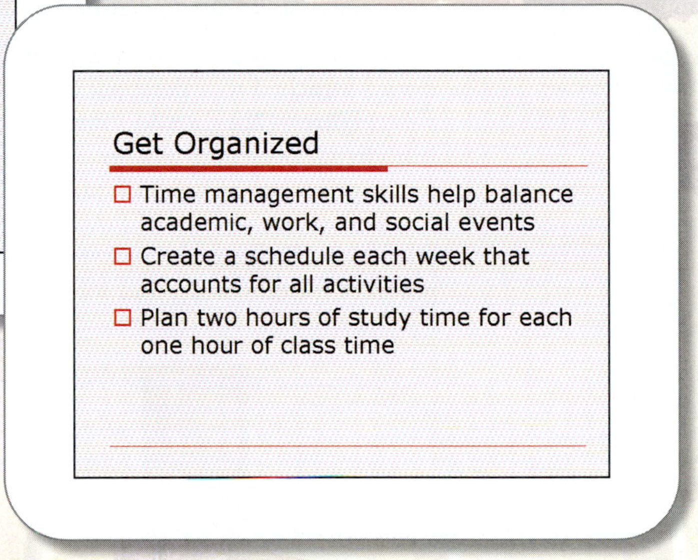

Strategies for College Success

Presented by
Lakemore Academic Skills Center

(b) Slide 2 (Single-Level Bulleted List)

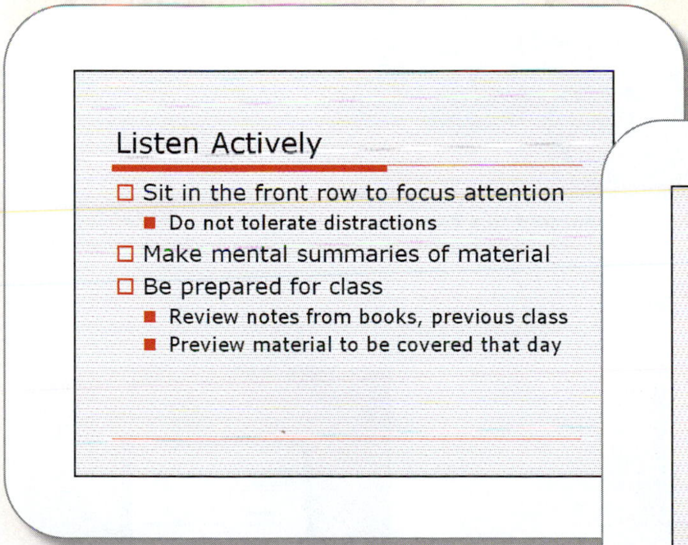

Get Organized

☐ Time management skills help balance academic, work, and social events
☐ Create a schedule each week that accounts for all activities
☐ Plan two hours of study time for each one hour of class time

(c) Slide 3 (Multi-Level Bulleted List)

Listen Actively

☐ Sit in the front row to focus attention
  ■ Do not tolerate distractions
☐ Make mental summaries of material
☐ Be prepared for class
  ■ Review notes from books, previous class
  ■ Preview material to be covered that day

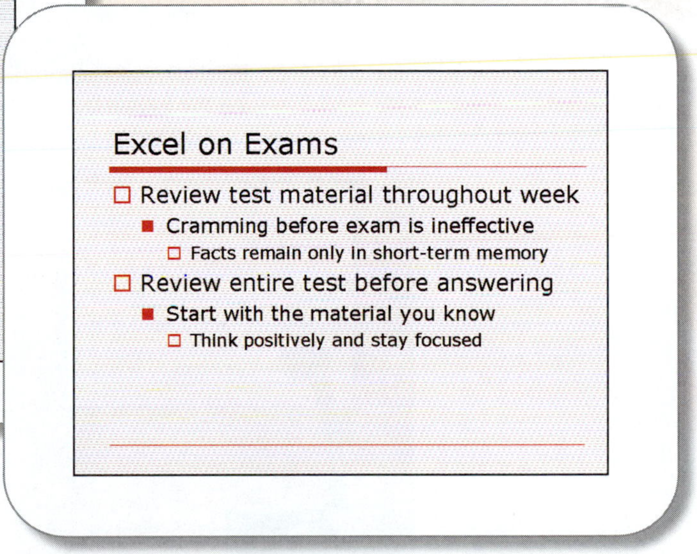

(d) Slide 4 (Multi-Level Bulleted List)

Excel on Exams

☐ Review test material throughout week
  ■ Cramming before exam is ineffective
    ☐ Facts remain only in short-term memory
☐ Review entire test before answering
  ■ Start with the material you know
    ☐ Think positively and stay focused

FIGURE 1-1

More About

Portable Projection Devices

New multimedia projectors weigh less than three pounds and can be held in one hand. Some projectors allow users to control the projector wirelessly from 300 feet away using a PDA. For more information about projectors, visit the PowerPoint 2003 More About Web page (scsite.com/ppt2003/more) and then click Projectors.

- **Web support** save presentations or parts of a presentation in HTML format so they can be viewed and manipulated using a browser. You can publish your slide show to the Internet or to an intranet.
- **E-mailing** send your entire slide show as an attachment to an e-mail message.
- **Using Wizards** create a presentation quickly and efficiently by answering prompts for specific content criteria. For example, the **AutoContent Wizard** gives prompts for the type of slide show you are planning, such as communicating serious news or motivating a team, and the type of output, such as an on-screen presentation or black and white overheads.

PowerPoint gives you the flexibility to make presentations using a projection device attached to a personal computer (Figure 1-2a) and using overhead transparencies (Figure 1-2b). In addition, you can take advantage of the World Wide Web and run virtual presentations on the Internet (Figure 1-2c). PowerPoint also can create paper printouts of the individual slides, outlines, and speaker notes.

This latest version of PowerPoint has many new features to make you more productive. It saves the presentation to a CD; uses pens, highlighters, arrows, and pointers for emphasis; and includes a thesaurus and other research tools.

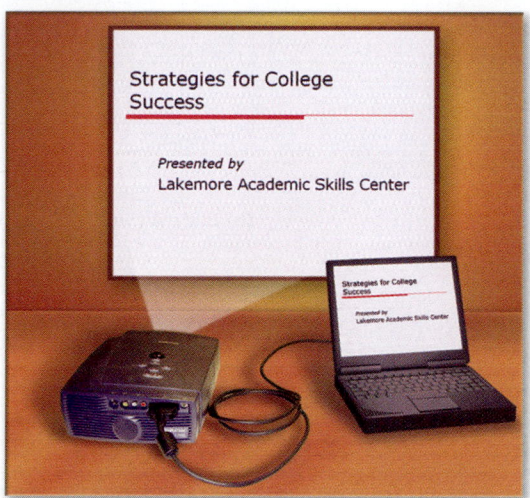

(a) Projection Device Connected to a Personal Computer

(b) Overhead Transparencies

(c) PowerPoint Presentation on the World Wide Web

FIGURE 1-2

Project One — Strategies for College Success

PowerPoint allows you to produce slides to use in an academic, business, or other environment. In Project 1, you create the presentation shown in Figures 1-1a through 1-1d. The objective is to produce a presentation, called Strategies for College Success, to be displayed using a projection device. As an introduction to PowerPoint, this project steps you through the most common type of presentation, which is a **text slide** consisting of a bulleted list. A **bulleted list** is a list of paragraphs, each preceded by a bullet. A **bullet** is a symbol such as a heavy dot (•) or other character that precedes text when the text warrants special emphasis.

Starting and Customizing PowerPoint

If you are stepping through this project on a computer and you want your screen to agree with the figures in this book, then you should change your computer's resolution to 800 × 600. To change the resolution on your computer, see Appendix D.

To start PowerPoint, Windows must be running. The quickest way to begin a new presentation is to use the Start button on the **Windows taskbar** at the bottom of the screen. The following steps show how to start PowerPoint and a new presentation.

To Start PowerPoint

1

• **Click the Start button on the Windows taskbar, point to All Programs on the Start menu, point to Microsoft Office on the All Programs submenu, and then point to Microsoft Office PowerPoint 2003 on the Microsoft Office submenu.**

Windows displays the commands on the Start menu above the Start button, the All Programs submenu, and the Microsoft Office submenu (Figure 1-3).

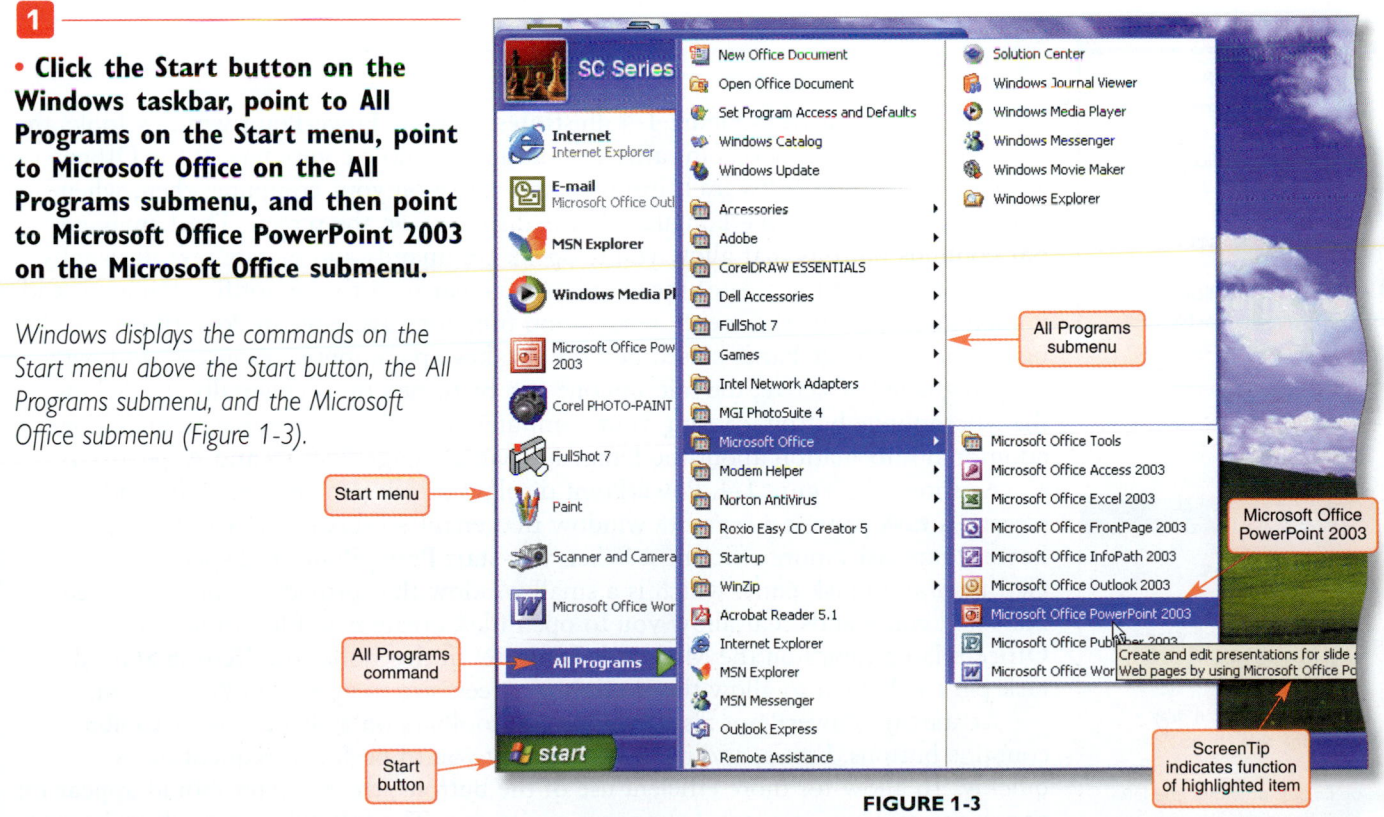

FIGURE 1-3

2

• **Click Microsoft Office
PowerPoint 2003.**

*PowerPoint starts.
While PowerPoint is
starting, the mouse pointer
changes to the shape of an
hourglass. After several seconds,
PowerPoint displays a blank
presentation titled Presentation1
in the PowerPoint window
(Figure 1-4).*

3

• **If the PowerPoint
window is not maximized,
double-click its title bar
to maximize it.**

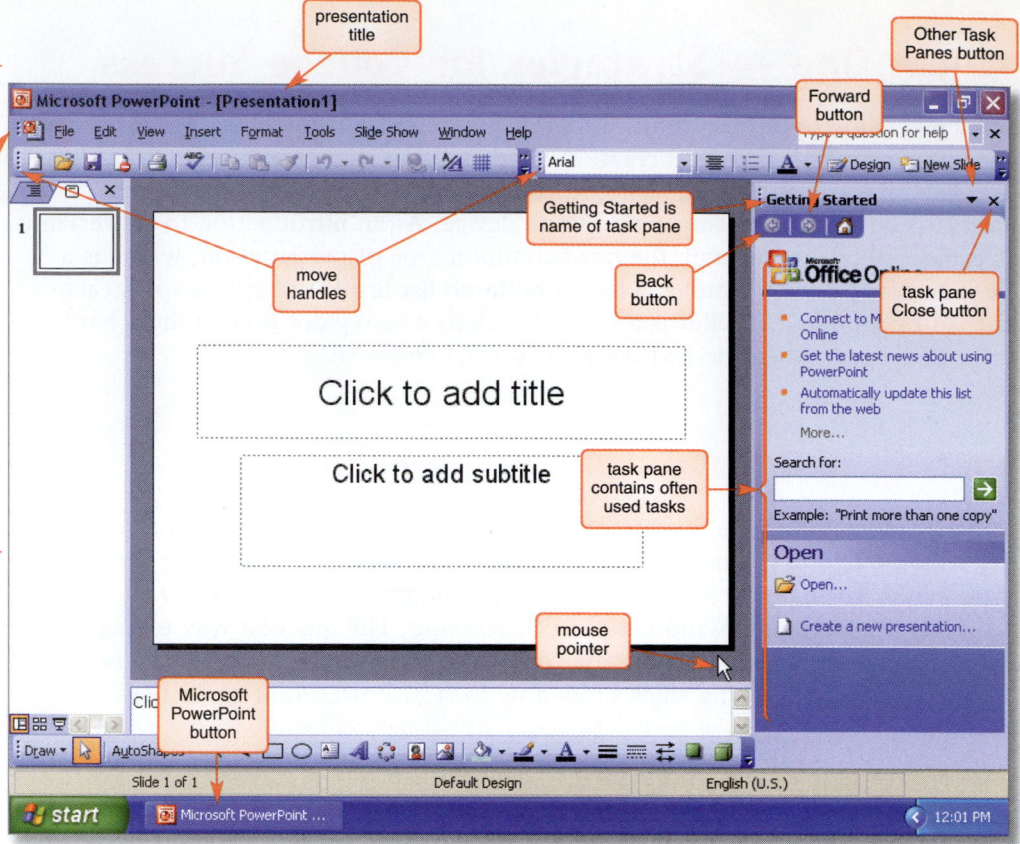

FIGURE 1-4

More About

Task Panes

When you first start
PowerPoint, a small window
called a task pane may be
docked on the right side of
the screen. You can drag a
task pane title bar to float
the pane in your work area
or dock it on either the left
or right side or the top
or bottom of a screen,
depending on your personal
preference.

The screen shown in Figure 1-4 illustrates how the PowerPoint window looks the first time you start PowerPoint after installation on most computers. If the Office Speech Recognition software is installed and active on your computer, then, when you start PowerPoint, the Language bar is displayed on the screen. The **Language bar** contains buttons that allow you to speak commands and dictate text. It usually is located on the right side of the Windows taskbar next to the notification area, and it changes to include the speech recognition functions available in PowerPoint. In this book, the Language bar is closed because it takes up computer resources, and with the Language bar active, the microphone can be turned on accidentally by clicking the Microphone button, causing your computer to act in an unstable manner. For additional information about the Language bar, see page PPT 16 and Appendix B.

As shown in Figure 1-4, PowerPoint displays a task pane on the right side of the screen. A **task pane** is a separate window that enables users to carry out some PowerPoint tasks more efficiently. When you start PowerPoint, it displays the Getting Started task pane, which is a small window that provides commonly used links and commands that allow you to open files, create new files, or search Office-related topics on the Microsoft Web site. In this book, the Getting Started task pane is hidden to allow the maximum screen size to appear in PowerPoint.

At startup, PowerPoint also displays two toolbars on a single row. A **toolbar** contains buttons, boxes, and menus that allow you to perform frequent tasks quickly. To allow for more efficient use of the buttons, the toolbars should appear on two separate rows, instead of sharing a single row. The following steps show how to close the Language bar, close the Getting Started task pane, and instruct PowerPoint to display the toolbars on two separate rows.

To Customize the PowerPoint Window

1

• **If the Language bar appears, right-click it to display a list of commands.**

The Language bar shortcut menu appears (Figure 1-5).

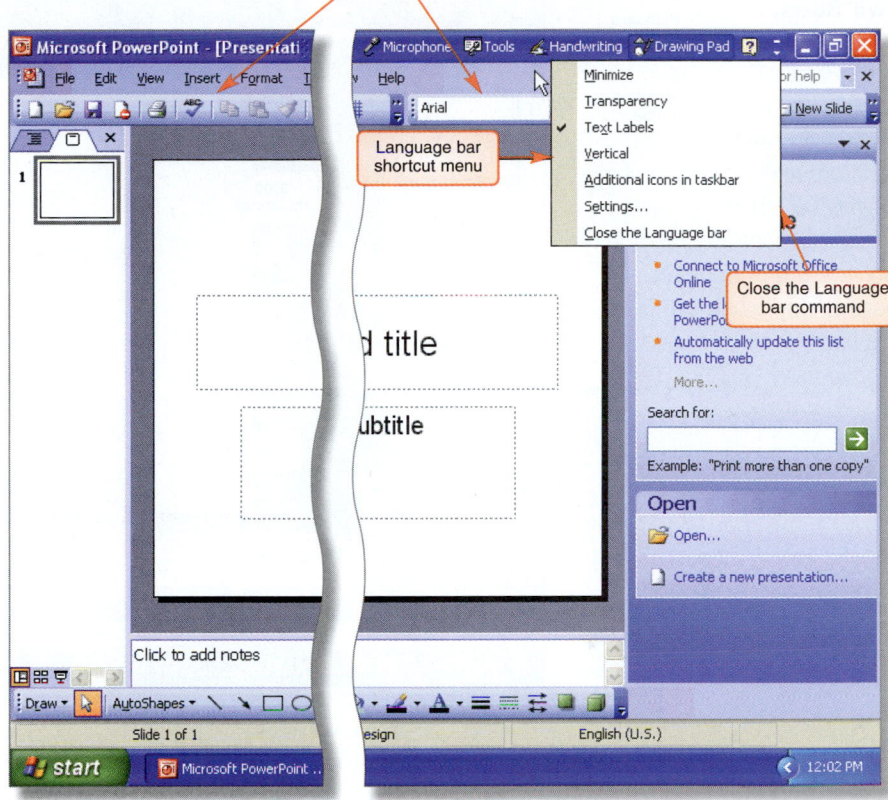

FIGURE 1-5

2

• **Click the Close the Language bar command.**

• **If necessary, click the OK button in the Language Bar dialog box.**

• **Click the Getting Started task pane Close button in the upper-right corner of the task pane.**

• **If the Standard and Formatting toolbars are positioned on the same row, click the Toolbar Options button on the Standard toolbar.**

The Language bar disappears. PowerPoint closes the Getting Started task pane and increases the size of the PowerPoint window. PowerPoint also displays the Toolbar Options list showing the buttons that do not fit on the toolbars when the toolbars are displayed on one row (Figure 1-6).

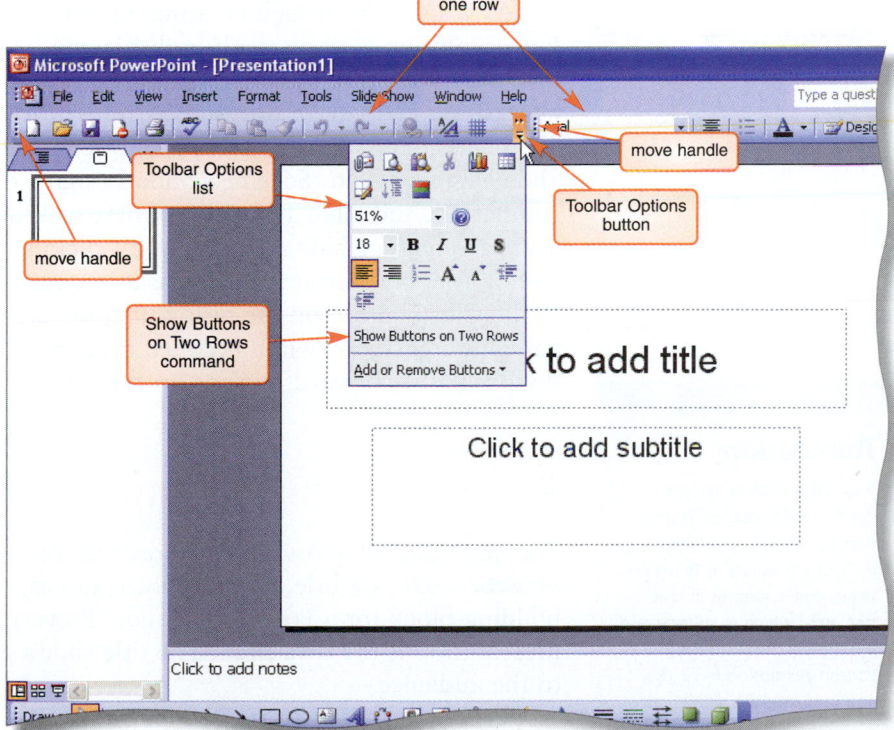

FIGURE 1-6

3

• **Click Show Buttons on Two Rows.**

PowerPoint displays the buttons on two separate rows (Figure 1-7). The Toolbar Options list shown in Figure 1-6 on the previous page is empty because all the buttons are displayed on two rows.

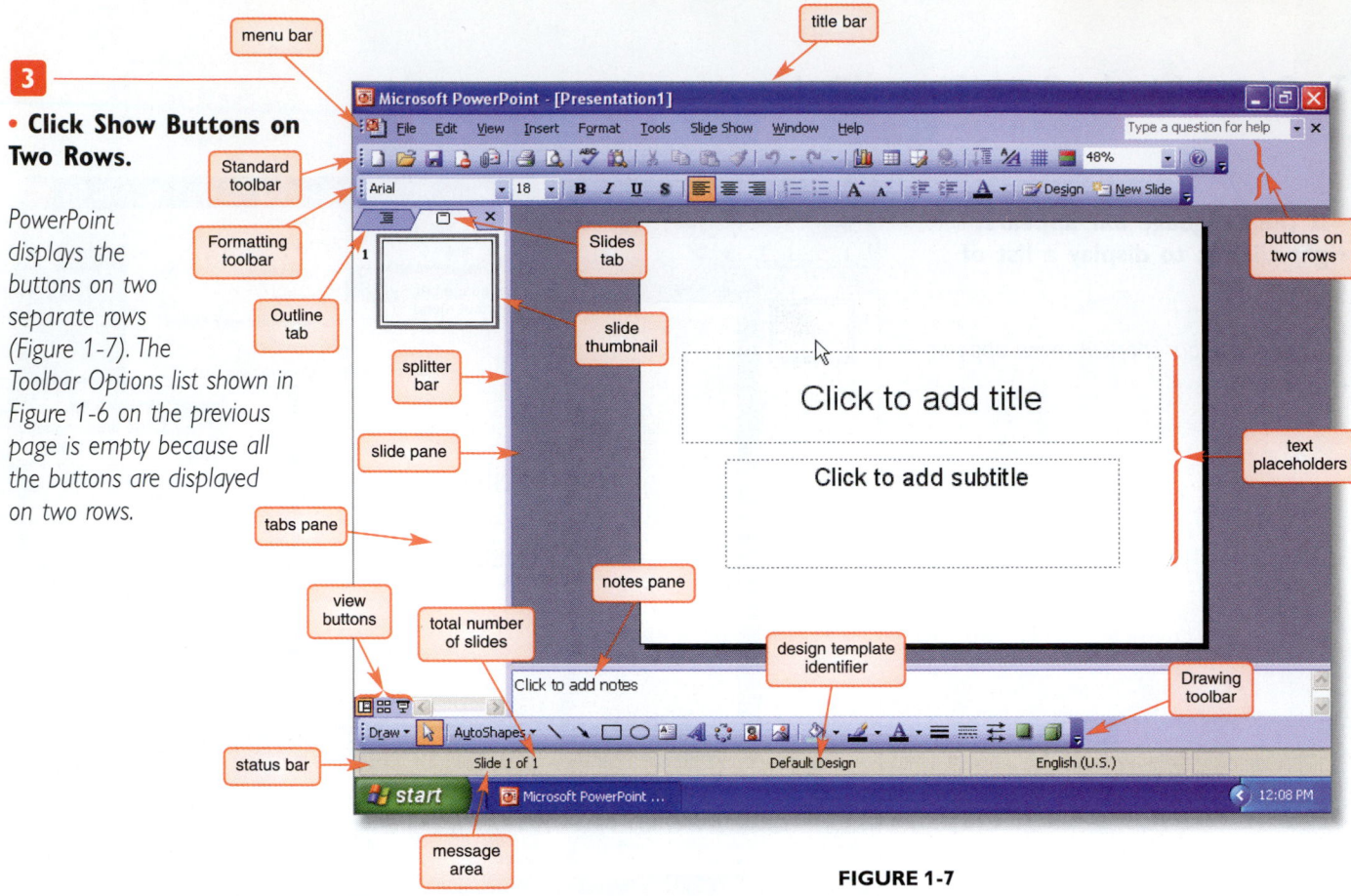

FIGURE 1-7

As you work through creating a presentation, you will find that certain PowerPoint operations result in displaying a task pane. Besides the Getting Started task pane shown in Figure 1-4 on page PPT 8, PowerPoint provides 15 additional task panes: Help, Search Results, Clip Art, Research, Clipboard, New Presentation, Template Help, Shared Workspace, Document Updates, Slide Layout, Slide Design, Slide Design - Color Schemes, Slide Design - Animation Schemes, Custom Animation, and Slide Transition. These task panes are discussed when they are used. You can show or hide a task pane by clicking the Task Pane command on the View menu. You can activate additional task panes by clicking the down arrow to the left of the Close button on the task pane title bar (Figure 1-4) and then selecting a task pane in the list. To switch between task panes that you opened during a session, use the Back and Forward buttons on the left side of the task pane title bar.

The PowerPoint Window

The basic unit of a PowerPoint presentation is a **slide**. A slide contains one or many **objects**, such as a title, text, graphics, tables, charts, and drawings. An object is the building block for a PowerPoint slide. PowerPoint assumes the first slide in a new presentation is the **title slide**. The title slide's purpose is to introduce the presentation to the audience.

In PowerPoint, you have the option of using the PowerPoint default settings or establishing your own. A **default setting** is a particular value for a variable that PowerPoint assigns initially. It controls the placement of objects, the color scheme, the transition between slides, and other slide attributes, and it remains in effect unless you cancel or override it. **Attributes** are the properties or characteristics of an object. For example, if you underline the title of a slide, the title is the object, and the underline is the attribute. When you start PowerPoint, the default **slide layout** is **landscape orientation**, where the slide width is greater than its height. In landscape orientation, the slide size is preset to 10 inches wide and 7.5 inches high. You can change the slide layout to **portrait orientation**, so the slide height is greater than its width, by clicking Page Setup on the File menu. In portrait orientation, the slide width is 7.5 inches, and the height is 10 inches.

When a PowerPoint window is open, its name appears in an icon on the Windows taskbar. The **active application** is the one displaying in the foreground of the desktop. That application's corresponding icon on the Windows taskbar is displayed recessed.

PowerPoint Views

PowerPoint has three main views: normal view, slide sorter view, and slide show view. A **view** is the mode in which the presentation appears on the screen. You may use any or all views when creating a presentation, but you can use only one at a time. You also can select one of these views to be the default view. Change views by clicking one of the view buttons located at the lower-left of the PowerPoint window above the Drawing toolbar (Figure 1-7). The PowerPoint window display varies depending on the view. Some views are graphical while others are textual.

You generally will use normal view and slide sorter view when you are creating a presentation. **Normal view** is composed of three working areas that allow you to work on various aspects of a presentation simultaneously (Figure 1-7). The left side of the screen has a tabs pane that consists of an **Outline tab** and a **Slides tab** that alternate between views of the presentation in an outline of the slide text and a thumbnail, or miniature, view of the slides. You can type the text of the presentation on the Outline tab and easily rearrange bulleted lists, paragraphs, and individual slides. As you type, you can view this text in the **slide pane**, which shows a large view of the current slide on the right side of the window. You also can enter text, graphics, animations, and hyperlinks directly in the slide pane. The **notes pane** at the bottom of the window is an area where you can type notes and additional information. This text can consist of notes to yourself or remarks to share with your audience.

In normal view, you can adjust the width of the slide pane by dragging the **splitter bar** and the height of the notes pane by dragging the pane borders. After you have created at least two slides, **scroll bars**, **scroll arrows**, and **scroll boxes** will be displayed below and to the right of the windows, and you can use them to view different parts of the panes.

Slide sorter view is helpful when you want to see all the slides in the presentation simultaneously. A thumbnail version of each slide is displayed, and you can rearrange their order, add transitions and timings to switch from one slide to the next in a presentation, add and delete slides, and preview animations.

Slide show view fills the entire screen and allows you to see the slide show just as your audience will view it. Transition effects, animation, graphics, movies, and timings are shown as they will appear during an actual presentation.

More About

Sizing Panes

The three panes in normal view allow you to work on all aspects of your presentation simultaneously. You can drag the splitter bar and the pane borders to make each area larger or smaller.

Table 1-1 identifies the view buttons and provides an explanation of each view.

Table 1-1	View Buttons and Functions	
BUTTON	**BUTTON NAME**	**FUNCTION**
	Normal View	Shows three panes: the tabs pane with either the Outline tab or the Slides tab, the slide pane, and the notes pane.
	Slide Sorter View	Shows thumbnail versions of all slides in a presentation. You then can copy, cut, paste, or otherwise change the slide position to modify the presentation. Slide sorter view also is used to add timings, to select animated transitions, and to preview animations.
	Slide Show View	Shows the slides as an electronic presentation on the full screen of your computer's monitor. Looking much like a slide projector display, this view can show you the effect of transitions, build effects, slide timings, and animations.

Placeholders, Text Areas, Mouse Pointer, and Scroll Bars

The PowerPoint window contains elements similar to the document windows in other Microsoft Office applications. Other features are unique to PowerPoint. The main elements are the placeholders, text areas, mouse pointer, and scroll bars.

PLACEHOLDERS **Placeholders** are boxes that are displayed when you create a new slide. All layouts except the Blank slide layout contain placeholders. Depending on the particular slide layout selected, placeholders are displayed for the slide title, body text, charts, tables, organization charts, media clips, and clip art. You type titles, body text, and bulleted lists in **text placeholders**; you place graphic elements in chart placeholders, table placeholders, organizational chart placeholders, and clip art placeholders. A placeholder is considered an **object**, which is a single element of a slide.

TEXT AREAS **Text areas** are surrounded by a dotted outline. The title slide in Figure 1-7 on page PPT 10 has two text areas that contain the text placeholders where you will type the main heading, or title, of a new slide and the subtitle, or other object. Other slides in a presentation may use a layout that contains text areas for a title and bulleted lists.

MOUSE POINTER The **mouse pointer** can become one of several different shapes depending on the task you are performing in PowerPoint and the pointer's location on the screen. The different shapes are discussed when they appear.

SCROLL BARS When you add a second slide to a presentation, a **vertical scroll bar** appears on the right side of the slide pane. PowerPoint allows you to use the scroll bar to move forward or backward through the presentation.

The **horizontal scroll bar** also may be displayed. It is located on the bottom of the slide pane and allows you to display a portion of the slide when the entire slide does not fit on the screen.

Status Bar, Menu Bar, Standard Toolbar, Formatting Toolbar, and Drawing Toolbar

The status bar is displayed at the bottom of the screen above the Windows taskbar (Figure 1-7). The menu bar, Standard toolbar, and Formatting toolbar are displayed at the top of the screen just below the title bar. The Drawing toolbar is displayed above the status bar.

STATUS BAR   Immediately above the Windows taskbar at the bottom of the screen is the status bar. The **status bar** consists of a message area and a presentation design template identifier (Figure 1-7). Generally, the message area shows the current slide number and the total number of slides in the slide show. For example, in Figure 1-7 the message area shows Slide 1 of 1. Slide 1 is the current slide, and of 1 indicates the slide show contains only one slide. The template identifier shows Default Design, which is the template PowerPoint uses initially.

MENU BAR   The **menu bar** is a special toolbar that includes the PowerPoint menu names (Figure 1-8a). Each **menu name** represents a menu of commands that you can use to perform tasks such as retrieving, storing, printing, and manipulating objects in a presentation. When you point to a menu name on the menu bar, the area of the menu bar containing the name changes to a button. To display a menu, such as the Edit menu, click the Edit menu name on the menu bar. A **menu** is a list of commands. If you point to a command on a menu that has an arrow to its right edge, a **submenu** shows another list of commands.

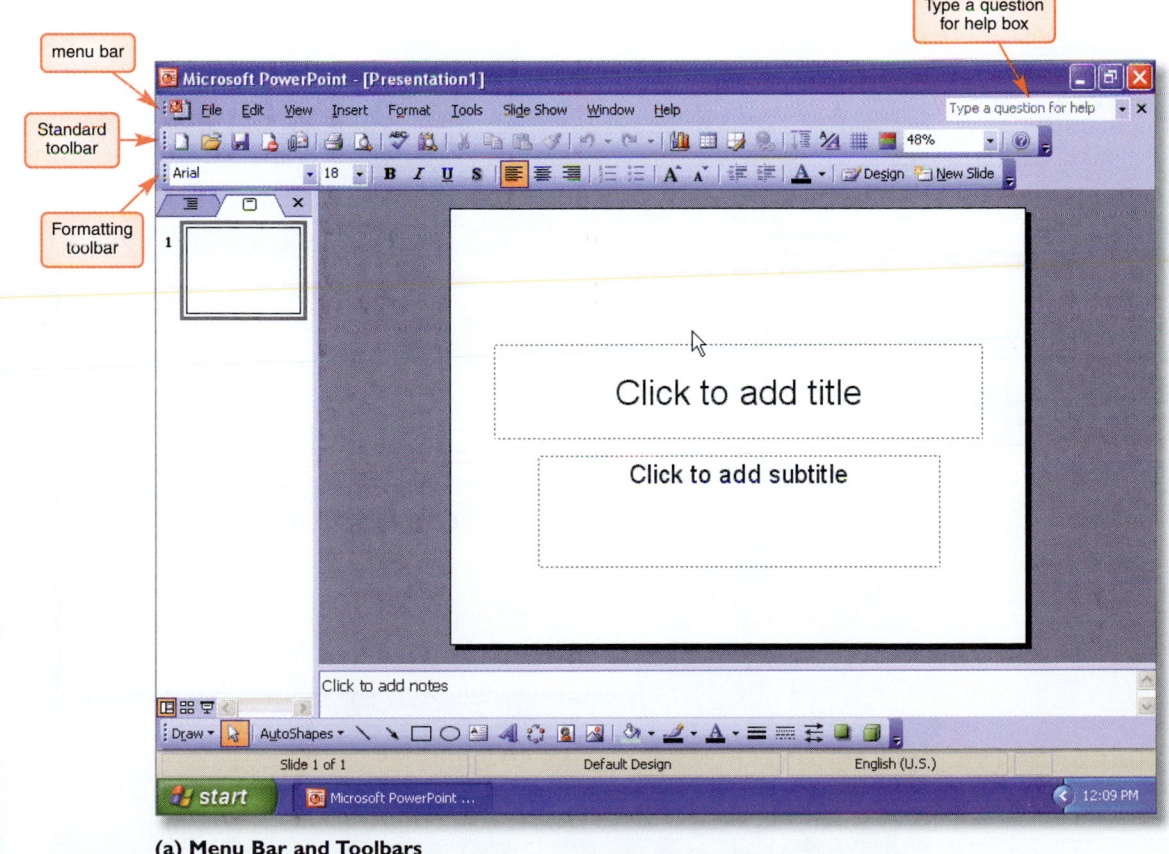

(a) Menu Bar and Toolbars

FIGURE 1-8

When you click a menu name on the menu bar, PowerPoint displays a **short menu** listing the most recently used commands (Figure 1-8b). If you wait a few seconds or click the arrows at the bottom of the short menu, it expands into a full menu. A **full menu** lists all the commands associated with a menu (Figure 1-8c). You also can display a full menu immediately by double-clicking the menu name on the menu bar. In this book, always have PowerPoint show the full menu by using one of the following techniques:

1. Click the menu name on the menu bar and then wait a few seconds.
2. Click the menu name on the menu bar and then click the arrows at the bottom of the short menu.
3. Click the menu name on the menu bar and then point to the arrows at the bottom of the short menu.
4. Double-click the menu name on the menu bar.

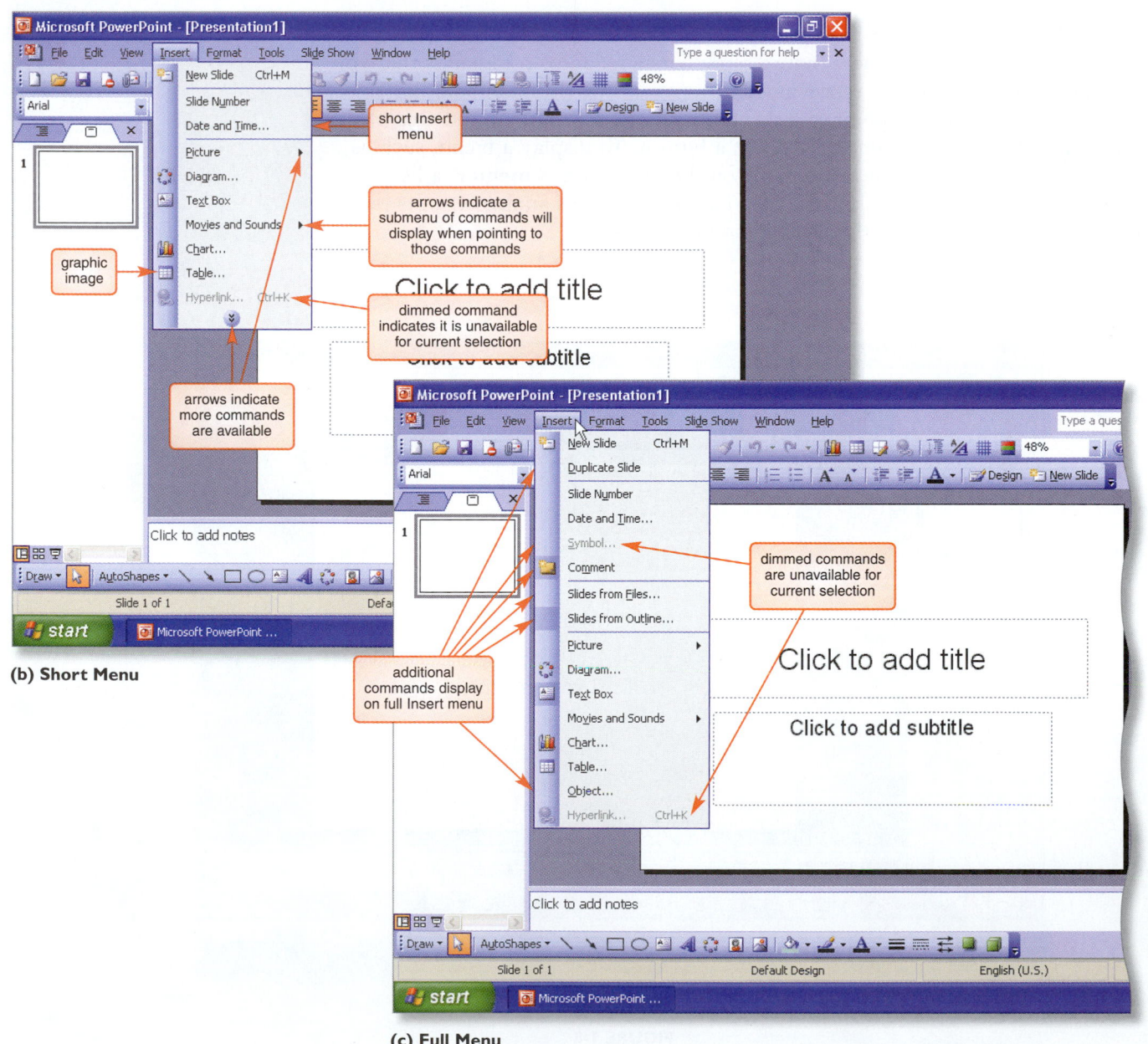

(b) Short Menu

(c) Full Menu

FIGURE 1-8 *(continued)*

Both short and full menus display some **dimmed commands** that appear gray, or dimmed, instead of black, which indicates they are not available for the current selection. A command with a dark gray shading to the left of it on a full menu is a **hidden command** because it does not appear on a short menu. As you use PowerPoint, it automatically personalizes the short menus for you based on how often you use commands. That is, as you use hidden commands, PowerPoint *unhides* them and places them on the short menu.

The menu bar can change to include other menu names depending on the type of work you are doing in PowerPoint. For example, if you are adding a chart to a slide, Data and Chart menu names are added to the menu bar with commands that reflect charting options.

STANDARD, FORMATTING, AND DRAWING TOOLBARS   The **Standard toolbar** (Figure 1-9a), **Formatting toolbar** (Figure 1-9b), and **Drawing toolbar** (Figure 1-9c on the next page) contain buttons and boxes that allow you to perform frequent tasks more quickly than when using the menu bar. For example, to print a slide show, you click the Print button on the Standard toolbar. Each button has an image on the button face that helps you remember the button's function. Also, when you move the mouse pointer over a button or box, the name of the button or box appears below it in a ScreenTip. A **ScreenTip** is a short on-screen note associated with the object to which you are pointing. For examples of ScreenTips, see Figures 1-3 and 1-13 on pages PPT 7 and PPT 19.

Figure 1-9 illustrates the Standard, Formatting, and Drawing toolbars and describes the functions of the buttons. Each of the buttons and boxes will be explained in detail when they are used.

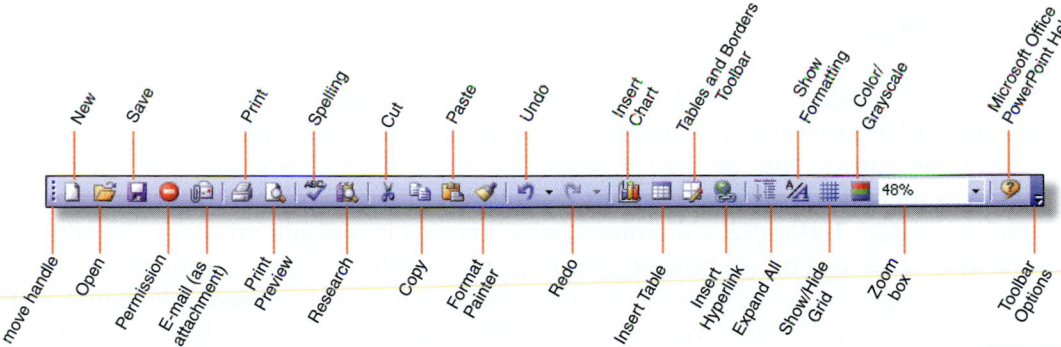

(a) Standard Toolbar

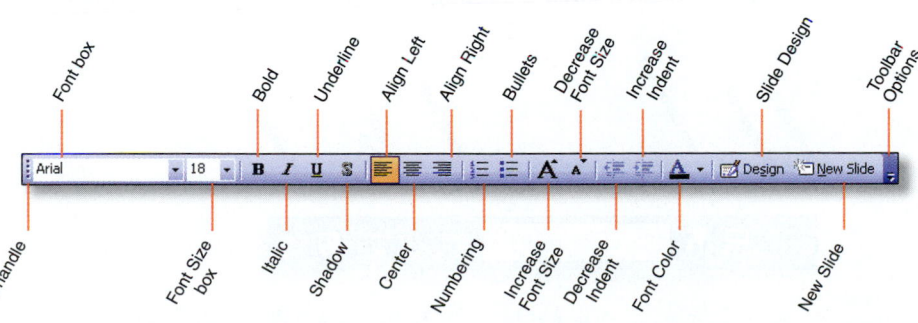

(b) Formatting Toolbar

FIGURE 1-9

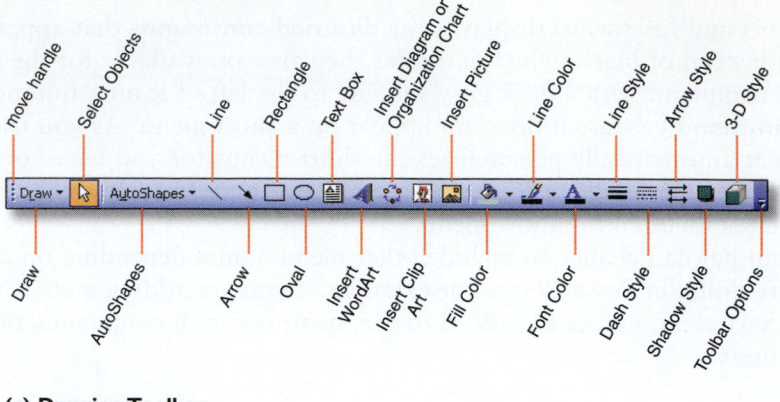

(c) Drawing Toolbar

FIGURE 1-9 *(continued)*

PowerPoint has several additional toolbars you can display by pointing to Toolbars on the View menu and then clicking the respective name on the Toolbars submenu. You also may display a toolbar by pointing to a toolbar and right-clicking to display a shortcut menu, which lists the available toolbars. A **shortcut menu** contains a list of commands or items that relate to the item to which you are pointing when you right-click.

Speech Recognition

With the **Office Speech Recognition software** installed and a microphone, you can speak the names of toolbar buttons, menus, menu commands, list items, alerts, and dialog box controls, such as OK and Cancel. You also can dictate words to fill the placeholders. To indicate whether you want to speak commands or dictate placeholder entries, you use the Language bar. The Language bar can be in one of four states: (1) **restored**, which means it is displayed somewhere in the PowerPoint window (Figure 1-10a); (2) **minimized**, which means it is displayed on the Windows taskbar (Figure 1-10b); (3) **hidden**, which means you do not see it on the screen but it will be displayed the next time you start your computer; (4) **closed**, which means it is hidden permanently until you enable it. If the Language bar is hidden or closed and you want it to display, then do the following:

1. Right-click an open area on the Windows taskbar at the bottom of the screen.
2. Point to Toolbars and then click Language bar on the Toolbars submenu.

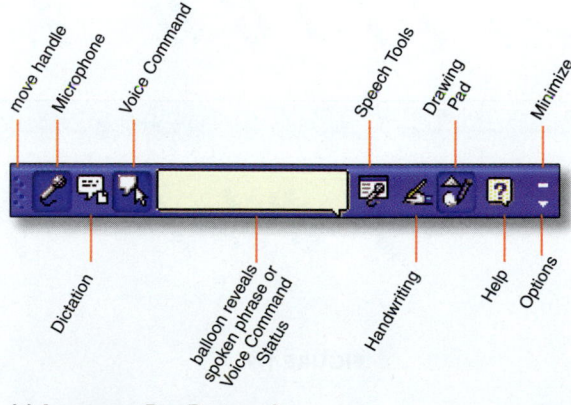

(a) Language Bar Restored

FIGURE 1-10

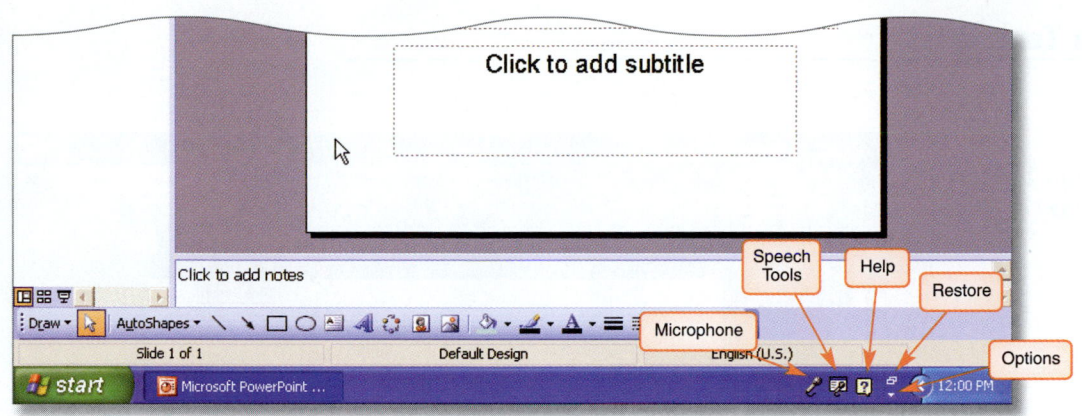

(b) Language Bar Minimized on Windows Taskbar

FIGURE 1-10 *(continued)*

If the Language bar command is dimmed on the Toolbars submenu or if the Speech command is dimmed on the Tools menu, the Office Speech Recognition software is not installed.

In this book, the Language bar does not appear in the figures. If you want to close the Language bar so that your screen is identical to what you see in the book, right-click the Language bar and then click Close the Language bar on the shortcut menu.

Additional information about the speech recognition capabilities of PowerPoint is available in Appendix B.

Choosing a Design Template

A **design template** provides consistency in design and color throughout the entire presentation. It determines the color scheme, font and font size, and layout of a presentation. PowerPoint has three Slide Design task panes that allow you to choose and change the appearance of slides in your presentation. The **Slide Design task pane** shows a variety of styles. You can alter the colors used in the design templates by using the **Slide Design – Color Schemes task pane**. In addition, you can animate elements of your presentation by using the **Slide Design – Animation Schemes task pane**.

In this project, you will select a particular design template by using the Slide Design task pane. The top section of the task pane, labeled Used in This Presentation, shows the template currently used in the slide show. PowerPoint uses the **Default Design** template until you select a different style. When you place your mouse over a template, the name of the template appears. Once a PowerPoint slide show has been created on the computer, the next section of the task pane displayed is the Recently Used templates. This area shows the four templates you have used in your newest slide shows. The Available For Use area shows additional templates. The templates are displayed in alphabetical order in the two columns.

You want to change the template for this presentation from the Default Design to Profile. The steps on the next page apply the Profile design template.

To Choose a Design Template

1

• **Point to the Slide Design button on the Formatting toolbar (Figure 1-11).**

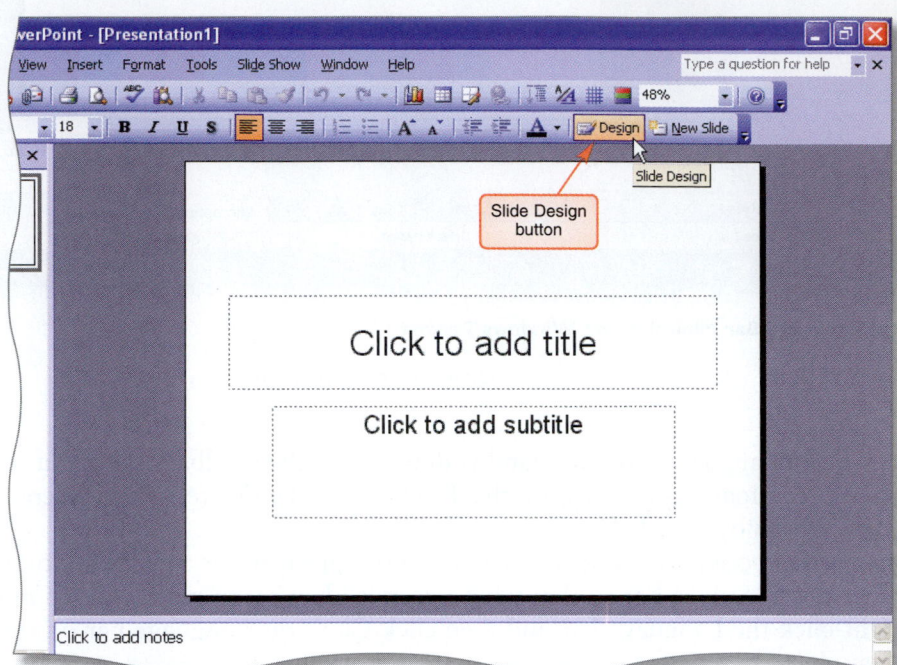

FIGURE 1-11

2

• **Click the Slide Design button and then point to the down scroll arrow in the Apply a design template list.**

The Slide Design task pane appears (Figure 1-12). The Apply a design template list shows thumbnail views of numerous design templates. Your list may look different depending on your computer. The Default Design template is highlighted in the Used in This Presentation area. Other templates display in the Available For Use area and possibly in the Recently Used area. The Close button in the Slide Design task pane can be used to close the task pane if you do not want to apply a new template.

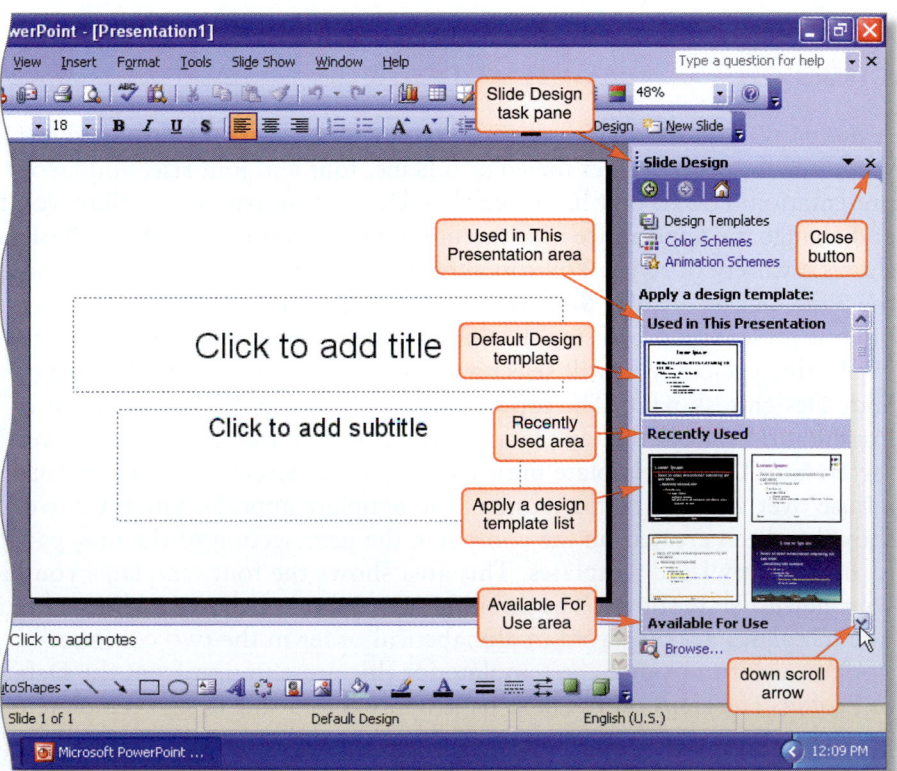

FIGURE 1-12

3

• **Click the down scroll arrow to scroll through the list of design templates until Profile appears in the Available For Use area. Point to the Profile template.**

The Profile template is selected, as indicated by the blue box around the template and the arrow button on the right side (Figure 1-13). PowerPoint provides 45 templates in the Available For Use area. Additional templates are available on the Microsoft Office Online Web site. A ScreenTip shows the template's name. Your system may display the ScreenTip, Profile.pot, which indicates the design template's file extension (.pot).

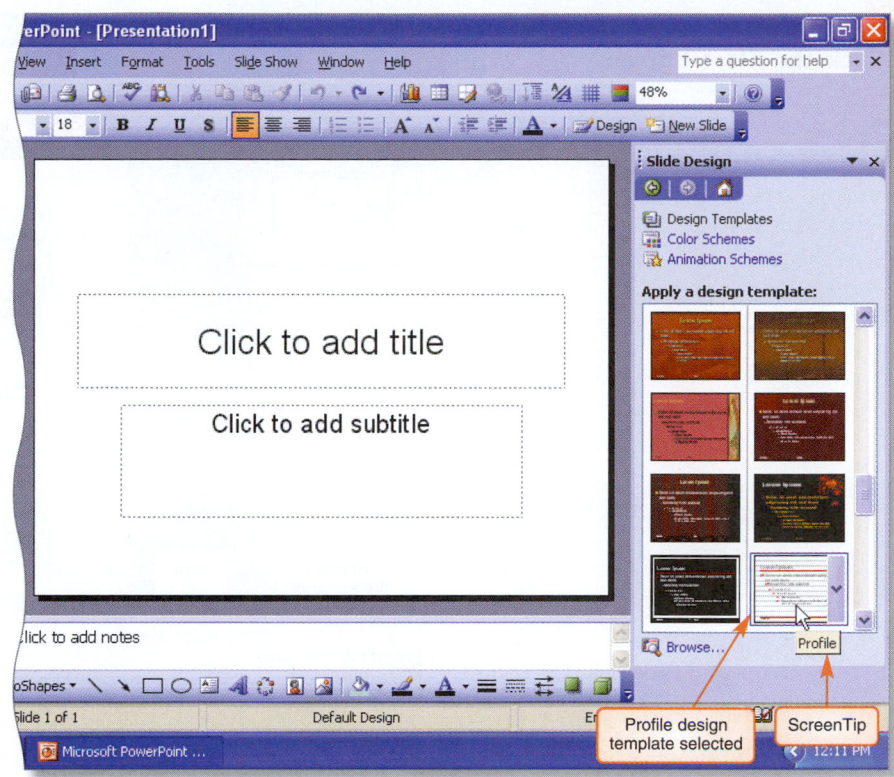

FIGURE 1-13

4

• **Click Profile.**

• **Point to the Close button in the Slide Design task pane.**

The template is applied to Slide 1, as shown in the slide pane and Slides tab (Figure 1-14).

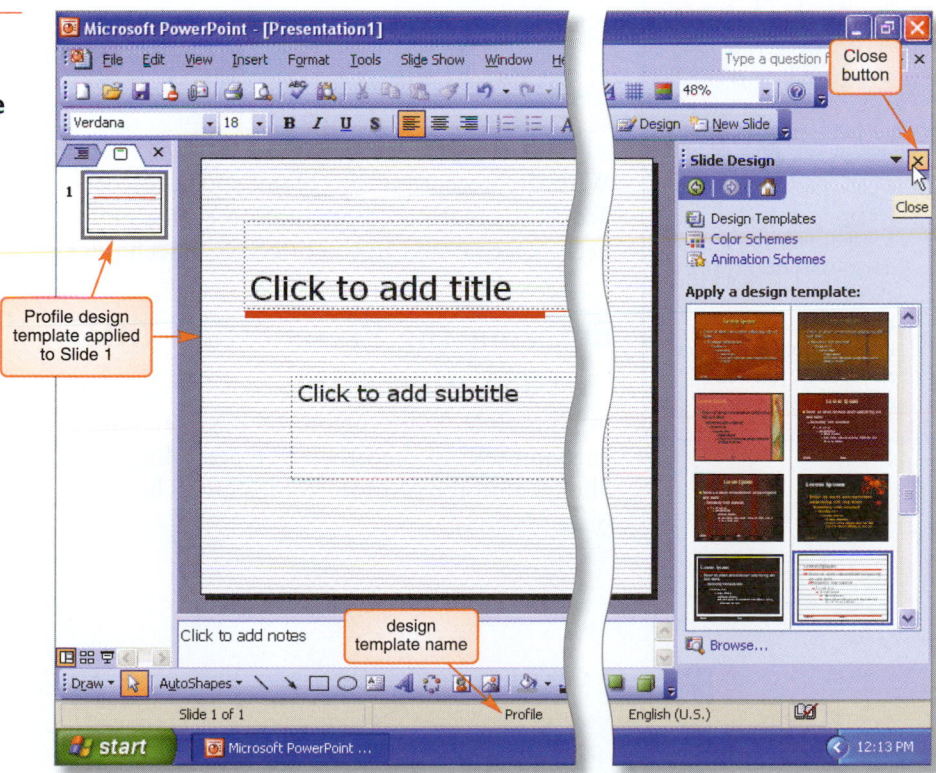

FIGURE 1-14

5

• **Click the Close button.**

Slide 1 is displayed in normal view with the Profile design template (Figure 1-15).

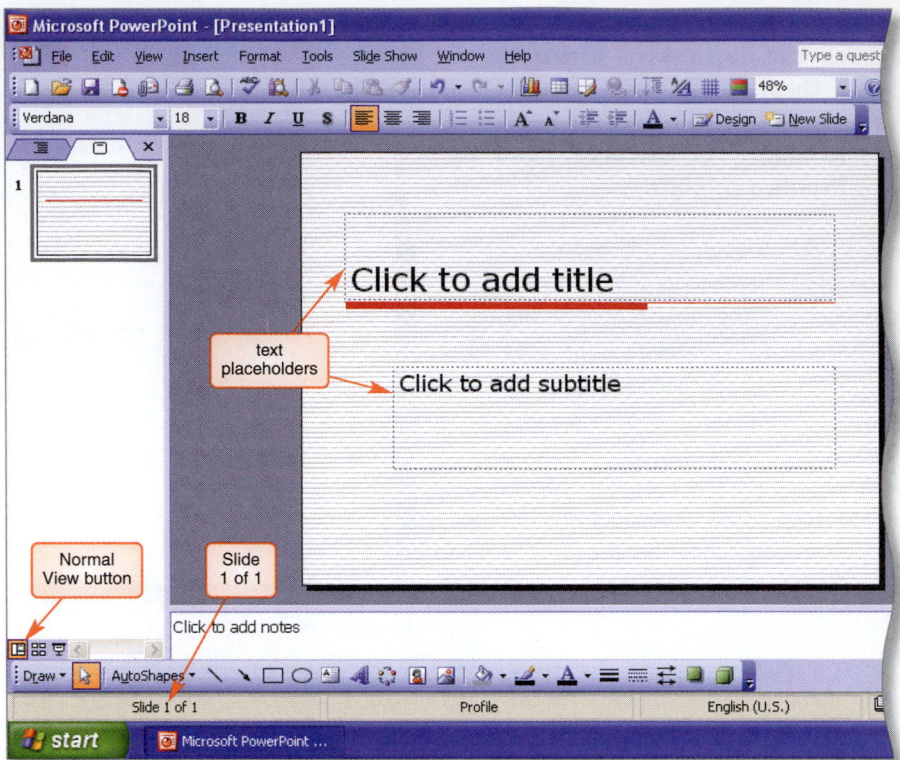

FIGURE 1-15

Creating a Title Slide

With the exception of a blank slide, PowerPoint assumes every new slide has a title. To make creating a presentation easier, any text you type after a new slide appears becomes title text in the title text placeholder.

Entering the Presentation Title

The presentation title for Project 1 is Strategies for College Success. To enter text in your slide, you type on the keyboard or speak into the microphone. As you begin entering text in the title text placeholder, the title text is displayed immediately in the Slide 1 thumbnail in the Slides tab. The following steps create the title slide for this presentation.

To Enter the Presentation Title

1

• **Click the label, Click to add title, located inside the title text placeholder.**

*The insertion point is in the title text placeholder (Figure 1-16). The **insertion point** is a blinking vertical line (|), which indicates where the next character will display. The mouse pointer changes to an I-beam. A **selection rectangle** appears around the title text placeholder. The placeholder is selected as indicated by the border and sizing handles displaying on the edges.*

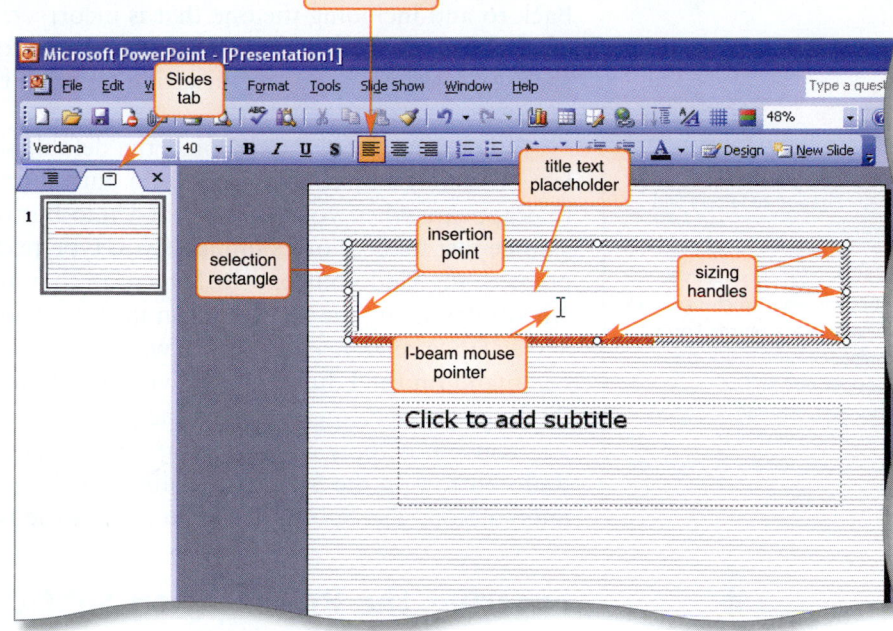

FIGURE 1-16

2

• **Type** Strategies for College Success **in the title text placeholder. Do not press the ENTER key.**

The title text, Strategies for College Success, appears on two lines in the title text placeholder and in the Slides tab (Figure 1-17). The insertion point appears after the final letter s in Success. The title text is displayed aligned left in the placeholder with the default text attributes of the Verdana font and font size 40.

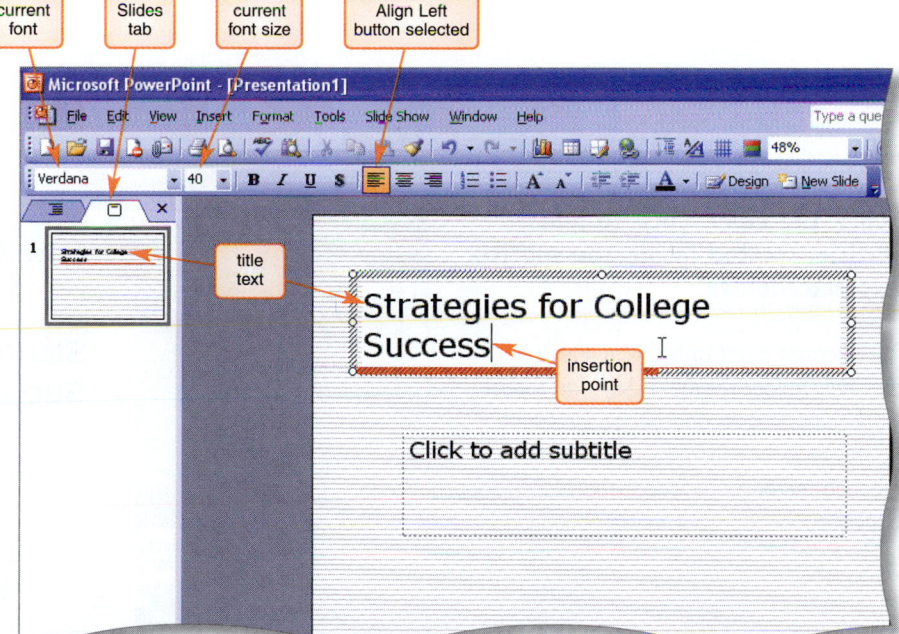

FIGURE 1-17

Other Ways

1. In Dictation mode, say "Strategies for College Success"

PowerPoint **line wraps** text that exceeds the width of the placeholder. One of PowerPoint's features is **text AutoFit**. If you are creating a slide and need to squeeze an extra line in the text placeholder, PowerPoint will prompt you to resize the existing text in the placeholder so the spillover text will fit on the slide.

Correcting a Mistake When Typing

If you type the wrong letter, press the BACKSPACE key to erase all the characters back to and including the one that is incorrect. If you mistakenly press the ENTER key after typing the title and the insertion point is on the new line, simply press the BACKSPACE key to return the insertion point to the right of the letter s in the word Success.

When you install PowerPoint, the default setting allows you to reverse up to the last 20 changes by clicking the Undo button on the Standard toolbar. The ScreenTip that appears when you point to the Undo button changes to indicate the type of change just made. For example, if you type text in the title text placeholder and then point to the Undo button, the ScreenTip that appears is Undo Typing. For clarity, when referencing the Undo button in this project, the name displaying in the ScreenTip is referenced. Another way to reverse changes is to click the Undo command on the Edit menu. As with the Undo button, the Undo command reflects the last type of change made to the presentation.

You can reapply a change that you reversed with the Undo button by clicking the Redo button on the Standard toolbar. Clicking the Redo button reverses the last undo action. The ScreenTip name reflects the type of reversal last performed.

Entering the Presentation Subtitle

The next step in creating the title slide is to enter the subtitle text into the subtitle text placeholder. Complete the following steps to enter the presentation subtitle.

To Enter the Presentation Subtitle

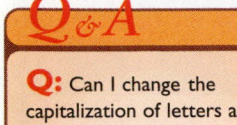

Q: Can I change the capitalization of letters and words?

A: Yes. Simply select the text you want to change, click Change Case on the Format menu, and then click the desired option. For example, you can change all uppercase letters to lowercase letters or capitalize the first letter in each word.

1

• **Click the label, Click to add subtitle, located inside the subtitle text placeholder.**

The insertion point appears in the subtitle text placeholder (Figure 1-18). The mouse pointer changes to an I-beam, indicating the mouse is in a text placeholder. The selection rectangle indicates the placeholder is selected.

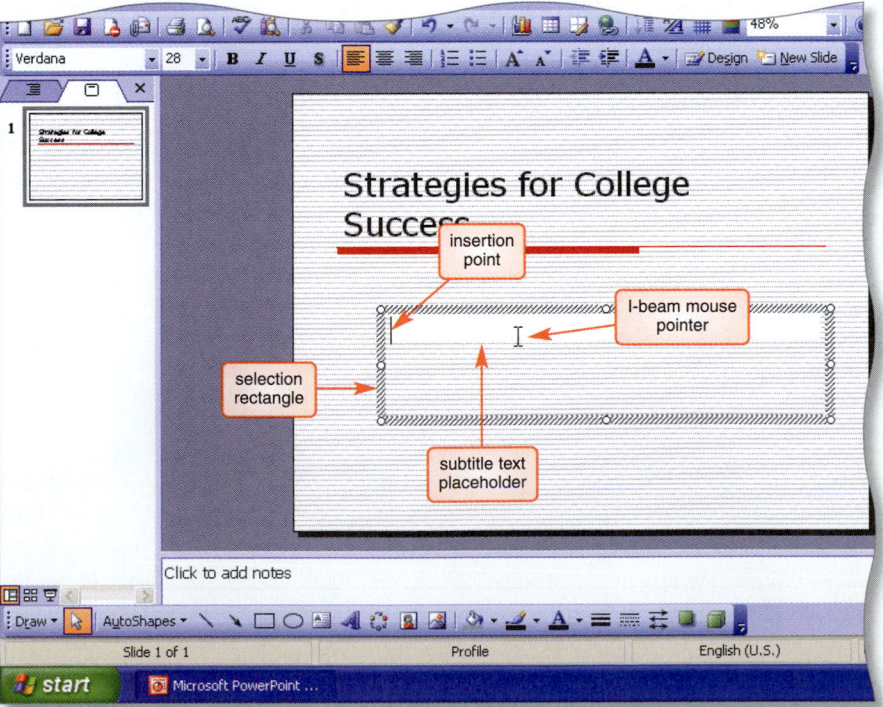

FIGURE 1-18

2

• **Type** Presented by **and then press the** ENTER **key.**

• **Type** Lakemore Academic Skills Center **but do not press the** ENTER **key.**

The subtitle text appears in the subtitle text placeholder and the Slides tab (Figure 1-19). The insertion point appears after the letter r in Center. A red wavy line appears below the word, Lakemore, to indicate a possible spelling error.

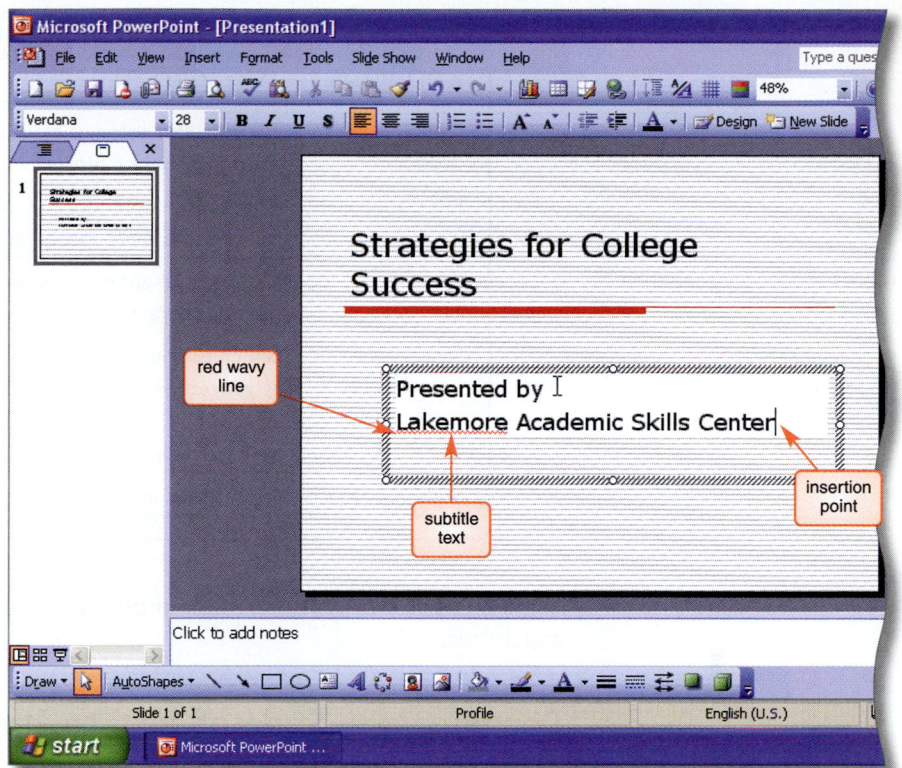

FIGURE 1-19

After pressing the ENTER key in Step 2, PowerPoint created a new line, which is the second paragraph in the placeholder. A **paragraph** is a segment of text with the same format that begins when you press the ENTER key and ends when you press the ENTER key again.

Other Ways

1. In Dictation mode, say "Presented by, New Line, Lakemore Academic Skills Center"

Text Attributes

This presentation uses the Profile design template. Each design template has its own text attributes. A **text attribute** is a characteristic of the text, such as font, font size, font style, or text color. You can adjust text attributes any time before, during, or after you type the text. Recall that a design template determines the color scheme, font and font size, and layout of a presentation. Most of the time, you use the design template's text attributes and color scheme. Occasionally, you may want to change the way a presentation looks, however, and still keep a particular design template. PowerPoint gives you that flexibility. You can use the design template and change the font and the font's color, effects, size, and style. Text may have one or more font styles and effects simultaneously. Table 1-2 on the next page explains the different text attributes available in PowerPoint.

More About

Text Attributes

The Microsoft Web site contains a comprehensive glossary of typography terms. The information includes a diagram illustrating text attributes. For more information, visit the PowerPoint 2003 More About Web page (scsite.com/ppt2003/more) and then click Attributes.

Table 1-2	Design Template Text Attributes
ATTRIBUTE	**DESCRIPTION**
Color	Defines the color of text. Printing text in color requires a color printer or plotter.
Effects	Effects include underline, shadow, emboss, superscript, and subscript. Effects can be applied to most fonts.
Font	Defines the appearance and shape of letters, numbers, and special characters.
Size	Specifies the height of characters on the screen. Character size is gauged by a measurement system called points. A single point is about 1/72 of an inch in height. Thus, a character with a point size of 18 is about 18/72 (or 1/4) of an inch in height.
Style	Font styles include regular, bold, italic, and bold italic.

The next two sections explain how to change the font size and font style attributes.

Changing the Style of Text to Italic

Text font styles include plain, italic, bold, shadowed, and underlined. PowerPoint allows you to use one or more text font styles in a presentation. The following steps add emphasis to the first line of the subtitle text by changing regular text to italic text.

To Change the Text Font Style to Italic

1

• **Triple-click the paragraph, Presented by, in the subtitle text placeholder, and then point to the Italic button on the Formatting toolbar.**

The paragraph, Presented by, is highlighted (Figure 1-20). The Italic button is surrounded by a blue box. You select an entire paragraph quickly by triple-clicking any text within the paragraph.

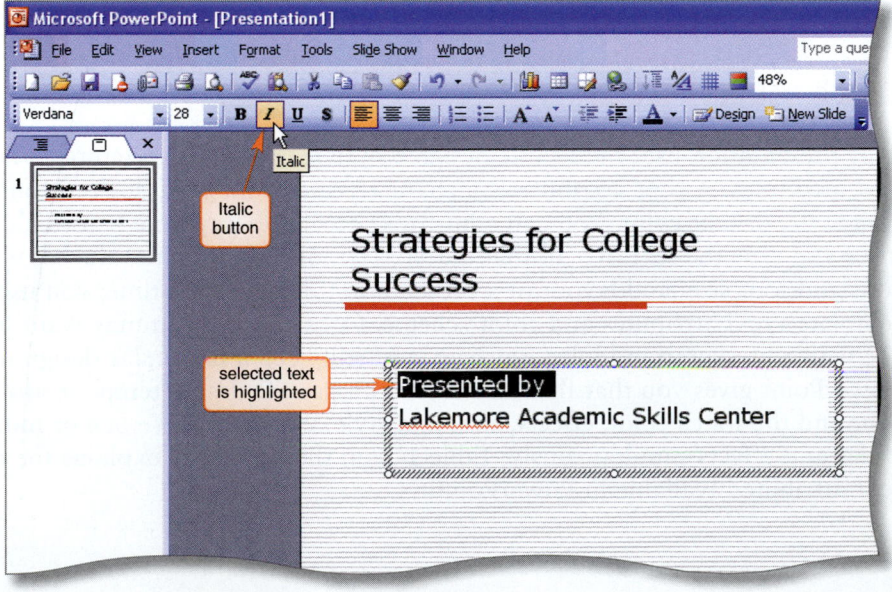

FIGURE 1-20

2

• **Click the Italic button.**

The text is italicized on the slide and the slide thumbnail (Figure 1-21).

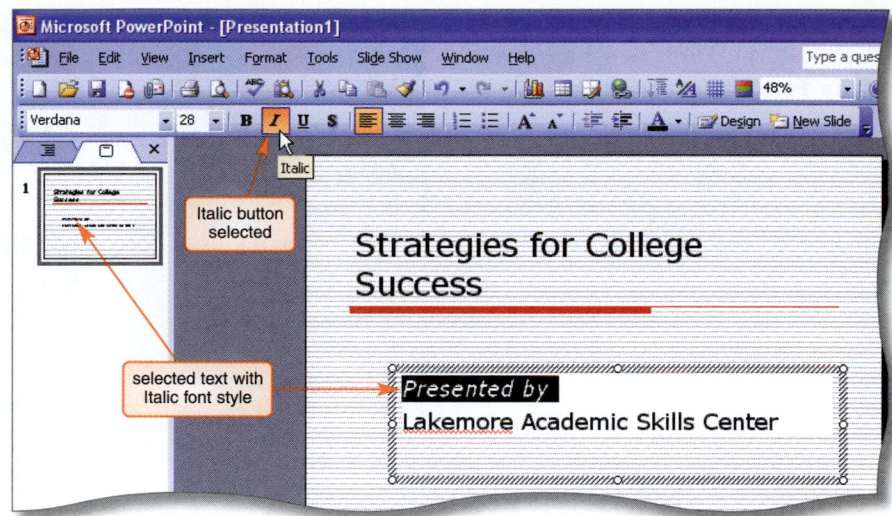

FIGURE 1-21

To remove the italic style from text, select the italicized text and then click the Italic button. As a result, the Italic button is not selected, and the text does not have the italic font style.

Changing the Font Size

The Profile design template default font size is 40 point for title text and 28 point for body text. A point is 1/72 of an inch in height. Thus, a character with a point size of 40 is 40/72 (or 5/9) of an inch in height. Slide 1 requires you to increase the font size for the paragraph, Lakemore Academic Skills Center. The following steps illustrate how to increase the font size.

To Increase Font Size

1

• **Position the mouse pointer in the paragraph, Lakemore Academic Skills Center, and then triple-click.**

PowerPoint selects the entire paragraph (Figure 1-22).

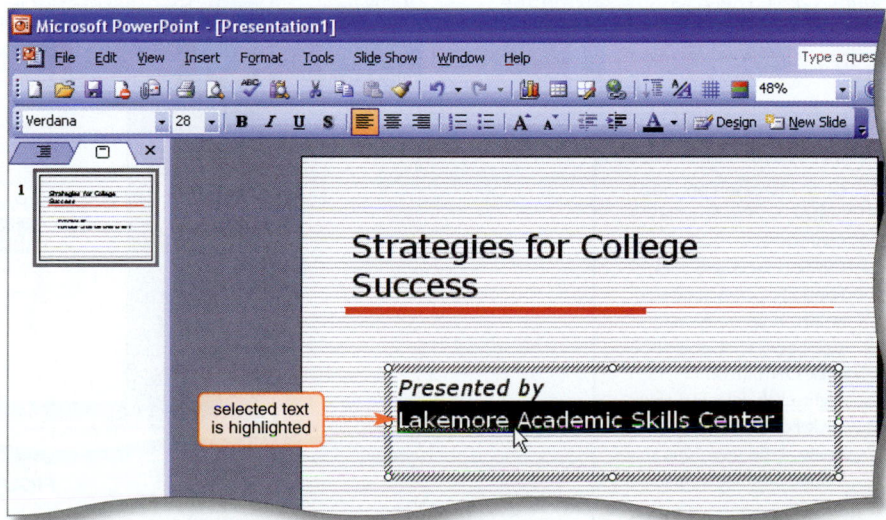

FIGURE 1-22

2

• **Point to the Font Size box arrow on the Formatting toolbar.**

*The ScreenTip shows the words, Font Size (Figure 1-23). The **Font Size box** is surrounded by a box and indicates that the subtitle text is 28 point.*

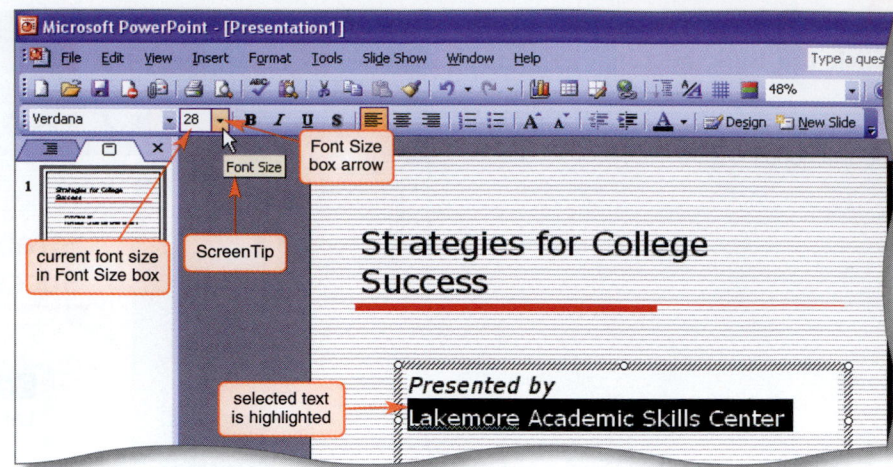

FIGURE 1-23

3

• **Click the Font Size box arrow, click the Font Size box scroll bar, and then point to 32 in the Font Size list.**

When you click the Font Size box, a list of available font sizes is displayed in the Font Size list (Figure 1-24). The font sizes displayed depend on the current font, which is Verdana. Font size 32 is highlighted.

FIGURE 1-24

4

• **Click 32.**

The font size of the subtitle text, Lakemore Academic Skills Center, increases to 32 point (Figure 1-25). The Font Size box on the Formatting toolbar shows 32, indicating the selected text has a font size of 32.

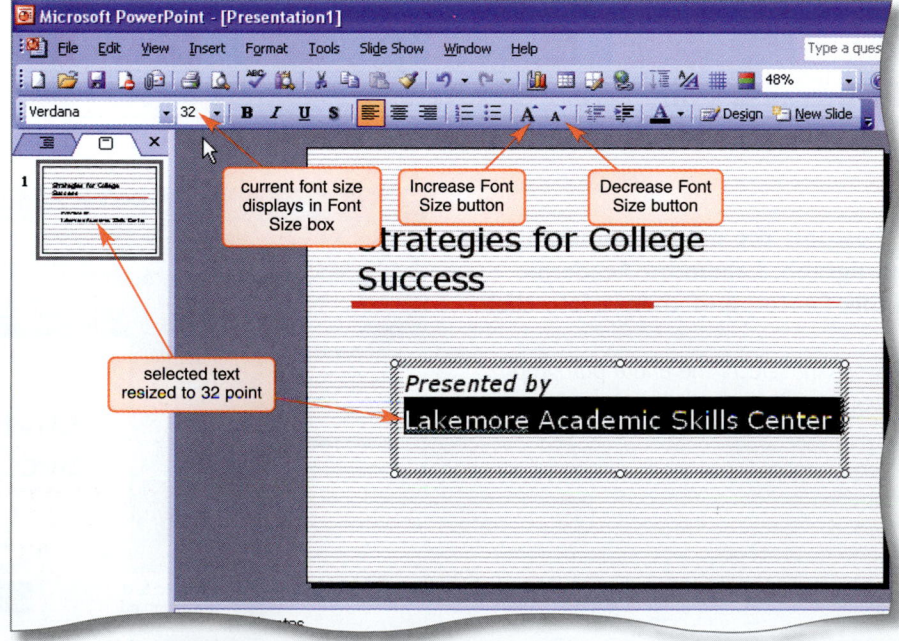

FIGURE 1-25

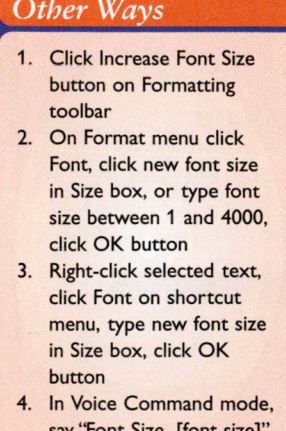

Other Ways

1. Click Increase Font Size button on Formatting toolbar
2. On Format menu click Font, click new font size in Size box, or type font size between 1 and 4000, click OK button
3. Right-click selected text, click Font on shortcut menu, type new font size in Size box, click OK button
4. In Voice Command mode, say "Font Size, [font size]"

The Increase Font Size button on the Formatting toolbar (Figure 1-25) increases the font size in preset increments each time you click the button. If you need to decrease the font size, click the Font Size box arrow and then select a size smaller than 32. The Decrease Font Size button on the Formatting toolbar (Figure 1-25) also decreases the font size in preset increments each time you click the button.

Saving the Presentation on a Floppy Disk

While you are building a presentation, the computer stores it in memory. It is important to save the presentation frequently because the presentation will be lost if the computer is turned off or you lose electrical power. Another reason to save your work is that if you run out of lab time before completing your project, you may finish the project later without starting over. Therefore, always save any presentation you will use later on a floppy disk or hard disk. A saved presentation is referred to as a **file**. Before you continue with Project 1, save the work completed thus far. The following steps illustrate how to save a presentation on a floppy disk in drive A using the Save button on the Standard toolbar.

To Save a Presentation on a Floppy Disk

1

• With a formatted floppy disk in drive A, click the Save button on the Standard toolbar.

The Save As dialog box is displayed (Figure 1-26). The default folder, My Documents, appears in the Save in box. Strategies for College Success appears highlighted in the File name text box because PowerPoint uses the words in the title text placeholder as the default file name. Presentation appears in the Save as type box. The buttons on the top and on the side are used to select folders and change the appearance of file names and other information.

Q&A

Q: Does PowerPoint save files automatically?

A: Yes. Every 10 minutes PowerPoint saves a copy of your presentation. To check or change the save interval, click Options on the Tools menu and then click the Save tab. Click the Save AutoRe cover info every check box and then type the specific time in the minutes box.

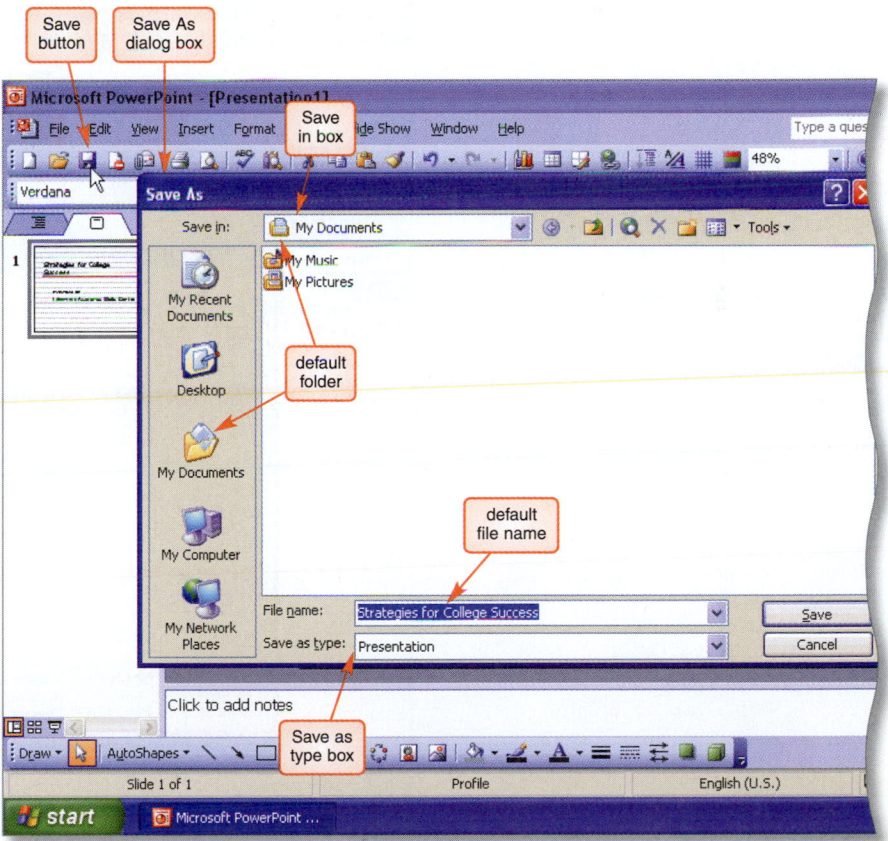

FIGURE 1-26

2

• **Type** College Success **in the File name text box. Do not press the ENTER key after typing the file name.**

• **Click the Save in box arrow.**

The name, College Success, appears in the File name text box (Figure 1-27). A file name can be up to 255 characters and can include spaces. The Save in list shows a list of locations in which to save a presentation. Your list may look different depending on the configuration of your system. Clicking the Cancel button closes the Save As dialog box.

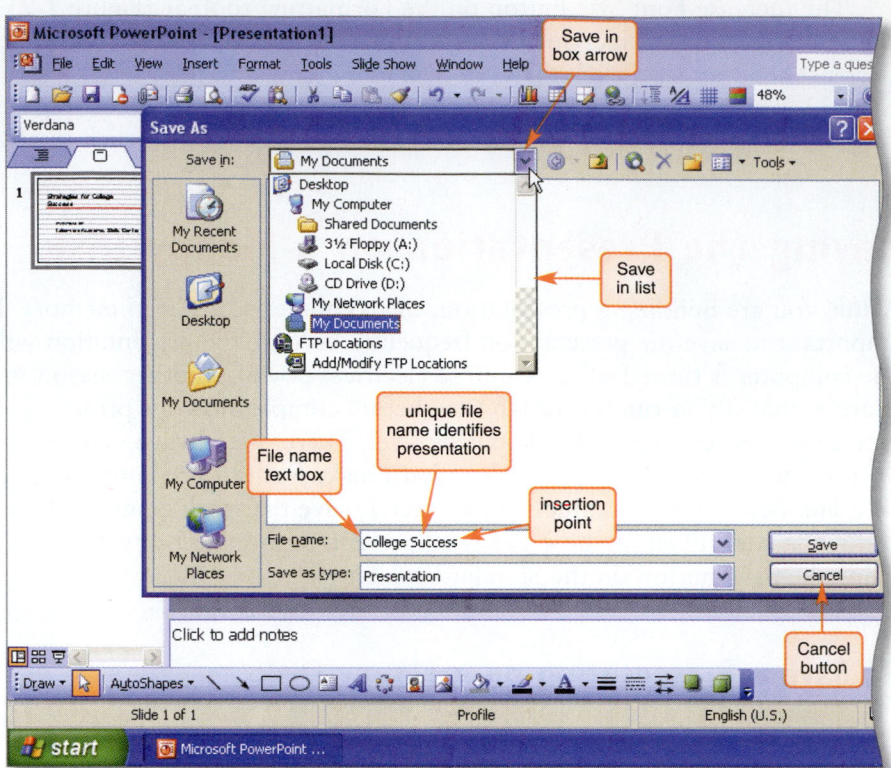

FIGURE 1-27

3

• **Click 3½ Floppy (A:) in the Save in list.**

Drive A becomes the selected drive (Figure 1-28).

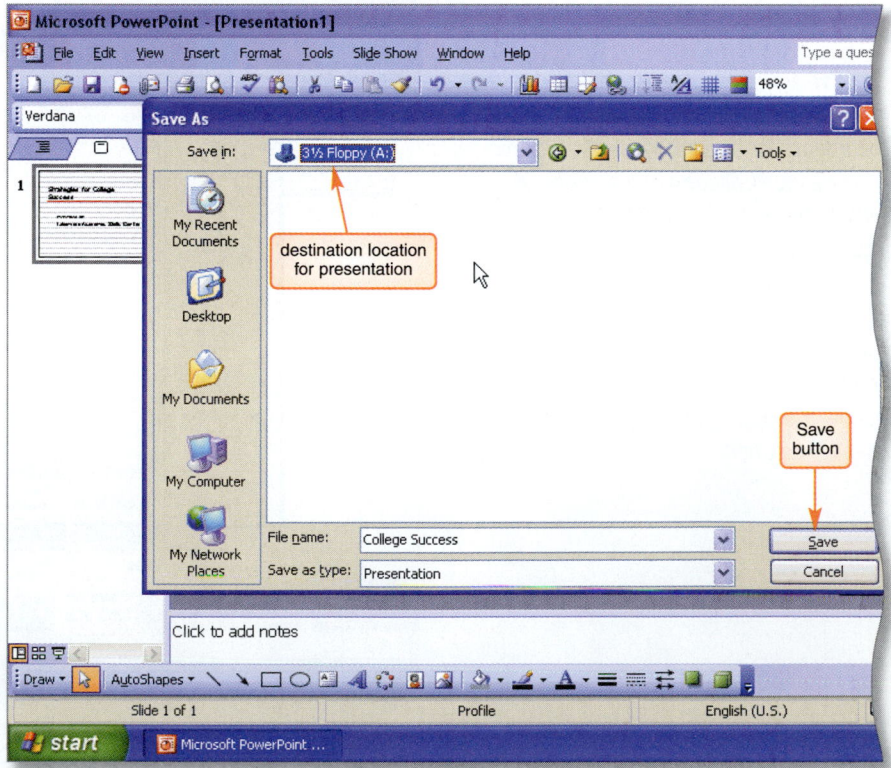

FIGURE 1-28

4

• **Click the Save button in the Save As dialog box.**

PowerPoint saves the presentation on the floppy disk in drive A. The title bar shows the file name used to save the presentation, College Success (Figure 1-29).

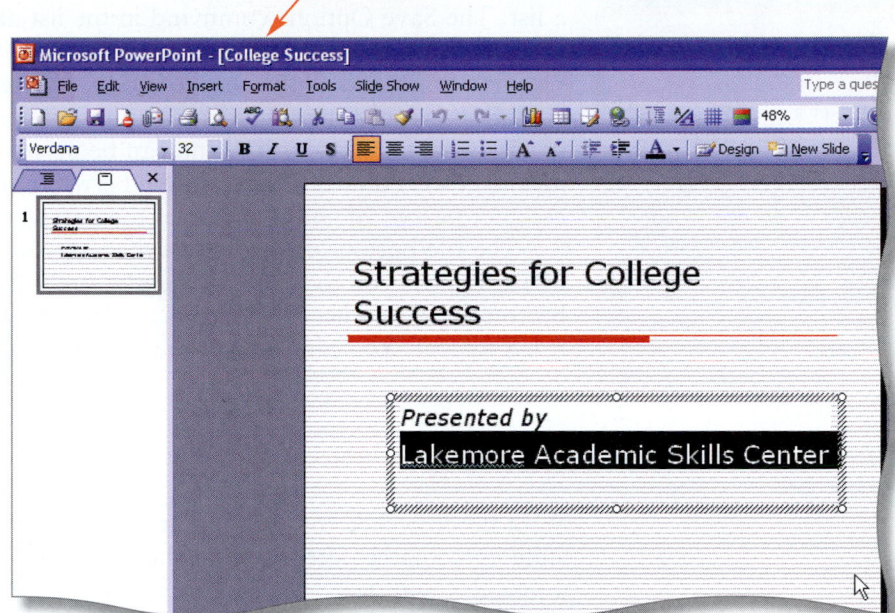

file name displays on title bar

FIGURE 1-29

PowerPoint automatically appends the extension .ppt to the file name, College Success. The **.ppt** extension stands for **P**ower**P**oin**t**. Although the slide show, College Success, is saved on a floppy disk, it also remains in memory and is displayed on the screen.

It is a good practice to save periodically while you are working on a project. By doing so, you protect yourself from losing all the work you have done since the last time you saved.

The seven buttons at the top and to the right in the Save As dialog box in Figure 1-28 and their functions are summarized in Table 1-3.

Other Ways

1. On File menu click Save As, type file name, select drive or folder, click Save button
2. On File menu click Save As, click My Computer button, select drive or folder, click Save button
3. Press CTRL+S or press SHIFT+F12, type file name, select drive or folder, click OK button
4. In Voice Command mode, say "File, Save As, [type desired file name], Save"

Table 1-3	Save As Dialog Box Toolbar Buttons	
BUTTON	**BUTTON NAME**	**FUNCTION**
	Default File Location	Displays contents of default file location
	Up One Level	Displays contents of folder one level up from current folder
	Search the Web	Starts browser and displays search engine
	Delete	Deletes selected file or folder
	Create New Folder	Creates new folder
	Views	Changes view of files and folders
	Tools	Lists commands to print or modify file names and folders

When you click the Tools button in the Save As dialog box, PowerPoint displays a list. The Save Options command in the list allows you to save the presentation automatically at a specified time interval and to reduce the file size. The Security Options command allows you to modify the security level for opening files that may contain harmful computer viruses and to assign a password to limit access to the file. A password is case-sensitive and can be up to 15 characters long. **Case-sensitive** means PowerPoint can differentiate between uppercase and lowercase letters. If you assign a password and then forget the password, you cannot access the file.

The file buttons on the left of the Save As dialog box in Figure 1-28 on page PPT 28 allow you to select frequently used folders. The My Recent Documents button displays a list of shortcuts (pointers) to the most recently used files in a folder titled Recent. You cannot save presentations to the Recent folder.

Adding a New Slide to a Presentation

With the title slide for the presentation created, the next step is to add the first text slide immediately after the title slide. Usually, when you create a presentation, you add slides with text, graphics, or charts. When you add a new slide, PowerPoint uses the Title and Text slide layout. Some placeholders allow you to double-click the placeholder and then access other objects, such as media clips, charts, diagrams, and organization charts.

The following steps add a new Text slide layout with a bulleted list. The default PowerPoint setting will display the Slide Layout task pane each time a new slide is added. Your system may not display this task pane if the setting has been changed.

To Add a New Text Slide with a Bulleted List

1

• **Click the New Slide button on the Formatting toolbar.**

The Slide Layout task pane opens. The Title and Text slide layout is selected. Slide 2 of 2 appears on the status bar (Figure 1-30).

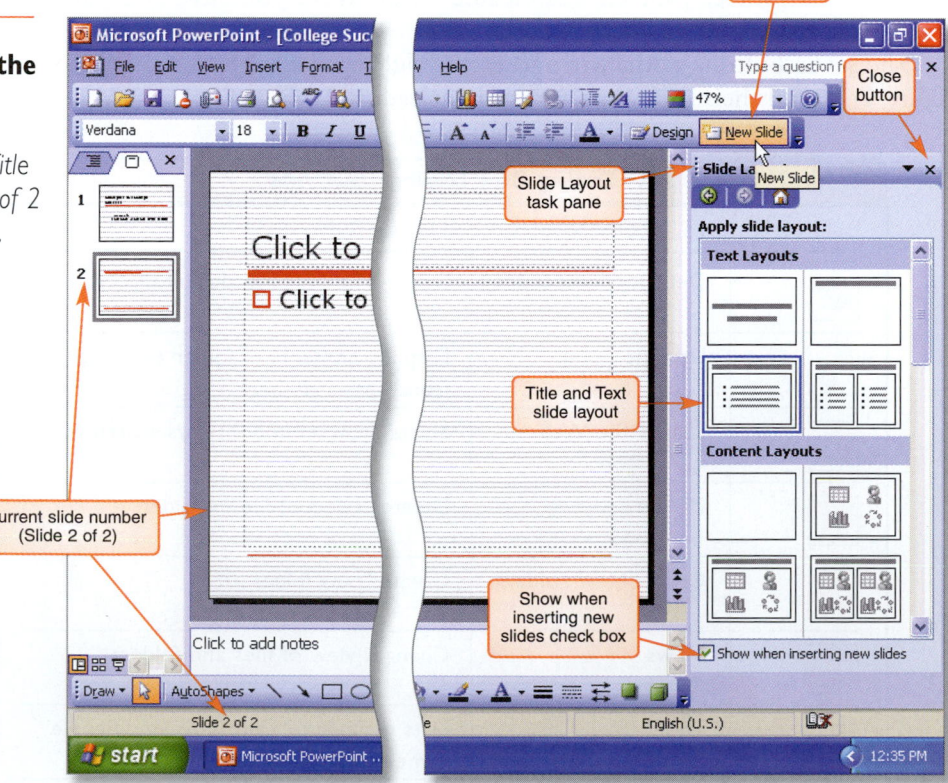

FIGURE 1-30

2

• **If necessary, click the Show when inserting new slides check box to remove the check mark, and then click the Close button on the Slide Layout task pane.**

Slide 2 appears in both the slide pane and Slides tab retaining the attributes of the Profile design template (Figure 1-31). The vertical scroll bar appears in the slide pane. The bullet appears as an outline square.

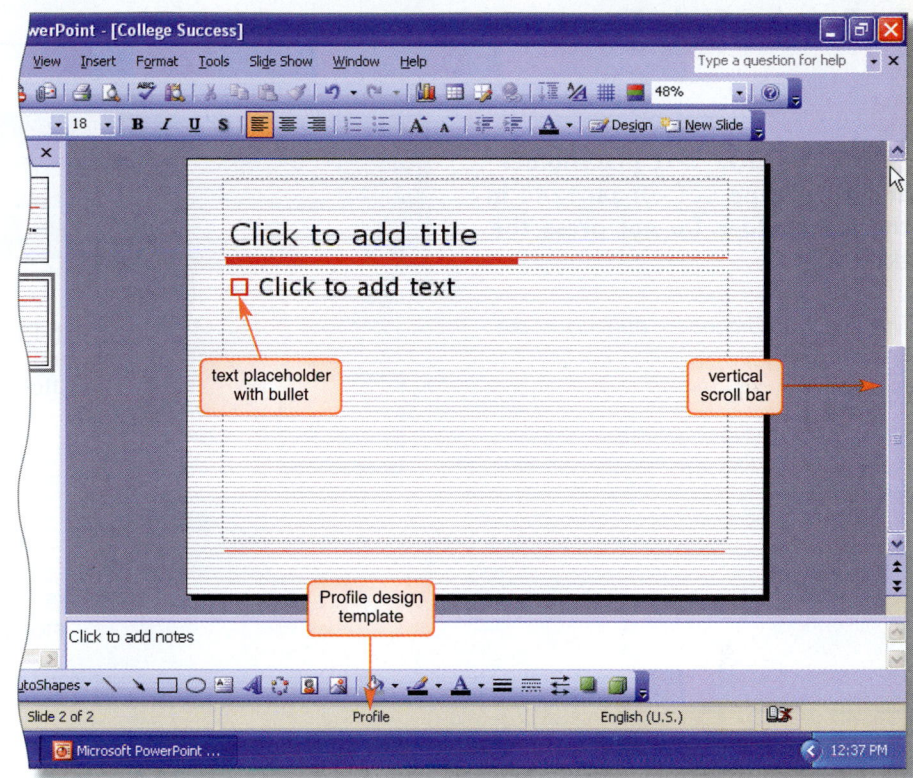

FIGURE 1-31

Slide 2 appears with a title text placeholder and a text placeholder with a bullet. You can change the layout for a slide at any time during the creation of a presentation by clicking Format on the menu bar and then clicking Slide Layout. You also can click View on the menu bar and then click Task Pane. You then can double-click the slide layout of your choice from the Slide Layout task pane.

Other Ways

1. On Insert menu click New Slide
2. Press CTRL+M
3. In Voice Command mode, say "New Slide"

Creating a Text Slide with a Single-Level Bulleted List

The information in the Slide 2 text placeholder is presented in a bulleted list. All the bullets appear on one level. A **level** is a position within a structure, such as an outline, that indicates the magnitude of importance. PowerPoint allows for five paragraph levels. Each paragraph level has an associated bullet. The bullet font is dependent on the design template.

Entering a Slide Title

PowerPoint assumes every new slide has a title. The title for Slide 2 is Get Organized. The step on the next page shows how to enter this title.

More About

Deleting Bullets

If you do not want bullets to display on a particular paragraph, select the paragraph and then click the Bullets button on the Formatting toolbar.

To Enter a Slide Title

1

• **Click the title text placeholder and then type** Get Organized **in the placeholder. Do not press the ENTER key.**

The title, Get Organized, appears in the title text placeholder and in the Slides tab (Figure 1-32). The insertion point appears after the d in Organized. The selection rectangle indicates the title text placeholder is selected.

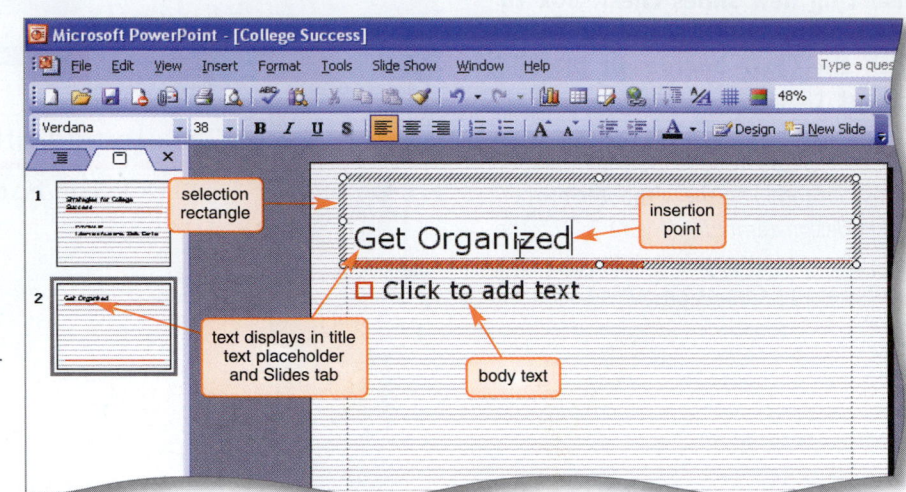

FIGURE 1-32

Selecting a Text Placeholder

Before you can type text into the text placeholder, you first must select it. The following step selects the text placeholder on Slide 2.

To Select a Text Placeholder

1

• **Click the bulleted paragraph labeled, Click to add text.**

The insertion point appears immediately to the right of the bullet on Slide 2 (Figure 1-33). The mouse pointer may change shape if you move it away from the bullet. The selection rectangle indicates the text placeholder is selected.

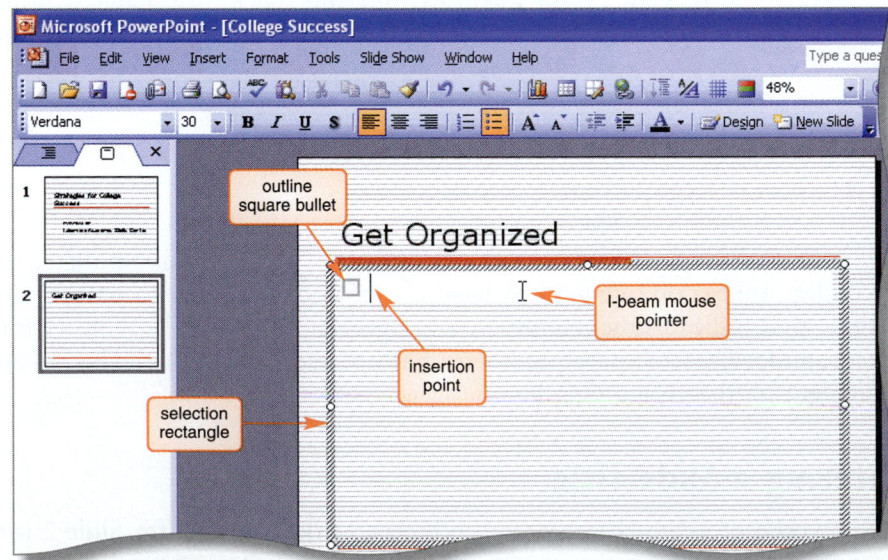

FIGURE 1-33

Typing a Single-Level Bulleted List

As discussed previously, a bulleted list is a list of paragraphs, each of which is preceded by a bullet. A paragraph is a segment of text ended by pressing the ENTER key. The next step is to type the single-level bulleted list, which consists of three entries (Figure 1-1b on page PPT 5). The following steps illustrate how to type a single-level bulleted list.

To Type a Single-Level Bulleted List

1

• **Type** Time management skills help balance academic, work, and social events **and then press the ENTER key.**

The paragraph, Time management skills help balance academic, work, and social events, appears (Figure 1-34). The font size is 30. The insertion point appears after the second bullet. When you press the ENTER key, PowerPoint ends one paragraph and begins a new paragraph. With the Title and Text slide layout, PowerPoint places an outline square bullet in front of the new paragraph.

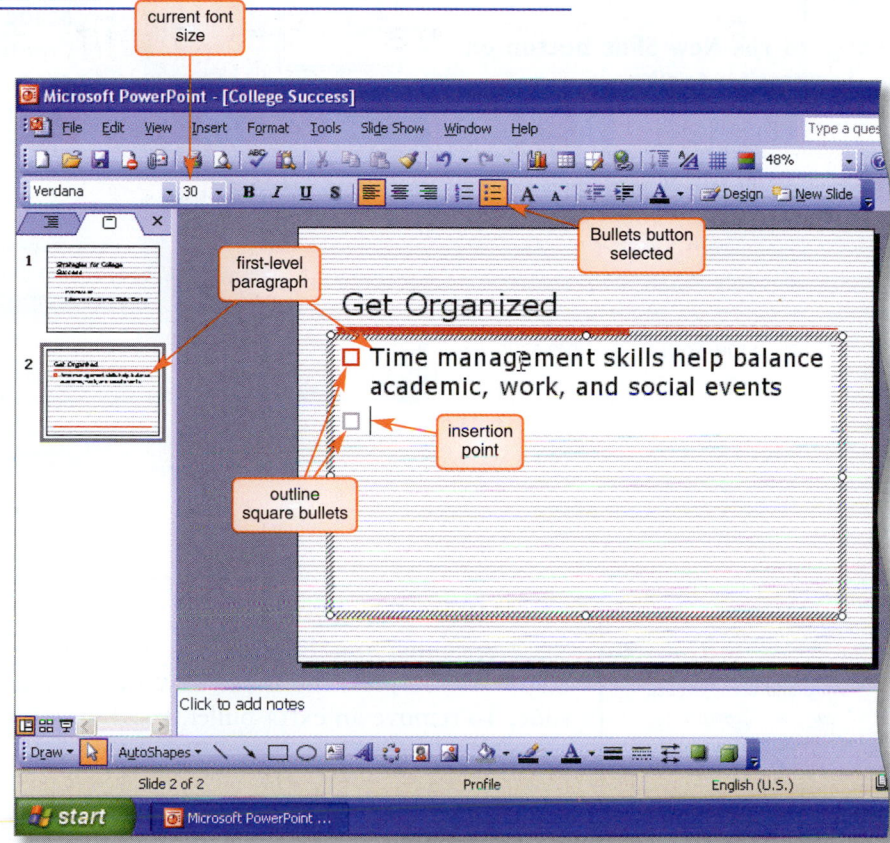

FIGURE 1-34

2

• **Type** Create a schedule each week that accounts for all activities **and then press the ENTER key.**

• **Type** Plan two hours of study time for each one hour of class time **but do not press the ENTER key.**

• **Point to the New Slide button on the Formatting toolbar.**

The insertion point is displayed after the e in time (Figure 1-35). Three new first-level paragraphs are displayed with outline square bullets in both the text placeholder and the Slides tab. When you press the ENTER key, PowerPoint adds a new paragraph at the same level as the previous paragraph.

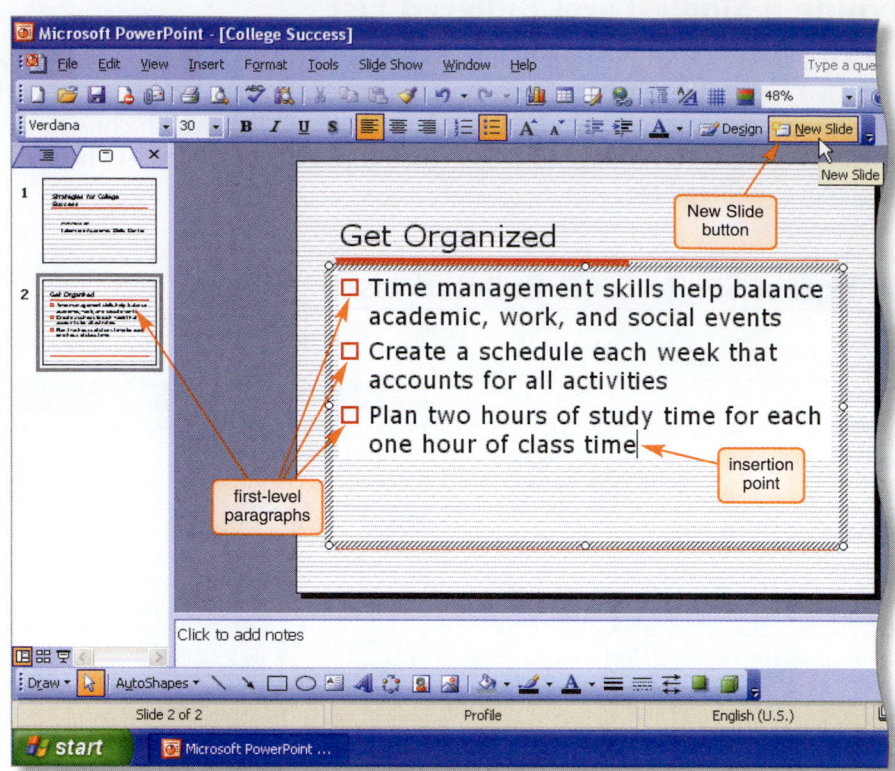

FIGURE 1-35

Notice that you did not press the ENTER key after typing the last paragraph in Step 2. If you press the ENTER key, a new bullet appears after the last entry on this slide. To remove an extra bullet, press the BACKSPACE key.

Creating a Text Slide with a Multi-Level Bulleted List

Slides 3 and 4 in Figure 1-1 on page PPT 5 contain more than one level of bulleted text. A slide that consists of more than one level of bulleted text is called a **multi-level bulleted list slide**. Beginning with the second level, each paragraph indents to the right of the preceding level and is pushed down to a lower level. For example, if you increase the indent of a first-level paragraph, it becomes a second-level paragraph. This lower-level paragraph is a subset of the higher-level paragraph. It usually contains information that supports the topic in the paragraph immediately above it. You increase the indent of a paragraph by clicking the Increase Indent button on the Formatting toolbar.

When you want to raise a paragraph from a lower level to a higher level, you click the Decrease Indent button on the Formatting toolbar.

Creating a text slide with a multi-level bulleted list requires several steps. Initially, you enter a slide title in the title text placeholder. Next, you select the body text placeholder. Then, you type the text for the multi-level bulleted list, increasing and decreasing the indents as needed. The next several sections explain how to add a slide with a multi-level bulleted list.

Adding New Slides and Entering Slide Titles

When you add a new slide to a presentation, PowerPoint keeps the same layout used on the previous slide. PowerPoint assumes every new slide has a title. The title for Slide 3 is Listen Actively. The following steps show how to add a new slide (Slide 3) and enter a title.

To Add a New Slide and Enter a Slide Title

1

• **Click the New Slide button.**

Slide 3 of 3 appears in the slide pane and Slides tab (Figure 1-36).

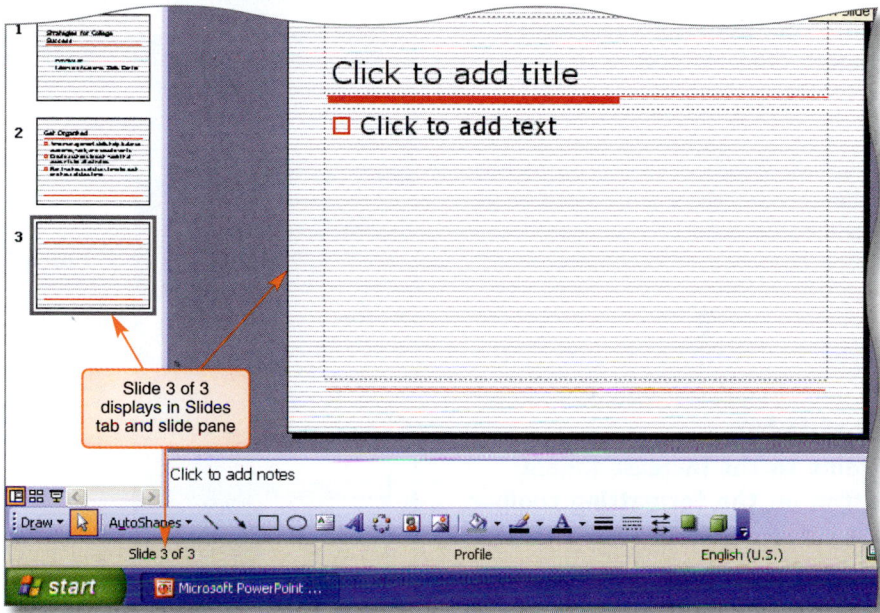

FIGURE 1-36

2

• **Type** Listen Actively **in the title text placeholder. Do not press the ENTER key.**

Slide 3 shows the Title and Text slide layout with the title, Listen Actively, in the title text placeholder and in the Slides tab (Figure 1-37). The insertion point appears after the y in Actively.

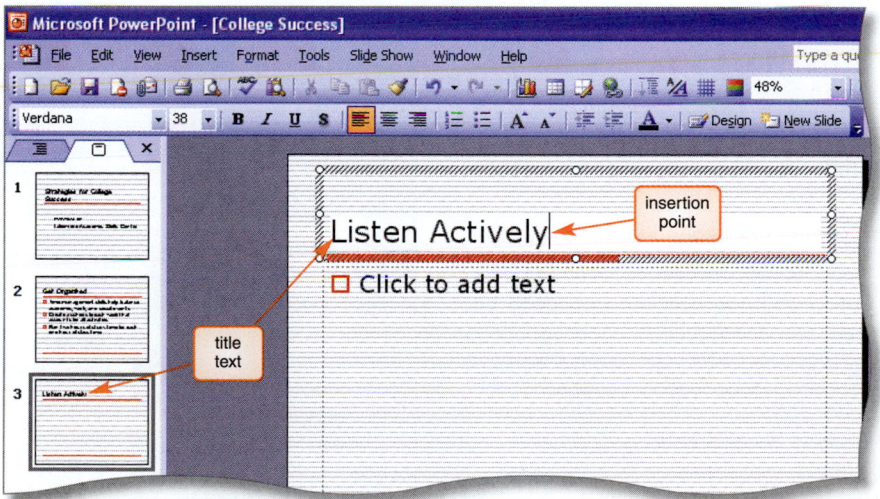

FIGURE 1-37

Slide 3 is added to the presentation with the desired title.

Other Ways

1. Press SHIFT+CTRL+M
2. In Dictation mode, say "New Slide, Listen Actively"

Typing a Multi-Level Bulleted List

The next step is to select the body text placeholder and then type the multi-level bulleted list, which consists of six entries (Figure 1-1c on page PPT 5). The following steps show how to create a list consisting of three levels.

To Type a Multi-Level Bulleted List

 1

• **Click the bulleted paragraph labeled, Click to add text.**

The insertion point appears immediately to the right of the bullet on Slide 3. The mouse pointer may change shape if you move it away from the bullet.

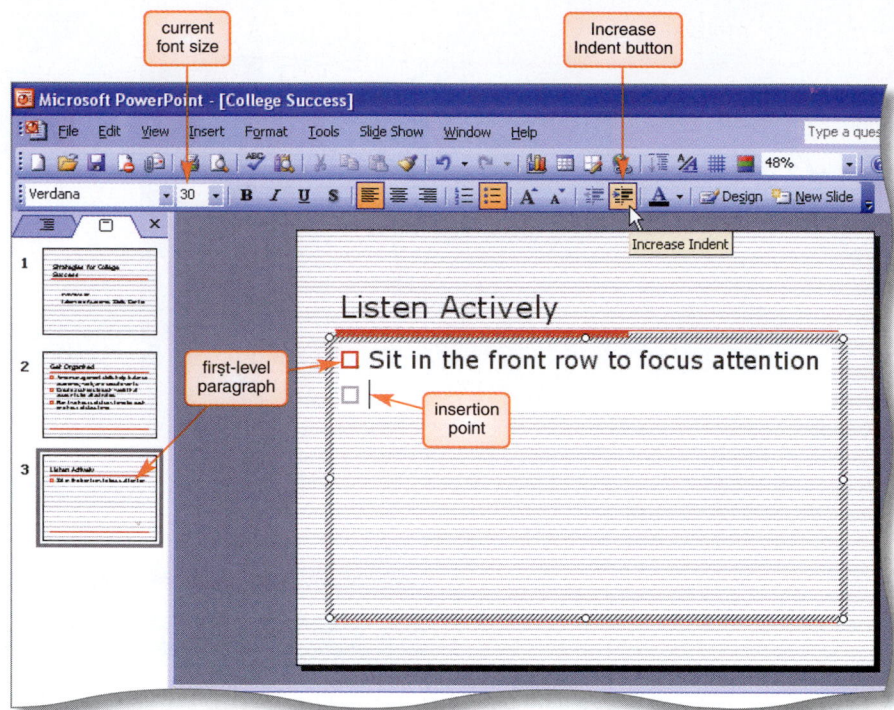

FIGURE 1-38

 2

• **Type** Sit in the front row to focus attention **and then press the ENTER key.**

• **Point to the Increase Indent button on the Formatting toolbar.**

The paragraph, Sit in the front row to focus attention, appears (Figure 1-38). The font size is 30. The insertion point appears to the right of the second bullet.

 3

• **Click the Increase Indent button.**

The second paragraph indents below the first and becomes a second-level paragraph (Figure 1-39). The bullet to the left of the second paragraph changes from an outline square to a solid square, and the font size for the paragraph now is 26. The insertion point appears to the right of the solid square.

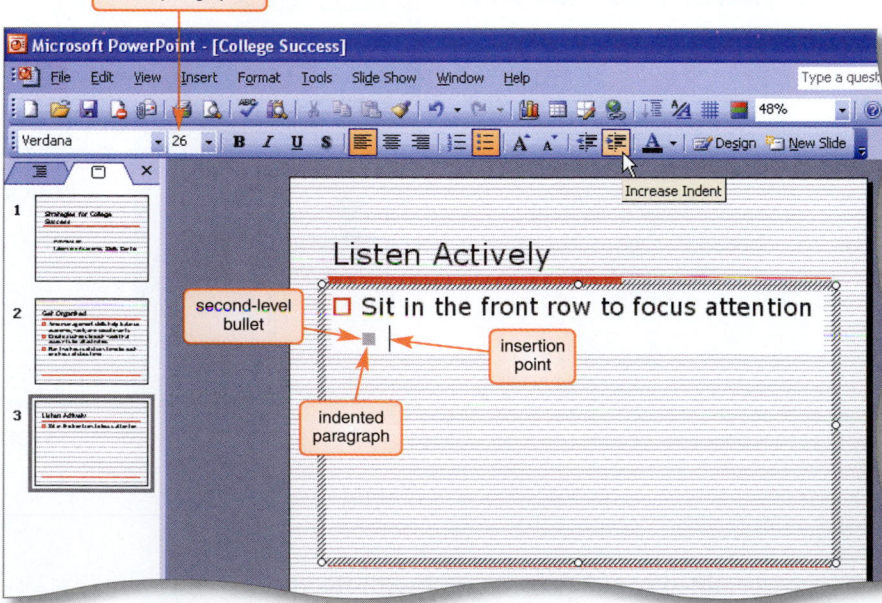

FIGURE 1-39

4

• **Type** Do not tolerate distractions **and then press the ENTER key.**

• **Point to the Decrease Indent button on the Formatting toolbar.**

The first second-level paragraph appears with a solid orange square bullet in both the slide pane and the Slides tab (Figure 1-40). When you press the ENTER key, PowerPoint adds a new paragraph at the same level as the previous paragraph.

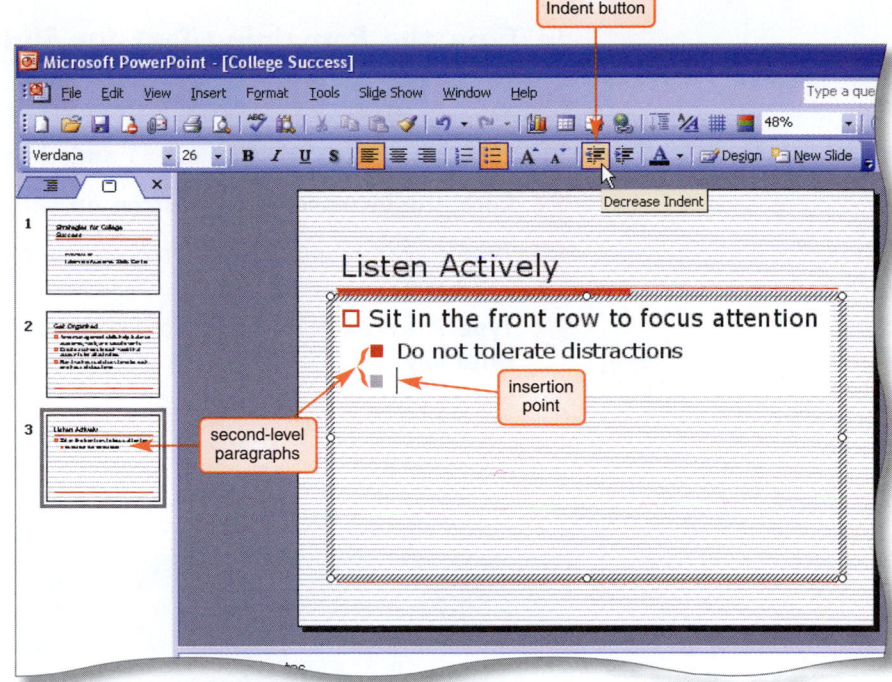

FIGURE 1-40

5

• **Click the Decrease Indent button.**

The second-level paragraph becomes a first-level paragraph (Figure 1-41). The bullet of the new paragraph changes from a solid orange square to an outline square, and the font size for the paragraph is 30. The insertion point appears to the right of the outline square bullet.

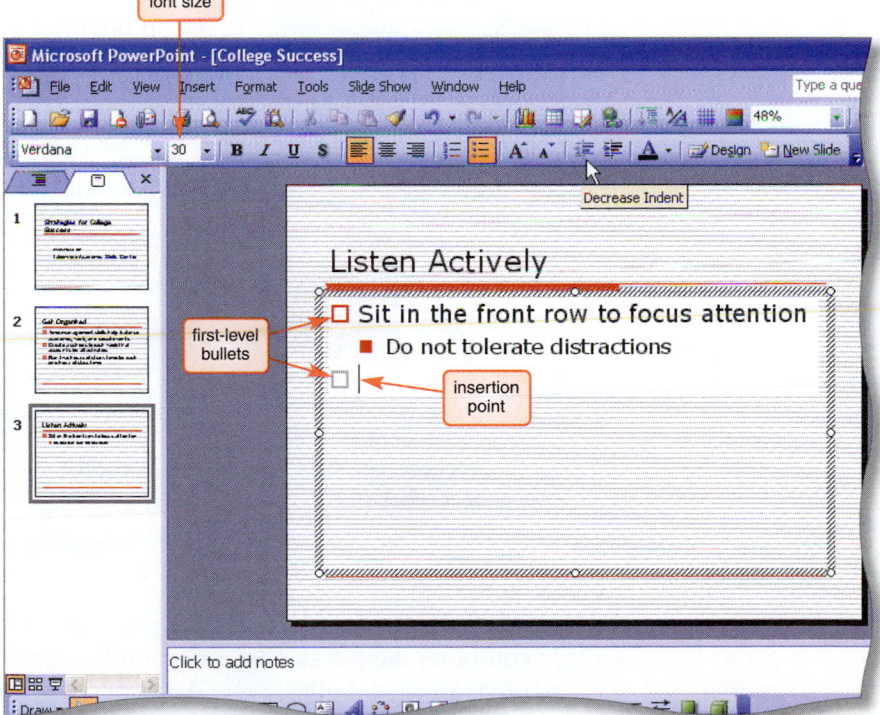

FIGURE 1-41

The steps on the next page complete the text for Slide 3.

To Type the Remaining Text for Slide 3

1 **Type** `Make mental summaries of material` **and then press the ENTER key.**

2 **Type** `Be prepared for class` **and then press the ENTER key.**

3 **Click the Increase Indent button on the Formatting toolbar.**

4 **Type** `Review notes from books, previous class` **and then press the ENTER key.**

5 **Type** `Preview material to be covered that day` **but do not press the ENTER key.**

Slide 3 is displayed as shown in Figure 1-42. The insertion point appears after the y in day.

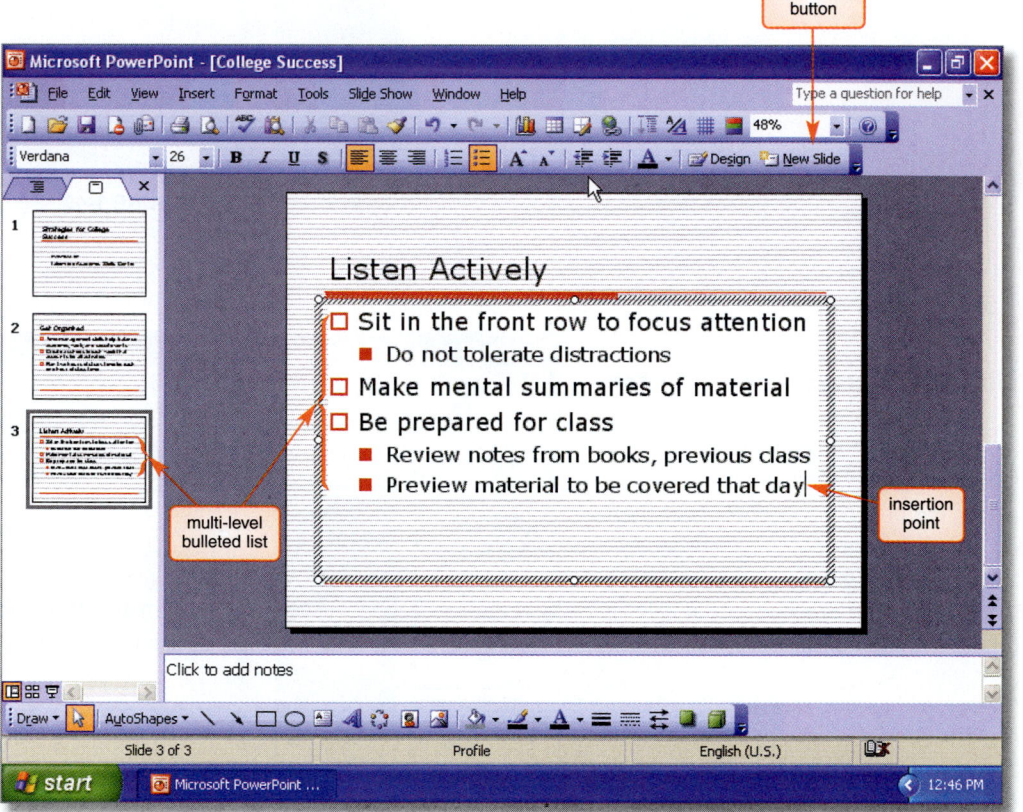

FIGURE 1-42

In Step 4 above, you did not press the ENTER key after typing the last paragraph. If you press the ENTER key, a new bullet appears after the last entry on this slide. To remove an extra bullet, press the BACKSPACE key.

Slide 4 is the last slide in this presentation. It also is a multi-level bulleted list and has three levels. The following steps create Slide 4.

To Create Slide 4

1 **Click the New Slide button on the Formatting toolbar.**

2 **Type** Excel on Exams **in the title text placeholder.**

3 **Press CTRL+ENTER to move the insertion point to the body text placeholder.**

4 **Type** Review test material throughout week **and then press the ENTER key.**

5 **Click the Increase Indent button on the Formatting toolbar. Type** Cramming before exams is ineffective **and then press the ENTER key.**

The title and first two levels of bullets are added to Slide 4 (Figure 1-43).

Other Ways

1. In Dictation mode, say "New Slide, Excel on Exams, [type CTRL+ENTER], Review test material throughout week, New Line, Increase Indent, Cramming before exams is ineffective"

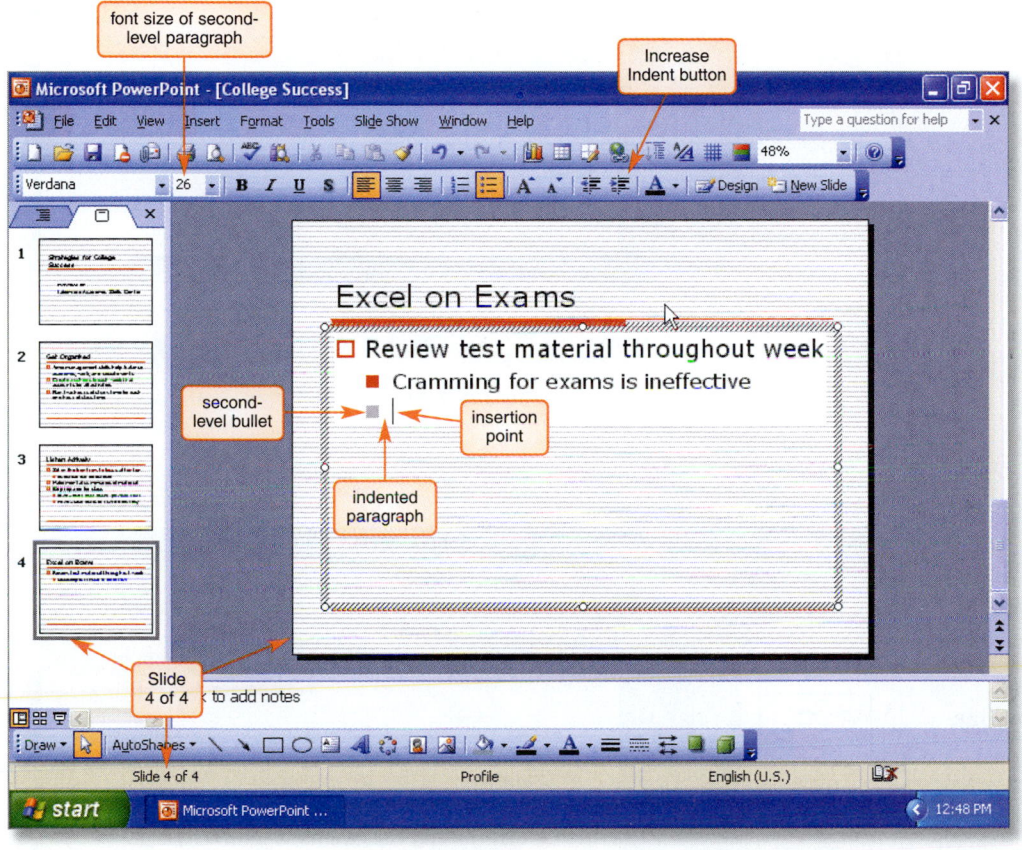

FIGURE 1-43

Creating a Third-Level Paragraph

The next line in Slide 4 is indented an additional level, to the third level. The steps on the next page create an additional level.

To Create a Third-Level Paragraph

1

• **Click the Increase Indent button on the Formatting toolbar.**

The second-level paragraph becomes a third-level paragraph (Figure 1-44). The bullet to the left of the new paragraph changes from a solid square to an outline square, and the font size for the paragraph is 23. The insertion point appears after the outline square bullet.

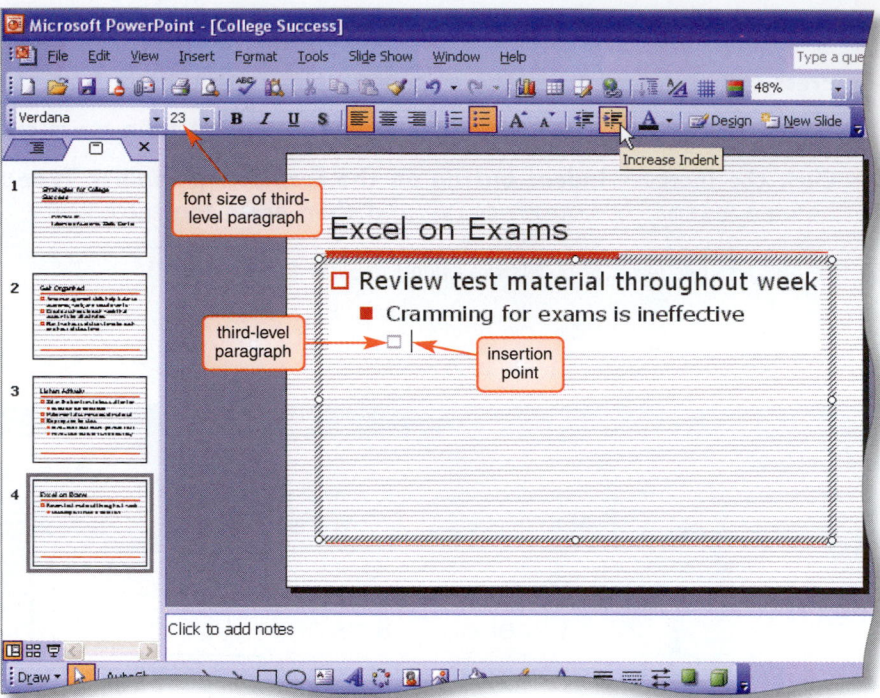

FIGURE 1-44

2

• **Type** Facts remain only in short-term memory **and then press the ENTER key.**

• **Point to the Decrease Indent button on the Formatting toolbar.**

The first third-level paragraph, Facts remain only in short-term memory, is displayed with the bullet for a second third-level paragraph (Figure 1-45).

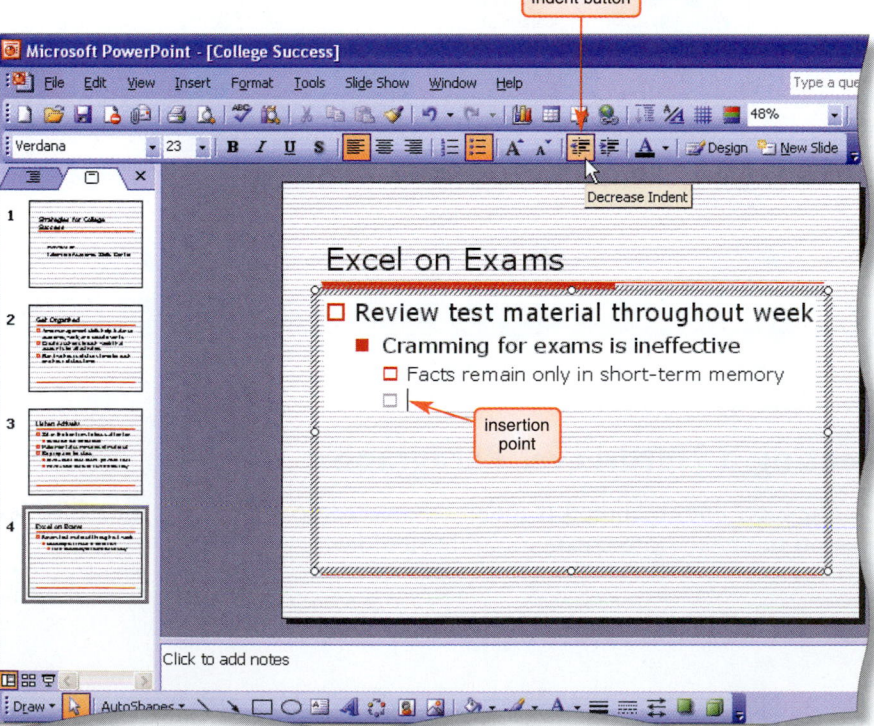

FIGURE 1-45

3

• **Click the Decrease Indent button two times.**

The insertion point appears at the first level (Figure 1-46).

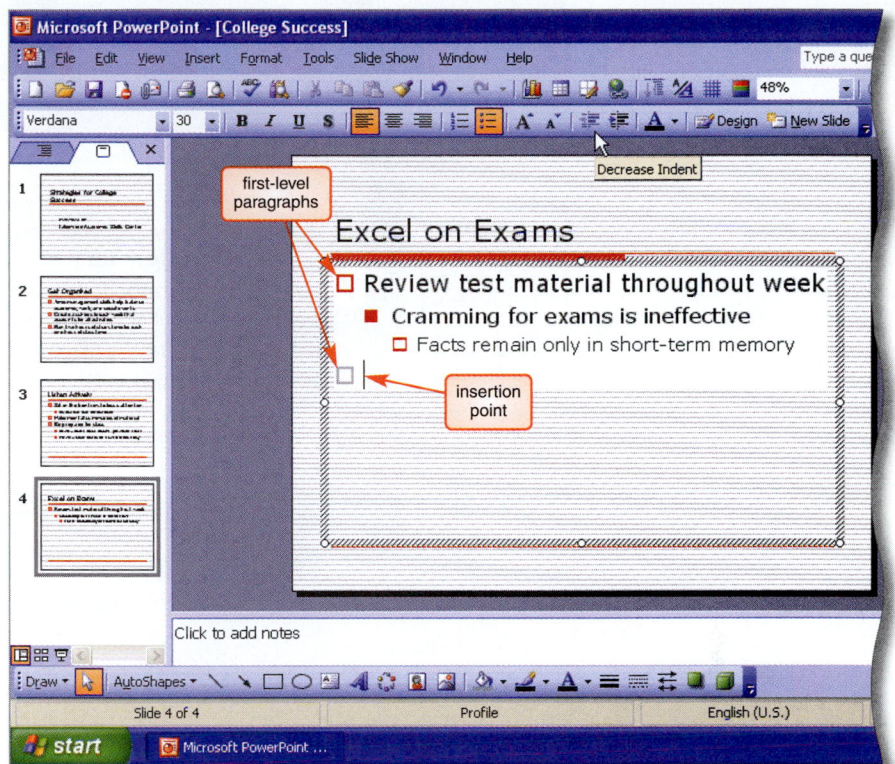

FIGURE 1-46

The title text and three levels of paragraphs discussing preparing for exams are complete. The next three paragraphs concern strategies for taking tests. As an alternative to clicking the Increase Indent button, you can press the TAB key. Likewise, instead of clicking the Decrease Indent button, you can press the SHIFT+TAB keys. The following steps illustrate how to type the remaining text for Slide 4.

To Type the Remaining Text for Slide 4

1 **Type** Review entire test before answering **and then press the ENTER key.**

2 **Press the TAB key to increase the indent to the second level.**

3 **Type** Start with the material you know **and then press the ENTER key.**

4 **Press the TAB key to increase the indent to the third level.**

5 **Type** Think positively and stay focused **but do not press the ENTER key.**

The Slide 4 title text and body text are displayed in the slide pane and Slides tabs (Figure 1-47 on the next page). The insertion point appears after the d in focused.

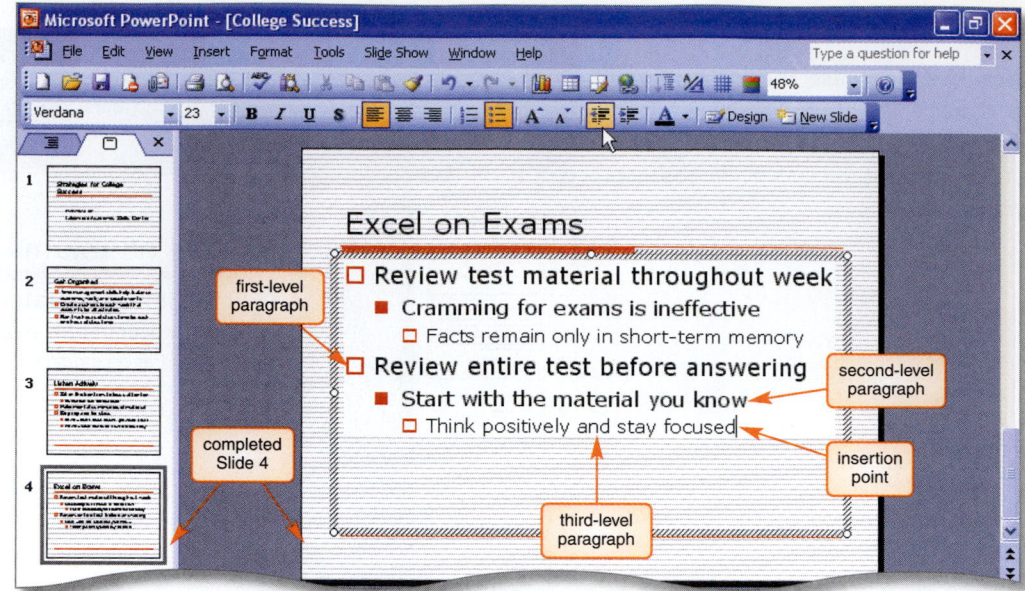

FIGURE 1-47

All the slides are created for the College Success slide show. This presentation consists of a title slide, one text slide with a single-level bulleted list, and two text slides with a multi-level bulleted list.

Ending a Slide Show with a Black Slide

After the last slide in the slide show appears, the default PowerPoint setting is to end the presentation with a black slide. This black slide appears only when the slide show is running and concludes the slide show gracefully so your audience never sees the PowerPoint window. A **black slide** ends all slide shows unless the option setting is deselected. The following steps verify that the End with black slide option is activated.

To End a Slide Show with a Black Slide

1

• Click Tools on the menu bar and then point to Options (Figure 1-48).

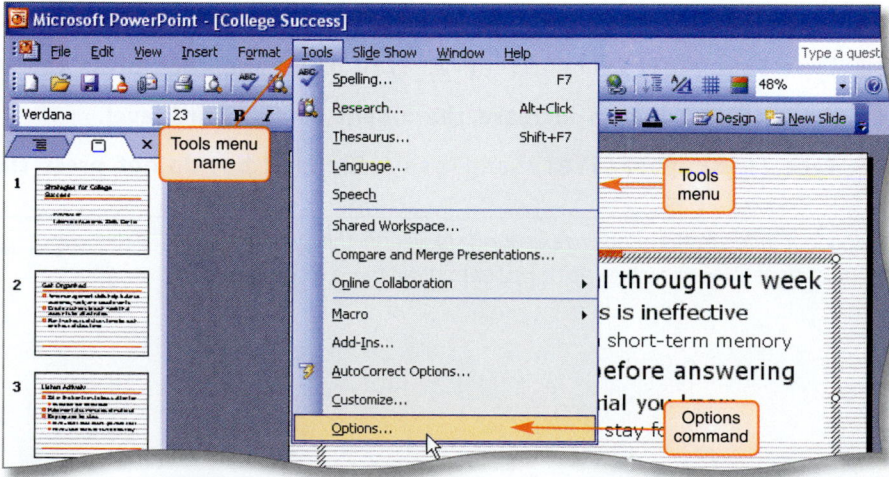

FIGURE 1-48

2

• **Click Options.**

• **If necessary, click the View tab when the Options dialog box appears.**

• **Verify that the End with black slide check box is selected.**

• **If a check mark does not show, click End with black slide.**

• **Point to the OK button.**

The Options dialog box appears (Figure 1-49). The View sheet contains settings for the overall PowerPoint display and for a particular slide show.

3

• **Click the OK button.**

The End with black slide option will cause the slide show to end with a black slide until it is deselected.

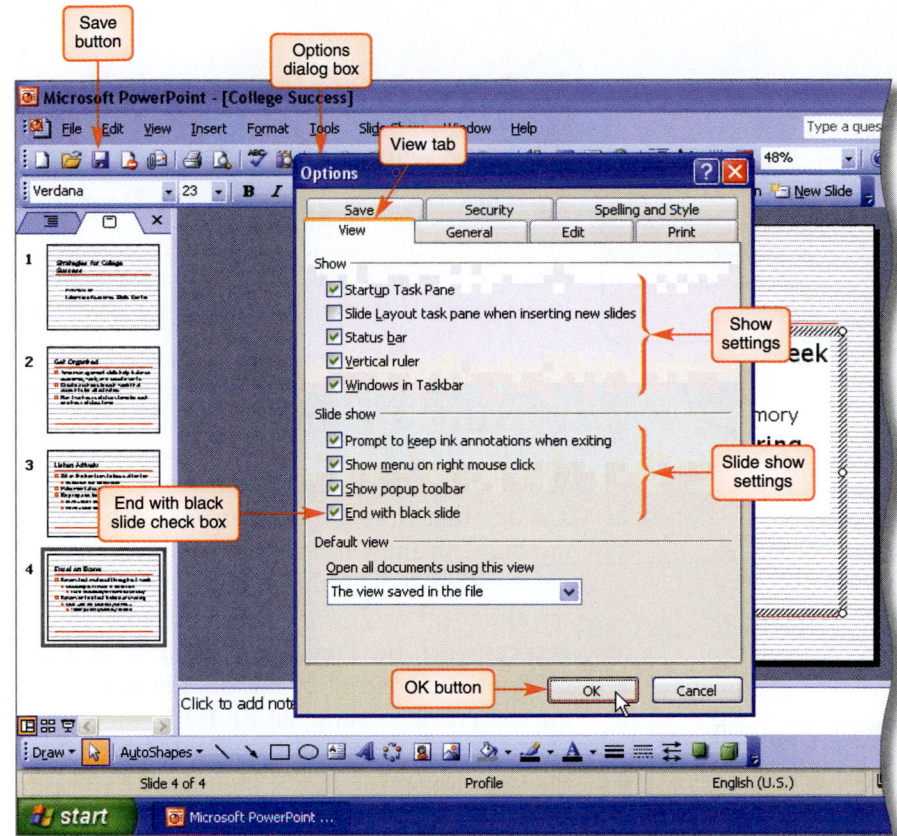

FIGURE 1-49

With all aspects of the presentation complete, it is important to save the additions and changes you have made to the College Success presentation.

Saving a Presentation with the Same File Name

Saving frequently cannot be overemphasized. When you first saved the presentation, you clicked the Save button on the Standard toolbar, and the Save dialog box appeared. When you want to save the changes made to the presentation after your last save, you again click the Save button. This time, however, the Save dialog box does not appear because PowerPoint updates the document called College Success.ppt on the floppy disk. The steps on the next page illustrate how to save the presentation again.

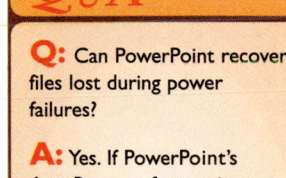

Q: Can PowerPoint recover files lost during power failures?

A: Yes. If PowerPoint's AutoRecover feature is turned on, files that were open when PowerPoint stopped responding may be displayed in the Document Recovery task pane. This task pane allows you to open the files, view the contents, and compare versions. You then can save the most complete version of your presentation.

To Save a Presentation with the Same File Name

1 Be certain your floppy disk is in drive A.

2 Click the Save button on the Standard toolbar.

PowerPoint overwrites the old College Success.ppt document on the floppy disk in drive A with the revised presentation document. Slide 4 is displayed in the PowerPoint window.

Moving to Another Slide in Normal View

When creating or editing a presentation in normal view, you often want to display a slide other than the current one. You can move to another slide using several methods. In the Outline tab, you can point to any of the text in a particular slide to display that slide in the slide pane, or you can drag the scroll box on the vertical scroll bar up or down to move through the text in the presentation. In the slide pane, you can click the Previous Slide or Next Slide button on the vertical scroll bar. Clicking the Next Slide button advances to the next slide in the presentation. Clicking the Previous Slide button backs up to the slide preceding the current slide. You also can drag the scroll box on the vertical scroll bar. When you drag the scroll box, the **slide indicator** shows the number and title of the slide you are about to display. Releasing the mouse button shows the slide.

A slide's **Zoom setting** affects the portion of the slide displaying in the slide pane. PowerPoint defaults to a setting of approximately 50 percent so the entire slide is displayed. This percentage depends on the size and type of your monitor. If you want to display a small portion of the current slide, you would zoom in by clicking the **Zoom box arrow** and then clicking the desired magnification. You can display the entire slide in the slide pane by clicking **Fit** in the Zoom list. The Zoom setting affects the action of the vertical and horizontal scroll bars. If Zoom is set so the entire slide is not visible in the slide pane, clicking the up scroll arrow on the vertical scroll bar shows the next portion of the slide, not the previous slide.

Using the Scroll Box on the Slide Pane to Move to Another Slide

Before continuing with Project 1, you want to display the title slide. The following steps show how to move from Slide 4 to Slide 1 using the scroll box on the slide pane vertical scroll bar.

To Use the Scroll Box on the Slide Pane to Move to Another Slide

1

• **Position the mouse pointer on the scroll box.**

• **Press and hold down the mouse button.**

Slide: 4 of 4 Excel on Exams appears in the slide indicator (Figure 1-50). When you click the scroll box, the Slide 4 thumbnail has no gray border in the Slides tab.

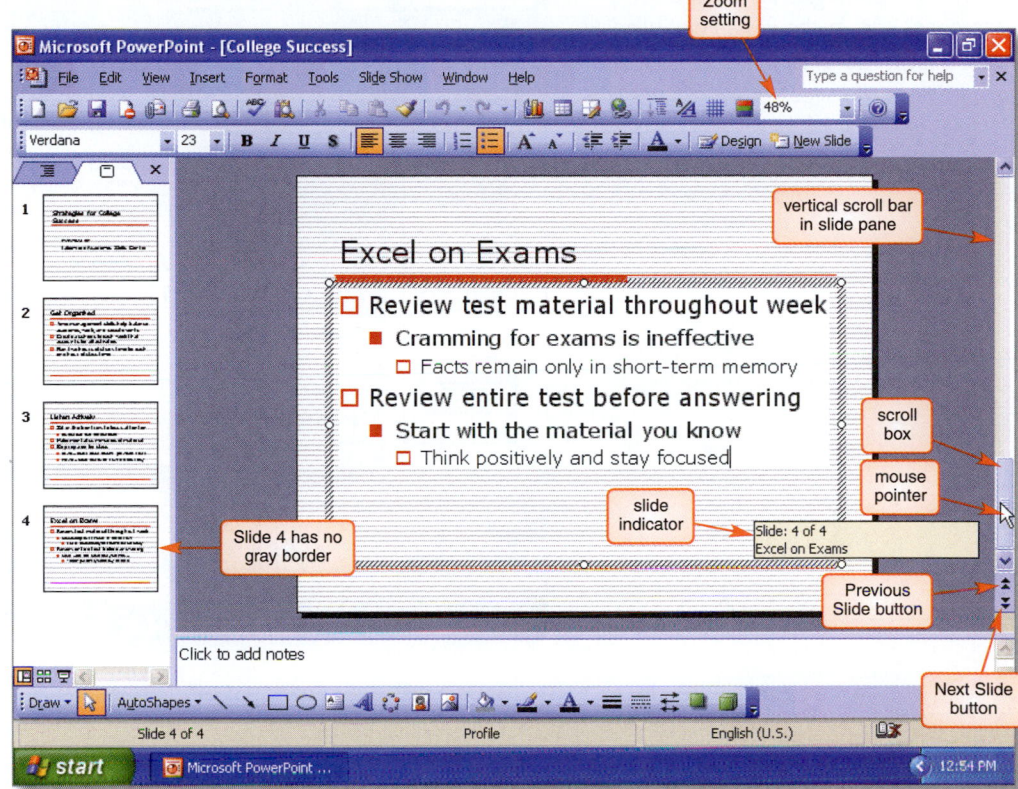

FIGURE 1-50

2

• **Drag the scroll box up the vertical scroll bar until Slide: 1 of 4 Strategies for College Success appears in the slide indicator.**

Slide: 1 of 4 Strategies for College Success appears in the slide indicator (Figure 1-51). Slide 4 still is displayed in the PowerPoint window.

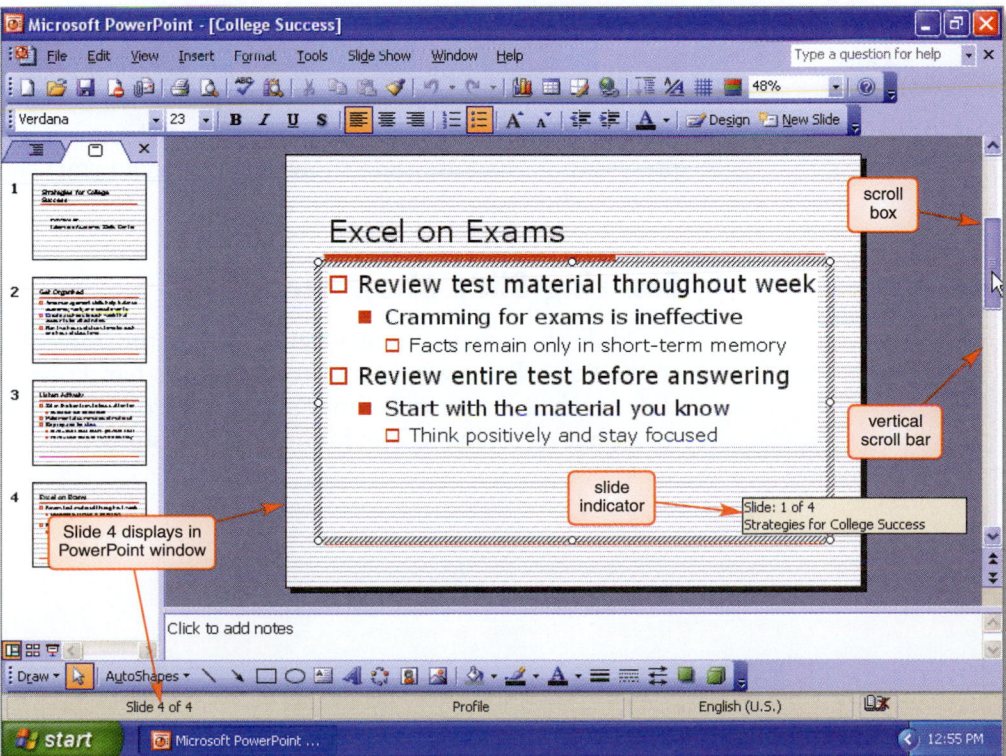

FIGURE 1-51

3

• **Release the mouse button.**

Slide 1, titled Strategies for College Success, appears in the PowerPoint window (Figure 1-52). The Slide 1 thumbnail has a gray border in the Slides tab, indicating it is selected.

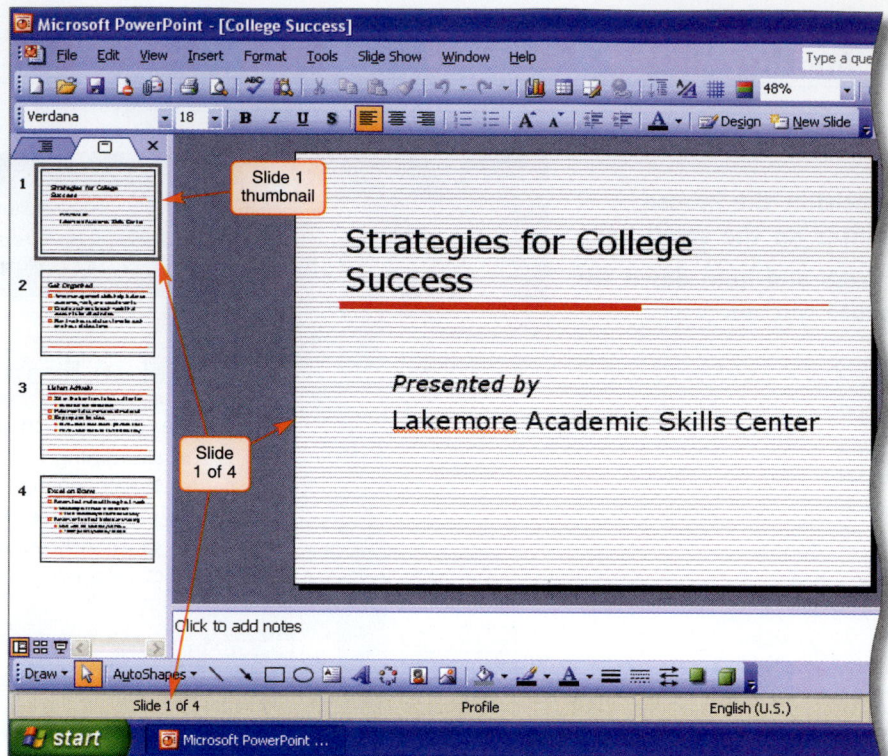

FIGURE 1-52

Viewing the Presentation in Slide Show View

The Slide Show button, located in the lower-left of the PowerPoint window above the status bar, allows you to show a presentation using a computer. The computer acts like a slide projector, displaying each slide on a full screen. The full-screen slide hides the toolbars, menus, and other PowerPoint window elements. When making a presentation, you use **slide show view**. You can start slide show view from normal view or slide sorter view.

Starting Slide Show View

Slide show view begins when you click the Slide Show button in the lower-left of the PowerPoint window above the status bar. PowerPoint then shows the current slide on the full screen without any of the PowerPoint window objects, such as the menu bar or toolbars. The following steps show how to start slide show view.

To Start Slide Show View

1

• **Point to the Slide Show button in the lower-left corner of the PowerPoint window above the status bar (Figure 1-53).**

FIGURE 1-53

2

• **Click the Slide Show button.**

A starting slide show message may display momentarily, and then the title slide fills the screen (Figure 1-54). The PowerPoint window is hidden.

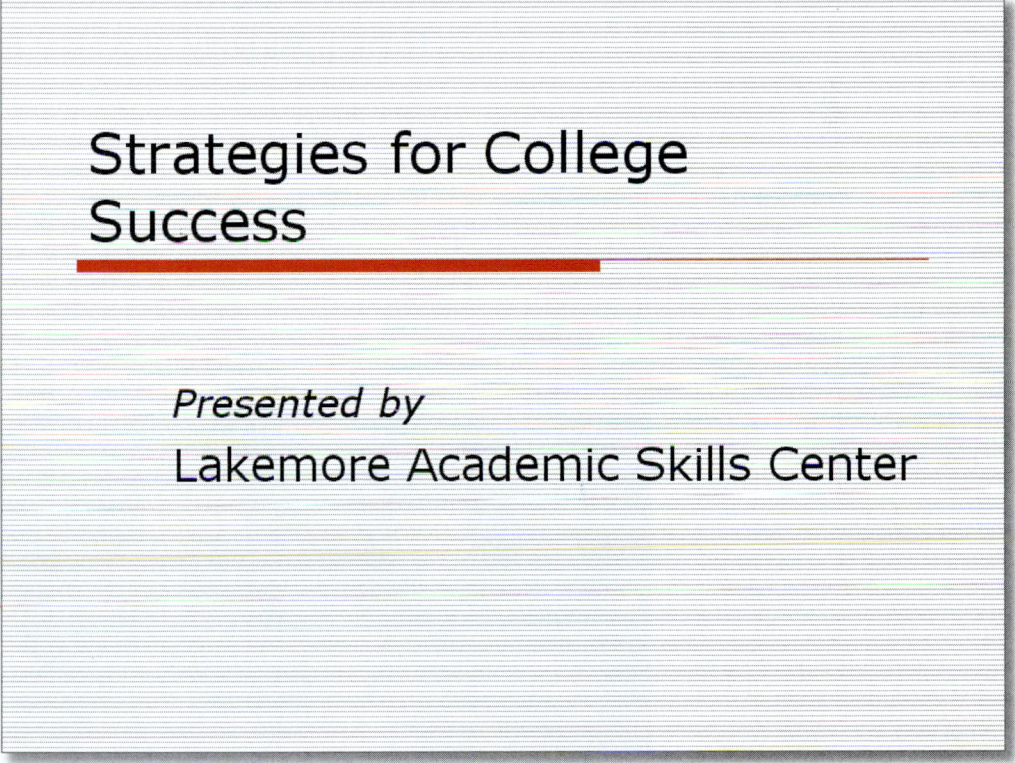

FIGURE 1-54

Other Ways

1. On View menu click Slide Show
2. Press F5
3. In Voice Command mode, say "View show"

Advancing Through a Slide Show Manually

After you begin slide show view, you can move forward or backward through the slides. PowerPoint allows you to advance through the slides manually or automatically. The steps on the next page illustrate how to move manually through the slides.

To Move Manually Through Slides in a Slide Show

1

- **Click each slide until the Excel on Exams slide (Slide 4) is displayed.**

Slide 4 is displayed (Figure 1-55). Each slide in the presentation shows on the screen, one slide at a time. Each time you click the mouse button, the next slide appears.

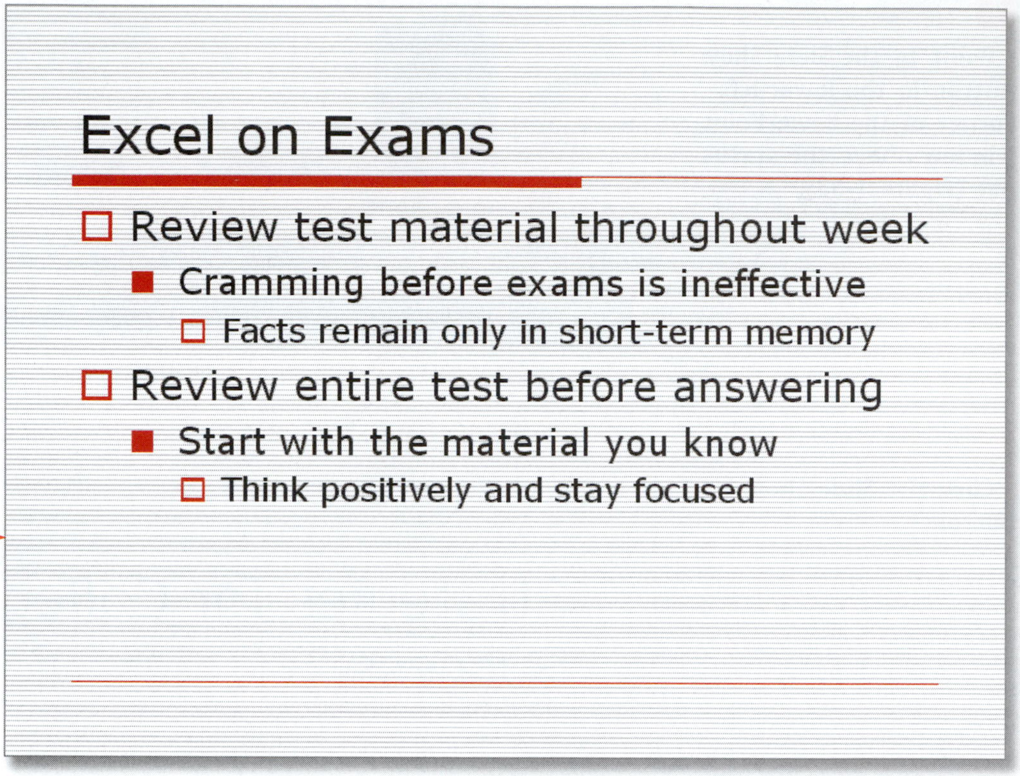

Excel on Exams
Review test material throughout week
Cramming before exams is ineffective
Facts remain only in short-term memory
Review entire test before answering
Start with the material you know
Think positively and stay focused
Slide 4 displays in slide show view

FIGURE 1-55

2

- **Click Slide 4.**

The black slide appears (Figure 1-56). The message at the top of the slide announces the end of the slide show. If you wanted to end the presentation at this point and return to normal view, you would click the black slide.

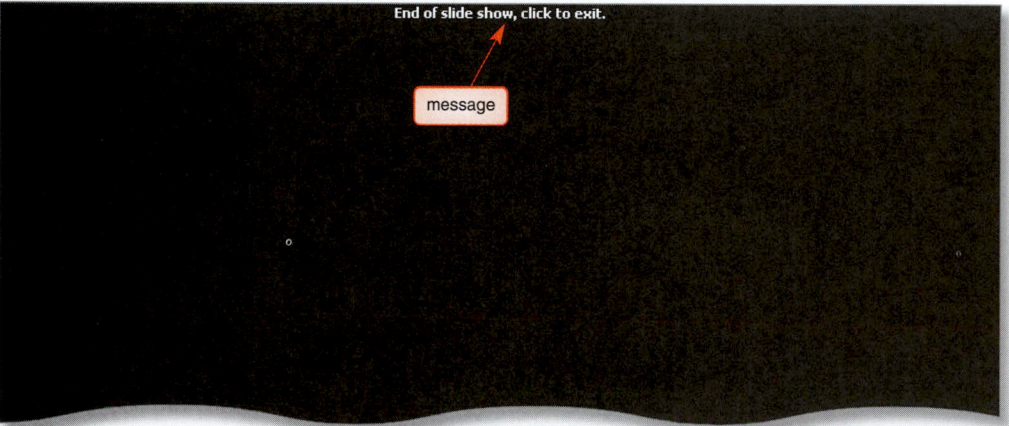

End of slide show, click to exit.
message

FIGURE 1-56

Other Ways

1. Press PAGE DOWN to advance one slide at a time, or press PAGE UP to go backward one slide at a time
2. Press RIGHT ARROW or DOWN ARROW key to advance one slide at a time, or press LEFT ARROW or UP ARROW key to go back one slide at a time

Using the Popup Menu to Go to a Specific Slide

Slide show view has a shortcut menu, called the Popup menu, that appears when you right-click a slide in slide show view. This menu contains commands to assist you during a slide show. For example, clicking the Next command moves to the next slide. Clicking the Previous command moves to the previous slide. Pointing to the Go to Slide command and then clicking the desired slide allows you to move to any slide in the presentation. The Go to Slide submenu contains a list of the slides in the presentation. You can go to the requested slide by clicking the name of that slide. The following steps illustrate how to go to the title slide (Slide 1) in the College Success presentation.

To Display the Popup Menu and Go to a Specific Slide

1

• **With the black slide displaying in slide show view, right-click the slide.**

• **Point to Go to Slide on the Popup menu, and then point to 1 Strategies for College Success in the Go to Slide submenu.**

The Popup menu appears on the black slide, and the Go to Slide submenu shows a list of slides in the presentation (Figure 1-57). Your screen may look different because the Popup menu appears near the location of the mouse pointer at the time you right-click.

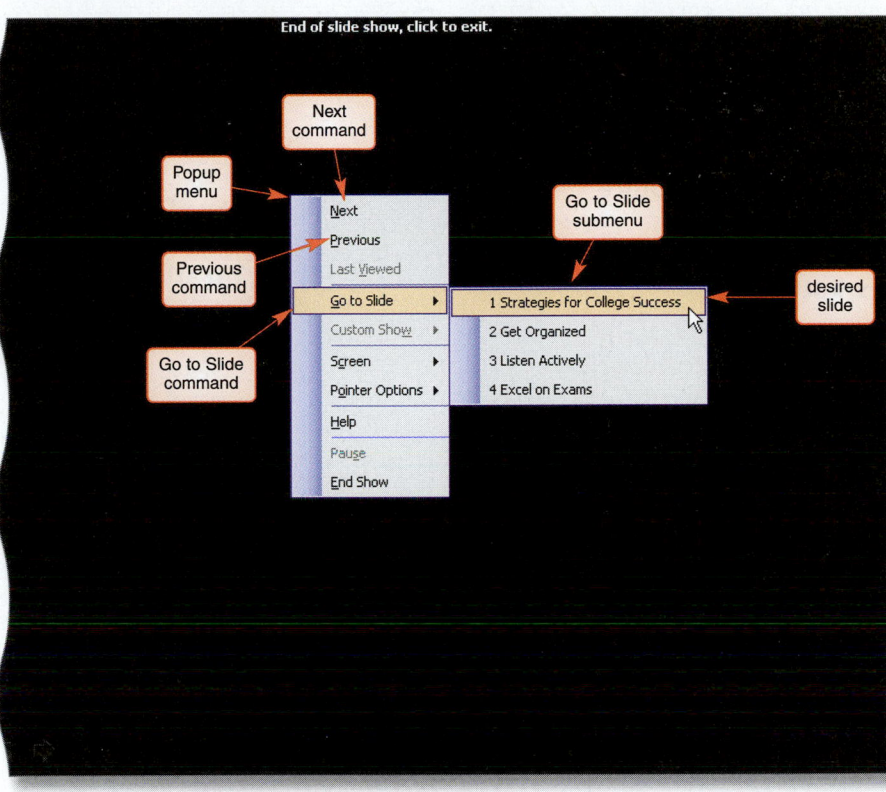

FIGURE 1-57

2

• **Click 1 Strategies for College Success.**

The title slide, Strategies for College Success (shown in Figure 1-54 on page PPT 47), is displayed.

Additional Popup menu commands allow you to change the mouse pointer to a ballpoint or felt tip pen or highlighter that draws in various colors, make the screen black or white, create speaker notes, and end the slide show. Popup menu commands are discussed as they are used.

Using the Popup Menu to End a Slide Show

The End Show command on the Popup menu ends slide show view and returns to the same view as when you clicked the Slide Show button. The steps on the next page show how to end slide show view and return to normal view.

To Use the Popup Menu to End a Slide Show

1

• **Right-click the title slide and then point to End Show on the Popup menu.**

The Popup menu appears on Slide 1 (Figure 1-58).

2

• **Click End Show.**

• **If the Microsoft Office PowerPoint dialog box appears, click the Yes button.**

PowerPoint ends slide show view and returns to normal view (shown in Figure 1-59 below). Slide 1 is displayed because it is the last slide displayed in slide show view.

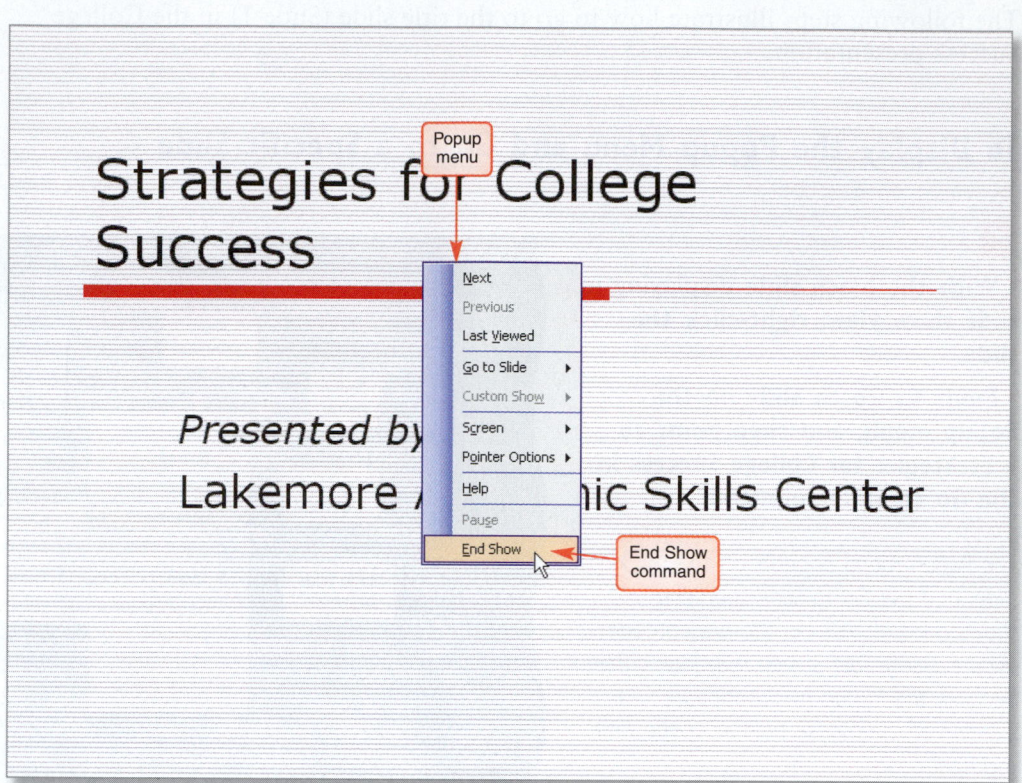

FIGURE 1-58

Quitting PowerPoint

The College Success presentation now is complete. When you quit PowerPoint, you are prompted to save any changes made to the presentation since the last save. The program then closes all PowerPoint windows, quits, and returns control to the desktop. The following steps quit PowerPoint.

To Quit PowerPoint

1

• **Point to the Close button on the PowerPoint title bar (Figure 1-59).**

FIGURE 1-59

2

• **Click the Close button.**

PowerPoint closes and the Windows desktop is displayed (Figure 1-60). If you made changes to the presentation since your last save, a Microsoft Office PowerPoint dialog box appears asking if you want to save changes. Clicking the Yes button saves the changes to the presentation before quitting PowerPoint. Clicking the No button quits PowerPoint without saving the changes. Clicking the Cancel button cancels the exit and returns control to the presentation.

FIGURE 1-60

Starting PowerPoint and Opening a Presentation

Once you have created and saved a presentation, you may need to retrieve it from the floppy disk to make changes. For example, you may want to replace the design template or modify some text. The steps on the next page assume PowerPoint is not running.

To Start PowerPoint and Open an Existing Presentation

1

• **With your floppy disk in drive A, click the Start button on the taskbar, point to All Programs, point to Microsoft Office, and then click Microsoft Office PowerPoint 2003 on the Microsoft Office submenu.**

• **When the Getting Started task pane opens, point to the Open link in the Open area.**

PowerPoint starts. The Getting Started task pane opens (Figure 1-61).

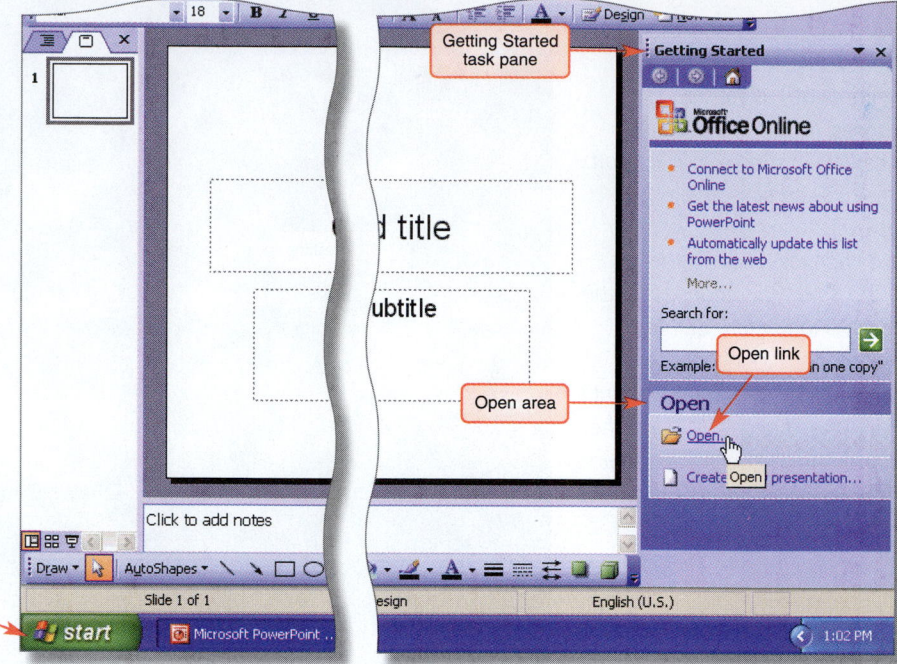

FIGURE 1-61

2

• **Click the Open link. Click the Look in box arrow, click 3½ Floppy (A:), and then double-click College Success.**

PowerPoint opens the presentation College Success and shows the first slide in the PowerPoint window (Figure 1-62). The presentation is displayed in normal view because PowerPoint opens a presentation in the same view in which it was saved. The Getting Started task pane disappears.

Other Ways

1. Right-click Start button, click Explore, display contents of drive A, double-click file name
2. Click Open button on Standard toolbar, select file name, click Open button in Open Office Document dialog box
3. On File menu click Open, select file name, click Open button in Open dialog box
4. In Voice Command mode, say "Open, [file name], Open"

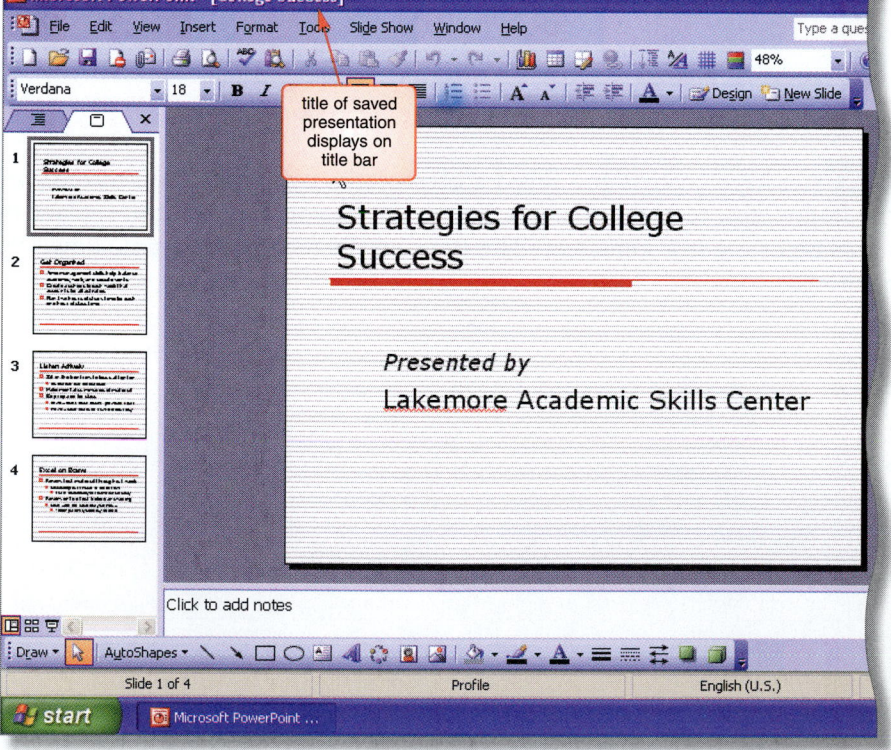

FIGURE 1-62

When you start PowerPoint and open the College Success file, the application name and file name are displayed on a recessed button on the Windows taskbar. When more than one application is open, you can switch between applications by clicking the appropriate application button. If you want to open a presentation other than a recent one, click the Open button on the Standard toolbar or in the Getting Started task pane. Either button lets you navigate to a slide show stored on a disk.

Checking a Presentation for Spelling and Consistency

After you create a presentation, you should check it visually for spelling errors and style consistency. In addition, you can use PowerPoint's Spelling and Style tools to identify possible misspellings and inconsistencies.

Checking a Presentation for Spelling Errors

PowerPoint checks the entire presentation for spelling mistakes using a standard dictionary contained in the Microsoft Office group. This dictionary is shared with the other Microsoft Office applications such as Word and Excel. A **custom dictionary** is available if you want to add special words such as proper names, cities, and acronyms. When checking a presentation for spelling errors, PowerPoint opens the standard dictionary and the custom dictionary file, if one exists. When a word appears in the Spelling dialog box, you perform one of the actions listed in Table 1-4.

Q & A

Q: Can I rely on the spelling checker?

A: While PowerPoint's Spelling checker is a valuable tool, it is not infallible. You should proofread your presentation carefully by pointing to each word and saying it aloud as you point to it. Be mindful of commonly misused words such as its and it's, through and though, and to and too.

Table 1-4 Summary of Spelling Checker Actions	
ACTION	DESCRIPTION
Ignore the word	Click the Ignore button when the word is spelled correctly but not found in the dictionaries. PowerPoint continues checking the rest of the presentation.
Ignore all occurrences of the word	Click the Ignore All button when the word is spelled correctly but not found in the dictionaries. PowerPoint ignores all occurrences of the word and continues checking the rest of the presentation.
Select a different spelling	Click the proper spelling of the word from the list in the Suggestions box. Click the Change button. PowerPoint corrects the word and continues checking the rest of the presentation.
Change all occurrences of the misspelling to a different spelling	Click the proper spelling of the word from the list in the Suggestions box. Click the Change All button. PowerPoint changes all occurrences of the misspelled word and continues checking the rest of the presentation.
Add a word to the custom dictionary	Click the Add button. PowerPoint opens the custom dictionary, adds the word, and continues checking the rest of the presentation.
View alternative spellings	Click the Suggest button. PowerPoint lists suggested spellings. Click the correct word from the Suggestions box or type the proper spelling. Then click the Change button. PowerPoint continues checking the rest of the presentation.
Add spelling error to AutoCorrect list	Click the AutoCorrect button. PowerPoint adds the spelling error and its correction to the AutoCorrect list. Any future misspelling of the word is corrected automatically as you type.
Close	Click the Close button to close the Spelling checker and return to the PowerPoint window.

The standard dictionary contains commonly used English words. It does not, however, contain proper names, abbreviations, technical terms, poetic contractions, or antiquated terms. PowerPoint treats words not found in the dictionaries as misspellings.

Starting the Spelling Checker

The following steps illustrate how to start the Spelling checker and check the entire presentation.

To Start the Spelling Checker

1
• **Point to the Spelling button on the Standard toolbar (Figure 1-63).**

FIGURE 1-63

2
• **Click the Spelling button.**
• **When the Spelling dialog box appears, point to the Ignore button.**

PowerPoint starts the Spelling checker and displays the Spelling dialog box (Figure 1-64). The word, Lakemore, appears in the Not in Dictionary box. Depending on the custom dictionary, Lakemore may not be recognized as a misspelled word.

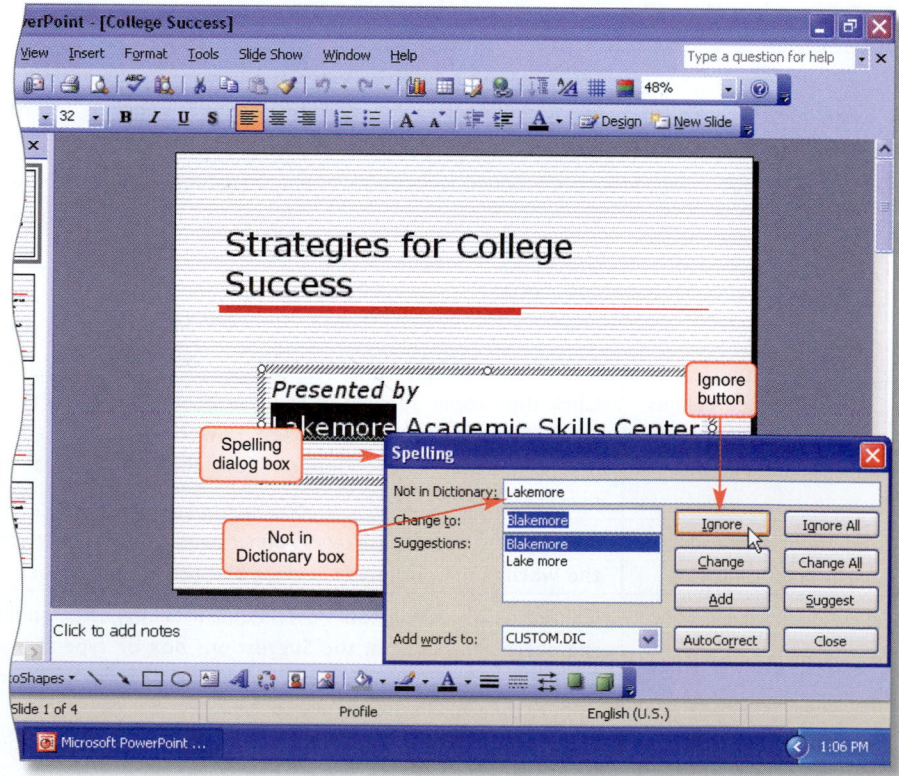

FIGURE 1-64

3

• Click the **Ignore** button.

• When the Microsoft Office PowerPoint dialog box appears, point to the **OK** button.

PowerPoint ignores the word, Lakemore, and continues searching for additional misspelled words. PowerPoint may stop on additional words depending on your typing accuracy. When PowerPoint has checked all slides for misspellings, the Microsoft Office PowerPoint dialog box informs you that the spelling check is complete (Figure 1-65).

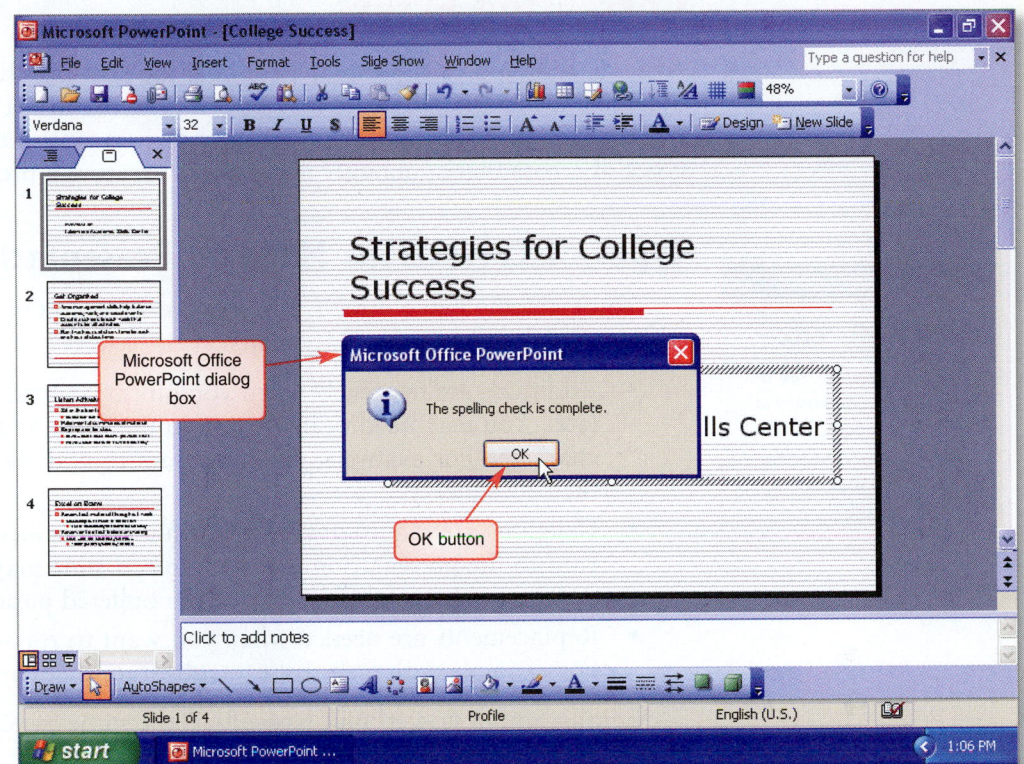

FIGURE 1-65

4

• Click the **OK** button.

• Click the slide to remove the highlight from the word, Lakemore.

PowerPoint closes the Spelling checker and returns to the current slide, Slide 1 (Figure 1-66), or to the slide where a possible misspelled word displayed.

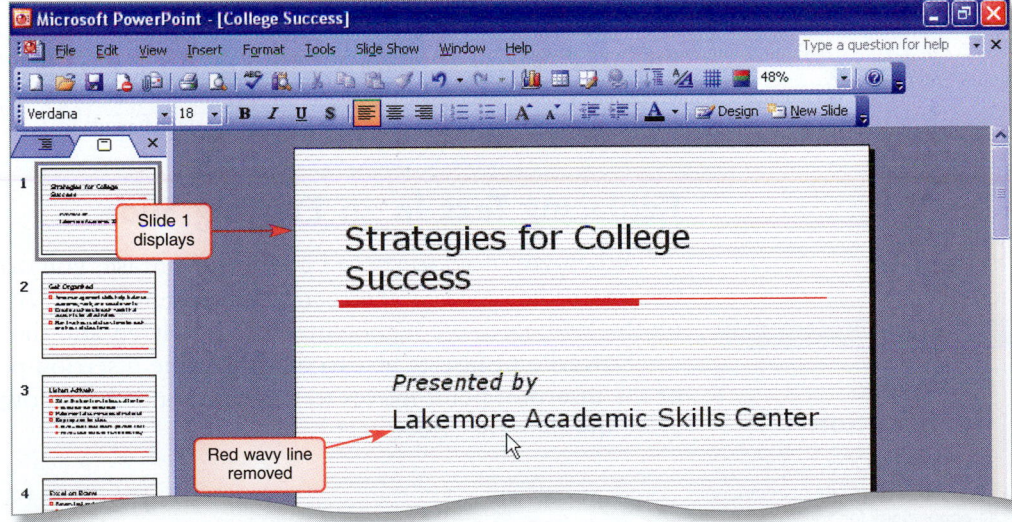

FIGURE 1-66

Other Ways

1. On Tools menu click Spelling
2. Press ALT+T, press S; when finished, press ENTER
3. Press F7
4. In Voice Command mode, say "Spelling"

The red wavy line below the word, Lakemore, is gone because you instructed PowerPoint to ignore that word, which does not appear in the standard dictionary. You also could have added that word to the dictionary so it would not be flagged as a possible misspelled word in subsequent presentations you create using that word.

Correcting Errors

After creating a presentation and running the Spelling checker, you may find that you must make changes. Changes may be required because a slide contains an error, the scope of the presentation shifts, or the style is inconsistent. This section explains the types of errors that commonly occur when creating a presentation.

Types of Corrections Made to Presentations

You generally make three types of corrections to text in a presentation: additions, deletions, and replacements.

- Additions are necessary when you omit text from a slide and need to add it later. You may need to insert text in the form of a sentence, word, or single character. For example, you may want to add the presenter's middle name on the title slide.
- Deletions are required when text on a slide is incorrect or no longer is relevant to the presentation. For example, a slide may look cluttered. Therefore, you may want to remove one of the bulleted paragraphs to add more space.
- Replacements are needed when you want to revise the text in a presentation. For example, you may want to substitute the word, their, for the word, there.

Editing text in PowerPoint basically is the same as editing text in a word processing package. The following sections illustrate the most common changes made to text in a presentation.

Deleting Text

You can delete text using one of three methods. One is to use the BACKSPACE key to remove text just typed. The second is to position the insertion point to the left of the text you wish to delete and then press the DELETE key. The third method is to drag through the text you wish to delete and then press the DELETE key. (Use the third method when deleting large sections of text.)

Replacing Text in an Existing Slide

When you need to correct a word or phrase, you can replace the text by selecting the text to be replaced and then typing the new text. As soon as you press any key on the keyboard, the highlighted text is deleted and the new text is displayed.

PowerPoint inserts text to the left of the insertion point. The text to the right of the insertion point moves to the right (and shifts downward if necessary) to accommodate the added text.

Displaying a Presentation in Black and White

Printing handouts of a presentation allows you to use them to make overhead transparencies. The Color/Grayscale button on the Standard toolbar shows the presentation in black and white before you print. Table 1-5 identifies how PowerPoint objects display in black and white.

Table 1-5 Appearance in Black and White View	
OBJECT	APPEARANCE IN BLACK AND WHITE VIEW
Bitmaps	Grayscale
Embossing	Hidden
Fills	Grayscale
Frame	Black
Lines	Black
Object shadows	Grayscale
Pattern fills	Grayscale
Slide backgrounds	White
Text	Black
Text shadows	Hidden

The following steps show how to display the presentation in black and white.

To Display a Presentation in Black and White

1

• **Click the Color/Grayscale button on the Standard toolbar and then point to Pure Black and White in the list.**

The Color/Grayscale list is displayed (Figure 1-67). Pure Black and White alters the slides' appearance so that only black lines display on a white background. Grayscale shows varying degrees of gray.

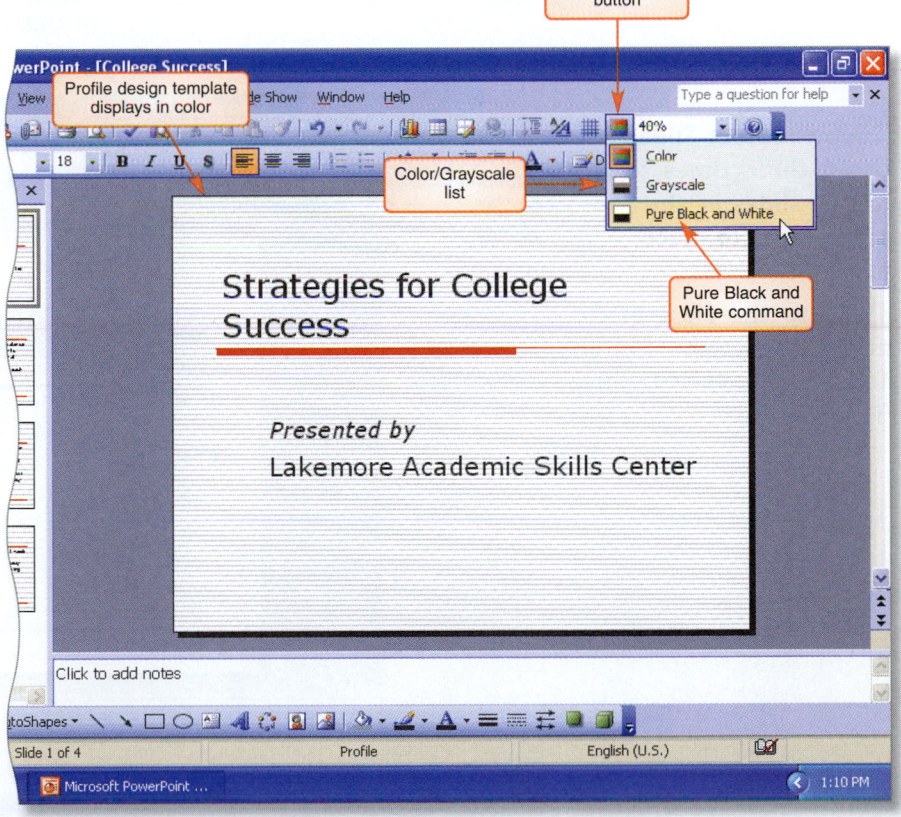

FIGURE 1-67

2

• **Click Pure Black and White.**

Slide 1 is displayed in black and white in the slide pane (Figure 1-68). The four thumbnail slides are displayed in color in the Slides tab. The Grayscale View toolbar appears. The Color/Grayscale button on the Standard toolbar changes from color bars to black and white.

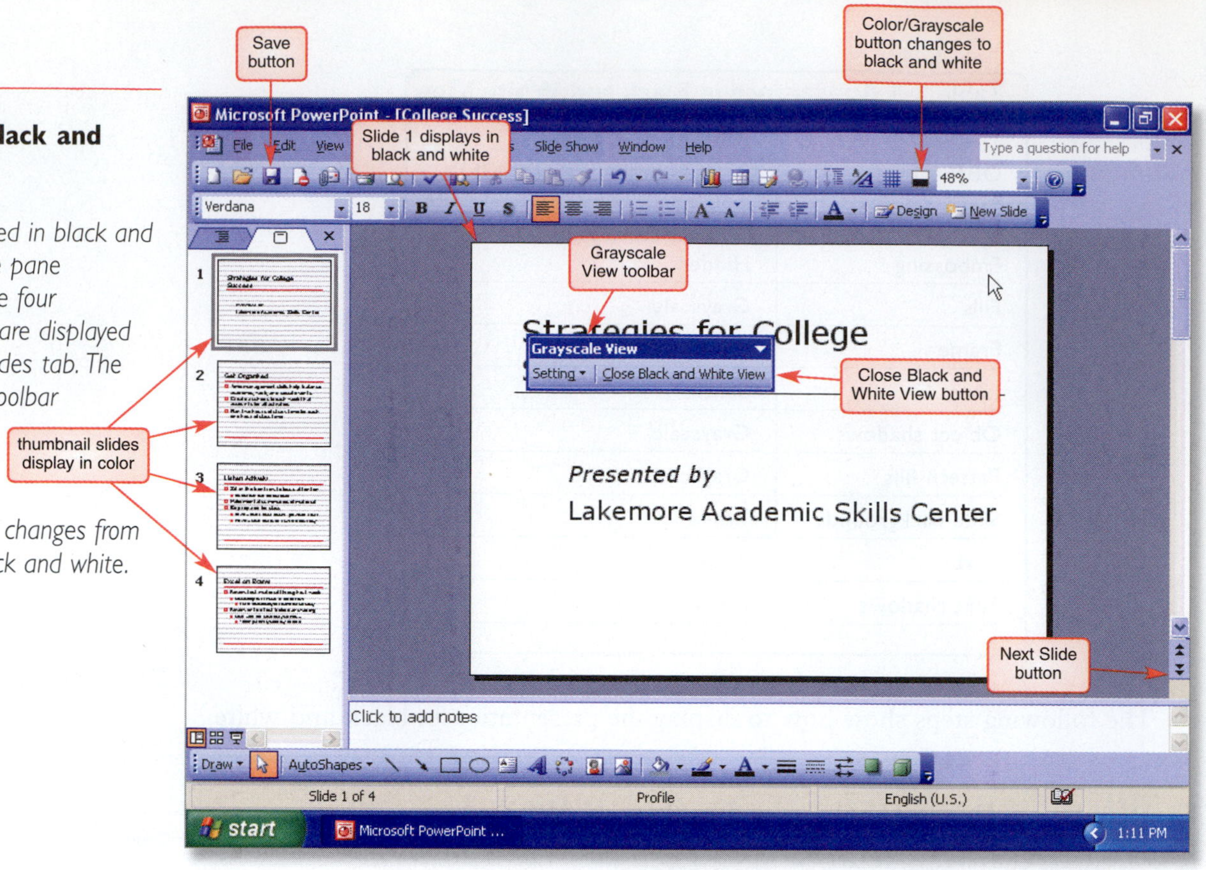

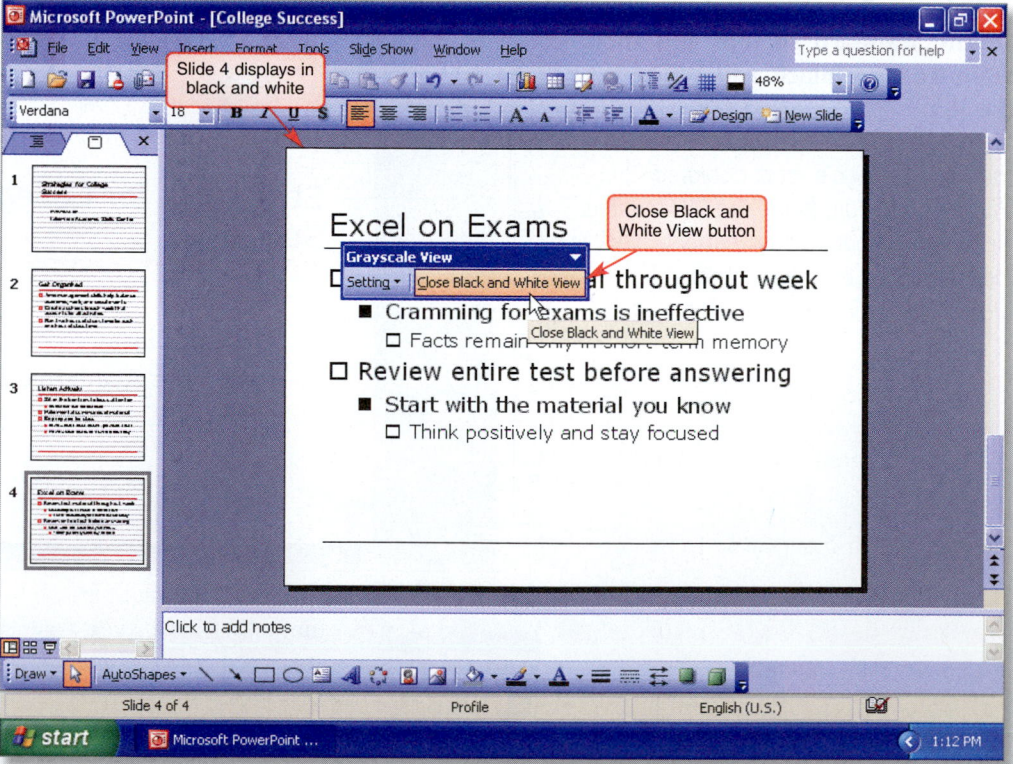

FIGURE 1-68

3

• **Click the Next Slide button three times to view all slides in the presentation in black and white.**

• **Point to the Close Black and White View button on the Grayscale View toolbar (Figure 1-69).**

FIGURE 1-69

4

- **Click the Close Black and White View button.**

Slide 4 is displayed with the default Profile color scheme (Figure 1-70).

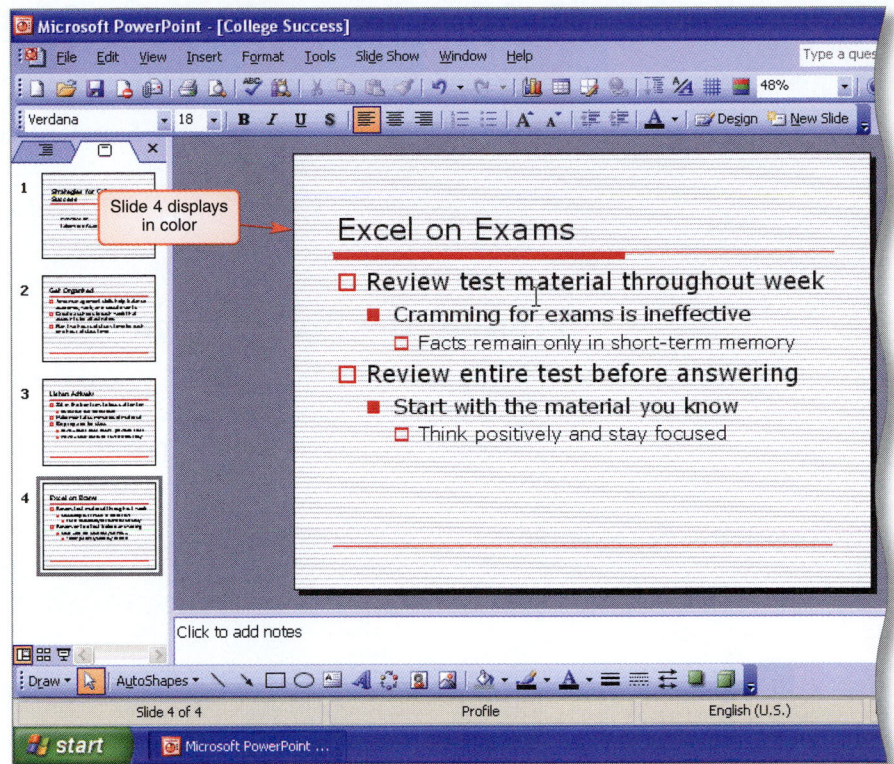

FIGURE 1-70

After you view the text objects in the presentation in black and white, you can make any changes that will enhance printouts produced from a black and white printer or photocopier.

Printing a Presentation

After you create a presentation, you often want to print it. A printed version of the presentation is called a **hard copy**, or **printout**. The first printing of the presentation is called a **rough draft**. The rough draft allows you to proofread the presentation to check for errors and readability. After correcting errors, you print the final copy of the presentation.

Saving Before Printing

Before printing a presentation, you should save your work in the event you experience difficulties with the printer. You occasionally may encounter system problems that can be resolved only by restarting the computer. In such an instance, you will need to reopen the presentation. As a precaution, always save the presentation before you print. The steps on the next page save the presentation before printing.

To Save a Presentation Before Printing

1 Verify that the floppy disk is in drive A.

2 Click the Save button on the Standard toolbar.

All changes made after your last save now are saved on the floppy disk.

Printing the Presentation

After saving the presentation, you are ready to print. Clicking the Print button on the Standard toolbar causes PowerPoint to print all slides in the presentation. The following steps illustrate how to print the presentation slides.

To Print a Presentation

1

• **Ready the printer according to the printer instructions.**

• **Click the Print button on the Standard toolbar.**

The printer icon in the tray status area on the Windows taskbar indicates a print job is processing (Figure 1-71). This icon may not display on your system, or it may display on your status bar. After several moments, the slide show begins printing on the printer. When the presentation is finished printing, the printer icon in the tray status area on the Windows taskbar no longer is displayed.

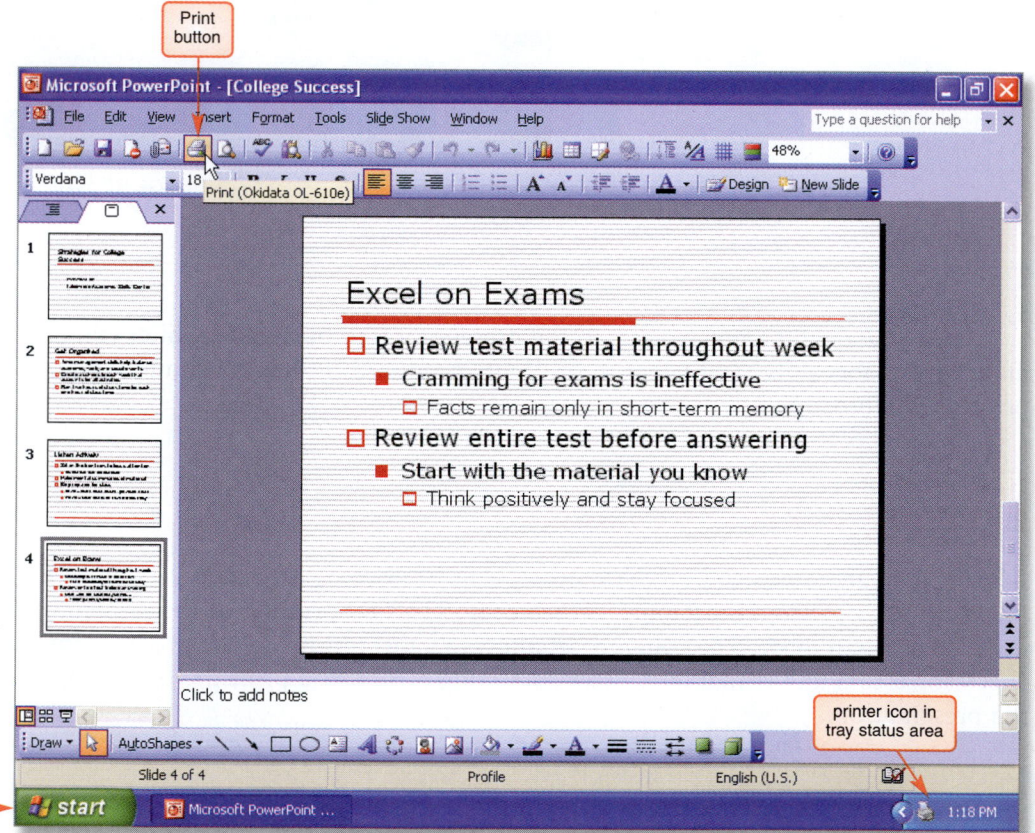

FIGURE 1-71

2

• **When the printer stops, retrieve the printouts of the slides.**

The presentation, College Success, prints on four pages (Figures 1-72a through 1-72d).

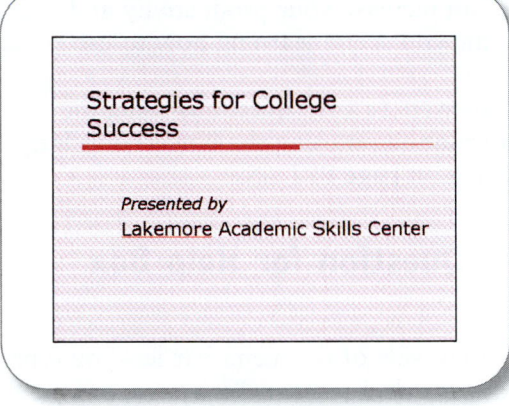

(a) Slide 1

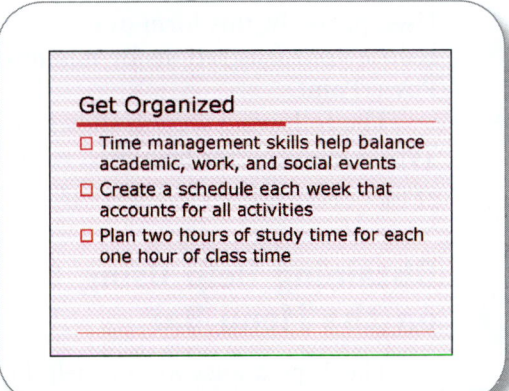

(b) Slide 2

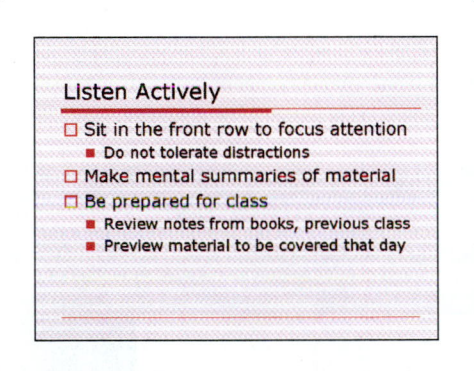

(c) Slide 3

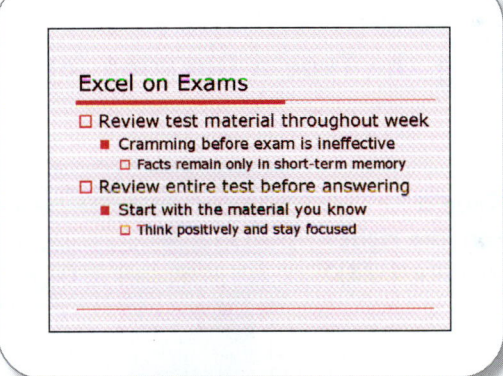

(d) Slide 4

FIGURE 1-72

You can click the printer icon next to the clock in the tray status area on the Windows taskbar to obtain information about the presentations printing on your printer and to delete files in the print queue that are waiting to be printed.

Other Ways

1. On File menu click Print
2. Press CTRL+P or press CTRL+SHIFT+F12
3. In Voice Command mode, say "Print"

Making a Transparency

With the handouts printed, you now can make overhead transparencies using one of several devices. One device is a printer attached to your computer, such as an inkjet printer or a laser printer. Transparencies produced on a printer may be in black and white or color, depending on the printer. Another device is a photocopier. Because each of these devices requires a special transparency film, check the user's manual for the film requirement of your specific device, or ask your instructor.

More About

**The PowerPoint
Help System**

Need Help? It is no further away than the Type a question for help box on the menu bar in the upper-right corner of the window. Click the box that contains the text, Type a question for help (Figure 1-73), type help, and then press the ENTER key. PowerPoint responds with a list of topics you can click to learn about obtaining help on any PowerPoint-related topic. To find out what is new in PowerPoint 2003, type what is new in PowerPoint in the Type a question for help box.

PowerPoint Help System

You can get answers to PowerPoint questions at any time by using the PowerPoint Help system. You can activate the PowerPoint Help system by using the Type a question for help box on the menu bar, by using the Microsoft PowerPoint Help button on the Standard toolbar, or by clicking Help on the menu bar (Figure 1-73). Used properly, this form of online assistance can increase your productivity and reduce your frustrations by minimizing the time you spend learning how to use PowerPoint.

The following section shows how to get answers to your questions using the Type a question for help box. Additional information on using the PowerPoint Help system is available in Appendix A and Table 1-6 on page PPT 65.

Obtaining Help Using the Type a Question for Help Box on the Menu Bar

The Type a question for help box on the right side of the menu bar lets you type free-form questions such as, *how do I save* or *how do I create a Web page*, or you can type terms such as, *copy*, *save*, or *format*. PowerPoint responds by displaying a list of topics related to what you typed. The following steps show how to use the Type a question for help box to obtain information on formatting bullets.

To Obtain Help Using the Type a Question for Help Box

1

• **Type** bullet **in the Type a question for help box on the right side of the menu bar (Figure 1-73).**

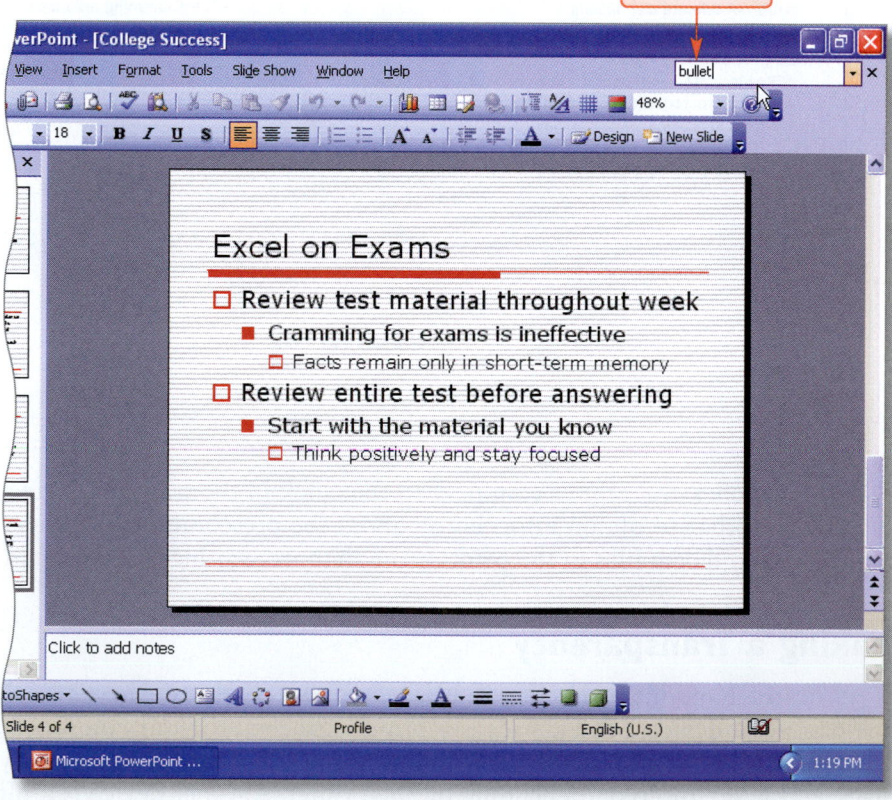

FIGURE 1-73

2

• **Press the ENTER key.**

• **When PowerPoint displays the Search Results task pane, scroll down and then point to the topic, Change the bullet style in a list.**

PowerPoint displays the Search Results task pane with a list of topics relating to the term, bullet. PowerPoint found 30 results from Microsoft Office Online. The mouse pointer changes to a hand, which indicates it is pointing to a link (Figure 1-74).

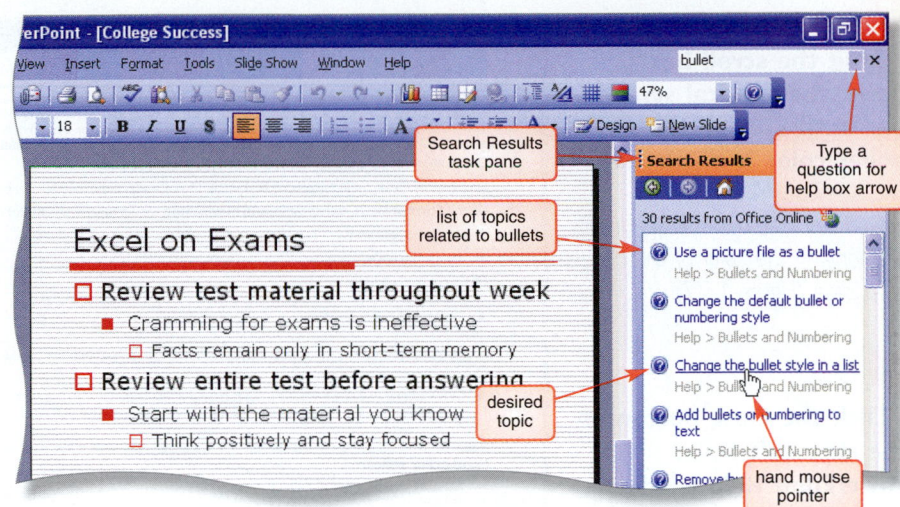

FIGURE 1-74

3

• **Click Change the bullet style in a list.**

• **When the Microsoft Office PowerPoint Help window is displayed, double-click its title bar to maximize it.**

A Microsoft Office PowerPoint Help window provides Help information about changing the bullet style in a list (Figure 1-75).

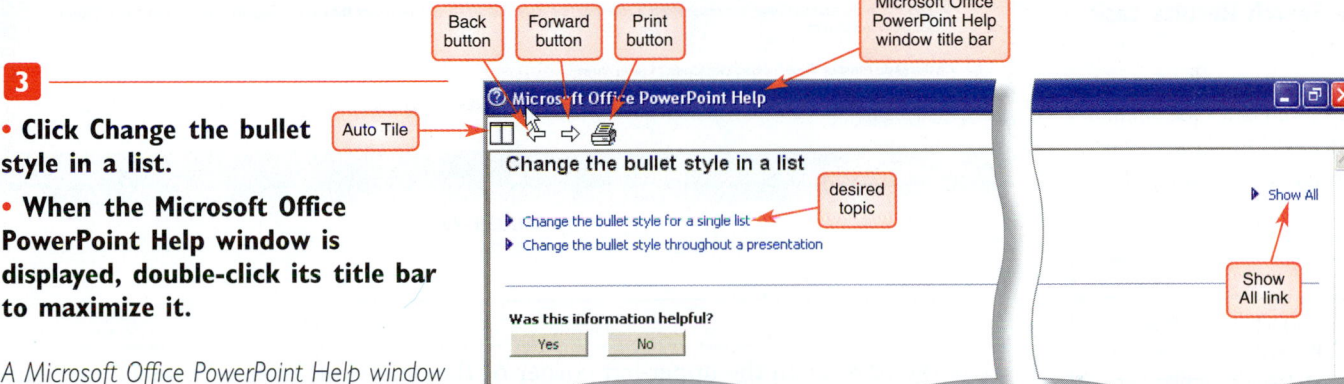

FIGURE 1-75

4

• **Click the Show All link.**

Directions for changing a bullet style for a single list are displayed. Options include change the bullet character, change the bullet size, and change the bullet color (Figure 1-76).

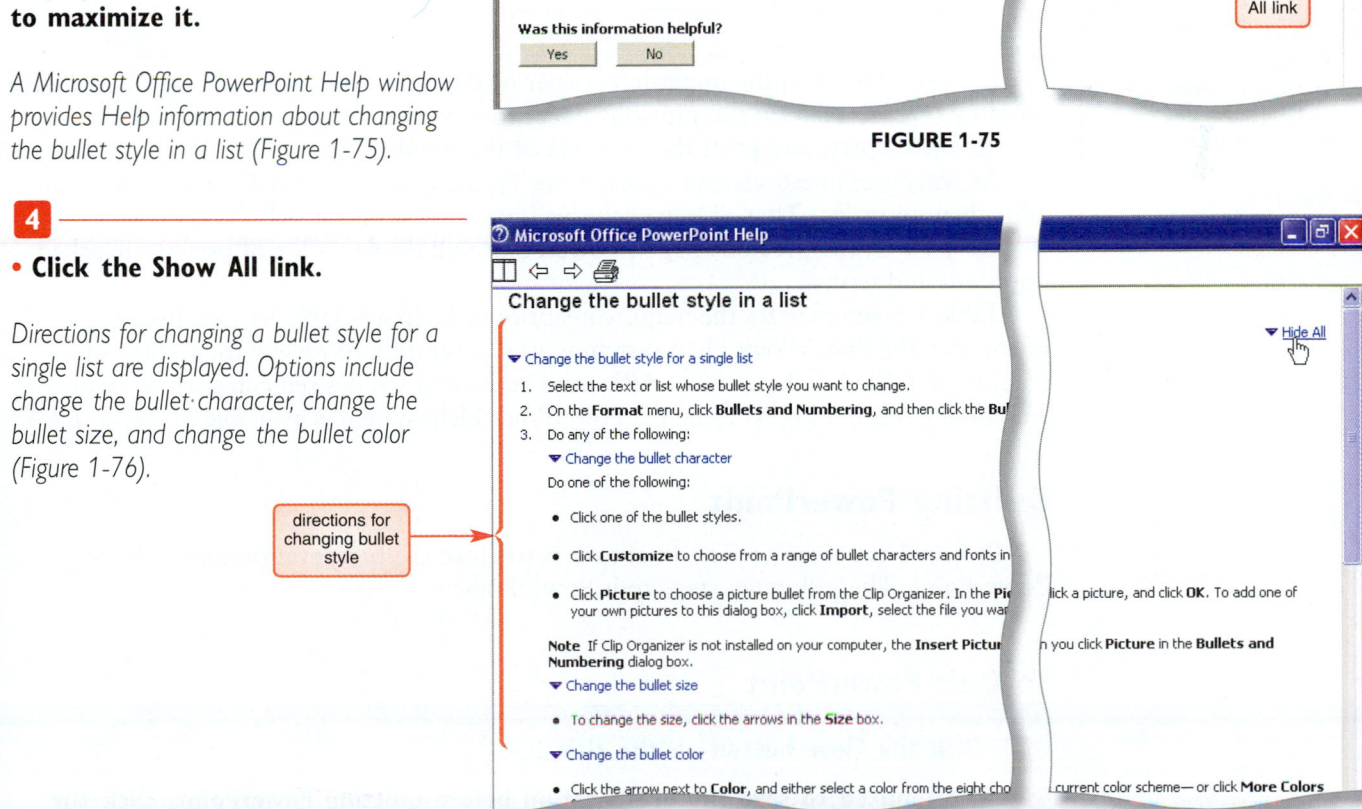

FIGURE 1-76

5

• **Drag the scroll box down the vertical scroll bar until Change the bullet color is displayed.**

PowerPoint displays specific details of changing the color of the bullets on a slide (Figure 1-77).

6

• **Click the Close button on the Microsoft Office PowerPoint Help window title bar.**

• **Click the Close button on the Search Results task pane.**

The PowerPoint Help window closes, and the PowerPoint presentation is displayed.

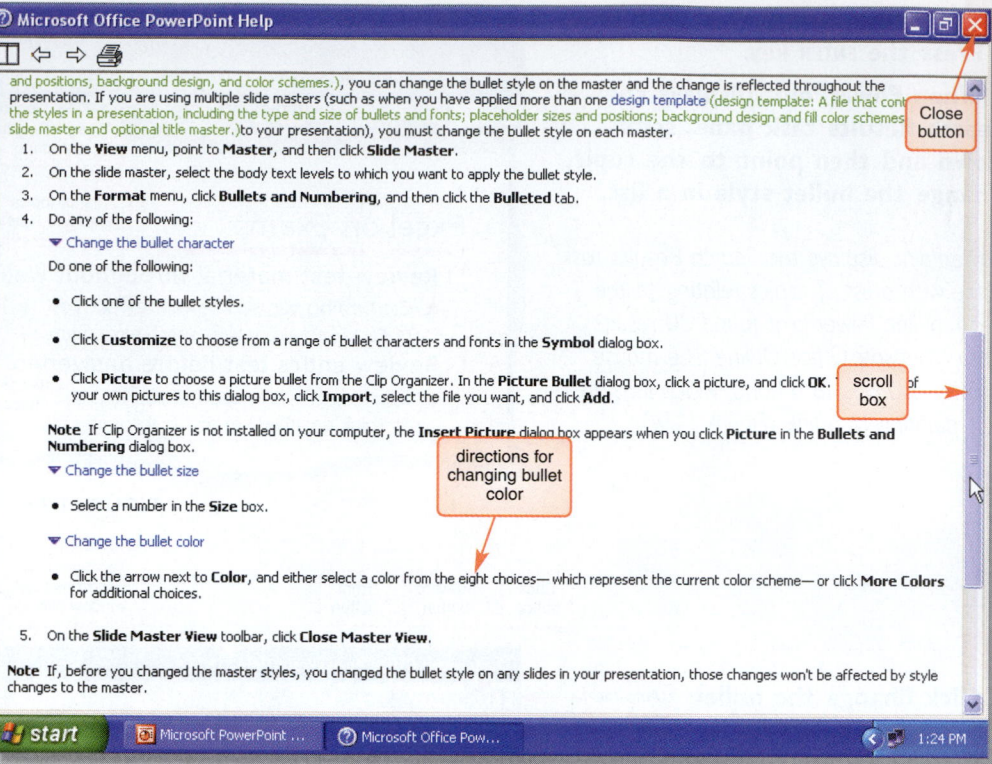

FIGURE 1-77

Other Ways

1. Click Microsoft Office PowerPoint Help button on Standard toolbar; or on Help menu click Microsoft Office PowerPoint Help
2. Press F1

Use the buttons in the upper-left corner of the Microsoft Office PowerPoint Help window (Figure 1-75 on the previous page) to navigate through the Help system, change the display, and print the contents of the window.

As you enter questions and terms in the Type a question for help box, PowerPoint adds them to its list. Thus, if you click the Type a question for help box arrow (Figure 1-74 on the previous page), PowerPoint will display a list of previously asked questions and terms.

Table 1-6 summarizes the major categories of Help available to you. Because of the way the PowerPoint Help system works, be certain to review the rightmost column of Table 1-6 if you have difficulties activating the desired category of Help. Additional information on using the PowerPoint Help system is available in Appendix A.

Quitting PowerPoint

Project 1 is complete. The final task is to close the presentation and quit PowerPoint. The following steps quit PowerPoint.

To Quit PowerPoint

1 **Click the Close button on the title bar.**

2 **If prompted to save the presentation before quitting PowerPoint, click the Yes button in the Microsoft Office PowerPoint dialog box.**

Table 1-6   PowerPoint Help System

TYPE	DESCRIPTION	HOW TO ACTIVATE
Microsoft Office PowerPoint Help	Displays PowerPoint Help task pane. Answers questions or searches for terms that you type in your own words.	Click the Microsoft Office PowerPoint Help button on the Standard toolbar or click Microsoft Office PowerPoint Help on the Help menu.
Office Assistant	Similar to the Type a question for help box. The Office Assistant answers questions that you type in your own words, offers tips, and provides help for a variety of PowerPoint features.	Click the Office Assistant icon. If the Office Assistant does not display, click Show the Office Assistant on the Help menu.
Type a question for help box	Answers questions or searches for terms that you type in your own words.	Type a question or term in the Type a question for help box on the menu bar and then press the ENTER key.
Table of Contents	Groups Help topics by general categories. Use when you know only the general category of the topic in question.	Click the Microsoft Office PowerPoint Help button on the Standard toolbar or click Microsoft Office PowerPoint Help on the Help menu, and then click the Table of Contents link on the PowerPoint Help task pane.
Microsoft Office Online	Used to access technical resources and download free product enhancements on the Web.	Click Microsoft Office Online on the Help menu.
Detect and Repair	Automatically finds and fixes errors in the application.	Click Detect and Repair on the Help menu.

Project Summary

In creating the Strategies for College Success slide show in this project, you gained a broad knowledge of PowerPoint. First, you were introduced to starting PowerPoint and creating a presentation consisting of a title slide and single- and multi-level bulleted lists. You learned about PowerPoint design templates, objects, and attributes.

This project illustrated how to create an interesting introduction to a presentation by changing the text font style to italic and increasing font size on the title slide. Completing these tasks, you saved the presentation. Then, you created three text slides with bulleted lists, two with multi-level bullets, to explain effective academic skills. Next, you learned how to view the presentation in slide show view. Then, you learned how to quit PowerPoint and how to open an existing presentation. You used the Spelling checker to search for spelling errors. You learned how to display the presentation in black and white. You also learned how to print hard copies of the slides in order to make handouts and overhead transparencies. Finally, you learned how to use the PowerPoint Help system to answer your questions.

 If you have a SAM user profile, you may have access to hands-on instruction, practice, and assessment of the skills covered in this project. Log in to your SAM account and go to your assignments page to see what your instructor has assigned.

What You Should Know

Having completed this project, you should be able to perform the tasks below. The tasks are listed in the same order they were presented in this project. For a list of the buttons, menus, toolbars, and commands introduced in this project, see the Quick Reference Summary at the back of this book and refer to the Page Number column.

1. Start PowerPoint   (PPT 7)
2. Customize the PowerPoint Window   (PPT 9)
3. Choose a Design Template   (PPT 18)
4. Enter the Presentation Title   (PPT 21)
5. Enter the Presentation Subtitle   (PPT 22)
6. Change the Text Font Style to Italic   (PPT 24)
7. Increase Font Size   (PPT 25)
8. Save a Presentation on a Floppy Disk   (PPT 27)
9. Add a New Text Slide with a Bulleted List   (PPT 30)
10. Enter a Slide Title   (PPT 32)
11. Select a Text Placeholder   (PPT 32)
12. Type a Single-Level Bulleted List   (PPT 33)
13. Add a New Slide and Enter a Slide Title   (PPT 35)
14. Type a Multi-Level Bulleted List   (PPT 36)
15. Type the Remaining Text for Slide 3   (PPT 38)
16. Create Slide 4   (PPT 39)
17. Create a Third-Level Paragraph   (PPT 40)
18. Type the Remaining Text for Slide 4   (PPT 41)
19. End a Slide Show with a Black Slide   (PPT 42)
20. Save a Presentation with the Same File Name   (PPT 44)
21. Use the Scroll Box on the Slide Pane to Move to Another Slide   (PPT 45)
22. Start Slide Show View   (PPT 47)
23. Move Manually Through Slides in a Slide Show   (PPT 48)
24. Display the Popup Menu and Go to a Specific Slide   (PPT 49)
25. Use the Popup Menu to End a Slide Show   (PPT 50)
26. Quit PowerPoint   (PPT 50)
27. Start PowerPoint and Open an Existing Presentation   (PPT 52)
28. Start the Spelling Checker   (PPT 54)
29. Display a Presentation in Black and White   (PPT 57)
30. Save a Presentation Before Printing   (PPT 60)
31. Print a Presentation   (PPT 60)
32. Obtain Help Using the Type a Question for Help Box   (PPT 62)
33. Quit PowerPoint   (PPT 64)

Learn It Online

Instructions: To complete the Learn It Online exercises, start your browser, click the Address bar, and then enter the Web address `scsite.com/ppt2003/learn`. When the PowerPoint 2003 Learn It Online page is displayed, follow the instructions in the exercises below. Each exercise has instructions for printing your results, either for your own records or for submission to your instructor.

1 Project Reinforcement TF, MC, and SA

Below PowerPoint Project 1, click the Project Reinforcement link. Print the quiz by clicking Print on the File menu for each page. Answer each question.

2 Flash Cards

Below PowerPoint Project 1, click the Flash Cards link and read the instructions. Type 20 (or a number specified by your instructor) in the Number of playing cards text box, type your name in the Enter your Name text box, and then click the Flip Card button. When the flash card is displayed, read the question and then click the ANSWER box arrow to select an answer. Flip through Flash Cards. If your score is 15 (75%) correct or greater, click Print on the File menu to print your results. If your score is less than 15 (75%) correct, then redo this exercise by clicking the Replay button.

3 Practice Test

Below PowerPoint Project 1, click the Practice Test link. Answer each question, enter your first and last name at the bottom of the page, and then click the Grade Test button. When the graded practice test is displayed on your screen, click Print on the File menu to print a hard copy. Continue to take practice tests until you score 80% or better.

4 Who Wants To Be a Computer Genius?

Below PowerPoint Project 1, click the Computer Genius link. Read the instructions, enter your first and last name at the bottom of the page, and then click the PLAY button. When your score is displayed, click the PRINT RESULTS link to print a hard copy.

5 Wheel of Terms

Below PowerPoint Project 1, click the Wheel of Terms link. Read the instructions, and then enter your first and last name and your school name. Click the PLAY button. When your score is displayed, right-click the score and then click Print on the shortcut menu to print a hard copy.

6 Crossword Puzzle Challenge

Below PowerPoint Project 1, click the Crossword Puzzle Challenge link. Read the instructions, and then enter your first and last name. Click the SUBMIT button. Work the crossword puzzle. When you are finished, click the Submit button. When the crossword puzzle is redisplayed, click the Print Puzzle button to print a hard copy.

7 Tips and Tricks

Below PowerPoint Project 1, click the Tips and Tricks link. Click a topic that pertains to Project 1. Right-click the information and then click Print on the shortcut menu. Construct a brief example of what the information relates to in PowerPoint to confirm you understand how to use the tip or trick.

8 Newsgroups

Below PowerPoint Project 1, click the Newsgroups link. Click a topic that pertains to Project 1. Print three comments.

9 Expanding Your Horizons

Below PowerPoint Project 1, click the Expanding Your Horizons link. Click a topic that pertains to Project 1. Print the information. Construct a brief example of what the information relates to in PowerPoint to confirm you understand the contents of the article.

10 Search Sleuth

Below PowerPoint Project 1, click the Search Sleuth link. To search for a term that pertains to this project, select a term below the Project 1 title and then use the Google search engine at google.com (or any major search engine) to display and print two Web pages that present information on the term.

11 PowerPoint Online Training

Below PowerPoint Project 1, click the PowerPoint Online Training link. When your browser displays the Microsoft Office Online Web page, click the PowerPoint link. Click one of the PowerPoint courses that covers one or more of the objectives listed at the beginning of the project on page PPT 4. Print the first page of the course before stepping through it.

12 Office Marketplace

Below PowerPoint Project 1, click the Office Marketplace link. When your browser displays the Microsoft Office Online Web page, click the Office Marketplace link. Click a topic that relates to PowerPoint. Print the first page.

Apply Your Knowledge

1 Searching on the World Wide Web

Instructions: Start PowerPoint. Open the presentation Apply 1-1 Internet Searching from the Data Disk. See the inside back cover of this book for instructions for downloading the Data Disk or see your instructor for information on accessing the files required for this book. The two slides in the presentation give information on tools to search the Web. Make the following changes to the slides so they appear as shown in Figure 1-78.

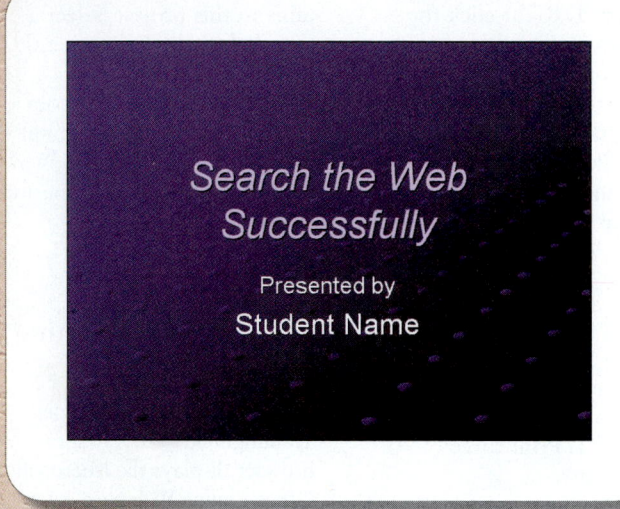

(a) Slide 1 (Title Slide)

(b) Slide 2 (Multi-Level Bulleted List)

FIGURE 1-78

Change the design template to Digital Dots. On the title slide, use your name in place of Student Name and change the font size to 40. Italicize the title text.

On Slide 2, increase the indent of the second and fourth paragraphs, Categorized lists of links arranged by subject and displayed in series of menus, and Requires search text: a word, words, phrase, to second-level paragraphs. Then change the last paragraph, Carefully craft keywords to limit search, to a third-level paragraph.

Display the revised presentation in black and white, and then print the two slides.

Save the presentation using the file name, Apply 1-1 Search Tools. Hand in the hard copy to your instructor.

In the Lab

Note: These labs require you to create presentations based on notes. When you design these slide shows, use the 7 × 7 rule, which states that each line should have a maximum of seven words, and each slide should have a maximum of seven lines.

1 Common Cold Concerns Presentation

Problem: The common cold is one of the most frequent health problems; more than one billion cases are reported each year. Although no remedy cures the runny nose or sore throat that accompany this illness, students can reduce their chances of catching a cold and feel better when they are sick. Dr. Larry Hopper is the head physician at your campus's health clinic. He has asked you to prepare a short PowerPoint presentation and handouts to educate students about how to thwart the common cold. He hands you the outline shown in Figure 1-79 and asks you to create the presentation shown in Figures 1-80a through 1-80f on the following pages.

I.) Coping with the Common Cold
Presented by
Larry Hopper, M.D.

II.) Cold Facts
- We have more than 1 billion colds annually
- No remedy cures the common cold
- You can reduce the chances of catching a cold
- You can feel better when you are sick

III.) When You Are Feeling Sick
- Get plenty of rest
- Drink lots of fluids
- Consume chicken soup

IV.) If Your Throat Is Sore
- Gargle with warm salt water
- Let a lozenge dissolve slowly in your mouth
  - Choose one with menthol and mild anesthetic

V.) If Your Nose Is Stuffy
- Try a decongestant
  - Shrinks blood vessels
  - Do not take for more than three days
- Try an antihistamine
  - Relieves a runny nose, itching, and sneezing
  - Has a drying effect

VI.) Avoid a Cold
- Stay away from other people with colds
- Wash your hands frequently
- Keep your hands away from your mouth and nose
- Dispose of tissues promptly

FIGURE 1-79

(continued)

Common Cold Concerns Presentation *(continued)*

Coping with the Common Cold

Presented by
Larry Hopper, M.D.

(a) Slide 1

Cold Facts

- We have more than 1 billion colds annually
- No remedy cures the common cold
- You can reduce the chances of catching a cold
- You can feel better when you are sick

(b) Slide 2

When You Are Feeling Sick

- Get plenty of rest
- Drink lots of fluids
- Consume chicken soup

(c) Slide 3

If Your Throat Is Sore

- Gargle with warm salt water
- Let a lozenge dissolve slowly in your mouth
  - Choose one with menthol and mild anesthetic

(d) Slide 4

FIGURE 1-80

In the Lab

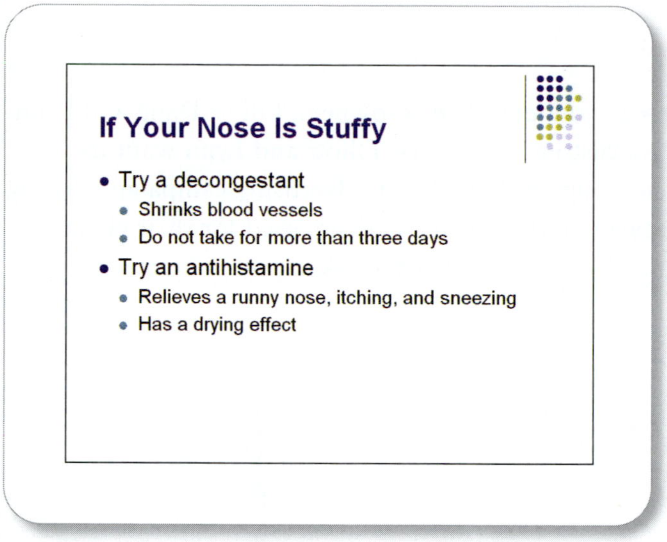

If Your Nose Is Stuffy

- Try a decongestant
  - Shrinks blood vessels
  - Do not take for more than three days
- Try an antihistamine
  - Relieves a runny nose, itching, and sneezing
  - Has a drying effect

(e) Slide 5

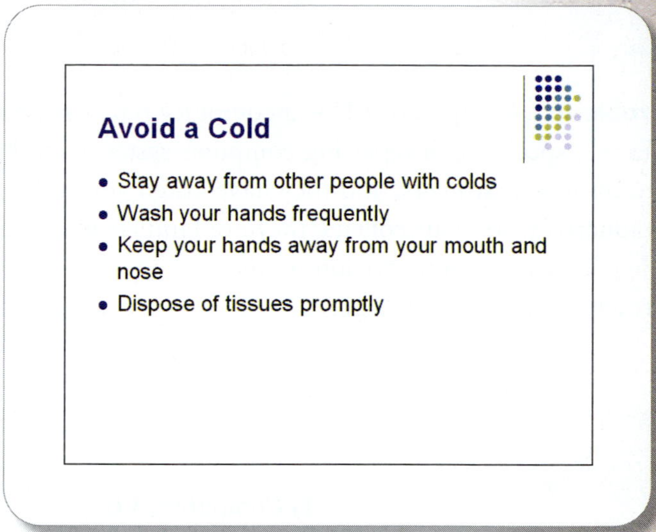

Avoid a Cold

- Stay away from other people with colds
- Wash your hands frequently
- Keep your hands away from your mouth and nose
- Dispose of tissues promptly

(f) Slide 6

FIGURE 1-80 *(continued)*

Instructions: Perform the following tasks.

1. Create a new presentation using the Network design template (row 14, column 2).
2. Using the typed notes illustrated in Figure 1-79 on page PPT 69, create the title slide shown in Figure 1-80a using your name in place of Larry Hopper. Italicize the title paragraph, Coping with the Common Cold, and increase the font size to 60. Increase the font size of the first paragraph of the subtitle text, Presented by, to 36. Italicize your name.
3. Using the typed notes in Figure 1-79, create the five text slides with bulleted lists shown in Figures 1-80b through 1-80f.
4. Click the Spelling button on the Standard toolbar. Correct any errors.
5. Drag the scroll box to display Slide 1. Click the Slide Show button to start slide show view. Then click to display each slide.
6. Save the presentation using the file name, Lab 1-1 Common Cold Concerns.
7. Display and print the presentation in black and white. Close the presentation. Hand in the hard copy to your instructor.

2 Computers 4 U Repair Store Presentation

Problem: Computers 4 U is a computer repair store near your campus. The co-owners, Elliott Dane and Lynn Verone, specialize in repairing computer systems and building custom computers. Elliott and Lynn want to attract new customers, and they have asked you to help them design a PowerPoint advertising campaign. Having graduated from your college, they are familiar with the hardware and software students need for their classes. They have typed information on their services for you (Figure 1-81), and they have asked you to create the presentation shown in Figures 1-82a through 1-82d.

1) Computers 4 U
Complete Repairs and Service
Elliott Dane and Lynn Verone

2) Hardware and Software
- Convenient in-store appointments
- On-site service
  - 24 hours a day
- Plan for future computer purchases
- Arrange financing for new systems

3) Complete Supplies
- Toner cartridges
  - All major printer brands in-stock
- Paper
  - Wide variety of patterns and colors
- Labels
  - Complete selection of sizes

4) Convenient Location
- Bremen Mall
  - 15800 South Wabash Street
  - Napier, Washington
  - 555-1123

FIGURE 1-81

In the Lab

(a) Slide 1 (Title Slide)

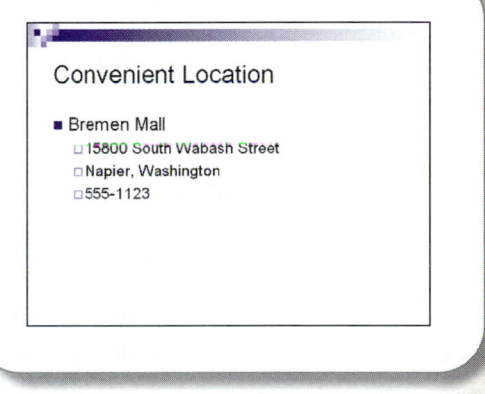

(b) Slide 2

(c) Slide 3

(d) Slide 4

FIGURE 1-82

Instructions: Perform the following tasks.

1. Create a new presentation using the Pixel design template (row 16, column 1).
2. Using the typed notes illustrated in Figure 1-81, create the title slide shown in Figure 1-82a using your name in place of Elliott Dane. Italicize both names. Increase the font size of the title paragraph, Computers 4 U, to 68. Decrease the font size of the first paragraph of the subtitle text, Complete Repairs and Service, to 30.
3. Using the typed notes in Figure 1-81, create the three text slides with bulleted lists shown in Figures 1-82b through 1-82d.
4. Click the Spelling button on the Standard toolbar. Correct any errors.
5. Save the presentation using the file name, Lab 1-2 Computers 4 U.
6. Display the presentation in black and white.
7. Print the black and white presentation. Close the presentation. Hand in the hard copy to your instructor.

3 Community Center Course Update

Problem: The Rivercrest Community Center has updated its winter classes and has included activities for town residents of all ages. For children, the new classes are Skateboarding Fundamentals, Tumbling for Toddlers, and Basketball Boot Camp. For adults, the new offerings are Yoga and Spinning. Seniors can enroll in Self-Defense and Flexibility.

Instructions Part 1: Using the outline in Figure 1-83, create the presentation shown in Figure 1-84. Use the Radial design template. On the title slide, type your name in place of Janice Jackson, increase the font size of the title paragraph, Rivercrest Community Center, to 50, and change the text font style to italic. Increase the font size of the subtitle paragraph, New Winter Classes, to 40. Create the three text slides with multi-level bulleted lists shown in Figures 1-84b through 1-84d.

Correct any spelling mistakes, and then view the slide show. Save the presentation using the file name, Lab 1-3 Part One Winter Classes. Display and print the presentation in black and white.

1. Rivercrest Community Center
New Winter Classes
Janice Jackson, Director

2. Children's Classes
- Skateboarding Fundamentals
  - Emphasizes safety and control
- Tumbling for Toddlers
  - Learn coordination while having fun
- Basketball Boot Camp
  - Features game strategies and conditioning

3. Adults' Classes
- Yoga
  - Enjoy a mind-body experience
    - Release external tensions and chaos
- Spinning
  - Learn proper bike set-up
  - Involves series of cycling techniques

4. Seniors' Classes
- Self-defense
  - Learn to avoid dangerous situations
- Flexibility
  - Improve range of motion, balance, posture
    - Helps to prevent falls
  - Instill your body with grace and movement

FIGURE 1-83

Rivercrest Community Center

New Winter Classes
Janice Jackson, Director

(a) Slide 1 (Title Slide)

Children's Classes

- Skateboarding Fundamentals
  - Emphasizes safety and control
- Tumbling for Toddlers
  - Learn coordination while having fun
- Basketball Boot Camp
  - Features game strategies and conditioning

(b) Slide 2

Adults' Classes

- Yoga
  - Enjoy a mind-body experience
    - Release external tensions and chaos
- Spinning
  - Learn proper bike set-up
  - Involves series of cycling techniques

(c) Slide 3

Seniors' Classes

- Self-defense
  - Learn to avoid dangerous situations
- Flexibility
  - Improve range of motion, balance, posture
    - Helps to prevent falls
  - Instill your body with grace and movement

(d) Slide 4

FIGURE 1-84

(continued)

Community Center Course Update *(continued)*

Instructions Part 2: The Rivercrest Community Center wants to update this presentation to promote the summer class schedule. Modify the presentation created in Part 1 to create the presentation shown in Figure 1-85. Change the design template to Glass Layers.

On the title slide, remove the italics from the title paragraph, Rivercrest Community Center, decrease the font size to 44, and center the text. Change the first subtitle paragraph to New Summer Classes. Then change your title in the second subtitle paragraph to Executive Director and decrease the font size to 28.

On Slide 2, delete the first-level paragraph regarding the basketball boot camp and replace it with the paragraph, Swimming Safely. Delete the last paragraph on the slide and replace it with the paragraph, Practice proper breathing and strokes.

On Slide 3, change the first subtitle paragraph to Yoga and Tai Chi. Then change the first first-level paragraph under Spinning to, Learn proper bike set-up and form.

On Slide 4, change the second-level paragraph under Self-Defense to, Learn to escape from an attacker.

Correct any spelling mistakes, and then view the slide show. Save the presentation using the file name, Lab 1-3 Part Two Summer Classes. Display and print the presentation in black and white. Close the presentation. Hand in both presentation printouts to your instructor.

In the Lab

(a) Slide 1

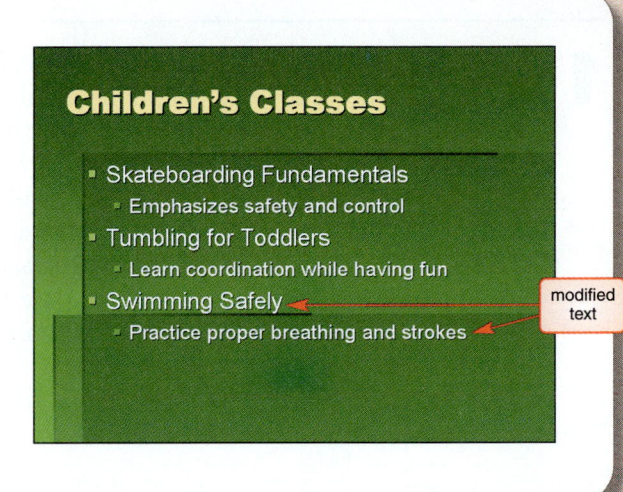

(b) Slide 2

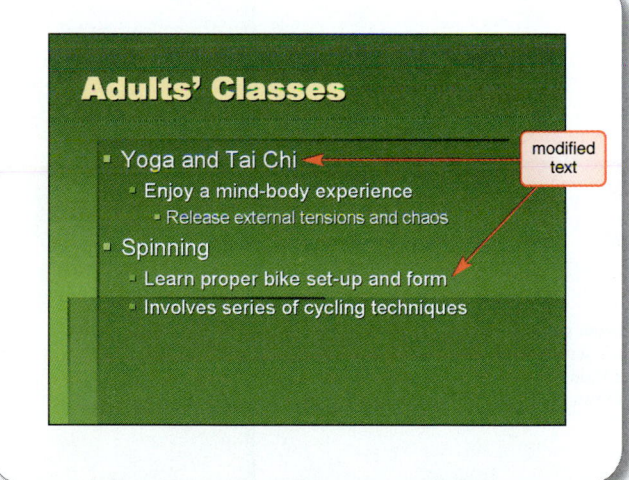

(c) Slide 3

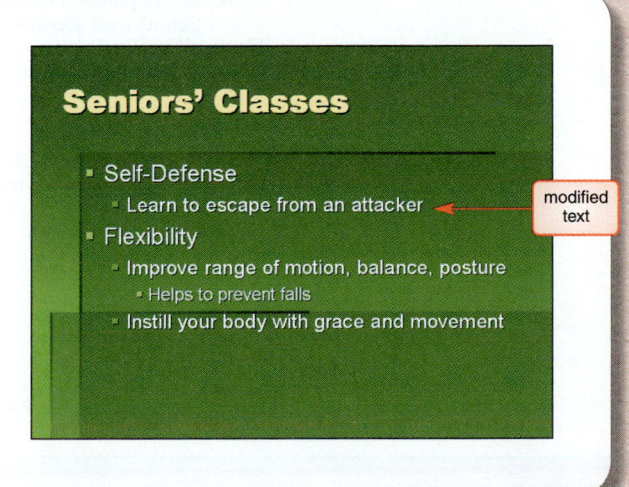

(d) Slide 4

FIGURE 1-85

The difficulty of these case studies varies: ■ are the least difficult and ■ ■ are more difficult. The last exercise is a group exercise.

Note: Remember to use the 7 × 7 rule as you design the presentations: a maximum of seven words on a line and a maximum of seven lines on one slide.

1 ■ The dispatcher at the Imperial Grove Police Station is noticing an increase in the number of calls made to the emergency 911 telephone number. These calls, unfortunately, are not always emergencies. Community residents have been calling the number to obtain information on everything from the times of movies at the local theatre to the names of the local city trustees. Police Chief Gina Colatta wants to inform homeowners of the importance of using the 911 service correctly. She created the outline shown in Figure 1-86 and asks you to help her prepare an accompanying PowerPoint presentation to show at the local mall and food stores. Using the concepts and techniques introduced in this project, together with Chief Colatta's outline, develop a slide show with a title slide and three text slides with bulleted lists. Print the slides so they can be distributed to residents at the conclusion of the presentation.

> **1) 911 – A Call for Help**
>   Presented by
>   Chief Gina Colatta
>   Imperial Grove Police Department
>
> **2) What It Is For**
>   When you need an emergency response
>   Fire
>   Police
>   Emergency Medical Personnel
>   When disaster occurs
>   Tornadoes, earthquakes, floods
>
> **3) How to Help**
>   Do not call for general information
>   Consult local telephone directories
>   If you call by mistake:
>   Tell the dispatcher you have misdialed
>   Wait if you hear a recording
>
> **4) Other Information**
>   Tell the telephone company if you change your name or address
>   This info displays on the dispatcher's screen
>   The dispatcher relies on this information
>   Be certain your house number can be seen from the street

FIGURE 1-86

Cases and Places

2 ■ Your school is planning a job fair to occur during the week of midterm exams. The Placement Office has invited 100 companies and local businesses to promote its current and anticipated job openings. The Placement Office director, Latasha Prince, hands you the outline shown in Figure 1-87 and asks you to prepare a presentation and handouts to promote the event. Use this list to design and create a presentation with a title slide and three text slides with bulleted lists.

1. Brookville College Career Fair
Presented by
Brookville College Placement Office
Latasha Prince, Director

2. Who Is Coming?
National corporations
Progressive companies looking for high-quality candidates
Local companies
Full-time and part-time
- Hundreds of jobs

3. When Is It?
Midterm week
Monday through Friday
Brookville College Cafeteria
Convenient hours
9:00 a.m. to 8:00 p.m.

4. How Should I Prepare?
Bring plenty of resumes
More than 100 companies expected
Dress neatly
View the Placement Office Web site
Up-to-date information
Company profiles

FIGURE 1-87

Cases and Places

3 ■■ In-line skating is a popular recreational sport throughout the world. In 1989, three million skaters spent $20 million on these skates and protective gear. In 1994, sales soared when nearly 14 million skaters spent $250 million. Today, the more than 27 million in-line skaters are purchasing more than $300 million in equipment yearly. Females account for 52 percent of skaters, and youths ranging in age from 7 to 17 are 58 percent of the total skaters. In-line skaters can participate more safely if they follow these steps: Wear full protective gear, including a helmet, wrist guards, and knee and elbow pads; practice basic skills, including braking, turning, and balancing, in a parking lot or other flat surface; always skate under control; and avoid hills until mastering speed control. The public relations director of your local park district has asked you to prepare a slide show emphasizing these safety tips and illustrating the in-line skating popularity surge. You decide to develop a slide show to run at the sporting goods store. Prepare a short presentation aimed at encouraging skaters to practice safe skating.

4 ■■ About 25 percent of the population suffers from the flu each year from October through May. Flu-related symptoms generally last for two weeks and include sudden headaches, chills, dry coughs, high fevers, and body aches. Serious complications are common, and an estimated 20,000 Americans die each year from the disease. Annual flu shots can help prevent the illness, and they are recommended for high-risk individuals such as the elderly and healthcare workers. Some drugs will help shorten the duration of the illness and decrease its severity if given within 48 hours after symptoms appear. General health tips include eating a balanced diet, getting enough rest, staying home when ill, exercising frequently, and washing hands frequently with warm, soapy water. Your campus' health services department wants to develop a presentation for students informing them about the flu and giving advice to stay healthy. Using the techniques introduced in the project, create a presentation about the flu.

5 ■■ **Working Together** Volunteers can make a contribution to society while they gain much fulfillment in return. Community organizations and non-for-profit businesses frequently seek volunteers for various projects. Have each member of your team visit or telephone several local civic groups to determine volunteer opportunities. Gather data about:

1) Required duties
2) Number of required hours
3) Contact person
4) Address
5) Telephone number

After coordinating the data, create a presentation with at least one slide showcasing the charitable organization. As a group, critique each slide. Hand in a hard copy of the final presentation.

Using the Outline Tab and Clip Art to Create a Slide Show

PROJECT

2

CASE PERSPECTIVE

For some students, the Healthy Eating Pyramid developed by the Harvard School of Public Health is as foreign as the Great Pyramid of Egypt. Eating a balanced diet seems as impossible as solving a quadratic formula. Obesity, hypertension, heart disease, and diabetes are soaring as a consequence of poor eating and lack of exercise, as two of every three Americans are classified as overweight or obese. Moreover, 25 percent of the U.S. population leads a completely sedentary lifestyle.

Cultural and social factors contribute to this unhealthy existence, so health care and fitness professionals need to educate adults and adolescents about adopting nutritious meals and daily exercise as the basis of a healthy lifestyle. Jessica Cantero, the Fitness Director at your college, realizes that students need to understand and apply simple measures they can take to help promote a healthy body. She wants to develop a series of workshops to motivate students to control their weight, exercise moderately, and release stress.

She knows that PowerPoint slide shows enhance speakers' presentations, so she asks you to assist her in developing a slide show to accompany her first workshop. This presentation will include nutritional information based on the Healthy Eating Pyramid, daily exercise guidelines, relaxation principles, and the advantages of maintaining a healthy lifestyle.

As you read through this project, you will learn how to use PowerPoint to add clip art and animation to increase the presentation's visual interest. You also will e-mail the completed presentation to Jessica.

MICROSOFT
Office PowerPoint 2003

Using the Outline Tab and Clip Art to Create a Slide Show

P R O J E C T

Objectives

You will have mastered the material in this project when you can:

- Start and customize a new slide show from an outline
- Add a slide and create a closing slide on the Outline tab
- Create text slides with multi-level bulleted lists on the Outline tab
- Save and review a presentation

- Insert and move clip art and change its size
- Add a header and footer to outline pages
- Animate clip art
- Add an animation scheme and run an animated slide show
- Print a presentation outline
- E-mail a slide show from within PowerPoint

Introduction

At some time during either your academic or business life, you probably will make a presentation. The presentation may be informative by providing detailed information about a specific topic. Other presentations may be persuasive by selling a proposal or a product to a client, convincing management to approve a new project, or influencing the board of directors to accept the new fiscal budget. As an alternative to creating your presentation in the slide pane in normal view, as you did in Project 1, PowerPoint provides an outlining feature to help you organize your thoughts. When the outline is complete, it becomes the foundation for your presentation.

Project Two — Healthy Eating, Healthy Living

Project 2 uses PowerPoint to create the five-slide Healthy Eating, Healthy Living presentation shown in Figures 2-1a through 2-1e. You create the presentation from the outline shown in Figure 2-2 on page PPT 84.

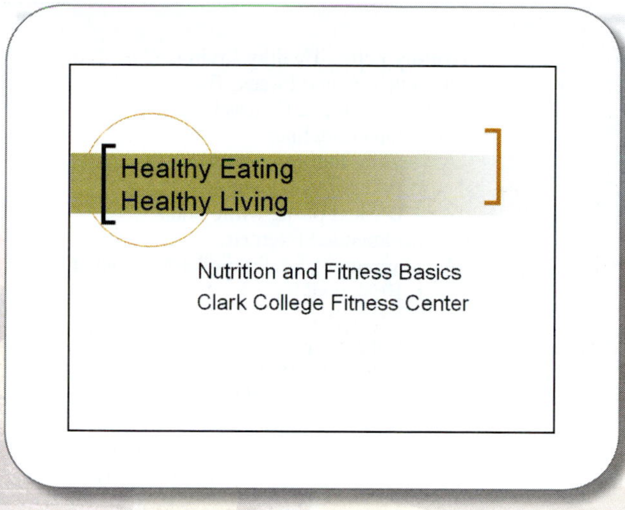

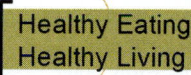

Healthy Eating
Healthy Living

Nutrition and Fitness Basics
Clark College Fitness Center

(a) Slide 1

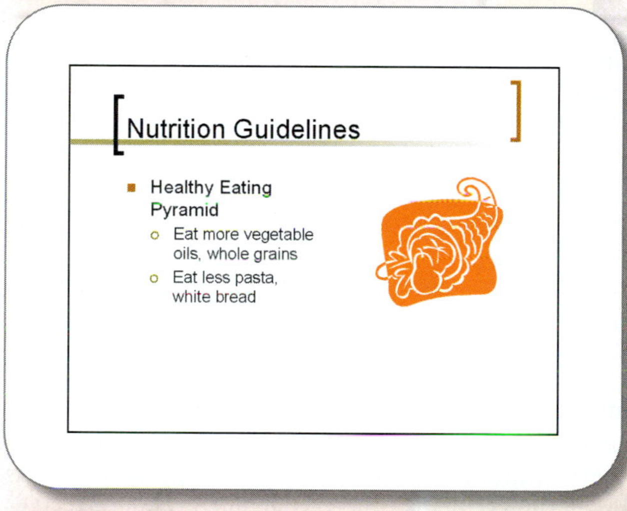

Nutrition Guidelines

- Healthy Eating
  Pyramid
  o Eat more vegetable
    oils, whole grains
  o Eat less pasta,
    white bread

(b) Slide 2

Recommended Exercise

- 30 minutes of daily
  moderate-intensity
  activity
  o Brisk walking
  o Bicycling
  o Gardening

(c) Slide 3

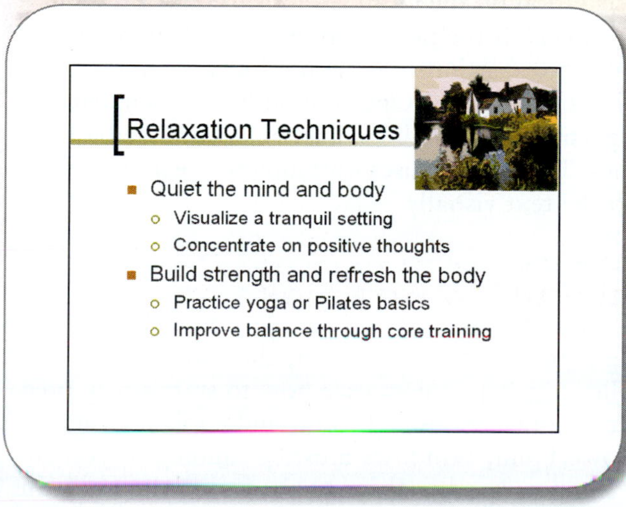

Relaxation Techniques

- Quiet the mind and body
  o Visualize a tranquil setting
  o Concentrate on positive thoughts
- Build strength and refresh the body
  o Practice yoga or Pilates basics
  o Improve balance through core training

(d) Slide 4

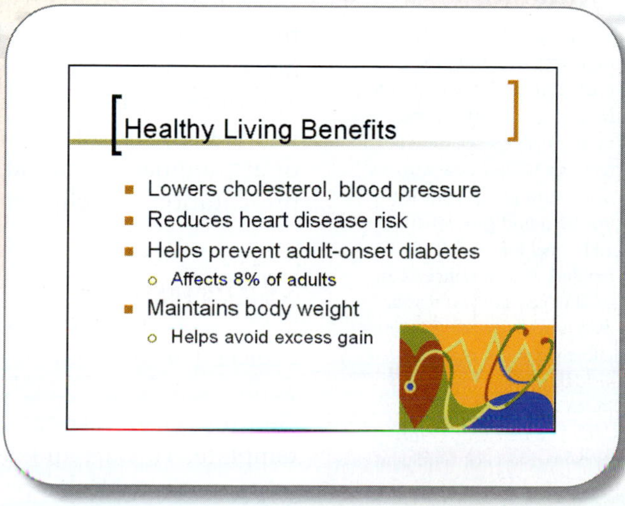

Healthy Living Benefits

- Lowers cholesterol, blood pressure
- Reduces heart disease risk
- Helps prevent adult-onset diabetes
  o Affects 8% of adults
- Maintains body weight
  o Helps avoid excess gain

(e) Slide 5

FIGURE 2-1

I. Healthy Eating Healthy Living
    A. Nutrition and Fitness Basics
    B. Clark College Fitness Center
II. Nutrition Guidelines
    A. Healthy Eating Pyramid
        1. Eat more vegetable oils, whole grains
        2. Eat less pasta, white bread
III. Recommended Exercise
    A. 30 minutes of daily moderate-intensity activity
        1. Brisk walking
        2. Bicycling
        3. Gardening
IV. Relaxation Techniques
    A. Quiet the mind and body
        1. Visualize a tranquil setting
        2. Concentrate on positive thoughts
    B. Build strength and refresh the body
        1. Practice yoga or Pilates basics
        2. Improve balance through core training
V. Healthy Living Benefits
    A. Lowers cholesterol, blood pressure
    B. Reduces heart disease risk
    C. Helps prevent adult-onset diabetes
        1. Affects 8% of adults
    D. Maintains body weight
        1. Helps avoid excess gain

FIGURE 2-2

You can create your presentation outline using the Outline tab. When you create an outline, you type all the text at one time, as if you were typing an outline on a sheet of paper. This technique differs from creating a presentation in the slide pane in normal view, where you type text as you create each individual slide and the text is displayed both in the slide pane and on the Outline tab. PowerPoint creates the presentation as you type the outline by evaluating the outline structure and displaying a miniature view of the slide. Regardless of how you build a presentation, PowerPoint automatically creates the three views discussed in Project 1: normal, slide sorter, and slide show.

The first step in creating a presentation on the Outline tab is to type a title for the outline. The **outline title** is the subject of the presentation and later becomes the presentation title text. Then, you type the remainder of the outline, indenting appropriately to establish a structure, or hierarchy. Once the outline is complete, you make your presentation more persuasive by adding **clips**, which are media files of art, animation, sound, and movies. This project uses outlining to create the presentation and clip art to support the text visually.

Starting and Customizing PowerPoint

Project 1 introduced you to starting a presentation document, choosing a layout, and applying a design template. The following steps summarize how to start a new presentation, customize the PowerPoint window, choose a layout, and apply a design template. To start and customize PowerPoint, Windows must be running. If you are stepping through this project on a computer and you want your screen to match the figures in this book, then you should change your computer's resolution to 800 × 600. For more information on how to change the resolution on your computer, see Appendix B.

More About

Outlining

Outlining helps you plan, organize, and design your presentation. When you start to create an outline, you often begin to see new possibilities and find new ways to divide and group your ideas. You also find gaps where additional information is needed. A final glance at an outline can tell you if your plan is appropriate. For more information on outlining, visit the PowerPoint 2003 More About Web page (scsite.com/ppt2003 /more) and click Outlining.

To Start and Customize PowerPoint

1 Click the Start button on the Windows taskbar, point to All Programs on the Start menu, point to Microsoft Office on the All Programs submenu, and then click Microsoft Office PowerPoint 2003 on the Microsoft Office submenu.

2 If the PowerPoint window is not maximized, double-click its title bar to maximize it.

3 If the Language bar appears, right-click it and then click Close the Language bar on the shortcut menu.

4 If the Getting Started task pane appears in the PowerPoint window, click its Close button in the upper-right corner.

5 If the Standard and Formatting toolbars are positioned on the same row, click the Toolbar Options button and then click Show Buttons on Two Rows.

6 Click the Slide Design button on the Formatting toolbar. When the Slide Design task pane is displayed, click the down scroll arrow in the Apply a design template list, and then click the Axis template in the Available For Use area.

7 Click the Close button in the Slide Design task pane.

If the Axis template is not displayed in the Slide Design task pane, ask your instructor about installing additional templates. The PowerPoint window with the Standard and Formatting toolbars on two rows appears as shown in Figure 2-3. PowerPoint displays the Title Slide layout and the Axis template on Slide 1 in normal view.

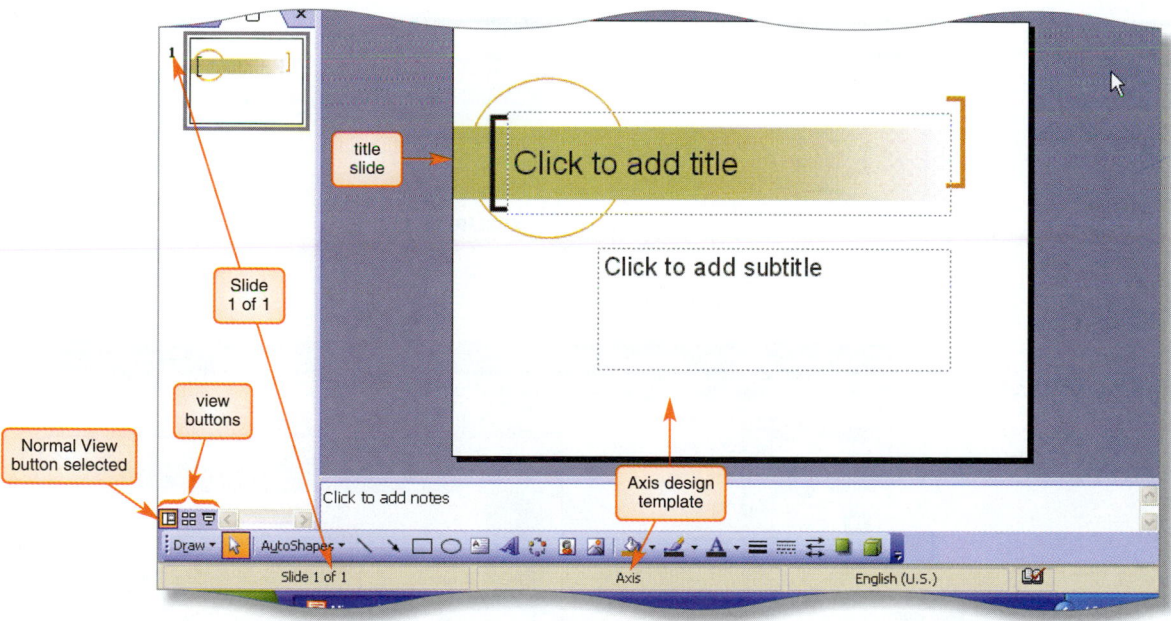

FIGURE 2-3

Using the Outline Tab

The **Outline tab** provides a quick, easy way to create a presentation. **Outlining** allows you to organize your thoughts in a structured format. An outline uses indentation to establish a **hierarchy**, which denotes levels of importance to the main topic. An outline is a summary of thoughts, presented as headings and subheadings, often used as a preliminary draft when you create a presentation.

The three panes — tabs, slide, and notes — shown in normal view also display when you click the Outline tab. The notes pane is displayed below the slide pane. In the tabs pane, the slide text appears along with a slide number and a slide icon. Body text is indented below the title text. Objects, such as pictures, graphs, or tables, do not display. The slide icon is blank when a slide does not contain objects. The attributes for text on the Outline tab are the same as in normal view except for color and paragraph style.

PowerPoint formats a title style and five levels of body text in an outline. The outline begins with the slide title, which is not indented. The title is the main topic of the slide. Body text supporting the main topic begins on the first level and also is not indented. If desired, additional supporting text can be added on the second through fifth levels. Each level is indented. Levels four and five generally are used for very detailed scientific and engineering presentations. Business and sales presentations usually focus on summary information and use the first, second, and third levels.

PowerPoint initially displays in normal view when you start a new presentation. To type the outline, click the Outline tab in the tabs pane. The following steps show how to change to the Outline tab and display the Outlining toolbar.

To Change to the Outline Tab and Display the Outlining Toolbar

1

• **Click the Outline tab located in the tabs pane.**

The Outline tab is selected. The tabs pane increases and the slide pane decreases in size. The tabs pane consists of the Outline tab and the Slides tab (Figure 2-4).

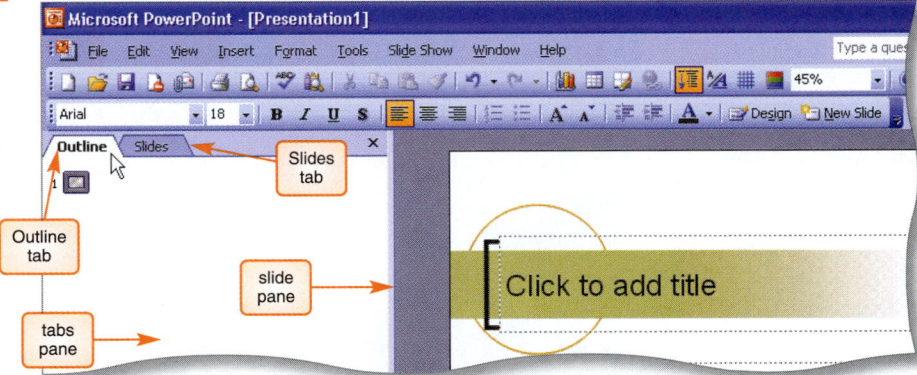

FIGURE 2-4

2

• **Click View on the menu bar and then point to Toolbars.**

• **Point to Outlining on the Toolbars submenu.**

The View menu and Toolbars submenu are displayed (Figure 2-5).

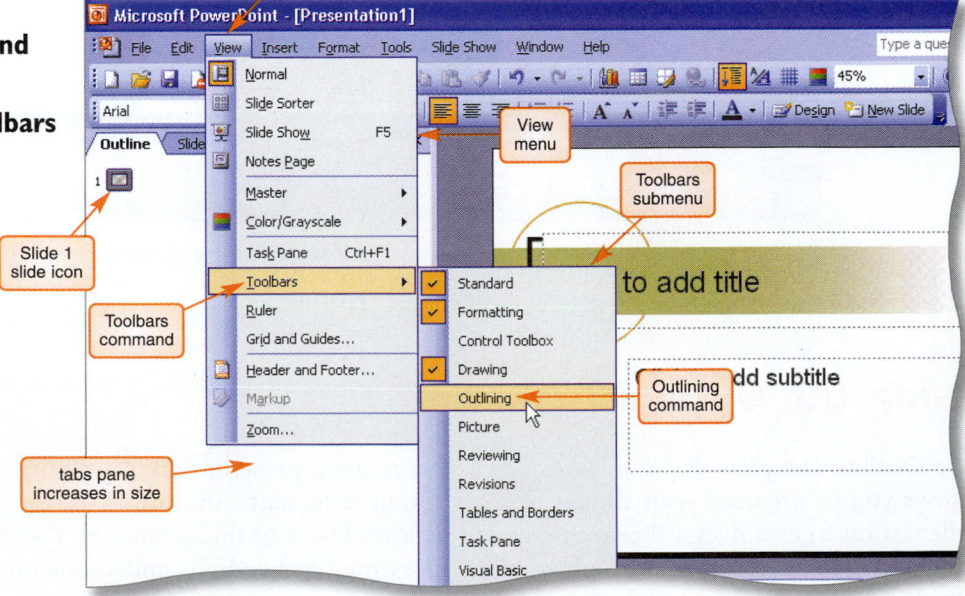

FIGURE 2-5

3

• **Click Outlining.**

The Outlining toolbar is displayed (Figure 2-6).

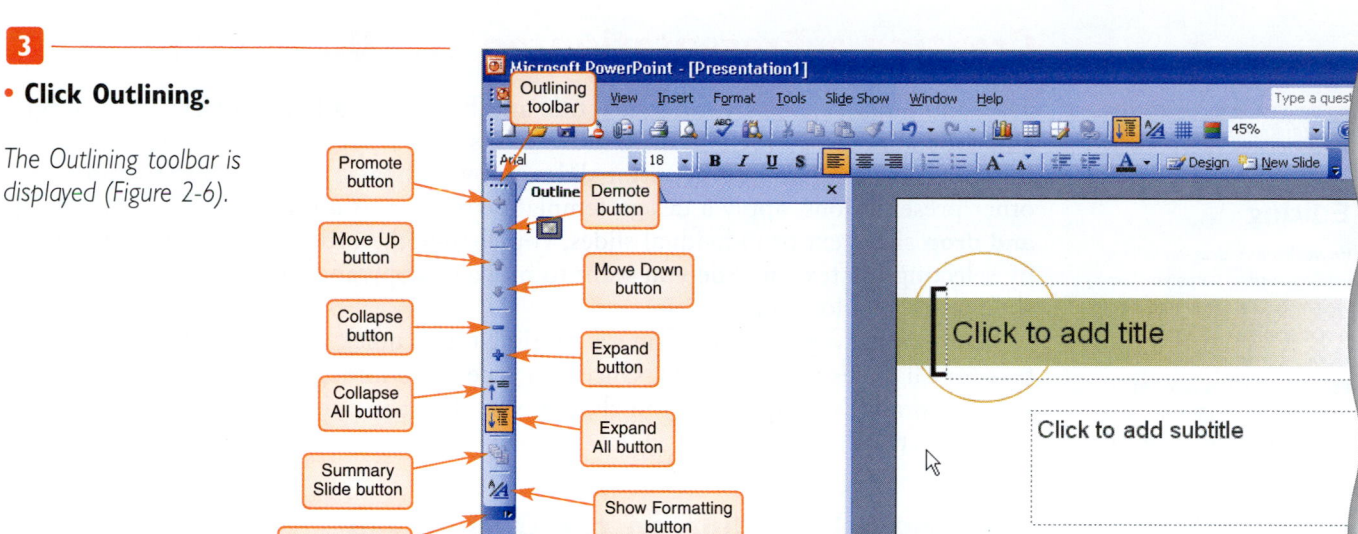

FIGURE 2-6

You can create and edit your presentation on the Outline tab. This tab also makes it easy to sequence slides and to relocate title text and body text from one slide to another. In addition to typing text to create a new presentation on the Outline tab, PowerPoint can produce slides from an outline created in Microsoft Word or another word processing application if you save the outline as an RTF file or as a plain text file. The file extension **RTF** stands for **R**ich **T**ext **F**ormat.

Table 2-1 describes the buttons on the Outlining toolbar.

Table 2-1	**Buttons on the Outlining Toolbar**	
BUTTON	**BUTTON NAME**	**DESCRIPTION**
	Promote	Moves the selected paragraph to the next-higher level (up one level, to the left).
	Demote	Moves the selected paragraph to the next-lower level (down one level, to the right).
	Move Up	Moves a selected paragraph and its collapsed (temporarily hidden) subordinate text above the preceding displayed paragraph.
	Move Down	Moves a selected paragraph and its collapsed (temporarily hidden) subordinate text down, below the following displayed paragraph.
	Collapse	Hides all but the titles of selected slides. Collapsed text is represented by a gray line.
	Expand	Displays the titles and all collapsed text of selected slides.
	Collapse All	Displays only the title of each slide. Text other than the title is represented by a gray line below the title.
	Expand All	Displays the titles and all the body text for each slide.
	Summary Slide	Creates a new slide from the titles of the slides you select in slide sorter or normal view. The summary slide creates a bulleted list from the titles of the selected slides. PowerPoint inserts the summary slide in front of the first selected slide.
	Show Formatting	Shows or hides character formatting (such as bold and italic) in normal view. In slide sorter view, switches between showing all text and objects on each slide and displaying titles only.
	Toolbar Options	Allows you to select the particular buttons you want to display on the toolbar.

Creating a Presentation on the Outline Tab

The Outline tab enables you to view title and body text, add and delete slides, drag and drop slide text, drag and drop individual slides, promote and demote text, save a presentation, print an outline, print slides, copy and paste slides or text to and from other presentations, apply a design template, and import an outline. When you **drag and drop** slide text or individual slides, you change the order of the text or the slides by selecting the text or slide you want to move or copy and then dragging the text or slide to its new location.

Developing a presentation on the Outline tab is quick because you type the text for all slides on one screen. Once you type the outline, the presentation fundamentally is complete. If you choose, you then can enhance your presentation with objects in the slide pane.

Creating a Title Slide on the Outline Tab

Recall from Project 1 that the title slide introduces the presentation to the audience. In addition to introducing the presentation, Project 2 uses the title slide to capture the audience's attention by using a design template with an interesting title. The following steps show how to create a title slide on the Outline tab.

More About

Drag-and-Drop Editing

PowerPoint's drag-and-drop editing setting helps you move text within a presentation, but it also can be used to move text from PowerPoint to another Microsoft Office program. To ensure the drag-and-drop editing setting is enabled, click Options on the Tools menu, click the Edit tab, and then click Drag-and-drop text editing if the check box is not checked.

To Create a Title Slide on the Outline Tab

1

• **Click the Slide 1 slide icon on the Outline tab.**

The Slide 1 slide icon is selected. You also could click anywhere in the tabs pane to select the slide icon (Figure 2-7).

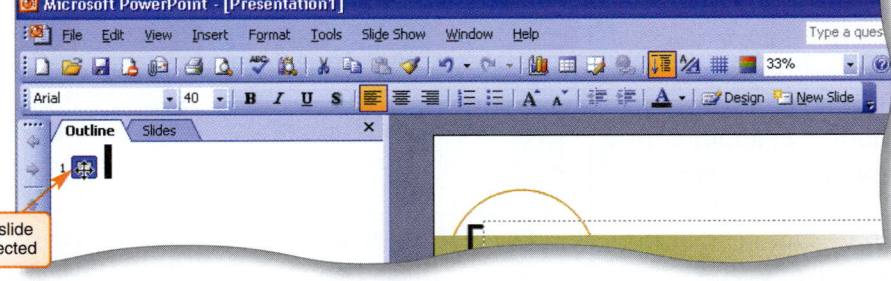

FIGURE 2-7

2

• **Type** Healthy Eating **and then press the SHIFT+ENTER keys.**

• **Type** Healthy Living **and then press the ENTER key.**

• **Point to the Demote button on the Outlining toolbar.**

The Demote ScreenTip is displayed (Figure 2-8). Pressing the SHIFT+ENTER keys moves the insertion point to the next line and maintains the same first level. The insertion point is in position for typing the title for Slide 2. The first-level font is Arial and the font size is 40 point.

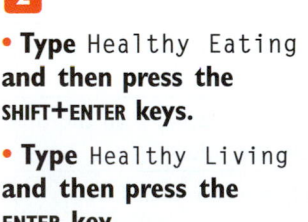
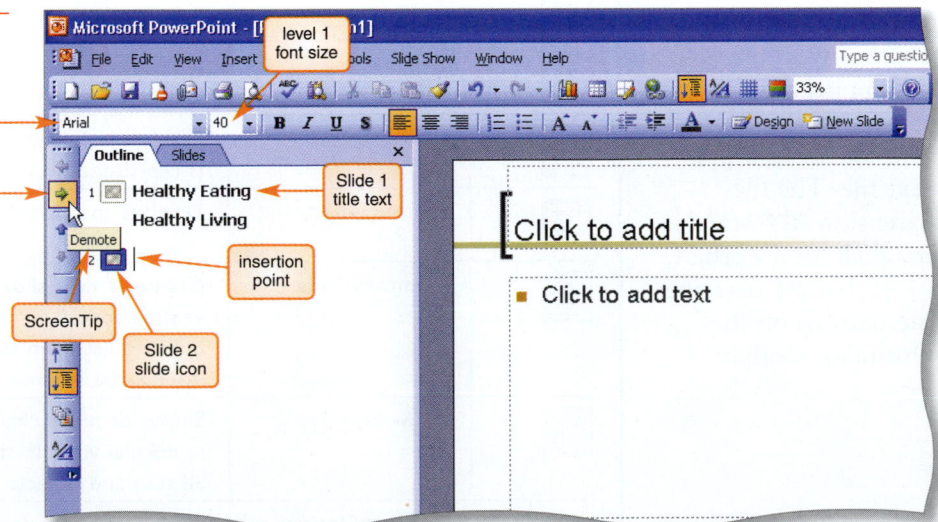

FIGURE 2-8

3

• **Click the Demote button on the Outlining toolbar.**

• **Type** Nutrition and Fitness Basics **and then press the ENTER key.**

• **Type** Clark College Fitness Center **and then press the ENTER key.**

The paragraphs, Nutrition and Fitness Basics and Clark College Fitness Center, are subtitles on the title slide (Slide 1) and demote to the second level (Figure 2-9). The second level is indented to the right below the first-level paragraph. The second-level font is Arial and the font size is 32 point.

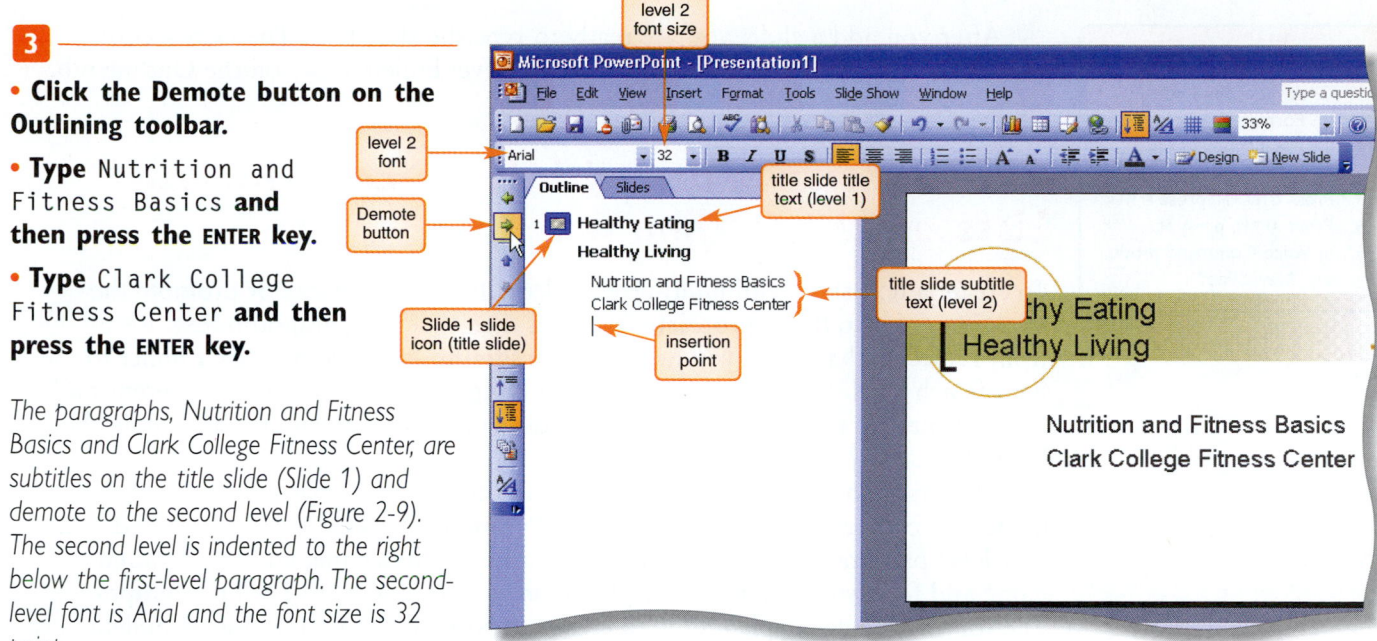

FIGURE 2-9

Other Ways

1. Type title text, press ENTER, click Demote button on Formatting toolbar, type subtitle text, press ENTER

2. Type title text, press ENTER, press TAB, type subtitle text, press ENTER

The title slide text for the Healthy Eating, Healthy Living presentation is complete. The next section explains how to add a slide on the Outline tab.

Adding a Slide on the Outline Tab

Recall from Project 1 that when you add a new slide in normal view, PowerPoint defaults to a Text slide layout with a bulleted list. This action occurs on the Outline tab as well. One way to add a new slide on the Outline tab is to promote a paragraph to the first level by clicking the Promote button on the Outlining toolbar until the insertion point or the paragraph is displayed at the first level. A slide icon is displayed when the insertion point or paragraph reaches this level. The following step shows how to add a slide on the Outline tab.

To Add a Slide on the Outline Tab

1

• **Click the Promote button on the Outlining toolbar.**

The Slide 2 slide icon is displayed, indicating a new slide is added to the presentation (Figure 2-10). The insertion point is in position to type the title for Slide 2 at the first level.

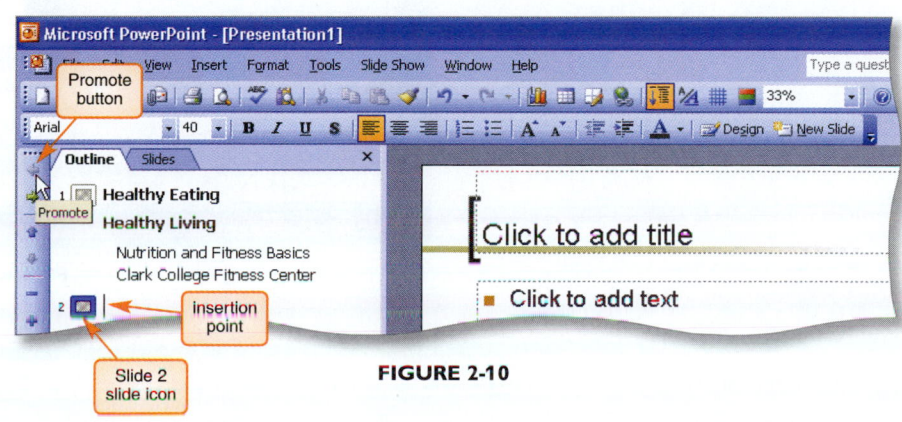

FIGURE 2-10

After you add a slide, you are ready to type the slide text. The next section explains how to create text slides with multi-level bulleted lists on the Outline tab.

Creating Text Slides with Multi-Level Bulleted Lists on the Outline Tab

To create a text slide with multi-level bulleted lists, you demote or promote the insertion point to the appropriate level and then type the paragraph text. Recall from Project 1 that when you demote a paragraph, PowerPoint adds a bullet to the left of each level. Depending on the design template, each level has a different bullet font. Also recall that the design template determines font attributes, including the bullet font.

The first text slide you create in Project 2 describes the basic nutritional guidelines comprising the Healthy Eating Pyramid. The slide title is displayed as a first-level paragraph on the Outline tab and in the slide pane, and the Pyramid name and food suggestions are displayed as second- and third-level paragraphs. The following steps explain how to create a text slide with a multi-level bulleted list on the Outline tab.

To Create a Text Slide with a Multi-Level Bulleted List on the Outline Tab

1

• **Type** Nutrition Guidelines **and then press the ENTER key.**

• **Click the Demote button on the Outlining toolbar to demote to the second level.**

The title for Slide 2, Nutrition Guidelines, is displayed and the insertion point is in position to type the first bulleted paragraph (Figure 2-11). A bullet is displayed to the left of the insertion point.

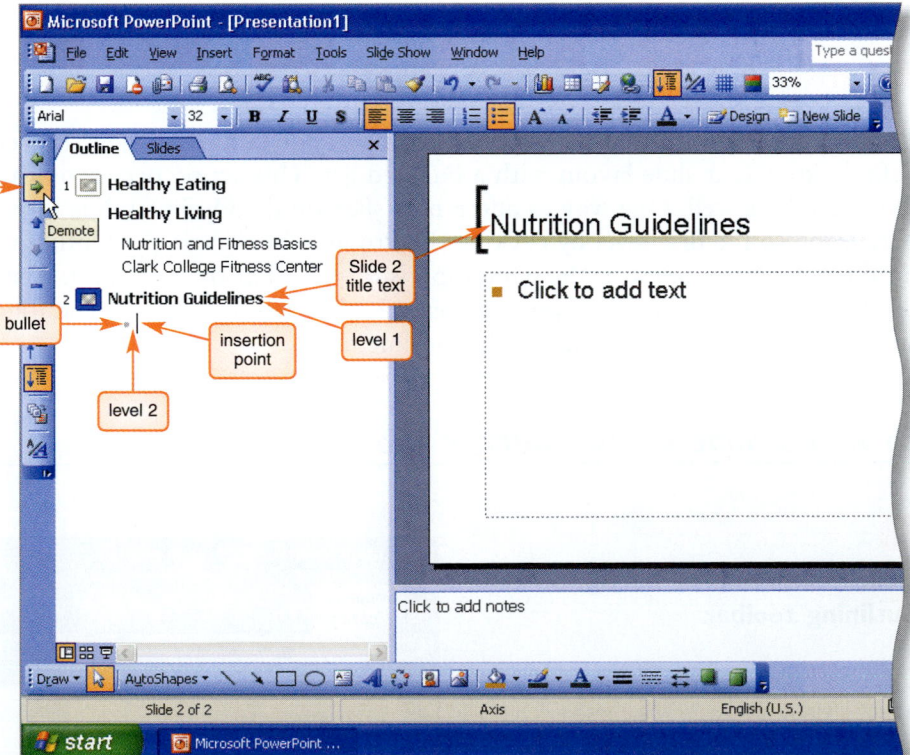

FIGURE 2-11

2

• **Type** Healthy Eating Pyramid **and then press the ENTER key.**

• **Click the Demote button on the Outlining toolbar to demote to the third level.**

• **Type** Eat more vegetable oils, whole grains **and then press the ENTER key.**

• **Type** Eat less pasta, white bread **and then press the ENTER key.**

Slide 2 is displayed with three levels: the title, Nutrition Guidelines, on the first level; the Pyramid name on the second level; and two bulleted paragraphs and the insertion point on the third level (Figure 2-12).

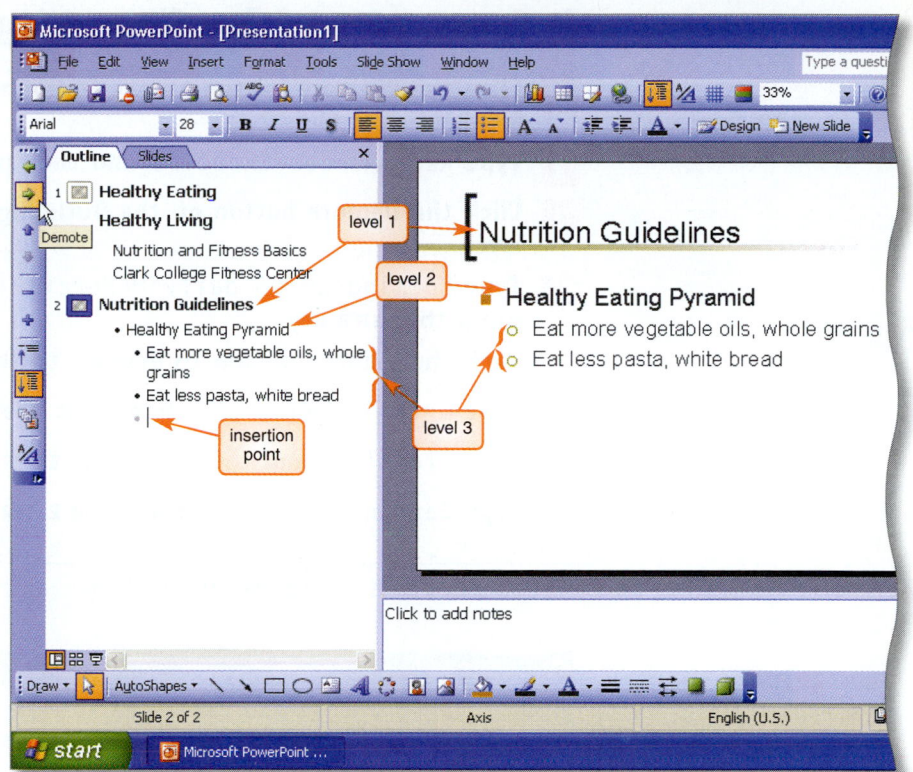

FIGURE 2-12

Slide 2 is complete. The text on this slide abides by the 7 × 7 rule. As you learned in Project 1, this rule recommends that each line should have a maximum of seven words, and each slide should have a maximum of seven lines. All slides in this slide show use the 7 × 7 rule.

The remaining three slides in the presentation contain multi-level bulleted lists. Slide 3 provides information about exercise guidelines, Slide 4 gives details about relaxation procedures, and Slide 5 lists the benefits of adhering to a healthy lifestyle. It is easy and efficient to type the text for these slides on the Outline tab because you can view all the text you type in the outline in the tabs pane to check organization.

Creating a Second Text Slide with a Multi-Level Bulleted List

The next slide, Slide 3, provides details about daily exercise. Experts recommend exercising moderately for 30 minutes each day. The steps on the next page show how to create this slide.

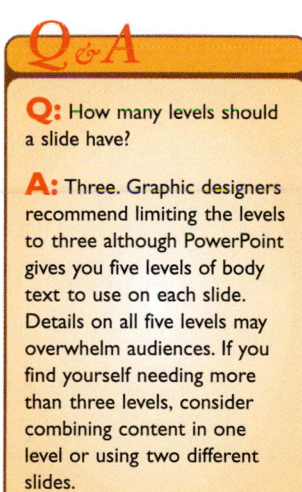

Q & A

Q: How many levels should a slide have?

A: Three. Graphic designers recommend limiting the levels to three although PowerPoint gives you five levels of body text to use on each slide. Details on all five levels may overwhelm audiences. If you find yourself needing more than three levels, consider combining content in one level or using two different slides.

To Create a Second Text Slide with a Multi-Level Bulleted List

1 Click the **Promote** button on the Outlining toolbar two times so that Slide 3 is added after Slide 2.

2 Type Recommended Exercise and then press the ENTER key.

3 Click the **Demote** button on the Outlining toolbar to demote to the second level.

4 Type 30 minutes of daily moderate-intensity activity and then press the ENTER key.

5 Click the **Demote** button to demote to the third level.

6 Type Brisk walking and then press the ENTER key.

7 Type Bicycling and then press the ENTER key.

8 Type Gardening and then press the ENTER key.

The completed Slide 3 is displayed (Figure 2-13).

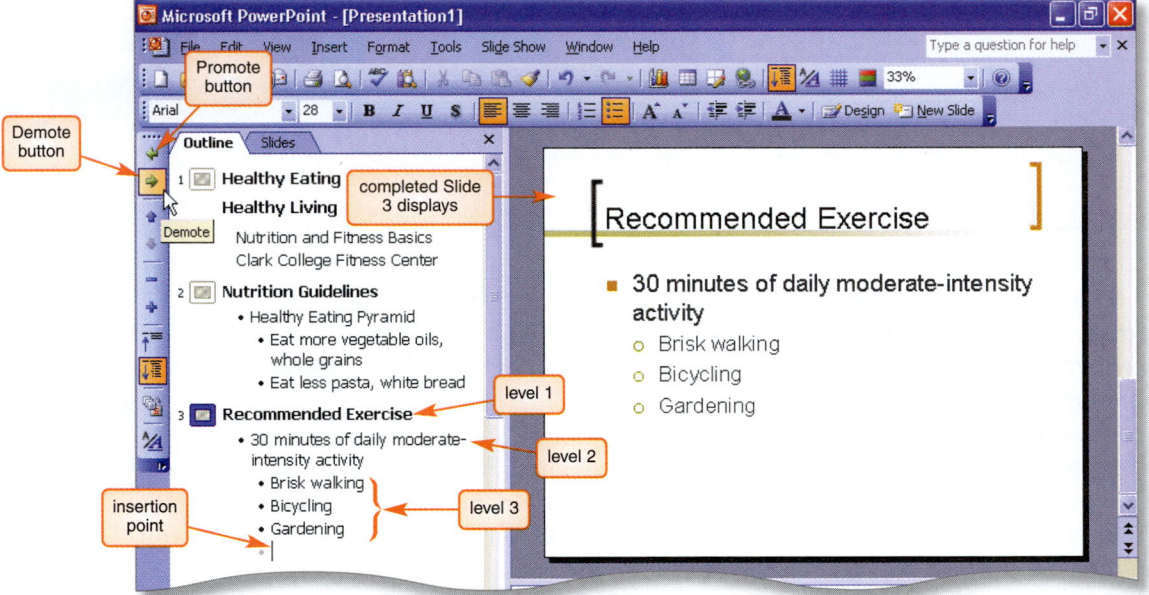

FIGURE 2-13

Creating a Third Text Slide with a Multi-Level Bulleted List

Slide 4 describes recommended relaxation techniques that should be practiced in conjunction with eating nutritional meals and exercising daily. The following steps show how to create this slide.

To Create a Third Text Slide with a Multi-Level Bulleted List

1 Click the **Promote** button on the Outlining toolbar two times so that Slide 4 is added after Slide 3.

2 Type Relaxation Techniques and then press the ENTER key.

3 Click the **Demote** button on the Outlining toolbar to demote to the second level.

4 **Type** `Quiet the mind and body` **and then press the** ENTER **key.**

5 **Click the Demote button to demote to the third level.**

6 **Type** `Visualize a tranquil setting` **and then press the** ENTER **key.**

7 **Type** `Concentrate on positive thoughts` **and then press the** ENTER **key.**

8 **Click the Promote button to promote to the second level.**

9 **Type** `Build strength and refresh the body` **and then press the** ENTER **key.**

10 **Click the Demote button to demote to the third level.**

11 **Type** `Practice yoga or Pilates basics` **and then press the** ENTER **key.**

12 **Type** `Improve balance through core training` **and then press the** ENTER **key.**

The completed Slide 4 is displayed (Figure 2-14).

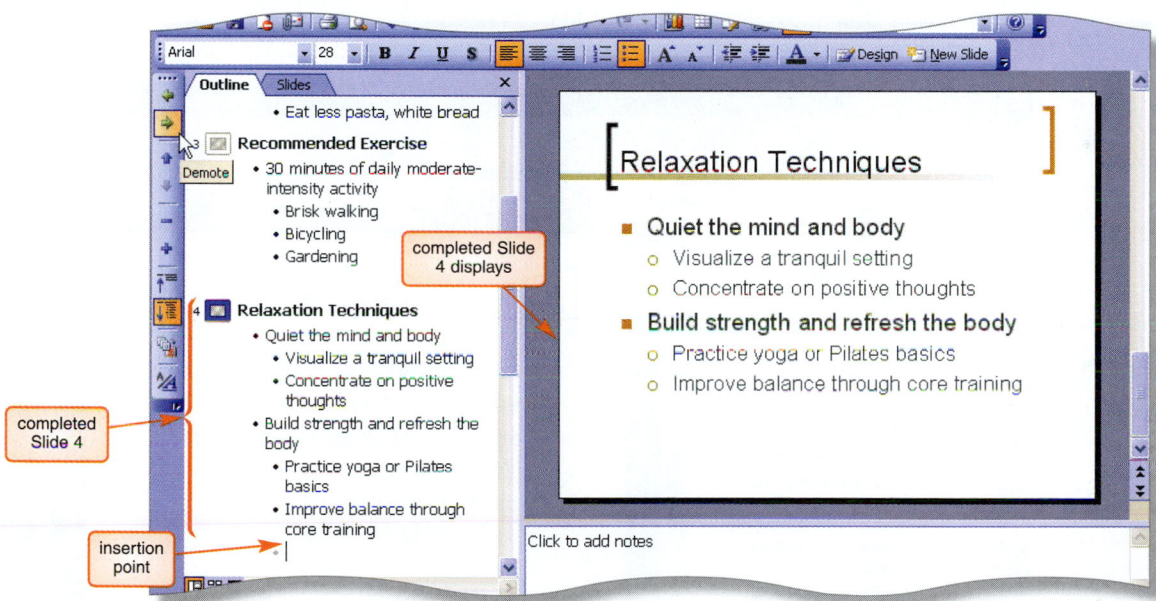

FIGURE 2-14

Creating a Closing Slide on the Outline Tab

The last slide in a presentation is the closing slide. A **closing slide** gracefully ends a presentation. Often used during a question and answer session, the closing slide usually remains on the screen to reinforce the message delivered during the presentation. Professional speakers design the closing slide with one or more of these methods:

1. List important information. Tell the audience what to do next.
2. Provide a memorable illustration or example to make a point.
3. Appeal to emotions. Remind the audience to take action or accept responsibility.
4. Summarize the main point of the presentation.
5. Cite a quotation that directly relates to the main point of the presentation. This technique is most effective if the presentation started with a quotation.

The last text slide you create in Project 2 describes the benefits of practicing a healthy lifestyle. The steps on the next page show how to create this closing slide.

To Create a Closing Slide on the Outline Tab

1 Click the **Promote button** on the Outlining toolbar two times to add Slide 5 after Slide 4. **Type** Healthy Living Benefits **and then press the** ENTER **key.**

2 Click the **Demote button** on the Outlining toolbar to demote to the second level. **Type** Lowers cholesterol, blood pressure **and then press the** ENTER **key.**

3 **Type** Reduces heart disease risk **and then press the** ENTER **key.**

4 **Type** Helps prevent adult-onset diabetes **and then press the** ENTER **key.**

5 Click the **Demote button** to demote to the third level. **Type** Affects 8% of adults **and then press the** ENTER **key.**

6 Click the **Promote button** to promote to the second level. **Type** Maintains body weight **and then press the** ENTER **key.**

7 Click the **Demote button. Type** Helps avoid excess gain **but do not press the** ENTER **key.**

The completed Slide 5 is displayed (Figure 2-15).

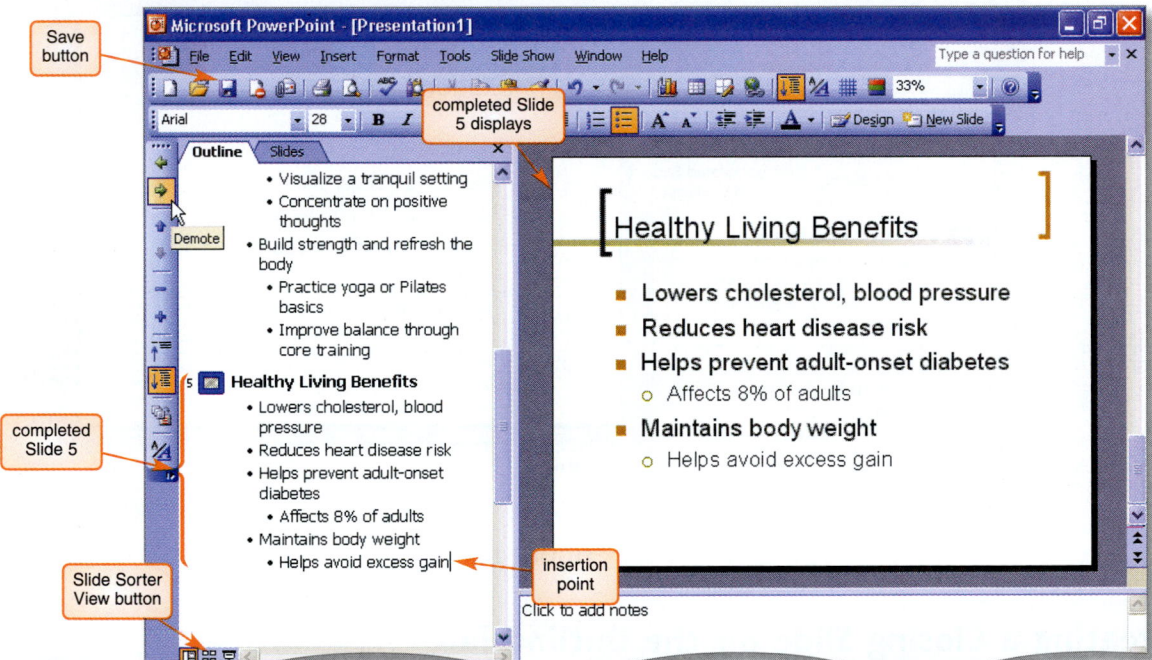

FIGURE 2-15

The outline now is complete and you should save the presentation. The next section explains how to save the presentation.

Saving a Presentation

Recall from Project 1 that it is wise to save your presentation frequently. With all the text for your presentation created, save the presentation using the following steps.

To Save a Presentation

1 Insert a formatted floppy disk in drive A and then click the Save button on the Standard toolbar.

2 Type Nutrition and Fitness in the File name text box. Do not press the ENTER key after typing the file name. Click the Save in box arrow.

3 Click 3½ Floppy (A:) in the Save in list.

4 Click the Save button in the Save As dialog box.

The presentation is saved with the file name, Nutrition and Fitness, on the floppy disk in drive A. PowerPoint uses the first text line in a presentation as the default file name. The file name is displayed on the title bar.

Reviewing a Presentation in Slide Sorter View

In Project 1, you displayed slides in slide show view to evaluate the presentation. Slide show view, however, restricts your evaluation to one slide at a time. The Outline tab is best for quickly reviewing all the text for a presentation. Recall from Project 1 that slide sorter view allows you to look at several slides at one time, which is why it is the best view to use to evaluate a presentation for content, organization, and overall appearance. The following step shows how to change from the Outline tab to slide sorter view.

To Change the View to Slide Sorter View

1

• Click the Slide Sorter View button at the lower left of the PowerPoint window.

PowerPoint displays the presentation in slide sorter view (Figure 2-16). Slide 5 is selected because it was the current slide on the Outline tab. The Slide Sorter View button is selected.

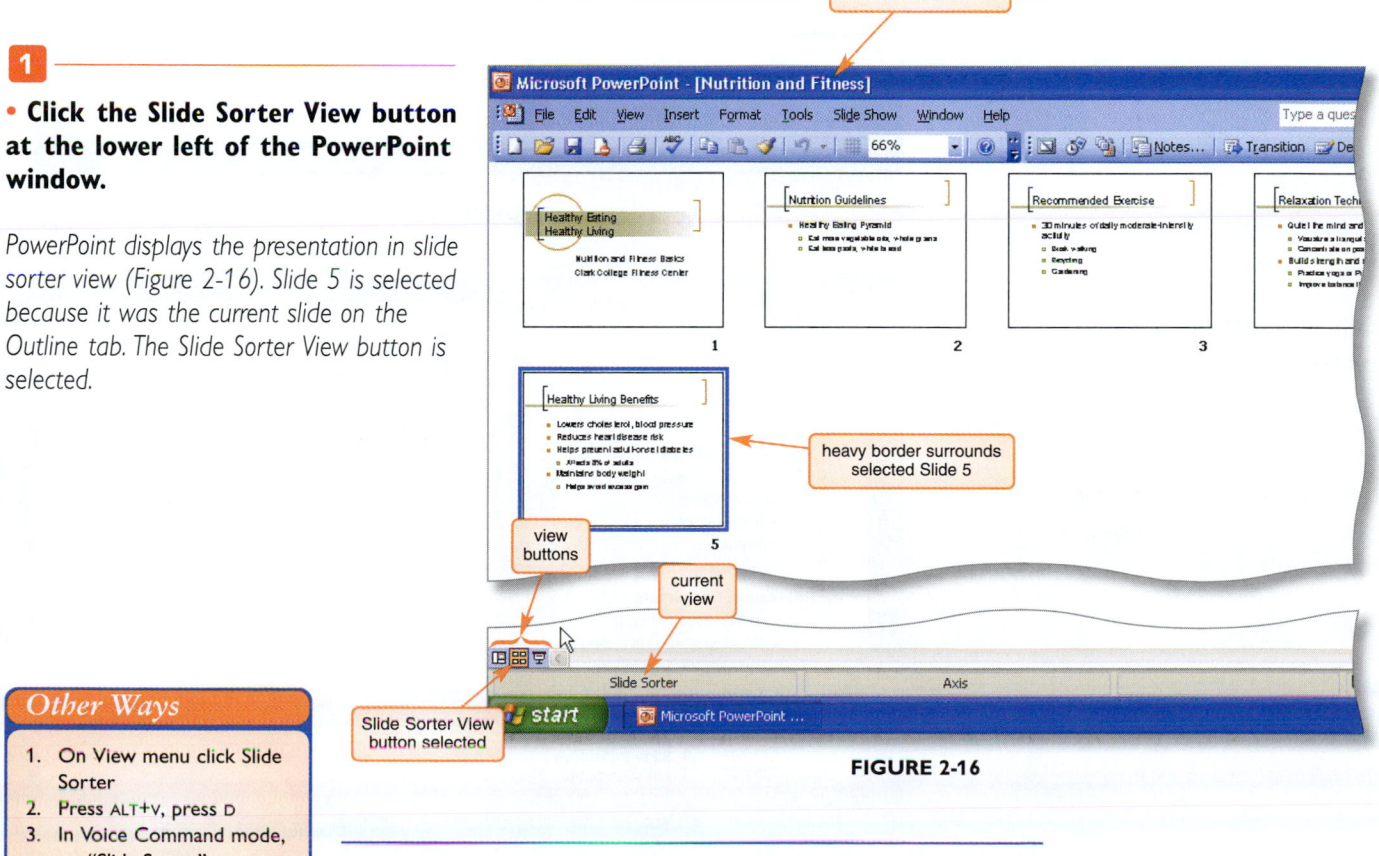

FIGURE 2-16

Other Ways

1. On View menu click Slide Sorter
2. Press ALT+V, press D
3. In Voice Command mode, say "Slide Sorter"

You can review the five slides in this presentation all in one window. Notice the slides have a significant amount of space and look plain. These observations indicate a need to add visual interest to the slides by using clips. The next several sections explain how to improve the presentation by changing slide layouts and adding clip art.

You can make changes to text in normal view and on the Outline tab. It is best, however, to change the view to normal view when altering the slide layouts so you can see the results of your changes. The following steps show how to change the view from slide sorter view to normal view.

To Change the View to Normal View

1

• **Click the Slide 2 slide thumbnail.**

• **Point to the Normal View button at the lower left of the PowerPoint window.**

Slide 2 is selected, as indicated by the thick blue border around that slide (Figure 2-17).

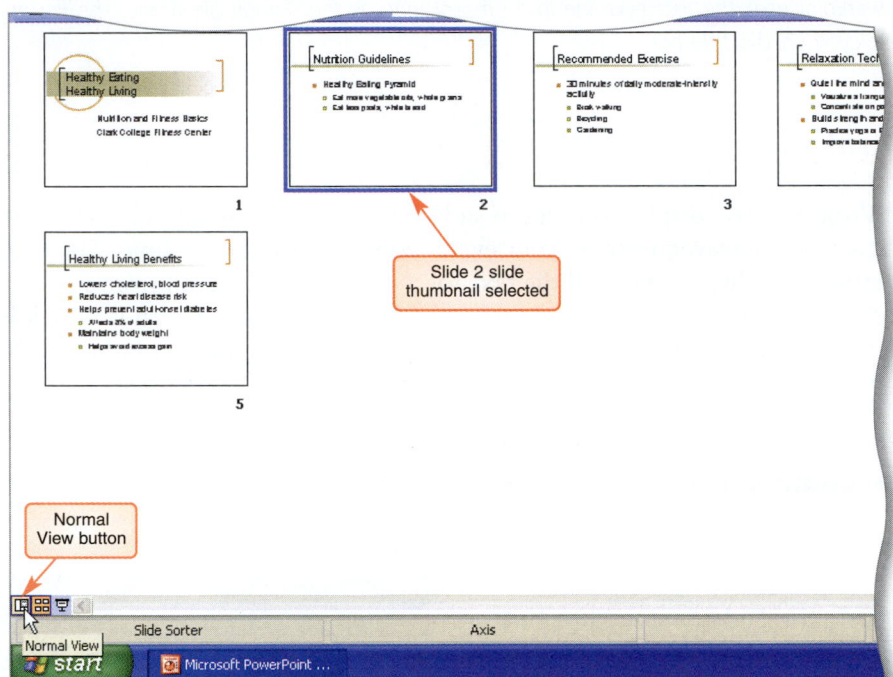

FIGURE 2-17

2

• **Click the Normal View button.**

The Normal View button is selected at the lower left of the PowerPoint window. The Slide 2 slide icon is selected in the tabs pane, and Slide 2 is displayed in the slide pane (Figure 2-18).

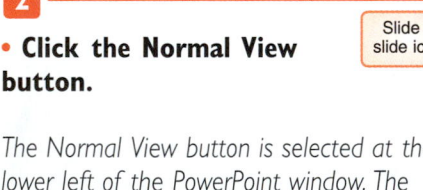

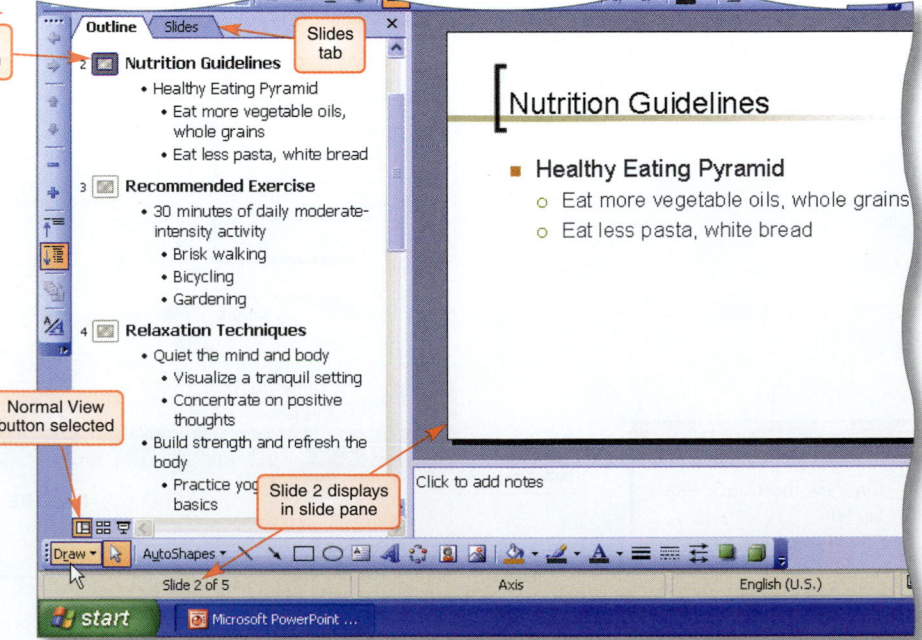

FIGURE 2-18

3

• **Click the Slides tab in the tabs pane.**

The tabs pane reduces in size. Slide thumbnails of the five slides are displayed (Figure 2-19).

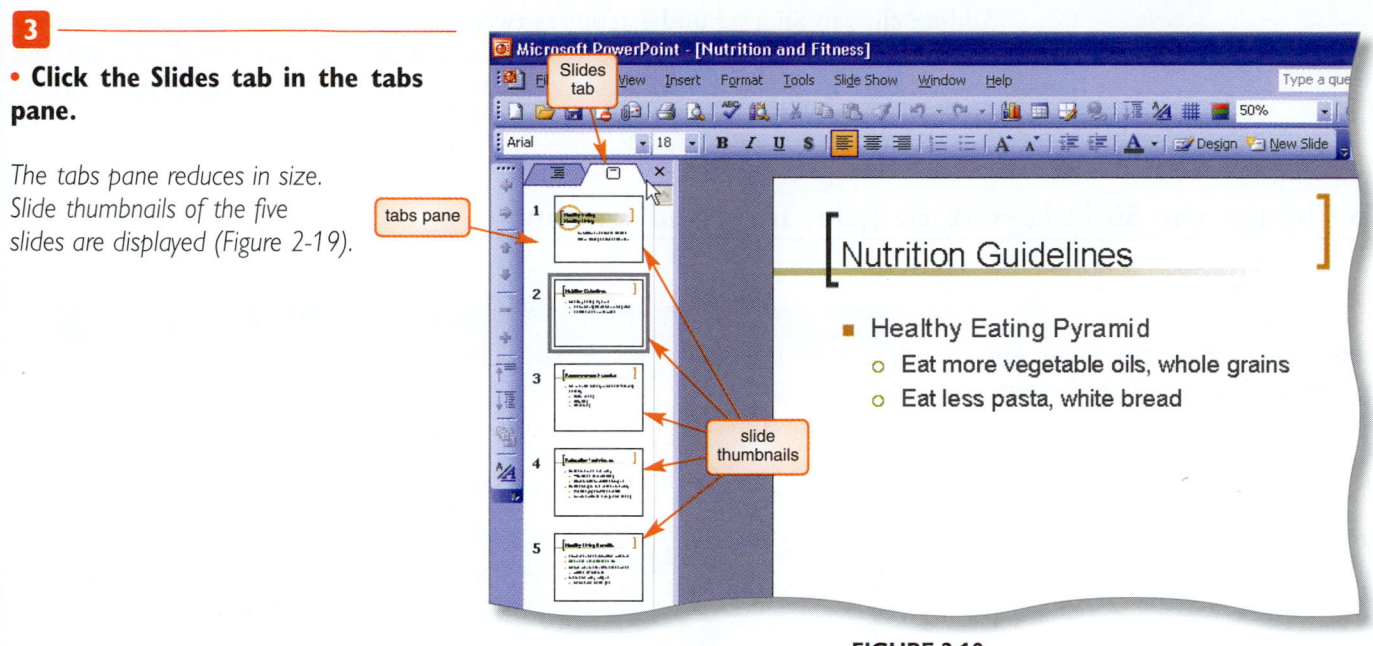

FIGURE 2-19

Switching between slide sorter view and normal view helps you review your presentation and assess whether the slides have an attractive design and adequate content.

Changing Slide Layout

When you developed this presentation, PowerPoint applied the Title Slide layout for Slide 1 and the Title and Text layout for the other four slides in the presentation. These layouts are the default styles. A **layout** specifies the arrangement of placeholders on a slide. These placeholders are arranged in various configurations and can contain text, such as the slide title or a bulleted list, or they can contain content, such as clips, pictures, charts, tables, and shapes. The placement of the text, in relationship to content, depends on the slide layout. The content placeholders may be to the right or left of the text, above the text, or below the text. You can specify a particular slide layout when you add a new slide to a presentation or after you have created the slide.

Using the **Slide Layout task pane**, you can choose a slide layout. The layouts in this task pane are arranged in four areas: Text Layouts, Content Layouts, Text and Content Layouts, and Other Layouts. The two layouts you have used in this project — Title Slide and Title and Text — are included in the Text Layouts area, along with the Title Only and Title and 2-Column Text layouts. The Content Layouts area contains a blank slide and a variety of placeholder groupings for charts, tables, clip art, pictures, diagrams, and media clips. The Text and Content Layouts have placeholders for a title, a bulleted list, and content. The Other Layouts area has layouts with placeholders for a title and one object, such as clip art, charts, media clips, tables, organization charts, and charts.

When you change the layout of a slide, PowerPoint retains the text and objects and repositions them into the appropriate placeholders. Using slide layouts eliminates the need to resize objects and the font size because PowerPoint automatically sizes the objects and text to fit the placeholders. If the objects are in **landscape orientation**, meaning their width is greater than their height, PowerPoint sizes them to the width of the placeholders. If the objects are in **portrait orientation**, meaning their height is greater than their width, PowerPoint sizes them to the height of the placeholders.

Adding clips to Slides 2 and 3 requires two steps. First, change the slide layout to Title, Text, and Content or to Title, 2 Content and Text. Then, insert clip art into the content placeholders. The following steps show how to change the slide layout on Slide 2 from Title and Text to Title, Text, and Content.

To Change the Slide Layout to Title, Text, and Content

1

• **Click Format on the menu bar and then point to Slide Layout (Figure 2-20).**

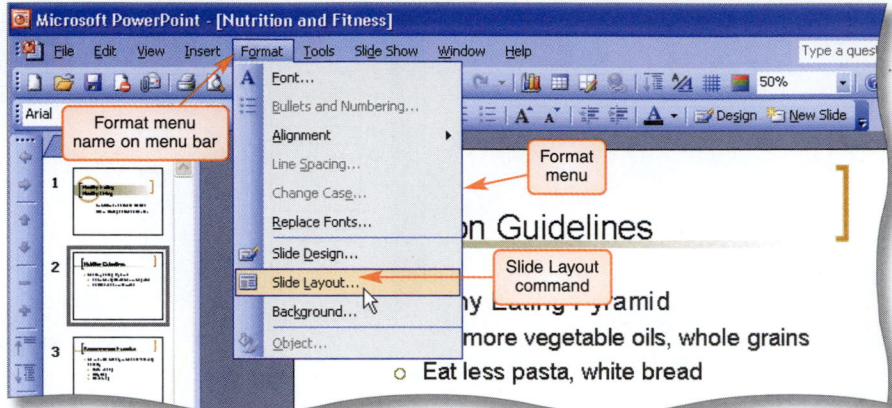

FIGURE 2-20

2

• **Click Slide Layout.**

• **Click the down arrow in the Apply slide layout area and scroll down until the Text and Content Layouts area displays.**

• **Point to the Title, Text, and Content layout in the Text and Content Layouts area.**

The Slide Layout task pane is displayed (Figure 2-21). The Title, Text, and Content layout is selected, as indicated by the blue box around the template, the ScreenTip, and the down arrow on the right side.

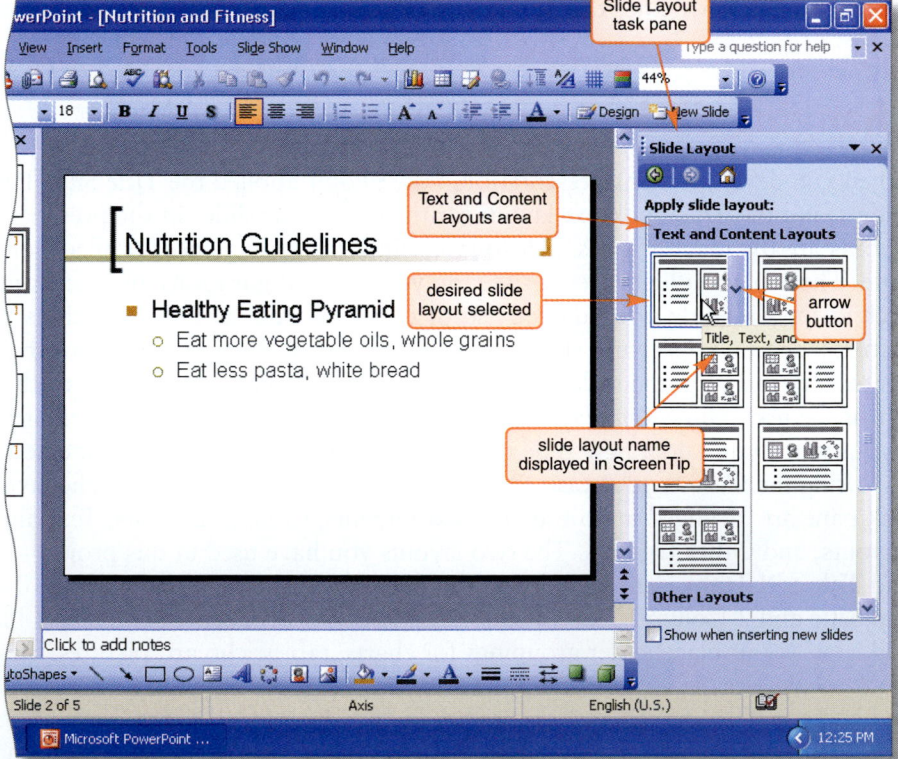

FIGURE 2-21

3

• **Click Title, Text, and Content.**

The layout is applied to Slide 2 (Figure 2-22). PowerPoint moves the text placeholder containing the bulleted list to the left side of the slide and automatically resizes the text. The content placeholder on the right side of the slide has the message, Click icon to add content.

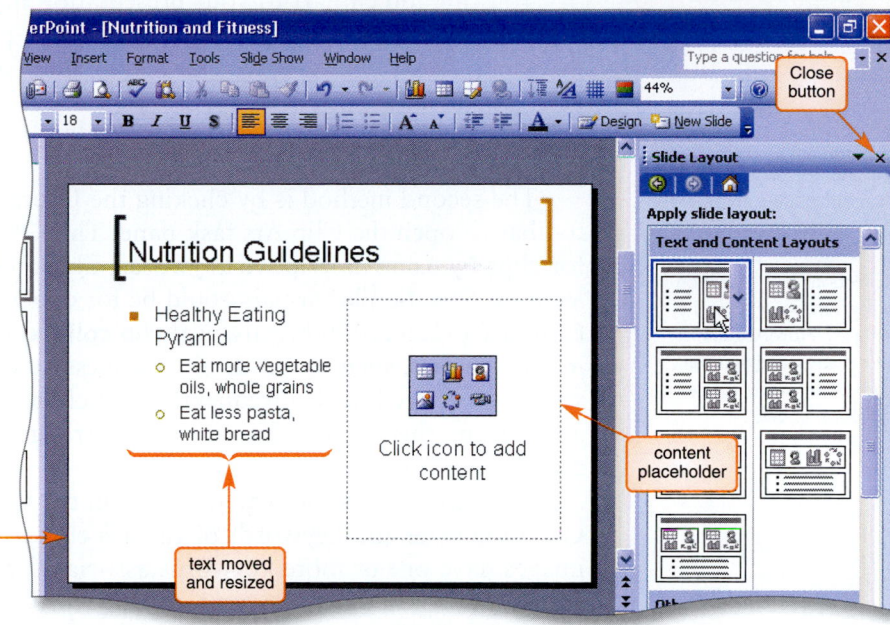

FIGURE 2-22

4

• **Click the Close button in the Slide Layout task pane.**

Slide 2 is displayed in normal view with the new slide layout applied (Figure 2-23).

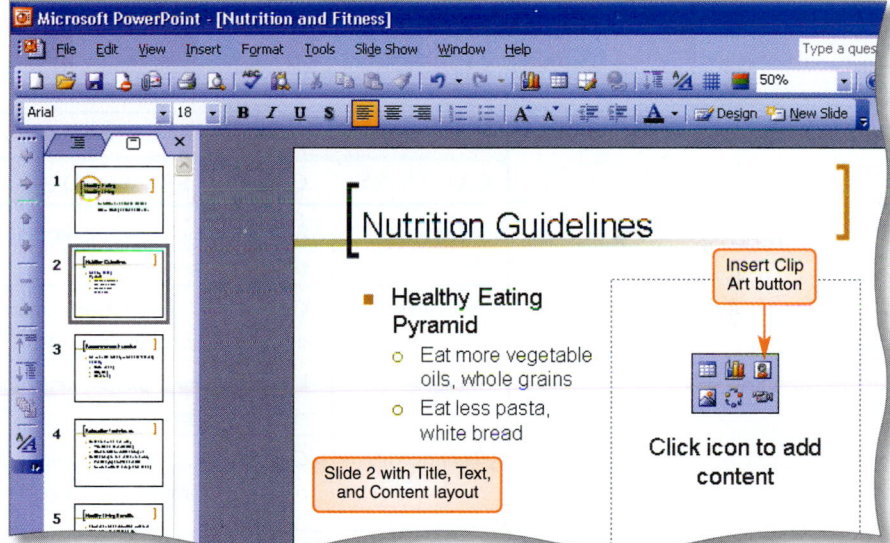

FIGURE 2-23

PowerPoint reduced the second-level text in the Slide 2 text placeholder from a font size of 32 point to 28 point so all the words fit into the placeholder.

Adding Clip Art to a Slide

Clip art helps the visual appeal of the Nutrition and Fitness slide show and offers a quick way to add professional-looking graphic images to a presentation without creating the images yourself. This art is contained in the **Microsoft Clip Organizer**, a collection of drawings, photographs, sounds, videos, and other media files shared with Microsoft Office applications.

Q: Can I add clips to the Clip Organizer?

A: Yes. You can add media files and objects created in Microsoft Office programs. The media files are stored in a new subcollection in the My Collections clip collection folder. The objects can be pictures, WordArt, and AutoShapes, and you can store them in any desired collection folder.

You can add clip art to your presentation in two ways. One way is by selecting one of the slide layouts that includes a content placeholder with instructions to open the Microsoft Clip Organizer to add content. You will add art to Slides 2 and 3 in this manner. Double-clicking a button in the content placeholder activates the instructions to open the Select Picture dialog box, which allows you to enter keywords to search for clips.

The second method is by clicking the Insert Clip Art button on the Drawing toolbar to open the Clip Art task pane. The **Clip Art task pane** allows you to search for clips by using descriptive keywords, file names, media file formats, and clip collections. Specific file formats could be for clip art, photographs, movies, and sounds. Clips are organized in hierarchical **clip collections**, which combine topic-related clips into categories, such as Academic, Business, and Technology. You also can create your own collections for frequently used clips. You will insert clip art into Slides 4 and 5 using this process. You then will arrange the clips on the slides without using a placeholder for content.

Table 2-2 shows four categories from the Office Collections in the Microsoft Clip Organizer and keywords of various clip art files in those categories. Clip art images have one or more keywords associated with various entities, activities, labels, and emotions. In most instances, the keywords give the name of the clip and related categories. For example, an image of a cow in the Animals category has the keywords animals, cattle, cows, dairies, farms, and Holsteins. You can enter these keywords in the Search text box to find clips when you know one of the words associated with the image. Otherwise, you may find it necessary to scroll through several categories to find an appropriate clip.

Table 2-2	Microsoft Clip Organizer Category and Keyword Examples
CATEGORY	**CLIP ART KEYWORDS**
Academic	Books, knowledge, information, schools, school buses, apple for the teacher, professors
Business	Computers, inspirations, ideas, currencies, board meetings, conferences, teamwork, profits
Nature	Lakes, flowers, plants, seasons, wildlife, weather, trees, sunshine, rivers, leaves
Technology	Computers, diskettes, microchips, cellular telephones, e-commerce, office equipment, data exchanges

Depending on the installation of the Microsoft Clip Organizer on your computer, you may not have the clip art used in this project. Contact your instructor if you are missing clips used in the following steps. If you have an open connection to the Internet, clips from the Microsoft Web site will display automatically as the result of your search results.

Inserting Clip Art into a Content Placeholder

With the Title, Text, and Content layout applied to Slide 2, you insert clip art into the content placeholder. The following steps show how to insert clip art of a cornucopia into the content placeholder on Slide 2.

To Insert Clip Art into a Content Placeholder

1

• **Point to the Insert Clip Art button in the content placeholder.**

The Insert Clip Art button is selected (Figure 2-24). A ScreenTip describes its function.

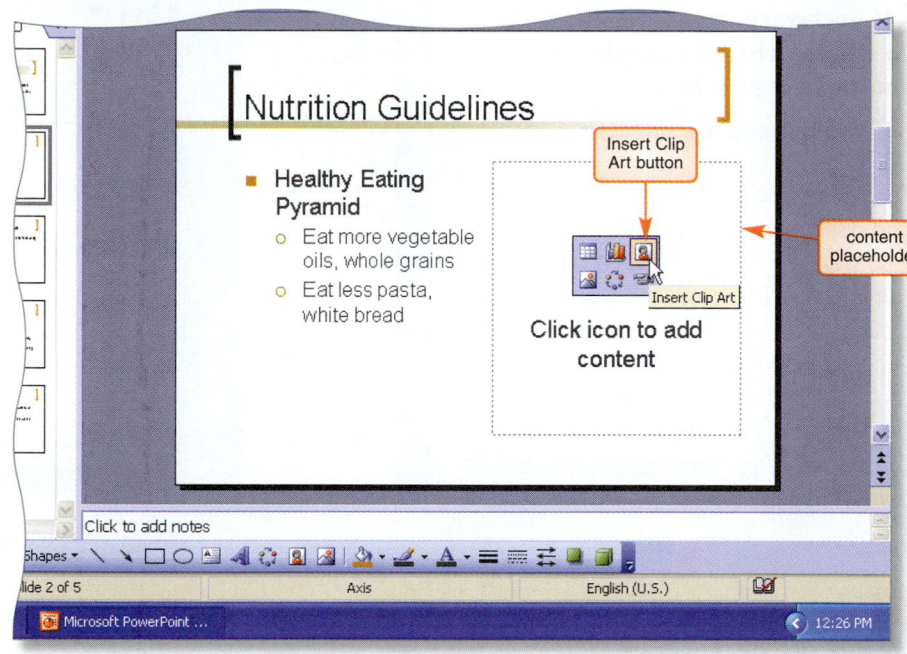

FIGURE 2-24

2

• **Click the Insert Clip Art button.**

• **Type** food **in the Search text text box and then point to the Go button.**

The Select Picture dialog box is displayed (Figure 2-25). The clips displaying on your computer may vary.

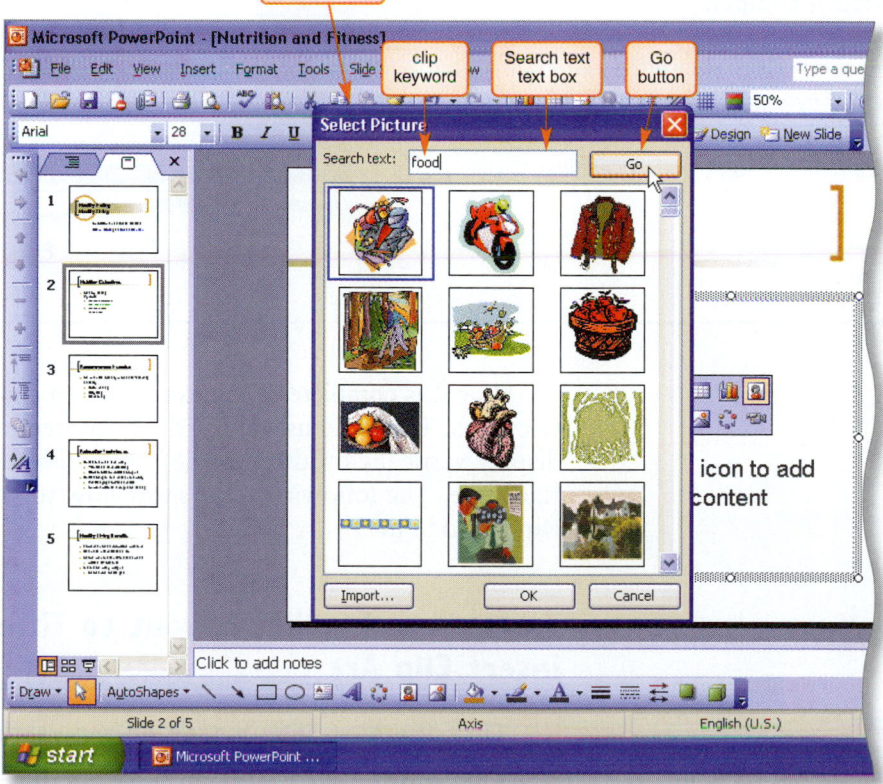

FIGURE 2-25

3

• **Click the Go button.**

• **If necessary, scroll down the list to display the cornucopia clip shown in Figure 2-26.**

• **Click the clip to select it.**

The Microsoft Clip Organizer searches for and displays all pictures having the keyword, food (Figure 2-26). The desired clip of a cornucopia is displayed with a blue box around it. Your clips may be different depending on the clips installed on your computer and if you have an open connection to the Internet, in which case you may need to obtain an appropriate clip from the Internet.

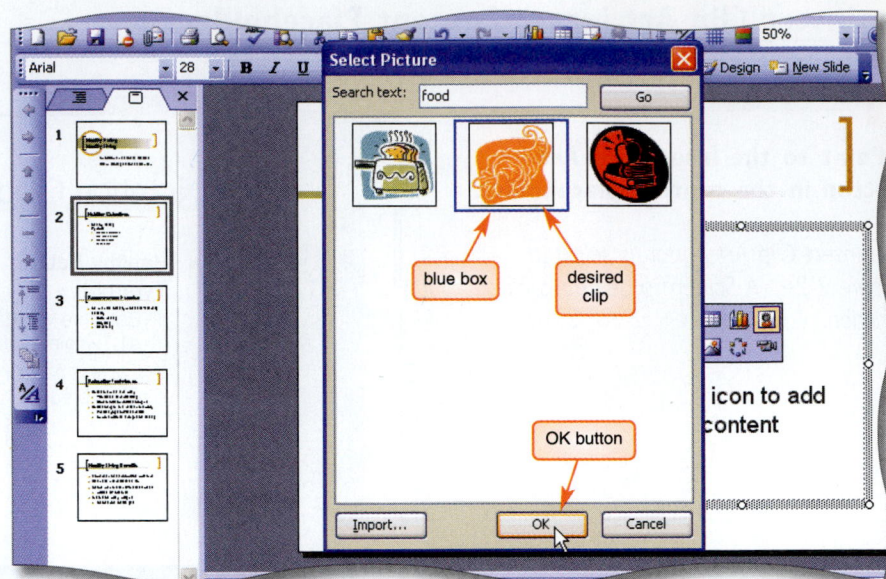

FIGURE 2-26

4

• **Click the OK button.**

• **If the Picture toolbar is displayed, click the Close button on the Picture toolbar.**

The selected clip is inserted into the top content placeholder on Slide 2 (Figure 2-27). PowerPoint sizes the clip automatically to fit the placeholder.

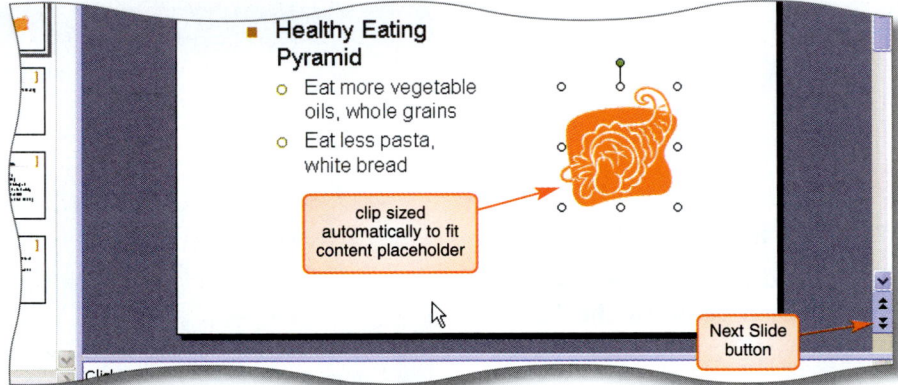

FIGURE 2-27

Slide 2 is complete. The next step is to change the Slide 3 layout and then add two clips. This slide uses the Title, 2 Content and Text slide layout so the two clips display vertically on the left side of the slide and the bulleted list is displayed on the right side. The following steps show how to change the slide layout and then add clip art to Slide 3.

To Change the Slide Layout to Title, 2 Content and Text and Insert Clip Art

1 Click the Next Slide button on the vertical scroll bar to display Slide 3.

2 Click Format on the menu bar and then click Slide Layout.

3 Scroll to display the Title, 2 Content and Text slide layout located in the Text and Content Layouts area of the Slide Layout task pane.

4 Click the Title, 2 Content and Text slide layout and then click the Close button in the Slide Layout task pane.

5 Click the **Insert Clip Art** button in the top content placeholder. Type woman in the **Search text** text box and then click the **Go** button.

6 If necessary, scroll down the list to display the desired clip of a woman walking and then click the clip to select it. Click the **OK** button.

The selected clip is inserted into the content placeholder on Slide 3 (Figure 2-28). The slide has the Title, 2 Content and Text slide layout.

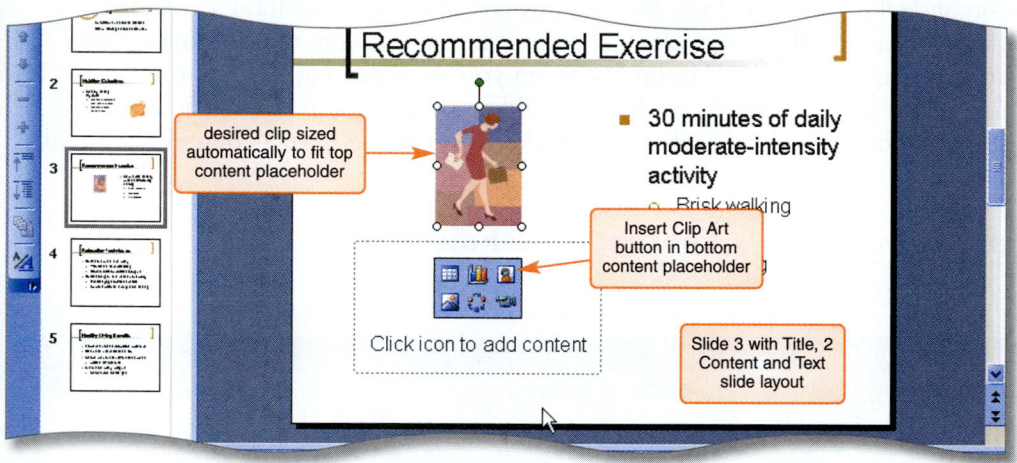

FIGURE 2-28

Inserting a Second Clip into a Slide

Another clip on Slide 3 is required to fill the bottom content placeholder. This clip should be the image of roses. The following steps show how to insert the roses clip into the bottom placeholder on Slide 3.

To Insert a Second Clip into a Slide

1 Click the **Insert Clip Art** button in the bottom content placeholder.

2 Type flowers in the **Search text** text box and then click the **Go** button.

3 If necessary, scroll down the list to display the desired clip of yellow roses, click the clip to select it, and then click the **OK** button.

The selected clip is inserted into the bottom content placeholder on Slide 3 (Figure 2-29). PowerPoint automatically sizes the clip to fit the placeholder.

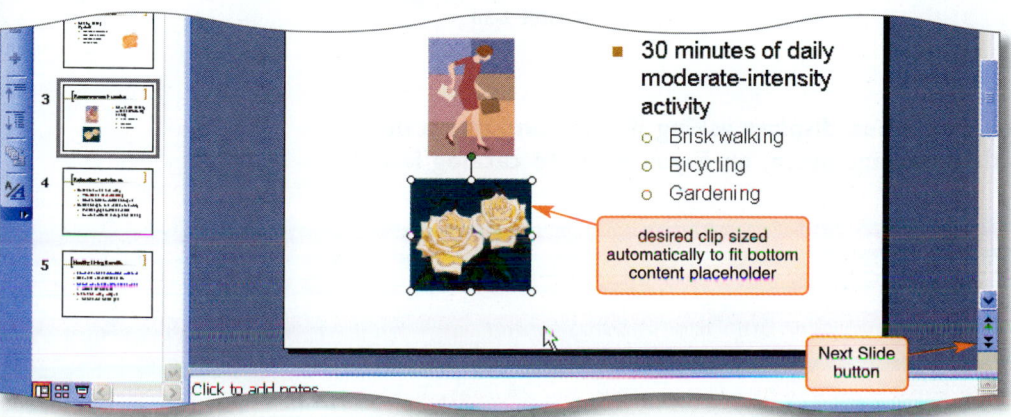

FIGURE 2-29

Slide 3 is complete. Your next step is to add a clip to Slide 4 without changing the slide layout.

Inserting Clip Art into a Slide without a Content Placeholder

PowerPoint does not require you to use a content placeholder to add clips to a slide. You can insert clips on any slide regardless of its slide layout. On Slides 2 and 3, you added clips that enhanced the message in the text. Recall that the slide layout on Slide 4 is Title and Text. Because this layout does not contain a content placeholder, you can use the Insert Clip Art button on the Drawing toolbar to start the Microsoft Clip Organizer. The clip for which you are searching has a house located by a lake. A few of its keywords are house, buildings, homes, and lakes. The following steps show how to insert this clip into a slide that does not have a content placeholder.

To Insert Clip Art into a Slide without a Content Placeholder

1

• **Click the Next Slide button on the vertical scroll bar to display Slide 4.**

• **Click Tools on the menu bar and then click AutoCorrect Options.**

• **If necessary, when the AutoCorrect dialog box displays, click the AutoFormat As You Type tab.**

• **Click Automatic layout for inserted objects in the Apply as you work area if a check mark does not display.**

• **Click OK.**

2

• **Click the Insert Clip Art button on the Drawing toolbar.**

• **If the Add Clips to Organizer dialog box displays asking if you want to catalog media files, click Don't show this message again, or, if you want to catalog later, click the Later button.**

The Clip Art task pane is displayed (Figure 2-30).

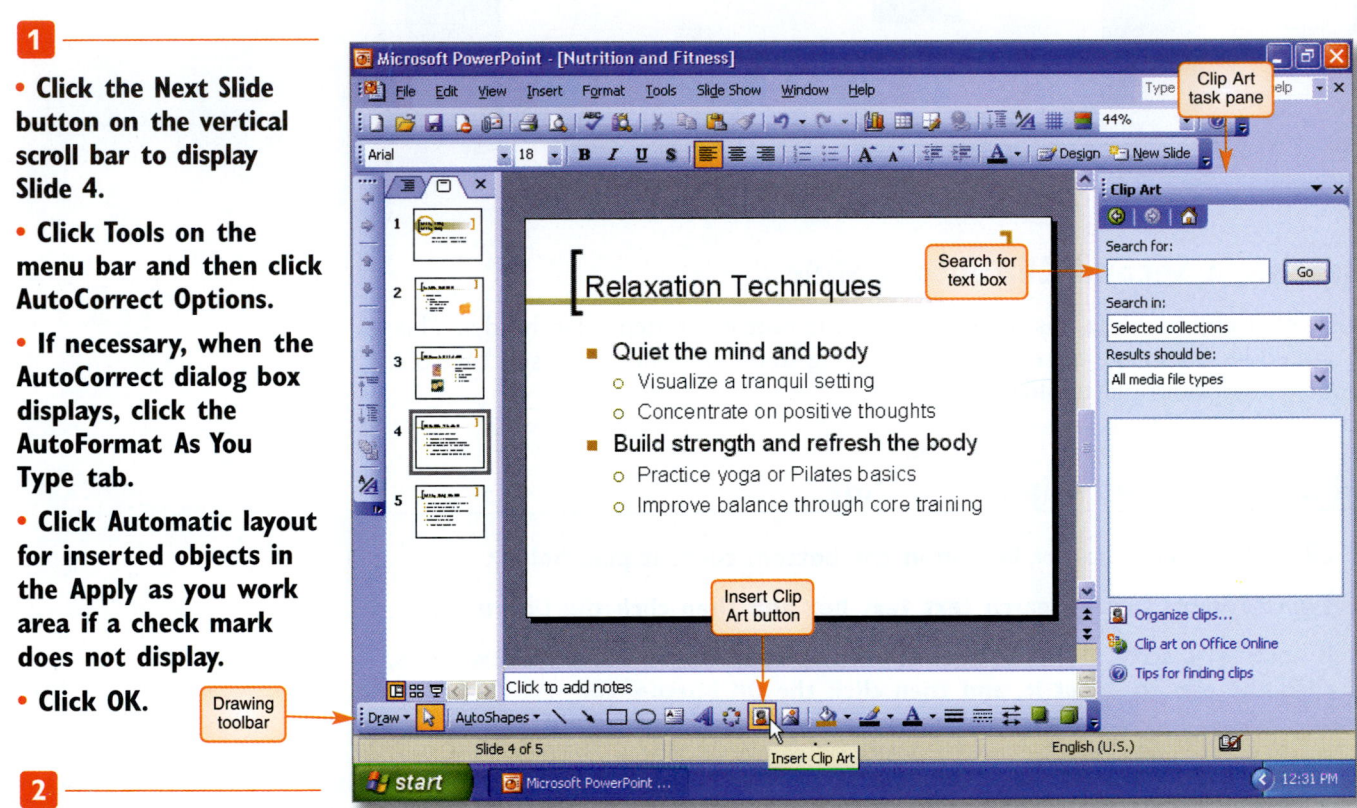

FIGURE 2-30

3

- **Click the Search for text box.**

- **Type** house **and then press the ENTER key.**

- **If necessary, scroll to display the desired clip of a house located beside a lake.**

- **Point to this image.**

The clip of a lake and house is displayed with any other clips sharing the house keyword (Figure 2-31). Your clips may be different. The clip's keywords, size in pixels (260 x 223), file size (33 KB), and file type (WMF) are displayed.

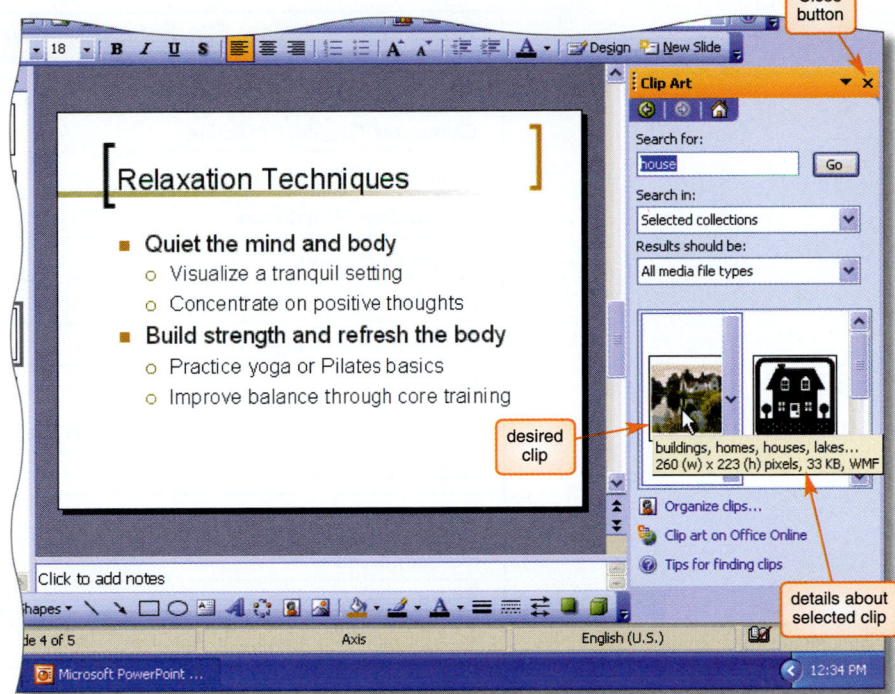

FIGURE 2-31

4

- **Click the desired clip.**

- **Click the Close button on the Clip Art task pane title bar.**

PowerPoint inserts the clip into Slide 4 (Figure 2-32). The slide layout changes automatically to Title, Text, and Content. The Automatic Layout Options button is displayed. If your slide layout does not change, then continue this project using the Moving Clip Art section on page PPT 108.

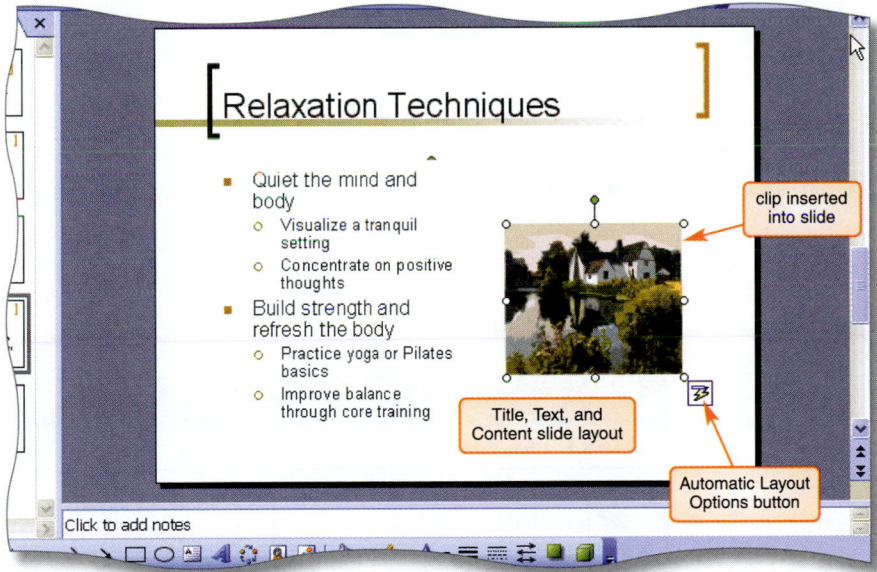

FIGURE 2-32

In addition to clip art, you can insert pictures into a presentation. These may include scanned photographs, line art, and artwork from compact discs. To insert a picture into a presentation, the picture must be saved in a format that PowerPoint can recognize. Table 2-3 (on the next page) identifies some of the formats PowerPoint recognizes.

You can import files saved with the .emf, .gif, .jpg, .png, .bmp, .rle, .dib, and .wmf formats directly into PowerPoint presentations. All other file formats require separate filters that are shipped with the PowerPoint installation software and must be installed. You can download additional filters from the Microsoft Office Online Web site.

| **Table 2-3   Primary File Formats PowerPoint Recognizes** | |
FORMAT	FILE EXTENSION
Computer Graphics Metafile	.cgm
CorelDRAW	.cdr, .cdt, .cmx, and .pat
Encapsulated PostScript	.eps
Enhanced Metafile	.emf
FlashPix	.fpx
Graphics Interchange Format	.gif
Hanako	.jsh, .jah, and .jbh
Joint Photographic Experts Group (JPEG)	.jpg
Kodak PhotoCD	.pcd
Macintosh PICT	.pct
PC Paintbrush	.pcx
Portable Network Graphics	.png
Tagged Image File Format	.tif
Windows Bitmap	.bmp, .rle, .dib
Microsoft Windows Metafile	.wmf
WordPerfect Graphics	.wpg

Smart Tags

A **smart tag** is a button that PowerPoint automatically displays on the screen when performing a certain action. The Automatic Layout Options button in Figure 2-32 on the previous page is a smart tag. In addition to the Automatic Layout Options button, PowerPoint provides three other smart tags. Table 2-4 summarizes the smart tags available in PowerPoint.

| **Table 2-4   Smart Tags in PowerPoint** | | |
SMART TAG BUTTON		MENU FUNCTION
	AutoCorrect Options	Undoes an automatic correction, stops future automatic corrections of this type, or displays the AutoCorrect Options dialog box.
	Paste Options	Specifies how moved or pasted items should display, e.g., with original formatting, without formatting, or with different formatting.
	AutoFit Options	Undoes automatic text resizing to fit the current placeholder or changes single-column layouts to two-column layouts, inserts a new slide, or splits the text between two slides.
	Automatic Layout Options	Adjusts the slide layout to accommodate an inserted object.

Clicking a smart tag button shows a menu that contains commands relative to the action performed at the location of the smart tag. For example, if you want PowerPoint to undo the layout change when you add a clip to a slide, click the Automatic Layout Options button to display the Smart Tag Actions menu, and then click Undo Automatic Layout on the Smart Tag Actions menu to display the initial layout.

Using the Automatic Layout Options Button to Undo a Layout Change

The Title and Text layout used in Slide 4 did not provide a content placeholder for the clip you inserted, so PowerPoint automatically changed the layout to Title, Text, and Content. If your slide layout did not change, then disregard this section and continue the project on the next page with the Moving Clip Art section. Because the text now violates the 7 × 7 rule with this layout and because you want to place the clip in a location other than the areas specified, you should change the layout to the Title and Text layout.

The Automatic Layout Options button is displayed because PowerPoint changed the layout automatically. If you move your mouse pointer near the changed object or text, the Automatic Layout Options button is displayed as an arrow, indicating that a list of options is available that allow you to undo the new layout, stop the automatic layout of inserted objects, or alter the AutoCorrect Options settings. The following steps show how to undo the layout change.

To Use the Automatic Layout Options Button to Undo a Layout Change

1

• **If your slide layout automatically changed to Title, Text, and Content, click the Automatic Layout Options button.**

• **Point to Undo Automatic Layout.**

The Automatic Layout Options list is displayed (Figure 2-33). Clicking Undo Automatic Layout will reverse the layout change.

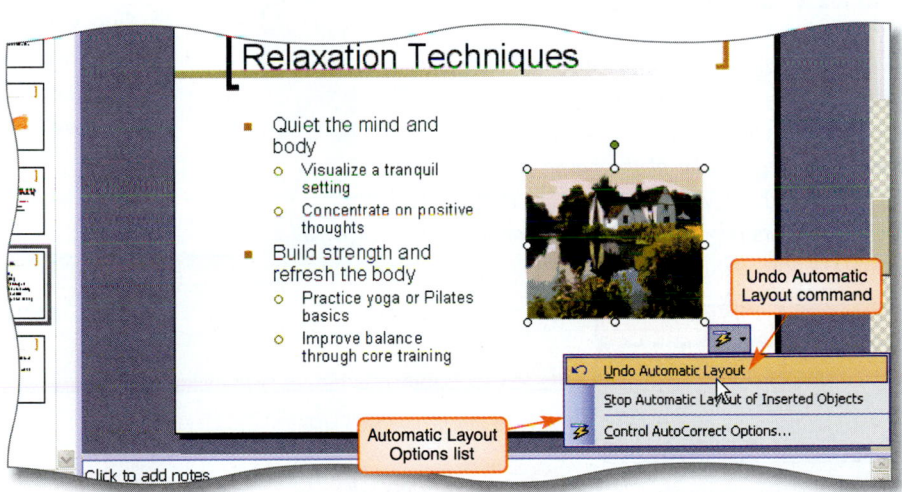

FIGURE 2-33

2

• **Click Undo Automatic Layout.**

The layout reverts to Title and Text (Figure 2-34).

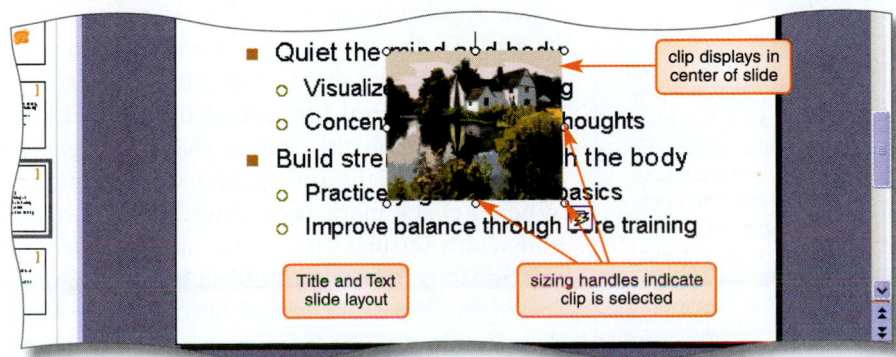

FIGURE 2-34

The desired clip is displayed in the center of Slide 4, which has the original Title and Text slide layout. The next step is to move the clip to the top-right corner of the slide.

Moving Clip Art

After you insert a clip into a slide, you may want to reposition it. The house clip on Slide 4 overlays the bulleted list. You want to move the clip away from the text to the upper-right corner of the slide. The following steps show how to move the clip to the upper-right corner of the slide.

To Move Clip Art

1

• **With the clip selected, point to the clip and then press and hold down the mouse button.**

• **Drag the clip to the upper-right corner of the slide.**

• **Release the mouse button.**

When you drag a clip, a dotted box is displayed. The dotted box indicates the clip's new position. When you release the left mouse button, the clip of the house is displayed in the new location and the dotted line disappears (Figure 2-35). Sizing handles display at the corners and along its edges.

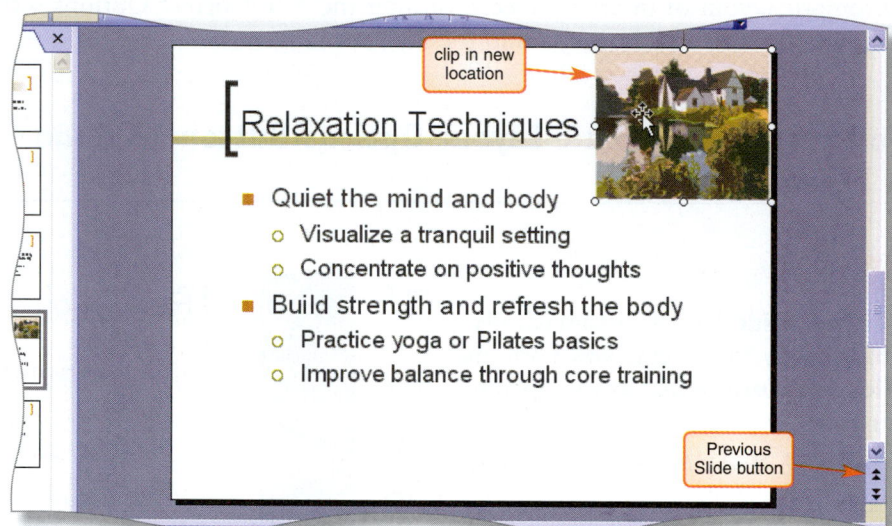

FIGURE 2-35

Changing the Size of Clip Art

Sometimes it is necessary to change the size of clip art. For example, on Slide 2 much space appears around the clip. To make this object fit onto the slide, you increase its size. To change the size of a clip by an exact percentage, use the Format Picture command on the shortcut menu. The Format Picture dialog box contains six tabbed sheets with several formatting options. The **Size sheet** contains options for changing a clip's size. You either enter the exact height and width in the Size and rotate area, or enter the height and width as a percentage of the original clip in the Scale area. When a check mark is displayed in the **Lock aspect ratio check box**, the height and width settings change to maintain the original aspect ratio. **Aspect ratio** is the relationship between an object's height and width. For example, a 3-by-5-inch object scaled to 50 percent would become a 1½-by-2½-inch object. The following steps describe how to increase the size of the clip using the Format Picture dialog box.

To Change the Size of Clip Art

1

• **Click the Previous Slide button on the vertical scroll bar two times to display Slide 2.**

• **Right-click the clip.**

• **Point to Format Picture on the shortcut menu.**

Sizing handles display at the clip's corners and along its edges (Figure 2-36).

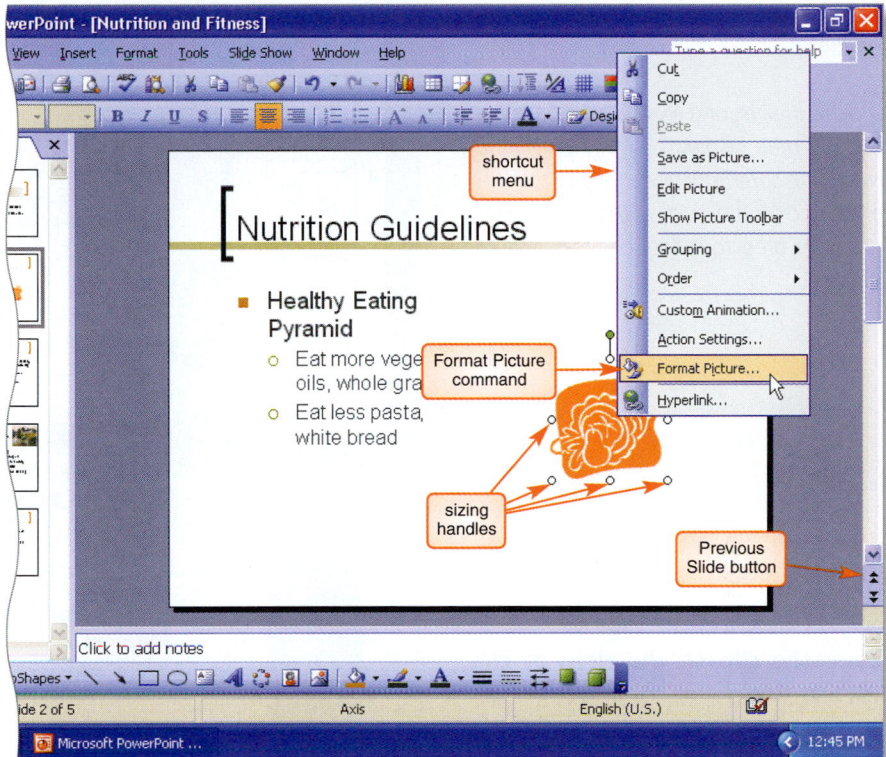

FIGURE 2-36

2

• **Click Format Picture.**

• **Click the Size tab when the Format Picture dialog box is displayed.**

The Size sheet in the Format Picture dialog box is displayed (Figure 2-37). The Height and Width text boxes in the Scale area display the current percentage of the clip, 100%. Check marks are displayed in the Lock aspect ratio and Relative to original picture size check boxes.

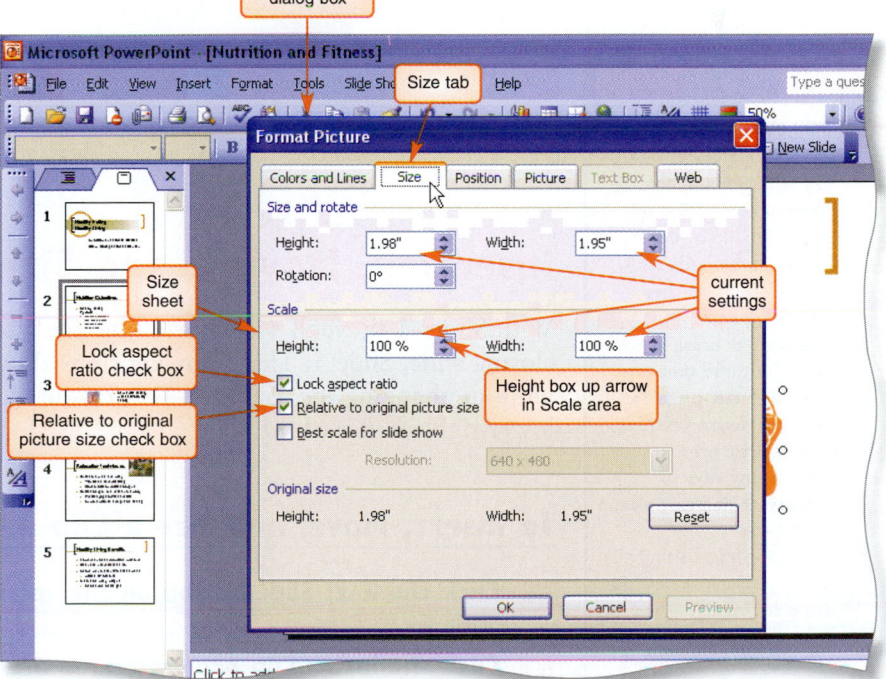

FIGURE 2-37

3

• **Click and hold down the mouse button on the Height box up arrow in the Scale area until 135% is displayed.**

Both the Height and Width text boxes in the Scale area display 135% (Figure 2-38). PowerPoint automatically changes the Height and Width text boxes in the Size and rotate area to reflect changes in the Scale area.

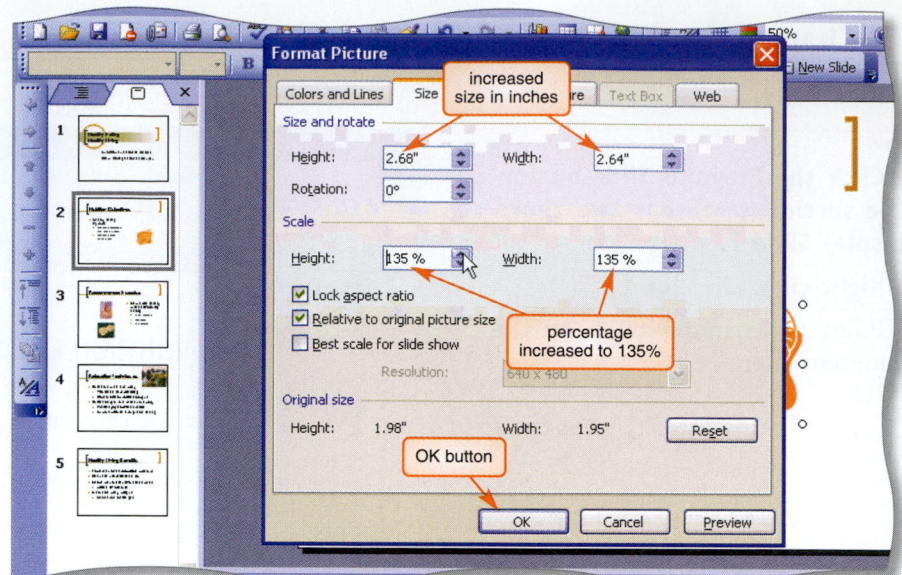

FIGURE 2-38

4

• **Click the OK button.**
• **Drag the clip to the right of the bulleted list.**

PowerPoint closes the Format Picture dialog box and displays the enlarged clip in the desired location (Figure 2-39).

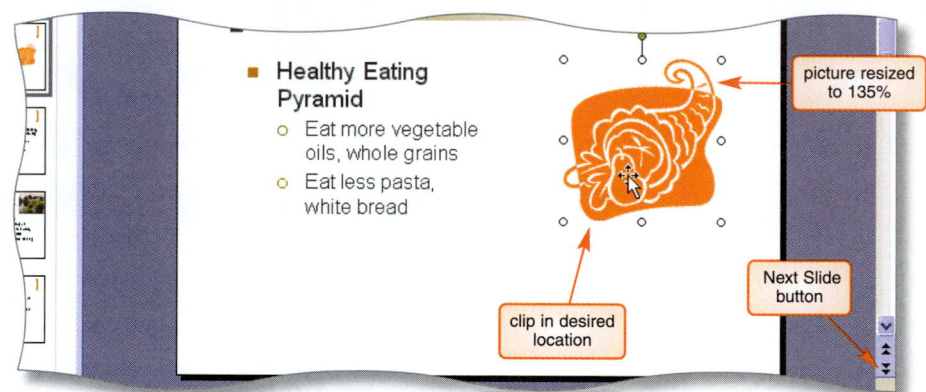

FIGURE 2-39

Other Ways

1. Click clip, on Format menu click Picture, click Size tab, click and hold down mouse button on Height box up or down arrow in Scale area until desired size is reached, click OK button
2. Press ALT+O, press I, press CTRL+TAB three times to select Size tab, press TAB to select Height text box in Scale area, press up or down arrow keys to increase or decrease size, press ENTER
3. Click clip, drag a sizing handle until clip is desired shape and size
4. Right-click slide anywhere except text placeholders, click Slide Layout on shortcut menu, double-click desired slide layout

Inserting, Moving, and Sizing a Clip into a Slide

With Slides 1 through 4 complete, the final step is to add the stethoscope clip to the closing slide, Slide 5. The following steps show how to add a stethoscope to Slide 5 without changing the Title and Text layout, size the clip, and then move it to the lower-right corner of the slide.

To Insert, Move, and Size a Clip into a Slide

1 **Click the Next Slide button on the vertical scroll bar three times to display Slide 5.**

2 **Click the Insert Clip Art button on the Drawing toolbar. Delete the word, house, in the Search for text box, type** stethoscope, **and then press the ENTER key. Click the stethoscope shown in Figure 2-40 or another appropriate clip. Click the Close button on the Clip Art task pane title bar.**

3 If the layout changes, click the **Automatic Layout Options** button and then click **Undo Automatic Layout**.

4 Right-click the stethoscope and then click **Format Picture** on the shortcut menu. Click the **Size** tab in the **Format Picture** dialog box, click and hold down the mouse button on the **Height** box up arrow in the **Scale** area until **160%** is displayed, and then click the **OK** button.

5 Drag the stethoscope to the lower-right corner of the slide.

The stethoscope is inserted, moved, and sized into Slide 5 (Figure 2-40).

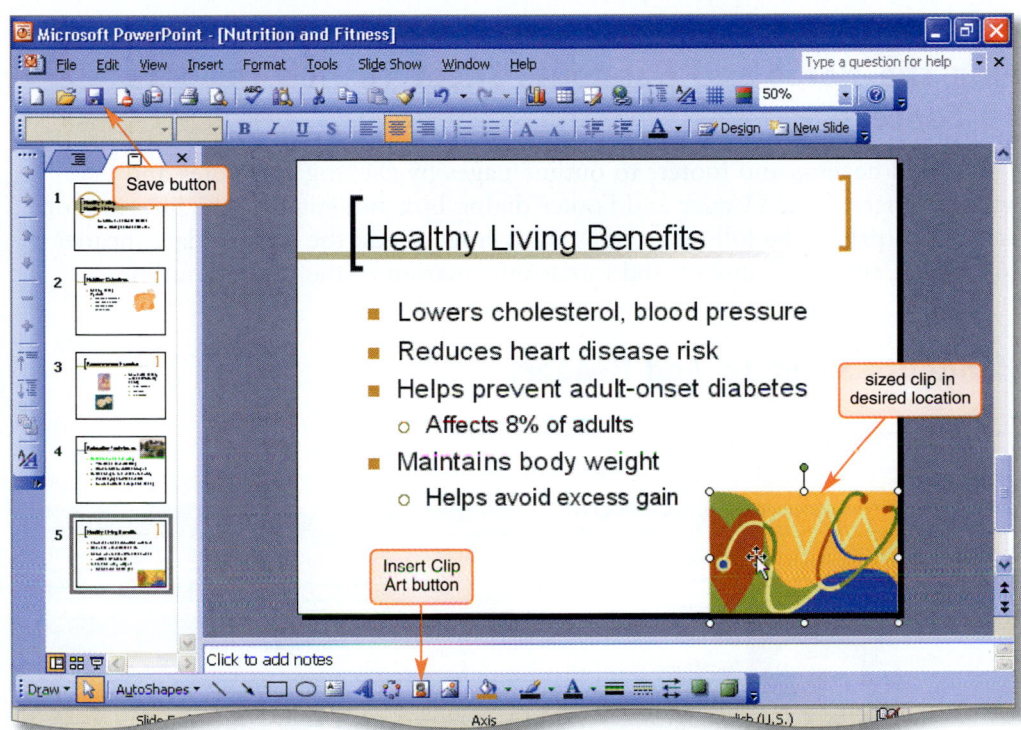

FIGURE 2-40

Saving the Presentation Again

To preserve the work completed, perform the following step to save the presentation again.

To Save a Presentation

1 Click the **Save** button on the **Standard toolbar**.

The changes made to the presentation after the previous save are saved on the floppy disk.

A default setting in PowerPoint allows for **fast saves**, which saves only the changes made since the last time you saved. To save a full copy of the complete presentation, click Tools on the menu bar, click Options on the Tools menu, and then click the Save tab. Remove the check mark in the Allow fast saves check box by clicking the check box and then click the OK button.

Adding a Header and Footer to Outline Pages

A printout of the presentation outline often is used as an audience handout. Distributing a copy of the outline provides the audience with paper on which to write notes or comments. Another benefit of distributing a copy of the outline is to help the audience see the text on the slides when lighting is poor or the room is too large. To help identify the source of the printed outline, add a descriptive header and footer. A **header** is displayed at the top of the sheet of paper or slide, and a **footer** is displayed at the bottom. Both contain specific information, such as the presenter's name or the company's telephone number. In addition, the current date and time and the slide or page number can display beside the header or footer information.

Using the Notes and Handouts Sheet to Add Headers and Footers

You add headers and footers to outline pages by clicking the Notes and Handouts sheet in the Header and Footer dialog box and entering the information you want to print. The following steps show how to add the current date, header information, the page number, and footer information to the printed outline.

To Use the Notes and Handouts Sheet to Add Headers and Footers

1

• Click View on the menu bar and then point to Header and Footer (Figure 2-41).

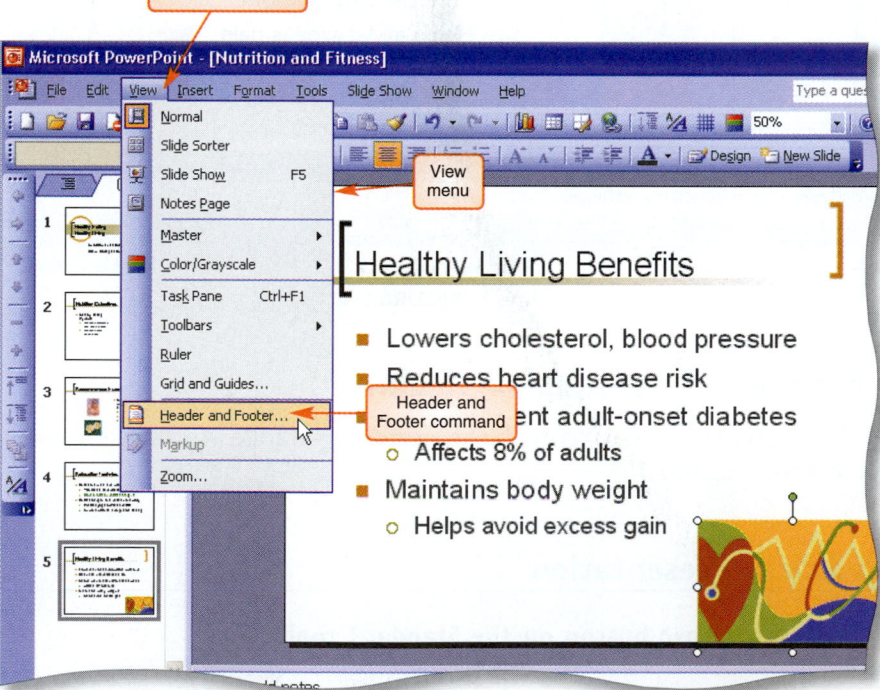

FIGURE 2-41

2

• **Click Header and Footer.**

• **Click the Notes and Handouts tab when the Header and Footer dialog box is displayed.**

The Notes and Handouts sheet in the Header and Footer dialog box is displayed (Figure 2-42). Check marks display in the Date and time, Header, Page number, and Footer check boxes. The Fixed option button is selected.

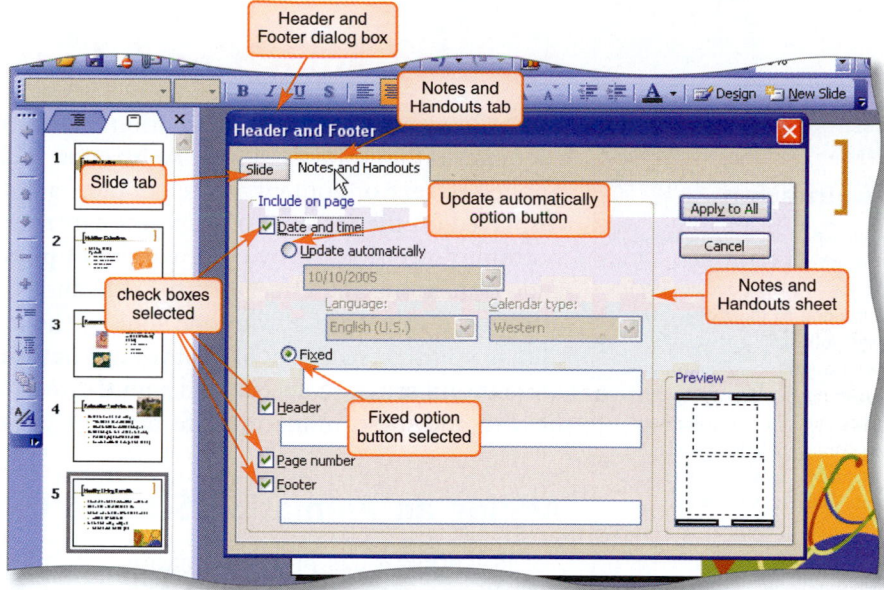

FIGURE 2-42

3

• **Click the Update automatically option button and then click the Header text box.**

• **Type** Healthy Eating, Healthy Living **in the Header text box.**

• **Click the Footer text box.**

• **Type** Clark College Fitness Center **in the Footer text box (Figure 2-43).**

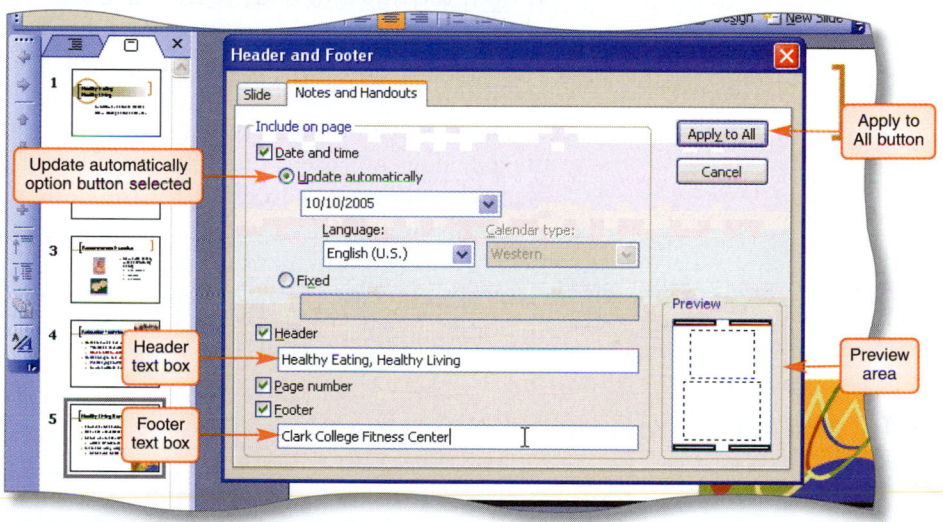

FIGURE 2-43

4

• **Click the Apply to All button.**

PowerPoint applies the header and footer text to the outline, closes the Header and Footer dialog box, and displays Slide 5 (Figure 2-44). You cannot see header and footer text until you print the outline (shown in Figure 2-60 on page PPT 124).

FIGURE 2-44

Applying Animation Schemes

PowerPoint provides many animation effects to add interest and make a slide show presentation look professional. **Animation** includes special visual and sound effects applied to text or content. For example, each line on the slide can swivel as it is displayed on the screen. Or an object can zoom in from the top of the screen to the bottom. PowerPoint provides a variety of **preset animation schemes** that determine slide transitions and effects for the title and body text. A **slide transition** is a special effect used to progress from one slide to the next in a slide show. PowerPoint also allows you to set your own **custom animation** effects by defining your own animation types and speeds and sound effects on a slide. The following pages discuss how to add these animation effects to the presentation.

Adding an Animation Scheme to a Slide Show

PowerPoint has preset animation schemes with visual effects that vary the slide transitions and the methods in which the slide title and bullets or paragraphs display on the slides. Not all animation schemes have the slide transition element or effects for both the title and body text. These schemes are grouped in three categories: Subtle, Moderate, and Exciting. The name of the animation scheme characterizes the visual effects used. For example, the Unfold animation scheme in the Moderate category uses the Push Right slide transition effect, the Fly In effect for the title text, and the Unfold effect for the body text. The Pinwheel scheme in the Exciting category does not use a slide transition effect, but it uses the Pinwheel effect for the title text and the Peek In effect for the body text.

In this presentation, you apply the Float animation scheme to all slides. This effect is added easily by using the Slide Design task pane, which you used earlier in this project to select a design template. The following steps show how to apply the Float animation scheme to the Nutrition and Fitness presentation.

To Add an Animation Scheme to a Slide Show

1

• **Click Slide Show on the menu bar and then point to Animation Schemes (Figure 2-45).**

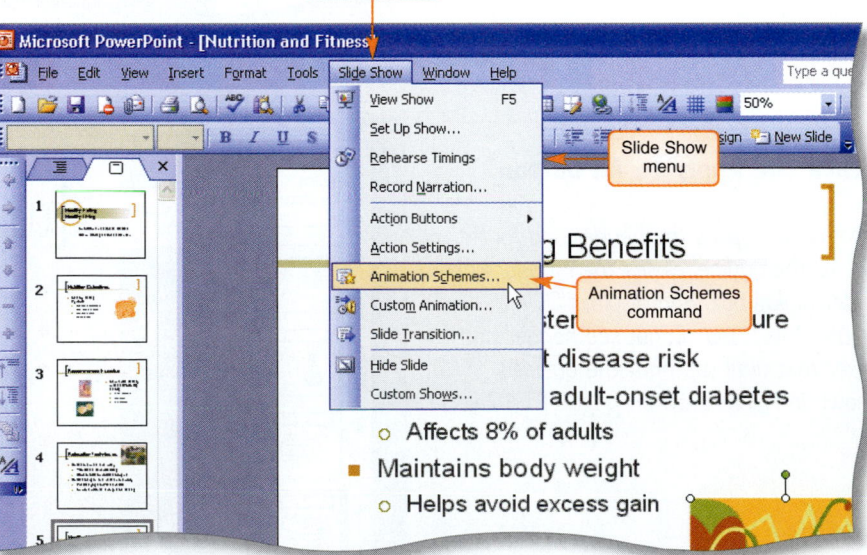

FIGURE 2-45

2

• **Click Animation Schemes.**

• **Scroll down the Apply to selected slides list and then point to Float in the Exciting category.**

The Slide Design task pane is displayed (Figure 2-46). The list of possible slide transition effects is displayed in the Apply to selected slides area. The Float ScreenTip shows that the Float animation scheme uses the Comb Horizontal slide transition, the Float effect for the title text, and the Descend effect for the body text.

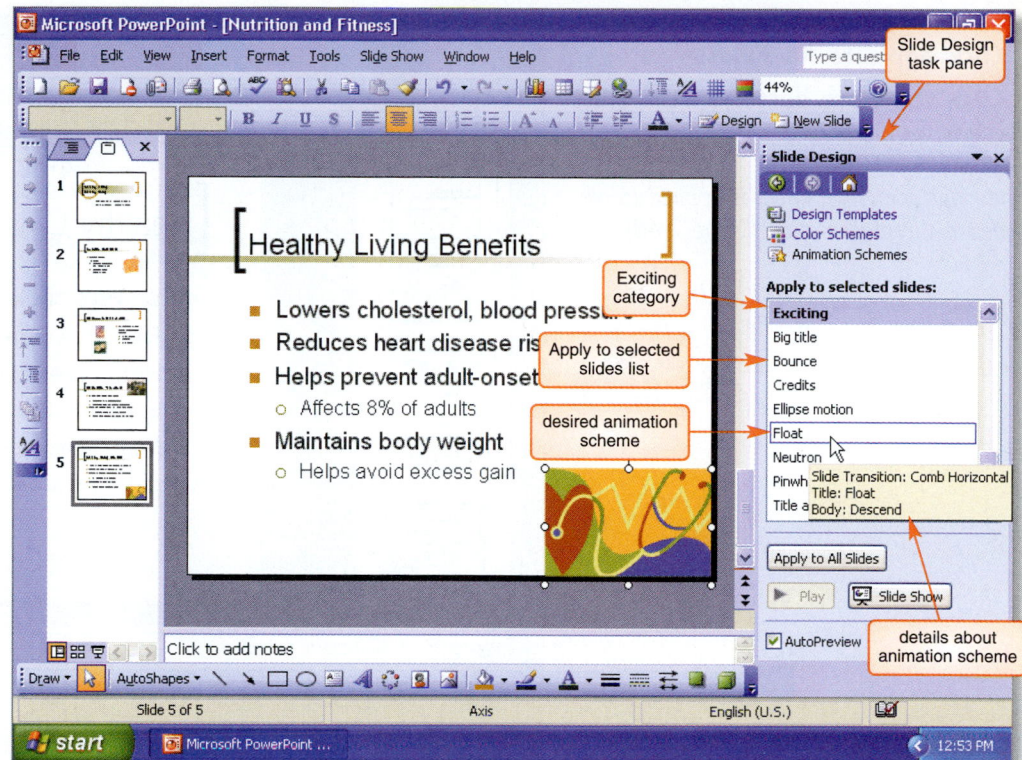

FIGURE 2-46

3

• **Click Float.**

• **Point to the Apply to All Slides button.**

PowerPoint applies the Float animation effect to Slide 5, as indicated by the animation icon on the left side of the Slide 5 slide thumbnail on the Slides tab (Figure 2-47). The Float animation effect is previewed because the AutoPreview check box is selected.

FIGURE 2-47

4

• **Click Apply to All Slides.**

• **Click the Close button in the Slide Design task pane.**

The Float animation effect is applied to all slides in the presentation (Figure 2-48).

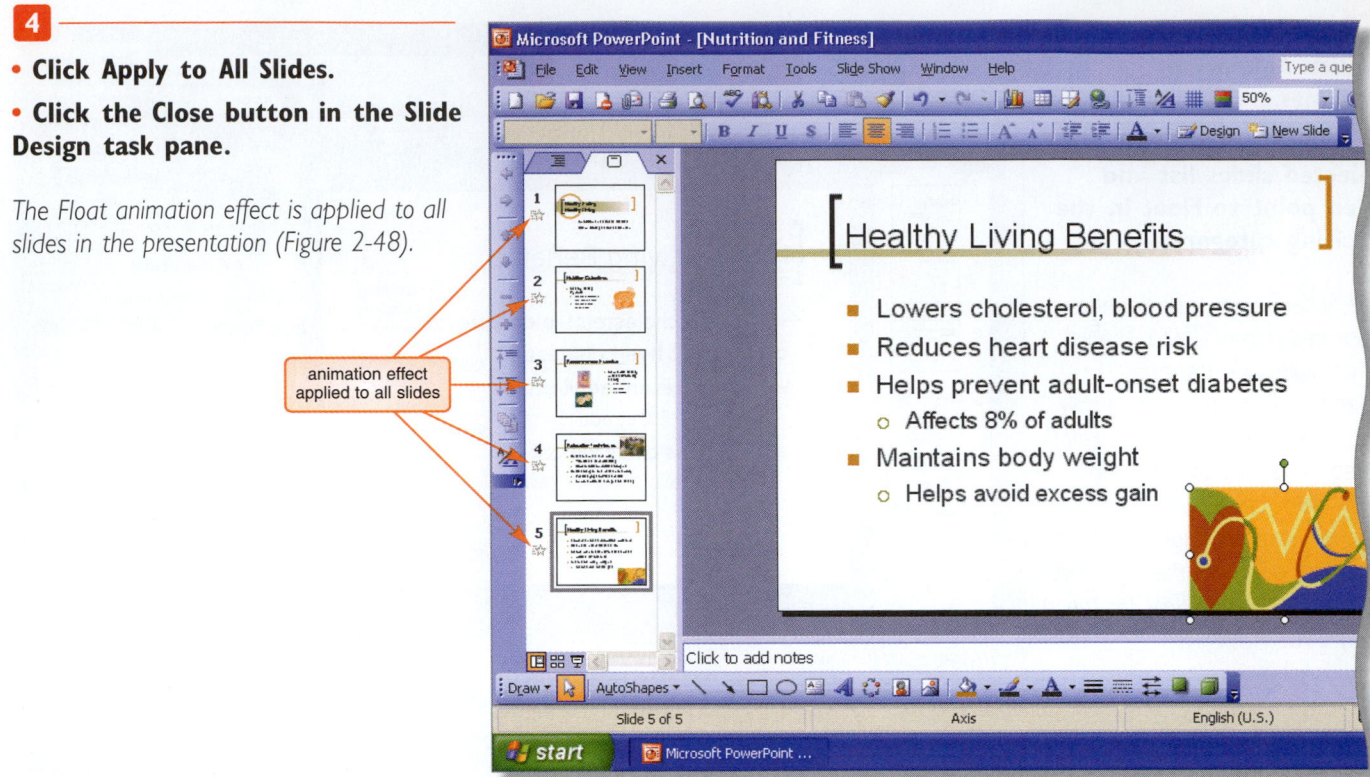

animation effect applied to all slides

FIGURE 2-48

Animating Clip Art

To add visual interest to a presentation, you can **animate** certain content. On Slide 5, for example, having the stethoscope appear in a diamond pattern on the screen will provide an interesting effect. Animating clip art takes several steps as described in the following sections.

Adding Animation Effects

PowerPoint allows you to animate clip art along with animating text. Because Slide 5 lists the benefits of maintaining a healthy lifestyle, you want to emphasize these facts by having the clip appear on the screen in a diamond pattern. One way of animating clip art is to select options in the Custom Animation dialog box. The following steps show how to add the Diamond animation effect to the clip on Slide 5.

To Animate Clip Art

1

• **Right-click the clip and then point to Custom Animation on the shortcut menu.**

The shortcut menu is displayed (Figure 2-49). The clip is selected, as indicated by the sizing handles that display at the corners and along its edges.

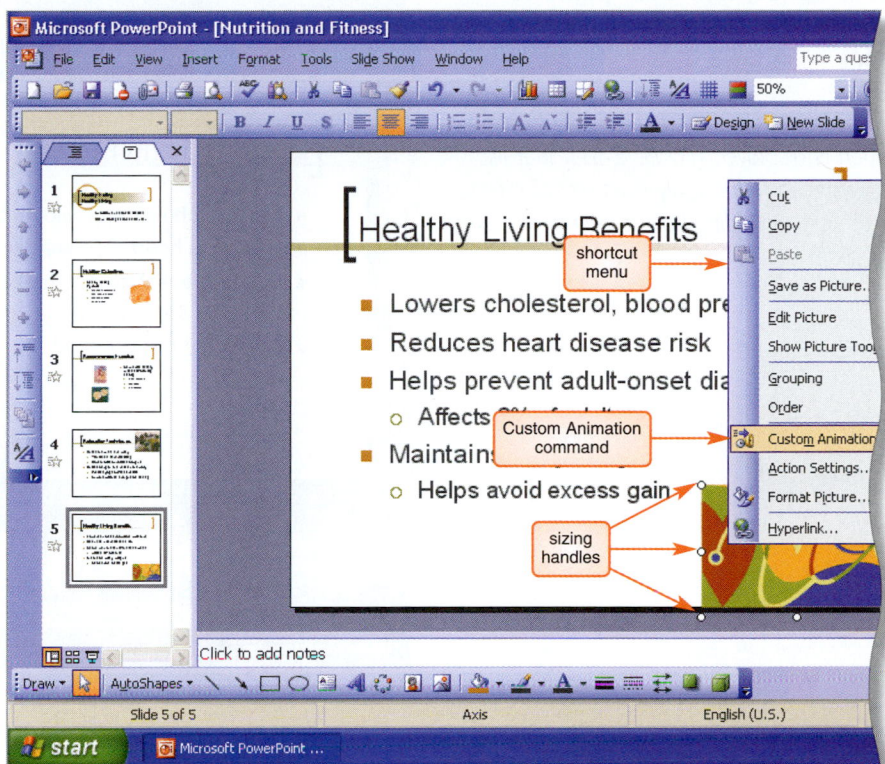

FIGURE 2-49

2

• **Click Custom Animation.**

• **Point to the Add Effect button.**

The Custom Animation task pane is displayed (Figure 2-50). Two animation effects have been applied to the title and body of the slide previously.

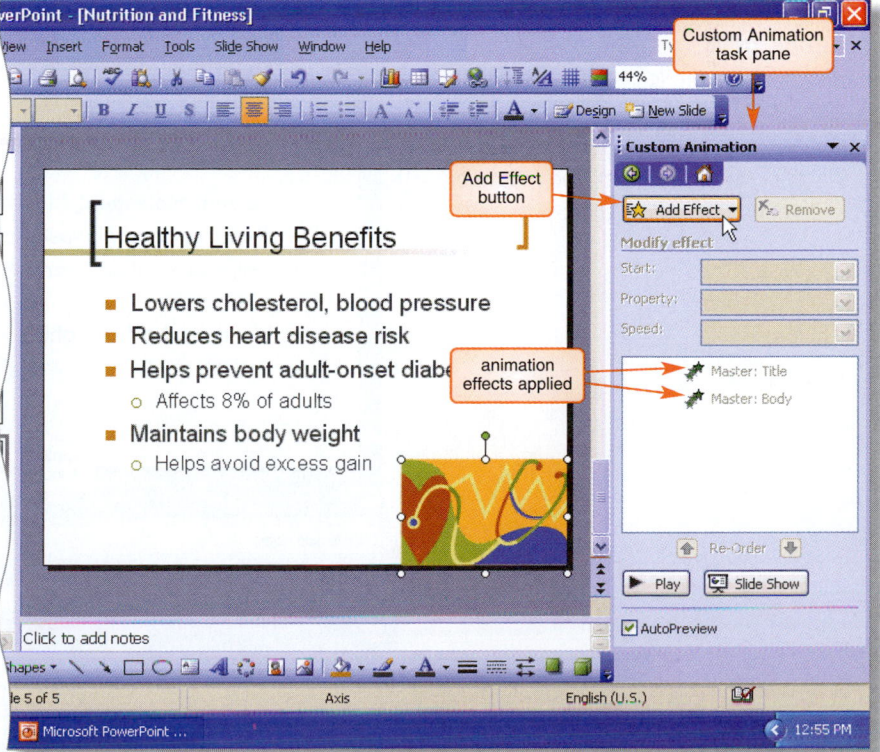

FIGURE 2-50

3

• **Click the Add Effect button, point to Entrance, and then point to Diamond in the Entrance effects list.**

A list of possible effects for the Entrance option is displayed (Figure 2-51). Your list may vary. You can apply a variety of effects to the clip, including how it enters and exits the slide.

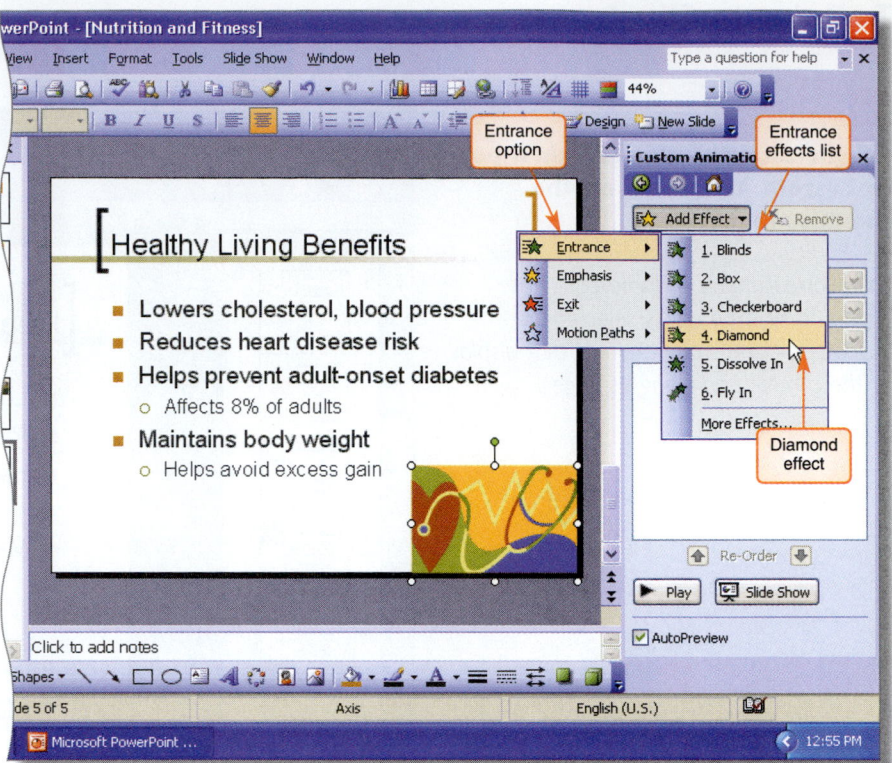

FIGURE 2-51

4

• **Click Diamond.**

The animation effect is applied to the stethoscope, as indicated by the number 1 icon displaying to the left of the clip and the corresponding 1 displaying in the Custom Animation list (Figure 2-52). You will see this effect when you click the mouse on that slide during your slide show.

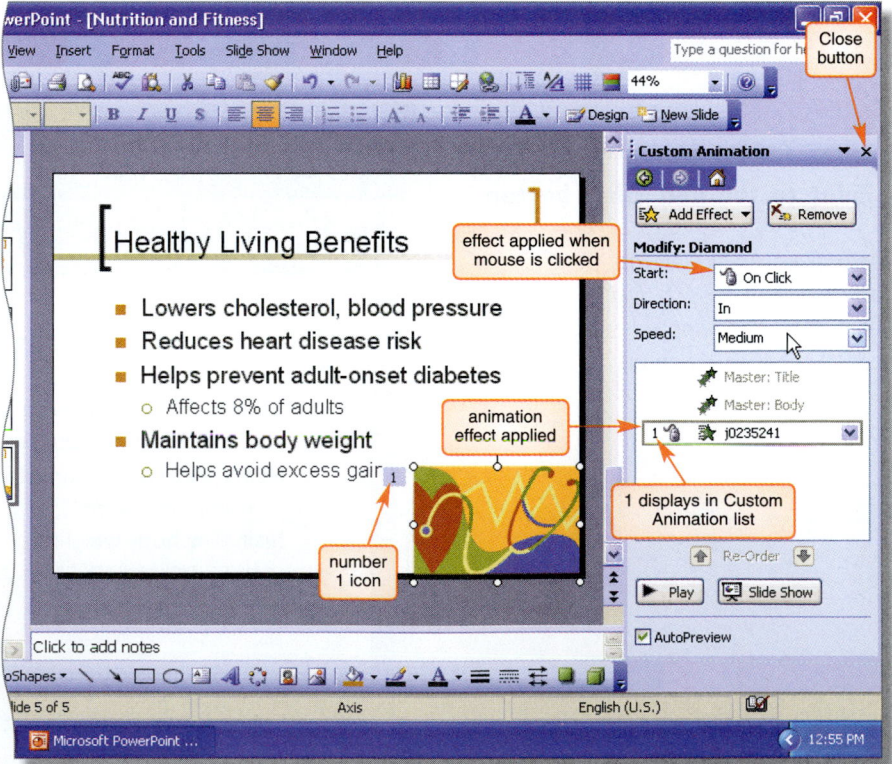

FIGURE 2-52

5

• **Click the Close button on the Custom Animation task pane title bar (Figure 2-53).**

The stethoscope clip will appear in the presentation using the Diamond animation effect during the slide show.

FIGURE 2-53

When you run the slide show, the bulleted-list paragraphs are displayed, and then the clip art will begin displaying on the slide in a diamond shape at the position where you inserted it into Slide 5.

Animation effects are complete for this presentation. You now can review the presentation in slide show view and correct any spelling errors.

Saving the Presentation Again

The presentation is complete. The following step shows how to save the finished presentation on a floppy disk before running the slide show.

To Save a Presentation

1 **Click the Save button on the Standard toolbar.**

PowerPoint saves the presentation on your floppy disk by saving the changes made to the presentation since the last save.

Running an Animated Slide Show

Project 1 introduced you to using slide show view to look at your presentation one slide at a time. This project introduces you to running a slide show with preset and custom animation effects. When you run a slide show with slide transition effects, PowerPoint displays the slide transition effect when you click the mouse button to advance to the next slide. When a slide has text animation effects, each paragraph level is displayed in the sequence specified by the animation settings in the Custom Animation dialog box. The following steps show how to run the animated Nutrition and Fitness presentation.

To Run an Animated Slide Show

1

• **Click the Slide 1 slide thumbnail on the Slides tab.**

• **Click the Slide Show button at the lower left of the PowerPoint window.**

• **When Slide 1 is displayed in slide show view, click the slide anywhere.**

PowerPoint applies the Comb Horizontal slide transition effect and shows the title slide title text, Healthy Eating, Healthy Living (Figure 2-54), using the Float animation effect. When you click the slide, the first paragraph in the subtitle text placeholder, Nutrition and Fitness Basics, is displayed using the Descend animation effect.

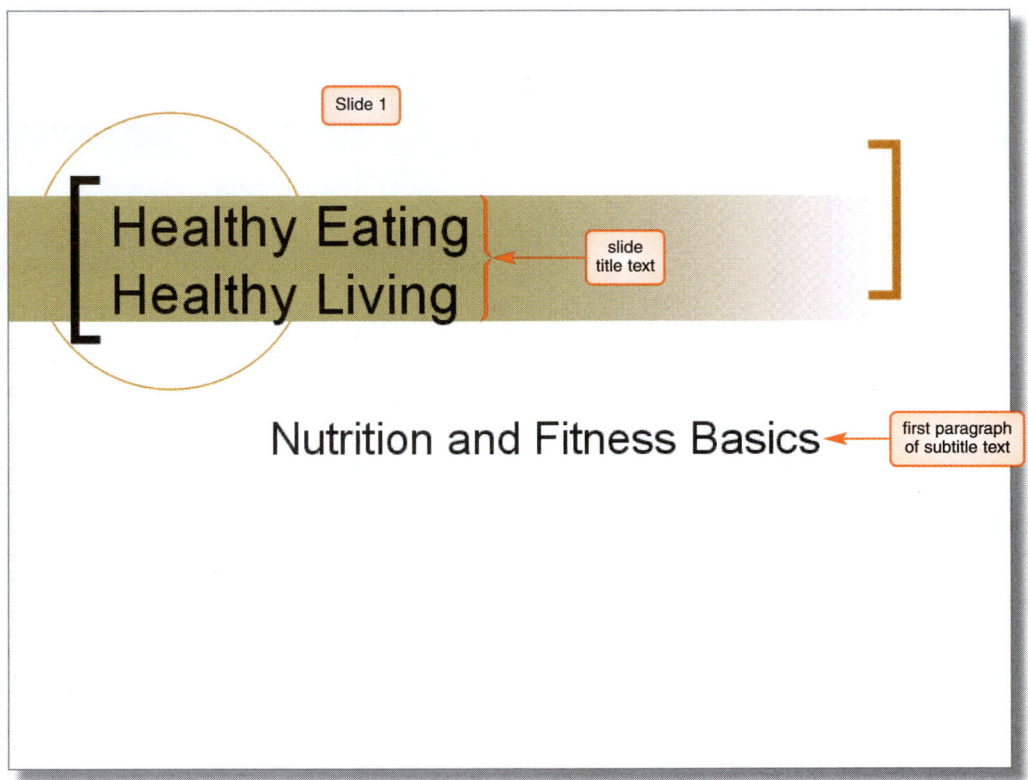

FIGURE 2-54

2

• **Click the slide again.**

PowerPoint displays the second paragraph in the subtitle text placeholder, Clark College Fitness Center, using the Float animation effect (Figure 2-55). If the Popup Menu buttons are displayed when you move the mouse pointer, do not click them.

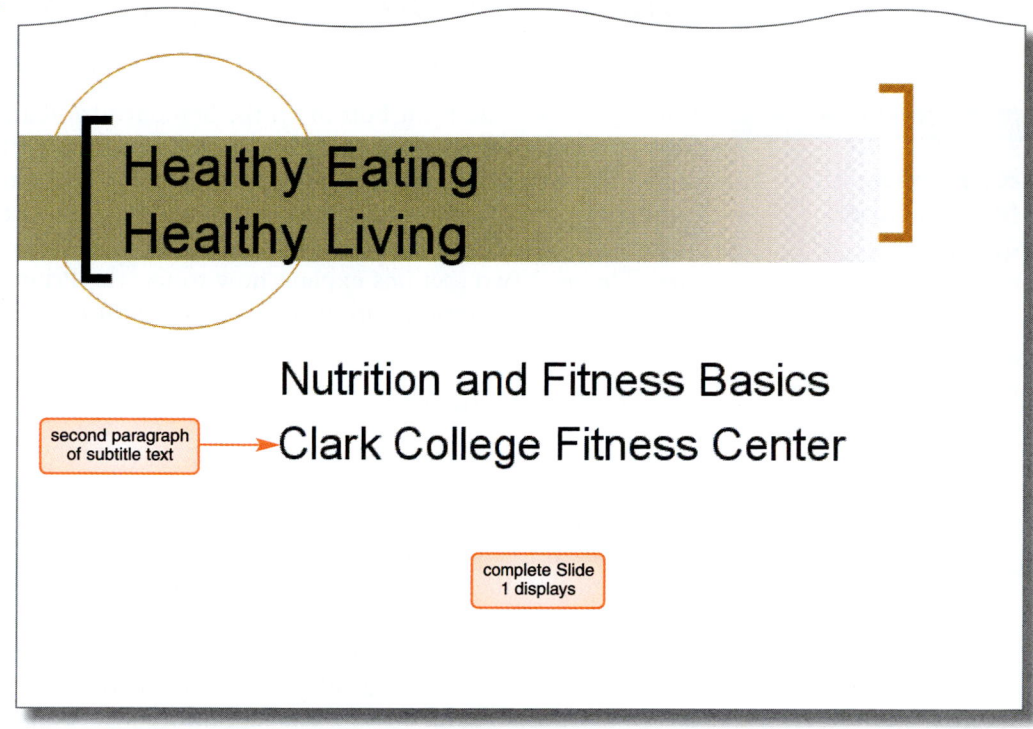

FIGURE 2-55

3

• **Continue clicking to finish running the slide show and return to normal view.**

Each time a new slide is displayed, PowerPoint first displays the Comb Horizontal slide transition effect and only the slide title using the Float effect. Then, PowerPoint builds each slide based on the animation settings. When you click the slide after the last paragraph is displayed on the last slide of the presentation, PowerPoint displays a blank slide. When you click again, PowerPoint exits slide show view and returns to normal view (Figure 2-56).

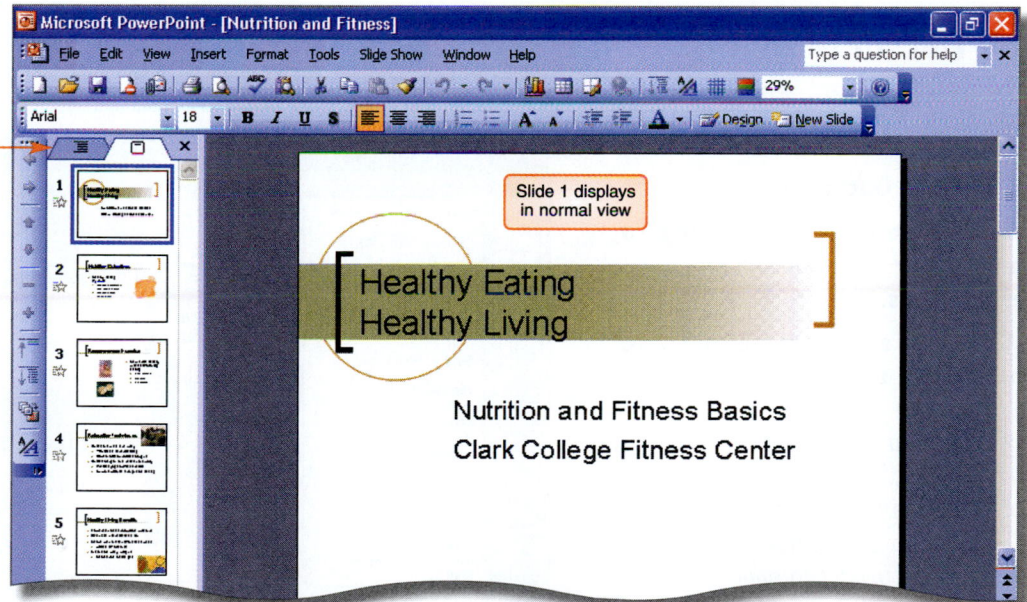

FIGURE 2-56

Other Ways

1. On Slide Show menu click View Show, click slide until slide show ends
2. Press ALT+D, press V, press ENTER until slide show ends
3. In Voice Command mode, say "Slide Show, View Show"

With the presentation complete and animation effects tested, the last step is to print the presentation outline and slides.

Printing a Presentation Created on the Outline Tab

More About

Remembering Information

Handouts and slides help audience members remember what they hear. People remember 10 percent of what they read, 20 percent of what they hear, 30 percent of what they see, and 70 percent of what they see and hear.

When you click the Print button on the Standard toolbar, PowerPoint prints a hard copy of the presentation component last selected in the Print what box in the Print dialog box. To be certain to print the component you want, such as the presentation outline, use the Print command on the File menu. When the Print dialog box is displayed, you can select the appropriate presentation component in the Print what box. The next two sections explain how to use the Print command on the File menu to print the presentation outline and the presentation slides.

Printing an Outline

During the development of a lengthy presentation, it often is easier to review your outline in print rather than on the screen. Printing your outline also is useful for audience handouts or when your supervisor or instructor wants to review your subject matter before you develop your presentation fully.

Recall that the Print dialog box shows print options. When you want to print your outline, select Outline View in the Print what list in the Print dialog box. The outline, however, prints as last viewed on the Outline tab. This means that you must select the Zoom setting to display the outline text as you want it to print. If you are uncertain of the Zoom setting, you should return to the Outline tab and review it before printing. The following steps show how to print an outline from normal view.

To Print an Outline

1

• **Click the Outline tab.**

• **Ready the printer according to the printer manufacturer's instructions.**

• **Click File on the menu bar and then point to Print.**

The File menu is displayed (Figure 2-57). The Expand All button on the Outlining toolbar is selected, so the entire outline will print. If you want to print only the slide titles, you would click the Collapse All button.

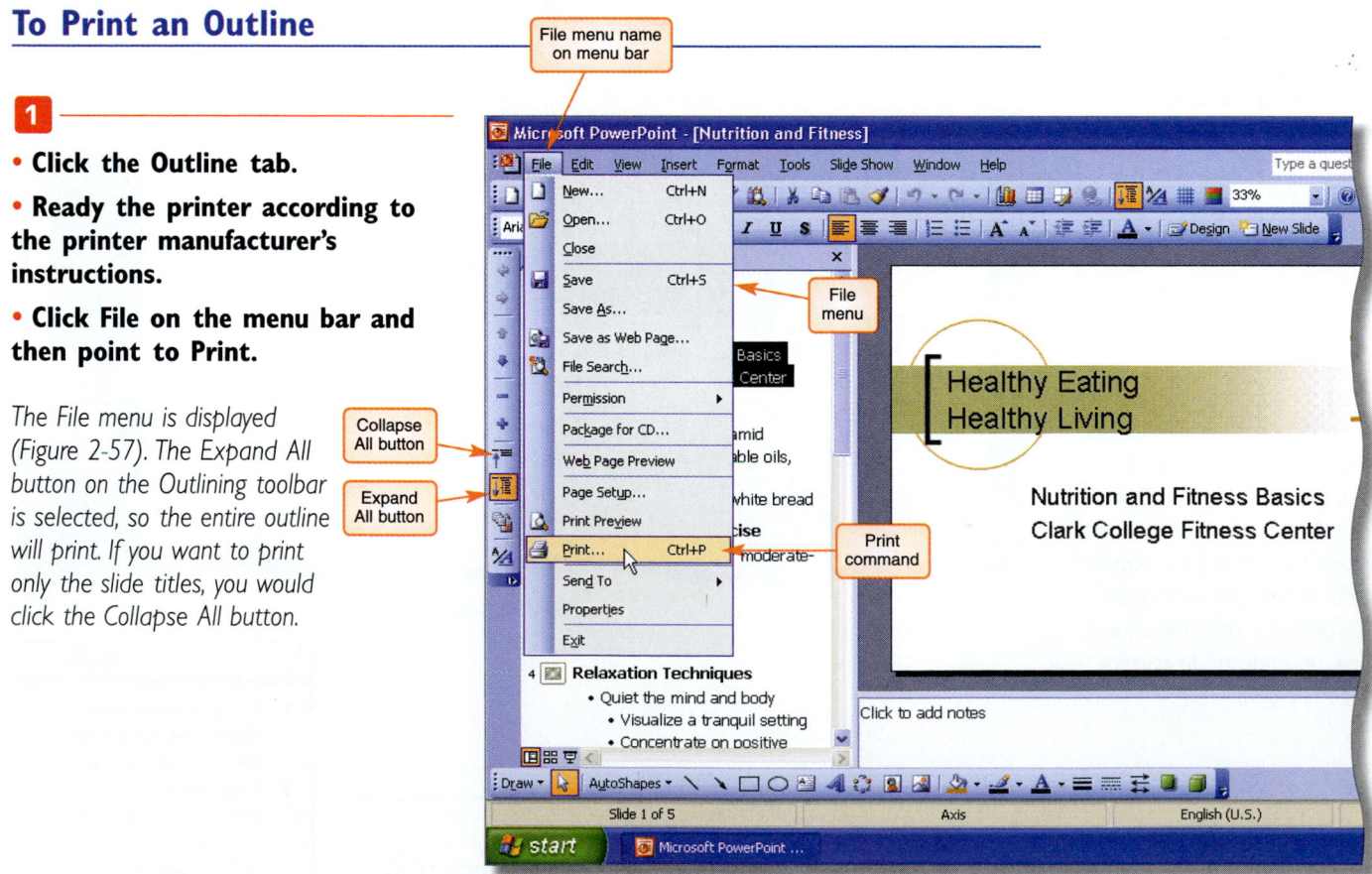

FIGURE 2-57

2

• **Click Print on the File menu.**

• **When the Print dialog box is displayed, click the Print what box arrow and then point to Outline View.**

The Print dialog box is displayed (Figure 2-58). Outline View is displayed highlighted in the Print what list.

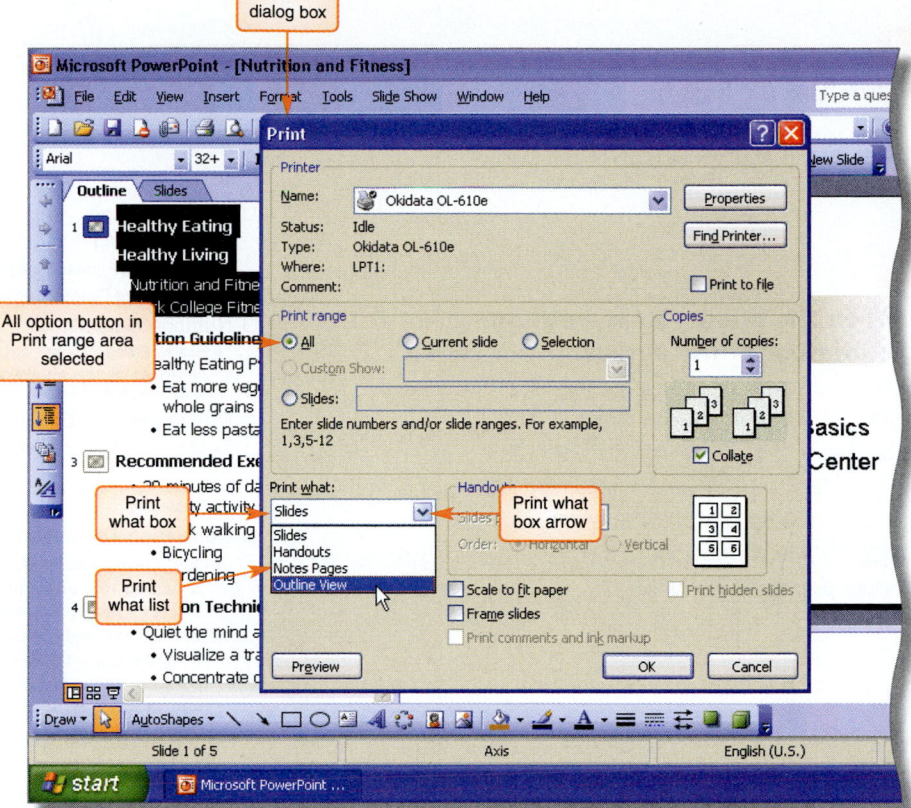

FIGURE 2-58

3

• **Click Outline View in the list (Figure 2-59).**

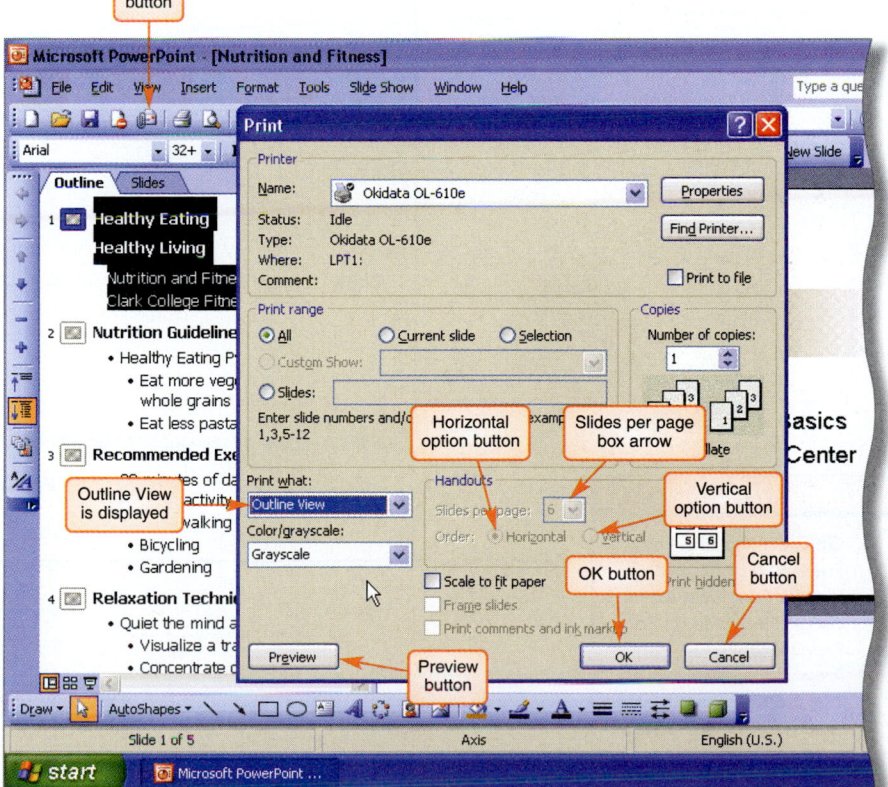

FIGURE 2-59

4

• **Click the OK button.**

To cancel the print request, click the Cancel button.

5

• **When the printer stops, retrieve the printout of the outline.**

PowerPoint displays the five slides in outline form (Figure 2-60). The words, Healthy Eating, Healthy Living, and the current date display in the header, and the words, Clark College Fitness Center, and the page number display in the footer.

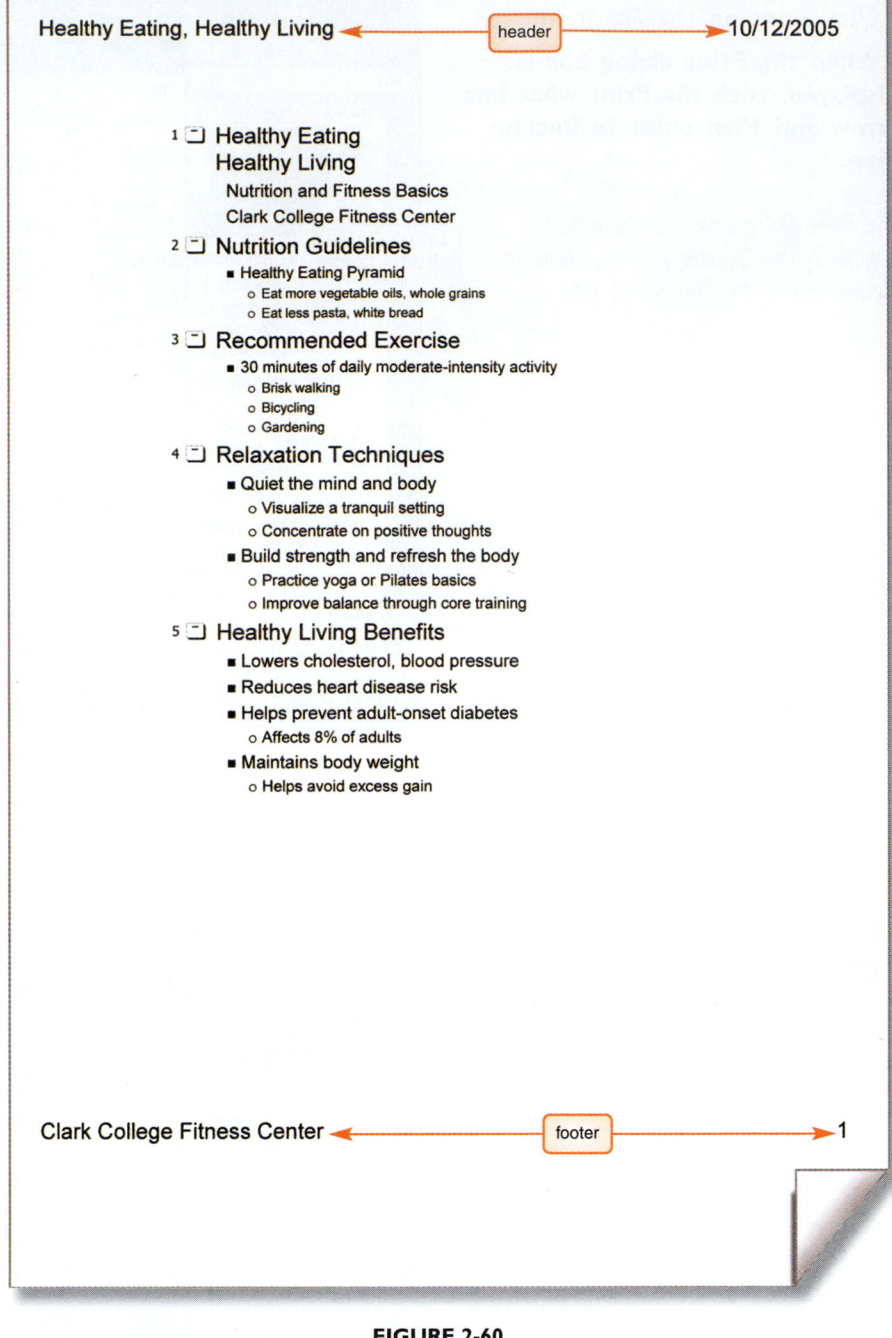

Healthy Eating, Healthy Living ← header → 10/12/2005

1 Healthy Eating
   Healthy Living
      Nutrition and Fitness Basics
      Clark College Fitness Center
2 Nutrition Guidelines
   ▪ Healthy Eating Pyramid
      ○ Eat more vegetable oils, whole grains
      ○ Eat less pasta, white bread
3 Recommended Exercise
   ▪ 30 minutes of daily moderate-intensity activity
      ○ Brisk walking
      ○ Bicycling
      ○ Gardening
4 Relaxation Techniques
   ▪ Quiet the mind and body
      ○ Visualize a tranquil setting
      ○ Concentrate on positive thoughts
   ▪ Build strength and refresh the body
      ○ Practice yoga or Pilates basics
      ○ Improve balance through core training
5 Healthy Living Benefits
   ▪ Lowers cholesterol, blood pressure
   ▪ Reduces heart disease risk
   ▪ Helps prevent adult-onset diabetes
      ○ Affects 8% of adults
   ▪ Maintains body weight
      ○ Helps avoid excess gain

Clark College Fitness Center ← footer → 1

FIGURE 2-60

Other Ways

1. On File menu click Print Preview, click Outline View in Print what list, click Print button on Print Preview toolbar
2. Press ALT+F, press P, press TAB, press W, press DOWN ARROW until Outline View is selected, press ENTER, press ENTER
3. In Voice Command mode, say "File, Print, Print What, Outline View, OK"

The **Print what list** in the Print dialog box contains options for printing slides, handouts, notes, and an outline. The Handouts area allows you to specify whether you want one, two, three, four, six, or nine slide images to display on each page. Printing handouts is useful for reviewing a presentation because you can analyze several slides displayed simultaneously on one page. Additionally, many businesses distribute handouts of the slide show before a presentation so the attendees can refer to a copy. To print handouts, click Handouts in the Print what box, click the Slides per page box arrow in the Handouts area, and then click 1, 2, 3, 4, 6, or 9. You can change the order in which the Nutrition and Fitness slides display on a page by clicking the Horizontal option button for Order in the Handouts area, which shows Slides 1 and 2, 3 and 4, and 5 and 6 adjacent to each other, or the Vertical option button for Order, which shows Slides 1 and 4, 2 and 5, and 3 and 6 adjacent to each other.

You also can click the Preview button if you want to see how your printout will look. After viewing the preview, click the Close button on the Preview window toolbar to return to normal view.

Printing Presentation Slides

At this point, you may want to check the spelling in the entire presentation and instruct PowerPoint to ignore any words spelled correctly. After correcting errors, you will want to print a final copy of your presentation. If you made any changes to your presentation since your last save, be certain to save your presentation before you print.

The following steps show how to print the presentation.

To Print Presentation Slides

1 Ready the printer according to the printer manufacturer's instructions.

2 Click File on the menu bar and then click Print.

3 When the Print dialog box is displayed, click the Print what box arrow.

4 Click Slides in the list.

5 Click the OK button. When the printer stops, retrieve the slide printouts.

The printouts should resemble the slides in Figures 2-61a through 2-61e.

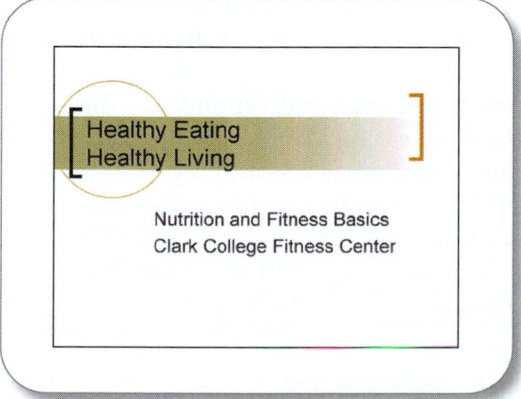

(a) Slide 1

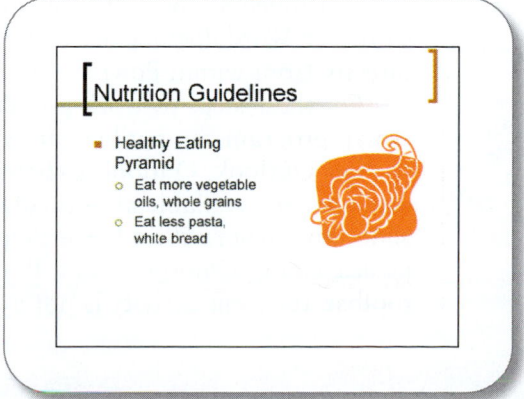

(b) Slide 2

FIGURE 2-61

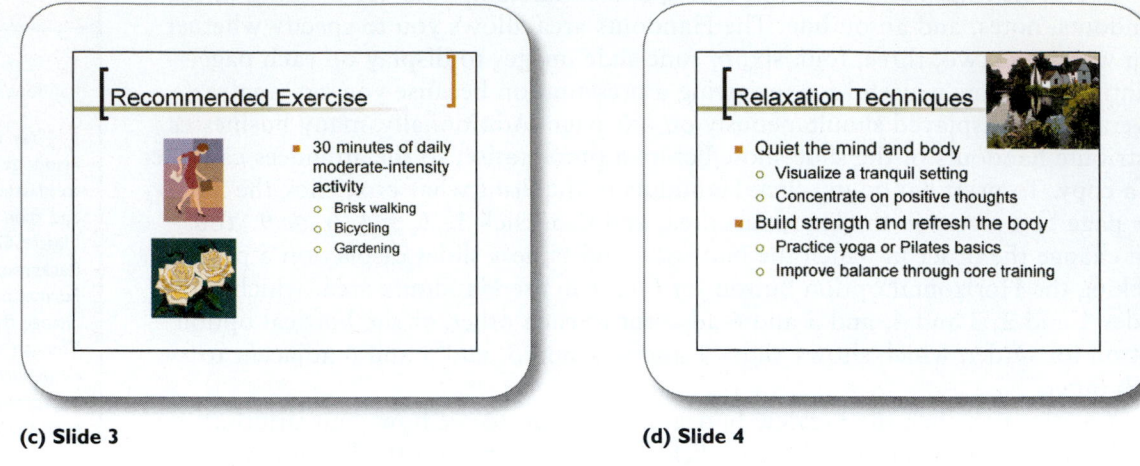

(c) Slide 3

(d) Slide 4

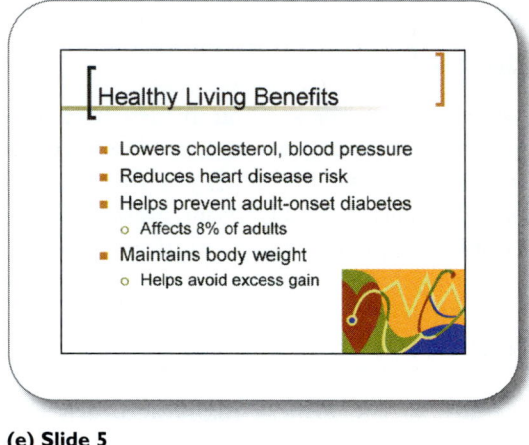

(e) Slide 5

FIGURE 2-61 *(continued)*

E-Mailing a Slide Show from within PowerPoint

More About

The Quick Reference

For more information, see the Quick Reference Summary at the back of this book, or visit the PowerPoint 2003 Quick Reference Web page (scsite.com/ppt2003/qr).

Billions of e-mail messages are sent throughout the world each day. Computer users use this popular service on the Internet to send and receive plain text e-mail or to send and receive e-mail content that includes objects, links to other Web pages, and file attachments. These attachments can include Office files, such as PowerPoint slide shows or Word documents. Using Microsoft Office, you can e-mail the presentation directly from within PowerPoint.

For these steps to work properly, users need an e-mail address and a 32-bit e-mail program compatible with a Messaging Application Programming Interface, such as Outlook, Outlook Express, or Microsoft Exchange Client. Free e-mail accounts are available at hotmail.com. The following steps show how to e-mail the slide show from within PowerPoint to Jessica Cantero. Assume her e-mail address is jessica_cantero@hotmail.com. If you do not have an E-mail button on the Standard toolbar, then this activity is not available to you.

To E-Mail a Slide Show from within PowerPoint

1

• **Click the E-mail (as Attachment) button on the Standard toolbar. See your instructor if the Choose Profile dialog box displays.**

• **When the e-mail Message window is displayed, type** `jessica_cantero @hotmail.com` **in the To text box.**

• **Select the text in the Subject text box and then type** Nutrition and Fitness slide show **in the Subject text box.**

• **Click the message body.**

PowerPoint displays the e-mail Message window (Figure 2-62). The insertion point is in the message body so you can type a message to Jessica Cantero.

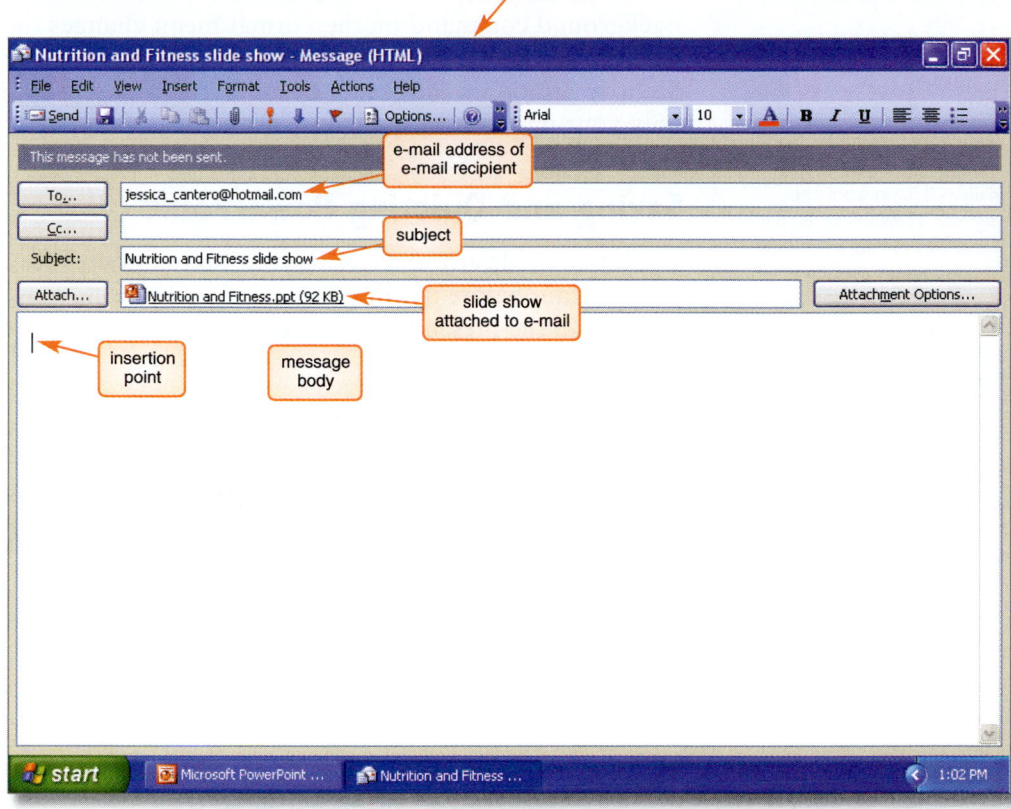

FIGURE 2-62

2

• **Type** Attached is the PowerPoint presentation you can use for your first workshop. **in the message body.**

• **Point to the Send button.**

The message is intended to help the recipient of the e-mail understand the purpose of your e-mail (Figure 2-63).

3

• **Click the Send button on the Standard toolbar.**

The e-mail with the attached presentation is sent to jessica_cantero@hotmail.com.

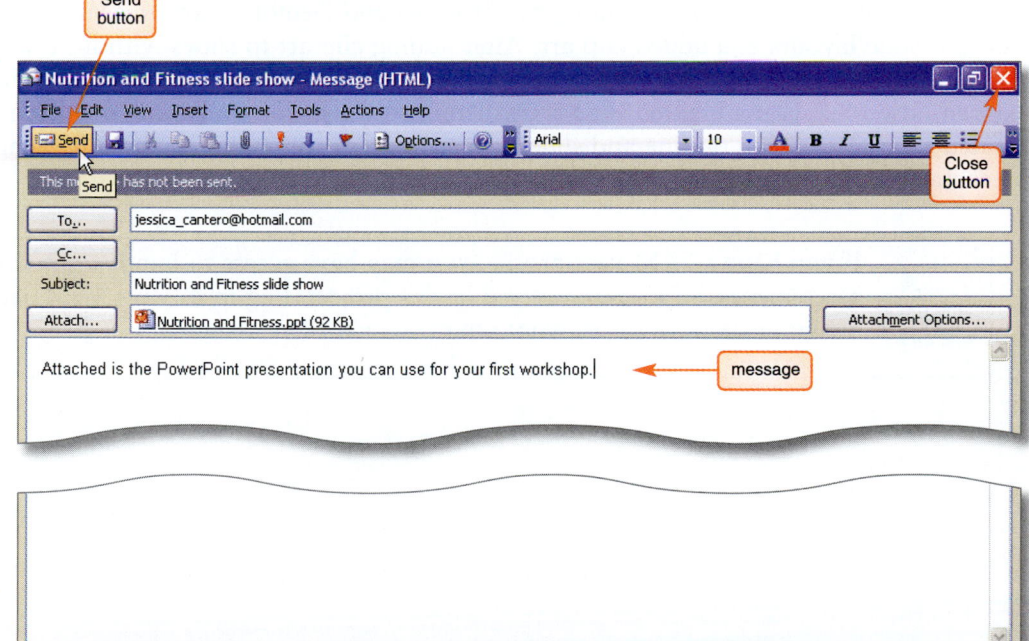

FIGURE 2-63

More About

E-Mail Messages

The first e-mail message was sent in 1969 from Professor Leonard Kleinrock to a colleague at Stanford University. Researchers estimate the number of messages sent daily will jump from the current 31 billion to 60 billion by 2006. For more information on e-mail messages, visit the PowerPoint 2003 More About Web page (scsite.com/ppt2003 /more) and click E-Mail.

Because the slide show was sent as an attachment, Jessica Cantero can save the attachment and then open the presentation in PowerPoint. You can choose many more options when you send e-mail from within PowerPoint. For example, the Background command on the Format menu changes the colors of the message background and lets you add a picture to use as the background. In addition, the Security button on the Standard toolbar allows you to send secure messages that only your intended recipient can read.

Saving and Quitting PowerPoint

If you made any changes to your presentation since your last save, you should save it again before quitting PowerPoint. The following steps show how to save changes to the presentation and quit PowerPoint.

To Save Changes and Quit PowerPoint

1 Click the Close button on the Microsoft PowerPoint window title bar.

2 If prompted, click the Yes button in the Microsoft PowerPoint dialog box.

PowerPoint saves any changes made to the presentation since the last save and then quits PowerPoint.

Project Summary

In creating the Healthy Eating, Healthy Living slide show in this project, you increased your knowledge of PowerPoint. You created a slide presentation on the Outline tab where you entered all the text in the form of an outline. You arranged the text using the Promote and Demote buttons. Once the outline was complete, you changed slide layouts and added clip art. After adding clip art to slides without using a content placeholder, you moved and sized the clips. You added preset animation effects and applied animation effects to a clip. You learned how to run an animated slide show demonstrating slide transition and animation effects. Finally, you printed the presentation outline and slides using the Print command on the File menu and e-mailed the presentation.

If you have a SAM user profile, you may have access to hands-on instruction, practice, and assessment of the skills covered in this project. Log in to your SAM account and go to your assignments page to see what your instructor has assigned.

What You Should Know

Having completed this project, you should be able to perform the tasks below. The tasks are listed in the same order they were presented in this project. For a list of the buttons, menus, toolbars, and commands introduced in this project, see the Quick Reference Summary at the back of this book and refer to the Page Number column.

1. Start and Customize PowerPoint   (PPT 85)
2. Change to the Outline Tab and Display the Outlining Toolbar   (PPT 86)
3. Create a Title Slide on the Outline Tab   (PPT 88)
4. Add a Slide on the Outline Tab   (PPT 89)
5. Create a Text Slide with a Multi-Level Bulleted List on the Outline Tab   (PPT 90)
6. Create a Second Text Slide with a Multi-Level Bulleted List   (PPT 92)
7. Create a Third Text Slide with a Multi-Level Bulleted List   (PPT 92)
8. Create a Closing Slide on the Outline Tab   (PPT 94)
9. Save a Presentation   (PPT 95)
10. Change the View to Slide Sorter View   (PPT 95)
11. Change the View to Normal View   (PPT 96)
12. Change the Slide Layout to Title, Text, and Content   (PPT 98)
13. Insert Clip Art into a Content Placeholder   (PPT 101)
14. Change the Slide Layout to Title, 2 Content and Text and Insert Clip Art   (PPT 102)
15. Insert a Second Clip into a Slide   (PPT 103)
16. Insert Clip Art into a Slide without a Content Placeholder   (PPT 104)
17. Use the Automatic Layout Options Button to Undo a Layout Change   (PPT 107)
18. Move Clip Art   (PPT 108)
19. Change the Size of Clip Art   (PPT 109)
20. Insert, Move, and Size a Clip into a Slide   (PPT 110)
21. Save a Presentation   (PPT 111)
22. Use the Notes and Handouts Sheet to Add Headers and Footers   (PPT 112)
23. Add an Animation Scheme to a Slide Show   (PPT 114)
24. Animate Clip Art   (PPT 117)
25. Save a Presentation   (PPT 119)
26. Run an Animated Slide Show   (PPT 120)
27. Print an Outline   (PPT 122)
28. Print Presentation Slides   (PPT 125)
29. E-Mail a Slide Show from within PowerPoint   (PPT 127)
30. Save Changes and Quit PowerPoint   (PPT 128)

Learn It Online

Instructions: To complete the Learn It Online exercises, start your browser, click the Address bar, and then enter the Web address scsite.com/ppt2003/learn. When the PowerPoint 2003 Learn It Online page is displayed, follow the instructions in the exercises below. Each exercise has instructions for printing your results, either for your own records or for submission to your instructor.

1 Project Reinforcement TF, MC, and SA

Below PowerPoint Project 2, click the Project Reinforcement link. Print the quiz by clicking Print on the File menu for each page. Answer each question.

2 Flash Cards

Below PowerPoint Project 2, click the Flash Cards link and read the instructions. Type 20 (or a number specified by your instructor) in the Number of playing cards text box, type your name in the Enter your Name text box, and then click the Flip Card button. When the flash card is displayed, read the question and then click the ANSWER box arrow to select an answer. Flip through Flash Cards. If your score is 15 (75%) correct or greater, click Print on the File menu to print your results. If your score is less than 15 (75%) correct, then redo this exercise by clicking the Replay button.

3 Practice Test

Below PowerPoint Project 2, click the Practice Test link. Answer each question, enter your first and last name at the bottom of the page, and then click the Grade Test button. When the graded practice test is displayed on your screen, click Print on the File menu to print a hard copy. Continue to take practice tests until you score 80% or better.

4 Who Wants To Be a Computer Genius?

Below PowerPoint Project 2, click the Computer Genius link. Read the instructions, enter your first and last name at the bottom of the page, and then click the PLAY button. When your score is displayed, click the PRINT RESULTS link to print a hard copy.

5 Wheel of Terms

Below PowerPoint Project 2, click the Wheel of Terms link. Read the instructions, and then enter your first and last name and your school name. Click the PLAY button. When your score is displayed, right-click the score and then click Print on the shortcut menu to print a hard copy.

6 Crossword Puzzle Challenge

Below PowerPoint Project 2, click the Crossword Puzzle Challenge link. Read the instructions, and then enter your first and last name. Click the SUBMIT button. Work the crossword puzzle. When you are finished, click the Submit button. When the crossword puzzle is redisplayed, click the Print Puzzle button to print a hard copy.

7 Tips and Tricks

Below PowerPoint Project 2, click the Tips and Tricks link. Click a topic that pertains to Project 2. Right-click the information and then click Print on the shortcut menu. Construct a brief example of what the information relates to in PowerPoint to confirm you understand how to use the tip or trick.

8 Newsgroups

Below PowerPoint Project 2, click the Newsgroups link. Click a topic that pertains to Project 2. Print three comments.

9 Expanding Your Horizons

Below PowerPoint Project 2, click the Expanding Your Horizons link. Click a topic that pertains to Project 2. Print the information. Construct a brief example of what the information relates to in PowerPoint to confirm you understand the contents of the article.

10 Search Sleuth

Below PowerPoint Project 2, click the Search Sleuth link. To search for a term that pertains to this project, select a term below the Project 2 title and then use the Google search engine at google.com (or any major search engine) to display and print two Web pages that present information on the term.

11 PowerPoint Online Training

Below PowerPoint Project 2, click the PowerPoint Online Training link. When your browser displays the Microsoft Office Online Web page, click the PowerPoint link. Click one of the PowerPoint courses that covers one or more of the objectives listed at the beginning of the project on page PPT 82. Print the first page of the course before stepping through it.

12 Office Marketplace

Below PowerPoint Project 2, click the Office Marketplace link. When your browser displays the Microsoft Office Online Web page, click the Office Marketplace link. Click a topic that relates to PowerPoint. Print the first page.

Apply Your Knowledge

1 Hiking for Family Fitness

Instructions: Start PowerPoint. Open the presentation Apply 2-1 Hiking Adventure from the Data Disk. See the inside back cover of this book for instructions for downloading the Data Disk or see your instructor for information on accessing the files required for this book. The four slides in the presentation give information on helping families plan for a hike through forest preserves and parks. Make the following changes to the slides so they appear as shown in Figure 2-64.

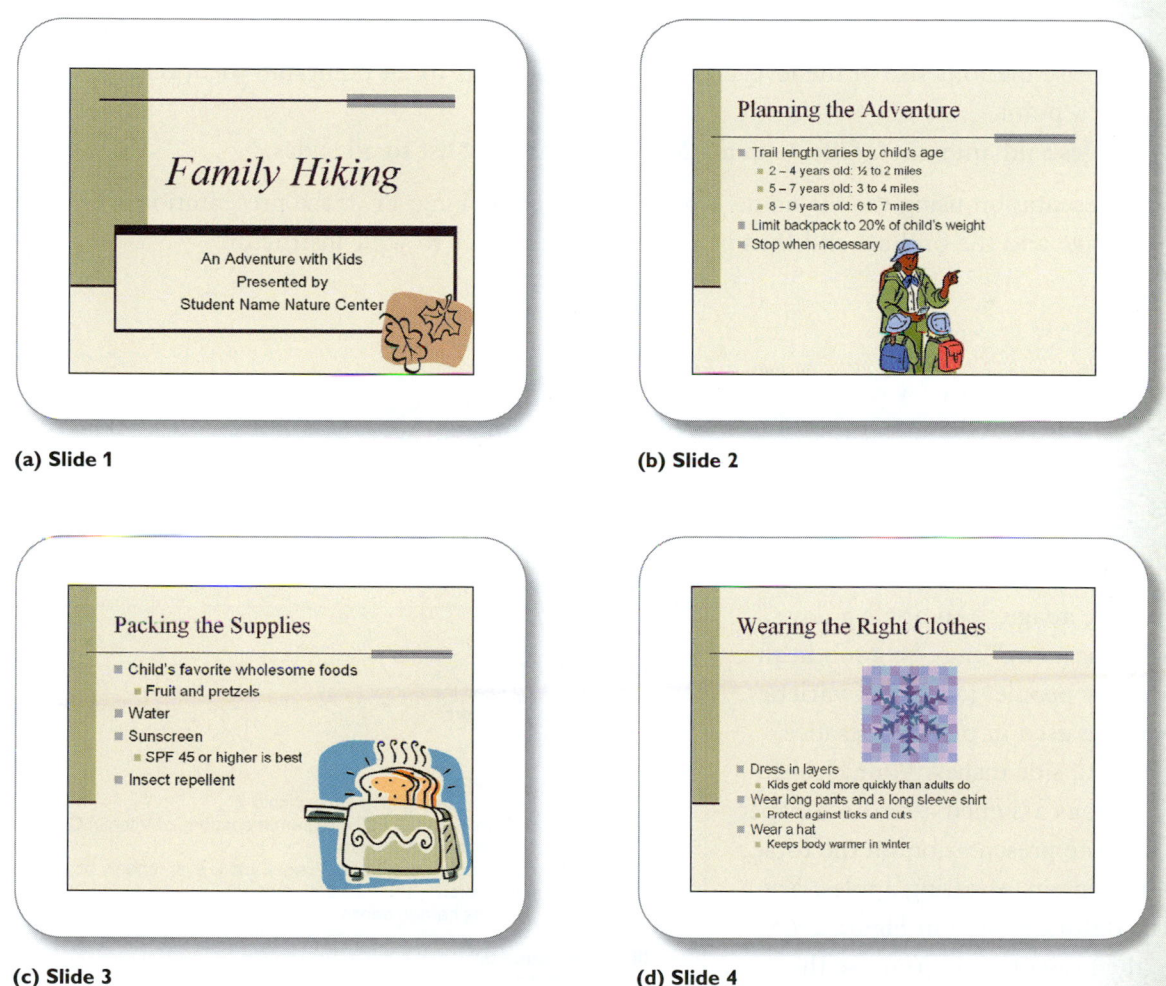

(a) Slide 1

(b) Slide 2

(c) Slide 3

(d) Slide 4

FIGURE 2-64

Change the design template to Layers. On the title slide, replace the words, Student Name, with your name. Then add the current date, page number, and your name to the notes and handouts footer.

On Slide 1, increase the font size of the Family Hiking paragraph to 72 point and then italicize this text. Insert the leaves clip shown in Figure 2-64a. Scale the clip art to 118% and then drag the clip to the bottom-right corner of the slide. Apply the Box Entrance custom animation effect to the clip.

(continued)

Hiking for Family Fitness (continued)

On Slide 2, change the slide layout to Title and Text over Content. Insert the backpacking clip shown in Figure 2-64b on the previous page. Change the size of the clip to 167% and then drag the clip to the bottom center of the slide.

On Slide 3, insert the toaster clip shown in Figure 2-64c. Undo the Automatic Layout if necessary, increase the clip size to 207%, and then drag it to the bottom-right corner of the slide. Apply the Blinds Entrance custom animation effect to the clip.

On Slide 4, change the slide layout to Title and Content over Text. Insert the snowflake clip shown in Figure 2-64d and then change the size of the clip to 120%. Apply the Spin Emphasis custom animation effect to the clip. Increase the font size of the level 2 body text paragraphs to 24 point and the level 3 body text paragraphs to 20 point.

Apply the Descend animation scheme in the Moderate category list to all slides.

Save the presentation using the file name, Apply 2-1 Family Hiking. Print the presentation with all four slides on one page and the outline, and then hand in the hard copies to your instructor.

1 An Apple a Day Presentation

Problem: The adage, "An apple a day keeps the doctor away" may be good health advice for many people. Dozens of varieties of apples can be used in pies, applesauce, juice, salads, and side dishes. Your Health 101 instructor has assigned a research paper and a five-minute presentation on the topic of the health benefits of eating apples. You generate the outline shown in Figure 2-65 to prepare the presentation. You use the outline to create the presentation shown in Figures 2-66a through 2-66d.

> **I. An Apple a Day...**
>   A. ...May Keep the Doctor Away
>   B. Nick Saunders
>   C. Health 101
>
> **II. Healthy Apple Facts**
>   A. Contains cancer-fighting antioxidants
>   1. More than a 1,500 milligram megadose of Vitamin C
>   2. Fight bad cholesterol
>   B. Complex carbohydrates give longer, more even energy boost
>   C. Contains boron
>   1. Helps harden bones
>
> **III. Apple Nutrients**
>   A. Pectin
>   1. Aids digestion
>   2. May help reduce cancer, heart disease
>   B. Fiber
>   1. Equal to bran cereal
>
> **IV. Cook or Baking Quantities**
>   A. 3 medium-sized apples equal 1 pound
>   B. 6-8 medium-sized apples fill a 9-inch pie
>   C. 1 pound makes 1½ cups applesauce

FIGURE 2-65

In the Lab

(a) Slide 1

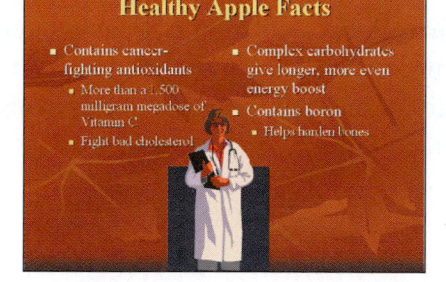

(b) Slide 2

(c) Slide 3

(d) Slide 4

FIGURE 2-66

Instructions: Perform the following tasks.

1. Use the Outline tab to create a new presentation. Apply the Maple design template.
2. Using the outline shown in Figure 2-65, create the title slide shown in Figure 2-66a. Use your name instead of the text, Nick Saunders. Decrease the font size of the class name to 24 point. Insert the caduceus clip art. Scale the clip to 150% and then drag the clip to the lower-left corner of the slide. Add the Blinds Entrance custom animation effect to the clip.
3. Insert a new slide. Change the slide layout on Slide 2 to Title and 2-Column Text. Using the outline in Figure 2-65, type the text for Slide 2. Insert the doctor clip art shown in Figure 2-66b. Scale the clip to 200% and then drag the clip between the two columns of text.
4. Using the outline shown in Figure 2-65, create the Slides 3 and 4 with the bulleted lists shown in Figures 2-66c and 2-66d.
5. Change the slide layout on Slide 3 to Title, Text, and Content. Insert the medicine clip art shown in Figure 2-66c. Scale the clip art to 210% and then center it in the space beside the text. Add the Diamond Entrance custom animation effect to the clip.
6. On Slide 4, change the slide layout to Title, Content and Text. Insert the apple clip art shown in Figure 2-66d, scale it to 200%, and then center it in the space beside the text. Add the Box Entrance custom animation effect.

(continued)

In the Lab

An Apple a Day Presentation *(continued)*

7. Add your name to the outline header and your school's name to the outline footer.
8. Apply the Title arc animation scheme in the Exciting category to all slides in the presentation.
9. Save the presentation using the file name, Lab 2-1 Apples.
10. Display and print the presentation with two slides on one page and the outline. Close the presentation. Hand in the hard copy to your instructor.

2 Financial Planning Advice

Problem: Credit card debt is at an all-time high, and many people are nearing retirement age with inadequate savings. Many students at your school have asked their instructors and members of the Accounting Club for advice on helping them gain financial security. To assist these students, the Accounting Club members have decided to prepare a PowerPoint presentation to show to these students. They have given you the outline shown in Figure 2-67. You create the text for the presentation on the Outline tab, and you decide to add animation effects to the slide show. The completed slides are shown in Figures 2-68a through 2-68d.

1. It Figures: Your Financial Future
    Build a Secure Fiscal Plan
    Midwest College Accounting Club

2. Prepare for Retirement Now
    Eliminate all debt
    Follow the 20/80 rule
        Live on 20 percent
        Save 80 percent
    Develop a financial plan

3. Realize Importance of Financial Planning
    Establish a monthly budget
    Develop an investment strategy
        Savings
        Low-risk investments
        High-risk investments

4. Use a Certified Financial Planner
    Helps prepare taxes
    Gives insurance advice
    Develops debt-reduction strategies
    Assists with estate planning

FIGURE 2-67

(a) Slide 1

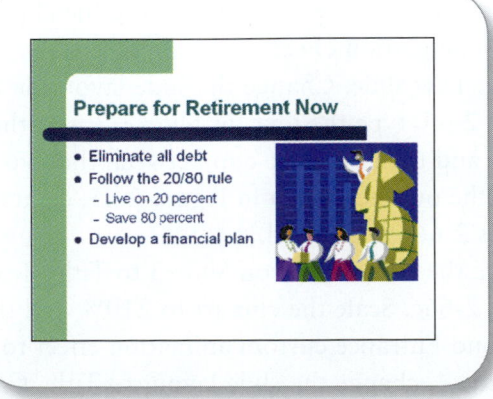

(b) Slide 2

FIGURE 2-68

In the Lab

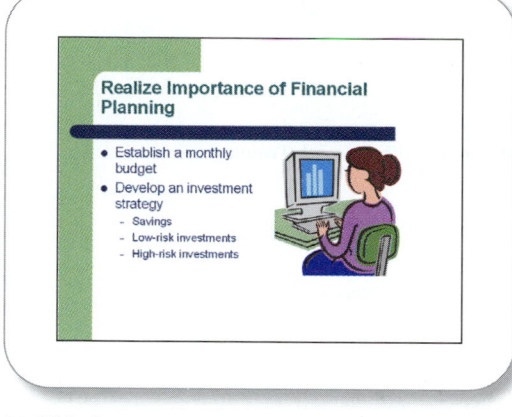

(c) Slide 3

(d) Slide 4

FIGURE 2-68 *(continued)*

Instructions: Perform the following tasks.

1. Use the Outline tab to create a new presentation from the outline shown in Figure 2-67. Apply the Capsules design template.
2. On the title slide, italicize the title text, It Figures: Your Financial Future. Increase the font size of the text, Build a Secure Fiscal Plan, to 36 point. Using Figure 2-68a as a reference, insert the dollar clip art shown, scale it to 105%, and then drag it to the upper-right corner of the slide.
3. On Slide 2, insert the clip art shown in Figure 2-68b and then, if necessary, click the AutoCorrect Options button to undo the layout change. Scale the clip to 230% and then drag it to the right of the text.
4. On Slide 3, change the slide layout to Title, Text, and Content. Insert the clip art shown in Figure 2-68c. Scale the clip to 160% and then move it to the location shown in the figure.
5. On Slide 4, change the slide layout to Title, Content and Text. Insert the clip art shown in Figure 2-68d, scale the clip to 195%, and then move it to the location shown in the figure.
6. Add the current date and your name to the outline header. Include Accounting Club and the page number in the outline footer.
7. Apply the Compress animation scheme in the Moderate category to all slides.
8. Animate the clip on Slide 1 using the Spin Emphasis custom animation effect, the clip on Slide 2 using the Fly In Entrance effect, and the clip on Slide 3 using the Box Entrance effect. Do not animate the clip on Slide 4.
9. Save the presentation using the file name, Lab 2-2 Financial Future.
10. Display and print the presentation with two slides on one page and the outline. Close the presentation. Hand in the hard copy to your instructor.

In the Lab

3 Strength Training for New Fitness Center Members

Problem: Strength training offers many positive benefits: it builds power, provides energy, decreases fatigue, and improves mood, self-confidence, and self-esteem. Additional advantages are helping to prevent osteoporosis, burn calories, and balance the body. Mary Halen, the director of your campus fitness center, wants new members to view a presentation on strength training. She gives you the outline shown in Figure 2-69. You create the text for the presentation on the Outline tab and then search for appropriate clip art to add to the slides. You are unable to find images that are part of the Microsoft Clip Organizer, so you connect to the Internet, obtain clips from the Microsoft Office Online Web site, and create the slides shown in Figure 2-70. The clips you find may vary from the clips shown in Figures 2-70a through 2-70d. You refine the presentation using an animation scheme and custom animation effects and then e-mail the presentation to Mary.

Gain More Than Muscles with Strength Training
    Presented by
    Mary Halen
    Central College Fitness Center

Build Power
    Increase performance in many sports
        Tennis and golf
    Increase endurance
        Running and swimming

Feel Energized
    Improve mood, confidence, and esteem
        Expand beyond sports into personal life
    Burn calories
        Even while resting
        Increase body's metabolism for up to 12 hours after exercising

Improve Health
    Help prevent osteoporosis
        Strengthen bones
        Build bone density
    Balance body by making both sides strong
        Normally one side is stronger than the other
        Balanced body is less prone to injuries

FIGURE 2-69

(a) Slide 1

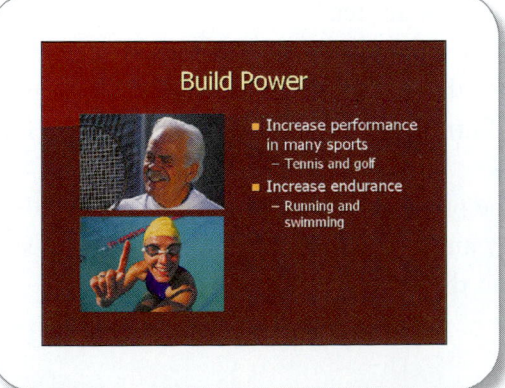

(b) Slide 2

FIGURE 2-70

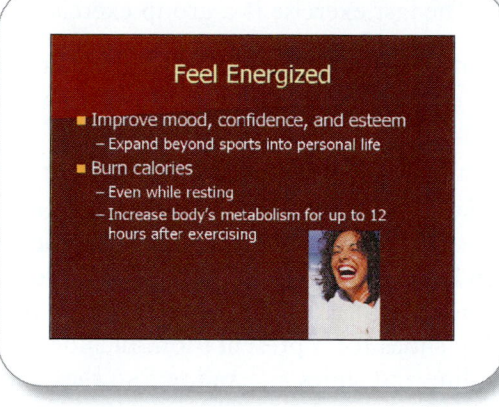

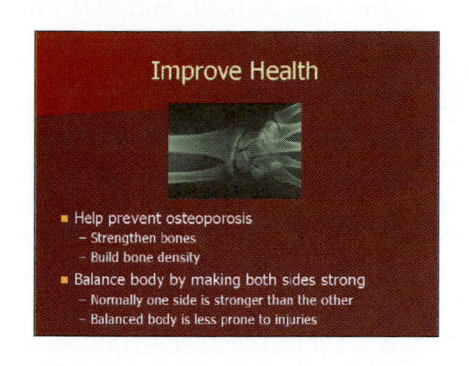

(c) Slide 3   **(d) Slide 4**

FIGURE 2-70 *(continued)*

Instructions: Perform the following tasks.

1. Create a new presentation using the Slit design template and the outline in Figure 2-69.

2. On the title slide, insert and size both clip art images shown in Figure 2-70a. Add the Fly In Entrance custom animation effect and change the speed to Medium.

3. On Slide 2, change the slide layout to Title, 2 Content and Text. Insert the clips shown in Figure 2-70b. Add the Fly In Entrance custom animation effect for the top image and change the direction to From Top. Add the Fly In Entrance custom animation effect for the bottom image. Size the clips if necessary.

4. On Slide 3, insert the clip shown in Figure 2-70c. Add the Spin Emphasis custom animation effect. Size the clip if necessary.

5. Change the slide layout on Slide 4 (Figure 2-70d) to Title and Content over Text. Insert the clip art image shown. Add the Box Entrance custom animation effect. Size the clip if necessary.

6. Display your name and the current date in the outline header, and display the page number and the name of your school in the outline footer.

7. Apply the Unfold animation scheme in the Moderate category to all slides.

8. Save the presentation using the file name, Lab 2-3 Strength Training.

9. Display and print the presentation with all four slides on one page and the outline. Close the presentation. Hand in the hard copy to your instructor.

10. E-mail the presentation to Mary using the address mary_halen@hotmail.com.

Cases and Places

The difficulty of these case studies varies:
■ are the least difficult and ■ ■ are more difficult. The last exercise is a group exercise.

Note: Remember to use the 7 × 7 rule as you design the presentations: a maximum of seven words on a line and a maximum of seven lines on one slide.

1 ■ One of the easiest methods of exercising is walking. Active walkers know that walking enhances the body and spirit. Paula Pearson, the director of recreation at your community's park district, wants to organize a walking club, and she has asked you to help her promote the idea. She hands you the outline shown in Figure 2-71 and asks you to create a slide show. Using the concepts and techniques introduced in this project, together with Paula's outline, develop slides for a presentation. Include clip art, animation effects, and an animation scheme. Print the outline and slides as handouts so they can be distributed to presentation attendees.

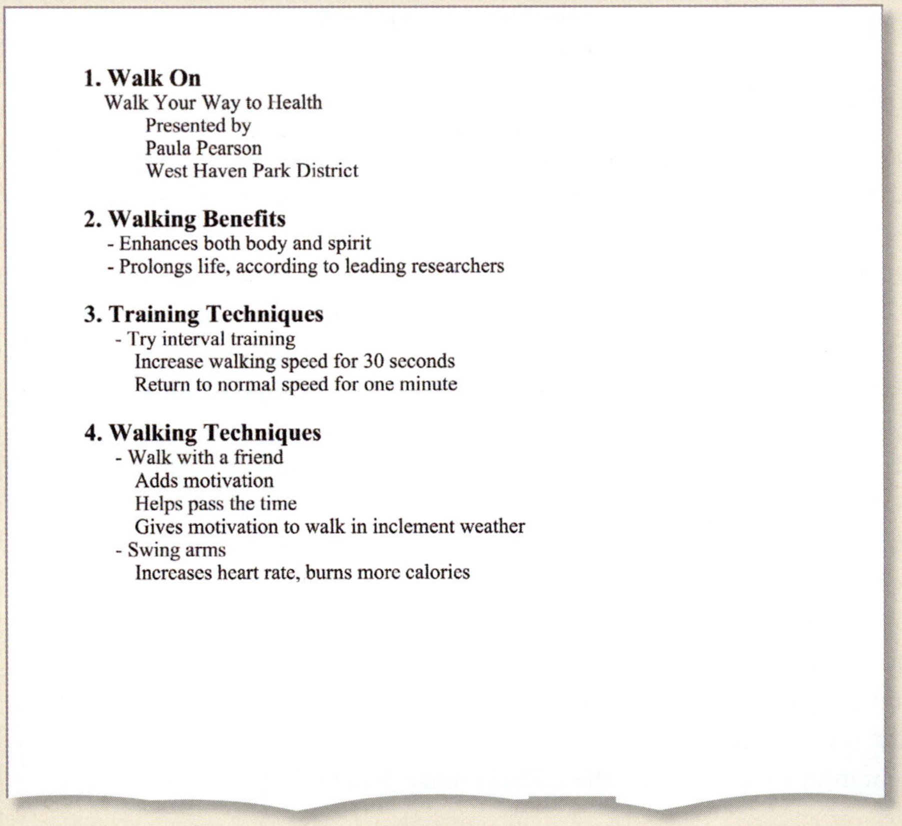

1. Walk On
    Walk Your Way to Health
        Presented by
        Paula Pearson
        West Haven Park District

2. Walking Benefits
    - Enhances both body and spirit
    - Prolongs life, according to leading researchers

3. Training Techniques
    - Try interval training
        Increase walking speed for 30 seconds
        Return to normal speed for one minute

4. Walking Techniques
    - Walk with a friend
        Adds motivation
        Helps pass the time
        Gives motivation to walk in inclement weather
    - Swing arms
        Increases heart rate, burns more calories

FIGURE 2-71

Cases and Places

2 ■ The community theater company in the town of Northern Shores is seeking subscribers and volunteers for the upcoming season. The public relations director has supplied the outline shown in Figure 2-72. You have been asked to help with the recruiting efforts. You decide to develop a presentation that includes information about the newly renovated theater, volunteer opportunities, and upcoming performances. Using the concepts and techniques introduced in this project, together with the outline, develop slides for a presentation. Include clip art, animation effects, and an animation scheme. Display the presentation title in the outline header and your name in the outline footer. Print the outline and slides as handouts.

A. Northern Shores Center for the Performing Arts
    The area's newest and finest theater company

B. Northern Shores Theater Venue
  Newly renovated building
    More than $7 million spent
    Improved sight lines and acoustics
    Full symphony orchestra pit
  Comfortable seating
    Accommodations for the disabled

C. Volunteer Opportunities
    Developing and distributing promotional materials
    Ushering at performances
    Participating in social activities throughout the year
    Assisting with Children's Theater

D. Upcoming Performances
    February 14 - Music for the Heart
    March 17 - Irish Favorites
    July 1 - Americana Folk Tales
    December 16 - Holiday Spectacular

FIGURE 2-72

Cases and Places

3 ■■ Many students on your campus visit the Health Clinic asking for antibiotics prescriptions. The doctors and nurses spend much time explaining that antibiotics are not necessarily the best medicine for the illnesses. You work in the clinic part time and volunteer to create a PowerPoint presentation that answers many of the students' common questions. You speak with the doctors on staff and learn that antibiotics are credited with changing modern medicine. They are used to kill bacteria, not viruses, and can control infectious diseases. Many bacteria, however, have become resistant to these drugs. Antibiotics are prescribed for bacterial infections, not viruses such as flu, colds, most coughs, and sore throats. Students can take antibiotics prudently by taking all doses of the medications exactly as prescribed. They should not stop taking drugs early, even if they feel fine. Antibiotic resistance occurs when the medications are taken unnecessarily. When the illness persists, additional drugs may be required to kill the germ. Some bacteria refuse to die, and super strains have been bred by overuse and misuse of antiobiotics. Using this information, develop a slide show. Choose an appropriate design template and add clip art, animation effects, and an animation scheme. Print the presentation slides and outline to distribute as handouts for patients.

4 ■■ The Healthy Eating Pyramid shows that a balanced diet contains daily servings of fruit and vegetables. Although fruit and vegetables are less costly than snack foods, many adults and children buy junk food rather than the vitamin-laden fruit and vegetable alternatives. Your school cafeteria manager has asked you to prepare a PowerPoint presentation explaining the ABCs of fruits and vegetables to students. Using the techniques introduced in the project, create a presentation about the virtues of eating these foods. Include clip art, animation effects, and an animation scheme to add interest. Print the outline and slides as handouts so they can be distributed to cafeteria diners.

5 ■■ **Working Together** Prospective employees often focus on salary and job responsibilities when they consider job offers. One area they often neglect, however, is benefit packages. Career counselors emphasize that these benefits can contribute significantly to salary levels and should be given serious consideration. Have each member of your team visit or telephone several local businesses, your campus placement center, or companies' Web sites to determine benefit packages. Gather data about:

  1) Retirement plans
  2) Stock options
  3) Life insurance coverage
  4) Health coverage
  5) Tuition reimbursement
  6) Signing bonuses
  7) On-site fitness facilities

After coordinating the data, create a presentation with at least one slide showcasing each company's benefit packages. As a group, critique each slide. Hand in a hard copy of the final presentation.

MICROSOFT
Office PowerPoint 2003

Creating a Presentation on the Web Using PowerPoint

CASE PERSPECTIVE

A home office can be the key to redefining the way we work. More than 54 percent of American households have a home office, and more than 46 million Americans work at home at least part time. These offices range from a desk and chair in the kitchen to a separate room complete with storage and ergonomic furniture.

Many people attempt to create an effective workspace only to realize that the space lacks comfort, connectivity, and convenience. The most important step in developing the home office is planning. Start by developing a budget, analyzing electrical needs such as the placement of outlets, and listing computer hardware and office equipment. Decisions need to be made about the optimal type of lighting, whether to buy modular or built-in furniture, and the arrangement of work materials to increase efficiency and minimize body strain.

Making these decisions can be daunting. Professional space planners know how to make functional and ergonomic workspaces. By analyzing their clients' unique needs, they can design environments that help workers be productive and comfortable. They arrange the equipment and furniture based on the clients' tasks and the rooms' dimensions and constraints.

Comfort @ Home, Inc., is a local business specializing in assisting home workers to develop the best office design for their needs. Kendra Linder, the owner of this business, wants to provide community residents with the guidelines for an effective home office design. She decides the most effective way to disseminate this information is to create a PowerPoint slide show (Figure 1 on the next page) and then have you publish the presentation on the World Wide Web.

As you read through this Web feature, you will learn how to create and display a Web page from a PowerPoint presentation, edit the results using a browser, and then publish the presentation.

Objectives

You will have mastered the material in this project when you can:

- Preview and save a presentation as a Web page
- Create a new folder using file management tools
- View a Web page using a browser
- Edit the Web page content through a browser
- Publish a presentation as a Web page

Introduction

The graphic design power of PowerPoint allows you to create vibrant presentations that convey information in a clear, interesting manner. Some of these presentations are created for small, specific audiences, such as a subcommittee planning a department retreat. In this case, the presentation may be shown in an office conference room. Other presentations are designed for large, general audiences, such as workers at a corporation's various offices across the country learning about a new insurance benefits package. These employees can view the presentation on their company's **intranet**, which is an internal network that uses Internet technologies. On a grand scale, you can inform the entire world about the contents of your presentation by posting your slide show to the World Wide Web. To publish to the World Wide Web, you need a **File Transfer Protocol (FTP)** program to copy your presentation and related files to an **Internet service provider (ISP)** computer.

PowerPoint provides you with two ways to create a Web page. First, you can start a new presentation, as you did in Projects 1 and 2 when you produced the Strategies for College Success and the Healthy

Eating, Healthy Living presentations. PowerPoint provides a Web Presentation template in the **AutoContent Wizard** option when you start PowerPoint. The wizard provides design and content ideas to help you develop an effective slide show for an intranet or for the Internet by opening a sample presentation that you can alter by adding your own text and graphics.

Second, the Save as Web Page command on the File menu allows you to **publish** presentations, which is the process of making existing presentations available to others on the World Wide Web or on a company's intranet. If you have access to a Web server, you can publish Web pages by saving them to a Web folder or to an FTP location. To learn more about publishing Web pages to a Web folder or FTP location using Microsoft Office applications, refer to Appendix C.

The Publish command allows you to create a Web page from a single slide or from a multiple-slide presentation. This Web Feature illustrates opening the Home Office presentation on the Data Disk (Figure 1a) and then saving the presentation as

FIGURE 1

a Web page using the Save as Web Page command. You will save the Web pages and associated folders on a floppy disk rather than to a Web server. At times, this saving process may be slow and requires patience. See the inside back cover of this book for instructions for downloading the Data Disk or see your instructor for information on accessing the files required in this book.

Then, you will edit the presentation, save it again, and view it again in your default browser. Finally, you will publish your presentation, and PowerPoint will start your default browser and open your file so you can view the presentation (Figures 1b through 1e).

Using Web Page Preview and Saving a PowerPoint Presentation as a Web Page

PowerPoint makes it easy to create a presentation and then preview how it will display on an intranet or on the World Wide Web. This action opens the presentation in your default Web browser without saving files. By previewing your slide show, you can decide which features look good and which need modification. The left side of the window includes the navigation frame, which is the outline of the presentation. The outline contains a table of contents consisting of each slide's title text. You can click the Expand/Collapse Outline button below the navigation frame to view the complete slide text. The right side of the window shows the complete slide in the slide frame. The speaker notes, if present, are displayed in the notes frame below the slide frame. Once the preview is acceptable, you then can save the presentation as a Web page.

Previewing the Presentation as a Web Page

Because you are converting the Home Office presentation on the Data Disk to a Web page, the first step in this project is to open the Home Office file. At any time while developing a presentation, you can preview it as a Web page by using the Web Page Preview command on the File menu. When you use the Web Page Preview command, your browser starts and the presentation is displayed as a Web page. The steps on the next page show how to use the Web Page Preview command.

More About

Home Office Planning

Assistance for designing an effective home office is available on various Web sites. Furniture companies, space planners, and ergonomics experts provide helpful advice for developing comfortable and useful workspaces. For more information on home office planning, visit the PowerPoint 2003 More About Web page (scsite.com/ppt2003/more) and click Offices.

More About

Viewing a Presentation

Saving the presentation in Web page format is an excellent vehicle for distributing the slide show to many viewers. Another method of sharing your file is by broadcasting, which allows audience members to view the slide show in real time on their computers while you control precisely what they see. You also can record a broadcast so viewers can watch the presentation at their convenience.

To Preview the Presentation as a Web Page

1

- **Insert the Data Disk in drive A.**
- **Start PowerPoint and then open the presentation, Home Office, on the Data Disk in drive A.**
- **Click File on the menu bar.**

PowerPoint starts and opens the slide show, Home Office, in normal view. The presentation is composed of four slides. PowerPoint displays the File menu (Figure 2).

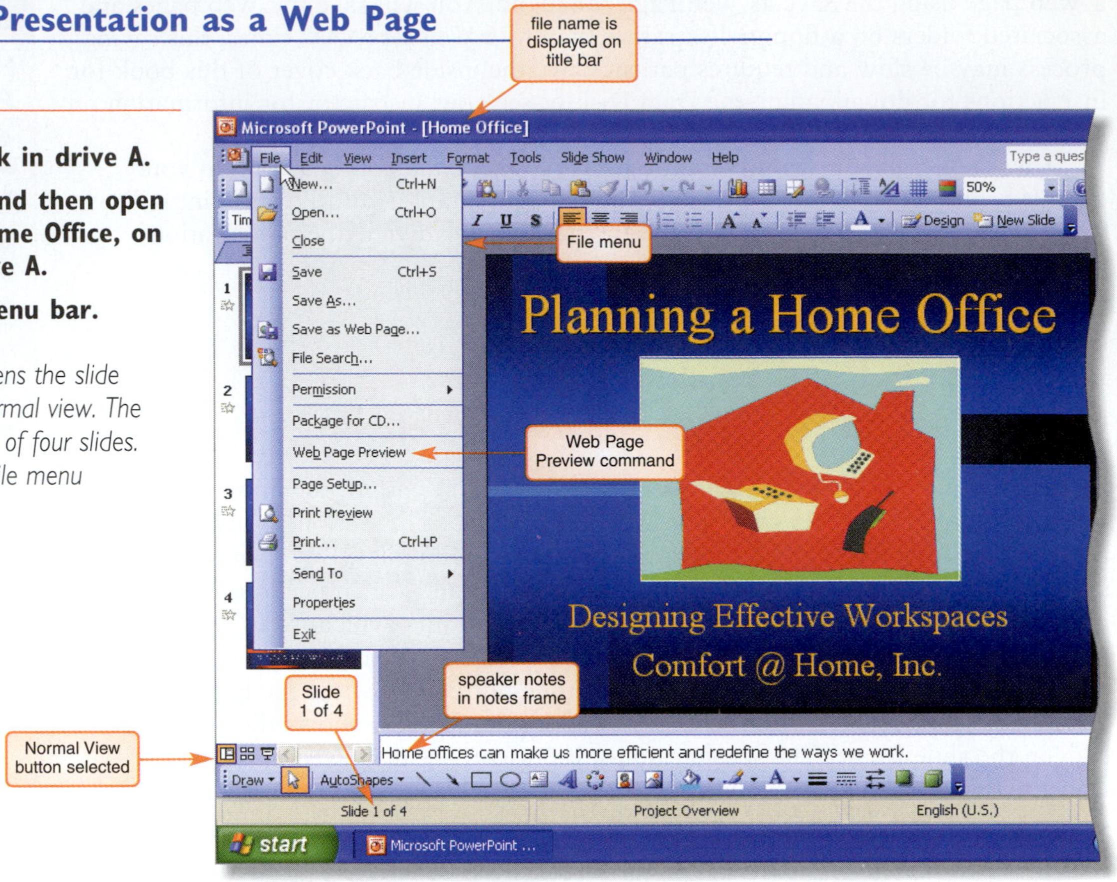

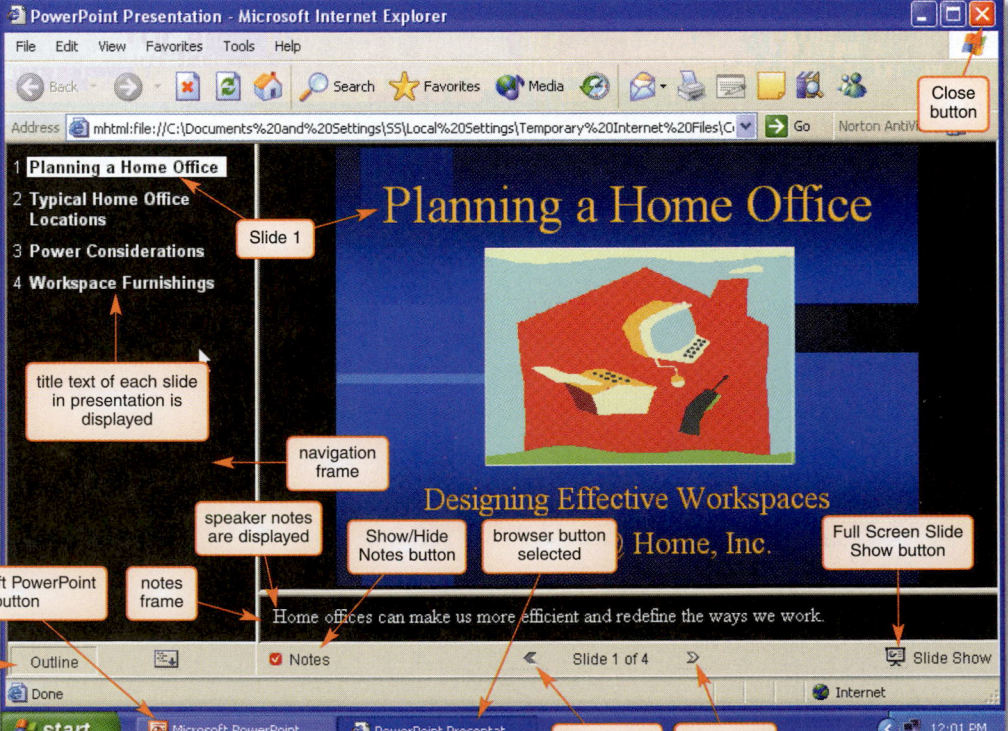

FIGURE 2

2

- **Click Web Page Preview.**

PowerPoint starts your browser. The browser displays a Web page preview of Slide 1 of the Home Office presentation in the slide frame in the browser window (Figure 3). The navigation frame contains the table of contents, which consists of the title text of each slide. The speaker notes are displayed in the notes frame. The Microsoft PowerPoint button on the taskbar no longer is selected. Windows displays a selected browser button on the taskbar, indicating it is active.

FIGURE 3

3

• **Click the Full Screen Slide Show button.**

Slide 1 fills the entire screen (Figure 4). The Slide 1 title text and clip art are displayed. The Web Page preview in the browser is nearly identical to the display of the presentation in PowerPoint.

Slide 1 title text and clip art

FIGURE 4

4

• **Click to display the first line of the subtitle text.**

The first line of the Slide 1 subtitle text is displayed.

5

• **Continue clicking each slide in the presentation.**

• **When the black slide is displayed, click it.**

Each of the four slides in the Home Office presentation is displayed. The message on the black slide, End of slide show, click to exit., indicates the conclusion of the slide show.

6

• **Click the Close button on the right side of the browser title bar.**

The browser closes, PowerPoint becomes active, and PowerPoint displays Slide 1 (Figure 5).

PowerPoint Home Office file active

Slide 1 is displayed

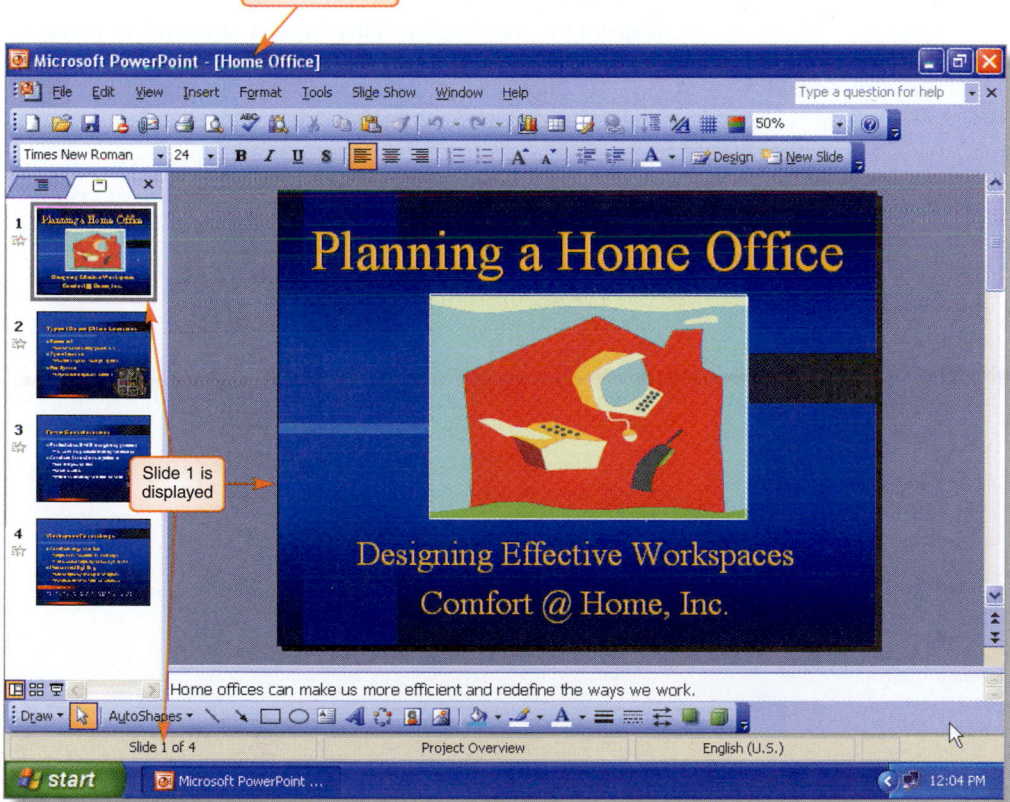

FIGURE 5

Q&A

Q: On what days are audience members most attentive?

A: Sundays, Mondays, and Tuesdays. Researchers believe these days are the best for delivering presentations because the viewers are more relaxed than at the middle and end of the week. As you choose to show or hide your outline and notes, consider your audience's attention span. You may need to provide more information via the outline and notes on the days when your audience is less focused.

The Web page preview shows that PowerPoint can produce professional-looking Web pages from presentations. You can alter the browser window by choosing to display or hide the navigation and notes frames. To hide the navigation frame, click the Show/Hide Outline button below the outline. Later, if you want to redisplay the navigation frame, click the Show/Hide Outline button again. Similarly, the Show/Hide Notes button below the slide frame allows you to display or conceal the speaker notes, if present, on a particular slide.

To advance through the Web page, you also can click the Next Slide button below the slide frame. Likewise, to display a slide appearing earlier in the slide show, click the Previous Slide button.

Saving a PowerPoint Presentation as a Web Page to a New Folder

Once the preview of a PowerPoint slide show is acceptable, you can save it as a Web page so you can view it in a Web browser. Microsoft Internet Explorer and Netscape Navigator are the two more common browsers installed on computers today.

You can save the presentation in one of two Web page formats. One format is called **Single File Web Page**, which saves all the Web page components in a single file with an .mht extension. This format is useful for e-mailing presentations in **hypertext markup language (HTML)**, which is a language browsers can interpret. The second format, called **Web Page**, saves the Web page in a file and some of its components in a folder. This format is useful if you need access to the components, such as clip art, that comprise the Web page. Both formats convert the slide show contents into HTML.

You can save and then view the presentation in two ways. First, you can save the entire presentation as a Web page, quit PowerPoint, open your browser, and open the Web page in your browser. Second, you can combine these steps by saving the presentation as a Web page, publishing the presentation, and then viewing the presentation as a Web page. In this case, PowerPoint will start the browser and display your presentation automatically. Later in this feature, the Publish button will be used to explain further how you can customize a Web page.

Experienced users organize their storage devices by creating folders and then save related files to a common folder. PowerPoint allows you to create folders in the Save As dialog box before saving a file. The following steps create a new folder on the Data Disk in drive A and then save the Home Office presentation in the Web Page format to the new folder.

More About

Browsers

In 1993, computer science students at the University of Illinois developed Mosaic, one of the first graphical Web browsers. Marc Andreessen and a friend worked 18 hours a day for 6 weeks to develop this browser. This success led to the organization of the Netscape Communications Corporation. For more information on graphical Web browsers, visit the PowerPoint 2003 More About Web page (scsite.com/ppt2003/more) and click Browsers.

To Save a Presentation in Web Page Format to a New Folder

1

• **With the Home Office presentation open, click the Next Slide button twice to view Slide 3.**

• **Click the notes pane and then type** More than 46 million Americans work at home at least part time; more than 54 percent of American households have a home office. **as the note.**

• **Click File on the menu bar.**

PowerPoint displays the File menu (Figure 6). The last four words of the speaker notes you typed appear in the notes pane.

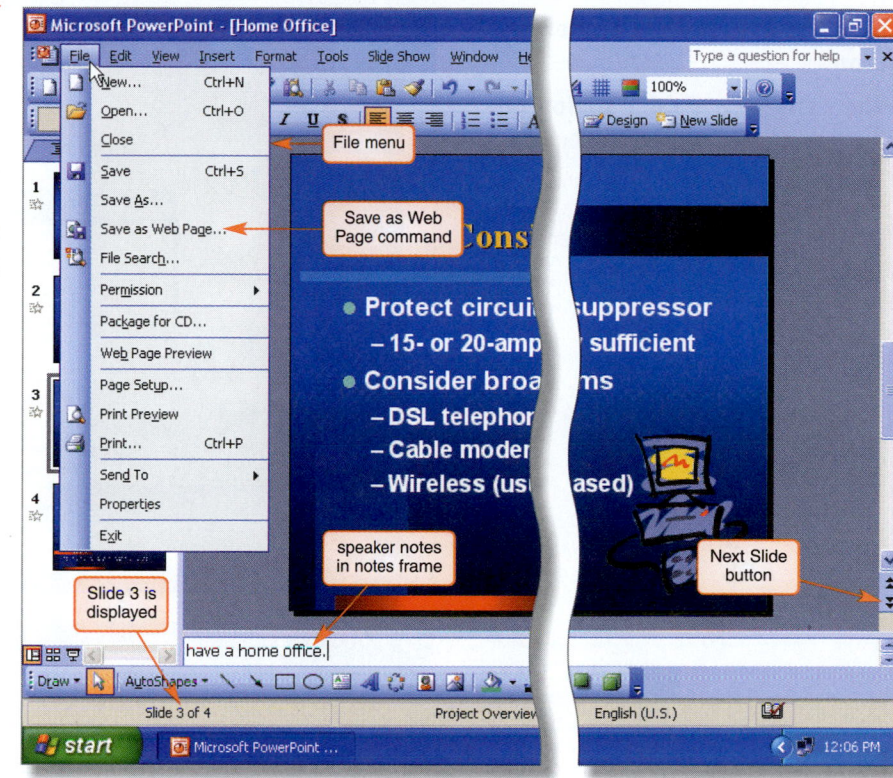

FIGURE 6

2

• **Click Save as Web Page.**

• **When the Save As dialog box is displayed, type** Home Office Web Page **in the File name text box.**

• **Click the Save as type box arrow and then click Web Page.**

PowerPoint displays the Save As dialog box (Figure 7). The default file format type is Single File Web Page.

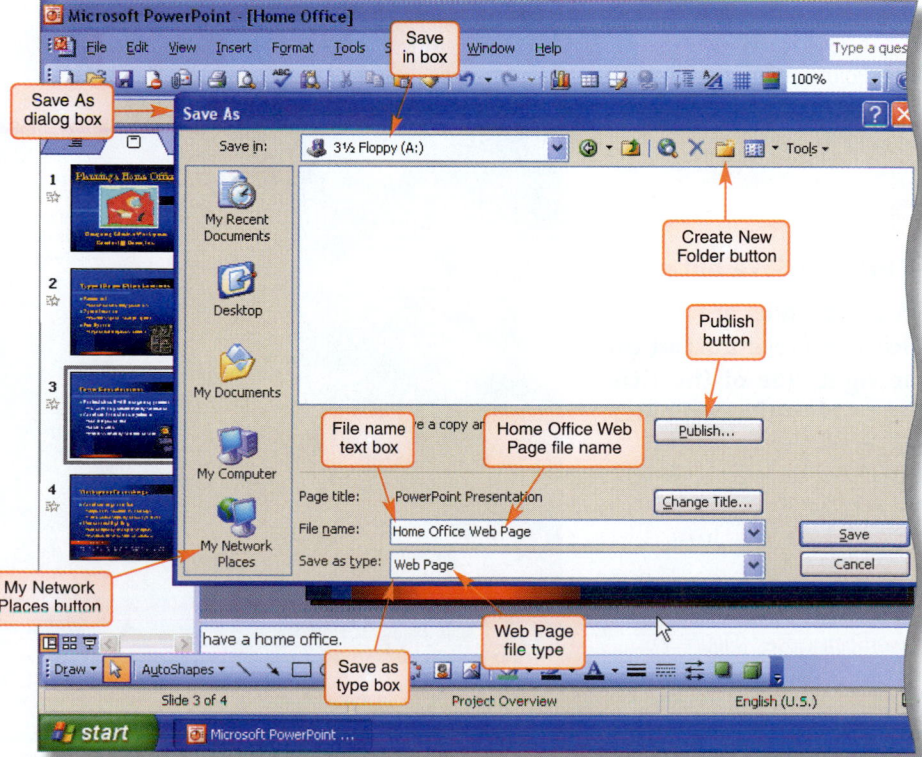

FIGURE 7

3

• **If necessary, click the Save in box arrow and select 3½ Floppy (A:).**

• **Click the Create New Folder button.**

• **When the New Folder dialog box is displayed, type** Web Feature **in the Name text box.**

PowerPoint displays the New Folder dialog box (Figure 8).

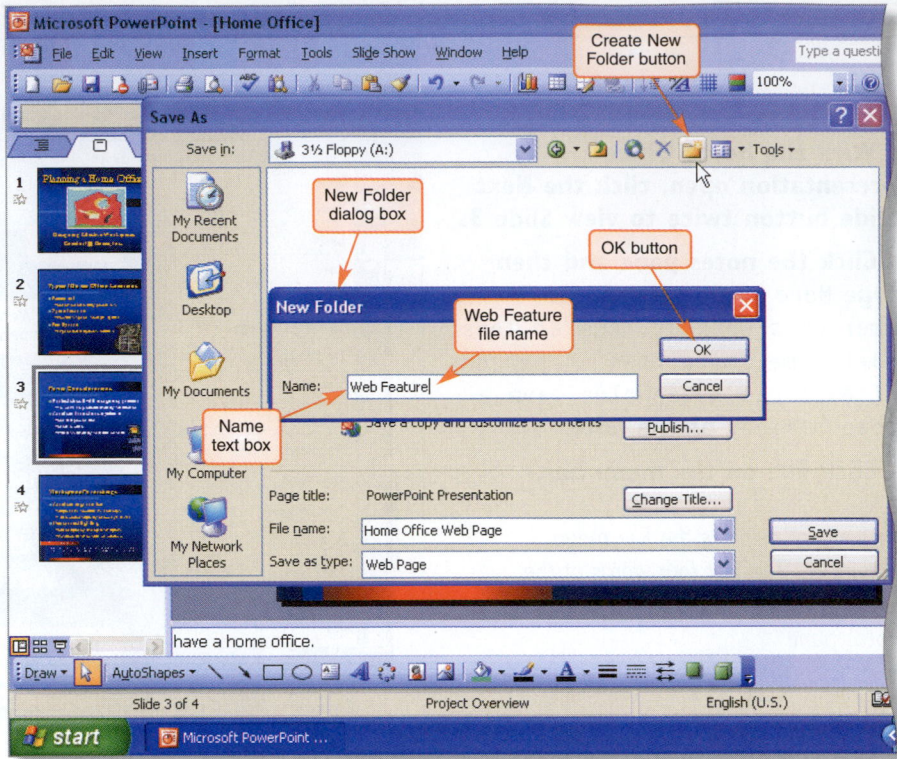

FIGURE 8

4

• **Click the OK button in the New Folder dialog box.**

PowerPoint automatically selects the new Web Feature folder in the Save in box.

5

• **Click the Save button.**

• **After all files are saved, click the Close button on the right side of the title bar to close PowerPoint.**

PowerPoint saves the presentation in HTML format on the Data Disk in drive A in the Web Feature folder using the file name Home Office Web Page.htm. PowerPoint closes (Figure 9).

FIGURE 9

The Save As dialog box that displays when you use the Save as Web Page command is slightly different from the Save As dialog box that displays when you use the Save As command. The Publish button in the Save As dialog box in Figure 7 on page PPT 147 is an alternative to the Save button and allows you to customize the Web page further. In the previous set of steps, the Save button was used to complete the save. Later in this feature, the Publish button will be used to explain further how you can customize a Web page.

File Management Tools in PowerPoint

Creating a new folder allows you to organize your work. PowerPoint automatically inserts the new folder name in the Save in box when you click the OK button in the New Folder dialog box (Figure 8). Once you create a folder, you can right-click it while the Save As dialog box is active and perform many file manager tasks directly in PowerPoint. For example, once the shortcut menu is displayed, you can rename the selected folder, delete it, copy it, display its properties, and perform other file management functions.

If you have access to a Web server that allows you to save files to a Web folder, then you can save the Web page directly to the Web server by clicking the My Network Places button in the lower-left corner of the Save As dialog box (Figure 7). If you have access to a Web server that allows you to save to an FTP site, then you can select the FTP site under FTP locations in the Save in box just as you select any folder in which to save a file. To save a presentation to a Web server, see Appendix C.

After PowerPoint saves the presentation in Step 5, it displays the HTML file — not the presentation — in the PowerPoint window. PowerPoint can continue to display the presentation in HTML format because within the HTML file that was created, PowerPoint also saved the formats to display the HTML file. This is referred to as **round tripping** the HTML file back to the application in which it was created.

Viewing the Web Page Using Your Browser

With the Home Office Web page saved to the folder, Web Feature, on the Data Disk in drive A, the next step is to view it using a browser, such as Microsoft Internet Explorer or Netscape, as shown in the steps on the next page.

To View the Web Page Using Your Browser

1

• **If necessary, insert the Data Disk in drive A.**

• **Click the Start button on the taskbar, point to All Programs, and then click Internet Explorer.**

• **When the Internet Explorer window displays, type** a:\web feature\home office web page.htm **in the Address bar and then press the** ENTER **key.**

The browser displays Slide 1 in the Web page, Home Office Web Page.htm (Figure 10).

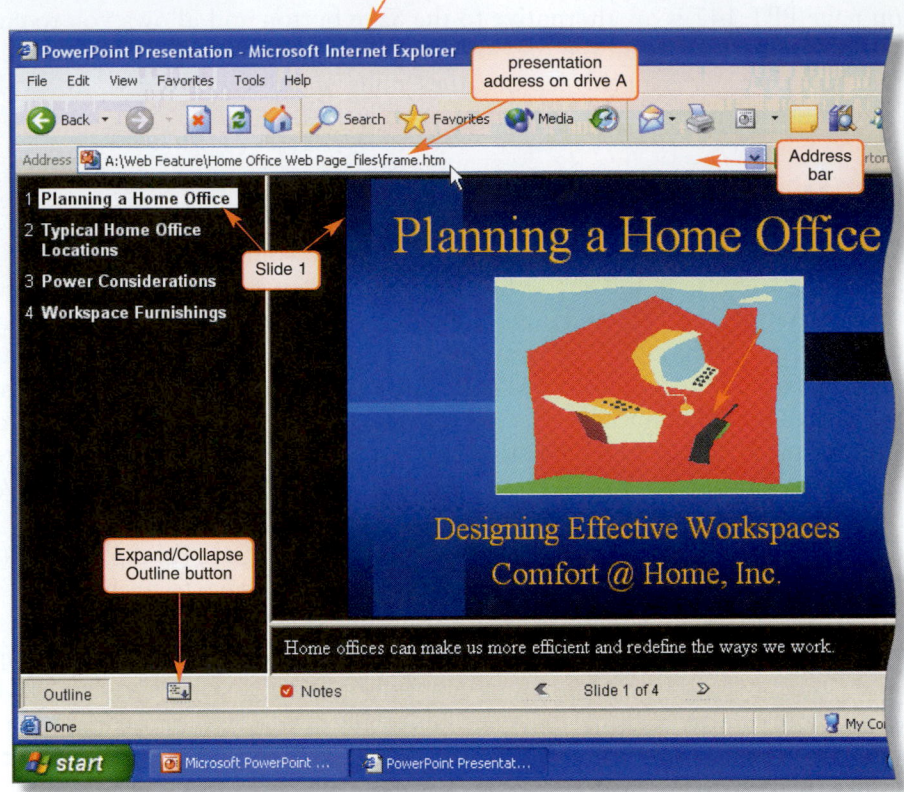

FIGURE 10

2

• **Click the Expand/ Collapse Outline button at the bottom of the window.**

The text of each slide in an outline appears in the navigation frame (Figure 11). To display only the title of each slide, you would click the Expand/Collapse Outline button again.

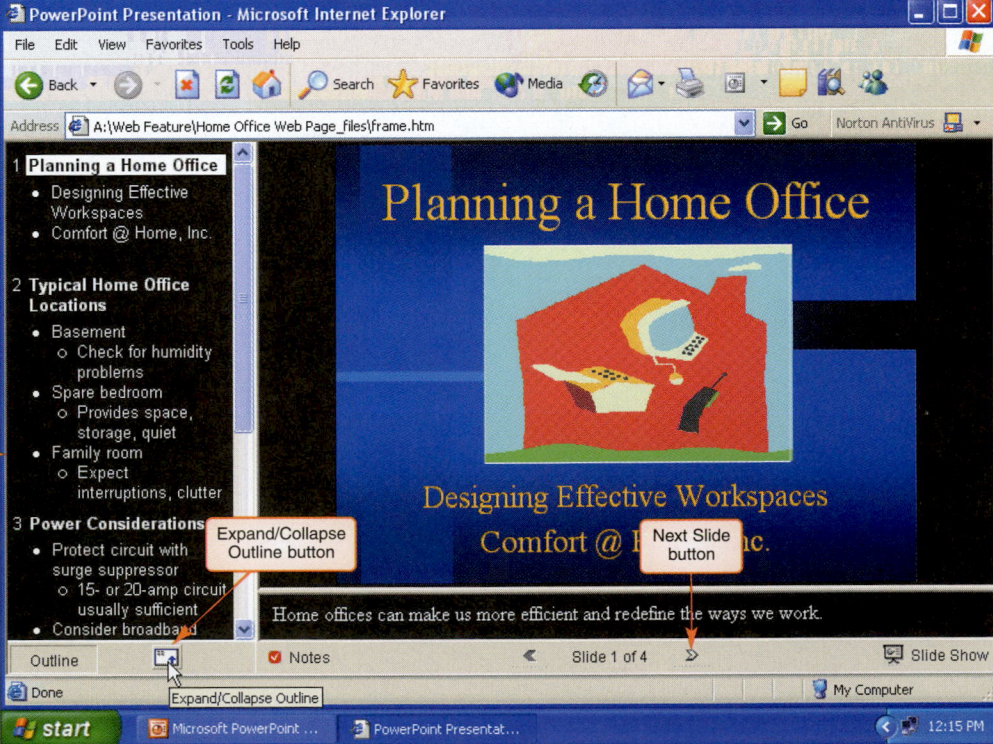

FIGURE 11

Editing a Web Page through a Browser • PPT 151

3

• **Click the Next Slide button three times to view all four slides.**

The browser displays each of the slides in the Home Office presentation. Slide 4 is displayed in the browser (Figure 12).

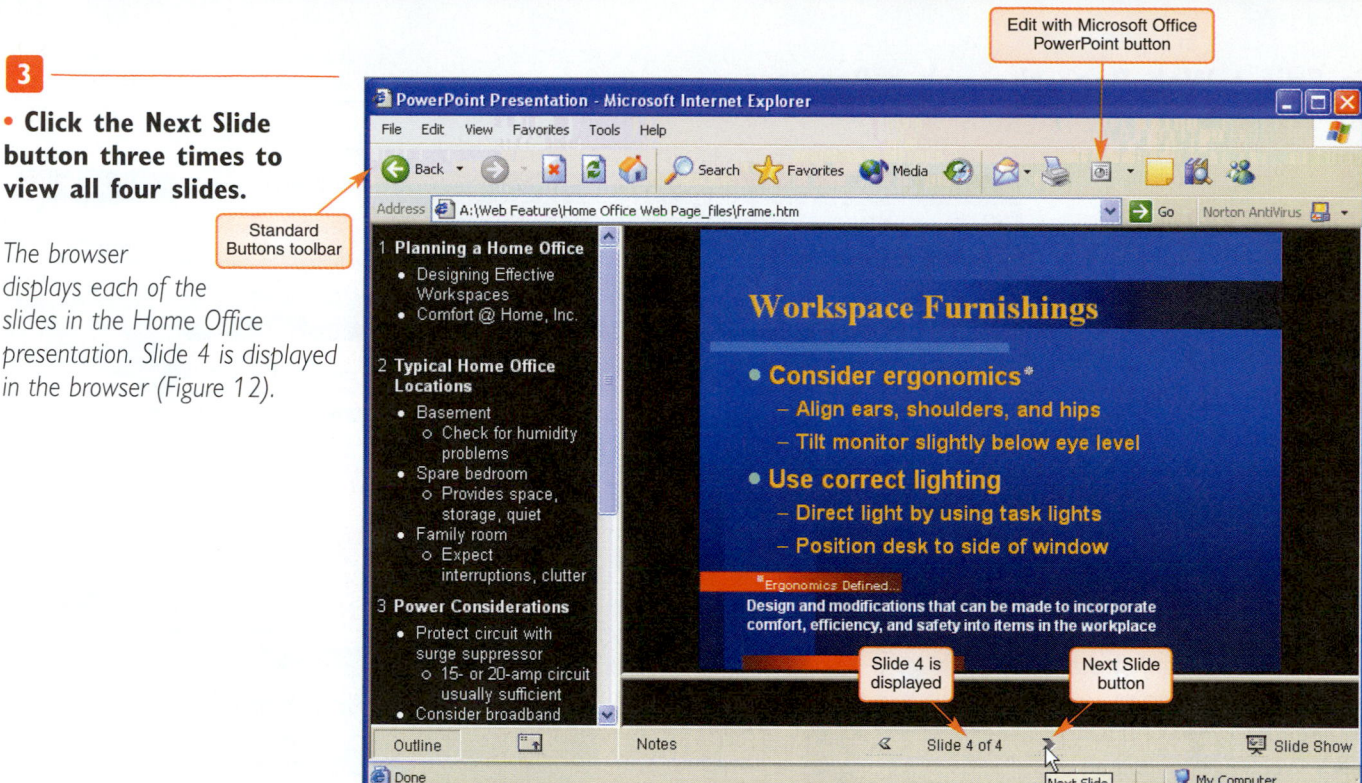

FIGURE 12

Figures 11 and 12 show that a Web page is an ideal medium for distributing information to a large group of people. The Web page can be made available to anyone with a computer, browser, and the address. The Web page also can be e-mailed easily because it resides in a single file, rather than in a file and folder.

If you want, you can use the Print command on the File menu in your browser to print the slides one at a time. You also can view the HTML source PowerPoint created by clicking Source on the View menu in Internet Explorer or Page Source on the View menu in Netscape.

Editing a Web Page through a Browser

You may want to modify your Web page by making small changes to the text or art on some slides. In this presentation, you want to change the title text in Slide 1 to reflect the fact that a home office can provide comfort as well as efficiency. You can modify the presentation using PowerPoint directly in the browser window. Your computer may indicate other editing options, such as using Windows Notepad. The steps on the next page modify the Title Slide title text.

More About

Printing

If your printer seems to print slowly, Microsoft suggests clearing at least two megabytes of space on your hard drive and also closing any unnecessary programs that are running simultaneously.

To Edit a Web Page through a Browser

1

• **Click the Edit with Microsoft Office PowerPoint button on the Standard Buttons toolbar.**

• **Select the words, Planning a Home Office, in the title text placeholder.**

When you click the Edit button, PowerPoint opens a new presentation with the same file name as the Web presentation file name, as indicated by the title bar and the selected Microsoft PowerPoint - [Home Office Web Page] button on the Windows taskbar (Figure 13). A selection rectangle appears around the title text place-holder. The four words are highlighted.

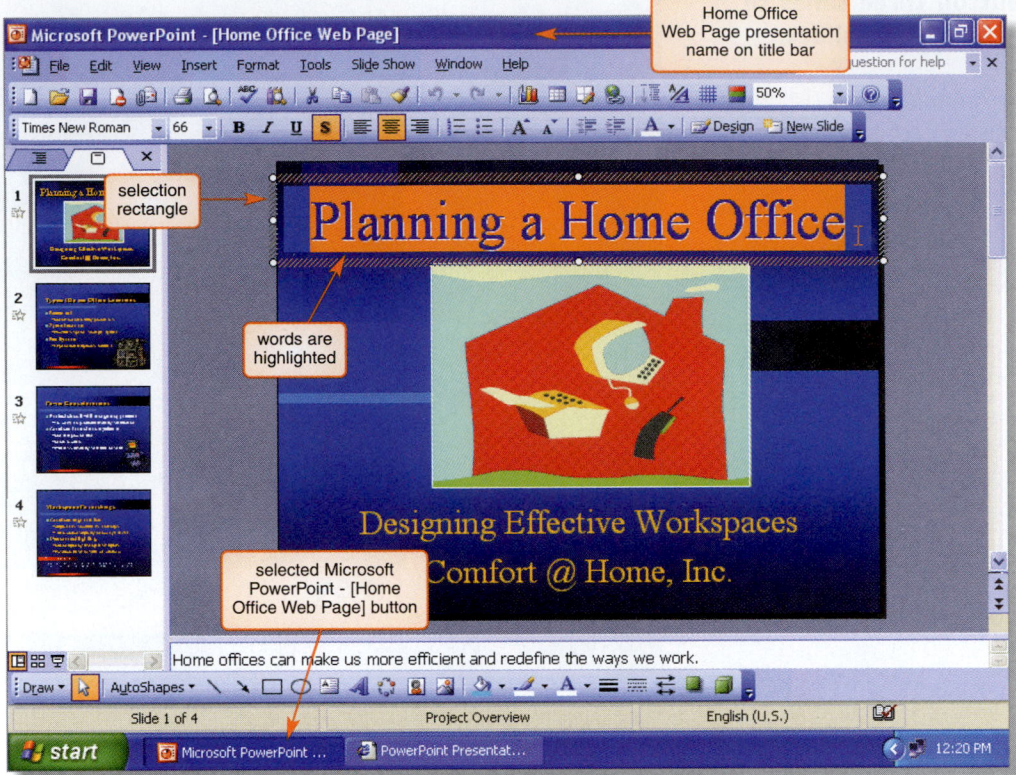

FIGURE 13

2

• **Type** The Comforts of Home **in the title text placeholder.**

The title text is modified (Figure 14).

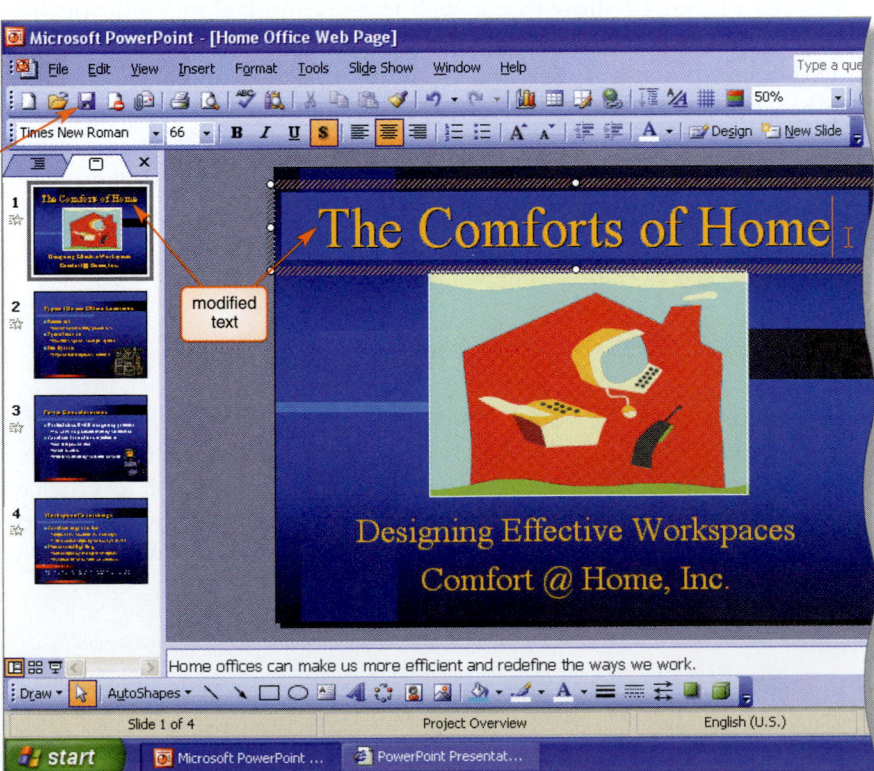

FIGURE 14

3

• **Click the Save button on the Standard toolbar.**

It takes several minutes for PowerPoint to save the changes to the Home Office Web Page.htm file on the Data Disk in drive A. The buttons on the taskbar indicate that the PowerPoint presentation and the browser are open.

4

• **Click the PowerPoint Presentation - Microsoft Internet Explorer button on the taskbar.**

• **Click the Previous Slide button three times to display Slide 1.**

The browser displays the revised title text on Slide 1 (Figure 15). If the revised text does not display, click the Refresh button on the Standard Buttons toolbar.

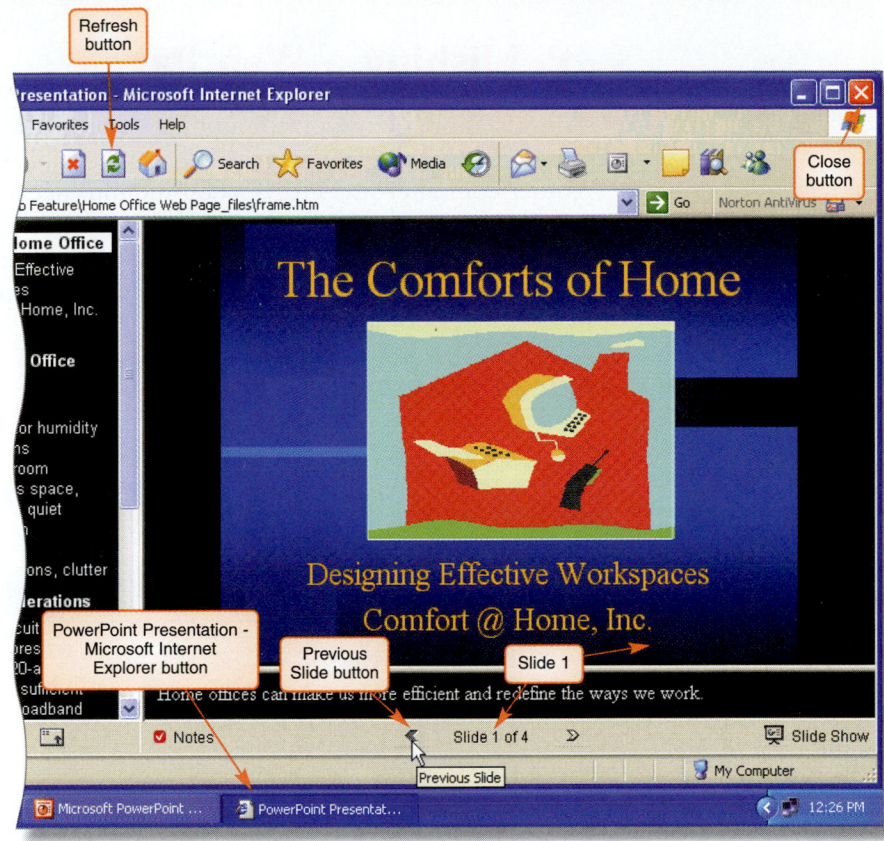

FIGURE 15

5

• **Click the Close button on the browser title bar.**

• **Click the Save button to save the revised PowerPoint Home Office Web Page.**

The browser closes, and the PowerPoint window displays in normal view with the modified Slide 1 of the Home Office Web Page presentation active (Figure 16).

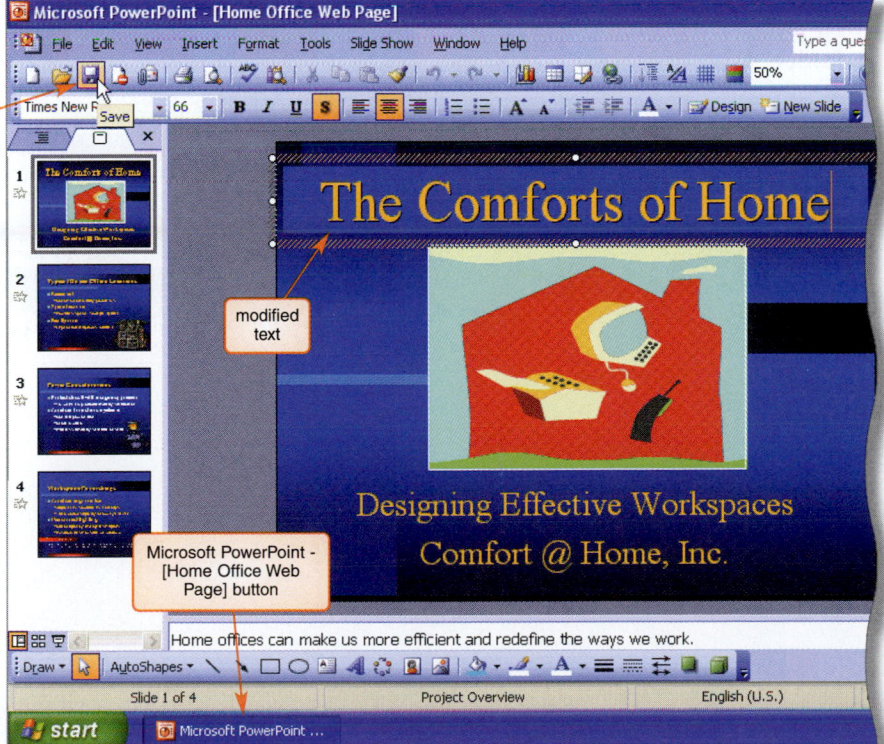

FIGURE 16

Publishing a Web Page

PowerPoint allows you to publish the presentation by saving the pages to a Web folder or to an FTP location. When you publish your presentation, it is available for other computer users to view on the Internet or by other means. Publishing a Web page of a presentation is an alternative to distributing printed copies of the slides. The following section uses the Publish button in the Save As dialog box, rather than the Save button, to illustrate PowerPoint's additional publishing capabilities.

To Publish a PowerPoint Presentation

1

• **Click File on the menu bar and then click Save as Web Page.**

• **Click the Save as type box arrow and then click Single File Web Page.**

• **Type** Home Office Single File Web Page **in the File name text box.**

• **If necessary, click the Save in box arrow, select 3½ Floppy (A:) in the Save in list, and then select the folder, Web Feature.**

The Save As dialog box is displayed (Figure 17). When you use the Publish button, PowerPoint will save the Web page in a single file.

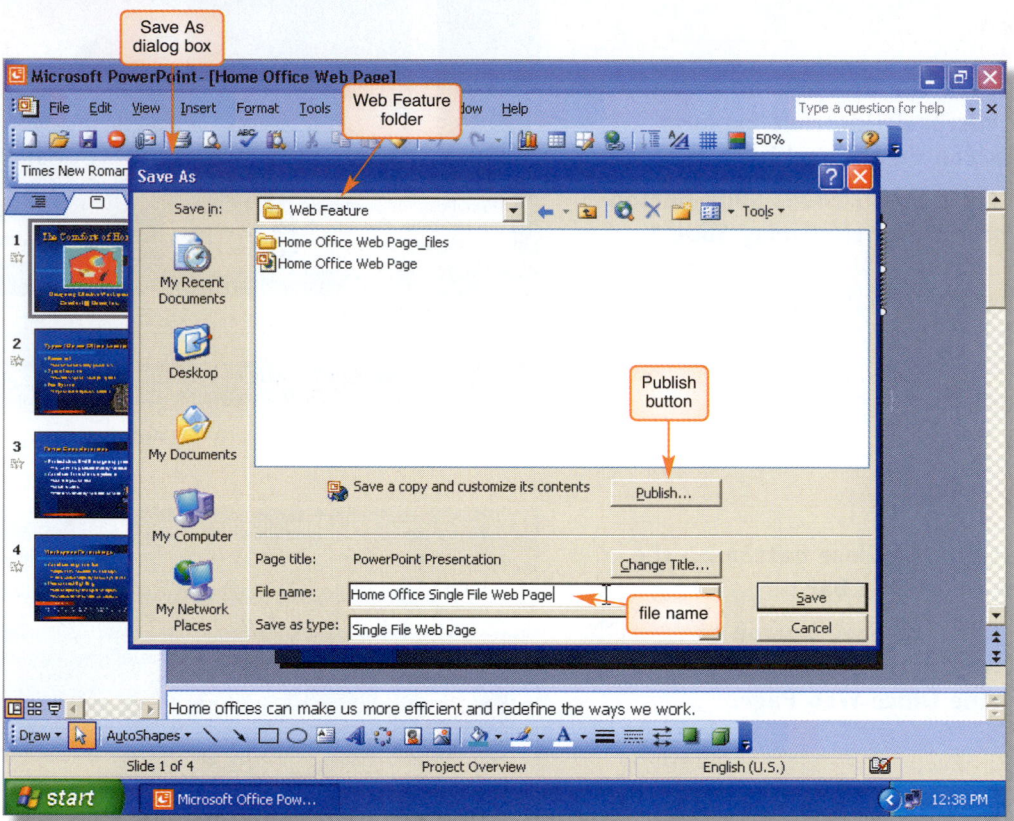

FIGURE 17

2

- **Click the Publish button.**
- **If the Office Assistant appears, click No, don't provide help now.**
- **If necessary, click Open published Web page in browser to select it.**

The Publish as Web Page dialog box is displayed (Figure 18). PowerPoint defaults to publishing the complete presentation, although you can choose to publish one or a range of slides. The Open published Web page in browser check box is selected, which means the Home Office Single File Web Page presentation will open in your default browser when you click the Publish button.

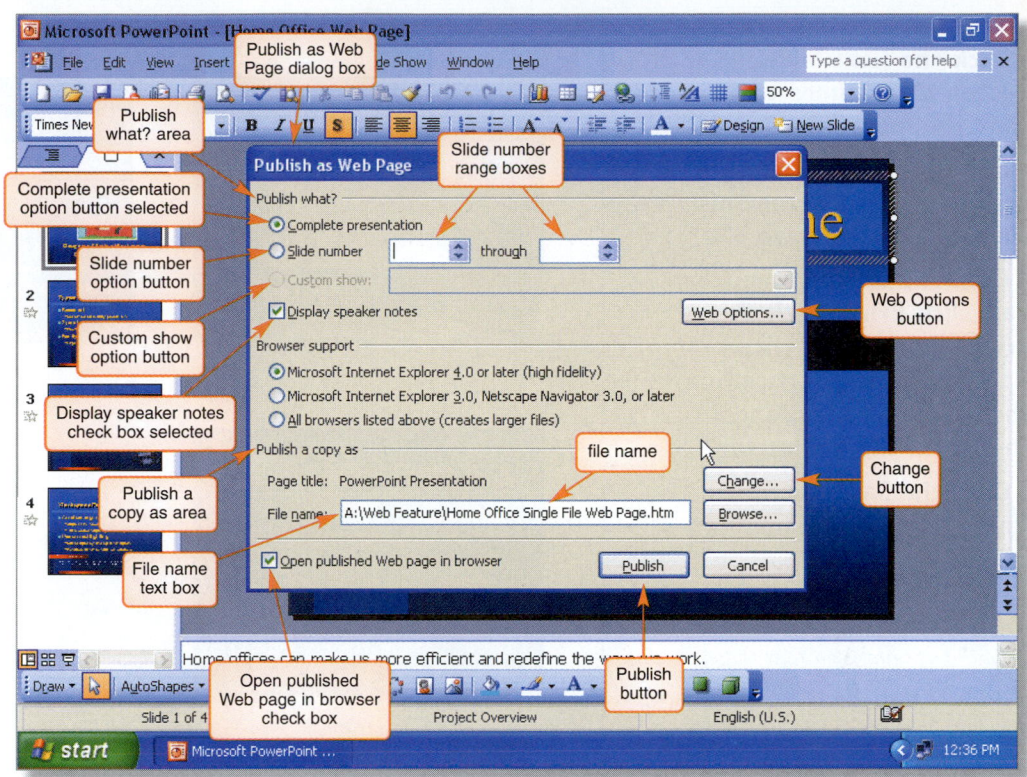

FIGURE 18

3

- **Click the Publish button.**

PowerPoint saves the presentation as a single file, Home Office Single File Web Page.mht, in the Web Feature folder on the Data Disk in drive A. After a few minutes, PowerPoint opens your default Web browser in a separate window (Figure 19). If the browser does not open, click the PowerPoint Presentation - Microsoft Internet Explorer button on the Windows taskbar.

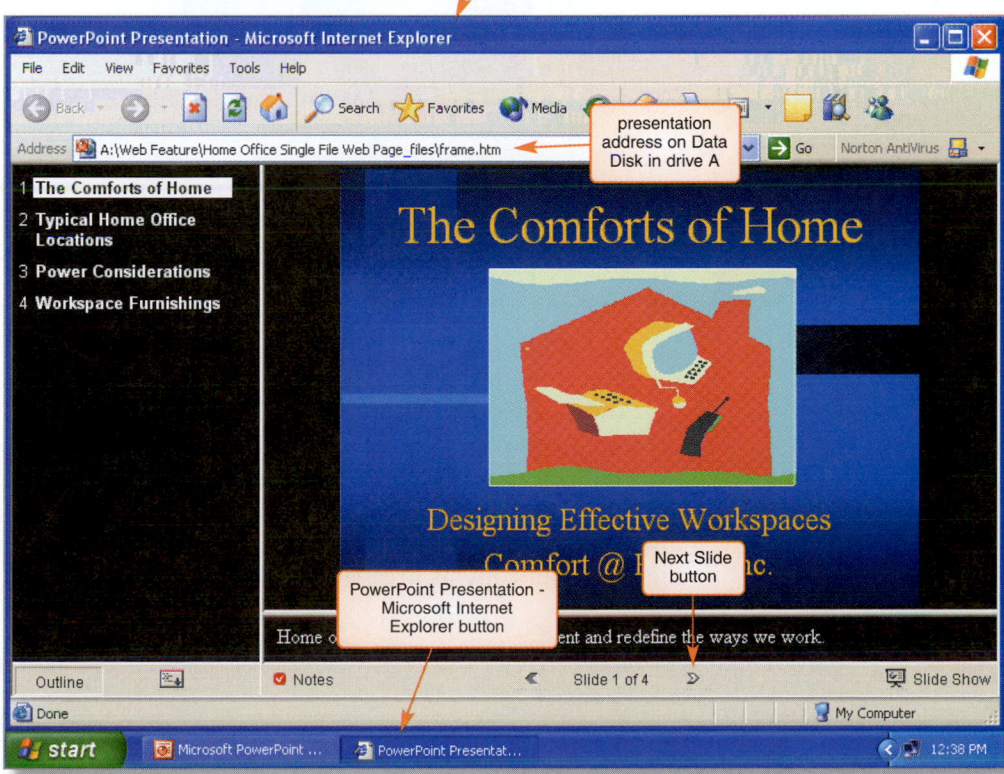

FIGURE 19

4

• **Click the Next Slide button three times to view the four slides.**

• **Click the Close button in the upper-right corner of the browser window.**

• **Click File on the menu bar, click Print, click the Print what arrow, click Handouts, click Vertical in the Handouts area, and then click the OK button.**

• **Click the Save button to save the revised Home Office Web Page.**

The browser closes, and PowerPoint prints the four slides as a handout (Figure 20). PowerPoint takes a few minutes to save the file to the Data Disk.

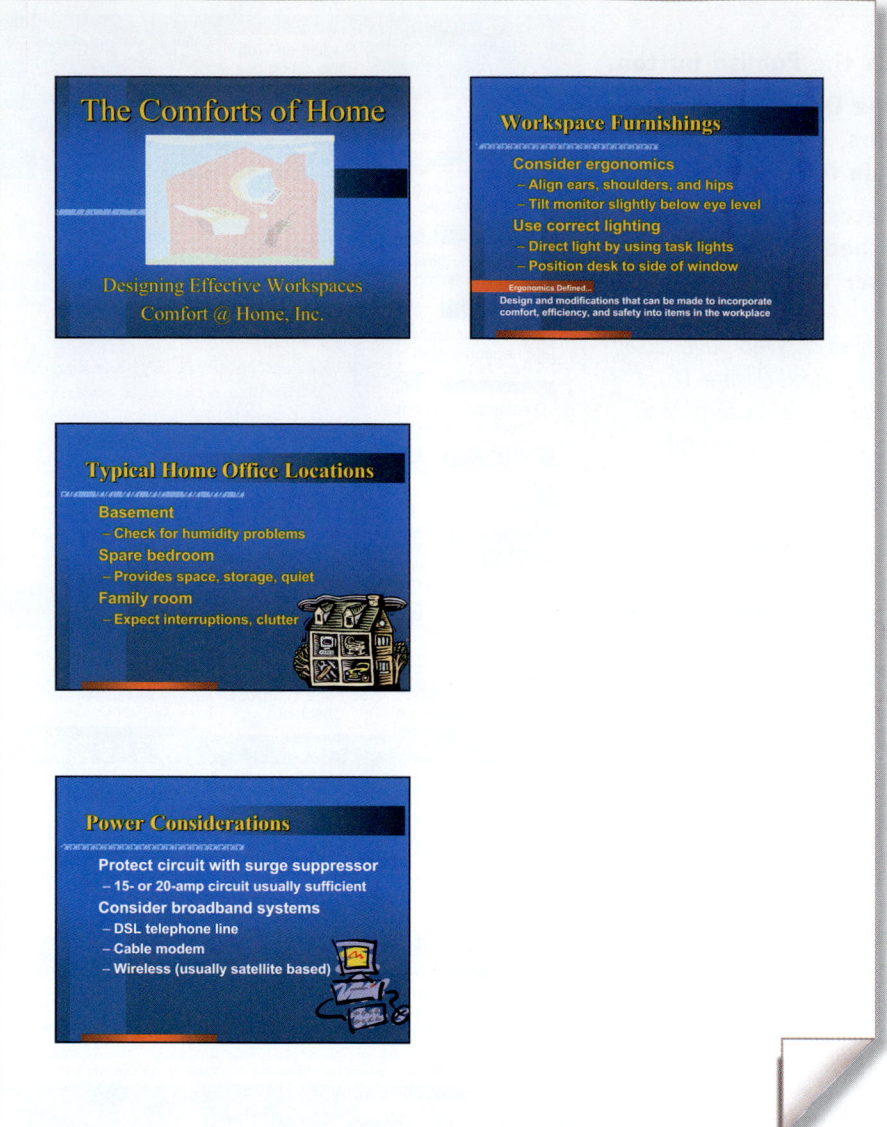

FIGURE 20

Publishing provides customizing options that are not available when you simply save the entire presentation and then start your browser. The Publish as Web Page dialog box provides several options to customize your Web page. For example, you can change the page title that displays on the browser's title bar and in the history list. People visiting your Web site can store a link to your Web page, which will display in their favorites list. To change the page title, you click the Change button in the Publish a copy as area (Figure 18 on the previous page) and then type a new title.

The Publish what? area of the Publish as Web Page dialog box allows you to publish parts of your presentation. PowerPoint defaults to publishing the complete presentation, but you can select specific slides by clicking the Slide number option button and then entering the range of desired slide numbers in the range boxes. In addition, you can publish a custom show you have created previously. A **custom show** is a subset of your presentation that contains slides tailored for a specific audience. For example, you may want to show Slides 1, 2, and 4 to one group and Slides 1, 3, and 4 to another group.

You can choose to publish only the publication slides and not the accompanying speaker notes. By default, the Display speaker notes check box is selected in the Publish what? area. You typed speaker notes for Slide 1 of this presentation, so the speaker notes will appear in the browser window. If you do not want to make your notes available to users, click the Display speaker notes check box to remove the check mark.

The Web Options button in the Publish what? area allows you to select options to determine how your presentation will look when viewed in a Web browser. You can choose options such as allowing slide animation to show, selecting the screen size, and having the notes and outline panes display when viewing the presentation in a Web browser.

The Web page now is complete. The next step is to make your Web presentation available to others on your network, an intranet, or the World Wide Web. Ask your instructor how you can post your presentation.

> *More About*
>
> ### Publishing Web Presentations
>
> Once a presentation is published, viewers can view the slide show and then offer comments about the document. Saving the presentation as an .htm or .mht Web-based format provides the most flexibility for these reviewers. The .mht format combines multiple pictures and slides into a single file called a Web archive. A Web archive works in the same manner as a Web page does in .htm format. For more information on publishing Web presentations, visit the PowerPoint 2003 More About Web page (scsite.com/ppt2003/more) and click Publishing.

Web Feature Summary

This Web feature introduced you to creating a Web page by viewing an existing presentation as a Web page in your default browser. The presentation then was saved as an HTML file. Next, you modified Slide 1. You then reviewed the Slide 1 change using your default browser and then published the slide show. With the Home Office presentation converted to a Web page, you can post the file to an intranet or to the World Wide Web.

 If you have a SAM user profile, you may have access to hands-on instruction, practice, and assessment of the skills covered in this project. Log in to your SAM account and go to your assignments page to see what your instructor has assigned.

What You Should Know

Having completed this project, you should be able to perform the tasks below. The tasks are listed in the same order they were presented in this project. For a list of the buttons, menus, toolbars, and commands introduced in this project, see the Quick Reference Summary at the back of this book and refer to the Page Number column.

1. Preview the Presentation as a Web Page (PPT 144)

2. Save a Presentation in Web Page Format to a New Folder   (PPT 147)

3. View the Web Page Using Your Browser (PPT 150)

4. Edit a Web Page through a Browser (PPT 152)

5. Publish a PowerPoint Presentation   (PPT 154)

1 Creating a Web Page from the College Success Presentation

Problem: Dr. Traci Johnson, the dean of the Academic Skills Center at Lakemore College, wants to expand the visibility of the College Success presentation you created for the Academic Skills Center in Project 1. Dr. Johnson believes the World Wide Web would be an excellent vehicle to help students throughout the campus and at other colleges, and she has asked you to help transfer the presentation to the Internet.

Instructions: Start PowerPoint and then perform the following steps with a computer.

1. Open the College Success presentation shown in Figure 1-1 on page PPT 5 that you created in Project 1. (If you did not complete Project 1, see your instructor for a copy of the presentation.)
2. Use the Save as Web Page command on the File menu to save the presentation in Web page format. Create a new folder called College Success Exercise and then save the Web page with the file name, Lab WF 1-1 Lakemore.
3. View the presentation in a browser.
4. Edit the Web page by using the words, Achieve Your Academic Personal Best, as the Slide 1 title text.
5. Change the last paragraph to the words, Turn off cellular telephone, on Slide 3.
6. View the modified Web page in a browser.
7. Print the modified presentation as a handout with the slides arranged vertically.
8. Ask your instructor for instructions on how to post your Web page so others may have access to it.

2 Creating a Web Page from the Nutrition and Fitness Presentation

Problem: The Nutrition and Fitness presentation you developed in Project 2 for Jessica Cantero, the Fitness director at your college, is generating much interest. Students are registering for the first workshop and are inquiring about additional seminars. Jessica has asked you to post the presentation to the school's intranet.

Instructions: Start PowerPoint and then perform the following steps with a computer.

1. Open the Nutrition and Fitness presentation shown in Figures 2-1a through 2-1e on page PPT 83 that you created in Project 2. (If you did not complete Project 2, see your instructor for a copy of the presentation.)
2. Use the Save as Web Page command on the File menu to save the presentation in Web Page format. Create a new folder called Healthy Exercise and then save the Web page using the file name, Lab WF 1-2 Nutrition.
3. View the presentation in a browser.
4. Modify Slide 1 by italicizing both subtitle lines.
5. On Slide 1, type Workshops are scheduled each Monday at 7 p.m. and Friday at noon. as the note.
6. Modify Slide 3 by changing the word, Bicycling, to the word, Golfing.
7. On Slide 4, type Yoga has been practiced actively for more than 5,000 years. as the note.
8. View the modified Web page in a browser.
9. Print the modified presentation as a handout with the slides arranged horizontally.
10. Ask your instructor for instructions on how to post your Web page so others may have access to it.

In the Lab

3 Creating a Personal Presentation

Problem: You have decided to apply for a position as a tutor in your college's academic assistance center. You are preparing to send your resume and cover letter to the dean of this area in your school, and you want to develop a unique way to publicize your academic skills and personality traits. You decide to create a personalized PowerPoint presentation emphasizing your scholarly achievements and your interpersonal communication skills. You refer to this presentation in your cover letter and inform the executive director that she can view this presentation because you have saved the presentation as a Web page and posted the pages on your school's Web server.

Instructions: Start PowerPoint and then perform the following steps with a computer.

1. Prepare a presentation highlighting your scholarly skills and personality strengths. Create a title slide and at least three additional slides. Use appropriate clip art and an animation scheme.
2. Use the Save as Web Page command to convert and publish the presentation as a single file Web page. Save the Web page in a folder named Tutoring Web File using the file name, Lab WF 1-3 Tutor Position.
3. View the presentation in a browser.
4. Print the Web page.
5. Ask your instructor for instructions on how to post your Web page so others may have access to it.

MICROSOFT OFFICE OUTLOOK

MICROSOFT
Office Outlook 2003

E-Mail and Contact Management with Outlook

PROJECT

1

CASE PERSPECTIVE

Maria Rosado is the captain of the Woodland Community College High Flyers championship women's basketball team. You attend several classes with Maria, and you always support her by attending the games. Maria's responsibilities as captain of the team include scheduling team meetings, notifying team members of schedule changes, and reporting team concerns and/or problems to the coach. She also likes to keep track of team and personal statistics, scores, standings, and home court winning streaks.

You work as a part-time Help desk specialist at the Woodland Community College computer lab, which has given you the opportunity to work with Outlook and become familiar with its information management and communications features. Maria has visited the Help desk and has watched you easily manage e-mail, contacts, and appointments. She knows that Outlook could help her, and she would like to use it to communicate with her teammates and coach and simplify team scheduling, but she needs some direction in getting started.

Maria has asked you to help her in familiarizing herself with Outlook's e-mail and contact management capabilities. She feels that becoming proficient with Outlook will make it easier to keep her teammates abreast of team meetings and schedule changes.

As you read through this project, you will learn how to use Outlook to open, read, create, send, and organize e-mail messages. You also will learn how to insert a file attachment to an e-mail message, and create and attach an electronic signature. In addition, you will learn how to create, organize, and print a contact list. Finally, you will learn how to create a distribution list and track activities of a contact.

MICROSOFT
Office Outlook 2003

E-Mail and Contact Management with Outlook

PROJECT

What Is Microsoft Office Outlook 2003?

Microsoft Office Outlook 2003 is a powerful communications and scheduling program that helps you communicate with others (Figures 1-1a through 1-1d), keep track of your contacts, and organize your busy schedule. Outlook allows you to send and receive electronic mail and permits you to engage in real-time messaging with family, friends, or coworkers using instant messaging. Outlook also provides you with the means to organize your contacts. Users easily can track e-mail messages, meetings, and notes with a particular contact. Outlook's Calendar, Contacts, Tasks, and Notes components aid in this organization. Contact information readily is available from the Outlook Calendar, Mail, Contacts, and Task components by accessing the Find a Contact feature. Personal information management (PIM) programs such as Outlook provide a way for individuals and workgroups to organize, find, view, and share information easily.

This latest version of Outlook has many new features, including a completely new look. The new Reading Pane takes the place of the Preview pane and allows for viewing twice as much information. A Junk E-mail filter has been added to help prevent unwanted messages. Quick flags make it easy to categorize and find your messages. Search Folders make it easy to find specific messages. Another new feature in Outlook allows you to have a unique signature for each e-mail account.

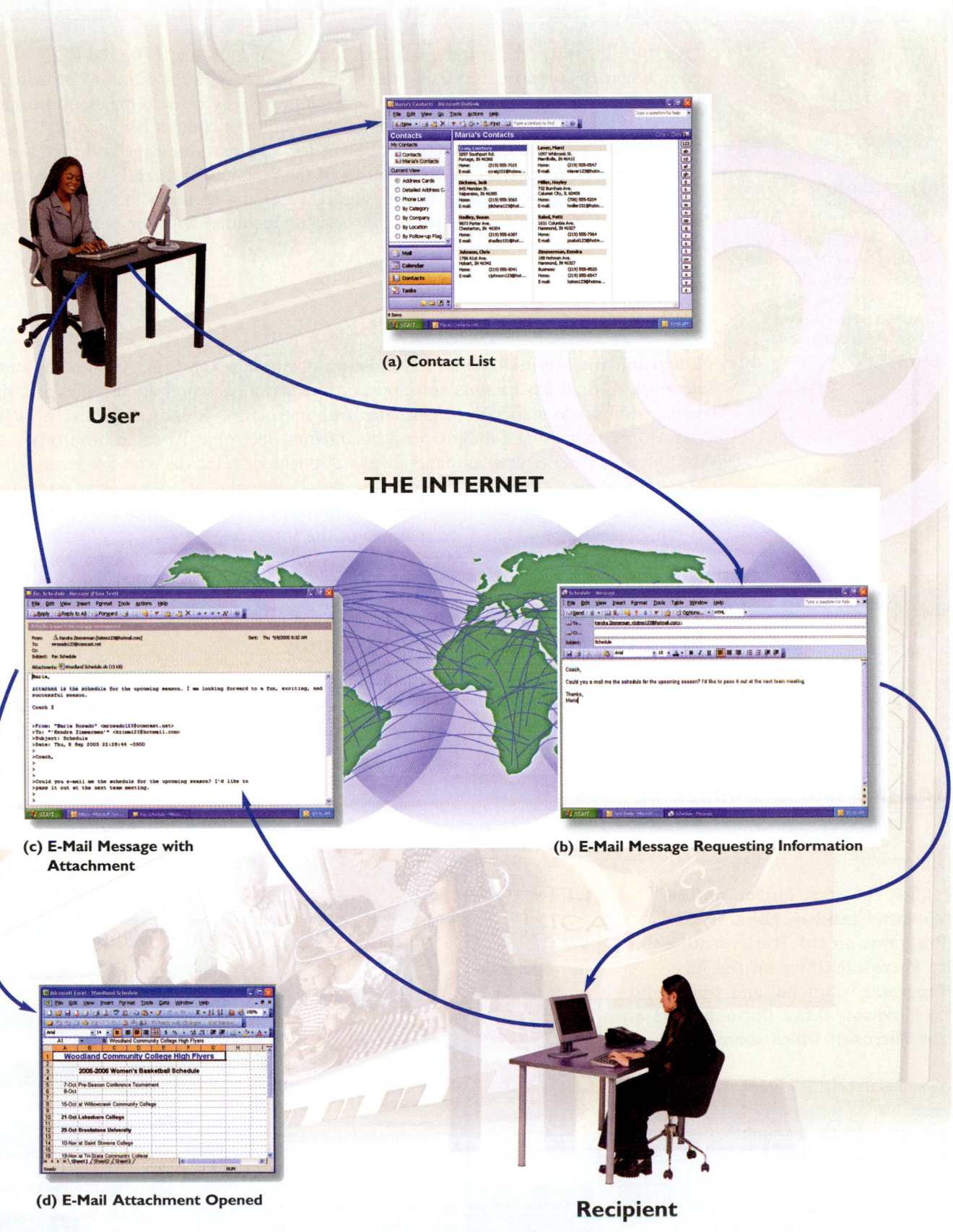

(a) Contact List

THE INTERNET

(c) E-Mail Message with Attachment

(b) E-Mail Message Requesting Information

(d) E-Mail Attachment Opened

User

Recipient

FIGURE 1-1

Project One — Communicating Over the Internet

Project 1 illustrates the communications features of Outlook using the Mail component to compose, send, and read e-mail messages. In addition to utilizing Outlook's communications tools, this project shows you how to create and organize a contact list using the Contacts component. Using the contact list (Figure 1-1a on the previous page), a user selects a recipient for an e-mail message and then sends an e-mail message requesting information from the recipient (Figure 1-1b). The recipient replies by sending an e-mail message (Figure 1-1c) and includes the requested information as an attachment (Figure 1-1d), or a file included with the e-mail message, that the recipient can open.

More About

Microsoft Outlook 2003

For more information about the features of Outlook 2003, visit the Outlook 2003 More About Web page (scsite.com/out2003/more) and then click Microsoft Outlook 2003 features.

Electronic Mail (E-Mail)

Electronic mail (**e-mail**) is the transmission of messages and files via a computer network. E-mail has become an important means of exchanging messages and files between business associates, classmates and instructors, friends, and family. Businesses find that using e-mail to send documents electronically saves both time and money. Parents with students away at college or relatives who are scattered across the country find that communicating via e-mail is an inexpensive and easy way to stay in touch with their family members. In fact, exchanging e-mail messages is one of the more widely used features of the Internet.

Outlook allows you to receive and store incoming e-mail messages, compose and send e-mail messages, and maintain a list of frequently used e-mail addresses.

Starting and Customizing Outlook

If you are stepping through this project on a computer and you want your screen to agree with the figures in this book, then you should set your computer's resolution to 800 × 600. The following steps start Outlook and customize its window.

To Start and Customize Outlook

1

• **Click the Start button on the Windows taskbar, point to All Programs on the Start menu, point to Microsoft Office on the All Programs submenu, and then point to Microsoft Office Outlook 2003 on the Microsoft Office submenu.**

Windows displays the Start menu, the All Programs submenu, and the Microsoft Office submenu (Figure 1-2).

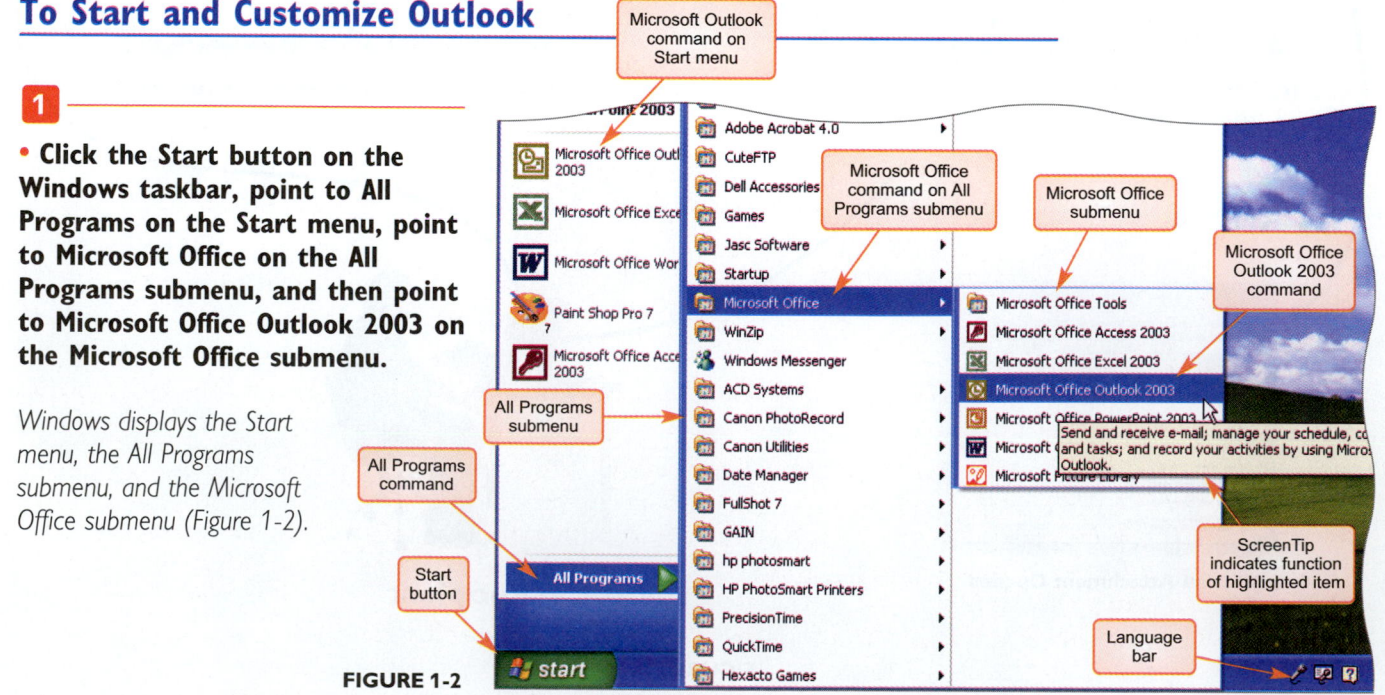

FIGURE 1-2

2

• **Click Microsoft Office Outlook 2003. If necessary, click the Mail button in the Navigation Pane and then click the Inbox folder in the All Mail Folders pane.**

• **If the Inbox – Microsoft Office Outlook window is not maximized, double-click its title bar to maximize it.**

• **Drag the right border of the Inbox message pane to the right so that the Inbox message pane and Reading Pane have the same width.**

• **If the Language bar shows, right-click it and then click Close the Language bar on the shortcut menu.**

Outlook starts and displays the Inbox – Microsoft Outlook window as shown in Figure 1-3.

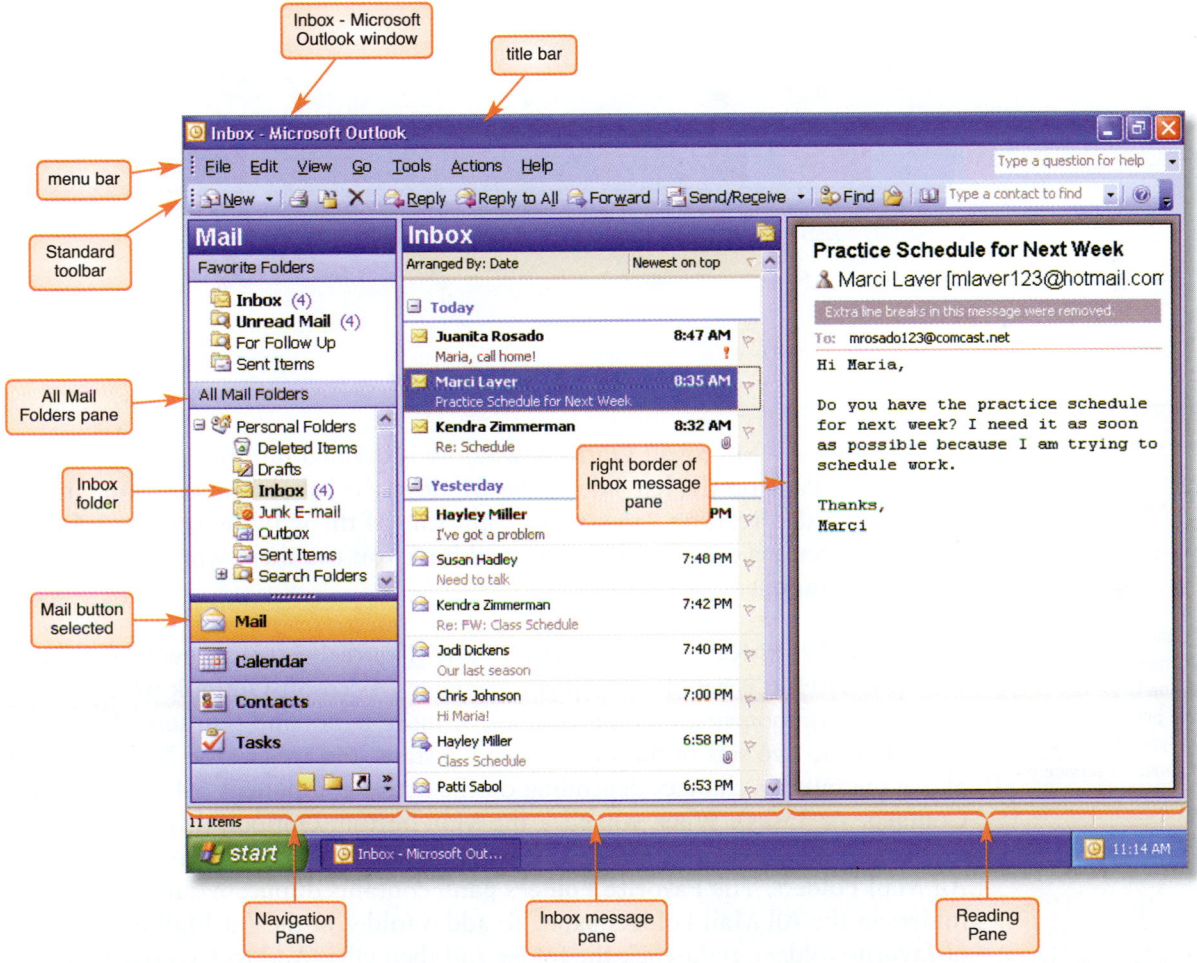

FIGURE 1-3

Other Ways

1. Double-click Microsoft Outlook icon on desktop
2. Click Start button on Windows taskbar, click Microsoft Outlook icon on Start menu

The screen shown in Figure 1-3 illustrates how the Outlook window looks the first time you start Outlook after setting up an e-mail account on most computers. If the Office Speech Recognition software is installed and active on your computer, then when you start Outlook, the Language bar may appear on the screen (Figure 1-2). The **Language bar** allows you to speak commands and dictate text. It usually is located on the right side of the Windows taskbar next to the notification area and changes to include the speech recognition functions available in Outlook. In this book, the Language bar is closed because it takes up computer resources and with the Language bar active, the microphone can be turned on accidentally causing your computer to act in an unstable manner.

The Inbox - Microsoft Outlook Window

The Inbox - Microsoft Outlook window shown in Figure 1-3 on the previous page comprises a number of elements that you will use consistently as you work in the Outlook environment. Figure 1-4 illustrates the Standard toolbar, located below the title bar and the menu bar. The Standard toolbar contains buttons specific to Outlook. The button names indicate their functions. Each button can be clicked to perform a frequently used task, such as creating a new mail message, printing, or sending and receiving mail.

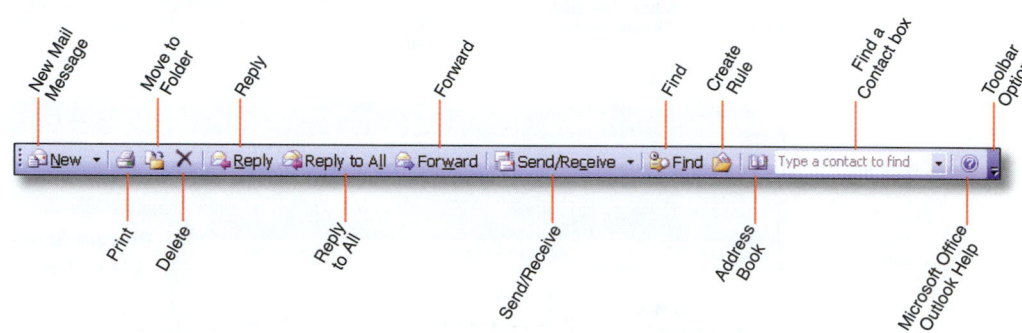

FIGURE 1-4

The Inbox – Microsoft Outlook window is divided into three panes: the Navigation Pane on the left side of the window, the Inbox message pane in the middle, and the Reading Pane on the right side of the window (Figure 1-5a). The following sections describe the panes and how you use them while working within the Mail component.

NAVIGATION PANE The **Navigation Pane** (Figure 1-5a) is a new feature in Outlook 2003. It is set up to help you navigate Microsoft Outlook while using any of the components. It comprises one or more panes and two sets of buttons. Although the two sets of buttons remain constant, the area of the Navigation Pane above the buttons changes depending on the active component (Mail, Calendar, Contacts, or Tasks). When you click the Mail button, Outlook displays Mail in the title bar of the Navigation Pane. This pane includes two panes: Favorite Folders and All Mail Folders. The **Favorite Folders pane** contains duplicate names of your favorite folders in the All Mail Folders pane. To add a folder in the All Mail Folders to the list of favorite folders, right-click the folder and then click Add to Favorite Folders.

Below the Favorite Folders pane, the **All Mail Folders** pane contains a set of folders associated with the communications tools of Outlook Mail (Deleted Items, Drafts, Inbox, Junk E-mail, Outbox, Sent Items, and Search Folders).

The **Deleted Items folder** holds messages that you have deleted. As a safety precaution, you can retrieve deleted messages from the Deleted Items folder if you later decide to keep them. Deleting messages from the Deleted Items folder removes the messages permanently. The **Drafts folder** retains copies of messages that you are not yet ready to send. The **Inbox folder** is the destination for incoming mail. The **Junk E-mail folder** is the destination folder for unwanted messages or messages of an unknown origin. You can customize the settings in Outlook to direct only messages that meet certain criteria to the Inbox folder. Messages not meeting those criteria are sent to the Junk E-mail folder. The **Outbox folder** temporarily holds messages you

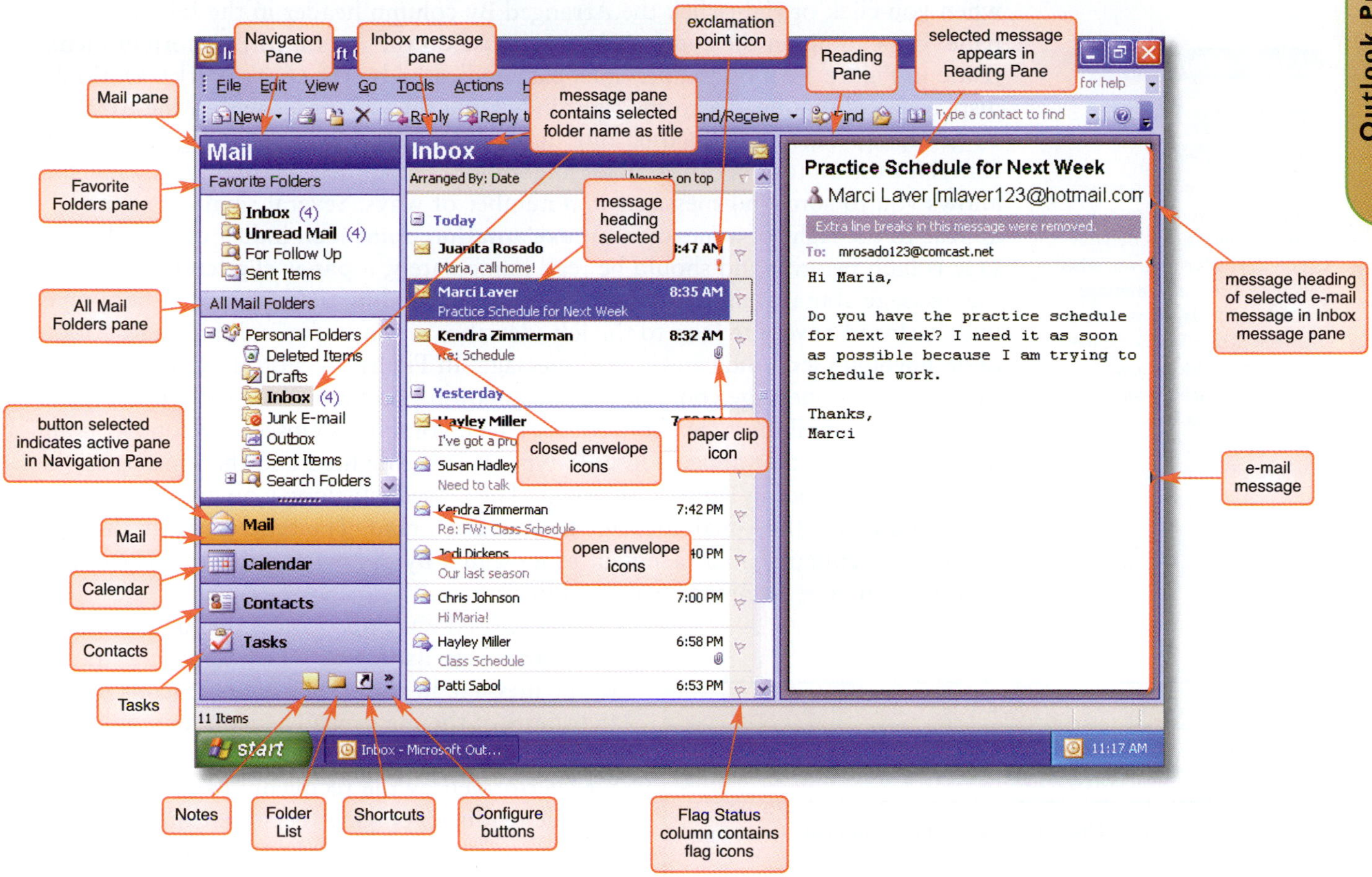

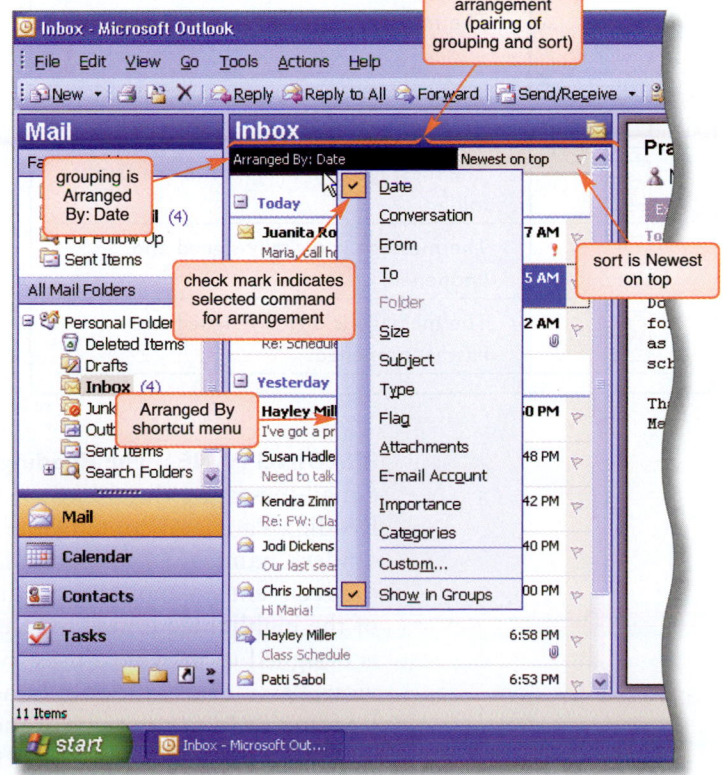

FIGURE 1-5a

send until Outlook delivers the messages. The **Sent Items folder** retains copies of messages that you have sent. The **Search Folders folder** is actually a group of folders that allows you to group your messages easily in one of three ways — messages for follow up, large messages, or unread messages.

Folders can contain e-mail messages, faxes, and files created in other Windows applications. Folders in bold type followed by a number in parentheses (**Inbox** (4)) indicate the number of messages in the folder that are unopened. Other folders may appear on your computer instead of or in addition to the folders shown in Figure 1-5a.

The two sets of buttons at the bottom of the Navigation Pane contain shortcuts to the major components of Outlook (Mail, Calendar, Contacts, Tasks, Notes, Folder List, Shortcuts, and Configure buttons).

MESSAGE PANE The Inbox **message pane** (shown in Figure 1-5a) lists the contents of the folder selected in the All Mail Folders pane. In Figure 1-5a, the Inbox folder is selected. Thus, the message pane lists the e-mails received. Figure 1-5b shows the Arranged By shortcut menu that appears

FIGURE 1-5b

when you click or right-click the Arranged By column header in the Inbox message pane. Depending on the command you choose on the Arranged By shortcut menu (Date in Figure 1-5b on the previous page indicated by the check mark), Outlook displays a column header to the right indicating the sort order within the Arranged By grouping. This predefined pairing of a grouping and a sort (Arranged By: Date/Newest on top) is called an **arrangement**. Using these predefined arrangements allows you to sort your messages in a number of ways. Several small icons may appear to the right of a message: an **exclamation point icon** indicates that the message is high priority and should be read immediately, a **paper clip icon** indicates that the message contains an attachment. A message heading that appears in bold type with a **closed envelope icon** to the left identifies an unread e-mail message. An **open envelope icon** indicates a read message. In Figure 1-5a on the previous page, the first e-mail message contains the exclamation point icon indicating it is urgent. The second e-mail message, from Marci Laver, contains a closed envelope icon and a message heading that appears in bold type. It is highlighted and therefore is displayed in the Reading Pane on the right. The closed envelope icon and bold message heading indicate the e-mail message has not been read. The third message shown in Figure 1-5a contains an attachment as indicated by the paper clip icon. The e-mail messages on your computer may be different.

The closed envelope icon is one of several icons, called **message list icons**, which appear to the left of the message heading. Message list icons indicate the status of the message. The icon may indicate an action that was performed by the sender or one that was performed by the recipient. The actions may include reading, replying to, forwarding, digitally signing, or encrypting a message. Table 1-1 contains a partial list of message list icons and the action performed on the mail message.

Flag icons are displayed when the Flag Status column is visible (Figure 1-5a). To the right of the message header, a **flag icon** indicates the status of the message. Outlook allows you to prioritize messages in a manner you choose using message flags. To set priorities, you right-click a flag icon and then choose colors and notes on the shortcut menu. To view the information about the message flag, point to the flag in the message heading and Outlook will display information about the message in a ScreenTip. Flagging and sorting e-mail messages using the Flag Status column are discussed later in this project.

Table 1-1	Message List Icons and Actions
MESSAGE LIST ICON	**ACTION**
	The message has been opened.
	The message has not been opened.
	The message has been replied to.
	The message has been forwarded.
	The message is in progress in the Drafts folder.
	The message is digitally signed and unopened.
	The message is digitally signed and has been opened.

READING PANE   The **Reading Pane** (Figure 1-5a) contains the text of the selected e-mail message (Marci Laver). The **message header** appears at the top of the Reading Pane and contains the e-mail subject (Practice Schedule for Next Week), the sender's name and/or e-mail address (Marci Laver [mlaver123@hotmail.com]), and the recipient's e-mail address (mrosado123@comcast.net). Outlook displays the text of the highlighted e-mail message below the message header. The new Reading Pane is designed to provide almost twice as much information as the preview pane in previous versions of Outlook. In addition, using the View menu, you can display the Reading Pane to the right of the message pane (vertically), as shown in Figure 1-5a, or you can display it at the bottom of the message pane (horizontally) according to your personal preference.

Note: If you are stepping through this project on a computer and you want your screen to appear the same as the figures in the Mail Component section of this project, then you should ask your instructor to assist you (or see page OUT 61) to import Maria's Inbox from the Data Disk. Once you have imported Maria's Inbox, click the plus sign (+) next to the Inbox folder in the All Mail Folders list, and then select the Maria's Inbox folder. See the inside back cover of this book for instructions for downloading the Data Disk or see you instructor for information about accessing files for this book.

Opening and Reading E-Mail Messages

In Figure 1-5a on page OUT 9, the message headings for each message appear in the message pane. Double-clicking the closed envelope icon in any heading opens the e-mail message and displays the text of the message in a separate window. The following step shows how to open the e-mail message from Marci Laver.

To Open (Read) an E-Mail Message

1

• **Double-click the Marci Laver message heading in the Inbox Message pane (Figure 1-5a) and then maximize the Practice Schedule for Next Week window.**

Outlook displays the maximized Message window (Figure 1-6). The Message window contains a menu bar, Standard toolbar, identifying information about the e-mail message, and message pane. The subject of the e-mail message (Practice Schedule for Next Week) becomes the window title.

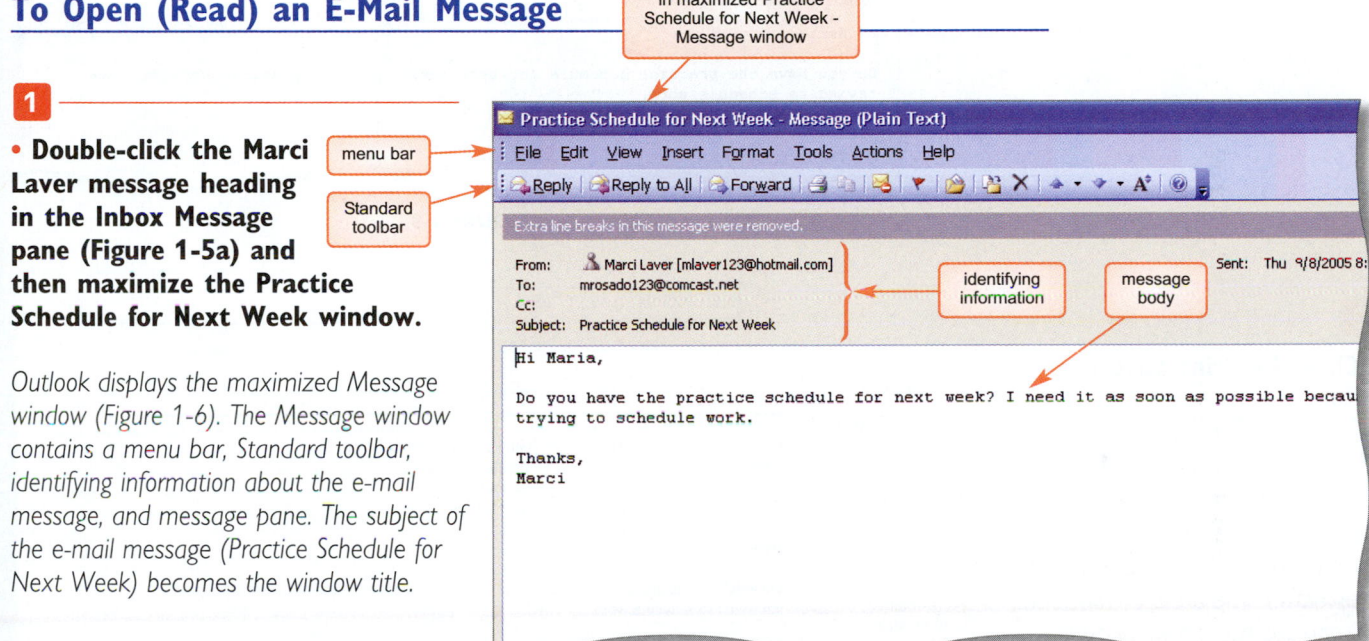

FIGURE 1-6

When you double-click a message heading in the message pane, Outlook displays the message in a separate window, changes the closed envelope icon to an opened envelope icon, and no longer displays the message heading in bold type.

Figure 1-7 illustrates the Standard toolbar in the Message window. The Standard toolbar is located below the title bar and menu bar. The buttons on the Standard toolbar allow you to select easily from a list of the most common responses to an e-mail.

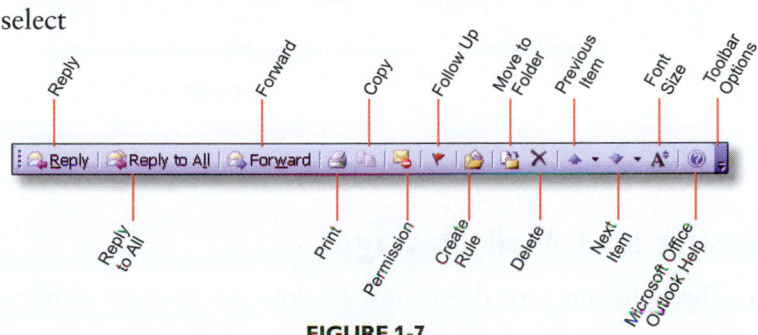

FIGURE 1-7

Other Ways

1. Right-click message heading, click Open on shortcut menu
2. Click message heading, on File menu point to Open, click Selected Items on Open submenu
3. Select message heading, press CRTL+O

Printing an E-Mail Message

You can print the contents of an e-mail message before or after opening the message. The following steps describe how to print an opened e-mail message.

To Print an Opened E-Mail Message

1

• **Point to the Print button on the Standard toolbar (Figure 1-8).**

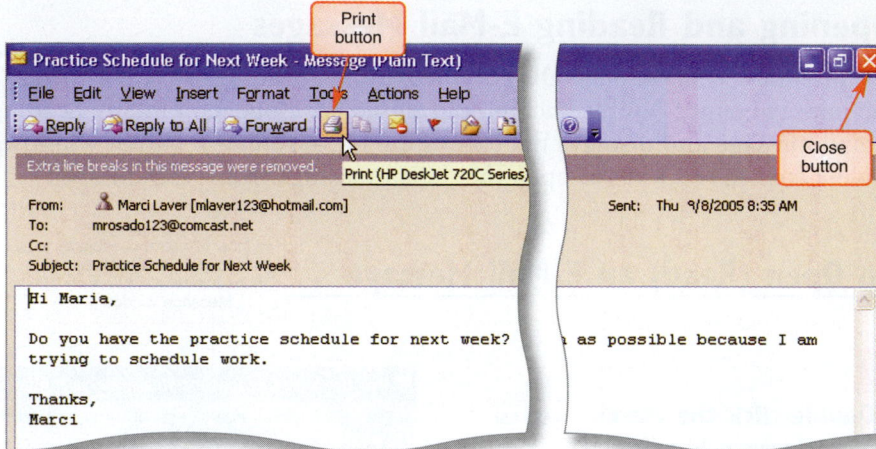

FIGURE 1-8

2

• **Click the Print button.**

Outlook prints the message (Figure 1-9). The printed message consists of a header at the top of the page, the recipient's name (Maria Rosado), and a horizontal line. Below the recipient's name are the From, Sent, To, and Subject entries, and the e-mail message. A footer at the bottom of the page contains the page number. The contents of the header and footer on your printout may be different.

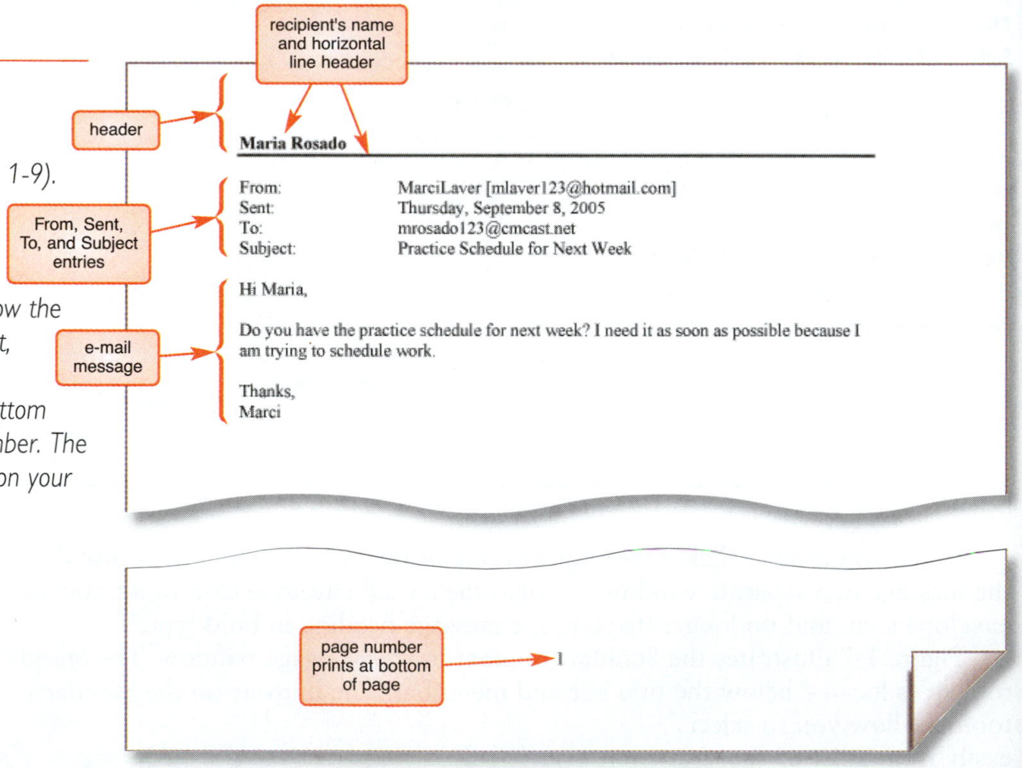

recipient's name and horizontal line header

header

Maria Rosado

From: MarciLaver [mlaver123@hotmail.com]
Sent: Thursday, September 8, 2005
To: mrosado123@cmcast.net
Subject: Practice Schedule for Next Week

From, Sent, To, and Subject entries

Hi Maria,

Do you have the practice schedule for next week? I need it as soon as possible because I am trying to schedule work.

Thanks,
Marci

e-mail message

page number prints at bottom of page

FIGURE 1-9

Other Ways

1. On File menu click Print, click OK button
2. Press ALT+F, press P, press ENTER
3. Press CTRL+P, press ENTER
4. In Voice Command mode, say "Print"

Closing an E-Mail Message

The following step shows how to close the Message window.

To Close an E-Mail Message

1

• **Click the Close button on the title bar (Figure 1-8).**

Outlook closes the Message window and displays the Inbox window (Figure 1-10).

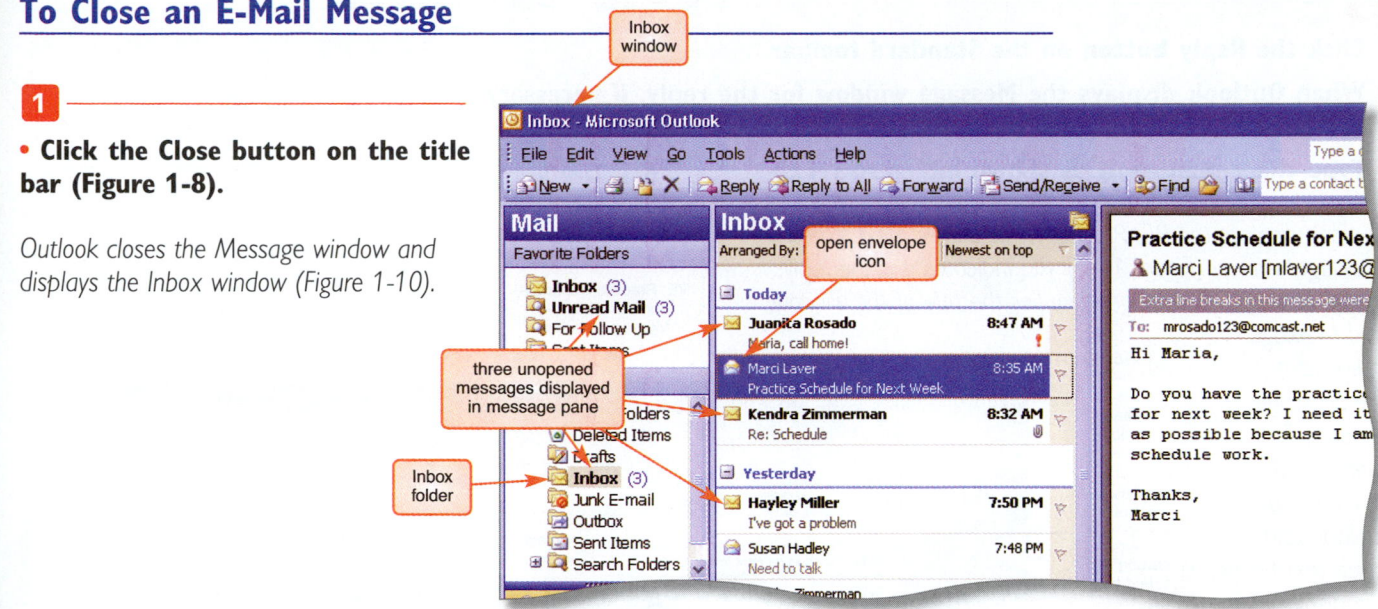

FIGURE 1-10

When you double-click a message heading with a closed envelope icon in the message pane, Outlook displays the corresponding message in the Message window. When you close the Message window, the Marci Laver message heading in the message pane no longer appears in bold type and the closed envelope icon changes to an open envelope icon to indicate the e-mail message has been opened. In addition, the Inbox folder in the All Mail Folders pane (Inbox (3)) indicates three e-mail messages remain unopened.

Replying to an E-Mail Message

The next step is to reply to the e-mail message from Marci Laver. The Reply button on the Standard toolbar in the Inbox window allows you to reply quickly to an e-mail message using the sender's e-mail address as shown in the following steps.

To Reply to an E-Mail Message

1

• **If necessary, click the Marci Laver message heading in the message pane (Figure 1-11).**

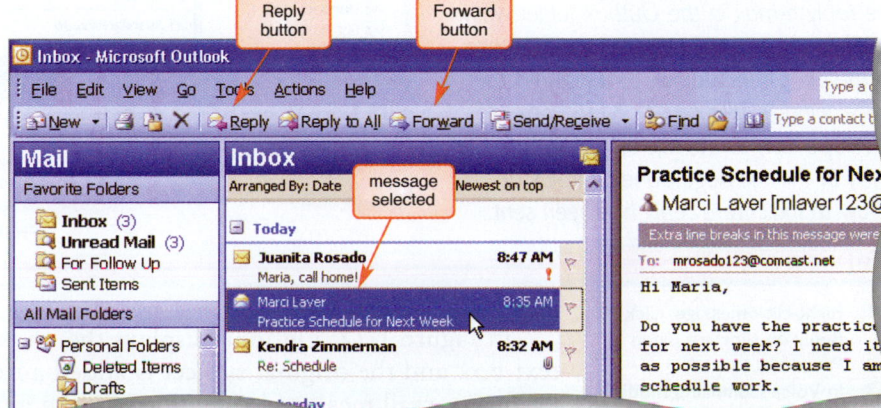

FIGURE 1-11

2

- **Click the Reply button on the Standard toolbar.**
- **When Outlook displays the Message window for the reply, if necessary, double-click the title bar to maximize the window.**
- **Type the e-mail reply as shown in Figure 1-12.**

Outlook displays the RE: Practice Schedule for Next Week - Message window (Figure 1-12). RE: indicates it is the reply, the subject of the message identifies the title of the window, and Message indicates it is the Message window. The menu, E-Mail toolbar, Mail toolbar, and three text boxes are displayed at the top of the window. The RE: entry and subject appear in the window title and Subject text box. The e-mail reply and original message appear in the message body.

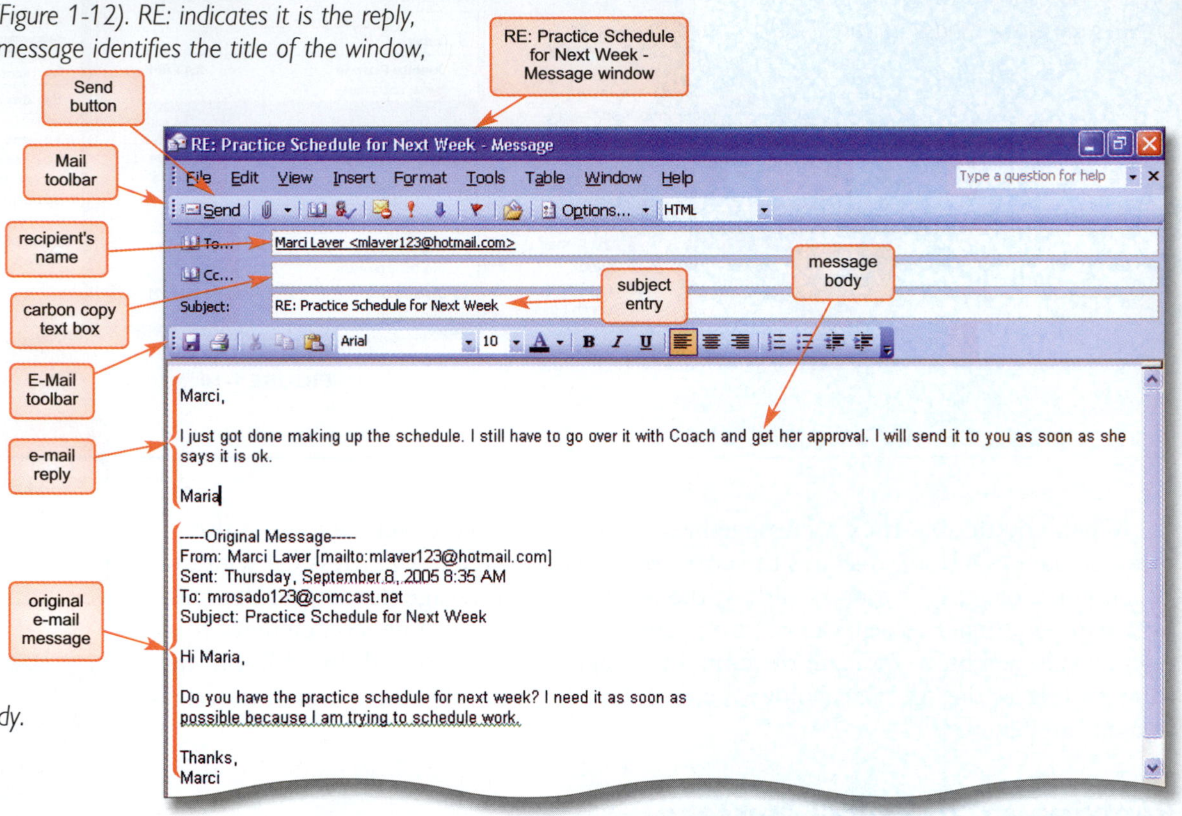

FIGURE 1-12

3

- **Click the Send button.**

Outlook closes the Message window, stores the reply e-mail in the Outbox folder while it sends the message, moves the message to the Sent Items folder, and displays the Inbox window (Figure 1-13). The opened envelope icon to the left of the Marci Laver entry in the message pane contains an arrow to indicate a reply has been sent.

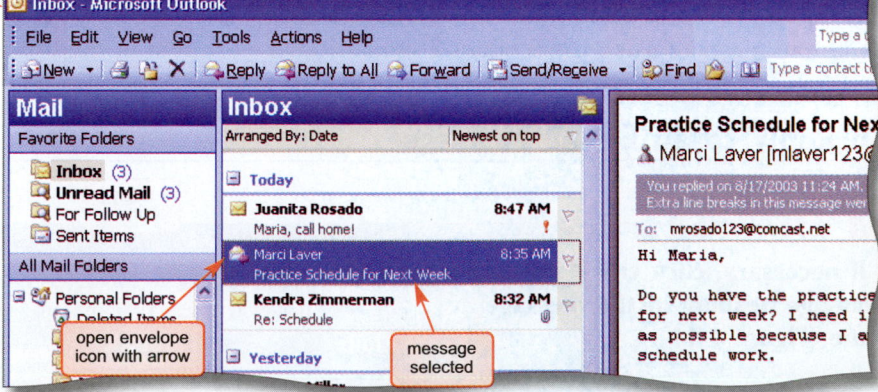

FIGURE 1-13

Other Ways

1. Right-click message, click Reply on shortcut menu
2. Press CTRL+R
3. In Voice Command mode, say "Message, Reply"

In Figure 1-12, Outlook displays the underlined Marci Laver name in the To text box and the original subject is added automatically to the Subject text box. The original e-mail message is identified by the words, Original Message, and the From, Sent, and To entries in the message body. In addition, the window

The E-Mail toolbar and Mail toolbar appear below the menu bar. The **E-Mail toolbar**, shown in Figure 1-14a, allows you to change the appearance, size, and color of text; bold, italicize, or underline text; create a numbered or bulleted list; change paragraph indentation or align text; and create a link or insert a picture in an e-mail message. Figure 1-14b illustrates the **Mail toolbar**, which includes buttons that are useful when replying to a message.

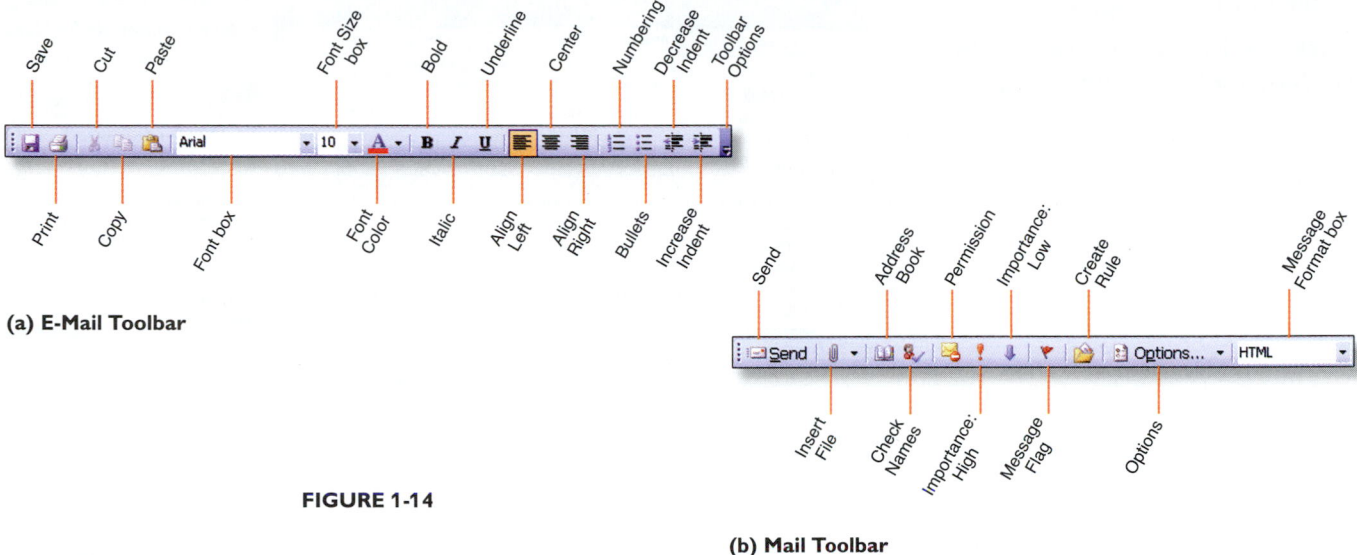

(a) E-Mail Toolbar

FIGURE 1-14

(b) Mail Toolbar

The Message Format box on the right side of the Mail toolbar is important because it allows you to change the format of the message. The options are HTML, Plain Text, and Rich Text and are summarized in Table 1-2. It is recommended that you use HTML format for your messages.

Table 1-2	Message Formats
MESSAGE FORMAT	**DESCRIPTION**
HTML	HTML format is the default format used when you create a message in Outlook. HTML supports the inclusion of pictures and basic formatting, such as text formatting, numbering, bullets, and alignment. HTML is the recommended format for Internet mail because the most popular e-mail programs use it.
Plain Text	Plain Text format is understood by all e-mail programs and is the most likely format to make it through a company's virus-filtering program. Plain text does not support basic formatting, such as bold, italic, colored fonts, or other text formatting. It also does not support pictures displayed directly in the message.
Rich Text	Rich Text Format (RTF) is a Microsoft format that only the latest versions of Microsoft Exchange Client and Outlook understand. RTF supports more formats than HTML or Plain Text, as well as linked objects and pictures.

Forwarding an E-Mail Message

In addition to replying to a message, you also can forward the message to additional recipients with or without adding additional comments as shown in the steps on the next page.

To Forward an E-Mail Message

1

• With the Inbox window active, click the Marci Laver message header in the message pane.

• Click the Forward button on the Standard toolbar (Figure 1-15).

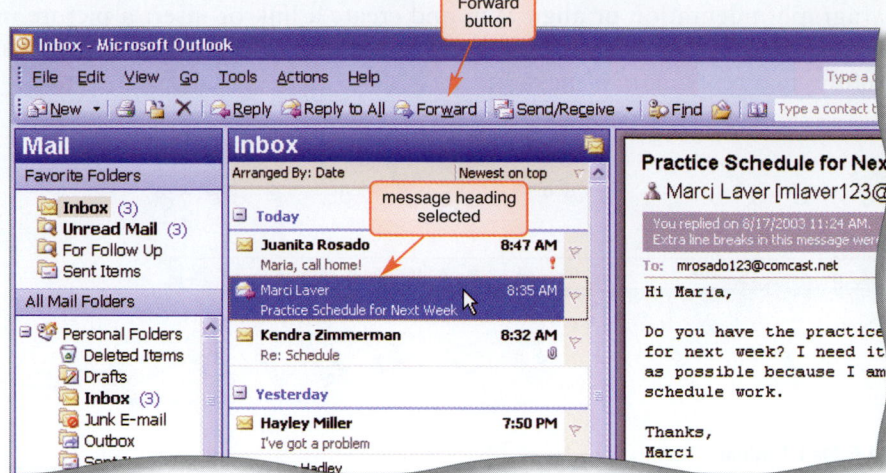

FIGURE 1-15

2

• When Outlook displays the Message window for the forwarded message, type kzimm123@hotmail.com in the To text box as the recipient's e-mail address. (If you are stepping through this task, use an actual e-mail address in the To text box.)

• Enter the forwarding message in the message body as shown in Figure 1-16.

Outlook displays the FW: Practice Schedule for Next Week - Message window as shown in Figure 1-16.

3

• Click the Send button.

Outlook closes the Message window, stores the reply e-mail in the Outbox folder while it sends the message, moves the message to the Sent Items folder, and displays the Inbox window.

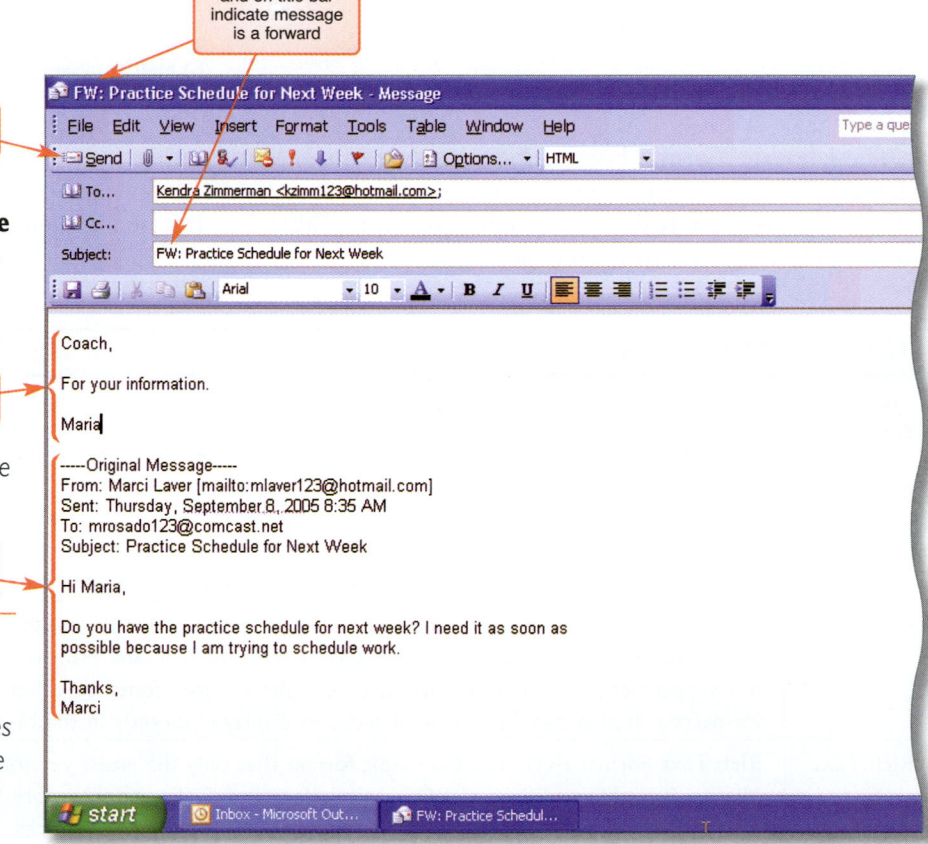

FIGURE 1-16

Other Ways

1. Right-click message heading, click Forward on shortcut menu
2. Press CTRL+F
3. In Voice Command mode, say "Message, Forward"

Deleting an E-Mail Message

After reading and replying to an e-mail message, you may want to delete the original e-mail message from the message list. Deleting a message removes the e-mail message from the Inbox folder. If you do not delete unwanted messages, large numbers of messages in the Inbox folder make it difficult to find and read new messages and wastes disk space. The following steps show how to delete the e-mail message from Marci Laver.

To Delete an E-Mail Message

1

• **With the Inbox window active, click the Marci Laver message heading in the message pane.**

The highlighted Marci Laver message heading appears in the message pane and the e-mail message appears in the Reading Pane (Figure 1-17). The open envelope icon contains an arrow to indicate you have replied to the message.

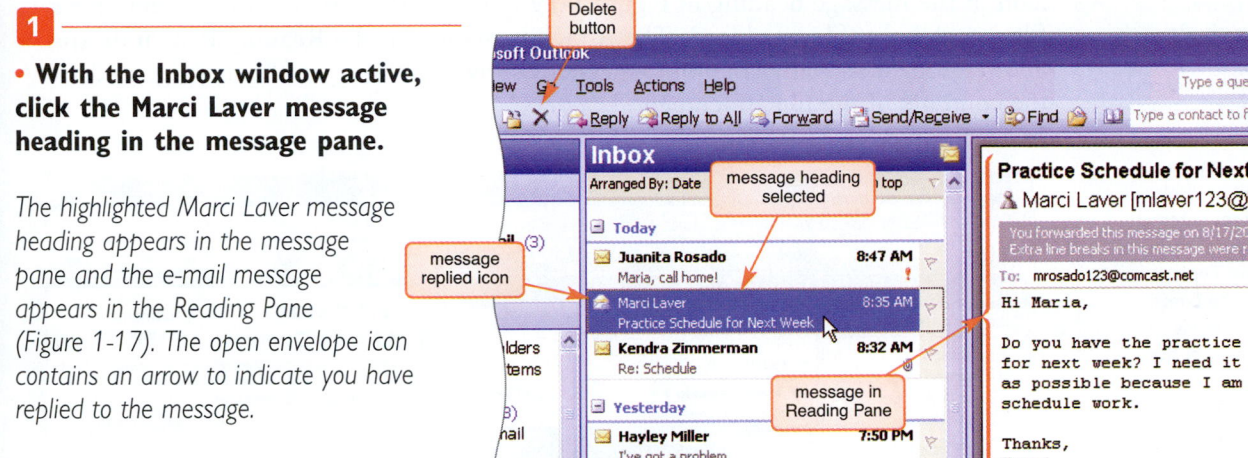

FIGURE 1-17

2

• **Click the Delete button on the Standard toolbar.**

Outlook moves the Marci Laver e-mail message from the Inbox folder to the Deleted Items folder and removes the e-mail entry from the message pane (Figure 1-18).

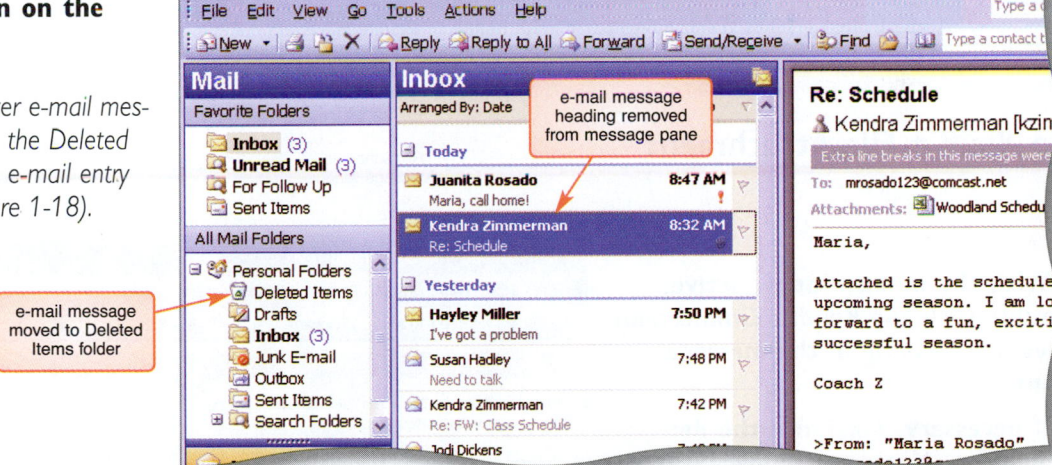

FIGURE 1-18

As you delete messages from the Inbox or Sent Items folders, the number of messages in the Deleted Items folder increases. To delete an e-mail message from the Deleted Items folder, click the Deleted Items folder icon in the All Mail Folders pane, highlight the message in the Deleted Items message pane, click the Delete button, and then click the Yes button in the Microsoft Office Outlook dialog box. You also can delete multiple messages at one time by clicking the first message and then holding

Other Ways

1. Drag e-mail message to Deleted Items folder in All Mail Folders pane
2. On Edit menu click Delete
3. Press CTRL+D
4. Click e-mail message, press DELETE key
5. In Voice Command mode, say "Edit, Delete"

down the SHIFT key or CTRL key to click one or more messages. Use the SHIFT key to select a list of adjacent messages. Use the CTRL key to select nonadjacent messages. Once the messages are selected, click the Delete button on the Standard toolbar or press the DELETE key.

Viewing a File Attachment

The message from Kendra Zimmerman contains a file attachment. The paper clip icon in the message heading in Figure 1-19 indicates the e-mail message contains a file attachment (file or object). The Attachments line in the Reading Pane indicates an attachment as well. The following steps show how to open the message and view the contents of the file attachment.

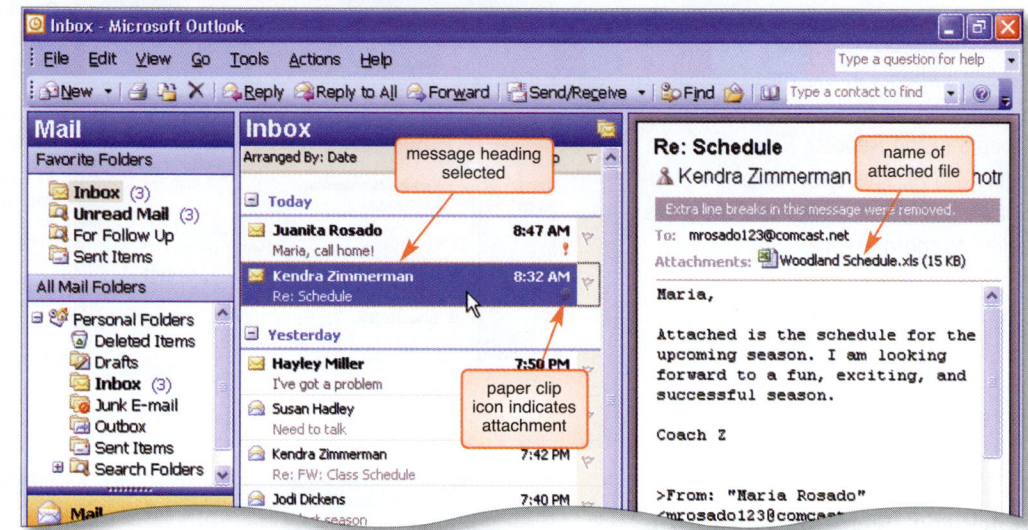

FIGURE 1-19

To View a File Attachment

1

• **With the Inbox window active, double-click the Kendra Zimmerman message heading in the message pane.**

• **If necessary, maximize the Re: Schedule - Message window.**

Outlook displays the Message window (Figure 1-20). The Attachments entry, containing an Excel icon, the file name (Woodland Schedule.xls), and the file size (15 KB) appear above the message body on the Attachments line.

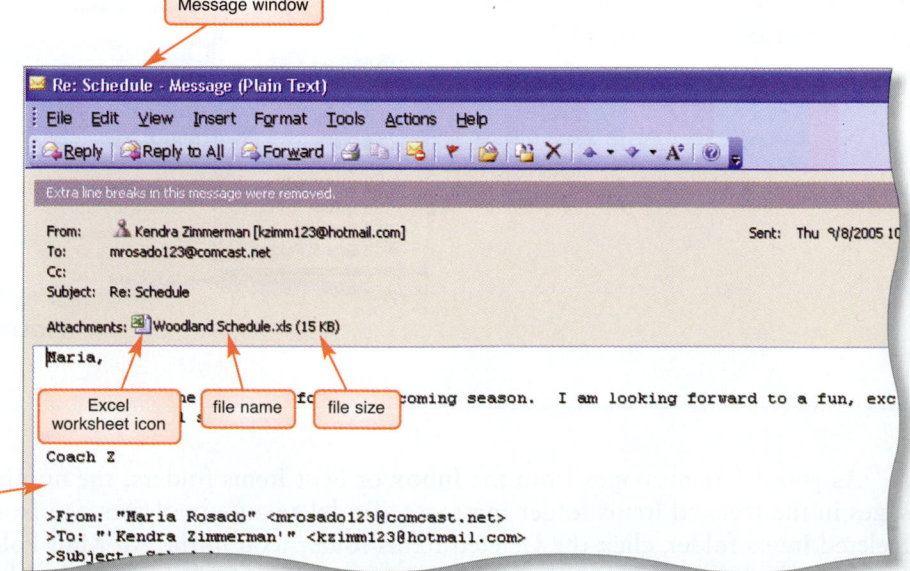

FIGURE 1-20

2

• **Double-click the Woodland Schedule.xls icon on the Attachments line.**

• **If Outlook displays the Opening Mail Attachment dialog box, click the Open button.**

The Microsoft Excel - Woodland Schedule window containing the schedule appears (Figure 1-21).

3

• **After viewing the worksheet, click the Close button on the right side of the title bar in the Excel window.**

• **Click the Close button in Message window.**

The Excel window and Message window close.

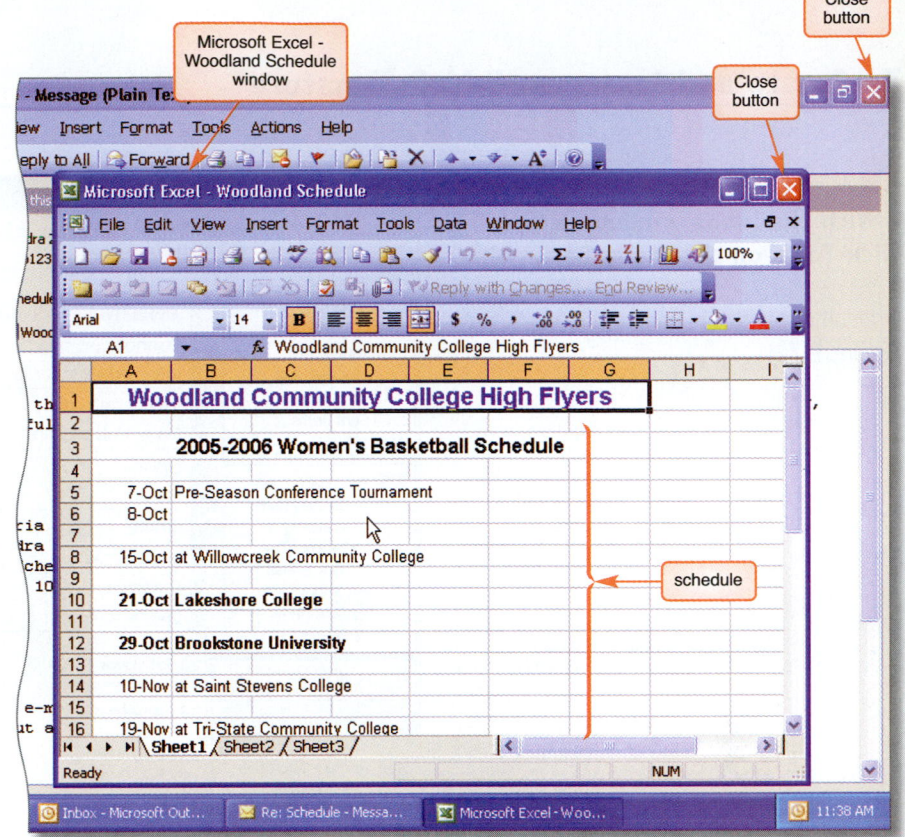

FIGURE 1-21

File attachments can be any type of file from worksheets to documents to presentations to pictures. Files can be viewed only if your computer has the appropriate software. For example, if your computer does not have Excel installed, then you cannot view an Excel file attachment. The Opening Mail Attachment dialog box in Step 2 gives you the option of viewing the attachment as you read the e-mail or saving it on disk to view at another time.

Creating an E-Mail Signature

An **e-mail signature** is a unique message automatically added to the end of an outgoing e-mail message. An e-mail signature can be much more than adding your name to the end of a message. It can consist of text and/or pictures. The type of signature you add may depend on the recipient of the message. For messages to family and friends, a first name may be sufficient, while messages to business contacts may include your full name, address, telephone number, and other business information. Outlook allows you to create a different signature for each e-mail account created in Outlook. The steps on the next page create and insert an e-mail signature in an e-mail message.

Other Ways

1. Double-click file attachment name in Reading Pane
2. Click Save button in Opening Mail Attachments dialog box to save attachment on disk
3. On File menu point to Save Attachments to save attachment on disk

To Create and Insert an E-Mail Signature

1

• **With the Inbox window active, click Tools on the menu bar.**

Outlook displays the Tools menu (Figure 1-22).

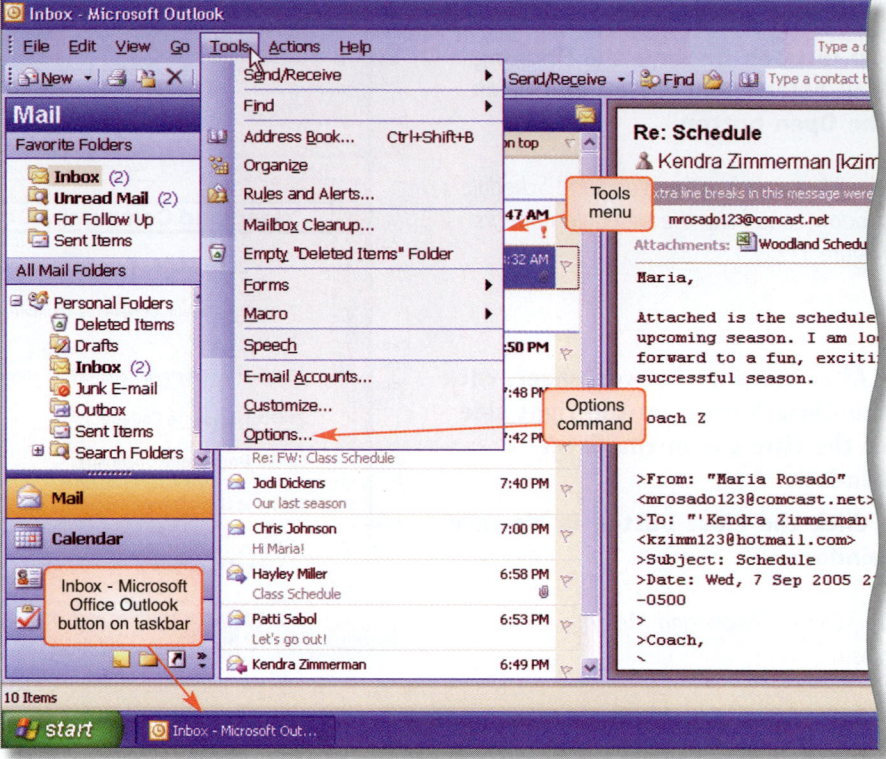

FIGURE 1-22

2

• **Click Options on the Tools menu.**

• **When Outlook displays the Options dialog box, click the Mail Format tab.**

Outlook displays the Mail Format sheet in the Options dialog box (Figure 1-23).

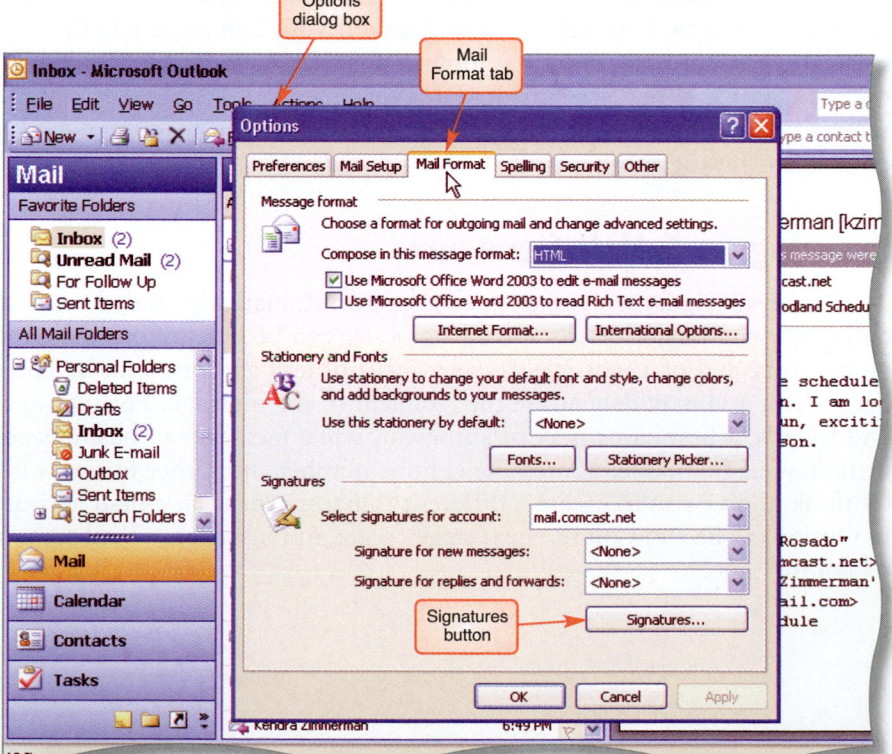

FIGURE 1-23

3

• **Click the Signatures button.**

Outlook displays the Create Signature dialog box (Figure 1-24).

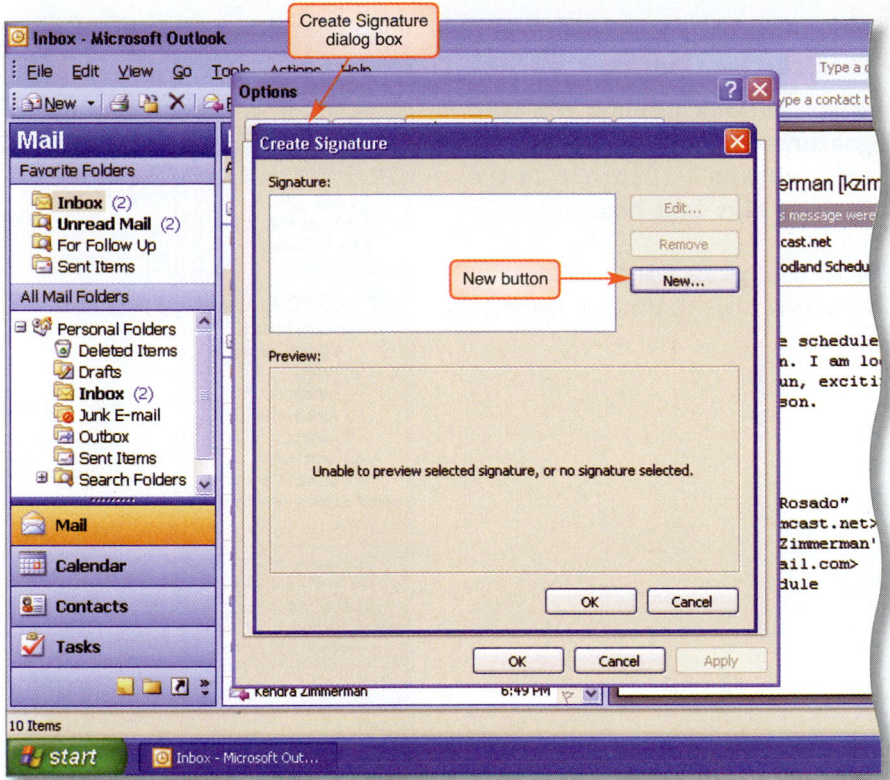

FIGURE 1-24

4

• **Click the New button.**
• **When Outlook displays the Create New Signature dialog box, type** Team **in the Enter a name for your new signature text box.**

Outlook displays the Create New Signature dialog box. Team is the name of the signature being created (Figure 1-25).

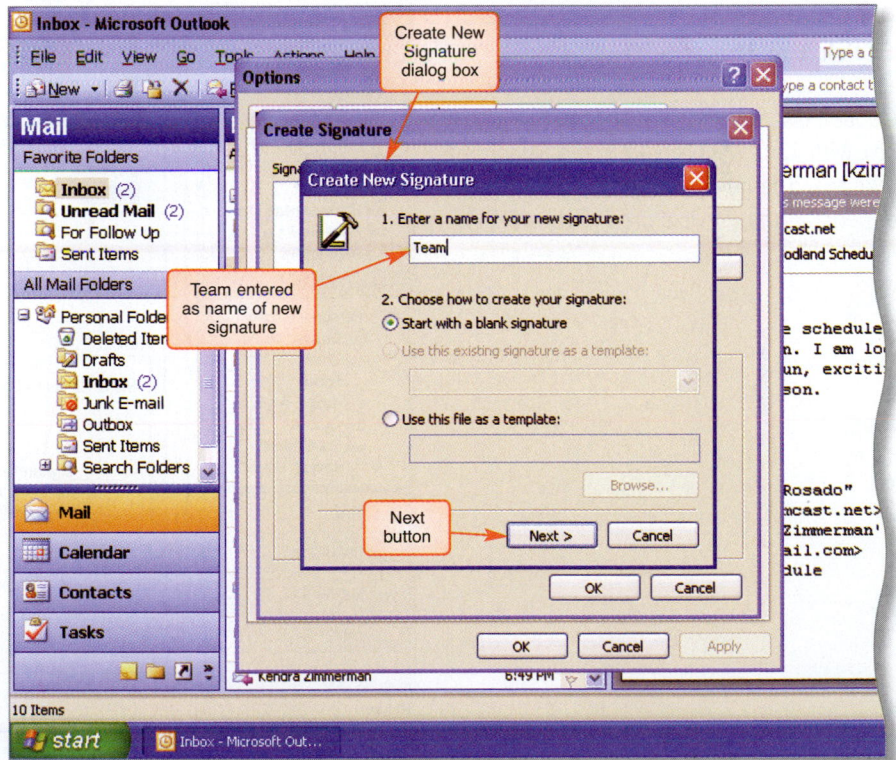

FIGURE 1-25

5

- **Click the Next button.**

- **When Outlook displays the Edit Signature – [Team] dialog box, type** `Maria Rosado - Captain` **in the Signature text text box.**

Outlook displays the Edit Signature – [Team] dialog box as shown in Figure 1-26.

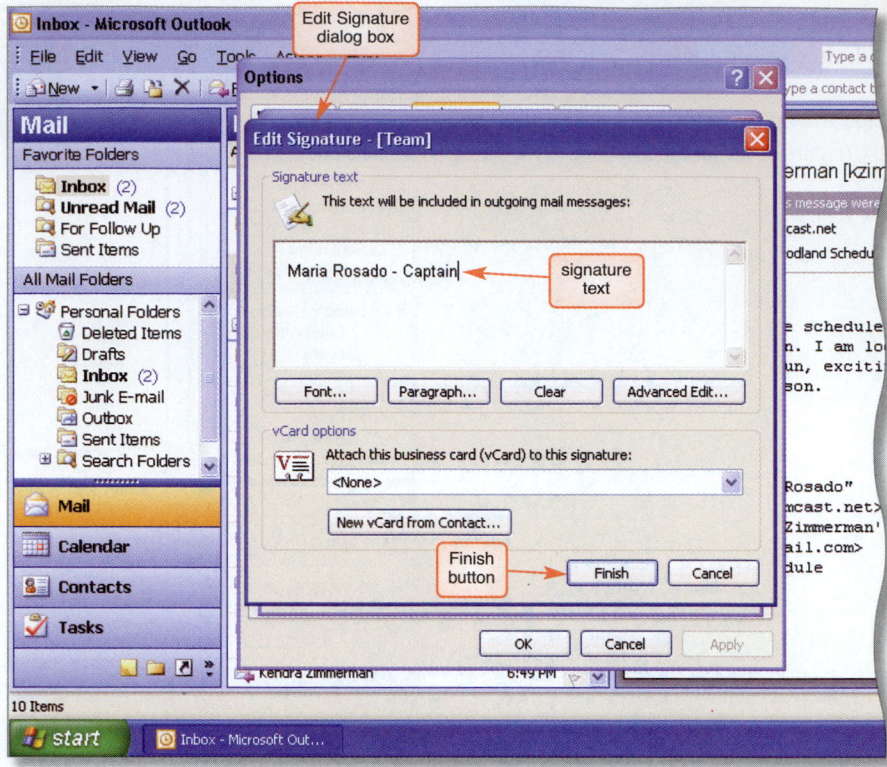

FIGURE 1-26

6

- **Click the Finish button.**

Outlook displays the Create Signature dialog box with Team highlighted in the Signature text box. The newly created signature appears in the Preview area (Figure 1-27).

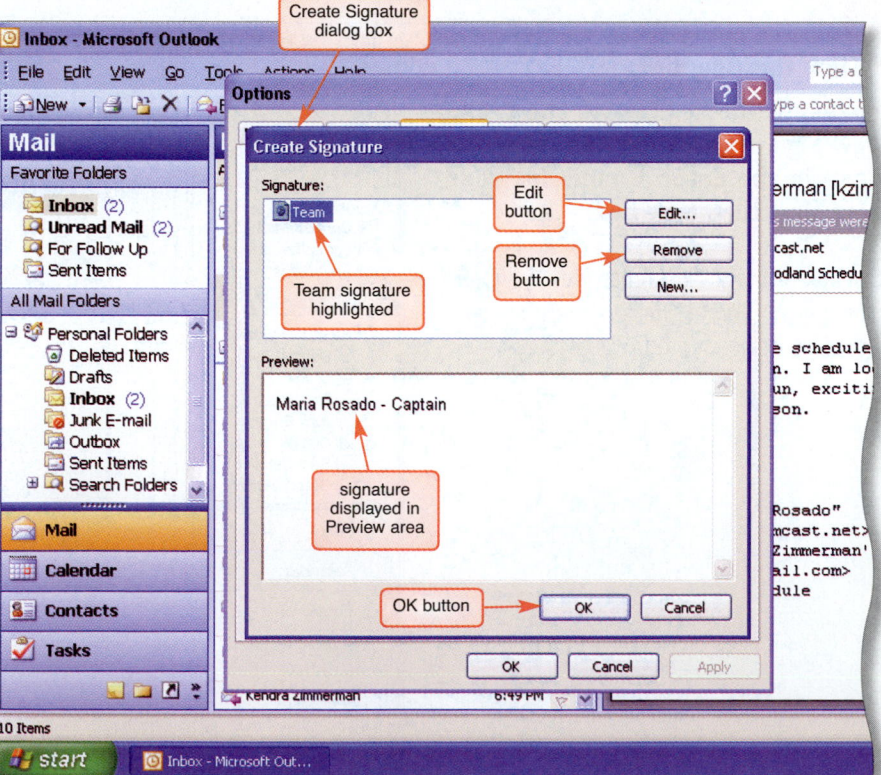

FIGURE 1-27

7

• Click the OK button.

• In the Signatures area of the Options dialog box, select the appropriate e-mail account (if you are stepping through this project, ask your instructor for the appropriate e-mail account).

• If necessary, select Team in the Signature for new messages box and the Signature for replies and forwards box.

Outlook displays the Options dialog box as shown in Figure 1-28. Team is selected as the signature for new messages and for replies and forwards.

8

• Click the OK button.

The signature settings are applied.

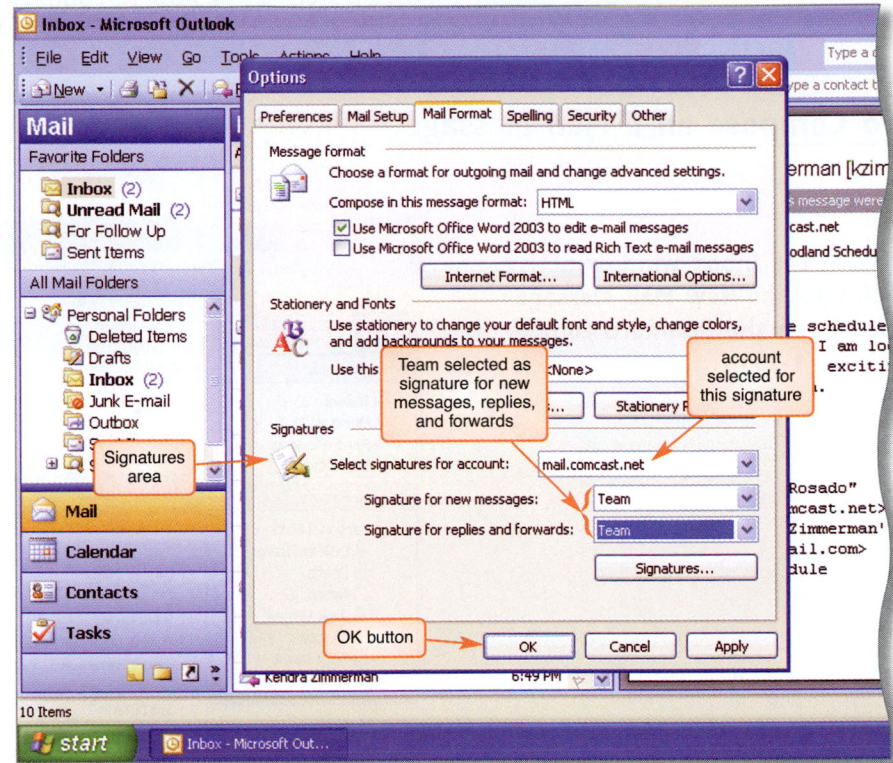

FIGURE 1-28

Other Ways

1. Press ALT+T, press O
2. In Voice Command mode, say "Tools, Options"

The signature Maria Rosado – Captain now will be inserted automatically in all new messages as well as reply messages and forward messages. Signatures can be modified or removed at anytime by clicking the Edit or Remove buttons in the Create Signature dialog box (Figure 1-27). You can add a variety of signatures to Outlook for different purposes that include any specific characteristics that you desire.

Creating Unique E-Mail Signatures for Multiple Accounts

You can create unique signatures for different accounts by adding new signatures and selecting a different account in the Signatures area of the Options dialog box (Figure 1-28). For one account, you may want to insert a personal signature. In another, you may want to include a business or professional signature with contact and other information.

Composing a New Mail Message

In addition to opening and reading, replying to, forwarding, and deleting e-mail messages, you will have many occasions to compose and send new e-mail messages. When you compose an e-mail message, you must know the e-mail address of the recipient of the message, enter a brief one-line subject that identifies the purpose or contents of the message, and then type the message in the message body.

You also can **format** an e-mail message to enhance the appearance of the message. Formatting attributes include changing the style, size, and color of the text in the document. As indicated earlier, Outlook allows you to choose from three formats: HTML, Plain Text, or Rich Text.

More About

E-Mail Signatures

Outlook allows you to add signatures to your e-mail messages that you create in Word 2003. Some of the advantages to creating them in Word is the ability to insert pictures and hyperlinks into the signature.

The following steps show how to compose a formatted e-mail message to Kendra Zimmerman with an attachment.

To Compose an E-Mail Message

1

• **With the Inbox window active, point to the New Mail Message button on the Standard toolbar (Figure 1-29).**

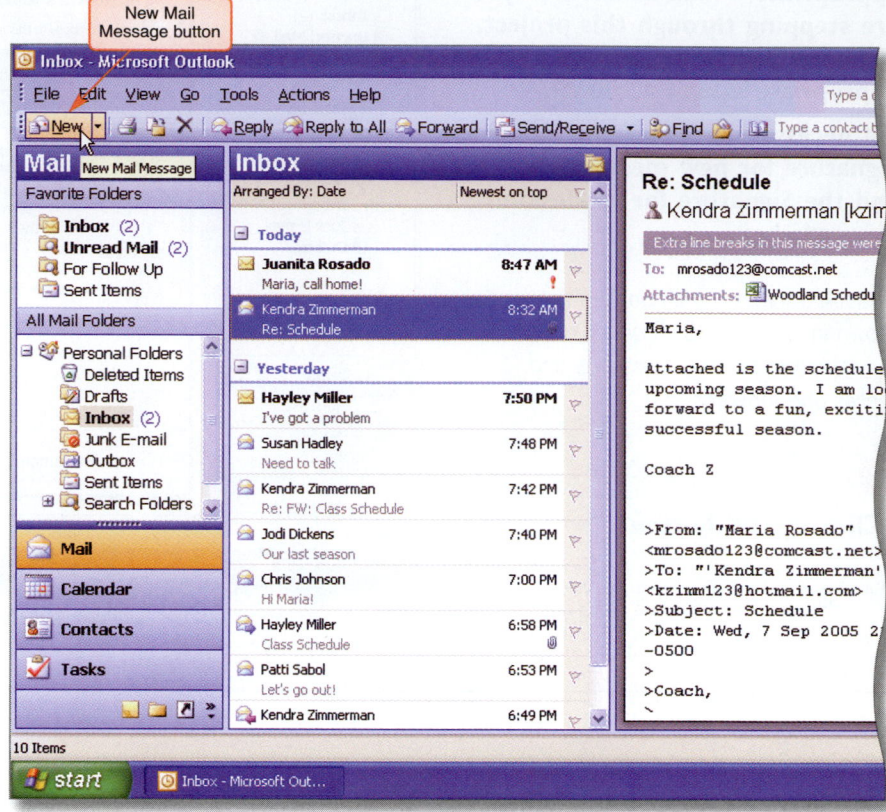

FIGURE 1-29

2

• **Click the New Mail Message button.**

Outlook displays the Untitled - Message window with the signature Maria Rosado - Captain (Figure 1-30). The Message window contains a menu bar, two toolbars, three text boxes, and the message body. Outlook positions the insertion point in the To text box.

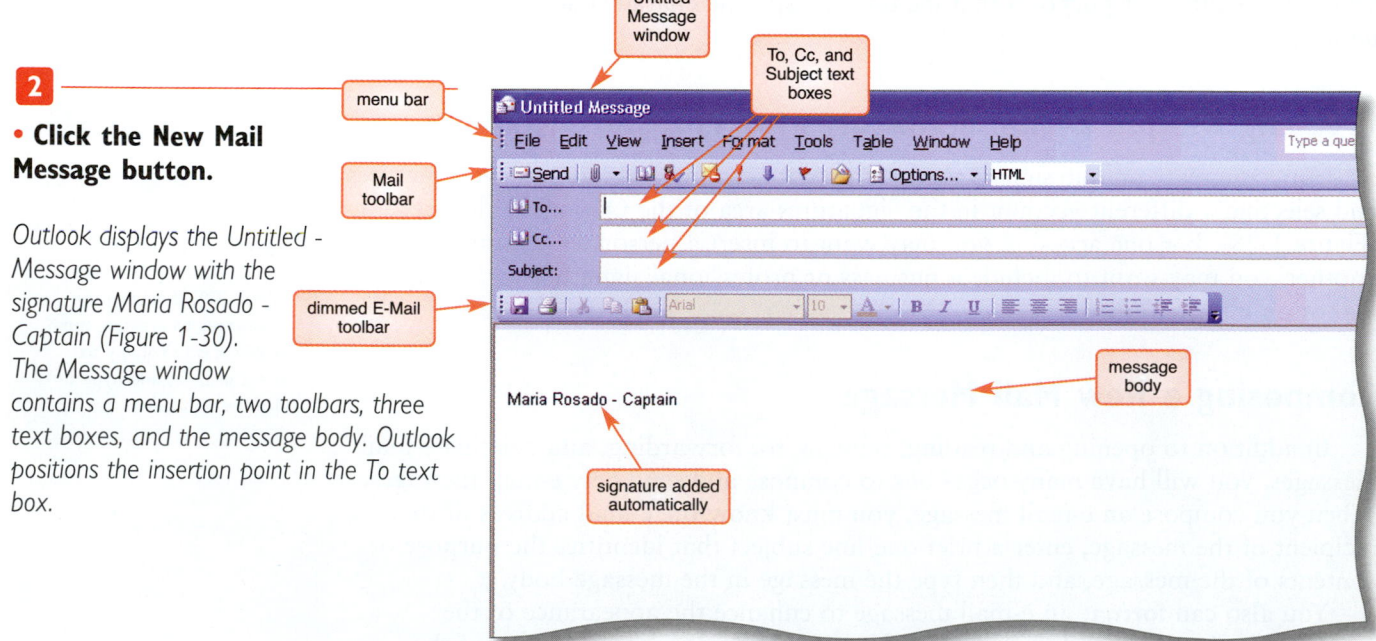

FIGURE 1-30

3

• **Type** kzimm123@hotmail.com **in the To text box, click the Subject text box, and then type** Updated Practice Schedule **in the Subject text box.**

• **Press the TAB key.**

The destination e-mail address appears in the To text box, and the subject of the message appears in the Subject text box (Figure 1-31). The title bar of the Untitled Message window now appears with the subject of the e-mail message (Updated Practice Schedule). The insertion point appears in the message body.

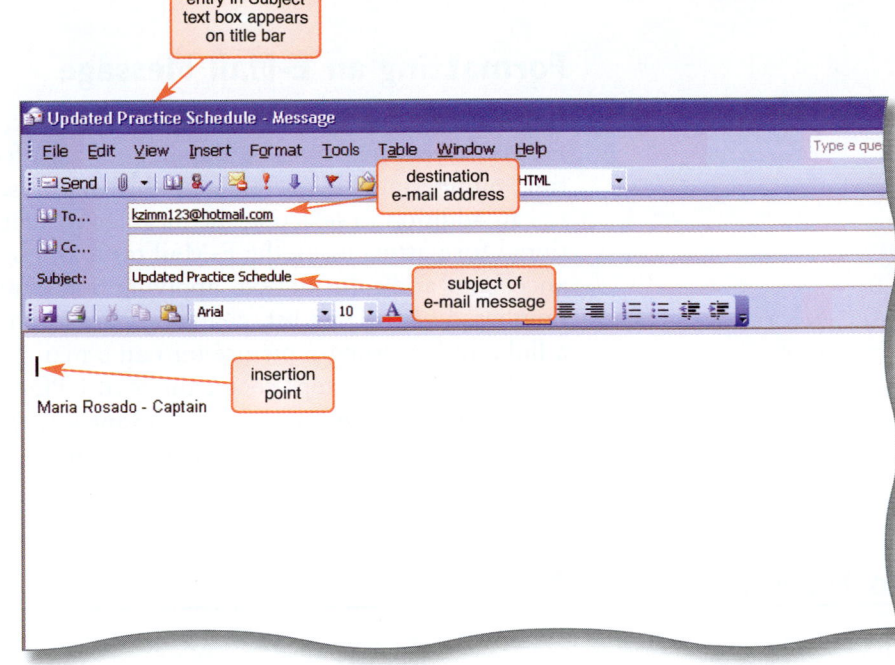

FIGURE 1-31

4

• **Type the e-mail message shown in Figure 1-32.**

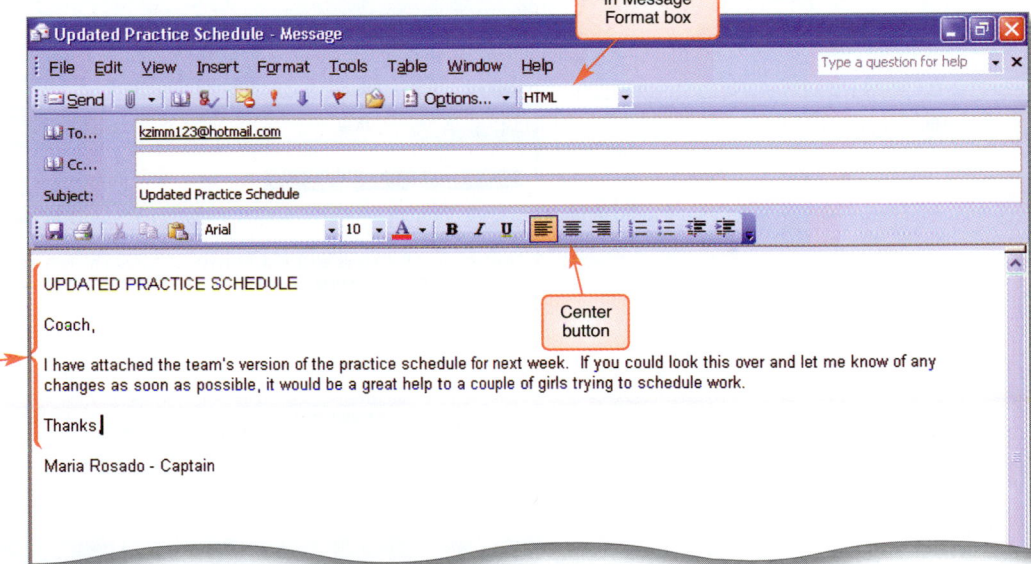

FIGURE 1-32

When you enter a message, you can use the DELETE key and BACKSPACE key to correct errors. Before pressing the DELETE key, select words, sentences, or paragraphs using the mouse. If you are using Microsoft Word as your e-mail editor and you have the appropriate Spelling options selected, then the spell checker will flag the misspelled words with a red wavy underline. Furthermore, the message will be spell checked before it is sent. To set the Spelling options, activate the Inbox window, click Tools on the menu bar, click Options on the Tools menu, and then click the Spelling tab in the Options dialog box.

Formatting an E-Mail Message

When you compose a message in Outlook, the default message format is **HTML** (**Hypertext Markup Language**). This format allows you to do text formatting, numbering, bullets, alignment, signatures, and linking to Web pages.

In addition to selecting the message format, Outlook allows you to apply additional formatting using the E-Mail toolbar. Formatting includes changing the appearance, size, and color of text; applying bold, italic, and underlines to text; creating a numbered or bulleted list, changing paragraph indentation or aligning text; creating a link, and inserting a picture into an e-mail message.

The following steps center the text, UPDATED PRACTICE SCHEDULE, and changes its font size to 36-point. A **font size** is measured in points. A **point** is equal to 1/72 of one inch in height. Thus, a font size of 36 points is approximately one-half inch in height.

To Format an E-Mail Message

1

• **Drag to select the text, UPDATED PRACTICE SCHEDULE, in the message body.**

The text, UPDATED PRACTICE SCHEDULE, is selected (Figure 1-33).

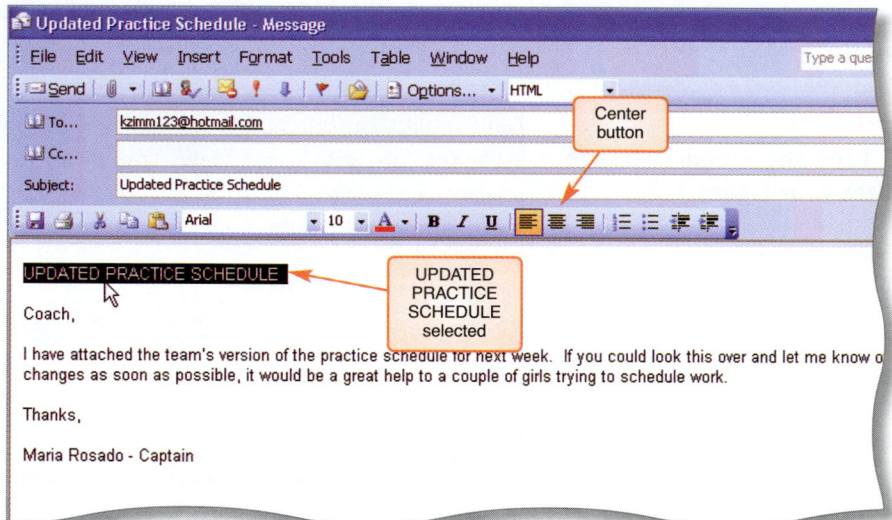

FIGURE 1-33

2

• **Click the Center button on the E-Mail toolbar.**

Outlook centers the text, UPDATED PRACTICE SCHEDULE, on the first line of the e-mail message (Figure 1-34). The current font size is the default 10-point.

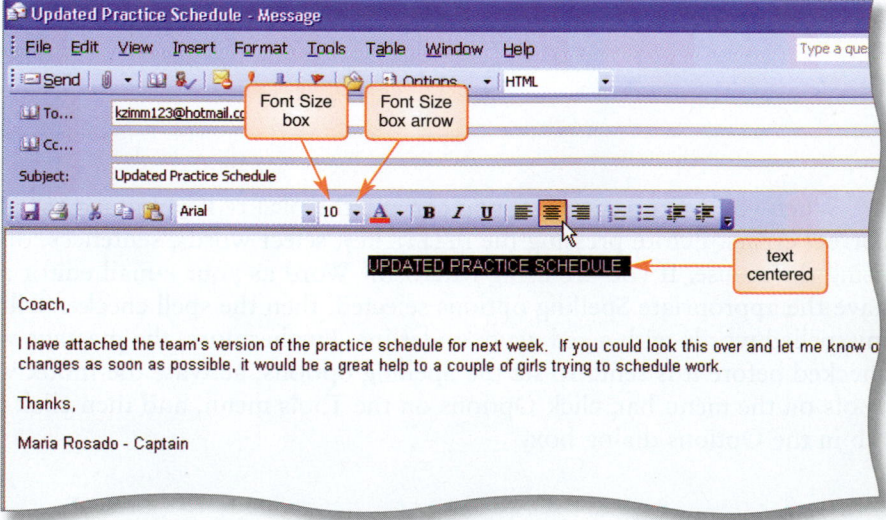

FIGURE 1-34

3

• **Click the Font Size box arrow on the E-Mail toolbar.**

Outlook displays the Font Size list (Figure 1-35).

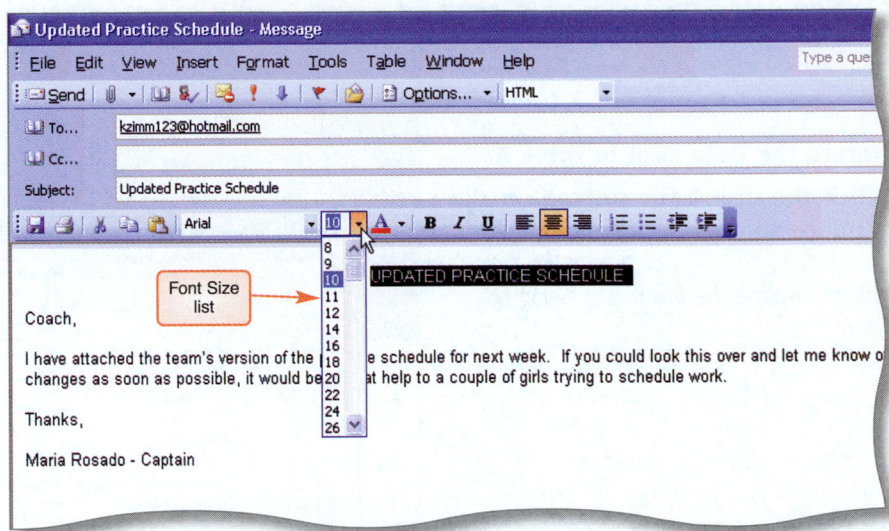

FIGURE 1-35

4

• **Scroll down the Font Size list, click 36, and then click the selected text to remove the selection.**

Outlook displays the text, UPDATED PRACTICE SCHEDULE, in 36-point font size (Figure 1-36).

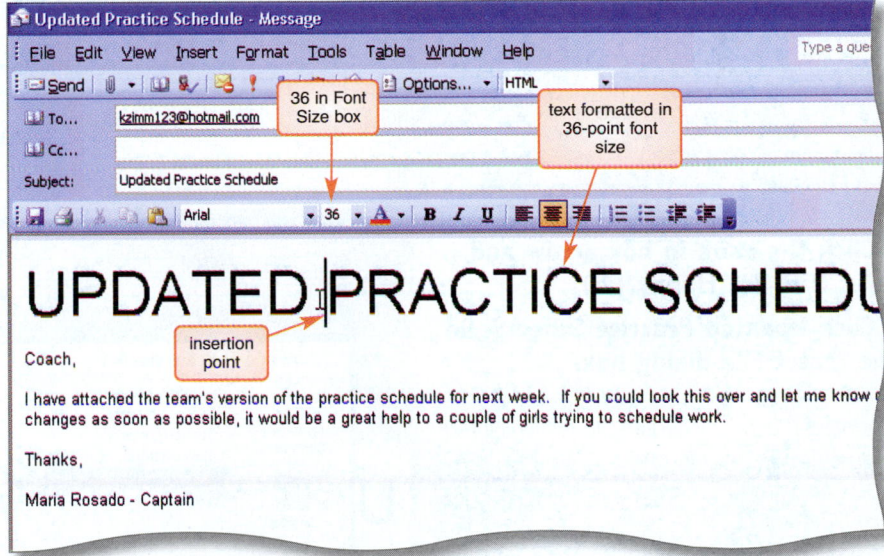

FIGURE 1-36

You do not have to select the text UPDATED PRACTICE SCHEDULE to center it on the line because centering is a paragraph format. All you have to do is click within the text, and then click the Center button on the E-Mail toolbar. Font size, however, is a character format; therefore, you must select all the characters in the text before you select the new font size.

Attaching a File to an E-Mail Message

In some situations, a simple e-mail message is not sufficient to get the required information to the recipient. In these cases, you may want to attach a file to your e-mail message. Outlook allows you to attach almost any kind of file to your message. You may need to send a Word document, an Excel worksheet, a picture, or any number of file types. The steps on the next page show how to attach the Updated Practice Schedule.xls file to the e-mail message.

More About

File Attachments

Outlook allows other ways for a file to be inserted into a message. You can drag a file from any folder on your computer to a message, or you can copy and paste a file into a message as an attachment by right-clicking the file, clicking Copy on the shortcut menu, then in the Outlook message, clicking Paste on the Edit menu.

To Attach a File to an E-Mail Message

1

• **Insert the Data Disk in drive A.**

• **Click the Insert File button on the Standard toolbar.**

Outlook displays the Insert File dialog box (Figure 1-37).

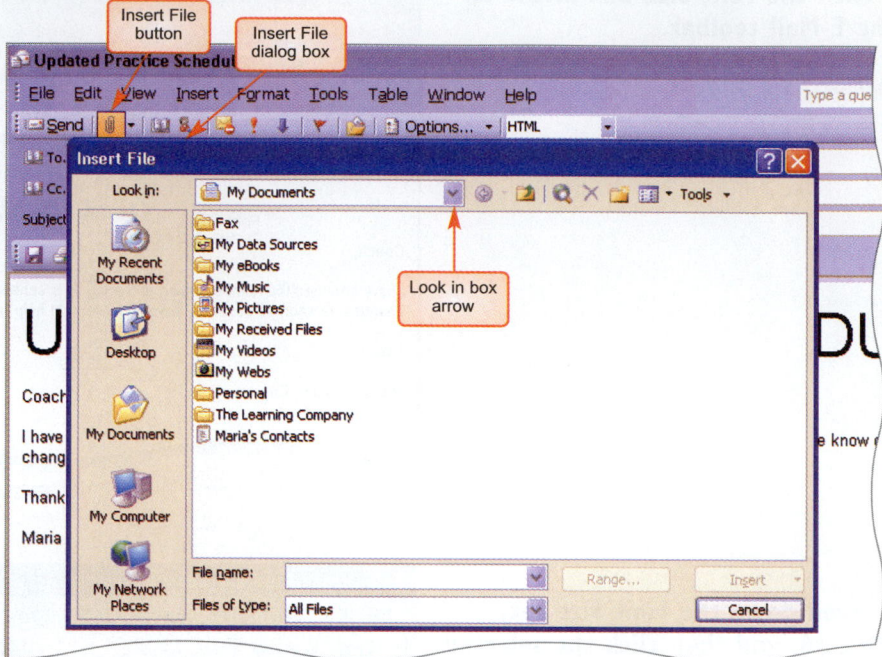

FIGURE 1-37

2

• **Click the Look in box arrow and then click 3½ Floppy (A:).**

• **Click Updated Practice Schedule in the Insert File dialog box.**

Updated Practice Schedule file is highlighted (Figure 1-38).

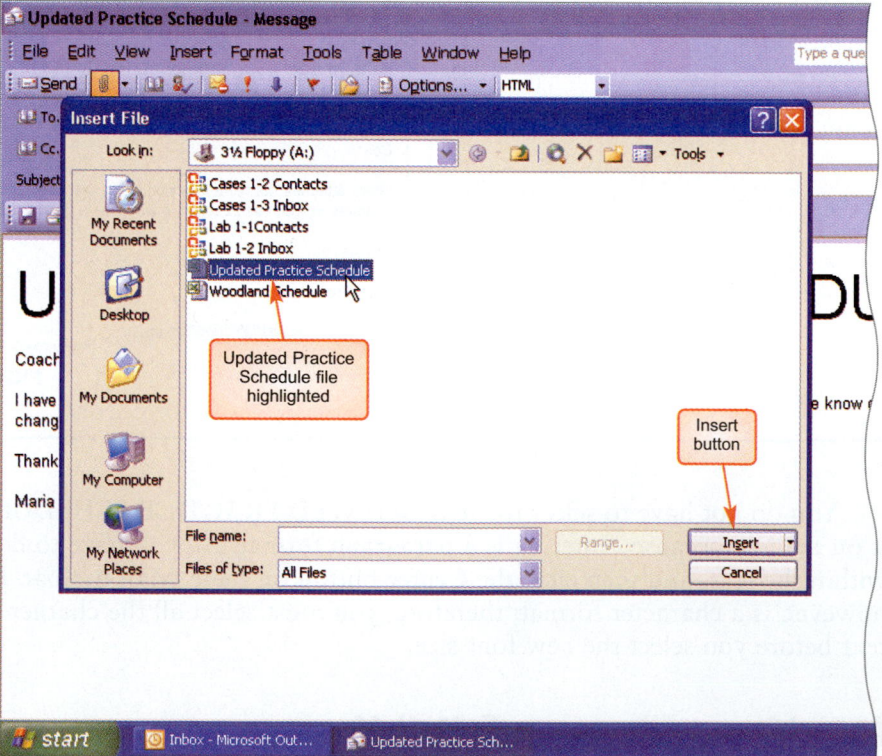

FIGURE 1-38

3

• **Click the Insert button in the Insert File dialog box.**

Outlook displays the name of the file, Updated Practice Schedule.xls, in the Attachment box, along with an Excel icon and file size (Figure 1-39).

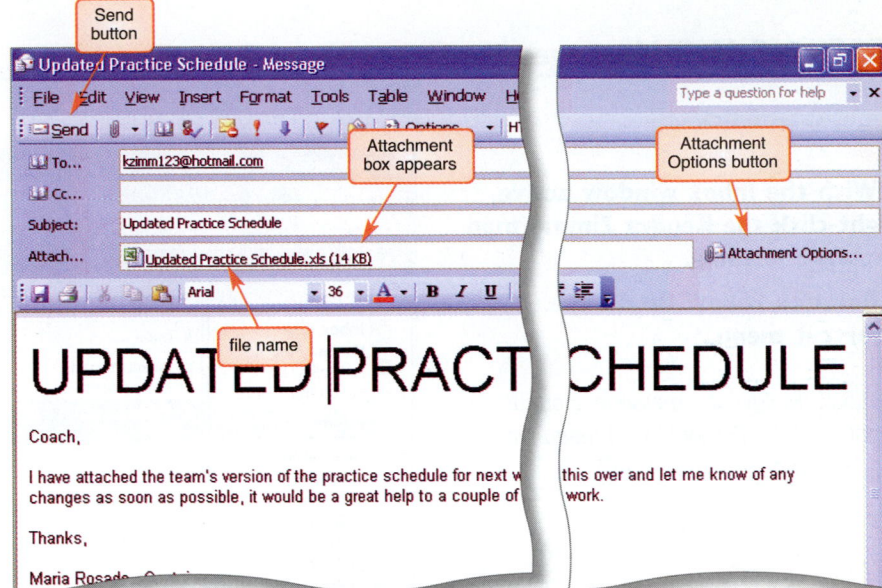

FIGURE 1-39

You can attach multiple documents to the same e-mail message. Simply perform the previous steps for each attachment. Keep in mind, however, that some Internet service providers have limits on the total size of e-mail messages they will accept. For example, if you attach pictures, which often are quite large, to an e-mail message, the recipient's service provider may not allow it to go through. In such cases, the sender is not informed that the e-mail message did not get through to the recipient. It is recommended that you keep the sum of the file sizes attached to an e-mail message less than 500 kilobytes.

Sending an E-Mail Message

After composing, formatting, and adding an attachment to an e-mail message, the next step is to send the message as illustrated in the following step.

To Send an E-Mail Message

1 **Click the Send button on the Standard toolbar.**

Outlook closes the Message window and temporarily stores the e-mail message in the Outbox folder while it sends the message, and then it moves the message to the Sent Items folder.

Flagging, Sorting, and Filtering E-Mail Messages

To the right of the message heading is the Flag Status column. The **Flag Status column** contains flags that can be assigned one of six different colors. One use for these flags could be to remind you to follow up on an issue. Color selection and the meaning of each color are entirely at the discretion of the user. For example, a red flag could mean the message needs immediate attention, a yellow flag may mean a response requires some information before you can reply, and a green flag simply may mean that the message requires a reply at your convenience (non-urgent). The steps on the next page show how to flag and sort e-mail messages.

To Flag E-Mail Messages

1

• **With the Inbox window active, right-click the Kendra Zimmerman message heading.**

• **Point to Follow Up on the shortcut menu.**

Outlook displays the message shortcut menu and the Follow Up submenu with the Flag commands (Figure 1-40).

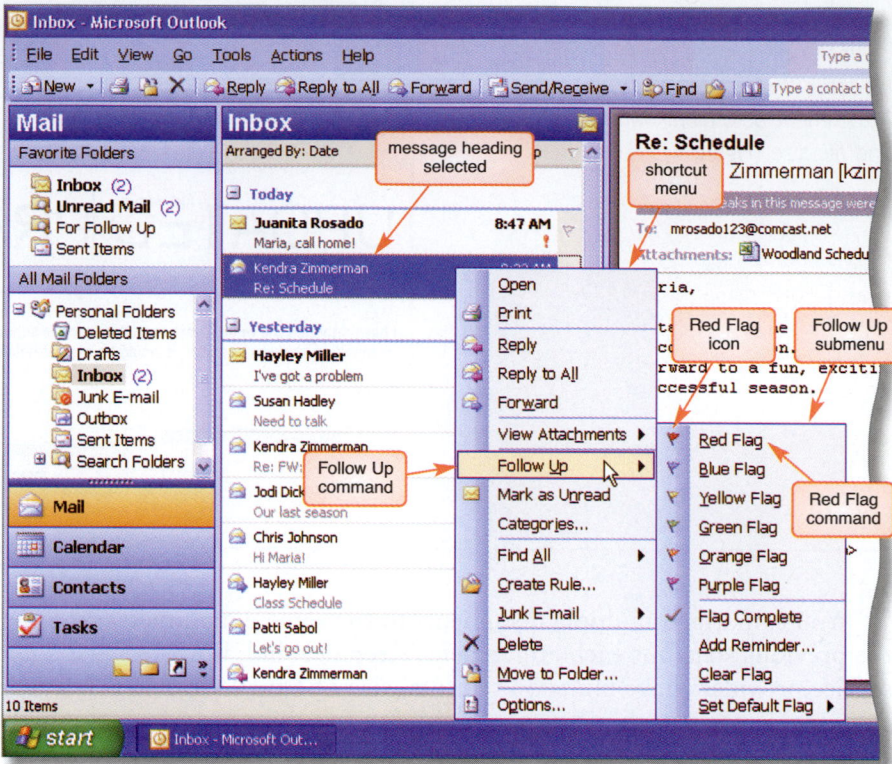

FIGURE 1-40

2

• **Click the Red Flag command on the Follow Up submenu.**

• **Repeat the Steps 1 and 2 to flag the remaining messages in the message pane.**

• **Select different colors as necessary.**

The Kendra Zimmerman message now displays a red flag icon in the Flag Status column (Figure 1-41). The remaining messages also display colored flag icons.

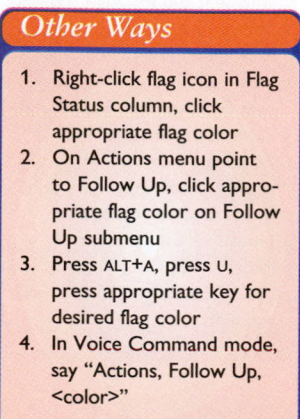

Other Ways

1. Right-click flag icon in Flag Status column, click appropriate flag color

2. On Actions menu point to Follow Up, click appropriate flag color on Follow Up submenu

3. Press ALT+A, press U, press appropriate key for desired flag color

4. In Voice Command mode, say "Actions, Follow Up, <color>"

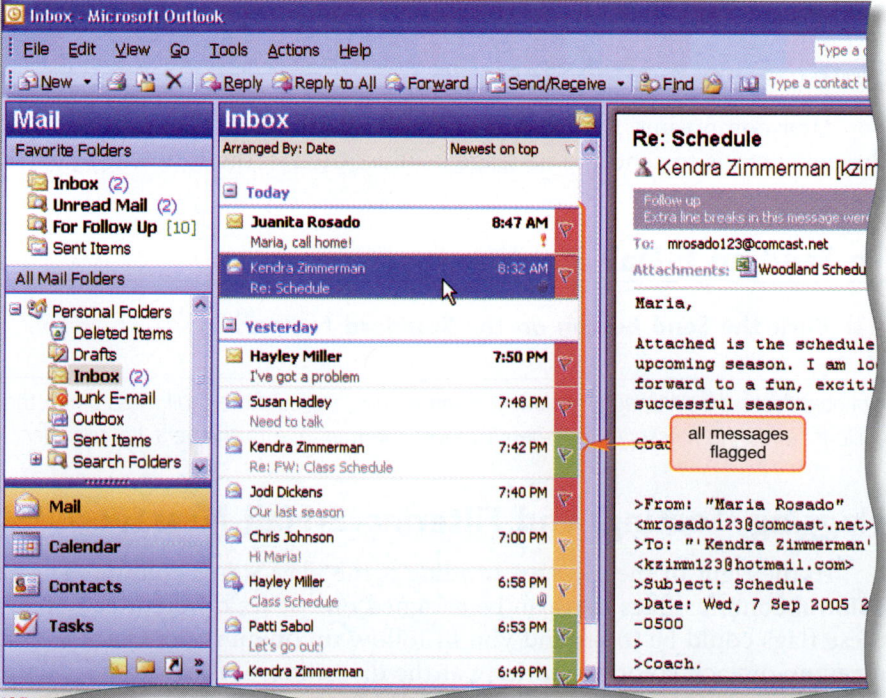

FIGURE 1-41

After flagging the appropriate messages, you can sort the messages by flag color. This is useful for grouping all the messages that require immediate attention as opposed to those messages that can be replied to at your convenience. The following steps show how to sort the messages by flag color.

To Sort E-Mail Messages by Flag Color

1

- **With the Inbox window active, click View on the menu bar and then point to Arrange By.**

Outlook displays the View menu and the Arrange By submenu (Figure 1-42).

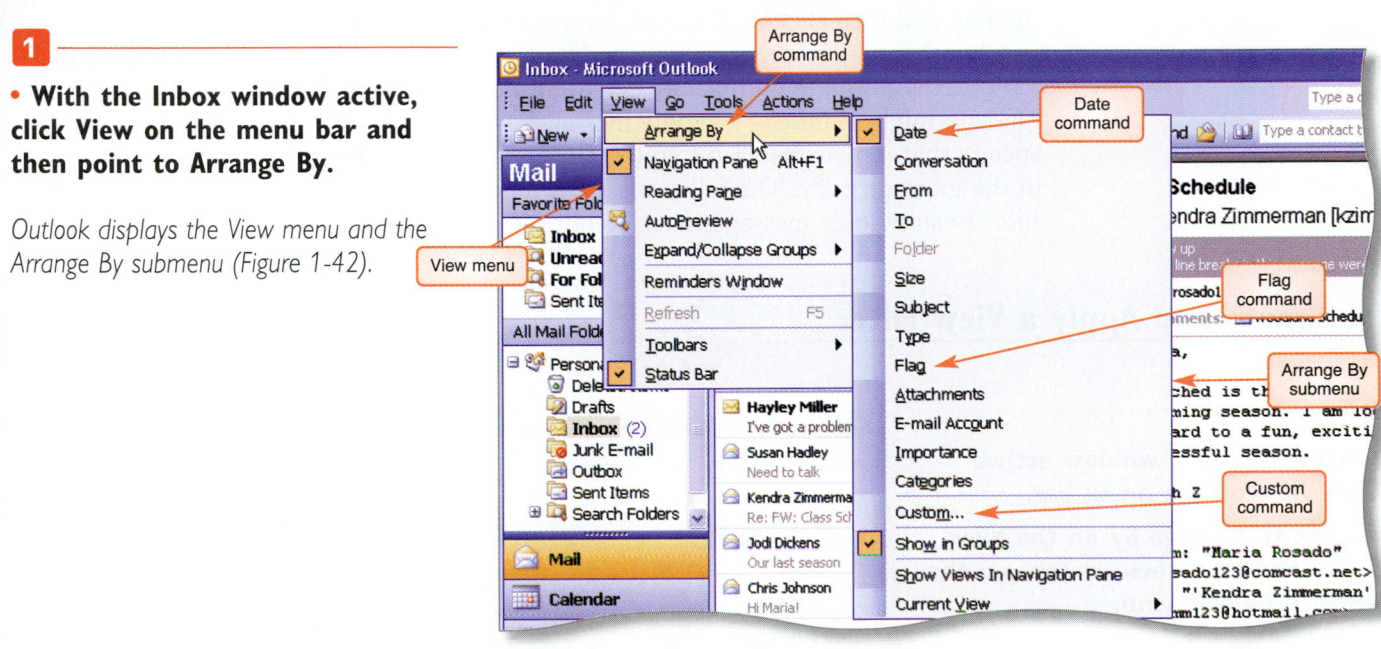

FIGURE 1-42

2

- **Click Flag on the Arrange By submenu.**

Outlook displays the Inbox window with messages arranged by flag and sorted by color (red on top) (Figure 1-43).

FIGURE 1-43

Other Ways

1. Press ALT+V, press A, press G
2. In Voice Command mode, say "View, Arrange By, Flag"

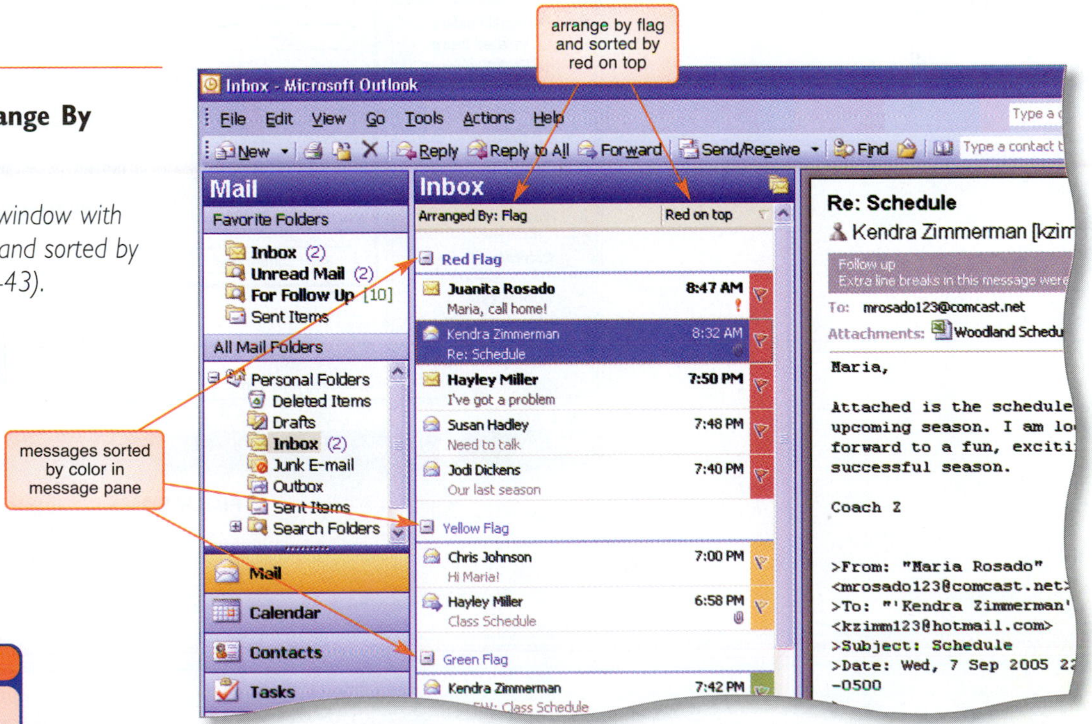

Outlook allows you to sort your messages several different ways using the Arrange By submenu (Figure 1-42 on the previous page). For example, you might want to see one particular person's messages. In this case, you would choose From on the Arrange By submenu. To return the messages to the default view, click Date on the Arrange By submenu.

After you have taken the appropriate action on a flagged message, you can indicate that no further action is required by changing the flag to a check mark by simply clicking the flag for that message. You also can remove the flag by right-clicking the flag and then clicking Clear Flag on the shortcut menu.

Another way to organize your messages is to use a view filter. A **view filter** displays items stored in Outlook folders that meet your specific conditions. For example, you might want to view only messages from Kendra Zimmerman. You would specify that only items with Kendra Zimmerman in the From text box should appear in the message body. The following steps illustrate how to create and apply a view filter to show only messages from Kendra Zimmerman.

To Create and Apply a View Filter

1

• **With the Inbox window active, click View on the menu bar.**

• **Point to Arrange By on the View menu and then click Custom on the Arrange By submenu.**

Outlook displays the Customize View: Messages dialog box (Figure 1-44).

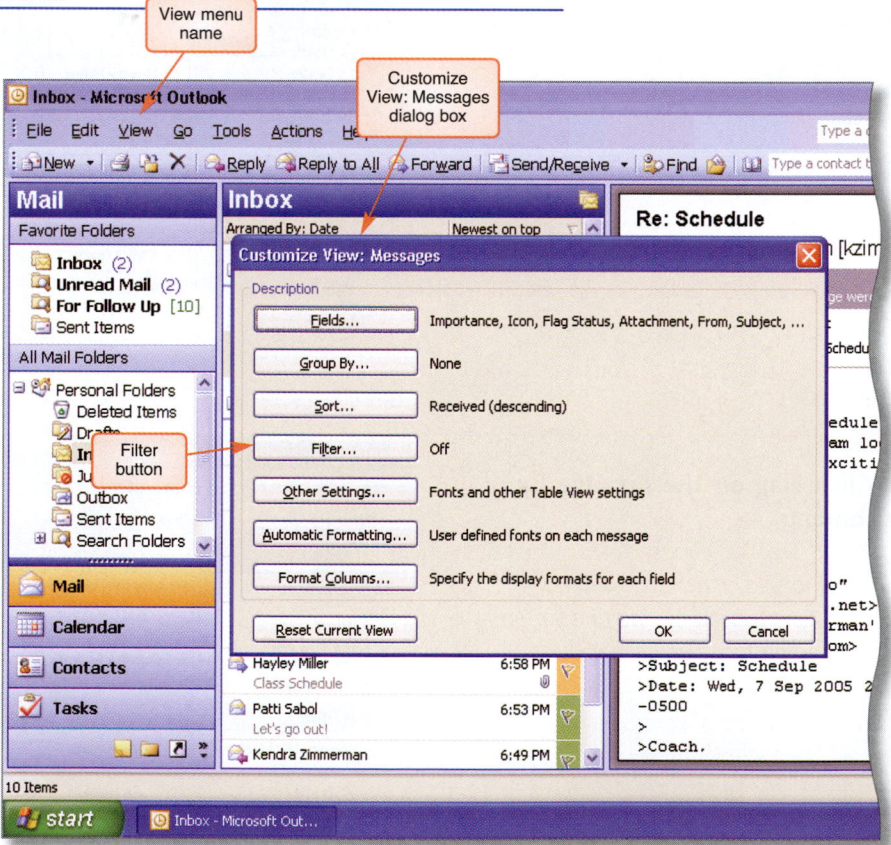

FIGURE 1-44

2

• **Click the Filter button.**

• **When Outlook displays the Filter dialog box, click the From text box.**

• **Type** Kendra Zimmerman **in the From text box.**

Outlook displays the Filter dialog box. The name, Kendra Zimmerman, appears in the From text box (Figure 1-45).

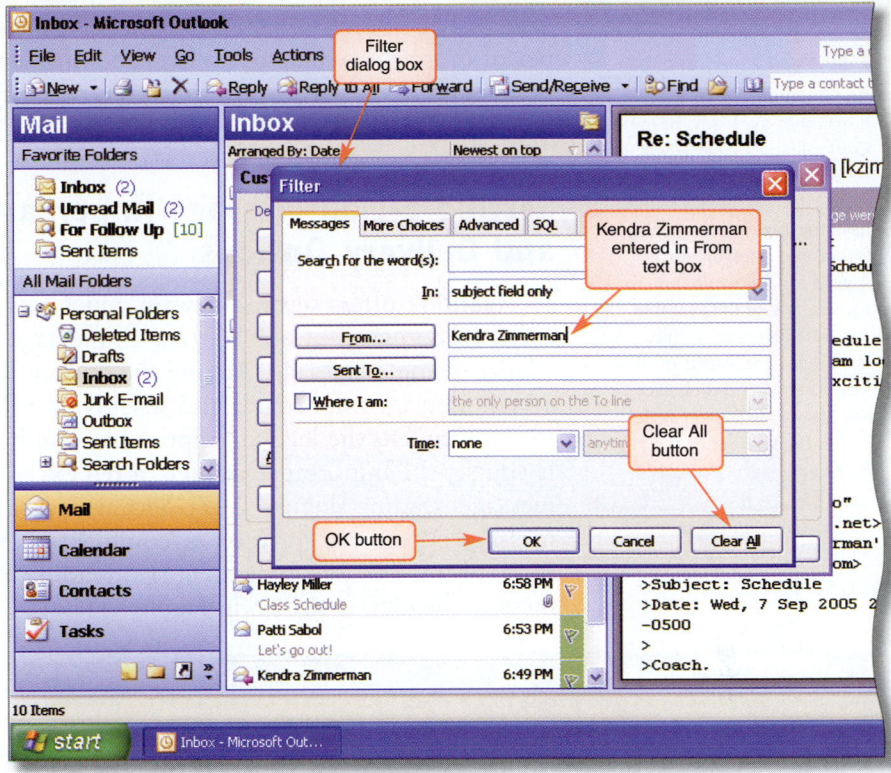

FIGURE 1-45

3

• **Click the OK button in the Filter dialog box and the Customize View: Messages dialog box.**

The Inbox window is redisplayed with only messages from Kendra Zimmerman showing in the message pane (Figure 1-46). The words, Filter Applied, appear on the status bar in the lower-left corner of the window.

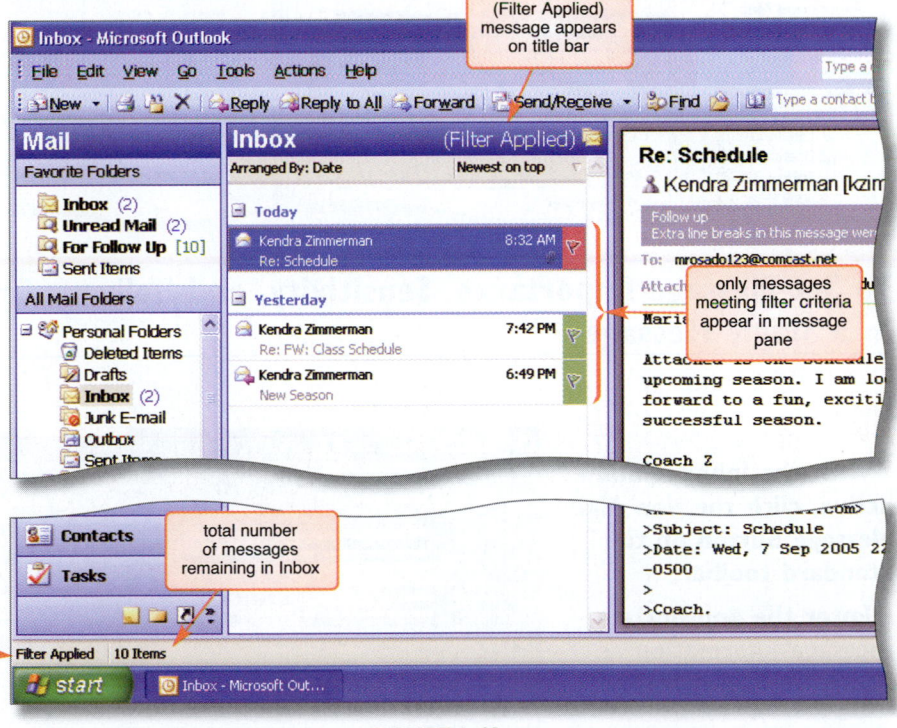

FIGURE 1-46

Outlook displays a Filter Applied message on the status bar and the Inbox pane title bar when a view filter is applied to a selected folder. It also shows the total number of messages remaining in the Inbox folder on the status bar. To remove a view filter, click the Clear All button in the Filter dialog box (Figure 1-45 on the previous page).

Setting E-Mail Message Importance, Sensitivity, and Delivery Options

Outlook offers several ways in which you can customize your e-mail. You can either customize Outlook to treat all messages in the same manner, or you can customize a single message. Among the options available through Outlook are setting e-mail message importance and sensitivity. Setting **message importance** will indicate to the recipient the level of importance you have given to the message. For example, if you set the importance at high, a red exclamation point icon will appear with the message heading (Figure 1-47). Setting **message sensitivity** indicates whether the message is personal, private, or confidential. A message banner indicating the sensitivity of the message appears in the Reading Pane below the sender's name in the message header as shown in Figure 1-47.

FIGURE 1-47

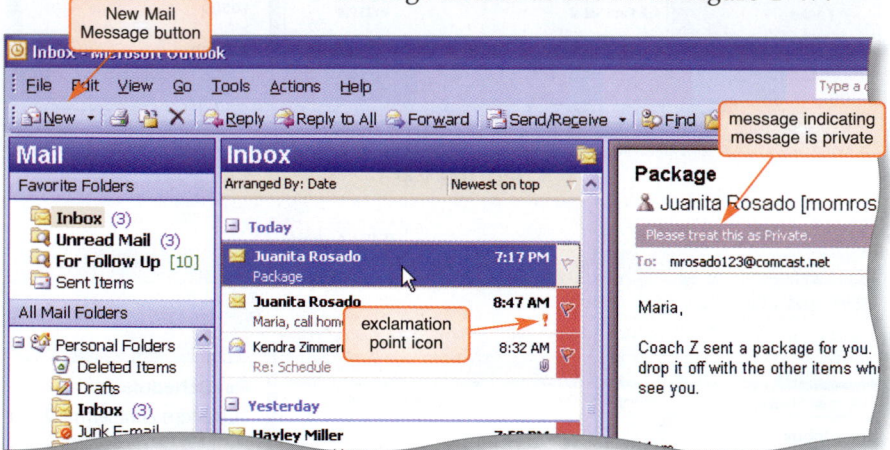

Along with setting importance and sensitivity, Outlook also offers several delivery options. You can have replies to your message automatically forwarded, save sent messages in a location of your choice (default is Sent Items folder), or delay delivering a message until a specified date and time.

The following steps illustrate how to set message importance, sensitivity, and delivery options in a single message.

To Set Message Importance, Sensitivity, and Delivery Options in a Single Message

 1

• **With the Inbox window active, click the New Mail Message button on the Standard toolbar.**

• **Enter the appropriate message information as shown in Figure 1-48.**

Outlook displays the Hayley Message window with the new message entered (Figure 1-48).

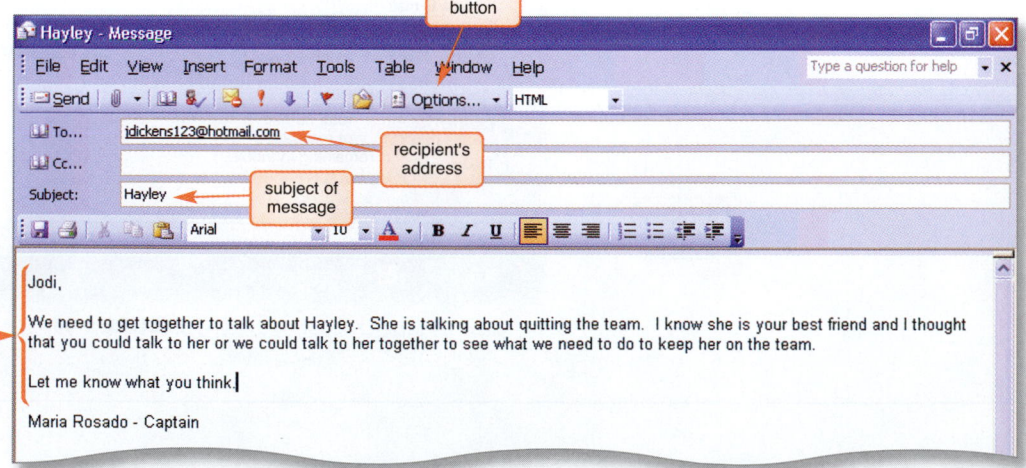

FIGURE 1-48

2

• **Click the Options button on the Mail toolbar (Figure 1-48).**

Outlook displays the Message Options dialog box (Figure 1-49).

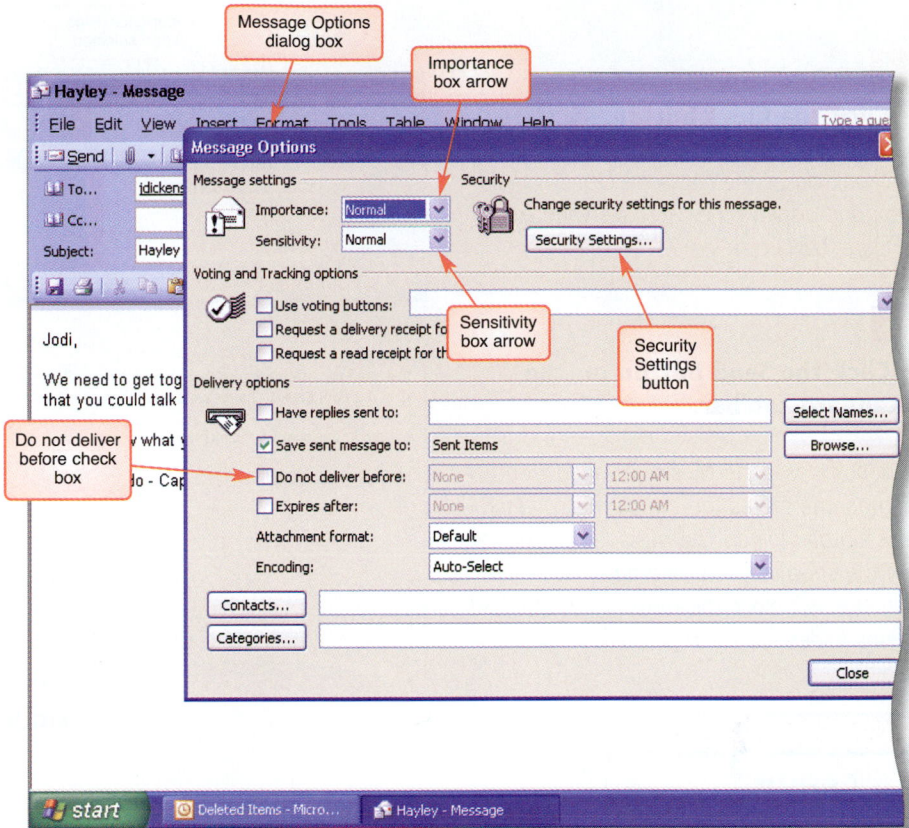

FIGURE 1-49

3

• **Click the Importance box arrow and then select High in the Importance list.**

• **Click the Sensitivity box arrow and then select Private in the Sensitivity list.**

• **Click Do not deliver before in the Delivery options area to select it.**

• **Select September 12, 2005 in the calendar and 12:00 PM as the time in the respective delivery boxes.**

Outlook displays the Message Options dialog box as shown in Figure 1-50. High is selected in the Importance box, Private is selected in the Sensitivity box, and the message delivery is set for 9/12/2005 at 12:00 PM in the date and time boxes.

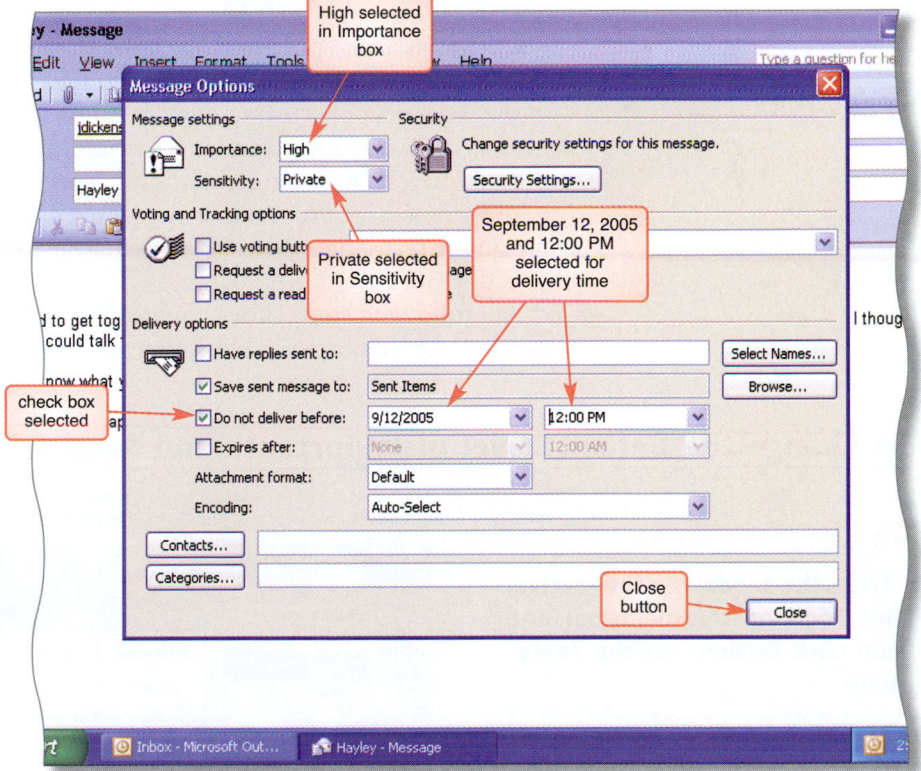

FIGURE 1-50

4

• **Click the Close button.**

Outlook closes the Message Options dialog box and displays the Message window (Figure 1-51).

5

• **Click the Send button on the Standard toolbar.**

Outlook closes the Message window and temporarily stores the e-mail message in the Outbox folder. The message will be sent on the specified date and time, and then Outlook will move the message to the Sent Items folder.

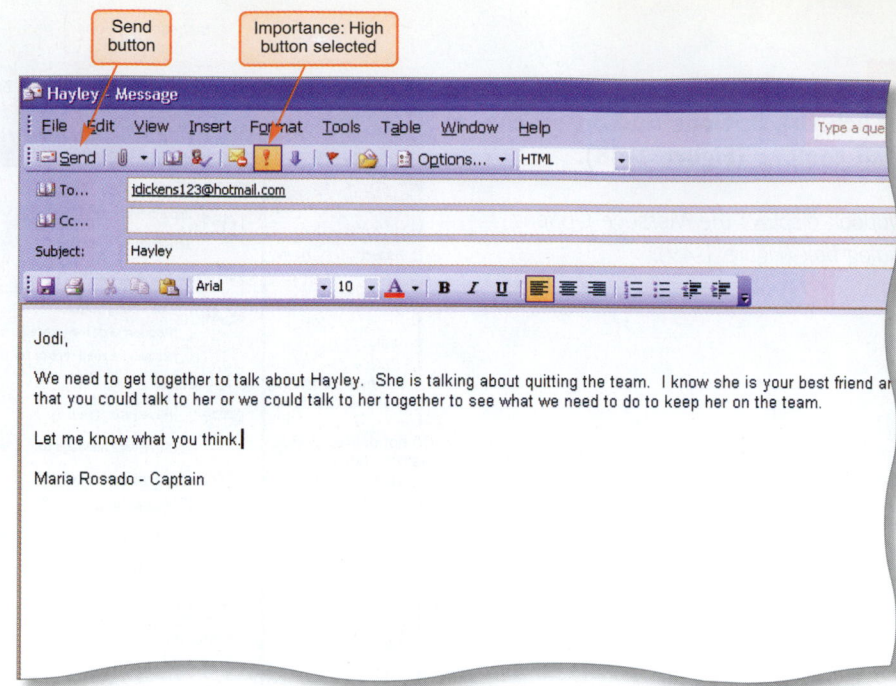

FIGURE 1-51

Other Ways

1. Press ALT+P
2. Right-click message heading in Inbox pane, click Options on submenu

The recipient of the message will receive the message with the red exclamation point icon and the message indicating the e-mail is private like the one shown in Figure 1-47 on page OUT 34.

As shown in the previous steps, the default level of importance and sensitivity is Normal. Outlook allows you to change the default level for either or both of these options. For example, you may want all of your outgoing messages to be treated as confidential by the recipients. It is important to know that marking an e-mail as personal, private, or confidential is advisory only. The recipient will still be able to forward the message to another person or copy the message into another e-mail. To learn about restricting the recipient's actions on a message, see the More About on page OUT 38.

The following steps show how to change the default level of importance and sensitivity for all outgoing messages.

To Change the Default Level of Importance and Sensitivity

1

• **With the Inbox window active, click Tools on the menu bar and then click Options on the Tools menu.**

Outlook displays the Options dialog box (Figure 1-52).

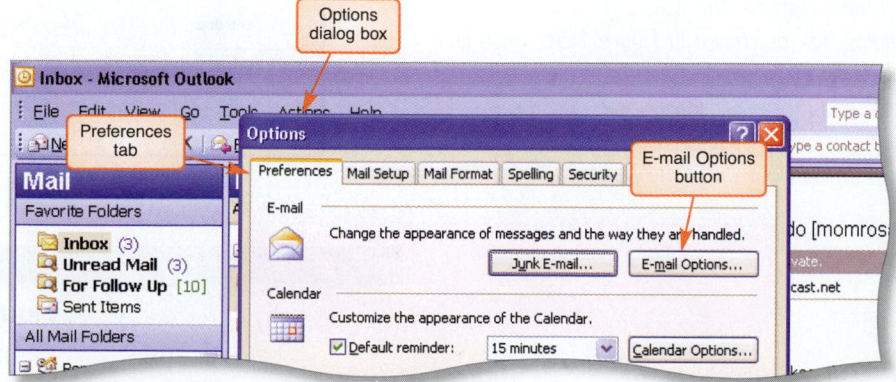

FIGURE 1-52

2

• **In the Preferences sheet, click the E-mail Options button.**

Outlook displays the E-mail Options dialog box (Figure 1-53).

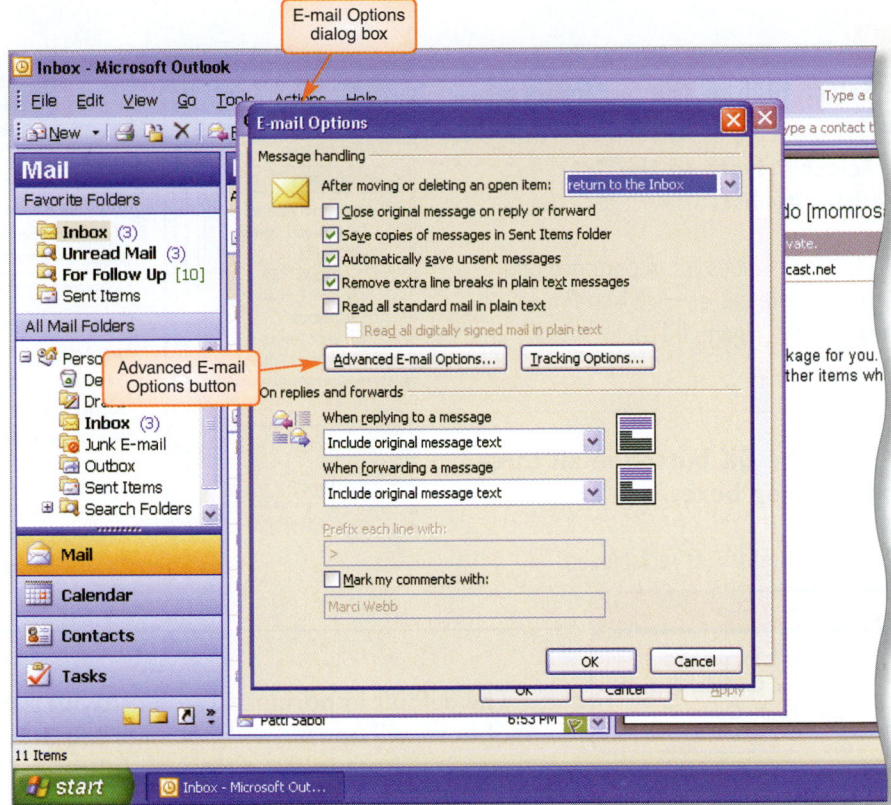

FIGURE 1-53

3

• **Click the Advanced E-mail Options button.**

• **When Outlook displays the Advanced E-mail Options dialog box, click the Set importance box arrow.**

Outlook displays the Advance E-mail Options dialog box with the Set importance list showing the available importance settings (Figure 1-54).

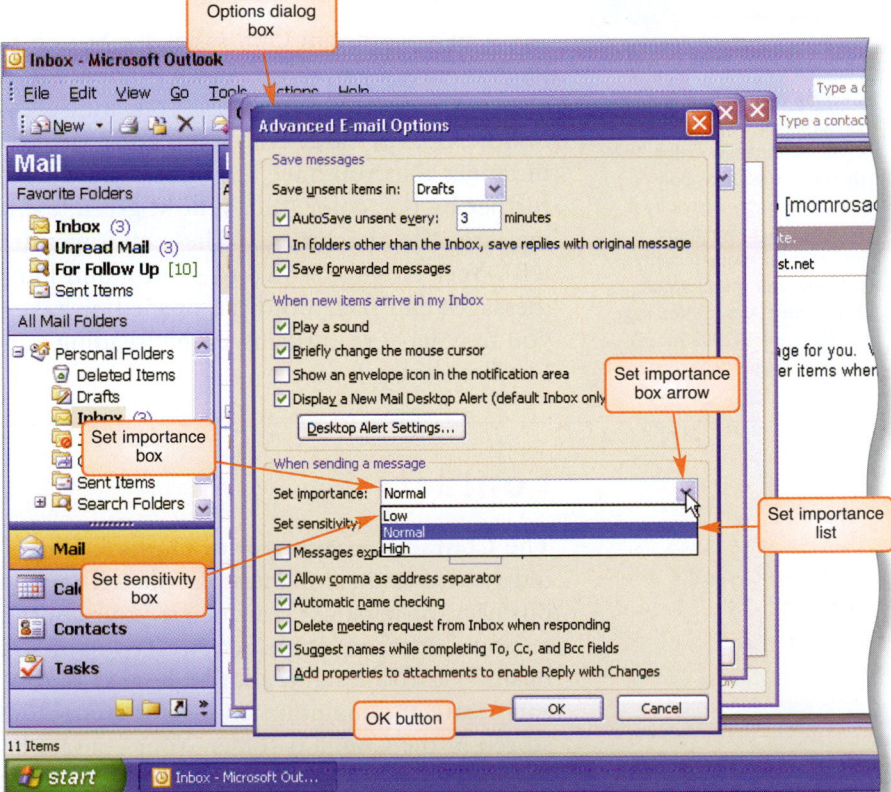

FIGURE 1-54

4

• **Select High in the Set importance list.**

• **Select Private in the Set sensitivity list.**

The default values for importance and sensitivity are set at High and Private, respectively (Figure 1-55).

5

• **Click the OK button in all three open dialog boxes.**

The Inbox window is redisplayed.

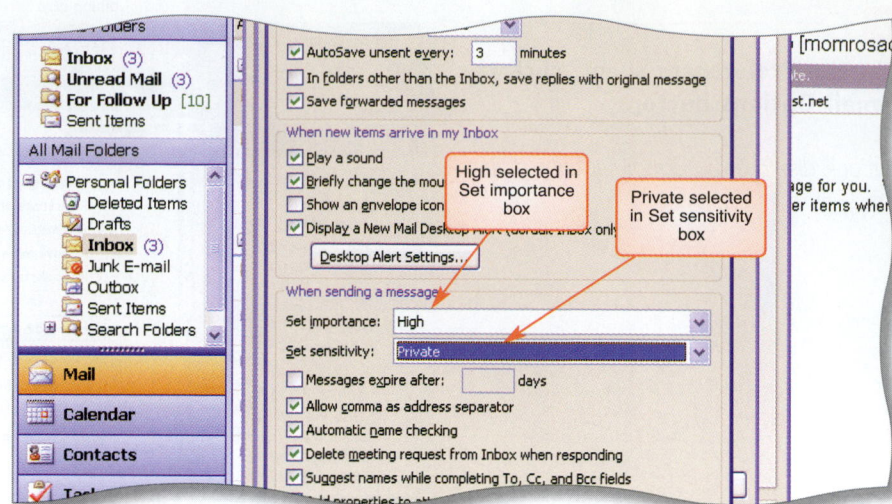

FIGURE 1-55

The default importance and sensitivity settings have been changed. Any outgoing e-mail now will appear with the high importance icon and the message indicating the message is private in the recipient's Inbox.

Using Search Folders to Display Categories of E-Mail Messages

A new feature in Outlook is the Search Folders folder in the All Mail Folders pane (Figure 1-56). The **Search Folders folder** includes a group of folders that allows you to group and view your messages quickly in one of three ways: (1) For Follow Up, (2) Large Messages, and (3) Unread Mail. **For Follow Up** messages are messages that you have flagged but have not taken action. These messages are sorted further by flag color (red, yellow, green, etc.). **Large Messages** are messages containing large file attachments. These messages are grouped by size: Large (100 to 500 KB), Very Large (500 KB to 1 MB), and Huge (1 to 5 MB). **Unread Mail** comprises messages that have not been opened or have not been marked as read even though you may have read them via the Reading Pane. Figure 1-56 shows messages in the For Follow Up folder.

Contacts

The **Contacts component** of Outlook allows you to store information about individuals and companies. People with whom you communicate for school, business, or personal reasons are your **contacts**. To help organize information about personal contacts, some people keep names, addresses, and telephone numbers in business-card files and address books. With the Outlook Contacts component, you can create and maintain important contact information in a **contact list**, which is stored in the Contacts folder. Your contact list is like an electronic address book that allows you to store names, addresses, e-mail addresses, and more. Once the information has been entered, your contact list can be retrieved, sorted, edited, organized, or printed. Outlook also includes a **Find option** that lets you search for a contact name in your address book while you are using the Calendar, Inbox, or other Outlook components.

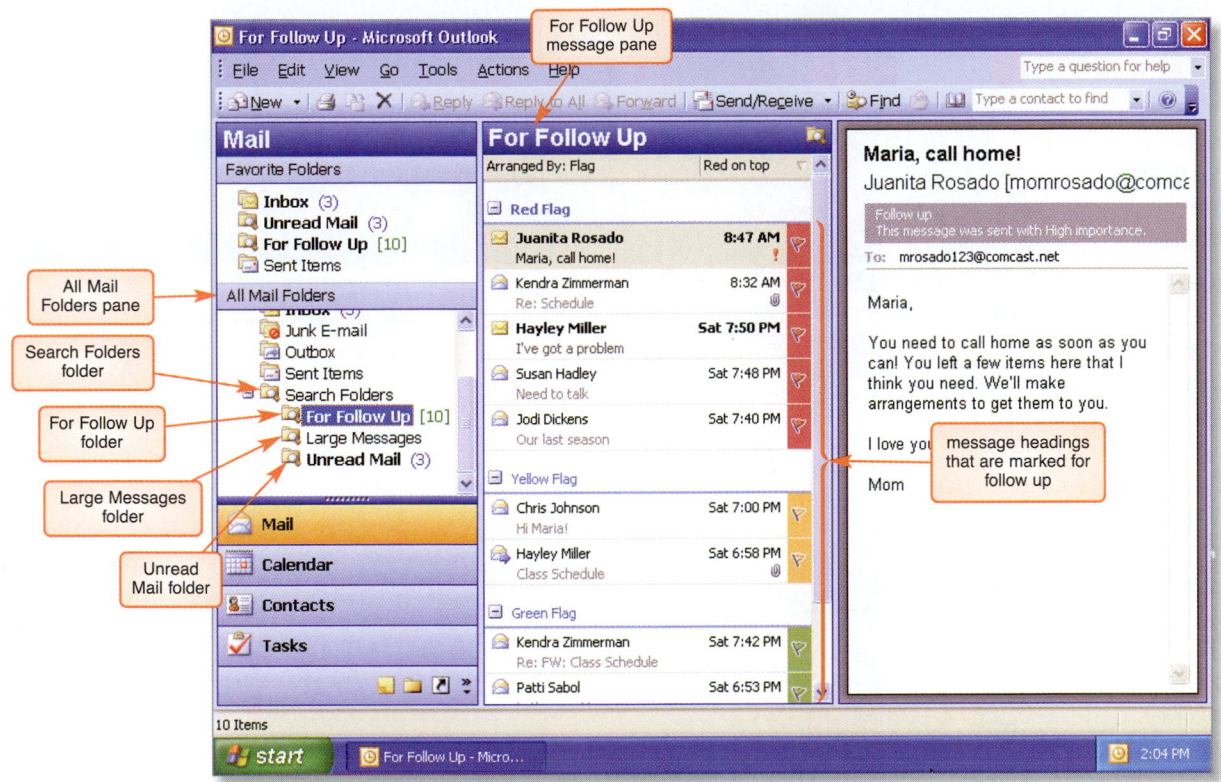

FIGURE 1-56

When the Contacts folder is open, information about each contact appears on an address card in the default **Address Cards view**. Each address card includes fields such as name, address, and various telephone numbers, as well as e-mail and Web page addresses. Choose which fields are displayed on the cards using the View menu.

Previously, an e-mail message was composed, signed, formatted, and sent to Kendra Zimmerman. Kendra's e-mail address was typed into the To text box (see Figure 1-31 on page OUT 25). The following sections show how to (1) create a personal folder; (2) create a contact list; (3) edit contact information; (4) print contact information; (5) send an e-mail to a contact; and (6) delete a contact.

Creating a Personal Folder

The first step in creating the contact list is to create a personal folder in which the contact list will be stored. When only one person is working on a computer, a contact list can be stored in Outlook's Contacts folder. If you share your computer with a roommate, lab partner, or coworker, you likely will want to store your contact list in a personal folder, which usually is added as a subfolder within the Contacts folder. The steps on the next page create a personal folder for Maria Rosado.

To Create a Personal Folder

1

• Click the Contacts button in the Navigation Pane.

• When Outlook displays the Contacts window, right-click Contacts in the My Contacts pane.

Outlook displays the Contacts - Microsoft Outlook window and the Contacts shortcut menu (Figure 1-57).

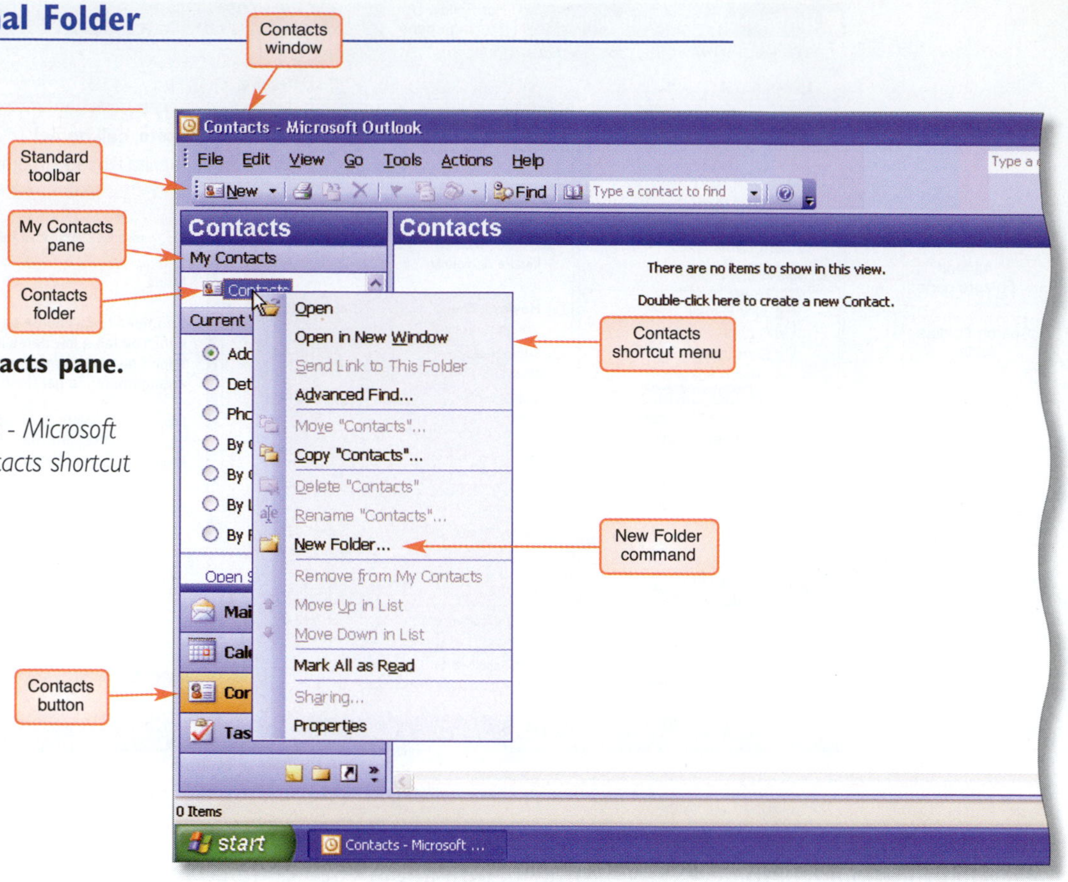

FIGURE 1-57

2

• Click New Folder on the My Contacts shortcut menu.

• When Outlook displays the Create New Folder dialog box, type Maria's Contacts in the Name text box.

• If necessary, select Contact Items in the Folder contains list.

• Click Contacts in the Select where to place the folder list.

The new folder, Maria's Contacts becomes a subfolder of the Contacts folder (Figure 1-58). Maria's Contacts appears in the Name text box.

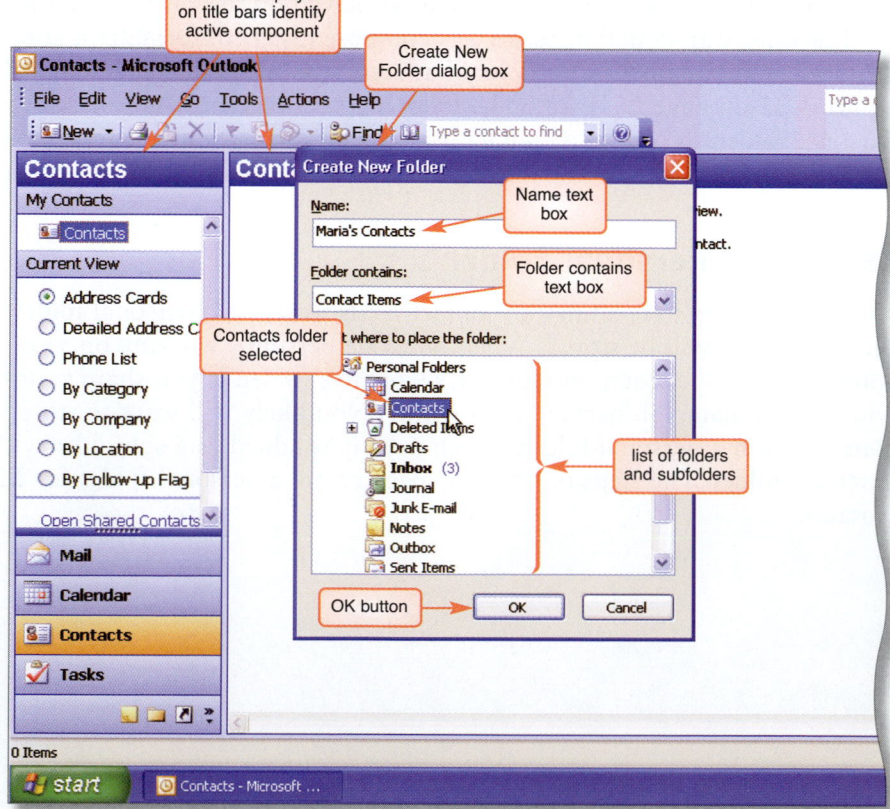

FIGURE 1-58

3

- Click the OK button.
- Click Maria's Contacts in the My Contacts list.

Outlook displays a list of available folders in the My Contacts pane and displays an empty Contacts pane (Figure 1-59).

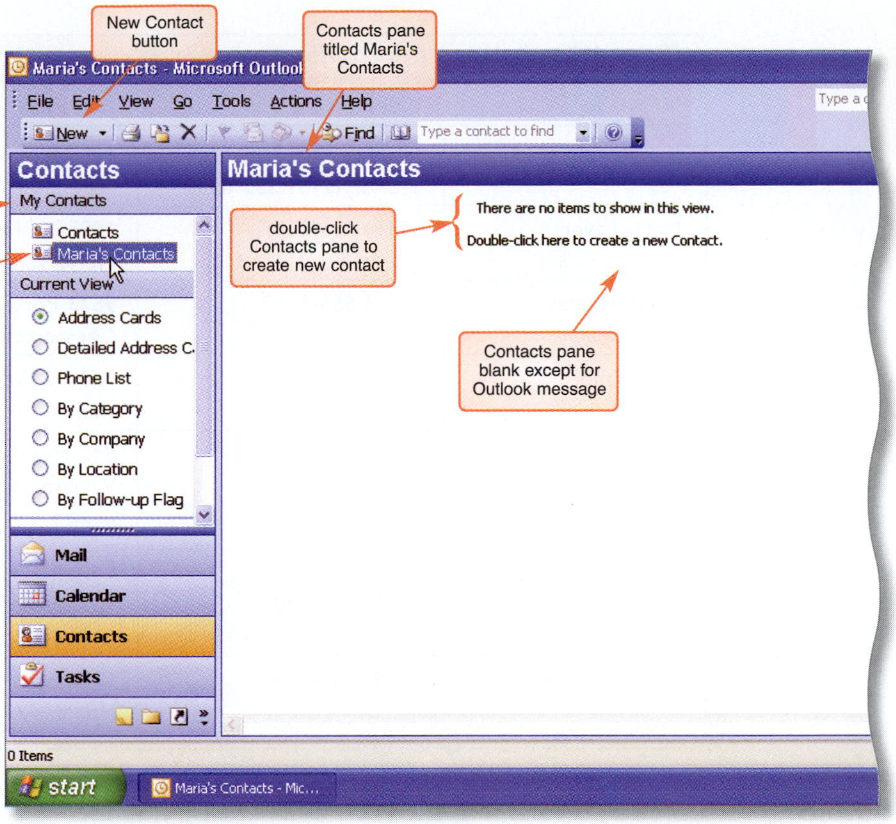

New Contact button

Contacts pane titled Maria's Contacts

My Contacts pane

Maria's Contacts folder

double-click Contacts pane to create new contact

Contacts pane blank except for Outlook message

FIGURE 1-59

As indicated in the previous steps, it is relatively easy to create folders for your contacts. Most Outlook users have one folder for all their contacts. But you can create a folder for your family, another for friends, another for business associates, and so on. The number of folders you use for your contacts will depend on what works best for you.

Figure 1-60 illustrates the Standard toolbar located below the menu bar in the Contacts window.

Other Ways

1. On File menu point to New, click Folder on New submenu
2. On File menu, point to Folder, click New Folder on Folder submenu
3. Press CTRL+SHIFT+E
4. In Voice Command mode, say "File, New Folder"

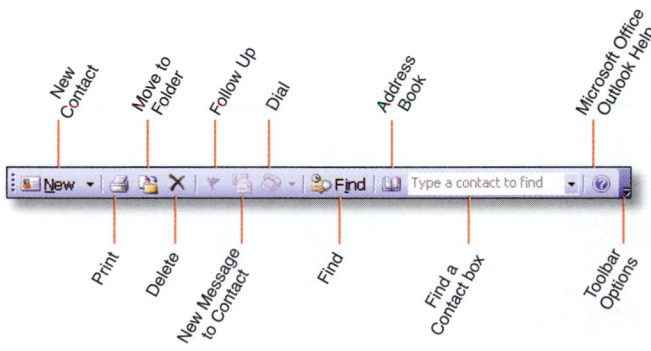

FIGURE 1-60

Creating a Contact List

The steps on the next page describe how to enter the contact information in Table 1-3 on the next page into the contact list.

Table 1-3   Contact Information

NAME	TELEPHONE	ADDRESS	E-MAIL ADDRESS
Kendra Zimmerman	Business: (219) 555-8520 Home: (219) 555-6547	188 Hohman Ave. Hammond, IN 46327	kzimm123@hotmail.com
Marci Laver	(219) 555-0547	1097 Whitcomb St. Merrillville, IN 46410	mlaver123@hotmail.com
Susan Hadley	(219) 555-6387	9873 Porter Ave. Chesterton, IN 46304	shadley101@hotmail.com
Patti Sabol	(219) 555-7964	1631 Columbia Ave. Hammond, IN 46327	psabol123@hotmail.com
Jodi Dickens	(219) 555-3060	845 Meridian St. Valparaiso, IN 46385	jdickens123@hotmail.com
Courtney Craig	(219) 555-7015	3287 Southport Rd. Portage, IN 46368	ccraig101@hotmail.com
Hayley Miller	(708) 555-5204	732 Burnham Ave. Calumet City, IL 60409	hmiller101@hotmail.com
Chris Johnson	(219) 555-8041	1786 61st Ave. Hobart, IN 46342	cjohnson123@hotmail.com

To Create a Contact List

1

• **With the Contacts window active and Maria's Contacts folder selected, click the New button on the Standard toolbar (Figure 1-59 on the previous page).**

• **When Outlook displays the Untitled - Contact window, if necessary, maximize the window.**

• **Type** Kendra Zimmerman **in the Full Name text box.**

• **Click the Business text box in the Phone numbers area.**

Notice that Outlook automatically fills in the File as box, last name first (Figure 1-61). The name on the title bar of the Contact window changes to the Kendra Zimmerman - Contact window.

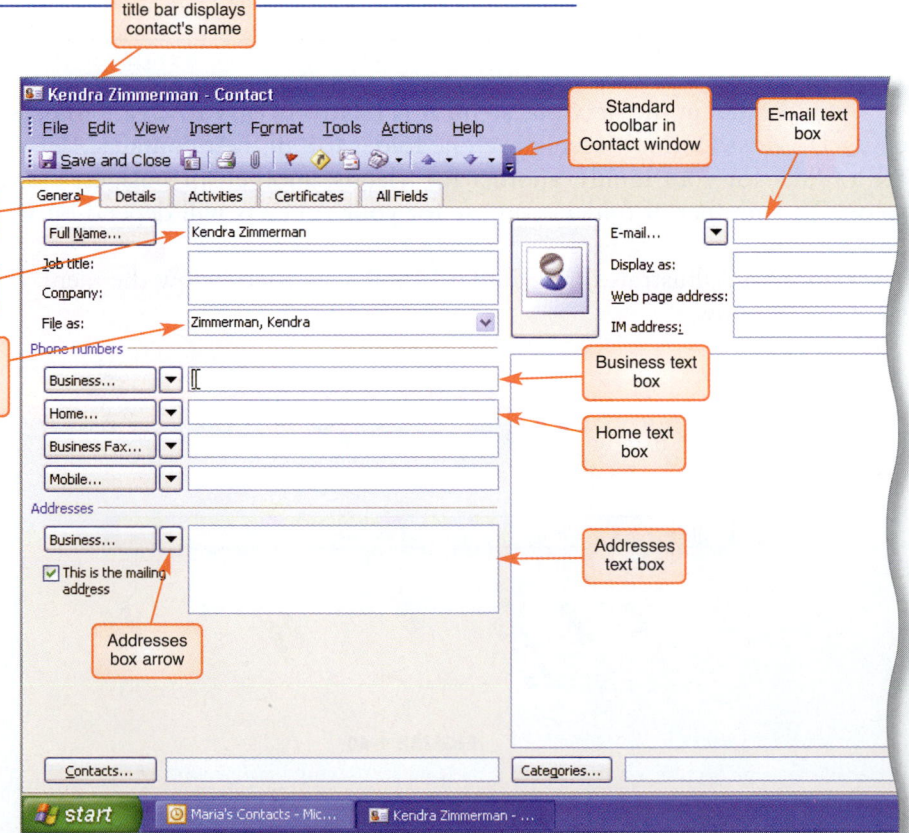

FIGURE 1-61

2

- **Type** 2195558520 **as the business telephone number and then click the Home text box.**

- **Type** 2195556547 **as the Home telephone number.**

- **Click the Addresses box arrow and select Home.**

- **Click the text box in the Addresses area, type** 188 Hohman Ave. **and then press the ENTER key.**

- **Type** Hammond, IN 46327 **to complete the address entry.**

- **Click the E-mail text box.**

- **Type** kzimm123@hotmail.com **as the e-mail address.**

Outlook displays the Kendra Zimmerman - Contact window as shown in Figure 1-62.

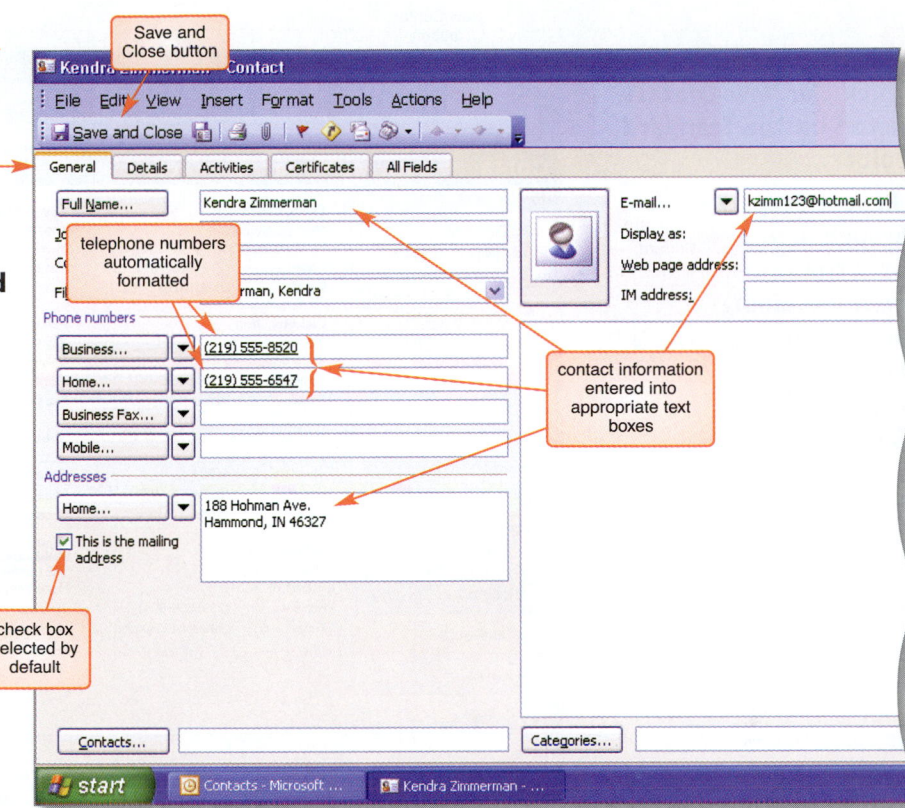

FIGURE 1-62

3

- **Click the Save and Close button on the Standard toolbar.**

Outlook displays the Kendra Zimmerman address card in Address Cards view in the Maria's Contacts pane (Figure 1-63). Address Cards is the current view by default.

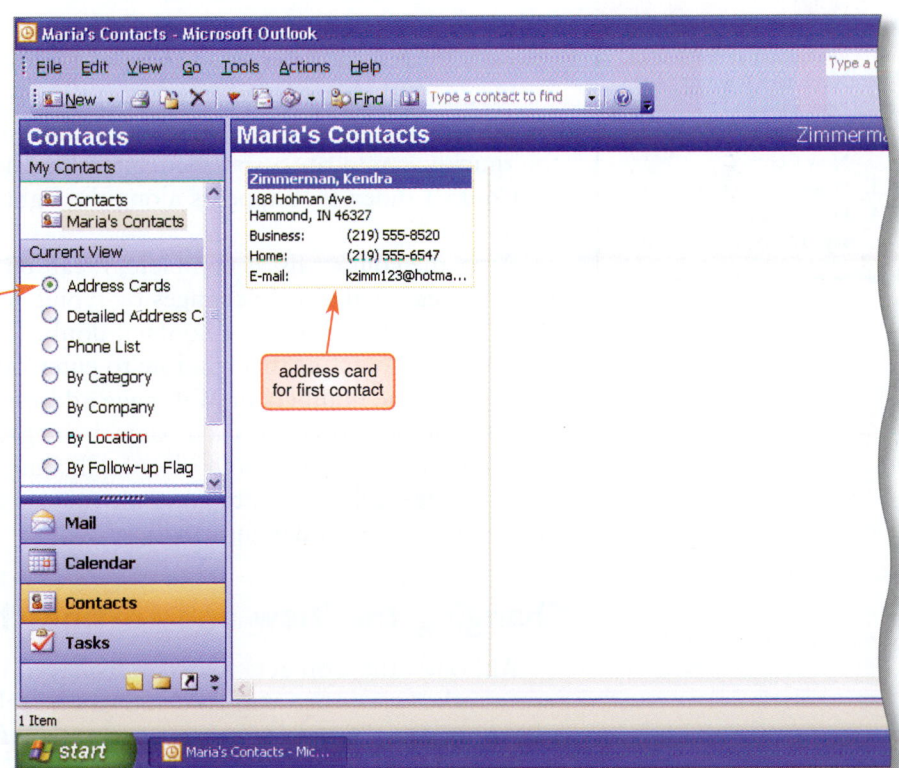

FIGURE 1-63

4

• **Click the New Contact button on the Standard toolbar.**

• **Repeat Steps 2 through 4 to enter the seven remaining contacts in Table 1-3 on page OUT 42.**

Outlook displays the contact list as shown in Figure 1-64. Outlook automatically lists the contacts in alphabetical order. The letters, Cra – Zim, that appear on the right side of the Maria's Contacts pane title bar indicate the range of contacts currently displayed (Craig to Zimmerman).

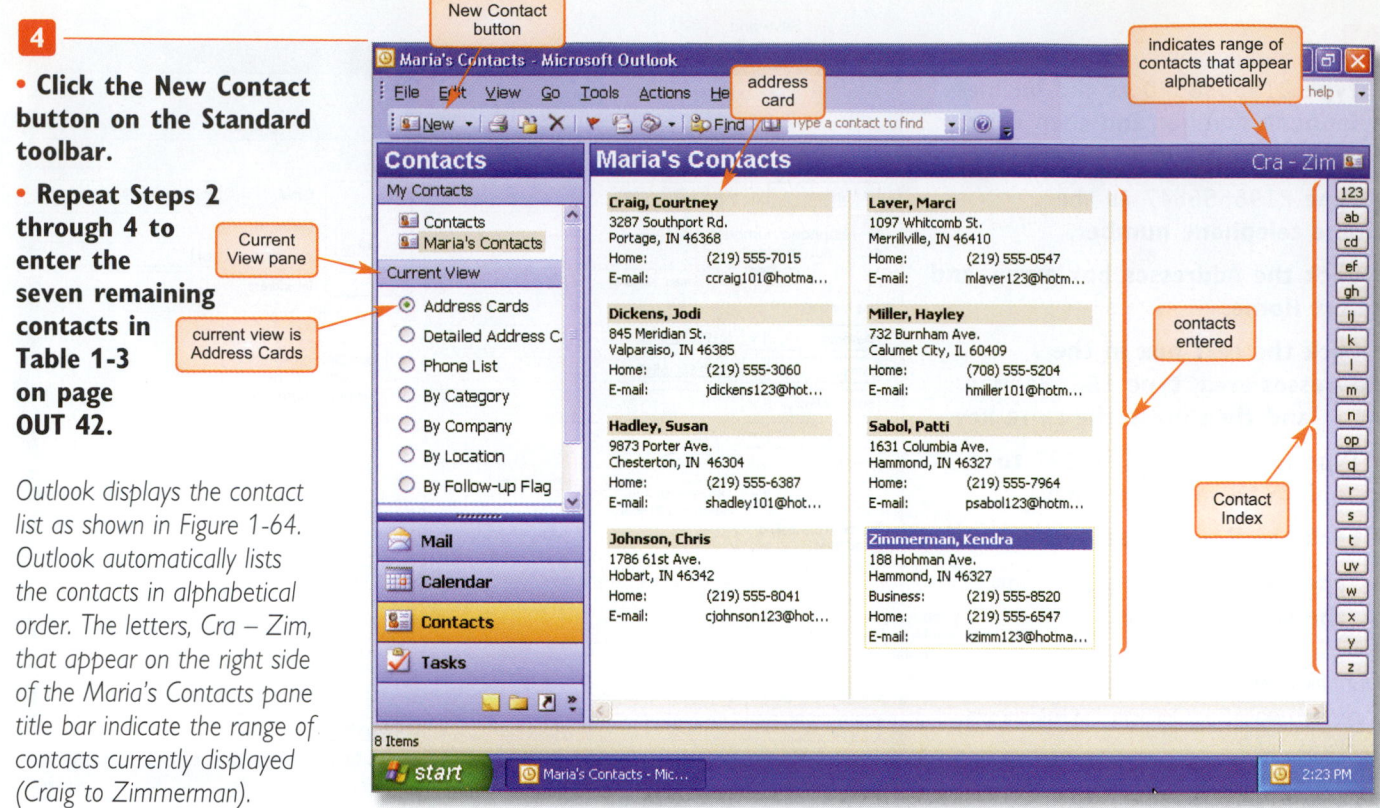

FIGURE 1-64

Because this contact list consists of only eight names, Outlook displays all of the contact names. The default view is Address Cards. With longer lists, however, you quickly can locate a specific contact by clicking a letters or numbers button on the **Contact Index** that appears along the right side of the Contacts window (Figure 1-64).

After the contact list is complete, it can be viewed, edited, or updated at any time. You can make some changes by typing inside the card itself. To display and edit all the information for a contact, double-click the address card to display the Contacts window. Use this window to enter information about a contact, such as home telephone numbers or Web page addresses. Up to 19 different telephone numbers can be stored for each contact categorized by location and type (business, home, fax, mobile, pager, and so on). Clicking the Details tab (Figure 1-62 on the previous page) allows you to enter a contact's department, manager's name, nickname, and even birthday information.

Changing the View and Sorting the Contacts List

Although the Contacts folder is displayed in Address Cards view by default, several other views are available and can be selected in the Navigation Pane. The following steps show how to change the view from Address Cards to Phone List, sort the contact list in descending sequence, and then change back to Address Cards view.

To Change the View and Sort the Contact List

1

- **With the Maria's Contacts - Microsoft Outlook window active, click Phone List in the Current View pane of the Navigation Pane.**
- **With the Phone List in ascending sequence by the File As field, click the File As column heading in the Contacts pane.**

Outlook changes the contact list view from Address Cards to Phone List and displays the contact list in descending sequence by last name (Figure 1-65). Notice the direction of the small arrow in the File As column heading.

2

- **After reviewing the contact list in Phone List view, click Address Cards in the Current View pane in the Navigation Pane.**

Outlook displays the contact list in ascending sequence in Address Cards view (Figure 1-64).

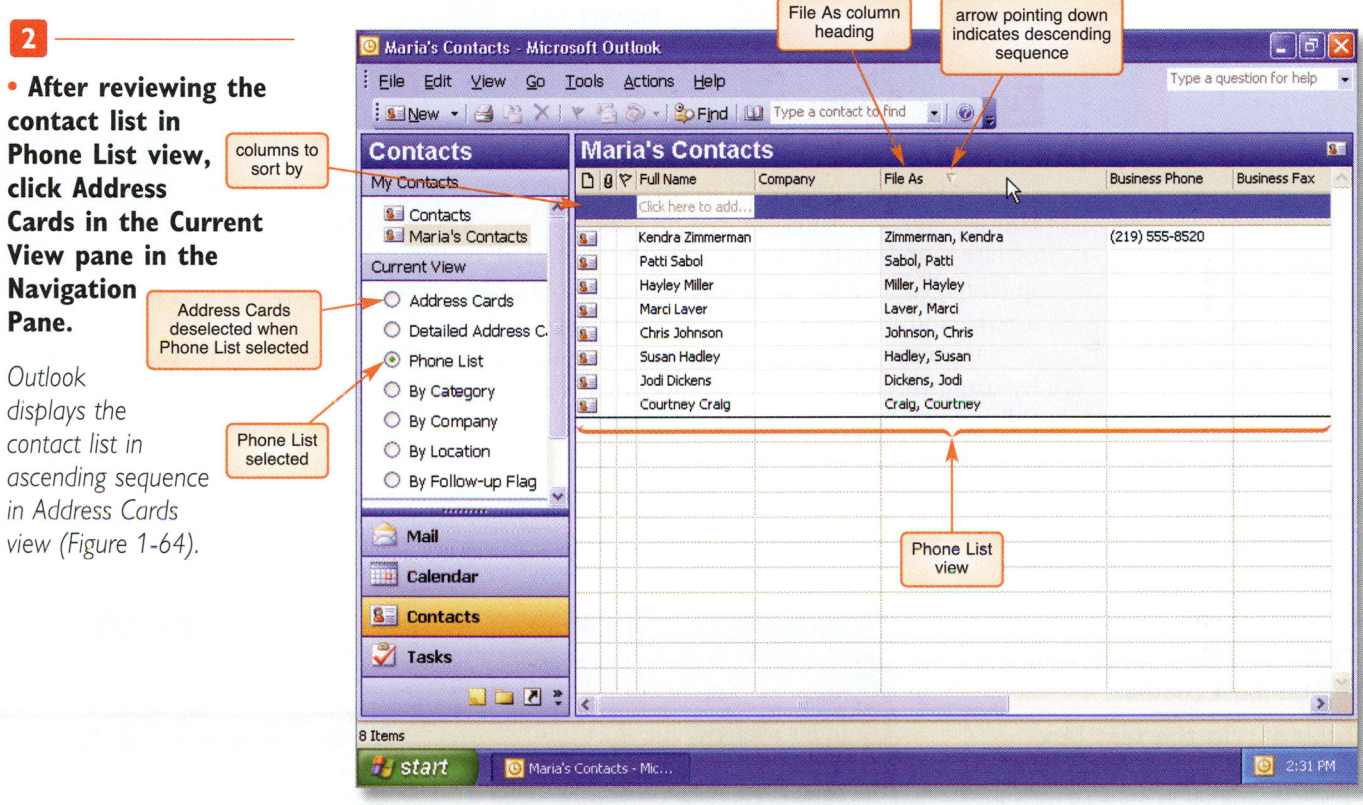

FIGURE 1-65

To see how easy it is to change views of the contact list, click one of the view options in the Current View pane in the Navigation Pane. You also can sort by any one of the column headings in the Contacts pane (Icon, Attachment, Flag Status, Full Name, Company, File As, Business Phone, etc.) just by clicking the column heading (see Figure 1-65). Click a column heading once and Outlook sorts the contacts list into descending sequence. Click the same column heading again and Outlook sorts the contact list into ascending sequence. The arrow in the middle of the column heading indicates whether the contact list is in ascending sequence or descending sequence. When you switch from one view to another, the sequence of the contact list reverts back to what it was the last time the view was used.

You can sort the views of the contact list, e-mail messages, and other Outlook information in many different ways. If you right-click a column heading in any Outlook component and point to the Arrange By command on the shortcut menu (Figure 1-66 on the next page) you can see the Arrange By commands.

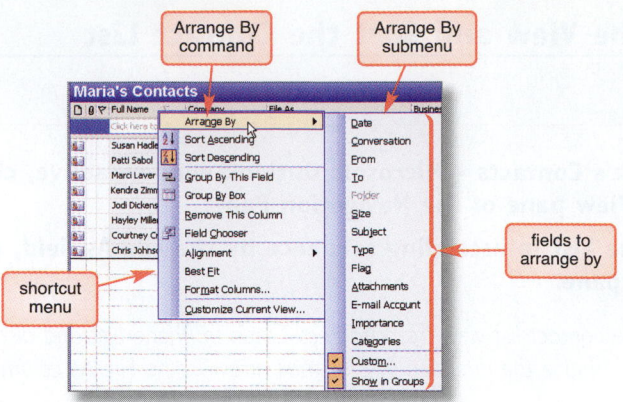

FIGURE 1-66

Finding a Contact

The contact list created in this project is small. Many Outlook users have hundreds of names stored in their contact lists. This section shows you how to find a contact quickly using the Find a Contact box on the Standard toolbar. Enter a first or last name, in full or partially. An e-mail alias also can be used to find a contact quickly. To locate a contact previously searched for, click the find a Contact box arrow, and then select a name in the list.

A contact record was created for Jodi Dickens. This record can be found easily by using the Find a Contact box to type a part of the contact name as shown in the following steps.

To Find a Contact

1

• **Click the Find a Contact box on the Standard toolbar.**

• **Type** dic **in the text box.**

The letters appear in the Find a Contact box (Figure 1-67). The letters, dic, are used to find the contact beginning with those letters.

FIGURE 1-67

2

• **Press the ENTER key.**

Outlook opens the Contact window (Figure 1-68). Currently, only one contact exists with the letters dic in its name.

3

• **Click the Close button on the right side of the title bar in the Contact window.**

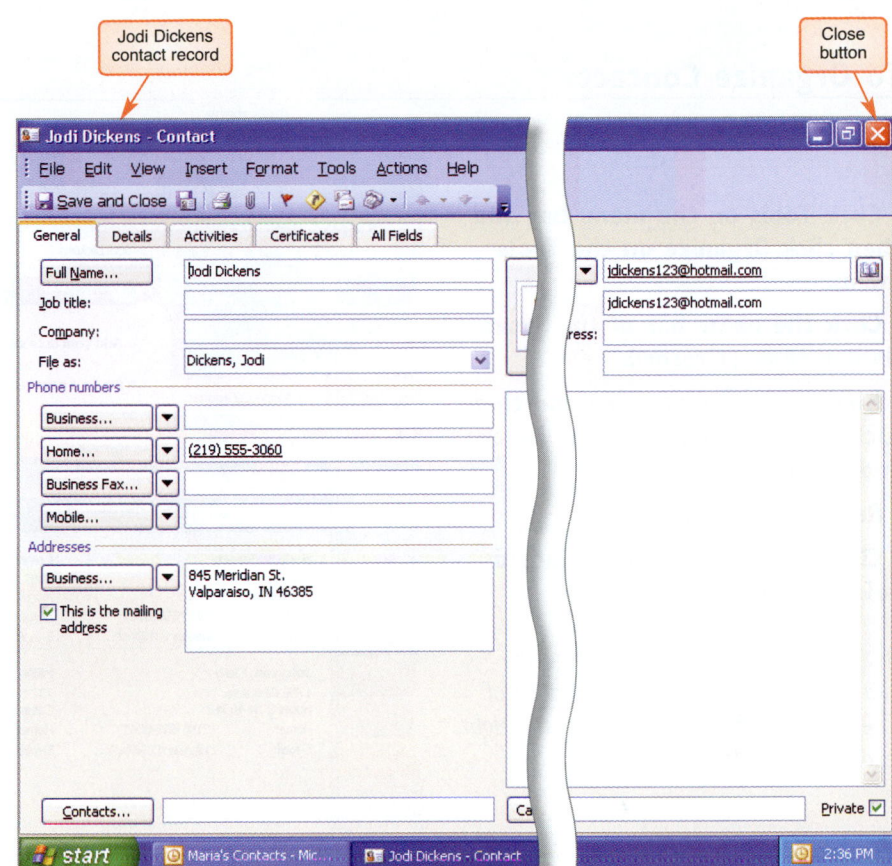

FIGURE 1-68

If more than one contact with the starting letters, dic, exists, Outlook displays a Choose Contact dialog box with the list of all contacts beginning with the string, dic. You then can select the appropriate contact from the Choose Contact dialog box.

Organizing Contacts

To help manage your contacts further, the contact list can be categorized and sorted in several ways. For example, you can group contacts into categories such as Key Customer, Business, Hot Contact, or even Ideas, Competition, and Strategies. In addition, you may want to create your own categories to group contacts by company, department, a particular project, a specific class, and so on. You also can sort by any part of the address; for example, you can sort by postal code for bulk mailings.

For the contact list created in this project, it is appropriate to organize the contacts in a personal category. You can do this by selecting the contacts and then adding them to the personal category of the contact list. The steps on the next page illustrate this procedure.

Other Ways

1. On Tools menu point to Find, click Find on Find submenu
2. Click Find button on Standard toolbar
3. Press CTRL+SHIFT+F
4. In Voice Command mode, say "Tools, Find"

More About

Contacts

You can organize contacts from one or more Contacts folders in a personal distribution list. Outlook also detects duplicates and provides the option to merge the new information with the existing contact entry. You also can filter your contact list and then use the filtered list to begin a mail merge from Outlook.

To Organize Contacts

1

• **Click Tools on the menu bar and then click Organize on the Tools menu.**

• **Click the name bar of the Susan Hadley contact record.**

• **Hold down the CTRL key and then click the name bar of Marci Laver and Patti Sabol.**

• **Release the CTRL key.**

• **Click the Add contacts selected below to box arrow.**

Outlook displays the Ways to Organize Maria's Contacts dialog box and a list of categories (Figure 1-69). Three of the eight records are selected.

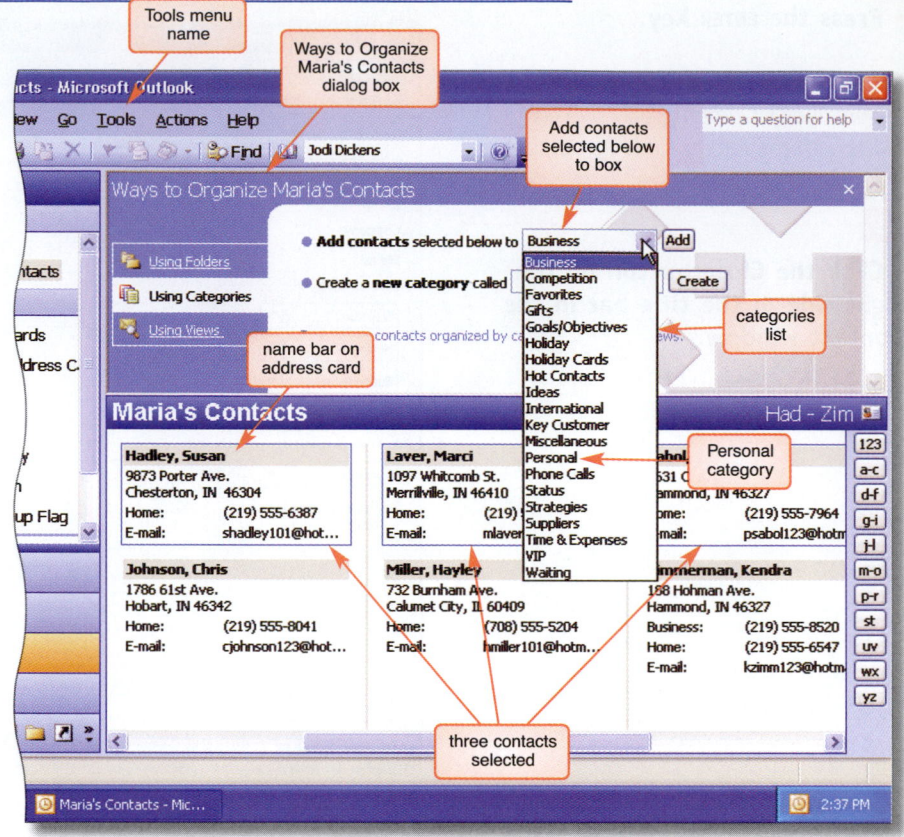

FIGURE 1-69

2

• **Click Personal in the list.**

• **Click the Add button.**

Outlook adds the selected records to the Personal category and the word Done! appears next to the Add button (Figure 1-70).

3

• **Click the Close button on the Ways to Organize Maria's Contacts dialog box.**

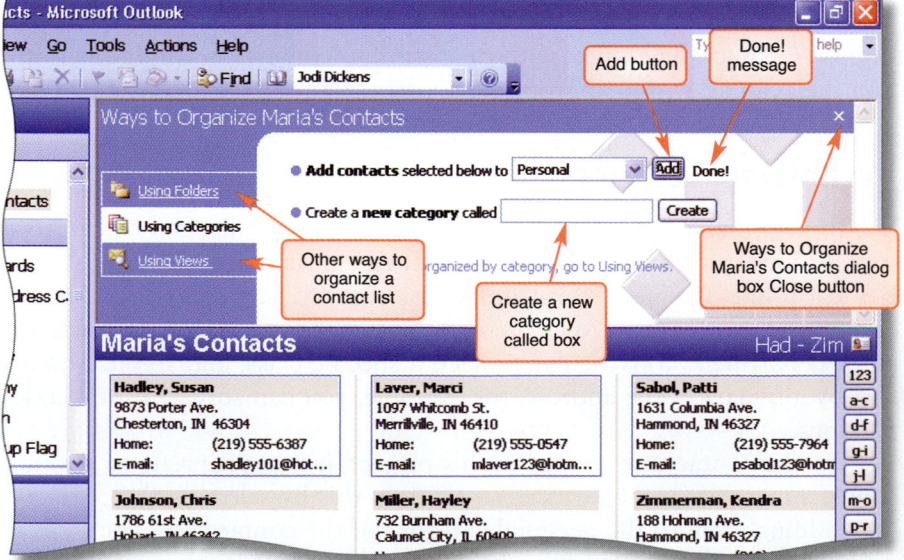

FIGURE 1-70

Other Ways

1. Press ALT+T, press Z
2. In Voice Command mode, say "Tools, Organize"

The three contacts are organized into a category called Personal. Organizing contacts in different categories helps make searching for groups of names easier.

Displaying the Contacts in a Category

By assigning the three contacts to a personal category, you can instruct Outlook to display only those contacts that belong to the category shown in the following steps.

To Display the Contacts in a Category

1

• **With the Contacts window active, click the Find button on the Standard toolbar.**

• **When Outlook displays the Find toolbar above the Contacts pane, type** Personal **in the Look for box.**

• **If necessary, click Maria's Contacts in the My Contacts pane so it appears in the Search In box.**

• **Click the Find Now button on the Find toolbar.**

Outlook displays the three contacts that belong in the Personal category (Figure 1-71).

2

• **After viewing the contacts in the Personal category, click the Find button on the Standard toolbar.**

Outlook displays all the contacts in the Maria's Contacts folder.

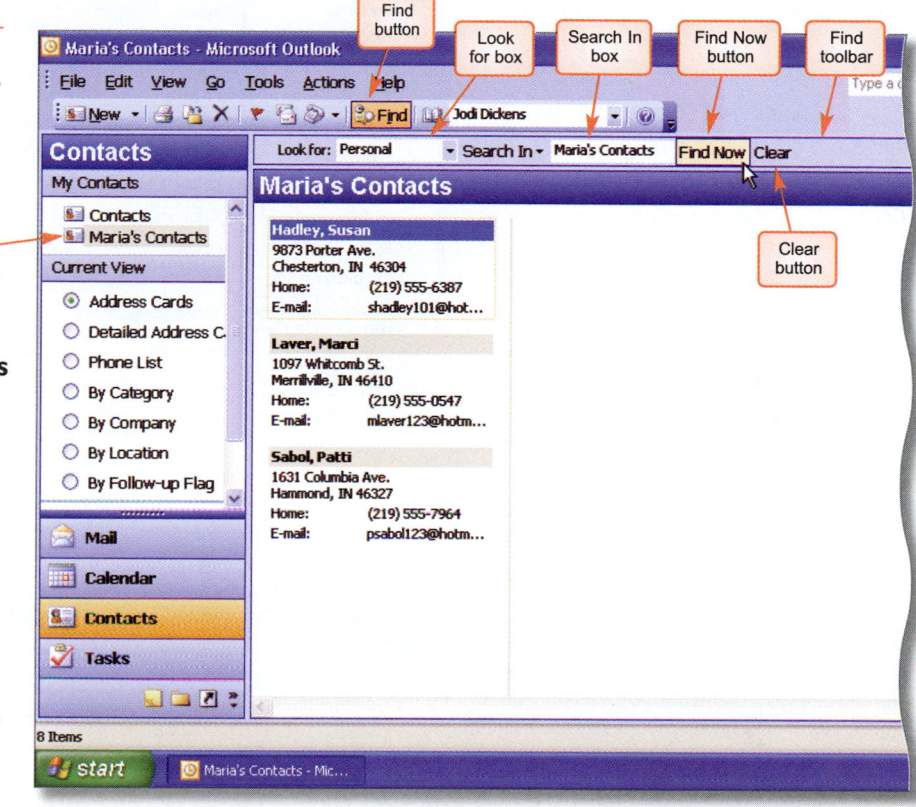

FIGURE 1-71

You can use the Find button on the Standard toolbar to find contacts when the Contacts component is active, messages when the Mail component is active, appointments when the Calendar component is active, and tasks when the Tasks component is active.

Previewing and Printing the Contact List

Printing the contact list is an easy way to obtain a listing of people you frequently contact. Previewing the contact list before you print it helps ensure the printed list can be used for business mailings, invitations to social gatherings, or even a telephone or Christmas card list. The step on the next page describes how to preview and print the contact list.

Other Ways

1. On Tools menu point to Find, click Find on Find submenu
2. Press CTRL+E
3. For advanced search, press CTRL+SHIFT+F
4. In Voice Command mode, say "Tools, Find, Find"

To Preview and Print the Contact List

1

• **With the Contacts window active, click the Print button on the Standard toolbar.**

Outlook displays the Print dialog box (Figure 1-72). In the Print dialog box you can select a format for the printout, print range, and number of copies. You can also change the orientation from portrait to landscape through the use of the Page Setup button.

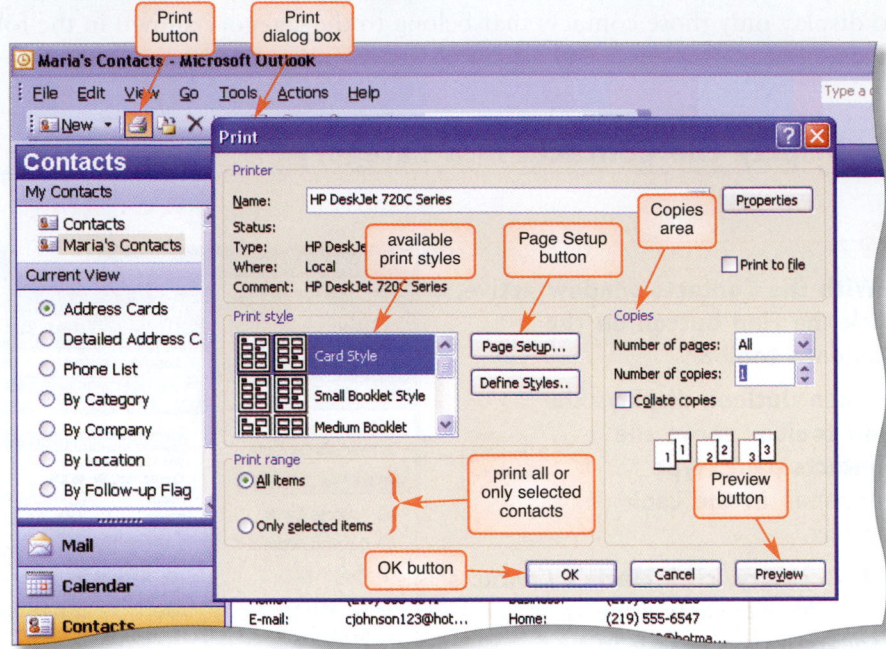

FIGURE 1-72

2

• **Click the Preview button.**

Outlook displays a preview of the printout (Figure 1-73).

3

• **After viewing the preview of the printed contacts list, click the Close button.**

• **If the preview is acceptable, ready the printer.**

• **Click the Print button on the Standard toolbar.**

• **When Outlook displays the Print dialog box, click the OK button.**

Outlook prints the contact list. The printout should resemble the preview in Figure 1-73.

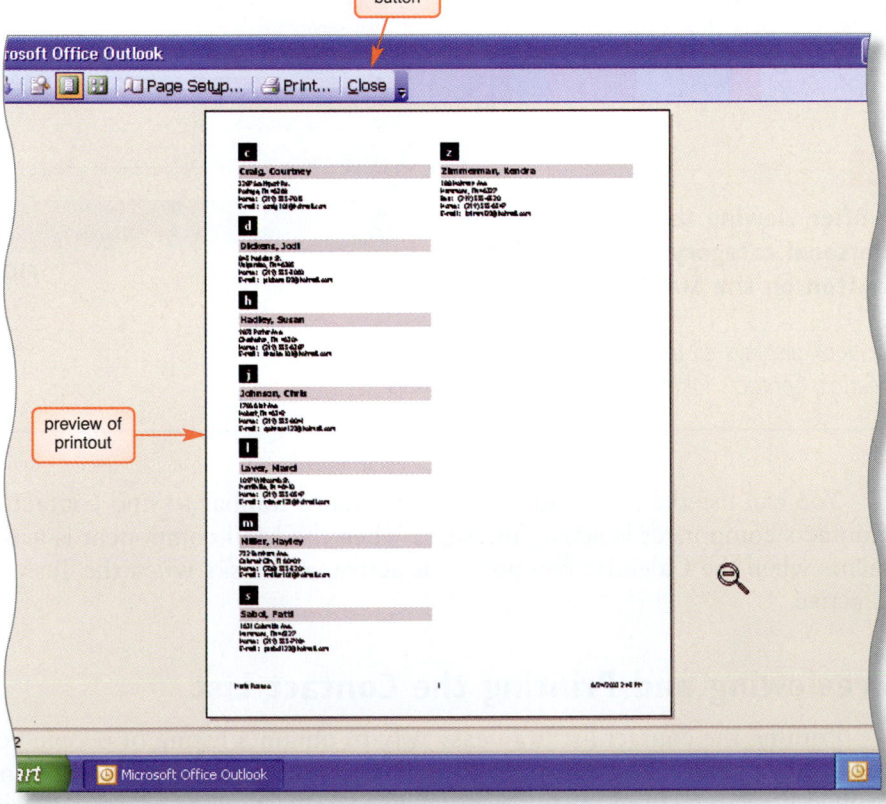

FIGURE 1-73

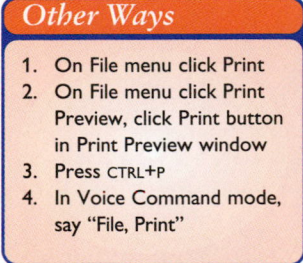

Other Ways

1. On File menu click Print
2. On File menu click Print Preview, click Print button in Print Preview window
3. Press CTRL+P
4. In Voice Command mode, say "File, Print"

If you display a category of contacts and then click the Print button, Outlook will print only the contacts in that category. A printout can be customized by changing the Print style in the Print dialog box. These styles let you choose from a variety of formats along with choices for paper orientation and size.

Using the Contact List to Address an E-Mail Message

When you address an e-mail message, you must know the e-mail address of the recipient of the message. Previously, when an e-mail message was addressed, the e-mail address was typed in the To text box in the Message window (see Figure 1-31 on page OUT 25). In addition to entering the e-mail address by typing the e-mail address, an e-mail address can be entered using the contact list. The following steps show how to use the contact list to address an e-mail message to Patti Sabol.

To Use the Contact List to Address an E-Mail Message

1

- **Click the Mail button in the Navigation Pane to display the Inbox window.**
- **Click the New Mail Message button on the Standard toolbar.**
- **When Outlook displays the Untitled Message window, if necessary, double-click its title bar to maximize it.**

Outlook displays the Untitled Message window (Figure 1-74) with the insertion point in the To text box.

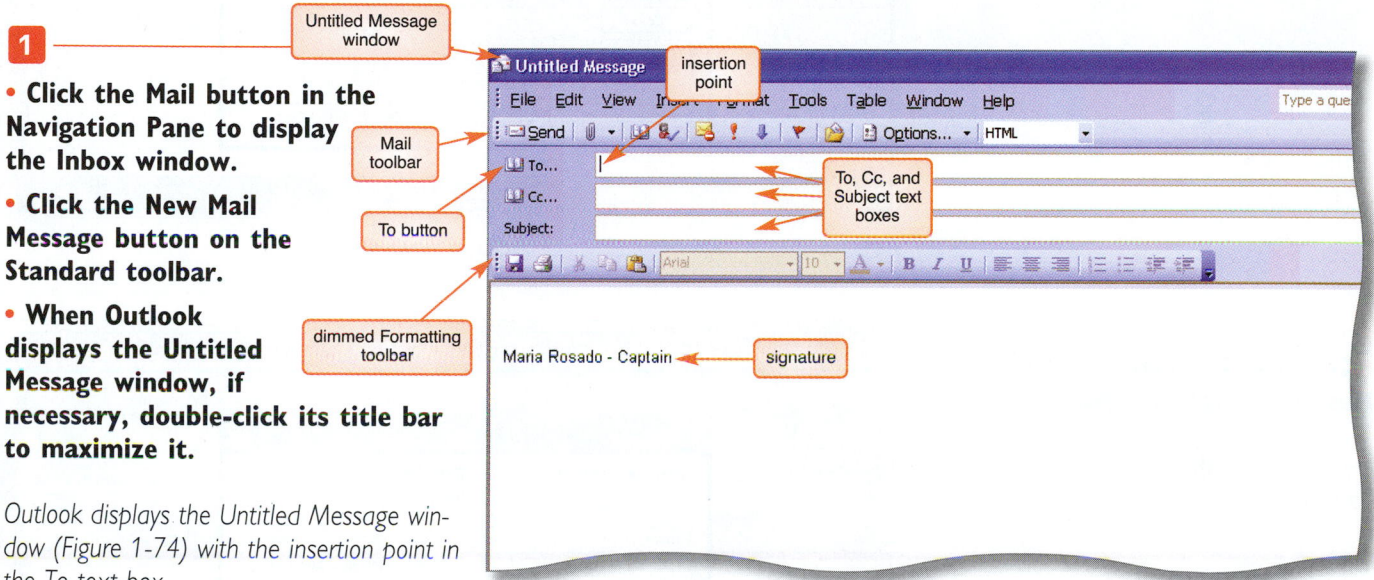

FIGURE 1-74

2

- **Click the To button on the left side of the Message window.**
- **When Outlook displays the Select Names dialog box, click the Show Names from the box arrow.**

Outlook displays the Select Names dialog box (Figure 1-75). The Show Names from the list displays the available contact lists from which to choose.

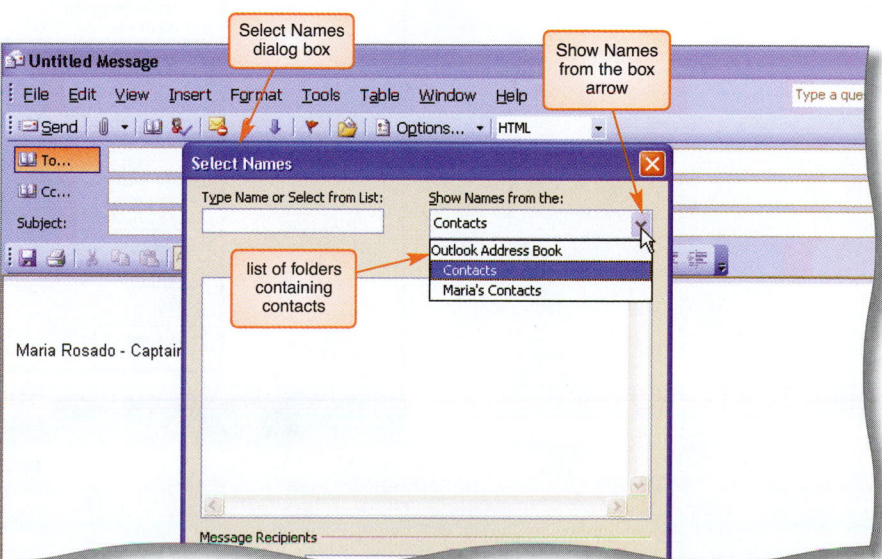

FIGURE 1-75

3

- **Click Maria's Contacts in the list.**
- **Click the Patti Sabol entry in the E-mail Address list box.**

The Patti Sabol entry in the E-mail Address list box is selected (Figure 1-76).

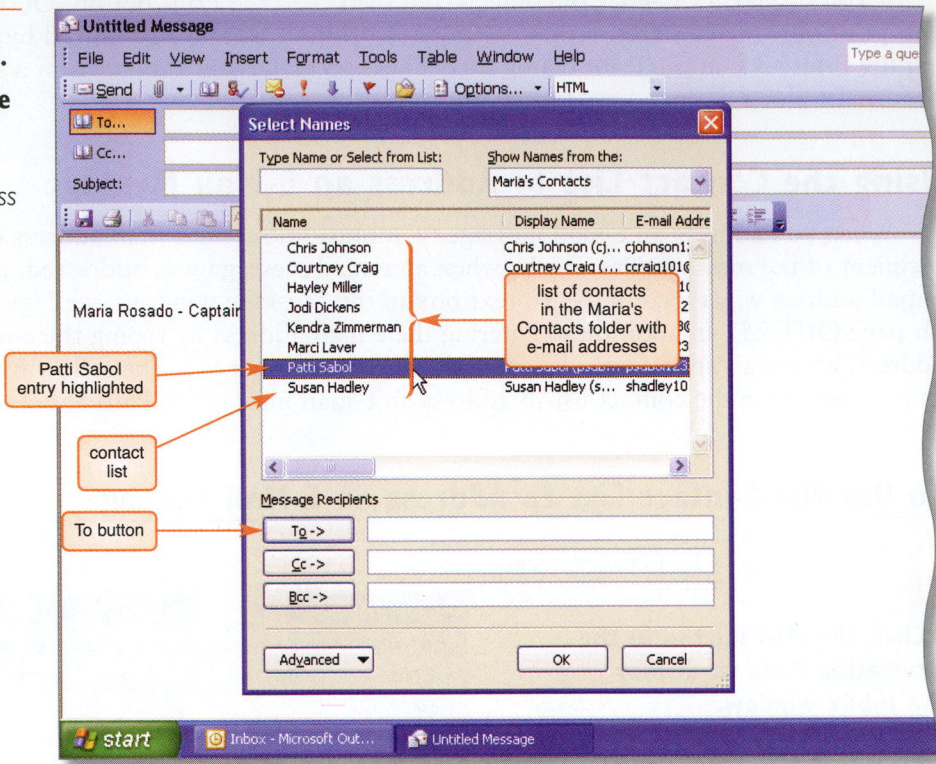

FIGURE 1-76

4

- **Click the To button in the Message Recipients area.**

Outlook displays the Patti Sabol entry in the To text box (Figure 1-77).

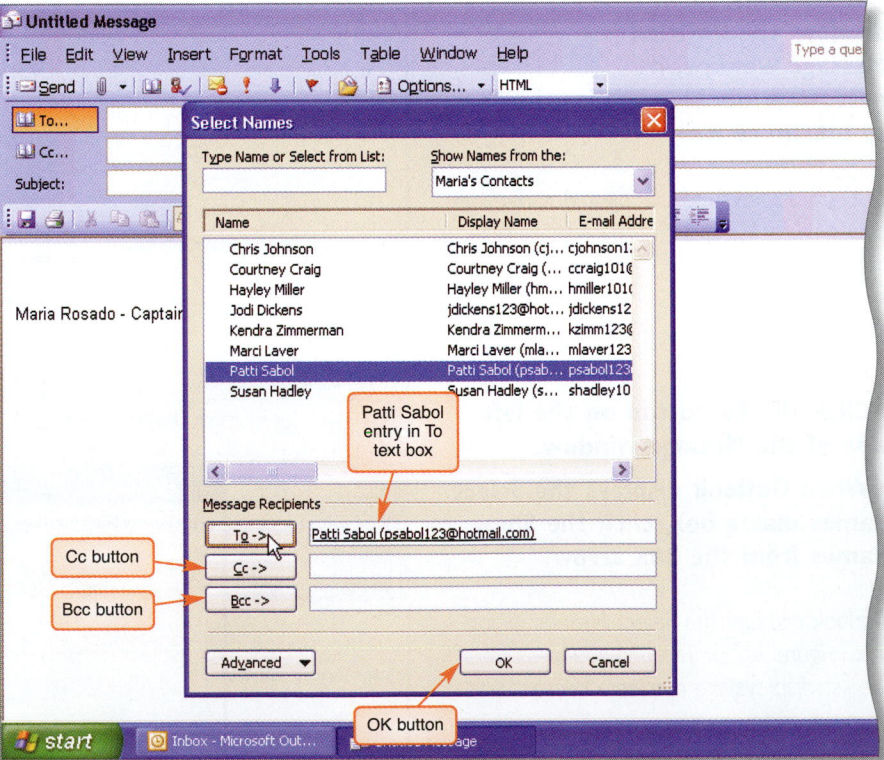

FIGURE 1-77

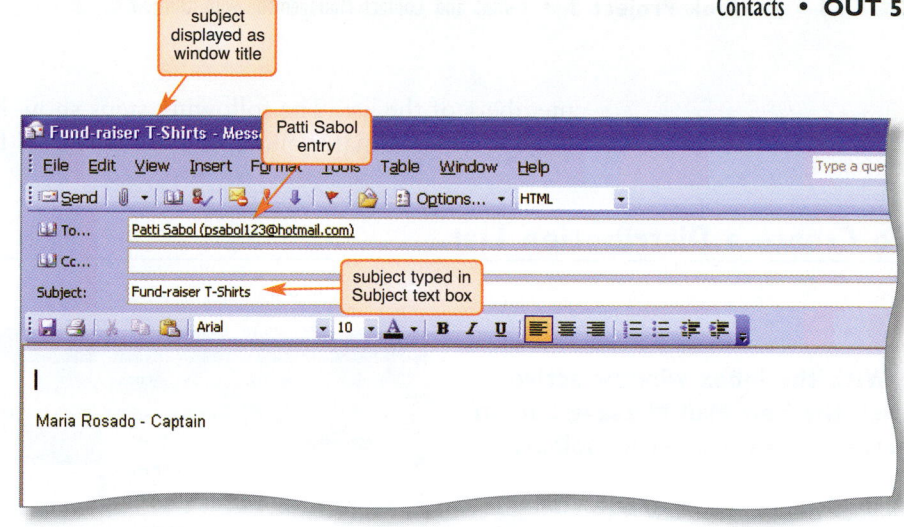

FIGURE 1-78

5

- Click the **OK** button.
- Click the **Subject** text box and then type Fund-raiser T-Shirts as the entry.
- Press the **TAB** key.

Outlook closes the Select Names dialog box, and displays the Patti Sabol entry in the To text box in the Message window (Figure 1-78).

6

- **Type** Patti, I need help! **and then press the** **ENTER** **key twice.**
- **Type** The T-shirts for the team fund-raiser will be ready at 2:00 p.m. on Friday. I will be in class at that time, so I will need you to pick them up.

Outlook displays the e-mail message in the message body (Figure 1-79).

7

- Click the **Send** button.

Outlook closes the Message window, displays the Inbox window, stores the e-mail message in the Outbox folder temporarily while it sends the message, and then moves the message to the Sent Items folder.

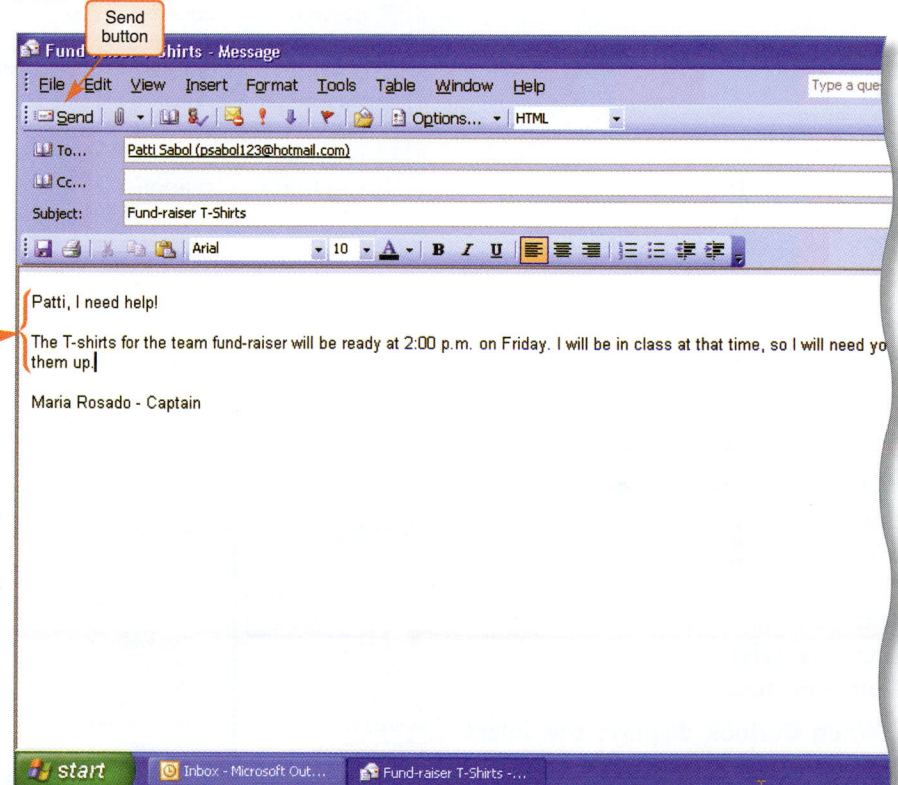

FIGURE 1-79

Other Ways

1. Click Address Book button on Mail toolbar

You can add as many names as you want to the To text box in Figure 1-77. You also can add names to the Cc text box. If you do not want those listed in the To text box or Cc text box to know you sent a copy to someone else, send a **blind copy** by adding the name to the Bcc text box.

Creating and Modifying a Distribution List

If you find yourself sending e-mail messages to the same group of people over and over, then you should consider creating a distribution list. A **distribution list** is similar to a category of contacts in that when you select the name of the distribution list as the recipient of an e-mail message, Outlook will send the message to all the

Microsoft Office
Outlook 2003

members of the list. The following steps show how to create a distribution list titled Computer Classmates and add three members from the Maria's Contacts list.

To Create a Distribution List

1

• **With the Inbox window active, click the New Mail Message button arrow on the Standard toolbar.**

Outlook displays the New Mail Message menu (Figure 1-80).

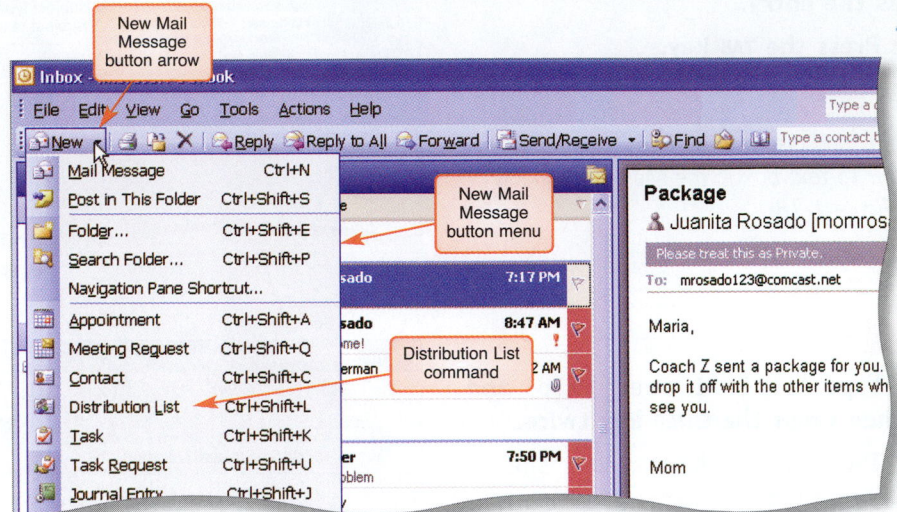

FIGURE 1-80

2

• **Click Distribution List.**

• **When Outlook displays the Untitled - Distribution List window, type** Computer Classmates **in the Name text box, and then click the Select Members button.**

• **When Outlook displays the Select Members dialog box, click the Show Names from the box arrow and click Maria's Contacts.**

• **Select Chris Johnson and then click the Members button.**

• **Add Hayley Miller and Susan Hadley in the same manner to the Members list in the Add to distribution list area.**

Outlook displays the three members to add to the Computer Classmates Members list (Figure 1-81). The Members list is displayed in the Add to distribution list area at the bottom of the Select Members dialog box.

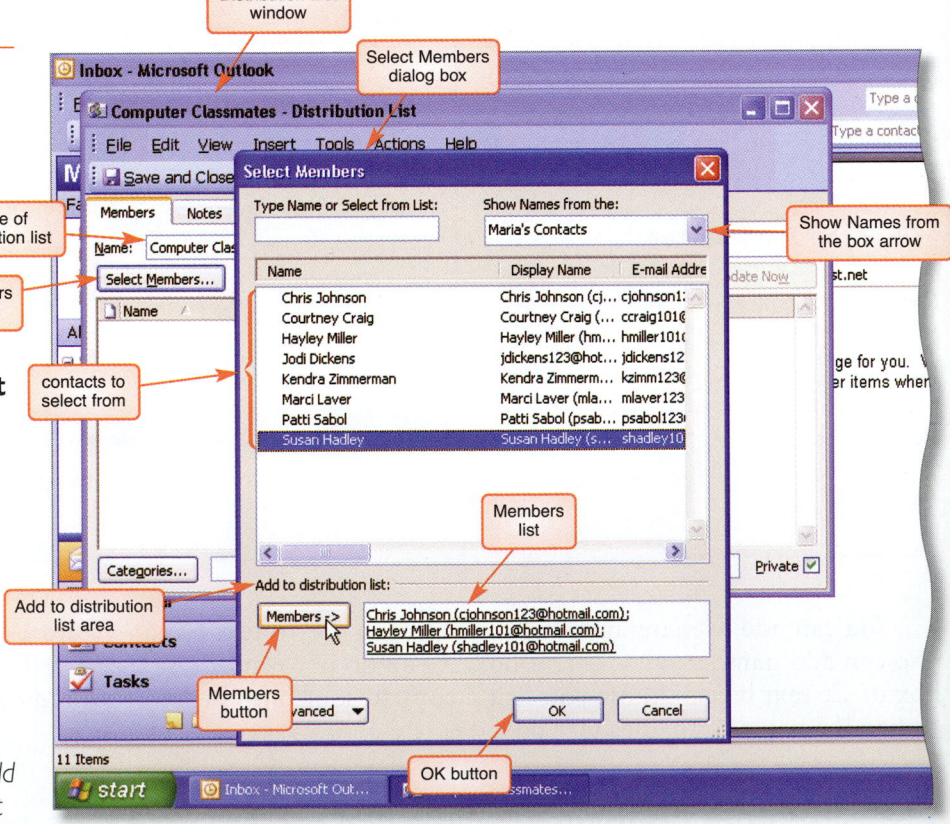

FIGURE 1-81

3

• **Click the OK button.**

Outlook displays the members of the Computer Classmates distribution list in the Untitled - Distribution List window (Figure 1-82).

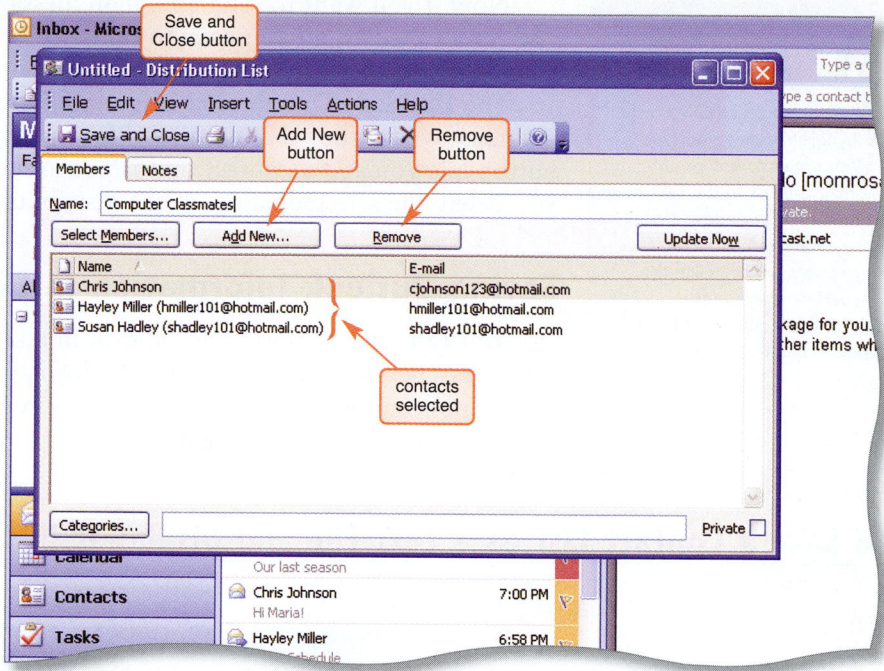

FIGURE 1-82

4

• **Click the Save and Close button on the Standard toolbar.**

Outlook closes the Untitled - Distribution List window, adds the new distribution list to the contact list, and activates the Inbox window.

5

• **Click the Address Book button on the Standard toolbar.**

Outlook displays the Address Book window, which includes the Computer Classmates distribution list (Figure 1-83).

6

• **Click the Close button on the right side of the title bar in the Address Book window.**

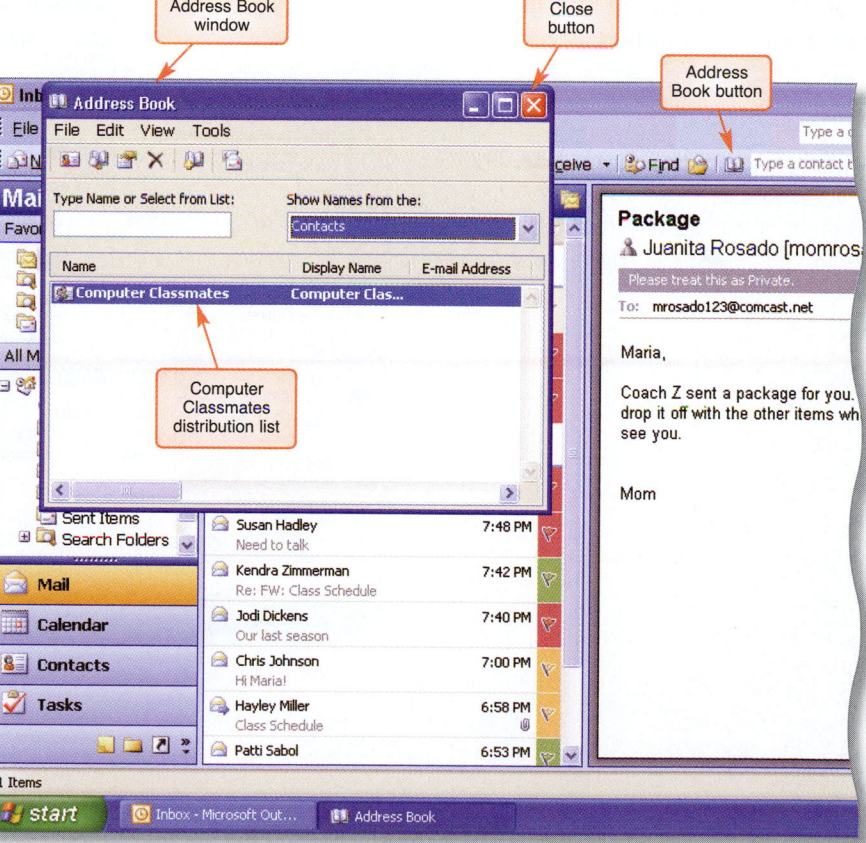

FIGURE 1-83

Now if you want to send an e-mail message to Chris Johnson, Hayley Miller, and Susan Dudley, all you have to do is select the distribution list Computer Classmates as the recipient of the e-mail message.

The Untitled - Distribution List window in Figure 1-82 on the previous page includes two buttons that are useful for modifying a distribution list. The Add New button lets you add a contact that is not in the contact list. The Remove button lets you delete the selected names in the distribution list.

Saving Outlook Information in Different Formats

You can save Outlook files on disk in a several formats. For example, you can save messages and contact lists in text format, which can be read or copied into other applications. The following steps show how to save a contact list on disk as a text file and display it in Notepad.

To Save a Contact List as a Text File and Display It in Notepad

1

• **Insert the Data Disk in drive A.**

• **With the Contacts window active, click the name bar of the first contact in the contact list.**

• **Press CTRL+A to select all the contacts.**

• **Click File on the menu bar.**

All the contacts are selected and Outlook displays the File menu (Figure 1-84).

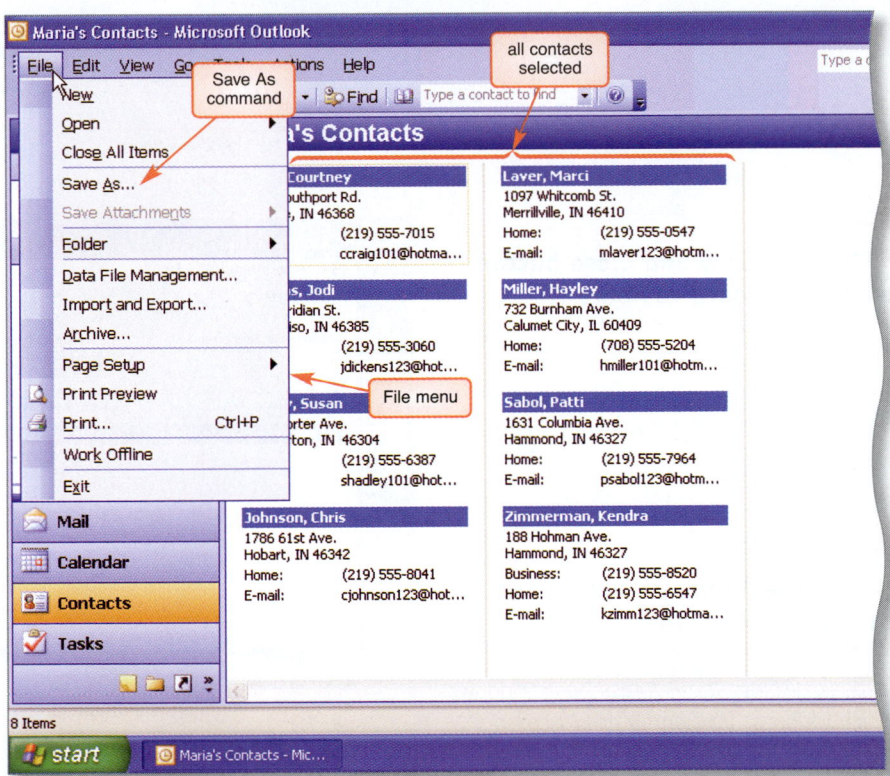

FIGURE 1-84

2
- Click Save As on the File menu.
- When Outlook displays the Save As dialog box, type Maria's Contacts in the File name text box.
- If necessary, select Text Only in the Save as type box.
- Click the Save in box arrow and then select 3½ Floppy (A:).

Outlook displays the Save As dialog box as shown in Figure 1-85.

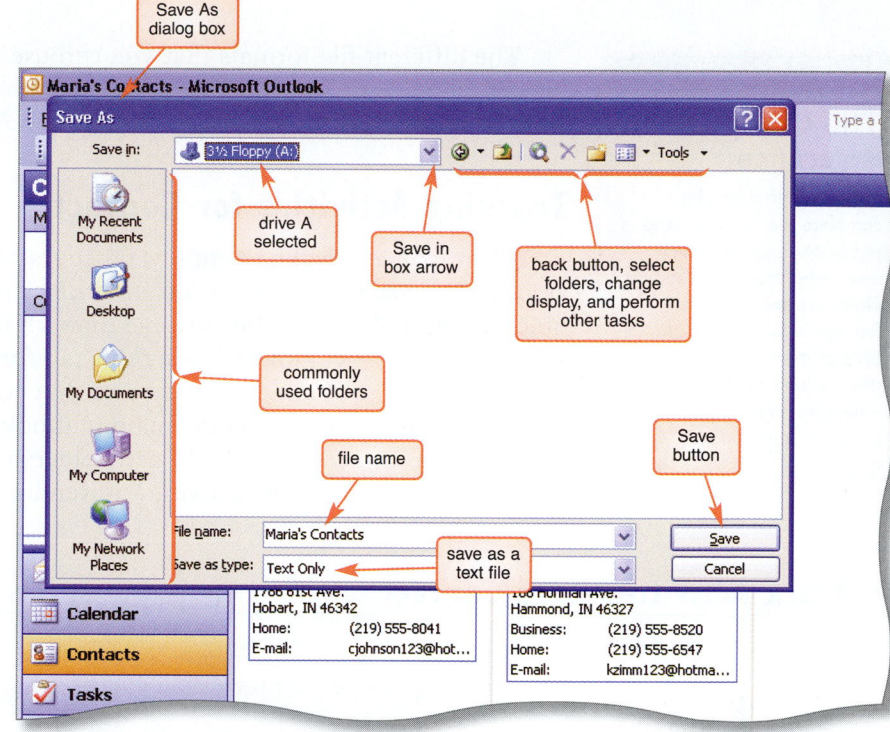

FIGURE 1-85

3
- Click the Save button in the Save As dialog box.
- Click the Start button on the Windows taskbar, point to All Programs on the Start menu, point to Accessories on the All Programs submenu, and then click Notepad on the Accessories submenu.
- When Notepad starts, click the Maximize button on the title bar, click File on the menu bar, and then click Open.
- When Outlook displays the Open dialog box, click the Files of type box arrow, click All Files, click the Look in box arrow, and then click 3½ Floppy (A:) in the Look in list.
- Double-click Maria's Contacts.

Notepad displays Maria's Contacts as a text file (Figure 1-86).

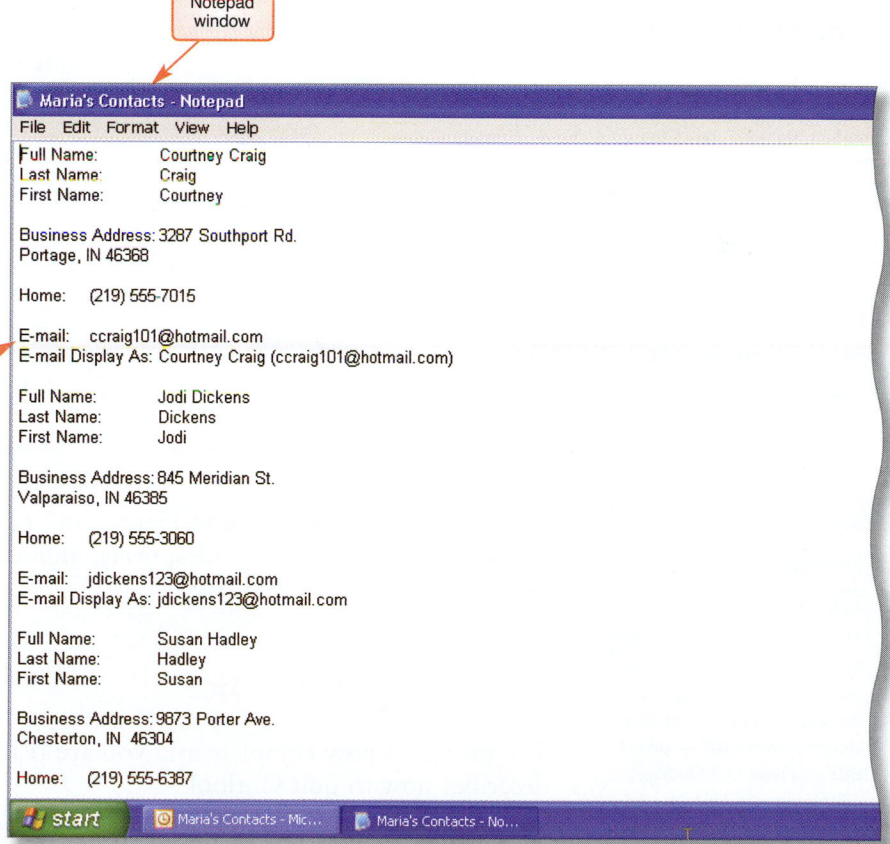

FIGURE 1-86

4
- After viewing the text file, click the Close button on the right side of the Notepad title bar.

More About

**The Quick
Reference**

For a table that lists how to
complete the tasks covered in
this book using the mouse,
menu, shortcut menu, and
keyboard, see the Quick
Reference Summary at the
back of this book, or visit
the Outlook 2003 Quick
Reference Web page
(scsite.com/out2003/
qr).

The different file formats that you can use to save information is dependent on the component you are working in. To view the different file formats for a component, click the Save as type arrow in the Save As dialog box.

Tracking Activities for Contacts

When you are dealing with several contacts, it can be useful to have all associated e-mails, documents, or other items related to the contact available quickly. Outlook makes this possible through the use of the Activities tab in the selected contact's window. Clicking this tab for any contact in your contact list will provide you a list of all items related to that contact. Outlook searches for items linked only to the contact in the main Outlook folders (Contacts, Calendar, etc.); however, you can create and add new folders to be searched. The following steps illustrate how to track the activities of Kendra Zimmerman.

To Track Activities for a Contact

1

• **With Contacts window active, double-click the Kendra Zimmerman contact heading.**

• **Click the Activities tab.**

Outlook displays the Kendra Zimmerman – Contact window with the Activities sheet showing a list of items related to Kendra Zimmerman (Figure 1-87).

2

• **Click the Close button on the Kendra Zimmerman – Contact window.**

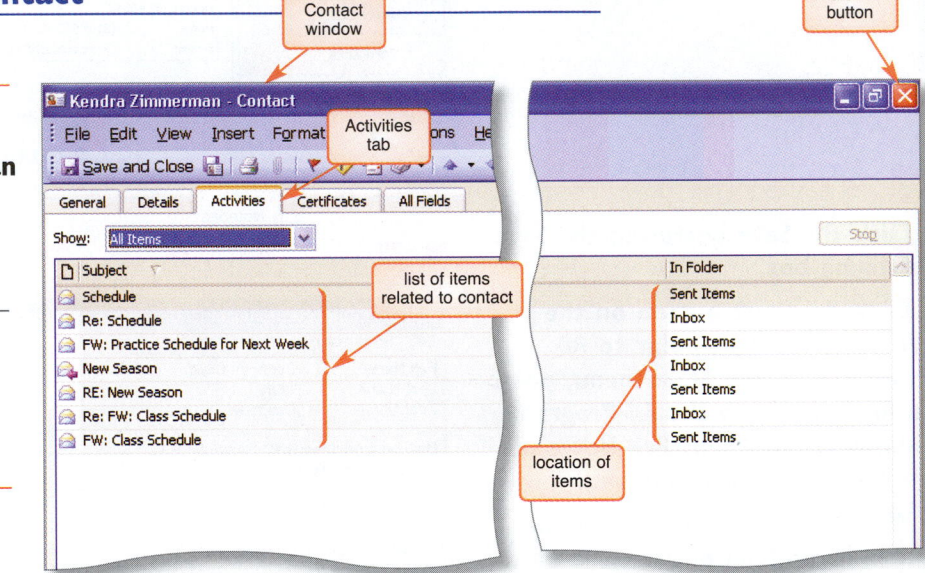

FIGURE 1-87

More About

**Microsoft
Certification**

The Microsoft Office
Specialist Certification program provides an opportunity
for you to obtain a valuable
industry credential — proof
that you have the Outlook
2003 skills required by
employers. For more information, see Appendix E or
visit the Outlook 2003
Certification Web page
(scsite.com/out2003/
cert).

The list of items shown in Figure 1-87 consists entirely of e-mail messages. You also can link items such as files, tasks, and appointments. E-mail messages are automatically linked to the contact.

Quitting Outlook

The project is now complete and you are ready to quit Outlook. The following step describes how to quit Outlook.

To Quit Outlook

1 **Click the Close button on the Outlook title bar.**

Outlook is closed, and the Windows desktop appears.

Project Summary

In this project, you learned to use Outlook to open, read, print, reply to, forward, delete, sign, compose, format, and send e-mail messages. You opened and viewed file attachments as well as attached a file to an e-mail message. You learned how to flag, sort, and set importance and delivery options to e-mail messages. You added and deleted contacts to a contact list. Finally, you used the contact list to create a distribution list and track activities of a contact.

What You Should Know

Having completed this project, you should be able to perform the tasks below. The tasks are listed in the same order they were presented in this project. For a list of the buttons, menus, toolbars, and commands introduced in this project, see the Quick Reference Summary at the back of this book and refer to the Page Number column.

1. Start and Customize Outlook (OUT 6)
2. Open (Read) an E-Mail Message (OUT 11)
3. Print an Opened E-Mail Message (OUT 12)
4. Close an E-Mail Message (OUT 13)
5. Reply to an E-Mail Message (OUT 13)
6. Forward an E-Mail Message (OUT 16)
7. Delete an E-Mail Message (OUT 17)
8. View a File Attachment (OUT 18)
9. Create and Insert an E-Mail Signature (OUT 20)
10. Compose an E-Mail Message (OUT 24)
11. Format an E-Mail Message (OUT 26)
12. Attach a File to an E-Mail Message (OUT 28)
13. Send an E-Mail Message (OUT 29)
14. Flag E-Mail Messages (OUT 30)
15. Sort E-Mail Messages by Flag Color (OUT 31)
16. Create and Apply a View Filter (OUT 32)
17. Set Message Importance, Sensitivity, and Delivery Options in a Single Message (OUT 34)
18. Change the Default Level of Importance and Sensitivity (OUT 36)
19. Create a Personal Folder (OUT 40)
20. Create a Contact List (OUT 42)
21. Change the View and Sort the Contact List (OUT 45)
22. Find a Contact (OUT 46)
23. Organize Contacts (OUT 48)
24. Display the Contacts in a Category (OUT 49)
25. Preview and Print the Contact List (OUT 50)
26. Use the Contact List to Address an E-Mail Message (OUT 51)
27. Create a Distribution List (OUT 54)
28. Save a Contact List as a Text File and Display It in Notepad (OUT 56)
29. Track Activities for a Contact (OUT 58)
30. Quit Outlook (OUT 58)

Learn It Online

Instructions: To complete the Learn It Online exercises, start your browser, click the Address bar, and then enter the Web address scsite.com/out2003/learn. When the Outlook 2003 Learn It Online page is displayed, follow the instructions in the exercises below. Each exercise has instructions for printing your results, either for your own records or for submission to your instructor.

1 Project Reinforcement TF, MC, and SA

Below Outlook Project 1, click the Project Reinforcement link. Print the quiz by clicking Print on the File menu for each page. Answer each question.

2 Flash Cards

Below Outlook Project 1, click the Flash Cards link and read the instructions. Type 20 (or a number specified by your instructor) in the Number of playing cards text box, type your name in the Enter your Name text box, and then click the Flip Card button. When the flash card is displayed, read the question and then click the ANSWER box arrow to select an answer. Flip through Flash Cards. If your score is 15 (75%) correct or greater, click Print on the File menu to print your results. If your score is less than 15 (75%) correct, then redo this exercise by clicking the Replay button.

3 Practice Test

Below Outlook Project 1, click the Practice Test link. Answer each question, enter your first and last name at the bottom of the page, and then click the Grade Test button. When the graded practice test is displayed on your screen, click Print on the File menu to print a hard copy. Continue to take practice tests until you score 80% or better.

4 Who Wants To Be a Computer Genius?

Below Outlook Project 1, click the Computer Genius link. Read the instructions, enter your first and last name at the bottom of the page, and then click the PLAY button. When your score is displayed, click the PRINT RESULTS link to print a hard copy.

5 Wheel of Terms

Below Outlook Project 1, click the Wheel of Terms link. Read the instructions, and then enter your first and last name and your school name. Click the PLAY button. When your score is displayed, right-click the score and then click Print on the shortcut menu to print a hard copy.

6 Crossword Puzzle Challenge

Below Outlook Project 1, click the Crossword Puzzle Challenge link. Read the instructions, and then enter your first and last name. Click the SUBMIT button. Work the crossword puzzle. When you are finished, click the Submit button. When the crossword puzzle is redisplayed, click the Print Puzzle button to print a hard copy.

7 Tips and Tricks

Below Outlook Project 1, click the Tips and Tricks link. Click a topic that pertains to Project 1. Right-click the information and then click Print on the shortcut menu. Construct a brief example of what the information relates to in Outlook to confirm you understand how to use the tip or trick.

8 Newsgroups

Below Outlook Project 1, click the Newsgroups link. Click a topic that pertains to Project 1. Print three comments.

9 Expanding Your Horizons

Below Outlook Project 1, click the Expanding Your Horizons link. Click a topic that pertains to Project 1. Print the information. Construct a brief example of what the information relates to in Outlook to confirm you understand the contents of the article.

10 Search Sleuth

Below Outlook Project 1, click the Search Sleuth link. To search for a term that pertains to this project, select a term below the Project 1 title and then use the Google search engine at google.com (or any major search engine) to display and print two Web pages that present information on the term.

11 Outlook Online Training

Below Outlook Project 1, click the Outlook Online Training link. When your browser displays the Microsoft Office Online Web page, click the Outlook link. Click one of the Outlook courses that covers one or more of the objectives listed at the beginning of the project on page OUT 4. Print the first page of the course before stepping through it.

12 Office Marketplace

Below Outlook Project 1, click the Office Marketplace link. When your browser displays the Microsoft Office Online Web page, click the Office Marketplace link. Click a topic that relates to Outlook. Print the first page.

Apply Your Knowledge

1 Creating a Contact List

Instructions: Start Outlook. Create a Contacts folder using your name as the name of the new folder. Create a contact list using the people listed in Table 1-4. Use the Department text box in the Details sheet to enter the student's grade level. Create a distribution list consisting of freshmen and sophomores. Sort the list by last name in descending sequence. When the list is complete, print the list in Card Style view and submit to your instructor.

Table 1-4	Contact Information			
NAME	TELEPHONE	ADDRESS	E-MAIL ADDRESS	GRADE LEVEL
Beth Thomas	(219) 555-6434	9865 Wexford	bthomas@isp.com	Sophomore
Jose Tinoco	(219) 555-6374	846 W. 5th	jtinoco@isp.com	Senior
David Price	(219) 555-1470	752 Calumet	dprice@isp.com	Senior
Kris Clark	(219) 555-0560	1853 Colonial	kclark@isp.com	Freshman
Judy Watson	(219) 555-5431	1548 Clay	jwatson@isp.com	Sophomore
Walter Stern	(219) 555-5415	2187 Porter	wstern@isp.com	Junior

In the Lab

Importing Subfolders for the In the Lab Exercises — Follow these steps to import subfolders for the following In the Lab Exercises:

1. Insert the Data Disk into drive A.
2. Click File on the Outlook menu bar and then click Import and Export.
3. In the Import and Export Wizard dialog box, click Import from another program or file and then click the Next button.
4. In the Import a File dialog box, click Personal Folder File (.pst) and then click the Next button.
5. In the Import Personal Folders dialog box, click the Browse button to access drive A, select the appropriate subfolder, click Open, and then click the Next button.
6. In the Import Personal Folders dialog box, select the appropriate folder to import from and then click the Finish button.

1 Creating a Distribution List and Sending E-Mail

Problem: You are the volunteer campaign chairperson of a friend's campaign for state senator. Part of your responsibilities is to solicit and organize campaign donations. To do so, you need to maintain and contact a list of past and potential donors.

Instructions Part 1: Import the Lab 1-1 Contacts folder (Figure 1-88 on the next page) into Outlook. Create two distribution lists; one consisting of past donors, the other consisting of potential donors. The status of each contact can be found in the Job Title text box. Print each distribution list and submit to your instructor.

(continued)

In the Lab

Creating a Distribution List and Sending E-Mail *(continued)*

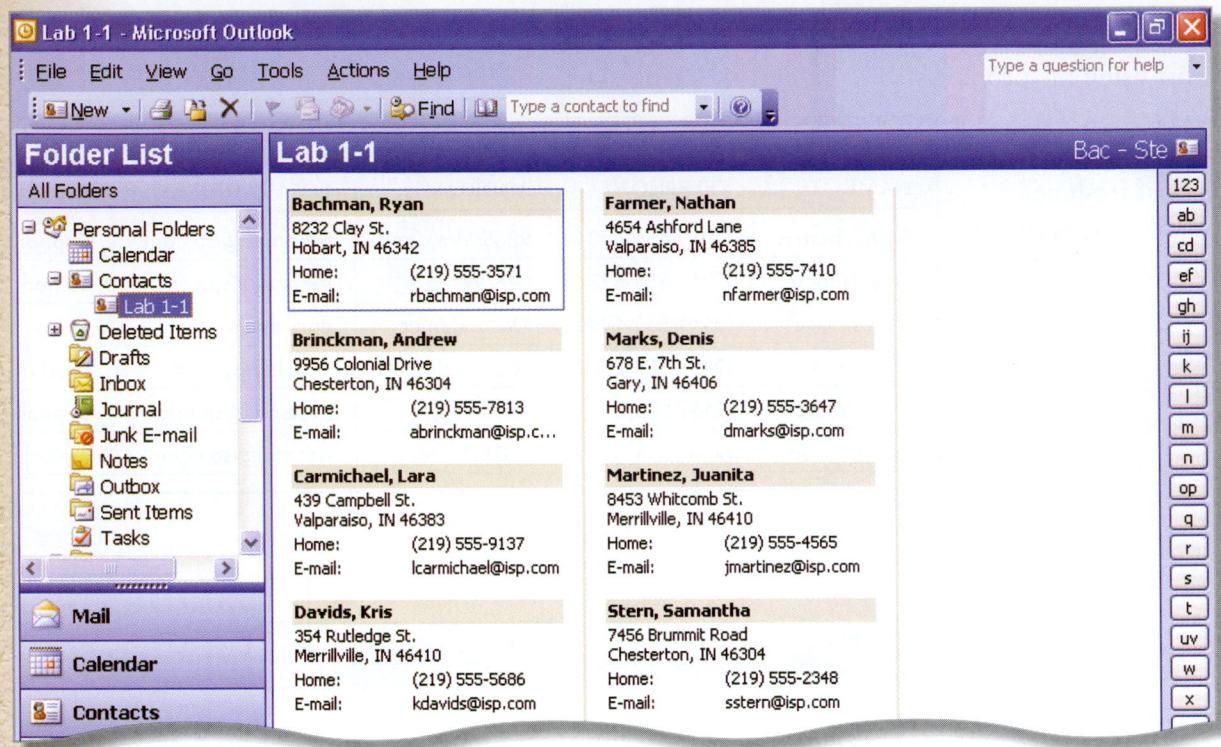

FIGURE 1-88

Instructions Part 2: Do the following:

1. Compose a message to each group created in Part 1. The message to past donors should thank them for their past support and request donations for this year's campaign. The message to potential donors should include a few reasons why it would be beneficial to have your candidate in office.
2. Set the sensitivity for each message as confidential.
3. Using Microsoft Word, create a document called Campaign Platform, and include this file as an attachment with your e-mail messages.
4. Set the delivery for each message to November 1, 2005 at 9:00 a.m.
5. Format your messages to past donors as Plain Text and your messages to potential donors as HTML.
6. Print each e-mail message and hand them in to your instructor.

Instructions Part 3: Save the Lab 1-1 contact list as a text file. Open the file using Notepad. Print the contact list from Notepad and hand it in to your instructor.

2 Flagging and Sorting Messages

Problem: As student director of the Computer Help Center, you are responsible for responding to questions received via e-mail. Some questions require a more timely response than others do, so you need a way to sort the questions first by urgency and then by when they were received. At that point, you will be able to address the questions in an orderly manner.

In the Lab

Instructions: Import the Lab 1-2 Inbox folder (Figure 1-89) into Outlook. Read through each message and appropriately flag each one. Use a red flag for messages requiring immediate attention, yellow for messages requiring information before you can respond and green for non-urgent, general questions. After you have flagged each message, sort the messages based on flag color.

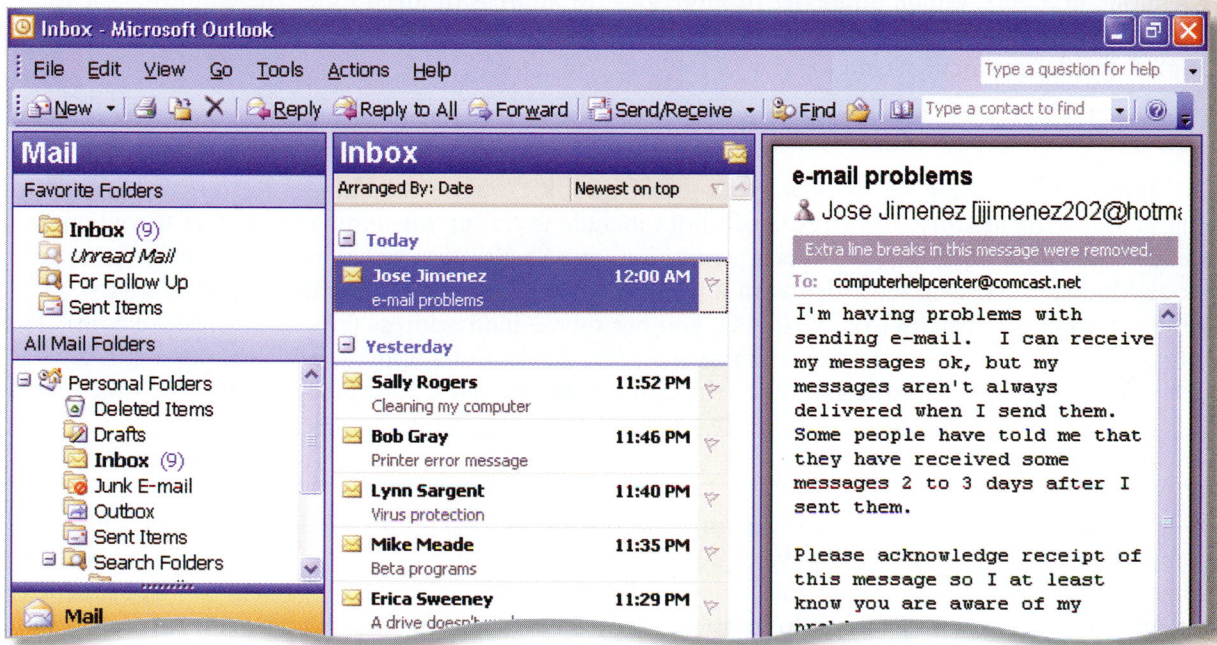

FIGURE 1-89

3 Creating an E-Mail Signature, Replying To, and Forwarding Messages

Problem: With all the messages sorted and flagged, you now have to respond to the messages. You need to perform this task in an efficient manner as it is the Computer Center's policy to respond to questions within 24 hours. It is also required that the name of the person responding, the Computer Center's telephone number, and its hours of operation appear on every reply.

Instructions Part 1: Create an e-mail signature consisting of your name, title (Director), a telephone number (555-1234), and hours of operation (8:00 a.m. – 8:00 p.m.). Click the New Message button on the Standard toolbar. Print the blank message containing the signature and hand it in to your instructor.

Instructions Part 2: Send a reply with the importance set at high to the messages flagged red. Forward the messages flagged yellow. You may use fictitious e-mail addresses for this exercise as the messages will not actually be sent. Hand in printouts of the replies and forwards to your instructor.

Instructions Part 3: Do the following:

1. Clear all the green flags from the non-urgent messages. Use Search Folders to display only the messages flagged for follow up. Make a list of the sender's name, subject, and flag color and hand it in to your instructor.

2. Using information from Microsoft Outlook Help, create a unique signature for a separate e-mail account. See your instructor about setting up a separate e-mail account.

3. Print a blank message containing the signature and hand it in to your instructor.

Cases and Places

The difficulty of these case studies varies:
■ are the least difficult and ■■ are more difficult. The last exercise is a group exercise.

1 ■ Create a contact list of your family, friends, and colleagues. Include their names, addresses, telephone numbers, e-mail addresses (if any), and IM address (if any). Enter the employer for each one, if appropriate. For family members, use the Detail sheet to list birthdays and wedding anniversaries (if any). Print the contact list and hand it in to your instructor.

2 ■ Import the Cases 1-2 Contacts folder into Outlook. You are the Human Resources Director for a large department store. Your responsibilities include updating the company contact list whenever someone changes positions, receives a promotion, etc. Sheila Weston has received a promotion to 3rd Floor Manager and was rewarded with a private office (Room 301), private telephone ((815) 555-0943) and fax number ((815) 555-0944), and her own e-mail address (sweston@bigstore.com). The information in her current record contains the general telephone number and store's e-mail. Find the Sheila Weston contact record and make the appropriate changes. Hand in a printout to your instructor.

3 ■ Import the Cases 1-3 Inbox folder into Outlook. You work in the IT department of a large company. Every day you receive several e-mail messages about various computer problems within the company. A coworker, Joe Smith, has been sending several e-mail messages to the IT department complaining that his problem has yet to be solved. You have been told to solve his problem. Apply a filter to the Cases 1-3 Inbox folder to display only the messages from Joe Smith. Respond to his latest e-mail message while sending a copy to your boss to show that you have found a resolution to Joe's problem. Hand in a printout of your reply to your instructor. Add Joe Smith to your contact list. Track the activities of Joe Smith. List the first five entries from the Activities list and hand it in to your instructor. After printing your reply message, delete all the messages from Joe Smith and remove the filter.

4 ■■ You recently accepted a position with an international construction company. Your first assignment is to make the main telephone and address file available to everyone in the firm. The file, which currently is maintained in a three-ring binder, contains names, addresses, telephone numbers, fax numbers, e-mail addresses, and Web site addresses of your company's subcontractors and vendors. You decide to create a contact list using Outlook so everyone can access the same information and automatically dial and send e-mail and access Web sites. Create a contact list that includes at least the names, addresses, and Web site URLs of seven construction companies. Use fictitious company names and addresses or look up construction companies on the Web using an Internet search engine. Create a Contacts subfolder in which to store the contact list. Categorize the contacts by subcontractor or vendor. Print the contact list and submit to your instructor.

5 ■■ **Working Together** Have each member of your team submit a design of a form for collecting contact information. Have them base the form on the available fields in the General and Details sheets in the Contact window. Have the team select the best form design. After selecting a form, Xerox copies for the entire class. Have your classmates fill out the form. Collect the forms and create a contact list from the collected information. Hand in printouts of the final contact list.

MICROSOFT OFFICE 2003
INTEGRATION

MICROSOFT
Office 2003 Integration

Integrating Office 2003 Applications and the World Wide Web

PROJECT

1

CASE PERSPECTIVE

Leland Mortgage is a mortgage broker for properties in several communities in Ohio. Loan agents find the right loans for borrowers, including borrowers who have income or credit difficulties. Lian Chang manages Leland Mortgage. In the past, the company enjoyed great success by being the only mortgage company in the area. Recently, the company's clientele has been using newer services, such as Internet-based mortgage companies and other local financial service providers.

Lian believes that the company's business would increase if she implements a marketing strategy that advertises the advantages Leland Mortgage has over competitors' services. Leland Mortgage offers nationally competitive interest rates and a simplified application process. In addition, Lian employs highly trained loan agents and a friendly staff. She is investigating ways to advertise these benefits in an efficient and cost-effective way. She thinks a Web site would be the answer, but she is inexperienced with the Internet. Lian knows that you are studying computer technology and asks you to help her create a Web site advertising Leland Mortgage.

Lian provides you with several files to get started, including the company's letterhead in a Word document, an Excel workbook that includes a chart, an Access database of the company's mortgage products, and a PowerPoint presentation that provides an overview of the company's mortgage application process. Using the information provided in these files, you are confident that you can create a compelling Web page that highlight's the company's strengths.

As you read through this project, you will learn how to use Office 2003 applications together to create a Web page.

Integrating Office 2003 Applications and the World Wide Web

Objectives

You will have mastered the material in this project when you can:

- Integrate the Office 2003 applications to create a Web site
- Add hyperlinks to a Word document
- Embed an Excel chart into a Word document
- Add scrolling text to a Web page created in Word
- Add a hyperlink to a PowerPoint slide
- Create Web pages from a PowerPoint presentation
- Create a data access page from an Access database
- Test a Web site in a browser

Introduction

Integration means joining parts so they work together or form a whole. In information technology, common usages can include the following:

1. Integration during product development combines activities, programs, or hardware components into a functional unit.
2. Integration in companies can bring different manufacturers' products together into an efficiently working system.
3. Integration in marketing combines products or components to meet objectives such as sharing a common purpose or creating demand. It includes such matters as consistent product pricing and packaging, advertising, and sales campaigns.
4. Integration in product design allows a unifying purpose and/or architecture, such as The Microsoft Office System. (The products also are sold individually, but they are designed with the same larger objectives and/or architecture.)

This Integration project will show you how you can use the functionality and productivity tools of the Microsoft Office System.

Integration Project — Leland Mortgage Web Site

Many businesses advertise their products and services on the Internet. Companies find it easy to create Web pages using information already saved in word processing, spreadsheet, database, or presentation software formats. The Web page creation capabilities of Microsoft Office 2003 make it simple for you to create an entire Web site using the information available. Word allows you to create and save a document as a Web page. PowerPoint provides the same capability and adds a navigation structure for browsing. In addition, an Access wizard helps you create data access pages that enable the Web page visitor to navigate through the database.

This project supplies the following four files of information to help you get started:

1. A Word document that contains the company letterhead, including logo images, company name, and company address (Figure 1-1a on page INT 6).
2. An Excel workbook with a Bar chart graphically illustrating the company's breakdown of mortgage type by mortgage amount (Figure 1-1b on page INT 6).
3. A PowerPoint slide show that contains general information about the company (Figure 1-1g on page INT 7).
4. An Access database that contains mortgage product information (Figure 1-1c on page INT 6).

The Leland Mortgage Web site should include the following:

1. A home page with a Bar chart that contains the mortgage type by mortgage amount (Figure 1-1e on page INT 7). Three hypertext links also are included on the home page: Application Process, Mortgage Products, and E-mail for Information.
2. The Mortgage Products data access page (Figure 1-1d on page INT 6) is created from the Access file. Clicking the Mortgage Products link on the home page accesses this Web page. On this Web page, visitors can scroll through the mortgage products, categorized by mortgage type.
3. The PowerPoint Web page (Figure 1-1g on page INT 7) displays information about the company's simplified application process. Clicking the Application Process link on the home page accesses this Web page.
4. Using the E-mail for Information hyperlink, you can create an e-mail message (Figure 1-1f on page INT 7). E-mail is sent to the e-mail address manager@isp.com.

The following pages contain a detailed explanation of these tasks.

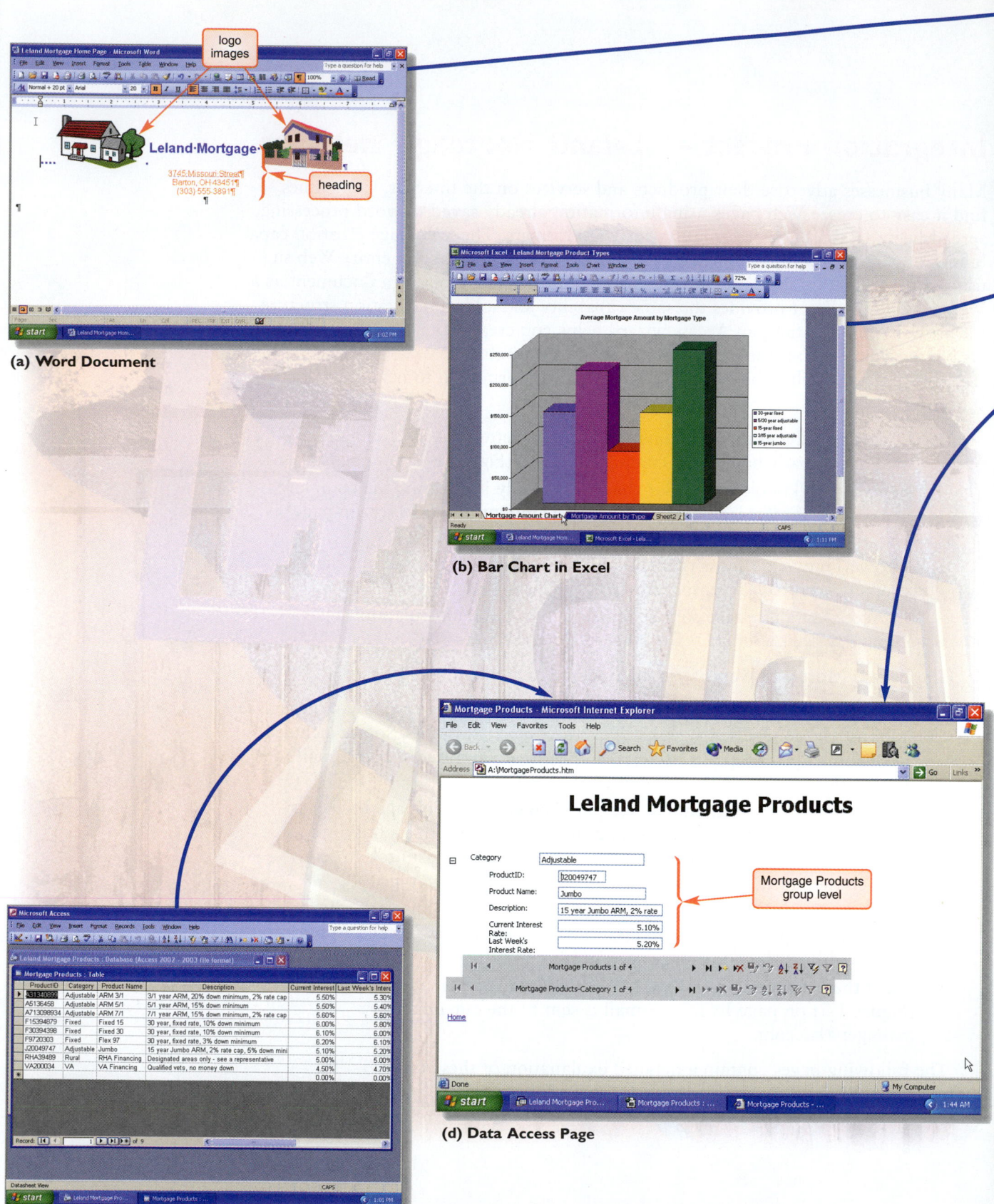

(a) Word Document

(b) Bar Chart in Excel

(c) Access Table

(d) Data Access Page

FIGURE 1-1

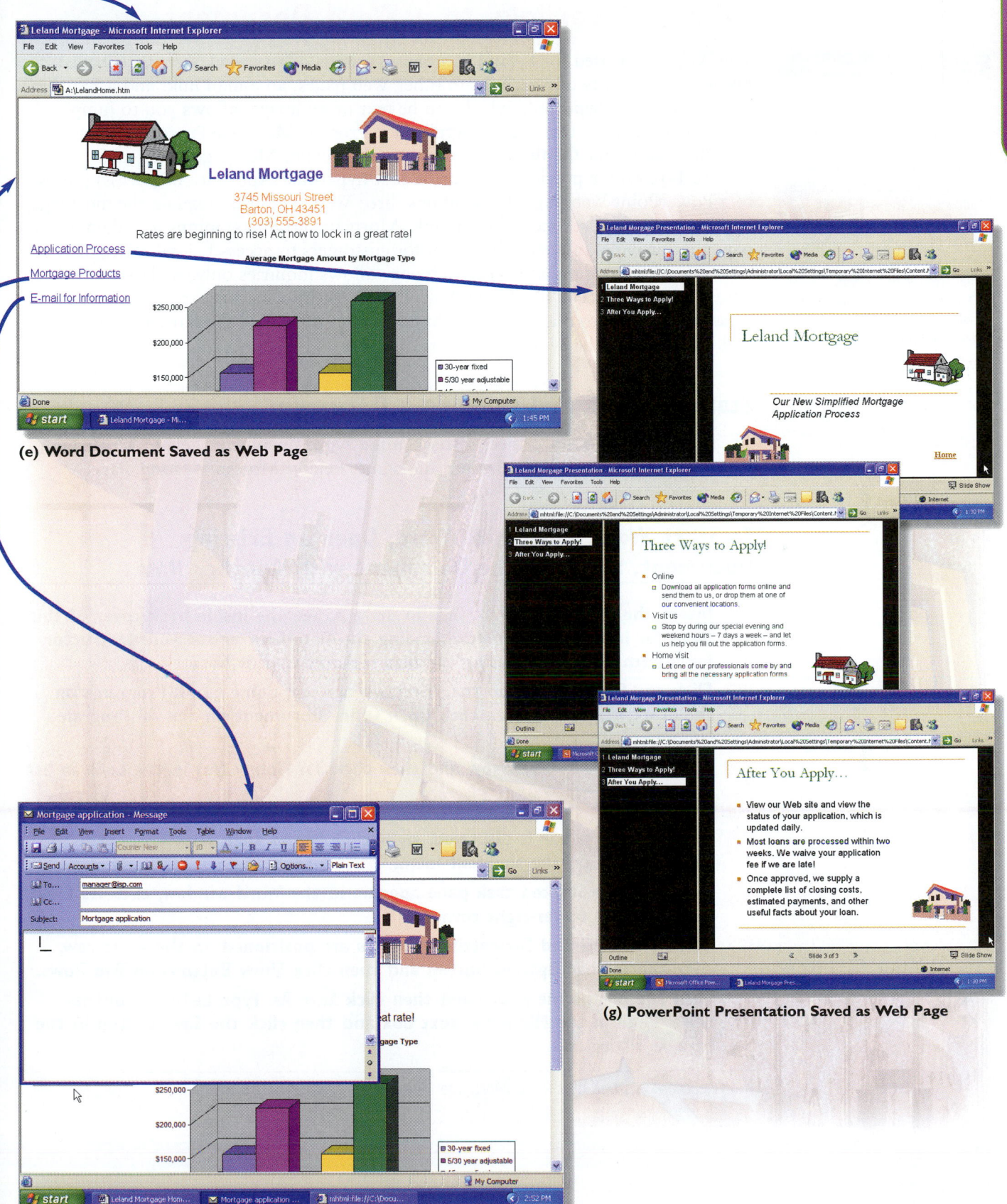

(e) Word Document Saved as Web Page

(g) PowerPoint Presentation Saved as Web Page

(f) New E-Mail Message Created from Hyperlink

Adding Hyperlinks to a Word Document

More About

Web Pages

Making information available on the Internet is a key aspect of business today. To facilitate this trend, the Office 2003 applications easily allow you to generate Web pages from existing files. An entire Web site can be created with files from Word, Excel, PowerPoint, or Access, using the Save as Web Page command on the File menu.

The Web site created for Leland Mortgage consists of an initial Web page, called the **home page**, with two hyperlinks to other Web pages, an e-mail link, and a Bar chart. Clicking a **hyperlink**, which can be text or an image, allows you to jump to another location. Text is used (Application Process, Mortgage Products, E-mail for Information) for the three hyperlinks on the Leland Mortgage home page (Figure 1-1e on the previous page). The first hyperlink (Application Process) jumps to a PowerPoint Web page that contains three Web pages that explain the mortgage application process. A second hyperlink (Mortgage Products) jumps to a data access page that provides inquiry capabilities for customers to access Leland Mortgage's mortgage product database. This Web page allows inquiries only; updating the database is prohibited. The third hyperlink (E-mail for Information) creates an e-mail message. In order to place the three hyperlinks to the left of the Bar chart, a table will be created in the Word document.

Starting Word and Opening a Document

The first step in this project is to open the Word document, Leland Mortgage Letterhead, and save it with the new file name, Leland Mortgage Home Page.

To Start Word, Customize Word, Open an Existing Document, and Save the Document with Another Name

1 Insert the Integration Data Disk in drive A. See the inside back cover of this book for instructions for downloading the Data Disk or see your instructor for information on accessing the files required in this book.

2 Click the Start button on the Windows taskbar, point to All Programs on the Start menu, and then click Open Office Document on the All Programs submenu.

3 Click the Look in box arrow and then click 3½ Floppy (A:) in the Look in list.

4 Double-click Leland Mortgage Letterhead.

5 If the Language bar is displayed, right-click it and then click Close the Language bar on the shortcut menu.

6 If the Getting Started task pane appears in the Word window, click its Close button in the upper-right corner.

7 If the Standard and Formatting toolbars are positioned on the same row, click the Toolbar Options button and then click Show Buttons on Two Rows.

8 Click File on the menu bar and then click Save As. Type Leland Mortgage Home Page in the File name text box and then click the Save button in the Save As dialog box.

The document is saved as Leland Mortgage Home Page (Figure 1-2).

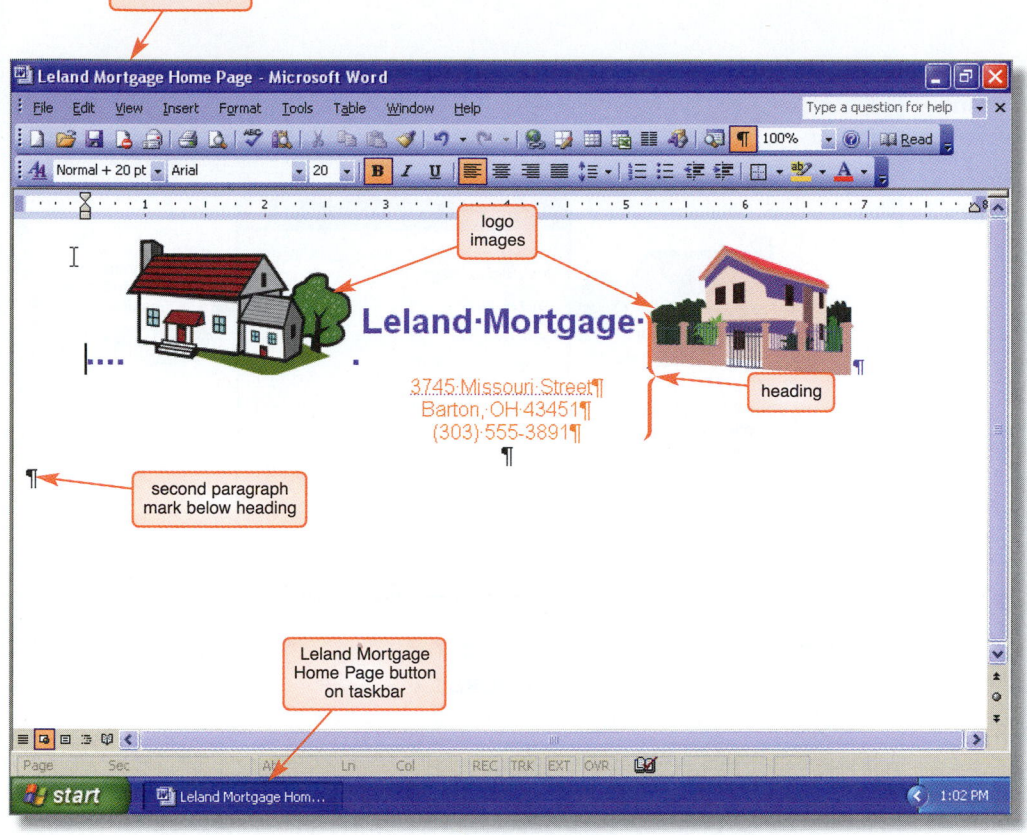

FIGURE 1-2

Inserting a Table into a Word Document

The next step is to insert a table with two columns and one row. The left column will contain three hyperlinks. The right column will contain the Bar chart.

The following steps add a table to the Leland Mortgage Home Page document.

To Insert a Table into a Word Document

1

• **Position the insertion point on the second paragraph mark below the company telephone number.**

• **Click Table on the menu bar, point to Insert, and then click Table.**

Word displays the Insert Table dialog box (Figure 1-3).

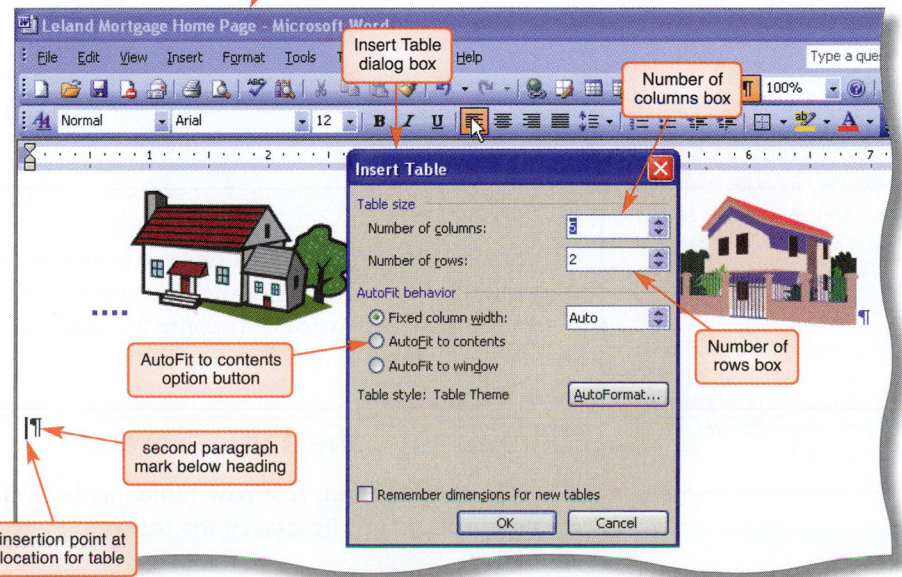

FIGURE 1-3

More About

Tables

You can use tables to create page layouts, such as side-by-side paragraphs, or to create text, graphics, and nested tables on a Web page. Tables are used frequently in Web pages to structure information and images.

2

• Type 2 **in the Number of columns box and then press the TAB key.**

• Type 1 **in the Number of rows box and then click AutoFit to contents in the AutoFit behavior area.**

The new settings appear in the Insert Table dialog box (Figure 1-4).

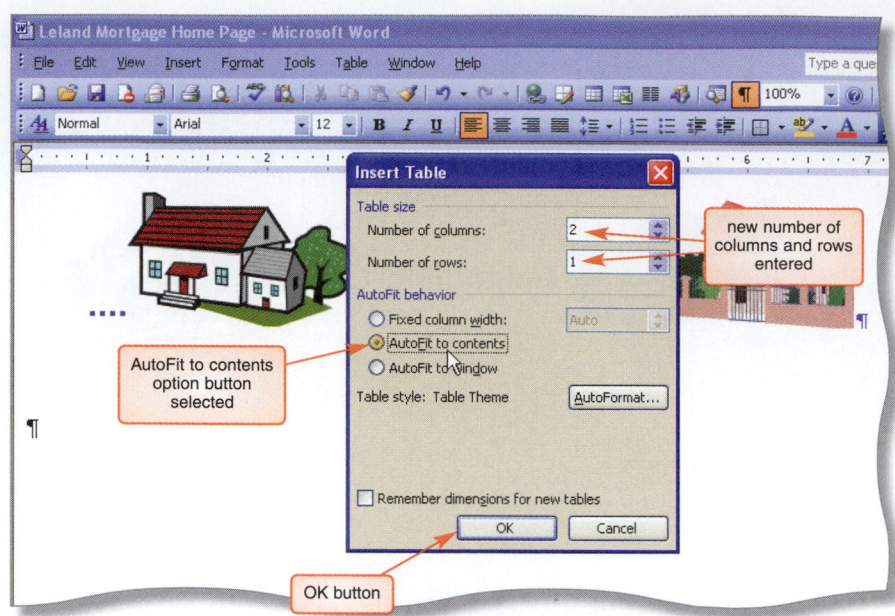

FIGURE 1-4

3

• **Click the OK button.**

Word displays the table in the document (Figure 1-5).

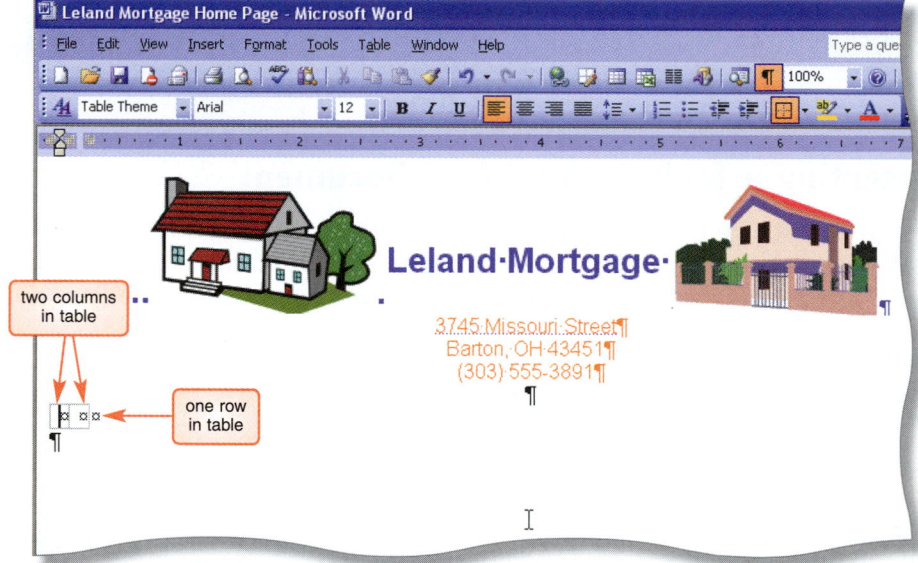

FIGURE 1-5

Step 2 instructed you to select AutoFit to contents. The **AutoFit to contents** option allows you to make the columns in a table fit the contents automatically. If you do not select AutoFit to contents, you can adjust the column widths manually using the sizing handles.

Eliminating the Table Border

The two-column, one-row table has been inserted into the Word document. The table border is not necessary for the Web page. The next steps remove the border of the table.

To Remove the Table Border

1

• Click **Table** on the menu bar and then click **Table Properties**.

• Click the **Borders and Shading** button in the **Table** sheet.

• When the **Borders and Shading** dialog box displays, if necessary, click the **Borders tab**.

Word displays the Borders and Shading dialog box (Figure 1-6).

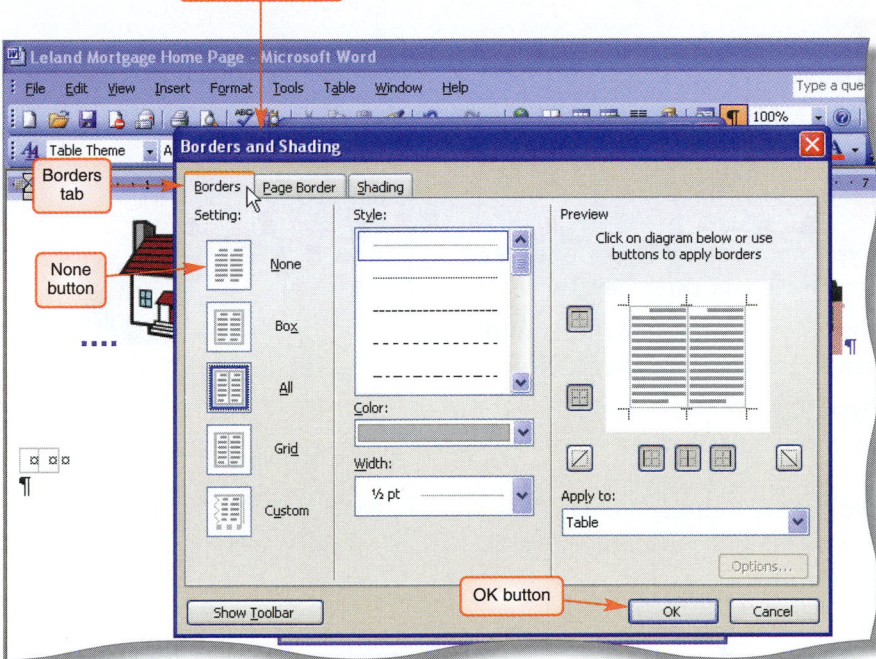

FIGURE 1-6

2

• Click the **None** button in the **Setting** area and then click the **OK** button in the **Borders and Shading** dialog box.

• Click the **OK** button in the **Table Properties** dialog box.

Word displays the borderless table (Figure 1-7).

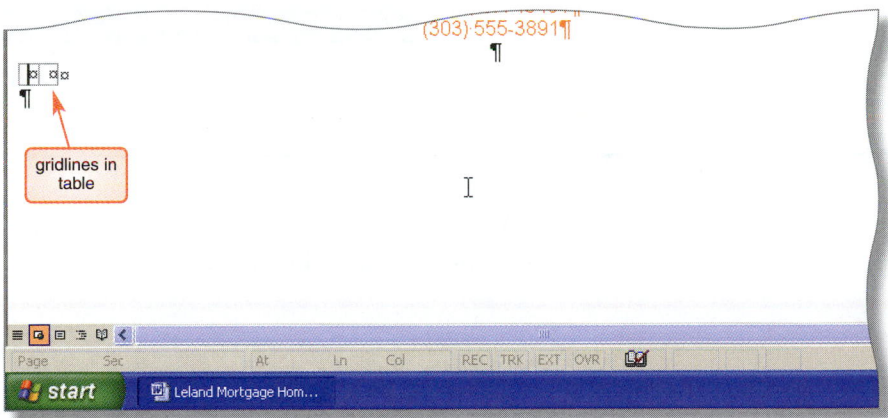

FIGURE 1-7

The border of the table displays with gridlines in the Word document. **Gridlines** can be used as a guide when entering text or images. When the document is viewed in your browser or printed, the gridlines do not display or print.

Inserting the Text for the Hyperlinks

After creating the borderless table, you must insert the three text phrases that will be used as hyperlinks on the home page. These phrases (Application Process, Mortgage Products, and E-mail for Information) allow the Web page visitor to jump to two other Web pages and create an e-mail message. The steps on the next page add the text phrases that are used as hyperlinks.

> *More About*
>
> ### Hyperlinks
>
> In addition to the way in which the hyperlinks are created in this project, you can copy and paste text as a hyperlink. Copy the text you want to the Clipboard, click where you want to insert the text, and then click Paste as Hyperlink on the Edit menu.

To Insert Text for Hyperlinks

1

• **If necessary, click the leftmost cell in the table.**

2

• **Type** Application Process **and then press the** ENTER **key twice.**

• **Type** Mortgage Products **and then press the** ENTER **key twice.**

• **Type** E-mail for Information **but do not press the** ENTER **key.**

Word displays the table with the three text phrases that will be used as hyperlinks (Figure 1-8).

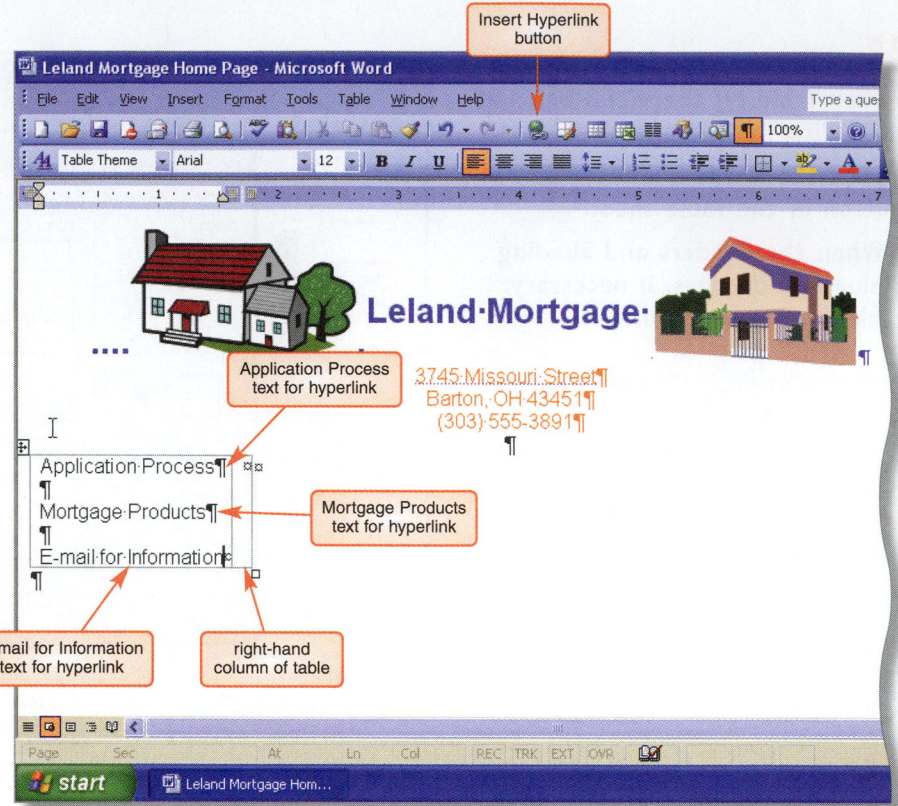

FIGURE 1-8

With the text phrases added, the next step is to select each text phrase and then insert the corresponding hyperlink.

Inserting a Hyperlink to PowerPoint Web Pages

The **Insert Hyperlink feature** provides the capability of linking to an existing file or Web page, to a place within the current document, to a newly created document, or to an e-mail address. In this project, two hyperlinks (Application Process and Mortgage Products) will be created that link to Web pages. The Application Process hyperlink will jump to a PowerPoint presentation that is saved as a Web page using the Web page name ApplicationProcess.htm. The Mortgage Products hyperlink will jump to a data access page using the Web page name MortgageProducts.htm. You will create the data access page later from an existing Access database. The third text phrase (E-mail for Information) links to an e-mail address, allowing the Web page visitor to send an e-mail message to the company's manager.

The following steps create a hyperlink for the first text phrase.

To Create a Hyperlink to PowerPoint Web Pages

1

• Drag through the text, Application Process, in the table.

• Click the Insert Hyperlink button on the Standard toolbar.

2

• If necessary, click the Existing File or Web Page button on the Link to bar.

• Type `ApplicationProcess.htm` in the Address text box.

The Insert Hyperlink dialog box is displayed with the name of the Web page in the Address text box (Figure 1-9).

3

• Click the OK button.

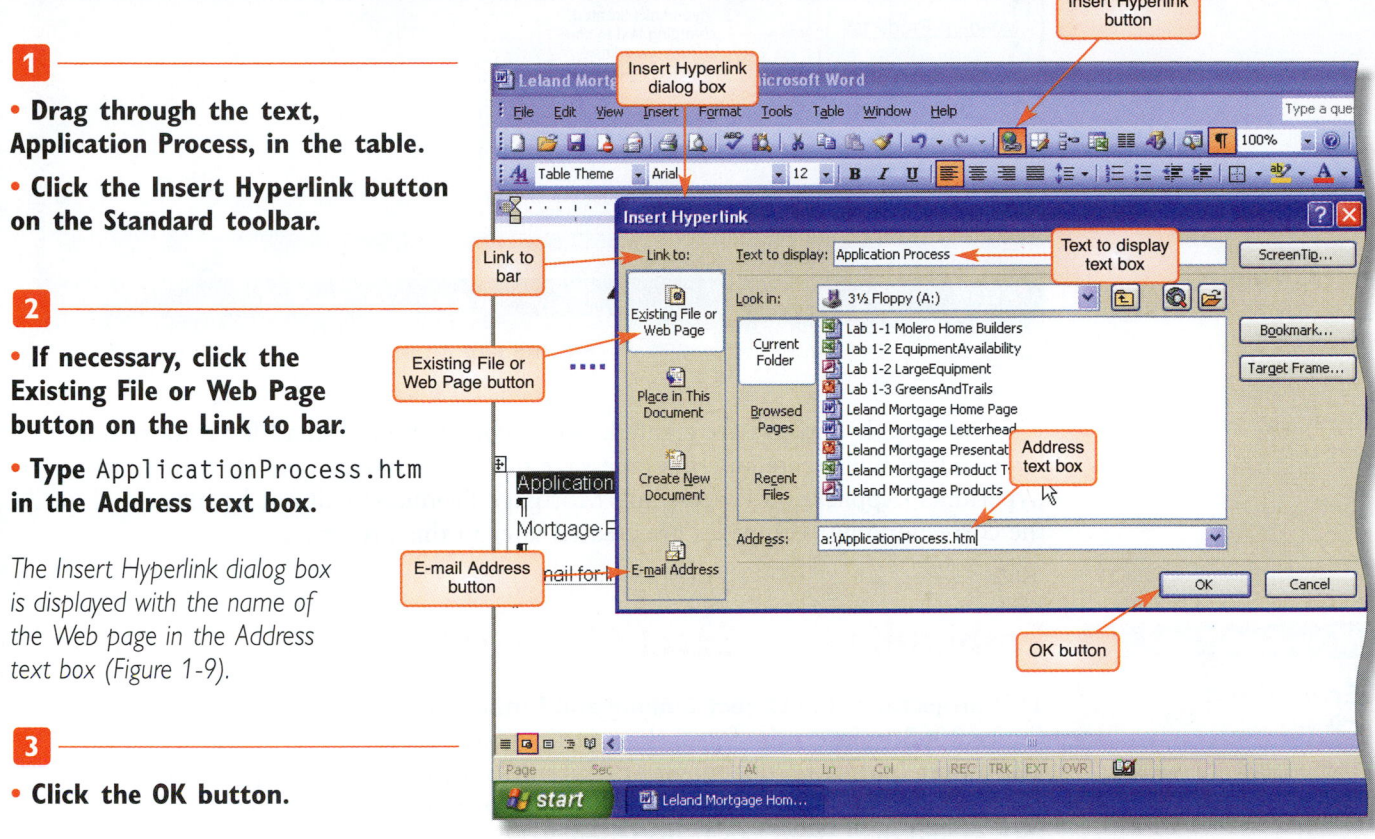

FIGURE 1-9

The hyperlink is assigned to the Application Process text phrase. After the Word document is saved as a Web page and the visitor clicks the text, Application Process, the ApplicationProcess.htm file on drive A is displayed. The following steps add the other two hyperlinks.

To Insert the Remaining Hyperlinks

1 Drag through the text, Mortgage Products, in the table. Click the Insert Hyperlink button on the Standard toolbar.

2 Type `MortgageProducts.htm` in the Address text box and then click the OK button.

3 Drag through the text, E-mail for Information. Click the Insert Hyperlink button on the Standard toolbar and then click the E-mail Address button on the Link to bar.

4 Type `manager@isp.com` in the E-mail address text box.

5 Type `Mortgage Application` in the Subject box and then click the OK button.

Word displays the table as shown in Figure 1-10 on the next page.

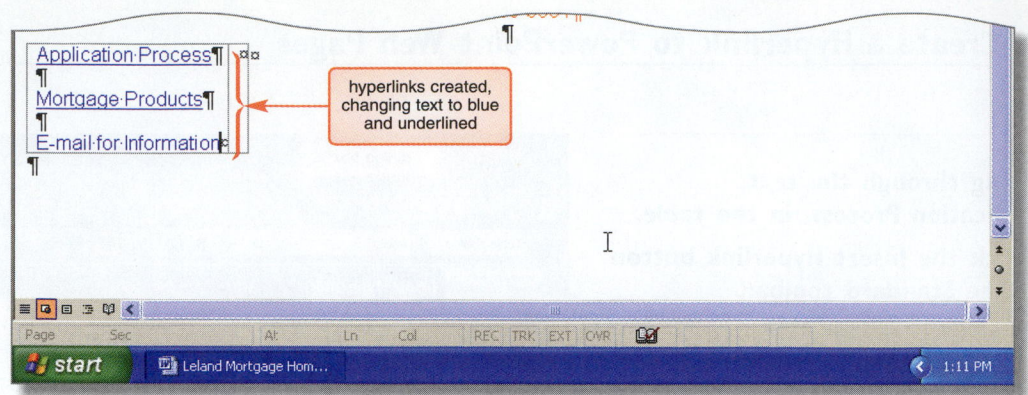

FIGURE 1-10

The three hyperlinks are created. When you click the E-mail for Information hyperlink, it will create an e-mail message to manager@isp.com. The other two hyperlinks (Application Process and Mortgage Products) will not be functional until the corresponding Web pages are created later in this project.

More About

Embedded Objects

The advantage of using an integrated set of applications, such as Office 2003, is the capability of sharing information among applications. The Object Linking and Embedding (OLE) features of Office 2003 make the integration process more efficient. A chart created in Excel can be included in a Word document using OLE. To edit the embedded object, double-click it. The source program then starts and opens the source object for editing.

Embedding an Excel Chart into a Word Document

This project uses the **Object Linking and Embedding** (**OLE**) feature of Microsoft Office 2003 to insert the Excel chart into a Word document. OLE allows you to incorporate parts of a document or entire documents from one application into another. The Bar chart in Excel is called a **source object** (Figure 1-1b on page INT 6) and the Leland Mortgage Home Page document is the **destination document**. After an object is embedded, it becomes part of the destination document. This project illustrates using the Paste Special command on the Edit menu to embed the Excel object. **Paste Special** inserts an object into Word, but still recognizes the **source program**, the program in which the object was created. When you double-click an embedded object, such as the Mortgage Amount by Mortgage Type worksheet, the source program opens and allows you to make changes. In this example, Excel is the source program. With the hyperlinks added to the Word document, the next step is to embed the Bar chart into the Word document. The following steps open the Excel workbook.

To Start Excel, Customize Excel, and Open an Existing Workbook

1 Click the Start button on the Windows taskbar, point to All Programs on the Start menu, and then click Open Office Document on the All Programs submenu.

2 If necessary, click the Look in box arrow and then click 3½ Floppy (A:) in the Look in list.

3 Double-click the Leland Mortgage Product Types workbook.

4 If the Language bar is displayed, right-click it and then click Close the Language bar on the shortcut menu.

5 If the Getting Started task pane is displayed in the Excel window, click its Close button in the upper-right corner. If the Chart toolbar is displayed, click its Close button.

6 If the Standard and Formatting toolbars are positioned on the same row, click the Toolbar Options button and then click Show Buttons on Two Rows.

The next two sections explain how to embed an Excel chart into a Word document and then resize it. The first section explains embedding a chart into a Word document. The following steps embed the Excel Bar chart into the Word document.

To Embed an Excel Chart into a Word Document

1

• **If necessary, click the Mortgage Amount Chart tab.**

The Bar chart is active and is displayed (Figure 1-11).

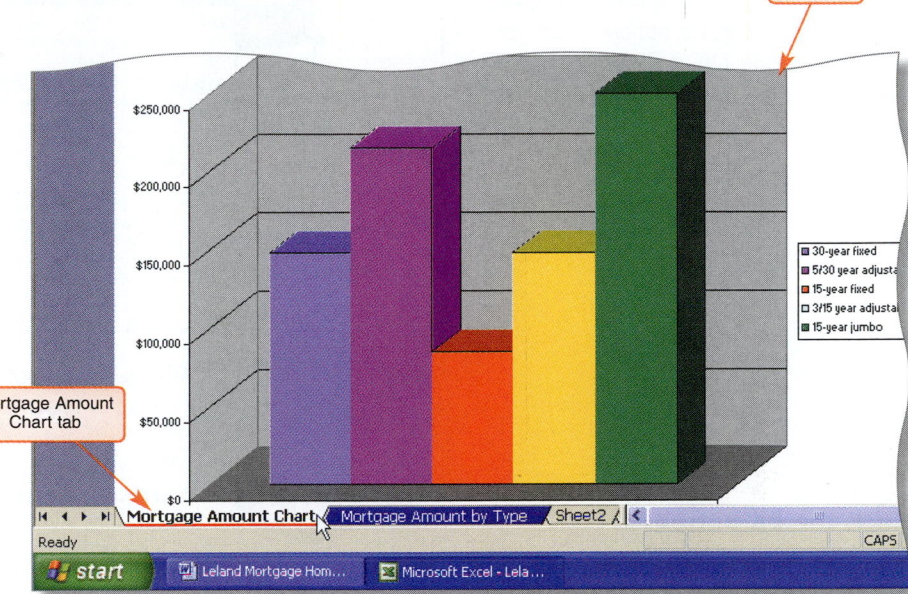

Bar chart

Mortgage Amount Chart tab

FIGURE 1-11

2

• **Click the white area around the chart area to select the chart and then click the Copy button on the Standard toolbar.**

Excel places a copy of the Bar chart on the Office Clipboard. A moving border is displayed around the chart area (Figure 1-12).

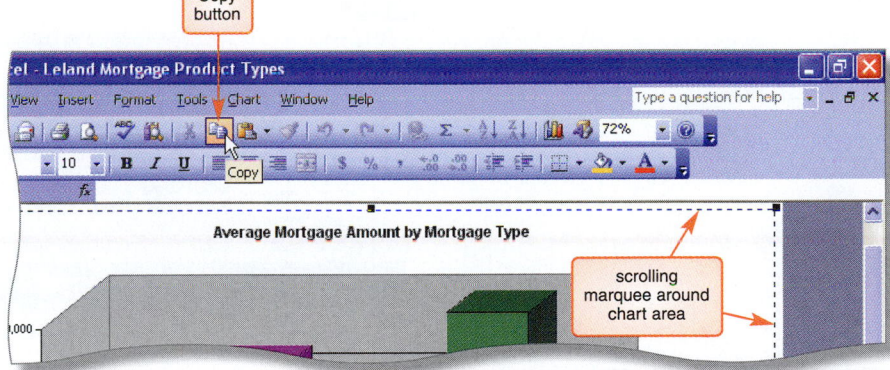

Copy button

scrolling marquee around chart area

FIGURE 1-12

• **Click the Leland Mortgage Home Page button on the taskbar.**

• **If necessary, click the right column of the table.**

• **Click Edit on the menu bar.**

The Edit menu is displayed (Figure 1-13).

Edit menu

Paste Special command

FIGURE 1-13

5

• **Click Paste Special.**

• **If necessary, click Microsoft Office Excel Chart Object in the As list.**

Word displays the Paste Special dialog box (Figure 1-14). The Paste option button is selected. Microsoft Office Excel Chart Object is selected in the As list.

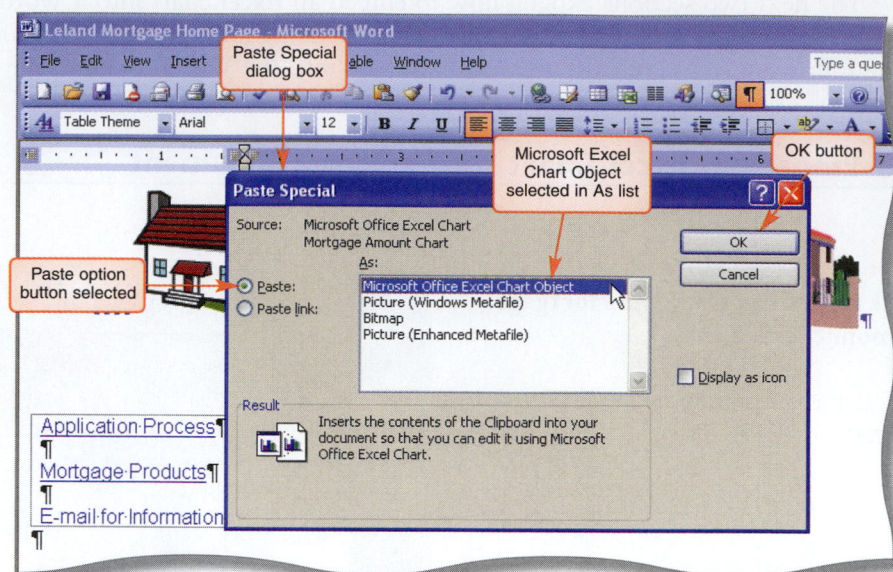

FIGURE 1-14

6

• **Click the OK button.**

Word embeds the Bar chart into the document (Figure 1-15).

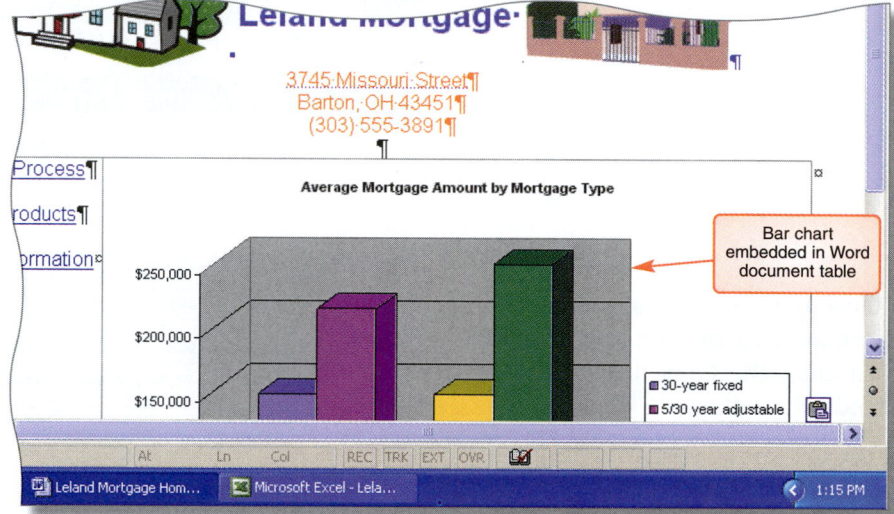

FIGURE 1-15

Other Ways

1. On Edit menu click Copy
2. Press CTRL+C
3. In Voice Command mode say, "Copy"

All Office 2003 applications allow you to use three methods to copy objects among applications: (1) copy and paste; (2) copy and embed; and (3) copy and link. The first method uses the Copy and Paste buttons. The latter two use the Paste Special command. Table 1-1 summarizes the differences among the three methods.

Changing the Size of an Embedded Object

The embedded Bar chart slightly exceeds the margins of the Leland Mortgage Home Page document. Reducing the size of the Bar chart will improve the layout of the document. In this project, you will use the Format Object dialog box to change the size of the chart.

Table 1-1   Copy Methods

METHOD	CHARACTERISTICS
Copy and paste	The source document becomes part of the destination document. An object may be edited, but the editing features are limited to those of the destination application. An Excel worksheet becomes a Word table. If changes are made to values in the Word table, any original Excel formulas are not recalculated.
Copy and embed	The source document becomes part of the destination document. An object may be edited in the destination document using source editing features. The Excel worksheet remains a worksheet in Word. If you make changes to values in the worksheet with Word active, Excel formulas will be recalculated. If you change the worksheet in Excel without the document open in Word, however, these changes will not display in the Word document the next time you open it.
Copy and link	The source document does not become part of the destination document, even though it appears to be. Instead, a link is established between the two documents, so that when you open the Word document, the worksheet displays within the document, as though it were a part of it. When you attempt to edit a linked worksheet in Word, the system activates Excel. If you change the worksheet in Excel, the changes also will display in the Word document the next time you open it.

The following steps reduce the size of the chart using the Object command on the Format menu.

To Change the Size of an Embedded Object

1

• **If necessary, click the Bar chart to select it.**

• **Click Format on the menu bar.**

The Bar chart is selected as indicated by sizing handles on the selection rectangle. The Format menu is displayed (Figure 1-16).

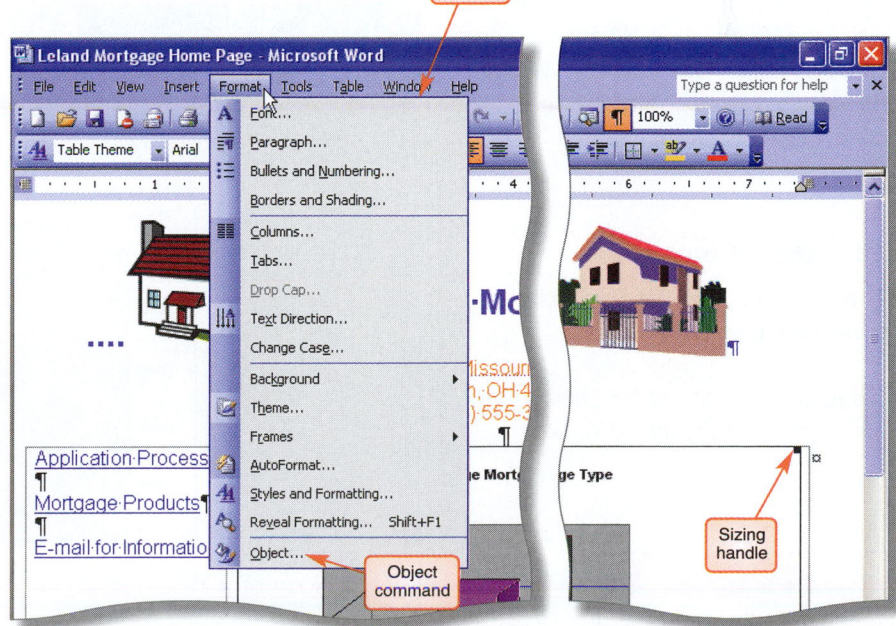

FIGURE 1-16

2

• **Click Object.**

• **If necessary, click the Size tab.**

The Format Object dialog box with the Size sheet selected is displayed (Figure 1-17).

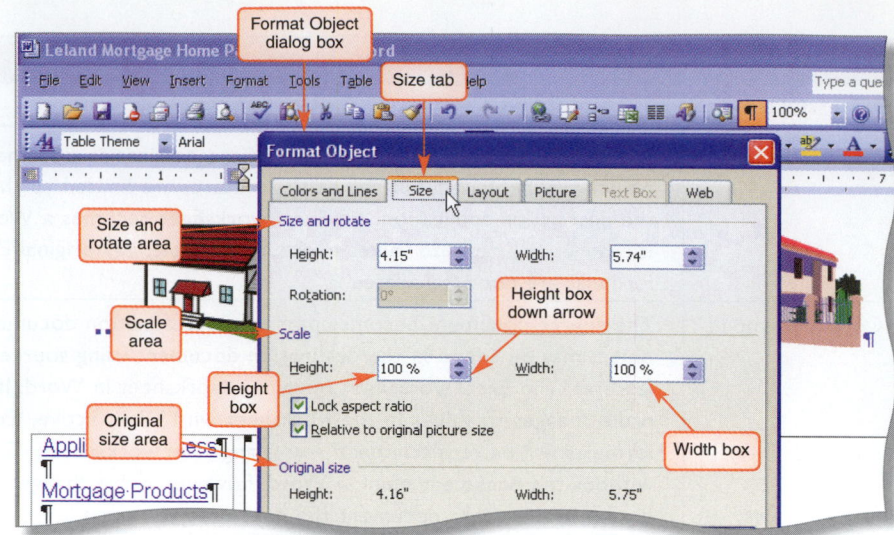

FIGURE 1-17

3

• **In the Scale area, if necessary, click the Height box up or down arrow or the Width box up or down arrow until 90 % appears in both the Height box and the Width box.**

The Height box and the Width box both display 90 % (Figure 1-18). Depending on the size of the object when it was pasted into the Word document, you either may need to scale up or down in the Scale area Height and Width boxes. When you change the value in either the Height or Width box, both values change because the Lock aspect ratio check box is selected.

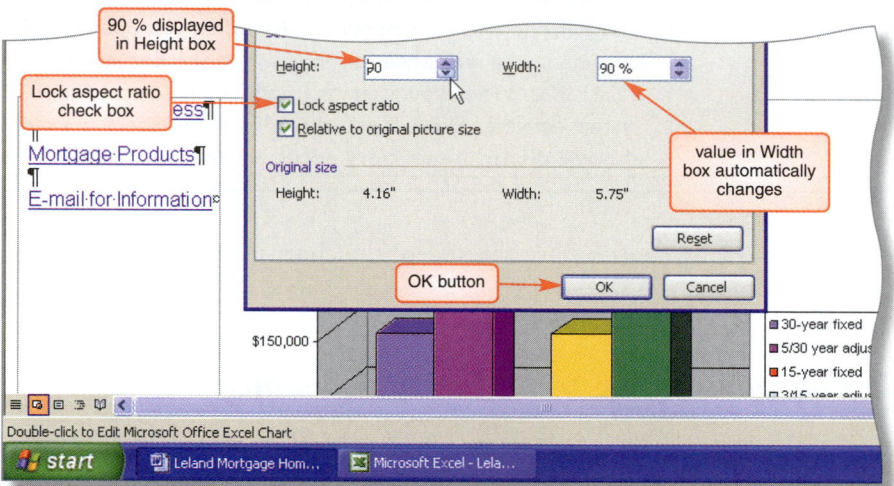

FIGURE 1-18

4

• **Click the OK button.**

• **If necessary, scroll to see the embedded chart.**

Word reduces the size of the chart to 90% of its original size (Figure 1-19).

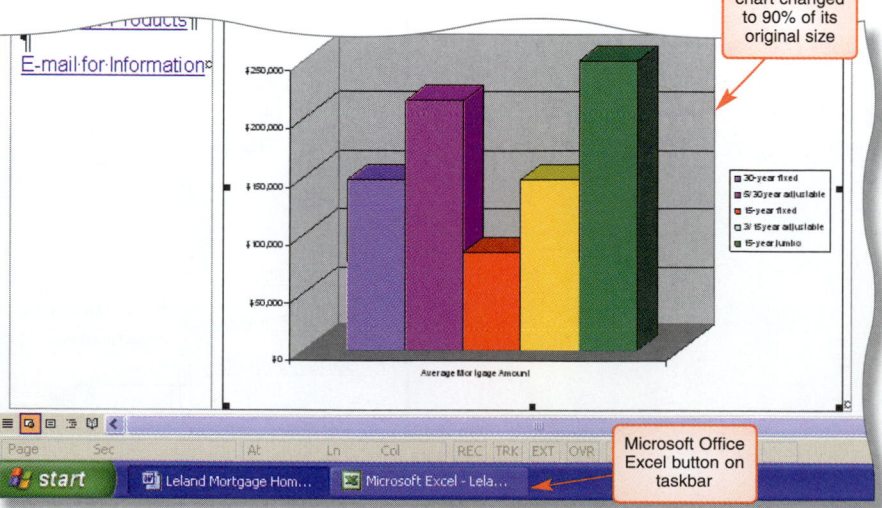

FIGURE 1-19

The Format Object dialog box (see Figure 1-17) contains two areas that can change the size of an object. The **Size and rotate area** allows you to increase or decrease the height or width of an object in inches. When available, it also allows you to rotate the object in degrees around an axis. The **Scale area** allows you to change the size of an object by a specific percentage while maintaining the height-to-width ratio. The height-to-width ratio is referred to as **aspect ratio**. You change the height and width independently by deselecting the Lock aspect ratio check box. The **Original size area** at the bottom of the Format Object dialog box displays the original height and width of the selected object.

Quitting Excel

With the Bar chart embedded in the Word document, you no longer need the Leland Mortgage Product Types workbook open. The following steps quit Excel.

To Quit Excel

1 **Right-click the Microsoft Office Excel - Leland Mortgage Product Types button on the taskbar. Click Close on the shortcut menu. If prompted to save changes, click the No button.**

2 **If the Microsoft Excel dialog box displays regarding saving the large amount of information on the Clipboard, click the No button.**

Adding Scrolling Text to a Word Document

The Word document is almost ready to be saved as a Web page. The final item that needs to be added is something that will capture the attention of your Web page visitors. One of the attention-grabbing techniques that Web developers use is scrolling text. **Scrolling text** is a line of text that moves across the Web page. Generally, scrolling text is used to highlight information about the Web site. With Word 2003, you can create scrolling text using the Scrolling Text button on the Web Tools toolbar. A scrolling marquee will be created just below the Leland Mortgage heading.

To create scrolling text, the Web Tools toolbar must display. The steps on the next page display the Web Tools toolbar.

Q&A

Q: What are some other methods to resize objects?

A: To resize an image proportionally from a corner, you can press and hold down the SHIFT key while dragging a corner sizing handle. To resize vertically, horizontally, or diagonally from the center outward, press and hold down the CTRL key while dragging a sizing handle. To resize proportionally from the center outward, press and hold down the CTRL+SHIFT keys and drag a corner sizing handle.

To Display the Web Tools Toolbar

1

• **If necessary, scroll to see the top of the document.**

• **Click View on the menu bar, point to Toolbars, and then click Web Tools on the Toolbars submenu.**

2

• **If necessary, point to the Web Tools toolbar title bar and then drag the toolbar to the center, right side of the window.**

The Web Tools toolbar is displayed (Figure 1-20).

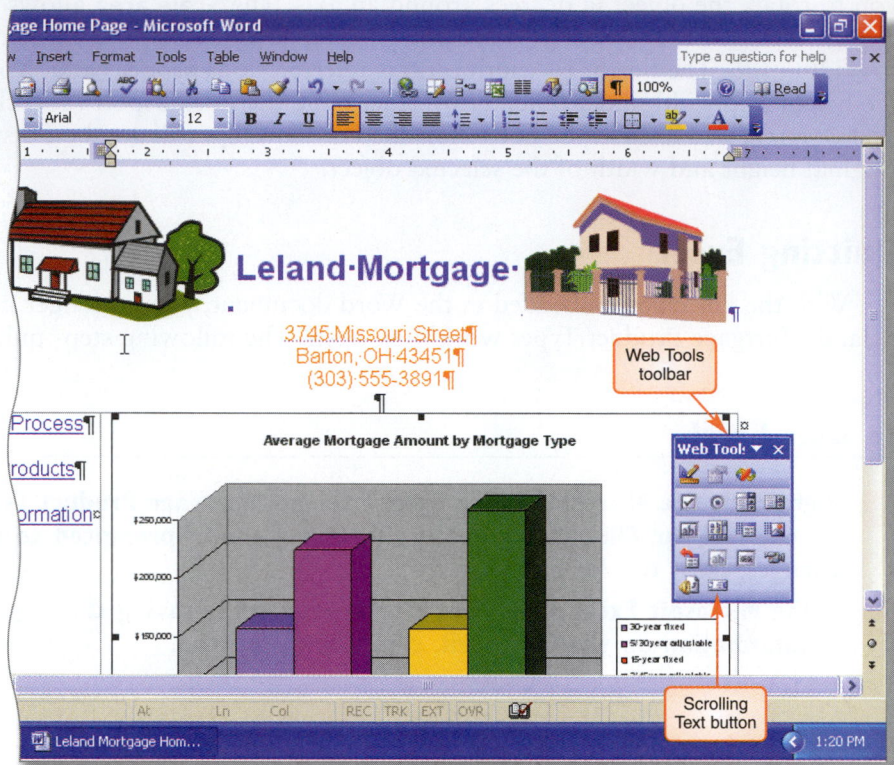

FIGURE 1-20

The Web Tools toolbar is used to create the scrolling text that moves below the Web page heading.

Inserting Scrolling Text

A number of options are available for scrolling text. The **behavior** of the text specifies the manner in which the text moves on the Web page. By default, the behavior of the line of text is to scroll. **Scrolling** moves the text in from one side and off the other side of the Web page. Another behavior option is to slide the text. Setting the behavior to **slide** moves the text in from one side of the Web page and stops as soon as the text touches the opposite side. The third option is to set text behavior to alternate. **Alternate** bounces the text back and forth in the margins of the marquee. The default behavior is scrolling text. In this project, the scrolling text behavior is changed to slide, as shown in the following steps.

To Insert Scrolling Text into a Word Document

1

• **Click the paragraph mark below the Leland Mortgage heading and then click the Scrolling Text button on the Web Tools toolbar.**

Word displays the Scrolling Text dialog box (Figure 1-21).

2

• **Click the Behavior box arrow and then click Slide in the list.**

3

• **Drag through the text, Scrolling Text, in the Type the scrolling text here text box.**

• **Type** Rates are beginning to rise! Act now to lock in a great rate! **as the scrolling text.**

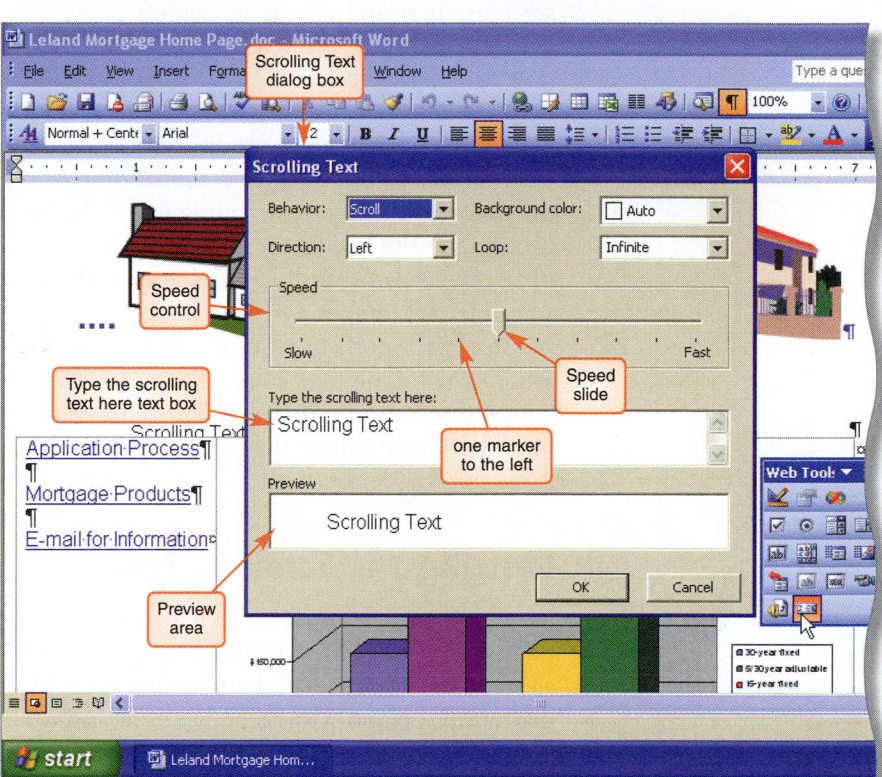

FIGURE 1-21

4

• **Drag the Speed slide one speed marker to the left and then click the OK button.**

The scrolling text is displayed (Figure 1-22).

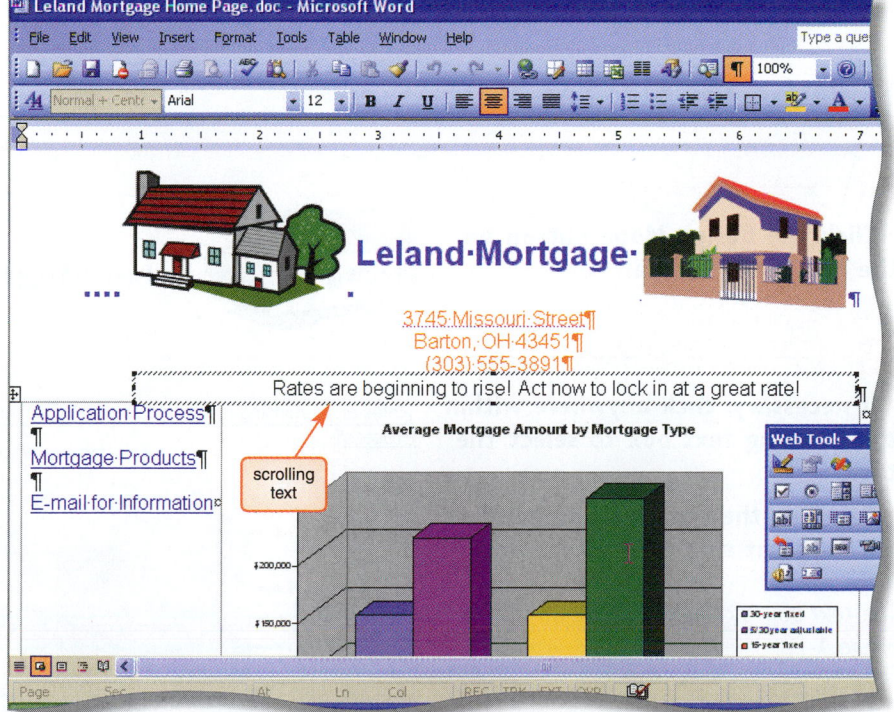

FIGURE 1-22

The **direction** of the text movement can be left to right or right to left. The direction attribute in the scrolling text options controls this movement. The default direction is to move right to left, so the text begins in the right margin of the line of scrolling text and moves to the left.

The **speed** of the scrolling text also can be varied from slow to fast. Scrolling the text too fast cancels the benefits of the scrolling text. If the Web page visitor cannot read the text because it scrolls too fast, the text serves no purpose.

Other options that can be controlled in scrolling text are background colors and the number of times to loop the scrolling text. The **background** attribute determines the color of the line of scrolling text. The background default is a transparent background, so the background of the line of scrolling text displays the background color of whatever is behind it. The **loop** attribute determines the number of times that the scrolling text moves across the Web page. The default is an **infinite loop**, which means the text will scroll indefinitely, but the loop can be set to a specific number of times.

The scrolling text inserted into the Word document uses the default direction, background color, and loop. The behavior selected for the scrolling text is Slide. The **Slide behavior** causes the text to scroll from the right margin and stop scrolling when it reaches the left margin. The next section explains how to resize the scrolling text.

Resizing the Scrolling Text

The default for scrolling text is to move the text all the way across the Web page from the right margin of the page to the left margin. Sometimes, it is better to shorten the distance of the scrolling text. In this project, the scrolling text is centered below the Leland Mortgage heading and address of the Word document. The Web page visitor sees the company name with address and telephone number information below it, followed by the scrolling message. This project uses the Design mode to change the size of the scrolling text. In general, **Design mode** allows you to rearrange and design the page in a user-friendly manner.

The following steps change the size of the scrolling text.

To Resize the Scrolling Text

1

• **Click the Design Mode button on the Web Tools toolbar.**

2

• **If necessary, click anywhere within the scrolling text box to select the text.**

• **Point to the center sizing handle on the right side of the text box.**

The text box is displayed as shown in Figure 1-23.

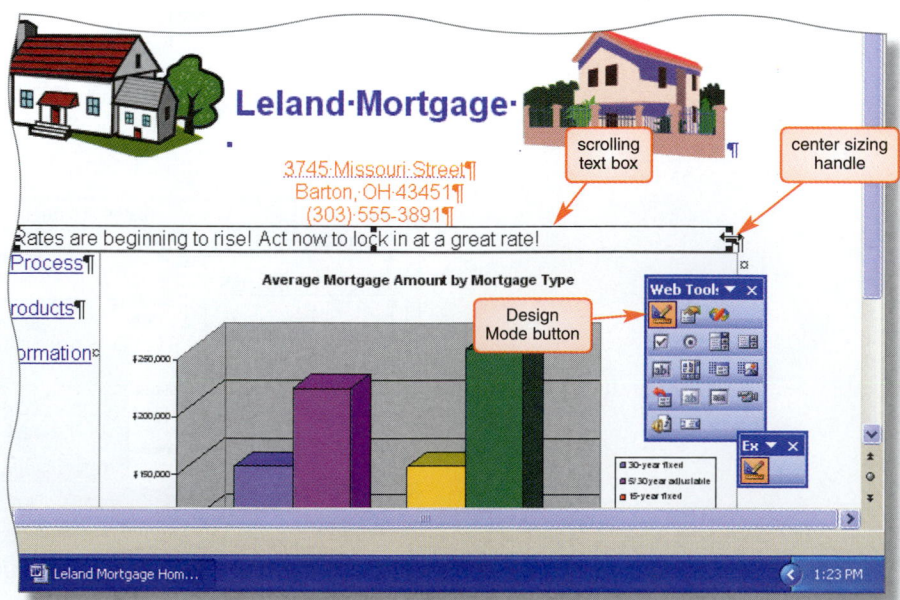

FIGURE 1-23

3

• **Drag the center sizing handle to the left, so that it is positioned approximately as shown in Figure 1-24, but do not release the mouse button.**

The dotted line shows the proposed size for the scrolling text.

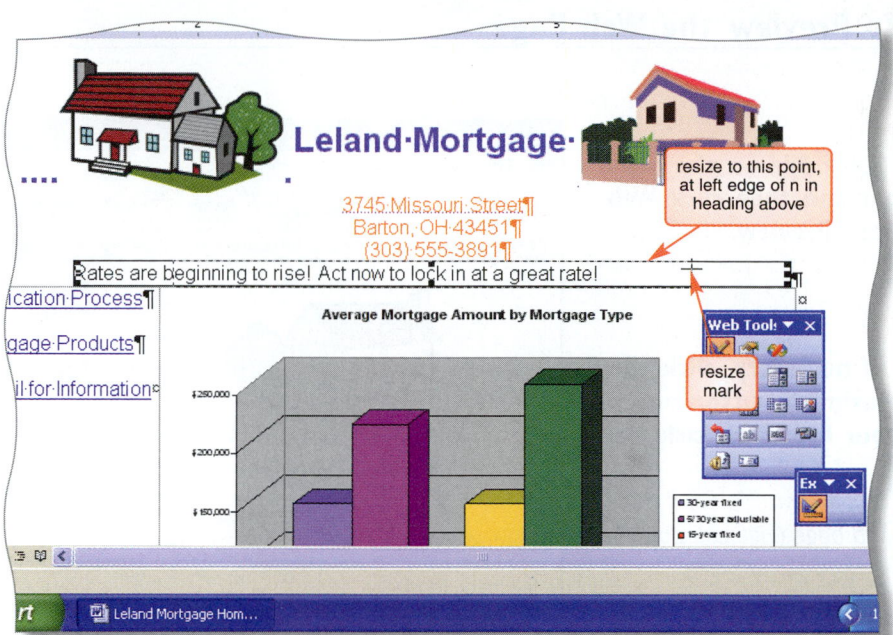

FIGURE 1-24

4

• **Release the mouse button.**

The scrolling text box is resized (Figure 1-25).

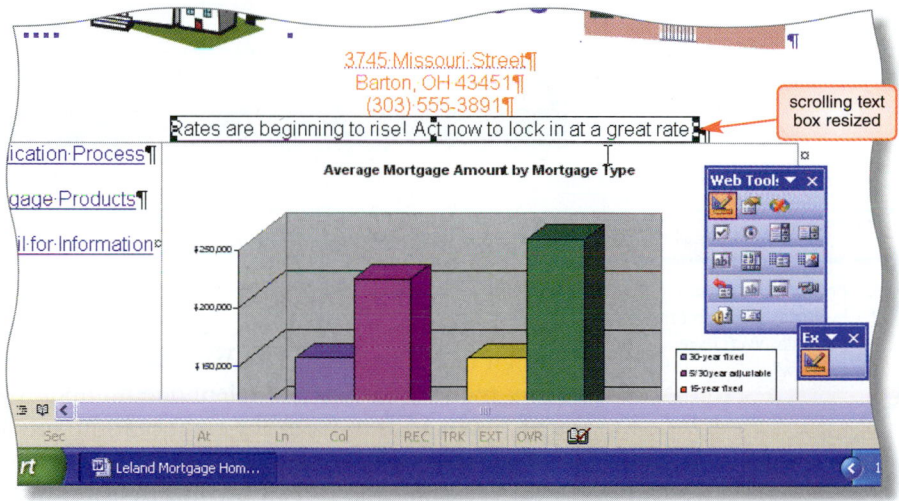

FIGURE 1-25

The home page for the Leland Mortgage Web site is complete.

Viewing the Word Document in Your Browser and Saving It as a Web Page

The next step is to view the Word document in your browser to verify that all information is accurate. After verifying its accuracy, you then can save the Word document as an HTML file. Saving the Word document as an HTML file makes it possible for it to be viewed using a browser, such as Internet Explorer.

The steps on the next page preview the document in the browser and then save the Word document as an HTML file.

More About

Web Page Formatting

Because Word provides formatting options that most Web browsers do not support, some text and graphics may look different when you view them on a Web page. When creating documents for the Web, using Web layout view will ensure that your graphics look the way you want them to when they are viewed as Web pages in a Web browser.

To Preview the Web Page

1
• **Click File on the menu bar and then click Web Page Preview.**

2
• **If necessary, click the Maximize button on your browser's title bar.**

The browser displays the Web page (Figure 1-26).

3
• **Click the browser's Close button.**

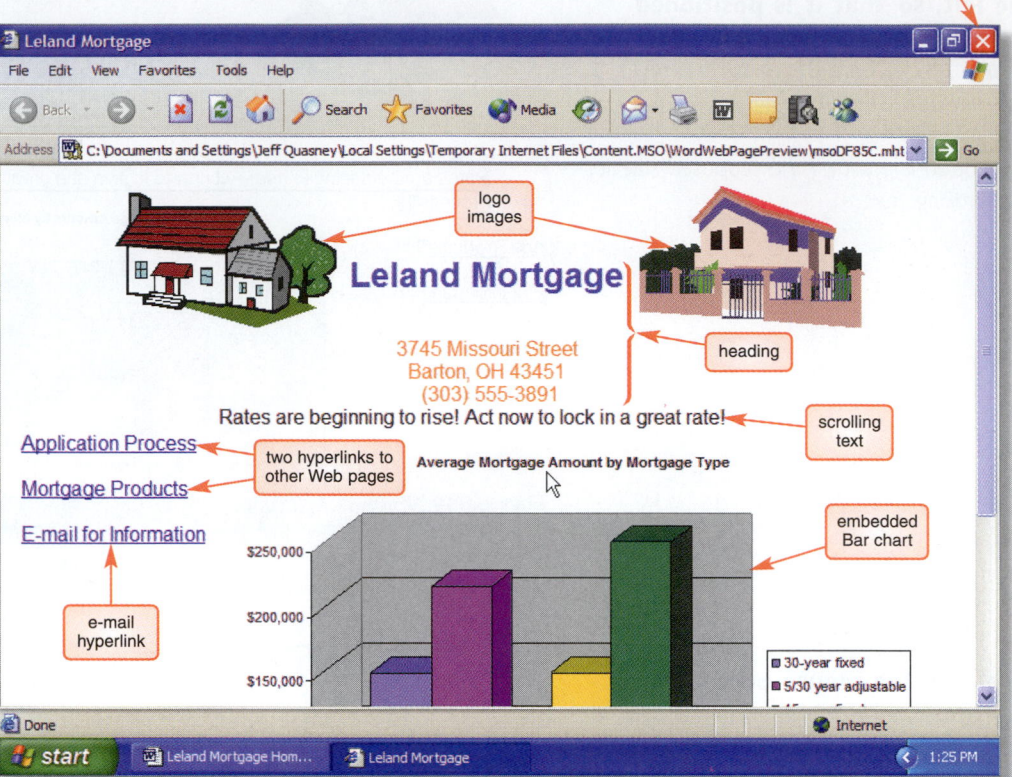

FIGURE 1-26

Verify that the Web page contains all information necessary and is displayed as shown in Figure 1-26. The Web page consists of a heading with images and the company name, address, and telephone number. Below that is a single line of scrolling text that scrolls in from the right margin and stops when it reaches the left margin. A borderless table displays three hyperlinks in the left column and a Bar chart in the right column. The E-mail for Information hyperlink should work appropriately when you click it, displaying a new message. The other two links, Application Process and Mortgage Products, do not work because the corresponding Web pages are not available until later in this project.

If the Web page is correct, save it on the Integration Data Disk as an HTML file. If changes need to be made to the Web page, return to the Word document and correct it. The following steps save the document as a Web page.

To Save a Document with a New File Name

1 Click File on the menu bar and then click Save as Web Page. If the Microsoft Office Word dialog box displays, click the Continue button.

2 Type LelandHome in the File name text box.

3 Select Web Page in the Save as type box.

4 If necessary, click the **Save in** box arrow and then click **3½ Floppy (A:)** in the Save in list.

5 Click the **Save** button in the **Save As** dialog box. If the **Microsoft Office Word** dialog box displays, click the **Continue** button.

Word displays the LelandHome Web page in the Word window (Figure 1-27).

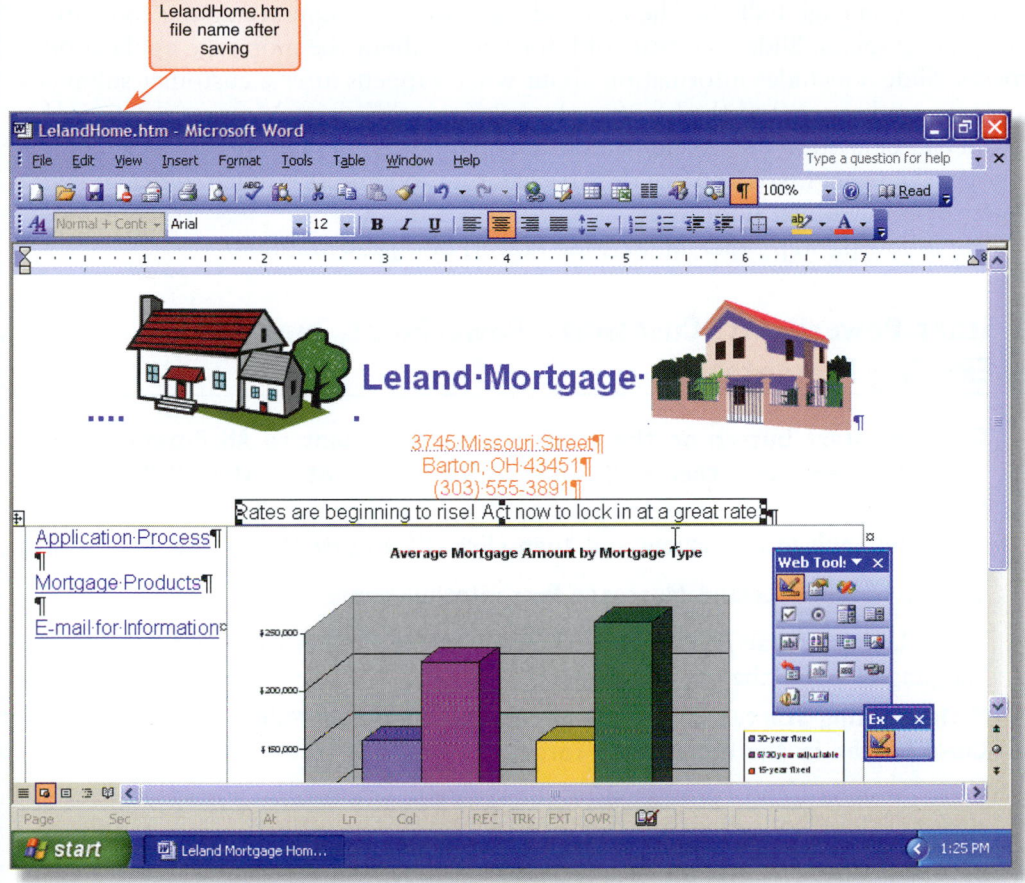

LelandHome.htm file name after saving

FIGURE 1-27

Saving an existing Word document as a Web page allows you quickly to get a Word document ready for copying to the Web or to an intranet. One alternative to this is to write the Hypertext Markup Language (HTML) to develop the Web pages. **HTML** is a programming language used for Web page creation. The home page created earlier in this project could be created by writing HTML tags (code). For documents that already are in Word format, the easier method is to use the Word Save as Web Page command. This essentially creates the HTML code for you and saves it in a file. The following step quits Word.

To Quit Word

1 Click the **Close** button on the **Microsoft Word** title bar.

The next step in creating the Web site for Leland Mortgage is to save a PowerPoint presentation as an HTML file. The sections on the next pages describe how to open a PowerPoint presentation, add a hyperlink to the first page, and save the presentation as an HTML file.

Creating a PowerPoint Presentation Web Page

PowerPoint is a powerful software tool often used to assist in the presentation of information to groups of people. **PowerPoint 2003** allows you to create Web pages from an existing PowerPoint presentation, using the Save as Web Page command. The presentation then can be viewed using your browser.

The PowerPoint presentation used in this project consists of three slides (Figure 1-1g on page INT 7). The first slide is a title slide, containing the company name and graphics. Slide 2 consists of information about the mortgage application process. Slide 3 includes information about what happens after a customer submits a mortgage application and the benefits of working with Leland Mortgage. This information can be used in its present format to enhance a presentation about the company. As Web pages, you can use this presentation to address a much wider, global audience on the World Wide Web.

The following steps open an existing PowerPoint presentation.

To Start PowerPoint, Customize PowerPoint, and Open an Existing Presentation

1 Click the Start button on the Windows taskbar, point to All Programs on the Start menu, and then click Open Office Document on the All Programs submenu.

2 Click the Look in box arrow and then click 3½ Floppy (A:) in the Look in list.

3 Double-click the Leland Mortgage Presentation name.

4 If the Language bar is displayed, right-click it and then click Close the Language bar on the shortcut menu.

5 If the Getting Started task pane appears in the PowerPoint window, click its Close button in the upper-right corner.

6 If the Standard and Formatting toolbars are positioned on the same row, click the Toolbar Options button and then click Show Buttons on Two Rows.

PowerPoint displays Slide 1 of the PowerPoint presentation (Figure 1-28).

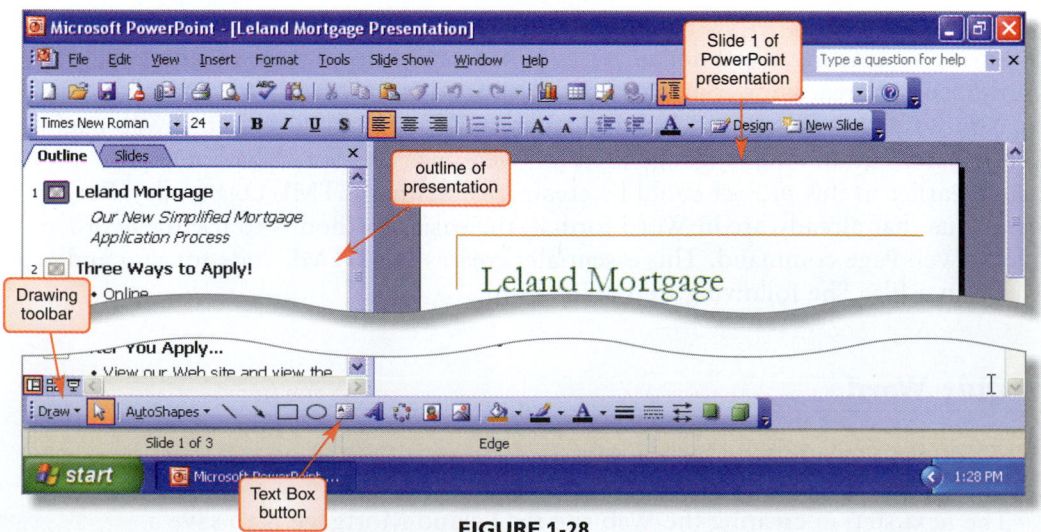

FIGURE 1-28

The PowerPoint presentation now is open. The next step is to add a hyperlink on Slide 1 that allows the Web page visitor to return to the Leland Mortgage home page.

Adding Text for a Hyperlink

One of the more important features of Web sites is their capability of linking from one Web page to another using hyperlinks. In earlier steps in this project, you added three hyperlinks to the Leland Mortgage home page. Once Web page visitors link to the PowerPoint Web pages, however, they cannot return to the home page without using the Back button on the browser's toolbar. This is not a convenient way for Web page visitors to navigate through the Web site. In this section, you will add a Home link to the first slide of the PowerPoint presentation (Figure 1-1e on page INT 7).

The following steps add the text that will be used as a hyperlink on the PowerPoint Web page.

To Add Text for a Hyperlink into a PowerPoint Presentation

1 **Click the Text Box button on the Drawing toolbar.**

2 **Click in the lower-right corner of Slide 1.**

3 **Type** Home **as the hyperlink text.**

The text box is displayed with Home as the text for the hyperlink (Figure 1-29).

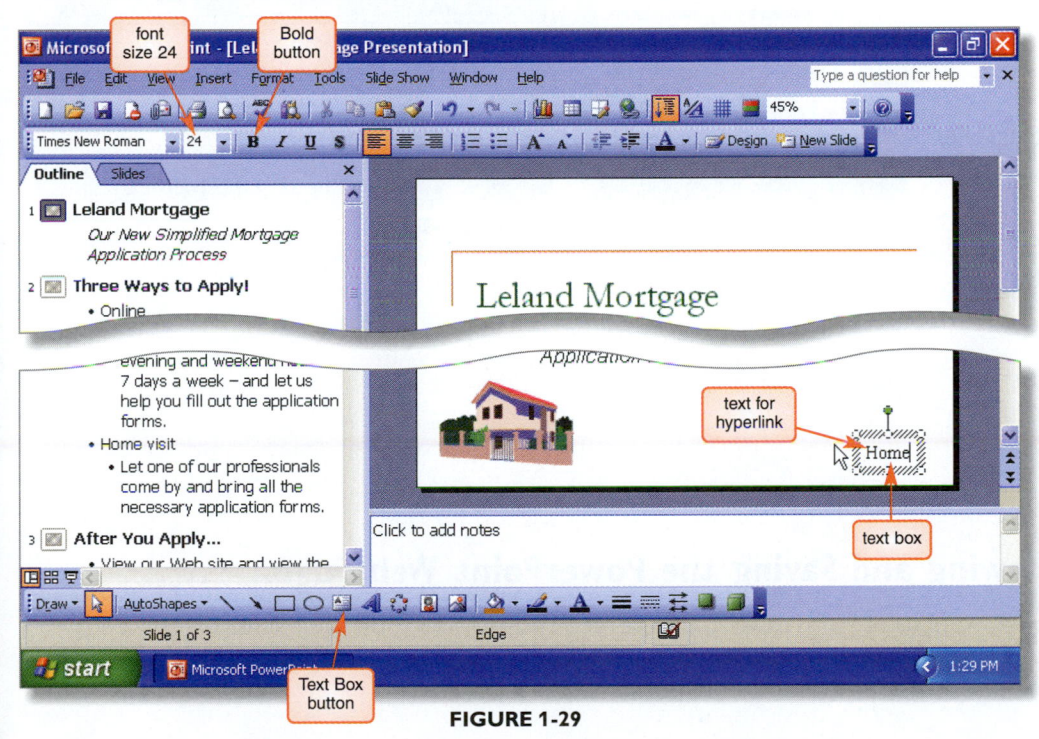

FIGURE 1-29

Creating a Hyperlink

After you enter the text for the hyperlink, you can create the hyperlink itself. When clicked, the hyperlink jumps to the Leland Mortgage home page created previously in this project and saved on drive A. To create the hyperlink, you will use the Insert Hyperlink button on the Standard toolbar.

The steps on the next page create the PowerPoint hyperlink.

To Insert a Hyperlink into a PowerPoint Presentation

1

• Double-click the word, Home, inside the text box you just inserted.

2

• If necessary, click the Font Size box arrow on the Formatting toolbar and then click 24.

• Click the Bold button on the Formatting toolbar.

3

• Click the Insert Hyperlink button on the Standard toolbar.

4

• If necessary, click the Existing File or Web Page button on the Link to bar.

• Type `a:\LelandHome.htm` in the Address text box. Click the OK button.

Slide 1 of the presentation is displayed as shown in Figure 1-30.

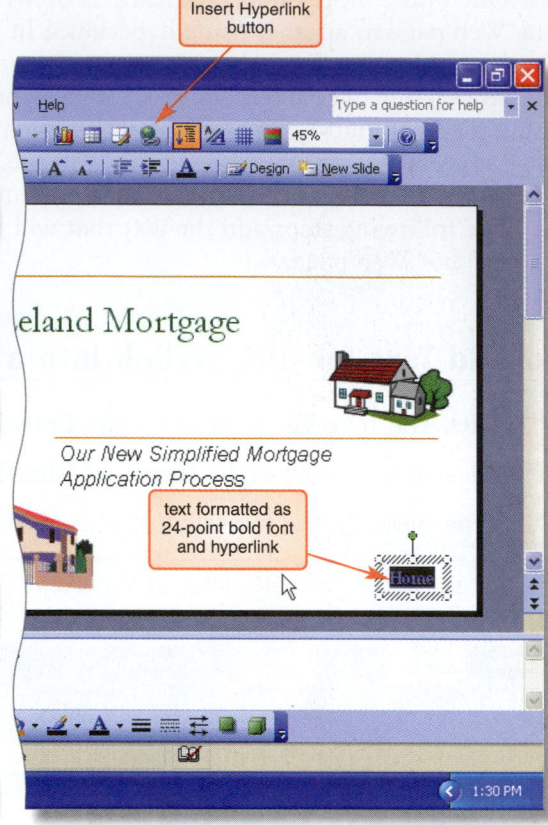

FIGURE 1-30

Other Ways

1. On Insert menu click Hyperlink
2. Right-click highlighted word, click Hyperlink on shortcut menu
3. Press CTRL+K
4. In Voice Command mode say, "Hyperlink"

Viewing and Saving the PowerPoint Web Page

Just as in the previous section of this project, the following steps display the Web page before saving it. It is important to verify all of the Web page navigation features before saving the file.

To View the Web Page in Your Browser

1 Click File on the menu bar.

2 Click Web Page Preview.

3 If necessary, click the Maximize button on your browser's title bar.

The browser displays the PowerPoint Web page (Figure 1-31).

Other Ways

1. Press ALT+F, press B
2. In Voice Command mode say, "File, Web Page Preview"

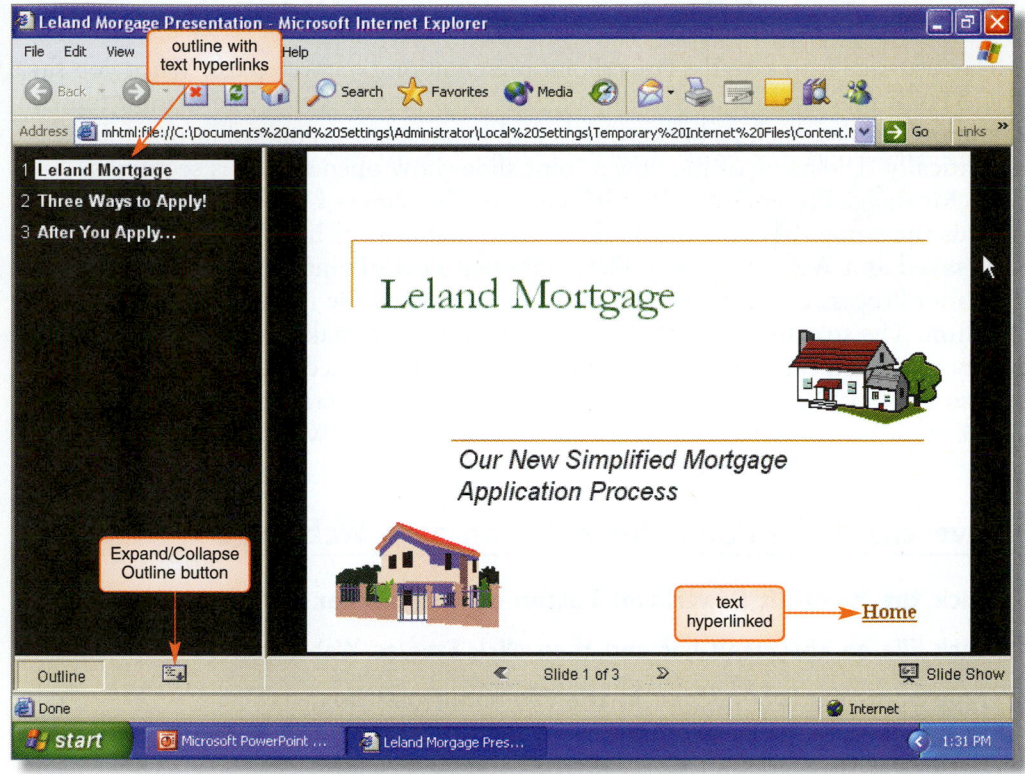

FIGURE 1-31

Slide 1 of the PowerPoint presentation Web page contains a hyperlink to the home page of the Leland Mortgage Web site. Although you created this hyperlink by adding a text box to the first slide, you also can create hyperlinks from existing text or images in a PowerPoint presentation. For example, one of the logo images on slide 1 could be used as a hyperlink to the home page of the Web site. Using one of those images, however, does not give the Web page visitor a clear idea of where the hyperlink will lead. It is more appropriate to create a hyperlink to the home page from text — for example, Home — that makes sense to the visitor.

In addition to any hyperlinks that are added to the presentation, PowerPoint automatically creates hyperlinks in the left column of the Web page, called the **outline**. Using the Expand/Collapse Outline button below the outline pane, you can expand or collapse the outline and navigate through the Web page presentation (Figure 1-31). The text in the heading of each slide is used as the phrases for these hyperlinks. When you click a link, you jump to that particular slide within the presentation. The ease of navigation within a PowerPoint Web page is valuable to the Web page visitor.

As well as being able to add your own hyperlink text, PowerPoint provides some ready-made action buttons that you can insert into your Web pages. **Action buttons** contain shapes, such as left and right arrows, that can be used to hyperlink to other Web pages within the presentation. You can insert symbols on the action buttons for going to the next (right arrow), previous (left arrow), first (beginning arrow), and last (end arrow) slides. PowerPoint also includes action buttons for playing movies or sounds. You insert these action buttons using the slide master feature of PowerPoint.

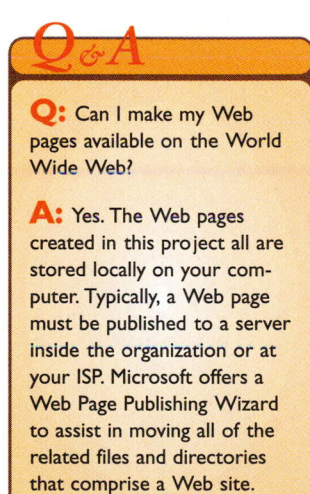

Q: Can I make my Web pages available on the World Wide Web?

A: Yes. The Web pages created in this project all are stored locally on your computer. Typically, a Web page must be published to a server inside the organization or at your ISP. Microsoft offers a Web Page Publishing Wizard to assist in moving all of the related files and directories that comprise a Web site.

Saving the PowerPoint Presentation as a Web Page

The next step is to save the PowerPoint presentation as a Web page. When you save a PowerPoint presentation as a Web page, the Web page is saved in a default folder. All supporting files, such as backgrounds and images, are organized in this folder automatically. The name of the PowerPoint slide show opened in this section is Leland Mortgage Presentation. PowerPoint uses the name of the saved Web page and adds the string, files, for the name of the new folder. When the current presentation is saved as a Web page, the folder name that PowerPoint Web creates is ApplicationProcess files. The default name for the first slide in the presentation is frame.htm. The structure used in the folder organization makes Web page publishing easier because you can keep track of all of the files associated with the Web page. You also can edit the files manually, rather than using PowerPoint.

The steps below save the PowerPoint presentation as a Web page.

To Save the PowerPoint Presentation as a Web Page

1 Click the Microsoft PowerPoint button on the taskbar.

2 Click File on the menu bar and then click Save as Web Page.

3 Type ApplicationProcess in the File name text box.

4 Select Web Page in the Save as type box.

5 If necessary, click the Save in box arrow and then click 3½ Floppy (A:) in the Save in list.

6 Click the Save button in the Save As dialog box.

The PowerPoint presentation is saved as a Web page.

The task of saving the PowerPoint presentation as a Web page is complete. The hyperlink has been added to Slide 1 of the presentation that jumps to the Web site home page when clicked. Standard Web page navigation was added automatically to the presentation that allows the Web page visitor to jump to any slide in the Web page presentation. All of the files necessary for the Web page were saved in a folder named ApplicationProcess_files.

After saving the PowerPoint presentation as a Web page, you can quit PowerPoint and close your browser as shown in the following steps.

To Quit PowerPoint and Close Your Browser

1 Click the Close button on the PowerPoint title bar.

2 Click the Close button on the browser title bar.

Creating a Data Access Page from an Access Database

The next step in the Leland Mortgage Web site creation is to use an Access database to create a data access page. A **data access page** is a special type of Web page that is designed for viewing and working with data. Similar to a form, a data access page is connected, or bound, directly to an Access database.

Q & A

Q: Can I hide the outline pane when viewing the presentation in a browser?

A: Yes. The outline pane is displayed by default when you view a presentation in a browser. To hide this pane, click the Outline button while in the browser. Click the Outline button again to redisplay the outline pane.

You can use data access pages to analyze data, enter and edit data, make projections, and review data. In addition, you can create a chart using the chart component to analyze trends, show patterns, and make comparisons on the data in the database. Then, you can add spreadsheet controls to allow the inclusion of formulas for calculations.

One of the more common purposes of data access pages is for viewing records in a database via a company's intranet or the World Wide Web. Data access pages provide a method to make inquiries of large amounts of data in a selective way. Groups of records can be expanded or collapsed so that Web page visitors can view the data they want to see.

The following steps open an Access database.

To Start Access and Open an Existing Database

1 Click the Start button on the Windows taskbar, point to All Programs on the Start menu, and then click Open Office Document on the All Programs submenu.

2 If necessary, click the Look in box arrow and then click 3½ Floppy (A:) in the Look in list.

3 Double-click the Leland Mortgage Products database name. If the Microsoft Office Access dialog box appears, click the Yes button.

4 If the Language bar is displayed, right-click it and then click Close the Language bar on the shortcut menu.

5 If the Getting Started task pane appears in the Access window, click its Close button in the upper-right corner.

Access starts and opens the Leland Mortgage Products : Database window (Figure 1-32).

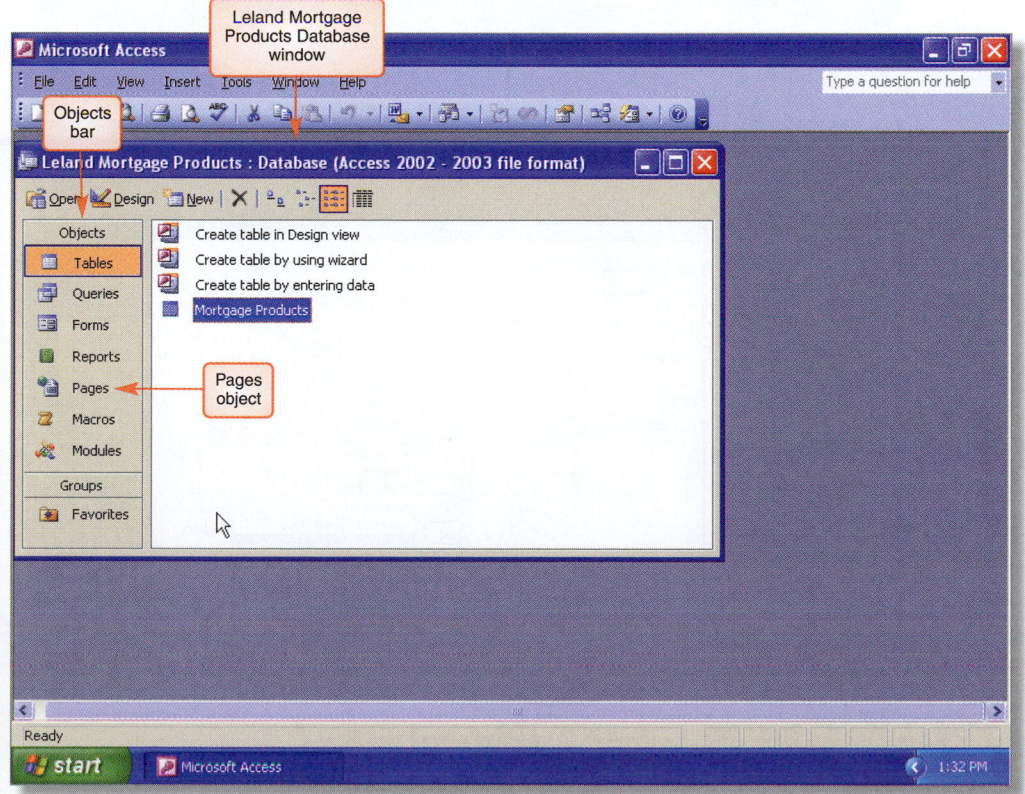

FIGURE 1-32

Creating a Data Access Page Using the Page Wizard

For the Leland Mortgage Web site, you do not want the database to be altered by the Web page visitor in any way. The visitors should be allowed to view only the data. Because of this, you must add a grouping level to the data access page. Adding **grouping levels** results in a read-only page. The Web page visitors can view all data and alter that view, but they cannot change the data itself.

The following steps use the Page Wizard to create a data access page.

To Create a Data Access Page Using the Page Wizard

1

• **Click the Pages object on the Objects bar.**

2

• **Double-click Create data access page by using wizard.**

Access displays the Page Wizard dialog box that includes options for setting up data access pages (Figure 1-33). The Mortgage Products table is selected automatically because it is the only table in the database. If more than one table exists, you would need to click the Tables object on the Objects bar and then select the appropriate table before clicking the Pages object in Step 1.

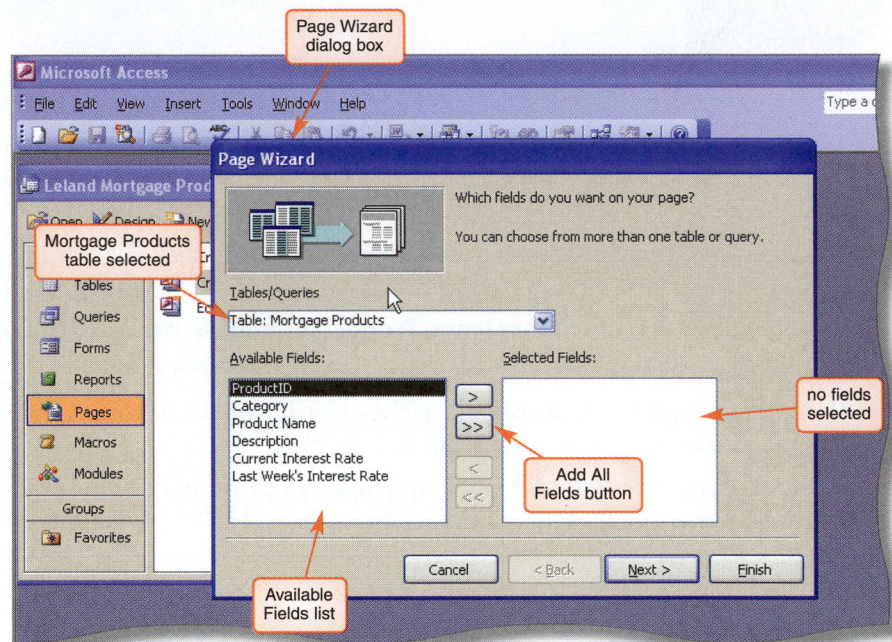

FIGURE 1-33

3

• **Click the Add All Fields button to add all the fields.**

The Selected Fields list displays all the fields in the table (Figure 1-34). This means you want to display all the fields on the data access page.

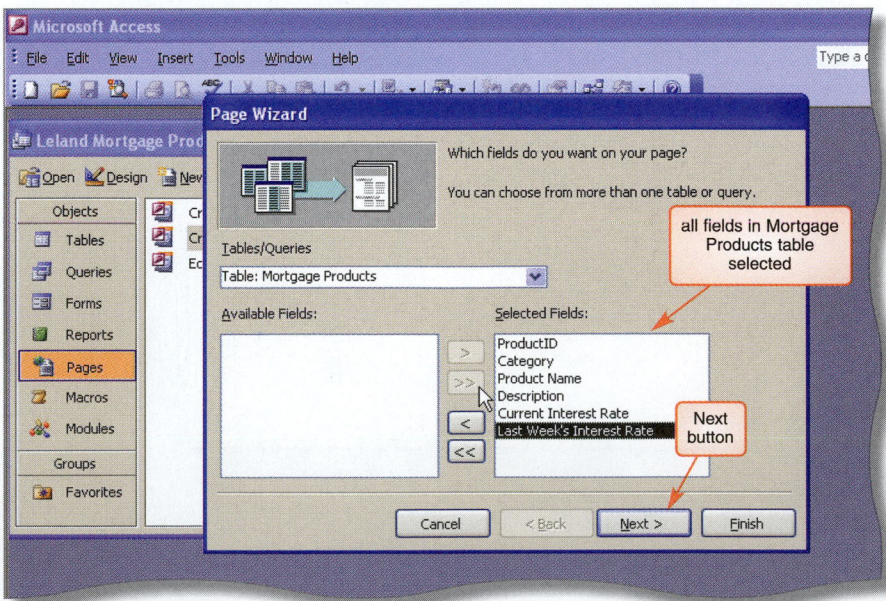

FIGURE 1-34

4

- **Click the Next button.**
- **Double-click Category in the box on the left.**

Adding a grouping level, such as Category, prohibits the data access page from being updated. Category is displayed in the upper-right box indicating it has been selected (Figure 1-35).

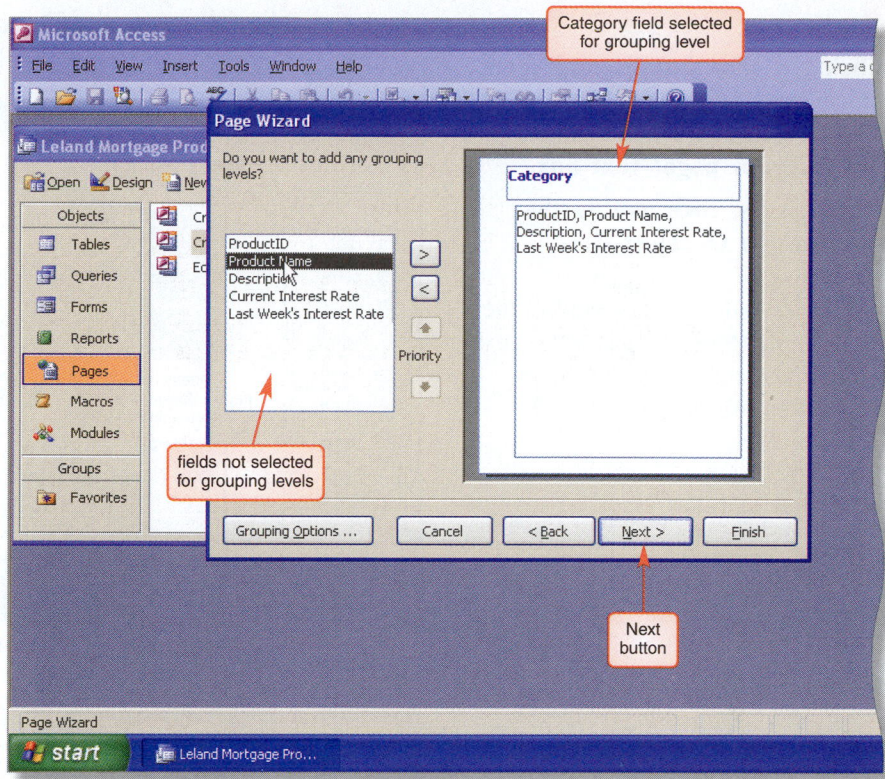

FIGURE 1-35

5

- **Click the Next button.**

The Page Wizard dialog box displays options for sorting records (Figure 1-36). No changes are required.

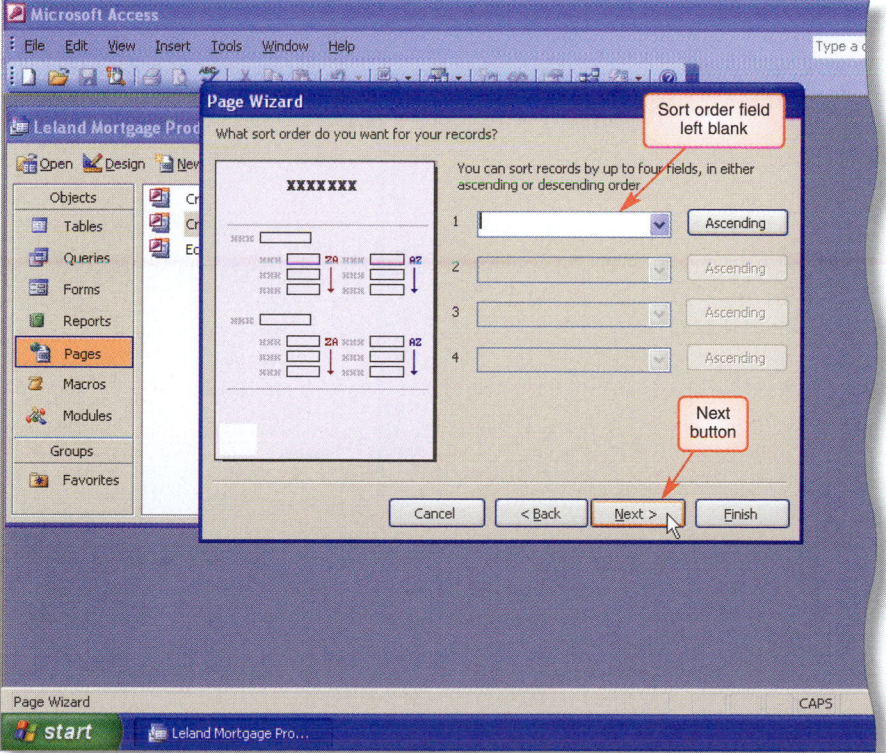

FIGURE 1-36

6

• **Click the Next button and then, if necessary, type** Mortgage Products **in the What title do you want for your page? text box.**

• **If necessary, click Modify the page's design to select it.**

The Page Wizard dialog box displays the page title, Mortgage Products, in the text box and the Modify the page's design option button selected (Figure 1-37).

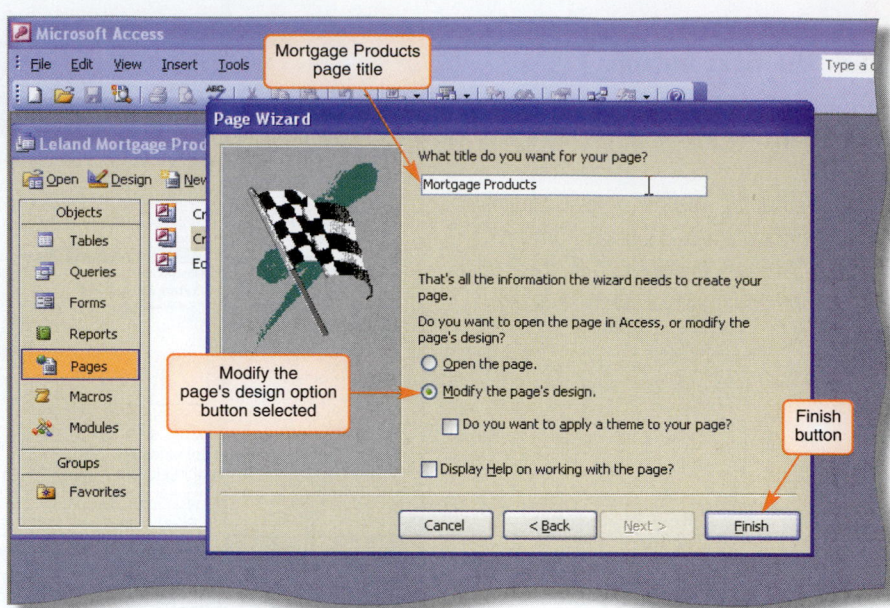

FIGURE 1-37

7

• **Click the Finish button.**

• **If necessary, close the Field List task pane.**

Access displays the data access page in Design view (Figure 1-38).

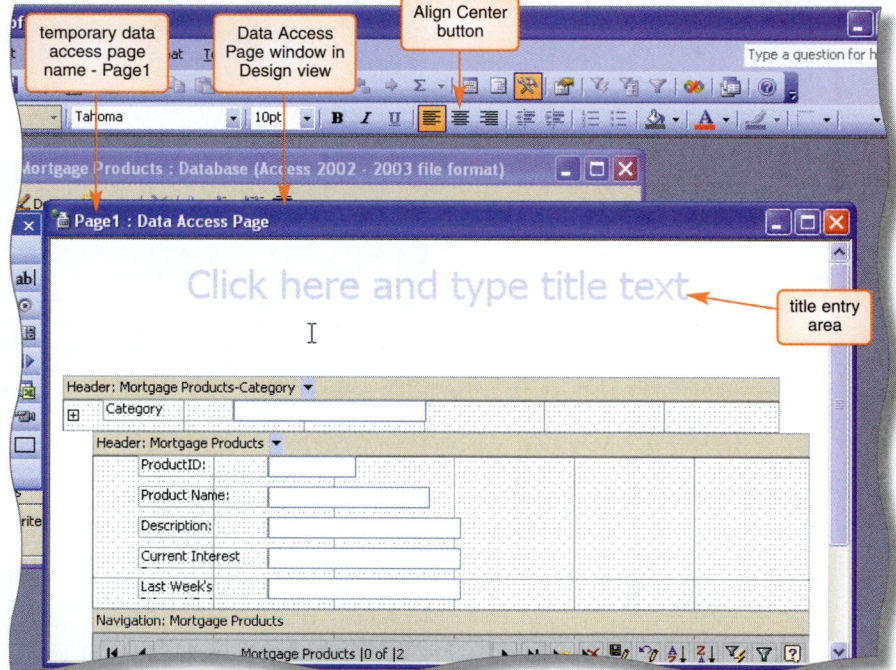

FIGURE 1-38

Adding a Title and Resizing a Label on a Data Access Page

The data access page is created, but additional information can be helpful for the Web page visitor. It is customary to insert a title at the top of the page that tells the visitor the purpose of the Web page. Resizing the Current Interest Rate label and the Last Week's Interest Rate label is necessary because the entire text of these labels does not show after completing the Data Access Page Wizard. The following steps add a title and resize two labels.

To Add a Title and Resize Labels on a Data Access Page

1

• **If necessary, scroll to the top of the data access page.**

• **With the data access page in Design view, click anywhere in the Click here and type title text entry area.**

• **Type** Leland Mortgage Products **as the title.**

Access displays the data access page as shown in Figure 1-39.

2

• **Click anywhere within the Current Interest Rate label in the Mortgage Products area of the data access page to select the label.**

• **Point to the lower-right sizing handle on the label.**

3

• **Drag the resize handle straight down so that it doubles in height.**

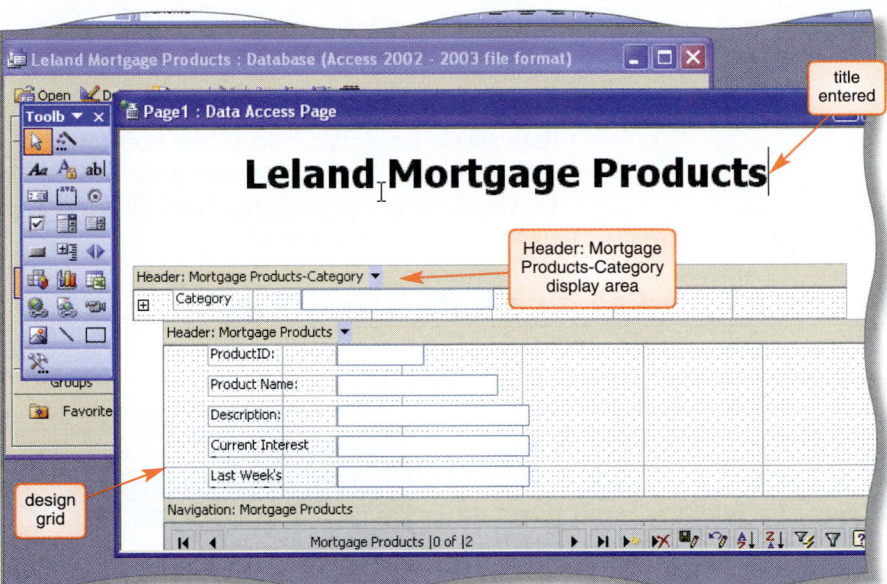

FIGURE 1-39

4

• **Click anywhere within the Last Week's Interest Rate label in the Mortgage Products area of the data access page to select the label.**

• **Point to the lower-right sizing handle on the label.**

5

• **Drag the resize handle straight down so that it doubles in height.**

The Current Interest Rate label and the Last Week's Interest Rate label are resized, and Access displays the data access page as shown in Figure 1-40.

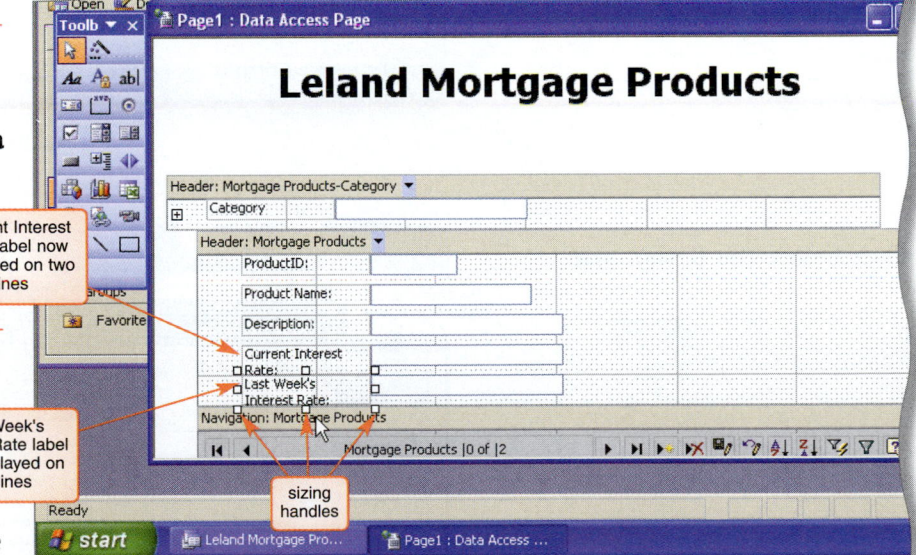

FIGURE 1-40

The data access page is created, a heading is positioned in the header, and the label is resized as shown in Figure 1-1d on page INT 6. The next step is to add a hyperlink that returns the visitor to the Web site home page.

Adding a Hyperlink to a Data Access Page

Just as you did on the PowerPoint Web page, you should add a hyperlink on the data access page that links to the home page. This allows the Web page visitor to return to the Leland Mortgage home page without having to click the Back button on the browser's toolbar repeatedly. The following steps add a hyperlink to the data access page.

To Add a Hyperlink to a Data Access Page

1

• **If necessary, click View on the menu bar and then click Toolbox to display the Toolbox. Scroll down so the bottom of the data access page displays.**

• **Click the Hyperlink button on the Toolbox and then point below the design grid.**

The hyperlink mouse pointer is displayed as shown in Figure 1-41.

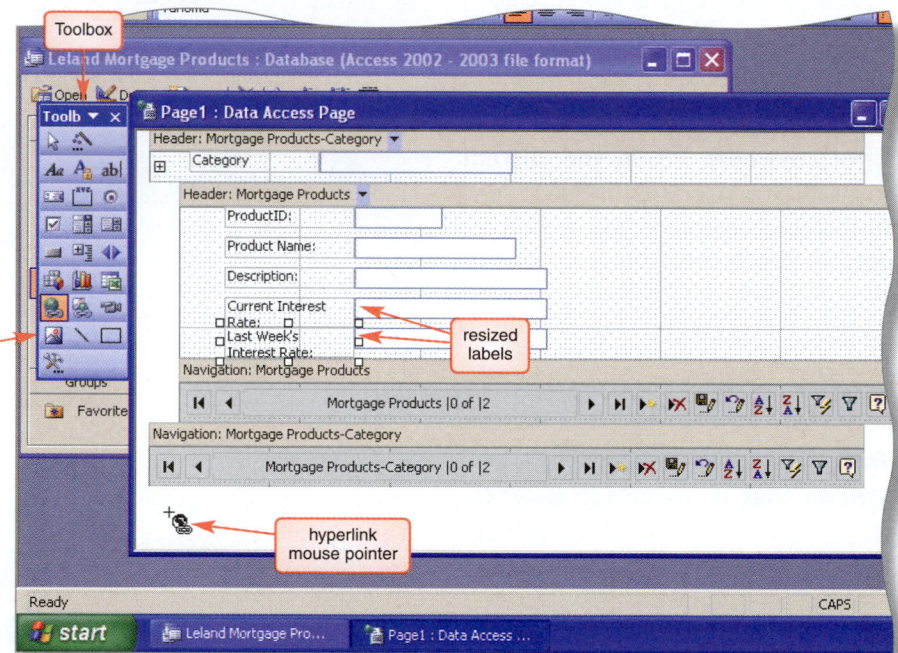

FIGURE 1-41

2

• **Click below the Design grid.**

The Insert Hyperlink dialog box is displayed (Figure 1-42).

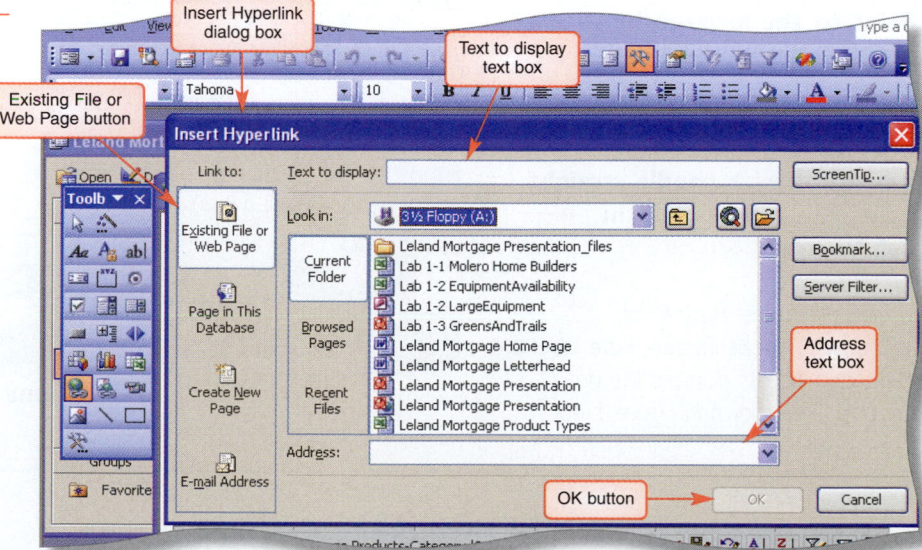

FIGURE 1-42

3

• If necessary, click the Existing File or Web Page button on the Link to bar.

• Type Home in the Text to display text box.

• Type LelandHome.htm in the Address text box and then click the OK button.

• If the Microsoft Office Access dialog box appears, click the OK button.

4

• Click anywhere on the data access page to deselect the hyperlink box.

Access displays the data access page as shown in Figure 1-43.

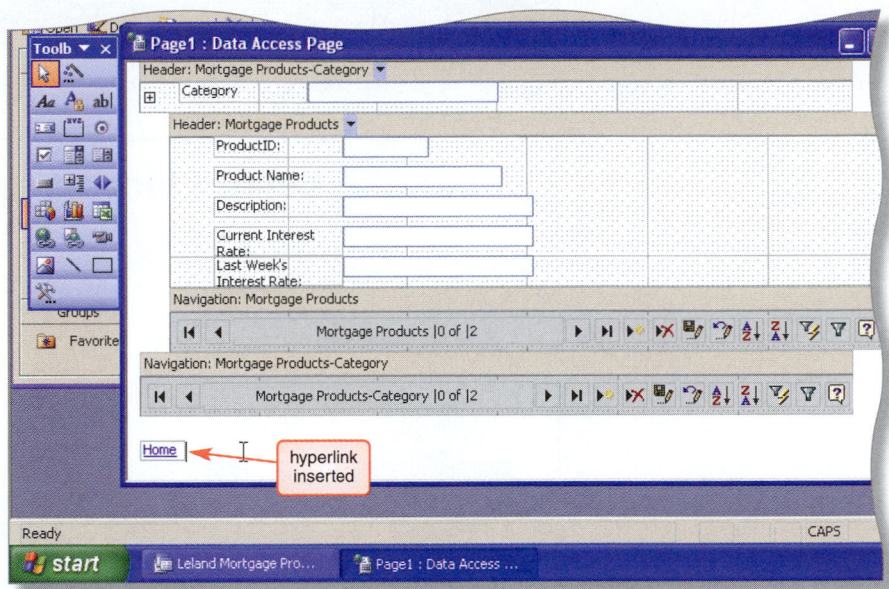

FIGURE 1-43

The data access page is complete. In the next section, you will save the page to the Integration Data Disk and view it in the browser.

Saving the Data Access Page and Viewing It

In other sections of this project, you have viewed the Web page, verified that it is correct, and then saved it on a floppy disk. Unlike Word and PowerPoint, you must save a data access page before you can preview it in your browser. As the Web page is being opened in your browser, Access displays a Databinding message on the status bar of your browser. This indicates that the data access page is connecting to the database that was open when the page was created (Leland Mortgage Products).

The following steps save the file on the Integration Data Disk and then open it for viewing in the browser.

To Save the Data Access Page and View It in Your Browser

1 Click File on the menu bar and then click Web Page Preview. When the Microsoft Office Access dialog box displays, click the Yes button.

2 When the Save As Data Access Page dialog box displays, if necessary, type MortgageProducts in the File name text box. If necessary, click 3½ Floppy (A:) in the Save in list.

3 Click the Save button in the Save As Data Access Page dialog box.

4 Click the Expand indicator to the left of the Category label to expand the display.

The browser displays the expanded data access page (Figure 1-44 on the next page).

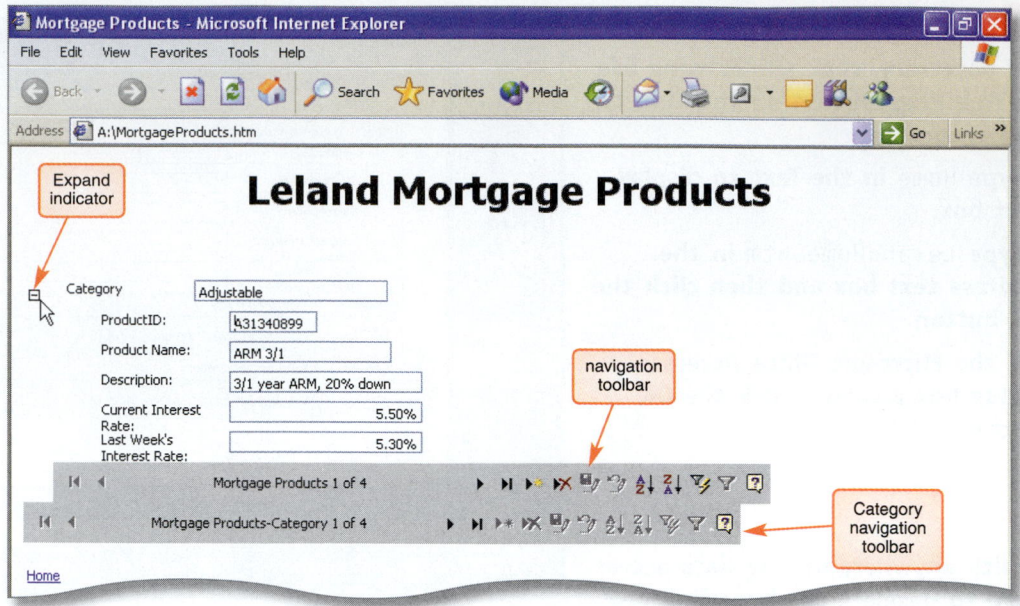

FIGURE 1-44

After you save the data access page, you can preview it and then quit Access and close your browser, as shown in the following steps.

To Close Your Browser and Quit Access

1 **Right-click the Leland Mortgage Products button on the taskbar and then click Close on the shortcut menu.**

2 **Click the Close button on the Access title bar to quit Access.**

More About

Microsoft Certification

The Microsoft Office Specialist Certification program provides an opportunity for you to obtain a valuable industry credential — proof that you have the Office 2003 skills required by employers. For more information, see Appendix E, or visit the Office Integration 2003 Certification Web page (scsite.com/int2003/cert).

Grouping records on a data access page is similar to grouping records on a report. You can group the data on this data access page in different ways, but the user cannot edit the data. The records in the data access page can be expanded or collapsed, using the **Expand and Collapse indicators**. This allows users to customize their view of the data and remove extra data from view that may not interest them. Using the **navigation toolbars** on the data access page, you can move, sort, and filter records and obtain Help.

Use the navigation toolbar to verify that the information in the database displays correctly. Click the link to the home page of the Web site to verify it.

Testing the Web Site

The Leland Mortgage Web site is complete. To ensure that all the links in the Web site are viable, the following steps open the home page and then thoroughly test the entire Web site.

To Test the Web Site

1 **Start your browser.**

2 **Click the Address bar of your browser.**

3 **Type** `a:\LelandHome.htm` **in the text box, and then press the ENTER key.**

The browser displays the home page of the Leland Mortgage Web site as shown in Figure 1-45.

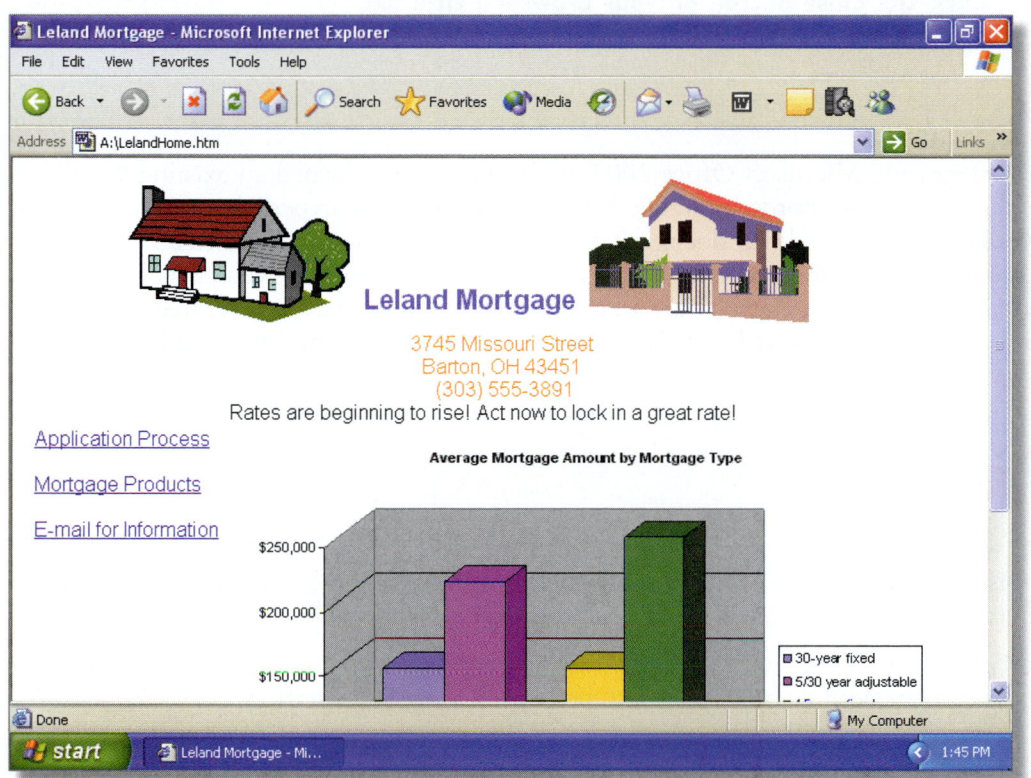

FIGURE 1-45

Verifying the Hyperlinks in Your Browser

All hyperlinks should be tested by clicking them and verifying that they jump to the correct Web page. Three hyperlinks are on the home page: Application Process, Mortgage Products, and E-mail for Information. The following steps test the links.

To Verify the Hyperlinks

1 **Click the Application Process hyperlink.**

2 **Click the navigation buttons to view all slides on the Web page.**

3 **On the first slide on the PowerPoint Web page, click the Home hyperlink.**

4 **Click the Mortgage Products hyperlink. Click the Expand and Collapse indicators and then scroll through the database using the navigation toolbars.**

5 **On the data access page, click the Home hyperlink.**

6 **Click the E-mail for Information hyperlink.**

A new e-mail message displays with manager@isp.com in the To text box.

With the hyperlinks verified, the steps on the next page quit the e-mail program and the browser.

To Quit E-Mail and Close Your Browser

1 Click the Close button on your e-mail program.

2 Click the Close button on your browser's title bar.

Project Summary

This project introduced you to integrating Microsoft Office 2003 applications. You opened an existing Word document and created a two-column, one-row, borderless table. You then inserted three hyperlinks, embedded a Bar chart from an existing Excel worksheet, and saved that document as an HTML file. You then opened an existing PowerPoint presentation, added a hyperlink to the first slide, and saved this presentation as a Web page. Finally, you opened an existing Access database and used the Page Wizard to create a data access page. You created a grouping level so the database could not be changed. You saved that data access page and viewed and tested all Web pages and hyperlinks.

What You Should Know

Having completed this project, you should be able to perform the tasks below. The tasks are listed in the same order they were presented in this project. For a list of the buttons, menus, toolbars, and commands introduced in this project, see the Quick Reference Summary at the back of this book and refer to the Page Number column.

1. Start Word, Customize Word, Open an Existing Document, and Save the Document with Another Name   (INT 8)

2. Insert a Table into a Word Document   (INT 9)

3. Remove the Table Border   (INT 11)

4. Insert Text for Hyperlinks   (INT 12)

5. Create a Hyperlink to PowerPoint Web Pages (INT 13)

6. Insert the Remaining Hyperlinks   (INT 13)

7. Start Excel, Customize Excel, and Open an Existing Workbook   (INT 14)

8. Embed an Excel Chart into a Word Document (INT 15)

9. Change the Size of an Embedded Object (INT 17)

10. Quit Excel   (INT 19)

11. Display the Web Tools Toolbar   (INT 20)

12. Insert Scrolling Text into a Word Document (INT 21)

13. Resize the Scrolling Text   (INT 22)

14. Preview the Web Page   (INT 24)

15. Save a Document with a New File Name (INT 24)

16. Quit Word   (INT 25)

17. Start PowerPoint, Customize PowerPoint, and Open an Existing Presentation   (INT 26)

18. Add Text for a Hyperlink into a PowerPoint Presentation   (INT 27)

19. Insert a Hyperlink into a PowerPoint Presentation   (INT 28)

20. View the Web Page in Your Browser   (INT 28)

21. Save the PowerPoint Presentation as a Web Page (INT 30)

22. Quit PowerPoint and Close Your Browser (INT 30)

23. Start Access and Open an Existing Database (INT 31)

24. Create a Data Access Page Using the Page Wizard (INT 32)

25. Add a Title and Resize Labels on a Data Access Page   (INT 35)

26. Add a Hyperlink to a Data Access Page (INT 36)

27. Save the Data Access Page and View It in Your Browser   (INT 37)

28. Close Your Browser and Quit Access   (INT 38)

29. Test the Web Site   (INT 38)

30. Verify the Hyperlinks   (INT 39)

31. Quit E-Mail and Close Your Browser   (INT 40)

Learn It Online

Instructions: To complete the Learn It Online exercises, start your browser, click the Address bar, and then enter the Web address scsite.com/int2003/learn. When the Office 2003 Learn It Online page is displayed, follow the instructions in the exercises below. Each exercise has instructions for printing your results, either for your own records or for submission to your instructor.

1 Project Reinforcement TF, MC, and SA

Below Office Integration Project 1, click the Project Reinforcement link. Print the quiz by clicking Print on the File menu for each page. Answer each question.

2 Flash Cards

Below Office Integration Project 1, click the Flash Cards link and read the instructions. Type 20 (or a number specified by your instructor) in the Number of playing cards text box, type your name in the Enter your Name text box, and then click the Flip Card button. When the flash card is displayed, read the question and then click the ANSWER box arrow to select an answer. Flip through Flash Cards. If your score is 15 (75%) correct or greater, click Print on the File menu to print your results. If your score is less than 15 (75%) correct, then redo this exercise by clicking the Replay button.

3 Practice Test

Below Office Integration Project 1, click the Practice Test link. Answer each question, enter your first and last name at the bottom of the page, and then click the Grade Test button. When the graded practice test is displayed on your screen, click Print on the File menu to print a hard copy. Continue to take practice tests until you score 80% or better.

4 Who Wants To Be a Computer Genius?

Below Office Integration Project 1, click the Computer Genius link. Read the instructions, enter your first and last name at the bottom of the page, and then click the PLAY button. When your score is displayed, click the PRINT RESULTS link to print a hard copy.

5 Wheel of Terms

Below Office Integration Project 1, click the Wheel of Terms link. Read the instructions, and then enter your first and last name and your school name. Click the PLAY button. When your score is displayed, right-click the score and then click Print on the shortcut menu to print a hard copy.

6 Crossword Puzzle Challenge

Below Office Integration Project 1, click the Crossword Puzzle Challenge link. Read the instructions, and then enter your first and last name. Click the SUBMIT button. Work the crossword puzzle. When you are finished, click the Submit button. When the crossword puzzle is redisplayed, click the Print Puzzle button to print a hard copy.

7 Tips and Tricks

Below Office Integration Project 1, click the Tips and Tricks link. Click a topic that pertains to Project 1. Right-click the information and then click Print on the shortcut menu. Construct a brief example of what the information relates to in Office Integration to confirm you understand how to use the tip or trick.

8 Newsgroups

Below Office Integration Project 1, click the Newsgroups link. Click a topic that pertains to Project 1. Print three comments.

9 Expanding Your Horizons

Below Office Integration Project 1, click the Expanding Your Horizons link. Click a topic that pertains to Project 1. Print the information. Construct a brief example of what the information relates to in Office Integration to confirm you understand the contents of the article.

10 Search Sleuth

Below Office Integration Project 1, click the Search Sleuth link. To search for a term that pertains to this project, select a term below the Project 1 title and then use the Google search engine at google.com (or any major search engine) to display and print two Web pages that present information on the term.

11 Office Integration Online Training

Below Office Integration Project 1, click the Office Integration Online Training link. When your browser displays the Microsoft Office Online Web page, click the Office Integration link. Click one of the Office Integration courses that covers one or more of the objectives listed at the beginning of the project on page INT 4. Print the first page of the course before stepping through it.

12 Office Marketplace

Below Office Integration Project 1, click the Office Marketplace link. When your browser displays the Microsoft Office Online Web page, click the Office Marketplace link. Click a topic that relates to Office Integration. Print the first page.

1 Creating a Web Page in Word with an Embedded Excel Chart

Problem: As vice president of Molero Home Builders, you have created a worksheet and chart in Excel to analyze the sales for the past year. Create a Web page in Word and embed the chart from the Molero Home Builders workbook on the home page. Add a link to a second Web page and an e-mail link to molero@isp.com below the chart. Create a second Web page in Word by embedding the Molero Home Builders worksheet.

Instructions: Perform the following tasks.

1. Start Excel by opening the Lab 1-1 Molero Home Builders workbook.
2. Start Word and create a new Web page. Add a title as shown in Figure 1-46. Select the Molero Home Builders chart in Excel, copy it, and use the Paste Special dialog box in Word to embed the Excel Chart Object. Resize the chart to 84% of its original size.

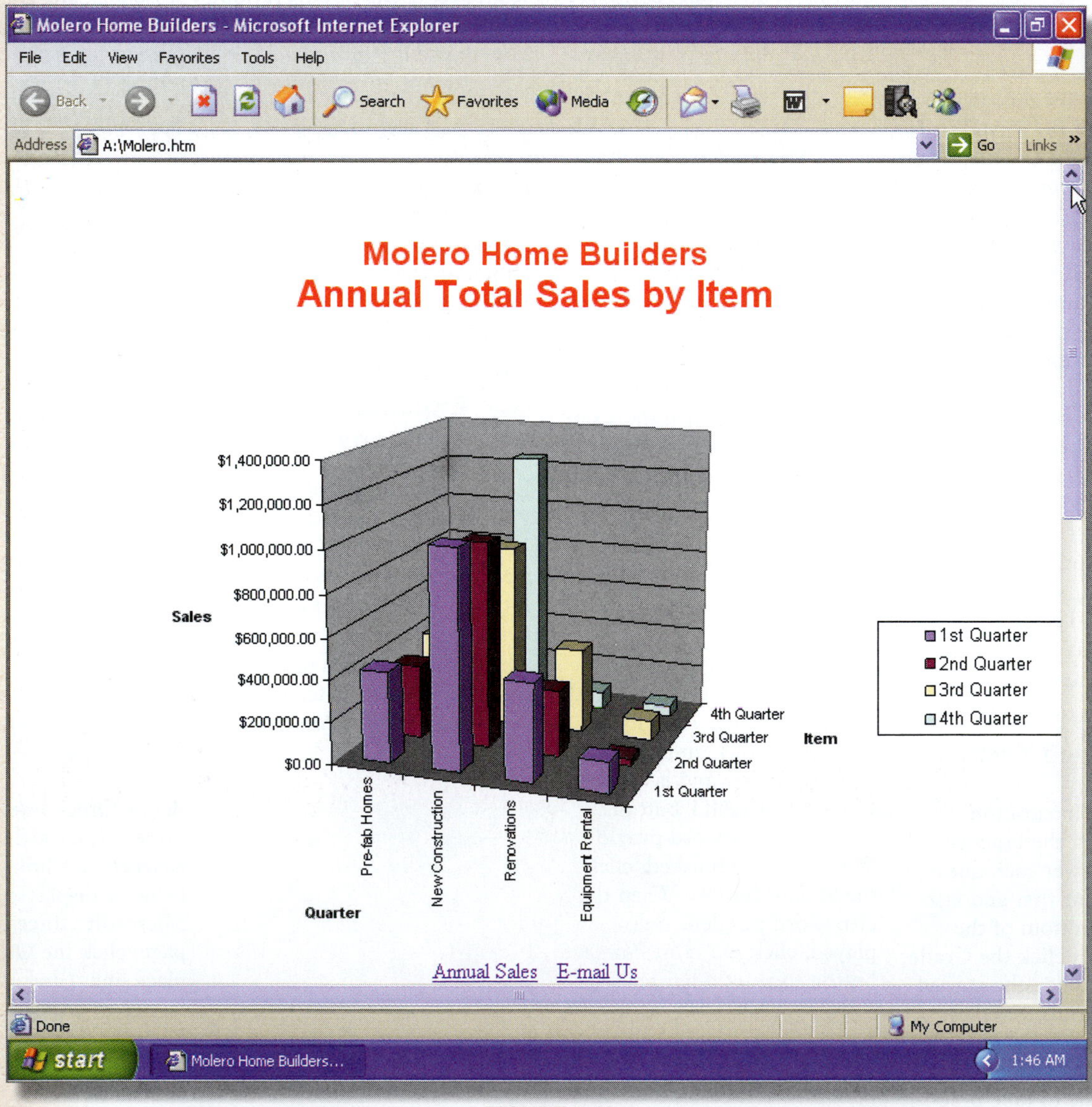

FIGURE 1-46

In the Lab

3. Add two hyperlinks to the bottom of the page in a centered, borderless table. The first hyperlink should jump to the Web page MoleroSales.htm, which is created next. The second hyperlink creates an e-mail message to molero@isp.com.
4. Save this file as Molero.htm.
5. Create a new Web page in Word.
6. Embed the Excel worksheet into the Word page. That is, switch to Excel, select the worksheet, copy the worksheet to the Clipboard, switch to Word, and use the Paste Special command on the Edit menu in Word to embed the Excel Worksheet Object.
7. Save this file as MoleroSales.htm.
8. View the Molero.htm file in your browser (Figure 1-46). Print the Web page. Click the Annual Sales link to navigate to the MoleroSales.htm page (Figure 1-47) and print it.

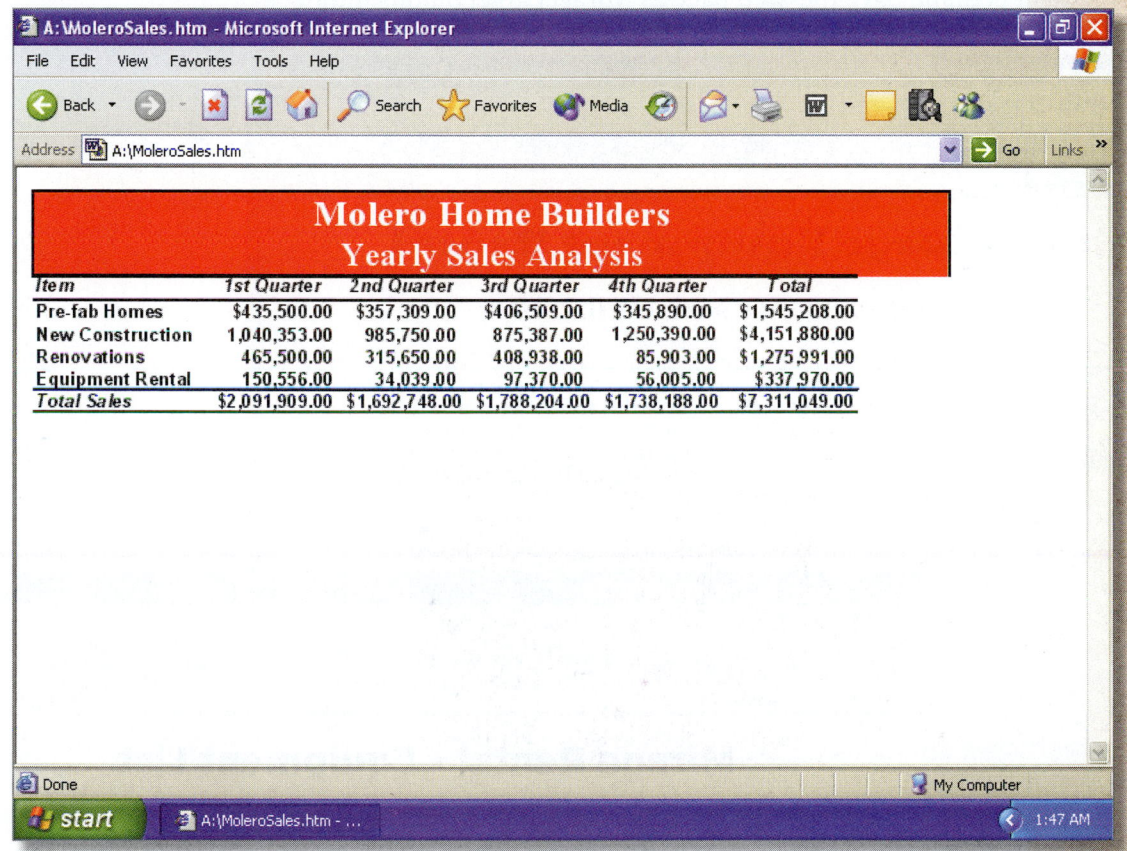

FIGURE 1-47

In the Lab

2 Mirage Rental Web Site with a Data Access Page and an Excel Worksheet

Problem: As the assistant manager of Mirage Rental, Tammie Glover is responsible for keeping track of large equipment that is rented on a per-day basis. She would like you to design a site that allows customers to view the availability of equipment for rent. She also wants an e-mail link for questions.

Instructions: Perform the following tasks.

1. Start Word. Create a home page for the Mirage Rental for Large Equipment Web site (Figure 1-48). Add a title and a borderless table below the title. In the left column, insert three hyperlinks. The first hyperlink should go to LargeEquipment.htm (Figure 1-49). The second hyperlink should go to EquipmentAvailability.htm (Figure 1-50). The third hyperlink should start an e-mail message to assistantmanager@isp.com. Type the text in the right column. Save the Web page as MirageLargeEquipment.htm.

FIGURE 1-48

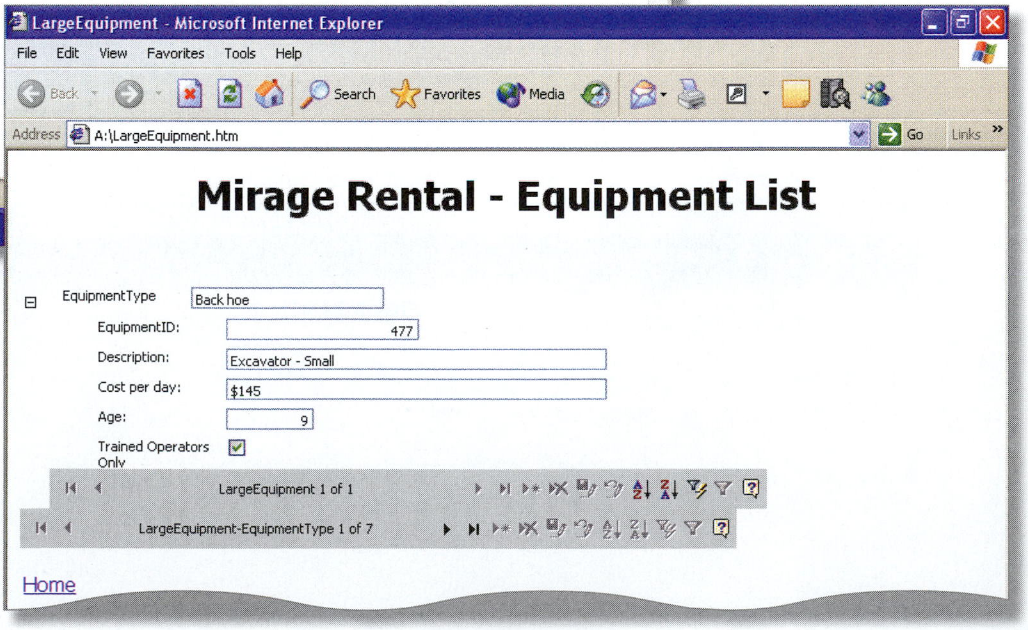

FIGURE 1-49

In the Lab

2. Start Access by opening the Lab 1-2 LargeEquipment.mdb database on the Integration Data Disk. Create a data access page from the LargeEquipment table. Create a grouping level using the EquipmentType field. Add a title as shown in Figure 1-49. Add a link named Home that links to the MirageLargeEquipment.htm home page at the bottom of the data access page. Save the data access page as LargeEquipment.htm.

3. Start Excel by opening the Lab 1-2 EquipmentAvailability.xls workbook on the Integration Data Disk. Create a Web page from the workbook by using the Save as a Web Page command on the File menu. Use the file name, EquipmentAvailability.htm.

4. View the MirageLargeEquipment.htm Web page in your browser. Verify that all links operate properly by clicking each one. Print all Web pages.

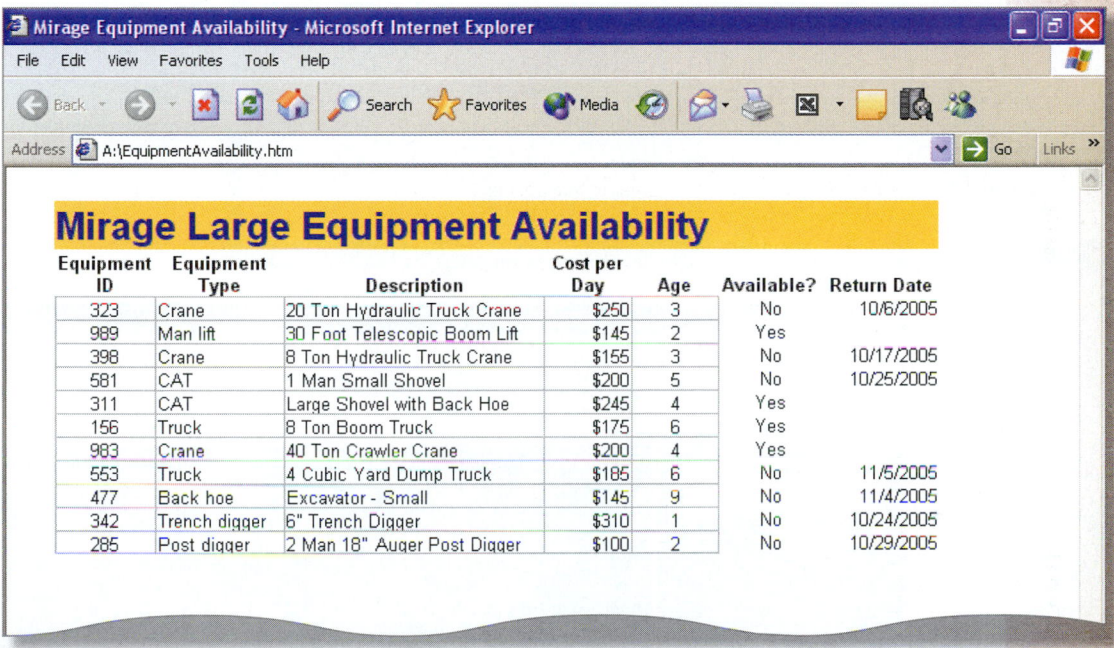

FIGURE 1-50

3 GreensAndTrails Association Information Web Site Incorporating PowerPoint Web Pages

Problem: As a volunteer with the GreensAndTrails Housing Association, you have offered to create a Web page that recruits residents to become board members of the association (Figures 1-51 and 1-52 on the next page). The specific information for the memberships is located in a PowerPoint presentation, which has four pages.

Instructions: Perform the following tasks.

1. Start Word. Create the Web page as shown in Figure 1-51. Include scrolling text below the Web page title. Insert two hyperlinks. The first hyperlink should link to GreensAndTrails.htm, and the second should link to an e-mail address at association@isp.com. Use clip art to insert the picture of a tree. Save this Web page as GATBoardRecruiting.htm.

(continued)

In the Lab

**GreensAndTrails Association Information Web Site Incorporating
PowerPoint Web Pages** *(continued)*

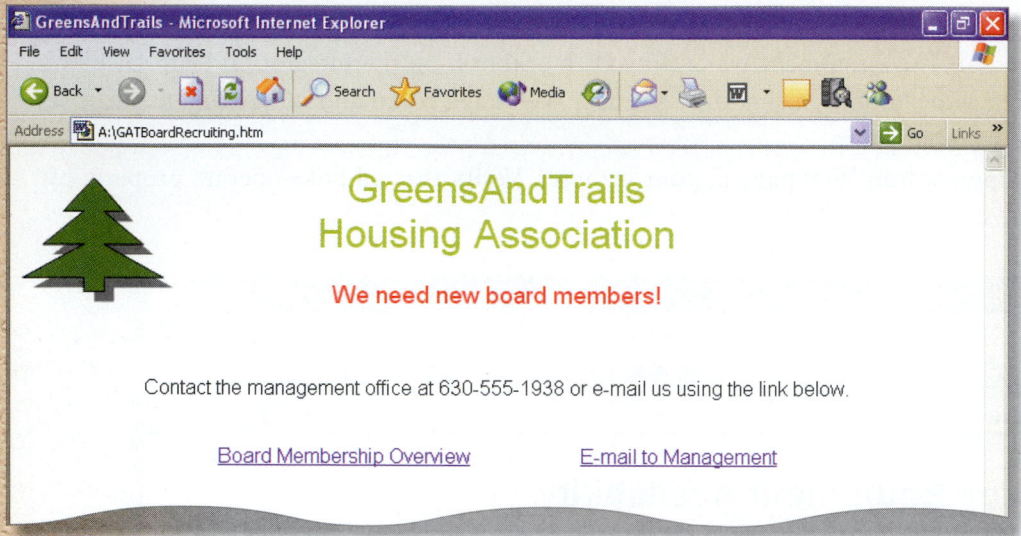

FIGURE 1-51

FIGURE 1-52

2. Open the Lab 1-3 PowerPoint presentation GreensAndTrails.ppt. Add a link named Home at the bottom of the first page of the presentation that jumps to the GATBoardRecruiting.htm Web page. Save the PowerPoint presentation as Web pages on the Integration Data Disk. Name the Web pages GreensAndTrails.htm.

3. View the Web pages in your browser. Print each page.

Cases and Places

The difficulty of these case studies varies:
■ are the least difficult and ■■ are the most difficult. The last exercise is a group exercise.

1 ■ You are working for a new ISP that offers wireless Internet access to local homes and businesses. The company offers three levels of service. The business plan has a startup fee of $100, a monthly charge of $75, and offers the highest speed and instant access to customer service. The residential plan has a startup fee of $50, a monthly charge of $40, and offers high speed, but with a limited amount of data that can be downloaded per day. The economy plan has a startup fee of $50, a monthly charge of $20, and offers a low-speed connection. Create a worksheet in Excel that summarizes each of these plans. Create a Web page using Word that embeds the Excel worksheet; the goal of the Web site is to inform new customers of the services provided. Make sure to include an e-mail address on the Web page.

2 ■ A local real-estate agent wants to advertise the child-friendly atmosphere of the area and has asked you for help. Research summer-time activities for area children under the age of 12 available from various groups and agencies in your area, and determine the following for each: organization name, program or activity name, number of weeks, contact name, contact telephone number, age range, and cost. Create an Excel worksheet and charts summarizing your data and graphing the age range and costs. Using Word, create a Web page and embed the worksheet on the home page of the Web site. Create another Web page, and embed the charts from Excel. Create a link to the Excel chart Web page and a link to each organization's Web page.

3 ■ You have started making extra money by selling some personal items on an online auction Web site. As the number of items you sell grows, you want to advertise your current items on your own Web site. Create an Access database and add ten items to it with the following information for each item: item name, category, description, condition, and sale price. From this table, create a data access page with inquiry capability only, using the category as the grouping level. Include item name, category, description, condition, and sale price in the data access page. Use a search engine to find relevant links about each category of items — such as sports memorabilia, comic books, and old coins — and create links to one Web page each for each category at the bottom of the data access page.

4 ■■ As a member of your school's Career Day organization team, you have been asked to create a Web page on which students can view information about speakers at this year's Career Day event. Create an Access database and add information about prospective speakers to the database. Include the following fields: name, area of expertise, job title, number of years in the field, and whether the person has spoken at Career Day in the past. From this table, create a data access page with inquiry capability only, using the area of expertise as the grouping level. Create a Web page using Word that will act as the Web page for the speaker list and create a link to the data access page. Be sure to include a link to your e-mail address on the Web page.

Cases and Places

5 ■■ **Working Together** Gather basic statistical data about the town or city in which you live, including population, important business and industry, and other demographic data. Have one member of your team create an Excel 3-D Bar chart to summarize the demographic information that you find. Have another member create a PowerPoint presentation that contains at least four major points regarding the town or city that may make the area interesting to outside businesses. A third member should create a data access Web page that includes information about local colleges. Embed the Excel chart into one of the PowerPoint slides. Create a link from one of the PowerPoint pages to the data access Web page. Save the PowerPoint presentation as Web pages. Include relevant links to Web pages regarding the area.

Appendix A

Microsoft Office Help System

Using the Microsoft Office Help System

This appendix shows you how to use the Microsoft Office Help system. At anytime while you are using one of the Microsoft Office 2003 applications, you can interact with its Help system and display information on any topic associated with the application. To illustrate the use of the Office Help system, you will use the Microsoft Word application in this appendix. The Help systems in other Office applications respond in a similar fashion.

As shown in Figure A-1, five methods for accessing Word's Help system are available:

1. Microsoft Office Word Help button on the Standard toolbar
2. Microsoft Office Word Help command on the Help menu
3. Function key F1 on the keyboard
4. Type a question for help box on the menu bar
5. Office Assistant

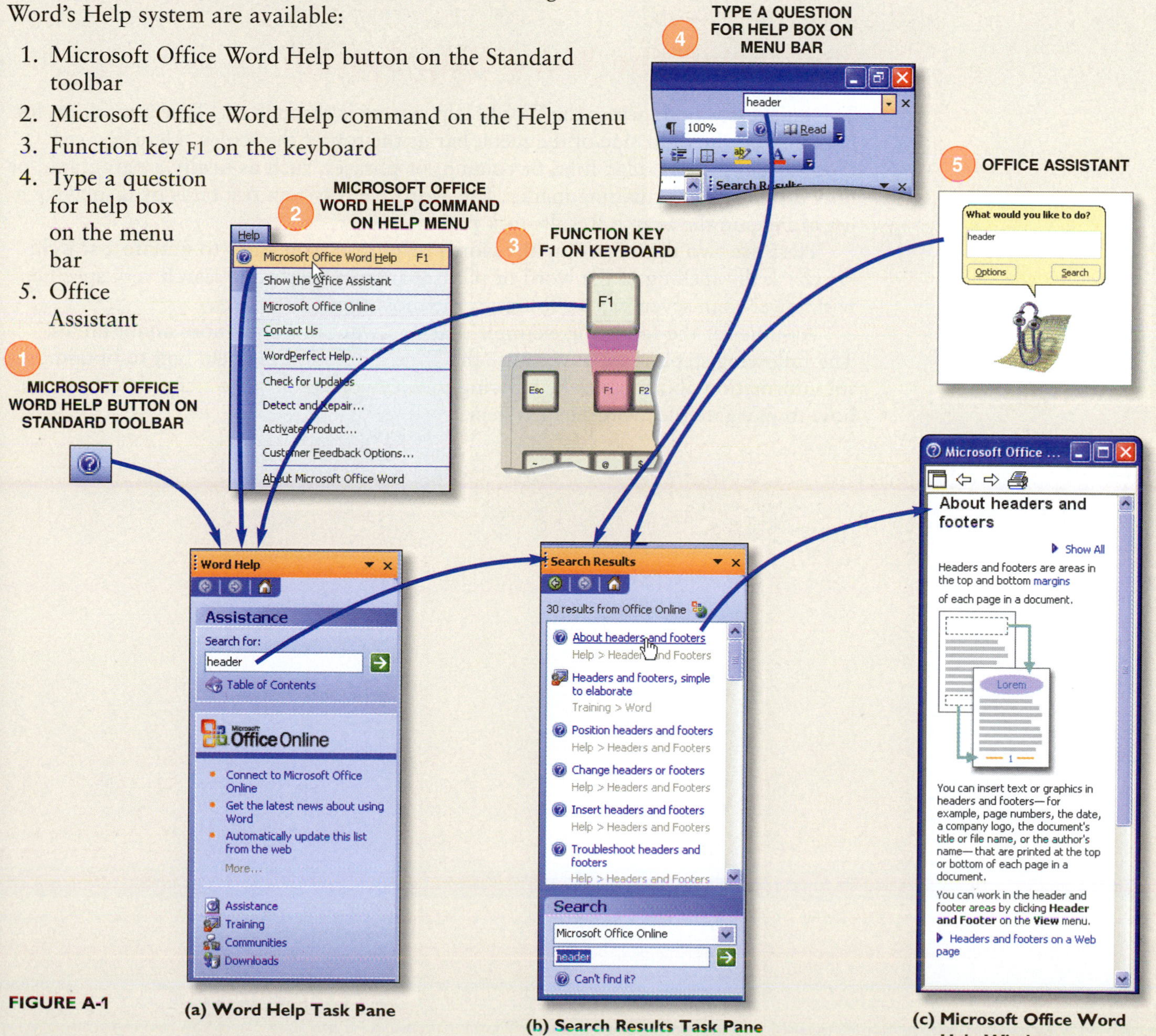

1 MICROSOFT OFFICE WORD HELP BUTTON ON STANDARD TOOLBAR

2 MICROSOFT OFFICE WORD HELP COMMAND ON HELP MENU

Help
- Microsoft Office Word Help   F1
- Show the Office Assistant
- Microsoft Office Online
- Contact Us
- WordPerfect Help...
- Check for Updates
- Detect and Repair...
- Activate Product...
- Customer Feedback Options...
- About Microsoft Office Word

3 FUNCTION KEY F1 ON KEYBOARD

F1

Esc   F1   F2

4 TYPE A QUESTION FOR HELP BOX ON MENU BAR

header
¶ 100% Read
Search Results

5 OFFICE ASSISTANT

What would you like to do?
header
Options   Search

Microsoft Office ...

About headers and footers
▶ Show All

Headers and footers are areas in the top and bottom margins of each page in a document.

Lorem
1

You can insert text or graphics in headers and footers—for example, page numbers, the date, a company logo, the document's title or file name, or the author's name—that are printed at the top or bottom of each page in a document.

You can work in the header and footer areas by clicking **Header and Footer** on the **View** menu.

▶ Headers and footers on a Web page

Word Help

Assistance
Search for:
header

Table of Contents

Office Online

- Connect to Microsoft Office Online
- Get the latest news about using Word
- Automatically update this list from the web

More...

- Assistance
- Training
- Communities
- Downloads

Search Results

30 results from Office Online

- About headers and footers
  Help > Headers and Footers
- Headers and footers, simple to elaborate
  Training > Word
- Position headers and footers
  Help > Headers and Footers
- Change headers or footers
  Help > Headers and Footers
- Insert headers and footers
  Help > Headers and Footers
- Troubleshoot headers and footers
  Help > Headers and Footers

Search
Microsoft Office Online
header

Can't find it?

FIGURE A-1   (a) Word Help Task Pane   (b) Search Results Task Pane   (c) Microsoft Office Word Help Window

All five methods result in the Word Help system displaying a task pane on the right side of the Word window. The first three methods cause the **Word Help task pane** to display (Figure A-1a on the previous page). This task pane includes a Search text box in which you can enter a word or phrase on which you want help. Once you enter the word or phrase, the Word Help system displays the Search Results task pane (Figure A-1b on the previous page). With the Search Results task pane displayed, you can select specific Help topics.

As shown in Figure A-1, methods 4 and 5 bypass the Word Help task pane and display the **Search Results task pane** (Figure A-1b) with a list of links that pertain to the selected topic. Thus, any of the five methods for accessing the Word Help system results in displaying the Search Results task pane. Once the Word Help system displays this task pane, you can choose links that relate to the word or phrase on which you searched. In Figure A-1, for example, header was the searched topic (About headers and footers), which resulted in the Word Help system displaying the Microsoft Office Word Help window with information about headers and footers (Figure A-1c on the previous page).

Navigating the Word Help System

The quickest way to access the Word Help system is through the Type a question for help box on the right side of the menu bar at the top of the screen. Here you can type words, such as ruler, font, or column, or phrases, such as justify a paragraph, or how do I display formatting marks. The Word Help system responds by displaying a list of links in the Search Results task pane.

Here are two tips regarding the words or phrases you enter to initiate a search: (1) check the spelling of the word or phrase; and (2) keep your search very specific, with fewer than seven words, to return the most accurate results.

Assume for the following example that you want to know more about tables. The following steps show how to use the Type a question for help box to obtain useful information about tables by entering the keyword table. The steps also show you how to navigate the Word Help system.

To Obtain Help Using the Type a Question for Help Box

1

• **Click the Type a question for help box on the right side of the menu bar, type** table**, and then press the ENTER key (Figure A-2).**

The Word Help system displays the Search Results task pane on the right side of the window. The Search Results task pane contains a list of 30 links (Figure A-2). If you do not find what you are looking for, you can modify or refine the search in the Search area at the bottom of the task pane. The topics displayed in your Search Results task pane may be different.

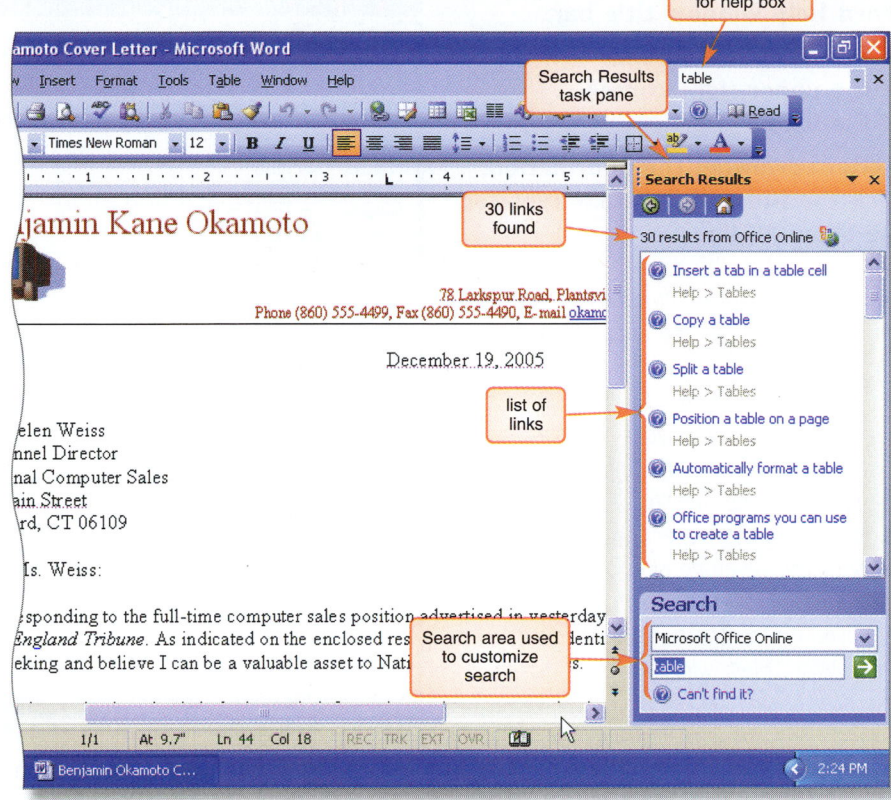

FIGURE A-2

2

Scroll down the list of links in the Search Results task pane and then click the About tables link.

• **When Word displays the Microsoft Office Help Word window, click its Auto Tile button in the upper-left corner of the window (Figure A-4 on the next page), if necessary, to tile the windows.**

Word displays the Microsoft Office Word Help window with the desired information about tables (Figure A-3). With the Microsoft Office Word Help window and Microsoft Word window tiled, you can read the information in one window and complete the task in the other window.

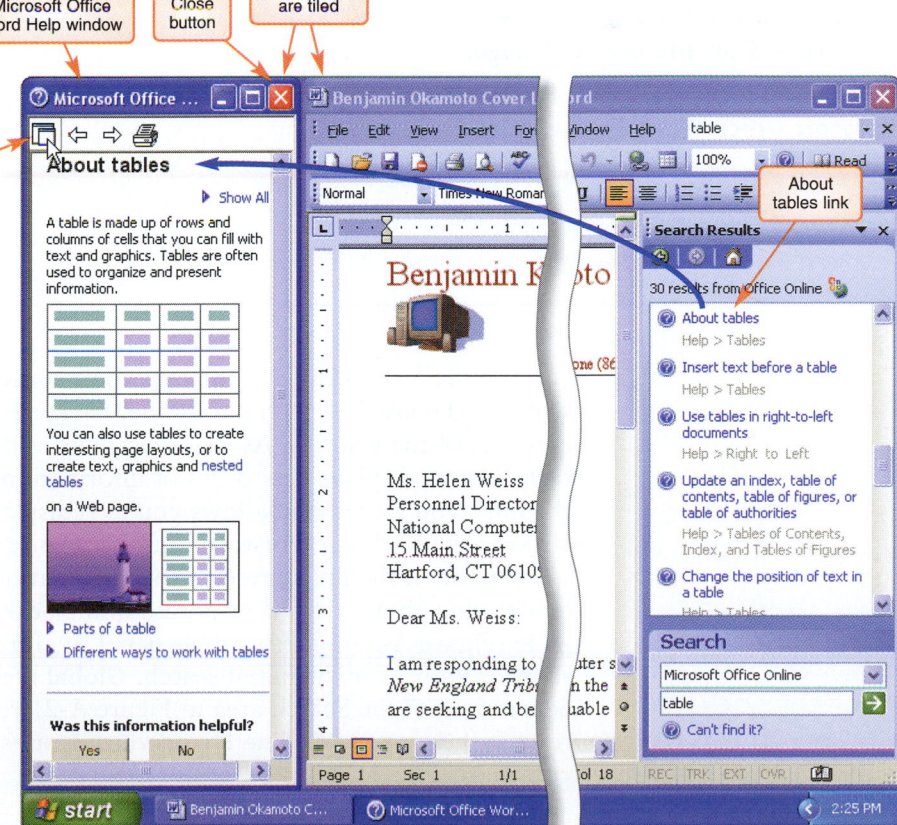

FIGURE A-3

3

• **Double-click the Microsoft Office Word Help window title bar.**

• **Click the Show All link in the upper-right corner of the window.**

• **After reviewing the information, click the Hide All link that replaced the Show All link.**

The Microsoft Office Word Help window is maximized so it fills the entire screen (Figure A-4). If you are connected to the Internet, you can give Microsoft your opinion as to whether the information was helpful by clicking the Yes or No button at the bottom of the page. The Show All link expands the coverage of information and the Hide all link condenses the information displayed on the topic in the Microsoft Office Word Help window.

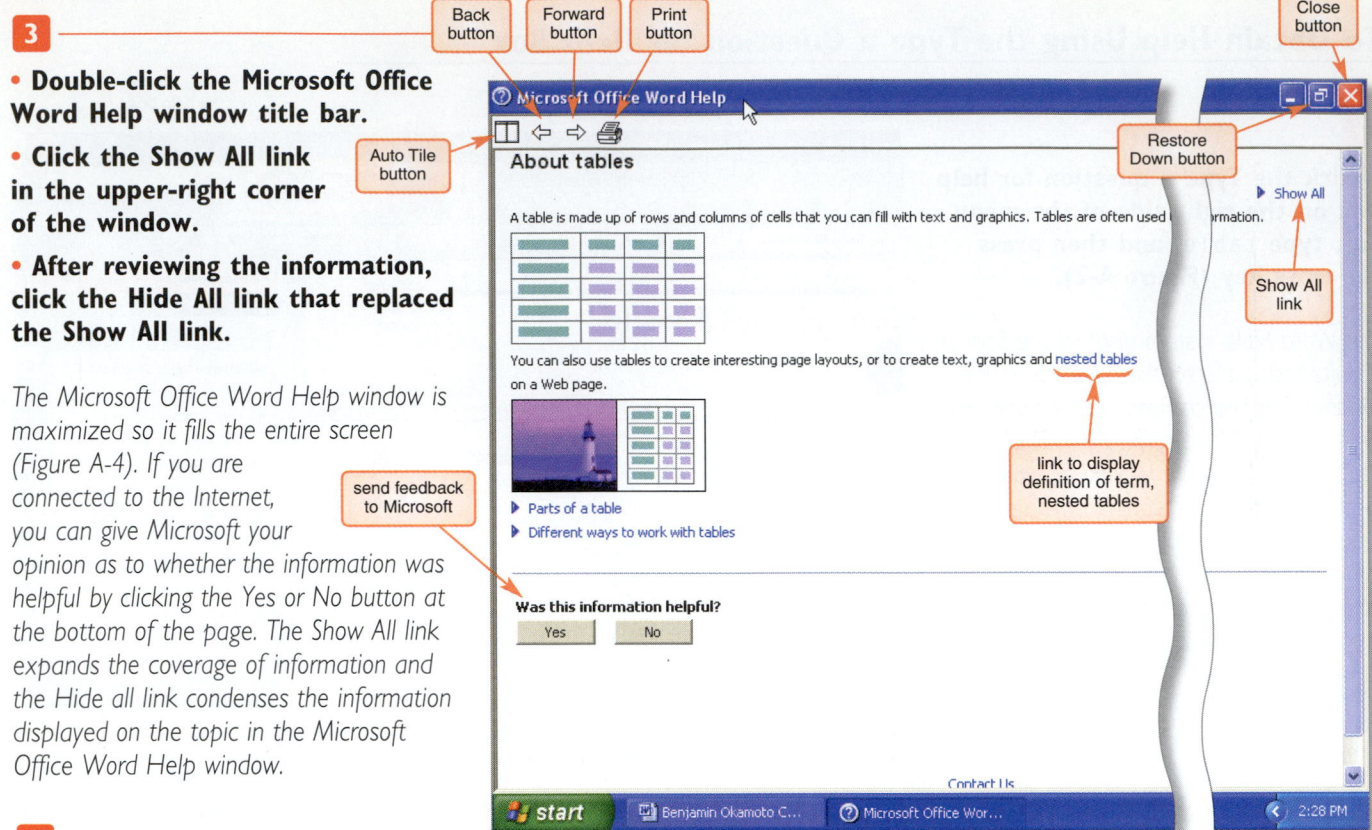

FIGURE A-4

4

• **Click the Restore Down button on the right side of the Microsoft Office Word Help window title bar to return to the tiled state shown in Figure A-3 on the previous page.**

• **Click the Close button on the Microsoft Office Word Help window title bar.**

The Microsoft Office Word Help window is closed and the Word document is active.

Use the four buttons in the upper-left corner of the Microsoft Office Word Help window (Figure A-4) to tile or untile, navigate through the Help system, or print the contents of the window. As you click links in the Search Results task pane, the Word Help system displays new pages of information. The Word Help System remembers the links you visited and allows you to redisplay the pages visited during a session by clicking the Back and Forward buttons (Figure A-4).

If none of the links presents the information you want, you can refine the search by entering another word or phrase in the Search text box in the Search Results task pane (Figure A-2 on the previous page). If you have access to the Web, then the scope is global for the initial search. **Global** means all of the categories listed in the Search box of the Search area in Figure A-2 are searched. For example, you can, restrict the scope to **Offline Help**, which results in a search of related links only on your hard disk.

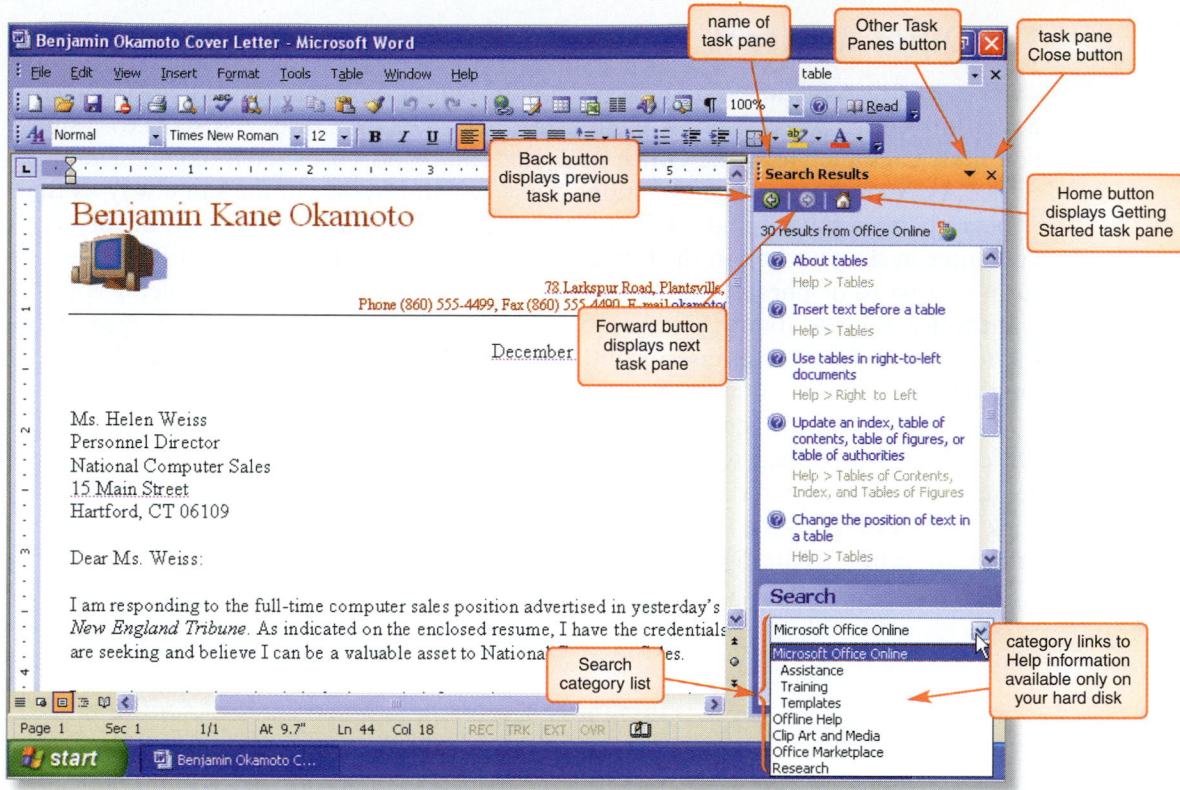

FIGURE A-5

Figure A-5 shows several additional features of the Search Results task pane. The Other Task Panes button and Close button on the Search Results task pane title bar allow you to display other task panes and close the Search Results task pane. The three buttons below the Search Results task pane title bar allow you to navigate between task panes (Back button and Forward button) and display the Getting Started task pane (Home button).

As you enter words and phrases in the Type a question for help box, the Word Help system adds them to the Type a question for help list. To display the list of previously typed words and phrases, click the Type a question for help box arrow (Figure A-6).

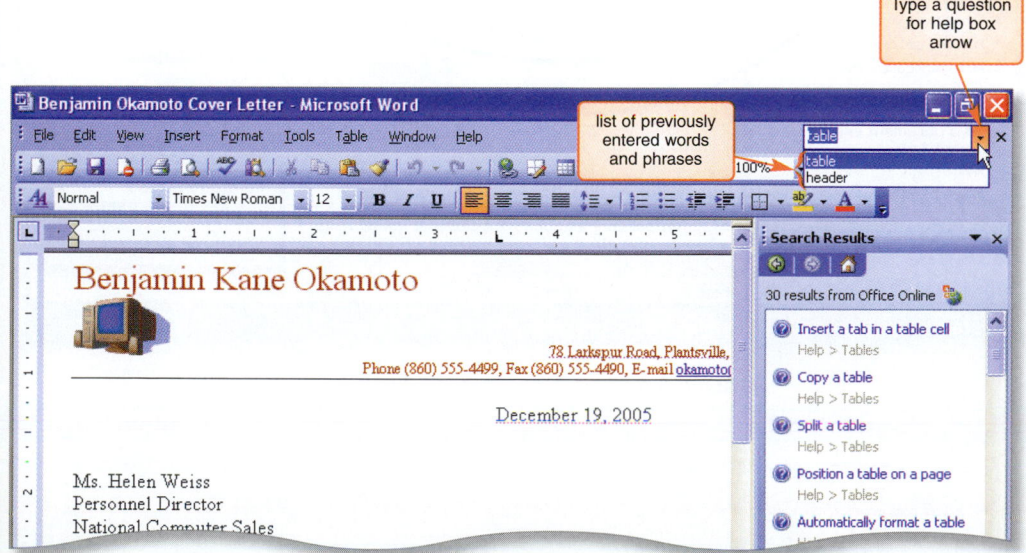

FIGURE A-6

The Office Assistant

The **Office Assistant** is an icon (middle of Figure A-7) that Word displays in the Microsoft Office Word window while you work. For the Office Assistant to display, you must click the Show the Office Assistant command on the Help menu. The Office Assistant has multiple functions. First, it will respond in the same way as the Type a question for help box with a list of topics that relate to the word or phrase you enter in the text box in the Office Assistant balloon. The entry can be in the form of a word or phrase as if you were talking to a person. For example, if you want to learn more about printing a file, in the balloon text box, you can type any of the following words or phrases: print, print a document, how do I print a file, or anything similar.

In the example in Figure A-7, the phrase, print a document, is entered into the Office Assistant balloon text box. The Office Assistant responds by displaying the Search Results task pane with a list of links from which you can choose. Once you click a link in the Search Results task pane, the Word Help system displays the information in the Microsoft Office Word Help window (Figure A-7).

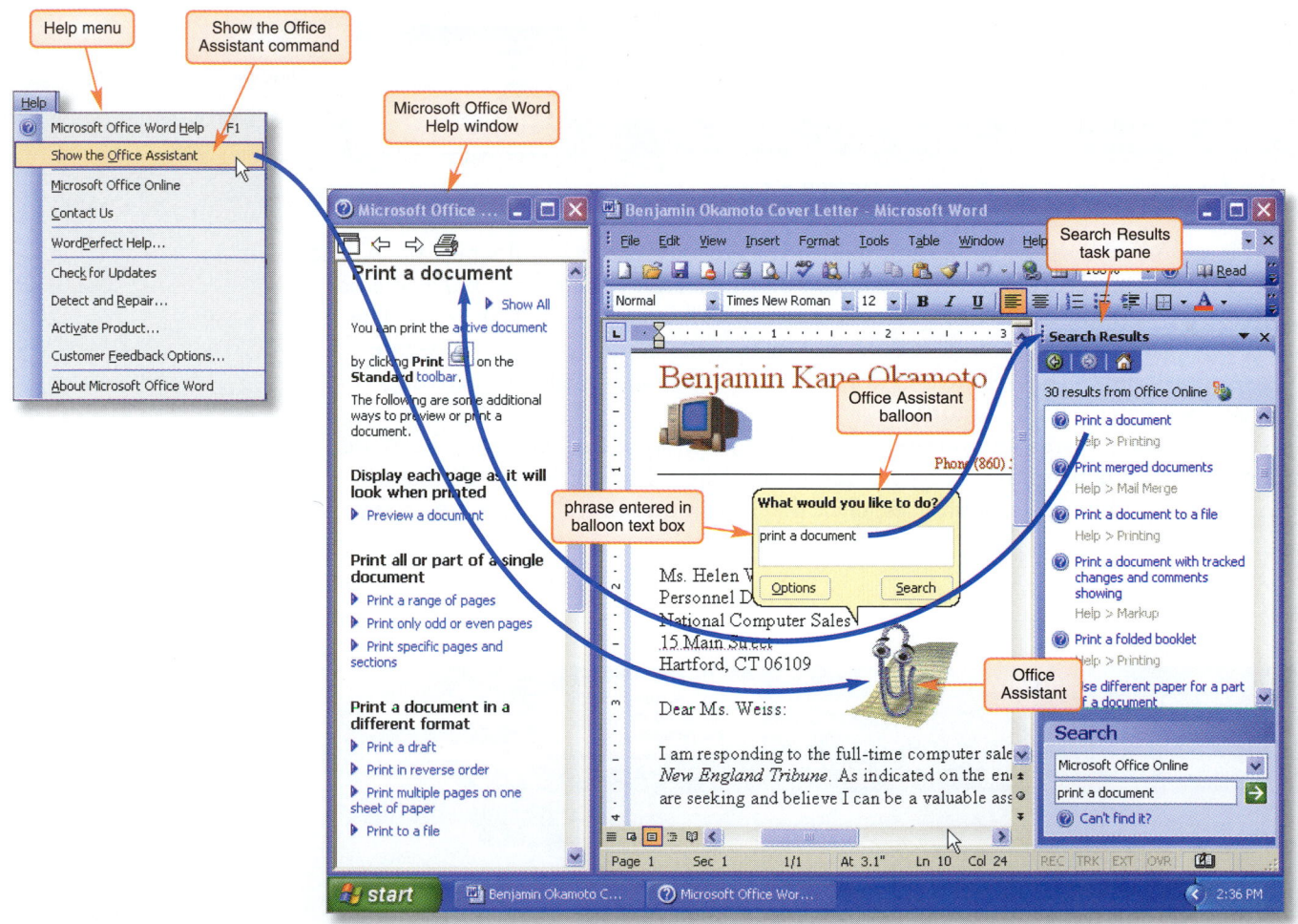

FIGURE A-7

In addition, the Office Assistant monitors your work and accumulates tips during a session on how you might increase your productivity and efficiency. The accumulation of tips must be enabled. You enable the accumulation of tips by right-clicking the Office Assistant, clicking Options on the shortcut menu, and then selecting the types of tips you want accumulated. You can view the tips at anytime. The accumulated tips appear when you activate the Office Assistant balloon. Also, if at anytime you see a light bulb above the Office Assistant, click it to display the most recent tip. If the Office Assistant is hidden, then the light bulb shows on the Microsoft Office Word Help button on the Standard toolbar.

You hide the Office Assistant by invoking the Hide the Office Assistant command on the Help menu or by right-clicking the Office Assistant and then clicking Hide on the shortcut menu. The Hide the Office Assistant command shows on the Help menu only when the Office Assistant is active in the Word window. If the Office Assistant begins showing up on your screen without you instructing it to show, then right-click the Office Assistant, click Options on the shortcut menu, click the Use the Office Assistant check box to remove the check mark, and then click the OK button.

If the Office Assistant is active in the Word window, then Word displays all program and system messages in the Office Assistant balloon.

You may or may not want the Office Assistant to display on the screen at all times. As indicated earlier, you can hide it and then show it later through the Help menu. For more information about the Office Assistant, type office assistant in the Type a question for help box and then click the links in the Search Results task pane.

Question Mark Button in Dialog Boxes and Help Icon in Task Panes

You use the Question Mark button with dialog boxes. It is located in the upper-right corner on the title bar of the dialog boxes, next to the Close button. For example, in Figure A-8 on the next page, the Print dialog box appears on the screen. If you click the Question Mark button in the upper-right corner of the dialog box, the Microsoft Office Word Help window is displayed and provides information about the options in the Print dialog box.

Some task panes include a Help icon. It can be located in various places within the task pane. For example, in the Clip Art task pane shown in Figure A-8, the Help icon appears at the bottom of the task pane and the Tips for finding clips link appears to the right of the Help icon. When you click the link, the Microsoft Office Word Help window is displayed and provides tips for finding clip art.

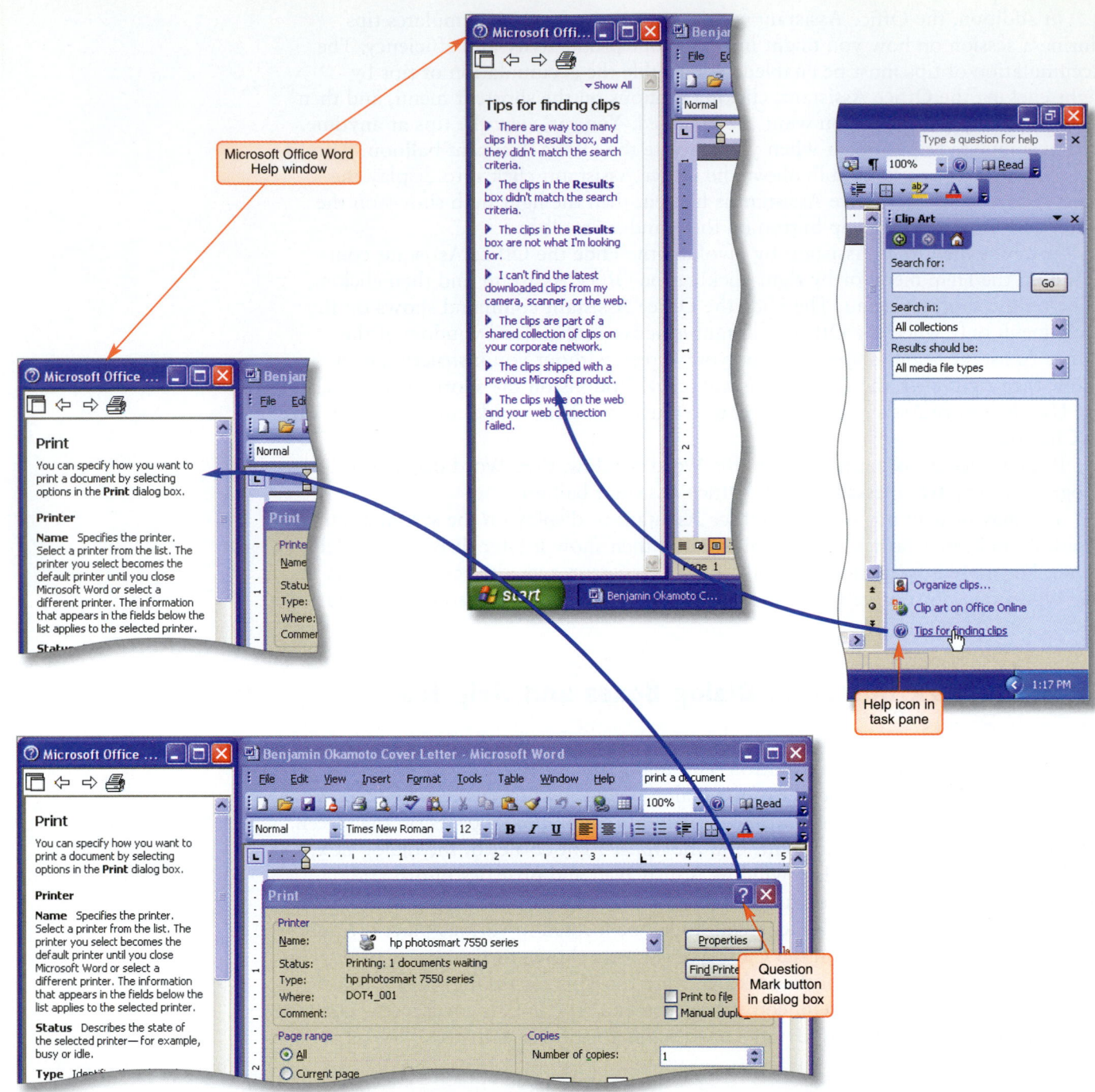

Microsoft Office Word Help window

Tips for finding clips

▶ There are way too many clips in the Results box, and they didn't match the search criteria.

▶ The clips in the **Results** box didn't match the search criteria.

▶ The clips in the **Results** box are not what I'm looking for.

▶ I can't find the latest downloaded clips from my camera, scanner, or the web.

▶ The clips are part of a shared collection of clips on your corporate network.

▶ The clips shipped with a previous Microsoft product.

▶ The clips were on the web and your web connection failed.

Help icon in task pane

Question Mark button in dialog box

FIGURE A-8

Other Help Commands on the Help Menu

Thus far, this appendix has discussed the first two commands on the Help menu: (1) the Microsoft Office Word Help command (Figure A-1 on page APP 1) and (2) the Show the Office Assistant command (Figure A-7 on page APP 6). Several additional commands are available on the Help menu as shown in Figure A-9. Table A-1 summarizes these commands.

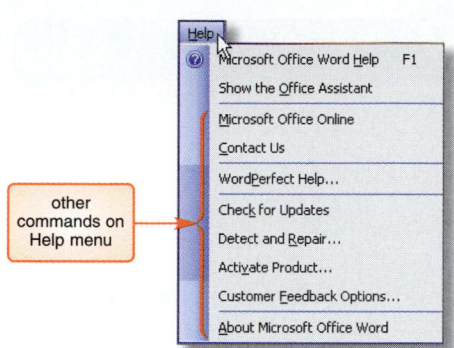

other commands on Help menu

FIGURE A-9

Table A-1 Summary of Other Help Commands on the Help Menu	
COMMAND ON HELP MENU	**FUNCTION**
Microsoft Office Online	Activates the browser, which displays the Microsoft Office Online Home page. The Microsoft Office Online Home page contains links that can improve Office productivity.
Contact Us	Activates the browser, which displays Microsoft contact information and a list of useful links.
WordPerfect Help	Displays the Help for WordPerfect Users dialog box, which includes information about carrying out commands in Word.
Check for Updates	Activates the browser, which displays a list of updates to Office 2003. These updates can be downloaded and installed to improve the efficiency of Office or to fix an error in one or more of the Office applications.
Detect and Repair	Detects and repairs errors in the Word program.
Activate Product	Activates Word if it has not already been activated.
Customer Feedback Options	Gives or denies Microsoft permission to collect anonymous information about the hardware.
About Microsoft Office Word	Displays the About Microsoft Word dialog box. The dialog box lists the owner of the software and the product identification. You need to know the product identification if you call Microsoft for assistance. The three buttons below the OK button are the System Info button, Tech Support button, and Disabled Items button. The System Info button displays system information, including hardware resources, components, software environment, and applications. The Tech Support button displays technical assistance information. The Disabled Items button displays a list of disabled items that prevents Word from functioning properly.

Use Help

1 Using the Type a Question for Help Box

Instructions: Perform the following tasks using the Word Help system.

1. Use the Type a question for help box on the menu bar to get help on adding a bullet.
2. Click Add bullets or numbering in the list of links in the Search Results task pane. If necessary, tile the windows. Double-click the Microsoft Office Word Help window title bar to maximize it. Click the Show All link. Read and print the information. At the top of the printout, write down the number of links the Word Help system found.
3. Click the Restore Down button on the Microsoft Office Word Help title bar to restore the Microsoft Office Word Help window.
4. One at a time, click two additional links in the Search Results task pane and print the information. Hand in the printouts to your instructor. Use the Back and Forward buttons to return to the original page.
5. Use the Type a question for help box to search for information on adjusting line spacing. Click the Adjust line or paragraph spacing link in the Search Results task pane. Maximize the Microsoft Office Word Help window. Read and print the contents of the window. One at a time, click the links on the page and print the contents of the window. Close the Microsoft Office Word Help window.
6. For each of the following words and phrases, click one link in the Search Results task pane, click the Show All link, and then print the page: page zoom; date; print preview; office clipboard; word count; and themes.

2 Expanding on the Word Help System Basics

Instructions: Use the Word Help system to understand the topics better and answer the questions listed below. Answer the questions on your own paper, or hand in the printed Help information to your instructor.

1. Show the Office Assistant. Right-click the Office Assistant and then click Animate! on the shortcut menu. Repeat invoking the Animate! command to see various animations.
2. Right-click the Office Assistant, click Options on the shortcut menu, click the Reset my tips button, and then click the OK button. If necessary, repeatedly click the Office Assistant and then click off the Office Assistant until a light bulb appears above the Office Assistant. When you see the light bulb, it indicates that the Office Assistant has a tip to share with you.
3. Use the Office Assistant to find help on undoing. Click the Undo mistakes link and then print the contents of the Microsoft Office Word Help window. Close the window. Hand in the printouts to your instructor. Hide the Office Assistant.
4. Press the F1 key. Search for information on Help. Click the first two links in the Search Results task pane. Read and print the information for both links.
5. Display the Help menu. One at a time, click the Microsoft Office Online, Contact Us, and Check for Updates commands. Print the contents of each Internet Explorer window that displays and then close the window. Hand in the printouts to your instructor.
6. Click About Microsoft Office Word on the Help menu. Click the Tech Support button, print the contents of the Microsoft Office Word Help window, and then close the window. Click the System Info button. If necessary, click the plus sign to the left of Components in the System Summary list to display the Components category. Click CD-ROM and then print the information. Click Display and then print the information. Hand in the printouts to your instructor.

Appendix B

Speech and Handwriting Recognition and Speech Playback

Introduction

This appendix discusses the Office capability that allows users to create and modify worksheets using its alternative input technologies available through **text services**. Office provides a variety of text services, which enable you to speak commands and enter text in an application. The most common text service is the keyboard. Other text services include speech recognition and handwriting recognition.

The Language Bar

The **Language bar** allows you to use text services in the Office applications. You can utilize the Language bar in one of three states: (1) in a restored state as a floating toolbar in the Word window (Figure B-1a or Figure B-1b if Text Labels are enabled); (2) in a minimized state docked next to the notification area on the Windows taskbar (Figure B-1c); or (3) hidden (temporarily closed and out of the way). If the Language bar is hidden, you can activate it by right-clicking the Windows taskbar, pointing to Toolbars on the shortcut menu (Figure B-1d), and then clicking Language bar on the Toolbars submenu. If you want to close the Language bar, right-click the Language bar and then click Close the Language bar on the shortcut menu (Figure B-1e).

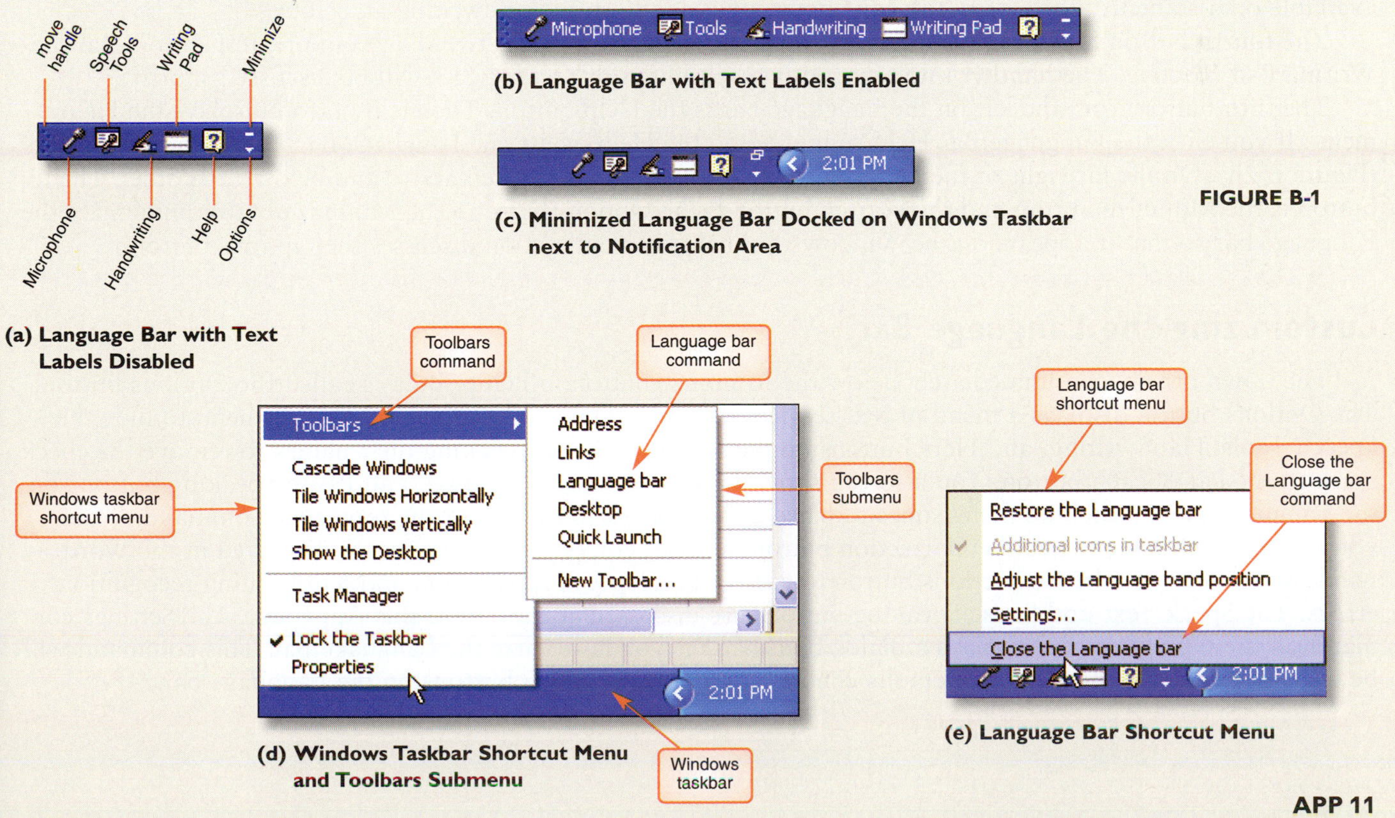

move handle · Speech Tools · Writing Pad · Minimize

Microphone · Handwriting · Help · Options

(a) Language Bar with Text Labels Disabled

Microphone · Tools · Handwriting · Writing Pad

(b) Language Bar with Text Labels Enabled

2:01 PM

(c) Minimized Language Bar Docked on Windows Taskbar next to Notification Area

FIGURE B-1

Toolbars command

Language bar command

Language bar shortcut menu

Windows taskbar shortcut menu

Toolbars
Cascade Windows
Tile Windows Horizontally
Tile Windows Vertically
Show the Desktop
Task Manager
Lock the Taskbar
Properties

Address
Links
Language bar
Desktop
Quick Launch
New Toolbar...

Toolbars submenu

2:01 PM

Windows taskbar

(d) Windows Taskbar Shortcut Menu and Toolbars Submenu

Close the Language bar command

Restore the Language bar
Additional icons in taskbar
Adjust the Language band position
Settings...
Close the Language bar

2:01 PM

(e) Language Bar Shortcut Menu

When Windows was installed on your computer, the installer specified a default language. For example, most users in the United States select English (United States) as the default language. You can add more than 90 additional languages and varying dialects such as Basque, English (Zimbabwe), French (France), French (Canada), German (Germany), German (Austria), and Swahili. With multiple languages available, you can switch from one language to another while working in Word. If you change the language or dialect, then text services may change the functions of the keys on the keyboard, adjust speech recognition, and alter handwriting recognition. If a second language is activated, then a Language icon appears immediately to the right of the move handle on the Language bar and the language name is displayed on the Word status bar. This appendix assumes that English (United States) is the only language installed. Thus, the Language icon does not appear in the examples in Figure B-1 on the previous page.

Buttons on the Language Bar

The Language bar shown in Figure B-2a contains seven buttons. The number of buttons on your Language bar may be different. These buttons are used to select the language, customize the Language bar, control the microphone, control handwriting, and obtain help.

The first button on the left is the Microphone button, which enables and disables the microphone. When the microphone is enabled, text services adds two buttons and a balloon to the Language bar (Figure B-2b). These additional buttons and the balloon will be discussed shortly.

The second button from the left is the Speech Tools button. The Speech Tools button displays a menu of commands (Figure B-2c) that allow you to scan the current document looking for words to add to the speech recognition dictionary; hide or show the balloon on the Language bar; train the Speech Recognition service so that it can interpret your voice better; add and delete specific words to and from its dictionary, such as names and other words not understood easily; and change the user profile so more than one person can use the microphone on the same computer.

The third button from the left on the Language bar is the Handwriting button. The Handwriting button displays the Handwriting menu (Figure B-2d), which lets you choose the Writing Pad (Figure B-2e), Write Anywhere (Figure B-2f), or the on-screen keyboard (Figure B-2g). The On-Screen Symbol Keyboard command on the Handwriting menu displays an on-screen keyboard that allows you to enter special symbols that are not available on a standard keyboard. You can choose only one form of handwriting at a time.

The fourth button indicates which one of the handwriting forms is active. For example, in Figure B-2a, the Writing Pad is active. The handwriting recognition capabilities of text services will be discussed shortly.

The fifth button from the left on the Language bar is the Help button. The Help button displays the Help menu. If you click the Language Bar Help command on the Help menu, the Language Bar Help window appears (Figure B-2h). On the far right of the Language bar are two buttons stacked above and below each other. The top button is the Minimize button and the bottom button is the Options button. The Minimize button minimizes the Language bar so that it appears on the Windows taskbar. The next section discusses the Options button.

Customizing the Language Bar

The down arrow icon immediately below the Minimize button in Figure B-2a is called the Options button. The Options button displays a menu of text services options (Figure B-2i). You can use this menu to hide the Speech Tools, Handwriting, and Help buttons on the Language bar by clicking their names to remove the check mark to the left of each button. You also can show the Correction, Speak Text, and Pause Speaking buttons on the Language bar by clicking their names to place a check mark to the left of the respective command. When you select text and then click the Correction button, a list of correction alternatives is displayed in the Word window. You can use the Corrections button to correct both speech recognition and handwriting recognition errors. The Speak Text and Pause Speaking buttons are discussed at the end of this Appendix. The Settings command on the Options menu displays a dialog box that lets you customize the Language bar. This command will be discussed shortly. The Restore Defaults command redisplays hidden buttons on the Language bar.

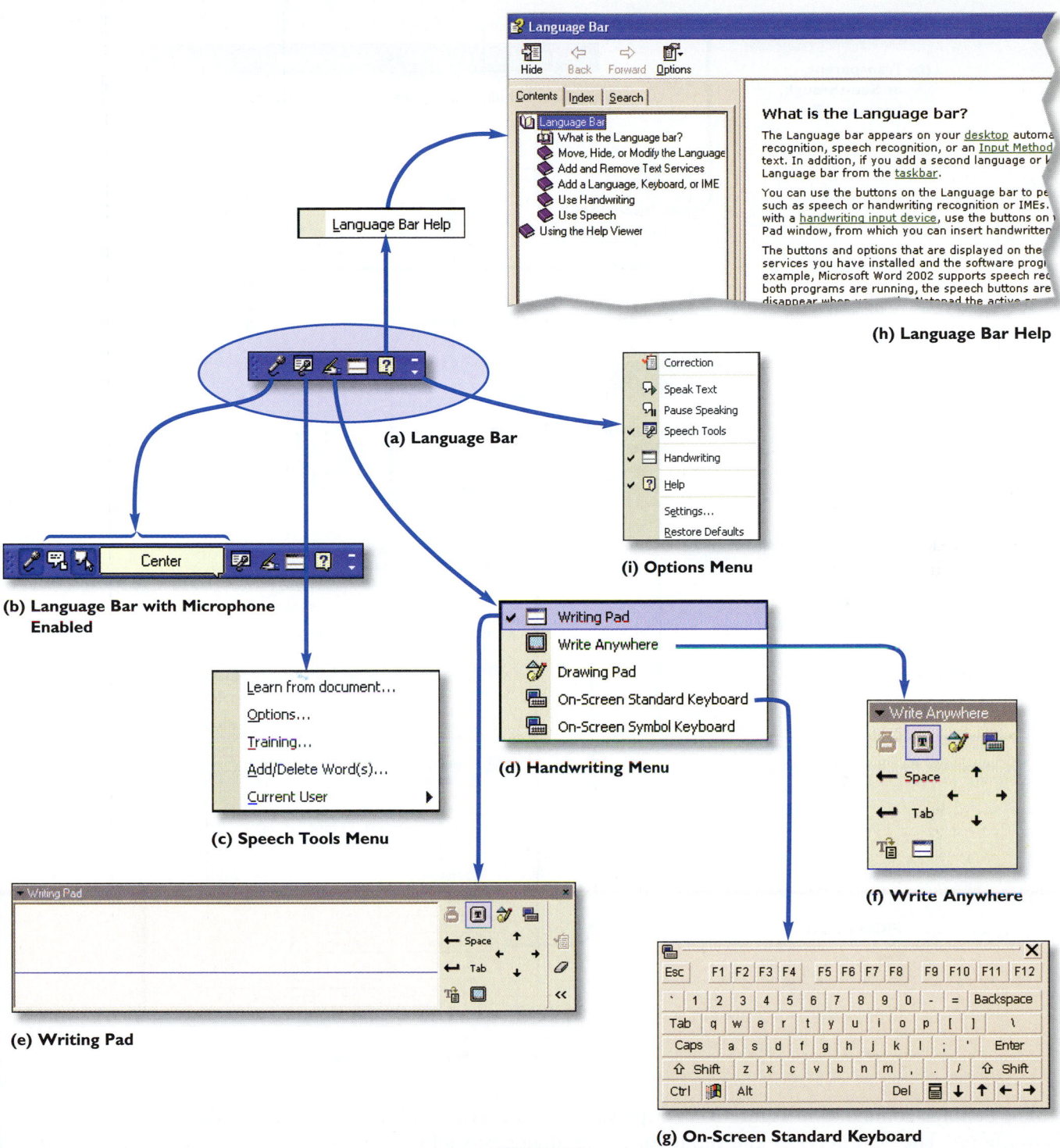

FIGURE B-2

If you right-click the Language bar, a shortcut menu appears (Figure B-3a on the next page). This shortcut menu lets you further customize the Language bar. The Minimize command on the shortcut menu docks the Language bar on the Windows taskbar. The Transparency command in Figure B-3a toggles the Language bar between being solid and transparent. You can see through a transparent Language bar (Figure B-3b). The Text Labels command toggles on text labels on the Language bar (Figure B-3c) and off (Figure B-3b). The Vertical command displays the Language bar vertically on the screen (Figure B-3d).

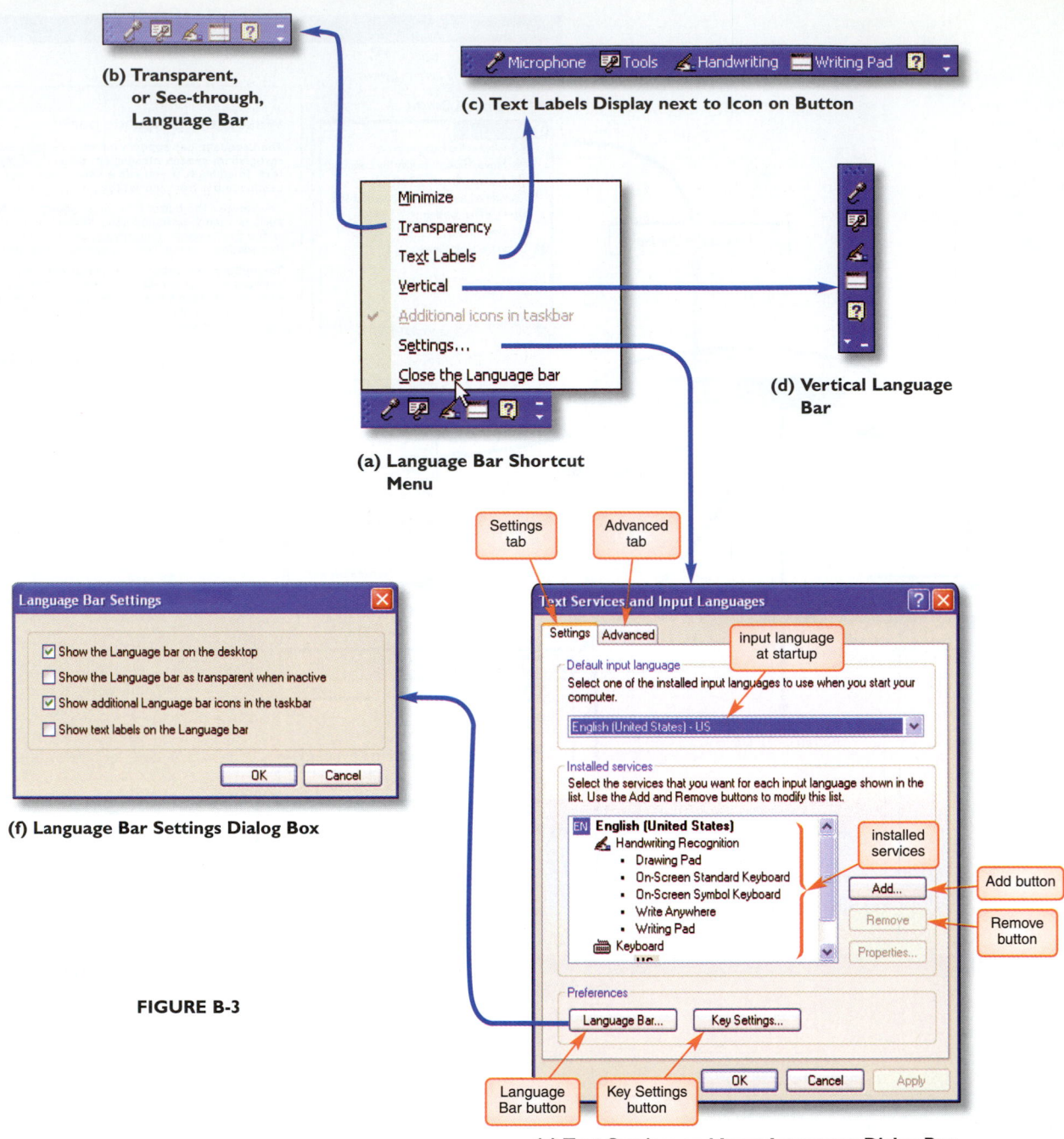

(b) Transparent, or See-through, Language Bar

(c) Text Labels Display next to Icon on Button

(a) Language Bar Shortcut Menu

(d) Vertical Language Bar

(f) Language Bar Settings Dialog Box

FIGURE B-3

(e) Text Services and Input Languages Dialog Box

The Settings command in Figure B-3a displays the Text Services and Input Languages dialog box (Figure B-3e). The Text Services and Input Languages dialog box allows you to add additonal languages, add and remove text services, modify keys on the keyboard, modify the Language bar, and extend support of advanced text services to all programs, including Notepad and other programs that normally do not support text services (through the Advanced tab). If you want to remove any one of the services in the Installed services list, select the service, and then click the Remove button. If you want to add a service, click the Add button. The Key Settings button allows you to modify the keyboard. If you click the Language Bar button in the Text Services and Input Languages dialog box, the Language Bar Settings dialog box appears (Figure B-3f). This dialog box contains Language bar options, some of which are the same as the commands on the Language bar shortcut menu shown in Figure B-3a.

The Close the Language bar command on the shortcut menu shown in Figure B-3a closes or hides the Language bar. If you close the Language bar and want to redisplay it, see Figure B-1d on page APP 11.

Speech Recognition

The **Speech Recognition service** available with Office enables your computer to recognize human speech through a microphone. The microphone has two modes: dictation and voice command (Figure B-4). You switch between the two modes by clicking the Dictation button and the Voice Command button on the Language bar. These buttons appear only when you turn on Speech Recognition by clicking the Microphone button on the Language bar (Figure B-5a on the next page). If you are using the Microphone button for the very first time in Word, it will require that you check your microphone settings and step through voice training before activating the Speech Recognition service.

The Dictation button places the microphone in Dictation mode. In **Dictation mode**, whatever you speak is entered as text at the location of the insertion point. The Voice Command button places the microphone in Voice Command mode. In **Voice Command mode**, whatever you speak is interpreted as a command. If you want to turn off the microphone, click the Microphone button on the Language bar or in Voice Command mode say, "Mic off" (pronounced mike off). It is important to remember that minimizing the Language bar does not turn off the microphone.

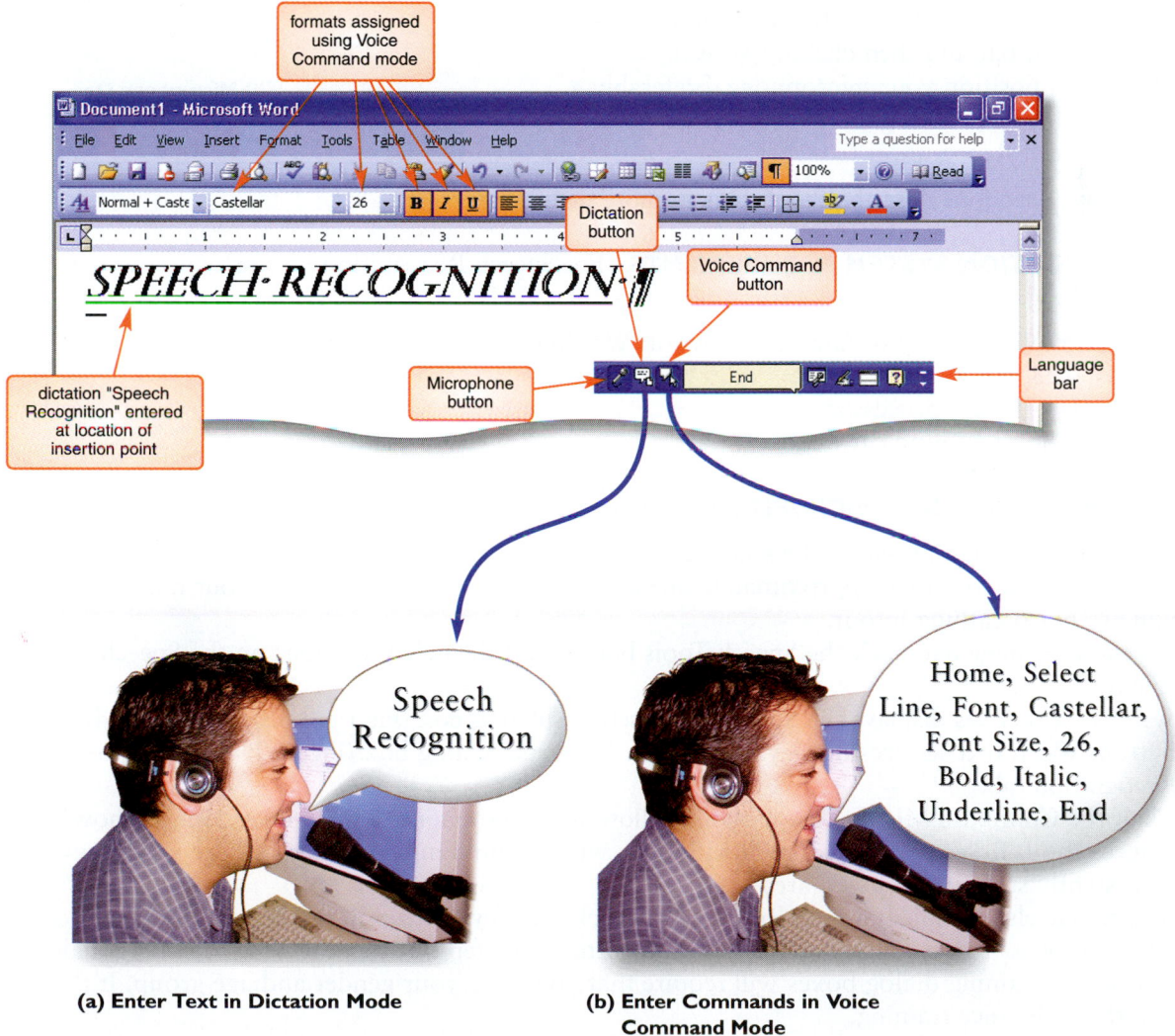

(a) Enter Text in Dictation Mode

(b) Enter Commands in Voice Command Mode

FIGURE B-4

The Language bar speech message balloon shown in Figure B-5b displays messages that may offer help or hints. In Voice Command mode, the name of the last recognized command you said appears. If you use the mouse or keyboard instead of the microphone, a message will appear in the Language bar speech message balloon indicating the word you could say. In Dictation mode, the message, Dictating, usually appears. The Speech Recognition service, however, will display messages to inform you that you are talking too soft, too loud, too fast, or to ask you to repeat what you said by displaying, What was that?

Getting Started with Speech Recognition

For the microphone to function properly, you should follow these steps:

1. Make sure your computer meets the minimum requirements.
2. Start Word. Activate Speech Recognition by clicking Tools on the menu bar and then clicking Speech.
3. Set up and position your microphone, preferably a close-talk headset with gain adjustment support.
4. Train Speech Recognition.

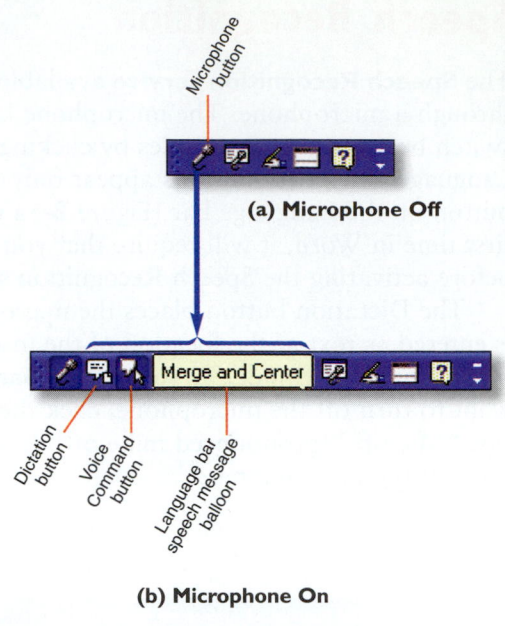

(a) Microphone Off

(b) Microphone On

FIGURE B-5

The following sections describe these steps in more detail.

SPEECH RECOGNITION SYSTEM REQUIREMENTS   For Speech Recognition to work on your computer, it needs the following:

1. Microsoft Windows 98 or later or Microsoft Windows NT 4.0 or later
2. At least 128 MB RAM
3. 400 MHz or faster processor
4. Microphone and sound card

SETUP AND POSITION YOUR MICROPHONE   Set up your microphone as follows:

1. Connect your microphone to the sound card in the back of the computer.
2. Position the microphone approximately one inch out from and to the side of your mouth. Position it so you are not breathing into it.
3. On the Language bar, click the Speech Tools button and then click Options on the Speech Tools menu (Figure B-6a).
4. When text services displays the Speech input settings dialog box (Figure B-6b), click the Advanced Speech button. When text services displays the Speech Properties dialog box (Figure B-6c), click the Speech Recognition tab.
5. Click the Configure Microphone button. Follow the Microphone Wizard directions as shown in Figures B-6d, B-6e, and B-6f. The Next button will remain dimmed in Figure B-6e until the volume meter consistently stays in the green area.
6. If someone else installed Speech Recognition, click the New button in the Speech Properties dialog box and enter your name. Click the Train Profile button and step through the Voice Training dialog boxes. The Voice Training dialog boxes will require that you enter your gender and age group. It then will step you through voice training.

You can adjust the microphone further by clicking the Settings button in the Speech Properties dialog box (Figure B-6c). The Settings button displays the Recognition Profile Settings dialog box that allows you to adjust the pronunciation sensitivity and accuracy versus recognition response time.

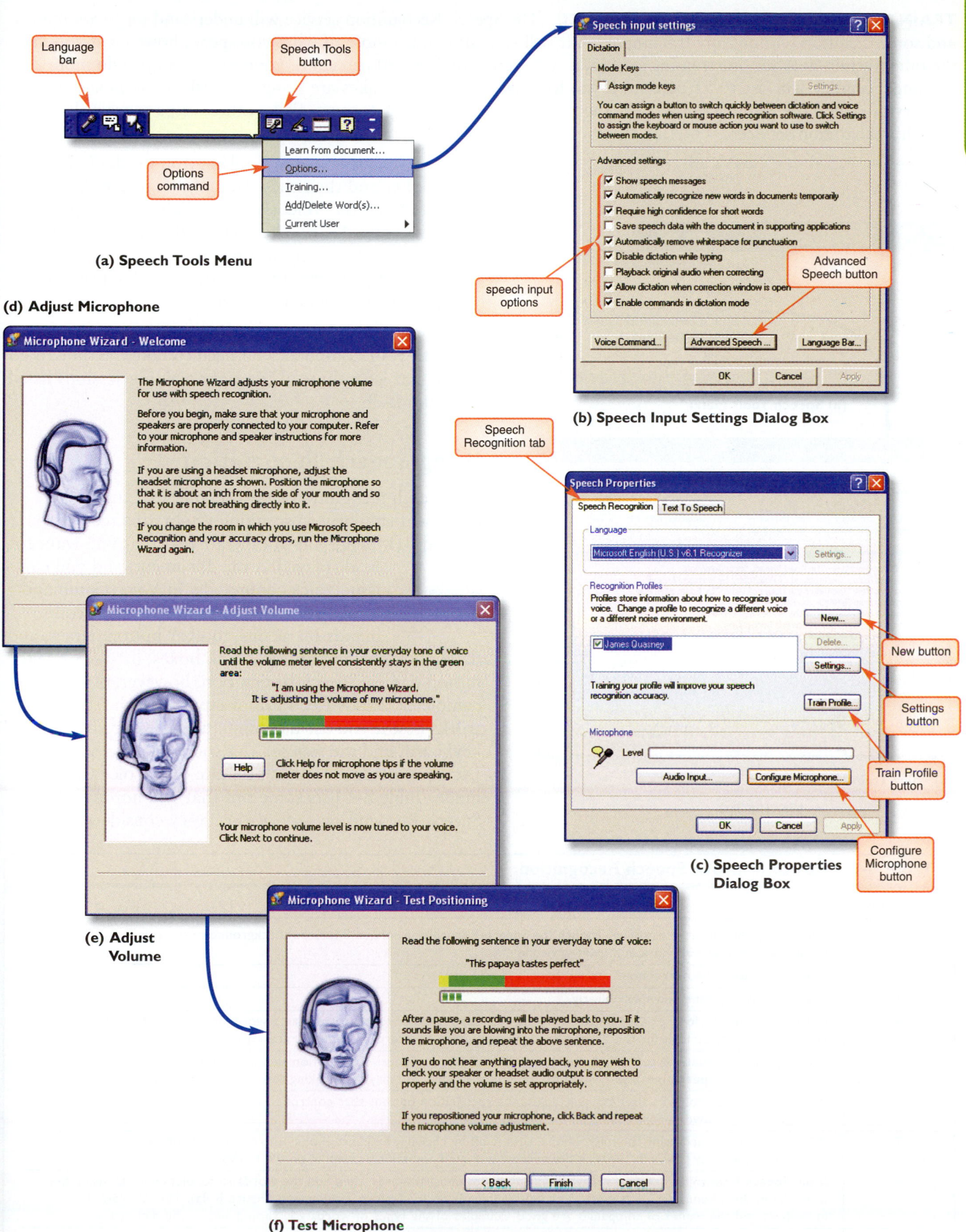

(a) Speech Tools Menu

(d) Adjust Microphone

(b) Speech Input Settings Dialog Box

(c) Speech Properties Dialog Box

(e) Adjust Volume

(f) Test Microphone

FIGURE B-6

TRAIN THE SPEECH RECOGNITION SERVICE The Speech Recognition service will understand most commands and some dictation without any training at all. It will recognize much more of what you speak, however, if you take the time to train it. After one training session, it will recognize 85 to 90 percent of your words. As you do more training, accuracy will rise to 95 percent. If you feel that too many mistakes are being made, then continue to train the service. The more training you do, the more accurately it will work for you. Follow these steps to train the Speech Recognition service:

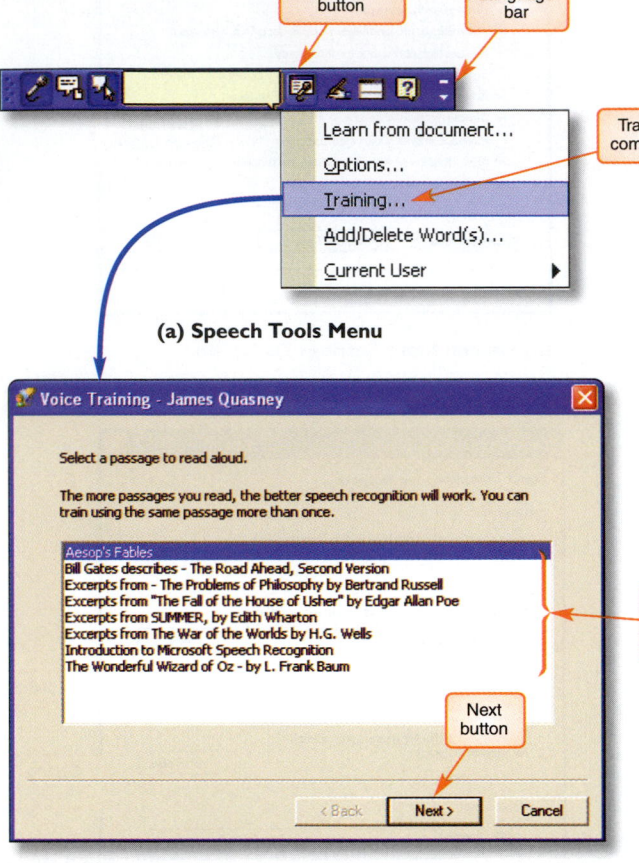

(a) **Speech Tools Menu**

(b) **Voice Training Dialog Box**

FIGURE B-7

1. Click the Speech Tools button on the Language bar and then click Training (Figure B-7a).
2. When the Voice Training dialog box appears (Figure B-7b), click one of the sessions and then click the Next button.
3. Complete the training session, which should take less than 15 minutes.

If you are serious about using a microphone to speak to your computer, you need to take the time to go through at least three of the eight training sessions listed in Figure B-7b.

Using Speech Recognition

Speech recognition lets you enter text into a document similarly to speaking into a tape recorder. Instead of typing, you can dictate text that you want to be displayed in the document, and you can issue voice commands. In Voice Command mode, you can speak menu names, commands on menus, toolbar button names, and dialog box option buttons, check boxes, list boxes, and button names. Speech recognition, however, is not a completely hands-free form of input. Speech recognition works best if you use a combination of your voice, the keyboard, and the mouse. You soon will discover that Dictation mode is far less accurate than Voice Command mode. Table B-1 lists some tips that will improve the Speech Recognition service's accuracy considerably.

Table B-1	Tips to Improve Speech Recognition
NUMBER	**TIP**
1	The microphone hears everything. Though the Speech Recognition service filters out background noise, it is recommended that you work in a quiet environment.
2	Try not to move the microphone around once it is adjusted.
3	Speak in a steady tone and speak clearly.
4	In Dictation mode, do not pause between words. A phrase is easier to interpret than a word. Sounding out syllables in a word will make it more difficult for the Speech Recognition service to interpret what you are saying.
5	If you speak too loudly or too softly, it makes it difficult for the Speech Recognition service to interpret what you said. Check the Language bar speech message balloon for an indication that you may be speaking too loudly or too softly.
6	If you experience problems after training, adjust the recognition options that control accuracy and rejection by clicking the Settings button shown in Figure B-6c on the previous page.
7	When you are finished using the microphone, turn it off by clicking the Microphone button on the Language bar or in Voice Command mode, say "Mic off." Leaving the microphone on is the same as leaning on the keyboard.
8	If the Speech Recognition service is having difficulty with unusual words, then add the words to its dictionary by using the Learn from document and Add/Delete Word(s) commands on the Speech Tools menu (Figure B-8a). The last names of individuals and the names of companies are good examples of the types of words you should add to the dictionary.
9	Training will improve accuracy; practice will improve confidence.

The last command on the Speech Tools menu is the Current User command (Figure B-8a). The Current User command is useful for multiple users who share a computer. It allows them to configure their own individual profiles, and then switch between users as they use the computer.

For additional information about the Speech Recognition service, enter `speech recognition` in the Type a question for help box on the menu bar.

Handwriting Recognition

Using the Office **Handwriting Recognition service**, you can enter text and numbers into Word by writing instead of typing. You can write using a special handwriting device that connects to your computer or you can write on the screen using your mouse. Four basic methods of handwriting are available by clicking the Handwriting button on the Language bar: Writing Pad; Write Anywhere; Drawing Pad; and On-Screen Keyboard. Although the on-screen keyboard does not involve handwriting recognition, it is part of the Handwriting menu and, therefore, will be discussed in this section.

If your Language bar does not include the Handwriting button, then for installation instructions, enter `install handwriting recognition` in the Type a question for help box on the menu bar.

Writing Pad

To display the Writing Pad, click the Handwriting button on the Language bar and then click Writing Pad (Figure B-9). The **Writing Pad** resembles a notepad with one or more lines on which you can use freehand to print or write in cursive. With the Text button enabled, you can form letters on the line by moving the mouse while holding down the mouse button. To the right of the notepad is a rectangular toolbar. Use the buttons on this toolbar to adjust the Writing Pad, select cells, and activate other handwriting applications.

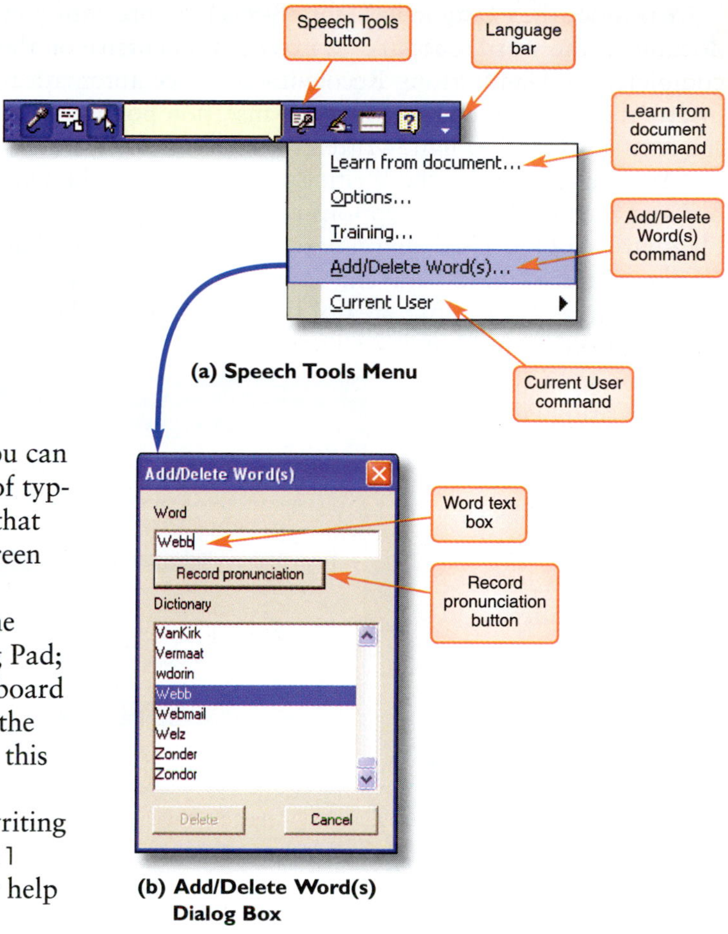

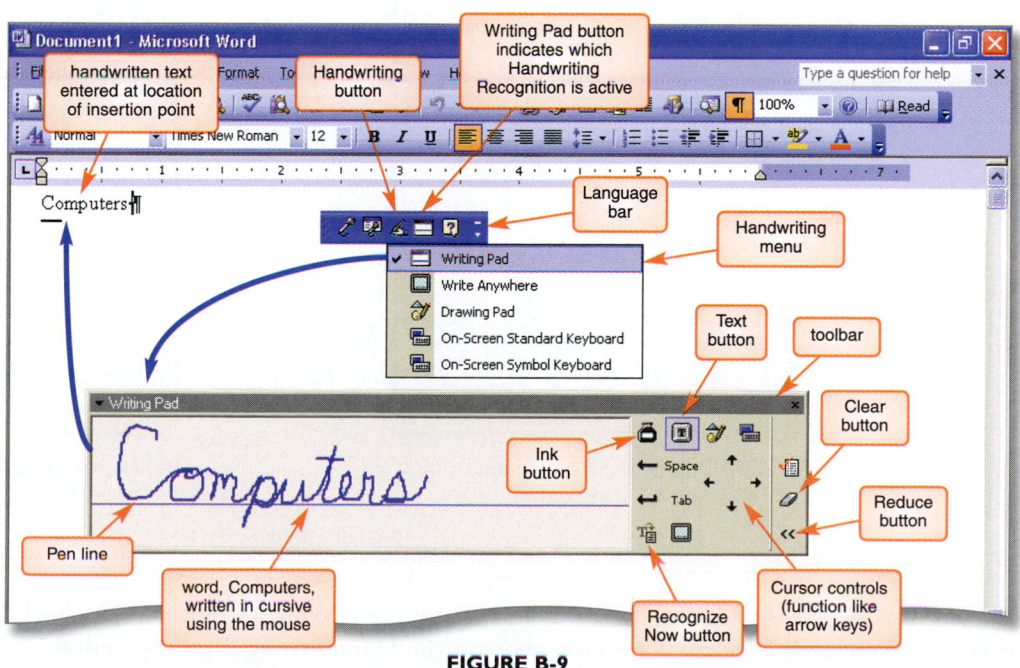

(a) Speech Tools Menu

(b) Add/Delete Word(s) Dialog Box

FIGURE B-8

FIGURE B-9

Consider the example in Figure B-9 on the previous page. With the insertion point at the top of the document, the word, Computers, is written in cursive on the **Pen line** in the Writing Pad. As soon as the word is complete, the Handwriting Recognition service automatically converts the handwriting to typed characters and inserts the text at the location of the insertion point. With the Ink button enabled, instead of the Text button, the text is inserted in handwritten form in the document.

You can customize the Writing Pad by clicking the Options button on the left side of the Writing Pad title bar and then clicking the Options command (Figure B-10a). Invoking the Options command causes the Handwriting Options dialog box to be displayed. The Handwriting Options dialog box contains two sheets: Common and Writing Pad. The Common sheet lets you change the pen color and pen width, adjust recognition, and customize the toolbar area of the Writing Pad. The Writing Pad sheet allows you to change the background color and the number of lines that are displayed in the Writing Pad. Both sheets contain a Restore Default button to restore the settings to what they were when the software was installed initially.

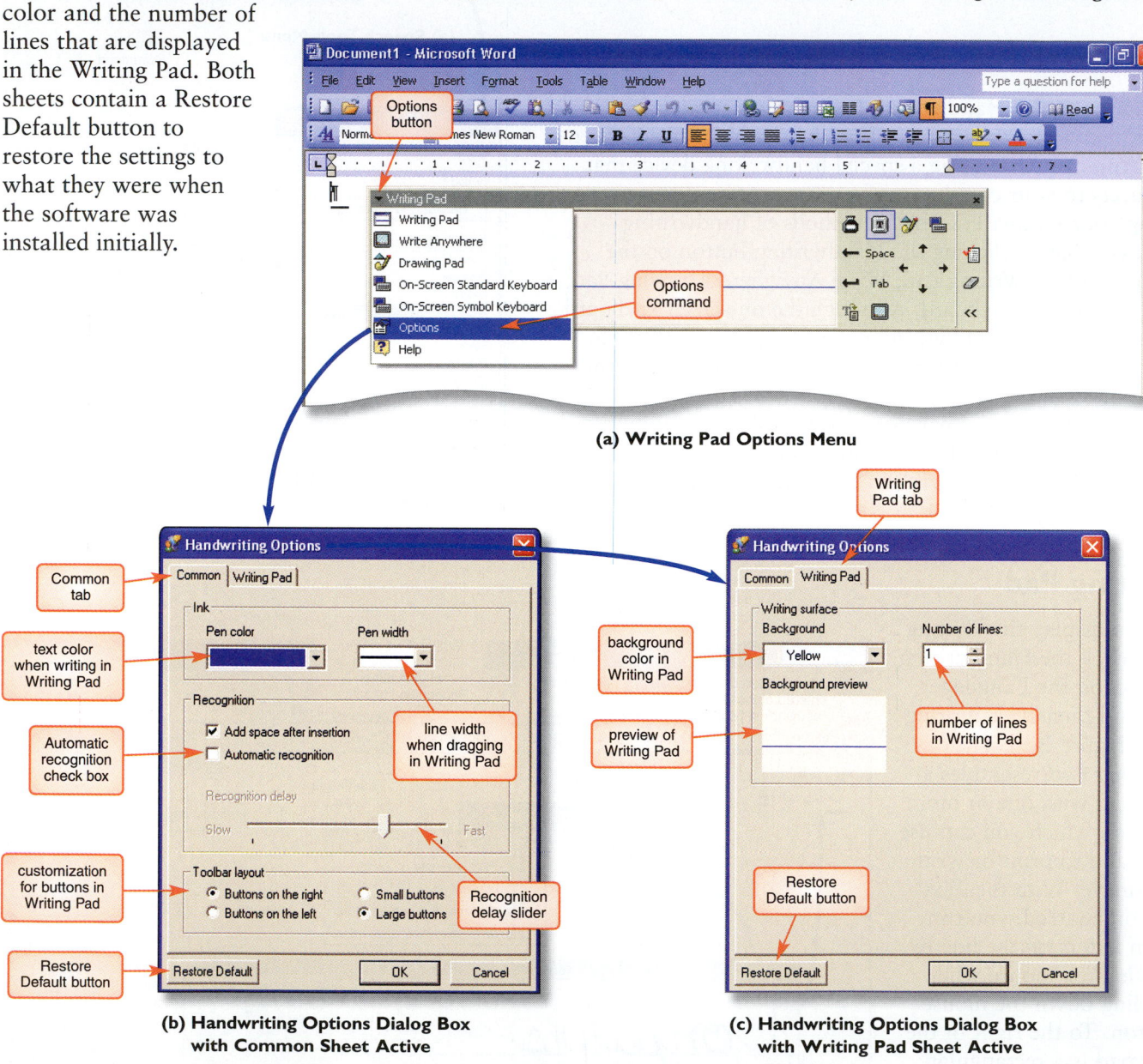

FIGURE B-10

When you first start using the Writing Pad, you may want to remove the check mark from the Automatic recognition check box in the Common sheet in the Handwriting Options dialog box (Figure B-10b). With the check mark removed, the Handwriting Recognition service will not interpret what you write in the Writing Pad until you click the Recognize Now button on the toolbar (Figure B-9 on the previous page). This allows you to pause and adjust your writing.

The best way to learn how to use the Writing Pad is to practice with it. Also, for more information, enter `handwriting recognition` in the Type a question for help box on the menu bar.

Write Anywhere

Rather than use Writing Pad, you can write anywhere on the screen by invoking the Write Anywhere command on the Handwriting menu (Figure B-11) that appears when you click the Handwriting button on the Language bar. In this case, the entire window is your writing pad.

In Figure B-11, the word, Report, is written in cursive using the mouse button. Shortly after the word is written, the Handwriting Recognition service interprets it, assigns it to the location of the insertion point, and erases what was written.

It is recommended that when you first start using the Write Anywhere service that you remove the check mark from the Automatic recognition check box in the Common sheet in the Handwriting Options dialog box (Figure B-10b). With the check mark removed, the Handwriting Recognition service will not interpret what you write on the screen until you click the Recognize Now button on the toolbar (Figure B-11).

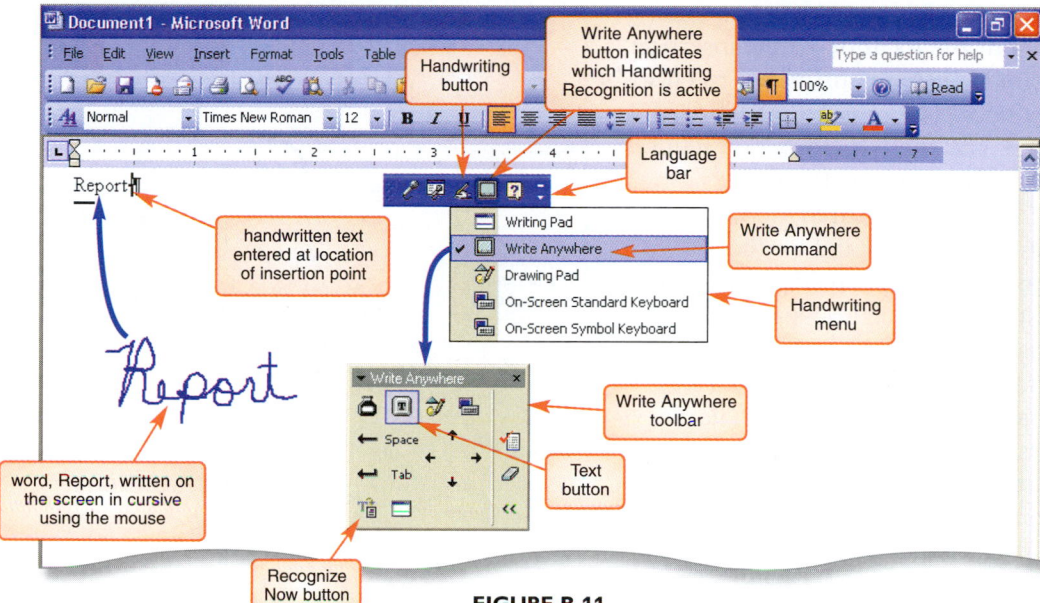

FIGURE B-11

Write Anywhere is more difficult to use than the Writing Pad, because when you click the mouse button, Word may interpret the action as moving the insertion point rather than starting to write. For this reason, it is recommended that you use the Writing Pad.

Drawing Pad

With the Drawing Pad, you can insert a freehand drawing or sketch in a Word document. To display the Drawing Pad, click the Handwriting button on the Language bar and then click Drawing Pad (Figure B-12). Create a drawing by dragging the mouse in the Drawing Pad. In Figure B-12, the mouse was used to draw a tic-tac-toe game. When you click the Insert Drawing button on the Drawing Pad toolbar, Word inserts the drawing in the document at the location of the insertion point. Other buttons on the toolbar allow you to erase a drawing, erase your last drawing stroke, copy the drawing to the Office Clipboard, or activate the Writing Pad.

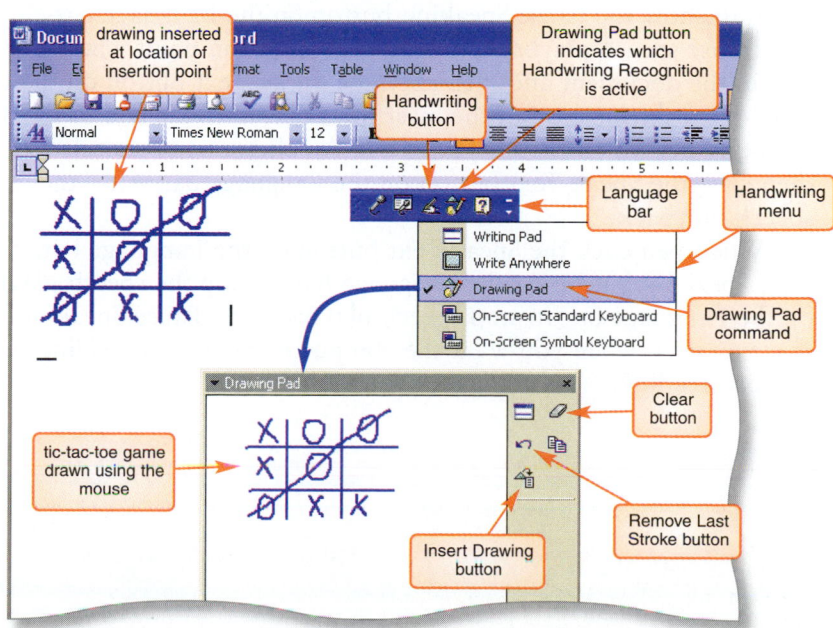

FIGURE B-12

The best way to learn how to use the Drawing Pad is to practice with it. Also, for more information, enter drawing pad in the Type a question for help box on the menu bar.

On-Screen Keyboard

The On-Screen Standard Keyboard command on the Handwriting menu (Figure B-13) displays an on-screen keyboard. The **on-screen keyboard** lets you enter data at the location of the insertion point by using your mouse to click the keys. The on-screen keyboard is similar to the type found on hand-held computers or PDAs.

The On-Screen Symbol Keyboard command on the Handwriting menu (Figure B-13) displays a special on-screen keyboard that allows you to enter symbols that are not on your keyboard, as well as Unicode characters. **Unicode characters** use a coding scheme capable of representing all the world's current languages.

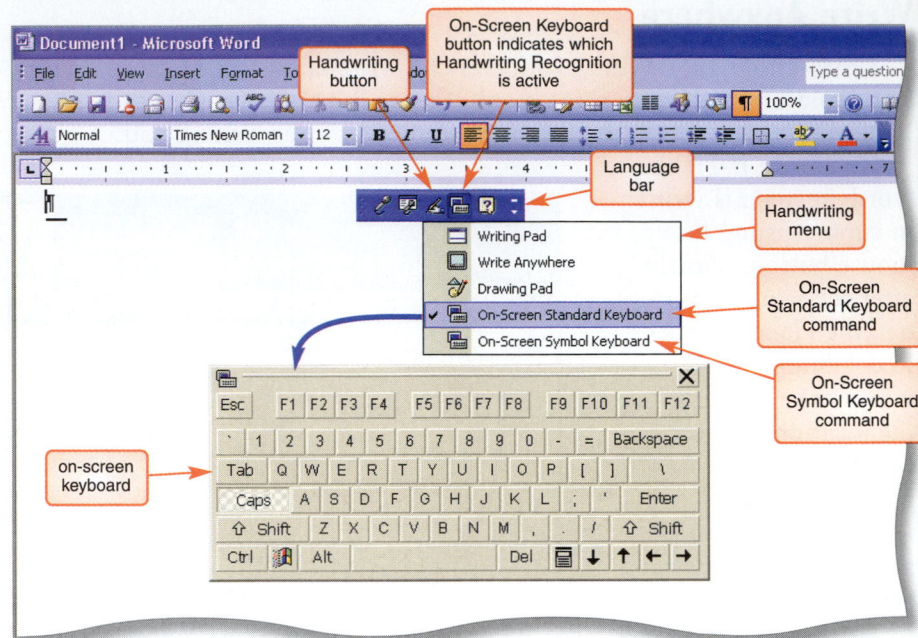

FIGURE B-13

Speech Playback

Using **speech playback**, you can have your computer read back the text in a document. Word provides two buttons for speech playback: Speak Text and Pause Speaking. To show the Speak Text button on the Language bar, click the Options button on the Language bar (Figure B-14) and then click Speak Text on the Options menu. Similarly, click the Options button on the Language bar and then click Pause Speaking on the Options menu to show the Pause Speaking button on the Language bar.

To use speech playback, position the insertion point where you want the computer to start reading back the text in the document and then click the Speak Text button on the Language bar (Figure B-14). The computer reads from the location of the insertion point until the end of the document or until you click the Pause Speaking button on the Language bar. An alternative is to select the text you want the computer to read and then click the Speak Text button on the Language bar. After the computer reads back the selected text, it stops speech playback.

When you click the Speak Text button on the Language bar, it changes to a Stop Speaking button. Click the Stop Speaking button on the Language bar to stop the speech playback. If you click the Pause Speaking button on the Language bar to stop speech playback, the Pause Speaking button changes to a Resume Speaking button that you click when you want the computer to continue reading the document from the location at which it stopped reading.

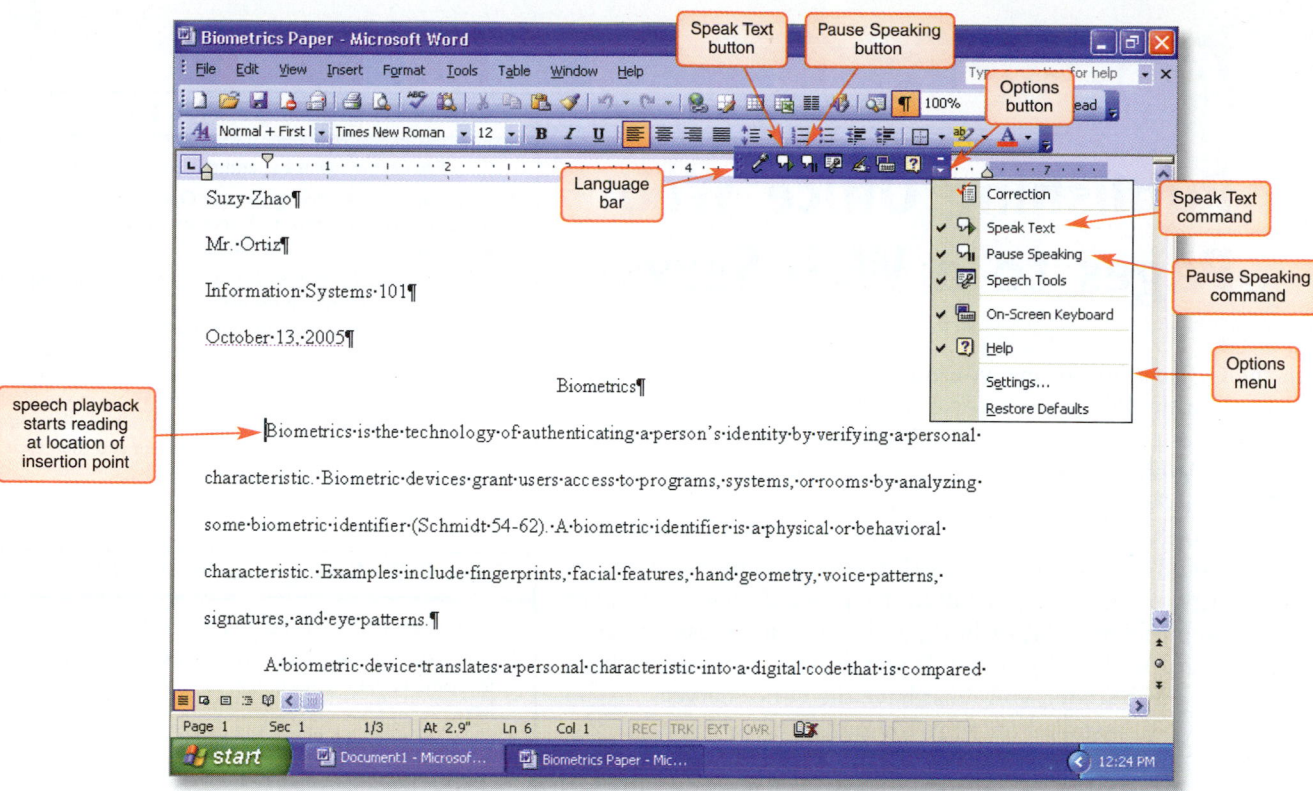

FIGURE B-14

Customizing Speech Playback

You can customize speech playback through the
Speech Properties dialog box. Click the Speech Tools button on
the Language bar and then click Options on the Speech Tools
menu (Figure B-6a on page APP 17). When text services displays
the Speech input settings dialog box (Figure B-6b), click the
Advanced Speech button. When text services displays the
Speech Properties dialog box, click the Text To Speech tab
(Figure B-15). The Text To Speech sheet has two areas: Voice
selection and Voice speed. The Voice selection area lets you
choose between two male voices and one female
voice. You can click the Preview Voice button to
hear a sample of the voice. The Voice speed area
contains a slider. Drag the slider to slow down
or speed up the pace of the speaking voice.

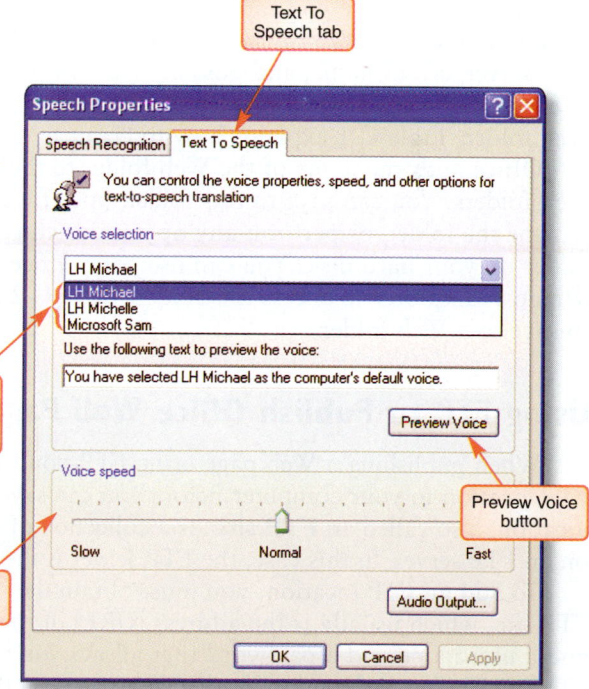

FIGURE B-15

Appendix C

Publishing Office Web Pages to a Web Server

With the Office applications, you use the Save as Web Page command on the File menu to save the Web page to a Web server using one of two techniques: Web folders or File Transfer Protocol. A **Web folder** is an Office shortcut to a Web server. **File Transfer Protocol** (**FTP**) is an Internet standard that allows computers to exchange files with other computers on the Internet.

You should contact your network system administrator or technical support staff at your ISP to determine if their Web server supports Web folders, FTP, or both, and to obtain necessary permissions to access the Web server. If you decide to publish Web pages using a Web folder, you must have the Office Server Extensions (OSE) installed on your computer.

Using Web Folders to Publish Office Web Pages

When publishing to a Web folder, someone first must create the Web folder before you can save to it. If you are granted permission to create a Web folder, you must obtain the URL of the Web server, a user name, and possibly a password that allows you to access the Web server. You also must decide on a name for the Web folder. Table C-1 explains how to create a Web folder.

Office adds the name of the Web folder to the list of current Web folders. You can save to this folder, open files in the folder, rename the folder, or perform any operations you would to a folder on your hard disk. You can use your Office program or Windows Explorer to access this folder. Table C-2 explains how to save to a Web folder.

Using FTP to Publish Office Web Pages

When publishing a Web page using FTP, you first must add the FTP location to your computer before you can save to it. An FTP location, also called an **FTP site**, is a collection of files that reside on an FTP server. In this case, the FTP server is the Web server.

To add an FTP location, you must obtain the name of the FTP site, which usually is the address (URL) of the FTP server, and a user name and a password that allows you to access the FTP server. You save and open the Web pages on the FTP server using the name of the FTP site. Table C-3 explains how to add an FTP site.

Office adds the name of the FTP site to the FTP locations list in the Save As and Open dialog boxes. You can open and save files using this list. Table C-4 explains how to save to an FTP location.

Table C-1 Creating a Web Folder

1. Click File on the menu bar and then click Save As (or Open).
2. When the Save As dialog box (or Open dialog box) appears, click My Network Places on the My Places bar, and then click the Create New Folder button on the toolbar.
3. When the Add Network Place Wizard dialog box appears, click the Next button. If necessary, click Choose another network location. Click the Next button. Click the View some examples link, type the Internet or network address, and then click the Next button. Click Log on anonymously to deselect the check box, type your user name in the User name text box, and then click the Next button. Enter the name you want to call this network place and then click the Next button. Click the Finish button.

Table C-2 Saving to a Web Folder

1. Click File on the menu bar and then click Save As.
2. When the Save As dialog box appears, type the Web page file name in the File name text box. Do not press the ENTER key.
3. Click My Network Places on the My Places bar.
4. Double-click the Web folder name in the Save in list.
5. If the Enter Network Password dialog box appears, type the user name and password in the respective text boxes and then click the OK button.
6. Click the Save button in the Save As dialog box.

Table C-3 Adding an FTP Location

1. Click File on the menu bar and then click Save As (or Open).
2. In the Save As dialog box, click the Save in box arrow and then click Add/Modify FTP Locations in the Save in list; or in the Open dialog box, click the Look in box arrow and then click Add/Modify FTP Locations in the Look in list.
3. When the Add/Modify FTP Locations dialog box appears, type the name of the FTP site in the Name of FTP site text box. If the site allows anonymous logon, click Anonymous in the Log on as area; if you have a user name for the site, click User in the Log on as area and then enter the user name. Enter the password in the Password text box. Click the OK button.
4. Close the Save As or the Open dialog box.

Table C-4 Saving to an FTP Location

1. Click File on the menu bar and then click Save As.
2. When the Save As dialog box appears, type the Web page file name in the File name text box. Do not press the ENTER key.
3. Click the Save in box arrow and then click FTP Locations.
4. Double-click the name of the FTP site to which you wish to save.
5. When the FTP Log On dialog box appears, enter your user name and password and then click the OK button.
6. Click the Save button in the Save As dialog box.

Appendix D

Changing Screen Resolution and Resetting the Word Toolbars and Menus

This appendix explains how to change your screen resolution in Windows to the resolution used in this book. It also describes how to reset the Word toolbars and menus to their installation settings.

Changing Screen Resolution

The **screen resolution** indicates the number of pixels (dots) that your computer uses to display the letters, numbers, graphics, and background you see on your screen. The screen resolution usually is stated as the product of two numbers, such as 800 × 600 (pronounced 800 by 600). An 800 x 600 screen resolution results in a display of 800 distinct pixels on each of 600 lines, or about 480,000 pixels. The figures in this book were created using a screen resolution of 800 × 600.

The screen resolutions most commonly used today are 800 × 600 and 1024 x 768, although some Office specialists operate their computers at a much higher screen resolution, such as 2048 x 1536. The following steps show how to change the screen resolution from 1024 × 768 to 800 × 600.

To Change the Screen Resolution

1

• **If necessary, minimize all applications so that the Windows desktop appears.**

• **Right-click the Windows desktop.**

Windows displays the Windows desktop shortcut menu (Figure D-1).

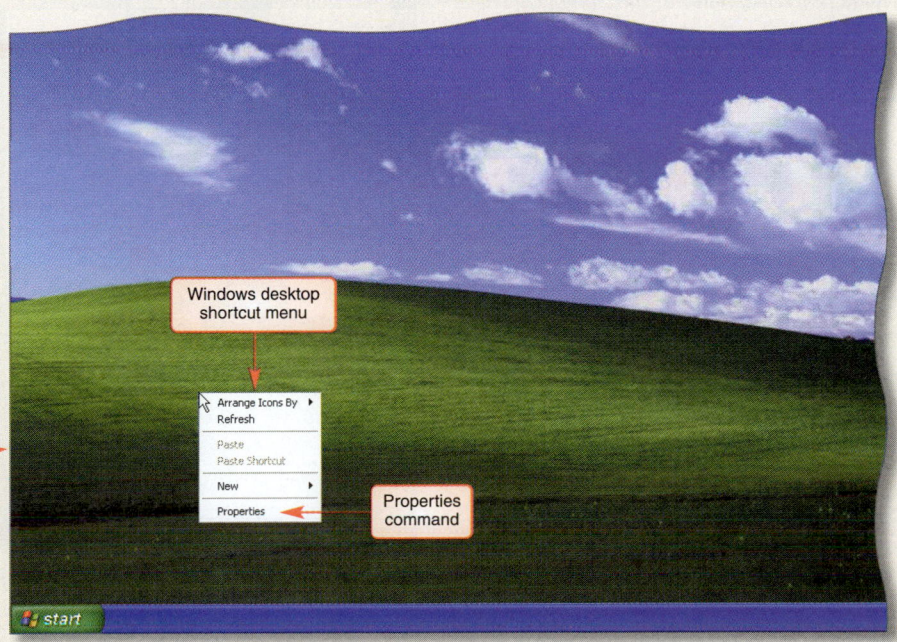

Windows desktop shown at 1024 ◊ 768 screen resolution

Windows desktop shortcut menu

Properties command

FIGURE D-1

2

• **Click Properties on the shortcut menu.**

• **When Windows displays the Display Properties dialog box, click the Settings tab.**

Windows displays the Settings sheet in the Display Properties dialog box (Figure D-2). The Settings sheet shows a preview of the Windows desktop using the current screen resolution (1024 x 768). The Settings sheet also shows the screen resolution and the color quality settings.

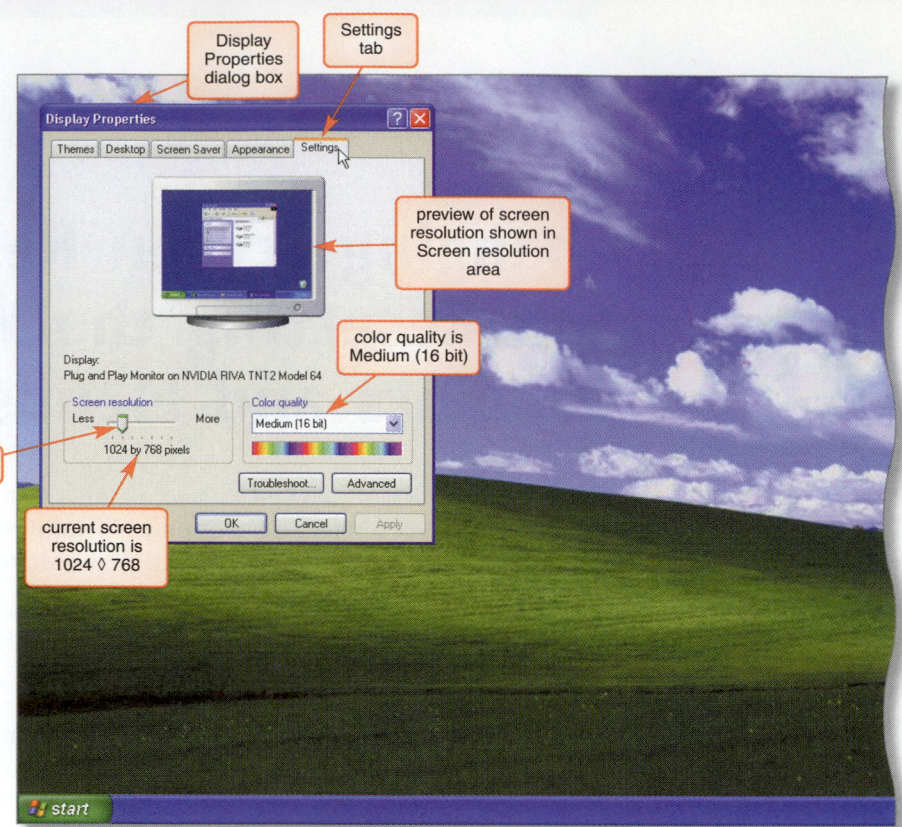

FIGURE D-2

3

• **Drag the slider in the Screen resolution area to the left so that the screen resolution changes to 800 x 600.**

The screen resolution in the Screen resolution area changes to 800 × 600 (Figure D-3). The Settings sheet shows a preview of the Windows desktop using the new screen resolution (800 × 600).

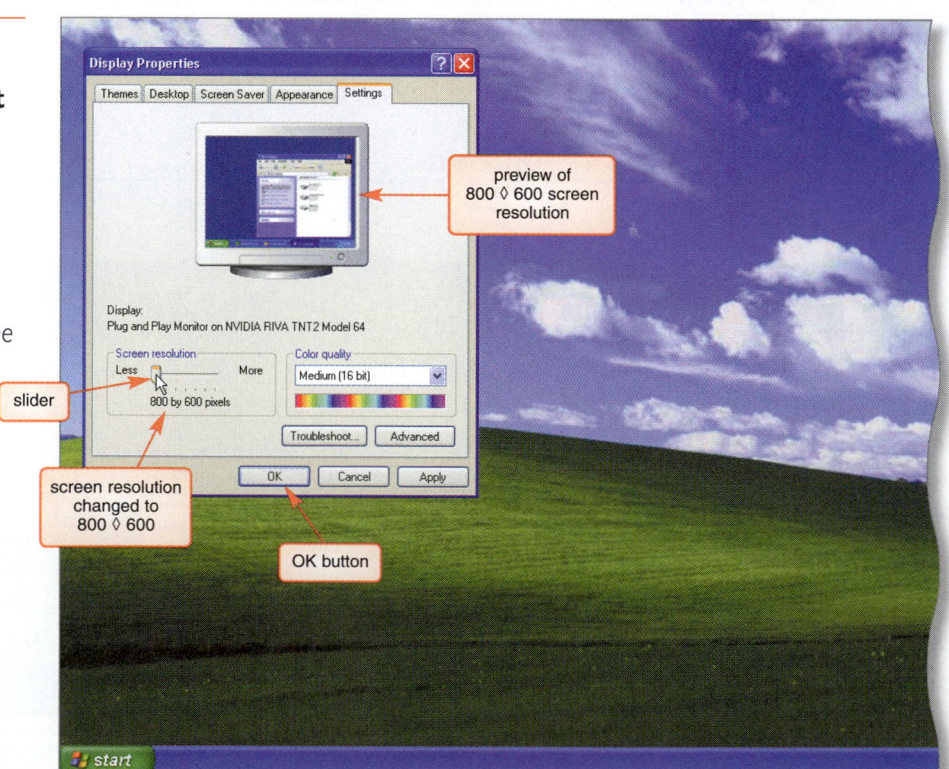

FIGURE D-3

4

• **Click the OK button.**

• **If Windows displays the Monitor Settings dialog box, click the Yes button.**

Windows changes the screen resolution from 1024 × 768 to 800 × 600 (Figure D-4).

800 ◊ 600 screen resolution

FIGURE D-4

As shown in the previous steps, as you decrease the screen resolution, Windows displays less information on your screen, but the information increases in size. The reverse also is true: as you increase the screen resolution, Windows displays more information on your screen, but the information decreases in size.

Resetting the Word Toolbars and Menus

Word customization capabilities allow you to create custom toolbars by adding and deleting buttons and personalize menus based on their usage. Each time you start Word, the toolbars and menus are displayed using the same settings as the last time you used it. The figures in this book were created with the Word toolbars and menus set to the original, or installation, settings.

Resetting the Standard and Formatting Toolbars

The steps on the next page show how to reset the Standard and Formatting toolbars.

To Reset the Standard and Formatting Toolbars

1

• **Start Word.**

• **Click the Toolbar Options button on the Standard toolbar and then point to Add or Remove Buttons on the Toolbar Options menu.**

Word displays the Toolbar Options menu and the Add or Remove Buttons submenu (Figure D-5).

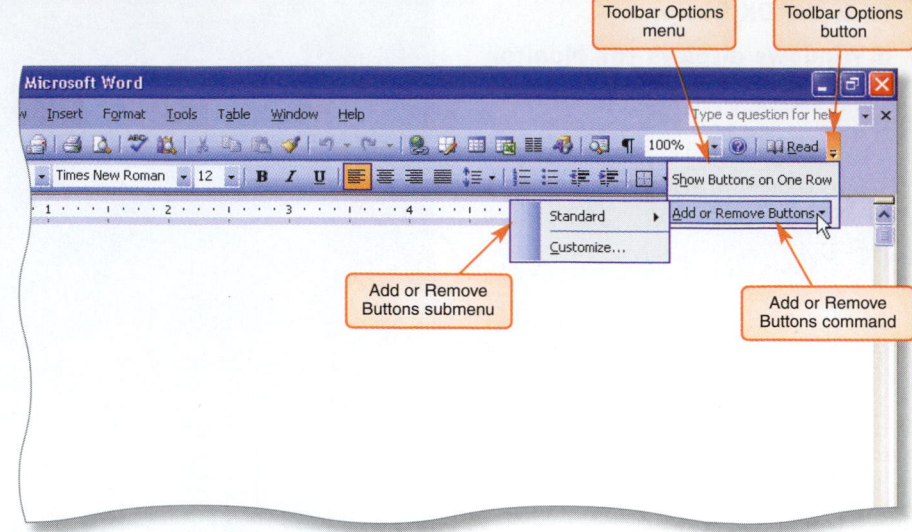

FIGURE D-5

2

• **Point to Standard on the Add or Remove Buttons submenu.**

• **When Word displays the Standard submenu, scroll down and then point to Reset Toolbar.**

The Standard submenu indicates the buttons and boxes that are displayed on the Standard toolbar (Figure D-6). To remove a button from the Standard toolbar, click a button name with a check mark to the left of the name to remove the check mark.

3

• **Click Reset Toolbar.**

• **If a Microsoft Word dialog box is displayed, click the Yes button.**

Word resets the Standard toolbar to its original settings.

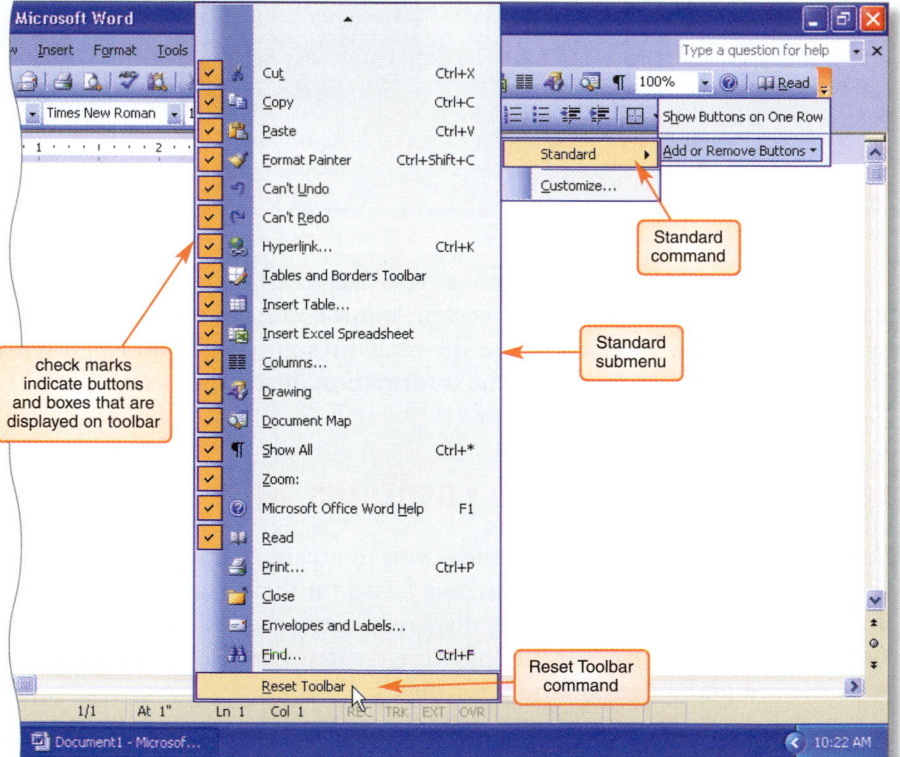

FIGURE D-6

4

• **Reset the Formatting toolbar by following Steps 1 through 3 and replacing any reference to the Standard toolbar with the Formatting toolbar.**

Not only can you use the Standard submenu shown in Figure D-6 to reset the Standard toolbar to its original settings, but you also can use it to customize the Standard toolbar by adding and deleting buttons. To add or delete buttons, click the button name on the Standard submenu to add or remove the check mark. Buttons with a check mark to the left currently are displayed on the Standard toolbar; buttons without a check mark are not displayed on the Standard toolbar. You can complete the same tasks for the Formatting toolbar, using the Formatting submenu to add and delete buttons from the Formatting toolbar.

Resetting the Word Menus

The following steps show how to reset the Word menus to their original settings.

Other Ways

1. On View menu point to Toolbars, click Customize on Toolbars submenu, click Toolbars tab, click toolbar name, click Reset button, click OK button, click Close button
2. Right-click toolbar, click Customize on shortcut menu, click Toolbars tab, click toolbar name, click Reset button, click OK button, click Close button
3. In Voice Command mode, say "View, Toolbars, Customize, Toolbars, [desired toolbar name], Reset, OK, Close"

To Reset the Word Menus

1

• **Click the Toolbar Options button on the Standard toolbar and then point to Add or Remove Buttons on the Toolbar Options menu.**

Word displays the Toolbar Options menu and the Add or Remove Buttons submenu (Figure D-7).

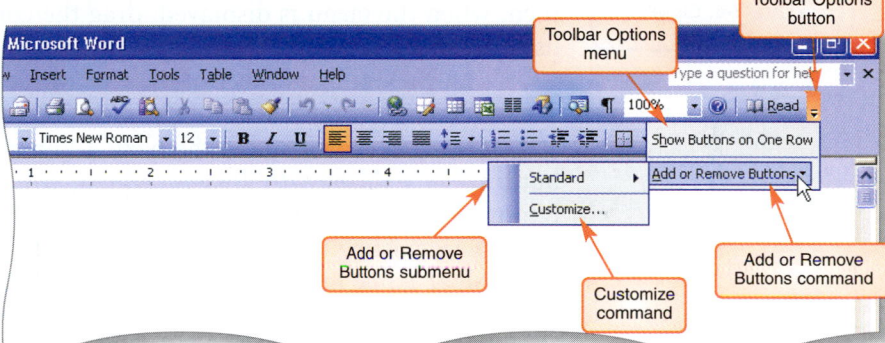

FIGURE D-7

2

• **Click Customize on the Add or Remove Buttons submenu.**

• **When Word displays the Customize dialog box, click the Options tab.**

The Customize dialog box contains three sheets used for customizing the Word toolbars and menus (Figure D-8).

3

• **Click the Reset menu and toolbar usage data button.**

• **When Word displays the Microsoft Word dialog box, click the Yes button.**

• **Click the Close button in the Customize dialog box.**

Word resets the menus to the original settings.

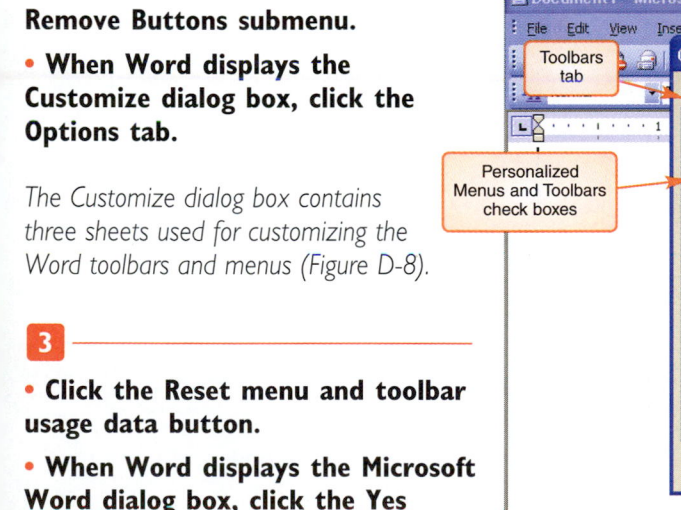

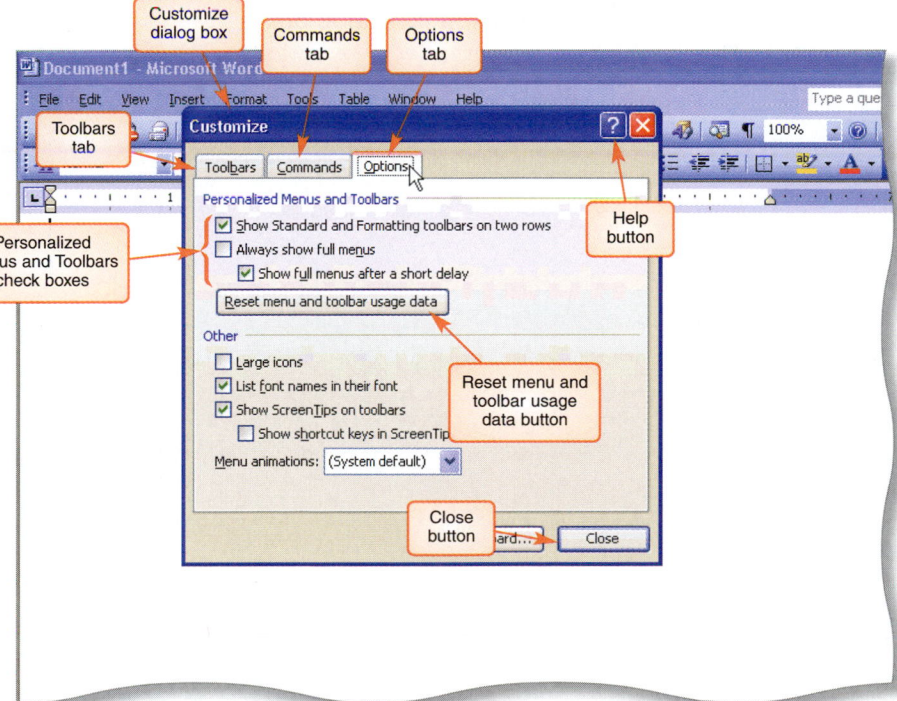

FIGURE D-8

Other Ways

1. On View menu point to Toolbars, click Customize on Toolbars submenu, click Options tab, click Reset menu and toolbar usage data button, click Yes button, click Close button
2. Right-click toolbar, click Customize on shortcut menu, click Options tab, click Reset menu and toolbar usage data button, click Yes button, click Close button
3. In Voice Command mode, say "View, Toolbars, Customize, Options, Reset menu and toolbar usage data, Yes, Close"

Using the Options sheet in the Customize dialog box, as shown in Figure D-8 on the previous page, you can select options to personalize menus and toolbars. For example, you can select or deselect a check mark that instructs Word to display the Standard and Formatting toolbars on two rows. You also can select whether Word always displays full menus or displays short menus followed by full menus, after a short delay. Other options available on the Options sheet including settings to instruct Word to display toolbars with large icons; to use the appropriate font to display font names in the Font list; and to display a ScreenTip when a user points to a toolbar button. Clicking the Help button in the upper-right corner of the Customize dialog box displays Help topics that will assist you in customizing toolbars and menus.

Using the Commands sheet in the Customize dialog box, you can add buttons to toolbars and commands to menus. Recall that the menu bar at the top of the Word window is a special toolbar. To add buttons to a toolbar, click a category name in the Categories list and then drag the command name in the Commands list to a toolbar. To add commands to a menu, click a category name in the Categories list, drag the command name in the Commands list to a menu name on the menu bar, and then, when the menu is displayed, drag the command to the desired location in the list of menu commands.

Using the Toolbars sheet in the Customize dialog box, you can add new toolbars and reset existing toolbars and the menu. To add a new toolbar, click the New button, enter a toolbar name in the New Toolbar dialog box, and then click the OK button. Once the new toolbar is created, you can use the Commands sheet to add or remove buttons, as you would with any other toolbar. If you add one or more buttons to an existing toolbar and want to reset the toolbar to its original settings, click the toolbar name in the Toolbars list so a check mark is displayed to the left of the name and then click the Reset button. If you add commands to one or more menus and want to reset the menus to their default settings, click Menu Bar in the Toolbars list on the Toolbars sheet so a check mark is displayed to the left of the name and then click the Reset button. When you have finished, click the Close button to close the Customize dialog box.

Appendix E

 # Microsoft Office Specialist Certification

What Is Microsoft Office Specialist Certification?

Microsoft Office Specialist certification provides a framework for measuring your proficiency with the Microsoft Office 2003 applications, such as Microsoft Office Word 2003, Microsoft Office Excel 2003, Microsoft Office Access 2003, Microsoft Office PowerPoint 2003, and Microsoft Office Outlook 2003. The levels of certification are described in Table E-1.

Table E-1 Levels of Microsoft Office Specialist Certification			
LEVEL	**DESCRIPTION**	**REQUIREMENTS**	**CREDENTIAL AWARDED**
Microsoft Office Specialist	Indicates that you have an understanding of the basic features in a specific Microsoft Office 2003 application	Pass any ONE of the following: Microsoft Office Word 2003 Microsoft Office Excel 2003 Microsoft Office Access 2003 Microsoft Office PowerPoint 2003 Microsoft Office Outlook 2003	Candidates will be awarded one certificate for each of the Specialist-level exams they have passed: Microsoft Office Word 2003 Microsoft Office Excel 2003 Microsoft Office Access 2003 Microsoft Office PowerPoint 2003 Microsoft Office Outlook 2003
Microsoft Office Expert	Indicates that you have an understanding of the advanced features in a specific Microsoft Office 2003 application	Pass any ONE of the following: Microsoft Office Word 2003 Expert Microsoft Office Excel 2003 Expert	Candidates will be awarded one certificate for each of the Expert-level exams they have passed: Microsoft Office Word 2003 Expert Microsoft Office Excel 2003 Expert
Microsoft Office Master	Indicates that you have a comprehensive understanding of the features of four of the five primary Microsoft Office 2003 applications	Pass the following: Microsoft Office Word 2003 Expert Microsoft Office Excel 2003 Expert Microsoft Office PowerPoint 2003 And pass ONE of the following: Microsoft Office Access 2003 or Microsoft Office Outlook 2003	Candidates will be awarded the Microsoft Office Master certificate for fulfilling the requirements.

Why Should You Be Certified?

Being Microsoft Office certified provides a valuable industry credential — proof that you have the Office 2003 applications skills required by employers. By passing one or more Microsoft Office Specialist certification exams, you demonstrate your proficiency in a given Office 2003 application to employers. With more than 400 million people in 175 nations and 70 languages using Office applications, Microsoft is targeting Office 2003 certification to a wide variety of companies. These companies include temporary employment agencies that want to prove the expertise of their workers, large corporations looking for a way to measure the skill set of employees, and training companies and educational institutions seeking Microsoft Office 2003 teachers with appropriate credentials.

The Microsoft Office Specialist Certification Exams

You pay $50 to $100 each time you take an exam, whether you pass or fail. The fee varies among testing centers. The **Microsoft Office Expert** exams, which you can take up to 60 minutes to complete, consist of between 40 and 60 tasks that you perform on a personal computer in a simulated environment. The tasks require you to use the application just as you would in doing your job. The **Microsoft Office Specialist** exams contain fewer tasks, and you will have slightly less time to complete them. The tasks you will perform differ on the two types of exams. After passing designated Expert and Specialist exams, candidates are awarded the **Microsoft Office Master** certificate (see the requirements in Table E-1 on the previous page).

How to Prepare for the Microsoft Office Specialist Certification Exams

The Shelly Cashman Series offers several Microsoft-approved textbooks that cover the required objectives of the Microsoft Office Specialist certification exams. For a listing of the textbooks, visit the Shelly Cashman Series Microsoft Office Specialist Center at scsite.com/winoff2003/cert. Click the link Shelly Cashman Series Microsoft Office 2003-Approved Microsoft Office Textbooks (Figure E-1). After using any of the books listed in an instructor-led course, you should be prepared to take the indicated Microsoft Office Specialist certification exam.

How to Find an Authorized Testing Center

To locate a testing center, call 1-800-933-4493 in North America, or visit the Shelly Cashman Series Microsoft Office Specialist Center at scsite.com/winoff2003/cert. Click the link Locate an Authorized Testing Center Near You (Figure E-1). At this Web site, you can look for testing centers around the world.

Shelly Cashman Series Microsoft Office Specialist Center

The Shelly Cashman Series Microsoft Office Specialist Center (Figure E-1) lists more than 15 Web sites you can visit to obtain additional information about certification. The Web page (scsite.com/winoff2003/cert) includes links to general information about certification, choosing an application for certification, preparing for the certification exam, and taking and passing the certification exam.

FIGURE E-1

Microsoft Office Specialist Certification Maps

The tables on the following pages list the skill sets and activities you should be familiar with if you plan to take one of the Microsoft Office Specialist certification examinations. Each activity is accompanied by page numbers on which the activity is illustrated and page numbers on which the activity is part of an exercise.

Microsoft Office Word 2003

Table E-2 lists the skill sets and activities you should be familiar with if you plan to take the Microsoft Office Specialist examination for Microsoft Office Word 2003. Table E-3 on the next page lists the skill sets and activities you should be familiar with if you plan to take the Microsoft Office Expert examination for Microsoft Office Word 2003. **ADV** means that the activity is demonstrated in the companion textbook *Microsoft Office 2003: Advanced Concepts and Techniques* (ISBN 0-619-20025-1 or ISBN 0-619-20026-X). **POST-ADV** means that the activity is demonstrated in the companion textbook *Microsoft Office 2003: Post-Advanced Concepts and Techniques* (ISBN 0-619-20027-8).

Table E-2 Microsoft Office Specialist Skill Sets, Activities, and Locations in Book for Microsoft Office Word 2003			
SKILL SET	**SKILL BEING MEASURED**	**SKILL DEMONSTRATED IN BOOK**	**SKILL EXERCISE IN BOOK**
I. Creating Content	A. Insert and edit text, symbols and special characters	WD 18-20, WD 22-27, WD 57, WD 58-59, WD 83, WD 107, WD 112-114, WD 118-120, WD 125, WD 152, WD 156-157, WD 154-155, WD 166-172, WD 180, **ADV**	WD 65 (Apply Your Knowledge Steps 1-4), WD 67 (In the Lab 1 Step 3), WD 69 (In the Lab 2 Step 3), WD 70 (In the Lab 3 Step 1), WD 78 (Cases and Places 1-3, last sentence), WD 129 (Apply Your Knowledge Steps 1, 7-8, and 10 - 3rd sentence), WD 131 (In the Lab 1 Steps 8-9), WD 133 (In the Lab 2, Part 1 Steps 3b and 4, Part 2 Step 1), WD 134 (In the Lab 3 Steps 2-3), WD 136 (Cases and Places 5 - 4th sentence from end), WD 199 (In the Lab 1 Steps 1-2), WD 202 (Cases and Places 5 - 3rd sentence from end), **ADV**
	B. Insert frequently used and pre-defined text	WD 84 (2nd paragraph), WD 89-90, WD 91-93, WD 177-179, WD 181-182	WD 129 (Apply Your Knowledge Step 10 - 4th sentence), WD 134 (In the Lab 3 Step 1 - 4th sentence), WD 135 (Cases and Places 1 - 2nd to last sentence), WD 200 (In the Lab 2 Step 2 - 3rd and 4th sentences)
	C. Navigate to specific content	WD 110-112, WD 116-117, **ADV**	WD 129 (Apply Your Knowledge Step 6), WD 131 (In the Lab 1 Step 11), WD 133 (In the Lab 2 Part 2 Steps 2 and 4), **ADV**
	D. Insert, position and size graphics	WD 46-50, **ADV**	WD 65 (Apply Your Knowledge Step 15), WD 68 (In the Lab 1 Steps 13-14), WD 60 (In the Lab 2 Steps 12-13), WD 70 (In the Lab 3 Steps 6-7), **ADV**
	E. Create and modify diagrams and charts	**ADV**	**ADV**
	F. Locate, select and insert supporting information	WD 118, WD 124, WD 125	WD 129 (Apply Your Knowledge Step 13), WD 134 (In the Lab 3 Step 3), WD 135 (Cases and Places 2-4)
II. Organizing Content	A. Insert and modify tables	WD 150-151, WD 182-187, **ADV**	WD 198 (Apply Your Knowledge Steps 4-13), WD 200 (In the Lab 2 Step 2), WD 200 (In the Lab 3 Step 2), **ADV**
	B. Create bulleted lists, numbered lists and outlines	WD 153-154, WD 156, WD 187-189, **ADV**	WD 70 (In the Lab 1 Step 5), WD 72 (Cases and Places 4 - next to last sentence), WD 199 (In the Lab 1), WD 200 (In the Lab 2), WD 200 (In the Lab 3 Step 2), WD 202 (Cases and Places 5 - 4th sentence), **ADV**
	C. Insert and modify hyperlinks	WD 108, WD 122, WD 174, WD 207, WD 212-213	WD 131 (In the Lab 1 Step 8), WD 133 (In the Lab 2 Step 3b), WD 200 (In the Lab 2 Step 2 - 2nd to last sentence), WD 216 (In the Lab 2 Steps 2 and 4)

Table E-2 Microsoft Office Specialist Skill Sets, Activities, and Locations in Book for Microsoft Office Word 2003 (continued)

SKILL SET	SKILL BEING MEASURED	SKILL DEMONSTRATED IN BOOK	SKILL EXERCISE IN BOOK
III. Formatting Content	A. Format text	WD 17, WD 34-36, WD 40-42, WD 44, WD 87, WD 117, WD 161, WD 173, WD 213, **ADV**	WD 65 (Apply Your Knowledge Steps 5-6, and 8-13), WD 67-68 (In the Lab 1 Steps 1, 5, and 8-11), WD 68-69 (In the Lab 2 Steps 1, 5, and 8-10), WD 70 (In the Lab 3 Steps 1, 3-4), WD 71 (Cases and Places 3 - 3rd & 4th sentences from end), WD 72 (Cases and Places 4 - 4th and 5th sentences from end), WD 129 (Apply Your Knowledge Steps 2 and 9), WD 198 (Apply Your Knowledge Steps 3 and 9), WD 200 (In the Lab 2 Step 2), **ADV**
	B. Format paragraphs	WD 37-38, WD 79-80, WD 82-83, WD 86-89, WD 104-105, WD 163-165, WD 172-173, WD 176-177, **ADV**	WD 65 (Apply Your Knowledge Steps 7 and 14), WD 67 (In the Lab 1 Steps 6-7, 12), WD 69 (In the Lab 2 Steps 6-7, 11), WD 129 (Apply Your Knowledge Steps 3-4), WD 131 (In the Lab 1 Steps 3, 5-8), WD 133 (In the Lab 2 Part 1 Steps 1-3, Part 2 Step 2), WD 134 (In the Lab 3), WD 135-136 (Cases and Places 1-5), WD 198 (Apply Your Knowledge Steps 1-2), WD 199-200 (In the Lab 2 Step 2), **ADV**
	C. Apply and format columns	**ADV**	**ADV**
	D. Insert and modify content in headers and footers	WD 81-84, **ADV**	WD 129 (Apply Your Knowledge Step 10), WD 131 (In the Lab 1 Step 4), WD 133 (In the Lab 2 Part 1 Step 1 - Part 3 Step 2), WD 134 (In the Lab 3 Step 1), WD 135-136 (Cases and Places 1-5), **ADV**
	E. Modify document layout and page setup	WD 77-79, WD 103, **ADV**	WD 131 (In the Lab 1 Steps 2 and 7), WD 133 (In the Lab 2 Part 1 Steps 1 and 2, Part 3 Step 2), WD 134 (In the Lab 3), WD 135-136 (Cases and Places 1-5), **ADV**
IV. Collaborating	A. Circulate documents for review	WD 123, **ADV**	WD 134 (In the Lab 3 Step 5), **ADV**
	B. Compare and merge documents	**ADV**	**ADV**
	C. Insert, view and edit comments	**ADV**	**ADV**
	D. Track, accept and reject proposed changes	**ADV**	**ADV**
V. Formatting and Managing Documents	A. Create new documents using templates	WD 142-148, WD 175 (More About Saving), **ADV**	WD 199 (In the Lab 1 Steps 1 and 2), WD 201-202 (Cases and Places 1-5), **ADV**
	B. Review and modify document properties	WD 100-101, WD 102, WD 193-194	WD 131 (In the Lab 1 Step 12), WD 133 (In the Lab 2 Part 1 Step 7, Part 2 Step 6, Part 3 Step 5), WD 134 (In the Lab 3 Step 4), WD 200 (In the Lab 2 Steps 3 and 6)
	C. Organize documents using file folders	**ADV**	**ADV**
	D. Save documents in appropriate formats for different uses	WD 30, WD 205, WD 206, **ADV**	WD 216 (In the Lab 1 Steps 2, 5-6), WD 216 (In the Lab 2 Step 2)
	E. Print documents, envelopes and labels	WD 53, WD 190-191, **ADV**	WD 65 (Apply Your Knowledge Step 17), WD 68 (In the Lab 1 Step 16), WD 69 (In the Lab 2 Step 15), WD 70 (In the Lab 3 Step 9), WD 131 (In the Lab 1 Step 12), WD 200 (In the Lab 2 Step 7), WD 200 (In the Lab 3 Step 3), **ADV**
	F. Preview documents and Web pages	WD 52, WD 158-159, WD 208-209	WD 70 (In the Lab 3 Step 7), WD 199 (In the Lab 1 Step 5), WD 200 (In the Lab 2 Step 5), WD 216 (In the Lab 1 Step 3), WD 216 (In the Lab 2 Step 5), **ADV**
	G. Change and organize document views and windows	WD 9 Step 4, WD 20-21, WD 77, WD 148-149, WD 169-170, WD 172, **ADV**	WD 67 (In the Lab 1 Step 2), WD 68 (In the Lab 2 Step 2), WD 71-72 (Cases and Places 1-5), WD 133 (In the Lab 2 Part 3 Step 1), WD 135-136 (Cases and Places 1-5), WD 199 (In the Lab 1 Step 2), **ADV**

Table E-3 Microsoft Office Expert Skill Sets, Activities, and Locations in Book for Microsoft Office Word 2003

SKILL SET	SKILL BEING MEASURED	SKILL DEMONSTRATED IN BOOK	SKILL EXERCISE IN BOOK
I. Formatting Content	A. Create custom styles for text, tables and lists	WD 96-98, **ADV**, **POST-ADV**	WD 133 (In the Lab 2 Part 1 Step 2, Part 2 Step 2), WD 135-136 (Cases and Places 2-5), **ADV**, **POST-ADV**
	B. Control pagination	WD 103, WD 154-155, **ADV**, **POST-ADV**	WD 131 (In the Lab 1 Step 7), WD 133 (In the Lab 2 Part 1 Step 2, Part 3 Step 2), WD 134 (In the Lab 3 Step 1), WD 135-136 (Cases and Places 1-5), WD 199 (In the Lab 1 Step 2), **ADV**, **POST-ADV**
	C. Format, position and resize graphics using advanced layout features	WD 49-51, **ADV**, **POST-ADV**	WD 69 (In the Lab 2 Step 13), WD 70 (In the Lab 3 Step 7), WD 199-200 (In the Lab 2 Step 1), WD 201 (Cases and Places 1), **ADV**, **POST-ADV**
	D. Insert and modify objects	**ADV**, **POST-ADV**	**ADV**, **POST-ADV**
	E. Create and modify diagrams and charts using data from other sources	**POST-ADV**	**POST-ADV**
II. Organizing Content	A. Sort content in lists and tables	WD 109-110, **ADV**, **POST-ADV**	WD 133 (In the Lab 2 Part 1, Step 3), WD 134 (In the Lab 3 Step 1 last sentence), WD 135-136 (Cases and Places 1-5), **ADV**, **POST-ADV**
	B. Perform calculations in tables	**ADV**	WD 198 (Apply Your Knowledge Step 7), **ADV**
	C. Modify table formats	**ADV**, **POST-ADV**	**ADV**, **POST-ADV**
	D. Summarize document content using automated tools	**POST-ADV**	**POST-ADV**
	E. Use automated tools for document navigation	**POST-ADV**	**POST-ADV**
	F. Merge letters with other data sources	**ADV**	**ADV**
	G. Merge labels with other data sources	**ADV**	**ADV**
	H. Structure documents using XML	**POST-ADV**	**POST-ADV**
III. Formatting Documents	A. Create and modify forms	**POST-ADV**	**POST-ADV**
	B. Create and modify document background	WD 207-208, **ADV**, **POST-ADV**	WD 216 (In the Lab 2 Steps 2-3), **ADV**, **POST-ADV**
	C. Create and modify document indexes and tables	**POST-ADV**	**POST-ADV**
	D. Insert and modify endnotes, footnotes, captions, and cross-references	WD 93-99, **POST-ADV**	WD 131 (In the Lab 1 Step 7), WD 133 (In the Lab 2 Part 1 Step 2, Part 2 Steps 3 and 4, Part 3 Steps 1-3), WD 134 (In the Lab 3 Step 1), WD 135-136 (Cases and Places 1-5), **POST-ADV**
	E. Create and manage master documents and subdocuments	**POST-ADV**	**POST-ADV**
IV. Collaborating	A. Modify track changes options	**ADV**	**ADV**
	B. Publish and edit Web documents	WD 205-215, WD 209-212, Appendix C	WD 216 (In the Lab 1 Steps 2-5), WD 216 (In the Lab 2 Steps 2, 7)
	C. Manage document versions	**POST-ADV**	**POST-ADV**
	D. Protect and restrict forms and documents	**POST-ADV**	**POST-ADV**
	E. Attach digital signatures to documents	**POST-ADV**	**POST-ADV**
	F. Customize document properties	**POST-ADV**	**POST-ADV**
V. Customizing Word	A. Create, edit, and run macros	**POST-ADV**	**POST-ADV**
	B. Customize menus and toolbars	**POST-ADV**	**POST-ADV**
	C. Modify Word default settings	WD 121, **ADV**, **POST-ADV**	WD 136 (Cases and Places 5), **ADV**, **POST-ADV**

Microsoft Office Excel 2003

Table E-4 lists the skill sets and activities you should be familiar with if you plan to take the Microsoft Office Specialist examination for Microsoft Office Excel 2003. Table E-5 on the next page lists the skill sets and activities you should be familiar with if you plan to take the Microsoft Office Expert examination for Microsoft Office Excel 2003. **ADV** means that the activity is demonstrated in the companion textbook *Microsoft Office 2003: Advanced Concepts and Techniques* (ISBN 0-619-20025-1 or ISBN 0-619-20026-X). **POST-ADV** means that the activity is demonstrated in the companion textbook *Microsoft Office 2003: Post-Advanced Concepts and Techniques* (ISBN 0-619-20027-8).

Table E-4 Microsoft Office Specialist Skill Sets, Activities, and Locations in Book for Microsoft Office Excel 2003			
SKILL SET	**SKILL BEING MEASURED**	**SKILL DEMONSTRATED IN BOOK**	**SKILL EXERCISE IN BOOK**
I. Creating Data and Content	A. Enter and edit cell content	EX 16-23, EX 50-53, EX 72-88, EX 151-154, **ADV**	EX 57 (Apply Your Knowledge 1), EX 58-64 (In the Labs 1-3 and Cases and Places 1-5), EX 212 (In the Lab 1 Step 2), **ADV**
	B. Navigate to specific cell content	EX 36-37, **ADV**	EX 57 (Apply Your Knowledge 1), EX 58-64 (In the Labs 1-3 and Cases and Places 1-5), **ADV**
	C. Locate, select and insert supporting information	**ADV**	**ADV**
	D. Insert, position, and size graphics	**ADV**	**ADV**
II. Analyzing Data	A. Filter lists using AutoFilter	**ADV**	**ADV**
	B. Sort lists	**ADV**	**ADV**
	C. Insert and modify formulas	EX 72-77, EX 79-80, EX 80-87, EX 168-172, EX 173, EX 174-175, **ADV**	EX 62 (In the Lab Part 3), EX 130 (In the Lab 1 Part 1), EX 130 (In the Lab 1 Part 1), EX 133 (In the Lab 1 Part 1 Steps 2 and 4), EX 135 (In the Lab 2 Part 1 Steps 3 and 5), EX 140-143 (Cases and Places 1-5), EX 211 (Apply Your Knowledge 1 Steps 5-8), EX 212 (In the Lab 1 Part 1), EX 217 (In the Lab 2 Part 1), EX 220 (In the Lab 3 Part 1 Step 11), **ADV**
	D. Use statistical, date and time, financial, and logical functions	EX 23-24, EX 26-27, EX 80-87, EX 165-167, EX 170-172, **ADV**	EX 59 (In the Lab 1 Step 2), EX 59 (In the Lab 2 Step 2), EX 130 (Apply Your Knowledge 1 Part 1), EX 133 (In the Lab 1 Part 1 Step 4), EX 135 (In the Lab 2 Part 1 Step 5), EX 212 (In the Lab 1 Part 1 Step 1), EX 216 (In the Lab 2 Part 1 Step 1), **ADV**
	E. Create, modify, and position diagrams and charts based on worksheet data	EX 38-41, EX 187-199, **ADV**	EX 59 (In the Lab 1 Step 6), EX 60 (In the Lab 2 Step 5), EX 62 (In the Lab 3 Part 2), EX 214 (In the Lab 1 Part 2), EX 217 (In the Lab 2 Part 2), **ADV**
III. Formatting Data and Content	A. Apply and modify cell formats	EX 28-36, EX 90-110, EX 177-186, **ADV**	EX 59 (In the Lab 1 Step 5), EX 60 (In the Lab 2 Step 5), EX 61 (In the Lab 3 Part 1), EX 63-64 (Cases and Places 1-5), EX 131 (Apply Your Knowledge 1), EX 133 (In the Lab 1 Steps 6-8), EX 135 (In the Lab 2 Part 1 Steps 6-9), EX 140-143 (Cases and Places 1-5), EX 214 (In the Lab 1 Step 8), EX 217 (In the Lab 2 Steps 8-10), **ADV**
	B. Apply and modify cell styles	**ADV**	**ADV**
	C. Modify row and column formats	EX 32-33, EX 91-94, EX 96-97, EX 107-111, EX 155-156, EX 159-162, **ADV**	EX 59 (In the Lab 1 Step 4), EX 60 (In the Lab 2 Step 3), EX 133 (In the Lab 1 Steps 6 and 7), EX 135 (In the Lab 3 Step 1), EX 135 (In the Lab 2 Step 6), EX 212 (In the Lab 1 Step 4), EX 216 (In the Lab 2 Steps 3 and 4), EX 219 (In the Lab 3 Steps 1-3), **ADV**
	D. Format worksheets	EX 124, EX 197-199, **ADV**	EX 135 (In the Lab 2 Step 10), EX 137-139 (In the Lab 3 Parts 1-4), EX 214 (In the Lab 1 Part 2), EX 217 (In the Lab 2 Step 11), **ADV**

Table E-4 Microsoft Office Specialist Skill Sets, Activities, and Locations in Book for Microsoft Office Excel 2003

SKILL SET	SKILL BEING MEASURED	SKILL DEMONSTRATED IN BOOK	SKILL EXERCISE IN BOOK
IV. Collaborating	A. Insert, view and edit comments	ADV	ADV
V. Managing Workbooks	A. Create new workbooks from templates	ADV	ADV
	B. Insert, delete and move cells	EX 24-27, EX 157-159, EX 161-162, EX 174-175, ADV	EX 62 (In the Lab 3 Part 3), EX 212 (In the Lab 1 Step 7), EX 216 (In the Lab 2 Step 6), EX 221 (In the Lab 3 Steps 1-3), ADV
	C. Create and modify hyperlinks	ADV	ADV
	D. Organize worksheets	EX 197-199, ADV	EX 214 (In the Lab 1 Part 2), EX 217 (In the Lab 2 Step 11), ADV
	E. Preview data in other views	EX 113-116, EX 228-230, ADV	EX 133 (In the Lab 1 Step 10), EX 137 (In the Lab 3 Part 2), EX 138 (In the Lab 2 Part 3), EX 239 (In the Lab 1 Part 1 Step 1), EX 240 (In the Lab 2 Part 1 Step 1), ADV
	F. Customize Window layout	EX 163-164, EX 175-176, EX 202-207, ADV	EX 215 (In the Lab 1 Part 3), EX 216-217 (In the Lab 2 Steps 2, 11, and 14), EX 219-220 (In the Lab 3 Steps 6 and 17), ADV
	G. Setup pages for printing	EX 113-116, ADV	EX 131 (Apply Your Knowledge 1), EX 133 (In the Lab 1 Step 11), EX 137 (In the Lab 3 Part 1), ADV
	H. Print data	EX 113-120, ADV	ADV
	I. Organize workbooks using file folders	EX 230-232	EX 240 (In the Lab 3)
	J. Save data in appropriate formats for different uses	EX 228-238, ADV	EX 239 (In the Lab 1 Parts 1 and 2), EX 240 (In the Lab 2 Parts 1 and 2), ADV

Table E-5 Microsoft Office Expert Skill Sets, Activities, and Locations in Book for Microsoft Office Excel 2003

SKILL SET	SKILL BEING MEASURED	SKILL DEMONSTRATED IN BOOK	SKILL EXERCISE IN BOOK
I. Organizing and Analyzing Data	A. Use subtotals	ADV	ADV
	B. Define and apply advanced filters	ADV	ADV
	C. Group and outline data	ADV	ADV
	D. Use data validation	ADV, POST-ADV	ADV, POST-ADV
	E. Create and modify list ranges	ADV	ADV
	F. Add, show, close, edit, merge and summarize scenarios	POST-ADV	POST-ADV
	G. Perform data analysis using automated tools	EX 204-208, ADV, POST-ADV	EX 215 (In the Lab 1 Part 3), EX 218 (In the Lab 2 Part 3), EX 221 (In the Lab 3 Part 2), EX 223-224 (Cases and Places 3-5), ADV, POST-ADV
	H. Create PivotTable and PivotChart reports	POST-ADV	POST-ADV
	I. Use Lookup and Reference functions	ADV	ADV
	J. Use Database functions	ADV	ADV
	K. Trace formula precedents, dependents and errors	POST-ADV	POST-ADV
	L. Locate invalid data and formulas	EX 89-90, EX 292-294, POST-ADV	EX 131 (Apply Your Knowledge 1 Part 1), ADV, POST-ADV

Table E-5 Microsoft Office Expert Skill Sets, Activities, and Locations in Book for Microsoft Office Excel 2003 *(continued)*

SKILL SET	SKILL BEING MEASURED	SKILL DEMONSTRATED IN BOOK	SKILL EXERCISE IN BOOK
	M. Watch and evaluate formulas	**POST-ADV**	**POST-ADV**
	N. Define, modify and use named ranges	**ADV**	**ADV**
	O. Structure workbooks using XML	**POST-ADV**	**POST-ADV**
II. Formatting z Data and Content	A. Create and modify custom data formats	**ADV**	**ADV**
	B. Use conditional formatting	EX 103-106, **ADV**	EX 133 (In the Lab 1 Step 8), EX 135 (In the Lab 2 Step 8), **ADV**
	C. Format and resize graphics	ADV	ADV
	D. Format charts and diagrams	EX 192-198, **ADV**	EX 214 (In the Lab 1, Part 2), EX 217-218, (In the Lab 2 Part 2), **ADV**
III. Collaborating	A. Protect cells, worksheets, and workbooks	**ADV, POST-ADV**	**ADV, POST-ADV**
	B. Apply workbook security settings	**POST-ADV**	**POST-ADV**
	C. Share workbooks	**POST-ADV**	**POST-ADV**
	D. Merge workbooks	**POST-ADV**	**POST-ADV**
	E. Track, accept, and reject changes to workbooks	**POST-ADV**	**POST-ADV**
IV. Managing Data and Workbooks	A. Import data to Excel	EX 120-123, **POST-ADV**	EX 136-139 (In the Lab 3), EX 143 (Cases and Places 5), **ADV, POST-ADV**
	B. Export data from Excel	**POST-ADV**	**POST-ADV**
	C. Publish and edit Web worksheets and workbooks	EX 225-239, **POST-ADV**	EX 239 (In the Lab 1), EX 240 (In the Lab 2), **POST-ADV**
	D. Create and edit templates	**ADV**	**ADV**
	E. Consolidate data	**ADV**	**ADV**
	F. Define and modify workbook properties	**POST-ADV**	**POST-ADV**
V. Customizing Excel	A. Customize toolbars and menus	**POST-ADV**	**POST-ADV**
	B. Create, edit, and run macros	**POST-ADV**	**POST-ADV**
	C. Modify Excel default settings	**ADV**	**ADV**

Microsoft Office Access 2003

Table E-6 lists the skill sets and activities you should be familiar with if you plan to take the Microsoft Office Specialist examination for Microsoft Office Access 2003. **ADV** means that the activity is demonstrated in the companion textbook *Microsoft Office 2003: Advanced Concepts and Techniques* (ISBN 0-619-20025-1 or ISBN 0-619-20026-X). Expert certification is not available for Microsoft Office Access 2003.

Table E-6 Microsoft Office Specialist Skill Sets, Activities, and Locations in Book for Microsoft Office Access 2003

SKILL SET	SKILL BEING MEASURED	SKILL DEMONSTRATED IN BOOK	SKILL EXERCISE IN BOOK
I. Structuring Databases	A. Create Access databases	AC 10	AC 56-64 (In The Lab 1, 2, 3; Cases and Places 1-5)
	B. Create and modify tables	AC 15, AC 159, AC 127-130	AC 63 (Cases and Places 3), AC 171 (Cases and Places 3), AC 167-172 (All Exercises)

Table E-6 Microsoft Office Specialist Skill Sets, Activities, and Locations in Book for Microsoft Office Access 2003

SKILL SET	SKILL BEING MEASURED	SKILL DEMONSTRATED IN BOOK	SKILL EXERCISE IN BOOK
	C. Define and modify field types	AC 130, AC 147	AC 169 (In The Lab 2 Step 5f, In The Lab 3 part 1), AC 172 (Cases and Places 5)
	D. Modify field properties	AC 127-128, AC 140, AC 141, 143, AC 142, AC 144, AC 160, **ADV**	AC 167-172 (All Exercises), **ADV**
	E. Create and modify one-to-many relationships	AC 151, AC 342	AC 171-172 (Cases and Places 1-4), **ADV**
	F. Enforce referential integrity	AC 152, **ADV**	AC 167 (Apply Your Knowledge Step 17), AC 169 (In The Lab 1 Step 13), AC 170 (In The Lab 2 Step 11), AC 170 (In The Lab 3 part 3), AC 171-172 (Cases and Places 1-4), **ADV**
	G. Create and modify queries	AC 34, AC 37, AC 104, AC 154,	AC 55 (Apply Your Knowledge Steps 3-6), AC 60 (In The Lab 2 Step 2), AC 62 (In The Lab Part 3), AC 63-64 (Cases and Places 3, 4), AC 109 (Apply Your Knowledge Step 8), AC 111 (In The Lab 2 Step 12), AC 112 (Cases and Places 5), AC 172 (Cases and Places 4), AC 171 (Cases and Places 3), AC 172 (Cases and Places 5), **ADV**
	H. Create forms	AC 38, **ADV**	AC 57 (In The Lab 1 Step 8), AC 61 (In the Lab 3 Part 1), AC 64 (Cases and Places 4), **ADV**
	I. Add and modify form controls and properties	**ADV**	**ADV**
	J. Create reports	AC 43, **ADV**	AC 55-64 (All Exercises), **ADV**
	K. Add and modify report control properties	**ADV**	**ADV**
	L. Create a data access page	**ADV**	**ADV**
II. Entering Data	A. Enter, edit and delete records	AC 23, AC 28, AC 116, AC 119, AC 125	AC 54-64 (All Exercises), AC 167-172 (All Exercises)
	B. Find and move among records	AC 27	AC 55 (Apply Your Knowledge Step 1), AC 57 (In The Lab 1 Step 9), AC 60 (In The Lab 2 Step 3), AC 62 (In The Lab 3 part 2)
	C. Import data to Access	AC 176-180	AC 191 (In The Lab 1)
III. Organizing Data	A. Create and modify calculated fields and aggregate functions	AC 96-97, AC 99-103	AC 110 (In The Lab 1 Step 11), AC 111 (In The Lab 3 part 3), AC 112 (Cases and Places 3), AC 110 (In The Lab 1 Steps 12, 13), AC 111 (In The Lab 2 Step 11, In The Lab 3 part 3), AC 112 (Cases and Places 1-4)
	B. Modify form layout	**ADV**	**ADV**
	C. Modify report layout and page setup	AC 30-31, **ADV**	AC 170 (In The Lab 3 Parts 2-3), **ADV**
	D. Format datasheets	AC 131-135	AC 171 (Cases and Places 2)
	E. Sort records	AC 86-89, AC 155, **ADV**	AC 167 (Apply Your Knowledge Step 15), AC 171-172 (Cases and Places 2, 4), **ADV**
	F. Filter records	AC 121, AC 123	AC 167 (Apply Your Knowledge Step 13), AC 169 (In The Lab 2 Step 9)
IV. Managing Databases	A. Identify object dependencies	**ADV**	**ADV**
	B. View objects and object data in other views	AC 23, AC 29-31, AC 42, **ADV**	AC 54-64 (All Exercises), AC 170 (In The Lab 3), **ADV**
	C. Print database objects and data	AC 29-31, AC 47, AC 72, **ADV**	AC 54-64 (All Exercises, AC 109-112 (All Exercises), **ADV**
	D. Export data from Access	AC 181, AC 183, AC 184, AC 185-187	AC 192 (In The Lab 2)
	E. Back up a database	AC 162-163	AC 167 (Apply Your Knowledge Step 18), AC 170 (In The Lab 2 Step 12), AC 171 (Cases and Places 1-2)
	F. Compact and repair databases	AC 163-164	AC 169 (In The Lab 1 Step 14), AC 170 (In The Lab 2 Step 12), AC 171 (Cases and Places 1-2)

Microsoft Office PowerPoint 2003

Table E-7 lists the skill sets and activities you should be familiar with if you plan to take the Microsoft Office Specialist examination for Microsoft Office PowerPoint 2003. **ADV** means that the activity is demonstrated in the companion textbook *Microsoft Office 2003: Advanced Concepts and Techniques* (ISBN 0-619-20025-1 or ISBN 0-619-20026-X). Expert certification is not available for Microsoft Office PowerPoint 2003.

Table E-7 Microsoft Office Specialist Skill Sets, Activities, and Locations in Book for Microsoft Office PowerPoint 2003

SKILL SET	SKILL BEING MEASURED	SKILL DEMONSTRATED IN BOOK	SKILL EXERCISE IN BOOK
I. Creating Content	A. Create new presentations from templates	PPT 18-43, PPT 85-11, PPT 111, **ADV**	PPT 69-71 (In the Lab 1 Steps 1-3), PPT 132-133 (In the Lab 1 Steps 1-4), **ADV**
	B. Insert and edit text-based content	PPT 20-24, PPT 31-42, PPT 53-55, PPT 56, PPT 88-94, **ADV**	PPT 69-71 (In the Lab 1 Steps 2-4), PPT 72-73 (In the Lab 2 Step 4), PPT 74-77 (In the Lab 3, Part 1 and Part 2), PPT 132-134 (In the Lab 1 Steps 2-4), **ADV**
	C. Insert tables, charts and diagrams	**ADV**	**ADV**
	D. Insert pictures, shapes and graphics	PPT 99-106, **ADV**	PPT 132-134 (In the Lab 1 Steps 2-3, 5-6), PPT 134-135 (In the Lab 2 Steps 2-5), **ADV**
	E. Insert objects	**ADV**	**ADV**
II. Formatting Content	A. Format text-based content	PPT 23-27, PPT 153-155, **ADV**	PPT 69-71 (In the Lab 1 Step 2), PPT 72-73 (In the Lab 2 Step 2), **ADV**
	B. Format pictures, shapes and graphics	PPT 108-111, PPT 116-119, **ADV**	PPT 132-134 (In the Lab 1 Steps 2-3, 5-6), PPT 134-135 (In the Lab 2 Steps 2-5, and 8), PPT 136-137 (In the Lab 3 Steps 2-5), **ADV**
	C. Format slides	PPT 17-20, PPT 85, PPT 97-99, PPT 144, **ADV**	PPT 69-71 (In the Lab 1 Step 1), PPT 131-132 (Apply Your Knowledge 1 Steps 3, 5), PPT 132-134 (In the Lab 1 Steps 3, 5, 6), PPT 134-135 (In the Lab 2 Step 1), **ADV**
	D. Apply animation schemes	PPT 114-116, **ADV**	PPT 131-132 (Apply Your Knowledge 1 Step 6), PT 136-137 (In the Lab 3 Step 7), **ADV**
	E. Apply slide transitions	**ADV**	**ADV**
	F. Customize slide templates	**ADV**	**ADV**
	G. Work with masters	PPT 112-113, **ADV**	PPT 132-134 (In the Lab 1 Step 7), PPT 134-135 (In the Lab 2 Step 6), PPT 136-137 (In the Lab 3 Step 6), **ADV**
III. Collaborating	A. Track, accept and reject changes in a presentation	**ADV**	**ADV**
	B. Add, edit and delete comments in a presentation	**ADV**	**ADV**
	C. Compare and merge presentations	**ADV**	**ADV**
IV. Managing and Delivering Presentations	A. Organize a presentation	PPT 30-31, PPT 89-97, **ADV**	PPT 69-71 (In the Lab 1 Step 3), PPT 132-134 (In the Lab 1 Steps 3-4), **ADV**
	B. Set up slide shows for delivery	**ADV**	**ADV**
	C. Rehearse timing	**ADV**	**ADV**
	D. Deliver presentations	PPT 46-50, **ADV**	PPT 74-77 (In the Lab 3 Part 1 Step 2, Part 2 Step 6), **ADV**
	E. Prepare presentations for remote delivery	**ADV**	**ADV**

Table E-7 Microsoft Office Specialist Skill Sets, Activities, and Locations in Book for Microsoft Office PowerPoint 2003

SKILL SET	SKILL BEING MEASURED	SKILL DEMONSTRATED IN BOOK	SKILL EXERCISE IN BOOK
	F. Save and publish presentations	PPT 146-149, PPT 154-157, Appendix C, **ADV**	PPT 158 (In the Lab 1 Steps 2-3, and 6), PPT 158 (In the Lab 2 Steps 2-3, and 8), PPT 159 (In the Lab 3 Steps 2-3), **ADV**
	G. Print slides, outlines, handouts, and speaker notes	PPT 56-61, PPT 122-126, **ADV**	PPT 69-71 (In the Lab 1 Step 7), PPT 72-73 (In the Lab 2 Steps 6-8), PPT 158 (In the Lab 1 Step 7), **ADV**
	H. Export a presentation to another Microsoft Office program	**ADV**	**ADV**

Microsoft Office Outlook 2003

Table E-8 lists the skill sets and activities you should be familiar with if you plan to take the Microsoft Office Specialist examination for Microsoft Office Outlook 2003. **ADV** means that the activity is demonstrated in the companion textbook *Microsoft Office 2003: Advanced Concepts and Techniques* (ISBN 0-619-20025-1 or ISBN 0-619-20026-X). Expert certification is not available for Microsoft Office Outlook 2003.

Table E-8 Microsoft Office Specialist Skill Sets, Activities, and Locations in Book for Microsoft Office Outlook 2003

SKILL SET	SKILL BEING MEASURED	SKILL DEMONSTRATED IN BOOK	SKILL EXERCISE IN BOOK
I. Messaging	A. Originate and respond to e-mail and instant messages	OUT 13-16, OUT 23-25, OUT 51-53, **ADV**	OUT 62 (In the Lab 1 Part 2 Step 1), OUT 63 (In the Lab 3 Part 2), OUT 64 (Cases and Places 3), **ADV**
	B. Attach files to items	OUT 27-29, **ADV**	OUT 62 (In the Lab 1 Part 2 Step 3), **ADV**
	C. Create and modify a personal signature for messages	OUT 19-23	OUT 63 (In the Lab 3 Part 1 and Part 3 Step 4
	D. Modify e-mail message settings and delivery options	OUT 15, OUT 29-31, OUT 34-38	OUT 62 (In the Lab 1 Part 2 Steps 2, 4-5), OUT 62 (In the Lab 2), OUT 63 (In the Lab 3 Part 2)
	E. Create and edit contacts	OUT 41-44, **ADV**	OUT 61 (Apply Your Knowledge 1), OUT 64 (Cases and Places 1-5), **ADV**
	F. Accept, decline, and delegate tasks	**ADV**	**ADV**
II. Scheduling	A. Create and modify appointments, meetings, and events	**ADV**	**ADV**
	B. Update, cancel, and respond to meeting requests	**ADV**	**ADV**
	C. Customize Calendar settings	**ADV**	**ADV**
	D. Create, modify, and assign tasks	**ADV**	**ADV**
III. Organizing	A. Create and modify distribution lists	OUT 53-56	OUT 61 (Apply Your Knowledge 1 and In the Lab 1 Part 1)
	B. Link contacts to other items	OUT 58	OUT 64 (Cases and Places 3)
	C. Create and modify notes	**ADV**	**ADV**
	D. Organize items	OUT 31-34, OUT 44-48, **ADV**	OUT 61 (Apply Your Knowledge 1), OUT 62 (In the Lab 2), OUT 64 (Cases and Places 3 and 5), **ADV**
	E. Organize items using folders	OUT 39-41, **ADV**	OUT 61 (Apply Your Knowledge 1), OUT 64 (Cases and Places 4), **ADV**
	F. Search for items	OUT 38, OUT 46-47	OUT 63 (In the Lab 3 Part 3 Step 2), OUT 64 (Cases and Places 2)

Table E-8 Microsoft Office Specialist Skill Sets, Activities, and Locations in Book for Microsoft Office Outlook 2003 (continued)

SKILL SET	SKILL BEING MEASURED	SKILL DEMONSTRATED IN BOOK	SKILL EXERCISE IN BOOK
	G. Save items in different file formats	OUT 56-58	OUT 62 (In the Lab 1 Part 3)
	H. Assign items to categories	OUT 47-49	OUT 64 (Cases and Places 4)
	I. Preview and print items	OUT 12, OUT 49-50, **ADV**	OUT 61-62 (Apply Your Knowledge 1, In the Lab 1 Part 1, and Part 2 Step 6), OUT 63 (In the Lab 3 Part 1, Part 2, and Part 3 Step 5), OUT 64 (Cases and Places 1-5), **ADV**

Index

Quick Reference Summary

In the Microsoft Office 2003 applications, you can accomplish a task in a number of ways. The following five tables (one each for Microsoft Office Word 2003, Microsoft Office Excel 2003, Microsoft Office Access 2003, Microsoft Office PowerPoint 2003, and Microsoft Office Outlook 2003,) provide a quick reference to each task presented in this textbook. The first column identifies the task. The second column indicates the page number on which the task is discussed in the book. The subsequent four columns list the different ways the task in column one can be carried out. You can invoke the commands listed in the MOUSE, MENU BAR, and SHORTCUT MENU columns using Voice commands.

Table 1 Microsoft Office Word 2003 Quick Reference Summary

TASK	PAGE NUMBER	MOUSE	MENU BAR	SHORTCUT MENU	KEYBOARD SHORTCUT
1.5 Line Spacing	WD 87	Line Spacing button arrow on Formatting toolbar	Format | Paragraph | Indents and Spacing tab	Paragraph | Indents and Spacing tab	CTRL+5
AutoCorrect Entry, Create	WD 91		Tools | AutoCorrect Options | AutoCorrect tab		
AutoCorrect Options	WD 90	AutoCorrect Options button			
AutoText Entry, Create	WD 179		Insert | AutoText | New		ALT+F3
AutoText Entry, Insert	WD 181		Insert | AutoText		Type entry, then F3
Blank Line Above Paragraph	WD 87		Format | Paragraph | Indents and Spacing tab	Paragraph | Indents and Spacing tab	CTRL+0 (zero)
Bold	WD 44	Bold button on Formatting toolbar	Format | Font | Font tab	Font | Font tab	CTRL+B
Border, Bottom	WD 172	Border button arrow on Formatting toolbar	Format | Borders and Shading | Borders tab		
Bulleted List	WD 187	Bullets button on Formatting toolbar	Format | Bullets and Numbering | Bulleted tab	Bullets and Numbering | Bulleted tab	* and then space, type text, ENTER
Capitalize Letters	WD 87		Format | Font | Font tab	Font | Font tab	CTRL+SHIFT+A
Case of Letters	WD 87				SHIFT+F3
Center	WD 38	Center button on Formatting toolbar	Format | Paragraph | Indents and Spacing tab	Paragraph | Indents and Spacing tab	CTRL+E
Center Vertically	WD 38		File | Page Setup | Layout tab		
Clip Art, Insert	WD 46		Insert | Picture | Clip Art		
Clipboard Task Pane, Display	WD 169	Double-click Office Clipboard icon in tray	Edit | Office Clipboard		
Close Document	WD 59	Close button on menu bar	File | Close		CTRL+W
Color Characters	WD 161	Font Color button arrow on Formatting toolbar	Format | Font | Font tab	Font | Font tab	
Copy (Collect Items)	WD 166	Copy button on Standard toolbar	Edit | Copy	Copy	CTRL+C
Count Words	WD 100	Recount button on Word Count toolbar	Tools | Word Count		
Custom Dictionary	WD 121		Tools | Options | Spelling and Grammar tab		
Date, Insert	WD 177		Insert | Date and Time		
Delete (Cut) Text	WD 59	Cut button on Standard toolbar	Edit | Cut	Cut	CTRL+X or DELETE
Demote List Item	WD 189	Decrease Indent button on Formatting toolbar			
Document Summary, Modify	WD 193		File | Properties | Summary tab		
Document Window, Open New	WD 160	New Blank Document button on Standard toolbar		File | New | Blank document	CTRL+N

Table 1 Microsoft Office Word 2003 Quick Reference Summary *(continued)*

TASK	PAGE NUMBER	MOUSE	MENU BAR	SHORTCUT MENU	KEYBOARD SHORTCUT
Double-Space Text	WD 80	Line Spacing button on Formatting toolbar	Format | Paragraph | Indents and Spacing tab	Paragraph | Indents and Spacing tab	CTRL+2
Double-Underline	WD 87		Format | Font | Font tab	Font | Font tab	CTRL+SHIFT+D
E-Mail Document	WD 123	E-mail button on Standard toolbar	File | Send To | Mail Recipient		
Envelope, Address	WD 190		Tools | Letters and Mailings | Envelopes and Labels		
Find	WD 117	Select Browse Object button on vertical scroll bar	Edit | Find		CTRL+F
Find and Replace	WD 116	Double-click left side of status bar	Edit | Replace		CTRL+H
File Properties, Display	WD 194	Views button arrow in Open dialog box			
First-Line Indent	WD 88	Drag First Line Indent marker on ruler	Format | Paragraph | Indents and Spacing tab	Paragraph | Indents and Spacing tab	
Font	WD 36	Font box arrow on Formatting toolbar	Format | Font | Font tab	Font | Font tab	CTRL+SHIFT+F
Font Size	WD 17	Font Size box arrow on Formatting toolbar	Format | Font | Font tab	Font | Font tab	CTRL+SHIFT+P
Footnote, Create	WD 94		Insert | Reference | Footnote		
Footnote, Delete	WD 99	Delete note reference mark			
Footnote, Edit	WD 99	Double-click note reference mark	View | Footnotes		
Footnotes to Endnotes, Convert	WD 99		Insert | Reference | Footnote		
Formatting Marks	WD 21	Show/Hide ¶ button on Standard toolbar	Tools | Options | View tab		CTRL+SHIFT+*
Formatting, Clear	WD 173	Style box arrow on Formatting toolbar			CTRL+SPACEBAR; CTRL+Q
Frame, New	WD 210	Desired button on Frames toolbar			
Frames Page, Create	WD 210		Format | Frames | New Frames Page		
Frame Properties, Modify	WD 214	Frame Properties button on Frames toolbar	Format | Frames | Frame Properties	Frame Properties	
Full Menu	WD 13	Double-click menu name	Click menu name and wait		
Go To	WD 111	Select Browse Object button on vertical scroll bar	Edit | Go To		CTRL+G
Hanging Indent, Create	WD 105	Drag Hanging Indent marker on ruler	Format | Paragraph | Indents and Spacing tab	Paragraph | Indents and Spacing tab	CTRL+T
Hanging Indent, Remove	WD 87	Drag Hanging Indent marker on ruler	Format | Paragraph | Indents and Spacing tab	Paragraph | Indents and Spacing tab	CTRL+SHIFT+T
Header, Display	WD 81		View | Header and Footer		
Help	WD 60 and Appendix A	Microsoft Office Word Help button on Standard toolbar	Help | Microsoft Office Word Help		F1
Highlight Text	WD 213	Highlight button arrow on Formatting toolbar			
HTML Source	WD 206		View | HTML Source		
Hyperlink, Convert to Regular Text	WD 174	AutoCorrect Options button | Undo Hyperlink		Remove Hyperlink	CTRL+Z
Hyperlink, Create	WD 108 and WD 212	Insert Hyperlink button on Standard toolbar		Hyperlink	Web address then ENTER or SPACEBAR
Hyperlink, Edit	WD 207	Insert Hyperlink button on Standard toolbar		Hyperlink	CTRL+K
Indent, Decrease	WD 87	Decrease Indent button on Formatting toolbar	Format | Paragraph | Indents and Spacing tab	Paragraph | Indents and Spacing tab	CTRL+SHIFT+M
Indent, Increase	WD 87	Increase Indent button on Formatting toolbar	Format | Paragraph | Indents and Spacing tab	Paragraph | Indents and Spacing tab	CTRL+M
Italicize	WD 41	Italic button on Formatting toolbar	Format | Font | Font tab	Font | Font tab	CTRL+I
Justify Paragraph	WD 87	Justify button on Formatting toolbar	Format | Paragraph | Indents and Spacing tab	Paragraph | Indents and Spacing tab	CTRL+J

Table 1 Microsoft Office Word 2003 Quick Reference Summary

TASK	PAGE NUMBER	MOUSE	MENU BAR	SHORTCUT MENU	KEYBOARD SHORTCUT
Leader Characters	WD 164		Format | Tabs		
Left-Align	WD 86	Align Left button on Formatting toolbar	Format | Paragraph | Indents and Spacing tab	Paragraph | Indents and Spacing tab	CTRL+L
Line Break, Enter	WD 154				SHIFT+ENTER
Mailing Label, Address	WD 191		Tools | Letters and Mailings | Envelopes and Labels		
Margins	WD 78	In print layout view, drag margin boundary on ruler	File | Page Setup | Margins tab		
Move Selected Text	WD 113	Drag and drop	Edit | Cut; Edit | Paste	Cut; Paste	CTRL+X; CTRL+V
Nonbreaking Hyphen	WD 180		Insert | Symbol | Special Characters tab		CTRL+SHIFT+HYPHEN
Nonbreaking Space	WD 180		Insert | Symbol | Special Characters tab		CTRL+SHIFT+SPACEBAR
Numbered List	WD 189	Numbering button on Formatting toolbar	Format | Bullets and Numbering | Numbered tab	Bullets and Numbering | Numbered tab	1. and then space, type text, ENTER
Open Document	WD 55	Open button on Standard toolbar	File | Open		CTRL+O
Outline Numbered List	WD 189		Format | Bullets and Numbering | Outline Numbered tab		
Page Break	WD 103		Insert | Break		CTRL+ENTER
Page Numbers, Insert	WD 83	Insert Page Number button on Header and Footer toolbar	Insert | Page Numbers		
Paste	WD 170	Paste button on Standard toolbar	Edit | Paste	Paste	CTRL+V
Paste Options, Menu	WD 115	Paste Options button			
Print Document	WD 53	Print button on Standard toolbar	File | Print		CTRL+P
Print Preview	WD 158	Print Preview button on Standard toolbar	File | Print Preview		CTRL+F2
Promote List Item	WD 189	Increase Indent button on Formatting toolbar			
Quit Word	WD 54	Close button on title bar	File | Exit		ALT+F4
Redo Action	WD 39	Redo button on Standard toolbar	Edit | Redo		
Repeat Command	WD 39		Edit | Repeat		
Research Task Pane	WD 124	ALT+click word in document	Tools | Research		
Research Task Pane, Insert text from	WD 125			Right-click selected text in task pane, click Copy; right-click document, click Paste	Select text in task pane, CTRL+C; click document, CTRL+V
Resize Graphic	WD 50	Drag sizing handle	Format | Picture | Size tab	Format Picture | Size tab	
Restore Graphic	WD 51	Format Picture button on Picture toolbar	Format | Picture | Size tab	Format Picture | Size tab	
Resume Wizard	WD 142		File | New | On my computer | Other Documents tab		
Right-Align	WD 37	Align Right button on Formatting toolbar	Format | Paragraph | Indents and Spacing tab	Paragraph | Indents and Spacing tab	CTRL+R
Ruler, Show or Hide	WD 11		View | Ruler		
Save as Web Page	WD 205		File | Save as Web Page		
Save Document - New Name or Format	WD 52		File | Save As		F12
Save Document - Same Name	WD 52	Save button on Standard toolbar	File | Save		CTRL+S
Save New Document	WD 28	Save button on Standard toolbar	File | Save		CTRL+S
Select Document	WD 113	Point to left and triple-click	Edit | Select All		CTRL+A
Select Graphic	WD 49	Click graphic			
Select Group of Words	WD 43	Drag through words			CTRL+SHIFT+ARROW
Select Line	WD 40	Point to left of line and click			SHIFT+DOWN ARROW
Select Multiple Paragraphs	WD 33	Point to left of first paragraph and drag down			CTRL+SHIFT+DOWN ARROW

Table 1 Microsoft Office Word 2003 Quick Reference Summary *(continued)*

TASK	PAGE NUMBER	MOUSE	MENU BAR	SHORTCUT MENU	KEYBOARD SHORTCUT
Select Paragraph	WD 113	Triple-click paragraph			
Select Sentence	WD 112	CTRL+click sentence			CTRL+SHIFT+ARROW
Select Word	WD 58	Double-click word			CTRL+SHIFT+ARROW
Single-Space Text	WD 87	Line Spacing button arrow on Formatting toolbar	Format | Paragraph | Indents and Spacing tab	Paragraph | Indents and Spacing tab	CTRL+1
Small Uppercase Letters	WD 87		Format | Font | Font tab	Font | Font tab	CTRL+SHIFT+K
Smart Tag Actions, Display Menu	WD 192	Point to smart tag indicator, click Smart Tag Actions button			
Sort Paragraphs	WD 109		Table | Sort		
Spelling and Grammar Check At Once	WD 119	Spelling and Grammar button on Standard toolbar	Tools | Spelling and Grammar	Spelling	F7
Spelling Check as You Type	WD 26	Double-click Spelling and Grammar Status icon on status bar		Right-click flagged word, click word on shortcut menu	
Style, Modify	WD 96	Styles and Formatting button on Formatting toolbar	Format | Styles and Formatting		
Styles and Formatting Task Pane, Display	WD 152	Styles and Formatting button on Formatting toolbar	View | Task Pane		
Subscript	WD 87		Format | Font | Font tab	Font | Font tab	CTRL+=
Superscript	WD 87		Format | Font | Font tab	Font | Font tab	CTRL+SHIFT+PLUS SIGN
Switch to Open Document	WD 166	Program button on taskbar	Window | document name		ALT+TAB
Synonym	WD 118		Tools | Language | Thesaurus	Synonyms | desired word	SHIFT+F7
Tab Stops, Set	WD 164	Click location on ruler	Format | Tabs		
Table AutoFormat	WD 187	AutoFormat button on Tables and Borders toolbar	Table | Table AutoFormat		
Table, Fit Columns to Table Contents	WD 185	Double-click column boundary	Table | AutoFit | AutoFit to Contents	AutoFit | AutoFit to Contents	
Table, Insert Empty	WD 183	Insert Table button on Standard toolbar	Table | Insert | Table		
Table, Insert Row	WD 184		Table | Insert | Rows Above/Below	Right-click selected row; Insert Rows	TAB from lower-right cell
Table, Resize Column	WD 186	Drag column boundary	Table | Table Properties | Column tab	Table Properties | Column tab	
Table, Select	WD 186	Click table move handle	Table | Select | Table		ALT+5 (on keypad)
Table, Select Cell	WD 186	Click left edge of cell			TAB
Table, Select Column	WD 186	Click top border of column			
Table, Select Cells	WD 186	Drag through cells			
Table, Select Row	WD 186	Click to left of row			
Task Pane, Display Different	WD 10	Other Task Panes button on task pane			
Template, Open	WD 175		File | New | On my computer		
Theme, Apply	WD 208		Format | Theme		
Toolbar, Dock	WD 82	Double-click toolbar title bar			
Toolbar, Float	WD 82	Drag toolbar move handle			
Toolbar, Show Entire	WD 14	Double-click toolbar move handle	Tools | Customize | Options tab		
Underline	WD 42	Underline button on Formatting toolbar	Format | Font | Font tab	Font | Font tab	CTRL+U
Underline Words	WD 87		Format | Font | Font tab	Font | Font tab	CTRL+SHIFT+W
Undo	WD 39	Undo button on Standard toolbar	Edit | Undo		CTRL+Z
User Information, Change	WD 194		Tools | Options | User Information tab		
Web Page Frame, Resize	WD 211	Drag frame border	Format | Frames | Frame Properties | Frame tab		
Web Page, Preview	WD 209		File | Web Page Preview		
White Space	WD 149	Hide or Show White Space button	Tools | Options | View tab		
Zoom	WD 21 and WD 169	Zoom box arrow on Formatting toolbar	View | Zoom		

Table 2 Microsoft Excel 2003 Quick Reference Summary

TASK	PAGE NUMBER	MOUSE	MENU BAR	SHORTCUT MENU	KEYBOARD SHORTCUT
AutoFormat	EX 34		Format | AutoFormat		ALT+O | A
AutoSum	EX 23	AutoSum button on Standard toolbar	Insert | Function		ALT+=
Bold	EX 30	Bold button on Formatting toolbar	Format | Cells | Font tab	Format Cells | Font tab	CTRL+B
Borders	EX 96	Borders button on Formatting toolbar	Format | Cells | Border tab	Format Cells | Border tab	CTRL+1 | B
Center	EX 97	Center button on Formatting toolbar	Format | Cells | Alignment tab	Format Cells | Alignment tab	CTRL+1 | A
Center Across Columns	EX 33	Merge and Center button on Formatting toolbar	Format | Cells | Alignment tab	Format Cells | Alignment tab	CTRL+1 | A
Chart	EX 39	Chart Wizard button on Standard toolbar	Insert | Chart		F11
Clear Cell	EX 52	Drag fill handle back	Edit | Clear | All	Clear Contents	DELETE
Close Workbook	EX 46	Close button on menu bar or workbook Control-menu icon	File | Close		CTRL+W
Color Background	EX 94	Fill Color button on Formatting toolbar	Format | Cells | Patterns tab	Format Cells | Patterns tab	CTRL+1 | P
Color Tab	EX 198			Tab Color	
Column Width	EX 107	Drag column heading boundary	Format | Column | Width	Column Width	ALT+O | C | W
Comma Style Format	EX 108	Comma Style button on Formatting toolbar	Format | Cells | Number tab | Accounting	Format Cells | Number tab | Accounting	CTRL+1 | N
Conditional Formatting	EX 104		Format | Conditional Formatting		ALT+O | D
Copy and Paste	EX 157	Copy button and Paste button on Standard toolbar	Edit | Copy; Edit | Paste	Copy to copy; Paste to paste	CTRL+C; CTRL+V
Currency Style Format	EX 98	Currency Style button on Formatting toolbar	Format | Cells | Number | Currency	Format Cells | Number | Currency	CTRL+1 | N
Cut	EX 159	Cut button on Standard toolbar	Edit | Cut	Cut	CTRL+X
Date	EX 166	Insert Function box in formula bar	Insert | Function		CTRL+SEMICOLON
Decimal Place, Decrease	EX 100	Decrease Decimal button on Formatting toolbar	Format | Cells | Number tab | Currency	Format Cells | Number tab | Currency	CTRL+1 | N
Decimal Place, Increase	EX 99	Increase Decimal button on Formatting toolbar	Format | Cells | Number tab | Currency	Format Cells | Number tab | Currency	CTRL+1 | N
Delete Rows or Columns	EX 161		Edit | Delete	Delete	
Drop Shadow	EX 184	Shadow Style button on Drawing toolbar			
E-Mail from Excel	EX 125	E-mail button on Standard toolbar	File | Send To | Mail Recipient		ALT+F | D | A
File Management	EX 232		File | Save As, right-click file name		ALT+F | A, right-click file name
Fit to Print	EX 118		File | Page Setup | Page tab		ALT+F | U | P
Folder, New	EX 230		File | Save As		ALT+F | A
Font Color	EX 32	Font Color button on Formatting toolbar	Format | Cells | Font tab	Format Cells | Font tab	CTRL+1 | F
Font Size	EX 31	Font Size box arrow on Formatting toolbar	Format | Cells | Font tab	Format Cells | Font tab	CTRL+1 | F
Font Type	EX 29	Font box arrow on Formatting toolbar	Format | Cells | Font tab	Format Cells | Font tab	CTRL+1 | F
Formula Assistance	EX 83	Insert Function box in formula bar	Insert | Function		CTRL+A after you type function name

Table 2 Microsoft Excel 2003 Quick Reference Summary *(continued)*

TASK	PAGE NUMBER	MOUSE	MENU BAR	SHORTCUT MENU	KEYBOARD SHORTCUT
Formulas Version	EX 118		Tools | Options | View tab | Formulas		CTRL+ACCENT MARK
Freeze Worksheet Titles	EX 163		Window | Freeze Panes		ALT+W | F
Full Screen	EX 11		View | Full Screen		ALT+V | U
Function	EX 81	Insert Function box in formula bar	Insert | Function		SHIFT+F3
Go To	EX 37	Click cell	Edit | Go To		F5
Goal Seek	EX 206		Tools | Goal Seek		ALT+T | G
Help	EX 53 and Appendix A	Microsoft Excel Help button on Standard toolbar	Help | Microsoft Excel Help		F1
Hide Column	EX 109	Drag column heading boundary	Format | Column | Hide	Hide	CTRL+0 (zero) to hide CTRL+SHIFT+) to display
Hide Row	EX 111	Drag row heading boundary	Format | Row | Hide	Hide	CTRL+9 to hide CTRL+SHIFT+(to display
In-Cell Editing	EX 50	Double-click cell			F2
Insert Rows or Columns	EX 160		Insert | Rows or Insert | Columns	Insert	ALT+I | R or C
Italicize	EX 186	Italic button on Formatting toolbar	Format | Cells | Font tab	Format Cells | Font tab	CTRL+I
Language Bar	EX 15 and Appendix B		Tools | Speech | Speech Recognition	Toolbars | Language bar	ALT+T | H | H
Merge Cells	EX 33	Merge and Center button on Formatting toolbar	Format | Cells | Alignment tab	Format Cells | Font tab | Alignment tab	ALT+O | E | A
Move Cells	EX 159	Point to border and drag	Edit | Cut; Edit | Paste	Cut; Paste	CTRL+X; CTRL+V
Name Cells	EX 37	Click Name box in formula bar, type name	Insert | Name | Define		ALT+I | N | D
New Workbook	EX 53	New button on Standard toolbar	File | New		CTRL+N
Open Workbook	EX 47	Open button on Standard toolbar	File | Open		CTRL+O
Percent Style Format	EX 103	Percent Style button on Formatting toolbar	Format | Cells | Number tab | Percentage	Format Cells | Number tab | Percentage	CTRL+1 | N
Preview Worksheet	EX 114	Print Preview button on Standard toolbar	File | Print Preview		ALT+F | V
Print Worksheet	EX 113	Print button on Standard toolbar	File | Print		CTRL+P
Quit Excel	EX 46	Close button on title bar	File | Exit		ALT+F4
Range Finder	EX 89	Double-click cell			
Redo	EX 52	Redo button on Standard toolbar	Edit | Redo		ALT+E | R
Remove Splits	EX 204	Double-click split bar	Window | Split		ALT+W | S
Rename Sheet Tab	EX 198	Double-click sheet tab		Rename	
Rotate Text	EX 151		Format | Cells | Alignment tab	Format Cells | Alignment tab	ALT+O | E | A
Row Height	EX 110	Drag row heading boundary	Format | Row | Height	Row Height	ALT+O | R | E
Save as Web Page	EX 230		File | Save as Web Page		ALT+F | G
Save Workbook, New Name	EX 42		File | Save As		ALT+F | A
Save Workbook, Same Name	EX 89	Save button on Standard toolbar	File | Save		CTRL+S
Select All of Worksheet	EX 53	Select All button on worksheet			CTRL+A
Select Cell	EX 16	Click cell			Use arrow keys

Table 2 Microsoft Excel 2003 Quick Reference Summary

TASK	PAGE NUMBER	MOUSE	MENU BAR	SHORTCUT MENU	KEYBOARD SHORTCUT
Select Multiple Sheets	EX 200	CTRL+click tab or SHIFT+click tab		Select All Sheets	
Series	EX 151	Drag fill handle	Edit | Fill | Series		ALT+E | I | S
Shortcut Menu	EX 92	Right-click object			SHIFT+F10
Spell Check	EX 112	Spelling button on Standard toolbar	Tools | Spelling		F7
Split Cell	EX 33	Merge and Center button on Formatting toolbar	Format | Cells | Alignment tab	Format Cells | Alignment tab	ALT+O | E | A
Split Window into Panes	EX 203	Drag vertical or horizontal split box	Window | Split		ALT+W | S
Stock Quotes	EX 121		Data | Import External Data | Import Data		ALT+D | D | D
Task Pane	EX 8		View | Task Pane		ALT+V | K
Toolbar, Dock	EX 182	Drag toolbar to dock			
Toolbar, Reset	Appendix D	Toolbar Options button on toolbar, Add or Remove Buttons, Customize, Toolbars tab		Customize | Toolbars	ALT+V | T | C | B
Toolbar, Show Entire	EX 13	Double-click move handle			
Toolbar, Show or Hide	EX 182	Right-click toolbar, click toolbar name	View | Toolbars		ALT+V | T
Underline	EX 187	Underline button on Formatting toolbar	Format | Cells | Font tab	Format Cells | Font tab	CTRL+U
Undo	EX 51	Undo button on Standard toolbar	Edit | Undo		CTRL+Z
Unfreeze Worksheet Titles	EX 176		Windows | Unfreeze Panes		ALT+W | F
Unhide Column	EX 109	Drag hidden column heading boundary to right	Format | Column | Unhide	Unhide	ALT+O | C | U
Unhide Row	EX 111	Drag hidden row heading boundary down	Format | Row | Unhide	Unhide	ALT+O | R | U
Web Page Preview	EX 228		File | Web Page Preview		ALT+F | B
Zoom	EX 201	Zoom box on Standard toolbar	View | Zoom		ALT+V | Z

Table 3 Microsoft Office Access 2003 Quick Reference Summary

TASK	PAGE NUMBER	MOUSE	MENU BAR	SHORTCUT MENU	KEYBOARD SHORTCUT
Add Field	AC 129	Insert Rows button	Insert | Rows	Insert Rows	INSERT
Add Group of Records	AC 139	Query Type button arrow | Append Query	Query | Append Query	Query Type | Append Query	
Add Record	AC 23, AC 116	New Record button	Insert | New Record		
Add Table to Query	AC 92	Show Table button	Query | Show Table	Show Table	
Advanced Filter/Sort	AC 124		Records | Filter | Advanced Filter Sort		
Apply Filter	AC 121, AC 123	Filter By Selection or Filter By Form button	Records | Filter		
Calculate Statistics	AC 100	Totals button	View | Totals	Totals	
Change Group of Records	AC 136	Query Type button arrow | Update Query	Query | Update Query	Query Type | Update Query	

Table 3 Microsoft Office Access 2003 Quick Reference Summary *(continued)*

TASK	PAGE NUMBER	MOUSE	MENU BAR	SHORTCUT MENU	KEYBOARD SHORTCUT
Clear Query	AC 75		Edit | Clear Grid		
Close Database	AC 26	Close Window button	File | Close		
Close Form	AC 39	Close Window button	File | Close		
Close Query	AC 73	Close Window button	File | Close		
Close Table	AC 21	Close Window button	File | Close		
Collapse Subdatasheet	AC 153	Expand indicator (-)			
Create Calculated Field	AC 96			Zoom	SHIFT+F2
Create Database	AC 10	New button	File | New		CTRL+N
Create Form	AC 38	New Object button arrow | AutoForm	Insert | AutoForm		
Create Index	AC 161	Indexes button	View | Indexes		
Create Query	AC 68	New Object button arrow | Query	Insert | Query		
Create Report	AC 43	New Object button arrow | Report	Insert | Report		
Create Snapshot	AC 184		File | Export, select SNP as file type	Export, select SNP as file type	
Create Table	AC 17	Tables object | Create table in Design view or Create table by using wizard	Insert | Table		
Crosstab Query	AC 104	New Object button arrow | Query	Insert | Query		
Default Value	AC 142	Default Value property box			
Delete Field	AC 130	Delete Rows button	Edit | Delete	Delete Rows	DELETE
Delete Group of Records	AC 138	Query Type button arrow | Delete Query	Query | Delete Query	Query Type | Delete Query	
Delete Record	AC 125	Delete Record button	Edit | Delete Record	Delete Record	DELETE
Exclude Duplicates	AC 87	Properties button	View | Properties | Unique Values Only	Properties | Unique Values Only	
Exclude Field from Query Results	AC 78	Show check box			
Expand Subdatasheet	AC 153	Expand indicator (+)			
Export Using Drag-and-Drop	AC 182	Drag object, then drop			
Export Using Export Command	AC 183		File | Export	Export	
Field Size	AC 19, AC 127	Field Size property box			
Field Type	AC 20	Data Type box arrow | appropriate type			Appropriate letter
Filter Records	AC 121, AC 123	Filter By Selection or Filter By Form button	Records | Filter		
Font in Datasheet	AC 133		Format | Font	Font	
Format	AC 144	Format property box			
Format a Calculated Field	AC 98	Properties button	View | Properties	Properties	
Format Datasheet	AC 134		Format | Datasheet	Datasheet	
Group in Query	AC 103	Totals button	View | Totals		

Table 3 Microsoft Office Access 2003 Quick Reference Summary

TASK	PAGE NUMBER	MOUSE	MENU BAR	SHORTCUT MENU	KEYBOARD SHORTCUT
Import	AC 177		File | Get External Data | Import	Import	
Include All Fields in Query	AC 74	Double-click asterisk in field list			
Include Field in Query	AC 71	Double-click field in field list			
Join Properties	AC 94		View | Join Properties	Join Properties	
Key Field	AC 19	Primary Key button	Edit | Primary Key	Primary Key	
Link	AC 180		File | Get External Data | Link Table	Link Tables	
Lookup Field	AC 147	Text box arrow | Lookup Wizard			
Move to First Record	AC 27	First Record button			CTRL+UP ARROW
Move to Last Record	AC 27	Last Record button			CTRL+DOWN ARROW
Move to Next Record	AC 27	Next Record button			DOWN ARROW
Move to Previous Record	AC 27	Previous Record button			UP ARROW
Open Database	AC 26	Open button	File | Open		CTRL+O
Open Form	AC 116	Forms object | Open button		Open	Use ARROW keys to move highlight to name, then press ENTER key
Open Table	AC 26	Tables object | Open button		Open	Use ARROW keys to move highlight to name, then press ENTER key
Preview Table	AC 30	Print Preview button	File | Print Preview	Print Preview	
Print Relationships	AC 151		File | Print Relationships		
Print Report	AC 47	Print button	File | Print	Print	CTRL+P
Print Results of Query	AC 72	Print button	File | Print	Print	CTRL+P
Print Table	AC 30	Print button	File | Print	Print	CTRL+P
Quit Access	AC 50	Close button	File | Exit		ALT+F4
Relationships (Referential Integrity)	AC 150	Relationships button	Tools | Relationships		
Remove Filter	AC 122	Remove Filter button	Records | Remove Filter/Sort		
Resize Column	AC 131	Drag right boundary of field selector	Format | Column Width	Column Width	
Restructure Table	AC 126	Tables object | Design button		Design View	
Return to Select Query Window	AC 72	View button arrow	View | Design View		
Run Query	AC 71	Run button	Query | Run		
Save Form	AC 39	Save button	File | Save		CTRL+S
Save Query	AC 80	Save button	File | Save		CTRL+S
Save Table	AC 21	Save button	File | Save		CTRL+S
Search for Record	AC 117	Find button	Edit | Find		CTRL+F
Select Fields for Report	AC 44	Add Field button or Add All Fields button			
Simple Query Wizard	AC 34	New Object button arrow | Query	Insert | Query		
Sort Data in Query	AC 86	Sort row | Sort row arrow | type of sort			
Sort Records	AC 155	Sort Ascending or Sort Descending button	Records | Sort | Sort Ascending or Sort Descending	Sort Ascending or Sort Descending	

Table 3 Microsoft Office Access 2003 Quick Reference Summary *(continued)*

TASK	PAGE NUMBER	MOUSE	MENU BAR	SHORTCUT MENU	KEYBOARD SHORTCUT
Switch Between Form and Datasheet Views	AC 41, AC 120	View button arrow	View | Datasheet View		
Top-Values Query	AC 89	Top Values button	View | Properties	Properties	
Use AND Criterion	AC 84				Place criteria on same line
Use OR Criterion	AC 85				Place criteria on separate lines
Validation Rule	AC 141	Validation Rule property box			
Validation Text	AC 141	Validation Text property box			

Table 4 Microsoft Office PowerPoint 2003 Quick Reference Summary

TASK	PAGE NUMBER	MOUSE	MENU BAR	SHORTCUT MENU	KEYBOARD SHORTCUT
Animate Text	PPT 114		Slide Show | Custom Animation | Add Effect button		ALT+D | M
Black Slide, End Show	PPT 42		Tools | Options | End with black slide		ALT+T | O | E
Check Spelling	PPT 54	Spelling button on Standard toolbar	Tools | Spelling		F7
Clip Art, Add Animation Effects	PPT 117		Slide Show | Custom Animation		ALT+D | M
Clip Art, Change Size	PPT 109	Format Picture button on Picture toolbar | Size tab	Format | Picture | Size tab	Format Picture | Size tab	ALT+O | I | Size tab
Clip Art, Insert	PPT 101, PPT 104	Insert Clip Art button on Drawing toolbar	Insert | Picture | Clip Art		ALT+I | P | C
Clip Art, Move	PPT 108	Drag			
Delete Text	PPT 56	Cut button on Standard toolbar	Edit | Cut	Cut	CTRL+X or BACKSPACE or DELETE
Demote a Paragraph on Outline tab	PPT 90	Demote button on Outlining toolbar			TAB or ALT+SHIFT+RIGHT ARROW
Design Template	PPT 18	Slide Design button on Formatting toolbar	Format | Slide Design	Slide Design	ALT+O | D
Display a Presentation in Black and White	PPT 57	Color/Grayscale button on Standard toolbar	View | Color/Grayscale | Pure Black and White		ALT+V | C | U
Edit Web Page through Browser	PPT 152	Edit button on Internet Explorer Standard Buttons toolbar	File on browser menu bar | Edit with Microsoft PowerPoint in browser window		ALT+F | D in browser window
E-Mail from PowerPoint	PPT 127	E-mail button on Standard toolbar	File | Send To | Mail Recipient		ALT+F | D | A
End Slide Show	PPT 50			End Show	ESC
Font	PPT 24	Font box arrow on Formatting toolbar	Format | Font	Font	ALT+O | F
Font Color	PPT 24	Font Color button arrow on Formatting toolbar, desired color	Format | Font	Font | Color	ALT+O | F | ALT+C | DOWN ARROW

Table 4 Microsoft Office PowerPoint 2003 Quick Reference Summary

TASK	PAGE NUMBER	MOUSE	MENU BAR	SHORTCUT MENU	KEYBOARD SHORTCUT
Font Size, Decrease	PPT 27	Decrease Font Size button on Formatting toolbar	Format | Font	Font | Size	CTRL+SHIFT+LEFT CARET (<)
Font Size, Increase	PPT 25	Increase Font Size button on Formatting toolbar	Format | Font	Font | Size	CTRL+SHIFT+RIGHT CARET (>)
Header and Footer, Add to Outline Page	PPT 112		View | Header and Footer | Notes and Handouts tab		ALT+V | H | Notes and Handouts tab
Help	PPT 62 and Appendix A	Microsoft PowerPoint Help button on Standard toolbar	Help | Microsoft PowerPoint Help		F1
Italicize	PPT 24	Italic button on Formatting toolbar	Format | Font | Font style	Font | Font style	CTRL+I
Language Bar	PPT 16 and Appendix B	Language Indicator button in tray	Tools | Speech | Speech Recognition		ALT+T | H | H
Move a Paragraph Down	PPT 87	Move Down button on Outlining toolbar			ALT+SHIFT+DOWN ARROW
Move a Paragraph Up	PPT 87	Move Up button on Outlining toolbar			ALT+SHIFT+UP ARROW
New Slide	PPT 30	New Slide button on Formatting toolbar	Insert | New Slide		CTRL+M
Next Slide	PPT 45	Next Slide button on vertical scroll bar			PAGE DOWN
Normal View	PPT 96	Normal View button at lower-left PowerPoint window	View | Normal		ALT+V | N
Open Presentation	PPT 52	Open button on Standard toolbar	File | Open		CTRL+O
Paragraph Indent, Decrease	PPT 37	Decrease Indent button on Formatting toolbar			SHIFT+TAB or ALT+SHIFT+LEFT ARROW
Paragraph Indent, Increase	PPT 36	Increase Indent button on Formatting toolbar			TAB or ALT+SHIFT+RIGHT ARROW
Preview Presentation as Web Page	PPT 144		File | Web Page Preview		ALT+F | B
Previous Slide	PPT 45	Previous Slide button on vertical scroll bar			PAGE UP
Print a Presentation	PPT 60	Print button on Standard toolbar	File | Print		CTRL+P
Print an Outline	PPT 122		File | Print | Print what box arrow | Outline View		CTRL+P | TAB | TAB | DOWN ARROW | Outline View
Promote a Paragraph on Outline tab	PPT 89	Promote button on Outlining toolbar			SHIFT+TAB or ALT+SHIFT+LEFT ARROW
Publish a Presentation	PPT 154		File | Save as Web Page | Publish | Publish		ALT+F | G | ALT+P | ALT+P
Quit PowerPoint	PPT 50	Close button on title bar or double-click control icon on title bar	File | Exit		ALT+F4 or CTRL+Q
Redo Action	PPT 22	Redo button on Standard toolbar	Edit | Redo		CTRL+Y or ALT+E | R
Save a Presentation	PPT 27	Save button on Standard toolbar	File | Save		CTRL+S
Save as Web Page	PPT 147		File | Save as Web Page		ALT+F | G
Slide Layout	PPT 98		Format | Slide Layout	Slide Layout	ALT+O | L
Slide Show View	PPT 47	Slide Show button at lower-left PowerPoint window	View | Slide Show		F5 or ALT+V | W

Table 4 Microsoft Office PowerPoint 2003 Quick Reference Summary *(continued)*

TASK	PAGE NUMBER	MOUSE	MENU BAR	SHORTCUT MENU	KEYBOARD SHORTCUT
Slide Sorter View	PPT 95	Slide Sorter View button at lower-left PowerPoint window	View | Slide Sorter		ALT+V | D
Spelling Check	PPT 54	Spelling button on Standard toolbar	Tools | Spelling	Spelling	F7
Task Pane	PPT 11		View | Task Pane		ALT+V | K
Toolbar, Reset	Appendix D	Toolbar Options button on toolbar, Add or Remove Buttons, Customize, Toolbars tab		Customize | Toolbars tab	ALT+V | T | C | B
Toolbar, Show Entire	PPT 9	Double-click move handle			
Undo Action	PPT 22	Undo button on Standard toolbar	Edit | Undo		CTRL+Z or ALT+E | U
Web Page, Preview	PPT 144		File | Web Page Preview		ALT+F | B
Zoom Percentage, Increase	PPT 44	Zoom Box arrow on Standard toolbar	View | Zoom		ALT+V | Z

Table 5 Microsoft Office Outlook 2003 Quick Reference Summary

TASK	PAGE NUMBER	MOUSE	MENU BAR	SHORTCUT MENU	KEYBOARD SHORTCUT
Address E-Mail Message	OUT 51	To button			CTRL+SHIFT+B
Attach File to E-Mail Message	OUT 28	Insert File button	Insert | File		ALT+I, L
Compose E-Mail Message	OUT 24	New button	File | New | Mail Message		CTRL+N
Create Contact List	OUT 42	New button	Actions | New Contact	New Contact	CTRL+N | ALT+A, N
Create Distribution List	OUT 54	New button	File | New | Distribution List		CTRL+SHIFT+L
Create E-Mail Signature	OUT 20		Tools | Options		ALT+T, O
Create Personal Folder	OUT 40		File | New | Folder	New Folder	CTRL+SHIFT+E
Create View Filter	OUT 32		View | Arrange By	Custom	ALT+V, A, M
Delete E-Mail Message	OUT 17	Delete button	Edit | Delete	Delete	CTRL+D
Display Contacts in a Category	OUT 49	Find button	Tools | Find		CTRL+E
Find a Contact	OUT 46	Find button	Tools | Find		CTRL+E
Flag E-Mail Messages	OUT 30		Actions | Follow Up	Follow Up	ALT+A, U
Forward E-Mail Message	OUT 16	Forward button	Actions | Forward	Forward	ALT+W
Open E-Mail Message	OUT 11		File | Open	Open	ALT+F, O
Organize Contacts	OUT 48	Organize button	Tools | Organize		ALT+T, Z
Print Contact List	OUT 50	Print button	File | Print		CTRL+P
Print E-Mail Message	OUT 12	Print button	File | Print		CTRL+P
Reply to E-Mail Message	OUT 13	Reply button	Actions | Reply	Reply	ALT+R
Save Contact List as Text File	OUT 56		File | Save As		ALT+F, A
Send E-Mail Message	OUT 29	Send button	File | Send To		ALT+S
Set Message Delivery Options	OUT 34	Options button			ALT+P
Set Message Importance and Sensitivity	OUT 34	Options button			ALT+P
Sort E-Mail Messages	OUT 31		View | Arrange By		ALT+V, A